on STREETS

D1716864

Noël Cochin, Fair at Guibray, near Falaise, Normandy [Paris, Bibliothèque Nationale]

on STREETS

Edited by Stanford Anderson
for The Institute for Architecture and Urban Studies

The MIT Press
Cambridge, Massachusetts, and London, England

First MIT Press paperback edition, 1986

Based on a project of The Institute for Architecture and
Urban Studies.

This work was done under a grant by the U.S. Department
of Housing and Urban Development under contract D-13.
The Institute wishes to acknowledge the help and consultation throughout the project of Howard Cayton, Ralph
Warburton, Michael Schneider, and all of the U.S. Department of Housing and Urban Development.

This book was set in VIP Times Roman by DEKR
Corporation, printed on Warren's Patina by Halliday
Litho Corp., and bound in Holliston Novelex Vellum
2693 by Halliday Litho Corp. in the United States of
America.

Designed by Abigail Moseley

Library of Congress Cataloging in Publication Data
Main entry under title:
On streets.
    "Based on a project of the Institute for Architecture and
Urban Studies."
    Bibliography: p.
    Includes index.
    1. Streets — Addresses, essays, lectures.
2. Streets — Design — Addresses, essays, lectures.
I. Anderson, Stanford.   II. Institute for Architecture and
Urban Studies.   III. Title: Streets.
HE331.05   711'.73   77-8175
ISBN 0-262-51039-1 (paper)

For Howard Cayton

Contents

Preface

Unclogging traffic-bound streets, restoring safety to streets, and feeling curiosity and fear about street culture and street-corner society are common issues. Equally familiar are the numerous entrenched expressions where "street" bears a negative connotation: "on the street," "streetwalker," "street crime." Streets then, present problems, and "street" is used as a metaphor for what is aberrant and fearful in the light of social norms.

Nevertheless, the actual and potential characteristics of streets are too little considered. Architects often bury themselves in individual building projects, ignoring any responsibility to the public space of the city; planners work at a scale where the street is seen only as a traffic channel or emphasize social and economic factors that cut through urban phenomena in such a way as to allow streets to remain unrecognized and lost in their negative connotations.

In the larger physical plans of architects and planners of this century, the amount, form, and organization of urban public space could not be ignored; but these planners largely shared, and played to, the societal fear of the street. The romance of unconstrained and rapid accessibility to all parts of a public space modeled on such socially positive terms as park, meadow, field, or campus led to the ideal schemes of a city-in-a-park, which simultaneously and intentionally killed the street.

This century's most pervasive models of the new city were ideal schemes of crystalline shelters in meadows with occasional ways but no streets — openness and transparency in an innocent and undomesticated nature. This gave us plans devoid of streets and of any metaphor for guile, secrecy, danger, fear, and, generally, the darker aspects of human nature and action. It was treated as a matter of some surprise that the removal of the street did not remove the darker aspects of human nature and action. Today, whatever our disappointments and fears in the use of streets, our strongest sense for most modern environments is of lost amenity and of fear so pervasive as to enforce total withdrawal from large parks and superblocks of single-use buildings in open space.

In the face of these events, architects and physical planners are alternately chastised for falsely holding that physical design could have any effect on human thought and action, and then damned for the social irresponsibility of creating the conditions which have led to a worsened urban life. The social critics cannot have it both ways. The authors of this book accept the damnation rather than the chastisement.

The problem of physical planning in general, and of the design of streets in particular, is to recognize the nature and limits of the interaction of people with their environment — not the polar conditions of presumed total irrelevance or absolute physical determinism. The physical environment must be seen as both a cultural system entailing the scope and qualifications of our aspirations and our resignation and a support system for our literal needs and actions — even if the interaction among these factors can only be partially distinguished for analytic purposes.

The essays of this book have their origin in a research project at the Institute for Architecture and Urban Studies which was funded by the U.S. Department of Housing and Development. However, in the diversity of their concerns and their varied development since the time of the research project, the essays reflect the complexity of the phenomenon under study, a complexity intensified by the perspectives of several disciplines. Perhaps the one feature that holds the essays together is their refusal to reduce the role of the street — a reductionism so sadly evident in much of the literature and in the actual design and transformation of streets. The volume is thus not a handbook for the design of a system of street types but rather a collection of essays that encourages a fuller understanding of the general problem of assessing and improving any particular street.

Since 1970, when the original research began, more sympathetic and comprehensive attitudes to public open space have appeared in the public and in the design professions. Evidence of this change will be found in the bibliography. If this book is out of season, it is because most of its authors and the institute from which it comes incline to a concern with the ideal and emphasize the development of conceptual frameworks and prototypical elements. The editor shares this concern — but more than most of the authors, perhaps, welcomes the selective development of any ideal configuration according to a broad range of both present and as yet unimagined human associations. The ideal and the real, the inherent and the self-imposed limits of physical design; these are difficult problems which are confronted throughout this book. The issues are admittedly unresolved; in my own contributions I have sought to intensify the dialectic of the ideal and the real as encountered in the environment — especially from the side of the real. Within the book itself, I have sought to intensify the dialectic among the authors.

Despite some differences, it is not an accident that these authors worked together. Most of them share certain hypotheses:

that the physical environment is a structurally integral part of society, simultaneously a support for literal needs and activities and a cultural system mutually interdependent with fundamental propositions about individuals and society;

that, in these roles, the physical environment is influential upon people — a satisfier of needs, a means of communication, a source of hurt or joy;

that, as planners and as a society, we have chosen and continue to choose among alternative environments and to select ways in which we use and interpret extant physical environments with as yet untapped, latent potential;

that, as planners and as a society, we must seek to enhance the range of these choices and the awareness of such opportunity to choose;

that new possibilities and their exploration may be constrained by certain limits inherent to human inquiry, but should not be constrained by currently powerful but arbitrary forces of economic or political power, land ownership, etc.;

that all of these matters, from individual learning behavior through social and political alternatives to the abstraction of a possible model of urban structure, are susceptible of more sustained inquiry than they have received.

In fairness to some of the authors of this volume, it should be acknowledged that these essays were assembled over a period of several years. I wish to thank all the contributors, but particularly those who met the original deadlines and then showed such forbearance about the delays in publication. These delays increased the already extensive work involved in the assembly of such a volume. Consequently I feel an especially heightened gratitude to many people at MIT Press and to a group of respected and beloved friends and associates: Sandy Heck in New York and Alice Paley, Susan Livada, and Katya Furse at MIT. Still other equally valued contributions are acknowledged in the context of the appropriate essays.

People in the Physical Environment: The Urban Ecology of Streets

Stanford Anderson

Streets, in concept and in reality, accord poorly with institutionalized categories of problems and professionals. "The economy of the street" is apt to strike us as a confusion of categories, even though every specialist is permitted to operate abstractly on the more inclusive environment of the city.

Graphically and conceptually the city is readily abstracted as a point or a field. Even the simplest representation of a street — a line necessarily marked with points or crossings that code potential arrival, movement, events, and access — is an index of the immediacy and insistent multiple readings of these urban spaces. The intermediate position of streets in the environment, intersecting public and private, individual and society, movement and place, built and unbuilt, architecture and planning, demands that simultaneous attention be given to people, the physical environment, and their numerous interrelations.

Consequently, the studies of this book do not take the course of reducing the street to an object that can be submitted to uniquely economic, social, physical, or cultural analysis. The ambition is rather to accept our sense of the ecological wholeness of streets — the spatial and temporal contexts within which complex events occur. Examination of this system may then contribute to a similar understanding of the city.

The rich texture of activities and significances associated with streets reinforces the difficulty but also the potential of a sociophysical examination of them. Streets are integral parts of our movement and communication networks; they are the places where many of our conflicts or resolutions between public and private claims are accessed or actually played out; they are the arenas where the boundaries of conventional and aberrant behavior are frequently redrawn. Although there are currently no means for dealing comprehensively with such a complex phenomenon, the studies reported here are, nevertheless, inquiries within the context of the multiple, interactive conditions that give rise to the complexities and ambiguities of the street. Rather than delineations of strictly constrained subproblems, these studies are a series of sketches for the methods and content of an ecology of streets. A relative emphasis on the street as a component of the physical environment accords with the potential contribution of an inquiry originated and conducted by architects, but does not imply a priority of this aspect within the entire system studied. I readily accept the reciprocities of users and their environments. Nevertheless, the belief that architects aggrandize themselves by conceiving their works to be powerfully deterministic of social behavior has such currency that it must be met at the outset.

An Architectural Inquiry Without Architectural Determinism?

Exaggeration of the significance of one's own field is one of the dangers of the specialization of disciplines. There have been so-called environmentalists (naive geographical determinists), naive economic determinists, and naive cultural determinists. As one finds such unilateral explanations inadequate, so one should also deplore architectural determinism. Still, in their ardor to correct architects on this point, social scientists may discourage inquiries into more subtle concepts of the interaction of people with the physical environment. The denunciation of such efforts as nonsense[1] traces less to a study of environment than to a destructive categorization of professional activities which grossly separates architects from social scientists. Robert Gutman, for example, perceives "the social role of the architect as practitioner and decision maker" as opposed to the "scholarly, academic, and scientific role of the behavioral scientist."[2] This failure to conceive of an architect reflecting critically on his activities or of a behavioral scientist playing a social role obscures the fact that both disciplines engage broad, intersecting ranges of human experience, thought, and production. Still more than the disciplines themselves, the environments within which they work and to which they refer are resistant to such antisystemic claims of the independence of elements. Ruling out a search for the interaction of physical with social, cultural, and cognitive factors as nonsense is dogmatic, encouraging the very professional chauvinism it purports to attack.

Similarly, Herbert Gans may appear to dismiss the physical environment as a factor in human situations:

. . . the physical environment has much less effect than planners imagine. Often it is thought to impinge, but people evade this effect through . . . "nonconforming use," that is, an evasion of the impingement in order to maintain or achieve behavior patterns that are in line with their predispositions. The social environment has considerably more effect.[3]

Upon consideration, however, Gans may be an architectural determinist. The concept of *nonconforming use* implies the existence of a recognized *conforming use*. A preferable account might well be that people choose to act innovatively within an environment that supports, or at least permits, both traditional and other activities.

It may be hypothesized that, happily, only rare, very special environments, if any, have physically determined conforming uses. Rather, physical environments allow ranges of activities and significances which are bounded by what are usually broad limits of the possible, successively narrowed to those uses and meanings that may be socioculturally coincident, collaborative, or symbiotic within the environment. These successive constraints are indeed of cultural or social origin, though interactive with the important issues of whether the physical environment suggested, supported, or merely tolerated newly defined uses.

Even the conforming use of a coffin is not determined by its physical form alone. Humor and horror movies remind us that one may sleep or lurk or eavesdrop or be smuggled in a coffin. Yet there are limits to the range of events that may occur in that environment. Its physical size and proportions, and the accretion of culturally constrained choices of materials and colors and symbols, assure that this environment will be selected only under certain unusual conditions of danger or radical gesture or madness — and will be understood by others as such. If, as here, environments do have a conforming use, they are to be explained by the interaction of physical and nonphysical variables. Rarely, if ever, will any one factor such as motivation, overt behavior, cultural norms, or physical characteristics determine use and meaning; but it is worth knowing what constraints are imposed by each factor and what may have been made possible by the constraints themselves. Indeed, as Gans's example suggests, the physical environment will ordinarily permit, and perhaps reinforce, a range of liberating actions outside any received system of social constraints.

Thus the concern of these studies is not to salvage either functionalism or determinism but to move toward a situation where one can better understand the interactions of factors — cognitive, cultural, social, psychological, environmental factors — that are involved in the relationships of people with their environments.

A more challenging concern than that of purely architectural determinism is whether the entire sociocultural system (including the physical environments it creates) is coercive of individuals and of society. Should not the concern be to destroy all constraints rather than merely to understand patterns of interactive constraints? Conceptually, this thorough subversion of the status quo has its appeal, yet the historical evidence suggests there are limits to the rate of both physical and cultural change. An ecological approach suggests itself as a way of avoiding blind commitment to the status quo while defining the conditions and rates of noncatastrophic or more protectively defined change.[4]

An Ecological Approach to People and the Physical Environment

Prominent branches of the social sciences maintain an unfamiliar, or even antagonistic, relation to the possibility that the physical environment is an operative factor in human relations. The ecological sciences, however, take as their field of study systems that include organisms and their environments. How helpful is the tradition of these sciences in addressing these questions?: Does the physical environment become an operative variable in the human ecological situation? If so, how? And how can these matters be investigated?

Early writings on human ecology, often emphasizing urban life, are those of the Chicago School of Robert Ezra Park, E. W. Burgess, R. D. McKenzie, and others. McKenzie defined human ecology as "a study of the spatial and temporal relations of human beings as affected by the selective, distributive and accommodative forces of the environment."[5] While distinguishing human ecology from animal ecology by the necessity of accounting for purposive action, McKenzie also stressed that the collective effects of individual actions — thus including most aspects of the city — are neither designed nor anticipated. This understanding that purposive actions also establish unintended systemic relations is a crucial insight[6] that must be constantly reasserted even if, for Park and McKenzie, it partially obscured both cultural forces and the individual within a study dominated by spatially arrayed economic relationships.[7] As this implies, the Chicago School treated the physical environment as a spatiotemporal field; thus even these ecologists largely failed to reveal the physical environment as an operative factor in human systems. Indeed, the latter part of McKenzie's article turns to surprisingly general observations on the growth of American towns.

Working in the tradition of the Chicago school, James Quinn recognized at least seven types of inquiry that had come under the rubric of human ecology.[8] The types ranged from studies that merely showed spatial distribution of social phenomena (a necessary but insufficient defining element) to the notion of an inclusive synthesis of the human sciences that aspired to an understanding of human beings and the environment and the relationships between people and the environment as "one definitely integrated whole."[9] Only the latter definition implicitly includes both the recognition of human beings as unique, volitional, cultural beings and an account of the environment that treats it as a physical and operative entity rather than merely as a socially differentiated field. These successive encouragements to an ever more inclusive characterization of the human environment are so correctly ambitious that even this tradition of human ecology provides more inspiration than guidance for the understanding of the possible relations of people with their physical environments.

William Michelson makes this last point still more emphatically and ascribes this failing of human ecology to, among other things, an incomplete conceptualization of the environment (treating space as a medium rather than as an ecological variable) and a fixation on aggregates (rather than individuals or small groups occupying specific places).[10] Michelson establishes an important position in calling for a study of people and the urban environment within what he calls an *intersystem congruence model*.[11] Equally important is his assertion that the most neglected parts of such a model are the concepts and techniques that would permit the description and analysis of the physical environment as one subsystem of the model.

Within a context that retains the awareness that space is a social product not only in the local, sentimental sense but also in the broadest political sense, the intention in this volume is to contribute to the closing of these gaps in the theory and method of human or, I would prefer to say, cultural ecology.[12]

The Physical Environment as the Setting for Sympatric Relations

Relative to human ecology, some animal ecologists give more detailed attention to the physical environment. Similarly, they also do greater justice to some interorganism relations, the parallels of which may be important for urban ecology.

The notion of territoriality, transferred from ethology, has played an increasingly prominent role in human ecology and in more narrowly defined studies of architecture. As in A. E. Parr's definition of territory, "space which an individual or close-knit group will defend,"[13] the concept necessarily involves a principle of competitive exclusion. Ethologists, however, have pointed to two extreme types of territory or "niche specificity." "In one the animal . . . requires to be spatially separate from its closest allies and competitors. . . . In the other the various species are structurally specialized to use different resources; they do not need to have behavioral mechanisms fixing them in place and in fact cross each other's paths."[14] Ecological sympatry, the sharing of the same region by different kinds of organism, is thus a concomitant of the description of territories. In the second type of niche specificity, competitive exclusion of one organism by another operates selectively, relative to only certain aspects of, or more specialized locales within, the environment. In spatial terms, the first type of niche specificity suggests a mosaic of defended areas; the second, a complex set of overlapping and variously defined networks and areas.

The literature developing the notion of territoriality among humans is by now extensive and includes diffuse formulations.[15] Consequently one cannot be categorical, yet the overwhelming dominance in this literature is of the more exclusionary pole of territoriality — the organism requiring "to be spatially separate from its closest allies and competitors." Perhaps this is not so surprising in those studies emphasizing the "body territory" that each organism carries with it. Even here the common image of body space as a bubble encourages attention to an exclusive space with its possible relations of resistance, deformation, and destruction rather than to a more nuanced space that also allows accommodation and sympatry.

It is still more remarkable that the strictly exclusionary pole should dominate the literature that examines territoriality in broader social relations. Goffman introduces certain complexities such as aggregation,

possession in the name of a collectivity, and the temporal discriminations involved in the possession of the space of a stall or the taking of a turn. His closest approximation to sympatry is in his recognition of space that is claimed by use; but it is passed over in a paragraph and the example is a particularly exclusionary one. The emphasis is always on possession and exclusion even if these qualities are now given a time dimension.[16] Hall reveals a fundamental mistrust of our cities, "our urban sinks." As a hope for the future he offers an encomium to Marina City (which, despite its name, is a pair of towers rising from a single set of platforms) in Chicago: "You don't need to go outside for anything."[17] The unstated, antisympatric, antisocial, antiurban corrollary of this ideal is "And others should stay in their exclusionary territories as well."

This tradition, together with the pressing problem of personal safety in some urban environments, encourages the formalization of exclusive territories in the city, as in Oscar Newman's *Defensible Space: Crime Prevention Through Urban Design*.[18] One must concede that strictly exclusionary territoriality does operate at some level for every organism, and Newman is addressing an immediate problem which may require that this trait be reinforced by specific provisions in the physical environment. Still, the way in which territoriality has entered the literature on human relations reflects both a cultural and a related intellectual bias. Intellectually, one observes the recurrence of notions such as architecturally determined behavior, functionally determined architecture, and strictly exclusionary territoriality (the requisite photograph of birds perched at equal distances from one another). The fervor of asserting or denying these positions rather than searching for a more articulate account of events reveals a fundamentally behaviorist prejudice searching for clear-cut cause and effect relations.

A proposal to analyze complex, interactive structures involving cognitive and cultural, as well as more tangible factors of environment and behavior, sounds — and is — complex. The recognition of sympatric relations of differentiated individuals, nuanced by intellect and will, has a sophisticated and urbane ring to it. An approach built on such notions is not the straightforward American defense of the individual — equal men with equal, identifiable shares. On the contrary, such an approach sympathetically studies exactly that which gives the city strength: an organized society of structurally specialized individuals who, to a significant degree, use different resources, provide different benefits, and appreciate different goods.

The homesteaders, spreading across this country — each family unit on its 160 acres and, at the outset, as self-sufficient as possible — provide the model for American individualism. As long as these people possessed and exploited the same resources, and cultural or social differentiation was slight, they were indeed one kind that could profit little and lose much from any erosion of their competitively exclusionary quarter-sections. Nevertheless, these agrarian settlements soon differentiated themselves. In contrast, recent suburban subdivisions with stratified social groups emulate, but provide only a degenerate form of, the original agrarian territoriality.

However true it may be that one of the needs of the city dweller is to be whole and to participate in a genuine and shared humanity, it is also a uniquely human quality that we have been able to differentiate ourselves, forming intricate, contributive, and challenging structures of society and culture. City dwellers individually and cities as environmental phenomena are the most dramatic manifestations of this aspect of human beings. If one is to construct analogies to territoriality in ethology, then, along with defensive territoriality (which operates primarily intraspecies), one must also emphasize the analogy with a complementary, interactive, even symbiotic territoriality (which operates, with patterns of conflict and competition as well as cooperation, among various kinds). Much of urban society, and perhaps even more in the possible and desirable urban society, is best analogized to this ecological sympatry.

There have been intimations of this point of view in the sociological literature. Park and Burgess recognized at least coexistence within the same region under the term commensalism.[19] Lyman and Scott recognize three types of territory beyond people's body space: public, home (club would be closer to their examples), and interactional territory. However, for these authors, the two latter territories are heavily constrained by explicit or implicit rules of access and egress while public territory remains rather amorphous in its characterization.[20] It is Hall who, in a statement that seemingly cannot be reconciled with his Marina City model, more happily advocates:

> One of man's most critical needs, therefore is for principles for designing spaces that will maintain a healthy density, a healthy interaction rate, a proper amount of involvement, and a continuing sense of ethnic identification. The creation of such principles will require the combined efforts of many diverse specialists all working closely together on a massive scale.[21]

In addition to the sympatric sense of this statement, it also evokes another important ecological principle — homeostasis, the self-maintenance of the system. While Hall's example suggests the cycling maintenance of what is globally the same system, such stability is not a necessary implication of a concern for homeostatic environments. Homeostasis may also be described in terms of a stable trajectory (as in an ecological succession; e.g., natural reforestation) in which there is an evolution of significantly different states.[22]

In suggesting an ecological approach to the understanding of people in their environments, there remains the danger of being interpreted as naively transposing studies of plant and animal communities to human communities, or of engaging primarily in behaviorist inquiries. Perhaps one must say again that people and the environments that they shape and use establish mutually interactive volitional, symbolic, cognitive systems manifested both at the level of the individual and in a hierarchy of social constructs. Although initial reference to the ecology of plants and animals is analogical, requiring appropriate transformation to accord with the volitional and cultural aspects of human communities, people are, nevertheless, organisms situated in environments, with reference to whom there can be a properly constituted ecology. For example, a hypothesis that suggests both continuities and discontinuities between plant ecology and cultural ecology would be that ecological succession is a valuable concept in both fields while cultural factors may preclude the transferral of the notion of a climax state. While research into such questions requires both hypotheses from whatever source and analytic divisions of the communities under study, the suggestiveness of the ecological approach remains its insistence on the extension of the notion of system as far as the community under study may require.

The preceding sections set a series of problems of descending generality that are summarized in the following paragraphs.

Beyond the ambition to understand various aspects of individuals and human associations (social, economic, cultural, cognitive, psychological, environmental), one must also seek to understand the interactions of these factors. I conceive this to be the problem of human, or cultural, ecology, which could be described more fully as: the theory and relational study of human activities and their products (including, but not limited to, signifying activities) within both their spatiotemporal environment and their inclusive organizing cultural universe (both of which universes are systemically interactive with one another and with particular activities and products).

To the extent that human ecology draws on the ethological concept of territoriality, the notion should receive critical examination in the context of human association, giving special attention to the complex, interactive territoriality of ecological sympatry. This would seem to be especially important for patterns of urban association.

Various forms of homeostasis in human communities should be studied, including the role of the environment in setting or relaxing the constraints that operate in such self-regulation.

Within the systemic study of people in the environment, the role of the physical environment deserves concerted investigation without the a priori assumption that such an inquiry automatically assigns priority to physical factors. Indeed, the hypothesis that calls for refinement and examination claims only that (1) the physical environment sets some, usually broad, limits to its possible uses and signification, and (2) that these limits may be significantly and progressively restricted through the impingement of cultural, social, and other factors.

The preceding ambitions for explanatory and projective capacities within human ecology require the development of adequately articulated techniques for the description of the physical environment and of human habitation within that environment.

The first three more general issues are given further consideration in the last part of this chapter (not including a further sketch of the more ambitious notions about cultural ecology, for that would be beyond the scope of this book). More specific explorations in the description and explanation of the urban environment are presented in my chapter on an ecological model of the urban environment.

Sympatry and Change in Community Relations; Robustness and Resilience in Environments: Toward an Account of the Form, Use, and Significance of the Physical Environment

Preceding sections reject concepts of functionally determined form or architecturally determined behavior. Recognizing inclusive, sympatric relations of people in the environment, one requires a model that will accommodate a loose fit among form, activity, and significance while also moving toward greater specificity in such notions as range of use, environmental support or inhibition, and limits of coexistent or symbiotic use.

These notions are reinforced by other observers, among them the highly sensitized psychological and social critic, R. D. Laing:

The physical environment unremittingly offers possibilities of experiences, or curtails them. The fundamental human significance of architecture stems from this. The glory of Athens, as Pericles so lucidly stated, and the horror of so many features of the modern megalopolis is the former enhances and the latter constricts man's consciousness.[23]

Physical environment as a source of support or inhibition is embedded in the work of the sociologist Herbert Gans too, even though he is among those who have argued that the physical environment has "little impact on the behavior patterns and values of people."[24] Gans's basic argument addresses itself to priorities. His primary attack devolves on economic, social, and political planners who deploy scarce resources for such questionable goals as new middle-class housing situated in urban areas where it must displace people who already have smaller resources and fewer opportunities. Gans also questions, but only at a secondary level, whether the physical planning of such projects is advantageous even for those "privileged" to receive the new units.

There is little doubt that public planning must be reassessed. Yet, irrespective of that reassessment, current inadequacies and maldistributions, together with changing demands, will require that the physical environment be restructured. One can quickly demonstrate that even Gans would agree that it *does* matter what is restructured and how it is done.

Gans's program was to make planning more responsive to people's needs by adjusting a perceived imbalance among the many types of planners. He saw physical planners as powerful and elitist; consequently, he is tendentious about physical planning. Emphasizing his own differences with physical planners, Gans relates:

. . . when I studied people and communities, it turned out that their notion of the good life also had little to do with land uses, public feasibilities, and expressways; they were concerned about work, income, health, family, neighbors, friends, church, and, if they were homeowners, space, comfort, status, and property values.[25]

Gans's distinction between the concerns of planners and those of people relies heavily on the distinction between what, in this context, are specific, denotative words such as *work, family,* and *church,* and an abstract term such as *land use*. If land use is, for example, translated back to schools and food shops, and thence to education and food acquisition, we have items that are also of major concern to people. Conversely, within Gans's list of people's concerns, at least *space* is a central concern of physical planners. Finally, Gans would have to agree that people are not indifferent to the existence and location of expressways.[26] In sum, Gans insinuates a generic conflict between people and physical planners when, at most, his evidence suggests the much more limited conclusion that planners may often be insufficiently aware of the relationship of their abstract terms to the specific needs of people.

At a deeper level, Gans's argument is still weaker. It is not only the planners' concepts that are artifacts. The people's notions of good life, work, income, even health and space — Gans's entire list — are social products that must be constantly reexamined for themselves and especially for their possible change or inversion in relation to a changing cultural universe. We constantly reconstruct these apparent simples of our social life; we also reaffirm these simples and use them to constrain more global change. The planner is not in possession of the answers, but neither are the people in possession of simple and immutable goods. We need discourse; we need one another.

Almost in spite of himself, Gans recurrently acknowledges the importance of physical planning. In an attack on those physical planners who support, and thereby extend, suburbia on the grounds that such arrangements constitute the societal norm, Gans asserts that some people prefer high-density urbanism. Clearly our society does not have a single norm, and one cannot allow for, or realize, such social choices without the development of physical alternatives.

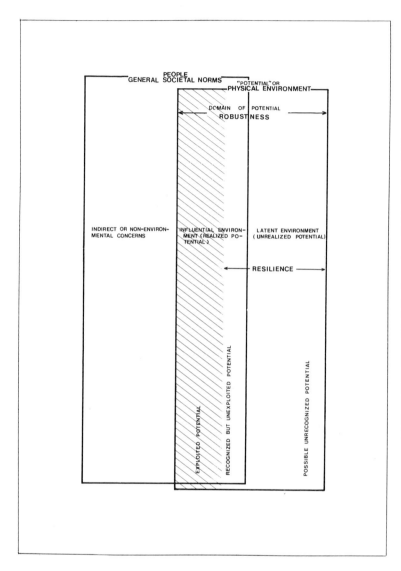

At a more detailed level, Gans wrote:

A park is a physical environment of flora, fauna, walkways, and facilities that are based on decisions about the way society or the planner defines a desirable park. Consequently, it is much more important to decide whose culture will be reflected in the planner's scheme than what kinds of material object will be incorporated into the park.[27]

The logical conclusion from these statements is not that one neglects physical planning but that one attempts to bring the physical environment and the culture of the users into greater congruence. One cannot separate the decisions of "whose culture" from the decisions on "choice and arrangement" of physical elements. At a deeper level, beyond the polemics, that seems to be Gans's position, too. Setting the polemic aside, then, one can profitably adapt several of Gans's formulations as hypotheses of people's relations to the physical environment.

Potential, Effective or Influential, and Latent Environments

In any given context there is a social system with its sets of societal values and norms that defines and evaluates "portions of the physical environment relevant to the lives of people involved, and structures the way people will use (and react to) this environment in their daily lives."[28]

The physical environment is an arena for *potential* actions and interpretations. This "potential environment" is reinterpreted by each user, thus yielding his or her subjective environment — the environment that is *effective* (or influential) for that person. Among the many members of a society, the patterns of use and meaning that are interdependent with the physical environment yield an intersubjective "effective (or influential) environment."

Returning to his example of the park, Gans argues:

. . . it is not the park alone but the functions and meanings which the park has for the people who are exposed to it that affect the achievement or nonachievement of the planner's aims. The park proposed by the planner is only a *potential environment*; the social system and culture of the people who will use it determine to what extent the park becomes an *effective environment*. Without the park, the emotional and aesthetic benefits predicted by the planner cannot be made available, but without use of the park by the people for whom it is planned, these benefits cannot be achieved either.[29]

Figure 1, in aiding the conceptualization of the environments posited by Gans, also leads to the conceptualization of an unrealized potential, or latent environment. Thus we have:

Potential environment. The physical environment; an arena for potential actions and interpretations. The extent of this potential might be termed the *robustness* of the environment.

1. Social and physical environments yield influential and latent environments.

Influential environment. The realized potential environment; that version of the potential environment that is manifestly or implicitly adopted by users. In this book dealing with the communally shared space of the street, "influential environment" will be used in a societal, intersubjective sense unless the context clearly indicates an individual's subjective influential environment. The potential environment must be presumed to divide into realms of exploited potential and recognized but unexploited potential. Such consciously unexploited potential may inflect our relations within the influential environment.

Latent environment. The unrealized potential environment; the degree of this latency together with the recognized but unexploited potential within the influential environment might be termed the *resilience* of the environment. Latency can be increased (or decreased) by physical change. Its availability and potential significance for society can be researched and communicated to society.

These environments permit some observations on how the physical environment relates to other concerns set out in this chapter.

The notion of multiple influential environments denies the concept of physical determinism. Within the same physical place, different individuals have different influential environments.[30] Similarly, the intersubjective influential environment of society changes over time without necessarily changing the physical form. The concept of multiple influential environments implies both that activity and significance are interdependent with the physical environment and that this is not a deterministic relation.

In turn, these observations on multiple, nondeterministic relations with the environment imply that the potential and influential environments will rarely approach coincidence (or "fit," as design method would have it).

Latency then assumes great importance. Latency in the environment allows for societal change without physical change. What can one know about the latent environment? In an extant environment, one person's influential environment may reveal what is latent for another. These differences may allow for noncompetitive sympatric relations. They may also teach us about opportunities that may result in new relations. Truly aberrant or innovative behavior may reveal an unexploited potential for the whole of society. Change over time yields historical information on environmental potential which may be currently unexploited. But can we discover previously unknown potential in an existing environment, or predict how proposed physical changes may decrease, increase, or otherwise alter latency? If this is to be accomplished, we need concepts and techniques for analysis of the physical environment itself, since behavioral studies can obviously come only after the fact. That is, we are encouraged to develop analytic capacities because the most inclusive of these environments, the potential environment, is more closely allied with the physical environment than with any set of behavior patterns. A means of describing physical environment in and for itself, independent of use, offers, in addition to methodological clarity, the best approach to recognizing and projecting environments with unexploited meanings and use.[31]

If it is assumed that a high degree of latency is desirable in the environment, how does one recognize these environments and how do they come about? One thing is sure: they are not environments with strictly prescribed use and meaning. Expressways, like the coffin, are such limited environments that they resemble instruments, highly constrained for specific utilitarian purposes. They may well continue to provide this instrumental service, or they may obsolesce. It is difficult to imagine more than a small part of the expressways evolving into another use.[32] Many old buildings and city sectors, with complex patterns of use and still more complex histories, provide examples of environments with high degrees of latency. Especially in the case of city sectors, these are rarely designed environments, but rather artifacts in the sense mentioned earlier — the products of human action, but not of human design.[33] These evolved environments, adjusting piece by piece over time to changing demands of use or signification, elude any globally prescribed use and meaning while incorporating many stimulating and sustaining parts.

One can design instruments and one can receive and manipulate artifacts; but can one design environments that meet, but are not constrained by, initial purpose? The answer is surely yes. Contributive, perhaps necessary, factors are complexity and articulation that allow for multiple and changing uses and meanings while also having the specificity to encourage and sustain them. Such environments can support the multiple and overlapping patterns of ecological sympatry. This resilience at any moment can also operate over time and thus contribute to a condition of homeostasis despite an extensive restructuring of activities within the environment.[34] Instances for the study of these notions occur in various environments at the scale of buildings that combine both articulation and a rich, ordered, but nonrepetitive, complexity.[35] The discussion of Savannah, in my chapter on an ecological model of the urban environment, begins an examination of this issue at the scale of the city, reinforcing the importance of articulation but suggesting that the design of an environment of high potential and latency (a robust and resilient environment, effective in terms of both sympatry and dynamic homeostasis) does not rely on inordinate complexity.

The relation of the description of physical form to activity and significance can be restated in the following way. The physical environment, as it exists at any point in time (but storing time reference information as well), is the potential environment. It is characterized by

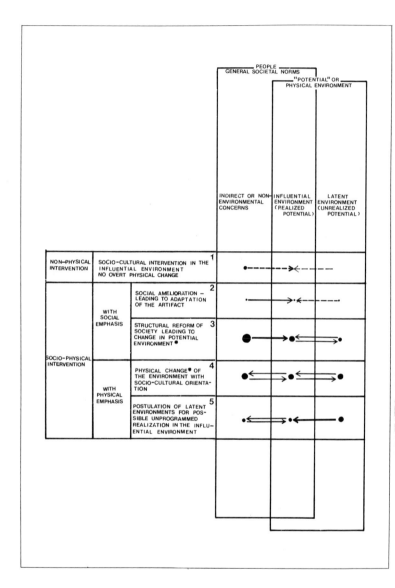

2. Types of planning intervention for change of the influential environment.

limits of activity and significance even if these can rarely be given an unalterable description. The influential environment is the actually observed pattern of use and meaning. This pattern relative to alternatives (that is, relative to the latency or resilience in the environment) is to be accounted for by its, to borrow Michelson's term,[36] "congruence" with other variables in the system (for example, law or tradition decrees that environments of this form are used in a particular way).

It may then be desirable to elaborate congruence into a number of more specific relations; for example, a space of certain ample dimensions and such and such other physical characteristics may have a virtually unlimited potential; given one limited use it may be capable of sustaining the relatively independent *coincidence* of a large but not indefinite number of other activities; its use as a church, for example, may establish levels of previously unrecognized meanings that are mutually reinforcing or *collaborative* between the environment itself and its use; its use for other kinds of large, sustained gatherings may make the purveying of food a requisite, *symbiotic* activity.[37]

This model of interacting physical and social environments also suggests some observations on modes of intervention. Giving particular attention to the influential environment, which can be changed by action on either the social or the physical environment, figure 2 reviews five types of environmental intervention:

Nonphysical intervention
   1. Sociocultural intervention in the influential environment leading to no overt physical change.
Sociophysical intervention with social emphasis
   2. Social amelioration leading to *adaptation* (physical amelioration) of the artifact.
   3. Structural reform of society leading to environmental
         restructuring
         or
         reformulation
Sociophysical intervention with physical emphasis
   4. Physical
         restructuring
         or
         reformulation
of the environment with sociocultural orientation.
   5. Postulation of latent environments for possible unprogrammed realization in the influential environment.

Of these five categories perhaps the most useful for an understanding of the recent past are the third and fourth: the difference between two and three may be defined as one of degree of intended social change, while categories one and five, the one purely social in its scope and the other physical/formal with previously unexplored social consequences, may be seen as extreme types bounding the middle categories.

In the modern period, the most ambitious positions classified under three and four — those subclassified as reformulations — were the province of social philosophers and architectural idealists respectively. The former sought to understand the physical environmental implications of the new social worlds they invented or struggled to realize, and even went further to say that the physical building of these worlds in architectural and urban form would, through the effects of the new environment on the user, tend to generate their desired society. The latter proposed new spatial and formal orders for cities, types of new environments that were conceived as social condensers — the agents of social change. The two more moderate positions concerning the restructuring of society or the physical order were perhaps the most typical modes of intervention, and usually remain, to planners and society alike, the most acceptable procedures.[38]

Figure 2 gives a graphic representation to these modes of intervention. At the right the two sets of social and physical environments are intersected to yield the common subset of the "influential environment" and also the subset of the latent environment (as in Figure 1). These boxes are crosscut by the five interventions. The dots and arrows at the right crudely sketch typical relations as follows:

Intervention 1 (Nonphysical). The action taken is directed to the social realm and has its impact on the influential environment without changing the physical environment. Since this change in the influential environment could be the fuller realization of the potential in the physical environment, there can be a shift from the latent environment to realized potential.

Intervention 2 (Social Amelioration). A modest approach that intends to ameliorate social problems. This is usually action taken with a modicum of social concern and with some intent to adapt the artifact. Here too the latent environment may be tapped or even slightly altered, but this is not an intent.

Intervention 3 (Structural Reform of Society). An ambitious approach that includes, but is not limited to, utopians. Fundamental interventions directed to social, political, and economic concerns, but with the awareness that the physical environment is interlocked with these structures. Thus change in the influential and latent environments is expected and even sought.

Intervention 4 (Physical Change with Social Awareness). The approach that encompasses the typical interventions of architects at their more enlightened moments — immediately directed to the physical environment but with intention to maintain awareness of the interactive sociophysical environment.

Intervention 5 (Postulation of Latent Environments). Action is intentionally directed to the latent environment — altering and usually increasing that latency in the interest of society's uncoerced, unprogrammed use of that latency.

In summary, four related points should be reemphasized. Within the inclusive definition of human or cultural ecology, a subcategory of urban ecology may be conceived that would examine the interrelations of people, their activities, and the urban environment. The principal concern of architects and physical planners is to improve what is currently a weak aspect of this field: the ability to describe and offer explanatory hypotheses about the physical environment as a variable within the total urban system.

The concept of sympatry assists in moving architects and social scientists from a static, defensive description of people in the city to a description that accounts for intersecting networks of relationships within the structured field of the physical city.

Homeostasis is fundamental to the continuity of a system; it can be defined dynamically in terms of a stable trajectory. Homeostasis is thus a concept that need not reinforce the status quo. However, the more dynamic we project or wish the social situation to be, the more the concept of homeostasis reinforces the importance of a robust and resilient environment.

Finally, the concept of environments that reveal variously employed robustness and unemployed resilience (or latency) breaks the determinist modes of architecturally determined activity or functionally determined architecture. It accords, rather, with the complex relations of sympatry and homeostasis, including the potential relations that are not currently realized. Through these several concepts we begin to be able to explain the environment without destructive oversimplifications.

Notes

In addition to work begun under a grant from the John Simon Guggenheim Foundation and continued as part of the "Streets Project" at the Institute for Architecture and Urban Studies under the sponsorship of the United States Department of Housing and Urban Development, I have had the privilege of continuing these studies in the Urban Ecology Program of the Department of Architecture at the Massachusetts Institute of Technology with support from the Ernest A. Grunsfeld Memorial Fund in Chicago. As the text evidences, I use "urban ecology" not primarily in the sense of the city in its natural setting but rather considering the city as a human environment that should be understood ecologically.

1. Participants in the work reported in this volume recurrently encountered the misunderstandings, verging on mistrust, between physical designers and social scientists. Usually this mistrust traced to the presumption of the other participant's tendency to conceptualize the entire system according to one professional insight. Robert Gutman, one of the contributors to this volume, criticized the "nonsense" of some of his collaborating architects (particularly the author of this chapter) with this assessment:

> The belief that design by itself can create community life, what is often referred to as "architectural determinism," is firmly lodged in the minds of many architects. Social research has overwhelmingly demonstrated that this doctrine is naive, yet it does not disappear. To some architects, the persistence of the idea indicated that if it were only restated or if research were only better designed, the idea would turn out to be valid. I believe this view is nonsense. (Robert Gutman, "The Street Generation," mimeo [New Brunswick, N.J.: Rutgers College, Department of Sociology, 1973], pp. 26-7.)

On the other hand, such sociological orthodoxy has resulted in the incompatible beliefs that the physical environment is simultaneously of little significance to human relations and that buildings designed by architects often seriously aggravate the human condition (as evidenced by the official dynamiting of modern apartment buildings in St. Louis).

I would like to make clear that I am not defending the architectural or planning professions toward which I also have a critical position. I am insisting that the physical environment will be changed, that it matters how we do (or do not) change it, and that we consequently need informed amateurs in the best sense of that word (among whom we may be fortunate to count some professionals).

The ambition of this work remains that of encouraging the replacement of determinism by relational principles and thus contributing to the conditions for a more reasonable collaboration of all people concerned with the sociophysical environment. Samuel Z. Klausner, *On Man in His Environment* (San Francisco: Jossey-Bass, 1971), provides a general discussion of the competing literatures of determinism as against "negotiation between man and environment." I am indebted to Aristide Esser for drawing my attention to this work as I completed this manuscript.

2. Robert Gutman, "The Questions Architects Ask," in his *People and Buildings* (New York: Basic Books, 1972), p. 338.

3. Herbert Gans, *People and Plans* (New York: Basic Books, 1963), p. 19. This is an idée fixe for Gans which by 1969 (and again 1974) took two forms in his writing that raise some question about the objectivity with which the issue is being engaged: "There is considerable evidence that the physical environment does not play as significant a role in people's lives as the planner believes." On the facing page, "Although research on the effects of the physical environment is still sparse, the data indicate so far that these effects are not as great as the planner believes." Gans, "Planning for People, not Buildings," in Frederick Sargent II, M.D., ed., *Human Ecology* (New York: American Elsevier, 1974), pp. 312-313. Gutman and Gans are not making sophisticated distinctions between the urban physical environment generally and architecture in a more limited sense — even if they do sometimes lash out at elitism among architects. Since our concern is streets, which only exceptionally are (and still less frequently remain) unilateral design objects, the general notion of physical environment seems preferable. The relation of evolved artifacts and design objects is, however, considered later.

4. A brief, concrete statement on the possible contribution of ecology to planning is that of C. S. Holling and M. A. Goldberg, "Ecology and Planning," *Journal of the American Institute of Planners*, 37 (1971), pp. 221-230.

5. R. D. McKenzie, "The Ecological Approach to the Study of Human Community," *American Journal of Sociology*, 30 (November 1924), pp. 287-301; reprinted in R. E. Park, et al., *The City* (Chicago: University of Chicago Press, 1925), pp. 47-62. See also Park and Burgess, eds., *Introduction to the Science of Society* (Chicago: University of Chicago Press, 1921), where the term *human ecology* was apparently introduced.

6. An insight that one encounters in Hayek's consideration of artifacts as products of human action but not of design. See F. A. Hayek, *Studies in Philosophy, Politics and Economics* (London: Routledge and Kegan Paul, 1967), pp. 96-105. With relation to the physical environment, see S. Anderson, "Environment as Artifact: Methodological Implications," *Casabella*, no. 359-360 (December 1971), pp. 71-77.

7. Milla Aïssa Alihan, *Social Ecology* (New York, 1938), and Walter Firey, *Land Use in Central Boston* (Cambridge, Mass.: Harvard University Press, 1947). Firey properly insists on the historically and culturally defined attachments of certain communities to certain areas of Boston; but, as the term *land use* in his title suggests, he still offers only a primitive sense of the physical environment as anything more than a spatiotemporal field differentiated by sociocultural energies.

8. James A. Quinn, *Human Ecology* (New York: Prentice-Hall, 1950), pp. 5-11.

9. This most inclusive view Quinn assigned uniquely to the botanist J. W. Bews, *Human Ecology* (London: Oxford University Press, 1935).

10. William Michelson, *Man and His Urban Environment* (Reading, Mass.: Addison-Wesley, 1970), pp. 17 ff. Despite these reservations, due consideration should be given to the contributions of: Maurice Halbwachs, *Morphologie sociale* (Paris: Armand Colin, 1938); A. Kardiner, et al., *The Individual and His Society* (New York: Columbia University Press, 1939); Firey, *Land Use* (1947); Amos H. Hawley, *Human Ecology* (New York: Ronald Press, 1950); Julian Steward, *Theory of Culture Change* (Urbana: University of Illinois Press, 1955); W. Firey, *Man, Mind and Land* (New York: Free Press, 1960); Leo F. Schnore, *The Urban Scene: Human Ecology and Demography* (New York: Free Press, 1965); Roger G. Barker, *Ecological Psychology* (Stanford: Stanford University Press, 1969); A. H. Hawley, *Urban Society* (New York: Ronald Press, 1971).

For further bibliography, see Otis Dudley Duncan and Leo F. Schnore, "Cultural, Behavioral and Ecological Perspectives in the Study of Social Organization," *American Journal of Sociology*, LXV (1959), pp. 132-146; the bibliographical notes of a recent reader, R. H. Moos and P. M. Insel, *Issues in Social Ecology, Human Milieus* (Palo Alto: National Press, 1974), and Michelson, *Man and His Urban Environment*.

11. Michelson, *Man and His Urban Environment*, pp. 23 ff. Although Michelson does not develop his "intersystem congruence model" in detail, I read his intent to be an operational, research-oriented characterization of the inclusive definition of human ecology presented in the preceding paragraph and of the position advocated in the preceding section of this chapter. Andrew F. Euston of the Department of Housing and Urban Development brought my attention to Michelson's work during the final stages of preparation of this manuscript.

12. Studies that are similar to this ambition, though not necessarily using the term "ecology," are more common in Europe than in the United States; for example, in Italy the writings of architects and architectural historians such as Carlo Aymonino, Maurice Cerasi, and Manfredo Tafuri, and in France the work of the social scientists Nicole Haumont, Henri Raymond, and Marion Segaud. A convenient entry point to both these literatures is through the special number of *Architecture d'aujourd'hui*, no. 174 (July-August 1974). German historiocriticism is also revealing the interdependence of concrete environments with the cultural models within which they are shaped; for example, Reinhard Bentmann and Michael Müller, *Die Villa als Herrschaftsarchitektur* (Frankfurt a. M.: Suhrkamp, 1970); Roland Günter, "Krupp and Essen," in M. Warnke, ed., *Das Kunstwerk zwischen Wissenschaft und Weltanschauung* (Gütersloh: Bertelsmann, 1970).

13. A. E. Parr, "In Search of Theory VI," *Arts and Architecture* (September 1965), pp. 2-3.

14. G. E. Hutchinson, *The Ecological Theater and the Evolutionary Play* (New Haven: Yale University Press, 1965), p. 55, relying, in turn, on R. MacArthur and R. Levins, "Competition, Habitat Selection, and Character Displacement," *Proceedings, National Academy of Science*, 51 (1964), pp. 1207-1210. In yet another terminology, Eugene P. Odum uses *habitat* to refer to "the organism's 'address'" and employs *niche* in a still more interactive, activity-oriented sense — namely, the organism's "'profession,' biologically speaking." See his *Fundamentals of Ecology* (Philadelphia: W. B. Saunders, 1953), p. 15.

15. See: Erving Goffman, *The Presentation of Self in Everyday Life* (Garden City, N.Y.: Doubleday, 1959), *Behavior in Public Places* (New York: Free Press, 1963), *Relations in Public* (New York: Harper & Row, 1972); E.

T. Hall, *The Silent Language* (Greenwich, Conn.: Fawcett, 1959), *The Hidden Dimension* (Garden City, N.Y.: Doubleday, 1969); Robert Ardrey, *The Territorial Imperative* (New York: Dell, 1966); Stanford M. Lyman and Marvin B. Scott, "Territoriality: A Neglected Sociological Dimension," *Social Problems*, 15 (1967), pp. 236–249; Robert Sommer, *Personal Space* (Englewood Cliffs, N.J.: Prentice-Hall, 1969), *Tight Spaces* (Englewood Cliffs, N.J.: Prentice-Hall, 1974); O. M. Watson, *Proxemic Behavior: A Cross-Cultural Study* (The Hague: Mouton, 1970); A. H. Esser, ed., *Behavior and Environment* (New York: Plenum, 1971); and C. B. Bakker and M. Bakker-Rabdau, *No Trespassing!* (San Francisco: Chandler & Sharp, 1973).

16. Goffman, *Relations in Public*, pp. 57, 32 ff.

17. Hall, *Hidden Dimension*, p. 127.

18. O. Newman, *Defensible Space* (New York: Macmillan, 1972).

19. R. E. Park and E. W. Burgess, *Introduction to the Science of Sociology* (Chicago: University of Chicago Press, 1921), p. 175.

20. Lyman and Scott, "Territoriality," reprinted in Robert Gutman, *People and Buildings* (New York: Basic Books, 1972), pp. 65–82. Bakker and Bakker in *No Trespassing!* include a chapter titled "Sharing Territory with Others," but this refers to "coterritory," sharing in the exclusion of others.

21. Hall, *Hidden Dimension*, p. 168.

22. Holling and Goldberg, *JAIP* (1971), p. 225.

23. R. D. Laing, *The Politics of Experience* (Harmondsworth: Penguin, 1967), p. 28.

24. Herbert Gans, *People and Plans*, p. ix.

25. Ibid., p. 1.

26. For a notable example in Cambridge, Mass., see Robert Goodman, *After the Planners* (New York: Simon and Schuster, 1971).

27. Gans, *People and Plans*, p. 5.

28. Idem.

29. Ibid., p. 6. The present study accepts and extends Gans's concept, but hereafter uses "influential" rather than "effective" since the latter term suggests both a deterministic cause-*effect* relationship and the satisfaction of users — a condition that may or may not have been achieved. The following concept of "latency" does not occur in Gans.

30. Holling and Goldberg, *JAIP* (1971), p. 255, point out that ecological systems that survive are those with a domain of stability broad enough to absorb the consequences of change. Acknowledging that such systems sacrifice efficiency in an optimizing sense for openness to change and resilience, they suggest that planning criteria be reoriented from forces that converge on equilibrium and maximize success to those that diverge from limits and minimize the chances of disaster.

31. The importance given to the potential environment here is another obvious contrast with Gans's comment on the park as "only a potential environment" (referenced at note 27). Of course, if the park provides little service, or a disservice, I agree there is a serious inadequacy in the design. But unpredicted use by people is not bad in itself, nor does it necessarily imply the nonexistence or irrelevance of the designer's potential environment which may be realized by some people now and by many people at another time.

32. This is not to argue we should have no instruments. I would argue, however, that we should consider whether problems can be met with more general-purpose artifacts.

33. See note 6. In juxtaposing these concepts of instrument and artifact, one should recognize evolved tools such as mallets or planes, which are artifacts by the above definition but serve a prescribed use. Perhaps originally instruments, they have evolved as artifacts because of the continuous need for the same operation within contexts that have changed radically.

34. Holling and Goldberg, *JAIP* (1971), p. 229, argue that "complexity is a goal in its own right." On complexity and order, see J. Roger Bray, "Notes Toward an Ecologic Theory," *Ecology*, 39 (1958), pp. 770–776, and F. A. Hayek, "The Theory of Complex Phenomena," in Mario Bunge, *The Critical Approach to Science and Philosophy* (New York: Free Press, 1964), pp. 332–349. Also, for a bridge to systems theory, see Royston Landau, "Complexity," a special number of *Architectural Design*, 42 (October 1970).

35. This book is not the place to pursue this suggested study, but perhaps one should give it some reference. In work of recent years, some of the buildings of Louis I. Kahn come to mind. Four active architects who provide distinctly different examples of such environments are Piet Blom (his student center at the Technical University Twente at Enschede, Holland, where, however, the pieces of the environment may be too specific in use and meaning to allow for many alternative readings); Maurice Smith (his own house at Harvard, Massachusetts, where the pieces of the environment are specific to timeless human activities such as sitting, lying, gathering in various numbers, and seeking isolation, but open to changing associations and organization); Herman Hertzberger (his office building at Apeldoorn, Holland, where a repetitive but highly articulated order establishes a range of environments for selective and adaptive use); and Peter Eisenman (his house series, in which he intentionally seeks to exclude received signification as an inducement to discovering the latency of the environment in potentially new relations to life).

36. See note 11.

37. Here again there are analogous ecological formulations; for example, that the ecological amplitude of a plant is much wider than is actually found in nature, with the selectivity among potential sites explained by preference for certain communities: Rudy W. Becking, "The Zürich-Montpellier School of Phytosociology," *Botanical Review*, 23 (1957), pp. 411–488.

38. Historical examples of these types of interventions will be found in the chapter by Anthony Vidler in this book.

Streets in the Past

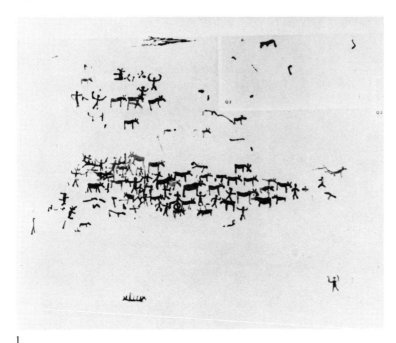

1

1. The hunted herd as road-makers. Rock carving,
Nämforsen, Sweden. [Gustaf Hallstrom in
*Monumental Art of Northern Sweden from the Stone
Age* (Stockholm: Almqvist and Wiksell, 1945), pl.
XX]

2. Paving of a Roman road, the Via Appia. After an
engraving by G. B. Piranesi, *Le Antichità Romane*
(1756). [G. B. Piranesi, *Le Antichità Romane*
(Rome, 1756), vol. 3, pl. III]

2

The Street: The Use of its History

Joseph Rykwert

For nearly a century, the street has been under persistent attack from several directions: the designers of *Siedlungen* and Garden Cities, the CIAM modern masters, and local government and welfare architects of Anglo-Saxon/Scandinavian countries have all attempted to postulate forms of urban settlement in which the street was deprived of its past function or analyzed out of existence. There has been a correlative attack by those followers of Haussmann who have subordinated all functions of urban settlement to the street itself, particularly to the street as a carrier of traffic. The most extreme of these was the Spanish urbanist, Arturo Soria y Mata, who envisaged a street-city linking Cadiz and Petersburg, Peking and Brussels; he arrogated to the street all those urban functions that it had never performed previously and therefore, like his fellows, overcharged it to the breaking point.

Soria y Mata, like so many of his contemporaries and predecessors, based his conception of the city on an analytic diagram of urban functions, dominated by transport. Such analytic diagrams, translated — usually more subtly — into vertical or horizontal schemas, underlie every concept of zoning: the taxonomic disease that has eroded all planning theory and urban utopias.

In spite of these utopian projects, building booms, and powerful technological innovations (rail, motorcar, elevator, television), the functions of the street have only been modified — not altered out of recognition — in existing cities. The expectation of daily human contact that the street uniquely offers, and offers in a pattern of exchanges without which the community would break down, is inhibited at the risk of the increasing alienation of the inhabitant from his city. The cost of this alienation is not easily calculable. It contributes to social stress generally; it generates wasted space and therefore urban blight; one of whose by-products is the rising crime rate. The community pays for this in an impoverishment of its life, in the destruction of public and private property, in the increasing cost of policing. Any cost calculation of street renewal (though this goes for urban renewal generally) in terms of fiscal effectiveness alone is shortsighted, not only socially but economically.

The state of affairs described in the last paragraph has concerned sociologists for several decades. Unfortunately, their discipline is not prescriptive: they describe, classify, determine causes. They do not solve social problems. The decisions that lead to a change in conditions are political and, to a lesser degree, formal. The sociologist cannot even tell us with any certainty what the social consequence of a given formal decision might be. He can only tell us, as a historian might, how certain social conditions and certain formal configurations of plan and volume were related in the past. Since such a relationship has existed, and in our past, he can tell us about ourselves and hope that with greater self-knowledge our political decisions might grow more mature and rational.

Paradoxically, this is particularly important at the moment because of the very strong impact of technology on street use. Both building and transport technology have had their transforming effect on it. Consequently, anyone concerned with the development of the street must postulate models for the future development of city patterns as well as street patterns. Urban renewal programs that are only remedies for street pathology are inadequate in the present situation. The urbanist must envisage the pressure he wishes to exert on technological progress in terms of his own vision of the most desirable future for the city. Of course, this raises the hoary problem of the urbanist as an elite specialist opposed to the operation of the general will. This very unreal objection need only be answered by those who equate the operation of the stock market with the general good. The urbanist is not in the position of a despot, however benevolent, but rather in that of a motorcar engineer who can choose whether he thinks it more proper to develop ever faster and larger motorcars or whether the consumer watchdog has a case and he should be thinking in terms of less powerful, smaller, safer, and cleaner vehicles. The decision — which of the two tendencies to follow — may be called economic but is ultimately political.

I should like at this point to consider what we expect of the street. The very words we use to describe it reveal something of our expectation. For the street is human movement institutionalized. An individual may clear or mark out a path in a wilderness: but unless he is followed by others, his path never becomes a road or street, because the road and the street are social institutions and it is their acceptance by the community that gives them the name and the function with which I am here concerned. The two words we use most commonly indicate a polarity. The word *street* is derived from the Latin *sternere,* to pave, and so relates to all Latin-derived words with the *str* root that are connected with building, with construction. It suggests that a surface is distinguished from its surroundings in some physical or at least notional way. It recurs in many European languages: the Italian *strada,* for instance, or the German *Strasse* suggest an area set apart for public use and can include spaces with simple, limited demarcations without necessary connections to other streets. It does not necessarily lead anywhere in particular therefore, but may finish in a plaza or in a blind alley.

Road, on the other hand, suggests movement to a destination and — incidentally — the transporting of people and commodities on foot, by pack animal, or vehicle. *Ride* is its Anglo-Saxon root (Old English *ridan*) and it denotes passage from one place to another. In this sense, it is identical with the French word *rue; via* in Latin and Italian, which is related to the Latin word *ire* and derives from the Indo-European word for bring or lead (Sanskrit *vahâmi,* from which *veho, Wagen,* and *waggon* also derive), is exactly analogous to *road* and *rue.* There are many other words to denote forms of passageway in English, as there are in other languages. All of these, however, whether described individually or classed into broader categories, elaborate the essential duality suggested by the two primary words. *Alley,* for example, always implies a narrow passage; *avenue,* a wide street with one or more lines of trees; *boulevard* again suggests a tree-lined street and is derived from the adaptation of sixteenth- and seventeenth-century defensive earthworks within the expanding street pattern of eighteenth- and nineteenth-century towns. The isolation of three groups of words suggests three different ways of considering the street.

First, terrace, row, arcade, embankment, or gallery display the way in which the street is physically constituted by its context. A second group includes words like path, track, parade, promenade, and mall, all of which are connected with ways of proceeding on foot — from picking out a route on totally unmarked ground (track), to sauntering along a well-defined, marked way, suggested by the word promenade; it even includes the walk through a path beaten by a recurrent walking game: mall.

The third and last group relates entirely to vehicular traffic and to the legal and engineering matters it involves: highway, artery, thoroughfare are such words. The term *high street* or *main street,* commonly a name of the principal street of many English and American towns, still carries the suggestion that a long distance route passes through a settlement, a built-up area. Often, before the days of bypasses, that is exactly what happened.

The variations on the ways in which traffic lanes are described have multiplied — and will continue to multiply as long as the volume of traffic grows and the legal complications that attend it increase. Both building and transport technology have contributed to transforming the fiscal and the legal notions connected with the street. What has lagged behind, however, is our understanding of the street as an essential carrier of communication, a thing deliberately created for that purpose and likely to continue in it. An essential attribute is that it is the most important component of the urban pattern: a pattern that is only consumed, learned, and acknowledged by its use. The extension of sea and air traffic seems to have abstracted the most obvious kind of communication — that is, getting from one place to another — from any tangible connotations. Nevertheless, air routes (particularly when they are much frequented), assume some of the notional characteristics and present some of the problems of terrestrial streets, which is also true of certain sea routes: they all share a recognized starting point, a definite aim, and a communicating channel.

Urban histories often account for the growth and prosperity of cities by their position at the crossroads of two trade routes: one is tempted to assume that such routes do not have stated goals but will go on crossing other trade routes indefinitely. It is as if a continent were a grid of such

roads, which lead further to ports and sea routes. A city grid plan also implies that the town street will connect with the road outside the gate or end in a blank wall or waterside; in a few exceptions there might be a square or a monument to impede and/or focus the street's progress.

Starting point and end are therefore not necessary physical attributes of the street or road but its notional attributes. The notional attribute impinges on physical structure: it is clearly essential for the street user that at whatever physical level its surface may be situated, its edges and boundaries may offer him sufficiently similar yet varied exit points to identify his particular aim with clarity. The unmediated passage between private and public, which is such a common feature of the twentieth-century street, seems to violate the primary condition of social intercourse in an urban milieu, which was previously assured by some form of private/public intermediate area: porch, gate, *cortile,* colonnaded street.

The very word *street,* as its etymology suggests, denotes a delimited surface — part of an urban texture, characterized by an extended area lined with buildings on either side. But the manner in which the notion of road or street is embedded in human experience suggests that it has reference to ideas and patterns of behavior more archaic than city building. Light is thrown on this by the way in which some preliterate societies, especially those with very elementary forms of shelter, use the street and also by the way in which children treat the space of play, suggesting a metamorphic notion of the street.

Track is the word that implies the most basic course along which movement may take place. To the uninitiated, whether they are members of an alien tribe or children excluded from a game, a track may even be invisible, may appear to be an undifferentiated part of a featureless landscape: but to those who are of its presence, the track will be evident. It may be marked out by small heaps of pebbles, by broken branches, or carved signs on trees, all tokens that signal the passage. At the most primitive technological level, the signals may show passage from one waterhole to another.

On a huge, monumental scale, the pilgrimage churches on the route to Compostela or the spires of the major cathedrals of Western Europe form an analogous tracking system in a countryside whose roads must otherwise have seemed undifferentiated. To the traveler who relies on landmarks, the sight of the spire provides a visual and ideational reference to the way he is to follow and to the faith he holds true. On a much smaller scale, there are passageways that assume, if only temporarily, definite characteristics of the street analogous to those followed by the pilgrim wayfarer. Such are the ceremonial areas of the several tribes in the Darling river valley of western Australia called *Bora* ground. These are sometimes just mounds of earth connected by a narrow passage that is bordered by shallow banks. These ceremonial

3

4

3. The notion of street as differentiated surface. Cleared site with pile of stones having totemic meanings (Yantruwanta tribe, southwestern Queensland). [A. P. Elkin, *The Australian Aborigines* (London and Sydney: Angus and Robertson, 1938), p. 219]

4. Communal activity as a basic concept of street. Nomadic African bushmen moving from one place of residence to another. [Mrs. Laurence K. Marshall, Cambridge, Mass.]

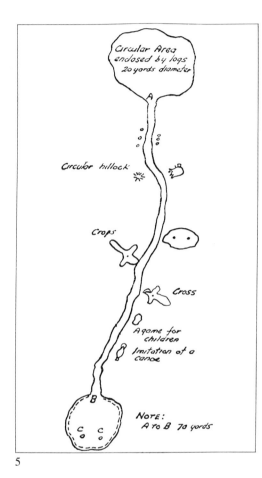

Circular Area
enclosed by logs
20 yards diameter

A

Circular hillock

Crops

Cross

A game for
children

Imitation of a
canoe

B

NOTE:
A to B 70 yards

C C

5

5. Diagram of a ceremonial ground in New South Wales, showing a marked path with a circular space (B) used for peacemaking between tribes. [Diagram by Surveyor General John Oxley at Moreton Bay, New South Wales; published in the *Journal of the Royal Society of New South Wales,* LIV (1920), pp. 74-78]

grounds were used for a number of purposes, such as peacemaking (the passage from war to peace), but their main use was for initiation rites. The track is specifically intended to mark a route for the boy who is being instructed about the ways and beliefs of his tribe. Lining the path are images cut with a digging stick directly in the ground, so that the way is always varied by the incidents these illustrations suggest. Along the path, and sometimes within the ground, the bark of living trees is carved to provide signposts or pointers in the ritual pattern. Unfortunately, too little is known about the value users attach to such images.

In central Australia an even more explicit usage is the construction of the *Apulla* ground: parallel lined banks are bracketed at either end by windbreaks of thicket. They are made for the circumcision ceremonies, which are the climax of *Arunta* initiation.

Initiation is a prominent feature of Australian aborigine life, though it is characteristic of social life generally. In Australia, it is visibly connected with the construction of special grounds involving signaled ways or roads of an elaborate nature in otherwise uninhabited territory. In all initiation, there is always a handing down of group secrets, most often closely linked with an account of the human predicament. In many primitive societies, there is also an explanation of the way in which the tribal heroes communicated such matters to their descendants and an explanation of the ground as a picture of the sky world.

The Darling valley tribes, like the *Arunta,* build little more than windbreaks as shelter. In South Africa, the *'Kung* set up villages of very fragile shelter, which may be moved and altered every day according to the mood of the inhabitants. These same tribes, like the Australian aborigines, build initiation enclosures that are linked to the village proper by a straight dance path usually about a quarter of a mile long and oriented as accurately as possible. Their ceremonies are performed between the village and the initiation ground. The passage from one to the other is the crucial feature of the ceremony.

In certain societies — in large tracts of Polynesia, for instance, and perhaps in the archaic Greece of the epic poets — the subject matter of initiation is itself a path, a way to escape the perils to the soul on its way to the underworld. Such customs suggest that human passage has always been metaphorically understood as part of the progress toward the "great perhaps" at a level where the notion of street or way was totally divorced from built form as its containment.

Megalithic fields and avenues represent still another kind of marked passageway. Their builders worked at a much higher technological level than either the Australians or the bushmen I described earlier, yet their use is unfortunately much more difficult to explain than that of the *Bora* or *Apulla* grounds, since no societies have survived with analogous constructions still in use.

The most spectacular of all such megalithic groupings are the long

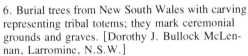

6

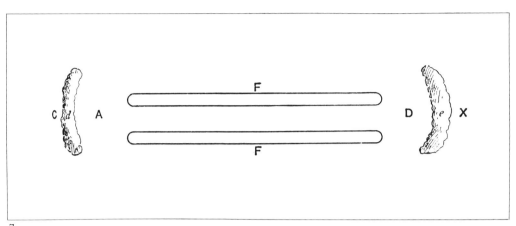

7

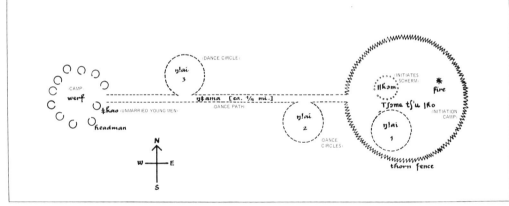

8

6. Burial trees from New South Wales with carving representing tribal totems; they mark ceremonial grounds and graves. [Dorothy J. Bullock McLennan, Larromine, N.S.W.]

7. Diagram of the Apulla ground for initiation ceremonies with a path between banks of the Apulla (F), Australia. [Spencer and Gillen, *Native Tribes of Central Australia* (New York: Dover Publications, 1899), p. 219]

8. Ritual path from settlement to initiation camp in Bushman *werf*, Kalahari Desert, Africa. [George Braziller, Inc., from *Village Planning in the Primitive World* by Douglas Fraser; reprinted with the permission of the publisher. Copyright 1968]

9

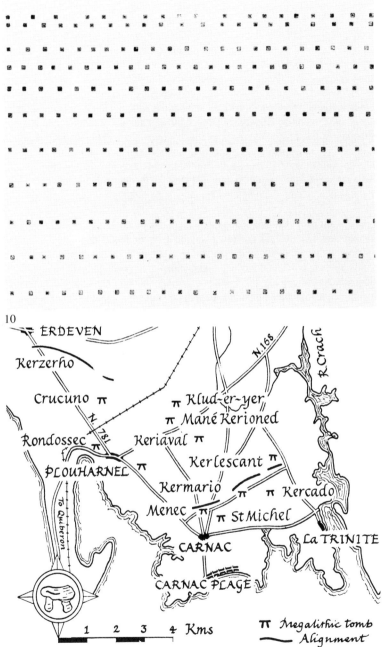

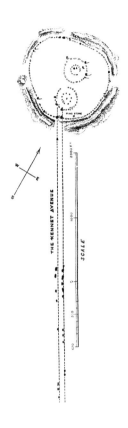

10

11

12

9. Carnac, Brittany. Megalithic alignments. Processional arrangement of stones suggests ceremonial purpose. [French Government Tourist Office, no. P653]

10. Carnac. Plan of alignments according to La Sauvagère, 1764. [David Roche, *Carnac* (Paris: Tchou, 1969), p. 116]

11. Location of main megalithic sites around Carnac. [Glyn Daniel, *Lascaux and Carnac* (Buildford: Lutterworth, 1955), p. 93]

12. Avebury, Wilts. Plan of Avebury Circle and Kennet Avenue. [Sir R. Colt Hoare, *Ancient Wilts* (1812), vol. II, pl. xiii]

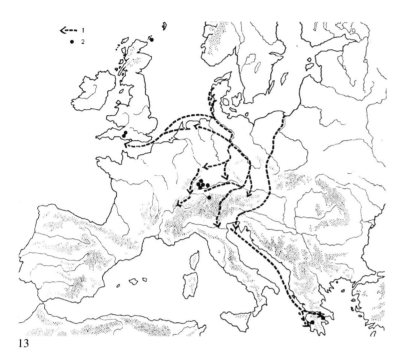

13

13. Europe, main routes of trade and exchange in
amber, mid-second millennium B.C. [Stuart Piggott,
Ancient Europe (Chicago: Aldine-Atherton, 1965),
p. 138]

14. Rock carvings of chariots or carts, horses and
wheels, late second-early first millennium B.C.,
Frännarp, Sweden. [Piggott, *Ancient Europe,*
p. 143]

15. Novgorod, Russia. The intersection of High and
Serf Streets at level 25 (laid 1006 A.D.). [M. W.
Thompson, *Novgorod the Great* (New York:
Praeger, 1967), fig. 17]

lines of densely packed stones, eleven thousand of them, at Carnac in southern Brittany. Although various astronomical explanations have been put forward for these constructions, there can be little doubt that such fields were built for a purpose important not only for a local group but for a much larger gathering at a national scale. Immemorial traditions associate them with processional and even perhaps initiatory occasions.

The efforts needed to build the megaliths of Carnac or Avebury or the many others found throughout the Mediterranean, western and central Europe, India, and Polynesia, certainly required a labor force recruited nationally. They suggest therefore the existence of national or even international travel routes, and this is further exemplified by the differing and sometimes very distant origins of the stones used in the construction.

Conceptually, the road or path may well preexist the permanence of human settlements. This may even be true of trade routes as a major channel of exchange. The transmission of certain definitely localized goods — for instance, amber, obsidian, or cowrie shells — suggests routes extending over thousands of miles in the Old and New World millennia before any permanent form of building appeared along them. The development from the notional street to the street as a surface and therefore as an object, particularly within the more permanent, explicit settlement, was a millenniary process.

Apparently remote, but nonetheless relevant, the interpretation of the life cycle as a way of progress governs many children's games. Throwing and skipping patterns devised by children may even have analogies with the dancing steps tapped out on the *Bora* grounds. On still another scale, reenactment of the daring that is rewarded and the chance that is a hazard in daily experience is also implicit in dice and token games, such as Monopoly, snakes and ladders, or the *gioco dell' oca*. Most of these have a further metaphorical quality, since they present a model of society. This in turn suggests that society itself is an entity, a landscape through which we proceed metaphorically.

From its inception, therefore, the road must have had both metaphoric and cognitive importance beyond its more obvious use. This nature of the street is witnessed by innumerable appearances in proverbs: everybody knows that the path to salvation is straight and the gate is narrow.

Movement along a set way, and even the delimitation of the way as an extended public space, are very deeply embedded in human experience. That is why the persistent prophecies of the end of the street's function as a *locus* of human communication have not been fulfilled. Nor has the invention of movies, the telephone, or television radically altered the need for the casual encounter as an essential element of human contact. It is perhaps a reaffirmation of this that the dropouts of the fifties, like the Hippies of the sixties, organized themselves into various subcultures limited to city areas, mostly downtown, and based on the street. The great ecstatic festivals (such as Woodstock) establish a new pattern of seasonal movement in the subculture rather than of day-to-day activity, which remains essentially city based.

I believe that the use of the street as a *locus* of personal exchange and communication can be promoted and that it is the business as well as the interest of public authority to promote such use, to which its more obvious functions, the carrying of traffic and the exchange of goods, should — at any rate conceptually — be subordinated. Failure to do this will not result in the death of a city — the large complexes of buildings will not be abandoned in a hurry, even if all services fail. Rather, if no major intervention occurs, the growning alienation of the city dweller from his physical environment — entailing all too familiar social problems — may well produce declining services and currently incalculable hazards.

At the present juncture, the mere treatment of the street at the face of the buildings that edge it will not do much good. In the modern city, and this is particularly true in the United States, the street has become a three-dimensional phenomenon. One inevitable by-product of nineteenth- and twentieth-century change is that this conceptual emphasis has to be translated into terms of built form. In some ways, the builders of the galleries and of nineteenth-century department stores were more acutely aware of the implications and possibilities inherent in the changes than most twentieth-century planners.

The piecemeal relegation of urban motor traffic to buried lanes and the raising of pedestrian platforms above them — on which promenades are built, ignoring the traffic below — is an image with disturbing psychological implications: that of repressing the whole problem of mechanized traffic. Any solution of urban street problems that will recognize the several aspects of the street will involve the city and the state in political decisions that might be unpopular in the short run. Such decisions might be about limiting private vehicles and improving public transport and furthering the development of three-dimensional street construction out of public funds, particularly of oblique mechanized surface carriers such as escalators and travelators. These are already in use widely in the subway stations of most metropolitan cities, in department stores, and in shopping centers. But so far, they have always been treated as mechanized staircases, their bulk awkwardly streamlined out of true scale. They have not been allowed to generate formal solutions of the kind that they inevitably suggest.

All these political matters have a corollary: that the provision of even the most minimal permanent social facilities (street surfaces, sewers) involves major formal decisions on the part of public authority, in the

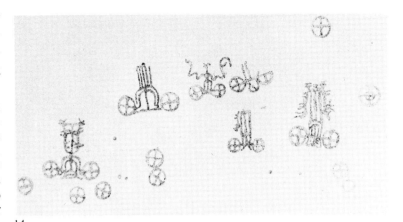

14

15

16

17

18

16,17. Biskupin, Poland. Remains of a breakwater, ramparts, houses, and corduroy circular road and cross streets of an early Iron Age settlement. Excavations conducted by Professors J. Kostrewski and Z. Rajewski. [Z. Rajewski, Director, State Archeological Museum, Warsaw]

18. Boys playing street game, "Tin Can Tommy," Workington, Cumberland. [Rev. Damian Webb, O.S.B., East Grinstead, Sussex]

sense that sewer and street surface must be in the public domain and are usually coaxial. The private domain is therefore often determined by the street/sewer layout and consequently all internal planning, whether by authority or by public speculator, or even by individual owners, is dependent on the initial decision about the layout of services.

If you extend the public domain into the third dimension, you are at once faced with the inevitable complication of a services network allied to structural support, which involves the developing authority, or the major private developer, in transforming services and surface into built form. In a three-dimensional city, therefore, the in-between realm, the belt between private and public, will assume an even greater importance. That is why we need to be clear about the nature of the street and its life, its apparent indestructibility. And that is why we must examine carefully the historical genesis of present street forms, as well as the conceptual origin of the street. It will teach us the limits of our possible intervention and the scale at which our intervention is essential.

Bibliography

Beguin, Jean-Pierre. *L'Habitat au Cameroun*. Paris: Publications de l'Office de la recherche scientifique outremer, Editions de l'Union française, 1952.

Black, Lindsay. *Burial Trees*. Melbourne: Robertson and Mullens, 1941.

————. *The Bora Ground*. Sydney: F. H. Booth, 1941.

Childe, Vere Gordon. *The Danube in Prehistory*. Oxford: Clarendon Press, 1929.

————. *Prehistoric Migrations in Europe*. Oslo: H. Aschenhoug, 1950.

Elkin, Adolphus Peter. *The Australian Aboriginees; How to Understand Them*. London: Angus and Robertson, 1938 (1964).

Fergusson, James. *Rude Stone Monuments in All Countries, Their Ages and Uses*. London: J. Murray, 1872.

Firth, Raymond William. *We the Tikopia*, A Sociological Study of *Kinship in Primitive Polynesia*. London: G. Allen and Unwin, 1936.

Fraser, Douglas. *Village Planning in the Primitive World*. New York: George Braziller, 1968.

Giedion, Sigfried. *The Eternal Present; A Contribution on Constancy and Change*, vol. 2, *The Origins of Architecture*. New York: Bollingen Foundation, distributed by Pantheon Books, 1962.

Griaule, Marcel. *Dieu d'eau; Entretiens avec Ogolommeli*. Paris: Editions du Chêne, 1948.

Janson, Sverker, and Harald Hvarfner. *Ancient Huntersand Settlements in the Mountains of Sweden*. Stockholm: Riksantikvarieämbetat, 1966.

Leroi-Gourhan, André. *Le Geste et la Parole*, vol. 1: *Technique et Langage*. Paris: A. Michel, c. 1964.

Mellaert, James. *Catal Hüjük*. London: Thames and Hudson, 1967.

Miln, James. *Excavations at Carnac, Brittany; A Record of Archaeological Researches in the Bossenno and Mont Saint Michel*. Edinburgh: David Douglas, 1877 (1881).

Morgan, Lewis Henry. *Houses and House-Life of the American Aborigines*. Chicago: University of Chicago Press, 1965.

Piggott, Stuart. *Ancient Europe, from the Beginnings of Agriculture to Classical Antiquity*. Chicago: Aldine Publishing, 1965.

Pope, C. D., Jr. *Ocmulgee National Monument, Georgia*, National Park Service Historical Handbook Series, No. 24. Washington, D.C.: U.S. Government Printing Office, 1956.

Spekke, Arnolds. *The Ancient Amber Routes and the Geographical Discovery of the Eastern Baltic*. Stockholm: M. Goppers, 1957.

Spencer, Baldwin, and F. J. Gillen, *The Native Tribes of Central Australia*. London: Macmillan, 1899.

————. *The Native Tribes of the Northern Territory of Australia*. London: Macmillan, 1914.

Thomas, Cyrus. ''Report on the Mound Explorations of the Bureau of Ethnology,'' in *Twelfth Annual Report of the Bureau of Ethnology*. Washington, D.C.: Government Printing Office, 1894.

Thompson, Michael Welmar. *Novgorod the Great*. London: Evelyn, Adams and Mackay, 1967.

Acknowledgment

I am grateful to Dr. Suzanne Frank for her work on the etymology of the street and road, as well as for her continuous assistance in the preparation of this document.

1

2

3

1. Sebastiano Serlio, *The Tragic Scene,* c. 1537.
[Jacob Burkhardt, *Die Kultur der Renaissance in Italien* (Vienna: Phiadon), pl. 294]

2. Sebastiano Serlio, *The Comic Scene,* c. 1537.
[Burkhardt, *Die Kultur,* pl. 295]

3. Sebastiano Serlio, *The Satyric Scene,* c. 1537.
[Burkhardt, *Die Kultur,* pl. 295]

The Scenes of the Street: Transformations in Ideal and Reality, 1750–1871

Anthony Vidler

Tout comme la société, la rue s'est transformée.
Gustave Kahn, The Aesthetic of the Street, *1897*

The cities are allowed to change
But you are not allowed to change.
Bertolt Brecht, Handbook for City-Dwellers, *1928*

The industrial revolution in England and the political revolution in France, each in different but ultimately interdependent ways, and in an incredibly short period of time, forced new forms of life and understanding on the inhabitants of the rapidly expanding cities. The radical effects of this huge overturning, the clash between the emerging forces of production and the rising political aspirations of those who would share, or were prevented from sharing, in its material benefits were displayed with particular intensity in the city streets.

City dwellers, architects, and philosophers — those who framed, so to speak, the discourse engendered by these transformations as they impinged on the urban environment — addressed the problems in ways that were sharply differentiated according to the interests they served. Architects, concerned with the order of the plan, the clear boundaries of space, responded to apparent chaos with constantly reelaborated ideal forms, initially inherited from their Renaissance tradition. Philosophers either dreamed of antiurban utopias, of the lost garden of Eden, or put forward practical schemes for the renewal and extension of cities that patently contradicted their ideals of civilization. As for the populace, where they were not served by the city of capital and luxury, they reacted as best they could, according to their needs, to the extent of their provocation, and to the immediate circumstances of their everyday life. Between submission to the intolerable and outraged revolt against it, they somehow defined a human existence within the walls and along the passages of their streets.

This discourse was bound together at its many, and often opposing levels, by the metaphors that served to characterize, assimilate, and organize the perception of these new realities. Manifested in urban form as well as in literary texts, certain dominant metaphoric devices set the tone for plan and riot alike, acting as the conscious mode of representation of the city to its inhabitants and rulers. In the late eighteenth and throughout the nineteenth century these metaphors were drawn immediately from the forms of industrial and scientific production; as art has ever been defined with reference to the nature it imitates, so the artifice of the city was seen according to the techniques of observation developed for natural science, or endowed with all the attributes of the new industrial organism. Thus cities were landscapes — sometimes jungles or forests — and later, gardens or parks; they were machines, engines, and factories that functioned according to laws of economics or inertia; they were bodies, healthy or sick, with characteristic symptoms of disease or fitness; they were sentient beings, however monstrous or deformed, with humors and psychologies that varied with the circumstances of their environment. And as these metaphors described the cities, so they prescribed remedies and forms for reconstruction. Nature should be tamed, engines repaired, bodies operated upon, humors therapeutically treated. Such were the determining images of planners and politicians, reformers and revolutionaries; at special moments, they even touched the consciousness of the people and rallied their defenses.

The scenes of the street depicted in the following essay are characteritic in this sense: taking as their frames of reference certain typical texts and paradigmatic spaces, either prescriptions for utopia or descriptions of reality, they attempt to follow the interlocking fate of each by means of the metaphoric structures that join them and determine their existence. Metaphors that produce form or describe life are thereby seen as the vehicles, or more often the masks, of the ideology they represent. In the continuing struggle for the space of the city these forms have reproduced themselves again and again, in different guises and in dialectical opposition, as the agents of reaction, reform, or revolution.

Prologue
From the Theater to the Street: The Three Scenes of Social Life

There are three kinds of scenes, one called tragic, second the comic, third, the satyric. Tragic scenes are delineated with columns, pediments, statues and other objects suited to kings; comic scenes exhibit private dwellings, with balconies and views representing rows of windows, after the manner of ordinary dwellings; satyric scenes are decorated with trees, caverns, mountains and other rustic objects delineated in landscape style.[1]

Serlio, interpreting the three scenes of Vitruvius for the Renaissance, depicted all three in the form of streets, drawn as elaborate exercises in frontal perspective: the tragic scene became a street of public buildings in the classical style, ending in a triumphal arch leading out of the city; the comic scene illustrated a residential street, less formal and in the gothic style, with arcades and stores on the street level, apartments above, and a church tower completing the view; the satyric scene was outside the city altogether — a path through the woods with rude woodcutters' huts in the trees to either side.[2] Together these three streets comprised the paradigmatic environments of the Renaissance, the public realms within which the dramas of city and country life were to be acted out; dramas of state and public ritual in the tragic street, of

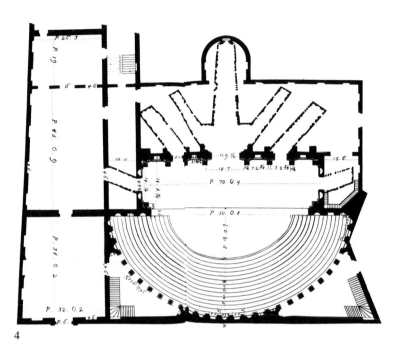

4

boisterous merchant and popular life in the residential street of comedy, and of bucolic manners and country sport in the forest path.

Not more than twenty-five years later, Palladio built three-dimensional versions of the streets of Olympus into the scaena of his theater in Vicenza.[3] This synchrony of street and theater was not coincidental but represented the double role of urban space and theatrical space in humanistic culture; even as the public realm of the street took on the functions of the theater of daily life — the city as a stage for the social action within its protecting walls — so did the theater retain its place as the mnemonic device, the ideal depiction of the world.[4] The building of the streets inside the theater brought the space of the real into the domain of the typical, the memory of the one allowing the observation and perhaps the critique of the other.

The art of perspective, by means of which this fictive insertion was achieved, itself retained a determining and formative role. For the laws of perspective were not only those of illusion, of depicting three dimensions in two, but fundamentally the constructive laws of space itself. Thus the street, subject to perspective representation in the ideal theater, was transformed by this technique and shaped by it. The assemblage of monuments, each individually typical of religious or secular activities common to the Roman and early Renaissance vision of the street, gradually gave place to the unifying vista that controlled the horizontals of each facade and subdued the erratic cornice line in favor of the point of view, the point of convergence of all horizontals.[5]

From the streets of Palladio and Serlio, to those of Vasari (Uffizi) and Fontana (Rome) the great perspective project of the Renaissance was logically realized. The salient projections that had marked the individual doorways of Palladio's street had disappeared in the Rome of Sixtus V. The long straight streets of Sixtus were primarily means of communication, joining the basilicas and providing access to a reclaimed countryside. The streets, reduced to corridors for public procession, became in a very real sense outdoor passages where the buildings that enclosed them were simply facades for an international city. The tragic street was thus the instrument of urban control and regulation, inserted at the will of the planner into a hitherto private realm. The streets of Fontana and the boulevards of Haussmann two and a half centuries later shared this common role.

The program for the planning of the Renaissance street had been already laid out by Alberti.[6] He had classified the differences between streets outside the town and those inside, as well as differentiating between those of importance within the walls.[7] The streets of the city were to be uniform in appearance — all doorways the same, all buildings the same height. At crossing points were to be arcades or triumphal arches — the doorways to these public rooms. Major streets and intersections should be protected by porticoes,

5

4. Andrea Palladio, *Teatro Olimpico*, begun 1580; plan. The streets of Olympus were built as permanent perspective sets, radiating from the center of the proscenium, forming a replica of the Renaissance ideal city within the theater. [*Le fabbriche e i disegni di Andrea Palladio, raccolti ed illustrati da Ottavio Bertotti Scamozzi* (Vincenza, 1796), with an introduction by J. Quentin Hughes (London: Alec Tiranti, 1968), pl. 1]

5. Andrea Palladio, *Teatro Olimpico*, elevation of Olympus; the five radial streets in forced perspective. [Palladio, *Le fabbriche*, pl. 2]

under which the old men may spend the heat of the day, or be mutually serviceable to each other; besides that, the presence of the fathers may deter and restrain the youth, who are sporting and diverting themselves in the other part of the place, from the mischievous folly natural to their age.[8]

Palladio repeated these prescriptions and distinguished roads outside the town by planting rows of trees on either side, "by their verdure to enliven our minds and by their shade to afford very great conveniency."[9] He recommended broad streets for the city as allowing greater ventilation, and also, understanding the problem of the frontally conceived facade on a perspective street, as permitting better views of each side. Porticoes would shelter the citizens from heat, rains, or snow, while paved sidewalks should be provided to separate pedestrians from vehicles. The tragic scene, no longer just a backdrop for civic activity, was being given technical specifications and rational classification. The street, planned as a building, was gradually absorbing the functions of circulation (of materials, goods, and people) as it retained its role as public scene.

As it was conceived in two-point perspective, so its typical form was envisaged in cross section from one public facade to the other, including the services running beneath its surface. Thus the theatrical street became, when realized in the city, a form of public order that at once demonstrated the unity of citizenship throughout the urban realm by means of its visual and technical artifice. It also incorporated the movement of the people into a general design planned to construct a world of symbols (monuments of religious and civic pride) and rites (processional paths) according to the vision of good government. Fontana even drew a plan of the routes and the monuments that left out the city fabric in between, as if the newly planned vistas in some way recreated a dream of the ancient Roman campagna: the tragic scene invested with rustic and antique virtue.[10]

The tragic scene was thus displaced from the theater of Memory to take its place among the instruments of rational order; but it nevertheless retained a supremely effective function within the emerging theater of Utopia, as the domain of noplace gradually asserted its new boundaries over those of an earlier, hermetic philosophy. That is, while the idea of Memory faded as the active agent of ideal themes in humanistic culture, and as the realm of Utopia, first defined by the principal memory artists, Andrae and Campanella, became less a world of icons and more a paradigmatic representation of reality, so the scenes of the street were given special significance as the carriers of meaning.

In general, planners and architects would be preoccupied, on behalf of the order they bring and the power they serve, with the forms of the tragic scene for the next three hundred years, while the comic scene would take on the role of an environment of the people, homely no

doubt, but disorderly and often insalubrious, and therefore to be contained or transformed by planning. Occasionally the inhabitants of this domain would take up arms to defend or appropriate it for themselves; at times it would be endowed with a semiheroic character on behalf of those who lived there. The rustic scene, increasingly as the critique of city life itself took hold in the eighteenth century, would emerge as the rallying stage of the radical and revolutionary transformation of state and life — the image of the disappearing city appealing to Rousseauesque individualist and anticapitalist alike. Here in these three scenes is illustrated, at the very inception of the classical discourse, the problem of street form in its potential transformations. This problem, not surprisingly, is stated at this point in terms that are irreducibly both physical and political; the space that defines the politics and the mode of political thought is also the real condenser of public political activity. The interpenetration of thought and life is complete, and the form of the street thereby embodies both as its characteristic mode of existence.

The City of Enlightenment Ideals
Morelly and the Geometries of Nature, 1750

What art your empires but an heap of Rubbish and of paltry Cabbins? amongst which, confusedly scattered, rise up some few great cities, Labyrinths of crooked, winding streets, composed of houses as unequal, as little uniform, as are the manners and conditions of their inhabitants.[11]

Overshadowed by Diderot, who was long given the credit for his major work, and distorted by his adoption into the canonical lineage of nineteenth-century utopian socialism, the Abbé Morelly, ambiguous *petit philosophe* and self-styled heir of Thomas More, nevertheless spoke directly from the mid-eighteenth century as the fabricator of Enlightenment utopia *par excellence*.[12] His was the true radicalism of the reason of nature, the material reason of Locke and Berkeley through Condillac, presented as an ideal for mankind that might finally engender an order to resolve all contradictions between progress and happiness, city and country, community and the individual. The fabulous kingdom he described in the *Basiliade* was in one sense a true utopia in the grand tradition of his namesake, of Campanella, Andrae, and Fénelon; set in "the midst of a vast sea," always calm, beneath "a pure and settled sky," the island he evoked was the very type of naturally abundant society. It was ruled by a wise prince, populated by a happy people, furnished with all they could desire and nature could provide, and accessible only in dreams. The laws, mores, and arts of this community were as paradigmatic as those of Utopia, and their cities as elegant as

6. Plan of *Karlsruhe*, built in 1715 as a hunting retreat for Karl Wilhelm, margrave of Baden. While the encircling ramparts that defined the ideal Renaissance city have disappeared, the circle remains, with the radials extending out into the prince's hunting forest on three sides, and into the town on the fourth. The center, no longer a public civic space, is now the point of authority and order; the enlightened, but absolute, ruler surveys his domain from a tower. Fourier will later transform this model into the Phalanstery of association, retaining the "Tower of Order." The radial *allées*, intersected by a rectilinear grid through the forest, form the prototype for Morelly's benign princedom, as well as exemplifying Laugier's metaphor of the "city as a park" of forty years later. Key:

A. Tower from which the Prince views the 32 routes, 9 of which form the streets of the town
B. Gallery
C. Château
D. Opera
E. Tennis court
F. The Prince's quarters
G. I,P, Stables
H. Riding School
K. Orangeries
L. Gentlemen's quarters
M. Salons
N. Menagerie
O. Hotels
Q. Houses
R. Lutheran Church
S. Calvinist Church
T. Catholic Church
V. Schools
W. Pumps
X. Reservoirs
Y. Orangeries
Z. Greenhouses
[Le Rouge, *Jardins a la mode* (Paris, 1776–88)]

those proposed by Mentor for Salentum. Indeed there is a hardly coincidental similarity between the city of More and that of Morelly: Aircastle, like the town depicted in the *Code de la Nature,* is square, planned on a grid, and its streets regularly and rationally planned. Both cities present in their form a three-dimensional model as it were of the perfect social structure of their inhabitants.

But between More and Morelly, between the paradigmatic utopia of sixteenth-century critical satire and the eighteenth-century realm of reason, there is a fundamental difference of instrumentality. Morelly, no matter how he dissimulated, in the end believed in the material possibility of his dream being achieved. The revolution in science, and the development of knowledge from Bacon and Newton, meant that nothing was beyond the bounds of control, and thereby of institution. And for this Locke had indicated the means. The power of environment over the mind, its effects on the body and the soul, was the basic forming and transforming force for man and society. Sensationalist philosophy, the primitive machine of behaviorism, taught that the surroundings of life were the first determinant of character, composed of ''an infinity of objects which form in each individual what we call his *state of mind.*''[13] From this it was an easy reversal to postulate that changes in environment would lead to changes in the state of mind; architects, princes, and philosophers were not slow to seize the delightful implications. What a wondrous invention for those who sensed the intractable qualities of existing society and grew impatient at its refusal to perceive its true path! The very form of the external world, over which material control was imminent, was in fact to be the agent of redemption. Environmental reconstruction was the logical precondition of moral regeneration and social happiness.

Thus, although a simple literary analogy on the surface, Morelly's comparison of the ''crooked, winding streets'' of past empires with the ''manners and conditions'' of their inhabitants was a direct statement of cause and effect. Given streets of order and light, the mores of the citizens would have remained strong and invincible, and the empires would have survived. The inequality and lack of uniformity of the street architecture was an immediate reflection, and more particularly the generator, of the unequal and chaotic social order it sheltered. In the island of the *Basiliade,* Morelly described the first act of the wise prince on his accession: he ''began to form large spacious roads, which led from one extremity of the kingdom to another,'' adding smaller ones, like branches to a tree, until he had completed a network of communication throughout the land. ''They cut through rocks, they levelled mountains and either filled up valleys or built bridges across them of a most noble structure.''[14] The countryside was filled with happy workers undertaking these grand projects. Along the roads they planted trees for shade, with arbors and alcoves of interwoven branches for the traveler's

rest. The whole island was regularly crossed by these routes, ''intersecting like threads which form a net,'' and to confirm the institution of order the rivers themselves were straightened and canals cut. The twin powers of symmetry and art converted the fields into pleasant gardens, and the order and distinction that was presented to the sight was a model to every citizen.

The prince had found his subjects living in ''an old and clumsy architecture''; their buildings were ''little uniform and so ill-arranged'' and correspondingly their mores were rude and unpolished.[15] These structures were destroyed, new ones erected in smooth and polished stone. The ''capricious monuments of the rich mans pride,'' for long so ugly next to the feeble efforts of the poor, were replaced by ''spacious buildings, simple indeed, but proper uniform and regular.'' Regularity was the dominant theme. Confusion, chaos, disorder were supplanted by an order and unity that reigned in the hearts and minds of men as the beneficent effect of their new architecture. The labyrinth was opened, the streets were straightened, and social disorder was dispelled.

All this, of course, was couched in the terms of a lyrical poem — hardly a model for social action in the present: ''some will say, perhaps,'' complained Morelly, ''that this is indeed a fine theoretical system to found the fable of a poem on, and will grant that all these things are true in Speculation but impossible in Practice.'' A more direct form was needed for the conversion of society, and this he provided in the *Code de la Nature* some two years later.[16] This code was no more nor less than a complete legislative system, a new constitution for a new society, whose adoption would immediately ''cut off at the roots the vices and the ills of society.'' The protocommunitarian and cooperative orders of his earlier poetic fable were now translated into the laws and directives that would ensure their support. And first in line was the construction of the communal settlement. Morelly drew up thirteen ''Laws of Building'' that described a complete model town, with its institutions and functions ordered according to an exact rule of placement that followed an encyclopedic classification of activities and their requisite zoning patterns.[17] The city's form was a precise map of its social structure: the units into which it was divided corresponded to social units, each quarter housing a tribe of fixed numbers. These were arranged symmetrically about a commercial and recreational center, ''a great square of regular shape.'' The whole was regularly divided by streets. Around the living areas were the workshops sheltered by continuous covered galleries; beyond these the agricultural workshops and barns spread out into the countryside.

Together, the *Basiliade* and the *Code de la Nature* presented a picture of the rationalist enlightenment model state, physically constructed in all respects to mirror the underlying geometrical perfection of nature. The differences between city and country, so marked in the Renaissance by virtue of the defensive rampart, which were to return again with idealistic force in the later part of the eighteenth century and with such environmental force with the industrial revolution, were, for a moment at least, suspended and held in balance by the hierarchic network of roads. Each division and subdivision of this grid rendered each part of the state a smaller or larger unit in the whole; towns were but larger occupations of the grid, as were community buildings larger units of private houses. Geometry would bring regularity, parity, and equality. Architecture would, so to speak, imbue society with its own aesthetic qualities; based in the first place on the imitation of natural order, its function was active and radically transforming. Morelly, disguised for the rest of the century as Diderot, had succeeded in joining architecture to mores, the form of the street to the forms of its social life, in a way that was at once recognized as radical; the primitive communist Gracchus Babeuf used the *Code de la Nature* as the source for his attack on property and the picture of its abundance as the image of a regenerated agriculture.[18] The utopian socialists of the early nineteenth century saw Morelly, more than Rousseau, as their forerunner. For he, alone of the radical egalitarians of the mid-eighteenth-century Enlightenment, had drawn up a tangible blueprint for the rational society.

Slowly, but inevitably, the architects were to realise the truly formative powers handed to them by Morelly's invention. Alberti might have served his Prince and mirrored the perfection of the social state in the perfection of his architecture; More might have demonstrated that the forms of his streets intimately reflected the social structures of Utopia, but only with materialist psychology was architecture invested with the final constructive role. The consciousness of what this meant for the reformulation of architectural theory and practice was to take a half century to emerge fully, but when, with Ledoux's monumental work, architects were finally presented to themselves as demigods, and to society as saviors, the readiness of social philosophy to embrace them and their structures as its own was in large measure the result of Morelly and his heirs.

Laugier and the Avenues of Enlightenment, 1755

Our towns are still as they were, a mass of houses piled up pell-mell without system, economy or design. This disorder is nowhere more evident and shocking than in Paris. The center of this capital has remained almost unchanged for three hundred years: there one still sees the same number of small, narrow and tortuous streets, exhaling nothing but dirt and filth, where the meeting of vehicles causes obstruction at every instant.[19]

The immediate problem posed to the philosopher of reason by the city of Paris was one of order — its complete lack of rational plan. The gap between the ideal model of Morelly and the reality of the capital was immense: from Rousseau in 1732 to Voltaire in 1749, the *philosophes* united in their reactions of disgust and horror at the conditions of life in this, the most potentially glorious of cities.[20] "How greatly did my first sight of Paris belie the idea I had formed of it," exclaimed Rousseau; "I had imagined a city of a most imposing appearance, as beautiful as it was large, where nothing was to be seen but splendid streets and palaces of marble or gold." Forming his impressions from his knowledge of Turin, the rationalist city par excellence, Rousseau had imagined Paris even finer in the beauty of its streets, the symmetry and alignment of the houses. His shock was profound and deeply formative on his future attitudes toward the cities of civilization: "As I entered through the Faubourg Saint-Marçeau, I saw nothing but dirty stinking little streets, ugly black houses, a general air of squalor and poverty, beggars, carters, menders of cloths, sellers of herb drinks and old hats."[21]

From this, the fall of the dream of a new Babylon, he was to develop a total aversion to the city per se. Even for those like Voltaire and Diderot who were more reconciled to the conceits of civilization, the sight of Paris was a continual reminder of an imperfect reality in the face of their symmetrical schemes for the right order.[22] But for the circle of Encyclopedists in general, the materialism and objective scientific attitudes that sustained their intellectual work was enough to give them hope that the city might finally be reconstructed in the image of their dream. For how could the Englightenment claim to be triumphant over the material order of the universe and the social order of man if it proved unable to constitute for itself a setting worthy of its brilliance? By the midcentury, the *philosophes* were impatient:

It is time for those who rule the most opulent capital in Europe, asserted Voltaire, to make of it the most comfortable and the most magnificent. There must be public markets, fountains which actually provide water and regular pavements. The narrow and infected streets must be widened, monuments that cannot be seen must be revealed and new ones built for all to see.[23]

The Abbé Laugier, a critic, historian, and member of the circle around Grimm and Diderot, was perhaps the first to embody the image of the Enlightenment city as a central concern in a treatise devoted to the restoration of a truly rational architecture. Writing in 1753, and influenced doubtless by his knowledge of Rousseau's *First Discourse* (1750), he evoked the celebrated picture of the primitive hut as the paradigmatic structure for an elemental, basic architecture that returned to principles of construction and form intended to be as immutable as those of Newton's physics. Readers of his lyrical account of primitive man engaged in a search for shelter and the final construction of the first cabin would have had no difficulty in relating it to Rousseau's own

7. *Map of the surroundings of Paris,* 1767; Paris surrounded by estates, forests, and gardens. Such a map, with its regular routes traced through the great hunting forests, implies that Paris itself would be susceptible to the same rational ordering. Hence Laugier's image. To the north and north-east are the forests of Montmorency and Ermenonville, later to provide shelter for Rousseau.

formulation of the emergence of society in the *Discourse on Inequality* (1755); the corresponding analogy of natural society with natural architecture was one that established the Arcadian environment centrally within the developing tradition of socially radical architecture.

But when he turned to the problems of the city, especially those of Paris, Laugier made it clear that he, at least, was not at all cynical about the end of civilization. A classicist at heart, he was only interested in natural origins as a conceptual tool; the final expression of man's humanity was through a highly refined and directed taste, not in any bucolic rusticity. Serlio's tragic scene was still the most serious of all.

If civilized taste had progressed in the conduct of private life during the eighteenth century, as everyone claimed, it was by no means evident in the public realm of the city — its streets. "We build new houses," Laugier argued, "but we do not change the bad distribution of the streets"; individualistic whim prevailed in the decoration of every building, so that an overriding impression of "deformed inequality" of confusion and disorder reigned where comfort, elegance, and magnificence should be the rule.[24] The terms were similar to those of Morelly; their aesthetic preferences were clear and common to those of his peers. Laugier, however, was concerned to guide the practice of architects rather than the speculation of social philosophers, and the solution appeared very simple: Paris was in great need of "embellishment," and to this it was infinitely susceptible.

"I am going to detail here," stated Laugier, "the principles according to which one must act, and the rules which it is essential to follow."[25] Classification being virtually synonymous with action to the midcentury Encyclopedists, he began by characterizing the three elements upon which the "beauty and magnificence" of a city depended: its entries, its streets, and its buildings. Wide and unobstructed avenues should lead to the entrances of the city, which should be themselves free and disengaged. The entrances in turn should give access to similarly wide avenues within the town: "it will even be desirable that at the entry to a large city one should find a great *place* pierced with many streets."[26] The gates of Saint Martin, Saint Jacques, and Saint Antoine, for example, should stand free in a square, with streets radiating from them distributing the traffic to the various quarters.[27] Anticipating the monumental *barrières* of Ledoux some thirty years later, Laugier proposed the triumphal arch as the model for such entries: "let us give to all the entries of our Capital this Roman air."

But the entries were only the first of the elements of Laugier's cityscape. Next, and no less important, were the streets themselves, and their principal function was to "render communication easy and comfortable." The narrow, twisting streets of Paris, "so tortuous, so full of bends and senseless angles" made it almost impossible to drive vehicles, or even sometimes to walk, within the different quarters, much less move from one to another. There were not enough bridges over the Seine; those that did exist were too narrow.[28] Indeed:

> Almost all the streets should be straightened and enlarged. They should be extended as much as possible to eliminate too frequent windings. New streets should be driven through all blocks that are longer than 600 feet. At all intersections of streets the corners should be rounded; at all crossroads there should be squares.[29]

And in response to these conditions, Laugier developed an idea that holds the same place in his theory as the hut in his principles of architecture: "One must conceive a town as a forest. The streets of the former are the routes of the latter; and ought to be cut in the same way."[30] At the very point when the formal, geometrical layouts of classical gardens and parks brought to perfection by Le Nôtre were being subjected to the implied and soon-to-be-stated criticism of the more naturalistic English landscape garden, Laugier introduced the model of a seventeenth-century hunting forest or pleasure park as the image of a city plan. "Let the design of our parks serve as the plan for our towns," he stated unambiguously. If a Le Nôtre could design the patterns of city streets as he laid out the alleys through a great park, taste and thought at once would be introduced into a realm of chaos and disorder. The park, alone of the large-scale environments of civilized man, had been able to develop rules for its planning unhampered by the exigencies of urban growth; a totality executed for a single client on a vast stretch of open landscape, it represented the full play of Enlightenment reason on nature, the real site of the ideal city of philosophy. Its aesthetic precepts were paradigmatic for the age:

> There one sees at the same time order and bizzarerie, symmetry and variety; here one perceives an *étoile*, there a crows-foot; on this side routes in a cluster, on the other routes in a fan shape; further away, parallel routes: every where cross-roads of different shapes and designs. The more choice, abundance, contrast, and even disorder there is in the compositon, the more the park will have piquant and delightful beauties.[31]

Here, departing from a strictly academic classical stance, Laugier demonstrated that he had not been entirely unmoved by the newly espoused principles of contrast and variety, the first intimations of pre-Romantic vision in the Enlightenment. Even the picturesque formed part of his criteria: "the picturesque can be found in the embroidery of a flower-bed, as well as in the composition of a picture." From a picture, and its rules of compositon, to the landscape and thence to the city was a shift that placed Laugier on the very edge of tendencies soon to become fully emergent. The aesthetics of sensation, of pictorial drama, of the sublime, to be such a powerful weapon in the hands of Boullée, Ledoux, and their peers, was hardly yet a conscious movement, nor was the landscape garden yet its environmental seat. For the moment,

Laugier was constrained to measure the parks of classical tradition with the potentially opposing canons of his sensibility. The result of this critically important fact was to freeze a specific formal image of the street, one based on the straight alleys of the classical park, into a concept of the city plan and its process of conception in a way that reinforced the continuing life of classicism as the mode of design suitable for cities for the next century or more. If Laugier had been writing some five or six years later, when Rousseau's *Nouvelle Héloïse* finally established the cult of landscape in France, and had applied the same metaphor, the implications for city form would have been drastically different. As it was, by the time Ledoux attempted to address the problem, Laugier's classical avenue was already firmly entrenched in urban compositional theory.

Laugier's analogy went beyond the varied patterns of streets and squares, however. The park was a holistic conception; its plan, although adapted to the terrain, was complete and imposed on nature from above. To apply the same methods to a city that already existed, as opposed to one in an ideal region of the mind, was to imply that the existing city was indeed a forest, a kind of natural phenomenon, to be seen as the ground for the architect's intervention. To submit this forest to the will of the designer, the terrain must be measured, the routes that will become streets and the crossroads that will become squares traced. The method of the gardener would thereby become the method of the planner in a very real sense:

> Paris; it is an immense forest, varied by the inequalities of the plain and mountain, cut right through the middle by a great river, which dividing itself into many arms forms islands of different size. Let us suppose that we were allowed to cut and prune at will, what means could not be drawn from so many advantageous diversities?[32]

The rural utopian image of Morelly has thus been reversed: from a landscape-city, which was no more than an immense garden spread out over the entire countryside, to a city-landscape, cultivated and cut out according to rational and aesthetic plan. Traces of this concept resonate in the plans of Patte, of Ledoux and the Visionaries, of David and the Revolutionary Commission of Artists, of Napoleon I, and finally of Haussmann: Laugier's dream of the ideal entry to the capital was to be realized in the Place de l'Etoile a century later:

> I imagine a grand avenue, very wide, in a straight line, and bordered with two or four lines of trees. It ends in a triumphal arch; from there one enters into a great semi-circular, or half oval or half polygonal place, pierced with many large streets branching in several directions, some leading to the center, others to the extremities of the city, all of which have a beautiful object terminating them.[33]

No sooner than the ideal form of the Enlightenment city had been concretized in the theory and practice of architects, it was adopted, fully

and with delight, into the literature of utopia again. Sebastien Mercier, that indefatigable critic and playright whose pictures of real Paris were the progenitors of Balzac and Zola, elevated the image of a newly reconstructed Paris (or perhaps he was slyly satirizing it) in his romance, the *Year 2240,* published in 1770,[34] symmetrically placed at the end of the eighteenth century, as Wells's *When the Sleeper Wakes* was to be for the nineteenth. Mercier had his hero awake in the Paris of four and half centuries hence. Not surprisingly, "everything has changed." The old familiar quarters were gone, submerged beneath new embellishment. But the most amazing transformation of all was that of the streets:

> I lost myself in grand and beautiful streets all perfectly aligned. I entered spacious cross-roads where such order reigned that I saw not the slightest obstruction. I heard none of those bizarre and confused cries which formerly grated harshly on my ear. I met no vehicles ready to crush me flat. A gouty old man would have been able to walk about with ease. The town had an animated air, but without disturbance and without confusion.[35]

As in many dreams there were no people; indeed, no sounds, smells, or untoward sights. The enlightenment was certainly triumphant: the volumes of the great Encyclopedia had been disseminated and tucked beneath every arm; children learned to read from the works of Rousseau, Montesquieu, Buffon, and Voltaire. Paris was full of light and quiet harmony, and the air was purified by greenery and ventilation. The heroic stage of the new order was calm, suspended between collective power and individual desire; the order was total — no disturbance, no confusion, and, presciently for its nineteenth-century successors, supremely silent. People, crowds, their cries, smells, and movement had been absorbed into the stable equilibrium of the rational street. In this street all would finally be at peace, subjected to a therapeutic space and dominated by the power of perspectives along avenues, limitless perspectives where vision, both physical and mental, would find its true home.

Techniques of Transformation
Patte and the Surgical Incision, 1765

> *Under the eyes of his listeners, he brought in the most seriously sick patients, classified their disease, analyzed its features, outlined the action that was to be taken, carried out the necessary operations, gave an account of his methods and the reasons for them, explained each day the changes that had occurred, and then presented the state of the cured patients.*[36]

Only twelve years after the second edition of Laugier's treatise, Pierre Patte published a Plan of Paris which in almost every detail seemed to correspond to the formal idea of the city as a park. Patte, a devoted pupil and colleague of the great academic teacher, Jacques-François Blondel, brought together on a single plan the various projects for *grandes places* that had been submitted in the competition for the placement of Louis XV's statue.[37] The assemblage of all the proposed plans combined in this way formed an image of a multifocal city, each quarter with its own square, arcades, and radiating avenues, with an implicit triangulation set up between the different centers. The variety of the squares, the uniqueness of each project, the cuts they inflected in the given terrain of the city, and the new scale of urban place they evoked all could well have been drawn in direct response to Laugier's description.

But, lest the fact that these were separate and isolated propositions detract from the overall idea of the Plan of Paris as a unified plan for intervention, Patte added a chapter entitled "The embellishments of Paris, general reflections on the means that could be employed to embellish this city in its totality," and "render it as confortable as it was agreeable." Like Voltaire, he castigated the narrow and tortuous streets and proposed to open up the Ile de la Cité, joining it to the Ile de Saint Louis as a grand center for the city. Such a plan, he claimed, might be accomplished in the short space of thirty years, given a consistent policy and the requisite funds. Paris would then become, as the center of Enlightenment culture, what Athens and Rome were for their own times, by means of works that contributed to the dignity of the state, to the comfort of the citizens, to the ease of communication, to the progress of trade and commerce, to the cleansing of the streets, all considered as interdependent systems.[38] As Blondel had stated on opening his school of architecture,

> Architecture views everything on the large scale; in our towns it prefers accessiblity and ease of communication to the decoration of façades; it is concerned with the alignment of streets, with squares and cross-roads, with the distribution of markets and public thoroughfares.[39]

Once the plan was introduced as a means of embellishment, the idea of a complete restructuring was a logical extension; one would therefore expect Patte, the technically minded, professional architect-urbanist to have developed comprehensive plans for the services and amenities of the new Paris, to be overlaid on the existing fabric with grand abandon. Could he not, after all, like Laugier's gardener, cut and prune at will? But this was not his perception of the architect's function nor of the process of planning. His very distinctive approach, while marking an important second stage in the transformation of the architect into social redeemer and the architect's forms into agents of social change,

nevertheless is as interesting for what it does *not* pretend to accomplish, especially so as the basic analogy of the plan itself is shifting. For if Laugier's architect was a gardener, Patte's was a surgeon. The city as a forest, to be tamed by the arts of cultivation, was now seen as a body in varying states of sickness and disease, to be cured by the arts of medicine. And, just as with a patient, radical surgery was the last resort of prolonged therapy.

We are witnessing in the last decades of the eighteenth century a fundamental transformation of the analogies that informed the arts of natural imitation — result, very simply, of the developing perceptions of the nature that was to be imitated. The principles of Renaissance design, based on the image of man, in symmetry and balance with the microcosmic forms of universal harmony, had reintroduced the Platonic idea of the perfect form as the most organic. Advances in the science of medicine had further redefined the spatial and mental attributes of human harmony in terms of balanced flows (blood), stress and tension (muscles), structure (skeleton), decay (tissues), and more recently a series of unseen, apparently unobservable phenomena like mental disorder, infection, and contagion. The effort to classify and to locate cause and effect in relation to this "unseen" led to the identification of agents, carrying and transmitting — the air with its newly discovered composition was a favorite culprit.[40] Now if the city was to be rebuilt in the image of man, and the city was exhibiting severe problems, it was no more than a sick body, to be diagnosed and treated as any man. Accordingly Patte saw the distribution system of cities as vicious, the air as in need of purification, the Hôtel-Dieu as an infectious center of disease, and the means of rectifying these illnesses as insertions and judicious cuts, not of the forester's axe but of the surgeon's knife.

Patte, like Laugier, stood at a pivotal edge of the transformation of one kind of knowledge to another. In 1770, it was still not possible to talk confidently, as we shall see the doctors of the nineteenth century talking, of a pathology of the city; nor was it too clear where the mechanical functions of human engineering stopped and where truly biological and chemical processes took over. It was not, after all, until the first ten years of the nineteenth century that the mind was finally selected as the seat and cause of insanity. So Patte was both technical and surgical, or rather his surgery was of a mechanical kind.[41] With meticulous care he determined the prototypical cut, the ideal form of the eighteenth-century street. In plan and in section it combined the systems of pedestrian and vehicular movement, sewage disposal, drainage, shelter, fresh water, and amenity (public conveniences, seats, for example), and with equal care specified their proper site and dimension. Every paving stone was drawn in loving outline. Light and ventilation were regulated too, with the width of the street proportioned to its height.[42] The means of construction were to be fireproof, and economic.

8

8. Pierre Patte, *Plan of Paris*, 1765; this plan, bringing together the various projects submitted in the
competition for an appropriate setting for a statue of
Louis XV (1748) as well as a number of other
proposals for embellishment, forms a transition between the forest analogy of Laugier and the more
incisive cutting of the *Plan des Artistes* developed
by the painter David and his Commission of 1793.
[Pierre Patte, *Monumens érigés en France à la
gloire de Louis XV* (Paris, 1765)]

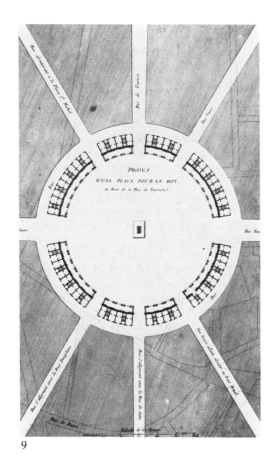

9

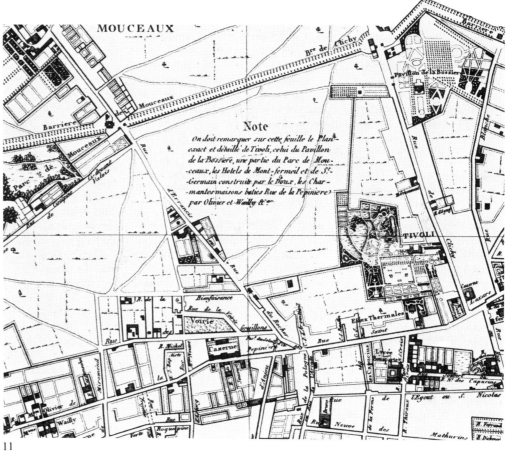

11

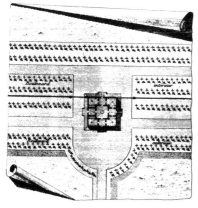

10

9. Polard, *Project for a circular place for Louis XV's statue*, 1748; from Pierre Patte, *Plan of Paris*. With its segmentally planned stores and continuous arcades, together with the radiating avenues, this plan anticipates Ledoux' plan for the Saltworks of Chaux and establishes the ideal city form once more in the center of the city.

10. Claude Nicolas Ledoux, *Plan of a prototypical tollgate* or *barrière*, 1785. Ledoux, commissioned by the farm-general to construct a wall and tollgates around the city of Paris, tried to seize the opportunity of embellishing the capital on a grandiose scale.

He projected a grand boulevard to run both inside and outside the wall, as well as eight large inns, to serve as recreation centers for the citizens. The tollgates, which were erected between 1785 and 1789, were for the populace a monumental symbolism of the oppression of the tax-farm and were sacked as the initial gestures of July 1789.

11. *The wall of the farmers-general*, 1808, showing the grand boulevard between the tollgates of Monçeaux and Blanche and the still undeveloped land inside the *barrières*. [Maire's *Plan de Paris*, 1808]

The street was to be washed down regularly, its rubbish carried outside the city, and its fountains numerous. Continuous porticoes would allow the resident to walk throughout the town protected from bad weather and the heat of the sun; where there were no arcades, stone posts would guard him from the passing vehicles. The instrument of recuperation was devised in a form that could be applied to any site in the city, and that, if diligently inserted over a period of several decades, might finally lead to the recovery of the complete system.

The Riot and the Festival, 1789

The Grande Rue du Faubourg is filled with platoons of citizens armed with pikes and a few old fashioned muskets; women are assembled in every street and are making a great noise.[43]

The medical analogy possessed another dimension altogether, which, for a brief instant, caused the analogy to disappear in favor of a basic identity between it and what it described; or, in other words, the total environment of the city, first seen as sick patient, was also seen as healing doctor. The city, with all the effects it was capable of producing in the minds of men and their society, was also capable of its own therapy. On the eve of the Revolution scientists and doctors turned their attention to the city as a whole, not just to cleanse its parts but to develop its innate therapeutic character. Ventilation, lighting, drainage, new hospitals, the removal of the old cemeteries were all functions of curing the urban disease; but the curing of the social disease was a political and, ultimately, a civic problem.[44] The influence of morals on health, the influence of political oppression on health, finally the influence of liberty itself on health, were all themes explored with increasing fervor in the last years of the *ancien régime.* The institution of the right ordered state, with its population trained from birth in habits of cleanliness, healthy exercise, and celebration of their freedom from social ills, would finally render medicine unnecessary. The city would then take on its rightful role as the site of health and its sustenance, and the street, the public room par excellence, would retrieve the civic and festive functions of a more natural age. The citizen would rise from his private sickbed and join his liberated peers in procession: like the Spartans of Rousseau's dreams, youth would run naked and age be undying. This dream of a "festive city, inhabited by an open air mankind,"[45] took the realm of planning (as every other professional realm) and lifted it at the moment of revolution bodily into the domain of politics, not as at its inception for the benefit of the Prince, but at last on behalf of all the citizens. There it remained, in theory at least, and throughout the next century and a half returned in practice to haunt the fears of order and to fire the hopes of people.

The great public festivals, processionals of the Revolutionary stage, carefully orchestrated, stage managed, and dressed by the architects of public ceremonial,[46] were ever poised uneasily on the edge of their most feared counterparts — the riot, the looting spree, the lynching, and perhaps even the massacre. If the Revolution needed the people of the streets *in* the streets as its most powerful and immediate weapon, it nevertheless was far from immune itself from the inherent cannibalism of the crowd whose hopes and frustrations were fired by each successive demonstration of revolutionary authority. Peaceful demonstrations (the Champ de Mars) might turn at an instant into bloody massacres; patriotic banquets (Champs-Elysées) could degenerate into fierce clashes; sudden shifts in the price of grain, causing the scarcity of bread, would consistently bring crowds into the streets and squares of the city in protest or in riot.[47] The Convention was threatened in its sessions by the guns of the people, terror (white and blue) was the instrument of control and counter revolution alike, and the all-pervading violence of the mob claimed its victims without respite.

The crowd in the street was at once demonstration of collective need and the temporary suspension of institutional control; as Georges Lefebvre noted, the worker, "in the crowds of the street, momentarily escapes the institutions which socialize his activities."[48] In the crowd one could lose oneself, as the *flâneurs* of the July Monarchy would find to their pleasure, but one was also fearful of the authority that remains ever ready to reimpose its structures of control. Between this joy — the joy of festive and public romp — and this fear — the fear of the forces of order — successive Revolutionary governments attempted to use the festival, the *cortège,* as both mediator and diversion.

"After times of disorganization," wrote the conservative functionary Jean-François Sobry in 1805, "nothing is more difficult than to reorganize well, because the ideas which tend towards reestablishment are in no way disengaged from those which have served to break down."[49] At this point the example of a public ceremony would serve to demonstrate to the citizen "the example of order, the happiness of order, the supremacy of order, the magnificence of order, the spectacle of order."[50] Architecture, for Sobry, became the necessary, even the indispensable, art for the maintenance of public order. Here he took the psychology of sensationalism, that primitive machine of behaviorism, as the key to its salutary effects: "the shortest route to reach the soul is through the eyes," he stated, paraphrasing Rousseau on eloquence. Accordingly, "ceremonial is the cement which binds to each other these stones, so differently cut, which make up the social edifice; it is in fact at the same time the totality and the strength, grace and solidity."[51] In this way, the revolutionary *cortège* was transformed into the instrument of the forces of order, the "dumb eloquence of the government," and the age of the festival had come to a close. Only in 1848 would a republican banquet again act as the catalytic event for an entire revolution.

12

13

12. Burning of the *Barrière des Bonshommes*, July 11, 1789.

13. The citizens of the faubourg Saint-Antoine and of the faubourg Saint Marçeau take to the streets to present a petition to the National Assembly, 20 June 1792. [L. Prudhomme, *Révolutions de Paris, dediées à la Nation* (Paris, 1792), no. 154, p. 548]

14

15

16

17

18

14. *Clash in the Champs Elysées* between Marseillais soldiers and supporters of Lafayette after Santerre's banquet of 30 July, 1792. [Prudhomme, *Révolutions,* no. 160, p. 194]

15. *Toppling the statue of Louis XV,* Place Louis XV, July 1792: "at the Place Louis XV and at the Hotel de Ville, the people make their own justice for the Kings of Bronze, throwing them to the earth. This example was followed in the 83 Departments." [Prudhomme, *Révolutions,* no. 161, p. 240]

16. "The National Assembly and the King climb the Altar of the fatherland, to preach a sermon." [Prudhomme, *Révolutions,* no. 158, p. 97., July, 1792]

17. Sunday, 22 July 1792: "amphitheaters were set up in the public squares and the magistrates of the people received enrollments without number from an ardent and vigourous youth." Following the state of emergency of 11 July, France was called to arms in defense against the Prussian and Austrian armies. [Prudhomme, *Révolutions,* no. 159, p. 138]

18. Funeral celebration in honor of citizens killed, 10 August 1792, [Prudhomme, *Révolutions,* no. 180, p. 569]

The Condensers of Community
Ledoux and the Porticoes of Arcadia, 1804

*Switzerland is the only place in the world which presents this mixture
of savage nature and human industry. The entire realm of Switzerland is, in a way, nothing more than a great city, whose streets,
longer and wider than the Faubourg Saint Antoine, are lost in the
forests and cut by the mountains, and whose houses, scattered and
isolated, are linked to each other solely by English gardens.*[52]

Paradoxically mingled with the dream of a disappearing medicine and
the society of open air life in the communal streets of the city were the
strains of its precise opposite, or perhaps its logical corollary: the image
of the city that itself disappears, and with it the ills, the very sites of
social and physical infection. Morelly had seen the future city of natural
equality as distributed equally across the landscape, but Rousseau had
seen the cities themselves as the receptacles of corruption: "it was on
the 9th of April 1756 that I left Paris," he wrote, "never to live in a
town again."[53]

The proper environment of natural society was nature, the only
surroundings that could reconstitute the individual soul in harmony with
himself and his fellows were natural, the only paths to a utopia situated
firmly within the personality were those of a *promeneur* through the
landscape, reflecting on Self and Other, and attempting to achieve a
state of transparent perception between both. *La Nouvelle Héloïse* was
written in seclusion from the city, and its environments were powerful
evocations of the healing forces of landscape.[54] Rousseau's hero Saint-
Preux climbs high in the Alps, his heroine Julie closes herself in the
elysium of a private *jardin-anglais;* both find themselves and thereby
each other as a result of the experience. Emile is withdrawn from the
city to protect him from the conceits and vices of civilization to a region
where "nothing shall strike his eye but what is fit for his sight." Men
are, by nature, Rousseau affirmed, "not meant to be crowded together
in ant hills, but scattered over the earth to till it."[55] The *Social Contract*
moved the argument from the personal and communitarian to the political:

People the territory evenly, extend the same rights to everyone, carry
the same abundance and life into every quarter — it is by these means
that the state will become at once the strongest and the best governed
that is possible. Remember that the walls of towns are made only
from the debris of rural houses.[56]

Such was the argument of the rural-revolutionary Babeuf to his
executioners; he and his conspirators for equality worked toward "the
extinction of those receptacles of vice, large cities; thus covering France
with villages adorned with immense and happy populations, whose

propagation and multiplying there would be nothing to retard."[57] Similar sentiments were voiced by that "Rousseau of the gutter," Restif de
la Bretonne, who warned of the "dangers of the city" in his series of
novels describing the moral fall of peasant boys and girls in the depravation of the towns.[58] And when the city had been dispersed, the street
would disappear in its turn, supplanted by the route connecting settlements or the pathway through the park connecting individual retreats.

In this way the social philosophy of equality was identified with the
environment of landscape, and, for the architects of the 1780s, the
particular forms of the English landscape garden. Encouraged by a
clientele of aristocratic landowners who played with the constructs of
the hermit of Montmorency as fashionable romanticisms and who saw a
certain physiocratic economic interest in the return to their ancestral
estates, the architects le Camus, Hubert Robert, François Barbier, and
above all Claude-Nicolas Ledoux, developed a completely new philosophy of architecture as they practiced the building of *fabriques* and
follies in carefully designed natural settings.[59]

Now, after more than twenty-five years the concealed message of
Laugier's Primitive Hut was understood; it was no longer a phenomenal
type of elemental architecture but a literal description of the proper
social habitat of man; Ledoux built it in the gardens of Mauperthuis,[60]
monumentalized it in fifty different ways around the walls of Paris,[61]
and idealized it in timber and stone for the woodcutters and charcoal
burners of his dream city of Chaux.[62] Hubert Robert painted it in
ruinous scenes and built it at Rambouillet; Le Camus made it Chinese
and gave it to the Duc de Choiseul on his forced retirement, and Barbier
endowed it with the forms of symbolic Freemasonry for the eccentric
François Racine de Monville.[63] This then was to be the final end of
equality: the "paltry cabbins" so despised by Morelly, given dignity,
artistic value, and the imprimatur of architecture as the isolated
monuments of individual idiosyncrasy. The street, a realm where the
private interest was ever merged for the public good, was no more.

For all intents and purposes the society implied by the landscape
conceits of the last decades of the eighteenth century was indeed more
like that of Rousseau's savage state, where each individual was isolated,
a world unto himself and running for survival in an alien world of
obstacles and beasts. The particular conditions for the creation of the
natural, domestic society, the "golden age," the *juste milieu* sung by
Rousseau at his most optimistic, were ignored. Appropriately so, for the
society expressed in the *fabriques* of fashion was an emerging, primitive
form of (high) bourgeois consumption where individual interest was
ever to subsume the common.

The precepts of Rousseau were ignored by most except, that is, by
Ledoux, who contrived to sustain a delicate balance between hierarchy
and levelling. His construction of the social street in a new form under

21

19

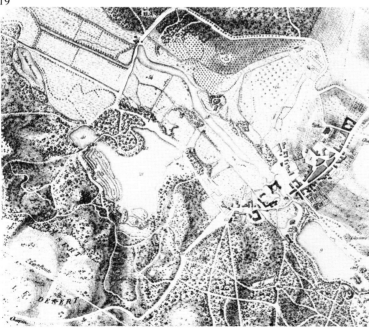

20

19. Jean-Jacques Rousseau, frontispiece to his *Discourse on Inequality,* 1755, detail showing the savage who refused civilized life in favor of his simple, natural existence with the tribe. "So long as men rested content with their rustic cabins . . . they lived free, healthy, honest and happy," wrote Rousseau, drawing an analogy with the "contemporary" savage and the quasi-anthropological ideal of "natural man" before property and society had disturbed his natural state.

20. *Plan of the Desert,* or landscape garden of the Marquis de Girardin at Ermenonville, where Rousseau died and was buried in 1788. The fashion for the English landscape garden had taken hold in the 1760s as a reaction to the formal, geometrical layouts of Le Nôtre. Girardin himself had written a treatise on garden designs in 1775, entitled *De la composition des paysages.*

21. The idealized landscape setting of Ledoux's Town of Chaux which he imagined developing around the Saltworks of Chaux (1774–79). This bridge over the river Loüe, a monumental version of the "bridge of boats" still used by military engineers in the eighteenth century, leads to the saltworks; in the background to the right another cluster of buildings forms the industrial and commercial center of the city. [Ledoux, *l'Architecture considérée sous le rapport de l'art, des moeurs et de la législation,* vol. 1. (Paris, 1804)]

22. *Temple of Friendship in the park of Betz,* c. 1780; a typical late-eighteenth-century *fabrique* in a landscape park. [A. de Laborde, *Description des nouveaux jardins de la France et de ses anciens châteaux* (Paris, 1808)]

23. Claude Nicolas Ledoux, the *Exchange of the Ideal Town of Chaux,* c. 1799. This idealized *fabrique* is typical of all the institutions of Ledoux' vision; set apart in clearings in the forest, they centralize the various functions of morality and government in many nuclei, joined by radiating routes through the landscape. The plan of such a city would resemble, in reverse, that of Pierre Patte for Paris. [Ledoux *l'Architecture*]

24. Country house for Ledoux' ideal town; like the institutions of the city, the houses are isolated and designed for their occupants' trades and crafts and given symbolic and functional plans accordingly. This one is for a grand master of waters and forests who desired to live near to his work, that is, within the forest itself. [Ledoux *l'Architecture*]

22

the exigencies of the landscape garden was an attempt — the last until
Morris — to maintain the community implied by city with the individuality allowed in the country without the shelter of the physical artifact,
city. This solution was the portico.

The realm in which Ledoux disposed the elements of his ideal city of
Chaux was a fertile and gently rolling plain, interspersed with clumps of
variegated trees and shrubs and irrigated by a limpid stream:

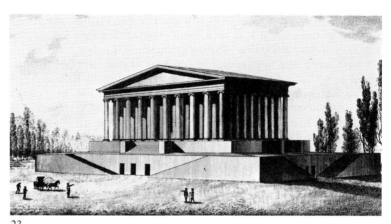

23

Agriculture, commerce, literature and the arts all have their meeting
halls; galleries, libraries and communal centers. Vast promenades
and medicinal fountains are set in the plain through which meander
the precious waters flowing from the mountains to irrigate the products of labor. Already the new social pact distributes its influence
everywhere.[64]

Streets, pavements, and the press of traffic no longer intruded on the
direct experience of nature. In their stead, pathways wandering through
the park-city joined building to building. In the forest, long avenues
formed of planted trees linked clearing to clearing, triangulating the
centers of social activity. This image was, in fact, the exact reverse of
Patte's plan for Paris and brought back Laugier's park to the country
from whence it came.

Even as nature and society were reconciled in this natural city, so on
the scale of the buildings themselves Ledoux was concerned to make an
explicit formal connection between the physical environment and public
social welfare. Indeed, with the disappearance of the street, the only
potentially public domain that remained was that narrow zone that acted
as interface between building and nature. The street was in a way
withdrawn to the outer skin of the house, even as the individual was
drawn to the very center of each private space. Thus withdrawn, and
pressed against the private wall, the public realm could be nothing else
but a portico. The portico, however, was not the colonnade that surrounded the Greek temple; it was not a defense against the penetration
of sacred *cella,* but rather a space of transition where the individual
could regain his social being and the crowd gradually break down into
its individual parts. Ledoux's porticoes were at once filters and covered
outdoor rooms in their own right. They surrounded every public building, and most private, and their autonomy was defined by their artificial
floor, the platform that extends from within as the base of the entire
monument:

24

A majestic building is dedicated to wisdom; multiplied porticoes
surround it. Children play there under cover, young people stroll
through them, the old meditate beneath them. There a school is
opened where man is taught his duties before being instructed in his
rights.[65]

The portico no longer simply embellishes, nor does it serve merely to
shelter the citizen from the rain — it is a positive instrument for

encouraging social activity, much in the way that Fourier was to conceive it in the year of Ledoux's death. Therein lies Ledoux's critical function in the constitution of social architecture. Laugier and Patte, as we have seen, were in some way hesitating on the edge of developments about to become dominant; Ledoux, a true student of Rousseau, received the awful responsibilities that were devolved upon the architect by the Enlightenment, first with equanimity, then with total acceptance, finally with transforming enthusiasm. With Ledoux, the promise of Locke through Condillac, of Shaftsbury through Burke, of Kent through Delille, of Morelly through Rousseau, and of architecture for society, was realized and embodied in the forms of a new architecture for a new society. The aspirations of the entire Enlightenment, whether against the city or for it, were, as it were, crystallized and deposited in the hermetic geometries of the *fabriques* of Chaux. And again and again Ledoux spoke of the porticoes, the endless arcades, the vaulted halls where his people would meet in final equanimity:

Porticoes where the inhabitant sheltering from the rain, seeks a way of continuing his useful activities. It is beneath these vaults, covered in the center to provide shade from the mid-day heat, open to the north for the refreshing air, that the hastening crowd will find health, and strengthen its lungs; it is beneath these vaults consecrated to mediation, to the discussion of individual interests, to science, to the collection of the best books, to games which occupy the mind without compromising morals, it is here, finally, that one will find the harmonious union of opposites.[66]

In the end, the portico is the aesthetic mode of reconciliation for society and for composition both; the tendencies toward variety and contrast that Laugier was conceding had developed too far to be unified in the matrix of classical geometry or proportional harmony. Only a device that could enfold and subsume without destroying individuality, that could act as a foil and a structure for the sharp and intense effects of elements imbued with character (and perhaps even a sublimity) of their own, could act as the public and general frame for bringing together private and particular elements. There are designs where Ledoux uses the portico as the formal setting for disparate, autonomous enclosures for private activities; there are plans where the portico is left empty, ready for its occupation by society. But always, the implication remains that the very form of the shelter will by its own example inform the actions of people. A multiplicity of columns unified in a grid, intersecting with nature on one side and with shelter on the other: such was Ledoux's vision. After this, the nature of architecture and the nature of society are inseparable considerations, despite all attempts by economics and elitists to stand in between. Ledoux was the first modern architect to entitle his treatise "Architecture considered *in relation to art, mores and legislation.*"[67]

Fourier and the Gallery-Streets of Community, 1808

The gallery streets are a means of internal communication which will be enough to put to shame all the palaces and fine towns of civilization.[68]

On his first visit to Paris in January 1790, Charles Fourier, accompanied by his brother-in-law — the future gourmand Brillat-Savarin — was amazed at the brilliance of the Palais Royale and its arcades: "The first time you see it," he wrote home to his mother, "you think you are entering a fairy palace. You find everything you could wish for there — spectacles, magnificent buildings, promenades, fashions."[69] If his taste for the art of eating was to be formed by his guide, his passion for architecture was immediately stimulated by this first vision of the social palace; the image of the Palais Royale was to be the inspiration and type for each succeeding project for social communitarian architecture throughout his life. At once a fairy palace, a realm of dreams and fantasy, and a real frame for social and commercial activity, the gardens, arcades, and galleries of the Palais provided Fourier with the essential ingredients, if not the desired results, for the peculiar mix he called first "Tourbillon" and then "Phalanstery."[70]

For it was not simply the architectural shell of the palace that excited the young student: barely six months after the storming of the Bastille, Paris, and especially the area around the Tuileries and Palais Royale, was seething with activity. In October the crowd had entered the Tuileries and it was this crowd, with its contrasts, costumes, and unceasing movement that attracted Fourier the *sociologue:* just before the onslaught of the Terror, and after the first ebullient steps of the Revolution, two worlds of Paris were juxtaposed, mingling in the gardens of the Palais. For a moment the Paris of duBarry and Necker lived side by side with the Paris of Balzac, concentrated in the shadow of the Galeries de Bois. The gardens in the center, surrounded by Philippe Egalité's galleries and apartments were political forum (Camille Desmoulins) and club house (Masonic sects); the arcades were filled with cafés, gambling houses, small traders of every description, and the heart of the publishing world. Here pamphlets were turned off the presses and distributed to the crowd almost simultaneously — the acts of conceiving, writing, printing, and communicating compressed into a single spatial domain. Here rich ladies and poor prostitutes strolled and paraded, gazed and exhibited, bought the wares of others and sold those of their own.

The Théâtre Français at one end of the garden, and the Théâtre du Palais Royale at the other, made the district the focus of Parisian entertainment. Cementing this heterogeneous and, to the casual visitor, incredible mélange were the gallery streets, the Galeries de Bois, and

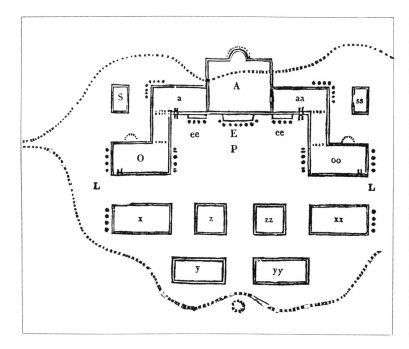

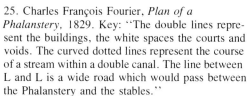

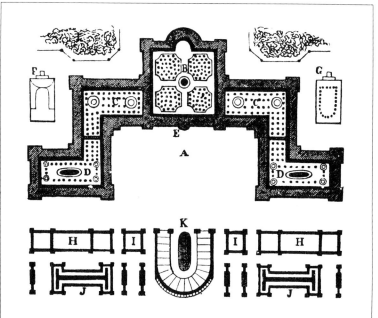

25. Charles François Fourier, *Plan of a Phalanstery,* 1829. Key: ''The double lines represent the buildings, the white spaces the courts and voids. The curved dotted lines represent the course of a stream within a double canal. The line between L and L is a wide road which would pass between the Phalanstery and the stables.''

P.   Parade ground at the center of the Phalanstery

A.   Court of honor forming a winter promenade planted with evergreen vegetation and giving shade all year round

a,aa Courts placed between the buildings
o, oo

•••• Colonnades and peristyles

x,y,z Courtyards for the rural buildings
xx, yy
zz

|| ||| Closed and heated porches, not projecting

E, ee Three porticoes, jutting out, for the different services

::   Double points, between two main buildings, are passages on columns at the first floor

[Charles Fourier, *Le Nouveau Monde industriel et sociétaire* (Paris, 1829)]

26. *Plan of a Phalanstery,* 1829, developed from Fourier's diagram:

''A.   Great parade ground at the center of the Phalanstery.

B.   Winter garden, planted with evergreens, surrounded by warm greenhouses.

C.,D. Interior service courts, with trees, fountains, pools.

E.   Great entry, grand stair, tower of order.

F.   Theater

G.   Church

H.,I. Great workshops, stores, granaries, sheds.

J.   Stables, mews, and rural buildings.

K.   Lower court.

Note. The rural buildings will generally be more extensive than in the figure. The great road passes between the dwelling palace and the work buildings. The gallery street is represented along the interior facades of the Phalanstery.'' [Fourier, *Le Nouveau Monde,* p. 123]

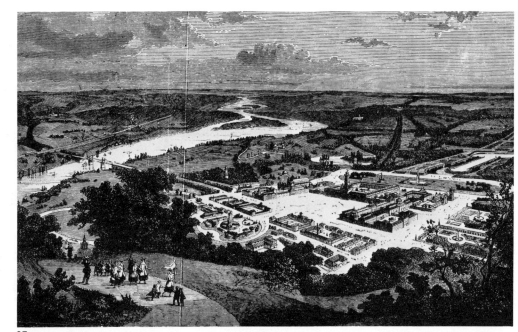

27. Victor Considerant, *Perspective view of a Phalanstery,* 1834. [*Description du Phalanstère* (Paris, 1834)]

28. Victor Considerant, *Perspective view of a Phalanstery,* 1834. [*Description du Phalanstère*]

27

28

the Galeries Vitrée, the ramshackle, leaky, and unplanned shelter that crossed the garden condensing commercial exchange (the Bourse) and social exchange within a physical form that was, some twenty years later, to emerge as the characteristic structure of the new consumer society. Of all the galleries the most spectacular, and the most short-lived, was the half sunken Circus, built in the middle of the garden in 1786 and destroyed by fire some twelve years later; an enormous colonnaded interior, lit from above by clerestory windows and a glazed roof, and terminated by apsidal arcades, it was used for spectacles and entertainment, balls and concerts.[71]

But, for Fourier, civilized consumption was pernicious, and the social commerce it generated even more so. The *actual* society he saw in the galleries was not his object; it was the principle of social condensation exemplified by the galleries that intimated the potential of architecture to reform the social world. If Fourier's major inventions, in economy, politics, social structure, and even gourmandism, all had their roots in his own experience, their forms were the dialectical opposite of their civilized counterparts. Even as the price of apples in Paris caused him to reflect on the social consequences that stemmed from the economy of a fruit that had been so scientifically useful to Newton, so it was the inconveniences of cities that generated the architecture of social harmony, and the need for gallery streets in particular. Above all Fourier hated the rain and the cold:

It must be possible to circulate day and night from one palace to another by means of heated and ventilated passages, so that one does not run the risk, as in the present order, of being ceaselessly soaked through, dirtied and beset by colds and inflammation of the lungs by the sudden transition from closed rooms to open streets.[72]

Social relations of pleasure and of business should, in order to operate freely and without inhibition, be protected from seasonal impediments, while social intercourse would be stimulated by the very possiblity of easy movement. Fourier's ideal city was a city of arcades, a continuous building, dedicated to play and festivals, a community fostered by communication. When man at last learned to use the gallery streets of the cities, then perhaps a new order would be born where cities themselves would no longer be the centers of civilization, and, in the decentralized units of Phalanstery the covered communications would take on their final role as the very instruments of community activity. In the Phalanstery palace, as in the Palais Royale, the gallery street would act as the binding agent, but now of a harmonious and unfettered world: "The most important of the interior arrangements of the palace, that which differs the most from civilized customs, is the covered communication by means of galleries, heated in winter and refreshed in summer."[73]

The promise of continuous communication, intimated by Fourier in

the idea of the transitional city, was fulfilled in the Phalanstery: the benefits of Fourier's social invention were self-evident: it would prevent ill health, link all the social activities of the community horizontally and vertically in time and space, and operate as the social center of the whole. It was also an architectural form that combined these advantages with that of being a readily understood symbol of the transformation of civilization into harmony: the jostling, licentiousness, and frantic world of consumption changed, with the fairy wand of architecture, into the luminous, bustling and intricately intermingling structures of association. Knowledge of the former allowed understanding of the latter, and the myth of the arcades thereby grew up imperceptibly side by side with their reality, long before the iron and glass halls of Louis Philippe's bourgeois shop windows.

As Fourier described his notion, as early as 1805, the gallery street was to run alongside the different blocks of building in the Phalanstery, sometimes above ground as it linked all the apartments and public rooms of the dwelling, sometimes below as it joined the workshops, stables, hotel, and opera: "In the combined order, one can in the height of winter go to the ball, to spectacles, plays, to the workshops, in colored shoes and flimsy dresses without noticing the cold or the humidity."[74] Gone would be the colds, inflammations, fevers, chills of the present; replacing them would be increased interrelationship of all the groups and sects of the community, day and night, moving, meeting, interchanging, regrouping, and developing every type of social and individual intercourse in life and love. The unchanging climate of these public rooms would ensure that virtually every activity might be carried on in comfort. If the citizens could not run naked through their city streets because of the weather, the gallery street would allow them to play like passionate children of nature among the flowers, aromatic plants, and festive tables of the new social green house.

In its vertical section the gallery would operate in the same way to join every story of the building. And here, in the complex sectional development of the gallery, we are presented with one of the most significant architectural interventions in the Phalanstery model. It occupies the entire vertical height of the building on one side; on the ground floor it runs along the various store rooms, kitchens, and service facilities, interrupted from time to time by porticoes and cross-openings to allow vehicular passage. On the first floor, though, it is continuous, three stories high, so that all the apartments look down into it on one side and over the countryside on the other. Stairs to these apartments climb up inside the space of the gallery itself, to the smaller attic rooms for the intellectuals and down to the lower mezzanine rooms for the children. The outside wall of the gallery is lit by high windows. The gallery, in this way, became for Fourier the critical element of Phalanstery; for having articulated the various activities of the community, only the gallery could act as the binding catalyst for the whole.

So important was this space to Fourier that no building would serve the purposes of harmony without it; "there is no way of using the buildings of civilization," [75] he wrote to his disciples, who proceeded to elevate the gallery into the prime instrument of ideal social change even as it found its perfect architectural form in the real galleries of iron and glass. Victor Considerant, military engineer, a graduate of the Ecole Polytechnique, established the gallery street once and for all in the conventions of social architecture:

> The gallery street is certainly one of the most characteristic organs of social architecture. It serves for great feasts and special gatherings. Adorned with flowers like the most beautiful glass-houses, decorated with the richest products of art and industry, the galleries and salons of the Phalansteries provide splendid permanent exhibitions for the artists of harmony. It is probable that they will often be constructed entirely of glass. [76]

Now invested with the display functions of the exhibition gallery, the technical advances of industrialization, and the organic analogies of the new biology, the gallery had become the repository of nineteenth-century social progressivism. In Considerant's eyes it had a life of its own, the independent existence of a natural organism. It was the "major artery," a "canal through which life circulates," it carried the blood of the community from the heart to all the veins, and finally, it was the unitary symbol of harmony, one linking all,

> Sometimes outside, sometimes inside the palace, sometimes widening out to form a wide rotunda, an atrium flooded with light, projecting its corridors across the courtyards on columns or light suspension bridges to join together the two parallel faces of the building, finally branching out to the great white stairways and opening up wide and sumptuous communication throughout. [77]

The great preoccupation of this organization, as Barthes has seen, was communication. [78] By means of unceasing, continually varied, and architecturally structured communication, mankind would attain a balanced and reconciled harmony. Every element, function, and space of the new social habitat was to be characterized, delineated, and placed within the total system: the gallery street would unify the whole. The grand party of Fourier would be realized in the grand glass houses of the industrial city; the dream and the ideal were insensibly merged throughout the nineteenth century. Adopted into the architecture of social habitat from Godin through Borie to Le Corbusier, [79] utilized as the shelter for the exhibitions of commercial progress and the promenades of *flâneurs*, by the end of the century it was virtually impossible to separate a glass-covered street from implications of social reform. Walter Benjamin was to write on *Fourier or the arcades* as if the two were interchangeable. [80]

Engines of Industrial Order
Bentham and the Galleries of Inspection, 1791

> *In a Panopticon-prison, one general problem applies to all: to extend to all of them, without exception or relaxation, the influence of the commanding principle. Cells, communications, outlets, approaches, there ought not anywhere to be a single foot square, on which man or boy shall be able to plant himself – no not for a moment – under any assurance of not being observed. Leave but a single spot thus unguarded, that spot will sure to be a lurking place for the most reprobate of the prisoners, and the scene of all sorts of forbidden practices.* [81]

Locke had proposed that the environment influenced the development of the faculties of men; Condillac and then Helvetius had converted this into a principle of psychology at the same time as Burke was transforming it under the guise of sensationalist aesthetics into a principle of sublime effect. The Enlightenment as a whole had placed the onus on the science and art of observation to reveal and instruct, to mediate between object and subject; the instrument of observation was the eye and its commanding quality — the faculty of vision. Bentham, with a passion for detail that would have fitted a new naturalist like Buffon, a mathematical precision that would have delighted a d'Alembert, and exhaustive specifications that would have satisfied an ironmaster in a machine shop, took all these ingredients and constructed a building out of them.

It was not just an ordinary building submitted to the traditional laws of proportion, or even to the new themes of sensation, but a building that while completely tactile and material (even the width of the railings was noted) was nevertheless a principle in itself and the instrument of that principle. The Panopticon was in fact an entire "mode of architecture" (named "from two Greek words — one of which signified everything, the other a place of sight") conceived explicitly to carry out the task of enlightenment — the provision of happiness with the tools of materialism — the power of sight and thereby of surroundings:"Morals reformed — health preserved — industry invigorated — instruction diffused — public burdens lightened — economy seated, as it were, upon a rock — . . . all by a simple idea in Architecture." [82]

The general form of this all-powerful principle was remarkably simple; Bentham had invented it on a visit to his brother Samuel in Russia; the occasion was the recalcitrance of shipyard workers to submit themselves to the discipline of the new technological routine. [83] What better form of control than to arrange the workshops radially from a central observation point where the inspector could immediately detect and suitably admonish laggardly conduct? [84] Thus the Panopticon, an idea

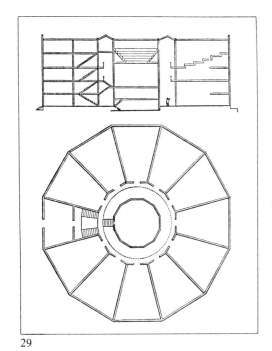

29

30

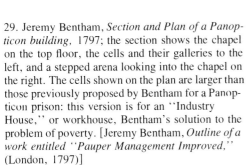

29. Jeremy Bentham, *Section and Plan of a Panopticon building,* 1797; the section shows the chapel on the top floor, the cells and their galleries to the left, and a stepped arena looking into the chapel on the right. The cells shown on the plan are larger than those previously proposed by Bentham for a Panopticon prison: this version is for an "Industry House," or workhouse, Bentham's solution to the problem of poverty. [Jeremy Bentham, *Outline of a work entitled "Pauper Management Improved,"* (London, 1797)]

30, 31. Augustus Welby Pugin; a Catholic town in 1440 contrasted with the same town in 1840; this celebrated pair of plates from the second edition of Pugin's *Contrasts* (1841), uses Bentham's Panopticon as the type of "the new jail" in the foreground of the industrial town.

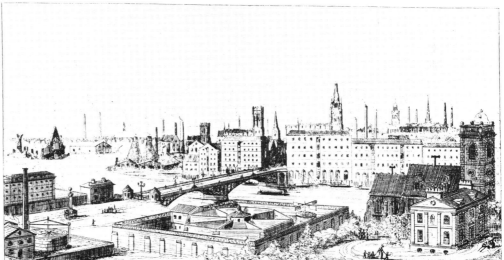

31

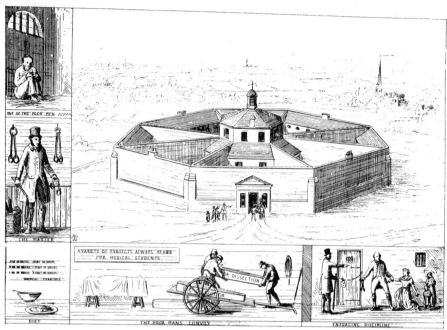

32

32, 33. Augustus Welby Pugin, *Modern Poor House,* 1841; again Pugin attacks Bentham in the contrast between a modern poorhouse and the medieval institution of monastic charity. Bentham, by the 1840s, had become the epitome of a technical, mathematical, mechanical solution to the ills of industrial society to those who, like Pugin, Carlyle, and later Ruskin, still held onto a dream of an organic medieval past reinstated, with all the human and spiritual values attributed to it, by means of a revived medieval architecture. [A. W. N. Pugin, *Contrasts,* with an introduction by H. R. Hitchcock (New York: Humanities Press, 1969)]

33

that Bentham first applied to the problem of the poor and the criminal. The building was to be circular, the cells of its inhabitants radially disposed around the perimeter; in the center was a circular house — the Lodge of the Inspector. Between the Lodge and the cells nothing would stand in the way of uninterrupted supervision of the inmates by the Inspector: "The more constantly the persons to be inspected are under the eyes of the persons who should inspect them, the more perfectly will the purpose of the establishment have been attained."[85]

The circular form ensured that one person centrally placed might view all the cells without changing position; the possibility of being seen at all times, as much as the fact of being so, would condition the behavior of every prisoner. At certain times the vision would extend the other way — toward, for example the salutary example of the Inspector eating with his well-regulated family. But the central function of the entire establishment was exercised by the annular galleries, the galleries of inspection: "In the three stories of the inspection tower, annular inspection galleries, low and narrow, surrounding in the lowermost story a circular inspection lodge."[86] The design criteria of these galleries was twofold: first, the necessity of seeing without being seen, then the economic need for speedy communication between all parts of the building. Bentham was particularly concerned with the precise techniques to be utilized in designing the gallery so as to protect the inspectors from being seen by the prisoners. He investigated the play of light and shade in the rotunda, the use of blinds and screens, the size of peep holes, the types of smoked glass available. In the end he settled for a gallery as narrow as possible, painted black on the inside, and shielded by blinds. The whole was calculated with mathematical accuracy:

> Station the inspector anywhere with his eye contiguous to the outer circumference of his ring, he can, without quitting the spot he stands or sits on, command a view of seven cells on each side. In the same ring, 46 feet may be described in walking without deviating from the right line: and 46 feet is the length of the chord subtending the space occupied in the circumference by 5 cells.[87]

If this were not enough, Bentham invented a further devise for observation: a lantern to be suspended in the center of the building, "shaped somewhat like two short-necked funnels joined together by their necks." Placed in this container, the inspector would be able to view, at will and unobserved, through small spy holes, and, when he entered the contraption from below through a trap door, his presence would remain undetected by the inmates.

Parallel to these galleries would be the access galleries to the cells, one above the other, again narrow, and protected with grills to prevent prisoners pushing the inspectors over. For cheapness, and for the overriding visual need of transparency, these gratings should be few and slender, surmounted by long slender spikes.[88] The galleries in this way

moved about the circle at every level, providing access and surveillance in equal degrees. Only one passage in the building was to run across and through its diameter: the "diametrical passage," serving the center lodge and the administrators, and moving out to the exit and the exercise yards.

These galleries were not confined to the inside, however: Bentham envisaged a complete colony of Panopticons, linked together around a central open space by covered arcades:

> Suppose two of these *rotundas* requisite: these two might, *by a covered gallery* constructed upon the same principles, be consolidated into one inspection house. And by the help of such a covered gallery the *field of inspections* might be dilated to any extent.[89]

That is, the extension of the covered gallery might extend the potential area of inspection. But always this realm would have to be centralized for the principle to be observed. Bentham proposed that the regular uncovered area thus opened to inspection might be circular, square, or oblong, according to local convenience: "a chain of any length composed of inspection houses adapted to the same or different purposes, might in this way be carried round an area of any extent." Hermetically sealed against outside influence or inside escape, the silent machines of Panopticon would stand as implements of social progress. Within them the aberrant, the deviant, the sick and the insane, the young and the aged, would be protected (for their own interest, of course) from the society that regarded them as an obstacle to its happiness.

Pain and pleasure being the sovereign masters of mankind, and quantity being the measure of satisfaction, the aim of "directing men's actions to the production of the greatest possible quantity of happiness" would be fulfilled automatically by rewarding pleasurably the greatest number according to their interests, and painfully reminding those who might not immediately conform that their own interests were involved integrally with the rest.[90] The preoccupation of good government, then, was to "promote the happiness of society, by punishing and rewarding," and all who for any reason, whether by accident of birth, misfortune, ill health, antisocial behavior, or criminal tendency interfered in any way with the accumulation of happiness by the majority were to be separated out, treated according to their condition, and perhaps rendered fit to return.

Utopias had presupposed an intolerable world of disorder and corruption and the escape of a few to preserve their sanity; the asylum provided by the ideal environment was protective against the infiltration of the outside and supportive of the mores within. Bentham, in a stroke, turned utopia inside out and utilized its structures of form and its functions of support on behalf of those outside. The great age of confinement had begun; from now, in quick succession, the hospital, the prison, the insane asylum, the old age home, the crèche, and the school would be conceived and built as the perfectly sealed capsules protecting society against its own peculiarities.[91] From now, a problem had only to be identified as socially irritant and situated within a group or classified according to a class for a building to be built as the institutional solution to that problem. And because it was utopia that had been reversed in this way, the internal structure of confinement — the life within — was itself duly beyond reproach.

Even as the conceptual form of utopia was adopted for these nuclei of social reform, so were the spatial characteristics of the ideal city adapted to the performance principles of the machine itself. The dominant centrality, the radiating lines, even the defensive wall of Panopticon were immediate translations of city form into building form, but with important differences; the radial lines, which in the ideal city were streets converging on the center, were now the partition walls of the cells; the center was no longer the common public place but the exclusive domain of the all-powerful inspector. Vision extended radially from the center; movement was forced into the concentric galleries that surrounded the hollow shaft of the Lodge, while only one route was privileged to pass diametrically through the plan, and at a single level — the single passage that gave access to the inspectors' quarters.

Rousseau had depicted early societies dancing, hands linked, about a tree, the symbol of natural order, or about a public space, the confirmation of their community. Ledoux had grouped the workers' dwellings of the city of Chaux in a semicircle around their common space. He had, it was true, placed a house of Surveillance at the center, but, with the factory sheds on either side, his plan still implied a reciprocal relationship between the director and his subjects. As in a theater, the plan of which Ledoux had self-consciously emulated, director as actor and worker as audience were bound to each other with mutual interest, and the community buildings of the workers acted as mediators between their social life and their political control. With Bentham, however, the triumph of order through vision had constituted the center as entirely occupied by authority, with the surrounding inhabitants forced into complete individuality and, thereby, subservience by their isolation. The role of the center was in this way inverted; the space of social control had been concretized in the guise of the community dwelling. The routes — galleries and passages — were solely means of fast communication or aids to more perfect observation. Trapped — the one in a cylindrical void, the others in wedge shaped cells — the inspector and the inmates were denied all connection save that of vision; social space, as conceived by Ledoux, and later by the utopian socialists, had been rendered nonexistent.

Saint-Simon and the Tracks of World Unity, 1819

Draining, clearing, the cutting of new roads and the opening of canals will be considered the most important part of this project.[92]

In 1819, Henri Saint-Simon announced the inception of his great project for world unity, a dream and a program that the nineteenth century was to fulfill almost literally, in material fact if not in social effect. As a young adventurer and business speculator, Saint-Simon had dabbled in the organization of stage coach routes from Paris to Bordeaux; a little earlier he had thrown himself into promoting ventures for canals in Panama and Spain.[93] When, in 1794, the Ecole Polytechnique was established to provide technical training for a new elite corps of engineers in the French army, Saint-Simon set himself up in an apartment across the street. There he held impromptu seminars for the students and faculty on the potential social transformations to be hoped for with the general application of science and technology to public works; for one out of the three years of education at the Ecole, a student had to study *communications*.[94] Thus identified with movement and its infrastructures, Saint-Simon developed a coherent and immensely influential doctrine of industrial progress, aided by the new routes of trade and commerce, which would finally bring peace and prosperity to a world divided through politics and self-interest.

His scheme was simple, and therein lay its appeal, especially as it coincided almost exactly with the emerging forces of change as industrial and political revolution transformed Europe: The French Revolution had failed; so indeed had the philosophical revolution of the eighteenth century. The English revolution, on the other hand, according to Saint-Simon, was advancing from strength to strength, together with the "liberal" constitution that appeared to guarantee freedom to its citizens. The aim of Saint-Simon was to install in France, along the lines of the Parliamentary system, an entirely new politics ordered on behalf of society by a new breed of professional, the *idéologue*.[95] From philosophical criticism to ideological positivism, from the development of knowledge to its application — this was the shared impulse of Monge, of Condorcet, and of Destutt de Tracy; the writings of Saint-Simon, from his quasi-Baconian "Letters from an Inhabitant of Geneva" to the "New Christianity" of 1825, developed the theme with passionate fervor.[96]

The plan of government that he proposed was entirely given over to the operations of industrial progress: a chamber of Inventions, a chamber of Review, and one of Execution would ensure the redemption of mankind through the works thus undertaken. The House of Invention, composed of two hundred civil engineers, together with assorted poets, artists, and architects, would be charged with submitting at the end of each year, "a program of public works to be undertaken to increase the prosperity of France and to ameliorate the lot of its inhabitants, taking into account utility and amenity in every case." [97]

The most important aspect of the projects conceived in this way was, of course, the construction of communication routes throughout France. The roads and canals to be built, while facilitating transport and thereby commerce and industry, should also be seen as public amenities in their own right: "their construction ought to be worked out in order to make them as pleasant as possible to travellers." [98] Fifty thousand acres of land, or more if necessary, would be selected and set aside from the regions crossed by the roads or canals, to be developed into vast cultural parks with artists' dwellings supported by the state, musicians to enliven the populace, and resting places for travelers: "the whole of France should become a superb English park, embellished with everything the fine arts can add to the beauties of nature." [99] Following Ledoux and perhaps even Babeuf, Saint-Simon saw the development of communications as a natural force of decentralization, a way of rendering luxury — hitherto confined and concentrated in the palaces and chateau of the rich — national in its distribution.

The movement he inspired, from his death in 1825 to the Revolution of 1848 and on into the Second Empire, was similarly dedicated to the opening up of communication routes — across continents and within cities. Père Enfantin, the leader of the Saint-Simonian sect, ended up as secretary general of the Paris-Lyons railway and encouraged Ferdinand de Lesseps in his Suez Canal project. Indeed, the manifesto of the movement, published from the community of Menilmontant in 1832, stated unequivocally:

> The aim is neither popular sovereignty, nor the legitimacy of the ancient regime, nor legality, but the development of industry, the organization of labor on a grand scale, the peaceful and progressive enfranchisement of the workers. And we have indicated the actual means of attaining this:
> 1. by beginning immediately the railroad from Paris to Marseilles;
> 2. by executing the project, for so long in existence, for a general distribution of water in Paris;
> 3. by piercing a street from the Louvre to the Bastille. [100]

Against the bloody uprising of the June days of that year, the provision of a complete drainage system for the capital, the cutting of a street that extended the east-west axis of the city, and the joining of the city to Marseilles were seen as the primary and peaceful steps in the establishment of a new social order. Perhaps the espousal of the cut in the city fabric was a survival from the Enlightenment projects of Laugier and Patte, but the dominant motive now was technical; no traces of aesthetic theory lingered in the practical proposals of the Saint-Simonians. Remembering that their own master had shifted his

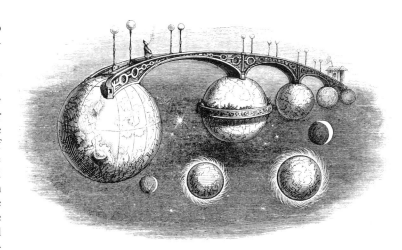

34. J. J. Grandville, *The Flâneur of the Universe*; a satirical engraving illustrating the popular vision of the Saint-Simonian view of progress through the development of universal communications. Here, the planets are united by an iron bridge, lit by gas, and observation galleries of iron and glass ring the earth, allowing uninterrupted vision of the solar system.

allegiance from Ecole Polytechnique to the Ecole de Chirurgie at the turn of the century, they talked of the "physiology" of society and the "biology" of the city in terms that extended the primitive mechanical surgery of Patte to the sophisticated terminology of the new schools of pathology and applied it to the reconstruction of the environment: Louis Blanc wrote, "Let these insanitary streets be torn down and spacious routes opened up! Let room be made for the sun in the darkest quarters, let lungs be given to Paris where it feels the need to breathe."[101] This was the program that was to inspire Louis Napoleon after 1851; but in 1832, the material aspects of social recuperation were still indissolubly merged with the spiritual in a cult that had a *New Christianity* for its principal text. The concentration on iron and glass, on railways and bridges, which characterized the late flowering of Saint-Simonianism in the Second Empire, was in this period of communitarian free love and social romanticisms imbued with a mystical cast that emerged most strongly in the poetry of Charles Duveyrier, as he portrayed the new Paris of the Saint-Simonians.[102]

Duveyrier, speaking on behalf of the brotherhood assembled in Menilmontant, began by castigating the "primitive chaos," the confusion of houses, churches, and buildings of old Paris, a veritable dance of death, with slaughterhouses, hospitals, prisons, cemeteries, and houses mingled without reason:

> And in the midst of this grand satanic dance, men and women, pell-mell, pressed together like ants, feet in mud, breathing an infested air, walking through all the obstructions of their streets and squares, buried in the rows of tall houses, black or dim, with neither hope nor care for anything better.[103]

The problem was to introduce this unhappy populace to the pleasures of an anticipated future with order, suitability, and beauty; the solution was to reform the entire city according to the image of the mores, customs, and civilization of the inhabitants. Accordingly (as society had not yet emerged from its unfortunately predominately male state), the city of Saint-Simonian future was to be in the shape of a gigantic man, lying prone along the Seine, with his head at the Ile de la Cité and his feet splayed around the Bois de Boulogne. This was to be a "living city" rising out of the morass of the old, with the power of the new industry. Its streets would be arcaded, galleried, wide, and tree-lined: "The streets are sinuous like interlaced rings; their walls are set on the ground, firm and puffed up like a pasha's turban, or suspended in the air, transparent and light in reed-like tresses."[104] Columns and vaults would cover them like fields of high plants with their leaves touching; the great circular places, with their irregular gardens, would act as centers of moving light and sound. From there the citizen could view all the marvels of advanced industrialism — the huge engines, clouds of vapor, sparks, and resounding din marking the progress of society as it lighted the sky of the city at night. Rising high in the midst of all this, finally, would be the Temple, a gigantic statue of triumphant Woman built of iron and glass, with galleries winding up and around her dress like filigreed lace.[105]

Model Towns for Health and Welfare
Owen and the Cloisters of Cooperation, 1820

> *As courts, alleys, lanes and streets create many unnecessary inconveniences, are injurious to health, and destructive to almost all the natural comforts of human life, they will be excluded.*[106]

Taking over the management of the cotton manufactory of New Lanark in January 1800, Robert Owen, enlightened, paternalistic, and one of the foremost young executives of the industrial revolution, transformed the hope of the eighteenth century into the pragmatic practice of the nineteenth. Environment and character were interdependent; environment was both mental and physical while character should be moral, and so Owen sent his factory children to a new school, stopped their parents from drinking by lecturing them at length every evening, and built more sanitary habitations for all.[107]

The illustrations for his first theoretical essays "on the principle of the formation of the human character" demonstrated the "application of the principle to practice." The ugly, squalid quarters of the working family, with husband fighting wife, child drinking gin, table collapsing, baby crying, were to be transformed into the book-lined salon of the harmonious society; musical instruments, busts of classical kind, and ornamental fruits would combine to generate familial love, mutual ties, and respect for learning in the very same individuals who had been set at each other's throats by misery.[108] Owen was convinced that "any general character" might be given to any community "by the application of proper means": these means were architectural and educational.[109]

By 1820, the architectural solution was clear. Bentham, his one time partner in New Lanark educational schemes, had designed the Panopticon; Owen proposed, in his turn, the Parallelogram.[110] In the former, the name, and the shape, referred to its active principle; in the latter, the name referred to its shape alone. The shift is significant as the space defined by parallelogram is both paradigmatic and active in its own right. No longer did the operations of the inhabitants depend on the fear of observation, of total control and visual inspectability, for the space itself was now the redeeming agent. By excluding streets, alleyways, and courtyards, it would naturally exclude the vices displayed in such environments; by emulating the form of the monastic precinct and the college court, it united the virtues of morality and learning and, by

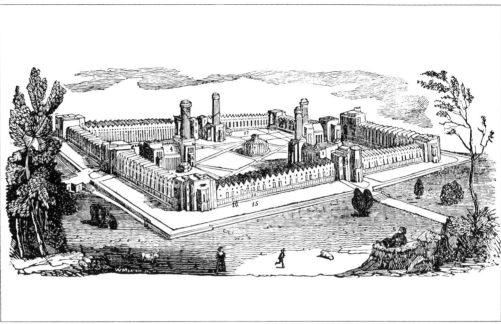

35. Robert Owen, *View of a Harmonious Community,* 1832. Key: "A design of a square building, for the accommodation of a Society of one thousand persons, combining on the principle of common property, joint labor, and united expenditure. The area of ground occupied by the buildings, promenades, and gardens of the establishment would be about thirty-three acres; that of the enclosed quadrangle, twenty-two acres; nearly three times as large as Russell Square. It is calculated to afford the inmates the advantages at once of a society and retirement, of town and of a country residence:

1. Gymnasiums or covered places for exercise, attached to the schools and infirmary.
2. Conservatory, in the midst of gardens, botanically arranged.
3. Baths, warm and cold, of which there are four for the males and four for the females.
4. Dining halls, with kitchens beneath them.
5. Angle buildings, occupied by the schools for infants, children, and youths and the Infirmary; on the ground floors are conversation rooms for adults.
6. Library, detached reading rooms, bookbindery, printing office.
7. Ball room and music rooms.
8. Theatre for lectures, exhibitions, discussions. With laboratory, small library.
9. Museum, with library of description and reference, rooms for preparing specimens.
10. The brewhouses, bakehouses, washhouses, laundries, arranged round the bases of the towers.
11. The refectories for the infants and children are on each side of the vestibules of the dining halls.
12. The illuminators of the establishment, clock towers, and observatories, from the elevated summits of which all the smoke and vitiated air of the buildings is discharged into the atmosphere.
13. Suites of adult sitting rooms and chambers.
14. Suites of chambers that may easily and quickly be made of any dimensions required; dormitories for the unmarried and children.
15. Esplanades one hundred feet wide, about twelve feet above natural surface.
16. Paved footpath.
17. The arcade and its terrace, giving both a covered and an open communication with every part of the building.
18. Subway, leading to the kitchen, along which meat, vegetables, coals are conveyed to the stores and dust and refuse brought out."

[Robert Owen and Robert Dale Owen, eds., *The Crisis,* 1832–33 (New York: Greenwood Reprint Corp., 1968), vol. ii, no. 5, Saturday, February 9, 1833]

No. 2. Vol. III.]   SATURDAY,   SEPTEMBER 14, 1833.   [Price 1½d.

THE CRISIS

AND

NATIONAL CO-OPERATIVE TRADES' UNION AND EQUITABLE LABOUR EXCHANGE GAZETTE.

36

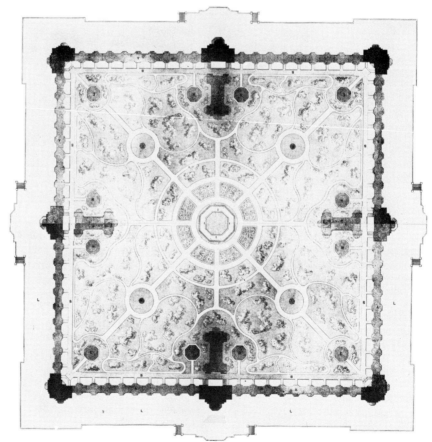

36. Robert Owen, *The Old Moral World and the New Moral World;* the frontispiece to the *Crisis,* September 1833, [Owen, *Crisis,* vol III., no. 2, Saturday, September 11, 1833]

37. Robert Owen, Plan of a *Self Supporting Home Colony,* 1841. Key:
A. Dwelling houses
B. Colonnade
C. Public buildings
D. Schools
E. Playgrounds and gymnasiums
F. Refectories
G. Towers
H. Baths
    Conservatory
K. Arbors
L. Terrace.
[Robert Owen, *A Development of the Principles and Plans on which to establish Self-Supporting Home Colonies* (London, 1841)]

37

providing a center toward which the entire community was turned, it concretized the very image of harmony and unity for the new social world. For the street, harbinger of every social ill, was substituted the cloister; the meditative walks of the past reinvoked for the secular purposes of the future:

> Running entirely around the interior of the square, at a short distance from the houses, will be a spacious cloister; by means of which access may be had to any apartment in the whole of this extensive range of buildings without going from under cover; and which will also present opportunities for sheltered exercise in very hot or wet weather.[111]

The overtly authoritarian order of Bentham had been replaced by a domestic order of apparent equality and union. Yet the controlling structures of materialist paternalism were not so easily dispensed with: the community gained its shape, specifically so that "the children can be better trained and educated under the eye of their parents" — playing in the court and undergoing "formation of character" in the centrally placed schools. Twenty years later these courts were to be lighted by high beacons throughout the night to ensure good behavior and facilitate the continuous process of industry.

Indeed, this first industrial new town, a model for the new factory villages of the next fifty years, was described by its author as a machine in its own right: "a machine it truly is, that will simplify and facilitate, in a remarkable manner, all the operations of human life."[112] As the invention of machines increased the power of labor, so the invention of the parallelogram machine would multiply the physical and mental powers of the whole society. But again the transition from Bentham is critical: from mechanistic galleries to harmonious cloisters, from the center occupied by the inspector to that occupied by education and recreation, indicates a movement toward the reciprocal obligations of teacher and pupil that was to inform the peculiar development of English socialism at its various levels for the next century. The village, once the site of natural yeoman virtue, was to be reconstituted in the guise of a rational monastery, bringing all classes together in peaceful reconciliation.[113]

The street eliminated, or at least transformed into a court: the title page of the *Crisis* (1832–1834) drew the picture graphically. Above was the shape of the old immoral world, below that of the New Moral World. The old comprised an unpaved street, dogs and cocks fighting, a beggar on crutches, flanked by the Public House on one side and the Lunatic Asylum on the other: its destination was the gallows-tree. In the new world, the street was no more; its space was paved over; it had fountains, carefully tended shrubs, children playing, adults strolling, and the clean lines of rational terraces, arcaded on the ground floor, framing the view. Even the sky had lightened:

> The artist has intended to represent the irrational and the rational arrangments of society. In the former we see the cumbrous buildings, inconvenient and crowded, of the old system; in the latter, the regular structures, scientifically disposed, of the new system.[114]

The power of the myth of a medieval past, while it might have suggested the basic form of the cloister, was not so great as to overwhelm the power of enlightened science. Rational instruction and planned order would serve the best interests of progress; science and technology, "the enormous powers of chemistry and mechanism," would enable mankind to "progress towards the highest degree of refinement, physical and mental which the human mind can rationally imagine or desire."[115]

In his proposition for "self-supporting home colonies," published seven years later, Owen developed the plans for Parallelogram in their most articulated form;[116] it is significant that, in the same year that saw the second edition of Pugin's *Contrasts,* at the height of the medieval revival in style and in ethical purpose, Owen remained wedded to the ideal of the monastery only insofar as it represented the paradigmatic space of community. The rest, with modern services, chimneys, and beacons, was an Enlightenment machine par excellence. The great square, some 1,650 feet long, was formed of four-story dwellings and closed at the corners with schools and colleges "for the scientific formation of superior character." At the midpoint of each side were assembly rooms, libraries, museums, laboratories, artists studios, and lecture halls, while projecting into the square were the four huge refectories with their kitchen smoke stacks rising to 240 feet, topped by astronomical observatories and powerful flood lights to illuminate the square at night.[117] In the green space of the courtyard were gymnasia, baths, kitchen gardens, and conservatories. The grand cloister ran around the inside of the parallelogram, pulled away from its walls for articulation, each entry way marked by its covered extension; the roof of the cloister was flat, at second-story level, with access from the apartments, for walking in fine weather. Outside the square, looking out on the three-thousand-acre estate, was a "noble terrace," a hundred feet wide, raised up from the ground on the first-floor level of the dwellings.

This plan, carefully elaborated by Owen's architect, would, according to its author, "realize more substantial and permanent happiness than has been promised in the 'New Jerusalem!'"[118]

Buckingham and the Colonnades of Morality, 1849

As a model house or lodging may lose half its good effects if placed in an unwholesome street full of pollutions and vitiating influences; whereas the benefits of a model street might derive a manifest augmentation if fortified by the general arrangements of a model town.[119]

As member of Parliament for Sheffield, with a mission to reform the poor by reforming their drinking habits, James Silk Buckingham introduced a bill empowering local authorities to establish recreational facilities for the public; walks, baths, playgrounds, halls, theatres, libraries, museums, and art galleries would, he stated, act naturally "to draw off by innocent pleasurable recreation and instruction all who can be weaned from habits of drinking."[120] As a direct result of his chairmanship of the Select Committee to inquire into the Causes of Drunkenness (1833), the teetotaler and ardent reformer was convinced that only a change in the cultural life of the poor would lead to the regeneration of their social life. The insanitary conditions of the towns, the state of working class housing and health, might well be contributing causes, but reform of these by themselves would have no real effect on the habits of the citizens. Parks and playgrounds should be opened, foot paths reestablished, public sports, games, and amusements should be organized, in order that the "mechanic who wanders forth on a holiday to breathe the fresh air of the country" should be able to "find a spot of green on which to rest his feet, or to see his children run about and gather flowers." Those who were condemned to take their exercise on foot must be provided with adequate facilities; families must be encouraged to visit public houses of culture rather than public houses of vice; the habitual patterns of the respectable middle class must be extended to the masses. Buckingham's plan was greeted with laughter, abuse, and defeat as at best "visionary and absurd."[121]

Thirteen years later, on the eve of the revolutions of 1848, he concluded that the diverse afflictions of mankind required a systematic answer for their solution: a complete model town that combined in its social organization, architectural plan, and institutional structures all the remedies for the national evils of the midcentury. Society was to be remodeled along entirely different lines, according to a plan of association, and housed in a remodeled environment that would sustain and structure its new forms, "A 'Model Society,' with its model farms, model pastures, model mines, model manufactures, model town, model schools, model workshops, model kitchens, model libraries, halls and places of recreation, enjoyment and instruction."[122]

The architectural model had supplanted, or better, subsumed, the social reform; if architectural change wrought social change then why could not society itself be designed, built, and function like a perfect building? Everywhere Buckingham saw evidence of the profound effect of environment on health, welfare, and morality. There was no town in the country that was adequately drained, or in which the dwellings were adequately ventilated — this had been well established by the Parliamentary Commissions including Buckingham's own — and consequently, "Premature deaths at all ages daily take place, and the very race itself becomes stunted and degenerated, from imperfect growth and development, arising from architectural and municipal defects alone."[123]

To remedy these defects Buckingham proposed the formation of a Model Town Association, for the purpose of building an entirely new town, "to combine within itself every advantage of beauty, security, healthfulness, and convenience, that the latest discoveries in architecture and science can confer upon it."[124] Its name would be Victoria, signifying both Queen and Victory; it would contain every improvement in siting, plan, drainage, ventilation, supply of light, water, and in architecture. A mile square, it would contain no more than 10,000 inhabitants. The entire gamut of nineteenth-century utopianism was brought to bear on the solution, once and for all, of society's problems. No beer, no prostitution, no swearing, no brawling, no child labor; these were the rules of the association, rules that encouraged the family in the regular pursuits of work, recreation, and instruction.

But, with all the regulations of the new society, the most important single instrument of reform was the plan itself, the very type of "order, symmetry, space and healthfulness" achieved with "the largest supply of air and light, the most perfect system of drainage, for the comfort and convenience of all classes." The prime requirement, not unexpectedly, was for "ready accessibility to all parts of the town, under continuous shelter from sun and rain when necessary." Buckingham had read Fourier, met Considerant, and absorbed this most important invention of social architecture into his scheme, not as a simple accommodation of pedestrian movement through the town, but as the overriding idea and physical structure of the plan. Victoria was to be a veritable city of arcades: "furnished with covered galleries, for shelter from the rain, wind, dust and sun, whenever it is desired to use them for this purpose; as to enable the residents to walk from any part of it to every other, perfectly free from exposure to any weather."[125] The purpose of these continuous arcades was, like the galleries of Fourier, to permit uninterrupted social intercourse prevented in cities by the intervention of bad weather. In this model town the arcades would be literally continuous, encircling each of the concentric rows of houses and workshops, and cutting into the center of the city along the diagonals of the square. The plan was much like a series of Parallelograms placed one inside the other, with their accompanying cloisters separated by "a large intermixture of grass lawn, garden ground and flowers," in which green spaces stood the various public buildings of the town.

The arcades were carefully graduated in form and architectural style to correspond to their specific place in the hierarchy of the town's functions; every variety of passage, gallery, cloister, and arcade in the repertory of the midcentury social architect was employed and carefully detailed.[126] The outermost range of buildings, row houses for the working classes, had a garden on one side, and on the inner front, facing onto

38. James Silk Buckingham, *Plan of Victoria*, 1849; "Plan of a Model Town for an Associated Temperance Community of about 10,000 inhabitants.

A. Outer square of 1,000 houses and gardens, 20 feet frontage, 100 feet deep.
B. Second square — Covered arcade for workshops, 100 feet wide.
C. Third square — 560 houses and gardens, 28 feet frontage, 130 feet deep.
D. Fourth square — Covered arcade for retail bazaars, 100 feet wide.
E. Fifth square — 296 houses and gardens, 38 feet frontage, 160 feet deep.
F. Sixth square — Covered arcade for winter promenades, 100 feet wide.
G. Seventh square — 120 houses and gardens, 54 feet frontage, 200 feet deep.
H. Central square — 24 mansions and gardens, 80 feet frontage, 260 feet deep.
I. Five churches or places of public worship, 200 feet by 130.
J. Library below and Gallery of the Fine Arts and Antiquities above.
K. University below and Museum of Natural History above.
Kk. Hall for public meetings below and concert room above.
L. 12 dining halls below and drawing rooms above, 100 feet by 65.
M. 12 public baths below and reading rooms above, 100 feet by 65.
N. 8 infant schools, gymnasium below, school above, 100 feet by 65.
O. 4 boys' schools for 5 to 10 years of age, same division and size.
P. 4 Girls' schools for 5 to 10 years of age — as above.
R. 4 Boys' schools for 10 to 15 years of age — same.
S. 4 Girls' schools for 10 to 15 years of age — same.
T. 8 avenues, 100 feet wide in the center, 20 feet colonnade each side.
U. 24 streets 100 feet wide in the center and 20 feet colonnade.
V. 24 open grass lawns for dining halls, baths, schools, 150 feet wide.
W. Inner Grass Lawns for Public Edifices, Churches, etc., 300 feet wide.
X. 8 fountains, 100 feet diameter, below and 50 feet jet.

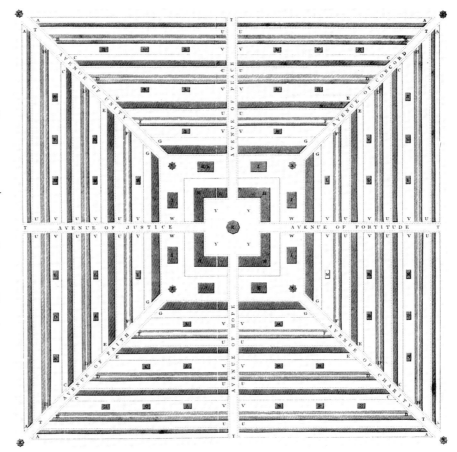

Y. Inner square or forum with porticoes and public offices, 700 feet square.
Z. Central tower for electric light, clock, and gallery, 300 feet high.

N.B. All large Manufactures using Steam Engines would be removed at least half a mile beyond the Town, as well as Abbatoirs or Slaughtering Houses, Cattle Markets, Reservoirs of Sewerage for Manure, the Public Cemetery, Hospital, Botanic Garden, Cricket Ground, and on the land to be attached to the Town for Agricultural and Horticultural purposes, Sites would be reserved for the building of Suburban Villas, by such residents as might desire it." [J. S. Buckingham, *National Evils and Practical Remedies* (London, 1849)]

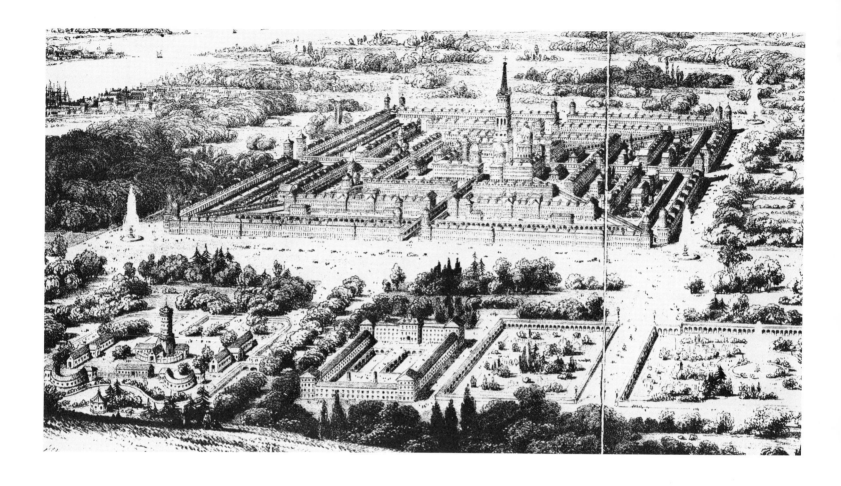

39. J. S. Buckingham, *Perspective view of Victoria,*
1849. [Buckingham, *National Evils*]

the first concentric roadway, there ran a "colonnade of the light Gothic order," twenty feet wide and one story high. Its flat roof allowed access from the second floor of the houses, forming a promenade in warm weather — and below a covered arcade for wet days. The next or second ring of buildings was itself a complete arcade structure modeled, in Buckingham's words, on the Burlington or Lowther arcades in London; it was to be some twenty feet wide, glazed and lit from above, running between single-story workshops, which themselves had flat roofs used as open walks on either side of the arcade proper. Then, moving toward the center of the town, there was another open green space for the major public buildings — dining halls, public baths, infant schools, reading rooms, and gymnasiums. The third square of houses, for middle-class occupants and therefore larger than the outer dwellings, had an arcade on its inner front of "the Gothic" order (as opposed to the "light" Gothic employed for the working classes), again with its open promenade roof. The fourth row was composed of shops, "a second covered gallery or Arcade, forming the Bazaar, for the Stores or Shops of all kinds in which the various articles made in and around the Town . . . arc disposed for exhibition."[127] This gallery, like the first, would be glazed over, and the shop roofs would be flat for promenades on both sides. The rows of dwellings for the professional classes in the next square would have a colonnade, but this time of the Ionic order.

The grandest arcade of all, the sixth row of buildings, was a covered gallery 100 feet wide that served as the major public promenade of the town,

> to be adorned as time and improved wealth may admit as the porticoes of the Romans and the Agora of the Greeks, with pictures and statuary and on every evening to have a Band, formed of the musicians of the town, to be open as a Public Promenade to all classes — sheltering them from rain, snow or sun, and enabling the youngest and most delicate to take walking exercise for health and pleasure at all hours, and on every day in the year.[128]

Thus was the portico of Ledoux, and the gallery street of Fourier, put to use as the central emblem of Victorian municipal progress, with the municipal band serenading the municipal population among municipal flowers and statues of municipal worthies. Within this arcade were rows of housing for the rich citizens, decorated with colonnades of the most highly decorated Corinthian order, and, to complete this scheme of graded architectural ornament,[129] the Grand Inner Square of the town was fronted by a magnificent arcade of the Composite order; each of the colonnades "growing more lofty and more elegant as they advance through the several gradations of the Gothic, the Doric, the Ionic, the Corinthian, and the Composite Orders of architecture." In the center of the whole town would rise a huge octagonal tower, like Fourier's Tower of Order, or Owen's Chimneys, three hundred feet high and surmounted

by an electric light for lighting the town, a clock, and bells.

Presented in description, in plan, and finally in bird's-eye view, the model Town of Victoria assembled in this way the architectonic elements of the romantic social utopia of the previous half century, but in a totally classical, almost mechanistic fashion. Closer perhaps to Morelly's communitarian city of the "Code of Nature" than to Fourier's Phalanstery, Buckingham's invention was marked by his belief in the final powers of Enlightenment reason, made operative through the combined effects of education and environment to overcome the problems of industrial society. His was the pragmatic reason of the ironmaster and parliamentary reformer rather than the idealistic reason of the communitarian utopist; his city was to be fireproof, built of iron throughout, and crimeproof, with literally no place for criminal or immoral activity:

> From the entire absence of all wynds, courts and blind alleys, or culs-de-sac, there would be no secret and obscure haunts for the retirement of the filthy and the immoral from the public eye, and for the indulgence of that morose defiance of public decency which such secret haunts generate in their inhabitants.[130]

The very sites of crime and immorality would be eradicated from the city; no secret haunts ergo no secret practices. If the circulation of pedestrians were encouraged throughout the town, either under the arcades or colonnades, or on the raised promenades themselves, joined by "light triumphal arches" bridging across the major avenues, then all the public spaces would be under continual public surveillance.

But if this seems like an eclectic and somewhat utopian plan, based on past dreams, it is nevertheless true that Victoria exercised a strong hold on the imagination of the reformers of the next half century, from Titus Salt to Ebenezer Howard.[131] Its critical role in the formulation of Victorian urban ideals and the practice of reform is a result not so much of its eclectic character but more particularly of its nature as model, a systematically conceived and synthetically designed structure for the sustenance of morality. Once built according to specification it would act to restore a balance to the disturbed social order through its architectural order, all classes would find their rightful place once more, and civic organization would regularly imitate its physical counterpart.

Buckingham had translated into urban terms the precepts of Bentham; nothing would prevent the construction of the full-scale model, once the scale prototype had been designed. Buckingham was supremely confident of the effects of building such a town:

> It is constantly contended that mankind are not to be improved by mere mechanical arrangements, and that their reformation must first begin within. But there is surely no reason why both should not be called into operation. A person who is well fed, well clad, cheerfully because agreeably occupied, living in a clean house, in an open and

well ventilated town with many objects of architectural beauty, would at least be more likely to be accessible to moral sentiments, generous feelings and religious and devout convictions and conduct, than in the teeming hives of iniquity, with which most of our large cities and towns abound.[132]

From this it was a short step to the idea that reform of conditions alone would act to reform morals and, despairing of an immediate change in human nature, the pragmatic materialists of the second half of the century worked with fervor to detail and to construct the well-planned, well-drained, well-ventilated, well-serviced environment that could be perfectly realized, if not in the old cities and industrial slums, at least in the model community of health and welfare.

The Pathology of Urban Form
Considerant and the Alleys of Infection, 1834

All these windows, all these doors, are so many mouths begging to breathe: and above all this you can see, when the wind is still, a leaden atmosphere, heavy, blue-grey, composed of all the filthy exhalations of the great sewer. This is the atmosphere that Paris breathes and beneath which it suffocates. Paris is an immense work-shop of putrefaction, where misery, plague and illness work in concert, where air and sun hardly penetrate.[133]

As early as 1783, Mercier had described the ''corrupted atmosphere'' of Paris, charged with its ''impure particles'' and trapped within the high and narrow street walls of the poor quarters; he had contrasted these ''infected exhalations'' to the pure air of the countryside — denied to the city dweller by virtue of the cadaverous odors of the cemeteries and the lack of sunlight and ventilation.[134] But, for Mercier, the pro-gressive hope of the Enlightenment, the hope that charged the very optimism of the medical gaze itself, in the schools and clinics of the turn of the century, still remained attached to the dream of a therapeutically reconstructed city. Writing some fifty years later, and two years after the cholera had claimed its eighteen and a half thousand victims, Victor Considerant was prepared to see the conjuncture of poverty, illness, epidemic, and environment as the symptomatic structure of an entire social order. While Victor Hugo climbed the towers of Nôtre Dame to reinvoke the picture of an organic, medieval Paris, Considerant found in the bird's-eye view (a new form of description, stimulated by the balloon and photography alike) a disturbing spectacle that intimately reflected its social state.[135] ''Architecture writes history'' he claimed, and the book of Paris, with its disorderly chaotic and insanitary streets, was no more than the story of a corrupt and dying civilization:

The great towns, and Paris above all, are thus sad spectacles to see especially for those who have any idea of order and harmony, for whoever thinks of the social anarchy that this shapeless mass depicts in three dimensions with a hideous fidelity.[136]

Ten years later Engels was also to characterize the problem of ''the great towns'' by reference to their physical condition; the unique con-tribution of Considerant and his utopian socialist peers (together with innumerable medical and social observers, novelists, and professionals) was to firmly establish the pathology of the city in the center of the discourse of the social problem.

In the last years of the Restoration and the first years of the July Monarchy, the special nature of this discourse was formed according to an analogy with medical diagnosis; or rather, was couched precisely in the terms of the medical discourse to the extent that the city as a physical organism, its inhabitants as a social organism, and their dual prob-lematic as sickness, disease, or death were perceived as living and interdependent systems:

How ugly Paris seems after an absence, as one suffocates in these dark, narrow and humid corridors that one would rather call the streets of Paris. One thinks one is in a subterranean town, the atmosphere is so heavy, the darkness so deep. And thousands of men live, move, press together in these liquid shadows, like reptiles in a marsh.[137]

The air, the light, the street, its inhabitants — all contributed to this frightful impression; and the entire city seemed moved with a single purpose and animated with a single natural law — that of putrefaction, suffocation, and death. All was concentrated in the narrow and con-densed space of the street: it was at once space of manifestation and of cause, its outward appearance, its very physical experience, simply revealing and confirming the condition of sickness that it created out of its very nature. Whether commentators spoke of the mud, the awful drains and their noxious exhalations, the rubbish, the dust, the poverty, beggary and crime, the maladies, the epidemics, the political manifesta-tions, the chaotic architecture, the dark and close walls, the smoke, the tragic scenes of death and misery, the comic scenes of picturesque thievery, the mysterious scenes of obscure depravity, they were attempt-ing to capture the tangible essence, the living presence of a human tragedy whose separate parts had not yet been separated out for clinical analysis. Just as the air perceptibly carried its diseases and entered every realm of the environment, penetrating each individual, so did the social infection stem from the continuous operations of a consuming and cannibalistic social order. Considerant posed the questions: ''Did God make Paris, or did man? Did God make cholera, or did man?'' If the effect was thus, then the cause was human in its origins.

In the face of such general disease, the single measures advocated by

40

41

40. *Bird's-eye View of Paris in the time of Louis XIII;* Victor Hugo describes such a view of a simple, neatly laid out vision of medieval Paris in *Nôtre Dame de Paris* (1831), Book iii., "Paris a vol d'oiseau." [Adolphe Joanne, *Paris Illustré* (Paris: Hachette, 1879), p. 21]

41. *Bird's-eye View of Paris in 1852:* a view of the city at the beginning of the Second Empire, such as Considerant describes in his *Considérations sociales sur l'architectonique* of 1834. [Edmond Texier, *Tableau de Paris* (Paris, 1852–53), in two vols., vol. I, frontispiece]

the planners seemed fruitless; a street from the Louvre to the Bastille would indeed be fine, but the hundred others, "in which the inhabitants are relegated like pariahs, in which the physiognomies are livid and cadaverous," remained untouched.[138] No piecemeal embellishment would serve to cure the organism, nor would a few judicious cuts of the surgeon's knife remove the cancer. The entire city was infected and must be rebuilt or replaced by another form of settlement. For Considerant, of course, the Phalanstery was the ready answer; for other Fourierists, like the engineer Perreymond and architect César Daly, reconstruction was still a possibility.[139] Perreymond published a new plan for Paris, detailing with precision the type of intervention to be made common practice by Haussmann under the Second Empire, while Daly investigated the possible forms of new social housing. Perhaps the most significant contribution of these romantic socialists, however, resided not in their solutions but in their *critique* that so graphically linked the description of social conditions with their underlying causes, using the environment as the frame of depiction:

> The greatest number of the streets of this marvellous Paris are mere trenches, dirty and always humid with infected water. Narrowly pressed between two rows of high houses, the sun never descends into them, and visits only the top of the chimneys that dominate them. A pale and sickly crowd moves through them ceaselessly, foot in the gutter, nose in infection, and the eye is struck at each corner by the most repulsive filth.[140]

Such were the streets of this city of burgeoning commerce, of bourgeois hegemony, of civilized culture; and if the streets of mid-eighteenth-century Paris had been incompatible with Enlightenment, these were surely, as the author of this description claimed, "incompatible with the Republic." Thus the politics of the street were directly read from its aspect in a way that was to inform the forms of public revolt for the next century or more. The identity of a poverty with a special realm had this double effect: while concretizing the motives of revolt about a visible cause, it also found the revolt identifying itself with a space to be defended, however miserable and dirty.

The lines between the sick, the poor, the political, and the criminal were not as clear in the world of pre-'48 Paris as they were to become in the Second Empire. The dangerous classes and the working classes were largely seen as one, as Chevalier has demonstrated, and together they possessed, or at least inhabited, this realm of Paris that constituted the dark, the choleric, the beneath — that mysterious underworld so eternally fascinating to the bourgeois. Fascinating, as the physiognomies of the romantic, picturesque novels and *feuilletons* depicted it, but also feared. An increasing population, its inherent propensity to crime and susceptibility to plague, its potential for political and perhaps revolutionary activity inherited from the bread riots of an earlier age, was

concentrated in the narrow, infected and, dirty streets of the center and east of the capital. Eugene Sue's "Mysteries of Paris" was written about this population of new "barbarians."

This localization of revolt, of public manifestation, had, of course, been present in the first Revolution, where the Faubourgs gained an identity for themselves, and even erected temporary barricades; but not until 1830 were the lines drawn so clearly in space that represented the boundaries of class. Increasingly, and in ever more violent forms, the domain of the street, defined by the barricade, took on the character of appropriated utopia. Perceptively, Hugo saw the barricades of June 1832 as natural extensions of the epidemic of the month before: the political continuation of a biological crisis, which in itself demonstrated the real conditions of social life with geographical precision. Long before 1848, and as a result of the successive manifestations of 1830 and 1832, the rationale behind certain projects for urban renewal had become clear. As Marx wrote in 1844, mysteries were more comfortable when confined to literary romance than to the urban precincts of ever-present criminality.

> The lairs of criminals are so great a *mystery*, not only for Parisians in general, but even for the Parisian police themselves that even at this very moment they cut clear and wide streets in the Cité to make these haunts accessible to the police.[141]

Engels and the Precincts of Poverty, 1844

The very turmoil of the streets has something repulsive, something against which human nature rebels.[142]

Little Nell, visiting Birmingham for the first time with her grandfather, felt "amidst the crowd, a solitude which has no parallel."[143] Successive revolutions in France had made of the crowd in Paris an essentially political and communal phenomenon; "the magnetism of enthusiastic crowds" was sensed by Hugo on the barricades of 1831, and Frederic, undergoing his sentimental education, on those of 1848.[144] The industrial and commercial revolution in England, concentrating in the great towns the masses of middle and working classes needed to sustain its appetite for ever-expanding production and consumption, had, for contemporary observers, engendered an entirely different type of experience, that of complete aloneness in the company of thousands. The incessantly moving throng, the lack of recognition of the individual in the multitude, the artificiality of the scene, lit by gas and framed by the new commercial streets, caused the sensitive visitor "to feel but an atom," and an atom, further, "in a mountain heap of misery."[145]

Like Little Nell, Engels, on his first visit to London, was repulsed by

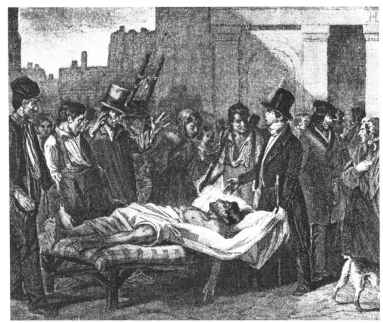

43

42. *A street in old Paris*, engraved by Gustave Doré. Less romantic than his later scenes of London streets, this engraving was published by Joanne to illustrate the contrast with Haussmann's avenues. [Joanne, *Paris Illustré*, p. 139]

43. ''The doctor raises the covers and says to the people, 'Here is a victim of cholera' ''; scene outside the Hôtel Dieu during the epidemic of 1832. Louis Blanc, Victor Hugo, and Considerant agreed in linking the uprising of June 1832 with the effects of the epidemic in which some 18,500 had died. — the political result of the conditions of life. [Louis Blanc, *Histoire des dix ans*, 1830–1840 (Paris, 1882), p. 497]

42

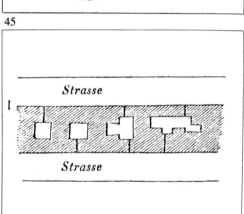

44

45

46

47

44. Friedrich Engels, *Plan of Manchester in 1844*. Plate from the second German edition of his *Condition of the Working Class in England* (1845) [Friedrich Engels, *Die Lage der Arbeitenden Klasse in England* (Stuttgart, 1892)]

45. Engels, the *Old Town of Manchester,* 1844: "Here the streets, even the better ones, are narrow and winding, as Todd Street, Long Millgate, Withy Grove, and Shude Hill, the houses dirty, old, and tumble-down, and the construction of the side streets utterly horrible." [Engels, *Die Lage,* p. 49]

46. Engels, street in the newer quarters of the Old Town of Manchester: "The space between the two streets is divided into more regular, usually square courts . . . [which] communicate with the streets by means of covered passages. If the totally planless construction is injurious to the health of the workers by preventing ventilation, this method of shutting them up in courts surrounded on all sides by buildings is far more so. The air simply cannot escape." [Engels, *Die Lage,* p. 56]

47. Engels, new contractors' cottages, Manchester, 1844: "By this method of construction, comparatively good ventilation can be obtained for the first row of cottages, and the third row is no worse off than in the former method. The middle row, on the other hand, is at least as badly ventilated as the houses in the courts, and the back street is always in the same filthy, disgusting condition as they." [Engels, *Die Lage,* p. 57]

the inhumanity of the scene: "The hundreds of thousands of all classes and ranks crowding past each other, are they not all human beings with the same qualities and powers and with the same interest in being happy?"[146] Notwithstanding, they crowded by one another, with nothing in common, each keeping to the right side of the pavement to separate the opposing streams of people; the effect of this, en masse, was to increase the individual's isolation, to separate out each as a monad, a Leibnizian atom, not for the purpose of self-development, as Rousseau would have hoped, but as the expression of private interest. The social war, hidden within the operations of consumption and production in the emerging world of capital, was in the street of the great city openly declared and revealed.[147]

And what was true in the broad streets of commerce was even more so in the narrow alleyways of poverty: in the areas assigned to the working classes, the conditions of the street furnished an index of the condition of the society it sheltered: "The streets are generally unpaved, rough dirty, filled with vegetable and animal refuse, without sewers or gutters, but supplied with foul, stagnant pools instead."[148] They were ill ventilated, owing to the "bad, confused method of building" of the whole quarter; they concentrated the poor in a space too small for their number. They served as drying grounds in good weather, market places, garbage dumps, sewers, and as the very dwelling of the outcast poor. The alleys and courts that led from these streets were even narrower, more filthy, worse ventilated, dark, and crime ridden. Engels described streets in London, in Dublin, and Glasgow; Leeds, Bradford, and Edinburgh: the conditions of the working classes and the conditions of their streets were everywhere the same. The streets were symptomatic of their entire lot. Those of Manchester were typical and furnished Engels with a detailed opportunity to construct a model of the social effects of industrial revolution through the study of its environments: if, as he was to state, toward the end of his analysis of Manchester, "the manner in which the need of a shelter is satisfied furnishes a standard for the manner in which all other necessities are supplied," then the street was likewise a vivid symptom, a complete pathology of the social disease.[149] Just as the doctors of Paris exhibited the condition of their patients in the public theaters of the Revolution, so the streets of Manchester publicly exhibited their content of private misery.[150]

The streets of Manchester had a distinct typology according to their use. Engels distinguished first those of the central commercial district, "abandoned by dwellers and lonely and deserted by night"; then the main thoroughfares cutting through this district, with their concentration of traffic and brilliant shops, active until late at night. Then beyond, an intermediate girdle of working-class dwellings, the regularly laid out streets of the middle classes and, further out, on the breezy hills around the city, the upper-class villas. It was possible for a person to pass daily from the middle- or upper-class quarters of the town right into the center without ever coming into contact with a worker, his dwelling, or his street; for the radial thoroughfares were lined continuously with shops sufficing effectively to "conceal from the eyes of the wealthy men and women of strong stomachs and weak nerves the misery and grime which form the complement of their wealth."[151] It was with these streets of misery and grime that Engels was principally concerned.

From the old town, with its dwellings irregularly crammed together defying all rational plan, to the more recently built labyrinths of the industrial areas, to the courts and straight streets of the new town, Engels persistently recorded and systematically analyzed the forms of social life enclosed. His description was, in his words, "far from black enough to convey a true impression of the filth, ruin and uninhabitableness, the defiance of all considerations of cleanliness, ventilation, and health which characterize the construction of this single district," but levels of his reading were profound. First, there was the confusion of the old town, characterized by its irrationality, its historically determined chaos. The visitor was lost, "He wanders from one court to another, turns countless corners, passes nothing but narrow filthy nooks and alleys until after a few minutes he has lost all clue, and knows not whither to turn."[152] It was an underworld, a Hell of Earth, whose filth, airlessness, and unhealthiness were an immediate function of the "planless, knotted chaos." Secondly, still in the old town, there were the newer rows of houses, built at least in straight lines and according to a plan: "But if, in the former case, every house was built according to caprice, here each lane and court is so built, without reference to the situation of the adjoining ones."[153]

An equal labyrinth, of equal squalor, was thus formed. Engels hesitated to use the word ventilation. The industrial epoch had allowed such sinks to be let for high rents to those who had nowhere else to look — no hole was so bad but that some poor creature must take it who could pay for nothing better. These were the old quarters, though, and badly constructed to start with; perhaps the newer streets furnish better conditions.

In the new town, "single rows of houses or groups of streets stand, here and there like little villages on the naked, not even grass grown clay soil."[154] The mud was thick in the lanes, which remain unpaved, and all semblance of city life or community was gone. The common method of building was to surround small, usually square, courts by the buildings, furnishing communication to the main street by covered passages. These courts had been compared by liberal reformers to a "multitude of little parks" improving ventilation and health; in fact, with no actual means of through ventilation, this method was even worse than the "totally planless construction" of the old town. The newer forms of "back to back" plan, adopted by contractors to economize in land and building materials, were hardly better in the

48

49

48. Gustave Doré, *Bishopsgate Street,* London: "another working day has fairly opened; and mighty and multi-form is the activity." Blanchard Jerrold's text to Doré's *London* appreciates the city and its inhabitants, rich and poor, as a picturesque scene rather than as an economic or social entity. [Doré, *London,* p. 115]

49. Gustave Doré, *Wentworth Street, Whitechapel:* "It is the striking and affecting feature of London especially, where in the lanes and alleys the houses are so full of children that, to use a wit's illustration,

you can hardly shut the street door for them. In the poorest of London districts the men, women and children appear, on entering, to have abandoned all hope. There is a desperate, ferocious levity in the air: and the thin, wan, woebegone faces laugh and jeer at you as you pass by." [Doré, *London,* p. 120]

50. Gustave Doré, *London street scene,* 1872: "On our way to the City on the tide of Labour, we light upon places in which the day is never aired. . . . Rents spread with rags, swarming with the children of mothers for ever greasing the walls with their

shoulders; where there is an angry hopelessness and carelessness painted upon the face of every man and woman." [Gustave Doré and Blanchard Jerrold, *London; a pilgrimage* (New York: Dover Publications, 1970), p. 116]

51. Gustave Doré, *Over London — by rail:* beneath the railway viaducts, the backyards of the slum houses are pressed together in filth and shadow. [Doré, *London,* p. 121]

50

51

resulting conditions provided, especially for the middle of the three rows of houses. Further, these new developments were built for a maximum period of forty years, often less, and deteriorated quickly after construction.

The critical archeology of dwelling that Engels provided, together with the social conditions he described, thus constitute the first systematic attack on the Enlightenment vision of progress, couched in precisely the Enlightenment's own terms. The planless chaos, the dirty, twisting streets, have been encountered before, from Rousseau onward; but it was always understood that the imposition of a rational plan, the development of a uniform mode of housing, would naturally shape the mores of the new inhabitants. Engels disposed of this myth and turned it right about, placing the blame for conditions squarely on the economics of the industrial system that created them. These conditions were, nevertheless, valuable analytical tools that precisely characterized the nature of social life, the results of the system of capital; in the end they revealed the ineffectivity of the environment by itself to produce a transformation in the social order.

One after the other, but with political conclusions less evidently and less precisely stated than in Engels, the writers of the midcentury called out the reality of the industrial ideal: one by one they traversed the same landscape of misery and in their own ways indicated the forms and ends of reform. Elizabeth Gaskell, opening *Mary Barton* with the graphic contrast of town and country, finds in the streets of Manchester the causes and the effects of the great division between rich and poor.[155] The picture of the "well-filled, well-lighted shops" side by side with the dim gloomy cellars of the Bartons' world, the "stagnant, filthy moisture" of the working-class streets oozing into their cellar rooms, and the clean, well-serviced drawing rooms of the employers; such contrasts were the literary translations of the statistics marsheled in her namesake's *Manufacturing Population of England*, a work used to such effect by Engels.[156]

More akin to Engels in moral fervor and political activity was Charles Kingsley. The setting of Alton Locke's conversion and the inferno of his revelation were the foul, chilly, foggy streets of London where the gas lamps flared and flickered, wild and ghastly. "Greasy parchments, odours, blood and sewer water crawled from under doors and out of spouts and reeked down the gutters amid offal."[157] Above, "hanging like cliffs," were the houses, with their teeming load of life, piled up "into the dirty choking night" along the streets, those "narrow, brawling torrents of filth and poverty and sin." Such were the scenes of Hell, with their attendant devils, the pawn broker's shop and the gin palace, "eating up men and women and bairns, body and soul." Kingsley had remarked that industrial capitalism was a form of mass cannibalism — here the street itself became the devourer, the image of the meat market

and the life that surrounded it conflated in a monstrously active maw, the mouth of consumption.

"The social state of a city," he wrote in 1857, "depends directly on its moral state," and the moral state in turn depends, to a yet uncalculated extent, "on the *physical state* of that city; on the food, water, air and lodging of its inhabitants."[158] Their life, existing on a level with their surroundings, was unable to rise above the physical and moral filth. The institutions so beloved of reformers — the reformatories, schools, hospitals, asylums — were now seen to be merely "the symptoms of the disease." The causes could only be touched by improving physical conditions for the entire working class.

Kingsley, while echoing the reform-through-reconstruction message of the earlier utopians, nevertheless recognized that it is the system of property, land values, and vested interests that has made, and continues to make, the rebuilding of cities an impossibility. But, idealist at heart, he prophesied that it was this very condition that would cause the building of "better things than cities"; prophetically for the later development of Marxist disurbanization, and perhaps even following the message of the Communist Manifesto of 1848, he proclaimed the need for "A complete interdependence of city and of country, a complete fusion of their different modes of life, and a combination of the advantages of both such as no country in the world has ever seen."[159] Dwellings would no longer be crowded into "ill built rows of undrained cottages," but would be combined in Fourieristic fashion in common blocks of building set in the heart of the country with rail lines connecting them to the workshops in the cities. In these remaining cities, "the old foul alleys will be gradually depopulated and replaced by the warehouses and workshops of commerce."

Thus was the pathology of the street conceived as a prelude to its disappearance: to abolish the foul air, foul water, foul lodging, and overcrowded dwellings that made a life of decency impossible was to abolish their seat and cause, the street. This message was clear in the writings of radical socialist and Marxist alike for the next century: what separated them was what divided (in the first place) Engels from Kingsley. The former insisted that cities were capital; that capital was the system of exploitation; that cities artificially separated the urban from the rural proletariat; and therefore they should be distributed into the country. The latter held that it was the living conditions in the cities that were evil and that living in the country was healthier; therefore the cities should be reserved for work alone. In both, the central problem of the nineteenth century, the unbearable rift between the country and the city, was to be healed again by the reestablishment of mankind within nature, not as Fourier and Owen would have had it, in autonomous and self-supporting agrarian communities, but in a continuous interspersion of agriculture and industry.

The City of Lost Illusions
Balzac and the Arcades of Commerce, 1837

Vast and solid galleries, very well ventilated and planned with art, have replaced those narrow, insanitary, muddy crossroads where, without order or taste, the daily provisions for 200,000 families were heaped up. Paris has become a manufacturing town, and the market place for all the manufactures of France.[160]

No urban structure so clearly epitomized the unequal dialectic between the utopian dream and the material reality of the first half of the nineteenth century as the Parisian arcade. From the Restoration the arcades were built increasingly of glass and iron, and thereby signified the apparent triumph of the new means of production in consort with the emerging world of consumption. A utopian might dream of a future made transparent with glass or fireproof with iron or socially harmonious with the gallery street; social reality concentrated the products of industrialism, the woven and printed goods of bourgeois households and mentalities, side by side with their consumers — these again pushing past their pariahs. The arcades were the haunts of thieves, vagabonds, and rapacious commercial interests, jostling humanity, bizarre physiognomy, frivolity, and misery — truly the microcosms of social and economic conditions. If Considerant had not reserved the galleries for his utopia, he would certainly have seen them as an example of the characteristic architecture of his epoch (even as he had seen the barracks and the prison). In their birth a product of speculation, the arcades nevertheless haunted the images of nineteenth-century progress; a double-sided, mirror image that posited potential ideality in the very space of the real.[161]

But these arcades did not come into being as fully fledged type-forms of the new marketplace overnight. It was their process of formation that at once crystallized and refracted the tensions between class and class, between the mode of production and the mode of construction, between, in fact, society and its culture, which had been forced by the industrial and political revolution. First there were the vauxhalls and porticoes of the *ancien régime;* then the great Circus of the Palais Royale and its accompanying galleries; then, following the burning of the circus, the appropriation by the people of Paris of the wooden galleries that crossed the gardens themselves. These were the Galeries de Bois, standing from the late 1780s until their replacement by the Galerie d'Orleans over forty years later. Balzac described them as they were in 1820:

They were barracks, or to be more exact, huts made out of planks, small, badly roofed, badly lighted from the court and from the garden by the casements called windows, but which resembled the dirtiest openings of the inns outside the barriers. A triple range of shops formed two galleries about twelve feet high. Shops sited in the middle opened onto the two galleries whose atmosphere gave them a mephitic air, and whose roof allowed little light to pass through the always dirty panes.[162]

These center shops, by reason of the double stream of passersby, gained an incredibly high value despite their minute size — not more than six feet wide. Outside, toward the gardens, the walls were plastered with peeling and falling stucco, covered with the "fantastic writings" or graffiti of the populace, piled high with garbage and discarded refuse, and soiled with excrement: a "noisome and disgusting approach" that might ward off those of a delicate and refined nature. But, despite their offensive aspect, the filth and mud of their floors, continually wet by the leaking roofs,

This sinister mass of mire, these glass panes encrusted with rain and dust, these flat-roofed huts covered outside by rags, the filth of the exterior walls, this assemblage of things like a gypsy camp or the barracks of a fair, or the temporary constructions with which they surround monuments yet to be built in Paris, this grimacing physiognomy went admirably with the different trades that swarmed beneath this lewd hangar.[163]

Even as the science of physiognomy provided the most fashionable, and perhaps the most characteristic, mode of perception of the age (the *physiognomies of Paris* were published and dissected in a multitude of popular tracts, guide books, and novels) so the Galeries de Bois acted as the setting for them all — the faces of commerce, of luxury, of poverty, of respectibility, of politics, money, and corruption, of pornography and depravity, of exoticism, and of criminality. They were the home of the Stock Exchange for twenty years, the center of speculation and stock dealing; they furnished a home to the printing trade and the cloth and fashion trades; finally, joining the two great theaters of Paris, they were themselves show rooms for humanity. As the whole space was open, with the shops along the center set up like the booths of a fair, the entire scene could be taken in at a glance, from one end to the other. Ladies of fashion could promenade, actors might pose, literary fops parade, and, "from all quarters of Paris a prostitute would come *to do the Palace.*" Indeed, its very name, "the Palace," signified the "temple of prostitution." Prostitutes in this period were the *flâneurs* of a later. These women drew such a considerable crowd to the Galeries de Bois in the evening that one was compelled to walk at a snail's pace, as in a procession or masked ball. This slowness, which troubled no one, allowed close examination.[164] This scene, exhibiting a collection of all the types of the street in a public room for the purposes of mutual display, was marked by its contrasts, the aesthetic criteria par excellence of romantic social ideology: it was both "horrible and gay," well-dressed mingled with raggedly poor, dark clothing set off white flesh "producing the most magnificent oppositions."

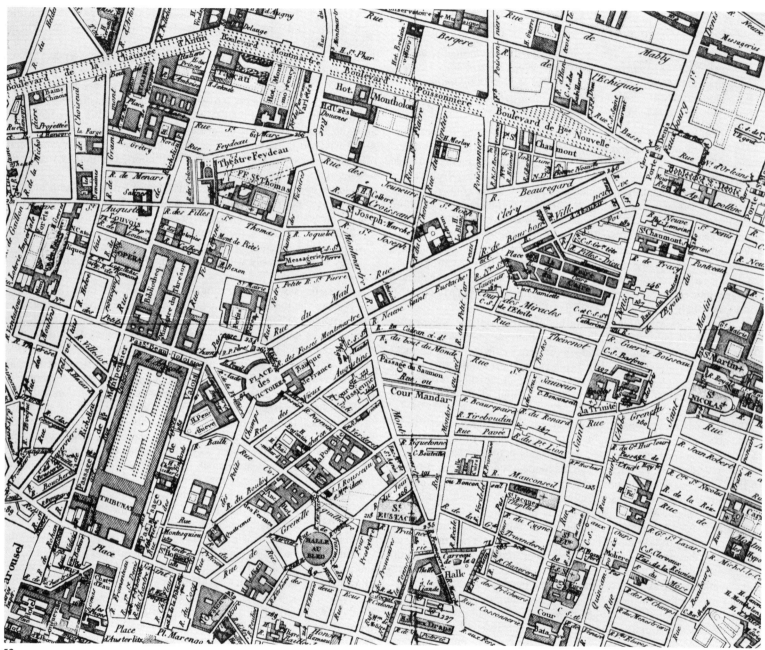

52

53

54

52. *Paris, the quarter of the Palais Royal,* from Maire's *Plan,* 1808. Between the gardens of the Palace and the old boulevards was the theater district, with the old Opéra, the Théâtre Feydeau, the Théâtre Italiens, the Variétés; next to this last was the Passage des Panoramas, and the first Panoramas themselves on the boulevard Montmartre.

53. *The Gallery d'Orleans,* Palais Royal, 1830; view from the gardens. "The most striking of the galleries is that to the south, called the Galerie d'Orleans, from its having been erected by the present king in 1830. It has the appearance of an oriental gallery of glass, the sides being entirely occupied by the windows of the shops and the intermediary panels being fronted with mirrors." [Galignani's *New Paris Guide* (Paris, 1839), p. 191]

54. *Interior of the gallery of the Palais Royal* (Galerie d'Orleans); drawn by A. Pugin (A. W. Pugin's father) for his *Paris et ses environs* (Paris, 1831). "The best time for seeing the garden and arcades is in the evening when they are brilliantly illuminated with gas, and when a continual tide of loungers fills them in every part. . . . There are many persons who pass not only days but years in ceaselessly sauntering through it. It is the perpetual residence of all that is idle and of the little *rentiers* of the capital. Improper characters of the other sex have of late years been excluded and a strict guard is kept up." [Galignani, *New Paris Guide,* p. 191]

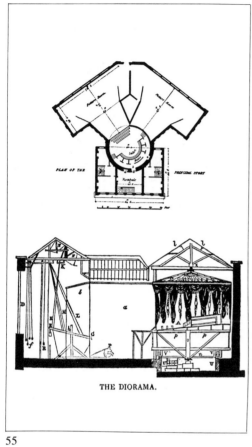

THE DIORAMA.

55

56

55. *Plan and section of a Diorama,* London, designed by A. Pugin (the elder) and J. Morgan, 1823.

56. *Interior view of a Diorama scene,* depicting St Paul-outside-the-walls, Rome, after a fire. [Texier, *Tableau,* vol. II, p. 297]

The spectrum of the social world was then presented to itself, so to speak, in a physical frame that served to condense and concentrate in order to heighten its special characteristics. This love of visual display, within an artificial environment that allowed its continuance day and night, unimpeded by the weather, was further reflected in the new entertainments that sprang up adjoining the arcades, the Panoramas, and the Dioramas; institutions that enclosed within their own circular space all the attributes of gallery while adding the dimension of travel, mystery, and romance.

The first Panoramas were built on the boulevard Montmartre at the turn of the century and gave their name to the passages that led to them from the Palais; significantly, their first scene was a "View of Paris," seen from the roof of the Tuileries. The city was presented in bird's-eye view to itself: the scene was astonishingly real. Painted in a circle and illuminated from above, it embraced the entire horizon for a spectator placed at the center; all sense of time and space was lost in the illusion. The painter David advised his pupils to study nature in the Panoramas — the triumph of the artificial — while the future inventor of photography, Daguerre, worked on their painting before transforming them into the Dioramas of the 1820s.[165] The Dioramas completed the illusion of nature by introducing changing lighting effects behind the translucent canvases, replacing cityscapes with landscape and gothic views, bringing all the apparatus of romantic association and sublimity to the city dweller. Art and nature had finally merged indistinguishably for the incredulous public who hotly disputed whether indeed they were witnessing mere paintings.[166] The perfect complement to the galleries, the Dioramas held the imagination of the people until the revolution of 1848, when the real city regained its importance as the theater of social action.

Both arcade and diorama were interiors par excellence, but, of course, public interiors; and if the arcade was seen as a city in miniature, then the Diorama extended this city to the entire world. Between 1830 and 1848, in the Paris of Louis-Philippe, the bourgeois monarch, the interior developed its characteristic role in consumer society as the realm of private fantasy, private wish fulfilment, and private display of private taste; decor might provide what social revolution had failed to deliver — the possibility of each to realize his individual utopia by populating his own interior world with the objects of his dreams, conveniently reproduced for him by the emerging industry of universal kitsch.

Correspondingly, it is not surprising that it was during this period, when the Dioramas were built on new and improved lines, that the arcade, as the exact conjuncture of public street and private interior, also received its typical definition. Now the arcades were built in the new materials, iron and glass, as complete buildings, with entrances and exits; their centers were public rooms, their shops and cafés semipublic rooms, and they were overlooked by the private apartments of the middle classes. In 1832 a guide book to the city referred to them in their most typical form: as "a rather recent invention of industrial luxury, glass covered marble panelled passageways through entire complexes of houses whose proprietors have combined for such speculations . . . such an arcade is a city, indeed a world, in miniature."[167]

In 1830, the architect Fontaine rebuilt the entire Galeries de Bois as the Galerie d'Orleans; Balzac describes it as "cold, lofty, a sort of greenhouse without flowers" and mentions the unanimous regret felt at the demolition of the old wooden shacks, "so much so that all Paris came there till the last moment, walking on the wooden planks with which the architect covered the cellars while he built."[168] The regret signified more than the passing of an old structure and the building of a new, however; with the introduction of the techniques of greenhouse construction into the sphere of commercial practice, an already emerging separation in public social life was reified. Greenhouses were for the artificial culture of nature, arcades for the artificial culture of society, but a society that was increasingly being divided from a common culture. The arcades gradually ceased to be instruments of social mingling and cultural diversity and became instead the means by which cultural difference was accentuated. The bohemian, the dandy, the *flâneur* were in a sense the middle-class response to the exclusion of the real differences from their world; self-consciously and artificially within a single dominant class the entire range of physiognomies might be recreated, again exhibited, and paraded for consumption. Real political eccentricity or radicalism was replaced by posture; real poverty aped, real criminality harmlessly imitated, in the same way as the real objects of past cultures were reproduced artificially. It is interesting that the arcades, the scene of this transformation, were built in the first artificial building materials. In the endlessly standardized units of the largest greenhouse of all, the Crystal Palace, Fourier's essentially bourgeois utopia found its real home in the very year of Louis Napoleon's own triumph. The domain of the people who filled the Palais of Balzac's Paris was, increasingly after 1827, confined to the streets and alleys of their own poverty. Like the small traders who set up shop in the huts of the wooden galleries, they too attempted to appropriate, with the materials to hand, the space of their confinement. This space now became recognizable as separate from the centers of luxury trade and entertainment, and as having its own pathology as the center of all ills. At this point the fragile glazing of the arcades was threatened by the powerful uprising of the barricades.

Hugo and the Barricades of Revolution, 1832

The eye which had viewed this mass of shadow from a height had perhaps glimpsed here and there, at different points, indistinct glimmers throwing into relief broken and strange lines, the profiles of strange constructions, something like lights coming and going in the ruins; there it was that the barricades stood.[169]

Victor Hugo had mounted the towers of Nôtre Dame to describe Paris in its medieval glory; in *Les Misérables* he again took to the heights to characterize the city in the throes of the insurrection of 1832, this time in the form of an owl, and at night.[170] It was, in contrast to the resplendent and almost magical vision of the fourteenth century, a "gloomy spectacle"; the old quarter of the markets, the streets of Saint Denis and Saint Martin, where the insurgents had established their redoubt, seemed like a city within a city, "an enormous dark hole hollowed out of the center of Paris." No lights shone in windows that might attract fire, no one stirred in the streets: "nothing but terror, grief, stupor in the houses, in the streets a kind of sacred horror." The only signs of the revolt were "strange constructions" and around them a few glimmers of light — the barricades.[171] The entire area was surrounded by a virtual wall of sabers and bayonets, turning it into a monstrous cavern — at once a shelter and a potential tomb for the invisible combatants, its inhabitants. From the haunts of crime, from the sick center of working-class misery, the political revolt had risen as its natural expression and confirmation, and the barricades had finally drawn the precise physical line that circumscribed this realm of poverty, crime, and plague. The laboring classes and the dangerous classes, the sick and the poor had appropriated the space of their subjection and traced its geography, as on a map, with buildings of their own made from the very fabric of their streets.

The barricade was not a characteristic structure of the '89 Revolution; in the first year at least, the crowd was intent on appropriating a new Paris for itself, entering previously forbidden realms, following the streets almost at random as assemblies turned into riots, riots into revolts. Paris was being opened up, not closed; even the parades of celebration and order were in some sense the ritual sanctions of a city made one for all its citizens. Only in 1827, some two centuries after their temporary appearance during the Fronde, did barricades block the public ways of Paris. The name came from the word *barrique* ("cask" or "barrel") and, in the celebration of the downfall of Villèle, they were also built of paving stones torn from the street itself.[172] In July 1830, they were erected again in the Faubourgs Saint Antoine and Saint Marcel, blocking the way from the Hotel de Ville to the Place de la Bastille. Two years later, in June 1832, they finally took on a distinct proletarian character as they defined an area of revolt roughly a third of that of Paris. Paradoxically enough, it was as a result of a cortège — the funeral of General Lamarque — that the barricades of June, the physical appropriation of the street, were built. On the same day (June 5) the red flag was borne through the streets by a mysterious horseman dressed in black.[173]

The barricades were erected quickly — in less than an hour Hugo notes; twenty-five rose out of the earth in the quarter of Les Halles alone; after 1848 Baudelaire was to refer to those "magic cobblestones that rise up to form fortresses." They were part of the process that transformed a riot into an insurrection:

The insurrection, brusquely, had built the barricades with one hand and with the other seized almost all the guard posts. In less than three hours like a train of powder set alight, the insurgents had invaded and occupied . . . a third of Paris.[174]

The space that the barricades formed was the space of combat and ambush; they were an attempt to make of an already impenetrable quarter an even more impenetrable labyrinth known only to the defenders: "The narrow, unequal, sinuous streets, full of corners and turns, were admirably chosen; the surroundings of les Halles in particular, a network of streets more entangled than a forest."[175] Within the space closed off by the barricades, the street took on the air of communal property, an open-air room adopted by the community as its own; cabarets were turned into guard posts, cafés into political and strategic headquarters.[176] But, whereas the July Revolution of 1830 had seen bourgeoisie and people fighting together, creating an almost festive atmosphere around and on top of the barricades, the June insurrection of 1837 was serious and somber, with the lines as clearly drawn as were the structures themselves. The barricade as theater had been replaced by the barricade as fortress. This pattern was to be repeated again only sixteen years later.

Indeed, the building of a barricade was a serious business, and its constructors became skillful as well as swift. First iron bars were wrenched from street railings, then the street paving was levered up; the base of the barricade was formed by an overturned cart or carriage, its contents (preferably casks) placed beneath the piles of paving stones. Other barrels were purloined and set beside the rest, while the whole *barrique* was buttressed by more stones and topped by beams torn from nearby houses. The resulting rampart was taller than a man. Passing vehicles were added to the original pile from time to time: "Rien n'est tel que la main populaire pour bâtir tout ce qui se bâtit en demolissant," observed Hugo.[177] The height of the barrier was such that the defenders might hide behind it, fire over it, or climb onto it by means of rough steps formed of paving stones inside; its aspect from outside was rough and unscalable. A red flag, or sometimes a red bonnet, capped the

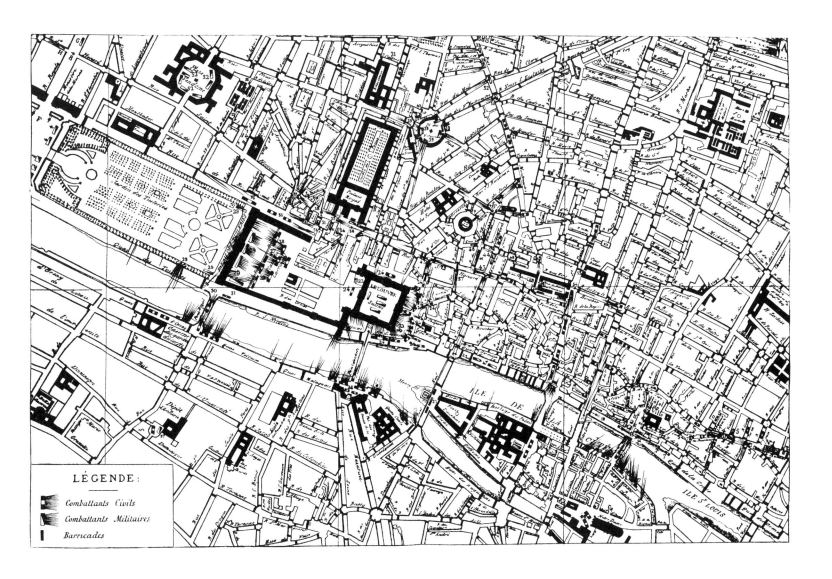

57. *Plan of Paris, during the three days of July, 1830;* showing the emplacements of barricades, and the lines of civil and military fire. [Blanc, *Histoire,* p. 76]

58

59

60

61

58. *A barricade, July 1830,* from an engraving by the radical artist Philippe Auguste Jeanron (1807–1877) for Blanc's *Histoire de dix-ans* (1846). Jeanron, a devoted painter of working-class scenes, portrays the defenders of the barricade in less idealistic a manner than that of Delacroix in *Liberty Leading the People* of the same year (1831). [Blanc, *Histoire,* p. 85]

59. *The Revolution of 1830 — combat in the rue Saint Antoine;* the entire street — roofs, windows, and ground — is taken over in the street fighting of the working-class quarters. [Blanc, *Histoire,* p. 46]

60. Victor Hugo, the *barricade in the faubourg Saint-Antoine,* 1848; engraved by Benett for the illustrated edition of *Les Misérables,* part 5, "Jean Valjean." Hugo compared this barricade to a petrified riot, made out of all the disparate objects of the misery and poverty of the quarter it defended. [Hugo, *Les Misérables,* p. 8]

61. Victor Hugo, the *barricade in the faubourg du Temple,* 1848; the barricade as architecture, "it was adjusted, clamped, imbricated, rectilinear, symmetrical and funereal." [Hugo, *Les Misérables,* p. 13]

whole edifice: "The street and the barricade remained plunged in darkness, and one saw only the red flag formidably lit by an enormous shaded lantern." The barricade completed, the long wait for the counter-attack began.

It was, of course, as the center of attack and defense that the barricade acted as the pivotal instrument of social knowledge and individual confrontation; face to face in the narrow street, divided only by a temporary wall of debris, the men and women of the revolt and the troops of authority were for a brief instant forced to recognize each other, even to speak and argue, before consciously firing. A "war within four walls," where the city wall had been replaced within the city by its popular type, was a domestic affair, a civil war in a civic space.[178]

If the barricades of July 1830 were epitomized by Delacroix' *Liberty leading the People,* and those of June 1832 by the appearance of the red flag, those of 1848, both in February and in June, were characteristically different in their turn.[179] First, they were bigger and more professionally built; Hugo and de Toqueville attest to the precision of their building. Schooled in '27, in '30, and in '39, Auguste Blanqui, the ardent defender of barricades through to '71, went so far as to dimension the thickness of each one to be built in the abortive revolt of 1839;[180] by 1848 masons and carpenters were using all the arts of their trade: "These barricades," recalled de Toqueville, "were skillfully constructed by a small number of men who worked industriously, like good workmen who wanted to do their job expeditiously and well." The public, he added, watched them passively, neither helping nor disapproving.[181]

Of course, this was de Tocqueville during February; the barricades of June were feverishly built through a single night and day, cutting Paris in half, dividing working class from bourgeoisie — the one in despair at the loss of even the token National Workshops, the other in fear of a finally red revolution. The territory of the workers was sharply separated from that of the bourgeoisie by the initial barricades of the Porte Saint Denis and the Cité: the critical line was the boulevard Saint-Martin. Hugo described this barricade in detail:

> The barricade Saint Antoine was monstrous; it was three floors high and seven hundred feet wide. It blocked from one corner to the other the vast mouth of the faubourg, that is to say, three streets; hollowed out, slashed, indented, hacked, crenellated with an immense fissure, shorn up with piles which were themselves bastions, pushing up points here and there, strongly leaning back against the two great promontories of the houses of the faubourg, it surged up like a cyclopean uprising at the foot of the redoubtable place which had seen the 14 of July. Nineteen barricades were ranged back in the depth of the streets behind this sheltering barricade.[182]

All the military science learned by the socialists in the Ecole Polytechnique was put to use in these gigantic structures.

Engels gave a military account of the fighting and the strategies of the Garde Mobile. The fortress of Saint Antoine was indeed the last to fall, the techniques of Vauban being employed on behalf of the workers. It was built in the form of an angle pointing inward, to provide a wider front of defensive cross fire and to present a weaker face to Cavaignac's cannons. The cross walls of the houses had been opened up, connecting the rows with each other and affording mobility to the defenders;

> The bridges and quays along the canal as well as the streets running parallel to it were also strongly fortified. In short the two faubourgs resembled a veritable fortress, in which the troops had to wage a bloody battle for every inch of ground.[183]

From hastily erected barriers of casks to the overturned carriages and paving stones of communal revolt to the fortresses of working-class defeat, the barricade had, like the arcade, found its type form, and, like the arcade, the form was that of a building,

> A strange wall reaching the second floor of the facades, a kind of treaty of union between the houses on the right with the houses on the left as if the street had turned back on itself with its highest wall to close itself off suddenly. This wall had been built with paving stones. It was right, correct, cold, perpendicular, levelled with the square, straightened with the line, aligned with the plumb.[184]

It was, in fact, architecture; its entablature was parallel to its base, its openings were regularly spaced, and together with the street it enclosed it formed a unified structure of almost permanent defense. To Hugo the barricade at the faubourg du Temple, was an awesome building, a "sepulchre," built by a geometer or a specter. The second characteristic of the barricades of 1848 was that they were (not all, but many) built by men who directed their designs from the outset.

The Triumph of Urbanism:
Haussmann and the Boulevards of Empire, 1853–1867

The Emperor was anxious to show me a map of Paris, on which one saw traced by Himself, in blue, in red, in yellow and in green, according to their degree of urgency, the different new routes that he proposed to have undertaken.[185]

Louis Napoleon, incarcerated in Ham prison, had dreamed Saint-Simonian dreams; that of a new and completely rebuilt Paris, according to Duveyrier and Enfantin, Perreymond and Daly, was perhaps the foremost task of the new Imperial regime. London, where he had been impressed by the rows, squares, and crescent of Georgian civility, was no longer to reign supreme as the urbane capital of Europe. Napoleonic ideas demanded a Paris in line with the promise of Enlightenment, so long deferred.[186] The conceptual schemes of Laugier and Voltaire, of David and the Commission des Artistes, of the first Napoleon, and of the technicians of the new industrial world were finally to be realized. Louis Napoleon's map, taken in hand by Haussmann, was to be the document by which dreams were deposited within the very heart of reality; a reality that corresponded to the triumphant march of commerce, industry, and science in the powerful hands of a truly hegemonic bourgeoisie. Between 1853 and 1870 (when responding to the pressures of this same bourgeoisie, Baron Haussmann was dismissed) the Emperor and his executive agent, the Prefect of the Seine, put into action the pent-up ideals of an entire century.

Having accomplished the reconstruction of the capital according to the guidelines of the eighteenth-century Enlightenment, Haussmann was finally unable to understand the opposition of his fellow citizens to such manifest improvements; if Voltaire, he wrote in 1890, "could enjoy the spectacle offered by the Paris of our own days, seeing all his wishes surpassed, he would not understand why in place of supporting the Administration that realized them so grandly, the Parisians, his sons, the heirs of his fine spirit, have criticized it, attacked it, fettered it."[187] How could it be that the Enlightenment vision, once realized, could be attacked from any point of view? Haussmann thus revealed himself as the last such heir of philosophic ideology; or at least as a prototype of the planner, who, schooled in the mechanisms of reason and order, faced with the intransigence of social life, remains bemused at human irrationality.

In this sense the Haussmannization of Paris may be seen as both the end of urbanism and its beginning. Carrying the techniques of rationalist analysis and the formal instruments of the *ancien régime,* as refurbished by the First Empire and its institutions, to their logical extreme, Haussmann joined them to the power released by the burgeoning consumer economies of speculative credit in a magnificent attempt to seal up disorder, and enshrine measured progress, in an aesthetic package derived from Beaux-Arts academic formulas realized with all the expertise of engineering science. It was in the city of Paris, finally, that the merging of Napoleon I's paradigmatic institutions of Ecole des Beaux Arts and Ecole Polytechnique effected the practice of urbanism, which was launched as the hope of the twentieth century, against revolution and poverty alike.

The new boulevard as the agent and form of this hope and this treaty between art and technique was perhaps the most urban product of the nineteenth century, and its final apotheosis; a tool of social, moral, and governmental progress; a monument to the ideal of a city as well as the site and provocation of its febrile economic life; a vista, a path of movement, a defense of order, a home for the alien crowds of the new urban landscape; the very epitome of social life as well as its implied critique, it precipitated the contradictions of its century in real life according to the substance of its dreams.

First in line for the accomplishment of any plan of public works was the preparation of an accurate plan of the city; Haussmann's geometers took to the skies on high scaffolds — "great wooden masts, higher than the highest houses" from whence they could "measure according to the methods of triangulation by means of the most perfect precision instruments, the angles formed by the sides of each of the triangles determined on the spot by the extension of the central shafts of these temporary constructions."[188] From such a triangulation was prepared the first detailed survey of the city, a basis for the instrumentalization of Louis Napoleon's plan of transformation. Many people, he observed, would still remember these strange masts; caricatures depicted the tightrope walker Madame Sacqui communicating with the platforms of each.[189] To determine a new network of communication for Paris, in other words, an abstract network of precise geometry was traced at a level far above the streets: in Haussmann's terms "to give a real existence to the Plan" meant no more nor less than bringing this imaginary intersection of lines, this horizontally perfect plan, down to earth, as traces through the existing city.

The geometer and the planner had been favored with the bird's-eye view hitherto reserved for the novelist and soon to be the privilege of the photographer; Nadar, ascending in a balloon, was to record the city indelibly from above so that the humblest citizen might share in this experience of Paris as a whole. Following Haussmann's work he might also view, on ground level, along the sight lines traced out by the planner, monument after monument, the isolated symbols of civic, national, and imperial pride: "They [the towers] had been placed in effect at the meeting points of absolutely straight streets or sections of streets."

Of course, the form of the Second Empire transformations had been predicated by countless plans of embellishment and amelioration from the revolutionary cuts of David after Patte in 1793 to the Saint-Simonian visions of Perreymond;[190] the difference lay in the mechanical precision, the rigor and relentless determination of the wielders of the instrument called triangulation. In a sense the holistic vision of an entire city brought into line, as opposed to the piecemeal creation of enclaves in districts, was only possible after this conscious conflation of method and experience. Technique and observation had been joined in the Enlightenment as instruments of progress; their joint triumph in effect had waited on the development of photography and cartography.

If the geometrical survey predicated the form of the new developments, the techniques of surgery provided the instruments of realiza-

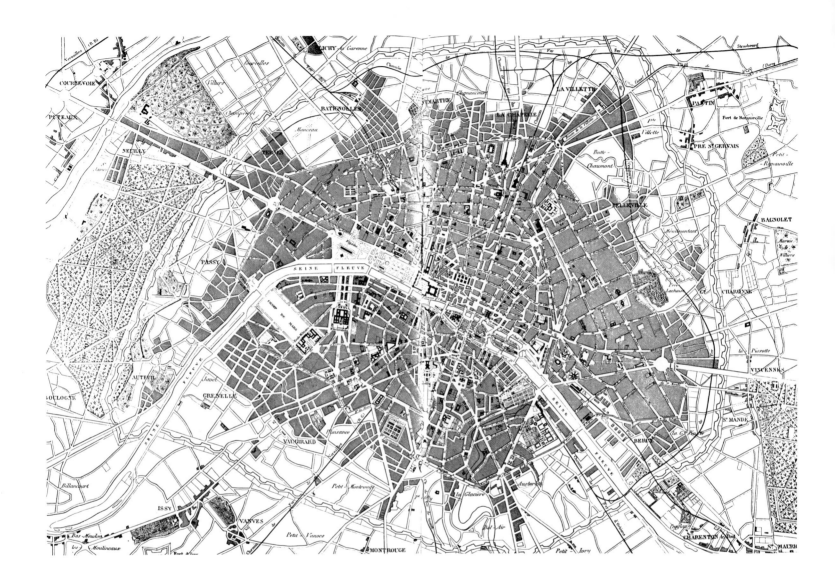

62. Galignani's *Plan of Paris*, 1839. Paris before
Haussmann's transformation: the Bois de Boulogne
to the west retains its old straight *allées,* the Buttes
Chaumont is still undeveloped, the *grands percées*
have not opened up the fabric of old Paris. The city
has still not developed to the limits set by the new
fortifications of the 1840s.

63. Joanne's *Plan of Paris,* 1876. Paris after
Haussmann's transformation. The Bois de Boulogne
and the Buttes Chaumont have been rendered as
English parks, the grand boulevards and avenues of
the first two networks have been completed (including the Avenue de l'Opéra), and the city has advanced toward the fortifications.

64

65

tion. After the prolonged pathology, the drawn-out agony of the patient, the body of Paris, was to be delivered of its illnesses, its cancers, and epidemics once and for all by the total act of surgery. "Cutting" and "piercing" were the adjectives used to describe the operation; where the terrain was particularly obstructed a "disembowelling" had to be performed in order that arteries be reconstituted and flows reinstated. The metaphors were repeated again and again by the pathologists, the surgeons, and even by their critics, becoming so firmly embedded in the unconscious analogies of urban planning that from that time the metaphor and the scientific nature of the action were confused and fused. Thus Haussmann spoke of the *eventrement* of the central quarters of the city, the cutting open of the tangled streets inaccessible to the circulation of vehicles.[191] A new requirement, "hygienic science," furthered by the piercing of streets, was to endow old and new quarters alike with "spaces, air, light, verdure and flowers, in a word, with all that dispenses health."[192] Such, according to Haussmann, was the primary objective of the Emperor. The horror of the old streets of the city must be exorcised once and for all; the "piled up, sordid, insanitary habitations, as much centers of poverty as of illness," the "horrible sinks" must be opened up to light and air, and perhaps just as important, to "public circulation."[193]

But the existence of enclaves of poverty, and thereby of illness, and above all criminality, was as much an affront to the dignity of the nation as it was a threat to public order. Even as Haussmann declared war on the quarters of old Paris, so he declared war on their inhabitants:

> The rue des Tenturiers was so narrow that the worm-eaten facade of one of its bordering houses, in panels of wood rough-cast with plaster, tried in vain to fall down: it could only prop itself up on that of the opposite house. And what a population lived there![194]

It was common knowledge and common fear that these slums "The filthy alleys and dead ends are the hideouts of the majority of released prisoners."[195] What was more troubling to an Emperor brought to power by the force of the barricades was the possibility of losing power in the same way. As Haussmann would note, the extension of the Rue de Rivoli was a "spacious, direct, monumental and above all a *strategic* route." This was certainly the argument used most tellingly in the City Council debate over the granting of the loan for the extension in 1851, two years before Haussmann's appointment:

> The interests of public order, not less than those of salubrity demand that a wide swathe be cut as soon as possible across this district of barricades. An intermediate line will be added to the great strategic line of the boulevards.[196]

Immediately after the coup d'etat such arguments held strong swaying power over the assembly; even Haussmann some five years later found it persuasive: the "disembowelling of old Paris, of the quarter of riots

66

64. *Building works at the place du Carrousel*, 1852; working on the completion of the Louvre and Tuileries gardens at the beginning of the Second Empire. [Texier, *Tableau*, vol. I. p. 340]

65. *The facades of the Boulevards des Italiens and Montmartre*, 1852, north side, showing the irregular and piecemeal development of the *anciens boulevards* before Haussmann. [Texier, *Tableau*, vol. I, p. 37]

66. *The facade of the new avenue de l'Opéra*, completed after Haussmann's resignation, in the late 1870s. The regular cornice line of the new boulevards. [Joanne, *Paris Illustré*, p. xliii]

67

67. Baron Haussmann, the *boulevard Saint Michel:* the southern end of the great north-south axis planned as the great crossing of Paris. The first network of Haussmann, 1853–1860. [Joanne, *Paris Illustré,* p. 67]

68. Baron Haussmann, the *avenue and place de Wagram:* an avenue of the second network, 1860–1863, developed as part of the radiating avenues from the replanned place de l'Etoile. The Arc de Triomphe is in the background. [Joanne, *Paris Illustré,* p. 69]

69. Baron Haussmann, the *boulevard Richard Lenoir,* built over the Canal Saint Martin, through the heart of the working-class quarters, 1861–1863.

70. *Perspective view of the boulevard Richard Lenoir,* from Alphand's *Promenades de Paris* (1867–1873). The space of the new boulevard, cut through the densely impacted old quarters. The juxtaposition of scales was dramatic — the final and monumental end to the baroque vision of perspective, vista, and order.

68

and barricades'' became a principal theme of his speeches. The prolonging of the Boulevard de Strasbourg had a ''utilité stratégique''; the Rue de Rivoli's straight alignment ''did not lend itself to the habitual tactic of local insurrections''; the covering of the Canal Saint Martin with the Boulevard Richard Lenoir, thus cutting through the most intransigent district of all, the Faubourg Saint Antoine, was dictated by the ''interests of public order,'' substituting ''in place of the defense offered by the canal to riots, a new access route in the habitual center of their manifestation.'' Paris was not only the home of the Parisian; it was the capital of a vast and centralized Empire; its order was the first condition of the order of the whole.[197]

The interests of strategic communication — the linking, for example, of the stations together and to the center of the city, allowing troops stationed outside the city to be recalled in times of civil unrest — were perhaps more convincing reasons in the rhetoric of debate than the underlying economic necessities pointed by the massive redevelopment projects. But, in the end, the requirements of commerce and industry, finance and employment were the dynamic agents of the transformation. Haussmann and Louis Napoleon, like Saint-Simon and his followers, believed in communication and circulation as the watchwords of progress; the center of commercial and industrial activity, Paris was ''a great market for consumption, an immense workshop, an arena of ambition.''[198] Direct and spacious communication would be furnished only by a coherent network of boulevards and avenues, the widening of streets, and their servicing with all the technical resources of modern science. The city had to be opened to itself and to the world. No longer should it take fifteen minutes to walk from rue Saint Denis to the Hôtel de la Ville. With a population that had doubled in fifty years, expanding suburbs that demanded access to the center, businesses that required efficient services, the entire infrastructure of old Paris was rendered hopelessly inadequate.

For all these reasons, and as many more as could be adduced to persuade an increasingly reluctant municipality to transform itself into a modern servant of social and commercial order, the networks of Haussmann came into being in the short space of fifteen years. The very word for urban reconstruction, once ''embellishment,'' was changed to ''transformation.'' And the artifact that contained within it the solution to all urban problems, that united technique and form, was, of course, the new boulevard.

In a space some thirty meters wide and up to two kilometers long, Haussmann concentrated the services and the circulation of the new commercial city. Paved with new macadam, lit with the latest design of gas light,[199] carefully planned to separate pedestrian, stroller, loiterer, ambling service vehicle, and rushing carriage, planted with rows of trees to ensure shade in summer, provided with underground piping for

69

70

71

72

73

rain water, sewage, and gas, cleaned with the aid of scientifically designed gutters, faced by the uniform height of the residences and stores of the *nouveau bourgeoisie,* and carefully sited to point toward a monument or vista as the object of civic pride or aesthetic pleasure, the boulevard of Haussmann was in effect the epitome and the condenser of Second Empire daily life: the modern artifact par excellence.

Its profiles and sections were calculated with a precision that had not been attempted since Pierre Patte had invented the Enlightenment avenue. Its plans were treated like buildings and its spaces like the outdoor rooms of a city that knew no secrets in its burgeoning prosperity. In a very real sense the street had become an interior — gas lit and policed; the crowd felt a safety in a domain where buildings and lights created an artificial sky at night. Its equipment was standardized and typified — from the bench to the lamp, the kiosk to the *pissoir,* the railing to the tree guard, the pavement to the drain — so that even as the trace of the route united a hitherto parceled-out city so did the objects of its use remind the citizen of one, uniformly governed Paris.[200] The bench in the Faubourg Saint Antoine was the same as that in the Champs-Elysées. All Paris was serviced, cleaned, and aesthetically embellished with the same techniques; all Paris was opened up to air, sun, and green on the one hand and uniform administration on the other. The sense of the city as an entity was never so strong; villages had congealed — districts had communicated with each other before, but the understanding of the city, from east to west, north to south, was now a part of the daily experience of every inhabitant of every quarter and not the special privilege of the poetic imagination of the *aérostier.*

Thus were the three great networks of Haussmann conceived and implemented; thus the great administrator dissociated himself from politics, from the disputes of special interests, to set himself up as the first "disinterested" planner, the rational technician, the benign servant of a benign administration, the accommodator of modernism, the subaltern to economic and commercial progress.

In the end, however, the boulevard, technical instrument that it was, also inserted its form and space into a fabric that had, save for the possible exceptions of the Champ de Mars or the *ancien* boulevards, never received such cutting, opening, and rupture. The boulevard was, finally, an aesthetic entity and recognized as such by its designers. The "giving satisfaction to the artistic instincts" of the inhabitants of Paris was, according to Haussmann, one of the primary aims of the Emperor:

> By beautiful perspectives, by the disengaging of ancient monuments and the isolation of new ones; by the opening of planted avenues, vast promenades, parks and public gardens, filling the eyes with a luxury of greenery and flowers without parallel.[201]

Herein are the aesthetic canons of Haussmann himself, inherited from the academic principles of late baroque and neoclassic, mediated by the

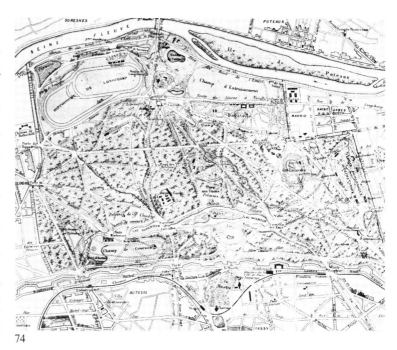

74

71,72,73. *Paris underground,* 1852–1867. The great sewers of Paris were a fascination to the public of the Second Empire, and an object of Haussmann's redevelopment, as part of the sanitation projects of drainage and water supply demanded by the rapidly expanding capital. Nadar, the photographer and balloonist, wrote on "Paris underground and Paris from the air," for the *Paris Guide* of 1867, the opening of the Great Exposition. [Joanne, *Paris Illustré,* pp. 909, 913, and Texier, *Tableau,* vol. II, p. 235, respectively]

74. The redesigned *Bois de Boulogne,* by Alphand, 1853–1858. The imperial answer to London's Hyde Park, with the double lake approximating the Serpentine. [Joanne, *Paris Illustré,* p. 186]

exigencies of modern materials and construction techniques, and styled according to the eclectic tastes of the bourgeois consumption of art. The first principle of boulevard planning was, of course, correct alignment; indeed, Haussmann claimed that the Emperor had reproached him for "sacrificing too much in the matter of alignments," of "searching too much for points of view to justify the direction of public routes."[202]

The preoccupation of the triangulator had been the joining of points by lines, the sighting from temporary tower to temporary tower; the preoccupation of the planner was the objective in view for a fitting end to every boulevard. Boulevards were, in keeping with their monumental status, far from being lines to infinity; at each end was the proper culmination of the axis: "In effect I have never ordered the tracing of any way whatsoever . . . without concerning myself with the point of view that one could give to it."[203] The disappointment of the Boulevard de Strasbourg, the line of which was set before Haussmann's administration, was that its axis missed by a very small dimension the culminating *point de vue* of the dome of the Sorbonne; instead he was forced to direct the construction of the Tribunal of Commerce to the Ile de la Cité so that its river facade ended the Boulevard and its dome remained on axis: "this new monument furnished me with the objective that I needed for the perspective of the Boulevard de Strasbourg." The monument had taken the place of the geometer's tower as the permanent witness to the mathematical construction of reality.

In this way was the vision of Laugier, the city as a forest with the avenues as the paths cut through it by professional foresters or garden designers, installed in Paris in monumental form. And even as the network of paths triangulated the walks through its otherwise inhospitable quarters, so the forest itself, the Bois de Boulogne and the Bois de Vincennes, was tamed and carefully redesigned to look like picturesque nature for the Sunday promenades of the rising middle classes. In this inversion of the relation between savage and tamed nature, the city was invested with the attributes of wilderness, ordered and defended by its routes with their impregnable and uniform walls — the sanctuaries of reason and light; the gardens were transformed from their earlier function as hunting forests, their straight *allées* eradicated in favor of peaceful and meandering paths around serpentine pools. The very garbage tips of the city were brought under cultivation in this way. In this sense the boulevards of Haussmann can be seen as monumental hunting routes; it is significant that Zola's novel of Haussmann was called *The Quarry*.

75. Victor Baltard, *the Central Markets*, interior, 1857–1858. The iron and glass interiors of what Emile Zola called the "stomach of Paris": the arcade monumentalized as a building in itself.

The City Consumed
Zola and the Spoils of the Street, 1871

> *It was the ripe and prodigious fruit of an epoch. The street invaded the apartment with its rumbling of carriages, its jostling of strangers, its license of language.*[204]

Zola, like Saint-Simon, had personified the city of Paris in the earlier volumes of the *Rougeon-Macquart* as a woman: sometimes fallen, sometimes a whore, often wounded and crying in the night, yet always full of heart for those needing comfort, an all-embracing and ultimately redeeming vision of golden fecundity and final perfection. He saw the Paris of Haussmann, however, disemboweled and bleeding, as the prey of speculation, the victim of all-consuming greed.[205]

Saccard, the anti-hero of *La Curée,* at once speculator and city hall functionary, spoke the double language of the planner and the hunter: assembled in his new residence, a miraculous replica of the new Louvre set in the Parc du Monçeau, were all the characters of the new Paris. The Municipal Councillor, a ''lean and important person'' (''the transformation of Paris will be the glory of the reign, to plough up Paris is to make it productive''); a contractor, newly rich and lately a bricklayer, not wanting to seem a traitor to his former class (''the alterations of Paris have given a living to the workman''); the provincial prefect, living most of the year in the capital, concerned with ''the artistic side of the question'' (''the new thoroughfares are majestic in their beauty''); the old baron, property owner (''as a landlord, whenever I have a flat done up and painted, I raise the rent''); a second contractor (''you see everything is fine so long as you make money by it''); all of them seeking ways in which to appropriate to their own fiscal ends the forms and functions of a city in the process of becoming modern.[206]

Saccard himself, the host of all, like a vulture hovering over the emerging city of capital in Zola's image, ''swept down on Paris and simply took possession of the city.'' He knew how to predict the increase in property values following the plan of improvements, how ''when throwing a boulevard across the belly of a quarter you juggle with six storied houses amidst the unanimous applause of your dupes.'' The districts of the city seemed no more to him than potential gold to be melted down for the enrichment of those who heat and stir the mortar. As he stood overlooking the city he spoke in the very words of Haussmann, but words invested by Zola with all the reality of the metaphors of the Transformation:

> From the Boulevard du Temple to the Barrière du Trône, that's one cutting; then on this side another from the Madeleine to the Plaine Monceau; and a third cutting this way, another that way, a cutting here, one further on, cuttings on every side, Paris slashed with saber cuts, its veins opened . . .[207]

Saccard's very hand seemed like a saber ''a living knife, those iron fingers mercilessly slicing'' as it hovered over the city, an unsuspecting prey. The speculator's hand had become the agent of urban surgery; ''without effort it tore asunder the entrails of the enormous city.'' Saccard saw himself as the agent of imperial interest (''the admirable strategic routes which will place the forts at the heart of the old quarters'') and of economic speculation (''in making the money dance . . . giving the laboring classes no time to think''). Under the speculator's greed Zola saw the map of Louis Napoleon as tracing the fall of the city in blood, in red slashes that cut even deeper than Saccard's hand.

If the city was to be consumed by capital so in turn it became all consuming of its inhabitants: caught in the fever following the hunt or trapped in the unfamiliar space of the boulevard, languishing in an unrecognizable milieu filled with aliens, the citizens participated in the agony of their wounded home. The life of the new street was rapacious and the invasion of the house was its natural consequence; the interior of bourgeois privacy, so much a part of the July Monarchy that Walter Benjamin could write of *Louis-Philippe or the Interior* as interdependent realms, was in the Second Empire subjected to the entrée of the brash and newly rich, the self-made man, the bricklayer turned contractor, rubbing shoulders with their partners of necessity, the older middle class and a failing aristocracy.

For Saccard's wife and her illicit lover, on the other hand, the life of the streets provided a welcome anonymity where their secret affairs might merge unnoticed. They relished ''the grey bands of wide interminable pavement,'' the ''stamping, swarming crowds'' where they might be lost in the melée.[208] The boulevard, a uniformly familiar realm throughout the city, became in a very real sense the lobby of their house.

Significantly, the camera, as well as the painting, recorded the life and forms of the street as seen from above, from the apartment that both witnessed and participated in the society below.[209] The monumentalization of the public realm had united facade with facade, public life and private, in a common space that no longer remained attached solely to the level of movement but was defined vertically by the uniform cornices and the perspective views. The lovers do not have to descend to street level to partake of its life; with the apartment window open they are at once within the public realm and voyeurs of it. The night life of the boulevard, passing through its own transformations of activity from the evening to the early morning, acts as the background to their private life, sets the tone of every moment, and characterizes the relations of two lovers even as it defines the states of the crowd, the forms of pleasure, and the daily life of individuals.

At ten in the evening, the night had barely commenced; Paris was yet

76

76, 77. *The Grand stair and entrance foyer of the Opéra,* by Charles Garnier, 1861–1874. Not completed until the Third Republic, Garnier's building nevertheless epitomized the high bourgeois aspirations of the Second Empire; its vast, eclectically decorated, semipublic interiors were the late-nineteenth-century substitute for the arcades of Louis Philippe. [Joanne, *Paris Illustré,* pp. 472, 475]

awakening, "prolonging the ardent day." Seen from above the dark rows of trees separated the whiteness of the sidewalk from the shadow of the roadway, lit fleetingly by the lamps of passing carriages. The kiosks of newsvendors and the lamps of cafés threw bands of light across the pavement. The gaze of the apartment dweller could span from one end of the boulevard to the other, along the entire perspective,

> into the noisy confused depths of the avenue, full of the black swarm of pedestrians, where the light became mere sparks. And the endless procession, a crowd strangely mixed and always alike, passed by with tiring regularity in the midst of the bright colours and patches of darkness, in the fairylike confusion and the thousand leaping flames that swept like waves from the shops.[210]

The endless crowd, all individuality lost in the eternal procession of movement, all physiognomies merged in the identity of the mass, was given unity by the space of uniformity; its faces were as many as the gas lights that illuminated them for fleeting moments.

The literature of the last Second Empire and the Third Republic, the literature of the transformed Paris, that is, remarked endlessly on the glimpse of the face in the crowd, the face seen once and forever lost, the infinite masses in movement along the modern ways; the noise and the rumble where sounds are indistinguishable, "The deafening noise that rose on high, a clamour, a prolonged monotonous rumbling like an organ note accompanying an endless procession of little mechanical dolls."[211] Engels had characterized the crowd in the London streets of 1844 as *monads,* disparate individuals following the rule of anarchic impulse. Now the crowd had attained its own identity, its own physiognomy. It was still a backdrop to the life of individuals, but individuals constrained to grow ever more heroic in order to stand out against the mass. Even when night triumphed and the boulevard emptied into vacancy, the inhabitants, knots of theatergoers returning late, prostitutes and their clients, still seemed unlike individuals; they remained "ghostly puppets," mechanical parts of the whole to the end. No matter how strident the cries of nostalgia, the perception of Haussmann as he planned for the alienated masses of the new city had been accurate. Paris, he had claimed, offending *Communard* and *archéologue* alike, was no longer the exclusive domain of the Parisian. The masses of immigrant workers were no more "than veritable nomads at the heart of Parisian society, absolutely deprived of municipal sentiment." Whereas, in the Paris of Balzac, the preoccupation with the face in the crowd, the physiognomy of the city, the types of inhabitant, was the favorite pastime of the *flâneur,* in the Paris of Zola, all faces were lost and indistinguishable. Even more saddening to the specialists in the *bohème* and the dandy was the eradication of the specifically Parisian type:

All is leveled, all is effaced, the *types* have disappeared, the characters have been dulled, and in this concert of peoples in this gigantic caravanserai where the whole world camps out, the Parisian born of the soil cramped between two sidewalks, enclosed by the glimmers of the gas light . . . now escapes analysis and dissection.[212]

The political implications of this leveling were as acute as the physical *percées* themselves; the small groups of dedicated insurrectionists, the meetings of workers and students, the rendezvous on narrow street corners, the world of bohemian, criminal, and political radical in the alleyways of old Paris, were now rendered impotent and consumed in the ever-growing *bizarrerie* of the crowd. In a mass where every individual became the same through difference, the difference of a few was imperceptible. The political *agitateur* was forced alone upon hostile streets; his quarters opened up and his movements traced by myriads of informers, he became more and more of a *flâneur* himself. In his alienation, but as the paradoxical mirror image of it, he was closer to the wandering dreamer of nostalgia than to the *sans culotte*. The black-caped figure of Auguste Blanqui mingled as conspicuously with the crowd as did the last wanderer, Edmond de Goncourt, lamenting the loss of self through the disappearance of environment: "I am a stranger to these new boulevards without turns, without incidents or perspective, implacable in their straight lines; no longer feeling like the world of Balzac, but bringing to mind some American Babylon of the future."[213]

In 1867, the year of the Universal Exposition and of Baudelaire's death, the new Paris was unveiled to the world. The great iron and brick galleries of the exhibition emulated the plan of Ledoux' ideal city of a less than century earlier, consecrating it in the new technology and filling it with the universe of products typical of the new consumer society. In some fourteen years Louis Napoleon, with his dreams of Saint-Simonian splendor, and Haussmann, with pragmatic efficiency and astonishing ingenuity, had transformed the Paris of Balzac into the Paris of Zola.

In this new city those who had known the old felt threatened and alien: Baudelaire, who had created an art out of losing himself in the crowd and gaining himself as its dandy, had written: "Old Paris is no more (the form of a city changes more quickly, alas, than the heart of a mortal)."[214] Goncourt felt like "a man merely passing through," while the *Paris Guide* in the year of the exhibition demonstrated a marked desire to recapture some of the past spirit of a lost city. The straight line had replaced the picturesque curve; the Rue de Rivoli was seen as the symbol of the new world — long, wide, and cold. One author proclaimed the final death of the street: "The street no longer exists in Paris, and the street once dead it is the reign of the boulevard and advent of the grand arteries."[215]

If there was a single image that best characterized the new boulevard space for the writers of the Second Empire, it was that of the desert. For

77

Zola, despite the clamor and incessant movement of its crowds, it was the space of his final alienation: "The avenue seemed unending. Hundreds of leagues ended in nothingness; the end of the road eluded him. The lanterns, lined up regularly spaced, with their short yellow flames, were the only life in this desert of death."[216] The visitor to this strange and mechanical world, empty of familiar jostling, where the walls of the street no longer pressed together against the sky, felt totally alone even in the center of a rushing crowd: "in the midst of a great silence and in the desert of the avenue."

For those who still retained their political hope, despite the repression of criticism and party activity, the options were few: some longed for a return to the secure haunts of the old Paris, those "peaceable obstructed quarters where the bohemians of the faubourg Saint Antoine took refuge,"[217] the cul-de-sacs of intrigue and subversive life. Others called for the complete reconstruction of what had already been transformed. Proudhon, in his last work, proposed the rebuilding of all the towns and villages of France, "and first in line the Paris of M. Haussmann."[218] Zola for his part saw and recorded the whole transformation as a grotesque *danse macabre;* one year before the Commune he pronounced its death: "autrefois le carneval passait en calèche sur les boulevards; aujourd'hui le carneval est mort."[219]

The Commune and the Theater of Combat, 1871

The working man's Paris, in the act of its heroic self holocaust involved in its flames buildings and monuments. While tearing to pieces the living body of the proletariat, its rulers must no longer expect to return triumphantly into the intact architecture of their abodes.[220]

The construction of the new quarter of Les Halles cut in half the population of this densely inhabited district in less than six years; the population of the old working-class quarter of the Faubourg Saint-Honoré fell by a third in the same period. At the same time a vast and desolate shanty town arose on the outskirts of the city to the north and north-east, increasing in size to some 140,000 by the end of Haussmann's ministry.[221] The first truly working-class district had been formed, not by any conscious act of paternalist planning, nor by the spontaneous efforts of the poor themselves, but solely as a result of the Haussmannization of Paris, as Engels was to term the great work. Without hospitals, schools, or public fountains, the workers lived as they could outside the walls, while their former city was opened up on behalf of their masters. On Tuesday, March 18, 1871, in victorious columns led by red banners, the workers marched back into the center of the city from the north and north-east and celebrated their reentry by a festival in front of the Hotel de Ville. They appropriated the edifice and in occupation declared the city theirs once more. The Proclamation and most of the brief life of the Commune was a festive affair, with the combined memory of the days of 1789, 1830, and 1848 and a renewed hope that this time, united, the mistakes and defeats of those former days would not be repeated.

With all the fervor of Enlightenment therapeutic vision, the men of 1796 had claimed the image of the asylum as their own to define the state and the space of their new republic. Extending the metaphor from isolated and healing retreat to the entire realm of Paris, they had cried, "the moment has come to found the Republic of Equals, this great asylum open to all men."[222] It was left to the reformers and the institutionalizers of the next fifty years to turn the concept of the asylum into the mechanism of control and the instrument of isolation. In the spring of 1871, the whole of Paris was again proclaimed an "asylum of equality" from the inside, but, pitifully for its inmates who were largely unconscious of their true condition of isolation, it was also seen from the outside as a very real asylum of another and more sinister kind. Its walls were confirmed first by the Prussian and then by the Versaillese armies, and its real defenses were never really in the hands of those who thought they were defending. From Versailles, the city was seen as a center of infection, a plague-ridden nest of political contagion to be encircled and isolated like any prison, workhouse, or insane refuge. Within, protected from this vision of their real state, the inhabitants celebrated their emancipation: "Everybody could enter freely; the streets swarmed with people, the cafés were noisy . . . the people were without anger because without fear."[223] It was a day of peace and joyous festivity, and two hundred thousand massed before the Hôtel de Ville and back into the Boulevard de Sebastopol while the new representatives read the Proclamation to the music of the old revolution.

In keeping with such an open revolution, the barricades of its inception, those of March 18, were temporary affairs, six feet high at most, and made almost entirely of *pavées*.[224] And in a continuing spirit of fearlessness the Communards were little concerned with the erection of a more permanent line of defense. Of course decrees were issued calling for the building of "a second enclosure behind the fortifications," and a chief of barricades, Napoléon Gaillard, was appointed to construct and oversee this work, as well as the creation of three "closed redoubts" or citadels on the Buttes Montmartre, the Trocadéro, and the Panthéon.[225] But Père Gaillard, the radical shoemaker, was more taken with his resplendent uniform and the picture of himself as the great defender than with the practical operations of a coordinated scheme for the protection of the municipalities. He invested all his time and some eighty thousand francs in the building of an admittedly formidable barricade across the Rue de Rivoli on the corner of the Place de la Concorde and the

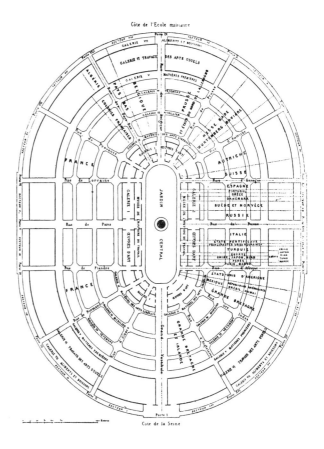

79

78

78. *The Universal Exposition*, central pavilion, 1867. The opening of Louis-Napoleon's new Paris saw the merchandise of the world assembled in an iron, glass, and brick version of Ledoux' ideal city of the Enlightenment. [Sigfried Giedion, *Space, Time and Architecture; the growth of a new tradition* (Cambridge, Mass.: Harvard University Press, 1941), p. 196]

79. *The Universal Exposition, 1867, plan*. Each of the interior streets is named after a country; the whole forms a model town of the arts and sciences in a true summary of the world at the end of the first industrial age.

80

81

80. *The construction of a barricade,* 18 March 1871. The barricades of the Commune were the tokens of a city that celebrated its liberation with a sense of invulnerability. They were, for the most part, no more than six or seven feet high and evenly built out of sandbags or paving stones. [Jules Clarette, *Histoire de la Révolution de 1870–71* (Paris, 1872), p. 581]

81. *The barricade of the place de la Concorde;* the defensive works of Père Gaillard. The only really substantial redoubts of the Commune, their lines of defense included ditches that exposed the underground sewers of the streets. [Clarette, *Histoire de la Révolution,* p. 645]

82. *The taking of a barricade by the Versaillese troops;* Clarette, who abhorred the Commune and its artifacts, takes pleasure in depicting the defenders routed, and the fragile barricade dispersed. [Clarette, *Histoire de la Révolution,* p. 681]

82

Tuileries gardens. Just before the days of May, he was to be seen standing before the huge ditch that divided the barricade from the Place, directing the National Guard to divert pedestrians while his photograph was being taken.[226] When it was already too late, a shocked member of the Commune angrily complained that Gaillard had spent all his money for the purchase of uniforms: "I understand that one could make barricades out of dung and sand; but with ratpickers!"[227] So confident were the Committee of Public Safety in the impregnability of worker-defended Paris, however, that they preferred to believe those who told of a city bristling with barricades. After all, the barricade was a temporary structure of war hardly befitting the open streets of a fraternal commune. If needed, "workers and engineers would work with such ardor that, in two or three days, these formidable works will be built."[228]

Beyond this, the Commune hardly identified with the discourse of monuments that had been used against it with such effect, edifices might be utilized according to exigency and appropriated in the service of a more equable state, but never again would the community build itself in the image of Imperial Paris. No plans were made for the reconstruction of the city as in the first revolution; the utopia was to be lived and experienced, not designed and walled in. Finally, and perhaps most pervasive of all the attitudes of unpreparedness, was the territorial sense of quarter so strongly embedded in the working people.[229] The myths and memories of preceding revolutions, carried through several generations, were those of a quarter taken over, a quarter barricaded, a realm marked out by daily life and defended to the death. If each *arrondissement* fought for its own soil with the passion fed by ownership and occupation, then Paris was truly impregnable: an assemblage of equally impenetrable communes, each a replication in miniature of the larger Commune, even as this in turn, was proposed as the model of a decentralized France.

Accordingly, when the Versaillese finally entered Paris on May 21, the sole defenses beyond those of the Rue de Rivoli were a few half-constructed barricades at the Bineau and Asnières gates. The Central Committee issued proclamations:

It is now a war of barricades, everyone to his quarter.

Let good citizens arise! To the barricades! . . . Let Paris bristle with barricades and from behind these improvised ramparts still hurl at her enemies her cry of war, of pride, of defiance, but also of victory; for Paris with her barricades is inexpugnable![230]

Thus, as Lissagaray demonstrated, hundreds of men returned to their quarter, there to barricade themselves in until the last, waiting for the enemy to overwhelm their positions. Nevertheless, the barricades arose with incredible speed and proliferated across Paris. In this art, if not in the precepts of tactical fighting, the population was instructed and

83

83. *Paris burned,* after the Commune; the sight of Paris in flames was the final demonstration to the right and its liberal apologists of the "barbarity" of the Communards. With shocked fascination the engravings record each of the sacred monuments of the Second Empire in ruins. Many of the scenes resemble those of Haussmann's own demolitions of fifteen years before. [Clarette, *Histoire de la Révolution,* p. 691]

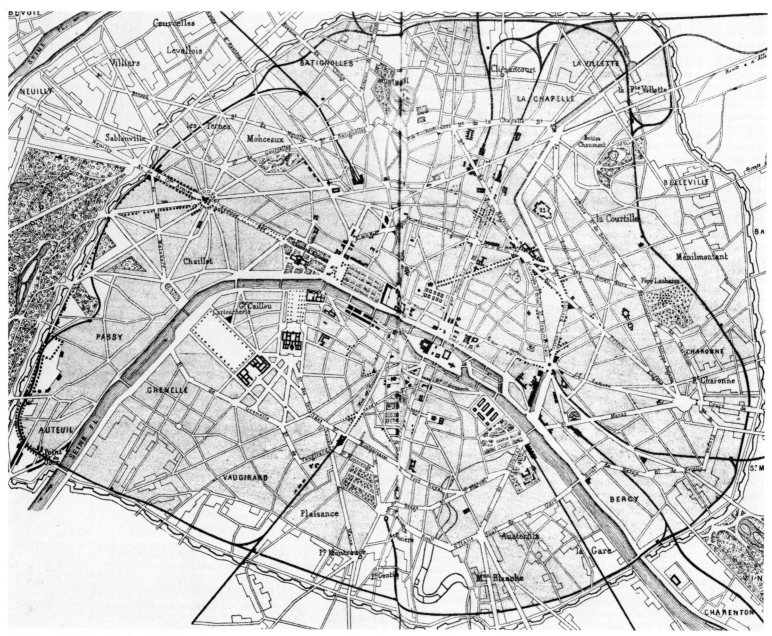

84. *Plan of Paris,* with the indication of the
monuments burned and the quarters bombarded,
1871. The final reckoning. Few cared to note that
the greatest area of destruction was clearly centered
in the eastern working-class quarters (the scene of
the last defense) and along the Champs-Elysées (the
route of Versaillese advance). [Clarette, p. 708.
Histoire de la Révolution, p. 708]

practised. Barricades again rose out of the earth like magic — on the Faubourg St. Honoré, the Rue de Suresne, the Boulevard Haussmann, throughout the ninth and thirteenth *arrondissements*. A particularly imposing structure was erected to protect the Hôtel de Ville at the corner of the Rue Saint Denis: "Fifty workmen did the mason work, while swarms of children brought wheelbarrows full of earth from the square. This work, several yards deep, six yards high, with fosses, embrasures was finished in a few hours."[231] This great wall, as large as Père Gaillard's four-week project, was, however, the only barricade of May to equal those of previous years; the rest were made of paving stones, mattresses thrown from windows, street gratings, perhaps with a cannon behind, and topped by the red flag. "Behind these shreds of ramparts" wrote Lissagaray, "thirty men held regiments in check."[232]

The barricade building continued throughout the day and the night of May; everyone was put to work — women, children, and passersby. The women of Les Halles were especially tireless in filling sacks full of earth and carrying wicker baskets; the barricade of the Place Blanche was, as found by the surprised reporter Maroteau, "perfectly constructed and defended by a batallion of women, about 120."[233] This was the "night of the barricades," and its memory was to haunt those who escaped; its fabrication was the prelude to the massacre of twenty-five thousand. Lissagaray described a scene strangely evocative of Hugo's some forty years before:

> The streets and boulevards, with the exception of the invaded quarters, had been lit as usual. At the entrance of the Faubourg Montmartre the light ceased abruptly, giving it the appearance of an enormous black hole. This obscurity was guarded by Federal sentinels . . . Beyond this only a menacing silence.[234]

Some six hundred barricades were constructed in the six days before the fall of the Commune, most without thought for any strategy of defense or covering fire. The flanking movements of the Versaillese troops easily countered Communards expecting only assault from the front, while each quarter, turned in on itself so to speak, refused to move to the aid of its neighbor. As a last resort, retreating into the north and east, the defenders began to fire the buildings that harbored snipers or provided cover for the troops. The fires that had started from the falling Versaillese shells were continued by the Commune. More than anything, it was this ultimate vandalism that shocked and provoked the forces of order: Paris seemed one sheet of flame, a macabre symbol of the devilish reign let loose within. To the Communards it was a fitting end to the monuments of monarchical power and a noble way to die. Marx compared the vandalism of the Commune to that of its predecessor Haussmann, the "razing of historic Paris to make way for the Paris of the sight-seer"; in time of war such "incendiarism" should be seen as good tactics:

The Commune used fire strictly as a means of defense. They used it to stop up to the Versailles troops those long straight avenues which Haussmann had expressly opened to artillery fire; they used it to cover their retreat, in the same way as the Versaillese, in their advance, used their shells which destroyed at least as many buildings.[235]

Against the fire power of the invader, advancing along the *percées*, which proved their use as cannon ranges, the embryo barricades were finally useless. Blanqui, who had criticized their building in '48, was nevertheless vindicated in his belief that the Parisian behind the barricade would fight with incredible tenacity. The last barricade of May to fall was in the Rue Ramponeau, defended by a single soldier for over a quarter of an hour.[236]

The triumph of the Versaillese was the signal for the massacre of the inmates of the rebellious city, a city declared a prison by Thiers and an asylum by its residents. The *Figaro* was clear in its imagery of slaughter,

> Never has such an opportunity presented itself for curing Paris of the moral gangrene that has been consuming it for the past twenty years. Today clemency equals lunacy. What is a republican? A savage beast. We must track down those who are hiding like wild animals.[237]

The hunting allées of Haussmann having served this purpose of purification, the urban space was reappropriated for its rightful owners by the rebuilding of every destroyed building in the same style. There was to be no visible or living memory of the time when the nation's capital had briefly become its largest correctional institution in riot.

With the defeat of the Communards and the regaining of the city by the forces of order, the last remnants of urban utopianism and communitarian idealism were dispelled. The radical critique of the city now turned, no longer toward the aim of its final reconstruction as the rightful home of a liberated community, but to its final destruction as the embittering symbol and symptom of the forms of advanced capitalism. Socialism directed its emerging political consciousness to the organization of its parties and the Second International and its critical energies to understanding the operations of economics and planning. Engels was as skeptical of Proudhon and his solution to the housing question as he was of Haussmann and the general mode of intervention he represented. The Parisian Haussmann, "breaking long, straight and broad streets through the closely built workers' quarters" had succeeded in his strategic and his economic intent — "to turn the city into a pure luxury city." Such was also the practice in other cities; it had, indeed, according to Engels, "now become general, quite apart from whether this is done from considerations of public health, for beautifying the town, or owing to the demand for big, centrally situated business premises, or owing to traffic requirements, such as the laying down of railways, streets, etc.''[238] Whatever the reasons in specific towns, the effect, argued Engels, was everywhere the same; ''The scandalous alleys and lanes disappear to the accompaniment of lavish self-praise from the bourgeoisie . . . but they appear again immediately somewhere else and often in the immediate neighborhood.''[239] Engels called this process ''Haussmannization.''

In the aftermath of the Commune, the ideal city of socialism was gradually restored to the countryside which had, from Rousseau to Babeuf, Fourier to Proudhon, been its first home. The call was for the abolition of the antithesis between town and country, as a precondition for the abolition of the division of social life through the division of labor. ''The first great division of labor'', wrote Engels in 1885, ''the separation of town and country, condemned the rural population to thousands of years of degradation and the people of the towns to subjection to each one's individual trade,'' a condition immensely exacerbated by the development of manufacture.[240] The theory of disurbanization, primitively embodied in the provisions of the *Communist Manifesto* of 1848, was now adopted as an essential prerequisite of balanced social relations of production; and incidentally the utopians were vindicated in their initial premises:

> The abolition of the separation between town and country is therefore not utopian, even in so far as it presupposes the most equal distribution possible of large scale industry over the whole country. It is true that in the huge towns civilization has bequeathed us a heritage to rid ourselves of which will take much time and trouble. But this heritage must and will be got rid of however protracted the process may be.[241]

The most radical of all such antiurban visions, that of William Morris, described with loving care the dismembering of ''the brick and mortar desert of London,'' and the ''big murky places which were once the centres of manufacture.''[242] The traveler from the nineteenth century found difficulty in recognizing the old urban places in the new landscape. The teeming metropolis had been invaded by orchards and lawns, woods and forests; the rows of badly built and ugly houses had been superseded by single cottages of brick and thatch, each set in spreading gardens. Only a few of the old monuments had remained, witness to the brutal prerevolutionary past. The streets of commerce and the unhealthy slums had been erased, overgrown with greenery, regaining their primitive state as tracks, pathways, and lanes, winding through an England of rustic harmony and childlike innocence. Industry might still perform the unwanted tasks of civilization, but out of sight and silent, freeing the population to engage in pursuits of art and craft, of making and embellishing, marrying hand and heart in the totally organic society:

> England was once a country of clearings amongst the woods and wastes, with a few towns interspersed, which were fortresses for the feudal army, markets for the folk, gathering places for the craftsmen. It then became a country of huge and foul workshops and fouler gambling-dens, surrounded by an ill-kept poverty stricken farm, pillaged by the masters of the workshops. It is now a garden, where nothing is wasted and nothing is spoilt, with the necessary dwellings, sheds, and workshops scattered up and down the country, all trim and neat and pretty. [243]

Morris, who had felt the despair of the Commune — sung wistfully in his ''Pilgrims of Hope'' — and who had marched with the rest to Trafalgar Square on Bloody Sunday, set himself resolutely against all the forms of life that denatured man and divided his life in labor.[244] Despite its inevitably medieval romanticisms, *News from Nowhere* remained the clearest and most uncompromising statement of the late-nineteenth-century postrevolutionary dream; a dream where the great divides of mechanical civilization were closed, the inhuman isolation and fragmentation bound up in a world of natural unity. In this world, Culture was no more divided from Society; the ''thought and the act,'' as Lethaby was to put it, were made one again, and, as a result — or perhaps as precondition — the city disappeared. Such a utopia, as successive revolutions have demonstrated, was to remain a dream in the face of the intractable machine of the great city.

1. Vitruvius, *The Ten Books on Architecture,* translated by Morris Hicky Morgan (New York: Dover Publications, 1960), p. 150.

2. Sebastiano Serlio, *I sette libri dell'architettura* (Venice, 1537–1557), illustrated in Helen Rosenau, *The Ideal City* (London, 1959), p. 50; Vitruvius' *Ten Books* had been published in Italy in 1486.

3. Andrea Palladio, the Teatro Olimpico in Vicenza; begun in the year of Palladio's death, 1580, the scenery was designed and carried out by Vicenzo Scamozzi. It is illustrated in *Le Fabbriche e i Disegni di Andrea Palladio,* edited by Bertotti Scamozzi (Vicenza, 1796), plates 1–4. See the reprint edition published by Alec Tiranti (London, 1968).

4. For the theater as a memory device in Renaissance humanism, see Frances Yates, *The Art of Memory* (London, 1966), especially chapter 16, and also her *Theatre of the World* (London, 1969).

5. Cf. Giulio Carlo Argan, *The Renaissance City* (New York: George Braziller, 1969), pp. 21–22.

6. Leon Battista Alberti, *Ten Books on Architecture,* Leoni edition edited by Joseph Rykwert (London: Alec Tiranti, 1965).

7. Ibid., p. 162.

8. Ibid., pp. 172–173: especially chapter VI, book VIII, "Of the principle Ways belonging to the City and the Methods of adorning the Havens, Gates, Bridges, Arches, Cross-ways and Squares."

9. Andrea Palladio, *The Four Books of Architecture.*

10. Print by G. F. Bordino illustrating a schematic view of the roads laid out in Sixtus V plan of Rome; in Argan, *Renaissance City,* plate 65.

11. Abbé Morelly, *Naufrage des Isles flottantes, ou Basiliade du célèbre Pilpaï* . . . ("Messine": Paris, 1753), translated by S. Hooper as *The Basiliade: Or the Book of Truth and Nature* (London, 1761), pp. 100–101.

12. Morelly's *Code de la Nature* (Paris, 1755) was published in the *Oeuvres de Diderot* (Amsterdam, 1773).

13. Abbé Morelly, *Essai sur l'esprit humain, ou principes naturels de l'éducation* (Paris, 1743), p. 25.

14. Morelly, *Basiliade,* pp. 110–111.

15. The history of the inhabitants of Morelly's utopian island was embodied in, and directly mirrored by, the history of their forms of shelter. The story of the evolution of the hut became in Morelly's terms the story of social and moral progress. In the earliest times the islanders lived in simple cabins or in hollows carved out of the rock; these dwellings were sufficient "indeed spacious and fit for their convenience," but unadorned and rustic in appearance. Later they learned to polish stone, give regular forms to their buildings, and to embellish the rude functionalism of these early houses. Only with the arrival of their enlightened prince, however, were the citizens of the *Basiliade* finally imbued with a true taste for reason; it was Prince Zeinzemin who miraculously caused the "love of regularity" to be born amongst his people.

16. Abbé Morelly, *Code de la Nature, ou le Véritable Esprit de ses Lois* (Paris, 1755).

17. See "Lois Ediles," in Morelly, *Code de la Nature,* edited with introduction and notes by Gilbert Chinard (Paris, 1950).

18. François-Noël Babeuf, called "Gracchus" (1760–1797), land-surveyor, journalist, organizer of the Conspiracy of the Equals, 1795. His program called for the equal division of the land and the distribution of its products in common. At his trial in 1796 he quoted freely from the *Code de la Nature* of "Diderot."

19. Abbé Laugier, *Essai sur l'Architecture* (Paris, 1753 and 1755), p. 209.

20. Cf. Thomas Cassirer, "Awareness of the City in the *Encyclopédie,*" *Journal of the History of Ideas,* XXIV, no. 3 (July–September, 1963). For a comparison of the ideals of the French *philosophes* and their European counterparts, see Carl E. Schorske, "The Idea of the City in European Thought: Voltaire to Spengler," *The Historian and the City,* Handlin and Burchard, eds. (Cambridge, Mass.: The MIT Press, 1963), pp. 95–114.

21. Jean-Jacques Rousseau, *The Confessions* (1781), translated with an introduction by J. M. Cohen (Harmondsworth: Penguin Books, 1954), p. 155.

22. Voltaire, "Des Embellissements de la ville de Cachemire" (1750), *Oeuvres Complètes* (Paris, 1879), XXIII, p. 473; also, "Des Embellissements de Paris" (1749), *Oeuvres Complètes,* p. 297.

23. Voltaire, "Des Embellissements de Paris," p. 297.

24. Laugier, *Essai sur l'Architecture,* p. 209.

25. Ibid., p. 210.

26. Ibid., p. 212.

27. Ibid., p. 213.

28. Ibid., p. 221.

29. Laugier, *Observations sur l'Architecture* (Paris, 1765).

30. Laugier, *Essai sur l'Architecture,* p. 222.

31. Ibid., p. 222.

32. Ibid., p. 224.

33. Ibid., p. 219. In 1753 this departure was regarded as novel and to a degree controversial. Although corresponding to Voltaire's own image of a polynuclear city (cf. Voltaire, "Des Embellissements de Paris," Note 38) Laugier's description was attacked by Grimm who maintained that there should only be one center for a city (cf. F. M. Grimm, *Correspondance Littéraire, philosophique, critique,* I [Paris, 1824], pp. 88–91. The plan of Karlsruhe (1715) with its centralized form and radiating avenues remained paradigmatic throughout the latter half of the century as Pierre Patte's description of an ideal town (1765) and even Ledoux's plan for the Saltworks of Chaux (1773) demonstrated.

34. Louis-Sebastien Mercier, *l'An 2440. Rêve s'il en fut jamais* ("à Londres", 1770).

35. Ibid., p. 14.

36. Description of the lessons in clinical surgery given by Desault in the Hôtel-Dieu in 1781, quoted in Michel Foucault, *The Birth of the Clinic* (London, 1973), p. 61.

37. Pierre Patte, *Monumens érigés à la gloire de Louis XV* (Paris, 1765).

38. Ibid., Chapter XVIII, "Des Embellissements de Paris."

39. Jacques François Blondel, *Cours d'Architecture,* I (Paris, 1771), p. xi.

40. Mercier, *Tableau de Paris,* I (Paris, 1783): "Narrow and ill pierced streets, houses too high which interrupt the free circulation of air, meat shops, fish shops, drains, cemeteries, make the atmosphere corrupt and charged with impure particles, so that this enclosed air becomes heavy and of malign influence."

41. Pierre Patte, in the first chapter of his *Mémoire sur les objets les plus importans de l'architecture* (Paris, 1769) under the heading "Considerations on the vicious distribution of towns and on the means of rectifying the inconveniences to which they are subjected," described his plan for an ideal city. Set out on a plain at the confluence of two navigable rivers, its overall form should be hexagonal or octagonal to facilitate policing and communication. All activities that produced noise, smell, or heavy traffic were to be placed outside the city limits and separated from it by an open zone or "cordon sanitaire." This band of greenery should completely encircle the city with a wide boulevard, pedestrian promenades, and four rows of trees. This *enceinte,* replacing the traditional ramparts, would act as a place of repose and recreation for the city dweller. Beyond would lie the industrial and commercial districts ringed by canals and roads for easy transportation. The whole city was to be planned according to scientific principles of ventilation and light.

42. Within fifteen years this type of provision had become the object of legislation: Royal Letters Patent issued in 1783 concerning the height of houses in the town and suburbs of Paris specified their height in relation to the width of the streets, "not only to render the air more healthy by easing its circulation, but also for the security of the inhabitants in case of fire." Patte's proposals for new techniques of building construction to reduce the risk of fire and its spread, his invention of means for cleaning and policing his ideal street were, in this way, gradually incorporated into real schemes for the reconstruction of Paris. Cf. *Lettres patentes du Roi* (25 August 1784) quoted in *La Vie Quotidienne à Paris dans la seconde moitié du XVIII siècle* (Paris: Archives Nationales, 1973). The decree established a height of 54 feet for streets 30 feet wide or more, and a height of 36 feet for streets 23 feet wide.

43. George Rudé, *The Crowd in the French Revolution* (London: Oxford University Press, 1959), p. 155. Police report of riot in Faubourg Saint-Antoine, 4th Prairial (23 May), 1795: "The guns of the rebels are trained on the city at the former Porte Saint-Antoine; the Grande Ru du Faubourg is filled with platoons of citizens armed with pikes and a few old-fashioned muskets; there are no armed pickets in the rues Charonne, Nicolas, Montreuil, Traversière, etc.; yet the citizens appear determined not to let themselves be disarmed. Women are assembled in every street and are making a great noise. Bread is the material cause of their insurrection; but the Constitution of 1793 is its soul."

44. In 1765, for example, the scientist and farmer-general, Antoine Lavoisier, proposed a new type of street lamp to the Academie Royale des Sciences that combined "clarity, ease of service and economy"; in 1774 he submitted another *mémoire* on the pumps and water supply of the city; he was active on commissions that studied the conditions of prisons, the siting of slaughter houses, the resiting of the Hôtel-Dieu, and he directed the study leading to the construction of the celebrated wall of the Farmers-General, built from 1784 by Ledoux.

45. Cf. Michel Foucault, *The Birth of the Clinic,* p. 34.

46. See Mona Ozouf, "Le Cortège et la Ville; les

itinéraires parisiens des fêtes révolutionnaires,'' *Annales E.S.C.*, (September–October 1971), n. 5, pp. 889–916; this is by far the most incisive account of the festivals and their routes through the city. Madame Ozouf traces these passages through meticulous research and analyzes the specific symbolic meaning of the places of rest, the particular processional patterns, and the architectural theory of the whole.

47. See Richard Cobb, *The Police and the People; French Popular Protest, 1789–1820* (London: Oxford University Press, 1970), especially part I, "The pattern of popular protest, 1795–1815."

48. Georges Lefebvre, ''Revolutionary Crowds'', in *New Perspectives on the French Revolution*, ed. Jeffry Kaplow (New York, 1965), pp. 173–190.

49. Jean François Sobry, *Discours sur le Cérémonial* (Paris, an XIII, 1805), p. 1. Sobry (1743–1820), although destined by his parents to be an architect, remained all his life a bureaucratic functionary of one kind or another. His best work, *De l'Architecture*, was published in 1776 and revised as the more celebrated *Poetique des Arts* of 1810. He turned from strong monarchical to strong revolutionary views, moving from a position as justice of the peace in Lyons (1794) to Commissioner of Police for the 10th arrondissement, Paris, 1800. This position simply confirmed him as one of the strongly conservative theoreticians of design (together perhaps with Bernard Poyet and Charles François Viel) of the Empire. In the case of Sobry, the political implications of architecture are made very explicit. His last writings were addressed to the police of his precinct, exhorting them to physical exercise as a guarantee of their health and preparedness.

50. Ibid., p. 5.
51. Ibid., p. 24.
52. Jean-Jacques Rousseau, ''Seventh Promenade,'' *Rêveries du Promeneur solitaire* (Paris, 1778), p. 146. The ''promenade,'' later to become the fashionable occupation of *flâneurs*, was favorite pastime of pre-Romantic poets and literary figures. Inevitably accompanied by daydreams or *rêverie*, it was a means of reexperiencing the primitive force of nature, long denied to civilized man.
53. J.-J. Rousseau, *Confessions*, Book IX, p. 375.
54. J.-J. Rousseau, *La Nouvelle Héloïse* (Paris, 1759).
55. J.-J. Rousseau, *Émile, ou de l'éducation* (Paris, 1762).
56. J.-J. Rousseau, *Le Contrat Social* (Amsterdam, 1762); translated as *The Social Contract*, by Maurice Cranston (Harmondsworth: Penguin Books, 1968), p. 38.
57. Babeuf's reply to a letter signed ''M.V.,'' Paris, 1796, in *Buonarroti's History of Babeuf's Conspiracy for Equality*, trans. J. B. O'Brien (London, 1836), from *Conspiration pour l'égalité dite de Babeuf*, by Philippe Buonarroti (Paris, 1828).
58. Nicolas Edme Restif de la Bretonne (1734–1806), popularly known as the ''Rousseau du ruisseau,'' or Rousseau of the gutter, a semimystic, moralistic, and futuristic writer, who contrasted the ''monde deprave'' of the city with the English landscape garden, where ''the earth itself is tilled to fulfill the noblest end of man'' (*La Famille Vertueuse*, Paris, 1767). In *Le Paysan Perverti, les dangers de la ville* (1775), he proposed a communal solution to city life in the image of a paternalistic settlement of

twenty-five families with a common refectory. Cf., ''Une ferme collective, Statuts du Bourg d'Oudun compose de la famille R**, vivant en commun,'' in Retif de la Bretonne, *La Vie de mon Père* (Paris: éditions Garnier Frères, 1970), pp. 242–249.
59. Cf. Johannes Langner, ''Ledoux und die *Fabriques*: voraussetzungen der Revolution-architektur im Landschaftsgarten,'' *Zeitschrift fur Kunst geschichte*, XXVI (1963).
60. Built for his patron, the general, poet and playwright, Anne-Pierre, Marquis de Montesquiou.
61. The *barrières*, or tollgates, of Paris, commissioned by the Farmers-General to improve the collection of city revenues and built between 1784 and 1789. Their monumental forms, combined with the wall that enclosed the boundary of the city, made them a target for the initial demonstrations of revolutionary fervor (11 July 1789).
62. This city, idealized as an outgrowth of the Salt Works of Arc-et-Senans, built by Ledoux in Franche-Comté between 1773 and 1779, was finally described in Ledoux' great *Architecture considerée sous le rapport de l'art, des moeurs et de la législation* of 1804.
63. Cf. Osvald Sirén, ''Le Desert de Retz,'' *Architectural Review*, 106, no. 135 (November 1949).
64. Claude-Nicolas Ledoux, *l'Architecture considerée sous le rapport de l'art, des moeurs, et de la législation* (Paris, 1804), volume I.
65. Ibid., p. 2.
66. Ibid., p. 102.
67. The idea that architecture might in some way work toward human progress by its very example, was proposed by critical utopians like Morelly as early as 1755, but it was some time before professional architects themselves realized the full implications of sensationalist philosophy on their work. Painting was perhaps the first of the arts to receive general attention in terms of its possible effects on the observer; Diderot, in his criticisms of the *Salons* from 1759, admired pictures that would, by their character and subject matter, ''instruct us, correct us and encourage us toward virtue.'' Ledoux similarly wrote, ''if he is enlightened, the artist engenders purifying mores by examples that have an effect on the mass of the people.''
68. François Marie Charles Fourier, *Traité de l'Association domestique-agricole*, II (Paris, 1882), chapter 4.
69. Fourier, Letter to his mother, Rouen, January 8, 1790; quoted in Charles Pellerin, *Charles Fourier, sa vie et sa théorie* (Paris, 1843), p. 175.
70. Fourier used the word ''tourbillon,'' or vortex, to describe the special and incessantly moving world of the passions in community; he finally adopted the more positive and less mystical title of ''phalanstère'' or home of the phalanx in 1816.
71. Cf. the painting by Meunier, ''Le cirque de Palais-Royal,'' illustrated in *Dessins Parisiens du XVIIIᵉ siècle* (Paris: Musée Carnavalet, 1971), p. 34. This circus was constructed by the duc d'Orleans in 1786 to replace the Opéra in the rue Saint-Honoré burned down in 1781.
72. Fourier, *Théorie des Quatre Mouvements et des Destinées Générales* (Paris, 1808), in *Oeuvres Complètes*, I (1846), p. 117.
73. *Publication des Manuscrits de Charles Fourier*, I (Paris, 1851), p. 86: text written between 1803 and 1808.

74. Ibid., p. 87.
75. Letter of Fourier to Just Muiron, 1819, Archives Nationales, 10AS, 25.
76. Victor Considerant, *Considérations Sociales sur l'Architectonique* (Paris, 1834), p. 63.
77. Ibid.
78. Roland Barthes, *Sade, Fourier, Loyola* (Paris, 1971), p. 118: ''The great preoccupation of this organization is communication. With what care and insistence Fourier describes the covered heated and ventilated galleries, the sand floored tunnels, and passages raised on columns by which the palaces or manors of neighboring tribes should communicate!''
79. Jean-Baptiste Godin, a friend of Considerant and follower of Fourier, whose *Familistère*, built after 1859 for the workers of his stove-founding plant at Guise in Northeastern France, became the paradigmatic realization of Association for the next half century; Henri-Jules Borie, a Saint-Simonian engineer whose *Aerodômes*, projects of 1865 anticipated in remarkable detail the *immeubles-villas* of Le Corbusier after 1922.
80. Walter Benjamin, *Charles Baudelaire: a Lyric Poet in the Era of High Capitalism*, trans. Harry Zohn (London: New Left Books, 1973), p. 117, ''Fourier or the Arcades.''
81. Jeremy Bentham, *Panopticon Postscript* (1791), in *Works*, ed. J. Bowring (London, 1843), vol. IV., p. 86.
82. Bentham, *Panopticon, or the Inspection House* (1791), in *Works*, IV, p. 39.
83. Samuel Bentham, a naval engineer, was working in the Ukraine for Prince Potemkin, building model dairies and industrial establishments.
84. A general problem faced by the managers of industry was, of course, the change in work habits and time schedules from rural or guild piecework to industrial production according to clocktime.
85. Bentham, *Works*, p. 40.
86. Ibid., p. 80.
87. Ibid., p. 81.
88. In a subsequent work, *Outline of a Work entitled ''Pauper Management Improved,''* Bentham summarized the principles upon which the Panopticon should be designed. These included health, comfort, industry, morality, and discipline. For the perfection of the latter, discipline, ''there should be Universal *transparency* and simultaneous inspectability at all times,'' *Works*, VIII, p. 375. Accordingly the building was to be built entirely from iron and glass: ''the edifice being circularly polygonal,'' wrote Bentham, ''glass was the sole material of which the boundary all round was composed, with the exception of the aggregate of the iron bars and leadings,'' *Works*, XI, p. 105. Bentham mentioned the great rotunda of Ranelagh House and contemporary garden conservatories as the prototypes for Panopticon.
89. Bentham, *Works*, IV, p. 43.
90. Bentham, *Introduction to the Principles of Morals and Legislation* (London, 1789), *Works*, I, p. 142.
91. For the philosophy of *confinement* cf. Michel Foucault, *Histoire de Folie à l'age classique* (Paris: Gallimard, 1972). The work of Robin Evans (see ''Bentham's Panopticon,'' *Architectural Association Quarterly* [London, August 1971]) has significantly added to our under-

standing of Bentham's philosophy of architecture, as also the recent study by Michel Foucault, *Surveiller et punir* (Paris: Gallimard, 1975).

92. Henri, Comte de Saint-Simon, *l'Organisateur,* in *Oeuvres de Saint-Simon,* vols. 19–22, p. 51.

93. For the life of Saint-Simon and a concise summary of his works, see Frank Manuel, *The New World of Henri Saint Simon* (Nôtre-Dame, 1963).

94. Formed in 1794 as the Ecole des Travaux Publics, constituted as the Ecole Polytechnique in 1795, this school became the single most important center for the technical instruction of civil and military engineers as well as architects in the empire and under the Restoration Monarchy.

95. For the origin and development of the *idéologue* out of the *philosophe* see George Lichtheim, *The Concept of Ideology and other Essays* (New York, 1967). The term *idéologue* was taken from A. Destutt de Tracy's *Eléments d'Idéologie* (1801–15) which attempted to inaugurate a science of ideas following Locke and Condillac.

96. Cf. *Henri Comte de Saint-Simon, Selected Writings,* edited by F. M. H. Markham (Oxford, 1952); ''Letters from an inhabitant of Geneva'' written in 1803, outlines a quasi-Baconian community of scientists, based on a Newtonian religion.

97. Saint-Simon, *Oeuvres,* p. 51.

98. Ibid.

99. Ibid., p. 52.

100. *Oeuvres de Saint-Simon et d'Enfantin,* VII (Paris, 1866), p. 119. Published by Charles Lemonnier in June of 1832, the manifesto called on Parisians to forego violence in favor of the Saint-Simonian program; ''the blood has run in Paris! The troops have camped in its streets.'' In their periodical, *Le Globe,* of April 1832, the Saint-Simonians called for the cutting of the street from the Louvre to the Bastille as a first step against cholera, which had swept the poorer quarters early in the year: ''This vast cut through the most unhealthy quarters, the narrowest streets, the worst built houses in Paris, has been projected for a long time. . . . This magnificent street, parallel to the Seine, will provide an outlet for the active circulation of these quarters, an outlet which becomes more necessary every day; it will shed light and air, passing a short distance from that Rue de la Mortellerie, which provided cholera its first and most numerous victims.''

101. Louis Blanc, quoted in Louis Hautecoeur, *Histoire de l'Architecture Classique en France.*

102. Charles Duveyrier, ''The New City, or Paris of the Saint-Simonians,'' in *Oeuvres de Saint-Simon et d'Enfantin,* vol. VIII, pp. 65–93.

103. Ibid., p. 67.

104. Ibid., p. 85.

105. Ibid., p. 88.

106. Robert Owen, *A New View of Society and Report to the County of Lanark,* edited with an introduction by V. A. C. Gatrell (Harmondsworth: Penguin Books, 1970), p. 229.

107. For a concise treatment of the educational, social, and economic thought of Owen, as well as a full ''industrial archeology'' of New Lanark with measured drawings of the buildings, see *Robert Owen, aspects of his life and work,* ed. John Butt (New York: Humanities Press, 1971),

especially chapters 2, 3, and 8.

108. Cf. Robert Owen, *Essays on the Formation of Human Character,* 1834 edition, containing two woodcuts illustrating the effects of good and bad circumstances; reprinted in Frank Podmore, *Robert Owen, a biography,* I (London, 1906), facing page 112.

109. Robert Owen, *Essays on the Formation of Human Character,* in Gatrell, *A New View,* p. 101.

110. The ''village of cooperation'' was first described by Owen in his ''Report to the Committee for the Relief of the Manufacturing Poor'' in March, 1817, and detailed in *Report to the County of New Lanark,* 1820. Like the Panopticon, this type form for a village community of some fifteen hundred inhabitants was developed in response to the problem of poverty and the administration of the Poor Laws following the drastic changes of the industrial revolution.

111. Robert Owen, *Self Supporting Home Colonies* (London, 1841), p. 39.

112. Owen, *Report to the County of Lanark,* p. 253.

113. Owen, like many of his contemporaries, shared a sense of loss for a past age of simplicity, reciprocal obligation between master and worker, and organic stasis. For Coleridge and Pugin in particular, this vision of a medieval golden age became a paradigmatic form by which to criticize industrial anarchy. Owen absorbed much of his dream of the past into his plans for the future; in his *Observations upon the effect of the Manufacturing System,* he characterized the social structure of this mythical state, one that bears resemblances to his own version of paternalistic capitalism: ''The lower orders experienced not only a considerable degree of comfort, but they had also frequent opportunities of enjoying healthy, rational sports and amusements . . . their services were willingly performed; and mutual good offices bound the parties by the strongest ties of human nature to consider each other as friends in somewhat different situations.'' (*The Life of Robert Owen, Supplementary Appendix* [London, 1858] pp. 38–41).

114. *The Crisis, and National Cooperative Trade's Union and Equitable Exchange Gazette,* vol. 3, no. 1 (September 7, 1833), frontispiece and explanation.

115. Ibid., p. i.

116. Robert Owen, *Self Supporting Home Colonies.*

117. ''From near their summits will be reflected at night, by powerful apparatus, the new Koniaphostic light, which will brilliantly illuminate the whole square.'' Ibid., p. 39.

118. Engels, recognizing the utopian nature of Owen's proposals, nevertheless perceived their curious quality of technical feasibility: ''and in his definite plan for the future, the technical working out of details is managed with such practical knowledge — ground plan, front and side and bird's eye views all included — that the Owen method of social reform once accepted, there is from the practical point of view little to be said against the actual arrangement of details.'' [Engels, *Socialism, Utopian and Scientific* (London, 1892), in *Engels: Selected Writings,* ed. W. O. Henderson (Penguin Books, 1967), p. 196.]

119. James Silk Buckingham, *National Evils and Practical Remedies, with the Plan of a Model Town* (London, 1849), p. 24. Buckingham is quoting a text by the Rever-

end Boone of Paddington to support his own scheme for a Model Town.

120. Cf. R. E. Turner, *James Silk Buckingham, a social biography* (New York, 1934), pp. 293–309.

121. Ibid., p. 307, quoting from *The British and Foreign Medical Review,* I (1836), p. 304, a journal that supported Buckingham's projects for temperance reform.

122. Buckingham, *National Evils,* p. 132.

123. Ibid., p. 110.

124. Ibid., p. 141; for a description of the antecedents to this plan and the involvement of Buckingham with John Minter Morgan and William Cooper, the Protestant reformers, see, W. H. G. Armytage, *Heavens Below, utopian experiments in England, 1560–1960* (London, 1961), pp. 209–223.

125. Ibid., p. 150.

126. Ibid., pp. 184–193.

127. Ibid., p. 187.

128. Ibid., p. 188.

129. The idea of ''graduated ornament,'' diminishing according to the fitness of its location in the town, was derived from Fourier who had proposed it in his *Traité de l'Association,* Note 68, in relation to his plans for a town that would act as a transitional environment between ''Civilisation and Harmony.'' Buckingham draws heavily on Fourier throughout his plan for Victoria, probably from his reading of *Cités Ouvrières,* a selection of Fourier's writings on town planning published by the Ecole Fourieriste in 1849.

130. Buckingham, *National Evils,* p. 193.

131. Titus Salt, cloth manufacturer and mayor of Bradford (1848), established a new works town at Saltaire for some 4,356 inhabitants. Opened in 1853, it was modeled on Trafford's model village in Disraeli's *Sybil;* like Buckingham, Salt was obsessed with temperance reformism, and the entrance to his town was surmounted with a huge sign that read, ''Abandon all beer, ye that enter here.'' It was said of him that ''no feudal lord could have opened his doors and offered his resources to the retainers of generations in the way he provided for those that labored under his direction.'' The town had wide, straight streets, with some 792 dwellings, all in the Renaissance style, as the style of reason and order. The glass galleries of Buckingham were put to use in the great weaving shed, the longest room in the world at the time, which produced some five thousand miles of cloth each year. Model towns of this kind were rapidly adopted by paternalistic industrial employers, like Cadbury (at Bourneville in 1878) and Lever (at Port Sunlight in 1887). Other utopists and social philosophers proposed improvements to the Buckingham model, including Robert Pemberton, the educationalist, whose *Happy Colony* was published in 1854, based on Ledoux' plan for the Ideal City of Chaux, but this time in iron and glass, and B. W. Richardson, the doctor and follower of Edwin Chadwick, whose *Hygeia* was first proposed in 1876. Ebenezer Howard, the dean of all the model-town enthusiasts and the most successful in practice, made use of all these proposals, but especially that of Buckingham, in his *Tomorrow, a peaceful path to real reform* of 1898.

132. Buckingham, *National Evils,* p. 224.

133. Victor Considerant, *Considérations Sociales sur*

l'Architectonique (1834), second edition (Paris, 1848), p. 42.

134. Sebastien Mercier, *Tableaux de Paris* (1783), vol. I, quoted in Louis Chevalier, *Classes Laborieuses et Classes Dangereuses* (Paris, 1958), p. 168.

135. Cf., Victor Hugo, *Nôtre Dame de Paris* (Paris, 1831), book III, ii, "Paris à vol d'oiseau." The peculiar aspect of the birds-eye view, allowing a view of the totality of a plan, was first exploited consciously in the ideal-city perspectives of Ledoux, but had been a favorite technique of cartographers since the Renaissance. The ability to actually ascend and verify the view hypothesized by perspective technique had of course existed since the first balloon flights of the mid-1780s.

136. Considerant, *Considérations Sociales*, p. 39.

137. Vicomte de Launay, 1838, quoted in Chevalier, *Classes Laborieuses*, p. 175.

138. *Édile de Paris*, 5 March 1833.

139. César Daly, architect, Fourierist, friend of Considerant and Flora Tristan, published his *Révue Générale de l'Architecture et des Travaux Publics* from 1840; it was undoubtedly the most influential architectural journal of the July Monarchy and the Second Empire.

140. Lecourturier, *Paris incompatible avec la République* (Paris, 1848), quoted in Chevalier, *Classes Laborieuses*, p. 180.

141. Karl Marx and Frederich Engels, *The Holy Family* (1845), French translation, *La Sainte Famille* (Paris: Editions Sociales, 1972), p. 72.

142. Frederich Engels, *The Condition of the Working Class in England* (1845), English edition, introduced by Eric Hobsbawm (London: Panther Books, 1969), p. 57.

143. Charles Dickens, *The Old Curiosity Shop* (London, 1840), chapter 44.

144. Gustave Flaubert, *Sentimental Education* (1869), translated and introduced by Robert Baldrick (Harmondsworth: Penguin Books, 1964), p. 292.

145. Dickens, *Old Curiosity Shop*, chapter 45.

146. Engels, *Condition of the Working Class*, p. 57.

147. Ibid., p. 58.: "And still they crowd by one another as though they had nothing in common, nothing to do with one another, and their only agreement is the tacit one that each keep to his own side of the pavement so as not to delay the opposing stream of the crowd. . . . The dissolution of mankind into monads of which each one has a separate principle and a separate purpose, the world of atoms is here carried out to its utmost extreme." The crowd in the street is here seen as the fullest expression of the social war, of "each against all." For a perceptive analysis of Engels's use of the crowd as a metaphor of capital, and a contrast with Baudelaire's observation of this new phenomenon in Paris, see Walter Benjamin, *Charles Beaudelaire*.

148. Engels, *Condition of the Working Class*, p. 60.

149. Ibid., p. 99.

150. This section of the article was completed before the publication of Steven Marcus's study of *Engels, Manchester and the Working Class* (New York, 1974), a methodologically challenging "reading of a reading" of the city.

151. Engels, *Condition of the Working Class*, p. 80: "And the finest part of the arrangement is this, that the members of this money aristocracy can take the shortest road through the middle of all the laboring districts to their places of business, without ever seeing that they are in the midst of the grimy misery that lurks to right and left."

In this way the facades of bourgeois respectability mask the reality and deprivation of the sources of middle-class wealth. The environment here acts as both the metaphor of capitalist development and the real confirmation of material conditions. Engels's reading of the city is at all points concerned with penetrating the appearance to discern the reality and to use the nature of the mask as a symptom of the condition of exploitation.

152. Ibid., p. 84.

153. Ibid., p. 85.

154. Ibid., p. 87.

155. Elizabeth Gaskell, *Mary Barton, a tale of Manchester life* (1848), edited and introduced by Stephen Gill (Penguin Books, 1970). For a thematic analysis of the city/country conflict in literature and in social life, see Raymond Williams, *The Country and the City* (London, 1973).

156. Peter Gaskell, *The Manufacturing Population of England . . .* (1833).

157. Charles Kingsley, *Alton Locke, tailor and poet* (1850), (New York, 1961), p. 117: "It was a foul, chilly, foggy Saturday night. From the butchers' and greengrocers' shops the gas lights flickered and flared, wild and ghastly, over haggard groups of slip shod dirty women bargaining for scraps of stale meat . . . Fish shops and fruit stalls lined the edge of the greasy pavement, sending up odors as foul as the language of sellers and buyers. Blood and sewer water crawled from under doors and out of spouts, and reeked down the gutters among offal, animal and vegetable, in every stage of putrefaction. . . . while above, hanging like cliffs over the streets — those narrow, brawling torrents of filth, and poverty, and sin — the houses with their teeming load of life were piled up into the dingy, choking night."

158. Charles Kingsley, *Sanitary and Social Lectures and Essays* (London, 1880), pp. 187 et seq. "Great Cities and their influence for good and evil," lecture delivered in Bristol, 1857.

159. Ibid., p. 189.

160. Dufey, *Mémorial d'un Parisien* (Paris, 1821).

161. Cf., Walter Benjamin, *Charles Baudelaire*, pp. 157–160.

162. Honoré de Balzac, *Illusions Perdues* (1837-1843), (Paris: Garnier, 1966), II, "Un Grand Homme de province à Paris," pp. 263 et seq.

163. Ibid., p. 265.

164. Ibid., p. 267.

165. See Helmut and Alison Gernsheim, *L. J. M. Daguerre, the history of the Diorama and the Daguerrotype* (New York: Dover, 1968). The panorama, invented by an Irish portrait painter, Robert Barker, was established in Paris by Pierre Prevost working for American investors who had built two rotundas on the Boulevard Montmartre. The first panorama, "A view of Paris," was displayed in June 1800.

166. Daguerre's first diorama, in a building erected to his design at the corner of the Place de la République and the Rue de la Douane, opened in July 1822 and represented "Canterbury Cathedral" and the "Valley of Sarnen." Cf.,

Gernsheim, pp. 14–47.

167. From an illustrated guide to Paris, 1832, quoted in Benjamin, *Charles Baudelaire*, p. 156.

168. Balzac, *Illusions Perdues*, p. 268.

169. Victor Hugo, *Les Misérables* (1862), (Paris: Garnier, 1963), vol. II, p. 353.

170. Ibid., "Paris a vol de Hibou."

171. Ibid., pp. 352-353.

172. The first barricades were built by the merchants and militia of Paris against the mercenaries of Henry III on May 12, 1588; built of barrels, paving blocks, and boards, they were set up at every intersection and encircled almost every quarter. During the Fronde of July 1648, Parlement and the merchants again barricaded the Ile de la Cité with paving stones and barrels to prevent the escape of Anne, regent of Louis XIV, and her chief minister, Mazarin.

173. Cf., Georges Duveau, *1848: the making of a Revolution* (New York: Vintage Books, 1968), pp. 161-181, "The Barricades."

174. Hugo, *Les Misérables*, p. 288.

175. Ibid.

176. Ibid.

177. Ibid., p. 328.

178. Ibid., "La Guerre entre Quatre Murs".

179. For a discussion of the art depicting the barricades and their successive transformations, see T. J. Clark's brilliant study, *The Absolute Bourgeois, Artists and Politics in France 1848-1851* (London, 1973), chapter I, "The picture of the Barricade."

180. Cf., Auguste Blanqui, *Textes Choisies*, ed. V. P. Volguine (Paris, 1955), especially pp. 214-220: "Instructions for an armed uprising," written in 1868 as a critique of the tactical errors of 1848.

181. *Alexis de Toqueville, Recollections*, ed. Mayer and Kerr (New York: Doubleday, 1970), p. 39.

182. Hugo, *Les Misérables*, p. 409.

183. Frederich Engels, "The June Revolution", *Neue Rheinische Zeitung*, nos. 31 and 32, July 1 and July 2, 1848; in Karl Marx and Frederich Engels, *The Revolution of 1848-49, articles from the Neue Rheinische Zeitung* (New York: International Publishers, 1972), p. 57.

184. Hugo, *Les Misérables*, p. 412.

185. *Mémoires du Baron Haussmann* (Paris, 1890), II, p. 53.

186. The relation of Louis Napoleon's *Idées Napoleoniennes* to the projects of his reign is discussed in H. N. Boon, *Rêve et réalité dans l'oeuvre économique et sociale de Napoleon III* (The Hague, 1936).

187. Haussmann, *Mémoires*, II, p. 533.

188. Ibid., III, p. 13: he is clear as to the significance of the operations of "triangulation, survey and levelling of the city" as the very instruments of the rational planner: "Before concerning myself with the piercing of the new public ways, whose network constitutes the most singular part of the Transformation of our great city, should I not, in effect, speak of the initial study for this long and laborious work and of the instruments which have served me to undertake this project in its entirety and its details; to determine on the spot the line of each avenue, boulevard or street to be opened up and to oversee the faithful execution of the whole?" (III, p. 1.)

189. Cf., Amédée de Noe, *Croquis Contemporains*

(Paris, n.d.), Part 3. The cartoon by de Noe ("Cham") of Madame Saqui, "the celebrated aerialist charged with maintaining communications among the surveyors," is illustrated in David H. Pinkney, *Napoleon III and the Rebuilding of Paris* (Princeton, 1958). This is perhaps the best general account of Haussmann's transformation in English.

190. For a reconstruction and analysis of the Plan des Artistes (1793) see Gaston Bardet, *Naissance et Méconnaissance de l'Urbanisme: Paris* (Paris, 1951). This plan was similarly preceded by an accurate triangulation of the city by Edmé Verniquet, between 1774 and 1790.

191. Haussmann, *Memoires,* III, p. 257.

192. Ibid., p. 28; a collection of attributes that have become almost synonymous with the Modern Movement since the founding of C.I.A.M. in 1928.

193. Ibid., II, p. 257.

194. Ibid., III, p. 27. Cardinal Morlot, the Archbishop of Paris and a strong supporter of Haussmann, was convinced of the intimate relation between the new works and the improvement of morality, "Your apostolate, he wrote, comes to the aid of mine. You indirectly but surely combat moral depravation by raising the conditions and the habits of life of the laboring classes. In wide and straight streets, inundated with light, they are not given the same freedom as in the narrow, tortuous and dark streets." (*Mémoires,* II, p. 257.)

195. Lanquetin, *Commission des Halles, Documents,* no. 4., p. 17. "The Ile de la Cité," he wrote, was "without possible contradiction one of the most deprived of elements of prosperity."

196. Leon Faucher, reporter of the bill empowering the city to float the 50-million franc loan for the Rue de Rivoli extension (1851); quoted in A. des Cilleuls, *Administration Parisienne,* vol. II, p. 192.

197. Haussmann, *Memoires,* III, p. 55, and II, p. 318: "The order of this queen of cities is one of the first conditions of general security . . . the very style of its public monuments excites attention." (*Memoires,* II, p. 203.)

198. Ibid., II, p. 197.

199. The emperor, styled by Saint Beuve "Saint-Simon on horseback," favored the new tar macadam surfaces for his horses; Haussmann, admitting it into the rides of the parks, preferred smooth granite *pavées,* as, of course, did those who were looking for barricade material. Gas lighting was introduced in 1861 — "cette revolution radicale" Haussmann called it, as he designed many new kinds of fixtures for its public use. He was more critical of the advent of electricity, however; writing his *Mémoires* in the 1880s (the first International Exposition of Electricity was held in Paris in 1881), he objected to its "unpleasant light" that in its extreme brightness hurts or tires the sight (*Memoires,* III, p. 163). The specific rhythm of light and shade so beloved of those who haunted the gas-lit boulevards was reinforced by the pace of the lamplighter; c.f., Benjamin, *Charles Baudelaire,* pp. 50–52.

200. Cf., the meticulous plans and sections of the boulevards and their typical furniture in A. Alphand, *Les Promenades de Paris* (Paris, 1867–1873), 2 vols. Alphand of course was responsible for the major park plans ordered by Haussmann.

201. Haussmann, *Memoires,* II, p. 271.

202. Ibid., p. 523.

203. Ibid., III, p. 530.

204. Emile Zola, *La Curée* (Paris, 1871); English edition, translated by A. T. De Mattos (New York, 1924), p. 124.

205. The great project of the Rougeon-Macquart had been conceived as a clinical examination of psychological cause and effect: how environment finally formed and transformed character. The transformation of Paris, the city of Zola's myth and reality, was perhaps the most shocking and fundamental rupture examined by the epic, beside that of the country and the city. One by one the novels scrutinized the change with scathing vision. From *Thérèse Raquin* (the failure of the arcades) to *Le Ventre de Paris* (the gluttony of the city), Zola portrayed the physical contexts and physiological agents of moral decay. In the preface to *Thérèse Raquin* he defined his object as studying "the profound modifications of organisms under the pressure of environment and circumstances."

206. Zola, *La Curée,* pp. 1–5.

207. Ibid., pp. 80–81.

208. Ibid., p. 204: "the gray bands of wide interminable pavements . . . amid the stamping, swarming crowds which filled them little by little with an absolute and entire contentment, with a feeling of perfection in the life of the streets. Every boulevard became a lobby to their house."

209. Cf., for example, Claude Monet's *Boulevard des Capucines* (1873) or Caillebotte's studies of the new urban landscape of Paris between 1875 and 1877. Linda Nochlin, in *Realism* (Harmondsworth: Penguin Books, 1971) compares these "cropped" views taken from above to the developing art of photography.

210. Zola, *La Curée,* pp. 150-155: the Boulevard des Italiens.

211. Ibid., p. 154.

212. *Paris Guide,* ed. A. Lacroix (Paris, 1867), II, p. 929.

213. Jules and Edmond de Goncourt, *Journals: 1851–1870* (Paris) p. 93.

214. Charles Baudelaire, *Les Fleurs du Mal,* ii, "Tableaux Parisiens," lxxxix, Le Cygne (Paris: Garnier, 1961), p. 95.

215. *Paris Guide,* p. 924.

216. Emile Zola, *Le Ventre de Paris* (1873), *Oeuvres Complètes,* II, p. 570.

217. *Paris Guide,* p. 294.

218. P.-J. Proudhon, *Du Principe de l'Art et de sa Destination Sociale* (1865), in *Oeuvres Complètes* (Paris: Riviere, 1939), p. 281.

219. Zola, *La Cloche,* February 13, 1870, in *Oeuvres Complètes,* 13, p. 259. Zola's articles on the transformation of Paris, written between 1868 and 1870, deserve serious analysis: they appeared in *La Tribune* of June 21, 1868; August 23, 1868; October 11, 1868; February 4, 1869, and *La Cloche* of April 22, 1870.

220. Karl Marx, *The Civil War in France,* in Karl Marx, *The First International and after,* Political Writings, volume III (New York: Vintage Books, 1974), p. 228.

221. Cf., Stewart Edwards, *The Paris Commune 1871* (London, 1971), p. 8; this is the best recent account of the short life of the Commune and its political significance.

222. Sylvain Maréchal, *The Manifesto of the Equals,* April 1796.

223. Lissagaray, *History of the Commune of 1871,* translated from the French by Eleanor Marx-Aveling (London, 1886), p. 127.

224. Edwards, *Paris Commune,* p. 144.

225. *Procès-Verbaux de la Commune de Paris,* ed. G. Bourgin and G. Henriot, II (Paris, 1945), p. 189; edict of 30 April 1871.

226. Edwards, *Paris Commune,* p. 312.

227. *Procès-Verbaux,* p. 418.

228. Ibid., p. 419.

229. A characteristic criticized by Blanqui some three years before. It was essential, he wrote, "above all not to become shut up each in his quarter, as all uprisings have failed to do, to their great loss."

230. Lissagaray, *History of the Commune,* p. 319.

231. Ibid., p. 320.

232. Ibid., p. 324.

233. G. Maroteau, *Salut Publique,* 23 May 1871; quoted in Lissagaray, *History of the Commune,* p. 324.

234. Lissagaray, *History of the Commune,* p. 323.

235. Marx, *Civil War in France,* p. 229.

236. Lissagaray, *History of the Commune,* p. 379.

237. Quoted in Edwards, *Paris Commune,* p. 340.

238. Engels, *The Housing Question* (1872), (New York: International Publishers), p. 74.

239. Ibid., p. 75.

240. Engels, *Anti-Duhring* (1885), trans. Emile Burns, ed. C. P. Dutt, (New York, 1972), p. 318.

241. Ibid., p. 323.

242. See William Morris, *News From Nowhere* (London, 1891), ed. A. L. Morton (New York: International Publishers, 1968), p. 250.

243. Ibid., p. 254.

244. "Pilgrims of Hope," published in the *Commonweal* between April 1885 and 1886, was written as a saga of the Paris Commune, described with true hope as a "glimpse of the coming day." Morris had taken an active part in the events of the free-speech march on Trafalgar Square on "Bloody Sunday," November 13, 1887.

Structure of Streets

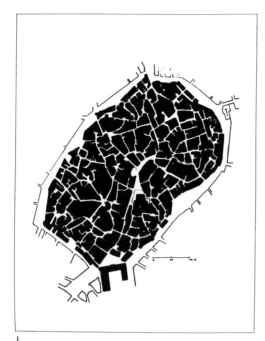

1

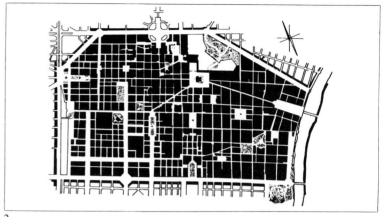

2

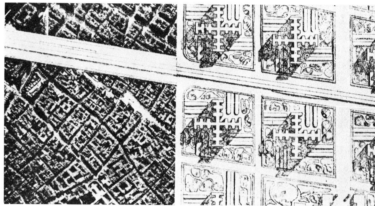

4

3

1. Martina Franca, Apulia, Italy, 927. [E. A. Gut-kind, *Urban Development in Southern Europe: Italy and Greece* (New York: Free Press, 1969), p. 401]

2. Turin, central sector today. [Gutkin, *Urban Development,* p. 251]

3. Finchingfield, Essex. [Thomas Sharp, *The Anatomy of the Village* (Harmondsworth: Penguin, 1946), p. 17]

4. Le Corbusier, Plan Voisin, 1925. [Le Corbusier, *The Radiant City* (New York: Orion Press, 1964), p. 207]

The Spatial Structure of Streets

William C. Ellis

Street . . . "A road in a town or village (comparatively wide, as opposed to a 'lane' or 'alley') running between two lines of houses; usually including the side walks as well as the carriage way. Also the road together with the adjacent houses."

The Oxford English Dictionary contains numerous such entries suggesting the particular, continuing, multiple nature of the street: at once a road and a place, inseparable from the buildings that flank it. The interdependency of these elements and functions underlies most of the essential qualities of the street, both good and bad. Through a cultural buildup over time, the street has evolved as an institution right up to the recent past. Today, however, streets have become less an integral part of our urban lives. By and large we question the street both as a conception and as an institution in our public urban structure. Yet streets have persisted in the face of technological and social change. As the many dictionary variations suggest, they still have the potential for enriching our individual activities and our collective conception of the urban surroundings we share. This provokes us to examine all facets of these basic urban elements, from their functions to their formal properties, to understand and use them better.

This essay isolates some formal properties of streets in order to make them more apparent and to form a basis for suggesting their desirability in our present-day cities. Its approach is reductive rather than proliferating: its subject matter is limited to urban streets, but it alludes to some intrinsic qualities of all streets. It omits roads, highways, and freeways, which fall outside the multiple nature of streets noted in the opening quotation. Its frame of reference is specific: the physical relation between buildings and open spaces in cities, reduced to a basic state of "solids" and "voids." This framework incorporates the conceptual component of perception; thus it helps us to deal with what we know as well as what we merely see. Also, it generates typological images without which it would be impossible either to represent or to understand most formal relationships between streets and buildings.

The essay is in two parts. The first compares two opposed physical conceptions of city: a traditional one with its streets in a system of differentiated open spaces and a contemporary one with its streets in a system of undifferentiated open space. It maintains that we can use both these conceptions; but because the traditional one is often thought to be obsolete, the argument emphasizes its particular kind of viability and the building/street relationships that characterize it. The second part describes in more detail some of these traditional relationships, considered under three topics: elemental street types, special streets in their contexts, and the interdependence of street walls and street space.

Purely formal analyses of entities as large and as ultimately utilitarian as our cities are problematic at best. Such analyses seem to make more sense as historical demonstrations than as programmatic proposals. Yet, as the following descriptions suggest, intellectual or formal ideas about the way our surroundings should be have often gone hand in hand with social conceptions and utilitarian goals. This will continue to be the case. The design of cities is hardly a matter confined merely to formal issues, but nevertheless we need a rational understanding of our cities as physical images, an understanding that coexists with, and even confronts, purely utilitarian concerns.

Cities and Streets as General Physical Conceptions

Present-day western cities are predominantly a combination of two generalized physical conceptions.[1] One could be described as a city that appears to have had its streets and open spaces carved out of what was once a solid mass of stuff (fig. 1). Because the spaces seem to have been given form within the more or less contiguous building pattern, the organization can be interpreted as a *structure of spaces*. This image corresponds to the traditional city. We think of it as a datum for physical cities in many cultures, and it can be represented by built-up cities from antiquity to the early twentieth century (fig. 2). The other conception is a city that appears to be open land — a park or a meadow — into which buildings have been introduced as objects sitting on a plane (fig. 3). Because the buildings are clearly the "generated" elements, the organization can be interpreted as a *structure of solids*. This image also corresponds to cities throughout time, but as an ideal it is usually thought to be a contemporary conception. In its most didactic form it can be represented by any of Le Corbusier's urban proposals (fig. 4).

These opposed conceptions form the basis for the following descriptions. They are meant to be referential only; and obviously, they have a historical as well as a typological existence. For instance, what is called here a "structure of spaces" is a conception referring to cities that more often than not have begun with the simple placement of a few isolated buildings on the ground. Their evolution into a complex arrangement of more or less contiguous buildings, which seem to form the spaces between them, has resulted from growth by infill rather than by expansion, reflecting such factors as their need to remain small and compact for efficient communication. This is not contradicted by the instances where cities with this physical arrangement have been built at a single stroke, using the contiguous, party-wall building unit that at the time represented the received way of building cities.

Alternatively, what is called here a structure of solids includes that early simple arrangement of isolated buildings; but it is also a reaction against the traditional city, and not only for technological or hygienic reasons. Variations on the idea of city as park extend back at least to the mid-eighteenth century. But for modernist architecture the pavilion

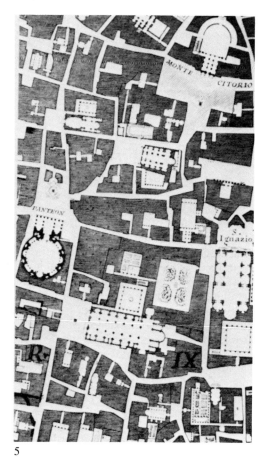

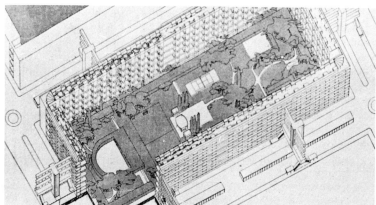

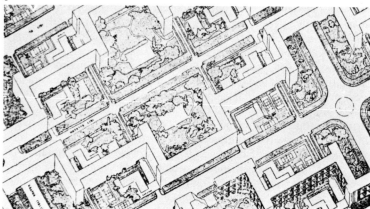

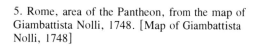

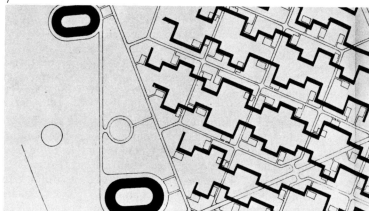

5. Rome, area of the Pantheon, from the map of Giambattista Nolli, 1748. [Map of Giambattista Nolli, 1748]

6. Le Corbusier, blocks of dwellings on the "cellular" system. [Le Corbusier, *The City of Tomorrow* (London: J. Rodker, 1929), p. 221]

7. Le Corbusier, dwellings with "setbacks." [Le Corbusier, *City of Tomorrow,* p. 233]

8. Le Corbusier, Antwerp project, 1933. [Wayne Copper]

building, free on all sides, became an ideal which replaced the traditional standard of contiguous urban buildings. Urban space came to be thought of ideally as providing light, air, and greenery, not only as a necessity which in most older cities had come to be in short supply (fig. 4).

But regardless of how these cities evolved or were conceived, they may be usefully considered as finished physical conceptions — useful not only because our present-day cities are arguably a combination of the two but also because they make more evident one of the essential relationships in our urban surroundings — that between buildings and open spaces, including streets. Moreover, they are useful because, as referential ideas, they are important components of the images that guide our actual designs, providing models at the level of basic, general choice.[2]

The traditional city, a structure of spaces, produces an elemental street whose basic spatial characteristic is felt volume. It is generated by and responds to the characteristics of the vertical wall planes that bound it on either side. Speaking of the medieval city, Françoise Choay observes that the buildings and the streets are inseparable; they define each other.[3] The elements of such a street — roadway, pedestrian way, and flanking buildings — exist interdependently with one another. Because of their well-defined characteristics of felt volume and their interdependent mix of elements and functions, these streets tend to act both literally and metaphorically as exterior rooms in the city. They function as places as well as links; they incorporate various social and operational activities into an integrated and somewhat unspecified mix, much as do the volumes interior to buildings. This condition is often elaborated into a complex of interior and exterior spaces of different configurations and uses, both public and private, linked together by a circuit of streets, itself a part of the differentiated system (fig. 5).

Choay's description of streets and buildings defining each other comes very close to the solid/void image being used here. But because of our familiarity with solid objects we find it difficult to conceive of voids generating or defining solids. In any organization of solids and spaces we tend to think of the solids as positive and the spaces as negative. However, in the city as a structure of spaces, the exterior spaces — including the streets — seem to have been generated by the buildings and thus resist interpretation as mere residue. We tend to interpret them as elements equivalent to the solids; in a sense they can be considered spatial objects. We attribute qualitative equivalence to the buildings and spaces of this kind of organization independent, within limits, of their actual ratio. For instance, figures 1 and 2 have substantially different ratios between their buildings and spaces; but in each the spaces seem to be configurations equivalent to the buildings.

Alternatively, the contemporary image of the city, interpreted as a structure of solids, produces an elemental street with few characteristics of felt volume: the street as road. The space between buildings is neither object nor residue, but rather is part of a continuum (figs. 3, 4). We tend to attribute to this kind of organization an inequality between the buildings and the surrounding space. The area covered by the buildings is comparatively small. But, like the equivalence between the elements of the traditional city, the inequality here is more a function of configuration than of actual ratio, mainly because the space is not generated by the buildings. For instance, figures 3 and 4 have substantially different ratios between their buildings and the surrounding space, but they can both be interpreted as organizations of objects in a spatial continuum. Moreover, in both these examples the roadway, pedestrian way, and flanking buildings are not only stretched apart, but exist independently of one another.

The functions of place and link have been separated. This represents the reduction of the idea of street to the concept of road marked out on the ground, a register of the evolving schism between collective urban space and public road as bearer of traffic. One product of this schism has been the progressive movement of public urban space into the interior of the buildings themselves, beginning in the nineteenth century with the great railroad terminals and department stores and the corresponding increase in importance of private domestic space, as people were driven off the street by the huge increase in vehicular traffic.[4]

Nevertheless, for architects in the early part of this century, the separation of road, pedestrian way, and flanking buildings developed into an intellectual program with a corresponding formal vision of the way things should be. This is well illustrated by the differences in Le Corbusier's earlier and later urban proposals: they exemplify the diminishing role of the vertical wall plane as the active, shared surface between solids and spaces. In his early scheme, *A City for Three Million Inhabitants,* he employed as a basic building type the Immeubles Villa (fig. 6). This type is in many ways similar to the traditional city block in that its vertical planes form two kinds of open space, between which it functions as both barrier and linking screen: on its exterior it articulates the street; on its interior it develops a kind of courtyard space. When replicated, it produces an idealized version of a system of traditional, differentiated urban spaces.

In his later proposals this building type seems to have been consciously discontinued. He continued to favor two other types: the linear *redant* housing evolved from Immeubles Villa (figs. 7, 8) and the point tower. Apparently these represented for Le Corbusier the means for transforming the city into a green park in which the inhabitants would live in a natural and healthful setting that at the same time would accommodate the automobile. These two favored prototypes embody a radically changed relationship to the streets and spaces around them:

they stand free, separated from the roads marked out on the ground as independent systems. They no longer define the street in space. This separation between building systems and street systems is the main characteristic of the contemporary street. There is no doubt these prototypes represent a grand vision, aspiring to accommodate both technology and a certain idea of nature. But they embody a second, problematic, distinction: they can only displace space; there is no means for their enclosing, surrounding, or shaping open space, and thus they lack the capacity to produce differentiated exterior spaces.

Apart from the advantages inherent in variety itself, it can be argued that undifferentiated open space is problematic in several ways. It makes difficult the development of a variety of open-space types and sizes, which can accommodate and encourage a range of uses from public to private, and it prevents absolutely the outright provision of private open space. The attempt to provide a variety of open spaces in this contemporary system must rely on landscaping alone, to subdivide what is actually one continuous open space — and thus often degenerates to a cosmetic treatment rather than a structural definition (fig. 9). This is another way of arguing that the design of our urban environment should engage not only building patterns but also exterior space patterns at a structural level.

The idea of differentiated exterior space is a distinction that depends for the most part upon the nature of the backs and fronts of buildings. In the traditional city, the structure of spaces, the typical block structure is made up of buildings that have a basically different condition of back and front (fig. 10). Fronts relate to fronts, forming a street space; backs relate to backs, generating a courtyard space. The space in the interior of the block may be developed or not; it may be broken up into individual rear lots corresponding to entrance doors; it may be a communal, semiprivate space; it may be simply a shaft for light and air; but it is recognized as part of the block structure. It is understood to be there by virtue of the dimensional discrepancy between the apparent depth of the total block and what we know to be the normal front to back depth of an average dwelling unit. So we see the range of buildings and spaces beyond the facade we happen to be looking at. We know that the depth of the block contains some kind of back-up structure; in this case, a courtyardlike space which may or may not be literally or even visually accessible to us. Simple as this relationship is, there is no basic unit in the contemporary version of city that can generate a comparable differentiation of open space.

This deficiency seems to be inherent in the confrontation between the point tower or the linear megastructure and the idea of street. In one sense, both the point tower and the linear megastructure are versions of the pavilion building: they stand essentially free in space. Their configurations provide ventilation and view equally to their occupants. Their

density is extremely high, freeing a large percentage of the ground for other uses. In a field of point towers the absence of differentiated open space is obvious. There is no distinction between fronts and backs; the configurations allow no means for enclosing or surrounding open space, and thus no means for articulating pieces of space from the surrounding continuum.

While this is not quite so obvious in a typical grouping of linear megastructures, the condition is much the same. They are often set out in parallel rows. Within this arrangement there are two typical relationships to the street grid: one in which the buildings only partially fill the grid segments (fig. 11a) and one in which the buildings more or less completely fill the grid segments, the building lines coinciding with the lot lines (fig. 11b). The first case displays many of the same properties as a field of point towers; the absence of differentiated open space is obvious. The latter case suggests the possibility of providing differentiation of the spaces between the buildings, but even here it is hardly possible. For instance, a project of 1926 by André Lurçat (fig. 12) appears to approximate the traditional relation between buildings and streets; but because the faces of the buildings are neither backs nor fronts, they produce what amounts to either a series of streets or a series of courtyards rather than a system containing both. There is no thickness to the buildings within which another category of open space could be generated, or which might allow one side of the buildings, and thus one intermediate space, to be different from another; and we read these buildings as seams stretching across one large open space. Where spatial differentiation is attempted at all, it occurs within the spaces themselves as a cosmetic treatment rather than as a function of their relationship with the buildings (fig. 13).

In Le Corbusier's *redant* buildings the condition is more complex because of their jointed or segmented configurations. Although they represent an evolution from the Immeubles Villa, breaking up and recombining its elements, (figs. 7, 8, 9), nevertheless they can be regarded as megastructures that have been "bent," or as a series of megastructures put together in sections. They form recesses that do begin to enclose space on three sides. But a recess on one side corresponds to an advance on the other. And because we know the buildings never vary in depth, and because we know there is no difference between front and back, we interpret that conceptually they are without depth; a folded plane, in fact, that alternatively seams together or divides two parcels of undifferentiated open space (cf. figs. 14, 15).

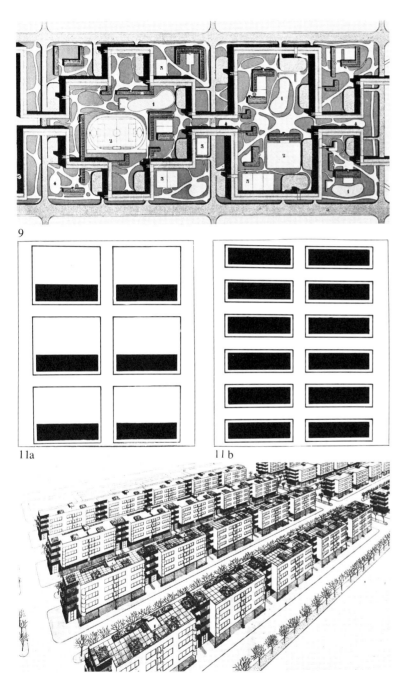

9

11a

11b

13

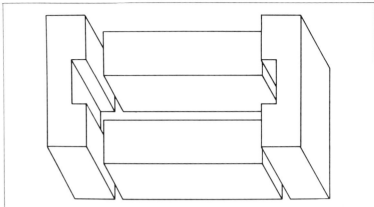

10

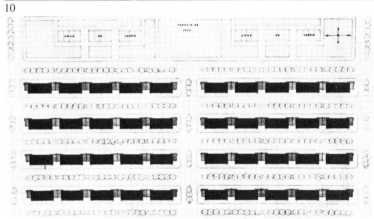

12

9. Le Corbusier, "La Ville Verte," 1930. [Le Corbusier, *Radiant City*, p. 163]

10. Diagram, typical city block. [William Ellis]

11a. Diagram, housing blocks set back from street.
[William Ellis]

11b. Diagram, housing blocks coincident with
street. [William Ellis]

12. André Lurçat, housing project, 1926, site plan.
[André Lurçat, *André Lurçat, Architecte, Projets et
Realisations* (Paris: Vincent, Fréal, 1929), p. 28]

13. André Lurçat, housing project, 1926, view.
[Lurçat, *André Lurçat*, p. 29]

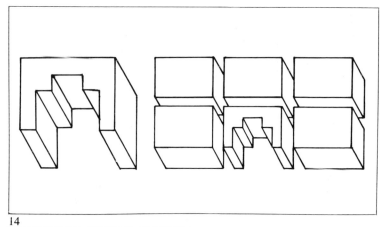

14

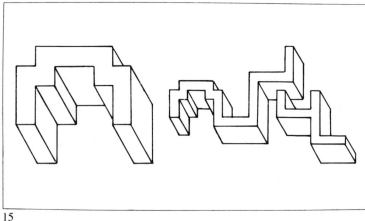

15

14. Diagram, building forms with fronts and backs coincident. [William Ellis]

15. Diagram, building forms with fronts and backs divergent. [William Ellis]

The Spatial Street
Elemental Types

Unity and equality between buildings and spaces, differentiated exterior space, and a different condition between fronts and backs are all characteristically absent from the city as a structure of solids and its roadlike street; together they form the very basis of the traditional, spatial street. There are two fundamental configurations of the traditional street: these can be called the *continuous development* and the *elongated courtyard*.[5] The first is a relatively straightforward conception, one that generally comes to mind when we think of streets: a route that proceeds along, restricted on one or both sides by buildings, apparently free of termination at its ends. It functions as both place and road. Partly because it is self-evident, we tend to forget that the very uniqueness of its configuration and function long ago caused its evolution into a common and replicated type of urban space; and because of these unique properties it still persists as an element of urban structure. It constitutes the pervading, principal element of the street grid; but because its terminations are often ill-defined, we usually think of its segments rather more than its total run; its problems of termination are often acute, as shown in figure 16. But for the most part its problems of termination are taken care of by the very unity between this street type and the grid itself. Sometimes it finds its way through a grid to extend gradually into the countryside; at other times it is turned back into its network with renewed definition through mergers, cranks, reversals, and so on. Thus the continuous development is continuous in its image as well as in its literal reality (fig. 1).

The nature of the continuous development depends on the properties of the street walls that bound it. Figure 17 illustrates the condition in which the street is almost literally a continuous channel of space. Here the transverse interruptions are neither numerous, strong, nor regular; they are so buried in the surrounding context that they may be thought of as being absent together. This gives a strength and contiguity to the walls of these boulevards that increase our tendency to see them as continuous linear spaces. The typical New York City avenue is also characteristically a continuous channel of space. But here the transverse interruptions are both numerous and regular, and the effect of this regular rhythm of breaks contributes to the articulation of the avenue itself (fig. 18). The repetitiveness and predictability of these breaks enhance the nature of the avenue as both a continuous sequence and a literal shaft of space. This sequential effect is bolstered by the occurrence of major crosstown streets at regular intervals, which break up the avenue into coherent segmental links. On the other hand, the typical small cross streets in New York City are so vitiated by the strong lines of the avenues that they can be said to be only technically continuous, in

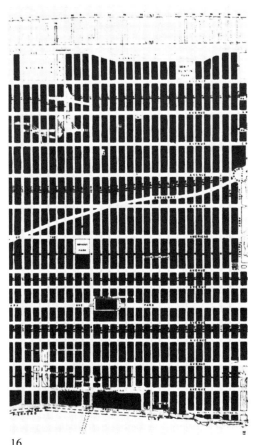

16

17

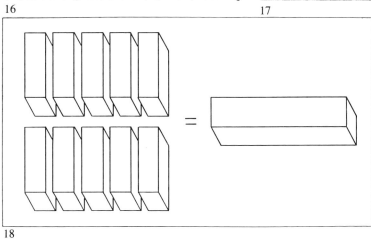

18

16. New York City, Manhattan, 34th Street to Central Park. [William Ellis]

17. Paris, Boulevard Beaumarchais and Boulevard Richard-Lenoir. [Sigfried Giedion, *Space, Time and Architecture* (Cambridge, Mass.: Harvard University Press, 1939), p. 752]

18. Diagram, Manhattan avenue with cross streets at regular intervals. [William Ellis]

19

20

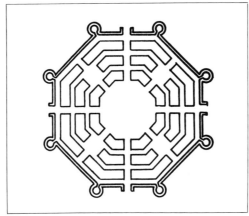

21

22

19. Courtyard street, colonnaded, attributed to Bramante. [Sibyl Moholy-Nagy, *Matrix of Man* (New York: Praeger, 1968), p. 139]

20. Florence, Piazza degli Uffizi. [Edmund Bacon, *Design of Cities* (New York: Viking, 1967), p. 98]

21. Francesco di Giorgio Martini, design for a fortress town. [Gutkind, *Urban Development,* p. 121]

22. Girolamo Maggi, design for ideal city, 1564. [Gutkind, *Urban Development,* p. 123]

the sense that their segments are highly discrete (fig. 16).

The street as elongated courtyard is in almost every way the opposite number to the street as continuous development. An idealized image of this type is provided by the drawing, attributed to Bramante, of a street view shown in figure 19. Here the street space is portrayed as enclosed volume to such an exaggerated degree that it becomes almost unrecognizable as street in the ordinary sense. But the Piazza degli Uffizi (fig. 20) embodies all the qualities of the courtyard street in that it exaggerates whatever roomlike attributes pertain to street space. It infers a configuration of street that has centralizing spatial characteristics and a strong sense of terminal closure. Where the continuous development represents a category of urban space unique to the street itself, the elongated courtyard represents a type of street space with characteristics we usually attribute to rooms or courtyards or piazzas. Thus it holds the qualities of link and place in a different balance. If the continuous development must have been originally a road around which buildings, and therefore place potential, began to develop, the elongated courtyard must be thought of as originally having been a place — a courtyard or a square — through which traffic began to flow.

Today we tend to think of streets more as roads than as places. If this way of thinking jeopardizes the kind of balance between link and place that characterizes the continuous development, it regards as anathema the emphasis on place typical of the elongated courtyard. Choay has pointed out, almost axiomatically, that closure is antagonistic to circulation, a statement that evidently applies at a general, abstract, systemic level.[6] Indeed, with very few exceptions, the elongated courtyard has never operated at the systemic level to facilitate vehicular traffic. Barring some unforeseen technological or social transformation in our urban surroundings, this condition is likely to continue. But to take Choay's observation too literally is to overlook the difference between actual and implied closure; thus the possibility for the exception to the rule. And we can say that a given street can imply spatial closure and still allow continuous traffic.

Some Functions of Streets in Their Contexts

Because the elongated courtyard is inward looking, centralizing, we attribute another characteristic to it: it is inevitably special in relation to a grid of generalized streets. This notion leads to the broader one of special streets versus generalized streets.

Although the elemental streets are not strictly separable from their relation to a context, most of the foregoing remarks have emphasized their autonomous properties. The notion of special streets is inherently one of relationships more than of properties. For example, Regent Street in London is a special street in terms of shopping and a famous street in

terms of its general reputation as a designed object; and so for the avenue des Champs-Elysée in Paris, the Via del Corso in Rome, Fifth Avenue in New York City, and so on. But these streets are also special parts of the physical structure of their cities. They tend to produce relative differentiation in the surrounding street systems. This structuring function tends to increase a sense of place in the organization of cities in that it helps to structure them into wholes; it tends to reduce the likelihood of random, limitless organization.

In this sense the idea of special street is notable for its absence in much of contemporary work, which often takes as a model the very concept of random limitless organization, whether thought of as acknowledging current technological imperatives or as an aesthetic ideal appropriate to the twentieth century because of its difference from the more consolidated organizations of the past. Nevertheless, most contemporary cities still embody special streets and generalized streets as existing, empirical conditions — not only the great world cities just mentioned but most built-up cities.

There are three categories of physical properties, any or all of which can obtain to give a street a special connotation relative to its context: special size, special configuration, and special position. Within these there are some very basic structuring functions, either geometric or topologic, that the special street traditionally serves. But these functions are in part explainable only in terms of the relation between a given context and the two elemental types of traditional street previously mentioned: the continuous development and the elongated courtyard.

It has been suggested that the continuous development is basically inseparable from the generalized street grid, and that the elongated courtyard is inevitably special to the street grid. But while the elongated courtyard is inherently special due to its configuration, the continuous development can have special qualities also — those deriving from its size and, moreover, from its critical position in a context, relative to the geometry or topology of the whole organization. For example, the boulevards Beaumarchais and Richard-Lenoir (fig. 17) act as special streets not only by virtue of their relative size but also in the sense that they serve to sector what would otherwise be an unstructured field of buildings and streets, much as Fifth Avenue, Park Avenue, and Broadway function in the context of New York City (fig. 16). More particularly, these streets can be interpreted as responding to what the overall geometry or topology of the organization itself seems to require in terms of internal structuring.

Some diagrammatic examples may make this idea more clear. For instance, one structuring function is the division of large fields by streets: the nature of the overall organizations in figures 21 and 22 pose geometrical conditions to which its internal divisions must, seemingly, respond. The square, the circle, the rectangle, and so on, each has a

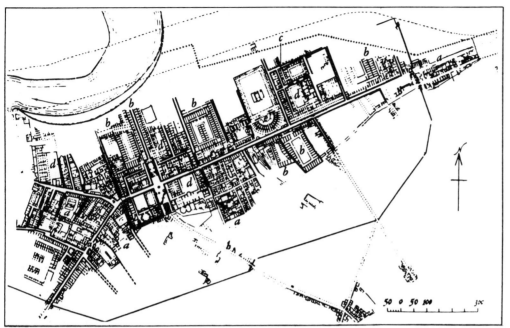

23

24

25

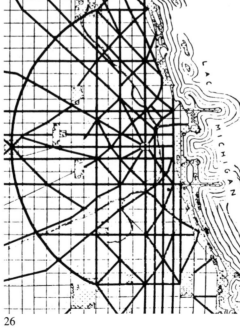

26

23. Ostia Antica. [M. A. Stein, *Caravan Cities* (1926–32)]

24. Palmanova, near Trieste. [Mario Morini, *Atlante di Storia dell'Urbanistica* (Milano: Ulrico Hoepli, 1963), p. 211]

25. Paris, Avenue de l'Opéra. [Giedion, *Space, Time and Architecture,* p. 756]

26. Daniel Burnham, diagram of plan for Chicago, 1909. [Moholy-Nagy, *Matrix of Man,* p. 238]

27. Florence, Piazza della Signoria and Piazza degli Uffizi, after Bacon. [William Ellis]

28. Florence, diagrammatic street plan, after Bacon. [William Ellis]

number of logical or at least conventional ways in which we expect them to be subdivided. They can be bisected, divided into quadrants, striated in any number of ways, divided radio-concentrically, or gridded without any particular reference to their center. Another structuring function is the aggregation of loosely related fields into a whole: in figure 23 the principal street can be seen to act as a seam — a linear center seemingly required for consolidation of the loose, multiple overall organization. A third function might be the definition of fields themselves: in figure 24 the street acts as an edge — an articulation of periphery that might be called for by some topographical condition, as a response to a strong condition of center, or as a final edge condition that signals a series of parallel internal striations. A fourth function is the linking of separate entities: in figure 25, the street acts to link two important entities within the overall structure; in figure 26, the linking function becomes the generator of a circuit of spaces, each of which would be somewhat meaningless without the internal linkage.

All these examples are diagrammatic and can be qualified. But they all have in common the characteristic of an internal response to geometric imperatives set by the latent structure of the overall organization. The shapes of cities as physical organizations are often far away from the simple geometry of squares and circles; but as the examples of Paris or London suggest, more complex overall shapes embody topological imperatives that demand internal responses in the same way: large fields need breaking up into smaller divisions, loosely connected fields suggest consolidation, and so on. The continuous development usually performs these topological functions, and we attribute special connotations to it when its size and position in the context are critical.

On the other hand, the elongated courtyard is special in terms of its configuration. It might be thought of as a set piece arbitrarily inserted into a generalized system. Rather than responding to the demands of its context, it seems to impose its own organization upon its surroundings. The Piazza degli Uffizi (figs. 20, 27, 28) is a good example of an elongated courtyard acting, along with a series of other set piece spaces, to organize a generalized context of building and streets (fig. 28). These set pieces are all self-conscious, closed, streetlike spaces. They aggregate around them what would otherwise be a fragmented heap of stuff. Their special configurations give unity and focus, creating an organization of differentiated parts in an arbitrary and imposed way, suggesting no particular reference to what the overall organization itself might have called for as an internal response. In the example of Burnham's plan for Chicago (fig. 26) the placement of the linked spaces seems inevitable, or at least logical, given the overall geometry. In the Florence example, the circuit of spaces might be strung out in a number of other patterns and still impose an organization that would successfully differentiate parts of the whole. We deduce then that this somewhat ineffable capac-

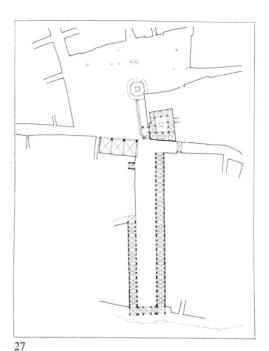

27

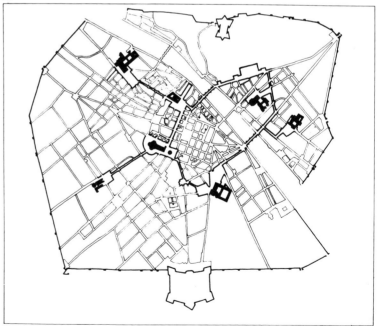

28

29

29. Genoa, Strada Nuova (Via Garibaldi), view, Palazzo Doria Tursi. [*Genova, Strade Nuova* (Genova: Vitali e Ghianda, 1967), p. 35]

30. Genoa, Strada Nuova (Via Garibaldi), roof plan. [Genova, *Strada Nuova*, p. 77]

31. Genoa, Strada Nuova (Via Garibaldi), *piano nobile*. [Genova, *Strada Nuova*, p. 71]

32. Genoa, Strada Nuova (Via Garibaldi), plan diagram. [Genova, *Strada Nuova*, p. 36]

33. Genoa, Strada Nuova (Via Garibaldi), air view. [Genova, *Strada Nuova*, p. 98]

ity of the courtyard street to impose organization depends in large part upon its special configuration relative to the generalized street.

The Street Wall and Street Space

Whether the traditional street is thought of as special or generalized, a continuous development or an elongated courtyard, the properties of the street wall constitute a third classification applicable in terms of the basic image — the city as an organization of solids and spaces. It cuts across both the elemental and the relational classifications; and within it there are two alternative conditions. The first can be called the street as unified wall; the other, the street as a series of pavilions. They are similar to, but independent of, the earlier, basic distinction between the structure of spaces and the structure of solids in that both fall within the idea of the spatial street. In both, the street space appears as a bounded configuration. But the unified wall produces a positive spatial configuration while the pavilion street produces a negative one. The differences between the two can be best understood through a direct comparison along common categories.

In the street as unified wall (figs. 17, 20, 27) the importance resides in the street space. The space is positive in the sense that it seems to have been generated into a purposeful figure by the buildings that flank it. It is the very illustration of the spatial objects referred to earlier (figs. 1, 2). Correspondingly, the buildings appear as the residue of a larger mass out of which the street has been carved. We tend to think of the street itself as a volumetric entity, seemingly separated from the other spaces of the city; and we think of the facades as belonging to the street more than to the flanking buildings.

In the street as a series of pavilions (fig. 29), the importance shifts from the street space to the flanking buildings. The street space is negative in that it does not seem to have been intended as a configuration produced by the flanking buildings. Because of the discontinuity of the street facade, the buildings read as autonomous objects — pavilions — each generated around some supposed center, standing free of each other, displacing more than forming space. We can see the continuity that exists around these buildings between the street space and the other adjacent streets. The individual differences of the building facades — detail, configuration, size, height, and relative placement — all devalue our understanding of the street space as a configuration in itself; and we suppose ourselves to be more outside the flanking pavilions than inside a street space. Thus the facade is assumed to belong more to the buildings than to the street.

There is some ambiguity in the examples given with respect to the descriptions they illustrate. This will almost always be so where abstract diagrams are not used. But, in particular, the example of the Strada

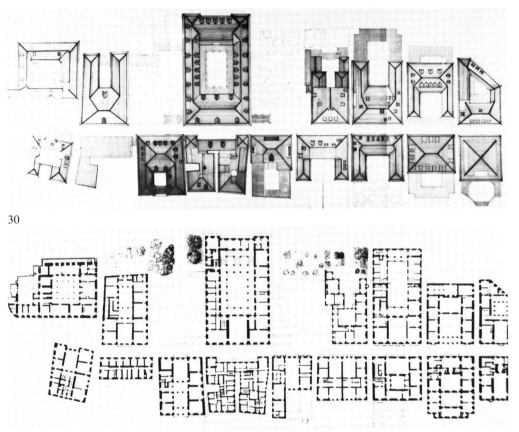

30

31

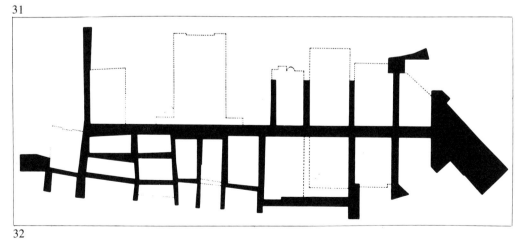

32

33

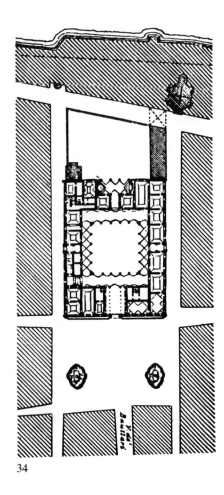

34

34. Rome, Palazzo and Piazza Farnese. [Gutkind, *Urban Development*, p. 145]

35. New York City, Manhattan, Park Avenue, looking south from 68th Street, circa 1940. [Vincent Scully, "The Death of the Street," *Perspecta 8* (New Haven: Yale School of Art and Architecture, 1963), p. 93]

Nuova (figs. 29–33) illustrates an ambiguous condition typical of many traditional streets: it is formed by free-standing pavilions that can also sustain interpretation as residual pieces of a formerly solid mass. This ambiguity arises not only because some of the pavilions are attached to adjacent buildings behind them but also because of the particular, ambiguous quality of the palazzos themselves: they seem to stand at that critical point in scale and configuration where their properties as individually generated objects merge with their metaphorical attributes as residual pieces of a larger mass.

There are some variations of this idea, most of which seem to depend on the similarity of size and configuration of the pavilions and the regularity of spacing between them. Because of this we might postulate a critical zone, rather than a point, along a scale of size and solidity within which this condition obtains. For instance, Park Avenue of, say, the 1940s represents a similar condition of ambiguity between the importance of the blocks as pavilions on the one hand and the importance of the street space they form on the other. The tendency is to regard the blocks as individual pavilions and at the same time to interpret them in their aggregate as forming two organized walls (fig. 35). This similarity between Strada Nuova and Park Avenue suggests some reason to regard the typical city block as a descendent of the urban palazzo (fig. 34), not only because they both differentiate street space from courtyard space, but also because of their ambiguity as both pavilion and components of a unified wall. Moreover, it can be suggested that an ambiguity such as this is a potentially fruitful one; in terms of a comparison between the two basic conceptions of city, it appears to be more intrinsic to the traditional one — the structure of spaces — than to the contemporary structure of solids.

Conclusion

At this point I have suggested that certain formal aspects of the traditional street are persistent, unique, and make it still viable. I have pointed out certain relationships between its structure, its accommodation of several elements and functions, its capacity to provide differentiated open space, its ability to create place qualities in a context, and its potentially fruitful ambiguity as a system of urban buildings and spaces. In the process, claims that have been inferred for the spatial street bear qualification. Judgment has been suspended in terms of its operational and social viability in order to set out in idea form some of its properties that might still be desirable. But the intention here is not to enshrine the traditional street. Rather it is to suggest there is merit in conceptions of street that often are considered antiquated and discounted as possibilities at the level of basic choice.

The notion of an equivalency between the solid and spatial elements of a city is an important one. The exterior spaces of the city are the rooms of the city, and the built structures are the walls of those rooms. These walls owe a responsibility to the formation of those rooms. The interior functional considerations of buildings can be coordinated to allow them to perform the function of creating exterior city space.

I recognize that the contemporary conception of city not only has a wide base in technological validity but also represents formal postulations that cannot be taken as simply negative concepts. At any rate, it constitutes a part of the stuff with which one must deal in manipulating environment. But one is led to search for a contemporary conception of city in which street, or streetlike space, is a positive element. And it can be suggested that a city viable both socially and operationally can grow out of traditional, as well as more recent, conceptions of physical city.

Notes

This essay is a shorter, substantially revised version of a draft treatise, part of a larger study done for the National Endowment for the Arts in 1969.

1. Colin Rowe et al., *The New City: Architecture and Urban Renewal* (New York: The Museum of Modern Art, 1967), p. 24. These and some of the other general classifications are attributed to Rowe.

2. See Alan Colquhoun, ''Typology and Design Method,'' *Arena: the Architectural Association Journal,* September 1967, for the uses of typological models.

3. Françoise Choay, *Espacements: essai sur l'evolution de l'espace urbain en France,* privately published, 1969.

4. Ibid.

5. The terms are attributable to Colin Rowe.

6. Choay, *Espacements.*

1. Stuyvesant Town and Peter Cooper Village, New
York City. From the Ville Radieuse model.
[Thomas Airviews, courtesy Metropolitan Life In-
surance Company]

Buildings and Streets: Notes on Configuration and Use   Thomas Schumacher

Street and Antistreet

Any discussion of contemporary American streets must weigh both the antistreet attitudes of this century and the technological developments that have reinforced those attitudes. Changes in American lifestyles that transformed public activities into private activities have reduced street use in existing neighborhoods and all but obliterated the street in many new developments. Some of these important daily activities that once had a less private reference are shopping, entertainment, incidental conversation, trips to school, and the traditional promenade. Twenty years ago a housewife would walk to the grocery store. Now she drives to the supermarket, thus confining all interactions to the market itself and none to the trip. Where entertainment was once a public event, it is now dominated by that singularly private mode of communication, television. In many American towns children are driven to school by their parents or taken by bus. Telephone calls have largely replaced the neighborly chat, and even the pedestrian promenade has, in many American environments, been replaced by the automobile promenade. Whether social interaction in public places has come to be so negative as to force a shift to private activity cannot be answered here. There is radical disagreement as to causes and effects in this area of social science. No definitive studies demonstrate the value (or lack of value) in providing generous opportunity for face-to-face contact throughout public urban space, indoor and outdoor. Do residents of environments that give preference to pedestrian choices rather than automobile-access choices experience a higher or lower degree of environmental satisfaction? The difficulty of giving a rigorous answer to this question is staggering. It may be impossible to produce environments for controlled experimentation on this problem. To find two neighborhoods where all the variables of class, origin, ethnic mix, age, economic status, and value systems among the inhabitants are the same would be difficult indeed, especially when the signs of upward mobility in the United States have been associated with greater exploitation of technological gadgets.

It may nevertheless be argued that an environment that provides a genuine diversity of choice (potential environment) would permit direct interaction by most inhabitants throughout a large portion of the public domain. I will assume that such possibilities for interaction in public open spaces are not only desirable but necessary for environmental satisfaction.[1]

We are interested, then, in getting people out into the street or, alternatively, out into some equivalent of the traditional street. Consider the inability of Americans to conceive of an environment where use of the street is desirable. An American says, "We live *on* Elm Street," while an Italian, for example, lives "*in* via Angelo Masina." The differences in terminology suggest differing conceptions. Italian urban life is dependent upon the street or piazza for social and economic organization. In the United States the street is used to locate private life, and little else. It is only in neighborhoods where a strong pre-twentieth-century physical context joins with a social structure of great stability (generally of first- and second-generation immigrants) that street activity occurs. Boston's North End and New York's Lower East Side are prime examples.

This essay concentrates primarily on the residential and mixed residential/commercial environments of American cities. Rather than take the traditional approach to housing as a problem of need, I will attempt to outline certain formal needs of streets where housing is *the* important land use.

Physical Planning Variables

Redevelopment of urban areas in the United States has been big-ball renewal. Great tracts of slums, streets, and new housing are built, generally on a model vaguely resembling the Radiant City of Le Corbusier (fig. 1).[2] Beyond the abrupt discontinuity of environmental form, the resulting configurations of buildings and uses are less adequate than the preexisting street systems in providing whatever it is that establishes the notion of community. Redevelopment on a wholesale basis results in interruptions in the context that the "set piece" of the typical housing project cannot mend; while one must admit that most American slum contexts are not models of urbanism, one must seek to understand which conditions are critical to the proper working of a given environment.

It may be possible to postulate contextual norms for predominantly residential streets. While the question "What makes a good street for a residential environment?" cannot be answered with any certainty — especially since so many factors enter into the variables of form and use that determine the influential environment — it is nevertheless possible to isolate certain factors that fall within the domain of the physical planner. Proposals are based on the previously stated premise that widespread use of street and public open space by pedestrians from a wide cross section of the population, for the greatest number of hours in the day and days in the year, is a positive environmental quality. Physical planning factors that appear most to influence street use are (1) user density, (2) land-use mix, (3) pedestrian/vehicular interaction, and (4) configuration of street and context.

User density. While research has failed to yield hard quantitative results, it is clear that street activity occurs only if it is convenient for large numbers of pedestrians to use the street in various ways. Streets are active when density is high enough to (1) inhibit use of the au-

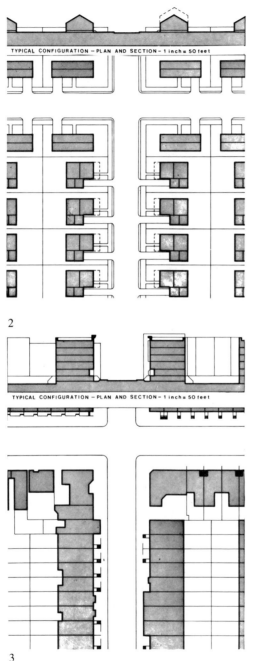

TYPICAL CONFIGURATION — PLAN AND SECTION — 1 inch = 50 feet

2

TYPICAL CONFIGURATION — PLAN AND SECTION — 1 inch = 50 feet

3

tomobile, (2) support goal-directed activities (shops, schools, for example, sufficiently close to each other and to the origins of pedestrian trips so that pedestrian orientation is clearly the preferred choice, and (3) employ the potential of the street space for unplanned, non-goal-directed activities. These factors immediately reveal the inadequacy of the suburban street. This can be illustrated by a comparison of two typical American streets: a low-rise, low-density, single-family, detached-house street in Cambria Heights, Queens, New York (fig. 2), and a low-rise, medium-density, multiple-family, attached-house street in Brooklyn, New York (fig. 3). There is virtually no pedestrian activity in the street in Cambria Heights except for occasional access to houses. The street in Brooklyn is used for recreation and sitting as well as pedestrian access to houses. The crucial difference in these examples is that goal-directed activities in the local context are easily accessible in the Brooklyn neighborhood, whereas in the Cambria Heights neighborhood those service activities (shopping, playgrounds, schools) are sufficiently distant to encourage the use of the automobile. In Cambria Heights most housewives shop by car and conceive of their community in such terms as "a ten-minute drive" to a particular goal.

It cannot be said that all variables except residential density are equal in these examples, but they do provide typical conditions for comparison between environments of low and medium-to-high density. Moreover, other variables (such as configuration) affect street use, often counteracting the positive effects of high density. This occurs in typical high-rise housing projects with large open spaces where, even if user density is high, a diffusion of pedestrian space and lack of concentration of users in the public domain prevent intensive street use. Frequently contrasting configuration and intensity of use can be found on either side of the same street (fig. 4).

Land-Use Mix. The inclusion of varied uses within an otherwise residential environment appears to be a necessary precondition for pedestrian street activity. While service activities and commercial uses tend to evolve within a medium- or high-density residential environment (fig. 5), the zoning of neighborhoods to exclude such activities often tends to reduce the possibility of use of, and consequently interaction in, the public domain.[3] In many public and private housing projects (fig. 6) the relegation of these goal-directed activities to the outside world creates a gap in continuity from the recognizable private domain to the specifically useful public domain. The resultant open space remains unused, at least partially, because there is no place of importance to go to.

Pedestrian/Automobile Interaction. The general norm of twentieth-century planning has been the separation of vehicular and pedestrian traffic. While separation of high-speed movement from pedestrian activity may be obviously necessary, total separation is often harmful to

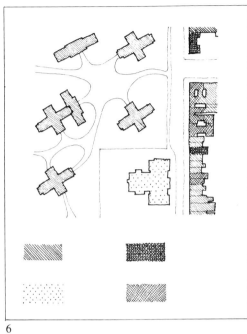

4

5

2. Cambria Heights, Queens. Plan of a typical street of houses, detached single family. [IAUS Streets Report, July 1971]

3. Brooklyn Heights. Plan of a typical street of houses, attached, multiple family. [IAUS Streets Report, July 1971]

4. Tenth Street, New York City. Different configurations and different scale of pedestrian activity. [Photo, Patricia Conway]

5. Broadway, Upper West Side, New York City. Mix of residential and commercial uses. [Photo Patricia Conway]

6. Robert F. Wagner, Sr., Houses, New York City, Plan. Goal activities are relegated to the outside world. [Schumacher]

6

7

7. Sketch of Madison Avenue, New York City, as a pedestrian mall. [New York City, Office of Midtown Planning and Development]

8. Bedford-Stuyvesant "Superblock." Street renovation by I. M. Pei and Paul Friedberg: cars penetrate partway into the block and are excluded only in specific activity areas. [I. M. Pei & Partners, Coordinating Architects; M. Paul Friedberg & Associates, Landscape Architects in Charge of Design, Travers Associates, Traffic Consultants]

9. The Madeleine, Paris. The object that displaces and occupies space.

8

street activity. The primary consideration in separating autos from pedestrians is pedestrian safety. Consequently, many central business districts and newer shopping centers adopt the pedestrian mall (fig. 7), often with notable success. Yet the success of a purely pedestrian domain of public open space is dependent both upon getting the pedestrians there and establishing the conditions that will keep them there. In primarily residential environments the pedestrian is already "there," in the dwelling, and we must view the relationship of street to goal in reverse, looking out from the dwelling rather than in from the street. Configurations in which the dwelling unit is isolated by extensive and underused spatial elements (path, lobby, elevator, corridor) occurring in the route from street to dwelling increase the incidence of danger and disorientation. A high degree of privateness for the dwelling unit may also enforce remoteness from the world outside. In projects dominated by the automobile, the car represents the link between the dwelling and the wider world. If the car is then taken from the immediate extension of the residence, the possible distancing, fear, and disorientation of the resident is further accentuated. These effects will vary with context, socioethnic group, and other factors; the development of an attitude toward the automobile must consider all the factors of pedestrian/auto interaction, not just traffic separation. Where conflict occurs it should be removed, without necessarily removing the cars.[4] (fig. 8)

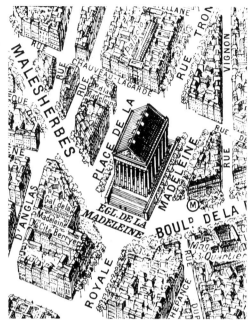

9

Configuration — Local Street: Street Space and Building Volume. The most difficult and elusive variable in terms of physical planning is the configuration of the public environment. In contemporary planning practice, the public street environment is what remains after private planning for individual land parcels along the street takes place.[5] When public open space is considered it is usually with the intention of creating plazas around buildings or removing streets to create superblocks. In this way, even when public open space is conceived as a positive design element, it still serves as the expression of pieces of the private environment.[6] Such widespread subservience of open space to building blocks is a singularly twentieth-century notion deriving from various antistreet attitudes that equate the *rue-corridor* with poor sanitary conditions[7] or assert the desirability of nonfrontal, volumetric, sculptural expression of building mass.[8]

In pre-twentieth-century urbanism the expression of "objectness" was reserved for certain of the community's most important buildings that might merit special expression, a dominance as great as or, perhaps, greater than the urban spaces to which they related (fig. 9). A building such as the church of the Madeleine in Paris could, as an object, occupy space and assume a figural form that easily established the cultural symbol its designers intended. Yet, most urban buildings before the twentieth century hold no such dominance over the urban fabric but must instead compete with the spaces to which they relate.

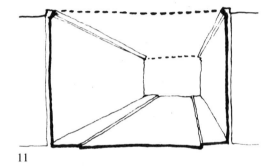

11

10

10. Piazza Navona, Rome. Church of Sant'Agnese: Ambiguity of figure and ground. [MIT, Rotch Library]

11. Diagram of Street Space as Figure. [Schumacher]

12. Strada Nuova, Genoa. Building facades relate to the public space of the street. [Strada Nuova, Genova, Vitali e Ghianda, Genoa, 1967]

13. Sixth Avenue, New York City. Street is "ground" to the buildings. [Photo, Leroy Heck]

14. Madison Avenue, New York City. Building is "ground" to the street space. [Photo, Schumacher]

12

The church of Sant'Agnese in Piazza Navona in Rome (fig. 10) exemplifies the ambiguity of building/space, figure/ground readings. In relation to Piazza Navona, a void that in its plan configuration is obviously a figure, the church acts both as a piece of facade for the piazza and as object-inserted-into-the-facade of the piazza.

The primacy of a figural reading for most public open spaces of communal meaning (including most streets), whether in Miletus or Haussmann's Paris, may be one of the most important factors in the use of public open space (read street). The capability of the user to perceive immediately the street as figure (fig. 11) not only promotes a sense of enclosure and orientation but also delimits the territory of the public realm as including its vertical binding surfaces, the facades of buildings. When a conscious effort is made to relate building facades to the public space thereby defined, the perception of that space as an outdoor room is further intensified (fig. 12).[9]

The territoriality of individuals or social groups is often studied, but not the territoriality of buildings — the idea that a building may possess a territory around or in front of itself. A building's territory has an important effect on the use of public open space. Does the building belong to the street, or does the street belong to the building? In Sixth Avenue, New York City (fig. 13), the new configuration of built form and open space is such that the open spaces appear to belong to the office towers along the street. Indeed, the street space and sidewalk also appear as a ground to the figure of the isolated point blocks. This reading of territory for the building is also enhanced by the fact that ground-level land uses are relatively private and relate to the buildings, but not to the street. While the street is called commercial on the land-use maps, the type of activity housed at ground level (elevator lobbies and banks) does not sponsor street activity. In Madison Avenue (fig. 14), by contrast, the land-use distribution, which places shops at street level, *is* conducive to street-related activity. In addition to this, the consistent facade and relatively constant cornice height allow the street space to be read as figure, and thus the buildings belong to the street.

While in commercial environments such as Madison Avenue or Sixth Avenue it could be argued that ground-level land-use distribution is the primary factor in street use, in mixed commercial and residential environments the relationship of binding surfaces to building volume and enclosed space becomes even more important. In Piazza Farnese (fig. 15) the facade of the Palazzo Farnese provides the completion of a figural void capable of holding incidental activities generated by the goal-directed activities in the other buildings which bind the public open space of the piazza.

But the incidence of private open space directly adjacent to the street may have helped to prevent incidental activities from occurring. A

13

14

15

15. Piazza Farnese, Rome, Palazzo Farnese. Completion of a "figural" void. [Paul Letarouilly, *Les Edifices de Rome Moderne*, Paris, 1841]

16. Typical American Suburban House. [Photo, Schumacher]

17. Diagrams of American Suburban House and Lawn. Lawn read as an illusionistic vertical plane. [Schumacher]

18. Palazzo Vidoni-Cafferelli, Rome. Facade with *piano nobile*. [Photo, Alinari-Anderson, Rome]

16

typical American residential street of single-family detached houses presents such an example (fig. 16). The front lawn may be perceived as a forecourt to the house by virtue of the fact that it is literally a horizontal plane. But a secondary — and for us, more important — reading is also apparent. The front lawn — which is not a contained space and which is made of grass and thereby inhibits walking — may be read as an illusionistic vertical plane. This effect is further enhanced by the common use of foundation planting, which blurs the joint between horizontal and vertical planes. In this sense, the lawn functions in the same manner as the ground floor of the Italian palazzo, which raises the principal level of the dwelling to the *piano nobile* (fig. 17).

This ambiguity has a negative effect on street use. Unlike the facade of the real palazzo (fig. 18) or town house, the lawn, read as an illustionistic vertical plane, does not function to enclose or define street space but only to isolate the street from the house. It is a no-man's-land, a miniature moat and city wall preventing access or use except at intervals.

The opposite effect is achieved in the typical row-house street with stoops (fig. 19). Here the vertical plane functions primarily to enclose street space, but the stoop also functions to subdivide the street space into parallel zones that roughly correspond to activity areas or settings. The ambiguity of reading of the zone between the front of the stoop and the actual vertical plane of the building facade works positively in this case. The connected row-house facades provide the primary spatial reading of enclosure and the exterior slot can easily be associated with the territory belonging to the street first and the building second.

From this discussion, enclosure of street space as an outdoor room or corridor would appear to emerge as a precondition for street activity. Yet one-sided, row-house streets (fig. 20) (that is, those that face parks or other open areas) also attract uses of an incidental nature, often without the provision of goal-directed activities in adjacent buildings. Thus, while some degree of spatial enclosure seems a necessary prerequisite for such activity, the alteration of such a principle to stipulate the necessity of the vertical plane or street facade is essential.

Residential environments of very high density, such as typical American public or private high-rise housing projects (fig. 4), fail to establish either spatial enclosure or a street facade. In such examples the activity present in public open space is minimal despite a generally high density of potential users. In some recent high-rise projects, an attempt to recreate street orientation for housing has led to new environments that react positively with their existing contexts (fig. 21). When a point block is placed into a neighborhood of three-story buildings, it may be impossible to avoid all the conditions of an object or set piece. Nevertheless, some means to bring the new building into a relationship with the existing context is possible (fig. 22).[10]

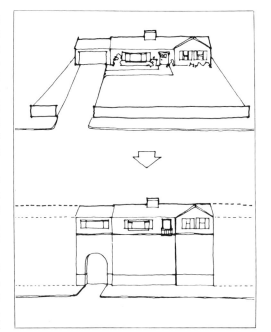

17

18

19

20

21

22

19. Willow Place, Brooklyn Heights. Street space is enclosed and subdivided. [Photo, Stanford Anderson]

20. Mosholu Parkway, Bronx, New York. Vertical plane defines, but does not enclose, the street space. [Photo, Schumacher]

21. Mixed-use development in Erba, Italy. Street-related uses at ground level adhere to rigid street facade pattern, while residential uses above are determined by the necessities of light and internal organization for efficient apartment planning. [Photo, Schumacher]

22. Columbus Avenue at 95th Street, New York City. Street continuity is supported shopping pavilion at grade. The scale of the street is maintained and the impact of a high-rise tower on the street space is minimized. [Photo, Victor Caliandro]

23. Piazza della Libertà, Faenza, Italy. The overlap and ambiguity of the formal structure and the use structure. [Photo, Schumacher]

24. Piazza della Libertà, Faenza, Section. The "zoning" of physical space is altered by the use structure, distinguishing a typology of physical use spatial types. [Diagram, Schumacher]

25. Bethlehem, Pennsylvania. Typical Street. Houses with porches. Private space is extended into public space. [Photo, Schumacher]

23

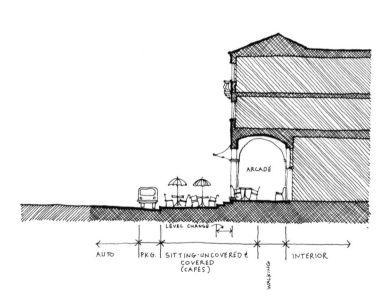

24

25

In the antistreet situation (figs. 4 and 6), while potential users abound, concentration of pedestrians does not occur, and no relationship between the user's dwelling and the public open space of the street exists. The lack of pedestrian concentration is a function of both the sheer size of public open space, street and street-space extension, and of its configuration. While the street space (vehicular and pedestrian channels) is a linear configuration, a narrow channel through which all pedestrians must pass, the rest of the public open space is an undefined entity that has no specific relationship of adjacency to either goal activities or a reference plane. There exists a piece of the local environment, between the recognizable interior environment and the understandable channel of movement, that has neither a specific configuration nor a specifiable social use.

Specific to such concepts of configuration, then, is the primary necessity for linearity in the street environment coupled with extension or subdivision of the street space in relation to that linearity, either parallel zones of space or perpendicular intrusions and extensions of space leading to the buildings that bind the street. Public open spaces that are centroidal in form — squares — may obviously still exist, but they depend on the widespread support of such linear space — streets.[11]

The extension and subdivision of space possesses yet another dimension, where the ambiguity of spatial reading in terms of form *and* land use encourages the development of activity settings. An example of such an ambiguity may be seen in the Piazza della Libertà, Faenza, Italy (fig. 23). The cross section of this square (fig. 24) distinguishes an arcade, a wide sidewalk outside the arcade at three steps below the arcade floor, a curb, and, finally, a roadway. Within the interior space adjacent to the arcade are shops and cafés. The use of this configuration is, however, only partially coincident with its physical structure. The sitting areas of the cafés exist both on the sidewalk outside the arcade and under the arcade proper. The primary circulation space is along the inside face of the arcade, adjacent to the shops. Thus, the single arcade space is divided into two activity spaces or zones, as is the open sidewalk. Such looseness of fit between form and use is one of the most important street-life characteristics eschewed by the Modern Movement, which postulated an attitude of "a place for everything, and nothing out of place."[12]

While this example represents a mixed-use, residential-above-commercial environment, one may see how the relationship of subdivisions of space can also affect purely residential situations. The Faenza example shows how street space is extended into the building. In a typical American street of pre-twentieth-century houses with porches, the opposite occurs: the interior space of the dwelling is extended out into the street (fig. 25). In both instances a zone of shared space, space that is neither totally private nor totally public, exists. This space allows for transition from public to private. (In the brownstone-with-stoop example in figure 19, the zone created by the existence of the stoop belongs primarily to the street; in the American house-with-porch example, the transition space, the porch, clearly belongs to the house). Critical to the usefulness of any of these configurations is the ambiguity of use that attaches to the forms. Such ambiguity must be considered in the very definition of street space, which in the context of this study is considered to be all the space of the public domain, indoors and outdoors, to which the pedestrian has access without ownership or invitation.[13]

The previous positive examples show instances of distinct continuity between the literal space of the street and the buildings along the street. The interlock and overlap of contiguous space, experientially and conceptually, may also be a primary characteristic of the local contexts of residential and mixed residential/commercial streets.

Link and Place Characteristics: Local Context

When you get there, there's no 'there' there. Gertrude Stein, writing about Oakland, California.

The preceding discussion elaborates local criteria for public open space and its use. However, whether a street will function as a "place"[14] cannot be determined solely by its own configuration and land uses, even assuming safety and adequate user density. The relation of the street to its local context is equally significant. While providing potential spaces for activity, streets also serve as "linkages" to and from the various goal functions of the urban environment.[15] They establish a variety of interface conditions with these other urban components. In most cases, the street space functions as the common shared element in the relations among separate goals: street and house, street and school, street and shop, street and work, street and transit system, street and park, and so on.

Streets are also related in a contiguous, pedestrian-oriented, hierarchical relationship: street to street. As such, streets enhance or inhibit contextual continuity. Contextual continuity appears to be critical to widespread pedestrian use and understanding of the public urban environment; the quality of "getting there" is central to the existence and quality of "there." Although the notion of spatial progression or promenade in architecture and urban design is one of modern theory's most belabored abstractions, the idea of "getting there," *not* as a prescribed "promenade architecturale" but as a choice system of understood multiple routes to multiple goals, is apparently essential.[16] Thus, the street system conducive to the existence of a useful, pedestrian context

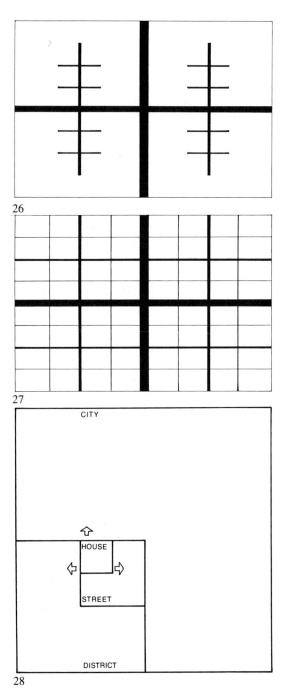

26

27

CITY

HOUSE

STREET

DISTRICT

28

would not be a treelike structure (fig. 26) of hierarchical relationships,[17] but would normatively appear, at the conceptual level, if not literally, as a net or plaid of hierarchical relationships (fig. 27).

Such a hierarchy of street relationships — that is, street to street — should find a corollary in a hierarchy of places based on an awareness of the environment expanding from house to street, to neighborhood, to district, to city. This hierarchy can be represented by a spiral diagram (fig. 28), which permits each of the direct relations of house to street, house to neighborhood, and house to district to be easily cognizable. One assumes all these potential relations should be realized; however, while one can usually place one's residence in the city, an effective sense that one's residence is also a piece of the district, neighborhood, and street is often missed in American cities.

Literal interpretation of such a hierarchy should, of course, be avoided. Flexibility for a normative hierarchy to include a spatial type like a mews (fig. 29) would be an obvious necessity. A configuration such as a mews in this context represents an extension of a normative hierarchy that further breaks down the relationship of the user to the street and city environment by the addition of yet another increment to that sequential hierarchy. Yet, it is the very configuration of the mews, a linear, street-like corridor, that contributes to its usefulness in enriching the choice system. Unlike the undefined foreground of the point block (fig. 6), but like the forecourt of the now virtually defunct medium-rise apartment block (fig. 30), the mews is a recognizable figural space and therefore can be clearly perceived as part of the sequence from house to city.

The perception of the local street environment by any user will naturally fall into a series of identifiable preferred choices. There may be instances where such preferences are, for example, a function of the specific location of a dwelling unit and therefore unique to that user and his influential environment. Within the hierarchy of even the most compact, antiautomobile environment there will naturally occur interruptions in contextual continuity. The users' perception of environmental hierarchy will necessarily be broken somewhere, whether at the level relating house to street or at the level relating district to city. It would appear imperative that those breaks in the hierarchy occur as infrequently as possible at the level relating house to street, and that continuity of perceived hierarchy be exploited to the highest possible degree throughout the residential environment. An attempt to reclaim the continuity is seen in an infill project by Laurence Halprin for the existing Penn Station South housing project (fig. 31). While the avowed intention of Halprin's scheme was to reduce the scale of urban spaces and make the existing physical environment more human, the corollary and necessary effect of relating the dwelling unit to a hierarchy of contiguous spaces has been schematically achieved.[18]

29

30

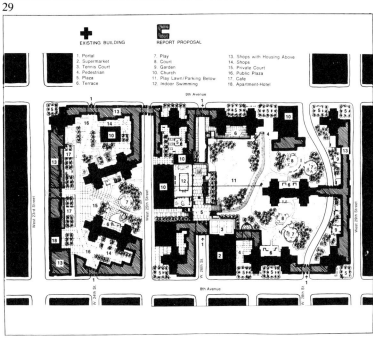

31

26. Treelike street hierarchy. Choice for movement is limited. [Schumacher]

27. Netlike street hierarchy. Choice for movement is expansive. [Schumacher]

28. Conceptual Hierarchy. Perception of the environment as an expanding hierarchy of places, not literally dependent upon, but acknowledging, the street as a component. [Schumacher]

29. Pomander Walk, New York City. Addition of further elaboration to the existing hierarchy of places. [Photo, Schumacher]

30. 2075 Grand Concourse, Bronx, New York. The forecourt is an extension of the street space and clearly defines an activity zone. [Photo, Schumacher]

31. Infill Project for Penn Station South by Laurence Halprin, Landscape Architect. [Halprin, New York, N.Y.]

If the idealization of street space as a normative condition as outlined is extended, similar relationships in the larger context may be appreciated. Viewing the town as a composition of solids *in* voids and voids *in* solids in some degree of equilibrium is essential to such extension.[19] But in American towns, where recognition of an urban core is quickly disappearing, such normative conditions rarely exist. Nor are they recognized as such. If one rejects "streetness" as a necessity of modern life, then there is no good reason to require any degree of spatial enclosure in public open space, much less a hierarchical norm to the local neighborhood environment.

One certainly cannot unreservedly suggest the norms as rigid constants of design or as necessarily improving life styles. However, if planners were to propose making a more economical and effective use of streets for the pedestrian, it would be necessary to intensify many American residential neighborhoods, in terms of residential density, building coverage, and multiplicity of uses. The implied configurational changes could often be incremental, economical relative to the changes in the influence of the environment on its users.[20]

Notes

For a general description of urban configuration relating to physical contexts, see T. Schumacher, "Contextualism: Urban Ideals and Deformations," *Casabella*, no. 359-360 (December 1971-January 1972), pp. 78-86.

1. The necessity for widespread pedestrian use of, and interaction in, the public environment is by no means generally accepted. The notion that modern life does not depend on, or does not exist within, a framework of contiguous space presenting physical proximity and propinquity as the defining elements of the physical or "potential" environment is presented by Melvin M. Webber, "Order in Diversity: Community without Propinquity," in L. Wingo, Jr., ed., *Cities and Space* (Baltimore: Johns Hopkins Press, 1963). See also Charles W. Moore, "Plug it in Ramses, and See if it Lights Up," *Perspecta* 11 (1967), pp. 33-43. Moore claims we do not have contiguous space, nor is it necessary. "Our own places, however, are not bound up with one contiguous space. Our order is not made in one discrete inside neatly separated from a hostile outside . . . Our new places, that is, are given form with electronic, not visual, glue." I disagree.
visual, glue." I disagree.

2. See Robert A. M. Stern, *New Directions in American Architecture* (New York: George Braziller, 1969), pp. 80-91 for a discussion of antiutopian and antiradiant city urban design views.

3. In public housing the bureaucratic need for simplification of administration seems to prevail and, thus, departments of housing tend to exclude uses other than habitation.

4. See the project for two streets in Bedford-Stuyvesant, Brooklyn, by I. M. Pei and Partners and Paul Friedberg Associates; the use of carefully considered physical barriers to rapid traffic permitted the inclusion of the automobile without negative effects. Stern, *New Directions in American Architecture*, p. 106.

5. This has often been the case in the history of planned urban development, but not always; for example, Haussmann's Paris, where the street space was so important that, in some cases, facades were constructed well before the buildings behind them.

6. See Schumacher, "Contextualism."

7. See Le Corbusier, *The Radiant City* (New York: Grossman, 1967), first published in French as *La Ville Radieuse* (Boulogne s. Seine: Editions de l'Architecture d'Aujourd'hui, 1935); and the essay by Vidler in this volume.

8. See Theo Van Doesburg, *Toward a Plastic Architecture* (Paris, 1923), reprinted in Ulrich Conrads, *Programs and Manifestoes of Twentieth Century Architecture* (Cambridge, Mass.: MIT Press, 1970).

9. See G. C. Argan, *The Renaissance City* (New York: George Braziller, 1969), p. 30: the notion of building form as related to open space surfaces on the example of Bernardo Rossellino's Piazza Pio in Pienza, where form is viewed as, ". . . not that of a solid volume whose facades suggest the internal structure, but of a cubic void whose facades are the enclosing walls."

10. Stern, *New Directions in American Architecture*, pp. 80-91.

11. Many medieval and Renaissance squares such as Piazza del Campo in Siena owe part of their existence to the fact that, in scale and configuration, they are centralized with a vertical axis as compared to the linear structures, with horizontal axes, characteristic of their surrounding contexts. See Schumacher, "Contextualism."

12. Such ambiguities have returned to favor in the architectural theory of the late 1960s and the early 1970s, through such influences as those of Team Ten and Robert Venturi, *Complexity and Contradiction in Architecture* (New York: The Museum of Modern Art, 1967); see particularly chapters 3, 4, and 5, pp. 27-45. In urban planning, notions relating form and use as noncorresponding, complementary, and only sometimes overlapping systems have been little studied. One such exploration is the ongoing work of Colin Rowe and Alfred H. Koetter of Cornell University.

13. See Anderson and Caliandro in this volume. Street space is said to extend to the "public/private [use] boundary," which should, in future planning, become the limit of street-planning control. Also in this volume, Eisenman and Schumacher in their essays on the IAUS case study.

14. By "place" characteristics or qualities I mean the ability of a street or other public open space to be understood and used as a setting for activity. A street possesses optimum place quality when the user can identify certain of his activities with a particular space and therefore personalize that space in a manner similar to the way he personalizes his dwelling.

15. By "link" qualities I mean the ability of a street or other public open space to be well understood as a preferred way of getting to a particular goal, or set of goals. These goals may be functions within buildings, open spaces adjacent to the street, or other streets.

16. I do not wish to subscribe to the viewpoints of either Camillo Sitte, *City Planning According to Artistic Principles* (New York: Random House, 1965), or Kevin Lynch, *Image of the City* (Cambridge, Mass.: MIT Press, 1960). On this point, see Kenneth Frampton, "America 1960–1970: Notes on Urban Images and Theory," *Casabella*, no. 359-360 (December 1971-January 1972), p. 24.

17. See Christopher Alexander, "The City Is Not a Tree," *Architectural Forum*, CXXII (April 1965), pp. 58-62, and (May 1965), pp. 58-61.

18. A similar proposal was made by Stanford Anderson, Robert Goodman, and Henry Millon as part of their project for an exhibition at the Museum of Modern Art in New York. See the catalog, *The New City* (New York: Museum of Modern Art, 1967).

19. The conceptual hierarchy is not literally a hierarchy of street types like Le Corbusier's "7-V's," although aspects of a literal street hierarchy may exist in contextual proposals.

20. See Schumacher, "Contextualism."

Street Form and Use:
A Survey of Principal American Street Environments

Victor Caliandro

Introduction

Contemporary urban life may be mirrored in the apparently accidental form of our cities; nevertheless there are certain environmental regularities that would permit a more intentional and consequential role for the urban street. Consequently, this survey[1] identifies typical urban street environments in the United States. By comparative analysis, these regularities of the form and use of streets emerge and aid in the formulation of policies and designs for a publicly responsible urban design.

Contemporary urban consciousness is divided between a longing for an environmental cohesion expressive of community and a sense of the disaggregation of the functions of contact and personal interchange within an environment that is progressively less dense and more private. The street and the activities in and along it promoted its role as a social condenser and as a locus of common interests. Similarly, the best-known streets and the city center came to symbolize the collective interests and values of the surrounding community. Today these public spaces have often been reduced to automobile rights-of-way. Satisfaction of the demands of private transportation and the management of traffic have usurped the principal role of the urban street—that of promoting an open setting for communications and exchange—and transferred this function to building interiors.

The idea of community in the United States finds its origins in certain ethnic, economic, social, religious, and historical values.[2] The functions a street may come to play within a community or neighborhood are often ambiguous and often purposely undefined.[3] An adequate definition of the term street is elusive and uncertain, and the concept of what constitutes a good street is even further removed from easy definition. Indeed, the street bears many negative connotations; in the minds of users and architects alike, the street is, at best, now considered a secondary and residual component of the city. The widespread use of the automobile, telephone, and television have drastically reduced street use; in many newly created contexts, the social and public role of the street has been obliterated.

Scope and Objectives

This survey set out to analyze the typical forms of existing streets, searching for the potential of these streets for human use and interpretation.[4] Specific objectives were (1) to determine the way in which street environments either permit or inhibit a certain range of social interaction; (2) to develop an analytic technique capable of revealing the social space of the street environment; and (3) to postulate alternative strategies for reformulation and restructuring based on the manner in which street environments affect social interaction.

This analysis of street environments depends on a classification of streets by principal land use, building density, and orientation of the buildings fronting the street. A primary reference for the study was the classification of street-oriented and non-street-oriented settings, a question of whether buildings depend directly on the street for accessibility and internal spatial organization.

With particular emphasis upon place-making in relation to pedestrian activities, another aspect of the street environment was analyzed by comparing the physical, legal, and activity boundaries of public space. The patterns of public activity often extend well into buildings, as in the case of stores and churches. The street front of buildings may favor or impede pedestrian interchange and access to activities along the street. The constraints of building form upon publicly accessible activities, analyzed in terms of a transition from public to private space, and the use made of this transition zone are critical descriptions of the street and its potential roles.*

Analysis of Street Types

The internal description of street types is summarized in five analytic categories, each of which is diagrammed. In the description of street phenomena, terms for objects and isolable events are commonplace, but the concepts of space, street, place, and link remain too general. The analytic terms presented here are signs for working definitions that should encourage a more thorough understanding of the street. Many of these terms should be augmented by quantitative descriptions.

I place special emphasis on the terms public-use boundary and activity setting. I identify a transition zone between the public realm and the private. The furthermost publicly accessible part of this zone is marked by a public-use boundary. Within this transition zone I have identified a variety of uses and activities that appeal to groups or individuals. Such activity settings are a partial measure of whether the transition zone is an active element in the use and meaning of the entire street space.[5]

Street Types

The following list summarizes principal American street types, listing specific streets that have been analyzed as models. Not every street is fully presented in the discussion, but the salient characteristics of each are brought out.

*See graphic key and *Notes on Method* on pp. 184–185.

Residential streets
1. Low-medium-rise buildings
   one-family detached, street oriented: Cambria Heights, Queens, New York City
   one-family detached, nonstreet-oriented: Tanglewood, Cheshire, Connecticut
   row house, street oriented: Willow Place, Brooklyn Heights, New York City
   row house, street- and park-oriented: Commonwealth Avenue, Boston, Massachusetts
   row house, garden apartment, non-street-oriented: Laurelton, New York
2. Medium-high-rise buildings
   apartment block, street-oriented: West End Avenue, New York City
   apartment block, street- and park-oriented: The Fenway, Boston, Massachusetts
   tower, non-street-oriented: Robert F. Wagner, Sr., Houses, New York City

Mixed residential and commercial streets
1. Low-medium-rise buildings
   row house and shops, street-oriented: Montague Street, Brooklyn Heights, New York City
2. Medium-high-rise buildings
   apartment block and shops, street-oriented: Broadway, New York City
   apartment block and shops, street- and park-oriented: Grand Concourse, Bronx, New York City

Commercial streets
1. Low-medium-rise buildings
   low-medium rise commercial, street-oriented: Broad Street, Bethlehem, Pennsylvania
   low-rise commercial strip, shopping center, non-street-oriented: Knoxville, Tennessee
   regional shopping center, non-street-oriented: Smith Haven Mall, Smithtown, New York
2. Medium-high-rise buildings
   metropolitan commercial, street-oriented: Fifth Avenue, New York City
3. Interior street environment
   above-grade system: Skyway, St. Paul, Minnesota
   below-grade system: Place Ville Marie, Montreal, Canada
   on-grade system: Midtown Plaza, Rochester, New York

The environments presented conform to major types of development common to cities. Pointing out the often complementary and interde-

pendent nature of different street types, I have tried to construct a series of development alternatives. They are not meant to be comprehensive and rigorously defined, but rather to signal the limitations that common and undue emphasis on building types and land-use planning have placed upon the form and use of streets.

Most urban design today exhibits a concern for a limited perceptual structure of urban forms rather than an analysis of their latent organization. This study investigates certain organizational schemes and conceptual qualities of the environment and initiates an inquiry into the formative process underlying the design of streets.

A number of design approaches are suggested in this discussion. Design typologies, however, must not be understood in a literal manner, which would limit a comprehensive synthesis of the forms and uses pertinent to street environments. As this survey demonstrates, it is seldom profitable to reduce environmental situations — and street design in particular — to a typologically basic form.

Streets in Low- to Medium-Density Settings

The low-rise, single-family, street-oriented residential area is representative of inner suburban developments whose acceptance was established in the early 1900s. It recurs as a quick answer to housing shortages. In turn, it spawned the growth of suburban commercial and professional centers. Although this type of development was originally served by rapid transit, it has adapted successfully to the automobile. The rapid-transit network is often supplanted by extensive highway and freeway networks. The example of this type is Cambria Heights, between 223rd and 225th Streets, in Queens, New York City.

The residential pattern in Cambria Heights is uniform across the landscape (fig. 1). Into it are inserted activity areas centered on specific community facilities (schools, churches, city administration, library), with shopping centers set along major arterial routes. Distances between residences and community facilities are usually long, precluding direct accessibility by most pedestrians. The relatively low density of this type of settlement is inefficient for public transit.

A uniform subdivision into streets and avenues is the primary reference of place and link within the entire settlement pattern. Its function is often limited to defining accessibility to each house.

The replication of similar houses facing undifferentiated streets and avenues relies upon variations in traffic intensity and signaling to create a perceived reference for potential place and link (fig. 2). Public buildings inserted into this pattern hint at localized pedestrian use but rely on associations at the scale of automobile movement. Except for these public buildings, there is no significant hierarchy of public exterior

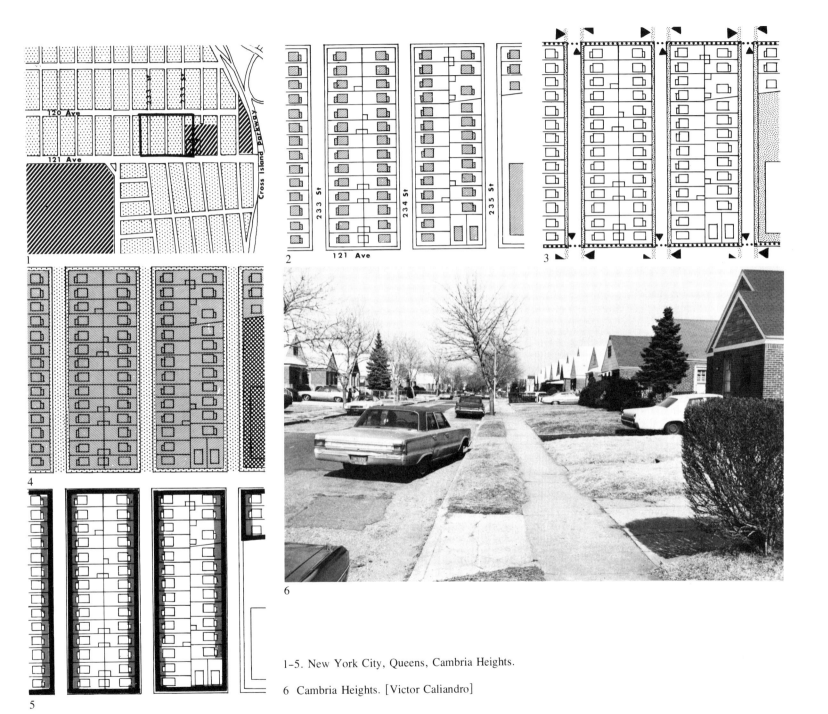

1-5. New York City, Queens, Cambria Heights.

6 Cambria Heights. [Victor Caliandro]

space. Link qualities of the streets are naturally high for cars but low for pedestrians; place qualities are low for both. Private open space is neither private nor open to use communally or publicly. However, the strong symbolic sense of the individual house and the uniform order of the area can diminish the potential for community identity.

Pedestrian circulation in Cambria Heights is limited mainly to children and the elderly and is directed toward the local school and church (fig. 3). Satisfaction of all other needs is primarily dependent on the automobile, requiring that a major portion of the public space be preserved for it (expressways, avenues, streets, driveways), with a consequent reduction of space available for pedestrian activities. Although the density of automobile movement is generally low, there is a potential conflict between automobile users and pedestrians for the use of public space. Curbside parking inhibits a more continuous use of the street frontage. Generally low link qualities and sparse nonresidential activities combine to induce little pedestrian movement along these streets.

Individual, random activities are concentrated around and in the house (fig. 4). Direct, goal activities are removed from the street setting and generally placed in shopping centers. Although few spontaneous activities contribute directly toward the place orientation of the street, those that center on the use and care of automobiles take precedence.

Streets in Cambria Heights, conceived as extensions of the private domain, are rarely used for direct personal contact. Those that are low in traffic are amenable to children's play, since place potential of such streets is relatively high. The public private boundary (figs. 5, 6) is conventionally recognized at the property line but the effect of public visual access reaches to the house fronts. A consequence is that the front yards of the houses are devoted to public show but may also be utilized as children's play spaces. These yards, though, are generally unused — at best a buffer between the street and the house.

Family and neighboring activities are often enclosed within the house or private backyard, leaving little scope for the street space to absorb these in the process of socialization.

The present differentiation between public and private exterior space is ambiguous. Therefore a reconfiguration of the public-use boundary to change the nature of the public/private interface would include the following alternatives: communal or public use of back yards — a green public zone; and communal use of front yards to create a public green space as an extension of the street.

An environment so dominated by the automobile demands a conscious change in land-use patterns to create activities and settings accessible and amenable to pedestrian use. This may be achieved in part by increasing the residential density to levels that will generate additional pedestrian-oriented activities and by creating car-free zones, children's

play parks, and truly local shopping facilities.

The built-form configuration does not lend itself easily to alteration, but several possibilities will be mentioned. The most drastic is conversion to row housing; the least radical is building low walls to redefine the public and private use of exterior space. Building row houses or low-rise slabs at the ends of blocks could effectively enclose the street space, establish a sense of spatial hierarchy, and increase density without major dislocation of current residents. The complete or partial closure of alternate streets would further this aim, as would the grouping of parking into walled garden subdivisions.

Few direct interventions would establish an active pedestrian realm, short of an increase in the residential density. There is, however, a series of possible ameliorations (such as street closings, benches, trees, lights, and play equipment) that seek to control the influence of the car and create more amenable spaces.

The street environment of Cambria Heights represents a significant, ongoing trend. The principal limitations of this street type arise not from the relation of individual buildings to the public space but from the dispersed, low-density development of which it is a part. This type of environment — the result of a desire to achieve the advantages of suburban living but emphasizing still more an escape from the disadvantages of urban living (such as overcrowding and lack of green space) — is representative of a shift in public consciousness away from an ideal of community toward greater individual fulfillment, symbolically represented in the detached house. Although ambivalent, not specifically antiurban in intention, this type of street environment is a step in the shift from an urban, pedestrian-oriented environment to a suburban environment in which the dichotomies between work and home and public and private spaces are exacerbated by an almost total dependence upon the automobile.

Examples of car-dependent environments are well known. The development of extensive suburbs and shopping centers has fostered a highly anticity and antistreet environment — one polarized between isolated, single-family houses and shopping centers surrounded by parking spaces.

The entire residential context of some suburban developments — illustrated here by Tanglewood, in Cheshire, Connecticut (fig. 7) — is composed of isolated houses in a wooded setting, removed from the immediate influence of any commercial development. One- and two-story houses are centered in one-half to two acre lots. Private open spaces, lawns, are conceived as interior-space extensions that do not cross into public space. In such a setting private property is the sole symbol of the environment, with public space understood only as an access route.

The shopping center is a type developed to replace the traditional,

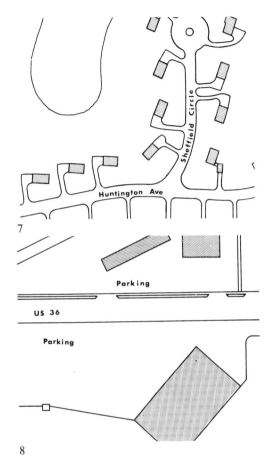

7. Cheshire, Connecticut, Tanglewood.

8. Knoxville, Tennessee, fragment of a strip.

9. Charleston, South Carolina, "Strip." [Stanford Anderson]

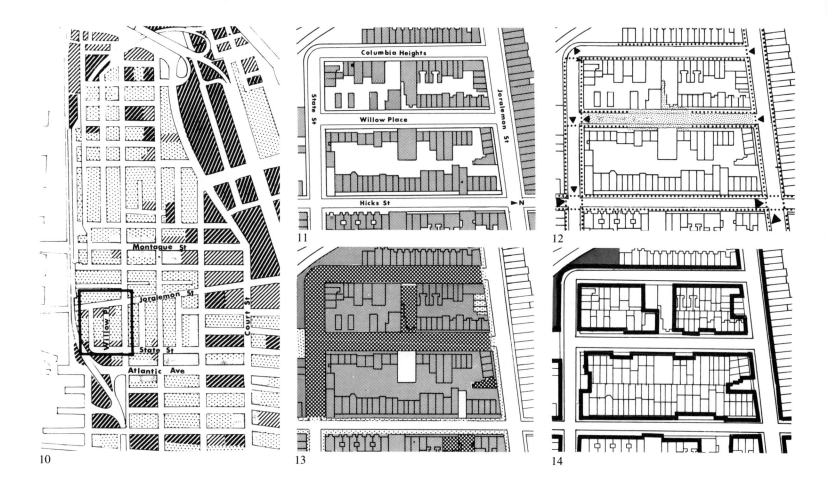

10. New York City, Brooklyn Heights.

11-14. New York City, Brooklyn Heights, Willow Place.

small-town shopping street. It offers a more direct car-to-store contact than the traditional form. The particular example shown here is a linear ''automobile shopping street'' (fig. 8), located in Knoxville, Tennessee, distended over the landscape to accommodate automobile traffic and access. It exists in a context of residential development, on an average of ten to fifteen minutes away by car. It also functions as a route for truck traffic. It combines car-oriented functions (service stations, car sales) with those that previously were pedestrian (supermarkets, drug stores, small shops). Figure 9 illustrates a similar strip near Charleston, South Carolina.

The buildings of such strip development break sharply with the residential surroundings. Buildings are removed from the road edge and set behind a parking lot. In general, zones of activity are defined in layered fashion by the perimeter road, parking lot, service lane, sidewalk, and shop front. Pedestrian activity is concentrated only on the sidewalk and at shop fronts. The potential for continuity of pedestrian access between residential developments and from shopping to residential areas is lacking because of the piecemeal nature of each development and to the extended space of the parking lots, which effectively negate any sense of significant space. Qualities of pedestrian place-making are overlooked in favor of spread-out automobile access.

The traditional row-house street, a medium-density setting little used in recent urban development, does not readily accommodate the automobile. It is still notable, however, for its potential to foster an urban, pedestrian-oriented environment with much face-to-face contact. It often includes desirable garden spaces behind the houses. The example of a street-oriented, row-house development is Willow Place, New York City, near the southern boundary of Brooklyn Heights, within easy walking distance of the shopping facilities of Montague Street, those of Atlantic Avenue, and the extensive retail facilities of downtown Brooklyn (fig. 10). Willow Place is one block long, a factor that distinctly aids its active street life. Nevertheless, there are similar one-block streets nearby that do not have the same degree of community activity. It can be assumed, therefore, that these streets are potential settings for communal life but do not in fact cause it.

Car access to Willow Place is from Joralemon Street, to the north. A parking garage at the south end of Willow Place accommodates some of the residents' cars, and garages built into several row houses provide additional parking. Most parking, however, is on the street. Rapid-transit stations on several major lines are within a few blocks.

Many activity choices are available to the user of this street, including corner stores at the end of the block. The high degree of pedestrianization of the entire context allows random individual and group activities to flourish. For example, a converted church in the center of the block is a community nursery by day and a playhouse by night.

Willow Place is a distinct element within its context. As such, its potential as a place is relatively high (automobile intrusions notwithstanding), in part because of its limited length, its proximity to a wide range of services and activities, and the intimate scale of the buildings.

The primary definition of the space of Willow Place is given by the slightly irregular, but continuous, facade of the houses along it, by the row houses on Joralemon Street to its north, and by the parking garage on State Street to the south (fig. 11). The community center, set back from the street wall, is a major focus of street activities. The hierarchy of the street space in its immediate context is clear. It is part of a descending regional order, from the Brooklyn-Queens Expressway to Atlantic Avenue to Hicks Street, Joralemon Street, and finally Willow Place itself. It is also part of a descending neighborhood order of streets including Court, Montague, Hicks, and Joralemon Streets, and Willow Place.

The uniform order of the street type creates a well-defined space into which individual buildings may be inserted. Continuity with the adjacent building fabric is established through variations on the same street type and building type. There are good scale characteristics to the facades; these include areaways, entries, stoops, enclosures to the areaways, continuous paving materials, planting, and building heights that vary only within a range that maintains easy relation to the street. These elements define a series of subsidiary spaces between the street and the house. Willow Place has strong place characteristics because of its spatial enclosure and the relatively dense use made of the street space.

Pedestrian circulation in Willow Place is relatively uninterrupted by outside traffic (fig. 12). The major portion of pedestrian movement is children coming to and from the day-care center and adults walking between Willow Place and rapid-transit stations, and after school hours it is a play street that attracts children from neighboring streets, although it is never closed to cars; the purely local character of the street, in conjunction with its short length, gives it a self-regulating aspect.

Automobile circulation is low-speed, local traffic only, serving no arterial role. Trucks are banned at all times. Continual curbside parking interferes, however, with children's playing in the street.

Local and context-directed pedestrian use of street space and adjacent stores is high; however, it has low linkage characteristics because it is not part of a preferential route system in Brooklyn Heights.

Willow Place is unusual because the street effectively functions as a communal space. This aspect is reinforced by the activity choices provided by the community center, such as day care, nursery school, a choir group, and theater groups. The activity space (fig. 13) is further extended by corner stores, a local YMCA youth center, and the parking

15. Willow Place. [Stanford Anderson]

16. New York City, Queens, Garden Apartments, Laurelton.

17. Laurelton. [Victor Caliandro]

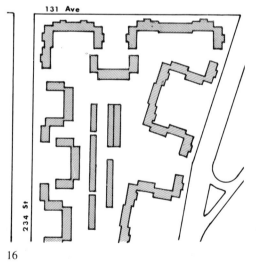

16

15

17

garage to the south. The areaways and stoops that simultaneously act as observation posts and as playground equipment, plus unobstructed areaways, garage entrances, and sidewalk curbs, help define local intimate activity places along the main street space.

Most activities that take place in the street are random ones founded on play and neighboring, but there are also such organized events as regular communal street washings and an annual, engaging street fair. Place characteristics are high because of the congruence between the physical configuration of the street and the activity settings along its length.

The public-use boundaries of Willow Place, external to the building face, are an example of a layer of private space extending to the exterior and serving, in its form and use, as a buffer and transition between house and street (fig. 14). This extension, a legal-spatial distinction, is achieved by the setbacks of the row houses from the property line and is made effective by changes in level at the areaways, by planting, and by the stoops. Entries, areaways, and stoops thus become the settings for the extension of private activities of the residents (gardening, sitting and watching, neighboring) and, when areaways are not fenced in, become small-scale spaces — or pockets — for street activities (fig. 15). The floor-through organization of many apartments helps to establish the house as part of a transition from the private, enclosed yards at the rear to the public space of the street.

The public-use boundaries on Willow Place alternate between the property line and the building fronts and include the community center buildings, thereby creating a street space that is varied and complex in outline. The control of this public-use boundary is subject to the individual user and to the intensity of use of the street, the community center activities, and the stores.

A use structure that has changed from single-family to multiple-family row-house occupancy engenders an ambiguous communal or public focus of the row houses — toward the street and toward the public or semipublic back yards or commons — establishing a new spatial hierarchy that reflects a new life-style. Although it is desirable to convert private yards to semipublic (that is, accessible to all the inhabitants of a house) or public open green space, the existing scale and enclosure of the street must be respected. The rear commons could be made accessible by stair balconies from each apartment, at the ends of the block, or by developing the areaways and ground floors of several row houses into subsidiary pedestrian channels connecting to the rear commons. Such modification of the public-use boundaries can effectively expand the public space and may suggest a future street type, one that interweaves residences, play areas, green commons, stores, and cars into a dominantly pedestrian experience.

The need to provide automobile access to large portions of an urban residential fabric has created a type of non-street-oriented row house in a garden setting that disperses throughout its fabric many of the pedestrian activities commonly associated with the street of the row-house.

In the following example — garden apartments, in Laurelton, Queens, New York (fig. 16) — the apartments are set within a landscape of trees and access roads and form part of a distended network of residences, shopping centers, professional centers, schools, clubs, and churches. Although built at a density greater than Cambria Heights in Queens, this type of development attempts to simulate many qualities of suburbia (fig. 17).

Within such a garden-apartment complex, pedestrian movement is directed onto access pathways and sidewalks, devoid of the usual street-related activites. Provisions for bicycle paths, sitting areas for the elderly and mothers with children, and children's playgrounds, often neglected or omitted entirely, are well within the confines of the development area and limited to it.

The buildings at Laurelton are used to define a series of courts and major boundary lines to the site. The buildings are of uniform order and scale but never aggregate to form dense clusters. The building type is articulated on its surface to provide subsidiary outside spaces, such as may occur in row houses with stoops and areaways. The individual blocks of buildings are dispersed so as to create several minor courts within the framework of a few larger courts, which are evenly placed across the whole site, without an apparent hierarchy.

The open space, although potentially the direct extension of the private dwelling space, remains under common scrutiny and hence under common control. These grounds, however, perform a symbolic function similar to that of the lawn in front of the single-family house. The place potential of such areas could be improved by the inclusion of community facilities such as schools, nurseries, laundromats, and small grocery stores, which would amplify both the public-use area and pedestrian activity. These suggested interventions highlight the ambiguity extant in the provision for public, semipublic, and semiprivate spaces. It is apparent that, without full consideration of the street as a potential reference for organizing public activities, this type of garden-apartment development will remain antiurban in its effect.

Streets and Building Types in Medium-Density Settings

Willow Place is an example of the interdependence between a building type and its physical context. The success of Willow Place as an urban residential place and street is contingent upon a congruence between the physical configuration and the activity choices — reinforced by a strong sense of enclosure, continuity with the adjacent building fabric, limited length, an identity within its immediate context, a clear dependence upon adjacent commercial and institutional facilities, and virtually no through vehicular traffic.

The row house has proven amenable to a variety of transformations and alterations to its intended function. The context role that a street must play is the most significant determinant of the use that will be made of the building type.

The evolution of an urban residential sector, however, may also influence changes in particular streets within its context. The gradual evolution of Back Bay, and the use made of Commonwealth Avenue, in Boston, is an example of the general urban role that a street may continue to perform despite changes in the characteristic use of its building type.

Commonwealth Avenue is the central spine of the 1860s development of the Back Bay area of Boston. It is the westward axial extension of the Boston Common and Public Garden and the principal ceremonial route to downtown Boston (fig. 18). Originally a residential street, Commonwealth Avenue is lined with large row houses that face a boulevard or parkway. The single-family dwellings are often of such generosity that present conditions encourage conversion to apartments or to completely different uses such as college classrooms, dormitories, and offices. There are at present no stores on Commonwealth Avenue. Formerly residents found grocery stores on parallel Newbury Street and on Massachusetts Avenue at the Western periphery of Back Bay. Today these small, dispersed shops have been largely replaced by a single supermarket in the Prudential Center at the southern periphery. Although little provision is made for satisfaction of the residents' immediate needs (such as food, medicine, or hardware), the context of Back Bay is rich in entertainment activities, regional retail facilities, small colleges, offices, and galleries.

The broad park along the center of Commonwealth Avenue is used for sitting and recreation, especially by elderly people and children. It remains, however, a formal and symbolic setting — the grand approach to downtown Boston. The 240-foot width of the avenue creates a distended space with respect to the building height (around 70 to 80 feet), emphasizing the park as the strongest defining element. The buildings contain the space of the park without dominating it.

The space of Commonwealth Avenue is strongly enclosed. The Common forms one end, and the shift in axis at the junction with Massachusetts Avenue creates a visual barrier at the other end. The primary definition of public space is made by the continuous facades of the row houses and by the continuum of the uniformly wide park.

Vehicular circulation on Commonwealth Avenue is a combination of downtown rush-hour traffic, traffic connection across Back Bay to the major arterial routes (Storrow Drive and the Massachusetts Turnpike),

and local traffic of shoppers and residents in Back Bay (fig. 19).

Pedestrian movement is mainly local, directed toward the park, adjacent streets, and rapid transit stops. There is a relatively high intensity of pedestrian flow from cross streets onto Commonwealth Avenue, which is part of a preferential route through Back Bay. Random movements are limited to the park, except for occasional groupings adjacent to churches and schools. Rerouting some of the district vehicular traffic might foster a greater continuity between the sidewalks and the central green space as well as offering the potential for including many more structured activities of benefit directly to students, children, and the elderly — a basis on which to increase further the residential and commercial uses along the avenue.

The character of the avenue changes when it is used for ceremonial parades and demonstrations. This use, if frequent, might conflict with the residential (private) nature of the street; at present, however, it is well accommodated on the avenue. The double roadway allows simultaneous parades and car traffic, and the park becomes a setting for watching, vending, and resting.

The medium building density is relatively uniform throughout the Back Bay. Variations in built form include different building types at the corners (churches, an occasional high rise), varied building setbacks, changes in levels at the setbacks, stoops, window bays, and widened sidewalk sections. Public/private distinctions are obscured because many public-devoted uses (colleges, schools) are contained in previously residential buildings. Only in churches does the public-use boundary encompass the whole building (fig. 20) and this obviously at selected times only.

Activity spaces adjacent to nonresidential buildings are formed mainly by the more traditional extensions of private interior space, as at Willow Place — entries, stairs, stoops, and setbacks — and not by street elements that penetrate the building line — sidewalks, benches, arcades, for example. These elements, if designed directly within and continuous with the street space, would aid in the grouping of people around activity spaces.

The generously proportioned, well-designed, and handsomely detailed row houses of Commonwealth Avenue have proven amenable to a wide range of alterations in use (fig. 21). Increasing economic pressures forced a new building type, the high rise, into Back Bay, threatening the entire fabric. This in turn has been stopped by the creation of a historic district.

At the southern edge of Back Bay, radical change continues. An increase in building density, accompanied no doubt by a shift in major land use from mixed residential/institutional to predominantly office/commercial will draw increasing automobile traffic from the entire metropolitan region. In an area where pedestrians enjoy relative free-

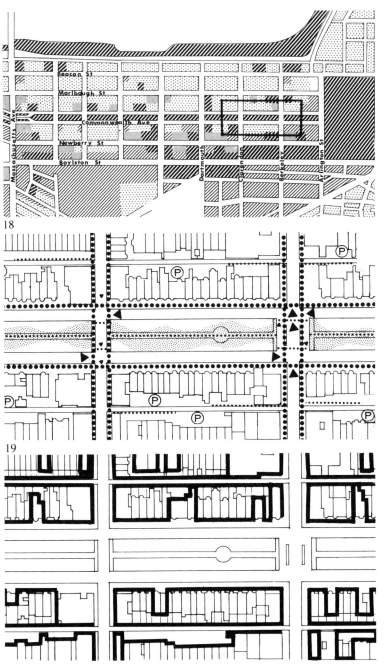

18

19

20

21

18. Boston, Back Bay.

19, 20. Boston, Back Bay, Commonwealth Avenue.

21. Commonwealth Avenue. [Stanford Anderson]

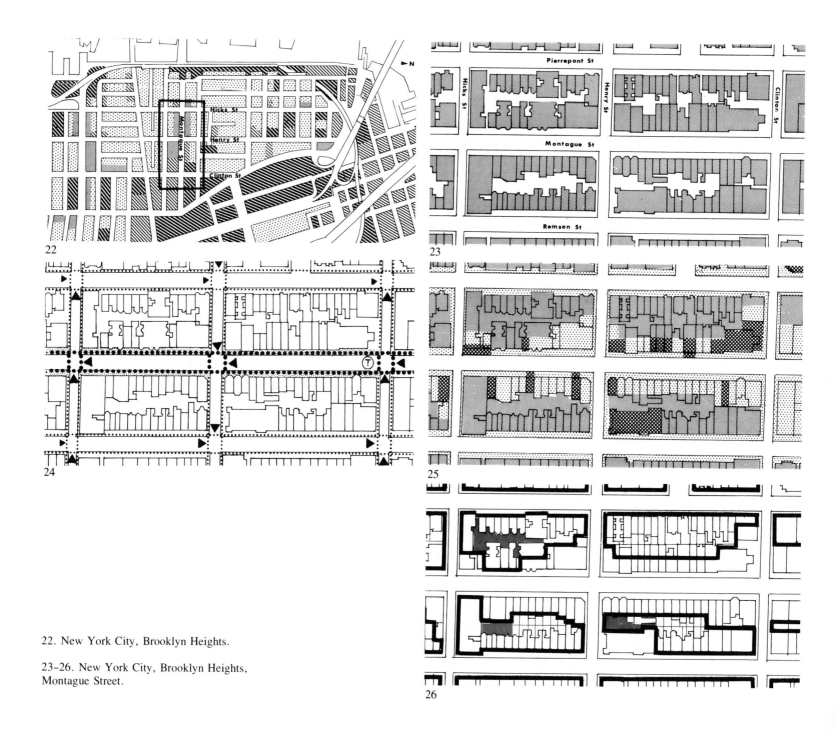

22. New York City, Brooklyn Heights.

23-26. New York City, Brooklyn Heights,
Montague Street.

dom of movement and easy access to shopping and entertainment, a substantial increase in automobile traffic and its attendant services would impair most of the positive street attributes that now exist. Instead, present arterial traffic should be syphoned off and pedestrian use of the center park augmented and reinforced, thereby making more accessible, and susceptible to intensified use, the urban qualities of the grand boulevard. In similar streets of this type, where preservation is not the obvious mode, new building types could be generated by an awareness of the intimate play between public and private activities, centered on full utilization of the street space.

The brownstone, row-house street that has been gradually transformed from a residential street into a street of mixed commercial and residential character, and has thereby assumed an increasingly important community role, highlights the flexibility and limitations of the building type as well as the social role that this type of street comes to play. Montague Street, in Brooklyn Heights, New York City, is one of several east-west streets connecting downtown Brooklyn with Brooklyn Heights. It is terminated at the west by the Promenade, a principal tourist attraction and an intensively used local park that overlooks the East River and downtown Manhattan. To the east it faces the judicial and administrative center of downtown Brooklyn and connects with the central retail and commercial area (fig. 22).

Montague Street serves several population groups, among them an elderly and poor group, artists, young professionals and their families, and long-established wealthy families. It also receives trade from tourists and from people who work and shop in downtown Brooklyn. A high density of activity choices on Montague Street is largely determined by its proximity to transportation facilities, the high population density of the area, the adjacency of retail and service facilities, a high level of residential amenities in the area, and its linkage to the major public attractions of the district. It is also in the center of the Heights.

The area of Brooklyn Heights is served by an elaborate network of subways — within five blocks of Montague Street there are four major lines. Principal access to Montague Street is by foot — a characteristic dependent not only on the high cost of car ownership and limited parking space but also on a relatively high residential density and the small-scale, intimate, and compact commercial and social activities adjacent to this residential area.

A typical segment of Montague Street includes in its row-house configuration two-level commercial facilities with apartments above. Buildings generally range in height from three to five stories, with a few one- and two-story commercial structures (fig. 23). Into this pattern are inserted several residential hotels. Toward the river the row houses have been replaced by large apartment blocks, the inexorable result of escalating land values. Toward downtown Brooklyn, high-rise office buildings introduce a larger scale that unfortunately breaks the pattern of stores and restaurants on two levels.

The decrease in the width of north-south blocks serves to emphasize Montague as the most important east-west collector. It also reduces the linear emphasis of the north-south streets. Increases in building density occur at the junction of the street to the Promenade and to downtown Brooklyn, emphasizing further the role of Montague Street as a principal link within the Brooklyn Heights area and hinting at its future form.

Traffic on Montague Street is a low-speed, one-way mix of service and maintenance vehicles and private automobiles. On-street parking reduces the effective width of the street and forces delivery vehicles to stop on the street, bringing all traffic to a standstill. There is no off-street parking directly on the street and little in the area.

North-south streets are major pedestrian collectors for Montague Street. Pedestrian movement is mixed — partly commuters going toward subway entrances, partly shoppers, browsers, women strolling with baby carriages, and others (fig. 24).

Activity settings (fig. 25) center on retail, service, and restaurant facilities. Goal-directed activities are also housed on the second level of brownstones, thereby allowing many non-goal-directed activities the possibility of direct access from the sidewalk. Goal-oriented, structured activities (supermarkets, cleaners, and such) are frequent, but since these are sufficiently open to the public and often adjacent to small-scale, non-goal-directed activities, users are engaged along the entire street front. In particular, children from the residential hotels play along the sidewalks, and the elderly use the restaurants and sitting places along the street.

Montague Street has a strong sense of place and link. The confluence of pedestrians and low-speed vehicles into a small-scale area, the articulation of activities along the street front, making for an easy continuity of choices, and the enclosure of the street space, enhance the activities clustered along it. The wide sidewalks, variations in setback, bay-window projections, level changes, and similar details create a rich interplay between public and private spaces.

The distribution and character of activities create a pedestrian public domain where space is extended into the buildings (fig. 26). Second-level stores further extend this domain. Entrances to residences frequently occur on the second story, through a lobby that often gives access to offices and shops as well (fig. 27).

In section, the public-use boundary splits to generate two levels of pedestrian movement in relation to commercial frontage. Above this level the public-use boundary coincides with the building face. The rear yards of the row-house type no longer operate as private open space because of the present multiple tenancy. This points to the need, as already discussed in the Willow Place example, to change the public-

27. Montague Street. [Victor Caliandro]

use boundary so as to reinterpret the private yards as a public system complementary to the street space. The buildings could be further modified to provide a service alley with off-street parking for residents and shoppers.

The future of urban collectors such as Montague Street depends on their ability to serve as commercial centers and as the foci for an active and mixed social life. Such multiple roles hinge upon a balance between activities of a mixed commercial, institutional, and recreational nature and an easy, almost spontaneous, access to them.

The limitations of the row-house building type are apparent in the context of Montague Street. The disadvantages of the private rear yard with respect to multiple tenancy, and in this case mixed use as well, have been discussed, but here building size and height limitations of the row-house type become crucial determining factors in its survival as an economically viable element. Several sections of Montague Street (and Commonwealth Avenue) have been replaced by high-rise structures — to the east by office and bank buildings and to the west by apartment blocks. These interventions militate against the streetscape by denying access and visual contact between residence and street or by zoning significant portions of the area as single-function spaces. By removing direct contact and control of the street space from large numbers of potential users and by segregating land-use types according to major functional characteristics (residences versus offices) the main role of the street as an urban collector is severely restricted and in fact often deliberately denied.

Although the derivation of an alternative building type has been proposed in conjunction with traffic controls, the examples of Montague Street and Willow Place make evident the need to reexamine our current concepts of residential development and building density in light of the limits in size and extent of services necessary, such as are characteristic of Brooklyn Heights, which can help create and maintain an urban street environment. The ability of the row house to define street spaces appears to offer many possibilities such as multiple variations in set-backs, widenings to create small plazas, changes in direction of the building fabric to accommodate differing street frontages, height and width changes, and the direct juxtaposition of dwelling and private yard. These are often overlooked today in favor of more economical building forms, as well as a need to reconfigure the environment around the demands of automobile use.

Originating as a typical street form in the eighteenth-century urban expansion, the row-house street usually was designed to accommodate only carriages and pedestrians, and the small scale of the houses was intended for single families.

The row house and its street section once afforded adequate street access and backyard open space. Subsequent multiple occupancy and crowding of the street with automobiles have thoroughly disrupted the access and open-space balance of the original section. Interventions that would alter this imbalance appear to be a restructuring of the use of the open spaces directly in front of and behind the building. These could create garages, service access, open green space, sitting and play areas, stores, or meeting halls.

Transformations in the public-use boundary present a key to the redevelopment of the row-house street type, contingent upon adequate control over the use of the automobile. But by far the most important to this redevelopment are the limitations over indiscriminate growth and control over segregated land-use parceling.

Streets in High-Rise Mixed Residential and Commercial Settings

The mixed residential and commercial high-rise building type is still being developed in dense urban centers despite recent tendencies to further separate commercial and residential uses. Although much recent commercial development has favored a move to shopping centers — in part to accommodate a largely car-oriented clientele — attempts to replicate the high-rise residential and commercial land-use mix as along Second and Third Avenues on the Upper East Side of Manhattan have been successful both economically and in terms of easy pedestrian access to goal-directed activities.

The specific examples chosen to represent the prevailing activity setting and building types are Broadway, between 86th and 91st Streets, and West End Avenue, between 93rd and 95th Streets, in New York City.

This section of Broadway is in a mixed land-use setting (fig. 28). The general context is a park along the Hudson River and a middle-class residential neighborhood on one side and institutional and lower-class residential users on the other. This disposition of special uses and residences in close proximity engenders an intense pedestrian flow. Furthermore, Broadway carries principal bus and subway lines connecting to midtown and downtown Manhattan.

Cross streets and north-south avenues to the west of Broadway are predominantly residential, with occasional commercial and institutional facilities. Broadway and north-south avenues to the east provide many residential buildings with ground-floor commercial space. Principal access is pedestrian; automobile access is possible but discouraged by insufficient parking facilities. Double and triple parking is common on cross streets.

Buildings rise from the property line in a continuous facade that varies in height from two stories (shops only) to sixteen stories (apartments with shops on the first floor). The commercial groupings at ground level are continuous, with apartment-house entrances generally on side streets. A tree-lined divider strip separates the two directions of traffic flow (fig. 29). The street space, contained by the continuous facades, tends to function as two separate, one-sided streets. The traffic lanes are not unusually wide, but the fenced-in center strip prevents pedestrian crossing except at breaks for cross streets. Wide sidewalks (16 to 20 feet in some cases) emphasize the presence of pedestrians and help reduce the impact of the automobile on pedestrian activities.

Throughout its length Broadway is perceived as a unique element in the spatial hierarchy of Manhattan streets, as a pedestrian collector and principal traffic artery, tying together a range of social and commercial services along its spine. Functions placed repetitively at intervals mark the unfolding of different community groups and activities of regional importance.

Automobile traffic is a combination of low- and high-speed flow, complicated by congestion at peak hours. Broadway appeals to local and through district traffic, whereas most of the cross streets serve slow residential traffic (fig. 30).

A high density of pedestrian activity, related to shopping and local residential areas, is reinforced by a range of random activities arrayed along Broadway and on the side streets. Pedestrian trips usually extend as much as ten to twenty blocks, beyond which buses and subways are used. Concentrations of activities at street corners, in conjunction with transit stops, help reinforce the pedestrian qualities of this area.

The mix of commercial and institutional facilities with a variety of residential settings — apartment blocks along Broadway and the avenues, with row houses on the cross streets — promotes a complex setting of structured and random activity settings (fig. 31). Goal-directed activities are confined mainly to interior spaces, with the exception of several specialty food and clothing stores that set up displays along their street fronts.

Children's play is generally confined to side streets, certain of which are closed by police lines during the day. Random activities — generated by individual encounter or by lack of suitable building spaces to house them — occur along the street. Benches at the ends of the center islands of Broadway are used as adult sitting areas. This setting, while isolated, is used intensively and obviously satisfies a need. Transferring these sitting areas to the sidewalk could reinforce its random qualities and foster the development of cafés and pleasant places to sit along its length.

At ground level, access to commercial spaces extends the usable public space (fig. 32). On the second level, restaurants further extend the potential public space of Broadway, although in general the distinctions between public and semipublic or semiprivate activities are not clearly set out. The distinctions are commonly made by simple door-

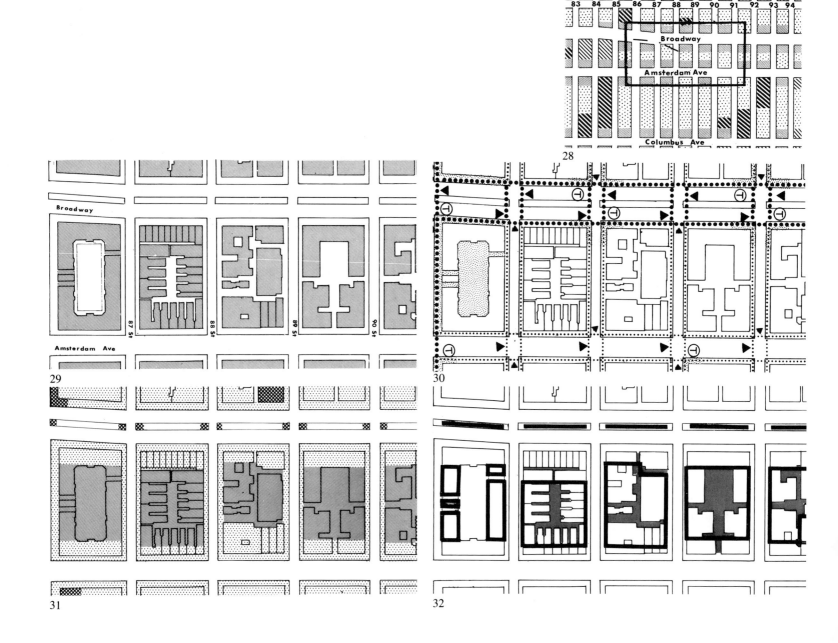

28

29   Broadway

Amsterdam Ave

30

31

32

ways and signs placed along the street front (fig. 33).

The public-use boundary and land use on side streets need to be changed to accommodate children's play areas. The permanent provision of play areas could be implemented by closing alternate side streets. The possible widening of sidewalk areas at street junctions — as at the 94th Street Urban Renewal Area — would help create public activity areas and control car access as well. A radical rerouting of district traffic in conjunction with the intermittent closing of one traffic lane along Broadway would increase the potential for residence-related as well as commercial and entertainment activities set within the entire space of the street. These types of interventions are aimed at balancing the needs of the pedestrian environment with the demands of automobile access and high-density residential development.

Much residential construction, dating mainly from the late 1920s and early 1930s but continued into the 1960s, followed the pattern of large apartment blocks that often occupied an entire city block. West End Avenue, parallel to Broadway, was developed as a high-rise replacement for a row-house street, providing large apartments with convenience to shopping and rapid transit. Along the segment of West End Avenue between 93rd and 95th Streets, public and private distinctions are clearly defined by building fronts without shops or provision for other public uses (fig. 34). The street space is primarily an access route. Most pedestrian activity is eventually drawn onto side streets and onto Broadway. Consequently neither public space nor private space is extended to interact with the other. Instead of a transition zone between interior and exterior public uses, between street and residence, there is a wall punctuated only by portals and canopies. This type of public-use boundary, coinciding with the building face, is reflected in the activity setting (fig. 35), which shows a juxtaposition of individual random activity spaces (the sidewalk and occasional setbacks, in this case) and the private space of the buildings. Interestingly, most ground-floor windows are blocked off or barred from direct visual contact with the street, an index of the limitation of West End Avenue to an access role (fig. 36).

Little should be done to modify the intense urban residential quality of this environment. The only significant change in land use on West End Avenue would be provision of open green spaces along the street for children's play areas and for transition spaces between the street and the apartment houses. Although this solution may appear to approach an ideal, that is, of buildings set in a park, the inclusion of park-oriented buildings can create an urban boulevard capable of sustaining a high degree of pedestrian contact in a pleasant setting.

Commonwealth Avenue and Fenway Park in Boston (fig. 37) show an activity setting that directly extends private residential activities into a collective open space. In Fenway Park (part of an original parkway

33

28. New York City, Upper West Side.

29–32. New York City, Upper West Side, Broadway.

33. Broadway at 87th Street. [Victor Caliandro]

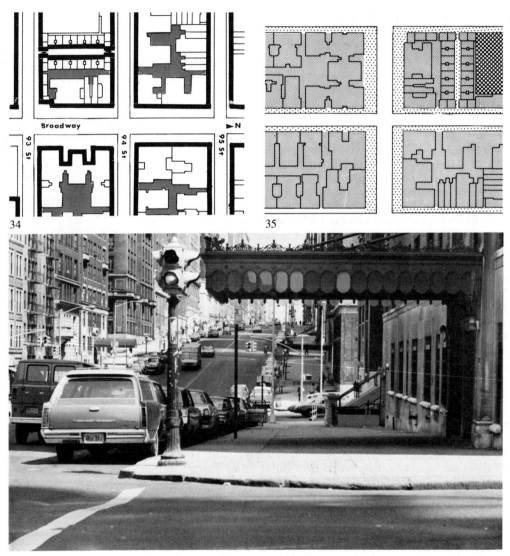

34

35

36

34, 35. New York City, Upper West Side, West End
Avenue and Pomander Walk.

36. West End Avenue. [Victor Caliandro]

system proposed and developed by Frederick Law Olmsted to create a green belt through the Boston area), activities are clustered around several major cultural institutions located in and along the park (fig. 38). This reinforces a sense of place and arrival within the park and marks major linkages through the city. Local, group-oriented activities (gardening, school lessons, softball, play groups) are also clustered around important pedestrian paths in the park. Yet the major pedestrian attractions are found on adjacent streets away from the park, thereby diminishing the potential impact that the park setting could exert in creating a car-free pedestrian realm. At present the Fenway, as part of a major arterial route to downtown Boston, creates a barrier between the residential sidewalk and the park.

A compelling intervention for the Fenway would be to restore primacy to pedestrian movement. The high degree of automobile conflict could be eliminated by rerouting much of the arterial traffic that passes through the park. The insertion of local commercial service and recreational activities along the park edge would stimulate pedestrian use and increase the linkage between the Fenway and the adjacent urban fabric.

The need to establish and maintain a high level of open pedestrian contact, through adequate provision of services and amenities, has been characteristic of many urban streets and the buildings fronting them. Whether through conscious planning and design intervention or through gradual accretion over time, activities and functions that take place in and along the street have come not only to satisfy necessary community services but also to act as social gathering mechanisms. The acceptance of street-related social functions and the dependence on them have traditionally been distinguishing characteristics of an urban culture.

Many of the preceding examples have illustrated, however superficially, the impact that the motor vehicle has had upon these traditional urban forms. But whereas total elimination of motor vehicles from urban centers is not feasible, selective control over the indiscriminate use of the car would aid in restoring the balance with pedestrian access and street-oriented life. To this end many solutions have been advanced, ranging from the creation of superblocks into which car access is strictly controlled to the proposals for new building types, such as Montreal's Habitat with its many pedestrian promenades in the air. Other solutions have envisioned totally controlled cityscapes within which advanced mass-transit systems supply all the needs for individual mobility. Most of these proposals have been allied to the need for large-scale urban housing. One must point out, however, that most large-scale, high-density housing developments have been consciously and deliberately antistreet. The purposeful negation of street-realted social and architectonic values has been fundamental to their planning and design. The example that follows documents some of these antistreet qualities.

The isolated, high-rise residential superblock is a building type allied

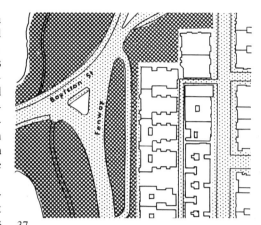
37

38

37. Boston, The Fenway.

38. The Fenway. [Stanford Anderson]

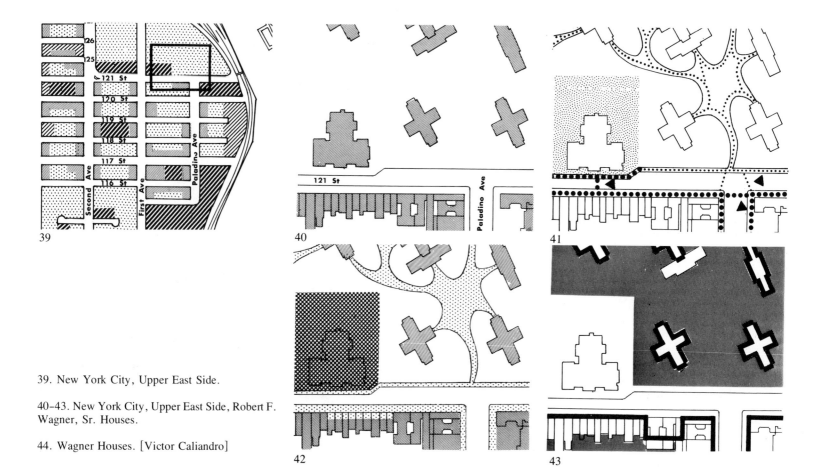

39. New York City, Upper East Side.

40-43. New York City, Upper East Side, Robert F. Wagner, Sr. Houses.

44. Wagner Houses. [Victor Caliandro]

39

40

41

42

43

to city-in-the-park planning ideas of the early twentieth century. Vast open spaces are the basic setting for large-scale, high-density urban housing. The example shown here, the Robert F. Wagner, Sr., Houses, in New York City, is typical of massive interventions that have disrupted local street patterns by creating superblocks of isolated tower and slab apartments.

The housing complex is an insertion into a mixed-use, street-oriented environment comprised of row houses and five- to seven-story apartment buildings. The surrounding area provides shopping, schools, and adult recreation facilities (fig. 39). The preexisting street system is, however, discontinuous with the tower apartments.

Where such insertions into the context of an existing grid occur, there are two main approaches to intervention. One is to extend this type of building-in-the-park until it becomes a new context in itself, at which point a new type of infill is possible — an infill that marks pedestrian circulation nodes and groups commercial and social functions. The second approach is to add infill between the towers and the street in an attempt to patch the division between the old context and the insertion.

The site displays a regular placement of cruciform towers of seven to fourteen stories, with green space between. Within the complex, meandering pathways connect the buildings to each other, to marked play areas (often fenced in), and to the perimeter streets (fig. 40).

Both site coverage and enclosure qualities are low in this classic antistreet pattern. This particular configuration is often wasteful of urban land and creates areas that are little used because they lack many of the psychologically reassuring qualities of place and link.

The built form is hardly amenable to significant modification. The public realm can be strengthened, however, by organization and articulation of the public open space so that movement, play, and recreation are much more differentiated and a landscaped transition from public to private is created.

Automobile traffic, low-speed and predominantly local, is segregated from the building context. Parking access is permitted, however. Pedestrian circulation is dispersed and thinly distributed throughout the open spaces. Local, goal-directed movement occurs at building entrances and at playgrounds, with little dependence upon the sidewalk along the street. Link qualities are perforce low, due to lack of clear goals or an articulated physical structure (fig. 41).

Group activities are programmatically limited to the adjacent "institutionalized" playgrounds (part of a public school), and individual interaction for adults is restricted to desultory movement along the interior paths (fig. 42). The site system attempts to provide a picturesque landscape of towers and parklands in the city, but it is not as well structured for activities as is the nearby street grid.

The public-use boundaries coincide with the built form (fig. 43) —

44

there are no transition spaces as such between exterior and interior, between public and private spaces. The exterior space belongs to everyone, but under such physical conditions that it is significant to no one (fig. 44).

Little can be done to relate these buildings to the street pattern of their context without a significant alteration of the public-use boundaries. These could be modified to include a controlled transition between public and private activities in conjunction with the insertion of pedestrian-oriented activities along preferred paths. An extension of the density and scale of the preexisting context by infill row housing, or, alternatively, by connecting the isolated towers into new slabs, would create a new American street-building type. Without a conscious effort to maintain and reinforce a pedestrian and architectural continuity with existing city structures, these towers-in-a-park are destined to remain antiurban.

Streets and Small City Centers

Antistreet attitudes conflicting with the revitalization of city centers find their most ardent and prolific spokesmen in motor vehicle users, however unaware they may be of this attitude. Insofar as urban residents are becoming more mobile through the use of the automobile, it is necessary that the structure of the city change to accommodate this random-route, personalized transport system. The choices for urban redevelopment, as currently conceived, are clearly set out in master plans that abound with large parking structures surrounding an exclusively commercial and financial core now known as the central business district (CBD).

The examples in this section and the next illustrate several renewal and development options typical for American cities. They range from a small-city shopping street (Broad Street, Bethlehem, Pennsylvania) to a metropolitan commercial center (Fifth Avenue, New York City), and include a series of prototypical suburban and center-city commercial developments designed to increase pedestrian access to shops and offices. These examples all represent a phenomenon of large numbers — planning for massive commercial ventures with parking for thousands of automobiles and relatively heavy pedestrian concentrations — and are discussed in order to suggest possible approaches toward a renewal of the city fabric.

Many of the intimate pedestrian qualities that characterized previous examples have little place in contemporary commercial centers. In efforts to accommodate large numbers of cars and shoppers and to concentrate as many high-revenue-producing services as possible, commercial centers have grown in scale until they resemble entire city centers. They have not, however, maintained the advantages of residential and recreational facilities adjacent to or integral with the traditional city center. Thus several important sources of urban pedestrian life have been deliberately omitted, reducing the vitality and psychological importance of these commercial centers and furthering a disaggregation of the urban fabric.

Broad Street, in Bethlehem, Pennsylvania (1970 population — 72,000), is an example of the traditional main street of small cities and towns that are gradually being revitalized. The containment of commercial facilities along a few blocks in the center of a long-established residential area has made this type amenable to pedestrian use. In the past, its linear configuration proved suitable for car-oriented shoppers. This type began to deteriorate, however, because of inadequate parking. Recently developed off-street parking has restored a certain measure of accessibility by car to Broad Street.

Broad Street is near the center of Bethlehem and is one of the principal east-west arterial connectors in the city (fig. 45). It is at the junction of a working- and middle-class neighborhood to the north and an upper-middle-class area to the south. Among its large residences, this southern area contains a civic center, a school campus, part of a college, a museum, various civic institutions, and clubs and fraternities. Broad Street and the intersecting Main Street, the principal retail streets for Bethlehem, are part of a long-established regional arterial network. Directly adjacent to this area is a recently completed expressway. The only public transit route has its terminus here; most shoppers, however, come by car (figs. 46, 47).

The major portion of the activities along Broad Street is contained in one long block. Alleys that run parallel to it allow access to parking areas and service to the stores. Although these commercial facilities are adjacent to residential areas, there is, in contrast to such diverse uses as those of Montague Street in Brooklyn or Broadway in New York City, little overspill of residentially oriented activities into Broad Street. A still stronger integration of intense residential and commercial use is seen in the Grand Concourse, Bronx, New York, a street that acts as a "Main Street" in a dense fabric of residential streets. Heavy district automobile traffic and mass-transit connections reinforce the use of the street for shopping and entertainment (fig. 48). The divider strips along the Concourse separate and recombine streams of fast and slow traffic at useful intervals — a potential advantage for other commercial streets such as Broad Street (fig. 49). The divider strips can supplement the pedestrian system and offer the opportunity of varying the width of the sidewalk, thereby enhancing the public-place use along store fronts. Divider strips may, however, discourage crossing from one side of the street to the other.

While there is a strong enclosure along Broad Street, achieved by a

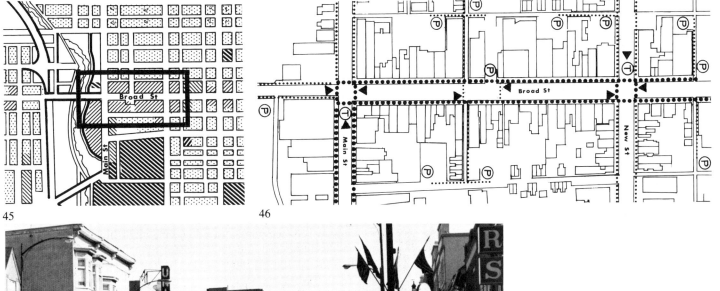

45. Bethlehem, Pennsylvania.

46. Bethlehem, Pennsylvania, Broad Street.

47. Broad Street. [Victor Caliandro]

48

49

relatively continuous street front, the public-use boundary extends from the sidewalk well into the shopping frontage (fig. 50). The parking lots and garages along the alleys behind Broad Street, together with those along the street itself, tend to isolate the street from its adjacent areas. Such parking barriers are often the real boundaries from which a ghetto development will begin.

Economic development of the Lehigh Valley region has created several shopping centers easily accessible by car from downtown Bethlehem. Although the vitality of this traditional type of urban center is threatened by direct competition, the redevelopment of a downtown commercial core can be undertaken to preserve and intensify local pedestrian movement. The Midtown Plaza in Rochester, New York, is an example of such redevelopment. Functioning as a commercial mall at ground level and as hotel and office space at higher levels, Midtown Plaza is an attempt to make a continuous, dense urban fabric (fig. 51) viable both for pedestrian users and automobile access. Pedestrian circulation within the mall space is uninterrupted by traffic, which is separated on grade and confined to parking structures at the edges of the complex. The downtown context into which this mall is inserted already has hotel facilities and some infill housing, which jointly serve to generate and maintain considerable local pedestrian movement.

Automobile drop-offs and the traffic system are only loosely related to the mall and its parking facilities, and there is no architectural relationship between public transit and the mall. In general, pedestrian and architectural ties to the total urban pattern need to be augmented in number and reinforced. Interventions such as this enclosed mall should either be treated as set pieces — and therefore endowed with an outstanding sense of architectonic place — or else become part of the general structure of the urban fabric, with arcades and malls extending throughout, as in the center of Bologna, Italy.

The Midtown Plaza is conceived as a supplementary system to the existing street-oriented fabric. Little use is made of the exterior public spaces, a condition that separates the mall both functionally and psychologically from its context and consequently reduces the impact that dense concentrations of activities can have upon maintaining an open and continuous street life. The traditional uses of the street/ building interface are resolved within the interior pedestrian network.

The development possibilities available to small cities and towns also include the total subjugation of the urban center to the regional shopping mall. Increasingly the car-oriented shopper is confronted with the ease of access and the convenience that the regional shopping center affords as well as by a high degree of user choice, emphasized by the compaction of public space within the mall.

The regional shopping center is a type that emerged during the 1950s and 1960s. It represents an attempt to bring CBD shopping facilities to

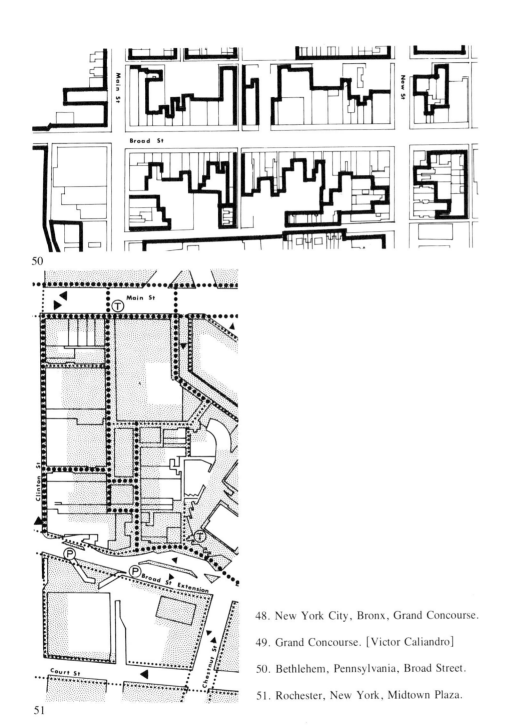

50

51

48. New York City, Bronx, Grand Concourse.

49. Grand Concourse. [Victor Caliandro]

50. Bethlehem, Pennsylvania, Broad Street.

51. Rochester, New York, Midtown Plaza.

suburban residents while still maintaining the capability of direct car access. Such a type tends to obviate the need to make special trips to downtown in order to shop with at least some range of choice and competition. The mall superimposes on an urban grid a supplementary pattern of traffic-free interior streets, cradled within a controlled or semicontrolled environment. Smith Haven Mall, in Smithtown, Long Island, is such an example.

Smith Haven Mall, an air-conditioned and totally enclosed marketing complex, is permeated by a cruciform shopping mall and an island within its surrounding parking lot. It is marooned in a loosely developed urban landscape, and there is no street context to which it would, through any intervention, establish a physical continuity.

The mall is located between a major suburban boulevard and a limited-access highway. It is surrounded at some distance by pockets of random, low-rise commercial facilities and by tracts of single-family houses (fig. 52). The mall provides general shopping facilities, in the form of small stores, a supermarket, and three chain department stores plus a movie theatre. The building complex forms a relatively low, irregular, rectilinear mass. This antistreet form has little or no relation to either access roads or adjacent development (fig. 53). There is little internal or external spatial hierarchy. The internal spatial enclosure is in marked contrast to the last of a positive definition of exterior space. Link qualities do not exist because of the isolation of the complex from its immediate environment. The cruciform shape of the mall unfortunately serves as a distributor to the parking lot and has none of the intense architectural, social, and symbolic significance commonly associated with such a form.

Pedestrian movement outside the mall space is between the entrance and parked cars; there is little possibility for random pedestrian encounters. In contrast, the mall space itself is subject to much random pedestrian movement. Individual activities take place in both the mall space and the shops, which are open along their entire frontage to the mall. The insertion of fixed benches and planters along the center of the pedestrian way, although providing a level of amenity not readily found on city streets, significantly constricts the free flow of people.

The mall space offers a high level of pedestrian amenities and an attractive setting that is often utilized when the stores are closed, but there seems to be an unresolved disjunction between the interior, sheltered environment and the unprotected access to cars outside, which are often quite distant.

Internally, the public-use boundary is extended from the mall space into the commercial space (fig. 54). Externally, the public-use boundary coincides with the building face; the perimeter sidewalk of the building is simply a strip that separates the parking area from a totally impermeable wall (fig. 55).

Because of the isolation of the shopping center within the urban fabric, the manipulation of the public-use boundary seems to offer little potential for achieving a significant change in the use of the space. The introduction of parking garages instead of parking lots would, however, be an initial step toward the transformation of the type. The provision of residential units and even office space in or near the site would be a further step toward a transformation into a new service/industry complex of truly urban character.

Streets and Metropolitan Centers

The development and preservation of metropolitan business and commercial centers in a manner compatible with intense pedestrian street use, and hence access to and mobility within this dense core, may well depend on limiting the horizontal expansion of these centers. The insertion of supplementary above-grade and below-grade pedestrian systems into the city grid can favor an intensive growth in the public use of the entire building section.

But whereas these supplementary pedestrian street forms require comprehensive planning and massive financial interventions, the metropolitan high-rise commercial development — associated with the skyscraper office tower — is still being replicated and intensified in large urban centers. When constructed as street-oriented buildings, such developments can aggregate office space and shopping facilities at high densities, attracting high concentrations of pedestrians. Within this metropolitan setting streets become symbols of the entire urban lifestyle — for example, Fifth Avenue in midtown Manhattan.

This section of Fifth Avenue is a commercial street of offices and shops, centrally located in a high-density, high-land-coverage context (fig. 56). Within this context there are certain variations in specific configurations and special land uses (for example, Park Avenue is partly residential and contains a few shops). Along Fifth Avenue there is a general and even distribution of goal-directed activities. No residential use occurs along this section of the avenue. Principal access to activity choices is by foot. The high pedestrian concentration congests the sidewalks at rush hours and at lunch time.

The buildings along Fifth Avenue rise seven to twenty-five stories, often from the site edge or with a marginal setback. Although some of the ground-level shop fronts are arcaded, most rely simply on setting back their entrances, increasing the effective shop-window surface. Thus the street space is locally extended into the buildings at intervals.

The spatial hierarchy of Fifth Avenue in its context is clear. This is due in part to the strong differentiation between north-south avenues and east-west streets. The crosstown streets, narrower than Fifth Avenue,

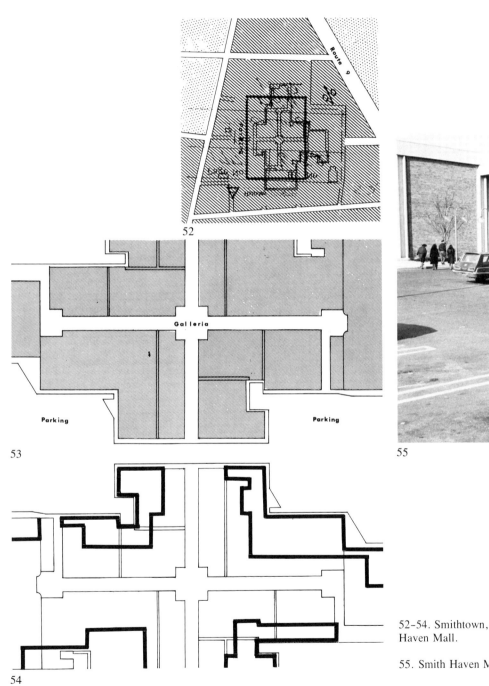

52–54. Smithtown, Long Island, New York, Smith Haven Mall.

55. Smith Haven Mall. [Victor Caliandro]

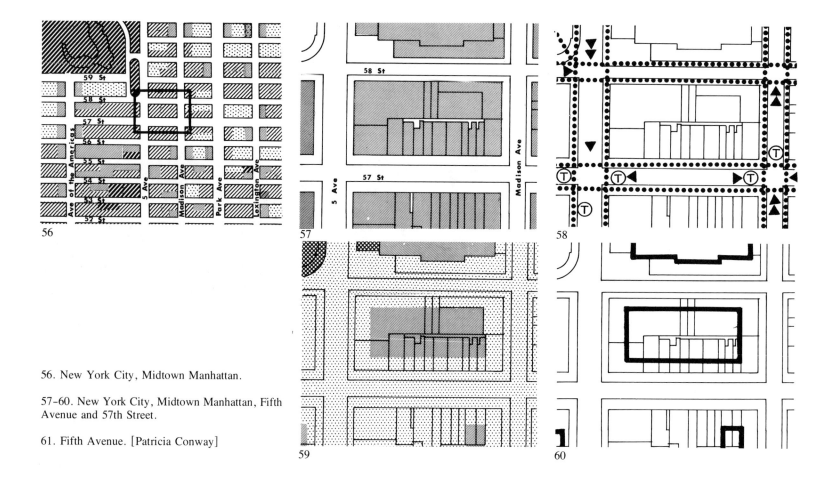

56

57

58

59

60

56. New York City, Midtown Manhattan.

57-60. New York City, Midtown Manhattan, Fifth Avenue and 57th Street.

61. Fifth Avenue. [Patricia Conway]

are lined with smaller, less important buildings fronting narrower sidewalks (fig. 57).

The enclosure qualities of Fifth Avenue are indeed strong, due partly to the relatively uniform facades of the buildings and partly to their height in relation to the width of the street space. Because of this emphatic corridor definition — a corridor that gives access to buildings along its length — and its prestige, Fifth Avenue is perceived as an important link in the fabric of Manhattan.

The qualities of place are perhaps secondary to the corridor definition, yet wide sidewalks contribute a partially realized potential for pedestrian amenities along Fifth Avenue. Unfortunately, the prestige of the Avenue has attracted numerous activities such as banks and airline offices, which do not significantly contribute to a rich and diversified pedestrian activity space. Fifth Avenue, once a promenade shopping street par excellence, is threatened; and the city encourages a guided restructuring by means of special zoning.

Local and district motor-vehicle traffic is intense. A mixture of high-density public transport with private vehicles and taxis tends to clog the junctions between the Avenue and its cross streets (fig. 58). High concentrations of pedestrians during business hours and on weekends reinforce the image of Fifth Avenue as an important link as well as a shopping street serving the metropolitan region. Yet a gross conflict exists between its roles as a shopping promenade and as a principal circulation artery in Manhattan.

Structured group activities, such as parades on special days, occur, owing to the symbolic character of Fifth Avenue as the most important street in New York. Individual activities that are goal directed appear to occur much more often than random (impulse) activities (fig. 59). Some random individual activity occurs in places within this context (such as Rockefeller Plaza, Paley Park, or in front of the Public Library and St. Patrick's Cathedral) that are set aside as public outdoor spaces.

Public/private distinctions are ambiguous at ground level; public space extends considerably into privately owned spaces and the degree and type of control is irregular (fig. 60, 61). Goal-directed activities take place almost exclusively in the private realm.

Although public-place potential is high — as defined by the built form — there is no extension of private spaces and activities into the public realm that permits strong place orientation toward the street space itself, such as a café terrace might provide. There is little opportunity at present for creating an inclusive transition zone between public and private activities, which might join the street space with the buildings. In part this lack may be due to the harsh weather conditions that demand climate control for most of the year, but it is also associated with the exclusive nature of the shops and services along the Avenue.

The scope of intervention at the public-use boundary is confined to

61

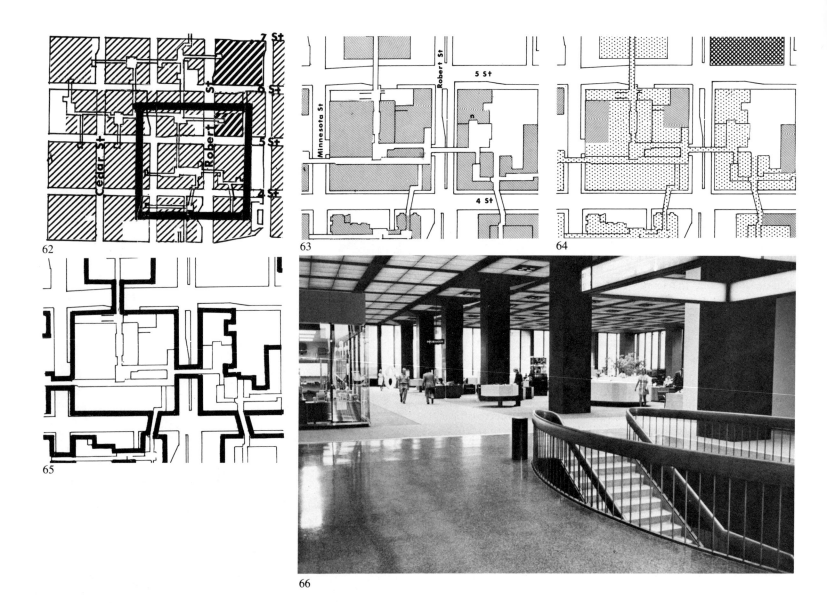

62-65. St. Paul, Minnesota, Skyway System.

66. Skyway Building. [Victor Caliandro]

manipulation of the sidewalk/street surface. Although incentive zoning has become crucial in controlling the built-form section of buildings along Fifth Avenue — to maintain the currently mixed promenade, shopping, and office use — provision must be made for augmenting the net sidewalk area and for reducing the impact of heavy traffic congestion.

Restrictions on truck traffic already exist, and access of private vehicles also could be restricted during peak traffic hours. The installation of some form of jitney-bus service could assist pedestrian movement along the Avenue. Authorities should consider the possibility of staggering office hours to reduce the highly crowded conditions that now occur at midday and at rush hours. Further possible alternatives are the widening of sidewalks and perhaps the total pedestrianization of Fifth Avenue, as has been proposed for nearby Madison Avenue. Retail shopping should be encouraged in favor of the present tendency of the street to attract service industries.

Transformations of the street surface that are intended to redress the imbalance between pedestrian needs and those of the automobile demand comprehensive planning interventions and new tools to implement them. The examples that follow present two design solutions to the problems of mediating pedestrian needs with those of automobile access in a high-density metropolitan center.

The skyway system for St. Paul, Minnesota, is proposed as a network of links and places within the downtown area (fig. 62). It has grown out of a need to increase the direct pedestrian linkage between major commercial and business facilities during inclement weather. The intensity of user choice is high, but the full range of choice is available to the user only when he enters this system.

The St. Paul Skyway is formed by a network of bridges that span the streets between buildings and by interior corridors connecting the bridges to places located at the cores of the buildings (fig. 63). Escalators and stairs connect these corridors and plazas to the ground and link the two-story commercial spaces. This system separates pedestrian and vehicular traffic into two competing orders, establishing a vast — perhaps impossibly vast — interface between public and private. Previous difficulties in sustaining the vitality of the commercial frontage of the city grid are now extended throughout the two systems. A possible response would be conversion of the skyway to include residential use, thereby substantially increasing pedestrian use and commercial activity.

When provided with glass-enclosed bridges, this above-grade system has the advantage of orienting the user at intervals to the city grid, but as with a below-grade system it is difficult to connect into the existing urban fabric.

A skyway system is able to operate in two ways. It can be the primary reference of movement and activity choices independent of the street; it can also serve as a secondary connector system, essentially private, that supplements the public orientation of movement and activity on the street below. It is typically organized on the basis of goal-oriented activities (fig. 64). The separation of pedestrian and vehicular traffic may well encourage the inclusion of many more non-goal-directed activities within the building fabric, in particular at the junction of the Skyway with vertical access routes and adjacent to the parking garage that connects to it directly.

The potential place qualities of the Skyway system are strong because every building has an associated series of interior plazas and nodes. It is perhaps unfortunate that these nodes do not occur in conjunction with important activities facing the street, a possibility that would greatly increase pedestrian awareness of the Skyway's place qualities and create a strong visual and symbolic link to the existing city fabric.

The difficulties inherent in public use of private spaces, especially when this use is conceived to be independent of the street system, pertain to the St. Paul Skyway system as well (fig. 65). The Skyway bridges are owned by the city and are under municipal authority, but the Skyway segments that extend into the private spaces enclosed in the buildings are under joint city and private control (fig. 66).

Place Ville Marie, Montreal, Canada, is typical as part of a private development complex that includes an interior pedestrian network around which commercial facilities are clustered. Above these interior walkways are offices and professional suites; below, parking and service facilities.

Place Ville Marie, while not specifically designed to serve a hierarchy of spaces, has slowly been adapted, through alterations, to accommodate the multiple needs of pedestrian flow to offices, to and from parking, and to the stores. The street system within it is formed solely by interior access requirements and is not dependent on nor related to existing streets (fig. 67, 68). The basic configuration of the interior streets is, as in the St. Paul Skyway, a locally continuous link interrupted by nodes or by points of vertical access to buildings above and to the "Place" above the pedestrian level. But the nonlinear qualities of the Place Ville Marie network seriously compromise a high link potential. Qualities of public place along the interior streets are subordinate to those of stores — a design strategy that reduces the very sense of street to commerciable commodity.

Activity settings, typically organized around provision of individual, goal-directed activities, fail to include the place potential of the interior street network nor do they open to the exterior street space.

The public-use boundary extends from the interior pedestrian street out toward the building line (fig. 69). Rarely does this boundary cross the building line and link the interior public realm with the exterior. The basic public/private distinctions are perfectly clear and nonambiguous,

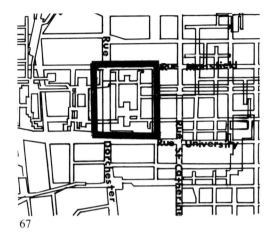

67

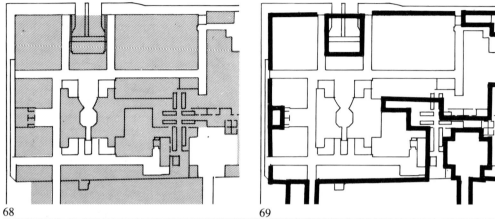

68   69

70

67. Montreal, Canada.

68, 69. Montreal, Place Ville Marie.

70. Place Ville Marie. [Victor Caliandro]

since the public pedestrian realm of the internal streets is contained within a private building form (fig. 70). In the introverted context of Place Ville Marie the relations to the existing city infrastructure could have been made more explicit if transitional extensions of the street level had been filtered into the internal network system. This would have made for a continuous street fabric rather than the superimposition of a network largely unrelated by activities, places, and form to the city grid.

The St. Paul Skyway and Place Ville Marie are both forms that have the potential to redress the imbalance between pedestrians and cars by providing a purely pedestrian realm that can operate in conjunction with the given downtown traffic network. Yet the increased concentration of parking and commercial establishment will aggravate traffic in surrounding streets. Without a direct and continuous dependence upon improved mass transit, these forms may very well be detrimental to a renewed pedestrian downtown.

Internal pedestrian systems limited to commercial facilities (such as the St. Paul Skyway and Place Ville Marie) are, I believe, ultimately counterproductive in relation to the whole urban fabric. They segregate a range of activities and therefore function for only part of daily and weekly cycles. It is not expedient or convenient to close such systems even though use often drops well below a desirable level. They do not act as social condensers associating people interested in many different goals, and thereby they also diminish the potential for access, interchange, and accidental encounter.

Conclusion

Many recent urban developments have eschewed the positive urban amenities and potentials of street-oriented structures and have internalized most commercial, social, and cultural functions. If such anti-street attitudes are fundamental to the present urban-planning process, the city moves toward an agglomeration of buildings and highways visited by automobile users and relinquishes those functions of individual contact and public interchange traditional to the urban street environment and its pedestrian constituency.

This survey of principal American street types, openly programmatic, focuses on the problems and potentials for maintaining a cohesive pedestrian-oriented city. The survey is presented in a discursive, exploratory manner because we still lack a thorough descriptive and analytic system capable of relating the multiple facets of the interdependence between man and his surroundings. Such a system is under continuing development; preliminary stages of that work are described in this volume by Stanford Anderson.

Throughout the discussion of these street environments, an effort has been made to place each example within a perspective that relates its impact to a larger physical context; that is, its ability to create a recognizable and identifiable order of streets and its capacity to sustain a certain level of pedestrian street activity throughout this context. It is this latter quality — the ability to sustain an autonomous and often indigenous street life (as at Willow Place) — that is the springboard for speculations about the future role such a street can have within an urban fabric. Yet the capacity to replicate through planning and design, under new conditions and with new building types, those qualities of scale, activity, enclosure, street/surface articulation, housing density, and context that promote a street life, is in its infancy. If the positive qualities of street environments are to be the programmatic basis for renewed cities, these must be sustained and developed not only through planning interventions but, more importantly, through the conscious efforts of those who seek an urban life-style.

The assumption that a street can be an effective element of the social life of urban Americans remains unchallenged in this study. I have hinted at an interdependence between the built form of the environment and prevalent lifestyles; the degree to which a street can be a greater part of this urban existence depends on the renewal of existing building types and the creation of definite pedestrian-oriented contexts within the cityscape.

The particular qualities of transition spaces and of public-use boundaries may provide a mechanism for understanding the interdependence between building type and street.

Street spaces, city blocks, and building types are mutually generative. The relationship of street space to block space is the result of various practical concerns for orientation, land division, density of building development, and communication and has produced a conceptual structure of the cityscape that is understood as a formal condition as well as an operational one. This relation is further modified by the public-use articulation of the building type. Specifically, a full consideration of the exposed edges of buildings, of the interior court spaces of city blocks, and their implications for street spaces, links the concept of public-use boundaries to that of the larger context; that is, the city conceived as a structure of streets integral with public and private open spaces.

Control over the form of public-use boundaries can be a direct means of establishing intimate relationships of use and form between activities and the rights-of-way, and therefore a renewed concept of the street may emerge — one that is capable of accommodating an urban lifestyle dependent on contact and interchange and of fostering an urban structure amenable to intense pedestrian life.

1972

CONTEXT- LAND USE

residential
commercial
institutional
mixed residential—commercial

1 inch = 1000 feet

BUILT—FORM CHARACTERISTICS

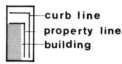
curb line
property line
building

1 inch = 200 feet

CIRCULATION

pedestrian
heavy
light
random

vehicular
heavy
light
Ⓟ parking
Ⓣ transit

1 inch = 200 feet

ACTIVITY SETTING

individual activity space
group activity space
private space

1 inch = 200 feet

PUBLIC—PRIVATE USE BOUNDARY

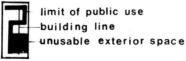
limit of public use
building line
unusable exterior space

1 inch = 200 feet

71. Key to plans of typical streets.

Notes on Method
Analytic Categories

The sequence in which the analytic categories are presented closely follows the method of study. A graphic notation of information isolated according to these categories appears in the text.

1. Context. The context summarizes the general built form in terms of dominant land uses. Particular context characteristics are scope of goals, intensity of goals, and context movement.

Scope of goals refers to the range of activities offered by a street. These activities include all types of commercial, institutional, and residential use. The scope of goals is wide when there are many choices of movement and exchange, narrow when a street offers a few choices. A narrow scope is generally attributable to the predominance of a single land use.

Intensity of goals is concentrated when available commercial, residential, and institutional services are located in close proximity and the choices among activities are clearly communicated to the pedestrian. The intensity is dispersed when the scope of available choices is not within the immediate realm of the pedestrian or is poorly communicated.

Context movement refers to the mode of access to the choices available on a street, whether predominantly by car or on foot.

2. Built-Form Characteristics. The figure/ground diagrams for this category show the built form versus open space at ground level. Further description of built-form qualities is developed as follows:

Spatial hierarchy is the evident rank ordering of a built street section in relation to the sections of streets immediately adjacent and diminishes to the local street section and its articulation or scale differentiation into coherent parts.

Enclosure of a street space is strong when the facades are continuous, the ratio of facade height to street width is regular, and the facade articulation is relatively uniform. The street enclosure is weak when none of the preceding conditions reinforces the street space; definition is then left to curb lines, topography, and landscaping.

Link qualities of a street are strong when its linear nature is emphasized by its volumetric enclosure and it is also a specific connector between two distinct goals.

Place qualities are strong when the street space articulates activity settings, be this by enclosure, variation in width, or other means and when this potential corresponds to social need. Place characteristics are weak when neither of the preceding conditions helps to define a street or area as different from another or when pedestrian activity does not enrich a particular physical setting.

Pedestrian potential is a measure of the ability of a street environment to generate and sustain pedestrian flow. It is said to be high when the density of users is high and sufficient activity choices are in close proximity. The capacity is low when there are few or no activity choices along designated pedestrian routes.

3. Circulation. Circulation diagrams show the presence and intensity of different movement systems; that is, the function of the street as link. A further description of circulation is developed as follows:

Automobile conflict is present when the volume of automobile flow or the density of parking limits the continuity of pedestrian paths and restricts pedestrian movement or use of the street.

Local traffic refers to automobile traffic principally within the context under study. The car in this instance is a partial substitute for the pedestrian realm.

District traffic refers to primary use of the automobile outside of the street complex under discussion.

Pedestrian flow within a street is of high or low intensity. It is said to be converging when the street functions as a collector and distributed when the street functions as an intermediate link between collector streets or when the entire context is lacking in intensity. Pedestrian flow may be highly directional to particular goals or include much random movement such as window shopping, playing, strolling, and observing. Pedestrian circulation may have strong link characteristics when it is directional between specific goals, weak when the street is used only by its residents and is not part of a preferred route.

4. Activity Setting. An activity setting is a space for public social interaction, including restaurants, parks, and entrance lobbies. The number and configuration of such settings is an index of the street as place. Up to a certain density of local activity, a place may still function as a link.

Activity types. Group activities occur either strictly in groups (such as certain sports) or as an aggregation of individuals in a setting. These activity settings include restaurants, movie theatres, and bars. Individual activities involve only individual-to-individual exchange of goods or information — shopping generally is an individual activity. A structured activity requires a particular physical setting with a specific, goal-directed nature. Structured activities include working, attending school, and some shopping but do not include strolling, reading, or playing (unless in an organized sport). Random activities are visually spontaneous in nature and require little by way of a special physical setting.

Activity location within the total extent of a public street space may be completely within a building (an enclosed shopping mall), oriented toward the street (shops along a downtown shopping street), or in the literal space of the street (sidewalk cafés).

5. Public/Private Use Boundary. These diagrams reveal the augmen-

tation or diminution of street space as located by the interface between public and private domains. The description of public-use boundaries is developed according to the following qualities:

Public-use boundary is distinct when the separation of public-use space and private space is defined by a wall or other obvious physical form. It is indistinct when the boundary is either unrelated to built form or not clearly defined within built form.

The analysis seeks to pinpoint transformations to particular streets and street contexts that would reintroduce or reinforce the potential for social contact and interchange. These design approaches are generally presented in a summary of the street type and according to possible manipulations of public-use boundaries.

The graphic key (fig. 71) applies to all the drawings presented. The diagrams based on the analytic categories are drawn over a base map with uniform outlines and curb and property lines. Unless otherwise indicated, north is the top of all plans.

Notes

1. This survey was carried out as part of the IAUS study on Streets as Elements of Urban Structure in the spring and early summer of 1971. The survey was developed and completed by Victor Caliandro, Gregory Gale, and Thomas Schumacher under the guidance of Stanford Anderson, William Ellis, and Kenneth Frampton.

2. I refer the reader to the following sources for an introduction to discussions of the idea of community, particularly the role that public spaces play in its formation and maintenance. In H. M. Proshansky, W. H. Ittleson, and L. G. Rivlin, ed., *Environmental Psychology: Man and His Physical Setting* (New York: Holt, Rinehart and Winston, 1970), the essays by Robert Beck (''Spatial Meaning and Properties of the Environment''), Robert Gutman (''Site Planning and Social Behavior''), Jane Jacobs (''The Uses of Sidewalks: Contact''), Anselm Strauss (''Life Styles and Urban Space''), and Melvin M. Webber (''Order in Diversity: Community without Propinquity'').

3. In particular, see the first essay by Stanford Anderson in this volume.

4. Ibid.

5. An analysis of the impact of these ideas on the form and use of streets has been further developed in the work of Stanford Anderson; see ''Studies toward an Ecological Model of the Urban Environment'' in this volume.

Bibliographic Notes

The bibliography and research material gathered for this study are extensive; I can only signal a few studies that have contributed in large measure to my work.

Special mention must be made of a recent study conducted by the San Francisco Department of City Planning, designed and supervised by Donald Appleyard. The *Street Livability Study* (San Francisco, 1970), surveyed the effects of traffic conditions on residential streets. This study furthermore develops several graphic approaches to the problem of representing the social space of streets. In the *AIP Journal* (March 1972), pp. 84–101. Donald Appleyard and Mark Lintell make a much more comprehensive presentation of this study, under the title ''The Environmental Quality of City Streets: The Residents' Viewpoint.''

The graphic material was compiled from many sources, including personal collections. In particular I am grateful to the New York City Planning Commission and the Office of Downtown Brooklyn Redevelopment (NYCPD) for assistance in locating and supplying maps and land-use information. All drawings are by members of the Institute for Architecture and Urban Studies.

Selected Bibliography

Alexander, Christopher. *The City as a Mechanism for Sustaining Human Contact*. Berkeley, Calif.: Institute for Urban and Regional Development, Working Paper no. 50, 1966.

Ewald, William R., Jr., ed. *Environment for Man: The Next Fifty Years*. Bloomington, Ind.: Indiana University Press, 1967.

Gans, Herbert. *People and Plans*. New York: Basic Books, 1968.

Goffman, Erving. *Behavior in Public Places: Notes on the Social Organization of Gatherings*. New York: The Free Press, 1963.

Hall, Edward T. *The Hidden Dimension*. Garden City, N.Y.: Doubleday Anchor, 1969.

Lewis, David, ed. *The Pedestrian in the City*. Princeton, N.J.: D. Van Nostrand, 1966.

Lynch, Kevin. *The Image of the City*. Cambridge, Mass.: The MIT Press, 1960.

Proshansky, Harold M., William H. Ittleson, and Leanne G. Rivlin. *Environmental Psychology: Man and His Physical Setting*. New York: Holt, Rinehart and Winston, 1970.

Rapoport, Amos. *House Form and Culture*. Englewood Cliffs, N.J.: Prentice-Hall, 1969.

Sommer, Robert. *Personal Space*. Englewood Cliffs, N.J.: Prentice-Hall, 1969.

Stein, Clarence S. *Towards New Towns for America*. Cambridge, Mass.: The MIT Press, 1969.

Tunnard, Christopher, and Boris Pushkaref. *Man-made America: Chaos or Control?* New Haven: Yale University Press, 1963.

Streets as Channels

1. Le Corbusier, Ville Contemporaine (1922). [Le Corbusier, *Une Ville Contemporaine* [1922]]

2. Process to Increase Street Capacity (1931). a. Present conditions: one moving line. b. With elevation of sidewalks: three moving lanes. c. With arcades for standing vehicles: six moving lanes. d. Deeper arcades provided in permanent construction: eight moving lanes. [*First Regional Plan of New York* (1930), p. 307]

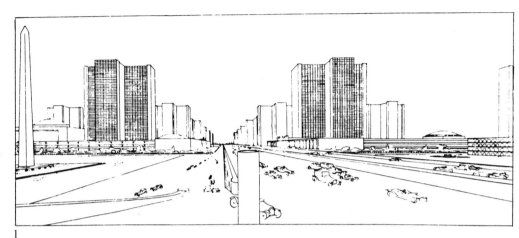

1

2a

2b

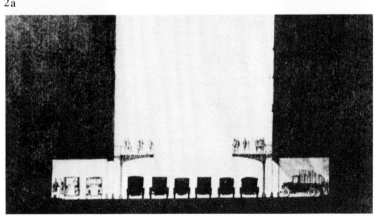

2c

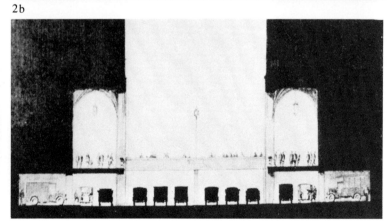

2d

Toward an Evaluation of Transportation Potentials for the Urban Street

Peter Wolf

Foreword

Obsession with the automobile by the postfuturist era is only now diminishing in a meaningful way. This obsession informed the vision of even the most thoughtful urbanists and architects in both Europe and America until the 1950s. In Europe, for example, Sant 'Elia's *Citta nuova* of 1914, Le Corbusier's only large-scale urbanistic projects of the 1920s and 1930s, Ville Radieuse, City for 3 Million Inhabitants, and the Algiers redevelopment proposal are dominated by the automobile (fig. 1). The highway becomes the core of the city. The public space of town is carelessly donated to the vehicle and to those who possess the car, a machine that inspired the imagination of progressive thinkers for many decades.

In the United States, in even the largest cities, it was assumed until only recently that the central problem of urban transportation was how to increase traffic capacity in the city center. For instance, principal recommendations of the First Regional Plan of New York City, issued in 1931, focus on suggested methods to increase street traffic capacity (fig. 2). The Committee of Architects led by Harvey Wiley Corbett suggested, with characteristic disregard for the public, that streets in Manhattan be widened to accommodate more cars; that they be used for truck access; indeed that they penetrate sidewalks and finally the first bay of buildings to assure ever greater traffic capacity. Until World War II few challenges existed to similar principles.

Only in the early 1950s, with Lou Kahn's provocative graphic analysis of Philadelphia street-use patterns and somewhat later Shadrach Woods's pedestrian-oriented "stem" concept for units of urban development and redevelopment, did even the most progressive urbanists and architects begin to reconsider the appropriate role of the urban street.

The street, after all, is the largest assemblage of public space in any and every city. It is meant to be available to all the people. It once served as the center for commerce, information, and recreation within cities. At the same time cities are larger than ever and people must be able to get around within them.

It is already clear that the technocracy of telecommunications is not going to replace the need for direct human interaction in commerce, recreation, education, and all other activities that dominate city life. Thus the question arises: how may urban streets serve as excellent communication and transportation channels and still serve as more? How may they once again become effective spaces for movement in cities and still be effective spaces for most people in the city? This essay is an attempt to approach these and other interrelated questions. Its focus is the complex, crowded, center-city urban street. And its purpose is to reveal, through systematic analysis to the extent possible, transportation options now available for the city center that would allow better urban design and a better urban environment in which to live.

Definitions, Scope and Focus

A number of specialized definitions are necessary. An *urban street* is a street in an urban place recognized as a "Main" street, and/or "The" street in which opportunity for a variety of communication, exchange, and interchange exists at a high level of intensity. The *influence zone* includes the urban street, abutting structures, and surrounding area served by a transportation mode. The zone includes open space, semipublic and private building interiors for distances that a pedestrian might logically travel to change from travel on foot to travel by another means. *Transportation* includes travel by all modes, including private automobile, private taxi, and all forms of communal and public vehicles or mechanisms. *Transit* refers to communal and public vehicles or mechanisms of all kinds and sizes.

A number of relatively obvious matters have been omitted from detailed consideration in this essay since they fail to promote inquiry into new territory, or function as understood relationships, or relate principally to material covered elsewhere in this book. Principal among these are the necessity of transportation for the existence of an urban street; transportation/development synergism on the urban street; economic impact and consequences of transportation on the urban street; social impact and consequences of transportation on the urban street; goods movement and service requirements imposed on the urban street; utility line linkage to transportation right-of-way.

Additional focus has been selected to sharpen considerations contained in this essay. As a working methodology the following restrictions were placed on the analysis that follows: (1) Transportation considerations that affect all street categories, as catalogued by the "user typology" (discussed elsewhere in this book), are outside of the possible scope of this inquiry. (2) This essay focuses on intense areas of change, interchange, and exchange where transit and transportation alternatives exist. These points or corridors create, define, or support urban streets. Here a relationship exists and grows between systems of transit and the influence zone. Here urban life for the individual is generally considered its most intense and special. And it is here that the demands generally asserted by transportation technology and planning are most often in conflict with optimum experience of the individual served by such transportation. In such areas the private vehicle has become a thoroughly recognized menace to the city and an inefficient travel means to the user. It is in such areas that innovative travel potentialities offer promise. (3) It is recognized that mobility in the city

Table 1

Trends in Transit Riding in the United States 1935–1968
Revenue Passengers (millions)

Year	Railway Transit			Trolley Coach	Motor Bus	Total Transit
	Street Cars	Subway & Elevated	Rail Total			
1935	5,156	2,252	7,408	77	2,297	9,782
1940	4,182	2,282	6,464	419	3,620	10,503
1945	7,081	2,555	9,636	1,001	8,345	18,982
1950	2,790	2,113	4,903	1,261	7,681	13,845
1955	845	1,741	2,586	869	5,734	9,189
1956	625	1,749	2,374	814	5,568	8,756
1957	491	1,706	2,197	703	5,438	8,338
1958	415	1,635	2,050	593	5,135	7,778
1959	378	1,647	2,025	517	5,108	7,650
1960	335	1,670	2,005	447	5,069	7,521
1961	323	1,680	2,003	405	4,834	7,242
1962	284	1,704	1,988	361	4,773	7,122
1963	238	1,661	1,899	264	4,752	6,915
1964	213	1,698	1,911	214	4,729	6,854
1965	204	1,678	1,882	186	4,730	6,798
1966	211	1,584	1,795	174	4,702	6,671
1967	196	1,632	1,828	155	4,633	6,616
1968	187	1,627	1,814	152	4,524	6,491

Source: American Transit Association, *Transit Fact Book,* 1969. Excludes commuter railroads, which account for less than one-tenth of one percent of transit patronage.

center poses requirements and constraints. Through analytic procedure and discussion, a number of pertinent postulations regarding this mobility are developed. (4) The total transportation trip, which may have a number of links, is from front door to office door. This reality is generally ignored by transportation planners because it is not recognized. In this study, that underlying reality is very much in mind. Concentration will not be on the total trip but the last link of it — interaction between movement system and dense, varied, multifunctional urban streets or areas.

For such a specialized viewpoint some background context framing evolutionary changes and current trends in transportation usage assists in underscoring circumstances that must be confronted. This background establishes the context of national trends that must be encountered if meaningful postulations and implementative work are to proceed.

Recent Transportation Trends in the United States

Over a long period of documented study it has been established that population size dictates intensity of area-wide travel demand that, in turn, because of the economic foundations upon which transportation feasibility is conventionally determined in the United States, dictates types of transportation networks and alternatives feasible in any area.

Three basic area scales have become established that give guidance as to transportation need. The largest area is the region with a major urban center and an approximate minimum population of 2 million people. There are seven of these in the United States. In them a wide variety of transportation modes generally exists, especially in older parts of the country where settlement is relatively dense. In such places approximately 70 percent of travelers who enter the central business district (CBD) daily use some form of public transit. In greater metropolitan areas of 500,000 to 2 million population, transit is generally limited to feeder buses and used more sparsely. The third category, cities with fewer than 500,000, generally cannot support major transportation variety. The automobile is the principal feeder mechanism to the central area.

Transit riding in the United States has been decreasing significantly for more than twenty years, as indicated in table 1. Although a number of circumstances temporarily distorted the trend during and just after World War II, it is clear that total transit riding decreased approximately 33 percent between 1935 and 1968. During the same interval, population of the country increased over 50 percent.

Nevertheless, significant numbers of people still use transit service in urban areas, as depicted in table 2, which surveys New York City and thirty-seven other major United States areas with populations exceeding 500,000. The smallest urban area in which rail rapid transit is in operation or under construction has approximately 1.8 million residents. These areas also have central-city population densities of 10,000 persons per square mile or more. Table 2 also suggests a strong relationship between the age of the city and transit riding. In general those cities that experienced major growth after the private car came into general use have the lowest transit usage and low central-city resident population densities, as would be expected.

The greatest deterrent to transit has been the dramatic increase in private car ownership and use. As shown in table 3, in the thirty-year period from 1935 to 1965 the nations's population increased by 52 percent, while private car registrations increased 233 percent and transit riding decreased 31 percent. The ratio of population to cars owned in the United States dropped from 5.7 in 1935 to 2.6 in 1965, while the average number of transit rides per capita decreased from 77 to 35 annually.

Simultaneously, because of increasing costs of labor and materials the cost of operating a transit vehicle has increased from 25 cents to over 80 cents per mile since 1935, as shown in table 4. The same table also shows that average passenger fares have not met operating costs since 1955.

Thus, by 1970, 96 percent of all daily passenger trips in urban areas in the United States were made by automobile, 3 percent by motor bus, and only 1 percent by rail and other means. However, these general statistics relevant to all daily travel in the county mask the importance of transit in larger cities, especially travel to the dense central areas. In New York, Chicago, and Philadelphia, where extensive rapid transit systems exist, more than 75 percent of all peak-hour passenger trips and over 50 percent of all daily trips to the central business district are made by some form of public transit.

As can be seen from this brief statistical review, over the past thirty years the freedom of movement permitted by the car, increasing levels of car ownership, and the increasing cost of transit operation have transformed the pattern and density of urban growth into configurations that often prove difficult to serve with mass carriers. This has contributed to the dissolution of urban centers. The result has been a rapid decline in the quality and amount of transit service in cities, the deterioration of urban life, growing isolation of those urban residents who prefer not to drive or do not have access to cars, and loss of city streets to almost all uses other than as conduits for vehicles.

Today there is increasing recognition that the private car, in spite of its great flexibility, is not the whole answer to urban transportation needs. Nor is it of conceivable value in retrieving a sense of place in cities or in designing new cities with urban areas of interest, of use, and

Table 2 Transit Riding in Major Urban Areas

Urban Area	Population (urbanized area)	Density[1] Central City	Density[1] Urban-ized Area	Transit Revenue Passengers[2] Total[3] (millions)	Transit Revenue Passengers[2] Rail Rapid Transit Number (millions)	Transit Revenue Passengers[2] Rail Rapid Transit Per Cent of Total
A. 1 to 7-million						
1. Los Angeles	6,489,000	5,500	4,700	160	—	—
2. Chicago	5,959,000	15,800	6,200	439	116	26.4
3. Philadelphia	3,635,000	15,700	6,100	214	68	31.8
4. Detroit	3,538,000	12,000	4,800	125	—	—
5. S.Francisco-Oakland	2,431,000	15,600	4,300	198	—	—
6. Boston	2,413,000	14,600	4,700	204[4]	95	46.6
7. Washington	1,808,000	12,400	5,300	153	—	—
8. Pittsburgh	1,804,000	11,200	3,400	111[4]	—	—
9. Cleveland	1,785,000	10,800	3,000	162[4]	17	10.4
10. St. Louis	1,668,000	12,300	5,200	91[4]	—	—
11. Baltimore	1,419,000	11,900	6,400	96	—	—
12. Minneapolis-St.Paul	1,377,000	7,400	2,100	62	—	—
13. Milwaukee	1,150,000	8,100	2,900	88	—	—
14. Houston	1,140,000	2,900	2,600	22[4]	—	—
15. Buffalo	1,054,000	13,500	6,600	50	—	—
Subtotal	37,670,000			2,175	296	13.6
B. 500,000 to 1-million						
16. Cincinnati	994,000	6,500	4,100	47	—	—
17. Dallas	932,000	2,400	1,400	31	—	—
18. Kansas City	921,000	3,700	3,300	25	—	—
19. Seattle	864,000	6,300	3,600	35	—	—
20. Miami	853,000	8,500	4,100	47	—	—
21. New Orleans	845,000	3,157	3,200	87	—	—
22. San Diego	836,000	3,000	3,000	15	—	—
23. Denver	804,000	7,000	4,800	19	—	—
24. Atlanta	768,000	3,800	3,100	52	—	—
25. Providence	660,000	11,592	3,500	19	—	—
26. Portland (Oregon)	652,000	5,546	3,387	18	—	—
27. San Antonio	642,000	3,662	3,337	24	—	—
28. Indianapolis	639,000	6,689	4,412	21	—	—
29. Columbus	617,000	4,300	4,259	25	—	—
30. Louisville	607,000	6,841	4,474	20	—	—
31. San Jose	603,000	3,747	2,702	6	—	—
32. Phoenix	552,000	2,343	2,222	7	—	—
33. Memphis	544,000	3,881	3,497	27	—	—
34. Birmingham	521,000	4,576	3,325	15	—	—
35. Norfolk-Portsmouth	508,000	6,612	4,676	22	—	—
36. Fort Worth	503,000	2,536	1,844	7	—	—
37. Dayton	502,000	7,808	4,029	18	—	—
Subtotal	15,367,000			587	0	0
Total — 500,000 to 7 million	53,037,000			2,762	296	10.7
C. New York City	14,114,927	23,321	7,462	2,126	1,288	60.6
Total	67,151,927			4,888	1,584	

[1]Resident population per square mile, 1960 census. [2]Passengers for dominant transit systems for latest available year. Excludes commuter railroads (one-tenth of one percent of transit total). [3]Includes small amount of street car and electric trolley bus operation. [4]Estimated on basis of passenger revenue and fare.

Source: *The Potential for Bus Rapid Transit*, Automobile Manufacturers Assn., 1970.

of delight to the individual. The car is essentially a transporter of the individual from independent origin to specific destination. As cities become larger, and public awareness grows, the potential is promising for improved forms of public transit that could supplement car travel in high-demand situations.

Clearly, as regions grow, if the intensively used street is to survive as a place of personal exchange and interchange, then the introduction of transit to it will be essential. The alternative is continued growth of extensive parking lots and activity dispersal instead of convenient and interesting urban areas in which streets are once again a true amenity within the public domain.

Travel Modes: Functional Criteria and Selection

Potentially acceptable modes of urban transportation have to be selected before evaluation of their impact on the urban street can be determined. For assistance in this selection of conventional and advanced travel modes a set of general criteria recently established through a study sponsored by the Urban Mass Transit Administration has been used selectively.[1] With these criteria as guidelines, seven conventional and advanced travel modes have been selected for comparative evaluation. These include private automobile, conventional taxi, public electric automobile, bus, fixed-track train, network cab, and pedestrian conveyor.

Criteria

In selecting these transportation types a variety of considerations related to the concept of this study were used for mode selection guideline purposes.

Basic Linkages. Center city distribution systems should serve two basic circulation needs:
1. Wholly intra-CBD circulation (for example, department store to office building).
2. Circulation between line-haul transportation terminals and major CBD destinations (largely home-to-work trips).

Range of Operations. Center-city distribution systems generally should be designed for a range of up to three miles. This range encompasses most central business districts (which are usually under two square miles in area). Greater ranges are generally best served by line-haul vehicles. Ranges of 500 to 1,000 feet are common in the center city and should be readily accommodated by belt-type as well as other technologies.

Route and Operating Flexibility. Ideally, a center-city distribution system should have a high degree of adaptability, subject to the practical constraints of right-of-way availability and cost.
1. The type of guideway could be fixed (rail or belt) or nonfixed (bus).
2. Systems should be able to negotiate grades and curves.
3. The ability to switch is essential — both between routes and between routes and storage areas (except, perhaps, for belt systems).
4. Vehicle storage (where needed) should be removed from central or core areas.
5. System design should allow for extension, as well as for possible accommodation of baggage and parcels.

Service Availability and Frequency. Because of the relatively short travel distance and high peaking characteristics, ready availability of service is more important than high sustained speeds.
1. Ideally, service should be continuously available, as in the case of belt-based technologies.
2. For headway or "intermittent" operations (buses, trains), average waiting times should not exceed 3 minutes (subject, of course, to patronage demands). This implies maximum headways (time between successive units) of 5 minutes. Headways of 1 to 2 minutes are desirable during periods of heavy demand.

Speeds and Trip Times. Overall portal-to-portal trip times, including walking, riding, and waiting times, should fall within a 5- to 10-minute range for center city trips. The following speed ranges appear desirable:

	Continuous Operation		
	Passengers on Belts	Passengers in Train-like Units	Headway Operation
Maximum	3 mph	15 mph	30 mph
Operating	1–1.5 mph[2]	12 mph	10–15 mph

Acceleration and Deceleration Limits. Acceleration and deceleration should be limited to levels compatible with passenger comfort and safety yet be high enough to allow efficient system performance. Thus, human acceptance limits should govern acceleration and deceleration rates. Normally, rates should not exceed 2.5–3 mph/sec where standing passengers are involved; maximum deceleration in emergency stops, 5 mph/sec.

Passenger Loading and Unloading Times. The time to enter or leave vehicles should be kept to a minimum. Ideally, these should be not more than 3 seconds per passenger, preferably 1 second.

Stop or Station Frequency. The frequency of stops depends on terrain traversed, land use, and type of system. In general, stops on continuous systems should be spaced at 150- to 400-foot intervals. Stops for center-city, headway-type distribution systems generally should be at 300- to 1,000-foot intervals.

Table 3
Changes in Transit Usage, Private Car Ownership, and Population 1935–1965

| Year | Transit Revenue Passengers | | | Private Passenger Cars Registered | | | Total Resident Population | | | Persons per Private Passenger Car | Transit Rides per Capita |
	Revenue Passengers (millions)	5-Year Change (percent)	Percent of 1935 Level	Passenger Cars Registered (millions)	5-Year Change (percent)	Percent of 1935 level	Resident Population (millions)	5-Year Change (percent)	Percent of 1935 Level		
1935	9,782	—	100.0	22.5	—	10.0	127.2	—	100.0	5.7	77
1940	10,504	+ 7.4	107.4	27.4	+21.7	11.8	132.5	+ 4.2	104.2	4.8	80
1945	18,982	+80.7	194.0	25.7	− 6.2	14.2	133.4	+ 0.7	104.9	5.2	143
1950	13,845	−27.0	141.5	40.2	+56.4	18.7	151.9	+13.9	119.4	3.8	91
1955	9,189	−33.6	94.0	52.0	29.4	21.1	165.1	+ 8.7	129.8	3.2	56
1960	7,521	−18.2	76.9	61.4	+18.1	22.9	179.9	+ 9.0	141.4	2.9	42
1965	6,798	− 9.6	69.5	74.9	+22.2	32.9	193.6	+ 7.7	152.4	2.6	35

Source: *Statistical Abstract of the United States, 1966* (population); Federal Highway Administration, Bureau of Public Roads, *State Motor Vehicle Registrations* (various tables); and American Transit Association, *Transit Fact Book 1968* (transit riders).

Table 4
Operating Expense per Mile and per Revenue Passenger
U.S. Transit Industry (1935–1968)

| Year | Operating Expense[1] | | Average Fare per Passenger (cents) |
	Per Vehicle Mile (cents)	Per Revenue Passenger (cents)	
1935	25.3	6.0	6.6
1940	25.4	6.3	6.7
1945	37.8	6.5	6.9
1950	46.1	10.0	10.0
1955	56.0	15.1	14.8
1960	64.2	18.3	17.7
1965	72.4	21.4	19.7
1968	81.0	24.8	23.6

[1]Excludes interest on debt service. Costs not adjusted for changes in the purchasing power of the dollar.
Source: American Transit Association, *Transit Fact Book,* 1969.

Horizontal Alignment. Systems should be able to negotiate curves. Turning radii should be as small as possible, consistent with safety, comfort, and land-use needs. Generally, a minimum radius of 25 to 30 feet will be desirable for center-city distribution systems. Minimum radii on line-haul systems depend on design speeds.

Vertical Alignment. Maximum gradients depend on system speeds and passenger limitations. The objective of maintaining a vertical passenger orientation is more significant than system grades per se. In this context, the following grades for people should not be exceeded:

1. Continuous operation (belts) 10 to 15 degrees from horizontal.

2. Headway operation (trains) 5 to 8 percent

Capacity[3] (service volume). Systems should provide adequate flexibility to serve a wide range of loads. One-way, peak-direction capacities of 3,000 to 5,000 persons per hour will generally meet most center-city requirements; however, in some cases (as where line-haul and distribution functions are provided by a common facility), capacities up to 15,000 persons per hour should be provided. Peak 15-minute flow rates, to be accommodated, should be twice the hourly capacity values. In all cases, stations must be adequately designed for peak loads.

Operating Costs. Operating costs should be minimized through maximum use of automation and a high rate of productivity per peak-hour employee. At current cost levels, this implies costs of about 1.0 cent or less per passenger — or seat-mile (for conveyor belts — per passenger place-mile). Ideally, maximum allowable costs — the estimated costs of bus operations — should be 1.5 cents to 2.5 cents per passenger — or seat-mile.

Service Dependability. Service dependability should be achieved through system operations on private rights-of-way wherever possible. Desirable performance objectives include:

1. *Schedule adherence* — Systems should be able to maintain schedules.

2. *Operational continuity* — Systems should have the ability to operate when parts of the system are being repaired or when vehicle units are disabled.

3. *Maintenance frequency and ease* — System way and vehicles should not require excessive or difficult maintenance.

4. *All-weather performance* — Systems should operate effectively during all weather conditions.

Passenger Safety. Maximum passenger safety must be assured and system design must comply with all codes, laws, ordinances, rules, regulations, and orders of appropriate public authorities. The system should be safe in terms of both entering, exit, and on-board conditions.

1. Passengers should not be required to cross any tracks or vehicle lanes to reach stations or loading areas.

2. Ideally, people should not enter moving vehicles or conveyances.

3. Ample fail-safe procedures should be provided, such as block signals and automatic train stops on rail rapid-transit lines.

4. Systems should be adequately monitored and free from unnecessary fire hazards.

Passenger Comfort and Ease of Operation. Passenger comfort should exceed that of existing automobile, bus, and rapid-transit vehicles. Systems should have attractive design qualities and have routing and service patterns that are easily comprehensible by passengers.

1. The elderly, physically handicapped, and people with small children must be able to use the system comfortably.

2. The internal noise level should be low — generally under 50 decibels.

3. Internal illumination should be adequate — 15 to 30 footcandles on the surface of reading materials would permit reading.

4. Complete climate control should be provided.

5. Internal vibrations should be kept to a minimum.

6. There should be no difficult ventilation requirements (such as experienced with diesel exhaust).

Environmental Qualities. The system should blend into the fabric of the urbanized area to the maximum extent possible.

1. It should have a pleasing appearance.

2. It should not produce air pollution, noise, or vibration in excess of the acceptable levels established for the particular locale.

3. It should be structurally safe — thereby affording safety to the nonuser as well as the user.

4. It should afford structural lightness. This quality is essential to allow more effective integration with major downtown buildings and developments. In this context, ideally it should be able to enter, penetrate, or append to buildings, as well as fit into joint developments.

Development Feasibility. The system should have no serious development problems. Ideally, it should be currently available or, at a minimum, have operating prototypes or be available within five years. These criteria are essential to assure early implementation in view of the normal research and development lag time of five to ten years.

Mode Characteristics

Each of the selected transportation modes, including the advanced systems — people movers, electric taxi, fixed guideway network cab, and modified caravan system — is considered to have either immediate application to the center city or a high degree of development feasibility.

Existing and innovative possibilities for center-city transit technologies fall into three broad categories: buses or multipassenger vehicles operating on existing streets; continuous service beltlike systems, operating continuously and always available for passengers to board; and train or fixed guideway vehicles.

It is evident that any of these could be made operational at any one level or on a combination of horizontal levels within the city. These roughly correspond to grade, below grade, and above grade. The implication of physical position for impact on urban areas will be considered later.

Detailed description and operating characteristics of each mode may be reviewed through descriptive reports and data published elsewhere. Special qualities implied by the presence of each, however, deserve mention here as they affect the evaluation of each mode against selected criteria related to interaction with the urban context.

Private automobile. Operationally the unique attribute to the car is that it operates on individual demand from origin to destination and is capable of following an arbitrary, random route. When not in use, however, storage of approximately 300 square feet is necessary. Conventional private vehicles in America also require lanes 12 feet wide — approximately the same as a railroad right-of-way. Capacity does not generally exceed 6 people, and the average automobile trip in America contains approximately 2 persons. Auto engine emission pollution control is a major environmental problem.

Taxi. The taxi includes all of the operational characteristics of the private automobile. However, multiple daily utilization eliminates parking requirements in the central city. In the urban context a high degree of convenience is due to random movement opportunity between any origin and destination without the necessity for a journey to find the vehicle and storage requirements at destination. With constant cruising auto engine pollution is an even greater issue than with the private automobile.

Public Automobile Service. This is one of the most highly developed and tested of the future transport concepts for local-area, central-city travel resulting from manufacturers' and government studies. It is reported and adequately documented in the final report on *Future Urban Transportation Systems: Descriptions, Evaluations, and Programs,* Stanford Research Institute, March 1968, to the U.S. Department of Housing and Urban Development.

This concept employs a small, electrically propelled surface vehicle on a multiuse rental basis. It can be left at any one of a number of stands within a given area, picked up by a second user, and so on continuously. The vehicle is projected to transport two adults plus children. It is expected to be 84 inches long, 54 inches wide, and about 60 inches high (fig. 3). It is expected that this system will be preferred by individuals able to drive, and their cotravelers, and would provide secure storage for parcels and baggage. It also appears feasible in this system to make

3. PAS Garage. [Stanford Research Institute, *Future Urban Transportation Systems: Descriptions, Evaluations and Programs*]

cars available on a speed-restricted basis to certain younger people and adults who are not allowed to drive standard automobiles.

It has been determined that daily utilization of 2.5 to 10 times that of similar private vehicles would achieve costs per trip acceptable to the general public and that such utilization is a reasonable expectation.

Public automobile service stands would be at curbside, parking lots, designated garages, or within large buildings. Operating characteristics include maximum speed of 25 miles per hour, limited range, maximum capacity of four people. Principal use is anticipated as feeder service to other line-haul transportation, short-range home-to-work trips, shopping, and business and commercial travel within the confines of the urban center.

It is currently suggested that vehicles could be battery powered. Local area travel implies frequent daily trips with intervals available for battery recharge; thus technical obstacles to electrically-driven, long-range vehicles are overcome.

Bus. A principal advantage of a bus system is that it serves both extended-area travel and local-area travel without required modal transfer. It also requires no special right-of-way and may modify its course as needed. Because of possible size variability a large number of urban and travel circumstances can be physically accommodated. The ratio of operation expense to income is variable, depending on load factors. Capacities on urban streets of 2,000 to 4,000 passengers per hour are commonly experienced.

Extended-area travel corridors in which one-direction, peak-hour demand is less than 4,000 persons creates a condition in which bus rapid transit has a clear economic advantage over rail as a means of large numbers of people entering urban areas. In the range between 4,000 to 8,000 peak-hour, one-way corridor transit riders, the economics of bus versus rail will depend upon specific local conditions. Both can obviously enter the central city on reserved rights-of-way including depressed or elevated levels. More and more frequently the bus is given special lane right-of-way outside of central areas, reducing travel times and increasing desirability.

Requirements for specialized and grade separated rights-of-way in the city center present problems of cost and engineering not unlike those imposed by rail. Problems of exhaust and noise, so long as diesel and gasoline engines are used, create additional environmental questions that are partially contained by establishing tunnel rights-of-way, but these add large cost increments and restrain the flexibility of the service itself.

Service by minibus only within urban local travel areas has proved popular in a number of demonstration experiments. For instance, in Washington, D.C., under sponsorship of the U.S. Department of Housing and Urban Development, small buses have operated on a fixed route and frequent schedule in a downtown shopping area for several years. Public reaction is overwhelmingly favorable. By the end of a recent one-year demonstration period, over 1.8 million passengers, twice the estimated patronage, used these buses.

Railed Train. As indicated previously, most circumstances still do not warrant most types of public transit, especially rail, which, in terms of fixed capital investment, is the most costly to develop and requires the highest ridership demand to justify. Indeed, conventional feasibility analysis indicates that rail transit systems have a difficult time finding adequate volumes to meet even minimum costs for system maintenance and operation.

At the turn of the century, a transit-oriented city with one million inhabitants could assure a viable market for a rail rapid-transit system. Today, city size is not an appropriate criterion upon which to predicate the need for, or success of, rail rapid transit. Rather, based on current experience, conditions under which operation or construction of rapid-transit rail systems appear feasible include: (1) High central-city population density — preferably 14,000 to 20,000 persons per square mile. (2) Strong central-city business district — with CBD employment exceeding 100,000, at least 50 million square feet of CBD floor space, and daily CBD destinations of 300,000 persons per square mile. (3) Each high-density travel corridor serving 70,000 or more persons daily (by all travel modes) with CBD destinations.

Rail systems do offer distinct advantages from an environmental viewpoint. Electric operations eliminate most effluent and many noise considerations. Rubber-wheeled coaches could reduce noise almost entirely, as they do in Paris, Moscow, Montreal, and Mexico City, although these do generate considerable heat during braking, which must be dissipated for passenger comfort.

Rail also offers distinct advantages of effective capacity over all other transit modes. Seating capacity of over 19,000 people per peak hour is possible with rail rapid transit. With buses, by comparison, it has been found on local streets in Chicago, New York, San Francisco, and elsewhere that seating capacity of about 8,000 per hour is the optimum expectation, with approximately 4,000 seats a more characteristic condition.

Fixed Guideway Local Area Systems.

1. Network Cab (fig. 4). Details of the network cab characteristics have been studied and published recently as the only candidate system of new transportation selected for central business district circulation by the *Society of Automotive Engineers, Case Studies of Seven New Systems of Urban Transportation,* 1969.

The network cab is designed to help preserve the CBD, reduce the presence of private cars and parking areas, and interlink effectively with radial routes and line-haul corridors to bring people and goods into the CBD.

The vehicles operate on a fixed guideway. They are small two-to-four-passenger cabs. Power is supplied by electric linear motors in the roadbed. Passengers enter the cab through doors that allow walk-in entry and comfortable seating. Heating, air conditioning, and all environmental control is provided.

The concept permits easy transportation of wheelchairs, perambulators, strollers, the placement of packages, and facilities used by the handicapped.

The vehicles are contained in a channel-shaped guideway and controlled by a remotely located command system that establishes routes, spacing, and distribution of cabs. It is considered likely that such a system could accommodate 100,000 to 1,000,000 daily trips, with a maximum peak-hour capacity of 26,400 passengers. Maximum speed is projected at 30 miles per hour, with average trip speed of about 24 miles per hour.

Each terminal would have a queue of available vehicles with a control unit adjacent to each vehicle. The passenger sets the control unit for his destination, enters the vehicle, and indicates readiness for departure. Cabs may be used privately or shared.

The network cab route could be placed below ground, at grade level, on elevated structures, or within larger enclosures.

2. Caravan Plan (fig. 5). Details of this concept are contained in a professional monograph, *The Caravan Midtown Circulation Plan — A Conceptual Plan for Midtown New York,* prepared by Mary Hommann, assisted by Joseph Jannone, New York, 1969. The caravan is a low-to-the-ground, electric-powered vehicle approximately 2.5 inches above the street with wide running boards. It would be capable of speeds of from 2 to 10 miles per hour, decelerating to 2 miles per hour at designated boarding and debarkation points.

The drive cable would be sunk into street surface and the caravan lane indicated by distinctive pavement marking. The rest of the street surface could be used for a large number of purposes other than transportation.

The caravan car would contain standing space plus two double rows of seats with a capacity of 27, and would not exceed 30 feet in length.

It is estimated that a one-way caravan system loop on paired crosstown streets could carry between 3,800 to 5,700 people from Second to Ninth Avenue in New York in about 13 minutes, even at peak travel periods. The present 49th and 50th Street crosstown bus systems in New York City carries approximately 657 people on a 16-minute schedule, which is rarely maintained. Thus, a capacity over five times current available transit at shorter time is envisioned.

Movement on streets and avenues would be directed one way. Ordinary traffic would be banned on caravan streets. Merchandise delivery

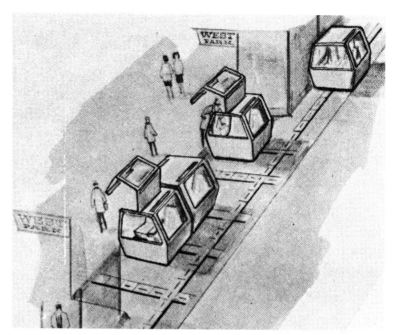

4. Network Cab and Guideway. [General Motors Corp., *Case Studies of Seven New Systems of Urban Transportation*]

and other service requirements would be permitted. At boarding points, approximately 800 feet apart, the caravan would slow down to 2 miles per hour, the maximum speed permitted by the American Elevator Code for electric sidewalks — and by New York City. Between slowdowns the speed would pick up to 10 miles per hour. A potential rider would step onto a broad running board, grasping a vertical pole. The transportation lane required by the caravan is about 11 feet wide, freeing a large proportion of the 30 to 35 percent of most cities now co-opted by street traffic.

Pedestrian Conveyor. The pedestrian conveyor possesses a special attribute of being a surface, not a vehicle. It is thereby a more versatile element for accommodation to urban design. It is commonly a continuous moving platform between points of high-intensity use and is especially appropriate when passengers are burdened with luggage or parcels. Generally, extensive routes have not been developed.

Pedestrian conveyors have been used successfully for specialized purposes since the beginning of the century. However, they are specially applicable for short-distance, high-volume situations. Pedestrian loading onto a moving belt continues to present a safety hazard not overcome by available design.

Evaluation of Impact of Transportation on the Urban Street

Specialized criteria have been developed to determine the impact of a given transportation system on the urban street as a place of communication, interchange, and access to spaces and structures in the transportation influence zone. Such an evaluation has never before been attempted. A three-dimensional reference frame is implied within the evaluation so that access is assumed at any level, and integration of transportation space use with other potential uses is encouraged. Desirable results from the viewpoint of improved street use and flexible urban design of any implemented urban transportation system should include:

1. Use of a large proportion of the street as a public space for nontransportation purposes.

2. Use of a large proportion of the street for pedestrian circulation.

3. Use of the street for direct access to abutting destinations.

4. Experience of the street as a place of acceptable noise levels.

5. Experience of the street as a place with acceptable air quality.

6. Experience of the street as a place of minimum danger to the pedestrian.

7. Ability of street to adapt to changes among its components.

8. Ability of street public space to interpenetrate with abutting private space, including joint development with arcades, mezzanines, and so forth.

5. Caravan Plan, Madison Avenue, New York City. [Mary Hommann, *The Caravan Midtown Circulation Plan* (1968)]

Table 5
Evaluation of Selected Travel Modes vs. Specialized Study Criteria

Mode		Criteria											Total	
		Public Space	Pedestrian Circula-tion	Direct Building Access	Noise	Air	Danger	New Config-urations	Inter-Pene-tration	Multi-Level	Non-Barrier	Transfer	Contrib-utes	Detracts
Private	S[1]	−	−	+	−	−	−	+	−	+	−	−	3	8
Auto	AS[2]	+	+	−	−	−	+	−	−	+	+	+	5	6
	SS[3]	+	+	+	+	−	+	+	+	+	+	−	9	2
Taxi	S	−	−	+	−	−	−	+	−	+	−	+	4	7
	AS	+	+	+	−	−	+	−	−	+	+	+	7	4
	SS	+	+	+	+	−	+	+	+	+	+	+	10	1
Public	S	−	−	+	+	+	+	+	−	+	−	+	7	4
Auto	AS	+	+	+	+	+	+	−	−	+	+	+	9	2
Service	SS	+	+	+	+	+	+	+	+	+	+	+	11	0
Bus	S	−	−	+	−	−	−	+	−	+	−	+	4	7
	AS	+	+	−	−	−	+	−	−	+	+	+	5	6
	SS	+	+	+	+	−	+	+	+	+	+	+	10	1
Railed	S	−	−	+	−	+	−	−	+	+	−	+	5	6
Train	AS	−	−	+	−	+	+	−	−	+	−	+	5	6
(subways, etc.)	SS	+	+	+	−	+	+	+	+	+	+	+	10	1
Network	S	+	−	−	+	+	+	−	+	+	−	+	7	4
Cab	AS	+	+	+	+	+	+	−	−	+	−	+	8	3
	SS	+	+	+	+	+	+	+	+	+	+	+	11	0
Caravan	S	+	−	−	+	+	+	−	+	+	−	+	7	4
	AS	+	+	+	+	+	+	−	−	+	−	+	8	3
	SS	+	+	+	+	+	+	+	+	+	+	+	11	0
Pedestrian	S	+	−	+	+	+	−	−	+	+	−	+	7	4
Conveyor	AS	+	+	+	+	+	+	−	−	+	−	+	8	3
	SS	+	+	+	+	+	+	+	+	+	+	+	11	0

		Total		Per Cent	
		+	−	+	−
Summary	S	44	44	50	50
	AS	55	33	62.5	37.5
	SS	83	5	94.3	5.7

[1] S = principal activity surface
[2] AS = above principal activity surface
[3] SS = below principal activity surface

9. Ability of street to involve multilevel organization.

10. Ability of street to function as activity surface rather than barrier to activities and interchange.

11. Ability of street zone to function for transportion intermodal transfer and directional transfer.

The extent to which each urban transportation system selected for consideration in this analysis contributes to or detracts from the urban street as described by criteria 1 through 11 is evaluated in table 5.

For this evaluation process no absolute quantitative system could be utilized. The criteria themselves are highly subjective. There has been no attempt to weight them, though obviously some are more important than others for various purposes and from various viewpoints. Also, the degree to which each transportation system might contribute or detract from each is a matter of personal judgement. It is determined, nevertheless, that an overall positive (contributes) or negative (detracts) assignment could be made for each mode in relation to the selected criteria. In addition, the influence of elevating above grade or depressing below grade of each mode is explored.

Evaluative Assumptions

A number of fundamental assumptions underlie the evaluative framework developed for this study and influence the evaluation of each mode chosen for analysis. Principal among these are:

1. The transportation is assumed to take place within a conventional street alignment rather than through structures, between midblocks, or any number of other possible configurations that might be postulated and will be considered in later phases of study.

2. Conventional transportation modes such as automobile, bus, taxi, and railed train are assumed to possess characteristics that now prevail in the United States.

3. Pedestrian activity is assumed to take place predominately on grade or street level as it now does and should in most urban places. Other configurations for pedestrian concourse levels exist and can be postulated in later phases of work.

4. Pedestrian activity, though a mode of transportation, is not evaluated as such in this framework. Rather, it is considered highly desirable and enjoyable activity. It is the implied programmed bias of this study that the most desirable mode of transportation in dense urban areas (were it so considered) is walking (assisted by vertical and horizontal lifts) as this is the only means of transportation that could satisfy all evaluative criteria at all physical levels.

5. Feasibility of implementation is recognized as a consideration premature to this phase of inquiry and one fundamental to later stages of work.

Evaluative Conclusions

Based on summary totals indicated in table 5, a number of basic conclusions emerge from this analysis of the degree to which each mode detracts and contributes to the urban street as a three-dimensional place of communication, interchange, exchange, and access to destination.

1. The automobile on grade is the most disruptive of all possibilities — and the one most commonly encountered.

2. The progression from surface to above surface to subsurface in every case leads toward higher goal realization. This indicates that central-city circulation quality depends very strongly on where it is positioned.

3. Desirability of subsurface transportation is indicated in aggregate as over 90 percent. Later work must focus constructively on design analysis and analysis of cost penalty to create and operate such facilities. These findings also suggest an attempt in implementative phase work to devise a strategy to offset, reduce, or reassess these costs.

4. Conventional means of elevating transportation above the principal pedestrian activity surface, in aggregate, improves goal realization only modestly. Improvement is restricted by imposed construction rigidity.

5. Four mode choices — public auto service, network cab, caravan, and pedestrian conveyor — indicate high degrees of goal achievement (approximately 63 percent) even on the surface. Consequently, it is relevant, when specific implementative site, goals, and framework are developed, to submit these to a refined analysis to determine what form of surface system or systems would be most desirable, especially if grade separation becomes infeasible or unwarranted.

Some Postulations Concerning Transportation and the Urban Street

With the dense urban center as the area of primary concern, a number of basic concerns emerge that form a postulative conclusion to this report.

1. It is clear from the preceding analysis that the question of level on which transportation takes place is a fundamental determinant of its urban design quality, or degree to which it satisfies the established evaluative criteria. Yet elevation causes a degree of inflexibility and thus reduces the street's ability to assume new configurations over time; traditional supports for elevated systems imply barriers to the pedestrian activity surface below. In addition, elevated systems within the street right-of-way, no matter how well designed, create environmental disadvantages.

2. A number of considerations should be kept in mind to assure a fully three-dimensional approach to the provision and design of urban

transportation integrated with the total built and space environment, especially if elevated systems are used. A number of possibilities exist. The integration of transportation into and through buildings is a noteworthy possibility. Buildings would become support for the system; public space would be served by lobbies that relate to street and structure if conventional streets were retained; and service to internalized channels of pedestrian activity would be greatly facilitated as shown, for example, in figure 6.

Subsurface transportation, well designed and fundamentally related to the built environment, as indicated in the evaluative analysis, is even more desirable. It is also the most costly means of inserting movement systems into urban areas. As indicated in figure 7, in 1967 rail transit or exclusive busways on the surface cost approximately 1.4 to 1.8 million dollars per lane mile. Elevated structures vary from about 2.0 to 2.4 million dollars. But underground rights-of-way imply a cost of ten times that amount, estimated at 20 to 25 million dollars per lane mile.

Given these facts, it is clear that conventional economic criteria, so long as they outweigh environment and urban design criteria in the presumptive framework of traditional cost-benefit analysis, will obviate the feasibility of subterranean and generally of multilevel urban potentialities. It is obviously necessary to establish a more comprehensive view of cost benefit components. Included among these should be added generally ignored and unquantified components such as social, environmental, design, and impact on long-term performance of urban areas. And, added to these newer and as yet unaccepted criteria, more emphasis should be given to recognized amenity values such as safety, decongestion, increased trip speed, liberation of land consumed by traffic lanes, and parking for productive (tax-generating) purposes and support to long-term stability of urban areas, as well as foundation for intense urban-center development.

Basic requirements of any multilevel urban system will certainly be provision of adequate horizontal and vertical linkages by elevator and escalator among all levels of activity, functions, public, semipublic, and private space. Only through acceptance of this principal can the necessary degree of integration be achieved.

Consequently, it is considered essential to discover, articulate, and quantify a development strategy, in consort with urban economists, legal authorities, and urban designers, that recognizes the fundamental consequences in terms of financial, functional, and aesthetic gains and benefits of subsurface and/or elevated transit systems integrated as a three-dimensional whole with the built environment. Such a methodology would clearly direct attention to new sources of funds from, for instance, building owners who benefit from development or presence of well-designed transit. It would also suggest means of realistically reallocating costs so that agencies responsible for health, welfare, and

6. Future Rapid Transit Systems. [*Westinghouse Engineer* (1970)]

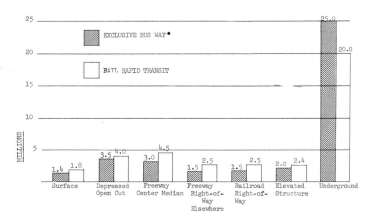

EXCLUSIVE BUS WAY*

RATT RAPID TRANSIT

MILLIONS

25 — 25.0

20 — 20.0

15 —

10 —

5 —

Surface 1.4 1.8
Depressed Open Cut 3.5 4.0
Freeway Center Median 3.0 4.5
Freeway Right-of-Way Elsewhere 1.5 2.5
Railroad Right-of-Way 1.5 2.5
Elevated Structure 2.0 2.4
Underground 25.0 20.0

* Exclusive busways constitute but a fraction of the bus transit systems; remaining route miles share freeways and arterial streets with other transportation.

SOURCE: Estimated from various rapid transit studies. Also see: Preliminary Report on Long-Range Transit Plan for the Minneapolis-St. Paul Area, June 1967, DeLeuw Cather and Company.

7. Approximate Capital Costs per Mile by Type of Construction (excluding land costs; 1967-68 price levels). [Estimated from various rapid transit studies]

safety would be able to share in the provision of such systems.

It is also recognized that funds, which now are collected based on assessment and tax of real estate and rent rolls in dense areas, could be recycled through accounting reform within government to substantially enhance the development of comprehensive movement systems in these areas. In addition, portions of the Highway Trust Fund could be allocated to urban-transit expenditures. In short, it is clear that pleasant, well-conceived urban centers served by proper and appropriate transit should and could become a recognized and manageable national priority. Through it housing, social needs, and transportation problems, which plague the United States and threaten to destroy its streets, could be effectively countered. Once such a goal is identified and recognized, the benefits of urban transit will be dramatically reassessed.

3. Transportation, and especially transit as an effective tool of urban design, should be ignored no longer. Considerable funds, which could be made available for transit design, would allow the simultaneous interlinkage of movement and destination. They present the possibility of establishing zones of intense activity where the complementary demands of people and spaces are met simultaneously.

Spatial zoning or urban areas into uniform districts of commercial, residential, and industrial precincts was popular during the industrial revolution and used in large measure to protect people from the hazards of commercial areas and the foulness of industrial districts. Three-quarters of the way through the twentieth century it is recognized that untenable land waste, unnecessary urban blandness, and undesirable transportation problems result from such a settlement pattern. We must respond with zoning-law changes and better urban design. We must support changes in business patterns and technology by rearranging urban areas to make them varied, vital, and desirable. To do this there must be properly planned transit that relates and interconnects zones and levels of employment commercial residential and recreation activity so that the city provides a unique locale for the continued change and interchange that takes place on the urban street.

4. Potential technological advances of the future are often presented as a reason to withold advanced transportation planning or new concepts in transportation organization. This is flawed and obstructionist reasoning. No development in the costly and complex areas of transportation can take place rapidly. No government will abandon its highway or transit system overnight to provide radically different systems of hardware, rights-of-way, operating controls, and financial bases. Rather, existing facilities can only gradually be retired or recycled. Indeed, the gradual implementation of new developments in transportation and other so-called public services is evident through the history of most countries. Consequently, it is germane to introduce a conceptual framework for transit planning that accounts for this reality and takes

advantage of it. And for this reason, long-term planning that recognizes the potential of staged development are redevelopment is necessary. At the same time, recognition of the potentialities inherent in the use of relatively permanent transportation corridors that service specified zones makes possible an evolutionary program. Such an approach utilizes a basic natural tendency. The permanence of major transportation corridors is one of the striking features of the history of cities.

5. The fact that it would seem logical and perhaps even economical, if analyzed in the terms of comprehensive feasibility suggested, to accommodate travel in urban areas predominately by public transit is no indication that this actually could take place in the future without strenuous, imaginative, and effective implementative devices. The personal mobility and freedom provided by the motor vehicle has become a way of life in the United States, and the public has grown to expect it. Arbitrary denial of this mobility, no matter how well intentioned, or the quality of provided substitutes, can stunt the growth of an area, redirect the pattern of growth, and even cause growth to take place elsewhere. Therefore, to achieve desirable characteristics of urban streets in viable urban areas in certain parts of the country, freedom of travel choice must not so much be dissolved but, rather, facilities and networks must be provided that will render choices freely made in favor of appropriate transit.

1. These criteria were initially developed by Wilbur Smith and Associates for a 1969–1970 study of innovations in center-city transportation technology.

2. Operating speeds for passenger belts is currently limited by present building codes to 1.0–1.5 miles per house.

3. Capacity is computed as follows:
Total Capacity
= (Total passengers per unit)
× (Units per hour passing a given point)
Seated Capacity
= (Seated passengers per unit)
× (Units per hour passing a given point)

Street as Locus of Communication
and Signification

New York City, Broadway at Cortland Street (c. 1883). [A.T. & T. Co. Photo Center, no. 1338]

The Street as a Communications Artifact

Thomas V. Czarnowski

In many areas of inquiry — behavioral psychology, linguistics, biology, or urban planning, for example — the term *communications* has evoked a certain common interest, touching on what is seen to be a fruitful way of describing the shared links between various human phenomena and promising, in its infancy, to develop eventually into a general theory with the power to synthesize a broad spectrum of knowledge about man the organism and his environment, both natural and man-made. Such promise is nevertheless tempered by hitherto unreconciled, and perhaps unreconcilable, modes of description emanating from each of these fields of inquiry, by the pitfall of using one set of phenomena as an analogue for another, and by the varying success of scientifically describing communication processes, due on the one hand to the uncharted nature of the territory and on the other to the probably innate indeterminancy of certain (largely social) human phenomena.[1]

It is in this context that in the past decade there have been several attempts at describing the city as an aggregate of open and sheltered spaces, of places of public gathering and passage that, by virtue of their multiplicity of use and their proximity, can be considered effective devices for sustaining maximum intensity and choice of communication among members of society.

In this view a society, or culture, is held to be "people in communication," and the great characteristic of the city — and one explanation for its phenomenal growth — is its unique capability to serve as a nodal point for regional communications and, internally, to provide physically for an easily accessible web of contacts and exchanges.[2]

At a regional scale this is a traditional view, and it has been frequently exercised in explaining the strategic location of towns primarily devoted to defense, the dissemination or exploitation of agricultural or mineral wealth, or the transshipment of manufactured goods, by reference to the position of such towns astride or at the edge of regional routes of communication. At a smaller scale, the scale of a town, this viewpoint has been invoked in describing the position of a palace, town hall, marketplace, or of commercial or manufacturing sectors whose position with respect to internal routes of communication are vital to or symbolic of their existence.[3]

Every town, by the geographical disposition of the physical elements that comprise it, can thus reveal the rough outline of a specific pattern of association, of intercommunication. This outline is usually clear enough for a visitor to comprehend a town new to his experience or for an archeologist to partially reconstruct the web of associations that once animated a dead town. But for a physical planner seeking to project future states on the basis of drawings and figures, such an outline is fragmentary, well developed in certain areas, such as highway design, but not in others, such as the communication needs of young children or of the old. On a critical issue, the interrelationships between physical patterns and man's social interactions, the outline is generally obscure, except in precise and very specific examples.[4]

It is against this landscape of fragmentary understanding that this article is placed. It focuses on the communicational role of the street and, more particularly, on that of the urban street. It is the urban street that from the first origins of settlements has acted as principal place of public contact and public passage, a place of exchange of ideas, goods, and services, a place of play and fight, of carnival and funeral, of protest and celebration. Its place in the web of associations that have sustained human society is therefore paramount. Yet today the urban street has too often become specialized, often largely a track for traffic; diffuse, an alternating sequence of monumentally isolated buildings and parking lots; and neglected, a no-man's-land of litter and crime. Today communication among members of society can take place in locations and by means remote from the street. Yet the street persists in our plans, in our imagination, and in our cities. Why? We contend that the urban street provides physically, probably uniquely, for a scale and range of communications vital to the life of society. It is the purpose of this article to trace very generally a background of concepts.

The web of communications that sustains and is created by urban life eludes a single method of categorization. Various writers have used the word *communication* in different senses when discussing the mass media, the structure of linguistic communication, or the development of modes of transport.[5] In this study I intend, for working purposes, to envelop with the single word *communication* every kind of dissemination or exchange, whether it be of persons, goods, messages, or energy, and whether it be transcribed, transported, or transmitted. My purpose is to delimit, within this array, those categories of communication for which the street serves as a physical locus. I will do this by discussing, in turn, categories of communication, the physical apparatus required to sustain certain of these modes of communication, and the place of the street in this array of physical artifacts that sustain communication.

Categories of Communication

The modes of communication that support social man vary broadly in type and in the manner in which they have been described. For convenience they will be traced at four levels of generalization. Into the first category can be put those modes of communication that, having biologically ancient roots, require personal participation but require no supporting physical artifact: the gestures, color, and temperature changes and distance-regulating functions that act as a primitive language; spoken language itself, generally accompanied by these protolinguistic signs; and terrestrial man's power of locomotion, enabling his displacement in space. At this level one finds the first expansions of man's range of nonwritten communication over distance and time: the functions of emissary and runner, of storyteller and instructor.[6]

Into a second category of communication modes can be placed the so-called extensions of man's linguistic and locomotive capabilities. Written language, relying in an earlier historical phase on physical transcription, on such artifacts as edicts, signs, letters, and accounts, has long depended for its dissemination either on being bodily transported or on being spatially fixed and strategically situated, relying on the mobility of the reader for exposure. The revolution in techniques of transcribing and disseminating language has come through familiarity: on the one hand the extension of transcription techniques by tape, film, recording, or computer memory, and on the other hand the magnification of the power of dissemination both by revolution in the methods of bodily transporting transcriptions and by the invention of the radio, television, telex, videophone, and laser.[7]

The extensions to man's locomotive power, which comprise transportation, have undergone generally familiar historical transformations and will not be enumerated, except to signal the profound effect upon urban structures by the nineteenth-century development of systems of public transport and by the twentieth-century development of systems of private transport.[8]

In a third category are placed the movement and exchange of goods. In three subcategories can be traced, first, the networks of supply and distribution of services, gas, electricity, heat, water; second, the transport of agricultural and manufactured goods whose supply sustains the life processes of the city and whose exchange constitutes the traditional market function; and third, by extension of the concept of goods and by borrowing from the transcription category the service industries, networks of supply and exchange of information and data.

Lastly, in a fourth category are assembled the by-products of the first three, generally thrown aside and therefore termed waste products, a category that some years ago would have merited little attention but that today can be seen to form a substantial and costly residue of the web of communications: discarded paper, garbage, sewage, lost energy, exhaust, and so on.

The categories of communication have been presented here in primary fashion, that is to say, with no reference to the myriad interconnections of the categories and subcategories that animate this still picture. Although no attempt will be made to map them, they make up the reality of the infinite and vital web of urban communications, and this caution ought to be retained in the consideration of artifact.

The Physical Apparatus That Sustains Communication

The historical development of the web of communications has left in its path a trail of physical constructions, of artifacts. In all its dimensions, this array of artifacts is the physical apparatus that is created by and that sustains the web of communications, and the term *communications artifact* is here used to indicate this functional interrelationship.

Physically the city could be seen as a vast conglomerate of communications artifacts: of places of passage — urban freeways, large and small streets, corridors, elevators, and stairs; subsurface pipes, cables, mains, subways, or sewers; of collection and distribution nodes — markets, radio stations, newsstands, switchboards, lobbies, and stations; of formal meeting places — auditoriums and stadiums; of informal meeting places — street corners and squares; of storage areas — warehouses, parking lots, and reservoirs. This list could be made extremely long and is made very complex by the many overlays and gradations of form and use that characterize the city. Thus on the one hand there are artifacts requiring great expenditure of space and materials — railway stations or elevator banks — while on the other hand there are merely designated operational areas, marked by signs or symbols — taxi ranks, bus lanes, or pedestrian crossings. The street itself is in its origins a designated surface, but in the course of its evolution it becomes a heavily built artifact not only on its surface but also in its subsurface and along its edges. At one end of the spectrum there are artifacts so specialized that they are capable of supporting a very narrow range of communication — traffic lights, for example. At the other extreme are found unspecialized artifacts, paramount among these the street — a classic example of the overlaying of functions: in its dual nature both a place of passage (path) and a place of gathering (mode), although it frequently performs the tertiary task of storage (parking, for example).

The Street As a Communications Artifact

The first observation that should be made is that these modes of communication and their supportive apparatus constitute the commonly shared communicational matrix of a society. Their role is therefore preeminently public. The particular role of the urban street is thus to fulfill, at a certain scale, the need for a place common to all other places, guaranteeing access of persons and machines, of goods, light, and air to those places. It is this scale of functioning, traditionally bounded by road scale and building scale, that is the unique domain of the communications artifact *street*.

But, as in the case of all other communications artifacts, the public life of the street can be a fragile one. The street is imparted a sense of ownership by the users of that street and can consequently be felt to be transgressed upon by an outsider. However, it is also concurrently felt to be not personal but common property and in a spirit of anonymity becomes a place for crime and garbage. The street is a generous recipient of historical events, but it suffers easily from congestion. And, to a military mind, just as, at a regional scale, control of a pass or of a river can mean control of a trerritory so, at an urban scale, control of a street can mean control of a portion of a city.

Thus, central to the functioning of this commonly held communicational matrix is its accessibility. In order to ensure this function, elaborate protective devices have evolved as guarantees of use to all. These have changed with social conditions and have become increasingly various with the development of mechanical and electrical extensions to the natural range of communication of biological man. These protective mechanisms can be traced at three levels of definition; they cut across the enumerated categories of communication.

At the most subconscious and biologically ancient level are the patterns in which man disposes himself in space so as to indicate a staked-out territory or varying degrees of social aloofness or intimacy. They are, broadly speaking, of two types: those of territoriality, by which man can assert possession of a piece of ground, a park bench, or a cafeteria table, and those of personal space, which describe the spatial envelope surrounding man, indicating strangers' or intimates' distance and regulating, for example, the average spacing of a crowd at a bus stop or along a sidewalk. In such ways, the neutral, public spaces of the street are made and remade into fluxing patterns of space held to be personal. A resident's street, a gang's turf, a stroller's sidewalk, and a sheltering doorway are thus temporarily imprinted with a sense of possession by the user and, conversely, frequently regarded as relatively anonymous and of no personal consequence to an outsider, transient, or visitor. Transgression into such personalized spaces is met with retreat, resistance, or, occasionally, force. The personal ''my street'' and the communal ''main street'' are extensions of this sense of identification.[9]

When such patterns of use have crystallized sufficiently to enter into a realm of social convention, they are made conscious and are deliberately expressed as social taboo, codes of conduct, or informal rule systems. Erving Goffman refers to the ''many rulings that restrict the right to be present in open, unwalled public places: in nineteenth-century London, for example, the exclusion of certain categories from some parks, and the informal exclusion of common people from riding promenades such as Rotten Row; in Islamic cities built on a *quartier* basis, the restriction of persons to their own neighborhood after dark . . .''[10] Tacitly understood queuing and pedestrian behavior, for example, although springing from the more ancient mechanisms of mutual adjustment, belong to this category.

These patterns, at an even greater degree of codification, form a third category: rules of trespass, laws regulating traffic, or zoning regulations restricting an individual's freedom to construct adjacent to the street. Having their counterpart in regulations controlling the use of the airwaves, the sea lanes, and the public services, these regulations have been formed by the gradual evolution that the legal mechanisms of contestation and precedent have provided. Perhaps the most lucid example of the principles at question here has been the litigation consequent to the erection of the elevated railways in New York in the 1880s, during which it was established that the air, light, and right of access that the street provides can be considered the property of abutting owners, even if no title were held to the street.[11]

The boundaries of the public life of the street are marked with signs and symbols — proclaiming ''keep off'' and ''no trespassing,'' declaring ownership of land (and the right to refuse entrance) in the shape of bollards, chains, doormen, plaques. These belong to the world of communications artifacts.

It is precisely because of the circumstances attendant to its scale of operation that the street, of all the communications artifacts, is the most long-lived. Although it may make sense to speak of the relative obsolescence of certain communications artifacts, such as the cart or the beacon, it is difficult to speak of the obsolescence of the street. Bound gradually on either side by private property deeds, receiving on its surface or in its subsurface the networks of transportation and transmission artifacts, the street as a place is endowed with a permanence that survives the physical evolution of the city, and even of its destruction.[12] But in spite of, and perhaps because of, its relative longevity, the street is in a process of continual transformation.

In a broad view, it is clear that the general patterns of communication that sustain human organization extend to urban artifacts well beyond the immediate context of the street. The relative role of the street as a location for certain of these patterns of communication has varied, and indeed the general historical trend has been for the street to play a diminishing role relative to the many artifacts that serve these patterns. This is not to say that the street is less used — street congestion is a characteristic of all of urban history — but rather that the street is used for less.

Accompanying the great growth of the newly industrialized western city came the technological developments that both caused and were created to serve this growth: the streetcars, elevated railways, and subways; applications of the railroad to the supposed relief of street congestion; the automobile; the telephone, telegraph, and later radio and television networks, radically new forms that enabled communication to be removed from the street. Attending these developments at every stage, one finds an ambivalent attitude toward the street: visions of trafficless streets by pedestrians, of pedestrianless streets by drivers; theories holding the street to be the breeding ground of social evils, attitudes investing the street with noble civic purpose.

By briefly considering the functions of movement (in the case of the street, of people, ideas, goods) and access (to goals either in or abutting the street), one can trace three aspects of the changed role of the street.

First, it is clear that, for certain ranges of communication, these functions can be and have been satisfied by other systems: the postal, telephone, or subway systems, for example. Whereas the extensions of man's linguistic powers (transcription and transmission) now function chiefly without demanding his presence in the artifact street, the extensions of his locomotive power (transportation) have, in urban contexts, taken place chiefly by superimposing themselves on the street. Thus, while the street is still a necessary place of movement from one part of the city to another, it is possible to converse with a neighbor, to receive news from down the street or from far away, to be entertained, or, if predictions are correct, to be able to shop without leaving one's home. This is not to say that those artifacts created to support the linguistic extensions bypass the street in the same manner as the communications themselves do. On the contrary, the street has served as a receptacle of many of these supporting artifacts: the telephone and telegraph cables, the transportation of mail, newspapers, or magazines. In an analogous manner, although it is no longer necessary to go into the street to gather water, the pipes that carry the water pass almost necessarily through the subsoil of the public street. So that whereas it has become possible to communicate on a linguistic level over great distances with no reference to a street or street pattern, the communications artifacts that support this capability, as well as those that extend man's range of mobility, are largely bound to the street or to its subsurface.

Second, it can be seen that a reliance on a mechanically aided mode of communication, such as the automobile, greatly expands the range of the movement function, greatly distends the spatial scale of the goal function, and may, when it shares the same channel with small-scale modes of movement and access such as pedestrian movement, generate environmental incompatibilities.

Third, depending on the scale, type, and distribution of varying modes of movement and access, alternate configurations of street have developed, resulting in regional patterns in which one can recognize a particular configuration to be a strip, a suburban tract, and so on.

The particulars of the impacts of modes of transport upon the street, especially that of the automobile, which in the twentieth century was to do for private transportation what the railroad in the nineteenth century did for public transportation, are best treated elsewhere. What one should recall is the obvious trend toward an independence of personal movement. This trend has been supported by a growing network of personalizable communication, the telephone, the growth of the mass media, indeed of the mass industrial product and of its attendant means of distribution[13] — which has allowed a widely dispersed population to exist with a lessened reference to the older urban centers and greater reference to a polynuclear structure of local nodes of meeting and exchange. As a result of these changes, the communicational functions of the street have been transformed, both in the old urban centers and in the new suburban areas that, almost by definition, have low density and scattered communicational intensity.[14]

These three events, the replacement of the street as a system of access and movement by other channels of communication, the alteration of the street by the superimposition of modes of communication requiring varying scales of operation, and the development of configurations of streets that rely on mechanized movement and form greatly distended regional patterns, constitute a metamorphosis and a narrowing of the role of the street as a locus for communication.

Beyond the street that binds buildings together lie the buildings themselves, grown in size to become complexes epitomized by the office block and the shopping center and dependent for their support on an enlarged net of communications artifacts that depend on the street for their physical accommodation but require little or no personal involvement with the street. Often the communicational operations of such a building complex are of sufficient scale to create within its body streetlike organizations of space and use that recapture, in isolated and usually enclosed situations, the scale and density of traditional streets.[15]

The second dimension of such complexes is their spacing along the street, which, even in extremely dense urban situations, is enlarged by virtue of their enlarged dimensions, by a desire for open space, and often by virtue of the appendages of parking storage. The distended patterns of urban fringes are familiar examples. But often the cores of the cities are made over to the new dimensions, so that the number of streets that can sustain a pedestrian scale of communication are few, and the prevalent pattern is of large building complexes, spaced at automobile scale, with internal streetlike distribution systems.[16]

Such an urban configuration, it could be argued, is the logical historical outcome of the extensions to man's communicational, capabilities. Such a configuration is tantamount to a series of small communities in close geographic proximity, both linked to and severed from each other by artifacts of personal mobility (communication of a limited kind): the highway and the strip.

It is certainly clear that such configurations demand inordinate amounts of land and disproportionate infrastructural investments. It may be too early to tell whether they can form lasting communities, although the verdict may well be negative, for the components — the residential or office complexes, the shopping or amusement centers, the corporate or manufacturing headquarters — if taken singly are not inclusive enough of man's physical or experiential needs and if taken as a whole are fragmented into physical and experiential discontinuities, with attendant problems of disorientation and anonymity.

The notion of environmental areas is not necessarily equivalent to and does not automatically produce neighborhoods. Wrongly sized and placed cellular divisions can create physical limits that do not correspond to the boundaries of a person's pattern of friendship or work and have, unfortunately, served to create ghettos (on both sides of the tracks). Such urban configurations, in which streets tend to become vestigial subjects of inwardly orienting residential or commercial organizations, lack the fine gradations and continuity of experience and social contact that a continuum of streets can bring as mediator between man and man, man and machine, building and building, private realm and public space.

Yet man is adaptable; over a period of years, the same physical configurations of a street or of a pattern of streets can be used and interpreted differently and can therefore play variable communicational roles, depending on the age, economic, or social composition of the residents or habitual users. Melvin M. and Carolyn C. Webber, in tracing the contrast between commonly held notions of space, territoriality, and distance among members of an elite and of a working class, clearly observe the problem:

> The long-term historical changes in industrial society have been toward an ever-increasing scale of the society, reflecting increasingly complex networks of interdependence, rising social mobility, lower transportation and communication costs, and, with it all, ever-increasing mileage distances of social interaction. Although in the United States public education and the mass media have exerted an important leveling effect, these changes have by no means touched all segments of the heterogeneous population. We find it sobering to be reminded that very large numbers of central-city and some suburban residents follow styles of life and adhere to systems of values that are in many respects unchanged from those that were brought over from the European peasant villages several generations ago. At the same time that social organization of cosmopolite groups is being largely freed from the restraints of territorial place, the "urban villagers" live out their lives in territorially bounded and territorially perceived societies.[17]

Thus the transformations of the street also take place at a fourth level — the experiential. In man's use of the street, in his memory of it, and in his anticipation of future events, the street is in a continual process of constitution and reconstitution. This occurs at a scale of yearly events, occupations, and seasonal change; at a scale of daily and nocturnal cycles of movement, noise, light, or unexpected event; and on a very immediate experiential scale, the scale of temporary identification with the street as one moves through it, the small and countless interchanges with strangers or acquaintances, the opposite experiences of leisure or haste. Such an experiential knowledge of the street is formed as the result of long exposure to the experiences of the street, but in a reciprocal relationship it also structures one's outlook toward the street, toward what one considers the role of the street to be. Urban renewal that fails to take this into account can concurrently shatter not only buildings and street patterns but entire structures of memory and expectation.

Finally, the street is in a continual state of construction and reconstruction in a purely physical and spatial sense. To this category one must give a communicational role analogous to that of the experiential structuring and restructuring. The entire assembly of communications artifacts — buildings; architectural styles; signs, banners, and symbols; the spaces, surfaces, and objects of the street in thier continual state of modification and remodification by successive users — acts as a great record of the activities of man, to be read, interpreted, and given meaning. By the gross character of the physical makeup of the street, one can read the rough outlines of the history and pattern of association of a city; by the more subtle modification of these forms and by their overlap in space can be read a finer grain of activity. Just as at an experiential level one's patterns of experience condition one's outlook and therefore predispose one toward future experience, so too do the physical forms of the street encourage or block patterns of use, of cognition and of re-cognition by which forms gain meaning. In this last sense the street is in its physical essence a communications artifact.

Notes

1. On pitfalls, see p. 2, Cherry (ref. 6); on indeterminancy, see Popper (ref. 21) and introductory material in refs. 15, 16, 22, 27.

2. Refs. 1, 8, 9, 18, 19, 31. See also introductory concepts in refs. 6, 15, 16, 27.

3. For an excellent regional example, see ref. 14, ch. 3: "The Continent's Economic Hinge."

4. On interrelationships between man and his physical surroundings, see refs. 12, 15, 16, 22, 26, 27.

5. Refs. 5, 6, 9, 24.

6. Refs. 15, 16, 22, 26, 27.

7. Refs. 10, 24, 25.

8. Refs. 5, 17, 23, 29.

9. Refs. 15, 16, 27.

10. Ref. 12, p. 10.

11. Refs. 3, 7, 28.

12. Postwar Frankfurt, for example, was rebuilt on its medieval street pattern through the combined pressures of surviving infrastructural elements and property deeds.

13. In ref. 20 Park contends that the growth of the department store was a function of the Sunday newspaper, of its advertising capacity, and of the housewife (shopper) as reader. The department store represents an early example of the internalization of functions (shops) that had previously given directly onto the street.

14. Refs. 10, 20, 5, 17, 24.

15. Ref. 13

16. The all-weather shopping centers outside Wayne, N.J., and Fairfax, Va.; the dream of the Ville Radieuse and its many public housing stepchildren; Los Angeles, Las Vegas, and North American cities from Kansas City to Toronto.

17. Ref. 30, p. 53.

References

1. Alexander, Christopher. "The City as a Mechanism for Sustaining Human Contact," in *Environment for Man*, Ewald, ed., 1967.

2. ———. "The City is Not a Tree," *Design*, no. 206, pp. 46–55.

3. Booth, Henry J. *A Treatise on the Law of Street Railways*. 1892.

4. Buchanan, Colin. *Traffic in Towns*. London: HM Stationery Office, 1963.

5. Campredon, Eugene. *Role Economique et Sociale des Voies de Communication*. Paris: Ch. Dunod, 1899.

6. Cherry, Colin. *On Human Communication*. Cambridge, Mass.: The MIT Press, 1957, 1966.

7. Demarest, Theodore F. C. *The Rise and Growth of Elevated Railway Law*. New York: Baker, Voorhis and Co., 1894.

8. Deutsch, Karl W. "On Social Communication and the Metropolis," in: Lloyd Rodwin, ed., *The Future Metropolis.*, London: Constable and Co., 1962.

9. *Ekistics*, 30, no. 179 (October 1970).

10. Ergmann, Raoul. "l'Influence des Moyens d'Information dans l'Economie Contemporaine," *Les Cours de Droit*. Paris, 1965.

11. Fleisher, Aaron. "The Influence of Technology on Urban Forms," in: Rodwin, ed., *Future Metropolis*.

12. Goffman, Erving. *Behavior in Public Places*. London: Macmillan, 1963.

13. Gottman, Jean. "Why the Skyscraper?," in: H. W. Eldredge, ed., *Taming Megalopolis*, vol. 1. Garden City, N.Y.: Doubleday, 1967.

14. ———. *Megalopolis*. Cambridge, Mass.: The MIT Press, 1961.

15. Hall, Edward T. *The Silent Language*. Greenwich, Conn.: Fawcett, 1959.

16. ———. *The Hidden Dimension*. Garden City, N.Y.: Doubleday, 1969.

17. Levasseur, Emile. "Des Changements Survenus au XIX Siecle dans les Conditions du Commerce par suite du Progres des Voies et Moyens de Communication," *Congres Internationale de Geographie Economique et Commerciale*. Paris, 1900.

18. Meier, Richard. *A Communications Theory of Urban Growth*. Cambridge, Mass.: The MIT Press, 1962.

19. ———. "The Metropolis as a Transactions Maximizing Device," *Daedalus*, 97 (February 1968).

20. Park, Robert E. "The Natural History of the Newspaper" (in Schramm, ref. 24).

21. Popper, Karl Raimund. "Of Clouds and Clocks." St. Louis: Washington University Press, 1965.

22. Proshansky, Harold, William H. Ittelson, and Leanne G. Rivlin. *Environmental Psychology: Man and His Physical Setting*. New York: Holt, Rinehart and Winston, 1970.

23. Ruhlmann, Henri. "Les Chemins de Fer Urbains," *Encyclopedie Industrielle et Commerciale*. Paris: Librarie de l'Enseignement Technique, 1936.

24. Schramm, Wilbur, ed. *Mass Communications*. Urbana University of Illinois Press, 1960.

25. ———. *The Process and Effects of Mass Communications*. Urbana: University of Illinois Press, 1961.

26. Searles, Harold F. *The Nonhuman Environment in Normal Development and Schizophrenia*. New York: International Universities Press, 1960.

27. Sommer, Robert. *Personal Space*. Englewood Cliffs, N.J.: Prentice-Hall, 1969.

28. Walker, James B. *Fifty Years of Rapid Transit*. New York: The Law Printing Co., 1918.

29. Warner, Samuel B. *Streetcar Suburbs*. Cambridge, Mass.: The MIT Press, 1962.

30. Webber, Melvin M. and Carolyn C. "Culture, Territoriality, and the Elastic Mile," in: Gottman, *Taming Megalopolis*.

31. Wingo, Loudon. *Cities and Space*. Baltimore: Johns Hopkins University Press, 1963.

Toward a Theory of Production of Sense in the Built Environment

Diana Agrest

What then does this catchword "interlocking" express? It merely expresses the most striking feature of the process going before our eyes. It shows that the observer counts the separate trees, but cannot see the wood. It slavishly copies the superficial, the fortuitious, the chaotic. It reveals the observer as one who is overwhelmed by the mass of raw material and is utterly incapable of appreciating its meaning and importance. Ownership of shares, the relations between owners of private property "interlock in a haphazard way." But underlying this interlocking, its very base, is the changing social relations of production. V. I. Lenin, "Imperialism, The Highest Stage of Capitalism"

Si j'avais à imaginer un nouveau Robinson, je ne le placerais pas dans une île désèrete mais dans une ville de 12 millions d'habitants dont il ne saurait déchiffrer ni la parole ni l'écriture: ce serait là, je crois, la forme moderne du mythe. Roland Barthes

On the Theoretical Practice

There are many ways in which one could approach the street as a subject of study. In this approach, the street as a public place, an urban configuration, brings forth particular issues concerning the social production of sense. In this article I intend to make some remarks on the production of sense in the built environment.

Each analytical work, irrespective of its content, implies a theoretical approach, which in turn is dependent on a particular representation of the world. On few occasions is this ideological set made explicit. Thus the real implication of the approach, or its essential differences from other approaches, is usually not made clear.

To render a theoretical instrumentality explicit, from the conception of a theory to its methodological procedures, is of major importance in analytical work, particularly at the juncture when this analysis enters the public realm, in order to avoid the ideological effects of such discourse. It is especially important now, when theory in architecture is practically nonexistent and when, paradoxically, there is an enormous amount of analysis which is often of great technical virtuosity but without clear indication of its origin, its ultimate orientation, its role in relation to theory. This article deals with the possibility of developing a theory of the built environment as social production of sense and not with the analysis of a particular case drawn from an already constituted theory, since such a theory has not yet been developed.

The explanation of the structure of this article is itself an intrinsic and theoretically important part of the article.

One must first broach the general problems that arise when undertak-

ing a theoretical work, namely, those concerning the conception of knowledge, a conception that is ultimately inseparable from the functioning of society.

An important aspect of the conception of knowledge underlying the majority of theories and one that is rarely made explicit is that of the relation of reality versus thought. It is necessary to consider this duality briefly in order to reveal the initial philosophical epistemological considerations that underlie the development of a theory.

To do this I recall Louis Althusser's analysis of the different conceptions of knowledge,[1] since his general formulation may be applied to environmental theories and particularly to those based on an empiricist conception of knowledge.[2] In the conception of knowledge that Althusser terms empiricist, science is seen as a process that develops between subject and object (out there) and that is based on the operation of abstraction. "To know is to abstract from the real object its essence the possession of which by the subject is then called knowledge." According to Althusser, for the operation of abstraction to be accomplished, the real object must be considered as something that "is made of two real essences, the pure essence and the impure essence, the gold and the dross, or, if you like (Hegelian terms), the essential and the inessential."[3]

In this conception the object of knowledge would be the part of the real object that is called pure essence; the process of knowledge would have as its function the distinction and separation of the two parts composing the real object (the essential and the inessential) and the elimination of the real inessential, leaving the subject in front of the essential part of the real object, which alone assures access to the knowledge of it. In this view, knowledge would be present completely, as a whole (object and process) in the real object. The object of knowledge is present in the real object as the part that Althusser calls "the pure essence." The process of knowledge would also be present in the real object as the difference between its two parts, one of which, the inessential, hides and envelops the essential— *"This investment of knowledge, conceived as a real part of the real object, in the real structure of the real object, is what constitutes the specific problematic of the empiricist conception of knowledge."*[4]

This conception of knowledge recognizes in some way that the object of knowledge is not identical to the real object, is only part of the real. However, while this difference is recognized, the object of knowledge remains obscure inasmuch as it is seen as a distinction between two parts of the same object. In this way the difference between two different objects, between the real object that exists outside the subject and the object of knowledge, is hidden and confused. "This difference should not only be established concerning the object but also between the different processes which should be considered as processes of production, namely, the transformation of a given primary matter (raw material) into a given product by means of the application of given means of production."[5]

As Althusser says: "While the production process of a given real object, a given real-concrete totality (e.g., a given historical nation) takes place entirely in the real and is carried out according to the real order of *real* genesis . . ., the production process of the object of knowledge takes place entirely in knowledge and is carried out according to *a different order,* in which the thought categories which 'reproduce' the real categories do *not* occupy the same place as they do in the order of real historical genesis, but quite different places assigned them by their function in the production process of the object of knowledge."[6]

This implies that knowledge is not a process that is developed between a subject and an object (the world) but is the "definite system of conditions of theoretical practice [which] assigns any given thinking subject [individual] its place and function in the production of knowledge."[7] This production of knowledge can be considered a theoretical practice in that it puts into operation theoretical means of production — a theory and a method — that are applied to a given raw material in order to produce concepts within given historical — theoretical, ideological, economic — relations.

Empiricism is based on an operation of reflection, on building a model of the real. In empiricism, reality and knowledge appear as equal and in this way the production of knowledge remains hidden. This approach implies an acceptance of a reality as it is given and it does not postulate any kind of questioning. It is of interest to recall some examples from the history of science such as those Babylonic instruments for navigation that reflected the position of the stars but did not explain their movements, nor the laws by which they moved, since (at that date) such concepts remained undeveloped. Then there is the example of Copernicus and Galileo in their fight to gain acceptance for concepts contrary to visual evidence; ideas that denied the whole ideology of the church. How was it possible that the earth was not the center of the universe and that it was not the sun that moved around it if that is what they saw? How was it possible that celestial bodies (such as the moon) could be matter? Giordano Bruno was burned by the church. Galileo was imprisoned. The common sense argument used at the time evoked a disjunction between what was seen and a logic of explanation that was not solely dependent on visual evidence.[8]

It should be remembered that theory "far from reflecting the immediate data of everyday experience and practice can only be constituted through challenging such data, to the extent that its results, once achieved, appear to contradict the experimental evidence of everyday practice rather than reflect it."[9]

An intrinsic characteristic of the ideology of architecture and urban planning is the reflection, rather than the challenge, of reality. Architectural theory should arise from a dialectical relationship to architectural ideology, yet should maintain a degree of radical opposition.

At the present time, architectural theory needs to be developed. It is necessary to acknowledge the critical nature of the two forms of raw material to be analyzed — the given general ideology and the environment itself. The means for theoretical production — concepts drawn from historical dialectical materialism and semiotics — and the different stages of analytical procedures must also be studied in the formulation of theory. The critical analysis of the ideological texts, revealing the nature of the ideological obstacle, thus allows for the development of theoretical models with which the built environment may be considered, in relation to culture, as a significant system.[10]

These models may be applied to the analysis of a second type of raw material — the street. For my purposes, the street is considered as a complex semiotic text, entering the theoretical process in order to produce concrete concepts.[11] It is clear that the issue is neither the description of the concrete nor the knowledge to be abstracted from a real street. Rather the complex process of production of the object of knowledge — the built environment as a production of significance — must provide the basis for further study.

Criticism of the Communications Ideology:
Communication/Signification

A work that deals with signification in the environment is linked inexorably to certain practices within the environment (architecture, urban design, urban planning) and thereby necessitates the use of some of the notions that appear in those practices. For this reason, I will deal initially with texts that approach the urban problem through one of the more advanced tendencies in architectural and urban ideology today: namely, through communication. Texts from planning and not from architecture were selected since the theme to be dealt with, the street, has to do with urban configuration as it affects those instances we call public places. The texts chosen for examination are those by Richard Meier and Melvin Webber.[12] Different kinds of criteria guided this choice. The first was that of generality. These texts are general enough to include almost every theoretical problem. Second, these texts have had a considerable influence over the practice of design. They constitute the point of departure for a new form of architectural ideology. As such their influence may be seen on designers as varied in their approach as Cedric Price and Robert Venturi. Furthermore, they are related to the dominant ideology of the present stage in the development of the capitalist mode of production.

These texts try to relate several physical/formal aspects to certain functional aspects, emphasizing the latter through their communications approach.

One may argue that these texts get very close to the problem of signification but still fail to acknowledge it. They deal mainly with the problem of communication. Although these two areas, communication and signification, are tightly linked, the difference between the development of these respective discourses remains quite radical. It is therefore necessary to establish the essential nature of their interrelationship. Four constituent elements of the communications model appear in the various works of Meier and Webber, sometimes explicitly in Meier, sometimes implicitly in Webber. These elements are: sender, receiver, information and channel.

In all these works two aspects of the model are consistently emphasized: (1) the channel, which allows for the transmission of information and (2) the quantity and distribution of information. The sender (that is, addresser) and receiver (that is, addressee) are mainly considered as the origin and destination of this information. The channel is seen by these authors as the basic element in the process of communication. The aspect emphasized in the communications process is the transportation of information. This paradigm successfully prevents these authors from inquiring into the nature of the information being communicated. Meier and Webber totally ignore the nature of the message or for that matter the language of which these messages are a part, as well as the structure of codes that make communication possible. In other words, even if the complete model is being used, there is no understanding of the positive theoretical implications of the notions of code and message and, therefore, little concern for the potential importance of these factors. This particular use of the communications model does not consider any aspects that are capable of rendering the communications model a theoretically positive concept. They ignore the potential of a complete model and particularly the role that message and code may play within a more complete model. The theoretical consequences of introducing the notions of message and code into an analysis of the built environment is a proposition that demands to be explored extensively and carefully.

If one focuses on the message instead of the channel, new dimensions are revealed. The notion of message emphasizes the fact that any communication implicates language — or, in more general terms, the use of some system of signs such as natural language, Morse code, traffic lights, and so on. When the built environment is conceived as a carrier of messages, every material object — its real appearance or its properties — becomes a sign; that is, in the process of communication it becomes something that designates something different from the designating thing. The fulfillment of this process requires the framework of a language to be accepted by both addresser and addressee, allowing the transmission of information about certain facts or thoughts or emotional states. In other words, in the process of communication, messages carried by the built environment are made according to the rules of the particular system of signs being used.

The analysis of the nature of this system of signs must be distinguished from their use in communication, since the latter, under the notions of channel and information, is the only aspect to be studied by the communications theories of the built environment. An analysis of the nature of a system of signs, or of a system of signification, must begin with the development of the most important element in the model, namely, the notion of code. An indirect way of expressing the need for the notion of code is to state that the sense is never an intrinsic property of the message. The realization that the information is never an exclusive property of that message indicates the need for the notion of code.[13] Information seen as the meaning of a message depends upon the possibility of being able to select from a repertory of other possible messages and combinations according to certain rules.

Why has this notion of code not been considered? Moreover, why has it been excluded from the communications theories of the built environment? In my opinion the answer to this question may be found in certain "ideological obstacles"[14] linked to the origins of these theories, which repress the acknowledgement of this notion of code.

If one examines the background of the communications theories of planning, one finds that the works I mention have a double origin. On the one hand they continue to develop problems that belong to the area of urbanism; in this respect they are linked to the problems of the design of the environment at an urban scale, based on previously established models in architecture and urban design. On the other hand, they introduce notions belonging to the social sciences, in particular to sociology and social psychology, as a means for solving function problems or, in general, dealing with nonphysical aspects of the built environment. The tradition that is followed in this instance, as it is related to the design disciplines of architecture and urbanism, is integral to the notion of functionalism. This tendency may be characterized by an overwhelming concern for fitness between form and function. These are seen as terms in a direct causal relationship in that the form can be derived from a function. Furthermore, this is regarded as a universal process in that any form may be considered to be the result of a function and to be natural inasmuch as the architect's role is to search for the form that ideally fits the function. This ideology is represented in the beginnings of urbanism in the work of people as diverse in orientation as Ebenezer Howard, Soria y Mata, and Le Corbusier.[15]

Concerning the notions incorporated from the social sciences, these also belong to a tendency known as functionalism, characterized by an approach preoccupied with causation and universalism.[16] The conjunction of the functionalist approaches of both architecture and the social sciences is the achievement of certain urban planning theories.

Design has always been based on a form/function polarity, oscillating between the two poles at different moments in history, emphasizing first one extreme and then the other. Our advanced ideological theories still play within this oscillation. In the case of the communications approach, the emphasis on information and its distribution results in an emphasis of the nonphysical or functional aspects. What is of major interest at this juncture is the fact that this functionalist conception of the environment relates to the form/function distinction; the underlying structural base of architectural ideology is thus certainly present in the communications approach to the urban environment.

The form/function distinction, which determines the design categories on which the activity of architecture has always been based, prevents the built environment from being approached in its signifying functions in a systematic way, either theoretically or practically. The functionalist approach presupposes a natural linkage between function and form, the latter being determined by the former. This preconception obstructs the development of the notion of code, the very notion that allows the functional relationship to be understood as only one of the structural links that determine the signifying nature of the built environment. In other words, to apprehend function, a set of forms must have been submitted to some kind of codification. Furthermore, function, though the most obvious, is not the unique meaning signified by the built environment.

There are several other meanings that, like function, are not linked in a direct way to form but are defined by the structural relations existing among different forms within a given culture. The use of an incomplete communications model is related to an operation wherein all the elements of the model contradictory to functionalist ideology — such as message and code—are deliberately eliminated. The notions of causal, dual, universal, and natural that define all relations between form and function in this ideology serve as an obstacle to the development of a more adequate theoretical base. The concepts code and message allow one to establish not only what is being communicated but also the structure of that which is being communicated; they predicate those organized repertories from which we may select and combine the messages, thus making it possible to establish specific relations, other than the functional, between form and meaning.

In examining the Meier/Webber communications approach one encounters at once the problem of defining the object of knowledge or theoretical object. What in their case is the theoretical object? Meier and Webber use a theory of communication that describes the causal relations existing between formal and functional aspects as manifest in an overall analysis of urban structure. However, the urban structure taken as a global whole cannot be considered a theoretical object; it is insufficient for this. What is called urban structure and to a lesser degree what is called the city, irrespective of any communications models, appear to us as wide sociocultural phenomena, as a sort of total social fact. Paraphrasing De Saussure one could say that one is free to analyze this environment from an economic point of view, from a sociological, a political, a psychological, and aesthetic, or even an exclusively technical point of view. It is the multidimensional character of this *structure* that indicates that it cannot be taken as a whole and be subjected to a rigorous and unitary study. Taken as a whole it can only be approached as a heteroclitous set of observations implying multiple and different points of view, a plurality of pertinences.

It happens because this structure is nothing but the pure essence of the real object city, the product of a typical empiricist approach. The reason that the definition of the theoretical object is not stated precisely lies in the empiricist approach of Meier and Webber, which is based on the description of reality. The structure in this approach is the description of communication as it appears in any urban center that is not productively developed because of ideological obstacles. The more advanced environmental design ideologies — of which the communications model is a prime example — proffer raw material for the production of a theory of production of signification in the built environment. In particular, the critical analysis of the ideological notion of function together with its subversion is an intitial stage that allows for the development of a concept that opposes and yet encompasses function. In this sense the concept of code appears as a more adequate (theoretical) model for the description of the built environment. But the concept of code is not enough to consider the built environment in terms of signification.

The consideration of the built environment or any other system as a system of signification implies that the information conveyed must be seen in terms of the culture that produces these objects. The notion of communication and the abstraction of universality are closely related.

Conversely, the notion of signification has its origin in an approach where the different systems of signs are defined in relation to a given culture. The sense of these signs is defined by the relations that link them to other signs, both within the specific system to which they belong and within an overall cultural system.

This work can only be carried out within a particular culture, since any object will have a different signification in different cultural contexts. In order to understand a cultural system one has to understand the cultural laws by which signification is produced by each, or in each, of the cultural subsystems that comprise the various systems of signification. The concept signification system introduces a new understanding of culture. ''The historical data on culture may be reexamined from the angle of significative information, as well as from the view of it being a system of social codes which allows information to be externalized as appropriate signs for entry into the public domains of a society.''[17]

Public places such as the street provide another segment of the material for the development of the theoretical object. Public places are those configurations where the complexity of a given culture is most densely manifested. It would be possible to characterize these places as clumps of specific articulations comprising various cultural and social codes. In order to describe and explain the structure of these clumps in its entire complexity, it is necessary to propose a specific model for analysis.

The object of study may be reformulated as the production of signification in the built environment through the articulation of various cultural codes within a culture and a mode of production.[18] I call this object *place*.

Signification I: Signification as Structure

The semiotic approach to the theory of the environment determines the need for incorporating theoretical instruments developed in areas distinct from architecture, mainly in linguistics. It is interesting to see that from a broad functional approach, still within the constraints of a communications model, it is possible to pass from a concern for communication to one for signification and to enter at once into the problem of culture and cultural codes in the built environment. At this point it is illuminating to evoke the model of the linguist Roman Jakobson which deals with the functions of the message.[19]

The linguistic model of the message as proposed by Jakobson is a concept that may be most strictly applied to oral messages or to speech. Only oral/verbal language offers precise indicators as to the predominance of each of the respective functions of this model. On the other hand, it is also true that this Jakobson model has had, and still has, a specific role in semiotics: namely, to make manifest the characteristic nature of any message. The procedure is to reveal the six basic functions or areas of signification that, according to their links with each of the necessary elements in each act of communication, are clearly distinguishable at a theoretical level.[20]

An understanding of these functions compels one to go back to the constitutive factors in any act of communication. The *addresser* sends a *message* to the *addressee*. To be operative the message requires a *context* referred to, that is, the ''referent,'' seizable by the addressee. The next prerequisite is the existence of a *code* fully, or at least partially, common to both the addresser and addressee — or, in other words, to the encoder and decoder of the message. Finally there is the essential condition of *contact:* a physical channel and psychological connection between sender and receiver of the message, enabling both of them to enter and stay in communication. All these factors may be schematized as follows:

	Context	
Addresser	Message	Addressee
	Contact	
	Code	

Each of these six factors determines a different function in language. This would also be true for the built environment, considered as signification. Although the six basic aspects of language are always present, one always tends to be emphasized at the expense of the others, depending on the context. The resultant diversity arises not out of a monopoly by one of these functions but through a different hierarchical ordering of these functions.[21]

When the message is set toward the referent, an orientation toward the *context,* it is called the *referential* function. It is the denotative aspect in language and although it is the predominant element in many messages, the other functions always have to be considered. If one regards this function as the equivalent to the ''functional'' aspect in the built environment — where a natural linkage occurs between form and function — it will seem as if a denotative relationship had appeared similar to that which occurs in language.[22] The so-called *emotive* or expressive function, focused on the *addresser,* aims a direct expression of the addresser's attitude toward what he is speaking about.[23]

When the orientation is towards the *addressee,* it is called the conative function; examples of this in language are the vocative and imperative (''Go out!'' ''Sit down!''). There are messages that serve primarily to establish, prolong, or discontinue communication, to check whether the channel works (''Hello, do you hear me?'' ''Are you listening?''). This emphasis on the *contact* is called the *phatic* function. Formulas or dialogues generated only for the purpose of establishing communication are other typical examples of it.[24] When the message is focused on the code, it performs a *metalingual* function; sometimes the addresser and the addressee need to check whether they are using the same code (''I don't follow you, what do you mean?''; or in anticipation of such a question, ''Do you know what I mean?'').[25] Finally the set toward the *message* itself, for its own sake, is the *poetic* function of language.[26] The study of the poetic function extends beyond the limits of poetry. The scheme of the factors may then be complemented by a corresponding scheme of their functions:

	Referential	
Emotive	Poetic	Conative
	Phatic	
	Metalingual	

Let us see how this model works in architecture by taking the case of the street as an example. If we approach the street from the point of view of the Webber/Meier communications model, the function that is emphasized is the referential. The referential function manifests itself here as a communication within the form of a channel, the media element linking origin and destination. Message and code are excluded by this emphasis, since there is neither concern for signification nor for the structure of messages. In a simplistic manner the street is considered merely as a channel where communication is solely transportation. The overriding concern is for the channel and not for the contact as opposed to Jakobson's model, where channel is considered in relation to the transmission of the messages between addresser and addressee.

In the traditional approach each element of the environment relates to a referent. But the referent is only one of the factors of the communication model, and the referential function only one of the functions. If one considers the street as a complex message rather than simply as a channel, other elements emerge which emphasize different functions. In the street as a complex message the functions manifest themselves as follows. The *referential* function is the act of circulating, wherein the street and a path in an open field are the same. The meaning circulation is here transmitted by a physical element, the surface of the ground, the horizontal plane, which in both instances functions as signifier.[27] With this referential function, the conative function regulates and imposes a mode of circulation by means of a system determining both permission and prohibition.

These controlling rules are brought into being through elements such as: sidewalk-street, crossings, block interruptions, traffic lights, and signs. Simultaneously, the *emotive* function also appears through elements that refer to an authorship: for example, the Paris Metro entrances designed by Guimard or the Parisian street as a whole in the avenues of Haussmann. Alternatively, such a function may be mediated through buildings; the Guggenheim Museum in New York is an example where the presence of the individual architect is strong. A comparable function may also be provided through graphic elements such as billboards. Elements that serve the conative function, such as traffic signs and lights or other kinds of signs, also possess a *metalingual* function through which every element insures the comprehension of another, referring to its code. This metaelement may be of very different constituent types, from language to objects that speak about objects. Thus a traffic light, by indicating "wait" and "walk," informs us that we are on a corner and also how we are supposed to act regarding this element in terms of traffic codes. A sign of a restaurant has the function of making sure that we understand the object as a restaurant.

There is also a metalingual function, present by connotation, in the case of display windows. The *phatic* function is one of the most difficult to find in a pure state in nonverbal cases. A good example, however, would be the advertising billboard, which, in view of the competition, tries to make sure that above all else contact is established. This is sometimes achieved with very strong lights, which are the first thing that attracts attention, even before communication is established through content. Finally, the poetic function is present in each and all of the examples given for the other functions. For example, the traffic sign system realizes a poetic function by means of design and color. Needless to say the poetic function plays a major role in the advertising code. In general, graphic advertising covers the conative function by means of the poetic; one may also cite sidewalk designs like the Copacabana strip in Rio de Janeiro or, alternatively, certain tree rhythms as examples.

None of these functions appear or exist in isolation. The elements never have just one function. The six are always present, though in varying hierarchical order. The definition of the model itself shows us the possibilities and limitations of its use. It is the case of a simple, exhaustive, and sufficiently abstract system of classification in order to allow extension to nonlinguistic areas.

However, a classification of signifying dimensions is not a theory for the mechanism by which they are produced. Jakobson's communication model permits us to view the built environment as a complex message and thereby to subvert the ideological notion of a single function through the discovery that each message must be seen as a sheaf of functions. Each of these functions implies a particular area of signification or meaning. The final understanding of these areas of signification is possible only when we apply the concept of code, since each function or area of signification is determined by a particular set of codes.

Through the use of the Jakobson model as a critical tool, it is possible to recognize the purely conventional, codified character of the form/function couple as the product of an extraordinary ideological set, operating in the technical or aesthetic realm, or in a combination of both.[28] At the same time Jakobson's model reveals the need for the systematization of the complex of cultural codes that are determined by the multiple functions implicit in the architectural object. However helpful the Jakobson model may be, it is insufficient for the specific study of the codes themselves.

From the foregoing initial stage we see that it is at least possible to consider the built environment in terms of signification, the different areas of signification corresponding to the different functions of the message. The next question is: What are the "elements and relationships" that make signification possible, that enable the signifying functioning of the built environment to come into being?

The study of the codes allows one to understand the mechanisms by which matter acquires the capability of transmitting meaning by establishing relations between matter and those different significations that are inscribed on it, thereby giving a configuration sense within a given culture. The study of codes has many sides and there are basically two ways in which it can be approached. On one hand we may analyze the codes as static structures. These structures are to be understood as different sets of rules combined in a particular way, underlying the built environment. On the other hand, these structures of sense have not always existed and are by no means immutable. These structures are produced and transformed in a process that is called *product of significa-tion*. This second kind of analysis, which constitutes a second stage, is our prime concern, but in order to realize it, it seems necessary to go through an analysis of structures, the first stage.[29]

Signification II

What have been described as stages are in fact not simply stages but two alternative options with which the semiotic project is confronted. The first option is to approach the built environment as systems of signification as structured by communication — that is, by the transmission and exchange of messages, which is done by the exchange of signs in a game both within the sign (signifiers and signifieds) and, mainly, between signs.

De Saussure affords us an economic metaphor that defines the sign through the notion of value: "For a sign (or an economic value) to exist — as its linguistic value — it must be possible, on the one hand, to exchange dissimilar things (work and wage) and, on the other, to compare similar things with each other. That is, one can exchange five dollars for bread or for soap or for cinema tickets, but one can also compare this five dollars with ten or fifty dollars, etc. In a similar way a 'word' can be 'exchanged' for an idea (that is for something dissimilar), but it can also be compared with other words (that is with something similar). In English the word mutton derives its value only from its coexistence with sheep; the meaning being truly fixed only at the end of this double determination: signification and value."[30] In the past few years in which the "analysis of sense" has been developing very fast, the ideological limitations of this structural approach to signification based upon the circulation of signs has become clear.[31]

The second option is that of approaching signification according to the possibilities initiated by the Marxist critique of economy and the consequent emphasis on the notion of productive work or production. Marx analyzes "value" in the circulation of merchandise, as a crystallization of social labor; that is, as the production previous to the circulation. Through this he reveals concepts such as surplus value which owe their existence to this production. This concept is "invisible" — Ricardo did not see it. It is hidden by the effect of the production; that

is, the circulation of merchandise. This analysis of production allows Marx to develop a criticism of a system based on the exchange and circulation of the product. A parallel criticism has only recently been developed in semiotics, analyzing the circulation of signs in an analysis comparable to that developed by Marx with respect to the circulation of money. "At the level of society, language functions as money, which allows the exchange of information but hides the production of sense."[32]

The whole dilemma facing architectural semiotics today seems to lie in the following area: either continue to formalize architecture as a semiotic system from the point of view of communication or else open, within the interior of the problem of communication (which inevitably constitutes the entire social problem), a whole other consideration, that which refers to the *production of sense previous to sense*. Referring to the current semiotic problem in literature, Kristeva states that ". . . it is effectively impossible to understand what such a semiology is speaking about when it formulates a problem of a production which is not equivalent to communication even if produced through it, if the breaking point which neatly separates the problematic of exchange from that of labor is not accepted."[33] In this field of analysis, a semiotic of the built environment, one has to develop and go through those two stages of exchange and production at the same time, since for architecture, unlike the field of literature, the first stage, a semiotic of the sign (in relation to communication), is virtually nonexistent. The brief analysis of the built environment considered as a sheaf of functions may be considered as one of the first steps toward a structural semiotic (or semiotic of the sign) in the built environment.

In the theoretical analysis I propose to develop, in the perspective of production (the second option), signification is not thought of as what the "thing" communicates but as the readings that, within a given culture, may be produced out of it — the readings that this culture allows. In this sense the street as one of the public places in our society appears as an extremely valuable material. It condenses, explains, reproduces the multiple sociocultural codes of our society. What we call culture is thought of as codes that organize different chains or systems, such as theater, gesture, politics, writing. These codes are no longer seen as the product of an analysis in front of the communicating object, as a classification and abstraction of an inventory that finds fixed and finite sets of regularities and rules. These codes are considered instead as forces in a dynamic process that both produces and transforms sense according to determined conditions of production.[34] The problem is then how to reveal these forces without reducing them to a system, to a closed construction.

From the problem of the codes as process one finds the need for analyzing an aspect that I believe is a priority. I am referring to the mode of articulating codes, which should be distinguished from the study of the codes themselves. If the study of the codes from the point of view of communication of meaning is based on the principle of unity, which allows one to recognize similarities and differences (value), what guides the work of reading is what could be called the principle of dispersion. This principle does not close a system, which is precisely what characterizes architecture and design, but opens it, allowing for an articulation of various readings as structured by the codes. This articulation between various readings constitutes a plural reading. Each reading develops a series of chains at the signifier level in a given context. This chain of signifiers then slides over a mosaic of signifieds belonging to the same context. It is as if points of a network were being linked neither by chance nor in accordance with a preconceived plan. It is this process of "chaining" that constitutes the structuring force.

The polysemy or multiplication of significations produced by this plural reading, that is, by an articulation of the codes, does not act as an addition to the old fixed structure, which remains untouched, but rather makes us enter a new dynamic space, that of work and the production of sense. One may think of the articulation between readings as that which opens the system, which forces the movement of sense; as that which allows us to enter into the production of signification and permits us to think of a practice based on the work on such mechanisms and on the structuring conditions of signification in the built environment.

1968 - 1972

Notes

This article is based on the work, "La Structure Urbaine; Communication, Pratique, Apprentissage" (developed under a Fellowship from the French government at the Centre de Recherche d'Urbanisme, Paris, in 1967-68), in which I analyzed the street as a system of signification. Most of the original content has been preserved. However, some changes have been made in order to put it in the context of this book and to incorporate some of the hypotheses that are in continuing development from the earlier work. Consequently, some quotations have a later date.

1. Louis Althusser and Etienne Balibar, *Lire Le Capital* (Paris: Maspero, 1967), references from the English edition, *Reading Capital* (London: NLB, 1970).

2. Developed in D. Agrest, "On the Ideology of Urban Planning," University of Buenos Aires, 1969, and in more detail in "Critical Remarks on Urban Planning Models," a lecture given at the Institute for Architecture and Urban Studies, New York, March 1972; in *Oppositions* 3 (1974).

3. Althusser, *Lire Le Capital*, p. 36.

4. Ibid., p. 38.

5. Ibid.; this passage, translated from the Spanish language edition (Buenos Aires: Ed. Siglo XXI, 1969, p. 44), remains only as a paraphrase in the English edition.

6. Ibid., p. 41; Althusser continues: "When Marx tells us that the production process of knowledge . . . takes place entirely in knowledge, in the 'head' or in thought, he is not for one second falling into an idealism of consciousness, mind or thought, for the '*thought*' we are discussing here is not a faculty of a transcendental subject or absolute consciousness confronted by the real world as *matter; . . .* This thought is the historically constituted system of an *apparatus of thought,* founded on and articulated to natural and social reality."

7. Ibid., pp. 41-42.

8. L. Althusser, "Practica Teorica y Lucha Ideologica," published in a collection of articles, *La Filosofia como Arma de la Revolucion* (Cordoba: Ed. Pasado y Presente, 1968), p. 37.

9. Ideology is a set of representations and beliefs (religious, moral, political, aesthetic), which refer to nature, to society, and to the life and activities of men in relation to nature and society. Ideology has the social function of maintaining the global structure of society by inducing men to accept consciously the place and role assigned to them by this global structure. In this way, ideology gives a certain distorted knowledge of the world; "ideology in a way alludes to reality, but it only offers an illusion of this reality." Architectural ideology — an ideological subregion — then can be seen as the summation of Western architectural knowledge in its entire range, from commonplace intuition to sophisticated theories and histories of architecture. This ideology has explicitly claimed to serve the practical needs of society by ordering and controlling the built environment. Nevertheless, I hold that the underlying function of this ideology is the pragmatic one of serving and preserving the overall structure of society in Western social formations — that is, the capitalist model of production and architectural practice as a part of it. D. Agrest and M. Gandelsonas, "Semiotics and Architecture: Ideological Consumption or Theoretical Work," *Oppositions* 1 (1973), pp. 93-100.

10. Semiotics, the theory of systems of signs, is considered to be only a first stage toward a future general theory of ideologies. In this stage semiotics not only can provide models but it can also suggest theoretical strategies in our battle against a specific ideology, architectural ideology.

11. Concrete concepts "'realise' theoretical concepts in the concrete knowledge about concrete objects" in a dialectical process. ". . . it is possible to say that the concrete knowledge about a concrete object presents itself to us as the 'synthesis' Marx speaks about. A synthesis of the necessary theoretical concepts (in a strict sense) combined with the elaborated . . ." concrete concepts. L. Althusser, "Acerca del Trabajo Teorico" in *La Filosofia Como Arma de la Revolucion*.

12. Richard Meier, *A Communications Theory of Urban Growth* (Cambridge, Mass.: The MIT Press, 1962); Melvin Webber, "Order in Diversity; Community Without Propinquity," in L. Wingo, Jr., ed., *Cities and Space: The Future Use of Urban Land* (Baltimore: Johns Hopkins University Press, 1963), and "The Urban Place and the Non-Place Urban Realm," in Webber, ed., *Explorations into Urban Structure* (Philadelphia: University of Pennsylvania Press, 1964).

13. W. Ross Ashby, *An Introduction to Cybernetics* (London: Chapman and Hall, 1956).

14. I refer here to function and functionalism as major ideological obstacles that will be partly explored.

15. The relationship between the functionalism of these urbanists and the functionalism underlying the work of the planners I criticize (among others) has been developed in research on the ideology of urban planning where I investigated its origins. D. Agrest, "La Ideologia del Planeamiento Urbano" [The Ideology of Urban Planning] (Universidad de Buenos Aires, 1969).

16. I refer to the functionalism of Emile Durkheim and the structural functionalism of Talcott Parsons. For a criticism of functionalism see Claude Lévi-Strauss, "Functionalist Theories of Totemism," *Totemism* (Boston: Beacon Press, 1963); *Structural Anthropology* (New York: Basic Books, 1963).

17. "The conception of culture as information determines certain methods of research. It authorizes in particular the analysis of cultural stages, as well as the set of historical and intellectual facts conceived as infinite texts; and it allows at the same time the use of methods of semiotics and structural linguistics." Jury M. Lotman, "Problèmes de la Typologie des Cultures," in *Essays in Semiotics* (The Hague: Mouton, 1971; my translation).

18. This will be part of a general theory that will study the nature of the functioning of ideological phenomena: in J. Kristeva's terms "a general theory of superstructure," the object of this theory being the social production of sense. Julia Kristeva, "La Semiologie comme science; Critique et/ou critique de la science," *La Nouvelle Critique*, 16 (1968). Eliseo Veron, "Vers une logique naturelle des mondes sociaus," *Communications*, 20 (1973), p. 247.

19. Roman Jakobson, "Linguistics and Poetics," closing statement in T. Sebeok, ed., *Style in Language* (Cambridge, Mass.: The MIT Press, 1960); page references, paperback edition, 1971.

20. Throughout this section I closely paraphrase Jakobson, "Linguistics," p. 354.

21. Idem.

22. Diana Agrest and Mario Gandelsonas, "Critical Remarks on Semiology and Architecture," *Semiotica,* IX (1972), pp. 252-271.

23. "The purely emotive stratum in language is presented by the interjections. . . . If we analyze language from the standpoint of the information it carries, we cannot restrict the notion of information to the cognitive aspect of language. A man, using expressive features to indicate his angry or ironic attitude, conveys ostensible information, and evidently this verbal behavior cannot be likened to such nonsemiotic, nutritive activities as 'eating grapefuit.'" Jakobson, "Linguistics," p. 354.

24. "'Well,' the young man said, 'well'' she said, 'well, here we are' he said, etc. The endeavor to start and sustain communication is typical of talking birds. It is also the first verbal function acquired by infants; they are prone to communicate before being able to send or receive informative communication." Ibid., p. 355.

25. The following dialogue is given by Jakobson as an example: "The sophomore was plucked." — "But what is plucked?" — "Plucked means the same as flunked." — "And flunked?" "To be flunked is to fail in an exam." — "And what is sophomore?" . . . "A sophomore is [or means] a second year student." Ibid., p. 356.

26. "The political slogan 'I like Ike', succinctly structured, consists of three monsyllables and counts three diphthongs/ay/ each of them symetrically followed by one consonantial phoneme, / . . . l . . . k . . . k/ . The make up of the three words presents a variation: no consonantial phonemes in the first word, two around the diphthong in the second, and one final consonant in the third." Ibid., p. 357. The secondary poetic function of this electional catch phrase reinforces its impressiveness and efficacy and covers the conative function. It is typical of advertising to cover the conative function with a poetic function.

27. I use "signifier" here, according to de Saussure, as one of the two sides of a sign. The sign is a two-sided linguistic unit that exists through the association of a sound image of *signifier* and a concept of *signified*. Ferdinand de Saussure, *Course in General Linguistics* (New York: McGraw-Hill, 1966).

28. Cf. D. Agrest, M. Gandelsonas, J. C. Indart, "On Semiotics, Perverse Objects and Ideological Texts" in *Summa* (Buenos Aires), no. 32 (1970); also, E. Veron "Semiotics and the Social Production of Knowledge," in *Structuralism Around the World,* Thomas Sebeok, ed. (The Hague: Mouton, in print).

29. Agrest and Gandelsonas, "Semiotics and Architecture."

30. De Saussure, *Course in General Linguistics*.

31. See criticism developed by J. Derrida, *De la Grammatologie* (Paris: Ed. du Minuit, 1967); Kristeva, "Semiology comme science"; E. Veron, "Pour une Semiologie des operations translinguistiques," *Versus,* 4 (1972).

32. Derrida, *De la Grammatologie*.

33. Kristeva, "Semiologie comme Science."

34. Roland Barthes, *S/Z* (Paris: Ed. du Seuil, 1970).

Social Aspects of Streets and
of Street Interventions

Anthropology and Sociology of Streets

Gloria Levitas

Introduction

An examination of the available literature on streets confirms an observation of Auguste Comte: "We reserve till last research into subjects closest to our social selves." Abundant studies of the street made by traffic engineers attest to our interest in increasing the speed and flow of traffic; observations of human beings on the street and analyses of how, when, and why they use them are virtually nonexistent.

Observations about street life in industrialized nations usually appear as notes incidental to the study of slums — a reflection of the fact that slum streets have retained some of their vitality and traditional social functions. Other information may be plucked from urban redevelopment studies and occasional analyses of pedestrian behavior in business districts.

While the studies of business districts make some attempt to link aspects of environment with behavior, the other research largely ignores the architectural aspect of what ought to be studies of social-environmental interaction; hence the architect or environmental researcher can learn little about man/environment relationships from these data.

The paucity of information derives at least partly from the dominant view of the street only in its role as a passage. Difficulty in research, on the other hand, is a reflection of our still primitive understanding of man/environment relationships. How do people or groups interact with their street environments? What aspects of the street — spatial dimension, availability of amenities, ease of transportation — have the most significant effects on human-use patterns? Is there any linkage between a rich street culture and a high degree of social cohesion and satisfaction? Do particular street layouts influence the patterns of human social interaction?

While such questions have rarely been raised about streets, similar questions have been posed by architects studying other environments. Even in more enclosed and tidy environments, where variables are more easily controlled, results of research have been disappointing. No general rules about human spatial behavior have emerged to provide guidelines for design; this failure in turn stems from the lack of a concept that would order the data and facilitate useful generalizations.

Man/Environment Studies: The Anthropological Perspective

Any attempt to understand the meaning of streets as well as their role in the processes of human communication and interaction requires a conception of the nature of the relationship between man and his environment, as well as some comprehension of the specific role or roles played by the street in this relationship. In the broadest sense, the problem of man/environment relationships and speculations on the effect of environment on behavior are as old as history. Early thinkers were much concerned with the effects of climate on race and thinking processes. The Roman architect Vitruvius contributed an exhaustive discussion of the problem in which he viewed people as passive recipients of climatic forces.

While most early thinkers did not concern themselves with the effects of the built environment on human beings, it is but a short step from Vitruvius's assignment of priority to nature to his Platonic faith that natural rules of symmetry and of dimension would ensure perfection and harmony. Vitruvius's Platonism became an article of faith for architects and designers. Eventually they did come to question how constructed environment affected human behavior; but even today, architects and planners tend to favor specific aesthetic ideals and to insist that these forms have a singular ability to make people happy, or to increase desirable social behaviors.

In a brief survey of the literature on man/environment relations, Amos Rapoport[1] concluded that designers' intuitions and rules of symmetry do not have the effects designers believe them to have. While cases did exist in which design appeared to have a potent effect on behavior and user satisfaction, such cases were rare, and most effects were far less significant than designers believed. Moreover, the effects that occurred appeared to involve social and psychological as well as physical determinants.

If this information comes as news to designers, it constitutes the very faith of most social scientists who have always maintained a profound skepticism regarding the ability of the physical environment to determine, or even significantly influence, human behavior. The social science position is best summed up by Herbert Gans, who assigns priority in the man/environment equation to human values, beliefs, and expectations, and who has continually asserted, along with most of his colleagues in the field, that ". . . the physical environment has much less effect than planners imagine. Often it is thought to impinge, but people evade this effect through . . . 'non-conforming use,' that is, an evasion of the impingement in order to maintain or achieve behavior patterns that are in line with their predispositions. The social environment has considerably more effect."[2]

In recent years, a number of psychologists and social psychologists have attempted to learn how physical and psychological factors interact. Those who deal with disturbed or abnormal people are not quite so certain that determinism flows from the social to the physical. Persons with impaired cognitive or emotional functions seem to be less able to impose their own cultural or personal order on the environment; they are often extraordinarily sensitive to the effects of environmental stimuli, and appear to be more easily coerced into useful or destructive behavior patterns by objects as well as spatial arrangements. Studies in mental hospitals indicate that such factors as room pattern and furniture arrangement not only affect, but often appear to determine, both the degree and patterns of socialization and withdrawal. Still other studies in ordinary hospital wards, school settings, and libraries[3] indicate that humans unconsciously structure their personal space to protect their privacy and thus control the amount and intensity of their interaction with others. Some of the studies also suggest that where space is structured for them, people tend to accept rules of behavior embedded in the spatial structure and will adopt roles more congruent with their position in space than with their personalities.[4] Because maneuvering is possible in most environments, people may unconsciously choose positions in the environment that reflect a particular view of self. Their relative dominance and their willingness to observe or participate is therefore often reinforced by their spatial positions.

These findings suggest, of course, that any simplistic view of man/ environment relationships will not yield an adequate picture of reality. But the research is not yet sophisticated enough to tell us how the objects or arrangements transmit messages or rules of behavior to users, nor do we understand the mental processes by which people make decisions to sit in one place rather than another, or to interpret a setting as formal or informal, social or economic, personal or impersonal. Like the rules of grammar this process seems to be embedded in our mental structures without our conscious awareness.

The dangers of generalizing on notions derived from studies in mental hospitals to normal people is well recognized; hence such studies may be more useful in establishing limiting cases of behavior patterns than in guiding environmental design outside the mental hospital. With care these studies may suggest useful hypotheses about design or design research, and thus psychology surely has contributions to make in the field of design. However, dialogue between the two fields appears to founder where the planner's or architect's need to create for mass use comes into conflict with the psychologist's emphasis upon individual differences.

Although some architects have shown an interest in anthropological data, citations from anthropological literature are conspicuously lacking in most of the literature on environment and behavior. Moreover, while anthropologists have in recent years conducted studies of the behavior/ environment interface, they have rarely communicated their findings to members of other professions. The failure of anthropologists to take the initiative probably reflects the fact that applied anthropology has had a very short history and that anthropologists, intent on the retrieval of data on rapidly disappearing non-Western and preliterate cultures, have paid little attention to complex Western societies.

What can anthropology offer architects and planners? For one thing, anthropologists have long been interested in learning how material cultures and spatial arrangements are related to social structure, to personality, and to human evolution. The interest derives from several sources: archeology has required information on the meaning of spatial organization in order to reconstruct the lifeways of people who left behind them only postholes, potsherds, and garbage heaps. Evolutionists, interested in understanding how man gradually differentiated himself from the ape, discovered that toolmaking preceded brain development and suggested that the process of toolmaking itself was necessary for human evolution. They envisioned man and his reactions in terms of a system that involved reciprocity and positive feedback.[5] From linguistics and the Sapir-Whorf hypothesis, which suggested that the structure of language determined the nature of human perception, anthropologists were drawn to explore the relationship between the mind and its material products.[6] This interest led to a search for innate structures of relationship that are believed to organize human perception of the environment.

Working within this linguistic tradition, Claude Lévi-Strauss sees culture as a reflection of a basic mental structure that, like a binary computer, appears to operate in terms of oppositions. Other structuralists, working within a parallel but less restrictive linguistic tradition, have applied the rules of linguistic analysis to other aspects of culture. Semiologists have recently begun research aimed at identifying the basic units of architectural meaning and the syntactic structures within which these units operate.[7] Success in this effort could provide architects with badly needed information on the ways and the extent to which architecture transmits messages. Interest in kinesics (nonverbal communication) and proxemics (communication through the ordering of space), pioneered by Raymond Birdwhistell[8] and Edward T. Hall[9] respectively, have underscored the role played by subliminal environmental cues in transmitting information. Input from ethology — the studies of animals in their natural habitats — has encouraged a search for unconscious species-specific mechanisms that appear to determine spatial relationships and operate to maintain group cohesion and the social order.[10]

A study by Segall, Campbell, and Herskovits provided information on the effects of a noncarpentered world on the thought processes of non-Western people.[11] And in the mid-nineteenth century, in "Houses and House Life of the American Aborigine," Lewis Henry Morgan embarked on an ambitious — if inaccurate — reconstruction of American Indian culture. Mistaking burial mounds for village remains, Morgan's work provides a cautionary lesson: relationships between artifacts and behavior, or spatial organization and culture, cannot be removed from cultural context. Commenting on Morgan's error at a research seminar on Archeology and Urbanization (London, December 1970), Mary Douglas demanded ''an ecological approach in which the structure of ideas and of society, the mode of gaining a livelihood and the domestic architecture are interpreted as a single interacting whole in which no element can be said to determine the other.''

Clearly, the most useful contribution made by the anthropologist to understanding the relationship between man and his natural and constructed environment stems from the anthropological perspective itself. Stressing participant observation, this approach has required the researcher to immerse himself in the culture he is studying in order to understand better the emotions and attitudes of his people. Furthermore, the anthropological perspective concerns itself with understanding cultures as coherent adaptive systems (including the interdependence of material and nonmaterial aspects of culture) — and to see these systems — as he sees the process of human evolution — as a continuous interactive process.

At the same time, the influence of structural relationship on behavior has served to replace the study of products with the study of processes. Following the program set out by Julian Steward, anthropologists have ''. . . focused analysis on the structural similarities which resulted from the interaction of habitats and cultures whose specific content mask a fundamentally similar ecological adjustment.''[12]

Anthropology and Design

While anthropologists have espoused holistic views and cautioned against application of ethnocentric theories, they have rarely been involved in planning: instead, they have been called upon after the fact to explain why a planning objective has not been realized. Those few who have conducted architecturally focused research have supplied a body of literature that provides support for recognition of the city as a multi-client organization and reflects growing concern with the number of different strategies with which people approach their environments in order to adapt to political and social as well as economic realities. These strategies may be very different from the conceptions of architects or planners. Cultural and subcultural rules, preferences, and values serve to alter the nature of the relationship between inhabitant and environment and the interpretations of a culturally naive planner may be at variance with the actual behavior of his subjects.

Evidence suggests that people will put up with all manner of discomfort to maintain the pattern of culture that gives meaning to their lives, even as it functions to adapt them to their habitat. By paying more attention to the organizational structures that underlie the culture and consequently influence housing patterns, the planner or change agent increases his chance of success. Unfortunately, we are often inclined to

regard other peoples' cultural patterns as capricious or meaningless. Mired in notions of our own cultural superiority, we tend to dismiss native practice as nonscientific and therefore nonvaluable. Anthropological research has indicated that even taboos and superstitions may play a crucial role in maintaining the health and welfare of a population. Where taboos and superstitions help define the rule system of a society, they must be accorded serious analysis.

The view of cultures as adaptive systems directs one's attention away from relatively trivial surface phenomena and toward the continuous interaction among technological, political, and other (for example, religious) structures in creating social and spatial forms. Moreover, by relieving researchers of the burden of specifying the direction of a determinate relationship, the approach encourages the focus upon processes of interaction.

How and where one imposes change should not depend upon some preconceived notion of the priority of the physical over the social, or of the social over the physical, but should rest on careful analysis of the process itself. Whether change is necessary at all depends upon our ability to judge whether or not the life of the people with whom we are involved is satisfactory to them and, at the same time, does not constitute an encroachment upon the rights and needs of others in the society. Where change is necessary, comprehension of the nature of social organization should aid us in deciding where to make the change, and how to accomplish it while monitoring other changes in the cultural fabric.

Although an argument persists in anthropology over whether changes in technological systems or ideational systems are more difficult to make, a consensus suggests that structural interventions altering the system of relationships that organizes a culture produce the most rapid change.[13] Such interventions are tantamount to opening Pandora's box and clearly should not be encouraged merely to satisfy the whim of the planner for his own kind of order.

On the other hand, where change *is* necessary because peoples' lives are not satisfactory (a fact most readily discerned in our own society by such indexes of distress as low income, high infant mortality, prevalence of crime and violence, and emotional disorder — and by the complaints of people themselves regarding their lives) our abilities must be directed toward altering the systems of relationship which maintain antisocial and antihuman patterns of adaptation. Intervention in the way in which a society organizes its work force and allocates its jobs is one way of effecting change. But where technology is crosscut and supported by political arrangements, it is equally necessary to alter power relationships among groups in such a way as to provide work opportunities. Only by so doing can one effect significant changes in social as well as the psychological structures.

By changing systems of relationships one can change cultural configurations; hence, an architecture that would hope to replace anomic with social attitudes, or one that aspires toward increasing personal satisfaction, must use its tools to maintain, where they already exist, satisfactory personal and group networks. At the same time, through judicious site planning as well as careful study of the symbolic message of space, time, and objects in the built environment, the architect and planner can strive to introduce more sociopetal environments.

In our zeal to produce environments that are true as well as beautiful, however, we must recognize that one of our best tools is not simply what we do for people, but how we make them active participants in their own lives. Changing streets so that they allow or limit access; changing the numbers and types of amenities on a street; changing boundary configurations or proportions or color or scale or circulation patterns can be important. But we must recognize that much of the social malaise we are striving to eliminate is, in good part, a result of the development of political systems which have gradually eroded the more organic social ties of the town and village and replaced them with superordinate legal and political systems. The stratified state system has developed complex methods to ensure that the differentially ranked groups within our society willingly accept their positions and adapt, as best they can, often to degrading physical environments and destructive social arrangements.

While state systems have allowed and encouraged the development of more and more efficient energy systems, and while they have increased peaceful contact among an ever-expanding network of human groups, they have succeeded only by exacting a severe price from the human beings who constitute the bottom layers of the system. Government policy which encourages spatial mobility and family instability has eroded the props once supportive of social interdependency even as it has limited the ability of many members of the lower classes to participate in the wider society. Such Government decisions also appear to have had profound, and not necessarily salutary, effects on those who do participate: increasing the need for privacy, encouraging the compartmentalization of personality, and training men in the image of the machine — they would appear to be both dehumanizing and destructive of precisely the attribute that differentiates men from animals: the need to learn and the ability to learn only in a social context.

If we are to study and change streets, then our first priority requires that we involve residents themselves in a new set of relationships with the government and change agents. Anthropological respect for cultural values is a first step toward this goal.

The Street as a Cultural Artifact

One could list numerous reasons for the decline in the proportion of daily social life that occurs in public urban space: the automobile; television; economic imperatives which make small, personal businesses unprofitable, forcing them to give way to large, impersonal supermarkets; increased crime and violence on the street, and so on. The thesis of this presentation is that streets, like any other aspect of culture, reflect the process of adaptation of culture to environment. The decline of our streets is comprehensible only in terms of the changing technological and sociopolitical configurations of our society (for example, industrialization and increasing centralization). Examination of the appearance and role of the street throughout history suggests that the street has always been both a tangible expression of the structure of relationships of the culture in which it appears and a tool by which the evident relationships could be considered and challenged or maintained.

The paucity of studies of the form, meaning, and use of streets requires that any review be conducted on the basis of hypotheses such as the foregoing — and in the spirit of a heuristic search for better hypotheses.

If we conceive of a street both as a locus of social interaction and a linear passageway linking destinations, then the street does not appear to exist at the simplest levels of human society. We can identify paths leading out of a village into the surrounding countryside; and we can find ritual ways, lanes reserved for menstruating women, and even tracks connecting settlements. But the street with boundaries that separate interior from exterior, private from public space does not exist in hunting and gathering societies. The compound or encampment or village itself, which seems to function as "a field of interaction,"[14] is not defined as a series of destinations in a linear system. This lack of street seems to correlate well with a similar nonlinear interpretation of time.

Nomadic or seminomadic tribes often inhabit circular villages. Their settlements tend to be temporary, made of natural materials, portable, and, while clearly distinguishable, an integral part of the surroundings. The absence of the street in circular villages appears to reflect no strongly felt need for boundaries between public and private behavior. Unity, interdependence, and cooperation are the rule; and the unit of cooperation is the coresident band — not the nuclear family.[15]

In such a society, even architecture is a mechanism of communication and can be utilized to inform the entire group of the state of interpersonal relationships and to set into motion the system of sanctions by which order is maintained. Among the Mbuti pygmies, for example, a woman may orient her hut door to express liking, indifference, or dislike for a neighbor; this positioning of the entranceway acts as any other communication device to arouse an appropriate response within the group.[16]

Even more permanent circular village compounds appear to exhibit a similar pattern. Though these are commonly found in horticultural societies, cultures that use them exhibit organizational systems remarkably similar to those found among hunters and gatherers. Here again, the basic unit of adaptation appears to be the compound itself, and linear streets do not exist. Generally, husbands and wives live in separate huts which are ranged in a rough circle within which most of the work of the compound is conducted. Depending upon the specific elements of the social structure, a man and his wives' huts may be clustered separately from those of his brothers, and occasionally the houses of husbands and wives may be connected by a covered passageway. Among the Massa, all the men's huts may be on one side of the circle while all the wives' huts may be on the other side.[17] A large compound may take in several families, a lineage, segment of a lineage, moiety, or even a clan. But what is most striking about these settlements is the public nature of life within them. Although smaller units of cooperation exist, and the household may function as a unit of production, the critical need for a larger cooperative group demands public food storage shared by all occupants of a compound. While the circular village may have a headman or men's club house, even the granaries of the headman or his senior wife are not private. For "in severe shortage, what food is held openly must be shared equally by all within a compound."[18] As long as a village remains circular in form one can generally infer that it is egalitarian both politically and economically, and that privacy — like private property — will be little in evidence. The beginnings of a concept of private family life may be seen in the use of a covered passageway (a private street) linking a man and his wives, but by and large the concept of family boundaries is little developed.

The village of rectangular houses presents a very different picture. In the Middle East where this form first appears, the houses seem to be designed to accommodate families rather than individuals. Although there may be a headman's granary or a village granary, each household has its own concealed, interior storage facilities, and the implication of these findings is that the individual household, rather than the compound or village, has now become the basic unit of production. Furthermore, it appears that since the household storage units are hidden from public view, the cultural imperative for sharing beyond the household itself either has been considerably weakened or no longer exists.[19] While disparities of wealth among members of a circular compound are virtually nonexistent, the opportunities for accumulation of resources within the family seem to be present in the rectangular house. Streets are very much in evidence in the rectangular village and function as the link between discrete, bounded units. But much of the activity that took

place in circular villages in the public communal center now takes place within the privacy of the household court.

A similar pattern — instructive because of its differences, however — is found among many horticulturalists who supplement their diets through fishing. Among these, each household is a unit of production, and village unity is required only intermittently — reflecting the need for occasional large-scale intensive cooperation during those periods of the year when fish spawn, when boats must be built, or forests cleared to replace exhausted soils. During the remainder of the time, the household is self-sufficient and the village expresses this self-sufficiency in its linear arrangement of individual homesteads, held together not simply by the need for intermittent cooperation but by what Emile Durkheim labeled "mechanical solidarity."[20] Since the inhabitants produce the same crops with the same cycles, fish the same grounds, and hunt the same animals, their daily, weekly, monthly, and yearly rounds tend to be identical. This identity is further consolidated through the development of shared religious systems which recognize the dual needs of the family or homestead and village by providing expression for both in the form of household as well as corporate deities. The presence of a corporate deity is signaled architecturally by the appearance of a village shrine.

Anthropologists have puzzled over the problems of cultural evolution for more than a century, and they have by and large sought the answers to their puzzle in the Middle East, where civilization appears to have emerged rather rapidly. While most theories involve some notion of the availability of a surplus with which the villagers were capable of supporting specialists, just how this surplus came into existence, and how it was translated into the development of complex urban political systems, remains somewhat of a mystery. Beyond such fundamental considerations as an assured water supply, it seems possible that the rectangular house-form and court of the Middle Eastern village allowed significantly more opportunity for privacy — thus permitting more enterprising families to accumulate wealth. At the same time, growth of religious and political leadership allowed an organizing body, through taxation and control of the populace, to tap this surplus for its own uses. The architecture of the village and its layout may be important clues to understanding the speed with which the Middle Eastern villages evolved into town, city, and state and the relatively slower pace of development in other parts of the world.

In both the rectangular house village of the Middle East and the linear maritime village we see the emergence of a change in the nature of human relationships which in turn depends upon technological ability and habitat. Both villages emphasize the family as the basic unit of production, and both have begun to grant privacy to the family.

Anthropologists have speculated that the linear village, often found strung out alongside roads and river banks, emerged because access to road or water coerces the form. While some linear villages clearly owe their origins to this need for shore access, many maritime villages consist of two facing rows of houses with the street between; and more often than not, the street is perpendicular, rather than parallel, to the water's edge. In a circle, all positions have equal access to the center, and information appears to be relatively equally distributed among all members. In studies of communication, social psychologists have learned that circular forms are egalitarian, that they seem to provide a sense of satisfaction for all their participants, and that they generally are not very efficient in performing tasks.[21] The linear arrangement may not only tend to limit the field of observation and increase the privacy of the household in its relationships to other households; it may also increase the ability of a spatially central chief, whose access to information is greater than that of the rest of the population, to substitute personal power for the organic system of the circular village.

While village plans and streets look very similar from one site to another, the kind and number of activities that take place on the street may be very different even for similar looking settlements, and the difference depends largely on particular social structures which, in turn, appear to reflect specific adaptational needs. Where a moiety system dominates, for example, members of each half may be ranged on opposite sides of the street. In this case, the street is not a focus for casual interaction but a spatial symbol of the separation of the moieties. It is, however, at the same time a symbol of the unity of the whole and frequently indicates this function by its inclusion at the center or toward one end of the street of those buildings that both symbolize village unity and operate to produce it — the chief's hut, village shrine or temple, communal granary, or men's club.

Other linear streets may express organization of subclans or lineage segments: in this case members of each subclan may be housed opposite as well as next to each other. Here the street may become the locus of daily, highly personal interactions, though these may be confined to particular segments of the street. In more complex organizations, sub-clan groups may be dispersed both laterally and lineally so that the whole street becomes the setting for interpersonal relationships for the whole village. Such a complex arrangement suggests the emergence of other social institutions which serve to form yet another means by which households may be held together beyond the bounds of kinship. Called sodalities, these organizations, which generally function as cooperative work groups and ceremonial organizations, cut across nuclear families and lineages to provide yet another source of cooperative village activity. Their presence has been confirmed for rectangular villages both in Mexico and the Near East.

The emergence of the street, then, seems to symbolize or express a gradual awareness of the separation of private and public, family and larger community. Competition and intensification of production rather than cooperation and stability of production emerge with the street. The state of disequilibrium prerequisite to change is thus apparent in spatial organization.

When we move from an examination of village to city streets, we find — within a field of far greater complexity — evidence of a similar linkage between street and social structure.

Cities exhibit a bewildering diversity of form. Some seem to be little more than superimpositions of a grid or other rationalized system on a village plan. Since presence of rationalized systems appears to correlate with the emergence of centralized power, it is not unlikely that such ordered plans are a response to administrative needs for order, predictability, and defense. Ordered forms include the orthogonally gridded city, which tends to break down into wards, and the radial city whose focus or center may well be correlated with increasing centralization of power.

Although we have only the most superficial notions of what life is like in such cities and how the form serves to organize or express social relationships, we do know that ward cities generally reflect political divisions based on religious, ethnic, or occupational differences. On the other hand, examination of caste-ridden Indian cities does not show congruence between caste and dwelling place — just as southern towns in the United States often mingle black and white dewellings. It seems possible that where social boundaries are clear and well supported by other institutions in the system, the need for physical boundaries may diminish. On the other hand, where the possibility of social interchange among two boundary systems is increased by development of crosscutting organizations or by the presence of superordinate authority, a system of physical boundaries may emerge to affirm and emphasize separation. Without careful examination, this notion must remain a hypothesis, but it would appear to be worth testing.

If the emergence of the street stands as a symbol of the separation of private from public domains, it nevertheless must also be the locus of the active definition of public and private. Furthermore, changes in economic and political organization can easily be observed in the changes in the street. Initially, presence of the city wall symbolized and supported the presence of a cooperative unit, operating principally through a system of interwoven kin, work, and religious networks. Within this walled city, activity was both public and social and economic activities were still embedded in the households; trade and social life were conducted together. In the medieval city, developing specialization in craft was marked as much by the appearance of specialized streets as by the presence of the guild hall. Church and state grappled for control over the emerging cities and indicated this tension in the spatial position of churches relative to major secular buildings within the town. The unity of life was expressed in the minimal separation that existed not only betwen workplace and home, but in the continuity of workplace and street. On pleasant days, work could be done in the street; in inclement weather, it was done inside. The barrier between interior and exterior was extremely penetrable, just as the barriers between age groups were virtually nonexistent; children as well as adults played street games, went to market, viewed the same entertainments, and dressed in identical clothing. The marketplace of the medieval town also reflected this unity: it provided an area for social interchange which included not only the exchange of goods for money but entertainment and the exchange of services as well. Physicians, barbers, scribes, and food vendors hawked their wares in the street and in the marketplace much as they do today in oriental cities.

Since the streets were open to all, and since no formal schools existed to remove children or adolescents from the streets, learning took place there and access to all the information of the society — except those skills guarded by the guild — was at least potentially available for the walking. Meanwhile, as long as the citizenry defined the market as essentially social, many of the phenomena that order today's street behavior were not present. As in the souks or the oriental markets of today, close physical contact, highly personal interchange, and crowding provided a festive environment which may have functioned to provide then, as it does now, a sense of excitement and adventure. The typical streaming behavior of modern pedestrian traffic on crowded streets, derived from the need for increased speed and efficiency, is conspicuously lacking — even today — in streets where economic and social functions are mixed.

As the growth of state systems and the concomitant development of new types of warfare and increasing trade destroyed the value as well as the need for city walls, the city itself and the streets within it took on new functions: again, both street and city reflect the role of the city in the new organizational framework. While the broad street, the perspective view, and the outlook over a wide area are often considered to be responses to military inventions, it is equally likely that they arose as tangible symbols of national power which turned the city outward toward the country as a whole and which used the capital city as a visible symbol of the state's power.[22] Changes in technology are reflected in increasing specialization of street function. The great streets, planned by military engineers or central planning agencies, became more than the locus of ordinary activity: settings for the symbols of national power (army and parade) and class distinctions (the horse and carriage). With the growth of nationalism, technology, capitalism, and state power, the guild hall and church lost their centrality; religious, kinship, and other spheres — once interwoven in a complex network of

mutual obligations — became separate and distinct. Differentiation in the use of the street by lower, middle, and upper classes reflected even as it helped to maintain the stratification of society. The upper classes used the great streets as a stage upon which to display their wealth and power. The lower classes used their streets (now, by comparison with new streets, mean, narrow, back streets) to escape the controls of constabulary or, in continuation of older practice, to extend their cramped living space. For the middle class, the street was increasingly *terra incognita* — a passageway utilized to get from home to work and otherwise avoided because of the potential violence that threatened there. The difference among the classes is obvious not only in their attitudes toward streets but their use of the streets, which were left at night to the upper and lower classes. The middle classes, in seventeenth-century Paris and in London until the eighteenth century, hesitated to venture forth at night except in dire emergency, a situation that was not unprecedented.[23]

It was only through the development of city constabulary that the dangers of the street were eventually countered. Emergence of city police accompanied increasing cohesion of the state and, as if reflecting the growing importance of international trade and alliances, the streets became more cosmopolitan in character. The *boulevardier*, equally at home in London, Paris, or Vienna, held court in the outdoor café and utilized the street for his amorous adventures. Entertainments of all kinds — including pleasure parks designed to simulate exotic places, dance halls, shopping arcades, and theatres brought nightly excitement — and, for the upper and now wealthy middle classes, the opportunity to participate in a wider world. Increasingly economically confined to their own neighborhoods, the poor exhibited in the novels of Dickens behaviors that suggest processes similar to those we observe today in our own slums: development of internal and highly personal communication systems on the street and the emergence of an expressive, rather than instrumental, personality. These processes appear to have adaptive value within the slum but severely limit the slum resident's ability to function within the larger social structure.

It seems apparent that the definitions and differentiations of systems of streets have grown increasingly complex as society itself has increased in complexity. Today, the role of the street and the nature and content of social interaction vary with class, ethnic group, age structures, and type of specialization of the neighborhood. It is clear, however, that increasing specialization and compartmentalization of society have removed indoors many of the socially cohesive activities once found in the street. Entertainment, marketing, information, and personal services, once available on the street, are now rarely there. With suburbanization, streets have disappeared; the physical sidewalk is often narrowed to a foot path, and in some developments there is no sidewalk.

In central areas of the city, the situation is much the same; in high-rise apartments, firm boundaries between building and street serve to maintain separation. Only in the slum and in the dwindling ethnic enclaves and blue-collar areas does the street still seem to function partially as a locus for public life. In the ethnic enclaves it often exhibits processes reminiscent of the village in which a moral order and its attendant values are enforced through gossip passed along in street networks.

The evolution of technology with its attendant economic pressures and proliferation of formal institutions, and the encroachment on the street of municipal and state functions, suggests that the role of the street is now rarely visualized in terms of an immediate neighborhood: acting as a link rather than a locus, the street now serves to maintain the order of larger political entitites. Increasingly, the street is recognized for its transit capabilities rather than for its ability to provide a setting for a range of rich and diversified human behaviors. Social controls, sanctions, rules, and laws reflect national rather than local norms; only those segments of our society denied access to the general culture or those with currently atypical devotion to community identity can maintain a system of norms specific to the neighborhood.

This brief and schematic view of the evolution of the street suggests that:

1. The street and settlement pattern of which the street is an integral part reflect and help to maintain particular forms of social organization necessary for adaptation. Streets maintain a particular way of life or structure or relationships by providing barriers and linkages that help regulate the amount of social interaction among groups. Streets and settlement patterns also appear to have some effect on limiting social interaction among groups. The importance of the street as a center of information wanes with the increase in literacy and the development of communication devices.

2. The emergence of the street marks the emergence of a concept of privacy, private property, and seems inseparable from the intensification of production necessary to create a surplus. The emergence of the street is vital to the emergence of the city and of civilization.

3. As we move along the scale of social organization and technology, specialization in other areas of life is reflected in growing specialization of the street. An increase in the number of institutions creates a cross cutting web of social relationships that helps knit society together; at the same time proliferation of organizations and sodalities creates more and more private or exclusive institutions. This development too is reflected in the street with the emergence first of guild streets and later of specialized work areas, separate residential zones, and streets used only for commercial or entertainment purposes.

4. Development of stratified class systems further specializes the streets, creating separate neighborhoods for different classes within the city. Streets that serve different classes reflect the classes they serve by the nature of their amenities and by differences in their daily, weekly, monthly, and yearly rhythms.

5. Increasing centralization of power asserts itself in rearrangement of the city form. Initially, the emergence of a separate political sphere correlates with the presence of grid systems or radial or ward plans. Later, streets are widened and perspective view and outlook favored. The city is no longer a self-contained entity but a node in a national network. The capital city, commonly radial in plan, symbolizes central power and control.

6. Just as old forms of adaptation and social organization are reflected in particular street forms and village and town layouts, so we might expect that new levels of technological adaptation and increasing centralized control will demand — and are demanding — adjustment throughout all our urban institutions. Gradual encroachment of central government functions into state and city affairs is apparent even now, and the effects of these shifts, as well as the effects of an automated technology, will be evidenced in the street. The success of automation raises the specter of the devolution of culture which may have emerged out of the need of human groups to allocate specific roles to males and females as a result of human development of the hunting way of life. Divested of work as a basis for mutual interaction and cooperation, man seems to face both a dangerous and promising void which demands that he find a new basis for social organization. Societies can be held together by increasingly centralized and powerful state systems and the dangers of such a development are only too obvious. Alienated from government, cut away from any system of mutual social obligations, and divested even of the labor that has given his life meaning, man appears to be cast adrift on an anomic sea. The influence of this centralization of power on the streets is only too obvious in the emphasis placed on the street as linkage rather than locus. Such an emphasis destroys smaller group boundaries and with them the organic relationships characteristic of these groups.

While it is possible that man is a plastic enough organism to survive even this turn of events, the prospects, based on extrapolation of evolutionary information, do not appear reassuring. Man, who evolved within small groups and who has few instincts to guide him, requires a close attachment to other men and to a primary reference group — at least during childhood — if he is to mature properly.[24] His ties to place, the frequently noted need for roots, seem to stem from his need for a relatively stable and predictable environmental setting in which he can learn both his limits and his powers, his boundaries and his possibilities. While it is possible to assure such environmental stability by creating a uniform worldwide environment and culture, such a device is extraordinarily dangerous. Adaptation to a single environment tends to eliminate genetic and cultural diversity. It is this ability to maintain diversity that has allowed man — unlike other animals — to remain a relatively generalized creature. Unprogrammed by rigid instinctive rules, he has been free to take advantage of his environment as has no other animal. Maintaining a degree of human diversity demands maintenance of a degree of environmental diversity; and both appear to be highly desirable. In nature, simple ecosystems are easily destroyed.

Moreover, maintenance of social interaction must now proceed without the familiar props of environmental necessity. If our technology does succeed in creating an automated society, man will no longer need to enmesh himself in a system of mutual social dependencies in order to get the work of his society done. He is thus potentially freed by technology to choose both the degree and nature of his social contacts. He is not yet free, however, of the processes of political authority which, as they have gradually absorbed the functions of his primary groups, have also encouraged development of smaller units of privacy and led to increasing isolation of human beings from one another. Man appears to be a social animal, requiring both physical contact and opportunity to learn from others; hence, increasing isolation appears to run counter to his nature. Indeed, psychological literature supports anthropology in attesting to the correlation between limited social networks and emotional instability. Man's sense of purpose and meaning derives from his relationships with others; if we remove the necessity of such relationships by providing a technology that supplies his wants, and a political system that imposes order upon him, we transform man from an active, inquisitive creature who makes himself into a passive victim of a self-created but all-powerful technocratic system. Our best attempts must be devoted to increasing social interaciton. This can best be done not only by creating a physical environment that permits and encourages contact but by some attempts to restore the social and economic functions of primary groups by investing some of the power of the state in local organizations. Only in this way can we hope to maintain an organic basis for human cooperation. Without such a base, social interaction may become, as it often is now, a series of ritual gestures that operate to maintain spatial separation but fail to provide adequate satisfaction or meaning for their users.

Projects and Slums: Streets for People

Most studies of slum streets, whether they are studies of slums as a whole or of juvenile gangs in particular, suggest that streets play a vital role in the slum by providing a locus for primary reference groups that give their members — otherwise unable to find meaningful attatchments — a sense of belonging and cohesion.[25] Slum streets also seem to function as a safety valve and provide the setting in which residents can achieve a certain amount of freedom from the pressures of domestic life. In *The Social Order of the Slum*, Gerald Suttles has suggested, in addition, that the street plays "an interstitial role that bridges the privacy of the areas family life and the seclusiveness of its internal segments. On the streets, age, sex, and territorial groups share boundaries that open them to mutual inspection, thus giving the occasion for transient interaction between groups, for gossip, and for interpretive observation. Street life, then, is a vital link in the communications network of the Addams area and, as a result, governs much of what the residents know of one another beyond the range of personal acquaintance."[26]

While street life functions as a communication network to link a variety of groups together, it also appears to help protect family privacy. As one woman explained: "I like to be able to talk to lots of people on the street, but not in the house. I don't want to get that involved."[27] Residents of the slum appear to have few devices for defending the privacy of the home; they have, moreover, little opportunity for privacy in the home — since crowded quarters, large families, and poor construction operate constantly to create intrusions. Social life, moreover, is so informal that, once started, "Domestic exchanges subject the residents either to unpredictable exposures or to additional confrontations from which they cannot easily retreat."[28]

Suttles's findings suggest that the street is also attractive because it offers the slum dweller an escape from the domestic world, provides a sense of color, freedom, and excitement, and an opportunity for a serendipitous and unscheduled experience.

Similar observations are offered by Elliot Liebow, Ulf Hannerz, Herbert Gans, William F. Whyte, and Lee Rainwater.[29] Whyte emphasized the supportive role played by the "Street Corner Society," while at the same time he perceived it as providing training in a relatively rigid and inflexible system of relationships that provided few techniques for operating in the larger society. Hannerz indicated that the informal gossip network did provide information about the outside world.

Suttles's most interesting finding about the urban slum is that there seems to be no general standard of morality, no general norm against which the individual may be evaluated. If Suttles is correct, the system of overlapping relationships, which appear to be necessary to create a moral order, does not exist in the slums. Instead, groups are separate, segregated by background and behavior. The tenuous connections they maintain with each other appear to derive from acquaintance on the street. The information circulated on the street is not utilized to maintain the community as a whole (except against external threat) but to maintain personal relationships. Ethnic group cohesion, therefore, is not

achieved through the workings of social sanctions but through a negative pact. Since everyone is jointly compromised by common disclo-
sures, everyone is obligated to protect the information. The group thus
shares knowledge of its own membership but keeps the information
from escaping the group.

Street gossip thus allows the slum dwellers to gain exact knowledge
of one another's personal character but limits the extent of the social
order, since there is a limit to the number of persons one may get to
know through private sources. Human ability to absorb information is
also limited: without a general system of moral categories, each personality must be memorized for itself; hence no person can get to know
more than a few others.[30]

It is likely that this concentration on discrete bits of internal information further inhibits the slum dweller's already diminished opportunity
to absorb additional information from outside. The result may be the
creation of a series of rigid categories or sterotypes about the larger
society that prevents the slum dweller from dealing with it realistically.
Nevertheless the studies suggest that even in the slum there must be
some degree of adaptation to a larger unit — a neighborhood made up of
a variety of ethnic and racial groups — and that the street is a vital link
in this adaptation.

While it is easy to denigrate the relatively rigid and tenuously connected segments of the lower- or working-class slum, comparison of its
structure with that of the Pruitt-Igoe housing in St. Louis (an initially
highly regarded but particularly unsuccessful urban-renewal project)
places into sharp relief the strengths of the slum and the role played by
the street in maintaining them. Divested of the organic structures that
accompany the growth of an ethnic neighborhood, deprived of the rich
street life of the working class slum, and blocked even from the
development of segmented groups, the project dweller is subject to
control by authorities above and beyond his own group. The project is
not held together by a system of social or group relationships but by a
superordinate authority that wields its power by virtue of its ability to
reward and punish project dwellers.

According to Lee Rainwater,[31] the project dweller develops social
and personal responses that tend to generate aggression toward self and
others. These responses are an understandable adaptation to the situation; clearly, they are neither socially nor personally desirable.

Within its limited street culture, the low-income project failed to
develop even the system of gossip that had acted as a negative focus for
community cohesion in the slum. Relationships in Pruitt-Igoe were so
agonistic and privacy so desperately defended that even the weeds of
gossip withered. Here, as in other projects whose residents are drawn
together by bureaucratic rather than human convenience, the basis for
community cohesion was extraordinarily weak. Strangers to begin with,
project residents were subject to administrative rules that increased the
atmosphere of distrust and suspicion in which they lived. Afraid that a
neighbor might report that her husband was visiting, that her morals
were questionable, or that she was earning money despite her welfare
status, the project woman attempted to avoid contact with her
neighbors. Similar fears motivated the behavior of the men who lacked,
in addition, any kind of organization that might provide training for
leadership, feelings of self-esteem, or opportunities to participate.

Conspicuously missing from the project were institutions that might
serve as a focal point for community cohesion. Street life in the project
was minimal and its principal function seemed to be provision of an
escape valve by which residents temporarily transcended their limited
self-definitions by developing a distinctive life style. This style, labeled
"expressive" in the literature, allowed project residents to assert some
control over their immediate environment but was not suitable for
extending the social network and inhibited the development of an
instrumental personality with which one might operate successfully in
the world outside the project.

The architecture of much low-income housing encourages anomie.
Separation from street is maximized in high-rise construction; in Pruitt-
Igoe, lack of physical streets with the usual groceries, candy stores,
repair shops, or other generators of social activity seemed to add to the
residents' woes. Though provision of amenities alone is not sufficient to
create social interaction, the bleak, streetless environment of the project
further eliminated possibilities of human encounter and thus helped to
maintain the hierarchical system of imposed power that might otherwise
be undermined — or at least questioned — by the development of
cooperative groups or strong local boundary systems.

Suttles's slum included a housing project and he noted that administrative rules forbade the moving of furniture onto the street; in the slum,
people often structured their own interaction by bringing chairs, tables,
and TV sets into the street. Prohibitions against such practices —
coupled with failure to provide equivalent facilities and the elimination
of stoops and steps used by slum residents — served to further diminish
opportunities in the project for social interaction. A system of interior
streets within the corridors, designed to facilitate childcare, worked
instead to scatter rather than condense people — again increasing
anomie and decreasing contact.

Analysis of the neighborhoods commonly labeled slums yields
similarities among them, and similarities between slums and lower-
income housing projects are evident where the projects collected their
residents from working-class or blue-collar populations. But even the
term *slum* conceals at least two clearly different sets of social organization — and it is obvious that these two do not exhaust the possibilities.

Both the lower-class slum described by Suttles and a variety of working-class or ethnic slums analyzed by Fried and Gleicher and by Herbert Gans[32] utilized the streets as part of a complex communication network. Both utilized the streets — and amenities along the streets — to develop and maintain valued and often valuable social contacts. The streets also functioned both to maintain communication within an area and to extend lines of communication among the various segments that appear to make up the slum.

Although at times the residents of Suttles's slum appeared to perceive the street simply as an extension of domestic space, more often they appeared to use it in a different way: as an arena in which to experiment with alternate life-styles and in which they might escape from a constricting domestic scene. Men seemed particularly in need of a place they could call their own, since the home was conceptualized and furnished as a woman's world. The more homogeneous ethnic slum, particularly if it had sufficient time dimension, used the streets in a less segregated manner. Here the street functioned as a setting for a web of overlapping behaviors; the segmentation and age, sex, and role separation were crosscut by ties of kinship, work, religious association, and neighboring, in a pattern that inspired Herbert Gans to call them "The Urban Villagers." Urban enclaves that are simultaneously street oriented, villagelike, and not markedly constrained economically or socially are also known.[33] Thus while the street may appear to play an ambiguous role for ethnic communities such as those described by Suttles, it can also demonstrably play an unambiguously positive role. The street is only one element of a larger slum structure that socializes the resident into an expressive rather than instrumental role and educates him into a rigid set of rule systems, while providing him with a security that limits both flexibility and the extent of his social network.

The Uses of Diversity

In *The Death and Life of Great American Cities,*[34] Jane Jacobs proposed that cities would be safer, more livable, and more attractive if their streets were zoned for an intricate mingling of different uses. Aside from aesthetic considerations, Mrs. Jacobs suggested that diversity of use aided in: (1) maintaining activity in an area during greater portions of day and night; (2) increasing safety by ensuring the presence of people on the street; (3) decreasing monotony; (4) and increasing public contact and cross use.

While most of Mrs. Jacobs's comments were based on her observation of her own and other neighborhoods, and while she is a careful and responsible observer, the mixed reception of her ideas indicates that some examination of her assertions — is both desirable and necessary. Very few such studies currently exist; therefore, support for the notion that diversity may be desirable must come from other quarters.

Prominent among those currently engaged in studying man/environment interactions are the ecological psychologists. Ecological psychology has suggested one solution of the man/environment dilemma by asserting, and attempting to describe, the presence of environmental units as bounded, internally differentiated, self-balancing organizations that operate according to rules specific for each setting and significantly shape the behavior of individuals inhabiting or using them. While ecological psychology has concentrated on behavior in school settings, some of its findings suggest that availability of a large number of behavioral settings has significant positive effects on satisfaction, morale, and participation.

Examining school settings,[35] the researchers began by contrasting behavior settings in small and large schools. While large schools seemed to exert particular pressures on students, the crucial factor did not appear to be size but rather different numbers of behavior settings available in each type of school. Undermanned settings — generally found in small schools — were associated with more satisfaction, more participation, and more self-confidence; they served a very important social function and, in allowing for much greater involvement of marginal students, provided higher levels of participation, satisfaction, and morale in this group. Large schools with relatively fewer behavior settings produced more vicarious watching behavior and a tendency for students to affiliate within a larger entity. Many participants who seemed content with their own passive behavior found the large schools satisfactory, but these schools were significantly less satisfactory to the marginal students.

The researchers suggested that an increase in the number of behavior settings within a large setting might be useful — but they warned that the large setting might be so overwhelming that participants would tend, despite opportunities available to them, to see the rules of the system as a whole as more coercive than the rules of any specific setting. Since streets are not schools — or total institutions — some of the problems raised by the school setting may be less important on the street. The proposed utilization of an increased number of behavior settings might be contributive in the freewheeling arena of the street.

The value of diversity of settings and of unprogrammed settings in general seems to lie in the ability of such settings to give people experience in a variety of roles and to provide many more opportunities for self-redefinition. They also create numerous opportunities for people to interact with a variety of other people — raising the possibility of conflict but also allowing for an increase in empathy and understanding. Since man is less a creature of instinct than of habit or culture, what he is and how he develops depends largely on the opportunities for interaction that are present in his environment.

Our ability to provide a diversity of behavior settings along a street has been seriously eroded by the demands of the marketplace. As many architects have pointed out, it is not sufficient to line a roadside strip or a street with a dozen different kinds of shops; indeed, such an interpretation of diversity leads to difference for difference's sake, masking an underlying monotony. Of course, a variety of small shops has its uses — but the focus on consumption activities in the street tends to restrict the definition of the participants either to salespersons or consumers.

Establishment of a variety of off-street behavior settings should stress construction not only of shops and restaurants but lecture halls, exhibit areas, clearly defined play areas, observation points, strolling lanes, and sitting zones that could accommodate both intimate pairs and more impersonal groups. Larger open areas might be suitable for serendipitous happenings, displays, and entertainments or opportunities to observe people at work. Lounges and cafés should accommodate teenagers as well as adults in their search for settings in which they can experiment with new definitions of self.

The ecological psychologists offer another proposition that deserves consideration — although, since it appears to have derived from the achievement-oriented school settings in which the ecological psychologists have done most of their research, it may bear reference primarily to highly structured environments. The proposition is simply that designers should plan settings not only to change people but simply to provide existential satisfaction. However, the implied criticism cuts deeper: as Barker and Gump point out, life is a process, and immediate actions and reactions are also important in assessing the worth of a setting. A behavior setting that provides immediate satisfaction improves the quality of life. As Gump asserts, planning should not aim primarily at improving the intellect or developing an idea of beauty but should increase the number and intensity of "smiles, involved postures, chats, exploration, and the assumption of responsibility."

Another study that seems to support a belief that diversity is valuable is John Gulick's "Images of an Arab City."[36] Utilizing some of Kevin Lynch's theories and techniques, the author set out to discover the "imageability" of the Lebanese city of Tripoli. Accoring to Lynch, imageability is a significant factor in creating a sense of city coherency; hence increased imageability would appear to provide an increased sense of place and order. Gulick had thirty-five college students draw a map of the city. The maps indicated that while individual buildings were unimportant, various sections of the city were vital to imageability. These sections were distinguishable because they had very distinctive visual and kinesthetic qualities. High on the list was the Tell — scene of intense, varied activities, an area containing a park surrounded by shops and coffee houses and filled with cars and pedestrians. Other important areas were differ en* in elevation; in others, one was subject to changes of light or spatial dimensions as one passed through them. While Gulick's sample of thirty-five college students is small, the findings corroborated those of other studies, which suggested that imageability requires distinctive sections with connecting paths, involves kinesthetic as well as visual factors, and emphasizes the presence of thronged sidewalks. The evidence is all the more persuasive because it was gathered in an Arab urban culture that has characteristically deemphasized community life while stressing an intense family life. Despite such cultural restrictions, the Lebanese students were most aware of and attracted by the dense, crowded Tell and by environments that offered changes in kinesthetic experience.

At the scale of individual streets, support for the notion that increased diversity of settings and activities offers positive human values comes from numerous psychological studies of stress, aging, and learning. Stress studies deal with extremes, of course — subjecting participants to total sensory deprivation or overstimulation. Under such extreme conditions human beings tend to break down, proving that there are limits to human ability to deal with the environment; these limits involve, at one end of the scale, the ability to process information and, at the other, to exist with minimal or no information.[37] While John Calhoun's studies of crowded rats have been widely applied by analogy to situations of human crowding, it seems clear that we do not have as yet any clear guidelines for analyzing an optimal environment or even for determining what degree of density is plausible or desirable or what dimensions of crowding create pathology in humans. While it is fashionable to believe that continued exposure to situations of high density leads to emotional problems, the data proving such a proposition are so confused and contradictory as to provide us with scanty information. On the one hand, we have numerous studies of the emotional and social pathology of the ghettos, the high incidence of disturbance in central-city areas, and the anomie that is assumed to be endemic in urban settings. Many of these settings, however, are not uniformly dense: in fact, they include bombed-out areas of relatively low density. Cultural patterns that militate against use of the street by women and children (in Spanish neighborhoods, for example) may serve to reduce street congestion while the dwellings are of statistically high density. Cultures differ enormously in the degree to which they perceive crowding and in the use of personal space.

To add to the problem we have numerous studies of Hong Kong, Tokyo, and India, which indicate that density by itself is not a sufficient explanation of social pathology. In Hong Kong, for example, Robert Schmitt found high density associated with low disease rates, relatively low infant mortality, and less mental disease and juvenile delinquency and crime than in far less crowded areas of the United States.[38]

Cultural expectations, rules, and adaptive techniques clearly play a major role in diminishing or exaggerating the effects of high density and consequent crowding. But most important perhaps is the nature of the boundary system. The gang boy may be delighted with close, intense, and crowded relationships within his territory, but he will feel — as the frequently uttered colloquialism ''don't crowd me'' suggests — crowded if his gang's territory is threatened by another group. Stanley Milgram has suggested the presence of psychological mechanisms that provide some protection against overstimulation or the reception of too much information from the environment.[39] Such mechanisms include the by now familiar ''supermarket syndrome'' or semihypnotic blinkless trance that symptomizes the presence of abundance and confusion in the supermarket. Others are the physical withdrawal and alterations in body position and tension that make it possible for people to crowd together in subways; another is avoidance of mutual eye contact. More profound, perhaps, is the phenomenon described by Georg Simmel as objectivity or intellectuality. Simmel laid out the paradox of urban mental life that demands the development of reserve, a blasé attitude, as the price of unprecedented personal freedom:

> The most profound reason, however, why the metropolis conduces to the urge for the most individual personal existence . . . appears to me to be the following: the development of modern culture is characterized by the preponderance of what one may call the ''objective spirit'' over the ''subjective spirit.'' . . . Indeed, at some points we notice a retrogression in the culture of the individual with reference to spirituality, delicacy and idealism. This discrepancy results essentially from a growing division of labor. For the division of labor demands from the individual an ever more one-sided accomplishment and the greatest advance in a one-sided pursuit all too frequently means death to the personality of the individual. In any case, he can cope less and less with the overgrowth of objective culture. The individual is reduced to a negligible quantity, perhaps less in his consciousness than in his practice, and in the totality of his obscure emotional states that are derived from this practice. . . . Here in buildings and educational institutions, in the wonders and comforts of space conquering technology, in the formations of community life and in the visible institutions of the state is offered such an overwhelming fullness of crystallized and impersonalized spirit that the personality, so to speak, cannot maintain itself under its impact. *On the one hand life is made infinitely easy for the personality in that stimulations, interests, uses of time and consciousness are offered to it from all sides . . . On the other hand, however, life is composed more and more of these impersonal contents and offerings which tend to displace the genuine personal colorations and incomparabilities.* This results in the individual's summoning the utmost in uniqueness and particularization in order to preserve his most personal core.[40]

As Simmel points out, we do not know whether such mechanisms are good or bad in themselves; however, if a good part of one's energy must be expended either in defense against contact or in the development of an inauthentic uniqueness, and if, moreover, personal relationships are less important than economic activity, then it seems likely that one is coerced into a role or, at any rate, has less control over his own role than he imagines. Freedom — on the ghetto street, for example — frequently involves the development of what Simmel called the blasé personality, what we know as ''cool.'' To ''keep his cool,'' to remain indifferent, allows the ghetto youngster — as it once allowed the boulevardier — to replace authentic personal colorations and incomparabilities with a superficial style.

From yet another vantage point, an amalgam of notions derived from theories about play and creativity, Amos Rapoport attempts to deal with the problems posed by perceptual overload in the environment.[41] Rapoport looks on both overload and understimulation as equally bad: both result in fatigue and shutdown, frequently in accidents. Rapoport believes that complexity is desirable and is a function of ''violated expectations.'' Such a conceptualization assumes the presence of expectation, an ordered rule system in the environment. Increased complexity aids in reducing monotony; it does not increase information if the elements themselves are unambiguous. Thus Rapoport states that the roadside strip, despite its superficial variety, is the visual equivalent of ''white noise'' (a concept that is embodied in the work of William Ewald on graphic design[42]).

At the moment we do not know the optimum amount of significant information necessary for human functioning. We know that people at different stages in their life cycles require different inputs: children whose perceptions of the world are not yet fully organized and whose attention mechanisms are not mature require environments somewhat different from those that might be suitable for an adult. At the same time, some research suggests that old people — whose perceptual apparatus is somewhat impaired — may need not only more environmental stimulus but stimulus that is more redundant and differently organized. Our information about age differences is far more detailed than that available about cultural difference in perception. While we know that every culture organizes the world differently, we know very little about the different rule systems of different groups, the spatial parameters of cultures, and how these affect both perception and classification of perception into meaningful units.

Generally, comparison of human and animal behavior under stress suggests that the development of the human brain, with its ability to organize perceptions into larger units, allows man more leeway in a crowded situation. Man's ability to symbolize and classify events is an effective method by which he reduces information and the stress involved in overload. At the same time, his brain seems to demand greater stimulation: when he is deprived of sufficient input, he hallucinates.

Variety and richness in his interior environment thus substitute for variety and richness in his exterior world. But concentration on interior stimulation tends to make the individual a closed system capable of generating only information he already possesses. His behavior loses its adaptive flexibility and is ruled instead by a series of repetitive compulsions that may maintain life at a minimal level but allow for nothing more. Just as the isolated individual has no way of defining himself, or even of conceiving himself as a person apart from his environment, so the isolated group or the group under stress (such as those in multiethnic neighborhoods) tends to specialize in the development of rigid boundary systems and compulsive social arrangements that limit both flexibility and adaptation. Such findings provide support for Rapoport's belief that optimum conditions are achieved when the environment can build up expectations (that is, develop a relatively stable rule system) and then depart from them. A variety of other evidence supports this hypothesis, just as it tends to support Jane Jacobs's formulations. These include time/motion studies of factory workers, analysis of the behavior of men in prison camps by Bruno Bettelheim,[43] the stress studies themselves,[44] research into the nature of play conducted by psychoanalysts, educational psychologists, and ethologists,[45] and learning theory which suggests that increase in learning takes place only after one is unsettled, forced to break set, and thus enabled to gain a new perspective on a problem. Ambiguity and violated expectations are not necessarily comfortable. However, it seems likely that man, whose evolution is not conceivable without his large brain and his symbol-making capacities, cannot exist without uncertainty. When it is lacking, he generates it psychically. At the same time, the uncertainty must be tied to a stable set of expectations: when a rule system and boundaries are lacking, he often falls back on ritual, magic, or a compulsive formula by which he attempts to create a predictable order within his environment.

Amassing arguments in favor of diversity that rest upon a human need for rules and surprise or attesting to demands created by the evolution of the human body does not, of course, demand that we create this diversity upon the street. A counterargument would be Melvin Webber's belief that a nonspatially oriented society can satisfy human needs through technology.[46] Webber's projections derive largely from the network analysis of today's upper middle class. This group spends little time in immediate surrounds, does not equate proximity with neighboring, and makes its friends among a far-flung society generally related by profession or business interests. Communication among them depends on media: they are the large consumers of the conference telephone and airline tickets. Fully stimulated by the amount of information they must process for their professions and to maintain their life-style, these men and women would appear to require very few of the amenities that have been suggested as appropriate to diversity on the street. Furthermore, it has been suggested that they represent the vanguard of the future, we must consider the possibility that scarce resources might be better spent on technological equipment than on streets and local developments.

While the argument is attractive and the number of people adopting this life-style is bound to grow, one must question the potentially damaging impact of such a technology on children, old people, the handicapped — as well as the large number of people who, in the foreseeable future, will neither be able to afford nor adjust to such a technology. The energy crisis foreseen by prominent scientists (became common property since this article was written) is another important factor: sufficient resources may not be available for this technological development. Committing all resources to more efficient distance communication or new forms of interior communication is not only psychologically and economically questionable; its political dangers are evident. Control by media is more easily effected over the individual isolated in his home than over the crowd in the street; and decisions as to what information is to be transmitted over the media are more likely to be controlled by the few than by the many.

But perhaps the most cogent argument against the universalization of this life-style derives from human biology and the examination of man as a species. Curious, specializing in generalization, and requiring both the presence of others to define himself and real physical contact from those others in order to maintain his sanity, man has developed as the creature who learns to learn. And he appears to learn best — or to function best — within a social context. Experiments with computer learning and television courses indicated that students absorbed significant amounts of information from media. In fact, it seemed that they actually accumulated more information in this way. However, despite their greater factual knowledge the students were less able to function within their learned disciplines.[47] For students to succeed, they had to absorb attitudes, facial expressions, body positions, behaviors, and numerous subtle clues about interpersonal relationships. Without this kind of personal social information, which required the physical presence of a teacher, they could not do as well as students with less information but greater opportunity for socialization into a discipline. Much that we have learned about education suggests that enormous energy is expended in this socialization process; it is, in fact, the development of this ability that both created and secured culture.

The possibility that culture may be transmitted solely through media, that learning information rather than socialization will become the aim of education, is, of course, quite real. Commentators, from Claude Lévi-Strauss[48] to George Steiner,[49] have recently predicted the end of culture. Nevertheless it seems unlikely that the lessons learned in two million years of evolution can be discarded without some major biological change in the organism. As a social animal, a ''medium-contact'' species, and an organism exquisitely sensitive to a variety of stimuli, man appears to require a broader social context for his activities than those admitted by the technological wizards.

Without dealing in questionable predictions of the shape of future evolution, one can firmly assert that the technological revolution, even if it should come about relatively rapidly, will not wipe out our ancient patterns overnight. These must be maintained for large groups in our society who lack either the physical, emotional, or financial wherewithal for immediate participation in the revolution. At worst, construction of a new order of streets will allow for a multidimensional perception of the social and physical reality and will be necessary for some time to come. At best, just as we use the radio as well as television, streets will remain with us because we need the variety of social as well as intellectual experiences they can uniquely offer.

Notes

1. Amos Rapoport, *House Form and Culture* (Englewood Cliffs, N.J.: Prentice-Hall, 1969).

2. Herbert Gans, *People and Plans* (New York: Basic Books, 1968), p. 19, relying in turn on Irving Rosow, "The Social Effects of the Physical Environment," *Journal of the American Institute of Planners*, 27 (May 1961), pp. 127-133.

3. H. M. Proshansky, W. H. Ittelson, and L. G. Rivlin, eds., *Environmental Psychology* (New York: Holt, Rinehart and Winston, 1970).

4. Erving Goffman, *Interaction Ritual* (Chicago: Aldine, 1967).

5. Richard Lee and Irving De Vore, *Man the Hunter* (Chicago: Aldine, 1968).

6. D. G. Mandelbaum, ed., *Selected Writings of Edward Sapir*, in *Language, Culture and Personality* (Berkeley: University of California Press, 1951), and J. B. Carroll, ed., *Language, Thought, and Reality: Selected Writings of Benjamin Lee Whorf* (Cambridge, Mass.: The MIT Press, 1957).

7. Charles Jencks and George Baird, *Meaning in Architecture* (New York: George Braziller, 1970).

8. Raymond Birdwhistell, *Introduction to Kinesics* (Louisville: University of Lousiville Press, 1952).

9. Edward T. Hall, *The Silent Language* (Garden City, N.Y.: Doubleday, 1959), and *The Hidden Dimension* (Garden City, N.Y.: Doubleday, 1966).

10. I. Eibl-Eibesfeldt, *Ethology: The Biology of Behavior* (New York: Holt, Rinehart and Winston, 1970).

11. Marshall H. Segall, Donald T. Campbell, and Melville J. Herskovits, *The Influence of Culture on Visual Perception* (Indianapolis: Bobbs-Merrill, 1966).

12. Andrew P. Vayda, *Environment and Cultural Behavior* (Garden City, N.Y.: Natural History Press, 1969).

13. William Mangin, ed., *Peasants in Cities: Readings in the Anthropology of Urbanization* (Boston: Houghton Mifflin, 1970).

14. Rapoport, *House Form and Culture*.

15. Lee and De Vore, *Man the Hunter;* Claude Lévi-Strauss, *The Elementary Structures of Kinship* (Boston: Beacon Press, 1969).

16. Douglas Fraser, *Village Planning in the Primitive World* (New York: George Braziller, 1968).

17. Paul Oliver, *Shelter and Society* (New York: Praeger, 1969).

18. Lee and De Vore, *Man the Hunter*.

19. Bruce G. Trigger, "Determinants of Urban Growth in Pre-Industrial Society," unpublished paper from Research Seminar on Archaeology and Related Subjects, London, December 1970.

20. Emile Durkheim, *The Division of Labor in Society* (New York: Free Press, 1933).

21. R. F. Bales, "Channels of Communication in Small Group Interaction," *American Sociological Review*, 16 (1951), pp. 461-468.

22. Irving Rouse, "Settlement Patterns," unpublished paper.

23. Ralph Nevill, *Night Life: London and Paris, Past and Present* (London: Cassell, 1926); Leon Bernard, *The Emerging City: Paris in the Age of Louis XIV* (Durham, N.C.: Duke University Press, 1970).

24. Herman Lantz, "Number of Childhood Friends as Reported in the Life Histories of a Psychiatrically Diagnosed Group of 1000," *Marriage and Family Living*, 28 (May 1956), pp. 107-108.

25. Louis Yablonsky, *The Violent Gang* (New York: Macmillan, 1962).

26. Gerald D. Suttles, *The Social Order of the Slum* (Chicago: University of Chicago Press, 1968), p. 73.

27. Ibid., p. 77.

28. Ibid., pp. 77-78.

29. Elliot Liebow, *Tally's Corner* (Boston: Little, Brown, 1968); Ulf Hannerz, *Soulside: Inquiries into Ghetto Culture and Community* (New York: Columbia University Press, 1969); Herbert Gans, *The Urban Villagers* (New York: Free Press, 1962); William Whyte, *Street Corner Society* (Chicago: University of Chicago Press, 1955); Lee Rainwater, "Fear and House-as-Haven in the Lower Class," *Journal of the American Institue of Planners*, 32 (1966), pp. 23-31.

30. Cf. Suttles, *Social Order*, pp. 6-9; also Gans on "person-oriented" modes of behavior, in *Urban Villagers*, pp. 89-103, 164-166, and 234-235.

31. Rainwater, "Fear and House."

32. Marc Fried and Peggy Gleicher, "Some Sources of Residential Satisfaction in an Urban Slum," *Journal of the American Institute of Planners*, 27 (November 1961), pp. 305-315; Gans, *Urban Villagers*.

33. A physically distinctive area of New York such as Brooklyn Heights succeeds, by local pride, community projects, and selective neighboring, in creating a relatively homogeneous community without kinship, religious, or narrowly defined work association. This kind of villaging has even spread to other parts of Brooklyn where restoring and enhancing the physical structure of the area becomes one of the inducements to cohesiveness. The residents of the areas are not economically deprived nor lacking in potential and real connections with the rest of the metropolis and outer world. Pleasure taken from street and community life and the social structure of a district or enclave are apparently not necessarily tied to ethnic groups or the deprived, who have no alternatives.

34. Jane Jacobs, *The Death and Life of Great American Cities* (New York: Random House, 1961).

35. Roger G. Barker, *Ecological Psychology* (Stanford, Calif.: Stanford University Press, 1968); R. G. Barker and Paul Gump, *Big School, Small School* (Stanford, Calif.: Stanford University Press, 1964).

36. John Gulick, "Images of an Arab City," *Journal of the American Institute of Planners*, 29 (1963), pp. 179-198.

37. Robert C. Schmitt, "Implications of Density in Hong Kong," *Journal of the American Institute of Planners*, 29 (1963), pp. 210-217.

38. Biderman's conclusion is relevant here: overcrowding is associated with pathology when the people involved lack optimism or group organization and is not so associated when the overcrowding is seen as necessary to a desired end. Reported in William Michelson, *Man and His Urban Environment* (Reading, Mass.: Addison-Wesley, 1970), pp. 153-154.

39. Stanley Milgram, "The Experience of Living in Cities," *Science*, 167 (1970), pp. 1461-1468.

40. Georg Simmel, "The Metropolis and Mental Life," in Kurt H. Wolff, *The Sociology of Georg Simmel* (New York: Free Press, 1964), pp. 409-424.

41. Susanna Millar, *The Psychology of Play* (London: Penguin Books, 1968); Amos Rapoport and Ron Hawkes, "The Perception of Urban Complexity," *Journal of the American Institue of Planners*, 36 (1970), pp. 106-111.

42. W. R. Ewald, Jr., *Street Graphics* (Washington: ASLA Foundation, 1971).

43. Bruno Bettelheim, *The Informed Heart* (Glencoe, Ill.: Free Press, 1961).

44. Mortimer H. Appley and Richard Trumbull, *Psychological Stress* (New York: Meredith, 1961).

45. Desmond Morris, ed., *Primate Ethology* (London: Weidenfeld and Nicholson, 1967).

46. Melvin Webber, "Order in Diversity, Community Without Propinquity," in L. Wingo, Jr., ed., *Cities and Space: The Future Use of Urban Land* (Baltimore: Johns Hopkins University Press, 1963).

47. Roy D'Andrade, personal communication.

48. Claude Lévi-Strauss, *The Scope of Anthropology* (London: Cape, 1967).

49. George Steiner, *Language and Silence* (New York: Atheneum, 1970).

Some Human Dimensions of Urban Design

Gary H. Winkel

Introduction

For years designers considered themselves the embattled protectors of an environment increasingly ravaged by technological philistines. The rapid emergence of environmental concern in the 1960s brought with it belated recognition of the activities of design professionals. This recognition, however, was curiously enough rather critical in nature. It stemmed from the alleged social insensitivity of designers whose clients were either an elite that delighted in the construction of personal monuments or governmental bodies that would build any monstrosity as long as it fit their misguided conception of fiscal responsibility. The final blow, however, was struck in an area where designers had traditionally felt themselves most secure — their concern for the human being. Critics maintained that architects actually spent very little time or effort attempting to understand how the built environment affected those who used it.

Some designers responded to these attacks with an admission that little was known about the relationships between the physical environment and behavior and argued that more attention should be paid to this question (Alexander, 1966; Van der Ryn and Silverstein, 1967; Goldberg, 1969). Others adopted an advocate position and placed themselves at the service of the poor who could neither afford professional services nor understand how alterations in the built environment could affect their lives.

These attempts to redefine the nature of design activity have introduced a small but intense degree of ferment in discussions of design theory and practice, which will probably become more widespread as students leave the university and enter careers oriented toward research or practice. If changes occur, they will do so against a backdrop of defensiveness on the part of a number of usually articulate architectural commentators who have responded with an uncharacteristic degree of confusion to recent events. This is well illustrated in the writings of the American architectural critic Wolf von Eckardt. In the *Social Impact of Urban Design,* von Eckardt's humanistic concerns become mixed with deep antipathy to the value systems of science (von Eckardt, 1971). He attacks science and technology while joining the ranks of those who serve as advocates of the poor and dispossessed whose lives are most likely to be disrupted by the massive physical changes that characterize life in many American cities. Von Eckardt expresses grave doubts about either the possibility or desirability of measuring the effects of design on behavior. He believes that even if this were possible the result would only be a further increase in the "acute aesthetic deprivation" that constitutes the "guts of the present urban crisis." This position easily highlights the belief shared by many designers that science and humanism are incompatible goals. Von Eckardt's solution for the problems facing designers is an intuitive urban design guided by social conscience. This approach, of course, is to be pursued without recourse to any kind of pseudoscientific evaluation. Von Eckardt's solution for the problems facing designers is an intuitive urban design guided by social conscience. This approach, of course, is to be pursued without recourse to any kind of pseudoscientific evaluation. Von Eckardt's social conscience finds it perfectly acceptable that a pedestrian mall will fail in one area while succeeding in another or that one area's density will be a boon while another's will be a disaster.

Even though the contradictions inherent in von Eckardt's position are easily identified, it would be a mistake to simply disregard some of his misgivings about "scientific" evaluation. We must recognize that the social sciences often epitomize the fears that have been expressed toward the deadening influence of a heavy-handed scientism. These fears are not entirely unjustified. I am certain that we have all experienced situations in which the richness of behavior in a natural setting has been stripped of its vitality through inappropriate applications of scientific procedure. An excessive preoccupation with proper technique combined with a limited imagination can quickly extinguish any excitement we might feel for better understanding man in his environment. The solution to the problems raised by von Eckardt and others is not more or less "science" but a greater concern for new approaches that contribute to the understanding of behavior in the man-made environment while respecting the uniqueness and departures from order that we will find there.

To accomplish these ends, three problems should be addressed directly if we are to create a setting within which the fears expressed by von Eckardt will be reduced. These are the limitations inherent in environmental determinism, the problem of nonhomogeneous populations having different design requirements, and the development and alternative methods that can be used by the design researcher.

Environmental Determinism Revisited

In its extreme form, environmental determinism posits a one-way flow of influence from the environment to behavior. In this essentially mechanistic model, environmental pushes and pulls are reflected in discernible behavioral changes. While applications of this model to real-world settings have resulted in some softening of hard-line determinism, the notion continues to haunt discussions of environment/behavior relationships (Sprout and Sprout, 1965; Broady, 1968).

Architects and planners are not immune to the influence of deterministic arguments. They seem to maintain a peculiar love/hate relationship to the concept. On the one hand there is militant support for the values of human freedom and reliance on intuition as the royal road to knowledge. On the other, designers are often fascinated by the prospect that their physical systems can actually change behavior. For example, when architects and planners ask behavioral scientists for assistance, their questions usually reflect assumptions that design can influence friendship formation, improve the social mix of ethnically or economically diverse groups, or make the city more knowable to its residents. Hidden under these kinds of questions is the belief that given any behavioral constellation of interest some unique design configuration must exist that will either encourage or discourage its expression.

The counterarguments to raw determinism place the locus of control in the human user of the environment. In this scheme, people make use of, interpret, adapt to, and change the environment to suit their own needs and purposes. Carried to an extreme, the flow of influence once again becomes one way — from behavior to environment.

The limitations of both types of determinism will become clearer when one examines the accumulated evidence in one area of central concern to planners and designers — community design.

Because of the importance attached to living together harmoniously, the processes involved in the development of community have preoccupied both European and North American philosophers, social scientists, and designers. From my admittedly parochial vantage point, it seems that North Americans in particular have become almost obsessed with the questions of how communities come into being, maintain themselves, and decline (Vidich et al., 1964; Stein, 1960; Seeley et al., 1963).

The notion of community carries a considerable amount of added meaning because of the emotional responses the term arouses. The depth of this feeling can easily be seen in works of social commentators who have engaged in savage polemics designed to show how North Americans have lost a sense of community. They are pictured as enmeshed in the pursuit of individualistic concerns centering on the acquisition of status, the perpetuation of an authoritarian family structure, an absence of concern for the needs of other members of the community, and the elevation of mediocrity to the level of high culture.

For those critics with a bent toward the physical environment, the suburb has become the focus of a special hostility. Reference is made to the cancerous spread of the suburbs over the landscape, the hopeless repetition of housing designs, the deadening uniformity of the landscaping, and so on. These physical characteristics of the suburbs are then linked to various social problems. No one, however, has really indicated just what it is about the suburban environment that leads to the "pathologies" described.

Whyte (1957) was among the first to be concerned explicitly about the physical environment of the suburbs. In his description of Park Forest, Whyte reported that the residents divided their days into partying, informal neighboring, and dealing with child-rearing problems. All these activities occurred within the context of a dizzying pursuit of improvement in social-class standing. Whyte was one of the first community researchers who suggested that the physical design of Park Forest, in particular the location of the homes relative to one another, was partially responsible for the observed patterns of social interaction. Indeed, evidence accumulated earlier by Festinger et al. (1950) and Merton et al. (1951) had already demonstrated that, under certain conditions, house orientation, the location of stairways, windows, entry points, and the presence of commonly used facilities could influence friendship formation.

It was Herbert Gans, however, who pointed to the important role that attitude, expectation, and social-class homogeneity play in the decision to engage in neighboring relationships (Gans, 1967). In his study of Levittown, New Jersey, Gans shows that patterns of neighboring are quite dependent on the degree of neighboring that the residents of the development consider desirable. Sheer physical proximity as a factor was important only during the early months of Levittown's existence, when some amount of neighboring was necessary to speed the town's completion. The significant design effects identified by Festinger et al. were dependent on the relative social homogeneity of the population they studied. Westgate and Westgate West were student housing units constructed for veterans returning from the war. Most of this group were young and only recently married. As a consequence there were a number of similarities in their life-style requirements. This factor combined with the design served to foster the development of friendship formation.

Although social-class homogeneity has been identified as critical to friendship formation, it does not follow that the presence of homogeneity will automatically allow design features to influence behavior. The effects of the suburb depend on the types of social interactions that the potential suburbanite has experienced in the past. Berger's (1960) work, for example, challenges the notion that suburban housing by itself will transform a non-middle-class person into a homogenized middle-class suburbanite. In his study of the working-class residents of a San Francisco suburb, Berger found that even with obvious improvements in economic condition this group retained life-styles that were quite similar to those they had experienced prior to moving. Membership in formal organizations was rare and there was very little semiformal visiting between couples. These people neither attended parties nor gave them. In contrast to the middle- and upper-middle-class residents of Crestwood Heights (Seeley et al., 1963) little anxiety was expressed about improvements in status position and almost no effort was made to become middle class. Thus, the social leveling effects of the suburbs have been rather dramatically overestimated. But there are other lessons to be learned from this research.

What these and other studies appear to demonstrate is that patterns of social living that people have adopted and adapted over generations of experience are extremely resistant to change through physical intervention alone. I believe that this generalization is correct only if another condition is met. Resistance to change is more likely in situations where the environmental options have been expanded with a corresponding increase in freedom of choice. In circumstances where options have been limited, either through economic circumstances or racial prejudice, the form of the physical environment can indeed have significant effects on behavior. Experience in the United States with urban renewal and the construction of major highways through central cities has indicated that these activities can fracture and fragment delicate social networks (Gans, 1962; Wilson, 1967; Fellman and Brandt, 1970, 1971). Evidence from England shows that the pub culture of working-class residents of London, who were relocated in new housing estates outside the city, underwent marked changes — in part because the environmental choices available to these residents were drastically different from those available in the city (Young and Willmott, 1962).

On the basis of these experiences it is possible to hypothesize that the saliency of the physical environment may actually decrease as environmental choice increases. This proposition holds that people seek out environments that they believe will support what they consider to be desirable social arrangements. A crudely stated environmental determinism must be changed to state that when we observe behavioral changes that appear to be caused by some environment, the changes are the result of an interaction between prior behavioral needs and values and the capacity of the environmental setting to meet those needs. An illustration of these propositions, which focuses on the way in which environments can be used to further social ends, will provide a counterpoise to the community studies cited earlier.

My work in conjunction with Emilie O'Mara of the Environmental Psychology Program on urban communes has shown, we believe, the effects that explicit social structure can have on the use of spaces that were designed to accommodate social interactions having little relation to the expanded family notions of the communards. Consider the use of multistoried buildings. The probability that there are significant between-floor social transactions is rather remote. People living on the same floor of an apartment building may not even know their neighbors. This is true even in settings where the social groups are fairly homogeneous in terms of activities, interests, and social class characteristics, as my work with Van der Ryn and Silverstein (1967) on high-rise student dormitories has shown. Yet, in communal settings, there is a considerable amount of interpersonal interchange regardless of the floor on which one happens to be located. The separation of floors can certainly inhibit the free flow of communication, but the commitment to an alternate style of life that stresses the primacy of interpersonal contact has the effect of partially reducing the barriers created by the stacking of floors. In these settings the influence of people's values concerning the use of the environment must be considered paramount. The living environment does not determine the types of behaviors that occur — it only operates in conjunction or disjunction with the values and needs that people are trying to realize in that environment.

There are limits, however, to the power of ideology to overcome environmental obstacles. In the same study, we also found instances of the ways in which the physical environment subtly operates to disrupt social organization. In one community we visited in Berkeley, California, older members of the commune lived approximately one and one-half blocks from a larger house where the younger members lived. This physical separation came to symbolize the gaps between the older and younger communards on other levels of social interaction. Even this short physical distance resulted in the development of another social structure in the larger house — a social structure in some ways antithetical to the purpose of the commune.

While these examples are instructive, I believe that a fuller understanding of the limitations of environmental determinism will come when a more ambitious program of comparative urban studies is undertaken. In the urbanized areas of developing countries, building schemes used in the industrialized nations of Europe and North America are often transplanted to an alien culture. In these instances I suspect that we will find very interesting examples of the ways in which these urbanized environments will be adapted or possibly even rejected by those who are not familiar with the hidden assumptions embodied in these building types about the nature of human interactions. This has already occurred in Corbusier's Chandigarh. Marked disjunctions exist between the use of the environment as apparently intended by the designer and the needs of the people who live there (Brolin, 1972).

The lesson for urban designers in all of this is that much closer attention must be paid to the social characteristics of the populations for whom design is undertaken, explicit statements about the presumed behavioral effects of design parameters must be more clearly specified, and simplistic deterministic statements that merely interfere with the development of more fruitful hypotheses must be avoided.

Now that we have considered some of the philosophical problems associated with design research we can turn directly to some of the issues that lie at the heart of urban design.

Urban Design — For Whom and for What Do We Design?

Urban design research in the United States has meant taking into account the changing nature of the central city's population. We can no longer speak of a heterogeneous urban population, since the bulk of our people now live in the suburbs that surround the central city. This means that the behavioral diversity that characterized cities of the past is beginning to narrow to the point where primary emphasis is placed on the commercial activities of the city. For many people the nonwork environment can no longer be found in the city. This has important implications for urban design.

Today the central city is largely inhabited by those who, because of their economic situation and/or skin color, are unable to join their more affluent neighbors in the flight to the suburb. One of the implications of this development is that the objectives of the urban designer must now be adapted to the special requirements of those residents who spend the majority of their daily lives in an urban context. This task presents problems for designers who are more often than not middle- and upper-middle-class professionals who probably cannot fully appreciate the nature of the demands that this new population of largely impoverished people places upon them.

The problem can be highlighted by an examination of the renderings that urban designers use to illustrate their proposals. The people in these drawings are generally depicted as well dressed and shown wandering through handsome environments with families who never seem to have more than two children. These people obviously enjoy the stimulating qualities of the city, the separation of pedestrian access from vehicles, and the opportunity to engage in leisure activities. If these delightful aspects of urban experience strike one as a bit incongruous with descriptions of ghetto existence, there should be little surprise. "Planners' people" are seldom confronted with dire poverty, the instability of family life, a concern for security from attacks against their person or property, or a pervasive sense of impending disaster from unexpected physical or social sources (Rainwater, 1971).

It would be foolish to suggest that urban designers could change these conditions alone. Clearly a social policy that stresses a more equitable system of income distribution, improved educational opportunities, the removal of barriers to employment, and increased control over the political forces that influence people's lives is needed. Within this context, however, the urban designer should not take for granted the problems that ghetto existence poses for those who must experience them. For example, greater attention should be paid to the problems that arise because of an inadequate concern for security. Both Rainwater (1966) and Yancey (1971) have indicated how areas external to the apartment may be redesigned to increase what they call "defensible space." These spaces can serve the function of allowing the development of informal networks of friends and relatives who can exercise some form of social control over the activities that transpire there. The problem of scale should be reconsidered so that parents can achieve a greater degree of control over the activities of their children and their friends. Finally, the designer may address himself more directly to the problem of the use of so-called common space outside the apartment. The question of who uses these spaces and for what purposes is not only a design problem. Still, we must try, with whatever means available, to consider ways in which internal and external space may be more carefully orchestrated to achieve not only a secure environment but one that may be used to advance the needs and desires of the residents of these areas.

While it would be foolish to underestimate the importance of security, it is clear that the designer and design researchers would be unduly limited if they concentrated their attention on this problem alone. If we are to use urban environments to the fullest it is important to recognize that we cannot confine our activities to the maximization of one or two factors to the exclusion of others. After all, even with the growth of uniformity of urban activities, the city still offers a number of learning potentialities. We can explore our environment, learning how it is organized and functions, what it may say about the people who were responsible for its realization, how it may relate to whatever historical knowledge we may possess, whether it is affectively pleasing, exciting, interesting, dulling, or deadening, how it might serve as a setting for self-expressive activities, and finally whether it allows us to play. Each of these human activities has an importance of its own, and it may be that efforts to improve the urban environment's capacity to meet these and other needs will have unintended positive benefits for other aspects of the urban resident's life. For example, if we paid greater attention to the problem of attracting people to spaces outside the dwelling unit for any one of the activities listed, we might simultaneously improve the general safety and security of the residents as a whole (Jacobs, 1961). I believe that I can illustrate how such a process might occur by considering urban design research concerned with the ways in which people come to know a city.

Kevin Lynch (1960) and his colleagues at the Massachusetts Institute of Technology have undertaken pioneering work on urban imageability. Lynch's original investigations have led to a number of more detailed studies designed to identify those physical characteristics of urban form that appear to be implicated in the development of conceptual maps of the city. For example, Carr and Schissler (1969) have isolated urban form components that appear to be influential for the clarity of the mental maps of urban trip makers. Appleyard (1969) has suggested a set of building characteristics that contribute to a person's memory for significant parts of a city. Steinitz (1968) has shown how the behavioral activities of urban residents relate to physical form characteristics and lead to differences of imageability. Appleyard's work has been particularly helpful in that he was able to make recommendations concerning the location of service functions such as hospitals, police stations, and schools, which would be more likely to give urban residents a sense of control over these very necessary services.

Important though urban knowledge may be to adults, it is even more critical for children who, in the course of developing their competence for dealing with the world, must come to terms with both their immediate environment and their extended surroundings. In the process of learning about the environment, children may not only be developing cognitively; they are also in a position where the physical environment provides a platform for social learning experiences. Moore (1972) has pointed to the possibility that subtle relationships exist between the child's cognitive development and his environmental experiences. Maurer and Baxter (1972) have been able to demonstrate how black, white, and Mexican-American children living in the same geographical area have different conceptions of that setting. What these studies have lacked, however, is an analysis of the ways in which social learning influences environmental cognition.

A research project that we currently have in preparation is addressed to an understanding of how children of varying ages make discriminations among private, semipublic, and public urban spaces. This study's purpose is twofold. We wish to know whether there is some age level at which the concept of public space/private space is first recognizable and whether the character of the physical environment has any influence on the concept's appearance and subsequent development. Our analysis of the problem has convinced us that social agents play an important role in mediating the nature of the public/private concept. By explicit and implicit rules these gatekeepers moderate and control space use. We hope to discover how the physical setting interacts with gatekeeper functions to influence the child's understanding both of the physical environment and the social agents who control that environment.

It should be clear that this study may have another outcome as well. To the extent that there is a mismatch between the definitions of space use provided by the gatekeepers and the activities of the children who are in or wish to use a space, it is possible to anticipate various sorts of conflicts. Recall that for ghetto residents it is important that they have some control over the area external to their dwelling units. One reason that such areas cease to be safe is that it is difficult to know who should take responsibility for them and under what conditions. The resulting conflicts can lead to a condition of no control, so that people are unable to defend spaces against unwelcome intrusions. We hope that this study will demonstrate the factors that are implicated in space control not only

for those living in ghetto settings but other urban areas as well. If we are successful, we can use a study designed to measure aspects of environmental cognition and determine whether the findings can also be applied to problems of security.

I believe very firmly that advances in urban design research will come only if we attempt to understand how the facets we happen to be investigating relate to other elements of urban life. For this reason I would like to turn now to questions concerning available methodologies.

Urban Design Research Strategies

Earlier I indicated a number of areas that would be appropriate subjects for urban design research. The type of research strategy we employ is obviously of considerable importance. If we are to avoid the misplaced scientism that von Eckardt warned of, we must develop our capacity for clear environmental description and be aware of alternative research strategies. This statement seems so obvious that it cannot even qualify for the banal. Yet there are altogether too many instances in which investigators have violated one or both of these dicta. Besides not advancing our knowledge, inappropriately conducted studies create a climate in which the utility of research is downgraded. I cannot hope to offer unequivocal rules for research, but I do believe that there are some factors all researchers must respect if any contribution to understanding in this immensely complex field is to be made.

I call the first of these factors key behavior analysis. Simply stated, this principle is that a listing should be made of the key behaviors expected to occur for any environmental system. This list may be drawn from the work of other investigators, anecdotal reports, the insights of sensitive observers such as artists or novelists, or personal experiences. Once this list is constructed, behaviors should be analyzed in terms of their congruence, unrelatedness, or conflict with one another. To the extent possible, behaviors should be grouped into generalized constructs that might lead to a more efficient description of the system under investigation. Efforts should be made to determine whether these behaviors could conceivably be under the control of factors outside the immediate environmental settings being examined. Finally, some priorities should be assigned to the various behaviors. In this sense priority means the importance of any class of behaviors to a better understanding of the environment. An example of how key behavior analysis operates can be drawn from research on housing satisfaction.

One of the most common approaches taken to housing satisfaction has involved asking a group of observers (usually college students) to rate the facades of different housing types through adjective checklists or Semantic Differential Scales (Osgood, 1962). The facades are usually shown in colored slides. Of course, the external appearance of a house represents only one component of the housing satisfaction. But judging external appearance does possess the advantage that it can be investigated without placing too many demands on the investigator. Colored slides can easily be taken and there are many available adjective checklists.

How well could this approach stand the scrutiny of a key behavior analysis of housing satisfaction? I suspect not very well, because housing satisfaction is obviously much more clearly related to the types of behaviors that internal space arrangements make possible, attitudes toward and use of space external to the dwelling unit, the ease with which needed goods and services can be obtained, the judged desirability of the social and physical characteristics of the neighborhood, whether the house is owned or rented, the factors surrounding the move into the house (was the resident forced to move or did he move voluntarily?), and finally the person's judgment concerning overall life satisfaction. The latter question must be asked because variations in the housing-related behaviors listed might better be accounted for by overall satisfaction rather than by any characteristics of the immediate housing environment.

The use of key behavior analysis can also be fruitfully applied to spaces external to the built environment. For example, if one were concerned with the development of an urban park, it would make little sense to ask people how they might like various landscaping arrangements. This approach already assumes that one of the major purposes of a park is the aesthetic enjoyment that landscaping may promote. A better initial strategy would be to determine how people actually make use of parks and for what purpose. Within the setting itself, one could identify various visitor types, learn more about the ways in which they use the park, determine the amount of the environment that visitors require to support various activities, question how uses relate to one another and how the park might better be adapted to visitor needs.

These very brief examples of key behavior analysis demonstrate how an investigator must identify each of the major behavioral possibilities an environment offers. The priorities assigned to these behaviors, judgments of the environment's adequacy in meeting them and their relationships to one another, must rest upon an empirical examination of different environmental alternatives. This process in turn implies that a single measuring technique is not adequate to illustrate the complexity of an environment.

The second principle thus states that one should employ multiple measuring devices to gauge the behaviors in which one is interested (Webb et al., 1969). For example, one is never certain about the reliability of information taken from a questionnaire. How does one

know whether a person actually behaves in the manner indicated? This question could not be answered if one relied solely on a questionnaire. If one only observed a person's behavior one might experience some difficulty in knowing what motivated the observed activity. Using questionnaires *and* observational techniques one would find the range of explanation considerably improved.

The use of multiple techniques can be illustrated through some research that my colleagues and I developed, at the University of Washington, to study Seattle, Washington's central business district (Grey et al., 1970). We did not rely only upon interviews and questionnaires designed to indicate the nature of people's desires for the future of downtown development because we also wanted to know how people actually used the central business district. This involved the location of central nodes of pedestrian activity located within various parts of the central city. From these points we were able to follow people from one activity to the next. These data allowed us to determine what behavioral land-use linkages existed, make estimates of the likely distances people would travel from land use to land use, measure the amount of time allocated to various activities, map the range of such activities, and describe the nature of the social exchanges characteristic of various settings. Through these techniques we learned that the central business district was not really a unitary area at all. Instead it was comprised of a set of subdistricts, each having its own internal character and rationale. We also found that people's activities were relatively restricted. Rather than make a trip that involved a mix of business, shopping, and recreation, people generally engaged in a single-purpose trip. These findings cast some doubt on the notion that people use the city for a diversity of purposes within the same general trip.

In this particular project we also discovered that there was a reasonably good match between the data taken from our interviews with downtown users and our observations of pedestrian behavior. For example, people often commented on a gaudy, potentially dangerous area around the downtown "slums." Our behavioral observations supported the distinctness of the "slum" district by showing that it was relatively isolated from the activities characteristic of other downtown areas. The behavioral vitality of the "slum" grew out of the activities of a quite different population. Had we relied only on questionnaires I doubt that we could have mapped the boundaries of these separate planning areas or indicated how each had a life of its own.

Much of the research undertaken in urban settings has implications for planning and design. This leads to the third principle. Wherever possible, the generation of research data should be judged in terms of its potential utility to decision makers. Let me hasten to add that I do *not* believe that theoretical issues should be ignored in our pursuit of that elusive concept "relevance." It is just that we would be remiss if we failed to consider how and in what form research data might be adapted to the needs of those who make the environmental decisions that ultimately affect us all.

I am afraid that I cannot offer instances of how such a process might be implemented, since research on environmental decision making is virtually nonexistent. Craik (1970) has identified the nature of the problem and it is now the responsibility of the growing body of environmental researchers to explore this uncharted and potentially controversial area.

In conclusion, I would like to say that I have really only begun to sketch out the outlines of what might be involved in better understanding the human dimensions of urban design. I hope that these observations will spur further discussion and stimulate some fruitful theory and research.

Bibliography

Alexander, C. (1966). *Notes on the Synthesis of Form*. Cambridge, Mass.: Harvard University Press.

Appleyard, D. (1969). "Why Buildings are Known: A Predestined Tool for Architects and Planners," *Environment and Behavior*, 1, pp. 131–156.

Berger, B. (1960). *Working Class Suburb: A Study of Auto Workers in Suburbia*. Berkeley: University of California Press.

Broady, M. (1968). *Planning for People*. London: Bedford Square Press.

Brolin, B. (1972). "Chandigarh was Planned by Experts but Something Has Gone Wrong," *Smithsonian*, 3, pp. 56–62.

Carr. S., and D. Schissler (1969). "The City as a Trip: Perceptual Selection and Memory in the View from the Road," *Environment and Behavior*, 1, pp. 7–36.

Craik, K. (1970). "The Environmental Dispositions of Environmental Decision Makers," *Annuals of the American Academy of Political and Social Services* (May), pp. 87–94.

Fellman, G., and B. Brandt (1970). "A Neighborhood a Highway Would Destroy," *Environment and Behavior*, 2, pp. 281–302.

———. (1971). "Working Class Protest Against an Urban Highway," *Environment and Behavior*, 3, pp. 61–80.

Festinger, L., et al. (1950). *Social Pressures in Informal Groups: A Study of Human Factors in Housing*. Stanford, Calif.: Stanford University Press.

Gans, H. (1962). *The Urban Villagers: Groups and Class in the Life of Italian Americans*. New York: Free Press.

———. (1967). *The Levittowners*. New York: Pantheon.

Goldberg, T. (1969). "The Automobile: A Social Institution for Adolescents," *Environment and Behavior*, 1, pp. 157–186.

Grey, A., et al. (1970). *People and Downtown*. Seattle, Wash.: College of Architecture and Urban Planning.

Jacobs, J. (1961). *The Death and Life of Great American Cities*. New York: Vintage Paperbacks.

Lynch, K. (1960). *The Image of the City*. Cambridge, Mass.: The MIT Press.

Maurer, R., and J. Baxter (1972). "Images of the City among Black, Anglo, and Mexican American Children," *Environment and Behavior*, 4, forthcoming.

Merton, R., et al. (1951). "Social Policy and Social Research in Housing," *Journal of Social Issues*, 7, nos. 1 and 2.

Moore, G. (1972). "Conceptual Issues in the Study of Environmental Cognition: An Introduction," in W. Mitchell, ed., *Proceedings of the Environmental Design Research Association*. Los Angeles: University of California, Department of Architecture.

Osgood, C. (1962). *The Measurement of Meaning*. Urbana: University of Illinois Press.

Rainwater, L. (1966). "Fear and the House as Haven in the Lower Class," *Journal of the American Institute of Planners*, 32, pp. 23–31.

———. (1971). "Poverty, Race and Urban Housing," in Center for Policy Studies, *Social Impact of Urban Design*. Chicago: University of Chicago Press.

Seeley, J. R., et al. (1963). *Crestwood Heights*. New York: John Wiley and Sons.

Sprout, H. and M. (1965). *The Ecological Perspective on Human Affairs*. Princeton: Princeton University Press.

Stein, M. (1960). *The Eclipse of Community*. New York: Harper & Row.

Steinitz, C. (1968). "Meaning and Congruence of Urban Form and Activity," *Journal of the American Institute of Planners*, 34, pp. 233–247.

Van der Ryn, S., and M. Silverstein (1967). *Dorms at Berkeley*. Center for Planning and Development Research, University of California, Berkeley.

Vidich, A., et al. (1964). *Reflections on Community Studies*. New York: Harper & Row.

Von Eckardt, W. (1971). "Our Design Behavior," Center for Policy Study, *The Social Impact of Urban Design*. Chicago: University of Chicago Press.

Webb, E., et al. (1966). *Unobtrusive Measures*. New York: Rand McNally.

Whyte, W. (1957). *The Organization Man*. New York: Doubleday Anchor Books.

Wilson, J. (1967). *Urban Renewal — The Record and the Controversy*. New York: Free Press.

Yancey, W. (1971). "Architecture, Interaction and Social Control: The Case of a Large Scale Public Housing Project," *Environment and Behavior*, 3, pp. 3–22.

Young, M., and P. Wilmott (1962). *Family and Kinship in East London*. Baltimore: Penguin Books.

Acknowledgment

This paper was originally delivered at the International Symposium, "Urban Design: Problems and Methods," University of Stuttgart, October, 1972.

The Street Generation

Robert Gutman

When we are young we do not immediately know where we shall hear those voices of our own time to which our virginal hearts will deeply and instinctively respond. They must come from figures of our own time, older than we are or they would not have found expression, but not old enough to have "arrived," so that we do not at once learn of their existence. Our teachers, as well as popular fame, thrust upon us the figures of the last generation, by whom they had themselves been inspired in youth, and these are, in general, precisely the figures to whom our instincts are most rebellious. Jane Addams, The Second Twenty Years at Hull-House *(New York: Macmillan, 1930, p. 1.)*

Until well into the nineteenth century, the concept of the street as a subject of intellectual discourse was mainly the property of architects. With the development of the industrial city, the concept of the street began to have some currency in other disciplines and social movements concerned with the city. Included among the former were civil engineering, landscape architecture, and, toward the end of the nineteenth century, after it emerged as a separate profession, city planning. The nineteenth-century movements for public health, housing reform, and urban improvement also began to refer to the street. Social science disciplines concerned with the city — in particular sociology, political science, and psychology — have only recently expressed interest in the idea of the street. The emergence of this academic interest is very important for understanding present-day thinking about the street, but in order to understand how present attitudes differ from past attitudes one must begin by understanding how the architectural tradition has viewed the street.

To say that until fairly recently architecture was the principal repository of sustained thinking about streets should not be interpreted to mean that the street existed only as an idea and not as a built form. Obviously, many urban forms one would recognize as streets, or at least as similar to streets in function, have existed since the first human settlements. The relationship between these forms and the ideas held by architects of the culture that built the forms has always been ambiguous and complex. In some cases the forms were built to fulfill architectural ideas; in other cases the ideas reflected the forms. As settlements grew in size and complexity, their street forms at any date reflected ideas that had emerged over many generations. Also, it should be understood that even though before the nineteenth century there were no established traditions other than architecture consistently concerned with streets, most urban cultures, from the Romans on, incorporated certain values and norms that were important determinants in shaping street environments.[1] Beginning with the Renaissance city, it is even possible to point to latent assumptions about the design of streets held by the elite groups of society.

In this paper, however, I will be primarily concerned with evidence of conscious cultural awareness of the idea of the street, in particular with the architectural idea of the street. I recognize, however, that the idea now belongs to other disciplines as well; furthermore, that it cannot be understood or discussed without noting that the street is also a social, a political, and a psychological fact. Certain common elements run through the architectural concept of the street, beginning with the end of the medieval period when "the cult of the street" first emerged as an ideological concern among architects, princes, guildsmen, clergy, and others responsible for laying out and building cities.[2]

The first common element is that the street is a social fact. No matter what the image of the street, it has always included a set of assumptions about who would own and control it, who would live on it or use it, the purposes for which it was built, and the activities appropriate to it. Streets proposed by baroque city designers, for example, were wide and presented long vistas. They were bordered by palaces and created for wealthy and powerful dukes, bankers, and merchants. These features were consistent with the assumption that these streets were to serve as settings for religious and civil processions and celebrations. To take another example, the arcades of Bologna, which are praised today for their splendid spatial qualities, were built for practical reasons: the government officials and merchants of Bologna conducted their affairs out of doors, and the arcades sheltered them from rain and sun.[3]

The second element is that the street is three dimensional. This may seem obvious, but it cannot be stressed too strongly. Otherwise there is an inevitable tendency to confuse the street as an architectural idea with the typical lay notion of the street as a two-dimensional link, a notion often held by those responsible for designing and managing our streets today — highway engineers, policemen, surveyors. When one speaks of the three-dimensional quality of the street, what one is pointing out is the fact that the street includes not just the road or sidewalk surfaces but the buildings located along it, the street furniture, the arches, and other ceremonial structures that mark its length or define its beginning and end. The quality of three dimensionality has been expressed in many ways in the course of architectural history: in the continuous facade seen in the street terraces of Georgian London; in the union of inside and outside space of the early baroque; in the notion of direction, as with the Romans; in the elimination of negative space, a phrasing common to contemporary formalist architects in the idea of the street as a building, which in Louis Kahn's conception extends below ground level;[4] or in the emphasis on providing ground access, a standard proposal in the housing schemes of recent English architects. Although these expressions are obviously very different and derive from very different cultures, what is important is the notion they all contain of the street as a three-dimensional space.

Third, definitions of the street assert that a street has two social functions. One of these is what sociologists today label *instrumental*. The purpose of the street is to provide a link between buildings, over which the goods and people necessary to sustain the agricultural, marketing, manufacturing, administrative, and military activities of the settlement can pass. Sometimes the emphasis has been on the circulation of pedestrians, but from the beginnings of urban civilization the street has also been designed to accommodate animals and vehicles.[5] The other function of the street is *expressive*. The street as a link between people facilitates communication and interaction, thus serving to bind together the social order of the *polis*, or what in current parlance would be called the local urban community. Its expressive function also includes its use as a site for casual social interaction, including recreation, conversation, and entertainment, as well as its use as a site for ritual observances, such as processions. In the baroque city the expressive function was met principally by encouraging processions on the major avenues leading to the palaces or the cathedrals.[6] It was not until the development of the "bye-law" streets of nineteenth-century England that serious thought was given to how the street might serve the more mundane activities of its residents.[7]

A fourth common element of the street, one that is closely related to the third, is that the street is a space that must be accessible to, and is intended to benefit, a group larger than a single household. This does not mean, of course, that the street is necessarily a public space in the contemporary sense of the term public; that is, owned by the state or municipality and therefore open for the use of all the resident population. Private streets were standard in cities in the past, and they are still found in the more affluent sections of major cities today. Also, streets can be, and in the baroque cities often were, subject to laws and codes that regulated their use according to season, month, day, hour, and by class and status; and there are still vestigial survivals of this ancient system in cities today, say, when grand routes are given over to parades. Still, despite these examples, which indicate the numerous ways in which accessibility to streets can fall short of any simple identification of it with modern ideas of public space, in all these cases the street is intended to serve many households and dwelling units rather than only one.

A fifth element found in almost all definitions of the street is that the street has two parts, one to be used principally by people and the other principally for passage by animals and vehicles. Until the middle ages, however, the dividing line was not clear (and often remains ambiguous today, especially in the towns and cities of developing countries). At first, the middle of the street was intended for pedestrians and the edges for animals and vehicles. As recently as the eighteenth century, however, there were no paved center areas, so pedestrians were often forced to the edges along with the offal and sewage while animals and vehicles took up the space supposedly reserved for pedestrians. Until the development of paved sidewalks, the intention of dividing the space for different activities was often expressed off the street itself. Facades were designed to include porticoes, roofs were built with overhangs, front stoops and yards marked off special spaces. The present pattern of street design, with the edges of the street paved differently from the road surfaces, and the former assigned to the pedestrian and the latter to other traffic, did not become standard until the middle of the nineteenth century. At that time the central paved area was divided and a curb added to prevent wheeled vehicles from veering into people and buildings.[8]

The sixth element is the assumption that the street is a closed system. This may seem curious, in view of the need for the street to provide for the continuous flow of traffic. Nevertheless, all discussions of streets from the late fifteenth century to the present have considered it appropriate to conceive of the street as a bounded form, which, at least for purposes of design, should be considered independent of the rest of the system of urban links. This aspect of the concept of the street became especially evident during the sixteenth century and may seem paradoxical in view of the fact that at this time the importance of the city's military function was diminishing. For the first time since the Roman period it became possible to think of the network of urban streets in relation to the network of territorial roads outside the city. But this very awareness seems to have made the baroque architects more self-conscious about the design of the urban street as such. From their proposals and from what was built between the sixteenth and eighteenth centuries, especially in France and Italy, it is clear that, whether they thought of a street in terms of landscape or in terms of buildings, they thought of it as a more or less closed system.

A seventh common element is the conception of the street as an urban space intermediate in scale between the individual building and the open space immediately surrounding it, such as the garden or courtyard, and the larger system of urban roads and avenues. This part of the definition is important because it suggests a way of thinking about the street that helps to establish a hierarchy of urban spaces and thus guides design theory in dealing with problems of urban form. This conception of the street scale is shared by solutions otherwise as different from each other as the formal geometry of the baroque street, the domesticity of the Georgian terrace, and the picturesque imagery of the street in English and American townscapes.[9]

These seven elements, then, constitute features common to definitions of the street in both the architectural and the urban cultures of the last five centuries — in other words, the period coterminus with the emergence of the city as the dominant settlement type of western civilization. What, then, is distinctive to the idea of the street as it is now being discussed by architects, planners, and social critics of urban life? What modifications have occurred in the importance attached to the different elements?

The first thing to be noted is that the street has once again become a subject of widespread interest. This was not the case twenty-five years ago, among either architects or other students of the city. Until recently modern architects were concerned principally with the design of individual buildings or the organization of the city or urban region as a whole, as seen in the writings and proposals of Le Corbusier.[10] Corbusier saw as the central problem of urban life the relationship between housing, in the form of superblocks and towers, and the urban freeway systems that made it possible for people to move between their homes and jobs. The intermediate scale of the street was examined superficially in his proposals. This was true not only for the *immeubles villas* and the cruciform towers, but also for the *blocs à redent*.[11] To the degree that he was concerned about spaces for the amenities ordinarily located in the street, he incorporated them in the building itself, as in the plans for the high-rise towers in the park in the Plan Voisin, in his proposals for Algiers, and in Chandigarh. Similar concepts mark the designs of other masters of modern architecture, including figures otherwise as different as Wright and Mies; the same is true of some of the progenitors of the urbanistic vision of modern architecture, such as Sant Elia.

In America the lack of interest in the street until very recently is even more striking. In the case of many architectural and urban theorists, antistreet attitudes have been associated with their reluctance to accept the city as a permanent or necessary form of social and physical existence. Wright's Broadacre City is probably the leading expression of this stance. In any conventional, certainly in any European, sense of the term, Broadacre is not a city at all. It is instead modeled on a Jeffersonian version of a rural community. Each family lives on its acre of ground; communication, exchange, and social interaction occur at settlement nodes, at which are located shopping centers, medical facilities, community halls, schools, and churches. People travel from their homes to these nodes by automobile, along safe, high-speed highways complete with overpasses and cloverleafs. Wright's view of the city reflects the existing pattern of low-density settlement in this country. It is a pattern that in recent years has been defended by many city planners who regard it as compatible with the highly differentiated and bureaucratized organizational structure of the United States, the wide distribution of car ownership, and the supposed shift from dependence on face-to-face contact to reliance on common occupational interests as the basis for community.[12]

But the lack of interest in the idea of the street also existed among Americans who were committed to city life, namely the real estate speculators, mortgage bankers, building developers, politicians, city planners, and civil engineers, who, for more than a century and a half, have been in charge of laying out, constructing, and supervising our cities. Their version of antistreet attitudes was of course different from that symbolized by Wright. This group obviously had a hand in designing and building many streets, but what they meant by the street, what they still mean by it, is a two-dimensional band. Their principal design criterion for a street is its capacity to stimulate the market for land values by accommodating swift and efficient surface and underground transportation. The kinds of buildings located on the street, the quality of life it can sustain, the sensory and aesthetic experience it affords — these concerns, which define the idea of the street in architectural history, were of only peripheral interest.[13]

A good argument can be made that this limited conception of the nature and potential of street design was also characteristic of the social reformers, who, in response to the sanitary investigations in Europe during the early nineteenth century and after the Civil War in the United States, were responsible for the introduction of higher standards in housing.[14] The English response to the sanitary investigations, for example, was to build wider streets, with curbs, sidewalk pavements, underground sewer installations, and the like, but the street itself was regarded only as a thoroughfare which, if cleaned up, would reduce infection. Little thought was given to what the adjoining buildings would look like or how the streets would fit with the surrounding areas. A similar attitude was found among American social workers and, later, sociologists. Not that they were antistreet; rather they did not regard the street as a means by which they could improve the health, reduce the poverty, or ennoble the family life of the immigrants and the native poor populations. Their emphasis throughout, right down to the end of the New Deal in this century, was on the quality of housing, with some attention paid to community halls, schools, and parks.

The revival of concern for the street began, as I say, about twenty-five years ago, especially in this country and in England.[15] Like the earlier antistreet or nonstreet attitudes it sprang forth in many disciplines concerned with city life and urban design. Because the concept of the street has continued to be most fully articulated within the architectural tradition, it is perhaps easiest to trace its reemergence there. Indeed, within the architectural tradition the revival of this interest has already been the subject of critical notice and historical investigation. Banham[16] has commented, for example, how the new interest in the street was part of the ideological revolt of the younger, especially English, members of the Congrès Internationaux d'Architecture Moderne (CIAM) against the ideas of Le Corbusier and the other founders of CIAM. The new attitude is most fully elaborated in the work of Team 10, and in the projects and buildings of the Smithsons in particular.[17] An American historian with

Banham's special relationship to the design culture could probably document a similar shift in this country.[18] It would undoubtedly have to focus on the projects and writings of Kahn and the Venturis.[19]

Because modern architecture did not really catch on in the United States until after the second world war, the interest in town building and populist urbanism evidenced by Kahn and the Venturis respectively was stimulated only in part by the reaction against Corbusier, Mies, Wright, and Gropius. In the United States the new attitude toward the street was also a reaction against the American version of Beaux-Arts formalism, the garden city and prosuburban ideology, and the commitment to urban sprawl of the city planning establishment. Since the influence of Corbusier affected American architects later than it did European architects, a fascination with Corbusier's urbanistic concepts has lingered on here longer than abroad. In the work of the New York City Urban Design Group or of many of the people associated with the Institute for Architecture and Urban Studies in that city or of Paul Rudolph, the street in the sense in which Team 10 discusses it is viewed ambivalently. These younger architects share the new belief in the importance of emphasizing the three-dimensional quality of the street in place of the prevailing American view of the street as part of a two-dimensional grid. They also acknowledge the importance of defining it as a multiuse space. But their designs and their rhetoric also suggest an infatuation with the baroque images of the processional street, which they are struggling to reconcile with their notion of the street as a place for the mundane activities of those who live along it.

A switch in opinion among social scientists runs parallel to the changes in the ideology of the architects. At the same time that a younger generation of architects here and in Europe were espousing positive views of the value of the street, sociologists, including Peter Willmott and Michael Young in England and Jane Jacobs and Herbert Gans in the United States, were conducting research and writing reports that argued against point blocks, highways through central cities, downtown urban renewal, and the general set of programs that assumed that new housing projects and more sunlight and better ventilation would solve the problems of the cities.[20] Much of this criticism was phrased in terms of the need to preserve old neighborhoods and the surviving social and physical fabric of cities. But in the case of Mrs. Jacobs, it was the street that was singled out as the spatial unit to be upgraded. She also was the leading figure among the social scientists to formulate her polemic using Le Corbusier and an older generation of architects as her foil. What began among the majority of the social critics as a more or less purely academic exercise directed against expert and professional opinion has since been transformed into a political movement. In the course of thirty years we have moved from a situation in which the idea of the street had little significance in any vocabulary except that of the land surveyor and traffic engineer to a time in which it is now a political rallying cry for the trapped poor population and those people in the middle class who still prefer the advantages of life in the inner city.

The revival of interest in the urban street has been accompanied by a wholly new emphasis in the view of the street's primary social function. Put simply, what sets the contemporary idea of the street apart from previous definitions is the conviction that the street should be designed and managed for the benefit of the community life of its residents. On numerous occasions, in defending their projects or in arguing against the older generation of modern architects, the Smithsons have expressed this emphasis by asserting that the problem of the city is no longer functional organization — the fitting together of places for work, residence, recreation, and the circulation system that connects them — but instead is the issue of human association — finding the patterns that will enable people to live together.[21] Probably because of the greater rootlessness and geographical mobility common to the United States, Kahn and the Venturis have emphasized somewhat different problems of community life, but the fundamental opposition of their ideas to the more mechanical conceptions of urban organization underlying Corbusier's proposals is similar to that of Team 10. Kahn, for example, was always eager to give people a sense of place, to enable them to achieve identity with their surroundings. These terms also have a role in the Venturis' thinking, but the sign for them that a community life exists or can be made to develop is that provision has been made in the plan for community participation. The residents of South Street in Philadelphia, for example, should be able to join in the rehabilitation of their area as well as in its street life later on. These notions are, of course, also prominent in the thinking of critics like Mrs. Jacobs and Professor Gans.

It may seem questionable that a concern for the street as a community should be singled out as a distinctive characteristic of today's definition of the street. Some critics may admit, for example, that the baroque architects and their princely clients were not much concerned with the ordinary day-to-day social life of the typical resident of Paris or London who flocked to the Tuileries or the Wren's streets to observe the public rituals. Still, readers may argue that the narrow crooked streets, which survived from medieval or Renaissance cities, were inhabited by people who knew each other, who worshipped at the same church, who helped each other out, who played together, and who generally enjoyed some kind of communal existence. However, it is important to realize that even though these communally oriented streets existed as part of the urban fabric, no provision for such streets was incorporated in the proposals of the baroque architects. Community life, in other words, may have existed on many streets, but it was not a concern of the architectural culture; indeed the explicit inclusion in city plans of the community oriented street does not become prominent until the nineteenth century. Such streets, for example, were proposed by Haussmann as part of his plans for the Paris boulevards, and the concept received its first theoretical treatment in the work of Sitte, published in 1889.[22]

Other readers may consider the emphasis overstated because they will argue, and quite rightly, that a belief in social order was assumed by the designers and builders of the baroque city. The streets radiating outward from the Piazza del Popolo, Wren's street pattern centering on the stock exchange — such plans were intended to symbolize the unity of the polis and the state. Each social class and each urban function was located in its own part of the city; by means of the street grid people were brought together on ritual occasions, often through the use of civil and religious processions. Indeed, in his wonderful essay on baroque building, Norberg-Schulz says that the baroque architect aimed at encouraging participation, the image was of an audience in a great theater, "where everybody was assigned a particular role."[23] Such popular involvement in a stratified, fairly rigid society is obviously far removed from the active advocacy role indicated by the new idea of the street, as well as from the democratic community life conceived of by the Smithsons and the Venturis.

It may also seem odd to assert that the concern for community life is a new emphasis, given that the resolution to improve the quality of life for the general run of urban residents had its origins in the nineteenth century. Even though the architectural tradition remained relatively aloof from wrestling with the problems of the industrial city until this century, many other professions and groups were concerned with these problems, among them social reformers, city planners, landscape architects, social scientists, and government officials. In part, the answer to the riddle is that these reformers did not think of the street as the space through which they might effect their reforms. Instead they focused on housing. But what is striking is that even in their discussions of housing, the terms "human association, identity, place participation" — the whole panoply of terms that crops up in today's discussions of community — do not appear.

Olmsted is especially notable in this respect because he was one of the few important figures of the nineteenth century who paid attention to street design. In fact, his writings on the street still are among the most penetrating sociological interpretations of the history of the form and function of the street that we have. Yet in all his commentary, Olmsted never once mentions community life as a problem of the street, focusing instead on the need to design the urban street system to facilitate the city resident's contact with the countryside and with recreational opportunities in a natural setting.[24] A similar absence of concern for the problem of human association characterized architecture and the other design disciplines once they began to study mass housing, public health, and urban traffic. In the various writings and projects of the Modern Movement, these problems were translated into issues of circulation systems, industrialized building, the provision of light and air, garden cities, suburbanization — in other words, into the very notions the current generation of architects and urban critics is reacting against.

Still another aspect of the current discussion of the street is worth noting. Not only is there a desire to evaluate street designs in terms of their contribution to community life but, in addition, architects in particular have often seemed to argue that the proper physical form for the street can somehow create that life where it may not have existed previously.[25] This emphasis is a new twist to an earlier architectural conception that, beginning with Ruskin,[26] asserted that architecture has the capacity to induce states of feeling, sentiment, and emotion. The contemporary view is more demanding, since it implies that the effect of the built environment can be extended to alter modes of behavior and stimulate urban dwellers to undertake new forms of social action. For example, in their discussion of such early postwar schemes as Golden Lane, the Smithsons claimed that the pedestrian balconies could bring about a pattern of association among the residents and produce a sense of community. Similarly, the Venturis argued that participation in the planning of South Street will *make* people develop a sense of identity with the area.

In fairness to these architects, it should be realized that the intellectual stance expressed in their assertions is widespread in other disciplines, including social work and social planning. In fact, one can go further and admit that what is reflected is a fundamental shift in intellectual and public attitudes. The belief that the most basic problems confronting the social order could be remedied by programs designed to manipulate the institutional framework of society, what Jane Addams called human engineering, first gained support in the nineteenth century and came gradually to be implemented by government policy in the twentieth. Social groups that were once thought inviolate, God-given, and universal, such as the family and the church, came to be regarded as ephemeral and transformable by organized human effort. At the same time it had come to be believed that the structure and categories of human thought were culturally determined and could be shaped by education, the newspaper, and advertising.[27] The new disciplines of sociology, anthropology, and psychology both resulted from and encouraged these beliefs. What is surprising about architecture, from this perspective, is not that it too now wishes to solve the problems of the community but rather that it has come relatively late to this position, at least in the sense of trying to use built forms as a means of social intervention. Other professions and disciplines exhibited a similar imperial stance in the past, but they have since acknowledged that modes of social action stem from a multitude of cultural, economic, and political influences, and that it is therefore essential to operate on several fronts at the same time.

Jane Jacobs's ideas about the street are a case in point. Consider the variety of factors she argues must be manipulated if the streets of large cities are to be made to function as cohesive communities. One must examine their physical characteristics, including their length, width, types of adjoining buildings, and accessibility to other parts of the city. One has also to take into account the spaces and building types provided along the street and the activities that go on in these buildings. Thought must be given to the people who inhabit the street, in terms of their income, ethnic background, and race. Finally, the politics of the street must be considered. How does this street as a political unit fit within the larger units of the neighborhood, the district, and the city as a whole?[28] This is a much more complex model for understanding the interaction between street form and community life than the approach that has been criticized as architectural determinism. It is also the model that an increasing number of architects have begun to adopt as they apply design concepts to the problems of the city.[29]

Three changes, then, have occurred in our attitude toward the idea of the street: a renewed interest in the subject; an emphasis on judging the street according to the life it generates; and the conviction that design can make a positive contribution to the quality of street life. Given the difference between these attitudes and the apathy toward the idea of the street only a generation ago, one is led to ask what accounts for the shift in sentiment.

City dwellers have probably always been interested in the street environment, if only because daily life for most of them was spent largely in the area immediately surrounding their houses. The house was "home"; it was often the workplace or very close to it, and it also was the locus for recreation and leisure activities. For this reason, it makes sense to assume that popular awareness of and interest in the street environment were more complete and extensive in preindustrial cities and were eroded only gradually as industrialization brought about the factory system, the nuclear family, and then finally modern transportation, especially the motor car. Although, as the result of these social changes, people today, except for the very poorest class, are less tied to their residential streets than many city people were just a few decades ago, the concern for the quality of the street still has firm underpinnings in the basic condition of human existence in urban areas. One can travel to work, one can go somewhere else to have fun, but almost every resident, regardless of social class, has to return to his dwelling and street to rest, to eat, to make love, to supervise children, to grow up, to be educated.

Given the close symbiotic relationship between the street and the human condition throughout time, the development only recently of working-class political activity in defense of the street must be attributed to popular democracy. In company with the spread of education, literacy, and job security, democracy has raised the city dweller's expectations about the amenities he deserves. Unions, political parties, district and street organizations are agencies through which he can address his demands to the mayor's office, planning and zoning commissions, and to the real estate industry.

The middle classes also have become concerned about the street. In the first place, the increasing size and density of many cities and almost all urban regions have made it harder to believe that some of the older concepts, such as neighborhood, in terms of which people have traditionally thought about cities, are really viable ideas. Neighborhoods are too large now, they include too many people, their residents are too diverse in terms of income, ethnic background, and race for their residents to have any sense of identification with them.[30] However, the street is still small enough to be comprehended and organized. Second, the interest in the street has become a metaphor for the concern of certain segments of the middle class in the revival and preservation of the city itself. Many middle-class families don't want to join the American exodus to suburban or rural communities. They want a style of life that will permit them to combine the cultural and economic opportunities of the city with a safe, pleasant, and easy environment in which to raise children. To make the streets work is a means of achieving these ambitions.

These impulses to make the street work, to make it into a community, some of which apparently are rooted in human nature, some of which are specific to the situation of the city today, have gained strength because, even in America, the residents of urban streets until recently regarded themselves as a relatively homogeneous population. This important point is often overlooked. We are concerned about the street community in large part because for the very first time in the history of cities the simple virtues and joys of urban life have been diminished for all social groups; and we connect this reduction in our level of satisfaction and safety with the breakdown of community.

Of course, for the upper social classes, there was never a street community. The residents of a Georgian terrace did not sit on the stoop chatting with neighbors, hold their parties on the pavement, or play bowls and cricket in the road. Their social life was carried on inside their town houses (and at their country homes) within the framework of an extended family and a complex domestic household. Many of the less affluent had a street life, of course, but this was the result of duress, not of choice. The poor spent a good deal of time on the streets adjoining their dwellings because there was too little space inside or because the rooms were dank and smelly or because other members of the household were ill with infectious diseases. They also spent a good deal of time on the grand streets of the cities, to beg or steal, as vendors or entertainers or just for the pleasure of observing the activities of the nobility and bourgeoisie. Often these activities were their only work and implied nothing whatsoever about whether the poor had a sense of belonging to the street. One of the curious effects of the sanitary and social reforms of the nineteenth century was that the poor were driven off the streets and into their homes; what this did was deprive them of a livelihood without necessarily affecting their local sense of belonging. This consequence was overlooked by the social workers and other advocates of the bye-law street who concentrated exclusively on the presumed benefit to the health and well-being of the poor that might accrue from better housing.[31]

In other words, the consequence of many of the reforms introduced to reduce the evils of the industrial city was to break up the prevailing social patterns and accepted routines of urban life. Well into this century, though, there were many areas where the sense of community remained, including the working-class neighborhoods of the slums of such cities as London and Manchester and the immigrant neighborhoods of New York and Chicago. Indeed, in the case of the United States, community life at the level of the street was stimulated by the great waves of immigration from southern and eastern Europe before the first world war. The sociologists who were studying American cities in the 20s and 30s noted this revival of urban neighborhood life. This was one reason why writers like Park and Wirth held up the Poles, the Italians, the Jews, and the Irish as models of the potential virtues of urban life, in opposition to the traditional antiurban attitudes of American writers.[32] It should be noted that many of the people who today are calling for a return to the city and for a revival of the street idea descend from these immigrant groups. A similar phenomenon has apparently occurred in England among the former residents of the East End and their descendants, although because Great Britain, like continental Europe, has long possessed ideological movements in favor of urban life, the pro-urban, prostreet attitudes draw their support from a broader variety of cultural and income groups.

The interest in the street, then, represents in part nostalgia for conditions of life that were common in cities before well-intentioned social reforms of the industrial city were institutionalized in laws and administrative codes. Events of the postwar world seem to have intensified the nostalgia. In England the people who moved to the Mark I and Mark II new towns complained that they missed the corner pub and the proximity of "mum" and other members of the extended family, and they found the commuter's life disturbing. A rash of sociological investigations documented this malaise and gathered evidence pointing to the deterioration in mental health consequent upon such moves. There followed the plans for the Mark III towns, which were intended both to provide people with transit systems that would enable them to adapt more efficiently to low-density settlements and to include town centers that would restore the texture of the slum areas they had left behind.

Similar problems resulting from the even more widespread suburban migration in the United States were identified during the 1950s. This was the period during which sociologists and critics in this country were denouncing split-level traps and what Riesman called the suburban dislocation.[33] It was the reaction to this reaction that led to major urban-redevelopment projects intended to provide housing for the middle and working classes closer to city centers and jobs. Then, when these programs failed to prove attractive and were denounced for depriving the poor and the blacks of the only housing they could afford, the new-town and planned-unit development movements emerged.

Of course, like most romantic ideologies, the nostalgia for the community life of the old bye-law streets and tenements ignores what was bad about the past. The industrial street had genuine hazards, which had given rise to the new town policy, suburban resettlement, the *Ville Radieuse*, and Broadacre City in the first place. Nostalgia has also produced a myth about the universal appeal of street life, which is not confirmed by what we know of the social structure and life-style of different classes in the Victorian and pre–World War I cities. For all the good sense Mrs. Jacobs makes in her defense of the virtues of street life and her call for its revival, even she falls into the trap of exaggerating the degree to which it suits the needs of all the residents of cities. As Gans has pointed out in a lengthy critique of her book, despite the fact that urban residents want a safe and convenient environment, the best of cities still presents real problems for mothers of young children.[34] Furthermore, in both England and America, there are many people who sincerely prefer the lower density and open space of the suburbs and are happy to pay for them by commuting to work. This was true in the last century too. Although the general exodus to the suburbs did not begin in this country until after the second world war, when federal housing policy made it easy to finance a home, the more affluent classes began settling in the inner-ring suburbs at the end of the last century, following the establishment of the commuter railways and streetcar lines.

There is considerable evidence that the bourgeoisie of Victorian England did not like their urban streets so much either. Most of their social life was carried out away from the street. In the Georgian terraces, the bedrooms and other private family rooms were on the upper floors or faced the rear of the house; the rooms adjoining the street were used for the kitchen and the servant quarters. The advocates of street life, who are so anxious to revive the open-air markets (or imitate those that still exist in continental cities), forget that those who were well enough off to make the choice did not patronize the stalls themselves but sent servants to do the shopping. Even as late as the end of the nineteenth century, the average member of the English middle class thought of the street as a place where he would suffer harassment by the rabble of the city wanting to entertain him or sell him a trinket.[35] Indeed, it was the fear of harassment that led the Victorians to ride in closed carriages.

To mention the romanticism connected with the new admiration for street life is not to denigrate the current concern for reviving it but to put the issue in perspective. We need to disentangle the more irrational justifications offered in defense of the street from the more realistic ones. Romantic nostalgia is dangerous because it draws our attention away from the fundamental social changes that account for the real difficulties we encounter in dealing with the urban street. For the problem of street life has been made more acute by the major influences operating on cities in recent times. The bonds of the street community have broken down not just because so many have moved away but because those who remain have been subjected to a variety of new forces that tend to destroy the social fabric and the capacity to reactivate it.

The blacks in the central cities of America today, if we accept the Moynihan thesis, are more vulnerable to the strains of urban life than were previous residents of the slums. It is consequently harder for them to engage in communal activities. The jobs available to slum residents are not usually in their neighborhood. When travel time is added to working hours, there is not much leisure left to develop or engage in street life. Education is relatively more important today, thus increasing the relative disadvantage of the urban poor. Also, the leaders in today's slums spend much of their time and energy trying to organize the population so that it can take advantage of the new popular democracy, again leaving little surplus time or energy for encouraging community life. In those American slums where racial diversity still exists, polarization has made communal life harder to attain. Despite the poverty of the inner-city residents, the availability of mass transit in some cities and the widespread ownership of cars make it much easier for people to get away for recreation, and there is therefore less desire to use the street space as the locus for casual social interaction. Add to this the omnipresence of television, which takes people off the street and into their homes, and the combination of forces inhibiting the development of communal life on the street seems overwhelming.

Architects, as citizens of this stage of industrial society, have been affected by the general social forces that have produced the revived interest in the street. But architects also have special orientations, traditions, ideologies, and interests that arise from the characteristics of their work and the position that designers hold in society. One feature of the distinctive architectural culture is especially relevant for understanding their version of interest in the idea of the street. This is that the ultimate test of the architect's theories takes place in making buildings that work. Yet it is fair to say that it is only since the second world war that modern theories of urban design have been put to any extensive test through buildings. Occasional one-off buildings, including some mass housing, were produced by the masters of modern architecture around the time of the first world war and in the twenties and thirties. Large-scale city projects, however, at least those projects that were constructed before the Great Depression hit the building industry, were designed mainly by architects still under the influence of the Beaux-Arts tradition and the dominant stylistic revivals of the turn of the century. Both in Europe and America, the greatest achievements of modern architecture between the two wars were achievements at the level of theory. The most important projects of Corbusier, Mies, even of Wright and Gropius, remained just that — projects — ideas that were never transformed into buildings.

There is no end to the list of ideas that never reached fulfillment, of competitions lost, of clients who at the last minute turned to more conventional designers: the St. Marks apartment tower, the Mies glass tower, the Paris plan for three million inhabitants, the League of Nations project, the Gropius-Meyer designs for the *Chicago Tribune* competition. It was because of this pattern of recurrent frustration that we all felt such excitement when, after the second world war, the masters of modern architecture finally began getting steady commissions for projects of larger scale or more permanence than villas and pavilions for exhibitions.

This history, though, is filled with irony. What happened when the Modern Movement's theories of urban design began to be tested on a significant scale? Their buildings turned out to be failures in many important ways. Looking back we can now see that the power and influence of the Ville Radieuse, of glass towers, of superhighways in the midst of the city, were achieved partly because these projects remained ideas. Regardless of whether or not Colin Rowe is correct in suggesting that the Plan Voisin was no more than a heuristic device that enabled Corbusier to set a believable stage for his ideas about buildings, and despite the merits of Banham's advice that younger architects ought to have paid more attention to what Corbusier did than to what he said he would do, these ideas did establish the antistreet framework in terms of which the architectural culture thought about design.[36] For example, Corbusier and his followers assumed they would be allowed to rebuild large parts of existing cities. Therefore it was appropriate to conceive of the city as a *tabula rasa*, a plain, the sort of landscape that was in fact made available to Corbusier for the Villa Savoye or the Unités, or, finally, on the required scale, in Chandigarh.

But on most occasions this ideal setting was not available. Instead, modern architects finally given a chance to build office towers, laboratory buildings, or housing slabs found themselves offered small lots in the middle of the city or campus. These lots were surrounded by other buildings of equivalent scale, designed according to other principles but sufficiently viable to generate a context that somehow had to be respected. Given this situation it is no wonder that a whole new set of concepts entered the architectural vocabulary, and this new set has in turn had a major influence in arousing an interest in the existing fabric of the street: ideas such as the Venturis' emphasis on "accommodation"; or the notion of the responsive environment, a popular term among architects who have been influenced by environmental psychology and other behavioral sciences; or the Smithsons' call to abandon the search for generalizable solutions and replace them by design concepts that acknowledge the special and accidental features of place.[37]

Modern architecture's relationship to government authorities was something else that did not work out as anticipated. Corbusier knew, for instance, that the implementation of his Paris plan could come about only if the government assembled the magnificent site he had in mind and razed the buildings. And he rather expected that this might eventually happen (although he also said that he would leave to "some specialist" the task of estimating its feasibility).[38] It was not uncommon during the 1930s for leading architects to look on public agencies in this way as their potential saviors — at the same time that they attributed their inability to get more work to the philistine and conservative orientation of the personnel in the ministries.

These contradictory beliefs were resolved by the continuing utopianism of this generation of architects, which allowed them at the same time to despise the existing bureaucracy while being convinced that the next incumbents, following the socialist revolution, would be sympathetic to advanced ideas. This was not just a French attitude but was common in England and in the United States, too. Many leading British architects, including at least one postwar president of the R.I.B.A. had been acknowledged communists during the 1930s. In the United States, those active in the housing movement, which was the principal vehicle through which modern architects expressed themselves politically, tended to be either socialist or adherents of the New Deal. Following the second world war, many modern architects in England took work with government ministries and, more importantly, with the London County Council. The major government programs for rebuilding the bombed-out cities were inaugurated at this time. In the United States a similar, but much less well-marked, trend occurred, the difference reflecting both the fragmentation of government authorities dealing with housing and the continuing dominance of the private sector over construction in this country.

When one looks back at the first postwar forays into urban rebuilding,

it is evident that the belief that government support would result in the implementation of advanced design ideas was confirmed. But it is another of the ironies of this history that the situation did not last long. Once the younger architects were established in the ministries they found themselves subjected to the usual political, economic, and legal constraints, which forced them to modify their ideas. Here was another source of their new respect for the existing urban context. In Great Britain, the shortage of housing was so severe that any proposal to prepare a flat site and start afresh, except where there was extensive bomb damage or where, as in Roehampton, the parklike setting already existed, was considered impractical. Government proposals were subject to parliamentary review, and it soon became evident that high-rise buildings were not always the fastest or most economical way to provide housing. Then too, a long established set of administrative rules and policies respecting the needs of the users existed in Great Britain. These were reinforced by the expansion of the Building Research Station and the establishment of other research groups in the ministries concerned with the building of schools, hospitals, housing and government offices. Architects were forced to become more responsive to the wishes of users. And user studies indicated considerable public resistance to such "modern" ideas as high-rise housing, large windows, and elevator flats.[39] Of course it should be added that there was always a curious contradiction between many Corbusian concepts and the English tradition in architecture, with its emphasis on picturesque landscape ideas.[40] To a degree the experience of modern architects in the ministries and county councils simply revealed the latent contradictions more fully. In the end, however, the younger architects in Britain shifted away from the continental tradition toward a smaller-scaled domestic view, which was more oriented to the street.

In the United States the timing of events was different and, because of the greater importance of private building and the more direct voice of the public in dealing with urban problems, the influences were also different.[41] Eventually, however, the result was the same. CIAM ideas were rejected in favor of the street. We see this very clearly in the recent work of the Institute for Architecture and Urban Studies, with its designs for low-rise, high-density housing in Brooklyn and Staten Island.[42] There is probably no group of architects in this country with closer ties to the Corbusian tradition or with better credentials to represent the main stream of the European architecture, but how firmly they have come out in favor of the street. Of course, in part they were following a line set for them by their client, the New York State Urban Development Corporation, which, while it still was operating, was the closest approximation we had in the United States to the public building authorities of England, the Low Countries, and Scandinavia. However, the inclination of Frampton and Eisenman to go along with, and even reaffirm the demands of, their client also stemmed from their familiarity and sympathy with the theoretical shift indicated by the ideas of Team 10. Perhaps it should also be mentioned that both the Institute and UDC were responding to the criticisms of social scientists and to the political activity of the ethnic and black populations of New York.[43]

One more irony in the history of the ideas of CIAM should be noted. Now that their housing proposals have been tested in the crucible of urban life, now that experience and research have shown that their view of urban problems is neither popular nor responsive to urban needs, it has become fashionable to accuse the founders of the Modern Movement of sociological naiveté. This accusation is exaggerated and unfair. Corbusier's notions may look inadequate now, but his emphasis on handling the problems generated by the automobile, on bringing sunlight into the house, on providing better ventilation, were perfectly reasonable responses to the problems of the industrial city as they were then understood. If the masters of modern architecture are to be labeled naive, then so should everyone else who talked about cities between the wars and earlier — city planners, landscape architects, social workers, social scientists, and politicians.

All these groups defined the central urban problems as public health, overcrowding, and traffic. These masters of modern architecture had a genuine social concern. Corbusier got many of his notions about the good society from the French syndicalists; Gropius and many other members of the Bauhaus were affiliated with German and central European Marxist ideologies and movements; Wright, although not a socialist, wanted to improve the lot of the average American citizen according to his version of Jeffersonian democracy (and this long before the Usonian house).

Given the social, also utopian, thrust behind their work and the emphasis on housing for the poor, how strange, and also sad, that their formal ideas should have been most widely adopted for entirely different building types and for luxury housing. The Lake Shore apartments, Society Hill Towers, and the John Hancock building in Chicago are not inhabited by the poor or even by the middle class. Furthermore, these buildings as well as the office buildings that fulfill the same formal ideas — Lever House, the Seagram building, the Pan Am building — are not run by the state for the benefit of the public; they are profit-making structures or are used by private corporations to enhance their public image.

None of the buildings mentioned pay much attention to the street. In fact the proliferation of the office tower along Park Avenue in New York City has played a considerable part in destroying what was one of the few grand baroque streets of that city.[44] Nevertheless, these buildings continue to be built. Despite their socialistically inspired origins they are able to serve other functions for the real estate and urban interests who own or rent land in the central cities of the United States. Tall buildings turn out to be economical in relation to land costs in downtown locations; their frame construction allows spatial flexibility for adjusting to changes in office organization within large bureaucracies; and their very size and monumentality apparently have positive symbolic value for the wealthy corporate client. Also, there are enough people in large cities who not only want to live close to their work but who can also afford apartment rents competitive with office use. These people can also afford the occasional servant and other amenities that make the high-rise luxury apartments livable.[45] It should be mentioned that although a similar tendency to build tower blocks exists in the private sector in England, in cities such as London and Manchester, they are much less common there. Also, their use is limited largely to offices; virtually no high-rise luxury apartments are being constructed.[46]

This account of the difficulties produced by the attempt to apply the leading concepts of modern architecture to the problems of the city is, of course, well known to the current generation of designers and is one source of their partial disenchantment with those architects who immediately preceded them. In coping with their disenchantment, the younger generation has not been content simply to be critics. However, the events of the immediate past have made them unusually self-conscious about the meaning of the architectural tradition and about the role of the designer in relation to the client, the user, and society in general. This self-consciousness has brought about a transformation in their approach to the process of design, which probably will endure long after the early failures of modern architecture have been forgotten.

One noteworthy characteristic of the new approach to design is its deliberate and often explicit use of the history of architectural form to guide the formulation of new proposals. In the case of the street, it is illustrated by the infatuation of English architects with the picturesque tradition, giving rise to the idea of townscape. Among younger architects in this country, there is the example of Philip Johnson and his many disciples and their fascination with Italian and baroque concepts of the street, the plaza, and the square. This reliance on earlier historical forms as a way of solving the problems of urban design is different from the method of the masters who argued that the problems of urban life could best be solved by liberating architecture from the ideas of the tradition.

The denial by men like Gropius of the value of historical studies was, of course, a reaction against the continuing influence of the Beaux-Arts tradition with its slavish attention to classical forms. Gropius's rejection of history went to the extreme of excluding historical studies from the curriculum first of the Bauhaus and then of the Harvard Graduate School of Design. As a result, many of today's mature architects trained in American professional schools when Harvard set the standard are unfamiliar with the history of modern architecture. The situation is quite different now. Modern architecture dominates the curriculum of schools, and the teaching of its history has become well established. But the younger generation does not seem to be able to find its way to new forms by reexperiencing the intellectual processes through which men like Mies or Le Corbusier arrived at their aesthetic positions. These men developed their architectural concepts more or less inductively. They began by defining a set of social and technological problems, analyzed the response of the existing tradition to these problems, and virtually in self-defense, as a polemical act, carved out the stances for which they became famous. The current generation is unable to do this. Instead, what they aim to do is begin where the masters ended, that is to say, to extract a set of ideas from the historical tradition.

The use of history can often be helpful to architects. Colquohoun has pointed out that designers, even when they claim to be empiricists and positivists, operate with some mental construct at the backs of their minds.[47] He argues that it is much better to admit this fact and to make the search for types explicit in the hope of conserving effort by profiting from the accumulated wisdom of the tradition. The realization of this point is now so widespread that we find Colquohoun's argument being praised by architects with antithetical attitudes toward design methodology.[48]

However, the resort to historical prototypes is laden with difficulties. When one is dependent on the past, there is an inevitable tendency to use it without qualifications as the model for the present. What does one do to compensate for the possibility that radical new forms of social life are constantly developing, perhaps so radical that no reasonable adaptations and adjustments in the stock of typologies will be adequate for dealing with them? An effective response to new conditions will be vitiated, then, by beginning an analysis with the street types available in cities of the past. Furthermore, there is the directly related difficulty of deciding which type from the past or which elements from past types should be used as the source for projecting new forms.

Both the virtues and the dangers of an historical approach are illustrated in current thinking about the street. The advantage is that it suggests to clients and to society at large possibilities that go beyond the current experience of cities. But the cost of depending on these images is that they distract the architect from addressing himself to the special problems of the urban street today. As an example, take the work of Gordon Cullen. It would be unfair to ignore his remarkable power to highlight the visual qualities of the existing English village and town and to present his insights in photographic images.[49] However, the implications of his presentation are absurd. Nothing we know about the history of cities or the way social forces now operate in cities could lead reasonable men to suppose that the replication today in London,

Sheffield or Milton Keynes of the spaces of Canterbury Close or the Poultry Cross in Salisbury will produce close-knit communities. In fact, the chain of explanation runs in the opposite direction. The charming spaces Cullen describes came about because of the prior existence of a coherent community; they did not then, nor could they now, by themselves bring about such a community. Some of the confusion here grows out of that same nostalgic romanticism that exalts the attractions of eighteenth-century urban life. Cullen's photographs of these spaces, in fact the spaces themselves when we visit them as tourists, undoubtedly rouse in us communitylike sentiments. But this is because we bring to them educated cultural memories and a strong desire to recover some of the feelings associated with the close community. Unfortunately it is also true that emotions generated by such visits tend not to survive when the tourist has returned home, even if some architect in his home city has attempted to recreate an identical setting. The reason is simply that the other conditions of contemporary life do not support the feelings the architecture is intended to elicit.

The difficulty of any attempt to draw on the past is of course that historical ideas arose in a historical context. Introduced into new social and cultural settings, they will not mean what they originally meant. If derivative forms are to work, then architects have to find some way to assure their clients and the public that the values these street ideas had in the past can still be communicated to the residents of today's cities, despite their different values, consciousness, social structure, and life experience. It might be nice to think this were possible, but there is very little evidence from the public's response so far to suggest the view is correct. If history is to be relied on by architects, it would be more helpful to use it to understand the political and social conditions that fostered the design concepts represented by the English village or the baroque city. Then it would be revealed that many of the solutions now being talked about were products of a social order that is not likely to be reconstituted and was not worth preserving anyway.

A second characteristic of the new architects of the street is their desire to collaborate with social scientists. As was the case with the reemergence of the emphasis on the street concept itself, the beginnings of this interest is associated with the formation of Team 10, and again the significant architectural office was that of the Smithsons, in England. As early as the 1950s the Smithsons were arguing that architects would not be able to solve the problems of urban rebuilding on their own but would need to borrow from the research and findings of sociologists.[50] Given the British background in producing council housing, a spate of reports by Royal Commissions from the first world war onward dealing with housing standards, and a well-established group of government agencies and research stations turning out information about building performance and user needs, the appeal by the Smithsons got a generally positive response.

The new generation's collaboration with social scientists must be seen as one of a more general series of changes in architectural practice and theory. For example, the willingness to seek the advice of sociologists is a specific example of the emergence of the concept of the design team, in which representatives of several disciplines work together to produce the final scheme. This is a very different approach to architectural practice from the mode utilized by masters such as Le Corbusier and Wright. Corbusier and Wright were in the grand tradition of highly individualistic designers who defined the program themselves and assumed that their own intellectual and imaginative resources were adequate for the solution of everything but major structural problems. The design team concept, however, is the current version of conditions of practice that were common before the first world war in government departments and also in some of the large industrial firms in Central Europe.

Men like Gropius were schooled in this tradition and adopted it for their own practices, initially in the state and municipal building ministries and, after they fled the Nazis, in private firms. It would be interesting to investigate the role of central European émigrés in diffusing this pattern of architectural organization to England and America, where it is now the dominant method for design. Whatever this role may have been, however, it also is obvious that the popularity of the team approach among the architects of the street is a necessary response to current demands: the increasing complexity of urban-design programs, the emergence of more demanding and more critical clients, and the rationalization of work processes that now affects all professions, not only architecture.

The team approach also is consistent with the rejection of the utopian tradition among the younger generation. Fewer architects still hold the view that nothing less than a radical restructuring of society and the building industry will allow design to achieve its social goals, a position advocated by many of the masters. The belief is more common now that enlightened state and municipal agencies concerned with housing, rather than posing an insurmountable threat to the achievement of what Wright called "Truth in architecture," instead offer the best hope that relatively humane projects can be built. This is a switch, of course, from the attitudes of the period immediately following the second world war when the architectural public, including the masters themselves, became discouraged by the negative response of agencies and user groups to their urbanistic proposals. But in the interim, architecture adopted the stance of sympathy for the idea of the street. This stance is much more compatible with the notion that extensive information about user needs and patient attention to client concerns can produce a reasonably good project.

The abandonment of utopianism also has its roots in the Central European architecture of the period between the wars. Men like Taut and Wagner, for example, learned through their experience in municipal departments that political rhetoric was not very helpful in managing the day-to-day difficulties that arose in carrying out a housing scheme. They also discovered that socialist systems of ownership and control of building production did not automatically remove the obstacles to an adequate supply of housing in war-ravaged and depressed economies. On the other hand, they came to realize that the lawyers, economists, social workers, and planners who also worked in the building departments possessed expert knowledge that helped to speed the programming and construction processes and provided inputs that resulted in a more useful product.[51] French, English, and American architects did not have the opportunities to learn these lessons until after the second world war. It is understandable that an awareness of the benefits accruing to architecture from operating in organizational settings has come to them much more recently.

It would be a mistake, however, to lean too heavily on the rise of a public architecture conducted under bureaucratic auspices to explain the popularity of the team approach. The problem that confronts the urban designer is unprecedented. Furthermore, the problem is one to which — or so it is reasonable to assume — the knowledge and research of the sociologists will prove relevant. With respect to the street, the central problem is how to create a community within its physical boundaries, when rarely before had the architect been expected to use his medium and expertise to create a social order where none existed. From the late Renaissance until recently, the architect could more or less assume that his client would represent a coherent user group and could present him with a reasonably well-defined program. His job was to provide the space and the form to fulfill the program. But today the street designer is faced with the problem of defining not only the program but the user group behind the program.

The expectation that collaboration with social scientists would rescue architecture from the dilemma presented by the street has not been fulfilled.[52] One basic difficulty is that the sociologist is no more able to solve the problem of community than the architect, in part because the sociologist, qua sociologist, is trained to describe and analyze social phenomena, not to design solutions to social problems. A second difficulty is that the problems the street designer faces are rooted in the fundamental human and technological conditions of our culture, which nobody, not just architects and sociologists, has been able to cope with effectively. A third difficulty is that even though interdisciplinary collaboration among members of the design team has made great strides, fiscal and political difficulties remain unresolved. For example, many of the management and social services that are required to make the street work are not budgeted and introduced at the same time that the housing and related urban spaces are built. These are not the kinds of difficulties that can be blamed on architects and sociologists especially, but have to do with the ongoing political and economic context in which design decision making is conducted.

Still, just as there are better and worse ways of using the examples of history, there are better and worse ways of using the findings of sociology. For example, it is important that architects make a serious effort to respect the findings of social research about the different life-styles of various social classes and ethnic groups as they relate to the use of the street. The danger arises, however, when, as in the work of the Brolin-Zeisel partnership, this information is translated into a scheme that reproduces in detail the amenities and spaces that many poor city dwellers already possess;[53] or when, as in so much work of the Venturis in Philadelphia, in New Haven, or in Las Vegas, new proposals artfully reproduce the vocabulary of forms and symbols with which the residents of these areas are already familiar. It is just as wrong for the "pop architects" to assume that the urban population can only respond to what it already knows from its present milieu as it is for the architect schooled in historical types to assume that a universal psychology of response will enable today's city dwellers to recapture the meaning of forms imported from other cultures. The latter ideology, whether right or wrong, is at least less patronizing to the Italians of the West End or the blacks of Philadelphia. The studies of sociologists like Gans suggest that the ambition of the poor is precisely to get away from their present milieus and into the houses and street forms we associate with higher income groups.[54] To design for the poor more of what they already have suggests that this is all they can ever attain; yet we know that their environments contain some of the least valued spaces and symbols of American society. Furthermore, the Venturis seem to forget that the vocabulary of styles that now surrounds the poor is often not *their* vocabulary. Instead what the Venturis are doing is reproducing hand-me-downs from other social groups. The urban poor often live in houses that were built earlier for richer groups and have passed on to the poor through the filtering process.

We have seen the difficulties that confront the generation of architects who are bent on creating a new idea of the street, one that will be relevant to today's cities. Recourse to history has its pitfalls and recourse to sociology its disappointments. Faced with a major challenge but finding it difficult to develop a solution that in some way can be accommodated within the architectural tradition, it is not surprising to find that some members of the prostreet generation reject the architectural culture itself.

One sign of this is the movement to break down architectural ideas into their constituent elements and to develop radically new concepts and geometries oriented to the building program. Alexander, for example, shares the view of many of the architects and critics discussed earlier that the problem of the street today is the problem of facilitating human contact. But instead of using types drawn from history, he develops his own "pattern language" to describe a set of physical elements that will, in his view, encourage the growth of community. The language is really a checklist of forms that will meet a set of twelve program specifications — for example, that the dwelling must be located next to a vehicular street or that it must contain a transparent communal room. He is not at all interested in whether what emerges will resemble conventional street types or how it might accommodate itself to the existing urban fabric.[55] Katz, in his analysis of American housing types, argues that the street is not a valid idea by itself but must be regarded as a special form drawn from a larger set of forms, all of which have to do with creating a sense of community. He describes a group of physical parameters that can help produce a community, including open space and enclosure, for example. Yet the street itself never reappears in his plans.[56] Lynch attacked the antistreet attitudes of his teacher, Wright, but he too removes the concept to a more abstract level in order to concentrate attention on the more general problem of achieving a sense of social order in the city through the provision of visual cues. His references to nodes, edges, paths, landmarks, and districts are ultimately addressed to the same problems that first brought about the new interest in the street, but it is noteworthy that his vocabulary does not include the word *street* itself.[57]

The approach of these "design methodologists" owes much to prevailing notions about how new knowledge is obtained in the sciences, and this faith in induction as the way to achieve new design ideas puts them at odds with the formalist street architects mentioned earlier who base their approach on history. However, because they approach design by considering programmatic issues first and hope that concepts of form will somehow arise through a consideration of the program, they are using a method that is really closer to the spirit of Gropius or le Corbusier than those who turn to history.

An antiarchitecture, prostreet attitude also characterizes the proposals of the visionary architects, including Habraken and Friedman in Europe and Price and the Archigram group in England. These people are also members of what we might call the street generation. Habraken's polemic, in *Supports,* against Corbusier and high-rise housing is explicit, as is his statement that the problem of urban design can be equated with the problem of restoring the urban resident's relationship to ground level.[58] Habraken in his book also eschews any attempt to propose a formal solution for the design of the urban infrastructure and the houses and other building types that rest on it. *Supports* deliberately avoids presenting any images of what the indeterminate city of the future will look like. The selection and arrangement of building elements is left to the consumer, to be chosen through what Friedman imagines will be a "flat typewriter." In this way Habraken hopes that the urban community, which he calls the natural relationship of man to building, will be restored. "The forms," he writes — and the suggestion is that he is thinking of social as well as physical forms — "will emerge almost by themselves. They will appear from all sides by the inventiveness and intelligence of all those concerned."[59]

Whatever the other merits or faults of Habraken's approach, there is some question whether the average urban dweller is as eager to design his own environment as Habraken suggests. Even if he is, how can this activity alone overcome the force of all the other factors that stand in the way of the revival of the local community? Nevertheless, the assumption has a powerful hold on many architects and offers an interesting rationale for those who, in their concern for the street, refuse to suggest specific contents for it.

The visionary architects can be classified among the members of the street generation because they disavow many of the formal ideas of the masters on the grounds that these ideas do not address the problem of community and restrict the user's choice of dwelling type. Nevertheless, they differ from most of the design methodologists in their continuing concern for the fact that the condition of the architectural culture is rooted in the state of the construction industry, the self-image of the profession, and the system of property relations. For Habraken's infrastructure and support system to be built, for example, major transformations would have to take place in the rules governing social and economic organization and in the manufacturing and distribution systems of the building industry. Also, Habraken's scheme is addressed only in part to finding a basis for collaboration between the architect, other professionals, and government departments concerned with building. He is interested equally in defining a unique role for the architect who, under his proposal, would be responsible for designing the urban infrastructure and also the components that the consumer assembles to make up dwelling units.[60]

Despite the many respects in which American and European architects adopt similar modes of thought and are concerned with similar issues, the approach represented by Habraken has not caught on yet in this country. However, both the populist impulse and the defiance of traditional emphases on form and geometry, which are part of this approach, have found expression in the United States. In fact, the striking thing about this country is not how far user participation and new design languages have been developed in theory but the extent to which they have been put into practice. Many American cities, particularly those with architecture schools, have workshops or design groups that provide free architectural services for the poor. These groups meet with their community clients, discuss with them the problems involved in design and building, and encourage their clients to "make many decisions that often are made by professionals."[61] The laymen who represent the client may be presented with alternative organizations for solving their housing needs and asked to choose the ones that fit their requirements best, or they may be stimulated to propose their own solutions. Reports on this new practice tell us little about whether the street and housing plans thus produced are any better than what the tradition can suggest or whether they work any better than the old solutions, but apparently some of the users and many of the architects have found the encounters stimulating and satisfying experiences.[62]

The satisfaction of these architects with the participation process is significant. It reveals that the architect feels the same sense of estrangement from society that has caused both the breakdown of the urban community and the new general interest in the street. However, the pleasure the architects find in making themselves dependent on the street users also suggests that it is not just the city that has lost the sense of community, it is the architectural profession as well. The new interest in the user also points up the architect's alienation from his clients. It was noted earlier that Corbusier and his generation had little chance to build their designs and this kept them from discovering how remote their proposals were from the needs of city dwellers. The greater opportunity today's architects have to build reveals still other gaps in their ideas and skills all too clearly. One way, and apparently in this country a common way, for the architect to get closer to the client is through a reversal of roles. The user has the ideas and does the design, while the architect acts as counselor. We thus end with a paradox: for many of the street generation the most effective way to solve the problem of street design is to forego a commitment to the architectural idea of the street and instead turn the job of architect over to the people of the street themselves.

Notes

1. Arthur Korn, *History Builds the Town* (London: Lund Humphries, 1953), p. 10.

2. See the discussion of the cult of the street in E. A. Gutkind, *Urban Development in Central Europe (International History of City Development,* vol. 1) (New York: Free Press, 1964), pp. 169 ff.

3. Bernard Rudofsky, *Streets for People: A Primer for Americans* (Garden City, N.Y.: Doubleday, 1969).

4. Oscar Newman, ed., *New Frontiers in Architecture: CIAM '59 in Otterlo* (New York.: Universe Books, 1961), pp. 205–216.

5. See pp. 22 ff. in S. B. Sutton, ed., *Civilizing American Cities. A Selection of Frederick Law Olmsted's Writings on City Landscapes* (Cambridge, Mass.: The MIT Press, 1971).

6. Korn, *History Builds the Town,* p. 54.

7. Thomas Sharp, *The English Panorama* (London: Architectural Press, 1950), p. 76.

8. Sutton, *Civilizing American Cities,* p. 32.

9. Heath Licklider, *Architectural Scale* (New York: George Braziller, 1966), p. 163.

10. See, for example, Charles Edouard Jeanneret-Gris (Le Corbusier), *The City of Tomorrow and its Planning* (3rd ed., translated from the 8th edition of Urbanisme by Frederick Etchells) (Cambridge, Mass.: The MIT Press, 1971) or *The Radiant City* (New York: Orion Press, 1967).

11. "In 1925, he [Le Corbusier] wrote a diatribe against the street; he hated its complex multiplicity and what seemed to him its mess and confinement." Vincent Scully, *American Architecture and Urbanism* (New York, Praeger, 1969), p. 167.

12. Melvin M. Webber, "Order in Diversity: Community without Propinquity," Lowdon Wingo, Jr., ed., *Cities and Space* (Baltimore: Johns Hopkins University Press, 1963), pp. 23–54.

13. This commercial view of the street was incorporated into the 1811 gridiron plan for New York City. See John W. Reps, *The Making of Urban America* (Princeton: Princeton University Press, 1965).

14. See Martin Pawley, *Architecture versus Housing* (New York: Praeger, 1971).

15. Obviously, some people maintained an interest in the street before the widespread increase in interest. In the United States, Lewis Mumford and members of the Regional Planning Association of America were concerned about the street. For a history of this group see Roy Lubove, *Community Planning in the 1920s; The Contribution of the Regional Planning Association of America* (Pittsburgh: University of Pittsburgh Press, 1964).

16. Reyner Banham, *The New Brutalism* (New York: Reinhold, 1966), pp. 70 ff.

17. Alison Smithson, ed., *Team 10 Primer* (Cambridge, Mass.: The MIT Press, 1968).

18. Scully suggests the beginnings of such a story but has yet to recount it in full. See Scully, *American Architecture and Urbanism,* passim, or "The Death of the Street," *Perspecta 8,* 1963, pp. 91–96.

19. For Kahn, see Scully, *Louis I. Kahn* (New York: George Braziller, 1962); for the Venturis, see Robert Venturi, Denise Scott-Brown and Steven Izenour, *Learning from Las Vegas* (Cambridge, Mass.: The MIT Press, 1962).

20. Herbert J. Gans, *The Urban Villagers* (New York: Free Press of Glencoe, 1962); Jane Jacobs, *The Death and Life of Great American Cities* (New York: Random House, 1961); Michael Young and Peter Willmott, *Family and Kinship in East London* (London: Routledge and Kegan Paul, 1957). Many of the findings and most of the ideas set forth in the books were discussed by these authors in scholarly periodicals, professional journals, and popular magazines five to ten years before the books appeared.

21. Alison Smithson, *Urban Structuring* (New York: Reinhold, 1967).

22. Camillo Sitte, *City Planning According to Artistic Principles,* trans. George R. and Christiane Crasemann Collins (New York: Random House, 1965).

23. Christian Norberg-Schulz, *Baroque Architecture* (New York: Abrams, 1972), p. 12.

24. Sutton, *Civilizing American Cities,* pp. 22 ff.

25. See Maurice Broady, "Social Theory in Architectural Design," and Robert Gutman, "The Questions Architects Ask," in Robert Gutman, ed., *People and Buildings* (New York: Basic Books, 1972), pp. 171–185 and 338–369, respectively.

26. See chapter 3 in John Ruskin, *The Seven Lamps of Architecture* (New York: Wiley, 1878).

27. Interestingly enough, those very philosophers who represent the shift in attitude toward culture change, the utilitarians for example, thought of the possibility of using the physical environment to produce new patterns of social action. But because they were not architects their work may not have attracted much attention. See Bentham's "Panopticon Papers" in Mary Peter Mack, ed., *A Bentham Reader* (New York: Pegasus, 1969), pp. 194–208.

28. Mrs. Jacobs's ideas have been an important source of the drive toward decentralization of the mayor's office in New York City and other cities.

29. Jon Lang and Charles Burnette, "A Model of the Designing Process," in Jon Lang, et al., *Designing for Human Behavior* (Stroudsburg, Pa.: Dowden, Hutchinson and Ross, 1947).

30. See Gerald D. Suttles, "The Defended Neighborhood," *The Social Construction of Communities* (Chicago: University of Chicago Press, 1972), pp. 21–43.

31. Although reformers were motivated by concern for the poor, many of the middle and upper classes who supported urban reform were simply anxious to get the poor off the streets.

32. See "The Plea for Community: Robert Park and John Dewey," in Morton and Lucia White, *The Intellectual versus the City* (New York: New American Library, 1964), pp. 159–180.

33. See Richard E. Gordon, Katherine K. Gordon, and Max Gunther, *The Split-Level Trap* (New York: Bernard Geis, 1961) and David Riesman, "The Suburban Dislocation," *Annals of the American Academy of Political and Social Science,* vol. 314 (November 1957).

34. Herbert J. Gans, "Urban Vitality and the Fallacy of Physical Determinism," in *People and Plans* (New York: Basic Books, 1968), pp. 25–33.

35. Alan Delgado, "Entertaining Streets," *Victorian Entertainment* (Newton Abbot, Devon: David and Charles, 1971), pp. 18–28.

36. See Colin Rowe, "Le Corbusier, Utopian Architect," *The Listener* (12 February 1959), p. 289, and Banham, *The New Brutalism,* p. 70 ff.

37. See Venturi et al., *Learning from Las Vegas;* Robert Sommer, *Design Awareness* (San Francisco: Rinehart Press, 1971); A. Smithson, *Urban Structuring.*

38. Jeanneret-Gris (Le Corbusier), *City of Tomorrow,* chapter XVI.

39. For reference to reports of research conducted by British government research groups, see Robert Gutman and Barbara Westergaard, "Annotated Bibliography," in Gutman, ed., *People and Buildings.*

40. Banham has also noted the connection between the domestic scale of recent British architecture and the picturesque tradition; *The New Brutalism,* p. 74.

41. Edward C. Banfield, "The Political Implications of Metropolitan Growth," in Lloyd Rodwin, ed., *The Future Metropolis* (New York: George Braziller, 1961), pp. 80–102.

42. This work was presented in an exhibition, New York City, Museum of Modern Art, *Another Chance for Housing: Low Rise Alternatives,* June 1973.

43. With the loss of population in New York City, land values have stabilized, and the UDC can now afford to build lower-density projects. Furthermore, they have become obsessed with the problems of safety and maintenance. They are now willing to spend more in the present in order to decrease future costs.

44. For a discussion of Park Avenue see Scully, "The Death of the Street."

45. See Janet Abu-Lughod, "A Survey of Center-city Residents," in Nelson N. Foote et al., *Housing Choices and Housing Constraints* (New York: McGraw-Hill, 1960), pp. 387–447.

46. Peter Cowan, *The Office: A Facet of Urban Growth* (London: Heinemann, 1969).

47. Alan Colquohoun, "Typology and Design Method," in Gutman, ed., *People and Buildings,* pp. 395–405.

48. Although ordinarily associated with the rationalist and formalist architects, Colquohoun is also quoted approvingly by the Venturis. See Venturi et al., *Learning from Las Vegas,* pp. 88–90.

49. I am of course referring to Gordon Cullen's extensive work on "Townscape," published in reduced form as *The Concise Townscape* (New York: Van Nostrand-Reinhold, 1961).

50. See Newman, *New Frontiers,* pp. 219 ff.

51. The discussion of the mode of architectural practice in central Europe, and Germany in particular, is based largely on Barbara Miller Lane, *Architecture and Politics in Germany, 1918–1945.*

52. The practical difficulties along with a method for dealing with them are discussed in Constance Perin, *With Man in Mind* (Cambridge, Mass.: The MIT Press, 1970).

53. See Brent C. Brolin and John Zeisel, "Mass Housing: Social Research and Design," *Architectural Forum,* vol. 129, no. 1 (July 1968), pp. 66–71.

54. Both Zeisel and the Venturis claim to be basing their projects on the findings of Gans. Apparently they have missed some of his conclusions. See his *The Levittowners* (New York: Pantheon, 1967) and *The Urban Villagers*

(New York: Free Press, 1962).

55. Christopher Alexander, "The City as a Mechanism for Sustaining Human Contact," in Gutman, ed., *People and Buildings,* pp. 409–434.

56. Robert Katz, *Design of the Housing Site, a Critique of American Practice* (Urbana: University of Illinois Press, 1966).

57. Kevin Lynch, *The Image of the City* (Cambridge, Mass.: Technology Press, 1960) and *Site Planning* (Cambridge, Mass.: The MIT Press, 1962).

58. N. J. Habraken, *Supports: An Alternative to Mass Housing,* trans. B. Valkenburg (New York: Praeger, 1972).

59. Ibid., p. 57.

60. See my review of *Supports,* "Simple-Minded Utopianism and Autocratic Nonsense," *Landscape Architecture,* vol. 63, no. 2 (January 1973), pp. 166–169.

61. Bernard Spring, *Planning and Design Workbook for Community Participation* (Princeton University, School of Architecture and Urban Planning: Research Center for Urban and Environmental Planning, 1969), p. 7.

62. This movement has been carried even further by those American architects who have worked in developing countries. See J. F. C. Turner and Robert Fichter, eds., *Freedom to Build* (New York: Macmillan, 1972). Other works are cited in the bibliography to Lance Jay Brown and Dorothy Whiteman, *Planning and Design Workbook for Community Participation — An Evaluation Report* (Princeton University, School of Architecture and Urban Planning: Research Center for Urban and Environmental Planning, 1973), pp. 45–48.

Streets within a Contextual Model

Studies Toward an Ecological Model of the Urban Environment

Stanford Anderson

Introduction

"H. G. Wells once said, coming out of a political meeting where they had been discussing social change, that this great towering city was a measure of the obstacle, of how much must be moved if there was to be any change. I have known this feeling, looking up at great buildings that are the centres of power, but I find I do not say 'There is your city, your great bourgeois monument, your towering structure of this still precarious civilization' or I do not only say that; I say also 'This is what men have built, so often magnificently, and is not everything then possible?'"[1]

To this rejection by Raymond Williams of the too easy association of the city with antipathetic political history, Murray Bookchin adds: "Can the bourgeois city be rescued from itself? Or, to ask a more basic question, can the high traditions of urbanism be instilled in the modern metropolis?"[2]

Sharing these thoughts, I would only shift the emphasis from the towering monuments to the everyday fabric of our cities. That fabric, humble as it may be, is still more extensive than the obvious bourgeois monuments — and harder to think away. We have inherited cities which, whatever the politics of their makers, today often function differently from what was envisioned when they were made. Current design is not so sound as to encourage wholesale reconstruction. Not only is there much about us that will change slowly; there is much that we should conserve or adapt. What the city is and how it has come to be is more important for our understanding of its potential than for simplistic association with previous political regimes.

It is refreshing that Williams and Bookchin help to break the politically naive rejection of the city; yet one finds that they too quickly reveal a greater trust in the country or in a dispersed urbanism. This advocacy deserts their own reexamination of the city and, if effected, would quite probably defeat their love of the country.

More than just realistically accepting the city because it is unwieldy, I find much that is good in it; but it is of little help to line up rejections and enthusiasms relative to the city. Is there, rather, a way in which we can recognize and guide preferred change within the sociocultural and physical environments of cities? To understand the multiple environments of beings is a problem accepted by ecologists. To do the same for human beings, the field must include cultural ecology. The present essay attempts a contribution within cultural ecology, an understanding of the contexts of city dwellers according to an urban ecology.[3]

City dwellers — people, as individuals and in groups — are special organisms in special environments. Human beings are unusually plastic, capable within certain limits of assimilating their environments. People are also unusually generative, adapting their environments to suit their wills and needs. These interactions between ourselves and our physical environments depend on our sociocultural settings and extend through time until both we and our environments are cultural artifacts — the results of human action but not of deliberate design.[4] These artifacts, cities and their people, are so extensive in time and space that even our largest interventions must be seen in context; and, on the other hand, systematic small-scale changes often affect the city more dramatically than these large interventions. A satisfactory urban ecology must account for all types of intervention in a spatial and temporal framework that includes historical time. Existing descriptive and analytic techniques, skipping from one specialized study to another, discourage a culture/ecological understanding of the city. Although a complex ecological model of urban systems will only be achieved through the efforts of many people, this chapter presents some hypotheses and models for the exploration of urban systems: the conjectural identification of elements and relational rules, accounting for change through transformational rules as well as the possible introduction of novel elements or rules. In this work, I have shifted back and forth between abstract structures and field observation, encouraging the impact of each on the other.

Concept and empirical observation, metropolitan systems and intimately experienced places, historical time and the present and future, people and sociophysical environments — the necessity and the difficult possibility of engaging all these issues is the message of this chapter.

In setting the problem of accounting for the physical environment as a variable in human situations, I accept the complications introduced by certain assumptions: (1) that the physical environment is neither deterministic nor irrelevant in human affairs (2) that, rather, the physical environment interacts with multiple complex patterns of activity and significance — both for individuals and groups, at any point in time, in certain cycles, and over time. These complex patterns of people in the physical environment might be termed the sympatry of human ecology.[5]

In an examination of cities, and of their streets and other elements as parts of ecological systems, Venice provides a provocative analogy. The regional hydraulic system of Venice is set by its lagoon, a large basin bordered by the low-lying mainland to the west and fragile sand bars (lidi) to the east. The mainland empties its streams and wastes into the lagoon. Breaks in the lidi release the run-off and admit the small but significant tidal flows. For Venice itself, these flows not only surround but penetrate it; major channels describe large islands, and a hierarchy of lesser channels further subdivide and serrate the islands. In its basic structure, Venice recalls primitive natural conditions; nevertheless, its channels and the stone-walled land that bounds them have long since become artifacts. The canals of late medieval and Renaissance times are simultaneously the product of natural and human energies and of demands both for mobility and for places — basins and quays and squares and buildings. The energies of nature that helped to create and serve Venice also remain a threat. Aside from the occasional major flood, there is the periodic, not fully explained phenomenon called *acqua alta,* high water. Water burbles up through the pavements, the canals overflow, and the pedestrian ways and major squares become tidal pools. Ground floors of buildings are inundated. Temporarily the location, the boundaries, the use, and the meaning of all the basic elements — canals and public ways and built spaces — change. And not only temporarily; the intervals of this periodicity are sufficiently frequent that patterns of use change permanently. Residential use at the ground floor is particularly discouraged. Pollution of the air and water is yet another factor. Relatively heavy industrialization of the mainland borders of the lagoon has introduced chemicals and microorganisms that carve away at the pilings and walls subtly but perhaps devastatingly.

We can choose to observe any of numerous interactions of structure and energy in this ecological system. We may see Venice as an entity relative to major flooding and the large context of the entire lagoon, its watershed, and the sea. We may emphasize the major canals and islands relative to the wake of large tankers. We may examine those parts of the city threatened by *acqua alta.* Or we may examine individual stones for their deterioration under adverse conditions. In the end, all of these must be seen together. The constant, subtle threat to stone and wood may be the critical factor in the collapse of Venice. The only response may be the alteration or elimination of regional or international industries. The underlying motivation for such action may be a cultural matter.

There are indeed many energy systems working here, often sympatrically, but at other times tending toward competitive exclusion of one another. Not only water and water-borne vehicles and pedestrian flows but also social and economic and cultural and conceptual energies distribute through the city, each with its own demands and all mutually interactive. Each of these energies laps at or creates different boundaries, which may be redrawn again even in short periods of time.

What is easily visualized in the canals and walkways of Venice is equally true for other factors in less unique places in the human environment. Our studies of the publicly accessible spaces of parts of Paris and of Cambridge, Massachusetts (see figs. 23 and 34), suggest something like a flood, the furthest dispersion of public action and energies in the physical environment, defining islands of private energy systems.

In Paris (fig. 23), this flood frequently penetrates the buildings, creating many small eddies of built, comparatively static communal space along the powerful channels. However, the buildings join one another to construct a continuous if eroded wall, separating the stream from the islands of private energy (in French, a block is an *ilot* —

"small island", from the Latin word that carries the same double meaning, *insula*). Another examination of these private islands reveals that they, too, have peculiar structures. Typically, despite their union against the external stream, they are composed of several, or even many, private parcels that share nothing with one another except the external energy systems. However, each of these private parcels will have its own, often complex, ecology — communically organized, sympatric households, and, frequently, semiprivate commerce and industry.

In Cambridge (fig. 34), as compared to Paris, the flood settles out through the planar surface. The channels are less well marked; most of the surface is inundated though not too intensely. There is a high degree of coincidence between the boundaries of the flood and the boundaries of built and unbuilt space. That is, little communal space is built volume; little open space is withheld from public view or access. The islands of privacy *are* the isolated buildings. They stand as symbols of this independence surrounded by space that always had the ambiguity of forecourt and void but increasingly serves as a moat between the communal and the private.

Is an ecological approach, then, to be reduced to mere metaphors? While metaphors may be more than "mere," there is also more to these initial comparisons that just an agreeable glow that everything relates to everything, and that different places can both illuminate one another and be distinguished. These initial observations are born of an aspiration to a more structured approach.

Urban Ecology: An Urban Model and Related Graphic Systems

There are serious dissatisfactions with existing relations between the physical city and our activities — our everyday use of the city as well as longer-term transformations.

Soundly operative parts of the city may be lost while the consequences of interventions are frequently miscalculated, often disastrously so. It is atypical that such negative impacts can be interpreted as malevolent. They arise rather from a lack of understanding of both broad systemic relations and of concrete environmental conditions which lead, in turn, to ill-conceived actions.

With such large, open systems as cities, it is unlikely that the search for understanding can set precision as a goal — certainly not as a proximate goal. We do not know what the atoms or simples or elements of the city are. We must begin from a concern for the organization of the entire system, and such an ambitious undertaking will obviously be hypothetical. Within such a conjectural organization we can examine the fruitfulness of its implicit relationships: do they elucidate the significance of parts of the city; explain certain connections; guide interventions; or even predict the results of such actions?

Since we do not know the ontology of the city, this approach through hypothesis is an exploration of alternative conventions. Nevertheless, through iterations between the hypothetical and the specific, we wish also to make the techniques of analysis as concrete and transferable as possible.

Social Space and Physical Space

Seeking to clarify alternative concerns about, and actions upon, the sociophysical environment, the first chapter of this book examined the general question of interrelations between people and the physical environment. The following distinctions were proposed. The whole of the physical environment is to be recognized as a ''potential environment''; the version of the potential environment that is manifestly or implicitly adopted by one or more users is that individual's or group's ''influential environment.'' The difference between the potential and influential environments forms what is, for that user, a ''latent environment.'' Aspects of that latency may or may not be recognized by that user, or by other users and observers; that is, latency may remain to be discovered. Modeling and other explanatory techniques should assist in clarifying these environments and their interrelationships.

Chapter one also argued that latency in the physical environment (and in other subsystems of the environment) is a social good. Since this latency, or at least those aspects of it that genuinely extend human sensibility and opportunity, is, by definition, not known through observing behavior, it would be desirable to have better means of exploring this phenomenon through the description and modeling of the physical environment per se. This ambition also reinforces an obvious methodological advantage of having an independent description of each subsystem under consideration.

William Michelson points simultaneously to this methodological demand and to the difficulty of meeting it. For example, totally accurate description of the microstructure of a segment of a city, while being a physical description relatively independent of behavioral analysis, would also not aid us at the level of biological integration with which we are primarily concerned.[6] How can we describe the physical, or ''potential,'' city relative to the ecological level of understanding?

The most commonly invoked general physical description of cities is that of built/unbuilt space treated as figure and ground (figs. 1, 2). This method has a venerable history. Camillo Sitte[7] used a version of it in which the solids were shaded in two ways, distinguishing both public buildings and the ordinary fabric of the city. The beautiful and justly famous Nolli map of Rome[8] made a similar distinction by showing the

1. Giambattista Nolli, Plan of Rome, Central area, 1748. [MIT., Rotch Library]

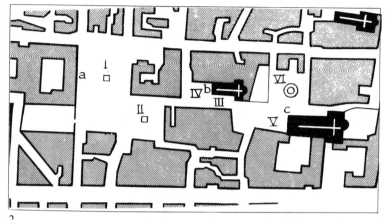

2

3

2. Camillo Sitte, Map of central section of Lucca, from his *Der Städtebau nach seinen künstlerischen Grundsatzen* (Vienna, 1899).

3. N. J. Habraken, Map of a Dutch urban area with "thematic" buildings in black, "non-thematic" buildings in gray, from *SAR 73*. [Eindhoven, Stichting Architecten Research, *SAR 73*, 1973, p. 22]

major interior spaces of public buildings as extensions of urban open space. Sitte thus compromises the fundamental figure/ground relationship in order to convey information about buildings of a certain category of use and meaning. Nolli conveys much the same information together with its significant internal spatial characteristics through a compromise of the built/unbuilt reference.

The purely abstract rendering of built volume as a figure/ground diagram has diffused throughout the architectural and design professions. Colin Rowe may be seen as its principal exponent on a theoretical level.[9] It has also served as a fundamental analytical device in the studies of urban tissue by N. J. Habraken and his colleagues. Habraken establishes four fundamental categories: built and unbuilt ("material and space"), and thematic and nonthematic.[10] In the associated mapping (fig. 3), graphic distinction is given to thematic and nonthematic buildings but not to thematic and nonthematic space. The mapping consequently has a similar appearance to that of Sitte. However, if one desires an abstract physical analysis, Habraken's distinction of thematic and nonthematic *morphological* elements is a clear advance over Sitte's social distinction of public and private buildings. Indeed, it is helpful to recognize thematic and nonthematic elements (I prefer to use *typical, atypical*) whether one is considering parceling or buildings or activity spaces or social factors; that is, the distinction elucidates both morphological and social analyses.

While Sitte and Nolli overtly conflated social and physical information, it may be noted that, even as advanced by Rowe and Habraken, built/unbuilt diagrams are neither purely physical nor very subtle. The drawings reveal certain social decisions such as size and/or continuity of material and spatial elements, preferred relationships, application of simple or complex geometries, and so on. Habraken also introduces parceling and distinguishes canals from other open spaces. Freestanding walls and important changes in level are instances of material factors that are omitted. Similarly, built spaces that operate continuously with open space are either ignored or rendered simply as space. Although a useful device at a certain scale of inquiry, the built/unbuilt diagram is obviously rather lacking in articulation, failing to make many material and spatial distinctions of rudimentary importance.

In the study of a sector of Paris, a rendering of physical structure that would be still more detached from social and functional reference was attempted. The commonly employed iconic designations for horizontal cuts through walls and columns were used. A description of building construction as found obviously incorporated such specific information as the sizes and interconnectedness of spaces and the relation of spaces to streets. With this slight information, one could already read many social and cultural characteristics. Figure 29 shows the next, relatively more abstract, step. Effectively, it approaches a representation of the spatial potential yielded by the civil engineering of this sector of Paris. Columnar buildings have only columns and no partitions. Walled buildings, however, present more problems. In Paris, walls are frequently broken through, from one cell to another and onto the street. Consequently, it seemed best to represent all walls as if they were interrupted at the greatest frequency that is statically possible, thus recording the minimal constraint imposed by construction. Pursued rigorously, the same rule would apply to walls on party lines. Indeed, Paris is distinctive for the relative ease with which uses do break through from one building to the next. However, as drawn in figure 29, the reinforcing factors of ownership, fire danger, and the commonly distinctive construction of party walls receive graphic representation in the continuity of the party-wall designation. Cool and physical as this drawing is (and even if one observed a rule which also broke the party walls), it still inevitably intrudes such information as land parceling, relative age of buildings, and available technologies. And of course there are physical environments and cultures in which one does not blithely break through walls. When to claim a wall is a wall? The answer to that question alone precludes a description of the physical environment that is wholly independent of information about the cultural factors that shape the influential environment.

Again, this last drawing is a useful device at a certain level of analysis. But, since I do not subscribe to architectural determinism, little can be done with either a figure/ground spatial diagram or an engineering diagram alone.

It is necessary to intersect these relatively physical descriptions with other ecological information. The most common next step is to divide urban space into movement channels and usable accessed spaces. Constantinos Doxiadis, who terms these elements "networks" and "shells," treats this division virtually as if it were a purely physical distinction.[11] The Center for Land Use and Built Form Studies at Cambridge University also makes "networks" and "adapted spaces" the first branching of the physical component in the tree of its urban model.[12] The semilattice of Christopher Alexander's "pattern language" is more subtle, but there too network and adapted space are fundamental distinctions.[13]

The network/adapted space distinction is not a purely physical demarcation — and Doxiadis's terms do not even describe the whole of space. A built/unbuilt, figure/ground diagram of a city (which is relatively physical and complete within its own rules) will usually permit one to distinguish the movement networks. However, in doing so one relies on the experience of the way in which cities are used; and one can easily be wrong. What looks like a movement channel may be a long, narrow courtyard or a series of independently used backyards. Some networks may penetrate buildings. The routes in sparsely built areas will

be indistinguishable. And even where the physical information is correctly read relative to its present use, it is a simple social act to withdraw a link in the network system from its use for movement. That is, a description of a network is already the record of social decisions.

Since this simple distinction of networks versus adapted spaces already intersects physical description with information on use and meaning, the question arises as to whether this is the most useful intersection directed toward understanding the relationships of form, activity, and significance.

I would argue it is not. A cursory examination of cities reveals that network channels serve not only directed movement but other activities such as strolling, meeting, vending, sitting, demonstrating, and fighting. Furthermore, many of the bordering accessed spaces are in such dynamic interaction with the channels that neither the channel nor these adapted spaces can be understood if they are analytically sliced apart.

The proposal here is that the analytic disaggregation of the city must employ distinctions that correspond as closely as possible with major distinctions in the ways in which we conceive and use the city. At the present state of this inquiry, I suggest three major operational subsystems which will be discussed in the last section of this chapter: spaces of public, dwelling, and occupational claims. Since these societal distinctions will usually not be mutually exclusive, descriptions of the complete set of subsystems will be partially redundant. Some spaces of the city, some activities, some symbolic structures will participate in more than one of the systems.

Global and Local Scale: Savannah as an Illustration

The last paragraphs anticipate the later sections of this chapter; but before pursuing those matters, it is necessary to insist on the frequently important impact of factors at one scale of the environment upon those of another. In the city there are not only the interactions of various factors such as cognition, culture, society, personality, and physical environment but also (and partially implied in these) the interactions of individuals and the various levels of urban aggregation and sociobiological integration. We need to know how the form, use, and meaning of local, small-scale elements of the environment inflect, and are inflected by, large structural characteristics of the environment. Savannah, Georgia, is a city that gives unusually tangible representation to many of the interactive forces that challenge our understanding and action. Savannah's systematic structure, partially through its very uniqueness, allows certain general issues to emerge clearly.

James Oglethorpe founded Savannah in 1733.[14] A regional plan established the site of the city (the six small rectangles below the center

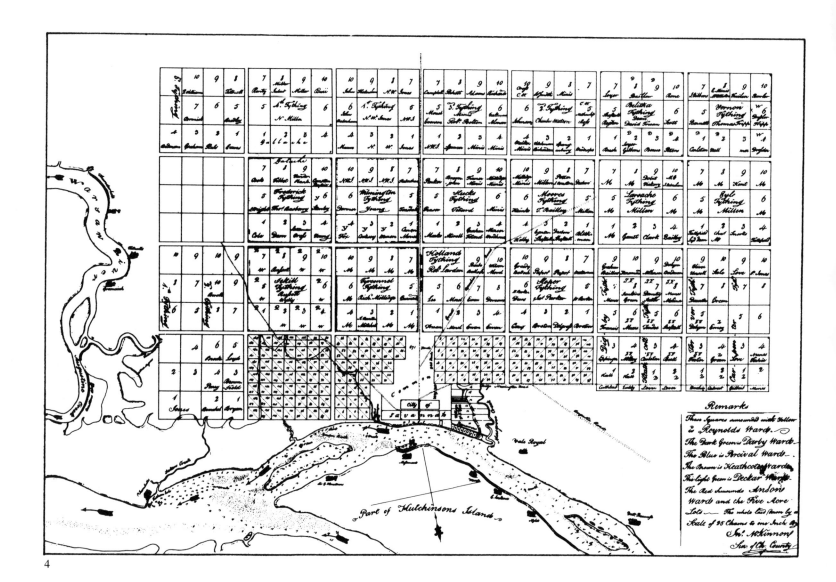

of the plan in figure 4) along the river with successive surrounding zones of common land, garden plots, and farm lands, which were assigned to the same settlers who received building lots in the town.

The basic unit of the town plan was a square "ward" with internal streets and a common open space at its center. The settlers immediately laid out four such wards; and, as figure 5 shows, the envisioned ward system was followed for more than one hundred years. Abstract geometry and pragmatic occupation, general system and local use interacted to establish the sociophysical structure of Savannah. Figure 6 shows the order of juxtaposed square wards each with its cross axes locating a central square. Figure 7 shifts the attention from the units to the assembly of units. It emphasizes that the edges of the units, the mere boundaries of centrally oriented wards, become the only uninterrupted routes through the agglomerated plan. The geometric order alone thus establishes one hierarchy which is internal to the ward and another which evolves in the additive growth of the city.

The analysis thus far involves a pure geometry with no preferred directions and without stipulated dimensions, site orientation, or use. But of course these decisions were made, and with them the abstract order becomes a structure with potentials for, and constraints on, its use and meaning. Figure 8 shows the parceling of a ward. Again, if we concentrate on a single ward there is a central focus, though not as strong as the abstract geometry might have suggested. Four "trustee lots" (parcels for public or communal uses) flank the central square to the east and west. The north and south sides of the central square become segments of continuous east-west streets which give access on one side to ordinary private development parcels — originally five sixty-by-ninety-foot parcels per block. Of the twenty private parcels along these interior streets, eight to twelve of them face on the variously sized central open places. The outer edges of the ward, no longer equal edges of a geometrical figure, are strongly differentiated. The north-south edges are still to be distinguished as the only straight routes in that direction while the east-west edges now share this characteristic with two streets skirting the central open spaces and with two alleys providing service at the rear of the private parcels. The north-south boundary streets give neither unique nor even principal access to any use parcels, while the east-west boundary streets have ten private development parcels each. These two sets of factors — movement and access patterns — serve to define the preferred role of the north-south boundaries for rapid movement through the system and the east-west boundaries for access to the localized activities of the city. When wards are added to one another, as one sees in figure 9, the east-west boundary streets cease to be mere collections of lots peripheral to the central squares and are rather recognized to be the only streets in the system that are continuously lined on both sides with private development parcels. This charac-

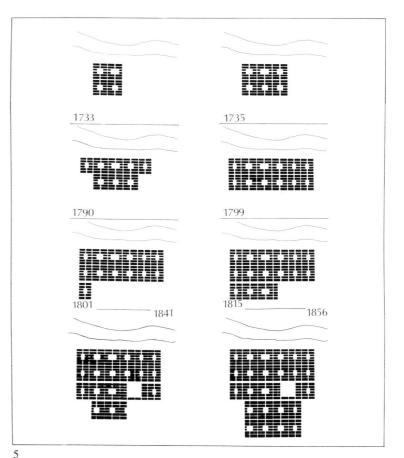

5

4. Savannah, Georgia. McKinnon Map, c. 1800. [Historic Savannah Foundation, *Historic Savannah*, p. 3]

5. Savannah. Sequence of growth of wards, 1733–1856. [*Historic Savannah*, p. 11]

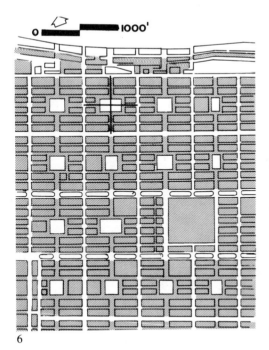

6

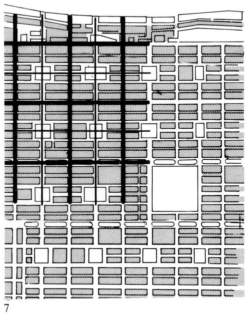

7

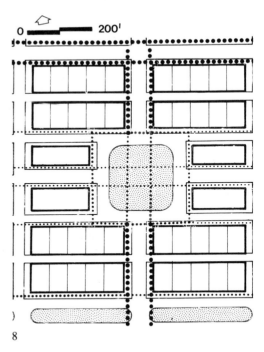

8

6. Savannah. Grid of wards. [Drawing, S. Anderson]

7. Savannah. Differentiation of principal elements. [Drawing, S. Anderson]

8. Savannah. Parceling and activity pattern of a ward. [Drawing, S. Anderson]

9. Savannah. Differentiation by schema of activity patterns. [Drawing, S. Anderson]

10. Savannah. Further differentiation by topography and actual activity patterns. [Drawing, S. Anderson]

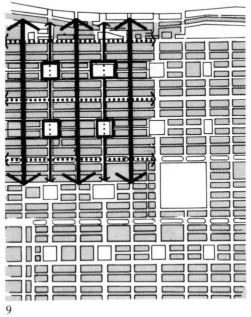

9

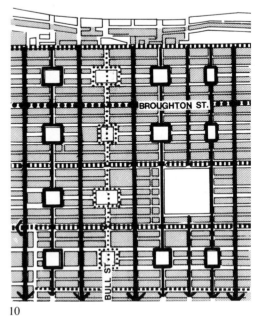

10

teristic has, in the multiward structure of the city, elevated these east-west boundary streets to the role of the most important streets in the city. Figure 9 helps to convey that the originally single-sided east-west street at the river took on distinctive local uses relating to the river and its critical role in the primary development of the city. The next east-west boundary street (Broughton Street, figure 11), lined on both sides with development parcels and centrally embedded in the early form of the city, quite naturally attracted the secondary commerce, the "main street" business of any community. The two principal commercial uses being satisfied, the third double-sided continuous street became the favored location for the finer dwellings. Since it had once been the line of a city wall, it was also possible to lay out this street in the form of a boulevard (Oglethorpe Street, figure 13).

This analysis reveals that movement along the east-west streets serves for continuous opportunities of access to similar uses; movement along north-south streets provides comparatively rapid access to the zones of alternative uses. In both figures 8 and 9, these observations are summarized, with solid lines referring to a primacy of wheeled traffic and broken lines referring to a primacy of pedestrian use. The main point is the intricate interaction of abstract geometry and use patterns, each modifying the other. The central east-west axis of the wards, which was a dominant element of the abstract ward geometry, has become the most redundant type of street in the system — it gives neither unique nor primary access to any parcel, and it is not important for movement since it is paralleled by six nearby continuous ways.

The decision to parcel the private development areas in a certain way (important features of which were the accessing of all such parcels on east-west streets; the establishment of no double-sided streets within a ward; the provision of as many private parcels at the edges as internal to the ward) established local use patterns that transformed the original arbitrary geometry into a structure filled with information. The small size of the wards and the importance of its periphery precluded the potential dominance of the central squares. Square, ward, and total structure each had their character and strength in attracting appropriate uses. It was not, as in most American grid cities composed of identical blocks, an arbitrary matter that one located a certain type of business or dwelling in one place or another. In Savannah, in growth, in decay, and in rebirth, energies knew where to flow first and from which to ebb last. Because the underlying structure is comparatively rich in information, the appearance and use of the various elements cannot be wholly arbitrary. Consequently, highly distinctive environments, serving their own uses and complementing one another, can lie around the corner from one another. This is seen most vividly in the juxtaposition of Savannah's main street (Broughton Street, figure 11) and the principal pedestrian route (Bull Street, figure 12) that accesses the main street.

11

11. Savannah. Broughton Street; the "Main Street," 1971. [Photo, S. Anderson]

12

12. Savannah. View in a square along Bull Street, 1971. [Photo, S. Anderson]

13. Savannah. Oglethorpe Street, 1971. [Photo, S. Anderson]

13

Broughton Street has accepted and served the same energies as most American main streets while the immediately surrounding elements could encourage and sustain desirable urban conditions that are unusual in the United States. Most comparable American cities today have weaker main streets and the surrounding area becomes a wasteland of machine space and derelict buildings undesired for either housing or business. In Savannah one turns from the brassy commercialism of Broughton Street immediately into the promenade of Bull Street cadenced with street walls and greens, houses, service buildings, and public monuments.

As Savannah continued to grow, special uses were too few to give such fine-grained differentiation to the trustee lots and the various street types. Similar dwellings were built throughout later wards, but the articulated ward plan contributed to environmental diversity and choice. In the longer term, the underlying structure provides for possible evolutionary change.

Even this meager sketch of what can be learned from Savannah insists on the complex reciprocities of urban structures and urban life. Certain impacts on local life structures can be deduced from overall ordering systems; but, equally, the local use patterns can differentiate the overall order into specific, and possibly evolving, use structures. Superimposed on this dialectic of order and use are the specifics of topography and historical development. Figures 4 and 10 give a cursory view of such matters: the importance of the waterfront for its critical commercial use and its constraint on growth in that direction; small streams to east and west constraining growth along the river were powerfully complemented by the differentiated movement system which also encouraged growth inland; the cemetery, originally peripheral to the city, becoming a permanent distortion of the order of the city; the single, small aberrant north-south street near the cemetery is a record of an irregularly positioned gate in the city wall which existed only briefly; the complex integrated pattern of uses of what was the entire early city has become a less differentiated sector which serves as the eccentric core of the modern city. No part of the city, at any point in time, can be understood without reference to its organizational, topographic, and historical context. Plans for the future, whether geared to preservation or development, also need such contextual understanding. Even massive urban actions are embedded in a collective environment where inidividual needs and actions should be seen in the context of social structures whose patterns of change — spatially and temporally — are usually rather slow.

A Model for the Study of Urban Structure and Transformations

With ecological organization and transformation of urban societies as our concern, the Savannah example suggests both the possibility of such an understanding and the complexity of such an inquiry.

The modeling of such complex environments is obviously difficult. The entire enterprise is subject to doubt, and I am aware of the limits of my own work. Still, there is every evidence that we currently act upon our cities and their life and other energy systems according to naively simple models; even modest advances would be contributive.

An inquiry into the form and use of streets, for example, will quickly convince one that most of the literature and most of the actual interventions are premised on a characterization of the street dominantly as a traffic channel. There is much expertise on street widening, widths of channels, effect of multiple lanes, on- and off-street parking, one-way traffic patterns, signaling, and the like. Even sophisticated researchers with broad concerns have tended to institutionalize such one-dimensional notions of the street. The model developed by the Cambridge University Center for Land Use and Built Form Studies[15] employs an organizational tree which first separates the social issues from the physical issues and then cleaves the physical elements into channels and spaces for use (adapted spaces, "stocks"). Such neat divisions can only reinforce the reductionism that characterizes so much modern action upon the city (fig. 14).

Enquiring into how streets are used and understood by people, I could make neither of these cleavages. Channels may include adapted spaces within their own volumes (figs. 15, 16). Every channel could be described, even for its movement characteristics, only if one accounted for what was accessed along its course — and with what frequency and in what way. Rather than a too simple model, even a more adequate description of streets as encountered might contribute to more considered actions. From the beginning, this study recognized the street as an organizational subsystem of the city. The street is neither merely a movement channel nor uniquely bounded (operationally, socially, conceptually, or physically) by a curb line or a property line or a building line. Each of these lines, or yet other limiting conditions, may mark the boundary of the intersubjective influential space of the street. And, of course, that boundary is redrawn at various times and for various users. For some users, or for all users in some locales, the street may extend into shops or churches or onto stoops. Consequently, I initiated my description with the recognition that the form and activity of the street space extend at least to a point where private control is asserted. In a residential row-house street such as that shown in figures 16, 17, and 18, the public/private boundary was conceived to run, typically, at the

14

14. Boston. Cambridge Street, 1973. One hundred years of technical progress. What Commonwealth Avenue is to Boston's nineteenth-century Back Bay development, Cambridge Street is to the twentieth-century development of Government Center and the West End. [Photo, S. Anderson]

15. Boston. Hanover Street, North End. Men and cars gather on a Sunday morning, 1973. [Photo, S. Anderson]

16. New York City. Willow Place, Brooklyn Heights. Street Fair, 1971. [Photo, S. Anderson]

17. Willow Place, Sunday street washing, 1971. [Photo, S. Anderson]

18. Willow Place, "Public/Private Boundary". [Drawing. IAUS. Victor Caliandro and Thomas Schumacher]

19. New York City. Montague Street, Brooklyn Heights. The "Main Street" of the district. "Public/Private Boundary." [Drawing. IAUS. Victor Caliandro and Thomas Schumacher]

15

16

17

18

19

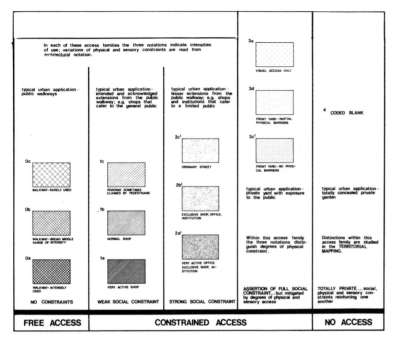

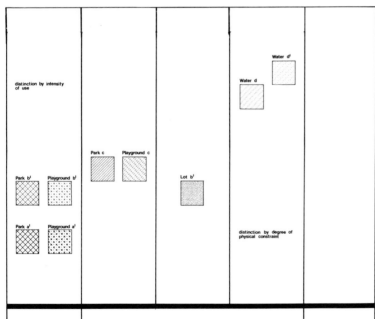

20. Key for detailed mapping of the "Space of Public Claim." [Drawing. MIT Urban Ecology Program]

face of the buildings. The stoops of the houses projected into public space. Occasionally a fence surrounded a smaller stoop which then existed in private space. The corner store and the midblock community center drew the public/private boundary inside the buildings.

A dominantly commercial street, such as that shown in figure 19, defines most of the adapted built space as an accessible part of the structure of the street, contrasting sharply with the privacy of the parallel residential streets. This contrast is the more startling when one adds the information that many of the commercial spaces are in converted residential buildings of the same type as those on the parallel streets.

This simple analytic device seems more adequate to the description of streets than either the distinction of network/adapted space or of built/open space; it also has distinct limitations. In instances (for example, most U.S. residential areas) where the public/private boundary exists in open space (whether established by social convention or by low or visually unobstructive markings), the public/private boundary notation implies that the open space beyond is not part of the street. A row of free-standing houses with private lawns maps, disappointingly, much as would a street of row houses. In complex environments with numerous accessible spaces, such as that in figure 19, the mapping included, on the public side of the line, without differentiation, spaces of widely varied significance.

Space of public claim: the concept; its mapping and analysis by graphs. These criticisms led to a generalized description system for the publicly accessible space of the city. The limit of this space was drawn to include all spaces that are in any way, directly or sequentially, accessible from the public realm, including spaces that are only visually accessible (fig. 23); it excludes spaces, even those of group use, where their existence or accessibility is not communicated to those spaces that are part of the publicly accessible space. This "space of public claim" is thus not uniquely bounded by buildings since it oftens extends into them; nor by ownership since private space can be publicly accessible, and publicly owned space can be withheld; nor by the limits of physical access since visually accessible spaces can be important elements in the form, activity, and significance of streets.

This most inclusive definition of the boundaries of the space of public claim was then analyzed for a limited set of included spatial types — the smallest set that would, nevertheless, facilitate critical distinctions about the structure of urban accessibility. Several interactions involving the field work of MIT students led to the sets of distinctions shown in figure 20. Each "family" of degree of accessibility is coordinated with a graphic pattern. White (unrendered surfaces) represents spaces that are totally inaccessible without privilege. At the other extreme, crosshatching denotes the spaces that are available to the public with the least degree of constraint within the society being analyzed (the relativity of this definition could be significantly clarified by describing to whom this accessibility is denied, for what reasons, and when). The two intermediate categories coded with diagonal lines represent those spaces that are subject to local control but which, in their normal condition, overtly seek continuity with the more public realm (coded with continuous lines and including, for example, active shops and some institutions) or communicate a more selective accessibility (coded with broken lines and including, for example, exclusive shops and many institutions). In each of these categories, the three densities of line denote intensity of use. The recognition of intensity was simplified to permit more rapid coding; but its very simplicity seems to preserve the most critical distinctions. The intermediate code denotes a broad range of medium intensity of activity that is bounded by two distinctive polar intensities: areas nearly devoid of activity and areas of such intense activity that users must regularly adjust to the behavior of others. The remaining category (fields of dots) records spaces that are visually but not physically available to those in the more public areas. In this instance, the graphic densities distinguish the areas most vulnerable to physical intrusion (highest density) from those that are clearly marked to those that are physically protected (for example, a visually open but secure fence or a marked change of level without mediation). The graphics thus run in a continuous gradation from unmarked publicly inaccessible areas to the darkest pattern which records spaces that have the highest degree of accessibility and are intensively used.

As employed in the analysis of several parts of Paris and of Cambridge, Massachusetts, this system records the accessibility and activity pattern of an urban sector — that is, what is available to at least some part of the public at some time of the day. In the terminology of chapter one, these maps show the intersubjective influential environment for public use. It is less general than the potential environment. It is more general that the influential environment of any individual or special group using the communal space — though these environments could be mapped in the same way for comparative purposes. Comparing this mapping of the area of Place d'Aligre in Paris (fig. 23) with a good conventional map (fig. 21), one sees how the public claim map differentiates among streets that are spatially similar, or even succeeds in emphasizing the activity and strong regional significance of rue d'Aligre (fig. 22), otherwise a minor street in terms of its size and lack of critical connectedness. The same recording system could be used to show the more constrained potential structure at certain times of the day or in cycles of the year. Cities, or districts of cities, might well be found to differentiate themselves on the basis of who has access to what percentage and which parts of the communal environments. The importance of such information for understanding, and often for policy, is obvious.

21. Paris. 12ᵉ arrondissement with the area of rue d'Aligre. [Map. City of Paris]

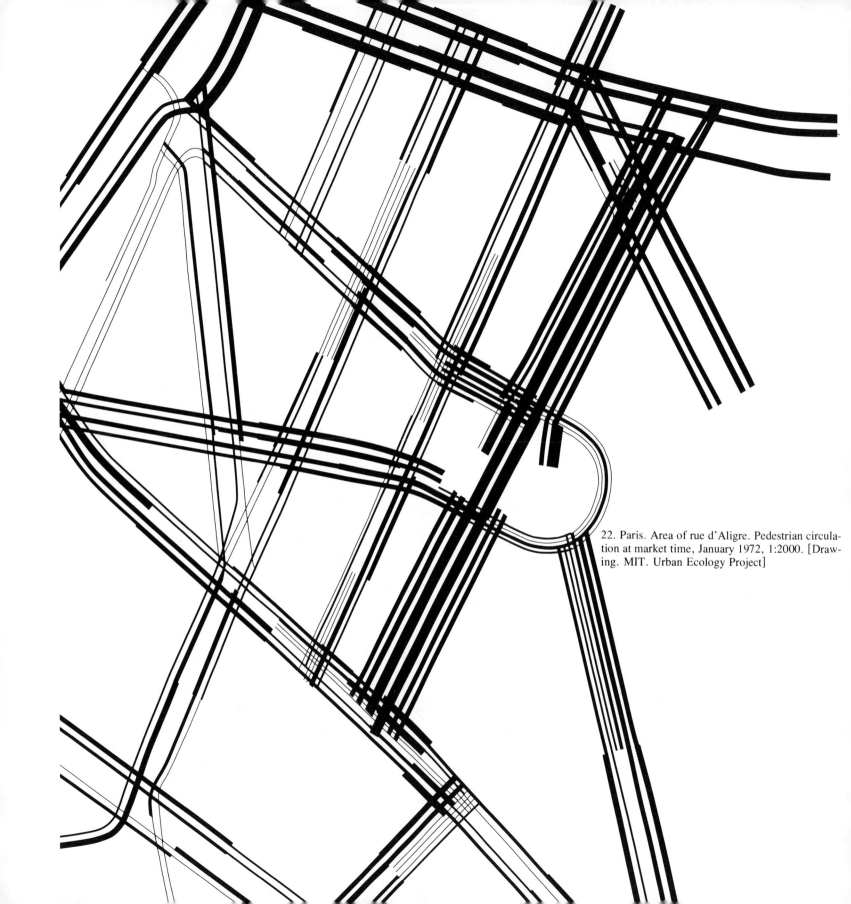

22. Paris. Area of rue d'Aligre. Pedestrian circulation at market time, January 1972, 1:2000. [Drawing. MIT. Urban Ecology Project]

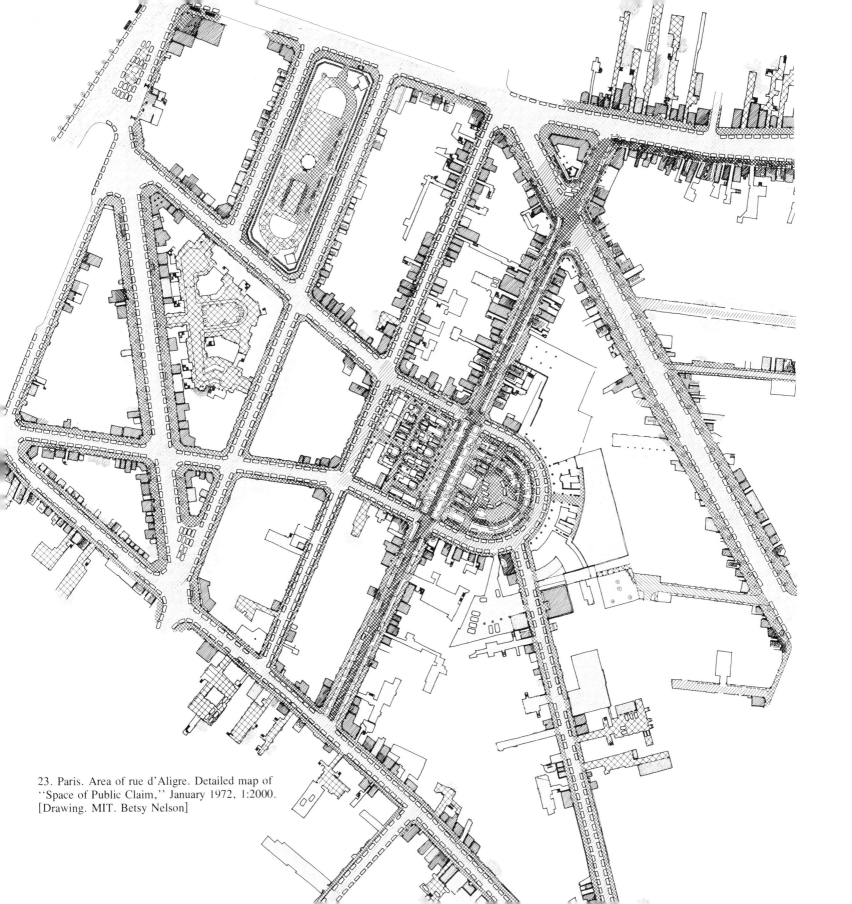

23. Paris. Area of rue d'Aligre. Detailed map of
"Space of Public Claim," January 1972, 1:2000.
[Drawing. MIT. Betsy Nelson]

Global comparisons of the North American and French examples (figs. 23, 30, and 34) reveal the marked differences in the elements and relations of each of the sociophysical structures. The Cambridge example records as a middle-gray field with white figures. This represents a continuous, dominantly accessible surface of the city upon which are placed free-standing buildings largely for private use. The open space is rarely intensively used, often is only visually accessible. In large parts of the Cambridge example, with a record (fig. 33) of the one type of urban space in which the public is given visual but not physical accessibility, a map reader could, from this limited information, reconstruct all of the streets, delineate most of the buildings, and make relatively accurate estimates of the age of the neighborhood, its population density, and other such factors. The same information about the Paris examples would, significantly, account for nothing in the dwelling environment except when ecologically atypical modern high-rise buildings have been introduced. The Paris examples rather show a space of public claim that is strongly tied to the street itself, is more limited in extent than we might have guessed from subjective experience, is often intensively used, often juxtaposes intensive public activity with total privacy, and rarely allows us to distinguish a building as an isolated urban element.

Even these cursory observations about parts of two cities as viewed in terms of the system of publicly accessible space suggest various hypotheses: Are there generalizable limits to the amount of urban space that can be made accessible if one wishes to reach certain levels of activity? If so, how is this relation modified by population density, mixture of uses, or culturally established mores? Relative to the same issues, is the length of the perimeter of publicly accessible space a better measure than area? (These questions bear on policy about limiting publicly accessible space by building street walls rather than free-standing buildings or on extending such space through multilevel public ways.) More questions: However problematic free-standing, high-rise buildings may be in general, are they a still more serious problem in an environment that has traditionally not employed urban free-standing buildings? Does the objectlike description of house and private property in the Cambridge example as compared to the communally structured Paris example contribute to significantly different cultural ecosystems for child rearing? Looking more carefully at the Cambridge example, does the reinforcement of "visually-accessible-only" spaces with hedges and fences reveal a stage of transformation from control by social conventions to control by physical design? Obviously, the drawings do not answer these questions. They do help to raise questions and to provide one body of information for the ensuing inquiry. As some of the questions are answered, further explanatory hypotheses may emerge and the drawings may yield more in the way of both description and desirable environmental policy.

Attempting to move from description to explanation and projection has directed our attention to two areas which can be presented here only briefly. One issue is how this information on the space of public claim can be understood more abstractly and in relation to other information. A related issue is putting this information back into the context of the entire ecosystem and into an urban model.

The simplest analysis of the public claim maps is by separations showing the various types of accessibility, singly or in selected combinations (fig. 33). While this may be suggestive, it is obviously a limited technique for a study of the relationships among such spatial elements or of the relationship between this organizational subsystem and other types of information such as vehicular and pedestrian circulation, open space, parceling, and ownership. For these purposes, it may be helpful to transform all such information into graphs that may be analyzed topologically; by retaining their metric, topographical reference may also be analyzed metrically or statistically.

Although we have already moved on to another formulation, the basic notion of comparable graphs starts from a "base graph" which is simply a linear street map — a graph generated by tracing center lines of streets and projecting them to their meeting points (as in figure 24a, Paris, area of Place d'Aligre). The vertices and edges of this graph are already the receptacles for some information — traffic circulation, bus routes, or concepts of street hierarchy. Maps that record information about areas (for example built space versus open space) can be transformed into linear graphs by tracing the centers of the largest circles that can be inscribed along or within the spaces. For example, the open space of the Place d'Aligre area of Paris permits the tracing of a graph (fig. 24b) that is very similar to the base graph but for the addition of points and small subgraphs generated by courtyards. Using the same technique, the map of the publicly accessible space of the area (fig. 23) yields a graph with many more points and with some completely new branches (fig. 24c). These vertices and edges can be used to store not only the designations of types of accessibility but also information that requires calculation (such as dimensions or areas of spaces) and related information that could not be shown on the map (for example, for commercial space, specific type of business, ownership structure of business and space, number of employees, dollar volume, and characteristics of customers). Such graphs may permit systematic and comparative descriptions of the transformational rules that relate one pattern of organization to another. In the present example, it is a simple transformation from the base graph to the open-space graph. From there to the graph of publicly accessible space is a transformation that changes the higher order vertices (those points where three or more edges meet) very little but adds many new second order (two-branch) vertices be-

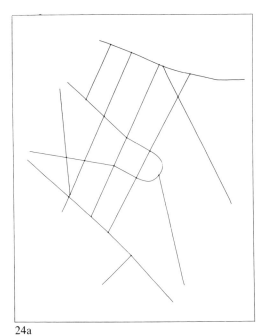

24a

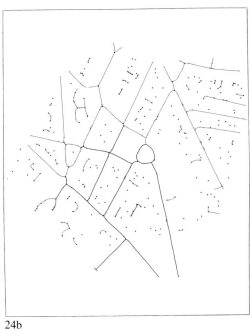

24b

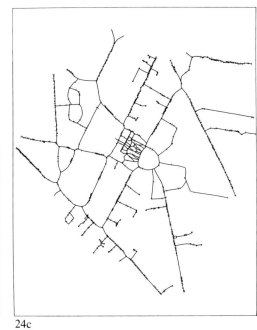

24c

24a. Paris. Area of rue d'Aligre. Base graph.
[Drawing. MIT. Aron Faegre]

24b. Paris. Area of rue d'Aligre. Graph of open
space. [Drawing. MIT. A. Faegre and Elizabeth
Hawley]

24c. Paris. Area of rue d'Aligre. Graph of public
claim. [Drawing. MIT. A. Faegre and E. Hawley]

tween the higher order vertices. New branches represent lines of continuous movement through built spaces. Imagining the same series for the Cambridge example (fig. 34), the base graph would not be significantly different from that of Paris. However, the transformation to the open-space graph would involve the generation of a highly complex web over the entire field, virtually obscuring the basis in the street layout. The graph of the space of public claim would be very similar to that of open space. A graph of space physically accessible to the public would, on the other hand, be closer to the base diagram than that in the Paris example. The graphs thus give promise of a rigorous means of describing the relations among various subsystems in one place or among similar subsystems over time or in various places.

The graphs also allow an exploration of what we take to be an important factor in understanding urban structure: the order of streets. In many cities, including much of Paris and New York, it is relatively easy to describe an order of streets which would be quite generally accepted in itself and in its implications for the activity and significance of the various streets. However, it is still a question as to what accounts for this order. In the Savannah example, we were concerned with the relative order of streets with reference to the original geometry, continuity, width, number of parcels accessed, intensity of circulation, reinforcement of certain characteristics over time, and other factors. The graphs would permit the assignment of a position to each street in all graphs according to a general order or the varying orders of streets according to the information stored in each graph.

Figure 25 shows how the graphs can be used to describe what might be called "communal space elements" out of which the total space is formed. The elemental spaces typically combine public and private ownership, built and unbuilt space, network and local-use functions. In rue d'Aligre one sees the repetitive, typical element and syntax, surviving from medieval times. In rue Crozatier one sees that a Haussmann street has the same syntax and that the elements vary only in size, not in organization. The most recent change, a supermarket forming a new route from rue d'Aligre to Place d'Aligre appears, on the contrary, as both a new type of element and a new syntax. Though the supermarket, unlike Haussmann's boulevards, is subtle in its change of Parisian open space, one may hypothesize that the radical change in the communal space element and syntax portends a more emphatic change in the sociophysical structure of Paris. The conditions imposed by postindustrial capitalism may well be ecologically more disruptive relative to the conditions of early industrial capitalism than were the latter relative to the pre-nineteenth-century organization of Paris. Finally, in the related graph of figure 24c one can also recognize the market building element which is atypical, a set piece, at this scale of environment, but could be seen as a dispersed, typical element in a larger view of the city.

It is my claim that the publicly accessible space of the city is an organizational subsystem of the city — and an important one which incorporates most of the channel or network spaces without being limited to the narrow definition of networks. The space of public claim is conceived with its boundary at what appears to be the most tangible boundary in the socially operative city. Nevertheless, one recognizes that any such boundary is an analytic device. If, for example, the space of public claim does include the stoop in front of a row house but draws a line at the wall of the building (fig. 18), it does also matter whether the domestic space beyond is for one or more families, whether kitchens or living rooms or bedrooms face the street, whether there are private gardens beyond the houses, and whether balconies or windows mitigate the closedness of a wall. That is, if we consider what is distinctly *not* the shared public space, we may observe, for example, that a private dwelling space may nevertheless send waves of its energy and psychic claims onto the sidewalk, the road surface, and into the neighborhood.

Some of these factors are handled in the architectural and use descriptions of the boundary of the publicly accessible space. Other of these factors and many more are internal to other organizational subsystems of the city which are partially consigned to the white areas of the maps of public claim. As with the private house, these elements may also project new and possibly conflicting information into the publicly accessible space with which they intersect. We are thus led to descriptions of subsystems of urban space that are analytically independent though often containing intersecting areas and redundant information. Two of these organizational subsystems are, then, the space of public claim already presented at length and the space of dwelling claim intimated in this paragraph. A third subsystem, termed the space of occupational claim, is the space of work places (including offices and closed institutions as well as industry and warehousing) to which the public does not have ready access. In this chapter, these subsystems will not be explored in detail but rather in their interrelations within an emerging urban model.

Urban Ecology Model. Alternating between generalized inquiries about urban ecology and field studies about different organizational subsystems of the city, we have also alternated between abstract models and empirical information. As noted before, we remain dissatisfied with earlier models that distinguish sharply between social and physical space, public and private ownership, built and unbuilt space, or network and adapted space.

In a recent state of our evolving model (fig. 26), we continue the attempt to reconcile the abstraction of the model, which incorporates the three organizational subsystems (P, Space of Public Claim; D, Space of Dwelling Claim; X, Space of Occupational Claim)[16] with the city as observed. The chart of the model mirrors a symbol for the actual city at

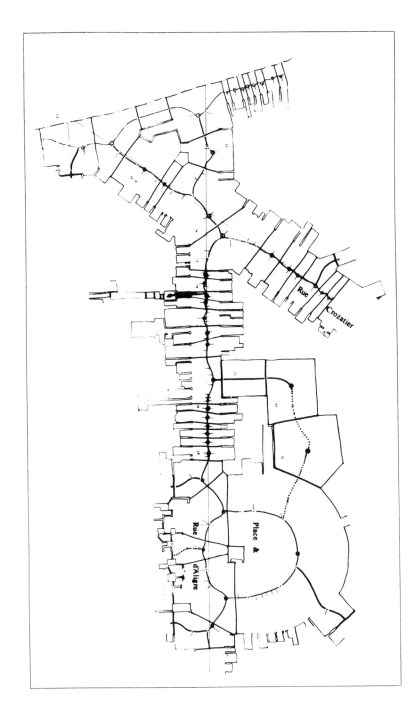

25. Paris. Area of rue d'Aligre. Spatial elements
defined by the graph of public claim. [Drawing.
MIT. S. Anderson]

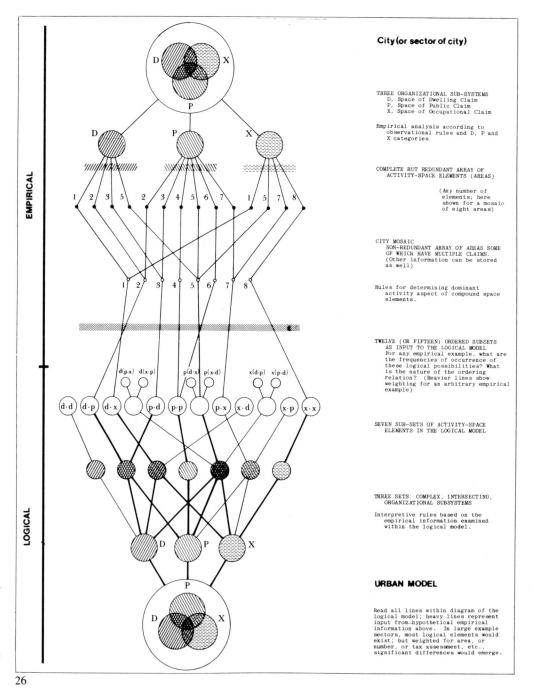

City (or sector of city)

THREE ORGANIZATIONAL SUB-SYSTEMS
    D, Space of Dwelling Claim
    P, Space of Public Claim
    X, Space of Occupational Claim

Empirical analysis according to
    observational rules and D, P and
    X categories

COMPLETE BUT REDUNDANT ARRAY OF
    ACTIVITY-SPACE ELEMENTS (AREAS)

                    (Any number of
                    elements; here
                    shown for a mosaic
                    of eight areas)

CITY MOSAIC
    NON-REDUNDANT ARRAY OF AREAS SOME
    OF WHICH HAVE MULTIPLE CLAIMS.
    (Other information can be stored
    as well)

Rules for determining dominant
    activity aspect of compound space
    elements.

TWELVE (OR FIFTEEN) ORDERED SUBSETS
    AS INPUT TO THE LOGICAL MODEL
    For any empirical example, what are
    the frequencies of occurrence of
    these logical possibilities? What
    is the nature of the ordering
    relation? (Heavier lines show
    weighting for an arbitrary empirical
    example)

SEVEN SUB-SETS OF ACTIVITY-SPACE
    ELEMENTS IN THE LOGICAL MODEL

THREE SETS: COMPLEX, INTERSECTING,
    ORGANIZATIONAL SUBSYSTEMS

Interpretive rules based on the
    empirical information examined
    within the logical model.

URBAN MODEL

Read all lines within diagram of the
logical model; heavy lines represent
input from—hypothetical empirical
information above. In large example
sectors, most logical elements would
exist; but weighted for area, or
number, or tax assessment, etc.,
significant differences would emerge.

26. Urban Ecology Model. Shadings serve as a key for figs. 31 and 32. [Drawing. MIT. Victor Karen]

27. Brooklyn Heights, southwest corner including Willow Place area. Detailed map of the Space of Dwelling Claim, 1972. [Drawing. MIT. Lawrence Speck]

26

the top against the sets of systems in the model at the bottom. Descending from the symbol, one encounters greater empirical specificity; ascending from the Venn diagram of the three subsystems is the more intricate structure of the model.

In the empirical section, the three, usually intersecting, organizational subsystems are acknowledged. Then, according to observational rules, mappings (such as those of figures 23, 30, 34) of the entire city are accomplished. This results in multiple complete mappings of the city which are redundant spatially (and usually in other terms too). A simple compiling operation permits, if desired, one, nonredundant mapping. At either of these stages, other empirical information can be stored with its spatial reference (demographic or economic data, social indicators, and the like).

The analytic and potentially explanatory and postulative stage of the work becomes the focus of the next stage where the empirical data and the model interact. The nonredundant spatial data would feed directly into the seven subsets of the model. However, for each city, one may learn some important organizational principles in determining how those spatial elements feed into the "twelve weighted inputs to the logical model"; in this case, one must determine whether and in what way a given space, mutually claimed by more than one subsystem, is in fact dominated by one subsystem or another.

This information flows according to the logic of the model. In the rudimentary example in our chart, the eight spatial elements do not, of course, match all the possible "weighted inputs." Consequently, the model is not fully occupied. This might be the case in the examination of small parts of the environment, such as dwelling prototypes. In looking at larger sectors of cities, all parts of the model would likely be utilized, but the nodes and branches could be weighted according to land area, tax base, and so on. In this way the diagram of the model would allow certain comparisons among sectors of cities or among different cities. However, the principal interest of the model is as an aid in searching the critical relational and transformational rules which pertain among urban elements at a given time and over time. Such inquiries might involve statistical or graph analyses as mentioned before. Here I shall present only a preliminary study of the interrelations revealed by the mappings of the various subsystems.

Interrelation of the spaces of the three subsystems of the urban ecology model. Each of the three subsystems can be mapped with appropriate internal differentiation. In what has been termed a "dwelling claim map" (figure 27, which has an internal structure roughly the inverse of the public claim maps), the most emphatic dark graphic is assigned to those parts of the urban fabric that are the physical and visual preserve of a single household. The intensity of the rendering is then diminished until one reaches the white areas where no domestic

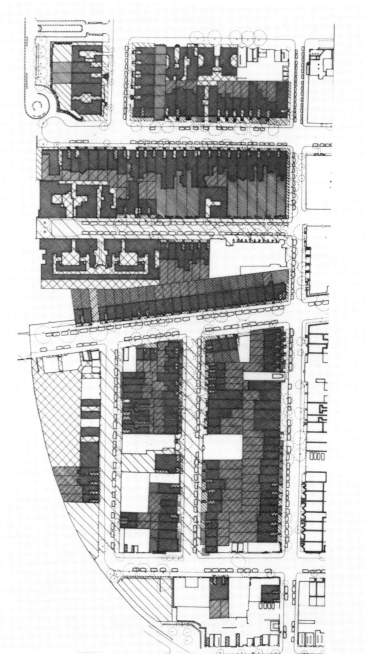

27

claim whatsoever is extended outward from the dwelling. A similar mapping for the space of occupational claim would grade off from the most privatized work areas.

As a first stage of studying the interrelations of these subsystem areas, we have made simplified maps that show the full areal extension of each of the three subsystems but without internal differentiation of each of the subsystems. Figures 31a–d[17] show the three subsystems superimposed and the three possible pairs of these subsystems for the Avenue Victor-Hugo area of Paris (figure 28); Figures 32a–d, the same combinations for a smaller section of Cambridge, Massachusetts. The model of figure 26 and its shadings provide a key for these two series of drawings.

Comparing the Paris and Cambridge areas, figures 31c and 32c (using, as all the other drawings in these series, the same graphic system and the same scale for both cities) show the full extension of public claim and of occupational claim. With this overlap of positively identified areas, the remaining white (uncoded) areas represent spaces that are *uniquely* claimed for dwelling purposes. A major distinction between the two examples is immediately obvious. In the Cambridge example, space unique to dwelling is strongly identified with the isolated building units, extending occasionally to visually private open space near these units. In the Paris example, built form is so continuous and mixed use so common that there is no experientially obvious physical identification of the space unique to dwelling. One would hypothesize that, within some limits, changing use is less disruptive to dwelling conditions in the Paris example than in the Cambridge example. The drawings assist one in characterizing, perhaps even quantifying, such differences.

If the meeting of spaces of public or occupational claim with spaces of unique dwelling claim is a socially and physically difficult juncture (or, in less pressured areas, a juncture with potential for private/communal association), it will be of interest to characterize this juncture — the edges of white areas in these drawings — qualitatively and quantitatively. The ratio of perimeter length to dwelling area is much higher for the Cambridge example.[18] Furthermore, the extensive perimeter in the Cambridge example is a far more penetrable boundary. In Paris, this boundary is usually either a rather closed wall against the street or, still more often, a wall buried behind a shop or against another building; access is, in fact, via a few designated places which are protected both physically and socially. In Cambridge, the boundary is typically of light walls with numerous windows and doors opening directly onto the dwelling spaces themselves. This relative openness is usually both extended and protected by a range of spaces with dual public and private claims: stoops or lawns, porches and verandas. The significance and the desirability of these areas with ambiguous claims

change in time and place. The front yards and porches, which were the active settings of a shared "lawn culture" in nineteenth-century America, may be the vacant moats or even threateningly vulnerable zones of the technologically internalized or dispersed families of mid-twentieth-century America.

Referring again to this same pair of drawings (figs. 31c and 32c), the Cambridge example shows the space of public claim extended throughout almost the whole of the open space. The spaces of public and occupational claim also extend into some buildings throughout the site (buildings ordinarily of identifiable form either from their origin or through physical readaptation to the street). In the Paris example, these claims are much more strongly related to the street (and very little coordinated with open space other than that of the street). Then too, while every street is marked out by these claims, they are also strongly differentiated by them. The broadest radiating street, Avenue Foch, has only public claim which is largely confined to the street space itself (with dwelling space beyond the walls and distinctive entry points). The next largest radiating street, Avenue Kléber, has extensive occupational claim (with virtual exclusion of dwelling claim) and thus periodic controlled meeting points where public and occupational claims intersect. The third radiating street, Avenue Victor-Hugo, has a complex pattern of all three claims. A recent significant change in this pattern is the insertion of a large uniquely occupational claim on the north side of Avenue Victor-Hugo. The fourth, minor radiating street, rue Lauriston, once had a pattern of all three claims working at a smaller, more dwelling-oriented scale. One sees how the power of the occupational claims of Avenue Kléber have virtually eliminated dwelling space from one side of rue Lauriston. Historical mapping would show the coincident successive elimination of the small units of simultaneous public/occupational claim (shops) along rue Lauriston.

A reasonable hypothesis is that, without purposive action by residents and the city, dwelling will be virtually eliminated from Avenue Kléber to just north of Avenue Victor-Hugo. The residences of Avenue Foch will be too few to support most of the services and shops that meet everyday needs; these residences will be increasingly reliant on the garages and shopping center already buried under Avenue Foch. The urban ecology of the district will be radically changed, serving an elite less well than the current (already stratified) population of the area. Returning to the analysis of the drawing itself, the distinctive and strong characterization of each of the radiating streets establishes their dominance over the circumferential streets. By comparison, these are ecologically ill-defined streets and would be still weaker environments were it not that the *ilots* are ordinarily so large as to require some access and local use along these streets. Viewed globally, the weakness of these streets may well prove to be part of a pattern that encourages intensity elsewhere and a desirable range of local environments. Finally, one also finds streets that are so unimportant within the pedestrian and vehicular circulation systems that they have become atypically uniform residential streets, resisting both public and occupational claims (although French urban decorum also discourages any strong claim of the street space by the abutting dwellers).

This last point is still better illustrated by the maps that show simultaneously the full extension of the dwelling and occupational claims (figs. 31a and 32a). These are the claims that emanate from private (or at least privatized) energy sources; consequently, it is not too surprising that, in the Paris example, these codings both exhaust and are coterminous with the property lines of the *ilot*. Uncoded areas (which in this case mean uniquely public areas) are the complementary street channels. However, one of the ways in which this elite Parisian area is atypical is in its paucity of commercial occupation of the street space (markets, extended shops, sidewalk cafés, and restaurants). The same mapping for rue d'Aligre (fig. 23) would have shown most of that street and parts of others under occupational claim. However, apart from truly private streets (one example of which appears near the corner of Avenue Victor-Hugo and rue Paul-Valery), it is rare for a dwelling claim to be extended into the Parisian street space. The opposite is true in the United States: occupational claim of the street is rare while the extension of dwelling claim is common.

The Cambridge example (fig. 32a) suggests some of the factors that encourage this extension of dwelling claim. The two most heavily trafficked streets are those along which one finds no claim extended outward from the property lines. The tendency toward domestic claim is inversely related to traffic flow — possibly extending to the sidewalk and parking areas of lesser streets and throughout the space of minor streets. Other factors are suggested: extension of claim is stronger from the entrance front of the house than from the side of a house on a corner site; isolated houses are less apt to extend claims than are rows of houses with the same entrance orientation; apartment houses with collective entrances are less apt to claim street space than are the rows of one- and two-family houses. Indeed, the residents of apartment houses in this example (the linked Y-shaped buildings near the center of figures 32a and 34) show a stronger sense of their own presence, a greater tendency to extend a dwelling claim than is typical for such dwellings. In such a mapping it would be more common to find only the building blocks (and perhaps not even their entrances) coded for dwelling claim while the entire site, or at least the entire periphery of the site, lost such claim. That this apartment group is atypical in this respect would deserve sociological study, but certain physical factors are plausibly contributive: the small extent of the project; that it is walk-up housing not radically disproportionate to its context; that the surrounding houses are

28. Paris. 16ᵉ arrondissement with the area of Avenue Victor-Hugo. [Map. City of Paris]

29. Paris. Area of Avenue Victor-Hugo. Engineering structure, January 1975, 1:2000. [Drawing. MIT. Wes Henderson]

30. Paris. Area of Avenue Victor-Hugo. Detailed map of ''Space of Public Claim,'' January 1973, 1:2000. [Drawing. MIT. Wes Henderson]

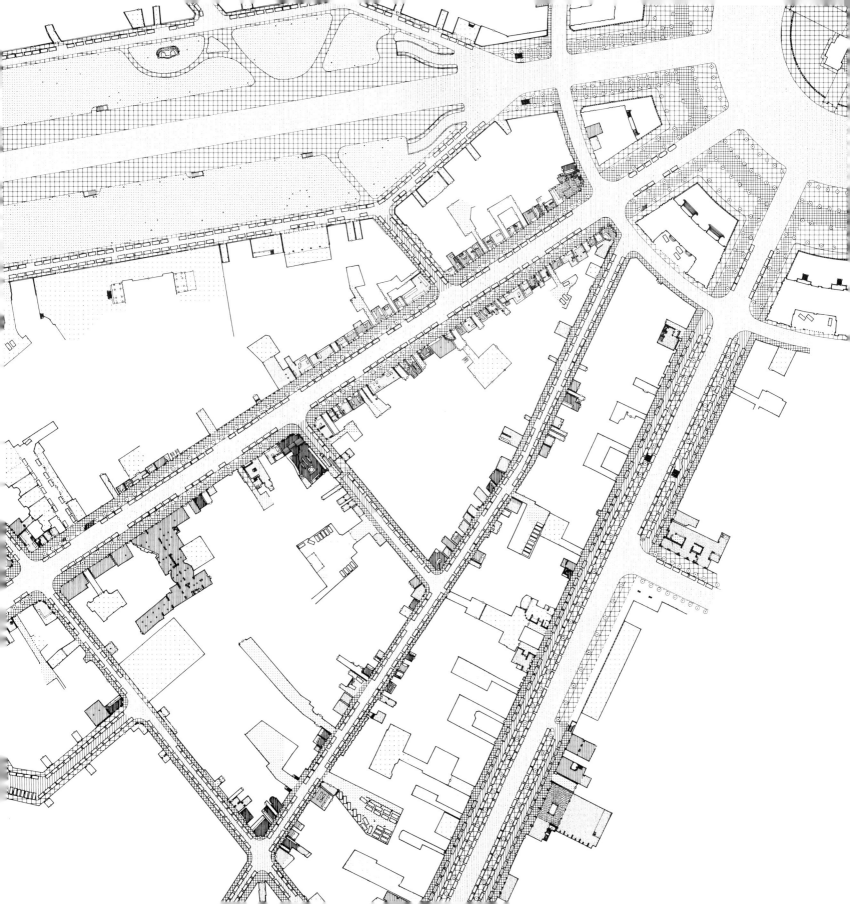

31a. Paris. Area of Avenue Victor-Hugo. Spaces of Dwelling and Occupational Claims, all drawings in this series January 1973, 1:2000. See figure 26 for key. [Drawing. MIT. Wes Henderson]

31b. Paris. Area of Avenue Victor-Hugo. Spaces of Dwelling and Public Claims. [Drawing. MIT. Wes Henderson]

D

X

D

P

31c. Paris. Area of Avenue Victor-Hugo. Spaces of
Public and Occupational Claims. [Drawing. MIT.
Wes Henderson]

31d. Paris. Area of Avenue Victor-Hugo. Spaces of
all three claims. [Drawing. MIT. Wes Henderson]

P

X

D

P

X

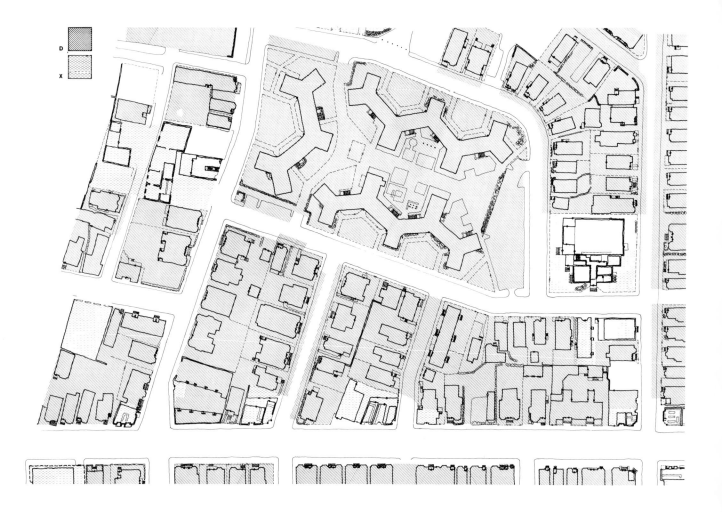

32a. Cambridge, Massachusetts. Part of Riverside
area. Spaces of Dwelling and Occupational Claims,
all drawings in this series 1972, 1:2000. See figure
26 for key. [Drawing. MIT. Wes Henderson]

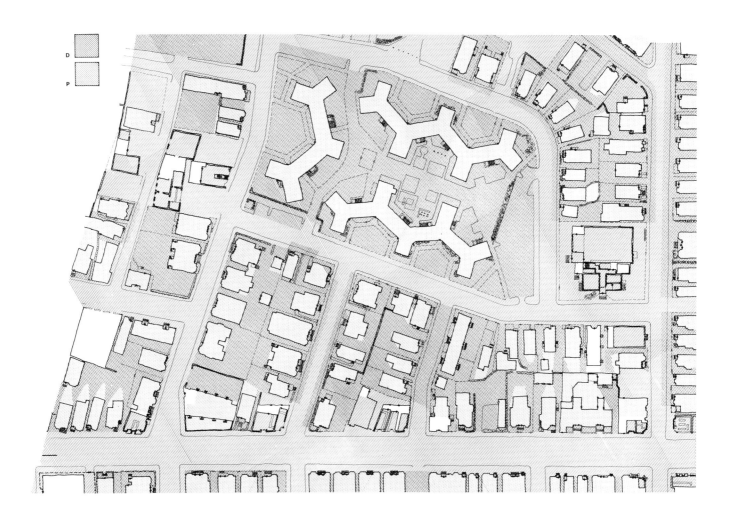

32b. Cambridge, Massachusetts. Part of Riverside area. Spaces of Dwelling and Public Claims. [Drawing. MIT. Wes Henderson]

32c. Cambridge, Massachusetts. Part of Riverside
area. Spaces of Public and Occupational Claims.
[Drawing. MIT. Wes Henderson]

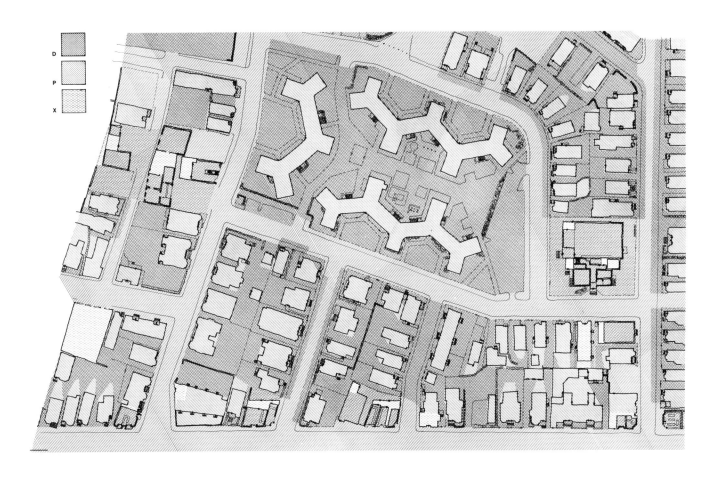

32d. Cambridge, Massachusetts. Part of Riverside
area. Spaces of all three claims. [Drawing. MIT.
Wes Henderson]

33

33. Cambridge, Massachusetts. Part of Riverside area. Separation showing areas from public claim map with visual access only. [Drawing. MIT. Wes Henderson]

34. Cambridge, Massachusetts. Part of Riverside area. Detailed map of Space of Public Claim, 1972, 1:2000. [Drawing. MIT. Marshall Audin]

also free-standing buildings with open space under dual public and dwelling claim; that at least the innermost open spaces of the project are furnished for play and are strongly defined as internal to the apartment group.

Figures 31b and 32b reveal characteristic differences between the French and American examples. In the latter (and this would be still more marked in many other American environments), there is an extensive intersection of the spaces of public and of dwelling claim. Most of the open space of the city — which is itself extensive — is under this ambiguous dual claim. In the Paris example these two claims are largely complementary and their rare intersections, upon investigation, are not ambiguous. In figure 31b, one can read off two typical and two atypical configurations of this intersection of public and dwelling claims: the typical entrance lobbies of apartment buildings along Avenue Foch and, in diminishing size with diminishing prestige, on some other streets in the area; the typical entrance courtyard which, under dual claim, occurs most frequently along Avenue Victor-Hugo; the atypical (for this area) private street mentioned before; and the atypical free-standing building with visible garden along Avenue Foch. In the two typical cases, the area of intersection is within the body of the building and has social as well as physical control; in the other two cases, although involving open space, there are such well-defined fences and gates as to once again eliminate ambiguity and permit social controls.

Reviewing this matter, it seems that the more viable American dwellings secure themselves by extending a sufficiently large, if somewhat ambiguous, area of territorial claim. The Parisian tendency is to withdraw dwelling claims from the public space and to draw the boundary between the two claims at a place where the line can be short and distinct. This strategy, in turn, usually implies a communal group and communal spaces on the private side of that boundary. What are the alternative configurations of each of these types? What densities do they sustain? How do they change domestic and public life for various age groups? What happens when the type that is characteristic of one culture is transferred to another?

The maps, which superimpose all three claims (figs. 31d, 32d), permit, of course, the recognition of those spaces that are simultaneously subject to all three claims. There are none such in the Cambridge example. The few such areas in the Paris example are all courtyards of buildings that house at least dwellings and places of work, and possibly shops as well. Even then the intersection is confined to the courtyard as access zone and does not extend to the working, dwelling, or commercial spaces per se. As in this case, characteristics defined by their absence in modern, Western, urban settings might be revealed or at least illuminated by comparison with similar mappings of smaller settlements or of cities in other cultures. In this instance, even the working-class

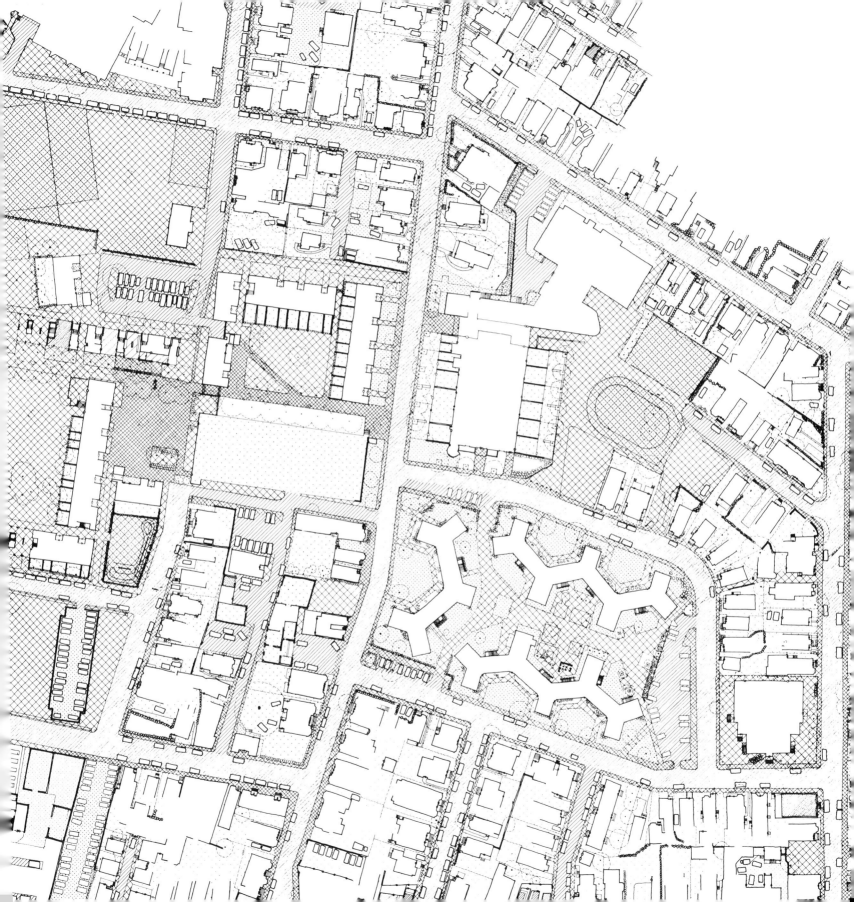

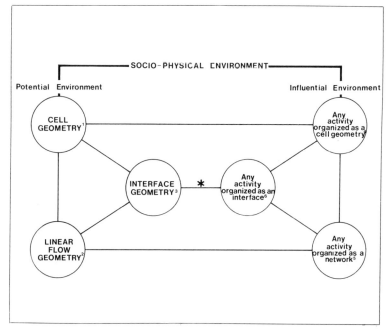

35. Urban Ecology model. Relation of analytic components. Key:

1. block, or block and parcelling geometry.
2. potential channel geometry.
3. potential access geometry.
4. in the Paris examples: D, Space of Dwelling Claim; X, Space of Occupational Claim.
5. in most examples: vehicular circulation; pedestrian circulation.
6. in the Paris examples: P, Space of Public Claim; C, Space of Communal Claim.
* What are the simples or units of urban space? Possibly the spatial units defined by interface graphs of the 'Space of Public Claim' (see Fig. 25).
[Drawing. MIT. Hong-Bin Kang and Lee Nason]

sectors of Paris would show a marked increase in such triple claims, and present-day central Naples would be dramatically different.

The discussion of this set of maps suggests that these observational and mapping systems allow us to objectify and, in some ways, to quantify characteristics of the physical environment and certain aspects of its use. The more we "read" them, especially in comparisons among settlements, the greater the chance that we discover other characteristics of which we were not aware. The reader is assisted in discovering and formulating hypotheses about sociophysical structure of cities, about cultural relations and historical evolution, and about subcultural or short-term cyclic variations. The same maps will remain a source, and a place for storage, of information — perhaps even a place for initial testing of such hypotheses. But clearly, most questions will demand other information and tools than that which is presented here or even in the urban ecology model of which these maps are simplified graphic illustrations.

In addition to this reminder of the proposed model and its potential for both storing other information and studying the relations of this information within an ecological framework, I would like to suggest a slight elaboration of the model.

The Urban Ecology Model elaborated to focus on one selected variable and its locational characteristics. As pointed out before, the mappings have thus far been conceived as representing the intersubjective influential environment for the entire community. Many of the questions we might wish to ask concern the relation, for example, of this generalized influential environment to the more constrained environment of one class of users. What nonprivate spaces dominantly serve children (further defined by age groups, class, time of day or year, as desired)? An appropriate fourth overlay to this Paris area (fig. 31d) might be almost blank while the Cambridge area would show extensive internal and external, public and private space accorded to children's use. What spaces are dominated by the users of motor vehicles? In the United States, private claims on public space are closely tied to private automobiles while Europeans more strongly emphasize commercial claims which in turn serve pedestrians. What spaces beyond the area of public claim are nevertheless under collective or communal social organization? In Paris, most open space associated with dwellings is of this type; in the Cambridge example, perhaps no space is uniquely defined in this way.

Even the proposed mapping system would extend to cover one, perhaps two such superimposed factors. The model shown in figure 26 can also be elaborated to accept additional factors.

The third dimension and the time dimension. It will be apparent that most of the urban representations discussed here remained two dimensional, in themselves incorporating neither the vertical dimension of space nor a temporal dimension. This observation seems to demand two responses. On the one hand, the long-term reliance on, and considerable success of, two-dimensional mappings of the human environment suggests that this limitation should not be unduly emphasized. Traditionally, the physical artifact and the conceptual grasp of what has here been termed the space of public claim seems particularly to rely on a two-dimensional configuration, though the surface may warp with the contours of the site or changes in building section. If dwellings and the spaces of occupational claim commonly have vertical dimensions of equal or greater magnitude than their planar dimensions, they also tend to be isolable spatial phenomena that often permit, from the viewpoint of urban structure, the projection of their descriptors onto a reference point or area in the two-dimensional representation.

On the other hand, a genuine facility in describing and analyzing the multidimensionality of the city is surely to be desired and, in increasing numbers of urban environments, virtually required by the layering of circulation and activity systems. Multidimensional representation is also particularly helpful as one moves to the postulation of new environments and their architectural realization. Multiple two-dimensional representations — in plan, section, and elevation — are a contribution. However, at the scale of the city and in its patterns of organization, elevations and sections usually seem particularly arbitrary and piecemeal. The demonstration project shows some attempts to diagram or design urban settings with the help of graphic techniques that represent three dimensions, in this case axonometric representations. Difficulties here are the rapid escalation of complexity of the drawing; the view of only one side of a street space; and, as buildings become only a few stories high, the overlapping and concealment of most of the ground surface and lower floors.

Attempts at rendering the temporal dimension of the urban environment[19] have thus far been notably one dimensional and thus either destructively reductionist in their descriptions or, at best, suited to particularly limited conditions. A type of choreographic notation allows one to record fragmentary information of a single person's movement trace through an environment. This takes on some interest if it is raised to an art form or supports a ceremonial use of the environment. It can also elucidate the required movement traces and experiences of many individuals in highly constrained movement instruments such as moving sidewalks or limited access roads. Although the utility of such instruments should not be denied, they are definitely not the subject of a study of streets. Indeed, if the multiple uses and significances of streets are valued, this is cause to advocate the most limited possible introduction of experientially constraining instruments.

As with the third spatial dimension, so we can describe changing temporal conditions in multiple planar representations. But in both these instances, the notion of graphs seems the most promising technique. Although it rapidly loses its iconic quality, a graph can immediately represent the three spatial dimensions and can store temporal information. At the very least, graphs will facilitate the systematic study of transformations of urban environments in time and space. While not precluded in other representations, graphs would also facilitate the storage of demongraphic, economic, cultural, or other information which could then be used in the search for congruences among these variables and spatial structures.

Organizational Summary

The foregoing attempt to deal broadly with a complex issue, combined with a respect for the criticism of people from several disciplines, led to all too many categories of environment and methods of study. At this point, with the help of figure 35, it may be possible to review, simplify, and order these notions.

The left hand of the diagram refers to the physical environment as the potential environment for human activity and significance. Here we would like to know whether various physical structures can be differentiated for their range of possible uses and meanings and for their varying degrees of resistance to change. Any values to be associated with these alternative degrees of adaptability is an issue that already requires a complex cultural analysis. Prior to this, the difficulty is in discussing the physical environment in terms of a potential that, we must presume, is not fully and overtly displayed to us. We may well assume that we shall never fully succeed in this enterprise, but some advance is worth seeking if we are to act and build in ways that preserve or encourage an openness to alternative futures. The present essay only hints at the work to be done in this area — primarily in the section on Savannah and in the discussion related to figures 1 through 3 and 29. As figure 35 shows, we anticipate that various topological analyses plus awareness of some limits set by dimensional thresholds are the most promising and systematic approaches to the characterization of the potential environment as it is actually used and interpreted. The right side of figure 35 refers to the influential environment — the potential environment as it is actually used and interpreted. This diagram preserves a generality by simply suggesting that representations of the influential environment may be analyzed by the same techniques as the potential environment. In this way, current and alternative relations between the two environments may be more easily studied. Most of this essay has been devoted to one general model and a graphic analysis of the collective, intersubjective influential environment of parts of two Western cities. The notes within the diagram suggest the techniques of analysis most appropriate to the representations of the influential environment that have emerged from the model. The influential environment of individuals or selected groups would involve the comparatively simple study of similar representations within the analytic space of the right side of this diagram.

The latent environment would be the difference between the representation of the potential and influential environments — a task made admittedly very difficult both by the problems of adequately accounting for potential and of comparing the necessarily somewhat different representations of potential and influential environments.

This summary has been stated in terms of the composite urban ecology model (fig. 26); it could be repeated for each of the organizational subsystems of that model: the spaces of public, dwelling, and occupational claim. Figures 31a–d and 32a–d and the related text sketch the kinds of analysis and discussion that emerge.

It must be abundantly clear that the work reported here is in an early phase of development. There are obvious reasons to see the effort as alternatively too simple relative to the city or too complex relative to its use. However, in its evolution it becomes less vulnerable to these criticisms; and, returning to the first section of this paper, the model can be supported as more adequate to the activity and significance of urban space than the simple models that stand behind current interventions in the city. The intent here is to understand environments sufficiently abstractly that we may both learn from existing environments and be encouraged to conceive new environments that incorporate valued characteristics.

This work began at the Institute for Architecture and Urban Studies in New York City under sponsorship of the Department of Housing and Urban Development. However, most of the work reported here has been done at the Massachusetts Institute of Technology, Cambridge, Massachusetts. I am especially grateful to numerous students, including Wes Henderson and others whose names appear in the drawing credits, to my colleagues, Lawrence Speck, Hong-Bin Kang, Alice Paley, and Susan Livada, and to the Ernest A. Grunsfeld Memorial Fund of Chicago for their continuing support.

1. Raymond Williams, *The Country and the City* (New York: Oxford University Press, 1973), p. 5.

2. Murray Bookchin, *The Limits of the City* (New York: Harper & Row, 1974), p. 94.

3. The emphasis here is on urban ecology as the study of city dwellers in their environments rather than the study of cities as artifacts within the natural landscape.

4. See note 6 of chapter one.

5. See note 14 of chapter one and the related text.

6. William Michelson, *Man and His Urban Environment: A Sociological Approach* (Reading, Mass.: Addison-Wesley, 1970).

7. Camillo Sitte, *City Planning according to Artistic Principles* (New York: Random House, 1965; first publ., Vienna, 1899).

8. *Nuova Pianta di Roma data in luce da Giambattista Nolli*, 1748.

9. See the essay by William Ellis in this volume.

10. SAR 73 (Eindhoven: SAR, 1973).

11. C. A. Doxiadis, *Anthropopolis. City for Human Development* (Athens: Athens Center for Ekistics, 1974.

12. Lionel March et al., "Models of Environment," *Architectural Design,* 41 (May, 1971), p. 278.

13. Christopher Alexander et al., *A Pattern Language which Generates Multi-Service Centers* (Berkeley: CES, 1968).

14. *Historic Savannah* (Savannah: Historic Savannah Foundation, Inc., 1968).

15. See note 12.

16. This notion is as yet little explored but would permit incorporation of information about those institutions and work places of a city to which one gains access only by membership, employment, or some other strongly controlling device.

17. All maps in this chapter were prepared from good base maps and extensive field surveys with the exception of part of the series numbered 31a–d. Within this series the extent of the spaces of dwelling and occupational claim were reconstructed from good base maps, published data, field notes, photographs, and recollections of field surveyors. It is believed the information is more than accurate enough for the general purpose it serves in this essay, but should not be considered a detailed document.

18. Planimeter readings from the maps in figures 31a–d and 32a–d permit the following calculations:
Columns d and c show that far less of the Paris district has some form of dwelling claim and yet it has half again more area that is uniquely claimed for dwelling (if this were continued into a three-dimensional account, the contrast would be still more sharp). This reversal of values ac-

Column	a	b	c	d	e	f	g	h
	Total Area	Total Dwelling Claim	Total Space Reserved Uniquely for Dwelling	Land Under Dwelling Claim	Land Uniquely Under Dwelling Claim	Land Under Dwelling Claim Plus Other Claim	Perimeter of c	Relative Perimeter Length
Unit	m^2	m^2	m^2	b/a %	c/a %	d-e %	m	%*
Paris (map series 29a–d) Area of Avenue Victor-Hugo and rue Lauriston	46,680	18,360	15,980	39	34	5	—	—
Same area plus side of Avenue Foch	65,780	27,560	23,060	42	35	7	4,900	75
Cambridge — Riverside (map series 30a–d) Area of Housing Project	8,820	7,160	1,680	81	19	62	700	147
Remainder of Area (Cambridge fabric)	26,400	18,640	5,680	71	22	49	3,340	208
Total of two areas	35,220	25,800	7,360	73	21	52	4,040	194

*These percentages are relative to an arbitrary standard taken as 100; namely, the perimeter to area ratio of an isolated, square building of 200 square meters; this is close to the size of the larger, approximately square units in the Cambridge maps. It would also be the approximate area of a generous American suburban house or of Frank Lloyd Wright's four-unit "Suntop" houses (Ardmore, Pa.). In column h, the relative difference in examples would remain with the adoption of other standards though the absolute difference in numbers could be made more or less striking.

counts for the especially sharp distinction between the two examples with relation to land simultaneously under dwelling and some other claim (column f).

Columns g and h engage the issue of how extensive is the boundary between areas of unique dwelling claim and other claims. If one assumes this boundary presents an important measure both for the boundary's potential role in community association and in fear and aggression, one sees that the two examples show a marked, and presumably significant, differentiation in values for perimeter relative to area (column h). This measure of the extent to which the condition is established, combined with physical descriptions of the way in which it is handled, would provide examples of how the potential environment establishes both opportunities and limits for the social structure of cities.

While I hypothesize that these differences are characteristic for many European and American environments — and significant for human activities — the intent here is not to use these two examples as a test or demonstration. They are offered rather as instances of the type of inquiry and comparative analyses that may be conducted.

19. Various systems were compiled, employed, and criticized in a master's essay within our program; see Premjit Talwar, "Notation Systems in Architecture," M. Arch. thesis, MIT, 1972.

1. Alison and Peter Smithson. Their 1952 Golden Lane Housing Prototype superimposed on bombed-out Coventry. The inherent problems of interface and urban continuity. [*Uppercase 3*, edited by Theo Crosby, Whitefriars Press Ltd., London, 1956]

The Generic Street as a Continuous Built Form

Kenneth Frampton

Most of the Paris arcades came into being during the decade and a half which followed 1822. The first condition for their emergence was a boom in the textile trade. . . . The manner in which they were fitted out displayed art in the service of the salesman. Contemporaries never tired of admiring them. For long after they remained a point of attraction for foreigners. An "Illustrated Paris Guide" said: "These arcades, a new contrivance of industrial luxury, are glass-covered, marble-floored passages through entire blocks of houses, whose proprietors have joined forces in the venture. On both sides of these passages, which obtain their light from above, there are arrayed the most elegant shops, so that such an arcade is a city, indeed a world, in miniature." These arcades were the setting for the first gaslighting. Walter Benjamin, Paris, Capital of the 19th Century, *1935*[1]

A high level post-civilized stable technology would almost have to be based on the oceans for sources, for its basic raw materials, as the mines and the fossil fuels will very soon be gone. There will, therefore, be some manufacturing concentrations around the shores of the world. We may even see a revival of the form of the classical city for pure pleasure where people can enjoy the luxury of walking and of face-to-face communication. Inequality of income in such a society is likely to be reflected in the fact that the poor will drive vehicles and the rich will walk. We are already, I think, beginning to see this movement in the movement of the rich into the city centers and the development of the mall. These cities, however, will be stage sets — they will arise out of the very freedom and luxury of the society rather than out of its necessities. Kenneth E. Boulding, The Death of the City: A Frightening Look at Post-Civilization, *1966.*[2]

Introduction: The Street and the Avant Garde

While the "nonplace urban realms"[3] as characterized by Boulding may be resistant to any kind of large-scale modification, the fact remains that an existential need for something that may be identified as a street seems to persist. In this respect, it is instructive to note that little more than twenty years separates the antistreet thesis of Le Corbusier from the prostreet preoccupations of Alison and Peter Smithson, a concern that first became evident in their Golden Lane Housing of 1952 (fig. 1). Where Le Corbusier, true to his Enlightenment heritage, castigated the traditional street for being, "no more than a trench, a deep cleft, a narrow passage,"[4] that in his opinion did nothing but oppress the spirit, the Smithsons by the early fifties had become acutely aware of the sociocultural vitality of the street — particularly as they had then experienced it in the still-existing London bye-law housing dating from the turn of the century (fig. 2).

Their appreciation of this street formulated for the first time in modern theory the idea of the generic street; that is, of a street that may not be recognizable as such but would have, nonetheless, many of the psychosocial attributes of the traditional street. Thus they wrote under a heading entitled *Patterns of Association* the following appreciation of the bye-law street:

In a tight knit society inhabiting a tight knit development such as the byelaw streets there is an inherent feeling of safety and social bond which has much to do with the obviousness and simple order form of the street; about 40 houses facing a common open space. The street is not only a means of access but also an arena for social expression. In these "slum" streets is found a simple relationship between house and street.[5]

What failed to follow from this appraisal of the street was a convincing idea as to how a generic form of this order could be generated within the prevailing megalopolitan milieu, and from this time onward the work of the Smithsons, together with that of the Team 10 formation, may be regarded as a loosely coordinated effort at inventing such a form.

What this form could validly be, in the increasingly abstract context of motopia was no clearer to the Smithsons than to any other member of Team 10, a fact that is brought home from the relative failure of Golden Lane's single-loaded access gallery (fig. 3) to function as a genuine substitute for the traditional street (cf. Parkhill Housing, Sheffield, of 1962). That the Smithsons were not capable at this time of sensing the existential and phenomenological limits of the street per se, namely, its essential doublesidedness[6] and its lateral continuity with the ground, not only points to the extent to which they, in their turn, were conditioned by the abstract rationality of the modern movement but also touches on another dilemma which has confronted architectural thought over the past decade. This parallel problematic essentially poses two questions: first, in what way may megastructural forms, such as the freeway, be used to impart landmark identity to the large-scale megalopolitan reality; and second, the related issue as to what may be an appropriate formulation for large urban elements such as mass housing, so that these will not only relate to the megalopolitan scale but at the same time "situate" man and provide for those fundamental needs of association and identity. That this dichotomous issue has led on occasion to the generation of poetic but operationally inconsistent models is evident from a good deal of architectural speculation over the last twenty years, as we may well judge from many of the designs projected by Team 10 during this period. Two projects stand out as being particularly exemplary of this dilemma — Louis Kahn's midtown Philadelphia proposal of 1953 (figs. 4 and 5) and the Smithsons' Hauptstadt Berlin competition entry of 1958 (fig. 6).

2

3

Where in the one instance the periphery of a pedestrianized center is shown as being lined by cylindrical parking silos, in the other a multi-leveled pedestrian esplanade, linking randomly placed office towers, is shown as being indifferent to the continuity of the "grain"[7] in the existing city despite its frequent connection to the sidewalk infrastructure through an elaborate system of escalator access. What is problematic about both these proposals is not only their mutual indifference to the historical limits of their respective urban contexts (which even in the case of Berlin still persists) but also their incapacity to formulate a convincing model for the generic interface between the automotive infrastructure and the pedestrian street. In these two projects, as in a great deal of our everyday urban reality, the separate realms of freeway and pedestrian street tend to cancel each other out, with the former invariably emerging as the dominant force.

But the most telling point about these examples is not their specific shortcomings — the vague differentiation made between automotive and pedestrian movement (which is particularly chronic in the case of Philadelphia; see figure 5) or the climatic and commercial inviability of the pedestrian decks in the case of Berlin (fig. 6) — but rather these disjunctive propositions as the manifestation of a general theoretical block, wherein the true limitations and needs of the present appear to be inimical to any kind of adequate formulation. At this juncture the endemic utopianism of the architectural profession seems to limit its creative and critical capacity, for the reality of the "nonplace urban realm" is hardly to be mediated by such imaginative, but ultimately inviable, essays in the grand-master manner. Ultimately, Kahn's Philadelphia looks more to Piranesi's Rome than it does to the existential realities of the American downtown, while the Smithsons' Berlin is more concerned with the iconography of San Gimignano than it is with the programming of public life in a convincing way. Their particular failure with regard to this last seems to be borne out by the absence of any viable public or commercial function on the podium of their Economist Building completed in London in 1965.[8]

It is clear that the responsibilities of the architect must increasingly lie with the realities of the past-in-the-present as they must with postulations for the immediate future, since he is the sole professional who is situated by definition in a mediatory historical role. This being so, the architect must endeavour to divest himself of a millenial view of history in which, at one and the same time, we overrate the future and underrate the past. For in the last analysis, the irreversibility of history has its own implacable but ambiguous meaning, namely, that while we cannot exchange one moment in time for some future or past golden age, we have nonetheless, by virtue of this, little choice but to integrate the past into the realizations of the present. Thus while we cannot hope to revoke the loss of the traditional street at a global level, we may hope still to

5

4

6

2. British Bye-Law Housing of the late nineteenth century. The prototype for the Bethnal Green Street. [Catherine Bauer, *Modern Housing,* Arno Press, New York, 1974]

3. Alison and Peter Smithson. Golden Lane Housing 1952. The street as an open-one-side deck. The original sketch of the Bethnal Green "generic" street. [*Uppercase 3,* edited by Theo Crosby, Whitefriars Press Ltd., London, 1956]

4. Louis Kahn. Midtown Philadelphia 1953. The problem of interface and urban continuity. [*Team 10*

Primer, edited by Alison and Peter Smithson. The MIT Press, 1968]

5. Louis Kahn. Garage and Shopping Tower for Midtown Philadelphia 1956–7. Sectional perspective showing the equally unresolved exit and entry interface of both cars and pedestrians. [Vincent Scully, *Louis I. Kahn,* Braziller, New York, 1962]

6. Alison and Peter Smithson and Peter Sigismond. Haupstadt Berlin 1958. Excessive layers of public movement without sufficient programmatic support. [Alison and Peter Smithson, *Urban Structuring,* Reinhold, New York, 1967]

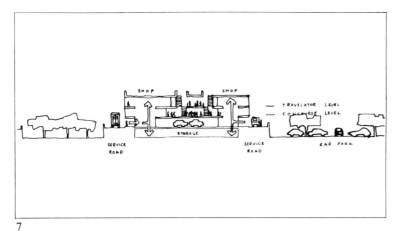

7

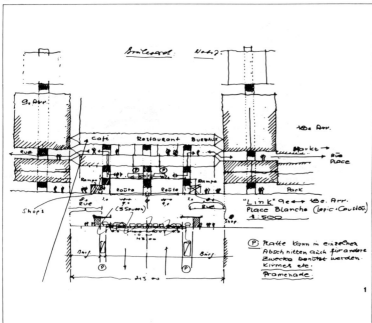

8

maintain within limits, those physical continuities that are capable of sustaining something of its living social history.

Furthermore, there seems to be a necessity to reintroduce into the abstract anonymity of the megalopolis type forms, which are capable of generating something of that sense of public space or rather place that has always characterized the denser parts of the traditional city; to engender, as it were, breaks in the abstract motopian system, which are identifiable and sustainable as public enclaves of varying density and capacity.

As was noted at the outset, such an approach is hardly original, since many members of the so-called avant garde have long since attempted to come to terms with this issue, not only Team 10 (the Smithsons in their London Roads Study of 1960, figure 7; or Stefen Werwerka in his Berlin U-Bahn megastructures of 1956, figure 8) but also the Japanese metabolists, men such as Maki and Ohtaka, in their ''group form'' proposals, their design for the Shinjuku district (fig. 9), and their prototypical shopping enclaves projected for Tokyo in 1962 (fig. 10).[9]

Two factors, however, have since become extremely self-evident from our experience of the recent past. The first concerns the whole technical and experiential problematic surrounding the viability and desirability of the megastructure per se; the second addresses itself to the limits and usefulness of the whole design strategy known by the name ''open aesthetic.'' In the first instance the megastructure itself guarantees very little, either from the point of view of its own realization in a reasonable time span or from the point of view of the appropriateness of its scale. Enough megastructures have already been built which, at one and the same time, not only establish a violent rift between their own form and the existing urban context but also engender an internal landscape of such a size and programmatic vacuity that the pedestrian is largely bereft of any ''living'' relation to his immediate context. In this perspective, there remains the possibility of the limited intervention of the generic street or enclave and it is to an examination of this possibility that the remainder of this chapter is devoted.

A Comparative Survey of Three Generic Street Alternatives:
The Perimeter Block, the Linear Arcade
and the Multilevel Megastructure
Criteria for Categories and Examples

While these three alternatives may appear to have been rather arbitrarily selected according to the abstraction of point, line, and plane, and while the first two may be developed by a simple process of extension into the third, they nonetheless seem to conform to the generic types available for immediate and limited intervention in the field of urban

7. Alison and Peter Smithson. London Roads Study 1960. The exploitation of the inner urban freeway as a route building. This attempt to establish a new scale of urban identity brings with it endemic interface problems between the existing fabric and the new intervention. [Alison and Peter Smithson, *Urban Structuring*]

8. Stefan Werwerka. Boulevard Building. Paris/Berlin. 1956. The traffic-system building as the constituent of a labyrinthine street intervention.

9. Maki and Ohtaka. Shinjuku District group form proposal, 1962. The exploitation of a traffic-system building as an artificial prodium. [Gyorgy Kepes, ed., *Vision and Value Series. Structure in Art and Science,* New York 1965]

10. Maki and Ohtaka. Prototypical shopping enclaves for Tokyo, 1962. The conversion of existing street frontage shopping into "enclaves" set back from the street. The model is clearly the nineteenth-century arcade. [Kepes, *Structure in Art and Science*]

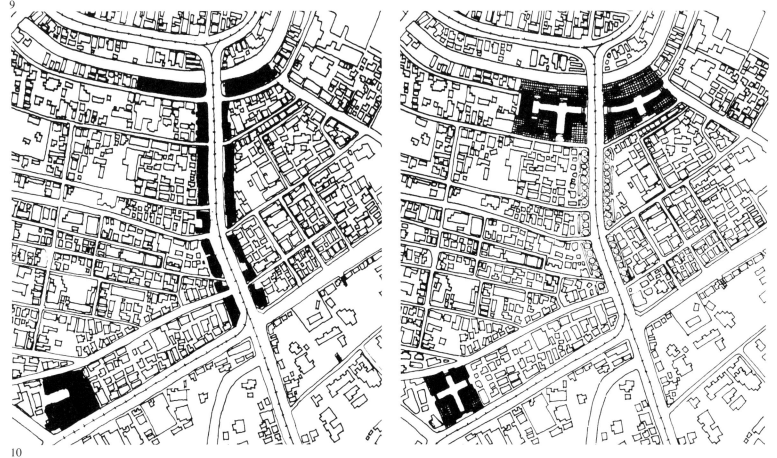

9

10

form. From the many projected and realized examples that could have been chosen, these three generic types are here primarily represented by the following examples:

The Perimeter Block: Spangen Housing, Rotterdam, by M. A. Brinkman, completed in 1919, and Cooper Square Housing, New York, by Roger A. Cumming, Architect, with Waldtraude Schleicher Woods, designed in 1974.

The Linear Arcade: Royal Mint Square Housing, London, by Nigel Greenhill and John Jenner, designed in 1974, and Students' Union Housing for the University of Alberta, Edmonton, Canada, by A. J. Diamond and Barton Myers, completed in 1973.

The Multilevel Megastructure: Frankfurt-Römerberg Center, Frankfurt-am-Main, designed in 1963 by Shadrach Woods and Manfried Schiedhelm of Candilis, Josic and Woods, and the Brunswick Center, London, by Patrick Hodgkinson, of 1973.

Some explanation is needed with regard to the emphasis that necessarily arises out of the selection of these particular examples. This selection pays direct homage to the work of the late Shadrach Woods, whose generic approach to the generation of urban form is now coming to be appreciated at its true worth. Hence two out of the six examples selected were designed under his direction or influence. The inclusion of Spangen may appear to be anomalous amid a set of examples that otherwise have been exclusively drawn from the work of the last decade. By way of justification, one can only assert that today, after over fifty years, Spangen still stands as one of the most remarkable examples of perimeter-block planning, not so much for its units, which have long since become substandard, but for the way in which it clearly differentiates between public, semipublic, and private space and for the manner in which it is able to maintain the continuity of the existing urban fabric.

Apart from these explanations, two criteria were generally applied to the selection of these models: (a) that they should demonstrate an evident capacity for maintaining social and physical continuity in relation to existing urban fabrics; (b) that they should be capable of differentiating identifiable and usable public space within their own aggregate built form.

Comparative Categories

Each of the above pairs will be freely compared to each other under three categories:

(1) *Scale and Basic Components:* The general size and organization of the types will be established under this category.

(2) *Continuity, Differentiation, and Interface:* The degree to which the types are able to maintain urban continuity and the way in which

they are able to differentiate between such categories as pedestrian/automobile, public/private, and so forth.

(3) *Applicability and Variation:* The apparent limits under which these type forms may be successfully applied and their relation to comparable variants that modify to a greater or lesser degree the essential attributes of the type.

The Perimeter Block: Spangen Housing, Rotterdam, 1919;
Cooper Square Housing, New York, 1974
Block: Scale and Basic Components

Spangen is a four-story scheme organized around an internal garden court and occupying a block measuring some 260 feet by 460 feet (fig. 11). There are three-bedroom apartments on the first and second floors, with three-bedroom duplexes over, served from a continuous elevated access gallery internal to the block.

Cooper Square, by contrast, is a nine- to fifteen-story scheme, with the perimeter profile stepping down to different heights within this range. It is simply organized about an internal open court, on a block measuring some 430 feet by 400 feet (figs. 12 and 13). Commercial-cum-service frontage and four-bedroom apartments on raised garden terraces alternately occupy the perimeter of the block at grade, with the one-, two-, and three-bedroom duplexes and apartments being stacked above. As in Spangen the upper units are served by a continuous system of gallery access, although the position of this access varies in Cooper Square. In response to a preferred orientation and to the relative noise levels of the adjacent streets, the access is either external or internal to the block. The arrangement is such that continuity of movement in the deck access necessitates changing levels at the corners where the elevators are located. The one exception to this is the sixth floor, which encircles the block at a median height without any change in level. This provision allows for midheight circulation from one elevator core to the next without having to descend to grade level.

Block: Continuity, Differentiation, and Interface

Spangen comprises a perimeter block that, for all of the complexity of its inner courtyards, resolves the problem of continuity and interface with the existing urban fabric in an extremely simple and effective manner. Since the private automobile barely existed at the time of its design, the few interruptions in the perimeter occur by virtue of providing vehicular access to the laundry block in the center. The continuous deck, elevated two floors above grade, maintains easy visual and aural contact with the ground and is consistently handled as an internal-access

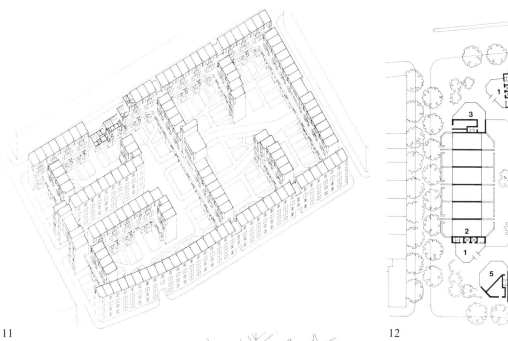

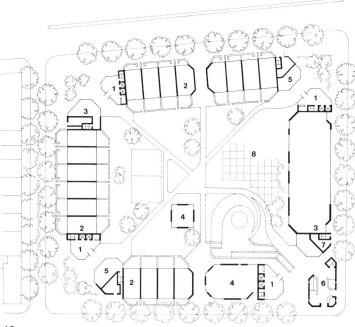

11

12

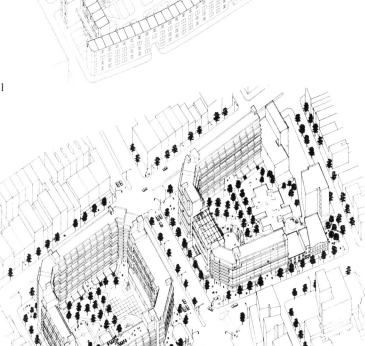

13

11. M. Brinkman. Spangen Housing, Rotterdam, 1919. The combination of the perimeter block with the elevated pedestrian deck. Designed after the urban precepts of Berlage, the hermetic perimeter here maintains the street space of the traditional city. [Axonometric drawing from *Modern Housing Prototypes* by Roger Sherwood, Cornell, 1971]

12. Roger A. Cumming, Architect, with Waltraude Schleicher-Woods, Cooper Square Housing, New York, 1974. Plan of main perimeter block at grade. 1. Elevator lobby. 2. apartments. 3. commercial. 4. community space. 5. laundry. 6. subway entrance. 7. compactor room. 8. tenants gardens. [the architects]

13. Roger A. Cumming, Architect, with Waltraude Schleicher-Woods, Cooper Square Housing, New York, 1974. Axonometric showing complete development. Note the alternation of access galleries from the exterior to the interior of the perimeter block. [the architects]

14

14. H. P. Berlage. Amsterdam South, 1917. The
perimeter block as a device for maintaining the
continuity of street space. Note the clear opposition
of tranquil court and active street. [Benevolo,
Leonardo, *History of Modern Architecture,* Vol I,
The MIT Press, 1966]

15. Prototypical perimeter block: Berlin, 1925. The
legal permitted maximum after 1925 for all outlying
districts. [Catherine Bauer, *Modern Housing,* Arno
Press, New York, 1974]

16. Kalesa and Gessner. Perimeter block prototype,
Vienna, 1919. This was the first of a series of twelve
housing enclaves built around the perimeter of
Vienna between 1919 and 1930. [Weiner Superblocks, Technische Universität, Berlin, 1966]

system, in opposition to the external street system encircling the perimeter. In Spangen this last is clearly maintained as a public continuum, integral with the urban fabric as a whole. Although a certain number of living units do in fact overlook this sidewalk at grade, the general effect of the built perimeter is to serve as a hermetic wall, separating the communal courtyard from the street space of the city. The internal garden courts and the elevated decks at Spangen clearly announce themselves in this context as varying levels of semipublic space. The garden layout itself, however, is broken down into small plots, according with the subdivision of the housing units, permitting semiprivate appropriation and maintenance of the plots.

In Cooper Square, continuity with the existing fabric and movement system of the city is assured in a very comparable manner, although continuity in usage and spatial containment along the perimeter itself varies to a much greater degree than at Spangen. The external frontage at Cooper Square is about equally divided between entrances, public facilities, and a containing perimeter wall. As a result, the internal court is decidedly more public, it being open to penetration not only from its four corners but also from the midblock position on its longer sides (fig. 12). In consequence, in contrast to Spangen, the surface is as much paved as it is planted, a treatment that reflects its highly public and open nature. The only exceptions to this are the tenants' gardens which, while comparable to the gardens in the courtyard at Spangen, are collectively grouped.

This tendency for the perimeter block to become a hermetic enclave, which is emphasized in Spangen but mediated by penetration in the case of Cooper Square, finds its paradoxical reflection in the location of public facilities. While these are centrally placed in Spangen, they are located on the diagonal corners adjacent to the elevator lobbies in the case of Cooper Square (fig. 12). It should be noted that out of a basic planning decision there happens to be just as little provision for the automobile in Cooper Square as there is in Spangen, although this omission is by no means a necessary element of the type form itself (cf. Wood's Karlsruhe proposal of 1971).

Block: Applicability and Variation

The applicability of Spangen in its own time was inseparable from the gridded European city extensions of the twenties when the perimeter block form became a generic housing prototype, as applicable to the new sections of Rotterdam as it then was to Amsterdam (fig. 14) or to Berlin (fig. 15). The greatest range of variation in this type occurred in the socialist housing built around the periphery of Vienna in the twenties (fig. 16).[10]

The subsequent mass ownership of the automobile has necessarily

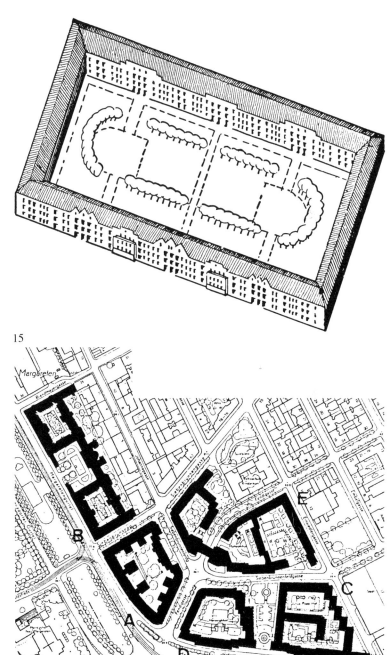

15

16

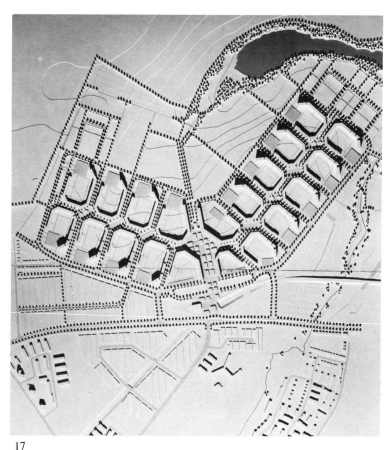

17

17. Shadrach Woods. Hamburg-Steilshoop, 1966. Site plan. Incomplete perimeter U-blocks grouped around a pedestrian spine and traversed by slow-moving, that is, cranked, access roads shown in black. Parking (shaded) at grade, to the rear of the U formations. Where at one level this may be regarded as a perimeter development, at another it is a linear spine with the typical front and back conditions that arise out of such a development. (c.f. Candilis, Josic and Woods, University of Bochum project, 1962). [the architects]

posed problems for the further application of this type, and variations have since been developed that have tried to come to terms with the integration of the automobile within the perimeter form. The reinvention of the perimeter block by Shadrach Woods, from his Hamburg-Steilshoop proposal of 1966 (fig. 17)[11] to his Karlsruhe project of 1971 (figs. 18, 19, 20, and 21) — the latter having been designed with Ilhan Zeybekoglu — are two attempts at just such an integration. The on-grade parking, which is only partially integrated into the Hamburg-Steilshoop proposal, becomes more fully incorporated in the subterranean parking of Karlsruhe. This is also true for an extension of the Karlsruhe concept, designed by Zeybekoglu for application to downtown Santiago as an entry to the Santiago international competition (figs. 22 and 23) of 1973.

Hamburg-Steilshoop, Karlsruhe, and Santiago represent three different variants of the same type, where the interface conditions between pedestrian movement, parking, and automobile access vary in each case. Hamburg-Steilshoop and Karlsruhe are two versions based on the same principle of intermixing restricted slow-moving service access with pedestrian street movement (fig. 19). These schemes differ not so much in respect of their approach to parking but rather in their attitude to the street space as volume; the continuous perimeter blocks of Karlsruhe assure continuity in the urban space (fig. 21). Santiago, on the other hand, relegates both parking and service to a volume immediately below grade and maintains the internal courts of the blocks as vehicular-free enclaves. In this respect the Cooper Square model is closely related to the Karlsruhe prototype but makes no provision whatsoever for either off-street parking or servicing.

A unique variation on the Spangen model, where the integration of the automobile was to result in an all but total disintegration of the perimeter form, was projected by J. Whitney Huber of Princeton University, in a low-rise, high-density housing scheme for Trenton, New Jersey (fig. 24). This scheme, which, unlike either Hamburg-Steilshoop or Karlsruhe, integrated the cars by distributing them over the site, sacrificed in the process of doing so the desirable proximity of built form and street. Thus while a vestigial perimeter still remained in the continuity of this aggregate form, it in itself was all but totally disassociated from the street: first, by a perimeter wall surrounding the site, and second, by a service road, which, apart from serving the cluster parking, would have acted like a moat, in dividing the built form from the continuity of the sidewalk (fig. 25). As the axonometric indicates, this arrangement would have tended to drain all pedestrian movement into the center of the site, despite the fact that regular cuts through the containing wall would have been maintained to the sidewalk. In many respects this version of the perimeter block has more in common with the walled mobile-home sites of the West Coast than it does with the

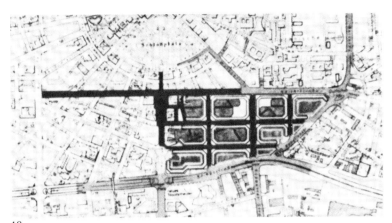

18

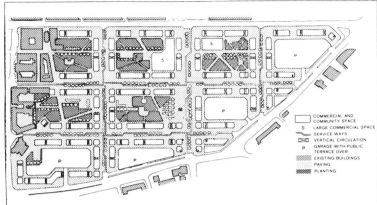

19

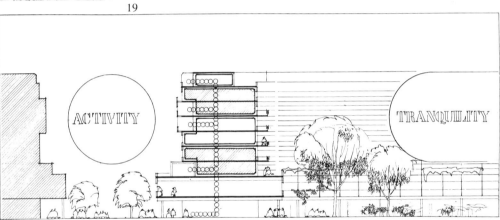

20

21

18. Shadrach Woods and Ilhan Zeybekoglu. Downtown Karlsruhe, 1971. Site Plan. Complete perimeter blocks, integrated as a coherent street system within the existing fabric. [the architects]

19. Shadrach Woods and Ilhan Zeybekoglu. Karlsruhe, 1971. Detailed site plan. Blocks of mixed use grouped about garden courts and served by a grid of pedestrian ways which are also accessible to service vehicles. [Shadrach Woods, *The Man in the Street*, Penguin Books, London/New York 1975).

20. Shadrach Woods and Ilhan Zeybekoglu. Karlsruhe, 1971. Section. Perimeter block. Commercial on the lower two floors with residential above. Conceptual separation between tranquil court and active street. [Woods, *The Man in the Street*]

21. Shadrach Woods and Ilhan Zeybekoglu. Karlsruhe, 1971. Model. [Shadrach Woods, *The Man in the Street*]

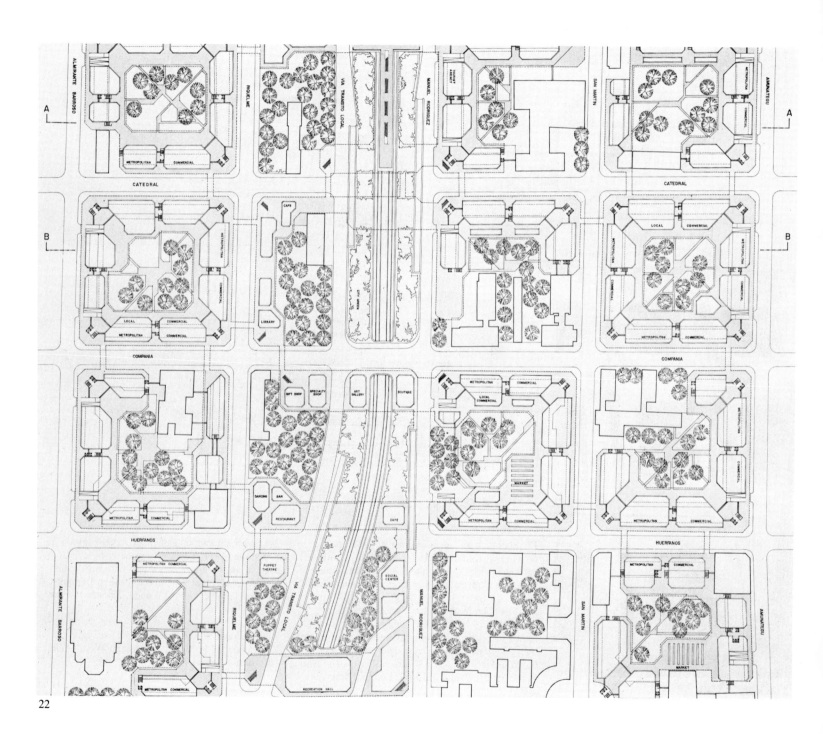

23

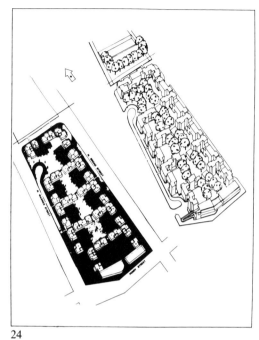

24

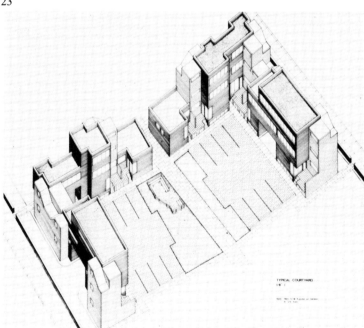

25

22. Ilhan Zeybekoglu. Downtown Santiago, 1973. Plan. Commercial for three floors at grade. Servicing below grade. [the architect]

23. Ilhan Zeybekoglu. Downtown Santiago, 1973. Model. [the architect]

24. J. Whitney Huber. Perry Street Housing, Trenton, 1972. Site axonometric. A service road continuously flanks the site on the east and west with a community building to the south. [the architect]

25. J. Whitney Huber. Perry Street Housing, Trenton, 1972. Axonometric. Note cluster parking served by perimeter access. [the architect]

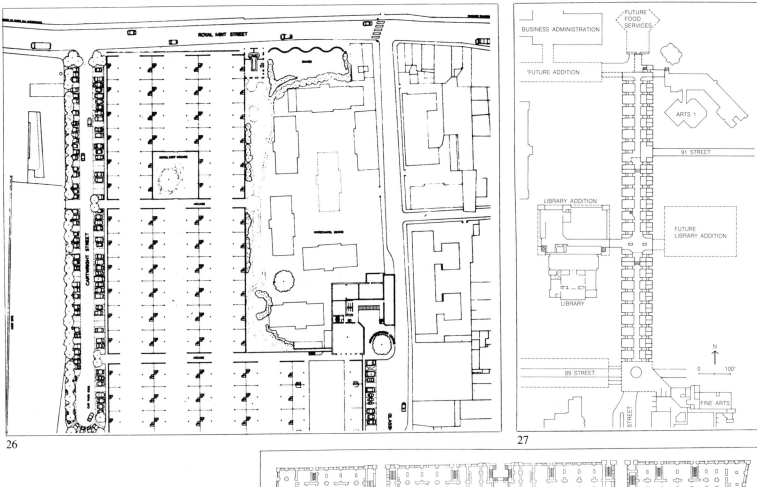

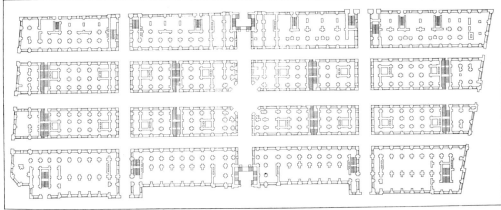

26. Nigel Greenhill and John Jenner. Royal Mint
Square Housing, London, 1974. Site plan. Note
perimeter parking with the linear arcade as the prime
pedestrian access. [the architects]

27. A. J. Diamond and Barton Myers. Students'
Union Housing, University of Alberta, Edmonton,
1972–74. Site plan at elevated access level, showing
linkage to library and future additions. [the ar-
chitects]

traditional perimeter model and a certain indifference to the living continuity of the urban fabric separates this scheme from the whole of the perimeter block sequence developed by Shadrach Woods.

The Linear Arcade: Royal Mint Square Housing, London, 1974; Students' Union Housing, Edmonton, Alberta, 1973
Arcade: Scale and Basic Components

The Royal Mint Square project is a two-story, glass-covered housing scheme occupying an irregular block measuring some 300 by 400 feet over its widest dimensions (fig. 26). This introverted scheme — comparable in certain respects to the Whitney-Huber scheme for Trenton — is structured about five linear arcades, of which the fifth is of double width due to variations in context and program. The primary introverted public circulation is along and across these glazed arcades.

The Edmonton complex is a seven-story glass covered student-housing scheme occupying a plan area some 100 feet wide by 950 feet in length and built over an existing campus street in the University of Alberta (fig. 27). The primary public circulation is along the length of this arcade (fig. 28), although the overall form can be penetrated laterally at numerous points throughout its length. Where the Royal Mint Square scheme tends toward becoming an arcaded network, comparable in its overall plan to the organization of the Gum Department Store in Moscow (fig. 29), the Edmonton complex is strictly linear in its organization.

Arcade: Continuity, Differentiation, and Interface

Royal Mint Square, like the nineteenth-century arcades and greenhouse structures from which it is obviously derived (fig. 30), is a totally introverted solution in which almost all of the internal pedestrian circulation is semipublic, in contradistinction to the potential public nature of the surrounding perimeter streets. It is in many respects a direct reinvention of the Bethnal Green play street (figs. 31 and 32) that had been the original point of departure for the Smithsons' 1952 Golden Lane Housing. While Royal Mint Square has none of the megastructural nor phenomenological characteristics of Golden Lane, it nonetheless still effects a major break in the continuity of the existing urban fabric. Like the Whitney-Huber scheme for Trenton, the interface conditions that it establishes, in respect of the immediate urban context, tend to be critical, even though a continuity of circulation at grade is maintained throughout. Unlike either Spangen or the Edmonton scheme, Royal Mint Square has no public elevation to speak of and, in that respect, it is able to contribute little to the public continuity of the city fabric. Like the Whitney-Huber scheme it integrates the car in such a way as to posit

28

28. A. J. Diamond and Barton Myers. Students' Union Housing, Edmonton. The linear arcade as the generic street flanked by shops and housing. [the architects]

29. Pomeranzew; Klein and Weber. Gum Department Store, Moscow, 1893. The linear arcade transformed into a network — the city in miniature. [J. F. Giest, *Passagen ein Bautyp des 19. Jahrhunderts*]

30. William Herbert. Lowther Arcade, London, 1830–31. Perspective. One of the earliest London arcades — 245 feet long, 20 feet wide and 35 feet high. [By courtesy of the British Museum Raymond McGrath, *Glass in Architecture and Decoration*, The Architectural Press, London, 1961]

31. Nigel Greenhill and John Jenner. Royal Mint Square Housing, London, 1974. Plan. The double-sided arcade as the generic street. [the architects]

32. Nigel Greenhill and John Jenner. Royal Mint Square Housing, London, 1974. Cross section through two typical arcades. [the architects]

33. A. J. Diamond and Barton Myers. Students' Union Housing, Edmonton, 1974. Typical cross section showing the closed and open sides of the arcade. [the architects]

34. A. J. Diamond and Barton Myers. Students' Union Housing, Edmonton, 1974. On one side the complex proffers a public facade with access at grade level. The original street, however, has been consumed by the building. [the architects]

30

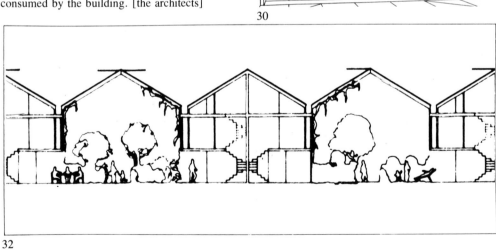

32

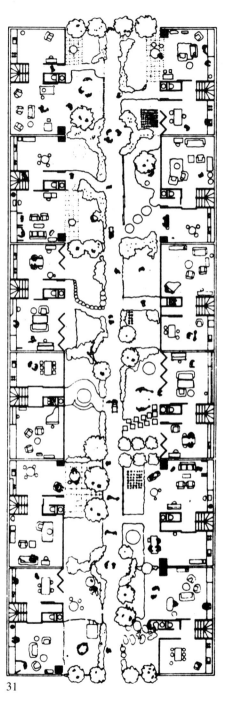

31

a suburban rather than an urban concept of space. This gesture is consummated, so to speak, by the containment of the entire complex within a continuous perimeter wall. It is of interest to note that in contrast to the Edmonton scheme, the play-street-cum-arcade, as developed here, totally fuses private and semiprivate space, recalling certain aspects of the American suburb (fig. 31).

While in contrast to Spangen the private garden plots are here strictly allocated at the ratio of one per unit, the bulk parking of automobiles on the flanking sides of the site establishes the whole as a form of collective and deprives it of the highly personalized cluster parking which is such a strong feature, say, in the Trenton housing (figs. 24 and 25).

In the Edmonton scheme, continuity with the existing urban fabric is only schematically maintained despite (or possibly even because of) the fact that the structure is built over an existing road. A fundamental break occurs in both plan and section (fig. 33) irrespective of the fact that the building presents a comprehensible public facade to the adjacent sectors of the campus (fig. 34). In effect, the building converts what had hitherto been a public street into a service and parking road (fig. 35), with all public pedestrian movement approaching the structure in a lateral direction rather than along its axis. A hiatus thus occurs between the public level of the campus at grade and the public level of the arcade raised some one and a half floors above the ground. In its present form the arcade is somewhat less public than the campus sidewalk system, although should this elevated structure be extended and connected to other public facilities at the higher level, as has in fact been projected (fig. 27), then an entirely new public level will be posited which will augment (and eventually compete with) the present campus network at grade. As it is, the asymmetrical section of the building has resulted in a preferred facade which faces the library and *centrum* of the campus. This distortion is reflected in plan, in the placing of the residential parking bays and major stairways (that is, the wider stairs for the first flight up to the arcade are located along this preferred edge; figure 37).

As the status of the arcade is much more public here than in the case of the Royal Mint Square scheme, the corresponding separation between public and private is more decisive. Thus, within the arcade itself, the perimeter shops constitute a natural and definite interface between the public arcade and the private rooms over, just as the continuous residential parking band forms a clear separation between the service street and the campus proper (fig. 36). Like the housing schemes for Trenton (fig. 24) and Royal Mint Square (fig. 26), the building is a permeable barrier between opposing flanks. However, should one in this instance wish to cross the barrier laterally at midpoint, then one would have no choice but to negotiate stairs and pass through the arcade itself, an awkward provision which is hardly offset by the frequency of the stair shafts by which this crossing may be effected.

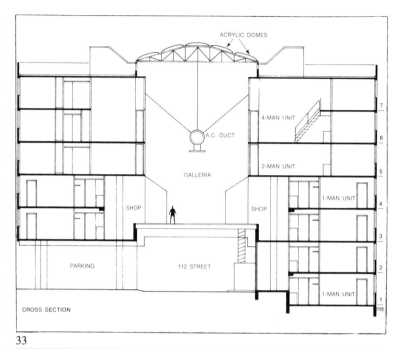

33

34

35

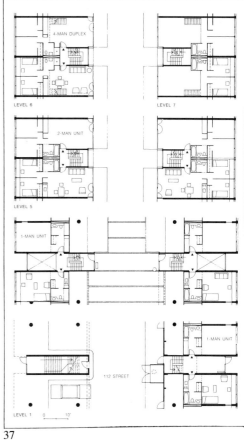

37

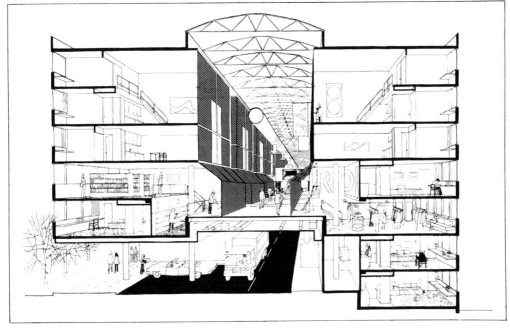

36

35. A. J. Diamond and Barton Myers. Students'
Union Housing, Edmonton, 1974. Note obvious
discontinuity between main pedestrian level and the
public level of the arcade. [the architects]

36. A. J. Diamond and Barton Myers. Students'
Union Housing, Edmonton, 1974. Perspectival section. [the architects]

37. A. J. Diamond and Barton Myers. Students'
Union Housing, Edmonton, 1974. Typical floor
plans. Note wider stairway from ground to arcade
level to the parking side of the building. [the ar-
chitects]

Arcade: Applicability and Variation

In morphological or topological terms the linear arcade appears as the inversion of the perimeter block, which, if it is extended, will tend to become transformed, as in the case of Moscow's Gum Store of 1893, into a network of introverted streets totally enclosed and lit from above. Where the perimeter block guarantees two contrasting spaces or places, as exemplified in the *outer active* and *inner tranquil* spaces of Woods' Karlsruhe scheme (fig. 20), the linear arcade only assures one; namely, the *inner active* realm (figs. 28 and 31). This city in miniature — the "unreal" counterform of the "real" city — has always gained its substance from being inlaid into the fabric of the city proper. The arcade or, more strictly, the galleria has invariably arisen like a parasitical labyrinth, dependent for its form on the public mass within which it is concealed. Where this context does not exist the arcade seems to have little capacity for contributing to the continuity of the exterior urban space. By virtue of its closure as a system it necessarily involves a break in the continuity of the open city, irrespective of the ease of its connection to the general level of circulation. This break is, of course, less marked where the normal sidewalk datum is maintained throughout, as in the case of most nineteenth-century arcades.

Thus we see that for all of its brilliance the student housing at Edmonton seems to possess little scope for general urban application, other than serving as a spine for a free-standing structure whose exterior facade would have the effect of reconstituting the continuum of the street space (cf. Spangen). And this, as we have seen, would be a paradoxical outcome since, on completing the elevated system of public circulation, the urban space at grade would no longer carry any significant movement. On the other hand there is little doubt that the arcade is capable of establishing a convincing sense of place through simulating the street experience of the traditional city, although this is perhaps less true of the model posited in the Royal Mint Square Housing where the private status of the flanking elements effectively determines the semiprivate nature of the enclosed space. Both the Edmonton student housing and the Candilis, Josic, and Woods design for the University of Bochum of 1962 make one aware of the space-creating limits of the arcade as a linear organizing spine. In Bochum, as in the Edmonton scheme, the only significant space, both volumetrically and operationally, is that which is internal to the arcade and its branchlike extensions (fig. 38). Once again the space external to the arcade — in the case of Bochum the open field of the unbuilt campus — is left bereft of both meaning and use — a sort of rustic no-man's-land surrounding the internal coherence of the arcaded artifact.

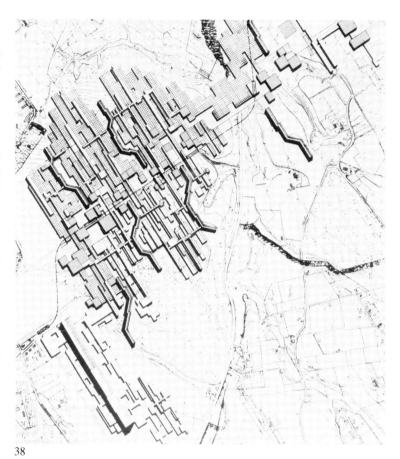

38

38. Candilis, Josic and Woods. University of Bochum, 1962. Plan of the main pedestrian spine with its branches. Note only the linear arcade has public significance since the irregular exterior is reduced to a meaningless perimeter. [Shadrach Woods, *Candilis, Josic and Woods. Buildings for People*, Praeger, New York, Washington, 1968]

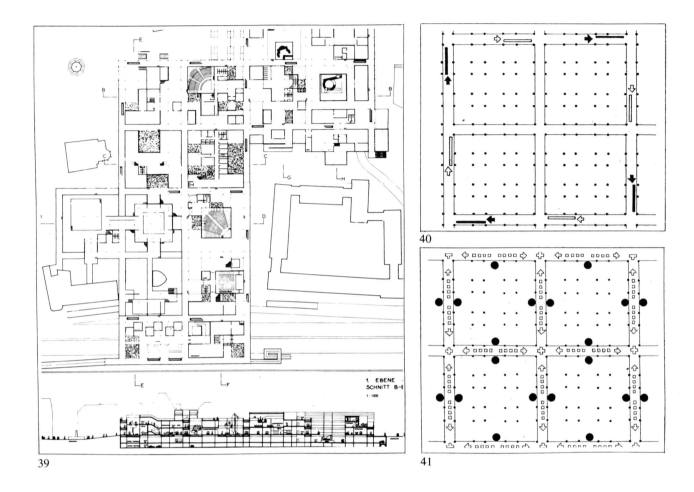

39

40

41

39. Shadrach Woods (Candilis, Josic, Woods). Frankfurt-Römerberg, Frankfurt-am-Main, 1963. Site plan at ground level and section. [Woods, *Buildings for People*]

40. Shadrach Woods (Candilis, Josic, Woods). Frankfurt-Römerberg. Typical tartan grid organization of loft infrastructure. White indicates up escalators and black down. [Woods, *Buildings for People*]

41. Shadrach Woods (Candilis, Josic, Woods).

Frankfurt-Römerberg 1963. Elevator service across (black dots) to loft space. [Woods, *Buildings for People*]

42. Shadrach Woods (Candilis, Josic, Woods). Frankfurt-Römerberg. Model. [Woods, *Buildings for People*]

43. Shadrach Woods (Candilis, Josic, Woods). Frankfurt-Römerberg. Model. Note the urban space created between the existing medieval fabric and the new intervention. [Woods, *Buildings for People*]

The Multilevel Megastructure: Frankfurt-Römerberg,
Frankfurt am Main, 1963; Brunswick Center, London, 1973
Megastructure: Scale and Basic Components

Frankfurt-Römerberg consists of a six-story, multilevel, gridded
megastructure rising to a maximum of four floors above grade and
extending to two floors below. This gridded orthogonal area, measuring
some 640 feet wide by 830 feet long, would have been broken down
into squares measuring 108 feet on their sides and separated by pedestrian rights-of-way, each twelve feet wide (fig. 39). The module of these
square bays would have corresponded to the size of the existing net of
pedestrian ways in the immediate vicinity of the site. Each of these bays
would be subdivided into a 25 foot 5 inch and 15 foot 8½ inch tartan
grid arranged according to an *a:b:a:b:a* rhythm (fig. 40). The architect's
description gives a clear idea of this open infrastructural organization,
intended for the accommodation of variations in both use and extent.
''The proposal consists of multi-level distribution grids containing the
mechanical services and corresponding to a circulation net or horizontal
or inclined ways. This organization serves as a basis for the determination of areas to be built up on a secondary, structural grid. It itself is
built only where it is needed to serve those parts of the complex which
are realized. Where it does not actually provide service, it exists only as
a right-of-way. The system, then, retains a certain potential for growth
and for change.''

The levels below grade were designed to provide for truck servicing
in the basement and parking in the subbasement (see section BB in
figure 39). The levels above grade would be capable of accommodating
a variety of uses, including in the competition entry for which the
scheme was designed: a historical museum, a music school, libraries, a
youth center, galleries, a cinema, a cabaret, restaurants, offices, shops,
cafés, and dwellings. The larger public volumes, requiring higher ceil-
ings, would be restricted to the ground level. The open labyrinthine
principle of space occupation was to have been fed by escalators
running along the rights-of-way (pedestrian access) (fig. 40) and by
elevators at the midpoint of each square bay (service) (fig. 41). The
interior spaces of the grid would have been illuminated where necessary
by light courts penetrating to different levels within the structure (figs.
42 and 43).

Brunswick Center consists of a ten-story, multilevel, gridded megastructure rising a maximum of eight floors above grade and extending
some two floors below. It occupies a strictly rectilinear area measuring
some 900 feet long by 400 feet wide, the latter dimension approximating to the length of the typical nineteenth-century block that in part still
constitutes the grain of the surrounding built-up area (fig. 44).

Based throughout on 20-foot square modules, Brunswick Center is

42

43

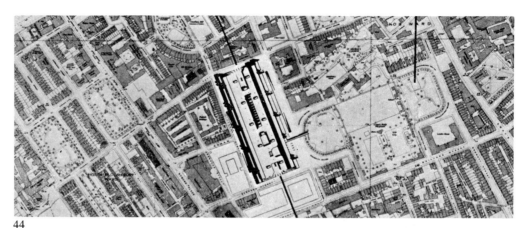

44

PLAZA LEVEL

SHOPPING LEVEL   N ← 0 30'

45

44. Patrick Hodgkinson, Brunswick Center, London, 1964–74. Site Plan. In spite of a formal inflection towards the main axis of Brunswick Square, this megastructure, while respecting the eighteenth century street grid, makes little acknowledgement to the scale of its context. [*A&U,* May 1973, Tokyo, Japan]

45. Patrick Hodgkinson. Brunswick Center, London, 1974. Shopping arcade and plaza levels. [*A&U,* May 1973, Tokyo, Japan]

46. Patrick Hodgkinson, Brunswick Center, London, 1974. Perspectival section. 1. apartments. 2. arcade access hall to apartments. 3. shopping arcade. 4. plaza level. 5. parking. 6. cinema. 7. service road. 8. arcade roof. 9. bridge from plaza to Brunswick Square. [A&U, May 1973, Tokyo, Japan]

organized about an internal shopping mall that is in effect the podium at grade upon which the rest of the scheme is built (fig. 45). The roof of this podium serves as a plaza-cum-planted space, which gives immediate access to the housing units flanking its eastern and western sides. These apartments are clustered in section about two linear entry arcades bounding the plaza on either side (fig. 46). On the outer perimeter these apartments are layered in five tiers in such a way that two fall below the plaza level and two rise above it, with the middle tier at the level of the entry hall. On the inner perimeter the apartments are stacked in setback formation for five floors above the entry level. Below the commercial podium there are two levels of parking, a cinema, and a ring road for the servicing of the shops and refuse disposal, for example.

Megastructure: Continuity, Differentiation, and Interface

Frankfurt-Römerberg comprises a megastructure that, for all the complexity and regularity of its grid, resolves the problem of the interface with the existing urban fabric in a remarkable way. The setback configuration of its modular plan form provides for the precise containment of urban space, as a volumetric interface between the old and the new (fig. 43). At the same time, the historical and living continuity of this space as a field for pedestrian movement is assured by the penetrability of the new intervention from every side; from the town hall square, the cathedral square, the old city, and the river bank. Continual pedestrian movement at grade — from old to new and vice versa — is maintained throughout with the aid of ramped courtyards. Separate access to servicing and parking, which is consigned to the double basement, can be immediately made from the riverside autoroute (fig. 47). This megastructure is literally a city in miniature, which at its perimeter restores the contained urban space of the city in its most traditional sense. By locating all the more public facilities at grade, a precise differentiation between public and private is established in section.

Brunswick Center, on the other hand, is a megastructure, which, for all its honorific gestures towards the axis of Brunswick Square (see figure 44), largely fails to maintain, or even to respond to, the continuity of the surrounding urban grain. Continuity in both urban space and life tends to be vitiated not only by the fortresslike nature of the street facades presented to the northeast and southwest but also by the cutoff fables of the scheme, situated to the northwest and southeast. In sum, the exterior perimeter contributes little to the life and visual continuity of the surrounding street space. It affords neither adequate enclosure nor any kind of continuum in respect of public activity. The setback facade, the sectional elevation (fig. 48), and the internalization of all public facilities effectively deprive the street of both definition and vitality.

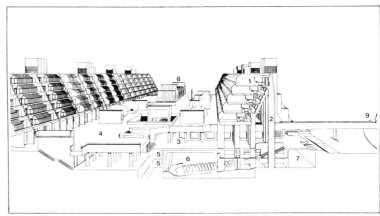

46

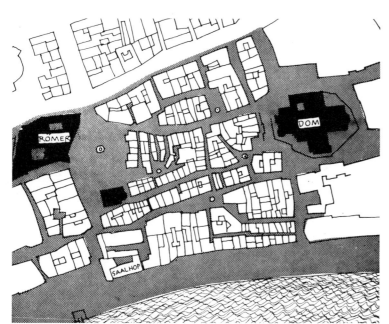
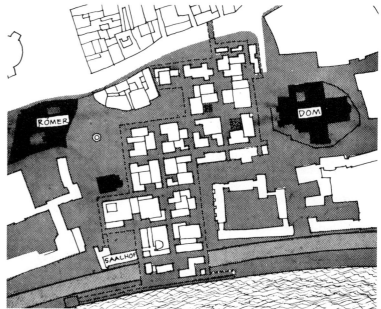

47

48

At the same time, the separation of public and private is not so clearly differentiated in section as in the Woods project for Frankfurt-Römerberg. This is most clearly revealed in the various interface conditions established in Brunswick Center for the residential units. Thus while in Frankfurt these units, raised clear of the street, open directly off the twelve-foot access way, often top-lit, in Brunswick Center they are served from a five-story, clerestory-lit interior hall (see 2 in figure 46), whose large size and scale provide insufficient gradation between public, semipublic, and private space. Here the pedestrian experiences all the architectonic grandeur of the megastructure but little that is capable of imparting structure and intimacy to his daily life. These hangarlike spaces seem to be both too large and undifferentiated to function as satisfactory interfaces between the street or public plaza and the private unit. Meanwhile an equally unsympathetic interface occurs on the perimeter at grade, where the lower units, deprived of an outside terrace, are set off from the street by a monument plinth (fig. 48).

Megastructure: Applicability and Variation

As stated at the beginning of this chapter, the megastructure is a paradigm for urban intervention that, apart from the difficulties attending its formulation, has rarely, if ever, been satisfactorily achieved. At the same time one has to admit that a precise definition of the term tends to prove elusive. José Luis Sert's Holyoke Center in Cambridge, Massachusetts, for example (figs. 49 and 50) would hardly qualify as a megastructure, but nonetheless it seems to achieve a satisfactory intervention at a megastructural scale.

In general, the megastructure with its intrinsic virtues of affording density and internal continuity is characterized by exactly those attributes that generally make for discontinuity in relation to an existing urban context. For all of its many virtues, Brunswick Center is exemplary of this, an enclave solution that appears, in its ingenious sectional organization, to be too closed and disassociative to be able to sustain any kind of adequate continuity at grade. Frankfurt-Römerberg, on the other hand, postulates a model of disarming simplicity that not only affords urban enclosure and continuity, but also posits a city-in-miniature whose internal order is appropriately differentiated according to status, scale and use. The range of urban situations to which the Woods/Scheidhelm Frankfurt model could be successfully applied seems to be both wide and varied, for while it affords a convincing sense of place in situations where the larger context is relatively discontinuous, it is equally capable of being integrated into a preexisting continuous whole. Where the specifics of the Frankfurt-Römerberg scheme are exemplary of the second condition, Woods's application of the same idea to his project for the Free University of Berlin of 1963 is clearly a demonstration of the first (fig. 51).

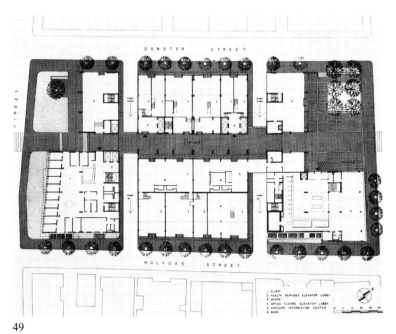

49

47. Shadrach Woods (Candilis, Josic, Woods). Frankfurt-Römerberg, 1963. Comparison between the pre-war fabric of traditional city and the proposed intervention. This strong sense of historical continuity assures continuity of both space and access. [Shadrach Woods, *Candilis, Josic and Woods. Buildings for People*, Praeger, New York, Washington, 1968]

48. Patrick Hodgkinson. Brunswick Center, 1964–74. General view of complex. [A&U, May 1973, Tokyo, Japan]

49. José Luis Sert. Holyoke Center, Cambridge, Massachusetts, 1963. Site plan.

50

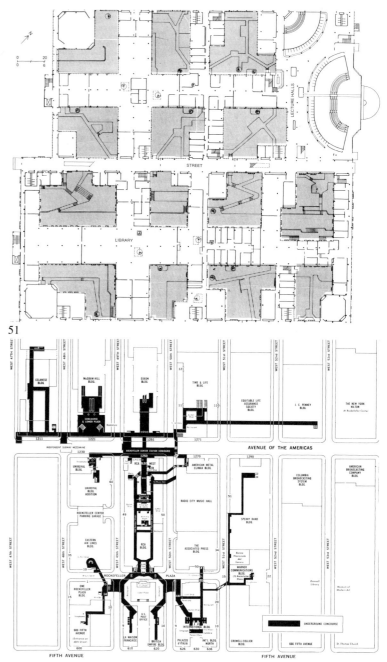

51

52

50. José Luis Sert. Holyoke Center, Cambridge, Massachusetts, 1963. General view.

51. Shadrach Woods (Candilis, Josic, Woods, Schiedhelm). Free University of Berlin 1963–73. Plan of first phase as built. [*Architecture Plus* International Magazine of Architecture Jan/Feb 1974]

52. Corbett, Harrison, Hood, and Fouilloux. Rockefeller Center, New York, 1932. Diagrammatic plan showing the present extent of the complex and the subterranean pedestrian system that connects the various free standing blocks into a continuous network.

53. Corbett, Harrison, Hood, and Fouilloux. Rockefeller Center, New York, 1932. General view. Continuity of pedestrian movement and street space.

54. Place Ville Marie and Place Bonaventure complexes. Montreal, 1967.

It may be argued that Frankfurt-Römerberg is a rationalization of a model for urban intervention that had first been posited in the 1932–1939 development of Rockefeller Center, New York, to the designs of Reinhard and Hofmeister, Corbett, Harrison, Hood, and Fouilloux. Despite major differences in scale, profile, structure, and, above all, in motivation, certain similarities obtain between the two models which are worthy of comment. In the first instance they are both irrigated by continuous systems of pedestrian access (fig. 52) which serve to unite a disparate series of identifiably different volumes and users. In the second they are equally articulated structures whose modular increments relate to the urban context and scale in which they are situated. The modulation of the Rockefeller Center profile along the Fifth Avenue frontage (fig. 53) has become a classic in this respect. By a similar token, its extensive mezzanine-concourse network has been copied in a number of recent urban developments, including Place Ville Marie and the Place Bonaventure complex, both built in Montreal in the mid-1960s (fig. 54).

Conclusion: The Rationale and Potential of the Generic Street

From the foregoing it is possible to develop the following argument for the use of the generic street as a device for urban intervention.

1. The traditional city can no longer be sustained or perpetuated. The prevailing mode of automotive distribution mitigates against the dense concentration of the traditional city.

2. *Tabula rasa* planning has already proven its ineffectiveness and inhumanity. The utopian a priori approach has invariably resulted either in the irrelevance of large scale schemes which are destined never to be realized or in the alienation of an abstract motopia. The corollary to *tabular rasa* planning, namely, the wholesale erosion of existing urban fabrics through the abrasive intrusion of the automobile, suggests the urgent need for alternative piecemeal strategies.

3. This false choice between two crude models of urban planning — namely, between abstract idealism and opportunist pragmatism — suggests that organic urban strategy must of necessity be incremental and hierarchically structured.

4. The success of any incremental transformation will be dependent on the creation of a significant hierarchical order. Such an order may be established through the application of a viable type that possesses certain concrete qualities.

5. In this respect there remains the possibility of creating and/or sustaining generic street forms of limited extent.

6. The generic street is here defined as a building that automatically engenders active street space, either adjacent to its perimeter or within

53

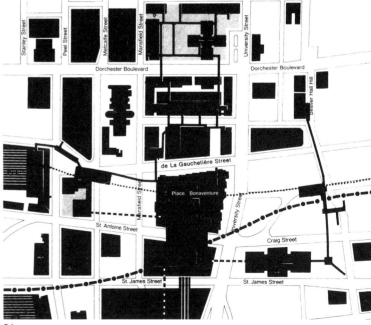

54

its own corporeal form. The oriental bazaar is the archetypical paradigm of such a street.

7. From the comparative analysis given earlier, it would seem that such generic forms should meet at least most, if not all, of the following criteria if they are to prove effective from both a social and a plastic point of view.

a. *Continuity:* Such forms should maintain as far as possible the existing urban continuity in terms of (i) pedestrian movement and activity, (ii) the sustenance of urban space as place, and (iii) the perpetuation of an urban grain that is compatible with the existing context.

b. *Hierarchy and Enclosure:* Such forms should engender a sense of enclosure and establish clearly a differentiation between public and private domains.

c. *Interface.* The interface conditions established by such forms are critical, in concrete terms, to the overall sense of hierarchy, enclosure, and continuity.

Notes

1. Walter Benjamin, "Paris, Capital of the 19th Century," translated by Ben Brewster, *The New Left Review,* no. 48 (March–April 1968), republished in *Perspecta 12* (1969). Benjamin was at work on various versions of this text between 1928 and 1935 and this final draft of 1935 bore the title of *Paris, die Haupstadt des XIX. Jahrhunderts.*

2. Kenneth E. Boulding, "The Death of a City: A Frightening Look at Post Civilization," in Oscar Handlin and John Burchard, eds., *The Historian and the City* (Cambridge, Mass.: The MIT Press, 1966).

3. See Melvin M. Webber, *Explorations into Urban Structure* (Philadelphia: University of Pennsylvania Press, 1964). Webber's coinage of the term "nonplace urban realm" has surely helped to further the ideology of the motopian open city, as has his rationalizing phrase, "community without propinquity."

4. See "La Rue" by Le Corbusier which appears in *Le Corbusier et Pierre Jeanneret. Oeuvre Complète de 1910-1929* (Zurich: Girsberger, 3rd edition, 1943) pp. 112-115. This by now famous antistreet polemic of Le Corbusier first appeared in the journal *l'Intransigeant* in May 1929.

5. A. and P. Smithson, *Urban Structuring,* (London: Studio-Vista, 1967). The text first appeared in *Uppercase 3,* ed. Theo Crosby (Tonbridge, Kent: Whitefriars Press, 1955).

6. *The Shorter Oxford English Dictionary,* 3rd edition, 1966, points to the essential double-sided nature of a street as a cultural phenomenon, as we may judge from the second definition. "2. A road in a town or village . . . running between two lines of houses of shops. Also the road together with the adjacent houses. Used for: the inhabitants of the street; also, the people of the street, late M. E."

7. For the concept of grain, see R. C. Stones, "Grain Theory in Practice: Redevelopment in Manchester at Longsight," *Town Planning Review,* 41 (October 1970), pp. 354-356. Although ultimately of picturesque origin, grain theory derives primarily from concern not only for the continuity of the street pattern but also for maintaining the general mass volume at a given sector of the city. (See also R. C. Stones, "Housing and Redevelopment," *Town Planning Review* 37 (January 1967), pp. 237-254.

8. See my essay, "The Economist and the Hauptstadt," *Architectural Design* (February 1965), pp. 61-62.

9. See Fumihiko Maki and Masato Ohtaka, "Some Thoughts on Collective Form" in *Structure in Art and in Science,* ed. Gyorgy Kepes (New York: George Braziller, 1965), pp. 116-127.

10. See Helmut Kunze, "Housing in Vienna in the 1920's," *Bauwelt* (1969, nos. 12-13), pp. 44-49.

11. The Hamburg-Steilshoop scheme, as requested by the city planning commission, only indicated access, building lines, perimeters, and height limits. Hamburg-Steilshoop has now been largely realized by various architects working within the guidelines established by Woods.

Demonstration Project

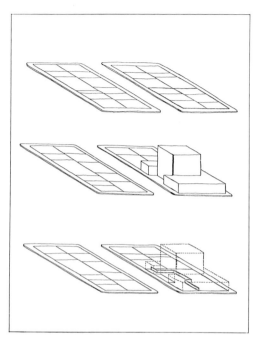

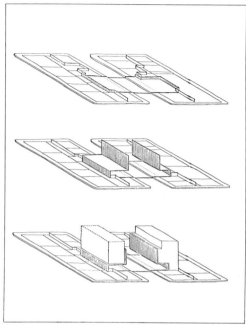

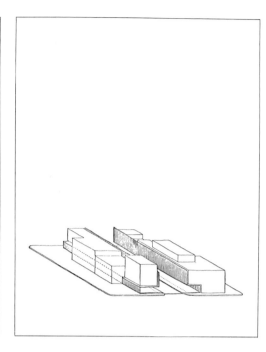

1. Parceling and the public/private boundary: Traditional concepts. (a) Traditional parceling. Parcels do not specifically concern the street. (b) Traditional development. Development limits and rule systems are determined by parcel limits. Street relationships are, at best, tenuously considered. (c) Public/private boundary. Public use of open space is not determined systematically and is without consistency. Breaks in the continuity of use of open space and accessible interior space is common.

2. Parceling and the public/private boundary: Proposed concepts. (a) IAUS proposed parceling concept. New parcels include the street and extend back to the public/private boundary to promote streets related development and continuity of use. (b) IAUS proposed public/private boundary. The new boundary is defined to include spatial defining elements of the street space. This helps to ensure a correlation of continuity of use with physical continuity within the public domain. New implementation devices accompany the new boundary definition. (c) IAUS proposed development system. Outside of the new public/private boundary, private development retains control of development subject to other zoning and program controls.

3. IAUS proposed development system extended to include additional parcels.

Streets in the Central Area of a Small American City

The Institute for Architecture and Urban Studies Project Team:
Peter Eisenman, Vincent Moore, Peter Wolf,
Victor Caliandro, Thomas Schumacher, Judith Magel

Background

This section is a condensed report of the IAUS case study, carried out in Binghamton, New York, during the second year of work on the comprehensive study of urban streets. In this phase of work many concepts presented in earlier chapters concerning street space and its relation to the built environment were tested in the field. The study was intended to demonstrate how, through an approach here termed the Design Process Model, a redefinition of public space can point to design solutions for the urban street.

One of the problems with planning and architecture today is that the spaces between buildings are rarely designed. This is especially true in the case of this century's Modern Movement in architecture. In contrast, planning in the seventeenth and eighteenth centuries was concerned with total composition and organization (whether for utilitarian, aesthetic, iconic, defensive, or, as in most cases, a complex of such reasons). In the nineteenth century, as buildings became more utilitarian in their organization, the notion of function was gradually displaced from the external spaces to the organization of internal space. A building tended to become, in itself, more of an object, separate from its context. However, even as late as 1920, buildings were still commonly thought of as a background and a context for public urban space. Prime examples can be found in many of the American college campuses planned and developed throughout the nineteenth and twentieth centuries. For example, at Yale and Princeton, most of the buildings, up until the 1920s were considered as the generators of a context; they defined the space rather than merely displaced it.

In the Modern Movement, the building as a free-standing element — the building-in-the-park idea of Le Corbusier — became a pervasive notion. Beyond its inherent limits, Le Corbusier's metaphor was initially abused by the production of objectlike buildings, whether they were "in the park" or not — objects standing on plazas in isolation, in parking lots, with public or street space poorly conceived and often merely left over. This concept reversed the older idea still evident in the denser parts of the nineteenth-century grid towns, where the buildings and the street network reinforced each other. The new tower buildings, devoid of necessary relationships to the street grid or context, destroyed the integrity of the street space. Public urban space more and more served a merely utilitarian function, that of getting people from Point A to Point B. The iconic function of the public urban space and the sense of space as place were forgotten; frequently, the only places of perceptible utility were the spaces inside buildings. The iconic function shifted to the buildings themselves; urban space was valued as little more than the locus of such objects. Thus, the original polemic of Le Corbusier had a reverse effect. Rather than yielding a parklike city, it produced, in case after case, a central city that was a wasteland; cities, pockmarked with the results of scavenger development, appeared more like bombed-out ruins than images of a twentieth-century utopia.

One motivation for this study was the desire to reverse this process again by conceiving of the street as a positive entity. By positive we do not mean the cosmetic treatments of decorative planting, cobblestones, and bollards inspired by rhetorical and nostalgic notions of the street. On the contrary, we have conceived of the street as a vital part of both the socio-physical structure of cities and the planning process. In our study, we have attempted to define how one might plan to use the street, the primary source of public urban space, as an operative element.

The earlier studies in the Streets Project emphasized that planning today often fails to take advantage of the potential for the public environment to provide both a symbolic and an operational structure for our cities. While much thought is given to traffic studies, to street closings, and to street amenities (signs, benches, lighting, and so on), only slight consideration has been given to phenomena that the street reveals dramatically and that are potentially fundamental bases for planning. Basically, these phenomena can be seen as the interface between the public and the private domain and can be described physically, symbolically, socially, economically, and politically. The basic premise of the following work is that although the legally defined street space, from property line to property line, has in past years been a limited factor in the design and renovation of our public environment, the public environment, far beyond what is implied in property ownership, land use, and zoning envelopes, is a major resource for planned urban improvements.

Public/Private Boundaries

The major factor underlying such a premise is the notion that the volume of the street space provides a complex hierarchy of symbolic and operational forces. The interface between the public environment and the private domain is a significant artifact, mutually interactive and therefore important to both. This phenomenon is too often ignored in the design process. Consequently, this interface, which we call the public/private boundary, became the focus of our study. The assumption was that this zone could be analyzed and designed to produce a more structured public environment, not in the traditional sense of street grid as structure but rather in terms of a hierarchy of spaces, serving as place and link, as transition from public to private, and as a container for a range of public uses. In such a conception, the street space is no longer simply the public open space of the street, but can be used freely by the pedestrian. The delineation of the public/private boundary suggests also that space which is under private ownership but is publicly used (for example, lobby space) can be responsive to public needs. Further public design and control of all space, from the traffic channel to the public/private boundary, might ensure that the configuration of this space would provide for an enhanced public use.

Normative Characteristics

Identification of the public/private boundary constituted one area of a larger investigation into the normative characteristics of the urban street. These norms may be divided into two categories: those concerned with the street's specific function (for example, as a residential or commercial street) and those related to its place in the overall structure. Planning methods are dominated by those normative conditions that shape streets according to standards for vehicular movement channels or for the proper light and air for surrounding buildings and pedestrian movement. Such things as the interrelationship between vehicle characteristics (weight, height, width, and speed) and the geometrics of the pathway utilized for movement (road alignments, sight distances on vertical or horizontal curves, pavement width, and so forth) are usually considered to be the basis for street design. However, there are other, qualitative characteristics of a street, such as the order in which its path and its built elements mass and create vistas and other welcomed variations in the urban environment, and these may have little to do with its function or with a quantification of its physical dimensions.

Street Types

Implicit in the development of a matrix of normative street characteristics is the delineation of street types. Once defined, these types, and their ascribed normative features, can become standards in a communal arbitration process. Such standards would militate against destructive communal violation of otherwise unrecognized street characteristics or specifications. In this way, the street itself would act as an arbitrative device. For example, a residential street and a shopping street in proximity to one another might generate conflicts: the merchants want to have parking on their streets; the neighborhood people do not, because they feel that parking is an activity not indigenous to their community and can make a potential play area unsafe. Given the normative relations for the street type involved, the decision-making body would have guidelines for action. To the interest group that wants to close the street, we might say: if you close this street there will be less traffic but also,

contrary to a generally perceived need, less monitoring of the public open space.

Use of Interventions

In these instances, one works back from a particular intervention to find the characteristics that accrue to such an intervention, but the process works in two ways. As in the example given, one confronts the advocacy of a particular intervention, e.g., closing a street; one demonstrates that the likely results of this action are inconsistent with stated goals; and thus one calls for either a reformulation of goals or alternative interventions. Perhaps the desired local action (more parking, street closing) is consistent with the characteristics of a nearby street and will, systemically, have the desired effects on the street first considered. Thus, one starts from a range of possible interventions and determines the best place to act. Alternatively, one starts at the other end and says: here is the street, here is its context; from analysis, here are the kinds of interventions that would apply to this particular street. In seeking to find normative conditions for a particular street, we might first examine significant issues for each of the streets in question. For example, What is the future of the shopping street and what are the alternative means of access? Is the residential street truly a good residential environment, and if not, why not? Are there places for, or already existing, mixed use that might be mutually beneficial to both a residential and a shopping street?

Background: Binghamton

Binghamton had a downtown community faced with the problem of strategically manipulating its street design to provide for and promote the use of off-street parking for its commercial community while at the same time preserving the integrity of a residential community. Without adequate parking facilities the downtown shops were losing business to suburban shopping centers in a pattern that was similar to other cities across the country. One way to generate enough activity downtown was to provide enough parking to accommodate the shops and also accommodate other agencies such as those housed in new office and civic facilities. A related problem for the residential community was that of cars using residential and neighborhood streets as parking areas or short cuts around peak-hour traffic routes. These two issues led to planning problems that were directly resolvable in terms of the way we would intervene on the street. Do we close certain streets? Do we widen certain streets? How can the integrity of the community and residential amenities be maintained while also providing adequate parking? Thus,

Binghamton provided us with a good case in which to test our model.

We were seeking the reasons for intervention in the street system relative to recognized community goals, reasons to, say, close or otherwise adapt a street, going beyond the rather arbitrary fashion in which streets are physically changed today in many cities. If street closing is one viable way to produce a better urban environment, how do you determine what streets are closed? For what length? At what times? What are the effects on adjacent streets? To provide a more objective model for dealing with design problems, to facilitate the reexamination of specific aspects or feedbacks in the planning process, and to evaluate alternative proposed street interventions, the findings of the Binghamton study served as a base for the development of the Design Process Model and the Process Matrix. The former is basically a flow chart of the planning process and as such is helpful in organizing the work and in presenting the major data-collection techniques (of which the streets game is probably the most innovative). It outlines the steps of the planning-making process without analyzing the decision-making process of each of these steps. The Process Matrix maps the development of an ideal concept model (concept model A) through the use of the Design Process Model.

We have seen how the street acts both as a major resource for physical intervention in the public sector and as a potential arbitrative mechanism in the resolution of conflicts of interest in the planning process. The architect/planner, having to deal with many interest groups (in Binghamton's case, the Model Cities Agency, the Urban Renewal Agency, the Mayor's office, the Broome County Planning Office, the Merchants Association, the Model Cities Community) as well as with the physical context of the street(s), assumes the role of arbiter. A design model such as the Process Matrix, which systematically outlines street data and graphically projects these data against a set of goals and pretested design solutions, provides him with a set of normative criteria for street design. In the analysis of the adjacent commercial and residential street problem, the architect/planner may seek design alternatives based on criteria provided by the Process Matrix. In the present case, the arbitrated decision might be that an existing residential street would serve better as a shopping street, and that a house eventually should be moved. Then, the first step toward this goal might be to increase the parking in that area so as to begin to generate a shopping street. In each case, the architect/planner's role in the arbitration would be based on what the street could do to generate, maintain, and articulate a better city structure in both its symbolic and functional senses. Our problem was to determine what kind of information was necessary to make such a decision and what other planning decisions could be made in this way.

In summary, in order for the arbitration process to work, certain

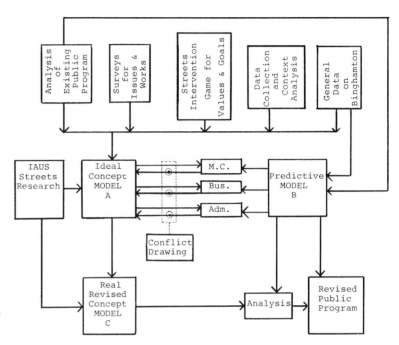

4. Design process model.

KEY
+ PROBABILITY OF A POSITIVE INTERACTION
− PROBABILITY OF A NEGATIVE INTERACTION
○ GENERALLY DESIRABLE RELATIONSHIP
● GENERALLY UNDESIRABLE RELATIONSHIP

PERFORMANCE RELATIONSHIPS MATRIX

CONTEXT SCALE

5. The process matrix.

normative specifications for the street have to be established. If streets are functional artifacts, then they should be designed so as to best accommodate the needs or goals (whether utilitarian, physical, social, or psychological) that have been ascribed to them. This phase of the project was intended to elucidate characteristics of the urban street other than those that solely satisfy functional requirements. Thus, it has sought to answer such questions as: What is a good street? How are the criteria for a residential or shopping street different? How does a street contribute to a better city structure and a better place in itself? Are there certain characteristics that may be necessary to a commercial street as opposed to a residential street? The characteristics or qualities that respond to these questions are the normative specifications for each street type. They define street characteristics relative to goals. For example, if the stated goal for a particular street was to facilitate movement from one place to another, the link characteristics must be respected in the overall plan so that it would fulfill this function. Other goals that ultimately affect the iconic potential of the environment are increasing the sense of enclosure or of spaciousness, increasing the surprise quality of a street, and so on. Thus, both functional and nonfunctional goals are recognized.

Once goals and interventions have been enumerated, the relationship between them can be quantified. If, for example, an increasingly simple order of the form leads to a corresponding increase in the link capacity of the street and in the overt structure of the context, then an increase in the variety of the form may result in a decrease in both the link capacity of the street and the apparent structure of the context.

The Process Matrix is used to develop the actual normative relationships for a particular street type; that is, the relationship between the normative goal intervention and a particular street type.

Issues and Goals

Working together, the IAUS team and the Binghamton Task Force developed a list of community objectives for downtown Binghamton and potential street interventions applicable within the context of the impact area. This list indicated the major tendencies in the downtown area that the community and the design team chose to reinforce or diminish, depending on which goals were to be met. Earlier phases of the IAUS Streets Study permitted the design team to make preliminary judgments as to the normative condition of different Binghamton streets, and these fell into categories enumerated in the street-type analysis.

Streets Game

In order to refine the range of community goals for a good public environment and possible corresponding street interventions, the Streets Game was developed. It consisted of a game board in the form of a map for the site area in Binghamton and two sets of chips: one set coded to represent a range of possible issues and goals involving streets; the other coded to represent a range of possible interventions on the street. The players of the game, either individually or in groups, were supplied with a list of interventions in a priority order from the most direct intervention on a street (a street closing) to the least direct intervention (land use in the adjacent buildings). Players were asked to place the various chips in what they considered to be appropriate places. They were asked to state the reason each chip was placed where it was. When a group or individual had placed all the chips desired, the resultant board set was photographed and then drawn as a record of a particular group's desire — for example, that this or that street be removed or this or that street receive an increase in its commercial uses.

When the game was first played, the moves represented thinking on the part of the individuals that was similar to traditional city planning and lacked any kind of overall strategy for putting chips down. Most people started out as if they were making a land-use diagram, putting an increased parking chip on one site, an increased shopping chip on the other site, and so on. Implicitly, they were saying that it was land use that had the major effect on the nature of the street, though only because land use was a familiar reference to them. In order to change the nature of their thinking — to get them to think about the street rather than the land use first — we changed the nature of the game. This was done through the development of a series of priorities for using chips. Land-use chips were made the last chips to be used. An individual started work directly from the street environment, employing direct street interventions such as closing a street or altering the width of a street. Then he had to think: Why should the street be wide? Should it act rather as a barrier? Do I want to get to my neighborhood from downtown via that street? Do I want others to do that? These are the kinds of questions we raised when we instituted a priority system for the way the game was to be played. The results that were recorded became part of the context analysis.

In this context, the street game represents a participatory aspect to the planning process. However, as a methodological control on the planning process, three theoretical models were developed. The first of these, Model A, describes an ideal situation in which a set of goals is directly translated into the corresponding set of interventions. The ideal nature of the model refers to the fact that the action of different interest groups and economic considerations, which ordinarily have a very real

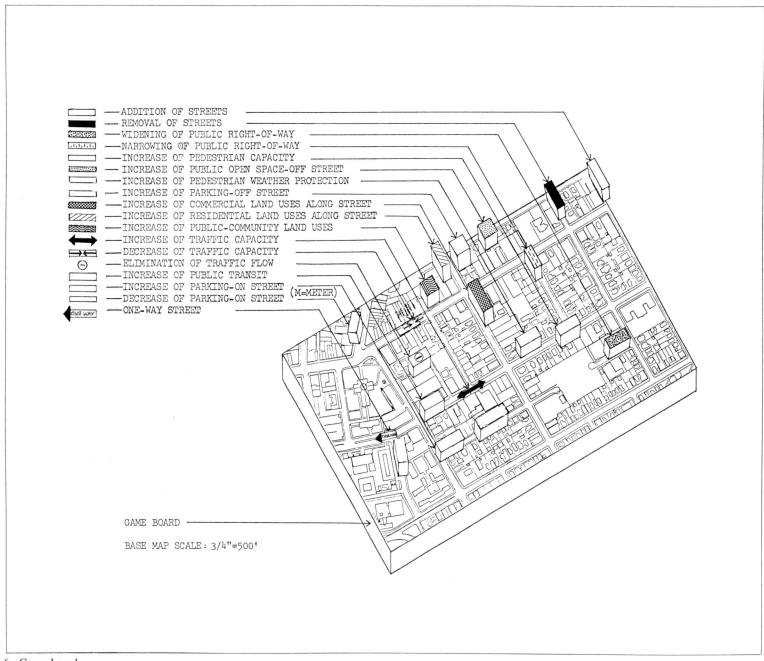

ADDITION OF STREETS
REMOVAL OF STREETS
WIDENING OF PUBLIC RIGHT-OF-WAY
NARROWING OF PUBLIC RIGHT-OF-WAY
INCREASE OF PEDESTRIAN CAPACITY
INCREASE OF PUBLIC OPEN SPACE-OFF STREET
INCREASE OF PEDESTRIAN WEATHER PROTECTION
INCREASE OF PARKING-OFF STREET
INCREASE OF COMMERCIAL LAND USES ALONG STREET
INCREASE OF RESIDENTIAL LAND USES ALONG STREET
INCREASE OF PUBLIC-COMMUNITY LAND USES
INCREASE OF TRAFFIC CAPACITY
DECREASE OF TRAFFIC CAPACITY
ELIMINATION OF TRAFFIC FLOW
INCREASE OF PUBLIC TRANSIT
INCREASE OF PARKING-ON STREET
DECREASE OF PARKING-ON STREET   (M=METER)
ONE-WAY STREET

GAME BOARD

BASE MAP SCALE: 3/4"=500'

6. Game board.

effect on planning proposals, is not considered. Model A is a straightforward equation of desired goals and planning interventions to yield an ideal urban context developed from the use of the street as the primary resource. As such, Model A serves as a lexicon of planning interventions. The second, Model B, describes those development projects that seem likely to occur in downtown Binghamton over the next few years if there are no new interventions. Thus, it provides an estimate of the minimum level of implementation resources available to the city over this time period and a base against which the ideal model can be compared.

Model C describes ''what could be'' in Binghamton. It is a synthesis of A and B. The proposals for Lisle Avenue in Binghamton, which are described later in this report, represent, on the street scale, part of Model C for this context.

Planning is a decision-making process. The IAUS study focuses on street-oriented planning, advocating a decision-making process that iteratively moves from the scale of context to that of individual street and from the street to the land parcel. Decisions at the context scale qualify rather than restrict physical planning since they are usually limited to large organizational decisions. Thus, a decision at the context level should not force a particular form on any particular parcel but rather should suggest a structure from which a range of specific configurations would be suitable. When interventions are applied in wholesale fashion at the context scale, the planning becomes locked into possible manipulations of the environment that may have negative effects on individual streets. The intention of the process presented here is to preserve flexibility in the planning process as one descends in scale so that each intervention may have a rationale at both the scale of the context and the scale of the street. Nevertheless, proposed design interventions for specific streets are ultimately based on previous analysis of the overall context within which such physical systems operate. The context scale for this particular study was downtown Binghamton.

Collection of Data Context Defined

In order to define this context, two types of surveys were taken. The first of these was a survey of the physical characteristics of the area. Data were collected on such things as the nature of intersections, traffic flow, and density. This information was mapped at both the macro-scale of context and the micro-scale of the individual street and was translated into a set of implications for street design.

The second survey involved a canvassing of individual residents' conceptions of their neighborhood and how they operated in it. Resi-

dents were asked such things as, What do you conceive of as your physical neighborhood? What do you consider downtown? Do you shop downtown? These questions refer to the context scale and were illustrated through context diagrams.

To find out the residents' conception of the individual streets in their neighborhood, the IAUS team asked them such questions as, Where is the edge of the street? Where do you park your car? Where do your children play? Once summarized, these data led to a set of street diagrams or maps.

The coding of both the context and the street maps reflect the hierarchical nature of the decision-making process. The mapping did not primarily deal with recording existing conditions, but served as a tool for analyzing these conditions in such a way as to reveal latent conditions that, given a set of specific goals such as the ones articulated for Binghamton, could be manipulated. Interventions in themselves are valueless. They must respond to a specified set of community-responsible goals.

Articulation of Goals

In addition to the two surveys, community goals were also determined through interviews with various community interest groups and through the playing of the Streets Game. This approach enabled the IAUS team to define accurately the downtown shopping area, Model Cities Neighborhood issues, specific street-related issues, and general community goals for the context area. In the Binghamton study, the street-scale investigation was predicated on the notion of the public/private boundary and the inadequacy and even detrimental effect traditional planning and zoning have had on the design of streets. An important objective in planning should be to make streets more responsive to their social as well as their physical context. Attention must be directed to the nature and sense of the public space and the contribution of the public/private boundary to them.

When the physical structure does not provide any form of notation in terms of what is public and what is private, it tends to create a psychic dislocation — a situation where the individual does not clearly conceptualize his environment and thus does not understand the physical signs present in that environment. He might feel alienated from what is supposed to serve as public space. However, the conception of zoning that exists does not have the capacity to make such physical signs available to him through the control of the interface between public and private spaces.

The IAUS's development of the concept of the public/private boundary was predicated on an idea that public space should be parceled in such a way that it would be controlled by a kind of public zoning. Under

7a. Alternative combinations of physical interventions: Court Street W.

Intervention Combinations: I₁ Court Street West

Intervention Types	Court Street	Exchange Street	Lisle Avenue	Tudor Street
Intervention Number — Type of Physical Intervention				
Changes to street system				
1. a. Addition of streets to pattern	●			
b. Removal of streets from pattern	●			
c. Intrusion of grids				
d. Interpenetration of grids				
Changes to individual streets				
2. a. Closing of streets	●			
b. Filling streets with buildings				
c. Removal of buildings along street				
d. Addition to existing buildings	●			
e. Placement of new buildings on vacant land	●			
f. Replacement of existing buildings	●			
g. Changes to street and sidewalk surface				
h. Widening of public right-of-way				
i. Narrowing of public right-of-way				
j. Creation of new public right-of-way				
Changes to Land-Use pattern				
3. a. Increase commercial land use	●			
b. Decrease commercial land use				
c. Increase residential land use	●			
d. Decrease residential land use				
e. Increase public land use				
f. Decrease public land use				
g. Increase industrial land use				
h. Decrease industrial land use				
Changes to circulation patterns				
4. a. Closing street to traffic	●			
b. Reduction of traffic capacity				
c. Increase of traffic capacity				
d. Making street one-way	●			
e. Increase of public transit				

7b. Alternative combinations of physical interventions: Court Street W.

Intervention Combinations: I₂ Court Street West

Intervention Types		Court Street	Exchange Street	Lisle Avenue	Tudor Street
Intervention Number	Type of Physical Intervention				
Changes to street system					
1. a.	Addition of streets to pattern	●			
b.	Removal of streets from pattern				
c.	Intrusion of grids				
d.	Interpenetration of grids				
Changes to individual streets					
2. a.	Closing of streets	●			
b.	Filling streets with buildings				
c.	Removal of buildings along street				
d.	Addition to existing buildings	●			
e.	Placement of new buildings on vacant land	●			
f.	Replacement of existing buildings	●			
g.	Changes to street and sidewalk surface				
h.	Widening of public right-of-way	●			
i.	Narrowing of public right-of-way	●			
j.	Creation of new public right-of-way				
Changes to Land-Use pattern					
3. a.	Increase commercial land use	●			
b.	Decrease commercial land use				
c.	Increase residential land use				
d.	Decrease residential land use				
e.	Increase public land use	●			
f.	Decrease public land use				
g.	Increase industrial land use				
h.	Decrease industrial land use				
Changes to circulation patterns					
4. a.	Closing street to traffic	●			
b.	Reduction of traffic capacity	●			
c.	Increase of traffic capacity	●			
d.	Making street one-way				
e.	Increase of public transit				

8a. Alternative combinations of physical interventions: Court Street E.

Intervention Combinations: II₁ Court Street East

Intervention Types		Court Street	Exchange Street	Lisle Avenue	Tudor Street
Intervention Number	Type of Physical Intervention				
Changes to street system					
1. a.	Addition of streets to pattern	●			
b.	Removal of streets from pattern	●			
c.	Intrusion of grids				
d.	Interpenetration of grids				
Changes to individual streets					
2. a.	Closing of streets				
b.	Filling streets with buildings				
c.	Removal of buildings along street				
d.	Addition to existing buildings				
e.	Placement of new buildings on vacant land	●			
f.	Replacement of existing buildings	●			
g.	Changes to street and sidewalk surface				
h.	Widening of public right-of-way				
i.	Narrowing of public right-of-way				
j.	Creation of new public right-of-way				
Changes to Land-Use pattern					
3. a.	Increase commercial land use	●			
b.	Decrease commercial land use				
c.	Increase residential land use	●			
d.	Decrease residential land use				
e.	Increase public land use				
f.	Decrease public land use				
g.	Increase industrial land use				
h.	Decrease industrial land use				
Changes to circulation patterns					
4. a.	Closing street to traffic				
b.	Reduction of traffic capacity				
c.	Increase of traffic capacity				
d.	Making street one-way				
e.	Increase of public transit				

8b. Alternative combinations of physical interventions: Court Street E.

Intervention Combinations: II₂ Court Street East

Intervention Types		Court Street	Exchange Street	Lisle Avenue	Tudor Street
Intervention Number	Type of Physical Intervention				
Changes to street system					
1. a.	Addition of streets to pattern	●			
b.	Removal of streets from pattern				
c.	Intrusion of grids				
d.	Interpenetration of grids				
Changes to individual streets					
2. a.	Closing of streets	●			
b.	Filling streets with buildings				
c.	Removal of buildings along street				
d.	Addition to existing buildings				
e.	Placement of new buildings on vacant land	●			
f.	Replacement of existing buildings	●			
g.	Changes to street and sidewalk surface				
h.	Widening of public right-of-way	●			
i.	Narrowing of public right-of-way				
j.	Creation of new public right-of-way				
Changes to Land-Use pattern					
3. a.	Increase commercial land use	●			
b.	Decrease commercial land use				
c.	Increase residential land use	●			
d.	Decrease residential land use				
e.	Increase public land use				
f.	Decrease public land use				
g.	Increase industrial land use				
h.	Decrease industrial land use				
Changes to circulation patterns					
4. a.	Closing street to traffic				
b.	Reduction of traffic capacity				
c.	Increase of traffic capacity				
d.	Making street one-way	●			
e.	Increase of public transit				

9a. Alternative combinations of physical interventions: Court Street W. and Exchange Street.

Intervention Combinations: III₁ Court Street West
Exchange Street

Intervention Types		Court Street	Exchange Street	Lisle Avenue	Tudor Street
Intervention Number	Type of Physical Intervention				
Changes to street system					
1. a.	Addition of streets to pattern		●		
b.	Removal of streets from pattern				
c.	Intrusion of grids				
d.	Interpenetration of grids				
Changes to individual streets					
2. a.	Closing of streets				
b.	Filling streets with buildings		●		
c.	Removal of buildings along street				
d.	Addition to existing buildings	●	●		
e.	Placement of new buildings on vacant land		●		
f.	Replacement of existing buildings				
g.	Changes to street and sidewalk surface				
h.	Widening of public right-of-way		●		
i.	Narrowing of public right-of-way				
j.	Creation of new public right-of-way				
Changes to Land-Use pattern					
3. a.	Increase commercial land use	●	●		
b.	Decrease commercial land use				
c.	Increase residential land use				
d.	Decrease residential land use				
e.	Increase public land use	●			
f.	Decrease public land use				
g.	Increase industrial land use				
h.	Decrease industrial land use				
Changes to circulation patterns					
4. a.	Closing street to traffic				
b.	Reduction of traffic capacity				
c.	Increase of traffic capacity				
d.	Making street one-way				
e.	Increase of public transit				

9b. Alternative combinations of physical interventions: Court Street W. and Exchange Street.

Intervention Combinations: III₂ Court Street West
Exchange Street

Intervention Types		Court Street	Exchange Street	Lisle Avenue	Tudor Street
Intervention Number	Type of Physical Intervention				
Changes to street system					
1. a.	Addition of streets to pattern				
b.	Removal of streets from pattern	●			
c.	Intrusion of grids				
d.	Interpenetration of grids				
Changes to individual streets					
2. a.	Closing of streets	●			
b.	Filling streets with buildings	●			
c.	Removal of buildings along street				
d.	Addition to existing buildings	●			
e.	Placement of new buildings on vacant land	●			
f.	Replacement of existing buildings	●			
g.	Changes to street and sidewalk surface				
h.	Widening of public right-of-way				
i.	Narrowing of public right-of-way	●			
j.	Creation of new public right-of-way				
Changes to Land-Use pattern					
3. a.	Increase commercial land use	●			
b.	Decrease commercial land use				
c.	Increase residential land use				
d.	Decrease residential land use				
e.	Increase public land use	●			
f.	Decrease public land use				
g.	Increase industrial land use				
h.	Decrease industrial land use				
Changes to circulation patterns					
4. a.	Closing street to traffic	●			
b.	Reduction of traffic capacity	●			
c.	Increase of traffic capacity	●			
d.	Making street one-way				
e.	Increase of public transit				

10a. Alternative combinations of physical interventions: Court Street E.

Intervention Combinations: IV₁ Court Street East

Intervention Types		Court Street	Exchange Street	Lisle Avenue	Tudor Street
Intervention Number	Type of Physical Intervention				
Changes to street system					
1. a.	Addition of streets to pattern	●			
b.	Removal of streets from pattern				
c.	Intrusion of grids				
d.	Interpenetration of grids				
Changes to individual streets					
2. a.	Closing of streets				
b.	Filling streets with buildings				
c.	Removal of buildings along street				
d.	Addition to existing buildings	●			
e.	Placement of new buildings on vacant land	●			
f.	Replacement of existing buildings	●			
g.	Changes to street and sidewalk surface				
h.	Widening of public right-of-way				
i.	Narrowing of public right-of-way				
j.	Creation of new public right-of-way				
Changes to Land-Use pattern					
3. a.	Increase commercial land use	●			
b.	Decrease commercial land use				
c.	Increase residential land use	●			
d.	Decrease residential land use				
e.	Increase public land use				
f.	Decrease public land use				
g.	Increase industrial land use				
h.	Decrease industrial land use				
Changes to circulation patterns					
4. a.	Closing street to traffic				
b.	Reduction of traffic capacity	●			
c.	Increase of traffic capacity	●			
d.	Making street one-way	●			
e.	Increase of public transit	●			

10b. Alternative combinations of physical interventions: Court Street E.

Intervention Combinations: IV₂ Court Street East

Intervention Types		Court Street	Exchange Street	Lisle Avenue	Tudor Street
Intervention Number	Type of Physical Intervention				
Changes to street system					
1. a.	Addition of streets to pattern				
b.	Removal of streets from pattern				
c.	Intrusion of grids				
d.	Interpenetration of grids				
Changes to individual streets					
2. a.	Closing of streets	●			
b.	Filling streets with buildings	●			
c.	Removal of buildings along street				
d.	Addition to existing buildings	●			
e.	Placement of new buildings on vacant land	●			
f.	Replacement of existing buildings	●			
g.	Changes to street and sidewalk surface				
h.	Widening of public right-of-way				
i.	Narrowing of public right-of-way	●			
j.	Creation of new public right-of-way				
Changes to Land-Use pattern					
3. a.	Increase commercial land use	●			
b.	Decrease commercial land use				
c.	Increase residential land use	●			
d.	Decrease residential land use				
e.	Increase public land use				
f.	Decrease public land use				
g.	Increase industrial land use				
h.	Decrease industrial land use				
Changes to circulation patterns					
4. a.	Closing street to traffic				
b.	Reduction of traffic capacity	●			
c.	Increase of traffic capacity	●			
d.	Making street one-way				
e.	Increase of public transit				

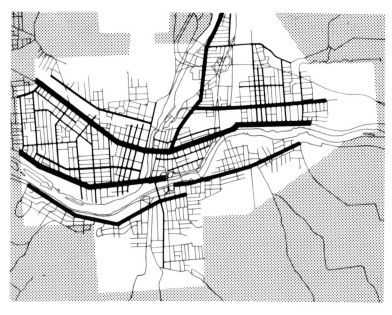

INTERSECTIONS PER STREET   PHYSICAL ANALYSIS

8-15
16-30
31-40
41+

11. Example of data collected.

such zoning the public/private boundary could be used as a control mechanism, providing physical signs or guidelines as to the nature and relationship of one street space to the next. The design of the street facade would become something other than mere design of the proportions of openings and the selection of materials. The privately contracted architect would be forced to recognize that he has a responsibility to the public as well as to the private domain when designing a street front, for the facade of a building can have a profound effect on the nature of a street. (It is conceivable that such responsibility should also extend into the lobby area since this area usually serves as a semipublic space). The physical volumes of the buildings would not have to conform to one another or relate to one another in scale; rather the bulk behind the public/private boundary could be designed to any kind of configuration in more purely functional terms. In this context, design is seen as primarily concerned with the vertical and horizontal surfaces that define the street volume. The facade becomes a containing envelope defining the public/private boundary.

Depending on the normative conditions set for a particular street type, there may be either a continuous or discontinuous public/private boundary, just as that boundary may or may not be coincident with the facade. Thus, the shape of the public environment is not the shape of the space external to the building. It is a product of the normative conditions for the street type involved and the extent to which these have been manipulated by the public and private sectors. The IAUS study proposes that the public environment is a positive entity with a facade and a horizontal surface that extends past the street bed and that does not necessarily stop at the traditional solid building envelope.

For each street type it is possible to define certain characteristics about the nature of the public volume and the public/private boundary. The street-scale analysis done in Binghamton sought to define the normative conditions for various street types. Lisle Avenue, because it seems amenable to change in the near future, was one of the streets selected for detailed development. The analysis of the transactional areas and space-defining qualities of its facades resulted in a set of proposals for physically transforming the street design. Segments of the street were drawn isometrically to show the critical relationships of space types to each other and to help in defining the nature of the public/private boundary.

Lisle Avenue was a deteriorating central-city street of residential-light industrial use. The IAUS study proposed it be redeveloped as a new type of park-street in the service of the neighborhood. The analysis of Lisle Avenue involved a consideration of the nature of housing in an urban context.

Housing is usually considered independently of its context. For example, much new housing is considered as prefabricated components

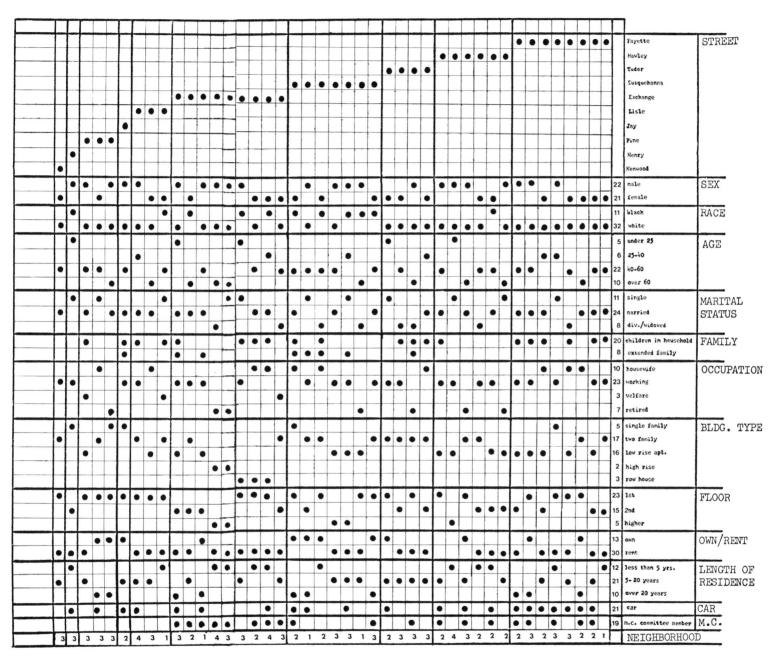

12. Characteristics of respondents. Example of resident/user survey.

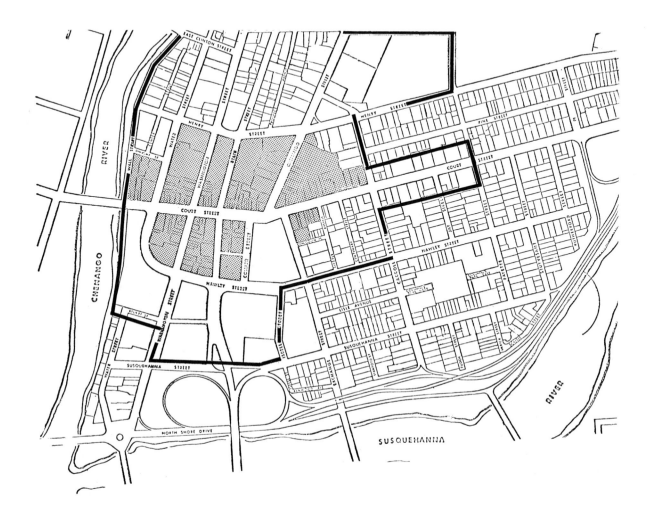

12a. Context diagram. Major fields, downtown.

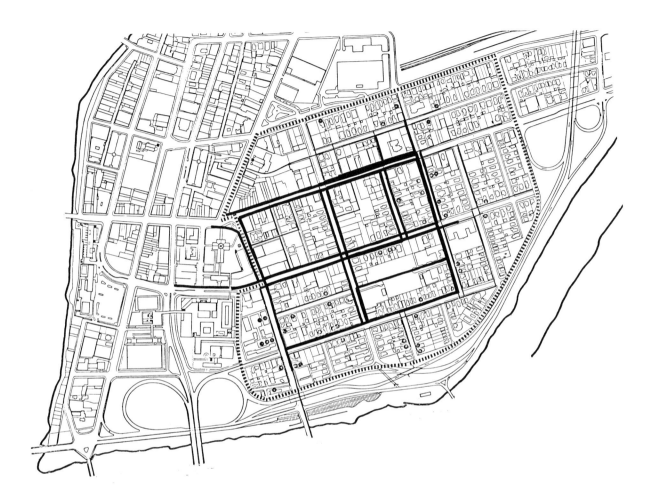

12b. Street diagram. Summary of walking routes.

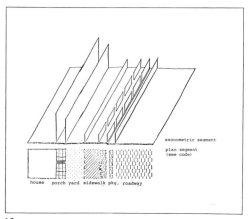

axonometric segment

plan segment
(see code)

house   porch yard sidewalk pkg. roadway

13

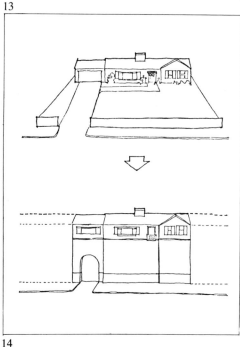

14

capable of being slotted into any environment. This attitude leaves a critical aspect unattended: the relationship of house to street or private boundary to public boundary. Lack of attention to this important interface has created a situation in which public street space and the house have become separated, the public space being thought of as belonging to someone else. Public space has therefore gradually become anonymous and unsafe.

On Lisle Avenue the IAUS proposed to consider the house and the street as an integral unit in the design of a street. That is, those portions of the house that relate to the public domain — its facade, its garages, its front stoop, its front lawn — were considered as part of the design of the street. Thus, the street became a three-dimensional element, the design of which was seen to include part of what was previously considered the private house. In a sense, the private house was seen as potentially attachable to this new street element, which may have different zoning, different administrative and economic structures, and different definitions of parcels for development.

The IAUS proposals for Lisle Avenue cannot be understood apart from their new conceptual context as based on general interventions prescribed for downtown Binghamton. These interventions, except for the closing and opening of streets, do not represent physical manipulations of the environment. Rather, the decisions made at the context scale, which form the basis of the intervention plans (concept Models A and C), explain intentions that can, at the smaller scale of the individual street project, be easily and responsibly converted into physical design.

In this manner, the individual street and the building types and forms within a street's domain may be programmed and designed in terms of a general streets plan. Lisle Avenue's existing place in the street structure of its local context is ambiguous in a negative way. It is a potential, but at present unused, link in a pedestrian system from the new government center and residential project on its west to Columbus Park on its east. The potential for Lisle Avenue may be realized by changing its relationship to other streets by context interventions in terms of alteration of the street pattern through the addition and removal of streets. Columbus Park can be effectively extended west by making Lisle Avenue into a small-scale urban parkway.

The context plan also calls for a general increase of residential land uses along Lisle Avenue. The present residential density is extremely low, with large gaps in the continuity of the built-form structure.

On the street scale, the IAUS proposal for Lisle Avenue calls for a continuous street facade on either side of a narrow park strip, providing a direct bridge connection to the housing project on the west and a greenbelt link with Columbus Park. The plan provides for housing as the primary land use, but the ends of the blocks allow for the mixing of housing with other activities.

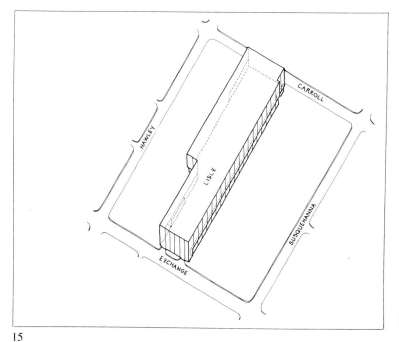

15

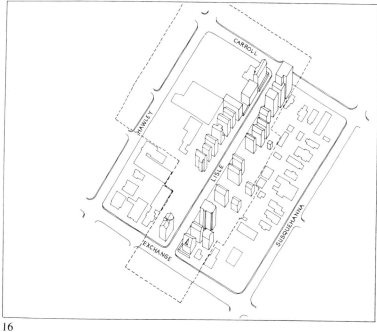

16

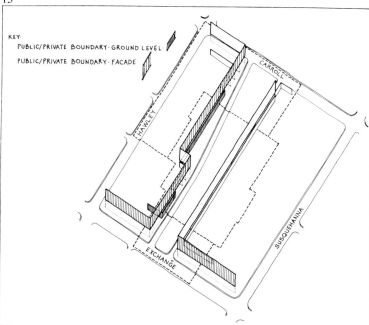

KEY
PUBLIC/PRIVATE BOUNDARY·GROUND LEVEL
PUBLIC/PRIVATE BOUNDARY·FACADE

17

13. Axonometric diagram showing spatial order on Lisle Avenue. Existing spatial zones do not provide "place" quality pedestrian space, only "link" quality pedestrian and automobile space.

14. Diagrams of typical American detached house. Lawn reads as an illusionistic vertical plane and serves as a barrier between public and private use, without enclosing street space.

15. Lisle Avenue, schematic street space drawn as solid.

16. Lisle Avenue, Binghamton. Existing built form configuration.

17. Lisle Avenue, proposed schematic location of the public/private boundary.

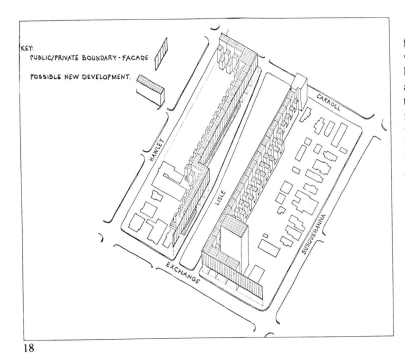

KEY:
PUBLIC/PRIVATE BOUNDARY - FACADE

POSSIBLE NEW DEVELOPMENT.

18

The street space of Lisle Avenue is defined by a consistent vertical facade plane on both north and south sides. These facades are consistent with the building mass and scale of the surrounding context. High-rise buildings are eschewed in the plan, as a result of community opposition and the IAUS context decisions concerning scale and density. Density is to be increased without drastically altering the scale of the residential neighborhood. In the IAUS proposal, the number of dwelling units is tripled to 124 using a low-rise, medium-density housing and row houses. Two housing types, A and B, were suggested for this avenue. Because of the emphasis placed on relating built environment to unbuilt environment, these units were designed to be especially street-related. Housing type A consists of groups of four units, two ground-level duplexes and two third-level duplexes, with all units directly related to the street through access. The entry stoop that makes its way up to the third level (one and one-half floors up) helps make these units appear more like town houses and thus enhances a relationship to the street. The zones of space developed at the facade, designed as the extension of private space into the street and simultaneously the extension of public space into the private realm, provide an ambiguity of territorial ownership, an aid in the promotion of incidental activities. The literal public/private boundary exists at the surface of the stoop, where a free beam may be introduced to further define this plane. The inclusion of a literal porch (balcony) on the uppermost level and an unprojected balcony at the entry level of the upper units further relate the upper units to the street.

The relationship of housing type B (town houses) to the street is effected by the intrusion of private into public — an extended canopy — and of public into private — a second-level porch carved out of the building volume. A setback from the plane that defines the public/private boundary helps to reinforce the ambiguity of spaces at the facades of the houses. That plane, shown as a free beam or as part of the upper-level facade, follows the site line at a diagonal, while the other facade elements follow an orthogonal relationship, thus maintaining a distinction between elements that belong to the street and those that belong to the building.

The redevelopment ideas for Lisle Avenue are only one example of how street design may be altered through a greater sensitivity to the public/private boundary. Another street that was singled out for intensive analysis was Washington Street (at the Court Street intersection.) Basically, the IAUS team and the community participants in the study wanted to redevelop it into a pedestrian street operating as the core of a commercial redevelopment project. Urban renewal programs have been conceived generally in terms of conventional land parcels, conventional street use, and conventional separation of public space and privately developed parcels. This conception has led to expensive public pro-

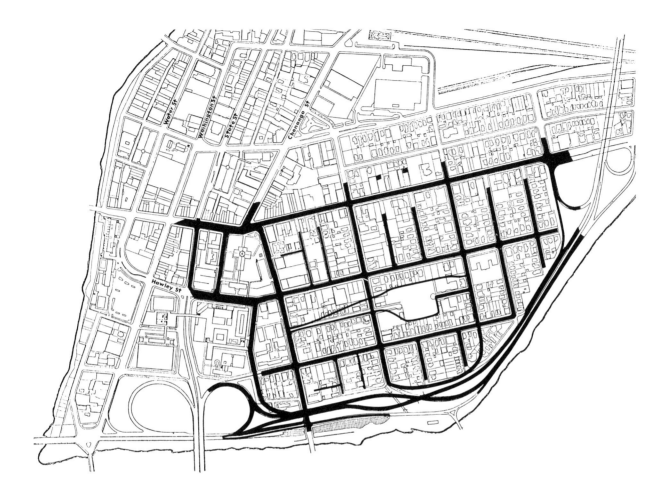

19

18. Lisle Avenue, diagram showing possible future development.

19. Proposed street system, IAUS concept model "C," Binghamton model neighborhood.

20

21

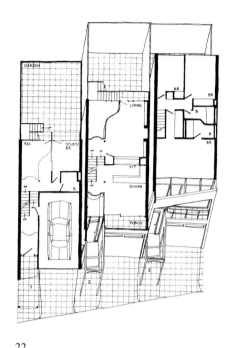

22

23

20. Lisle Avenue, housing type A, plans.

21. Lisle Avenue, axonometric view, housing type A.

22. Lisle Avenue, housing type B, plans.

23. Lisle Avenue, axonometric view, housing type B.

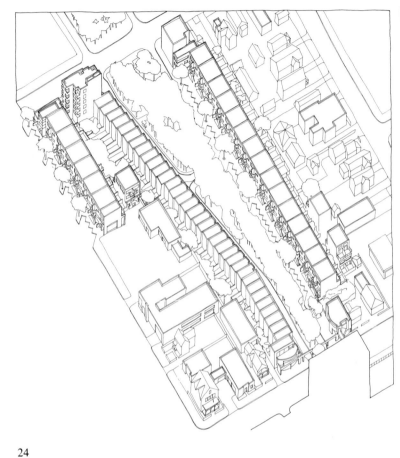

24

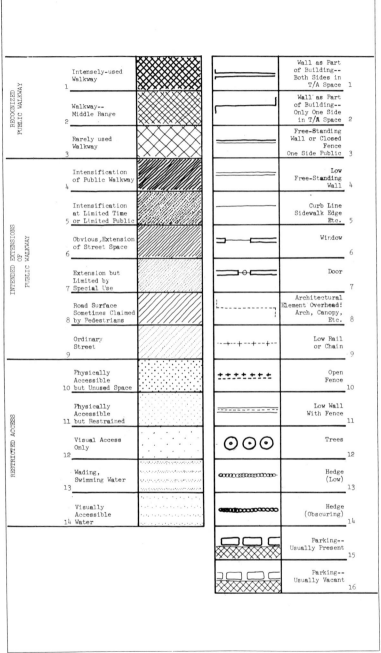

24. Lisle Avenue, axonometric general view.

25. Lisle Avenue, diagrammatic plan showing transactional space analysis.

25a. Key transactional space analysis.

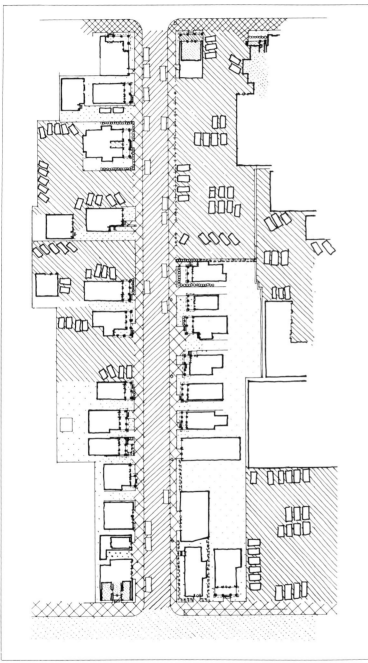

25a

grams from which rebuilding occurs as a mirror image of older, conventional, and, in many cases, unsuccessful land-development patterns.

The IAUS Streets Study was designed to discover and, it is hoped, to implement a new approach to urban development, an approach that focuses on public space as a physical, economic, and administrative component of the total urban fabric. With this approach, the design of places in which people walk, transact business, and congregate is given a priority heretofore denied. These transactional spaces, which are in reality the life blood of a successful central business district, are the focal point for the proposal of a new kind of urban street for Washington Street, the central spine of a middle-sized regional center.

The IAUS Streets Project sought to expand the concept of street design to a consideration of planning ideas beyond the random closing of a street or the addition of park benches and new street lighting. Such factors as the social, economic, and administrative integration of the public and private domain, implemented through a design process, extend what was previously thought to be the street space (in its conventional, wall-bounded sense) to include both physical and social continuity and access to private buildings. This expanded conception requires the implementation of new urban-planning devices that will provide for new parceling and zoning.

Rethinking the Urban Street: Its Economic Context

Peter Wolf

Foreword

This essay sets out means for implementing new redevelopment suggested elsewhere in this book. The most imaginative proposals are destined to be lost and forgotten unless accompanied by workable implementative devices. The fascinating history of fantasy, illusion, and utopianism throughout the history of architecture and urbanism exists principally because important ideas were released without any notion of how they might be achieved.

With this in mind, the economic implementative strategies outlined in the following essay largely accept contemporary American political and social realities that do not appear susceptible to change in the intermediate future. Most important among these is the evident, and increasingly disadvantaged, position of cities with respect to political and economic resources compared to suburban areas and state government. Thus, in my judgment, any realizable strategy must discover methods to utilize whatever economic and legislative powers are available to city authorities and still provide reasonable inducement to the private sector to build and rebuild our cities. In many of our cities, and in all of the most viable ones, private interest produces necessary urban development vitality; private investment decisions produce necessary risk capital for construction and redevelopment. Without such forces, urban design ideas such as those proposed in this book cannot be realized; and without them conventional contemporary development in both the public and private sectors will continue to provide less than desirable, less than optimally humanistic cities.

Considering the nature of capital investment feasibility analysis and land ownership patterns in this country, it is also presumed that large-scale, long-term, incrementally accomplished urban design and urban redevelopment goals for the urban street can only be achieved with the assistance and intervention of public authorities. The structure of our economic systems, of our capital resource decisions, and of our social attitudes makes this conclusion both self-evident and inevitable.

The Existing Context

Through a long and well-known history of private initiative in urban and suburban development, the street has become a corridor of access (people, vehicles, utilities) crucial to creating marketable value to abutting private and public property.[1] At the same time the street is conceptually and administratively subsumed within the public domain, shorn of a mechanism for evaluation and of a constituency to advocate the development of its physical and economic potential. It is a residual artifact in the public domain with no coherent program other than the satisfaction of demands placed upon it by the public and private sector for services of many sorts. These services primarily benefit either abutting property owners or people who use the street as a conduit for vehicular transport.

Progressive evolutionary development of concept and design of the urban street has been, in part, restricted by the unavailability of appropriate economic concepts to stimulate realization.[2] These limitations are evident if one recognizes that

1. The field of interaction relevant to the urban street is principally the interpenetration of public and private interests.

2. Public and private financing and value manipulating mechanisms such as loans, mortgages, taxes, and zoning have remained relatively static and inflexible.

3. The acceptable economic unit for finance and construction is still the individual building lot. Few economic devices are generally available for coordinated treatment of large areas under multiple ownership or within the public domain such as the street.

4. Financing, tax, and economic plans are geared to vertical organization from land assessment through assessment of improvements. Mortgages, the basic financial instrument in real estate, are typically only on land and improvements. No device generally exists for horizontal financing that would make it possible in terms of the urban street to consider the multicontiguous building lot that might incorporate the street.

5. Regulations, codes, and administration of streets pertain principally to them as functional channels. Their role as resources of immense economic significance is generally not recognized or reflected in administrative organization or in public resource allocation. Economically, streets are accorded the status of residual urban artifacts — not that of a major resource.

6. The few relevant, flexible, economically based devices such as tax abatement, land write-down, and incentive zoning are not fully utilized to benefit street planning and design. Exceptions on a limited basis are the Special Planning Districts in New York and San Francisco. In most cases, however, few publicly prepared planning and design goals even exist for the urban street.

7. The shared public/private inability to recognize the economic potential of the urban street for people typically deforms most feasibility and cost/benefit analyses in cases that actually require the urban street. For instance, road costs are generally considered only from the viewpoint of right-of-way construction, and benefits are assumed to be principally those derived by the vehicle passenger in such terms as time-saving. Some consideration of social cost and benefit has occurred recently. But cost and benefit to the community at large, to the pedestrian, and to the abutting property owner are not often included. As a result, evaluation of value lost and value gained through use or rede-

velopment of the urban street is narrowly defined. The role of the urban street as a generator of value does not appear. At the same time, the role and full cost of vehicle occupation of the urban street in terms of maintenance and signal costs, police and traffic services, land lost to taxable purposes, and wider public use are hidden. These are not charged in analysis at all, and are certainly not allocated to the specific beneficiary whether it is the private user or public operating authority; yet these are real costs to the community, subsidized by the community as its contribution to the urban street.[3] Other possible allocation of these funds, or reoriented distribution of funds, to the urban street for greater, or even different, kinds of public benefit are not now generally considered because no guidelines have been developed, consciousness of other possibilities is rare, no administrative mechanism exists, and there is no public constituency that recognizes the enormous potential of reconsideration of the economic context of the urban street.

As it now stands, there is currently no parity between funds earned by the urban street as an enormously significant generator of value and funds returned to the street so that a wide variety of services it might render to the urban community could be realized.

Recent Efforts to Modify the Existing Context

Inequities, disfunction, and disincentives of public economic policy related to the street have not gone totally unrecognized. Indeed in recent years a number of significant special programs have been reexamined or developed and tested, which attempt to reorder aspects of public programs and private actions that affect urban development. A number of these either embody principles applicable to the urban street or specifically focus on the street itself. While interaction between public and private sectors is at the core of these, an attempt is made for purposes of focus and clarity to divide them according to source of initiation, whether public, private, or mixed public/private.

Public Sector Policies

Public sector policies of importance, which use flexible economic considerations as a manipulative tool, include incentive zoning, real estate tax incentives, and condemnation variants. In each case, private willingness to develop urban real estate is supplemented by a policy that allows higher potential economic return to the private developer in exchange for amenities considered in the public interest by public planning authorities. Whether the amenities identified are actually in the public interest is not at issue here. The means of intervention based on economic principles and their utility to the street is the issue. Briefly, these manipulative tools may be described as follows.

Incentive Zoning. This is an administrative device that allows the private developer to build more than the legally zoned maximum of floor space on a building plot in return for provision of a specific public amenity. A broad range of amenities has been covered in such legislation in both New York and San Francisco, where this procedure has been used effectively over the past ten years.[4] These amenities have included plazas, arcades, shopping galleries, legitimate theaters, subway entrances, pedestrian tunnels, and rooftop observation platforms. Obviously, wherever pressure to develop exists, incentive zoning is a possibility for contributions to the urban street, such as arcades, moving sidewalks, linkage to structures and public transportation, and recreation and open space. But this pressure to develop exists only in the most limited parts of urban America, so only scattered and intermittent amelioration of the physical context of the urban street is possible through such a program. In addition, careful and even wise administration is required to avoid misplacement and proliferation of amenities beyond useful or well-considered numbers, scale, location, or quality.

The most appealing aspect of incentive zoning is that the city obtains significant improvements at no apparent cost to itself. Indeed the bonus in permissible built space on a fixed amount of land area (known as floor area ratio bonus or FAR bonus) results in increased real estate tax assessment with consequent higher property tax revenue for the city. However, this benefit is often offset by increased density, which requires higher investment in infrastructure, public services, and street use.

Real estate tax incentives. Approximately 20 to 25 percent of commercial, industrial, residential, and office building gross income must be allocated to pay real estate tax. This politically favored indirect tax, which seems to affect only landlords and home owners, actually affects everyone in the form of higher rent, reduced salary, or diminished profit. Abatement of this tax has been used over the years to encourage specified private development and to subsidize various public or quasi-public institutions and services.

Since there is no specific recognition of the value of the public street to the private beneficiary (abutting property owner, vehicle passenger) or community at large in the form of an identifiable and quantified tax, the opportunity of tax abatement to induce new or better utilization of the street is entirely lost. However, such specific benefit exists and could be identified in taxing policies.

It should be recognized, at the same time, that tax abatement is a very costly incentive device. Full-value dollars, which would otherwise be income to the taxing authority, are lost. The only real advantage of tax abatement is that it hides the cost of public support to exempt property. A specific cash subsidy to churches, hospitals, schools, low- and middle-income housing projects, and government property are likely to be less complacently accepted by taxpayers. One wonders, on the other hand, if such subsidies were granted, how much and for what purpose would the public demand that funds be allocated to the urban street, the one amenity used by all city residents at all stages of the life cycle and regardless of social, economic, or racial status. Required disclosure of subsidy granted through tax abatement compared to budget expenditures for public use of streets would reveal, among other things, the very small per capita street allocation for community benefit, as opposed to vehicle owner benefit.

Condemnation variants. Condemnation of property is a privilege and power of government. When public purpose is accepted, the right of public condemnation of private property exists in this country. Traditionally, this legal power has been used to accumulate large areas of urban land, clear it, and transform its use to rights-of-way for streets and highways, for public buildings, or for housing principally, as outlined in Title I of the Housing Act of 1949 and later the Housing Act of 1954. After assembly and clearance, land is sold to a developer in the private sector below acquisition plus clearance cost so that economically feasible projects, which fulfill the original public intention, such as new low-cost housing and limited commercial development to replace slum areas, can be built. Federal and local subsidy in the form of below-cost cleared land and mortgage guarantees that reduce borrowing costs were expected to induce publicly desirable improvements. Again the generally accepted goals and the results of condemnation programs as practiced traditionally — though much could be said of them, and much would be critical — are not at issue here. Only the mechanism and its possible improved use in the economic context of the urban street is considered.

An interesting modification of the traditional condemnation procedure combined with tax relief has been successfully pioneered in Missouri and has prompted energetic redevelopment of the St. Louis downtown/waterfront area. In this program the city does not acquire land but rather lends its power to eminent domain to the developer for an acceptable project. This short-circuits costly and time-consuming government delay. After a twenty-five year graduated period taxes on land and improvements are based on full value.[5]

The write-down of property value for tax purposes could be applied to the urban street, and to buildings or parts of buildings that abut the street. In this way a public subsidy could be provided to induce owners to conform to particular urban design goals such as the linking of lobbies, the provision of arcades, and so forth. This subsidy might very well not have to be precisely equivalent to the owner's tax saving if persuasive analysis proved that the urban design concept and particular amenity would materially improve the value of the property in question. Alternatively, the city could condemn certain portions of buildings such

as lobbies or facades and reduce assessments and tax accordingly to the owner. These building elements, which are used by the public or very much affect the public's experience of the street and abutting spaces, would then be available as coherent segments of the city susceptible to public control and to large-scale urban design goals. Condemnation in this case does not require or even imply destruction. It refers, on the contrary, to a method of reclaiming or at least establishing control over parts of the built urban environment that are crucial to developing better urban streets and adjacent spaces for more of the urban population.

Private-Sector Policies

Within the private sector a number of economically based concepts exist and are proven which could be converted into effective mechanisms to alter the existing economic context of the urban street.

Amenity cooperatives. The cooperative ownership and maintenance of residential apartments is a recognized mechanism whereby tenants or user groups aggregate resources to replace a single owner or landlord. The result (among others) is that all shared space and amenities become the property and responsibility of those who use and benefit from them. The amenity cooperative is also used in planned urban (or surburban) developments in which entrepreneurs build a set of houses or apartments that forego some degree of private land in favor of an aggregate common or public space for use by the cooperative.

The concept of the amenity cooperative could be applied to the urban street at two scales. The most obvious is the scale of a particular street, or segment of a street. Property owners, if convinced that a particular amenity is desirable, could cooperatively develop such an amenity, own it, and maintain it. Examples such as shopping arcades, shuttle bus service, and even landscape planting and good lighting come to mind as possible candidates on a commercial street. These could be supported if abutting owners were convinced that capital investment and operating maintenance costs would be more than offset by increased rent, increased value, and/or increased profit from induced patronage. In a slightly modified form, benefit assessment, voluntarily established by property owners along Nicollet Mall in Minneapolis for maintenance and capital construction bond repayment, is an existing and working example of such a procedure. A mechanism of real estate tax abatement on improvements and value added by the amenity, as well as special depreciation write-off schedules, might be combined as a public subsidy to such voluntary cooperatives. At this scale, however, the voluntary cooperative depends on a narrow economic formula in which the public benefits only at specific locations.

At the wider scale, all property owners along streets could be considered required members of amenity cooperatives. Legislative, administrative, and fiscal adjustments would have to be made to enact such a program. The program itself might even be structured so that it did not have to benefit the cooperative property owner directly. Instead, it could be considered a device for compensatory adjustment of the economic benefit provided by the street to all adjacent property. To a greater or lesser degree, public subsidy could be granted depending on detailed calculation and determination of public interest improvements provided by and perhaps required of the amenity cooperative. Furthermore, devices such as zoning bonus or development rights above specific street amenities could be made available to help support the street amenity cooperative.

Block or street association. This is a private economic unit defined in physical terms. It assumes joint interests because of topographic proximity. Examples abound: the neighborhood block association, the Fifth Avenue Association and the Avenue of the Americas Association in New York, and Nicollet Mall Association in Minneapolis. These groups recognize their mutual interest and have even defined it in some cases in terms of the street itself. Thus block associations attend to tree planting, building appearance and maintenance, public services, and the like. Street associations acknowledge the value of public attitudes stimulated by public amenities on the commercial and social success of the street. This recognition, often taken for granted and exclusively channeled toward long-run private benefit, is actually one of the few cases in which the value of the urban street as a public amenity is openly and administratively acknowledged. Such recognition, in collaboration with more effective public policies such as the Investment Partnership and Operation Main Street, could begin renewed recognition of the possibilities of the urban street in the economic context through private leadership.

Mixed Private/Public Sector Policies

In recent years pertinent mixed public/private economic interaction has evolved. In broad terms, these can be classified as joint development, investment partnerships, and air rights. Each involves complex and rather new relationships between public and private interests. Each depends for implementative success on new administrative formulas. And each involves techniques of economic analysis so new that real agreement of offsetting value is both difficult to achieve and so subject to variation that no specific explanation can be attempted here.[6] Within each approach, certain qualities are worthy of consideration in terms of the urban street.

Air rights and air rights transfer. Air-rights development involves the evaluation and subsequent sale or lease of unused air space. The air space might be privately held above a building or a railroad yard; or it

might be publicly owned above a street, waterway, highway, or government property. Wherever it is, a public/private interaction is certain, for it is public limitation on buildable space and height that directly or indirectly imbues the unused air space with value. What is especially relevant about air rights, however, is that they are a specific example of the once unused, unvalued, residual space becoming a positive entity in some cases sought out for new and previously unconceived uses.

In most cases, of course, it is the private sector that attempts to acquire air-rights space for private use and profit. The air space is dormant in terms of value unless it is sought after, as it is not taxed, it has no operational economic power, and is not recognized as an active ingredient in the urban economic picture until it is wanted. Streets themselves, which comprise 30 to 35 percent of the city surface, are in much the same position, and, of course, streets generally possess air space of greater or lesser value depending on the use to which such space could be put. However, the possibility of this space being of value for public benefit is not usually recognized, though private interests are quick to perceive its value for private development. The use of air rights could become operative in terms of streets if street space were viewed as a positive, usable resource that remains unutilized or underutilized for public benefit in certain circumstances. One circumstance could be the public commitment to build second-level pedestrian promenades and parks by decking over the present street level. In such an instance the lower level could still serve as a pedestrian arcade and also be used to obtain accessible utility channels to serve the city, an invisible amenity now generally unavailable and one that limits city services in many ways. Were such a goal set, then street air space would acquire a value that could be manipulated in public/private negotiations, tax policies, and planning in a way that would promote the development of such an amenity.

In addition, if streets' air rights were made transferable within set zones and constraints, a wide range of public benefit from physical development to financial contributions could be realized.

Joint development. Cooperative and unconventional economic partnerships between the private sector and public authorities are now being explored, especially in relation to transportation centers. For instance, many airports are owned by public authorities which pay no tax. They in turn lease space to private airline operators. The tax-exempt status of the public authority assures a lease rent considerably less costly than land purchase, facility development, and full tax payment would be to private carriers. In addition, the cooperative shared nature of the facility assures a measure of reduced cost to each carrier, better service to the public, and a coordinated planning concept.

Another kind of public/private joint development gaining prominence is construction of private buildings above or in conjunction with publicly owned and operated facilities. Private offices or apartments above public schools, private office structures adjacent to or above a post office, and other combinations have appeared recently. The public facilities enjoy tax-free use of land, which in turn makes it possible to build private for-profit buildings above this tax-free land at reduced capital and operating costs. In addition, the tax-exempt property can be assigned some of the foundation and structural costs, thus reducing the effective capital investment and subsequent tax assessment of the private structure. In return, the private structure does provide a tax source where none might otherwise exist.

The mutual benefit from public and private viewpoints, which joint-use development accomplishes, has a potential corollary for the urban street. For if the street were recognized as a major public economic resource, new combinations of interaction with the private sector for interpenetration and interaction of an economic, physical, and administrative nature would become possible. It is not difficult to imagine, as an example, that the lobby of a building could be defined as a penetration of the public street into private property. As a consequence some of the cost of the lobby (one of the most expensive increments of any building) could be considered available for subsidy, or even reimbursement. Any number of possibilities could be imagined as goals of this program, such as through block pedestrian connectors, internal arcades, and many more. Districtwide implementive possibilities exist to redirect consideration of the economic position and possibilities of the urban street through imaginative and sound use of joint-development concepts that now apply at limited scale to certain conventional building types.

Investment partnership. Investment partnerships between the private and public sector for limited and narrowly defined improvement of the street already exist. In some cases they are initiated by the private sector, in rarer instances by the public sector. Private funding by the Avenue of the Americas Association in New York, for instance, led to public help to improve street lighting along Sixth Avenue. A share was contributed by the private association, but the work and much of the cost were contributed by the city. In other cases it is the city that takes the initiative. Operation Mainstreet is one of the few cases in point.[7] For a commercial street that qualifies, the Department of Commerce and Industry spends two dollars of public funds for every one dollar of private expenditure on certified public improvements. This is a working program, but one that only works in particular spots. A strong private association is necessary. The street itself must conform to specific criteria set by the city. Street choice is subject to political pressure and unrecognized conflict of economic interest. Finally, this form of partnership, which requires cash outlay, can have only limited impact in the context of financially strained government budgets. Such a program would only be meaningful at large scale if accompanied by a new formula of resource allocation based on a much more fundamental redefinition and recognition of the true economic role of the urban street.

Postulations: Toward a Redefinition of
the Economic Context of the Urban Street

As discussed earlier, the current economic context of the urban street results from neglect. The redirection of this context, to the extent that it is attempted at all, usually depends on intermittent possibilities or only local area influence. Longer-term effective economic programs are needed. This requires not just a change in implementative programs but a fundamental redirection of attitude.

A number of basic attitudinal shifts and realizations could lead to an entirely new economic concept of the street.

1. The street should be recognized, through fiscal policy, not as a mere residual space but as a community resource, a positive urban asset that should benefit the entire community most directly. In addition, the street should be recognized as a part of the total urban context with its own possibilities for improved design, functional redefinition, and physical reorganization.

2. Let the urban street become an active protagonist on the urban economic scene. Give it economic powers to penetrate into the fabric of public and nonpublic space, just as the opposite dynamic exists and is constantly at work in air rights and superblock buildings.

3. Long-term, coherent definition and goals for the urban street must be set in accordance with overall urban evolution or development concepts. These must be coupled with sound economic precepts and analysis to facilitate realization.

4. These goals must be attainable through evolutionary transformation over a considerable time lapse if applied to existing cities because of the conservative nature of capital investment, the realities of depreciation value, and the complex new private/public economic and administrative operations envisioned.

5. Economic incentives must underlie any program that depends on voluntary cooperation within the private sector.

6. Economic benefit derived from the urban street must be more accurately revealed and these benefits converted to acceptable public amenities in a greater degree than now exists.

7. Differentiation of goals and role for the urban street in different locations must be developed in specific conjunction with relevant economic and administrative feasibility and in association with economic and administrative devices for orderly goal realization.

Were these realizations achieved, a number of ongoing economically based, long-term implementative mechanisms could be developed to fulfill new goals for the role, design, and function of the urban street. These would include, but certainly not be limited to, such considerations as:

1. Establishment at local, state and federal levels of an economic development agency for streets to intervene, represent, and develop a constituency and programs that recognize and utilize the economic clout of the collectivity of public street space for public benefit. This should be part of a single coordinated agency or department of HUD, constituted to develop policies and administrate plans for the urban street. Besides economic competency it should contain operational, urban-design, and implementative ability. Such an agency, at the outset, could define its service area in a sufficiently comprehensive way to include its functional area, which now includes much semiprivate and private space.

2. Development of federal tax incentives for the private sector calculated to stimulate improvement to property along the street or to fulfill new street concepts themselves. Currently, federal subsidies are available to induce capital expenditures through capital gains on investment, depletion allowances for natural resource exploration, and accelerated depreciation in exchange for the purchase of new equipment, to cite a few examples. It is time to apply the well-proven economic leverage of the tax laws to benefit the cities and the people who live in them. Preferential treatment to capital expenditures for approved street redevelopment, if properly rewarded, could lead to far-flung private programs to improve street quality according to revised concepts.

3. Promotion of a program of reverse penetration in which public space is encouraged to intrude into the private and semiprivate domain according to a long-term, well-developed, citywide plan. This program could be implemented through tax relief, assessment reduction, incentive zoning, or any combination of mechanisms already available. Program criteria would include a citywide reference frame and long-term guarantees, which allow basic investment decisions to be made confidently in relation to public goals established by the reverse penetration plan.

4. Development of conclusive proof of the conditions under which the unconventional acceptance of the urban street in a new context actually benefits the owner of private property, and to what extent. This would take the form of objective, publicly supported economic analyses of the interaction of federal, state, and local taxation opportunities, investor behavior, real estate market trends, and street influence on basic property value and annual cash flow. Such studies could document parameters of value increment assignable to interiorized shopping streets, continuous pedestrian levels through commercial structures, agreeable open space, and the like. If such studies were reliable, they could become effective tools to induce private sector reconstruction of the urban street in specific and appropriate locations in accordance with areawide or citywide goals and objectives at no public cost. A part of this program could include, as well, tax abatement on the capital value added and even preferential treatment of related generated income, if such inducements were found to be necessary to generate specific private investment.

5. Sound economic principles should be developed to permit horizontal financing and operation of public or private space that abuts or interpenetrates with an unlimited number of conventional building lots at any one or a number of levels, including below grade, street level, and upper areas. Zoning incentives and capital commitment incentives of all sorts should be reviewed to this end; favorable treatment of operating income, depreciation, and other possibilities should also be evaluated to accomplish this new financing potential, as should opportunities for joint development and air-rights utilization in an effective way.

6. State and federal governments should directly and indirectly finance improvements or fundamental changes in streets in downtown urban areas that serve regional needs. This support could be as direct as capital grants or as indirect as provisions in federal tax legislation. Existing federal agencies such as the Department of Housing and Urban Development, the Department of Transportation, and the Internal Revenue Service should make programs available that focus on new potential for the urban street. State organizations which have strong financial and financing resources specifically mandated to work as a catalyst with the private sector, should become involved in the urban street in cities.

7. Taxation subsidies provided through tax abatement should be revealed according to property type, ownership, and amount per capita. These subsidies should be reviewed in relation to the total budget available to streets and the effective expenditure for community benefit per capita. Such exposure might very well lead to a more equitable distribution of public funds to reflect the service and amenity value of the street.

Conclusion

The foregoing essay is but an initial effort to reveal the perilous extent to which the economic context and potentialities of the urban street have been ignored. The consequence has been a gradual depletion of the economic, political, and administrative interest in streets in urban and suburban America. Unless new recognition and new definition of the economic potential of the urban street occur, the tools so necessary to the smooth and coherent increase in its vitality and role as the principal public space of every city will not be forthcoming.

Notes

1. The term *street*, in addition to its inclusive redefinition implied throughout this book, refers specifically in an economic context to non-tax-generating public rights-of-way and the access influence zone in a three-dimensional field to which it is linked.

2. Within this essay the term *economic* is understood to mean those questions and rules relative to generation and dispersal of funds, as well as initiation or conceptualization of fiscal programs.

3. The idea of costs that are not borne by those responsible for them originated in the distinction drawn by the economist A. C. Pigou between private and social costs. See A. C. Pigou, *The Economics of Welfare* (London, 1926).

4. For more detailed discussion of incentive zoning, see Jonathan Barnett, *Urban Design as Public Policy* (New York, 1974), and Norman Marcus and Marilyn Groves, *New Zoning: Legal, Administrative, and Economic Concepts and Techniques,* and the New York City and San Francisco Zoning Resolutions.

5. For a rather full discussion of the Missouri experience, including profit limitations, see "Planners Notebook," American Institute of Planners, May 1971. The program was made possible by legislative modification of chapter 353 of the Revised Statutes of Missouri, 1949, as amended.

6. For discussions see *Joint & Collateral Development Complexes,* Urban Design Concept Associates, 1968; *Metro Property Utilization,* Larry Smith & Company, Inc., 1969; *A Report on the Status of Multiple Use and Joint Development,* U.S. Department of Transportation, 1968; *Air Rights and Highways,* The Urban Land Institute Technical Bulletin No. 64, Washington, 1969; *A Study of Airspace Utilization,* U.S. Department of Transportation, Washington, 1968.

7. Operation Mainstreet was developed by the New York City Department of Commerce & Industry. For operational details and criteria see "Operation Main Street, N.Y.C.," Economic Development Administration, City of New York, New York, 1970.

A Bibliography

Stanford Anderson

Contents

An Expository Introduction with Bibliography

Compiling a bibliography on streets poses a dilemma. Works devoted to streets, narrowly conceived, are not sufficiently rich to justify the exercise. Broadly conceived, "streets" is a topic that opens to extensive literatures in many fields. Some works which never use the word *streets* may then appear more pertinent than others which carry the word in their titles.

Being devoted to a broad social, cultural, and physical understanding of streets, this book must tend toward the extensive bibliography, pruned back by some selective criteria. It seems best that these criteria be as obvious as possible; consequently, the first section of the following bibliography is set forth within an exposition. The reader is also referred to the notes of appropriate chapters, for here I make only selections from the authors' sources while adding works to which the authors did not have cause to refer.

The first effort of this bibliography is to note a few major publications for which the authors of this book have respect but from which they have consciously attempted certain departures.

Browne, Kenneth. "Street Scape with Furniture," *Architectural Review*, 123 (May 1958), pp. 312–324.

Cullen, Gordon. *Townscape*. New York: Reinhold, 1961.

Ewald, William R. *Street Graphics*. Washington, D.C.: American Society of Landscape Architects, 1971.

Ferebee, Ann. "The Street: Shall We Have Asphalt Jungles or Gardens of Beauty and Delight?", *Industrial Design*, 6 (November 1959), pp. 36–51.

Malt, Harold Lewis. *Furnishing the City*. New York: McGraw-Hill, 1970.

Rudofsky, Bernard. *Streets for People*. New York: Doubleday, 1969.

"Street Furniture," sp. no. of *Landscape Architecture*, 58 (July 1968), pp. 307–326.

Rudofsky's book, giving graphic documentation of his eye for congenial urban places, received wide acceptance and contributed to the notably extended concern with streets that appeared in the seventies. The book is marred by its bitterness that America is not Europe. Subtitled "A Primer for Americans," it nevertheless does not attempt to account for why these places are as they are, nor how or to what extent such principles would be transferable across time and space to the Americans. Consequently, Rudofsky's book easily feeds the older Anglo-Saxon tradition of "Townscape" which too readily identifies a concern for surface elements (quality, design and placement of street furniture, signs, lights, surfacing materials, and so on) with a concern for sound, liveable places. A notable failure of this townscape approach was the Johnsonian beautification of F Street in Washington, D.C. (1968). The latter concern appears to the authors of the present book to require difficult and continuing inquiry into the social, cultural, and fundamental physical characteristics of places that are taken as exemplary or upon which intervention is contemplated.

Lynch, Kevin. *The Image of the City*. Cambridge, Mass.: The MIT Press, 1960.

The Modern Movement in architecture developed in such a way as to emphasize the separate identity of each building, often according to degenerating formal principles that were no longer in discourse with the sociocultural setting, nor even, reflexively, with themselves. The city, especially its open space and its users, was neglected. Lynch's book of 1960 immediately stimulated a widespread reexamination of the urban context. Yet Lynch himself acknowledged that his method offered a strangely thin context — almost total emphasis on one characteristic of the environment, the "legibility" of its "visual quality," and on one aspect of users' experiences, "mental images" of the city. Relative to "townscape," Lynch offered a method of codifying a larger and more abstract aspect of urban experience; nevertheless, attempts at applying the method foundered on its one dimensionality, its tenuous relation to historical, cultural, and social factors, patterns of use, or even a finer scale of physical organization.

On the other hand, despite his fundamentally visual method, Lynch stopped far short of giving visual phenomena fundamental importance in the environment. He worked with the mental images of sample populations as they serve "legibility" rather than with a more specifically visual set of principles through which we might expand our sensibilities.

Over the relative significance of these two criticisms of Lynch's work (that it is inadequate either to social and functional or to visual criteria), the authors of the present book, in their basic orientations, split. Nevertheless, most of them have attempted positions that learn from both criticisms.

A small sample of other studies of users' impressions of the open space of cities, often inspired by Lynch, are:

Appleyard, Donald, Kevin Lynch, and John R. Myer. *The View from the Road*. Cambridge, Mass.: The MIT Press, 1966.

deJong, Derk. "Images of Urban Areas," *Journal of the American Institute of Planners*, 28 (1962), pp. 266–276.

Vigier, François C. "An Experimental Approach to Urban Design," *Journal of the American Institute of Planners*, 31 (February 1965), pp. 7–20.

Jacobs, Jane. *The Death and Life of Great American Cities*. New York: Random House, 1961.

Through this work, Jacobs exerted a profound influence on both large- and small-scale planning. In her exposition, the street took on density as a social and physical phenomenon. Her attack was directed at the physical planners not because they attended to the physical environment but because they, in real-life terms of many dimensions, attended to it destructively. While Jacobs too did not provide the methods by which her insights could be readily generalized from selected, extant communities and environments, the tangibility of her argument contributed to the stabilization of some of those communities and to the encouragement of fresh thought about people and their urban environments.

Among recent complementary studies are the following, of which that by Stein is an excellent review of major American community studies since the 1920s:

Duhl, Leonard J., ed. *The Urban Condition: People and Policy in the Metropolis*. New York: Basic Books, 1963.

Fried, Marc, and P. Gleicher. "Some Sources of Residential Satisfaction in an Urban Slum," *Journal of the American Institute of Planners*, 27 (November 1961), pp. 305–315.

Gans, Herbert. *The Urban Villagers: Group and Class in the Life of Italian-Americans*. New York: Free Press of Glencoe, 1962.

————. *The Levittowners: Ways of Life and Politics in a New Suburban Community*. New York: Pantheon, 1967.

————. *People and Plans*. New York: Basic Books, 1968.

Glass, Ruth, "Urban Sociology," chap. 26 in A. T. Welford et al., eds. *Society: Problems and Methods of Study*. London: Routledge and Kegan Paul, 1962.

Gutman, Robert, ed. *People and Buildings*. New York: Basic Books, 1972.

————., and David Popenoe, eds. *Neighborhood, City and Metropolis: An Integrated Reader in Urban Sociology*. New York: Random House, 1970.

Hannerz, Ulf. *Soulside: Inquiries into Ghetto Culture and Community*. New York: Columbia University Press, 1969.

Keller, Suzanne. *The Urban Neighborhood: A Sociological Perspective*. New York: Random House, 1968.

Liebow, Elliot. *Tally's Corner*. Boston: Little, Brown, 1967.

Stein, Maurice R. *The Eclipse of Community*. Princeton: Princeton University Press, 1960; expanded edition, 1972.

Suttles, Gerald. *Social Order of the Slum*. Chicago. University of Chicago Press, 1969.

————. *The Social Construction of Communities*. Chicago: University of Chicago Press, 1972.

Whyte, William F. *Street Corner Society*. Chicago: University of Chicago Press, 1955.

Willmott, P., and M. Young. *Family and Class in a London Suburb*. London: Routledge and Kegan Paul, 1960.

Yablonsky, Louis. *The Violent Gang*. New York: Macmillan, 1962.

These and other studies by social scientists contain valuable insights, though one is disappointed at how frequently they are marred by a curious ambivalence about the role of the physical environment — gloating over the failures of physical planners which have caused so much human suffering while assuring us that successful communities owe little or nothing to the physical environment. Since these authors are in the service of better communities, they often conclude (logically enough from inconsistent premises) that they need not go into detail in understanding the physical environment. Even by their argument, knowing enough to avoid disaster would seem to be desirable; the multidisciplinary bibliography that follows includes works that forthrightly inquire into possible relations of social and physical environments.

In contrast to the frequently conservative, individualistic nature of the works already cited, the foundation works of urban sociology and another body of recent studies are more overtly political, emphasizing collective phenomena:

Bookchin, Murray. *The Limits of the City.* New York: Harper & Row, 1974.

Castells, Manuel. *La Question Urbaine.* Paris: F. Maspero, 1973.

Durkheim, Emile. *Division of Labor in Society.* (First published in French, 1893.) Glencoe, Ill.: Free Press, 1933.

Engels, Friedrich. *Condition of the Working Class in England in 1844.* (First published in German, 1845.) New York: J. W. Lovell, 1887.

————. ''Zur Wohnungsfrage'' (1872–1873), vol. 18, pp. 209–287, in *Marx-Engels Werke.* Berlin (Ost), 1971.

Fathy, Hassan. *Architecture for the Poor.* Chicago: University of Chicago Press, 1973.

Halbwachs, Maurice. *Morphologie Sociale.* (First published 1938.) Paris: Armand Colin, 1970.

————. *La Memoire Collective.* Paris: Presses Universitaires de France, 1950.

————. *La Population et les Traces des Voies à Paris un Siècle.* Paris: Presses Universitaires de France, 1928.

Lefebvre, Henri. *Everyday Life in the Modern World.* New York: Harper & Row, 1971.

————. *La Revolution Urbaine.* Paris: Gallimard, 1970 (and an extensive work in French).

Marcus, Steven. *Engels, Manchester, and the Working Class.* New York: Random House, 1974.

Simmel, Georg. ''The Metropolis and Mental Life,'' *The Sociology of Georg Simmel*, Kurt Wolff, ed. New York: Free Press, 1950.

Weber, Max. *The City.* Don Martindale and Gertrude Neuwirth, eds. New York: Free Press, 1958.

Despite the brilliance of many of the works selected above, none is adequate with regard to our concern to understand the physical environment as one — not the determinant, nor even usually the dominant, but nevertheless a potentially significant — factor in patterns of human association. That concern suggests several disciplines as areas for further search: archeology, anthropology, ecology, geography, and architecture and planning.

Archeology has only recently begun to consider modern environments, anthropology the urban environments, with which this book is primarily concerned. With reference to ecology, a more extensive bibliography appears in the notes to Stanford Anderson's opening chapter in this book but the following would introduce the reader to the origins of human ecology and its early concern with cities:

Park, Robert E., Ernest W. Burgess, and Roderick D. McKenzie. *The City.* Chicago: University of Chicago Press, 1925.

Park, Robert Ezra. ''Human Ecology,'' *American Journal of Sociology*, 42 (July 1936), pp. 1–15.

Reiss, A. J. *Louis Wirth on Cities and Social Life.* Chicago: University of Chicago Press, 1964.

Stein, Maurice R. *The Eclipse of Community.* Princeton: Princeton University Press, 1972.

A major critique of Parkian ecology for its Darwinism, inadequate incorporation of sociocultural factors, and weak methodology is:

Alihan, Milla Aissa. *Social Ecology: A Critical Analysis.* New York: Columbia University Press, 1938.

Commentary and bibliography on the late nineteenth- and early twentieth-century contributions to human geography of such men as Jean Brunhes, Lucien Febvre, C. Daryll Forde, Friedrich Ratzel, Carl O. Sauer, and Paul Vidal de la Blache may be found in Philip L. Wagner and Marvin W. Mikesell, *Readings in Cultural Geography* (Chicago: University of Chicago Press, 1962), but a slightly later work deserves specific mention for its more direct influence on postwar study of the urban environment:

Sorre, Maximilien. *Les Fondements de la Géographie Humaine.* Paris: Armand Colin, 3 vols., 1943–1952.

A work that is both a critique of some of the foregoing works and the exposition of a suggestive methodology is:

Steward, Julian. *Theory of Culture Change.* Urbana: University of Illinois Press, 1955.

Multidisciplinary Studies of Urban Space as Human Environment

Since the second world war, the boundaries of such fields as archeology, anthropology, ecology, geography, and sociophysical planning, never distinct, have virtually disappeared. Archeology is shifting its attention from isolated artifacts to settlement patterns over an increasing range of times. The Parkian origins of urban ecology are obscured and revitalized by cultural ecology and urban anthropology. Within a number of disciplines, one now finds works that recognize the wholeness and complexity of people in their environments. Attempts are made to bridge traditional disciplines or at least to carry out more specialized studies within a nonexclusive context.

Such works are closest to the spirit of this book; consequently a more extensive bibliography follows in this section. While the list includes many, not always compatible, positions, their relations and intersections are so complex that within the context of a short bibliography it seems better not to separate these items by discipline or orientation.

Appleyard, Donald. *Street Livability Study*. San Francisco: Department of City Planning, 1970.

Auzelle, Robert. *Plaidoyer pour une Organisation Consciente de l'Espace*. Paris: Vincent, Fréal, 1962.

Aymonino, Carlo, et al. *La Città di Padova. Saggio di Analisi Urbana*. Rome: Officina, 1970.

Barker, Roger G. *Ecological Psychology*. Stanford, Calif.: Stanford University Press, 1968.

Beazley, E. *Design and Detail of the Space Between Buildings*. London: Architectural Press, 1961.

Bell, Gwendolyn D., Edwina Randall, and Judith E. R. Roeder, eds. *Urban Space and Human Behavior: An Annotated Bibliography*. New York: John Wiley, 1973.

Bettelheim, Charles, and Suzanne Frère. *Une ville française moyenne: Auxerre en 1950. Etude de structure sociale et urbaine*. Paris: Armand Colin, 1950.

Brambilla, Roberto, ed. *More Streets for People*. New York: Italian Art and Landscape Foundation, n.d. [c. 1974].

Buttimer, Anne. "Social Space in Interdisciplinary Perspective," *The Geographical Review*, 59 (July 1969), pp. 417–426 [a bibliographic article].

Caplow, Theodore. "The Social Ecology of Guatemala City," *Social Forces*, 28 (1949), pp. 113–133.

———. "Urban Structure in France," *American Sociological Review*, 17 (1952), pp. 544–549.

Carr, Stephen. "The City of the Mind," *Environment for Man: The Next Fifty Years*, pp. 197–231. Bloomington: Indiana University Press, 1967.

———, and Kevin Lynch. "Where Learning Happens," *Daedalus*, 97 (Fall 1968), pp. 1277–1291.

Cerasi, Maurice. *La lettura dell'ambiente*. Milan: clup, 3rd ed., 1973.

[———.] *Città e periferia*. Milan: clup, 1973.

Cervellati, P. L., and R. Scannavini, eds. *Bologna: politica e metodologia del restauro nei centri storici*. Bologna: il Mulino, 1973.

Chermayeff, Serge, and Christopher Alexander. *Community and Privacy*. Garden City, N.Y.: Doubleday, 1963.

———, and Alexander Tzonis. *Shape of Community*. Baltimore: Penguin Books, 1971.

Chombart de Lauwe, Paul-Henri. "The Social Sciences, Urbanism and Planning," *International Journal of Comparative Sociology*, 4 (1963), pp. 19–30. And an extensive bibliography in French; notably:

———. *La Vie quotidienne des familles ouvrières*. Paris: Centre National de la Recherche Scientific, 1956.

———. *Des hommes et des villes*. Paris: Payot, 1965.

———. *Paris, Essais de sociologie. 1952–1964*. Paris: Editions Ouvrières, 1965.

———, et al. *Paris et l'agglomeration parisienne*. Paris: Presses Universitaires de France, 2 vols., 1952.

Conrads, Ulrich. *Architektur — Spielraum für Leben. Ein Schnellkurs für Stadtbewohner*. Munich: Bertelsmann, 1972.

Cooper, Clare C., "Fenced Back Yard — Unfenced Front Yard — Enclosed Front Porch," *The Journal of Housing*, 5 (1967), pp. 268–274.

Craik, Kenneth. *New Directions in Psychology*. New York: Holt, Rinehart and Winston, 1970.

———. "The Comprehension of the Everyday Physical Environment," *Journal of the American Institute of Planners*, 34 (January 1968), pp. 29–37.

Devillers, Christian. "Typologie de l'habitat et morphologie urbaine," *Architecture d'aujourd'hui*, 174 (July–August 1974), pp. 18–22.

Dickinson, Robert Eric. *City and Region: A Geographical Interpretation*. London: Routledge and Kegan Paul, 1964.

Dubos, René J. "Humanizing the Earth," *Science*, 179 (February 23, 1973), p. 769.

Duncan, Otis Dudley, and Leo F. Schnore, "Cultural, Behavioral and Ecological Perspectives in the Study of Social Organization," *American Journal of Sociology*, 65 (1959), pp. 132–146.

Eindhoven. Van Abbemuseum. *De Straat*. Eindhoven: Van Abbemuseum, 1972.

Eindhoven. Stichting Architekten Research. *SAR '73*. Eindhoven: SAR, 1973.

Environment and Behavior. Beverly Hills, Calif.: Sage Publications, vol. 1, 1969 ff.

Environmental Design Research Association. *Proceedings*, vol. 1, 1970 ff.

Fava, Sylvia Fleis, ed. *Urbanism in World Perspective*. New York: Thomas Y. Crowell, 1968.

Firey, Walter. "Sentiment and Symbolism as Ecological Variables," *American Sociological Review*, 10 (1945), pp. 140–148.

———. *Land Use in Central Boston*. Cambridge, Mass.: Harvard University Press, 1947.

Friedmann, Georges, ed. *Villes et campagnes: Civilisation urbaine et civilisation rurale en France*. Paris: Armand Colin, 1952.

Geertz, Clifford. *The Interpretation of Cultures*. New York: Basic Books, 1973.

Goffman, Erving. *Behavior in Public Places. Notes on the Social Organization of Gatherings*. New York: Free Press, 1963.

———. *Relations in Public . Microstudies of the Public Order*. New York: Basic Books, 1971.

Goodman, Paul and Percival. *Communitas*, 2nd ed. New York: Vintage, 1960.

Grassi, Giorgio. *La costruzione logica della architettura*. Padua: Marsilio, 1967.

Hall, Edward T. *The Silent Language*. Greenwich, Conn.: Fawcett, 1959.

———. *The Hidden Dinension*. Garden City, N.Y.: Doubleday, 1966.

Halprin, Lawrence. *RSVP Cycles*. New York: George Braziller, 1974.

Hammel, Pietro. *Unsere Zukunft: die Stadt*. Frankfurt: Suhrkamp, 1972.

Haumont, Nicole. "Habitat et modèles culturels," *Revue Française de Sociologie*, 9 (July–September 1968), pp. 180–190.

Hauser, Philip M., and Leo F. Schnore, eds. *The Study of Urbanization*. New York: John Wiley, 1965.

Hertzberger, Herman. "Huiswerk voor meer herbergzame Vorm," *Forum*, 24 (1973).

Hirsch, Werner Z. *Urban Life and Form*. New York: Holt, Rinehart and Winston, 1963.

Holling, C. S., and M. A. Goldberg. "Ecology and Planning," *Journal of the American Institute of Planners*, 37 (1971), pp. 221–230.

Jackson, J. B. *Landscapes*. Amherst: University of Massachusetts Press, 1970.

Jonassen, C. T. "Cultural Variables in the Ecology of an Ethnic Group," *American Sociological Review*, 14 (1949), pp. 32–41.

deJong, F. M., H. Van Olphen, and M. F. Th. Bax. "Drie fasen van een stedebouwkundig principe," *Plan*, 2 (1972), pp. 10–31.

Kennedy, Declan and Margrit I., eds. *The Inner City*. London: Elek, forthcoming.

Klausner, Samuel. *On Man and His Environment*. San Francisco: Jossey-Bass, 1971.

Labasse, Jean. *L'organization de l'espace: Éléments de géographie volontaire*. Paris: Hermann, 1966.

Lerup, Lars. "Environmental and Behavioral Congruence as a Measure of Goodness in Public Space: The Case of Stockholm," *DMG-DRS Journal*, 6 (April–June 1972), pp. 54–78.

Lewis, David, ed. *Urban Structure*. London: Elek, 1968.

———. *The Growth of Cities*. London: Elek, 1971.

Lynch, Kevin. *What Time Is This Place?* Cambridge, Mass.: The MIT Press, 1972.

McHarg, Ian L. *Design with Nature*. Garden City, N.Y.: Doubleday, 1969.

Mesmin, Georges. *L'Enfant, l'architecture et l'espace*. Brussels: Casterman, 1971.

Meyer-Heine, Georges. *A Human Approach to Urban Planning*. Paris: International Federation for Housing and Planning and Centre de recherche d'urbanisme, 1968.

Michelson, William. *Man and His Urban Environment*. Reading, Mass.: Addison-Wesley, 1970.

Miller, Jonathan, guest ed. "Metaphoropolis," sp. no. of *Architectural Design*, 38 (December 1968).

Moos, Rudolf H., and Paul M. Insel, eds. *Issues in Social Ecology. Human Milieus*. Palo Alto, Calif.: National Press, 1974.

New York, City of, Urban Design Council. Alexander Cooper, Exec. Dir. *Housing Quality. A Program for Zoning Reform*. New York: The Urban Design Council of the City of New York [1973].

Opie, Iona and Peter. *Children's Games in Street and Playground — Chasing, Catching, Seeking, Hunting, Racing, Duelling, Exerting, Daring, Guessing, Acting, Pretending*. Oxford: Clarendon Press, 1969.

Palmade, Jacqueline. "Symbolism and Practice in Context of Living Space," pp. 40–52 in National Swedish Institute for Building Research. *Open Space in Housing Areas*. Stockholm: Svensk Byggtjänst, 1972.

Perin, Constance. *With Man in Mind*. Cambridge, Mass.: The MIT Press, 1970.

Peters, Paulhans. *Stadt für Menschen*. Munich: Callwey, 1974.

Platt, Robert S. "Environmentalism vs. Geography," *American Journal of Sociology*, 53 (1947–48), pp. 351–358.

Proshansky, Harold M., William H. Ittleson, and Leanne G. Rivlin. *Environmental Psychology: Man and His Physical Setting*. New York: Holt, Rinehart, 1970.

de Radkowski, G. H. "Les caractéristiques formelles de l'habitat dans les sociétés nomades, sédentaires et industrielles," *Cahiers d'Etudes des Sociétés Industrielles et de l'Automation*, 6 (1964), pp. [199]–4213.

Rapoport, Amos. *House Form and Culture*. Englewood Cliffs, N.J.: Prentice-Hall, 1969.

———. "Designing for Complexity," *Architectural Association Quar-*

terly, 3 (Winter 1971), pp. 29–33.

Rasmussen, Steen Eiler. *Towns and Buildings*. (First published in Danish, 1949). Cambridge, Mass.: Harvard University Press, 1951.

Raymond, Henri. "Habitat, modèles culturels, et architecture," *Architecture d'aujourd'hui*, 174 (July–August 1974), pp. 50–53.

Ripley, Dillon, and Helmut K. Buechner. "Ecosystem Science as a Point of Synthesis," *Daedalus*, 96 (Fall 1967), pp. 1192–1199.

San Francisco, City and County. Department of City Planning. *The Urban Design Plan*. San Francisco, 1971.

Schnore, Leo F. "Social Morphology and Human Ecology," *American Journal of Sociology*, 63 (1958), pp. 620–634.

Segaud, Marion. "Anthropologie de l'espace: catalogue ou projet?", *Espace et Société*, 9 (July 1973), pp. 29–38.

Settlement Patterns and Urbanisation. Research Seminar on Archeology and Related Subjects. London: Institute of Archeology, 1970.

Seymour, Whitney North, Jr., ed. *Small Urban Spaces*. New York: New York University Press, 1969.

Smithson, Alison, ed. *Team 10 Primer*. Cambridge, Mass.: The MIT Press, 1968.

———. *Ordinariness and Light*. Cambridge, Mass.: The MIT Press, 1970.

———, and Peter. *Urban Structuring*. New York: Reinhold, 1967.

Sorokin, Pitirim A. *Sociocultural Causality, Space, Time*. Durham, N.C.: Duke University Press, 1943.

Steward, Julian. *Theory of Culture Change*. Urbana: University of Illinois Press, 1955.

Tafuri, Manfredo. *Architecture and Utopia. Design and Capitalist Development*. (First published in Italian, 1973). Cambridge, Mass.: The MIT Press, 1976.

Tricart, J. *Cours de géographie humaine, I — L'habitat rural; II — L'habitat urbain*. Paris: Centre de Documentation Universitaire, 1951.

Vayda, Andrew P. *Environment and Cultural Behavior*. Garden City, N.Y.: Natural History Press, 1969.

Wächter, Klaus. *Wohnen in der städtischen Agglomeration des zwanzigsten Jahrhunderts*. Stuttgart: Karl Krämer, 1971.

Wapner, Seymour, Bernard Kaplan, and Saul B. Cohen. "An Organismic-Developmental Perspective for Understanding Transactions of Men and Environment," *Environment and Behavior*, 5 (September 1973), pp. 255–289.

Williams, Raymond. *The Country and the City*. New York: Oxford University Press, 1973.

Wingo, Lowdon, *Cities and Space*. Baltimore: Johns Hopkins University Press, 1963.

Woods, Shadrach. *Candilis, Josic, Woods*. Stuttgart: Krämer, 1968.

———. *Urbanism is Everybody's Business*. Stuttgart: Krämer, 1968.

———. *The Man in the Street. A Polemic on Urbanism*. Hammondsworth: Penguin, 1975.

Znaniecki, Florian. *Cultural Sciences*. Urbana: University of Illinois Press, 1952.

Semiotics of Urban Space

Among the preceding works are those that incorporate a concern with urban space (or specifically the street) as a symbolic structure. For works devoted more narrowly to this approach, see the chapter by Diana Agrest and:

"Arredo inurbano," sp. no. of *Casabella*, nos. 339–340 (August–September 1969).

Barthes, Roland. "Sémiologie et Urbanisme," *Architecture d'aujourd'hui*, 153 (December 1970–January 1971), pp. 11–13.

Choay, Françoise. "Remarques à propos de sémiologie urbaine," *Architecture d'aujourd'hui*, 153 (December 1970–January 1971), pp. 9–10.

Gouvion, Colette, and François van de Mert. *Le Symbolisme des rues et des cités*. Paris: Berg International, 1974.

Paris. Groupe 107 [Manar Hammad et al.]. *Sémiotique de l'espace*. Paris: Groupe 107, 1973.

Takeyama, Minoru, ed. "Street Semiology," sp. no. of *Kenchiku-Bunka*, 30 (February 1975).

Venturi, Robert, Denise Scott Brown, and Steven Izenour. *Learning from Las Vegas*. Cambridge, Mass.: The MIT Press, 1972.

The scope of urban semiotics is not yet defined. For an inclusive concept of the city within the theory of communications, see the chapter by Thomas Czarnowski in this book and the seminal work on which that chapter, in turn, relies:

Meier, Richard. *A Communications Theory of Urban Growth*. Cambridge, Mass.: The MIT Press, 1962.

Studies Contributive to a History of Streets

While the social and physical history of streets has yet to be adequately addressed, there are many works that contribute to such a study. For eighteenth- and nineteenth-century France and England, see the exemplary chapter by Anthony Vidler. The following list includes both historical studies proper and works that, though intended as practical works directed to either the social or physical environment, today serve as historical documents.

Abercrombie, Sir Patrick. *A Civic Survey and Plan for Edinburgh.* London: Oliver and Boyd, 1949.

————. *Town and Country Planning,* 3rd ed. London: Oxford University Press, 1959.

Addams, Jane. *The Spirit of Youth and the City Streets.* New York: Macmillan, 1909.

Aymonino, Carlo. *Origini e sviluppo della città moderna.* Padua: Marsilio, 1965; fifth ed., 1974.

Bacon, Edmund. *Design of Cities.* New York: Viking, 1967.

Bardet, Gaston, *Le nouvel Urbanisme.* Paris: Vincent Fréal, 1948.

————. *L'urbanisme.* Paris: Presses Universitaries de France, 1959.

Behrendt, Walter C. *Die einheitliche Blockfront als Raumelement in Stadtbau.* Berlin: B. Cassirer, 1911.

Benedetta, Mary, and Laszlo Moholy-Nagy. *Street Markets of London.* London: J. Miles, 1936.

Benevolo, Leonardo. *The Origins of Modern Town Planning.* Cambridge, Mass.: The MIT Press, 1967.

Berlage, Hendrik Petrus. "De Kunst in Stedenbouw." *Bouwkundig Weekblad,* 12 (1892), pp. 87–91, 101–102, 121–127.

Berty, F. A., et al. *Histoire Générale de Paris. Topographie historique du Vieux Paris.* 6 vols., Paris: Imprimerie Impériale and Imprimerie Nationale, 1866–1897.

Bobek, Hans, and Elisabeth Lichtenberg. *Wien, Bauliche Gestalt und Entwicklung seit der Mitte des 19. Jahrhunderts.* Graz/Köln: H. Böhlau, 1966.

Booth, Charles. *Charles Booth's London.* New York: Random House, 1968.

Bournon, Fernand. *La Voie publique et son décor.* Paris: Laurens, 1909.

Brinckmann, A. E. *Deutsche Stadtbaukunst in der Vergangenheit.* Frankfurt a. M.: Frankfurter-Verlag, 1921.

————. *Platz und Monument als künstlerisches Formproblem.* Berlin: E. Wasmuth, 1923.

Burke, Gerald L. *The Making of Dutch Towns, A Study of Urban Development from the Tenth to the Seventeenth Centuries.* London: Cleaver-Hume Press, 1956.

Burke, Thomas. *The Streets of London through the Centuries.* London: Charles Scribners, 1940.

Cacciari, Massimo. *Metropolis: Saggi sulla grande città di Sombart, Endell, Scheffler e Simmel.* Rome: Officina, 1973.

Castagnoli, Ferdinando. *Orthogonal Town Planning in Antiquity.* Cambridge, Mass.: The MIT Press, 1971.

Chapman, J. M., and Brian. *The Life and Times of Baron Haussmann: Paris in the Second Empire.* London: Weidenfeld & Nicholson, 1957.

Chastel, André. "Du Paris de Haussmann au Paris d'aujourd'hui," in Guy Michaud, gen. ed., *Paris: Présent et avenir d'une capitale.* Paris: Institut Pédagogique National, 1964.

Choay, Françoise. *Espacements.* (Privately printed in France, 1969).

————. *The Modern City: Planning in the 19th Century.* New York: George Braziller, 1969.

Ciucci, Giorgio, et al. *La città americana.* Bari: Laterza, 1973.

Collins, George R. "Linear Planning throughout the World," *Journal of the Society of Architectural Historians,* 43 (October 1959).

————, and C. C. *Camillo Sitte and the Birth of Modern City Planning.* New York: Random House, 1965.

Coolidge, John. *Mill and Mansion.* New York: Columbia University Press, 1942.

Creese, Walter L. *The Legacy of Raymond Unwin. A Human Pattern for Planning.* Cambridge, Mass.: The MIT Press, 1967.

David, A. C. "Innovations in the Street Architecture of Paris," *Architectural Record,* 24 (August 1908), pp. 109–128.

Davis, Philip. *Street-Land. Its Little People and Big Problems.* Boston: Small, Maynard, 1915.

Detti, Edoardo, et al. *Città murate e sviluppo contemporaneo.* Lucca: CISCU, 1968.

Dickinson, Robert E. *The West European City.* London: Routledge and Kegan Paul, 1951–1962.

Dresden. Deutsche Städtebauaustellung 1903. *Die deutschen Städte.* 2 vols., Dresden, 1904.

Dyos, H. J. *Victorian Suburb.* Leicester: Leicester University Press, 1966.

Egorov, I. A. *The Architectural Planning of St. Petersburg.* Athens, Ohio: Ohio University Press, 1969.

Fanelli, Giovanni. *Firenze. Architettura e Città.* Florence: Vallecchi, 1973.

Fassbinder, Horant, Imgrid Krau, and Irmgard Lensing. *Berliner Arbeiterviertel 1800–1918.* Berlin: Verlag für das Studium der Arbeiterbewegung, 1974.

Forster, Kurt W. "From 'Rocca' to 'Civitas': Urban Planning at Sabbioneta," *L'Arte,* 5 (March 1969).

Fritsch, Theodor. *Die Stadt der Zukunft.* Leipzig: T. Fritsch, 1896.

Gauldie, Enid. *Cruel Habitations. A History of Working-Class Housing 1780–1918.* London: George Allen and Unwin, 1974.

Geddes, Patrick. *Cities in Evolution.* London: Williams and Norgate, 1915.

Giedion, Sigfried. *Space, Time and Architecture*. Cambridge, Mass.: Harvard University Press, 1941 and later editions.

Goetz, W. *Die Verkehrswege im Altertum und Mittelalter*. Stuttgart, 1888; reprinted Amsterdam, 1969.

Grote, Ludwig, ed. *Die deutsche Stadt im 19. Jahrhundert*. Munich: Prestel, 1974.

Günter, Roland. "Krupp und Essen," in Martin Warnke, ed., *Das Kunstwerk zwischen Wissenschaft und Weltanschauung*. Gütersloh: Bertelsmann, 1970.

Gutkind, E. A. *The International History of City Development*. 8 vols., New York: Free Press, 1964 ff.

Habel, Heinrich, et al. *Münchener Fassaden*. Munich: Prestel, 1974.

Halbwachs, Maurice. *La population et les tracés de voirie à Paris*. Paris: Alcan, 1928.

Haussmann, Baron Georges. *Mémoires*. Paris: V. Havard, 1890-1893.

Hegemann, Werner. *Der Städtebau nach den Ergebnissen der allgemeinen Städtebau-Ausstellung in Berlin 1910*. Berlin: Wasmuth, 1911-1913.

———. *Das steinerne Berlin*. Berlin: Ullstein, 1963.

———, and Elbert Peets. *The American Vitruvius. An Architect's Handbook of Civic Art*. New York, 1922; reprinted New York: B. Blom, 1972.

Hénard, Eugène. *Rapport sur l'avenir des grandes villes*. Actes du premier Congrès international d'urbanisme, 1910.

Hiorns, Frederick R. *Town Building in History*. London: G. G. Harrap, 1956.

Hitzer, Hans. *Die Strasse*. München: D. W. Callwey, 1971.

Lavedan, P. *Histoire de l'Urbanisme*. 4 vols., Paris: Laurens, 1926-1952.

Léon, Paul. *Paris. Histoire de la Rue*. Paris: La Taille Douche, 1947.

Merten, Klaus, and Christoph Mohr. *Das Frankfurter Westend*. Munich: Prestel, 1974.

Morris, A. E. J. *History of Urban Form*. London: George Godwin, 1972.

Mumford, Lewis. *The Culture of Cities*. New York: Harcourt, Brace and World, 1938.

———. *The City in History*. New York: Harcourt, Brace and World, 1961.

Muratori, Saverio. *Studi per una operante storia urbana di Venezia*. Roma: Istituto Poligrafico dello Stato, 1960.

Olsen, Donald J. *Town-Planning in London, the Eighteenth and Nineteenth Centuries*. New Haven: Yale University Press, 1964.

Ostwald, Hans, ed. *Groszstadt Dokumente* [an extensive series]. Berlin, c. 1905 ff.

Pastor, L. Von. *Sisto V, il Creatore della Nuova Roma*. Rome: Tipografia Poliglotta Vaticana, 1922.

Pinkney, David H. *Napoleon III and the Rebuilding of Paris*. Princeton: Princeton University Press, 1958.

Rasmussen, Steen Eiler. *London, the Unique City*. London: Jonathan Cape, 1937.

Rauda, Wolfgang. *Raumprobleme in europäischen Städtebau*. Munich: Callwey, 1956.

Reps, John. *The Making of Urban America*. Princeton: Princeton University Press, 1965.

Riis, Jacob. *How the Other Half Lives*. New York: Scribners, 1890.

Roberts, Kate L. *The City Beautiful: A Study of Town Planning and Municipal Art*. New York: H. W. Wilson, 1916.

Robinson, Charles M. *Modern Civic Art*. New York: Putnam, 1903.

———. "The Sociology of a Street Layout," *American Academy of Political and Social Science Annals* (1914), 192-199.

———. *City Planning*. New York: Putnam, 1916.

Rönnebeck, Thomas. *Stadterweiterung und Verkehr im neunzehnten Jahrhundert*. Stuttgart: Karl Krämer, 1971.

Ronzi, Renzo. *Bologna, una città*. Bologna: Cappelli, 1960.

Rykwert, Joseph. "The Idea of a Town," *Forum*, 3 (1963), pp. 99-148; enlarged as *The Idea of a Town*. Princeton: Princeton University Press, 1976.

Saalman, Howard. *Haussmann: Paris Transformed*. New York: George Braziller, 1971.

Saulnat, E. de, and A. P. Martial. *Les Boulevards de Paris*. Paris: Paris-Gravé, 1877.

Savannah. Historic Savannah Foundation. *Historic Savannah*. Savannah: Historic Savannah Foundation, 1968.

Scheffler, Karl. *Die Architektur der Grossstadt*. Berlin: B. Cassirer, 1913.

Schmidt, Jürgen. "Strassen in altorientalischen Wohngebieten," *Baghdader Mitteilungen*, 3 (1964), pp. 125-147.

Schreiber, Hermann. *Sinfonie der Strasse*. Düsseldorf and Vienna: Econ-Verlag, 1959.

Scott, Mel. *American City Planning*. Berkeley: University of California Press, 1969.

Sisi, Enrico. *L'Urbanistica negli Studi di Leonardo da Vinci*. Firenze: G. Cencetti, 1953.

Sitte, Camillo. *Der Städtebau nach seinen künstlerischen Grundsätzen*. Vienna: Carl Graeser, 1889; trans. G. R. and C. C. Collins as *City Planning According to Artistic Principles*. New York: Random House, 1965.

Soria y Mata, Arturo. *La Ciudad Lineal, Antecedentes y datos varios acerca de su construcción*. Madrid: Est Tipográfico "Succesores de Rivadenegra," 1894.

Stein, Clarence S. *Toward New Towns for America.* New York, 1950; reprinted, Cambridge, Mass.: The MIT Press, 1971.

Stokes, I. N. Phelps. *The Iconography of Manhattan Island.* 6 vols., New York: Arno Press, 1915-1928.

Stübben, J. *Der Städtebau.* Darmstadt: Bergstrasser, 1890 (and later editions).

————. "Die südliche Stadterweiterung von Amsterdam," *Deutsche Bauzeitung,* 52 (February 16, 1918), p. 65 ff.

Summerson, Sir John. *Georgian London.* Baltimore: Penguin Books, 1962.

Sutcliffe, Anthony. *The Autumn of Central Paris. The Defeat of Town Planning 1850-1970.* London: Edward Arnold, 1970.

Tafuri, Manfredo. "Austromarxismo et città «Das rote Wien»," *Contropiano,* 2 (1971), pp. 259-311.

Tarn, John Nelson. *Five Per Cent Philanthropy. An Account of Housing in Urban Areas between 1840 and 1914.* Cambridge: Cambridge University Press, 1973.

Tunnard, Christopher, and Boris Pushkarev. *Man-Made America: Chaos or Control?* New Haven: Yale University Press, 1963.

————. and Henry Hope Reed. *American Skyline.* New York: Houghton Mifflin, 1953.

Turin. Istituto di Architettura Tecnica del Politecnico di Torino. *Forma urbana ed architettura nella Torino barocca.* Turin: Unione Tipografico-Editrice Torinese, 3 vols. 1968.

Unwin, Raymond. *Town Planning in Practice: An Introduction to the Art of Designing Cities and Suburbs.* London: Unwin, 1909.

Warner, Samuel B. *Streetcar Suburbs.* Cambridge, Mass.: The MIT Press, 1962.

Whiffen, Marcus, ed. *The Architect and the City.* Cambridge, Mass.: The MIT Press, 1966.

White, Morton and Lucia. *The Intellectual Versus the City.* Cambridge, Mass.: Harvard University Press, 1962.

Wilson, Samuel, Jr. *The Vieux Carré, New Orleans. Historic District Demonstration.* New Orleans: Marcou, O'Leary, and Associates, 1968.

Wolf, P. *Städtebau. Das Formproblem der Stadt in Vergangenheit und Zukunft.* Leipzig: Klinkhardt and Biermann, 1919.

Wolf, Peter. *Eugène Hénard and the Beginnings of Urbanism in Paris. 1900-1914.* Paris: International Federation for Housing and Planning and Centre de recherche d'urbanisme, 1968.

Wright, Henry C. *The American City: An Outline of Its Development and Functions.* Chicago: McClurg, 1916.

Wurster, Catherine Bauer. "The Social Front of Modern Architecture," *Society of Architectural Historians Journal,* 24 (March 1965), pp. 48-52.

Zeitler, Julius. "Über Künstlerischen Städtebau," *Kunstgewerbeblatt,* 17 (January 1906), pp. 71-82.

Zevi, Bruno. *Biagio Rossetti: Architetto ferrarese, il prima urbanista moderna europea.* Turin: Einaudi, 1960.

Zucker, Paul. *Town and Square. From the Agora to the Village Green.* New York: Columbia University Press, 1959.

Corpus: Information on Famous or Typical Streets

Collections (See also Rudofsky and Eindhoven, Van Abbemuseum.)

Caminos, Horatio, John F. C. Turner, and John A. Steffian. *Urban Dwelling Environments.* Cambridge, Mass.: The MIT Press, 1969.

Davis, Richard Harding, et al. *The Great Streets of the World.* London: Scribners, 1892.

Geist, Johann F. *Passagen. Ein Bautyp des 19. Jahrhunderts.* Munich: Prestel, 1969.

Katz, Robert D. *Design of the Housing Site. A Critique of American Practice.* Urbana: University of Illinois, Building Research Council, 1966.

Lässig, Konrad, et al. *Strassen und Plätze.* Munich: Callwey, 1968.

Lavedan, Pierre. *Géographie des Villes.* Paris: Gallimard, 1936.

Morini, Mario. *Atlante di storia dell'urbanistica.* Milan: Hoepli, 1963.

Reilly, C. H. "Street by Street: A Critical Tour of Famous Thoroughfares," *Architectural Review,* 79 (1936), pp. 35-37, 134-136, 473.

Individual Streets (See also the more general urban histories.)

Alphande, Adolphe. *Les promenades de Paris.* 2 vols., Paris: J. Rothschild, 1868-[1873].

Brown, Henry Collins. *Fifth Avenue Old and New, 1824-1924.* New York: Fifth Avenue Association, 1924.

Chastel André, and Françoise Mallet. "L'îlot de la rue du Roule et ses abords," *Paris et Ile-de-France,* pp. 16-17 (1965-1966).

Genoa. Universitá degli Studi di Genova, Istituto di Elementi di Architettura e Rilievo dei Monumenti. *Genova, Strada Nuova.* Genoa: Vitale e Ghianda, 1967.

Hillairet, Jacques. *La rue Saint-Antoine.* Paris: Minuit, 1970.

House, J. W., and B. Fullerton. "City Street: A Half Century of Change in Northumberland Street–Pilgrim Street, Newcastle-upon-Tyne. 1891-1955," *Planning Outlook,* 3 (1955), pp. 40-62.

James, Theodore, Jr. *Fifth Avenue.* New York: Walker, 1971.

Lichtenberger, Elisabeth. *Wirtschaftsfunktion und Sozialstruktur der Wiener Ringstrasse.* Graz: H. Böhlau, 1970.

Poleggi, Ennio. *Strada Nuova. Una lottizzazione del Cinquecento a Genova*. Genova: Segep Editrice, 1972.

Salerno, Luigi, Luigi Spezzaferro, Manfredo Tafuri. *Via Giulia*. Rome: Aristide Staderini, 1975.

Scully, Vincent, "The Death of the Street [New York, Park Avenue]," *Perspecta 8* (1963), pp. 91–102.

Pedestrianization and Auto-Restricted Zones

Barton-Aschman Associates, Inc. *Auto-Free Zones: A Methodology for Their Planning and Implementation*. Washington, D.C.: Department of Transportation, July 1972.

Benepe, Berry. "Pedestrian in the City," *Traffic Quarterly* (January 1965), pp. 28–42.

Breines, Simon, and William J. Dean. *The Pedestrian Revolution. Streets without Cars*. New York: Random House, 1974.

Brunmayr, Erich, et al. "Fussgängerfreundliche Zonen," sp. no. *Transparent*, 6, no. 2–3 (1975).

Contini, Edgardo. "Anatomy of the Mall," *Journal of the American Institute of Architects*, (February 1969), pp. 42–50.

Füspök, Làszlò, et al. "Fussgänger Manifest" [I and II], *Umwelt-Design*, 46 (March 1974) and 60 (May 1975).

Gray, John G. *Pedestrianized Shopping Streets in Europe*. [Edinburgh]: Pedestrians Association for Road Safety [1965].

Grey, Arthur L. *People and Downtown*. Seattle: University of Washington, College of Architecture and Urban Planning, 1970.

Gruen, Victor. *The Heart of Our Cities: The Urban Crisis — Diagnosis and Cure*. New York: Simon and Schuster, 1964.

Lewis, David, ed. *The Pedestrian in the City*. London: Elek Books, 1965.

London. Greater London Council. Traffic and Developments Branch. Policy Group. *Pedestrianised Streets*. London: Greater London Council, 1973.

Mills, D. Dewar. "Pedestrian Network," *Architectural Review*, 112 (July 1952), pp. 20–29.

Older, S. J. "Movement of Pedestrians on Footways in Shopping Streets," *Traffic, Engineering and Control* (August 1968), pp. 160–163.

Regional Plan Association, Inc. *Walking Space for Urban Centers*. Prepared by Boris Pushkaref with Jeffrey Zupan. New York: Regional Plan Association, 1971.

Spector, David Kenneth. *Urban Spaces*. Greenwich, Conn.: New York Graphic Society, 1974.

Stuart, Darwin C. "Planning for Pedestrians," *Journal of the American Institute of Planners*, 34 (January 1968).

Thompson, Brenda, and Peter Hart. "Pedestrian Movement. Results of Small Town Survey," *Journal of the Town Planning Institute*, 54 (July/August 1968), pp. 338–342.

Tyrwhitt, Jacqueline. "The Pedestrian in the Megalopolis: Tokyo," *Ekistics*, 25 (February 1968), pp. 73–79.

Wolfe, M. R. "Shopping Streets and the Pedestrian Rediscovered," *Journal of the American Institute of Architects*, 37 (May 1962), pp. 33–42.

Wood, A. A. "The Pedestrianization of Traditional Central Areas," *Architect's Yearbook 12*. London: Elek Books, 1968, pp. 182–193.

Rethinking the Urban Street and How Buildings Make It

See also the chapters by Kenneth Frampton and Victor Caliandro.

Air Rights and Highways, Real Estate Research Corporation in cooperation with Office of Research and Development, Bureau of Public Roads. Washington, D.C.: The Urban Land Institute, 1969.

Dixon, John Morris. "Student Street [University of Alberta]," *Progressive Architecture*, 55 (February 1974), pp. 46–51.

Doshi, B. V., and Christopher Alexander. "Main Structure Concept," *Landscape*, 13 (Winter 1963–64), pp. 17–20.

Friedman, Yona. *Toward a Scientific Architecture*. Cambridge, Mass.: The MIT Press, 1975.

Habraken, N. J. "de ontwikkeling van een taal: the pursuit of an idea," [Dutch and English], *Plan*, 3 (1970), pp. 160–209.

———. *Supports: An Alternative to Mass Housing*. New York: Praeger, 1972.

———, et al. *Variations. The Systematic Design of Supports*. Cambridge, Mass.: Laboratory of Architecture and Planning at MIT, 1976.

Kahn, Louis I. "Toward a Plan for Midtown Philadelphia," *Perspecta*, 2, 1954), p. 10 ff.

Maki, Fumihiko, and Masato Ohtaka. *Investigations in Collective Form — Three Paradigms*. St. Louis: Washington University, School of Architecture, 1964.

Martin, Leslie, and Lionel March. *Urban Space and Structures*. Cambridge: Cambridge University Press, 1972.

New York City. Office of the Mayor. Office of Lower Manhattan Development. *Special Greenwich Street Development District*. New York, n.d. [1973].

Smithson, Alison and Peter. *Team 10 Primer; Urban Structuring*.

Smithson, Alison. "Mat-building: how to recognise and read it," *Ar-*

chitectural Design, 44 (September 1974), pp. 573-590.

Ungers, O. Mathias. "Grossform," *Architecture d'aujourd'hui,* 57-58 (October 1967), pp. 108-113.

Woods, Shadrach. *Candilis, Josic, Woods; Urbanism is Everybody's Business; The Man in the Street.*

Streets as Networks and as Generators of Structured Areas

Alexander, Christopher. "The City is Not a Tree," *Architectural Forum,* 122 (April/May, 1965).

Buchanan, Colin, and Partners. "South Hampshire Study," *Architects' Yearbook 12.* London: Elek, 1968, pp. 25-41; an abridgment from the full report of the same name, London: HMSO, 1966.

LeRicolais, Robert. "The Trihex: New Pattern for Urban Space," *Progressive Architecture,* 49 (February 1968), pp. 118-119.

March, Lionel, and Marcial Echenique. "Models of Environment," sp. no. of *Architectural Design,* 41 (May 1971).

Reichow, Hans Bernard. *Die autogerechte Stadt.* Ravensburg: Otto Maier, 1959.

Wright, Henry, et al. "Realistic Replanning," *Architectural Forum,* 61 (July 1934), pp. 49-55.

Streets and Networks as Traffic Channels:
The Automobile and Alternative Transport Systems

Alexander, Christopher. "The Pattern of Streets," *Architectural Design,* 37 (November 1967), pp. 528-537.

American Transit Association. *Transit Fact Book.* Washington, D.C.: American Transit Association, issued annually.

Branch, Melville C. *Transportation Developments, Cities, and Planning.* Chicago: American Society of Planning Officials, 1965.

Buchanan, Colin, et al. *Traffic in Towns.* London: HMSO, 1963; abbreviated version, Hammondsworth: Penguin, 1964.

Canty, Eugene T. *Transportation and Urban Scale.* Ann Arbor, Mich.; General Motors Research Laboratories, 1969.

Doxiadis, C. A. "Man, City, and Automobile," *High Speed Ground Transportation Journal,* 3 (January 1969), pp. 1-33.

Gakenheimer, Ralph. *The Impact of the Motor Vehicle on the Environment.* Cambridge, Mass.: The MIT Press, forthcoming.

George, Patricia Conway, ed. "Mass Transit: Problems and Promise," *Design Quarterly,* 71 (1968).

Great Britain. Minister of Transport. *Cars for Cities.* London: HMSO, 1967.

"Innovations in Mass Transit," *Journal of the American Society of Transportation Modes.* Washington, D.C.: Institute of Traffic Engineers, 1964.

Lang, Albert S. *Urban Rail Transit: Its Economics and Technology.* Cambridge, Mass.: Joint Center for Urban Studies, 1964.

Meyer, John R., J. F. Kain, and M. Wohl. *The Urban Transportation Problem.* Cambridge, Mass.: Harvard University Press, 1965.

"Milton Keynes," sp. nos. of *Architectural Design,* 43 (June 1973) and 44 (August 1974).

Mitchell, Robert B., and Chester Rapkin. *Urban Traffic: A Function of Land Use.* New York: Columbia University Press, 1954.

Mumford, Lewis. *The Highway and the City.* New York: Harcourt, Brace and World, 1963.

Owen, Wilfred. *The Metropolitan Transportation Problem.* A Brookings Institution Study. Garden City, N.Y.: Doubleday, 1966.

————. "Urban Housing and Transportation: A New Partnership," *Current History,* 59 (November 1970), pp. 290-295.

Princeton University. *Urban Development and Urban Transportation.* Conference Report. 1957.

Reische, Diana, ed. *Problems of Mass Transportation.* New York: H. W. Wilson, 1970.

Richards, Brian. *New Movement in Cities.* New York: Reinhold, 1966.

Ritter, Paul. *Planning for Man and Motor.* London: Pergamon, 1964.

"Road Space Required for Traffic in Towns," *Town Planning Review,* 33 (January 1963), pp. 279-292.

Smith, Wilbur, and Associates. *Transportation and Parking for Tomorrow's Cities.* Report to Automobile Manufacturers Association. New Haven: Wilbur Smith and Associates, 1966.

Stanford Research Institute. *Future Urban Transportation Systems* [a group of publications]. Menlo Park, Calif.: Stanford Research Institute, 1967 ff.

Tetlow, J., and A. Goss. *Homes, Towns and Traffic.* New York: Praeger, 1965.

Traffic Engineering Handbook. (John E. Baerwald, ed.; prepared under the direction of the Traffic Engineering Handbook Editorial Board). Washington, D.C.: Institute of Traffic Engineers, 1965.

U.S. Department of Housing and Urban Development. *A Summary of Urban Mass Transportation Demonstration Projects.* Washington, D.C.: U.S. Department of Housing and Urban Development, 1968.

————, *Tomorrow's Transportation — New Systems for the Urban Future.* Leon Monroe Cole, ed., Harold W. Merritt, technical ed. Washington, D.C.: U.S. Department of Housing and Urban Development, 1968.

Van Ginkel Associates. *Movement in Midtown.* New York: Office of Midtown Planning and Development, 1970.

Warburton, Ralph, ed. ''New Concepts in Urban Transportation Systems,'' sp. no. of *Journal of the Franklin Institute,* 286, no. 5 (November 1968).

Antistreet Architecture and Urbanism

Congrès Internationaux d'Architecture Moderne. *La Charte d'Athenes.* Paris: Plon, 1943; in English as *The Athens Charter* (New York: Grossman, 1973).

———. *The Heart of the City.* New York: Pellegrini and Cudahy, 1952.

Evenson, Norma. *Le Corbusier: The Machine and the Grand Design.* New York: George Braziller, 1969.

Garnier, Tony. *Une Cité industrielle. Etude pour la construction des villes.* Paris: A. Vincent, 1917.

Jeanneret, Charles-Edouard (Le Corbusier). *Urbanisme.* Paris: Crès, 1923; in English as *The City of Tomorrow and Its Planning* (London: Architectural Press, 1929).

———. ''La rue,'' *L'Intransigent* (May 1929).

———. ''Mort de la rue,'' *Plan,* 5 (May 1931), pp. 49–64.

———. *La ville radieuse.* Paris: Crès, 1935; in English as *The Radiant City* (New York: Orion, 1968).

———. *Quand les cathédrales étaient blanches.* Paris: Plon, 1937; in English as *When the Cathedrals Were White* (New York: Reynal and Hitchcock, 1947).

———. *Les Plans Le Corbusier de Paris 1956–1922.* Paris: Minuit, 1956.

Newman, Oscar, ed. *New Frontiers in Architecture. CIAM '59 in Otterlo.* New York: Universe, 1961.

Pawlowski, Christophe. *Tony Garnier.* Paris: Centre de recherche d'urbanisme, 1967.

Sert, J. L. *Can Our Cities Survive?* London: Oxford University Press, 1942.

Tubbs, Ralph. *Living in Cities.* Hammondsworth: Penguin, 1942.

Wiebenson, Dora. *Tony Garnier: The Cité Industrielle.* New York: George Braziller, 1969.

Antistreet Regionalism

Abercrombie, Patrick. *Greater London Plan.* London: HMSO, 1944.

Barlow Report. *Report of Royal Commission on Distribution of Industrial Population.* London: HMSO, 1940.

Caro, Robert A. *The Power Broker. Robert Moses and the Fall of New York.* New York: Knopf, 1974.

Gropius, Walter. *Rebuilding Our Communities* (Institute of Design Book). Chicago: Paul Theobald, 1945.

Howard, Ebenezer. *Garden Cities of Tomorrow* (originally published in 1898 as *Tomorrow: A Peaceful Path to Real Reform*). Cambridge, Mass.: The MIT Press, 1965.

Macfadyen, Dugald. *Sir Ebenezer Howard and the Town Planning Movement.* Manchester: Manchester University Press, 1933; reprinted Cambridge, Mass.: The MIT Press, 1970.

Mumford, Lewis. *The Culture of Cities.* New York: Harcourt, Brace, 1938.

Osborn, Frederic J. *Green-Belt Cities.* London: Faber and Faber, 1946.

———, and Arnold Whittick. *The New Towns: The Answer to Megalopolis.* New York: McGraw-Hill, 1963.

Regional Plan Association, Inc. *Regional Plan of New York and Its Environs: Planning of the New York Region.* New York: Regional Plan Association, 1927.

Stein, Clarence S. *Toward New Towns for America.* 1951; reprinted Cambridge, Mass.: The MIT Press, 1969.

Webber, Melvin, ed. *Explorations into Urban Structure.* Philadelphia: University of Pennsylvania Press, 1964.

Wright, Frank Lloyd. *When Democracy Builds.* Chicago: University of Chicago Press, 1945.

———. *The Living City.* New York: Horizon Press, 1958.

Wright, Henry. *Rehousing Urban America.* New York: Columbia University Press, 1935.

Wright, Henry N. ''Radburn Revisited,'' *Architectural Forum,* 135 (July–August 1971), pp. 52–57.

Streets: Dark Sides

Addams, Jane. *The Spirit of Youth and the City Streets.* New York: Macmillan, 1911.

Bechtel, Robert B. ''The Discovery of Areas of Potential Social Disturbance in the City,'' *The Sociological Quarterly,* 12 (Winter 1971), pp. 114–121.

Cuthbert, Sidney John. *We Shall Fight in the Streets: A Guide to Street Fighting.* Boulder, Colo.: Panther Publications, 1965.

Dyos, H. J., and Michael Wolff, eds. *The Victorian City: Images and Realities.* London: Routledge and Kegan Paul, 1974.

Nevill, Ralph. *Night Life: London and Paris, Past and Present.* London: Cassell, 1926.

New York Press. *Night Side of New York.* New York: B. J. C. Harfe, 1866.

Newman, Oscar. *Defensible Space. Crime Prevention through Urban Design*. New York: Macmillan, 1972.

Night People's Guide to New York. New York: Darien House, 1965.

Powell, E. H. "The Evolution of the American City and the Emergence of Anomie: A Culture Case Study of Buffalo, New York, 1810–1910," *British Journal of Sociology*, 13 (1962), pp. 156–168.

Environmental Conditions: Noise, Wind, Light, Microclimate

Bona, Enrico. "The Sound and Noises of the City," *Casabella*, 339–340 (August–September 1969), pp. 60–64.

Branch, Melville Campbell, with R. Dale Beland. *Outdoor Noise and the Metropolitan Environment*. Los Angeles: Department of City Planning, 1970.

Branch, Melville Campbell, with R. Dale Beland. *Outdoor Noise and the Metropolitan Environment*. Los Angeles: Department of City Planning, 1970.

Edwards, A. Trystan. "Sunlight in Streets," *Town Planning Review*, 8 (1920), pp. 93–97.

Klausner, Samuel. *On Man and His Environment*. San Francisco: Jossey-Bass, 1971.

Lynch, Kevin. *Site Planning*. Cambridge, Mass.: The MIT Press, 1962.

———, and Michael Southworth. "Environmental Standards for Street Quality," *MIT-LES Working Paper*, April 6, 1972.

The Economics of Preservation and Development

The economic effect of alternative regulatory and administrative structures is so strong that this and the next section of the bibliography should be reviewed together.

Bernard, Michael. *Airspace in Urban Development — Emergent Concepts*. Washington, D.C.: Urban Land Institute Technical Bulletin, July 1963.

Costonis, John J. *Space Adrift: Saving Urban Landmarks through the Chicago Plan*. Urbana: University of Illinois Press, 1974.

Downs, Anthony. "Alternative Forms of Future Urban Growth in the United States," *Journal of the American Institute of Planners*, 36 (January 1970), pp. 3–11.

Frieden, Bernard J. *The Future of Old Neighborhoods. Rebuilding for a Changing Population*. Cambridge, Mass.: The MIT Press, 1964.

Hoyt, Homer. *Dynamic Factors in Land Values*. Urban Land Institute Technical Bulletin no. 37. Washington, D.C.: ULI, 1960.

Jacobs, Jane. *The Economy of Cities*. New York: Random House, 1969.

Kunzmann, Klaus Rainer. *Grundbesitzverhältnisse in historischen Stadtkernen und ihr Einfluss auf die Stadterneuerung*. Wien: Springer-Verlag, 1972.

Marcus, Norman, and Marilyn Groves. *New Zoning: Legal, Administrative, and Economic Concepts and Techniques*. New York: Praeger, 1970.

Netzer, Richard. *Economics of the Property Tax*. Washington, D.C.: Brookings Institution, 1966.

Pickard, Jerome P. *Changing Urban Land Uses as Affected by Taxation*. Urban Land Institute Research Monograph No. 6. Washington, D.C.: ULI, 1962.

Rawson, Mary. *Property Taxation and Urban Development*. Urban Land Institute Research Monograph No. 4. Washington, D.C.: ULI, 1961.

Real Estate Research Corporation. In cooperation with Office of Research and Development, Bureau of Public Roads. *Air Rights and Highways*. The Urban Land Institute Technical Bulletin No. 64, Washington, D.C.: ULI, 1969.

———. *A Study of Airspace Utilization*. Report to California Division of Highways. U.S. Department of Transportation, Federal Highway Administration, Bureau of Public Roads. Washington, D.C.: U.S. Department of Transportation, 1968.

Reskin, Melvin A., and Patrick J. Rohan. "Nichol's the Law of Eminent Domain." *Condemnation Procedures and Techniques*, vol 7. Matthew Bender, ed.

Swanson, Carl V., and Raymond J. Waldmann. "A Simulation Model of Economic Growth Dynamics," *Journal of the American Institute of Planners*, 36 (September 1970), pp. 314–322.

Teitz, Michael B. "Cost Effectiveness: A Systems Approach to Analysis of Urban Services," *Journal of the American Institute of Planners*, 34 (September 1968), pp. 303–311.

U.S. Department of Transportation. *A Report on the Status of Multiple Use and Joint Development*. Washington, D.C.: U.S. Department of Transportation, 1969.

Ziegler, Arthur P., Jr., Leopold Adlèr II, and Walter C. Kidney. *Revolving Funds for Historic Preservation: A Manual of Practice*. Pittsburgh: Ober Park Associates, 1975.

Regulatory and Administrative Structures
for Preservation and Development

Anderson, Robert Milford. *American Law of Zoning: Zoning, Planning, Subdivision Control*. Rochester, N.Y.: Lawyers Cooperative

Publishing Co., 1968.

Architectural Forum, Editors of special number on effects of first (1916) zoning law in New York City, *Architectural Forum,* 35 (October 1921).

Barnett, Jonathan. *Urban Design as Public Policy: Practical Methods for Improving Cities.* New York: Architectural Record Books, 1974.

Berkeley, E. "Zoning in a Three Dimensional World." *Architectural Forum,* 133 (November 1970), pp. 48–51.

Bookchin, Murray. "The Myth of City Planning," *Liberation,* 18 (September/October 1973), pp. 24–42.

Brooks, Mary. *Bonus Provisions in Central City Areas.* Chicago: American Society of Planning Officials, 1970.

Cervellati, P. L., and R. Scannavini, eds. *Bologna: politica e metodologia del restauro nei centri storici.* Bologna: il Mulino, 1973.

Comer, John Preston. *New York City Building Control, 1800–1941.* New York: Columbia University Press, 1942.

Kotler, Milton. *Neighborhood Government: The Local Foundations of Political Life.* Indianapolis: Bobbs-Merrill, 1969.

Kriken, John. *Urban Design Mechanisms for San Antonio.* San Antonio: City Planning Department, October 1972.

Long, Norton. *The Unwalled City: Reconstituting the Urban Community.* New York: Basic Books [1972].

Manheim, Marvin L. "Reaching Decisions about Technological Projects with Social Consequences: A Normative Model," Cambridge, Mass.: MIT ILP Symposium Paper, December 10, 1970.

New York, City of, Board of Estimate and Apportionment. Height of Buildings Commission. *Report to the Committee on the Height, Size, and Arrangement of Buildings.* New York, 1913.

————. Planning Commission. Department of City Planning. *Zoning Handbook.* New York, 1961.

————. Planning Commission. *Plan for New York City.* New York, 1967.

————. Planning Commission. *Community Planning Districts.* New York, 1968.

————. Planning Commission. *The Planning Commission's Report Adopting the Zoning Amendment Permitting the Transfer of Development Rights.* New York, 1968.

————. Planning Commission. *Planned Unit Development.* New York, 1968.

————. Planning Commission. *An Amendment to the Zoning Resolution Relating to Section 86-00 Establishing a Special Lower Third Avenue Development District Which Provides an Incentive for Construction of New Housing for All Income Levels.* New York, 1970.

————. Urban Design Council. *Housing Quality: A Program for Zoning Reform.* New York: City of New York, Urban Design Council, 1973.

Pooley, Beverley J. *Planning and Zoning in the United States.* Ann Arbor: University of Michigan Law School, 1961.

Reilly, William K., ed. *The Use of Land: A Citizens' Policy Guide to Urban Growth.* New York: T. Y. Crowell, 1973.

Reps, John W. "Requiem for Zoning," *Planning,* (1964), pp. 56–57.

San Francisco, City and County of. City Planning Commission. *San Francisco Downtown Zoning Study.* San Francisco: City Planning Commission, 1966.

Scharpf, Fritz W. *Planung als politischer Prozess. Aufsätze zur Theorie der planenden Demokratie.* Frankfurt: Suhrkamp, 1973.

Siegan, Bernard H. *Land Use Without Zoning.* Lexington, Mass.: Lexington Books, 1972.

Sittler, Helen Bush. "A Contextual Approach to Preservation." M. Arch. thesis, Massachusetts Institute of Technology (June 1975).

Toll, Seymour I. *Zoned American.* New York: Grossman Publishers, 1969.

Turner, John F. C., and Robert Fichter. *Freedom to Build. Dweller Control of the Housing Process.* New York: Macmillan 1972.

Warburton, Ralph. "Progressive Approach to Zoning and Building Codes," *Systems Building News.* Atlanta: July 1971.

Willhelm, S. M. *Urban Zoning and Land Use Theory.* Glencoe, Ill.: Free Press, 1962.

Williams, Frank B. *The Law of City Planning and Zoning.* New York: Macmillan, 1922.

Streets: Notation Systems, Representation

Appleyard, Donald, Kevin Lynch, and John R. Myer. *The View from the Road.* Cambridge, Mass.: The MIT Press, 1964.

Architecture d'aujourd'hui. (sp. no. on urban space), 153 (December 1970–January 1971).

Bretez, Louis. *Le plan de Louis Bretez dit Plan de Turgot.* (engraved, Paris, 1734–39); reprint, Paris: Yeux Ouverts, 1966.

Fillipetti, H. *Recherche d'une methodologie pour l'étude de l'animation des rues.* Paris: Ecole Normale Superieure des Beaux-Arts, U.P. No. 6, 1972.

Hall, E. T. "A System for the Notation of Proxemic Behavior," *American Anthropologist,* 65 (1963), pp. 1003–1026.

Halprin, Lawrence. "Notation," *Progressive Architecture,* 46 (July 1965), pp. 126–133.

Hauser, P. M., and L. F. Schnore. *The Study of Urbanization.* New York: John Wiley, 1965; see bibliographic footnote 50 on p. 106.

Horvath, Ronald J. "Machine Space," *The Geographical Review*, 64 (April 1974), pp. 167–188.

Lynch, Kevin. *The Image of the City*. Cambridge, Mass.: The MIT Press, 1960.

Nolli, Giambattista. *Roma*. (Famous map, engraved Rome, 1748.)

Passonneau, Joseph R., and Richard S. Wurman. *Urban Atlas: 20 American Cities*. Cambridge, Mass.: The MIT Press, 1966.

Takeyama, Minoru, ed. "Street Semiology," sp. no. of *Kenchiku-Bunka*, (February 1975).

Talwar, Premjit. "Notation Systems in Architecture." M. Arch. Thesis, Massachusetts Institute of Technology (June 1972).

Thiel, Philip. "A Sequence-Experience Notation," *Town Planning Review*, 32 (April 1961).

———. "Notes on the Description, Scaling, Notation and Scoring of Some Perceptual and Cognitive Attributes of the Physical Environment," pp. 593 ff. in Harold M. Proshansky et al., eds., *Environmental Psychology*. New York: Holt, Rinehart and Winston, 1970.

Wray, James R., et al. "Photo Interpretation in Urban Area Analysis," Chap. 12 in *Manual of Photographic Interpretation*. Washington, D.C.: American Society of Photogrammetry, 1960.

A Supplementary Bibliography for the Paperback Edition
Stanford Anderson (1986)

Multidisciplinary Studies of Urban Environment

"Architecture and Public Spaces," a special issue of *The Public Interest*, no. 74 (Winter 1984).

Gouvion, Colette, and François van de Mert. *Le Symbolisme des rues et des cités*. Paris: Berg International, 1974.

Hillier, Bill, and Julienne Hanson. *The Social Logic of Space*. Cambridge: Cambridge University Press, 1984.

Jackson, John Brinkerhoff. *Discovering the Vernacular Landscape*. New Haven: Yale University Press, 1984.

Jacobs, Allan. *Looking at Cities*. Cambridge: Harvard University Press, 1985.

Lynch, Kevin. *A Theory of Good City Form*. Cambridge: The MIT Press, 1981.

New York, Cooper-Hewitt Museum (Lisa Taylor, ed.). *Cities. The Forces that Shape Them*. New York: Rizzoli, 1983.

———. *Urban Open Spaces*. New York: Rizzoli, 1980.

Rapoport, Amos. *Human Aspects of Urban Form. Towards a Man-Environment Approach to Urban Form and Design*. Oxford: Pergamon Press, 1979.

Studies Contributing to a History of Streets

Benevolo, Leonardo. *The History of the City*. Cambridge: The MIT Press, 1980.

Castex, Jean, et al. *Formes urbaines: De l'îlot à a la barre*. Paris: Dunod, 1977.

Ciucci, Giorgio, et al. *The American City. From the Civil War to the New Deal*. Cambridge: The MIT Press, 1979.

Collins, George R., and Christiane Crasemann Collins. *Camillo Sitte. The Birth of Modern City Planning*. Revised edition (including the Collins' translation of Sitte's *Der Städtebau*), New York: Rizzoli, 1986.

Crouch, Dora, et al. *Spanish City Planning in North America*. Cambridge: The MIT Press, 1982.

Evenson, Norma. *Paris: A Century of Change, 1878–1978*. New Haven: Yale University Press, 1979.

Fehl, Gerhard, and Juan Rodriquez-Lores. *Städtebau um die Jahrhundertwende. Materialien zur Entstehung der Disziplin Städtebau*. Cologne: Deutscher Gemeindeverlag und Verlag W. Kohlhammer, 1980.

Girouard, Mark. *Cities and People. A Social and Architectural History*. New Haven: Yale University Press, 1985.

Guidoni, Enrico. "Street and Block. From the Late Middle Ages to the Eighteenth Century," *Lotus* 19 (1978), pp. 4–19.

Rasmussen, Steen Eiler, *London: The Unique City*. Revised edition, Cambridge: The MIT Press, 1982.

Reps, John W. *Cities of the American West. A History of Frontier Urban Planning*. Princeton: Princeton University Press, 1979.

Sutcliffe, Anthony, ed. *Metropolis 1890–1940*. Chicago: University of Chicago Press, 1984.

Corpus: Information on Famous or Typical Streets

Boudon, Françoise, et al. *Systéme de l'architecture urbaine. Le Quartier des Halles à Paris*. Paris: CNRS, 1977.

Castex, Jean, et al. *Lecture d'une ville: Versailles*. Paris: Moniteur, 1980.

Ciucci, Giorgio. *La Piazza del Popolo. Storia architettura urbanistica*. Rome: Officina Edizioni, 1974.

Geist, Johann Friedrich. *Arcades: The History of a Building Type*. Cambridge: The MIT Press, 1982.

Hobhouse, Hermione. *A History of Regent Street*. London: Queen Anne Press, 1975.

Liebs, Chester H. *Main Street to Miracle Mile*. Boston: New York Graphic Society/Little, Brown, 1985.

Tobriner, Stephen. *The Genesis of Noto. An Eighteenth Century Sicilian City*. Berkeley, CA: University of California Press, 1982.

Pedestrianization and Auto-Restricted Zones

Appleyard, Donald, *Livable Streets*. Berkeley, CA: University of California Press, 1981.
London, Design Council. *Street Furniture: A Design Council Catalogue*. London: Design Council, 1979.

Rethinking the Urban Street and How Buildings Make It

Alexander, Christopher, et al. *The Timeless Way of Building*. New York: Oxford University Press, 1979.
————. *A Pattern Language. Towns, Buildings, Construction*. New York: Oxford University Press, 1977.
Baird, George, and Barton Myers. "Vacant Lottery," sp. no. of *Design Quarterly*, no. 108 (1978).
"City Segments," sp. no. of *Design Quarterly*, no. 113–14 (1980).
Culot, Maurice, and Leon Krier. *Contreprojets. Controprogetti. Counterprojects*. [Brussels]: Archives d'Architecture Moderne, 1980.
Culot, M., et al. *Les Espaces publics Bruxellois. Analyse et projets*. Brussels: Fondation Roi Baudouin, 1981.
Ellis, William. "Type and Context in Urbanism: Colin Rowe's Contextualism," *Oppositions* 18 (Fall 1979), pp. 1–27.
Habraken, N. John, et al. *The Grunsfeld Variations. A Report on the Thematic Development of an Urban Tissue*. Cambridge, MA: Massachusetts Institute of Technology, Department of Architecture, 1981.
————. *The Appearance of the Form* (Cambridge, MA: Awater Press, 1985).
Koetter, Fred. "On Robert Venturi, Denise Scott Brown, and Steven Izenour's *Learning from Las Vegas*," *Oppositions* 3 (May 1974), pp. 98–104.
Koolhaas, Rem. *Delirious New York. A Retroactive Manifesto for Manhattan*. New York: Oxford University Press, 1978.
Krier, Leon. "Cities within the City," sp. no. of *a+u* (Tokyo), 83 (1977).
Krier, Rob. *Urban Space*. London: Academy Editions, 1979.
————. *Rob Krier on Architecture*. London: Academy Editions, 1982.
————. *Rob Krier: Urban Projects. 1968–1982*. New York: Rizzoli, 1982.

London, Design Council. *Streets Ahead*. New York: Whitney Library of Design, 1979.
Rossi, Aldo. *The Architecture of the City*. Cambridge: The MIT Press, 1982.
————. *Aldo Rossi: Three Cities. Perugia, Milan, Mantua*. New York: Rizzoli, 1985.
Rowe, Colin, and Fred Koetter. *Collage City*. Cambridge: The MIT Press, 1978.
Shane, Graham. "The Revival of the Street," *Lotus* 24 (1979), pp. 103–14.
Vernez-Moudon, Anne. *Built for Change. Neighborhood Architecture in San Francisco*. Cambridge: The MIT Press, 1986.
Vernez-Moudon, A., and Pierre Laconte, eds. *Streets As Public Property. Opportunities for Public/Private Interaction in Planning and Design*. Seattle, WA: University of Washington, 1983.
Von Eckardt, Wolf. *Back to the Drawing Board! Planning Livable Cities*. Washington, DC: New Republic Books, 1978.

Regulatory and Administrative Structures for Preservation and Development

Barnett, Jonathan. *An Introduction to Urban Design*. New York: Harper & Row, 1982.
Craycroft, Robert. *Revitalizing Main Street. Small Town Public Policy*. Starksville, MS: Mississippi State University, 1982.
Plunz, Richard ed. *Housing Form and Public Policy in the United States* (New York: Praeger, 1980)

List of Contributors

Diana Agrest is an architect and a Fellow of the Institute for Architecture and Urban Studies, New York City.

Stanford Anderson is Professor of History and Architecture at the Massachusetts Institute of Technology. He is a Fellow of the Institute for Architecture and Urban Studies.

Victor Caliandro teaches architecture and urban design at Columbia University and at Lehigh University.

Thomas Czarnowski is an architect in the office of E. L. Barnes, New York City.

Peter Eisenman is an architect and director of the Institute for Architecture and Urban Studies, New York City.

William C. Ellis practices architecture in New York City and teaches at the City College of New York and the Cooper Union. He is a Fellow of the Institute for Architecture and Urban Studies.

Kenneth Frampton is Lecturer, Royal College of Art, London. He is a Fellow of the Institute for Architecture and Urban Studies.

Robert Gutman is Professor of Sociology at Rutgers University and Class of 1913 Lecturer in Architecture and Urban Planning at Princeton University.

Gloria Levitas is Instructor of Anthropology at Queens College, City University of New York.

Judith Magel is a student in urban planning at the University of Pennsylvania.

Vincent Moore is Vice-President of The Saratoga Associates, a private interdisciplinary consulting firm.

Joseph Rykwert is Professor of Art at the University of Essex and an editor of *Lotus*.

Thomas Schumacher is Assistant Professor of Architecture at Princeton University.

Anthony Vidler is Professor of Architecture at Princeton University where he also teaches in the European Cultural Studies Program. He is a Fellow of The Institute for Architecture and Urban Studies.

Gary H. Winkel is Associate Professor in the Environmental Psychology Program at the Graduate Center of the City University of New York.

Peter Wolf is a planning consultant and Chairman of the Board of Fellows of the Institute for Architecture and Urban Studies.

Index

COMPUTER-INTEGRATED SURGERY

Technology and Clinical Applications

edited by Russell H. Taylor, Stéphane Lavallée, Grigore C. Burdea, and Ralph Mösges

THE MIT PRESS
CAMBRIDGE, MASSACHUSETTS
LONDON, ENGLAND

This book was set in Baskerville by Asco Trade Typesetting
Ltd., Hong Kong and was printed and bound in the United
States of America.

Library of Congress Cataloging-in-Publication Data
Computer-integrated surgery : technology and clinical
 applications / edited by Russell H. Taylor ... [et al.].
   p.   cm.
 Includes bibliographical references and index.
 ISBN 0-262-20097-X
 1. Surgery—Data processing. 2. Surgery—Computer
simulation. 3. Robot hands. I. Taylor, Russell H.
 [DNLM: 1. Surgery, Operative—methods. 2. Computer
Systems. 3. Man-Machine Systems. 4. Image Processing,
Computer-Assisted. 5. Robotics. WO 500 C738 1995]
RD29.7.C65   1995
617.9′0285—dc20
DNLM/DLC
for Library of Congress   94-27743
                                              CIP

To Beverley and Samuel, for their patience and understanding for all the long nights when Daddy was working on this project.
—Russell Taylor

To Philippe Cinquin, pioneer of computer-integrated surgery, for having introduced me to this field ten years ago.
—Stéphane Lavallée

To my dear wife, Haigui.
—Grigore Burdea

To our patients, who trust in medical progress and thereby make it achievable.
—Ralph Mösges

CONTENTS

INTRODUCTION

An emerging partnership

THE SUBJECT OF this book is an emerging active partnership between people and machines to do certain skilled tasks *better* than either can do alone. The book is targeted both at technologists (engineers and scientists) and at clinicians (surgeons, radiologists, dentists, etc.) in the hope that it can provide the information necessary to expedite progress in technical development and effective application of this rapidly evolving discipline.

For clinicians, this human-machine partnership is important because it offers the possibility both of significantly improving the efficacy, safety, and cost-effectiveness of existing clinical procedures and of developing new procedures that cannot be performed at all otherwise. For technologists, this partnership offers real, challenging applications with articulate end users. Furthermore, incremental progress is possible. Even relatively simple uses of new technology can make significant differences clinically, and the lessons learned can then be applied to harder problems.

In exploring a partnership involving complementary capabilities, it is useful to consider the strengths and weaknesses of each party. Human surgeons have, of course, many capabilities. They are very dexterous, quite strong, and fast, and are highly trained to exploit a variety of tactile, visual, and other cues. They are adaptable and can exercise these skills over a surprisingly wide range of geometric scales. "Judgmentally" controlled, they understand what is going on in the surgical procedure and use their dexterity, senses, and experience to execute the procedure. They can analyze their own performance and apply the lessons learned— that is, they can improve with practice.

However, surgeons do have limitations. They are not geometrically accurate. In other words, they cannot easily place an instrument at an exact, numerically defined location relative to the patient and then move it through a defined trajectory, nor are they very good at exerting *exactly* a predefined force in a particular direction. They do not tolerate ionizing radiation well and are understandably not eager to be exposed to it on a daily basis. They get clumsy if forced to work in very confined spaces or over long periods of time. They may have small hand tremors that limit their ability to operate on very delicate structures. They get tired and make mistakes. They get old and lose some of their skill. Unfortunately, many of these limitations affect the efficacy of certain surgical procedures, especially in cases where great geometric accuracy is required or in which the surgeon's direct use of his or her senses or manual dexterity are impaired.

Fortunately, machines have complementary capabilities that can remedy some of these defects. Machines are very precise and untiring. They can be equipped with any number of sensory feedback devices and can measure and position instruments very accurately in six degrees of freedom. Numerically controlled machines can move a surgical instrument through an exactly defined trajectory with precisely controlled forces. Potentially, they can be miniaturized to function in very confined spaces and can be hardened to withstand significant doses of ionizing radiation. When properly maintained, they are reliable, and their every move can be recorded for subsequent analysis. Viewed in this light, even very sophisticated computer-controlled machines such as robots are simply better surgical tools. As such, they do not pose any significant threat to replace surgeons, but they *can* help surgeons to work better.

Nonetheless, the computer control required to achieve many of these advantages of machines introduces important questions. Because surgeons are responsible for everything that goes on in the operating theater, they are naturally wary of any entity—be it a scrub nurse, intern, resident, or machine—that may not respond to their wishes in exactly the desired manner and at exactly the right time. Surgeons have learned (more or less) to trust human assistants, who can be trained to respond to verbal and nonverbal commands and to exercise some judgment in carrying out assigned tasks. Machines, on the other hand, are very literal-minded, possessing a very limited ability to interpret human language. Furthermore, much of the information needed to exploit the geometric precision of machines is not easily described linguistically. How can surgeons tell a machine what it is supposed to do? How can they be sure that the machine "understands"? They *must* rely on the machine to provide precision or access to otherwise inaccessible parts of the patient's anatomy. How can they keep track of what it is doing when their own senses are inadequate? How can they trust it not to harm the patient? How can the machine help them to perform a tricky, precise maneuver or possibly warn them when human error may hurt the patient?

None of these questions are easily answered. Indeed, all are the subjects of ongoing research. We hope that the work reported in this book will give the reader a better understanding both of the underlying issues and of potential areas for improvement.

The synergy between planning and execution

A related theme is the significant synergy that can be achieved between computer methods for presurgical planning and an enhanced ability actually to execute the plans developed. This book has many examples of systems that extract information from medical images to model anatomic structures in live patients and to help clinicians use this information in diagnosis and treatment planning. For these systems to have value, it is essential that surgeons actually be able to carry out the surgical plans developed. If a plan is primarily a qualitative preoperative simulation, it may be possible for a surgeon simply to rehearse ahead of time and then carry the results into the operating room in his or her head. However, the usefulness of such a simulation may be greatly enhanced if the system is capable of following the progress of the actual surgery and of providing the surgeon with an interactive real-time display as a reference. If the plan involves quantitative information, such as the shape and position of a tumor or desired positions and orientations of osteotomy fragments, then the ability to achieve the necessary geometric accuracies intraoperatively becomes even more important. Again, many of the chapters in this book describe systems designed to provide appropriate real-time information about surgical plans or to execute precise geometric plans. The availability of such systems, in turn, makes the computational effort required to plan the surgery much more worthwhile. Furthermore, the consistency of computer-assisted surgical execution means that comparative studies involving several subjects become more meaningful.

A structuring architecture

The figure below illustrates, in a general way, our view of the key architectural components required to support such human-machine partnerships in surgery. In a sense, it represents our view of what a comprehensive future system of computer-integrated surgery might include.

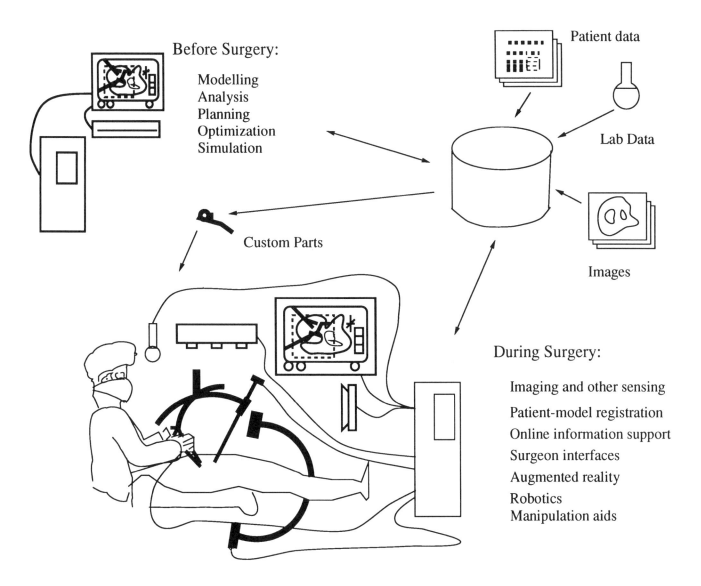

A *unified database*, eventually will contain essentially all information about a patient. Much of this data will be in the form of *medical images* gathered from a variety of sensors and modalities. Powerful *presurgical planning* and *postsurgical analysis systems* will process patient data. A key element of this processing will be the derivation of three-dimensional (3D) engineering models of the patient's anatomy and the use of these models to assist the physician in analyzing the patient's condition. This processing will include both precise quantitative computations (e.g., numeric optimizations, finite elements, etc.) and qualitative analysis augmented by powerful graphics and visualization hardware. Surgeons will use this analysis to plan an optimal surgical procedure, to simulate its execution, and (possibly) to simulate future healing by the patient. If necessary, they will use these data in consultation with engineers to design appropriate custom implants or surgical aids, which will then be fabricated in an automated manufacturing facility. The systems used to plan surgical procedures also will interact with the hospital information system to order any necessary consumable items, schedule the operating room and surgical personnel, and instruct the hospital staff on any preoperative procedures needed for the patient.

For postoperative follow-up, similar systems will assist in analyzing intraoperative and postoperative medical images and assessing how well the planned surgical procedure was carried out and how well the patient's recovery is proceeding. They will assist in planning additional rehabilitation procedures or any follow-up surgery that might be required. Finally, the results of individual procedures will be combined back into larger databases that can be used to analyze and compare the efficacy of different procedures. This statistical analysis, in turn, may be used to suggest and optimize new surgical procedures with measurable benefits to patients.

Intraoperative systems will have access to all data about the surgical plan (and, indeed, all the data about the patient) to assist the surgical team carrying out the procedure. *Sensing subsystems* will provide information needed to register the virtual reality of the presurgical models with the actual reality of the patient on the operating table. Many sensing modalities, including conventional computer vision, real-time radiography, ultrasound devices, special-purpose geometric sensors, force sensors, voice recognition systems, intraoperative magnetic resonance imaging, and computerized tomography, will be available and may be used either individually or in combination. A key responsibility of the surgical workstation will be the management of all these data. It must select appropriate inputs and then combine and interpret data in the light of what it "knows" about the surgical plan and patient's anatomy. *Surgeon interface subsystems* will use a variety of modalities (e.g., graphics, synthesized voice, tonal cues, programmable impedance of manipulator joints) to provide on-line, real-time "advice" to the surgeon, based on the sensed relationship between the surgical plan and surgical execution. Eventually, such subsystems will become very sophisticated, with the ability to monitor progress of the surgical plan and use this information to customize displays, select appropriate sensor-tracking modes, and help interpret inputs from the surgeon. In an advanced system, a see-through stereo display might be used to project the surgical advice directly onto the surgeon's visual field, and the surgeon would use voice input to tell the system what he or she wants. A simpler initial system might provide very simple real-time graphics and auditory cues for alignment advice, coupled with an on-line 3D model display to provide somewhat more detailed "snapshots" of patient-to-model registration.

Manipulation aids are provided to assist the surgeon in precisely aligning his or her instruments relative to the patient or in executing the mechanical parts of the planned procedure. Such aids will run the gamut from passive devices of various degrees of sophistication, to point-to-point robots and motorized stereotactic frames, to teleoperated devices, to semiautonomous, continuously controlled robots. Indeed, some surgical procedures may well employ a variety of such devices, all interfaced to a common control and information management system.

Of course, this dream is not yet a reality. In particular, the *integration* of such systems would represent a very serious challenge even if the individual subsystems were fully developed. Indeed, the challenges are not even all purely technical. Issues such as regulatory approval, compensation, interface standards, deployment into existing infrastructure, and hospital and clinical working relationships must be faced and are likely to have a major impact on the evolution of such systems. For example, the technical problems required to make all relevant clinical information (images, laboratory studies, etc.) about a patient available to a surgeon in the operating room are relatively well defined, even if full solutions will require considerable implementation effort. However, radiologists and surgeons must learn to cooperate in new ways for this technologic possibility to be converted to effective clinical deployment.

Nevertheless, elements of this architecture may be found in existing or emerging systems, many of which are reported in this book. Indeed, several of these systems have evolved to the point where they may be viewed as prototypical instances of this more general architecture.

What's in a name?

As is typical of any technical field that is not yet fully structured, there is often a certain amount of redundancy between component concepts and subdisciplines. In reading the book, the same or related concepts will come up several times, often with different names and with slightly different emphasis. This is a natural consequence of parallel evolution of a common set of core technologies in multiple application domains that are just now beginning to recognize the significant synergies and opportunities that exist. Indeed, there is no consensus on what the field ultimately will be called. Among the names that have been proposed thus far are *computer-assisted surgery*, *image-guided operating room robotics*, *medical robotics*, *computer-assisted medical interventions*, *computer-integrated medicine*, *information-intensive surgery*, and *computer-integrated surgery*. Each of these names has a slightly different connotation, in some cases narrowly focusing on particular technologies, in other cases encompassing more or less all of modern medicine. We have chosen *computer-integrated surgery* (CIS) because it is reasonably short and, by analogy with the use of the term *computer-integrated manufacturing*, emphasizes the integration of presurgical planning and analysis, computer-based systems in surgical execution, and postoperative follow-up and quality control. However, the name is much less important than the emerging reality of these new systems.

Structure of the book

In the balance of this book, we will use the themes developed in this introduction (of surgeon-machine partnerships, the synergy between planning and execution, and common architectural elements emerging from evolving applications and systems) as organizing principles for our discussion. The remainder of the book is organized into two parts. In turn, each part is divided into a number of sections, each consisting of a short introduction and one or more chapters that provide an in-depth treatment of the relevant material. Most of the chapters were written by the authors for this book, although we have also included several contributions reprinted from prior publications.

The 19 chapters in part I, Technology, explore the essential technologic components that are the basis of computer-integrated surgery. The discussion is divided into six major sections: Data Acquisition and Segmentation, Registration, Basic Tools for Surgical Planning, Human-Machine Interfaces, Robotic Manipulators, and Safety. For technology researchers wanting to get into CIS, these sections provide essential background material needed to get up to speed on current work. For those who are already active in the field, we hope that these chapters provide a convenient collection of important material in one place for ready reference and for broadening one's understanding of this evolving discipline. For clinicians, we hope that the material will provide an understanding of what is possible today and an awareness of the problems yet to be solved. Further, we hope that such an understanding can significantly facilitate more effective communication between clinical users and technologists in defining what is to be tried next.

The 39 chapters in part II, Applications, are organized into sections covering eight clinical areas and a concluding section on the future of high technology in the operating room. Each of these sections contains at least one chapter on requirements and opportunities, written by a leading clinician in the clinical area being discussed. We hope these chapters will be especially useful to technologists in understanding both where they may make contributions and the environment in which real clinical problems must be solved. In addition, we hope this part of the book will be valuable to both technologists and clinicians in understanding current trends and systems.

The eight clinical sections are Neurosurgery, Orthopaedics, Eye Surgery, Dentistry, Minimal-Access Surgery, Ear, Nose, and Throat Surgery, Craniofacial Surgery, and Radiotherapy. This list is not exhaustive. Although we have attempted to be reasonably comprehensive in our coverage, the field of CIS is expanding very rapidly, and we have had to stop somewhere to avoid the continued growth of this book without limits (except perhaps those of MIT Press's patience). Although some exciting areas (e.g., cardiovascular surgery) have been left out, at least for this edition, we hope the areas covered provide a strong indication of the progress of CIS.

The concluding section, The High-Tech Operating Room, includes a chapter by another leading research team in CIS. Although their specific categorical breakdown differs slightly from the one provided in this introduction, we were pleased to find that their vision is substantially similar to ours, as discussed further in the section introduction.

We should also mention one important logistic detail. When we first discussed this book with the editors at MIT Press, we had hoped to avoid extensive use of color illustrations. However, it soon became apparent that this was not entirely practical in light of the extensive use of color in surgical planning displays and the importance of color in intraoperative procedures. To control costs, we have consequently included the color illustrations in a single plate section. References to each color plate will be found in the appropriate chapter or chapters. We apologize to readers for any inconvenience that this may cause and also extend our thanks to our contributors for their cooperation.

Finally, we would like to thank the many people who have contributed to this book. Like the field of Computer-Integrated Surgery, it grew from relatively modest beginnings into a complex project involving 58 chapters and more than 150 co-authors. We are very grateful to every one of these authors for their patience, flexibility, and forbearance in coping with the inevitable minor snags, delays, and short deadlines that are encountered in such endeavors. We also want to express our particular thanks to our friends at MIT Press, and especially to Bob Prior and Katherine Arnoldi, for their continued encouragement and support throughout all phases of this project.

I TECHNOLOGY

Data Acquisition and Segmentation

THIS IS THE FIRST of three sections devoted to the flow of information emerging from basic data and ending at the surgical planning step. Data acquisition and pre-modeling (or segmentation) are addressed in this section, whereas registration of data is described in the next section, and basic tools for surgical planning are presented in the last section of these three. Although some surgical augmentation systems, especially those that rely primarily on simple teleoperation, can function successfully with only intraoperative data, the use of preoperative models derived from medical images is a central theme of our overall architecture. Indeed, even simple teleoperative systems can be significantly enhanced by the availability of such models and by their registration with intraoperative reality.

Current technology is far from providing general modeling tools for any application. However, the discipline is young and progress is rapid. Consider that deformable models, magnetic resonance angiography, and anatomy-based registration are less than a decade old. Moreover, the purpose of this research is not to find the unique best modeling system but rather to build a framework of modeling, including a battery of powerful tools assembled in a comprehensive toolbox, where the possibilities and limits of each tool are defined precisely. Progress is as dependent on experimentation and integration as much as on novel algorithms.

In the first chapter of this section, Mösges and Lavallée detail the multimodal information potentially available for computer-integrated surgery (CIS) sys-tems. They begin with a general summary, which can be skipped by the reader who already has a knowledge of medical imaging and modeling technology. The authors continue with a more specific discussion describing and comparing various technologies for intraoperative three-dimensional (3D) position sensing. Such sensing is a crucial technology for CIS systems, as the goal is not simply to plan a surgical procedure but also to carry it out. Examples of the use of such intraoperative tools are pervasive throughout the second part of this book.

The integration of information from multiple pre-operative and intraoperative sources, especially image sources, is crucial if the information is to be used effectively in CIS systems. Such integration is greatly facilitated if the various medical imaging devices can communicate via communication networks with suitable image databases. The management of such networks is a major concern. In the second chapter of this section, Greinacher describes current progress in picture archiving and communication (PAC) systems and their integration into larger hospital information systems. The chapter begins by discussing the needs and requirements of PAC systems and then discusses a specific example (the Siemens system) in greater detail.

Once basic image data have been acquired, the aim of an advanced CIS system is to extract relevant information for surgical planning, visualization, and registration. Image segmentation, or the association of each element of an image with a label corresponding to a tissue type, anatomic structure, or the like, is a crucial first step in construction of the higher-level representations used for further analysis. Two chapters present different approaches to this problem, as applied to 3D images. The chapter, "Imaging Transforms for Volume Visualization," by Udupa and Gonçalves, does not address only the problem of visualization. The authors propose a general methodology of image processing that starts at the pixel level and ends at the 3D view of structures. This necessarily encompasses the segmentation of images into structures. Their methodology is based on a sequential combination of basic imaging transforms, which include most of the known image-processing techniques such as filtering, volume interpolation, shape-based interpolation, partitioning, and volume and surface rendering. The authors describe how these tools can be used in a variety of possible combinations and also propose a method for comparing different visualization strategies.

The next chapter, "Segmentation of Complex Three-Dimensional Medical Objects," by Ayache et al., focuses on automated contouring of structures, which many researchers consider to be, arguably, the most difficult problem in 3D image processing. When the data can be segmented by simple thresholding, an algorithm such as "marching cubes" or one of its extensions [1] yields a triangulated surface of the desired structure without much trouble. One example of such successful segmentation is the reconstruction of bone models from closely spaced computerized tomography (CT) slices, although thin bony plates or close proximity of bones, as in a hip or knee joint, can still be a problem. In other cases, manual assistance from a human technician using a mouse or other indicating device usually is required. The general problem remains unsolved. Ayache et al. present both current standard and novel approaches to the problem. Standard segmentation techniques discussed include detection of maximal gradients, region growing, and the like. Even when they are not a complete solution, these basic techniques always are useful as a first step for further processing. Typically, a Canny-Deriche filter on an image produces a set of probable edge points. Then, a higher-level process has to build a surface that goes through some of the edge points and that corresponds to the anatomic structure to be segmented. The second part of this chapter presents two related approaches to 3D segmentation using deformable models: the finite element-based approach of INRIA's Project Epidaure and the spline 3D snake approach of the TIMC Group at Grenoble University. We chose to cite this work because deformable models seem to represent a very promising approach. However, only partial results have been achieved, and many problems remain to be solved in that domain.

We close this introduction with two thoughts. First, we reiterate the observation that automated or even semiautomated segmentation of medical imaging data is effectively available today in only a relatively few application domains. For some time, the choice of segmentation technique is likely to be highly application-dependent. Second, it is necessary to consider models with real physical and physiologic properties instead of pure geometric models. This, in turn, will require the ability to integrate information from many different sensory modalities and will also require considerable biomedical engineering research. Indeed, many of the same modeling and registration capabilities being designed for CIS applications are also likely to be crucial in the conduct of such research.

REFERENCE

[1] KALVIN, A., 1992. A survey of algorithms for constructing surfaces from 3D volume data. *IBM Research Report RC 17600*, January 16.

1 Multimodal Information for Computer-Integrated Surgery

RALPH MÖSGES AND STÉPHANE LAVALLÉE

COMPUTER-INTEGRATED surgery (CIS) is based on a partnership between surgeon and machine. Both have to share information coming from various sources. The quality of this information affects the quality of the operation. For a long time, surgeons had only their senses as sources of information to help them operate. With the founding of medical schools, surgeons could integrate more and more knowledge acquired by anatomic and postoperative studies (generic information) with the interpretation of only clinical symptoms (specific information). The body of anatomic and clinical knowledge has not stopped growing. Surgeons today must interpret an increasing volume of specific information for each case, mainly due to the emergence of new imaging systems. However, the adequate use of images and data for therapeutic purposes remains problematic. It is the aim of systems for CIS to make available to the surgeon all the information that exists for a given patient and for a given pathologic process.

This chapter delineates the information available for surgery as a source for decision making and action. This information is multimodal at three distinct levels. First, the various modalities convey different physical properties (attenuation to x-ray, magnetic properties, acoustic or electric impedances, etc.). Second, they also have different representations in space and in time, ranging from single-point static information to a 3D set of data evolving with time. Third, the information-gathering modalities may be preoperative or intraoperative, and all convey information that is relevant from a medical point of view, ranging from standard morphologic or functional information to technical information such as position and force. Although it is very difficult to classify, we divide multimodal information into two categories: *Standard medical data* (images, signals, models) are presented in the second section of this chapter, and new trends in imaging are discussed in the next section. Finally, *technical information* (position, force, etc.)

applicable to surgery is described in the last section, with an emphasis on intraoperative sensing technologies.

Medical information: Images, signals, models

In this section, medical imaging modalities and sources of biosignals are briefly characterized. Models derived thereof are described.

VARIOUS PHYSICAL PROPERTIES

A classification of medical imaging technology is based on physical properties, including x-rays, magnetic properties, nuclear medicine, ultrasound, video signals, and various others [1].

X-RAY BASED IMAGES The measurement of x-rays emitted by a punctiform source and transmitted through the human body depends on the integral of the radiologic density along rays, which is a function of the mean atomic number. These measurements are made on films or on image intensifiers, which can be linear or planar detectors. Differentiating between high and low densities is used primarily to image bony structures but also to image the evolution of contrast agents such as iodine in structures (e.g., blood vessels).

Projections on planes can be digitized directly, through digitization of the signal output from the image intensifier, or indirectly, through laser scanning or video digitization of x-ray films. With direct digitization, images taken at different times can be subtracted from one another. This direct method is used in digitized subtraction angiography (DSA) to improve the quality of angiograms by subtracting images without contrast agents from images obtained with contrast agents. Many different techniques have been introduced for the direct digitization process. There is usually a difference in quality between devices employed in radiology departments and standard x-ray intensifiers that can be found in surgical theaters.

Rotation of the source and the detector around the longitudinal axis of the patient produces projections that can be used for tomographic reconstruction, with typical series of parallel sections of 512×512 pixels. As this reconstruction process provides a correct approximation of tissue densities and not integrals of tissue densities as in x-ray projections, CT images accurately differentiate bony and soft tissues. The advent of CT in the seventies initiated computer-assisted surgical planning techniques. Now, the technology is evolving in two directions. First is high-speed image acquisition. For instance, the commutation of multiple fixed x-ray sources and detectors yield ultrafast techniques that allow for efficient real-time 3D cardiac imaging (acquisition of a slice in 50 msec) [2]. A slower but now common technique, the spiral CT, uses a continuous rotation of the x-ray source (coupled with the 2D detector) synchronized with a linear continuous motion of the patient [3]. This technique provides slices in approximately 1 sec. Second is the use of planar detectors for real 3D volumetric reconstructions instead of standard reconstructions of series of 2D sections. One method uses a series of fixed x-ray detectors [4], but a less expensive method makes use of only one fast rotating x-ray system [5].

MAGNETIC RESONANCE IMAGING Magnetic resonance imaging (MRI) provides information about properties of tissues [6]. A body first is set into an intense constant magnetic field (ranging from 0.1 Tesla to a few Teslas). MRI studies the way tissues behave when they are submitted to a weak perturbation of the magnetic field: Radio frequency pulses induce motions of spins that come back to an equilibrium. Using a select sequence of perturbations, information is provided about the densities of atoms (mainly hydrogen) and about the physicochemical environment. During a single acquisition, several components of the received signals usually are used (proton densities, response times T_1 and T_2). Actually, an almost infinite set of acquisition sequences is possible. MRI is a true 3D imaging technique as the selection of gradients of magnetic fields gives access to any point of the volume studied. However, most standard devices provide series of parallel sections in sagittal, coronal, and axial planes. Devices having homogeneous spatial resolution are becoming increasingly popular. This feature is very important for modeling information in CIS. It is much easier to model a homogeneous volume of $256 \times 256 \times 256$ voxels than a series of 256×256 slices with a pixel resolution of 1 mm and an interslice resolution of 3 mm or even 12 mm.

A major breakthrough of MRI is magnetic resonance angiography (MRA), which produces clear images of blood vessels noninvasively. Techniques for MRA are based on two physical principles—inflow and phase effects [7]. Inflow effects are due to motion of spins (entry slice phenomenon). Phase effects are a consequence of motions of spins along the direction of the field gradients employed for imaging.

Magnetic resonance spectroscopy (MRS) allows for metabolic studies of complex biologic systems: Spectra in the frequency domain correspond to the composition of molecules of a region. Since the advent of whole-body magnets, clinical applications are possible; these use magnetic field gradients coupled with selective pulse sequences. The main nuclei that can be observed in vivo are the proton, phosphorus $31\,(^{31}\mathrm{P})$ and carbon $13\,(^{13}\mathrm{C})$. Recently, chemical shift imaging techniques (multivoxels spectroscopy) have been developed [8], but much work is still necessary before these will be ready for routine clinical use. Miniaturization of coils is another interesting trend in research [9].

NUCLEAR MEDICINE In nuclear medicine, or scintigraphy, a source of photons (gamma) or positrons (beta) is associated with a specific vector and injected inside the body. The emission of such radioactive elements is studied by external line or plane detectors, preceded by collimators. An image corresponds to an orthogonal projection of the density of radioactive elements, which is related to the metabolism of the studied region. A rotation of the gamma-camera around the patient provides a set of projections that is fed into tomographic algorithms. The result is a 3D volume of data, the tomoscintigraphy or single photon emission computed tomography (SPECT). A more complex strategy studies the emission of positrons (negative electrons): Each emitted positron collides with an electron of the environment and gives rise to two photons that go in opposite directions. A ring of detectors set around the patient detects these two photons at very near instants. Thus, the associated event is on a straight line between these two corresponding detectors. The intersection of such lines gives rise to the 3D region of emission. Such is the technique of positron emission tomography (PET). Thus far, PET requires an expensive device and is not very widespread compared to SPECT. Both SPECT and PET have poor spatial resolution when compared with CT or MRI (typically a set of 64^3 or 128^3 voxels is obtained), but these methods provide functional information that is not available with other techniques. Note that PET scanners also provide some transmission images that coincide with functional images: They are low-resolution morphologic images obtained through standard tomographic reconstruction with external x-ray sources.

ULTRASOUND After the emission of an ultrasound wave from a piezoelectric element, the signal reflected by the discontinuities of acoustic impedances of tissues is analyzed. Measurement of the time of flight gives spatial information of such discontinuities, provided that the speed of the ultrasound is constant. Selection of the frequency depends on a standard trade-off of resolution versus attenuation. Analysis of the signal in one spatial direction is the A-mode. Mechanically or electronically moving the direction of ultrasound allows one to obtain a 2D image of the discontinuities (B-mode). Echography is a real-time imaging system with an average resolution (typically 1 mm). Images are corrupted by a rather strong texture noise, due to a speckle phenomenon, and by distortions, due to nonconstant velocities in inhomogeneous tissues.

Standard devices are 2D ultrasound probes, but it is also possible to acquire 3D or pseudo-3D data (see Hottier and Billon [10] for a description of different techniques). One solution is to mount a 3D coordinate localizer (mechanical, ultrasound, electromagnetic, or optical; see the section Intraoperative position sensing) on a standard 2D probe [11, 12], which gives sets of registered 2D images. Another solution is to extend 2D probes to 3D, either mechanically, which raises problems of acquisition time and some constraints of usage, or by using array detectors, which is a very promising solution that still raises technical problems.

The analysis of blood vessel velocities is achievable through the use of Doppler probes. Standard probes give 1D signals, and some miniaturized probes can now be mounted at the tip of a needle. A new imaging modality is the color Doppler or color-coded duplex sonography, which produces a 2D image of velocities in color superimposed on a standard 2D ultrasound image.

VIDEO SIGNALS Standard video signals are used widely in medical imaging. They yield an important amount of information, potentially usable in computer-integrated surgery. Color image output from microscopes and endoscopes can be digitized and processed to control microsurgery and endoscopy. This is particularly helpful in the case of stereo-endoscopy and stereomicroscopy. Such information is practical only with relative or absolute registration of images. Therefore, some localizing system must be connected to the microscope or endoscope to register the location of the image with other images or with preoperative images or surgical tools or probes. It is complicated to extract relevant information from these images in order to define, update, or control a surgical strategy.

OTHER IMAGES AND SIGNALS Various other images include magnetoencephalography (MEG) that uses SQUID (superconducting quantum interference device) detectors to detect magnetic fields corresponding to active brain regions [13] or electrical impedance tomography with surface electrodes [14], transmission ultrasound images, transmission laser images, passive microwave imaging (maps of temperature), 3D active microwave imaging, and pressure imaging. Similarly, signals produced by body activities can carry useful information for the surgeon. Among these are electrocardiograms, electroencephalograms, and basically all electrical signals, pressures, and temperatures. An interesting development is the increasing use of miniaturized biosensors [15].

CLINICAL DATA Clinical data must not be forgotten. To date, they can be interpreted only by physicians. The development of integrated information systems for hospitals should make these data accessible to machines, which will collect patient files, including history of the patient, data and observations taken by nurses and physicians, reports of radiologists, and documentation of previous surgery.

MODELS

In the previous section, we presented specific information that is available for each patient. Generic information will also be taken into account by the surgeon.

This section will show that part of this a priori information can be modeled and used by CIS systems.

ANATOMIC KNOWLEDGE Anatomophysiologic studies of organs give general knowledge of normal and pathologic structures on both the morphologic and functional levels. It seems unrealistic to build a database that would include all the current medical knowledge, first because the amount of information is considerable, second because different physicians may have different interpretations of similar phenomena, and third because access to such a database would be difficult. Building image databases is also a problem but is more realistic. However, anatomophysiologic knowledge can be very useful for computer-based therapeutic systems. For instance, segmentation of images can benefit from this; known items are easier to delineate.

More generally, there exists some a priori knowledge that can be integrated directly into CIS systems—namely, the knowledge about a geometric component. This includes geometric models of anatomy, geometric rules, and recorded postoperative information.

ANATOMIC GEOMETRIC MODELS OR ATLAS Anatomic geometric models can help to define a surgical plan. Typically, a brain atlas details the morphology of functional regions, which cannot be seen with imaging techniques. It can be a set of histologic sections such as the Talairach or Schaltenbrandt atlas, digitized with scanners or video cameras, and segmented in order to obtain a set of labeled regions. These models have the disadvantage of corresponding to a particular single case, assumed to be representative and stable. Another kind of atlas is provided by a collection of registered sets of 3D images. For instance, an elastic registration of normal brain MRI images of multiple patients can provide an *average brain*, which can serve as reference for pathologic brains. Thus far, the statistical value of these models has been poorly studied; one problem is finding representations for the variability of the model. Updating these models with patient data will allow the recording of surgical planning descriptions and postoperative results in a common database. The correlation of recorded signals coming from electrodes implanted in the brain through stereo-electroencephalography (SEEG) procedures with a brain atlas is a large and dense research field [16].

EMPIRIC GEOMETRIC RULES Many surgeons use empiric geometric rules daily. For instance, an intervertebral disc puncture can be performed using a trajectory with an entry point lying on the skin at a specified number of centimeters from the middle sagittal plane, or an anterior cruciate knee ligament replacement can be performed by drilling a tunnel in the femur that is a defined distance posterior to the roof of the notch. Such strategies are already established as geometric rules, but they often remain inaccurate because the reference structures are difficult to define accurately by all their components of position and orientation, and also because anatomic studies report some discrepancies about the parameters of the defined distances. Such rules provide a basis for modeling in CIS. However, more general solutions, based on optimization of precisely defined criteria, can make these rules obsolete in some cases.

RECORDED POSTOPERATIVE INFORMATION A major potential strength of CIS systems is their ability to record and compare postoperative clinical results versus surgical planning. Thus far, previous postoperative results have been evaluated differently by each surgeon, which is part of individual experience. Moreover, this knowledge often is not quantified. Recording in a database both surgical planning parameters and clinical results would allow definition of some probabilities of success for a proposed surgical plan. For instance, in stereotactic functional neurosurgery, a trajectory can be defined with the Guiot rule [17] by three or four parameters with respect to some anatomic landmarks. The regions of success can be defined in the parameter space using a series of postoperative clinical results. For a particular patient, a score can be attributed to any proposed trajectory, which in turn will update the database postoperatively. This scientific approach can be seen as an extension of the work to build image databases in radiology that merge images and medical reports. Information retrieval can then be directed by high-level requests [18].

New trends

DIGITIZATION AND POOLING OF INFORMATION

Physicians experience a change from analogous to digital systems on a broad level (i.e., in all imaging modalities). In many fields, conventional tomography has been replaced by CT. MRI, SPECT, and PET, among others, have no analogous equivalent but were developed originally as digital techniques. In conventional x-ray radiology, we notice an increasing change to digitization. In this case there is a severe lack of refinement and loss of positional resolution and therefore loss of radiologic information, but this is generously compensated by many new advantages of digital images such as histodifferentiation and the ability to combine various imaging modalities. The compilation of different primary information about a patient (pooling) makes high demands on technical equipment. Current forms of presentation (picture box, alternator) cannot meet these demands sufficiently; a new orientation is needed. Just as different partial functions of industrial production processes have been integrated into computerized manufacturing (computer-integrated manufacturing [CIM]), computer-integrated radiology—consisting of digital image generation, computer-assisted image generation, computer-assisted image integration, and knowledge-based image interpretation—has begun to be developed. The most important presupposition for this is a picture archiving and communication (PAC) system, which still exists in only rudimentary form at selected centers.

MULTIMODAL INFORMATION

A major trend in medical imaging is the increasing use of several imaging techniques for the same patient, each one of them giving specific information. Accurate registration between these various modalities is needed, and important work is being done in this domain (see chapter 5). To illustrate, we will focus on examples in the ear, nose, and throat (ENT) domain.

MRI permits accurate tumor localization and delimitation of the lesion's surrounding tissues. Osseous geometries that are required for radiotherapeutic planning as well as osseous barriers that are crucial for biopsy can be best visualized in CT. In preoperative diagnosis before cochlea *implantation*, the osseous structure of the petrous bone can be shown by CT, whereas MRI gives evidence of an endolymph-filled cochlea [19]. CT information determines the surgical strategy, and MRI permits elimination of anatomic irregularities. CT and MRI are also complementary in the assessment of parotid gland tumors. CT sialography provides evidence of penetration of the tumor into Stensen's duct [20], whereas MRI offers assessment of

soft-tissue infiltration, by which dimensions of the processes can be evaluated [21]. In the case of neuroma of the acoustic nerve, MRI shows evidence of tumors of smallest size, down to 1 mm in diameter [22].

For surgical planning, CT is absolutely indispensable for visualizing osseous barriers in the petrous bone. As a complement to CT, ultrasound imaging (also known as *sonography* or *echography*) can be employed and provides additional information on soft-tissue processes [23–25]. A combined application of sonography and CT allows for tumor staging (TNM classification [26]) of tongue cancer and carcinoma of the floor of the mouth. These techniques have priority in TNM classification and are characterized by certainty factor C2 [27]. The combination of ultrasound image visualization and scintigraphic functional analysis can indicate the need for biopsy, surgery, or drug therapy of thyroid processes [28]. Salivary gland calculi can be visualized with accuracy by B-mode ultrasound images [29]. In combining information obtained from sonography with pantomography and the unmodified x-ray films of the floor of the mouth, superior diagnostic accuracy can be achieved for salivary gland calculi of the submandibular gland [30].

Diagnostics of vessel abnormalities and tumorous alterations in the head and neck region offer another example of combining 3D techniques such as CT and MRI. In this case, arterial DSA can provide additional information [31]. Higher diagnostic accuracy also can be achieved by combining a 2D real-time technique with a 1D method. By A-mode ultrasound scanning, tumors of the orbit can be analyzed in a tissue-differentiated way, whereas B-mode sonography permits topographic classification [32].

REDUCED USE OF IONIZING RADIATION

Among other events, the nuclear power plant disaster in Chernobyl has made many people aware of the effects of ionizing radiation. One "side effect" of the disaster has been the comparison of natural radioactivity, industrially caused radiation (e.g., that which was released from the damaged reactor), and the radioactivity generated by radiodiagnostic modalities. On the one hand, the heightened sense of awareness of the damaging effects of radiation, especially in the medical profession, has led to improved documentation of irradiation ("x-ray passport"). On the other hand, this awareness has resulted in an increased application of radiodiagnostic imaging techniques that dispense with the use of ionizing radiation (e.g., ultrasound imaging and MRI).

During the past 10 years, the technique of ultrasonography widely expanded from the domain of inpatient care into the sector of outpatient clinics and private practices. Sonography has proved successful in the diagnosis of abdominal diseases, in gastroenterology, and in abdominal surgery. It has proved useful as well for the assessment of arthropathy in orthopaedics, for cardiologic diagnostics, and for gynecologic and urologic disciplines. In head and neck surgery, the diagnosis of abnormalities of the paranasal sinuses and orbits however, require radiologic findings initially. The sonographic image is successful also for documenting the course of a disease [32, 24].

The initial optimism about completely replacing roentgenologic methods with sonography and MRI within a few years' time could not be maintained [33, 34]. MRI remains time-consuming and costly. MRI studies often require supplementation by CT findings [35]. To date, 70% of all radiologic studies have been carried out using conventional radiography. In these cases, digital radiography can lead to a 50% reduction of exposure to radiation without any detrimental effect on diagnostic quality. Even invasive imaging techniques are important in the range of radiologic methods.

ABANDONMENT OF INVASIVE METHODS FOR DIAGNOSTICS

As a maxim for a physician's action, a diagnosis should be made with the least possible use of invasive methods. This especially applies when imaging techniques are used.

MRI not only reduces the use of ionizing radiation but also avoids invasive methods in the diagnostic workup. In the region of the cranium, the osseous bar is readily surmounted. In this as in other regions of the body, the differentiated visualization of soft tissue serves as a basis for detailed assessments of pathologic processes. In some cases, obtaining biopsy specimen can be avoided by histodifferentiation and tissue characterization in MRI. Tissue characterization is possible with unmovable organs using variable pulse sequences. Tolxdorff et al. [36] report the possibility of differentiating between recurrences of tumors and surgical scars in operated mastocarcinoma by a combination of short and long magnetic echosequences using multiecho-

sequence. The analysis of recorded echosequences implies much calculating and can be optimized by an expert system.

Differentiate diagnosis among lesions of the petrous bone, cerebellopontine angle tumors, and other central nervous system (CNS) diseases is possible with the help of MRI [37]. The invasive method of air cisternography for studies of the internal auditory meatus has therefore become superfluous [38]. With the contrast medium gadolinium-DTPA, the sensitivity of the method can be increased to almost 100% even for the smallest intrameatal tumors [39, 40]. This intravenous contrast medium is employed also for the visualization of jugular glomus tumors. MRI has replaced the formerly used combination of CT and angiography, clearly showing the simultaneous abandonment of radiation exposure and invasive methods.

There is a general tendency nowadays to replace some examinations that employ angiographic techniques with MRA, although MRA still has some severe limitations (e.g., in small vessels). Likewise, MRI permits noninvasive diagnosis of encephalocele [41]. Preoperatively, the surgeon is offered information that he or she otherwise could obtain only through surgical exposure of the skull base.

As a noninvasive routine technique for the examination of cardiac action, color Doppler was shown to be successful. It makes assertions on function parameters possible that formerly could be established only by cardiac catheter examinations. Color Doppler sonography is used also in angiology, where it renders possible the quantification of stenoses. In case of pretherapeutic diagnostics when large-vessel obstruction, is suspected, this modality can replace invasive examination methods such as angiography [42, 43].

High-resolution CT also contributes to a reduction of invasive diagnostic procedures in the ENT arena. According to Oberascher et al. [44], it is possible to dispense with the usual second-look surgery for cholesteatoma because residua can be reliably detected by high-resolution CT. CT makes possible a well-founded indication for revision surgery [45]. After stapedectomy with prosthetic insertion, complications such as too-long, too-short, and dislocated prostheses can be visualized on CT [46, 47]. This works on the presupposition that radiopaque prostheses have been inserted [48]. A labyrinthine fistula causing acute dizziness is visualized in 3D reconstructed CT of the petrous bone; tympanoscopy can be employed more effectively [49].

When choanal atresia is suspected, sounding of the meatus of the nose in the neonate can be abandoned. By employing CT of the nasal cavity instead [50], differentiation between osseous and chondric choanal atresia is possible. Hence, planning of subsequent surgery is facilitated. CT also has a high value in the differential diagnosis of tumors of the larynx.

The technique of digital substraction sialography permits use of a reduced amount of injected contrast medium [51]. Digital image processing leads to reliable demonstration of concrements with minimal diagnostic invasion [52]. Indication for sialolithotripsy can also be based on this method [53, 54]. This example clearly demonstrates how minimal invasive diagnostic methods can serve as a base for a noninvasive therapeutic procedure.

REAL-TIME PROPERTIES AND INTERVENTIONAL IMAGING

The development of techniques for real-time imaging is, to a certain degree, opposed to the abandonment of invasive methods in image processing. The diagnostician seeks contact with the pathologic process, delineates its function, and increasingly acts also as a therapist. Interventional radiography sometimes competes with surgical methods, as in ballooning of stenosed vessels, and at other times complements such methods, as in embolization of tumor vessels.

Sonography is the most important imaging technique with real-time properties. It tolerates studies of movable organs under functional conditions. In contrast to tomographic techniques, the plane of the 2D section can be changed with B-mode sonography in an interactive way and according to findings. This facilitates studies of deglutition [55], cardiac action (especially valvular function), and joint action.

Sonography has already proved successful in prenatal cardiologic diagnosis. Prenatal ultrasound diagnosis of airway obstruction is new and is possible through further heightened positional resolution. In cases of severe obstruction, a head and neck surgeon can be consulted prepartum [56].

Sonography offers special advantages for fine-needle biopsy. Under ultrasound control, material can be obtained from solid, mural parts of metastatic cystic lymph nodes [57]. Therefore, analysis of insufficient, necrotic lymph node material is prevented. This leads to increased sensitivity of cytologic diagnostics. The same is true of ultrasound-controlled biopsy of sialoma

[58]. This technique is superior to fine-needle biopsy under palpation as well as to CT-controlled biopsy [59].

Fluoroscopy is the classic real-time imaging technique. It involves high radiation exposure that can be reduced by use of digital image intensifiers and digitization with image processing. By this technique, the spectrum of indications has expanded once again. In a modified fashion, fluoroscopy is used for dysphagia diagnostics as digital high-frequency cinematography [60]. The same is true of angiography, another classic real-time technique in imaging. As arterial DSA [61], it has crucial importance in embolization of tumor-supplying vessels. This is done under screen control for pretherapeutic interventional procedures for head and neck tumors [31].

Muscular movements, especially those of the myocardium, for a long time could not be visualized by 3D techniques. The image scanning frequency necessary for such studies made high demands on the design of the x-ray source. Cine-CT, which is now available in several centers, conquers this technologic obstacle. This method can produce 17 images/sec with an exposure time of 50 msec [62]. Functional studies of moving organs in space have become possible. Thus, myocardial function under contrast medium enhancement can be assessed.

VISUALIZATION OF FUNCTIONAL PARAMETERS

New perspectives for visualizing pathologically altered structures are offered by imaging techniques that can delineate, quantify, and demonstrate metabolic processes in combination with the morphologic image. By employing these techniques, differences between tumors present themselves in different ways. The metabolism of tumor and metastases become accessible to evaluation. Thereby, follow-ups under treatment are possible. The change-over from mere morphologic assessment to metabolic function evaluation offers new perspectives in oncologic aftercare [63]. Scintiscanning is the classic 2D technique of nuclear medicine for visualizing the metabolism of organs. Its applications include thyroid diagnostics and bone scanning for differentiating between metastatic and degenerative osseous alteration. In addition, it is used for myocardial scanning that permits detailed assessment of the metabolic situation in ischemic cardiopathy or in infarction. Studies of metabolism of organs, especially of the localized function of metabolism in three dimensions, can be made by PET or SPECT.

As a consequence of the increasing use of real-time imaging, functional parameters corresponding to motions of organs are increasingly studied. The increasing digitization of images enable computers to extract more and more easily quantified parameters from images (functional parameters, volumes, distances, etc.). Also, more and more information is 3D instead of 2D, which means that volume data are acquired directly. Hence, dimensional visualization is no longer a problem. This is very important for CIS systems, because CIS is based on a link between information about a patient and the surgical action on that patient. A prerequisite for this is 3D representation.

Technical information: Position and forces

Obtaining quantified 3D information offers new possibilities for CIS. New tools that help one easily and accurately to manipulate, register, and use all the information intraoperatively must be developed. This is a twofold problem. In some cases, information contained in standard medical data is sufficient to be used by a CIS system. In that case, user interface and algorithmic problems must be solved. In others, it may be necessary or preferable to add new information, not relevant from the medical point of view but useful for manipulation and registration of information. To some extent, such additional technical information may exceed its primary purpose and will be used not only by the machine but also by the surgeon. Intraoperative sensing systems might help the surgeon to locate himself or herself, to navigate using multimodal medical information, and to sense physical properties of tissues during the intervention. In this section, we discuss all systems dealing with position and force information. These represent technical information, not medical information. Here we focus briefly on the technology related to it. We distinguish three main techniques: shape acquisition, intraoperative position sensing and, finally, force and tactile sensing.

Shape acquisition

In computer vision, many techniques have been developed to identify shapes of visible objects for multiple applications, as in robotics, pattern recognition, and so on. The medical profession can benefit from these developments. Automatic acquisition of shape can be useful in many cases. For instance, the surface of the patient's face or the surface of an organ exposed intraoperatively can be used as an anatomic reference structure for subsequent registration by different imaging systems. Obtaining an image can also be very useful to quantify the effects of reconstructive surgery, during revision surgery, or for follow-up.

Basically, we can differentiate passive and active methods for 3D reconstruction of shapes in computer vision (see, for instance, Kanade [64]). The most suitable case of *passive vision* for the medical field is trinocular vision, which makes use of three video cameras and stereoscopic principles [65]. In principle, a feature point identified on three video images corresponds to a 3D point computed as the intersection of the three corresponding projection lines. However, this kind of technique will be used effectively only to extract position and shapes of nonanatomic objects (surgical tools, reference landmarks, etc.). To yield 3D information about smooth anatomic shapes, it is necessary to create some detailed information about the shape—for instance, using a simple random projection of light on the surface. Other techniques of passive vision, such as shape from shading and shape from motion, are usually less robust. The second class of vision methods is *active vision*, in which the sensor has an active component (a projector of structured light, for example) related to a passive one (e.g., a camera) both components making an angle ranging from 20–60°. Such systems rapidly can provide range images, which are sets of accurate coordinates of 3D surface points (see [66, 67]). A typical system is made of a laser plane (a laser beam going through a cylindric lens) moving with 1 degree of freedom (dof), intersecting the surface to be digitized. A video camera is watching the moving curved line created by the intersection between the laser plane and the surface. Triangulation techniques associated with accurate calibration methods allow one to obtain 3D coordinates of the surface points in a few seconds [68]. The principle of triangulation is that 3D point coordinates are given by the intersection between projection lines of the camera and the light plane (their geometry roughly corresponds to a triangle). The laser plane moving with 1 dof can also be replaced by a laser beam moving in 2 dof, or by a laser beam reflected by a mirror mounted in 2 dof. A second type of system, also based on triangulation techniques, consists of a video camera and a slide projector, in which a controlled semitransparent LCD slide is projected to create specific patterns on the surface. With this technology, the acquisition time is limited only by the acquisition of approximately 8 or 16 video images. More sophisticated techniques (for instance, using Moire patterns) exist, but standard techniques meet most medical requirements and are simple and cost-effective.

INTRAOPERATIVE POSITION SENSING

Intraoperative position-sensing systems are called *3D digitizers*, *3D localizers*, or *3D navigation systems*. Such systems give the 6D coordinates (three components of translation, three components of rotation) of one or several points or rigid bodies in real time. The number of applications of such systems is quickly growing. Their main task is to encode the 6D position of a surgical tool, to register the coordinate frame of the position sensor with some preoperative 3D medical images using anatomic or material landmarks, and thus to display in real time the location of the surgical tool on preoperative images. The position sensor can be mounted on a standard surgical tool, a guide, a simple tip used to digitize points, a 2D ultrasound probe (in order to collect relative locations of ultrasound image planes), a rigid endoscopic tube, or a microscope, or it can be rigidly linked to one or several bones to track some motions. Alternatively, it can be fixed at the end of a robot to check its location redundantly.

MECHANICAL PASSIVE MANIPULATOR   One robust way to obtain 6D coordinates is to use a 6-dof passive manipulator. Each joint variable is given by a potentiometer, an optical encoder, or a resolver. Simple forward kinematics of the arm transforms these joint variables into position and orientation coordinates. Some reduced versions of this method using only four or five axes are also practical. To be easily handled by surgeons, either the system must be light enough (which is usually difficult to achieve for sufficiently large work spaces) or each articulation must be balanced with counterweights or springs. However, there always remains some friction that makes them not as easy to move as free objects. On the other hand, some of these systems can include mechanical, electromechanical, or pneumatic brakes, which allow the operator to rest and to put some tool or sensor in a fixed position. The resolution of passive manipulators only is limited by the resolution of the encoders, which is usually better than the required accuracy (typically less than ± 0.1 mm in x, y, z). Because it is always difficult to determine complete models of mechanical systems (static and dynamic deformations, backlashes, misalignments, etc.), their *absolute* accuracy is strongly dependent on the size of the work space in the six dimensions [69]. Typically, an accuracy of ± 0.5 mm is easily achieved in a volume of $(200 \text{ mm})^3$ with a few rotations, whereas errors up to 10 mm can be observed if a large work space of approximately 1 m^3 is used. Note that standard mechanical technology would allow one to achieve better accuracies for smaller working volumes (e.g., in microsurgery, dentistry). An advantage of mechanical digitizers over noncontact sensors (described in the rest of this section) is their constant activity: They cannot be obscured. Obviously, the disadvantage of this feature is that they further obstruct the field of operation. Another strong drawback is that one passive manipulator is necessary to encode the location of each rigid body of interest, so that an application that would use four rigid bodies would require four manipulators. Sterile coatings must cover the arm during this instrument's use in surgery.

Several mechanical systems have been designed that are used in the medical field. In chapter 23, Reinhardt describes such systems in neurosurgery (see also [70–74]). Mösges et al. report an ENT application [75]. As previously mentioned, the use of these systems has also been studied to register multiple 2D ultrasound images (see [10]). A potential advantage of mechanical systems is their ability to be dynamically constrained or braked, in order to help the operator to reach predefined positions or to follow imposed trajectories [76].

ULTRASOUND 3D DIGITIZERS   A cheap and simple technology that has been used for 3D localization is based on the measurement of times of flight of ultrasound. A system encompasses $N \geq 3$ receivers (microphones) and M emitters (piezoelectric components or spark emitters). For a given emitter, the time of flight of the ultrasound wave between the emitter and each receiver is measured using a simple synchronization technique. Assuming that the ultrasound speed in the air is known and constant, the lengthes $l_1, l_2, \ldots l_N$ between the receivers and the emitter are computed. If the relative locations of the receivers are known, one can compute the 3D coordinates of the emitter as the intersection of the spheres centered at the receivers and of respective radius $l_1, l_2, \ldots, l_N$. Then the combination of the emitters with rigid bodies (using at least three emitters per rigid body) allows the computation of all the degrees of freedom of each rigid body. Standard commercial systems can reach spatial resolution of up to ± 0.1 mm for large volumes, at a rate of up to 100 3D points/sec. Absolute accuracy with such standard systems is poor, typically ± 5 mm. These values are mainly due to the influence of temperature on ultrasound velocity, air displacements, air inhomogeneities, and large sizes of emitters. These problems can be partially solved by on-line calibration, limitation of distances between emitters and receivers, and use of spark emitters, which are then inverted with receivers (see chapter 23 for more detail). An absolute accuracy of ± 1 mm in a volume of $(200 \text{ mm})^3$ can be achieved.

Ultrasound offers the advantages of a noncontact technology: totally free motion of rigid bodies, detection of multiple points or rigid body locations, and no obstruction of the surgical field. Unless some remote infrared transmission is used, note that there are still wires connecting emitters, receivers, and the system. However, the sensors can be obscured by objects between the emitters and the receivers, which usually defines a very large area. Moreover, both emitters and receivers have limited angles of activity (this problem can be solved using emitters spread around a rigid body but, in turn, it needs more computation time). Although it remains possible in theory, submillimeter accuracies have not yet been achieved with ultrasound localizers.

OPTICAL 3D DIGITIZERS Optical technology probably offers the greatest potential in terms of accuracy and speed of acquisition, at the expense of slightly more complex components than for ultrasound localizers. The use of multiple cameras is a well-known triangulation technique for 3D acquisition. In standard computer vision, the segmentation of reference features (passive targets) in images and the computation of 3D coordinates from these extracted image points has been widely studied. It remains a difficult problem in the general case. To overcome this difficulty, active systems have been proposed in which a series of small infrared lights emit *sequentially* some pulses or short-time modulated signals, and the cameras are synchronized with the emitters so that each of the cameras receives only one specific signal at a time. Three system configurations have been proposed.

The first involves at least two charge-coupled detector (CCD) cameras. If cameras are made of standard lenses with CCD sensors, the location of each light on the corresponding 2D image defines a 3D line in space. Using at least two cameras permits the acquisition of 3D coordinates by computing the intersection of the two corresponding projection lines. Adams [77] reports the use of this technology using 512×512 CCDs and a third camera for redundancy, which improves both the reliability and the accuracy. The accuracy is approximately ± 0.5 mm in volumes of $(500 \text{ mm})^3$. The main drawback of this approach is that dedicated processors are necessary to process the pixel data from each image (300 Kbytes per frame) in order to obtain real-time measurements.

In a second system configuration, at least two position-sensitive device (PSD) sensors are employed. With cameras made of standard lenses with analogic PSD sensors the analogic signal given by each sensor corresponds to the coordinates x and y of each light spot centered in the image plane. Therefore, a simple digitization of the PSD signals of each camera gives the same information as in the previous configuration. These sensors, however, are faster with a much simpler technology, but they are hindered by the fact that reflections on metallic objects can mislead detection because the true and reflected signals are merged. The accuracy is approximately ± 0.5 mm in volumes of $(500 \text{ mm})^3$.

A third system configuration involves at least three linear cameras. If cameras are made of cylindric lenses and a high-resolution linear CCD sensor (typically 4096 elements), the spot on each 1D signal corresponds to a plane in three dimensions. Three cameras provide 3D coordinates as the intersections of three planes. This technology provides the best accuracy, for there are just three 1D signals to process, and this is accomplished with numeric processing that enables the rejection of false reflections by thresholding. An accuracy of ± 0.2 mm in volumes of $(500 \text{ mm})^3$ can be reached.

Optical localizers have the same advantages and disadvantages as noncontact technologies for ultrasound systems. They are, however, most accurate, and they can be more reliable than ultrasound-based devices. Using appropriate lenses, the accuracy is proportional to the size of the working volume, the only actual limitation for obtaining less than 0.1 mm is the size of standard emitting diodes.

TRANSBODY TECHNOLOGIES Mechanical, ultrasound, and optical systems discussed in the preceding sections cannot localize objects through the human body. This capability is desirable, though, in many applications (e.g., to locate the extremity of flexible catheters and flexible endoscopes). Other technologies can be used here, but there is a concomitant loss in accuracy. For instance, in electromagnetic systems, each generator coil defines a spatial direction, and small detector coils detect low-frequency magnetic fields that can be transmitted through soft tissues. This technology is well-known in computer graphics animation, for which 6D mouses are required. Commercial systems give spatial coordinates with a typical accuracy of ± 3 mm. Kato et al. [78] used such a device for neurosurgery. The main drawback of these systems is their sensitivity to the introduction of any metal object in the work space, as it induces strong perturbations of magnetic fields. In still more prospective work, radio-frequency techniques and propagation of ultrasound through soft tissues are being studied. Finally, for localization of the tip of a flexible tube (endoscope, catheter, etc.), information about the length of the insertion coupled with information about bending can be studied.

ABOUT THE TIP OF POINTING DEVICES For many applications, 3D localizing technologies are used to acquire, with specific pointing devices, point locations. In such a case, a pointing system is mounted on a rigid body located with a 3D sensor or at the end of a passive arm. Several solutions can be used to design such a pointing system. A simple method is to use a rigid pointed rod, but more sophisticated techniques can be more accurate and practical. For instance, to digitize a discrete set of points, a contact switch mounted on the tip can detect automatically contact between the pointer and the surface to be digitized. Noncontact detection can also be useful or necessary. For instance, interferometry lasers provide distances to surfaces with an extremely high accuracy (a few micrometers), so that a laser telemeter can replace the rigid bar. Accurate calibration of a varying focal lens in microscopes can also be used to estimate a distance along the optical axis, whereas the orientation of the optical axis can be known through encoders or external sensors, as previously described [79]. Finally, imaging ultrasound probes are also good pointers, using either 1D signals (see [80]) or 2D probes (see chapter 24). In the latter case, some manual interaction may be

necessary to detect points on images, but such probes have the advantage of being a percutaneous pointing device.

OTHER SENSING TECHNOLOGIES

When an active surgical tool is used, more general feedback than simple position feedback is necessary. If the tool is computer-controlled, detailed feedback is mandatory and, if the surgeon manipulates the active tool, such information is very helpful for him or her. At one extreme of active tools, advanced teleoperation requires that many signals be detected, processed, filtered, and fed back to the operator.

A first important category of sensing is force and tactile measurement. Many standard technologies can be used to detect forces and torques (strain gauges, pressure measurements, etc.). For instance, if a motorized rotating drill is intended to drill or cut bone, analyzing the current consumed by the motor gives measures related to the torque, which then can be used to ensure safety, perhaps by stopping the motor if the torque exceeds a certain threshold [81]. Alternatively it can serve to control a motorized linear displacement of the drill that pierces a bone, stopping the linear motion when the torque rapidly decreases [82]. In a more interactive manner, force feedback could be used simply as a way to distinguish spongious bone from cortical bone in orthopaedics. For teleoperation with multiple degrees of freedom, complete forces and torques can also be measured, as in the fingertip force sensing developed by Salisbury [83]. Local distributions of forces on a surface can be quantified through the use of *tactile sensors* [84]. Again, many transducing technologies are feasible for that purpose (piezoresistive, magnetic, and electromagnetic, capacitive, electrooptic, and ferroelectric polymer sensors). Tactile sensors allow discrimination among different mechanical properties of sensed regions, with an opportunity to model complex interactions between a surgical tool and human tissues.

Both for differentiation between tissues and control of action, one can speculate that all available sensing technologies could be used for delicate surgery, integrating information about many physicochemical properties of tissues (chemical composition, temperature, pH, color, resistance, motions, elasticity, stiffness, fragility, stickiness, etc.). Though this is only a vision currently, general trends of sensing technology are *min-*

iaturization and *integration*. For instance, conventional biosensors composed of a detector and immobilized catalysts (oxygen, hydrogen peroxide, and pH electrodes) are replaced by microelectrodes that use ion-sensitive field effect transistors (ISFET) [15]. An example of impressive integration is found in Ikuta et al. [85], including application of an active endoscope. It is important to note that these general trends of miniaturization in sensor technology are found also in actuation technology (see a description of many microelectromechanical systems in Benecke and Petzold [86]).

Conclusions

In this chapter, we provide an overview of techniques that can be integrated in CIS to acquire information complementary to the natural visual and tactile senses of the surgeon. Primary developments are multimodal information (all specificities of various information is used), less invasive and real-time techniques, and digitized data to replace analogous data (which allows for quantification and 3D or 4D imaging).

In this framework of multimodal information, the emerging importance of intraoperative sensing and use of systems that do not present conventional medical information but that help to manipulate and integrate information in many ways is enhanced. This yields the basis for computer-integrated surgery.

Questions concerning these sources of information in surgery remain: How can such different data be registered? How can useful models be extracted? How can machines communicate with one another and with users? What solutions can be found for storage and data management? The following chapters address these questions.

REFERENCES

[1] WEBB, S., 1988. *The Physics of Medical Imaging* (Medical Science Series). Bristol, UK: IOP Publishing.

[2] BOYD, D. P., J. L. COUCH, S. A. NAPEL, K. R. PESCHMANN, and R. E. RAND, 1987. Ultra cine-CT for cardiac imaging: Where have we been? What lies ahead? *Am. J. Cardiac Imag.* 1(2):175–185.

[3] KALENDER, W., A. POLACIN, G. MARCHAL, and A. L. BAERT, 1992. Current status and new perspective in spiral CT. In *Advances in CT: Second European Scientific User Conference*. Berlin: Springer-Verlag, pp. 85–94.

[4] RITMAN, E. L., J. H. KINSEY, R. A. ROBB, L. D. HARIS, and B. K. GILBERT, 1980. Physics and technical considerations in the design of the D.S.R.: A high temporal resolution volume scanner. *A.J.R.* 134:369–374.

[5] SAINT-FELIX, D., et al., 1993. A new system for 3D computerized x-ray angiography: First in vivo results. In *IEEE Engineering in Medicine and Biology Society Proceedings*. San Diego: IEEE, pp. 2051–2052.

[6] MANSFIELD, P., and P. G. MORRIS, 1982. *NMR Imaging in Biomedicine*. London: Academic.

[7] LOEFFLER, W. K., 1990. Magnetic resonance imaging. In *NATO ARW, Vol F60: 3D Imaging in Medicine*, K. H. Höhne, ed. Berlin: Springer-Verlag, pp. 3–19.

[8] BROWN, T. R., B. M. KINCAID, and K. UGURBIL, 1982. N.M.R. chemical shift imaging in three dimensions. *J. Natl. Acad Sci.* 79:3523–3526.

[9] PECK, T. L., L. LaVALLE, R. L. MAGIN, I. ADESIDA, B. C. WHEELER, and P. C. LAUTERBUR, 1993. RF microcoils patterned using microlithographic techniques for use as microsensors in NMR. In *IEEE Engineering in Medicine and Biology Society Proceedings*. San Diego: IEEE, pp. 174–175.

[10] HOTTIER, F., and A. COLLET BILLON, 1990. 3-D echography: Status and perspective. In *NATO ARW: Vol F60: 3D Imaging in Medicine*, K. H. Höhne, ed. Berlin: Springer-Verlag, pp. 21–41.

[11] WATKIN, K. L., and J. M. RUBIN, 1989. Pseudo three dimensional reconstruction of ultrasonic images of the tongue. *J. Acoust. Soc. Am.* 85:496–499.

[12] MORITZ, W. E., A. S. PEARLMAN, D. H. McCABE, D. K. MEDEMA, M. E. AINSWORTH, and M. S. BOLES, 1983. An ultrasonic technique for imaging the ventricle in three dimensions and calculating its volume. *IEEE Trans. Biomed. Eng.* 30:482–492.

[13] SINGH, M., R. R. BRECHNER, and V. W. HENDERSON, 1992. Neuromagnetic localization using magnetic resonance images. *IEEE Trans. Med. Imag.* 11(1):129–134.

[14] HUA, P., E. J. WOO, J. WEBSTER, and W. TOMPKINS, 1991. Iterative reconstructions methods using regularization and optimal current patterns in electrical impedance tomography. *IEEE Trans. Med. Imag.* 10(4):621–630.

[15] KARUBE, I., 1990. Micro biosensors. In *Twelfth IEEE Engineering in Medicine and Biology Proceedings*. Philadelphia: IEEE, pp. 5–6.

[16] LIPINSKY, H. G., 1989. New trends in computer graphics and computer vision to assist at neurosurgery. *Stereotact. Funct. Neurosurg.* 52:234–241.

[17] TAREN, J., G. GUIOT, P. DEROME, and J. C. TRIGO, 1968. Hazards of stereotaxic thalamotomy. Added safety factors in corroborating x-ray target localization with neurophysiological methods. *J. Neurosurg.* 29(4):173–182.

[18] BERRUT, C., and P. CINQUIN, 1989. Natural language understanding of medical reports. In *IFIP-IMIA Conference on Computerized Natural Medical Language for Knowledge Representation*, J. R. Scherrer, ed. North-Holland: pp. 129–137.

[19] ROSENBERG, R. A., N. L. COHEN, and D. L. REEDE, 1987. Radiographic imaging for the cochlea implant. *Ann. Otol. Rhinol. Laryngol.* 96:300–304.

[20] HANSSON, L. G., C. C. JOHANSEN, and A. BJOERKLUND, 1988. CT sialography and conventional sialography in the evaluation of parotid gland neoplasms. *J. Laryngol. Otol.* 102:163–168.

[21] GADEMANN, G., J. HAELS, W. SEMMLER, and G. VAN KAIK, 1988. Magnetic resonance imaging in parotid gland diseases. *Laryngol. Rhinol. Otol.* 67:211–216.

[22] LINDERMANN, J. A., W. STEINBRICH, G. FRIEDMANN, and K.-G. ROSE, 1987. MR tomography in neurinomas of the acoustic nerve. *Laryngol. Rhinol. Otol.* 66:440–443.

[23] SCHRADER, M., 1988. Improved diagnosis of laryngeal lipomas by CT scan. *HNO* 36:161–163.

[24] ROCHELS, R., 1987. Echography in orbital complications of inflammatory paranasal sinus diseases. *Laryngol. Rhinol. Otol.* 66:536–538.

[25] ZUNA, I., 1985. Computerized ultrasonic tissue characterization: Methods and clinical use. In *CAR '85*, H. U. Lemke et al., eds. Berlin: Springer, pp. 155–163.

[26] RADKE, C., P. GUNDLACH, B. HAMM, and H. SCHERER, 1989. Imaging procedures in tumour staging—their usefulness in the case of the head and neck region. *Klinikarzt* 4:196–199.

[27] HEDTLER, W., C. BERCHTOLD, and W. WEY, 1988. The use of computed tomography and ultrasound in staging of cancer in the tongue and the floor of the mouth. *HNO* 36:33–39.

[28] TIEDJEN, K. U., and H. HILDMANN, 1988. Ultrasound imaging of the neck: Indications and clinical value. *HNO* 36:267–276.

[29] EICHHORN, T., H.-G. SCHROEDER, and W. B. SCHWERK, 1988. Experiences with B-scan sonography in the diagnosis of soft tissue tumors of the head and neck. *HNO* 36:16–21.

[30] HOEHMANN, D., and P. LANDWEHR, 1990. Wertigkeit der Sialographie in der Speicheldrsendiagnostik. *Eur. Arch. Otorhinolaryngol.* 247:113 (Suppl 2).

[31] GREVERS, G., and T. VOGL, 1988. Intraarterial and intravenous digital subtraction angiography—how to use in otorhinolaryngology. *Laryngol. Rhinol. Otol.* 67:221–225.

[32] BLEIER, R., and R. ROCHELS, 1987. Echographic diagnosis of paranasal sinus tumours invading the lacrimal pathways. *Laryngol. Rhinol. Otol.* 66:539–542.

[33] BACHUS, R., 1988. Zukunftsperspektiven der MR-Tomographie und der Spektroskopie. *Nuklearmediziner* 11:163–168.

[34] HEUCK, A., M. REISER, C. WAGNER-MANSLAU, J. GMEINWIESER, and M. HERZOG, 1988. Tomographie des Gesichtsschaedels und Halses. *Roentgenraxis* 41:155–161.

[35] CLOSE, L. G., M. MERKELL, D. K. BURNS, and S. D. SCHAEFER, 1986. Computed tomography in the assessment of mandibular invasion intraoral carcinoma. *Ann. Otol. Rhinol. Laryngol.* 95:383–388.

[36] TOLXDORFF, T., H. HANDELS, F. UPMEIER, H. DRIESSEN, and R. REPGES, 1989. Data and methodbase management software system (RAMSES) for image processing in tissue characterizing magnetic resonance imaging. In *Proceedings of the Sixth Conference of Medical Informatics*, B. Barber et al., eds. Amsterdam: North-Holland, pp. 1132–1135.

[37] VALVASSORI, G. E., 1988. Diagnosis of retrocochlear and central vestibular disease by magnetic resonance imaging. *Ann. Otol. Rhinol. Laryngol.* 97:19–22.

[38] HOUSE, J. W., V. WALUCH, and R. K. JACKLER, 1986. Magnetic resonance imaging in acoustic neuroma diagnosis. *Ann. Otol. Rhinol. Laryngol.* 95:16–20.

[39] MEES, K., and T. VOGL, 1989. Computed tomography and magnetic resonance imaging of the head and neck. *Eur. Arch. Otorhinolaryngol.* 246:1340 (Suppl 1).

[40] SCHRADER, M., M. LENZ, G. SCHROTH, and H. KOENIG, 1987. NMRI: A new tool in the diagnosis of the petrous bone and the cerebello-pontine pathology. *Laryngol. Rhinol. Otol.* 66:45–53.

[41] LUSK, R. P., and V. D. DUNN, 1986. Magnetic resonance imaging in encephaloceles. *Ann. Otol. Rhinol. Laryngol.* 95:432–433.

[42] JAHNKE, V., U. FLESCH, and H. WITT, 1988. Angiodynography: A new diagnostic imaging in otorhinolaryngology. *Laryngol. Rhinol. Otol.* 67:217–222.

[43] KENN, R.-W., H. HOTZEL, R. HUBER, and K. J. PFEIFER, 1985. A new method of evaluating vessel stenosis with the digital subtraction angiography. In *CAR '85*, H. U. Lemke et al., eds. Berlin: Springer, pp. 143–148.

[44] OBERASCHER, G., M. GROBOVSCHEK, and K. ALBEGGER, 1988. The use of high-resolution computed tomography to exclude cholesteatoma recurrence: Is second-look operation necessary? *HNO* 36:181–187.

[45] VOGL, T., M. BAUER, G. FENZL, K. MEES, and J. LISSNER, 1985. Optimiertes diagnostisches Procedere bei Erkrankungen des Felsenbeines. In *CAR '85*, H. U. Lemke, et al., eds. Berlin: Springer, pp. 17–21.

[46] OBERASCHER, G., and M. GROBOVSCHEK, 1987. High-resolution middle ear computed tomography in stapes surgery. *HNO* 35:255–261.

[47] GROBOVSCHEK, M., and G. OBERASCHER, 1987. High-resolution computed tomography of the temporal bone. *Laryngol. Rhinol. Otol.* 66:547–553.

[48] OBERASCHER, G., and M. GROBOVSCHEK, 1988. Identification of middle ear implants in high-resolution computed tomography. *Laryngol. Rhinol. Otol.* 67:17–22.

[49] BATES, G. J. E. M., G. M. O'DONOGHUE, P. ANSLOW, and T. HOULDING, 1988. Can CCT detect labyrinthine fistulae pre-operatively. *Acta Otolaryngol.* 106:40–45.

[50] GREVERS, G., and T. VOGL, 1988. CT presentation of choanal atresia. *Laryngol. Rhinol. Otol.* 67:221–225.

[51] GMELIN, E., B. HOLLANDS-THORN, and E. RINAST, 1987. Digital subtraction sialography. *Laryngol. Rhinol. Otol.* 66:445–447.

[52] BRAUNSCHWEIG, R., H. HERMES, and K. BOHNDORF, 1990. Sialography with digital screens. *HNO* 38:338–341.

[53] IRO, H., T. SCHNEIDER, N. NITSCHE, G. WAITZ, and C. ELL, 1990. Extracorporal piezoelectric lithotripsy of salivary stones. *HNO* 38:251–255.

[54] KNIGSBERGER, R., J. FEYH, A. GOETZ, V. SCHILLING, and E. KASTENBAUER, 1990. Endoscopically controlled laser lithotripsy on sialolithiasis. *Laryngol. Rhinol. Otol.* 69: 322–323.

[55] WEIN, B., S. KLAJMAN, W. HUBER, and W. H. DOERING, 1988. Ultrasound analysis of disturbed coordination in tongue movements during swallowing. *Nervenarzt* 59:249–256.

[56] HOLINGER, L. D., and J. C. BIRNHOLZ, 1987. Management of infants with prenatal ultrasound diagnosis of airways obstruction by teratoma. *Ann. Otol. Rhinol. Laryngol.* 96:61–64.

[57] TOVI, F., Y. BARKI, and H. ZIRKIN, 1987. Ultrasonic diagnosis of metastatic cystic lymph node. *Ann. Otol. Rhinol. Laryngol.* 96:716–717.

[58] BLEIER, R., and R. ROCHELS, 1988. Echographic differential diagnosis of tumours of the salivary gland. *Laryngol. Rhinol. Otol.* 67:202–210.

[59] MANN, W., and W. WACHTER, 1988. Sonography of the salivary glands. *Laryngol. Rhinol. Otol.* 67:197–201.

[60] KAHLE, G., F. SCHAUSS, J. P. HAAS, and W. DRAF, 1990. Digitale Hochfrequenz Roentgenkinematographie des Schluckaktes. *Eur. Arch. Otorhinolaryngol.* 247:184.

[61] SCHNEIDER, S., and U. KRETSCHMAR, 1988. Erfahrungen mit der intraarteriellen digitalen Subtraktionsangiographie in der neurologischen Routinediagnostik. *Roentgenpraxis* 41:84–91.

[62] JASCHKE, W., M. J. LIPTON, R. G. GOULD, and M. GEORGI, 1988. Cine-CT. *Roentgenpraxis* 41:205–211.

[63] SEMMLER, W., F. GAECKEL, P. BACHERT-BAUMANN, and G. VAN KAL, 1989. In vivo Magnetresonanzspektroskopie. *Aerzteztg* 87:4–6.

[64] KANADE, T., 1987. *Three-Dimensional Machine Vision.* Norwell, Mass.: Kluwer Academic.

[65] AYACHE, N., 1991. *Artificial Vision for Mobile Robots: Stereo Vision and Multisensory Perception.* Cambridge, Mass.: MIT Press.

[66] BESL, P. J., 1988. *Active Optical Range Imaging Sensors.* New York: Springer-Verlag.

[67] BOLLES, R. C., J. KREMERS, and R. CAIN, 1983. Projector-camera range sensing of three-dimensional data. *Machine Intelligence Research Applied to Industrial Automation SRI International* 12:29–43.

[68] CHAMPLEBOUX, G., S. LAVALLÉE, P. SAUTOT, and P. CINQUIN, 1992. Accurate calibration of cameras and range imaging sensors, the NPBS method. In *IEEE International Conference on Robotics and Automation.* Nice, France: IEEE, pp. 1552–1558.

[69] HOLLERBACH, J. M., 1989. A survey of kinematic calibration. *The Robotic Review* 1:207–242.

[70] KOSUGI, Y., E. WATANABE, and J. GOTO, 1988. An articulated neurosurgical navigation system using MRI and CT images. *IEEE Trans. Biomed. Eng.* 35(2):147–152.

[71] FINLAY, P., 1992. Neurobot: Steps towards the development of an advanced surgery robot. In *Proceedings of the Fourteenth IEEE Engineering in Medicine and Biology Conference.* Paris: IEEE, pp. 1081–1082.

[72] GIORGI, C., F. BELTRAME, F. LUZZARA, and G. MARCENARO, 1992. Integration of a real-time localizer and 3D imaging for stereotactic neurosurgery. In *Proceedings of the Fourteenth IEEE Engineering in Medicine and Biology Conference.* Paris: IEEE, pp. 1083–1084.

[73] LOUHISALMI, Y., J. ALAKUIJALA, and J. OIKARINEN, 1992. Development of a localization arm for neurosurgery. In *Proceedings of the Fourteenth IEEE Engineering in Medicine and Biology Conference.* Paris: IEEE, pp. 1085–1086.

[74] TAYLOR, R. H., C. B. CUTTING, Y. Y. KIM, A. KALVIN, D. LAROSE, B. HADDAD, D. KHORAMABADI, M. NOZ, R. OLYHA, M. BRUUN, and D. GRIMM, 1991. A model-based optimal planning and execution system with active sensing and passive manipulation for augmentation of human precision in computer-integrated surgery. In the *Second International Workshop on Experimental Robotics.* Toulouse, France: Springer-Verlag.

[75] MÖSGES, R., G. SCHLONDORFF, L. KLIMEK, D. MEYER-EBRECHT, W. KRYBUS, and L. ADAMS, 1989. Computer assisted surgery: An innovative surgical technique in clinical routine. In *Computer Assisted Radiology, CAR '89,* H. U. Lemke, ed. Berlin: Springer-Verlag, pp. 413–415.

[76] TROCCAZ, J., S. LAVALLÉE, and E. HELLION, 1993. Padyc: A passive arm with dynamic constraints. In *Proceedings of the International Conference on Advanced Robotics.* Tokyo. Tokyo: JIRA Pub., pp. 361–366.

[77] ADAMS, L., A. KNEPPER, W. KRYBUS, D. MEYER-EBRECHT, G. PFEIFFER, R. RUGER, and M. WITTE, 1992. Orientation aid for head and neck surgeons. *ITBM: Innovation Tech. Biol. Med.* (special issue) 13(4):409–424.

[78] KATO, A., T. YOSHIMINE, T. HYAKAWA, Y. TOMITA, T. IKEDA, M. MITOMO, K. HARADA, and H. MOGAMI, 1991. Armless navigational system for computer assisted neurosurgery. *J. Neurosurg.* 74:845–849.

[79] ROBERTS, D. W., J. W. STROHBEIN, and J. F. HATCH, et al., 1986. A frameless stereotaxic integration of computerized tomographic imaging and the operating microscope. *J. Neurosurg.* pp. 545–549.

[80] LEWIS, J. T., and R. L. GALLOWAY, 1992. A-mode ultrasonic detection of subcutaneous fiducial markers for image-space registration. In *Proceedings of the Fourteenth IEEE Engineering in Medicine and Biology Conference.* Paris: IEEE, pp. 1061–1062.

[81] TAYLOR, R. H., H. A. PAUL, C. B. CUTTING, B. MITTELSTADT, W. HANSON, P. KAZANZIDES, B. MUSITS, Y. Y. KIM, A. KALVIN, B. HADDAD, D. KHORAMABADI, and D. LAROSE, 1992. Augmentation of human precision in computer-integrated surgery. *ITBM: Innovation Tech. Biol. Med.* (special issue) 13(4):450–468.

[82] VILLOTTE, N., D. GLAUSER, P. FLURY, and C. W. BURCKHARDT, 1992. Conception of stereotactic instruments for the neurosurgical robot Minerva. In *Proceedings of the Fourteenth IEEE Engineering in Medicine and Biology Conference,* Paris: IEEE, pp. 1089–1090.

[83] SALISBURY, K., 1984. Interpretation of contact geometries from force measurements. In *Robotics Research,* M.

Brady and R. Paul, ed. Cambridge, Mass.: MIT Press, pp. 567–577.

[84] DARIO, P., 1989. Tactile sensing for robots: Present and future. *The Robotics Review*. Cambridge, Mass.: MIT Press, pp. 133–146.

[85] IKUTA, K., M. TSUKAMOTO, and S. HIROSE, 1988. Shape memory alloy servo actuator system with electric resis-

tance feedback and application to active endoscope. In *Proceedings of the IEEE Conference on Robotics and Automation*. Philadelphia: IEEE, pp. 427–430.

[86] BENECKE, W., and H. C. PETZOLD, eds., 1992. *Proceedings of IEEE Microelectromechanical systems '92 Workshop*. Travemunde, Germany: IEEE.

2 Information Systems for Imaging Modalities

CHRISTIAN F. C. GREINACHER

THE DEVELOPMENT of digital imaging systems for radiology and the penetration of computer-supported management and information systems into hospitals inspire users' wishes for a computer-supported information system for the radiology department. In addition to advantages for the patients, doctors, and nursing staff, cost savings in hospital administration are expected from such systems.

Computer-supported management systems for radiology departments, generally known as *radiology information systems* (RISs), were introduced early in the eighties [1–3]. These systems collect, process, and store alphanumeric information but not radiologic images. Image information systems for radiology, developed in the mid-eighties, have been used successfully not only within the radiology department but also for image communication between radiology and other service departments in the hospital and between remotely situated hospitals [4–6].

Combination of information in radiology

The complex, informal dependencies within a radiology department can be modeled in two partial systems (figure 2.1). In the image information system, image-oriented information is exchanged. The body of information begins with the patient examination and terminates with the archival record of the images generated during this examination. The radiologic images are central. The management information system is, to a large extent, separate from this. Here the flow of administrative information, from admissions through the scheduling of the individual examination room and equipment to assistance with billing, is covered.

The solutions originally proposed for pure computer-aided image information systems, known as a *picture archiving and communication system* (PACS) [7, 8], today merge with the administratively oriented RIS into in-

tegrated information systems for radiology [9]. From a user's standpoint, the division into RIS and PACS is losing importance. In English-speaking countries, this combination of information in radiology has come to be called the image management, archival, and communication system (IMACS). In the next section, we concentrate on the image-oriented features of these information systems—that is, on PACS.

THE IMAGE INFORMATION SYSTEM

An image information system supports the following radiologic functions within the radiology department: image generation, image processing, image communication, image reporting, image storage, and archival, plus the distribution of images to the required hospital departments. The exchange of images among various locations in a hospital [10] or among experts from different institutions is known as *teleradiology* [11] and is gaining in importance.

Of special interest for a digital image information system are those imaging modalities wherein the images are prepared digitally and stored intermediately in the examination unit or those in which an image, initially not digital, can be rapidly converted, with adequate spatial and contrast resolution, into a digital image (as, for example, in digital luminescent radiography [DLR]).

The image information content displayed can be matched to the specific diagnostic problem by using digital postprocessing. Basically, image processing can be divided into *temporal* and *spatial filtering* (feature extraction) and *quantitative image evaluation* (length, area, volume, and angle).

Image communication takes place within the radiology department as well as between x-ray and requesting departments in the hospital. After reporting, various images must be sent to the ward (in the case of in-

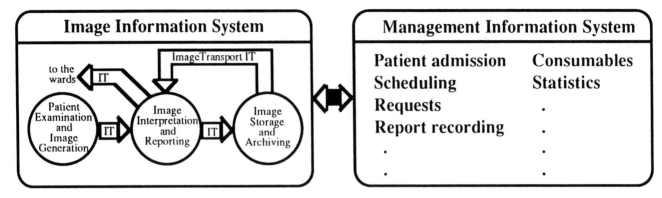

FIGURE 2.1   Image and management information system for a radiology department.

patients) or made available to the surgeons when an operation is planned. Timely image communication in emergency cases is critical.

Image interpretation and reporting requires use of both the current images and images from previous examinations. The radiologist dictates his or her report, has it typed in the office, and then signs it off. Very often today, reports are drawn up using computer-assisted text systems. This is beneficial in that the report can be made directly available to the reporting section of an RIS. After reporting, all images must be stored and archived.

Image storage means keeping the images easily and rapidly accessible during the inpatient's stay. *Image archiving* is retaining the images over long periods of time (up to 30 years) after the patient has been discharged from hospital. The access rate for archived images is very low in comparison and the access time, therefore, can be longer.

THE MANAGEMENT INFORMATION SYSTEM

Today's commercially available management or radiology information systems support the work of:

- Patient admission and card index management
- Patient appointment planning
- Room occupancy planning
- Patient flow control
- Supervision of film transport
- Report recording
- Support of the report function
- Documentation of the report
- Examination data recording for long-term documentation

- Recording procedure statistics to assist in billing
- Evaluation of procedure statistics
- Equipment workload statistics
- Equipment downtime statistics
- Consumables statistics

This relieves the doctors and radiology technicians from the increasing administrative load. In addition, such systems provide information to optimize the economic operation of a radiology department.

INFORMATION NETWORKING WITH THE HOSPITAL ADMINISTRATION

The range of application for administrative systems in hospitals extends from patient admission to bookkeeping, procedure recording, and billing, pharmacy and material stock keeping to salaries and wages. Two of these areas are closely coupled with the events in a radiology department.

Patient data recorded in the admissions department of the hospital is also required in the radiology department, and the procedures carried out on each patient must be relayed to the administration for billing purposes. At least partial cooperation between the image information system and the hospital administrative system is desirable to avoid duplicating the recording of data.

INFORMATION NETWORKING WITH THE HOSPITAL INFORMATION SYSTEM

For each inpatient, numerous reports accumulate during the hospital stay (e.g., laboratory test results, electrocardiographic reports). The indication for a given radiologic examination as well as the reporting of the resulting images can depend on these previous findings, so they must be made known to the radiologist. The ideal, therefore, would be to combine information hospitalwide via an integrated *hospital information system* (HIS), in which all patient-related data are administered. Partial systems such as RIS and PACS must take this concept into consideration [9].

PACS

The main aim in introducing a PACS is optimization of patient care, sequence of working steps in the radiology department, image distribution within the hospital, provision of images for research and teaching, and image archiving.

Conventional operation with films can lead to delays in the radiologic examination, reporting, or commencement of therapy because a given film may not always be available on time or it may even be missing. PACS should prevent images from being lost, reduce search times to a minimum, and supply the images and reports to the requesting doctor at the earliest possible time.

Rapid communication of images to the radiologist's place of work means that he or she can assess the quality of a series of images that have just been generated and, as the results from an actual examination can be immediately viewed, a decision can be made immediately to extend the examination or modify it if necessary. Direct access from the reporting desk to previous examination results that are stored shortens the reporting time. Thus, the work process is accelerated, patient care is expedited, and the stress on individual patients is reduced.

Computer-assisted access to images and reports opens up new possibilities for research and teaching staff for preparing and organizing conferences and teaching seminars. Multiple access to digitally stored images and reports prevents the occurrence of any collision with patient care requirements.

Digital archiving allows images to be accessed with short search times. Today's archival media fulfill the requirement that the storage medium (optical disk, optical tape) remain stable over the archive lifetime (≥ 30 years). I believe that the requirement for the storage medium to be readable over its lifetime, despite advancing technology and at a reasonable cost, should be qualified. Frequency of access to archival images diminishes drastically after 2 years [12] and, after

5 years, it is well under 1% so that access to images stored in "old" technology could be by means of a converter, even allowing for the increase in access time, without disturbing the radiologic work pattern.

THE SYSTEM CONCEPT

The basic elements of a PACS are shown in figure 2.2: The *image-generating systems* pass the images on to an *image communication network* in the form of electric signals. These images then are collected in an *image storage and archiving system*. Stored images are requested by multiple *image work stations and viewing stations*, in various locations, at different times during the day, where they are displayed on monitors for reporting, consultation, research, and teaching. There they can be postprocessed and compared to one another and with the results of previous studies. The doctor who requested the examination can have the end results sent over the digital communication network and displayed on viewing stations. Because it is not always possible to send images of every case over the network to every location (e.g., outpatients must be given images on conventional film), *laser cameras* connected to the communication network allow the image data to be documented on film. Connection with an RIS allows patient data and service data to be exchanged. An actual system architecture will be discussed later, using SIENET as the example.

STANDARDIZATION

Individual modules of a PACS can originate from different suppliers. Subsystems are, for example, the image-generating systems (modalities), the communication network, the database, the image processing and viewing stations, and the laser cameras. To guarantee the compatibility of these subsystems, supplier-independent standards must be generated for the equipment interfaces, the image header and image format, the communication protocol, and the storage format, as well as for the control elements and the syntax of the user interface. National and international bodies of experts are working to produce standards. For RISs, the most important are OSI, DICOM, and IPI.

The open systems interconnect (OSI) is an international standardized software architecture model in which communication-oriented partial functions are systematically structured in seven functional layers

Image generating systems (modalities)

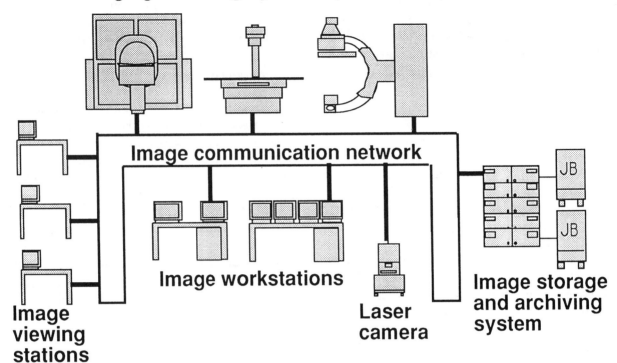

Image communication network

Image workstations

Image viewing stations

Laser camera

Image storage and archiving system

FIGURE 2.2   Basic structure of a PACS.

[13]. Within each layer, the rules, sufficient for the related communication functions, are defined as communication protocols and guarantee that communication partners on the network can understand one another.

The two most common communication networks and protocols available today, standardized in accordance with OSI, are the transport control protocol–internet protocol (TCP/IP) on Ethernet, with a signal rate of 10 megabits per second (Mbit/sec) and TCP/IP on fiber digital data interconnect (FDDI) with a signal rate of 100 Mbit/sec.

Digital imaging and communication (DICOM) is the result of cooperation between the American College of Radiology (ACR) and the National Electrical Manufacturers Association (NEMA) [14]. DICOM standardizes the structure of the formats and the accompanying parameters for radiologic images and commands for the exchange of such images between two units as well as the description of other data objects (e.g., image series, examination series, reports). The description of various methods of image data compression are also detailed in DICOM.

The image processing and interchange standard (IPI) is a comprehensive image-oriented standard for general data processing and communications applications [15, 16] and is supported worldwide by the appropriate industry. DICOM can describe the context-specific characteristics within IPI.

SYSTEM DATA TO BE HANDLED

In a PACS, personnel data, request data, physical examination data, image data, and reports must be recorded, communicated, and stored. Estimates of the average data volume for the radiologic images generated from one patient vary greatly (table 2.1). We choose as an average value 30 images per radiologically examined patient during his or her inpatient stay, with an average of 1 Mbyte image information per image. Individual cases range from 8 kbyte per nuclear medicine image or 2 Mbyte per digital subtraction angiography image up to 8 Mbyte per image for digital luminescent radiography.

In our example, we consider a department with 15 examination rooms. Twenty patients are examined daily per room, and 20 images are generated per examination on average. Thus, for such a department, 6000 digital images (15 × 20 × 20) are generated per day.

TABLE 2.1

Structure and volume of patient data (30 Mbyte + 9 kbyte)

Data	Volume
Personal	1 kbyte
Name	
Birthday	
Sex	
Profession	
Identification	
Request	1 kbyte
Organ	
Requesting ward	
Requesting physician	
Preliminary diagnoses	
Risks	
Physical examination	6 kbyte
Exposure dose	
Field of exposure	
Image	30 Mbyte
Image header	
Pixel values	
Graphic overlays	
Textual overlays	
Findings	1 kbyte
Reports	

This rough estimate is in line with the values reported for 700- to 900-bed hospitals [17, 18]. Estimating an average value of 1 MB per image, this means a daily image data volume of 6 gigabytes (Gbyte). However, this estimated data volume can be greatly exceeded at peak times or with special examinations (e.g., cardiologic radiographic studies). We will, therefore, use an average daily generated data volume of 10 GB in the following calculation.

According to Templeton and Dwyer [17], each image of a patient is accessed up to 14 times in the first 3 days of the hospitalization. With 10 Gbyte daily, this means translates to a throughput of 140-Gbyte image transfer. Eighty percent of this load is concentrated within 5 working hours. This translates to an average network load of approximately 6 Mbyte/s during the 5 hours.

In addition to the frequency of access to new images, access to previously archived images is also of interest. A study in a 540-bed hospital showed that 2.47% of the 409,661 film envelopes in the archive (5 years) were pulled each year [12, 17]. In absolute terms, this is

10,120 film envelopes per year or, with an average of 25 images per envelope, 1000 images per day that have to be collected from the archive. Hence, approximately 1 year's radiologic images must be retained in a storage system that permits direct access.

SYSTEM REQUIREMENTS

Based on the data from the preceding section for an inpatient stay of 13 days, the required storage capacity has an image data volume of 150 Gbyte, to which direct access is needed. Archiving the images with direct access for 1 year requires a storage capacity of approximately 2.5 Tbyte (2.5×10^{12} bytes). Using an optical storage medium, an archive with this capacity can be realized today. Data compression can be used to reduce the storage capacity by a factor of 2.5 : 1.

The *average* network load during the main load period, as shown in the previous section, is approximately 6 Mbyte/sec. However, a higher rate of 8 Mbyte/sec, resulting from the need to transmit one single image (8-Mbyte image information) on demand in 1 second, is sought. According to our studies, FDDI, with a signaling rate of 100 Mbit/sec today, will reach a throughput of approximately 3 Mbyte/s. Although one can expect that communication networks with higher throughputs will be available in the future, we have chosen a system architecture for our SIENET product (see next section) that reduces the bottlenecks in data throughput owing to its conceptional approach [19].

In daily routine, limited downtime, error tolerance, and absolute data security are demanded from a PACS. This means that data storage and archiving and the network configuration must be laid out redundantly.

The Siemens SIENET system

SIENET—STRUCTURED SYSTEM ARCHITECTURE

Earlier, the basic system concept for a PACS was delineated. In real life, the configuration must be matched to the individual user requirements. The radiology department (or, more correctly, the imaging department), with its subdepartments such as CT, angiography, nuclear medicine, trauma department, consultation, and clinical demonstration, and special areas such as cardiology and oncology require specific solutions to their problems. SIENET is made up of many hardware

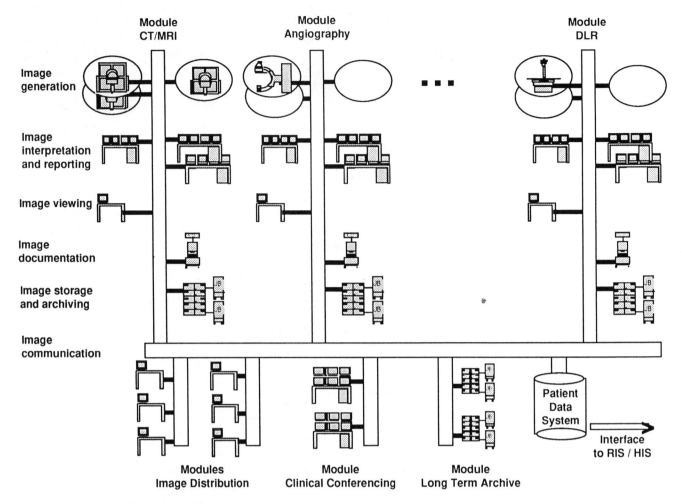

FIGURE 2.3   SIENET system architecture.

and software components (products), individually configured in a modular structured system architecture (engineering), and thus it is capable of being matched to different needs (figure 2.3). Each module is itself a miniature stand-alone PACS and is optimized to the special demands of its subsection. The integration of the individual modules to a complete system uses the "backbone network" and the comprehensive patient data system (PDS) (figure 2.4).

This structured system architecture offers the following advantages [20]:

• The complete system can be expanded in stages.

• The operational availability of the complete system is increased. Even if one module fails, the other parts of the system can continue undisturbed.

• Bottlenecks in image communication are avoided. Data communication is distributed over several subnetworks.

• Each module can be optimally matched to the requirements of its area. For example, transport of the (relatively low) data quantities of CT or MR modalities to their workstations can use Ethernet, whereas digital luminescent radiography or angiography scenes can use FDDI.

• Access to the stored data is accelerated because of the hierarchic data structure.

• The system architecture is retained even when integrating OEM systems.

IMAGE STORAGE AND ARCHIVING IN SIENET

In SIENET, a hierarchic data storage and archival system is realized (figure 2.5). It is divided into five levels, as follows:

• Level 1   Imaging modalities
• Level 2   Image-reporting consoles

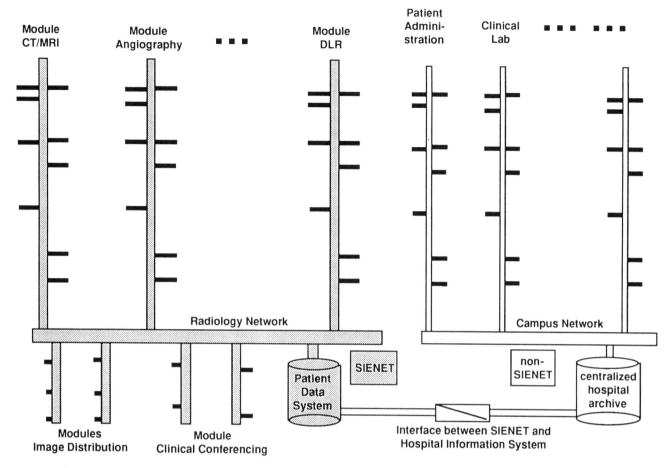

FIGURE 2.4   System architecture of a hospital information system.

- Levels 3 & 4   Image storage on rapid magnetic discs
- Level 5   Image archiving on optical media on- and off-line

Levels 3, 4, and 5 are known collectively as *image storage and archiving* (ISA). Newly acquired images are always initially stored simultaneously at two of these levels (modality and reporting console, or reporting console and ISA) until they are permanently stored on optical disks in the archive. This guarantees a high degree of data security.

Additional security is offered by the redundant array of independent disks (RAID) architecture used for the storage hardware [21]. The principle is shown in figure 2.6.

A *conventional* image store, with, for example, 8 GB of storage capacity, is constructed from eight individual Winchester disks of 1 GB each. Image matrices, com-

prising $n \times m$ pixels, each with 2 bytes, are stored sequentially (initially on disk 1 and, when this is full, disk 2, and so on). If one disk fails, all images on this disk are no longer available and, if the disk crashes, they are lost forever. In a RAID configuration, however, each of the Winchester disks receives one bit from each byte. An additional error reconstruction bit is added to each byte and stored on Winchester disk no. 9. In the event of any Winchester in the configuration failing, then the complete reconstruction of every byte in any image can be guaranteed by the error bit.

In this example, the RAID architecture is error tolerant with an additional expenditure of only 12.5% in comparison to the necessary expenditure if all the data were to be mirrored on a redundant storage system. A RAID also increases the write-read speed as all the bits in a byte are written and read at the same time, in parallel. In theory, this should lead to an increase by a factor of 8 but, in practice, only 60% or so of this gain

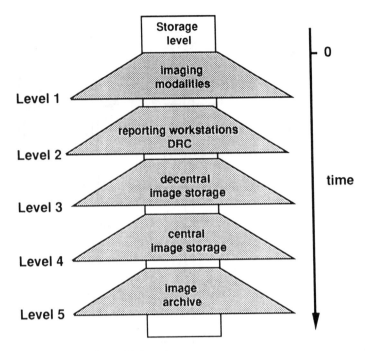

FIGURE 2.5 Hierarchic data storage and archiving in SIENET.

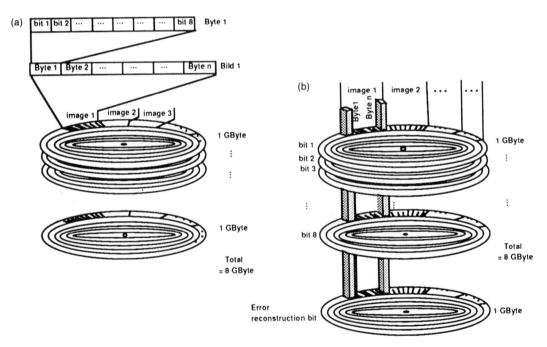

FIGURE 2.6 Architecture of a redundant array of independent disks (RAID). (a) Conventional image storage, with eight drives, each 1GB. (b) RAID image storage, with nine drives, each 1GB.

is realizable. In practice, four disks plus one with various error correction algorithms are usual, instead of the eight plus one shown here.

To control such large data quantities while maintaining fast access, data storage and archiving in SIENET is distributed over the individual modules. Each module in figure 2.3 can support one or more ISAs. Structuring the image storage in the following categories permits the shortest possible search and access times to all patient examinations:

- Not yet reported patient examinations, stored at the reporting consoles (level 2)
- Actual reported patient examinations, stored in the central store of the respective module (level 3)
- Complete patient folders of current patients, including all previous examinations, stored in a fast store (level 4)
- Long-term storage of all patient folders on optical disks (level 5)

So as not to bother the user explicitly with this distributed data storage, a central database, PDS, administers levels 3, 4, and 5. PDS administers not only the on-line images but also the off-line images in level 5. Naturally, for reasons of data safety, the PDS database is administered in a fail-safe system (e.g., RAID) and also is backed up at regular intervals on off-line media.

The communication network in SIENET

TCP/IP is used as the communication protocol in SIENET, on Ethernet as well as FDDI. Ethernet is a cost-effective solution to be used when a signal rate of 10 Mbit/sec with point-to-point throughput of approximately 600 kbyte/sec is sufficient. A typical example would be the transfer of images of a CT examination from the CT device over the network to the related workstation.

The situation is different when several users want to send data over the network at the same time. Collisions between the different data packages and the necessary repeating of the protocol lead to a drastic reduction in the data throughput of Ethernet. Therefore, for connections between image workstations and image storage systems, the FDDI network is used so that the protocols avoid collisions, even in the case of multiple users accessing the network simultaneously. The higher throughput also is required in the case of larger data

quantities (e.g., for chest radiographs using digital luminescent radiography (an exam consists of three images of 8 Mbytes each) or for angiographic examinations (where an examination comprises 20 images of 2 MB each). Because SIENET uses the same protocol TCP/IP in Ethernet as in FDDI networks, the two networks can be easily connected with one another by bridges.

SIENET workstations

In SIENET, workstations with high output and image quality are available for image viewing and reporting. The platform consists of a host computer (Sparc with UNIX operating system), a local image storage capacity together with a standardized modular library for the image-processing programs, and an operating surface. To increase the computing power for complicated image processing, the host is assisted by a fast SMI 5 image processor (Siemens Medical Imaging System, fifth generation). Workstations support the functions shown in table 2.2.

High-contrast monitors SIMOMED (54-cm screen diagonal, 1280 lines, and 1024 pixels) offer highest image quality. The workstation is modular and available with between two and six monitors (figure 2.7). The image representation on the monitors is configurable. In addition to this representation in *diagnostic view*, image series (i.e., the sequential sections of a CT study) can be arranged in a *stack view*. The viewer can then interactively page through the stack, thereby gaining a quasi-3D impression of the information content. A quick overview of the contents of a film envelope can be obtained by displaying them as heavily minified images. This flexibility is required in order to match the workstation, insofar as is possible, to the demands of the various locations where it is in use.

Image distribution in SIENET

Images have only to be viewed and not further manipulated at many locations inside and outside the radiology department. Therefore, SIENET includes viewing consoles based on the same architecture as the reporting consoles but not including the high-performance SMI 5 component. The system software, user software, and user interface remain identical.

The fast distribution of images to the consoles within the radiology department takes place over Ethernet or

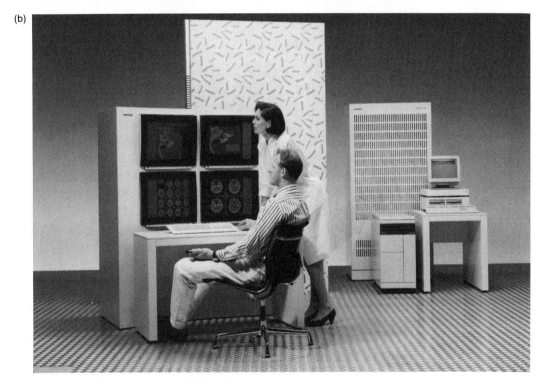

FIGURE 2.7 Workstations. (a) SIENET reporting console with two monitors. (b) SIENET reporting console with four monitors.

TABLE 2.2
Main functions of a SIENET diagnostic reporting console

Administrative functions
User identification
Password
Modality-specific configuration
Work lists
Report visualization
Reference folders
Access to central database
Archive files

Image display functions
Token view
Diagnostic view
Scratch view
Stack view
Delete/duplicate images
Scroll and page

Image evaluation functions
Gray-scale windowing
Gray-scale inversion
magnifying glass
Magnification, reduction
Pixel lens
Geometric measurements
ROI and statistics
Addition, subtraction
Rotate, mirror
Link images
mark and label details
3D surface reconstructions
Multiplanar reconstruction

DLR-specific functions
Nonlinear windowing
Edge enhancement
Configuration of processing parameters

FDDI networks, depending on requirements. However, it is not always possible to distribute images to every recipient in hospital over a network. Also, for outpatients, images must be handed to the requesting doctor as hard copies on film. For these purposes, digitally stored images from SIENET can be documented using a laser camera or film printer. To permit the connection of cameras from different suppliers, a camera server is available in the SIENET range. The camera server adapts the various cameras to the SIENET protocol.

Conventional films such as those brought by outpatients must be entered into SIENET. Film digitizers scan the existing films and pass on system-conformable digital images to SIENET.

System planning, realization, and operation

The previously described system architecture and the individual components of a PAC system are the building blocks for a user's solution. To realize a PACS in a given environment, the necessary components must be selected, supplied, and matched to the individual organization with its specific working processes. The individual products must, of necessity, be flexible, especially in regard to modifying the parameters of the user software. In addition, a team of experts from the users and suppliers must draw up a binding *project plan*, clearly structured in phases and milestones. The main phases of such a master plan are system planning, system realization, and system operation [22].

Whereas the supplier is responsible for the development, manufacture, marketing, supply, and maintenance of the hardware and software system components, system planning, realization, and operation must be realized as a system-specific achievement, with the user and supplier working in close cooperation. In addition to software and hardware, system engineering is the deciding factor for the quality of the system.

ACKNOWLEDGMENT This chapter will be published in the original German language version as "Informationssysteme für die bildgebenden Systeme" in *Bildgebende Systeme für die medizinische Diagnostik*, 3rd edition, H. Morneburg, ed. Berlin-Munich: Siemens.

REFERENCES

[1] DECrad: The DECmed radiology system—overview (product information), 1983. Digital Equipment Corporation, Medical Systems Group, Marlboro, Mass. EA-23295-14/83.
[2] GIERE, W., H. E. RIEMANN, and U. LOERCHER, 1980. Reasons for the introduction of a radiological department system. *Comp. Diagn. Radiol.* 266–270.
[3] LIEBER, H., W. BUCHSTEINER, and W. OFFENMÜLLER, 1991. RIS—Ein Radiologie-Informationssystem, Einführung und Nutzen in der Röntgenabteilung des Krankenhauses Straubing. *Electromedica* 59:89–97.
[4] First International Conference and Workshop on Picture Archiving and Communication Systems (PACS) for Medical Applications, 1982. *Proc. S.P.I.E.* 318.
[5] Second International Conference and Workshop on Picture Archiving and Communication Systems (PACS II) for Medical Applications, 1983. *Proc. S.P.I.E.* 418.
[6] GREINACHER, C. F. C., et al., 1984. Digitale Bildinformationssysteme in der Radiologie—Stand und Entwicklungstendenzen. *Digitale Bilddiagnostik* 4:87–104.

[7] *Understanding PACS*, 1992. Harrisburg, Penn.: Society for Computer Applications in Radiology, ed.

[8] PETERS, P. E., and W. WIESMANN, 1991. Digitale Bildarchivierungs—und Kommunikations—systeme (PACS). Dt. Ärzteblatt 88(24):1932–1942.

[9] Lecture notes, 1988. In *Medical Informatics*, Vol. 37, O. Rienhoff and C. F. C. Greinacher, eds. Berlin: Springer-Verlag.

[10] FELIX, R., M. LANGER, F. ASTINET, and W. ZENDEL, 1990. Das Berliner Radiologie-Kommunikations-Projekt. *Fortschr. Röntgenstr.* 152(6):667–672.

[11] TEMPLETON, A. W., et al., 1991. A dial-up digital teleradiology system: Technical considerations and clinical experience. *A.J.R.* 157:1331–1336.

[12] BROLIN, I., and K. H. HOLMDAHL, 1984. Arkivering av röntgenfilm. SPRI report 6/70.

[13] Information processing systems—open systems interconnection: Basic reference model (ISO IS 7498), 1984.

[14] Digital imaging and communications, 1985. ACR-NEMA Standards public. no. 300.

[15] CLARK, A. F., 1992. Image processing and interchange—the imaging model. *Proc. S.P.I.E.* 1659:106–116.

[16] Information technology, computer graphics and image processing, image processing and interchange (ISO/IEC Committee Draft [CD] 12087), May 1992.

[17] TEMPLETON, A. W., and S. J. DWYER III, et al., 1982. A peripheralized digital image management system: Prospectus. *A.J.R.* 139:979–984.

[18] HRUBY, W., et al., 1992. Datenvernetzung in einem neu errichteten Röntgeninstitut am Beispiel des Donauspitals Wien. *Röntgenpraxis* 45:103–110.

[19] GREINACHER, C. F. C., D. FUCHS, and J. PERRY, 1986. Product related advantages of a structured PACS architecture. *Proc. Computer Appl. Med. Care* 296–305.

[20] GREINACHER, C. F. C., B. LUETKE, and G. SEUFERT, 1987. Digital image information systems in radiology. *Siemens Forsch. Entwickl. Ber.* 16:22–29.

[21] Understanding disk arrays (part no. 800-7549-11). SUN Microsystems Inc.

[22] GREINACHER, C. F. C., E. F. BACH, et al., 1990. Practical experience from Siemens PACS installations. *S.P.I.E.* 1234:370–376.

3 Imaging Transforms for Volume Visualization

JAYARAM K. UDUPA AND ROBERTO J. GONÇALVES

THREE-DIMENSIONAL imaging in medicine encompasses visualization, manipulation, and analysis of structure information captured in 3D (and higher-dimensional) digital images. In recent years, this activity has become an established discipline in medical imaging. The fast pace of development in this field is evidenced by the frequency of conferences held and papers published on this subject recently. As further testimony to the brisk activity in this field, three books on this subject [1–3] have been published in a 1-year period.

The subject of this chapter is mainly *visualization*—that is, processes relating to how the 3D structural information may be presented on a computer display screen to a human observer. Although *manipulation*—relating to how structures may be altered—and *analysis*—concerning how structures may be quantified—are equally important operations, there is significantly less published work on these topics than on visualization.

Visualization methods may be grouped into two classes, the *surface-* and *volume-rendering* methods. While this nomenclature is widely accepted in the literature, the meaning that each of these phrases conveys is not unique. We may consider as the surface-rendering class all methods wherein a surface representation of the structure first is created and subsequently a rendition of the structure is generated by rendering the surface elements. Similarly, all methods that render the entire volume (region) occupied by the structure by rendering the volume elements forming the region can be considered to belong to the volume-rendering class. In both, the basic elements are assigned an opacity value and renditions are created by determining the intensity of light reaching the points (pixels) in a viewing plane under certain assumed illumination conditions. In volume rendering, it is not necessary for each volume element to have a fixed opacity value (in fact, the power of volume rendering comes from such a consideration). However, every surface element in a given surface in surface rendering should necessarily have a fixed opacity value (usually 100% unless the structure is viewed with other structures and it is desirable to make it semi-transparent). Surface rendering thus appears to be a special case of volume rendering. In a strict mathematic sense, however, a surface occupies zero volume (although the volume enclosed by the surface usually is nonzero) and the particularity becomes questionable. In the digital situation, surface elements that each have zero volume (e.g., voxel faces) or nonzero volume (e.g., voxels themselves) can be used to represent a surface [4, 5]. Therefore, whether this particularity becomes meaningful depends on the situation. Conversely, we may use a set of surfaces—say voxel faces as surface elements—to represent a volume, for example, by making each surface an isodensity surface for a distinct image density value. To render the volume, we may render the collection of surfaces, assigning a fixed opacity value to each surface [6]. Of course, among them the surfaces may have different opacity values. When surface rendering is viewed in this more general fashion, the distinction between the two methodologies begins to disappear. Without digressing further, for the purpose of this chapter, we assume a somewhat general definition of the two methodologies: A rendering method that requires the explicit creation of a surface description will be called *surface rendering* and that which does not will be classified as *volume rendering*.

The preceding argument brings out an important point relating to one of the main purposes of this chapter. It hints at borrowing an important idea from volume rendering into surface rendering. In biomedical visualization, often the functionally independent operations in a rendering method are integrated among themselves or with the rendering method for computational efficiency. This is especially true in computer implementations. Yet freeing the individual basic operations from the idiosyncrasies of the rendering method and viewing them in a more general setting can lead to very powerful functionalities resulting from combining these operations in ways that have not been envisaged when they are first designed. Our first objective is to demonstrate the richness resulting from a bewildering array of rendering methods that can be generated when the individual operations are identified appropriately and combined properly. Because the effectiveness of a rendering method often depends on the data, the usefulness of the richness of the environment cannot be overstated. We introduce an operator notation to describe concisely the individual basic operations and the resulting rendering methods. We do not attempt an exhaustive examination of the possible sequences of operations (i.e., rendering methods) simply for want of space. We introduce several new operations, demonstrate the improved renditions resulting from sequences using such operations, and describe many new rendering methods with potential for improved rendition.

This discussion naturally leads us to the question of how rendering methods are to be compared, which is the second topic of importance in this chapter. One method objectively comparing renditions is to use observer studies [7]. A main difficulty with observer studies, however, is that they are very expensive. Most rendering methods have a number of independent parameters. The selection of optimal values (optimal from the point of view of the underlying medical question to which an answer is being sought through imaging) for these parameters for a given rendering method is itself an evaluation problem. If the studies to compare rendering methods have also to take into account these variables, the number of variables involved will be so large that conducting observer studies becomes impractical. Hence, much sifting of the parameters and methods should be done first using observer-independent techniques, and observer studies should be used only as the final arbiter of competing methods. The approach we suggest consists of using carefully prepared mathematic phantoms, putting them through image reconstruction processes emulating the image acquisition situation as realistically as possible [8], applying the 3D operator sequence to the resulting data, and then quantitatively comparing with the truth those aspects that determine the appearance of specific object features in renditions. We will see that such quantification of visual entities and subsequent comparison of rendering methods us-

ing derived numbers allow close scrutiny of individual operations used in rendering.

Basic transforms

In this section, we describe the basic transforms that have commonly been used in 3D imaging and introduce a few new transforms. Each transform will be identified with an operator. The operators are generic in the sense that they do not distinguish between the different variants of the same class of transforms. For example, 3D image interpolation is a transform that converts one 3D image into another with volume elements of possibly a different size. It will be represented by a single operator, although many interpolating functions—linear, bilinear, trilinear, and various cubic forms—can be used with the transform.

SOME DEFINITIONS

In visualization, in general, the 3D image data available to us constitute a digitized and quantized representation of a vector-valued function of three independent variables. In medical imaging, typically the function is scalar-valued and represents the distribution of some anatomic or physiologic property value over a 3D region of the body. We call this function a *body function* and assume the 3D region to be a cuboid of finite size in Euclidean 3D space. The digitization operation can be considered to partition this cuboid into smaller cuboids by three sets of mutually orthogonal planes. The quantization operation separates the aggregate property value within each smaller cuboid into one of a finite set of numbers. We call the small cuboids *voxels*, the quantized value associated with them their *density*, the set of all smaller cuboids together with their densities a *scene*, the (bigger) cuboid region the *scene region*, and the set of all smaller cuboids the *scene domain*.

We associate a fixed *scene coordinate system* (x^s, y^s, z^s) with the scene to describe the location of the voxels in the scene and determine a fixed *imaging device coordinate system* (x^d, y^d, z^d) with respect to which the position and orientation of the scene coordinate system is described. The scene coordinate system is chosen such that its axes are parallel to the edges of the cuboid representing the scene region.

We consider a scene D to be a pair (V, f), where V is the scene domain, and f, called the *density function*, is a mapping that assigns to every voxel in V a number in the closed interval $[L, H]$ called the *density range*, where L and H are real numbers. When $L = 0$ and $H = 1$ are the only numbers in the range, we call D a *binary scene*. Otherwise, D will be referred to as a *gray-level scene*. V essentially represents a *digitization* of the scene region.

The voxels in V sometimes are not of identical size, but usually all voxels have identical, square cross-sections in planes parallel to the $x^s y^s$ plane, and voxels with the same z^s coordinate for their centers have, in addition, the same size in the z^s direction. Therefore, voxels in V can be completely specified by the coordinates of their centers together with the size of the square cross-section (usually referred to as *pixel size*) and the voxel size in the z^s direction for each layer of voxels with the same z^s coordinate of their centers. We call the subset of voxels of V with a fixed z^s coordinate of their centers, together with their densities, a *slice of D*. If the subset constitutes the *i*-th layer, the corresponding slice will be referred to as the *i-th slice*.

The set of all scenes will be called the *scene space*. Note that the scenes in a scene space need not have for their scene domains the same size, orientation with respect to the imaging device coordinate system, or digitization. The purpose of acquiring scene data usually is to study the form and function of certain structures, called *objects*, about which information is captured in the scene. Objects are geometrically described via their boundary or region representations as sets of points, line segments, area elements, or volume elements. Associated with every object is an *object coordinate system* (x^o, y^o, z^o) whose location and orientation relative to the scene coordinate system, and hence to the imaging device coordinate system, is known. We call the set of all objects the *object space*. One of the main goals of visualization is to create 2D images, called *renditions*, depicting some 3D information of interest captured in a given scene. We consider a rendition to be a pair $(\mathcal{P}, g)$ where $\mathcal{P}$, a rectangular array of pixels, is the *rendition domain*, and g, an *intensity function*, associates with every pixel in $\mathcal{P}$ a scalar-valued intensity from a gray scale given by $\{0, 1, \ldots, U\}$ or a vector-valued intensity from a color scale $\{0, 1, \ldots, U_r\} \times \{0, 1, \ldots, U_g\} \times \{0, 1, \ldots, U_b\}$. We call the set of all renditions the *view space* and associate with every rendition a *view coordinate system* (x^v, y^v) whose location and orientation relative to the scene or object coordinate system is known. Imaging transforms discussed in this section transform information from one space to the other among scene, object, and view spaces.

In the following discussion, we group basic imaging transforms into two classes: *scene-related*, which operate mainly on scenes, and *structure-related*, which operate mainly on objects extracted from scenes.

SCENE-RELATED TRANSFORMS

The transforms described in this section are applicable to both gray-level and binary scenes, although their applicability to binary scenes sometimes is trivial. Throughout we denote the input and output scenes by $D = (V, f)$ and $D' = (V', f')$, their density range by $[L, H]$ and $[L', H']$, and the scene space by $\mathcal{D}$.

VOLUME OF INTEREST (A) Volume of interest (A) is a scene space–to–scene space transform:

$$A: \mathcal{D} \to \mathcal{D} \qquad (1)$$

such that $V' \subset V$, $[L', H'] = [L, H]$, and f' is a restriction of f to V'. This is often the first in a sequence of operations, and its purpose is to reduce the size of data that need to be processed subsequently to create a rendition.

FILTERING (F_s) Filtering (F_s) may be described most generally by the following transform:

$$F_s: \mathcal{D} \to \mathcal{D} \qquad (2)$$

such that $V' = V$. The form of f' is determined by the nature of the filter. Many forms of smoothing and enhancing filters have been used in picture processing [9], which readily generalize to 3D scenes. We consider one example of a (Gaussian) smoothing filter that will be used in the next section:

$$f'(v) = \sum_{v' \in \mathcal{N}(v)} h(v' - v) f(v') \qquad (3)$$

where $\mathcal{N}(v)$ is the subset of voxels of V in an appropriate (say, the $3 \times 3 \times 3$) neighborhood of v (including v), and for all $t = (t_1, t_2, t_3) \in R^3$

$$h(t) = \frac{1}{\sigma \sqrt{2\pi}} \exp\left(-\frac{t_1^2 + t_2^2 + t_3^2}{2\sigma^2}\right) \qquad (4)$$

The role of scene filtering in visualization has not been studied much. As we will demonstrate in the next section, it is a powerful operation that forms a bridge between surface- and volume-rendering methodologies.

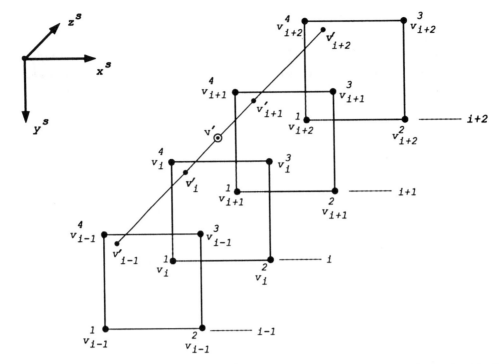

FIGURE 3.1 Illustration of bilinear-cubic density interpolation. The density of voxel v' (only the centers of voxels are shown to simplify drawing) of the output scene is determined by unicubic interpolation of the estimated densities at points v'_{i-1}, v'_i, v'_{i+1}, and v'_{i+2}. Each of these densities is determined, in turn, via bilinear interpolation of the densities of four voxels whose centers are closest to these points in the input scene.

INTERPOLATION (I_s, I_b) Interpolation (I_s, I_b) is a scene space–to–scene space transform in which the scene regions of input and output scenes remain the same but their domains differ: That is,

$$I_s: \mathscr{D} \to \mathscr{D} \qquad (5)$$

such that $V' \neq V$ (except when I_s is an identity operator) and f' is a sampling of an interpolant of f. Various forms of interpolating functions have been used to determine the density values of voxels in V': unilinear [10], bilinear, trilinear [11–14], various forms of unicubic [13, 14], bicubic, and a combination of linear and cubic forms [15]. An example of the latter form, which we call *bilinear-cubic*, is illustrated in figure 3.1. For simplicity, we have shown only the centers of relevant voxels: $v' \in V'$ represents (the center of) the voxel whose density is to be determined; $v'_{i-1}, v'_i, v'_{i+1}, v'_{i+2}$ are the projections of the center of v' onto the two closest slice planes (a slice plane is the plane that contains the centers of all voxels in the slice) of D in the $+z^s$ and $-z^s$ directions relative to v'; $v^k_t, 1 \leq k \leq 4$, are the four voxels in V closest to the point v'_t, for $i-1 \leq t \leq i+2$. The density value at v'_t is determined via bilinear inter-

polation of the four voxel densities of v_t. The density of v' is determined by a cubic spline type of interpolation of the values at v'_t: The interpolating function is such that its values at v'_i and v'_{i+1} equal the densities at v'_i and v'_{i+1}, respectively, and its derivative at v'_t, for $t = i$, $i + 1$, is density at v'_{t+1} − density at $v'_{t-1}/z^s_{t+1} - z^s_{t-1}$, z^s_{t+1} and z^s_{t-1} being the z^s coordinate of v'_t and v'_{t+1}, respectively. Imaging transforms using this form of interpolation will be illustrated in later sections.

Recently, binary scene interpolation methods have been investigated and a method called *shape-based interpolation* [13] has been introduced and its variants [16, 17] developed. These (and other shape interpolation methods [18]) have been shown to produce more accurate results than gray-level scene interpolation in many situations. The basic idea here is first to convert the given binary scene into a gray-level scene and then to interpolate the latter. The conversion is done by assigning to every voxel in the scene domain the shortest distance to the voxel from the boundary between 0 and 1 voxel regions in the binary scene, the distance being taken to be positive for 1-voxels (voxels with density 1) and negative for 0-voxels (voxels with density 0). The distance usually is computed within the same slice that contains the voxel in question and from the 2D boundary in that slice (though there is no reason why this cannot be generalized to a 3D distance). A practical motivation for shape-based interpolation comes from situations where interactive outlining on slices is the only possible method of identifying objects. Clearly, object identification followed by interpolation would save a great deal of user time, especially when dealing with 4D scenes, compared to interpolation followed by object identification. We denote shape-based interpolation by the operator I_b:

$$I_b : \mathscr{D}_b \rightarrow \mathscr{D}_b \qquad (6)$$

where $\mathscr{D}_b$ represents the set of all binary scenes. We will indicate later how other operators can be combined with the scene interpolation operator I_s to give effects similar to that of I_b.

SEGMENTATION   We identify two types of segmentation operators S_b and S_g. In *binary segmentation*,

$$S_b : \mathscr{D} \rightarrow \mathscr{D}_b \qquad (7)$$

such that $V' = V$ and $[L', H']$ is the set $\{0, 1\}$.

In *gray segmentation*,

$$S_g : \mathscr{D} \rightarrow \mathscr{D}_p \qquad (8)$$

such that $V' = V$ and $[L', H']$ is $[0, 1]$. Here $\mathscr{D}_p$, a subset of the scene space, is the set of all scenes with voxel densities in the interval $[0, 1]$.

Thresholding is the most commonly used binary segmentation operator, which can be defined by

$$f'(v) = \begin{cases} 1 & \text{if } f(v) \in [T_l, T_h] \\ 0 & \text{otherwise} \end{cases} \qquad (9)$$

where T_l and T_h are fixed numbers. Clustering based on multiparametric scene data (that is, scenes in which voxel density is vector-valued as in MRI of the brain using multiple magnetic resonance properties) is another popular method of binary segmentation. This approach seems to be capable of reproducible results with proper user training [19–23]. Binary segmentation being as hard as it is, and yet being a crucial operation in visualization, manipulation, and analysis, a variety of general methods as well as application-specific approaches are being investigated (see the articles on segmentation in Ezquerra et al. [24]).

Gray segmentation is a generalization of binary segmentation, the idea being to assign density to voxels in the output scene that reflects the likelihood of the voxel

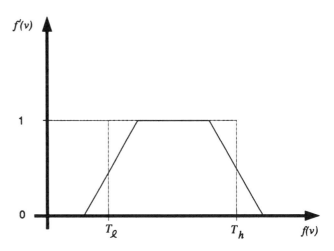

FIGURE 3.2   Gray segmentation via thresholding. T_l and T_h are fixed lower and upper thresholds that determine a decision boundary in a one-dimensional feature space; $f'(u)$ is a function of the distance of the density of v from the decision boundary.

being in the structure that is being segmented. In the terminology of pattern classification [25], treating segmentation as a voxel classification problem, this likelihood can be chosen to be a function of the distance from the decision boundary. For example, in thresholding, the decision boundary is given by $f(v) = T_l$ and $f(v) = T_h$, and the distance function may be chosen to be that shown in figure 3.2 [26]. This idea can be generalized to higher-dimensional feature spaces, in particular to the clustering approaches mentioned previously. It should be emphasized that the introduction of fuzziness in the result of segmentation by itself does not make the segmentation problem easier to solve. It only allows a flexibility to retain the uncertainties inherent in the scene data in the segmentation result, but the problem itself remains as difficult as binary segmentation.

MASKING   The purpose of masking (M_s) is to "clip" the input scene so that objects of no interest are excluded in the clipped scene. Alternatively, by applying a segmentation technique to the clipped scene, the object(s) of interest may be identified automatically. Masking is a scene space–to–scene space transform

$$M_s : \mathscr{D} \rightarrow \mathscr{D} \qquad (10)$$

such that $V' = V, H' = H$, and L' is any number less than L, and

$$f'(v) = \begin{cases} f(v) & \text{if } v \in V_1 \subset V \\ L' & \text{otherwise} \end{cases} \qquad (11)$$

V_1 may be specified in a variety of ways. Usually this is done interactively [27, 28], by having the user either draw or paint the region occupied by V_1 slice by slice or cut the scene domain via some form of 3D display. Automatic mask generation to aid in segmentation seems simpler than solving the segmentation problem itself in many situation, although it does not appear that it has been attempted.

STRUCTURE DEFINITION (O_s, B_s) The purpose of the structure definition transforms (O_s, B_s) is to generate a 3D object or surface description from the given scene. These are scene space–to–object space transforms

$$O_s: \mathscr{D} \to \mathscr{Q}$$
$$B_s: \mathscr{D} \to \mathscr{S} \qquad (12)$$

where $\mathscr{Q}$, a subset of the object space, is the set of all object descriptions (in the form of region representation), and $\mathscr{S}$, also a subset of the object space, is the set of all surface descriptions. A variety of methods (representing O_s) are available for obtaining object descriptions from scenes, which differ mainly in how the objects are represented—simply as an array of voxels constituting the object [29–33] or as other specialized schemes that encode sets of voxels via segment end [34, 35], skewed array [36], semiboundary [37], or various forms of octree representations [38–40]. A greater variety of techniques (representing B_s) are available for obtaining boundary surface descriptions from scenes, including methods of surface detection in gray-level scenes [4, 15, 41–48], and surface tracking and formation in binary scenes [5, 49–54]. Some methods express the surface as a connected set of faces of cubic voxels. Others approximate the surface via polygonal elements, in particular triangles. Some of these methods are guaranteed to produce "closed" surfaces, and some produce nonclosed surfaces. The closure of surfaces is important because otherwise they do not correspond to physically realizable objects. Closure is essential in some of the new structure-related transforms we introduce in the next section.

CLASSIFICATION The classification transform (C) creates (an opacity scene) from a given scene by assigning opacity values to voxels:

$$C: \mathscr{D} \to \mathscr{D}_p \qquad (13)$$

Here $V' = V, [L', H'] = [0, 1]$ (note that this represents an interval of real numbers), and $\mathscr{D}_p$ is the set of all scenes with the density range $[0, 1]$. The purpose of this transform is to create a semitransparent volume that may subsequently be volume-rendered.

To perform classification adequately so as subsequently to create accurate renditions is not an easy task. In fact, this is as difficult a problem as segmentation. As outlined in the section Segmentation, classification is indeed analogous to gray segmentation. The existing classification techniques [12, 26] have drawbacks similar to those of the simple segmentation techniques.

VOLUME RENDERING $(R_{vs}, R_{vbs}, R_{vbo}, R_{vo}, R_{vbv})$ Given an object description either explicitly—as, for example, an array of binary-valued voxels—or implicitly as an opacity scene, volume rendering $(R_{vs}, R_{vbs}, R_{vbo}, R_{vo}, R_{vbv})$ to create a rendition of the object consists of two distinct operations: projection and pixel intensity calculation. Projection is done via either ray casting [12, 55–60] or direct projection of object elements [26, 29, 30, 32–40, 61]. Pixel intensity calculation is done by a variety of methods that differ mainly in how the unit normal vector to the alleged object surface in the volume is estimated. The methods of projection differ mainly in their computational requirements. Differences in the quality of renditions attributable to the methods of projection are subtle. Although ray casting allows more complex illumination models than does voxel projection, it has not been demonstrated that the added complexity improves diagnostic information. The quality of rendition is determined mainly by the method of estimating the unit normal vectors. Therefore, in the following definition of volume-rendering transforms, we consider only this latter aspect and ignore the differences due to the method of projection.

Depending on the space in which the data used for estimating the normal vector are defined, we classify normal estimation methods as *scene space*, *object space*, and *view space methods*. Consider the scene density function:

$$w = f(v) = f(x^s, y^s, z^s) \qquad (14)$$

where we have represented voxel v by the coordinates of its center (x^s, y^s, z^s) in the scene coordinate system. If f is known at every point within the scene region and if its partial derivatives exist at (x^s, y^s, z^s), then its gradient at that point is given by

$$\nabla w = i \frac{\partial f}{\partial x^s} + j \frac{\partial f}{\partial y^s} + k \frac{\partial f}{\partial z^s} \qquad (15)$$

Scene space methods operate on the principle that if the object boundaries are characterized by sharp changes in voxel density, then the direction of most rapid density change at points in the vicinity of the boundary should be approximately normal to the boundary. (For isodensity surfaces, it is a known mathematic fact that the gradient vector is normal to the boundary at points on the boundary.) For high-contrast boundaries (such as bone surfaces in scenes obtained from CT), these conditions are mostly satisfied well, and therefore a unit vector in the direction of ∇w forms a good estimate of surface normal [57]. Since f is not known at every point in the scene region, an appropriate interpolating function may be used instead of f in equation 15 or, as is usually done, the partial derivatives are approximated by central differences of voxel densities in the three directions [12, 15, 26, 31, 43–45, 57]. What forms a good approximation to ∇w at points on (near) isodensity surfaces is an interesting problem that is yet to be fully explored. The following example is an approximation we will use again later.

To estimate ∇w at any point $P = (x_o^s, y_o^s, z_o^s)$ in the scene region (not necessarily voxel centers), we determine 26 neighboring points $P_1, \ldots, P_{26}$ forming the vertices, centers of edges, and centers of faces of an $\alpha \times \alpha \times \alpha$ cube centered at P, with its edges parallel to the scene coordinate axes. The density at each neighboring point is determined using the bilinear-cubic scene interpolation method described earlier (see figure 3.1). Let L_{x^s} be the set of straight-line segments l such that l passes through P, l does not lie in the plane $x^s = x_o^s$, and l's end points are in $\{P_1, \ldots, P_{26}\}$. Define L_{y^s} and L_{z^s} similarly. Then

$$\nabla w \approx iPD_{x^s} + jPD_{y^s} + kPD_{z^s} \qquad (16)$$

where

$$PD_{x^s} = \sum_{l \in L_{x^s}} \frac{1}{|l|} CD(l) \qquad (17)$$

$$PD_{y^s} = \sum_{l \in L_{y^s}} \frac{1}{|l|} CD(l) \qquad (18)$$

$$PD_{z^s} = \sum_{l \in L_{z^s}} \frac{1}{|l|} CD(l) \qquad (19)$$

and $|l|$ represents the length of line segment l and $CD(l)$ is the central difference (from the positive side of the plane to its negative side) of the density of the two end points of l.

Volume-rendering methods employing scene space normal estimation may be characterized by the following transforms:

$$R_{vs} : \mathcal{D}_p \times \mathcal{D} \to \mathcal{V} \qquad (20)$$

$$R_{vbs} : \mathcal{D}_b \times \mathcal{D} \to \mathcal{V} \qquad (21)$$

where $\mathcal{V}$ denotes the view space. R_{vs} represents rendering methods that use nonbinary volumes (opacity scenes) [12, 26, 55, 58–61] and R_{vbs} represents rendering methods that use binary volumes [29–40]. R_{vs} and R_{vbs} both require the given scene for estimating the surface normal (equation 15) in addition to an appropriate object description (an element of $\mathcal{D}_p$ for R_{vs} and of $\mathcal{D}_b$ for R_{vbs}).

Object space methods estimate normals based on the local geometry of the surface in the object-surface description [10, 38, 62–66]. Rendering methods employing such normal estimation techniques have been used to render mainly binary volumes. They may be characterized by the following transform:

$$R_{vbo} : \mathcal{D}_b \to \mathcal{V} \qquad (22)$$

Object space methods can also be used to render nonbinary volumes (though we are not aware of any such method reported in the literature). One possible approach is the following: Suppose we quantize the density range of a given opacity scene into a finite number of discrete levels. (Because the density range of scenes usually consists of only integers, there is an obvious quantization.) We compute an isodensity surface for each of these discrete opacity values, estimate surface normals using object space methods for each surface, and then volume render the set of surfaces. Obviously, a variety of methods can be used both for determining the surface and for estimating the normals. Accordingly, such volume-rendering methods can be described by the following transform:

$$R_{vo} : \mathcal{D}_p \to \mathcal{V} \qquad (23)$$

View space methods operate on the assumption that the distance to the object surface from the viewpoint is known for all visible parts of the surface to be captured in the rendition. (This distance is available as a byproduct or is otherwise easily calculated during the projection operation in both classes of projection methods.) If this distance map is expressed as the following function—

$$z^v = d(x^v, y^v)$$

or

$$w = d(x^v, y^v) - z^v \qquad (24)$$

then from equation 15

$$\nabla w = i \frac{\partial d}{\partial x^v} + j \frac{\partial d}{\partial y^v} - k \qquad (25)$$

As d is known only at pixel centers in the rendition domain, view space methods [24] use various approximations [11, 46, 61] to estimate the partial derivatives in equation 25 to determine a unit vector in the direction of ∇w, which is taken to be the surface normal at the point (x^v, y^v, z^v).

View space normal estimation methods have been used to render only binary volumes. We characterize such rendering methods by the following transform:

$$R_{vbv}: \mathscr{D}_\ell \to \mathscr{V} \qquad (26)$$

It is not clear how the view space method can be used to render nonbinary volumes especially, because the normal estimated at a point on the surface depends on the view point.

Clearly, the filtering (F_s) and gray-level scene interpolation (I_s) operators can be modified to operate in view space on renditions. We denote these modified operators by F_v and I_v, respectively.

STRUCTURE-RELATED TRANSFORMS

The transforms described in this section are applicable to object descriptions.

STRUCTURE CONVERSION $(O_o, O_{so}, B_o, B_{os})$ The purpose of the structure conversion transforms $(O_o, O_{so}, B_o, B_{os})$ is to convert one form of object-boundary description to another. We identify four types of transforms:

$$O_o: \mathscr{Q} \to \mathscr{Q}$$
$$O_{so}: \mathscr{S} \to \mathscr{Q}$$
$$B_o: \mathscr{S} \to \mathscr{S} \qquad (27)$$
$$B_{os}: \mathscr{Q} \to \mathscr{S}$$

O_o converts one form of object description into another —for example, a segment-end [34] or run-length code description into an octree [38]. O_{so} converts a surface description into an object description—for example, a discrete surface [50] into an octree [39]. B_o converts one form of surface description into another—for example, from a polygonal form into a triangular form

[52]. This conversion often is very useful since modern workstations have graphics engines that allow rapid rendering of triangles. Another class of methods exemplifying B_o is the so-called tiling approach, by which a surface description in the form of a stack of contours defined on slices [87] is converted into an enveloping surface by tiling triangular [71–77], square [27], or other polygonal elements [78] between contours in successive slices. B_{os} converts an object description into a surface description (e.g., an octree object representation into a surface form) [79].

The need for structure conversion operators comes from the fact that a form of object representation useful for one operation may not be appropriate for another. For instance, a particular polygonal representation of a surface may be appropriate to create high-quality renditions of a structure, yet if we wish to create a physical model of the surface (say, for manufacturing a prosthesis), it has to be converted into a stack of contours for driving a numerically controlled milling machine [80].

GRAY TRANSFORM (G_s, G_o) This new operation, the gray transform (G_s, G_o), allows converting an object or surface description into a scene. Accordingly, we have:

$$G_o: \mathscr{Q} \to \mathscr{D}$$
$$G_s: \mathscr{S} \to \mathscr{D} \qquad (28)$$

The scene domain V is such that the object or surface is properly contained in it. The density function f is such that $f(v) = H$ if $v \in V$ is in the interior of the object or surface, and $f(v) = L$ if $v \in V$ is not in the interior of the object or surface. As an example of G_o, suppose the object is simply a set Q of voxels. Then V is chosen such that $Q \subset V$ and f is given by

$$f(v) = \begin{cases} H & \text{if } v \in Q \\ L & \text{if } v \in V - Q \end{cases} \qquad (29)$$

As an example of G_s, consider a closed surface S. $G_s(S)$ is a scene (V, f) such that

$$f(v) = \begin{cases} d_1(v, S) & \text{if } v \text{ is in the interior of } S \\ -d_1(v, S) & \text{if } v \text{ is in } V \text{ but in the exterior of } S \\ 0 & \text{if } v \text{ is in } V \text{ and intersects } S \end{cases}$$
$$(30)$$

where $d_1(v, S)$ is an appropriate measure of distance of v from S. This may be the 2D distance from S in the slice containing v or a 3D distance from S.

Clearly, in order that the "interior" of a surface S be well-defined, it should be closed: That is, S should partition V into two subsets, an interior set and an exterior set, such that it is not possible to get to the exterior from the interior without crossing S (see [49, 50, 54] for a precise definition of such notions in the digital space). G_s is not defined for surfaces that do not satisfy this condition.

As we will demonstrate in the next section, these operations lead us to a variety of powerful operations on objects and surfaces including interpolation, filtering, and volume rendering.

DIGITIZATION (T_o, T_b, T_s) Often, parametrically defined continuous geometric objects have to be dealt in conjunction with digital entities such as scenes, objects, and surfaces in applications such as prosthesis design and radiotherapy planning [80, 81]. Recently, algorithms have been developed [82, 83] to digitize such continuous descriptions into digital object representations (T_o, T_b, T_s). Once the digital representations are obtained, the complete battery of structure-related operations are available to visualize, manipulate, and analyze these objects in conjunction with scene-derived objects and surfaces. This digitization operation may be characterized by the following transforms: T_o and T_b:

$$
\begin{aligned}
T_o &: \mathcal{Q}_c \to \mathcal{Q} \\
T_b &: \mathcal{S}_c \to \mathcal{S}
\end{aligned}
\tag{31}
$$

where $\mathcal{Q}_c$ and $\mathcal{S}_c$ are, respectively, the set of all parametric object and surface descriptions.

We suggest that the digitization operation should attempt to retain the inaccuracies accompanying this operation in the digitized representation. If the digitized object is represented as a set of voxels, this retention can be done naturally by assigning to voxels a membership value that reflects the fraction of the total voxel volume occupied by the continuous object in the voxel. Instead of assigning an all-or-none membership value as in [82, 83], the voxels now have values in the range $[0, 1]$: That is, a digitization transform T_s creates a scene (much like in gray segmentation) from a continuous object or surface description:

$$
T_s : \mathcal{Q}_c \cup \mathcal{S}_c \to \mathcal{D}_p
\tag{32}
$$

If the continuous object or surface is a sphere, for example, the region of the resulting scene is a cube that encloses the sphere. The sphere is digitized such that the voxels that lie completely inside or outside the sphere are assigned the density 1 or 0, respectively, and

those intersecting the boundary are assigned the fraction of the voxel volume intersected by the sphere.

SURFACE RENDERING Given an object or surface description explicitly as a (hard) set of volume or surface elements, these operations create renditions of the object or surface. (Note that rendering methods that operate on [hard] surfaces as well as on the more redundant [hard] volumetric descriptions are considered here under the topic Surface Rendering. Recall that methods for rendering hard volumetric descriptions were considered under the topic Volume Rendering. This dichotomy reflects the unsettled nature of the otherwise well-accepted terminology.) We identify three types of operations—scene space (R_{ss}), object space (R_{so}), and view space (R_{sv})—depending on the method used for estimating the unit surface normal vector.

$$
R_{ss} : (\mathcal{Q} \cup \mathcal{S}) \times \mathcal{D} \to \mathcal{V}
\tag{33}
$$

$$
R_{so} : \mathcal{Q} \cup \mathcal{S} \to \mathcal{V}
\tag{34}
$$

$$
R_{sv} : \mathcal{Q} \cup \mathcal{S} \to \mathcal{V}
\tag{35}
$$

The three normal estimation methods are exactly as described under Volume Rendering. Again, as before, a projection or a ray-casting method may be used for creating projections of volume and surface elements.

Derived transforms and 3D imaging methodologies

The operators defined in the previous section represent some of the basic imaging transforms used in visualization, manipulation, and analysis of 3D structures. They are generic, in the sense that each operator stands for a whole class of similar operators. In this section, we study how these basic operators may be combined to generate useful *composite* operators that perform more sophisticated scene- and structure-related transforms, and how the basic operators may be chained to produce a wide variety of complete 3D imaging methodologies which, when given a scene, enable us to create its renditions. We will not attempt here to cover exhaustively all possible composite transforms or complete imaging methodologies. We will give examples only, to illustrate the richness of the resulting environment. We will identify specific complete imaging sequences that we have found to produce better renditions than commonly used approaches. These improvements are substantiated in the next section using our evaluation methods. In addition, we point out a host of new methodologies that seem to have the potential for improved rendition. Owing to space limitations of this text, these methods are not evaluated here.

COMPOSITE TRANSFORMS

SCENE PREPROCESSING (I_sF_s and F_sI_s) We assume throughout that the order of operation is right to left. The output scene created by the transforms I_sF_s and F_sI_s for an input scene D is thus given by

$$D_1 = I_s[F_s(D)]$$
$$D_2 = F_s[I_s(D)]$$

Of course, generally, $D_1 \neq D_2$.

OBJECT OR SURFACE FILTERING The first transform, $O_sF_sG_o$, converts a given object $Q \in \mathcal{Q}$ into a scene $G_o(Q)$ (say, using equation 29) and then filters this scene. The filtered object Q' is determined from the filtered scene $F_s[G_o(Q)]$. (If F_s is a smoothing filter, O_s may be a threshold operator, the actual threshold determined from a knowledge of L and H in equation 29.) The second transform, $B_sF_sG_s$, converts a given surface $S \in \mathcal{S}$ into a scene $G_s(S)$ (say, using equation 30) and subsequently filters this scene. The filtered surface S' is determined from the filtered scene using an appropriate surface detector B_s. Note that although S' and a surface detected from Q' may represent the same underlying continuous surface, they may differ because of different filtering effects.

OBJECT OR SURFACE INTERPOLATION The basic idea here is first to convert the object or surface into a scene, then to interpolate the scene, and subsequently to extract the interpolated object or surface using object or surface definition operators. This can be accomplished using two possible composite transforms: ($O_sI_sG_o$, $B_sI_sG_s$). Conversion to scene may be done using equation 29 or, preferably, 30. The latter actually allows capturing some aspects of the shape of the object or surface and therefore permits interpolation of the shape.

Both the previously cited class of filtering operators and the interpolation operators are very powerful when appropriately used and lead to significant improvements in visualization methods, as we will later demonstrate.

GLOBAL-LOCAL SEGMENTATION One of the most difficult tasks in scene segmentation is to design global criteria that can ward off errors due to local decision making. One approach to specifying global guidelines (perhaps the most commonly used) is to indicate interactively a subset of V to which automatic segmentation must be confined [27]. When such a masking operation is implemented properly, user interaction time required can be kept to a minimum (a shell around the boundary is often all that is needed). Recently, we have had considerable success in automatically finding globally optimal boundaries using 2D dynamic programming [84] when the search is confined to a mask. Because this method seems to work in a variety of different applications, automatic mask generation seems to be a useful problem to pursue. The composite transforms for global-local segmentation are S_gM_s and S_bM_s.

FUZZY BOUNDARY DEFINITION The transform for fuzzy boundary definition is $G_sB_sM_s$. Suppose M_s is such that V_1 in equation 19 is a shell around the boundary of interest and that B_s finds an optimal boundary [84] within the shell. Then G_s creates a scene $D_p \in \mathcal{D}_p$ such that voxels in V_1 are assigned the boundary likelihood value used in finding the optimal boundary and voxels not in V_1 are assigned a 0 value.

It is clear by now how other composite operators may be designed along similar lines. The study of the grammar [85] defining the permissible ways the basic operators may be combined is an interesting exercise.

IMAGING METHODOLOGIES

EXISTING METHODOLOGIES Early methods developed for rendering scenes, objects, and surfaces may be described by the following operator sequences:

(1) $R_{so}B_sI_s$

(2) $R_{so}B_oB_s$
    $R_{so}B_oB_sS_bI_s$

(3) $R_{so}B_sS_bI_sA$
    $R_{so}B_sS_bF_sI_sA$
    $R_{so}B_sS_bM_sI_s$

The method in expression (1) [10] is based on scene interpolation, surface detection, and surface rendering using object space normals. Expressions in (2) represent methods based on contour tiling and object space normals for surface rendering [27, 71, 73, 86]. Early software packages [87, 88] for medical 3D imaging incorporated the approaches expressed in (3) [27, 49, 50, 62, 63].

In the quest for speed, a variety of rendering methods for binary volumes were subsequently developed. These can be described by the following expressions:

(4) $\quad R_{so}O_{s}S_{b}I_{s}$

(5) $\quad R_{so}B_{s}I_{s}$

(6) $\quad R_{vbv}S_{b}I_{s}A$
$\quad\quad R_{vbv}O_{s}S_{b}I_{s}$
$\quad\quad F_{v}R_{sv}B_{s}S_{b}I_{s}A$

Expression (4) represents an early method that was incorporated into hardware [38] based on an octree representation of the binary segmented objects defined in interpolated scenes. Expression (5) represents a class of techniques based on contour-defined objects [70, 89–91] that use object space normals. The idea of using the entire binary volume or some encoded version of it is expressed in the sequences shown under (6) [29–37]. A view space normal estimation method was introduced in this connection [67], which has subsequently been modified by others [65, 69].

Scene space normal estimation was introduced in Höhne and Bernstein [36] for surface rendering. This rendering method, characterized by expression (7), used ray casting and binary segmentation to determine object boundary locations. This normal estimation method has been used in later surface-rendering techniques [43–46] [expression (8)] and has also been improved further [14, 15, 92].

(7) $\quad R_{vbs}(S_{b}I_{s}, I_{s})$

(8) $\quad R_{ss}(B_{s}I_{s}, I_{s})$.

Given a scene D, the above (and similar) expressions should be interpreted as follows:

$$R_{vbs}(S_{b}I_{s}, I_{s})(D) = R_{vbs}[S_{b}I_{s}(D), I_{s}(D)]$$

$$R_{ss}(B_{s}I_{s}, I_{s})(D) = R_{ss}[B_{s}I_{s}(D), I_{s}(D)]$$

Volume-rendering methods were introduced in Levoy [12] and Drebin et al. [26]. These methods use scene space normals and can be described by the following expressions (the third expression in (9) corresponds to the method of Levoy [93]):

(9) $\quad R_{vs}(CI_{s}, I_{s})$
$\quad\quad R_{vs}(I_{s}C, I_{s})$
$\quad\quad I_{v}R_{vs}(CI_{s}, I_{s})$

Shape-based interpolation is a recent addition [13, 16, 17] to 3D imaging. It has been used mainly for surface rendering, and the visualization methods investigated using this operator [13, 69, 94] are as follows:

(10) $\quad F_{v}R_{sv}B_{s}I_{b}S_{b}M_{s}$
$\quad\quad R_{ss}(B_{s}I_{b}S_{b}, I_{s})$
$\quad\quad R_{ss}(O_{s}I_{b}S_{b}, I_{s})$

The digitization operators may be used [82, 83] if mathematically defined objects or phantoms are to be rendered alone or in combination with the objects scanned by an imaging device. In the latter case, the two object or surface descriptions should be combined prior to rendering.

(11) $\quad R_{so}B_{os}T_{o}$
$\quad\quad R_{sv}T_{b}$
$\quad\quad R_{so}[B_{os}T_{o}(Q_{c}) \cup B_{os}O_{s}I_{s}(D)]$

In the last example in expression (11), D and Q_{c} are, respectively, a scene and a continuous object description.

NEW METHODOLOGIES   It is clear how even limiting oneself to the operators used by existing methodologies, it is possible to generate a variety of new methodologies. Some examples are given here.

(12) $\quad R_{vbv}I_{b}S_{b}$
$\quad\quad R_{vbo}I_{b}S_{b}$
$\quad\quad R_{so}B_{s}I_{b}S_{b}$

The use of the digitization operator T_{s} is illustrated here:

(13) $\quad R_{ss}(B_{s}T_{s}, T_{s})$
$\quad\quad R_{vs}(T_{s}, T_{s})$

The main thrust of this section is the use of operators F_{s}, G_{o}, and G_{s} in conjunction with other scene- and object-related operators. These three operators lead us to a host of new methodologies, each having its own interesting features, as we shall see. We encourage the reader to examine carefully the expressions representing these methodologies as they embody a variety of ideas expressed very compactly.

To systematize our discussion, we consider structures to be visualized as belonging to one of two classes—robust and frail. A structure is *robust* in a scene if first it has consistently well-defined boundaries in the scene and second if, in the vicinity of the structure boundary, the scene density changes most rapidly in the direction normal to the boundary. A structure is *frail* in a scene if it is not robust in the scene. Bone in CT scenes is a good example of a robust structure (although there are some aspects of bony structures, such as thin parts, that are closer to being frail than robust; we shall come back to this point later). Bone in MRI scenes is an example of a frail structure. Frail structures usually do not satisfy both the preceding conditions.

The main purpose of introducing this classification is to suggest that the transforms that prepare a structure for (volume or surface) rendering should be treated independently of the methods of estimating normals. This separation allows us to select the operations best suited for structure preparation and normal estimation individually, so that the resulting renditions are optimal for the given situation. For example, suppose we have a frail structure that can be segmented (either automatically or, in the worst case, interactively) that does not satisfy the second condition for robustness. Clearly, scene space normal estimation methods that use the given scene would generate unreliable normals. Nonetheless, we can create scenes—for example, using a combination of operators F_s, G_o, and G_s on the segmented object—that can be used for scene space normal estimation which is more reliable. On the other hand, the segmented object may be filtered in a variety of ways (e.g., to smooth it) and still the normals may be estimated from the given scene if the second condition for robustness is satisfied. These points will become clearer in the following expressions. We treat robust and frail structures separately.

Robust structure rendering Because robust structures satisfy the second condition, we retain the original scene for normal estimation but suggest that the structure itself may be prepared in numerous ways via combinations of interpolation, gray transform, and filtering operations to minimize digitization effects.

Use of F_s *only*

(14) a. $R_{ss}(B_s F_s S_b I_s, F_s I_s)$
     b. $R_{vbs}(S_b F_s S_b F_s I_s, I_s)$
     c. $R_{vs}(F_s C I_s, I_s)$

(15) a. $R_{ss}(B_s I_s S_b F_s, I_s)$
     b. $R_{ss}(B_s F_s I_b S_b, I_s)$
     c. $R_{ss}(B_{os} O_s F_s I_b S_b F_s, I_s)$
     d. $R_{vs}(S_g F_s I_b S_b, I_s)$

(16) a. $R_{vo} F_s T_s$
     b. $R_{vs}(T_s, F_s T_s)$

Expressions in (14) illustrate how scene filtering may be used to filter a structure. Expressions (14)a and b show how the result of binary segmentation may be filtered to create a filtered (hard) structure while (14)c suggests that the result of classification may be filtered to create a filtered version of fuzzily defined structures.

Expressions in (15) show how filtering may be combined with structure (shape-based) interpolation to create possibly even smoother representations of structures both for hard (a, b, c) and fuzzily defined (d) structures. The method in (15)d is particularly interesting. It suggests that the shape-interpolated binary scene on filtering (which results in a gray scene) be gray-segmented, which essentially creates a shell around the object boundary, and be (gray) volume-rendered.

Expressions in (16) show how filtering may be used in conjunction with fuzzily digitized continuous parametrically defined objects.

Use of G_o, G_s *with* F_s

(17) a. $R_{ss}(B_s F_s G_o O_s I_s, I_s)$
     b. $R_{ss}(B_s F_s I_s G_s B_s, I_s)$
     c. $R_{vs}(S_g I_s F_s G_o O_s, I_s)$

(18) a. $R_{ss}(B_s F_s G_o O_s I_b S_b F_s, I_s)$
     b. $R_{vbs}(S_b F_s G_s B_s I_b S_b, F_s I_s)$
     c. $R_{vs}(S_g F_s G_s B_s I_b S_b F_s, I_s F_s)$

(19) a. $R_{so} B_s F_s G_s T_b$
     b. $R_{vs}(S_g F_s G_o T_o, T_s)$

Examples of G_s and G_o given in equations 29 and 30 allow us to create an effect similar to that of shape-based interpolation [60] when combined with F_s. Expressions (17)a and b use G_o and G_s with F_s to smooth the surface, whereas (17)c smooths the structure for volume rendering in a fashion similar to (15)d. Expressions in (18) combine the effects of G_o, G_s and I_b (shape interpolation) with scene filtering (F_s) to prepare the structure that is being rendered. Expression (18)c, which is similar to (15)d and (14)c, is an interesting volume-rendering method. Expressions (19)a and b show how G_s, G_o, and F_s may be combined for rendering digitized continuous objects.

Frail structure rendering In methods for rendering robust structures, we concentrated mainly on how the structure may be appropriately prepared while relying mostly on scene space methods applied to the given scene for normal estimation. Frail structure rendering is more challenging because normals estimated in that fashion are not reliable. The following expressions therefore emphasize the need to prepare the scene carefully if scene space normal estimation were to be used, in addition to preparing the structure appropriately, as in robust structure rendering.

Use of F_s *only*

(20)   a. $R_{ss}(B_sF_sS_bI_s, F_sS_bI_s)$
         b. $R_{vbv}(S_bI_sF_sS_b)$
         c. $R_{vs}(S_gF_sS_bI_s, I_sF_sS_b)$

(21)   a. $R_{ss}(B_sI_bS_b, F_sI_bS_b)$
         b. $R_{ss}(B_sS_bF_sI_bS_bF_s, F_sI_bS_b)$
         c. $R_{so}(B_sF_sI_bS_b)$
         d. $R_{vs}(S_gF_sI_bS_b, F_sI_bS_b)$

Expressions in (20) show how F_s alone may be used to prepare the structure as well as to create a scene artificially for computing scene space normals. Expression (20)c is an interesting method that shows how a binary scene may be brought into the gray volume-rendering paradigm by filtering the binary scene and subsequently doing gray segmentation and using the filtered binary scene for normal estimation. Expressions in (21) combine shape-based interpolation with F_s, both for preparing the structure and for creating the scene used for normal estimation. View space and object space methods [(20)b, (21)c] may also be appropriate for normal estimation. Expressions (20)c and (21)d embody the shell idea referred to earlier for (gray) volume rendering.

Use of G_o, G_s *with* F_s

(22)   a. $R_{ss}(B_sF_sI_sG_oO_s, I_sF_sG_sB_s)$
         b. $R_{ss}(B_sI_sF_sG_sB_sS_b, F_sI_bS_b)$
         c. $R_{vbv}(S_bF_sG_sB_sI_s)$
         d. $R_{vs}(S_gF_sI_sG_sB_s, F_sI_sG_oO_sI_s)$

(23)   a. $R_{ss}(B_sF_sG_sB_sI_bS_bF_s, F_sF_sI_bS_s)$
         b. $R_{sv}(B_sF_sG_oO_sF_sI_bS_b)$
         c. $R_{vbs}(S_bF_sG_sB_sF_sI_bS_bF_s, F_sG_sB_sF_sI_bS_b)$
         d. $R_{vs}(S_gF_sS_gF_sI_bS_bF_s, F_sG_oO_sI_bS_bF_s)$

Expressions in (22) show how operators G_s and G_o may be combined with F_s for preparing the structure for rendering, as well as for estimating normals from specially created scenes [(22)a, b, d]. Expressions in (23) show how G_o, G_s, and F_s may be combined with I_b for structure preparation and normal estimation.

We can realize in our current implementation many of the methodologies outlined earlier for specific instances of the individual generic operators. However, owing to space limitations, we will not attempt here to illustrate with an example every methodology. We nevertheless intend to demonstrate the improvements that are possible both for robust and for frail structures over commonly used techniques. The new methods were selected based on our own intuition and somewhat limited experience of their performance. We have not yet studied them systematically to grade them. To keep the number of images manageable, we have selected two scenes: one representing a robust structure (a dry skull in a $256 \times 256 \times 68$ CT scene with identical voxels of size $0.8 \times 0.8 \times 3.0$ mm) and the other representing a frail structure [one of the four bones (talus) at the midtarsal joint of a normal human volunteer in an MRI scene with a $256 \times 256 \times 62$ scene domain and identical voxels of size $0.7 \times 0.7 \times 1.5$ mm]. The methods selected are as follows:

- Robust structure rendering
   R1. $R_{sv}B_sI_bS_b$
   R2. $R_{ss}(B_sI_bS_b, I_s)$
   R3. $R_{vs}(I_sC, I_s)$
   R4. $R_{ss}(B_s'I_s, I_s')$
   R5. $R_{ss}'(B_sF_sI_b'S_b, I_s')$
- Frail structure rendering
   F1. $R_{ss}(B_s'I_s, I_s')$
   F2. $R_{sv}B_sI_bS_b$
   F3. $R_{sv}B_sF_sS_bI_s$
   F4. $R_{ss}(B_sS_bF_sI_b'S_b, F_sI_b'S_b)$
   F5. $R_{vs}(CF_sI_b'S_b, F_sI_b'S_b)$
   F6. $R_{ss}(B_sS_bF_sG_sB_sI_b'S_b, F_sG_sB_sI_b'S_b)$

The operators used in these methods are as follows:

I_s Trilinear scene interpolation
I_s' Bilinear-cubic scene interpolation (see figure 3.1)
I_b Shape-based binary scene interpolation using city block distance [13]
I_b' Shape-based binary scene interpolation using a more accurate approximation to Euclidean distance [16]
S_b Segmentation using thresholding
B_b Surface detection in binary scenes [50] with integer coordinate for boundary faces
B_s' Surface detection using a threshold in gray scenes with real coordinates for boundary faces [15], the

location of the face determined by computing exactly where the threshold is satisfied in a direction perpendicular to the face

C Classification based on voxel density and gradient magnitude [12]

R_{sv} Surface rendering using view space normals [69]

R_{ss} Surface rendering using scene space normals estimated from central differences of density at six points equally spaced from the center of the boundary face [94]

R_{ss}' Surface rendering using the scene space normal estimation method described in equations 16–19

R_{vs} Volume rendering using scene space normals estimated as in R_{ss} (but from center of voxels)

F_s Scene filtering as in equations 3 and 4

G_s Gray transform as in equation 30, with 2D distance from boundary in the slice

Figure 3.3 shows renditions created by methods R1–R5 of the robust structure. R4 has been our best method for rendering robust structures, and we have previously shown their rendition quality to be as good as that of high-quality gray volume-rendering techniques [15]. R5 seems to be a further improvement of this method as it allows better approximation of surface shape via a combination of shape-based interpolation and surface filtering. The "slicing artifact" seems to be reduced and some of the sutures (especially in the temporal region) seem to be better defined compared to the rendition created by R4 (objective criteria for comparing renditions are described in the next section). We expect a further improvement of R5 when B_s is replaced by B_s' in R5. Unfortunately, because our implementation in the existing programs is not designed around the basic operators, such modifications are not trivial. We will come back to this point later.

Figure 3.4 shows renditions of the frail structure created by methods F1–F6. Note that although F1 is identical to R4, which undoubtedly produces excellent results for robust structures, F1 clearly produces the poorest rendition of the frail structure, mainly because the two conditions mentioned earlier that characterize robust structures are not fulfilled by the MRI scene of the midtarsal joint. Of the remaining methods, F3–F6 all have a clear advantage over F2, which demonstrates considerable digital artifacts (which often camouflage real features). We will come back to these points later. In summary, F5 seems to produce better renditions than F3, F4, and F6.

Evaluation of rendering methods

The evaluation of rendering methods is one area in medical 3D visualization that calls for considerably more work. Comparisons usually are made visually, much as was described in the preceding section. Recently, the subject of comparing rendering methods has drawn some attention [7, 15, 92, 95–99].

Considering the genericness of the operators and the fact that each method given by an expression has itself a number of independent parameters whose optimal selection often is not trivial, the enormity of the problem becomes clear. Conduction of observer studies [100] would be simply impractical at the global level of grading methods, even for a specified small set of tasks. We suggest a two-tiered approach. Given the set of tasks that form the basis for comparison [e.g., how well ridges, small holes, and fine separations (such as sutures and fine fractures) are portrayed, how well smoothness of surfaces is retained], the first tier consists of creating mathematic phantoms that embody the task-related features, subjecting the phantoms to image reconstruction processes [101] to simulate tomographic scanning realistically, and then applying to the resulting scenes the visualization methods to be compared. Because reality is known precisely, how well it is portrayed in renditions can be quantified (as described later), and therefore rendering methods can be quantitatively compared objectively and graded, of course, for the chosen tasks. The second tier then consists of resolving among closely competing methods via observer studies. The size of the problem will now have been drastically reduced because not only is the number of methods to be compared reduced but optimal parameter settings will have been determined and therefore they will not enter into observer experiments.

There is a definite advantage to using mathematic phantoms instead of physical phantoms in the first tier. It may be very difficult (even impossible) to quantify certain aspects of reality using physical phantoms. For example, as already seen, surface normal plays a crucial role in determining the quality of renditions, and therefore it is vital to be able to know true normals at points on the physical object surface. Still, it is difficult to establish a correspondence between points on the modeled surface and points on the physical surface and harder even to determine true normal at points on the physical surface. Although this difficulty does not arise in mathematic phantoms, these phantoms sometimes

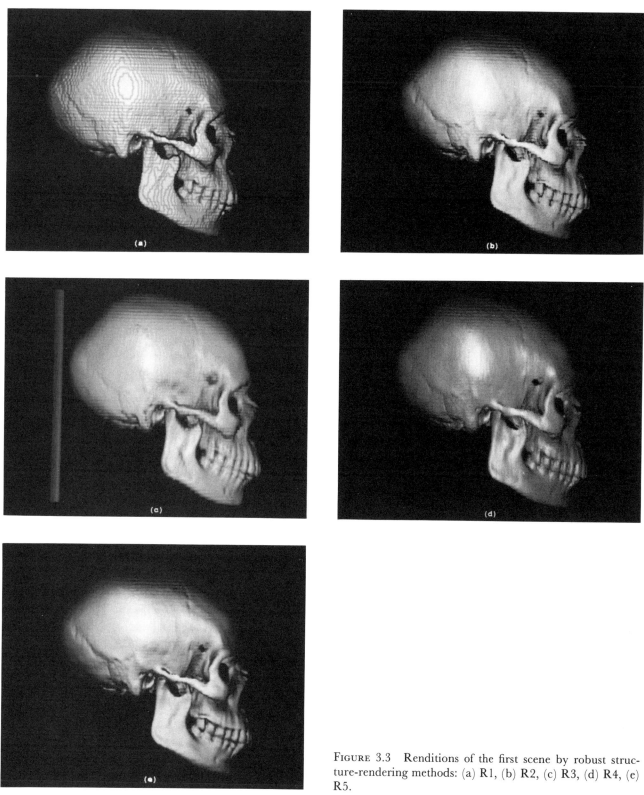

FIGURE 3.3 Renditions of the first scene by robust structure-rendering methods: (a) R1, (b) R2, (c) R3, (d) R4, (e) R5.

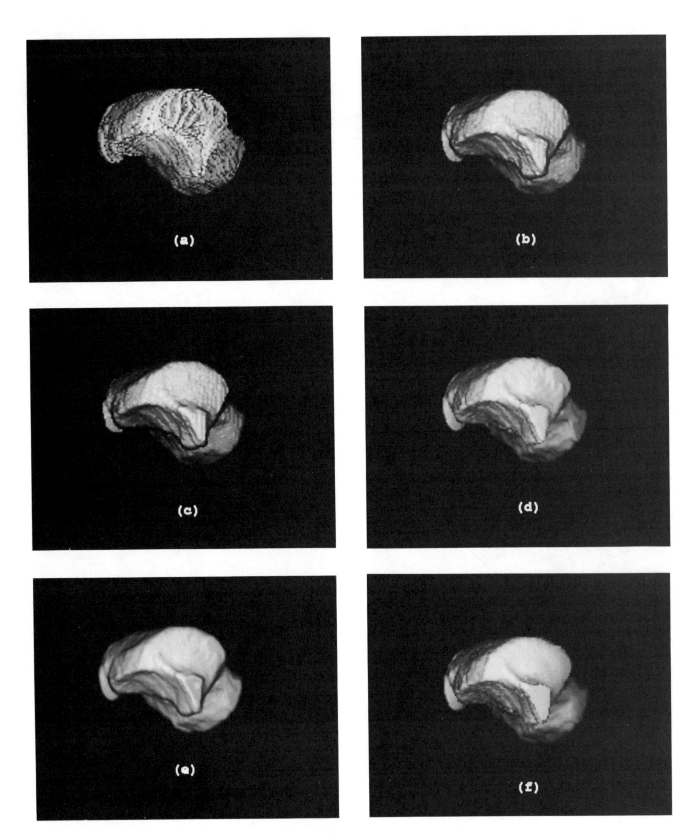

FIGURE 3.4   Renditions of the second scene by frail structure rendition methods: (a) F1, (b) F2, (c) F3, (d) F4, (e) F5, (f) F6.

have a different disadvantage in that it may not be possible to capture the reality adequately in the phantoms either geometrically or in simulating the scanning process. Despite this drawback, we believe that there are many situations in which comparison based on mathematic phantoms can shed light on the effectiveness of imaging transforms.

We first concentrate on surface (and binary volume) rendering for quantifying the quality of portrayal and later indicate how the ideas may be generalized to nonbinary volume-rendering methods. Our ideas are best described using the ray-casting paradigm. For a given viewing direction ω, imagine a ray emanates (orthogonal to the viewing plane) from the center of each pixel p in the rendition domain $\mathscr{P}$ into the modeled object or surface. We compute the value of a number of features, $\phi_1, \ldots, \phi_n$, of the object or surface at the point of entry of the ray into the object or surface. (When the ray does not intersect the object or surface, we assign a 0 value for each of the features.) For identical viewing conditions for the same ray, we determine the feature values for the mathematic object or surface. We define a disparity function $\delta_i(\phi_i)$ for each feature that expresses the disparity between the modeled and the true object or surface for each ϕ_i. (When the ray is nearly tangential to the surface, it may intersect only one among the modeled and mathematic surfaces and not both. Such rays clearly do not provide reliable disparity information. See comments on this issue later.) Thus, for a given ω, we arrive at a *disparity image*:

$$E_\omega(p) = \begin{bmatrix} \delta_1(\phi_1) \\ \vdots \\ \delta_n(\phi_n) \end{bmatrix}_{\omega, p}, p \in \mathscr{P} \qquad (36)$$

We define *pose disparity* $\rho(\omega)$ as the vector resulting from taking the componentwise root mean squared value of the disparity image over all pixels:

$$\rho(\omega) = \begin{bmatrix} \rho_1(\omega) \\ \vdots \\ \rho_n(\omega) \end{bmatrix} = \begin{bmatrix} \sqrt{\dfrac{1}{n_p} \sum_p [\delta_1(\phi_1)]^2} \\ \vdots \\ \sqrt{\dfrac{1}{n_p} \sum_p [\delta_n(\phi_n)]^2} \end{bmatrix} \qquad (37)$$

where n_p is the number of pixels in $\mathscr{P}$. Finally, we define the *portrayal disparity* Δ of the given visualization method over a given solid angle Ω of viewing directions to be simply the componentwise integral of the pose disparity vector over all $\omega \in \Omega$:

$$\Delta = \begin{bmatrix} \displaystyle\int_\Omega \rho_1(\omega)\, d\omega \\ \vdots \\ \displaystyle\int_\Omega \rho_n(\omega)\, d\omega \end{bmatrix} \qquad (38)$$

For better rendering methods, we expect E_ω, ρ, and Δ to have componentwise smaller values.

Potential features are properties of the surface that are locally determinable at specified points, such as orientation of surface normal (consideration of normals for comparing renditions was suggested earlier by Tiede et al. [92]), distance of the surface point from a fixed view point, and principal curvatures at the surface point or other properties derived from them such as mean and Gaussian curvatures. We illustrate the use of the first two features in this chapter. In our actual implementation, we have replaced the integral in equation 38 by summation, and we have used the following disparity functions for the two features:

$$\delta_1(\phi_1) = \sin\frac{\phi_1}{2}$$

$$\delta_1(\phi_2) = \frac{\phi_2}{\phi_{2\,\max}} \qquad (39)$$

where ϕ_1 is the angle between the normal to the modeled and to the mathematic surface, and ϕ_2 is the distance between the two surfaces along the ray. We use $\phi_{2\,\max}$ to represent a scaling constant that we have chosen to be the diameter of the sphere that just encloses the phantom.

It is not always necessary to compute pose disparity and portrayal disparity over the whole rendition domain, as pointed out earlier. In fact, it may be useful to scrutinize closely specified regions of interest in $\mathscr{P}$ to determine how good portrayal is in those regions. For example, we may be interested in determining how good a method is in portraying ridges. Once the disparity images for desired ω are computed, the user may outline a region of interest containing ridges in appropriate renditions of the modeled object or surface. The computation of pose and portrayal disparity confined to this region will indicate the effectiveness of the method in displaying ridges. This approach also alleviates the difficulty associated with considering those pixels in the disparity image whose rays are almost tangential to the object or surface.

It is much more difficult to devise evaluation methods for nonbinary volume-rendering approaches because there are no obvious physical models corresponding to the commonly used volume-rendering techniques. We suggest a generalization to the preceding approach (we have not yet implemented this generalization). Continuing with the ray-casting paradigm, we determine the values of the feature along each ray at the most likely surface point (of the modeled object or surface) that is closest to the view point and then proceed as before. Alternatively, we may determine the disparity function value $\delta_i(\phi_i)$ at each sampled point along the ray and take a weighted sum of the disparity values, the weight chosen to be an appropriate function of the opacity value of the point. The first approach seems more reasonable, although we cannot give sound justification for either of these methods.

The mathematic phantom we created (figure 3.5) consists of a cylindric base with a hemispherical top. The base consists of a number of curved and straight slits (mimicking suture and fracture lines) of varying width (1, 1/2, 1/3, and 1/4 pixel) and small structures of circular cross-section (mimicking gyrations). The hemisphere has four small spherical holes (2-, 1-, 1/2- and 1/4-pixel diameter) at its base (mimicking foramina).

Simulation of x-ray projection and image reconstruction is done using the SNARK89 package [8] developed in our group. The scanner geometry, noise characteristics, resolution, and other properties are chosen to mimic closely the data collection and reconstruction processes of the General Electric CT/T 8800 scanner [101]. Figure 3.5a and b show a rendition of the true geometric phantom obtained via ray casting and using the Phong shading model [102], and figure 3.5c shows a reconstructed cross-section through the cylindric base of the phantom.

Renditions of the phantom created by methods R1–R5 are shown in figure 3.6a–e. Disparity images for the first view in figure 3.6a, b, and e are shown in color plate 1. Figure 3.7 shows pose disparity as a graph for

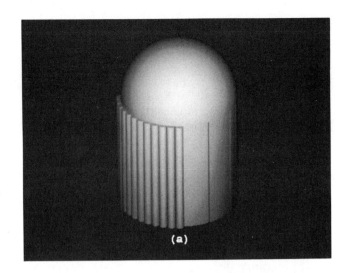

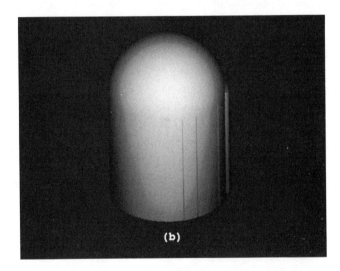

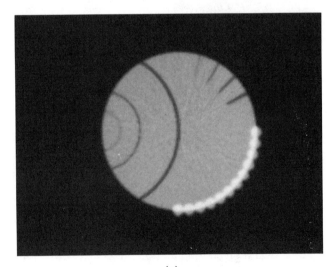

FIGURE 3.5 The mathematic phantom used in our evaluation. (a, b) A rendition of the true geometric phantom by ray tracing. (c) A reconstructed cross-section through the lower cylindric base part of the phantom. The cross-sections in this cylindric part are more or less identical. The upper part of the phantom consists of a hemisphere with small holes near its base.

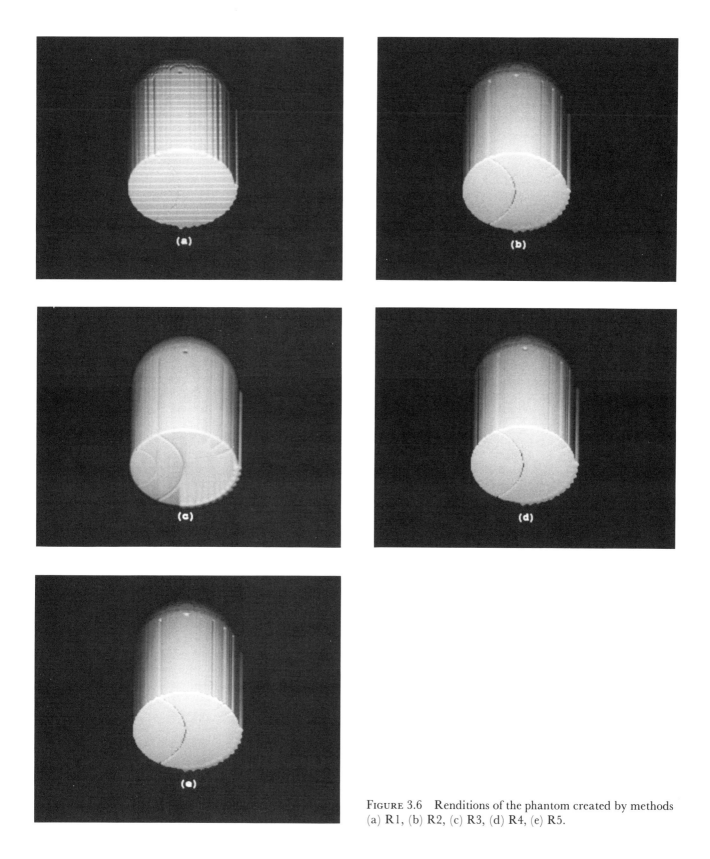

FIGURE 3.6 Renditions of the phantom created by methods
(a) R1, (b) R2, (c) R3, (d) R4, (e) R5.

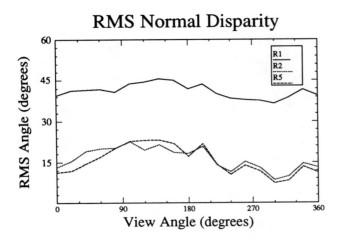

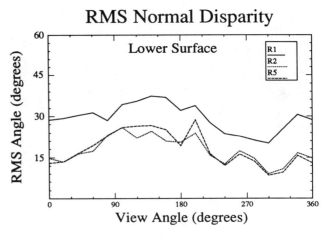

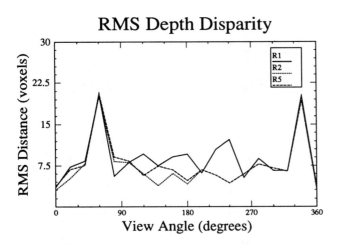

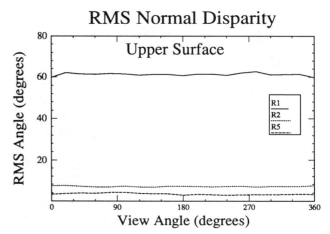

FIGURE 3.7 Pose disparity for a complete 360° rotation for the methods R1, R2, and R5.

FIGURE 3.8 Regional pose disparity for a complete 360° rotation for methods R1, R2, and R5.

the methods illustrated in plate 1 for the different views in a complete 360° rotation. Viewing angles shown in figure 3.7 (and all similar graphs) are illustrated in figure 3.5c. Figure 3.8 shows pose disparity in ϕ_1 (normal) separately for the upper spheric part and the lower cylindric part for the different views in a complete 360° rotation for the three methods. Table 3.1 lists por-

trayal disparity for the three methods over the views illustrated in figures 3.7 and 3.8. We also carried out several "region-of-interest" portrayal disparity analyses by selecting rectangular regions in $\mathscr{P}$ in the region of one of the foramina, straight and curved slits, and of the gyrations. The results are summarized in table 3.2 for the three methods for these regions.

Clearly, R2 and R5 produce more accurate estimation of surface normal and location than R1. R5 produces more accurate normals than R2 for smooth regions of the surface with little detail, as seen in figures 3.7 (top) (roughly from 210° to 90°; see figure 3.5c and in figure 3.8 (top). Its accuracy in estimation of location is comparable to that of R2 for smooth aspects of the surface (figure 3.7, bottom). However, in corrugated regions and regions with subtle details (especially between 90° and 180°; see figure 3.5(c), R5 is inferior to R2 in the estimation of surface normal and

TABLE 3.1

Portrayal disparity over the viewer illustrated in figure 3.7 for methods R1, R2, and R5

| Method | Entire surface | | Upper surface | Lower surface |
	$\phi1$	$\phi2$	$\phi1$	$\phi2$
R1	39.6	9.9	62.12	29.80
R2	15.6	8.6	7.19	18.22
R5	15.9	8.9	3.45	19.00

Method	Foramen		Straight slits		Gyrations		Curved slits	
	$\phi1$	$\phi2$	$\phi1$	$\phi2$	$\phi1$	$\phi2$	$\phi1$	$\phi2$
R1	19.2	3.87	29.48	8.57	32.22	7.8	25.9	6.75
R2	12.46	2.92	17.42	7.72	25.27	3.85	13.74	6.47
R5	16.9	3.85	19.2	7.47	31.26	7.67	9.73	6.82

location (see bottom panels, figures 3.7 and 3.8). The reason for this behavior is that, in such regions, the composite operator $B_sF_sI_s'S_b$ tends to shift the surface from its true location (because of the filtering effect), and therefore, in addition to location, the estimated normal can be expected to be wrong. This phenomenon is further illustrated in table 3.2, which lists portrayal disparity for regions with small details. Combining the best features of R2 and R5, we can create the following method: $R_{ss}(B_sI_bS_b, I_s')$. This method should produce overall better surface normal and location than R2 and R5. Unfortunately, our current implementation does not allow the flexibility needed in producing such composite methods. [It is also due to an implementation issue that we did not include R4 in our comparison of pose disparity, although we believe that its performance (as measured by pose disparity) will be very comparable to that of the method expressed by the above-mentioned sequence.] In response to this flexibility issue, we have been developing a data-, machine-, and application-independent software system called 3DVIEWNIX [103, 104], for the visualization, manipulation, and analysis of multidimensional images; the design of this system is based on the principles described in this chapter.

The phantom used in this section represents a robust structure, and therefore the analysis and the associated remarks just made apply mostly to robust structures. However, a similar methodology can be used to construct phantoms depicting frail structures and to evaluate the effectiveness of rendering methods for such structures.

Concluding remarks

The main contributions of this chapter are as follows: We have introduced an operator notation to describe concisely the basic 3D imaging transforms commonly used in biomedical 3D visualization. We have also identified a comprehensive set of basic transforms. Several new basic transforms for filtering and interpolating structures and scenes and for rendering surfaces and volumes have been described. The power of the principle of treating 3D imaging methodologies as comprising an appropriate combination of the basic operators has been demonstrated. We have shown how such a treatment leads to a great variety of new rendering methods, and we have demonstrated how many such methods can lead to improved portrayal. We also have developed a comprehensive evaluation method to compare objectively rendering methods based on mathematic phantoms, which makes possible the grading of rendering methods for specified medical tasks. Finally, we have developed separate transform sequences to render robust and frail structures (i.e., structures represented in scenes with well- and ill-defined boundaries, respectively) optimally. Of the methods we have evaluated, those labeled R5 and F5 seem to produce the best portrayal of robust and frail structures, respectively.

When a rendering method is expressed as a sequence of operators, there is no implication that that is how the method should be implemented. Often, it is computationally more efficient to combine basic operators in the implementation. Consider method F3 as an example. It can be implemented in two modules, one doing $B_sF_sS_bI_s$ and the other R_{sv}. Clearly, as the determination of surface location using B_s is based on local information in the scene, and the computation of the result of F_s, S_b, and I_s also depends only on local information, all four operators can be combined in the implementation as follows. The surface detection operator B_s starts from a specified initial surface element and looks for neighboring elements. In determining the actual location of these new elements, we need to determine the density of a few voxels in the neighborhood. Each of these densities can be determined by interpolation, segmentation, and filtering of a few voxel densities in a small neighborhood. Thus, the operations I_s, S_b, and F_s can be confined to a thin shell around the surface that is being detected. Clearly, this is vastly more efficient than applying each of the operators on the whole scene because most of the voxels interior or exterior to the surface do not enter into any computation. However, the flexibility of combining the individual operators to realize other rendering methods is lost in the efficient implementation. One solution to this dilemma is to identify the basic and often-used composite operators (such as $B_s F_s S_b I_s$) and have each of them efficiently implemented as a single operator. These composite operators now become available for chaining with other basic or composite operators, providing a rich and powerful environment retaining efficiency.

ACKNOWLEDGMENTS This work is supported by National Institute of Health grants CA56071, CA50851 and a National Science Foundation grant IRI 90-13341. We are grateful to Ms. Hsiu-Mei Hung for assistance with some of the volume-rendering programs and to Mary A. Blue for typing the manuscript.

REFERENCES

[1] UDUPA, J. K., and G. T. HERMAN, eds., 1991. *3D Imaging in Medicine*. Boca Raton, Fla.: CRC Press.

[2] KAUFMAN, A., ed., 1990. *A Tutorial on Volume Visualization*. Los Alamitos, Calif.: IEEE Computer Society Press.

[3] HÖHNE, K. H., H. FUCHS, and S. M. PIZER, ed., 1990. *3D Imaging in Medicine: Algorithms, Systems, Applications*. Berlin: Springer-Verlag.

[4] LIU, H. K., 1970. Two- and three-dimensional boundary detection. *Comput. Grapics Image Process.*, 6:123–134.

[5] UDUPA, J. K., S. N. SRIHARI, and G. T. HERMAN, 1982. Boundary detection in multidimensions. *IEEE Trans. Pattern Anal. Mach. Intell.* (PAMI) 4:41–50.

[6] HERMAN, G. T., and J. K. UDUPA, 1982. Display of multiple surfaces. In *Proceedings of the World Federation of Nuclear Medicine and Biology*, Paris, Third World Congress. New York: Pergamon Press, pp. 2165–2168.

[7] VANNIER, M. W., C. F. HILDEBOLT, J. L. MARSH, T. K. PILGRAM, W. H. McALISTER, G. D. SHACKELFORD, C. J. OFFUTT, and R. H. KNAPP, 1989. Craniosynostosis: Diagnostic value of three-dimensional CT reconstruction. *Radiology* 173:669–673.

[8] HERMAN, G. T., R. M. LEWITT, D. ODHNER, and S. W. ROWLAND, 1989. SNARK89—a programming system for image reconstruction from projections. *Tech. rep. MIPG160* (Medical Image Processing Group). Philadelphia: Department of Radiology, University of Pennsylvania.

[9] HALL, E. L., 1979. *Computer Image Processing and Recognition*. New York: Academic Press.

[10] HERMAN, G. T., and H. K. LIU, 1979. Three-dimensional display of human organs from computed tomograms. *Comput. Graphics Image Process.* 9:1–29.

[11] GOLDWASSER, S. M., R. A. REYNOLDS, D. TALTON, and E. WALSH, 1986. Real-time display and manipulation of 3-DCT, PET, and NMR data. *SPIE Proc.* 671:139–149.

[12] LEVOY, M., 1988. Display of surfaces from volume data. *IEEE Comput. Graphics Appl.* 8(3):29–37.

[13] RAYA, S. P., and J. K. UDUPA, 1990. Shape-based interpolation of multidimensional objects. *IEEE Trans. Med. Imaging* 9:32–42.

[14] CHUANG, K. S., J. K. UDUPA, and S. P. RAYA, 1980. High-quality rendering of discrete three-dimensional surfaces. Tech. rep. MIPG130 (Medical Image Processing Group). Philadelphia: Department of Radiology, University of Pennsylvania.

[15] UDUPA, J. K., H. M. HUNG, and K. S. CHUANG, 1991. Surface and volume rendering in 3D imaging: A comparison. *J. Digital Imaging* 4:159–168.

[16] HERMAN, G. T., J. ZHENG, and C. A. BUCHOLTZ, 1992. Shape-based interpolation. *IEEE Comput. Graphics Appl.* 12(3):69–79.

[17] HIGGINS, W. E., C. MORICE, and E. L. RITMAN, 1990. Shape-based interpolation technique for three-dimensional images. In *Proceedings of IEEE 1990 International Conference on Acoustics, Speech and Signal Processing*, Albuquerque, N.M., April 3–6, IEEE Computer Society. Los Alamitos, Calif.: pp. 1841–1844.

[18] LIN, W. C., C. C. LIANG, and C. T. CHEN, 1988. Dynamic elastic interpolation for 3-D medical image reconstruction from serial cross sections. *IEEE Trans. Med. Imaging MI* 7:225–232.

[19] VANNIER, M. W., R. L. BUTTERFIELD, D. L. RICKMAN, D. M. JORDAN, W. A. MURPHY, and P. R. BIONDETTI, 1987. Multispectral magnetic resonance image analysis. *CRC Crit. Rev. Biomed. Eng.* 15:117–144.

[20] KOHN, M. I., N. K. TANNA, G. T. HERMAN, S. M. RESNICK, P. D. MOZLEY, R. E. GUR, A. ALAVI, R. A. ZIMMERMAN, and R. C. GUR, 1991. Analysis of brain and cerebrospinal fluid volumes with MR imaging: I. Methods, reliability and validation. *Radiology* 178:115–122.

[21] RUSINEK, H., M. J. DE LEON, A. E. GEORGE, L. A. STYLOPOULOS, R. CHANDRA, G. SMITH, T. RAND, M. MOWRINO, and H. KOWALSKI, 1991. Alzheimer's disease: Measuring loss of cerebral gray matter with MR imaging. *Radiology* 178:109–114.

[22] TANNA, N. K., M. I. KOHN, D. N. HORWICH, P. R. JOLLES, R. A. ZIMMERMAN, W. M. ALVES, and A. ALAVI, 1991. Analysis of brain and cerebrospinal fluid volumes with MR imaging: Impact on PET data correction for atrophy. II. Aging and Alzheimer dementia. *Radiology* 178:123–130.

[23] SNELL, J. W., and M. B. MERICKELL, 1991. Tissue labelling of MRI using recurrent artificial neural networks. In *Proceedings of the Thirteenth Annual International Conference of the IEEE Engineering in Medicine and Biology Society*, 13(1): 66–67.

[24] EZQUERRA, N., E. GARCIA, and R. ARKIN, eds., 1990. *Proceedings of the First Conference on Visualization in Biomedical Computing*. Los Alamitos, Calif.: IEEE Computer Society.

[25] DUDA, R. O., and P. E. HART, 1973. *Pattern Classification and Scene Analysis*. New York: Wiley.

[26] DREBIN, R. A., L. CARPENTER, and P. HANRAHAN, 1988. Volume rendering. *Comput. Graphics* 22:65–74.

[27] UDUPA, J. K., 1982. Interactive segmentation and boundary surface formation for 3D digital images. *Comput. Graphics Image Process.* 18:213–235.

[28] ROBB, R. A., and C. BARILLOT, 1989. Interactive display and analysis of 3-D medical images. *IEEE Trans. Med. Imaging* MI8:217–226.

[29] FRIEDER, G., D. GORDON, and R. A. REYNOLDS, 1985. Back-to-front display of voxel-based objects. *IEEE Comput. Graphics Appl.* 5:52–60.

[30] FARRELL, E. J., W. C. YANG, and R. A. ZAPULLA, 1985. Animated 3D CT imaging. *IEEE Comput. Graphics Appl.* 5:26–32.

[31] SCHLUSSELBURG, D. S., W. SMITH, D. J. WOODWARD, and R. W. PARKEY, 1988. Use of computed tomography for a three-dimensional treatment planning system. *Comput. Med. Imaging Graphics* 12:25–32.

[32] YASUDA, T., Y. HASHIMOTO, S YOKOI, and J. TORIWAKI, 1990. Computer system for craniofacial surgical planning based on CT images. *IEEE Trans. Med. Imaging* MI9:270–280.

[33] YLÄ-JÄÄSKI, J., F. KLEIN, and O. KÜBLER, 1991. Fast direct display of volume data for medical diagnosis. *CVGIP: Graphical Models and Image Processing* 53:7–18.

[34] TRIVEDI, S. S., 1986. Interactive manipulation of three-dimensional binary scanners. *The Visual Computer* 2:209–218.

[35] REYNOLDS, R. A., D. GORDON, and L. S. CHEN, 1987. A dynamic screen technique for shaded graphics display of slice-represented objects. *Comput. Vision, Grapics, Image Process.* 38:275–298.

[36] KAUFMAN, A., and R. BAKALASH, 1988. Memory and processing architecture for 3-D voxel-based imaging. *IEEE Comput. Graphics Appl.* 8:10–23.

[37] UDUPA, J. K., and D. ODHNER, 1991. Fast visualization, manipulation, and analysis of binary volumetric objects. *IEEE Comput. Graphics Appl.* 11(6):53–62.

[38] MEAGHER, D., 1982. Geometric modeling using octree encoding. *Comput. Graphics Image Process.* 19:129–147.

[39] GARGENTINI, I., H. H. ATKINSON, and G. F. SCHRACK, 1991. Multiple-seed 3D connectivity filling for inaccurate borders. *CVGIP. Graphical Models and Image Processing* 53(6):563–573.

[40] WILHELMS, J., and A. V. GELDER, 1990. Octrees for fast isosurface generation. *Comput. Graphics* 24(5):57–62.

[41] ZUCKER, S. W., and R. A. HUMMEL, 1978. An optimal three-dimensional edge operator. In *Proceedings of the IEEE Computer Science Conference on Pattern Recognition and Image Processing*, pp. 162–168.

[42] MORGENTHALER, D., and A. ROSENFELD, 1981. Multi-dimensional edge detection by hypersurface fitting. *IEEE Trans. Pattern Anal. Mach. Intell.* (PAMI) 3:482–486.

[43] CLINE, H. E., W. E. LORENSON, S. LUDKE, C. R. CRAWFORD, and B. C. TEETER, 1987. Two algorithms for the three-dimensional reconstruction of tomograms. *Med. Physics* 15:320–327.

[44] BAKER, H. H., 1988. Building, visualizing and computing on surfaces of evaluation. *IEEE Comput. Graphics Appl.* 8(4):31–41.

[45] WYVILL, G., C. McPHEETERS, and B. WYVILL, 1986. Data structures for soft objects. *The Visual Computer* 2:227–234.

[46] PAYNE, B. A., and A. W. TOGA, 1990. Surface mapping brain function on 3D models. *IEEE Comput. Graphics Appl.* 10(2):41–53.

[47] CAPPELLETTI, J. D., and A. ROSENFELD, 1989. Three-dimensional boundary following. *Comput. Vision. Graphics Image Process.* 48(1):80–92.

[48] WALLIN, A., 1991. Constructing surfaces from CT data. *IEEE Comput. Graphics Appl.* 11(6):28–33.

[49] ARTZY, E., G. FRIEDER, and G. T. HERMAN, 1981. The theory, design, implementation and evaluation of a three-dimensional surface detection algorithm. *Comput. Graphics Image Process.* 15:1–24.

[50] GORDON, D., and J. K. UDUPA, 1989. Fast surface tracking in three-dimensional binary images. *Comput. Vision Graphics Image Process.* 45:196–214.

[51] UDUPA, J. K., and V. G. AJJANAGADDE, 1990. Boundary and object labelling in three-dimensional images. *Comput. Vision Graphics Image Process.* 51:355–369.

[52] KALVIN, A. D., 1991. Segmentation and surface-based modeling of objects in three-dimensional biomedical images. Doctoral thesis, Department of Computer Science, New York University, New York, N.Y.

[53] SHU, R., and A. KRUGER, 1991. A 3D surface construction algorithm for volume data. In *Proceedings of the International Computer Graphics Conference*. Cambridge, Mass.: Massachusetts Institute of Technology, pp. 221–226.

[54] ROSENFELD, A., T. Y. KONG, and A. Y. WU, 1991. Digital surfaces. *CVGIP: Graphical Models and Image Processing* 53(4):305–312.

[55] HARRIS, L. D., R. A. ROBB, T. S. YUEN, and E. L. RITMAN, 1978. Non-invasive numerical dissection and display of anatomic structure using computerized x-ray tomography. *SPIE Proc.* 152:10–18.

[56] TUY, H. K., and L. TUY, 1984. Direct 2D display of 3D objects. *IEEE Comput. Graphics Appl.* 4:29–33.

[57] HÖHNE, K. H., and R. BERNSTEIN, 1986. Shading 3D images from CT using gray-level gradients. *IEEE Trans. Med. Imaging* MI 5:45–47.

[58] KAJIYA, J. T., and B. P. VON HERZEN, 1884. Ray tracing volume densities. *Comput. Graphics* 18(3):165–174.

[59] SABELLA, P., 1988. A rendering algorithm for visualizing 3D scalar fields. *Comput. Graphics* 22:51–58.

[60] MEINZER, H. P., K. MEETZ, D. SCHEPPELMANN, U. ENGELMANN, and H. J. BAUR, 1991. The Heidelberg ray tracing model. *IEEE Comput. Graphics Appl.* 11(6):34–43.

[61] UPSON, C., and M. KEELER, 1988. V-buffer: Visible volume rendering. *Comput. Graphics* 22:59–64.

[62] HERMAN, G. T., and J. K. UDUPA, 1981. Display of 3D discrete surfaces. *SPIE Proc.* 283:90–97.

[63] CHEN, L. S., G. T. HERMAN, R. A. REYNOLDS, and J. K. UDUPA, 1985. Surface rendering in the cuberille environment. *IEEE Comput. Graphics Appl.* 5:33–43.

[64] LENZ, R., B. GUDMUNDSON, B. LINDSKOG, and P. E. DANIELSSON, 1986. Display of density volumes. *IEEE Comput. Graphics Appl.* 6:20–29.

[65] COHEN, D., A. KAUFMAN, B. BAKALASH, and S. BERGMAN, 1990. Real-time discrete shading. *The Visual Computer* 6(1):16–27.

[66] WEBBER, R. E., 1990. Ray tracing voxel data via biquadratic local surface interpolation. *The Visual Computer* 6:8–15.

[67] GORDON, D., and R. A. REYNOLDS, 1985. Image-space shading of three-dimensional objects. *Comput. Vision Graphics and Image Process.*, 29:361–376.

[68] LENZ, R., P. E. DANIELSSON, S. CONSTROM, and B. GUDMUNDSSON, 1986. Presentation and perception of 3D images. In *Pictorial Information Systems in Medicine* (NATO ASI), K. H. Höhne, ed., Berlin: Springer-Verlag, pp. 459–465.

[69] RAYA, S. P., J. K. UDUPA, and W. A. BARRETT, 1990. A PC-based 3D imaging system: Algorithms, software, and hardware considerations. *Comput. Med. Imaging Graphics* 14:353–370.

[70] UDUPA, J. K., H. M. HUNG, and L. S. CHEN, 1986. Interactive display of 3D medical objects. In *Pictorial Information Systems in Medicine* (NATO ASI), K. H. Höhne, ed., Berlin: Springer-Verlag, pp. 445–457.

[71] FUCHS, H., Z. M. KEDEM, and S. P. USELTON, 1977. Optimal surface reconstruction for planar contours. *Comm. ACM* 20:693–702.

[72] COOK, L. T., S. J. DWYER III, S. BATNITZKY, and K. R. LEE, 1983. A three-dimensional display system for diagnostic imaging applications. *IEEE Comput. Graphics Appl.* 3:13–19.

[73] CHRISTIANSEN, H. N., and T. W. SEDERBERG, 1978. Conversion of complex contour line definitions into polygonal element mosaics. *Comput. Graphics* 12:187–192.

[74] SHANTZ, M., 1981. Surface definition for branching contour-defined objects. *Comput. Graphics* 15:242–259.

[75] GANAPATHY, S., and T. G. DENNAHY, 1982. A new general triangulation method for planar contours. *Comput. Graphics* 16(3):69–74.

[76] SHAW, A., and E. L. SCHWARTZ, 1988. Automatic construction of polyhedral surfaces from voxel representation. Tech. rep. robotics rep. RR-150. New York: Courant Institute of Mathematical Sciences, New York University.

[77] SHINAGAWA, Y., and T. L. KUNII, 1991. Constructing a Reeb graph automatically from cross sections. *IEEE Comput. Graphics Appl.* 11(6):44–50.

[78] MAZZIOTTA, J. C., and K. H. HUANG, 1976. THREAD (three-dimensional reconstruction and display) with biomedical applications in neuron ultrastructure and computerized tomography. *Am. Fed. Info. Process. Soc.* 45:241–250.

[79] ATKINSON, H. H., I. GARGANTINI, and M. V. S. RAMANATH, 1984. Determination of the 3D border by repeated elimination of internal surfaces. *Computing* 32:279–295.

[80] ROBERTSON, D. D., 1991. Three-dimensional modelling and the design of hip and knee prostheses. In *3D Imaging in Medicine*, J. K. Udupa and G. T. Herman, eds. Boca Raton, Fla.: CRC Press.

[81] ROSENMAN, J., 1991. 3D imaging in radiotherapy treatment planning. In *3D Imaging in Medicine*, J. K. Udupa and G. T. Herman, eds. Boca Raton, Fla.: CRC Press.

[82] KAUFMAN, A. 1987. Efficient algorithms for 3-D scan conversion of parametric curves, surfaces, and volume. *Comput. Graphics* 21:171–179.

[83] COHEN, D., and A. KAUFMAN, 1991. Scan conversion algorithms for linear and quadratic objects. In *Volume Visualization*, A. Kaufman, ed. Los Alamitos, Calif.: IEEE Computer Society Press, pp. 280–301.

[84] MORSE, B. S., W. A. BARRETT, J. K., and R. P. BURTON, 1991. Trainable optimal boundary finding using two-dimensional dynamic programming. Tech. rep. MIPG180 (Medical Image Processing Group). Philadelphia: Department of Radiology, University of Pennsylvania.

[85] AHO, A. V., and J. D. ULLMAN, 1972. *The Theory of Parsing, Translation and Compiling, Vol. 1. Parsing.* Englewood Cliffs, N.J.: Prentice Hall.

[86] LEDLEY, R. S., and C. M. PARK, 1977. Molded picture representation of whole body organs generated from CT scan sequences. In *Proceedings of the First Annual Symposium of Computer Applications in Medical Care.* Washington, D.C.: IEEE, pp. 363–367.

[87] UDUPA, J. K., 1983. DISPLAY82—a system of programs for the display of three-dimensional information in CT data. Tech. rep. MIPG67 (Medical Image Processing Group). Philadelphia: Department of Radiology, University of Pennsylvania.

[88] UDUPA, J. K., G. T. HERMAN, P. S. MARGASAHAYAM, L. S. CHEN, and C. R. MEYER, 1986. 3D98: A turnkey system for the display and analysis of 3D medical objects. *SPIE Proc.* 671:154–168.

[89] DEV, P., S. L. WOOD, J. P. DUNCAN, and D. N. WHITE, 1983. An interactive graphics system for planning reconstructive surgery. In *Proceedings of the Fourth Annual Conference and Exposition of the National Computer Graphics Association*, pp. 130–135. Fairfax. Va.: National Computer Graphics Association,

[90] HEFFERNAN, P. B., and R. A. ROBB, 1985. A new method for shaded surface display of biological and medical images. *IEEE Trans. Med. Imaging* MI 4:26–38.

[91] VANNIER, M. W., J. L. MARSH, and J. O. WARREN, 1983. Three-dimensional computer graphics for craniofacial surgical planning and evaluation. *Comput. Graphics* 17:263–274.

[92] TIEDE, U., K. H. HÖHNE, M. BOMANS, A. POMMERT, M. RIEMER, and G. WIEBECKE, 1990. Investigation of

medical 3D rendering algorithms. *IEEE Comput. Graphics Appl.* 10:41–53.

[93] LEVOY, M., 1990. Efficient ray tracing of volume data. *ACM Trans. Graphics* 9:245–261.

[94] RAYA, S. P., 1989. SOFTVU—a software package for multidimensional medical image analysis. Tech. rep. MIPG148 (Medical Image Processing Group). Philadelphia: Department of Radiology, University of Pennsylvania.

[95] GILLESPIE, J. E., 1991. Three-dimensional computed tomographic reformations: Assessment of clinical efficacy. In *3D Imaging in Medicine,* J. K. Udupa and G. T. Herman, eds. Boca Raton, Fla.: CRC Press.

[96] RUSINEK, H., N. S. KARP, and C. B. CUTTING, 1990. A comparison of two approaches to three-dimensional imaging of craniofacial anomalies. *J. Dig. Imaging* 3:81–88.

[97] UDUPA, J. K., and G. T. HERMAN, 1989. Volume rendering versus surface rendering. *Comm. ACM* 32:1364–1366.

[98] LANG, P., P. STIEGER, and T. LINDQUIST, 1990. Three-dimensional reconstruction of magnetic resonance images: Comparison of surface and volume rendering techniques.

In *Proceedings of SCAR90, Computer Applications to Assist Radiology*, R. L. Arenson and R. M. Friedenberg, eds., Carlsbad, Calif.: Symposia Foundation, pp. 520–526.

[99] S. L., Wood, 1992. Visualization and modeling of 3-D structures. *IEEE Eng. Med. Biol. Magazine* 11 (2):72–79.

[100] SWETS, J. A., and PICKETT, R. M., 1982. *Evaluation of Diagnostic Systems*. New York: Academic.

[101] HERMAN, G. T., 1980. *Image Reconstructions from Projections: The Fundamentals of Computerized Tomography*. New York: Academic.

[102] PHONG, B. T., 1975. Illumination for computer generated images. *Comm. ACM* 18:311–317.

[103] UDUPA, J. K., H. M. HUNG, D. ODHNER, and R. GONCALVES, 1992. Multidimensional data format specification: A generalization of the American College of Radiology—National Electric Manufacturers Association standards. *J. Dig. Imaging* 5(1):26–46.

[104] UDUPA, J. K., H. M. HUNG, D. ODHNER, R. J. GONÇALVES, and S. SAMARASEKERA, 1992. 3DVIEWNIX: A data-, machine-, and application-independent software system for multidimensional data visualization and analysis. *SPIE Proc.* 1653:185–191.

4 Segmentation of Complex Three-Dimensional Medical Objects: A Challenge and a Requirement for Computer-Assisted Surgery Planning and Performance

NICHOLAS AYACHE, PHILIPPE CINQUIN,
ISAAC COHEN, LAURENT COHEN, FRANÇOIS LEITNER,
AND OLIVIER MONGA

ADVANCED SURGERY planning relies mostly on 3D imaging modalities, such as CT or MRI. These devices provide images of anatomic or pathologic structures that form the basis on which surgery planning may be performed. Quantitative decisions (e.g., direction of a needle) will be made. It is therefore essential that the objects be accurately segmented. This accuracy requirement will be evident also when anatomy-based registration is considered. Each imaging modality is characterized by image features that will be obtained by a segmentation process. An error in this stage would, of course, dramatically affect the registration itself, implying poor performance of the intervention.

Segmentation must also be as user-friendly as possible. Modern imaging systems provide almost isotropic volumes, defined as a set of tens of slices. A user cannot be expected to track structures on each of these slices, for it is very time-consuming, but automatic segmentation is not always possible because medical objects have complex shapes, combining flat parts, sharp edges, holes, and other topologic difficulties. There is currently no ideal system that minimizes user time in all situations.

A designer of a computer-integrated surgery system will have to devise a solution to the segmentation problem. Therefore, we propose in this chapter a review of segmentation methods. Deformable models are a class of methods that are characterized by their user-friendliness. The latter half of this chapter is devoted to these methods, two of which are detailed.

Multidimensional image segmentation:
State of the art

The goal of computer vision is to extract from digital images the information useful for a given task. David Marr [1] proposed three levels to describe a vision system:

1. What is the image information really useful to solve this task (i.e., what to compute)?

2. What are the algorithms to compute this information (i.e., how to compute)?

3. What are the devices to implement these methods (i.e., biologic or electronic)?

These levels can be applied to either a whole vision system or each of its components.

The fields of applications are numerous, among them medical images, robotics, satellites and aerial images, and seismic images. In addition, images can be

2D or 3D (CT, MRI, depth maps, etc.) or even 4D when dealing with temporal sequences (as time is the fourth dimension).

A generic approach in building a vision system consists in producing intermediate descriptions of images corresponding to increasing symbolic levels toward a final goal. Segmentation is usually the first stage of such a system. It is specified by the characterization of the suitable information (an analytic model) as well as by the algorithms used to extract this information (an algorithmic solution). Much work has been devoted to image segmentation because of the various kinds of images, the difficulty of the task, the various backgrounds of researchers, the evolution of computer performances, and some empiricism to evaluate results.

Whatever its origin, an image represents entities: for example, organs of the human body, cells, seismic surfaces, or objects of an indoors scene. The goal of any segmentation algorithm is to extract features characterizing these entities. Classically, the features that are considered are points or areas of interest—edges or regions. Edge detection consists in searching local discontinuities of the gray-level function of the image. Region segmentation deals with the extraction of homogeneous areas in the image. For instance, in the case of CT images, edges correspond to boundaries of body structures and regions to their areas. These two approaches —*edge detection* and *region extraction*—are dual because a region defines a line (a surface in 3D) with its boundary and a closed line (a closed surface in 3D) defines a region. Nevertheless, they lead to completely different algorithms and do not provide the same results. Therefore, multidimensional image segmentation is naturally split into these two parts; edge detection and region extraction. We may note that few algorithms actually combine a dual approach.

Edge detection

In a 2D or 3D image, the boundaries of the structures correspond to local gradient extrema or to Laplacian zero crossings of the gray-level function. The main problems set by edge detection come from the degradation of the images (sensor noise, irregularity of object surfaces, discretization, etc.). This leads to the differentiation of an nD noisy signal. To solve it, a classic scheme is to define some performance criteria of an operator, including characterization of the edges and the noise. In a second stage, a set of optimal filters can

be derived from these criteria. The third stage deals with implementation of these filters. This filtering step provides labeling of the pixels where edge points are marked, but generally this representation is too poor to be used by the next processing stage of the vision system. It usually is necessary to structure the edge detection result, using chaining, polygonal and polyhedral approximation, or interpolation [2].

FILTERING STAGE

Statement Most techniques use linear filters. In the case where no a priori knowledge about the nature of the noise is available, this method leads to efficient algorithms, providing satisfactory results. Nevertheless, from a theoretic point of view, linear filtering can be efficient only if the noise mean is close to zero. In most images, the hypothesis of a centered white Gaussian noise is reasonable. However, if not, an ordering filter (e.g., a median filter) can be used in a preliminary stage [3].

Usually, it is admitted that edges correspond to discontinuities of order zero in the image (step model). We may notice that some edges are located at discontinuities of order 1 (roof model). Most published works deal with the first model and propose two main approaches:

- *Gradient approach*: Gradient computation and extraction of the local extrema of its magnitude along its direction
- *Laplacian approach*: Laplacian computation and determination of its zero crossings

The first approach consists in finding the zero crossings of the second derivative in the gradient direction that are different from the zero crossings of the Laplacian. Practically, these two methods provide very similar results.

First approaches Several linear filters to approximate the gradient or the Laplacian have been proposed. Owing to properties of the convolution product, these two schemes can be reduced to finding a smoothing filter.

The first approaches proposed 3×3 convolution masks to compute gradient components in two orthogonal directions [3]. These methods are efficient if the image is not too noisy and if no multiple edge points exist. Otherwise, it is of interest to use larger convolution masks [3, 4] or to discretize the orientations to define a derivative mask for each direction. Unfortunately, these principles lead to methods of high algorithmic complexity, particularly in the case of 3D images. Moreover, these algorithms are not justified by an edge model and a noise characterization. For these reasons, much effort has been devoted to define theoretically the performances of an edge detector and to find optimal filters that can be implemented efficiently [5–7].

Optimal filters The most popular model to evaluate the performances of an edge detector was introduced by Canny [5]. In his simulation model, Canny has made noise a central concern in his investigation for edge finding. He first considers the 1D case with the traditional model of a step corrupted by additive white Gaussian noise. He formulates precisely the criteria for effective edge detection: good detection, good localization, one response to one edge. Using the calculus of variations, he derived a general solution for an optimal operator, proposing to use the first derivative of a Gaussian whose performances are close to the optimal operator.

Further work was done to seek an impulse response closer to the optimal one that could be implemented more efficiently. Shen and Castan [6] proposed a derivative filter that is an optimal solution for the first part of Canny's criteria. It corresponds to the best trade-off detection-localization. Deriche [7] pointed out that Canny's design was developed for finite impulse response (antisymmetric) filters (FIR) and derived an optimal solution in the case of infinite impulse response filters (IIR).

Implementation The filters of Deriche [7] and Shen [6] share the interesting property of being separable and recursive and therefore of efficient implementation. This is particularly important for 3D data because the huge size of images makes the algorithmic complexity and the storage requirement crucial. In particular, the size of the convolution masks used to implement the operator cannot be too large in order to avoid very prohibitive computing times. The convolution of a 3D image dim $x \times$ dim $y \times$ dim z by a mask $n \times n \times n$ costs $\sigma(n^3 \times$ dim $x \times$ dim $y \times$ dim $z)$. For example, this complexity makes it almost impossible to use masks of a size larger than $5 \times 5 \times 5$ for an image $256 \times 256 \times 64$. Therefore an important limitation of many

3D edge detectors has been the use of small convolution masks, which are very sensitive to noise. Recursive and separable filtering, recently introduced for 3D edge detection, does not suffer from these limitations [8, 9].

From gradient or Laplacian to 3D edges In the case of a first derivative approach, one computes the gradient at each point of the image. In the first approaches [3], a thesholding stage allows one to mark points whose gradient magnitude is higher than a given threshold. However, if the gradient magnitude at the edge points varies strongly in the image, there exists no single threshold value that allows for selecting exactly the correct edge points. A way to avoid this problem is to proceed in two steps [5, 6, 10]. First, extract local maxima (of the gradient magnitude) in the gradient direction, thus providing thin edges one pixel wide. Second, eliminate spurious points while keeping high connectivity of edge chains, by hysteresis thresholding. This technique provides thin and well-connected contours of one-pixel width.

In the case of a second derivative approach, one computes an estimation of the Laplacian at each image point [1, 4, 9, 11]. We assume that edge points are located at Laplacian zero crossings. Therefore, one simply marks points where the sign of the Laplacian changes. A last thresholding stage is also necessary to remove points whose gradient magnitude is too low.

Discussion Generally, computation of the second derivative is more sensitive to noise than computation of the first derivative. In addition, the computation complexity is higher for the gradient than for the Laplacian, because the gradient estimation requires that each of its components be computed. However, the thresholding stage in both approaches requires computation of the gradient magnitude (only at zero crossing points for a second derivative approach). The experimental edge localization is roughly the same. We note that the Laplacian approach tends to smooth angles due to the isotropy of the operator. These problems are studied by Hildreth [12], Torre and Poggio [13], and Berzins [14].

EDGE TRACKING AND CLOSING METHODS Even with hysteresis thresholding, it is difficult to obtain perfect edge chains; they must be improved. Generally, it is easier to extend uncompleted contours than to validate true contours in a noisy edge image. Thus, it is of interest to choose high thresholds to remove false edge points and then to use a tracking and closing algorithm. This kind of algorithm could also be used to close open contours. Recently, Deriche and Cocquerez [15] have proposed an efficient 2D closing algorithm based on the search of optimal paths between extremities of open contours. Monga et al. [9] proposed a 3D extension of this method by applying it on each plane xy, yz, zx, and by combining the three edge images obtained.

HIGHER-LEVEL REPRESENTATIONS OF EDGES For many applications, the matrix description provided by the filtering stage is not sufficient. It then is necessary to define higher-level representations of edges.

Linking 2D edges The goal of edge linking is to chain connected edge points to structure the boundaries of objects.

Among the different techniques proposed recently in the litterature, Giraudon [16] proposed a linking algorithm based on an efficient data structure.

Approximations by polygonal and planar patches Linking provides structure but does not compact the edge information. A way to reduce the amount of edge is to represent 2D edges by a polygonal approximation and 3D edges by a polyhedral approximation. An interesting way to describe 3D edges is to compute a triangulation of the surfaces they define. This may be done by the following steps: First, accomplish linking and polygonal approximation of edges on a set of parallel planes. Then connect edge segments between pairs of adjacent planes using a triangulation algorithm.

For the second stage, the triangulation method introduced by Fuchs et al. [17] may be used. The key point of this method is to look for the triangulation that minimizes the sum of the length of the edges. This is performed by searching an optimal path in the triangulation graph. The method does not work if the object is decomposed into several connected components in one or several cross-sections. For this case (very frequent in practice), Boissonnat [18] introduced a reconstruction method whose principle is first to compute the Delaunay triangulation of the segment endpoints and then to remove the tetrahedra that produce singularities. The results are good even with very complex shapes.

Optimal boundaries In some cases, one wants to include in the linking process a function to optimize. The basic principle of such methods is to look for an optimal path in the adjacency graph where each point is attached to its gradient magnitude. For instance, a method proposed by Martelli [19] consists in searching for a connected path extending from the bottom to the top of the image that maximizes the sum of the gradient magnitudes. Generally, such methods use dynamic programming to solve the optimization problem.

More recently, active contours have been introduced by Kass et al. [20], who propose a global approach to determine the position of a whole chain of edge points. These techniques will be discussed later.

REGION EXTRACTION

The goal of regional segmentation is to find image partitions corresponding to real objects of the corresponding scene. It may be considered in the more general context of data segmentation. The basic problem of data segmentation is the following: What are given are a set of entities, a set of features characterizing these entities, and relational features between these entities. One defines a quality criterion attached to a partition, and the segmentation task consists in maximizing these criteria.

For the specific problem set by image segmentation, entities are image points (2D or 3D), features are the spatial position and the gray level, topologic relationships are four-connectivity or eight-connectivity, and relational features are characteristics of the borders between two entity sets. Therefore, an image segmentation task can be specified by a set of homogeneous criteria defining the properties of the image partition (analytic model) and an algorithm using these criteria to segment the image (algorithmic problem). Thus we must cope with two basic problems: to define *specific* segmentation criteria for each given segmentation task and to define a *generic* strategy by which to use these segmentation criteria.

We note that if the homogeneity properties of the regions are simple, it is possible to derive an edge detector that finds the regions' boundaries. Regions can then be extracted thanks to a closing edges method. However, it is not always possible to find efficient filters to detect transitions of a homogeneity property. This problem has motivated the vast amount of work devoted to region image segmentation.

The existing methods can be divided into two classes, *classification* (including region splitting) and *region growing*. The main difference between these two approaches is based on the use of the luminance space and of the spatial relationships existing between pixels. The basic principle of the classification algorithms is first to define a partition of the luminance space and then to use connectivity to determine regions. The region-growing scheme consists of combining these two kinds of information.

CLASSIFICATION METHODS   First, these methods determine a partition of the luminance space by using the gray-level distribution in the image. To each pixel is attached the corresponding gray-level class. The regions are defined by maximal sets of connected pixels belonging to the same class. Generally, the homogeneity properties are not explicitly defined.

Most methods use the luminance histogram for classification. The picks and the corresponding valleys of the histogram are determined. Gaps between valleys define classes. This principle works for images including a few objects having well-separated gray-level distributions.

Olhander et al. [21] have improved this idea by adding a recursive classification that makes the algorithm work even in complex scenes. At each step, only the best histogram pick is selected, and the procedure is applied recursively to the two corresponding classes. A class is depicted only if the histogram has one mode. Ohta, Kanade, and Sakai [22] have adapted this algorithm for color image segmentation.

In case the image contains one object and a background, many classification techniques by adaptive thresholding have been developed [23–26]. These methods combine connectivity and luminance information to set thresholds.

Chow and Kaneko [23] compute at each point a threshold depending on the luminance histogram in a neighborhood. A squared neighborhood measuring 33×33 or 65×65 is used to determine these local histograms. To avoid computing a histogram at each point, the image is split in blocks and a histogram is determined for each block. An adapted thresholding is defined for each block, and then a linear interpolation of the thresholds yields an adaptive threshold for each pixel.

Weszka, Nagel, and Rosenfeld [25] proposed to take into account only low-gradient pixels. Then only gray levels inside homogeneous areas are considered. Watanabe [24] chooses a threshold that maximizes the gradient sum of all pixels whose gray level is equal to the threshold.

These classification methods are efficient if the gray-level distribution is sufficient to characterize the homogeneous regions of the image. In the case of images representing objects with different luminances in front of a background, this kind of approach works well, but if the images are noisy and contain a lot of objects, the classification is difficult to use. It then is necessary to use connectivity relationships from the beginning of the segmentation process. This is the main idea of region-growing algorithms.

REGION-GROWING ALGORITHMS

Introduction   Region-growing methods consist in iteratively merging sets of connected points in larger regions, using conditions depending on homogeneity properties. The key point of these approaches is to find merging criteria and merging strategies to obtain homogeneous regions. Spatial relations are therefore used from the beginning of the segmentation process. These methods can be divided into two classes, *aggregation of points* and *iterative merging*.

Aggregation of points   Here the basic principle is to attach to each pixel a feature vector. Two pixels are merged if their feature vectors are similar enough. The segmentation result is the obtained connected components. Many feature vectors and similarity measures have been proposed.

The simplest heuristic consists in merging two pixels if the difference between their gray levels is low. Bryant [27] normalizes this difference by the mean of all differences computed for all adjacent points in the image. Asano and Yokoya [28] merge two pixels if the difference between their gray levels is low with respect to the biggest difference existing between a pixel and its neighbors in a small squared neighborhood. Nagao and Matsuyama [29] apply this kind of algorithm for color image segmentation. A pixel is merged with a seed region if its color vector (red, green, blue) is similar enough to any color vector of a point of the seed region. A point-by-point expansion yields a set of regions in which the step variation of the points' luminance with respect to the red, green, and blue component is less than a given threshold.

More sophisticated merging criteria, using a feature vector depending on a squared neighborhood centered at the pixel, have also been proposed [30, 31]. Often the feature vector comes from an edge detection operator. Two adjacent pixels are merged if there are no edges between them. Of course, the obtained results depend on the type of edge detector used.

The limitation of the aggregation of points approach is that the merged entities (pixels) do not carry enough information. The basic principle of this method is to merge points to seed regions. The only information used for merging are features of the seed region and the gray level of the involved point. Iterative merging allows one to use richer information to build regions.

Iterative merging The key point here is to define a sequence of image partitions by merging iteratively connected regions. These strategies allow one to use merging heuristics depending on similarities of region properties.

The first approach, proposed by Muerle and Allen [32], merges two adjacent regions if their gray-level distributions are similar enough. These authors proposed using the Kolmogorov-Smirnov test.

Brice and Fennema [33] perform region growing by first partitioning an image in an initial set of similar gray levels. Then they merge sequentially pairs of adjacent regions such that a significant border part has a low contrast.

Horowitz and Pavlidis [34] use a quadtree to represent the image. A merging and splitting strategy then is applied. They obtain a set of regions such that the gray-level variation amplitude is less than a given threshold. This method can be directly extended to 3D by using an octree.

The approach developed by Pong et al. [35] is based on the sequential use of two algorithms: The image first is segmented by using a sloped facet model [36], and then this initial segmentation is the input of a region-growing algorithm. Two adjacent regions are merged if a similarity criterion is satisfied.

Most of these methods iteratively merge pairs of adjacent regions verifying similarity conditions. The merging process stops when no pair of adjacent regions satisfying the fusion conditions exists. In general, the result depends on the order in which regions are merged and not on the data alone. An interesting principle is to define merging hierarchies. These ideas are developed in the work by Monga and Deriche [8]. A general framework to solve segmentation problems is presented. First, a new definition of a segmentation problem is proposed by adding to the classic one the optimization of a global quality function. This definition leads to a NP-complete problem. An algorithm that enables one to derive a suboptimal solution is described. This algorithm proceeds by the optimization of a local quality function in the whole image. Its originality is to use, in an optimal way, a sequence of merging criteria. Then assumptions are made about the merging criteria. These conditions yield an implementation of low algorithmic complexity. This approach can tackle various segmentation tasks, it is applied to the segmentation of 2D monochromatic and color images and to the segmentation of 3D images [37, 38].

CONCLUSION

Segmentation is the first stage of any vision task and therefore must contend with the image reality, a matrix of pixels originating from a mixture of various geometric and physical phenomena. Moreover, the image representation it provides is used by the subsequent processing stages, so much effort must be extended to improve this primary process.

The goal of image segmentation is to extract information about the real world described by images. Thus it is necessary to establish the links between the properties of the observed universe and its image representation. This implies that an image must be considered not like any signal but like the representation of a physical world. The complexity of the image formation process explains why only a few segmentation algorithms take the complexity of the image formation process into account. Nevertheless, the more efficient models rely implicitly on physical reality. For instance, modeling an edge by a perfect step with an additive Gaussian noise or a region by a low-variance area has physical foundations.

Therefore, evaluating a segmentation algorithm is meaningful for a particular context only. A way to estimate the results of a method is to consider a complete system realizing a specific task—for instance, to evaluate the performance of segmentation with respect to the requirements of computer-integrated surgery. Among all the methods that have been overviewed, snakes seem to be particularly suitable to meet the requirements of computer-integrated surgery, because they have the following features: flexibility, reasonable user-interactivity, reasonable cost, 3D objects handling, possibility of a priori knowledge integration, and representation of complex structure boundaries by continuous surfaces. We will therefore analyze two typical approaches using snakes.

3D segmentation by deformable models

Active contours, or snakes, have proved a very efficient method for 2D image segmentation [39, 40], whether completely automatic or semiautomatic. The generalization of these methods to 3D images instigates difficult problems regarding the complexity of the system needed to minimize the 3D generalization of the energy defining the border of the object.

This complexity may be dealt with by solving the 3D classic problem by finite elements. Another solution is to simplify the 3D problem, by embedding part of the minimization of the energy in the choice of spline functions. These two approaches lead to continuous and differentiable representation of the border of the object and will now be described.

Finite elements, deformable surfaces

We propose a deformable 3D shape model that can be used to extract reliable surfaces in 3D images and infer a differential structure on them. Usually, 3D images are given as a set of intensity voxels (volume elements). A 3D edge detector, after a *local* image analysis [8, 41], provides a set of 3D *edgels* (edge elements). These edgels can be considered as the trace of a certain number of surfaces. One then is confronted with a dual problem: to select edgels belonging to the same surface trace (this is the segmentation problem) and to recover a continuous and differentiable description of each surface (this yields a path between the original sparse discrete data and the ability to compute a differential structure useful for interpretation) [42, 43].

Both questions were analyzed by Sander and Zucker [44] who proposed to solve by a connectivity analysis and by the fitting of a set of local quadratic models. However, difficulties arise when the connectivity analysis fails because edges are too sparse and also when the model is too local to describe a complex shape reliably.

Another approach to solve a similar problem in 2D consists in introducing an active deformable model [45], which solves the segmentation problem, assuming an initial estimate is provided (an initial solution might be provided by several means, including user interactivity, which usually is encouraged in medical applications), and the interpolation problem when the curve is expressed in a basis of continuous functions [46]. Such models were generalized in $2\frac{1}{2}$D and 3D [39, 47], where the deformable surface is evolving under the forces computed on a 2D image or a set of 2D images.

In contrast with the methods of reconstruction based on a 2D slice-by-slice approach [46, 48, 49], we use, in this chapter, a 3D deformable model that evolves in 3D images under the action of internal forces (describing some elasticity properties of the surface) and external forces attracting the surface toward some detected edgels. This formalism leads to minimization of an energy that is expressed as a functional. We use a variational approach and a conforming finite element method to express the surface in a discrete basis of continuous functions. This method allows "adaptive subdivision" of the parameterization domain without adding nodal points and, consequently, without increasing the size of the linear system we solve. This leads to reduced computational complexity and better numeric stability than a classic finite difference method.

ENERGY-MINIMIZING SURFACES   A 3D image is given by a set of intensity voxels or as a set of successive 2D cross-sections. In our first work [46, 49] we processed 3D images as a set of successive 2D images. This is a familiar approach that is used also in tracking methods, but it is not effective and cannot take into account the spatial homogeneity of the data. In the following, we consider the 3D image data as a set of pixels, and the boundaries of a 3D image are described by a set of surfaces [50]. A deformable surface model allows one to characterize these surfaces [39, 47]. The characterization consists in determining the location and shape of the surface.

In the following, we restrict ourselves to parameterized surfaces, as any 3D surface has a local parameterization. This model is defined by a space of admissible deformations (Ad) and a functional E to minimize. This functional E represents the energy of the model. A surface v is defined by a mapping:

$$\Omega = [0, 1] \times [0, 1] \rightarrow R^3$$

$$(s, r) \mapsto \mathbf{v}(s, r) = [x(s, r), y(s, r), z(s, r)]$$

The associated energy E is given by:

$$E: Ad \rightarrow R$$

$$\mathbf{v} \mapsto E(\mathbf{v}) = \int_{\Omega} w_{10} \left| \frac{\partial \mathbf{v}}{\partial s} \right|^2 + w_{01} \left| \frac{\partial \mathbf{v}}{\partial r} \right|^2 + 2w_{11} \left| \frac{\partial^2 \mathbf{v}}{\partial s \partial r} \right|^2$$

$$+ w_{20} \left| \frac{\partial^2 \mathbf{v}}{\partial s^2} \right|^2 + w_{02} \left| \frac{\partial^2 \mathbf{v}}{\partial r^2} \right|^2 + P(\mathbf{v}) \, ds \, dr$$

where P is the potential associated with the external forces. The external forces refer to the forces that allow the surface to localize the image attributes. Therefore, if we want the surface to be attracted by 3D edge points, the potential P will be expressed in terms of a 3D gradient image. The internal forces acting on the shape of the surface depend on the coefficients w_{ij} such that the elasticity is determined by (w_{10}, w_{01}), the rigidity by (w_{20}, w_{02}), and the resistance to twist by w_1. The coefficients w_{ij} determine the mechanical properties of the surface. These coefficients are also called *regularization parameters*. We can constrain the surface structure by adjusting boundary conditions (for instance, to create a cylinder or a torus).

A local minimum $\mathbf{v}$ of E satisfies the associated Euler-Lagrange equation:

$$\begin{cases} -\dfrac{\partial}{\partial s} \left(w_{10} \dfrac{\partial \mathbf{v}}{\partial s} \right) - \dfrac{\partial}{\partial r} \left(w_{01} \dfrac{\partial \mathbf{v}}{\partial r} \right) + 2 \dfrac{\partial^2}{\partial s \partial r} \left(w_{11} \dfrac{\partial^2 \mathbf{v}}{\partial s \partial r} \right) \\[2mm] \quad + \dfrac{\partial^2}{\partial s^2} \left(w_{20} \dfrac{\partial^2 \mathbf{v}}{\partial s^2} \right) + \dfrac{\partial^2}{\partial r^2} \left(w_{02} \dfrac{\partial^2 \mathbf{v}}{\partial r^2} \right) = -\nabla P(\mathbf{v}) \\[2mm] + \text{boundary conditions} \end{cases} \quad (1)$$

which represents the necessary condition for a minimum $(E'(\mathbf{v}) = 0)$. A solution of equation 1 can be seen either as realizing the equilibrium between internal (or regularizing) and external forces or reaching the minimum of the energy E. The boundary conditions constrain the surface structure by specifying different properties of the surface at the boundaries of the parameterization domain $\Omega = [0, 1] \times [0, 1]$.

Because the energy function is not convex, there may be many local minima of E. The Euler-Lagrange equation (equation 1) may characterize any such local minimum but, as we are interested in finding a 3D contour in a given area, we assume that we have a rough *prior* estimation of the surface. This estimate is used as initial

data for the associated evolution equation in which we add a temporal parameter t:

$$\begin{cases} \dfrac{\partial \mathbf{v}}{\partial t} - \dfrac{\partial}{\partial s} \left(w_{10} \dfrac{\partial \mathbf{v}}{\partial s} \right) - \dfrac{\partial}{\partial r} \left(w_{01} \dfrac{\partial \mathbf{v}}{\partial r} \right) + 2 \dfrac{\partial^2}{\partial s \partial r} \left(w_{11} \dfrac{\partial^2 \mathbf{v}}{\partial s \partial r} \right) \\[2mm] \quad + \dfrac{\partial^2}{\partial s^2} \left(w_{20} \dfrac{\partial^2 \mathbf{v}}{\partial s^2} \right) + \dfrac{\partial^2}{\partial r^2} \left(w_{02} \dfrac{\partial^2 \mathbf{v}}{\partial r^2} \right) = -\nabla P(\mathbf{v}) \\[2mm] \mathbf{v}(0, s, r) = \mathbf{v_0}(s, r) \text{ initial estimation} \\[2mm] + \text{boundary conditions} \end{cases} \quad (2)$$

A solution to the static problem is found when the solution $\mathbf{v}(t, s, r)$ converges as t tends to infinity; then the term $\partial \mathbf{v}/\partial t$ vanishes, providing a solution of the static problem.

This evolution equation can also be seen as a gradient descent algorithm, starting with the initial estimate $\mathbf{v}_o$ (see [50]). The potential P is such that the force $F(\mathbf{v}) = -\nabla P(\mathbf{v})$ has to attract the surface to the image attributes for which we are looking. Our main goal is the extraction of "good" edge points (i.e., to be able to remove spurious edge points while ensuring connected contours). Thus the surface has to be attracted by edge points and to minimize the energy:

$$E_{ext} = \int \int_{\Omega} P[\mathbf{v}(s, r)] \, ds \, dr \quad (3)$$

For this purpose, Kass, Witkin, and Terzopoulos [45] set the potential $P = -|\nabla \mathcal{I}|^2$ so that edge points will minimize E_{ext}, where $\mathcal{I}$ is the 3D image convolved with a Gaussian function. For numeric stability (a complete discussion is given in [46, 49]) we normalize the force:

$$F(\mathbf{v}) = -k \frac{\nabla P}{\|\nabla P\|}$$

where k is a parameter that allows one to tune the attraction force. Now all the edge points, including spurious ones, have the same ability to attract the surface, but spurious points generally form small connected components in 3D images. Consequently, when the surface converges toward the real contours, all these points first attract the surface and then are ignored by the regularization effect of the algorithm.

The solution of equation 2 is done in two steps. First we solve the static problem (equation 1) with a conform finite element method (FEM) [51], and then we solve the evolution problem with a finite difference method. This can be done because the space variables (s, r) and the temporal variable (t) are independent.

SOLUTION OF THE STATIC PROBLEM: THE VARIATIONAL
PROBLEM   The solution of equation 1 done through a
variational method. This consists in defining a bilinear
form $a(\mathbf{u}, \mathbf{v})$ and a linear form $L(\mathbf{v})$ such that solving
equation 1 is equivalent to solving the associated varia-
tional problem: Find a function $\mathbf{v}$ in the Sobolev space
$H_0^2(\Omega)$ such that:

$$a(\mathbf{v}, \mathbf{u}) = L_{\mathbf{v}}(\mathbf{u}) \qquad \forall \mathbf{u} \in H_0^2(\Omega) \qquad (4)$$

where $H_0^2(\Omega)$ is the space of functions such that
$\int_\Omega |D^m \mathbf{v}|^2 < +\infty$ for $m = 0, 1, 2$ where $D^m \mathbf{v}$ is the mth-
order derivative of function $\mathbf{v}$. Such a formulation can
be easily obtained [50] from equation 1 by defining:

$$a(\mathbf{u}, \mathbf{v}) = \int_\Omega w_{10} \frac{\partial \mathbf{u}}{\partial s} \frac{\partial \mathbf{v}}{\partial s} + w_{01} \frac{\partial \mathbf{u}}{\partial r} \frac{\partial \mathbf{v}}{\partial r} + w_{20} \frac{\partial^2 \mathbf{u}}{\partial s^2} \frac{\partial^2 \mathbf{v}}{\partial s^2}$$
$$+ 2w_{11} \frac{\partial^2 \mathbf{u}}{\partial s \partial r} \frac{\partial^2 \mathbf{v}}{\partial s \partial r} + w_{02} \frac{\partial^2 \mathbf{u}}{\partial r^2} \frac{\partial^2 \mathbf{v}}{\partial r^2} \, ds \, dr$$

remark that $a(\mathbf{u}, \mathbf{v})$ is defined only for $\mathbf{u}, \mathbf{v} \in H_0^2(\Omega)$]
and

$$L_{\mathbf{v}}(\mathbf{u}) = -\int_\Omega \nabla P(\mathbf{v}) \, \mathbf{u} \, ds \, dr$$

We can further show that equation 4 has a unique
solution as long as the bilinear form $a(\mathbf{u}, \mathbf{v})$ is symmetric and definite positive, providing the parameters w_{ij}
are positive.

A well-known approach for approximating such
problems is Galerkin's method [51], which consists in
defining a similar discrete problem over a finite dimensional subspace (V_h) of the Sobolev space $H_0^2(\Omega)$.

The conforming FEM provides an efficient tool for
defining the space V_h. It is characterized by three
aspects:

• A tessellation is established over the parameterization set $\Omega = [0, 1] \times [0, 1]$.
• The functions $\mathbf{v_h} \in V_h$ are piecewise polynomials.
• There exists a basis in the space V_h whose functions
have a small support.

This last feature is very important as it defines the
structure of the linear system we solve. Choosing
functions with a small support induces a very sparse
linear system and leads to a reduced computational
complexity.

In the following, we choose rectangular patches and
Bogner-Fox-Schmit (BFS) elements, which define for
every $\mathbf{v_h} \in V_h$ the identity:

$$\mathbf{v_h} = \sum_{i,j=0}^{N_s-1, N_r-1} \mathbf{v_h}(a_{ij}) \varphi_{ij} + \frac{\partial \mathbf{v_h}}{\partial s}(a_{ij}) \psi_{ij}$$
$$+ \frac{\partial \mathbf{v_h}}{\partial r}(a_{ij}) \eta_{ij} + \frac{\partial^2 \mathbf{v_h}}{\partial s \partial r}(a_{ij}) \zeta_{ij}, \qquad (5)$$

where $a_{ij} = (ih_s, jh_r)$ are the nodal points and φ, ψ, η,
and ζ are the BFS basis functions. Equation 5 gives us
a $\mathscr{C}^1$ analytic solution over the set Ω.

Finally, the solution of the discrete problem associated with equation 1 is equivalent to a solution of the
linear system:

$$\mathbf{A} \cdot \mathbf{V} = \mathbf{L} \qquad (6)$$

where the matrix $\mathbf{A}$ is symmetric, definite positive, and
tridiagonal per bloc.

In figure 4.1, we use a deformable surface constrained by boundary conditions (cylinder type) to segment the inside cavity of the left ventricle.

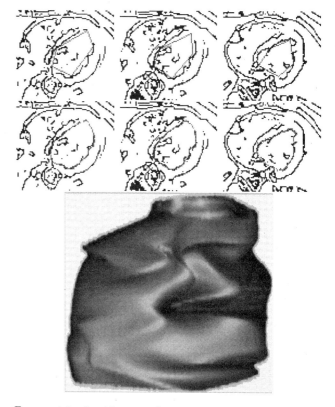

FIGURE 4.1   In this example, we use a deformable surface
constrained by boundary conditions (cylinder type) to segment the inside cavity of the left ventricle. There are overlays
of some cross-sections (in gray) of the initial estimation (top)
and the obtained surface (bottom) and a 3D representation
of the inside cavity of the left ventricle.

SOLUTION OF THE EVOLUTION PROBLEM In the previous section, we have shown that solving equation 1 can be done by solving a linear system $\mathbf{A} \cdot \mathbf{V} = \mathbf{L}$. Consequently, the discrete form of the evolution equation 2 is:

$$\frac{\partial \mathbf{V}}{\partial t} + \mathbf{A} \cdot \mathbf{V} = \mathbf{L_V}$$

This equation is solved by an implicit scheme:

$$\begin{cases} \dfrac{\mathbf{V}^t - \mathbf{V}^{t-1}}{\tau} + \mathbf{A} \cdot \mathbf{V}^t = \mathbf{L}_{\mathbf{V}^t} \\ \mathbf{V}^0 = v_0 \text{ initial estimation,} \end{cases} \quad (7)$$

where τ is the time step. The scheme is difficult to solve because the term $\mathbf{L}$ is complex. Thus we have chosen an implicit scheme for $\mathbf{V}^t$ and an explicit scheme for the forces $\mathbf{L}$. This leads to the solution of the linear system:

$$(\mathbf{Id} + \tau \mathbf{A}) \cdot \mathbf{V}^t = \mathbf{V}^{t-1} + \tau \mathbf{L}_{\mathbf{V}^{t-1}} \quad (8)$$

Finally, to find a solution to equation 2, we solve a sparse linear system with a conjugate gradient method.

EXPERIMENTAL RESULTS In figure 4.2, we show an application of the 3D deformable surfaces to segment magnetic resonance images. This figure represents some cross-section of the surface once we have reached a minimum of the functional E. Note that the model characterizes accurately the 3D edge points. In figure 4.3, a 3D representation of the solution is given.

The evolution of the surface toward the solution is shown in figure 4.4.

SNAKE SPLINES

In the previous approach, it was shown that the energy E to minimize consisted in two parts: an external potential $\mathbf{P}$ and an internal energy term. We will now show that it is possible to consider only the potential $\mathbf{P}$ provided that the internal energy is embedded in the border representation. We will present the characteristics of this representation and its application to adaptive deformation.

BORDER REPRESENTATION The border of a 3D object is a surface that we will represent with parametric spline functions. We discuss first the characteristics and interest of this representation. Then we describe its implementation and, finally, we analyze the problems posed by the local refinement of this representation.

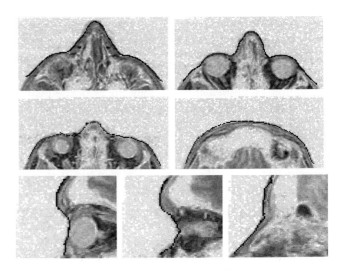

FIGURE 4.2 Here we represent the surface once we have reached a minimum of the energy E. Some vertical and horizontal cross-sections of the surface are given. They show an accurate localization of the surface at the edge points.

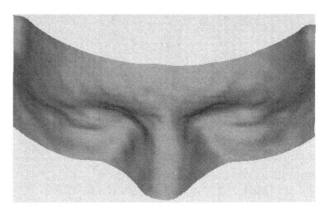

FIGURE 4.3 A 3D representation of the surface depicted in figure 4.2.

Characteristics of the parametric spline representation of the border Spline functions have long been a popular way to represent free-form curves or surfaces [52]. These functions are interesting in the frame of active contours because most of them have variational properties [53] that make them useful candidates for representing surfaces that are supposed to minimize some sort of intrinsic energy. In two dimensions, this stems very clearly from the comparison between the energy minimized by active contours and the energy minimized by splines.

Variational properties of spline curves Let C be the active contour, parametrically represented by

$$\forall y \in [1, m], \mathbf{M_j} = \sum_{i=1}^{n} B_{ij} \boldsymbol{\alpha}_i$$

where $\boldsymbol{\alpha}_i \in R^2$ and $B_{ij} = B_i[\,(j-1)/(m-1)\,]$.

This can be written under a matrix form as $\mathbf{M} = \mathbf{B}\boldsymbol{\alpha}$, where $\mathbf{M} \in R^m \times R^m, \mathbf{B} \in R^m \times R^n, \boldsymbol{\alpha} \in R^n \times R^n$.

Finding $\boldsymbol{\alpha}$ when $\mathbf{M}$ is given is a least-squares problem, in which $\|\mathbf{M} - \mathbf{B}\boldsymbol{\alpha}\|^2$ is minimized, thus implying $\boldsymbol{\alpha} = (\mathbf{B}^t\mathbf{B})^{-1}\mathbf{B}^t\mathbf{M}$, which we shall rewrite as $\boldsymbol{\alpha} = \mathbf{B}^{-1}\mathbf{M}$. Let $\mathbf{N}_i = \mathbf{M}(u_i)$, with $u_i = [\,(i-1)/(m-1)\,], i = 1, \dots, m$. A classic result for spline functions is that $\mathbf{M}(u) = [x(u), y(u)]$ minimizes

$$\int_0^1 \left\{ [x''(u)]^2 + [y''(u)]^2 \right\} du \qquad (9)$$

for all $\mathbf{M}$ belonging to $H^2([0,1]) \times H^2([0,1])$ and satisfying $\mathbf{M}(u_i) = \mathbf{N}_i, i = 1, \dots, n$.

The ratio n/m defines the "smoothing power" of the spline: If $n = m$, the spline is the interpolating spline. The smoothing is all the more important as n/m decreases. Later this feature will allow for adaptive segmentation.

Variational properties of snakes Active contours are not assigned to pass through given points. In fact, they are required to minimize the following energy:

$$\int_0^1 \alpha\left\{ [x'(u)]^2 + [y'(u)]^2 \right\} + \beta\left\{ [x''(u)]^2 + [y''(u)]^2 \right\}$$
$$+ \gamma E\{f[x(u), y(u)]\}\, du \qquad (10)$$

In this equation, f represents the initial image and E is some sort of energy adapted to image segmentation (e.g., $-\|\nabla(f)\|^2$), α, β, and γ are parameters that can be optimized to find a compromise among bending, length, and extrinsic energy.

The snake spline The expression minimized in problem 10 can be split into an intrinsic energy (involving the derivatives of the contour) and an extrinsic energy (which involves the image itself). As opposed to splines, the intrinsic energy involves first derivatives, which results in controlling the length of the contour. This effect is particularly interesting when, for some reason, the border of the object to segment does not attract the active contour (which may typically happen in flat regions of the image, where no gradient can attract the active contour). The absence of first-derivative terms in problem 9 is not dramatic, if some technique for moving the curve in those flat regions is

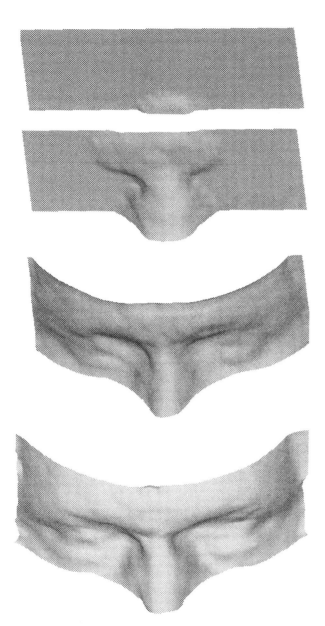

FIGURE 4.4   Evolution of the 3D surface "falling" on a 3D MRI image of a head. The initial surface is a plane on the border of the image.

$$\forall u \in [0, 1], \mathbf{M}(u) = \sum_{i=1}^{n} B_i(u) \boldsymbol{\alpha_i}$$

where

$$\boldsymbol{\alpha_i} \in R^2.$$

The B_i are the basis spline functions. For cubic spline functions, they are piecewise third-degree polynomials, which differ only by translations. This implies provided. We will see that this is possible and, more-over, in a local way. The second derivative terms are the most interesting as they are responsible for the smooth aspect of the active contour. Obviously, these terms are identical in problems 9 and 10. This stresses the proximity between active contours and splines.

The basic idea of a snake spline is therefore to minimize only the extrinsic energy, looking for the solution in an appropriate spline space that will embed minimization of some intrinsic energy. We will define a *snake spline* as the element of a spline space that minimizes

$$\int_0^1 E\{f[x(u),y(u)]\}\, du \qquad (11)$$

where f is the image and E is an extrinsic energy. A later section of this chapter proposes a constructive implementation of this definition.

The major advantage of snake splines over classic active contours lies in the fact that problem 11 is much simpler than problem 10 for two principal reasons: First, the dimension of the space is dramatically reduced. Indeed, the dimension of the functional space in problem 10 is infinity, whereas it can be completely controlled in problem 11 (the interesting adaptive consequences of this versatility will be emphasized in later section). Second, the system to solve is much simpler as it no longer involves the derivatives of the parametric representation of the border of the object. We will show further that it results in an ordinary differential equation that can be solved very easily.

PRACTICAL EVALUATION OF A SNAKE SPLINE   Each of the numerous spline functions designed for a computer-aided design (CAD) system can be adapted to become a snake spline, according to problem 11, yet the most interesting will be those that minimize an energy with a strong physical meaning or those that are computationally interesting. Besides, an adequate representation of the snake spline must be selected.

Depending on the use of the spline, various representations have been proposed [54, 55]. Representations based on control vertices, initially popularized by Bezier [56] have proved very interesting from a computational point of view, because recursive subdivision algorithms, which can easily be optimized on computers [57, 58], perfectly suit this representation. We will present more details on such a representation, briefly reviewing a 2D instance and its generalization to 3D through tensorial products and finally analyzing how

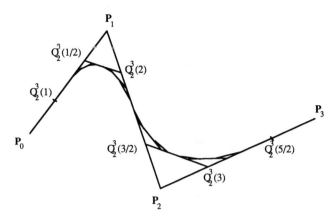

FIGURE 4.5   Subdivided control polygon $\{R_k\}$ formed from the initial control polygon $\{P_k\}$, for a second-degree spline curve.

surfaces with poles can be dealt with, because the next section of this chapter will employ this representation as a basis for adding more flexibility to the spline.

2D spline subdivision algorithm   Let us consider a piecewise quadratic spline, which will therefore be C^1. This spline is represented initially by a control polygon of $n+1$ vertices $\{\mathbf{P}_i\}$, $i = 0, n$. The subdivision algorithm consists in dividing each segment $\mathbf{P}_i\mathbf{P}_{i+1}$ into three subsegments of equal length, thus providing $2n$ vertices $\{Q_i\}$, $i = 0, \ldots, 2n - 1$ (figure 4.5). This process can be iterated. It can easily be proved that the set of points that it generates converges toward the spline, and this technique can be generalized to higher-order splines.

Surface representation through tensorial products of splines When the object we have to segment lies in a 3D space, its border is a surface that we will parametrically represent by $\mathbf{M}(u,v) = [x(u,v), y(u,v), z(u,v)]$, with

$$(u,v) \in [0,1] \times [0,1]$$

The values of x, y, and z will be obtained by tensorial products of unidimensional splines [e.g., $x(u,v) = s_u(u) \times s_v(v)$, where s_u and s_v are unidimensional splines]. The interest of these functions is that they can be very easily constructed. The previous subdivision algorithm readily applies: One merely has to subdivide first the lines and then the set of columns corresponding to the new mesh obtained by the first subdivision.

The drawback of these approaches is that the minimization properties satisfied by these tensorial splines usually have no physical meaning. For instance, in the case of a bicubic spline x, it minimizes

$$\int_{[0,1]\times[0,1]} \left| \frac{\partial^4 x}{\partial^2 u \partial^2 v} \right|^2 du\, dv$$

However, we will see further that this regularizing energy is sufficient and that it is not necessary to use "thin-plate splines" [59], which actually minimize the real generalization of the bending energy:

$$\int_{[0,1]\times[0,1]} \left| \frac{\partial^2 x}{\partial u^2} \right|^2 + 2 \left| \frac{\partial^2 x}{\partial u \partial v} \right|^2 + \left| \frac{\partial^2 x}{\partial v^2} \right|^2 du\, dv$$

Indeed, the corresponding spline is not separable and is defined with log functions. This is an important drawback for our application, because such functions have infinite support, which makes computation time-consuming and which we will prove would be inconvenient for adaptive local refinement.

We showed in previous work [60] that such splines can also be applied to closed surfaces, even when "holes" are present.

LOCAL REFINEMENT OF A SNAKE SPLINE   As opposed to classic splines, which are used to represent a given function and are not supposed to evolve with time, snake splines are supposed to move progressively toward an a priori unknown shape. Besides, classic splines have a "bending energy" (corresponding to problem 9) that is a priori completely controlled by the number and position of the control vertices. In the case of snake splines, the desired flexibility is not known. It can depend on local characteristics of the border (which may be smooth for some parts of the object, thus requiring few control vertices, and rough for some other parts, which would imply more control vertices). We therefore need a refinement algorithm, which will give more flexibility to the initial spline. We propose to modify slightly the initial subdivision algorithm, to turn it into the desired snake spline refinement algorithm.

In the subdivision algorithm, the control vertices are completely defined at each level of subdivision by the set of vertices of the previous level and by proportionality rules that correspond to the type of spline. To provide flexibility, the refinement algorithm will only give their "autonomy" to some selected control vertices, which means that instead of being strictly defined by proportionality rules, these control vertices will become real degrees of freedom, as the $n + 1$ initial control points. We will call the set of the initial control vertices, completed with these freed control points, a

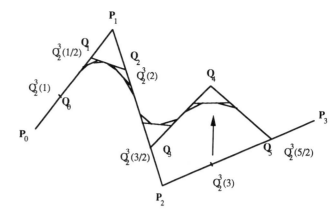

FIGURE 4.6   Refined control polygon $\{R_k\}$ formed from previous control polygons $\{P_k, Q_k, R_k\}$, for a second-degree spline curve. The generalized set of control points is $\{P_0, P_1, P_2, P_3, Q_2, R_3\}$.

generalized set of control points. Figure 4.6 shows such a refinement, where vertices $\mathbf{Q}_2$ and $\mathbf{R}_3$ have been freed. The rest of the algorithm is not modified. It can therefore easily be seen that the new curve keeps the same continuity characteristics as the initial spline but that locally more flexibility has been provided. This technique can, of course, be generalized to spline surfaces with no major difficulty.

We now have to make use of this new flexibility, which will be described in the following section.

EVOLUTION OF A SNAKE SPLINE IN A STRENGTH FIELD   We saw in the previous section that a snake spline minimizes problem 11 in the functional space defined by a generalized set of control points and by a subdivision algorithm. We shall now see how such a snake spline can be constructed, which are the adaptive features of the proposed method, and how it is possible to represent topologically complex objects.

Dynamic construction of the snake spline   For the sake of simplicity, we shall present this construction in the 2D case. The tensorial product structure makes generalization to 3D images very easy. The image f in problem 11 is usually discrete. It therefore is not inconvenient to use a discrete version of this equation, which reads:

$$\sum_{i=1}^{m} E[f(\mathbf{M_i})] = \sum_{i=1}^{m} V(\mathbf{M_i}) \qquad (12)$$

where $\mathbf{M} = \{\mathbf{M_i}, i = 1, m\}$ is the image of a set of m equidistant points in the parametric space and where V

corresponds to the potential from which the strength field derives.

To minimize equation 12, we would like each point $\mathbf{M_j}$ to move into the direction of strength $\mathbf{F_j} = -\|\nabla V(\mathbf{M_j})\|^2$. We shall consider that the position of $\mathbf{M_j}$ depends on time t. Deriving $\mathbf{M_j}$ with respect to t, this implies:

$$\forall j \in \{1, m\}, \frac{d\mathbf{M_j}}{dt} = \mathbf{F_j}$$

or, in matrix form,

$$\frac{d\mathbf{M}}{dt} = \mathbf{F}$$

Let $\mathbf{P} = \{\mathbf{P}_i, i = 1, k\}$ be the generalized set of control points. The subdivision algorithm ensures that $\mathbf{M} = \mathbf{BP}$, where $\mathbf{B}$ is a matrix that characterizes the subdivision algorithm at the chosen precision level. $\mathbf{P}$ can be considered to be the solution to the minimization of $\|\mathbf{M} - \mathbf{BP}\|^2$, known to be $\mathbf{P} = (\mathbf{B}^t\mathbf{B})^{-1}\mathbf{B}^t\mathbf{M}$, which can be rewritten as $\mathbf{P} = \mathbf{B}^{-1}\mathbf{M}$. Therefore, if $\mathbf{M}$ depends on time, $\mathbf{P}$ also depends on t and can be derived with respect to t. We then obtain:

$$\frac{d\mathbf{P}}{dt} = \mathbf{B}^{-1}\frac{d\mathbf{M}}{dt} = \mathbf{B}^{-1}\mathbf{F} \qquad (13)$$

This means that if the curve C is put into a strength field, it will evolve with time until a balance position is found. As with the classic snake approach, two kinds of energy account for the final shape of C: the energy corresponding to the strength field (extrinsic energy) and the energy corresponding to the minimization of the sum of the squares of the second derivatives of the spline functions (intrinsic energy). However, unlike in the classic snake methods, it is not necessary to deal explicitly with the intrinsic energy, as it is self-contained in the definition of the spline. Therefore, the resulting systems will be much easier, because they will take into account only the extrinsic energy.

Adaptive evolution of the snake spline We have seen previously how a spline can evolve in a strength field deriving from V. Introducing V into equation 13, we obtain:

$$\frac{d\mathbf{P}}{dt} = \mathbf{B}^{-1}\frac{d\mathbf{M}}{dt} = \mathbf{B}^{-1}\mathbf{F} = \mathbf{B}^{-1}\mathbf{V}(\mathbf{M}) = \mathbf{B}^{-1}\mathbf{V}(\mathbf{BP}) \quad (14)$$

This is an ordinary differential equation, in which the unknowns are the control vertices $\mathbf{P}$.

The initial values of $\mathbf{P}$ will depend on the knowledge on the object. If no a priori knowledge is available, the initial curve will fit roughly the limits of the image. For 3D image segmentation, we will take the aforementioned spherical mesh of $n = 6$ control points as a starting point. The method will then behave adaptively. The differential system represented by equation 14 is solved with n coefficients, corresponding to n knots $\mathbf{M_j} = 1, \ldots, n$ until they stop evolving. At that time, the refinement algorithm is applied. Two kinds of stop criteria can be used: testing a cost of the contour (e.g., integral of the potential along the contour) or testing the evolution of the coefficients $\boldsymbol{\alpha}$. We have found the latter easier to implement.

Two other adaptive features of the method, which have not yet been tested, might prove interesting. First, it is possible to adapt the number m of points on which the strengths are computed according to the number of knots of the spline. Then, the kind of function g to use as a convolution with the initial potential should also depend on the number n of knots: When n is low, the curve is supposed to be far away from the correct position. Therefore, g should be broad, to increase the sensitivity of the curve to the high but potentially distant gradients. On the contrary, when n is high, g should be more narrow, to be able to fit mean gradients.

A priori knowledge can be input in the form of a CAD model of the object to segment. This has not yet been tested but should prove interesting. In that case, the first problem is to estimate as well as possible the six parameters (translations and rotations) for fitting the model with no modification to the real image. This is a rigid matching problem, for which solutions have been proposed. Once this rigid matching has been done, an elastic matching can take place, using the method previously described.

This approach may be modified (see [60]) to take into account topologically complex objects. The method was tested on sets of parallel slices of CT or MRI scans. The CT slices were 1 mm thick and discretized in 512×512 pixels, each of which covered approximately 0.25 mm^2 in surface area. We processed 50 such slices. Figure 4.7 shows the deformation of the surface toward its aim.

This snake splines method has proved very efficient for topologically complex object representation and segmentation. It presents interesting features in terms of hierarchic representation of an object that make it a promising candidate for interactive design of

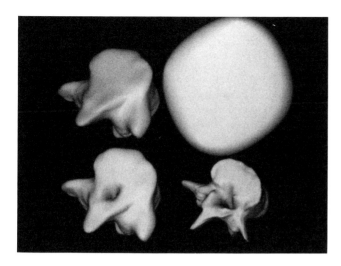

FIGURE 4.7   Segmentation of vertebra defined by a set of CT slices. Four steps of the deformation of a roughly spherical snake spline toward the vertebra are shown.

complex surfaces. In addition, it has intrinsic properties of parallelism that allow for massively parallel implementation.

Conclusion

Efficient 3D segmentation is a critical requirement for any integrated surgery system, as it is the basis for both surgical planning and anatomy-based registration. Some specific tools are becoming available in which user interaction is minimized. Such tools are user-friendly, yet much work remains to allow for a flexible and generic semiinteractive 3D segmentation method. A promising issue with respect to this challenge is the possibility of unifying segmentation and fusion, which is exhibited by nonrigid matching [61].

ACKNOWLEDGMENTS   This research is supported in part by Digital Equipment Corporation.

REFERENCES

[1] MARR, D., 1982. *Vision.* Cambridge, Mass.: MIT Press.

[2] AYACHE, N., J. D. BOISSONNAT, E. BRUNET, L. COHEN, J. P. CHIEZE, B. GEIGER, O. MONGA, J. M. ROCCHISANI, and P. SANDER, 1989. Building highly structured volume representations in 3D medical images. In the *Third International Symposium on Computer Assisted Radiology,* Berlin. H. U. Lemke, ed. Berlin: Springer-Verlag.

[3] ROSENFELD, A., and A. KAK, 1976. *Digital Image Processing.* New York: Academic.

[4] MARR, D., and E. HILDRETH, 1980. Theory of edge detection. *Proc. R. Soc. Lond. [B]* 207:187–217.

[5] CANNY, J., 1983. Finding edges and lines in images. Technical rep. 720. Cambridge, Mass.: MIT Artificial Intelligence Laboratory.

[6] SHEN, J., and S. CASTAN, 1986. An optimal linear operator for edge detection. In *Conference on Vision and Pattern Recognition.* IEEE.

[7] DERICHE, R., 1987. Using Canny's criteria to derive a recursively implemented optimal edge detector. *Int. J. Comput. Vision* 1(2).

[8] MONGA, O., and R. DERICHE, 1989. 3D edge detection using recursive filtering. In *IEEE Proceedings of Computer Vision and Pattern Recognition.* San Diego: IEEE.

[9] MONGA, O., R. DERICHE, G. MALANDAIN, and J. P. COCQUEREZ, 1990. Recursive filtering and edge closing: Two primary tools for 3D edge detection. In *First European Conference on Computer Vision,* Nice, France. (Research rep. INRIA 1103.)

[10] MONGA, O., and R. DERICHE, 1986. A new three dimensional boundary detection. In *International Conference on Pattern Recognition,* Paris.

[11] DERICHE, R., 1989. Fast algorithms for low level vision. *IEEE Trans. Pattern Anal. Mach. Intell.*

[12] HILDRETH, E. C., 1980. Implementation of a theory of edge detection. Tech. rep. AI-TR-579. Cambridge, Mass.: MIT.

[13] TORRE, V., and T. POGGIO, 1986. On edge detection. *IEEE Trans. Pattern Anal. Mach. Intell.*

[14] BERZINS, V., 1984. Accuracy of laplacian edge detectors. *Comput. Vision Graphics Image Proc.* 27:195–210.

[15] DERICHE, D., and J. P. COCQUEREZ, 1988. An efficient method to build early image description. In *International Conference on Pattern Recognition.*

[16] GIRAUDON, G., 1987. An efficient edge chaining algorithm. In *Fifth Scandinavian Conference on Image Analysis,* Stockholm.

[17] FUCHS, H., Z. M. KEDEM, and S. P. USELTON, 1977. Optimal surface reconstruction from planar contours. *Graphic Image Proc. Comm. ACM,* Vol. 20, pp. 693–702.

[18] BOISSONNAT, J. D., 1986. Shape reconstruction from planar cross-sections. Tech. rep. 546, I.N.R.I.A., Centre de Rocquencourt.

[19] MARTELLI, A., 1972. Edge detection using heuristic search methods. *Comput. Graphics Image Vision Proc.* Vol. 1.

[20] KASS, M., A. WITKIN, and D. TERZOPOULOS, 1987. Snakes: Active contour models. In *Int. J. of Computer Vision,* pp. 1:321–331.

[21] OLHANDER, R., K. PRICE, and D. R. REDDY, 1978. Picture segmentation using a recursive region splitting method. In *Comput. Graphics Image Proc.* (8):313–333.

[22] OHTA, Y., KANADE, and T. SAKAI, 1980. Color information for region segmentation. *Comput. Graphics Image Proc.* (13):222–241.

[23] CHOW, C. K., and T. KANEKO, 1972. Boundary detection of radiographic images by a thresholding method. In *Frontiers of Pattern Recognition,* S. Watanebe, ed. New York: Academic, pp. 61–82.

[24] WATANABE, S., and CYBEST Group, 1974. An automated apparatus for cancer prescreening: Cybest. In *Comput. Graphics Image Proc.* (3):350–358.

[25] WESZKA, J. S., R. N. NAGEL, and A. ROSENFELD, 1974. A threshold selection technique. *IEEE Trans. Comput.* (C-23): 1322–1326.

[26] WESZKA, J. S., 1978. A survey of threshold selection techniques. *Comput. Graphics Image Proc.* (7):259–265.

[27] BRYANT, J., 1979. On the clustering of multidimensional pictorial data. *Pattern Recogn.* (11):115–125.

[28] ASANO, T., and N. YOKOYA, 1981. Image segmentation schema for low level computer vision. In *Proceedings of International Conference on Pattern Recognition* (14):267–273.

[29] NAGAO, M., and M. MATSUYAMA, 1983. Structural image analysis.

[30] HARALICK, R. M., and I. DINSTEIN, 1995. A spatial clustering procedure for multi-image data. *IEEE Trans. on Circuits and Systems.*

[31] HARALICK, R. M., and S. G. SHAPIRO, 1985. Survey: Image segmentation techniques. *Comput. Vision Graphics Image Proc.* (29):100–132.

[32] MUERLE, J., and D. ALLEN, 1968. Experimental evaluation of techniques for automatic segmentation of objects in a complex scenes. In *Pictorial Pattern Recognition*, G. Cheng et al., eds. Washington, D.C.: Thompson, pp. 3–13.

[33] BRICE, C., and C. FENEMA, 1970. Scene analysis using regions. *Artif. Intell.* (1):205–226.

[34] HOROWITZ, S. L., and T. PAVLIDIS, 1976. Picture segmentation by a tree transversal algorithm. *Assoc. Comput. Machine* 23:368–388.

[35] PONG, T. C., L. G. SHAPIRO, L. T. WATSON, and R. M. HARALICK, 1980. Experiments in segmentation using a facet model region grower. *Comput. Vision Graphics Image Proc.* (25), 1980.

[36] HARALICK, R. M., and L. T. WATSON, 1981. A facet model for image data. *Comput. Graphics Image Proc.* (15): 113–129.

[37] MONGA, O., and N. KESKES, 1986. A hierarchical algorithm for the segmentation of 3-D images. In *Proceedings of the Eighth International Conference on Pattern Recognition*, Paris.

[38] Monga, O., 1989. An optimal region growing algorithm for image segmentation. *Int. J. Pattern Recogn. Artif. Intell.* 1(3):351–376.

[39] TERZOPOULOS, D., A. WITKIN, and M. KASS, 1988. Constraints on deformable models: Recovering 3D shape and nonrigid motion. *A.I.J.* 36:91–123.

[40] TERZOPOULOS, D., 1987. On matching deformable models to images. In *Topical meeting on machine vision* (Technical Digest Series) Vol. 12. Optical Society of America, pp. 160–163.

[41] ZUCKER, S. W., and R. M. HUMMEL, 1981. A three-dimensional edge operator. *IEEE Trans. Pattern Anal. Mach. Intel. (PAMI)* 3(3):324–331.

[42] AYACHE, N., J. D. BOISSONNAT, L. COHEN, B. GEIGER, O. MONGA, J. LEVY-VEHEL, and P. SANDER, 1990. Steps toward the automatic interpretation of 3d images. *NATO ASI Series on 3D Imaging in Medicine*, F 60:107–120.

[43] GUÉZIEC, A., and N. AYACHE, 1992. Smoothing and matching of 3D-space curves. In *Proceedings of the Second European Computer Vision*. Santa Margherita Ligure, Italy. Berlin: Springer Verlag, pp. 620–629.

[44] SANDER, P. T., and S. W. ZUCKER, 1990. Inferring surface trace and differential structure from 3-D images. *IEEE Trans. Pattern Anal. Mach. Intell.* 12:833–854.

[45] Kass. M., A. Witkin, and D. Terzopoulos, 1987. Snakes: Active contour models. In *Int. J. of Computer Vision*, pp. 1:321–331

[46] COHEN, L. D., and I. COHEN, 1990. A finite element method applied to new active contour models and 3-D reconstruction from cross sections. In *IEEE Proceedings of the Third International Conference on Computer Vision*, Osaka, Japan, pp. 587–591.

[47] TERZOPOULOS, D., A. WITKIN, and M. KASS, 1987. Symmetry-seeking models for 3D object reconstruction. In *Proceedings of the First International Conference on Computer Vision*, pp. 269–276.

[48] BOISSONNAT, J. D., 1988. Shape reconstruction from planar cross-sections. *Comput. Vision Graphics Image Proc.* 44: 1–29.

[49] COHEN, L. D., 1991. On active contour models and balloons. *Comput. Vision Graphics Image Proc.* 53(2):211–218.

[50] COHEN, I., D. COHEN, and N. AYACHE, 1992. Using deformable surfaces to segment 3-D images and infer differential structures. *Comput. Vision Graphics Image Proc.* 56(2):242–263.

[51] CIARLET, P. G., 1987. *The Finite Element Methods for Elliptic Problems*. Amsterdam: North-Holland.

[52] LE MÉHAUTE, A., P. J. LAURENT, and L. L. SCHUMAKER, 1991. *Curves and Surfaces*. New York: Academic.

[53] LAURENT, P. J., 1987. *Approximation et Optimisation*. Paris: Hermann.

[54] DE BOOR, C., 1978. *A Practical Guide to Splines*. Berlin: Springer-Verlag.

[55] BEATY, J. C., R. H. BARTELS, and B. A. BARSKY, 1987. *Mathématiques et CAO, B-Splines*. Paris: Hermes.

[56] BÉZIER, P., 1987. *Mathématiques et CAO, Courbes et Surfaces*. Paris: Hermes.

[57] COHEN, E., T. LYCHE, and R. F. RIESENFELD, 1978. Discrete b-splines and subdivision techniques in computer aided design and computer graphics. *Comput. Graphics Image Proc.* 1 14:87–111.

[58] SABLONNIÈRE, P., 1978. Spline and bézier polygons associated with a polynomial curve. *Computer Aided Design* 10: 257–261.

[59] DUCHON, J., 1976. Interpolation des fonctions de deux variables suivant le principe de la flexion des plaques minces. *RAIRO Analyse Numérique* 10:5–12.

[60] LEITNER, F., and P. CINQUIN, 1993. From snake and splines to snake-splines. In *Lecture Notes in Computer Science 708: Geometric Reasoning for Perception and Action*, C. Laugier, ed. Berlin: Springer-Verlag, pp. 264–281.

[61] SZELISKI, R., and S. LAVALLÉE, 1993. Matching 3-D anatomical surfaces with non-rigid deformations using octree splines. In *Proceedings S.P.I.E. Geometric Methods in Computer Vision*, San Diego. SPIE, 306–315.

Registration

THIS SECTION IS devoted to the problem of matching all the geometric data available for a patient in a unique coordinate system. This problem is commonly referred to as *registration*, although other words, such as *co-registration*, *matching*, and *fusion*, also are used. Registration is a crucial technology in computer-integrated surgery for three reasons. First, the registration of medical data allows the surgeon to plan an operation using all the available information. Second, registration of preoperative and postoperative data is crucial for individual patient follow-up and statistical analysis of results. Third, registration of preoperative and intraoperative data provides the crucial step required to relate the "virtual patient" of surgical planning with the actual patient on the operating table. Ideally, all patient data should be correlated with the physical space of the real surgery and made available to the surgeon. Once intraoperative registration is accomplished, the results are used in several ways. In navigation systems, the position of a surgical tool is typically depicted on a 2D or 3D intraoperative display. For such displays, it is essential to link images and surgical tools accurately.

In this section, three chapters present the basic concepts and algorithms for registration. However, many chapters in the second part of this book, applications, deal with this crucial problem and present some techniques that allow for effective linking between the surgical planning and the patient during surgery. Such examples may be found especially in the sections devoted to neurosurgery, orthopaedics, and ear, nose, and throat surgery. In the first chapter, "Registration for Computer-Integrated Surgery," Lavallée reviews the registration problem. A general framework is

presented that includes three steps: definition of a relation between reference systems, extraction of reference features, and minimization of a disparity function between features. Existing methods are reviewed according to the geometric representations of the selected features. For instance, several classes of 3D surface registration are presented.

The second chapter, "Correlative Analysis of Three-Dimensional Brain Images," by Evans et al., focuses on registration of brain images. Results obtained at the Montreal Neurological Institute (MNI) over several years using registration of positron emission tomography (PET), MRI, and atlas images are presented in this chapter. The correlation of brain images for neurologic and neurosurgical purposes is detailed. In particular, authors discuss the need for registration between morphologic images such as CT or MRI, which give the shape of anatomic structures, and functional images such as single photon emission computed tomography (SPECT) and PET, which give information about the activity of a region. The correlative technique is used routinely clinically at MNI.

The third chapter, "Anatomy Based Registration of Three-Dimensional Medical Images, Range Images, X-Ray Projections, and Three-Dimensional Models Using Octree Splines," by Lavallée et al., relates the possibility of using only reference anatomic structures to register images and physical spaces. This is extremely important as it avoids the need for using external fiducial markers. For instance, authors demonstrate how a pair of x-rays can be used to register the position of the patient during surgery with preoperative images. The chapter presents algorithms for rigid registration of 3D surfaces with 3D surfaces or with 2D projections. Extensions to the nonrigid case also are proposed. This general method of anatomy-based registration can be used in many applications.

In conclusion, this section demonstrates that accurate rigid registration truly is possible and that it has been tested in many cases. The real issue now is to provide efficient solutions for elastic registration—for instance, to track deformations due to surgery, respiration, and evolution of structures. This is a much more difficult and open problem than rigid registration but, in view of its potential clinical payoff, it will be the focus of considerable future research.

5 Registration for Computer-Integrated Surgery: Methodology, State of the Art

STÉPHANE LAVALLÉE

IN CIS, REGISTRATION of all the information available for a given patient is an essential step. Making all the information available in the surgical theater through the use of more or less advanced picture archiving and communication systems is necessary but not sufficient. Particularly, for most of the systems presented in this book, a crucial step is to estimate an accurate relation between preoperative images and intraoperative systems. Some authors have proposed the use of heavy imaging devices such as CT or MRI directly in the surgical theater (see, for instance, Huck and Baer, 1980; Kwoh et al., 1988). This approach removes the need for any registration. However, these devices are not easily available in standard surgical theaters, and imaging systems of radiology departments already have difficulty meeting current demands. Another approach is to move the patient until some reference position relative to imaging systems or operating reference systems is reached. For instance, in external radiotherapy, registration of the patient during all irradiation sessions often is reached through the use of crosses or lines drawn on the patient's skin and aligned with laser planes that give the irradiation coordinate system. These methods are robust, but they obviously lack accuracy. A more convenient approach is to use intraoperative sensors, which can be systems already available in surgical theaters (e.g., x-ray radioscopy, ultrasonography, microscopic or endoscopic imaging systems) or low-cost vision sensors (see chapter 1), followed by the use of software registration techniques presented in this chapter to make preoperative images virtually available during surgery.

In many applications, using only one type of information intraoperatively is insufficient. Registration procedures then are required to allow the surgeon or the physician to take the specificity of each information into account. The advantages for diagnostic purposes of such registration between multimodal information has already been described by many authors. For instance, positron emission tomography (PET) or single photon emission computed tomography (SPECT) images provide functional information that is necessary to correlate with anatomic images such as CT or MRI (Pelizzari et al., 1989; Kramer et al., 1992). The registration of several MRI scans taken at different times for the same patient enables one to follow the evolution of a tumor. Likewise, the registration of vertebra models derived from CT with dynamic x-rays can be employed to observe accurately the motion of spine without any approximation (Brunie and Lavallée, 1992).

Registration for CIS requires more accuracy than for diagnosis. In addition, not only images but also operating systems and tools must be registered (mechanical or noncontact intraoperative navigation systems, robots, irradiation systems, etc.). Therefore, the problem addressed in this chapter is not only to match images but also to register physical spaces. A typical instance is stereotactic neurosurgery where in preoperative MRI and CT provide accurate information about the location of a lesion, intraoperative or preoperative angiograms enable the surgeon to find some safe path for a biopsy needle, a brain atlas gives statistical information required for functional neurosurgery and, finally, some guiding system linked to all images enables the surgeon to follow the planned trajectory (Henri, Collins, and Peters, 1991; Lavallée et al., 1992).

Basically, several kinds of data may have to be registered:

- Preoperative data

Medical images are usually 2D or 3D images: x-ray, ultrasound images, CT, MRI, PET, SPECT, and so on. They often constitute the basis of the surgical planning.

Models are usually 3D atlases, or surface models, and they have a statistical relevance.

Preoperative positioning information is linked directly to medical images and its unique purpose is to provide information for subsequent registration between medical images and intraoperative systems. This is necessary only when such positioning information is not available on medical images. A typical instance is functional imaging (e.g., SPECT, magnetoencephalography [MEG]).

- Intraoperative data

Medical images obtained intraoperatively give information useful to CIS for three reasons. First, they help the surgeon complete the surgical planning (for instance, intraoperative angiograms help to define a safe path). Second, they provide a real-time intraoperative control of the surgery (e.g., some vascular or other incidents that may occur during surgery are sometimes detectable on intraoperative images). Third, they give positioning information that can be used for registration purposes.

Intraoperative positioning information, provided by various sensors in 3D, indicates the position of organs so that an accurate registration can be performed via optical, ultrasound, mechanical, or electromagnetic 3D localizers, range imaging systems, and the like.

Intraoperative guiding systems, which may be passive 3D localizers or active robots, have to be registered with the images on which the surgical planning has been defined.

- Postoperative data, which is similar to preoperative data, have to be registered to measure the efficiency of an intervention and to update the models.

Obviously, not all applications need to register all the types of information mentioned. A typical application will have to register preoperative CT images with a 3D passive or active manipulator during surgery.

We can now make an important distinction between registration and extrinsic calibration. For each modality of information, pre-, intra-, and postoperative medical imaging system, anatomic atlas, and intraoperative system, a coordinate system is defined. The purpose of calibration and registration is to link the coordinate systems together—that is, to build a graph of relations among all the coordinate systems. If two coordinate systems are rigidly connected to a same object, then their relation will be estimated through calibration procedures; if these coordinate systems are totally independent, they are linked through registration procedures. For instance, to estimate a relation between an intraoperative x-ray device and an intraoperative robotic arm is a calibration problem, whereas to estimate a relation between preoperative CT and preoperative MRI is a registration problem. This chapter focuses on registration problems, which are specific to CIS, while reference to calibration problems can be found in many books and articles on robotics and computer vision.

Over the past few years, many solutions have been proposed to deal with image-matching problems in general, not only in the medical field but also in computer vision (see Besl and Jain, 1985; Besl, 1990; for surveys in that field). A framework and a survey of image registration techniques in general is presented in Brown (1992). However, in this chapter, we are concerned with registration of 3D spaces. The registration of 2D images is not addressed.

In the following sections, we propose a general framework for registration based on three steps:

1. Definition of a relation between coordinate systems

2. Segmentation of reference features and definition of a disparity (or similarity) function between extracted features

3. Optimization of the disparity (or similarity) function

Once this framework is defined, we will review existing methods according to the different classes of reference features. Finally, a typical algorithm for 3D/3D registration is presented.

Definition of a relation between reference systems

DEFINITION OF REFERENCE SYSTEMS

Registration between two modalities of information (A and B) is defined by the estimation of a relation between two coordinate systems (Ref_A and Ref_B) associated with each mode of information. The first step is to define a coordinate system for each information modality and to have a model that links raw sensor data to coordinates given in the defined coordinate system, through intrinsic calibration procedures. CT, SPECT, and PET images usually are assumed to present no distortion and to be accurately calibrated, but this is not always the case for MRI and digital radiography. To use MRI for accurate surgical planning, distortions could be compensated in two ways: A first solution is to place a calibration cage around the patient and to compute a 3D warping function from images of calibration points (see, for instance, Schad et al., 1987, and Gastambide, 1992, for preliminary attempts). A second solution, not yet developed, would be to use CT images as reference images and to perform an elastic matching between CT and MRI, in order to transform magnetic resonance images in the nondistorted CT space. Both solutions need further investigation. Thus far, the only requirement with MRI is to tune the device accurately in order to make the images as linear as possible, which was shown to be accurate in many cases (e.g., see Zhang et al., 1990, and Maurer et al., 1993). To use digital radiography (or equivalent radioscopy) for surgical planning or for registration, it is necessary to correct distortions of these images. For instance, the $\mathcal{N}$-planes bicubic spline (NPBS) method uses spline approximation to correct local distortions (Champleboux et al., 1992).

To give an example, we associate a coordinate system, $\mathrm{Ref_{3D}}$, with CT preoperative images, and a coordinate system, $\mathrm{Ref_{sensor}}$, with an intraoperative sensor (for instance, x-ray images). Now, the objective is to estimate the transformation $\mathbf{T}$ between $\mathrm{Ref_{sensor}}$ and $\mathrm{Ref_{3D}}$.

DEFINITION OF A RELATION

In the most general case, the transformation $\mathbf{T}$ is simply a function that transforms coordinates $\mathbf{M_B} = (X_B, Y_B, Z_B)$ in $\mathrm{Ref_B}$ into coordinates $\mathbf{M_A} = (X_A, Y_A, Z_A)$ in $\mathrm{Ref_A}$, taking an index t into account, which is usually the time:

$$(\mathbf{M_A}) = \mathbf{T}(\mathbf{M_B}, t) \tag{1}$$

However, the evolution of transformations with time has not been widely studied yet (except for strictly modeling applications). Therefore, we limit our survey to static transformations (or discrete series of transformations).

RIGID-BODY TRANSFORMATIONS In most registration problems, the transformation $\mathbf{T}$ is a transformation between the same structures observed by different sensors; therefore, it is a rigid-body transformation. A transformation can be considered as rigid provided that deformations are negligible with respect to the required accuracy. Typically, the registration between preoperative CT, MRI, and SPECT images and intraoperative images taken at the beginning of an operation is modeled by rigid-body transformations.

Rigid-body transformations can be represented by a three-parameter translation vector $\mathbf{t}$ and a 3×3 rotation matrix $\mathbf{R}$ that depends on three parameters. Several possibilities exist to represent rotation matrices. The most popular representation uses Euler angles corresponding to three successive rotations with angles ϕ, θ, ψ, around x, y, and z axes (or z, x, and z with true Euler notations):

$$\mathbf{R} = \begin{bmatrix} \cos\psi\cos\theta & -\sin\psi\cos\theta & \sin\theta \\ \cos\psi\sin\theta\sin\phi + \sin\psi\cos\phi & -\sin\psi\sin\theta\sin\phi + \cos\psi\cos\phi & -\cos\theta\sin\phi \\ -\cos\psi\sin\theta\cos\phi + \sin\psi\sin\phi & \sin\psi\sin\theta\cos\phi + \cos\psi\sin\phi & \cos\theta\cos\phi \end{bmatrix} \tag{2}$$

The drawbacks of the Euler representation are first, that the matrix coefficients are very nonlinear and, second, that this representation is not differentiable at some singular values (where $\theta = -\pi/2$) (Ayache, 1991).

Another well-known representation makes use of unit quaternions (Faugeras and Hebert, 1986). The unit quaternion is a four-component vector $\mathbf{q} = [q_0 q_1 q_2 q_3]^t$, where $q_0 \geq 0$, and $q_0^2 + q_1^2 + q_2^2 + q_3^2 = 1$. Each unit quaternion corresponds uniquely to a 3×3 rotation matrix:

$$\mathbf{R} = \begin{bmatrix} q_0^2 + q_1^2 - q_2^2 - q_3^2 & 2(q_1 q_2 - q_0 q_3) & 2(q_1 q_3 + q_0 q_2) \\ 2(q_1 q_2 + q_0 q_3) & q_0^2 + q_2^2 - q_1^2 - q_3^2 & 2(q_2 q_3 - q_0 q_1) \\ 2(q_1 q_3 - q_0 q_2) & 2(q_2 q_3 + q_0 q_1) & q_0^2 + q_3^2 - q_1^2 - q_2^2 \end{bmatrix} \tag{3}$$

Unit quaternions have some advantages, among which are simple derivatives and efficient formulations to find direct rotation matrices for points-matching problems (Faugeras and Hebert 1986; Horn, 1987; Besl and McKay, 1992). However, for more general applications, it is necessary to use a nonminimal four-parameter representation, which requires to normalize quaternions at repetitive steps of a minimization algorithm.

Therefore, it is recommended one use another much less known representation that is minimal and avoids singularities: the rotation vector $\mathbf{r} = (r_x, r_y, r_z)$, where the direction of $\mathbf{r}$ is the rotation axis and the norm of $\mathbf{r}$ is the rotation angle (see all details in Ayache, 1991).

ELASTIC TRANSFORMATIONS   In other cases, the transformation $\mathbf{T}$ has to take deformations into account. However, elastic matching is a wide area with many applications. Therefore, to define elastic transformations, it is necessary first to detail which are the applications. The main objectives of elastic matching in CIS are as follows:

• To register data of different patients in the same database. Therefore, it becomes possible to perform statistical analysis (e.g., to study the correlation between postoperative results and surgical planning).

• To match atlases with patient data in order to infer the position of structures only visible on atlases. Typically, in functional neurosurgery, the position of some functional regions is known on brain atlases only. Therefore, registration of MRI with an atlas yields the position of these regions on patient data.

• To study a time-varying deformation. Off-line, it can serve to quantify the progression of a tumor, for instance, or to study local motions of a beating heart. On-line, an ultimate goal is to track deformations during surgery.

• To help segmentation procedures using the a priori knowledge of a geometric model.

Such deformations can be global or local, microscopic or macroscopic, elastic or plastic, varying quickly with time or not. Therefore an infinite set of models can be used to define a nonrigid transformation $\mathbf{T}$. A first global deformation can be defined by merely adding scaling factors to a rigid-body transformation (see, for example, Bajcsy and Kovacic, 1989). More generally, a global polynomial transformation from $\mathscr{R}^3$ to $\mathscr{R}^3$ of order 2 to 5 can be used (see, for example, Schiers, Tiede, and Hohne, 1989). Another possibility for global transformations is to use warping functions that interpolate the deformation vectors computed at eight corners of a cube that contains the region of interest (Jacq and Roux, 1993). However, such global transformations do not often model deformations of anatomic structures, which are intrinsically local. Piecewise polynomial approximations of deformations seem more suitable to model local deformations: Spline functions are very appropriate. The simple format of

3D spline transformations is given by spline coefficients $\alpha x, \alpha y, \alpha z$ and basis spline function B.

$$\begin{cases} x_B = \Sigma_{i,j,k}\, \alpha x_{i,j,k} B_{i,j,k}(x_A, y_A, z_A) \\ y_B = \Sigma_{i,j,k}\, \alpha y_{i,j,k} B_{i,j,k}(x_A, y_A, z_A) \\ z_B = \Sigma_{i,j,k}\, \alpha z_{i,j,k} B_{i,j,k}(x_A, y_A, z_A) \end{cases} \quad (4)$$

Many variations of this format exist (Laurent, Le Mehaute, and Schumaker, 1991). In Evans et al. (1991) and Bookstein (1989), authors use a set of N thin-plate Duchon splines to register two sets of N landmarks coming from images and atlases. This approach is highly appropriate when the number N is small. The possible incorporation of edge information at landmarks has also been presented in Bookstein and Green (1992). Adaptive hierarchic representations for such local deformations have been studied by Szeliski and Lavallée (1993).

Another approach is to set up the problem using physics theory of deformable models (Bajcsy and Kovacic, 1989): The function is defined by a set of 3D displacement vectors and a linear interpolation can be computed on a regular grid of displacement vectors. Smoothing between all the displacement vectors is, in fact, implicit as it appears in some terms of the equation that rule the evolution of the function.

A restriction to the previously defined formulation appears when the problem is to deform a surface model instead of a volume. A 3D displacement vector is computed in each surface point of the model. The transformation $\mathbf{T}$ is a function $(dx, dy, dz) = \mathbf{T}(u, v, t)$ that transforms parametric surface coordinates (u, v) into displacement vectors $(dx, dy, dz) = (x_B - x_A, x_B - x_A, x_B - x_A)$, and a time parameter can be taken into account. See, for instance, 3D snakes in chapter 4 or Terzopoulos and Metaxas (1991), and Terzopoulos, Witkin, and Kass (1988).

Related work in other disciplines is also promising for potential applications to medical images and models. In computer graphics, nonrigid deformations are widely used for modeling and animation purposes (Barr, 1984; Witkin and Welch, 1990). In computer vision, nonrigid deformations have been used for surface reconstruction by fitting flexible models to both image and range data (Burt, 1981; Terzopoulos and Metaxas, 1991; Terzopoulos, Witkin, and Kass, 1988).

Elastic deformations truly based on a physical modeling of interactions between anatomic structures and surgical tools have yet to be studied. Very little work has been done in that domain (e.g., see chapter 11 and Hanna et al., 1992), though it is important for designing intervention simulators for educational purposes and also, in our registration framework, for tracking real deformations during surgery.

Definition and optimization of a disparity function between extracted features

Once a relation between Ref$_A$ and Ref$_B$ has been defined, the second step is to extract corresponding features in Ref$_A$ and Ref$_B$ and, at the same time, to define a disparity function (or a similarity function) between these features. Reference systems Ref$_A$ and Ref$_B$ will be assumed to be registered when the defined disparity function (or similarity function) will be minimal (or maximal). Such an optimization will constitute the last step of the registration process. Obviously, the choice of reference features and of the corresponding optimization method is the heart of any registration strategy; most methods differ at this level.

In this section, we will first present disparity functions and their corresponding optimization methods. Then we will review the different methods according to the geometric representation of the reference features that are used.

DEFINITION OF A DISPARITY FUNCTION

Let's assume a set of reference features $\mathscr{F}_A = \{F_{Ai}, i = 1 \ldots \mathcal{N}\}$ have been extracted in Ref$_A$, with a corresponding set of features $\mathscr{F}_B = \{F_{Bj}, j = 1 \ldots M\}$ in Ref$_B$. The possible features representations will be analyzed later. The disparity function must involve some function of the distances between features F_{Ai} and the features F_{Bj} transformed by the transformation $\mathbf{T}$ we are seeking.

A first problem is to find corresponding features in both sets $\mathscr{F}_A$ and $\mathscr{F}_B$. However, for most medical applications, there is a low number of reference features; therefore, this matching problem often is solved using a priori knowledge or user interaction. Usually, the disparity function is not symmetric in A and B: Typically, if one set contains more features than the other, it will constitute the model A. Then, all features F_{Bj} of $\mathscr{F}_B$ constitute the data that will all be matched on $\mathscr{F}_A$; hence, some elements of $\mathscr{F}_A$ can remain unmatched. There still remain some cases where the correspondence between features must be determined simultane-

ously with the geometric registration; then some local strategy that makes a hypothesis and check hypothesis with feedback must be used. This will be discussed briefly in the next sections.

Now, we assume that the correspondence between features is known and we introduce a local disparity function D between corresponding features (a particular cost function). Many disparity functions D can be proposed: For instance, here are some simple examples of global criteria:

$$D = \sum_i w_i \{distance[F_{Ai}, \mathbf{T}(F_{Bi}, t)]\}^2 \qquad (5)$$

where w_i are scalar weights

$$D = MAX_i \{distance[F_{Ai}, \mathbf{T}(F_{Bi}, t)]\} \qquad (6)$$

$$D = MEDIAN\{distance[F_{Ai}, \mathbf{T}(F_{Bi}, t)], i = 1 \ldots \mathcal{N}\} \qquad (7)$$

$$D = Card\{distance[F_{Ai}, \mathbf{T}(F_{Bi}, t)] < threshold\} \qquad (8)$$

where Card(E) represents the number of elements in E

Once one of these criteria D has been selected, the real problem is to define and implement a *distance* function between features. If features are points, the Euclidean distance is perfect, but the problem is more complex for higher-level features. The minimum Euclidean distance d_{min} between two geometric features F_{Ai} and F_{Bi} may not always be suitable:

$$d_{min}(F_{Ai}, F_{Bi}) = MIN_{P_a \in F_{Ai}, P_b \in F_{Bi}}[d_{eucl}(\mathbf{P_a}, \mathbf{P_b})] \qquad (9)$$

where $d_{eucl}(\mathbf{P_a}, \mathbf{P_b})$ is the Euclidean distance between points $\mathbf{P_a}$ and $\mathbf{P_b}$.

For instance, what distance must we define between two straight lines? In the case of two straight lines that intersect but make an angle, the minimum Euclidean distance is zero while features are very different. The Hausdorff distance solves this problem: It is defined by the maximum of the minimum Euclidean distances between each point of a feature and the other feature. However, the Hausdorff distance is difficult to use in practice because usually, corresponding features match only partially. Therefore, there is no universal distance to use; it is problem-dependent. Moreover, features to be matched do not always have the same geometric representation: For instance, in Lavallée, Szeliski, and Brunie (1991), a distance between a 3D surface and tangent projection lines is defined. Reducing optimization time is a serious requirement in the medical field; therefore, implementation of the computation of the distance functions usually is a deciding factor. Using distance maps in which minimum Euclidean distances have been precomputed for a given model is very attractive to speed up registration algorithms that must be applied at the beginning of an operation, for instance (Danielson, 1980; Borgefors, 1984; Jiang, Robb, and Holton, 1992; and chapter 7 in this book).

The general formulation we propose can include registration techniques based on correlation (Bajcsy and Kovacic, 1989; Brown, 1992; Gerlot-Chiron and Bizais, 1992). Then the features are just sets of pixels or voxels and, instead of a disparity function, we have local similarity functions given by the correlation coefficients between regions.

Most methods minimize a weighted least-squares criterion of the type in equation 5. In that case, weights w_i must be set to the inverse of the a priori variance σ_i of the noise associated with measurements i. These weights can be useful to allot influence to data in regions where sensors are not well calibrated (usually the frontiers of the working space) or to data segmented with less certainty than others (e.g., using the gradient norms of edges in images). As is well-known, a least-squares criterion corresponds to the maximum likelihood when the noise is Gaussian (Press et al., 1986). In registration problems, the noise is generated by the sensors, the errors of the feature extraction procedures, and the phenomena not taken into account in the model of the transformation $\mathbf{T}$. If a non-Gaussian noise distribution is observed, it is likely that the sensors are not calibrated with enough accuracy, that edges are segmented with poor accuracy, or that the model is not good enough. However, one usual exception is to observe *outliers*, which correspond to false detection problem (i.e., features of $\mathscr{F}_B$ that have no corresponding feature in $\mathscr{F}_A$). Then, robust statistics must be applied (Huber, 1981), at least using elementary procedures such as rejection of data above a given threshold.

Previous considerations open the discussion about the particular case of elastic matching. Indeed, elastic matching tends to deform a model A until it fits perfectly with a model B. Therefore, it tries to reduce errors to zero, which conflicts with the existence of noise. Moreover, there is usually an infinite set of solutions for $\mathbf{T}$ that make such a perfect elastic matching. For instance, let's assume that we have to match two sets of n^3 voxels A and B (e.g., $n = 256$) and that we have extracted two sets of m corresponding points (e.g., $m = 1000$). If we try to estimate directly a dis-

placement vector in each voxel of A, we have only $3m$ equations for $3n^3$ unknowns. The problem is ill-posed. To deal with such an ill-posed problem, it is necessary to set some constraints. A first solution is to set constraints directly on the transformation $\mathbf{T}$ by limiting the number of degrees of freedom or parameters that are necessary to define an elastic transformation $\mathbf{T}$. For instance, $\mathbf{T}$ can be defined as a second-order polynomial transformation from $\mathscr{R}^3$ to $\mathscr{R}^3$ (Schiers, Tiede, and Hohne, 1989) or as an adaptive hierarchic spline function (Szeliski and Lavallée, 1993). A second solution is to set constraints during the optimization process, using regularization theory (Terzopoulos and Fleischer, 1988; Terzopoulos, 1988; Bookstein, 1989). In that case, the criterion to be minimized is a weighted sum of the errors between features and a regularization (smoothing) term.

OPTIMIZATION OF A DISPARITY FUNCTION

Once a disparity function (or similarity function) has been defined, we must find a method to minimize (or maximize) it. It is difficult to classify optimization methods because there are many distinguishing features among them.

GLOBAL VERSUS LOCAL MATCHING   First, there are two main categories: global and local methods. In global methods, only one criterion depends on the searched parameters, and this criterion takes all features of $\mathscr{F}_A$ and all features of $\mathscr{F}_B$ into account. Typically, the sum of squares of distances between segmented features of $\mathscr{F}_A$ and segmented features of $\mathscr{F}_B$ is minimized as a function of six parameters that define a rigid-body transformation between Ref_A and Ref_B. In local methods, features of $\mathscr{F}_A$ are matched individually with features of $\mathscr{F}_B$, and each matched pair of features gives directly some possible parameters of the transformation $\mathbf{T}$ or at least gives some constraints between these parameters. For example, with generalized Hough transforms (Ballard and Brown, 1982), an accumulator corresponding to a discretization of the parameter (or Hough) space, is incremented in all points that are possible matching parameters for a given pair of corresponding features. This is repeated for each pair of features, and the winner is simply the point of the Hough space that has the maximum value. Usually, Hough transforms are difficult to implement for high-dimension spaces. In a later section of this chapter, we describe a typical example of an efficient local method using *hashing tables*. Roughly, local methods are useful when there is a large number of features and, most of all, when correspondences between features are unknown.

NONLINEAR OPTIMIZATION   Very few methods give a direct solution: This is the case only for rigid registration of points or planes (Faugeras and Hebert, 1987). Therefore, minimization techniques often require nonlinear optimization using iterative procedures. In a general case, a standard conjugate gradient descent technique can be used. However, each time a least-squares criterion is used, the very powerful Levenberg-Marquardt algorithm can be applied (Press et al., 1986), which is a weighted combination of a gradient descent technique with a Newton method, where the Hessian is approximated using only first-order derivatives through the least-squares formulation. See this algorithm's use in registration problems in Lowe (1991) and Lavallée, Szeliski, and Brunie (1991). An equivalent approach uses the generalized Kalman filter (Ayache, 1991).

LOCAL MINIMA   When iterative optimization is used, there is always a risk that the method falls into a local minimum. If we focus on rigid-body registration, two qualitative kinds of local minima can be observed. A first class contains series of many local minima spread in a small neighborood of the true global minimum. Such phenomena are reported for a surface-matching algorithm in Oghabian and Todd-Pokropek (1991), and this problem is solved by authors using a multi-level minimization technique. In general, such local minima are difficult to deal with; however, they are inherent to discretization problems in the data or in the implementation of the distance functions between features. Typically, these minima occur when registration is performed between two surfaces that differ only for fine details. Therefore, they can and must be avoided by an appropriate discretization. A second category includes large local minima, which are quite far away from the true global minimum. Their existence, location, and number is very shape-dependent. However, for applications in the medical field, there is always some a priori knowledge about the region where the minimum has to be searched. This comes from the fact that physicians, surgeons, and radiologists already use a reference system, the patient reference system.

Typically, for registration between MRI and CT of the head, the rotation matrix between both volumes is known with uncertainties of approximately ± 30 degrees around each axis. For translation components, using an initial translation that makes centroids of features coincident is usually suitable. Therefore, time-consuming global minimum search methods, such as simulated annealing or genetic algorithms, usually are not required in the medical field. In applications where a few local minima are still observed in the search space, starting an iterative search from a few points may be sufficient, but using multilevel minimization seems more efficient: Such a hierarchic search strategy first performs a matching for data resampled at a low resolution and then uses the result as the initial point for matching at a higher resolution, and so on. It has been successfully applied to 2D image registration (Borgefors, 1988) and 3D surface registration (Oghabian, and Todd-Pokropek, 1991; Jiang, Robb, and Holton, 1992). For elastic registration, as the parameter space has a much higher dimension, local minima are more likely to occur. Then, it is possible to use a stochastic method to find the global minimum. For instance, optimization in a 24-parameter search space has been achieved through the use of genetic algorithms (Jacq and Roux, 1993). However, multiresolution algorithms also provide an efficient and simple solution: See a successful application to elastic volume registration in Bajcsy and Kovacic (1989).

In the general framework of registration, it is interesting to note that there is an obvious link between local minima problems obtained with global methods and combinatorial problems of feature matching obtained with local methods. For instance, let's consider the estimation of a rigid-body transformation **T** between two sets of points $\{P_{Ai}, i = 1 \ldots \mathcal{N}\}$ and $\{P_{Bj}, j = 1 \ldots M\}$, where correspondences between points are unknown (we just assume that all points P_{Bj} have a corresponding point in the other set). A typical global search method will minimize the cost function: $D = \sum_j \{min_i [d_{eucl}(P_{Ai}, TP_{Bj})]\}^2$. It is easy to imagine a large number of local minima. Without knowledge of a good initial estimate of the transformation, this solution would be expensive, but if a good initial estimate is known, the convergence is very fast and it finds the global minimum. Actually, for that particular points-matching problem without correspondences, an elegant global method based on correlation of Dirac-based functions has been proposed in Lin et al. (1986).

On the other hand, a typical local method will try all the possible pairs of points and then will register them by a direct method such as the SVD algorithm (Arun, Huang, and Blostein, 1987). Actually, some processes have been proposed that use the coherence between possible pairs in order to speed up such an exhaustive search—for instance, using relaxation methods (Ranade and Rosenfeld, 1980), clustering techniques (Stockman, Kopstein, and Benett, 1982), dynamic programming (Maitre and Wu, 1987). Such a comparison on this simple example explains why local matching is much more developed in computer vision than in the medical field, where global minimization often is used.

REFERENCE FEATURES

In this section, we review the existing registration methods according to the geometric representation of the involved reference features, where the expression *reference feature* is defined broadly. The purpose is to extract and match some *reference features* common to the same anatomic or material structure in each coordinate system. These features do not necessarily have the same representation in each modality. Algorithms that allow one to extract such features are not described in this chapter, as segmentation is a full research topic partially presented in another chapter of this book and in many other books and conference proceedings. However, we discuss the ability of a method to detect selected features automatically or semiautomatically, which is obviously important from a practical point of view.

MATCHING 3D POINTS WITH 3D POINTS The registration of two sets of corresponding points is a well-known problem for which authors have proposed iterative solutions (Huang, Blostein, and Margerun, 1986) or direct methods using quaternion theory (Faugeras and Hebert, 1987) or singular value decomposition [see Umeyama (1991) for a slight modification of the original method of Arun, Huang, and Blostein (1987) that avoids obtaining reflections instead of rotations]. See also Chen (1992) for a parameter-clustering approach located between least-squares minimization and Hough transforms, which seems suitable in the case where few outliers appear. Hence, mathematics do not raise any problem except in the case where correspondences between points are not known, which is more compli-

cated but rarely happens for medical applications. In that particular case, methods that match points on surfaces provide some solutions. The real problem is to extract such reference points, and this will be described now.

Anatomic landmarks segmented interactively A standard and very simple approach to extracting reference points consists of selecting interactively some pairs of corresponding points in two 3D examinations. This approach has been applied to the head by many authors, using reference points such as the nasion and the top of the head. Chen, Kessler, and Pitluck (1985), Schiers, Tiede, and Hohne (1989), and Toennies et al., (1990) use this method to register CT with MRI. Singh, Brechner, and Henderson (1992) register MRI with SQUID neuromagnetometer images (using a digitizing probe to register the neuromagnetometer coordinate system with some reference points taken on the skin). Kosugi, Watanabe, and Goto (1988) register MRI or CT with the coordinate system of a mechanical navigation system used for stereotactic neurosurgery. Peifer, Garcia, and Cooke (1992) register SPECT of the myocardium with arteries reconstructed from biplanar x-ray angiograms. In all these methods, the achieved accuracy is a few millimeters. In this book, Evans and colleagues (chapter 6) propose to match 3D points manually extracted on MRI and PET images. Such reference points can be defined also on a 3D brain atlas, which allows one to use spline interpolation to obtain an elastic registration between the atlas and MRI images. This approach is appropriate in that case because atlas models and functional and morphologic images are very different and thus difficult to register automatically. In the general case, however, such methods usually are inaccurate and require much time and experience on the part of the operator.

External landmarks A second approach is to fix fiducial markers on the patient. Some authors have designed systems in which just a few pins or balls are fixed to the patient during preoperative image acquisition. During surgery, a 3D mechanical or optical localizer enables the surgeon to detect the position of such landmarks, and the system can easily compute the corresponding rigid transformation. For instance, a system successfully used in ENT surgery relies on a registration performed through little balls pasted on the patient's skin and manually detected with a passive mechanical arm

(Mösges et al., 1989) or with an optical infrared sensor (Adams et al., 1992). Authors obtain millimetric accuracy. After such a registration, the mechanical or optical sensor indicates in real time the location of a surgical tool with respect to the preoperative images.

In Koivukangas et al. (1993), balls are taped on the skin at locations defined by tattooed ink points: Balls are detected on preoperative images, but they are withdrawn just after MRI acquisition. During surgery, a mechanical localizer is used to detect the tattooed ink points. An accuracy of 3 mm is reached using four points.

In a successful system designed for robotic hip replacement surgery (Taylor et al., 1992), the preoperative and intraoperative registration is performed through metallic pins implanted into the femur prior to CT examination and sensed with a semiautomatic robotic procedure during surgery; submillimetric accuracy is reached. Similarly, Lewis and Galloway (1992) propose that small permanent fiducial markers be implanted under the skin into the skull, these markers could be easily localized on CT or MRI scanning, and they could be detected during surgery using an A-mode ultrasonic probe mounted at the end of a mechanical localizer.

In Roberts et al. (1986), the registration is performed using at least three radiopaque 5-mm beads attached to the patient's scalp, localized on CT images and detected during surgery with the focal axis of an operating microscope targeting the beads, the location of which is known with an ultrasonic 3D localizer. However, several millimeters of error have been observed.

A submillimetric registration is reached for brain images in Mandava et al. (1992) with four markers for registration among CT, MRI, PET, and a 3D mechanical localizer. See other examples of using markers for SPECT/CT registration in Pohjonen et al. (1992; brain images), Kramer et al. (1992; chest and pelvis images, accuracy of approximately 5 mm), and in Hill et al. (1990; wrist and brain images, accuracy of approximately 5 mm). For all these methods, the accurate detection of the landmarks in 3D images is not obvious (Mandava et al., 1992): For example, the global centroid of the centroids of the landmarks segmented on each slice may not coincide exactly with the true 3D centroid of the landmarks because of slice thickness and spacing.

All these approaches still raise the problem of adding some material structures on the patient before CT, MRI, or SPECT acquisition. They might be inaccurate in some applications when these structures are just pasted on the skin, and they imply an invasive operation before the planned operation when the reference structures are fixed to the bones.

Anatomic landmarks segmented automatically A more practical method would be to identify singularity points automatically in images and to match them, but we are not aware that such work has been reported in the case of medical structures. However, methods to obtain such singularity points do exist (e.g., see Sander and Zucker, 1992).

MATCHING 3D POINTS WITH 2D POINTS Registration of points has also been used widely to register 3D images with 2D projections. For instance, in stereotactic neurosurgery, some frames or head-holders are composed of acrylic plates containing radiopaque markers: It is then possible to register the stereotactic frame coordinate system with standard x-rays and digital subtraction angiography (DSA) images (Henri, Collins, and Peters, 1991; Kall, 1992; Suetens et al., 1992). In these cases, x-ray projections are modeled by simple perspective transformations so that just a few points are used to calibrate the projections and to perform the registration simultaneously: The result is a perspective matrix that links x-ray pixels to 3D coordinates of the stereotactic frame. The frame is then registered with 3D images (see next paragraph), and an articulated guide accurately attached on the frame allows one to match the position of surgical tools with all images.

Actually, the stereotactic frame is not strictly necessary in this approach. For instance, in Grzeszczuk et al. (1992), scalp markers are used to register a patient coordinate system with standard angiograms. Using a 3D localizer and a surface-matching technique, the patient coordinate system also is registered with magnetic resonance angiography (MRA) images, so that the transformation among MRA and angiograms can be computed.

As for 3D/3D points matching, it is possible to register 3D points with 2D points identified interactively. For instance, in Henri et al. (1992), MRI and DSA are registered using only anatomy based landmarks.

MATCHING STRAIGHT LINES OR PLANES It is quite difficult to encounter straight lines or perfect planes in the anatomy, even for a very abnormal patient! Thus, many methods that make use of such features and were developed for matching in computer vision are not usable in our case. The only exception occurs when such features are fixed to the patient. The typical instance is the registration of stereotactic frames or head-holders made of N-shaped fiducial markers, visible on several imaging systems (Kelly, 1986; Wilson and Mountz, 1989; Henri, Collins, and Peters, 1991). The detection of opaque rods on CT, MRI, SPECT sections, or x-ray images is usually an automated or semiautomated procedure. Some simple geometric relations allow one to compute the location of image planes directly from the coordinates of the intersections between the image plane and the opaque rods that constitute the N-shaped markers (Goerss et al., 1982; Peters et al., 1986; Zhang et al., 1990). More generally, the registration of arbitrary 3D straight lines can be solved by using only iterative methods (Faugeras and Hebert, 1987). However, a trick is to build two sets of "virtual points" that are the intersections of each possible pair of lines and then to register these two sets of points by direct point-matching techniques (here, the intersection between two lines is defined by the nearest point from the two lines) (Peria et al., 1993).

For registration of planes or planar patches, a number of methods have been developed to recognize or localize manufactured objects in computer vision (Grimson and Lozano-Perez, 1984; Besl and Jain, 1985; Faugeras and Hebert, 1987). See, for instance, an extension of line Hough transforms to 3D planes in Krishnapuram and Casasent (1989).

MATCHING 3D CURVES WITH 3D CURVES   There are a few cases in which reference features can be 3D curves. As these curves do not coincide exactly from start to finish, most curve-matching techniques match, in a first step, shape signatures that are invariant by translation and rotation (usually using curvature and torsion) and then register matched pieces of curve. For robustness purposes, these two steps can be merged. [See examples in Kehtarnavaz and deFigueiredo (1988), Wolfson (1990), and Guéziec and Ayache (1992).] In practice, there are three cases in which 3D curves can be used as reference features:

• A first possibility is to fix wires or opaque catheters on the patient in order to register two examinations where these curves are visible. An advantage over registration based on points such as balls is that it is not necessary to obtain slices that go exactly through these landmarks or contiguous slice. [An application to SPECT-CT registration of chest images is presented in Dubois, Brut, and Cinquin (1992).]

• A second case is to consider some anatomic structures that can be represented with 3D curves by their very nature. For instance, one could imagine registering blood vessels segmented in preoperative MRI or MRA, with the corresponding vessels segmented in intraoperative Doppler ultrasound images spatially registered using 3D localizers. Generally, the axes of all kinds of canals, ducts, and vessels could be used as reference features, with potential applications in tracking deformations of soft tissues.

Another recent method for 3D/3D registration is based on the extraction of singularity curves on isodensity surfaces. This is the approach of Ayache and coworkers described in the last section of this chapter (see also Thirion et al., 1992; Monga, Benayoun, and Ayache, 1992; and Guéziec and Ayache, 1992).

MATCHING SURFACES WITH SURFACES OR SURFACE POINTS   A very general and useful feature is the 3D boundary surface of a reference anatomic structure. Typically, one surface can be the result of a 3D segmentation algorithm on 3D images (CT, MRI, etc.) or a 3D surface model obtained from anatomic sections or merged collections of segmented structures. How to obtain such segmented surfaces is not described in this chapter but, in practice, skin and bones can be segmented automatically in most cases on CT and MRI scanning, whereas automated segmentation of soft tissues remains a challenging problem. This first surface will have to be registered with a second data surface, which can be another surface segmented on 3D images, but which can also be a set of surface patches or points acquired with a large variety of sensors. For instance, if the chosen reference structure is visible (i.e., in the case of skin surfaces or for open surgery), standard vision sensors—stereovision or range-imaging sensors, 3D localizers (optical, ultrasound, or mechanical)—can be used. The great advantage of such sensors is that their output is a direct set of surface points ready to be matched without further segmentation. Ultrasound images spatially registered together using 3D localizers (which constitute 2.5D ultrasound images) also yield invaluable information about surface points localization. However, automated segmentation of ultrasound images remains a very difficult problem in the general case.

Surfaces can provide basic features for 3D rigid registration as well as 3D elastic matching. However, surface-based elastic matching is still delicate, and few results are reported in the literature for medical applications. (See the section, Elastic Transformations.) In this section, we review existing work on surface-based rigid registration, for which many different approaches have been proposed and many results exist.

In computer vision, there is a large body of literature on the problem of matching a surface model with surface data, but most of these techniques have addressed limited classes of shapes. First, much of the work on 3D pose extraction focuses on polyhedral objects (see, for example, Grimson and Lozano-Perez, 1984). Second, for free-form shape matching, most authors rely on the existence of specific simple features within shapes or make assumptions about the global shape [see Besl and Jain (1985) and Besl (1990) for an extensive review]. For instance, the work of Faugeras and Toscani (1986) assumes the existence of reasonably large planar regions on the surfaces. In Fan, Medioni, and Nevatia (1989), the authors use surface patches delimited by 3D curves corresponding to surface discontinuities. Generalized cylinders are the basic representation used in Nevatia and Binford (1977). Representations of surfaces with extended Gaussian images (based on surface normal histograms) are well adapted to registration of more or less convex shapes (Brou, 1984; Kang and Ikeuchi, 1993).

However, some of the work described in computer vision may be applicable in registration of anatomic surfaces. The main requirement is that the surface representation be one of the representations that 3D segmentation of smooth objects can provide—namely, spline surfaces, faceted surfaces (sets of triangles), sets of connected voxels, sets of planar curves corresponding to parallel cross-sections, or simply collections of 3D points. In this framework, methods that make use of small surface patches with stable differential properties are interesting (Stein and Medioni, 1992). Decomposition of 3D surfaces into distance profiles centered at singular points could also be used to reduce the surface-matching complexity (Radack and Badler, 1989). If reference surfaces are closed and have continuous representations, a simple approach is to reconstruct the 3D transformation from bidimensional transformations computed on three orthogonal projections of the surfaces to register (Huang et al., 1991; Flifla et al., 1992).

Actually, there is a simple and general approach that solves the free-form surface registration problem, which consists simply in the minimization of a distance between a model surface $\mathscr{S}_A$ and a data surface $\mathscr{S}_B$:

$$D = distance[\mathscr{S}_A, \mathbf{T}(\mathscr{S}_B)] \qquad (10)$$

At least three classes of algorithms follow this approach. Their main difference lies in the different definitions of the distance functions between two surfaces.

Head and hat algorithm   In the medical field, the most famous method of surface registration is probably "head and hat" matching (Levin et al., 1988; Pelizzari et al., 1989). This algorithm originally was developed for PET registration with CT or MRI (using the skin surface of the head as a reference segmented on both PET transmission images and CT images) and then was applied to SPECT images (using both scalp surfaces and brain surfaces as reference features) (Holman et al., 1991). A study of the accuracy of this method is presented in Turkington et al. (1993). The starting point is a model surface $\mathscr{S}_A$ represented by a set of planar contours segmented on CT or MRI slices, and a second surface $\mathscr{S}_B$ represented by 3D data points P_{Bj}, $i = 1 \ldots M$. The algorithm estimates the rigid-body transformation $\mathbf{T}$ that minimizes the quantity D:

$$D = \sum_j [d_S(\mathscr{S}_A, \mathbf{T}\mathbf{P_{Bj}})]^2 \qquad (11)$$

Once the centroid $\mathbf{G}$ of the surface $\mathscr{S}_A$ has been computed, the distance d_S between a surface S and a point $\mathbf{P}$ is defined by the Euclidean distance between the point $\mathbf{P}$ and the intersection point $\mathbf{Q}$ that lies between the surface S and the line $(\mathbf{GP})$. The criterion D depends on six parameters that define $\mathbf{T}$, and it is minimized iteratively from a starting point quite close to the final solution. This minimization is performed with a standard gradient descent technique of Powell.

The method has three drawbacks. First, it has been reported that the search could fall into local minima, possibly due to the particular implementation of the distances or to the inaccuracies of the segmentation of SPECT or PET brain contours. In that case, user interaction is required. Second, because the definition of the *distance from the centroid* used in equation 11 uses the centroid $\mathbf{G}$, it implies that the surface be more or less spherical. Third, this distance can be used only if surfaces are close to one another all along the iterative process. These major drawbacks have been partially eliminated by replacing the centroid with a central curved axis for more or less cylindric shapes, which was found efficient for registering 3D images using bony structures as references (Pelizzari, Chen, and Du, 1992). Nonetheless, this does not yet yield a general method.

Surface matching using distance maps To overcome the previously mentioned drawbacks, some authors have proposed to minimize a more general distance. Let the data surface $\mathscr{S}_B$ be represented by 3D data points $\mathbf{P_{Bj}}$, $j = 1 \ldots M$. Any surface representation can be transformed into such a simple point representation. First, we assume that, after registration, $\mathscr{S}_B$ is included in $\mathscr{S}_A$. The problem is to estimate the rigid-body transformation $\mathbf{T}$ that minimizes the quantity D defined in equation 11, where the distance d_S between a surface S and a point $\mathbf{M}$ is defined by the minimum Euclidean distance:

$$d_S(S, \mathbf{M}) = min_{P_i \in S} d_{eucl}(\mathbf{P_i}, \mathbf{M}) \qquad (12)$$

To compute the distance d_s between a point and a surface, many algorithms have been developed in the literature, but they all depend on the chosen surface representation (Besl and McKay, 1992). For Instance, let's consider a parametric surface representation of the following type:

$$\begin{cases} x = f_x(u, v) \\ y = f_y(u, v) \\ z = f_z(u, v) \end{cases} \qquad (13)$$

where f_x, f_y, f_z can be spline functions. Then, for each point $\mathbf{M}$, the distance $d_{eucl}(\mathbf{P_i}, \mathbf{M})$ in equation 12 is a function of u and v; therefore, $d_S(S, \mathbf{M})$ can be computed with a nonlinear bidimensional minimization in u and v, using derivatives of f_x, f_y, f_z. However, to avoid local minima during this minimization, it is necessary to find first a suitable initial point (u_0, v_0). A solution is to add a dual higher-level representation, which can be a description of concave and convex regions or an approximation of the surface by facets, for instance. Whatever the approach for complex shapes, this is a time-consuming approach.

Therefore, several authors have suggested precomputing and storing the distances $d_S(S, \mathbf{M})$ on a lattice of a volume V containing S: The result is a 3D distance map. Once the distance map has been built, for any point $\mathbf{M}$ inside V, the distance $d_S(S, \mathbf{M})$ is approxi-

mated by a combination of the distances computed at the lattice points neighboring M (usually a simple trilinear interpolation of the eight nearest lattice points is used).

To build such 3D distance maps, it is possible to compute exact point-to-surface distances at lattice points using previously cited methods. Again, this suffers from expensive computations and surface representation dependence. A much better approach is to extend in three dimensions the standard 2D chamfer distance maps (or *distance transforms*) (Barrow et al., 1977; Borgefors, 1984). This solution has been followed by several authors simultaneously (Brunie, 1992; Jiang, Robb, and Holton, 1992; Malandain and Rocchisani, 1992; Mangin et al., 1993). In that case, the model surface is represented by a set of voxels inside the 3D image array. Then, Euclidean distances in the 3D image are approximated by propagating a mask of local distances, each local distance being associated with an elementary displacement in the lattice. However, for anisotropic voxels (still the most general case in medical imaging), the presence of artefacts near the surface has been observed (Mangin et al., 1993), which led authors to build correction tables. To optimize memory space and accuracy of the distance map near the surface, octree-spline distance maps have been introduced by Lavallée, Szeliski, and Brunie (1991). (See a detailed presentation in chapter 7.)

Interestingly, different optimization methods have been reported to minimize the criteria of equation 11: In Jiang, Robb, and Holton (1992), the authors use a simple gradient descent of Powell. However, to avoid local minima, a multilevel minimization is performed. Accurate results are presented for registration of MRI with PET, MRI with SPECT, MRI with CT, and $MRI(T_1)$ with $MRI(T_2)$. For all these examples, the reference feature is the brain surface segmented semiautomatically.

In Mangin et al. (1993), the authors use a pragmatic approach based on a downhill search applied iteratively to separated rotation and translation components. These investigators emphasize the fact that local minima are avoided because initial conditions are always close enough to the final solution. For PET and MRI brain images, a very effective strategy allows one to perform the registration fully automatically: First, the scalp surface is easily segmented on PET transmission images and then on MRI images. The result of the registration between the two scalp surfaces is used to initialize a second swift registration between the brain surface segmented on PET images and all edge points of MRI scans (which includes brain surface points). This "trick" allows authors to avoid the difficult problem of automated brain surface segmentation.

It can be shown that the term D of equation 11 can be seen as the potential energy of a system of springs attached to data points and moving without friction on the surface (Brunie, Lavallée, and Szeliski, 1992). In Malandain and Rocchisani (1992), authors use the dynamics law of such a system to minimize the energy D. A damping factor is added to prevent oscillations. Actually, this intuitive physical approach is very close to standard mathematic minimization techniques. Unfortunately, local minima still exist. This approach has been sucessfully tested on registration of two CT examinations of a same skull automatically segmented by simple thresholding, as well as on registration of PET with MRI using the brain surface segmented semiautomatically via mathematic morphologic operators.

In Lavallée, Szeliski, and Brunie (1991), the authors use the powerful Levenberg-Marquardt algorithm to minimize the function D. These investigators do not address problems of local minima because enough a priori knowledge is available to initialize the minimization at correct points. The method is very general as it can be used to register not only medical images but also surface points extracted with 3D sensors. See chapter 7 in this book for its application to registration of automatically segmented scalp surfaces on MRI and CT, or Peria et al. (1993) for automated SPECT/MRI registration using an intermediate range-imaging sensor. See also in this book chapter 32 for registration of vertebral surfaces semiautomatically segmented on CT images and manually segmented on ultrasound images.

Iterative closest point algorithm In Besl and McKay (1992), the authors reduce the general nonlinear minimization previously presented to an iterative point-matching problem. Starting from an initial position and orientation, the iterative closest point (ICP) algorithm first searches for each data surface point P_{Bj}, $j = 1 \ldots M$ and the corresponding nearest point P_{Aj} on the surface model. Then the rigid transformation that matches both point sets P_{Aj} and P_{Bj} is computed by a direct method using quaternions (a singular value decomposition [SVD] method could have been used

also). The result is applied to data surface points, and the whole procedure is iterated. The resulting transformation is given by the product of the transformation matrices computed at each iteration. Although this elegant solution can be applied to any surface, it requires the findings of nearest points on the model surface very quickly, which is not obvious for complex shapes (authors report execution times of 10 minutes to 1 hour for complex shapes).

For all described formulations, it is important to note that the registration is not symmetric. One has to match the smallest surface patch (the data) on the largest surface patch (the model). Therefore, care must be taken to extract the most possible points for the model surface and the least possible points for the data surface. This rule makes segmentation processes easier, as there is no real need for exact segmentation but rather for undersegmentation or oversegmentation.

However, some data surfaces may overlap model surfaces. Therefore, there exists a simple strategy to deal with that case: Remove data for which distances exceed a threshold, or remove a given percentage of the worst data, either at each iteration or at the end of a series of iterations. See an example in Bittar, Lavallée, and Szeliski (1993).

MATCHING A 3D SURFACE WITH 2D PROJECTIONS In computer vision, many standard approaches can match edges extracted on 2D images with 3D models (see, for example, Dhome et al., 1989, and Lowe, 1991). In the medical field, edges extracted on 2D x-ray projection images represent valuable features for registration with 3D models. However, for smooth surfaces, inferring the contour generators (i.e., the curves that belong to the surface and that form the image contours) can be very difficult (Kriegman and Ponce, 1990). Very few reports deal with this problem, and none of these methods has been used in the medical field. For instance, the method described by Kriegman and Ponce (1990) is restricted at present to objects modeled by a few patches. The method developed in a later paper (see Lavallée, Szeliski, and Brunie, 1991) uses octree-spline distance maps, exactly as for 3D surface registration. This allows one to compute quickly and accurately a distance between projection lines and a 3D surface (the distance is minimum when projection lines are tangent to the surface). It has been tested on vertebral and skull surfaces interactively segmented on a pair of calibrated x-rays projections and semiautomatically segmented on CT data.

In Terzopoulos, Witkin, and Kass (1988), a 3D model can be deformed to fit with 2D projections. Although this work is restricted to generalized cylinders and makes assumptions about some symmetry in the deformation, the approach seems interesting to follow to track anatomy deformation during surgery using x-ray projections.

MATCHING INERTIA MOMENTS OF VOLUMES   Still in the field of 3D/3D matching, moments of inertia of volumes corresponding to reference structures can be used. Once two corresponding volumes have been extracted, inertia matrices are computed and eigenvectors are extracted for each one. Then the matching process just aligns the corresponding eigenvectors or principal axes (see the application to brain matching in Gamboa-Aldeco, Fellingham, and Chen, 1986; Alpert et al., 1989; and Bajcsy and Kovacic, 1989).

This approach suffers from two drawbacks. First, volumes usually do not strictly coincide but rather overlap. To overcome this problem, an iterative procedure that eliminates parts that do not overlap at each iteration has been proposed (Arata and Dhawan, 1992). This solution remains limited to the case of almost coincident volumes. The second drawback is related to the reduction of information involving the use of inertia matrices. Some complex shapes can have an inertia matrix with three quasi-identical eigenvalues, which will make the shape equivalent to a sphere; thus, it will be impossible to register it in orientation. Methods based on surface matching do not have such a drawback as local information is preserved.

CORRELATING GRAY LEVELS   Correlation of gray levels has been studied for intramodal registration (i.e. when the information that must be matched together has been or can be set to the same density values) (Cerchiari et al., 1986; Bajcsy and Kovacic, 1989).

A typical 3D/3D registration algorithm: Automatic registration of 3D voxel images using crest lines

In this section, we present an elegant solution developed in the Epidaure project at Institut National de la Rechenche en Informatique et Automatique (INRIA), France, for automated registration of volumetric images of the same patient taken at different times and in different positions. [For details, refer to Thirion et al. (1992), Thirion (1993), Ayache et al. (1993), and Ayache (1993).] This is necessary, for instance, to study the evolution of a pathologic process such as multiple sclerosis (MRI images) or the efficiency of a treatment against a cancerous lesion (MRI or scanner images). Because of potential occlusions, the two data sets cannot be registered globally, using, for instance, the centroids and axes of inertia. Also, volumetric images generally are quite large, and high-resolution images of the head typically can represent 20 MB or more. According to the framework presented in this chapter, the three steps of the method are as follows:

1. The searched relation between data sets is defined by a standard six-parameter rigid-body transformation.

2. The reference features are typical lines of high curvatures, called *ridges* or *crest lines*, on the surface of reference objects in each volumetric image. The ridge lines convey very rich and compact information, typically 10,000 times more compact than the original image, which tend to correspond to the natural anatomic features. Crest lines of a surface are the loci of the maxima of the maximal curvature, in the associated principal directions. Computing these ridges requires computation of the differential properties of the surfaces up to the third order. This computation is carried out by two different methods:

a. A presegmentation of a volumetric image is done with deformable models or gradient analysis, providing a set of points on the surface (see chapter 4). Then a parametric model (splines) is fit to this set of points and provides the required differential properties.

b. Assuming the surface corresponds to an isointensity surface defined in the volumetric image by the implicit equation $I(x, y, z) = $ constant, it is possible to compute the required differential properties by differentiation of the intensity function. This is obtained by filtering the intensity function, combining smoothing with derivation (see Thirion et al., 1992).

3. Once ridges are computed, it is possible to compute locally Euclidean invariants on these curves, such as the curvature, torsion, normal curvature, geodesic curvature, and geodesic torsion. These invariants are used to match the whole sets of ridges. First, a trihedron is associated with each point of the ridges (it can be the Frenet trihedron defined by the curve or the principal directions and normal of the underlying iso-

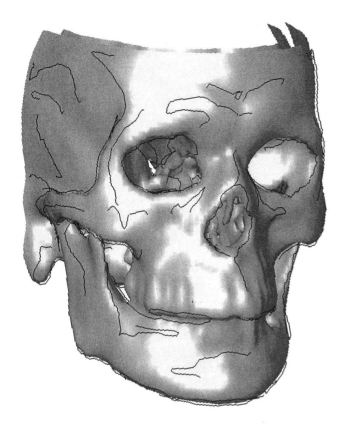

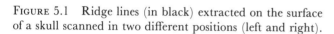

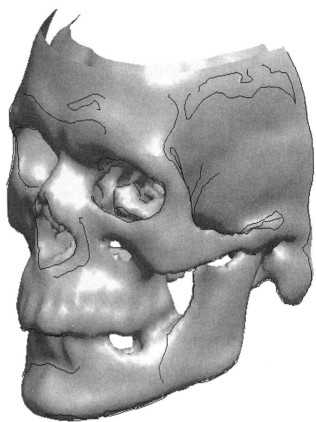

FIGURE 5.1   Ridge lines (in black) extracted on the surface of a skull scanned in two different positions (left and right).

Original 3D images are produced by a GE CT scan. (Courtesy of the Epidaure Project at INRIA.)

surface). A correspondence between two points of the two images, along with their associated trihedrons, defines without ambiguity a rigid motion between the two points. This geometric transformation has 6 degrees of freedom; therefore, it can be represented as a single point in the six-dimensional parametric space that represents any possible rigid motion. For each point taken along a curve, there is a vote for all possible correspondences that are stored in the buckets of a *hash table* representing the 6D parametric space. The bucket with the highest number of votes gives the most likely geometric transformation between the two line sets (Guéziec and Ayache, 1992). This method is very robust because it is not necessary that sets of ridge curves coincide globally; a partial overlapping of curves is sufficient.

Figures 5.1 and 5.2 show experimental results on the entirely automatic registration of CT images of high resolution in the three dimensions (approximately 1 mm), with subvoxel registration accuracy. The com-

puting time, once ridges are extracted, is a few seconds on a DEC station 5000/200.

Conclusions

A first conclusion is that the technology of registration can be used in CIS in the rigid case (i.e., when operated structures are bones or attached to bones, as in orthopaedics or craniofacial surgery) or when the motions of the operated structures are weak compared to the desired accuracy (e.g., the brain in stereotactic neurosurgery). In that case, software packages are now commercially available (e.g., the ANALYZE software presented by Robb in chapter 10, and the MEDIAN library of Focus Med, 4 chemin de Maupertuis, 38240 Meylan, France). Practically, two classes of registration methods exist and work in the rigid case:

• *Material-based registration*: Using frames, pins, and beads fixed to the patient allows one to perform multimodal registration automatically, accurately, and with robustness.

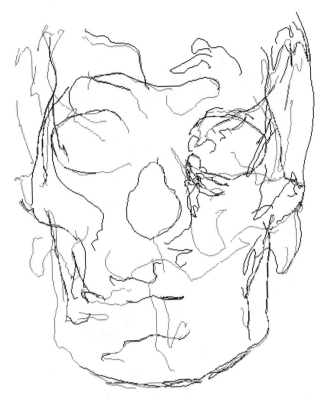

FIGURE 5.2 Automatic registration of the two sets of ridge lines (respectively, bold and plain lines), allowing a subvoxel comparison of the two original 3D images. (Courtesy of the Epidaure Project at INRIA.)

• *Anatomy-based registration*: Using reference features segmented on patient data allows one to perform multimodal registration accurately.

Drawbacks of the first approach are obvious for both the patient and the medical staff, but this is not true of the second class of methods. However, the cost of this second very attractive approach is twofold. First, for registration of patient data with an intraoperative coordinate system, this approach implies the use of intraoperative sensors. These sensors often are available in surgical theaters, and they also are useful to update the surgical planning and to control the surgery itself. Second, it may require semiautomatic or even manual segmentation of reference features. Thus far, fully automated segmentation is restricted to the best cases: bones on CT data, skin surfaces on CT or MRI scans and, obviously, surface points extracted with 3D localizers. However, in the future, it is hoped that segmentation and registration will not be considered separately (using iterative feedback of registration on segmenta-

tion) so that difficult cases could be solved automatically also.

Regarding safety, two issues must be considered. First, it is necessary to measure the real accuracy of any registration method. Here the best solution is to perform surgery on phantoms, which necessitates a registration step: Measuring the errors on the result of surgery gives an upper boundary of the inaccuracies of registration. At least some phantom studies must be performed by comparing the result of a registration method with a known transformation determined with any 3D sensor or an articulated mechanical system or a standard material-based registration method. Once the accuracy of the registration is known, it provides an estimation of uncertainties that must be updated for each case; for instance, some minimization algorithms can yield rough estimates of uncertainties of registration parameters.

Then it is necessary to detect any failure for each case. Automatic detection of misregistration is a delicate task. The observation of residual errors is insufficient. For instance, rough symmetries can lead to misregistered data with low root mean squares (rms) values. Thus far, the only valid solution is visual feedback from the physician: Each registration case must be validated by a careful visual examination of superimposed raw data. However, research work must be performed in that field, first to reduce misregistration risks (using redundant registration with different algorithms and different features whenever possible and detecting local minima by looking at statistical distributions of local errors), and second to simplify the validation task (submitting only representative information for validation).

In this chapter, we focused on algorithmic methods for registration in order to avoid some iterative and inaccurate positioning of the patient and to avoid the use of molded masks or bite pieces with dental impression or any other repositioning systems. However, there are other alternatives. One very simple solution is to perform registration fully interactively: A specific user interface can allow one to control the parameters of the searched transformation, while superimposed segmented or raw data are displayed from several viewpoints simultaneously. Typically, a 6D mouse (or a standard 2D mouse with three buttons) can be used to modify interactively the six parameters that define a rigid transformation, while the user is looking at three orthogonal views of a moving surface superimposed on a fixed 3D image, with a transparency effect. This requires practice on the part of the user, but it may be applicable in difficult cases, where segmentation is delicate.

Another instance of interactive registration consists of moving a real video camera that gives a view of an intraoperative scene until the video image fits visually with a realistically rendered image computed from a preoperative CT or MRI model. Both real video and computer images can be displayed on the same screen, with a transparency effect. This approach has been proposed for spine surgery in Mazier, Lavallée, and Cinquin (1990) and for neurosurgery in Wells et al. (1993). A still less algorithmic but very clever registration method for orthopaedics is presented in chapter 33, in which the authors suggest one build individual templates for each patient at the surgical planning step. The template is the negative part of the operated bone, and a guide corresponding to an optimal trajectory for surgery is also built in the template. During surgery, the template is manually fitted to the bone (this is the matching step), so that the guide is finally at the optimal location.

For elastic registration, methods are much less mature. There are some generic tools, such as 3D snakes, developed mainly in the field of computer vision. Their application to CIS, however, requires much work. Nevertheless, elastic registration of brain images with atlases, modeling of the beating heart, modeling of facial deformities, and so on yield successful examples. Research in this field is very active, and the day when 3D ultrasound images correlated to miniaturized stereo-endoscopic images and preoperative MRI scans will allow us to track in real time deformations and destructions of soft tissues may be close at hand.

ACKNOWLEDGMENT We are grateful to Nicholas Ayache, Epidaure Project–INRIA, for his helpful contribution to this chapter.

REFERENCES

ADAMS, L., A. KNEPPER, W. KRYBUS, D. MEYER-EBRECHT, G. PFEIFFER, R. RUGER, and M. WITTE, 1992. Orientation aid for head and neck surgeons. *ITBM: Innovation Tech. Biol. Med.* (special issue) 13(4):409–424.

ALPERT, N. M., J. F. BRADSHAW, D. KENNEDY, and J. A. CORREIA, 1989. The principal axes transformation: A method for image registration. *J. Nucl. Med.* 31(10):1717–1722.

ARATA, L. K., and A. P. DHAWAN, 1992. Iterative principal axes registration: A new algorithm for retrospective correlation of MR-PET brain images. In *IEEE Engineering in Medicine and Biology Society Proceedings*, J. P. Morucci, ed. Paris: IEEE, pp. 2776–2777.

ARUN, K. S., T. S. HUANG, and S. D. BLOSTEIN, 1987. Least-squares fitting of two 3-D point sets. *IEEE Trans. Pattern Anal. Mach. Intell.* PAMI-9(5):698–700.

AYACHE, N., 1991. *Artificial Vision for Mobile Robots: Stereo Vision and Multisensory Perception.* Cambridge, Mass.: MIT Press.

AYACHE, N., 1993. *Volume Image Processing—Results and Research Challenges* (tech. rep. 2050). France: INRIA.

AYACHE, N., A. GUEZIEC, A. GOURDON, J. P. THIRION, and J. KNOPLIOCH, 1993. Evaluating 3D registration with crest lines. In *Mathematical Methods in 3D Medical Images.* San Diego.

BAJCSY, R., and S. KOVACIC, 1989. Multiresolution elastic matching. *Comput. Vision Graphics Image Proc.* 46:1–21.

BALLARD, D. H., and C. M. BROWN, 1982. *Computer Vision.* Englewood Cliffs, N.J.: Prentice-Hall.

BARR, A. H., 1984. Global and local deformations of solid primitives. *Comput. Graphics (SIGGRAPH '84)* 18(3):21–20.

BARROW, H. G., J. M. TENENBAUM, R. C. BOLLES, and H. C. WOLF, 1977. Parameteric correspondence and chamfer matching: Two new techniques for image matching. In *Proceedings of the Fifth International Joint Conference on Artificial Intelligence*, Cambridge, Mass., pp. 659–663.

BESL, P. J., 1990. The free-form surface matching problem. In *Structure Transfer Between Sets of Three-Dimensional Medical Imaging Data*, H. Freeman, ed. New York: Academic.

BESL, P. J., and R. C. JAIN, 1985. Three-dimensional object recognition. *ACM Comput. Surv.* 17(1):75–145.

BESL, P. J., and N. D. MCKAY, 1992. A method for registration of 3-D shapes. *IEEE Trans. Pattern Anal. Mach. Intell.* 14(2):239–256.

BITTAR, E., S. LAVALLÉE, and R. SZELISKI, 1993. A method for registering overlapping range images of arbitrarily shaped surfaces for 3-D object reconstruction. *S.P.I.E. Proc.* 2059.

BOOKSTEIN, F. L., 1989. Principal warps: Thin-plate splines and the decomposition of deformations. *IEEE Trans. Pattern Anal. Mach. Intell.* 11(6):567–585.

BOOKSTEIN, F. L., and W. D. K. GREEN, 1992. Edge information at landmarks in medical images. *S.P.I.E. Proc.* 1808:242–258.

BORGEFORS, G., 1984. Distance transformations in arbitrary dimensions. *Comput. Vision Graphics Image Proc.* 27:321–345.

BORGEFORS, G., 1988. Hierarchical chamfer matching: A parametric edge matching algorithm. *IEEE Trans. Pattern Anal. Mach. Intell.* 10:849–865.

BROU, P., 1984. Using the gaussian image to find the orientation of objects. *Int. J. Robotics Res.* 3(4):89–125.

BROWN, L. G., 1992. A survey of image registration techniques. *ACM Comput. Surv.* 24(4):326–376.

BRUNIE, L., 1992. Fusion d'images medicales multi-modales: Application a l'etude tridimensionnelle dynamique de la colonne vertebrale (in French). Doctoral thesis, Grenoble University.

BRUNIE, L., and S. LAVALLÉE, 1992. Three-dimensional dynamic imaging of the spine. In *MEDINFO '92*, Geneva, Switzerland. K. C. Lun, ed. Amsterdam: Elsevier Science Pub.

BRUNIE, L., S. LAVALLÉE, and R. SZELISKI, 1992. Using force fields derived from 3D distance maps for inferring the attitude of a 3D rigid object. In *Proceedings of the Second European Conference on Computer Vision (ECCV '92)*, G. Sandini, ed. Santa Margherita, Italy, pp. 670–675. Berlin: Springer-Verlag.

BURT, D. J., 1981. A dynamic model for image registration. *Comput. Graphics Image Proc.* 15:102–112.

CERCHIARI, U., G. DEL PANNO, C. GIORGI, and G. GARIBOTTO, 1986. 3-D correlation technique for anatomical volumes in functional stereotactic neurosurgery. In *Time-Varying Image Processing and Moving Object Recognition*, V. Cappellini, ed. Firenza, Italy, pp. 147–152.

CHAMPLEBOUX, G., S. LAVALLÉE, P. SAUTOT, and P. CINQUIN, 1992. Accurate calibration of cameras and range imaging sensors, the NPBS method. In *Proceedings of the IEEE International Conference on Robotics and Automation*, Nice, France, pp. 1552–1558.

CHEN, G. T. Y., M. KESSLER, and S. PITLUCK, 1985. Structure transfer between sets of three dimensional medical imaging data. In *Computer Graphics*, R. C. Bower, ed. Dallas: pp. 171–175.

CHEN, X., 1992. *Vision-based geometric modeling*. Doctoral thesis, Telecom, Paris.

DANIELSON, P. E., 1980. Euclidean distance mapping. *Comput. Vision Graphics Image Proc.* 14:227–248.

DHOME, M., M. RICHETIN, J. T. LAPRESTE, and G. RIVES, 1989. Determination of the attitude of 3D objects from a single perspective view. *IEEE Trans. Pattern Anal. Mach. Intell.* 11(12):1265–1278.

DUBOIS, F., A. BRUT, and P. CINQUIN, 1992. Mise en correspondance d'images tomoscintigraphiques de perfusion pulmonaire avec des images tomodensitometriques a l'aide de catheters externes (in French). In *32eme Colloque de Medecine Nucleaire*, Clermont-Ferrand, France.

EVANS, A. C., W. DAI, L. COLLINS, P. NEELIN, and S. MARETT, 1991. Warping of a computerized 3-D atlas to match brain image volumes for quantitative neuroanatomical and functional analysis. *S.P.I.E. Proc.* 1445:236–247.

FAN, T. J., G. MEDIONI, and R. NEVATIA, 1989. Recognizing 3D objects using surface properties. *IEEE Trans. Pattern Anal. Mach. Intell.* 11(11):1140–1157.

FAUGERAS, O. D., and M. HEBERT, 1986. The representation, recognition and locating of 3D objects. *Int. J. Robotic Res.* 5(3):27–52.

FAUGERAS, O. D., and M. HEBERT, 1987. The representation, recognition, and positioning of 3-D shapes from range data. In *Three-Dimensional Machine Vision*, T. Kanade, ed. New York: Kluwer Academic, pp. 301–353.

FAUGERAS, O. D., and G. TOSCANI, 1986. The calibration problem for stereo. In *Proceedings of the IEEE Computer Society Conference on Computer Vision and Pattern Recognition (CVPR '86)* Miami Beach, Fla., pp. 15–20.

FLIFLA, J., J. L. DILLESENGER, P. HAIGRON, and J. L. COATRIEUX, 1992. Quaternion based registration method in medical imaging. In *Proceedings of International Biomedical Engineering Days*, Istanbul, pp. 161–165.

GAMBOA-ALDECO, A., L. FELLINGHAM, and G. CHEN, 1986. Correlation of 3D surfaces from multiple modalities in medical imaging. *S.P.I.E. Proc.* 626:467–473.

GASTAMBIDE, I., 1992. *Utilisation des splines pour le calibrage d'images IRM (in French)* (technical rep.). Grenoble: TIMB-IMAG.

GERLOT-CHIRON, P., and Y. BIZAIS, 1992. Registration of multimodality images using a region overlap criterion. *Comput. Vision Graphics Image Proc.* 54(5):396–406.

GOERSS, S. J., P. J. KELLY, B. A. KALL, and G. J. ALKER, 1982. A computed tomographic stereotactic adaptation system. *Neurosurgery* 3(10):375–379.

GRIMSON, W. E. L., and T. LOZANO-PEREZ, 1984. Model-based recognition and localization from sparse range or tactile data. *Int. J. Robotics Res.* 3(3):3–35.

GRZESCZCZUK, R., N. ALPERIN, D. N. LEVIN, Y. CAO, K. K. TAN, and C. A. PELIZZARI, 1992. Multimodality intracranial angiography: Registration and integration of conventional angiograms and MRA data. In *IEEE Engineering in Medicine and Biology Society Proceedings*, J. P. Morucci, ed. Paris: IEEE, pp. 2783–2784.

GUÉZIEC, A., and N. AYACHE, 1992. Smoothing and matching of 3-D space curves. In *Proceedings of the Second Conference on Computer Vision (ECCV '92)*, G. Sandini, ed. Santa Margherita, Italy: pp. 620–629. Berlin: Springer-Verlag.

HANNA, K. D., F. E. JOUVE, G. O. WARING, and P. G. CIARLET, 1992. Computer simulation of arcuate keratotomy for astigmatism. *Refract. Corneal Surg.* 8:152–163.

HENRI, C. J., D. L. COLLINS, and T. M. PETERS, 1991. Multimodality image integration for stereotactic surgical planning. *Med. Phys.* 18(2):167–177.

HENRI, C. J., A. ČUKIERT, D. L. COLLINS, A. OLIVIER, and T. M. PETERS, 1992. Towards frameless stereotaxy: Anatomical-vascular correlation and registration. *S.P.I.E. Proc.* 1808:214–224.

HILL, D., D. J. HAWKES, E. D. LEHMANN, and J. E. CROSSMAN, 1990. Registered high resolution images in the interpretation of radionucleide scans. In *Proceedings of the IEEE Engineering in Medicine and Biology Society Conference*, Philadelphia: IEEE, pp. 143–144.

HOLMAN, B. L., R. E. ZIMMERNAN, K. A. JOHNSON, P. A. CARVALHO, R. B. SCHWARTZ, J. S. LOEFFLER, E. ALEXANDER, C. A. PELIZZARI, and G. T. Y. CHEN, 1991. Computer-assisted superimposition of magnetic resonance and high-resolution technetium-99m HMPAO and thallium-201 SPECT images of the brain. *J. Nucl. Med.* 32:1478–1484.

HORN, B. K. P., 1987. Closed-form solution of absolute orientation using unit quaternions. *J. Optom. Soc. Am.* 4(4): 629–642.

HUANG, T. S., S. D. BLOSTEIN, and E. A. MARGERUN, 1986. Least-squares estimation of motion parameters from 3-D correspondences. In *Proceedings of the IEEE Conference on Computer Vision and Pattern Recognition*, Miami, pp. 24–26.

HUANG, Y., H. STEINMETZ, U. KORR, and H. HERZOG, 1991. 3D matching of structural (CT, MR) and functional (PET) brain image data. In *Computer Assisted Radiology (CAR '91)*, H. U. Lemke, ed. Berlin: Springer, pp. 229–233.

HUBER, P. J., 1981. *Robust Statistics*. New York: Wiley.

HUCK, W., and U. BAER, 1980. A new targeting for stereotaxis procedures within the CT scanner. *Neuroradiology* 19: 13–17.

JACQ, J. J., and C. ROUX, 1993. Automatic registration of 3D images using a simple genetic algorithm with a stochastic performance function. In *IEEE Engineering in Medicine and Biology Society Proceedings*. San Diego: IEEE, pp. 126–127.

JIANG, H., R. A. ROBB, and K. S. HOLTON, 1992. A new approach to 3-D registration of multimodality medical images by surface matching. *S.P.I.E. Proc.* 1808:196–213.

KALL, B. K., 1992. Comprehensive multimodality surgical planning and interactive neurosurgery. In *Computers in Stereotactic Neurosurgery*, P. J. Kelly and B. A. Kall, eds. Boston: Blackwell Scientific, pp. 209–229.

KANG, S. B., and K. IKEUCHI, 1993. The complex EGI: A new representation of 3D pose determination. *IEEE Trans. Pattern Anal. Mach. Intell.* 15(7):707–721.

KEHTARNAVAZ, N., and R. J. P. DEFIGUEIREDO, 1988. Recognition of 3D curves based on curvature and torsion. In *SPIE Digital and Optical Shape Representation and Pattern Recognition*, Vol. 938, pp. 357–365.

KELLY, P. J., 1986. Technical approaches to identification and stereotactic reduction of tumor burden. In *Biology of Brain Tumour*, M. D. Walker, and D. G. T. Thomas, eds. pp. 237–343. Boston: Martinus Nijhoff.

KOIVUKANGAS, J., Y. LOUHISALMI, J. ALAKUIJALA, and J. OIKARINEN, 1993. Ultrasound-controlled neuronavigator-guided brain surgery. *J. Neurosurg.* 79:36–42.

KOSUGI, Y., E. WATANABE, and J. GOTO, 1988. An articulated neurosurgical navigation system using MRI and CT images. *IEEE Trans. Biomed. Engin.* 35(2):147–152.

KRAMER, E., M. NOZ, G. MAGUIRE, J. SANGER, C. WALSH, and E. MILLAN, 1992. Fusing of immunoscintigraphy SPECT with CT or MRI for improved multimodality image interpretation. In *IEEE Engineering in Medicine and Biology Society Proceedings*, J. P. Morucci, ed. Paris: IEEE, pp. 1805–1806.

KRIEGMAN, D. J., and J. PONCE, 1990. On recognizing and positioning curved 3-D objects from image contours. *IEEE Trans. Pattern Anal. Mach. Intell.* PAMI-12(12):1127–1137.

KRISHNAPURAM, R., and D. CASASENT, 1989. Determination of three-dimensional object location and orientation from range images. *IEEE Trans. Pattern Anal. Mach. Intell.* 11(11):1158–1167.

KWOH, Y. S., J. HOU, E. A. JONCKHEERE, and S. HAYATI, 1988. A robot with improved absolute positioning accuracy for CT guided stereotactic brain surgery. *IEEE Trans. Biomed. Engin.* 35(2):153–160.

LAURENT, P. J., A. LE MEHAUTE, and L. L. SCHUMAKER, 1991. *Curves and Surfaces*. San Diego: Academic.

LAVALLÉE, S., R. SZELISKI, and L. BRUNIE, 1991. Matching 3-D smooth surfaces with their 2-D projections using 3-D distance maps. In *S.P.I.E. Proc.* 1570:322–336.

LAVALLÉE, S., J. TROCCAZ, L. GABORIT, P. CINQUIN, A. L. BENABID, and D. HOFFMANN, 1992. Image guided robot: A clinical application in stereotactic neurosurgery. In *Proceedings of the IEEE International Conference on Robotics and Automation*, Nice, France: IEEE, pp. 618–625.

LEVIN, D. N., C. A. PELIZZARI, G. T. Y. CHEN, C. T. CHEN, and M. D. COOPER, 1988. Retrospective geometric correlation of MR, CT, and PET images. *Radiology* 169(3): 817–823.

LEWIS, J. T., and R. L. GALLOWAY, 1992. A-mode ultrasonic detection of subcutaneous fiducial markers for image-space registration. In *Proceedings of the Fourteenth IEEE Engineering in Medicine and Biology Conference*. Paris, IEEE, pp. 1061–1062.

LIN, Z. C., T. S. HUANG, S. D. BLOSTEIN, H. LEE, and E. A. MARGERUM, 1986. Motion estimation from 3-D points sets with and without correspondences. In *IEEE Computer Society Conference on Computer Vision and Pattern Recognition (CVPR '86)*, Miami, pp. 194–197.

LOWE, D. G., 1991. Fitting parameterized three-dimensional models to images. *IEEE Trans. Pattern Anal. Mach. Intell.* 13(5):441–450.

MAITRE, H., and Y. WU, 1987. Software tools to standardize and automate the correlation of images with and between diagnostic modalities. *Pattern Recogn.* 20(4):443–462.

MALANDAIN, G., and J. M. ROCCHISANI, 1992. Registration of 3D medical images using a mechanical based method. In *Proceedings of the IEEE Engineering in Medicine and Biology Society Conference*. Rennes, France: IEEE, pp. 91–95.

MANDAVA, V. R., J. M. FITZPATRICK, C. R. MAURER, R. J. MACIUNAS, and G. S. ALLEN, 1992. Registration of multimodal volume head images via attached markers. *S.P.I.E. Proc.* 1652:271–282.

MANGIN, J. F., V. FROUIN, I. BLOCH, J. LOPEZ-KRAHE, and B. BENDRIEM, 1993. *Fast nonsupervised 3D registration of PET and MR images of the brain* (tech. rep. 93C006). Paris: Telecom Paris.

MAURER, C. R., J. M. FITZPATRICK, M. Y. WANG, and R. J. MACIUNAS, 1993. Correction of geometrical distorsion in MR image registration. In *IEEE Engineering in Medicine and Biology Society Proceedings*. San Diego: IEEE, pp. 122–123.

MAZIER, B., S. LAVALLÉE, and P. CINQUIN, 1990. Computer assisted interventionist imaging: Application to the vertebral column surgery. In *IEEE Engineering in Medicine and Biology Society Proceedings*. Philadelphia: IEEE, pp. 430–431.

MONGA, O., S. BENAYOUN, and N. AYACHE, 1992. From partial derivatives of 3D density images to ridge lines. In

IEEE Computer Society Conference on Computer Vision and Pattern Recognition (CVPR '92). Champaign, Ill., pp. 354–359.

MÖSGES, R., G. SCHLÖNDORFF, L. KLIMEK, D. MEYER-EBRECHT, W. KRYBUS, and L. ADAMS, 1989. Computer assisted surgery: An innovative surgical technique in clinical routine. In *Computer Assisted Radiology (CAR '89)*, H. U. Lemke, ed. Berlin: Springer, pp. 413–415.

NEVATIA, R., and T. O. BINFORD, 1977. Description and recognition of curved objects. *Artif. Intell.* 8:77–98.

OGHABIAN, M. A., and A. TODD-POKROPEK, 1991. Registration of brain images by a multi-resolution sequential method. In *Lectures Notes in Computer Science*, Vol. 511: *Information Processing in Medical Imaging*. Berlin: Springer-Verlag, pp. 165–174.

PEIFER, J. W., E. V. GARCIA, and C. D. COOKE, 1992. 3-D registration and visualization of reconstructed coronary arterial trees on myocardial perfusion distributions. *S.P.I.E. Proc.* 1808:225–234.

PELIZZARI, C. A., G. T. Y. CHEN, and J. DU, 1992. Registration of multiple MRI scans by matching bony surfaces. In *Proceedings of the Fourteenth IEEE Engineering in Medicine and Biology Conference*. Paris: IEEE, pp. 1972–1973.

PELIZZARI, C. A., G. T. Y. CHEN, D. R. SPELBRING, R. R. WEICHSELBAUM, and C.-T. CHEN, 1989. Accurate 3-D registration of CT, PET, and-or MR images of the brain. *J. Comput. Assist. Tomogr.* 13(1):20–26.

PERIA, O., S. LAVALLÉE, G. CHAMPLEBOUX, A. F. JOUBERT, J. F. LEBAS, and P. CINQUIN, 1993. Millimetric registration of SPECT and MR images of the brain without head-holders. In *IEEE Engineering in Medicine and Biology Society Proceedings*. San Diego: IEEE, pp. 14–15.

PETERS, T. M., J. A. CLARK, A. OLIVIER, E. P. MARCHAND, G. MAWKO, M. DIEUMEGARDE, L. MURESAN, and R. ETHIER, 1986. Integrated stereotaxic imaging with CT, MR imaging and digital substraction angiography. *Med. Phys.* 161(3):821–826.

POHJONEN, H., A. KIURU, P. NIKKINEN, and P. KARP, 1992. Registration of anatomical and functionnal 3D data sets. In *IEEE Engineering in Medicine and Biology Society Proceedings*, J. P. Morucci, ed. Paris: IEEE, pp. 2239–2240.

PRESS, W. H., B. P. FLANNERY, S. A. TEUKOLSKY, and W. T. VETTERLING, 1986. *Numerical Recipes: The Art of Scientific Computing.* Cambridge, Engl.: Cambridge University Press.

RADACK, G. M., and N. I. BADLER, 1989. Local matching of surfaces using a boundary-centered radial decomposition. *Comput. Graphics Image Proc.* 45:380–396.

RANADE, S., and A. ROSENFELD, 1980. Point pattern matching by relaxation. *Pattern Recogn.* 12:269–275.

ROBERTS, D. W., J. W. STROHBEIN, and J. F. HATCH, et al., 1986. A frameless stereotaxic integration of computerized tomographic imaging and the operating microscope. *J. Neurosurg.* 65:545–549.

SANDER, P. T., and S. W. ZUCKER, 1992. Singularities of principal direction fields from 3D images. *IEEE Trans. Pattern Anal. Mach. Intell.* PAMI-14(3):309–320.

SCHAD, L. R., R. BOESECKE, W. SCHLEGEL, G. H. HART-MANN, V. STURM, L. G. STRAUSS, and W. J. LORENZ, 1987. Three dimensionnal image correlation of CT, MR and PET. Studies in radiotherapy treatment planning of brain tumors. *J. Comput. Assist. Tomogr.* 11(6):948–954.

SCHIERS, C., U. TIEDE, and K. H. HÖHNE, 1989. Interactive 3D registration of image volumes from different sources. In *Computer Assisted Radiology (CAR '89)*, H. U. Lemke, ed. Berlin: Springer, pp. 667–669.

SINGH, M., R. R. BRECHNER, and V. W. HENDERSON, 1992. Neuromagnetic localization using magnetic resonance images. *IEEE Trans. Med. Imaging* 11(1):129–134.

STEIN, F., and G. MEDIONI, 1992. Structural indexing: Efficient 3-D object recognition. *IEEE Trans. Pattern Anal. Mach. Intell.* PAMI-14(2):125–145.

STOCKMAN, G. C., S. KOPSTEIN, and S. BENETT, 1982. Matching images to models for registration and object detection via clustering. *IEEE Trans. Pattern Anal. Mach. Intell.* PAMI-4:229–241.

SUETENS, P., D. VANDERMEULEN, J. M. GYBELS, G. MARCHAL, and G. WILMS, 1992. Stereotactic arteriography and biopsy simulation with the BRW system. In *Computers in Stereotactic Neurosurgery*, P. J. Kelly and B. A. Kall, eds. Boston: Blackwell Scientific, pp. 249–258.

SZELISKI, R., and S. LAVALLÉE, 1993. Matching 3-D anatomical surfaces with non-rigid deformations using octree-splines. *S.P.I.E. Proc.* 2031:306–315.

TAYLOR, R. H., H. A. PAUL, C. B. CUTTING, B. MITTELSTADT, W. HANSON, P. KAZANZIDES, B. MUSITS, Y. Y. KIM, A. KALVIN, B. HADDAD, D. KHORAMABADI, and D. LAROSE, 1992. Augmentation of human precision in computer-integrated surgery. *ITBM: Innovation Tech. Biol. Med. (special issue)* 13(4):450–468.

TERZOPOULOS, D., 1988. The computation of visible-surface representations. *IEEE Trans. Pattern Anal. Mach. Intell.* PAMI-10(4):417–438.

TERZOPOULOS, D., and K. FLEISCHER, 1988. Deformable models. *The Visual Computer* 4(6):306–331.

TERZOPOULOS, D., and D. METAXAS, 1991. Dynamic 3D models with local and global deformations: Deformable superquadrics. *IEEE Trans. Pattern Anal. Mach. Intell.* 13(7):703–714.

TERZOPOULOS, D., A. WITKIN, and M. KASS, 1988. Constraints on deformable models: Recovering 3D shape and nonrigid motion. *Artif. Intell.* 36:91–123.

THIRION, J. P., 1993. *The marching line algorithm: New results and proofs* (tech. rep. 1881). France: INRIA.

THIRION, J. P., O. MONGA, S. BENAYOUN, A. GUEZIEC, and N. AYACHE, 1992. Automatic registration of 3D images using surface curvature. In *IEEE International Symposium on Optical Applied Science and Engineering*, San Diego.

TOENNIES, K. D. J. K. UDUPA, G. R. HERMAN, I. L. WORNOM III, and S. R. BUCHMAN, 1990. Registration of 3-D objects and surfaces. *IEEE Comput. Graphics Appl.* 10(3):52–62.

TURKINGTON, T. G., R. J. JASZCZAK, C. A. PELIZZARI, C. C. HARRIS, J. R. MACFALL, J. M. HOFFMAN, and R. E. COLEMAN, 1993. Accuracy of registration of PET, SPECT and MR images of a brain phantom. *J. Nucl. Med.* 34(9): 1587–1594.

UMEYAMA, S., 1991. Least-squares estimation of transformation parameters between two point patterns. *IEEE Trans. Pattern Anal. Mach. Intell.* PAMI-13(4):376–380.

WELLS, W., R. KIKINIS, D. ALTOBELLI, and W. LORENSEN, 1993. Video registration using fiducials for surgical enhanced reality. In *IEEE Engineering in Medicine and Biology Society Proceedings*. San Diego: IEEE, pp. 24–25.

WILSON, M. W., and J. M. MOUNTZ, 1989. A reference system for neuroanatomical localization on functional reconstructed cerebral images. *J. Comput. Assist. Tomogr.* 13(1): 174–178.

WITKIN, A., and W. WELCH, 1990. Fast animation and control of nonrigid structures. *Comput. Graphics (SIGGRAPH '90)* 24(4):243–252.

WOLFSON, H., 1990. On curve matching. *IEEE Trans. Pattern Anal. Mach. Intell.* 12(5):483–489.

ZHANG, J., M. F. LEVESQUE, C. L. WILSON, R. M. HARPER, J. ENGEL, R. LUFKIN, and E. J. BEHNKE, 1990. Multimodality imaging of brain structures for stereotactic surgery. *Radiology* 175(2):435–441.

6 Correlative Analysis of Three-Dimensional Brain Images

ALAN C. EVANS, D. L. COLLINS, P. NEELIN, AND
T. S. MARRETT

IN RECENT YEARS, there has been rapid growth in the use of 3D correlative imaging (also described as *image registration*, *co-registration*, *matching*, or *fusion*) in studies of the human brain. The wide appeal of such techniques has found applications in the areas of disease diagnosis, longitudinal monitoring of disease progress or remission, preoperative evaluation and surgery planning, radiotherapy treatment planning, functional neuroanatomy of sensorimotor and cognitive processes, and morphometric analysis of neuroanatomic variability. Based on the strategy of resampling one image such that it becomes coextensive with another, the underlying methods fall into two broad categories—crossmodality and within-modality registration. The former operation usually is performed for image volumes taken from the same individual. The latter may involve registering data from the same subject that has been acquired minutes or years apart, or it may demand the optimal spatial superposition of data from different individuals under the constraints imposed by the allowed geometric transformation (e.g., linear or nonlinear deformation).

A particularly active area of cross-modality imaging combines functional images with the corresponding anatomic images from MRI or CT. Tomographic imaging of cerebral physiology with positron emission tomography (PET) and single photon emission computed tomography (SPECT) scanning provide in vivo measurement of a wide variety of functional parameters on a regional basis in the human brain, including local hemodynamics, metabolism, pharmacokinetics, tissue pH, and the distribution of chemotherapeutic agents (Phelps, Mazziotta, and Schelbert, 1986). In practice, such images often are limited in their ability to yield accurate anatomic information because of poor spatial resolution, poor counting statistics, and often because the distribution of the radiolabel does not adequately reflect underlying anatomic variation. This latter limitation may be due to the relatively uniform distribution of the functional parameter in brain (as for tissue pH, oxygen extraction fraction, and water partition coefficient), or because of a lack of differential uptake between normal brain and pathologic tissue (as may occur in low-grade tumors). The lack of precise anatomic localization of tracer has often compromised the qualitative interpretation of functional images for diagnostic purposes and has severely hampered attempts to obtain reliable quantitative results from in vivo research. The need to augment the functional data with structural knowledge has therefore become paramount (Mazziotta and Koslow, 1987).

Intramodal registration is a simpler problem than cross-modal matching, because the corresponding features from each image will exhibit similar properties of contrast, noise, and spatial resolution as a result of the imaging process. Although strategies for how best to register data from the same individual differ, most methods seek to minimize some summed residual expressing measure of the intensity discrepancy between the two volumes at each voxel. Long-term monitoring of volumetric changes in lesion volume or tissue atrophy are salient diagnostic examples of this work. There are also many applications in which it is crucial to ensure that different image volumes from a single subject are exactly registered, notably studies of the slight regional changes in cerebral blood flow during some mental task. When dealing with data from different individuals, such as in studies of neuroanatomic variability, overall feature correspondence methods can be used (e.g., Collins et al., 1992; Collins, Peters, and Evans, 1992) or homologous landmarks may be identified in each volume for linear (Fox, Perlmutter, and Raichle, 1985; Talairach and Tournoux, 1988; Steinmetz and Seitz, 1991; Evans et al., 1992a,b) or nonlinear (Bookstein, 1991; Evans et al., 1991b) superposition within a standardized space.

In this chapter, we describe the 3D imaging environment developed at the Montreal Neurological Institute (MNI) for these two domains of image registration and present examples of their application in research and diagnostic brain studies. We describe our own experience over 4 years with a landmark-matching algorithm and briefly compare this with another popular method. Finally, we describe the integration of the separate elements of correlative imaging within a standardized brain space for quantitative analysis of physiology and anatomy across subject populations (i.e., brain mapping). A more comprehensive overview of the current status of multimodal correlation and analysis is presented in Evans (1993).

Cross-modality matching

BACKGROUND

Numerous approaches to multimodality correlation have been reported. Despite numerous attempts to obtain matched image planes at acquisition time (e.g., Evans et al., 1988), the majority of groups performing multimodality registration now favor a post-hoc analysis, resampling one image volume to obtain a new set of image planes that are coincident with those of the other volume. The most popular approaches to date have employed surfacematching (Pelizzari et al., 1989; Levin et al., 1989), homologous landmark matching (Evans et al., 1989, 1991a; Hill et al., 1991), or some form of solid modeling of the objects to be registered, using geometric properties of the derived object (e.g., principal axes) to define the required transformation (e.g., Alpert et al., 1990). Recent developments (Collins et al., 1992; Collins, Peters, and Evans, 1992; Van den Elsen, Maintz, and Viergever, 1992) suggest that a combination of all these methods within a general feature-matching approach might be more robust against defects in the raw data resulting from incomplete object coverage, intensity distortion, geometric distortion, lack of contrast, and image noise.

POINT MATCHING   Point-matching registration methods require the matching of a set of 3D points in one image with a homologous set in the other image. These points can be obtained from external fiducial markers attached to the head-holder or preferably to the head itself, or from internal anatomic landmarks.

External fiducials often consist of small capsules, visible in each modality, that are attached to the head but can also include more structured fiducial attachments, particularly for stereotactic surgical applications (Bergstrom et al., 1981; Kelly, Kall, and Goerss, 1984; Peters et al., 1986, 1989; Kall, Kally, and Goerss, 1987; Zhang et al., 1990). Problems can arise with external fiducials in functional imaging, particularly in tracer uptake studies, as the fiducial signal must match that in each image to preserve dynamic range in the image data. Also, for correlative studies, the fiducials must stay in place during the set-up procedure for both machines and, possibly, for some extended period between the functional and anatomic scans.

The use of internal landmarks, identified by hand in each image, have the advantages of no special prescan procedures and possible retrospective matching of data. However, the applicability of the method rests on the ease with which image volumes can be searched to tag corresponding landmarks in each volume. Hence, its success depends on the local implementation of the user interface as much as on fundamental considerations of algorithmic robustness, image contrast, and noise. The landmarks can also provide the raw data for image matching by nonlinear 3D image warping, either in the same patient for body imaging (Maguire et al., 1986) or across subjects in studies of morphometric variability (Bookstein, 1991; Evans et al., 1991b).

SURFACE MATCHING   A method that has gained acceptance recently in a number of centers is the "head and hat" approach for matching surfaces from the different modalities (Levin et al., 1988, 1989; Pelizzari et al., 1989; Neiw et al., 1991). The surface of a 3D object that can be identified in both modalities, usually the brain surface, is extracted as a set of 2D contours by an automatic edge-finding operator applied to each slice. One set of contours, usually from the higher-resolution data (MRI or CT), constitutes a rigid-body "head" while the other set is a rigid-body "hat." Fitting the hat on the head determines the best affine transformation between the two data sets. The algorithm achieves this by minimizing the volume between the two surfaces by an iterative nonlinear least-squares procedure, varying either six (three translation, three rotation) or nine (including anisotropic scaling) affine parameters.

MNI IMPLEMENTATION OF LANDMARK-MATCHING PROCEDURES

At the MNI, co-registration of MRI and PET is performed for every PET study. Between 1988 and 1993, more than 500 such procedures have been completed using the landmark-matching approach. Of these, approximately 400 have been studies of cerebral blood flow (CBF), predominantly in normal brain. For purposes of intersubject averaging (see the section, Stereotactic Transformation) where anatomic variability prevents exact superposition of equivalent structures from different subjects, CBF images have been reconstructed to a lower resolution (18 mm), than for single-subject analysis, in which the reconstructed resolution is typically 10 mm.

DATA COLLECTION

PET PET data are acquired with a Scanditronix PC-2048B system with 15 slices and 3D resolution of $5 \times 5 \times 7$ mm (Evans et al., 1991c). Images are reconstructed as 128×128 or 256×256 matrices with 2-mm or 1-mm square pixels, respectively. Phantom measurements indicated no significant geometric distortion over the imaging field of view. PET images are obtained using ^{18}F-fluorodeoxyglucose (FDG) for measurement of regional glucose metabolism, $H_2^{15}O$ for measurement of regional blood flow (Herscovitch, Markham, and Raichle, 1983), or ^{18}F-fluoroDOPA, a tracer for dopaminergic neurotransmission (Garnett, Firnau, and Nahmias, 1983; Gjedde et al., 1991).

MRI All MRI studies are performed on a Philips Gyroscan 1.5 tesla superconducting magnet system. Using 3D spin-echo acquisition, 64 nonoverlapped T_1-weighted (Repetition Time $T_R = 400$ msec, Echo Time $T_E = 30$ msec) image planes are collected at 2-mm intervals over the whole brain. MRI data are stored as 256×256 images with 1-mm square pixels. Measurements of the dimensions of an MRI calibration phantom indicate negligible geometric distortion through the central portion of the MRI imaging field (Peters et al., 1988).

Computing All images are reconstructed on local VAX systems and transferred via Ethernet to the Neuro-Imaging Laboratory. For analysis, PET images are expanded by pixel copying to 256×256 format. The 3D imaging systems used are a PIXAR-1, hosted by a SUN 3/180, or SGI 4D/35 and Indigo systems.

PROCEDURE

To obtain registration of the MRI and PET image volumes, a 3D image-processing package has been developed that allows the following:

- Arbitrary rotation, translation, and scaling of image volumes
- Real-time triplane display through two volumes, which are independently controllable, and through the corresponding merged volume
- Interactive identification of equivalent 3D points in two image volumes via cursor
- Linear least-squares optimization to calculate the affine transformation that minimizes the root mean square distance between two ensembles of paired points
- Oblique sectioning through a volume using trilinear, quadratic, or cubic spline interpolation
- Compositing of two image volumes by opacity weighting

The registration procedure requires that two sets of equivalent points be defined, one in each volume, and is based on the Procrustes algorithm (Sibson, 1978; Golub and Van Loan, 1983) which finds the "best" solution, in a least-squares sense, by minimizing the rms distance between all paired points. During the procedure, any three cardinal planes can be selected through each of the MRI, PET, and MRI/PET composite images, and the nine resultant images displayed simultaneously. Typically, 10–20 point pairs are tagged in 20–30 minutes, and the transformation that best matches the two point ensembles is obtained by minimizing some distance norm, usually in a least-squares sense. The landmarks selected depend on the tracer being used but generally include centers of obvious structures and features such as points of maximum curvature. For a typical CBF or regional glucose metabolism (CMRGlc) study, where tracer accumulates in gray matter, the landmarks selected include head of caudate, thalamus, frontal temporal and occipital poles, sylvian fissure, occipitocerebellar junction, and the superolateral aspect of the parietal lobe. For tracers that provide less anatomic detail, such as fluoroDOPA, which accumulates significantly only in caudate and putamen, we combine points from the fluoroDOPA image and from the PET transmission image. The transmission image, acquired immediately before the emission study, is in essence a CT scan of density but acquired with 511-keV gamma rays and a PET detector geometry. While lacking the fine detail of true CT, such images identify petrous bones, sinus cavities, and skull landmarks that can be correlated with the MRI data. Validation studies (discussed later) indicate that such procedures do not significantly degrade registration accuracy.

Color plate 2 shows a single slice through a 3D example of matched MRI/FDG data, whereas plate 3 shows a composite fluoroDOPA and MRI image. Plate 4 shows an MRI/FDG composite after each image volume had been volume-rendered (Drebin, Carpenter, and Hanrahan, 1988) to enhance surfaces.

VALIDATION STUDIES OF REGISTRATION ACCURACY

In landmark-matching algorithms, the residual rms error between apparently homologous points is not a measure of registration accuracy as it also includes the error in identifying truly equivalent landmarks, referred to as the *homology error*. This error often is significantly larger than the true error in placing equivalent points in register. To measure the registration error alone, one may use attached fiducial markers but, because of looseness of the skin, it is difficult to fix the fiducial position between scans to the required tolerance of 1–2 mm. Hence, to determine the number of pairs and the accuracy of point localization needed to obtain a given accuracy in registration, simulation studies were performed using random point ensembles (Evans et al., 1989, 1991a). Recently, we have extended these experiments using simulated 3D PET data and results from more than 360 MRI/PET registrations performed in our laboratory to generate more realistic point ensembles and 3D transformations (Neelin et al., 1992).

SIMULATED IMAGES Simulated PET images were generated as follows: 3D gradient-echo MRI data ($T_R = 75$ msec; $T_E = 14$ msec; flip angle $= 60°$; slice thickness $= 3$ mm) were collected over the whole brain. A model-based 3D tissue classification algorithm (Kamber et al., 1992) was used to identify gray matter, white matter, cerebrospinal fluid (CSF), and bone. Idealized PET images corresponding to blood flow or glucose metabolism were created by assigning gray-white-CSF voxel

TABLE 6.1
Error in registration of simulated PET images with MRI (standard deviations for 79 registrations)

	σ_x	σ_y	σ_z	Mean
Rotation error (deg)	1.9	1.5	1.6	1.67 ± 0.08
Translation error (mm)	0.9	1.5	1.4	1.27 ± 0.06
Error at 75 mm (mm)	2.7	3.2	2.6	2.83 ± 0.13

intensities a ratio of $4:1:0$. The volume was then sampled to generate planar projection PET data, taking into account the 3D point spread function, sampling geometry, scatter, randoms, gamma-ray attenuation, and Poisson noise in the projections (Ma, Rousset, and Evans, 1992). Projection data were then reconstructed using filtered backprojection to generate a PET data set registered by definition with the MRI. Applying a known realistic transformation to the MRI and performing the landmark identification procedure for registration yielded a direct measure of registration accuracy in the presence of realistic image contrast and noise characteristics. Table 6.1 shows the results obtained for 79 such simulated registrations, indicating an average registration error of 1.27 mm at the centroid and 2.83 mm at a distance of 75 mm from the centroid (approximating the brain surface distance). The corresponding rms error in identifying equivalent points averaged 4.9 mm in each dimension, with no preferred direction.

POINT SIMULATION In a complementary study, a set of N points was taken to represent landmark positions identified in MRI. A random linear transformation was applied to generate corresponding PET landmarks and Gaussian noise added to each coordinate to simulate homology errors (i.e., uncertainty in identifying these equivalent landmarks). The apparent inverse transformation then was determined and, after application of this transformation to the *noise-free* ensemble, the rms error in recovering the original landmark positions provided a measure of registration accuracy that could be assessed for different N and increasing levels of injected homology error. In contrast to earlier random point-ensemble simulations (Evans et al., 1989, 1991), the landmarks and applied transformation were drawn from actual image registration procedures, either the 79 examples described in the preceding section or from 360 real MRI/PET registrations (mostly

TABLE 6.2

	Simulated PET	CBF	FDG	FluoroDOPA
Simulations/point	7900	6380	800	3300
Homology error (mm)	4.66	4.14	3.92	4.51
Rotation error (deg)	1.23	1.19	1.16	1.19
Centroid error (mm)	1.18	1.06	1.00	1.16
Error at 75 mm (mm)	1.81	1.66	1.61	1.73

Note: Values quoted are for 16 points. Distance measures are average of each dimension.

CBF studies; see table 6.2). For each ensemble, a subset of N point pairs, from 3 to a possible 16, was used for registration and the registration error measured on 4 of the omitted point pairs. For each N, 100 (for 8 FDG and 33 fluoroDOPA cases) or 20 (for 319 CBF cases) runs were performed at each noise level to generate stable estimates of registration error as a function of N. As shown in figure 6.1 for an injected homology error of 5 mm, registration error falls rapidly with N at first and then adopts a $1/\sqrt{N}$ dependence after N of 8–10. Similar curve shapes were obtained for injected noise levels of 2.5, 5.0, 10, and 15 mm, the error scaling linearly with noise level.

These simulation results, where both the registration error and the homology error are known, were then used to interpret the residuals obtained with real image data where only the overall error is known, thereby extracting the registration error in real data. The ratio of overall error for real data to that of simulated data was constant with N for each class of image (see table 6.2), confirming the adequacy of the simulation for predicting error propagation and allowing a direct estimate of typical homology and registration error in each case. Table 6.2 summarizes the results for our typical N of 16, indicating the registration error to be typically 1.1 mm at the centroid and typically 1.7 mm at the brain surface (75 mm from the centroid). Interestingly, no strong dependence was observed on image type for registration error or for uncertainty in landmark identification, which was 4–4.5 mm (note that measurements are 1D; multiplying by $\sqrt{3}$ gives approximate 3D values).

Translational errors measured in tables 6.1 and 6.2 are very similar, averaging 1.2–1.3 mm, but rotation errors are 40–50% bigger in table 6.1 (typically 1.7° versus 1.2°). This is partially due to a smaller N (mean

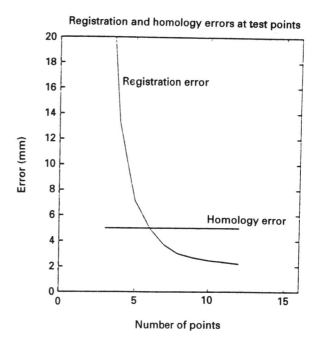

FIGURE 6.1   Registration error, σ_r, as a function of the number of landmark pairs, N, used in the Procrustes algorithm for a given uncertainty in identifying truly equivalent landmarks in each image volume (i.e., rms homology error = σ_h, set at $\sigma_h = 5$ mm). The registration error scales with input homology error, such that for $N > 8$–10, σ_r is proportional to $\sigma_h/\sqrt{N}$.

of 14.4 versus 16) but also depends on the limited quality of the simulated images, where imperfect tissue segmentation, particularly in cerebellum, degraded the resultant PET image. The use of an isotropic model for homology error may also be an oversimplification as, in some cases (e.g., the frontal pole), the landmark is well defined in the radial direction but poorly defined in the tangential direction. Such factors may adversely affect the rotational stability of the registration obtained from image-derived landmarks compared with point simulations. Nevertheless, the results overall indicate a typical 3D registration error of 2.5–3.5 mm, averaged over the whole brain when using 16 landmarks.

COMPARISON OF LANDMARK MATCHING WITH
SURFACE MATCHING

Inherent in the landmark-matching method is the disadvantage of a manual step needed to identify the landmarks. Landmark identification requires some anatomic training, although the problem rapidly becomes a pattern-recognition issue rather than a biologic issue. Anatomic definition from functional images is not straightforward, particularly where the tracer distribution is disrupted by a pathologic process or where the tracer is confined to specific regions (e.g., with receptor-transmitter mapping of basal ganglia). As discussed previously, it is possible to obtain additional anatomic information from the PET transmission scan acquired before (Evans et al., 1991a) or simultaneously (Ranger, Thompson, and Evans, 1989; Thompson et al., 1991) with the emission study, to measure gamma-ray attenuation.

The strength of the surface matching is its potential for automatic operation or, at least, its operation by a trained technologist. Care must be taken to ensure that the extracted contours properly represent a continuous 3D surface and that the effects of variable image contrast (e.g., from cold lesions), noise, and reconstruction artifacts (e.g., streaking) have been removed. This may require manual editing. Also, the method does not require a sophisticated user interface to extract the 2D contours and, therefore, it can be readily set up at remote sites. Problems can occur with missing data; for instance, the top of the "head" may be missing in one set of contours. The iterative nature of the algorithm occasionally leads it to settle into a local minimum on the parameter surface, which necessitates operator intervention to "nudge" the algorithm toward the global minimum. Pelizzari et al. (1989) quote registration accuracy for various permutations of two modalities (MRI, CT, and PET) on the order of 0.7–2.5 mm in 2D images, depending on the pixel size for the lower-resolution data set and the slice thickness. The PET/MRI value of 2.5 mm is comparable to the 3D estimate obtained in our own simulation studies. Recently, Neiw et al. (1991) improved this method by automating the surface-detection operation, precomputing some of the geometric information relating surface points in each volume to the corresponding centroid, and using a simulated annealing algorithm for the parameter optimization that, while requiring much longer to converge, is less sensitive to problems related to local minima.

The head and hat algorithm minimizes the mean distance between "hat" points and the "head" surface. In MRI/PET-correlation studies, the method yields residual rms distances between "hat" points and "head" surface of the order of 1–2 mm. The method differs from landmark-matching methods in that it minimizes a point-to-surface residual, whereas the Procrustes algorithm performs a point-to-point minimization. The methods therefore cannot be compared directly in terms of residual because, for example, a "hat" point may be moved parallel to the adjacent "head" surface without affecting its distance from that surface. The point-to-point mapping approach uses more specific constraints at the expense of requiring that equivalent points first be identified.

Pelizzari et al. (1991a) recently compared a landmark-based method with this surface-matching procedure for PET/MRI correlation in three different types of PET image: FDG CMRGlc reconstructed to 8-mm resolution, H_2O CBF study reconstructed to 20 mm, and a transmission study reconstructed to 10 mm. They concluded that the methods produced very similar results in each case and that a 2-mm registration error represented a practical lower bound for both methods.

Intramodal matching

It is often important to align data sets acquired at different times from a single subject to monitor and quantify disease progress (e.g., tumor growth and remission, proliferation of multiple sclerosis lesions, surgical assessment from preoperative and postoperative scans). There is also increasing interest in optimal alignment of data from different subjects, such that normal variability in anatomy or function can be measured. Diagnostic decisions can then be made by direct comparison of individual images with an image or images that express the normal range of image intensities.

In stereotactic transformation, 3D image data are linearly mapped into a standardized brain-based coordinate space (Talairach et al., 1967; Talairach and Tournoux, 1988) such that all brains have the same extent in three orthogonal directions and each plane of the resliced volume can be compared directly with an anatomic atlas. The Talairach transformation is based on the identification of the anterior posterior commissural (AC-PC) Line, extended to the cortical edge in the anteroposterior (AP) direction, and a set of perpendiculars to this line from the AC and PC points to the cortical edge. Strict application of the method (Lemoine et al., 1991) requires the proportional scaling to be partitioned into three piecewise linear components in the AP direction (pre-AC, AC-PC, post-PC) and two in the craniocaudal direction (above and below AC-PC) and to be independent for each hemisphere. This is intended to overcome problems introduced by nonlinear morphometric variability among individuals. Most centers either have retained a single scale along each dimension or have applied full nonlinear warping techniques to address the nonlinearity issue directly.

Originally developed for use with pneumoencephalographic studies of brain step and periventricular structures, this method has become central to so-called functional brain-mapping studies (Fox, Perlmutter, and Raichle, 1985) and general multimodal surgical applications (Barillot et al., 1990; Lemoine et al., 1991). In the simplest form of brain-mapping studies, CBF is measured in a baseline state and during some form of cerebral activation (e.g., primary sensory stimulus, cognitive task, psychological challenge). Regional CBF changes indicate brain areas involved in stimulus processing. These changes often are too small ($<10\%$) to be discerned from a single subject, and so the experiment is repeated in a series of individuals. The results are averaged after mapping all volume data into stereotactic space.

At the MNI, the Talairach space is used both for anatomic analysis with MRI data and for functional activation studies with PET, using a preregistered MRI image for defining the required transformation. Because the AC and PC points are close (approximately 25 mm apart) and difficult to identify reliably even on MRI, significant errors can be introduced that are magnified at the cortex. We therefore select a series of five well-separated midline landmarks that yield a least-squares fit approximation to the AC-PC line (Evans et al., 1992a). Validation studies in 37 young normal brains indicate an angular discrepancy of $-0.24 \pm 2.9°$ and a vertical translational error of 1.2 ± 1.0 mm. Using this strategy, a database of more than 300 MRI volumes, each comprising 64 contiguous 2-mm-thick image planes, have been collected from young normal right-handers (Evans, Collins, and Milner, 1992). The average intensity MRI data set obtained from the database illustrates the effect of anatomic variability in different brain areas and serves as a low-resolution, large sample atlas of gross neuroanatomy in Talairach space. Figure 6.2 illustrates selected slices from this MRI atlas, which is composed of 80 planes separated by 1.5 mm in Talairach coordinates.

Recently, we have implemented an automated method for mapping data into stereotactic space, using a general multiscale feature-matching technique discussed in more detail later (Collins et al., 1992; Collins, Peters, and Evans, 1992). This strategy uses a 3D cross-correlation residual to match a single MRI volume to the 300-brain MRI composite. When appropriate, the corresponding transformation is also applied to the previously registered PET scan.

LANDMARK-DRIVEN ATLAS AND IMAGE WARPING

At the MNI, a 3D volume-of-interest (VOI) atlas has been constructed by manual outlining of individual brain regions on sixty-four 2mm-thick adjacent MRI slices. Sixty structures in each hemisphere are identified, including deep gray-matter structures, major gyri, ventricles, and white-matter zones. The data exist as a tessellated geometric model that can be resliced along any 2D plane or warped in three dimensions to fit an image volume. Usually, the template is matched to MRI before being applied to a correlated PET image for functional measurement (Marrett et al., 1989; Evans et al., 1991a).

ATLAS WARPING We have implemented a procedure for deforming the entire 3D atlas under landmark-driven constraints, by application of the "thin-plate" spline procedure of Bookstein (1989). This method determines the continuous coordinate transformation

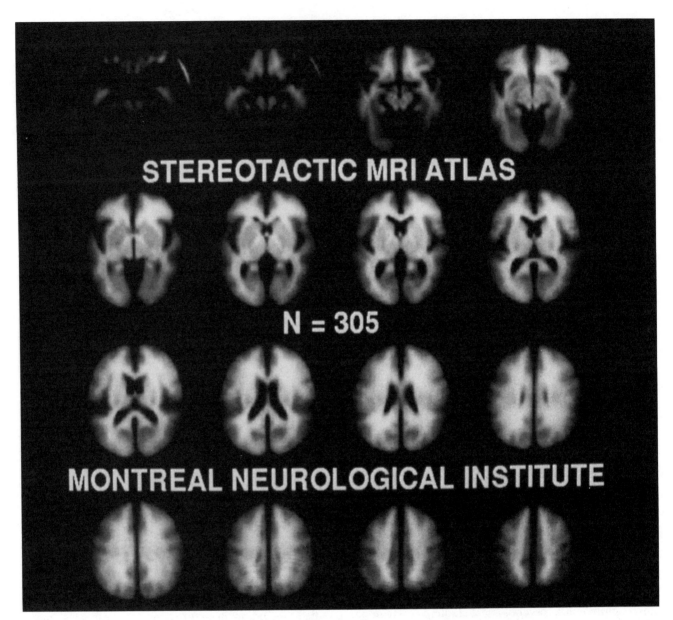

FIGURE 6.2 Mean MRI data set drawn from 305 young normal volunteers. The data set can be used as an anatomic atlas for locating functional activation data in Talairach space. It also provides a visual impression of local anatomic variability and an indication of how well a particular functional measurement can be localized.

that maps one set of 3D coordinates onto an equivalent set of homologous points. The procedure decomposes the overall deformation into a series of principal warps of decreasing geometric scale. In two dimensions, this is mathematically analogous to the bending energy required to deform a thin metal sheet so that a set of points on the sheet have a defined height above corresponding points on a flat surface. To assess the algorithm, we applied it to MRI from 16 young, normal subjects (Evans et al., 1991b).

LANDMARK IDENTIFICATION Using the landmark-tagging procedure, a set of anatomic features in each MRI study was matched to corresponding structures in the master MRI volume from which the VOI atlas originally was derived. Each point was also identified by its coordinates within the Talairach stereotactic atlas for consistent reference among subjects, because a particular landmark could be identified in many ways (e.g., center of thalamus). These homologous point pairs were used to define the linear or nonlinear mapping of the VOI atlas from the master MRI data set to the current MRI data. A set of 26 points was identified in each MRI volume using the following rationale. Points at the extremities (frontal and occipital poles, brain vertex, pons and midbrain notch) were selected to constrain the overall size of the fitted atlas. Deep nuclei were identified by their approximate centroid as defined by the selected Talairach coordinates. These combined with the anterior and posterior horns of the lateral ventricles constrained the distortion of periventricular brain. Finally, a limited set of gyral and sulcal landmarks were selected to constrain the topology of the cortical mantle.

LINEAR AND NONLINEAR MODEL COMPARISON By restricting the number of terms in the warping algorithm to only affine transformations, including anisotropic scaling, the mapping operation was reduced to a linear model in which the solution was effectively a least-squares residual between master and target ensembles. Mapping the VOI atlas into a single MRI volume by both linear and nonlinear solutions allowed a direct comparison of the two solutions for that volume. However, because each brain had different dimensions, the pooling of results across all subjects would not have been straightforward. Instead, by first fitting a volume with the nonlinear solution and then performing a numeric inverse solution but allowing only linear terms, all measurements were established in the master frame. This procedure was applied to the 16 data sets, and the center of gravity for each of the structures in the VOI atlas was used to assess the local inadequacy of the linear model.

In general, the warped atlas fitted the central brain regions well, owing to the number of landmarks identifiable in the periventricular regions (caudate, thalamus, anterior and posterior commissures, corpus callosum, lateral ventricles). In cortical regions, the relative lack of identifiable landmarks limited the extent to which local cortical adjustments could be both initially specified and subsequently evaluated. The lack of specific cerebellar landmarks resulted in unsatisfactory fits of that region. Such problems must be dealt with by additional cerebellar constraints. The results in table 6.3 indicate that a substantial component of normal anatomic variation cannot be accommodated within a linear model. The overall 3D center of gravity shift between linear and nonlinear models of 6–7 mm is considerable for applications that seek to localize spe-

TABLE 6.3

RMS distance (mm) of regional 3D center of gravity from target position following linear warping of VOI atlas to target space

Distance (R)	SD	Region
6.34	3.15	Superior frontal gyrus
7.69	2.27	Middle frontal gyrus
5.86	2.40	Inferior frontal gyrus
5.83	2.14	Precentral gyrus
5.05	2.35	Postcentral gyrus
4.50	1.91	Superior temporal gyrus
4.47	1.65	Middle temporal gyrus
5.19	2.07	Inferior temporal gyrus
5.38	2.19	Amygdala
5.22	2.26	Hippocampus
9.18	3.52	Head of caudate nucleus
7.14	2.99	Putamen
7.80	3.15	Globus pallidus
7.63	2.94	Thalamus
6.52	3.16	Total (60 structures)

Note: RMS distance indicates residual anatomic variability not handled by the linear model [60 regions total (14 shown); 16 subjects].

cific structures with respect to other anatomic fiduciary markers based on principles of linear stereotaxy (e.g., biopsy or depth electrode placement).

IMAGE WARPING The landmark-driven warping algorithm can also be used for nonlinear 3D deformation of individual image volumes. Using the same 26 landmarks as previously, an inverse 3D warp was performed to map the individual MRI images into the atlas space using either the full nonlinear interpolation or the first three terms only, which define the affine component of the overall transformation. Figure 6.3 illustrates a single slice through the central region of the 16-brain average normalized intensity image using either linear or nonlinear transformation. The nonlinear transformation exhibits a sharper appearance and more detail than the linear version, reflecting the superiority of the nonlinear approach for bringing homologous structures in the neighborhood of individual landmarks into precise alignment.

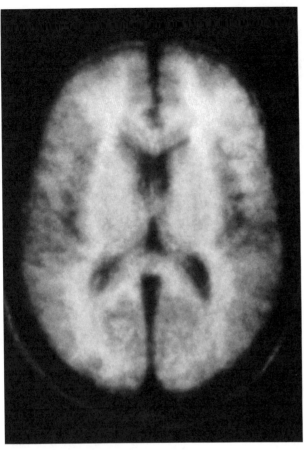

(a)

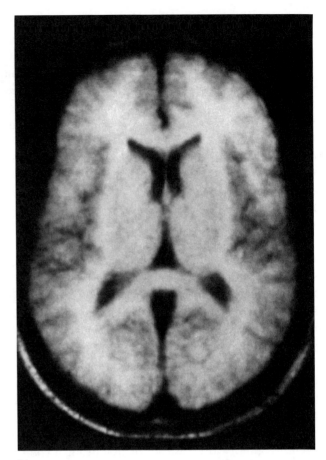

(b)

FIGURE 6.3 Comparison of the average MRI brain obtained from 16 subjects using a (a) linear and (b) nonlinear model of anatomic variability.

FEATURE MATCHING

A problem of some concern with interactive landmark-based approaches is the subjectivity of landmark choice (i.e., the dependence of the resultant deformation on the number and distribution of landmarks selected and the behavior of the algorithm in regions distant from any landmark). An alternative approach that avoids the need for potentially time-consuming landmark tagging but sacrifices explicitly defined point correspondence is that of feature matching (e.g., Bajcsy, Lieberson, and Reivich, 1983; Bajcsy and Kovacic, 1989). In this context, image features are local properties of the image intensity that can be extracted automatically by neighborhood operators (e.g., edges, zones of relatively homogeneous intensity, or particular shapes).

We have implemented a 3D feature-matching procedure that employs repetitive evaluation of the feature cross-correlation function (FCCF) between two images (Collins et al., 1992; Collins, Peters, and Evans, 1992). The global maximum FCCF hypersurface, indicating the required transformation, is found by nonlinear optimization using the SIMPLEX algorithm. The algorithm operates in a multiscale loop, beginning with a heavily smoothed version of each image and successively sharpening the images at each iteration. The use of blurred images for obtaining approximate transformation parameters reduces the likelihood of encountering local minima during the search and is approximately four times faster than single-stage high-resolution optimization. At each stage, the original image is first convolved with a 3D Gaussian smoothing kernel before the best transformation is determined by

TABLE 6.4

*Simulation of intrasubject registration (20 repeats, 17 subjects):
errors in affine parameters for rotation and translation only (exp. 1), and with scaling (exp. 2)*

	RMS error				Standard deviation		
	x axis	y axis	z axis	avg.	x axis	y axis	z axis
Experiment 1							
Rotation (deg)	0.0766	0.0958	0.0773	0.0832	0.0487	0.0612	0.0466
Translation (mm)	0.0959	0.1027	0.1081	0.1022	0.0576	0.0675	0.0639
Experiment 2							
Rotation (deg)	0.0787	0.1010	0.0874	0.0890	0.0500	0.0640	0.0513
Translation (mm)	0.1055	0.1034	0.1218	0.1102	0.0628	0.0678	0.0760
Scale	0.0012	0.0011	0.0018	0.0014	0.0009	0.0007	0.0011

maximizing the FCCF at scales (SD of Gaussian kernel) of 32, 16, 8, 4, and 2 mm. For affine transformation, the method uses only image intensity as a feature but, for nonlinear image warping, gradient vector fields are needed.

To measure intrasubject registration accuracy, 20 random linear transformations (only translations and rotations) were applied to each of 17 MRI (T_1-weighted gradient-echo sequence, 3-mm thick) volumes of the head from normal volunteers (27 ± 3 years old), and the algorithm was applied to recover the transformation. For each trial, two measures of registration error were calculated: the rms difference between input and recovered parameters and the rms registration error between 48 landmarks, manually identified in each volume. Over the 340 trials (table 6.4), the rms errors for rotation, translation, and landmark distance were less than or equal to 0.1°, 0.1 mm, and 0.2 mm, respectively. Adding anisotropic scaling to the simulations had a negligible impact on these values.

For intersubject registration, each data set in turn was identified as the target, and the other 16 volumes were registered to it. Over the 272 trials, the linear transformation recovered by multiresolution registration yielded an rms landmark distance of 6.65 mm. Note that this measure is dominated by nonlinear anatomic variability and not by landmark homology error among MRI volumes. This value agrees well with the mean measure of anatomic variability of 6.52 mm in table 6.3, determined with a different technique in different subjects.

To compare this result to manual landmark registration, we submitted the 48 landmarks to the Procrustes procedure (see the previous section, Procedure). With an isotropic scale variable, the rms residual was 5.94 mm, whereas with anisotropic scaling, it was 5.79 mm. Although these values are smaller than the 6.65 mm obtained for the automatic approach, the comparison is biased because the points used to define the Procrustes transformation are the same as those used to measure the error. Nevertheless, the values indicate that the automatic feature-matching approach performs as required.

The applicability of the method for cross-modal matching depends on the extent to which equivalent features can be extracted from the two images which, in turn, depends on the tracer distribution of the functional image. Rizzo et al. (1991) obtained encouraging results in two dimensions for MRI/PET correlation using a tracer (FDG) that distributes preferentially in gray matter. Similar results could be expected with blood flow tracers.

REGIONAL SEGMENTATION

We currently are developing a procedure for automatic identification of individual brain regions (e.g., caudate, superior temporal gyrus) that combines multiscale feature matching, the concept of stereotactic space, and the VOI atlas. The VOI atlas and the MRI volume on which the VOI atlas originally was defined are now resident in stereotactic space. Hence, mapping an individual MRI volume into this space by feature

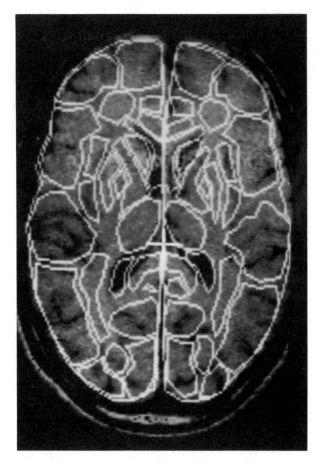

FIGURE 6.4 An example of the fit between VOI atlas and target MRI data set in a plane passing through the basal ganglia.

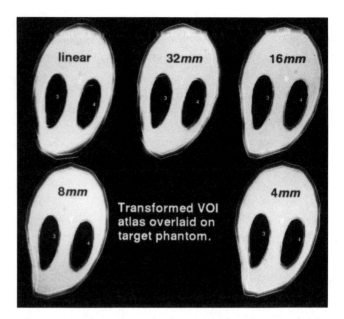

FIGURE 6.5 Results of the nonlinear registration and segmentation feature-matching algorithm using a simple multiellipsoid phantom. The original 3D phantom, composed of four separate ellipsoids, was first deformed to a pear shape using thin-plate spline warping based on manually defined landmarks. The automatic feature cross-correlation was then maximized at successively finer scales to register the original phantom with this new object. Using the object contours for clarity, these five panels show the progress from a linear fit to a nonlinear fit at 32-, 16-, 8-, and 4-mm scales.

matching against the resident MRI also fits it to the VOI atlas. A trivial inverse transformation fits the VOI atlas to the new MRI in its original space. Figure 6.4 shows such a fit in stereotactic space.

The multiscale nature of the feature-matching algorithm facilitates the recursive application of the linear cross-correlation optimization to individual neighborhoods defined on a 3D grid with a dimension equal to the current scale. Hence, an overall nonlinear transformation is obtained by successive local linear transformations. Figure 6.5 shows application of the algorithm to recover the original shape of a 3D multiellipsoid brain phantom following application of a known deformation via a thin-plate spline 3D warp (Bookstein, 1989). Using as a measure of accuracy a distance residual for 296 points distributed over all phantom surfaces, the linear method yielded an rms registration error of 9.21 mm. The most recent version of the nonlinear algorithm reduced this value by 80%.

Discussion

In this chapter, we have described various aspects of 3D correlative imaging in progress at the Montreal Neurological Institute, including both cross-modal and intramodal registration. Although the applications described refer to MRI and PET data, most of the discussion applies equivalently to the CT (for MRI) or SPECT (for PET) settings.

A precise knowledge of the individual anatomy of each patient corresponding to the physiologic image is essential for accurate and reproducible results in both the neurologic and neurosurgical settings. For example, in cerebrovascular disease, hemodynamic changes often precede metabolic dysfunction which, in turn, may be measurable long before anatomic images manifest observable changes. Conversely, the interpretation of functional data in the vicinity of the ischemic or infarcted region may be extremely difficult because of a lack of anatomic cues and noisy data. The combination of the anatomy and function from correlated

MRI, PET, and CT images (Heiss et al., 1986) and the further possibility of using an anatomically customized region-of-interest (ROI) atlas to obtain regional measurements is of obvious benefit (Evans et al., 1988). Figure 6.1 illustrates a 2D merged MRI/PET data set in a case of bilateral parieto-occipital ischemia, in which the corresponding anatomic image shows a corresponding lesion on only one side.

For tumor studies, the ability to observe a heterogeneous functional profile in the context of a correspondingly complex neoplastic mass has immediate benefits for subsequent management of the patient. Increased uptake may signal tumor recurrence or invasion of the surrounding parenchyma. Apparent metabolic depression of the tumor may be due to tumor necrosis or surrounding edema. Color plate 5 illustrates a temporal lobe oligodendrocytoma using PET, MRI, and merged PET/MRI. In analogous fashion, the superposition of radiotherapy dose distributions on the correlated anatomy and functional images provides a more complete picture of the expected and actual outcome of treatment.

The rapidly developing area of functional and anatomic brain mapping employs a number of correlative imaging methods described earlier. The transformation of individual brain image volumes into Talairach space allows for their correlation with each other or with some form of knowledge base for anatomic interpretation. This may take the form of a book containing an example or a schematic representation of a brain in Talairach space (Talairach et al., 1967; Fox, Perlmutter, and Raichle, 1985; Talairach and Tournoux, 1988). In addition, a computerized atlas may be used to identify regions of this standardized brain space. We correlate each subject's MRI and PET volumes and then transform both into Talairach space, providing a customized anatomic template for the functional image, which consists of a sparse map of significant CBF changes. The differences between an idealized representation and the true underlying anatomy provided by MRI can sometimes be crucial to the interpretation of the data (Drevits et al., 1988). The availability of correlated atlas or MRI data also offers the possibility of untangling the purely anatomic component from the variability in location of the response to a given stimulus observed among a population (Steinmetz and Seitz, 1991). In addition, the use of MRI is vital in interpreting activation data obtained where there are likely to be morphologic changes (e.g., Alzheimer's disease,

normal aging, space-occupying lesions). Color plate 6 illustrates this type of anatomic-functional correlation.

The facility for assessing the functional status of a proposed operative site is likely to assume increasing importance as these techniques become easier. In epilepsy surgery, it is often crucial to establish whether a seizure focus, often apparent in the functional image as a region of interictal hypometabolism, is in or near the motor strip. The use of correlated MRI data, in the form of a 3D surface rendering, usually can resolve this question prior to surgery. Conversely, in situations where the underlying anatomy is distorted from normal, the precise assessment of functional neuroanatomy is extremely difficult. Here, the use of functional brain-mapping techniques become important. For instance, the mapping of language or motor areas in the vicinity of vascular malformations or neoplastic lesions has already begun to figure in the surgeon's decision making and now combines MRI and PET in the process (Leblanc and Meyer, 1990; Leblanc et al., 1992). Similarly, the ability to localize early tumor recurrence or evaluate tissue viability, using correlated image data, is likely to be more in demand. In all these situations, representing the multimodal data in a realistic 3D setting wherein the surgeon can rehearse the procedure will offer major advantages. Surgical practice is rapidly adopting multimodal techniques in which the images are correlated not only with one another but also with the patient's head and neurosurgical tools (Lavallée and Cinquin, 1990; Lemoine et al., 1991; Pelizzari et al., 1991b).

Beyond simple superposition of anatomy and functional data for visual inspection, the ability to endow each voxel (more correctly, each voxel's neighborhood, as defined by the aperture function of the lower-resolution image) with independent characteristics drawn from complementary modalities offers a number of possibilities for improved quantitative analysis of the functional and anatomic properties of an individual brain. For quantitative procedures, the structural image becomes the medium for defining anatomic 2D ROIs or 3D VOIs from which an average functional measure is obtained by averaging the enclosed pixels (voxels in 3D) from the correlated functional image. This approach can be augmented by the use of a previously defined geometric model that is adapted to the current anatomic image. Alternatively, the anatomic image can be segmented automatically on a pixel basis into tissue classes and class-specific measurements obtained from the functional image. Tissue classification can also be used in various ways to modify the functional image and increase the accuracy of physiologic measurements by, for example:

• Incorporating anatomic prior information into the functional image reconstruction process.

• Providing accurate information about the heterogeneity of gamma-ray attenuation through the object and its subsequent correction.

• Correcting the functional image for underlying tissue heterogeneity (e.g., tissue atrophy or differences in tracer transfer coefficients for gray and white matter).

• Statistical analysis of brain-mapping data involves a continuing problem of multiple comparison when searching over the whole brain for significant activation foci. The use of a correlated and segmented MRI data set permits a search space restricted to some anatomic zone (e.g., left temporal lobe) or tissue class (e.g., gray matter) when automatically processing the PET data (Worsley et al., 1992).

• Modeling and correcting for errors introduced by the PET scanner geometry (e.g., scattered events, spill-over fraction from adjacent structures and, possibly, signal recovery losses) (Kim et al., 1992; Ma, Rousset, and Evans, 1992; Rousset et al., 1992).

In the area of intramodal correlative imaging, the ability to examine repeated studies on the same subject, collected over extended periods, has many applications in disease progression (e.g., multiple sclerosis, cerebrovascular disease, and neoplastic growth). Similarly, the ability to align precisely preoperative and postoperative 3D images for quantitative assessment of the amount and location of excised tissue is a relatively new procedure with considerable promise. This presents special problems for automatic procedures as it may be necessary to exclude some subvolume, where changes have occurred, from the registration procedure. Such exclusion is easily performed with manual identification of landmarks. If the changes, functional or anatomic and from developmental or surgical causes, not only affect some well-defined zone but also introduce generalized distortion in the brain, then nonlinear techniques become mandatory. It may still be necessary to exclude the region that is not topologically equivalent in both volumes (e.g., a tumor mass) before these approaches can be employed.

The intersubject comparison of 3D brain images is presently being used principally in studies of gross neuroanatomy and functional mapping of normal brain. However, as the field develops, it is likely to find increasing application in diagnostic settings. For instance, the use of normative data on the location of specific gyri and sulci, when expressed within a standardized brain space, may aid in the identification of cortical dysplasia as a basis for epileptogenesis or for developmental problems in cognitive skills or language acquisition. The nonlinear mapping of presegmented brain models, in the form of raster volumes or 3D, geometric atlases, onto individual data sets is an area of intense interest in many centers worldwide. The eventual goal in such cases is the automatic labeling of each structure within the brain according to some predefined anatomic hierarchy.

In conclusion, it is apparent that correlative imaging has come of age. It is no longer a procedure performed occasionally by computer engineers but a medical procedure that is increasingly demanded. Nevertheless, we have only scratched the surface of the potential that is evident in the integration of complementary information, both patient-specific image data and prior knowledge about the brain.

ACKNOWLEDGMENTS The authors wish to thank their colleagues within the McConnell Brain Imaging Centre for many helpful comments and insights in the development of this work, notably Drs. Terry Peters and Albert Gjedde, staff Weiqian Dai, Sylvain Milot, and Youpu Zhang, and students David Macdonald, Yilong Ma, Micheline Kamber, and Olivier Rousset. We also thank Drs. John Crossman and David Hawkes from Guy's and Thomas' Hospitals, London, for their collaboration in the simulation studies.

REFERENCES

ALPERT, N. M., J. F. BRADSHAW, D. N. KENNEDY, and J. A. CORREIA, 1990. The principal axis transformation: A method for image registration. *J. Nucl. Med.* 31(10):1717–1722.

BAJCSY, R., and S. KOVACIC, 1989. Multiresolution elastic matching. *Comput. Vision Graphics Image Proc.* 46:1–21.

BAJCSY, R., R. LIEBERSON, and M. REIVICH, 1983. A computerized system for the elastic matching of deformed radiographic images to idealized atlas images. *J. Comput. Assist. Tomogr.* 7(4):618–625.

BARILLOT, C., D. LEMOINE, B. GIBAUD, P. J. TOULEMONT, and J. M. SCARABIN, 1990. A PC software package to confront multimodality images and a stereotactic atlas in neurosurgery. *Proc. S.P.I.E. (Medical Imaging IV)* 1232:188–199.

BERGSTROM, M., J. BOETHIUS, L. ERIKSSON, T. GREITZ, T. RIBBE, and L. WIDEN, 1981. Head fixation for reproducible position alignment in transmission CT and positron emission tomography. *J. Comput. Assist. Tomogr.* 5:136–141.

BOOKSTEIN, F., 1989. *Principal warps:* Thin-plate splines and the decomposition of deformations. *IEEE Trans. Patt. Anal. Mach. Intell.* 11(6):567–585

BOOKSTEIN, F., 1991. Thin-plate splines and the atlas problem for biomedical images. In *Lecture Notes in Computer Science 511: Information Processing in Medical Imaging*, A. C. F. Colchester and D. J. Hawkes, eds. Heidelberg: Springer-Verlag, pp. 326–342.

COLLINS, D. L., W. DAI, T. M. PETERS, and A. C. EVANS, 1992. Model-based segmentation of individual brain structures from MRI data. *Proc. S.P.I.E.* 1808:10–23.

COLLINS, D. L., T. M. PETERS, and A. C. EVANS, 1992. Non-linear multi-scale image registration and segmentation of individual brain structures from MRI. In *Proceedings of IEEE Symposium on Advanced Medical Image Processing in Medicine*, pp. 105–110.

DREBIN, R., L. CARPENTER, and P. HANRAHAN, 1988. Volume rendering. *ACM Comput. Graphics* 22(4):65–74.

DREVITS, W. C., T. O. VIDEEN, A. K. MACLEOD, J. W. HALLER, and M. E. RAICHLE, 1988. PET images of blood flow changes during anxiety: Correction. *Science* 256:1696.

EVANS, A. C., 1993. Multi-modality correlation and analysis. In *Principles of Nuclear Medicine*, H. Wagner, ed.

EVANS, A. C., C. BEIL, S. MARRETT, C. J. THOMPSON, and A. M. HAKIM, 1988. Anatomical-functional correlation using an adjustable MRI-based region-of-interest atlas with positron emission tomography. *J. Cereb. Blood Flow Metab.* 8(4):513–530.

EVANS, A. C., S. MARRETT, D. L. COLLINS, and T. M. PETERS, 1989. Anatomical-functional correlative analysis of the human brain using three-dimensional imaging systems. *Proc. S.P.I.E.* (Medical Imaging III) 264–274.

EVANS, A. C., W. DAI, L. COLLINS, P. NEELIN, and S. MARRETT, 1991b. Warping of a computerized 3-D atlas to match brain image volumes for quantitative neuroanatomical and functional analysis. *Proc. S.P.I.E.* (Medical Imaging V) 1445:236–247.

EVANS, A. C. S. MARRETT, D. L. COLLINS, and T. M. PETERS, 1989. Anatomical-functional correlative analysis of the human brain using three-dimensional imaging systems. *Proc. S.P.I.E.* (Medical Imaging III) 264–274.

EVANS, A. C., S. MARRET, P. NEELIN, L. COLLINS, K. WORSLEY, W. DAI, S. MILOT, E. MEYER, and D. BUB, 1992a. Anatomical mapping of functional activation in stereotactic coordinate space. *NeuroImage* 1(1):43–63.

EVANS, A. C., S. MARRETT, J. TORRESCORZO, S. KU, and L. COLLINS, 1991. MRI-PET correlative analysis using a volume of interest (VOI) atlas. *J. Cereb. Blood Flow Metab.* 11(2):A69–A78.

EVANS, A. C., T. M. PETERS, D. L. COLLINS, C. J. HENRI, T. S. MARRETT, G. B. PIKE, and W. DAI, 1992b. 3-D correlative imaging and segmentation of cerebral anatomy, function and vasculature. *Automedica* 14(1):65–80.

EVANS, A. C., C. J. THOMPSON, S. MARRETT, E. MEYER, and

M. MAZZA, 1991c. Performance characteristics of the PC-2048: A new 15-slice encoded-crystal PET scanner for neurological studies. *IEEE Trans. Med. Imag.* 10(1):90–98.

FOX, P. T., J. S. PERLMUTTER, and M. E. RAICHLE, 1985. A stereotactic method of anatomical localization for positron emission tomography. *J. Comput. Assist. Tomogr.* 9(1):141–153.

GARNETT, E. S., G. FIRNAU, and G. NAHMIAS, 1983. Dopamine visualized in the basal ganglia of living man. *Nature* 305:137–138.

GJEDDE, A., J. REITH, S. DYVE, M. DIKSIC, A. C. EVANS, and and H. KUWABARA, 1991. DOPA decarboxylase activity in the living human brain. *Proc. Natl. Acad. Sci.* 88:2721–2725.

GOLUB, G. H., and C. F. VAN LOAN, 1983. Matrix Computations. Baltimore: Johns Hopkins University Press.

HERSCOVITCH, P., J. MARKHAM, and M. E. RAICHLE, 1983. Brain blood flow measured with intravenous $H_2^{15}O$ I. Theory and error analysis. *J. Nucl. Med.* 24:782–789.

HILL, D. L. G., D. J. HAWKES, J. E. CROSSMAN, M. J. GLEESON, T. C. S. COX, E. E. BRACEY, A. J. STRONG, and P. GRAVES, 1991. Registration of MR and CT images for skull base surgery using point-like anatomical features. *Br. J. Radiol.* 65:1030–1035.

KALL, B., P. J. KELLY, and S. GOERSS, 1987. Comprehensive computer-assisted data collection, treatment planning and interactive surgery. *Proc S.P.I.E.* 767:509–514.

KAMBER, M., D. L. COLLINS, G. S. FRANCIS, R. SHINGHAL, and A. C. EVANS, 1992. Model-based 3D segmentation of multiple sclerosis lesions in MRI data. *Proc. S.P.I.E.* 1808: 590–600.

KELLY, P. J., B. KALL, and S. GOERSS, 1984. Functional stereotactic surgery utilizing CT data and computer generated stereotactic atlas. *Acta Neurochir. (Suppl.)* 33:577–583.

KIM, H.-J., B. R. ZEEBERG, F. H. FAHEY, E. J. HOFFMAN, and R. C. REBA, 1992. 3-D SPECT simulations of a complex 3-D mathematical brain model: Effects of 3-D geometric detector response, attenuation, scatter and statistical noise. *IEEE Trans. Med. Imag.* 11(2):176–184.

LAVALLÉE, S., and P. CINQUIN, 1990. Computer Assisted Medical Interventions. NATO ARW, Vol. F60, 3D Imaging in Medicine. K. H. Höhne, ed., Berlin: Springer-Verlag, pp. 301–312.

LEBLANC, R., and E. MEYER, 1990. Functional PET scanning in the assessment of cerebral arteriovenous malformations. *J. Neurosurg.* 73:615–619.

LEBLANC, R., E. MEYER, D. BUB, R. ZATORRE, and A. C. EVANS, 1992. Language mapping with activation PET scanning. *Neurosurgery* 31(2):36–373.

LEMOINE, D., C. BARILLOT, B. GIBAUD, and E. PASQUALINI, 1991. An anatomical-based 3D registration system of multi-modality and atlas data in neurosurgery. In *Lecture Notes in Computer Science 511: Information Processing in Medical Imaging*; A. C. F. Colchester and D. I. Hawkes, eds. Heidelberg: Springer-Verlag, pp. 154–164.

Levin, D. N., X. Hu, K. K. Tan, S. Galhotra, C. A. Pelizzari, G. T. Y. Chen, R. N. Beck, C.-T. Chen, M. D. Cooper, J. F. Mullan, J. Hekmatpanah, and J.-P. Spire, 1989. The brain: Integrated three-dimensional display of MR and PET images. *Radiology* 172:783–789.

Levin, D. N., C. A. Pelizzari, G. T. Y. Chen, C.-T., Chen, and M. D. Cooper, 1988. Retrospective geometric correlation of MR, CT and PET images. *Radiology* 169:817–823.

Ma, Y., O. Rousset, and A. C. Evans, 1992. Three-dimensional MRI-based simulation of PET images. In *Proceedings of IEEE Symposium on Advanced Medical Image Processing in Medicine*, pp. 141–146.

Maguire, G. Q., M. E. Noz, E. M. Lee, and J. H. Schimpf, 1986. Correlation methods for tomographic images using two- and three-dimensional techniques. In *Proceedings of the Ninth International Symposium on Information Processing in Medical Imaging*, S. L. Bacharach, ed. pp. 266–279.

Marrett, S., A. C. Evans, L. Collins, and T. M. Peters, 1989. A volume of interest (VOI) atlas for analysis of neurophysiological image data. *Proc. S.P.I.E.* (Medical Imaging III) 467–477.

Mazziota, J. C., and S. H. Koslow, 1987. Assessment of goals and obstacles in data acquisition and analysis from emission tomography: Report of a series of international workshops. *J. Cereb. Blood Flow Metab.* 7:S1–S31.

Neelin, P., J. Crossman, D. Hawkes, Y. Ma, and A. C. Evans, 1992. Evaluation of MRI/PET registration using simulated PET brain images. In *Proceedings of IEEE Symposium on Advanced Medical Image Processing in Medicine*, pp. 73–78.

Neiw, H. M., C.-T. Chen, W. C. Lin, and C. A. Pelizzari, 1991. Automated three-dimensional registration of medical images. *Proc. S.P.I.E.* (Medical Imaging III) 1445: 259–264.

Pelizzari, C. A., G. T. Y. Chen, D. R. Spelbring, R. R. Weichselbaum, and C.-T. Chen, 1989. Accurate three-dimensional registration of CT, PET and/or MRI images of the brain. *J. Comput. Assist. Tomogr.* 13:20–26.

Pelizzari, C. A., A. C. Evans, P. Neelin, C.-T. Chen, and S. Marrett, 1991a. Comparison of two methods for 3D registration of PET and MRI images. *Proc. IEEE Eng. Med. Biol. Soc.* 13(1):227–228.

Pelizzari, C. A., K. K. Tan, D. N. Levin, G. T. Y. Chen, and J. Balter, 1991b. Interactive 3-D patient-image registration. In *Lecture Notes in Computer Science 511: Information Processing in Medical Imaging*, A. C. F. Colchester and D. J. Hawkes, eds. Heidelberg: Springer-Verlag, 132–141.

Peters, T. M., J. A. Clark, A. Olivier, E. P. Marchand, G. Mawko, M. Dieumegarde, L. V. Muresan, and R. Ethier, 1986. Integrated stereotaxic imaging with CT, MR imaging and digital subtraction angiography. *Radiology* 161:821–826.

Peters, T. M., J. A. Clark, G. B. Pike, C. Henri, L. Collins, D. Leksell, and O. Jeppsson, 1989. Stereotactic neurosurgery planning on a personal-computer-based workstation. *J. Digit. Imag.* 2(2):75–81.

Peters, T. M., M. Drangova, J. A. Clark, and G. B. Pike, 1988. Image distortion in MR imaging for stereotactic surgery. Presented at the SMRM annual meeting, San Francisco.

Phelps, M. E., J. C. Mazziotta, and H. R. Schelbert, 1986. Positron Emission Tomography and Autoradiography. New York: Raven.

Ranger, N. T., C. J. Thompson, and A. C. Evans, 1989. The application of a masked orbiting transmission source for attenuation correction in PET. *J. Nucl. Med.* 30(6): 1056–1068.

Rizzo, G., P. Pasquali, M. C. Gilardi, S. Cerutti, V. Bettinardi, G., Lucignani, G., Scotti, and F. Fazio, 1991. Multimodality biomedical image integration: Use of a cross-correlation technique. *Proc. IEEE Eng. Med. Biol. Soc.* 13(1):219–220.

Rousset, O., Y. Ma, M. Kamber, and A. C. Evans, 1992. Simulation of striatal ^{18}F-fluoroDOPA uptake: Sensitivity of quantitative estimates to axial position. In *Proceeding of IEEE Symposium on Advanced Medical Image Processing in Medicine*, pp. 167–172.

Sibson, R., 1978. Studies in the robustness of multidimensional scaling: Procrustes statistics. *J. Statist. Soc.* 40:234–238.

Steinmetz, H., and R. J. Seitz, 1991. Functional anatomy of language processing; Neuroimaging and the problem of individual variability. *Neuropsychologia* 29(12):1149–1161.

Talairach, J., G. Szikla, P. Tournoux, A. Prossalentis, M. Bordas-Ferrer, L. Covello, M. Jacob, A. Mempel, P. Buser, and J. Bancaud, 1967. *Atlas d'Anatomie Stereotaxique du Telencephale*. Paris: Masson.

Talairach, J., and P. Tournoux, 1988. Co-Planar Stereotactic Atlas of the Human Brain: 3-Dimensional Proportional System—An Approach to Cerebral Imaging. Stuttgart: Thieme Verlag.

Talbot, J. D., S. Marrett, A. C. Evans, E. Meyer, M. C. Bushnell, and G. H. Duncan, 1991. Multiple representations of pain in human cerebral cortex. *Science* 251:1355–1358.

Thompson, C. J., N. Ranger, A. C. Evans, and A. Gjedde, 1991. Validation of simultaneous PET emission and transmission scans. *J. Nucl. Med.* 32:154–160.

Van den Elsen, P., J. B. A. Maintz, and M. A. Viergever, 1992. Image fusion using geometric features. *Proc. S.P.I.E.* 1808:172–186.

Worsley, K. J., A. C. Evans, S. Marrett, and P. Neelin, 1992. Determining the number of statistically significant areas of activation in subtracted activation studies from PET. *J. Cereb. Blood Flow Metab.* 12(6):900–918.

Zhang, J., M. F. Levesque, C. L. Wilson, R. M. Harper, J. Engel, R. Lufkin, and E. J. Behnke, 1990. Multimodality imaging of brain structures for stereotactic surgery. *Radiology* 175:435–441.

7 Anatomy-Based Registration of Three-Dimensional Medical Images, Range Images, X-Ray Projections, and Three-Dimensional Models Using Octree-Splines

STÉPHANE LAVALLÉE, RICHARD SZELISKI, AND LIONEL BRUNIE

ONE OF THE CLASSIC problems in model-based vision is the estimation of the pose (i.e., the location and orientation) of a 3D object with respect to a scene described by sensory data (2D images or 3D range data). Expressed formally, the problem is: Given an object in a coordinate system Ref_{3D} and sensory data (2D image contours or 3D range images) in a coordinate system Ref_{sensor}, estimate the six-component vector $\mathbf{p}$ that defines the rigid-body transformation $\mathbf{T}(\mathbf{p})$ between Ref_{sensor} and Ref_{3D}. When using 2D contours, although this problem can theoretically be solved for a single projection, in practice two or more projections are necessary to achieve a sufficiently accurate estimate. For range data, a single image often can produce a good pose estimate.

Although the method we will describe has many applications, our primary interest is in solving multimodal medical image-matching problems [1]. In that case, a general formulation of the problem is also the registration of two coordinate systems, Ref_{3D} and Ref_{sensor}. Ref_{3D} is a coordinate system associated with 3D images (MRI, CT, range images, etc.) whereas Ref_{sensor} can be associated with other 3D images [MRI, CT, range images, single photon emission computed tomography (SPECT), positron emission tomography (PET), magnetoencephalography (MEB)], but also with 2D x-ray projections, localized ultrasound images, or a 3D point localizer. To perform this registration, we first segment some reference anatomic structures (e.g., vertebrae, brain ventricles, skull) both in Ref_{3D} and in Ref_{sensor}. For most of our applications, the existence of a reference structure is confirmed. However, in some particular cases, this assumption is not true (for instance, if Ref_{sensor} is a SPECT imaging system). Then, we add an external sensor, $Ref_{external}$ (e.g., a range-imaging system, localized ultrasound images, x-ray system, 3D point localizer) to the device, Ref_{sensor}, that we want to register with Ref_{3D}. This external sensor is chosen according to its ability to provide information about a reference anatomic structure observed in Ref_{3D}. Then this external sensor is calibrated with the device associated with Ref_{sensor} (which is always possible). Finally, we register $Ref_{external}$ with Ref_{3D} using a reference structure; thus, the registration between Ref_{sensor} and Ref_{3D} is obtained by transitivity. Note that this approach allows one to consider the case in which Ref_{sensor} is associated with any device, which is not necessarily a sensor (e.g., a robot, an external irradiation system, a navigator).

How to extract a reference structure from images (2D and 3D segmentation problems) is not addressed in this chapter as these problems constitute separate, expansive research topics [2–4]. In our general formulation, we assume that a smooth surface of an organ or a bone has been segmented in 3D in Ref$_{3D}$ and that some partial data of this structure have been extracted in Ref$_{sensor}$. These partial data can be other 3D surface points (then we have a 3D/3D registration problem) or 2D contours of projections (in which case we have a 3D/2D registration problem). Our purpose is to estimate a transformation between Ref$_{3D}$ and Ref$_{sensor}$.

An instance of an application of this formulation is the registration of preoperative 3D CT scans with intraoperative x-ray projections for computer- or robot-assisted surgery. For instance, prior to a surgical operation, a simulated intervention procedure is performed on 3D CT images of the patient. Then, at the beginning of the operation, x-ray images of the patient lying on the operating table are taken from two or three viewpoints. The geometry of the x-ray projections is related to the robot's reference frame using standard calibration techniques [5]. To perform robot-assisted surgery accurately based on the preoperative simulation, the exact position of the patient must be determined by matching the reference system Ref$_{3D}$ associated with the preoperative images with the reference system Ref$_{sensor}$ associated with the x-ray images taken in the operating room [6, 7]. Figure 7.1 illustrates this 3D/2D matching problem.

Another medical application of our technique of 3D/2D matching is to register the vertebrae of a spinal segment in x-ray images of a standing scoliotic patient with models derived from CT data (where the patient was reclining) in order to provide 3D *dynamic* imaging

of the spine [8] and to allow 3D measurements of the scoliosis [9].

Similarly, the surface of the skin of a patient can be segmented on 3D images (MRI or CT) and can be acquired with range-imaging sensors linked to other imaging devices or operating robots [7]. Thus, a 3D/3D smooth surface–matching technique is needed to register the various imaging systems and robots: CT with MRI, CT or MRI with range images, MRI with MRI over time, and so on. In other applications, 3D data can be sets of 3D surface points extracted from series of spatially registered ultrasound images or 3D surface points manually digitized with optical or mechanical digitizers. Our technique can also be applied to nonmedical robotics, where the position of a smooth free-form object within the robot's work space must be determined. This problem has been receiving increased attention in computer vision, techniques having been proposed for matching an object both with its 2D projections (silhouettes) in video images [10] and with range data [11].

For all these applications, the main requirements are (1) to perform the matching process for arbitrary free-form smooth surfaces; (2) to achieve the best accuracy possible for the six rigid-body transformation parameters; (3) to compute an estimate of the uncertainties in the six parameters; and (4) to perform the matching process in a reasonable time. In this chapter, we focus on the 3D/2D matching problem, which is more difficult to solve with our defined requirements. Later in this chapter, we show that our method can easily be modified to solve the more commonly investigated 3D/3D matching problem with good accuracy.

Previous work

Estimating the pose of a 3D rigid object from sensor data has been widely studied in both medical data processing and computer vision. In medical imaging, the problem of image registration has usually been solved using external fiducial markers placed on the body of the patient [12–14] or by interactively selecting pairs of matching points [15–17]. An automated algorithm for matching 3D surfaces with other 3D surfaces (such as the head skin surface) has been developed by Pelizzari et al. [18]. Methods based on the registration of singular 3D curves have also been proposed [19, 20]. The automated matching of 3D medical images with x-ray projections has not been studied previously.

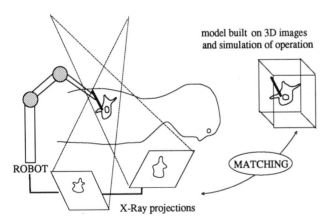

FIGURE 7.1 In computer- and robot-assisted surgery, it is necessary to match 3D medical images (MRI or CT) with 2D x-ray projections.

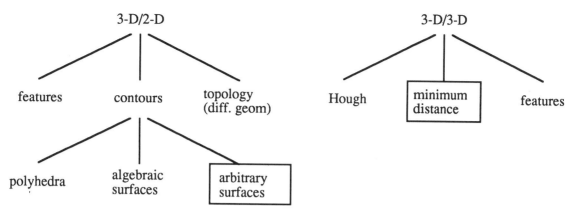

FIGURE 7.2 A (partial) taxonomy of pose estimation algorithms. (The boxed techniques are the ones used in this chapter.)

In computer vision, the recovery of pose information from both 2D images and 3D range data has been widely studied. The more general problem of *elastic matching* has also received much attention [21–25]. For the method we present, we will assume that a complete representation of the 3D surface of the object is known but will not assume anything about the existence of edges or particular points or curves on the object. First let us review methods for pose estimation from 2D images, followed by a review of techniques based on 3D range data.

Techniques for recovering pose from 2D images (the 3D/2D matching problem) can be classified into three general categories, based on the matching primitives used (figure 7.2). The first class of techniques is based on matching features identified on the surface of the object [26]. The correspondence between features can be computed using either direct or coarse-to-fine procedures. These approaches resemble stereo matching algorithms and are particularly well-suited to formulation using the theory of graphs [27–29]. Reducing the space of the possible poses [30] and using contextual knowledge [17, 31] can speed up the matching.

A second, more global, approach estimates the pose by aligning the extreme contours of the object with the available projections. For objects modeled as a set of polygonal surface patches, Lowe [32] describes an iterative approach for aligning the projected extreme contours with edges found in the image. His approach is similar to ours in that it uses nonlinear least squares. It differs in measuring errors in the image plane and assuming a polyhedral model (which may not be suitable for complex anatomic surfaces).

For smooth surfaces, inferring the contour generators (i.e., the curves that belong to the surface and that form the image contours) can be difficult [10]. A traditional approach is to restrict the shape of the object —for example, to objects of revolution [33] or generalized cones [34]. Ponce and Kriegman [10] have used rational parametric surface patches, implicit algebraic equation [35], and elimination theory to obtain analytic expressions for the projected contours. However, their method is restricted at present to objects modeled by a few patches.

By comparison, our approach can deal with objects of arbitrary shape and complexity because it does not need to compute the projected contours explicitly. In fact, our approach is close to classic chamfer matching [36], which maximizes the correlation between 2D features in the image and the projections of 3D object features. However, our distance measure is computed in 3D, which, as we will see, removes the need to identify 3D object features.

A third approach to 3D/2D matching uses a topological analysis of the object based on catastrophe theory [37–39] and differential geometry [40]. Unfortunately, no one has yet been able to develop an algorithm using these concepts. Recent analysis of aspect graphs for smooth objects [41] further demonstrates the high complexity of this approach.

By comparison, pose estimation based on 3D range data is better understood. In addition to the work in medical images [18–20], Besl and McKay [11] have recently proposed a technique for matching points to surfaces. Their method is similar to ours [42] but does not address the complex issue of rapidly finding the nearest point on a surface. Additional methods for registering 3D images include the Hough transform [43] and feature-based approaches (the *relative orientation* problem [44]).

Problem formulation

In this section, we first introduce the representation and notation chosen for the rigid-body transformations. We then briefly underline the importance of sensor calibration and present our formulation of the matching problem as the minimization of an energy.

Transformation and parameters

Using the notation defined earlier, the problem is to estimate the transformation $\mathbf{T}$ between $\mathrm{Ref}_{\mathrm{sensor}}$ and $\mathrm{Ref}_{3\mathrm{D}}$. $\mathbf{T}$ is called the *final pose* of the object and can be defined by a translation vector $\mathbf{t} = (T_x, T_y, T_z)^t$ and a 3×3 rotation matrix $\mathbf{R}$. Several representations can be used for $\mathbf{R}$ (e.g., Euler angles, quaternions, or rotation vectors [42]). We have chosen to use Euler angles $(\phi, \theta, \psi)^t$, where R is constructed from three rotations around axes x, y, and z with angles ϕ, θ, ψ.

$$\mathbf{R} = \begin{bmatrix} \cos\psi\cos\theta & -\sin\psi\cos\theta & \sin\theta \\ \cos\psi\sin\theta\sin\phi + \sin\psi\cos\phi & -\sin\psi\sin\theta\sin\phi + \cos\psi\cos\phi & -\cos\theta\sin\phi \\ -\cos\psi\sin\theta\cos\phi + \sin\psi\sin\phi & \sin\psi\sin\theta\cos\phi + \cos\psi\sin\phi & \cos\theta\cos\phi \end{bmatrix}$$
$$(1)$$

The Euler representation is valid only if some restrictions on Euler angles are applied [2]. In our case, the Euler angles remain in a single domain during the convergence because the initial estimates are not too far away from the solution.

If we gather the six parameters of the transformation $\mathbf{T}$ into a six-component vector

$$\mathbf{p} = (T_x \, T_y \, T_z \, \phi\theta\psi)^t \qquad (2)$$

and use homogeneous coordinates, $\mathbf{T}(\mathbf{p})$ can be represented by a single 4×4 matrix:

$$\mathbf{T}(\mathbf{p}) = \begin{pmatrix} \mathbf{R} & \mathbf{t} \\ 0 & 1 \end{pmatrix} \qquad (3)$$

The relation between a point $\mathbf{q} = (x\,y\,z\,1)^t$ [or vector $\mathbf{v} = (x\,y\,z\,0)^t$] in $\mathrm{Ref}_{\mathrm{sensor}}$ and the corresponding point $\mathbf{r} = (X\,Y\,Z\,1)^t$ [or a vector $\mathbf{u} = (X\,Y\,Z\,0)^t$] in $\mathrm{Ref}_{3\mathrm{D}}$ can be written as follows:

$$\mathbf{r} = \mathbf{T}(\mathbf{p})\mathbf{q}$$

or $\qquad\qquad\qquad\qquad\qquad\qquad (4)$

$$\mathbf{u} = \mathbf{T}(\mathbf{p})\mathbf{v}$$

Relationship between 2D image and 3D scene coordinates

Because one of our requirements is accuracy in the recovered parameters, accurate sensor calibration is very important [46]. Therefore, we cannot use approximations such as orthography or weak perspective (also called *scaled orthography*). Moreover, we must model any image distortions that deviate from the perspective model. To take such *local* distortions into account with good accuracy, we have extended the two-planes method [47, 48] to the N-planes bicubic spline (NPBS) method [5]. By not limiting ourselves to the simplified perspective mathematic model, we can obtain an extremely accurate and simple method, using a wide array of calibration measurements and spline approximations of the calibration functions. The result of these calibration processes is a calibration function, $\mathscr{C}(\mathscr{P}_i) = L_i$, that associates every pixel ($\mathscr{P}_i$) of each projection with a 3D line whose representation is known in $\mathrm{Ref}_{\mathrm{sensor}}$. Each line $L_i = (\mathbf{q}_i, \mathbf{v_i})$ is given by a point $\mathbf{q}_i$ and a vector $\mathbf{v}_i$, which represent the set of points $\mathbf{q}_i + \lambda\mathbf{v}_i$. In principle, we obtain a function $\mathscr{C}$ for each one of the N_P projections but, in practice, we can gather all these N_P functions into one general function valid for any pixel of any projection. Note that we can use this sensor model for both video cameras and x-ray projection systems. In Champleboux et al. [5], this NPBS model is extended also to calibrate range-imaging sensors.

Energy minimization (mechanical analogy)

Given N_P projection contours of an object S, we first select a set of M_P pixels $\{\mathscr{P}_i, i = 1 \ldots M_P\}$, that belong to the N_P contours. This means that we do not need to segment perfectly the projection contours of S. Instead, only some pixels $\mathscr{P}_i$ that lie on the contours with a high certainty need to be known. Each pixel $\mathscr{P}_i$ corresponds to a 3D *matching line* (L_i) given in $\mathrm{Ref}_{\mathrm{sensor}}$ through the function $\mathscr{C}$ defined previously. The transformation of each line $L_i = (\mathbf{q}_i, \mathbf{v}_i)$ in $\mathrm{Ref}_{\mathrm{sensor}}$ by $\mathbf{T}(\mathbf{p})$ into a line $l_i(\mathbf{p})$ in $\mathrm{Ref}_{3\mathrm{D}}$ is given by the following formula:

$$l_i(\mathbf{p}) = [\mathbf{T}(\mathbf{p})\mathbf{q}_i, \mathbf{T}(\mathbf{p})\mathbf{v}_i] = [\mathbf{r}_i(\mathbf{p}), \mathbf{u}_i(\mathbf{p})] \qquad (5)$$

In the final pose $\mathbf{T}^*$, every matching line is tangent to the surface S of the object. We can reasonably suppose that for complex objects, in a large neighborhood of an initial estimate of $\mathbf{T}^{(0)}$, $\mathbf{T}^*$ is the only 3D pose of S leading to such a geometric configuration (this will later be confirmed in our experiments). Based on this important assumption, we design an algorithm that moves the surface S toward the matching lines (or equivalently, moves the rigid set of matching lines toward the surface) until S is in contact with all these lines.

An intuitive idea of how to perform this task is to imagine a mechanical device in which a spring (of null minimal length and of elasticity k_i sliding along each matching line L_i) is attached between the line L_i and the point of S the closest to it.[1] Clearly, the surface will globally be attracted toward the matching lines (i.e., the distance from S to the set of lines will decrease). When the object is placed in a force field in which a spring-type force is applied on the object from every matching line, the mechanical motion in the 3D space of such an isolated system is defined by Newtonian dynamics. During this motion, the potential energy of the system is minimized continuously until the system reaches a local minimum where the resultant forces cancel each other. At any instant, the energy $E(\mathbf{p})$ depends on the current pose of S and is defined by the following:

$$E(\mathbf{p}) = \sum_{i=1}^{M_P} \frac{k_i}{2} [d(l_i(\mathbf{p}), S)]^2 \qquad (6)$$

where $d[l_i(\mathbf{p}), S]$ is the Euclidean distance from $l_i(\mathbf{p})$ to S (i.e., the length of the ith spring).

The main drawback of using mechanical modeling is that the system may take a long time to converge to its minimum energy configuration. Therefore, for reasons of *robustness and efficiency*, we will use a least-squares method, as described in the next section.

LEAST-SQUARES FORMULATION

To formulate the least-squares problem, we need a function that estimates the distance from any matching line to S. We first define the 3D *unsigned distance* between a point $\mathbf{r}$ and the surface S, $d_E(\mathbf{r})$, as the minimum Euclidean distance between $\mathbf{r}$ and all the points of S. If we define the distance between a line $l_i(\mathbf{p})$ and the surface S as the minimum of $d_E(\mathbf{r})$ over all the points that belong to $l_i(\mathbf{p})$, then the distance associated

with a line piercing the surface would be zero even though the line would not be tangent to S. To avoid this problem, we define the *signed distance*, $\tilde{d}(\mathbf{r})$, between a point $\mathbf{r}$ and a closed surface S as $d_E(\mathbf{r})$ if $\mathbf{r}$ is exterior to S, and as the negative of this distance if $\mathbf{r}$ is interior to S. We thus define the signed distance between a line $l_i(\mathbf{p})$ represented in Ref_{3D} and the surface S, $\tilde{d}_l[l_i(\mathbf{p})]$, as the minimum of $\tilde{d}(\mathbf{r})$ over all the points that belong to $l_i(\mathbf{p})$:

$$\tilde{d}_l[l_i(\mathbf{p})] \equiv \min_\lambda \tilde{d}[\mathbf{r}_i(\mathbf{p}) + \lambda \mathbf{u}_i(\mathbf{p})] \qquad (7)$$

Therefore, although the minimum unsigned distance along a line piercing the surface may be zero, the signed distance will be negative. Thus, whether the line $l_i(\mathbf{p})$ passes through the surface or not, because we look for the minimum value of the signed distance along $l_i(\mathbf{p})$, the absolute value of $\tilde{d}_l[l_i(\mathbf{p})]$ indicates whether the line $l_i(\mathbf{p})$ is *close* and *tangent* to S (figure 7.3).

When the final pose is reached, every line $l_i(\mathbf{p})$ is tangent to S, and every signed distance $\tilde{d}_l[l_i(\mathbf{p})]$ is therefore zero. The energy minimized in a least-squares model, $E(\mathbf{p})$, is:

$$E(\mathbf{p}) = \sum_{i=1}^{M_P} \frac{1}{\sigma_i^2} [\tilde{d}_l(l_i(\mathbf{p}))]^2 \qquad (8)$$

where σ_i^2 is the variance of the noise of the measurement $\tilde{d}_l[l_i(\mathbf{p})]$ (compare equation 6).

Given an initial estimate $\mathbf{p} = \mathbf{p}_0$ of the 3D/2D transformation parameters, we will use the Levenberg-Marquardt algorithm (see the section, Least-Squares Minimization) to perform the minimization. The next three sections detail the steps involved in this method.

Fast distance computation using octree-splines

The method described in the previous section relies on the fast computation of the distances $\tilde{d}$ and $\tilde{d}_l$. If the surface S is discretized in n^2 points, the computation of the distance $\tilde{d}$ is a $O(n^2)$ process. Similarly, if a line $l_i(\mathbf{p})$ is discretized in m points, the computation of the distance $\tilde{d}_l$ is a $O(mn^2)$ process. To speed up this process, we precompute a 3D *distance map*, which is a function that gives the signed minimum distance to S from any point $\mathbf{q}$ inside a bounding volume V that encloses S. In practice, a scale factor k is selected such that this bounding volume V is k times greater than the smallest parallelepiped that contains S. The next few paragraphs describe several 3D distance maps that we

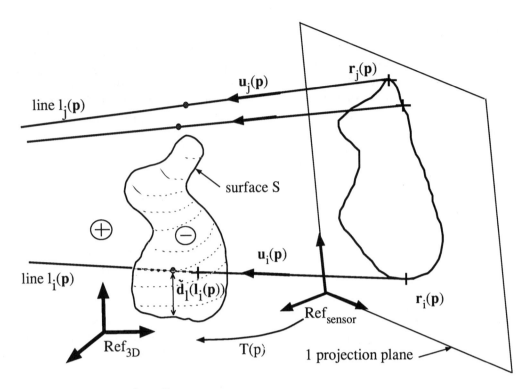

FIGURE 7.3 Projection line-to-surface distance computation.

Uniform 3D distance maps

The first representation that we studied and implemented was a uniform 3D distance map. At each point $\mathbf{q}$ on a regular grid of $\mathcal{N}^3$ points that describe V, the distance $\tilde{d}(\mathbf{q})$ is computed and stored. First, we look for the unsigned Euclidean distance $d_E(\mathbf{q})$ between $\mathbf{q}$ and S by computing exhaustively the minimum value of the distance between $\mathbf{q}$ and all points $\mathbf{s}_i$.

$$d_E(\mathbf{q}) = \min_{\mathbf{s}_i} d(\mathbf{q}, \mathbf{s}_i) = d(\mathbf{q}, \mathbf{s}_{i_{\min}}) \qquad (9)$$

where d is the Euclidean distance. To set negative values inside the surface, two solutions have been studied.

USING SURFACE NORMAL VECTORS If the surface normal vector $\hat{\mathbf{n}}_i$ is known at each point $\mathbf{s}_i$ (this is the case when the initial surface representation is parametric)

and if this normal vector can be oriented toward the exterior of the surface, then $\tilde{d}(\mathbf{q})$ is computed by the following:

$$\tilde{d}(\mathbf{q}) = \text{sign}[\hat{\mathbf{n}}_{i_{\min}} \cdot (\mathbf{q} - \mathbf{s}_{i_{\min}})]\, d(\mathbf{q}, s_{i_{\min}}) \qquad (10)$$

Another possibility would be to use this equation:

$$\tilde{d}(\mathbf{q}) = [\hat{\mathbf{n}}_{i_{\min}} \cdot (\mathbf{q} - \mathbf{s}_{i_{\min}})]\, d(\mathbf{q}, s_{i_{\min}}) \qquad (11)$$

Both equations 10 and 11 can be used for surfaces that are not closed. Unfortunately, if the surface is not discretized finely enough or if the normal vectors are not accurate enough, this method leads to artifacts such as negative values far away from the surface.

SPREADING A SIGN FROM AN EXTERIOR POINT In this method, $\tilde{d}$ is computed in two passes. In the first pass, each $\tilde{d}(\mathbf{q})$ is set to $-d_E(\mathbf{q})$ using equation 9. Then, a positive sign is spread from an initial exterior point.[2] This recursive spreading of the positive sign from points to their neighbors is terminated at points close to the surface [using a threshold on the distance $d_E(\mathbf{q})$]. Once $\tilde{d}$ has been computed for all points on the regular grid, the distance $\tilde{d}$ can be computed at arbitrary points $\mathbf{q}$ inside the volume V by interpolating grid values. Both

have studied and implemented. In each of the following methods, the representation chosen for the input surface is a set of n^2 points $\mathbf{s}_i, i = 1 \ldots n^2$. This choice is motivated by the fact that any surface representation can be converted into this point representation.

trilinear interpolation and tricubic interpolation with tensorial spline functions have been implemented.

In the preceding method, because computing the distance map has a $O(n^2 \mathcal{N}^3)$ complexity, computation times rapidly become prohibitive. To reduce these computation times, we have used the classic *chamfer algorithm* [49–51] in three dimensions, which requires only two sweeps of V. Unfortunately, uniform distance maps are not well suited to finding quickly the minimum distance along a line $\tilde{d}_l$ (see the section, Line-to-Surface Distance Minimization). Moreover, achieving acceptable accuracy can be prohibitively expensive in terms of memory space (typically 128^3 nodes).

OCTREE-SPLINE DISTANCE MAPS

In looking for an improved trade-off among memory space, accuracy, speed of computation, and speed of construction, we have developed a new kind of distance map that we call the *octree-spline*. The intuitive idea behind this geometric representation is to have more detailed information (i.e., more accuracy) near the surface than far away from it. We start with the classic octree representation associated with the surface S [52] and then extend it to represent a continuous 3D function that approximates the signed Euclidean distance to the surface. This representation combines advantages of adaptive spline functions and hierarchic data structures.

As with the previously described distance maps, the input to the octree-spline construction algorithm is a set of n^2 points $\mathbf{s}_i$ regularly spread on the surface S. The algorithm performs the following steps:

1. *Surface point octree construction*: First, the octree associated to the set of points $\mathbf{s}_i$ is built according to classic octree subdivision [52]. Starting from the initial cube V, each node that contains points (gray node) is recursively split into eight subcubes until it contains no points (white node) or it has the maximal selected resolution (black node) (figure 7.4). For our applications, the octree typically has six to eight levels, corresponding to a resolution of $1/64$ to $1/256$. At the end of this step, each node (gray, black, or white) contains the list of surface points that are inside the node.

2. *Subdivision (refinement)*: The octree previously computed may have large empty nodes near the surface, because no rules about subdivision near the surface have been introduced. To overcome this problem, we perform a further subdivision of the octree to ensure that two nodes that are neighbors along a face, edge, or corner differ in size by, at most, a factor of k_S (in practice, we choose $k_S = 2$). To compute the 26

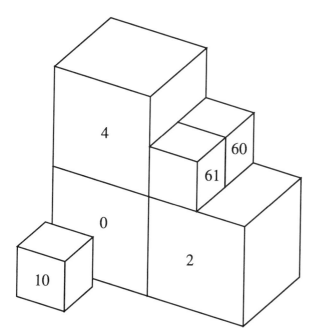

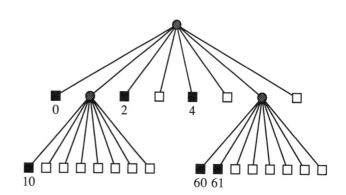

FIGURE 7.4 A simple two-level octree and its tree representation.

neighbors of any node in the octree, we use the technique described in Garcia [53]. Our refinement then is performed by traversing the octree in a bottom-up breadth-first fashion. The resulting structure is called a *restricted octree* [54].

3. *Corner distance computation*: For each corner **c** of each terminal node (white or black), the distance $d(\mathbf{c})$ is computed according to equation 9. The spatial organization of surface points created by the octree makes this process much faster as we can use an efficient search technique to find the minimum distance between **c** and all the points $\mathbf{s}_i$. For each corner $\mathbf{c} = (U_c, V_c, W_c)$ of a node $\mathcal{N}$, the octree is visited starting at $\mathcal{N}$ and recursively visiting the parents and neighbors of $\mathcal{N}$. A best value, d_{best}, for the minimum distance is maintained during this process. If a candidate node has central coordinates (U, V, W) and a size s such that

$$|U - U_c| > d_{best} + \frac{s}{2} \quad \text{or} \quad |V - V_c| > d_{best} + \frac{s}{2}$$

$$\text{or} \quad |W - W_c| > d_{best} + \frac{s}{2} \tag{12}$$

the points $\mathbf{s}_i$ lying inside this node are not tested because the minimum distance would be guaranteed to be greater than d_{best}. Finally, after the distance values for the corners of the terminal nodes have been computed, they are reported to the appropriate parents that share the same corners to reduce duplicate computation.

4. *Signed distance computation*: To compute $\tilde{d}$ from d_E, the two different methods described for uniform distance maps have been implemented for octree-splines. As in that previous case, we prefer the recursive spreading of a sign starting from an exterior point. Here, the recursive spreading stops when a black node is encountered (rather than when a low threshold on distances is passed). This works if the black nodes constitute a connected set of nodes. This condition is valid if the discretization of the surface S is such that the distance between two neighboring points of S is not greater than the resolution of the octree.

5. *Crack elimination (continuity enforcement)*: Because the signed distance is computed at any point **q** by an interpolation based on the eight corner values of the terminal node that contains **q** (see later), discontinuities or *cracks* can appear if we simply interpolate the true corner distance values. Several solutions can be used to suppress the cracks [53]. We chose the following process for its simplicity: If a corner **c** of a node $\mathcal{N}_1$ of size s_1 lies on a face or an edge of another node $\mathcal{N}_2$ of size $s_2 > s_1$, then the distance value of the corner **c** is simply replaced by the distance computed at **c** by interpolation inside $\mathcal{N}_2$. This method is applied to the octree with a top-down breadth-first traversal. Note that this process introduces only a small loss of accuracy as the octree had been previously *restricted* at step 2. After the previous steps have been performed, $\tilde{d}(\mathbf{q})$ can be computed for any point **q** by first finding the terminal node $\mathcal{N}$ that contains the point **q** (using classic binary search) and then using a trilinear interpolation of the eight corner values $\tilde{d}_{ijk}$. If $(u, v, w) \in [0, 1] \times [0, 1] \times [0, 1]$ are the normalized coordinates of **q** in the cube $\mathcal{N}$,

$$\tilde{d}(\mathbf{q}) = \sum_{i=0}^{1} \sum_{j=0}^{1} \sum_{k=0}^{1} b_i(u)\, b_j(v)\, b_k(w)\, \tilde{d}_{ijk} \quad \text{with}$$

$$b_l(t) = \delta_l t + (1 - \delta_l)(1 - t) \tag{13}$$

We can compute the gradient $\nabla \tilde{d}(\mathbf{q})$ of the signed distance function by simply differentiating equation 13 with respect to u, v, and w. Because $\tilde{d}$ is only C^0, $\nabla \tilde{d}(\mathbf{q})$ is discontinuous on cube faces. However, these gradient discontinuities are relatively small and do not seem to affect the convergence of our iterative minimization algorithm.

One additional preprocessing step is required in order to speed up the line minimization algorithm presented in the next section:

6. *Lower bound estimation*: Compute for each node $\mathcal{N}$ of the octree a function B_N that is a lower bound on the function $\tilde{d}$ inside $\mathcal{N}$,

$$\forall \mathbf{q} \in \mathcal{N}, B_N(\mathbf{q}) < \tilde{d}(\mathbf{q}) \tag{14}$$

A suitable choice for a bound function, with a good trade-off between simplicity and accuracy, is the following linear approximation:

$$B_N(\mathbf{q}) = au + bv + cw + d \tag{15}$$

Because trilinear interpolation (equation 13) is used to compute $\tilde{d}_l(\mathbf{q})$, the inequality (equation 14) can be solved recursively (bottom-up) for (a, b, c, d) using a modified simplex algorithm.

Line-to-surface distance minimization

This section describes how the signed distance from a line to the surface $\tilde{d}_l[l_i(\mathbf{p})]$, defined in equation 7, can be rapidly computed using the octree-spline. One possible approach to computing the minimum expressed in equation 7, which works for any representation of the distance map, would be to use classic one-dimensional functional minimization. Because the function $f(\lambda) = \tilde{d}(\mathbf{r} + \lambda\mathbf{u})$ may have several local minima, global search techniques such as simulated annealing may have to be used. Another alternative that works with a discretized distance map would be to search exhaustively all cells that the line intersects. For a uniform discretization of the distance map, this takes $O(\mathcal{N})$ steps, which may be prohibitively slow.

Our approach is to take advantage of the octree-spline to develop an optimized search technique that requires approximately $O[\log(\mathcal{N})]$ steps (where $\mathcal{N}$ is the resolution of the octree). Because our octree representation of the distance map is tree-based, we could use a variety of tree-search techniques. We have chosen to use a best-first search, with lower bounds computed for each node (interior and terminal) of the octree-spline (figure 7.5). A best-first search requires a priority queue, which we implement using a heap. In our algorithm, a candidate line $l_i(\mathbf{p})$ is recursively split by the octree cube boundaries into smaller line segments $\Sigma = [\mathbf{a}, \mathbf{b}]$ until the line segment with minimum distance is found. During this process, the current minimum distance d_{best} is maintained, and an estimated lower bound on the distance

$$B_{\mathcal{N}}(\Sigma) = \min[B_{\mathcal{N}}(\mathbf{a}), B_{\mathcal{N}}(\mathbf{b})] \qquad (16)$$

is computed for each new segment before it is pushed onto the priority queue. As segments are popped from the queue in order of smallest lower bound, they are either split into smaller segments (if the associated node is nonterminal) or tested to determine whether the minimum attainable distance

$$\tilde{d}_l(\Sigma) = \min[\tilde{d}(\mathbf{a}), \tilde{d}(\mathbf{b})] \qquad (17)$$

is lower than d_{best} (in which case $\mathbf{a}$ or $\mathbf{b}$ becomes the new minimum point). Note that while equation 17 is not the exact minimum distance over the line, the approximation is good, especially near the correct pose, where the line segments Σ are tangent to the surface S and the corresponding nodes $\mathcal{N}$ are of minimal size. The best-first search is terminated when the smallest lower bound on the priority queue is greater than d_{best}. The algorithm is summarized in table 7.1.

Least-squares minimization

This section describes the nonlinear least-squares minimization of the energy or error function $E(\mathbf{p})$ defined in equation 8. Least-squares techniques work well

Initialization:
    clip the line $l_i(\mathbf{p})$ to the root node V, $\Sigma \leftarrow \text{clip}(l_i(\mathbf{p}), V)$
    initialize the minimum distance value, $d_{best} \leftarrow \infty$
    push the initial line segment and root node, $\text{push}(pqueue, (d_{best}, \Sigma, V))$
    while $(B_{\mathcal{N}}(\Sigma), \Sigma, \mathcal{N}) \leftarrow \text{pop}(pqueue)$ **and** $B_{\mathcal{N}}(\Sigma) \le d_{best}$
        (Σ is the line segment $[\mathbf{a}, \mathbf{b}]$, $B_{\mathcal{N}}(\Sigma)$ is the lower bound estimate,
        and $\mathcal{N}$ is the corresponding node)
      If $\mathcal{N}$ is a terminal node **then**
        compute the minimum of $\tilde{d}$ along Σ, $d_\Sigma \leftarrow \min(\tilde{d}(\mathbf{a}), \tilde{d}(\mathbf{b}))$
          (this is only approximate, but has good accuracy when
          the line segment is tangent to the true surface)
        if $d_\Sigma < d_{best}$ **then**
          $d_{best} \leftarrow d_\Sigma$, **best** $\leftarrow \mathbf{a}$ or $\mathbf{b}$
        endif
      else ($\mathcal{N}$ is an interior node)
        for each child C of $\mathcal{N}$ **do** (push sub-segments)
        if $\Sigma_C \leftarrow \text{clip}(\Sigma, C)$ **then**
          compute the lower bound, $B_{\mathcal{N}}(\Sigma) \leftarrow \min(B_{\mathcal{N}}(\mathbf{a}), B_{\mathcal{N}}(\mathbf{b}))$
          $\text{push}(pqueue, (B_{\mathcal{N}}(\Sigma), \Sigma_C, C))$
        endif
      endif
    endwhile

FIGURE 7.5 Algorithm for line-to-surface distance minimization.

when we have many uncorrelated noisy measurements with a normal (Gaussian) distribution.[3] To begin, we will make this assumption, even though noise actually comes from calibration errors, 2D and 3D segmentation errors, the approximation of the Euclidean distance by octree-spline distance maps, and nonrigid displacement of the surface between $\text{Ref}_{3\text{D}}$ and $\text{Ref}_{\text{sensor}}$. (In our application, 2D and 3D segmentation errors usually predominate because accurate sensor calibration is always feasible, and the resolution of the octree can be selected high enough to meet this requirement. A rough estimate of σ_i^2, in equation 8 can thus be obtained from $\sigma_{2\text{D}}^2 + \sigma_{3\text{D}}^2$, where $\sigma_{2\text{D}}^2$ is the variance of the segmented contours on the projection images and $\sigma_{3\text{D}}^2$ is the variance of the 3D segmentation. These values can either be fixed to some fraction of the pixel-voxel size or derived from the image gradient and the edge operator [55].)

To perform the nonlinear least-squares minimization, we use the Levenberg-Marquardt algorithm because of its good convergence properties [56]. Merging equations 5, 7, and 8, we get:

$$E(\mathbf{p}) = \sum_{i=1}^{M_P} \frac{1}{\sigma_i^2} [e_i(\mathbf{p})]^2$$

$$= \sum_{i=1}^{M_P} \frac{1}{\sigma_i^2} \left[\min_{\lambda} \tilde{d}(\mathbf{T}(\mathbf{p})\mathbf{q}_i + \lambda \mathbf{T}(\mathbf{p})\mathbf{v}_i) \right]^2 (18)$$

To compute the gradient and Hessian matrix of $E(\mathbf{p})$, the Levenberg-Marquardt algorithm requires the first derivatives of each $e_i(\mathbf{p})$.[4] For any component p_j of $\mathbf{p}$, we obtain

$$\frac{\partial e_i(\mathbf{p})}{\partial p_j} = [\nabla \tilde{d}[\mathbf{T}(\mathbf{p})(\mathbf{q}_i + \lambda_{\min}\mathbf{v}_i)]]$$

$$\cdot \left[\left(\frac{\partial \mathbf{T}(\mathbf{p})}{\partial p_j} \right) (\mathbf{q}_i + \lambda_{\min}\mathbf{v}_i) \right] \quad (19)$$

where $\lambda_{\min}$ is the value of λ in which the minimum is reached in equation 18. The appendix shows that the variation of $e_i(\mathbf{p})$ does not depend on λ. Thus, computing the six-component gradient of $E(\mathbf{p})$ requires computing only the gradient of the octree-spline distance $\tilde{d}$ (by differentiating equation 13) and computing the three derivatives of $\mathbf{T}(\mathbf{p})$ with respect to the three Euler angles; the three derivatives of $\mathbf{T}(\mathbf{p})$ with respect to translational components are simple constants.

The end of the iterative minimization process is reached when $E(\mathbf{p})$ is lower than a fixed threshold,

when the difference between parameters $|\mathbf{p}^{(k)} - \mathbf{p}^{(k-1)}|$ at two successive iterations is below a fixed threshold, or when a maximum number of iterations is reached. At this point, we compute a robust estimate of the parameter $\mathbf{p}$ by throwing out the measurements where $e_i^2(\mathbf{p}) \gg \sigma_i^2$ and performing additional iterations [57]. This process removes the influence of the *outliers*, which are likely to occur in the automatic 2D and 3D segmentation processes (e.g., a partially superimposed object on x-ray projections can lead to false contours). The threshold for outlier rejection must be fixed according to application-specific knowledge or by experimentation. In our case, we chose to set this threshold to 3σ, where σ is a mean a priori standard deviation of the noise.

When using a gradient descent technique such as Levenberg-Marquardt, there is a possibility that the minimization might fail because of local minima in the six-dimensional parameter space. However, for the experiments we have conducted (see the section, 3D/2D Matching with Simulated Sensor Data), false local minima were few and always far from the solution. Because in our application we have a good initial estimate of the parameters, these other minima are unlikely to be reached. Moreover, an initial least-squares estimate of the translation parameters based on image moments allows us to avoid most of the false local minima far from the solution. We have also found that first estimating the pose based on a small number of matching lines and then adding more lines shows an improved robustness to false local minima.

At the end of the iterative minimization procedure, we estimate the uncertainty in the parameters. The covariance matrix $\text{Cov}(\mathbf{p})$ is computed by inverting the final Hessian matrix, and eigenvalue analysis of $\text{Cov}(\mathbf{p})$ is performed [56]. The result is an ellipsoid of uncertainties in the six-dimensional parameter space, which could be used in further processing to quantify the uncertainty in other geometric measures. For example, when we specify a 3D line in the data, we could also display its associated uncertainty envelope. The distribution of errors after minimization is also computed, in order to check that it is Gaussian.

Pose estimation from 3D range data

Our 3D/2D matching algorithm can easily be extended to solve 3D/3D matching problems. Here we look for the transformation $\mathbf{T}(\mathbf{p})$ between a surface S

known in Ref_{3D} and a set of M_P points $\mathbf{q}_i$ known in $\text{Ref}_{\text{sensor}}$ (we make the assumption that most of the points $\mathbf{q}_i$ match to the surface).

The formulation we introduced previously can be used for the 3D/3D matching problem. The error measure, equation 18, is now replaced by

$$E(\mathbf{p}) = \sum_{i=1}^{M_P} \frac{1}{\sigma_i^2} [e_i(\mathbf{p})]^2 = \sum_{i=1}^{M_P} \frac{1}{\sigma_i^2} [\tilde{d}(\mathbf{T}(\mathbf{p})\mathbf{q}_i)]^2 \quad (20)$$

The gradient of $E(\mathbf{p})$ is computed using the following:

$$\frac{\partial e_i(\mathbf{p})}{\partial p_j} = [\nabla \tilde{d}(\mathbf{T}(\mathbf{p})\mathbf{q}_i)] \cdot \left[\left(\frac{\partial \mathbf{T}(\mathbf{p})}{\partial p_j} \right)(\mathbf{q}_i) \right] \quad (21)$$

As in 3D/2D matching, the distance map $\tilde{d}$ is also built and represented using an octree-spline. In 3D/3D matching, however, because the distance need not be signed (negative inside and positive outside), the octree-spline can be built for nonclosed surfaces and without knowledge of surface normal vectors. However, using a signed distance remains preferable as the zeros of the 3D function $\tilde{d}$ coincide more accurately with the 3D surface than the minima of the unsigned distance function (Szeliski and Lavallée, manuscript in preparation).

Experimental results

The octree-spline construction and the matching algorithm have been implemented in C, using X Windows on a DECstation 5000/200. Computation times expressed in the following sections are given for this machine.

As part of our implementation, we have developed a suite of real-time interactive 3D graphic tools that helped us to develop our algorithms, to visualize their performance, and to explore various parameter settings. Our graphic programming environment has been used to visualize both the octree-spline construction process and the iterative matching process. We can selectively visualize any object at any time: 3D surface, projection frames, projection curves, projection lines, and octree frame at different resolutions (figures 7.6–7.8). The viewpoint can be interactively modified to perform rotations, translations, or zooms of the scene, or it can be set to coincide with one of

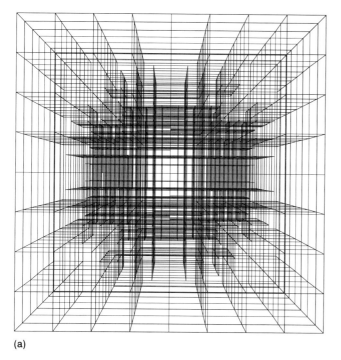

(a)

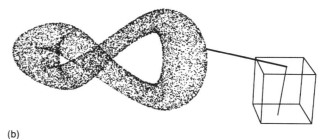

(b)

FIGURE 7.6 Octree frame and line-to-surface distance. (a) Octree frame for surface S_2 (only five resolution levels are displayed). (b) Line-to-surface distance computation: For an interactively selected line, the node where the minimum

signed distance to the surface is found is displayed and the gradient vector at this point is drawn with a length equal to the minimum distance.

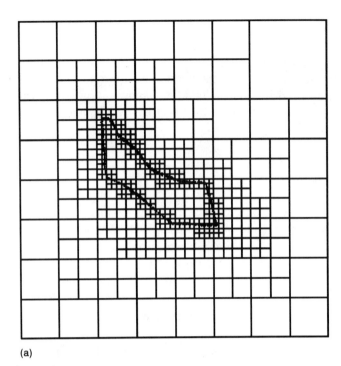

(a)

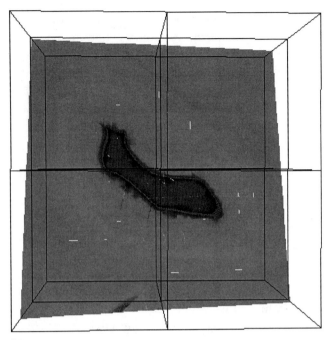

(b)

FIGURE 7.7   Two-dimensional slice of the octree-spline (surface S_1) showing the intersection between a plane interactively selected by the user and the octree spline. (a) Slice of the octree frame and intersection curve between the plane and S_1. (b) Slice of the octree-spline in pseudocolor: shaded red (dark gray) for negative values inside S_1 and shaded green (light gray) for positive values outside.

the real conic projection viewpoints (figure 7.9). Two-dimensional slices of the octree-spline can be computed in real time, and the quadtree decomposition of the slice or a pseudocolored rendering of the signed distance function $\tilde{d}$ can be displayed (see figure 7.7). Individual components of the algorithms can also be tested. For example, the distance value $\tilde{d}$ can be interactively displayed for any point on a slice or, for interactively selected lines, the minimum value $\tilde{d}_l$ can be computed in real time, and the octree node where the minimum is reached can be displayed (see figure 7.6b).

3D/2D MATCHING WITH SIMULATED SENSOR DATA

In this section, we describe our experiments with 3D/2D matching. We have performed tests on both real anatomic surfaces (surface S_1; see figure 7.8) and on simulated surfaces (surface S_2; figure 7.10). The projection curves of these surfaces were obtained by simulation in order to know "ground truth" for the parameters $\mathbf{p}^*$. (Tests on real projections are given in the section, 3D/2D Matching with Real Sensor Data.) The different steps of our experiments are as follows:

1. Simulate a transformation $\mathbf{T}(\mathbf{p}^*)$ applied to S and compute the $\mathcal{N}_P$ silhouettes of the transformed surface $S'(\mathbf{p}^*)$ by projecting all the surface points.

2. Extract the $\mathcal{N}_P$ contours of the silhouettes of $S'(\mathbf{p}^*)$.

3. Randomly select M_P pixels on the $\mathcal{N}_P$ contours (a percentage of all the contour pixels is chosen, typically 10%, or 30–40 points). For each selected pixel, compute the corresponding projection line according to the calibrated projection parameters (simulated perspective projection).

4. Compute the octree-spline $\tilde{d}$ associated with the original surface S.

5. Starting from an initial estimate $\mathbf{p}^{(0)}$, use the Levenberg-Marquardt algorithm to minimize iteratively the function $E(\mathbf{p})$ defined by equation 18, using the gradient expressions given in equation 19. At each iteration k, compute and display the error $\Delta\mathbf{p} = \mathbf{p}^{(k)} - \mathbf{p}^*$ between the current parameters $\mathbf{p}^{(k)}$ and the simulated parameters $\mathbf{p}^*$. Compute the error transformation

$$\Delta\mathbf{T}^{(k)} = [\mathbf{T}(\mathbf{p}^{(k)})][\mathbf{T}(\mathbf{p}^*)]^{-1} \qquad (22)$$

and extract the translation error

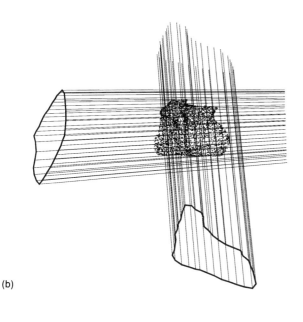

(a)

(b)

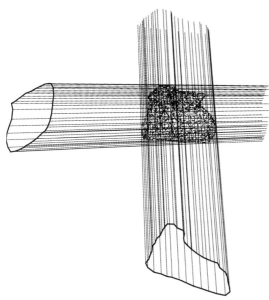

(c)

$$\Delta \mathbf{t}^{(k)} = g - \Delta \mathbf{T}^{(k)} \mathbf{g}$$

where $\mathbf{g}$ is the center of gravity of the surface points in $\mathrm{Ref_{3D}}$. Extract $\Delta \alpha^{(k)}$, which is the angle of the rotation component $\mathbf{R}$ of $\Delta \mathbf{T}^{(k)}$. The values of $\|\Delta \mathbf{t}^{(k)}\|$ and $|\Delta \alpha^{(k)}|$ are displayed to monitor the convergence of the algorithm toward the optimal solution.

6. Perform robust estimation by removing the outliers and performing some more iterations.

7. Perform error analysis: Compute the covariance matrix and the corresponding eigenvalues and eigenvectors; compute and display the error distribution.

Figures 7.8–7.11 show the results of some of the experiments that we have conducted. Figures 7.8 and 7.9 show the state of the iterative minimization algorithm for surface S_1 after zero, two, and six iterations. Figure 7.8 shows the relative positions of the projection lines and the surface from a general viewpoint. Figure 7.9 shows the same state from the viewpoints of the two cameras. Figure 7.10 shows similar results for surface S_2. A plot of the algorithm convergence (energy, translation error, and rotation error) is shown in figure 7.11. A plot of the region of convergence (number of steps to convergence versus starting error) is shown in figure 7.12. In this figure, only initial rotations were tested, as the translation always is initialized based on image moments (see the section, Least-Squares Minimization). As we can see from this figure, the algorithm always converges when started within 20° of the correct solution and often converges from as far away as 60°.

Table 7.1 shows some results for the computation times of $\tilde{d}_l$ and how they vary according to the choice of search strategy and octree resolution. As we can see from these results, the algorithm very quickly finds the optimal match between the surface and its projections.

3D/3D MATCHING WITH SIMULATED SENSOR DATA

Experiments have also been conducted to test the 3D/3D matching method on synthetic data. For a real ana-

FIGURE 7.8 Convergence of the algorithm observed from a general viewpoint (surface S_1 is represented by a set of points). Two sets of projection lines evolve in the 3D potential field associated with the surface until each line is tangent to S_1: (a) Initial configuration. (b) After two iterations. (c) After six iterations. For this case, the matching is performed in 1.8 sec using 77 projection lines, and in 0.9 sec using 40 projection lines.

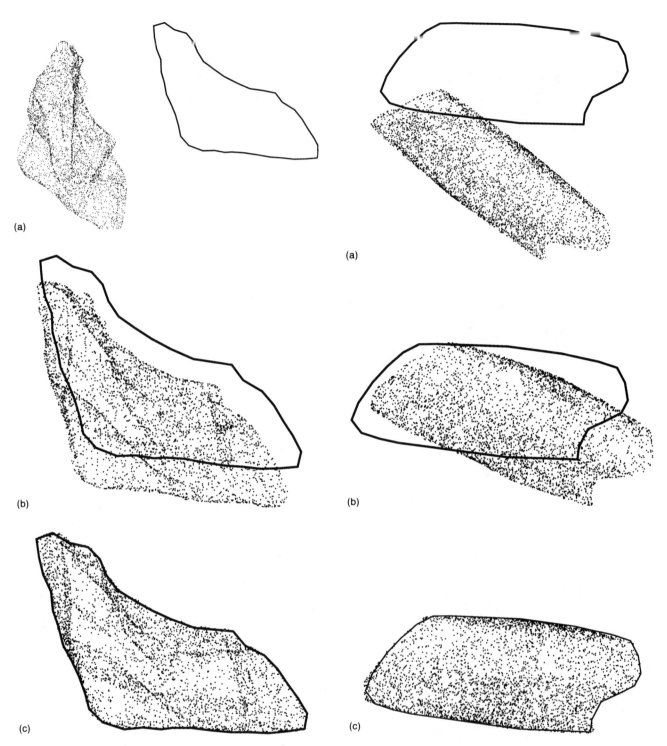

FIGURE 7.9 Convergence of algorithm for surface S_1 observed from the two projection viewpoints. The external contours of the projected surface end up fitting the real contours.

(a) Initial configuration. (b) After two iterations. (c) After six iterations.

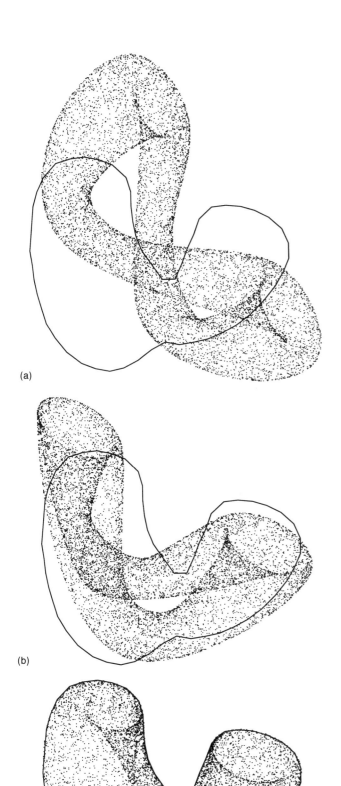

(a)

(b)

(c)

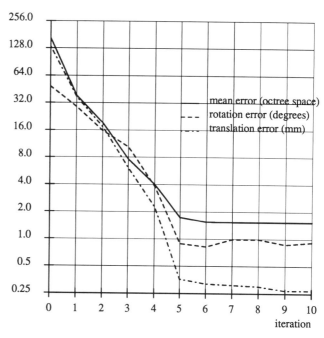

FIGURE 7.11 Typical convergence curves of the matching algorithm (surface S_1) showing the mean error $E(\mathbf{p}^{(k)})/M_P$ (in voxels), translation error $\|\Delta t^{(k)}\|$ (in mm), and rotation error $|\Delta\alpha^{(k)}|$ (in degrees) as a function of iteration number k.

tomic surface S_3 (surface of a vertebra, figure 7.13), we compute the associated octree-spline and select a sub-sampled set of M_P surface points $\mathbf{q}_i$. A transformation $\mathbf{T}(\mathbf{p}^*)$ is applied to this set of points, and the robust estimation of the parameters is performed as for the 3D/2D matching by minimizing the energy $E(\mathbf{p})$ expressed in equation 29. The results of this minimization for surface S_3 are shown in figure 7.13.

3D/2D MATCHING WITH REAL SENSOR DATA

The accuracy and robustness of our 3D/2D matching algorithm has also been verified on real data. In this experiment, we prove that the matching is correct

FIGURE 7.10 Convergence of algorithm for surface S_2 (twisted torus) observed from a general viewpoint. For this case, the matching is performed in 5 sec using 135 projection lines, and in 1 sec using 15 projection lines. (a) Initial configuration, $E(\mathbf{p}^{(0)})/M_P = 63.87$, $\|\Delta\mathbf{t}^{(0)}\| = 44.10$ mm, $|\Delta\alpha^{(0)}| = 48.25°$. (b) After two iterations, $E(\mathbf{p}^{(2)})/M_P = 13.33$, $\|\Delta\mathbf{t}^{(2)}\| = 10.72$ mm, $|\Delta\alpha^{(2)}| = 14.75°$. (c) After 10 iterations. $E(\mathbf{p}^{(10)})/M_P = 0.91$, $\|\Delta\mathbf{t}^{(10)}\| = 0.21$ mm, $|\Delta\alpha^{(10)}| = 0.16°$.

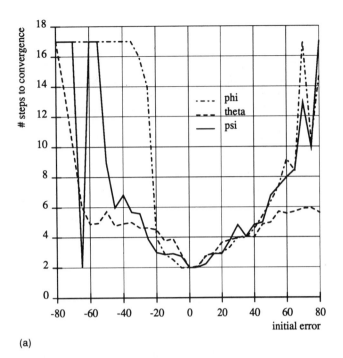

(a)

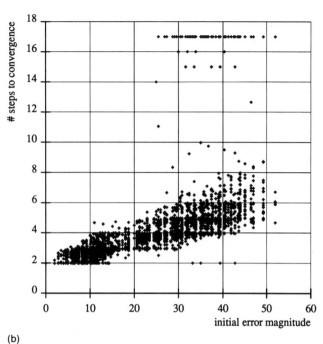

(b)

FIGURE 7.12   Typical convergence behavior for the matching algorithm (surface S_1). The plots show the number of iterations required to converge to within 5% of the final error as a function of the starting error in orientation (a) for the three Euler angles and (b) for all orientations sampled on a rectangular grid. Data points above 14 indicate a failure to converge (false local minimum).

TABLE 7.1

Number of nodes visited and computation times (msec) for various algorithms and resolutions

Octree resolution	Constant bound		Linear bound		Depth first		Error
	Nodes visited	Time	Nodes visited	Time	Nodes visited	Time	Rot./Trans.
32	1494	195	1098	179	2827	243	1.02°/0.25 mm
64	2200	251	1353	212	4002	330	0.89°/0.28 mm
128	2800	381	1973	300	5371	455	0.32°/0.43 mm

Note: The computation times are per iteration, averaged over the last 10 iterations. The three algorithms tested are (1) best-first search with constant lower bounds, (2) best-first search with linear lower bounds, and (3) depth-first (exhaustive) search. The choice of algorithm does not affect the accuracy of the results (last column), which depends only on the resolution.

using a complete robotics system (see chapter 32 for more details). The test object used is an isolated vertebra that was pierced with two tubular 3-mm holes. A 3D CT scan of this vertebra is obtained, and the positions of the hole axes $A1$ and $A2$ are computed. The 3D surface of the object then is segmented in the CT image. The result is a set of 200,000 points, which is used to build a six-level octree-spline.

For each experimental trial, the vertebra is placed in the fields of view of two calibrated cameras. Figure 7.14 shows two typical images of the vertebra. A simple edge extraction algorithm gives a set of between 10 and 200 contour points on each image. The 3D/2D matching algorithm then is applied. Figure 7.15 shows a typical convergence from one viewpoint. Figure 7.16 shows the iterative evolution of the energy that we

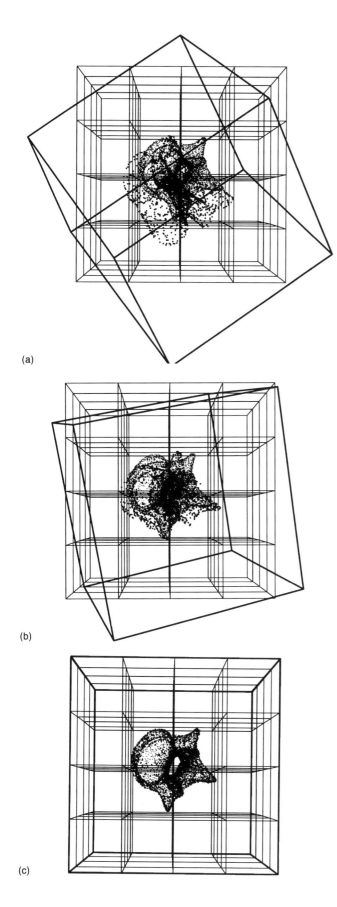

(a)

(b)

(c)

minimize for that case. Note that the vertebra is partially occluded by the edge of the video camera so that only a few points are used in the minimization.

At the end of the convergence, we obtain the final pose **T**. We then use a six-axis robot carrying a laser beam and calibrated with the pair of cameras to align the laser beam with either hole axis $A1$ or $A2$. We visually determine whether the laser beam has passed through the 3-mm hole. The observed result is that in all our experiments, the matching was visually perfect, which corresponds to a submillimeter accuracy. If we move the vertebra, 1–4 seconds are needed to perform a new matching and to move the robot (no human intervention is required).

The 3D/2D matching method has also been validated on CT/x-ray registration based on the skull. Four 2-mm opaque catheters are inserted inside a "rando" phantom head that has the exact characteristics of a real head. In one instance, we segmented the skull's external surface on a set of 2-mm-spaced CT sections, and we determined the locations of the barycenters of the four catheters on these CT images. In another instance, we interactively segmented the contours of the skull on two frontal and sagittal calibrated x-rays. The barycenters of the projection of the catheters were segmented also on both x-rays and were reconstructed as 3D points using our calibration techniques. Then a 3D/2D registration was performed, using only the skull 3D surface and 2D edges as reference structures. The convergence of the algorithm is shown in figure 7.17. At the end of the convergence, we could compute the distance between the four catheters known in Ref_{3D} and their positions in Ref_{sensor} transformed by the result of the registration algorithm. The result was an average distance of 2 mm, with a maximum of at 2.5 mm. Note that these values include errors of the accuracy test, mainly due to the segmentation of 2-mm catheters on 2-mm-spaced CT sections. Thus the real error of the registration must still be

---

FIGURE 7.13 Convergence of 3D/3D matching algorithm for surface S_3 (vertebra) segmented from a 3D CT image. For this case, the matching is performed in 2 sec using 130 data points. (a) Initial configuration, $E(\mathbf{p}^{(0)})/M_P = 113.47$, $\|\Delta\mathbf{t}^{(0)}\| = 125.23$ mm, $|\Delta\alpha^{(0)}| = 48.25°$. (b) After two iterations, $E(\mathbf{p}^{(2)})/M_P = 38.58$, $\|\Delta\mathbf{t}^{(2)}\| = 25.97$ mm, $|\Delta\alpha^{(2)}| = 20.53°$. (c) After six iterations. $E(\mathbf{p}^{(6)})/M_P = 4.20$, $\|\Delta\mathbf{t}^{(6)}\| = 0.75$ mm, $|\Delta\alpha^{(6)}| = 0.32°$.

LAVALLÉE ET AL.: ANATOMY-BASED REGISTRATION USING OCTREE-SPLINES   131

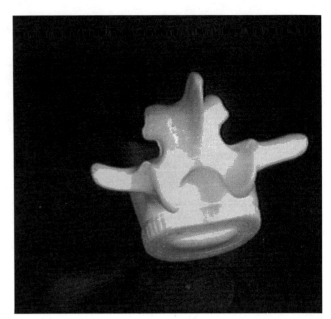

FIGURE 7.14   Typical video images used as data in the 3D/2D matching algorithm.

better than this result, which is already sufficient for many of our applications.

3D/3D MATCHING WITH REAL SENSOR DATA

The accuracy and robustness of our 3D/3D matching algorithm has been assessed also on real data. In this experiment, we demonstrate that the matching is correct using an accurate articulated system with 3 degrees of freedom (Θ, Φ, T) for both sensor calibration and match checking. First, a laser range finder is calibrated with an articulated device [14]. Next, a polystyrene head (phantom) is placed on the articulated plate. For a recorded position (Θ_1, Φ_1, T_1) of the head on the plate, a range image of the face is acquired. A known transformation then is applied to the head. For this second head position (Θ_2, Φ_2, T_2), a second range image is taken. For both images, the range data are given in the coordinate system $\mathrm{Ref_{sensor}}$ linked to the base of the articulated device. Thus the true rigid-body transformation $\mathbf{T}(\mathbf{p}^*)$ between the two head surface locations is known in $\mathrm{Ref_{sensor}}$.

Next, we applied our 3D/3D matching algorithm to the two range images. The first image is used to build an octree-spline that constitutes the model. We start our iterative minimization algorithm from an initial transformation very far from the solution. Since we

know the exact real transformation, we are in the same situation as for simulated data. Thus at each iteration k, we can compute the error transformation $\Delta\mathbf{T}^{(k)}$ and extract the norm of translation error $\|\Delta\mathbf{t}^{(k)}\|$ and $\|\Delta\alpha^{(k)}\|$, the angle of the rotation component of $\Delta\mathbf{T}^{(k)}$.

Figure 7.18 shows a typical convergence of the algorithm toward the real solution. The octree-spline is built from 7500 points (first range image). We use 2700 points from the second range image. In approximately 10 seconds on a DECstation 5000/200, the algorithm reaches a first minimum. At this point, the rotation error is $0.7°$ and the translation error is 2.9 mm. After the outliers are automatically removed (34 points are suppressed), the algorithm is restarted and attains an accuracy of nearly $0.4°$ in rotation and 1.2 mm in translation. This accuracy is similar in magnitude to the resolution of the range-imaging sensor. Therefore, we conclude that not the calibration process with the NPBS method, nor the object modeling with the octree-spline, nor the robust minimization algorithm introduce appreciable inaccuracies. Two other identical experiments have been made, with similar orders of accuracy for both rotation (approximately $0.5°$) and translation (approximately 1 mm).

The 3D/3D matching algorithm has also been used on 3D images of patients, first for CT/MRI registration, and then for SPECT/MRI registration. In these

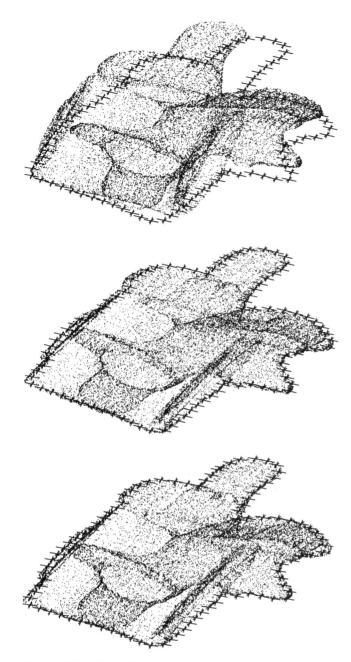

FIGURE 7.15 Typical convergence for the vertebra observed from one viewpoint.

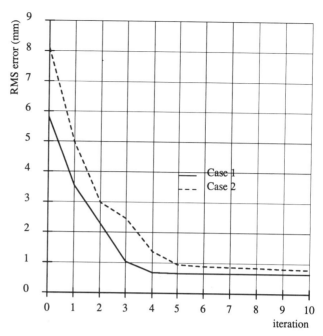

FIGURE 7.16 Typical convergence curve for the 3D/2D matching on a vertebra showing the mean error $E(\mathbf{p}^{(k)})/M_P$ (in voxels) as a function of iteration number k.

cases, the accuracy could be validated only by a visual interpretation of composite or superimposed images: For a given MRI image, we compute for each pixel the nearest corresponding pixel in the volume of CT or SPECT images after registration, and we interlace these MRI pixels with their corresponding CT or SPECT pixels, in a chessboard format. Both images can be displayed separately as well, but then the comparison is made using an elastic cursor.

CT/MRI REGISTRATION For CT/MRI registration, a simple way to proceed is to use the skin surface of the patient as a reference structure. As we use a least-squares formulation, small local displacements of the skin between CT and MRI do not affect very much the registration accuracy. Obviously, if important trauma create important modifications of the skin surface, such an assumption is no longer valid. For instance, we could note some displacements of ears between CT and MRI, but this did not affect the registration at all, as is shown in color plate 7.

SPECT/MRI REGISTRATION For SPECT/MRI registration of the head, no reference structure is available in both modalities for most of cases. Thus we used the idea, mentioned previously, of adding an external sensor (a range-imaging system) to the SPECT device and calibrating this sensor with the SPECT images. For that calibration, we designed a specific calibration template, which is a known object having reference external surfaces and reference linear catheters that can be filled with radioactive elements. By this method, we could also use a part of the skin surface as a reference anatomic structure: MRI easily provides the whole skin surface, and the range-imaging sensor provides 3D data points that lie on the face (from the

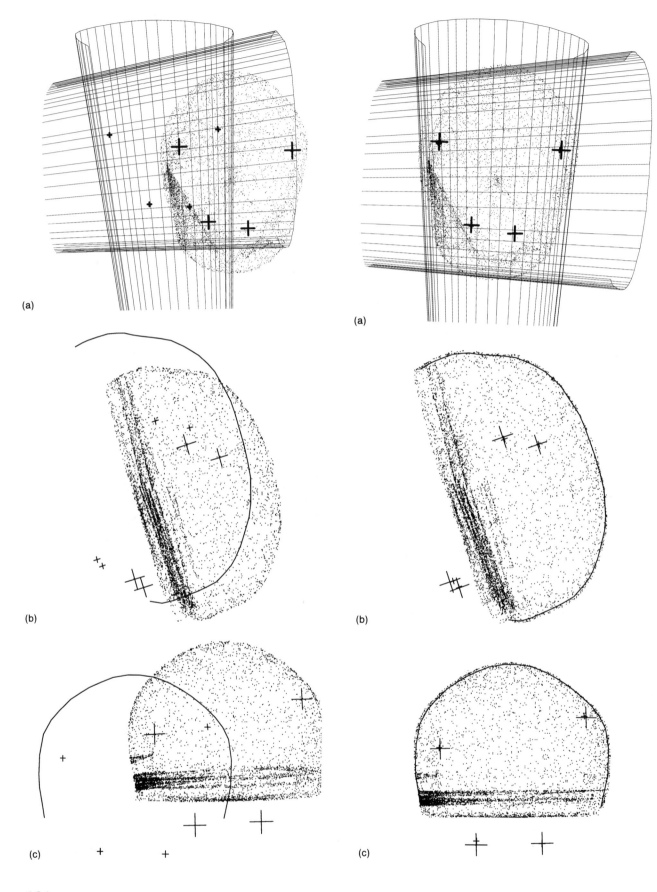

(a)

(a)

(b)

(b)

(c)

(c)

134   REGISTRATION

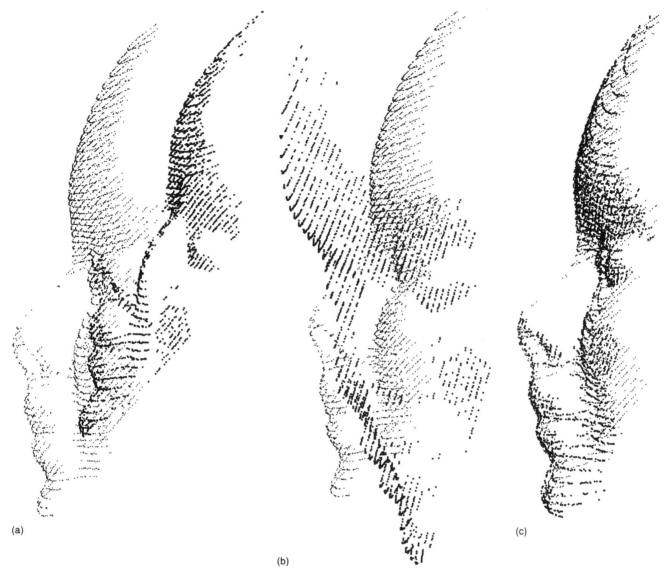

(a)

(b)

(c)

FIGURE 7.18 Convergence of 3D/3D matching algorithm for surface S_4 (phantom face). (a) Initial configuration, $E(\mathbf{p}^{(0)})/M_P = 38.0$, $\|\Delta\mathbf{t}^{(0)}\| = 58.5$ mm, $|\Delta\alpha^{(0)}| = 21.5°$. (b) After five iterations, $E(\mathbf{p}^{(5)})/M_P = 27.0$, $\|\Delta\mathbf{t}^{(5)}\| = 52.7$ mm, $|\Delta\alpha^{(5)}| = 12.2°$. (c) After nine iterations. $E(\mathbf{p}^{(9)})/M_P = 1.6$, $\|\Delta\mathbf{t}^{(9)}\| = 2.8$ mm, $|\Delta\alpha^{(9)}| = 0.7°$.

middle of the nose to the upper part of the forehead). This technique has been used on several patients, and color plate 8 shows a typical instance of SPECT/MRI registration.

FIGURE 7.17 3D/2D registration between CT sections and two frontal and sagittal x-rays of a phantom skull. Left images show the relative positions of contour points and the 3D surface before convergence. Right images show the result after convergence. With this registration, we could measure a mean error of 2 mm on some reference catheters placed inside the phantom skull before the test.

Discussion

MATCHING BY DISTANCE MINIMIZATION

In this chapter, we have developed two new algorithms for 3D surface–to–2D contour matching and for 3D surface–to–3D surface matching based on nonlinear least squares. Our procedure performs a minimization of the 3D distance between the data (projection lines or points) and the surface. This approach is both simple and particularly useful when no simple geometric description can be determined for the shape of the model, which is the case for anatomic structures. Our method is very general as it does not depend on any particular analytic representation of the surface; it merely requires a collection of 3D data points. The simplicity of this problem formulation is enhanced by the fast computation of distances using the octree-spline representation.

The energy that we minimize corresponds to a sum of distances from each individual data point to the model, and not vice versa. Thus our algorithm can work with poor-quality data, provided that the accuracy of the model is high. Furthermore, the σ_i terms in equations 18 and 20 enable us to take into account uncertainties in the segmented data. Our experiments have demonstrated that only a moderate number of data points are necessary to obtain an accurate match. Finally, robust estimation allows us to deal with outliers. In applications where the data are x-ray images, this ability to perform matching with poor-quality data is important, because edge extraction of a complete anatomic structure often is difficult.

A drawback of our approach, compared with methods that rely on feature matching, is that local minima of the energy may exist. However, as mentioned earlier, our method is intended to be used when a rough initial estimate of the object pose is known, which is the case in most medical applications. Moreover, our graphics software enables us easily to determine an initial pose for the object by interactively aligning the model with the data in 3D perspective views of the scene or in 2D projections of the scene. In applications where such approaches are not feasible, more work would be needed to develop a strategy for finding the global minimum.

An advantage of the our method is that it easily solves the problem of sensor fusion when 2D data and 3D data must be matched to a 3D model. For example, if a sensor is made of $\mathcal{N}$ x-ray sensors and M range-imaging systems, the data are $\mathcal{N}$ projections and M range images (A practical interesting case would be to have $\mathcal{N}$ and M each equal 1.) Each type of data gives an energy of the type in equation 18 or equation 20. Merging all these data is solved by minimizing the sum of these energies:

$$E(\mathbf{p}) = \sum_{i=1}^{M_P} \frac{1}{\sigma_i^2} [\tilde{d}(\mathbf{T}(\mathbf{p})\mathbf{q}_i)]^2$$
$$+ \sum_{i=1}^{M_P} \frac{1}{\sigma_i^2} \left[\min_{\lambda} \tilde{d}(\mathbf{T}(\mathbf{p})\mathbf{q}_i' + \lambda \mathbf{T}(\mathbf{p})\mathbf{v}_i) \right]^2 + \cdots$$
$$(23)$$

3D/2D MATCHING METHOD

A new algorithm for 3D surface-to-2D contour matching has been developed in this chapter, based on a minimization of the 3D distance between the projection lines and the surface. In earlier work, we had implemented a method that iteratively projected the surface S transformed by $\mathbf{T}(\mathbf{p})$ onto the image plane and minimized the 2D distance between the contours C_S of these simulated projections and the contours C_R segmented on the real input images. What, then, are the advantages of our new method with respect to this alternative approach (which is closer to traditional chamfer matching [5])?

First, computing the silhouette contours of the surface is more time-consuming than looking for the minima of the octree-spline along a set of projection lines. When projection models have to take local distortions into account, a fast way of computing the silhouette contours of a projection of S is to use a function that tests for any pixel if the corresponding projection line intersects the surface (this is equivalent to our minima search along projection lines). However, this function must be computed at each iteration for all pixels on the contour and for all of their neighbors [58]. In our method, only a few pixels on the contours are used.

Second, the distance measure between two arbitrary 2D contours that may only partially overlap can be difficult to define and to minimize. It may be possible to use some *global* characteristics such as angles between inertia moments of contours and to minimize this distance [58], but this relies on a full 2D segmentation of real contour projections, which can be difficult, especially for x-ray projections. Moreover, these characteristics are reliable only for more or less convex objects. A sum of local distances is thus more appropriate. Because fast computation is a requirement, a 2D distance map must be computed for each real contour projection [36]. However, 2D segmentation errors will be propagated to the distance map, which may lead to unpredictable results. Moreover, solving the minimization problem using the Levenberg-Marquardt algorithm requires the distances be computed at points of the real edge, which implies the need to recompute distance maps at each iteration. An alternative would be to use a less efficient classic minimization of multivariate functions instead [56]. Finally, in this alternative technique, gradient components cannot be computed analytically (whereas in our new method, we can use equations 19 and 21). Hence, approximation of the gradient by finite differences is required, which means computing six more projection contours at each iteration and weakening the convergence owing to inaccurate gradients.

A potential weakness of our method is that we use only the contour information in the projected images. In x-ray images, the gray levels give us information about the integral of the density along the corresponding projection line. The octree-spline representation used in this chapter could be extended to model such densities and would help in rapidly computing the integrals. Our method also ignores the discontinuities in the projected contours, which must coincide with some event in the projected 3D scene [38]. It would be interesting to determine how to add this information to our matching process.

OCTREE-SPLINES

The octree-spline representation introduced in this chapter has proved to be very effective at solving our matching problem. We are currently studying how to extend the octree-spline and how to use it as a general modeling tool for a variety of applications.

First, we are studying how to construct octree-splines from inputs more sophisticated than unordered point lists. Examples of such input surface representations include parametric splines [43], arbitrary triangulations, and level crossings in volumetric (voxel) data. Second, we are examining how to speed up the computation of the distance map $\tilde{d}$ at the corners of the octree,[5] using generalizations of chamfer distances to octrees as well as approximate techniques based on fast $\mathcal{N}$-body solvers [59].

Finally, we are studying methods for extending the continuity of the octree-spline from C^0 to C^1 and higher-order continuities. The difficulty here is to merge overlapping spline basis functions with the octree representation. This new representation can be viewed as the combination of 3D adaptive meshes [60], hierarchic B-splines [61], and hierarchic data representations (pyramids) [62]. Compared with these other representations, octree-splines have the potential to be less space-consuming and to permit the rapid evaluation of certain geometric operations. Possible novel applications for the octree-spline include obstacle avoidance in robotics using potential field methods; fast computation of intersection curves between two complex 3D

surfaces; and surface interpolation of arbitrary point sets, using the zero-crossings of a C^k octree-spline to represent the surface implicitly.

Extensions to elastic registration

Recently, we extended our technique to recover smooth nonrigid deformations between 3D surfaces. Details can be found elsewhere [63]. In this chapter, we briefly present the method and some preliminary results.

Our approach is based on describing the deformation as a warping of the space containing one of the surfaces. In particular, we use a multiresolution warp or displacement field based on concepts from free-form deformations [64], octree-splines [42], and hierarchic basis functions [62]. Our approach enables us to adapt the resolution of the deformation field locally to bring the two surfaces into registration, while maintaining smoothness and avoiding unnecessary computation. The result is a rapid and efficient registration algorithm that does not require the extraction (manual or automatic) of features on the two surfaces and that can work on arbitrarily shaped surfaces with highly complicated deformations.

The main application of our technique is model-based segmentation of 3D medical images. Although unsupervised segmentation based on purely local operators can be very difficult, the a priori knowledge contained in anatomic models can make the segmentation process easier and more robust. Such anatomic models can either be digitized from textbooks or can be built by elastically registering data sets from many patients.

A second application of our technique is in quantification of normal anatomic structures and deviations from normal—*morphometrics* [65] (e.g., studies of brain asymmetry)—and in deviation from self over time (e.g., changes in liver tumors). In some cases, a volume registration between a patient data set (e.g., a 3D MRI data set) and a model (e.g., a brain atlas) is made possible by the existence of some common reference surfaces in both data sets (e.g., the surface of brain ventricles). This registration can be used to *infer* the location of specific features (e.g., thalamic brain nuclei) on the patient data set.

Another application of our technique is the calibration of nonlinear distortion in medical imaging devices such as MRI through elastic registration with CT images, which do not have such distortions. Our technique can also be used in other applications of deformable model-based vision (e.g., in the tracking of deformable objects such as the beating heart [24] or animate motion [25]).

OVERVIEW OF THE METHOD FOR ELASTIC REGISTRATION

For elastic registration of two surfaces, we keep the same problem formulation as for rigid registration and, in particular, we still use equation 20. However, the main difference is that the transformation $\mathbf{T}(\mathbf{p})$ between Ref_{3D} and Ref_{sensor} is no longer defined by only six parameters. In fact, the nonrigid deformation is decomposed in two parts: First, a global polynomial transformation is applied to points of Ref_{sensor} (this transformation is affine, trilinear, or quadratic). Then, in a second step, we model local deformations using a family of volumetric tensor product splines:

$$\mathbf{T}(\mathbf{p}) = \sum_{j,k,l} \mathbf{d}_{jkl} B_j(x_i) B_k(y_i) B_l(z_i) \quad (24)$$

where the $\mathbf{d}_{jkl}$ are the spline coefficients that comprise the parameter vector $\mathbf{p}$, and B_j, B_k, and B_l are B-spline basis functions [64]. The final transformation is the composition of the global and local transformations.

In fact, the benefits of using a hierarchic data structure for representing the distance map can be extended to the representation used for the tensor-product (local deformation) displacement spline. In this case, the coefficients associated with the spline are 3D vectors representing the displacement between the model and sensor reference frames. As in the distance octree-spline, we use the octree to determine at what resolution the spline coefficients are interpolated. To ensure continuity, we must enforce "crack filling." In this case, however, because the coefficients in the octree-spline are unknown parameters being estimated, this is equivalent to controlling which coefficients are free variables and which are determined by their parents' values.

Elastic transformations are modeled by many more than six parameters; thus the inner update loop of the Levenberg-Marquardt algorithm for parameters estimation requires the solution of a large system of linear equations. Because direct methods are prohibitive, we use the iterative conjugate gradient descent algorithm. To accelerate its convergence, we wish to use a *hierarchic basis* representation of the octree-spline [62, 66]. In this representation, displacement values at finer levels are added to the displacements interpolated from the parents, making this a *relative* or *offset representation* [61, 67]. In a true hierarchic basis representation, only nodes not coincident with their parents in location have a nonzero offset, which keeps the number of variables in the hierarchic and regular (*nodal*) representations the same [66].

In our implementation, we keep both the hierarchic and nodal representations, as well as map between the two as required. For accumulating the distances and gradients required in equations 20 and 21, we compute the interpolated displacements and the derivatives with respect to the parameters in the nodal basis. We then use the hierarchic basis to *smooth* the residual vector before selecting a new conjugate direction and computing the optimal step size (for details, Szeliski [62]). The hierarchic basis also makes it easier to understand the influence that the octree has on which displacement parameters are free to change. In the hierarchic basis, a node is free to change (has nonzero value) if all the cubes within its support region have been subdivided to at least its level. In other words, a basis function associated with a nonzero node cannot extend into a larger cube where its influence would not be accounted for.

To use the hierarchic octree-spline for modeling deformations, we still have to devise a strategy for deciding how to subdivide the octree-spline adaptively. The heuristic we use is to measure the average squared distance for all the points inside a given octree cube and to subdivide those cubes that exceed a threshold. This in itself often will not suffice as a node is not freed up to take on a nonzero value unless all the cubes it influences have been subdivided. We therefore mark all neighboring cubes for subdivision as well (the extent of the neighborhood depends on the order of the spline). We proceed in a top-down fashion, subdividing all cubes within a given level before increasing the finest resolution level.

The hierarchic octree-spline favors smoother displacement solutions because it tries to account for deformations at the coarsest (most global) level possible. In many situations, however, we may still wish to add an *elastic* smoothness constraint on the deformation spline [23]. This can be done in one of two ways—either by adding a regular regularization term on the interpolated displacement field [23, 62] or by penalizing each node in a hierarchic basis independently. We are currently investigating the trade-offs between these two approaches.

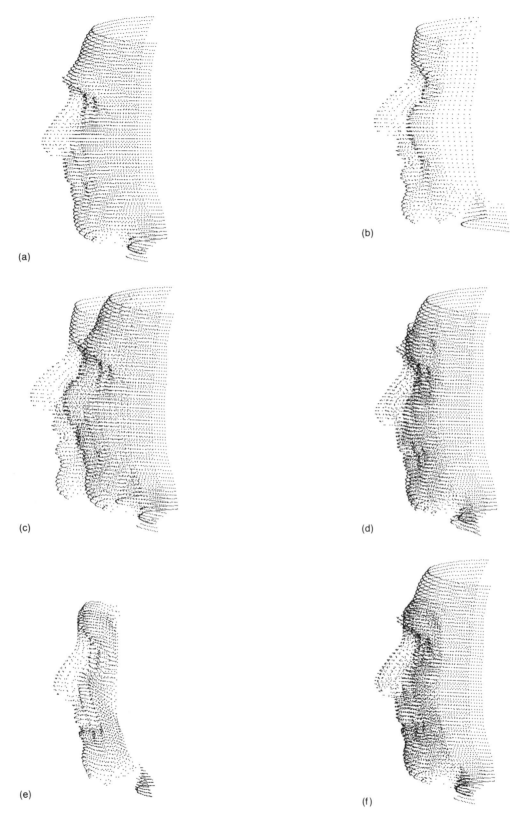

FIGURE 7.19   Registration of two face data sets: (a) model data set (george1) and (b) sensor data set (heidi). (c) Both data sets overlayed (initial position). (d) After affine registration. (e) Final deformed sensor data. (f) Final registered data sets.

To demonstrate the local nonrigid matching, we use two different sets of range data acquired with a Cyberware laser range scanner (figure 7.19a,b). In their initial positions, the data sets overlap by approximately 50% and differ in orientation by approximately 10° (figure 7.19c). Here, the octree-spline distance map is computed on the larger of the two data sets (`georgel` in figure 7.19a), and the smaller of the two data sets is deformed (`heidi` in figure 7.19b). After eight iterations of rigid matching and eight iterations of nonrigid affine matching, the registered data sets appear as in figure 7.19d. We then perform eight iterations at each level of the local displacement spline for one, two, three, and four levels. The finest octree-spline level has $(2^4 + 1)^3 \approx 5000$ nodes for a total of nearly 15,000 degrees of freedom.[6] Even with this large number of parameters, the algorithm converges very quickly, because it is always in the vicinity of a good solution (a typical iteration at the finest level takes approximately 2 seconds). From figure 7.19f, we see that the two data sets are registered well, except for the eyebrows, which would require a more detailed deformation. We also note that the deformed face of `heidi` (figure 7.19e) resembles that of `georgel` (see figure 7.19a) more than its former (undeformed) self (see figure 7.19b).

As a final example of our algorithm, we matched the surface of a real patient vertebra to the surface of a plastic phantom vertebra (both 3D images sets were acquired with a CT scanner). Figure 7.20 shows the result of our matching. After affine registration, a fair amount of discrepancy remains. After the local spline registration, most of the patient vertebra (contour lines) matches the phantom model (cloud of dots), except for the tips of the vertebra that have not been pulled into registration; this may be an artifact of the asymmetric nature of the cost function.

Conclusions

In this chapter, we have presented a new method for estimating the pose of a 3D surface by matching it with

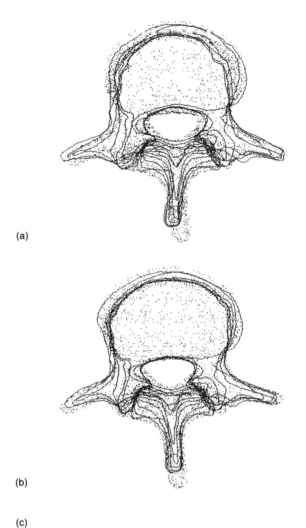

(a)

(b)

(c)

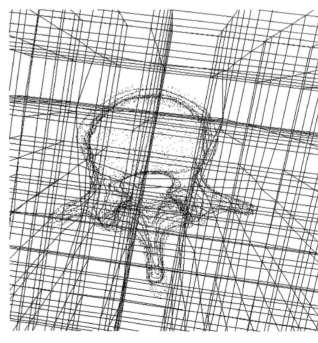

FIGURE 7.20 Registration of patient vertebra with plastic "phantom" (a) after affine registration and (b) after final local spline registration. (c) Selected lines in deformation spline.

a set of 2D projections or a set of 3D points. We have demonstrated the performance of this approach on a number of examples (simulations and real data). The four requirements presented in the introduction have all been met. First, the matching process works for any free-form smooth surface, as no a priori assumptions (symmetry hypotheses, algebraic forms, or special curves) are used. Second, we achieve a very high accuracy for the estimation of the six parameters in **p**, because the octree-spline representation we use approximates the true 3D Euclidean distance with an error smaller than the segmentation errors in the input data. Third, we provide an estimate of the uncertainties of the six parameters, using least-squares estimation with the Levenberg-Marquardt algorithm to compute these uncertainties. Fourth, we perform the matching process rapidly, using the octree-spline to compute a signed distance from a line to the surface very quickly. Finally, we extend the method to take nonrigid deformations into account (using a second octree-spline to model the transformation), and some preliminary results have been presented.

The real practicability of our simple method has been studied and demonstrated on many examples for many system configurations. Registration of x-ray with CT images, CT with MRI, and SPECT with MRI has been exhibited. We believe that this approach has many advantages over registration techniques that use only a few landmarks or material structures. This methodology of using only reference anatomic structures is easy to apply to CIS because, in most cases, the sensors used for registration (x-rays, ultrasound, 3D localizers, etc.) are available in surgical theaters or they are inexpensive. So we hope that this work will enhance the possibilities and interest of computer-integrated surgery, in a way that is comfortable for both the patient and the medical staff.

ACKNOWLEDGMENT We are very grateful to Professor Philippe Cinquin for his contribution to the idea of setting the 3D/2D matching problem in 3D.

NOTES

1. If L_i penetrates the surface S, the spring must be attached from the point of L_i inside S the farthest from S.
2. It is always possible to find automatically a point q_0 lying outside the surface S, whereas it may be more difficult to find an interior point for a complex surface.

3. Under these assumptions, the least-squares criterion is equivalent to maximum likelihood estimation.
4. Although it is not strictly necessary, we have found it beneficial in terms of accuracy, computation time, and stability of convergence to compute the gradient of the error functions analytically rather than performing approximations with finite differences. This computation is explained later in the text.
5. This off-line preprocessing operation currently takes approximately 7 minutes on a DECstation 5000/200 for a seven-level octree with 40,000 points.
6. In our current implementation, the octree is subdivided uniformly throughout.

REFERENCES

[1] LAVALLÉE, S., L. BRUNIE, B. MAZIER, and P. CINQUIN, 1991. Matching of medical images for computer and robot assisted surgery. In *Proceedings of the IEEE EMBS Conference*, Orlando, Fla.: pp. 39–40.
[2] LEITNER, S., I. MARQUE, S. LAVALLÉE, and P. CINQUIN, 1991. Dynamic segmentation: Finding the edge with spline snakes. In *Curves and Surfaces*, P. J. Laurent, ed. Chamonix: Academic.
[3] MARQUE, I., 1990. Segmentation d'Images Medicales Tridimensionnelles Basee sur une Modelisation Continue du Volume (in French). Doctoral thesis, Grenoble University, France.
[4] MONGA, O., R. DERICHE, G. MALANDAIN, and J. P. COCQUEREZ, 1990. Recursive filtering and edge closing: Two primary tools for 3D edge detection. In *First European Conference on Computer Vision (ECCV '90)*, Antibes, France. Berlin: Springer-Verlag, pp. 56–65.
[5] CHAMPLEBOUX, G., S. LAVALLÉE, P. SAUTOT, and P. CINQUIN, 1992. Accurate calibration of cameras and range imaging sensors, the NPBS method. In *IEEE International Conference on Robotics and Automation*, Nice, France, pp. 1552–1558.
[6] LAVALLÉE, S., and P. CINQUIN, 1990. Computer assisted medical interventions. In *NATO ARW: Vol. F60. 3D Imaging in Medicine*, K. H. Höhne, ed. Berlin: Springer-Verlag, pp. 301–312.
[7] CHAMPLEBOUX, G., S. LAVALLÉE, R. SZELISKI, and L. BRUNIE, 1992. From accurate range imaging sensor calibration to accurate model-based 3-D object localization. In *IEEE Computer Society Conference on Computer Vision and Pattern Recognition (CVPR '92)*, Champaign, Ill.
[8] BRUNIE, L., and S. LAVALLÉE, 1992. Three-dimensional dynamic imaging of the spine. In *MEDINFO '92*, Geneve, Switzerland.
[9] BRUNIE, L., 1992. Accurate 3D modelization of the scoliosis by matching 3D images (MR, CT) with 2D x-rays. In *International Symposium on 3D Scoliotic Deformities*, J. Dansereau, ed. Berlin: Fischer Verlag, pp. 11–17.
[10] KRIEGMAN, D. J., and J. PONCE, 1990. On recognizing and positioning curved 3D objects from image contours.

IEEE, Trans. Patt. Anal. Mach. Intell. PAMI-12(12):1127–1137.

[11] BESL, P. J., and N. D. McKAY, 1992. A method for registration of 3-D shapes. *IEEE Trans. Patt. Anal. Mach. Intell.* 14(2):239–256.

[12] KALL, B. A., P. J. KELLY, and S. J. GOERSS, 1987. Comprehensive computer-assisted data collection treatment planning and interactive surgery. *Proc. S.P.I.E.* (Medical Imaging) 767:27–35.

[13] MÖSGES, R., G. SCHLÖNDORFF, L. KLIMEK, D. MEYER-EBRECHT, W. KRYBUS, and L. ADAMS, 1989. Computer assisted surgery: An innovative surgical technique in clinical routine. In *Computer Assisted Radiology (CAR '89)*, H. U. Lemke, ed. Berlin: Springer-Verlag, pp. 413–415.

[14] PEUCHOT, B., A. TANGUY, and M. SAINT-ANDRE, 1992. Video tracking of vertebral displacement for intra-operative evaluation of scoliosis correction—principles and methods. In *International Symposium on 3D Scoliotic Deformities*, J. Dansereau, ed. Berlin: Fischer Verlag, pp. 38–41.

[15] SCHIERS, C., U. TIEDE, and K. H. HÖHNE, 1989. Interactive 3D registration of image volumes from different sources. In *Computer Assisted Radiology (CAR '89)*, H. U. Lemke, ed. Berlin: Springer-Verlag, pp. 667–669.

[16] STOKES, I., 1989. Axial component of thoracic scoliosis. *J. Orthop. Res.* 7:702–708.

[17] BEAUCHAMP, A., J. DANSEREAU, J. DE GUISE, and H. LABELLE, 1992. Computer-assisted digitization system for scoliotic spinal stereo-radiographs. In *International Symposium on 3D Scoliotic Deformities*, J. Dansereau, ed. Berlin: Fischer Verlag, pp. 18–25.

[18] PELIZZARI, C. A., G. T. Y. CHEN, D. R. SPELBRING, R. R. WEICHSELBAUM, and C.-T. CHEN, 1989. Accurate 3-D registration of CT, PET, and/or MR images of the brain. *J. Comput. Assist. Tomogr.* 13(1):20–26.

[19] GUÉZIEC, A., and N. AYACHE, 1992. Smoothing and matching of 3-D space curves. In *Second European Conference on Computer Vision (ECCV '92)* (LNCS series vol. 588), G. Sandini, ed. Berlin: Springer-Verlag, pp. 620–629.

[20] MONGA, O., S. BENAYOUN, and N. AYACHE, 1992. From partials derivatives of 3D density images to ridge lines. In *IEEE Computer Society Conference on Computer Vision and Pattern Recognition (CVPR '92)*, Champaign, Ill., pp. 354–359.

[21] WITKIN, A., K. FLISCHER, and A. BARR, 1987. Energy constraints on parameterized models. *Comput. Graphics* 21(4):225–232.

[22] TERZOPOULOS, D., A. WITKIN, and M. KASS, 1988. Constraints on deformable models: Recovering 3D shape and nonrigid motion. Artif. Intell. 36:91–123.

[23] BAJCSY, R., and S. KOVACIC, 1989. Multiresolution elastic matching. *Comput. Vision Graphics Image Proc.* 46:1–21.

[24] HOROWITZ, B., and A. PENTLAND, 1991. Recovery of non-rigid motion and structure. In *IEEE Computer Society Conference on Computer Vision and Pattern Recognition (CVPR '91)*. IEEE Computer Society Press, pp. 325–330.

[25] TERZOPOULOS, D., and D. METAXAS, 1991. Dynamic 3D models with local and global deformations: Deformable superquadrics. *IEEE Trans. Patt. Anal. Mach. Intell.* 13(7): 703–714.

[26] DEMAZEAU, Y., 1986. Niveaux de repésentation pour la vision par ordinateur; indices d'image et indices de scène. Doctoral thesis, Institut National Polytechnique de Grenoble, Grenoble University, France.

[27] LOWE, D. G., 1985. *Perceptual Organization and Visual Recognition.* Boston: Kluwer Academic.

[28] LIU, Y., T. HUANG, and D. FAUGERAS, 1990. Determination of camera location from 2D to 3D line and point correspondences. *IEEE Trans. Patt. Anal. Mach. Intell.* 12: 28–37.

[29] HORAUD, R., 1987. New methods for matching 3D objects with single perspective views. *IEEE Trans. Patt. Anal. Mach. Intell.* 9(3):401–412.

[30] DHOME, M., M. RICHETIN, J. T. LAPRESTE, and G. RIVES, 1989. Determination of the attitude of 3D objects from a single perspective view. *IEEE Trans. Patt. Anal. Mach. Intell.* PAMI-11(12):1265–1278.

[31] GRANGER, C., 1985. Reconnaissance d'objets par mise en correspondance en vision par ordinateur. Doctoral thesis, Nice University, France.

[32] LOWE, D. G., 1991. Fitting parameterized three-dimensional models to images. *IEEE Trans. Patt. Anal. Mach. Intell.* 13(5):441–450.

[33] GLACHET, R., M. DHOME, and J. T. LAPRESTE, 1992. Finding the pose of an object of revolution. In *Second European Conference on Computer Vision (ECCV '92)* (LNCS series vol. 588), G. Sandini, ed. Berlin: Springer-Verlag, pp. 681–686.

[34] BROOKS, R., 1981. Symbolic reasoning among 3D models and 2D images. *Artif. Intell.* 17:285–348.

[35] SEDERBERG, T. W., D. C. ANDERSON, and R. N. GOLDMAN, 1984. Implicit representation of parametric curves and surfaces. *Comput. Vision Graphics Image Proc.* 28: 72–84.

[36] BARROW, H. G., J. M. TENENBAUM, R. C. BOLLES, and H. C. WOLF, 1977. Parameteric correspondence and chamfer matching: Two new techniques for image matching. In *Fifth International Joint Conference on Artificial Intelligence* IJCAI-77:659–663.

[37] ARNOLD, V. I., 1994. *Catastrophe Theory.* Berlin: Springer-Verlag.

[38] KERGOSIEN, Y. L., 1987. Projection of smooth surfaces: Stable primitives. In *MARI-COGNITIVA*, pp. 447–454.

[39] THOM, R., 1981. *Modèles Mathématiques de la Morphogénèse.* Paris: Bourgeois.

[40] DEMAZURE, M., 1989. *Catastrophes et Bifurcations.* Paris: Ellipses.

[41] PONCE, J., S. PETITJEAN, and D. J. KRIEGMAN, 1992. Computing exact aspect graphs of curved objects: Algebraic surfaces. In *Second European Conference on Computer Vision (ECCV '92)* (LNCS series vol. 588), G. Sandini, ed. Berlin: Springer-Verlag, pp. 599–614.

[42] LAVALLÉE, S., R. SZELISKI, and L. BRUNIE, 1991. Matching 3-D smooth surfaces with their 2-D projections using 3-D distance maps. *Proc. S.P.I.E.* 1570:322–336.

[43] KRISHNAPURAM, R., and D. CASASENT, 1989. Determination of three-dimensional object location and orientation from range images. *IEEE Trans. Patt. Anal. Mach. Intell.* 11(11):1158–1167.

[44] HORN, B. K. P., 1990. Relative orientation. *Int. J. Comput. Vision* 4(1):59–78.

[45] AYACHE, N., 1991. *Artificial Vision for Mobile Robots: Stereo Vision and Multisensory Perception.* Cambridge, Mass: MIT Press.

[46] TSAI, R. Y., 1989. Synopsis of recent progress on camera calibration for 3D machine vision. *Robotics Rev.*, 1:147–160.

[47] MARTINS, H. A., J. R. BIRK, and R. B. KELLEY, 1981. Camera models based on data from two calibration planes. *Comput. Graphics Image Proc.* 17:173–179.

[48] GREMBAN, K. D., C. E. THORPE, and T. KANADE, 1988. Geometric camera calibration using systems of linear equations. In *IEEE International Conference on Robotics and Automation*, Philadelphia, pp. 562–567.

[49] DANIELSON, P.-E., 1980. Euclidean distance mapping. *Comput. Graphics Image Proc.* 14:227–248.

[50] BORGEFORS, G., 1984. Distance transformations in arbitrary dimensions. *Comput. Vision Graphics Image Proc.* 27:321–345.

[51] BORGEFORS, G., 1986. Distance transformations in digital images. *Comput. Vision Graphics Image Proc.* 34:344–371.

[52] SAMET, H., 1989. *The Design and Analysis of Spatial Data Structures.* Reading, Mass.: Addison-Wesley.

[53] GARCIA, G., 1989. Contribution a la modelisation d'objets et a la detection de collisions en robotique a l'aide d'arbres octaux. Doctoral thesis, Nantes University, France.

[54] HERZEN, B. V., and A. H. BARR, 1987. Accurate triangulations of deformed, intersecting surfaces. *Comput. Graphics* 21(4):103–110.

[55] MONGA, O., N. AYACHE, and P. T. SANDER, 1991. From voxel to curvature. In *IEEE Computer Society Conference on Computer Vision and Pattern Recognition (CVPR '91)*, Maui, Hawaii, pp. 644–649.

[56] PRESS, W. H., B. P. FLANNERY, S. A. TEUKOLSKY, and W. T. VETTERLING, 1986. *Numerical Recipes: The Art of Scientific Computing.* Cambridge, Engl.: Cambridge University Press.

[57] HUBER, P. J., 1981. *Robust Statistics.* New York: Wiley.

[58] LAVALLÉE, S., 1989. Geste Medico-Chirurgicaux Assistes par Ordinateur: Application a la Neurochirurgie Stereotaxique. Doctoral thesis, Grenoble University, France.

[59] BARNES, J., and P. HUT, 1986. A hierarchical $o(n \log n)$ force-calculation algorithm. *Nature* 324:446–449.

[60] TERZOPOULOS, D., and M. VASILESCU, 1991. Sampling and reconstruction with adaptive meshes. In *IEEE Computer Society Conference on Computer Vision and Pattern Recognition (CVPR '91)*, Maui, Hawaii, pp. 70–75.

[61] FORSEY, D. R., and R. H. BARTELS, 1988. Hierarchical B-spline refinement. *Comput. Graphics (SIGGRAPH '88)* 22(4):205–212.

[62] SZELISKI, R., 1990. Fast surface interpolation using hierarchical basis functions. *IEEE Trans. Patt. Anal. Mach. Intell.* 12(6):513–528.

[63] SZELISKI, R., and S. LAVALLÉE, 1993. Matching 3-D anatomical surfaces with non-rigid deformations using octree-splines. *Proc. S.P.I.E.* (Geometric Methods in Computer Vision II) 2031:306–315.

[64] SEDERBERG, T. W., and S. R. PARRY, 1986. Free-form deformations of solid geometric models. *Comput. Graphics (SIGGRAPH '86)* 20(4):151–160.

[65] BOOKSTEIN, F. L., 1989. Principal warps: Thin-plate splines and the decomposition of deformations. *IEEE Trans. Patt. Anal. Mach. Intell.* 11(6):567–585.

[66] YSERANTANT, H., 1986. On the multi-level splitting of finite elements spaces. *Numerische Mathematik* 49:379–412.

[67] SZELISKI, R., 1988. Bayesian Modeling of Uncertainty in Low-Level Vision. Doctoral thesis, Carnegie-Mellon University, Pittsburgh.

APPENDIX: WHY THE GRADIENT DOES NOT DEPEND ON λ

To see that $\partial e_i / \partial p_j$ in equation 19 does not depend on λ, let

$$f(\mathbf{p}, \lambda) \equiv \tilde{d}[\mathbf{T}(\mathbf{p})\mathbf{q}_i + \lambda \mathbf{T}(\mathbf{p})\mathbf{v}_i]$$

The $e_i(\mathbf{p})$ in equation 18 can be written as

$$e_i(\mathbf{p}) = f[\mathbf{p}, \lambda_{\min}(\mathbf{p})]$$

where $\lambda_{\min}$ is the value of λ at the point of the line closest to S. Therefore, $\lambda_{\min}$ satisfies the implicit equation

$$\frac{\partial f}{\partial \lambda}[\mathbf{p}, \lambda_{\min}(\mathbf{p})] = 0$$

We thus have for any parameter value $\mathbf{p}_0$

$$\begin{aligned}
\frac{\partial e_i(\mathbf{p})}{\partial p_j}(\mathbf{p}_0) &= \frac{\partial f[\mathbf{p}, \lambda_{\min}(\mathbf{p})]}{\partial p_j}(\mathbf{p}_0) \\
&= \frac{\partial f[\mathbf{p}, \lambda_{\min}(\mathbf{p}_0)]}{\partial p_j}(\mathbf{p}_0) \\
&\quad + \frac{\partial \lambda_{\min}(\mathbf{p})}{\partial p_j}(\mathbf{p}_0) \frac{\partial f(\mathbf{p}_0, \lambda_{\min})}{\partial \lambda_{\min}}(\mathbf{p}_0) \\
&= \frac{\partial f}{\partial p_j}[\mathbf{p}_0, \lambda_{\min}(\mathbf{p}_0)]
\end{aligned}$$

which shows that the variation of $\lambda_{\min}$ with respect to p_j can be ignored when computing $\partial e_i / \partial p_j$.

Basic Tools for Surgical Planning

THIS IS THE THIRD of three sections devoted to data modeling for CIS. Once basic information has been acquired and modeled, it is necessary to provide suitable tools to visualize and manipulate the modeled data. These tools must be integrated in surgical planning systems that are specific to each application. In the second part of this book, particularly the sections devoted to neurosurgery, orthopaedics, craniofacial surgery, and radiotherapy will provide many instances of surgical planning integration. This section focuses on basic technology used in a surgical planning system.

The first chapter, "Surgical Planning Using Computer-Assisted Three-Dimensional Reconstructions," from Kikinis, Gleason, and Jolesz serves as an introduction. It presents a typical surgical planning application in neurosurgery. The chapter shows how image manipulation and visualization can help a surgeon plan an intervention and provides an illuminating particular example. The basic tools that are used are detailed further in other chapters in this section. The authors describe a situation in which surgeons register mentally surgical planning with the real world of the operating room. Although this example demonstrates the current usefulness of high-level surgical planning tools, accurate registration appears to be an important requirement.

The chapter "Three-Dimensional Imaging in Medicine," by Pommert et al., briefly reviews the modeling problem of medical images in general and then focuses on visualization techniques. Surface-based and volume-

rendering methods are presented and discussed. The particular problem of 3D visualization techniques is also discussed by Udupa and Gonçalves in chapter 3. Both chapters focus on the visualization of 3D scenes on standard monitor screens. The possibility of using alternative display technologies is discussed elsewhere, notably in the section Human-Machine Interfaces and, briefly, in a subsequent chapter of this section.

In the chapter "The ANALYZE Software System for Visualization and Analysis in Surgery Simulation," Robb and Hanson describe the integration of multiple modeling and interactive manipulation techniques into a comprehensive software package. This chapter can be viewed as a summary of the first three chapters of this book as it covers various topics such as interactive 2D and 3D display, segmentation, registration, and quantitative measurement. Many illustrations provide a clear presentation of most of the basic tools, which are shown to be easily integrated in specific surgical planning applications. However, in this work, surgical planning itself is considered to be the goal. The purpose is more to quantify and analyze a series of images rather than to define accurately a surgical strategy that will be reproduced through the use of CIS systems. In this sense, ANALYZE, although itself an integrated software package, also must be seen as a toolbox that must be integrated in a complete CIS system.

The last chapter of this section, "Synthetic Muscular Contraction on Facial Tissue Derived from Computerized Tomography Data," presents a modeling system that can take tissue deformations into account. Keith Waters proposes to extract the bone and skin surface from CT data and then build a three-layer model of the skin that includes some muscles. The action of a synthetic muscle yields a deformation of the face that can be observed in three dimensions. This work offers a basic tool that may find immediate applications in craniofacial surgical planning. It also provides an idea of what is currently feasible on realistic deformable models.

In conclusion, many generic basic tools for surgical planning do exist and can be used in numerous surgical applications. Typically, visualization, analysis, manipulation, and cutting of rigid segmented structures is feasible. However, much work remains to be done on realistic deformable models, taking real physical properties into account, in order to simulate complex surgical strategies acting on soft tissues. Multimodal images and signals and anatomic studies provide data that contain enough information to build such models, but long-term research still is necessary before all these data can be fully exploited clinically.

8 Surgical Planning Using Computer-Assisted Three-Dimensional Reconstructions

RON KIKINIS, P. LANGHAM GLEASON, AND
FERENC A. JOLESZ

PLANNING SURGERIES with 3D computer reconstructions of diagnostic images is a relatively new concept. In the past, technologic limitations made such reconstructions difficult to produce and time-consuming to display graphically. The ability to segment and render such images rapidly arose in the 1980s owing to several advances in computer science, in particular increased hardware computational speed and improved graphics software [1–3]. In the future, such 3D reconstructions will eclipse standard 2D images as the standard for planning complex surgeries.

Background

Traditionally, clinicians have had to envision mentally the actual 3D pathologic processes portrayed in standard 2D radiographic images. For instance, the task of interpreting and integrating multiple image data streams during surgery (e.g., correlating the preoperative and intraoperative imaging studies with the surgeon's view of the operative field) was left to the mind's eye. This ability to conceptualize pathologic anatomy three-dimensionally plays a particularly important role in the field of craniofacial surgery, which first used the reconstruction techniques described here. In the past, craniofacial surgeons studied the 2D information provided by plain skull x-ray films plus CT scans and imagined the steps necessary to correct the deformities.

Similarly, neurologic surgeons require a clear 3D conception of the pathologic and normal anatomy, it is crucial to the successful execution of delicate brain surgeries. Skull base tumors with complicated relationships to the surrounding cerebral arteries, cranial nerves, and brain stem challenge even the most skilled neurosurgeon. Lesions of the cerebral hemispheres in or adjacent to functionally significant cortex require careful mapping to delineate not only their anatomic but also their physiologic locations. Given recent advances in therapeutic technologies such as microsurgery, computerized stereotaxis, laser surgeries, and radiosurgery, surgeons need to know more than just the cross-sectional (2D) extent of a lesion. Precise definition of a lesion's various components, such as neoplastic tissue, edema, necrosis, and hemorrhage, must be clearly portrayed preoperatively, along with the relationship of critical surrounding structures such as the white matter tracts and deep nuclei.

To address these needs, the Brigham & Women's Hospital surgical planning laboratory, Boston, was established within the MRI division of the radiology department in conjunction with various other clinical departments, including neurosurgery and plastic surgery. The laboratory consists of more than a dozen computer workstations and two supercomputers linked to the magnetic resonance scanners and to the operating suite over a computer network. Radiologists, craniofacial surgeons, neurosurgeons, urologists, cardiologists, neuropsychologists, and technicians work side by side with computer scientists and programmers, both within the lab and at the General Electric Corporate Research and Development Center in Schenectady, New York, and the Massachusetts Institute of Technology's media laboratory, Cambridge. This group developed multistep algorithms to three-dimensionally segment data from CT and MRI, scans and render the segmented images rapidly to allow manipulation in real time [4–9]. The techniques described in this chapter were executed on workstations (SUN Microsystems, Mountain View, California) using data from a 1.5-tesla General Electric Signa MR Scanner (GE Medical Systems, Milwaukee, Wisconsin).

Data acquisition

To facilitate the reconstructions, optimized scanning techniques are used to gather the image data [10]. Maximal contrast between tissues of interest simplifies the segmentation process so that the choice of pulse sequences is critical. An initial sagittal localizer image defines the region of interest, particularly for subsequent magnetic resonance angiography (MRA), which has a field-of-view limit smaller than the entire head. An axial spin-echo, double-echo sequence then is acquired to bring out the contrast between the cerebrospinal fluid (CSF) and various soft-tissue signals. One hundred eight slices on 54 levels with half-Fourier sampling (0.5 number of excitations) are acquired in 12 minutes using 192 phase-encoding steps. The echo times are 30 and 80 msec, to provide T_2 and proton density contrast, respectively, and the repetition time is 3000 msec. A gradient-moment-nulling flow-compensation technique reduces flow artifacts [11, 12]. The images are acquired with no intervening gaps in a 24-cm field of view with a 256×256–pixel matrix by combining twenty-seven 3-mm slices from each of 2 interleaved sequences covering the entire brain. Ideally, isotropic voxels (volumes of pixels) would be used, in which the thickness equals the width and length. The resulting anisotropic voxels measure $0.975 \times 0.975 \times 3$ mm. Additional acquisitions used include Gradient Acquisition in Steady State (GRASS) and Spoiled Gradient (SPGR) images with T_1 contrast. At times, intravenous contrast (i.e., gadolinium pentate) is used to help highlight the distinction between tissues protected by the blood-brain barrier, such as the normal brain, and those that are not, such as tumor core. Finally, phase-contrast MR has been helpful in portraying neurovascular anatomy [10].

Image processing

DATA TRANSFER AND FILTERING

After image acquisition, the data are transferred from the scanner's console over an Ethernet computer network to a SUN workstation in the surgical planning laboratory. The first step in image processing is noise reduction in order to reduce extraneous artifacts and bring out real borders. An anisotropic diffusion filter accomplishes this without blurring important morphologic details [7, 9, 13]. To implement the filter, the user specifies two empirically determined parameters: the number of filter iterations and the threshold constant for distinguishing signal from noise (k value). After repeatedly segmenting an image data set, these two parameters were found to be optimized at three iterations and a k value of 8.

SEGMENTATION

Next, the medically relevant components contained in the images must be identified, a procedure known as *segmentation*. We approached this task using a supervised tissue classification followed by a statistical multivariate analysis (using the coparametric parzen windows algorithm) to calculate the tissue classifiers [4, 5, 8, 14, 15]. First, the operator isolates the intracranial cavity (ICC). This is accomplished on the double-echo series with each echo displayed simultaneously by training on several "seed points" representing the various intracranial contents (e.g., gray and white matter, CSF, tumor, vessels) as a single tissue class, along with the background and skin as separate classes. The computer then calculates a parzen map and, from that map, creates a segmentation image of each slice. The operator studies this preliminary segmentation to determine whether the various tissues are represented correctly. If editing is necessary, additional points can be selected and the parzen map recalculated. The operator then restudies the segmentation to see if further editing is required. A mask of the ICC is formed by eroding the intracranial tissue class to break the narrow, soft-tissue bridges crossing the skull (e.g., vessels and cranial nerves). Connectivity and island removal algorithms then are applied to remove extraneous tissue classes, followed by dilation to make up for the eroded volume [14].

The next step involves creating a detailed segmentation of the intracranial cavity. The operator produces a second segmentation of the head by training for each of the various intracranial tissue classes (e.g., gray and white matter, tumor, CSF, vessels). Again this map can be edited by selecting additional points as needed. The ICC mask is applied to this second segmentation to yield a detailed segmentation of the ICC [4, 5]. A connectivity algorithm is used to define various subsets of each class, such as intraventricular CSF versus sub-arachnoid CSF [4–6]. The skin can be segmented by resetting the ICC tissue value to that of the skin and segmenting the head as a solid volume, as only the surface will be rendered ultimately. Some manual editing is necessary to close off cranial openings to the external world, such as the external auditory canals and nares.

RENDERING

After segmentation, the computer-processed image must be translated into a readily appreciated form in order to plan the surgical approach. Several strategies, reference frames, and tools for data manipulation have been devised to facilitate the surgical planning process [16–20]. A surface rendering is generated from the results via the dividing cubes algorithm [4, 6, 10, 21, 22]. The 3D reconstructions are available on computer monitors for display and in various printout forms such as slides or color prints.

In general, registration of the real world with the computer-generated reconstructions still must be carried out mentally by the surgeon. (One noteworthy exception is stereotactic neurosurgery, in which a reference frame is attached to the patient's head prior to neuroimaging [23–29].) To facilitate this process in our hospital, the neurosurgeons review the 3D reconstructions in the surgical planning laboratory to formulate the surgical strategy in advance. This allows them to simulate different angles of approach and to optimize the exposure of the lesion while minimizing the risk of damage to normal neural structures. In addition, the SUN workstation is brought to the operating suite and connected over the hospital's computer network to the surgical planning lab. This permits intraoperative visual reference to the reconstruction to guide the dissection.

VOLUMETRIC ANALYSIS

In addition to offering a detailed depiction of the 3D relationships of the intracranial structures, the reconstructions permit precise measurement of each segmented component's volumes [8, 10, 30, 31]. Volumetric analysis can be performed automatically by multiplying the number of voxels for each tissue class by the volume per voxel. This allows clinicians to quantify tumor responses to treatments, be they surgical resection, radiotherapy, or chemotherapy.

ESTIMATED ERROR

Segmentation of a phantom brain slice using these techniques has shown the range of error to be between 4 and 6% [10].

Illustrative case

In the case illustrated here, a 37-year-old right-handed man presented with several months of ninth and tenth cranial palsies on the left. His symptoms included hoarseness of speech and a depression of the left gag reflex. The initial MRI scan demonstrated an intradural, extraaxial mass anterior to the cervicomedullary junction. The axial T_2-weighted image through the level of the foramen magnum shows the relationship of the tumor anterior to the left vertebral artery and displacing the medulla slightly to the right within the foramen magnum (figure 8.1). A second axial T_2-weighted image through the posterior fossa shows the tumor displacing both the left vertebral artery and the brain stem to the right (figure 8.2). In the axial flow-weighted image, blood moving within vessels appears bright. Thus, the left vertebral artery appears to be encased by the tumor in conjunction with a small cyst posteriorly (figure 8.3).

The segmentation image shown corresponds to the flow-weighted image (figure 8.4). Different colors are assigned to the structures that have been segmented

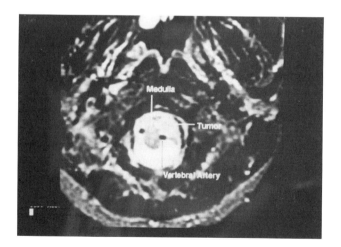

FIGURE 8.1   The axial T_2-weighted image through the level of the foramen magnum shows the relationship of the tumor anterior to the left vertebral artery and displacing the medulla slightly to the right within the foramen magnum.

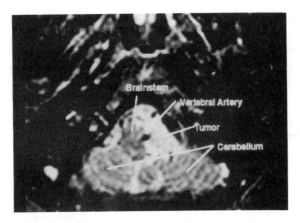

FIGURE 8.2   Axial T$_2$-weighted image through the posterior fossa showing the tumor displacing both the left vertebral artery and the brain stem to the right.

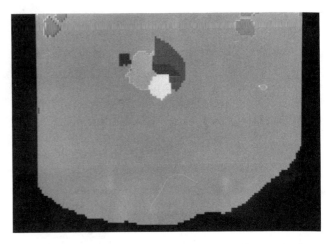

FIGURE 8.4   Segmentation image corresponding to the flow-weighted image.

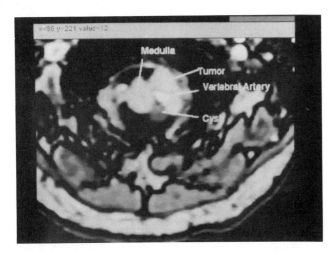

FIGURE 8.3   Axial flow-weighted image in which blood moving within vessels appears bright. The left vertebral artery appears to be encased by the tumor in conjunction with a small cyst posteriorly.

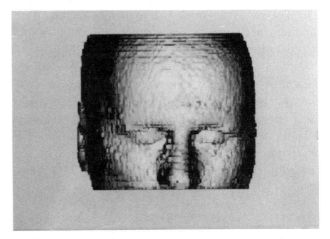

FIGURE 8.5   Frontal view of the segmentation of the patient's skin.

(brain stem, vertebral arteries, solid and cystic portions of the tumor, carotid arteries, jugular veins, connective tissue). In this case, the important information to gather from the preoperative 3D reconstruction is the relationship of the tumor to the left vertebral artery and, if possible, to cranial nerves IX, X, and XI on the left side. Figure 8.5 is a frontal view of the segmentation of the patient's skin. In figure 8.6, the skin has been removed and the intracranial structures enlarged to show detail, including the tumor, brain stem, cerebellum, vertebrobasilar arteries, carotid arteries, and jugular veins. Figure 8.7 shows a simulation of the operative exposure with the patient lying prone and the

right side of the head at the top of the image. The cyst can be seen to overlie the verterbral artery in this view.

The intraoperative photograph was taken from a videotape of the patient being positioned on the operating table (figure 8.8). In the foreground, the patient lies on the operating table awaiting final positioning. The SUN workstation stands in the background with the 3D reconstruction on display to assist the surgeon in planning the surgery (figure 8.9). Having studied the 3D images, the surgeon positions the patient's head and the operating microscope to facilitate the surgical approach. Throughout the operation, the surgeon has access to the 3D images with the ability to manipulate the images in real time in order to fit the exact viewing angle of the dissection. The SUN workstation remains

FIGURE 8.6 Frontal view of the segmentation in which the skin has been removed and the intracranial structures enlarged to show detail.

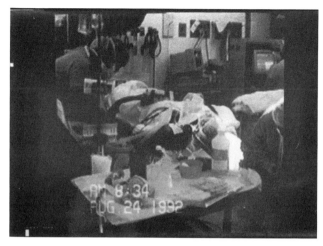

FIGURE 8.8 Intraoperative photograph from a videotape of the patient being positioned on the operating table. In the foreground, the patient lies on the operating table awaiting final positioning. The workstation can be seen in the background on the right.

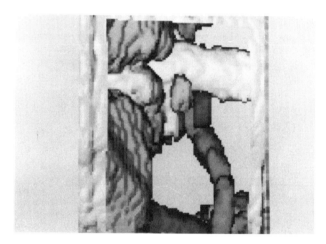

FIGURE 8.7 Simulation of the operative exposure with the patient lying prone and the right side of the head at the top of the image. The cyst can be seen to overlie the verterbral artery.

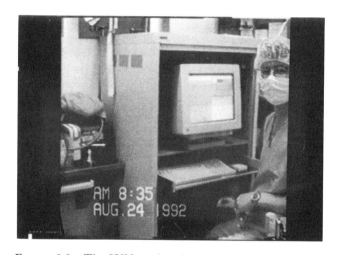

FIGURE 8.9 The SUN workstation is mounted on a mobile cart to allow movement of the computer to different locations within the operating room depending on the configuration of the operating table and anesthesia machines.

in the operating room while the hospital's computer network allows access to relatively bulky, sophisticated hardware available in the surgical planning laboratory. That equipment includes a prototype hardware accelerator board, custom-designed for the dividing cubes algorithm. The hardware accelerator board renders medical image data sets orders of magnitude larger than technical CAD/CAM drawings on a subsecond scale [10].

The image of the operative field was taken from the surgeon's perspective through the operating microscope (figure 8.10). This magnified view shows the

inferior cerebellar structures on the left and the brain stem in the upper midfield on the right. The relatively translucent cyst in the center of the picture obscures the underlying cranial nerves and the vertebral artery. Nonetheless, the surgeon knows from the preoperative reconstructions that the left vertebral artery lies just deep to the cyst. At higher magnification, the spinal component of the eleventh cranial nerve is identified exiting the upper cervical spinal cord and running

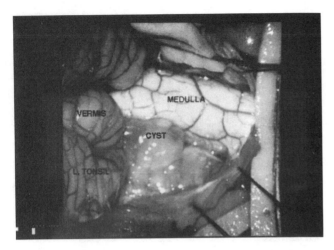

FIGURE 8.10 Image of the operative field taken from the surgeon's perspective through the operating microscope. This magnified view shows the inferior cerebellar structures on the left and the brain stem in the upper midfield on the right. The relatively translucent cyst in the center of the picture obscures the underlying cranial nerves and the vertebral artery.

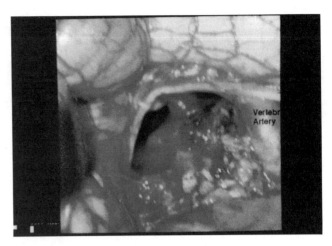

FIGURE 8.12 After the surgeon removes the cystic portion of the tumor, the left vertebral artery is seen clearly. The remaining solid component of the tumor lies behind that artery adjacent to the tenth cranial nerve.

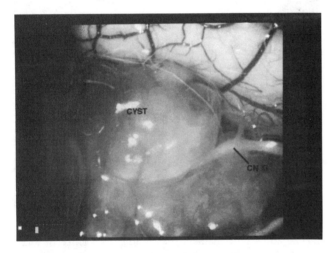

FIGURE 8.11 At higher magnification, the spinal component of the eleventh cranial nerve is identified exiting the upper cervical spinal cord and running superiorly just behind the cyst.

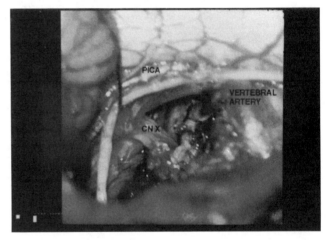

FIGURE 8.13 View through the operating microscope after removal of the cystic and solid components of the tumor. The vertebral artery now is seen clearly, with the posterior inferior cerebellar artery branching off and coursing superiorly into the fourth ventricle. The tenth cranial nerve can be seen exiting the brain stem.

superiorly just behind the cyst (figure 8.11). After the surgeon removes the cystic portion of the tumor, the left vertebral artery is seen clearly (figure 8.12). The remaining solid component of the tumor lies behind that artery adjacent to the tenth cranial nerve. In this image, one sees the view through the operating microscope after removal of the cystic and solid components

of the tumor (figure 8.13). The vertebral artery now is seen clearly, with the posterior inferior cerebellar artery branching off and coursing superiorly into the fourth ventricle. The tenth cranial nerve can be seen exiting the brain stem. Figure 8.14 shows the 3D segmentation of the expected appearance of the operative field after removal of the tumor. The tenth cranial nerve can be seen exiting the medulla.

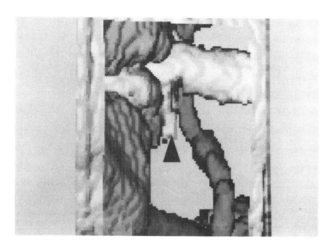

FIGURE 8.14   3D segmentation of the expected appearance of the operative field after removal of the tumor. The arrowhead points out the tenth cranial nerve exiting the medulla, as can be seen in the intraoperative photo shown in figure 8.13.

Results

Thus far, we have three-dimensionally segmented 56 neurosurgical cases. Twenty-four of these were used preoperatively to help plan the surgical approach. Since installing the operating room's Ethernet connection, an additional 52 cases have been reviewed intraoperatively as well as preoperatively.

Our experience with 3D reconstructions of neurosurgical cases suggests that they facilitate planning the operative approach. In addition, the intraoperative viewing of such reconstructions improves the surgeons' ability to understand the relationship of intracranial lesions to the surrounding critical structures such as the cranial nerves, cerebral vessels, and vital neural structures. The improved understanding of the anatomy holds the potential for shortened anesthesia risk and decreased operating room time charges, thus yielding benefits for the patient and the health care cost system once the techniques are perfected.

Outlook for the future

The technologies used in 3D reconstructions require further improvements. Currently, the resolution of the original image data stands as one principal barrier to obtaining higher-quality 3D segmentations. Ideally, the neurosurgeon would like to know the position of tiny but vital anatomic structures, such as cranial

nerves measuring as little as 1 mm in diameter. The resolution of segmented images is limited by the resolution of the original gray-scale data, and so improvements in this area will require improved scanner technologies and parameter optimization.

Automation of the segmentation process will be important to make these techniques practical and available to surgeons outside of large university research settings. Current 3D renderings lack plastic deformability. To model surgical dissection techniques accurately, image-rendering methods that allow elastic image deformation must be developed. This will better simulate intraoperative retraction of tissues and thus better portray the actual intraoperative appearance of the surgical field as the procedure progresses. Other potential innovations include projection of the images into the operating microscope after registration and the use of intraoperatively derived video information to update the display.

In summary, currently available resources make the 3D segmentation and rendering of brain MRI scans feasible and enhance the neurosurgical planning process by better displaying complex 3D anatomic relationships. In the future, further technologic advances will be needed to make such renderings more practical and even more useful.

REFERENCES

[1] LEVIN, D. N, X. HU, K. K. TAN, et al., 1989. Surface of the brain: Three-dimensional MR images created with volume rendering. *Radiology* 171:277–280.

[2] HU, X., K. H. TAN, D. N. LEVIN, et al., 1990. A volume-rendering technique for integrated three-dimensional display of MR and PET data. Proceedings of the NATO advanced workshop in Travemuende, Germany, June 1990. In *3D Imaging in Medicine (NATO ASI Series F): Computer and Systems Sciences*, Vol. 60, K. H. Höhne, H. Fuchs, and S. M. Pizer, eds. Berlin: Springer, pp. 379–397.

[3] EHRICKE, H. H., L. R. SCHAD, G. GADEMAN, B. WOWRA, R. ENGELHART, and J. LORENZ, 1992. Use of MR angiography for stereotactic planning. *J. Comput. Assist. Tomogr.* 16(1):35–40.

[4] CLINE, H. E., C. L. DUMOULIN, H. R. HART, Jr., et al., 1989. 3D reconstruction of the brain from magnetic resonance images using a connectivity algorithm. *Magn. Reson. Imag.* 5:345–352.

[5] CLINE, H. E., W. E. LORENSEN, R. KIKINIS, et al., 1990. 3-D segmentation of MR images of the head using probability and connectivity. *J. Comput. Assist. Tomogr.* 14(6): 1037–1045.

[6] CLINE, H. E., W. E. LORENSON, S. LUDKE, C. R. CRAWFORD, and B. C. TEETER, 1988. Two algorithms for the three-dimensional reconstruction of tomograms. *Med. Phys.* 15:320–327.

[7] GERIG, G., R. KIKINIS, and O. KUEBLER, 1990. Significant improvement of MR image data quality using anisotropic filtering (tech. rep. BIWI-TR-124). Zurich: Eidgenoessischen Technischen Hochschule.

[8] KIKINIS, R., F. A. JOLESZ, G. GERIG, et al., 1990. 3D morphometric and morphologic information derived from clinical brain MR images. Proceedings of the NATO advanced workshop in Travemuende, Germany, June 1990. In *3D Imaging in Medicine (NATO ASI Series F): Computer and Systems Sciences*, Vol. 60, K. H. Hoehne, H. Fuchs, and S. M. Pizer, eds. Berlin: Springer, pp. 441–454.

[9] PERONA, P., and J. MALIK, 1987. Scale space and edge detection using anisotropic diffusion. In *Proceedings of the IEEE Workshop on Computer Vision, Miami, Florida, 1987.* Washington, D.C.: IEEE Computer Society Press, pp. 16–22.

[10] CLINE, H. E., W. E. LORENSEN, S. P. SOUZA, et al., 1991. 3D surface rendered MR images of the brain and its vasculature. *J. Comput. Assist Tomogr.* 15(2):344–351.

[11] JOLESZ, F. A., R. B. SCHWARTZ, G. T. LECLERQ, et al., 1990. Half Fourier spin echo imaging in routine clinical brain and cervical spine protocols [abstr.]. *Magn. Reson. Imag.* 8(Suppl. 1):62.

[12] SHENTON, M. E., R. KIKINIS, R. W. MCCARLEY, et al., 1991. Application of automated MRI volumetric measurent techniques to the ventricular system in schizophrenics and normal controls. *Schizophr. Res.* 5:103–113.

[13] GERIG, G., O. KUEBLER, R. KIKINIS, and F. A. JOLESZ, 1992. Nonlinear anisotropic filtering of MRI data. *IEEE Trans. Medi. Imag.* 11(2):221–232.

[14] GERIG, G., W. KUONI, R. KIKINIS, et al., 1989. Medical imaging and computer vision: An integrated approach for dagnosis and planning. In *Proceedings of the Eleventh DAGM Symposium, Mustererkennung, Hamburg, FRG, Oct. 2–4, 1989* (Fachberichte IFB 219). Berlin: Springer, pp. 425–433.

[15] LEVIN, D. N., C. A. PELIZZARI, G. T. Y. CHEN, et al., 1988. Retrospective geometric correlation of MR, CT, and PET images. *Radiology* 169:817–823.

[16] KOSUGI, Y., E. WATANABE, J. GOTO, et al., 1988. An articulated neurosurgical navigation system using MRI and CT images. *IEEE Trans. Biomed. Eng.* 35(2):147–152.

[17] KWOH, Y. S., J. HOU, E. A. JONCKNEERE, et al., 1988. A robot with improved absolute positioning accuracy for CT guided stereotactic brain surgery. IEEE Trans. Biomed. Eng. 35(2):153–160.

[18] LAVALLÉE, S., and P. CINQUIN, 1990. Computer assisted medical interventions. Proceedings of the NATO advanced workshop in Travemuende, Germany, June 1990. In *3D Imaging in Medicine (NATO ASI Series F): Computer and Systems Sciences*, Vol. 60, K. H. Hoehne, H. Fuchs, and S. M. Pizer, eds. Berlin: Springer, pp. 301–312.

[19] ADAMS, L., J. M. GILSBACH, W. KRYBUS, et al., 1990. CAS a navigation support for surgery. Proceedings of the NATO advanced workshop in Travemuende, Germany, June 1990. In *3D Imaging m Medicine (NATO ASI Series F): Computer and Systems Sciences*, Vol. 60, K. H. Hoehne, H. Fuchs, and S. M. Pizer, eds. Berlin: Springer, pp. 411–423.

[20] LEVIN, D. N., X. HU, K. K. TAN, et al., 1989. The brain: Integrated three-dimensional display of MR and PET images. *Radiology* 172:783–789.

[21] KIKINIS, R., F. A. JOLESZ, H. E. CLINE, W. E. LORENSEN, G. GERIG, D. ALTOBELLI, D. METCALF, and P. M. BLACK, 1991. The use of computerized imaging and image processing for neurosurgical planning. Presented at the American Society of Neuroradiology Twenty-Ninth Annual Meeting, June 9–14, 1991, Washington, D.C.

[22] YLAE-JAEAESKI, J., O. KUEBLER, and R. KIKINIS, 1987. Real-time interactive three-dimensional display of CT and MR imaging volume data. Seventy-Third Scientific Assembly and Annual Meeting of the RSNA. *Radiology* 165(P):421.

[23] APUZZO, M. L., and J. K. SABSHIN, 1983. Computed tomographic guidance stereotaxis in the management of intracranial mass lesions. *Neurosurgery* 12:277–285.

[24] BROWN, R. A., 1979. A computerized tomography-computer graphics approach to stereotaxic localization. J. Neurosurg. 50:715–720.

[25] HEILBRUN, M. P., T. S. ROBERTS, M. L. APUZZO, et al., 1983. Preliminary experience with Brown-Roberts-Wells (BRW) computerized stereotaxic guidance system. J. Neurosurg. 59:217–222.

[26] KELLY, P. J., B. A. KALL, S. GOERSS, et al., 1986. Results of computer-assisted stereotactic laser resection of deep-seated intracranial lesions. *Mayo Clin. Proc.* 61:20–27.

[27] KELLY, P. K., 1986. Computer-assisted stereotaxis: New approaches for the management of intracranial intra-axial tumors. *Neurology* 36:535–541.

[28] KELLY, P. K., B. A. KALL, S. GOERSS, et al., 1986. Computer-assisted stereotaxic laser resection of intra-axial brain neoplasms. *J. Neurosurg.* 64:427–439.

[29] KALL, B. A., P. K. KELLY, S. GOERSS, et al., 1985. Cross-registration of points and lesion volumes from MR and CT. Proceedings of the IEEE/Seventh Annual Conferences of the Engineering in Medicine and Biology Society, pp. 939–942.

[30] SHENTON, M. E., R. KIKINIS, F. A. JOLESZ, S. D. POLLAK, M. LEMAY, C. G. WIBLE, H. HOKAMA, J. MARTIN, D. METCALF, M. COLEMAN, and R. W. MCCARLEY, 1992. Abnormalities of the left temporal lobe and thought disorder in schizophrenia: A quantitative magnetic resonance imaging study. *N. Engl. J. Med.* 327(9):604–612.

[31] MATSUMAE, M., R. KIKINIS, A. V. LORENZO, T. SANDOR, M. S. ALBERT, P.McL. BLACK, and F. JOLESZ, 1994. Intracranial compartment volumes in ventriculo-megalic patients assessed by MRI based image processing. Unpublished manuscript.

9 Three-Dimensional Imaging in Medicine: Methods and Applications

ANDREAS POMMERT, MARTIN RIEMER,
THOMAS SCHIEMANN, RAINER SCHUBERT,
ULF TIEDE, AND KARL HEINZ HÖHNE

MEDICAL IMAGING technology has experienced a dramatic change over the past two decades. Previously, only x-ray radiographs were available, which showed the depicted organs as superimposed shadows on photographic film. These images suffered from poor contrast and, even more importantly, gave no information on the depth of an object. With the advent of modern computers, new tomographic imaging modalities such as CT and MRI could be developed, which deliver cross-sectional images of a patient's anatomy and physiology. These images show with unprecedented precision different organs free from overlays (figure 9.1). Even the 3D structure of organs can be recorded if a sequence of parallel cross-sections is taken.

In current practice, the individual cross-sectional images of a tomographic study are inspected visually in order to establish a diagnosis. This procedure is suitable for typical radiologic investigations such as the detection of a tumor. For many clinical tasks such as surgical planning, however, it is necessary to understand complex and often malformed 3D structures. Experience has shown that the "mental reconstruction" of objects from cross-sectional images is extremely difficult and depends strongly on the observer's training and imagination. For these cases, it is certainly desirable to present the human body as a surgeon or anatomist would see it.

The aim of 3D imaging in medicine is to create precise and realistic views of objects from medical volume data. The resulting images, even though they are, of course, 2D, are often called *3D images* or *3D reconstructions* to distinguish them from 2D cross-sections or conventional radiographs. The first attempts date back to

the late 1970s [1, 2], with the first clinical applications reported on the visualization of bone from CT in craniofacial surgery and orthopedics [3–6]. Methods and applications have since been extended to other subjects and imaging modalities. Recently, the same principles have also been applied to sampled and simulated data from other domains, such as fluid dynamics, geology, and meteorology. As a general expression, the term *volume visualization* now is widely accepted [7].

Related fields

3D imaging has its roots in three other fields of computer science—image processing, computer vision, and computer graphics. *Image processing* deals with any image-to-image transformation, such as filters or geometric transformations [8]. Most steps in 3D imaging can therefore be considered as the application of special image-processing methods.

The aim of *computer vision*, also known as *image understanding*, is to create symbolic descriptions (in terms of names, relationships, etc.) of the contents of an image [9, 10]. In 3D imaging, the more low-level functions of image segmentation and interpretation are used to identify different parts of a volume, which may be either displayed or removed. This has to be strictly distinguished from higher-level functions such as the automatic detection of lesions or even computer-aided diagnosis, which are investigated in *artificial intelligence* [11].

Computer graphics provides methods to synthesize images from numeric descriptions [12]. These techniques were developed originally for the realistic display

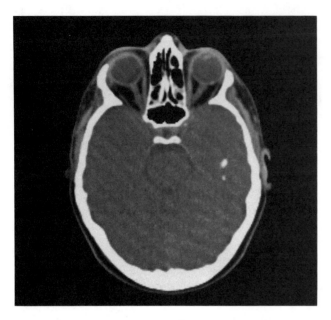 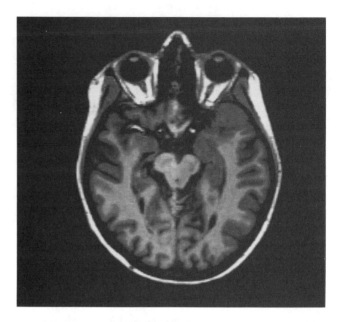

FIGURE 9.1 Tomographic images of a head. (Left) X-ray computerized tomography. (Right) Magnetic resonance imaging. These modalities show widely complementary aspects of the human anatomy.

of human-defined objects, such as technical models from computer-aided design (CAD). Objects in 3D space usually are represented by infinitely thin surface patches such as triangles or higher order curves. Contributions of computer graphics to 3D imaging include data structures, projection techniques, and shading models.

Imaging modalities

Medical imaging technology is based on various physical phenomena, such as x-ray attenuation in CT [13], the relaxation of magnetized hydrogen nuclei in MRI [14], sound reflections in ultrasonography [15, 16], or radioactive decay of injected markers in positron emission tomography (PET) and single photon emission computed tomography (SPECT) [17]. The resulting images show widely complementary aspects of the patient's anatomy (structure) and physiology (function). CT is especially suitable for showing high-density objects such as bone. MRI, In contrast, is very sensitive to variations in soft tissue (see figure 9.1). Compared to these, ultrasonography offers rather a low image quality; the depicted structures are mainly borders between different organs. PET and SPECT are used to visualize the metabolism of a patient.

All the imaging modalities mentioned are fully computerized and deliver the images in digital form as a matrix of currently typical 128^2 to 1024^2 picture elements. The intensity (also called *gray level*) of a picture element (or *pixel*) represents the physical property of the object in question, measured in a small rectangular volume element (or *voxel*) in 3D space. In CT and MRI, a pixel size of less than 1 mm can be achieved. Intensity resolution is typically 12 bits, equivalent to 4096 different gray levels.

For 3D imaging, it is important whether different tissue types can be automatically identified. In CT, major classes of tissue type such as background, soft tissue, and bone show characteristic intensity ranges. At the borders of these areas, however, the so-called *partial volume effect* occurs where two or more tissues are present within one voxel. The resulting intermediate intensity value indicates the percentages of the different materials.

In contrast to CT, the intensity ranges of different tissue types in MRI images typically overlap or are even identical. However, MRI can generate multiparameter images of the same anatomy which, to some extent, compensates for this problem. Each parameter shows a different aspect, such as proton density or various relaxation times (so-called T_1- and T_2-weighted images). The recently introduced magnetic resonance angiography (MRA) emphasizes flow effects and thus is particularly suitable for visualizing blood vessels [18].

Methods

OVERVIEW

In this chapter, we present a survey of 3D imaging methodology. Figure 9.2 provides an overview. After the acquisition of a series of tomographic images from a patient, the data usually undergo some preprocessing for data conversion and image filtering. From this point on, one of several paths may be followed.

The dotted line in figure 9.2 represents an early approach in which an object is reconstructed from its contours on the cross-sectional images. This method is briefly reviewed later. All other methods, represented by the solid line, start from a contiguous data volume. If required, equal spacing in all three directions can be achieved by interpolation. Like a 2D image, a 3D volume can be filtered to improve image quality.

The next step is to identify the different objects represented in the data volume so that they can be removed or selected for visualization. This involves first segmentation and second interpretation. The simplest way is to binarize the data with an intensity threshold (e.g., to distinguish bone from other tissues in CT). Especially for MRI data, however, more sophisticated segmentation methods are required.

After segmentation, there is a choice of which rendering technique is to be used. The more traditional surface-based methods first create an intermediate surface representation of the object to be shown. It may then be rendered with any standard computer graphics method. Mare recently, voxel-based methods have been developed which create a 3D view directly from the volume data. These methods use the full gray-level information to render surfaces, cuts, or transparent and semitransparent volumes. Both surface- and voxel-based methods have their merits; the decision regarding which one should be used for a particular application depends both on the available memory and computing power and on the visualization goals.

Two sections of this chapter are devoted to some extensions to the 3D imaging pipeline presented thus far. The objective of multimodal matching is to register data volumes from different sources. Manipulation of volume data is used, for example, for surgical simulation systems.

The final sections of the chapter address the accuracy of the resulting 3D images and some hardware and software considerations for implementing a 3D imaging system. Applications are also discussed.

PREPROCESSING

DATA CONVERSION   The first step in the 3D processing pipeline after image acquisition is usually data conversion. Besides a change of the data format, which may be required, this involves a number of measures for data reduction to save storage space and processing time.

3D imaging usually deals with huge amounts of data. A typical CT study of 80 cross-sections with 512×512 pixels each takes up 40 MB of memory. Furthermore, if an explicit interpolation step is performed, the amount of data may be multiplied (see the section, Interpolation). The following are some common techniques for data reduction:

- *Cutting*: A region of interest is chosen; other parts (e.g., outside the body) of the images are cut.
- *Reduced spatial resolution*: The matrix size is reduced (e.g., by averaging from 512^2 to 256^2 pixels).
- *Reduced intensity resolution* (e.g., from 16 to 8 bits): An intensity window is chosen that represents most of the contrast in the images. This usually is done on the basis of a histogram that shows the distribution of the gray levels [8].

The latter two points generally will cause some loss of information; they should therefore be used with care.

FILTERING   Another important aspect of preprocessing is image *filtering* [8], which is rather a general term for all kinds of image-processing routines that are used to smooth or enhance the information contents of a given image. A typical example is the improvement of the signal-to-noise ratio, especially in MRI and ultrasonographic images. Well-known noise filters are average, median, and Gaussian filters. These filters, however, tend to smooth out small details as well. Better results are obtained with anisotropic diffusion methods [19]. Other filter types are applied to emphasize special aspects of an image (e.g., to enhance edges).

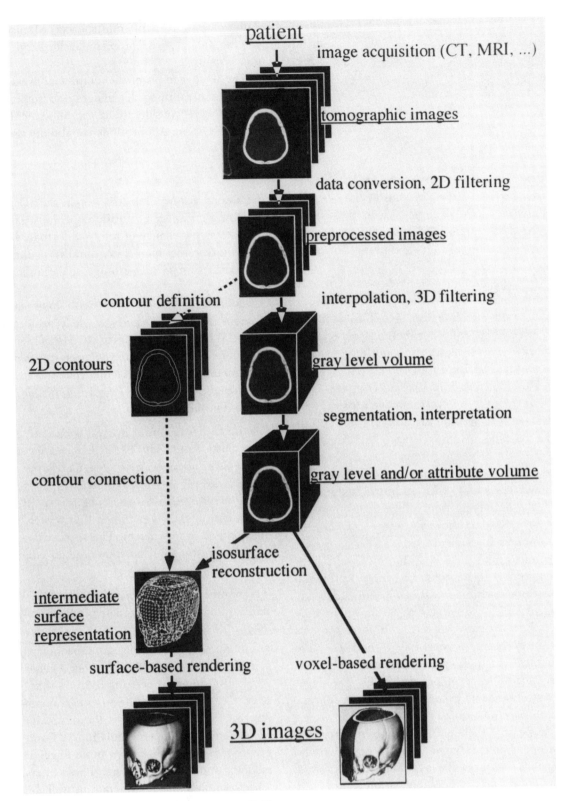

patient

image acquisition (CT, MRI, ...)

tomographic images

data conversion, 2D filtering

preprocessed images

contour definition

interpolation, 3D filtering

2D contours

gray level volume

segmentation, interpretation

contour connection

gray level and/or attribute volume

isosurface reconstruction

intermediate surface representation

surface-based rendering

voxel-based rendering

3D images

FIGURE 9.2   Overview of the 3D imaging pipeline. Individual processing steps may be left out, combined, or reversed in order by a particular method.

INTERPOLATION   At this point, the data are still a stack of 2D images. If they are put on top of each other, a contiguous gray-level volume is obtained. The resulting data structure is an orthogonal 3D array of voxels, each representing an intensity value. This is called the *voxel model*.

Many algorithms for 3D imaging work on *isotropic* volumes, in which the sampling density is equal in all three dimensions. In practice, however, only very few data sets have this property. CT images often are obtained with considerable and varying spacing between the cross-sections so that the resolution in the image plane is much better than perpendicular to it. In these cases, the missing information has to be reconstructed in an *interpolation* step. A very simple method is image replication [6]. Better results are obtained with linear interpolation of the intensities between adjacent images. Higher-order functions such as splines may be used as well [20]. An alternative approach is shape-based methods [21]; however, in these most of the original gray-level information is lost (see also the section Surface Reconstruction from Contours).

DATA STRUCTURES FOR VOLUME DATA   There are a number of different data structures for volume data. The most important are as follows:

• *Binary voxel model*: Voxel values are either 1 (object) or 0 (no object). This very simple model is not much used any more. To reduce storage requirements, binary volumes may be subdivided recursively into subvolumes of equal value; the resulting data structure is called an *octree* [22].

• *Gray-level voxel model*: Each voxel holds intensity information. Octree representations have also been developed for gray-level volumes [23].

• *Generalized voxel model*: In addition to intensity information, each voxel contains *attributes*, describing its membership to various objects, or data from other sources (e.g., MRI and PET). This data structure is the basis for many advanced applications [24, 25].

Segmentation

A gray-level volume usually represents a large number of different structures. To display a particular one, we thus have to decide which parts of the data we want to use or ignore. Ideally, selection would be done with a command such as "show only the brain". This, however, requires that the computer know which parts of

the volume (or, more precisely, which voxels) constitute the brain and which do not. This information also is needed for morphometric measurements of distances, angles, or volumes.

A first step toward object recognition is to partition the gray-level volume into different regions that are homogeneous with respect to some formal criteria and corresponding to real (anatomic) objects. This process is called *segmentation* [9]. The generalized voxel model is a suitable data structure for representing the results. In a further *interpretation* step, the regions may be identified and labeled with meaningful terms such as *white matter* or *ventricle*.

All segmentation methods can be characterized as either binary or fuzzy, corresponding to the principles of binary and fuzzy logic, respectively [10]. In *binary segmentation*, the question of whether a voxel belongs to a certain region is always answered yes or no. This information is a prerequisite, for example, for creating surface representations from volume data (see the section Surface-Based Rendering). However, a drawback, is that cases wherein a small object takes up only a fraction of a voxel (partial volume effect) cannot be handled properly. For example, a very thin bone would appear with false holes on a 3D image. Strict yes-no decisions are avoided in *fuzzy segmentation*, in which a set of probabilities is assigned to every voxel, indicating the evidence for different materials. Fuzzy segmentation is closely related to the so-called volume-rendering methods discussed later.

Currently, a large number of segmentation methods for 3D medical data are being developed. The major directions of research are presented in the following subsections. Division into three classes—point-, edge-, and region-based methods—roughly follows that in Ballard and Brown [9]. Many of the methods described have been tested successfully on a number of cases, but experience has shown the results should always be viewed critically.

POINT-BASED SEGMENTATION   In point-based segmentation, a voxel is classified depending only on its intensity, no matter where it is located. A very simple but nevertheless important example that frequently is used in practice is *thresholding*. A certain intensity range is specified with lower and upper threshold values; a voxel belongs to the selected class if and only if its intensity level is within the specified range. Thresholding is a common method for selecting bone or soft tissue in

CT. In voxel-based rendering, it often is performed during the rendering process itself so that no explicit segmentation step is required.

To avoid the problems of binary segmentation, Drebin, Carpenter, and Hanrahan [26] use a fuzzy maximum likelihood classifier, which estimates the percentages of the different materials represented in a voxel, according to Bayes's rule. This method requires that the gray-level distributions of different materials be different from one another and be known a priori. This is very nearly the case in musculoskeletal CT.

Unfortunately, these simple segmentation methods are not suitable if different structures have overlapping or even identical gray-level ranges, as frequently occurs —for example, in the case of soft tissues from CT and MRI. The situation is somewhat simplified if multiple-parameter data, such as T_1- and T_2-weighted images in MRI, are available. In this case, individual threshold values can be specified for every parameter. To somewhat generalize this concept, voxels in an *n*-parameter data set can be considered as *n*-dimensional vectors in an *n*-dimensional *feature space*. In *pattern recognition* [27], this feature space is partitioned into arbitrarily shaped subspaces, representing different tissue classes or organs. This is the *training phase*: In supervised training, the partition is derived from feature vectors that are known to represent particular tissues [28–31]. In unsupervised training, the partition is generated automatically [29]. In the subsequent *test phase*, a voxel is classified according to the position of its feature vector in the partitioned feature space.

Pattern recognition methods have successfully been applied to considerable numbers of two- or three-parametric MRI data volumes of the human head [28, 29, 31] and chest [30]. Quite frequently, however, isolated voxels or small regions are incorrectly classified (e.g., subcutaneous fat in the same class as white matter). To eliminate these errors, a connected component analysis often is applied (see Region-Based Segmentation).

A closely related method based on recent *neural network* methodology has been developed by Kohonen [32]. Instead of an *n*-dimensional feature space, a so-called *topological map* of $m \times m$ *n*-dimensional vectors, is used. During the training phase, the map iteratively adapts itself to a set of training vectors, which may represent either selected tissues (supervised learning [33]) or the whole data volume (unsupervised learning [34]). Finally, the map develops several relatively homogeneous regions, which correspond to different tissues or organs in the original data. The practical value of the topological map for 3D MRI data seems to be generally equivalent to that of pattern recognition methods.

EDGE-BASED SEGMENTATION   The aim of edge-based segmentation methods is to detect intensity discontinuities in a gray-level volume. These edges (in 3D, they are actually surfaces; it is, however, common to speak about edges) are assumed to represent the borders between different organs or tissues. Regions are subsequently defined as the enclosed areas.

A common strategy for edge detection is to locate the maxima of the first derivative of the 3D intensity function. A method that very accurately locates the edges was developed by Canny [35]. All algorithms using the first derivative, however, have the drawback that the detected contours usually are not closed (i.e., they do not separate different regions properly). To repair broken edges, combinations with region-based methods are currently being investigated [36].

An alternative approach is to detect zero-crossings of the second derivative. The Marr-Hildreth operator convolves the input data with the Laplacian of a Gaussian; the resulting contour volume describes the locations of the edges [37]. With a 3D extension of this operator, Bomans et al. [38, 39] segmented and visualized the complete human brain from MRI for the first time. A similar approach was presented in Kübler, Ylä-Jääski, and Hiltebrand [40]. Occasionally, however, this operator creates erroneous "bridges" between different materials, which have to be removed interactively. Furthermore, curved surfaces are dislocated outward. Methods of correcting these errors are discussed in Bomans et al. [38].

REGION-BASED SEGMENTATION   Region-based segmentation methods consider whole regions instead of individual voxels or contours. Because we are actually interested in regions, this approach appears to be the most natural. Properties of a region are, for example, its size, shape, location, variance of gray levels, and its spatial relation to other regions.

A typical application of region-based methods is to postprocess the results of a previous point-based segmentation step. A *connected component analysis* is applied to determine whether the voxels that have been classified as belonging to the same class are part of the

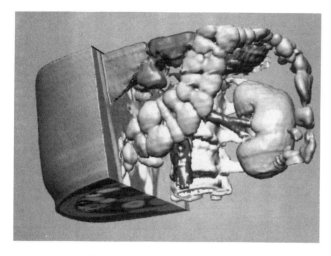

FIGURE 9.3   3D image of an upper abdomen from CT. Eighteen objects (e.g., kidney, intestine, spine) were defined using an interactive segmentation system.

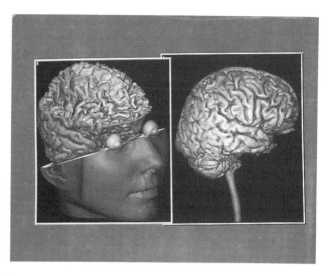

FIGURE 9.4   3D images of a head from MRI. (Left) Brain with white matter partly unveiled. (Right) Brain in a lateral view. For segmentation, a set of object hypotheses was created and tested for every voxel.

same (connected) region. If not, there will often have been errors in classifying the voxels in some of the regions. On the other hand, *region-growing* algorithms can be used to split and merge greater regions, according to certain criteria [9].

Region-based methods often combine segmentation and interpretation steps into a single algorithm. The knowledge required may be provided interactively by a human user or automatically by a model. Cline et al. [41] have developed an algorithm that grows a region from a user-selected seed voxel. Höhne and Hanson [42, 43] propose an interactive segmentation system based on mathematic morphology [44]. Regions are defined initially with thresholds; the user can subsequently apply simple but fast operations such as erosion (to remove small bridges between erroneously connected parts), dilation (to close small gaps), connected component analysis, region fill, or Boolean set operations. After each step, segmentation results are immediately inspected on a 3D image (figure 9.3).

A different interactive method developed by Pizer et al. [45] first creates a multiscale hierarchy of volume representations, based on higher-order features such as symmetry axes. Finally, the user can interactively select, add or subtract regions, or move to larger "parent" or smaller "child" regions in the hierarchy.

There are also many automatic systems for region-based segmentation and interpretation. For example, Raya and Udupa [46] use a rule-based system to generate successively a set of thresholds. Brummer et al.

[47] encode the knowledge required to detect brain contours in a fixed sequence of morphologic operations. Bomans [48] generates a set of hypotheses for every voxel, depending on its gray level. Location, surface-volume ratio, and so on of the resulting regions are compared to some predefined values, and the regions are modified accordingly (figure 9.4). Menhardt [49] uses a rule-based system that models the anatomy with relations such as "brain is inside skull." Regions are defined as fuzzy subsets of the volume, and the segmentation process is based on fuzzy logic and fuzzy topology. A number of other approaches are reviewed in [50].

The problem with automatic segmentation and interpretation systems is, of course, that the results may be wrong if the underlying model does not represent the data properly. The models used thus far are not adequate to handle all data (e.g., various pathologies).

SURFACE-BASED RENDERING

The first techniques for volume visualization, which evolved in the late 1970s, were closely related to conventional computer graphics methods. The key idea of these so-called surface-based methods is to extract an intermediate surface description of the relevant objects from the volume data. Only this information then is used for rendering.

A clear advantage of surface-based methods is that a very high data reduction from volume to surface representations may be achieved. This affects both memory requirements and computing times. Views from different angles can thus be generated quickly. Computing times can be further reduced if the surface representations are based on common data structures such as triangle meshes, which are supported by computer graphics workstations. Another advantage in this case is that standard computer graphics software can be used.

On the other hand, the surface reconstruction step throws away most of the valuable information on the cross-sectional images [51]. Once the surface representation is created, there is no way of getting back to the original intensity values. Even simple cuts are meaningless because there is no information about the interior of an object. Furthermore, every change of surface definition criteria requires a recalculation of the whole data structure.

The following subsections focus on how to reconstruct surface descriptions from tomographic images. The subsequent rendering is based largely on standard computer graphics methods and will therefore be reviewed only briefly.

SURFACE RECONSTRUCTION FROM CONTOURS In 1975, Keppel [52] presented an algorithm to reconstruct a surface representation from a stack of planar contours. This method has since been modified by various groups [2, 53–55]. In a first step, a set of object contours is defined on every tomographic image (see figure 9.2, dotted line). This may be done either interactively or with an edge-detecting operator. In a second step, the contours from adjacent cross-sections are connected to form a 3D structure. If triangles are used as surface elements, this process is called *triangulation*.

The crucial step with this method is to connect the different contours properly. Especially for medical data, shapes often are extremely complex and vary greatly from one cross-section to the next. With general solutions lacking, contour connection is based on heuristic rules; it is, however, questionable whether they will apply in every case. Therefore, surface reconstruction from 2D contours is not used much in practice today.

SURFACE RECONSTRUCTION FROM VOLUMES In contrast to contour connection, surface reconstruction from vol-

FIGURE 9.5   3D image of a fractured vertebra from CT. The image was created using the cuberille model, with shading based on the surface normals of the visible voxel faces.

umes is a true 3D operation. Given a certain intensity level, its goal is to create an *isosurface*, representing all points where this intensity is found in the original gray-level volume. Alternatively, the surface can be defined using object attributes.

The first method to be used widely in clinical practice, known as the *cuberille model* (figure 9.5), was developed by Herman et al. in the late 1970s [1, 3, 56–58]. The gray-level volume is first binarized with an intensity threshold. Then a list of square voxel faces is created, which denote the border between voxels inside and outside the object, using a surface-tracking algorithm. It can be shown that the resulting surfaces are always well defined and closed.

A surface description created with this algorithm is simple in the sense that all faces are the same size and shape, with only six different orientations. Of course, this is only a rough approximation of the actual object form. The resulting 3D images therefore miss many fine details.

More recently, methods have been described that utilize the full gray-level information. The *marching cubes* algorithm developed by Lorensen and Cline [59, 60] basically considers a cube of $2 \times 2 \times 2$ contiguous voxels in the data volume. Depending on whether one or more of these voxels are inside the object (i.e., above a threshold value), a surface representation of up to four triangles is placed within the cube. The exact location of the triangles is found by linear interpolation of the intensities at the voxel vertices. The result is a highly detailed surface representation with subvoxel resolution. Surface orientations are calculated from gray-level gradients (see the section Shaded Surfaces). Meanwhile, an entire family of similar algorithms has been developed [61–63].

Applied to clinical data, the marching cubes algorithm typically creates hundreds of thousands of triangles. As has been shown, these numbers can be reduced considerably by a subsequent simplification of the triangle meshes, without much loss of information [64, 65].

A somewhat simplified approach to surface reconstruction developed by the same group uses points instead of triangles [59]. This method, called *dividing cubes*, subdivides a group of $2 \times 2 \times 2$ contiguous voxels into smaller cubes, whereby the intensities are interpolated. The surface description is made from the cubes that approximate the threshold value. As with the marching cubes algorithm, surface orientations are calculated from gray-level gradients.

SHADING   After the surface representation has been created with one of the methods just described, it is mapped to a raster image display to make the final 3D image. This so-called rasterization step consists of scan conversion, hidden surface removal, and shading [12]. Scan conversion and hidden surface removal are standard problems of computer graphics and will therefore not be covered here. For surface shading, however, a number of nonstandard methods are used. A more detailed survey of shading methods for 3D imaging is found in Kaufman [7].

In general, *shading* is the realistic display of an object, based on the position, orientation, and characteristics of its surface and the light sources illuminating it [12, 66]. The reflective properties of a surface are described with an *illumination model* such as the Phong model, which uses a combination of ambient light, diffuse (like chalk), and specular (like polished metal) reflections. A key input into these models is the local surface orientation, described by a normal vector perpendicular to the surface.

In principle, the surfaces created with the cuberille method can be rendered with any of the methods developed in computer graphics. Due to the low dynamic range of only six different surface orientations, however, the images appear more or less jagged (see figure 9.5). An alternative approach is to use the information

in the *z-buffer*. This 2D array describes the local depth of a scene (i.e., the distance between image plane and object surface). In *distance shading*, the intensity of a pixel is a function only of the corresponding value in the z-buffer [6, 67]. A more realistic impression is obtained if the z-buffer is used to estimate the local surface normal vectors. This distance gradient shading method was first used by Gordon and Reynolds [68], and a number of variations have since been published [7, 57, 69]. Still, image quality is low, compared to other methods.

The original marching cubes algorithm calculates the surface normal vectors from the gray-level gradients in the data volume. This method was developed originally for voxel-based surface rendering (see Shaded Surfaces). Alternatively, the surface normal vectors of the triangles can be used directly. Both versions deliver highly detailed images, where the latter variation shows some staircase artifacts. Images produced with these two methods are compared in [69, 70].

VOXEL-BASED RENDERING

In voxel-based rendering, images are created directly from the volume data, without any intermediate surface representations. The first algorithms working on binary voxel data were developed by Oswald et al. [71] and Tuy and Tuy [72]. In 1984, Lenz et al. [73] presented the first algorithm for voxel-based rendering of gray-level volumes. This technique has since gained enormous popularity. Compared to surface-based methods, the major advantage is that all gray-level information that has originally been acquired is kept during the rendering process. As shown by Höhne et al. [24, 25, 74], this makes it an ideal technique for interactive data exploration. Threshold values and other parameters that are not clear from the beginning can be changed interactively. Furthermore, voxel-based rendering allows a combined display of different aspects such as opaque and semitransparent surfaces, cuts, and maximum intensity projections.

A current drawback of voxel-based techniques is that the large amount of data that has to be handled does not allow real-time applications on present-day computers. With dedicated hardware, however, several frames per second can already be created. As computing power continues to increase, this problem will be overcome in a few years.

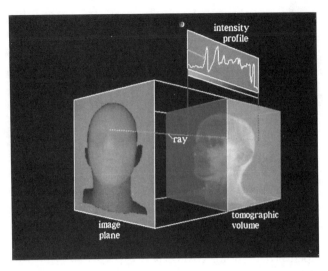

FIGURE 9.6   Principle of ray casting for volume visualization. The image also shows how a surface is found using an intensity threshold.

SCANNING TECHNIQUES   In voxel-based rendering, we basically have a choice between two scanning strategies: pixel by pixel (image order) or voxel by voxel (volume order). These strategies correspond to the image and object order rasterization algorithms used in computer graphics [12].

In *image order* scanning, the data volume is sampled on rays along the view direction [72, 73]. This method is commonly known as *ray casting*:

FOR each pixel on image plane DO
    FOR each sampling point on associated viewing
        ray DO compute contribution to pixel

The principle is illustrated in figure 9.6. Along the ray, visibility of surfaces and objects is easily determined. The ray can stop when it meets an opaque surface. Recently, Yagel et al. [75] extended this approach to a full ray-tracing system, which follows the viewing rays as they are reflected on various surfaces. Multiple light reflections between specular objects can thus be modeled.

Ray casting is a very flexible and easily comprehensible scanning strategy. Integration of opaque, semitransparent, and transparent rendering methods is comparatively easy. Furthermore, image order scanning can be used to render both voxel and polygon data at the same time [76, 77]. Image quality can be adjusted by choosing smaller (oversampling) or wider (undersampling) sampling intervals [78, 79]. Unless

stated otherwise, all 3D images shown here were rendered with a ray-casting algorithm.

Performance of ray-casting algorithms is limited by both marked memory and computing requirements. To allow views from various directions, the whole input volume must be available for random access. Furthermore, for oblique rays, interpolation of the intensities at the sampling points is required. A strategy to reduce computation times is to prerotate the whole volume so that the rays for a given viewing angle scan along the lines of the voxel array [25, 26]. Even if several images are rendered from this view, interpolation thus is required only once. A different speed-up technique is to start with a coarse sampling density to generate a view quickly. If the user does not specify any changes, sampling density is progressively refined to full resolution [80].

In *volume order* scanning, the input volume is sampled along the lines and columns of the 3D array, projecting a chosen aspect onto the image plane in the direction of view:

FOR each sampling point in volume DO
    FOR each pixel projected onto DO
        compute contribution to pixel

The volume can be traversed in either back-to-front (BTF) order [81], from the voxel with maximal distance to the voxel with minimal distance to the image plane, or vice versa, in front-to-back (FTB) order [68]. In both cases, several voxels may be projected to the same pixel. If an opaque surface is to be shown, the visible parts thus have to be determined. In BTF, pixel values are simply overwritten so that only the visible surface appears. In FTB, pixels that have already been written are protected using a z-buffer.

Scanning the input data as they are stored, these techniques are reasonably fast even on computers with small main memories and are especially suitable for parallel processing. Then far, ray-casting algorithms still offer a higher flexibility in combining different display techniques. However, volume-rendering techniques (see the section Volume Rendering) working in volume order have already been developed [82].

SHADED SURFACES   Using one of the described scanning techniques, the visible surface of an object can be determined with a threshold or an object attribute. For shading, any of the methods developed for the cuberille model, such as distance or distance gradient shading, can be applied (see earlier section, Shading).

As shown by Höhne and Bernstein [83] and independently by Barillot et al. [84], a much more realistic and detailed presentation is obtained if the gray-level information present in the data is taken into account. Due to the partial volume effect, the gray levels in the 3D neighborhood of a surface voxel represent the relative proportions of different materials inside these voxels. The resulting gray-level gradients can thus be used to calculate surface inclinations (unless stated otherwise, this method was used for all 3D images shown here). The simplest variant is to calculate the components of a gradient G for a surface voxel at (i, j, k) from the gray levels g of its six neighbors along the main axes as follows:

$$G_x = g(i + 1, j, k) - g(i - 1, j, k)$$

$$G_y = g(i, j + 1, k) - g(i, j - 1, k)$$

$$G_z = g(i, j, k + 1) - g(i, j, k - 1)$$

Scaling G to unit length yields the surface normal [85]. The gray-level gradient may also be calculated from all 26 neighbors in a $3 \times 3 \times 3$ neighborhood, weighted according to their distance from the surface voxel [85, 86]. Thus, aliasing patterns are almost eliminated.

In the case of very small objects such as thin bones, the gray-level gradient does not correspond to the actual surface inclination any more. Pommert et al. [69, 70] proposed an adaptive gray-level gradient method, which chooses only three to six meaningful neighbors. The basic idea is to maximize the gradient magnitude. This algorithm yields smooth images even for thin objects.

CUT PLANES   Once a surface view is available, cutting is a very simple and effective method to visualize interior structures. When the original intensity values are mapped onto the cut plane, they can be better understood in their anatomic context [24, 25, 74]. A special case is selective cutting, in which certain objects are excluded (figures 9.3, 9.4, 9.7).

INTEGRAL AND MAXIMUM INTENSITY PROJECTION   A different way to look into an object is to integrate the intensity values along the viewing ray. If applied to the whole data volume, this is a step back to the old x-ray projection technique [73, 74]. If applied in a selective way, it is nevertheless helpful in certain cases [25, 69].

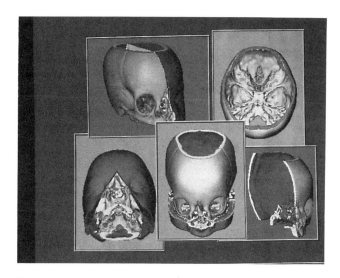

FIGURE 9.7   3D image (from CT) of a child with a congenital facial cleft. Soft tissues and bone were detected with threshold values and rendered as opaque surfaces. Cuts visualize the original intensity values.

For small bright objects such as vessels from MRA, *maximum intensity projection* (MIP) is a suitable display technique (figure 9.8). Along each ray through the data volume, the maximum gray level is determined and projected onto the image plane [87]. The advantage of this method is that neither segmentation nor shading is needed, which may fail for very small vessels. There are some drawbacks, however: Because light reflection is ignored entirely, MIP does not give a realistic 3D impression. Spatial perception can be improved by rotating the object or by a combined presentation with other surfaces or cut planes [24].

VOLUME RENDERING   *Volume rendering* is the visualization equivalent of fuzzy segmentation. This method was first described in 1988 by Drebin, Carpenter, and Hanrahan [26], Levoy [78], Sabella [88], and Upson and Keeler [89] and has since been modified by various groups [23, 24, 82, 90, 91]. A commonly assumed underlying model is that of a colored, semitransparent gel with suspended reflecting particles [92]. Illumination rays are partly reflected and change color while traveling through the volume [93].

Each voxel is assigned a color and an opacity. This opacity is the product of an object weighting function and a gradient-weighting function. The object-weighting function usually depends on the gray level,

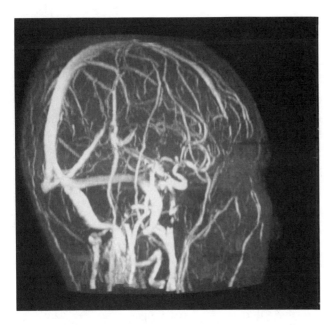 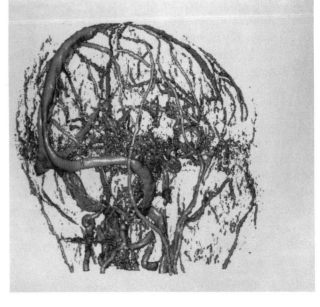

FIGURE 9.8   3D images of head vessels from magnetic resonance angiography. Although the maximum intensity projection (left) shows more details, spatial perception is much better for thresholding segmentation and surface shading (right).

but it can also be the result of a more sophisticated fuzzy segmentation algorithm. The gradient-weighting function emphasizes surfaces for 3D display. All voxels are shaded, using the gray-level gradient method. The shaded values along a viewing ray are weighted and summed up. A somewhat simplified basic equation modeling frontal illumination with a ray-casting system is given as follows:

I Intensity of reflected light

p Index of sampling point on ray
        $(0 \ldots$ maximum depth of scene$)$

l Fraction of incoming light $(0.0 \ldots 1.0)$

α Local opacity $(0.0 \ldots 1.0)$

s Local shading component

$$I(p,l) = \alpha(p) \cdot l \cdot s(p)$$
$$+ [1.0 - \alpha(p)] \cdot I\{p + 1, [1.0 - \alpha(p)] \cdot l\}$$

The total reflected intensity as displayed on a pixel of the 3D image is given as $I(0, 1.0)$.

Because binary decisions are avoided in volume rendering, the resulting images are very smooth and show a lot of fine details (figure 9.9). Another important advantage is that even coarsely defined objects can be rendered with acceptable quality. The fetus shown in figure 9.10 was rendered from ultrasonographic data

for which binary segmentation proved worthless. Other examples can be found in [69].

On the other hand, the more or less transparent images produced with volume-rendering methods often are difficult to understand so that their clinical use may be limited [69, 70]. Spatial perception can, however, be improved by rotating the object. Another serious problem is the large number of parameters that must be specified to define the weighting functions. A good mapping is difficult to find, and even small variations can completely change the image. Finally, volume rendering is comparably slow because weighting and shading operations are performed for many voxels on each ray. If certain values such as gradients are precalculated, a substantial speed-up can be achieved at the cost of higher memory requirements [26].

MULTIMODAL MATCHING

It often is desirable to combine information from different imaging modalities to improve the available information to the clinician. For example, PET images show only physiologic aspects; for their interpretation, it is necessary also to know the anatomy, as shown in MRI.

In general, different data sets do not match geometrically. It therefore is necessary to *register* the volumes

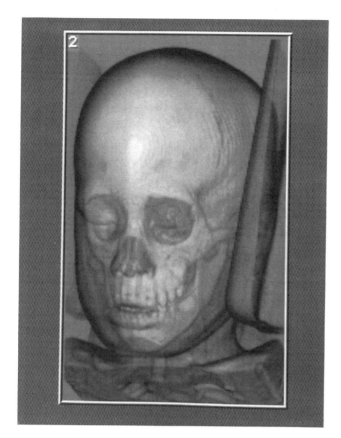

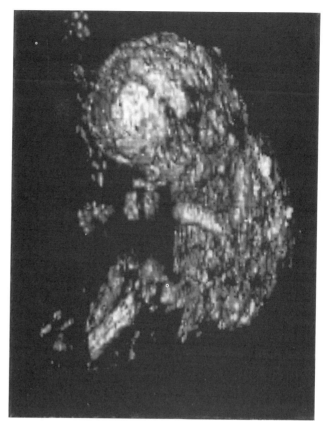

FIGURE 9.9 Volume-rendered image, from CT, of a child with a craniosynostosis (trigonocephalon). Semitransparent visualization shows a lot of different aspects such as skin and bone surface, but spatial perception is difficult.

FIGURE 9.10 Volume-rendered image, from ultrasonography, of a 12-week-old intrauterine fetus. The image shows some fine details such as legs (bottom), arms (center), and the head with mandible, nose, and sutures (top).

in relation to one another. This is a difficult task; to make it somewhat easier, external markers can be attached to the patient that will be visible on the different modalities. Their positions in the respective volumes define the geometric transformation. Without this additional information, it is necessary to define corresponding features in both data sets. A very robust method that registers the 3D skin surface of the patient has been developed by Pelizzari et al. [94]. Other approaches use corresponding landmarks, which are interactively defined on 3D images [95].

MANIPULATION

Thus far, we have focused on merely visualizing the data. A further step is to manipulate the data at the computer screen for simulation of surgery. These techniques are especially useful for craniofacial surgery in which a skull is dissected into small pieces and then rearranged to achieve a desirable shape. Several sys-

tems have been designed that allow the user interactively to draw closed curves onto the screen, which are interpreted as cuts into the volume [96–98]. The resulting segments can be inspected from other view directions and individually moved and rearranged in 3D space. The system by Yasuda et al. [98] can even predict roughly the resulting face. Whereas most of today's 3D manipulation systems are based on binary data, Pflesser, Tiede, and Höhne [99] developed an algorithm that handles full gray-level volumes. Thus, all features of voxel-based rendering, including cuts and semitransparent rendering of objects obscuring or penetrating one another, may be used.

IMAGE FIDELITY

For clinical applications, it is, of course, important to ensure that the 3D images show the true anatomic situation, or at least to know about their limitations. A common approach for investigating image fidelity is to compare 3D images rendered by means of different algorithms [100]. This method, however, is of limited value because the "truth" usually is not known.

A different approach is to apply 3D imaging techniques to simulated data [69, 70, 101, 102] and to data acquired from corpses [103–107]. In both cases, the actual situation is available for comparison. Using the first technique, the accuracy of different shading algorithms, for example, has been shown. Results of the latter studies include visibility of sutures or fracture gaps as a function of acquisition parameters and object size. The diagnostic performance of 3D imaging, tomography, and conventional radiography has been compared using the *receiver operator characteristic* (ROC) analysis [108].

IMPLEMENTATION ASPECTS

Acceptance of volume visualization systems in a clinical environment strongly depends on both computing time and the availability of user-friendly interfaces. To speed up image generation, a number of dedicated hardware systems have been developed that allow near-real-time applications even for volume data (e.g., Cube by Kaufman and Bakalash [109], Pixel-Planes 5 by Fuchs [110]). A key idea of these systems is to support parallel operation on numerous processors. A survey of major systems, both research and commercial, is presented in Kaufman [7].

Although dedicated hardware systems are not yet commonly used, a large number of software packages already are available that run directly on scanner or general-purpose workstations. Advanced window and menu techniques are widespread, but handling the whole process from data conversion to 3D imaging still seems too complicated for the nontechnical user.

Applications

At first glance, one might expect diagnostic radiology to be the major field of application for 3D imaging. This is not the case, however. One reason is clearly that radiologists are especially skilled in reading cross-sectional images. Another is that many diagnostic tasks, such as tumor detection and classification, can be done well from tomographic images. Furthermore, 3D visualization of these objects from MRI requires robust segmentation algorithms that are not yet available.

The situation generally differs in all fields where therapeutic decisions most be made by nonradiologists on the basis of radiologic images [111]. A major field of application for 3D imaging methods is craniofacial surgery [58, 112–114]. 3D imaging not only facilitates understanding of pathologic conditions but also is a helpful tool for planning optimal surgical access and cosmetic results of an intervention. Typical cases are shown in figures 9.7 and 9.9.

Another important field of application is traumatology (see figures 9.5, 9.11). Due to the emergency situation, planning times are usually very short. With new, faster imaging modalities available and computing power ever increasing, 3D imaging techniques are being introduced for difficult cases. Especially in pelvic surgical cases, in which the morphology is difficult to assess, 3D imaging is considered most advantageous [115, 116].

An application that is becoming more and more attractive with the increasing resolution and specificity

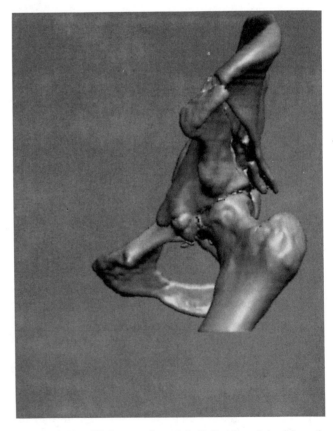

FIGURE 9.11 3D image of a pelvis (left side only) with multiple fractures. Image was created from CT in a lateral view.

of MRI is neurosurgical planning. Here the problem is to choose a proper access path to a lesion. 3D visualization of brain tissue from MRI and blood vessels from MRA before surgical intervention allows the surgeon to find in advance a path with minimal risk [79, 117]. In combination with a 3D coordinate digitizer, the acquired information can even be used to guide the surgeon during the intervention [118]. In conjunction with functional information from PET images, localization of a lesion is facilitated [94].

Another potential application that reduces the risk of a therapeutic intervention is radiotherapy planning. Here, the objective is to focus the radiation to the target volume while avoiding radiation to healthy organs. 3D visualization of target volume, organs at risk, and simulated radiation dose allows a realistic rehearsal of the treatment procedure (figure 9.12). Work in this field is being done by several groups [119, 120].

Applications apart from clinical work include such areas as medical research and education [121, 122]. The 3D brain atlas shown in figure 9.13 is based on an MRI data set wherein every voxel has interactively been labeled with an attribute, describing its membership to an anatomic or functional constituent of the brain [123, 124]. It allows dissection and surgical training on the computer screen.

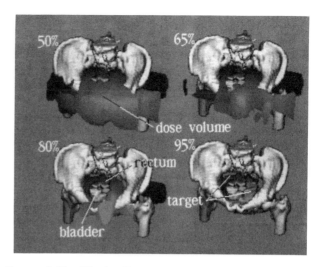

FIGURE 9.12   3D visualization of different isodose levels of a radiation treatment plan, calculated from CT volume data. The study shows how the dose volume covers target (prostate) and organs at risk (rectum and bladder). The latter regions have been outlined by a radiologist.

Conclusions

Medical 3D imaging has come a long way from the first experiments to the current highly detailed renderings. As the rendering algorithms are improved and

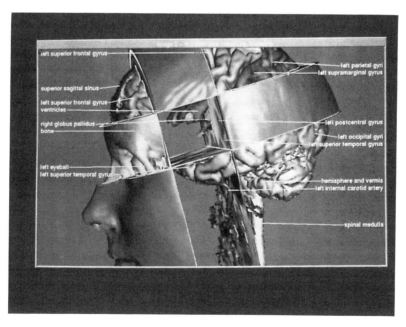

FIGURE 9.13   Anatomy teaching by dissection on the computer screen. The volume may be arbitrarily rotated and cut. By pointing to a visible surface, the selected region can be highlighted and annotated. Objects to be displayed may also be selected from an alphabetic list.

the fidelity of the resulting images is investigated, 3D images are not just pretty pictures but a powerful source of information for the clinician. In certain areas such as craniofacial surgery or traumatology, 3D imaging is increasingly becoming a component of the standard preoperative procedure.

A number of problems still hinder an even broader use of 3D imaging methods. First, current workstations are not yet able to deliver 3D images fast enough. For the future, it is certainly desirable to be able to interact with the workstation in real time, instead of just looking at static images or precalculated movies. With the further increase of computing power, it is expected that this problem will be overcome in a few years.

The second major problem is the design of a user interface that is suitable for the clinician. Currently, there are numerous rather technical parameters (e.g., for controlling segmentation and shading). Acceptance in the medical community will depend heavily on progress in this field.

A third problem is the augmentation of a volume into meaningful parts representing different objects. To date, there are no reliable automatic methods that perform well in every case, especially for MRI. As has been shown, research in several directions is ongoing.

In the near future, 3D imaging is likely to see the surface-based rendering methods widely replaced by the much more powerful and flexible voxel-based rendering methods. Furthermore, a number of applications beyond mere visualization will become operational (e.g., surgical simulation systems and educational systems). In all these cases, experimental setups are already available.

The more distant future may see functional information (e.g., motion, force) included and even dynamically changing over time (4D imaging). Another intriguing idea is to combine 3D imaging with current efforts in virtual reality systems, which will enable the clinician to walk around or even fly through a virtual patient [110, 125]. The future will show which of these new techniques are truly useful for clinical work.

ACKNOWLEDGMENTS We are grateful to B. Pflesser and C. Seebode (both of the Institute of Mathematics and Computer Science in Medicine), our former colleague M. Bomans (now Rheinisch-Westfölische Elektrizifäte RG/DEA, Hamburg), and Dr. D. Friboulet (Institut National des Sciences Appliquées, Lyon) for many discussions and practical assistance. We also thank I. Gulens and K. Pommert for their help in drafting the manuscript.

Tomographic raw data were provided kindly by Dr. F. Hottier, Philips Paris (Figure 9.10), and Siemens Medical Systems, Erlangen (figures 9.3, 9.4, 9.8, and 9.13). Applications are in cooperation with Prof. W.-J. Höltje, Department of Craniofacial Surgery (figures 9.7 and 9.9), Prof. W. Lierse, Department of Anatomy (figure 9.13), Dr. R. Schmidt, Department of Radiotherapy (figure 9.12), and Dr. A. Wening, Department of Traumatology (figures 9.5 and 9.11).

Work at the Institute of Mathematics and Computer Science in Medicine is supported by the Werner Otto Foundation, Hamburg.

REFERENCES

[1] HERMAN, G. T., and H. K. LIU, 1979. Three-dimensional display of human organs from computed tomograms. *Comput. Graphics Image Proc.* 9:1–21.

[2] SUNGUROFF, A., and D. GREENBERG, 1978. Computer generated images for medical applications. *Comput. Graphics* 12(3):196–202.

[3] HEMMY, D. C., D. J. DAVID, and G. T. HERMAN, 1983. Three-dimensional reconstruction of craniofacial deformity using computed tomography. *Neurosurgery* 13:534–541.

[4] HERMAN, G. T., and J. K. UDUPA, 1983. Display of 3-D digital images: Computational foundations and medical applications. *IEEE Comput. Graphics Appl.* 3(5):39–46.

[5] TEMPLETON, A. W., J. A. JOHNSON, and W. H. ANDERSON, 1985. Computer graphics for digitally formatted images. *Radiology* 152:527–528.

[6] VANNIER, M. W., J. L. MARSH, and J. O. WARREN, 1983. Three dimensional computer graphics for craniofacial surgical planning and evaluation. *Comput. Graphics* 17(3): 263–273.

[7] KAUFMAN, A., ed., 1991. *Volume Visualization.* Los Alamitos, Calif.: IEEE Computer Society Press.

[8] ROSENFELD, A., and A. C. KAK, 1982. *Digital Picture Processing* (2nd ed.). New York: Academic.

[9] BALLARD, D. H., and C. M. BROWN, 1982. *Computer Vision.* Englewood Cliffs, NJ: Prentice-Hall.

[10] TANIMOTO, S. L., 1987. *The Elements of Artificial Intelligence.* Rockville, Md.: Computer Science Press.

[11] SCHWARTZ, W. B., R. S. PATIL, and P. SZOLOVITS, 1987. Artificial intelligence in medicine: Where do we stand? *New Engl. J. Med.* 316(11):685–688.

[12] FOLEY, J. D., A. VAN DAM, S. K. FEINER, and J. F. HUGHES, 1990. *Computer Graphics: Principles and Practice* (2nd ed.). Reading, Mass.: Addison-Wesley.

[13] LEE, J. K. T., S. S. SAGEL, and R. J. STANLEY, eds., 1989. *Computed Body Tomography with MRI Correlation* (2nd ed.). New York: Raven.

[14] STARK, D. D., and W. G. BRADLEY, 1988. *Magnetic Resonance Imaging.* St. Louis: Mosby.

[15] HOTTIER, F., and A. COLLET BILLON, 1990. 3D echography: Status and perspective. In *3D-Imaging in Medicine: Algorithms, Systems, Applications,* K. H. Höhne et al., eds. Berlin: Springer-Verlag, pp. 21–41.

[16] Wells, P. N. T., 1977. *Biomedical Ultrasonics*. New York: Academic.

[17] Bernier, D. R., P. E. Christian, J. K. Langman, and L. D. Wells, 1989. *Nuclear Medicine: Technology and Techniques*. St. Louis: Mosby.

[18] Edelman, R. R., 1992. Basic principles of magnetic resonance angiography. *Cardiovasc. Intervent. Radiol.* 15(1):3–13.

[19] Gerig, G., O. Kübler, R. Kikinis, and F. A. Jolesz, 1992. Nonlinear anisotropic filtering of MRI data. *IEEE Trans. Med. Imag.* 11(2):221–232.

[20] Parker, J. A., R. V. Kenyon, and D. E. Troxel, 1983. A Comparison of interpolating methods for image resampling. *IEEE Trans. Med. Imag.* MI-2(1):31–39.

[21] Raya, S. P., and J. K. Udupa, 1990. Shape-based interpolation of multidimensional objects. *IEEE Trans. Med. Imag.* MI-9(1):32–42.

[22] Meagher, D. J., 1982. Geometric modeling using octree encoding. *Comput. Graphics Image Proc.* 19(2):123–147.

[23] Laur, D., and P. Hanrahan, 1991. Hierarchical splatting: A progressive refinement algorithm for volume rendering. *Comput. Graphics* 25(4):285–288.

[24] Höhne, K. H., M. Bomans, A. Pommert, M. Riemer, C. Schiers, U. Tiede, and G. Wiebecke, 1990. 3D visualization of tomographic volume data using the generalized voxel model. *Visual Comput.* 6(1):28–36.

[25] Höhne, K. H., M. Riemer, and U. Tiede, 1987. Viewing operations for 3D-tomographic gray level data. In *Computer Assisted Radiology (CAR '87)* H. U. Lemke et al., eds. Berlin: Springer-Verlag, pp. 599–609.

[26] Drebin, R. A., L. Carpenter, and P. Hanrahan, 1988. Volume rendering. *Comput. Graphics* 22(4):65–74.

[27] Duda, R. O., and P. E. Hart, 1993. *Pattern Classification and Scene Analysis*. New York: Wiley.

[28] Cline, H. E., W. E. Lorensen, R. Kikinis, and F. Jolesz, 1990. Three-dimensional segmentation of MR images of the head using probability and connectivity. *J. Comput. Assist. Tomogr.* 14(6):1037–1045.

[29] Gerig, G., J. Martin, R. Kikinis, O. Kübler, M. Shenton, and F. A. Jolesz, 1991. Automating segmentation of dual-echo MR head data. In *Information Processing in Medical Imaging (Proc. IPMI '91)*, A. C. F. Colchester, and D. Hawkes, eds. Berlin: Springer-Verlag, pp. 175–187.

[30] Merickel, M. B., T. Jackson, C. Carman, J. R. Brookeman, and C. R. Ayers, 1990. A multispectral pattern recognition system for the noninvasive evaluation of atherosclerosis utilizing MRI. In *3D-Imaging in Medicine: Algorithms, Systems, Applications*, K. H. Höhne et al., eds. Berlin: Springer-Verlag, pp. 133–146.

[31] Vannier, M. W., C. M. Speidel, D. L. Rickman, L. D. Schertz, L. R. Baker, C. F. Hildeboldt, C. J. Offutt, J. A. Balko, R. L. Butterfield, and M. H. Gado, 1988. Multispectral analysis of magnetic resonance images. In *Proceedings of the Ninth International Conference on Pattern Recognition* (ICPR '88). Washington, D.C.: IEEE Computer Society Press, pp. 1182–1186.

[32] Kohonen, T., 1988. *Self-Organisation and Associative Memory*. (2nd ed.). Berlin: Springer-Verlag.

[33] Vaske, E., 1991. Segmentation von Kernspintomogrammen mit der topologischen Karte zur 3D-Visualisierung (IMDM tech. rep. 91/1). Hamburg, Germany: Institute of Mathematics and Computer Science in Medicine, University of Hamburg.

[34] Saurbier, F., D. Scheppelmann, and H. P. Meinzer, 1989. Segmentierung biologischer Objekte aus CT- und MR-Schnittserien ohne Vorwissen. In *Proceedings of the Eleventh DAGM Symposium, Mustererkennung 1989*, H. Burkhardt et al., eds. Berlin: Springer-Verlag, pp. 210–215.

[35] Canny, J., 1985. A computational approach to edge detection. *IEEE Trans. Patt. Anal. Mach. Intell.* 8(6):679–698.

[36] Brelstaff, G. J., M. C. Ibison, and E. J. Elliot, 1990. Edge-region integration for segmentation of MR images. In *Proceedings of the British Machine Vision Conference* (BMVC '90), pp. 139–144.

[37] Marr, D., and E. Hildreth, 1980. Theory of edge detection. *Proc. R. Soc. Lond. [B]* 207:187–217.

[38] Bomans, M., K. H. Höne, U. Tiede, and M. Riemer, 1990. 3D segmentation of MR images of the head for 3D display. *IEEE Trans. Med. Imag.* MI-9(2):177–183.

[39] Bomans, M., M. Riemer, U. Tiede, and K. H. Höhne, 1987. 3D segmentation von Kernspin-Tomogrammen. In *Proceedings of the Ninth DAGM Symposium, Mustererkennung*, E. Paulus, ed. Berlin: Springer-Verlag, pp. 231–235.

[40] Kübler, O., J. Ylä-Jääski, and E. Hiltebrand, 1987. 3-D segmentation and real-time display of medical volume images. In *Computer Assisted Radiology (CAR '87)*, H. U. Lemke et al., eds. Berlin: Springer-Verlag, pp. 637–641.

[41] Cline, H. E., C. L. Dumoulin, H. R., Hart, W. E., Lorensen, and S. Ludke, 1987. 3D reconstruction of the brain from magnetic resonance images using a connectivity algorithm. *Magn. Reson. Imag.* 5:345–352.

[42] Höhne, K. H., and W. A. Hanson, 1992. Interactive 3D segmentation of MRI and CT volumes using morphological operations. *J. Comput. Assist. Tomogr.* 16(2):285–294.

[43] Schiemann, T., M. Bomans, U. Tiede, and K. H. Höhne, 1992. Interactive 3D segmentation. In *Proc. S.P.I.E.* 1808:376–383.

[44] Serra, J., 1982. *Image Analysis and Mathematical Morphology*. New York: Academic.

[45] Pizer, S. M., T. J. Cullip, and R. E. Fredericksen, 1990. Toward interactive object definition in 3D scalar images. In *3D-Imaging in Medicine: Algorithms, Systems, Applications*, K. H. Höhne et al., eds. Berlin: Springer-Verlag, pp. 83–105.

[46] Raya, S. P., and J. K. Udupa, 1990. Low-level segmentation of 3-D magnetic resonance brain images—a rule-based system. *IEEE Trans. Med. Imag.* MI-9(3):327–337.

[47] Brummer, M. E., R. M. Mersereau, R. L. Eisner, and R. R. J. Lewine, 1991. Automatic detection of brain contours in MRI data sets. In *Information Processing in Medical Imaging*, A. C. F. Colchester, and D. J. Hawkes, eds. Berlin: Springer-Verlag, pp. 188–204.

[48] Bomans, M., 1994. Vergleich verschiedener Verfahren und Entwicklung eines kombinierten Verfahrens zur Segmentation von Kernspintomogrammen des Kopfes. Doctoral thesis, Department of Computer Science, University of Hamburg. In preparation.

[49] Menhardt, W., 1988. Image analysis using iconic fuzzy sets. In *Proceedings of the European Conference on Artificial Intelligence*. London: Pitman, pp. 672–674.

[50] Stiehl, H. S., 1990. 3-D image understanding in radiology. *IEEE Eng. Med. Biol.* 9(4):24–28.

[51] Tessier, P., and D. Hemmy, 1986. Three dimensional imaging in medicine: A critique by surgeons. *Scand. J. Plast. Reconstr. Surg.* 20:3–11.

[52] Keppel, E., 1975. Approximating complex surfaces by triangulation of contour lines. *IBM J. Res. Develop.* 19(1): 2–11.

[53] Boissonnat, J. D., 1988. Shape reconstruction from planar cross sections. *Comput. Vision Graphics Image Proc.* 44(1):1–29.

[54] Chen, S.-Y., W.-C. Lin, C.-C. Liang, and C.-T. Chen, 1990. Improvement on dynamic elastic interpolation technique for reconstructing 3-D objects from serial cross sections. *IEEE Trans. Med. Imag.* MI-9(1):71–83.

[55] Fuchs, H., Z. M. Kedem, and S. P. Uselton, 1977. Optimal surface reconstruction from planar contours. *Commun. ACM* 20(10):693–702.

[56] Artzy, E., G. Frieder, and G. T. Herman, 1981. The theory, design, implementation and evaluation of a three-dimensional surface detection algorithm. *Comput. Graphics Image Process.* 15(1):1–24.

[57] Chen, L. S., G. T. Herman, R. A. Reynolds, and J. K. Udupa, 1985. Surface shading in the cuberille environment. *IEEE Comput. Graphics Appl.* 5(12):33–43.

[58] David, D. J., D. C. Hemmy, and R. D. Cooter, 1990. *Craniofacial Deformities: Atlas of Three-Dimensional Reconstruction from Computed Tomography*. New York: Springer-Verlag.

[59] Cline, H. E., W. E. Lorensen, S. Ludke, C. R. Crawford, and B. C., Teeter, 1988. Two algorithms for three-dimensional reconstruction of tomograms. *Med. Phys.* 15(3):320–327.

[60] Lorensen, W. E., and H. E. Cline, 1987. Marching cubes: A high-resolution 3D surface construction algorithm. *Comput. Graphics* 21(4):163–169.

[61] Baker, H. H., 1989. Building surfaces of evolution: the Weaving Wall. *Comput. Vis.* 3:51–71.

[62] Wallin, Å., 1991. Constructing isosurfaces from CT data. *IEEE Comput. Graphics Appl.* 11(6):28–33.

[63] Wilhelms, J., and A. van Gelder, 1990. Topological considerations in isosurface generation. *Comput. Graphics* 24(5):79–86.

[64] Schroeder, W. J., J. A. Zarge, and W. E. Lorensen, 1992. Decimation of triangle meshes. *Comput. Graphics* 26(2):65–70.

[65] Wilmer, F., U. Tiede, and K. H. Höhne, 1992. Reduktion der Oberflächenbeschreibung triangulierter Oberflächen durch Anpassung an die Objektform. In *Proceedings of the Fourteenth DAGM-Symposium, Mustererkennung 1992*, S. Fuchs and R. Hottmann, eds. Berlin: Springer-Verlag, pp. 430–436.

[66] Hall, R., 1986. A characterization of illumination models and shading techniques. *Visual Comput.* 2:268–277.

[67] Herman, G. T., and J. K. Udupa, 1981. Display of three-dimensional discrete surfaces. *Proc. S.P.I.E.* 283:90–97.

[68] Gordon, D., and R. A. Reynolds, 1985. Image space shading of 3-dimensional objects. *Comput. Vis. Graphics Image Proc.* 29:361–376.

[69] Tiede, U., K. H. Höhne, M. Bomans, A. Pommert, M. Riemer, and G. Wiebecke, 1990. Investigation of medical 3D-rendering algorithms. *IEEE Comput. Graphics Appl.* 10(2):41–53.

[70] Pommert, A., U. Tiede, G. Wiebecke, and K. H. Höhne, 1990. Surface shading in tomographic volume visualization: A comparative study. In *First Conference on Visualization in Biomedical Computing*. Los Alamitos, Calif.: IEEE Computer Society Press, pp. 19–26.

[71] Oswald, H., W. Kropatsch, and F. Leberl, 1982. A perspective projection algorithm with fast evaluation of visibility for discrete three-dimensional scenes. In *Proc. ISMIII '82, International Symposium on Medical Imaging and Image Interpretation*, Silver Spring, Md.: IEEE Computer Society Press, pp. 464–468.

[72] Tuy, H. K., and L. T. Tuy, 1984. Direct 2-D display of 3-D objects. *IEEE Comput. Graphics Appl.* 4(10):29–33.

[73] Lenz, R., P. E. Danielsson, S. Cronström, and B. Gudmundsson, 1986. Presentation and perception of 3-D images. In *Pictorial Information Systems in Medicine*, K. H. Höhne, ed. Berlin: Springer-Verlag, pp. 459–468.

[74] Höhne, K. H., R. L. DeLaPaz, R. Bernstein, and R. C. Taylor, 1987. Combined surface display and reformatting for the 3D-analysis of tomographic data. *Invest. Radiol.* 22:658–664.

[75] Yagel, R., D. Cohen, and A. Kaufman, 1992. Discrete ray tracing. *IEEE Comput. Graphics Appl.* 12(5):19–28.

[76] Kaufman, A., R. Yagel, and D. Cohen, 1990. Intermixing surface and volume rendering. In *3D-Imaging in Medicine: Algorithms, Systems, Applications*, K. H. Höhne et al., eds. Berlin: Springer-Verlag, pp. 217–227.

[77] Levoy, M., 1990. A hybrid ray tracer for rendering polygon and volume data. *IEEE Comput. Graphics Appl.* pp. 33–40.

[78] Levoy, M., 1988. Display of surfaces from volume data. *IEEE Comput. Graphics Appl.*, 8(3):29–37.

[79] Pommert, A., M. Bomans, and K. H. Höhne, 1992. Volume visualization in magnetic resonance angiography. *IEEE Comput. Graphics Appl.* 12(5):12–13.

[80] Levoy, M., 1990. Volume rendering by adaptive refinement. *Visual Comput.* 6(1):2–7.

[81] Frieder, G., D. Gordon, and R. A. Reynolds, 1985. Back-to-front display of voxel-based objects. *IEEE Comput. Graphics Appl.* 5(1):52–59.

[82] Westover, L., 1990. Footprint evaluation for volume rendering. *Comput. Graphics* 24(4):367–376.

[83] HÖHNE, K. H., and R. BERNSTEIN, 1986. Shading 3D images from CT using gray level gradients. *IEEE Trans. Med. Imag.* MI-5(1):45–47.

[84] BARILLOT, C., B. GILBAUD, L. M. LUO, and J. M. SCARABIN, 1985. 3-D representation of anatomic structures from CT examinations. *Proc. S.P.I.E.* 602:307–314.

[85] TIEDE, U., M. RIEMER, M. BOMANS, and K. H. HÖHNE, 1988. Display techniques for 3D tomographic volume data. *Proc. NCGA '88* 3:188–197.

[86] ZUCKER, S. W., and R. A. HUMMEL, 1981. A three-dimensional edge detector. *IEEE Trans. Patt. Anal. Mach. Intell.* PAMI-3(3):324–331.

[87] EHRICKE, H.-H., and G. LAUB, 1990. Combined 3D display of cerebral vasculature and neuroanatomic structures in MRI. In *3D-Imaging in Medicine: Algorithms, Systems, Applications*, K. H. Höhne et al., eds. Berlin: Springer-Verlag, pp. 229–239.

[88] SABELLA, P., 1988. A rendering algorithm for 3D scalar fields. *Comput. Graphics* 22(4):51–58.

[89] UPSON, C., and M. KEELER, 1988. V-BUFFER: Visible volume rendering. *Comput. Graphics* 22(4):59–64.

[90] MEINZER, H.-P., K. MEETZ, D. SCHEPPELMANN, U. ENGELMANN, and H. J. BAUR, 1991. The Heidelberg ray tracing model. *IEEE Comput. Graphics Appl.* 11(6):34–43.

[91] ROBB, R. A., and C. BARILLOT, 1989. Interactive display and analysis of 3-D medical images. *IEEE Trans. Med. Imag.* MI-8(3):217–226.

[92] BLINN, J. F., 1982. Light reflection functions for simulation of clouds and dusty surfaces. *Comput. Graphics* 16(3):21–29.

[93] KAJIYA, J. T., and B. P. VON HERZEN, 1984. Ray tracing volume densities. *Comput. Graphics* 18(3):165–173.

[94] PELIZZARI, C. A., G. T. Y. CHEN, D. R. SPELBRING, R. R. WEICHSELBAUM, and C. CHEN, 1989. Accurate three-dimensional registration of CT, PET, and/or MR images of the brain. *J. Comput. Assist. Tomogr.* 13(1):20–26.

[95] SCHIERS, C., U. TIEDE, and K. H. HÖHNE, 1989. Interactive 3D registration of image volumes from different sources. In *Computer Assisted Radiology (CAR '89)*, H. U. Lemke et al., eds. Berlin: Springer-Verlag, pp. 666–670.

[96] ARRIDGE, S. R., 1990. Manipulation of Volume Data for Surgical Simulation. In *3D-Imaging in Medicine: Algorithms, Systems, Applications*, K. H. Höhne et al., eds. Berlin: Springer-Verlag, pp. 289–300.

[97] UDUPA, J. K., and D. ODHNER, 1991. Fast visualization, manipulation and analysis of binary volumetric objects. *IEEE Comput. Graphics Appl.* 11(6):53–62.

[98] YASUDA, T., Y. HASHIMOTO, S. YOKOI, and J.-I. TORIWAKI, 1990. Computer system for craniofacial surgical planning based on CT images. *IEEE Trans. Med. Imag.* MI-9(3):270–280.

[99] PFLESSER, B., U. TIEDE, and K. H. HÖHNE, 1991. Volume based object manipulation for simulation of hip joint motion. In *Computer Assisted Radiology* (CAR '91), H. U. Lemke et al., eds. Berlin: Springer-Verlag, pp. 329–335.

[100] UDUPA, J. K., H. M. HUNG, K. S. CHUANG, 1991. Surface and volume rendering in 3D imaging: A comparison. *J. Dig. Imag.* 4:159–168.

[101] MAGNUSSON, M., R. LENZ, and P. E. DANIELSSON, 1991. Evaluation of methods for shaded surface display of CT volumes. *Comput. Med. Imag. Graph.* 15(4):247–256.

[102] POMMERT, A., U. TIEDE, G. WIEBECKE, and K. H. HÖHNE, 1989. Image quality in voxel-based surface shading. In *Computer Assisted Radiology (CAR' 89)*, H. U. Lemke et al., eds. Berlin: Springer-Verlag, pp. 737–741.

[103] DREBIN, R. A., D. MAGID, D. D. ROBERTSON, and E. K. FISHMAN, 1989. Fidelity of three-dimensional CT imaging for detecting fracture gaps. *J. Comput. Assist. Tomogr.* 13(3):487–489.

[104] HEMMY, D. C., and P. L. TESSIER, 1985. CT of dry skulls with craniofacial deformities: Accuracy of three-dimensional reconstruction. *Radiology* 157(1):113–116.

[105] NEY, D., E. K. FISHMAN, D. MAGID, D. D. ROBINSON, and A. KAWASHIMA, 1991. Three-dimensional volumetric display of CT data: Effect of scan parameters upon image quality. *J. Comput. Assis. Tomogr.* 15(5):875–885.

[106] POMMERT, A., W.-J. HÖLTJE, N. HOLZKNECHT, U. TIEDE, and K. H. HÖHNE, 1991. Accuracy of images and measurements in 3D bone imaging. In *Computer Assisted Radiology (CAR '91)*, H. U. Lemke et al., eds. Berlin: Springer-Verlag, pp. 209–215.

[107] RUSINEK, H., M. E. NOZ, G. Q. MAGUIRE, A. KALVIN, B. HADDAD, D. DEAN, and C. CUTTING, 1991. Quantitative and qualitative comparison of volumetric and surface rendering techniques. *IEEE Trans. Nucl. Sci.* 38(2):659–662.

[108] VANNIER, M. W., C. F. HILDEBOLT, J. L. MARSH, T. K. PILGRAM, W. H. MCALISTER, G. D. SHACKELFORD, C. J. OFFUTT, and R. H. KNAPP, 1989. Craniosynostosis: Diagnostic value of three-dimensional CT reconstruction. *Radiology* 173:669–673.

[109] KAUFMAN, A., and R. BAKALASH, 1988. Memory and processing architecture for 3D voxel-based imagery. *IEEE Comput. Graphics Appl.* 8(11):10–23.

[110] FUCHS, H., 1990. Systems for display of three-dimensional medical image data. In *3D-Imaging in Medicine: Algorithms, Systems, Applications*, K. H. Höhne et al., eds. Berlin: Springer-Verlag, pp. 315–331.

[111] HÖHNE, K. H., M. BOMANS, B. PFLESSER, A. POMMERT, M. RIEMER, T. SCHIEMANN, and U. TIEDE, 1992. Anatomic realism comes to diagnostic imaging. *Diagn. Imag.* 1:115–121.

[112] MARCHAC, D., ed., 1987. *Craniofacial surgery: Proceedings of the First International Congress of the International Society of Cranio-Maxillo-Facial Surgery*. Berlin: Springer-Verlag.

[113] VANNIER, M. W., 1987. Despite its limitations, 3-D imaging here to stay. *Diagn. Imag.* 9(11):206–210.

[114] ZONNEVELD, F. W., S. LOBREGT, J. C. H. VAN DER MEULEN, J. M. VAANDRAGER, 1989. Three-dimensional imaging in craniofacial surgery. *World J. Surg.* 13:328–342.

[115] FISHMAN, E. K., D. R. NEY, and D. MAGID, 1990. Three-dimensional imaging: Clinical applications in orthopedics. In *3D-Imaging in Medicine: Algorithms, Systems, Applications*, K. H. Höhne et al., eds. Berlin: Springer-Verlag, pp. 425–440.

[116] NEY, D., E. K. FISHMAN, D. MAGID, and R. A. DREBIN, 1990. Volumetric rendering of computed tomography data: Principles and techniques. *IEEE Comput. Graphics Appl.* pp. 24–32.

[117] CLINE, H. E., W. E. LORENSEN, S. P. SOUZA, F. A. JOLESZ, R. KIKINIS, G. GERIG, and T. E. KENNEDY, 1991. 3D Surface rendered MR images of the brain and its vasculature. *J. Comput. Assist. Tomogr.* 15(2):344–351.

[118] ADAMS, L., W. KRYBUS, D. MEYER-EBRECHT, R. RUEGER, J. M. GILSBACH, R. MÖSGES, and G. SCHLÖNDORFF, 1990. Computer-assisted surgery. *IEEE Comput. Graphics Appl.* 10(3):43–51.

[119] SCHLEGEL, W., 1990. Computer assisted radiation therapy planning. In *3D-Imaging in Medicine: Algorithms, Systems, Applications,* K. H. Höhne et al., eds. Berlin: Springer-Verlag, pp. 339–410.

[120] SCHMIDT, R., T. SCHIEMANN, K. H. HÖHNE, and K.-H. HÜBENER, 1992. Three-dimensional treatment planning for fast neutrons. In *Advanced Radiation Therapy: Tumor Response Monitoring and Treatment Planning,* A. Breit, ed. Berlin: Springer-Verlag, pp. 643–648.

[121] MANO, I., Y. SUTO, M. SUZUKI, and M. IIO, 1990. Computerized three-dimensional normal atlas. *Radiat. Med.* 8(2):50–54.

[122] TOGA, A. W., ed., 1990. *Three-Dimensional Neuroimaging.* New York: Raven.

[123] HÖHNE, K. H., M. BOMANS, M. RIEMER, R. SCHUBERT, U. TIEDE, and W. LIERSE, 1992. A 3D anatomical atlas based on a volume model. *IEEE Comput. Graphics Appl.* 12(4):72–78.

[124] TIEDE, U., M. BOMANS, K. H. HÖHNE, A. POMMERT, M. RIEMER, T. SCHIEMANN, R. SCHUBERT, and W. LIERSE, 1993. A computerized three-dimensional atlas of the human skull and brain. *Am. J. Neuroradiol.*

[125] BAJURA, M., H. FUCHS, R. OHBUCHI, 1992. Merging virtual objects with the real world: Seeing ultrasound imagery within the patient. *Comput. Graphics* 26(2):203–210.

10 The ANALYZE Software System for Visualization and Analysis in Surgery Simulation

RICHARD A. ROBB AND DENNIS P. HANSON

HUMAN VISION provides an extraordinarily powerful and effective means for acquiring information. Much of what we know about ourselves and our environment has been derived from images—images produced by various instruments, ranging from microscopes to telescopes, which extend the range of human vision into realms beyond that which is naturally accessible. The traditional disciplines of biological and medical science are grounded significantly in the observation (i.e., images) of living structures and in the measurement of various properties of these structures (e.g., their functions). Ever since the invention of the microscope and the discovery of x-rays, physicians, surgeons, and life scientists have been using images to diagnose and treat disease and to understand better basic physiology and biology. The imaging modalities used in biology and medicine are based on a variety of energy sources, including light, electrons, lasers, x-rays, radionuclides, ultrasound, and nuclear magnetic resonance. The objects imaged span orders of magnitude in scale, ranging from organelles and cells to organ systems and the full body.

The process of forming an image involves the *mapping* of an object, or some property of an object, into or onto what is called *image space*. This space is used to visualize the object and its properties and may be used to characterize quantitatively its structure or function. *Imaging science* may be defined as the study of these mappings and the development of ways to understand them better, to improve them, and to use them productively. The challenge of imaging science in biomedical research is to provide advanced capabilities for acquisition, processing, visualization, and quantitative analysis of biomedical images in order to increase substantially the faithful extraction of useful information that they contain. The challenge of imaging science

in clinical applications is to provide realistic and faithful displays, interactive manipulation and simulation, and accurate, reproducible diagnostic and therapeutic measurements. However, the full scientific, educational, or clinical value of these images, although profoundly significant, remains largely unexploited. This is due primarily to the lack of objective, quantitative methods to analyze fully the intrinsic information contained in the images. The need for resolution of this problem will become increasingly important and pressing as advances in imaging and computer technology enable more complex objects and processes to be imaged and simulated. The ANALYZE[1] software system has been developed to meet this need effectively.

Background

The Biomedical Imaging Resource at the Mayo Clinic has been involved since the early 1970s in the design and implementation of computer-based techniques for the display and analysis of multidimensional biomedical images. The Resource is a unique and technologically advanced facility for support of multimodal, multidimensional biomedical imaging investigations. It is associated with a comprehensive array of biomedical laboratories and patient clinical facilities within the Mayo Clinic and maintains a variety of extramural research collaborations nationally and internationally. The Resource has a multidisciplinary professional and skilled technical staff with an established record in pioneering imaging research. The staff is committed to development, evaluation, and dissemination of new and improved technology, techniques, and systems for scientific visualization and multidimensional biomedical image display and analysis.

The algorithms and programs developed through this Resource have been integrated into a comprehensive software system called ANALYZE, useful in a variety of multimodal, multidimensional biomedical imaging and scientific visualization applications. The ANALYZE system features integrated, complementary tools for fully interactive display, manipulation, and measurement of multidimensional image data. It has been applied to data from many different imaging modalities, including CT, MRI, PET, SPECT, ultrasonography, and digital microscopy. The software runs efficiently within X-windows on standard UNIX workstations without the need for special-purpose hardware, including systems from Sun Microsystems, Silicon Graphics, International Business Machines, Hewlett Packard, Digital Equipment Corporation, and Apple Computer Corporation.

The ANALYZE software system is written entirely in the C language and utilizes several features of the UNIX operating system to facilitate its modular architecture. The system comprises more than 60 individual programs, each representing a particular imaging function, all of which are built from a base of 12 libraries of functions to provide a common level of functionality to all programs. In total, the ANALYZE source code is approximately 500,000 lines of code for all programs and libraries.

Five complementary attributes of ANALYZE make it a uniquely powerful visualization workshop. First, it is *comprehensive* and generic, containing a large number of intelligently and synergistically *integrated tools* for display, manipulation, and measurement of multimodal images. Second, it has several *original algorithms* that deal directly and accurately with multidimensional image data. Third, it is highly *operator-interactive*; most operations are performed in fractions of a second while preserving accuracy and image quality. Fourth, it is *intuitive and easy to use*; surgeons, physicians and basic scientists can use it productively with little knowledge of computers. Finally, it is *extensible and transportable*; its modular design facilitates expedient enhancements, additions and workstation implementations.

Features of the ANALYZE software system

Image data management

The ANALYZE system contains many image data management tools, including:

- Support for image information recorded in several commercial scanner formats
- Management tools for standard file operations such as Delete, Copy, Rename, and Archive to standard Unix tar files on selected media
- File display from disk for preview prior to loading data into workstation memory
- Image compression and decompression for reduction of storage requirements and high bandwidth data transfer
- Image conversion to and from several common image file formats (e.g., TIFF, Sun Rasterfile, SGI RGB, PPM)

The *Load Images* program enables the selection of an image file, specification of processing options, and display of the processed images. Processing options include the extraction of subregions, scaling the data to a specific dynamic range, and trilinearly interpolating the image volume to new voxel dimensions, usually to create isotropic voxels. When the selected volume is loaded into memory, it becomes available to all ANALYZE programs.

The *Save Images* program copies the images from the shared image memory to a named image file. The images can be subregioned, scaled, or orthogonally reformatted as they are transferred from memory to disk.

The *Film File Manager* program provides data management facilities, including backup and restoring files to and from UNIX tar format tapes, deleting files from disk, compressing and decompressing files using several algorithms, changing the current directory, creating new directories, removing directories, and reporting disk usage information.

The *Header Edit* program can be used as an editing tool to change values in an ANALYZE image header file or to create a new ANALYZE image header file, which is useful when importing image data from other sources for use in ANALYZE.

The *Tape Read* program reads images from 1/2-inch magnetic tape onto the me system. Formats from several imaging vendors currently are supported, with format determination done automatically. Tape drives configured within a network of systems can be accessed across the network directly from ANALYZE.

The *Convert Images* program provides file conversion utilities for several common file formats, including 24-bit image files. These formats include multiple scanner disk file formats (e.g., GE9800CT, GE Signa MRI) and common single-image file formats (e.g., TIFF, Sun Raster, SGI RGB, PPM). Images can be rescaled during the conversion process.

IMAGE GENERATION AND DISPLAY

2D DISPLAY FUNCTIONS   The tools for interactive 2D image display in the ANALYZE system include the following:

• Interactive display of multiple images with variable size control
  • Interactive intensity windowing
• Rapid generation of orthogonal images from 3D image volumes (i.e., multiplanar reformatting)
• 3D volume image display as a cube, with control of size, intensity range, angle of view, and interactive dissections along orthogonal planes
• Generation and display of arbitrary oblique planar images through 3D volume images with interactive control of the orientation of the plane
• Generation of parallel oblique images for image volume reformatting along an arbitrary axis
• Interactive generation of "curved" images or radial image sections through regions traced on orthogonal images
• Rapid display of images in cine movie loops using multiple simultaneous panels with interactive control of speed and stop/start points

The *Multiplanar Sections* program allows rapid computation and display of multiplanar orthogonally reformatted images, including transverse, coronal, and sagittal images (figure 10.1). Basic processing facilities are provided to enable viewing the volume data in a variety of ways, including arbitrary sizing, flexible formatting, and intensity windowing, thresholding, smoothing, inverting, contouring, and rotating.

The *Oblique Sections* program extracts arbitrarily oriented image planes from the volume image. Planes can be interactively generated by flying—that is, moving the oblique plane relative to its current position with well-defined maneuvers (pitch, roll, yaw, elevate, slip, slide). Oblique planes may also be absolutely specified in terms of a plane perpendicular to a specified line segment, a plane passing through three specified points, or a center point and two perpendicular vectors. Sequences of oblique images can be written to a new image file to reformat an entire image volume prior to subsequent analysis.

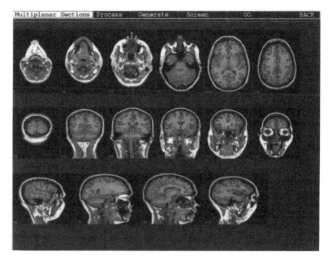

FIGURE 10.1   Multiplanar reformatting of a 3D MRI volume image of the head can be accomplished with the *Multiplanar Sections* program. Multiple images in the original transaxial plane of acquisition (top row) and the orthogonally reformatted coronal plane (middle row) and sagittal plane (bottom row) can be interactively computed and displayed. Variable format control can be applied to the images as they are displayed, including size, position, and windowing.

The *Curved Sections* program generates and displays curved planar images by interactively tracing on an orthogonal reference image while each point along the trace generates a line perpendicular to the image through the volume. Each of these lines becomes a horizontal line in the curvilinear image (figure 10.2). Straight lines can also be used to generate radial sections from a specific anchor point.

The *Cube Sections* program enables interactive generation and display of orthogonal sections in a 3D cubic viewing environment. The orthogonal sections are displayed as the three visible faces of a cube, as depicted in color plate 9. Like a microtome, planes can be interactively sliced away in the three orthogonal orientations to reveal interior sections of the cube. Buttons and slide bars are used to control the cube orientation and orthogonal sectioning.

The *Contours* program displays contours of objects that have been previously extracted by other ANALYZE programs, usually in preparation for surface rendering. A contour is defined as the coordinates of the edges of a surface that lie on any one orthogonal slice. These contours can be stored in an ASCII file.

The *Intensity Grid* program generates wire-mesh displays of images, where the wire mesh is a plot of the intensities in the image. Wire-mesh displays can also be

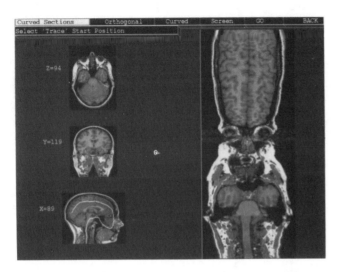

FIGURE 10.2 The *Curved Sections* program interactively generates curved planar images through 3D volume images. A trace along an arbitrary path on any orthogonal image (left column, lower sagittal image) interactively generates and displays the curved planar image sampled through the 3D volume image along that trace (right).

created where the brightness of a pixel is a function of the depth at which the first occurrence of a specified intensity occurs.

The *Movie* program rapidly displays images in a fixed frame to create an animation effect. This program is used most commonly to show sequences of rendered images. Showing rotation sequences of these images is an effective way to view 3D structures. Time sequences may also be displayed to view changes in structure or function. Multiple movie loops can be displayed in a multipanel display.

3D DISPLAY FUNCTIONS   The ANALYZE system contains powerful tools for interactive computation and display of 3D images. Volume rendering using ray casting to display 3D images from volumetric image data contains fully interactive options for the following:

- Depth and gradient shaded surfaces
- Voxel and object compositing
- Transparency for overlying surface structures
- Variable illumination and angle of view
- Variable render masks and dynamic preview modes
- Radial cylindric and stereo-pair rendering
- Numeric projection images (summation, brightest voxel, and surface)
- Multiplanar dissection and subregioning

- Generation of orthogonal and oblique sections depicting intersection with displayed surfaces
- Manual and automatic editing of objects
- Combined display of multiple segmented objects using different rendering parameters and colors
- Dynamic viewpoint manipulations
- Interactive spatial manipulations on independently rendered objects
- Mirror images
- Linear and curvilinear surface measurements
- Direct surface area and volumetric measurements

One of the most powerful and versatile modules within the ANALYZE system is the *Volume Render* program. This program contains several algorithms that all are based on a ray-casting model. To render an image, the output pixel values are assigned appropriate intensities based on the algorithm being used to sample the voxels along the ray path, in conjunction with a set of ray-casting control parameters. There are several algorithms implemented in two classes of rendering algorithms: reflection (surface) algorithms and transmission (projection) algorithms. The reflection algorithms model the image voxels as light reflectors and require the detection of surfaces within the volume. The basic reflection algorithms consider the first voxel along the ray path within the constraints of the rendering parameters (threshold, cutting depth, etc.) as the surface voxel to be rendered and differ in how the detected surface voxels are rendered into the output image. Advanced reflection algorithms map the grayscale threshold range to a continuum of opacity values between fully transparent and fully opaque, compositing a surface shading value by accepting weighted contributions from all voxels having nonzero opacity. Transmission algorithms model the image voxels as light emitters and do not involve explicit surface detection. A rendered image pixel's value is computed as a function of the ray passing through a set of voxels. Each of these algorithms has an associated set of control parameters that alter the ray conditions and the rendered output pixel values. This provides a rich set of rendering functionality through which various structures from multiple modalities can be interactively visualized. Examples of these algorithms are shown in figure 10.3.

In visualization applications, it is desirable to visualize individual structures in the volume image in a way that separates each structure. A method has been

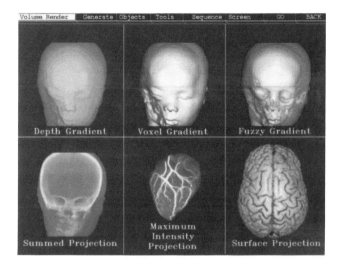

Depth Gradient   Voxel Gradient   Fuzzy Gradient

Summed Projection   Maximum Intensity Projection   Surface Projection

FIGURE 10.3 Rendering algorithms in the *Volume Render* program are divided into two classes: reflection (upper row) and transmission (lower row). The reflection algorithms render surfaces using several shading models, including depth gradient shading (upper left), voxel gradient shading (upper middle), and fuzzy gradient shading (upper right). The transmission algorithms create projections, including summed voxel projection (lower left), maximum intensity projection (lower middle), and integrated surface projection (lower right).

developed to allow the interactive specification and manipulation of individual structures in rendered volume images. This method provides functions to classify voxels specifically in the original volume image into user-defined objects, to assign names and attributes to the objects, and independently to manipulate the objects in the rendered image. The basis for this functionality is a secondary volume data set of the same size and dimension as the original volume image, called an *object map*. The object map forms a one-to-one map of the voxels in the original volume image to objects defined by the object map. The set of voxels in the object map that have a specific value constitute the complete object without regard to spatial connectivity of the voxels (e.g., object maps can contain multiple structures within a single object, or objects can simply be a set of spatially unrelated voxels that have other criteria motivating their definition as an object). In this way, the object map provides direct classification of voxels in the volume image into distinct structures. The construction of an object map requires either the prerendering segmentation of structures from the volume image or the interactive editing and specification of structures directly from the rendered image.

Once structures have been defined in an object map, attributes can be assigned to each individual structure, including visibility, color, spatial position, and orientation, as shown in color plate 10. Visibility controls the inclusion or exclusion of the object voxels in the ray-casting process. The color attribute assigns a specific color to the object and the number of color shades used to represent the surface of the object, with the number of shades available for all objects equitably divided across all objects to produce the most effective rendered display. An opacity attribute can be assigned to each object to effect multicolored transparent displays of the multiple objects. Spatial position attributes can be assigned to each independent object, allowing for independent spatial manipulation of structures in the volume image. Translation provides for the positioning of an object at a specific 3D location within the volume-rendering space. The rotation attribute will allow the rotation of objects around a specified center of rotation. Individual objects can be mirrored across any of the orthogonal volume image axes. Increments can be established for each of the translation and rotation values used, in conjunction with sequence generation to produce rendered sequences of spatial manipulations.

The rendering process provides a rendered image that can be utilized as the visualization reference for further analysis. The ANALYZE volume-rendering program provides tools that interact directly with the rendered image in three categories: display tools, manipulation tools, and measurement tools. These tools provide powerful complementary support for surgery simulation and planning.

The display tools use the rendered image as a reference for resectioning the original volume image. Orthogonal sections in the transverse, coronal, and sagittal planes can be interactively computed and displayed using a cursor to indicate the point of intersection for the orthogonal planes on the rendered surface (see plate 10). The rendered image can further be used as the visualization reference for the orientation of an arbitrarily oriented oblique plane sectioning through the volume image. Interactive maneuvers for plane orientation can be selected as the display of the plane updates its intersection with the rendered image. The rendered surface and the image on the oblique plane can be made transparent, so as to visualize the internal structures sectioned with the oblique plane as intersecting with the surface (see plate 10). The display of the rendered surface can be used to define subregions to be selectively rendered with different parameters. After definition of a traced region on the surface, rendering parameters can be altered to render only the portion of the volume image inside the trace, creating combined renderings of multiple objects or multiple algorithms (i.e., a transmission rendering inside a surface rendering).

The manipulation tools apply transformations to the structures in the rendered image. Region growing can be invoked by selecting a seed point on a structure in the rendered image, with the voxels subsequently deleted from the volume image or saved to an object map. Structures can be manually traced, and all voxels found in the traced region throughout the 3D volume image can be found and deleted from the original volume image. Contours can be extracted from the currently rendered surface and stored in a contour file for further analysis, bridging the gap between the volumetric description of the structure and a geometric description.

Several measurement tools are available for direct application to the rendered image. Points can be selected from the rendered surface, with the 3D coordinates and voxel values stored to a file. Linear distances can be measured between two points selected on the rendered surface, including both the 3D linear distance between the points and the curvilinear distance along the surface between the two points (see plate 10). The planar surface area cut through the rendered image and the surface area on the rendered surface can be tracked and measured by drawing a trace directly on the rendered image. Volumes can be measured by selecting a seed point on a particular structure in the rendered image and counting all connected voxels to the seed point using 3D region growing.

All spatial manipulations and attribute control can be performed interactively using the workstation's mouse and a multipanel, multiviewpoint display of the rendered structures, as shown in plate 10. Interactive manipulations are important to various biomedical imaging applications, including surgery simulation and planning.

IMAGE PROCESSING, SEGMENTATION, AND FUSION

IMAGE PROCESSING Images in the ANALYZE system may be modified through the following kinds of transformations:

- Linear combinations of images computed from user-specified formulas
- 3D matrix operations for full geometric volume transformations
- Linear and adaptive histogram operations
- Spatial and frequency domain image processing including filtering
- Interactive, graphic-based design of custom filters or modifications of classic filters
- 2D and 3D fast Fourier transform (FFT) and deconvolution routines
- Image transformation and compression using wavelets

The *Image Algebra* program facilitates algebraic manipulation of images through user-defined formulas, which may be specified as a combination of volume image identifiers and various mathematic, logical, Boolean, and transcendental operators. Geometric and densitometric processing can also be applied, including functions for interpolation, rotation, translation, subregioning, windowing, and scaling. The *Matrix Ops* program performs arbitrary geometric transformations on a volume image using a cumulative transformation matrix sequentially built by the user through specification of the transforms (rotation, translation, scale) and application of matrix math.

The *Histogram Operations* program performs three basic point operations that alter the shape of the gray-level histogram of an image: histogram preservation, flattening, and matching. In general, the program will map gray levels from the input range into any output range having the same or fewer levels. Histogram preservation will preserve the distribution of values when images are converted to a different dynamic range. Histogram flattening will attempt to give equal frequency representation to all values within the dynamic range. Histogram matching will match the histogram of one image set to that of another. The *Adaptive Histo* program performs *adaptive histogram equalization*, a process of adjusting the gray-scale values of an image based on the histogram or count of pixel values in a localized region of the image. This process enhances the viewable contrast in all areas of the image without regard to maintaining any strict mathematic relationship in any gray-scale value by creating a histogram for each set of predefined regions within the image and adjusting the gray scale within each region to increase the contrast locally. This method is particularly effective when used to view images that have subtle detail in both very bright and very dim regions of the image.

The *Spatial Filter* program enables the application of 2D and 3D filters as convolutions in the spatial domain to any region of a volume image, with independent kernel sizes in each dimension. Filter functions include low pass, unsharp mask, Sobel, median, VSFmean, gradient, and sigma. The *Filter Designer* program is a general-purpose image-processing tool that performs convolution and deconvolution in the frequency domain using the FFT. A unique feature of this program is an interactive filter designer that operates as an interactive graphic equalizer for images, providing up to a 40-decibel boost or suppression at each individual digital frequency in the image, demonstrated in color plate 11. *3D FFT/Deconv* performs 2D and 3D forward and inverse FFTs, convolutions, and deconvolutions on image data. Advanced deconvolution techniques (nearest-neighbor slice-by-slice deconvolution and constrained iterative deconvolution) commonly used in optical and confocal microscopy are implemented in this program.

The *Wavelet* program provides a variety of 1D, 2D, and 3D forward and inverse wavelet transforms that can be used on image data, usually for image compression. Like the frequency spectrum obtained by a Fourier transform, a wavelet transform represents the information in an image in a different way—in this case, as responses to a hierarchic set of wavelet functions, which are all translations and scalings of each other. Real-world images expressed on a wavelet basis usually carry most of their information in a relatively small number of wavelet coefficients, and a large number of coefficients can be truncated to zero (effectively thrown away) with relatively little effect on the appearance of the image. Because only the important coefficients need to be stored, a very natural form of image compression is possible. The *Wavelet* program is designed for interactive experimentation with different degrees of compression on an image, including the specification of particular regions of the image that are to be preserved with maximum fidelity in the compression process.

SEGMENTATION Segmentation of features from images in the ANALYZE system may be accomplished using the following kinds of functions:

- Interactive manual object segmentation using thresholding, tracing, and erasing
- Semiautomated, interactive boundary detection for object segmentation
- 2D and 3D region growing for object segmentation
- 2D and 3D math morphology for interactive segmentation
- Automatic edge contour extraction
- Multispectral image classification tools

The *Image Edit* program enables the editing of images to isolate 3D structures using efficient manual segmentation tools and semiautomated object definition and feature extraction. Manual segmentation is accomplished by manually editing structures from the data using erasing and tracing interactions. The semiautomated mode uses a region-growing method in which the user selects a seed point and then interactively manipulates the threshold range about the selected seed pixel. As the region growing takes place, pixels that fall outside the threshold range (above and below) are selected for boundary pixels, with a neighbor-connectivity constraint imposed to ensure a continuous boundary, demonstrated in color plate 12.

The *2D Morphology* program applies 2D mathematic morphologic transformations (e.g., Erode, Dilate, Open, Close) to the images in the volume image data set. Each of these transformations can be performed with one of the structuring elements provided (e.g., rectangle, circle, diamond), or user-defined structuring elements can be imported. The transformations can be chained together by creating a sequence of steps. The *3D Morphology* program applies 3D mathematic morphologic transformations and object topology operations. The transformations include Threshold, Erode, Dilate, Max, Min, Open, and Close, all of which use various 3D structuring elements. Other transformations include Conditional Dilate, Nonmax Suppression, Ultimate Erosion, Complement, Umbra, 3D Connect, 2D Connect, Deletes Holes, Thinning, and Homotopic Thickening. These morphologic tools provide the basis for powerful automated 3D segmentation utilities, as demonstrated in the 3D MRI structures shown in color plate 13.

The *Connect* program segments a binary volume image by performing 3D region growing from a user-specified seed pixel, finding the set of all pixels adjoining the seed pixel that are set until the entire 3D region is found. The *Extract Contours* program extracts surface contours from a binary volume. The surface description formed by this process consists of the x, y, z coordinates of the surface points and an estimate of the surface normals at each face. This usually is done in preparation for surface rendering or to export the contours to other software packages.

The *Multi-Spectral* classification program provides manual tools for exploring and classifying two-spectrum images and automated measurement space classification algorithms that will operate on images of any number of spectra. Multispectral images consist of voxels that are actually vectors of values, usually reflecting measurements of different physical quantities from multiple imaging modalities, such as correlated MRI/CT or CT/PET/MRI. Multispectral images may also be made up of derived measures from a single original volume image, like gradients or texture features for each voxel. The promise of multispectral analysis is that the dimensionally expanded measurement space will allow differentiations to be made that are impossible in any of the component images. The manual tools in the *Multi-Spectral* program include display of the single-channel component images, along with a vector-histogram of the two-channel image, a linked cursor which shows the same location in both channel images, the ability to sample the channel images and observe the location of the sampled pixels in the measurement plane, and the ability to define regions of the measurement plane and observe the regions of the channel images that meet that measurement criterion, depicted in color plate 14. The automated algorithms include five common classification techniques—Gaussian clustering, neural network, nearest neighbor, k-nearest neighbor, and Parzen windows—which differ in complexity and basic approach. All the automated algorithms assume that certain voxels have been defined by the user as belonging to certain classes, and these voxels are used as samples of these classes. Unassigned voxels then are classified (or are left unclassified) based on the estimated likelihood of their belonging to each of the defined classes.

FUSION   Image fusion means automated spatial registration and integrated display of multimodal image data sets. This is accomplished in ANALYZE using a surface-matching approach. The *Surface Matching* program determines 3D geometric transformation parameters (translation, rotation, scale) which can be used spatially to register two volume images. As input to the program, a surface is extracted from both a "base object" and a "match object," which are preprocessed from the "base volume" and "match volume," respectively. The matching process will search through the parameter space to determine the parameter set that minimizes the mean square distance between surfaces (using Chamfer distance). The initial best-guess transformation and search range parameters are supplied by the user. The search starts from grid points in parameter space uniformly distributed within the search range, with a specified rotational search interval and a calculated translational search interval. A pyramid multiresolutional approach is used in the searching process. Once the transformation that gives the smallest mean square distance is found, the transformation is stored in an ANALYZE matrix file and can be applied to one of the input volume images. The transformed volume, spatially correlated to the other volume, can be displayed in conjunction with the other volume image using color overlays and linked cursors to visualize the match, as in color plate 15. Fusion can be performed on multimodal volume images (plate 16) or on volumes within a single modality that reflect different scan times or scanning parameters (plate 17).

IMAGE MENSURATION AND QUANTITATIVE ANALYSIS

The ANALYZE system contains several tools for mensuration and quantitative analysis of image features. These tools include the following:

• Interactive plotting of line and trace profiles with linear measurement capabilities, including 3D tracing
• Interactive definition of multiple regions of interest using analytic shapes, arbitrary traces, or semi-automated boundary definition
• Selection and automatic sampling of regions of interest with image parameter output to data files
• Interactive regional surface area and volume calculation
• Regional shape and texture analysis, in two and three dimensions
• Output data file format selection for several numeric analysis packages
• Data plotting and statistical analysis

The *Line Profile* program interactively samples and plots image intensities from single-dimension profiles, straight lines, and curvilinear traces. The *Tree Trace* program provides a method of unambiguously tracing branching 3D tree structures, such as dye-filled blood vessels. Such traces can be used to compute segment lengths, branching angles, and oblique images. Four maximum-intensity projection images are displayed at different angles of view. Each voxel in the projection image is identified with a unique 3D coordinate in the original volume. The cursor can be placed in any of the projections, and its position is indicated in the other three projections corresponding to the same 3D coordinate. Points can be interactively selected and line segments drawn to generate a tree with multiple branching points and segments of varying length that describe the spatial distribution of the structure being traced.

The *Region of Interest* program is used to define interactively and sample regions of interest (ROIs). Multiple regions can be defined using analytic shapes (e.g., rectangles and ellipses), tracing a free-form area on the image, or using semiautomated boundary definition. Image information within these regions can be interactively sampled by user selection or sampled automatically by region name. Information provided by the area sampling includes the maximum and minimum values, mean and standard deviation, the calibrated area, the integrated brightness-area product, and the fractal signature. The fractal dimension is calculated for the specified regions by placing an envelope both above and below the gray-scale surface and then calculating the volume that is contained between them. When these calculations are completed over a desired range of scales, a log-log plot of surface area versus scale is generated and a least-squares estimate of the linear regression line for this plot is calculated. The linear correlation coefficient of this fit is given in the statistics output, and the slope of the fit is reported as the fractal signature for the region. Shape measures for selected regions also are reported, as shown in color plate 18.

The *Volume Estimator* program measures and estimates the volume of an arbitrary 3D object using a probabilistic model. A user-specified number of voxels are randomly marked in the volume image and displayed as color-coded points overlying selected images. A square cursor of varying size can be used with the mouse to select the marked voxels overlying the structure for which the volume is to be calculated. The ratio of selected voxels to the total number of marked voxels is employed to estimate the volume of the object. The *Stereology* program provides similar volume estimation

functions but adds surface areas and line attributes as well.

The *Plot* program plots information sampled from the mensuration programs in ANALYZE. Selected analysis functions can be applied to the data, including regression analysis and mathematic combinations of the information prior to plotting.

OTHER PROGRAMS

Several other programs constitute unique features of the ANALYZE system:

- Configuration of workstation environment
- Configuration for connection to networked peripherals
- Screen editor with interactive options for cut, paste (with proportional scaling), overlays, text, labels, and graphics for full-screen slide composition
- Hard-copy output control for printing text and images, including color
- A facility for automatic recording and playback of sessions

The *Configure* program permits the ANALYZE run time environment and workstation environment to be configured to specific preferences, including menu appearances (font size, type, and color), device types and locations, and printer types. Menu structure and program parameter default values can be changed to suit personal needs and preferences. Network location and names of peripheral devices are configured in this program.

The *Screen Edit* program provides the ability to prepare presentation slides with ANALYZE screens. Flexible typesetting and drawing facilities are provided for adding special text and graphics effects to ANALYZE screens, as demonstrated in color plate 19.

The Macro Record option creates an ANALYZE macro containing a recorded session. The macro capability is based on a very simple design, allowing many types of actions to be recorded, such as tracing or pointing. The Macro Play option is designed to play back a recorded ANALYZE session.

ANCILLARY TOOLS

A rich suite of ancillary tools and useful utilities is available throughout the entire ANALYZE package and can be invoked from any ANALYZE program. Among these ancillaries are the following:

- Magnifying glass for interactive magnification of areas of the screen at selectable sizes
- Extensive interactive color manipulation
- Screen region capture capability for saving to image files
- Screen measurement tools
- File viewer for quick display of any image file from within any module
- Editor for session notes, attachable to image files
- On-line, context sensitive help documentation
- On-screen calculator and clock
- Multiple session feature for multiple image, multiple process analyses

The Magnifying Glass tool can be invoked to magnify regions of the screen interactively, display histograms of the regions, or view the underlying screen pixel values. The region size and magnification factor are controlled with mouse buttons, and the magnified image can be interpolated and inverted without compromising the interactivity (figure 10.4).

The Interactive Color tool enables interactive assignment of colors to the display lookup table, producing different mappings of the colors to the images displayed on the screen. The user can change interactively the number and location of multiple bins to seg-

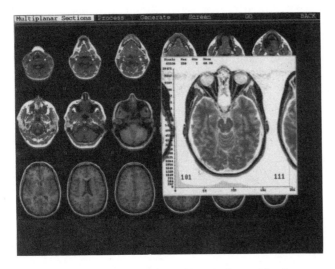

FIGURE 10.4 The *Magnifying Glass* tool provides interactive positioning and magnification of a region of the screen. Region size, magnification factor, and screen position can be interactively specified. The magnified image may be bilinearly interpolated and inverted (as shown). A histogram of the values within the magnified region may be plotted and dynamically updated as the region is moved. Individual voxel values may also be examined.

ment the range of gray scale values in the image and then, within each bin, the color components of the color map can be individually adjusted. Color reference bars can be displayed for reference between colors and specific image values.

The Caliper tool enables geometric measurements to be performed on the screen. Distance measurements in pixels along an interactively specified straight line or curvilinear trace can be made. A shape is presented initially allowing the measurement of multiple linear distances and angles between line segments.

The Image Viewer enables the display of images from ANALYZE image files without disturbing the currently loaded images. Color map differences are maintained between the currently loaded image data and the images displayed in the viewer, making it possible to verify output results of processing and segmenting functions within the currently running program.

The Snapshot tool can be used to capture an ANALYZE screen and store it as an image, raster, or screen file. The screen can be captured interactively or manually.

The Hardcopy tool enables the display and printing of text files, image files, screen files, and any portion of the ANALYZE screen. Several types of printers can be driven by this program, including standard PostScript and color PostScript devices.

The Text Editor tool is a full-screen, mouse-controlled text editor suitable for most simple text-editing tasks. The Calculator tool is an on-screen simulation of a simple hand-held calculator. It can be used to perform quick on-line computations. The UNIX Shell tool starts a UNIX shell to allow direct interaction with the operating system using UNIX commands. This shell is invoked using the "rlogin" command on the local system. A completely new ANALYZE session can be started using the New Session tool. When multiple ANALYZE sessions have been invoked, sessions can be toggled using this selection. The ANALYZE Reference Manual has been placed on-line for reference from any of the ANALYZE programs. The *Help* facility is context-sensitive, providing the manual pages for the currently running program, with options to switch to other parts of the manual.

Surgical simulation and planning applications

The ANALYZE system has been successfully applied to a variety of surgical planning and simulation applications, including certain applications that utilize multiple biomedical imaging modalities. Some of these applications will be described here.

CRANIOFACIAL SURGERY

Craniofacial surgery involves surgery of the facial and cranial skeleton and soft tissues. These operations are performed to correct congenital deformities or for the treatment of deformities caused by trauma, resection of tumors, infections, and other acquired conditions. Surgical treatment of these deformities requires both quantitative and qualitative knowledge of the anatomy of the face and skull. Currently, the most faithful source of this information is x-ray CT scanning for the skeleton and MRI scanning for the soft tissues. Although the data presented by the scanners themselves are useful, the information obtained is significantly increased by analysis of the image data using the measurement and visualization features of the ANALYZE software system.

Assessment of postoperative results in craniofacial surgery often is qualitative, consisting primarily of comparison of preoperative and postoperative photographs. Visualization and quantitative analysis of postoperative CT and MRI scans allows accurate, objective assessment of the results of craniofacial surgery. Effects of such uncontrollable factors as growth in children, resorption of bone grafts, and the tendency of moved segments of bone to return to their original positions can be quantitatively evaluated. Quantitative assessment of the results of craniofacial surgery is required if statistical methods are to be applied to the analysis of results and for quality assurance. Quantitative methods also are used to establish normative values, a necessary step to facilitate analysis of pathologic conditions.

The risk of complications in craniofacial surgery has been shown in several studies to be directly related to the duration of operations. Precise presurgical planning minimizes the duration of the surgical procedure, thus minimizing the risks. With interactive computer planning and simulation of the surgical procedure (figure 10.5 and plate 20), it is possible to prepare an accurate preoperative plan, minimizing the need to spend time designing these complex operative plans while the patient is already anesthetized and the intracranial contents exposed.

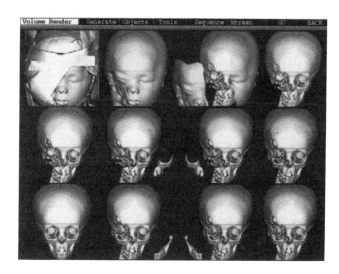

FIGURE 10.5 Craniofacial surgical planning with ANALYZE. Top row shows realistic 3D rendering from CT scan data showing different surfaces (e.g., skin and bone) in head of trauma patient. Center row shows damaged skull (left), design of prosthetic implant by mirror imaging of contralateral normal maxilla (middle two panels), and placement of simulated implant (right). Bottom row shows full-skull mirror image (left), design of prosthetic implant by mirror imaging of contralateral normal mandible (middle two panels), and placement of simulated implant (right).

ORTHOPAEDIC SURGERY

ANALYZE visualization and analysis tools have been successfully used in several orthopaedic surgical applications, as shown in figures 10.6 and 10.7 and plates 21 and 22. Transparency is employed to examine relationships between cartilage and bone (see plate 21). Oblique sectioning is used to capture the extent and intersections of fracture paths (see figure 10.6), and object manipulation is used to simulate possible approaches to corrective surgery (see figure 10.7). Quantitative measurements of bars in the growth plate of long bones is an inherently difficult problem but yields to accurate analysis using ANALYZE rendering and measurement techniques (see plate 22).

NEUROSURGERY

Neurosurgical planning is facilitated by accurate segmentation and visualization of brain tissues, (figure 10.8). Accurate resection of parenchymal brain to control epilepsy (plate 23) and of intracranial tumors (plate 24) is optimally planned using ANALYZE visualization and mensuration tools. Not uncommonly,

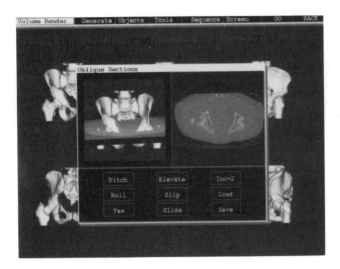

FIGURE 10.6 Using the volume-rendered image as a reference for structure localization, the *Oblique Sections* tool in the *Volume Render* program can be used to generate a section at an arbitrary angle through particular structures of interest. Although the image is here reproduced in black and white the oblique image (right) depicts the original x-ray CT data with the femur colored yellow (same as in rendering), to show its location, and with the fracture shown in the acetabulum.

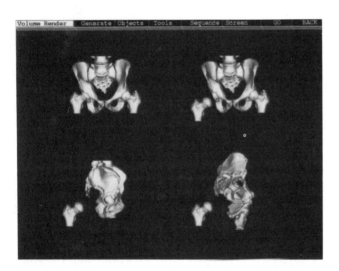

FIGURE 10.7 Volumetric x-ray CT of skeletal structures provides image information for direct visualization of various structures in orthopaedic applications, including visual inspection of trauma damage. The rendered images shown here are from x-ray CT data through the hip of a trauma patient with an intra-acetabular fracture. This fracture cannot be visualized from the initial antero-posterior rendering (upper left) but, by segmenting the head of the femur, defining it as a separate object, and translating it away from the hip (upper right), the hip is allowed to rotate independently (lower left) to permit visualization of the fracture (lower right).

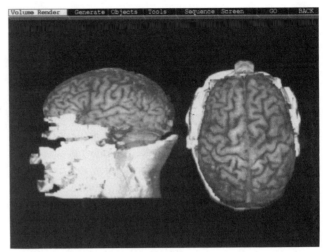

FIGURE 10.8 Automated segmentation and realistic rendering of the brain are important for neurosurgical planning and simulation applications. These renderings were created by first automatically segmenting the cortical surface of the brain using 3D morphologic processing, followed by rendering using a surface projection algorithm that integrates the contributions of several voxels to each surface point for a selected depth into the brain, thus providing a highly detailed rendering of the cortical surface.

neurosurgical resections of brain tumor are augmented with radiotherapeutic planning when it is not possible to remove all of the tumor due to location, size, type, or other factors. In such instances, adjunct planning of 3D radiotherapy treatment can be carried out with ANALYZE as shown in plate 25.

OTHER APPLICATIONS

ANALYZE is also being used as an educational adjunct to surgery (plate 26), providing computer-assisted teaching of anatomy to surgical trainees and residents.

ANALYZE has been used to plan the successful separation of conjoined twins, as illustrated in figure 10.9. Volume rendering and the interactive tools associated with realistic 3D visualization, manipulation, and measurements in ANALYZE were used to plan this operation. Full-body CT scans reveal joined sternum, abdomen, and liver. 3D renderings can be viewed and dissected from any orientation to evaluate anatomic spatial relationships accurately. The Oblique Plane tool was used interactively to determine the optimal approach to surgical bisection. After simulating the bisection, the surgical openings can be accurately mea-

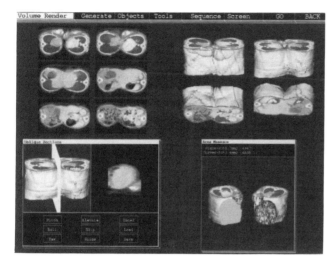

FIGURE 10.9 Surgical separation of conjoined twins using ANALYZE. Upper left panel shows original CT scans through trunk of joined bodies. Upper right panel shows different 3D visualizations rendered from CT scans. Lower left panel shows interactive dissection plane to simulate surgical separation. Lower right panel shows measurement of surface area of body openings following simulated separation, used to estimate the amount of skin required to cover the openings.

sured to estimate the quantity of skin and grafting material required to cover the openings. This operation is a concrete and complete example of the three major components of biomedical visualization needed to support surgical planning—namely, realistic display, interactive manipulations (editing), and quantitative measurement. This successful result is prototypical of the growing evidence that 3D visualization and analysis of medical images have bridged the gap from science to practice, from the computer laboratory to the operating room, heralding a new era in the field of surgery.

ACKNOWLEDGMENTS The authors are grateful to their colleagues in the Mayo Biomedical Imaging Resource without whom this work would not be possible. Special recognition is given to the software development staff that designs, implements, debugs, and maintains the ANALYZE software system: Ron Karwoski, Al Larson, Ellis Workman, and Margret Ryan. Recognition is given also to the systems staff of the Biomedical Imaging Resource who integrate and maintain the computational resources need to support this work: Mahlon Stacy, Mark Korinek, Russ Moritz, and Bruce Cameron. Appreciation is expressed to Jon Camp, imaging scientist in the Biomedical Imaging Resource, for his expertise and advice. Thanks to Gina Croatt for her assistance in the preparation of this manuscript. Finally, the authors would like to acknowledge the contributions of many imaging collaborators at the Mayo Foundation and Clinic and at other national and international medical institutions.

NOTE

1. ANALYZE is a trademark of the Mayo Foundation. It has been filed with the U.S. Patent and Trademark office.

BIBLIOGRAPHY

BAUMANN, O., T. KITAZAWA, and A. P. SOMLYO, in press. Laser confocal scanning microscopy of the surface membrane/T-tubular system and the sarcoplasmic reticulum in insect striated muscle stained with DilC18(3). *J. Structural Biol.* 105:154–161, 1990.

BENTLEY, M. D., and R. A. KARWOSKI, 1988. Estimation of tissue volume from serial tomographic sections using a statistical random marking method. *Invest. Radiol.* 23(10): 742–747.

BITE, U., and I. T. JACKSON, 1985. The use of three-dimensional CT scanning in planning head and neck reconstruction. *Plast. Surg. Forum* 3:461–476.

BOURLAND, J. D., 1990. A finite-size pencil beam model for three-dimensional photon dose calculations. Doctoral dissertation, University of North Carolina at Chapel Hill, Chapel Hill, N.C.

CHEN, G. I. Y., and C. A. PELIZZARI, 1989. Image correlation techniques in radiation therapy treatment planning. *Comput. Med. Imag. Graphics* 12:235–240.

COATRIEUX, J. L., and C. BARILLOT, 1990. A survey of 3D display techniques to render medical data. In *3D Imaging in Medicine* (NATO ASI series F), Vol. 60, K. H. Höhne, H. Fuchs, and S. M. Pizer, eds. Berlin: Springer-Verlag, pp. 175–195.

DREBIN, R., L. CARPENTER, and P. HARRAHAN, 1988. Volume rendering. *SIGGRAH '88* pp. 65–74.

FARRELL, E. J., T. J. WATSON, R. A. ZAPPULLA, and M. SPIGELMAN, 1987. Imaging tools for interpreting two and three dimensional medical data. *Proc. NCGA* 3:60–68.

FUKUTA, K., I. T. JACKSON, C. N. McEWAN, and N. B. MELAND, 1990. Three-dimensional imaging in craniofacial surgery: A review of the role of mirror image production. *Eur. J. Plast. Surg.* 13:209–217.

GREENLEAF, J. F., 1989. Review of multidimensional ultrasonic imaging. International Electronic Imaging Exposition and Conference, Pasadena, Calif., April 10–13, pp. 512–513.

GULLBERG, G. T., G. L. ZENG, P. E. CHRISTIAN, B. M. W. TSUI, and H. T. MORGAN, 1991. Single photon emission computed tomography of the heart using cone beam geometry and noncircular detector rotation. *Inform. Proc. Med. Imag.* 511:123–138.

HARALICK, R. M., S. R. STERNBERG, and X. ZHUANG, 1987. Image analysis using mathematical morphology. *IEEE Trans. Patt. Anal. Mach. Intell.* PAMI-9:532–550.

HARRIS, L. D., 1981. Identification of the optimal orienta-tion of oblique sections through multiple parallel CT images. *J. Comput. Assist. Tomogr.* 5:881–887.

HARRIS, L. D., R. A. ROBB, T. S. YUEN, and E. L. RITMAN, 1978. Non-invasive numerical dissection and display of anatomic structure using computerized x-ray tomography. *Proc. S.P.I.E.* 152:10–18.

HAWKES, D. J., D. L. G. HILL, E. D. LEHMANN, G. P. ROBINSON, M. N. MAISEY, et al., 1990. Preliminary work on the interpretation of SPECT images with the aid of registered MR images and an MR derived 3D neuro-anatomical atlas. In *3D Imaging in Medicine* (NATO ASI series F), Berlin: Springer Verlag, Vol. 60, K. H. Höhne, H. Fuchs, and S. M. Pizer, eds. Pp. 241–251.

HEFFERNAN, P. B., and R. A. ROBB, 1985. A new method for shaded surface display of biological and medical images. *IEEE Trans. Med. Imag.* 4:26–38.

HÖHNE, K. H., and R. BERNSTEIN, 1986. Shading 3-D images from CT using grey-level gradients. *IEEE Trans. Med. Imag.* MI-15:45–47.

HÖHNE, K. H., M. BOMANS, A. POMMERT, M. RIEMER, U. TIEDE, et al., 1990. Rendering tomographic volume data: Adequacy of methods for different modalities and organs. In *3D Imaging in Medicine* (NATO ASI series F), Berlin: Springer Verlag, Vol. 60, K. H. Höhne, H. Fuchs, and S. M. Pizer, eds. Pp. 333–361.

HÖHNE, K. H., M. RIEMER, U. TIEDE, and M. BOMANS, 1987. Volume rendering of 3D tomographic imagery. In *Proceedings of the Tenth IPMI International Conference*, Utrecht, The Netherlands, pp. 403–412.

JACK, C. R., JR., W. R. MARSH, K. A. HIRSCHORN, F. W. SHARBROUGH, G. D. CASCINO, et al., in press. Electro-physiologic mapping onto 3-D surface display images of the brain. *Radiology*.

JACK, C. R., JR., C. K. TWOMEY, A. R. ZINSMEISTER, F. W. SHARBROUGH, R. C. PETERSON, et al., 1989. Anterior tem-poral lobes and hippocampal formations: Normative volu-metric measurements from MR images in young adults. *Radiology* 172:549–554.

KAUFMAN, A., R. YAGEL, and D. COHEN, 1990. Intermixing surface and volume rendering. In *3D Imaging in Medicine* (NATO ASI series F), Vol. 60, K. H. Höhne, H. Fuchs, and S. M. Pizer, eds. Berlin: Springer Verlag, pp. 217–227.

KERMODE, A. G., P. S. TOFTS, A. J. THOMPSON, D. G. MACMANUS, P. RUDGE, et al., 1990. Heterogeneity of blood-brain barrier changes in multiple-sclerosis: An MRI study with gadolinium-DTPA enhancement. *Neurology* 40:229–235.

KÜBLER, Q., and G. GERIG, 1990. Segmentation and analysis of multidimensional data-sets in medicine. In *3D Imaging in Medicine* (NATO ASI series F), Berlin: Springer Verlag, Vol. 60, K. H. Höhne, H. Fuchs, and S. M. Pizer, eds. Pp. 63–81.

LECHLEITER, J., S. E. GIRARD, E. G. PERALTA, and D. E. CLAPHAM, 1991. Spiral calcium wave propagation and annihilation. *Science* 252:123–126.

LEVIN, D., X. HU, K. K. TAN, S. GALHOTRA, C. A. PELIZ-ZARI, et al., 1989. The brain: Integrated three-dimensional display of MR and PET images. *Radiology* 172:783–789.

LEVOY, M., 1988. Display of surfaces from volume data. *Comput. Graphics Appl.* 8(3):29–37.

LUECK, C. J., S. ZEKI, K. J. FRISTAN, M.-P. DEIBER, P. COPE, et al., 1989. The colour centre in the cerebral cortex of man. *Nature* 340(6232):386–389.

MARSH, J. L., M. W. VANNIER, S. J. BRESINA, and K. M. HEMMER, 1986. Applications of computer graphics in craniofacial surgery. *Clin. Plast. Surg.* 13:441.

MOHAN, R., F. BAREST, L. J. BREWSTER, C. S. CHUI, G. J. KUTCHER et al., 1988. A comprehensive three-dimensional radiation treatment planning system. *Int. J. Radiat. Oncol. Biol. Phys.* 15:481–495.

PELEG, S., J. NAOR, R. HARTLEY, and D. AVNIR, 1984. Mul-tiple resolution texture analysis and classification. *IEEE Trans. Patt. Anal. Mach. Intell.* PAMI-6(4):518–532.

PIZER, S. M., T. J. CULLIP, and R. E. FREDERICKSEN, 1990. Toward interactive object definition in 3D scalar images. In *3D Imaging in Medicine* (NATO ASI series F), Berlin: Springer Verlag, Vol. 60, K. H. Höhne, H. Fuchs, and S. M. Pizer, eds. Pp. 83–105.

RHODES, M. L., 1990. Computer-assisted orthopaedic sur-gery. In *Proceedings of Digital Imaging in Orthopaedic Surgery: A Dialogue Between Physician and Engineers*, p. 38.

ROBB, R. A., 1990. A software system for interactive and quantitative analysis of biomedical images. In *3D Imaging in Medicine* (NATO ASI series F), Vol. 60, Berlin: Springer Verlag, K. H. Höhne, H. Fuchs, and S. M. Pizer, eds. Pp. 333–361.

ROBB, R. A., and C. BARILLOT, 1988. Interactive 3-D image display and analysis. *Proc. S.P.I.E.* 939:173–202.

ROBB, R. A., and C. BARILLOT, 1989. Interactive display and analysis of 3-D medical images. *IEEE Trans. Med. Imag.* 8(3):217–226.

ROBB, R. A., and D. P. HANSON, 1990. ANALYZE: A soft-ware system for biomedical image analysis. In *Proceedings of the First Conference on Visualization in Biomedical Computing*, Atlanta, Ga., May 22–25, pp. 507–518.

ROBB, R. A., and R. L. MORIN, 1991. Principles and instru-mentation for dynamic x-ray computed tomography. In *Cardiac Imaging—A Companion to Braunwald's Heart Disease*, M. L. Marcus, D. J. Skorton, H. R. Schelbert, and G. L. Wolf, eds. Philadelphia: Saunders, Chapter 32.

SEHGAL, C. M., D. G. LEWALLEN, J. A. NICHOLSON, R. A. ROBB, and J. F. GREENLEAF, 1989. Ultrasound transmis-sion and reflection computerized tomography for imaging bones and adjoining soft tissues. *IEEE 1988 Ultrasonics Symposium* 2:849–852.

SHEROUSE, G. W., J. D. BOURLAND, K. REYNOLDS, H. L. MCMURRY, T. P. MITCHELL, et al., 1990. Virtual simula-tion in the clinical setting: Some practical considerations. *Int. J. Radiat. Oncol. Biol. Phys.* 19:1059–1065.

SMITH, D. K., T. H. BERQUIST, K.-N. AN, R. A. ROBB, and Y. S. CHAO, 1989. Validation of three-dimensional recon-struction of knee anatomy: CT vs. MR imaging. *J. Comput. Assist. Tomogr.* 13(2):294–301.

TALTON, D. A., S. M. GOLDWASSER, R. A. REYNOLDS, and E.

188   BASIC TOOLS FOR SURGICAL PLANNING

S. Walsh, 1987. Volume rendering algorithms for the presentation of 3D medical data. *Proc. NCGA* 3:119–128.

Valente, R. M., H. S. Luthra, and R. A. Robb, 1989. Quantitative analysis of joint images for patients with rheumatoid arthritis. In *Proceedings of the Eleventh Annual International Conference of the IEEE/EMBS.* 11:1971–1972.

Vannier, M. W., B. Brunsden, C. F. Hildebolt, D. Falk, J. M. Cheverud, et al., 1991. Quantification of brain cortical surface sulcal lengths by 3-D MR. *Radiology* 80: 479–484.

Vannier, M. W., J. L. Marsh, and J. O. Warren, 1984. Three-dimensional CT reconstruction images for craniofacial surgical planning and evaluation. *Radiology* 150:179–184.

11 Synthetic Muscular Contraction on Facial Tissue Derived from Computerized Tomography Data

KEITH WATERS

TRADITIONAL craniofacial surgical planning relies on the surgeon's experience to select the most appropriate procedure. Typically, preoperative planning involves manipulating 2D radiographs to simulate surgery. In this process, the skeletal bone is rearranged and, once the bone is displaced, the 3D soft-tissue deformation becomes difficult to predict. High-performance graphics workstations and general-purpose parallel architectures provide a powerful resource to simulate surgical procedures. However, the most significant advantage of computerized surgical planning is the ability to simulate surgical procedures in advance of the actual operation.

Emulating muscle and skin activity using physically based models has proved promising, allowing a wide range of facial articulations to be computed at high screen refresh rates on a graphics workstation (Waters and Terzopoulos, 1991, 1992). Typically, the geometry for these physical models is acquired from stereophotogrammetry or optical surface scanners that collect several thousand range and color samples in a few seconds (Cyberware Laboratory, 1990). The skeletal geometry can be created directly from the surface data by estimating skin tissue depth from polygon size and orientation (Waters and Terzopoulos, 1990). Although this is an acceptable simplification for the purposes of animation, it does underestimate the influence of skin thickness on the tissue simulation. A geometric model of facial tissue extracted from CT data improves the skin tissue simulation by using accurate skin tissue depths. Furthermore, deformations by synthetic muscles provide a tool for observing, analyzing, and predicting soft-tissue mobility on the face.

Facial tissue is a complex biologic solid, and its mechanical behavior is primarily due to the physical properties of elastin, collagen, and ground substance (Larrabee, 1986). In addition, the mechanics of skin depend on tissue depth, which varies significantly over the face. On the forehead, it is only a few millimeters deep, whereas at the base of the nose it is relatively thick. Facial tissue also has a variety of subcutaneous attachments. For example, the tissues that form the cheek and mouth cavity are completely devoid of skeletal attachment; this is in contrast to regions, such as the root of the nose, where the tissue has a more rigid attachment to bone. To simulate facial tissue successfully, the geometric and mechanical properties have to be incorporated into a physical model.

Tissue simulations to date have been limited to small idealized patches of skin, ignoring skin tissue depths and subcutaneous attachments (Deng, 1988; Pieper, 1989). Although the results from a finite element approach are accurate, it can be computationally expensive (Larrabee, 1986; Deng, 1988; Piper, 1991). Physically based models consisting of nonrigid curves, surfaces, and solids construct elements from springs connected to point masses (Greenspan, 1973). The underlying simplicity of these elements allows composite units to be chained together to assemble complex surfaces or volumes (Terzopoulos and Fleischer, 1988a,b). In addition, these models are attractive because solutions can be computed in real time, even on modest hardware.

This chapter describes an experimental system that uses a geometric representation of facial tissue derived directly from CT data. The geometric representation captures the surface curvature of the face and provides realistic tissue thicknesses for the physical simulation. A simple but effective interaction solution is achieved with two discrete models: a surface model to process the facial skeleton and a solid model for the skin tissue. Both models are integrated in an interactive user interface and a parallel implementation on a fine-grained single instruction multiple data (SIMD) architecture is developed.

Skin tissue mechanics

Human skin has a layered structure consisting of the epidermis, the dermis, and the subcutaneous cellular tissue. The epidermis, a superficial layer of dead cells, is approximately one tenth the thickness of the dermis that it protects. These skin tissue layers are nonhomogeneous and nonisotropic, with lower stiffness along Langer's lines than across them [Kenedi et al., 1975; Larrabee and Sutton, 1986).

As stated earlier, the mechanical properties of human skin are primarily due to the physical properties of elastin fibers, collagen fibers, and ground substance. Dermal tissue is composed of collagen (72%) and elastin (4%) fibers forming a densely convoluted network in a gelatinous ground substance (20%). Under low stress, dermal tissue offers low resistance to stretch but, under greater stress, the uncoiled collagen fibers resist stretch much more markedly. This yields a biphasic stress-strain curve, as seen in figure 11.1, where the strain indicated by A is due to the deformation of the delicate elastin network, that of B is due to a gradual straightening of the collagen fibers, and that of C occurs when the majority of collagen fibers are elongated in the direction of the stress (Kenedi et al., 1975).

The incompressible amorphous matrix or ground substance retards the motion of the fibers and thereby gives rise to time-dependent viscoelastic behavior: stress relaxation at constant strain, strain creep at constant stress, and hysteresis under cyclic loading. Finally, the elastin fibers act like elastic springs that return the collagen fibers to their uncoiled condition under zero load.

The deformable model

Deformable models use point node masses connected by discrete spring units. Spring lattice topologies are simulated using Lagrange equations of motion and an explicit Euler time-integration procedure (Greenspan, 1973). Lattices with several thousand springs and nodes can be computed and displayed on dedicated

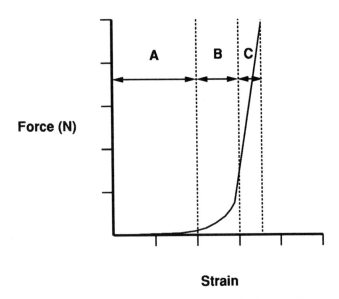

FIGURE 11.1   A typical stress-strain curve for human tissue.

graphics workstations in real time, providing to the user not only valuable feedback but also the facility to interact directly with the model. Furthermore, the node spring element lends itself to parallel computation, enabling even larger, more complex lattices to be computed.

A single node i has a point mass m_i and a three-space position $\mathbf{x}_i(t) = [x_i(t), y_i(t), z_i(t)]^t$. The velocity of the node is described by $\mathbf{v}_i = d\mathbf{x}_i/dt$ and its acceleration by $\mathbf{a}_i = d^2\mathbf{x}_i/dt^2$. A single spring unit k is constructed by connecting node i to node j. The spring has natural length l_k and stiffness c_k. The actual length of the spring is $\|\mathbf{r}_k\|$, where $\mathbf{r}_k = \mathbf{x}_j - \mathbf{x}_i$ is the vector separation of the nodes. The deformation of the spring is $e_k = \|\mathbf{r}_k\| - l_k$, and the force the spring exerts on node i can be described as follows:

$$\mathbf{s}_k = \frac{c_k e_k}{\|\mathbf{r}_k\|} \mathbf{r}_k \qquad (1)$$

The discrete Lagrange equation of motion for the dynamic node-spring system is the system of coupled, second-order ordinary differential equations:

$$m_i \frac{d^2\mathbf{x}_i}{dt^2} + \gamma_i \frac{d\mathbf{x}_i}{dt} + \mathbf{g}_i = \mathbf{f}_i; \quad i = 1, \dots, \mathcal{N}, \qquad (2)$$

where

$$\mathbf{g}_i(t) = \sum_{j \in \mathcal{N}_i} \mathbf{s}_k \qquad (3)$$

is the total force on node i due to springs connecting it to neighboring nodes $j \in \mathcal{N}_i$ and where $\mathbf{f}_i$ is a net force acting on node i. The quantity γ_i is a velocity-dependent damping coefficient dissipating the kinetic energy of the deformable lattice through friction. The profile of γ_i can be varied to produce an overdamped behavior in much the same way that skin tissue behaves.

To simulate the dynamics of a deformable lattice, we provide initial positions $\mathbf{x}_i^0$ and velocities $\mathbf{v}_i^0$ for each node i for $i = 1, \ldots, \mathcal{N}$, and numerically integrate the equations of motion forward through time. At each time step, we must evaluate the forces, accelerations, velocities, and positions for each node. A simple and quick time-integration procedure is the explicit Euler method (Press et al., 1986).

Facial tissue construction

The tissue simulation depends on the existence of a lattice topology that reflects the surface curvature of the face and realistic skin tissue thicknesses. To create a compact node lattice configuration, two radial images of the bone and skin tissue are used. These radial projections are unique because they embed a 3D space in two dimensions.

CT scan data consist of contiguous slices of 3D Hounsfield values, from which a number of geometric representations can be constructed (Wyvill, McPheeters, and Wyvill, 1986; Bloomenthal, 1987; Baker, 1989). For example, the marching cubes algorithm creates a polygonal representation from CT data by a sequential tessellation of a logical voxel (Lorensen and Cline, 1987), and carefully selected threshold values can isolate the skin and bone tissues (figure 11.2). A data set of 256^2 pixels by 113 slices typically generates approximately 500,000 polygons per isovalue, which is excessive if the numeric simulation and the display device are to achieve a near-real-time response.

RADIAL MAPPING

Isovalue surface algorithms generate both the inner and outer surfaces of bone tissue. For facial tissue modeling, only the outermost surface is needed for the bone and skin; therefore, a technique is required to extract only the exosurface for a specified isovalue.

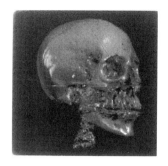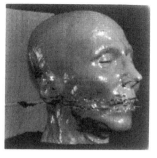

FIGURE 11.2   Three-dimensional isovalued surface of the skull and skin (CT data: 256^2 pixels × 113 slices).

The human face maps conveniently into a cylindrical coordinate system because the face is, for the most part, convex with limited line-of-sight shadowing. This is why a rotating laser scanner can create a nearly complete panoramic range image of the human head. A scanner typically creates range data at each point $f(\theta, y)$, and a complete image contains 256 equally spaced samples in y and 512 samples in θ from 0 to 2π (Cyberware Laboratory, 1990). Thus, the range data embed a 3D space, parameterized in two dimensions. This parameterization has significant advantages for facial tissue modeling because global and local operations can be performed on the 3D data in a 2D space. To map a 3D world coordinate $\mathbf{p}$ into a cylindric system $\mathbf{c}$, the following straightforward transformation can be used:

$$\mathbf{c} = [atan2(\mathbf{p}_x, \mathbf{p}_z), y] \qquad (4)$$

where $atan2$ is the C language math library function returning the arctangent of x/z in the range $-\pi$ to π. The inverse transformation is simply $\mathbf{p} = [r\cos(\theta), y, r\sin(\theta)]$.

Creating a radial image of the polygons formed by the marching cubes algorithm is straightforward: First, we create a z-buffer image of size $-\pi$ to π by n CT slices, then convert the centroid of each polygon into cylindric coordinates, compare each x, y image location z-depth to the current range value and, finally, update the z-depth if the range data have a value greater than the previously stored value.

Though this produces acceptable results, a more efficient solution uses the original 2D CT data slices. In essence this technique involves 2D ray tracing (figure 11.3). For each CT data plane, which represents an image row in the radial image, a ray is cast to the

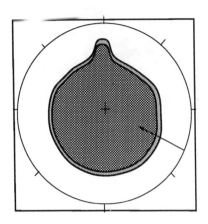

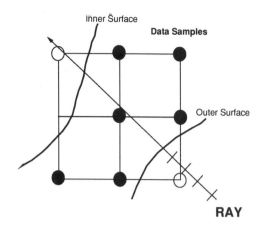

FIGURE 11.3   Two-dimensional image plane tracing.

center of the image at regular $2\pi/x$ radial intervals. From the circumference, the ray increments by Δ_i, sampling cells of image data. At each increment, the four surrounding data samples are tested for a surface traversing the cell, in much the same way that the marching cubes algorithm operates. If a surface occupies the current cell, the value is bilinearly interpolated and tested against the selected isovalue. The tracing terminates when the first intersection occurs, at which point the radial depth is stored in an image array (figures 11.4, 11.5). Essentially, this produces the same results as that of casting polygons into the image domain; however, this process is more computationally efficient.

EXTRACTING A CONTINUOUS SKELETAL SURFACE

The radial image surfaces (see figure 11.5) can have holes and artifacts when cast into radial coordinates; this is particularly evident around the eye orbits, nasal cavities, and the upper part of the mandible. Although these features are anatomically correct, they do present a problem for the surface-fitting method. It is desirable to have a continuous surface representation for the skeletal foundation and skin because large depressions create undesirable motion artifacts when simulated. Artifacts collected in the original CT data, such as x-ray reflections off fillings in the teeth, also produce undesirable spikes in the data (see figure 11.2). One solution is to ensure that sampling nodes do not access these areas at all by approximating the region by interpolation. This may be sufficient for a small number

FIGURE 11.4   Radial data of the skull. Image size 512 × 256 pixels.

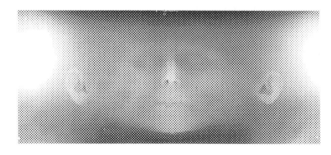

FIGURE 11.5   Radial data of skin. Image size 512 × 256 pixels.

of pixels but, for large regions, such as the orbits, an alternative solution is required.

An interactive *physical mesh* has been developed to capture the shape where it is known and provide a continuous smooth surface where there are omissions in the data. A *face mask* is created at the resolution of the simulation lattice to isolate those nodes in corrupt or hole

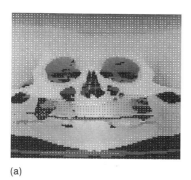
(a)

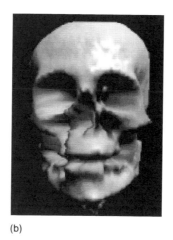
(b)

(c)

FIGURE 11.6 The face mask (a), and the prelattice (b) and postlattice (c) relaxation. Lattice resolution 64 × 64 pixels.

Notice how the eye sockets have been filled with a smooth surface.

regions (figure 11.6a). The mask is used to determine lattice node mobility: Nodes at holes are determined to be mobile, whereas nodes at bone are determined to be fixed. Additionally, the user can interactively fix nodes and release nodes from data observation. Once the face mask has been created, the simulation is computed using equation 2, and the lattice minimizes its energy in the mobile regions, filling the holes with a smooth surface (figure 11.6c). The result is a complete mesh approximating the skeletal foundation without any holes. It should be noted that the geometric model illustrated in figure 11.2 is approximately 200 times the resolution of the model shown in figure 11.6.

Physical model of facial tissue

Once the epidermis and skeletal subsurface are generated, a complete physical model can be constructed. Both the epidermis and the skeletal surfaces are regular lattices and require no further modification. The muscle layer, between the epidermis and bone, acts as a mobile zone to which the muscles are attached and articulated. The nodes of the lattice are constructed as follows: (1) The regular lattice of the epidermis, muscle, and bone layers is strutted diagonally to resist shearing forces (figure 11.7); (2) each node of the epidermis element is projected to the muscle layer (equidistant between the layers); and (3) a node is projected onto the skeletal bone and is rigidly attached. Nodes that do not have skeletal attachment are assumed to be free. The stiffness of the muscle layer elements c_k is set to be lower than that of the epidermis, reflecting the

mechanical properties of subcutaneous tissue (Larrabee, 1986; Kenedi et al., 1975). In addition, a biphasic spring can be used to emulate the stress-strain relationship, as seen in figure 11.1. A biphasic spring is defined by the stiffness

$$c_k = \begin{cases} \alpha_k & \text{when } e_k \leq e_k^c \\ \beta_k & \text{when } e_k > e_k^c \end{cases}$$

where α_k is smaller than β_k. Similar to dermal tissue, the biphasic spring is readily extensible at small strains but exerts rapidly increasing restoring stresses past a critical strain e^c.

Synthetic muscles

To date, three primary muscles types have been considered for facial synthesis: linear, sphincter, and sheet (Waters, 1987). In this section, the primary function of the linear muscle is described. In two dimensions, the linear muscle operates in an arc of influence; in three dimensions, it operates in a cone of influence on the muscle layer only.

Synthetic facial muscles are modeled as bundles of contractile muscle fibers. These fibers reside in the muscle layer and attach to bone. When the muscles contract, they pull the soft tissue toward the place where the muscles emerge from the underlying skeletal framework. The resulting perturbation places those nodes not influenced by the muscle contraction in an unstable state, and unbalanced forces propagate through the deformable tissue lattice, establishing a new equilibrium position.

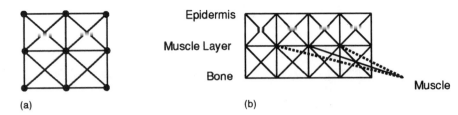

FIGURE 11.7 (a) Plane view of epidermis, muscle, and bone layer. (b) Cross-section of the tissue model.

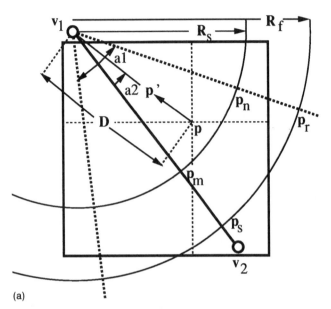

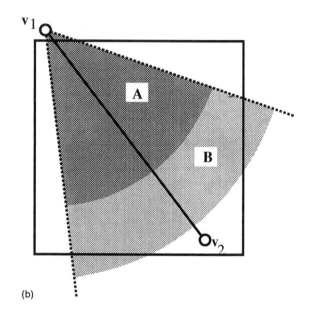

FIGURE 11.8 Description of the linear muscle zones of influence.

For a linear muscle, it is necessary to compute how adjacent tissue, such as the node **p** in figure 11.8a, is affected by a muscle vector contraction. It is assumed that there is no displacement at the point of insertion in the bone and that maximum deflection occurs at the point of insertion into the skin. Consequently, a dissipation of the force is passed to the adjoining tissue, across both sectors A and B in figure 11.8b.

To compute the displacement of an arbitrary node **p** to **p**′, within the segment $(\mathbf{v}_1, \mathbf{p}_r, \mathbf{p}_s)$, toward $\mathbf{v}_1$ along the vector $(\mathbf{p}, \mathbf{v}_1)$, the following expression is employed:

$$\mathbf{p}' = \mathbf{p} + akr\frac{\mathbf{pv}_1}{\|\mathbf{pv}_1\|} \qquad (5)$$

Here the new location **p**′ is a function of an angular displacement parameter

$$a = \cos(a2) \qquad (6)$$

where $a2$ is the angle between the vectors $(\mathbf{v}_1, \mathbf{v}_2)$ and $(\mathbf{v}_1, \mathbf{p})$, D is $\|\mathbf{v}_1 - \mathbf{p}\|$, r is a radial displacement parameter

$$r = \begin{cases} \cos\left(\dfrac{1-D}{R_s}\right); & \text{for } \mathbf{p} \text{ inside sector } (\mathbf{v}_1\mathbf{p}_n\mathbf{p}_m\mathbf{p}_1) \\[2ex] \cos\left(\dfrac{D-R_s}{R_f-R_s}\right); & \text{for } \mathbf{p} \text{ inside sector } (\mathbf{p}_n\mathbf{p}_r\mathbf{p}_s\mathbf{p}_m) \end{cases}$$

$$(7)$$

and k is a fixed constant representing the elasticity of skin. Figure 11.9 illustrates the contraction of a linear muscle with an increasing contraction factor.

Parallel implementation

The node lattice simulation performs reasonably well with several hundred nodes and lattice connections on

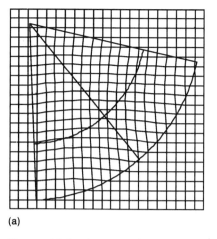 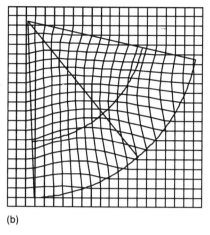 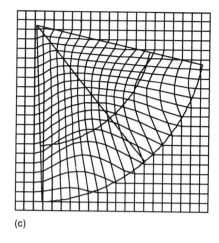

(a)   (b)   (c)

FIGURE 11.9 A progressing sequence of muscle contraction
with a linear cosine activity.

a workstation. However, a fine-grained lattice with
several thousand nodes and lattice connections requires
much larger-scale computations. Architectures such as
the massively parallel SIMD DECmpp 12000/Sx lend
themselves to such data parallel applications.

A crucial component of data-oriented parallel computation concerns the mapping of data to *processing elements* (PE). Mappings that fail to capitalize on the PE
layout often are penalized by inefficient interprocessor
communication. Therefore, the 3D tissue lattice uses
the most efficient mapping possible, where each PE
stores a single data node for the bone, muscle, and skin
layers, respectively (figure 11.10). This data layout
reduces the interprocessor communication to nearest-
neighbor and on-processor communication. In addition, the regularity of the lattice (see figure 11.10)
permits the construction of pentahedral networks that
reflect in a stable physical geometry (see figure 11.7)
with a low overall computational overhead.

A 4K DECmpp 12000 Sx was used for the parallel
implementation, with a single data node for each PE.
At each time step in the simulation, every processor
computes all forces acting on the current node $\mathbf{x}_i(t)$
from all the lattice connections in parallel with the X-
Net construct (Digital Equipment Corporation, 1992).
The X-Net construct is used to access PEs that are a
uniform step away from the current PE along any of
the eight directions; in this case, we use only the nearest
neighbor (see figure 11.10). The sequence of parallel
operations is as follows: (1) Compute forces from all
nodes in the muscle, epidermis, and the mobile bone
layers; (2) propagate forces between the layers; (3)

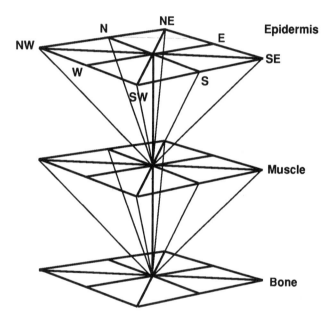

FIGURE 11.10 Parallel data layout and PE communication
along eight directions.

resolve the forces into velocities; (4) and calculate the
displacements. The final parallel displacement vectors
then are converted into a serial array and shipped to
the remote host. At the remote host, the 3D lattice data
are converted into polygons and are displayed.

Examples

Using the linear muscle deformation in combination
with the physically based tissue simulation results in a
time sequence such as that depicted in figure 11.11.

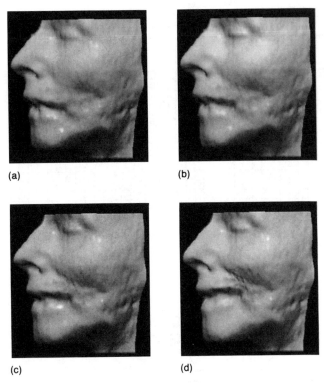

(a)   **(b)**

(c)   **(d)**

Figure 11.11 A focused face mask on half of the face at a 64^2 resolution provides a finer data sampling over the cheek. The four frames illustrate a zygomatic contraction that draws the corner of the mouth upward toward the outer margins of the zygomatic arch.

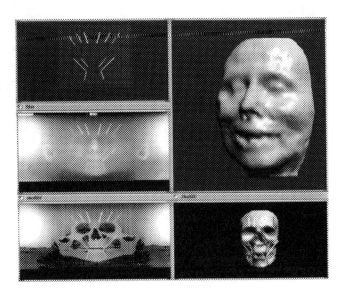

Figure 11.12 The interface.

Here the contraction of the zygomatic major muscle draws the corner of the mouth upward toward the zygomatic arch. Figure 11.12 illustrates the interface as it appears on the workstation. To the left are the radial image maps for the bone and skin tissue, whereas the top window displays the computational lattice geometry. In these windows, six paired linear muscle vectors are displayed. To the right, the windows display the 3D aspects of the data. In the bottom window is the skull with 3D vectors describing the muscle attachments, whereas the top window displays the 3D epidermal skin tissue.

Conclusion

A synthetic facial tissue model, derived from CT data and deformed under the influence of synthetic facial muscle, has been demonstrated to generate realistic skin tissue deformations. Although this interface is experimental, it does demonstrate the ability to observe, analyze, and predict facial tissue mobility in advance of surgical procedures.

The simplicity of the deformable volume lattice model allows the rapid creation and simulation of muscular deformation. Furthermore, extensions to data parallel architectures are straightforward, thereby providing the necessary computational requirements for future large-scale tissue simulation.

REFERENCES

BAKER, H. H., 1989. Computation and manipulation of three-dimensional surface from image sequences. In *Visualization in Scientific Computing*. Nielson G. M., Shriver B. D. ed. Los Alamitos, Calif.: IEEE Computer Society Press, pp. 109–127.

BLOOMENTHAL, J. 1987. Boundary representation of implicit surfaces (tech. rep. CSL-87-2). Palo Alto, Calif.: Xerox PARC.

Cyberware Laboratory Inc., 1990. 4020/RGB 3D scanner with color digitizer. Monterey, Calif.: Cyberware Laboratory Inc.

Digital Equipment Corporation, 1992. *DECmpp Programming Language User's Guide*. Maynard, Mass.: Digital Equipment Corporation.

DENG, X. Q., 1988. A finite element analysis of surgery of the human facial tissue. Doctoral thesis, Columbia University, New York City.

GREENSPAN, D., 1973. *Discrete Models*. Reading, Mass.: Addison Wesley.

KENEDI, R. M., T. GIBSON, J. H. EVANS, and J. C. BARBENEL, 1975. Tissue mechanics. *Phys. Med. Biol.* 20(5):699–717.

LARRABEE, W., 1986. A finite element model of skin deformation: I. Biomechanics of skin and soft tissue: A review. *Laryngoscope* 96:399–405.

LARRABEE, W., and D. SUTTON, 1986. A finite element model of skin deformation: II. An experimental model of skin deformation. Laryngoscope, 96:406–412.

LORENSEN, W. E., and H. E. CLINE, 1987. Marching cubes: High resolution 3D surface construction algorithm. Computer Graphics, 21(4):163–169.

PIEPER, S. D., 1989. More than skin deep: Physical modeling of facial tissue. Master's thesis, Massachusetts Institute of Technology, Media Arts and Sciences, Cambridge.

PIEPER, S. D., 1991. CAPS: Computer-aided plastic surgery. Doctoral thesis, Massachusetts Institute of Technology, Media Arts and Sciences, Cambridge.

PRESS, W., B. FLANNEY, S. TEUKOLSKY, and W. VERTTERING, 1986. *Numerical Recipes: The Art of Scientific Computing*. Cambridge, Engl.: Cambridge University Press.

TERZOPOULOS, D., and K. FLEISCHER, 1988a. Deformable models. *Visual Comput.* 4(6):306–331.

TERZOPOULOS, D., and K. FLEISCHER, 1988b. Viscoelasticity, plasticity and fracture. *Comput. Graphics* 22(4):269–278.

WATERS, K., 1987. A muscle model for animating three-dimensional facial expressions. *Comput. Graphics* (SIGGRAPH '87) 21(4):17–24.

WATERS, K., and D. TERZOPOULOS, 1990. A physical model of facial tissue and muscle articulation. In *Proceedings of the First Conference on Visualization in Biomedical Computing*, pp. 77–82.

WATERS, K., and D. TERZOPOULOS, 1991. Modeling and animating faces using scanned data. *J. Visualization Animation* 2(4):123–128.

WATERS, K., and D. TERZOPOULOS, 1992. The computer synthesis of expressive faces. *Philos. Trans. R. Soc. Lond. [Biol.]* 355(1273):87–93.

WYVILL, B., C. MCPHEETERS, and G. WYVILL, 1986. Data structures for soft objects. *Visual Comput.* 2:227–234.

Human-Machine Interfaces

THE CONTINUALLY increasing level of technology in all fields of life underscores the importance of human-machine interactions. If a system is efficient but the operator controlling it does not know how to use it, then time and productivity are lost. Conversely, a system design is poor if it does not take into consideration the human abilities, specifically intelligence and adaptability. These general considerations are equally important for medicine and especially for the modern operating room environment. For these reasons, we have chosen to include a section dedicated to the design of human-machine interfaces and their application in surgical training and diagnostic procedures.

The analysis of human-machine communication has as its goal determining the most efficient and safe way to present information to, and read input from, the operator. When the distance between the operator and the controlled system is large, good interfaces have to ensure success despite long transmission delays.

The complexities of human behavior make impractical at the present time a comprehensive mathematic simulation of the human-machine system. Thus, the interface design is at best an empiric "art," mastered by teams of engineers, scientists, and psychologists who perform "human-factor" (or ergonomic) tests in which tasks and communication modalities are changed, and the corresponding operator error rate and learning time are measured. It is a trial-and-error process.

In the first chapter of this section, "Aspects of Ergonomic System Design Applied to Medical Work Systems," Rau et al. examine ways to reduce the stress and strain on the medical staff and patient while simultaneously increasing the safety and efficiency of the system through high-performance user interfaces. The authors argue against corrective design of isolated components, such as increasing equipment performance at the expense of larger fatigue and stress on the operator of that equipment. What is needed is a comprehensive system design that considers three subareas of personnel, equipment, and environment. In a medical work system, the patient represents an additional human component, so the overall work system must be oriented toward the patient. Rau et al. distinguish three basic steps in system design—analysis, synthesis, and evaluation—which are supported by modern computer simulation tools. They illustrate the proposed approach by presenting three case studies in the areas of anesthesia information systems, dental operating units and, finally, minimally invasive surgery. An additional chapter by Tendick et al. (chapter 44) reports human factors research applied specifically to the problems of minimally invasive surgery.

The second chapter in this section, "Human Factors in Telesurgery" by Sheridan, analyzes the human factors associated with telesurgery. Telesurgery is an extension of telerobotics to the operating room. Its goal is to allow a specialist to perform a consultation or surgical procedure remotely while assisted locally by nurses and robots. Many of the visual inspection and manipulation problems of telesurgery are also present in minimally invasive surgery or in microsurgery under direct viewing. Remote visual inspection through a desktop or head-mounted TV display, requires good depth perception. Stereo displays are superior to monoscopic ones, but other considerations are also important. The author describes tests showing that in simple manipulation tasks, performance depends on image frame rate, its resolution, and gray scale combined (or bits per second). Also important are superposed graphic diagrams and instructions designed to make visible parts of objects or organs that are otherwise occluded from view. In the third part of his chapter, Sheridan describes factors involved in actual remote manipulation. Such factors are the presence or absence of force and touch feedback from the remote robot to the operator, as well as communication delays to the remote operating site. Force feedback has proved beneficial for short time delays, but otherwise it brings system instability. Several solutions are described, based largely on the experiments of the US National Aeronautics and Space Administration (NASA) with space teleoperation and the use of "supervisory" control for delays of more than 0.5 sec.

NASA has played a leading role in the development of another form of high-end human-machine interface, namely virtual reality, which is the subject of the next chapter, "Virtual Reality and Surgery." In this chapter, Rosen, Lasko-Harvill, and Satava first introduce the basic terminology related to user input and output (I/O) tools, such as sensing gloves, head-mounted displays, and 3D sound generators. The underlying computing hardware needs to be very powerful in order to ensure realistic and fast simulations. These authors show how this new technology can revolutionize the way medical students and residents are taught anat-omy and pathology. They cite as a case study the first surgical simulator for gallbladder removal developed by the US Army, as well as work on leg surgery simulation done by NASA.

Virtual reality can also be used in other areas of medicine such as remote consultation and diagnosis. The last chapter in this section, by Bajura, Fuchs, and Ohbuchi, describes such an application in ultrasound patient imagery. In "Merging Virtual Objects with the Real World," the authors describe the system developed by the group at the University of North Carolina, which uses a standard ultrasound scanner but which is integrated with a computer system that stores and re-displays several image "slices" registered with the patient body. Graphics are merged with real-time video, resulting in the ability of the clinician effectively to see into the patient's body. The advantage demonstrated by this feasibility project is the ability to bring images in front of the clinician, thus reducing stress involved with display on a TV, plus the ability to reconstruct virtual 3D organs from real 2D images in quasi real-time.

These chapters help the reader gain an understanding of the problems and complexities involved in human-human and human-machine interactions in the operating room. Because this is an active research area, the examples given here are by no means exhaustive. The technologies described, as well as their evaluation procedures, are continually evolving. The potential of modern human-machine interfaces will become more apparent through the examples given in the Applications part of this book.

12 Aspects of Ergonomic System Design Applied to Medical Work Systems

GÜNTER RAU, KLAUS RADERMACHER, BERNHARD THULL, AND CLETUS VON PICHLER

IN RECENT YEARS, there has been dramatic progress in medical diagnosis and therapy. The use of new physical effects and the improvement of existing procedures and systems are pushed by the technologies available but also pulled by the medical needs and applications. Nuclear magnetic resonance imaging and computerized tomography as well as complex automatic laboratory analyzers are good examples of increasing technical support (and dependency) in medical diagnostics. Microprocessor and information technology has opened new ways to process, correlate, and store various qualities of information with increasing complexity and quantities, ranging, for example, from on-line measured patients' vital parameters and laboratory values up to complete images (picture archiving and communication systems, 3D image processing). Laser application for treatment of retinal detachment, pacemaker therapy, extracorporeal dialysis, use of artificial heart valves, customized implants, extracorporeal shockwave lithotripsy (ESWL), technologies of minimally invasive surgery, automatic stereotactic mammabiopsy and computer-assisted stereotactic skull-base or brain surgery are examples of some of the most recent major efforts. However, there is still a lag between the technologic standards of technical support of therapeutic procedures in the operating room on the one hand and the diagnostic, as well as therapeutic, equipment outside the operating theater on the other. In clinical routine, there is to date no possibility of interlinking the 3D image-processing and therapy-planning procedures directly to surgical intervention in the operating room. In most cases (e.g., in orthopaedic surgery), the surgeon uses relatively simple instruments of a low technical level, such as hand-held drills and saws.

A conceptual ergonomic system design of the work-system "operating room" leads to the possibility of utilizing complex technologies and supportive devices such as surgery-assisting manipulators, computer-integrated therapy planning and performance, or computer-based documentation and information systems for such functions as anesthesia and intensive care. In general, the aim is to reduce the stress and strain for the medical staff and patient and, at the same time, to increase the efficiency and safety of the system by means of implementing technical support devices with high-performance user interfaces.

Ergonomics

Ergonomics deals with the interaction between humans and the technical environment. Introducing ergonomics into system design means taking a true multidisciplinary approach by understanding humans as an additional nontechnical but essential system component. Thus far it is not possible to give a comprehensive quantitative description of this human system component with regard to human physiology, psychology, and behavior structure. "Ergonomics, therefore, relies on empiric procedures and heuristic methods" (Rau, 1990). In general, structure and function of the whole human-machine system and the interaction between its components must be analyzed. System ergonomics describe, analyze, and integrate all elements, information, and interactions of its three subareas—personnel ergonomics, equipment ergonomics (*anthropotechnique*), and environmental ergonomics (figure 12.1) (Bernotat and Rau, 1980). *Personnel ergonomics* deals with the adaptation of human to machine (and, in case of team-

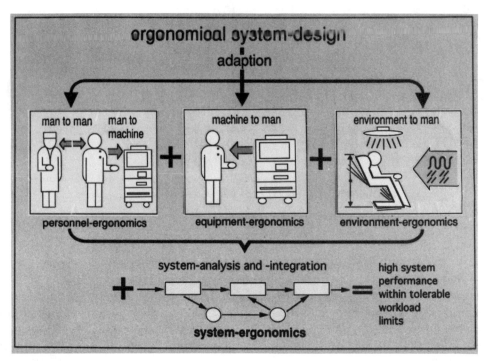

FIGURE 12.1   Three subareas of system ergonomics—personnel, equipment, and environment. (Reprinted from Bernotat and Rau, 1980, by permission.)

work, of human to human) by selection and training. The aim is to help human operators achieve the necessary physical and mental requirements and develop the skills for operation. *Equipment ergonomics* tries to match machine or system and whole process to human, to the user's characteristics, capabilities, and limitations. This area of concern takes into account anthropometric factors, design of suitable visual and acoustic displays, selection, arrangement and combination of control elements as input media, and allocation of functions to human and machine. *Environmental ergonomics* is concerned with the physical, chemical, biologic, and even social environment and its adaptation to working personnel, including such factors as vibration, noise, illumination, radiation, smell, and danger of infection or toxification.

A comprehensive conceptual ergonomic system design ("conceptual ergonomics") leads to far better system performance than an isolated corrective design of some already existing components (figure 12.2) (Rau, 1990). This fact becomes increasingly important if the work system becomes more complex. When looking at a work system that already exists in part (e.g., the integration of a 3D localizer system or equipment for minimally invasive surgery into the operating theater), elements of conceptual and corrective ergonomics must be combined, for organizational, technical, economic, psychological, social, and traditional reasons. Established systems and methods often cannot be totally replaced by new conceptually designed systems but have to be correctively optimized in their several components. In every ergonomic approach, it is critical to keep the whole system in mind and therefore to start with analysis of the existing system and with definition of performance of the overall system.

Mathematic models and handbooks describing the results of ergonomic research on human capabilities, functions, and limitations; anthropometric, physiologic, and psychological relationships; and models and statistics such as methods for analysis, synthesis, and evaluation are available (see the references).

SYSTEM ANALYSIS AND DESCRIPTION

In the first step, the whole system and the break down into its individual components have to be characterized and analyzed, with special regard to its bottlenecks. The consideration of components supports a better study and classification of causes and effects. The criteria of this analysis are the effectiveness and security of

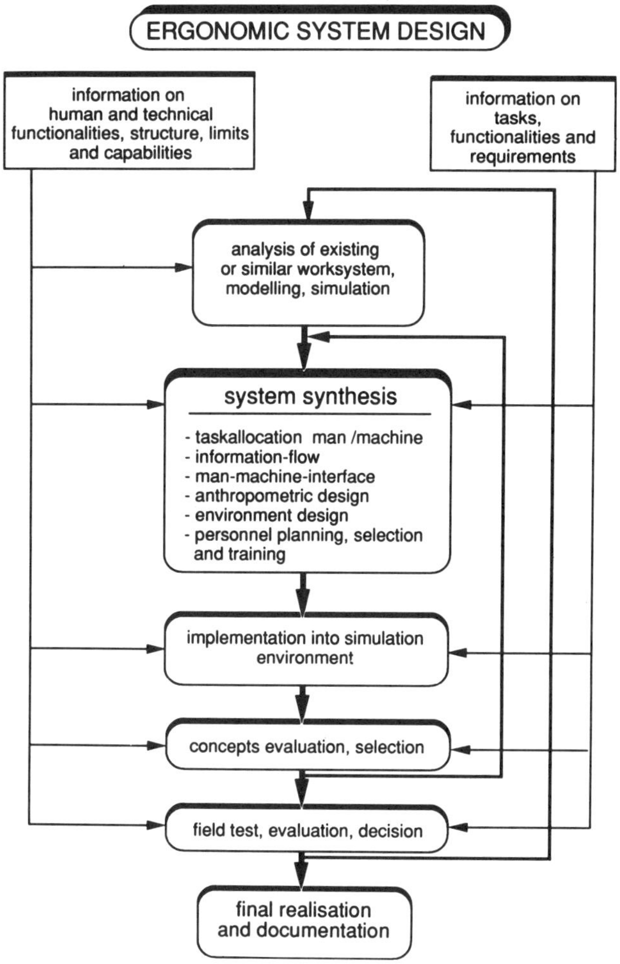

FIGURE 12.2 Ergonomic system design. Basic steps are analysis, synthesis, and evaluation. (Derived from Bernotat and Rau, 1980.)

the entire work process, as well as the stress and strain of the human user participating as a system component in the process. Various scientific methods are available for this first step of an ergonomic system design. Structured interviews and observations within the work process using so-called paper-and-pencil methods such as the Ovako Working-posture Analyzing System or OWAS (Stoffert, 1985), AET (Rohmert, 1989), and MAS (Rohmert, 1989], Linkanalysis (Rohmert, 1989), and Harmonography (Rohmert, 1989), as well as subjective rating methods (Shackel, Chidsey, and Shipley, 1969; Nitsch, 1976; Hancock and Meshkati, 1988) are very effective, reliable, and rather inexpensive tools. Furthermore, the measurement of physiologic parameters (electromyography, electrocardiography, etc.), physical and chemical values, videosomatography, and

motion analysis up to the computer-based modeling and simulation are suitable methods for analyzing a work system.

Analysis of a system leads mostly to model approaches because of the fact that the human user needs a model, at least a mental model, for a better understanding of a process of which he or she becomes a part. Simulation may be an additional support to understanding and describing the process. A simulator also can be used for evaluating and testing new design approaches. It can consist of hardware as well as a software-simulation environment (i.e., a computer simulation as well as a mock-up of the workplace in the laboratory). System analysis may be supported by the comparison of a model simulation and the real process. The closer a simulation gets to the real process, the better the real process can be described and the more realistic is the simulation environment for the testing of new system components.

In the past, the computer-based simulation was restricted mainly to simple relationships and had to be programmed by using standard programming languages such as Basic, Fortran, or Pascal. Recently, special modern simulation languages such as STELLA (Richmond, 1985), EMSIG (Knäuper and Kraiss, 1986), or SIMKIT (IntelliCorp, 1984) have been developed that allow an interactive graphic simulation of work systems and processes, interfaces, and dialogue sequences, as well as evaluation and documentation of the results of a simulation. System components and their dynamic functionality are realized in the form of software modules and are represented in the form of icons displayed on the screen. These icons can be composed and connected interactively on the screen. In this way, the structure of the whole system with its logical and functional relations can be represented. By means of the interconnection of the corresponding software modules, a quantitative dynamic simulation of the system can be performed and documented adequately.

One special difficulty must be recognized in simulating the interaction between different system components with both discontinuous and continuous behavior: It is due to and occurs in cognitive processes and control activities of a human user. A comprehensive description of the performance of some languages for the simulation of human-machine systems, and especially for the simulation of human behavioral patterns —languages such as SAINT (Seifert and Döring, 1981), SLAM, and HOPROC (Lane et al., 1980) is

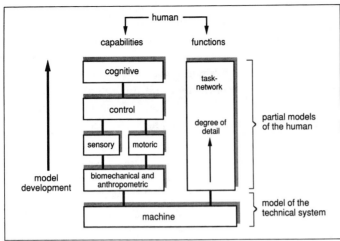

FIGURE 12.3 Human operator modeling. (Reprinted from Bernotat and Rau, 1991, by permission.)

given in Kraiss (1986). The analysis of cognitive tasks of a human user is very difficult, but nevertheless it is very important for the understanding of a work system and its ergonomic design. Even in very simple cases, the simulation of mental information processing remains a big problem. In general, it should be considered that the human being is too complex to be thoroughly measured or described by models or simulations. Only certain specific aspects can be analyzed and described in experiments or model simulation (figure 12.3) (Bernotat and Rau, 1991). A comprehensive survey of existing models is given in McMillan et al., (1989) or Kaster (1986).

Therefore, in the phases of analysis, synthesis, and evaluation, it is necessary to measure and analyze the behavior parameters of a sufficiently large number of representative users of existing similar systems both in model simulations of the technical equipment and under field conditions. Furthermore, it is in no way

sufficient to optimize the equipment performance only on the criteria of overall system performance. For example, temporarily measured high system performances may result from a compensating higher effort of a human operator, with appreciable stress resulting in high strain, fewer reserve capacities, fatigue, probability of user errors, even long-term damage for the user, and certainly a decreasing long-term system performance (figure 12.4) (Rohmert et al., 1983).

For the measurement of human stress and strain in the course of an ergonomic analysis or concept evaluation, physiologic parameters are not comprehensive indicators on which one can rely solely. It can be assumed that subjective rating methods have a high reliability and validity (Shackel, Chidsey, and Shipley, 1969; Nitsch, 1976; Hancock and Meshkati, 1988), which can be amended by physiologic parameters.

SYNTHESIS OF ALTERNATIVE CONCEPTS

Once the work system and the work process have been analyzed and modeled and, optionally, a simulation environment has been developed, the synthesis of a new or modified work system with new or optimized components can be performed. For a conceptual design, several scientific tools, methods, and even some handbooks as well as hardware and software tools for a computer-based design and simulation are available (figure 12.5).

For the optimization and synthesis of a conceptual system design approach, the cooperation of engineers, ergonomics researchers, and experienced users of already existing or similar work systems or components is indispensable. The decoupling of tasks and subprocesses in order to study parameters and to optimize components may be helpful (figure 12.6).

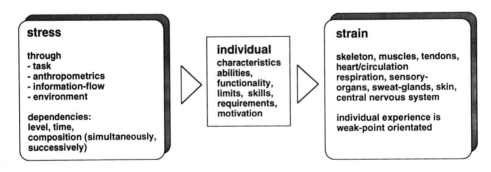

FIGURE 12.4 Stress-strain concept. (Adapted from Rohmert et al., 1983.)

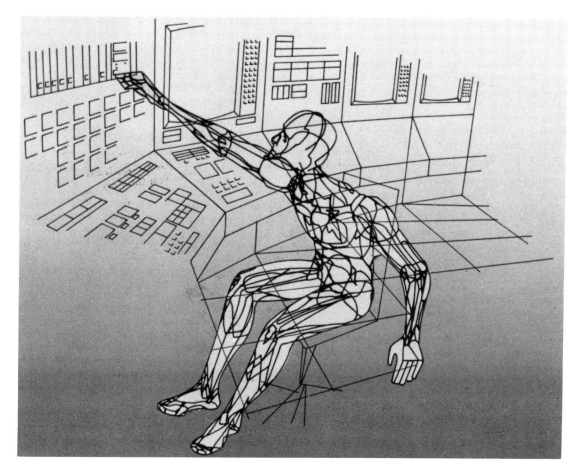

FIGURE 12.5 CAD-somatographic study in the course of an ergonomic system synthesis. (Reprinted from Kraiss, 1986, by permission.)

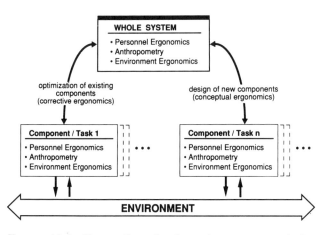

FIGURE 12.6 Decoupling of tasks and components during design process.

The selected design approach always must be integrated and verified within the whole system. Additional system components that may be necessary or useful in the course of additional work tasks or technical progress can basically be designed in a conceptual (noncorrective) manner.

In general, stress and strain should be taken into account in the design and evaluation process. Therefore, the consideration of stress and strain, caused by inconvenient working postures, static holding work, and mental and sensory or sensorimotor workload is very important. A long-term overload or the exceeding of damage limits may result in diseases of organs or organ systems and will lead to a suboptimal system performance.

In modern work systems, the interaction between the user and the technical system concentrates increasingly on a visual display workstation. The quality of the herein realized displays and control and interaction functions, focusing all relevant functionalities, is decisive for overall system performance. Especially for the nontechnical user, such as medical users, a self-explanatory user guide inherent to the system is particularly important.

For visual display workstations, a computer-based graphic interactive rapid-prototyping approach—as described, for instance, in Langen et al. (1989)—provides a favorable solution. It is possible to design a complete supervisory workplace on the screen, simulating hardware displays, analog control elements, and dials with their connection to the simulated process. One great advantage of the rapid-prototyping approach is that different concepts can be simulated, evaluated, and selected very quickly in cooperation with experienced users. Nevertheless, a final evaluation in a field test must be performed because the possibilities of modeling and simulation in the laboratory environment alone are insufficient for a reliable and definite statement concerning the ability and benefits of an ergonomic design concept (Bernotat and Rau, 1980).

In conclusion, the ergonomic system design methodology leads to a better understanding of a work process by way of analysis and to a systematic and effective synthesis and evaluation of user-friendly high-performance human-machine systems, accepting human needs, abilities, skills, and limits. With the increasing complexity of instrumentation in medicine, it becomes more and more necessary to apply the methods of ergonomic system design. Before giving some examples of ergonomic approaches in medicine, it will be useful to discuss some special characteristic aspects of ergonomics in medicine.

Special aspects of ergonomics in medicine

Apart from the high complexity of medicotechnical systems, the following additional factors recommend an ergonomic system approach in designing medical work systems (figure 12.7).

In a medicotechnical work system the patient, apart from the medical staff, represents an additional but essential human component. Through the interaction of this component with the system, an additional human-machine interface (and even an additional human-human interface) must be taken into account in the course of ergonomic system design. In most cases (especially in surgery), the patient can be formally de-

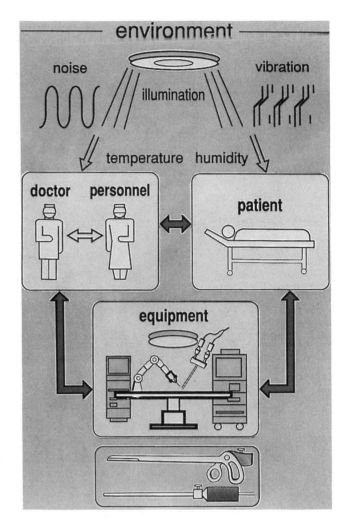

FIGURE 12.7 Typical situation of a medical work system.

scribed as a system component while at the same time he or she is the object of work.

The patient and his or her illness are very complex system components and can even be considered objects that cannot be changed or adapted in any way. The ergonomic design and optimization must focus on the technical process, to relieve the medical staff of avoidable activities and to design technical support devices that do not require the users' attention intrinsically.

The overall work system must be oriented toward the patient who, because of illness, is in a situation of extreme psychological and physiologic stress. The instrumentation of a medical work system should require only a minimum of attention from medical staff and has to achieve the requirements of medical staff and patient. (In contrast, ergonomic design of the cockpit of an aircraft must consider only the requirements of the pilots, who can pay undivided attention to the complex technical system and the mission.) Nonetheless, the distinction should be made in the medical arena between a true physician-patient-machine work system (e.g., operating room, workplaces for medical therapy and diagnostics) and a technical work system with more or less technical users (e.g., laboratory, orthopaedic workshop, 3D image processing, and 3D planning systems for surgical interventions). Therefore, it is very important during the phases of task allocation to consider not only the distribution of tasks between human and machine (relieving humans of avoidable activities and strain) but also among different medical work systems (e.g., preoperative and operative phases). In this context, the importance of an ergonomic design approach becomes evident, taking into account the whole system and its environment. If it is possible (e.g., by means of a shift of tasks into the preoperative planning and preparation phase) to release the operating team from intraoperative time-consuming complex and stressing interactions with technical equipment, the support of complex technical systems can be used without additional loading of the critical intraoperative work process of the surgeon-patient-machine system.

From the personnel ergonomic viewpoint, there are very restrictive marginal conditions concerning the possibility of technical training of physicians or medical staff. In some cases, technical specialists already are involved in the therapeutic process. The cooperation of physicist and physician during a radiation treatment, or the intraoperative assistance of an orthopaedic artificer or engineer during orthopaedic operations, are solutions that already exist. The introduction of robotics into the operating theater certainly will require an operating assistant with a special technical education. It should be considered that apart from the additional costs, an additional human system component requiring interfaces, interactions, and information flow must be taken into account. With an increasing number of interfaces (especially interfaces between human and machine or human and human), the complexity, the necessity for communication, and the probability of errors is increasing exponentially. The new generation of ESWL or the systems for semiautomatic mammobiopsy are good examples for well-prepared robotoid systems. Ultrasound or x-ray image acquisition, target point localization and calculation, and the automatic or semiautomatic positioning of the end effector

can be performed by the physician during ambulant clinical routine. The principles of the interactive procedures (stereotaxy, biplanar x-radiation, or localization via ultrasound) are known from conventional clinical education.

Clearly, the design of efficient user interfaces with a self-explanatory user guide and optimally adapted forms and sequences of interaction are especially important for the effectiveness of a medical work system design and overall systems performance.

In addition to the discussed pecularities of a medical technical work system, there are some additional boundary conditions in the operating theater, especially concerning environmental ergonomics (e.g., clothing, illumination, danger of infection, conditions of sterility, temperature). In most cases, the surgeon is working under enormous pressures of time, action, and reaction, because of medical reasons. The surgeon must concentrate attention primarily on the operating field. In addition, his or her hands must not leave the sterile area. Interactions with the nonsterile equipment must be performed through sterile barriers (e.g., flexible plastic tubes) using foot-operated switches, speech input, or dialogue (additional human-human interface!) with a person assisting in the nonsterile area. At the same time, the surgeon's work requires extreme concentration, dexterity of hands, and eye-hand coordination, as well as 3D thinking and orientation. It represents mental and visually guided fine sensorimotor work on a high level. Any additional interactive load with complex technical processes must be avoided. The introduction of new components can be performed only with limitations and on the basis of an ergonomic integration and optimization of the entire work system.

It should be noted, however, that surgical intervention is only one step in a computer-integrated surgical procedure. Assuming that a typical procedure consists of the basic steps of preoperative image acquisition, 3D image processing and visualization, planning (and programming) of intervention, preparation and, finally, execution of surgical intervention, it must be considered that only during the first and the last step does the patient have to be present (i.e., directly involved the procedure). The workplaces or systems for image processing, planning, and preoperative preparation (and, for example, for the programming or manufacture of operation support devices) have to fulfill different marginal conditions. In view of the nontechnical education of the medical staff, these systems also must have an effective self-explanatory user interface, but they can be more complex, and the physician can focus his or her full attention on the process. In most cases, the user does not work under the same pressures of time as during a surgical intervention. Furthermore, it is possible to delegate technical subtasks to the technical staff without the necessity of direct intraoperative cooperation.

For an ergonomic system approach, only design and evaluation procedures, guidelines, marginal conditions, and empiric values can be formulated. A general solution for an ergonomic system design cannot be given. It is for these reasons that even today tables in handbooks are of limited value only. Therefore, the main aspects and typical methodology of ergonomic system design will be presented in more detail in the following three totally different examples of ergonomic applications in the operating room.

Examples of ergonomic design approaches applied in the operating room

ANESTHESIA INFORMATION SYSTEM

The task of the anesthetist is to prepare the patient for an operation, to administer the anesthetic, and to bring the patient around after the operation. Particularly during the anesthesia while the surgical operation is taking place, the administration of drugs must be regulated so that the patient is subjected to as little strain as possible by the anesthesia while the surgeon is nevertheless able to operate under ideal conditions. The Anesthesia Information System (AIS) (Klocke et al., 1986) is intended to support the anesthetist in monitoring and documenting the course of the anesthesia and to provide greater opportunity for direct involvement with the patient (e.g., for visual observation, administering drugs, or taking samples) (figure 12.8).

The concept of the AIS is determined by the requirements resulting from the tasks and the procedures as well as marginal conditions. The patient's vital parameters measured during anesthesia (blood pressure, pulse, temperature, etc.) and the therapeutic measures of the anesthetist (drugs, stored blood, respiration, etc.) must be represented in a suitable form first. Because not every piece of information must be presented continuously and simultaneously, an interactive system is required that allows the data to be called corresponding to the current events in the operating theater (i.e.,

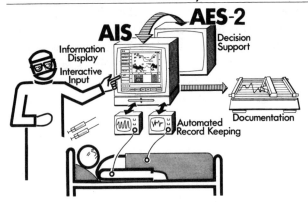

FIGURE 12.8   The Anesthesia Information System (AIS).

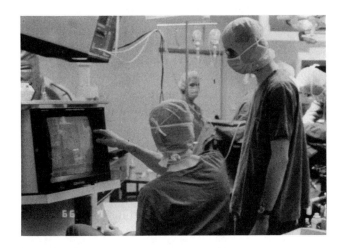

FIGURE 12.9   AIS in the operating room.

corresponding to the particular phase of the operation) (figure 12.9). The following requirements must therefore be fulfilled: First, the information provided must be unambiguous and clearly represented and logical relationships among various parameters must be recognizable. Second, the interaction must be task-oriented and have suitable user guidance. The design of the user interface and the interaction sequences between the user and AIS is therefore of major significance. The concept was created in close consultation with future users and it was checked continuously during the stages of its development.

IMPLEMENTATION OF THE USER INTERFACE OF THE AIS The interaction between the doctor and AIS takes place exclusively via a touch-sensitive, high-resolution color monitor (Rau and Trispel, 1982). The most im-

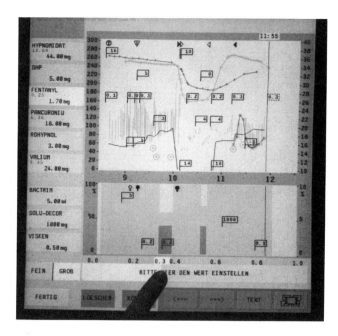

FIGURE 12.10   User interface of the AIS. (Reprinted from Rau, 1990, by permission.)

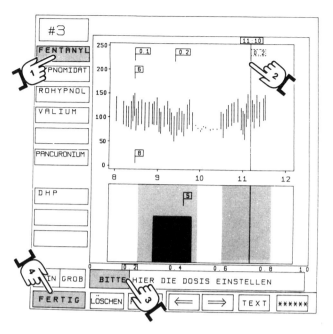

FIGURE 12.11   Example of a typical interaction sequence of AIS. (Reprinted from Klocke et al., 1986, by permission.)

portant vital parameters of the patient, such as blood pressure and pulse, are automatically measured by monitoring systems in the operating theater, transferred to the AIS, and displayed on the monitor. The operating controls for entering data are implemented in the screen as virtual controls that are operated by touching the surface of the monitor screen (i.e., by placing a finger on the required information or item. The integration of the information display and information input in this form is known as *direct manipulation* (Rau, 1979; Shneiderman, 1982; Rau and Trispel, 1982).

The representation of the information on the screen has a structure based on previous analyses of the requirements (figure 12.10). The central section is a data window in which all collected data are visible over the time in which the system displays the indispensable vital parameters to be monitored. Automatically acquired patient parameters (blood pressure, pulse, etc.) and manually entered parameters are compiled and displayed in different colors.

The manually entered parameters include blood analysis values (ascertained in the laboratory), drugs (more than 120 are stored in the AIS), infusions, results, events, and observations. The lower part of the display window indicates the setting of the respirator and the respiratory gas composition. The proportion of

nitrous oxide and oxygen can be recognized immediately by the color coding (Klocke et al., 1986).

Each parameter can be input into the AIS as a triplet of term-time-amount: The interaction sequence is indicated in figure 12.11 by the numbers 1 through 4. The recording of a therapeutic measure, "medicine fentanyl was administered at 11:30 in a dose of 0.2 mg", is used as an example:

1. The user activates the item fentanyl by pressing the virtual function key Fentanyl.

2. The user enters the time when the drug was administered by moving a *time value slider* (time line) with his or her finger to the required position on the screen. This step can be omitted, in which case the time entered is the current time.

3. The user sets the dose of the drug by moving an analogue slider with his or her finger to the required value. The value set can be read from the dynamically adjusted scale and is also displayed as a small flag in the vital parameter window with the time according to the time line.

4. The user completes the input cycle by pressing the virtual Enter key. If the Fentanyl key is pressed again before the Enter key, the input cycle is abandoned and all the input steps are cancelled (undo function).

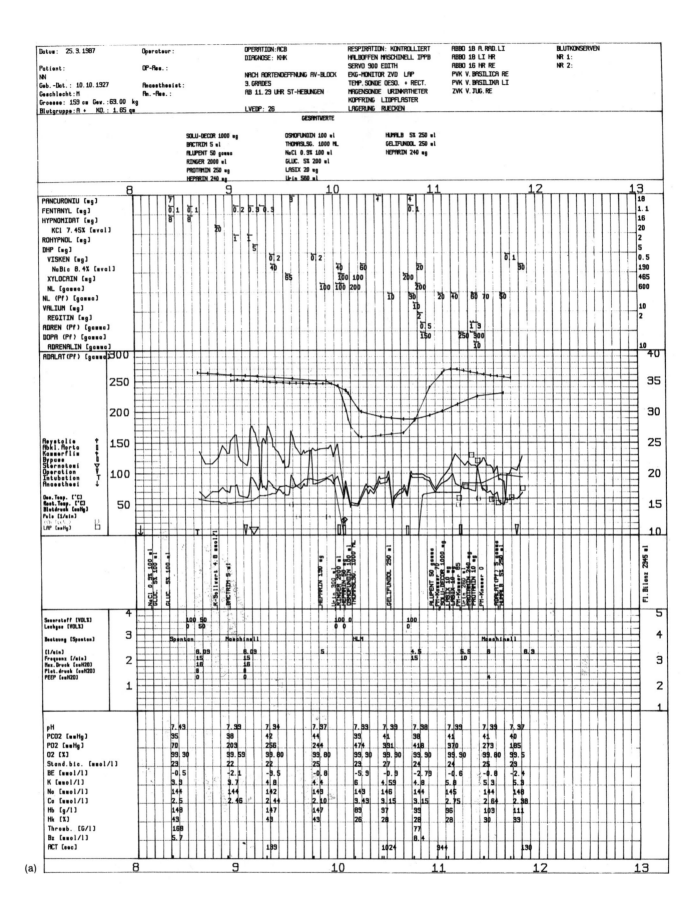

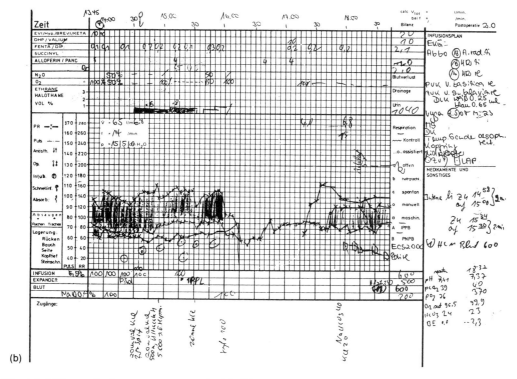

(b)

FIGURE 12.12 (a) AIS anesthesia report compared with (b) the anesthetist's report prepared by hand. (Reprinted from Rau, 1990, by permission.)

Almost all data can be entered in this way. Even measured data, which are normally read into the AIS automatically from the measuring instruments, can be entered in a similar fashion if an instrument develops a failure. It is also possible to enter text such as patient data or comments in this way (Klocke et al., 1986).

The time line as a movable analogue control element that can be adjusted continuously within the vital parameter display can be set not only according to the exact time but also relative to the changes in the vital parameters (process-related). Accordingly, the entry could be, for example, "Fentanyl was administered at 11:20" or "Fentanyl was administered at the last rise in blood pressure but one." Anesthetists prefer the entry to be made relative to the changes as the exact time usually is no longer known when the entries are made subsequently. However, the therapeutic measures are determined by the pattern of changes, and so the pattern of the vital parameter display is known. This is the great advantage of input into the process display by direct manipulation (Rau and Trispel, 1982).

A touch to a key that cannot be activated at the present moment in time is ignored by the system.

Routines to handle operator errors are not required with this concept; syntactically incorrect inputs are excluded by the user guidance system. This provides users (especially those with little technical knowledge) with a feeling of security. To become familiar with the AIS and the interaction, the user does not need to work through operating instructions. Instead, the user can learn quickly the interaction modes by "playing" with the system (i.e., by pressing virtual keys and recognizing the next possible steps by means of the color coding). In laboratory experiments with anesthetists, the participants learned the principles of the interaction within a few minutes (Trispel et al., 1982).

STRUCTURE AND REPRESENTATION OF THE INFORMATION The total information in the AIS acquired during the anesthesia is represented in one level of several equal-priority *display pages* or *working pages* (Klocke et al., 1986). A distributor page contains the terms of all the available pages and each page can be called directly from the distributor page. Access to any page therefore requires a maximum of two input steps.

The distributor page provides an overview of all the information available in the AIS. The items corresponding to the information can be seen on the virtual keys that call the working pages. When a key is pressed to select a required page (e.g., "working page with drug fentanyl") the selected page appears on the screen. Nevertheless, the vital parameter window always remains visible. The graphic and colored design and the interaction mode is the same for all working pages, leading to an optical "pacification" during paging. This structuring of the information proved to be superior to hierarchic menu structures. Loss of orientation or unnecessary paging is therefore avoided. This strategy is considered particularly "transparent" by the users.

It should be pointed out that the AIS allows the individual user to select his or her own individual information structure on the working pages (configuration). In this way, parameters (including drugs) can be grouped together on pages especially for specific types of operation.

PREPARING REPORTS FOR DOCUMENTATION   One important aspect is the generation of a comprehensive and clear report for documentation purposes—in our example, an anesthesia report. The information about the state of the vital parameters, the administration of drugs, blood, and so on, the machine parameters for respiration and other recorded events, and entered laboratory data are recorded in chronologic order, for example, with the aid of a 10-color digital plotter.

Compared to preparation of the normal anesthetist's report prepared by hand, which is a time-consuming task, the automatic report is a considerable improvement (figure 12.12) (Klocke et al., 1986). The report is generated continuously on the plotter during the anesthesia. If the information system breaks down for any reason, the paper report can be taken from the unit and can be completed manually to document the remaining events during the anesthesia.

ERGONOMICS OF DENTAL OPERATING UNITS

Another typical area of interest in ergonomic design is the dental operating chair, in order to reduce physicians' as well as patients' stress. This example demonstrates the advantages of the ergonomic approach in dental medicine. Ergonomic and especially anthropometric studies showed a direct relationship between the

physician's posture during therapeutic treatment and a physician's strees and bodily ailments as a dentist aged (Rohmert, Mainzer, and Zipp, 1988; Rohmert and Bruder, 1991). The range of variations in positions of the physician as well as the positioning of the patient were analyzed (Rohmert, Mainzer, and Zipp, 1988; Rohmert and Bruder, 1991). This cooperation between an ergonomic research department and a specific industrial development department involved all typical steps of an ergonomic system design, from analysis and synthesis up to the design of an industrial prototype of a dental operating unit.

The research program began with interviews of 466 dentists and assistants (Rohmert and Bruder, 1991). Subjective measurement of strain through measurement of electrophysiologic parameters (myoelectric activity) and subjective rating methods had been performed in field tests. In addition to these field studies, laboratory experiments with mock-ups of elements of the dental equipment were built. Anthropometric design of dental workplaces was investigated with conventional somatographic methods (figure 12.13) and the CAD-somatographic human model (Rohmert, 1989).

The 3D positioning of the tooth face to be treated is a determining factor for the dentist's working posture during treatment (figure 12.14). The dentist's work is visually controlled fine sensorimotor work. The operating chair must be able to cover the range of optimal heights at the work site, which can be defined according to Kirchner and Rohmert (1974), for sitting as well as for standing work, taking into account the combination of the body heights of dentist and patient (DIN 33402, 1986). Furthermore, the required leg room for the dentist and the dentist's assistant must be respected during treatment and during movement of the operating chair. The positions and movements of the chair concerning accelerations and vibrations as well as the physiologic range and kinematics of movements must be tolerable for the patient. Especially among trunk, pelvis, and legs, or among head, neck, and shoulder, nonlinear and geometrically nontrivial kinematic relations must be taken into consideration. On the other hand, the time for moving between different positions should be minimized. The user interface must be self-explanatory and reachable without alteration of the whole body posture. In consideration of hygienic problems, a transfer of some interactions to a foot-operated switch could be useful. A multifunctional foot-operated mouse is one current topic of ergonomic

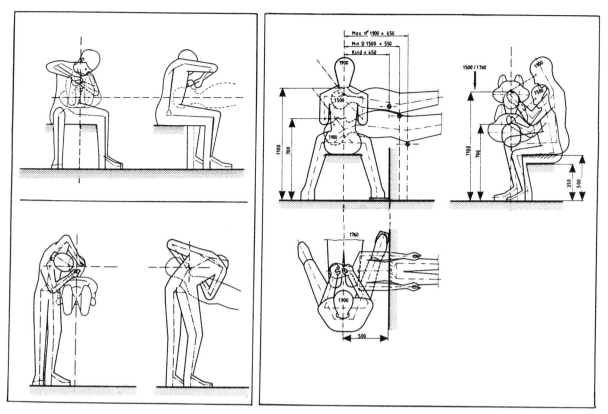

FIGURE 12.13 Example of somatographic studies of dental work. (Reprinted from Rohmert, Mainzer, and Zipp, 1988, by permission.)

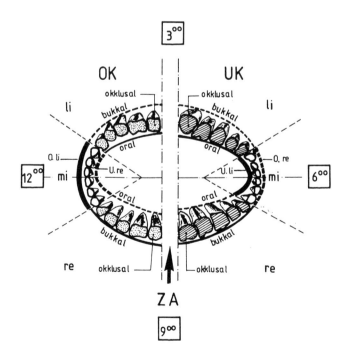

FIGURE 12.14 Orientation of different tooth faces. (Reprinted from Rohmert, Mainzer, and Zipp, 1988, by permission.)

research. Hence, the main points of interest of the ergonomic design of a dental operating chair can be summed up as follows: location and range of adjustability, sufficient leg room and adequate accessibility to the patient, position and design of control elements, and design of the backrest and head support (Rohmert and Bruder, 1991).

The process of syntheses and design was supported by computer-aided design (CAD) and computer network–based model simulations for the rapid prototyping of an anthropometric workplace design and graphic user interfaces with the connected functionalities, dynamics, and kinematics. Furthermore, this simulation environment was used for testing a new computer-based

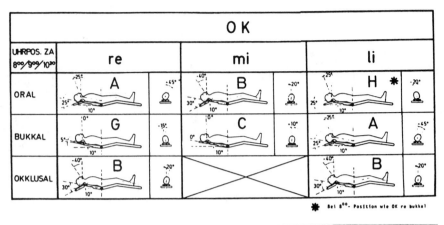

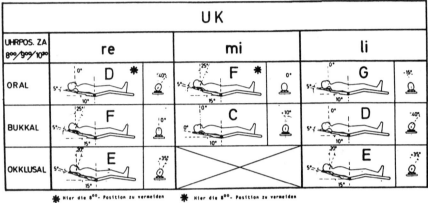

FIGURE 12.15 Basic set of positions of dental operating chair. (Reprinted from Rohmert, Mainzer, and Zipp, 1988, by permission.)

control system for the automatic adjustment of programmable positions of the operating chair.

Depending on the physician's and the patient's stature (which can be fed to the system interactively), a basic set of 16 positions of the dental chair, optimal for the majority of dental treatments (Rohmert and Bruder, 1991), is transformed and adapted to the given combination of patient and physician (figure 12.15). Each of these individually calculated optimal positions is realized automatically when called up by the physician during a dental therapy session (Radermacher, 1988). The dental operating chair just described, together with new instruments and techniques of dental therapy and diagnosis, required high-performance user interfaces between the dentist and the control elements of the dental workplace. These were realized using a touch-sensitive graphic monitor. Finally, this application of principles of an ergonomic system design led to an industrial prototype of a new generation of dental operating chairs using modern technologies to benefit humans.

ERGONOMIC ANALYSIS AND APPROACHES IN MINIMALLY INVASIVE SURGERY

Surgical interventions through rigid endoscopes with small working channels can all be described as *minimally invasive surgery* (Buess et al., 1990). These mostly very complex manipulations require a high degree of dexterity and practice on the part of the physician, an extremely developed ability to "think" in three dimensions, and a high technical standard of instrumentation. Based on observations during endoscopic operations, analyses of work sessions, and discussions with surgeons and medical staff as well as with technical experts, we identified nearly 70 problems arising in different fields of medical engineering (devices, endoscopic suturing, laser and high-frequency technology, optics, materials, etc.). After a specific ergonomic analysis of the work system operating room for minimally invasive surgery, we concluded that many problems arising in the course of endoscopic operations are caused by an insufficient ergonomic system design.

ANALYSIS OF THE WORK SYSTEM OPERATING ROOM FOR MINIMALLY INVASIVE SURGERY   The goal of our investigation was to optimize safety and efficiency of endoscopic operations and to reduce stress and strain for both the surgical team and the patient. To define several starting points for ergonomic optimization, we performed work analysis with observations, questioning, and discussions with doctors and surgical staff, particularly in the field of laparoscopic surgery. We used the selective OWAS method (Stoffert, 1985) to analyze 14 different laparoscopic operations. The evaluation showed the contribution of static and dynamic working postures and holding work, with a ranking of urgency for optimizing anthropometric design. Furthermore, we performed a work-sequence analysis to measure the chronologic and spatial structure of manipulation and observation activities. We used the questionnaire methods of Nitsch (1976) and Shackel, Chidsey, and Shipley (1969) to measure subjective strain of surgeons before, during, and after the surgical procedure. The results can be summed up as follows (Radermacher, von Pichler, and Rau, 1992a,b): There is a high contribution of critical static working postures observable during endoscopic operations (especially postures of trunk, head, arms, and hands). They are caused by a disadvantageous arrangement of the equipment in the operating theater and the patient's positioning, which is either unsuitable or even missing arm and hand supports, and nonergonomic user interfaces (handles) of endosurgical instruments. Particularly, the assisting surgeon is additionally stressed by static holding work (support of endoscopes and cameras, retractors, forceps, etc.) caused by the lack of suitable support devices and intelligent holder systems (a task allocation problem between human and machine).

Three-dimensional orientation and precise coordinated working is carried out without direct view of the operating site. The surgeon must work with a monocular 2D image. By use of a videoendoscopy device, the working postures of head and trunk may be optimized. Furthermore, it is possible for all members of the operating team (human-human interaction) to observe the image of the operating site so that coordinated working

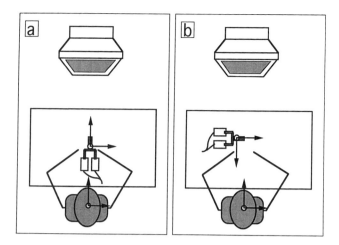

FIGURE 12.16   (a) Zero-degree arrangement; compatibility of vectors of movement of eye-hand coordinate system. (b) Ninety-degree misarrangement; incompatibility of vectors of movement of eye-hand coordinate system.

during the surgical procedure becomes easier. However, monocular 2D images still are flat projections of an image because the display on a video monitor is 2D. The introduction of modern stereo video technologies will provide the possibility to realize a 3D videoendoscopic display.

In both cases (mono or stereo videoendoscopy), a spatial misarrangement of endoscope and video monitor may result in problems of hand-eye coordination caused by incompatibilities of the vectors of movement in the hand-eye coordinate systems (figure 12.16). This can be addressed as the incompatibility of the *manipulating space* and the *visual-perceptual space*. Furthermore, effects of interaction among the operating team members have to be considered. The dexterity of the operator is influenced, for example, by the dexterity and symptoms of fatigue of the assistant guiding and holding the videoendoscope. In addition, it is necessary to take a look at the problems of tactile or "mental" (mental matching of the endoscopic image with environment coordinates or image coordinates) 3D orientation in the operating site. The realization of an artificial fingertip at the distal end of an endoscopic instrument could be one approach for supporting the tactile orientation of the operator (Dario and Bergamasco, 1988). To support the mental correlation between the operating site and, for example, MRI or CT image data, 3D localizers for neurosurgery and base-skull surgery have been developed that could also be useful for laparoscopic or arthroscopic applications.

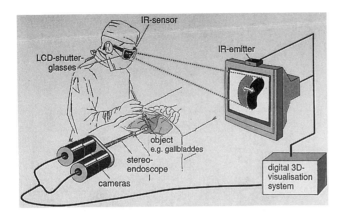

FIGURE 12.17   Principle of 3D videoendoscopy.

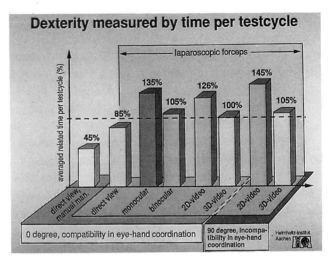

(a)

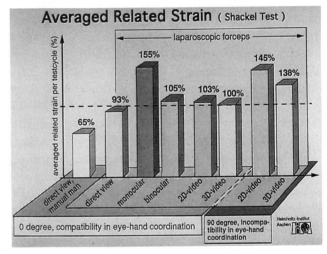

(b)

FIGURE 12.18   (a) Dexterity of endoscopic manipulations measured by time per test cycle. (b) Results of subjective ratings of stress and strain (Shackel test) during endoscopic manipulations. (Reprinted from Radermacher, von Pichler, and Rau, 1992, by permission.)

The dexterity of the operator or the operating team has a strong influence on the security and accuracy of positioning and moving of high-frequency probes, taking and clamping of vessels, manipulation of needles, and preparation with scalpels and scissors. Dexterity is determined by the state of training, by the ability of 3D orientation and hand-eye coordination, by the contribution of unsuitable static working postures and holding work and, finally, by the resulting strain and stress with related symptoms of fatigue.

MODELING, SYNTHESES, AND SIMULATION   The next step of our study was to separate components for a model simulation and an analysis of isolated problem areas and parameters. To investigate the influence of a stereo videoendoscopic display of the operating site on the dexterity and accuracy of the surgical team, we built test equipment on the base of 3D LCD shutter technology (figure 12.17).

We developed an automatic dexterity test procedure especially adapted to the conditions of endoscopic operations. With 20 test subjects (16 students and 4 surgeons), we carried out tests under the varying conditions of (1) direct view (with and without laparoscopic forceps), (2) monocular and (3) binocular endoscopic view, (4) mono and (5) stereo videoendoscopic view, and with variations of the spatial relations between endoscope, test subject, and video monitor. The test subjects had to work with laparoscopic forceps. For the measurement of individual subjective strain during operation, the test subjects were questioned according to the listed subjective rating methods (Nitsch, 1976; Shackel, Chidsey, and Shipley, 1969).

Dexterity and positioning accuracy were measured by the time per test cycle (100 task performances each). Typical results of our investigations are shown in figure 12.18. The dexterity of test subjects working with the monocular optic or mono videoendoscope improved by approximately 60–80%, whereas using a stereoscopic optical system afforded approximately a 25–30% improvement compared to the monoscopic systems. It was proved that the use of a stereo videoendoscopic system leads to a significant increase in dexterity and positioning accuracy during endoscopic manipulations.

In addition, the subjective strain of tested subjects was diminished in this case. Furthermore, it must be noted that the compatibility of vectors of movement in eye-hand coordination is a very important factor influencing the dexterity and strain during laparoscopic operations (Radermacher, von Pichler, and Rau, 1992a). The 3D videotechnology must be improved. The relatively small decrease of subjective strain using the 3D videoendoscopic system compared with the use of a 2D videoendoscope may be explained by the better resolution of the 2D image (zero degree arrangement, compatibility of eye-hand coordination).

To investigate the influence of stereo videoendoscopic viewing on dexterity and spatial orientation, the model simulation of endoscopic manipulations allowed us to study some parameters of coordinated 3D working with endoscopic instruments. It demonstrates a typical procedure with a decoupling of system components for the analysis and synthesis of parameters or components, respectively.

After the adaptation of the stereo videoendoscopy equipment to the requirements of the operating theater, the demonstrated effects must be proved in a real working environment. Together with the results of our approaches in the field of anthropometrically designed operating units, holder systems, and standardized training procedures, the modified working system must be re-analyzed in clinical routine.

Conclusions

Technical progress and social changes can serve as a motive for the design of new workplaces. Although there is a broad spectrum of handbooks and methods describing results of ergonomic research, often even complex workplaces are designed without regard for basic ergonomic demands. The availability of highly complex technical systems demands a high amount of information flow and exchange between the user and the technical systems. Hence, a comprehensive design of the user interface is crucial for the usability of complex technical systems. The introduction of CIS into operating theaters does not tolerate a design approach based on the principle of trial and error. Such systems must be planned with the methodology of conceptual ergonomic design. All three subareas of system ergonomics have to be considered, and the system must be designed as a whole. Cooperation and testing with ex-

perienced human users seems to remain indispensable. The solutions selected in the laboratory must be verified in field tests. The overall aim must be to increase system performance, reliability, and security while reducing stress and strain imposed on the medical staff as well as on the patient. The principal aim and task for ergonomics is to design human labor in order to obtain the maximum benefit from technical progress and full development of human abilities while keeping as its fundamental value advantages for humans and their environment. The principles of ergonomic system design must be applied to the design of modern medical work systems. Specific aspects of ergonomics in medical application must be taken into account. Only this approach will permit the use of complex technical equipment such as CIS to the benefit of both patient and medical staff.

ACKNOWLEDGMENTS We would like to thank Prof. G. Kalff, M.D., Department of Anesthesiology, Prof. G. Jakse, M.D., Department of Urology, and Prof. V. Schumpelick, M.D., Department of Surgery, and their staff at the Aachen University Hospital for their friendly and helpful cooperation.

BIBLIOGRAPHY

BERNOTAT, R., and G. RAU, 1980. Ergonomics in medicine. In *Perspectives in Biomechanics*, H. Reul, D. N. Ghista, and G. Rau, eds. New York: Harwood Academic Publishers, pp. 381–398.

BERNOTAT, R., and G. RAU, 1991. Man-machine interaction. In *Proceedings of the First European Conference on Biomedical Engineering*, February 17–20, Nice, France.

BOFF, K. R., L. KAUFMANN, and J. P. THOMAS, eds., 1986. *Handbook of Perception and Human Performance*, Vol. 1. New York: Wiley.

BUESS, G., et al., 1990. Endoskopie. Köln: Deutscher Ärzte-Verlag.

CARD, S., T. P. MORAN, and A. NEWELL, 1983. *The Psychology of Human-Computer Interaction*. Hillsdale, N.J.: Erlbaum.

VAN COTT, H. P., and R. G. KINKADE, 1963. *Human Engineering Guide to Equipment Design*. New York: McGraw-Hill.

DARIO, P., and M. BERGAMASCO, 1988. An advanced robot system for automated diagnostic tasks through palpation. *IEEE Trans. Biomed. Eng.* 35(2).

DIN 33402, 1986. *Körpermasse des Menschen*. Berlin: Beuth Verlag.

DIN 66234, 1988. *Bildschirmarbeitsplätze*. Berlin: Beuth-Verlag.

DUTTON, J. M., and W. H. STARBUCK, 1971. *Computer Simulation of Human Behaviour*. New York: Wiley.

GULICK, W. L., 1976. *Human Stereopsis, A Psychophysical Analysis*. Oxford: Oxford University Press.

HANCOCK, P. A., and MESHKATI, eds., 1988. *Human Mental Workload* Amsterdam: Elsevier.

IntelliCorp., 1984. The Knowledge Engineering Environment (computer program). Mountain View, Calif.: IntelliCorp.

JOHANNSEN, G., and J. G. RIJNSDORP, eds., 1983. *Analysis, Design and Evaluation of Man-Machine Systems.* Oxford: Pergamon.

KASTER, J., 1986. The artificial operator in variable system environments—an approach to analyze and evaluate man-machine interfaces. In *Proceedings of the Second IAO Workshop on Cognitive Modelling and HCI,* July, Stuttgart.

KIRCHER, J. H., and W. ROHMERT, 1974. *Ergonomische Leitregeln zur menschlichen Arbeitsgestaltung.* München: Hanser.

KLOCKE, H., S. TRISPEL, G. RAU, U. HATZKY, and D. DAUB, 1986. An anaesthesia information system for monitoring and record keeping during surgical anaesthesia. *J. Clin. Monitoring* 4:256–261.

KNÄUPER, A., and K.-F. KRAISS, 1986. An interactive graphic system for the design and evaluation of human-machine interfaces. In *Human Decision Making and Manual Control,* H.-P. Willumeit, ed. Amsterdam: Elsevier (North Holland), pp. 125–134.

KRAISS, K.-F., 1986. Rechnergestützte Methoden zum Entwurf und zur Bewertung von Mensch-Maschine Schnittstellen. In *Arbeitsorganisation und Neue Technologien,* R. Hackstein, F.-J. Heeg, and F. von Below, eds. Berlin: Springer, pp. 435–457.

LANE, N. E., M. I. STRIEB, F. A. GLENN, and R. Y. WHERRY, 1980. The human operator simulator: An overview. In *Proceedings of the Conference on Manned Systems Design—New Methods and Equipment,* Freiburg, September 22–25, pp. 1–39.

LANGEN, M., B. THULL, Th. SCHECKE, G. RAU, and G. KALFF, 1989. Prototyping methods and tools for the human interface design of a knowledge-based system. In *Designing and Using Human Computer Interfaces and Knowledge-Based Systems,* G. Salvendy and M. J. Smith, eds. Amsterdam: Elsevier, pp. 861–868.

LAURIG, W., 1980. *Grundzüge der Ergonomie.* Berlin: Beuth-Verlag.

MCCORMICK, E. J., 1976. *Human Factors in Engineering and Design.* New York: McGraw-Hill.

MCEWEN, J. A., C. R. BUSSANI, G. F. AUCHINLECK, and M. J. BREAULT, 1989. Development and initial clinical evaluation of pre-robotic and robotic surgical retraction systems. In *Proceedings of the Eleventh Annual International Conference of IEEE EMBS,* pp. 881–882.

MCMILLAN C. R. et al., eds., 1989. *Application of Human Performance Models to System Design.* New York: Plenum.

MEISTER, D., 1986. *Human Factors Testing and Evaluation.* New York: Wiley.

MILSUM, J. H., 1966. *Biological control systems analysis* (Electronic Sciences Series). New York: McGraw-Hill.

MURREL, K. F. H., 1969. *Ergonomics.* London: Chapman and Hall.

MUTER, P., and C. MAYSON, 1986. The role of graphics in item selection from menus. *Behav. Inform. Tech.* 5:89–95.

NAS VAN, F. L., 1986. Space, colour and typography on visual terminals. *Behav. Inform. Tech.* 5(2):99–118.

NEUMANN, J., and K. P. TIMPE, 1976. *Psychologische Arbeitsgestaltung.* Berlin: VEB-Verlag der Wissenschaften.

NITSCH, J. R., 1976. Die Eigenzustandsskala—Ein Verfahren zur hierarchisch-mehrdimensionalen Befindlichkeitsskalierung. In *Beanspruchung im Sport,* J. R. Nitsch, and I. Udris, eds. Bad Homburg: Limbert, pp. 81–102.

RADERMACHER, K., 1988. Die mathematische Beschreibung der Kinematik eines dentalen Behandlungsstuhles. Internal publication of the Institute for Human Factors, Darmstadt University of Technology.

RADERMACHER, K., C. VON PICHLER, and G. RAU, 1992a. Aspects of ergonomics in minimally invasive surgery—analysis and approaches. In *Proceedings of the Fourteenth Annual International Conference of the IEEE Engineering in Medicine and Biology Society,* October 29–November 1.

RADERMACHER, K., C. VON PICHLER, and G. RAU, 1992b. Aspekte der Minimal Invasiven Chirurgie—Analyse und Ansätze im Bereich der Ergonomie. In *Proceedings of the Twenty-Sixth Annual Conference of the German Society for Biomedical Engineering.* Hannover, Germany, pp. 210–211.

RAU, G., 1979. Ergonomische Überlegungen bei der Gestaltung komplexer medizinischer Instrumentierung unter Einsatz von Mikroprozessoren. *Biomed. Technik* 24:10–15.

RAU, G., 1990. *Ergonomics and Aspects of Its Applications in Medicine.* Knittlingen: R. Wolf GmbH.

RAU, G., and S. TRISPEL, 1982. Ergonomic design aspects in interaction between man and technical systems in medicine. *Med. Progr. Technol.* 9:153–159.

RICHMOND, B., 1985. A User's Guide to STELLA. Lyme, N. H.: High Performance Systems, Inc.

ROEBUCK, J. A., K. H. KROEMER, and W. G. THOMSON, 1975. *Engineering Anthropometry Methods.* New York: Wiley.

ROHMERT, W., 1989. *Arbeitswissenschaftliche Methodensammlung.* Darmstadt: Institute for Human Factors, Darmstadt University of Technology.

ROHMERT, W., and R. BRUDER, 1991. Ergonomic research and work design for the dentist. In *Ergonomics, Health and Safety—Perspectives for the Nineties,* W. T. Singleton and J. Dirks, eds. Leuven University Press, pp. 121–142.

ROHMERT, W., J. MAINZER, and P. ZIPP, 1988. *Der Zahnarzt im Blickfeld der Ergonomie.* Köln: Deutscher Ärzte-Verlag.

ROHMERT, W., J. RUTENFRANZ, et al., 1983. *Praktische Arbeitsphysiologie.* Stuttgart: Thieme Verlag.

SALVENDY, G., 1987. *Handbook of Human Factors.* New York: Wiley.

SCHMIDTKE, H., ed. 1981. *Ergonomie.* München: Hanser Verlag.

SEIFERT, D. J., and B. DÖRING, 1981. SAINT—ein Verfahren zur Modellierung, Simulation und Analyse von Mensch-Maschine-Systemen. *Angew. Systemanalyse* 2:127–135.

SHACKEL, B., K. D. CHIDSEY, and P. SHIPLEY, 1969. Assessment of chair comfort. In *Sitting Postures,* E. Grandjean, ed. London: Taylor and Francis.

SHERIDAN, T. B., and W. R. FERRELL, 1974. *Man-Machine Systems. Information, Control and Decision Models of Human Performance.* Cambridge, Mass.: MIT Press.

SHNEIDERMAN, B., 1982. The future of interactive systems and the emergence of direct manipulation. *Behav. Inform. Tech.* 3:237–256.

STOFFERT, G., 1985. Analyse und Einstufung von Körperhaltungen bei der Arbeit nach der OWAS-Methode. Zeitschrift fur Arbeitswissenschaft 1:31–38.

TRISPEL, S., H. KLOCKE, K. GÜNTHER, and G. RAU, 1982. Operation simulation for the evaluation and improvement of a medical information system. In *Proceedings of the Symposium on Analysis, Design and Evaluation of Man-Machine Systems*, Baden-Baden, pp. 233–239.

WICKENS, C., 1984. *Engineering Psychology and Human Performance*. Columbus, Ohio Charles E. Murrel.

13 Human Factors in Telesurgery

THOMAS B. SHERIDAN

Definitions

TELESURGERY IS a natural extension of developments in teleoperation, defined as "the extension of human inspection and manipulation capability to remote or otherwise inaccessible locations." A teleoperator is a device that has sensors (such as video) and actuators (hands for grasping and arms for positioning and conveying forces to the hands, plus some means of mobility), which are combined with a means of communicating information to and from the human operator (figure 13.1). For telesurgery or other forms of telediagnosis, the actuators usually are electric motors rather than hydraulic or pneumatic pistons, because the latter pose safety hazards (power that can be released very quickly) that electric motor-drive systems do not pose, and they can leak and be messy. A manual knife, clamp, or similar instrument used under direct vision is not normally called a *teleoperator*, although strictly it does fit the formal definition.

A teleoperator that has also a computer that can process the sensory information locally and determine some simple control actions, under supervision from the human operator, is called a *telerobot*. (A *robot*, strictly defined, is a completely autonomous system; no human operator is needed except to install some initial program. Robots for surgery are not now conceivable.)

This chapter addresses the problems of teleoperation and telerobotics in surgery and telediagnosis from the perspective of the human factors or human-machine systems.

Endoscopy, laparoscopy, and other telescopic surgical procedures

Primitive forms of telesurgery are now being performed routinely and successfully. Most utilize some form of telescopy, wherein either a rigid or a flexible fiberoptic bundle is inserted into a natural opening (e.g., gastrointestinal tract) or entered through a sealed cannula that is inserted by piercing with a trocar. Typically, air

is introduced under slight pressure to push back surrounding tissue and create a space. Laparoscopy (for gallbladder removal), colonoscopy (for inspection of the colon and biopsy or removal of polyps), and arthroscopy (to inspect trauma to knee and other joints and removal of cartilage, etc.) are common forms of telescopy. The proved advantage of all these forms of telescopic surgery is that minimal cutting and opening of the body, and therefore minimal exposure to bacteria, is required. Hospital stays are reduced from many days to several hours, resulting in very large cost savings.

Many enhancements of telescopic surgery are promising. Producers of fiberoptic bundles are continuing to make endoscopes and laparoscopes smaller and with higher resolution. Stereo imaging is being developed (Virtual Reality, Inc., Pleasantville, N.Y.). Many developments have to do with improving the capability to manipulate the end of the scope more freely. More flexible end-point manipulation is desirable for three reasons: (1) need to steer the flexible endoscope as it is being inserted so as to minimize damage to tissue; (2) need to control the point and orientation of view more accurately for better inspection; and (3) need for greater capability to perform surgical tasks through the tubes in the endoscope or laparoscope for biopsy and other procedures.

Microsurgery under direct viewing

Some telesurgical procedures are not performed through an endoscope inserted into a body cavity or through a pierced opening into the body. Rather, the surgeon is remote (*tele*) in the sense that the surgical task is on a very small scale. Retinal surgery is an example. In this case, visual inspection is enlarged by means of optics or through a miniaturized charge-coupled devices (CCD) camera and a video display. The surgeon's hand and finger movements for such surgery must be scaled down kinematically in both displacement and force (Green, 1993).

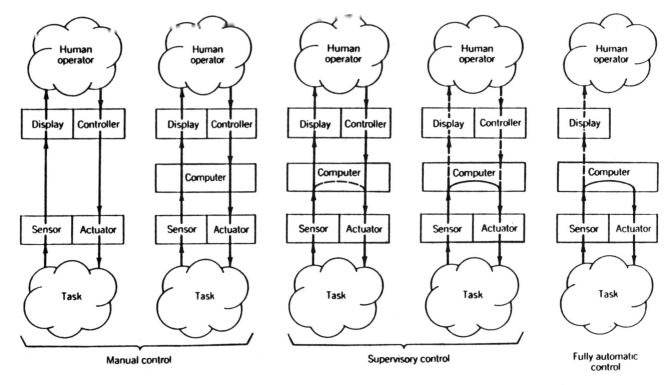

FIGURE 13.1   The spectrum of control modes. (Reprinted from Sheridan, 1992a, by permission.)

Consultation from a distance

In the first two categories of telesurgery, the surgeon is located spatially with the patient, as close as the endoscope or the apparatus for visual magnification and manipulation minification will allow. This third category of telesurgery, often called *telemedicine*, is that in which the patient is unavoidably separated by many miles from the surgeon, and the telecommunication is primarily for visual inspection of the patient and consultation with the paramedic or physician's assistant who is with the patient. Such displacement between surgeon and patient would occur because there is no time for the patient to travel to the surgeon or vice versa (e.g., in an emergency). This is especially true in military operations or civil disasters.

In telemedicine, at least in the near future, the surgeon would likely be viewing the patient over a video link and talking over an audio link. Possibly, the patient is viewing the surgeon as well. The surgeon may be reading x-rays and pointing to certain locations on the patient's body with a laser pointer. In a few years, however, in any endoscopic, laparoscopic, or other

telescopic surgery or microsurgery where a video image is the primary display, the motor actions of the surgeon will be transformed into forces and motions on an endoscope or on surgical instruments directly: That is, the distance per se need not preclude accomplishing the surgical task.

The remainder of this chapter provides more detail about the problems of visual inspection and of surgical manipulation and cutting, whether or not by telescopy and whether or not the surgeon is close to the patient or half a continent away. If the patient and surgeon are linked by electronic means, especially over a communication satellite, there is likely to be a significant time delay in the control loop, which poses very special problems that will be discussed later.

Televisual inspection

DEPTH PERCEPTION

Achieving satisfactory depth perception is one of the most difficult problems of telesurgery or, indeed, teleoperation of any kind. One conventionally thinks of stereo imaging as the way to achieve depth perception. In fact in ordinary daily living, stereo is only one of several cues we use to give a sense of depth. Indeed, binocular stereo is helpful only at relatively short distances, say several feet. Another cue is parallax, the ability to move our heads from side to side, achieve a different image with each different viewing position, and correlate the images with how we moved. A third cue is shadows cast by a light source (especially if the light source can be moved under the observer's control. A fourth cue is "size constancy," knowing the relative absolute sizes of viewed objects, so that relative depth can be judged from the apparent sizes calibrated to the known sizes.

Stereo television is relatively well developed and has been applied quite successfully to telemanipulation in recent years. Parallel images can be brought independently from two video cameras to two video displays to the two eyes (usually miniature cameras and displays). Alternatively, images from two cameras can be frame-buffered and sampled alternately (at least 30 Hz) by one communication channel and displayed on a single screen. A human observer, wearing liquid crystal spectacles that are alternately changed from transparent to opaque electronically, in synchrony with the sampling the two images, sees a stereo picture. The older techniques of red and green color filters or orthogonal polarization can also be employed to separate the stereo images at the eyes.

Color and other bandwidth considerations

There are three primary ways in which signal bits per second are converted to visual images: frames (width pixels times height pixels = pixels per frame), frame rate (frames per second), and bits of gray scale (bits per pixel). It can be seen that the product is bits per second. There are, of course, others consumers of bandwidth. Each pixel can have three color components, so that instead of gray scale it can be the level (in bits) of intensity of each CRT gun.

Experiments by Ranadive (1979) showed that in simple manipulation tasks, as frame rate, resolution, and gray scale were increased with the levels of the other two variables held constant, performance (measured in terms of both time and accuracy) increased but then leveled off with further increases: That is, there was a definite saturation effect. Further, it was shown that within a certain range of the three vari-

ables, performance was a direct function of bits per second, independent of the particular combination of frame rate, resolution, and gray scale.

Experiments by Murphy et al. (1974) showed that in remote diagnosis of skin disease by both specialists and nonspecialists over a television channel, color made surprisingly little difference compared with resolution.

Superposed diagrams and instructions

Superposition of computer-based text and graphics on television images enables an actual video image of an operation to be combined (overlaid) with instructional material (e.g., a step-by-step checklist), or an image of an outline of a given organ at a previous observation (e.g., to compare size or shape change over time), or a reference shape, or a scale used for measurement.

The new technology also enables the surgeons or other examining physicians who are remote from the patient to coordinate their attention with one another and possibly even with a nurse or paramedic who is with the patient. This can be done, for example, by each using a different and separately identified cursor overlayed on the common video image to "point" to different locations on the body or to make drawings on the same). Alternatively, by means of a remotely controlled pan and tilt device, the physician can control the position of a laser pointer such as is commonly used by speakers in slide presentations.

Visual telepresence

Telepresence means "sensing that one is present at a location other than where one actually is." Such a sensation can be brought about in a number of ways, but the head-mounted video display (HMD) is what has brought on most of the current excitement about telepresence. When an HMD is instrumented so that head position drives a remote video camera into a corresponding position and orientation, movements of the head produce visual images that correspond to what one would see if one were positioned at the location of the camera. Current HMD technology is limited primarily with respect to size and weight of the device (producing encumbrance and fatigue), picture resolution (number of pixels), stereopsis (crude stereo systems do exist), and the time lag and smoothness of the servomechanism that drives the remote camera to follow head movements (the environment does not move

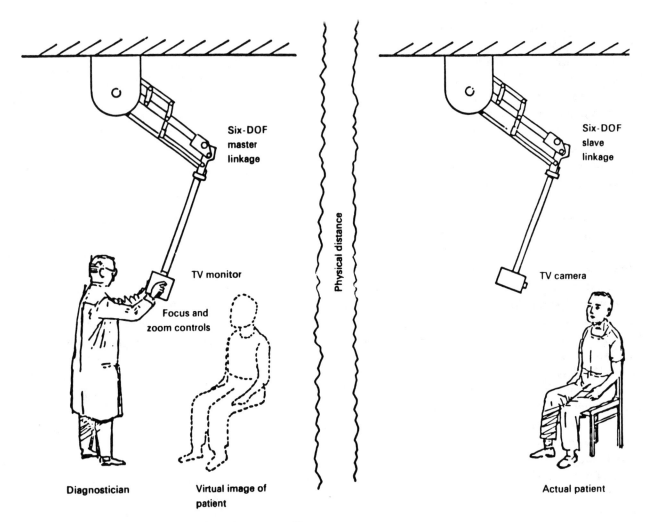

FIGURE 13.2 Medical telediagnosis using telepresence. (Reprinted from Sheridan, 1992a, by permission.)

instantaneously when one moves one's head and is jerky). Other chapters of this book discuss HMDs in more detail.

An alternative mode, originally developed by Goertz (1965) in the mid-1960s and tried by the author in 1969 (*New York Times*, Dec. 14) is to have a video monitor mounted on a counterbalanced arm having 6 degrees of freedom (dof) but flexible enough to be positioned at any angle and place within a work space. This gets the display off the head but requires overt action by the operator to move the display (which can, in this case, be thought of as a kind of "magical picture frame" for the remote environment). Figure 13.2 illustrates medical telediagnosis through telepresence (Sheridan, 1992a).

TELECOMMUNICATION BETWEEN PEOPLE

In most foreseeable situations, some other trained person would be with the patient undergoing telediagnosis or telesurgery. That person (as well as the patient himself or herself if sufficiently able) must communicate with the remote physician. Naturally, ordinary audio methods go a long way for voice communication. Vocal messages, however, must be augmented by something visual, some means of pointing to locations on the patient's body. This may be done in two ways: A first is to have the physician remotely control (in pan and tilt) a low-power laser pointer such as is used in slide presentations. The nurse or paramedic can use his or her finger. A second means is for both the remote physician and the nurse or paramedic to have his or her own cursors that each can move by means of a mouse or trackball.

PATIENT REACTIONS

There have been few studies of how patients react to telediagnosis or telesurgery. Telediagnostic experiments conducted 20 years ago between a medical clinic at Boston's Logan Airport and several of the major downtown hospitals revealed that patients largely accepted the system. A psychiatrist who interviewed patients there over the closed-circuit video system commented to the author that patients actually preferred the video to face-to-face communication. The video gave patients a sense of being "off in a different world" with the psychiatrist.

Telemanipulating

HISTORY AND SAFETY OF MASTER-SLAVE SYSTEMS

Electric master-slave manipulation systems having 6 dof (plus at least 1 dof for a gripper) date back to Goertz and Thompson (1954) at the Argonne National Laboratory. The first hydraulic servomanipulators were developed by Mosher and Wendel (1960) 6 years later. Although the most dexterous current system is that of Jacobsen et al. (1989), the hydraulic servomanipulator is not advisable for telediagnosis or surgery because hydraulic servo devices tend to be less safe. Errors in electric signals or mechanical valving can cause rapid unwanted movements of the slave. In addition, hydraulic oil can leak. Electric motors usually are small and geared, inherently limiting the speed and power of erratic excursions. Thus, there is little danger unless motors are very large as these would be used in the direct-drive mode, without gears. Electric control signals are low-power and can be insulated reliably.

KINEMATIC AND DYNAMIC TRANSFORMATIONS OF SURGEON'S HAND MOVEMENTS

It is not necessary that all telediagnosis or telesurgery be done with master-slave systems (a *master-slave system* means, essentially, that the position of the slave corresponds to the position of the master). For certain applications, a rate-control joystick (which means that the position of the slave corresponds to the time integral of the position of the master) may be more convenient

and positioning may be more accurate. This may be true especially where very fine positioning is desirable. In this case, it may be useful to have two joysticks with three axis each (as is done on the Space Shuttle to drive the long telemanipulator) rather than a single six-axis joystick. The latter is available, but it is difficult, when concentrating on moving one or two axes, not to inadvertently cause movement in some other axis. Alternatively, the movements of the physician's hand may be scaled down in a kinematic sense so that, for example, for 50 mm of hand movement, the slave moves only 2 mm.

FORCE FEEDBACK

Force feedback means that the surgeon or other human operator of a teleoperator system feels in his a her own tendons and muscles the forces that are being applied to the patient. This occurs naturally if the surgeon is using an instrument in a direct mechanical way, whether it is rigid or flexible. However, if the teleoperator is not direct (an artificial sensor is measuring the surgeon's hand position or force), and this is communicated to an artificial motor that applies the actual force, then there must be other means provided in order that the forces are felt on the surgeon's hand. The force applied to the patient must be measured (by the current generated in the motor, by strain gauges, or by some other means) and motors provided at the master end driven in proportion to this signal to create a force back on the surgeon's hand. This force can be scaled up to greater than one (to make the hand more sensitive than it normally would be) or down (to make it possible to exert forces greater than is normally possible) (Raju, Verghese, and Sheridan, 1989).

Although force feedback was built into even the early master-slave prototypes of Argonne National Laboratory, high-resolution force feedback still is not easy to implement. This is because electric motors, if they respond quickly (high bandwidth) can exert only low levels of force, and vice versa. Gearing does not help, as it adds static friction. Direct-drive teleoperators usually are used where good "feel" is desired. To convey well the sensation of touching a hard object—because the force level must increase from zero to a palpable force in almost zero time—requires a system that is essentially impossible with today's technology. Approaching the required level of bandwidth by use of high gain risks control-loop instability. In fact, *contact instability* (a chattering that occurs when a rigid object suddenly is contacted) is a common phenomenon with a master-slave teleoperator system.

One way around this problem is to display contact or force information to the ears or eyes rather than to the muscles (Massimino and Sheridan, 1992). This avoids instability, but such sensory substitution poses its own problems of "not seeming natural."

TOUCH FEEDBACK

The layperson does not always differentiate resolved force feedback (the geometric resultant of all the forces applied at a point) from touch but, in fact the two are very different and should be distinguished in considering teleoperation. Whereas in the human body Golgi and other receptors in the tendons and muscles mediate resolved force feedback, those in the skin (Meissner, Merkel, Pacinian, and Ruffini sensors) mediate touch. Resolved force magnitude sensitivity exhibits a much smaller differential threshold operating over a wider force range than in touch, whereas touch exhibits a differential sensitivity in the plane of the skin surface down to roughly 1 mm.

There are many occasions in performing remote manipulation when touch would be useful (e.g., discriminating edges, textures, slippage of grasped object), but touch has not been highly developed or much used in remote handling. Part of the problem is that good touch sensors are only recently available (arrays of electric resistive and capacitive and fiberoptic elements are now commercially marketed), but there is no acceptable display that presents force pattern information to the skin. The latter remains a very difficult engineering problem, for much the same reason as high-bandwidth force sensing remains difficult (see later). Display of touch (i.e., spatial-temporal-magnitude patterns of force) to the eyes is relatively easy by means of computer graphics, and currently this seems the only viable option (Ellis, 1991).

TIME-DELAY PROBLEMS WITH LONG-DISTANCE TELESURGERY

Long-distance communication in the past has been noisy, but today's satellite and fiberoptic communication systems have permitted much higher bandwidths than before. One remaining problem is that of transmission time delay, owing to the combination of speed of light (sometimes to communicate up to satellites and back) and time required to push bits through shift registers in electronics at several relay points in the round-trip communication circuit. Experience with the National Aeronautics and Space Administration's TEDRIS system has evidenced delays of several seconds, just for communicating round-trip between one point on Earth to another point on Earth.

Ferrell (1965) showed that to avoid instability when the delay is longer than roughly 0.5 sec, one must adopt a move-and-wait strategy (making an open loop move as far as one deems "safe," then stopping and waiting for the visual feedback to "catch up"). In essence, the task completion time increases over the no-delay case by the number of open-loop moves (the more complex the task, the more moves) times the time delay. Task-time increases may be ameliorated through use of a predictor display, in which the human control commands are sent to a computer-graphic model of the manipulation task, and the human sees the results instantaneously (Noyes and Sheridan, 1984; Hashimoto, Sheridan, and Noyes, 1986).

Supervisory control in telesurgery

Supervisory control refers to a human communicating instructions to a computer about goals, obstacles, and other constraints and procedures, and the computer executing the instructions automatically through machine sensors and effectors (see figure 13.1). The human supervisor must plan the desired actions and instructions, which generally involves developing a good reference model of the process to be controlled or the action to be taken, as well as the criteria (objective function) or trade-off between the (usually multiple) attributes of goodness or badness (Park, 1991). The supervisor then must decide what intention to communicate to the computer and how to code the instructions and must monitor the automatic execution to ensure that it goes well. In the event of any failure, he or she must intervene to make minor adjustments, take over to effect direct manual control, or stop the operation completely. Finally, the human supervisor must learn from experience so as to improve future operations. Examples of supervisory control are piloting an aircraft with an autopilot, doing word processing on a personal computer, and operating a washing machine or an elevator. See Sheridan (1992a,b) for a full discussion.

In the context of telesurgery and medical telediagnosis, supervisory control might offer advantages over more conventional teleoperation if:

1. Greater precision than the physician could provide is required for positioning and applying force to an instrument relative to the patient.

2. Some preprogrammable timing or sequencing is required and is more complex than what the physician could reliably remember.

3. Some operation must be executed consistently for a longer time than the physician could sustain attention.

4. The transmission time delay is greater than 0.5 sec (see last section). Because, with supervisory control, the continuous loop closure is local to the patient, there is no instability.

In such cases, the computer and telerobotic manipulator or instrument must be programmed and tested, and the supervisory interface must also be tested to ensure that it is working properly.

In some sense, conventional CT and MRI scans are specialized forms of supervisory control. Experiments with supervisory control are currently being conducted by orthopaedic surgeons to machine cavities in bones for fitting of artificial sockets and by neurosurgeons for precisely matching telerobotic incisions to previously made images of defective tissue.

REFERENCES

ELLIS, S. R., ed., 1991. *Pictorial Communication in Virtual and Real Environments.* New York: Taylor and Francis.

FERRELL, W. R., 1965. Remote manipulation with transmission delay. *IEEE Trans. Hum. Factors Electr.* HFE-6(1).

GOERTZ, R. C., 1965. An experimental head-controlled television system to provide viewing for a manipulator operator. In *Proceedings of the Thirteenth RSTD Conference*, p. 57.

GOERTZ, R. C., and R. C. THOMPSON, 1954. Electronically controlled manipulator. *Nucleonics* pp. 46–47.

GREEN, P., 1993. Personal communication, Stanford Research Institute, Menlo Park, Calif.

HASHIMOTO, T., T. B. SHERIDAN, and M. V. NOYES, 1986. Effects of predicted information in teleoperation through a time delay. *Jpn. J. Ergonomics* 22(2).

JACOBSEN, S. C., E. K. IVERSEN, C. C. DAVIS, D. M. POTTER, and T. W. MCLAIN, 1989. Design of a multiple degree-of-freedom, force-reflective hand master/slave with a high mobility wrist. In *Proceedings of ANS/IEEE/SMC Third Topical Meeting on Robotics and Remote Systems*, March 13–16, Charleston, SC.

MASSIMINO, M., and T. B. SHERIDAN, 1992. Sensory substitution for force feedback in teleoperation. In *Proceedings of the Fifth IFAC Symposium on Analysis, Design and Evaluation of Man-Machine Systems*, June 9–11, The Hague. Netherlands.

MOSHER, R. S., and B. WENDEL, 1960. Force reflecting electro-hydraulic servo-manipulator. *Electro-Technology* 66: 138.

MURPHY, R. L. H., T. B. FITZPATRICK, H. A. HAYNES, K. T. BIRD, and T. B. SHERIDAN, 1974. Accuracy of dermatological diagnosis by television. *Arch. Dermatol.* 105:833–835.

NOYES, M. V., and T. B. SHERIDAN, 1984. A novel predictor for telemanipulation through a time delay. In *Proceedings of Annual Conference on Manual Control*, Moffett Field, Calif., NASA Ames Research Center.

PARK, J. H., 1991. Supervisory control of robot manipulators for gross motions. Doctoral thesis, Massachusetts Institute of Technology, Cambridge.

RAJU, G. J., G. VERGHESE, and T. B. SHERIDAN, 1989. Design issues in 2-port network models of bilateral remote manipulation. In *Proceedings of IEEE International Conference on Robotics and Automation*, Scottsdale, Ariz., May 14–19, pp. 1316–1321.

RANADIVE, V., 1979. Video resolution, frame-rate, and gray scale tradeoffs under limited bandwidth for undersea teleoperation. Masters thesis, Massachusetts Institute of Technology, Cambridge.

SHERIDAN, T. B., 1992a. *Telerobotics, Automation, and Human Supervisory Control.* Cambridge, Mass.: MIT Press.

SHERIDAN, T. B., 1992b. Musings on telepresence and virtual presence. *Presence: Teleoperators and Virtual Environments* 1(1):120–127.

14 Virtual Reality and Surgery

JOSEPH M. ROSEN, ANN LASKO-HARVILL, AND
RICHARD SATAVA

Introduction to virtual reality systems

VIRTUAL REALITY allows a user to enter a 3D environment generated by computers and to actively move and interact as if he or she were there. This experience of "there-ness" affords a powerful and highly intuitive modality for interacting with data of all kinds, and particularly with complex sets of visual, spatial, and quantitative information. These computer-generated displays replace sight, sound, and touch from the physical world. This kind of simulation is different from the simulation seen in movies (in which the viewer is passive) and in video games (in which the viewer is active but the environment is not realistic). Elements in a virtual world look realistic; they change their characteristics and have real-world unpredictability.

Virtual reality has progressed from the first demonstration of a virtual cube more than two decades ago by Sutherland (1965) to the present demonstrations of complex realistic interactive virtual worlds. Virtual reality has become important in the fields of education, communication, the military, entertainment, and medicine. This chapter is concerned with the components of a virtual reality system and its applications to surgery.

The basic components of a virtual reality system are a computer, computer software, a head mounted display, and input devices such as a whole-hand measuring device (figure 14.1). With these components, the 3D world of virtual reality is created by immersing the user's senses—visual, auditory, and manual—in the simulated world. The software provides an operating system and the objects that make up the surgical world, including the operating room, the tools and, most importantly, the virtual patient.

COMPUTER

The simulated world is animated in real time, which means that frames of the projected image move fast enough so the eye cannot detect a flicker (30 frames/sec). This animation is created by high-end graphic workstations, such as the Silicon Graphics Iris computers (Mountain View, Calif.). Everything that is rendered in sound or picture is recalculated many times per second based on the unpredictable actions of the user. This is far different from movie special effects sequences, which may take hours or days to render but last only seconds on the screen. Real-time rendering places tight constraints on the simulation in terms of the complexity of the models. As the model becomes more complex, more computer power is needed to calculate the simulation and display the results.

SOFTWARE

A number of software tasks must be performed in concert to create a smooth simulation. First, a physical model of the initial conditions of the simulation must be created. This includes the description of the structure and appearance of the virtual world, as well as the rules by which it behaves. For example, principles of Newtonian physics, such as gravity, may or may not be modeled in a given virtual environment, depending on its intended use. Second, during *run time*, when a user is active within the virtual environment, these initial conditions will be continuously modified based on those rules and on the user's actions. The system must constantly monitor the input devices that signal the user's actions and combine that information with internally derived data to form and reform the everchanging model of the world. Finally, many times per second the system produces the appropriate feedback to the user —an entirely recomputed set of graphics, synthesized sound, and perhaps tactile or force feedback—to reflect the new state of the virtual world.

APPLICATION AND THE PLATFORM   The platform software creates dynamic behavior of the virtual environment by coordinating user inputs, computer simulations, and renderings. An example of a software

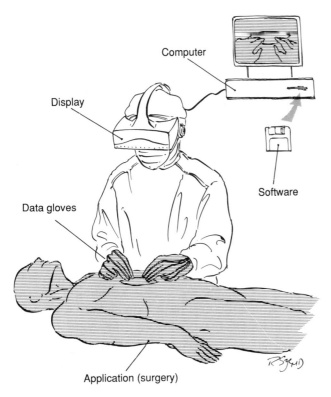

Computer

Display

Data gloves

Software

Application (surgery)

FIGURE 14.1 Virtual reality system showing its components. Viewer: head-mounted display (EyePhones). Interface: whole-hand controller (DataGloves). Application: virtual cadaver (software). Computer: image engine. Software provides an operating platform and specific applications.

platform for a virtual reality system is BodyElectric by VPL Research (Palo Alto, Calif.). BodyElectric, a graphic data flow language, is the portal through which the real world flows into the virtual world. It directs the computer to acquire the data streaming in from the user interface devices and uses this information to drive the behavior of objects in the simulation. Users can employ BodyElectric interactively to create specific applications, such as the one for surgical simulation.

GEOMETRIC MODELS Because in many fields immense databases of 3D models have already been developed for computer-aided design (CAD) and computer-aided manufacturing (CAM), geometric modeling of the virtual worlds generally is accomplished by software that is separate from that which determines the dynamic behavior. The way in which 3D structures are represented within the system has a great impact on the performance. There are several different methods, each capable of displaying different information and each requiring a different amount of computation. Because the success of the virtual reality interface requires a minimum number of complete frames every second, the computational overhead of the model becomes critically important.

Surface geometries are models of the outer surfaces of the structures in the virtual world and are described as a patchwork of polygons approximating the overall shape. Shading algorithms blend these facets into the appearance of a smooth surface. Attributes of each whole object, such as color or size, can be addressed and modified dynamically by the application software. For each new frame, the computer must determine the new position of the vertices of each polygon; thus, a greater number of polygons requires a greater number of computations, often causing the simulation to run more slowly. In general, however, polygonal models run faster and require far less power to compute than other 3D representation methodologies.

Volumetric data, such as CT or MRI data, are also 3D models of great interest in surgical applications of virtual reality. New algorithms must be developed to use this computationally intensive data effectively within virtual reality.

Another 3D representation, called *finite-element systems*, describes surfaces as a network. Rules can dynamically reshape the network based on feedback, such as changing forces and the elasticity of a given component. Finite-element systems are used extensively in biomechanical modeling. Although the computational costs are high, these systems offer great capabilities for simulation.

Models of a virtual patient may be 3D, developed in 3D modeling packages, such as Swivel (Paracomp, San Francisco, Calif.), or created in mathematic terms through finite-element systems. Most 3D models used today are constructed of rigid-surface geometry with links to multiple objects. The links provide constraints of motion between the multiple objects. This may be done in a hierarchic manner. The Swivel system RB2 was used to create the bowel model described later. However, by using finite-element systems, it is possible to create more realistic models that allow for material continuums which more accurately represent the physical characteristics of the objects being created. This is especially important regarding the deformation of object models. As the models become more realistic, the computations become more complex.

Force feedback

Tactile, or tangible, displays are those that can be felt with the body rather than heard or seen. These displays include systems with vibrating "tactors," which produce sensations on the skin (cutaneous), and devices that apply force to the hand or to the whole arm. Researchers at the University of North Carolina have shown that the difficult task of the molecular chemist searching for "dockings," or fit, between molecules can be significantly improved with the aid of force feedback (Brooks, 1992). Burdea and his colleagues (1992) have developed a mechanical force-feedback device that retrofits to an existing whole-hand input device, such as a DataGlove (VPL Research, Redwood City, Calif.) The goal is to provide the feedback necessary for telerobotic and other applications.

The neurophysiologic elements of tangible feedback are complex and so are difficult to simulate. For example, when a cup is held in the hand, the pressure from the cup is felt at the site of contact between hand and cup and is felt also as joint reaction forces at the wrist, elbow, and shoulder. A simulation would have to incorporate this wide range of tactile experiences. Also, the body rapidly adjusts to cutaneous tactile sensation, such as that caused by a vibrating element. This adjustment decreases sensitivity to the sensation, an effect that would also have to be simulated.

With each task, the feedback needs of the user change. As a corollary, there are changes in the information that must be transduced, or sensed, from the user and from other aspects of the physical world. When systems are used to control robotic or other remote operations (telepresence), tangible displays become important, as does the ability to monitor and display information about the system being controlled. This is especially true for surgical simulators and telesurgery.

Physiologic sensors and alternative input

There are many sensors used to monitor physiologic conditions, such as temperature, heart rate, and blood pressure. When these sensors are applied to a virtual world, they offer a new level of personal inclusion. For example, eye-tracking devices that determine the direction of the user's gaze could more finely tune the tracking systems. Devices that can help the user manipulate the virtual world include pneumatic mouth-actuated controllers, eye trackers, and dispersed switches. In virtual reality, we are all disabled to the extent that we cannot participate without assisting devices and, conversely, there is no limit to what we can accomplish with them.

Head-mounted displays

To experience the sights and sounds of the virtual world, the user wears a head-mounted, or head-coupled, display. There are two different kinds of displays. The first type uses two video screens (one for each eye) with mounted lens assemblies that fuse the two screens into a single stereo view of the scene. The second type uses a head-tracking system, which allows the system to display a view that coordinates with the direction in which the user is looking. The tracking systems includes two magnetic devices. One device allows the computer to adjust the simulation display as the user looks around, whereas the second device registers the motion of the hand.

In opaque systems, such as the EyePhone (VPL Research, Mountain View, Calif.), these displays completely occlude the user's view of the physical world, reinforcing the experience of immersion, or presence. There are also heads-up, or transparent, displays that project the image on a window through which the user also can see the physical world. These are most often used to add instrumentation data, such as targeting, to the user's field of view. The device itself may actually be worn on the head (head-mounted), as in the case of the traditional EyePhones, or it may be externally supported as is the BOOM, which is a stand-mounted display fashioned after a prototype developed at NASA Ames (Mountain View, Calif.) during the virtual environment workstation (VIEW) project and which is made by Fake Space (Menlo Park, Calif.) (Fisher et al. 1986; Fisher, 1989). The term *head-coupled* covers both types of displays. In either case, it is important to maintain the proximity of the video displays to the eyes and especially the consistency of the head tracking.

The number of discrete picture elements, or pixels, in the video display of each eye is defined as the *resolution*. It determines the sharpness of the image and sets limits on the level of detail that can be displayed. Resolution is a key numeric standard for head-mounted displays, and its definition requires close attention. Color LCDs, such as those used in the EyePhone, are composed of closely packed triads of red, blue, and green triangles. Therefore, the number of *colored* pixels of any given display is three times that of its actual monochrome effect.

The LCDs are used more often than are cathode ray displays because of their lighter weight, more compact size, and relative freedom from electromagnetic-induced radiation. However, the manufacture of LCDs is far more difficult. Resolution frequently is cited as one of the key criteria for improving head-mounted displays, and resolution will improve as new display technologies are developed.

INPUT DEVICES

The hand is the most natural tool for acting on the world. Thus, it is with the hand that we act on most of the interface devices we use, such as joysticks, keyboards, buttons, and knobs. Input devices allow a user to manipulate virtual objects. Whole-hand manipulation allows the user to operate intuitively and naturally in the virtual world. The DataGlove is an input device for whole-hand manipulation. Worn like any glove, the DataGlove measures the bends of the fingers using fiberoptic sensors that trace the backs of the fingers. A magnetic tracking sensor transmits the motion of the entire hand in space, similar to the way that the EyePhone head-mounted display tracks the head. The user's gestures control the actions of a virtual hand which becomes the user's proxy in the virtual world. This identification strongly reinforces the psychological experience of presence, or of actually being inside the virtual world. Another whole-hand input device, the Exos Dexterous Hand Master (Exos, Inc., Lexington, Mass.), uses mechanical coupling to measure the degree of freedom of the hand.

Surgical applications

Virtual reality technology can be used in many areas of surgery, such as teaching, training, planning and performing surgical operations, and predicting the outcomes of operations (figure 14.2). Significant progress has been made in each of these areas and, in some areas, fully operational systems now are available. However, some areas are still only in the pilot stages. Each of these application areas and the progress in developing virtual reality systems for them are described in the following sections. Also discussed are areas that

© MMS 1992

FIGURE 14.2 Applications of virtual reality to medicine. In the central circle, a user wears a head-mounted display, stereo sound headphones, and a whole-hand controller. (Upper left) Anatomy teacher demonstrates arm anatomy on a virtual cadaver. (Upper right) Application to planning nasal reconstructive surgery. (Lower left) Application of telepresence to telesurgery. (Lower right) Application to predicting outcomes of surgery.

must be addressed to provide more realistic surgical simulation environments.

VIRTUAL REALITY SURGICAL TEACHING

Teaching surgical anatomy through virtual reality progresses beyond the present methods of using textbooks and real cadavers. A virtual reality system allows the student to enter and tour the body to see how organs or systems function. For example, a student could become part of a neurotransmitter to see how the synapse works. It also is possible to increase viewing magnification so that an object can be enlarged and examined more closely, and it is possible to overlay or "map" additional information onto the real cadaver.

The virtual reality system can provide a unique environment for two or more surgeons to interact with a virtual cadaver. The two surgeons could be in two different locations and could be linked with the presence of the virtual environment. Ultimately, with improvements in artificial intelligence, one surgeon could perform an operation while the second surgeon, or teacher, could be a computer-generated mentor (Minsky, 1991).

Anatomic systems that use 2D displays and basic elements of an expert system have been used to teach students about anatomic structures (Chase, 1989). A similar system has been created specifically for teaching rhinoplasty (Constantian, Ephrenpreis and Sheen, 1987). To develop a realistic 3D surgical simulator, a detailed physical model of the entire body must be developed. A complete kinematic model of the human skeleton has been described by Zeltzer (1984). Specific parts of the body, including the skeleton with attached tendons, have also been developed. A model of the hand allows realistic tendon transfers for patients with nerve palsy (Thompson and Giurintano, 1989) and a newly developed model of the lower extremity allows doctors to predict the outcomes of reconstructive surgery (Delp, 1990; Delp et al., 1990). This model was first used for osteotomies around the hip joint and has progressed to muscle and tendon reconstructions.

This lower-extremity musculoskeletal model was used to demonstrate the usefulness of practicing surgery within a 3D virtual environment instead of on a 2D screen (figure 14.3) (Pieper et al., 1990). This model was used to study the different approaches to visualizing and interacting with a virtual environment.

A similar 3D model of the soft tissue is necessary to create plastic and reconstructive surgery simulators. Mathematic dynamic models of skinlike materials have been developed (Terzopoulos et al., 1987; Terzopoulos and Fleischer, 1988) and research is now under way to develop more realistic dynamic skin and soft-tissue models (Pieper, 1989; 1992).

A *virtual cadaver* is the central component of a virtual reality anatomy trainer. The virtual cadaver may consist of 3D models of the anatomy and layers of simulation software that approximate various attributes of the anatomy, including biomechanics and physiologic and pathologic processes. Students can navigate through the virtual cadaver, beginning in one place and following a functional pathway through the body. For example, a student could follow the path of vision by en-

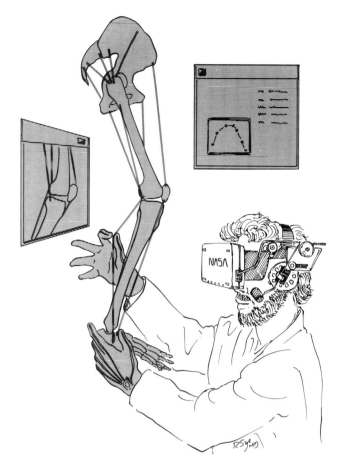

FIGURE 14.3 Anatomy teaching system for demonstrating the anatomy and biomechanics of the lower extremity. A user manipulates tendons on the 3D leg model. By moving the origin or insertion of a tendon, the user can determine the function of the muscle in a new position and can see display windows that can show traditional biomechanical graphs and radiologic images. (Reprinted from Pieper, 1991).

tering the body through the globe of the eye, entering the retina, and traveling up the optic nerve to the brain. By changing the magnification scale, the student can watch the neurotransmitters being released at the synapses as the electric impulses are communicated to the brain.

This kind of simulation provides a unique tool for teaching surgeons-in-training about anatomy, physiology, and the effects of an operation. The simulation also permits a change in scale similar to that in the operating room, where the surgeon has the option to increase the magnification through loupes and then through the operating microscope (VPL Research, 1992).

A virtual reality anatomy trainer could also overlay, or map, a virtual cadaver onto a real cadaver (Fuchs, 1992). By using a heads-up display during dissection, the surgeon-in-training could see through the skin at the underlying structures while dissecting the real cadaver. This would superimpose a virtual map of the body onto the real cadaver.

Because surgeons must also explore pathologic conditions, especially in cases of congenital anomalies, the virtual reality anatomy trainer could have a stored library of congenital anomalies. These virtual cadavers could present, for example, the anatomy of rare facial clefts. This stored library would allow the surgeon-in-training to dissect anomalies that might otherwise be encountered only a few times in an entire career.

While training on the virtual cadaver and exploring the body, the surgeon can also access other data, including volumetric data, physiologic data, or historic data. Volumetric data, for example, can be superimposed in the virtual cadaver to give a better understanding of the relationship between 3D structures and the data of a CT scan and MRI (Cutting et al., 1986; Marsh et al., 1985; Tessier, 1986; Vannier, 1984).

VIRTUAL REALITY SURGICAL SIMULATOR

The virtual abdomen has been created to teach medical students specific anatomic details of abdominal organs (virtual cadaver) and to instruct surgical residents in performing surgical techniques and operative procedures (virtual patient). Each area can be used in a teaching (predetermined, automatic presentation to the student) and learning (practice and exploring) mode. For example, in teaching surgical anatomy of the gastrointestinal tract, a tour can be created from the esophagus to the rectum that delineates the individual organs and their relationship to other organs (e.g., spleen, pancreas) and demonstrates intraluminally through the gastrointestinal tract the same view as an endoscopic procedure. As certain areas are entered, specific features can be highlighted. When coupled with a multimedia database, touching the gastric mucosa could bring a histologic view of the mucosa, a video tape of gastric motility, or a history of the signal events in gastric surgery (such as Billroth's first gastrectomy or Dregstadt's discovery of vagal stimulation of gastric secretion) (Miller, 1987).

Once the tour is complete, the student can explore the gastrointestinal tract and learn the interrelationships of organs. The bile duct, which passes between the pancreas and the duodenum, could be visualized without dissection by "flying" through the bile duct or through the pancreas. Thus, organs would not have to be removed from the cadaver as is necessary in traditional cadaver dissection. This would eliminate the cost required to obtain, maintain, and store cadavers. More importantly, the student learns by doing; once the basics are learned, exploring is a more powerful educational tool than prescribed didactics.

The same methods can be used to teach surgical technique and procedures. A typical surgical procedure can automatically be played for the resident, demonstrating key factors in the operative procedure. The organs could be rotated to show the location of hidden nerves or arteries and could show the technique of isolation or ligation. Variations of a gastric resection, such as Billroth or Roux-en-Y, can be demonstrated, or common congenital anomalies can be simulated. Once the correct surgical technique has been learned, the resident can practice the operation until proficient, free to make mistakes or to try different techniques. It is an ideal synthesis of a book, which can be read as many times as needed but has no manipulation, or a cadaver, which allows actual practice of a procedure but only once.

The current virtual reality surgical simulator has been created on the RB2 system and consists of a torso with a stomach, duodenum, liver, bile ducts, gallbladder, pancreas, and colon. Surgical instruments have been provided, including scalpels, clamps, and needle holders. The level of graphics is only cartoon quality; however, the interactivity and display are real-time without lag.

There are five distinct areas necessary for a realistic simulation: (1) fidelity—the image must have enough high resolution to appear real; (2) object properties (e.g., morphing)—the organs must deform when grasped and must fall with gravity; (3) reactivity—the organs must have appropriate reactions to manipulation or cutting, such as bleeding or leaking fluids; (4) interactivity—the surgeon's hand and surgical instruments must interact realistically with the organs; and (5) sensory input—force feedback, tactile input, and pressure must be felt by the surgeon. To render each of these areas in real time, the power of a supercomputer is required. Therefore, present simulation must be a trade-off and balance of each of these components; priority has been given to interactivity.

As the computer power increases, the image will become more realistic (approaching video quality), the organs will react naturally, and the surgical resident will get the feel of surgery. The simulator uses the conventional, immersive approach of helmet-mounted display (HMD) and the DataGlove. This is an excellent approach for learning anatomy but is not a natural environment for a surgical procedure: Surgeons do not operate with a helmet or glove; they use Virtual reality and surgery instruments and look into a video monitor. One likely modification will be to export the virtual abdomen world to a telepresence surgery system (discussed later), which uses a "through-the-window" approach with a 3D monitor instead of an HMD and uses the handles of actual surgical instruments instead of the DataGlove. This would result in the ideal surgical simulator because the same controls that are used for a simulation are used for the actual surgical procedure. After more than 40 years of flight simulation, pilots now train on flight simulators that are superrealistic, and a pilot cannot begin flying without hundreds of successful takeoffs and landings: It is hoped that the surgical simulator will achieve this level of realism in a shorter time period (Haber, 1986; Rolfe and Staples, 1986).

© J Rosen,MD 1991

FIGURE 14.4 A present-day reconstructive surgeon plans a complex jaw and cheek reconstruction using CAD storyboards and radiologic aids. The user holds a 3D model of the jaw, which was produced on a lathe, generated from volumetric data. The model shows the defect, and the computer screen displays a 2D image of the 3D data. The x-ray view box shows a radiologic 2D image of the skull and the boney defect in the jaw. The storyboard in the background displays the steps of obtaining a complex flap from the back and transforming it into a new jaw and cheek. (Reprinted from Rosen, 1991).

VIRTUAL REALITY PLANNING

An important part of performing surgery is the planning and preparation for the operation. The planning of an operation is central to its successful outcome. The present-day surgeon planning a complex operation takes advantage of drawings and photographs, montages, radiologic data, and CAD tools (figure 14.4). For a complex cosmetic or plastic surgery operation, a storyboard may be created to help plan the optimal number of steps of the reconstruction. These steps may span a course of treatment lasting several weeks or months and may include multiple operations, with each operation including several procedures (McDowell, 1987).

For a complex mandible and cheek reconstruction, many more steps may be necessary to create an aesthetic and functional cheek, jaws, and lips. In addition, the surgeon must visualize the transformation of one part of the body for use elsewhere, such as taking muscles or skin from the back to use in reconstructing the face (see figure 14.4). This transfer and transformation of tissue from one part of the body to another is one of the most complex procedures performed in reconstructive surgery (Rosen, 1991).

For example, a nasal reconstruction may require several operations (figure 14.5). Because the virtual environment allows the surgeon to interact with a virtual patient, each step of the operation can be planned and performed in 3D. In the past, this planning was performed with clay models and other plastic materials (McDowell, 1987). Currently, surgeons are increasingly using CAD tools. In the future, virtual reality tools could provide a more realistic and productive environment. The mathematic computational physical models developed for the CAD systems could be viewed with a virtual reality system (Mann, 1991; Pieper, 1992).

VIRTUAL REALITY TELESURGERY SIMULATION AND HYBRIDS

Telepresence was one of the first applications of virtual environments (figure 14.6). Through telepresence, the surgeon can control a distant system (Fisher, 1989; Fisher et al., 1986; Green, 1992). Telepresence is being

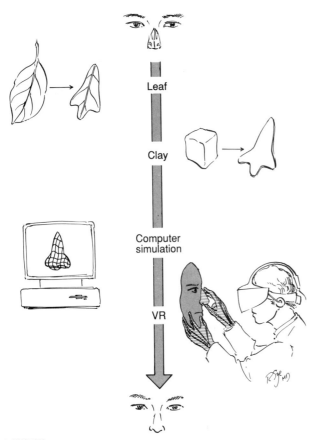

© MMS 1992

FIGURE 14.5 Evolution of nasal reconstruction planning from early methods to virtual reality (*VR*). (Top) A nasal defect. (Upper left) A leaf was used in India 3000 years ago as the first template for planning a forehead flap to reconstruct the nose. (Upper right) Clay then was used to help plan the reconstruction in 3D. (Lower left) More recently, CAD has been used to simulate the new nose. (Lower right) A user plans the nasal reconstruction in a virtual reality environment. (Bottom) Final result in each case is complete nasal reconstruction.

used to perform actual surgical procedures. Although there are many similarities to virtual reality, *telepresence* refers to manipulating objects or performing tasks in the real world, whereas virtual reality pertains to interacting with imaginary objects in a virtual world.

The Green Telepresence Surgery System was developed at SRI International (Menlo Park, Calif.) by Philip Green. This system was produced in response to the inadequacies of current laparoscopic surgery ("keyhole" surgery, in which the surgeon removes or repairs internal organs without cutting the patient open). These deficiencies include the absence of stereoscopic vision, the lack of dexterity in the instruments,

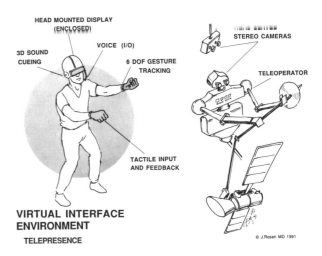

FIGURE 14.6 Telepresence and teleoperations using a virtual reality system, a human master, and a slave robot. The human master is controlling the operations of the robot through the virtual reality system. The head-mounted display allows the master to see into the 3D environment of the robot. The master can see either through the stereo cameras of the robot or through the head-slaved stereo cameras. The whole-hand controller of the master controls the motion of the hands of the robot. What the robot "feels" is transmitted to the master through tactile input and feedback. The 3D sound cueing allows the master to hear into the 3D sound environment of the robot. The master is controlling the robot that is fixing a satellite in space. (Courtesy of the National Aeronautics and Space Administration.)

and poor sensory (tactile, force, pressure) feedback. There are two basic components to the system: the operative work site where the actual surgery occurs, and the surgical workstation from which the surgeon directs the operative procedure. At the operative site, there is the remote manipulator with the surgical instrument, the stereoscopic camera, and even a stereophonic microphone. At the surgical workstation, the 3D image is displayed on a monitor that is seen with simple polarized glasses. The surgeon grasps the handle of an actual surgical instrument that receives the tactile, pressure, and force feedback and transmits precise remote manipulation. The stereophonic sound adds a dimension of multisensory input that rarely is appreciated during routine surgery. The result is a convincing realism, as if the surgeon were actually in the remote site performing the surgical procedure.

The surgical workstation is the core technology that has permitted the implementation and integration of current, future, and potential applications in surgery. Not only can it receive real input from actual surgical procedures, but it also can accept digital imaging from diagnostic or monitoring devices (e.g., CT scans or vital signs monitors) to overlay the real-time video image. It can also import graphics simulation, such as the virtual abdomen (Hoffman, 1987). In essence, this is the ideal simulator because the same instruments (i.e., surgical workstation) are used to perform both the practice and the actual surgery, perhaps even with a flip of a switch. In addition to the great versatility in receiving input, the surgical workstation permits the performance of procedures other than operations, such as endoscopy, ophthalmology, or (with a simple change of scale) potentially microscopic or cellular surgery (Hunter, 1992). With the ever-expanding global telecommunications network of fiberoptic cables and satellites, any of these can be performed at places too dangerous or distant (e.g., space station, third-world countries) for routine procedures. Both telepresence and virtual environments are constructed for multiple persons with interactivity. Thus, surgical procedures or simulations can, for example, involve an "expert" surgeon from a medical center assisting a rural surgeon in a complicated case, or can teach a new operative procedure to many residents at different hospitals at the same time. However, as with all new technologies, the successful implementation frequently is determined not by the technical feasibility but by other considerations, such as political reality, economic feasibility, or even social acceptability.

Telesurgery, which evolved from work with telepresence, is another application of virtual reality. Telesurgery was first proposed by NASA in the 1980s (figure 14.7) with the goal of performing surgery from earth on an astronaut in an orbiting space station (Fisher, 1989; Fisher et al., 1986). However, before telesurgery can become a reality, several obstacles must be overcome, such as problems with the significant time delay, the limits of present force-feedback whole-hand controllers, and the medicolegal issues of telepresence errors for the patient and the surgeon.

Most of these problems can be avoided by using virtual reality only for simulators. At NASA, a simulator for leg surgery was used for an operation within the virtual environment (Pieper et al., 1991). This was one of the first demonstrations of a virtual reality simulator for surgery. Other simulators have addressed orthopaedic surgery (Delp, 1990; Delp et al., 1990; Mann, 1985; 1991) plastic surgery of the face (Pieper 1989, 1992) hand surgery (Thompson and Giurintano, 1989) and, most recently, abdominal surgery (Satava, 1992).

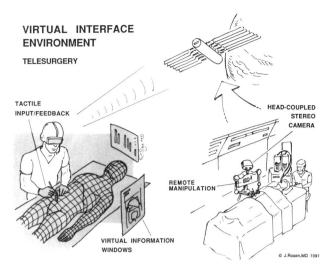

FIGURE 14.7 Telesurgery. A surgeon on the ground operates on a patient in a space station that is orbiting the earth. The surgeon on the ground performs surgery on a patient (astronaut) by remotely manipulating a robot surgeon in the space station. The virtual environment places the surgeon on the ground in the presence of the robot surgeon in the space station. (Reprinted from Fisher, 1989.)

The virtual reality surgical trainer has three basic components: the physical model, the interface, and the computer. The physical model is a realistic mathematic representation of the patient and the surgeon's tools. The interface uses the DataGlove to allow the user to manipulate the surgical tools and the patient model (Foley, 1987; Sturmin, Zeltzer and Pieper, 1989). The computer provides the software and hardware to run the model in real time or near real-time, allowing the surgeon to practice and rehearse surgery in the virtual computer environment.

ABDOMINAL SURGERY PILOT STUDY

The authors currently are exploring the development of a fully operational virtual reality simulator for abdominal surgery. This project was first designed as a prototype for testing virtual reality as a means to train surgeons in the use of a bowel anastomotic device (American Cyanamid Co., 1991). The device is used to join the ends of bowel that remain when a section has been surgically removed. Applying the bowel coupler required several steps and specific maneuvers that were identified and then simulated in the virtual reality environment. The specific tools were created, including a syringe, purse-string clamp, and needles.

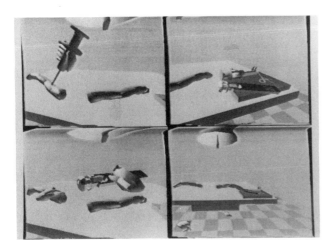

FIGURE 14.8 Four-part video capture showing Davis and Geck project and VALTRAC coupler for bowel.

The goal of the simulator was to provide surgeons with a substitute for animals or cadavers on which to practice new abdominal surgical procedures. The bowel simulator provided a limited operating room environment (figure 14.8). This included the operating table, lights, an instrument table, basic instruments, and a model of the bowel. We also developed a model of the coupling device and its specialized tools. These were all developed in Swivel, which creates rigid objects, for the virtual reality system.

To create a true surgical simulator, several elements must be fashioned: a virtual operating room, including lights, tables, and other required furniture; a virtual patient who has anatomic structures with realistic properties (e.g., bowel that bleeds when cut); and surgical tools that respond accurately and realistically. Each of these parts must demonstrate sufficient realism both in form and function to allow the simulator to operate effectively.

APPARATUS The abdominal simulation was developed on the RB2 virtual reality system at VPL Research using two Silicon Graphics 310 VGX Iris computers. The system included standard left and right DataGloves. Although all interactions were modeled for a single user with two hands, provisions have been made to add a second "surgeon" to the environment as an assistant or trainer.

BUILDING THE 3D MODEL A 3D model of the relevant anatomy and the surgical environment was built inter-actively in RB2 Swivel, a 3D software modeler. Because each object was modeled as a rigid object, some anatomic structures, notably the bowel itself, were modeled as a hierarchically linked set of objects. Object deformation, such as the conformation of tissue over the bowel anastomosis ring (BAR) device as the sutures were drawn tight, was handled either by relative motion of segments or by successively making objects of different shape visible and invisible, reminiscent of animation effects. The clamplike action of the purse-string device closely paralleled that of the physical device, as it was composed of two separate objects linked and constrained at the pivot joint. The color, surface qualities, rendering style (or quality of shading), and object geometry were defined in Swivel. The model then was optimized for rendering frame rate by reducing the total number of polygons used to define the object's geometry or shape.

The structures modeled in this initial simulation included the surgeon's right and left hands, distal and proximal bowel segments, Valtrac BAR, Valtrac applicator handle, Valtrac purse-string device (suturing clamp), lidocaine hypodermic, needle and sutures, operating environment, surgical table, adjustable-height surgical lamp, and a floor-defining virtual operating space.

DESCRIPTION OF THE SIMULATION The model just described includes all the necessary information about the structure and appearance of all objects in the virtual environment. Their behavior was designed in BodyElectric. In the first iteration, the anatomic model was limited to the two bowel sections that would be coupled. This is consistent with conventional training methods in which foam tubing represents the bowel sections during practice sessions (the fact that practice using animal bowel may also be required has been a motivation for developing a replacement simulation methodology). It was assumed that users of the simulator would be trained surgeons already familiar with resection of the bowel and its antecedents. Some highly specific, sequential surgical tasks required simulation.

Performing these surgical tasks presents some difficulty in physical reality. To simulate these difficulties, they were modeled and appropriate feedback was given for both correct and incorrect actions. Audio feedback was used as an analogue to touch to indicate contact and successful grip of an object. Visual feedback for the

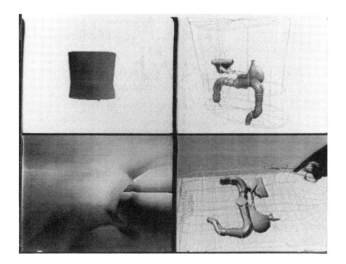

FIGURE 14.9 Four-part video capture (Ethicon project) showing the outside of the abdomen, an operation on the abdomen, the inside of the bowel, and an operation on the bowel.

successful completion of a task included the coupled bowel section turning wireframe so that the encapsulated BAR device could be visually inspected.

Gestural controls, such as grasping, had to be refined from the generic "grab" gesture used in most VPL-designed worlds. Different forms of grasp were modeled for each instrument with regard to the angle of grip and "hit-test," or intersection, between the tool and the portion of the hand and fingers that initiate the grip.

A second, more complete abdominal simulator later was created to examine general surgical procedures on a wider set of organs, including the gallbladder, stomach, and intestines (figure 14.9). The simulator included a more complete virtual patient created in Swivel. It also included an abdominal wall, several internal organs, and additional tools. It was encumbered with some of the same problems as the first abdominal simulator, but it also had the advantages of fly-through and see-through to enable the surgeon better to visualize and navigate the abdominal space and organs. For example, the exact placement of the purse-string sutures within the four layers of the bowel is of the highest import. Within the simulated environmen, it is possible to change scale, either by shrinking the operator or expanding the object, so that details of these layers and the proper dispensation of suture between them can be demonstrated clearly.

RESULTS Many significant human-factor issues were identified during the course of the project. Historically, surgery has been a highly manual activity that requires a broad range of motor skills. Simulating these activities presented new problems in both input gathering and user feedback. Although audio feedback was successful in some cases in substituting for touch, the basic tactility of the actual surgical task was not recreated.

This pilot study demonstrated the overall feasibility of building a simulator for training surgeons on a new surgical device. It demonstrated the unique features of fly-through and see-through, which were especially important in seeing how the bowel coupler worked. However, there were specific limitations to achieving realism in the bowel model, in the interactivity of the tools, and in the interface of the surgeon with the virtual operating room. A truly flexible model of the bowel could not be created with Swivel, and instead only a linked model was built. The bowel model only approximately captured the geometry of the bowel, and there are many characteristics of the bowel that still must be simulated. In addition, a more realistic model could be created that would show physical reactions, such as bleeding when the bowel is cut. The simulated surgical tools were limited in what they could accomplish. For example, passing a needle through the purse-string device was only a gross approximation of the real motor activity. The manipulation of the tools was limited by the DataGlove worn by the surgeon. This was particularly apparent because of the lack of force feedback in the present DataGloves.

AVENUES FOR FUTURE WORK: HYBRIDS

For the future, the authors propose to use a combination of virtual reality simulation with concrete apparatus to form a hybrid training system. Trainees would hold and manipulate real devices in their hands while performing the procedures in virtual reality. Instrumentation of these props would make them, in effect, interface devices that will provide highly accurate tactile feedback. This will then leave the system free to simulate and display more aspects of the surgery that cannot be experienced in the real world.

To be truly useful in training surgeons, future simulators will need to be improved, including an increased resolution of the HMDs and improvements in the glove interfaces, which should allow better contact and inter-

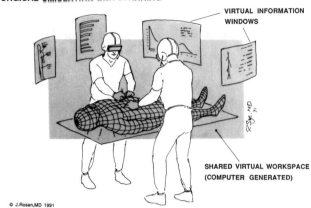

VIRTUAL INFORMATION WINDOWS

SHARED VIRTUAL WORKSPACE (COMPUTER GENERATED)

© J.Rosen,MD 1991

FIGURE 14.10   Future abdominal simulator.

activity for the surgeon. Eventually, the touch and feel will be improved with force feedback in the gloves. More accurate and rapid tracking devices would provide a more realistic presence in the surgical environment.

Although much progress has been made toward a virtual cadaver, the present models of the abdomen are limited. Rigid 3D models do not adequately simulate the motion of the bowel and abdomen. Finite-element models will provide more accurately the necessary realism of the bowel and abdomen, but these models have not yet been created. Knowledge and experience gained from building the finite-element models of the leg and face could be used to address the difficult task of building finite-element models of soft tissues in the abdomen.

These are only the first steps toward virtual reality surgical simulators. Many of the original concepts for this work came from pioneering work in computer-aided surgery by Robert Mann (1991), who said, "The ultimate simulator will be virtual reality—a computer environment in which a surgeon will not only see but 'touch' and 'feel' as if actually performing a surgery" (figure 14.10).

PREDICTING THE OUTCOME OF SURGERY

CAD evolved into computer-aided surgery (CAS) under the influence of Mann. His goal was to use these systems to predict the outcomes of surgery (Mann 1985, 1991). The CAS systems present either numeric 2D or 3D visual data output on a 2D display. Virtual

reality systems would provide a more realistic presentation of the data and greater ease of interaction.

As originally envisioned by Mann (1985) the ideal predictor would allow the surgeon to perform an operation and then turn the clock ahead to evaluate the functional outcome months or years later. The present leg simulator would require several improvements to achieve this ideal, including the operation on and the testing of a walking patient (McKenna, 1990). Prior to the testing, model would need to incorporate the wound-healing process. For example, in the case of orthopaedic surgery, this might include healing of bone, incorporating an implant, and remodeling the soft tissues as a result of the operation (Collier, 1992). The surgeon could choose between multiple operations and try one on the virtual patient. The virtual patient would recover, leave the room, and then return some time later to be evaluated. The surgeon could evaluate the numeric data, view the screen or, in the virtual reality environment, interact with the virtual patient and touch, feel, and see the functional result.

Although we are on the path to such a possibility, more conventional methods are required first to provide the data for the virtual reality system to display. The future of virtual reality will see increased use of these systems in all aspects of surgery to improve planning, performance, and prediction of outcomes.

ACKNOWLEDGMENTS   This chapter was written in part with the support of Davis and Geck and Endo-Ethicon.

REFERENCES

AMERICAN CYANAMID Co. 1991. Valtrac Biofragmentable Anastomosis Ring Instruction Manual. Davis and Geck Medical Device Division.

BROOKS, F., 1992. Proceedings of the 1992 Symposium on 3D Graphics. Comput. Graphics (special issue), pp. 127–134.

BURDEA, G., J. ZHUANG, E. ROSKOS, D. SILVER and N. LANGRANA, 1992. "A Portable Dextrous Master with Force Feedback," Presence—Teleoperators and Virtual Environments, 1(1), pp. 18–27.

CHASE, R., 1989. Report of the Ad Hoc Committee on Computers in Medical Education at Stanford University School of Medicine. SUMMIT.

COLLIER, J., 1992. Personal communication.

CONSTANTIAN, M., C. EPHRENPREIS, and J. SHEEN, 1987. The expert teaching system: A new method for learning rhinoplasty using interactive computer graphics. Plast. Reconstr. Surg.

CUTTING, C., F. L. BOOKSTEIN, B. GRAYSON, L. FELLINGHAM,

and J. G. McCarthy, 1986. Three-dimensional computer-assisted design of craniofacial surgical procedures: Optimization and interaction with cephalometric and CT-based models. *Plast. Reconstr. Surg.*

Delp, S., 1990. Surgery simulation: A computer-graphics system to analyze and design musculoskeletal reconstructions of the power limb. Doctoral thesis, Stanford University.

Delp, S., Loan, M. Hoy, F. Zajac, P. E. Topp, and J. Rosen, 1990. An interactive graphics-based model of the lower extremity to study orthopaedic surgical procedures. *IEEE Trans. Biomed. Eng.* 37:8.

Fisher, S., 1989. Virtual environments, personal simulation and telepresence. In *Implementing and Interacting with Real-time Microworlds* (ACM SIGGRAPH '89 course notes no. 29).

Fisher, S., M. McGreevy, J. Humphries, and W. Robinett, 1986. Virtual environment display system. In *Proceedings of the 1986 ACM Workshop on Interactive Graphics*, October 23–24, Chapel Hill, N.C., pp. 77–87.

Foley, D., 1987. Interfaces for advanced computing. *Sci. Am.* pp. 127–135.

Fuchs, H., 1992. *Proceedings of SIGGRAPH*, July, Chicago.

Green, P., 1992. *Proceedings of the Virtual Reality Meets Medicine Conference*, June, San Diego.

Haber, R. N., 1986. Flight simulation. *Sci. Am.* pp. 96–103.

Hoffman, C., 1987. Simulation of physical systems from geometric models. *J. Robotics Automation*, RA-3(3):194–206.

Hunter, I., 1992. Personal communication.

Mann, R., 1985. Computer-aided surgery. In *Proceedings of the RESNA Eighth Annual Conference*, Memphis, Tenn.

Mann, R., 1991. Scalpel! Clamp! Floppy Disk! *Technol. Rev.* pp. 66–71.

Marsh, J., et al., 1985. Surgical simulation. *Clin. Plast. Surg.*

McDowell, F., 1987. *The Origin of Rhinoplasty*. Austin, Tex.: Silvergirl, Inc.

McKenna, M., 1990. Dynamic simulation of autonomous legged locomotion. *Comput. Graphics* 24(4): 29–38.

Miller, M.D., 1987. Simulations in medical education: A review. *Medical Teacher* 9(1):35–41.

Minsky, M., 1991. Personal communication.

Pieper, S., 1992. CAPS: Computer-aided plastic surgery. Doctoral thesis, Massachusetts Institute of Technology, Cambridge.

Pieper, S., 1989. More than skin deep: Physical modeling of facial tissue. Master's dissertation, Massachusetts Institute of Technology Media Lab, Cambridge.

Pieper, S., S. Delp, J. Rosen, and S. Fisher, 1990. A virtual environment system for simulation of leg surgery. *S.P.I.E.* 1457: 188–197.

Rolfe, J., and K. Staples, 1986. Flight simulation. Cambridge, Engl.: Cambridge University Press.

Rosen, J., 1991. Search for a composite free flap. In *Procedures in Plastic and Reconstructive Surgery*, L. M. Vistnes, ed. Boston: Little, Brown, pp. 686–698.

Satava, R., 1992. Virtual reality surgical simulator: The first steps. In *Proceedings of the Virtual Reality Meets Medicine Conference*, June, San Diego.

Sturmin, D., D. Zeltzer, and S. Pieper, 1989. Hands-on interaction with virtual environments. In *Proceedings of UIST '89: the Symposium on User Interface Software and Technology* (ACM SIGGRAPH/SIGGHI), November 13–15, Williamsburg, Va., pp. 19–24.

Sutherland, I. E., 1965. The ultimate display. In *Proceedings of the IFIP Congress 65, Symposium Summary*, pp. 506–508.

Terzopoulos, D., and K. Fleischer, 1988. Modeling inelastic deformation: Viscoelasticity, plasticity, fracture. *Comput. Graphics*, Vol. 22.

Terzopoulos, D., J. Platt, A. Barr, and K. Fleischer, 1987. Elastically deformable models. *Comput. Graphics*, Vol. 21.

Tessier, P., 1986. Three-dimensional imaging in medicine. *Scand. J. Plast. Reconstr. Surg.* 3(11): 4–11.

Thompson, D., and D. Giurintano, 1989. A kinematic model of the flexor tendons of the hand. *J. Biomech. Eng.* 22:327–334.

Vannier, M. W., 1984. Three-dimensional CT reconstruction images for craniofacial surgical planning. *Radiology* pp. 179–184.

VPL Research Inc., 1992. *Brain Tour*.

Zeltzer, D., 1984. Representations and control of three-dimensional computer animated figures. Doctoral thesis, Ohio State University.

15 Merging Virtual Objects with the Real World: Seeing Ultrasound Imagery Within the Patient

MICHAEL BAJURA, HENRY FUCHS, AND
RYUTAROU OHBUCHI

WE HAVE BEEN working toward an "ultimate" 3D ultrasound system that acquires and displays 3D volume data in real time. Real-time display can be crucial for applications such as cardiac diagnosis, which need to detect certain kinetic features. Our "ultimate" system design requires advances in both 3D volume data *acquisition* and 3D volume data *display*. Our collaborators, Dr. Olaf von Ramm's group at Duke University, are working toward real-time 3D volume data acquisition (Smith, 1991; von Ramm, 1991). At the University of North Carolina at Chapel Hill, we have been conducting research on real-time 3D volume data visualization.

Our research efforts at UNC have been focused in three areas: (1) algorithms for acquiring and rendering real-time ultrasound data, (2) creating a working virtual environment that acquires and displays 3D ultrasound data in real time, and (3) recovering structural information for volume rendering specifically from ultrasound data, which has unique image-processing requirements. This third area is presented in Lin (1991) and is not covered here.

The next section of this [chapter] reviews previous work in 3D ultrasound, and the section following it discusses our research on processing, rendering, and displaying echographic data without a head-mounted display. Since the only real-time volume data scanners available today are 2D ultrasound scanners, we try to approximate our "ultimate" system by incrementally visualizing a 3D volume data set reconstructed from a never-ending sequence of 2D data slices (Ohbuchi, 1990, 1991). This is difficult because the volume consisting of multiple 2D slices needs to be visualized incrementally as the 2D slices are acquired. This incremental method has been successfully used in off-line experiments with a 3-degrees-of-freedom (dof) mechanical arm tracker and is extensible to 6 dof (e.g., a 3D translation and a 3D rotation) at greater computational cost.

The fourth and fifth sections present our research on video see-through head-mounted display (HMD) techniques involving the merging of computer-generated images with real-world images. Our video see-through HMD system displays ultrasound echography image data in the context of real (3D) objects. This is part of our continuing see-through HMD research, which includes both optical see-through HMD and video see-through HMD. Even though we concentrate here on medical ultrasound imaging, applications of this display technology are not limited to it (see the section, Other Applications).

Previous research in 3D ultrasound

The advantages of ultrasound echography are that it is relatively safe compared with other imaging modalities and that images are generated in real time (Wells, 1977). This makes it the preferred imaging technique for fetal examination, cardiac study, and guided surgical procedures such as fine-needle aspiration biopsy

Previously published in Computer Graphics 26(2):203–210.

of breast tumors (Fornage, 1990). Ultrasound echography offers the best real-time performance in 3D data acquisition, although slower imaging modalities such as MRI are improving.

The drawbacks of ultrasound imaging include a low signal-to-noise ratio and poor spatial resolution. Ultrasound images exhibit "speckle," which appears as grainy areas in images. Speckle arises from coherent sound interference effects from tissue substructure. Information such as blood flow can be derived from speckle but, in general, speckle is hard to utilize (Thijssen, 1990). Other problems with ultrasound imaging include attenuation that increases with frequency, phase aberration due to tissue inhomogeneity, and reflection and refraction artifacts (Harris, 1990).

3D ULTRASOUND IMAGE ACQUISITION

Just as ultrasound echography has evolved from 1D data acquisition to 2D data acquisition, work is in progress to advance to 3D data acquisition. Dr. Olaf von Ramm's group at Duke University is developing a 3D scanner that will acquire 3D data in real time (Shattuck, 1984; Smith, 1991; von Ramm, 1991). The 3D scanner uses a 2D phased array transducer to sweep out an imaging volume. A parallel processing technique called *Explososcan* is used on return echoes to boost the data acquisition rate.

Since such a real-time 3D medical ultrasound scanning system is not yet available, prior studies on 3D ultrasound imaging known to the authors have tried to reconstruct 3D data from imaging primitives of a lesser dimension (usually 2D images). To reconstruct a 3D image from images of a lesser dimension, the location and orientation of the imaging primitives must be known. Coordinate values are explicitly tracked acoustically (Brinkley, 1978; King, 1990; Moritz, 1983), mechanically (Geiser, 1982a, 1982b; Hottier, 1989; McCann, 1988; Ohbuchi, 1990; Raichelen, 1986; Stickels, 1984), or optically (Mills, 1990). In other systems, a human or a machine makes scans at predetermined locations and/or orientations (Collet Billon, 1990; Ghosh, 1982; Itoh, 1979; Lalouche, 1989; Matsumoto, 1981; Nakamura, 1984; Tomographic Technologies, 1991).

A particularly interesting system under development at Philips Paris Research Laboratory is one of the closest yet to a real-time 3D ultrasound scanner (Collet Billon, 1990). It is a follow on to earlier work, which

featured a manually guided scanner with mechanical tracking (Hottier, 1990). This near-real-time 3D scanner is a mechanical sector scanner, in which a conventional 2D sector scanhead with an annular array transducer is rotated by a stepper motor to get a third scanning dimension. In a period of 3 to 5 seconds, 50 to 100 slices of 2D sector scan images are acquired. Currently, the annular array transducer in this system provides better spatial resolution, but less temporal resolution, than the real-time 3D phased array system by von Ramm et al., mentioned earlier. A commercial product, the *Echo-CT* system by Tomographic Technologies, uses the linear translation of a transducer inside a tube inserted into the esophagus to acquire parallel slices of the heart. Image acquisition is gated by respiration and an electrocardiograph to reduce registration problems (Tomographic Technologies, 1991).

3D ULTRASOUND IMAGE DISPLAY

One should note that 3D image data can be presented not only in visual form but also as a set of calculated values (e.g., a ventricular volume). The visual form can be classified further by the rendering primitives used, which can be either geometric (e.g., polygons) or image-based (e.g., voxels). Many early studies focused on noninvasively estimating the volume of the heart chamber (Brinkley, 1978; Ghosh, 1982; Raichelen, 1986; Stickels, 1984). Typically, 2D echography (2DE) images were stored on video tape and manually processed off-line. Since visual presentation was of secondary interest, wire frames or a stack of contours often were used to render the image.

An interesting extension to 2D display is a system that tracks the location and orientation of 2D image slices with 6 dof (King, 1990). On each 2D displayed image, the system overlays lines indicating the intersection of the current image with other 2D images already acquired. The authors claim that these lines help the viewer understand the relationship of the 2D image slices in 3D space. Other studies reconstructed 3D gray-level images preserving gray scale, which can be crucial to tissue characterization (Collet Billon, 1990; Hottier, 1989; Lalouche, 1989; McCann, 1988; Nakamura, 1984; Pini, 1990; Tomographic Technologies, 1991). [The work by] Lalouche (1989) is a mammogram study using a special 2DE scanner that can acquire and store 45 consecutive parallel slices at 1-mm intervals. A volume is reconstructed by cubic-spline interpolation and then is volume-rendered. McCann (1988) performed gated acquisition of a heart's image over a cardiac cycle by storing 2DE images on video tape and then reconstructing and volume rendering them. *Repetitive low-pass filtering* was used during reconstruction to fill the spaces between radial slices, which suppressed aliasing artifacts. Tomographic Technologies (1991) provides flexible re-slicing by up to six planes as well as other imaging modes. Collet Billon (1990) uses two visualization techniques: re-slicing by an arbitrary plane and volume rendering. The former allows faster but only 2D viewing on a current workstation. The latter allows 3D viewing but often involves cumbersome manual segmentation. The reconstruction algorithm uses straightforward low-pass filtering.

Incremental volume visualization

We have been experimenting with volume rendering as one alternative for visualizing dynamic ultrasound volume data. Standard volume rendering techniques that rely heavily on preprocessing do not apply well to dynamic data, which must be visualized in real time (Levoy, 1988; Sabella, 1988; Upson, 1988). We review here an incremental, interactive, 3D ultrasound visualization technique that visualizes a 3D volume as it is incrementally updated by a sequence of registered 2D ultrasound images (Ohbuchi 1990, 1991).

Our target function is sampled at irregular points and may change over time. Instead of directly visualizing samples from this target, we reconstruct a regular 3D volume from this time series of spatially irregular sample points. This places a limit on storage and computation requirements, which would grow without bound if we retained all the past sample points. The reconstructed volume then is rendered with an incremental volume-rendering technique.

The reconstruction is a 4D convolution process. A 3D Gaussian kernel is used for spatial reconstruction followed by a temporal reconstruction based on simple autoregressive moving average (ARMA) filtering (Haddad, 1991). Time stamps are assigned to each 3D voxel, which are updated during reconstruction. The time stamp difference between a reconstructed voxel and an incoming sample is used to compute coefficients for the ARMA filter. The 3D Gaussian filter is loosely matched to the point spread function of the ultrasound transducer and is a good choice because it minimizes

the product of spatial bandwidth and spatial frequency bandwidth (Hildreth, 1983; Leipnik, 1960).

An image-order, ray-casting algorithm based on Levoy (1988) renders the final images incrementally. Rendering is incremental and fast only if the viewpoint is fixed and if the updated volume is relatively small. Shading and ray sampling are done only for voxels proximate to incoming data. The ray samples are stored in a 3D array in screen space called a *ray cache* for later use. The ray cache is hierarchic so that a small partial update of the ray cache can be composited quickly $[O(\log(n))]$ (Ohbuchi, 1991). The hierarchic ray cache also allows fast rendering of polygons properly composited with volume data, which can enhance the volume visualization (Levoy, 1990; Miyazawa, 1991). This incremental volume-rendering algorithm is not restricted to ultrasound and is applicable to other problems that update volume data incrementally (e.g., interactive volume modeling by sculpting) (Galyean, 1991).

To test this visualization technique, we acquired a series of 2D images with a manually guided conventional 2DE scanhead attached to a mechanical tracking arm with 3 dof (two translations and one rotation). As we scanned various targets in a water tank, their images and their corresponding geometry were stored off-line. We then ran the incremental volume visualization algorithm on a DECstation 5000 with 256 MB of memory using this data. With a reconstruction buffer size of $150 \times 150 \times 300$ and an image size of 256×256, it took 15–20 seconds to reconstruct and render a typical image after insertion of a 2D data slice. This time varied with reconstruction, shading, and viewing parameters.

Figure 15.1 shows two of ninety 2D images of a plastic toy doll phantom, which is visualized in figure 15.2. The 2D images were produced by an ATL Mark-4 Scanner with a 3.5-MHz linear scanhead. The 2D images overlap but are roughly parallel at approximately 2-mm intervals.

Virtual environment ultrasound imaging

Various medical ultrasound imaging applications require a registration of ultrasound images with anatomic references (e.g., in performing a fine-needle aspiration biopsy of a suspected breast tumor) (Fornage, 1990). A virtual environment that displays images acquired by ultrasound equipment in place within a

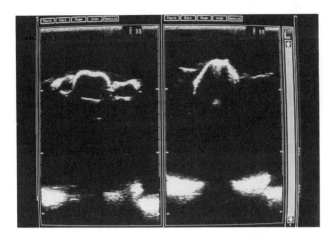

FIGURE 15.1   Two of 90 2D ultrasound echography images of a plastic toy doll phantom that was scanned in a water tank. The scans shown are at the torso (left) and at the head (right). The clouds at the bottom of the scans are artifacts due to reflections from the bottom of the water tank.

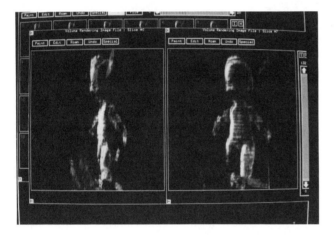

FIGURE 15.2   Reconstructed and rendered image of the toy doll phantom using incremental volume visualization.

patient's anatomy could facilitate such an application. We have developed an experimental system that displays multiple 2D medical ultrasound images overlaid on real-world images. In January 1992, after months of development with test objects in water tanks, we performed our first experiment with a human subject.

Our virtual environment ultrasound imaging system works as follows (note that this is a different system than our older one described in the previous section): As each echography image is acquired by an ultrasound scanner, its position and orientation in 3D world space are tracked with 6 dof. Simultaneously, the posi-

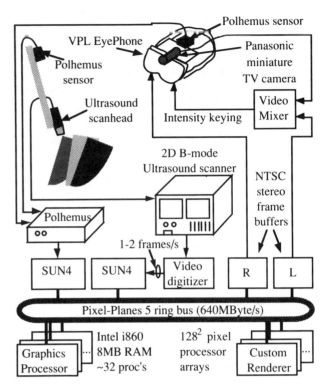

FIGURE 15.3   Hardware block diagram for the virtual environment ultrasound system.

tion and orientation of an HMD are also tracked with 6 dof. Using this geometry, an image-generation system generates 3D renderings of the 2D ultrasound images. These images are video mixed with real-world images from a miniature TV camera mounted on the HMD. The resulting composite image shows the 2D ultrasound data registered in its true 3D location.

Figure 15.3 is a block diagram of our system's hardware. There are three major components: (1) an image-acquisition and tracking system, which consists of an ultrasound scanner and a Polhemus tracking system, (2) an image-generation system, which is our Pixel-Planes 5 graphics multicomputer, and (3) an HMD, which includes a portable TV camera, a video mixer, and a VPL EyePhone. Each component is described in more detail in the following three subsections.

IMAGE ACQUISITION AND TRACKING

Two-dimensional ultrasound images are generated by an IREX System III echography scanner with a 16-mm aperture, 2.5-MHz phased array transducer. These images are digitized by a SUN 4 with a Matrox MVP/S real-time video digitizer and transferred to our Pixel-

Planes 5 graphics multicomputer (Fuchs, 1989). The SUN 4 operates as a 2DE image server for requests from the Pixel-Planes 5 system. Images are distributed among the graphics processors (GPs) on a round-robin scan-line by scan-line basis. Due to the bandwidth limitations of the SUN 4 VME bus, transfer of the 512 × 480 × 8 bits/pixel images is limited to 2 Hz.

A Polhemus system with one source and two receivers is used for tracking (Polhemus, 1980). One receiver tracks the HMD. The other tracks the ultrasound transducer. The Polhemus system is mounted in non-ferrous materials away from magnetic interference sources such as the ultrasound transducer, HMD, and other lab equipment. A calibration procedure is used to relate both the ultrasound transducer to its Polhemus receiver and the HMD TV camera to its Polhemus receiver mounted on the HMD. This calibration procedure is described later.

Image generation

Images are generated by the Pixel-Planes 5 system based on geometry information from the tracking system. Pixel-Planes 5 runs a custom Programmer's Hierarchical Interactive Graphics System (PHIGS) implementation, which incorporates a facility to update display structures asynchronously from the display process. This separates the interactive virtual environment update rate from the 2D ultrasound image data acquisition rate. Images in the virtual environment are registered to the real world within the update-rate limit of the tracking and display system and not within the acquisition-rate limit of the image-acquisition system.

Pixels from the 2D ultrasound images are rendered as small, unshaded sphere primitives in the virtual environment. The 2D ultrasound images appear as space-filling slices registered in their correct 3D position. The ultrasound images are distributed among the GPs where they are clipped to remove unnecessary margins and transformed into sphere primitives, which are then sent to the renderer boards for direct rasterization. Pixel-Planes 5 renders spheres very rapidly, even faster than it renders triangles, more than 2 million per second (Fuchs, 1985, 1989). Final images are assembled in double-buffered National Television System Committee (NTSC) frame buffers for display on the HMD. To reduce the number of sphere primitives displayed, the ultrasound images are filtered and subsampled at every fourth pixel. Due to the low resolution of the HMD and inherent bandwidth limitation of the ultrasound scanner, this subsampling does not result in a substantial loss of image quality. An option to threshold lower-intensity pixels in 2D ultrasound images prior to 3D rendering can suppress lower-intensity pixels from being displayed.

Video see-through HMD

A video see-through HMD system combines real-world images captured by head-mounted TV cameras with synthetic images generated to correspond with the real-world images. The important issues are tracking the real-world cameras accurately and generating the correct synthetic images to model the views of the cameras. Correct stereo modeling adds concerns about matching a pair of cameras to each other as well as tracking and modeling them. Robinett (1991) discusses stereo HMD in detail and includes an analysis of the VPL EyePhone.

A Panasonic GP-KS102 camera provides monocular see-through capability for the left eye in our current system. Images from this camera are mixed with synthetic images from the Pixel-Planes 5 system using the luminance (brightness) keying feature on a Grass Valley Group Model 100 video mixer. With luminance keying, the pixels in the output image are selected from either the real-world image or the synthetic image, depending on the luminance of pixels in the synthetic image. The combined image for the left eye and a synthetic image only for the right eye are displayed on a VPL EyePhone.

Calibration

Two transformations, a *transducer transformation* and a *camera transformation*, are needed to calibrate our test system. The transducer transformation relates the position and orientation of the Polhemus tracker attached to the ultrasound transducer to the position and scale of 2D ultrasound image pixels in 3D space. The camera transformation relates the position and orientation of the head-mounted Polhemus tracker to the HMD TV camera position, orientation, and field of view.

Both transformations are calculated by first locating a calibration jig in both the lab (real) and tracker (virtual) 3D coordinate systems. This is accomplished by performing rigid-body rotations with the transducer tracker about axes that are to be fixed in both the real and virtual coordinate systems. Two samples from the tracker, each consisting of both a position and an orientation, are sufficient to fix each calibration axis. The transducer transformation is computed by taking an ultrasound image of a target of known geometry placed at a known position on the calibration jig. By finding the pixel coordinates of point targets in the ultrasound image, the world coordinates of pixels in the ultrasound image can be found. From this relationship and the location of the Polhemus tracker attached to the ultrasound transducer at the time the target was imaged, the transducer transformation is derived. Similarly, the camera transformation is found by placing the HMD TV camera at known positions and orientations relative to the calibration jig. The field of view of the TV camera is known from camera specifications. Manual adjustments are used to improve the camera transformation.

Experimental results

In January 1992, we conducted an experiment with a live human subject using the method just described. We scanned the abdomen of a volunteer who was 38 weeks pregnant. An ultrasound technician from the Department of Obstetrics & Gynecology of the UNC Hospitals performed the ultrasound scanning.

Figure 15.4 is a scene from the experiment. A person looks on with modified VPL EyePhone with the miniature video camera mounted on top and in front. Figure 15.5 shows the left eye view from the HMD, a composition of synthetic and real images. Figure 15.6 is another view from the left eye of the HMD wearer, which shows several 2D ultrasound images in place within the subject's abdomen.

Conclusions and future directions

The results presented so far are the initial steps in the first application of what we hope will be a flourishing area of computer graphics and visualization.

Remaining technical problems

conflicting visual cues   Our experiment (see figures 15.5, 15.6) showed that simply overlaying synthetic images on real ones is not sufficient. To the user, the ultrasound images did not appear to be *inside* the subject, so much as pasted on *top* of her. To overcome this

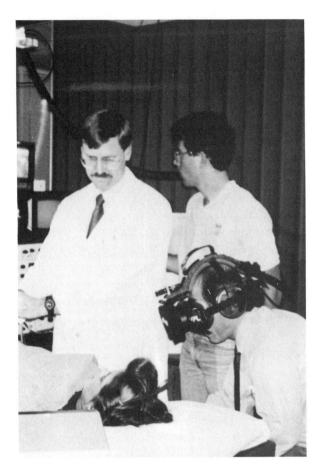

FIGURE 15.4 An ultrasound technician scans a subject while another person looks on with the video see-through head-mounted display (HMD). Note the miniature video camera attached to the front of the VPL EyePhone HMD.

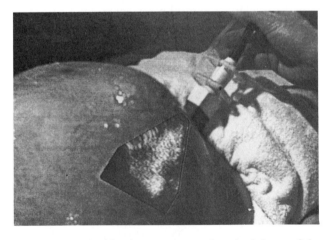

FIGURE 15.5 A video image presented to the left eye of the HMD showing a view of the subject's abdomen with a 2D ultrasound image superimposed and registered. Note the ultrasound transducer registered with the image acquired by it. The 2D image is from the antero-inferior view.

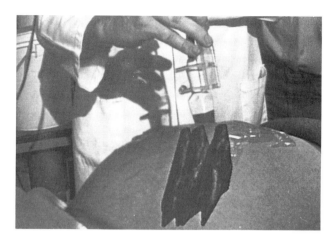

FIGURE 15.6 Another video image presented to the HMD showing several 2D image slices in 3D space within the patient's abdomen. The image slices are from the anterior view.

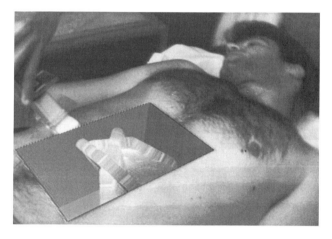

FIGURE 15.7 An image showing a synthetic hole rendered around ultrasound images in an attempt to avoid conflicting visual cues. Note the depth cues provided by occlusion of the image slices by the pit walls and shading of the pit. Also note the incorrect obscuration of the ultrasound transducer by the pit wall. (RT3200 Advantage II ultrasound scanner courtesy of General Electric Medical Systems.)

problem, we now provide additional cues to the user by making a virtual hole in the subject (figure 15.7) by digitizing points on the abdominal surface and constructing a shaded polygonal pit. The pit provides occlusion cues by obscuring the abdominal surface along the inside walls of the pit. Shading the pit provides an additional cue. Unfortunately, this does not completely solve the problem; the pit hides *everything* in the real image that is in the same location (in 2D) as the pit, including real objects that are closer in 3D than the

pit. (Note in figure 15.7, the edge of the transducer is hidden behind the pit representation even though it should appear in front of it.)

To solve this problem, the systems needs to know depth information for both the real and synthetic objects visible from the HMD user's viewpoint. This would make it possible to present correct occlusion cues by combining the live and synthetic images with a z-buffer-like algorithm. An ideal implementation of this would require real-time range finding from the viewpoint of the HMD user—a significant technical challenge. Graphics architectures that provide real-time depth-based image composition are already under development (Molnar, 1992).

Another remaining problem is the visualization of internal 3D structure in data captured by the ultrasound scanner. Neither our incremental volume-rendering algorithm (see the section Incremental Volume Visualization) nor multiple explicit image slices in 3D space (see figure 15.6) solve this problem well. A combination of multiple visualization methods will probably be necessary in the future. We suspect that this problem is difficult because the human visual system is not accustomed to seeing structure within opaque objects, and so our development cannot be guided by the "gold standard" of reality that has been used so effectively in guiding other 3D rendering investigations.

SYSTEM LAG Lag in image generation and tracking is noticeable in all head-mounted displays, but it is dramatically accentuated with see-through HMD. The "live video" of the observer's surroundings moves appropriately during any head movement but the synthetic image overlay lags behind. This is currently one of our system's major problems, which prevents it from giving the user a convincing experience of seeing synthetic objects or images hanging in 3D space. A possible solution may be to delay the live video images so that their delay matches that of the synthetic images. This will align the real and synthetic images but won't eliminate the lag itself. We are also considering predictive tracking as a way to reduce the effect of the lag (Liang, 1991). Developers of some multimillion-dollar flight simulators have studied predictive tracking for many years, but unfortunately for us, they have not, to our knowledge, published details of their methods and their methods' effectiveness. For the immediate future, we are planning to move to our locally developed "ceiling tracker" (Ward, 1992) and use predictive tracking.

TRACKING SYSTEM RANGE AND STABILITY Even though we arc using the most popular and probably most effective commercially available tracking system from Polhemus, we are constantly plagued by limitations in tracking volume and tracking stability (Liang, 1991). The observer often steps inadvertently out of tracker range and, even while keeping very still, the observer must cope with objects in the synthetic image "swimming" in place. We are eagerly awaiting the next generation of tracking systems from Polhemus and other manufacturers that are said to overcome most of these problems. Even more capable tracking systems will be needed in order to satisfy the many applications in which the observer must move about in the real world instead of a laboratory, operating room, or other controlled environment. Many schemes have been casually proposed over the years, but we know of no device that has been built and demonstrated. Even the room-size tracker we built and demonstrated for a week at SIGGRAPH '91 still needs special ceiling panels with infrared LEDs (Ward, 1992).

HEAD-MOUNTED DISPLAY SYSTEM RESOLUTION For many of the applications envisioned, the image quality of current head-mounted video displays is totally inadequate. In a see-through application, a user is even more sensitive to the limitations of his or her head-mounted display than in a conventional non-see-through application because he or she is painfully aware of the visual details being missed.

MORE POWERFUL DISPLAY ENGINES Even with all the preceding problems solved, the synthetic images we would like to see—for example, real-time volume visualization of real-time volume data—would still take too long to be created. Much more powerful image generation systems are needed if we are to be able to visualize usefully detailed 3D imagery.

OTHER APPLICATIONS

VISION IN SURGERY In neurosurgery, ultrasound is already used to image nearby arteries that should be avoided by an impending surgical incision.

BURNING BUILDINGS With close-range, millimeter-wavelength radar, rescuers may be able to "see through" the smoke in the interior of burning buildings.

BUILDING GEOMETRY Geometry or other structural data could be added to a "live" scene. In the above burning-building scenario, parts of a building plan could be superimposed onto the visual scene, such as the location of stairways, hallways, or the best exits out of the building.

SERVICE INFORMATION Information could be displayed to a service technician working on complicated machinery such as a jet engine. Even simpler head-mounted displays, ones without head tracking, already provide information to users on site and avoid using large cumbersome video screens. Adding head tracking would allow 3D superimposition to show, for instance, the location of special parts within an engine or the easiest path for removal or insertion of a subassembly.

ARCHITECTURE ON SITE Portable systems could allow builders and architects to preview buildings on site before construction or to visualize additions to existing architecture.

With the work presented here and the identification of problems and possibilities for further research, we hope to encourage applications not only of "virtual environments" (imaginary worlds) but also applications that involve an "enhancement of vision" in our real world.

ACKNOWLEDGMENTS We would like to thank the following people: David Chen and Andrew Brandt for experimental assistance; General Electric Medical Systems (and especially R. Scott Ray) for the loan of an ultrasound scanner; Stefan Gottschalk for much assistance with video acquisition, editing, and printing; Professor Olaf von Ramm (Duke University) for donation of the IREX ultrasound scanner; ultrasound technician George Blanchard, RDMS, for scanning the subject; David Harrison and John Hughes for video and laboratory setup; Andrei State for experimental assistance; John Thomas for fabrication of a custom camera mount; Terry Yoo for video tape editing; Vern Katz, M.D., for assistance with multiple ultrasound machines and scanning experiments; Nancy Chescheir, M.D., for loan of an ultrasound machine and arrangements with the ultrasound technician; Warren Newton, M.D., and Melanie Mintzer, M.D., for finding our subject; Warren Robinett and Rich Holloway, for consultation with HMD optics and software; Professor Stephen Pizer and Charlie Kurak for consultation on the difficulty of enhancing ultrasound images; David Adam (Duke University) for instruction in the use of the IREX scanner; and our subject and her husband for their time and patience.

This research is partially supported by DARPA ISTO contract DAEA 18-90-C-0044, NSF ERC grant CDR-86-22201, DARPA ISTO contract 7510, NSF grant MIP-9000894, NSF cooperative agreement ASC-8920219, and NIH MIP grant PO 1 CA 47982, and by Digital Equipment Corporation.

REFERENCES

BRINKLEY, J. F., W. E. MORITZ, and D. W. BAKER, 1978. Ultrasonic three-dimensional imaging and volume from a series of arbitrary sector scans. *Ultrasound Med. Biol.* 4:317–327.

COLLET BILLON, A., 1990. Philips Paris Research Lab. Personal communication.

FORNAGE, B. D., N. SNEIGE, M. J. FAROUX, and E. ANDRY, 1990. Sonographic appearance and ultrasound guided fine-needle aspiration biopsy of brest carcinomas smaller than 1 cm³. *J. Ultrasound Med.* 9:559–568.

FUCHS, H., J. GOLDFEATHER, J. P. HULTIQUIST, S. SPACH, J. AUSTIN, F. P. BROOKS, JR., J. EYLES, and J. POULTON, 1985. Fast spheres, textures, transparencies, and image enhancements in Pixel Planes. *Comput. Graphics (Proc. SIGGRAPH '85)* 19(3):111–120.

FUCHS, H., J. POULTON, J. EYLES, T. GREER, J. GOLDFEATHER, D. ELLSWORTH, S. MOLNAR, and L. ISRAEL, 1989. Pixel Planes 5: A heterogeneous multiprocessor graphics system using processor-enhanced memories. *Comput. Graphics (Proc. SIGGRAPH '89)* 23(3):79–88.

GALYEAN, T. A., and J. F. HUGHES, 1991. Sculpting: An interactive volumetric modeling technique. *Comput. Graphcs (Proc. SIGGRAPH '89)* 25(4):267–274.

GEISER, E. A., M. ARIET, D. A. CONETTA, S. M. LUPKIEWICZ, L. G. CHRISTIE, and C. R. CONTI, 1982a. Dynamic three-dimensional echocardiographic reconstruction of the intact human left ventricle: Technique and initial observations in patients. *Am. Heart J.* 103(6):1056–1065.

GEISER, E. A., L. G. CHRISTIE, D. A. CONETTA, C. R. CONTI, and G. S. GOSSMAN, 1982b. Mechanical arm for spatial registration of two-dimensional echographic sections. *Cathet. Cariovasc. Diagn.* 8:89–101.

GHOSH, A., C. N. NANDA, and G. MAURER, 1982. Three-dimensional reconstruction of echo-cardiographics images using the rotation method. *Ultrasound Med. Biol.* 8(6):655–661.

HADDAD, R. A., and T. W. PARSONS, 1991. *Digital Signal Processing, Theory, Applications, and Hardware.* New York: Computer Science Press.

HARRIS, R. A., D. H. FOLLETT, M. HALLIWELL, and P. N. T. WELLS, 1990. Ultimate limits in ultrasonic imaging resolution. *Ultrasound Med. Biol.* 17(6):547–558.

HILDRETH, E. C., 1983. The detection of intensity changes by computer and biological vision systems. *Comput. Vis. Graphics Image Proc.* 22:1–27.

HOTTIER, F., 1989. *Philips Paris Research Lab.* Personal communication.

HOTTIER, F., and A. COLLET BILLON, 1990. 3D echography: Status and perspective. In *3D Imaging in Medicine.* Berlin: Springer-Verlag, pp. 21–41.

ITOH, M., and H. YOKOI, 1979. A computer-aided three-dimensional display system for ultrasonic diagnosis of a breast tumor. *Ultrasonics*, pp. 261–268.

KING, D. L., D. L. KING JR., and M. Y. SHAO, 1990. Three-dimensional spatial registration and interactive display of position and orientation of real-time ultrasound images. *J. Ultrasound Med.* 9:525–532.

LALOUCHE, R. C., D. BICKMORE, F. TESSLER, H. K. MANKOVICH, and H. KANGARALOO, 1989. Three-dimensional reconstruction of ultrasound images. *SPIE '89, Medical Imaging*, pp. 59–66.

LEIPNIK, R., 1960. The extended entropy uncertainty principle. *Info. Control* 3:18–25.

LEVOY, M., 1988. Display of surface from volume data. *IEEE CG&A* 8(5):29–37.

LEVOY, M., 1990. A hybrid ray tracer for rendering polygon and volume data. *IEEE CG&A* 10(2):33–40.

LIANG, J., C. SHAW, and M. GREEN, 1991. On temporal-spatial realism in the virtual reality environment. In *User Interface Software and Technology, 1991*, Hilton Head, S.C., U.S.A., pp. 19–25.

LIN, W., S. M. PIZER, and V. E. JOHNSON, 1991. Surface estimation in ultrasound images. *Information Processing in Medical Imaging 1991*, Wye, U.K. Heidelberg: Springer-Verlag, pp. 285–299.

MATSUMOTO, M., M. INOUE, S. TAMURA, K. TANAKA, and H. ABE, 1981. Three-dimensional echocardiography for spatial visualization and volume calculation of cardiac structures. *J. Clin. Ultrasound* 9:157–165.

MCCANN, H. A., J. S. SHARP, T. M. KINTER, C. N. MCEWAN, C. BARILLOT, and J. F. GREENLEAF, 1988. Multidimensional ultrasonic imaging for cardiology. *Proc. IEEE* 76(9):1063–1073.

MILLS, P. H., and H. FUCHS, 1990. 3D ultrasound display using optical tracking. In *First Conference on Visualization for Biomedical Computing*, Atlanta, Ga., IEEE, pp. 490–497.

MIYAZAWA, T., 1991. A high-speed integrated rendering for interpreting multiple variable 3D data. *SPIE* 1459(5).

MOLNAR, S., J. EYLES, and J. POULTON, 1992. Pixel Flow: High-speed rendering using image composition. *Comput. Graphics (Proc. SIGGRAPH '92)* 26(2).

MORITZ, W. E., A. S. PEARLMAN, D. H. MCCABE, D. K. MEDEMA, M. E. AINSWORTH, and M. S. BOLES, 1983. An ultrasonic techinique for imaging the ventricle in three dimensions and calculating its volume. *IEEE Trans. Biomed. Eng.* BME-30(8):482–492.

NAKAMURA, S., 1984. Three-dimensional digital display of ultrasonograms. *IEEE CG&A* 4(5):36–45.

OHBUCHI, R., and H. FUCHS, 1990. Incremental 3D ultrasound imaging from a 2D scanner. In *First Conference on Visualization in Biomedical Computing*, Atlanta, Ga., IEEE, pp. 360–367.

OHBUCHI, R., and H. FUCHS, 1991. Incremental volume rendering algorithm for interactive 3D ultrasound imaging.

Information Processing in Medical Imaging 1991 (Lecture Notes in Computer Science), Wye, U.K., Berlin: Springer Verlag, pp. 486–500.

PINI, R., E. MONNINI, L. MASOTTI, K. L. NOVINS, D. P. GREENBERG, B. GREPPI, M. CEROFOLINI, and R. B. DEVEREUX, 1990. Echocardiographic three-dimensional visualization of the heart. *3D Imaging in Medicine*, Travemünde, Germany, F 60. Berlin: Springer-Verlag, pp. 263–274.

POLHEMUS, 1980. *3Space Isotrak User's Manual.*

RAICHELEN, J. S., S. S. TRIVEDI, G. T. HERMAN, M. G. SUTTON, and N. REICHEK, 1986. Dynamic three dimensional reconstruction of the left ventricle from two-dimensional echocardiograms. *J. Am. Coll. Cardiol.* 8(2): 364–370.

ROBINETT, W., and J. P. ROLLAND, 1991. A computational model for the stereoscopic optics of a head-mounted display. *Presence* 1(1):45–62.

SABELLA, P., 1988. A Rendering algorithm for visualizing 3D scalar fields. *Comput. Graphics (Proc. SIGGRAPH '88)* 22(4):51–58.

SHATTUCK, D. P., M. D. WEISHENKER, S. W. SMITH, and O. T. VON RAMM, 1984. Explososcan: A parallel processing technique for high speed ultrasound imaging with linear phased arrays. *JASA* 75(4):1273–1282.

SMITH, S. W., S. G. PAVY, JR., and O. T. VON RAMM, 1991. High-speed ultrasound volumetric imaging system: Part I. Transducer design and beam steering. *IEEE Transaction on Ultrasonics, Ferroelectrics, and Frequency Control* 38(2):100–108.

STICKELS, K. R., and L. S. WANN, 1984. An analysis of three-dimensional reconstructive echocardiography. *Ultrasound Med. Biol.* 10(5):575–580.

THIJSSEN, J. M., and B. J. OOSTERVELD, 1990. Texture in tissue echograms, speckle or information? *J. Ultrasound Med.* 9:215–229.

Tomographic Technologies, 1991. *Echo-CT.*

UPSON, C., and M. KEELER, 1988. VBUFFER: Visible volume rendering. *ACM Comput. Graphics (Proc. SIGGRAPH '88)* 22(4):59–64.

VON RAMM, O. T., S. W. SMITH, and H. G. PAVY, JR., 1991. High-speed ultrasound volumetric imaging system: Part II. Parallel processing and image display. *IEEE Transaction on Ultrasonics, Ferroelectrics, and Frequency Control* 38(2): 109–115.

WARD, M., R. AZUMA, R. BENNETT, S. GOTTSCHALK, and H. FUCHS, 1992. A demonstrated optical tracker with scalable work area for head-mounted display systems. In *1992 Symposium on Interactive 3D Graphics*, Cambridge, Mass., ACM, pp. 43–52.

WELLS, P. N. T. 1977. *Biomedical Ultrasonics*. London: Academic.

Robotic Manipulators

INFORMATION without the ability to act is of limited value. Although in many cases the provision of information allows the surgeon to provide the necessary action, it is not always easy for the surgeon to act unaided, even if there is perfect feedback. Robotic manipulators are extensions of computer systems that allow programmed physical interaction with the environment. This section describes robotic manipulators used today in various tasks, including surgery, where the environment is the patient, the operating room, and the surgical team. Even in those cases where surgeons continue to provide the motive element, manipulation aids exploiting many of the technologies in active systems are essential for surgical applications.

Recent years have seen an increased interest on the part of the robotic research community in the development of special-purpose designs for medical use. Before going into particular robotic geometries required for surgery, it will be useful to familiarize the reader with the general-purpose robot manipulator. These manipulators are widely used today in many fields, from industrial production to service and military. The first chapter in this section, by Burdea, is a short survey of general-purpose manipulators. It introduces the specific terminology as well as the manipulator's components and its work envelope, end-effectors (tools), and control. "General-Purpose Robotic Manipulators" further describes various actuators that power today's robotic arms, (hydraulic, electric, or pneumatic). This chapter leaves out the detailed matricial mathematics involved in manipulator kinematics and trajectory planning. Interested readers can consult several textbooks on robotics, such as Fu, Gonzales, and Lee (1987).

Also important for manipulators is their control using data from external sensors. Use of external sensors gives robots a degree of flexibility and adaptability (sometimes called *intelligence*). Sensor noise and drift, however, can affect manipulator accuracy. While manipulators repeatability is excellent, their accuracy may be poor and needs to be checked (by manual calibration). Accuracy becomes even more critical in tasks that involve close contact with the environment, such as the cutting and drilling associated with surgery.

The area of special-purpose surgical manipulators is new and under active research. The use of robots in surgery poses additional requirements in terms of the patient's safety. These requirements are discussed in the second chapter in this section, "Special-Purpose Actuators and Architectures for Surgery Robots," by Khodabandehloo, Brett, and Buckingham. In Khodabandehloo's opinion, concern for the patient's safety dictates some changes in manipulator geometry and actuator control. Fail-safe brakes must be incorporated into the actuators so that the manipulator does not collapse on the patient during unexpected power outages. The manipulator's work envelope must be easily recognized by the members of the surgical team, so that it becomes clear to them when the patient is placed inside the volume reached by the manipulator tool. The spherical manipulator described in this chapter has a design that satisfies this safety requirement. This special-purpose manipulator also has independent control for the last joint, allowing "manual" retraction of the tool by the surgeon. Robotic safety issues are discussed further in chapter 19 and in a number of chapters in Part II of this book.

Surgical requirements may also result in changes to the generic manipulator in terms of the actuator technology used. For certain applications, electric, hydraulic, or pneumatic actuators may not be at all adequate, and new solutions are needed. The third chapter, by Ikuta, Tsukamoto, and Hirose describes novel actuators that use shape-memory metals. These alloys change shape in an amount proportional with the electric current that passes through them. They have excellent power-weight ratios and are compact, light, and noiseless. Because of these characteristics, they have been used in many other fields besides medicine, such as for active construction materials in civil engineering and for micromechanics. Ikuta's group describes a surgical application of shape-memory metals to a novel active endoscope capable of up to 60° bending. Its major advantage is the use of shift control, which minimizes the patient's discomfort by reducing the push against the colon walls. Alternative design approaches are described in chapter 48.

There are still many unresolved issues in the design of surgical robot manipulators. Some may be solved by technologists, others by wide acceptance of this new technology and its use in hospitals. This section is not an exhaustive presentation but rather an introduction to the complexities of robotic technology, which may prove to be a very powerful new surgical tool. Specific surgical procedures that are presently being robotized are discussed at length in the Applications part of this book.

REFERENCE

Fu, K. S., R. C. Gonzolez, and C. S. G. Lee, 1987. *Robotics: Control, Sensing, Vision, and Intelligence.* New York: McGraw-Hill.

16 General-Purpose Robotic Manipulators: A Short Survey

GRIGORE C. BURDEA

THE ROBOTIC Institute of America defines a robot as "a reprogrammable, multifunctional manipulator designed to move materials, parts, tools or specialized devices through variable programmed motions for the performance of a variety of tasks" (Critchlow, 1985). A robotic system, however, is more than a mechanical manipulator. The special-purpose computer that interprets operator inputs and controls the manipulator motions is the *robot controller*. Operator inputs are sent to the controller through an *operator interface*; that term refers to the console terminal as well as the teach pendant used for manual control. The robot controller samples *external sensors* that detect changes in the robot's environment. The robotic system also includes equipment such as conveyors, feeders, part bins, and fixtures that help in the performance of the automated process. Finally, in cases where tasks involve heavy computational loads, the robot controller is interfaced with powerful host computers. These machines perform most of the number-crunching operations and communicate with the robot controller through communication lines (serial, ethernet, etc.) (Burdea and Wolfson, 1991).

Manipulators

The robot manipulator is the principal component of the robotic system. The manipulator, in turn, is composed of a *base, links, actuators*, and an *end-effector*. The base usually is fixed to a supporting surface and prevents the manipulator from toppling at high rates of speed. The base also provides a fixed reference system, which helps in robot programming. The manipulator links are its movable segments (usually in an open kinematic chain). Links are numbered in ascending order starting with the base (link 0) and ending at the wrist. The links are also called the *trunk, shoulder, upper arm,* and *forearm*, as shown in figure 16.1.

The motion of the manipulator is made possible by joints that connect adjacent links. Joints may be prismatic or revolute, depending on their geometry. Prismatic joints allow relative translation of two links, whereas revolute joints have rotation but no translation. The number of manipulator joints corresponds to its number of degrees of freedom (dof). If a robot needs only to place but not to orient objects in space, then 3 dof are sufficient. Therefore such a manipulator has only three joints. If, however, the manipulated object must be oriented, then the manipulator needs at least 6 dof. Robots with more than 6 dof are called *redundant*. The extra degrees of freedom are used to pick up objects behind obstacles in the work space and in tight places where a nonredundant manipulator cannot reach. The increased dexterity comes at a price; the control of redundant manipulators is more complicated than of manipulators with six joints or less. Therefore this is still an area of active research (Lovass-Naghy and Schilling, 1987).

The first three joints (starting from the manipulator base) are called the *major* joints. Depending on the type of major joints (prismatic or revolute), manipulators are *Cartesian, cylindrical, spherical, scara,* or *revolute*, as shown in figure 16.2. The work envelope of a manipulator is the 3D space wherein the robot can reach and perform its programmed task. A robot has a Cartesian work envelope if all its major joints are prismatic. If one major joint is revolute, the robot is cylindrical; spherical and scara manipulators have two revolute major joints. If all three major joints are revolute, the robot has a revolute work envelope. Examples of various robot configurations are IBM 7565 (Cartesian), GMF Robotics M-1 (cylindrical), Prab Robots Inc. P-42 (spherical), IBM 7547 (scara), and Puma 560 (revolute) (Society of Manufacturing Engineers, 1985).

The last three joints allow the manipulator to orient the grasped object in space. These are the *minor* joints,

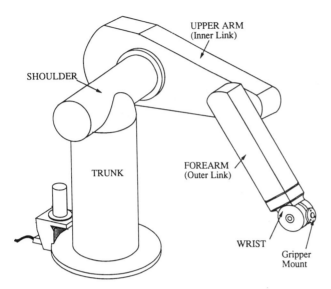

FIGURE 16.1 Manipulator components (Puma 560 robot). (Adapted from Fu, Gonzalez, and Lee, 1987.)

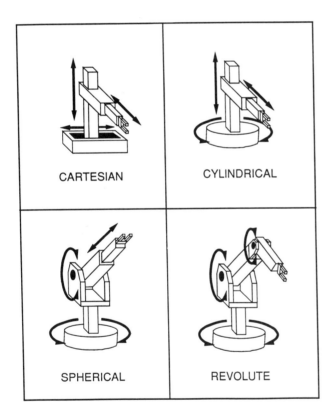

FIGURE 16.2 Manipulator work envelopes.

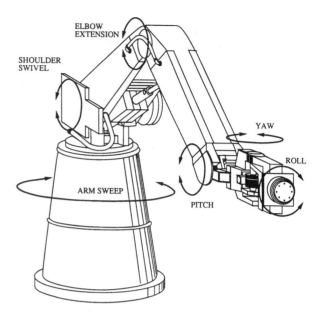

FIGURE 16.3 Manipulator wrist axes. (Adapted from Fu, Gonzalez, and Lee, 1987.)

Other important components of the manipulator are its actuators and its internal sensors. Actuators are used to move the manipulator to the desired position and orientation whereas internal sensors are measuring joint positions to reduce control errors. Depending on the type of actuator used, a manipulator may be classified as *hydraulic*, *electric*, or *pneumatic*. Hydraulic actuators use high-pressure oil as hydraulic fluid. Due to the incompressibility of oil, these actuators produce very large forces or torques with high control bandwidth. Hydraulic actuators are therefore used in manipulators designed for very large payloads. The disadvantages of hydraulic manipulators are that they are not "clean" (due to oil leaks), they are noisy (due to the oil pump), and they are difficult to install (due to the extensive piping required). These drawbacks make hydraulic manipulators unsuitable for use in an operating room environment.

Most of today's manipulators use electric actuators (either AC or DC). These electric manipulators have small to medium payloads, are clean, and are easier to install and maintain. Recent advances have allowed electric manipulators to be used in very humid environments without fear of short circuits. An example are the water-tight Adept One manipulators used in food packaging, where they are cleaned by water hose after each shift (Kassler, 1990).

Electric robots, however, cannot be used in explosive environments (such as munitions factories and storage

called *roll*, *pitch*, and *yaw*. Due to the requirement to have an analytic (closed-form) solution for the robot position control, the axes of the three minor joints intersect at the wrist, as shown in figure 16.3.

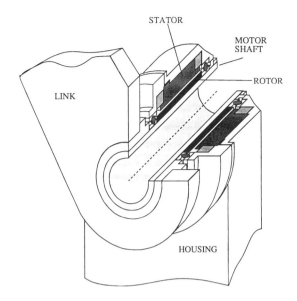

FIGURE 16.4 Direct-drive electric actuator. (Adapted from Asada and Youcef-Toumi, 1987.)

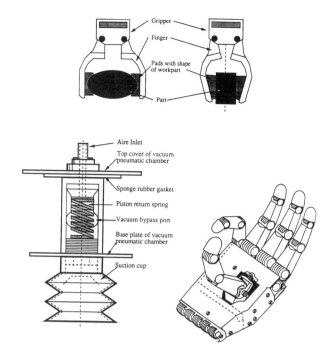

FIGURE 16.5 Manipulator end-effectors.

facilities). These settings use pneumatic robots, which are clean and reduce the chance for explosions. Their major drawback is a low control bandwidth due to the compressibility of air.

Actuators have traditionally been placed remote from the joints they move due to the limited space available inside the manipulator. Motion and torques are then transmitted from the actuator shaft to the joint through cables, pulleys, and belts. This mechanical assembly suffers from backlash and friction, with adverse effects on the control accuracy of the manipulator. Modern designs use *direct-drive* actuators, which are placed coaxial with the (revolute) joints (Asada and Youcef-Toumi, 1987). These actuators are high-performance brushless DC motors, as in the Matsushita Direct-Drive Robot HDD-1. Each component of the motor is installed directly at the joint housing, the rotor on a hollow shaft, and the stator at a case, as shown in figure 16.4. This results in improved control and simpler manipulator geometry.

End-effectors

A manipulator interacts with the task it has to complete through the end-effector (or tool) mounted on its wrist. Depending on their geometry, end-effectors may be *grippers*, *specialized tools*, or *dextrous hands*, as shown in figure 16.5. The factors involved in selecting a given end-effector are the task to be handled, the actuation

method, the power and signal transmission, and the operating environment.

Grippers have the simplest construction, with only two moving fingers (in either a parallel or an angular motion). Grippers may have their own actuators, allowing for a programmed degree of opening or closing of the fingers, or may have just two positions (fully opened, fully closed). When grasping cylindric or spherical objects, gripper fingers must be fitted with pads that maximize the contact surface for a more stable grasp (Cutkosky, 1985). Grippers may have their own sensors, such as LEDs that detect part presence before closing the fingers. More advanced grippers have force and touch sensors that monitor forces during part grasping and manipulation. Thus, robots can prevent part slippage during transport and can identify grasped parts based on touch information.

Other tasks may require drilling, welding, or picking up thin objects (such as computer chips or glass sheets). In these cases, where a gripper cannot be used, the end-effector becomes a drill, a welding gun, or a vacuum cup respectively. When the task is such that robots are required to change end-effectors for each subtask, then the manipulator wrist is fitted with an adaptor. A second adaptor is coupled with tools in a *tool library* in a modular fashion. The manipulator can then change tools automatically.

The greatest degree of flexibility for performing a task is obtained when the robot end-effector is a dextrous hand. These robotic hands are similar to the human hand in geometry and dexterity (Venkataraman and Iberall, 1990), with higher force and quicker response capability. The newer robotic hand models have placed the actuators inside the palm and wrist (Ali and Engler, 1991) and therefore are compact enough to be installed directly on the robot wrist. The hand control is done by a dedicated *hand controller*, which is separate from the robot controller (Clark et al., 1989). Therefore, the improved manipulator dexterity also increases the overall system's complexity and cost.

Sensors

As robotics evolved and tasks had to be performed in unstructured environments (with many unknowns), it became apparent that the manipulator internal sensors were not sufficient to ensure success. External sensors are needed to provide information on changes in the work space and to allow the robot a degree of adaptation to these changes. External sensors are also needed when the manipulator tracks moving targets or must avoid colliding with obstacles.

External sensors can be classified as *vision sensors* (Pugh, 1986a; Fairhurst, 1988) or *nonvision sensors* (Pugh, 1986b). Vision sensors are solid-state cameras mounted above the work envelope (fixed) or on the manipulator arm (mobile). These cameras are compact and light enough that their weight does not produce a significant increase in the manipulator payload. When the field of view needs to be inside the robot gripper, cameras can be fitted with optic fibers incorporated in the gripper fingers or wrist (an "eye-in-hand" arrangement). Camera electric signals are first processed in an interface box that subsequently relays vision information to a host computer (not the robot controller). The host computer then "understands" the image by applying high-level vision algorithms for object recognition, and transmits new motion commands to the manipulator controller (Fu, Gonzalez, and Lee, 1987).

Nonvision sensors are force sensors, touch sensors, ultrasound range finders, proximity sensors, 3D position trackers, limit switches, and the like. Force sensors are typically wrist sensors that measure three forces and three moments at the robot wrist (Piller, 1986).

Touch sensors are thin arrays of sensing elements that are layered on the manipulator fingers. Whereas force sensors measure total force, touch sensors can discretize the contact area, thus giving more meaningful sensing data (closer to where the force is actually generated) than do wrist force sensors. Proximity sensors are used to detect a part or an obstacle at close range. These are Hall-effect transducers (for metallic surfaces), micro-air jets, or LEDs (Cheung and Lumelsky, 1988). 3D position trackers are noncontact sensors that use low-frequency magnetic fields to measure the position and orientation of a moving probe versus a fixed system of coordinates (An et al., 1988). If the probe is attached to a moving target, the robot can use this data to track that target in real time (Burdea et al., 1991).

Control

The low-level manipulator control involves servo loops, each controlling a manipulator joint using internal sensors. The high-level manipulator control has three layers, namely (in increasing order of complexity) manual control, off-line control, and task-level control. Manual control is accomplished by moving the manipulator using push-buttons on a teach pendant connected to the robot controller. This is the simplest and most frequent way of teaching a new task (no programming skills are needed). The robot stores the taught positions and then "plays back" during task execution. The disadvantages are safety risks (the operator must be close to the robot to observe its end-effector) and the difficulty of integrating external sensing commands into the "program."

A more advanced way of controlling the robot is through off-line programming in one of numerous robotic languages (Blume and Jakob, 1986). This allows easy integration of external sensing data as well as manipulator control at faster speeds than those achieved with manual control, with increased safety to the operator. Off-line programming does, however, require computer programming skills, and it entails lengthy debugging, typically through a graphics simulator (Schilling and White, 1990).

The most advanced method of robot control is through high-level, natural-language programming. Rather than specifying each manipulator motion, task-level programming describes only the task to be done, regardless of what manipulator is used. Therefore task-level programming is more general in nature than off-line programming, which depends on the specific model of manipulator used. The added complexity required to translate high-level programming to specific robotic languages makes this an area of current research (Craig, 1989; Koivo, 1989).

In a surgical task implementation, it is unreasonable to rely totally on robot reasoning and action without some form of human supervision. The kind of control that allows the robot to perform some (or most) of the tasks automatically, but still gives the human operator the possibility to take over at any time, is called *supervisory control* (Vertut and Coiffet, 1986a,b; Sheridan, 1992). This form of control combines the manipulator's high force capacity and good repeatability with human adaptability and intelligence.

Accuracy and repeatability

Manipulator accuracy is crucial for the successful performance of tasks that involve control based on external sensing data. *Accuracy* refers to the degree by which the robot end-effector's actual position differs from the commanded one. The manipulator's *repeatability* is its ability to return to a given location repeatedly (whether or not that location was the commanded one). These two attributes are illustrated in figure 16.6.

Robots have excellent repeatability, on the order of 0.1 mm (Groover et al., 1986). However, their accuracy is much poorer, such that the tool position may be as much as 5–6 cm and 4°–5° away from its intended position and orientation. These inaccuracies are due to a number of factors, including manipulator design, control errors, and external sensing errors. Although controllers and sensors can be improved and noisy data filtered, there is not much that can be done about the manipulator design. Each joint has tolerances, and too tight a fit is not possible. These tolerances add up, because manipulators are (in general) open-loop kinematic chains.

Manipulator inaccuracies result in an "arm signature" specific to each individual robot within a given model population. These position errors are reduced by the process of *calibration*, which may be done by the robot manufacturer but usually is carried out at the manipulator task site (Veitschegger and Wu, 1988). This process is tedious but unavoidable for high-precision tasks, such as robot-assisted surgery.

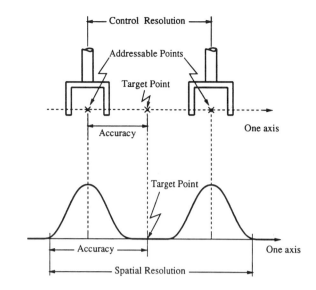

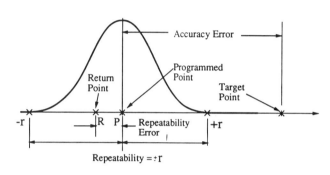

FIGURE 16.6 Manipulator accuracy and repeatability. (Adapted from Groover et al., 1986.)

Conclusion

This chapter has described the configuration of general-purpose robotic manipulators, considering their degrees of freedom, work envelopes, end-effectors, and types of actuators. These manipulators are integrated in a robotic system that uses a robot controller, external sensors, and host computers. The resulting system is adaptable and has machine intelligence, which increases the likelihood of successful task performance.

REFERENCES

ALI, M. S., and C. ENGLER JR., 1991. System description document for the Anthrobot-2: A dextrous robot hand, *NASA Technical Memorandum 104535*, National Aeronautics and Space Administration.

AN, K.-N., M. C. JACOBSEN, L. J. BERGLUND, and E. Y.

CHAO, 1988. Application of a magnetic tracking device to kinesiologic studies. *J. Biomechanics* 21(7):613–620.

ASADA, H., and K. YOUCEF-TOUMI, 1987. *Direct-Drive Robots: Theory and Practice.* Cambridge, Mass.: MIT Press.

BLUME, C., and W. JAKOB, 1986. *Programming Languages for Industrial Robots.* Berlin: Springer-Verlag.

BURDEA, G. C., S. DUNN, M. MALLIK, and C. IMMENDORF, 1991. Real-time sensing of tooth position for dental digital subtraction radiography. *IEEE Trans. Biomed. Eng.* 38(4): 366–378.

BURDEA, G. C., and H. WOLFSON, 1991. Solving jigsaw puzzles using a robot. In *Intelligent Robotic Systems*, S. Tzafestas, ed. New York: Marcel Dekker, pp. 637–671.

CHEUNG, E., and V. LUMELSKY, 1988. Motion planning for robot arm manipulators with proximity sensing. In *Proceedings of the 1988 IEEE International Conference on Robotics and Automation.* Philadelphia: IEEE Press.

CLARK, D., J. DEMMEL, J. HONG, G. LAFFERRIERE, L. SALKIND, and X. TAN, 1989. Teleoperating the Utah/MIT Hand with a VPL DataGlove: II. Architecture and applications. In *Proceedings of the 1989 Conference on Robotics and Automation.* IEEE Press.

COIFFET, P., 1991. Personal communication.

CRAIG, J. J., 1989. *Introduction to Robotics: Mechanics and Control*, 2d ed. Reading, Mass.: Addison-Wesley.

CRITCHLOW, A. J., 1985. *Introduction to Robotics.* New York: Macmillan.

CUTKOSKY, M. R., 1985. *Robotic Grasping and Fine Manipulation.* Boston: Kluwer.

DARIO, P., and M. BERGAMASCO, 1988. An advanced robot system for automated diagnostic tasks through palpation. *IEEE Trans. Biomed. Eng.* 35(2):118–125. IEEE Press.

FAIRHURST, M., 1988. *Computer Vision for Robotic Systems: An Introduction.* New Jersey: Prentice Hall.

FU, K. S., R. GONZALEZ, and C. S. G. LEE, 1987. *Robotics: Control, Sensing, Vision, and Intelligence.* New York: McGraw-Hill.

GRAHAM, H. J., ed., 1987. *Computer Architectures for Robotics and Automation.* New York: Gordon and Breach.

GROOVER, M. P., M. WEISS, R. N. NAGEL, and N. G. ODREY, 1986. *Industrial Robotics: Technology, Programming, and Applications.* New York: McGraw-Hill.

HARWIN, W., A. GINIGE, and R. JACKSON, 1988. A robot workstation for use in education of the physically handicapped. *IEEE Trans. Biomed. Eng.* 35(2):127–131.

KASSLER, M., 1990. Introduction to the special issue on robots and food-handling. *Robotica* 8:267–268.

KOIVO, A. J., 1989. *Fundamentals for Control of Robotic Manipulators.* New York: Wiley.

KWAH, Y., I. REED, J. CHEN, H. SHAO, and T. TRUONG, 1985. A new computerized tomographic-aided robotic stereotaxis system. *Robotics Age*, June, 17–21.

LOVASS-NAGHY, V., and R. SCHILLING, 1987. Control of kinematically redundant robots using {1}-inverses. *IEEE Trans. Systems Man Cyber.* SMC-17(4):644–649.

PILLER, G., 1986. A compact six-degree-of-freedom force/torque sensor for assembly robots. In *Robot Sensors: Tactile and Non-Vision*, A. Pugh, ed. IFS Publications; pp. 67–74.

PREISING, B., T. HSIA, and B. MITTELSTADT, 1991. A literature review: Robots in medicine. *IEEE Eng. Med. Bio.* 10(2):13–22.

PUGH, A., ed., 1986a. *Robot Sensors*, Vol. 1: *Vision*. IFS Publications.

PUGH, ed., 1986b. *Robot Sensors*, Vol. 2: *Tactile and Non-Vision.* IFS Publications.

SCHILLING, R. J., and R. B. WHITE, 1990. *Robotic Manipulation: Programming and Simulation Studies.* Englewood Cliffs, N.J.: Prentice Hall.

SHERIDAN, T. B., 1992. *Telerobotics, Automation, and Human Supervisory Control.* Cambridge, Mass.: MIT Press.

Society of Manufacturing Engineers, 1985 *Industrial Robots.* Dearborn, Mich.: Society of Manufacturing Engineers.

VEITSCHEGGER, W., and C. H. WU, 1988. Robot calibration and compensation. *IEEE J. Robotics Automation* 4(6):643–656.

VENKATARAMAN, S. T., and T. IBERALL, eds., 1990. *Dextrous Robot Hands.* New York: Springer-Verlag.

VERTUT, J., and P. COIFFET, 1986a. *Teleoperation and Robotics*, Vol. 1: *Evolution and Development.* Englewood Cliffs, N.J.: Prentice Hall.

VERTUT, J., and P. COIFFET, 1986b. *Teleoperation and Robotics*, Vol. 2: *Applications and Technology.* Englewood Cliffs, N.J.: Prentice Hall.

17 Special-Purpose Actuators and Architectures for Surgery Robots

KOOROSH KHODABANDEHLOO, PETER N. BRETT, AND R. O. BUCKINGHAM

THERE ARE A growing number of examples of robot systems in which integration of the manipulator, sensory, and expert system technologies has increased the system level of autonomy and its ability to cope automatically with variation in working conditions. Examples include the sheep-shearing robot (Trevelyan, 1988) where the cutter is able to react to variations in sheep's geometry and its moving surface; robot systems for fruit picking (Marchant, 1988) and poultry packaging (Khodabandehloo, 1990) involving the identification of objects of varying size and geometry to guide a manipulator to pick and place; and a robot for playing a game of snooker (Rennell and Khodabandehloo 1989). These innovations demonstrate the increasing scope of potential applications for robot technology.

Surgery is one such area of application. Difficulties are imposed by the complex working environment, the extreme safety requirements, and the limitations of the current state of technology. Although it is accepted that the capabilities of the surgeon cannot be fully replaced, there are some applications where benefits can be realized in the near future. In such applications, the use of robotic technology can alleviate the difficulties of recognition, location of the working point, and dealing with nonrigid tissues. It is important that these abilities be identified and demonstrated successfully in order for robotics to be accepted for use in surgery.

The fundamental advantages of the use of robots in surgery are as follows:

- Repeatable tool position and trajectory
- Steady motion
- Ability to react rapidly to changes in force level
- Remote operation
- Ability to remain poised in a fixed position

Because of such attributes, the use of robots can lead to more effective treatment. In the case of contagious diseases, reducing human contact lowers the risk of infection. In other cases robots can reduce risks to the patient by offering the potential of less invasive surgery.

There are examples of robots used without physical contact with patients. In these cases the noninvasive action of the robot has avoided some of the safety concerns, reducing the possibility of litigation while providing some of the benefits discussed earlier. More recent investigations are exploring human contact using a robotic device (Finlay, 1990). Research in France is directed toward developing a robotic system to assist in spinal surgery procedures (McEwan et al., 1989), and an automated retraction system is undergoing research in Canada (Drake et al., 1991). Recently, a purpose-built device has been developed for transurethral resection of the prostate (Davies et al., 1991); this invasive machine has successfully completed clinical trials.

A number of areas of technology must be considered before a suitably autonomous device can be developed, not least the role of "expert systems" for high-level system control. It is not considered reasonable that a robot system should operate without continuous backup from a surgeon who is in a position to define and check the step-by-step progress of the task and to override the system in case of unforeseen difficulties. The robotic device would be driven to an acceptable start under position control by the surgeon and, on instruction, would perform the defined task, prompting the surgeon at each stage. The system would be required to react to given situations in real time by comparison of actual behavior with reference models of characteristic behavior of the medium during cutting or handling. Such reference data can assist in identifying material properties or anticipating undesirable behavior requiring remedial action.

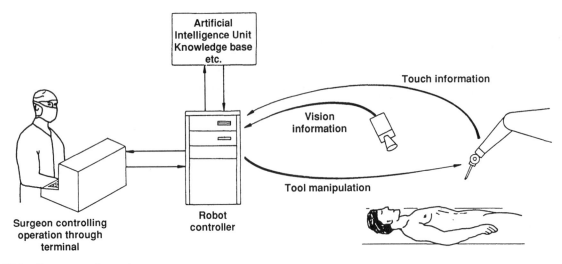

FIGURE 17.1   System configuration.

An appropriate system configuration is shown in figure 17.1. The system is rich in sensors. At the tool or end-effector, torque and force measurements would be combined with vision data. The expert system provides high-level control in relation to progress and task description. By comparison with behavioral reference models, the planning of manipulator motion can be achieved. The low-level controller of joint motion will have to react to tool force levels as well as velocity and position. The nature of surgical procedure is such that descriptions of techniques tend to be qualitative rather than quantitative. Therefore considerable cooperation is required between physicians and engineers to produce technical specifications for a robot and the associated tools, reflecting manipulation requirements and acceptable force levels.

Consideration of intracranial surgery

Much of the pioneering work on the surgery of brain tumors was carried out in the last century by a German-born surgeon, Ernst von Bergmann (1836–1907). In "A System of Practical Surgery" (1904) he wrote: "No matter how much one might wish for better results for removal of brain tumours than are obtained at present, it must be borne in mind now and in the future that surgical treatment is the only treatment that can save the patient from an otherwise incurable disease. Even the most benign tumour within the skull will be fatal due to its growth, and on account of the space it occupies with operation there is only one termination —death."

Primary CNS (brain and spinal cord) neoplasms are important because although they account for only 2.2% of all cancer deaths, they affect younger age groups more than most other types of cancer and in fact cause 22% of cancer deaths in the under-15 age group and 10% in those aged between 15 and 35 years. Primary neoplasms arise from various types of tissue in the CNS and are classified according to their cell of origin. The two most important groups are the gliomas, which account for 50% of the primary tumors and can occur virtually anywhere within the brain substance; and meningiomas (15%), which arise from the meningi, or membranes covering the surface and folding into the crevices of the brain. Fifty percent of brain tumors are metastases—that is, secondary tumors arising from other primary sites, typically the breast, the lung, or a melanoma of the skin.

Despite the use of and continued research into chemotherapy (Grunberg et al. 1991; Krischer et al., 1991) and radiotherapy to treat various types of brain tumor, these techniques are used only if resection is inadvisable due to the condition of the patient or the position of the tumor. The aim of any surgical resection of a tumor will be one of the following:

1. Removal of the tumor in its entirety, causing as little damage to surrounding brain tissue as possible. This is possible only with well-demarcated tumors such as meningiomas.

2. Removal of the tumor with some surrounding normal brain to ensure adequate resection margins (nonvital areas of the brain only). This technique is

used for gliomas that spread by infiltration so that their boundaries are impossible to define.

3. Removal of the bulk of the tumor while disturbing the surrounding brain as little as possible. This would be used in palliative rather than curative treatment of gliomas or metastases.

The development of CT, MRI (Douglas et al., 1991), ultrasound, and angiography have been invaluable in the diagnosis of tumor type and localization and in giving information about the blood supply of the tumor, thus aiding the planning of surgical techniques. Recently, they have been used intraoperatively to give continued anatomic information where adequate surgical exposure is not possible and differentiation between normal and abnormal tissue is difficult. Furthermore, information from these pictures can be used by computer-assisted navigational systems (Epstein et al., 1991; Watanabe et al., 1987; Kato et al., 1991).

Gliomal tumors are resected through a transcortical incision of the shortest route. The skull opening (craniotomy) is therefore placed to provide optimum access. Having reflected a skin flap, the piece of bone then is removed by drilling small bore holes through the skull and sawing between them. The dura (the outermost of the meninges) is opened, and a brain cannula is used to locate the tumor, which is then exposed by a cortical incision that is gradually widened. The tumor is removed by suction or by ultrasonic aspirator until more firm or normal areas are reached where the brain architecture is preserved. The dura is repaired as far as possible and the bone flap replaced.

The craniotomy for removal of a meningioma is similar; however, the piece of skull may be saved and replaced at a later date to allow for some postoperative swelling of the brain. The tumor may have begun to infiltrate the undersurface of the skull, in which case a blunt instrument is inserted under the flap and the tumor is dissected off it. Great care must be taken not to distort the underlying brain or tear blood vessels. A circular incision is made in the dura at the tumor margin. A small hole then is made in the middle of this piece of dura, and the central part of the tumor is sucked out, avoiding undue thinning of the remaining thickness of tumor capsule, and possible penetration of inversion, by means of palpation at intervals with blunt forceps. Small blood vessels must be coagulated or tied off. The location of vessels will have been shown

by the arteriogram. The tumor can now be gently peeled away from the brain surface, and the nutrient arteries, once it has been confirmed that their distribution is confined to the tumor, are clipped or coagulated. It is obviously important throughout the procedure to maintain hemostasis—that is, to prevent bleeding by laser, by electric coagulation, or by tying the arteries. Failure to do this will result in hemorrhage and clot formation with potentially severe neurologic consequences. It is also important to avoid drainage to the brain, either by traction and distortion or indirectly by interference with arteries and veins. This will minimize the amount of postoperative edema and hence compression of brain tissues. Edema can be limited by the use of steroid treatment.

It may be useful to carry out a biopsy of the lesion through a bore hole, either for histologic diagnosis or to decompress a tumor in those patients unsuitable for craniotomy. A tumor cyst may be drained by this method. The tumor is approached by the shortest route from the surface, avoiding passage through important areas if possible. After the meninges are incised, a blunt side-holed brain cannula is introduced. The distance of insertion will have been estimated previously from radiologic information. A stereotactic method of biopsy is essential for tumors located deep in the brain, in the thalamus or basal ganglia or around the third ventricle.

The preceding descriptions are necessarily brief and generalized. A detailed account of methods of tumor resections in their wide variety of locations in the brain would assume a detailed knowledge of neuroanatomy and is beyond the scope of this chapter.

To summarize, the basic aims of most intracranial surgery are (1) maximum tumor resection, (2) minimum damage to normal brain tissue, (3) maintenance of hemostasis, and (4) reduction in complication rate.

Manipulator design for intracranial surgery

In the case of the manipulator, the design objectives are driven by the required access and manipulation of tools, accuracy of position, and force level control. High safety standards must be observed because the robot system is to operate in close proximity with the patient and the team of surgical theater staff. A potential hazard is a "runaway" joint. The risk can be reduced by selecting a suitable manipulator configuration. The following criteria are considered important:

• At the working site, tool motion should be achieved by moving a minimum number of joints.

• Tool motion should be achieved by decoupled joint motion at the end-effector.

• The facility for tool and end-effector position should be deduced simply by visual inspection of joint positions.

• By manual override, the tool and end-effector should be extracted and withdrawn from the working site safely by moving one joint at a time.

• The work space of the manipulator should be discernible by theater staff. This is best achieved if the work space is internal to the structure of the manipulator.

• The patient should be outside of the work space available to the manipulator when the end-effector is moved to the working site.

• Manipulator structure should enable reasonable access to the patient.

It is unlikely that a manipulator will satisfy such constraints and be suitable for general use. It will more likely be dedicated to a particular procedure or to working on a specific region of the body.

The configuration shown in figure 17.2, for example, is suited to working on an area of the head. The design features three linear drives, a rotary axis, and a curved

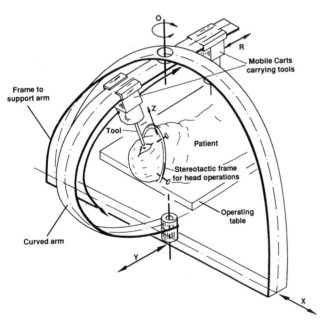

FIGURE 17.2 Stereotactic biopsy: manipulator configuration.

rail on which carriages supporting specialized end-effectors can be moved. Many procedures require two working points of contact in the manipulation of tissue or the use of tools. Safety considerations are reflected in the method of operating the manipulator. Initially, drives X and Y are moved to align the manipulator with the operating table. In some procedures, the patient must be supported such that his or her position is assured with respect to a reference position. In that case, the end-effector is moved to the correct position and the manipulator joints are locked in that position. Tool motion can then be controlled by drives actuated at the end-effector. The movement of the joints of the manipulator can be restricted to avoid contact with the patient when the manipulator is moved into position. The fact that the robot cannot move outside of its well-defined work envelope, given by the curved members, also reduces the risk to theater staff. End-effector motion can be achieved by decoupled joint motion such that end-effectors can be removed manually, easily and quickly, without risk to the patient.

When considering the application of mechanisms to the task of assisting a surgeon in head surgery, it is important to consider some elements of the design process in detail. In particular, the safety aspects of robot designs will come under extreme scrutiny. A failure of any description and, at worst, an error resulting in the death of a patient on the operating table, will certainly delay the application of this useful technology to surgical practice. A key part of the development of such a system will be the testing and evaluation of the risks involved. In addition, it is highly unlikely that advanced, autonomous mechanisms will be used from the outset. In the first instance, it is expected that a surgeon will use a mechanism such as that shown in figure 17.2 in a similar manner to stereotactic frames. This puts great emphasis on the user interface between the surgeon and the mechanism. From a technical standpoint, it has been proved that an autonomous system, with input data from CT and MRI, can locate and remove intracranial neoplasms with great accuracy, reliability, and speed (Kall et al., 1992).

The improvements that surgeons would like to see in operative techniques include the following:

1. More exact tumor location
2. Increased ability to reach the desired location with minimum damage to the intermediate and surrounding normal brain tissue

3. Increased ability to reach the desired location in a controlled manner at a predefined and most appropriate orientation

4. Reduction in the size of the skull flap

5. Reduction in operating time

6. Reduction in the duration of postoperative care

7. Increased range of possible operations

A high-accuracy mechanism that enables a specified position and orientation to be reached reliably and repeatedly, on the basis of previously scanned data, offers the capability to achieve all these goals.

SURGICAL MOBILITY REQUIREMENTS AND CURRENT STEREOTACTIC FRAMES

The basic surgical maneuver is to move a tool to a certain depth in a certain direction defined by two orientation angles, from a start position defined by three Cartesian $x, y,$ and z coordinates. Therefore, to achieve complete flexibility of tool motion, the robot must have at least 5 degrees of freedom (dof). Current stereotactic support devices generally have only 2 dof, which allow the tool to lie along any radius of a hemisphere where the center of the hemisphere is fixed in relation to the skull.

The robot requires the following pieces of information to define its required motion:

• A datum from which all measurements are known
• The position of the tumor in the brain with respect to the datum (x_t, y_t, z_t)
• The required approach orientation $(\alpha_\tau, \beta_\tau)$
• The standoff position (x_s, y_s, z_s)

Given this information, the robot can be moved to the standoff position and orientation and the correct penetration depth calculated. This is illustrated in figure 17.3.

A REVOLUTE DESIGN

Figure 17.4 shows a revolute mechanism that has much in common with the majority of current robot designs. The robot consists of a linear axis (x_1), four rotary joints $(\theta_2, \theta_3, \theta_4, \theta_5)$, and a final linear axis (T_6) in line with the approach vector of the surgical tool. The motions of the rotary joints are coupled, in the sense that the achievement of end-effector motion in the most important direction requires the concurrent interaction of more than one joint. In this case, straight-line end-

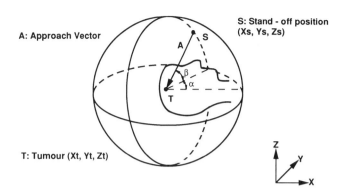

FIGURE 17.3   Standoff sphere.

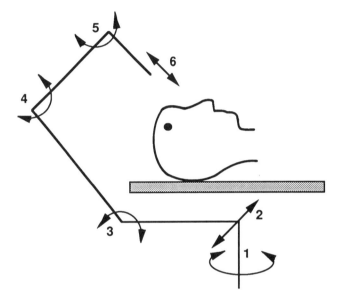

FIGURE 17.4   Revolute design.

effector motion in the y or z planes requires the interaction of at least joints 3, 4, and 5. With the linear motion in the x axis and the base rotation about the z axis, the tool can take up any line of action that intersects with the base-rotation z axis. The first five joints are capable of driving the tool along the approach vector without having an extra tool drive—that is, T_6 is redundant. T_6 is included for safety reasons.

The normal method of driving the links of the robot is to mount an electric motor on each of the joints. This enables large torques to be generated, giving robots great strength. Similarly, an encoder or resolver can be fitted to each joint in order to measure accurately the angle of one joint relative to the next. The information defining the tumor position and standoff position

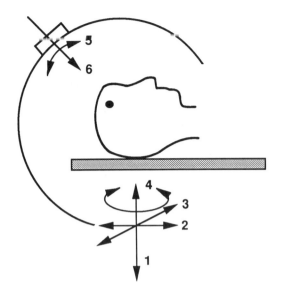

FIGURE 17.5   Spherical design.

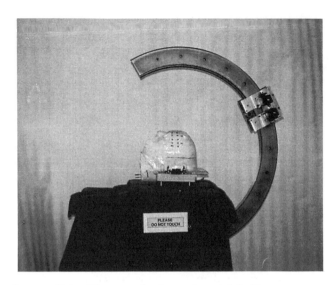

FIGURE 17.6   Photograph of experimental facility.

(see figure 17.3) must be transformed into information to drive the joints of the robot. The mathematic equations for these transformations are not simple to derive, and in this instance there are at least two solutions for each desired tool position. These correspond to the "elbow-up" and "elbow-down" solutions. In addition, with respect to the correspondence of velocities required at the joints to produce velocities at the tool, there are singularities within the work envelope. These singularities are the positions at which a robot of this design can become unstable and uncontrolled. The analysis of these singularities is beyond the scope of this chapter.

A SPHERICAL DESIGN

The design of the robot shown in figure 17.5 is intrinsically different from the revolute design. The robot still has five driven joints and a sixth tool drive. The joints will be identified as z_1, x_2, and y_3 linear motion and a rotation about the z_4 axis; these occur below the operating table. The final two axes of motion are the motion along the circular slide C_5 and along the tool axis T_6, which is normal to C_5. The important difference between the revolute and spherical designs is that each of the joints in the spherical design produces an independent motion—that is, the x travel does not cause any y or z motion of the tool. This makes the control of the robot simpler and also has profound safety advantages. One advantage is that the Jacobian of this design is diagonal and always invertible—that is, there are no

singularities. In addition, there is a direct correspondence between the definition of the tumor location and standoff point and the information required to drive the axes of the spherical mechanism.

The similarity between this robot and the stereotactic frames currently in use is intentional; the motion of the robot will not be unfamiliar to the surgeon, and the positions and angles can be double-checked using reference scales that are provided on the axes of motion. The spherical robot can also be designed to have a number of tool carriages running concurrently on the C slide. Often more than one tool must be held along the axis of the current tool for a supporting task. A spherical robot based on this design has been built and is currently being investigated at the University of Bristol (figure 17.6); it will be used for safety and reliability trials on models.

Safety considerations

Mechanisms as just described can be designed to be powerful, fast, and silent. A number of fatal accidents have occurred in industry using industrial robots, usually when the operator of the robot enters the work space of the robot to carry out maintenance and becomes trapped between the robot and another fixed machine (Dhillon, 1992). Robot accidents can occur due to the malfunction of some component of the hardware or software or, as seems more typical, due to operator error (Khodabandehloo et al. 1985).

The first safety technique that should be employed with all moving machinery is to restrict access in order to keep humans out of the working area of the machine. In the case of surgery, it is quite feasible to keep the operator out of the interaction zone. However, the patient must be placed within this zone. For the patient, the danger zone is better defined as the volume contained within the surface of the head. Therefore, for surgery mechanisms, the first line of safety is to ensure that entry into and exit from this danger zone is conducted in a completely controlled manner at the appropriate time. Systematic analysis of robot safety and reliability can also lead to more realistic consideration of the technical and practical issues (Khodabandehloo et al., 1991).

All mechanical and electric components will at some stage fail. It is therefore necessary to assign a probability of failure to each component of the mechanism and to assign an importance to each of these failures in terms of the system. Techniques such as calculating the mean time to failure and failure mode effects analysis can be applied to such mechanisms to provide reliability and safety information. The accuracy of such techniques is dependent on the accuracy of the data collected during the testing of the mechanism. However, the best method of ensuring safe operation of a mechanism is to design for fail-safe operation.

The principal type of error that can be expected is location of a joint in an incorrect position. This can occur due to backlash, friction, limitations of achievable positional accuracy, power failure, motor component failure, software error, or operator error. The incorrect position may or may not be known to the operator. Of all the causes listed, it is the operator errors that are the most difficult to inhibit. In a comparison between the revolute and the spherical robot, a number of features give the spherical robot a clear safety advantage:

1. A failure of any of the joints of the spherical robot, except the tool axis (i.e., uncontrolled motion of a joint) cannot bring the tool into contact with the patient. In contrast, a failure of joints 3, 4, or 5 of the revolute robot could cause the tool to enter the danger zone. Such failures do occur and can occur very quickly. (The motion of the spherical mechanism's C slide can be made safe by providing mechanical end stops to limit travel.)

2. The spherical design has no singularities.

3. The motion of the spherical robot is easily quantified by the operator—that is, the total required motion of the mechanism can be broken down into clearly defined individual motions.

4. The motion of the spherical robot will be more accurate than that of the revolute robot, because small angular errors of joints $\theta_2, \theta_3, \theta_4$, and θ_5 of the revolute robot can add up to produce a compound error in orientation and position of the tool. The errors produced in the spherical configuration are all independent and are much more easily quantifiable.

5. The main drive motors for the spherical robot are all located below the operating table. This means that access to the patient is maximized. In comparison, it may be difficult to design a revolute type arm that does not restrict necessary access of the surgeon or anesthetist during the operation.

One safety feature can be applied to either mechanism: The motion of the first five joints of the robot can be locked (power removed and a fail-safe brake applied) before any motion of the tool axis is allowed. This action can be overseen by a number of interlocks. In addition, mechanical end stops can be provided so that the depth of penetration of the tool into the patient's brain can be limited to a known amount.

These observations demonstrate that it is possible to design a mechanism that can be relied on, even taking into account operator error, to perform head surgery tasks with minimal (but as yet unquantified) risk. A spherical mechanism as defined is an obvious starting point. Example illustrations of the design and simulation studies are presented in figure 17.7.

Automated drilling of a stapedotomy

THE STAPEDOTOMY PROCEDURE

Stapedotomy is a procedure applied to the middle ear to restore hearing when excess growth of new bone occurs over the flexible ligament around the flat portion of the stapes (known as the *footplate*; figure 17.8). This condition, named *otosclerosis*, reduces movement of the stapes and therefore the transmission of sound disturbances to the cochlea (see figure 17.8). The surgical process involves working within the deep and narrow access of the passage of the outer and middle regions of the ear to drill a hole 0.6 mm in diameter through the stapes footplate, into which a piston-type prosthesis supported on a moving part of the ossicular chain

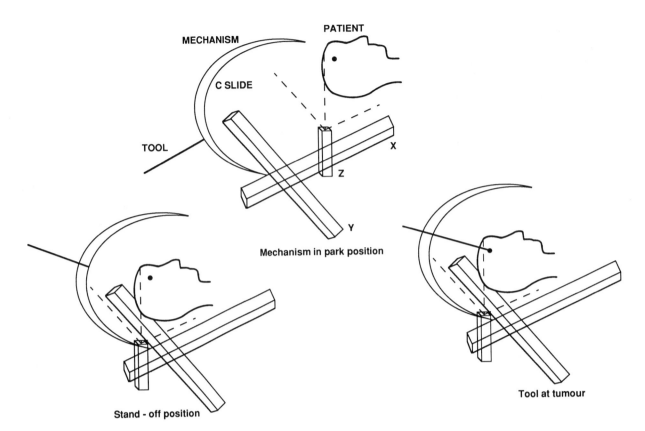

MECHANISM

PATIENT

C SLIDE

TOOL

X

Z

Y

Mechanism in park position

Stand - off position

Tool at tumour

FIGURE 17.7   Simulation studies of the spherical mechanism.

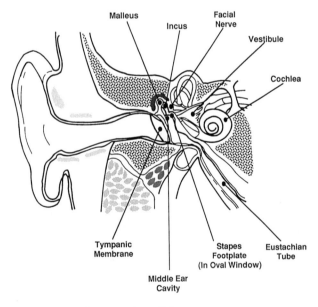

Malleus

Incus

Facial Nerve

Vestibule

Cochlea

Tympanic Membrane

Stapes Footplate (In Oval Window)

Eustachian Tube

Middle Ear Cavity

FIGURE 17.8   Cross-section of the ear.

moves to restore transmission of sound disturbances (figure 17.9).

The footplate of the stapes is of unknown thickness, typically 0.2 mm to 2.5 mm thick, and the surgeon has the difficult task of penetrating the bone without perforating the membrane containing the endolymph in the inner ear beyond the medial surface of the footplate. This involves minimizing penetration of the tool beyond this surface, keeping it to less than 0.2 mm. Because the bone is compliant, there is the added complication of compensating for bone behavior on breakthrough. The bone and surrounding tissues will resume their neutral position, adding risk of damage to the membrane containing endolymph. Currently, many surgeons prefer to employ picks for the boring process, but these produce a poor-quality aperture. Hand-held microdrills are also available; however, when using these it is difficult to control the breakthrough process.

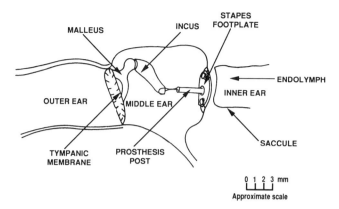

FIGURE 17.9 Configuration of the middle ear after stapedotomy operation.

There is a need for an automatic device that is able to recognize the state of the drilling procedure from force and torque sensory information and to react appropriately.

THE EXPERIMENTAL DRILLING DEVICE

Current techniques of stapedotomy have evolved to minimize disturbance of the vestibular contents and to maximize audiologic gain. A precision stapedotomy with hand-held perforators or a microdrill requires delicate manipulation through a footplate that may vary from 0.6 mm to 2.4 mm thick. Excessive forward pressure may cause fragmentation or disrupt the stapedovestibular ligament to leave a floating footplate. The laser has overcome these complications, though it is not without problems. Furthermore, the decline in the number of stapedotomies has had a significant impact on training and the maintenance of technical expertise.

A robotic device for use in stapedotomy is being developed through collaboration between the departments of otolaryngology of the Bristol Hospitals and the Robotics Research Group at Bristol University. In the first instance, the device is being used to investigate suitable sensing and actuation schemes for automated drilling through the stapes footplate. Automation of the process offers the potential to increase positional accuracy and repeatability and to reduce reaction time to changes in force level compared with manual methods. The device copes with any thickness and has demonstrated that it is possible to anticipate the critical condition of drill-tip "breakthrough" automatically.

The examples of robotic devices employed in surgical procedures described earlier can operate successfully by carefully measuring the location of the work site relative to some datum and positioning the tool with great accuracy. This is true of stereotactic procedures and some orthopaedic procedures. A manipulator is employed as a tool support to locate the invasive tool because without repeatable, accurate positioning, many of the benefits offered by automation technology would be lost. For example, by combining force and displacement information with deformation models, it is possible to anticipate the behavior of the medium.

The following subsections describe an example of such a tool able to perform the controlled penetration of a compliant bone. The tool is designed as a microdrill used to penetrate the stapes footplate, a small bone in the middle ear. The technique developed can also be employed to penetrate other flexible layers of unknown thickness. The experimental device has been deployed on cadavers in experimental trials in a procedure to produce a stapedotomy.

The tool that has been developed is currently laboratory-based and is able to perform the following functions:

• Measure the force characteristics associated with drilling the stapes.

• Demonstrate control strategies for minimum penetration of the drill beyond the far surface of the stapes by reacting to force sensory information.

• Demonstrate the accuracy to which axial distances can be measured using precise positional feed information and tactile sensing. This is particularly valuable in sizing the length of prosthesis.

• Determine deflection characteristics of joints within the ossicular chain. This information offers the potential to assist in identifying the freedom of motion of the moving parts before further surgery is carried out.

A device to automate this procedure must reflect the skill of the operator in judging the progress of cutting through the stapes in order to anticipate penetration and to allow for deflection. The construction is shown in figure 17.10 and features a single-degree-of-freedom drive carriage supporting the drilling mechanism along the feed axis. A DC servo controls feed position by driving the lead screw. Carriage alignment with the axial direction is ensured because the carriage runs on

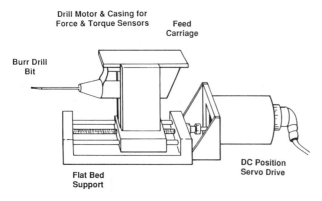

FIGURE 17.10 Demonstration device for drilling a stapedotomy.

two parallel slide rails. The drill bit is driven by a DC motor suspended on brass shims within the carriage to enable small relative motion of the drill bit relative to the carriage in the axial direction. This is necessary to deflect the stiff piezo resistive force transducer. The force transducer is used to determine the feed force exerted on the drill bit. The selection of a particularly mechanically stiff transducer is preferable because feed displacement measurements are required to high accuracy. By setting a preload, using the adjustment screw, the contact between the motor and sensor is maintained both for positive and negative forces acting along the feed axis. The rotational speed of 120 rpm is comparable to that of a number of other hand-held devices applied to the ear that are in current use. Drill-bit torque is derived from the measurement of motor current.

The low-level control of feed position is achieved using the hard-wired DC servo system that responds to velocity demand signals from the high-level control computer. Feed position measurement is obtained using a shaft potentiometer on the lead screw. The high-level controller executes the drilling strategy automatically, as would be required in an operating theater. The computer interfaces with the user via screen, keyboard, and joystick, and with the device through analog-to-digital (A/D) and digital-to-analog (D/A) channels. The high-level control program responds to the positional and force data and controls the feed velocity in the following operating sequence:

1. Surgeon prepares access to stapes footplate.
2. Drill axis is aligned with required feed trajectory.
3. Drill is driven into position under manual control.
4. Drill feed automatic control is activated by surgeon to approach bone surface with care.

5. Drill-to-bone contact is detected and indicated to surgeon.
6. Device determines stiffness of the stapes on application of feed force by the drill with drill bit stationary.
7. Drill bit automatically withdraws a known clearance from the bone surface.
8. Drill bit rotation is activated.
9. Device drills into stapes footplate.
10. On detection of the onset of tip breakthrough, feed force is reduced in order to reduce deflection of stapes.
11. Feed is stopped on detection of tip breakthrough and drill is withdrawn.

In the case of a prototype tool, the alignment of the drill with the desired hole center through the prepared access could be checked using a low-powered visible laser. During laboratory trials on cadavers, an operating theater binocular microscope was used to assist in guiding the tip of the drill bit to a suitable position above the stapes. The machine then was activated and followed the previously cited sequence automatically, pausing only between stages 4 and 5 before confirmation of drilling.

Drill-to-bone contact is indicated on obtaining a feed force of 0.05 N. This feed position, x_d, is recorded. The value of stiffness measured at this stage can be used to provide an indication of the level of mobility of the footplate. This information can be interpreted by the surgeon as the level of difficulty and risk involved in drilling the footplate. A rigid footplate, produced by massive buildup of otosclerosis, is the least difficult to tackle. In addition, the stiffness measurement provides the relationship needed to estimate the true depth of the hole in the stapes by taking the deflection under the action of the feed force into consideration. The estimated deformation can be used to avoid excessive penetration of the drill bit beyond the far surface of the stapes by first detecting the onset of breakthrough and then reducing, or even reversing, feed velocity such that breakthrough occurs with low feed force.

EXPERIMENTAL MEASURES

The form of typical force and torque characteristics for drilling the stapes is shown in figure 17.11. On entering the bone (stages 1 and 2), there is a rapid rise in force and a gradual rise in torque. The asymptote represents the stiffness of the bone or ligament and the restraint holding the temporal bone. When the full diameter of

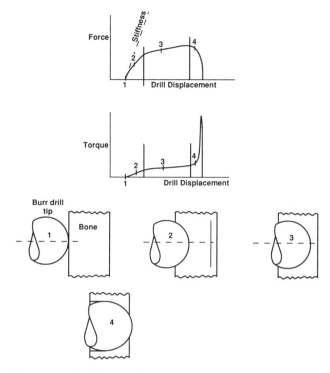

FIGURE 17.11   Force and torque characteristics.

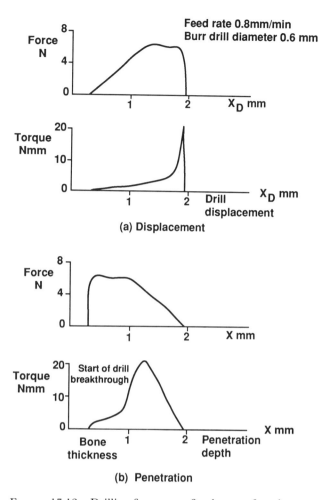

(a) Displacement

(b) Penetration

FIGURE 17.12   Drilling forces on a fixed stapes footplate.

the burr has entered the bone, the rise in force is constant (stage 3). A rise in force indicates that the compliant bone is being deflected in the feed direction. It is possible for the system to reduce the feed rate at this point such that there is no further increase in feed force. Under these conditions the rate of material removal corresponds with the advance of the drill relative to the fixed base of the drilling machine. There is no further deflection of the bone; therefore, there is no increase in force. On approaching breakthrough, there is a fall in force (stage 4), gradual at first as the tip reaches the far surface. There is also a rapid rise in torque and force, interpreted by the system as the tip reaching the far surface. Full breakthrough is achieved in a short space of time and must produce rapid reaction to ensure that the tip does not protrude unnecessarily beyond the far surface as the bone resumes its neutral position. These characteristics are repeatable insofar as the distinct features described are produced regardless of bone thickness and the operating speed of the device.

Measurements corresponding with drilling a fixed stape are given in figure 17.12a, showing the characteristics mentioned earlier. In figure 17.12a, the results are plotted as a function of drill displacement x_d; this is in contrast with the plot shown in figure 17.12b, where

the results plotted are presented as a function of penetration depth x. This information is produced automatically, showing the progress of drilling by applying a simple model to the raw data of figure 17.12a. Using this data, it is possible to identify bone thickness from known features on the graph. In this case, the bone is approximately 0.5 mm thick.

Compared with manual techniques, the automated device produces a hole of higher quality. The penetration of the drill past the far surface of the stapes footplate is controlled to be the radius of the burr drill tip and could be less if so desired. The results shown are typical of a rigidly held stape with a severe condition of otosclerosis. In the case of a stapes where the ligament is free to deflect, the procedure is much more delicate and involves lower forces, peaking at around 0.7 N and a feed rate of 0.3 mm/min. The device has successfully drilled stapes under these conditions with a 100%

success rate. Many otolaryngologists would admit difficulty in tackling a bone in this state.

STATUS OF WORK ON STAPEDOTOMY

An experimental automated surgical tool has been devised for microdrilling in the stapedotomy procedure. Using both drilling force and torque sensory data, it has demonstrated automatic controlled penetration of flexible bones of unknown thickness. The device has also demonstrated the potential for the application of automation technology in an invasive tool for diagnostic and sizing information. These benefits offer the surgeon the potential to achieve greater precision, leading to a higher success rate and quality of result. There is also a lower skill requirement placed on the surgeon in carrying out this particularly delicate procedure.

The techniques described are applicable also to the controlled penetration of other compliant mediums in surgery and could be extended to other industries, such as in food preparation and manufacturing, where there is a need to automatically control breakthrough of layers of unknown thickness.

Conclusions

Despite considerable effort in the field, automatic or robotic tools that assist surgeons in the execution of surgical procedures have not been developed with the anticipated speed. The work presented in this chapter represents new breakthroughs for mechatronic devices. Such devices are likely to be tested with real patients within the next decade. Stapedotomy and intracranial surgery will be only two examples of what technology can bring to the operating theater. Success in improving the quality of life for those unfortunate enough to need such operations will require team effort. We must strive to bridge the gap and strengthen the already established links between surgeons and engineers. As described, the technology can be safe, reliable, and—most important—effective.

ACKNOWLEDGMENT   The input from M. V. Griffiths, J. Blanshard, D. L. Baldwin, M. Wood-Collins, R. A. Buckingham, and R. Fawcett must be acknowledged. The interest of Mr. Dhasmara, Mr. Hutter, Mr. Sandeman, and Mr. Potts of Frenchay Eye Hospital is much appreciated. We thank the DTI for its support in the early parts of the research in this field at the University of Bristol.

REFERENCES

VON BERGMANN, E., 1904. A system of practical surgery. In *Surgery of the Head*, 2d ed. New York: Lea Bros., pp. 17–337.

BRETT, P. N., and K. KHODABANDEHLOO, 1991. Use of robots in surgical procedures. *IMACS-IFAC Symposium, PD Com.*, Corfu, Greece.

BUCKINGHAM, R. O., R. A. BUCKINGHAM, M. E. C. WOOD-COLLINS, P. BRETT, K. KHODEBANDEHLOO, 1992. Kinematic analysis of advanced mechanisms for intra-cranial surgery. In *Proceedings of the First International Workshop in Mechatronics in Medicine and Surgery*, Malaga, Spain.

DAVIES, B. L., R. D. HIBBERD, W. S. NG, A. G. TIMONEY, and J. E. A. WREXHAM, 1991. A surgeon robot for prostatectomies. In *ICAR Proceedings of the Fifth International Conference on Advanced Robotics*, Pisa, Italy, pp. 871–875.

DHILLON, B. S., 1992. *Robot Reliability and Safety*. New York: Springer-Verlag.

DOUGLAS et al. 1991. Characterization of astrocytomas, meningiomas, and pituitary adenomas by phosphorus magnetic resonance spectroscopy. *J. Neurosurg.* 74:447–453.

DRAKE, J. M., M. JOY, A. GOLDENBERG, and D. KREINDLER, 1991. Computer and robotic assisted resection of brain tumours. In *ICAR, Proceedings of the Fifth International Conference on Advanced Robotics*, Pisa, Italy, pp. 888–892.

EPSTEIN, F., et al. 1991. Intra-operative ultrasonography: An important surgical adjunct for intra-medullary tumours. *J. Neurosurg.* 74:729–733.

FINLAY, P. A., 1990. SARAH: An advanced robot for assisting in precision surgery. In *Proceedings of the Conference on Robotics in Medicine*. IMechE HQ, London.

GRUNBERG, S. M., et al., 1991. Treatment of unresectable meningiomas with the antiprogesterone agent mifepristone. *J. Neurosurg.* 74:861–866.

KALL, et al 1992. Computer-assisted stereotactic neurosurgery: Functional design and clinical applications. In *Proceedings of the International Conference IEEE EMBS*, Paris.

KATO, A., et al., 1991. A frameless, armless navigational system for computer-assisted neurosurgery. *J. Neurosurg.* 74:845–849.

KHODABANDEHLOO, K., 1990. Robotic handling and packaging of poultry products. *Robotica* 8:285–297.

KHODABANDEHLOO, K., et al., 1985. Safety integrity assessment of robot systems. In *Safety of Computer Systems*, IFAC Publication. Elmsford, N.Y.: Pergamon, pp. 132–141.

KHODABANDEHLOO, K., et al., 1991. *Safety and Reliability of Robots in Human-Robot Interface*. New York: Taylor and Francis, pp. 121–160.

KRISCHER, P., et al., 1991. Nitrogen mustard, vincristine procarbazine, and prednisone as adjuvant chemotherapy in the treatment of medulloblatome: A paediatric oncology group study. *J. Neurosurg.* 74:897–904.

MARCHANT, J., 1988. *The Use of Robots in the Agricultural and Food Industries*. Bedford, U.K.: National Institute of Agricultural Engineering.

McEWAN, J. A., C. A. BUNAMS, G. F. AUCHINLECK, and M. J. BREAULT, 1989. Development and initial clinical evaluation of pre-robotic and robotic retraction systems for surgery. In *Proceedings of the IARP Second Workshop on Medical and Healthcare Robotics*, Newcastle, U.K.

RENNELL, I. J, and K. KHODABANDEHLOO, 1989. Development of skilled robots: A new approach in robotics. Presented at the Twentieth ISIR, Tokyo.

TREVELYAN, J. P., 1988. Sheep handling and manipulation for automated shearing. In *Proceedings of the Nineteenth International Symposium and Exposition of Robots*, Sydney, Australia.

WATANABE, et al., 1987. Three-dimensional digitizer (neuro-navigator): New equipment for computed tomography-guided stereotactic surgery. *Surg. Neuro.* 1(27):543–547.

18 Shape Memory Alloy Servo Actuator System with Electric Resistance Feedback and Application for Active Endoscope

KOJI IKUTA, MASAHIRO TSUKAMOTO, AND
SHIGEO HIROSE

RECENTLY, SHAPE memory alloy (SMA) has attracted much attention from various fields because of its unique characteristics. In the field of robotics, several trials have been made to realize a servo actuator system for robots [1–3]. However, unfortunately, most of them could not go beyond the model to demonstrate its usefulness. SMA has not yet been practically tried for robot actuators. The authors believe that more fundamental investigations are needed to reach the final goal. On this account, we have been conducting a series of studies [4, 5].

As a result, the optimum material property of SMA as a servo actuator and the optimum condition of heat treatment have been discovered [6]. Moreover, basic concepts for designing and driving a system were established [7]. In the first part of this chapter, a new control scheme of an antagonistic-type SMA actuator with electric resistance feedback is proposed and verified by some experiments. In the later part, these techniques are applied to a superminiature SMA servo actuator system for an active endoscope.

Antagonistic-type resistance feedback control scheme

The driving configuration of SMA servo actuators to achieve cyclic motion can be classified into two types. The first type consists of one SMA actuator for contraction and one bias spring for expansion. The second is an antagonistic-type actuator, which consists of a pair of SMA actuators arranged antagonistically. The second one is more controllable and has a better response property than the first one, because we can control the motion in two directions actively. Therefore, we will advance resistance feedback control for antagonistic-type SMA actuators.

INTRODUCTION OF NORMALIZED ELECTRIC RESISTANCE

Before discussing the control scheme, we would like to introduce a new nondimensional variable λ named *normalized electric resistance* in order to facilitate handling of the electric resistance of SMA. We have already obtained a relationship between electric resistance and temperature [4]. Most feasible SMA (Ti-Ni alloy) annealed to have the optimum property for SMA actuators exhibit similar relationships between temperature and resistance, as shown in figure 18.1.

From the knowledge of past material investigations, it can be discerned that the high-resistance area corresponds to *R*-phase and the low-resistance area to parent phase. In the intermediate area, this curve has a

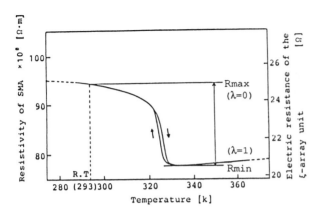

FIGURE 18.1 The definition of R_{max} and R_{min} in relation to the electric resistance and operational temperature.

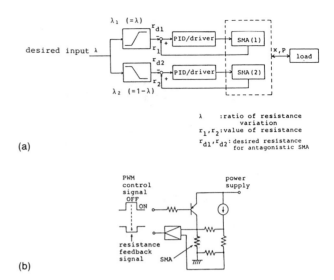

(a)

λ : ratio of resistance variation
r_1, r_2 : value of resistance
r_{d1}, r_{d2} : desired resistance for antagonistic SMA

(b)

FIGURE 18.2 (a) Block diagram of antagonistic-type resistance feedback control system of SMA servo actuator. (b) PWM driver with SMA resistance detector.

negative slope and some hysteresis. Therefore, we normalize electric resistance values between R_{max} and R_{min} by the following equation:

$$\lambda = (R_{max} - R)/(R_{max} - R_{min})$$

where $R_{min} \leq R \leq R_{max}$; R_{max} is the resistance value at room temperature; and R_{min} is the lowest resistance value.

Because electric resistance corresponds to phase transformation, this λ can be thought of as a quantitative index that means "ratio of transformation" (ratio of parent phase in all volumes) [2]. Therefore, $\lambda = 1$ corresponds to SMA in 100% R-phase (0% parent phase) and $\lambda = 0$ corresponds to SMA in 100% parent phase (0% R-phase).

ANTAGONISTIC-TYPE RESISTANCE FEEDBACK CONTROL

The resistance monitoring was made easier by introducing the ξ-array configuration [2]. (This is one of the basic design concepts we proposed.) It means to connect SMA wires mechanically in parallel but electrically in series, and it can increase the absolute value of the electric resistance of SMA without any reduction of its other performance. Hence, the resistance feedback control scheme became feasible. This eliminates the need for such sensors as potentiometers and encoders to realize superminiaturization of actuators.

Past approaches never tried such an accordant control scheme using electric resistance of antagonistic-type SMA actuators as feedback signals. Therefore, the authors tried an approach that changed λ_1 from 0 to 1 while steadily satisfying the relation $\lambda_1 + \lambda_2 = 1$, as shown in figure 18.2a. This resistance feedback system

includes a Proportional-Integrative-Derivative (PID) controller in the feedback loop. The driving circuit in figure 18.2b has the ability not only to supply electric current to an SMA from a Pulse Width Modulation (PWM) driver, but also to measure electric resistance of an SMA simultaneously when the current is off.

EXPERIMENTAL EVALUATION OF CONTROL SCHEME

This approach produced good position-control characteristics over a broad range of strain with relatively little hysteresis without any position feedback loop, as shown in figure 18.3.

To evaluate this result, we compared it with the result obtained by the conventional control method not using any resistance feedback. Figure 18.4 shows the experimental result obtained by controlling only the duty ratio of the PWM driver antagonistically. A large nonlinear hysteresis appears, and it cannot be neglected.

Next, we will focus on the dynamic property of electric resistance feedback control. Though response speed is not very high, good step response can be seen in figure 18.5. Figure 18.6 shows another important response when cooling air was suddenly shut off under certain displacement (see figure 18.6a). Despite such drastic change of the cooling condition, the resistance feedback system worked well to adjust the heating cur-

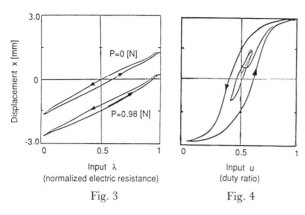

Fig. 3

Fig. 4

FIGURE 18.3 The experimental results of using antagonistic-type resistance feedback control under two load (P) conditions.

FIGURE 18.4 The experimental results of using antagonistic-type duty ratio without electric resistance feedback.

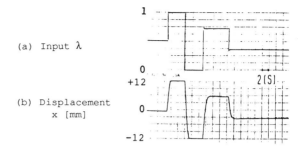

FIGURE 18.5 The step response of SMA actuator using antagonistic-type resistance feedback control.

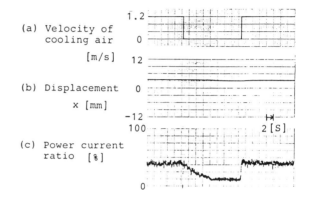

FIGURE 18.6 The response of SMA actuator when the cooling condition changed drastically.

rent simultaneously, as shown in figure 18.6c, so that the actuator displacement changed little, as shown in figure 18.6b.

According to the results just cited, it was made clear that antagonistic-type resistance feedback control produced the following advantages, which were previously impossible:

- Reducing hysteresis of SMA actuator
- Avoiding overheating of SMA
- Drastic improvement for robustness against changes of heating and cooling conditions
- Sensor function for position control

The first three advantages are indispensable to realize a feasible SMA servo actuator. Moreover, the fourth is needed to make a miniature servo actuator system, such as an active endoscope (see next section).

Test production of a real-size active endoscope

Endoscopes or fiberscopes are indispensable tools in today's medical and industrial fields. One of the bottlenecks is the difficulty of insertion when the path is narrow or of a complicated nature. Especially, much improvement is required for a fibersigmoidoscope to abate the discomfort of the patients at insertion. The endoscopes themselves are mostly stiff in construction. Even when a scope has an active moving section, the section is limited to the tip area and the degree of freedom is low [8]. For instance, the current most

advanced fibersigmoidoscope has only 2 degrees of freedom.

Significant improvement will be possible if the whole stem of the endoscope could be actively operated along the narrow and winding path of the colon. SMA actuators allowed these authors to design and produce such an endoscope, named the *active endoscope*.

UTILIZATION OF SMA ACTUATOR WITH ELECTRIC RESISTANCE FEEDBACK

The SMA actuator is especially suitable for the active endoscope because (1) miniature actuator systems, just like muscle, can be realized due to their high power-weight ratio and (2) the energy efficiency and response speed are not the crucial requirements for the actuation function.

To design the SMA actuator for an active endoscope, systematic experimental investigations were conducted by the authors. As a result, we succeeded in obtaining the material properties of SMA and finding the optimum annealing condition for the actuator

TABLE 18.1

Specifications of the produced five-segment real-size active endoscope
(SMA-ACM II)

1. Dimension	$\phi 13 \times 215$ mm		
2. Total weight (for one segment)	32	g	
	6.4	g)	
3. Maximum bending angle	60	deg	(for one segment)
4. Maximum produced torque	6.9	Nm	(for one segment)
5. Electric resistance	$12 \sim 13$		(for one ξ-array)
6. Maximum bending velocity	30	deg/sec	(for one segment)
7. Power source—maximum PWM duty ratio	12V–1A		(for one ξ-array)
	0.33		
8. Flow rate of cooling water	0.13	ml/sec	

material. Detailed discussions of this problem are presented elsewhere [6, 7].

SPECIFICATIONS OF THE ACTIVE ENDOSCOPE

The basic design of the active endoscope model was determined by considering its application to a fiber-sigmoidoscope. For this purpose, it should have mechanical compliance to pass smoothly through the sigmoid colon at its smallest radius of curvature. Also, it should be able to guide a fiberscope. Specifications were set for the external diameter and maximum flexing angle to satisfy those needs. The diameter of the current experimental model (13 mm) is satisfactory in comparison with the diameter of endoscopes on the market now (10–20 mm). The specifications are summarized in table 18.1.

According to the 2D arrangement of the colon, an endoscope is expected to bend mostly on the plane dividing a human body into front and back sides. In this connection, the test production model was designed to have five segments, comprising four segments with flexibility in the same direction on a plane and one segment at the tip that can bend orthogonally to this plane.

Figure 18.7 shows the constructed real-size active endoscope and its maneuver joystick.

MECHANISM OF INDIVIDUAL SEGMENTS

The driving mechanism of each segment, same as the primary model [9], consists of a stainless steel coil

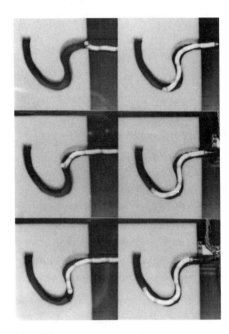

FIGURE 18.7 Test-produced real-size active endoscope using SMA servo actuators (SMA-ACM II).

spring which forms a main skeleton at the center of a joint, and a series of SMA coil springs arranged around it for the driving function. In this model, one segment has 1 degree of freedom, so that a pair of SMA actuators capable of antagonistic motion are arranged in symmetry with respect to the axis, as shown in figure 18.8. The ξ-array configuration is sufficiently served by power-supplying lead, thinner than 0.1 mm in external diameter, including Teflon coating. The lead wires are

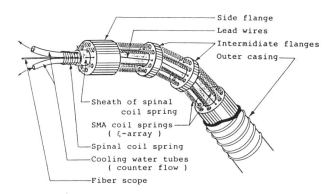

FIGURE 18.8   Inner structure of active endoscope (for unit segment).

TABLE 18.2
Specifications of SMA actuator used in active endoscope

1. Composition	Ti-50.2 at % Ni		
2. Annealing condition	350°C 2.5 hours		
3. Diameter of wire	d	=	0.2 mm
4. Diameter of coil spring	D	=	1.0 mm
5. Maximum strain	max	=	0.06
6. Minimum strain	min	=	0.043

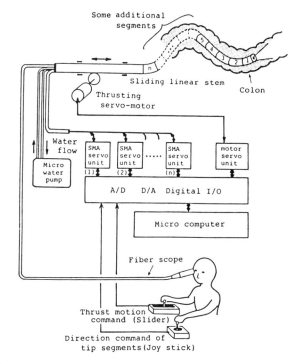

FIGURE 18.9   Total control system of the test-produced active endoscope.

arranged along the main skeleton so that they do not interfere with the motion of the segment.

To enhance the response speed and safety, a cooling water tube is set. The water flows back and forth in a fine tube (made of silicone rubber) held in a coil spring located in the center of the segment to indirectly cool the SMA.

Based on the knowledge obtained previously [6], the driving characteristic is ameliorated by using an SMA coil spring of optimum specifications (table 18.2) in terms of annealing temperature and strain range. The sheath (external jacket) is required to bend pliably without buckling and isolation. At this time, an artificial vein of PTFE serves best for this object.

CONTROL SYSTEM

Basic architecture of the control system is shown in figure 18.9. A couple of SMA actuators of each segment are microcomputer-controlled via respective resistance measurement and driving circuits. The microcomputer also receives commands from a joystick to control the bending angle of the first and second tip

segment and from a direct-motion servo system, which advances and retracts the whole endoscope.

For insertion into the colon, a medical doctor, watching the images fed by the fiberscope, operates the joystick to control manually the two tip joints and simultaneously pushes in the scope at the desired speed by hand.

The two kinds of command (i.e., the command for tip segment bending angle given by manual operation and the direct-motion command given by hand at the base of the scope) are translated, via the microcomputer, to the shift command. The shift command consecutively transmits the manually given bending angles at the tip segment, synchronous with the direct-motion speed, to the hind segments. We called this control method *shift control*; it enables pliable motion of the whole stem as it follows the winding path, instead of motion by reactive force of the entire pairs.

The measuring and driving circuits are set for each pair of SMA actuators at each segment. Introduction of ζ-array configuration enables stable and effective feedback of electric resistance values to prevent overheating, to detect short circuiting, and to keep the control characteristic free of external interferences.

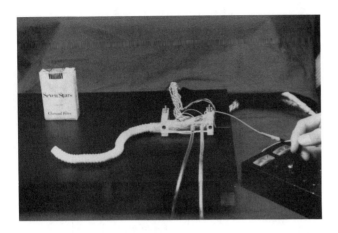

FIGURE 18.10 Sequential motion of the text-produced active endoscope as it enters into sponge-rubber colon model under shift control.

DRIVING EXPERIMENT

To verify the basic performance of this device, the driving experiment was conducted in a colon model environment. The active endoscope proved to offer pliable motion with approximately 30°/sec. up to a designed maximum angle (60°) at a high enough responding speed for the purpose.

The shift control characteristic of all segments synchronous with backward and forward motions also was confirmed to be effective, as exhibited in figure 18.10. Most of the discomfort is caused by pushing strongly against the wall of the colon. However, as this active endoscope can avoid pushing against the wall by using shift control, we believe that the patient feels much better than with conventional sigmoidoscopy. The temperature of the sheath during the experiment was approximately 30°C in continuous operation at a room temperature of approximately 15°C.

In summary, the active endoscope using SMA actuators is regarded to serve sufficiently the practical purpose for which it was designed.

Conclusion

For the purpose of realizing practical SMA servo actuator systems, several kinds of feedback control schemes were discussed. As a result, antagonistic-type electric resistance feedback control was proposed, and its effectiveness was verified by some experiments. Finally, this servo actuator system was successfully applied to an active endoscope, which will be available for industrial use.

ACKNOWLEDGMENT   We would like to thank Prof. Y. Umetani of the Tokyo Institute of Technology, Dr. Y. Suzuki and Mr. H. Tamura of Central Research Lab, and Furukawa Electric Co., Ltd., Tokyo, for their valuable advice and offer of Ti-Ni alloy. One of the authors, K. Ikuta, wishes to thank Prof. Gerardo Beni and Prof. Susan Hackwood for giving him the opportunity to continue this research on an SMA actuator at the Center for Robotics of the University of California at Santa Barbara.

REFERENCES

[1] HONMA, D., Y. MIWA, and N. IGUCHI, 1983. Application of SME to digital control actuator (in Japanese). *Trans. JSME-C*, 49(448):2163–2169.

[2] HIROSE, S., K. IKUTA, and Y. UMETANI, 1984. A new design method of servo actuators based on the shape memory effect. In *Proceedings of the Fifth RO.MAN.SY. Symposium*, Udine, Italy, pp. 339–349.

[3] HOSODA, Y., FUJIE, KOJIMA, 1983. Three fingered robot hand by using SMA (in Japanese). In *Proceedings of the First Annual Conference of Robotic Society of Japan*, p. 213.

[4] HIROSE, S., K. IKUTA, and Y. UMETANI, 1986. Development of shape memory alloy actuator (performance evaluation and introduction of a new design concept) (in Japanese). *J. Robotics Soc. Jap. (JRSJ)* 4-2:15–26.

[5] HIROSE, S., K. IKUTA, and K. SATO, 1986. Development of shape memory alloy actuator (improvement of output performance by the introduction of a sigma-mechanism) (in Japanese). *J. Robotics Soc. Jap (JRSJ)* 4-6:28–38.

[6] HIROSE, S., K. IKUTA, and M. TSUKAMOTO, 1987. Development of shape memory alloy actuator (characteristics measurements of the alloy and development of an active endoscope) (in Japanese). *J. Robotics Soc. Jap. (JRSJ)* 5-2:3–17.

[7] IKUTA, K. 1987. Study of servo actuator using shape memory alloy. Doctoral dissertation, Tokyo Institute of Technology.

[8] BEYOND, W. E., et al., 1967. *Proceedings of the Twelfth SPIE Technical Symposium*, pp. 49–53.

[9] HIROSE, S., K. IKUTA, M. TSUKAMOTO, and Y. UMETANI, 1984. *Proceedings of the Second Annual Conference of the Robotics Society of Japan* (in Japanese), pp. 123–126.

Safety

"Do no harm" is a fundamental principle in any surgeon's training, and surgeons are naturally very concerned about the safety aspects of any device used in the operating room. With simple hand tools, the issues are fairly straightforward. For example, is the device likely to break in use or leave debris inside the patient? Can sterility be assured? Are there sharp edges that might cut the surgeon or the patient in unintended ways? As devices become more complicated, the questions get harder. For example, if electricity is involved, is there any way that the patient or operating room staff can be shocked or burned unintentionally? Over time, the medical device industry, in cooperation with the surgical community and government regulatory agencies, has developed a reasonable consensus on how many of these questions should be addressed [1].

Although there are some standards for devices that rely on computer software for significant aspects of their function [2], systems for computer-assisted surgery are still novel. Safety considerations are, and should be, of crucial importance in the design of such systems. The challenge from a surgeon's perspective is especially great, as such systems can seem both complex and mysterious in their internal workings. One of the principle themes of this book is the ability of machines to augment human capabilities to enable surgeons to improve significantly the efficacy of surgical procedures. The challenge is that in order to exploit the machine's capabilities, the surgeon must give up a certain amount of control. The machine may have *better* precision, access, or sensory capabilities than the surgeon, but it has little judgment. How can the surgeon trust it not to harm the patient? Although there is

no simple answer to this question, it is one that must be considered for essentially every system reported in this book. Rather than repeat the entire discussion here, we will touch on a few high points.

One useful way of thinking about safety of computer-controlled systems is to consider the relative degree of autonomy of the system's function and the criticalness of the surgical task being performed. At one extreme are presurgical planning systems, which provide the surgeon with some qualitative insight into what is to be done in the operating room or perhaps some stereotactic coordinates. A number of such systems are described in this book (see chapters 3, 9, 10, 54). Here, the crucial requirements are that the simulation not be misleading, that the surgeon understand the limitations, and that any geometric information provided be accurate to within specified tolerances.

At the other extreme are active robots that perform complex tissue removal operations. Significant portions of two companion chapters (chapters 28 and 29) in the Orthopaedics section of this book are devoted to discussion of safety measures for a robot designed to machine bone for orthopaedic surgery. Some additional general discussion may be found in the Robotic Manipulators section of this book.

In between are a spectrum of systems. Some rely entirely on the surgeon for motive power. Others function essentially as motorized stereotactic frames. Still others perform very simple continuous motions or do not come into critical contact with the patient. Passive navigation aids, which simply report the intraoperative position of surgical instruments relative to preoperative images of the patient's anatomy, are an important subclass of passive systems. Examples in this book can be found in chapters 22, 23, 32, and 50. In addition to usual concerns related to matters such as sterility and electric safety, the key issue for such systems is accuracy. Does the position reported on the surgical display correspond to the actual position of the instrument relative to the patient?

Other systems augment navigational assistance with a passive or semiactive mechanical manipulation aid to hold the desired alignment. One example in this book is described in chapter 52, "Applications of Simulation, Morphometrics, and Robotics in Craniofacial Surgery", by Cutting et al. The primary concern again is accuracy, together with means to ensure proper fixation and monitoring that will notify the surgeon if the alignment changes. An interesting variation on such passive alignment systems is the use of computer-controlled braking to assist the surgeon in achieving a desired alignment or simple trajectory [3–5]. In such systems, the surgeon is constrained to go toward a position or follow a trajectory but provides all the energy for motion. Here the issues are roughly the same as for any passive system, with perhaps additional attention required for electric safety issues.

The next step up are systems that use an active robotic device to position a passive instrument guide but in which all motion of the robot is disabled after the position is achieved but before any instrument is applied to the patient. In one of the first widely reported uses of an industrial robot in surgery, Kwoh et al. [6] used this approach. Examples in this book include two systems of Lavallee et al. (chapters 24 and 32) and that of Kienzle et al. (chapter 30). Additional safety considerations in such systems include making sure that the robot does not accidentally collide with the patient or the surgical team, that motion is truly disabled when the passive guide is in use, and that accuracy is maintained when the robot switches from computer-controlled to motion-disabled mode.

In any active system, redundant safety checking and control becomes especially important. It is very important that no single component failure should cause the machine to behave in a way that is harmful to the patient. In cases where such redundancy is not practical, great care must be taken to minimize the probability of such single-point failures. A crucial form of redundancy is the surgeon's ability to monitor what the machine is doing, exercise judgment, and intervene if necessary. Appropriate human-machine interfaces for

this purpose must be provided. Adequate reaction time is important for both machine-detected and human-detected failures. Consequently, the maximum speed of surgical robots often is severely restricted.

Assistant teleoperated systems such as those described in the section on laparoscopy present their own challenges. In these systems, the surgical instrument is often a camera, which usually does not contact the patient's internal organs. This is a help in terms of safety, because accuracy may be less crucial and because there is again more time to react. It is important to realize that other instruments (retractors, staplers, etc.) that a surgeon might manipulate by a laparoscopic "assistant" robot are, in fact, designed to be used in contact with the target anatomy. Further, even simple cameras often must pass through a narrow entry portal, and it is important that the robot not exert excessive lateral force on the patient at that point. This may represent a significant challenge for systems that rely on conventional manipulators as such systems usually depend on tightly coordinated joint motion to achieve a desired instrument motion. Because high relative joint speeds often are required even for slow instrument motions, it is not always practical to "detune" such robots as much as one would like for safety-checking purposes. Further, small joint motion disparities can affect the accuracy of instrument path motions. For this reason, many of the robotic systems discussed in this book have specially designed manipulators. For example, the AESOP system of Sackier and Wang (chapter 45) uses two instrumented passive joints to implement the constraint that no lateral force be applied to the patient at the entry portal. Similarly, the surgical assistant robot of Taylor et al. (chapter 46) provides a remote center of motion or "fulcrum" point at which the natural motions of the instrument align with individual joint motions.

Active systems, whether used as point-to-point positioning devices or as continuous-path therapy devices, often include one or more means to prevent excessive force from being applied to the patient. Typical means include passive "mechanical fuses," usually part of the robot's instrument holder, torque-limited clutches, and actively monitored force-torque sensors. All such devices involve trade-offs. For example, a breakaway instrument holder can cause the robot to drop the instrument rather than push it into the patient. However, once this happens, control over the instrument is lost and it may do considerable damage on its own. Similarly, clutches can cause loss of accuracy, and force-torque sensors require additional software and calibration procedures that must be verified.

In the chapter that follows, "A Discussion of Safety Issues for Medical Robots," Brian Davies provides a similar perspective derived from his development of a special-purpose robot for prostatectomies, reported in chapter 47 of this book, together with a possible classification scheme for systematically considering systems with varying degrees of autonomy.

REFERENCES

[1] ESTRIN, N. F., ed., 1990. *The Medical Device Industry: Science, Technology, and Regulation in a Competitive Environment.* New York: Marcel Dekker.

[2] FRIES, R. C., G. T. WILLINGMYRE, D. SIMONS, and R. T. SCHWARTZ, 1990. Software regulation. In *The Medical Device Industry: Science, Technology, and Regulation in a Competitive Environment,* N. F. Estrin, ed. New York: Marcel Dekker, pp. 557–569.

[3] TAYLOR, R. H., C. B. CUTTING, Y.-Y. KIM, A. D. KALVIN, D. LAROSE, B. HADDAD, D. KHORAMABADI, M. NOZ, R. OLYHA, N. BRUUN, and D. GRIMM, 1991. A model-based optimal planning and execution system with active sensing and passive manipulation for augmentation of human precision in computer-integrated surgery. In *Proceedings of the 1991 International Symposium on Experimental Robotics,* Toulouse, France, June 25–27. Berlin: Springer-Verlag.

[4] LEWIS, M. A., and G. A. BEKEY, 1992. Automation and robotics in neurosurgery: prospects and problems. In *Neurosurgery for the Third Millenium,* M. L. J. Apuzzo, ed. American Association of Neurological Surgeons. 1992.

[5] TROCCAZ, J., and S. LAVALLEE, 1993. An alternative to actuated robots and passive arms in medical robotics. *Proc. IEEE EMBS,* Nov.: pp. 934–935.

[6] KWOH, Y. S., J. HOU, E. JONCKHEERE, and S. HAYATI, 1988. A robot with improved absolute positioning accuracy for CT guided stereotactic surgery. *IEEE Trans. on Biomed. Eng.* Feb.:153–161.

19 A Discussion of Safety Issues for Medical Robots

BRIAN L. DAVIES

MEDICAL ROBOTS, unlike industrial robots, do not have clear safety guidelines. The health and safety requirements for industrial robots suggest that they should not operate in contact with people but should be isolated in a cell with safety interlocks, for example on the doors, to prevent the robot functioning while people are in the cell. The only exception to this is that the robot may be programmed by a skilled operator in the cell. During programming, the robot can move only under reduced speed conditions while the operator keeps out of reach of the moving arm. If medical robots were to operate under the same requirements as industrial robots, they clearly would be very limited in their capability and application.

Medical robots, like domestic robots, are a new application. To be fully effective, they must operate in contact with people, and appropriate safety procedures have yet to be defined that will allow them to carry out their functions with adequate safety levels. On the other hand, such safety levels should not require the robots to be so complex and expensive that they are priced out of the market. The concept of how adequate the safety must be and how safe *is* safe is a matter that needs to be discussed by the community at large. It generally is recognized that even where safety is of overriding importance (e.g., in the Space Shuttle), there is no such thing as 100% safety and errors in software and failures of hardware do occur, despite duplication of systems and the very high costs that ensue. What is needed is recognition that the benefits to be obtained from medical robots are such that a small amount of risk is inherent in their use. This is justifiable and acceptable. This is not to say that unsafe or unsound medical robot systems should be utilized. Of course, every effort should be taken to ensure that the system is as safe as possible. Yet having done this, it is likely that some risk, no matter how small, will still be present. However, the area of medical robots is almost never a case where a robot's failure to function will result in a life-damaging situation. Provided that the medical robot is designed to fail in a safe manner and come to a controlled halt so that it can be removed and the procedure completed manually, no danger to life will ensue. This is unlike the case of, say, a military aircraft that could not be flown manually if the computer control system failed. Medical robots can generally be removed and the procedure completed manually without any risk to the patient. Thus, what is required is for the robot to come to a controlled stop in the event of a failure, rather than to have very long mean-time-between-failures (MTBFs), which is a less important criterion.

Possibly the only exception to this general rule is in certain aspects of neurosurgery, where very critical regions of the anatomy are being operated on. In such operations, the exact trajectory of the tool and the accuracy of placement may be required to be so great that it is not possible to intervene manually without some detrimental outcome. This may be because the removal of the tool from the robotic system, and subsequent removal from the patient, is so difficult that it cannot be performed accurately and safely enough. Alternatively, in the case of critical locations deep within the brain, it is probable that the only way to achieve the required accuracies is to use a robot, and the necessary accuracies cannot be achieved with the use of stereotactic frames and jigs, even assuming that such jigs can be subsequently brought into position and determined to the required accuracy. In such cases, more emphasis will need to be placed on a high MTBF value than on failing with a safe mode that allows the device to be readily removed.

The justification for use of medical robots is not easy to quantify. In the early days of the motor car, it was considered necessary for a man to walk in front with a red flag. It is accepted nowadays that motor cars bring sufficient benefit that their unconstrained use when driving at high speed down roadways is considered acceptable and the benefits justify the number of injuries and deaths that occur annually. If a medical robot allows a life-saving operation to be performed, such as brain tumor removal, a process that could not be carried out as accurately manually, then one could argue that, provided all reasonable safety measures have been taken so that failure of the system is rare, the overall use of the robot is justified. Because its use would save lives that would otherwise be lost, the use of very expensive safety measures would also be easy to justify. However, such arguments do not generally apply to the majority of robotic surgery applications or to those of manipulators in the rehabilitation field. Here the robots generally are functioning as a replacement for human activity, simply because they are more accurate, are faster, or do not require the continual attendance of a person. Hence, the benefits that accrue are generally less easy to quantify and are concerned with cost savings or convenience. Such benefits are not critical to life, and so the safety measures needed and how much they can be justified in terms of complexity and cost are less clear. It is important that the medical community make recommendations for a level of safety that is acceptable, with the various implications discussed, so that users, helpers, relatives, and the public at large can come to a consensus about what is an acceptable standard.

If such a consensus is not achieved, then the development of medical robots (and domestic robots) will continue to be slow. Companies are reluctant to develop new products for which the required safety levels and attendant legal issues are ill-defined. It appears that in the United Kingdom and, to some extent, in Europe, an adequate defense in the event of an accident resulting from equipment failure is for the equipment to have been designed and manufactured to "best current practice." However, as such standards of best current practice have yet to determined, the issues remain unclear and would have to be tested in law before they can be clarified. The situation in the United States, which is a potentially large and lucrative market, is even less clear. Concerns about the legal implications of their work and uncertainties about how safe products should be has caused manufacturers to drag their feet in developing medical robots.

Surgical assistant robots

ESTABLISHING ACCEPTABLE SAFETY LEVELS

One approach to the safety of surgical assistant robots has been to suggest that their safety levels be better than those achieved by conventional surgery. This is an attractive proposition because it would appear that the robot would be safer than the human surgeon. However, in practice, this concept would give rise to considerable difficulties. First, the exact safety record of traditional surgery in specific applications is very difficult to obtain. Second, statistical estimates of robotic surgical safety would not be acceptable; it would be necessary for the robot to perform safely a number of operations greater than that expected by a human surgeon. However, if a failure did occur earlier than this predicted time, which is statistically possible, it would be difficult to argue a case in a court of law on the basis of statistics. No matter when a robot failure occurred, if it resulted in an accident it is unlikely that the damaged parties would waive their rights to sue the robot supplier simply on the basis of statistical probability. A further aspect to this problem is that when surgeons use simple tools and an error occurs, it is seldom that those tools and the manufacturers are blamed. It generally is accepted that surgery is a risky business and, unless the surgeon has been negligent, no court case results. However, when the surgeon uses a relatively autonomous piece of equipment, such as a robotic assistant, it is likely that the surgeon will not be considered totally liable. For this reason, the author believes it is essential, when using robotic assistant surgeons, to involve the human surgeon wherever possible in confirming decisions throughout the surgical procedure. On the basis of the information displayed by the sensor systems and the human-computer interface, it would be the surgeon's decision about whether to proceed with an operation.

One successful approach to these difficulties has been undertaken by the group in Grenoble for head surgery [1]. Here the robot was used to carry a jig or fixture close to the head of the patient. When the fixture is at the correct position and orientation, a series of cutting instruments are clipped to the jig and used by the surgeon manually. Thus, the robot is reduced to a preliminary role as a positioning jig and not for direct intervention. The safety of the robot is further ensured by introducing a very large reduction gear ratio to each of the motor output drives. This means that in the event that something goes wrong with the robot, there is plenty of time to hit the emergency off button, because the robot is moving so slowly. Another approach has been suggested in which a standard robot uses only high-level software to monitor the motions of the robot. This may present other safety problems because the monitoring is at a high level rather than at the hardware servo level and so may be slow to act. It is possible to imagine a scenario in which the servo is moving in a straight line when failure causes it to try to take off at high speed in the same direction. The inertia of the system may cause the robot arm to travel some distance before the fault is detected by the high-level monitor and the brakes can bring the arm to a halt. It could be argued that only hardware monitoring at the servo level will give the necessary speed of response to avoid damage in critical instances, even though the robot is restricted to the role of carrying a jig or fixture.

Liability

A further consideration in the safety arena is that manufacturers of the industrial robot seldom will make available to suppliers of the medical robotic system all the specific details of software and hardware in the industrial robot. Nonetheless, only if such full details are supplied can the medical group assure themselves that the necessary safety features are in place so that they can take responsibility for the system they propose to supply. It is also likely that industrial robot manufacturers will not sanction the use of their systems in juxtaposition to people, as the devices were not designed with that specific application in mind and hence do not have the appropriate safety features. In such a case, it is the author's opinion that it would be foolhardy for researchers to use such unmodified robots for rehabilitative or surgical applications. Although it may be acceptable to use a standard robot for feasibility study purposes to try out concepts and ideas prior to the implementation of a special-purpose medical robot, care should be taken to protect the researchers. In the author's view, if the powered robot comes within range of the research worker, then similar safety features should be incorporated as would be used in the final device on a patient. If, for example, a researcher in the laboratory holds the end of six-axis force sensor mounted on a powered-up robot and "leads" the robot tip to a datum position for simulated surgery on a cadaver,

then that robot should offer the same safety protection features for the researcher as would be desirable if the application were by a surgeon for use on a patient.

Redundant systems

Some redundancy in sensors and software systems also is desirable for reliability. Dual sensors, one on each servo motor and one on each output drive, could act as a check that the drive output system is not slipping and that encoder integrity is being maintained. Dual software systems running on separate transputers in parallel are another means of checking for errors. Additionally, all software codes must be ensured. Although dependable computing systems have made great strides, complex software still cannot be guaranteed to be entirely safe. One answer to these computing problems could be to have two software systems running simultaneously on two different pieces of hardware. For further integrity, the software would need to have been independently generated by separate groups using completely different language systems. The two systems would need to be run in parallel and come to the same conclusion before an action could be taken. The cost and complexity of such a system would be likely to prohibit its use from all but the most life-critical robotic surgical assistance.

Special-purpose robots

One solution has been to design a special-purpose robot for a particular surgical procedure to operate within a localized region. Associated with this concept is that of a mechanical constraint that physically prevents motion outside a limited area. This approach was arrived at because it was felt that the use of anthropomorphic robots capable of reaching a large-volume space (the very feature that makes them attractive to industry) could, in the event of failure, fly off in any direction, causing damage to patients, surgeons, and other bystanders. A further implication of this approach is that, where possible, axes should be moved sequentially, one at a time rather than in parallel, to minimize the volume of space that can be swept out by an unforeseen motion. This implies that complex shapes resulting from the interaction of many axes of motion may need to be approximated by a series of simple shapes, resulting from a sequence of single axes' motions. In addition to the usual sensor-based software

Table 19.1

A potential hierarchy of systems for holding and manipulating surgical tools

Code	Type of System
1	Hand-held tools
2	Hand-held tools with a spatial location system
3	Arm-mounted tools with a spatial location system
3.1	As for 3, but target location is updated with patient movement intraoperatively
4	Arm mounted tools with spatial location system *and* powered brakes (used passively)
4.1	As for 4, but arm is used actively to insert/move tools
4.2	As for 4, but arm adapts to patient/organ movement intraoperatively
5	Tools mounted on powered robot arm equipped with position measurement (used passively)
5.1	As for 5, but robot is used actively to insert/move tools
5.2	As for 5, but robot adapts to patient/organ movement intraoperatively
6	Tools mounted on powered robot arm equipped with force and position control (used passively)
6.1	As for 6, but robot is used actively to insert/move tools
6.2	As for 6, but robot adapts to patient/organ movement intraoperatively

Code	General Notes
1	Surgeon holds/moves tools freehand using only human innate sensing (touch, vision, etc).
2	Freehand-held tools, but surgeon can track a target using, e.g., cameras plus LEDs on tool, or magnetic field source and sensors.
3	Arm is moved by surgeon, which to some extent constrains the sense of "feel" and freedom of motion. Joint motions are usually monitored.
3.1	Usually a second (passive) arm is strapped to patient to monitor patient motion. Target location on a quantitative model is updated in real time to allow surgeon to track target with tool on arm.
4	The addition of powered brakes to arm permits arm to be locked in position, e.g., to permit long-term treatment at target location.
5	Tools can be moved on the powered arm, either actively (as in 5.1) to enter the patient using the rbot or passively (as in 5). In the latter case it acts as a stationary jig that locates the tools so that the surgeon can manually insert them into the patient. The ability to adapt, on-line, to

patient motion (as in 5.2) provides the possibility of errors that cannot be trapped at a planning stage.

6	The addition of force control permits the robot to switch between position control and force control so that the robot can yield to a given force level in prescribed locations.

limits on motion, mechanical stops may need to be positioned for each programmed size of cut, to restrict the range of motion physically to a safe and acceptable limit should anything unforeseen occur. This concept of a special-purpose robot with mechanical constraint has been developed at Imperial College Robotics Centre, for the design of a surgical assistant for prostatectomies [2, 3].

COMPUTER-ASSISTED SURGERY

Many of the safety implications of robotic surgery are being avoided in the short term by the use of computer-assisted surgery (CAS). A typical example is that at Aachen where ENT surgery is being carried out [4]. Here a passive arm is used to carry tools. Each joint on the passive arm is instrumented and, in some instances, can be locked using electromagnetic brakes. Because the surgeon is holding the tool and moves it directly to provide its power, he or she is in control of the process and relies on the computer system for tracking information. Thus, the possible malfunction of robot arm servo systems is removed from the activity. The accuracy of the arm pointing system and the associated database can be checked beforehand, thus minimizing problem areas to those of advising the surgeon rather than carrying out operations for him or her.

AVAILABLE TOOLS

There is thus a host of tools potentially available to the surgeon, ranging from simple hand-held tools, through various levels of CAS, to the fully powered autonomous robot. An attempt has been made to classify them into types, as shown in table 19.1. It can be seen that, as the hierarchy moves from simple hand-held tools toward autonomous robots, the surgeon's direct control of the system diminishes and control becomes embedded in a hardware and software system that is under the control of engineers. Consequently, there inevitably will be more questions as to who is in control

TABLE 19.2

A coding system for imaging and modeling

	Preoperative imaging		Intraoperative imaging		Postoperative imaging	
	Qualitative	Quantitative	Qualitative	Quantitative	Qualitative	Quantitative
No model	A	D	G	J	M	P
2D model	B	E	H	K	N	Q
3D model	C	F	I	L	O	R

of the system (and who is responsible legally should errors occur) as the hierarchy proceeds toward fully automated systems. For this reason, the author believes there will be a tendency for the CAS systems to be favored and used more frequently in the early years of robotic surgery, because they will more easily obtain ethics committee approval. However, the very features that leave total control in the hands of the surgeon are also those that result in imprecise information and control. Provided that adequate safety features are incorporated into fully robotic systems and that they are fully developed to be free of errors, such robotic systems are potentially safer than CAS systems, which rely on the surgeon's motions. For this reason, it is essential that these safety issues be widely discussed and a consensus view developed concerning how safe is safe.

In addition to tools that are instrumented and supported in some way, safe robotic surgery is highly dependent on the ability to image the patient correctly and form a concept (or model) of what the imaged data represents. These imaging systems can be categorized according to the three stages of surgical procedure: the preoperative (or planning) phase; the intraoperative phase (or on-line verification), and the postoperative phase to monitor patient progress. Each phase may produce either qualitative or quantitative data. In addition, the data may be incorporated into a qualitative or quantitative model. Such models may be 2D, giving information in only one plane at a time, or a 3D reconstruction of either the surface or the complete volume. A coding system for the hierarchy of imaging and modeling is shown in table 19.2, and the range and uses of imaging and modeling systems are outlined in table 19.3. Some examples of the application of the coding systems are given in table 19.4 for both tools and imaging and modeling. One reason for including a hierarchy of imaging and modeling systems is that they are the source of data on which the robotic system func-

TABLE 19.3

A range of imaging and modeling systems

Qualitative	Quantitative
Preoperative imaging gives picture for preop process planning and training	Preoperative imaging allows dimensions to be taken for setting up manual jigs and robot systems
3D modeling gives 3D pictures and sectioned views	3D modeling gives 3D pictures and dimensional data
Intraoperative imaging allows qualitative cuts using "eyeball" judgment	Intraoperative imaging allows quantitative cuts using hand tools with jigs or robots
Postoperative imaging provides qualitative check on process	Postoperative imaging provides dimensioned check on system accuracy and performance

tions. Thus, if there are errors or sources of imprecision in either the images or the models, then the robotic surgery performance will be similarly affected and safety will be reduced. In the case of imaging and modeling, we see that, as for robots as the hierarchy moves from qualitative imaging with no model toward quantitative imaging with a full 3D model, so the surgeon (and the robot) has more precise data on which to base decisions and actions. However, this same hierarchy implies that the information and data are correct. The more complex the system, the more do we depend on the quality of software and hardware that is provided by the engineers. Just as for robotics, we may see a tendency for a surgeon to rely on simple 2D images from which he or she builds a 3D model in the mind's eye rather than passing control to the engineer and relying on the integrity of complex systems in which he or she has not been part of the development team.

TABLE 19.4

TABLE 19.4

Examples of classification of systems

Code	Examples
1(A + G + M)	A preliminary x-ray shows the site of a tumor (A). A hand-held tool (1) is used by the surgeon while observing the process using x-ray (G). Postoperative x-rays check that all is well using subjective assessment (M).
1(D + G + P)	Preoperative CT scans used to define dimensioned images (D). Hand-held tools (1) (with additional jigs or fixtures) remove precise quantities of tissue while monitoring the process on-line using qualitative x-rays (G). Postoperative CT scans are used to provide dimensioned images (P).
2(F + L + M)	A preoperative CT scan provides data for a fully dimensioned 3D model (F). A camera-observed system allows a hand-held tool, fitted with LEDs (2) to locate a tumor in 3D space by matching the current location of the tool to the model reference framework and to the preop model (L). Qualitative postoperative x-rays (M) check that all is well.
3(F + L + M)	As for 2(F + L + M), but the tool is held on an articulated arm (3) without brakes.
4(F + G + M)	A preoperative CT scan gives a fully dimensioned 3D model of the brain (F). An articulated arm with measurement of joint angles moves to a datumed position above the skull and is locked by brakes in position (4). The surgeon uses the arm as a jig to locate a hand-held drill. X-rays are used intraoperatively to give a subjective assessment of the process (G). Postoperative x-rays (M) give a qualitative measure of the outcome. [If 4.1 were used in place of 4, then an example would be as for 4, but the last link of the arm could be unlocked separately to give a single axis motion to the drill in the required direction, but still powered by the surgeon.
5(F + L + R)	A preoperative scan using CT and subsequent modeling provides a 3D dimensional model (F). A fully powered robot moves to a position above the patient and is held by its motors at that location to act as a jig (5). The surgeon powers a hand drill while x-ray monitors with 3D modeling give a reconstruction in real time of what is happening (L). A full model with CT scan provides quantitative postoperative data (R). 5.1 would do the same task as 5, but the robot would actively insert the drill into the patient. An example of 5.2 would be where a second passive arm updates the current 3D model of the target location (e.g., as the patient breathes). The target "cross" could then be tracked dynamically by the powered robot under adaptive control.

However, the long-term safety of such complex imaging and modeling systems is likely to be much higher than that of the unenhanced surgeon, although the issues of reliability, safety integrity, and legal responsibility need to be clarified to ensure their optimal use.

Medical robots in rehabilitation

MANIPULATOR-PATIENT CONTACT

Medical robots are frequently being used to assist the disabled. Potential locations for the manipulator relative to the patient range from no contact to full contact with the user. The former emulates the industrial set-up, so that the medical manipulator is part of a workstation with an envelope of reach that is always out of contact with the use. In this manner, potential safety problems are largely avoided. In this application, the robot can only place items onto surface from which the

user can then take them. Unfortunately, although this is potentially a very safe solution, it also is most limited in its benefits to the user. In addition, it will be necessary to fence off the manipulator arm, away from both helpers and the public.

The next safe concept is one in which only the extreme reach of the extended manipulator arm comes near the user. This is often a workstation configuration in which the arm is used as a feeding aid, presenting food at its full reach for the user to move the head, for example, to eat from a spoon. Although this is a fairly safe solution, it seldom is possible rigidly to fix the user location. If, say, the user slumps down in a wheelchair, then the user will be within the envelope of arm motions. Similarly, long tools held in the gripper could also strike the user.

An alternative solution would be to provide the arm with very low force and speed, not just limited by software or force control but also by the intrinsic capabilities of the arm. This has some merit because the disabled user usually is content with a slow motion, as long as there is not a long delay before an observable motion starts. However, the low-force capability usually implies that the arm must be capable of lifting the heaviest design load at the longest reach. Thus, when the arm is in a bent configuration with a light load, it will still be capable of exerting a significant force. Also, even if the arm were so lightly powered that it could be pushed away with the chin, the resulting force capability could still damage the eye if the gripper were carrying a sharp object.

A further possible configuration is to place the arm totally within reach of the user (e.g., on the arm of a wheelchair). This has the advantage of being of considerable benefit to the user, particularly if the arm can also reach to the floor and a high shelf. However, it can potentially reach (and hence damage) not only the user but helpers and passersby. This can be partially guarded against by designating "no-go" areas for the patient—for example, operating at slowest speed when the arm configuration is near the head and totally preventing motion where the arm could strike the head. However, as mentioned earlier, it is very difficult to so constrain the user that the no-go areas are constant with reference to the chair. Though this objection could be overcome with additional sensing that can dynamically adapt the no-go areas to suit the user's current posture, it implies considerable extra complexity and cost and does nothing for the public passing by, who can adopt any position and circumnavigate no-go concepts. For them, more sensing all over the arm would be needed to warn of an impending collision and stop the arm. All such emergency procedures will require elaborate safety status checks before the arm can be re-initialized. It can be seen that as further systems are added to take care of potentially unsafe situations, the cost and complexity rises until the system becomes unlikely to be used. At some level of complexity, it is likely that we must all accept that medical manipulators are potentially hazardous devices, and reasonable care will be needed during their use.

The medical manipulator becomes more of a hazard when it is part of a complex control system (e.g., involving a powered wheelchair with powered adjustable seat position and an environmental controller). The integrated control system needs to take account not only of the individual devices but also of the potential unsafe outcome of a combination of the devices

(e.g., attempting to pass through a doorway at speed while the arm is extended, or trying to turn the chair abruptly while the arm is carrying a load at full reach).

THE TIDE PROJECT

Many of the problems of this type of complex system have come to light in a European TIDE project concerned with medical mobile manipulator systems, in which the author is concerned with safety issues [5]. Although this TIDE project has been primarily concerned with the specification of an international bus structure for a collection of subsystems (powered wheelchairs, manipulator, and environmental controller), it has also highlighted the particular problems for medical manipulators in this role. For the wheelchair and other systems, a "dead-man switch" (DMS) has been recommended whereby for any prime mover to continue to act, a switch has to be positively held in an on position. The moment that the DMS is released, the power is removed from the local prime mover power relays. However, such a severe stop would be disadvantageous for the smooth control of a manipulator, so instead it is proposed that the manipulator have a DMS linked to a zero-velocity command fed into the normal control system. This has the disadvantage that the DMS is now reliant on the integrity of the control system, but it is probably the best overall compromise.

This concept is further supplemented in the TIDE proposal by a speed cut-off directly at the prime movers if the zero-velocity control command fails to act within a certain time span. Safety integrity is also enhanced by the use of safety monitoring, both of the central control functions and at the subsystem power module levels. The safety monitors would remove power from different areas, depending on the fault, and report back to the central display unit. In addition to the continuous action of closing a DMS, there is also need for a large red button, prominently displayed, as a final emergency off switch. Figure 19.1 shows an example of the communication and safety signals used for a mobile medical manipulator system employing a number of input systems that can control a number of outputs via a central BUS structure. In this instance, the bus (M3S BUS) uses a "CAN BUS" for its control data and command structure whose integrity is continuously checked by a positive polling action, together with a Dead Man Switch DMS, a DMS line, and a key line. The key line ensures that the system can be turned

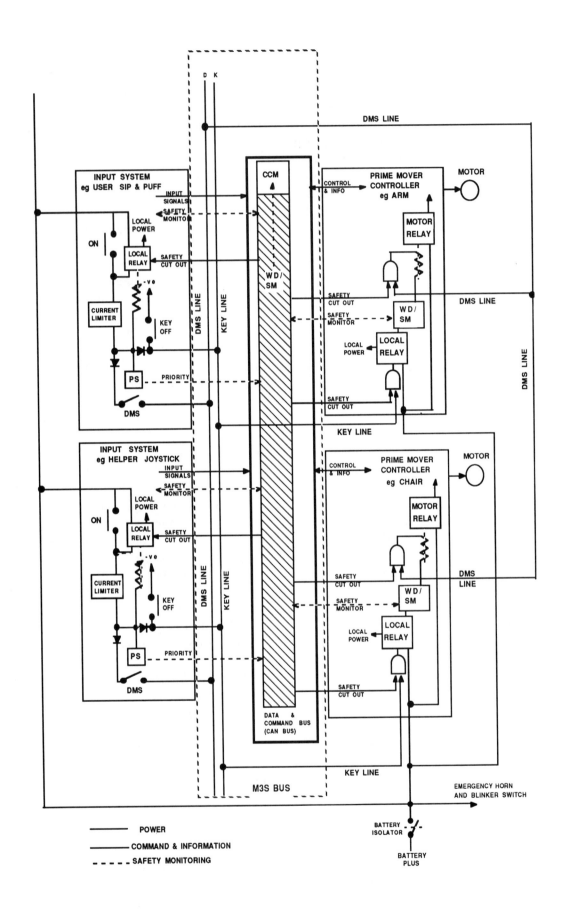

off and then restarted from any of the input systems. It also allows any of the local power relays to be turned off, independent of the local processor systems, and it allows the complete isolation of a faulty subsystem without turning off the whole system.

Probably the most unpredictable environmental configuration is when the manipulator arm is placed on a free-roving mobile robot. The whole system then is so complex that a simple but safe human-computer interface is difficult to achieve. Also, the arm can be carried by its mobile platform into many different configurations, out of sight of the user, who then has to rely on the partial view obtained from camera systems attached both to the mobile platform and to the manipulator arm. The use of "islands of safety" (e.g., implemented by light curtain) may become necessary, in addition to the normal safety features used on automated guided vehicles operating in public places.

Some safety guidelines

The author's experiences, both with the TIDE project and with the clinical implementation of surgical robots, suggest that, where possible, the use of the following features could be beneficial in improving safety levels:

1. Provide safety sensors, monitors, and isolation systems at a servo level as well as a supervisory level.

2. Use a dead-man switch concept (i.e., a continuous positive signal is required to proceed) rather than just an emergency button. The latter requires a positive action first to locate the button and then activate it, whereas a DMS simply requires the cessation of a continuous action.

3. Use a safety monitor at both a servo level and a supervisory level.

4. Provide a facility to cut out prime movers independently while still keeping microprocessors powered up. Such a facility should be provided at a local (servo) level as well as at a systems level.

5. Duplicate sensors. Monitor at the output motion as well as the motor shaft.

6. Avoid adapting software models and motions online. Try to check out all motions and models in a preprocess planning phase.

7. Avoid the use of artificial intelligence systems except for preliminary planning phases.

8. Arrange force levels to be inherently limited to just satisfying the required tasks rather than relying only on force sensors and software systems.

9. Use mechanical constraints to limit motions to a safe volume or trajectory in case all else should fail.

10. In the event of failure, (a) ensure the system can fail only in a safe, predictable manner; (b) ensure the system can be readily removed; and (c) ensure that when the system is restarted, it has not moved relative to the patient (e.g., use absolute position measurement. Monitor the position of the patient in-line reference to a robot datum).

11. Use a key switch and key line to power up the system, with full safety status checks at power-up.

12. Use single-axis motions sequentially where possible, rather than compound-axis motions, to limit the number of possible outcomes (range, motions, etc.) should a failure occur.

13. Give the user clear error messages indicating the current status of the system. Keep the human-computer interface as simple as possible to avoid confusion.

Conclusions

From the preceding discussion, it can be seen that the greatest potential for benefit tends to come from medical robot systems, which put the user and public at the most risk. Although it is possible to guard these systems with additional software and sensing, the penalty this carries is increased cost and complexity. The integrity and fail-safe nature of software and hardware (including sensors) has to be rigorously considered, with an evaluation of the additional potential to be gained from formal methods of software development, duplication of software and hardware, and the use of such analytic techniques as failure mode effect analysis and fault tree analysis. These may well require the presence of separate positive, continuously acting dead-man switches and kill lines to provide a hardware stop independent of the software and computer-based control system. All this usually will need to be accompanied by a large red button to turn everything off in an emergency.

FIGURE 19.1 Communications and safety signals for a typical mobile medical manipulator system.

REFERENCES

[1] LAVALLÉE, S., 1989. A new system for computer assisted neuro-surgery. In *Proceedings of the IEEE Engineering in*

Medicine and Biology Society Eleventh International Conference, pp. 926–927.

[2] DAVIES, B. L., R. D. HIBBERD, W. S. NG, A. TIMONEY, and J. E. A. WICKHAM, 1991. Development of a surgeon robot for prostatectomies. *J. Eng. Med., Proc. Inst. of Mech. Eng.* 205:35–38.

[3] DAVIES, B. L., R. D. HIBBERD, W. S. NG, A. TIMONEY, and J. E. A. WICKHAM, 1991. A surgeon robot for prostatectomies. In *Proceedings of the Fifth International Conference on Advanced Robotics,* Pisa, Italy, June 1991.

[4] ADAMS, J., J. GILSBACH, K. KRYBUS, D. EBRECHT, and R. MOSGES, 1989. CAS—a navigation support for surgery. In *Proceedings of the IEEE Engineering in Medicine and Biology Society Eleventh International Conference.*

[5] TIDE Project No. 128, 1992. A general purpose multiple master slave, intelligent interface for the rehabilitation environment. E.C.E. DGX111/C3, Brussels.

II APPLICATIONS

Neurosurgery

Neurosurgery is very demanding in terms of accuracy. For surgery of the convexity of the brain, visual landmarks are relatively rare, and they are completely missing within the gray matter. If a critical structure is injured because of a minor positioning error, the results for the patient can be severe functional impairment or death. On the other hand, the brain is relatively fixed with respect to the skull, therefore allowing for accurate and stable reference, and 3D medical imaging of the brain is well developed. For these reasons, neurosurgery has historically been one of the leading-edge applications driving the development of computer-integrated surgery.

Computers have been used heavily in neurosurgery since the late 1970s, almost from the very first development of CT. The use of CT images to visualize pathologic processes and provide precise targeting information for stereotactic interventions met a real need. The systems described in this section reflect considerable technologic progress since those early days, but the idea remains the same: Use medical images to guide surgery with increased accuracy.

We present seven chapters overall that reflect the evolving state of the art in computer-assisted open and stereotactic neurosurgery. The first two chapters provide insights into requirements from two neurosurgeons who have been leaders in the development of neurosurgical CIS applications. The next four chapters provide extensive descriptions of four of the most successful present-day systems, each of which has been used in hundreds of clinical cases in Japan, Switzerland, the United States, and France. The last chapter presents a more futuristic view of neurosurgery. Again,

the field of computer-integrated neurosurgery is now becoming very well established, with many academic and commercial efforts worldwide, and this section does not pretend to detail or discuss *all* the improvements of each of these systems. Several excellent recent books (e.g., Kelly and Kall [1]) provide a more extended review.

In the first chapter, "Computer-Assisted Neurosurgery," Kelly relates the evolution of his work in computer-assisted neurosurgery performed at the Mayo Clinic over the last decade. He uses this experience to provide the context for describing what he sees as the requirements for upgrading and improving current systems. The main points discussed include fast data transfers, frameless stereotaxy, anatomy-based registration, computers' speed, realistic and fast display, registration of microscope positions, and the use of robotics. Kelly also develops some of the reasons why computer systems are or are not likely to be accepted by neurosurgeons. According to the author, the vision proposed in this chapter is mainly a "predictable extension of what is already possible," and surgeons must keep a very open mind to new technologies.

In the second chapter, "Computers and Robotics in Neurosurgery," Fukushima and Gruen extend the presentation of Kelly to a more general application of computers and technology in neurosurgery. These authors insist that "appropriate use of computers in surgery requires an understanding of what computers can do that people cannot." Then they present a vision of the computer-assisted neurosurgery room, which is based mainly on several tools developed or being developed by Fukushima. The main points discussed include the computer-assisted operating table and lighting, articulated navigation systems, intraoperative C-arm DSA control, adjustable and maleable arms, dynamic retractors, intraoperative monitoring of electroencephalogram and transcranial Doppler signals, facial nerve monitoring, video microscopes, databases, expert systems, and simulation systems for education. In this presentation, the authors finally advance two general requirements. First, computer-assisted systems must be flexible enough to adapt to specific needs at a given site. Second, simplicity of user interfaces and data management is essential to avoid to innundating the surgeon with irrelevant data.

The next five chapters in this section detail implementations of specific systems. In all of them, the idea of image-guided surgery is present. Their main difference lies in the degree of relative autonomy of action for the surgical aids. Chapters 22 and 23 present passive systems, chapters 24 and 25 show semiactive systems (although the Mayo Clinic system can also be considered active), and chapter 26 proposes an active system.

In "The Neuronavigator," Watanabe details an articulated arm that allows for navigation through MRI or CT preoperative images. The system tells you where you are. Note that the registration is performed using only three anatomic landmarks selected on the skin surface. This gives errors of a few millimeters but is sufficient for open-skull surgery, according to the authors.

Reinhardt may have been the first to propose a navigation system for neurosurgery. In "Neuronavigation: A 10-Year Review," he focuses on technologies for navigation systems. Reinhardt describes an impressive route that led his group from a first version of a mechanical arm in 1983 to an efficient noncontact ultrasound localizer. His group also is currently studying optical infrared localizers. Answering one of Kelly's requirements, Reinhardt proposes a system in which the location of a video microscope is registered continuously with preoperative images.

Lavallée and colleagues, in "Image-Guided Operating Robot," describe the work performed at Grenoble University to build a semiactive neurosurgical system that integrates a modified industrial robot. The surgeon defines a trajectory relative to medical images, the robot positions a guide at the given location and,

finally, the surgeon introduces tools inside this guide. The main advantage of a robot over a standard articulated frame in such systems is to offer more flexibility and easy and reliable guide positioning. This chapter should be read in conjunction with a related article by Kwoh, et al. [2] that describes the use of a standard industrial robot linked to a CT system. We consider this latter work to be a precursor in that domain. Unfortunately, the system of Kwoh was used only for approximately 50 cases before work was stopped. The Grenoble system has been used for more than 600 cases since 1989 and it is still in use. The other strong point of the Grenoble system is that it relies on anatomy-based registration methods, discussed in chapter 7.

In the chapter "Computer-Assisted Surgical Planning and Robotics in Stereotactic Neurosurgery," Kall presents the Compass System, which he developed with Patrick Kelly at Mayo Clinic and which they have improved over the past 15 years. This system is by far the most widely used such system, with more than 3000 clinical interventions thus far. Compass is a motorized system that allows for accurate point-in-space or volumetric stereotactic neurosurgery. User-friendly interfaces permit interactive specification of anatomic targets, trajectories, or positions of a cylindric retractor, based on multimodal images registered with a stereotactic frame. Compared with the Grenoble system, the Cartesian robot used here probably is less flexible and more cumbersome near the operating field, but it provides superior rigidity and accuracy.

The last chapter in this section, "Magnetic Stereotaxis," presents some fascinating possibilities to move capsulae through the brain using external magnetic fields, thus allowing for nonlinear trajectories. In the long term, one can imagine using such magnetic fields to carry microrobots instead of passive capsulae to the appropriate workplace.

REFERENCES

[1] KELLY, P., and B. KALL, 1992. *Computers in Stereotactic Neurosurgery*. Boston: Blackwell Scientific.

[2] KWOH, Y. S., J. HOU, E. JONCKHEERE, and S. HAYATI, 1988. A robot with improved absolute positioning accuracy for CT guided stereotactic surgery. *IEEE Trans. Biomed. Eng.* Feb.: 153–161.

20 Computer-Assisted Neurosurgery: Needs and Opportunities

PATRICK J. KELLY

BEFORE THE ADVENT of CT, traditional neurosurgery was a qualitative technical exercise: free-hand techniques based on the hand-eye coordination of the surgeon and indirect information derived from projection radiography (e.g., ventriculography, pneumoencephalography, and angiography) and clinical findings elicited by neurologic examination. Surgical exposures were much larger than necessary in order to permit one to find the lesion, and sometimes it still was difficult to localize the lesion.

Computer-based medical imaging—CT and, later, MRI—revolutionized not only radiology but also neurosurgery. Surgeons now could actually "see" the lesion responsible for their patients' neurologic problems. However, until the incorporation of stereotactic techniques, little changed in the operating room: Surgical exposures still were larger than required. When employing free-hand neurosurgical techniques, maintainence of 3D surgical orientation is tenuous below the cortical surface, so there remained some difficulty in finding lesions located there. In addition, the histologic boundary between tumor and surrounding normal brain tissue, particularly in glial neoplasms, is not always clear to a surgeon at an open operation.

The incorporation of computer-based medical imaging data into stereotactic techniques helped surgeons localize lesions by point-in-space methods. These were mathematically simple and convenient to use in an operating room environment, and ensured that a surgeon could at least find a subcortical lesion. However, expansion of the method beyond simple point-in-space localization for any more than a few target points becomes mathematically cumbersome, time-consuming, and not practical during the course of a surgical procedure. Furthermore, point-in-space stereotaxis does not deal with the problem of identifying intraoperatively the boundaries of a lesion, even though the interface between tumor and brain parenchyma seems clearly apparent on computer-based medical imaging.

Our group developed a method for volumetric stereotaxis and described this in 1979 (Kelly, 1991).[1] In that method, slices of a stereotactic CT-defined (and later, MRI-defined) tumor volume, sliced perpendicular to the stereotactically defined view line, were presented to a surgeon during the course of a stereotactic surgical tumor resection. The position of stereotactically directed instruments could then be plotted on these slice images. Initially, the instruments were catheters holding a radionuclide source for interstitial brachytherapy. Later we incorporated a carbon dioxide laser whose beam was directed from the stereotactic frame for open vaporization of the tumor slice by slice, extending from the most superficial slices to the deepest.

We soon found that manual methods for deriving the stereotactic tumor volume and slice images were far too cumbersome and time-consuming to be practical on a day-to-day basis. We therefore incorporated a computer into the instrumentation and wrote the software necessary to execute these manual methods conveniently for CT-derived tumor volume reconstruction, tumor slice reformatting, and monitoring the stereotactic position of the stereotactically directed CO_2 laser on these slice images.

In addition to the display of slice images, we found the computer useful for other surgical applications. First, through a digital-to-analogue output to X and Y galvanometers, each of which controlled mirrors mounted on the stereotactic frame, the computer could control the laser beam accurately in regular sweeps across the tumor defined by the computer-generated slice images. This probably was the first use of a robotic system in neurosurgery in general and for the removal of brain tumors in particular. However, the operating room computer system had other uses as well. Multimodal image cross-correlations of target points and volumes among different imaging modalities (e.g., CT and angiography) were possible.

Nevertheless, computer-assisted stereotactic methods were not rapidly accepted by other groups. Capacious high-speed computers of the type required for efficient image processing were too expensive for the average neurosurgical group, which did not anticipate using the technology often enough to justify the cost. Furthermore, no stereotactic software existed; it had to be produced on a custom basis. In addition, physicians tend to be suspicious of things they do not understand (few could see use for a computer in the operating room), and there is a general reluctance in the medical community to change procedures that work. Fortunately, the practical bases for all these objections are now being resolved!

Operating room computer systems

Advances in computer capacity and speed and reduction of cost has made computer technology available to many neurosurgeons. Other groups have incorporated high-capacity computer workstations into imaging-based stereotactic techniques to facilitate target point and trajectory calculations, multimodal-image target-point registration, and presentations in stereotactic preoperative planning. In addition, it now is generally evident that because of operating room computer systems, stereotaxis can progress from point-in-space stereotactic procedures to volumetric procedures: CT- or MRI-defined lesions can be represented as a volume in space and presented to a surgeon during the course of an operation. The computer display can also demonstrate the position of stereotactically directed instruments with respect to the displayed image that represents the lesion.

Basically, computer-assisted stereotactic neurosurgery comprises three phases: (1) database acquisition, (2) surgical planning and simulation, and (3) interactive surgery. Each will be described separately.

DATABASE ACQUISITION

The purpose of the database acquisition phase is to *define* pathologic lesions (which must be removed or treated) in spatial relationship to the patient's normal anatomy (which must be preserved.) Many available modalities define the lesion, normal anatomy, and even functional anatomy. These include MRI, digital projection angiography, magnetoencephelography (MEG), positron emission tomography (PET), scalp and cortical surface electroencephalography, somatosensory evoked potentials, motor evoked responses, stereotactic brain atlases, ultrasonography, intraoperative radiographs, and others. Many of these modalities provide computer-based data. Others can be digitized and the data manipulated by computer.

IMAGE TRANSFER   Our group most commonly uses CT, MRI, digital angiography, and computer-resident stereotactic atlases in our work. Some modalities are not available at our institution (e.g., PET), and others have not provided enough useful information at this stage to justify the labor they require. Specifically, we need a uniform way of conveniently reading data from a wide variety of sources into an operating room workstation.

One problem is that various manufacturers for the computer-based medical imaging equipment currently use different display formats that often are proprietary. The American College of Radiology (ACR) and the National Electronic Manufacturing Association (NEMA) have proposed a standard for display hardware and formats. If universally adopted, this problem will be obviated.

Another problem is the need for a convenient means for transferring images to an operating room workstation that is not labor-intensive. Film digitizers (video digitizers and flatbed scanners) are not time-efficient. Data tape transfer probably is the most reliable but requires personnel. High-speed data links from imaging computers to the operating room computer would be the ideal solution but are not practical at all institutions. High-speed fiberoptic data transfer or Ethernet connections between radiology computers and the operating room may provide the best alternatives for transfer of preoperative planning data to an operating room workstation. The key factors to general acceptance of all technology within the operating room are convenience and time efficiency. If it is inconvenient, it will not be used, even if available.

IMAGE CROSS-REGISTRATION   A reliable yet convenient method for multimodal image registration and correlations is required. Stereotactic frames and external fiducial marker systems are simple and accurate. However, placing a stereotactic frame requires a separate (albeit simple) surgical procedure that necessitates setup and procedure time. Imaging examinations (even though already performed for diagnostic purposes) must then be repeated in stereotactic conditions. This increases the cost and adds to patient discomfort.

Various frameless stereotactic methods for cross-registration between various imaging modalities have been proposed. However, the problem of image registration to the surgical field is not insignificant. Several solutions have been proposed. First, scalp markers applied to the patient during imaging (CT, MRI, PET, etc.) are identified on the images and by a digitizer at surgery. This provides a means of translating coordinate systems from one imaging database to another as well as to the patient on the operating table. However, there are some inaccuracies with this method because the scalp and markers can move with respect to the underlying skull and brain. Alternatively, markers can be implanted through the scalp and into the patient's skull. However, this seems as inconvenient and may be as time-consuming as placing a stereotactic head frame.

A more ideal solution may be to use the unique configuration of the patient's head. All imaging-based data about the brain and its pathology is contained within a fixed envelope (i.e., the scalp and skull). Both of these can be defined automatically from the imaging database by automatic segmenting programs. An imaging-based terrain-matching program could be used that employs a least-squares-fit alogrithm which will match the imaging database with the surface of the patient's scalp. Contour-matching programs can fit one surface (or volume) into another as a hand fits into a glove. This could provide a means for image cross-registration between imaging modalities. In addition, the surface of the scalp defined in the surgical field by a digitizer provides a means for translating the image coordinate systems to the surgical coordinate system.

SURGICAL PLANNING

The role of surgical planning is to define the safest possible approach to an intracranial lesion, one that inflicts the least possible damage to normal anatomic structures. In general, surgical approaches to subcorti-

cal lesions should be through nonessential brain tissue parallel to white matter projections and in the least invasive manner available. All the preoperative imaging modalities provide information as to the localization of the pathalogic process as well as to its spatial relationship to normal anatomic structures. However, different modalities demarcate different aspects of the lesion and surrounding anatomy. For example, CT displays bone anatomy well, MRI defines the normal gray and white matter brain anatomy, and projection angiography defines vascular anatomy in the greatest detail possible. In addition, modalities such as MEG and high-field fast MRI can establish the function of CT- and MRI-defined anatomic regions for noninvasive brain mapping. All preoperative databases are fused into a uniform computer matrix that corresponds to the individual patient's brain. The fixed database can then be presented to a surgeon in a single display for efficient surgical planning and computer-based surgical simulations that will render surgery safer and more time-efficient. These displays may also prove useful in the training of young surgeons and medical students and in patient teaching.

However, for realistic computer simulations of surgical procedures, we require significantly greater computer power and capacity than that available in the average workstation. Because medical professionals are able to afford and justify the cost of relatively inexpensive computers having limited BUS capacity, specially designed computers featuring capacious random access memory (RAM) and parallel and voxel processers are necessary for complex, real-time, high-resolution volumetric image processing. Higher-capacity RAM will improve resolution of the database and allow increased speed in computations and user interaction. More voxels within the 3D computer surgical planning matrix will improve image quality to generate more lifelike and real-time displays.

DISPLAY MODALITIES We are trying to display 3D databases on 2D screens, which is a significant problem. Our group reported the display of reformatted slice images through a volumetric matrix along a defined stereotactic view line. Three-dimensional shaded graphics make pretty pictures but at the present time are not very useful. Stereoscopic pairs can be presented on a computer screen. However, few surgeons can "cross their eyes" to appreciate the fine detail in a stereoscopic pair.

Three-dimensional displays of the vibrating mirror type have been tried but currently have limited resolution. However, virtual reality simulations, in which right and left views of a computer-generated stereoscopic image are transmitted to LCD viewing screens for each eye, present an exciting possibility, assuming that the host computer has sufficient speed to allow almost real-time rotations of a huge volumetric or surface display database.

HOLOGRAPHY   Computer slice images can be used to create a hologram of the preoperative database. In the past, the production of holograms has taken days or weeks to produce. However, in a new process, holograms can be produced in approximately 20 minutes. These may be adequate for a surgeon to appreciate anatomic relationships but will have no value in making stereotactic calculations. Unfortunately, we cannot computer-interact with a static hologram: A holographic computer terminal is needed.

Computer-generated holograms are not new. However, limited computer capacity and computational speeds have produced modest results. As computers have gotten faster and more capacious, an interactive holographic terminal is possible. In fact, a prototype system has been developed at the Computer Science Department of the Massachusetts Institute of Technology, Cambridge, Mass. Nevertheless, resolution in this unit must improve significantly to be useful in an operating room for surgical planning.

INTERACTIVE SURGERY   The surgical planning step is useful in conceptualizing the surgical approach and defining a plan of action. However, unless there can be translation of the coordinate system of the imaging database to the real-world environment of the patient on the operating table, all the plans will be qualitative only. This would represent a tragic waste of the precise quantitative information that imaging databases provide.

In computer-assisted stereotaxis, a stereotactic frame establishes the coordinate system for the surgical field and defines the approach trajectory, target points, and volumes. Intraoperatively, the computer displays stereotactic frame settings and, by cursor or some other defined indicator, the placement of instruments directed by that frame on an appropriate computer-generated image. However, this procedure is somewhat cumbersome as a human interface is required: Someone must manually enter certain parameters from the surgical field to the computer so that the computer can calculate and display the position of the instruments directed by the stereotactic device. For example, in arc-quadrant stereotaxis, one must enter arc and collar angles and probe depth in order to have the computer calculate the 3D position of its tip and indicate its position on the appropriate image display.

FRAMELESS STEREOTAXIS   The concept of the stereotactic frame is sacred to stereotactians and oppressive to nonstereotactic neurosurgeons. Stereotactic frames impede the freedom of motion that makes open surgery an art form. Many surgeons are intimidated by the mechanics and mathematics involved in stereotaxis, which may explain why many surgeons have never incorporated this technology in their practice. In fact, stereotactic frames are cumbersome and stereotactic calculations time-consuming. In addition, stereotactic frames require a database acquisition procedure that necessitates repeating CT, MRI, and angiographic examinations that may have already been performed in making the initial diagnosis. Could the diagnostic imaging be used as a stereotactic database and the stereotactic frame be eliminated?

If we can define a common coordinate system for patient and database, digitizers in the operating room could be used to touch precise points on the patient's scalp or skull that would then be registered on CT or magnetic resonance images. At present, two such digitizer systems are in beta-testing phases. The first is a multijointed digitizer arm with optical encoders on each joint (ISG Technologies, Toronto, Ontario). The second employs a tuned, low-frequency, magnetic field transmitter source and a sensor-pointer for real-time read-out of stereotactic coordinates (Regulus System, Stereotactic Medical Systems, Rochester, Minn.).

The operating microscope could provide a frameless stereotactic system, provided that the operating microscope were indexed into the surgical coordinate system so that its field of view is known in 3D surgical space. The stereotactic computer-generated images could be transmitted to the surgeon by means of a "heads-up" display into the operating microscope.

Before any innovation is universally accepted, it must be convenient, produce instantaneous results, and be totally free of any human interface: The surgeon moves the instrument, and the computer display immediately and accurately shows that movement with respect to the preoperative imaging database. Neurosurgeons truly need systems that will give stereotactic coordinates within the operative field for hand-held instruments. This instrument could be a simple pointer but could also be an instrument that a surgeon needs to use in the procedure, such as a sucker or a bipolar forceps. For example, ideally the position of these instruments would be detected by the computer and displayed with respect to imaging-defined tumor boundaries.

The position of these tools within the surgical work envelope might be digitized in a number of ways. The following are some examples.

Fiberoptic calibration systems such as those developed by the National Aeronautics and Space Administrations (NASA) and the Ames Research Laboratory quantitatively measure light deflection in fiberoptic bundles. Basically, the system detects where the fiberoptic shaft is being bent, how far it is being deflected, and in what direction. It is thus theoretically possible to obtain 3D coordinates of the tip of the fiberoptic shaft. At present, this technology is used in virtual reality and some telepresence systems. For example, a digitizing glove worn by an astronaut is used to control robotic devices in space machinery.

This technology could be applied to obtain the 3D position of any surgical instrument connected by a flexible cord. Several of these bundles could be incorporated into the electric cord of a bipolar cautery, for example, or onto a suction tubing to provide coordinates and deflection information in three or more planes. Supplied with these data and given the length of forceps and suction tip, the computer could calculate coordinates of their tips in 3D surgical space.

Machine vision techniques could also be used to detect the position of dissectors, scissors, or forceps in the surgical field. Here the instrument would be fitted with two microbattery-powered LEDs having specific emitting frequencies. The distance between the LEDs would be known, as would be the length and configuration of the instrument. Biplanar videocameras could transmit to the operating computer system the images of the surgical field viewed from precise projections. The images would be placed in 2D image matrices by frame grabbers, and sensitivity detection scan would determine the position of each LED in the two planes. By triangulation, the computer then could calculate the position in surgical space of each LED and thus determine the inclination between the two LEDs. Because the length and configuration of the instrument would be known (this could be relayed to the computer by a bar code), the computer could determine the position of the tip of the instrument within the surgical field.

ROBOTICS In all robots, each joint for movement is electronically controlled by stepper motors or servomotors. In addition, feedback of joint position is supplied to the host computer by means of an optical encoder on each joint. Some robot types could be adapted for surgical applications. The Compass stereotactic system (Stereotactic Medical Systems, Rochester, Minn.) is, in fact, a Cartesian robot. Others have adapted articulated coordinate industrial robots as a replacement for stereotactic frames. Robots can be used to hold probes for biopsy or retractor systems.

However, the use of off-the-shelf industrial robots in stereotaxis is neither safe nor practical for several reasons, not the least of which is that surgeons require accuracy, whereas industrial robots provide reproducibility. A surgical robot should be designed from the ground up with specifications that provide safety, backup systems, and accuracy—that is the ability to assess a defined x, y, z point reliably within an imaging-defined work envelope.

An operating microscope could be suspended from a surgical robot. The robotic device would position the microscope in precise 3D space. The position of the microscope and thereby its field of view would be known and transmitted to the surgical computer system. The computer then could display, with respect to the position of the actual surgical field defined by the robotic work envelope, the preoperatively defined image of what the surgical field should look like, as gathered from the fused preoperative imaging database.

An imaging-based rendition of the surgical field scaled for the particular magnification being used can be displayed to the surgeon in several ways. One efficient method far this is by means of the "heads-up" display device that we have used since 1986. The surgeon will be able to overlay a scaled image of the surgical field on the actual surgical field in order to identify tumor boundaries, anticipate important blood vessels that may be near or beneath the plane of surgery, and so on. Voice-activated computer commands would prompt image updates and microscope movements.

Conclusions

The preceding represents only a short list of the many possible applications of computers and robotic technology in computer-assisted neurosurgery. These developments are a predictable extension of what is already possible and indeed is operational in various nonmedical industries. However, we cannot predict the impact on stereotaxis of revolutionary developments in other disciplines that may be easily adapted for stereotactic surgery. New computer systems, optical storage devices, and efficient means of electronic data transfer are being developed at a rapid rate. Neurosurgeons must keep abreast of high-technology developments and keep an open mind regarding how such developments can be useful in the operating room.

NOTE

1. A fuller description of the results of the evolution of this system may be found in chapter 25.

REFERENCE

KELLY, P. J., 1991, *Tumor Stereotaxis*. Philadelphia: W. B. Saunders.

21 Computers and Robotics in Neurosurgery

TAKANORI FUKUSHIMA AND PETER GRUEN

REVOLUTIONARY advances in computer and information science are transforming medicine and surgery. In no specialty are these advances more apparent than in neurologic surgery. Although occasionally inappropriately used, sometimes placed more as props than as functional accessories in the operating room, computers have become essential parts of monitoring, instrumentation, and data management.

In preoperative evaluation, operative technique, intraoperative monitoring, and data collection and manipulation, computational power enables effective application of technologies requiring high-resolution visualization and precise control and manipulation of physiologic parameters.

Appropriate use of computers in surgery requires an understanding of what computers can do that people cannot. Computers perform calculations and manipulate information at great speed. They are not susceptible to mental fatigue and therefore make far fewer computational errors than comparably worked humans. The programs that control how computers process information can be modified to suit particular needs. They can be programmed to do tasks that meet specific needs and, as these needs change, can be modified accordingly. These machines are versatile adjuncts to the neurosurgeon and his or her assistants.

Preoperative assessment of neurosurgical patients

Preoperative evaluation of every surgical patient includes a battery of laboratory tests, including blood cell count, urinalysis, and screening panels measuring levels of metabolites and other physiologically important substances. Automated testing of huge numbers of specimens requires computer regulation of quantities of reagents and precise control of reaction times. The massive amounts of data generated on large numbers of patients with many tests repeated several times during a patient's hospital stay requires increasingly sophisticated data collection, storage, and retrieval systems.

For billing and other administrative reasons, hospitals collect large amounts of demographic and financial information on patients. Quality assurance considerations are adding pressure for more complete documentation of patient encounters and charting of each patient's in-hospital course. An efficient functional electronic data management system may soon be part of the requirement for hospital accreditation.

The volume of data generated in hospitals is monumental. Increasingly, hospitals are employing user-friendly software "front ends" to allow nursing staff, physicians, and ancillary personnel to keep up with charting demands. Systems that allow nurses to chart directly into computers are being supplemented by systems in which data is automatically captured from monitoring devices in technology-intensive areas such as intensive care. The entire team treating neurosurgical patients relies on computer-controlled data generation and collection systems to initiate the peoperative evaluation.

During the past two decades, remarkable progress has been made in neuroradiologic imaging techniques utilizing computer technology. The ease, simplicity, and noninvasive nature of these new imaging modalities has made them a great boon to patient evaluation pre-, post-, and intraoperatively. Few neurosurgical procedures are performed without a thorough neuroradiologic workup employing computer-intensive equipment and techniques.

DIGITAL SUBTRACTION ANGIOGRAM

Angiography, in which radiopaque dye is injected into the patient's vascular system and filmed with x-rays while circulating therein, provides an accurate image of the cerebral, head and neck, and other vasculature. Advanced computer technology permits digitization of these images so that they can be stored on magnetic tape and, if desired, be magnified and otherwise enhanced with computer graphics techniques.

Using digital subtraction angiography (DSA) to eliminate bone and metal objects, it is possible to visualize selectively the cerebrovascular images. Any phase of serial angiograms—arterial, capillary, or venous—can be visualized on a television screen with just the pushing of certain buttons on the control panel. Computerized DSA has stimulated important technical advances in the emerging specialty of interventional neuroradiology. More accurate visualization enables production of highly detailed vascular "road maps" of patients' cerebral vasculature, which serves as the basis for guidance of catheters used in such applications as "superselective" catheterization for exquisitely precise infusion of embolization material or pharmacologic or chemotherapeutic agents [1].

Computerized tomography

The density-dependent differential absorption of x-rays is the basis for images obtained by exposure of photographic plates placed beyond an object subjected to energy from an x-ray source. This technique has been refined to produce images that provide information about different densities of tissue within pathologic lesions. Computers can combine thousands of x-rays shot simultaneously from an arc of x-ray ports surrounding any structure. The computer then can construct tomographic or slice images through tissues, providing high-fidelity pictures noninvasively. This differential density information obtained in the living person is undoubtedly the greatest single advance in medical and, specifically, brain imaging in the modern era.

Previously, surgeons had to rely on indirect phenomena, such as abnormalities of patterns of distribution within the ventricular system of air injected into the subarachnoid space around the brain or spinal cord, or of irregular displacements of vessels as viewed on angiograms. With the advent of CT scanning, cerebral tissue and lesions within it could be directly visualized. With experience, the radiographic appearance of different types of tumor, clots of different ages, brain swelling, and many other images were defined and quite reliably diagnosed in vivo. The intravenous infusion of contrast agent that crossed the blood-brain barrier in certain pathologic states and, by its radiopacity,

showed up brightly was an important addition to the neuroradiologist's diagnostic armamentarium.

Preoperative planning also was greatly facilitated by CT scanning. Smaller incisions and skull flaps were possible as surgeons could more precisely localize lesions and determine optimal trajectories to reach them.

Magnetic resonance imaging

MRI is based on the magnetic properties of hydrogen bipoles in living tissue. The changes in frequency of bipoles pulsed to change their alignment in an imposed magnetic field, returning from the higher frequency to a resting state, is the basis for this newest generation of computer-derived images. MRI differs from CT in that it images differences in tissue based on chemical rather than density properties. It differs also in its far more intensive use of computers for mathematic calculations to generate its images. The sensitivity of MRI is greater than that of CT, and it provides images in the sagittal plane and of the posterior fossa, which are obtained only with great difficulty by CT and, if obtained thus, are of far poorer quality.

In terms of resolution and accuracy, MRI is far superior in most instances. CT is helpful still for visualizing certain aspects of tissue such as collections of calcium but, some notable exceptions aside, MRI is much better for visualizing cerebral anatomy and will continue to play the major role in neurodiagnostic examinations.

On machines equipped with very high tesla magnets, magnetic resonance spectroscopy can be used to supplement standard anatomic images, providing information about the location of certain metabolites and energy-storing molecules. This can be important information in differentiating among tissue types and pathologic states.

Positron emission tomography and single photon emission computed tomography

CT scanning techniques have been modified for scanning following the injection of radionuclide-labeled pharmacologic and metabolic agents. The distribution of these materials in tissue provides useful information about the metabolic function of activated sites, which gives important clues to pathophysiologic processes taking place. Positron emission tomography (PET) and Single photon emission computed tomography

(SPECT) functional visualization of brain slices are performed routinely at the University of Southern California (USC) University Hospital as part of the evaluation of patients with brain tumors, stroke, epilepsy, and other neurologic disorders.

ELECTROENCEPHALOGRAPHY

Electroencephalography (EEG) has many applications in the evaluation of patients with tumors, traumatic lesions, cerebrovascular diseases, or seizure disorders. It provides important localization information as well as an indication of the extent of abnormal electrophysiology. Using high-speed computers, conventional waveforms can be Fourier-analyzed to produce a 2D image to a screen. In the neurosurgical intensive care unit, so-called compressed spectral arrays are used to provide a means of continuous monitoring of ongoing EEGs in patients with severe head injury or stroke.

Magnetoencephalography is a new technology that will enable combining functional cortical mapping with MR for localization of such "eloquent" areas as speech and voluntary movement [2].

Computers and robotics in operative neurosurgery

Computers have a role not only in preoperative evaluation of neurosurgical patients. All aspects of surgical intervention now require the assistance of computational systems.

THE NEUROSURGICAL OPERATING ROOM

Recently constructed hospitals such as the USC University Hospital incorporate sophisticated systems into their infrastructure [3]. Computers control not only laboratory data accumulation and transfer but also the patient food delivery system and other services.

The USC University Hospital was designed with the aid of sophisticated computers for drawing plans and testing out various structural scenarios. The foundation of the building was designed to tolerate severe shocks during an earthquake. This system was tested with computer simulations. The inner environment is computer-controlled. Automatic temperature regulation and flow of air is coordinated centrally within the building.

LAMINAR FLOW   The operating rooms are equipped with additional specialized equipment for environmental manipulation, supplementing systems in place throughout the building. Airborne fungi and bacteria that have the potential to infect open surgical wounds are controlled with laminar flow air circulation systems.

AUTOMATION   Lighting is essential to accurate surgical maneuvers. Focusing of lighting is automated so that sensors in the lights can be directed into the appropriate portion of the surgical field.

An automated, remotely controlled, hydraulically driven operating table was pioneered by Fukushima in 1981. The cordless, battery-operated device, in addition to motors for elevating and lowering parts of the patient's body, has an adjustable step for the assisting nurse, ensuring his or her optimal height with respect to the surgeon and operative field. The instrument table that sits over the patient's body also can move up and down with a hydraulic motor driven in combination with the movement of the operating room table (figure 21.1).

INTRAOPERATIVE SURGICAL GUIDANCE

To avoid damage to neural tissue, intraoperative surgical guidance is provided by a variety of high-tech instruments.

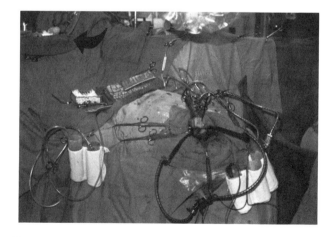

FIGURE 21.1 Advanced neurosurgical operating setup. Operating table controlled with battery-powered, remote-controlled, hydraulic system provides for a variety of patient positions with ease of setup and modifications. Table for surgical instruments and nurse's step also automatically controlled (arrow).

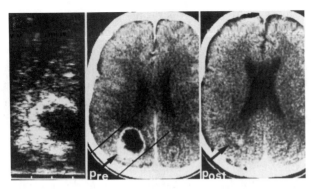

FIGURE 21.2 Intraoperative ultrasound visualization and guidance. Noninvasive localization of a subcortical tumor using a 2.5-cm miniprobe linear electronic scanner. Utilizing this ultrasound real-time guidance, the surgeon can enter the brain through a minimal cortical opening.

ULTRASOUND SCANNING AND COLOR DOPPLER IMAGING Despite the use of advanced neuroradiologic techniques, localization of small subcortical lesions intraoperatively is often difficult. The advent of real-time B-mode ultrasound scanning has solved this problem, allowing noninvasive precise imaging of the brain surface and subcortical tissue, which permits accurate localization and characterization of subcortical lesions during neurosurgical operations. In 1980, Fukushima [4] developed a special 2.5-cm miniprobe with a linear electronic scanning system for neurosurgery (figure 21.2).

By combining the technique of B-mode scanning with color Doppler imaging, it is possible to visualize noninvasively from the surface of the brain an arteriovenous malformation located at some depth (see color plate 27).

ARTICULATED NEURAL NAVIGATION SYSTEM An articulated neural navigation system has been developed using 3D CT or magnetic resonance images [5, 6]. Following determination of several key cranial surface landmarks such as the glabela, bregma, or ear canal, CT or magnetic resonance images are obtained with markers at these landmarks, which then can serve as reference points for a navigational system. Intraoperatively, the surgeon moves the articulated arm pointing in succession to the key landmarks. The computer analyzes the movement of the articulated joints to determine the relative location of the landmarks and uses them as reference coordinates. When a probe attached to the articulated arm is used to point in any direction toward the target, the computer can simultaneously localize on a television image the exact trajectory from the probe into the target. This innovative technology is a refinement of the stereotactic concept. It is being used in the development of frameless stereotactic targeting systems.

INTRAOPERATIVE C-ARM DSA CONTROL Formerly, the surgeon who had clipped an aneurysm or resected an arteriovenous malformation had to move the patient out of the operating room to a separate suite to assess the completeness of his or her work. Technologic advances have included the development of portable DSA x-ray machines that can be used to obtain intraoperative angiography for confirmation of surgical results before closure of the wound [7] (figures 21.3, 21.4).

STEREOTACTIC SYSTEMS

In stereotaxis, coordinates of a lesion with respect to external reference landmarks are used to guide the trajectory of instruments precisely to biopsy, resect, or ablate the lesion. CT enables direct visualization of the target. Following attachment of an immovable base ring to the skull with reference bases of known orientation, fiducial coordinates are recorded along with the coordinates of the proposed target. A separate computer then generates the coordinates to enter onto a stereotactic frame to which the biopsy cannula is affixed and which thereby guides the trajectory along which the cannula moves on its way to the target. Not only is the patient spared an open craniotomy, but unnecessary damage to brain tissue is minimized by the predetermined sure trajectory to the lesion.

UTILIZATION OF HIGH-TECH SURGICAL TOOLS

Instrumentation in neurosurgery is high-tech as well. Designers apply every possible innovation to the operative endeavor. High-speed pneumatic drills with fine cutting and diamond burrs enable neurosurgeons to dissect structures from the confines of the skull base. The ultimate high-powered drilling system for universal application, including routine craniotomy, difficult skull-base exposure, spinal and even orthopaedic procedure, has been developed by Fukushima at the USC Skullbase Laboratory in cooperation with engineers from Zimmer-Hall Instruments.

The cavitron ultrasonic aspirator (CUSA) is a state-of-the-art instrument that uses high-frequency sound

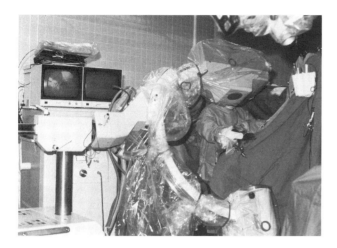

FIGURE 21.3 C-arm portable image intensifier with computerized DSA unit in use for intraoperative angiographic control.

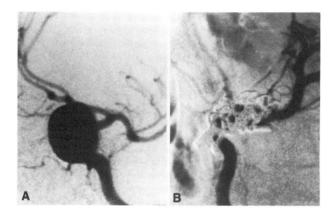

FIGURE 21.4 (A) Giant paraclinoid carotid aneurysm causing visual loss in a 45-year-old woman. (B) Intraoperative DSA picture demonstrating successful obliteration of aneurysm with seven clips preserving all normal vasculature.

waves to disrupt tissue. The sound-generating tip is surrounded by a tube that simultaneously irrigates and aspirates the microscopic tissue fragments.

Nowadays, the majority of neurosurgical procedures are performed under a microscope to obtain magnified views with detailed anatomy and high-intensity illumination. The mechanics of these operating microscopes have been refined, employing free-moving, floating motions with joints having electromagnetic locking systems, which facilitate rapid changes of the operative view of the surgeon and aid in microcopic surgery in the depths with a rapidly changing viewing angle.

ROBOTIC INSTRUMENTS

Robotics is the use of machines to perform a sequence of tasks. Robotics relies heavily on the technology of cybernetics—control and feedback. Computers enable rapid processing of feedback information with generation of an appropriate response command to drive the action of the robot.

Refinement of the means of visualization (microscopes) and of increasingly precise instruments enables microsurgical manipulations of smaller and smaller objects in increasingly delicate and often previously unexplored anatomic locations in brain and other nervous tissue. The limiting factor in microsurgery is increasingly human frailty. The precision and stability of human hand movements is limited by the physiologic and anatomic engineering constraints of the eyes, arms, and fingers. Physiologic tremor of no consequence in gross everyday movement takes on unsettling proportions when seen under a microscope with a sharp or hot instrument poised proximate to a small but crucial vessel critical to the survival of a vital neural structure.

Robot arms are not vulnerable to surprise, anxiety, or other environmental factors that can magnify human weakness under the operating microscope. Yasargil [8] was the first to develop a flexible self-retaining retractor system. The simple concept of an L-shaped metal rod, the long arm of which was attached to the operating room table, with a short arm that extended onto the sterile field and that could be adjusted at will, has become the central supporting element of complex self-retaining retractor systems.

Fukushima [9] has developed a system of robotic adjuncts for neurosurgery that provide the neurosurgeon with an assistant for some purposes more reliable, or at least more stable, than the surgeon himself or herself (figure 21.5).

Adjustable, malleable arms can be positioned in the operative field to direct irrigation fluid (figure 21.6). Human assistants performing this job often get in the way or irrigate the wrong place. Unlike humans, such static robot arms do not fatigue and remain stably fixed once placed in proper position. Other similar neurosurgical support systems or craniotomy frames have been developed and applied to clinical neurosurgery [10, 11].

A dynamic robot arm for brain retraction connected to sensors of cerebral blood flow and pressure is under development at the USC Skullbase Laboratory (figure

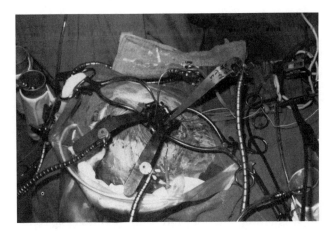

FIGURE 21.5 Neurosurgical operating setup showing robot arm and retraction system.

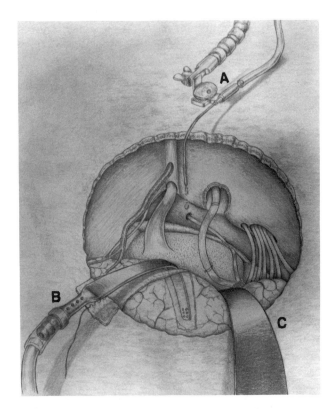

FIGURE 21.6 Static robot arm system holding automatic irrigation needle (A), automatic suction-retractor (B), and malleable brain retractor (C) during tumor resection and cranial nerve anastomosis.

21.7). The retractor is connected to an arm that makes rotational and translational movements in response to feedback instructions from EEG and regional cerebral blood flow monitors. The sensors are able to detect and

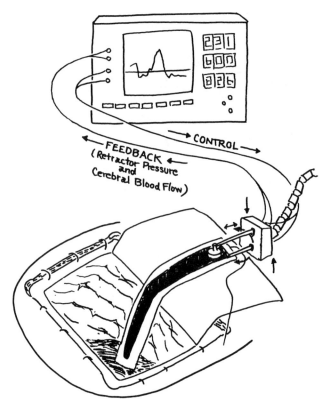

FIGURE 21.7 Scheme for dynamic robot arm system with holding arm able to make translational, elevation-depression, and rotational movements, automatically controlled by feedback from retractor pressure and cerebral blood flow monitors.

monitor parameters that humans cannot. Previous reports from this country and Denmark have emphasized that excessive brain retraction can result in radiographically apparent brain damage all too frequently associated with neurologic deficit [12, 13].

In cooperation with researchers from the California Institute of Technology, we are developing a pressure-sensitive device for placement between retractor and brain tissue. Such a device would serve as a continuous feedback to the surgeon, with appropriate alarms for excessive or protracted pressure on brain tissue.

Intraoperative monitoring

Signals from recordings in continuously changing biologic systems appear in the form of waves with spikes, peaks, and troughs. To store this information and to analyze it, these smooth waveform signals must be digitized—that is, the value of points at predetermined intervals along the wave must be assigned and then stored in a retrievable form. The speed and computational capacity of microcomputers is essential to the development of this technology. The same computer can collect data and then tap the resulting database repository when asked to reproduce any recorded waveform or to perform statistical analyses on those in its memory.

ELECTROENCEPHALOGRAPHY

In surgery that may require resection of brain tissue in proximity to eloquent cortex, such as that for seizures, it is essential to know what is functionally inexpendable tissue. In addition to improvements in standard EEG technology, electrodes have been designed that can be placed directly on the cortex for localization of seizure foci preoperatively and during the course of seizure surgery as well. In addition, it is possible to "map" certain brain functions such as language and voluntary movement by performing procedures with the patient sedated but awake and therefore able to cooperate. Using computers for data storage and analysis, intraoperative maps are constructed that aid the surgeon in knowing where he or she can safely resect.

In cerebrovascular surgery, continuous monitoring of EEG activities has become a standard procedure to prevent ischemic complications [14]. During aneurysm surgery, endarterectomy, vascular repair, or bypass anastomosis, the neurosurgeon needs temporarily to occlude the parent vessels, causing decreased flow and potential ischemia to the areas of the brain they supply. Neuropharmacologic agents are being used to minimize the metabolic consequences of this decreased flow, and EEG monitoring is essential for accurate titration of brain-protective pharmacologic agents.

EVOKED POTENTIALS

Evoked EEG potentials to various peripheral stimuli can be summated and averaged for 100 to 1000 times to show the pattern of wave peaks and troughs. The latency between various peaks is characteristic for different neuroanatomic pathways within the spinal cord and brain. Operative manipulations and pharmacologic interventions can alter the way that impulses travel along the various pathways and thus can affect the latency of the waveforms as seen on the evoked potential monitoring screens.

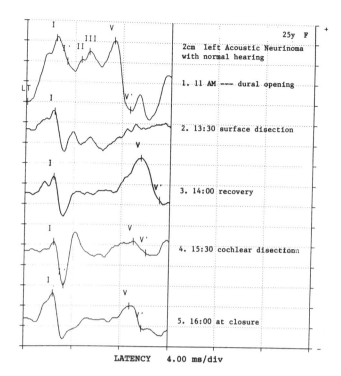

LATENCY   4.00 ms/div

FIGURE 21.8   Serial auditory brainstem response recordings demonstrating prolongation of latencies and diminution of amplitude of waveforms by manipulation of acoustic nerve (cranial nerve VIII) during resection of acoustic tumor.

Evoked potential monitoring has become standard practice in the majority of neurosurgical procedures. The somatosensory evoked potentials (SSEPs) [15–17] and auditory brainstem response (ABR) [18–20] are the most frequently monitored responses (figure 21.8). Occasionally, visual evoked potential monitoring is performed [21, 22] and, more recently, motor evoked potentials have been tried with noninvasive magnetic stimulation [23, 24]. In addition to extracranial recording, evoked potentials can be also recorded from the depths of the brain to determine the appropriate placement of electrodes during functional stereotactic operations [25].

In most neurosurgical operating rooms, technicians are required to watch the ongoing real-time monitoring so that they can alert the surgeon in the event that he or she is doing something that causes significant alterations in the latency or waveform seen on the monitor. In 1987, Fukushima [26] developed a system of automatic peak detection and a latency measurement automatic warning system in the evoked potential monitoring. The computer can be programmed to take the evoked potential waveforms as they are

Auditory Brain Stem Response (ABR)
Computer-aided monitoring of waveform/peak latency

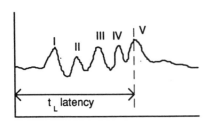

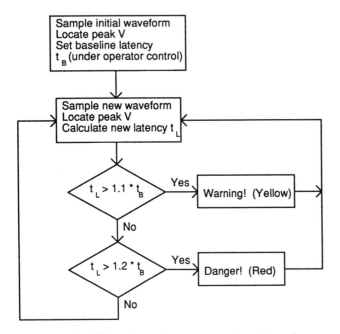

FIGURE 21.9 Flow chart for computer detection of wave V peak latency with thresholds for generation of warning signals.

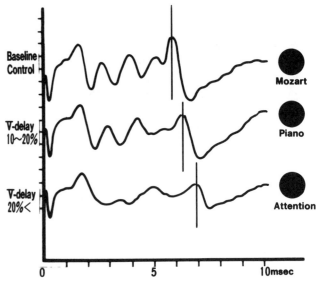

FIGURE 21.10 Ongoing brainstem response continuously checked by computer monitoring system, which delivers signals for safe range, warning, or danger. Signals can be transformed to generate different styles of music in the operating room, such as Mozart for the safe range, Beethoven piano for warning, and Souza march for danger.

TRANSCRANIAL DOPPLER ULTRASONOGRAPHY

Transcranial Doppler ultrasonography has been utilized in the neurosurgical intensive care unit to monitor noninvasively the cerebrovascular circulation, particularly the flow and velocity of the middle cerebral artery [27, 28]. The technique has proved to be very useful to monitor cerebral blood flow in patients with head injury or cerebrovascular stroke. This technology has recently been applied to the intraoperative monitoring of cerebrovascular flow during carotid endarterectomy at USC (figure 21.11). Clinical applications include monitoring the course of cerebral vasospasm following subarachnoid hemorrhage, following severe head trauma, and during intraoperative temporary carotid occlusion.

Recently, direct measurement of cerebrocortical blood flow has been reported using a thermistor plate electrode that will help to measure the amount of cerebral circulation during aneurysm surgery or bypass surgery [29]. In the event of an acute alteration in blood flow, due to such events as temporary clipping or inadvertent rupture of an aneurysm, the change in cerebral blood flow can be accurately charted and will influence the surgeon's management strategy (e.g.,

produced and to compare these to control waveforms (figure 21.9). In the event that there is a prolongation of the latency of any particular peak, the computer issues a warning signal. The intensity or quality of the signal can be programmed to reflect the degree of prolongation of the latency. If the prolongation in latency is within 10%, the computer can produce a "safe" signal or green light or soothing music. If the latency is prolonged by 10–20%, the signal becomes "attention" or a yellow light or gloomy music. Once the latency reaches the 20% threshold, the signal is "danger" or a red light or a stirring march (figure 21.10).

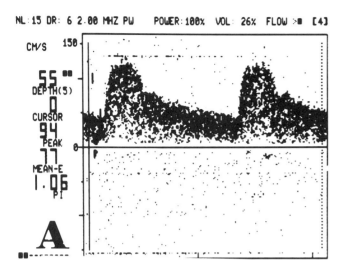

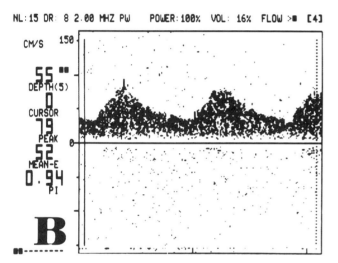

FIGURE 21.12 A 7-kg high-definition television camera is mounted on a floating microscope for recording of microsurgical events (the system tested in Tokyo in 1988 by the author).

FIGURE 21.11 Transcranial Doppler monitoring of middle cerebral artery (MCA) flow during carotid endarterectomy in a 67-year-old man with left carotid stenosis. (A) Doppler spectrum preclamp. (B) Fifth percent reduction of MCA flow following carotid clamping.

more time to complete operation, asking neuroanesthetist to increase brain protection).

FACIAL NERVE MONITORING

Surgery on cranial nerves requires means of stimulation and of recording elicited responses. Facial nerve stimulators, whereby touching the facial nerve with a probe elicits a response from a recording electrode in the face, are used routinely during resection of tumors of the eighth cranial nerve to avoid confusion between this and the adjacent seventh (or facial) nerve.

Visualization and preservation of neurosurgical procedures

Recent advances in imaging technology have revolutionized neurosurgery both in diagnostics and operative planning and execution. CT and MRI are two examples.

Computers have the capacity to convert graphic images into various digital formats that can then be reformulated to produce enhanced graphics images. One-dimensional images can be digitally enhanced, and images in different planes can be combined to give 3D images, which can then be enlarged, zoomed in on, or rotated. Although the applicability of these technologies to current neurosurgical operative procedures is limited, it holds great promise as other technologies advance.

Advances in computer technology have been paralleled by improvements in optical system design, which has stimulated a revolution in video technology. In 1987, Fukushima developed a high-resolution 3D television system using a pair of three chip (CCD) cameras with a 120-Hz liquid crystal panel. In 1988, he first utilized the high-definition television camera mounted on a floating microscope for microneurosurgical visualization and recording (figure 21.12).

All phases of operative event, from patient positioning to skin incision to microscope dissection, can be visualized simultaneously on monitors in or at a distance from the operating room. Surgical assistants and technicians can help the operating surgeon effectively by watching on a monitor without needing to look through the microscope. All that occurs can be recorded for later playback. Such documentation of intraoperative events is increasingly important for quality assurance as well as for educational purposes. Medical students, nurses, and paramedical personnel can benefit from review of operative films. Exchanges and presentations at specialty and scientific meetings also are facilitated by video demonstrations.

At USC, construction of an operative suite dedicated to stereotactic and microneurosurgery was supervised by neurosurgery professor Michael L. J. Apuzzo who worked closely with the USC Department of Computer Science and Cinematography to determine the most effective application of the latest in 3D and image reconstruction graphics technology to surgery.

Information management

DATABASES

Computerized data management offers an alternative to paper-based record keeping. Data in virtually unlimited quantities can be stored and retrieved with just a few keystrokes. Such electronic databases enable clinical investigators to access specific pieces of information without having to sift through masses of undesired recorded information.

Computers have serious limitations as applied to medicine. Biologic systems are complex. Although every discipline attempts to quantify as much as possible, it remains true that many scales and parameters are arbitrary. An important goal in developing means of monitoring must be the establishment of ranges of safety.

Another consideration in the development of computerized measurement and monitoring systems for biologic applications is the fact that biologic systems are dynamic with multiple variables, sometimes described as chaotic. These systems are only beginning to be described mathematically, which limits their ability to be simulated by computers.

The USC neurosurgery service admits more than 200 victims of head trauma every year. Due to adverse socioeconomic and logistic factors, many of these patients are lost to follow-up, and records of their in-hospital course are obtained only through recourse to paper records, which frequently are voluminous and often irretrievable. Culling specific pieces or categories of information from these records sometimes is prohibitive due to the number of person-hours required. The educational value of such menial searching is questionable.

At USC, we used a commercially available database, Advanced Revelation. This package was chosen for its versatility, programmability, and modifiability. We prepared a head trauma database sheet and gave it to the residents caring for patients. Entry of information into the database was initially a house officer responsibility, but we envision this function being performed by medical students or clinical research nurses. The first version of the database sheet was a skeletal minimal patient information form. We reasoned that it was important initially for the residents to gain confidence in their ability to interact with the software package and to realize that their time investment for patient data entry would not be too great.

Once the database was up and running, we were able to expand its scope incrementally—recording data relevant to particular aspects of our head trauma victims' clinical courses. Some categories of information were later omitted once it became apparent that such information would not be useful for more effective management or for inclusion in clinical research reports. Using the industry standard System Query Language (SQL), we were able to construct queries requiring linkage of operative and clinical demographic information filed in three separate portions of the database. The Advanced Revelation software also permits ready exportation of data to spreadsheet programs so that we can generate charts and graphs for morbidity and mortality conferences.

EXPERT-SYSTEMS

We are currently working on an expert system for analysis of head trauma data. Based on rules derived from a review of pertinent literature as well as from the collective experience of our house and attending staff, the computer makes a determination as to whether an operation is indicated in any given patient case. The expert system is *not* used to replace informed clinical judgment but rather as a source of feedback. It ensures that certain basic criteria are considered prior to any surgical intervention.

Discrepancies between surgeon and expert system decision rarely have resulted from inadequate consideration of relevant factors by the surgeon. Most often the problem has been the necessity to consider a factor for which a rule was not included in construction of the expert system.

The system "learns" by trial and error: At each encounter, the surgeon has the opportunity to "teach" the system by revising rules and introducing new ones that make it more inclusive. The teaching works both ways. The surgeon can assess his or her thought process in comparison to that of the expert system. Medical students can test their knowledge of neurosurgery in the setting of real patients they are following on our service.

Expert systems are programs that allow users to enter and store heuristics or rules of thumb relevant to any particular field requiring decision making. The expert's rules are "taught" to the machine such that, according to these rules, the system evaluates any inquiry put to it. The strength of the expert system is that it can "remember" many rules or criteria and apply them to any situation. More advanced (and expensive) systems have the capacity for rules to be weighted and prioritized; others can generate new rules when given information relevant to a particular clinical question.

Perhaps most exciting of all are developments in artificial intelligence. Using various computer science algorithms, programs have been constructed whereby computers can actually "learn." Different varieties of so-called expert systems have been developed based on user-supplied rules of multilevel complexity. In the future, computers may offer valuable second opinions on operative strategy and patient management.

With a burgeoning neurosurgical literature beyond the grasp of even the most dedicated reader, expert systems may provide a means whereby the latest advances are culled, sorted, analyzed, and prioritized so that any neurosurgeon, whether at a major medical center or out in the community, could enjoy the full benefit of what was in the literature.

SIMULATION

Finally, and perhaps most importantly, computer technology, in all of its forms as previously discussed, offers the possibility of a major breakthrough in neurosurgical education, both resident and continuing, academic and community. Self-assessment on personal computers is a precursor to surgical simulation. Initially, this will probably take the form of something akin to video games, but soon this will be supplanted by such technologies as simulation and virtual reality.

Computer simulation is a powerful tool for the analysis of dynamic systems. Any technology that enables a surgeon to practice an operation *before* opening a patient's head must improve safety.

Computers and neurosurgeons

It is not enough to engage computer consultation services when designing a new neurosurgical suite or upgrading an older one. Consultants have knowledge about what computers can do and about available technology but, unless they are neurosurgeons themselves, consultants cannot fully understand the requirements for computer technology in neurosurgery. Without experiencing physical contact with neural tissue or, perhaps more important, without an intraoperative misadventure, lay concepts of neurosurgery are based on fantasies.

Analogous to the problem of what is the appropriate realm for application of computer technology is that of determining how much information to capture and store. More is not necessarily better. Too much information, if irrelevant, can result in confusion and disorientation.

In establishing linkages among computers, the question again is how to capture adequate information without becoming overwhelmed by its implications. The role of the clinician in determining this is obvious.

REFERENCES

[1] BARNWELL, S. L., C. F. DOWD, et al., 1993. Endovascular therapy for cerebral arteriovenous malformations. In *Brain Surgery*, M. L. J. Apuzzo, ed. New York: Churchill Livingstone, pp. 1225–1242.

[2] WOOD, C. C., et al., 1985. Electrical sources in human somatosensory cortex: Identification by combined magnetic and potential recordings. *Science* 227:1051–1053.

[3] APUZZO, M. L. J., 1989. Surgery of intracranial tumors: Aspects of operating room design with integration and use of technical adjuvants. *Clin. Neurosurg.* 35:185–214.

[4] FUKUSHIMA, T., 1992. Intraoperative ultrasound localization of small subcortical lesions with a newly developed 2.5 cm linear mini-probe; In *Recent Advances in Neurosonology*, M. Oka, ed. Amsterdam: Elsevier, pp. 487–491.

[5] KOSUGI, Y., E. WATANABE, J. GOTO, T. WATANABE, S. YOSHIMOTO, K. TAKAKURA, and J. LKEBE, 1988. An articulated neurosurgical navigation system using MRI and CT images. *IEEE Trans. Biomed Eng.* 35:147–152.

[6] WATANABE, E., T. WATANABE, S. MANAKA, Y. MAYA-NAGI and K. TAKAKURA, 1987. Three dimensional digitizer (neuro-navigator): A new equipment for CT guided stereotaxic surgery. *Surg. Neurol.* 27:543–547.

[7] MARTIN, N. A., J. BENTSON, et al., 1990. Intraoperative digital subtraction angiography and the surgical treatment of intracranial aneurysms and vascular malformations. *J. Neurosurg.* 73:526–533.

[8] YASARGIL, M. G., and J. L. FOX, 1974. The microsurgical approach to acoustic neurinomas. *Surg. Neurol.* 2:393–398.

[9] FUKUSHIMA, T., and K. SANO, 1980. Simple retractor holder for the Mayfield skull clamp. *Surg. Neurol.* 13:320.

[10] KANSHEPOLSKY, J., 1977. Extracranial holder for brain retractors (tech. note). *J. Neurosurg.* 46:835–836.

[11] SUGITA, K., T. HIROTA, T. MIZUTANI, N. MUTSUGA, M. SHIBUYA, and R. TSUGANE, 1978. A newly designed multipurpose microneurosurgical head frame (tech. note). *J. Neurosurg.* 48:656–657.

[12] ALBIN, M. S., L. BUNEOIN, et al., 1975. Brain retraction pressure during intracranial procedures. *Surg. Forum* 26:499–500.

[13] ROSENORN, J., 1989. The risk of ischaemic brain damage during the use of self-retaining brain retractors. *Acta Neurol. Scand.* 79 (suppl.):120.

[14] RAMPIL, I. J., 1983. Prognostic value of computerized EEG and analysis during carotid endarterectomy. *Anesth. Analg.* 62:186–192.

[15] ALLEN, A., et al., 1981. Assessment of sensory function in the operating room utilizing cerebral evoked potentials: A study of fifty-six surgically anesthetized patients. *Clin. Neurosurg.* 28:457–481.

[16] WANG, A. D., et al., 1984. Somatosensory evoked potential monitoring during the management of aneurysamal SAH. *J. Neurosurg.* 60:264–268.

[17] WHITTLE, I. R., et al., 1986. Recording of spinal somatosensory evoked potentials for intraoperative spinal cord monitoring. *J. Neurosurg.* 64:601–612.

[18] OJEMANN, R. G., R. A. LIEVINE, et al., 1984. Use of intraoperative auditory evoked potentials to preserve hearing in unilateral acoustic neuroma removal. *J. Neurosurg.* 61:938–948.

[19] STOCKARD, J. H., V. S. ROSSITER, T. A. JONES, and F. W. SHARBROUGH, Effects of centrally acting drugs on brainstem auditory responses. *Electroencephalogr. Clin. Neurophysiol.*

[20] STOCKARD, J. J., F. W. SHARBROUGH, et al., 1978. Effects of hypothermia on the human brainstem auditory responses. *Ann. Neurol.* 3:368–370.

[21] WILSON, W. B., et al., 1976. Monitoring of visual function during parasellar surgery. *Surg. Neurol.* 5:323–329.

[22] WRIGHT, J. E., et al., 1973. Continuous monitoring of the visually evoked response during intraorbital surgery. *Trans. Ophthalmol. Soc. U.K.* 93:311–314.

[23] BARKER, A. T., I. L. FREESTON, et al., 1987. Magnetic stimulation of the human brain and peripheral nervous system: An introduction and the results of an initial clinical evaluation. *Neurosurgery* 20:100–109.

[24] MILLS, K. R., N. M. F. MURRAY, et al., 1987. Magnetic and electrical transcranial brain stimulation: Physiological mechanisms and clinical applications. *Neurosurgery* 20:164–168.

[25] FUKUSHIMA, T., Y. MAYANAGI, and G. BOUCHARD, 1976. Thalamic evoked potentials to somatosensory stimulation in man. *Electroencephalogr. Clin. Neurophysiol.* 40:481–490.

[26] FUKUSHIMA, T., 1989. Automatic warning system in monitoring auditory brainstem response during microvascular decompression surgery. In *Abstract of the Ninth World Congress of Neurosurgical Societies*, October, New Delhi, India.

[27] AASLID, R., T. M. MARKWALDER, and H. NORNES, 1981. Noninvasive transcranial Doppler ultrasound recording of flow velocity in basal cerebral arteries. *J. Neurosurg.* 57:764–774.

[28] AASLID, R., P. HUBER, and H. NORNES, 1984. Evaluation of cerebrovascular spasm with transcranial Doppler ultrasound. *J. Neurosurg.* 60:37–41.

[29] CARTER, L. P., and J. R. ATKINSON, 1973. Cortical blood flow as measured by thermal diffusion. *J. Neurol. Neurosurg. Psychiatry* 36:906–913.

22 The Neuronavigator: A Computer-Controlled Navigation System in Neurosurgery

EIJU WATANABE

ONE OF THE most important factors in neurologic surgery is good orientation. With the rapid development of computer-assisted diagnostic imaging modalities, including CT, MRI, positron emission tomography (PET), and magnetoencephalography (MEG), the diagnostic scene in neurosurgery has change greatly. These image data provide a neurosurgeon with accurate coordinates and size of lesions and functionally important areas. It is a natural outcome that CT and MRI have become the main diagnostic tools in preoperative diagnosis as well as in surgical planning.

Nevertheless, the method of applying CT- or MRI-derived 3D information of a lesion to the actual operating field remains to be improved. The only practical method that has been routinely used is CT- or MRI-guided stereotaxy. Numerous systems have been invented to localize intracranial lesions for facilitating needle biopsy [1, 2]. Specially designed head frames are used to localize the lesion. However, these are not suited for open-cranium surgery because their arc system interferes with conventional surgical procedures and considerable manual tasks are required for targeting even one single point.

It sometimes is difficult to obtain exact orientation during deep-seated tumor surgery, even for an experienced surgeon. The surgeon will, in such a moment, be anxious to ascertain whether he or she has moved in a wrong direction, passing the lesion. Some kind of spatial monitoring system is greatly needed.

To solve this problem, we have invented a frameless stereotactic guiding device, named a *neuronavigator*, which is a computer-assisted system that provides a surgeon with real-time information about the location of the operating site [3–5]. This chapter deals with the principle of this system, its clinical utility, and future developments.

Principle of the neuronavigator system

STRUCTURE

The neuronavigator (figure 22.1) consists of a personal computer (PC-9801RX, 16-bit, 80386-based computer [NEC, Japan], run on MS-DOS with a math coprocessor), a multijoint sensing arm, and an image scanner (figure 22.2). The computer software was programmed using C language and a macroassembler. The user interface is via a mouse with which one selects menu items and enters points as required. Requirements for point input are announced by voice signal generated by a sound card so that the surgeon can continue his or her maneuvers in the operating field without looking at the CRT prompt. The image monitor displays CT or magnetic resonance images in eight gray scales and a color cursor. The sensing arm has six joints, and each joint is equipped with a high-resolution potentiometer (50K ohm; nonlinearity: 0.1%). A stabilized direct-current potential is loaded to the potentiometer to obtain an angle-related output potential, which is sampled by the computer via an analog-digital converter. The 3D coordinates of the arm tip are calculated using the angle of each joint and the length of each segment.

CT or magnetic resonance images are first printed on conventional film, which then is loaded onto the computer via an image scanner. This method has been selected so that the system works with any available CT or MRI scanner. A set of six transverse CT images (figure 22.3), one lateral angiogram, and one MRI

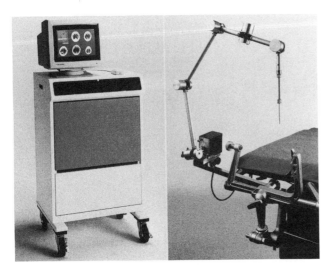

FIGURE 22.1 The neuronavigator consists of a personal computer, a multijoint sensing arm, and an image scanner.

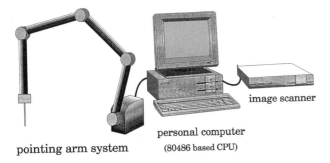

pointing arm system

personal computer
(80486 based CPU)

image scanner

FIGURE 22.2 A diagram of the neuronavigator.

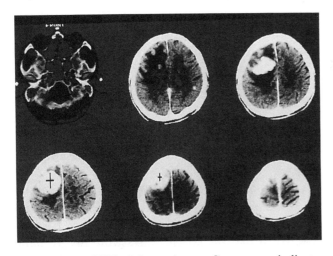

FIGURE 22.3 CRT of the navigator. Cross cursor indicates the location of the arm tip.

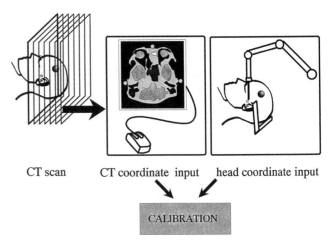

CT scan   CT coordinate input   head coordinate input

CALIBRATION

FIGURE 22.4 Calibration is done using three points on the patient's head. We use the nasion and bilateral tragi for this purpose.

sagittal scan are alternately displayed on the CRT monitor, with the switching made via a mouse.

CALIBRATION

The basic function of the navigator is to obtain the location of the arm tip within a surgical field and to translate it into the CT coordinates. To fulfill this function, the patient's head should initially be related to the CT coordinates. The relationship is established by the following calibration process. Calibration is made on the basis of three points on the patient's head (figure 22.4). We use the nasion and bilateral tragi for this purpose, because these points move minimally with the movement of the scalp when the head is anchored to the head-holder.

PREOPERATIVE PROCEDURE Preoperative CT is undertaken with small metal balls taped on the patient's nasion and bilateral tragi. The scanning angle is selected so that these three points appear on one single plane. The selection is completed easily using the localizing beam projected from the CT gantry. The scanning thickness is set to 10 mm when the target is larger than 2 cm, and 5 mm when smaller than 2 cm. As long as the patient is cooperative, no invasive head-holders are required. The same principle is applied when MRI is used for navigation. We use capsules that contain a fat-soluble substance such as vitamin A as a fiducial marker. After the capsules are taped onto the nasion and the tragi, as in the case of CT scan, sagittal MRI sections are taken to show these three points. The cutting angle for transverse section then is adjusted based on the sagittal images of these markers, so that these three points appear on a single transverse image.

IN THE OPERATING THEATER   After the introduction of general anesthesia, the patient's head is fixed firmly by a Mayfield skull clamp as in conventional craniotomy. The navigator arm is secured to the head-holder. The surgeon touches three fiducial points on the patient's head with the navigator tip, and their locations are registered on the computer. The locations of the corresponding points on the CT or magnetic resonance images also are registered using the mouse. The conversion matrix is calculated using the coordinates of the two sets of the fiducial points. The location of the navigator tip is automatically converted thereafter into CT coordinates and projected onto the corresponding CT slice on the computer screen, represented by cross-shaped cursors.

Two cursors are displayed on the screen in order to display the fine movement of the navigator tip within the slice thickness, as follows: When the navigator tip is situated between two planes, the distances between the tip and each plane are indicated by the change of the size of the cross-shaped cursor. When the tip is located between two slices, two crosses appear on both planes. The size of each cross is determined according to the distance to each plane (i.e., the nearer to the slice, the bigger the size of the cross, and vice versa). When the tip is located exactly in the midpoint of the slice, only one cross cursor of the maximum size appears on the corresponding plane.

VALIDATION   Calibration of the head is the most important step in the whole procedure of our navigation system. When the calibration is improper, the navigation will be incorrect. We validate the calibration by examining whether the cursor moves exactly on the outline of the skin on CT when the surface of the patient's scalp is traced with the navigator tip.

SLIPPAGE COMPENSATION

Sometimes the skull on the Mayfield skull clamp slips when strong pressure is applied to the head, such as during craniotomy. This inevitably causes crucial error in coordinate conversion. Intraoperatively, however, it is almost impossible to recalibrate the head location as the fiducial points are inaccessible, being hidden under the draping.

To recover from this situation, our system employs additional software to make up for the coordinate conversion error due to cranial slippage. This software works as follows: After calibrating the coordinate with respect to the standard fiducial markers, we additionally choose three marker points on the skull that are situated in the accessible area after sterile draping of the patient's head (e.g., in the vicinity of the possible burr holes on the skull). We usually mark these points on the cranium with an air drill (2 mm in diameter). By touching these new fiducial points with the navigator tip, each coordinate is stored in the computer. When unexpected slippage is suspected, one may select the recalibration menu and access the new fiducial points with the arm tip; the computer then calculates the coordinate reconversion matrix to be used for conversion from the slipped coordinate back to the original coordinate system. When another slippage occurs, one can call the recalibration menu again. Because the reconversion matrix represents the positional relation between the original cranial position and the latest cranial position, the error due to the recalibration procedure is not accumulated even after many efforts at recalibration.

VIRTUAL TIP

The system thus provides information on the location of the arm tip in terms of CT coordinates, which guides the surgeon during the operation. We invented a small trick that we call the *virtual* tip. When the pointing tip is shortened by some length, the system still indicates the location of the tip that it assumed before shortening (figure 22.5). It is this theoretical point that is designated the *virtual tip*. As this point has a theoretic existence, it can be freely introduced into the tissue before actual invasion. If the virtual tip reaches the tumor, it means that the tumor will be found at the known length ahead of the actual tip. This is particularly useful when a surgeon searches for a tumor from the brain surface. It is also useful in specifying the exact location of a tumor from outside the head. The surgeon can easily track the tumor edge with the virtual tip in designing a proper position and size for the craniotomy (figure 22.6).

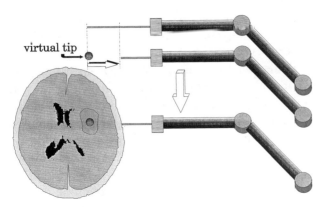

FIGURE 22.5 Virtual tip. When the pointing tip is shortened by some length, the system still indicates the location of the tip that it assumed before shortening. We call this theoretic point the *virtual tip*, which can be introduced into the brain before craniotomy.

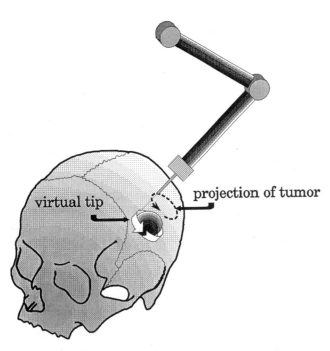

virtual tip

projection of tumor

FIGURE 22.6 The virtual tip is also useful in specifying the exact location of a tumor from outside the head. The surgeon can track the tumor edge easily with this tip in designing a proper position and size for the craniotomy.

DRESSING

When the operation begins, the tip segment of the arm is replaced with a sterilized piece and the arm is covered with a sterilized polyethylene dressing.

Various applications

COMBINATION WITH ANGIOGRAPHY

Once the tip location is translated into CT coordinates, it is easily projected onto the lateral view of an angiogram. The angiogram is obtained preoperatively as follows: The patient's head is taped so that both tragi lie on the horizontal line. This is achieved easily using the water level. Three metallic markers are taped to the nasion and both tragi just as for CT scanning. Angiograms contain image distortion inherently because x-ray beams are not parallel. To solve the distortion problem, the center of the x-ray beam also is marked with a fourth marker taped onto the patient's head. The distance between the nasion and the x-ray source emitter is measured. The lateral projection of the angiogram is fed into the computer with an image scanner.

At the beginning of operation, after calibration of the patient's head, the computer screen is switched from CT images to the lateral view of the angiogram. The positions of nasion and both tragi and the center of the x-ray beam on the angiogram are loaded to the computer using the mouse. The size of the angiogram to be used for this purpose is determined by the distance between the nasion and the center of both tragi. Next, an imaginary x-ray tube and x-ray film are projected onto the CT coordinates in proper relation to the CT data of the patient's head. When the CT coordinates of the navigator tip are obtained, the tip position projected on the angiogram is computed by tracing the x-ray beam within the CT coordinates. By this process, the inherent image distortion is corrected.

COMBINATION WITH MEG

The brain-generated currents that produce the potentials measured by the electroencephalogram also produce magnetic fields that can be measured by MEG. An N20-compatible evoked field after median nerve stimulation is known to be generated in primary sensory cortex. Using MEG with 37-channel SQUIDs (BTI, USA), a current dipole is back-traced that corresponds to the sensory cortex. When the dipole is projected onto the magnetic resonance image of the same patient, the primary sensory cortex is identified precisely in the magnetic resonance image. These data were used as the key images for the navigator. Representative cases of this method are described later (patients 1 and 2).

COMBINATION WITH A TRANSCRANIAL DOPPLER FLOWMETER

The directional, pulsed-wave transcranial Doppler (TCD) device operating at 5 MHz [6] can be used for the examination of intracranial blood flow. The probe of a TCD flowmeter is mounted at the tip of the navigator. The axis of the TCD probe and that of the end segment of the navigator arm should coincide with each other. The probe is so mounted that the measuring point of the probe is placed at the virtual tip of the navigator. The system then translates the location of the measuring point of the TCD flowmeter into CT coordinates and projects it onto the corresponding CT image. When the TCD probe is placed at the patient's head, the navigator immediately displays the location of the measuring point on the CT images.

Four normal volunteers participated in the experiment with a TCD flowmeter. A contrast-enhanced CT scan was obtained with a 2-mm slice thickness, including three fiducial marks and the basal cistern. The TCD probe was mounted on the navigator arm tip, and the head was taped down to the plastic headrest. The probe was placed at the temporal acoustic window, and the points where the peak flow velocity is captured, which are assumed to represent major arteries, are plotted on CT slices. Figure 22.7 shows the distribution of peak points on a CT scan in one representative case. The distances between the center of the

circles and the central line of the arterial image on the CT scan fall within 3 mm. Translation of measured points of the TCD into CT coordinates was performed rapidly enough to trace smoothly the TCD probe movement.

3D SURGICAL SIMULATION

Pseudo-3D rendering of reconstructed data of CT or MRI were realized on a personal computer [1]. The 80486-based PC9801RA (driven at 40 MHz, NEC, Japan) was used. A 24-bit, full-color graphics board (Hyperframe, Digital Arts, Tokyo, Japan) was installed. The software was written by the author using C language. CT or MRI data were loaded to the computer via an image scanner as for the neuronavigator or via Ethernet. The data representing the cranium and the tumor were extracted separately by a semiautomated method with density thresholding or a feature extraction routine. Extracted data were segmented and handled as voxel data. They are processed with the volume-rendering routine. The fine profile of the surface was exaggerated by a shadowing technique. In figure 22.9, the cranium was represented in gray scale, and the tumor was represented in red scale.

Three-dimensional parameters representing viewing angle and cursor location are transmitted to the computer from the computer controlling the navigator program via an RS-232C network cable. The navigator generates the 3D coordinates corresponding to the navigator arm tip. These coordinates are transferred to the

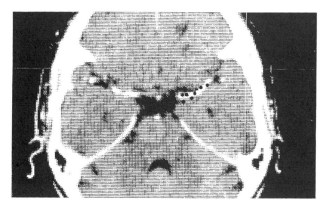

FIGURE 22.7 The distribution of peak points of TCD flow on CT scan in one representative case.

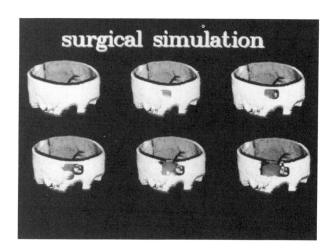

FIGURE 22.8 3D surgical simulation. Small resections are simulated on the skull, exposing the intracranial tumor.

computer for 3D display. The viewing angle is defined by pointing at two points on the viewing line with the navigator tip in the actual space around the patient's head. These coordinates then are transferred to the computer for 3D display, and the viewing angle is calculated. After the 3D surface appears on the screen, a cursor is displayed on-screen that is driven by the movement of the navigator tip in actual space. This also is realized by transferring the 3D coordinates of the arm tip via the RS-232C cable between the two computers. When the surgeon pushes a button on the navigator arm, a small cubic volume is removed at the cursor on the surface display, realizing surgical simulation (figure 22.8). This enables the rehearsal of craniotomy or simulation of tissue removal. As this simulation routine is accomplished in less than 1 second, the real-time and intraoperative surgical rehearsal is possible just before the actual surgical procedure is executed.

Cases

PATIENT 1

A 74-year-old woman was operated on for a tumor in the left precentral area (figure 22.9). Preoperative MEG was used to study the sensory evoked magnetic field following electrical stimulation of the median nerve. N20-compatible current dipole at the latency of 20 msec was traced and projected onto the magnetic resonance image. The central sulcus was identified according to the dipole, which revealed that the tumor was located in the postcentral gyrus. Surgery was conducted under neuronavigator guidance to remove the tumor, intending to save the motor strip. The MEG-defined hand area and the MRI-defined tumor boundary were projected onto the cortex after the dura was opened. Cortical evoked potentials also were recorded at four points around the MEG-defined hand area following median nerve stimulation. As they all coincided with one another, the motor strip was identified easily and protected in the operating field. The tumor was successfully removed, inducing no motor paresis.

PATIENT 2

A 44-year-old woman with a convexity meningioma was operated on. Under neuronavigator guidance, craniotomy was designed with the virtual tip extending 3 cm ahead of the actual tip. When the tumor boundary was traced with the virtual tip before craniotomy, the retracted actual tip delineated the projected tumor margin on the scalp. The craniotomy so designed proved to be proper in placement and size.

PATIENT 3

A boy with drug-resistant epilepsy underwent anterior callosotomy (figure 22.10). During the operation, the extent of the incision of the corpus callosum was monitored with the navigator. We were able to carry out the section with sufficient accuracy.

Error analysis

Accuracy of the system has been evaluated by means of phantom simulation and clinical application. The total system error, including nonlinearity of potentiometers, arm bending, and imaging distortion error, were evaluated with an artificial target placed in a cranial phantom made of plastic. The error measurement was repeated 30 times, and the averaged error was calculated in terms of the standard deviation, which was 1.33 mm.

The error during clinical application was studied with reference to the skull-base structures, which are clearly identifiable both on CT and in the operating field. The edge of the anterior clinoid process and the sphenoid ridge were used for this purpose. The sphenoid ridge was used to examine the accuracy in the sagittal and vertical directions. The maximum error

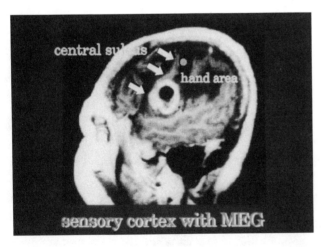

FIGURE 22.9   MEG of patient 1. A filled circle indicates the sensory dipole after median nerve stimulation. Arrowheads point to the central sulcus, which was proved to be running anterior to the tumor.

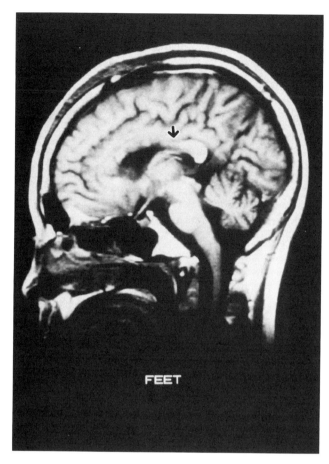

FIGURE 22.10 Sagittal navigation display of callosotomy (patient 3). The arrow indicates the posterior limit of the callosotomy.

tested during operation turned out to be 2.5 mm in 30 trials, an accuracy level that proved to be sufficient for open microsurgery. In open surgery, an accuracy of less than 2 mm gives no practical benefit because the brain tissue and the target inevitably move during surgical procedures. The thickness of the CT slice is the largest limiting factor for accuracy. When we utilize the variably sized cursor, 10-mm-thick slices are sufficient for a lesion larger than 20 mm. When high accuracy is needed in targeting, one can simply use the 2-mm-thick slice, although we find this unnecessary for normal open surgery. What is required above all is the flexibility of any monitoring device, such that it does not become an obstacle to conventional surgical procedures. Our navigator fulfills this requirement as one can move it away from the operating field when it is not needed.

Discussion

MECHANISM

We utilized a mechanical arm structure to obtain 3D coordinates. Similar trials were reported by other authors using a mechanical arm [8]. Ultrasonic detection also was tried to direct the operating microscope [9, 10] or a probe [11] toward the lesion. It is reported that the detection error increased when the room temperature changed. A magnetic field sensor was utilized by Kato et al. [12], who reported a maximum 4-mm error unless iron material is placed between the magnetic source and the sensor. All these trials and ours have been performed to apply the stereotactic approach to open surgery.

Each of these methods has its own problems in detection error and a similar level of accuracy. Among them, our mechanical method is the most stable with respect to detection error in various surgical circumstances.

SLIPPAGE

In seven cases, the patient's head slipped within the Mayfield skull clamp during craniotomy. The skull slipped when the three skull pins were situated too high on the skull. In all those cases, the recalibration software successfully recovered the situation. Because of those accidents, we have made it a rule to place the fixation pins low enough to generate counterforce against the pressure from the drilling burr.

BRAIN SHIFT

As our navigation is based on preoperative diagnostic images, intraoperative tissue distortion causes error of interpretation. This occurs when the brain is retracted, when a large tumor mass is removed, or when the cerebrospinal fluid is lost. We have observed that dural opening resulting from craniotomy of routine size does not necessarily cause a significant brain shift. We also know from experience that this type of navigation method is not properly applied to intraventricular lesions, because brain tissue sinks considerably after a ventricle is opened. At present, the most practical method to overcome these problems is implanting marking thread or a tube into the tissue as soon after the brain is exposed as possible. Intraoperative CT scanning may solve the problem in the near future.

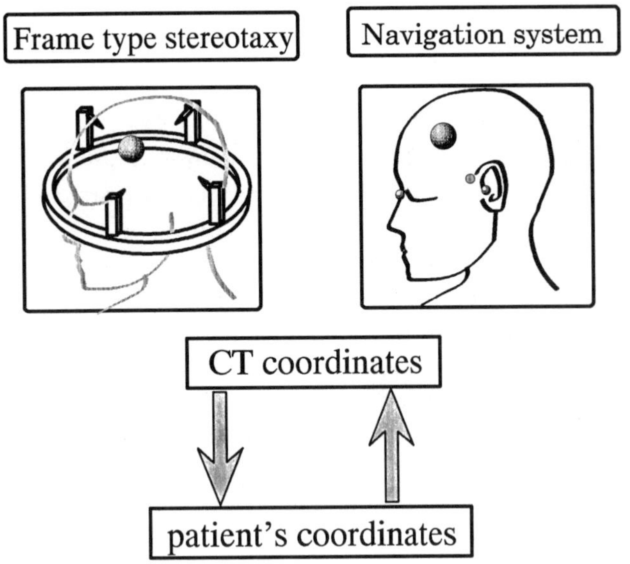

FIGURE 22.11   The greatest difference between the navigator and conventional CT-guided stereotaxy is the direction of the conversion of spatial information.

Software simulation of brain distortion may also be possible if the performance of microcomputers further improves.

NEURONAVIGATOR VERSUS STEREOTAXIS

The greatest difference between the neuronavigator and conventional CT-guided stereotaxy is the direction of the conversion of spatial information (figure 22.11). In the conventional system, the CT coordinates of a lesion are measured and translated into a patient's coordinates. The surgeon then sets the frame parameters corresponding to the patient coordinates to reach the lesion. With the navigator, we first place the arm tip on the patient's head to obtain the patient's coordinates. The computer automatically translates these into the CT coordinates and moves the cursor onto the corresponding CT image. In short, in the stereotactic system, the spatial information is translated from CT coordinates into patient's coordinates, whereas in the navigator system the information is translated from a patient's coordinates into CT coordinates. When we target one particular point in the cranium, as in needle biopsy, the former method is reasonable. The procedure is similar missile launching. However, when we want to monitor our direction of approach or monitor our location, the latter method is more comfortable. The direction from patient coordinates to CT coordi-

nates is similar to the flow of information in a surgeon's own thought processes when trying to orient himself or herself in the intracranial space.

The other difference between the two systems is that the stereotactic system locates the lesion relative to the head frame but not to the patient's head. The navigator uses fiducial points on the patient's biologic landmarks. Hence, the navigator does not require a head frame. Biologic landmarks have both advantages and disadvantages. Because no head frame is necessary during preoperative CT scanning, the patient is spared unnecessary pain. The reproducibility of the biologic landmarks is, however, poorer than the head frame—embedded fiducial points, which produces the fundamental error of localization.

From these difference, it is reasonable to conclude that the conventional CT stereotactic system is suitable for accurate biopsy of a small lesion, whereas the neuronavigator serves better in open-cranium surgery, providing global orientation in the intracranial space. In the latter situation, several millimeters of error is not a critical problem in the face of the advantages of rapid and convenient feedback of spatial information.

Conclusion

According to the rapid development of computer technologies, the time has come when the computer directly assists a surgeon in the operating theater. Our navigational system is a tool that provides a missing link between the diagnostic image and open-cranium surgery. This opens the door to future developments in computer-assisted surgery such as robotic surgery.

REFERENCES

[1] BROWN, R. A., 1979. A computerized tomography–computer graphics approach to stereotaxic localization. *J. Neurosurg.* 50:715–720.
[2] KELLY, P. J., B. A. KALL, and S. J. GOESS, 1988. Results of computed tomography–based computer-assisted stereotactic resection of metastatic intracranial tumors. *Neurosurgery* 22:7–17.
[3] KOSUGI, Y., E. WATANABE, J. GOTO, T. WATANABE, S. YOSHLMOTO, K. TAKAKURA, and J. IKEBE, 1988. An articulated neurosurgical navigation system using MRI and CT images. *IEEE Trans. Biomed. Eng.* 35:147–152.
[4] WATANABE, E., T. WATANABE, S. MANAKA, Y. MAYANAGI, and K. TAKAKURA, 1987. Three dimensional digitizer (neuro-navigator): A new equipment for CT guided stereotaxic surgery. *Surg. Neurol.* 27:543–547.

[5] WATANABE, E., Y. MAYANAGI, Y. KOSUGI, S. MANAKA, and K. TAKAKURA, 1991. Open surgery assisted by the neuronavigator, a stereotactic articulated, sensitive arm. *Neurosurgery*, 28:792–800.

[6] AASLID, R., T. M. MARKWALDER, and H. NORNES, 1982. Noninvasive transcranial Doppler ultrasound recording of flow velocity in basal cerebral arteries. *J. Neurosurg.* 57: 769–774.

[7] WATANABE, E., T. IDE, A. TERAMOTO, and Y. MAYANAGI, 1991. Three-dimensional CT reconstructed system on a personal computer. *Neurol. Surg.* 19:247–253.

[8] MÖSGES, R., and G. SCHLOENDORFF, 1988. A new imaging method for intraoperative therapy control in skullbase surgery. *Neurosurg. Rev.* 11:245–247.

[9] FRIETS, E. M., W. STROHBEHN, J. F. HATCH, and D. W. ROBERTS, 1989. A frameless stereotactic operating microscope for neurosurgery. *IEEE Trans. Biomed. Eng.* 36:608–617.

[10] ROBERTS, D. W., J. W. STROHBEHN, J. F. HATCH, W. MURRAY, and H. KETTENBERGER, 1986. A frameless stereotaxic integration of computerized tomographic imaging and the operating microscope. *J. Neurosurg.* 65:545–549.

[11] REINHARDT, H., H. MEYER, and E. AMREIN, 1988. A computer-assisted device for the intraoperative CT-correlated localization of brain tumors. *Eur. Surg. Res.* 20:51–58.

[12] KATO, A., T. YOSHIMINE, T. HAYAKAWA, Y. TOMITA, T. IKEDA, M. MITOMO, K. HARADA, and H. MOGAMI, 1991. A frameless, armless navigational system for computer-assisted neurosurgery. *J. Neurosurg.* 74:845–849.

23 Neuronavigation: A Ten-Year Review

HANS F. REINHARDT

"COMPARED WITH the automobile industry, CAS is now in about the year 1910. Almost all the important discoveries had already been made by then. Nevertheless, cars were still an impractical toy of the privileged classes." This comparison by Schlöndorff [1] in 1992 hits the nail on the head for the present situation in computer-assisted surgery (CAS). Many different navigation systems have been developed, from simple, modified stereotactic frames to interactive robots—one might say from the bicycle with auxiliary motor to the aristocratic coach. However, what is missing is the Model T, an economical vehicle that runs without complaining and can transport everything from a bag of potatoes to one's mother-in-law.

To continue with this analogy, even the network of filling stations remain inadequate. Siemens and Philips, market leaders in Europe, still supply CT, MRI, and digital subtraction angiography (DSA) systems without standard interfaces. Every CAS user would be satisfied with a simple Ethernet or SCSI output which, as primary equipment including a small software module, would scarcely have any effect on the final price. However, both companies sell the additional equipment for tens of thousands of dollars. It is hoped that industrial management will soon see that these devices not only serve as simple image generators but also are valuable interactive information systems for the surgeon.

In Basel, all three main CAS types—modified stereotactic frames, armlike digitizers, and interactive nonmechanical systems—were constructed and tested. In our opinion, the surgical robot is still a new method in search of an application, still too expensive for the technically trivial stereotaxy and too critical in terms of safety for open-brain operations. In contrast, we have constantly worked toward smaller, more compact targeting devices that provide the (neuro)surgeon with a maximum of spatial information while at the same time guaranteeing him or her complete freedom of movement. The aim was and is a simple targeting tool that can be used simultaneously in any difficult operation without a great deal of further complexity, the computers and screens required in any case also being used for many other tasks in the operating theater (see the last section of this chapter).

In the hope that certain developers might benefit from our earlier successful designs and from our failures, we describe in this chapter our CAS systems over the past 10 years [2–4] and attempt an extrapolation into the near future with our latest equipment, the (ultra)sound-assisted microstereometry system [5–7] and the digital operating microscope [18].

The ET project

The impetus to construct the first navigation system came at the end of 1982 from two directions. On the one hand, the first industrial robots began to make the headlines. We too dreamed at that time of developing a miniature robot for stereotaxy, for positioning tasks in open-brain surgery, and possibly even for image-assisted tumor resection with the aid of ultrasonic aspiration, a research item in Basel [9] that was still new at that time.

On the other hand, we used the ^{32}P tumor marker for the first time in operations on brain tumors [10, 11]. We soon found that, although it was possible to detect remote tumor ramifications in this way, visual orientation based on anatomic landmarks in the depth of large tumor cavities was unsuccessful. This gave rise to the desire for an additional navigational aid.

The development was based on our first Apple-2 microcomputer and the four-axis 3D digitizer TM-4 from Micro Control Systems (Vernon, Conn.), which also had a surprisingly efficient small software package written by M. Pelczarski (The Complete Graphics System, Penguin Software, Geneva, Ill.). The 1983 film by Steven Spielberg gave the project its name: ET, the experimental targeting device.

Only two interactive, image-assisted systems were known at that time. The most advanced was the device of Kelly [12], which already had a very efficient computer system and included a spatially locatable operation microscope. The simpler device from Jacques, Shelden, and McCann [13] also anticipated many later developments. The common feature of both was that they were based on conventional, partially motorized, arc-centered stereotactic frames.

In contrast, our aim was to dispense with restrictive frame systems. We intended to use only a stable halo ring for firm head fixation and, from the end of 1985, also for a coordinate base, with which a freely movable, small measuring arm could be docked.

The first multijoint measuring arm: ET-01

Initial experiments were concerned with the accessibility of intracranial targets with a limited number of axes of rotation in order to reduce mechanical inaccuracy. We found that most intracranial targets could be reached with a four-axis arm system that could also be rotated along the halo head ring (4.5 degrees of freedom; figure 23.1).

Investigations with regard to the most advantageous reference system between the previously recorded CT data set (EMI Medical Systems, EMI-1010) and the patient's head during surgery initially led in the wrong direction. We believed that sufficient accuracy could be achieved by the use of small lead marks and ink spots at the root of the nose, lateral palpebral fissures, and earlobes, which were tapped with the measuring arm at the beginning of the operation. As a result of

the unavoidable movement of skin during positioning of the head, we achieved a reproducibility of only ±3 mm in five exactly measured cases, making superfluous a major part of the efforts for improved mechanical accuracy.

A transport stretcher with a vacuum mattress and integrated headrest therefore was constructed in 1985 (figure 23.2), the patient, fixed with sharp pins, remaining in a completely unchanged position for imaging and the operation. The precisely precalibrated measuring arm then was fixed onto one of five fixed positions on the ring and brought to the zero position by tapping a lead mark that had a sterile covering and was firmly screwed to the ring. It then was possible to begin the intraoperative measurements. The reference accuracy between CT and patient was thus reduced to ±2 mm, but the overall accuracy of the system (coarse image matrix + mechanical inaccuracies + deviations of the angular sensors) of ±3–4 mm in the central measuring field was unsatisfactory in the long term.

The first measuring arm (figures 23.2–23.4, table 23.1) was constructed initially in the author's clockmaker's workshop and subsequently in the labs and workshops of the Basel University Clinic by a small three-man team consisting of a mechanic, a neurosurgeon, and a part-time information scientist. We aimed at the following properties:

FIGURE 23.1   Laboratory version of the first frameless navigation device (worldwide?), 1983.

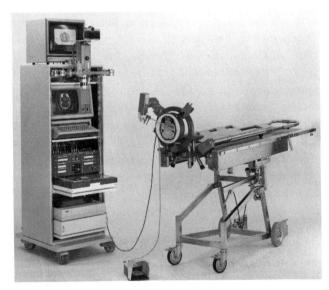

FIGURE 23.2   General view of the ET-01 system. The measuring arm (left) is mounted on a stretcher and can be moved on a carriage.

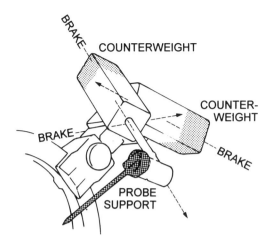

FIGURE 23.3   Mechanical principle of ET-01.

FIGURE 23.4   The ET-01 measuring arm with 4.5 degrees of freedom.

• Miniaturized design, fully gas-sterilizable (chloralform) in a medium-size standard tray

• Capable of being used as a pointing instrument as well as an instrument support (tumor marker probes, stereotaxy needles, etc.)

• Easily operating central axes largely balanced by counterweights

• Axes locked by lock-and-spring brakes and pneumatically released (dead-man's principle: automatic blocking on interruption of energy supply, in order to prevent sinking into the brain)

TABLE 23.1

Data on the first measuring arm ET-01, 1983–1986

4.5 degrees of freedom: four axes of rotation and five position (45°) on 25-cm halo ring

Weight: 1600 g; dimensions folded: 19 × 33 × 6 cm; measuring volume: ≈ 15 × 15 × 15 cm

Spring-locked, pneumatically released brakes, two arm segments with counterweights, end axis as interchangeable instrument support or pointer

Angular sensors: 22-mm potentiometers (Sakae, Japan), 0.25% linearity

20 × 30-cm CT films; video camera: Panasonic WV-1500/Q; video mixer: IVC KM 1500-II

Apple-II 48 kbyte; 192 × 290 pixel graphics; STRATOS overlay software in C

Duration per measurement: 2 sec; accuracy of measurement: ± 2–4 mm

Option: adapter for ^{32}P tumor-measuring probes; beta-counter values integrated in graphics

• No heavy-current electrical equipment (patient safety)

• Measuring inputs optoelectronically separated

• Potentiometric angular sensors that can be replaced with Portescap miniature stepping motors for subsequent robotics developments (not pursued)

The functional principle was simple: CT images (EMI-1010) were recorded by means of six polyvinyl-chloride rods inserted into the halo ring. Intraoperatively, the intracranial target was aimed at and the software gave the position in the z axis, including the number of the CT slice to be underlaid. The image foils then were exactly centered on a film platform and recorded by a video camera, the image of which was displayed on a 12-in. monochrome monitor via a video mixer. At the same time, an overlay with the x/y values of the measuring arm was fed into the mixer by the computer and thus integrated into the video image. In early 1986, the images were scanned beforehand via a four-bit frame grabber, and image change was automatic. This improvement was superseded after a few months by the second measuring system.

Intraoperative trials with 10 patients in 1985–1986 were not conclusive. Although possible to demonstrate the feasibility of the measuring arm principle, the limited overall accuracy of at best ± 3 mm and the considerable loss of time for data processing and the manual image changing with CT film transparencies prevented wider clinical use. At the end of 1986, we therefore decided to design a second system, focusing on greater accuracy and stability of the measuring arm at the expense of weight and miniaturization. In particular, the device was intended also to hold an endoscope or ventriculoscope, including a CCD-color video camera, reliably in position. Furthermore, it was planned to use a more advanced computer and to achieve higher image resolution (CT and MRI) and faster data handling by direct digital image transfer.

MEASURING ARM OF THE SECOND-GENERATION ET-02

The design principle was retained. The arm lengths were increased, and a linear transmitter with an extension of 90 mm was inserted between the second and third joint (the so-called lower arm). All axes of rotation and translation were mounted on ball bearings, and the brakes with spring blocking and pneumatic release were replaced by simpler, manually lockable, over-dimensioned disk brakes. Instead of the small 22-mm potentiometers with 0.25% linearity, 45-mm precision potentiometers with 0.05% linearity were used. The total weight increased to 3.9 kg, and the rigidity corresponded to that of the best industrial robots. The end joint (or hand) contained a 20-mm hollow axis in which a sterilizable aluminum sleeve system with two plastic bag passages was fixed. This provided a maximum bearing of 15 mm for endoscopes, needles, probe holders, and the like. The entire arm was covered by a sterile plastic bag.

An IBM AT-02 computer with a large hard disk was used as a measurement and graphics computer. The CT data were transferred from the Siemens DRH CT scanner to the IBM computer from 8-in. floppy disks (software from Flagstaff Engineering, Flagstaff, Ariz.) (figure 23.5). From 1989 on, it was also possible to transfer MRI data from the 2-tesla Siemens magnetome via Ethernet. The EGA graphics provided 16 false colors in the original matrix of 256 × 256 pixels. The movement of the space cursor and image change took place in real time (80 msec). Oblique and 3D reconstructions were dispensed with for the sake of speed and better resolution.

As there was no longer any need for an external operator, a small control console (figure 23.6) with a sterile covering and joystick (menu up/down, menu function on/off) and three buttons (menu level, virtual

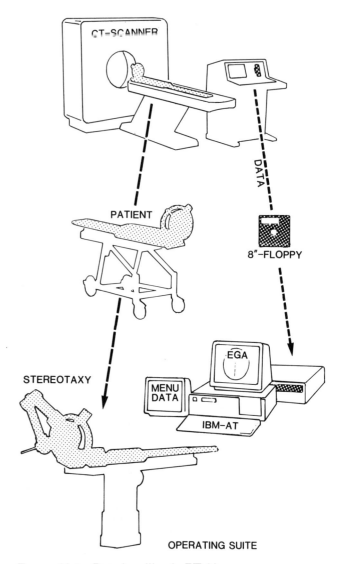

FIGURE 23.5 Data handling in ET-02.

offset of end segment, CT [MRI] window) was placed in the surgeon's working area.

The measuring arm was calibrated a single time by the teach-in method on the baseplate (figure 23.7). Before the beginning of each operation, all that was necessary was a zero check at a zero mark (lead cross fastened to the base ring close to the operation opening and shown on the CT scan). As in the case of ET-01, the patient's head was anchored with sharp spindles on the stable aluminum base ring and remained in the identical position during data acquisition and during the operation. This permitted an absolute accuracy of measurement of ±2 mm in the central 20 × 20 × 20–cm measuring volume (figure 23.8, table 23.2).

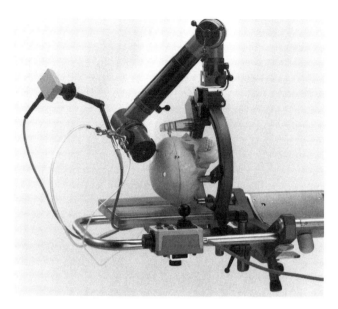

FIGURE 23.6 Digitizer of the second generation with ventriculoscope and docked video camera. (Center bottom) Control console.

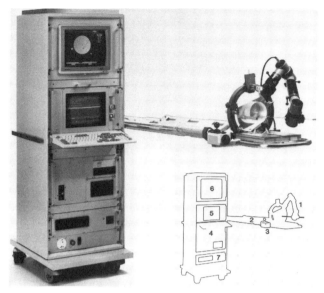

FIGURE 23.8 Overview of the ET-02 system: (1) measuring arm; (2) stretcher; (3) control console; (4) industrial computer; (5) data monitor; (6) graphics monitor; (7) 8-in. floppy drive.

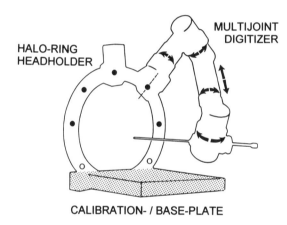

HALO-RING HEADHOLDER

MULTIJOINT DIGITIZER

CALIBRATION- / BASE-PLATE

FIGURE 23.7 Four and one-half degrees of freedom in ET-02.

The clinical trial was difficult, although all functions worked satisfactorily. There was only a small number of opportunities for an application in combination with the ventriculoscope. Compared with a conventional frame, there were no major advantages in stereotaxy. In open-brain operations, the measuring arm was too heavy and inconvenient for use, although the accuracy would now have been sufficient even for smaller lesions. Soon after completion of ET-02 in 1987–1988, we therefore began looking for new methods of mea-

TABLE 23.2

Data on the second measuring arm ET-02, 1986–1988

$5\frac{1}{2}$ degrees of freedom: four axes of rotation, one translation, five positions (45°) on 25 cm halo ring

Weight: 3900 g; dimensions folded: $38 \times 18 \times 10$ cm; measuring volume: $\approx 20 \times 20 \times 20$ cm

Five over-dimensioned manual disk brakes without reset effect

Four angular sensors: 45 mm diameter potentiometers (Midori, Japan), with 0.05% linearity

90-mm linear potentiometer 0.1% (Genge and Thoma, Switzerland)

digital image data transfer via 8-in. diskettes (CT) or Ethernet (MRI); matrix 256×256 pixel, eight bit

IBM-AT02; EGA graphics; 16 false colors; extended STRATOS software in C measurement, frequency; 80 msec/position; accuracy of measurement: ± 2 mm

Option: various adapters up to 16 mm diameter on end joint; load capacity, 800 g

surement that would be particularly suitable for open microsurgery.

Because optical methods of measurement require a great deal of equipment and computation, the technically surprisingly simple measuring method with ultrasound appeared to us to be particularly suitable for

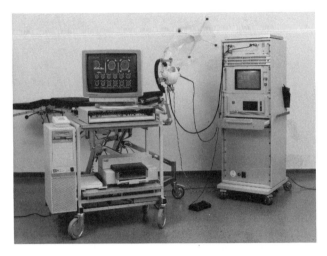

FIGURE 23.9   First sonic digitizer: system overview. Graphic computer (left), head-holder, sonic system (middle), SAC device, measuring computer (right).

intraoperative application. While we were evaluating the Science Accessories Corporation's (SAC) sonic system, we read about a first application of this device by Roberts [14] for the spatial, image-assisted localization of an operating microscope.

SONIC MICROSTEREOMETRY: ET-03

The Sonic Digitizer GP8-3D from SAC (Science Accessories Corp., Stratford, Conn.) formed the basis of this frameless and armless measuring system. Sound impulses at 24 kHz were generated by means of small spark gaps and were received by miniature microphones (figure 23.9). By determining the traveling time of the sound and the trigonometry of emitters and receivers, it was possible to determine the spatial position of the spark equipped targeting instrument. The advantages of the sonic system are the technical simplicity and the possible miniaturization, whereas the main disadvantage is the sensitivity to reflected sound and environmental influences, such as temperature changes or air turbulence.

While the SAC device, designed for 3D computer-aided design (CAD) tasks, was being converted for medical application, we encountered many difficulties. Finally, approximately 30% of the measuring device and the entire operative environment with head-holder, measuring panel, and targeting tools were newly designed. The acquisition, evaluation, and correction of the measured data were transferred to a dedicated computer, and a graphic workstation was used

FIGURE 23.10   SPOCS with emitter panel (top), head-holder with detachable calibration frame, and supported targeting instrument (below left).

for imaging. In the devices of the subsequent generation (ET-04/SPOCS), the entire measuring technology was entirely redesigned in cooperation with industry.

Following problems with the previous aluminum construction with regard to use in MRI, the head-retaining system (similar to figure 23.10) was constructed from nonferromagnetic materials. The 32-cm halo ring consisted of glass-fiber composite with cemented-in bronze bushes, and the posts of polycarbon (Lexan ICI) were fixed on the ring with 8-mm titanium screws. Micrometrically measured Talairach-Leksell type carbon-fiber pins drilled into the tabula externa of the skull guarantee precise repositioning of the ring even after temporary removal. This two-stage procedure (figure 23.11), allowing an interval of days to weeks between data acquisition and operation, permitted a careful simulation of the operation on our laboratory workstation.

The image data were recorded with reference marker boxes screwed onto the halo head ring. The N-shaped markers consisted of 1.5-mm diameter aluminum rods for CT and iron sulphate–filled glass tubes of 2.5–4 mm diameter for MRI. For the operation, a panel with

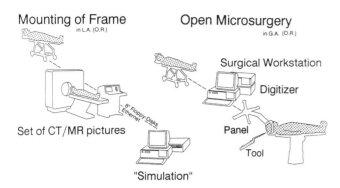

FIGURE 23.11 Sonic microstereometry. Data acquisition and operating procedure.

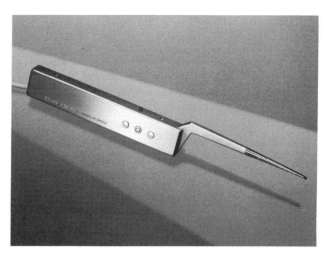

FIGURE 23.12 Bayonet-shaped standard measuring tool.

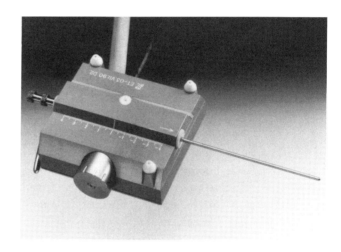

FIGURE 23.13 Measurement platform with four emitters for stereotaxy.

three microphones was docked with the ring at the same time, immediately after image data acquisition, or in a separate second procedure (see figure 23.11). The system was calibrated with a calibration panel containing three emitters, which were screwed temporarily to the ring. On the basis of the CT or MRI calibration marks, the software determines the exact position of each individual image relative to the calibration panel or base ring (first matrix operation) and then calculates the spatial relationship with the microphone panel (second matrix operation). The position of the targeting tool (one to four emitters) relative to the panel is determined finally in a third matrix operation.

The effect of interfering thermal factors could be largely eliminated by means of a measuring distance between the foot of the panel close to the head-retaining ring and the panel. Before each measuring cycle, a reference signal was emitted by the reference emitter and reached the panel microphones approximately 60 cm away in a known time of travel. Deviations (e.g., owing to temperature shifts) were taken into account automatically. In the case of large deviations, the entire measurement cycle was discarded. Influences owing to air turbulence were greatly reduced by means of the relatively short measurement distance (60–75 cm transmitter-to-receiver distance) and a saillike design of the panel with a sterile plastic bag stretched between the panel arms. Reflections were separated out by means of filter algorithms.

Several medical tool types were developed. A 120-g, 23-cm-long targeting instrument with two emitters 10 cm apart and a bayonetlike tip (shape similar to figure 23.12) proved most suitable for microsurgical operations. A platform with four emitters was con-

structed for stereotaxy (figure 23.13), three emitters being used for position determination and the fourth transmitting the needle advance. Simple one-emitter pointers give an ideal, extremely simple 3D mouse that can be sterilized and used for intraoperative software control.

This first microstereometry system (table 23.3) was tested successfully in a pilot study comprising 20 brain operations [1]. Thanks to the high accuracy of nearly ± 1 mm, even very small, deep-seated tumors and vascular malformations could be reliably found and removed. On the basis of this positive experience, an improved system was developed in early 1991 in concern

TABLE 23.3

Data on sonic microstereometry, SAC-based device; 1988–1991

Complete freedom of movement; assuming free transmission distance: setting angle of up to ≤90° possible between panel and targeting instrument

Weight of targeting instrument: 110 g; length: 22 cm; two sound emitters

Panel 70 × 35 × 35 cm, 2.5 kg, covered with sterile plastic bag, screwed to halo ring in 10 positions (12.5°); three microphones, one emitter (reference distance)

Measurement volume: 30 × 30 × 30 cm; measuring frequency: 50–80 msec; accuracy of measurement: not more than ±2 mm

Sonic digitizer SAC GP-8 3D, modified

Digital image transfer (Ethernet, 8-in or 3½-in floopy disks, 44-MB cartridges)

i286/287 measuring computer connected to i386/387 graphics computer via RS-232

Positioning and visualization software in Turbo-Pascal 6.0 (DOS 4.1)

sVGA graphics (Eizo MDB-10: 600 × 800 pixels, eight-bit color/64 shades of gray)

Option: various localizers (one to four emitters) for stereotaxy, aspiration tubes, and so on

TABLE 23.4

Data on SPOCS (a sonic microstereometry system), ET-04 (prototype)

Complete freedom of movement (assuming free transmission distance)

Targeting instrument: weight, 210 g including SMD electronics; length, 26 cm; two microphones at 100-mm distance; bayonet-shaped tip, 130 mm

Emitter panel (PE) folded 39 × 30 × 16 cm; two locking joints, gas-sterilizable; weight, 2.4 kg; can be clamped in ±75° angle on 32-cm halo ring head ring (PE/steel or aluminium); three emitters; one reference microphone

Measurement volume: 20 × 20 × 20 cm, on the outside used for menu functions (3D mouse)

Custom-made electronics from dipl. Ing. F. Hüthe and Aesculap/Leukhardt

i386/387 measuring computer connected to i486 workstation via RS-232

TIGA graphics (Elsa Gemini 10, max. 1024 × 1280 pixels, 24-bit); 16–21-in. RGB-monitors

Positioning and visualization software in C++

Option: various localizers (pointers, aspiration tubes, adapters for endoscopes, etc.)

with industry, attention being focused on more professional medical technology, user-friendliness, and patient safety. A further increase in the accuracy of measurement (e.g., by increasing the frequency) or a more sensitive method of measurement was deliberately ignored in favor of the error tolerance.

SPOCS FOR MICROSTEREOMETRY, ET-04

SPOCS, the Surgical Planning and Operation Computer System, originally was advanced planning software from Aesculap AG (D-7200 Tuttlingen, Germany) that lacked an interactive navigational system. Microstereometry therefore was a welcome addition. Joint developmental work over 2 years resulted in a further improved system with completely new measurement electronics and radically revised instrumentation (table 23.4).

The main change consists in an inversion of the measurement principle. Instead of the safety-critical 1.5-kV spark emitters, the measurement tools (see figure 23.12) now contain subminiature low-voltage microphones. The control buttons, preamplifiers, and part of the measurement logic are located in the handpiece.

The high-voltage module for sound generation is now housed in the measurement panel and is multiply insulated, far away from the patient's head (see figures 23.10, 23.14). The spark emitters were retained owing to the previously unachieved small size (pointlike sound radiation through 0.6-mm electrode spacing). Subminiature microphones from hearing-aid technology with an integrated impedance converter serve as receivers.

For measurement, an Intel 386/387-based industrial computer is used. The measuring software written in C++ calculates a coordinate vector in real time (80 msec with a two-microphone instrument) which then is transmitted to the i486 graphics computer, together with tool identification code and check sum, via a serial interface. The whole system is now housed in one desktop personal computer–size case.

The CT and magnetic resonance image data acquisition by fiducial marker boxes mounted on a halo ring and the calibration are simplified and mostly automated. The calibration between the base coordinate system on the halo ring and the measuring panel is performed by means of a temporarily screwed-on calibration panel with two three-microphone arrays. The entire calibration procedure takes a few seconds.

The graphic software, written in Borland C++ (figure 23.15), is trimmed for visual simplicity and

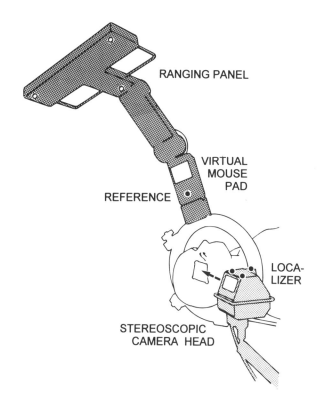

FIGURE 23.14 Camera of the operating microscope, optionally localizable with SPOCS.

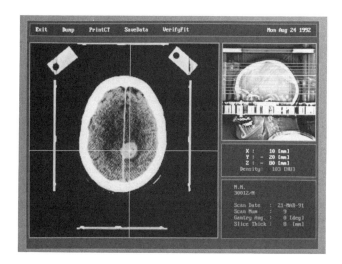

FIGURE 23.15 Simple, fast graphic software.

optimal speed (cursor in real time; image change, 400 msec). Although 3D reconstructions and the like also were developed, only original sections have thus far been routinely used. More efficient graphic workstations (Intel-based EISA personal computers, Silicon-Graphics Personal-Iris, SGI Indigo) and graphics pro-

grams (ISG Allegro, BrainScan) are currently being evaluated.

Laboratory tests indicated an absolute accuracy of measurement of ±1 mm, the accuracy being better in most measuring positions and poorer in extremely inclined positions. When 512 × 512 matrix CT scans with a 2-mm slice thickness are used and if a mechanical inaccuracy of ±1 mm is included for the head-retaining system, a *total accuracy* of approximately ±2 mm is obtained. This is sufficient even for very small, deeply seated intracranial processes.

Outside the central measuring volume, the target instrument serves as a 3D mouse: Software functions can be controlled by touching eight fields on an aluminum plate at the foot of the panel (virtual mouse pad; see figure 23.14).

SPOCS currently is undergoing clinical trials in neurosurgery (Neurosurgical University Clinic, Basel, Switzerland) and in ENT surgery (Dr. Nitsche, ENT Department, Klinikum rechts der Isar, TU Munich), and the initial results are favorable. However, many improvements in detail will be necessary before the system is ready for series production. Moreover, further clinical trials are required before a detailed assessment can be made.

The compactness of the receivers and of the measurement electronics permits the installation of small localization elements in a wide range of surgical instruments or handpieces. A suction-aspiration tube with two microphones and a three-microphone platform for pin-type instruments (endoscope, biopsy needles, Laser, etc.) have been realized already. A miniaturized stereo operating microscope based on completely novel technology has also been developed for this purpose.

NEURONAVIGATION WITH OPTICAL DIGITIZER
(SPOCS II)

Since the second half of 1993 an optical measuring system was developed in addition to sonic stereometry and successfully applied in 16 neurosurgical procedures. In principle, the microphones were replaced by infrared LEDs, the sonic panel was substituted by a ceiling-mount boom assembly of three CCD line-scan cameras manufactured by Pixsys Inc. (Boulder, CO, USA). Therefore most of the former equipment could be used. Whereas for electronic sonic microphones even plasma sterilization was critical, selected IR-LEDs tolerate ethylene-oxide and (to a certain extent)

TABLE 23.5

Data on the stereo-video operating microscope

Two miniature Y/C CCD camera modules (Matsushita/Kappa)

6 × motor zoom; working distance: 25–40 cm (interchangeable front lenses; LEICA)

Coaxial halogen illumination with 6-mm optical wave guide

Weight, 1.6 kg; housing, 12 × 12 × 15 cm with eight-switch keypads on both sides

Pneumatically lockable, flexible ball-chain stand

20-in. RGB monitor 100 (2 × 50) Hz Y/C (Taxan) with LCD stereo shutter (Tektronix) mounted on solenoid stand and to be operated by sterile handles

19-in. 9 HE electronics module with stereo camera electronics (Kappa), illumination (Kolpi Intralux 6000), pneumatic control, s-VHS video recorder (Hitachi)

Under development: SPOCS (Aesculap) three-microphone sonic localizer correlated with focal point, with second monitor for CT or MRI position and additional information

Planned: one-screen solution with overlay technique, pop-up windows, and so on

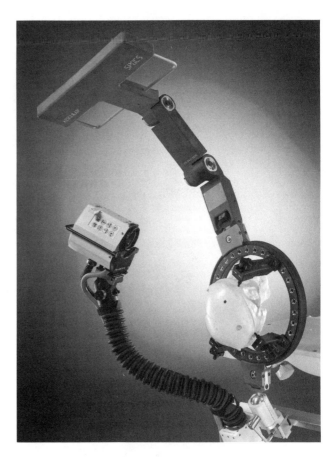

FIGURE 23.16   Stereo-video camera of the operating microscope.

steam sterilization. Again, measuring accuracy lies within a range of ±1 mm.

THE STEREO-VIDEO OPERATING MICROSCOPE, ET-05

The functional model of a stereo-video operating microscope has been constructed jointly with LEICA-Heerbrugg, Switzerland, over the past 2 years (table 23.5) [8]. The experience gained in endoscopy in recent years showed that operations can be carried out in small body cavities using even flat, low-resolution screens. Our tests in 1989–1990 with a Toshiba Stereo Camcorder (SK-3D7, Toshiba Corp., Tokyo, Japan) directly connected to the oculars of a Zeiss OPMI-1 operating microscope (C. Zeiss, AG, Oberkochen, Germany) showed that it is possible to perform precise technical work (e.g., the dismantling and reassembly of a chronometer) via a stereoscopic screen without a long period of familiarization. To be able to test the new optoelectronic technique in demanding neurosurgical operations, a miniaturized stereo camera with a stereo monitor adapted for use in the operating theater was developed.

The system consists of a stereo-video camera on a flexible stand (figure 23.16), a 19-in. electronics unit,

and a stereo monitor on a solenoid stand (figure 23.17). As an option, the camera can be localized in space with CT or MRI correlation using SPOCS.

The camera head is the size of a small 8-mm camcorder and consists of two CCD units, including a subminiature preamplifier (Kappa Messtechnik GmbH, D-3407 Gleichen, Germany), a stereo zoom optical system, and a housing with the control elements for optics, stand, and video technology (LEICA AG, CH-9435, Heerbrugg, Switzerland). It is mounted on a novel, pneumatically controlled, ball-chain stand, and is freely movable in space (see figure 23.16).

The 100-Hz stereo image in Y/C or SVHS quality is viewed with slightly tinted Polaroid spectacles on an RGB monitor (20-in. Taxan UV-1095 Autoscan) with an LCD stereo shutter (Tektronix Display Products, Beaverton, Oreg.). (see figure 23.14). The 40-kg monitor is mounted on a weight-compensated stand with magnetic brakes and can be easily positioned by means of sterile handles. A 19-in./9 HE supply unit on castors,

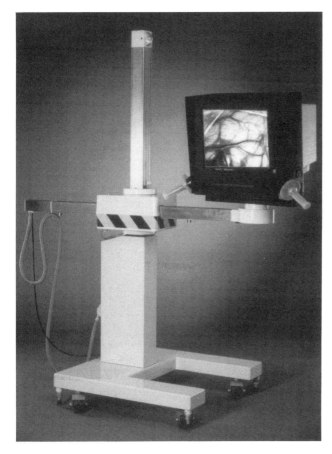

FIGURE 23.17   Stereo monitor on solenoid stand.

with camera electronics, halogen lighting, stand pneumatics, and an SVHS video recorder, is pushed under the operating table.

A narrow (8-mm) array of three microphones mounted at right angles 10 cm apart is located on top of the camera and allows the focal point of the optical system to be localized on CT or magnetic resonance images with millimeter accuracy. At present, this position information is displayed on a second stereo monitor (16-in. with LCD shutter, Fimi-Philips, Sqronno, Italy). A digital version with a fast frame grabber and integration of video image with additional information, using the window technique and overlays on one working monitor, is in preparation.

The images of this first video operating microscope, still based on standard components, are already of astonishing brilliance and definition. In the future, through specially calculated optical systems, optimized illumination, and improved video technology, it will be possible to increase the quality further. The size and weight can be reduced considerably.

The advantages of the optoelectronics and of the digital technology are evident. Conventional operating microscopes have grown recently into real monsters as a result of increasingly convenient auxiliary optical systems, beam splitters, and the like (including floating stands weighing up to 120 kg!). In contrast, video camera technology has been experiencing rapidly advancing miniaturization. This will permit an ergonomic improvement with today's increasingly smaller surgical openings. Thanks to the digitization of the operating image, integration of a navigating system and of additional computer information is highly facilitated.

Clinical trials of the camera based entirely on video technology have just begun. Owing to its unusual flexibility, use of this camera requires a period of familiarization, but surprisingly good microsurgical work can be performed with little practice. However, it is necessary from the outset to avoid comparing this visualization technique with the conventional operating microscope. It is a new technique that ranges between the conventional operating microscope and endoscopy and is especially tailored to minimally invasive surgery with very small access openings and refined intraoperative orientation aids.

Outlook

Industry already makes extensive use of the networking of information and production machines, and computer-integrated manufacturing workstations are the rule. In contrast, the surgeon still works today in largely the same way as he or she did 60 years ago. Although techniques have been refined and instruments and magnification aids have been optimized, his or her activity is still entirely a handicraft. However, the emergence of "alien" monitor-oriented operative techniques, such as endoscopy and endovascular invasive radiology, shows that the surgeon too must urgently adopt smaller approaches and new ablation techniques. Until now, the surgeon could scarcely rely intraoperatively on the rapidly advancing diagnostic methods such as CT, MRI, and DSA.

Thanks to these improved diagnostics, it is hoped that pathologic processes can be discovered at an early stage. Interactive navigation aids will make it possible to localize even very small, deep-seated processes and to remove them under gentle conditions. Unfortunately, there is still a large variety of navigation systems, predominantly arm type digitizers (more than 12 constructions known [15–17]), all of which have interesting design details but most of which are not yet suitable for routine use. We hope that SPOCS comes a little closer to this aim—a sort of Model T of the targeting devices. CCD optics, laser interferometry, radio frequency, and the like could be the measuring principles of the future. In Basel, an optical system with CCD line-scan cameras is already in an advanced stage of preclinical testing.

Digital visualization not only permits considerable miniaturization of the optical aids but also simplifies the integration of additional information, including the navigation system, in the operating procedure. Papering the walls with hundreds of small CT, MRI, and DSA pictures is of little use during operation! The possibility of retrieving radiologic image data from a Picture Archiving and Communication System and displaying it intraoperatively on a computer screen should already be a matter of course. Stereo microvision also permits visualization of stereoscopic angiographs and stereo 3D reconstructions of CT, MRI, and positron emission tomography pictures. A status line with values of the anesthesia system (blood pressure [aneurysms], pulse [cerebral pressure, posterior cranial fossa], and water loss [hypothalamus, pituitary]) is relatively simple to implement and helpful in many neurosurgical operations. The settings of routinely used (coagulation, power center, aspiration pressure, ultrasonic resection) and rarely used devices (micro-Doppler, laser, neuromonitoring, tumor markers, etc.) can be displayed on the working monitor and varied on demand by input-output interfaces.

The following on-line aids could be realized as well: a scalable brain atlas within the navigation system, an intelligent database providing textbook type information (typical accesses, procedures, parallel cases, therapy guidelines, alternative and adjuvant treatments, etc.), or a video link to the pathologist's microscope for rapid evaluation of the frozen sections.

The medical engineer and information scientist are faced with the challenge of overcoming the flood of data without further burdening the surgeon with additional sensory impressions. Everything should be available at a critical instant with a minimum of effort, discreetly, providing information rapidly and without distraction. An intermediate stage between diagnostics and operation—simulation on the workstation—may help the surgeon plan the operation and then perform it in the most specific manner under mild conditions.

This also might be an important tool for training future surgeons, an aid that entails little risk for the patient!

The surgeon-machine interface is largely unresearched but has become very topical with the advent of the operating computer. In our opinion, what is needed today is not so much a robot that performs trivial surgical manipulations at immense expense but systems that are simple to operate and that make the diagnostic advances of our time directly available to the surgeon. Research in surgical robotics is entirely justified for the future, but it is surprising how many trivial problems remain to be solved in daily work with "simple" interactive navigation systems. Even the simplest targeting devices are still much too complicated. Managing the data glut (CT, MRI, DSA, 3D reconstructions, etc.) often is impractical and confusing. Calibration is critical and time-consuming. Reliable matching algorithms should be written that, by using any data set, would make superfluous special recordings with time-consuming and often too-invasive marker systems. Instrumentation and information technology still have a long way to travel.

REFERENCES

[1] SCHLÖNDORFF, G., 1992. Workshop 207: computer assisted surgery. In *Medinfo 92, Proceedings of the Seventh World Congress on Medical Informatics*, Geneva, September 8.

[2] REINHARDT, H., H. MEYER, and E. AMREIN, 1986. Computer aided surgery: Robotik für Hirnoperationen? *Polyscope Plus* 6:1–6.

[3] REINHARDT, H., H. MEYER, and E. AMREIN, 1988. A computer assisted device for the intraoperative CT-correlated localization of brain tumors. *Eur. Surg. Res.* 20:51–58.

[4] REINHARDT, H. F., and H. LANDOLT, 1989. CT-guided real-time stereotaxy. *Acta Neurochir. Suppl.* (Wien) 46:107–108.

[5] REINHARDT, H. F., and H. J. ZWEIFEL, 1990. Interactive SONAR-operated device for stereotactic and open surgery. *Stereotact. Funct. Neurosurg.* 54/55:393–397.

[6] REINHARDT, H. F., G. A. HORSTMANN, and O. GRATZL, 1991. Mikrochirurgische Entfernung tiefliegender Gefässmissbildungen mit Hilfe der Sonar-Stereometrie. *Ultraschall Med.* 12:80–83.

[7] REINHARDT, H. F., G. A. HORSTMANN, and O. GRATZL, 1993. Ultrasonic stereometry in microsurgical procedures for deep seated brain tumors and vascular malformations. *Neurosurgery* 32:51–57.

[8] REINHARDT, H. F., G. A. HORSTMANN, R. SPINK, E. I. AMREIN, and P. FORRER, 1993. Stereo-microvision: devel-

opment of an opto-electronic operating microscope. *Bildgebung/Imaging* 60:105–109.

[9] KRATTIGER, B., H. REINHARDT, and H. J. ZWEIFEL, 1990. Technische Aspekte der Ultraschallaspiration. *Ultraschall Med.* 11:81–85.

[10] REINHARDT, H., D. STULA, and O. GRATZL, 1985. Topographic studies with ^{32}P tumor marker during operations of brain tumors. *Eur. Surg. Res.* 17:333–340.

[11] REINHARDT, H, 1989. Surgery of brain neoplasms using 32-P tumour marker. *Acta Neurochir.* (Wien) 97:89–94.

[12] KELLY, P. J., G. J. ALKER, and S. GOERSS, 1982. Computer assisted stereotactic laser microsurgery for the treatment of intracranial neoplasms. *Neurosurgery* 14:172–177.

[13] JACQUES, S., C. H. SHELDEN, and G. D. McCANN, 1980. A computerized microstereotactic method to approach, 3-dimensionally reconstruct, remove and adjuvantly treat small CNS lesions. *Appl. Neurophysiol.* 43:176–182.

[14] ROBERTS, D. W., J. W. STROHBEHN, J. F. HATCH, and W. MURRAY, H. KETTENBERGER, et al., 1986. A frameless stereotaxic integration of computerized tomographic imaging and the operating microscope. *J. Neurosurg.* 65:545–549.

[15] GUTHRIE, B. L., R. KAPLAN, and P. J. KELLY, 1990. Neurosurgical stereotactic operating arm. *Stereotact. Funct. Neurosurg.* 54/55:497.

[16] MÖSGES, R., and G. SCHLÖNDORFF, 1988. A new imaging method for intraoperative therapy control in scull base surgery. *Neurosurg. Rev.* 11:245–247.

[17] WATANABE, E. T., S. WATANABE, S. MANAKA, Y. MAYANAGI, and K. TAKAKURA, 1987. Three-dimensional digitizer (neuronavigator): New equipment for CT-guided stereotaxic surgery. *Surg. Neurol.* 27:543–547.

[18] ZWEIFEL, H. J., H. F. REINHARDT, G. A. HORSTMANN, and E. AMREIN, 1990. CT/MRI-korrelierte Stereometrie mit Ultraschall für Hirnoperationen. *Ultraschall Med.* 11:72–75.

24 Image-Guided Operating Robot: A Clinical Application in Stereotactic Neurosurgery

STÉPHANE LAVALLÉE, JOCELYNE TROCCAZ,
LINE GABORIT, PHILIPPE CINQUIN,
ALIM LOUIS BENABID, AND
DOMINIQUE HOFFMANN

Computer-assisted medical interventions

MAJOR EFFORTS are continually made to improve the effects of surgery and to minimize the related trauma by observing three criteria: (1) making surgery as minimally invasive as possible by reducing, whenever possible, the approach to so-called keyhole surgery, (2) minimizing the intervention duration, and (3) optimizing the intervention by making its actual effects match as closely as possible the expected ones. This is particularly true in neurosurgery, for which the susceptibility of the brain tissue has naturally led to new surgical procedures such as stereotactic neurosurgery. Such an advance is made easier thanks to computerized imaging technologies that enable one to locate with high precision 3D anatomic structures that a surgeon or physician wants to access using a needle or a beam or that the practitioner wants to modify surgically in shape or relation to other structures. By means of computerized tools, the surgeon or physician can see these structures, prepare the surgical strategy, visualize the expected results, validate the strategy, or iteratively modify it. The surgical stage itself can be assisted, providing the surgeon with some guiding systems in order to place the instrumentation in the planned location.

A general methodology of computer-assisted medical interventions aimed at providing these tools to the surgeon has been developed in our laboratory (see Lavallée and Cinquin [1] for a more detailed description of this methodology). It can be decomposed in four nonsequential parts:

- *Data acquisition* Different modalities of sensory data are provided by a set of accurately calibrated sensors. The major pieces of information are given by preoperative or intraoperative medical images produced by CT, MRI, radiography, or ultrasound. Medical a priori knowledge (e.g., an anatomic atlas) as well as video images or different types of signals (Doppler, electrophysiology, etc.) can also be used.
- *Registration* The reference systems associated with the different modalities are related by rigid or elastic transforms. A major stage consists in determining the 6-degrees of freedom (dof) relations among the operative reference system, the preoperative reference system, and the guiding-system reference system.
- *Surgical strategy definition* The operator (surgeon or physician) can manipulate the model (matched data) to define the surgical strategy that is simulated (the functional or anatomic consequences are visualized) and can be modified.
- *Performing the surgical strategy* Different types of guiding systems can be used to execute the strategy. *Passive systems* enable the surgeon to compare the actual intervention with the planned one. This is the case with the system described in Adams et al. [2] in which the position of the surgical instrument is visualized in real time on CT images. The instrument is fixed on an encoded passive articulated arm, and it is moved by the surgeon. Mazier, Lavallée, and Cinquin [3] describe a system in which a synthesis image is superimposed on a video intraoperative image and enables the surgeon to correct the current position according to the expected one. *Semiactive systems* enable the physical guiding of

the instrument that is still controlled by the operator, which is the case, for example, of the stereotactic neurosurgical system described in this chapter. This is also the case for the system described in Taylor et al. [4], which makes use of a passive encoded articulated arm whose brakes are computer-actuated when the surgeon goes away from the planned target (the application is reconstructive plastic surgery). Finally, *active systems* execute part of the intervention. Kelly [5] developed a system in which a laser is used for brain microsurgery. The laser shot is directed toward a tumor that has been localized by MRI. The laser is telemanipulated until a synthesis image built from MRI data can be superimposed on an intraoperative video image. Taylor et al. [6] describe such a system based on the use of an IBM robot for hip replacement surgery in dogs. Davies' group [7] presents a system for the removal of prostatic tissue. An interesting feature of the system is the ability to constrain the motions of the robot for safety purpose. A physical device has been designed such that the cutter held by the robot can move only inside a cone that corresponds to the shape of the removed tissue.

Stereotactic neurosurgery is a typical case for which computer-assisted medical interventions is required and possible: Repetitive handling of multimodal pictures, numerous geometric calculations, guiding the tip of a probe through a small burr into the brain without any direct visualization, and good accuracy (<1 mm) are the essential requirements of stereotactic brain neurosurgery, which involves biopsies of tumors, isotope implants, introduction of brain-stimulating and recording electrodes, and cyst removal.

Overview of the system

SYSTEM ARCHITECTURE

Figure 24.1 is a sketch of the system architecture. From the medical point of view, the system consists mainly of a Talairach stereotactic frame in which the patient's head is fixed by four screw pins. The function of the frame is to maintain a rigid relationship between the patient's skull and brain and the operative reference system. This is absolutely necessary for interventions demanding a submillimetric accuracy. Two x-ray systems enable lateral and frontal radiography. From the computational point of view, the central computer is a DEC workstation connected to different computers via

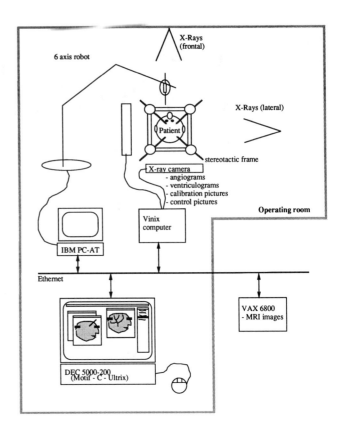

FIGURE 24.1 System components.

Ethernet. The application relies on multiprocess programming running on the workstation. One can classify the applications to three nonsequential components:

• *Image acquisition* A Vinix computer enables the digitization and storage of the intraoperative x-ray images. Preoperative images (MRI) are stored on a VAX 6800 computer (Digital Equipment Corporation). Any of them can be transmitted to the workstation as soon as the operator requests it.

• *Image processing* This is completely supported by the workstation. It is the most intervention-dependent part of the application. The operator defines his or her surgical strategy using the corresponding interface and its tools (figure 24.2).

• *Robot control* A personal computer is connected to a six-axis robot. It communicates with the workstation, from which it receives its queries. The interventions performed using this system require only 5 dof as the task consists in placing a probe along a line. The sixth degree of freedom is used as a redundant degree in order to find an orientation of the robot (and, there-

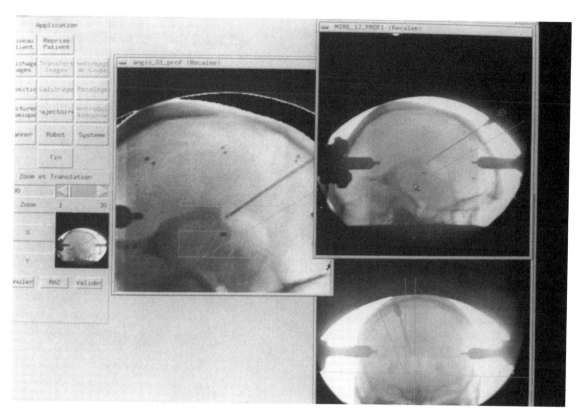

FIGURE 24.2   Interactive definition of a target and a 3D line on calibrated x-ray images.

fore, of the instrument) that produces no collision of the arm with the environment (see the subsection, Trajectory Generation).

In the following sections, we detail each of these three stages.

DATA ACQUISITION

As mentioned earlier, the surgeon makes use of preoperative magnetic resonance images (especially for biopsies of tumors). Intraoperative images are produced by two x-ray systems. Different types of images are acquired during the interventions; each type is obtained using both frontal and lateral x-ray tubes. Calibration images enable the calibration of the x-ray systems (intrinsic and extrinsic parameters) and the calibration of the robot reference system with respect to the operative reference system (see the section, Registration). Ventriculograms are acquired after injection of a contrast liquid in the ventricular system of the brain. The purpose of this operation, which is considered by surgeons to be easy, is to register preoperative

and intraoperative images as the ventricular system can be seen in both modalities of images. Another possibility would have been to practice the preoperative acquisition with the stereotactic frame on the patient's head, using the frame as the registration feature. Removing the frame between these two phases would introduce errors. It implies that the patient must keep the frame between the preoperative phase and the intervention, which has many practical and psychological drawbacks. Angiograms are necessary in order to find a target for which the probe does not intersect the vessels. Additional projections are acquired after having rotated the stereotactic frame 10° with respect to the double x-ray device. These series of successive images make possible visualization of projections of the vascular tree. Finally, control images are acquired for verifying the location of the robot with respect to the target. Some small relative motions can be executed if the surgeon is not satisfied with the current location. Such errors can occur, for example, because of the mouse inaccuracy when clicking the target on the images or due to uncertainty propagation.

Surgical strategy definition

DEFINITION OF THE TARGET

As explained previously the problem is to reach a particular point within the brain, giving a particular orientation to the probe. Thus, the target is defined by a 3D point and an orientation vector in the operative reference system. A target must verify three constraints:

1. The tip of the probe must be located in an area whose size depends on the intervention (several millimeters for tumor biopsies and ± 0.5 mm for an electrode placement).

2. There must be no intersection between the probe trajectory and the brain vessels (and other critical anatomic structures) once the robot is located at its final position.

3. There must exist a collision-free trajectory for the robot with respect to the environment that makes it possible to reach this final position.

The first constraint determines the 3D point location, whereas the second constrains the orientation vector. The third must be verified for each point-vector pair. The system interactive tools existing in the image-processing module provide some help in satisfying the first two constraints. The third one is automatically managed by the system. For some interventions (e.g., isotope implants) the surgeon must specify a collection of targets; in this case, the same constraints must be verified for each.

ADDING AN ESSENTIAL PIECE OF INFORMATION: ANGIOGRAMS

A major problem for the surgeon consists of choosing a trajectory for the instrument in the brain that does not intersect the vessels. By injecting a contrast product into the carotid artery, we obtain x-ray images of the vascular tree. Using these projections, our aim is to test whether the selected trajectory of the instrument intersects the vessels. Remember that the surgeon has at his or her disposal two sequences of pairs of orthogonal images. The second one is obtained after the rotation of the frame. Each pair is acquired using the two orthogonal x-ray tubes. A whole sequence of images illustrates the diffusion of the liquid in the vascular tree observed from a given viewpoint.

Most authors who have dealt with this problem use a pair of stereoscopic images and try to make a 3D

model of the vascular tree [8]. However, this remains difficult for automatic processing. Our method relies on some interactive tools. On each image, the calibration process enables us to compute the projection of a selected trajectory. The surgeon specifies the 3D trajectory, which can be projected in four windows containing a frontal image, a lateral image, a frontal rotated image, and a lateral rotated image. An elastic cursor enables the surgeon to move along the trajectory of the probe from an initial point to the target on one image. This elastic segment is simultaneously echoed on the other images. When the current extremity of the segment intersects a vessel on one image, the surgeon can verify on the other images whether the echoed extremity intersects a vessel also. If several intersections are found on the images, the surgeon can reject the trajectory unless he or she knows perfectly that the 2D intersected vessels found on the images do not correspond to the projection of a single 3D vessel. Such an approach can lead to false detections, but no true intersection can be omitted. Another possibility consists of defining a target such that the orientation vector is aligned with the lateral x-ray trajectories. In this case, intersection checking is made easier for the surgeon. This strategy is possible only for interventions demanding a lateral approach, which is not the case for midline neurosurgery.

TRAJECTORY GENERATION

The system must generate a collision-free trajectory for the robot from the definition of the target. In the following discussion, we will call *destination* the position of the robot for which the target is reached by the instrument. The potential obstacles are mainly the stereotactic frame and the patient's head. The robot has to move very close to them. Our choice has been to develop a method adapted to this particular problem. Indeed, classic configuration space approaches of robot motion planning [9, 22] are ill-adapted to this problem. In the case of robots having 6 dof, many authors plan the robot trajectories in the configuration space for the three first axes, whereas the last three links are enclosed in a volume and considered a rigid link. The volume is defined so as to contain the wrist moving from its initial configuration to its final one. This is practicable in the context of gross motions for pick-and-place operations [10]. In the neurosurgical context, it is not usable because potential collisions come from these last three links. A way this approach differs from many existing approaches is that we do not generate a continuous path. The planning system implemented on the workstation generates a trajectory, defined as a discrete set of via points, and communicates it to the robot control system supported by the personal computer. The trajectory is generated such that if a free motion is used by the robot controller between two successive points, no collision will occur. From the communication point of view, this has the advantage of decreasing the amount of transmitted data between the workstation and the personal computer.

Because the robot moves in a constant environment, there is no need for a method that generates a trajectory from the ready position to the destination. The basic idea is to have a collection of collision-free approach trajectories that have been learned once and for all. These trajectories, defined as a set of via points, enable the robot to come without any collision from its ready position to some position close to the stereotactic frame, keeping a constant type of configuration (one among eight possible). Therefore, the problem is to choose the best trajectory such that there will be no collision between its ending point and the destination using a free motion. We will call this nonlearned part of the robot motion *target trajectory*.

The stereotactic frame enables five access areas (figure 24.3). The target determines which area must be used. With each configuration-area pair—1 among 40—is associated a set of approach trajectories. Being given a destination of the robot (point **PT** and orientation vector $\vec{\mathbf{A}}$), the Cartesian position of the wrist can be determined for each possible type of configuration of the robot as soon as we have chosen a slide orientation vector $\vec{\mathbf{S}}$ (represented by an angle S and $\vec{\mathbf{A}}$) (figure 24.4).

Thus, the algorithm has to choose a value of $\vec{\mathbf{S}}$ for the destination, a configuration of the robot, and an approach trajectory. Our algorithm determines the best choice of $\vec{\mathbf{S}}$ such that there is a collision-free approach trajectory and there is no collision along the target trajectory. This last condition is checked using distance computation algorithms applied to the frame components and the head with respect to the wrist components. (Note that the head is modeled as an ellipsoid from data input by the operator on the images.) No attention is paid to the first three axes both because they are far from the obstacles and because the variations of the first three articular values are very small along the target trajectory. The criterion that is opti-

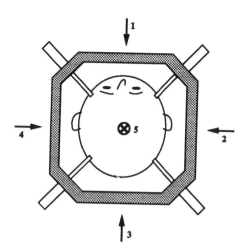

FIGURE 24.3   Access areas enabled by the stereotactic frame.

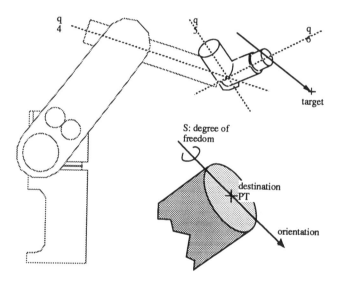

FIGURE 24.4   Determining the position of the wrist.

mized is defined as a function of (1) the minimum distance to the obstacles along the target trajectory, (2) the articular distance between the initial and final positions of the target trajectory, and (3) the robot configuration, as the robot is more precise for some of them (see the subsection, On Solving the Accuracy Problem).

Some experiments have been conducted using a potential field approach for collision-free trajectory planning. This method, based on a fast distance computation [11], has proved to be very efficient in this case, although obstacles are very close to the target. This is owing to the fact that the target is underconstrained

FIGURE 24.5   Collision-free trajectory planning under ACT.

FIGURE 24.6   The calibration cage held by the robot.

and the method allows one to specify such undercon-strained Cartesian goals. Figure 24.5 shows an output of the method implemented in the ACT system.

Registration

REGISTRATION OF THE X-RAY REFERENCE SYSTEM WITH THE OPERATIVE REFERENCE SYSTEM

The aim of this stage is to determine the intrinsic and extrinsic parameters of the two x-ray systems in order to determine the target coordinates in the operative reference system from data extracted from the x-ray images. The method is inspired by the two-planes method designed for camera calibration [12]. Our ap-proach is based on the use of a calibration cage made of two pairs of parallel planes, each of the planes containing nine opaque metallic beads. The cage is held by the robot, which brings it in the spot of the x-ray system (figure 24.6). Then both a lateral image and a frontal image are acquired. This operation is executed at the beginning of each intervention.

Let us consider one x-ray system and therefore one image and one pair of parallel Plexiglass planes. We want to compute the projection line associated with any point defined on the image. Each plane P_j ($j = 1, 2$) of the cage may be defined in the robot end-effector refer-ence frame by an equation similar to $Z = Z_{0_j}$. For each plane P_j, we search for a 3×2 matrix A_j such that

$$(X_i \, Y_i) = (1 \, u_i v_i) \cdot A_j$$

where $(X_i \, Y_i \, Z_{0_j})$ are the coordinates of a point $\mathbf{M_{ji}}$ of P_j in the robot end-effector frame and $(u_i v_i)$ are the coor-

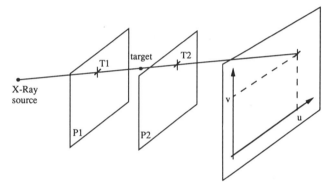

FIGURE 24.7   Two-planes calibration.

dinates of the projection of $\mathbf{M_{ji}}$ in the image reference frame. If we write this system for the case of the metal-lic beads, the 3D location of which is known in the robot end-effector frame, that leads to a system in which A_j is the unknown. A linear least-squares method gives the best fit for A_j. Now, if a target is given by its projection $(u \, v)$ on the image, matrix A_1 (resp. A_2) en-ables one to compute one point T_1 (resp. T_2) on plane P_1 (resp. P_2). Finally, T_1 and T_2 define the projection line of the target (figure 24.7). Doing the same pro-cessing for the other x-ray source, we obtain another line. The target is defined as the intersection of these two lines.

This process is sufficient in the case of x-ray films. When using digitized images, a supplementary process is necessary to deal with the image distortion. Another calibration device is used in order to include this dis-tortion in the x-ray system model. This process is based on the N Planes B-Spline method described in Champleboux, Lavallée, Cinquin [13].

REGISTRATION OF PREOPERATIVE AND INTRAOPERATIVE IMAGES

MRI preoperative images are registered with intraoperative images using anatomic structures that can be seen in both modalities. That is the case in particular for the ventricular system but also for the skull, some of the arteries, and other regions. The surgeon can draw one of these structures on one image using some Macintosh-like drawing tools. For example, he or she can draw on one magnetic resonance image the tumor region and some of the typical structures just cited. Then the surgeon can superimpose this drawing on another image (typically, an x-ray image on which the tumor cannot be seen) by registering the anatomic structures. Registration of different x-ray images (or drawings on these images) is done automatically using the screw pins by which the head is fixed on the frame. Because they keep a constant relationship to the x-ray cameras and they can be seen on each x-ray image they can be used as a registration feature.

Registration of preoperative and intraoperative images could be done automatically. It requires both 3D and 2D segmentation tools and 3D-2D matching tools. From 3D images of the brain reconstructed from MRI, the ventricular system must be segmented; 2D projections on the ventricular system have also to be segmented on x-ray images. Then a rigid transform must be found that enables one to superimpose the 3D object with its projections. Such tools have already been developed in our laboratory. Cinquin [14] developed a 3D reconstruction algorithm using tricubic spline functions to describe a volume as a continuous function giving the density for a 3D position (x, y, z). This basic function enables one to compute cuts, views, or projections of a volume. Segmentation algorithms are based on elastic patterns [15], whereas 3D-2D registration [16] is based on the computation of a distance map represented by an octree-spline.

LINKING THE OPERATIVE REFERENCE SYSTEM WITH THE REFERENCE SYSTEM OF THE ROBOT

At the end of the definition of a target, we know the exact location of the selected trajectory with respect to the calibration cage (as discussed earlier). Because the

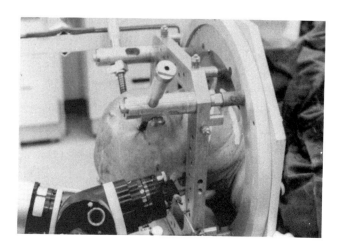

FIGURE 24.8   Strategy execution.

cage was held by the robot during the calibration process, the trajectory is known with respect to the robot coordinate system. Hence, the operator merely replaces the cage with a simple guide that is placed by the robot at the desired location. Finally, the surgeon has only to push the instrument forward into the guide, as shown in figure 24.8.

Performing the surgical strategy

ON SOLVING THE ACCURACY PROBLEM

The robot is a modified, industrial, 6-dof manipulator robot. Its particular design has been considered suitable for surgical use. According to the robot repeatability of ± 0.2 mm and the limitations in accuracy of images sensors, our objective was to reach a submillimeter overall accuracy. Therefore, we referred to related works in order to deal with the inaccuracies of the robot model [17–19], and we developed our own method to calibrate the robot in the whole system. Lavallée [20] describes this stage in full details.

ON SOLVING THE SAFETY PROBLEM

The first way to solve the safety problem is to reduce as much as possible hardware breakdowns. We have found it very useful to cut down significantly the reduction ratio of each joint, thus creating one of the slowest robots in its category. First, overheating is significantly reduced and, second, it is easier to stop the robot in case of unlikely undesirable motion. Another point consists of considering remaining possible breakdowns and preventing them using software. Several software tests have been added to check the normal behavior of the robot. For instance, position errors are checked continuously with respect to a threshold. Once the robot has reached the destination, as we expect no motion, the differences among the articular variables are tested: Any motion first triggers a beep and then cuts the power off, according to its magnitude. Moreover, thanks to the reduction ratios, the robot is irreversible —that is usual human forces cannot move it. Thus, the operator can cut the power off before introducing a needle in the guide. The robot does not move and no outcome can result from any mechanical, hardware, or software problem. During this stage, position errors are still tested such that if any deviation occurs because of an unusual force, a message advises the surgeon to remove the needle from the brain. Then he or she can restart the power and begin positioning anew. Although no failure has been observed since the robot has been in clinical practice, this procedure is used still.

Conclusion

The system described here has been in routine clinical use since March 1989 [21], and approximately 600 interventions have been performed. The surgical team has been able to use the system with no assistance after a first training period of nearly 150 interventions. Some statistics have been compiled during the first 14 months of use in the stereotactic operating room. They are representative of the whole range of interventions practiced in everyday neurosurgery: 141 tumor biopsies, 14 stereo-electroencephalographic (SEEG) investigations of epileptic patients, 5 brachytherapeutic procedures (introduction of permanent ^{125}I seeds or ^{192}Ir wires), and 36 midline stereotactic neurosurgical procedures (including 29 patients suffering from Parkinson's disease, 5 suffering from chronic pain, and 2 suffering from deafferentation pain). From the surgical point of view, no complication could be attributed to the use of the robot. As stated in Benabid et al. [21]: "During this clinical experience the robot was found to be as safe as conventional stereotactic procedures. Moreover, the flexibility of its positioning, made the choice of trajectories easier and thus, the overall procedure safer."

This system is highly representative of the uses to which a robot can be put now in many medical and surgical applications. It is potentially very useful because it can be seen as a human-computer interface that physically and accurately links the surgeon or physician to the computerized data needed to perform the planned strategy. Even though the field of medical robotics is advancing steadily, very few systems are used in routine clinical practice. As far as we know, Kelly's [5] and our systems are the only ones. That is no doubt due to safety problems. Using a robot as a more active device to perform complex tasks and motions cannot be envisioned until the safety issue is carefully analyzed and some robust solutions are found.

REFERENCES

[1] LAVALLÉE, S., and P. CINQUIN, 1991. IGOR: Image guided operating robot. In *Proceedings of the Fifth International Conference on Advanced Robotics*, Pisa, pp. 876–881.

[2] ADAMS, L., W. KRIBUS, D. MEYER-EBRECHT, R. RUEGER, J. GILSBACH, R. MÖSGES, and G. SCHLOENDORFF, 1990. Computer assisted surgery. *IEEE Comput. Graph. Appl.* May: 43–51.

[3] MAZIER, B., S. LAVALLÉE, and P. CINQUIN, 1990. Computer assisted interventionist imaging: Application to the vertebral column surgery. In *Proceedings of the Annual International Conference of the IEEE Engineering in Medicine and Biology Society*, Philadelphia, 12(1):430–431.

[4] TAYLOR, R. H., C. B. CUTTING, Y. Y. KIM, A. D. KALVIN, D. LAROSE, B. HADDAD, D. KHORAMABADI, M. NOZ, R. OLYHA, N. BRUUN, and D. GRIMM, 1991. A model-based optimal planning and execution system with active sensing and passive manipulation for augmentation of human precision in computer-integrated surgery. Presented at the Second International Workshop on Experimental Robotics, Toulouse, France, June.

[5] KELLY, P. J., 1986. Technical approaches to identification and stereotactic reduction of tumor burden. In *Biology of Brain Tumor*, M. D. Walker and D. G. T. Thomas, eds. Pp. 237–343.

[6] TAYLOR, R. H., H. A. PAUL, B. D. MITTLESTADT, W. HANSON, P. KAZANZIDES, J. F. ZUHARS, E. GLASSMAN, B. L. MUSITS, W. L. BARGAR, and W. WILLIAMSON, 1990. An image based robotic system for hip replacement surgery. *J. Robotics Soc. Jpn.* Oct.: 111–116.

[7] DAVIES, B. L., R. D. HIBBERD, W. S. NG, A. G. TIMONEY, and J. E. A. WICKHAM, 1991. A surgeon robot for prostatectomies. In *Proceedings of ICAR: International Conference on Advanced Robotics*, Pisa, pp. 871–875.

[8] FUDJII, S., Y. TSUKAMOTO, M. FUJII, Y. KANEDA, M. MATSUO, and K. YAMAZAKI, 1986. Three dimensionalization of cerebral arteries from cineangiograms. In MedInfo: *Proceedings of the Fifth Conference on Medical Informatics*, Washington, pp. 700–704.

[9] LATOMBE, J. C., 1991. *Robot Motion Planning*. Boston: Kluwer Academic.

[10] BELLIER, C., C. LAUGIER, E. MAZER, and J. TROCCAZ, 1991. A practical system for planning safe trajectories for manipulator robots. Presented at the Second International Workshop on Experimental Robotics, Toulouse, June.

[11] MAZER, E., J. TROCCAZ, B. FAVERJON et al., 1991. ACT: A robot programming environment. Presented at the IEEE Conference on Robotics and Automation, Sacramento.

[12] GREMBAN, K. D., C. E. THORPE, and T. KANADE, 1988. Geometric camera calibration using systems of linear equations. In *Proceedings of the IEEE International Conference on Robotics and Automation*, Philadelphia, pp. 947–951.

[13] CHAMPLEBOUX, G., S. LAVALLÉE, and P. CINQUIN, 1992. Accurate calibration of cameras and range imaging sensors, the NPBS method. In *Proceedings of the IEEE Conference on Robotics and Automation*, Nice, France, pp. 1552–1558.

[14] CINQUIN, P., 1987. Application des fonctions splines au traitement d'images [in French]. Thèse d'Etat es Sciences Mathématiques, Grenoble University, 1987.

[15] LEITNER, F., I. MARQUE, S. LAVALLÉE, and P. CINQUIN, 1991. Dynamic segmentation: Finding the edges with snake-splines. In *Curves and Surface*, New York: Academic Press, pp. 279–284.

[16] LAVALLÉE, S., R. SZELISKI, L. BRUNIE, 1991. Matching 3D smooth surfaces with their 2D projections using 3D distance maps. In *Proceedings of the SPIE Conference on Geometric Methods in Computer Vision*, San Diego, pp. 322–336.

[17] ROTH, Z. S., B. W. MOORING, and B. RAVANI, 1987. An overview of robot calibration. *IEEE J. Robotics Automation* 3(5):377–385.

[18] HAYATI, S., K. TSO, and G. ROSTON, 1988. Robot geometry calibration. In *Proceedings of the IEEE International Conference on Robotics and Automation*, Philadelphia, pp. 1400–1406.

[19] VEITSCHEGGER, W. K., and C. H. WU, 1987. A method for calibrating and compensating robot kinematics errors. In *Proceedings of the IEEE Conference on Robotics and Automation*, Raleigh, pp. 39–44.

[20] LAVALLÉE, S., 1989. Gestes médicaux-chirurgicaux assistés par ordinateur: Application à la neurochirurgie stéréotaxique [in French]. Doctoral thesis, Université Joseph Fourier, Grenoble.

[21] BENABID, A. L., D. HOFFMANN, S. LAVALLÉE, P. CINQUIN, J. DEMONGEOT, J. F. LE BAS, and F. DANEL, 1991. Is there any future for robots in neurosurgery. In *Advances and Technical Standards in Neurosurgery*, vol. 18, L. Symon et al., eds. Berlin: Springer-Verlag, pp. 3–40.

[22] KODITSCHEK, D. E., 1989. Robot planning and control via potential functions. In *The Robotics Review*, O. Khatib, J. J. Craig, and T. Lozano-Pérez, eds. Cambridge, Mass.: MIT Press, pp. 349–368.

25 Computer-Assisted Surgical Planning and Robotics in Stereotactic Neurosurgery

BRUCE A. KALL

By this means every cubic millimeter of the brain could be studied and recorded.
—Robert Henry Clarke and Sir Victor Horsley, 1906

THE STEREOTACTIC technique was devised by Horsley and Clarke in the early twentieth century as a mechanical method for placing probes and electrodes in precise locations in the brain of animals. It was not until 1947 that the first reported human stereotactic procedure was reported [1]. A positive contrast ventriculogram (a two-dimensional x-ray image taken after injecting a contrast agent) was used to derive targeting information by measuring the target's distance (and adjusting for magnification) from anatomic landmarks. These techniques were adopted by many centers around the world, primarily for the treatment of movement disorders. The applications for stereotactic surgery increased with the development of computerized digital medical imaging, specifically CT in the early 1970s and, more recently, MRI, digital subtraction angiography (DSA), and positron emission tomography (PET). The precise 3D databases made possible by these technologies enable the surgeon to visualize and treat intracranial tumors and aid in the performance of procedures for movement disorders.

Several methods to transform coordinates from imaging slice coordinates to stereotactic coordinates have been developed. These typically involve scanning the patient following placement of three reference marks on the patient's scalp or skull (frameless) or attaching a fiducial reference system to a stereotactic head frame. These markers or fiducials are then related to an instrument that defines a coordinate system in the operating room. In either technique, mathematic transformations are determined to translate between scan and operating room (stereotactic) coordinate systems. The calculations to transform a single point from an imaging modality into a stereotactic coordinate system can be performed by hand, with a calculator, with graph paper, or by placing calibrated transparent overlays onto films generated from CT, MRI, DSA, and PET scans. While generally straightforward, these methods take a considerable amount of time and may be prone to human error as the number of calculations increases. Calculations to transform and treat an irregularly shape 3D volume (volumetric stereotaxis) are not practical utilizing manual techniques.

Our group began the development and use of computer-assisted surgical planning and interactive surgery more than 15 years ago [2, 3]. This has evolved into the Compass system (Compass International, Inc., Rochester, Minn.) which provides computerized image –directed stereotactic surgical planning, an interactive robotic surgical positioning system for point-in-space, and, more uniquely, volumetric stereotactic procedures. Target points and safe surgical trajectories may be rapidly calculated and correlated between modalities for point-in-space procedures such as biopsy, third ventriculostomy, Ommaya reservoir placements, and functional stereotactic procedures. Volumetric stereotactic procedures involve localization, reconstruction, and integration of 3D volumes in stereotactic space. In our system, 3D volumes are reconstructed and integrated from planar CT and MRI slices into 3D stereotactic space. These volumes may be rendered in a manner useful to the surgeon for planning and removing intracranial lesions during craniotomy and for planning interstitial irradiation procedures.

Our group has also developed Regulus (Compass International, Inc.) a hardware and software device that allows performance of some surgical procedures with or without the use of the stereotactic frame. This device maintains the usefulness of preoperative surgical planning and interactive surgical control while enabling rapid registration of the location of instruments in the surgical field to preoperatively collected radiologic images and volumetric reconstructions. This aids the physician in maintaining the spatial relationship of the instruments to the intended intracranial target or volume.

Our computer and imaging system is accessible from the physician's office, from a treatment planning area adjacent to surgery, or from the operating room on monitors suspended from the operating room ceiling. All interaction is performed with a mouse and on-screen menus or a voice recognition system. The interactive robotic positioning system is moved and monitored by the computer under direct physician control as the surgery progresses.

Computer-assisted surgical planning and interactive surgery not only allows the surgeon to plan and implement the safest and least invasive surgical procedure, but allows the surgery to be performed in less time because the entire process has been simulated before the patient ever enters the operating room. This chapter will review our developments in computer-assisted surgical planning and the use of robotics in stereotactic neurosurgery.

The Compass system

The Compass system consists of a robotically controlled arc-quadrant positioner and a multimodality treatment planning and interactive surgery system with custom stereotactic software.

CARTESIAN ROBOTICS DEVICE

Our stereotactic device utilizes the *arc-quadrant* concept, which entails rigid fixation of the patient's head onto a 3D translation mechanism in order to position intracranial targets and volumes into the focal point of a sphere of a defined radius. Probes, surgical retractor, and other surgical interventions are directed perpendicular to a tangent of the sphere. The target point is accessed when the instrument is introduced to a depth equal to the radius of the sphere.

The Compass surgical system and robotics device (figure 25.1) was developed primarily for volumetric stereotactic procedures but is also used for point-in-space procedures. In this system, the patient is immobi-

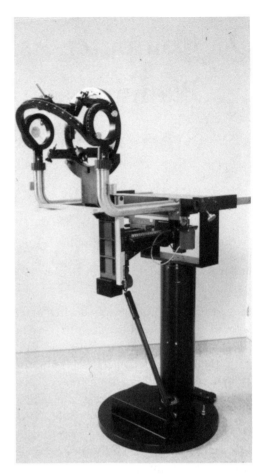

FIGURE 25.1 The Compass Cartesian robotics device consists of a stepper-motor-controlled three-axis positioner and a manual 160-mm arc system. Optical encoders on each axis allow the computer to monitor the current coordinates of the positioner. Patient movements within this arc-quadrant system are performed under computer control when a foot pedal is pressed by the surgeon.

lized in a stereotactic head frame that allows positioning in decubitus, supine, prone, or any other orientation comfortable for the surgeon and beneficial to the patient. A stepper-motor-controlled Cartesian robot moves the patient within a 160-mm sphere. Optical encoders on each axis allow the computer to monitor interactively the position of each axis. Trajectories are described by three rotation angles: collar (horizontal), arc (vertical), and rotation of the patient's head in the positioner's receiving yoke. The trajectory angles and patient orientation are selected so that the surgeon has a comfortable working situation and is able to access the target point or volume through brain along an optimal trajectory in a pre-planned manner. The 6 degrees of freedom (x, y, z, collar, arc, and patient orientation) allow an unlimited number of approaches to any intracranial target.

IMAGE-DIRECTED STEREOTACTIC SURGICAL PLANNING

Our computer-assisted stereotactic procedures are performed in three stages: imaging data collection; treatment planning and simulation; and finally the interactive surgical procedure. Prior to surgery, the patient is fitted with a replaceable modality-compatible head frame and undergoes a CT, MRI, or DSA study under local anesthesia. Stereotactic fiducial localization methods are employed during each study so that the computer will be able to relate points and volumes from each study to one another as well as to the Compass stereotactic device. The imaging data is transferred to the operating room computer system by tapes or network. After the data are collected, the head frame is removed and the patient returns to his or her room. The head frame is then reapplied on the day of surgery, in exactly the same location, using our micrometer-based reapplication technique. This allows optimal use of the surgeon's and operating room time.

Surgeons perform preoperative surgical planning in their offices on a single-screen, multiwindowed workstation, or adjacent to surgery at our multiscreen treatment planning console (figure 25.2). Both systems use Sun Microsystems (Sunnyvale, Ca.) SPARCstation technology. Our custom stereotactic software is developed in C language and utilizes the X Window System from MIT. The system has the capability to store 10 different targets, each having up to three different preplanned trajectories and a variety of integrated multimodal lesion volumes. All interaction with the software is performed via on-screen menus and a mouse or by voice recognition. The computer initially registers each radiologic image into the coordinate system of the stereotactic device. This is automatically performed by locating fiducial reference markers on the CT, MRI, and DSA images and calculating transformations to translate any pixel on each image into the stereotactic coordinate system. In the case of a DSA image, an elastic pincushion correction also must be applied because of the nature of the distortion introduced by the image intensifier in the DSA unit.

Point-in-space procedures, such as biopsy, third ventriculostomy, pallidotomy, and cyst aspirations, require safe access to a single point within the brain along a safe trajectory. Target determination in the Compass

FIGURE 25.2 Preoperative planning and surgical simulation is performed at a custom three-screen imaging console. The surgeon selects and correlates targets, trajectories, and 3D volumes among all modalities in order to simulate and derive an optimal surgical plan.

system is similar whether from CT and MRI. The surgeon displays any image on which the target is evident and simply moves the cursor over the location and presses a button on the mouse. The surgeon enters the patient orientation in the receiving yoke of the Compass positioner and the system instantly displays the target coordinates. A vascular target may also be determined from DSA by selecting corresponding locations on a lateral and anteroposterior (AP) images. Once a target is determined on any modality, the system then can automatically correlate it to the closest pixel on the closest slice from any other imaging study and determine its stereotactic coordinates [5]. The system then measures the 3D distance between the selected target and correlated target and displays both images on the computer screen (figure 25.3). An entry location may similarly be determined and correlated to be used for trajectory determination.

Surgical trajectories may likewise be determined on any imaging modality. The system may calculate directly the collar and arc angles between a previously selected target and entry location. In most cases though, the surgeon will want to visualize the target and entry locations in relationship to the vascular structures on arterial and venous DSA images. The target and entry point are projected onto the arterial, venous, or mask (unsubtracted) DSA images (figure 25.4), alternating between lateral and AP projections. The surgeon moves

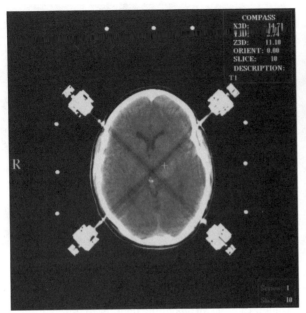 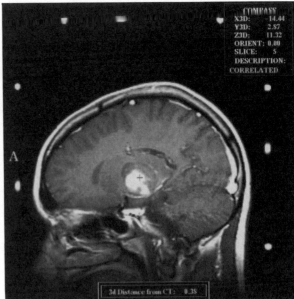

FIGURE 25.3 Target points can be selected and correlated between modalities (left, CT; right, MRI). The 3D distance between the two correlated points is also annotated.

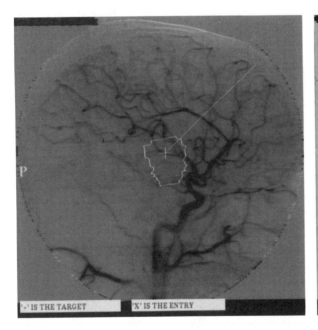

FIGURE 25.4 Trajectories can be interactively determined on DSA images (left, lateral; right, anterior/posterior) that

are annotated with the surgical target (+), cross-sections of the lesion volume, and intended surgical trajectory (line).

the cursor on any image and the system interactively determines the collar and arc angles between the projected target location and the current position of the cursor. The surgeon selects the avascular angles by

pressing a button on the mouse. Once a set of collar and arc angles are calculated, a probe path may then be simulated on the CT and MRI images. This trajectory may be coplanar or oblique to any of the original

356   NEUROSURGERY

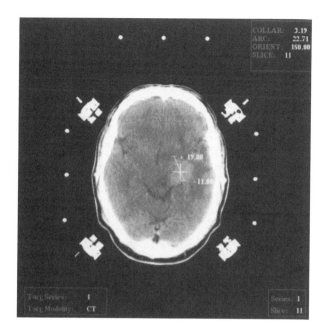

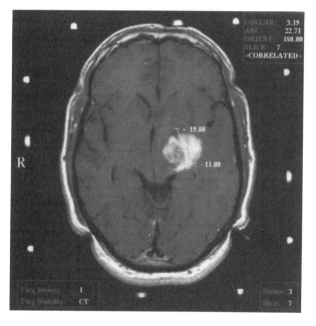

FIGURE 25.5 Surgical trajectories are displayed and confirmed on CT (top) and MRI (bottom) images indicating the probes path or the location of serial biopsies. Negative distances are proximal to the lesion target.

images. When the trajectory is coplanar, the entire surgical path may be annotated on one image (figure 25.5). Oblique trajectories are visualized by displaying a cursor at the precise location where a probe would pierce each slice.

Volumetric stereotaxis involves reconstruction, integration, and visualization of a multimodal lesion vol-ume in addition to selecting a target reference and surgical trajectory. Volumes are selected and reconstructed from contour outlines on serial CT and MRI images by techniques that have been described elsewhere [7–11]. Briefly, the surgeon identifies the contour of the lesion on any sequential CT and MRI slices exhibiting the lesion (Figure 25.6). This establishes a series of contours for each modality that may be suspended in stereotactic space at various levels corresponding to the slice thickness of the image on which the contour was traced. Intermediate contours of each lesion volume are created by linear interpolation so as to create evenly spaced contours at 1-mm levels. All contours are then filled with 1-mm cubes, classified by a code indicating the modality each was derived from, and integrated into a 3D computer matrix in relationship to the stereotactic target. This integrated volume can then be displayed and differentiated by different colors and gray scales on cross-sections or on 3D rendered images (figure 25.7).

The target, trajectory, and volume information are also useful in planning interstitial irradiation implants and other noninvasive radiation treatments [11, 12]. A simulation routine allows the surgeon to select the locations of radioactive ^{125}I seeds or shots from a linear accelerator or gamma knife so as to cover the lesion volume optimally with an isodose volume. This can be visualized on the serial cross-section images or on the CT and MRI images. The software displays the isodose volume as a series of contours that are percentages of the total dose. The location of each source or shot can be retained, integrated, and displayed with other seeds or shots that make up the total dose. Individual seeds or shots can be added, deleted, moved, or modified until the isodose best fits the lesion volume. The software then determines the stereotactic coordinates of each seed or shot, corresponding to the preplanned parameters, so that they may be accurately accessed with the Compass arc-quadrant system during the surgical or noninvasive procedure.

Interactive neurosurgery

The interactive surgical procedure involves monitoring and interacting with the surgical plan as the procedure progresses. The head frame is replaced onto the patient and the robotics positioner is automatically moved to the selected x, y, z target coordinates by the computer. The patient is placed under general anesthesia and posi-

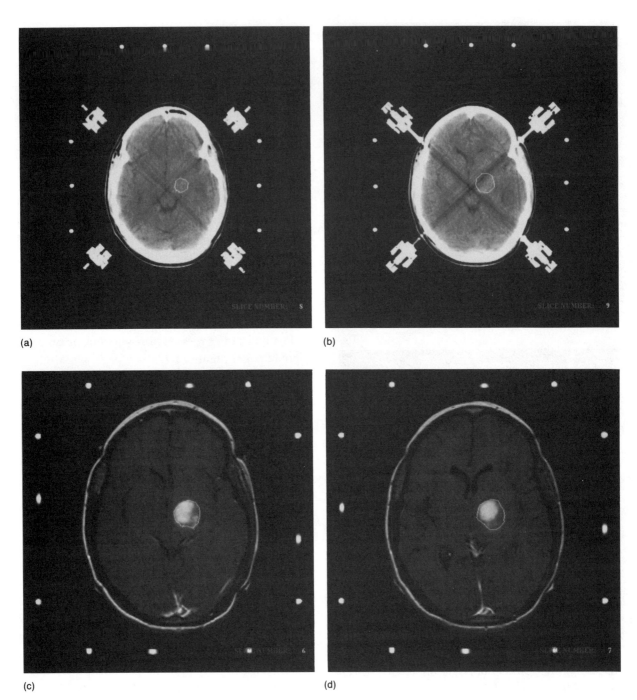

(a)   (b)

(c)   (d)

FIGURE 25.6 The surgeon outlines the lesion on serial CT (a, b) and MRI images (c, d). The computer interpolates intermediate outlines and integrates all volumes into a composite imaging matrix. These may then be sliced orthogonal to the surgical trajectory at any level and piped into an intra-microscope display device so as to provide a template for the surgeon to follow during tumor removal.

tioned on the receiving yoke of the Compass positioner. The surgeon interacts with the computer and robotics device in the operating room, using a mouse and menus on the screen or, alternatively a voice recognition sys-tem focused on the surgeon's voice. The operating room system is used to monitor the progression of the surgical plan, displaying corresponding images annotated with targets, trajectories, and lesion volumes as well as

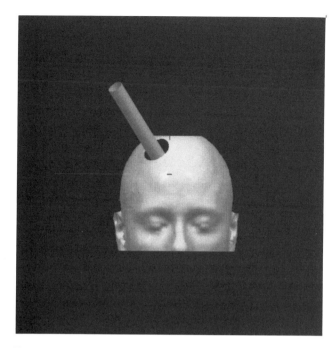

FIGURE 25.7 Three-dimensionally rendered images also help the surgeon to visualize global relationships between the scalp, skull, lesion, and stereotactic retractor.

the position of stereotactically directed surgical instruments. Fixed-tube teleradiography is used to confirm targets and probe positions and provide other feedback to the surgeon.

Volumetric stereotactic procedures are the most interactive. The surgeon removes intracranial volumes through a stereotactically directed cylindric retractor [13] by viewing cross-sections of the reconstructed and integrated lesion volume registered to the surgical field within the heads-up intramicroscopic display system. This system consists of a beam splitter and a tiny monitor attached to the surgical microscope. Successive slices of the lesion volume, sliced perpendicular to the current surgical trajectory, are updated into the heads-up display as the procedure progresses. These cross-sections are scaled to actual size and are superimposed onto the surgical field. The position and size of the surgical retractor is also displayed. The surgical retractor creates a shaft from the brain's surface and maintains exposure to the tumor. Because the retractor is directed from a known tangent on the arc-quadrant sphere and has a fixed length and radius (two cylindric retractors are available: 2-cm and 3-cm diameters), the end of the retractor within the brain is at a known

plane. Cross-sections of the integrated CT/MRI lesion volume on the plane of the retractor are interactively displayed within the intramicroscope display device and are utilized as a template to excise the lesion.

The system can also be used to remove tumors that are larger than the diameter of the surgical retractor (figure 25.8). The surgeon may make angular adjustments in the trajectory of the surgical retractor in order to reach areas outside the sphere of the retractor. Alternatively, a series of small translations in the orthogonal x-y coordinate plane of the cross-sections may be performed to bring areas of the lesion beneath the retractor. x, y, z translations are calculated to move the patient to the corresponding location. When the surgeon steps on a foot pedal, the stepper-motor-controlled Cartesian robot moves to the new position so that the operative field and the template of the lesion in the heads-up display correspond.

Alternatively, some interactive surgical procedures can be performed using Regulus. The Regulus device and interactive software enables interactive registration of surgical probes and instruments within the surgical field. The Regulus device defines a 3D coordinate system that encompasses the surgical field. The tip of the probe or instrument can be rapidly located in the surgical field and displayed as a cursor on the closest imaging slice or volumetric cross-sections utilizing stereotacic and frameless registration techniques. This further aids the surgeon in maintaining his or her spatial relationship to the intended intracranial target or volume.

Discussion

Stereotactic tumor biopsy and tumor resections may be performed without a computer and a robotic surgical device. Procedures can be planned and performed based on manual calculations. However, the computer, combined with stereotactic software, allows rapid and easy manipulation of the multitudinous diagnostic information presented to the surgeon. Furthermore, manual modification of a surgical plan based on considerations occurring intraoperatively is not practical because of time constraints.

The Compass computer-assisted planning and interactive surgical system allows the surgeon to plan and perform various procedures in a rapid and efficient manner. This makes optimal use of the surgeon's time

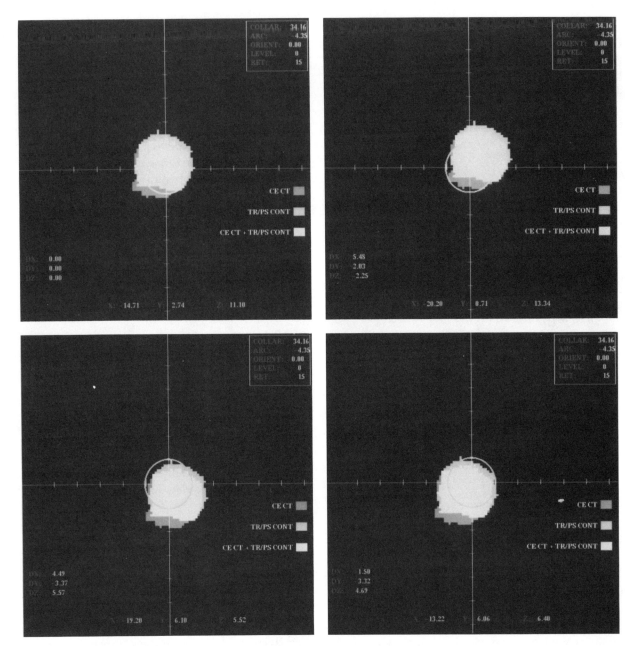

FIGURE 25.8 Cross-sections of the integrated lesion volume orthogonal to the surgical trajectory are displayed. A lesion larger than the cylindrical retractor may be removed by ap-plying orthogonal translations of the image and correspond-ing movements by the robotics positioner. This brings other areas underneath the retractor.

and operating room time. Point-in-space procedures include biopsy, cyst aspiration, third ventriculostomy, Ommaya reservoir placement, and functional proce-dures for movement disorders. Most importantly, the Compass system allows the surgeon to perform volu-metric stereotactic procedures. Compass volumetric procedures allow the surgeon to reach the intended intracranial target locations and maintain the sur-geon's orientation as the procedure extends below the surface of the brain. The approach may be simulated beforehand in order to select the path that is least disruptive to normal brain tissue. Thus the volumetric capabilities of the system aid the surgeon with three principal functions: localization, 3D visualization, and spatial orientation. A surgeon's 3D orientation de-grades as the procedure proceeds below the surface of the brain. The computer-interactive method helps the surgeon to find the lesion. Second, tumors are not simple spheres nor rectangles; they are often irregular in shape. The system aids the surgeon in visualizing the lesion. Finally, the boundary between normal brain and the tumor is frequently unclear intraoperatively. The interactive method aids the surgeon in maintaining their spatial orientation within the lesion during surgery.

Compass computer-assisted stereotactic techniques provide a number of patients with a surgical alternative that may not be offered using conventional neurosurgical means. The system allows the surgeon to derive the safest and least invasive procedure preoperatively, thereby increasing operative efficacy. There is no need to hold open an operating room while patients are scanned because the head frame is replaceable, enabling data acquisition, treatment planning, and surgery to be performed at different times. Computer-assisted stereotactic procedures can be performed in less time because the entire procedure is planned, simulated, and rehearsed before the patient enters the operating room.

Operatively, biopsies are performed with the Compass system through $\frac{1}{8}$-in. twist drill holes rather than the conventional burr hole used with other systems. Compass volumetric craniotomies are performed using the smallest trephine that the stereotactic retractor will traverse. Recovery time for patients undergoing computer-assisted volumetric lesion removal is typically shorter than those patients who undergo conventional craniotomy. Patients are usually released from the hospital sooner, decreasing the associated costs for the hospital and the patient. At the Mayo Clinic during the period from July 1984 to July 1993, 3142 stereotactic surgical procedures were performed. These include 1463 biopsies, 1024 interactive volumetric craniotomies, 107 thalamotomies, 112 third ventriculostomies, 27 Ommaya reservoir placements, 114 cyst aspirations, 21 P^{32} installations, 23 amygdalohippocampectomies, 41 depth electrode placements, and 210 miscellaneous stereotactic procedures.

NOTE

"Compass" and "Regulus" are trademarks of Compass International, Inc., of Rochester, Minnesota.

REFERENCES

[1] SPIEGEL, E. A., H. T. WYCIS, O. R. MARKS, et, al., 1947. Stereotaxis apparatus for operations on the human brain. *Science* 106:349–350.

[2] KELLY, P. J., and G. J. ALKER, 1981. A stereotactic approach to deep-seated central nervous system neoplasms using the carbon dioxide laser. *Surg. Neurol.* 15(5):331–334.

[3] KELLY, P. J., G. J., ALKER, JR., and S. GOERSS, 1982. Computer-assisted stereotactic laser microsurgery for the treatment of intracranial neoplasms. *Neurosurgery* 10(3):324–331.

[4] KALL, B. A., P. J. KELLY, S. J. GOERSS, and F. EARNEST, 1985. Cross-registration of points and lesion volumes from MR and CT. In *Proceedings of the Seventh Annual Conference of the IEEE Medicine and Biology Society*, Chicago, pp. 939–942.

[5] KALL, B. A., 1992. Comprehensive multimodality surgical planning and interactive neurosurgery. In *Computers in Stereotactic Neurosurgery*. Cambridge, Mass.: Blackwell Scientific, pp. 209–229.

[6] KELLY, P. J., B. A. KALL, and S. J. GOERSS, 1984. Transposition of volumetric information derived from computed tomography scanning into stereotactic space. *Surg. Neurol.* 21:465–471.

[7] KALL, B. A., P. J. KELLY, and S. J. GOERSS, 1985. Interactive stereotactic surgical system for the removal of intracranial tumors utilizing the CO_2 laser and CT-derived database. *IEEE Trans. Biomed. Eng.* BME-32:2, 112–116.

[8] KELLY, P. J., B. A. KALL, S. GOERSS, and F. EARNEST, 1986. Computer-assisted stereotaxic laser resection of intra-axial brain neoplasms. *J. Neurosurg.* 64:427–439.

[9] KELLY, P. J., B. A. KALL, and S. J. GOERSS, 1986. Computer-assisted resection of posterior fossa lesions. *Surg. Neurol.* 25:530–534.

[10] KELLY, P. J., F. W. SHARBROUGH, B. A. KALL, and S. J. GOERSS, 1987. MRI-based computer-assisted stereotactic resection of hippocampus and amygdala in patients with temporal lobe epilepsy. *Mayo Clinic Proc.* 62:103–108.

[11] KELLY, P. J., B. A. KALL, and S. J. GOERSS, 1984. Preoperative computer determination of interstitial iridium 192 source placement into CNS tumor volumes. *Acta Neurochir.* 33:377–383.

[12] KALL, B. A., P. J. KELLY, S. O. STIVING, and S. J. GOERSS, 1992. Preoperative computer-assisted simulation of interstitial ^{125}I source placements into CNS lesion volumes. *Stereotact. Funct. Neurosurg.* 59:1–4, 205.

[13] KELLY, P. J., S. J. GOERSS, and B. A. KALL, 1988. The stereotaxic retractor in computer-assisted stereotaxic microsurgery. *J. Neurosurg.* 69:301–306.

26 Magnetic Stereotaxis: Computer-Assisted, Image-Guided Remote Movement of Implants in the Brain

R. C. RITTER, M. S. GRADY, M. A. HOWARD III, AND G. T. GILLIES

THE USE OF magnetic fields to guide small objects through the body for therapeutic purposes has been discussed in the literature and studied experimentally for many years [1]. Most of the previous attempts at in vivo magnetic manipulation have focused on the towing of catheters through the vasculature, for the thrombosis of intracranial aneurysms, for instance. However, there have also been some attempts at magnetic guidance through tissues and organs rather than the vasculature. [2–6]. With the exception of the proposal by Oldendorf [7], though, there has been little discussion of and no previous attempt at magnetically guiding small objects through the bulk (parenchymal) brain tissues. In 1984, Howard, Grady, and Ritter envisioned that, should this be possible, one might have at hand a new stereotactic modality for delivering hyperthermia to deep-seated brain tumors. This would be done via the noncontact radio-frequency (RF) induction heating of the implanted object (called a *seed*) once it had been maneuvered inside of the tumor mass. Moreover, the same method might also be used to magnetically tow a flexible catheter into the brain to deliver drugs stereotactically for the treatment of other types of focal neurologic disorders, such as Parkinson's disease.

Once the early laboratory studies [8, 9] confirmed the feasibility of intraparenchymal magnetic manipulation, a series of advanced studies were carried out to demonstrate the workability of image-guided magnetic

stereotaxis [10, 11]. In what follows we describe the key features that underlie the magnetic stereotaxis system (MSS), discuss the types of therapies that can be delivered to points within the brain via the MSS, and assess the status of the development of the instrumentation.

Principles of operation

Because patient safety is the highest concern in any neurosurgical procedure, a minimum-risk method had to be identified for guiding the implanted seed around the critical brain structures and blood vessels. In traditional stereotaxis, this is accomplished by imaging the patient's brain with respect to a fiducial reference frame attached rigidly to the skull. The safest straight-line path to the intracranial target then is established in terms of the reference frame's coordinates, and the probe is inserted into the brain via a guideway aimed precisely along this path.

In magnetic stereotaxis, the fiducial frame is left on the head continuously, but only in the form of a few small skull marker screws as opposed to a large and heavy circumferential assembly. A magnetic resonance or CT brain scan is taken, and the resulting atlas of images is stored in the MSS host computer. Following this, a small burr hole is opened in the skull under local anesthesia, and the seed is inserted through it onto the pial surface of the brain.

The patient's head then is positioned inside the MSS "helmet" (described later) such that it is centered within a set of three orthogonally oriented pairs of superconducting coils and a biplanar x-ray system. The host computer is then initialized such that the x-ray-derived locations of the seed and markers are superimposed onto the sagittal, axial, and coronal magnetic resonance images of the brain and markers, with the results displayed on the computer monitor. In effect, this gives the neurosurgeon a "road map" against which the seed movement can be monitored and controlled. The movement sequences consist of selecting the desired direction and length of seed movement, and then executing the movement by computer-commanding the helmet's coils to pull the seed magnetically to the desired location.

With this strategy, one set of preoperative magnetic resonance or CT images serves for the full procedure and, simultaneously, the x-ray dose acquired by the patient can be kept small. The latter is possible by virtue of the large density difference between the biologic tissues on the one hand and the seed and markers on the other: The x-ray system need produce only enough intensity for threshold detection of the seed and markers; it is not required to resolve anatomic details within the brain. We estimate that for a 2-hour procedure, during which the x-ray tubes are triggered at a rate of four pulses per second, the MSS skull entrance rate requirements are such that the dose can be kept to approximately 0.1 R [12].

The MSS enables the neurosurgeon to perform *nonlinear* stereotaxis in that the probe—that is, the magnetically manipulated seed—is not constrained to follow a straight line to the target. Instead, it can be maneuvered as necessary, even along tightly curved paths within the brain. (In the present version of the MSS, the smoothness of the curve the seed follows is limited by the step size of the movement selected by the neurosurgeon. It may eventually be possible to control the superconducting coils in the helmet in such a way that continuously curved movement of the seed becomes feasible.)

Potential applications

Hyperthermic treatment of brain tumors

The MSS was conceived within the context of efforts to provide neurosurgeons with a new tool for treating ma-

lignant neoplasms within the brain. Surgical resection is presently the modality of choice, although survival probability is seldom significantly enhanced by either the operation itself or by follow-on courses of radiotherapy [13]. Hyperthermia has often been held out as a promising adjuvant therapy in such cases. However, it has always been a difficult task to confine the applied heat to the tumor without thermally damaging the surrounding healthy tissues. This is so whether the heat has been generated by interstitially implanted microwave antennae, induction-driven thermoseed arrays, or any other geometric arrangement of sources relied on to create therapeutic isothermal volumes within the tissues.

The MSS introduces a new variable into such schemes: movement of the source of heat. By having a single inductively heated implant that can be freely repositioned within the tumor, the neurosurgeon can balance seed location, RF power level, and duration of heating to achieve dynamic control over the boundary of thermally driven cell death. The principles of "dynamic boundary hyperthermia" have been studied in our laboratories by Molloy [14]. She found that it was possible to obtain uncertainties of less than 1 mm in the boundary of cell-kill in living brain tissue using an RF induction hyperthermia system capable of delivering approximately 1 W to the implant [15]. The design details of the RF induction heating system used in those studies are available elsewhere [16]. Table 26.1 presents for comparison the characteristics of several recently built RF induction heating systems [17–23], including that of this work.

The integration of the RF hyperthermia subsystem into the already rather complex MSS apparatus is not without its difficulties. For instance, the induction coil must surround the upper part of the patient's head to ensure that the seed will be heated as efficiently as possible. This means that the coil must be radiographically transparent enough to enable passage of the x-ray beams used to identify the location of the seed in the brain.

Arguably, more serious problems arise from the fact that the coil will of necessity be positioned in the inner cavity of the magnetic manipulation helmet (as that is where the patient's head will be). In essence, then, the coil will be surrounded by stainless steel surfaces and, during operation, much of the energy in the coil's field will inevitably be dissipated. This type of loading stands to greatly reduce the efficiency of the hyper-

TABLE 26.1

Characteristics of various radiofrequency induction heating systems

	Operational frequency (kHz)	Plate input power (kW)	Coil design	Seed material	Seed dimensions	Characteristic temperature (°C)	Heating efficiency (%)
Burton et al., 1966	380	20	elliptical single turn, 20 cm ID, water-cooled	430 stainless steel	8 mm long, 1.6 mm diameter	104° (in air) after 3 minutes	10–0.1
Stauffer et al., 1984a	1900	1	5-turn solenoid, water-cooled Faraday shield, 38 cm ID	430 stainless steel	10 mm long, 1.5 mm diameter	65° at implant surface	0.02 (1 cm long seed)
Brezovich et al., 1984	90	1.5	elliptical 9-turn, 48 cm major axis ID, air-cooled	Ni-Cu alloy	7 to 25 mm long, 0.9 mm diameter	50° cut-off point	∼0.007 (1 cm long seed)
Moidel et al., 1985	37.2	—	14-turn copper coil	carbon steel, Hysterloy	10 mm long, 0.5 mm diameter	37°–39° for up to 2 hour periods	—
Kimura and Katsuki, 1986	20–30	1	cylindric coil, 23 cm ID	copper	192 mm long, 0.2 mm diameter (braided wire lopp)	43°–44° for 20 minutes in vivo	—
Kobayashi et al., 1989	100–500	0.2	6 copper tubing windings, 15-cm ID, water-cooled	Fe-Pt alloy	10 mm long, 0.8 mm diameter	45° for 30 minutes in vivo	—
Molloy et al., this work	640	1.5 (measured forward 410 W–630 W)	9-turn, square winding cross-section, copper tubing windings	Ni high-purity Fe, steel	4.8 mm diameter sphere, 4.8 mm × 9.6 mm ellipsoid	50° after 4 minutes, 2 mm from seed surface	0.1
Ameritherm, SP-15 1988	50–200	25	4-turn copper, water-cooled	magnetic steel	5 mm diameter rod (length unpublished)	870° to harden steel	—

thermia system unless an almost lossless flux return path can be designed to solve the problem. The flux return path, however, must be made in such a way that it, like the induction coil, is not radiographically opaque. Moreover, it must not significantly affect the precise magnetic force fields.

It is not clear yet, but the conflicting requirements of nonradiopacity and the need for a flux return path may turn out to be completely mutually exclusive. If so, the alternative may be to move the seed with the MSS and then heat it at a separate hyperthermia station designed uniquely for that purpose. Fractionation of treatments in this manner is not uncommon in neurosurgery; for instance, many types of radiotherapies are delivered in this way.

MSS-based drug delivery

Approximately 400,000 persons in the United States, and many more worldwide, suffer from Parkinson's disease, and a large number of them receive only marginal benefit from the existing drug therapies. This is in part due to complications arising from the blood-brain barrier, a biophysical mechanism that selectively screens many types of substances (including therapeutic medications) from passage through the capillaries of the brain.

With the MSS, it may be possible to avoid the screening effect of the blood-brain barrier by delivering the drug directly to the brain tissues themselves. The approach calls for the magnetically manipulated seed to tow a thin, flexible catheter tube into the striatum of the brain. The tube would be made of a semipermeable membrane that would permit the chemical transport of the catheter contents into the caudate nucleus and putamen of the striatum, or other dopaminergic site, as appropriate [24]. With the catheter in place, delivery of the drug (via passage through the membrane wall) would take place in a smooth, continuous manner similar to the way in which, say, dopamine is naturally secreted.

There are additional potential advantages to this type of drug delivery, particularly when compared to the standard stereotactic surgical procedures. For instance, at present, multipass stereotaxis often is required to ensure adequate placement of tissue grafts,

TABLE 26.2

Properties of the five different MSS magnetic manipulation systems used to date

MSS coil generation	1	2	3	4	5
Coil type	Wire-wound "neck-loop"	Circular cross-section cropper tubing	Square cross-section copper tubing	Superconducting	Multicoil superconducting system
Power supply	Hewlett-Packard 6434B (2 each)	Lincwelder DC-250-MK motor-generator	Cableform MK-10 pulse-modulating controller and deep cycle batteries	Electronic measurements EMP-100-200-1211 with static bypass switch	Electronic measurements EMP-100-200-1211 with switching contactors and supply drivers
Ramp-time to full current	< 1 sec	< 1 sec	< 1 sec	10 sec	300 sec
Mounting system	Two-degree goniometer (manual)	Hand-adjustable cradle	Five-degree goniometer (manual)	Four-degree goniometer (computerized)	Static floor-mounted
Protocol to use	Brain phantom gelatin	in vivo	in vivo	Brain phantom gelatin	Primates, human trials
Dates of operation	1/87 to 9/87	11/87	7/88 to 8/88	4/90 to 8/90	6/91 to present
Reference number	9	29	10	30	27

cell slurries, or pharmaceutical compounds of the type used to treat Parkinson's disease. As a result, the layers of brain overlying deep-seated targets sometimes sustain nontrivial levels of damage due to the various passes of the stereotactic probe. In some cases, glioblastoma has even been associated with the Parkinson's treatment of this type [25]. The MSS methodology, though, requires only one pass of the seed through the brain because the towed catheter can be laid out exactly along the entire length of the targeted brain structure.

Besides being used to treat Parkinson's disease, such a concept might also be employed to deliver the drugs needed to treat chronic pain disorders, to place chemotherapeutic agents directly into brain tumors, and to provide phototherapy to points inside the brain via towed, laser-pumped optical fibers. One can also envision the MSS being used with different kinds of seeds (without catheter) that could take biopsy samples, deliver radiotherapies, neutralize epileptic foci, and so on [26].

Status of the instrumentation development

The magnetic manipulation system has gone through five generations of development, as described in table 26.2. In its earliest versions, room-temperature, water-cooled coils were used in the feasibility studies that demonstrated the safety of magnetically manipulating a small (≈ 5 mm maximum dimension) object through in vivo canine brain. The latest version, the fifth generation, is the multicoil magnetic manipulation system that will ultimately be used in human clinical trials of both hyperthermia and drug delivery.

As shown in figure 26.1, it consists of a large, box-shaped stainless steel cryostat in which the six superconducting coils are mounted. The patient's head is inserted through the open bore of the coil on the front of the cryostat. The biplanar x-ray generators are mounted such that the x-ray beams pass through the open bores of the coils on the upper sides of the cryostat, continue on through the patient's head, and then emerge through the open bores of the coils on the lower side of the cryostat where they are transduced by detectors. Further details about the structure and dimensions of the MSS helmet are available elsewhere [27].

The x-ray detection chain consists of a phosphor target, a light-gathering lens, a microchannel plate image intensifier, and a solid-state camera that captures the

FIGURE 26.1   The MSS helmet with reserve and fill dewars, and with the biplanar x-ray imaging systems attached to the sloped sides of the helmet.

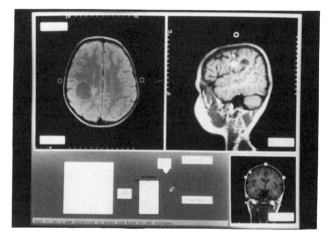

FIGURE 26.2   Split-screen presentation of magnetic resonance images, including skull markers and seed.

resulting image [12]. The microchannel plate intensifier and the camera are coupled via a fiberoptic taper.

The image formed on the CID camera is transferred into an ANDROX ICS-400 image processing system that, via a Sun 4/110 SPARC workstation, runs software that identifies and locates the seed and the markers [28]. The coordinates for these objects are then passed to the user-interface part of the program [27] where representations of them are superimposed onto the preoperatively stored MRI scans, as shown in figure 26.2. Given this visual feedback, and a thorough

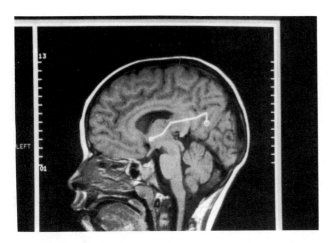

FIGURE 26.3 The user-interface software projects the path traveled by the seed onto the magnetic resonance slices.

knowledge of the brain's structure, the neurosurgeon can then guide the seed along whatever path is appropriate to achieve its placement in the target location. The user-interface software is able to track and display the path of movement, as suggested in figure 26.3 (the path shown there was arbitrarily chosen for demonstration purposes only).

Future work

The MSS is still in the early stages of development, and much work remains to be done. Projects now in progress include the implementation of a new algorithm that will permit accurate, relatively fast control of the ramp rates of the six independent superconducting coils; a front-to-back safety analysis of the software and computer operating system; installation and calibration of the low-dose, biplanar fluoroscopy system; design of the flux return path of the RF induction hyperthermia system; and, finally, integration of all these components into a fully functional MSS apparatus capable of achieving uncertainties of less than 1 mm in the absolute value of seed movement. Following acceptance testing, the apparatus will be used in clinical trials of a primate model of Parkinson's disease and in preliminary human trials of the hyperthermic treatment of brain tumors.

ACKNOWLEDGMENTS The authors thank their colleagues M. A. Lawson, K. G. Wika, J. A. Molloy, E. G. Quate, P. A. Ramos, S. W. Allison, A. J. Cheng, K. Wu, and W. C. Broaddus, M. D., for their numerous and ongoing contributions to the development of the MSS. We also thank the many individuals and private foundations that have funded the work, including the Huston Foundation, the Kopf Foundation, the Sachem Fund, the Margaret W. and Herbert Hoover Jr. Foundation, and all the others. The commercial development of the MSS is now being made possible by Sanderling Ventures of Menlo Park, California, in cooperation with the Virginia Center for Innovative Technology, Wang NMR, Inc., and the Universities of Virginia, Washington, and Iowa.

REFERENCES

[1] DRILLER, J., and E. H. FREI, 1987. A review of medical applications of Magnet Attraction and Detection. *J. Med. Eng. Technol.* 11(6):271–277.

[2] MCCARTHY, H. F., H. P. HOVNANIAN, T. A. BRENNAN, P. BRAND, and T. J. CUMMINGS, 1961. Magnetic guidance of gastrointestinal probes. In *Digest of the 1961 International Conference on Medical Electronics*. Washington, D.C.: McGregor and Werner, 134.

[3] GROB, D., and P. STEIN, 1969. Magnetically induced function of heart and bladder. *J. Appl. Physics* 40(3):1042–1043.

[4] RAM, W., and H. MEYER, 1991. Heart catheterization in a neonate by interacting magnetic fields: A new and simple method of catheter guidance. *Cathet. Cardiovasc. Diagn.* 22(4):317–319.

[5] WEBER, H., and G. LANDWEHR, 1982. A new method for the determination of the mechanical properties of the vitreous. *Ophthalmic Res.* 14:326–334.

[6] BERARDINIS, L. A., 1990. A closer look at magnetically assisted eye surgery. *Machine Design* 62(23):36–37.

[7] OLDENDORF, W. H., 1962. Speculations on instrumentation of the nervous system. In *Proceedings of the San Diego Symposium on Biomedical Engineering*, vol. 2. San Diego: San Diego Society of Biomedical Engineers, 274–280.

[8] GRADY, M. S., et al., 1988. Initial experimental results of a new stereotaxic hyperthermia system. *Surg. Forum* 39: 507–509.

[9] MOLLOY, J. A., 1988. A device for delivering a highly localized hyperthermia treatment to deep-seated brain tumors. Master's thesis, University of Virginia.

[10] GRADY, M. S., M. A. HOWARD, J. A. MOLLOY, R. C. RITTER, E. G. QUATE, and G. T. GILLIES, 1990. Nonlinear magnetic stereotaxis: Three-dimensional, in vivo remote magnetic manipulation of a small object in canine brain. *Med. Phys.* 17(3):405–415.

[11] GRADY, M. S., M. A. HOWARD, W. C. BROADDUS, J. A. MOLLOY, R. C. RITTER, E. G. QUATE, and G. T. GILLIES, 1990. Magnetic stereotaxis: A technique to deliver stereotactic Hyperthermia. *Neurosurgery* 27(6):1010–1016.

[12] RAMOS, P. A., J. A. MOLLOY, S. W. ALLISON, M. A. LAWSON, E. G. QUATE, K. G. WIKA, G. T. GILLIES, R. C. RITTER, M. S. GRADY, and M. A. HOWARD, 1991.

Design studies of a fluoroscopic imaging system for the video tumor fighter. University of Virginia (tech. rep. UVA/640419/NEEP91/113), pp. 9–10.

[13] QUIGLEY, M. R., and J. C. MAROON, 1991. The relationship between survival and the extent of the resection in patients with supratentorial malignant gliomas. *Neurosurgery* 29(3):385–389.

[14] MOLLOY, J. A., 1990. Brain tumor hyperthermia with static and moving seeds. Doctoral dissertation, University of Virginia.

[15] MOLLOY, J. A., et al., 1991. Thermodynamics of movable inductively heated seeds for the treatment of brain tumors. *Med. Phys.* 18(4):794–803.

[16] MOLLOY, J. A., R. C. RITTER, M. S. GRADY, M. A. HOWARD, E. G. QUATE, and G. T. GILLIES, 1991. RF induction heating system for dynamic boundary hyperthermia (University of Virginia tech. rep. no. UVA/640419/NEEP91/110).

[17] BURTON, C. V., et al., 1966. Induction thermocoagulation of the brain: A new neurosurgical tool. *IEEE Trans. Biomed. Eng.* 13:114–120.

[18] STAUFFER, P. R., et al., 1984. Observations on the use of ferromagnetic implants for inducing hyperthermia. *IEEE Trans. Biomed. Eng.* 31:76–90.

[19] BREZOVICH, I. A., et al., 1984. Local hyperthermia with interstitial techniques. *Cancer Res.* 44:(Suppl.) 4752s–4756s.

[20] MOIDAL, R. A., et al., 1975. Chemothermal therapy of brain tumors: Heating characteristics of materials in the radio-frequency electromagnetic (RFEM) field. In *Proceedings of the San Diego Biomedical Symposium*. San Diego: San Diego Society of Biomedical Engineers, pp. 315–319.

[21] KIMURA, I., and T. KATSUKI, 1986. VLF induction heating for clinical hyperthermia. *IEEE Trans. Magnet.* 22:1897–1900.

[22] KOBAYASHI, T., et al., 1989. Interstitial hyperthermia of experimental brain tumor using implant heating system. *J. Neurooncol.* 7:201–208.

[23] Ameritherm, Inc. 1988. Applications note for Model SP-15 Induction Heater. Scottsville, N. Y.: Ameritherm, Inc.

[24] LAITINEN, L. V., 1985. Brain targets in surgery for Parkinson's disease. *J. Neurosurg.* 62(3):349–351.

[25] DEMBITZER, F. R. et al., Glioblastoma following stereotaxic implantation of autologous adrenal medulla for young-onset familial Parkinsonism: An autopsy case. *J. Neuropathol. Exp. Neurol.* 49:346.

[26] HOWARD, M. A., R. C. RITTER, and M. S. GRADY, 1989. Video tumor-fighting system. U.S. Patent no. 4,869,247.

[27] WIKA, K. G., et al., 1991. A user interface and control algorithm for the video tumor fighter. (University of Virginia tech. rep. no. UVA/640419/NEEP91/112).

[28] LAWSON, M. A., et al., 1991. Near real time Biplanar fluoroscopic tracking system for the video tumor fighter. In *Proceedings of the Institute of Photo-Optical Instrumentation Engineers* 1445:265–275.

[29] GRADY, M. S., M. A. HOWARD, J. A. MOLLOY, R. C. RITTER, E. G. QUATE, and G. T. GILLIES, 1989. Preliminary experimental investigation of in vivo magnetic manipulation: Results and potential application in hyperthermia. *Med. Phys.* 16(2):263–272.

[30] QUATE, E. G., et al., 1991. Goniometric motion controller for the superconducting coil in a magnetic stereotaxis system. *IEEE Trans. Biomed. Eng.* 38(9):899–905.

Orthopaedics

THE CHAPTERS IN this section focus primarily on systems that enable orthopaedic surgeons to carry out accurately surgical procedures planned from preoperative images. As we shall see, the relatively good contrast for bone in radiographic images, together with the relative rigidity and macroscopic nature of the skeletal system, makes orthopaedics a natural application domain for the development of computer-assisted or robotically enhanced surgical methods.

The first chapter, "Computer- and Robot-Assisted Orthopaedic Surgery," by Stulberg and Kienzle, introduces orthopaedic surgery and discusses requirements and opportunities for the robotic systems in orthopaedics. The authors define five key requirements for robotic surgical devices: (1) safety, (2) accuracy, (3) sterility, (4) general integration into the operating room, and (5) provision of measurable benefits to the surgeon and patient, such as reduced time required in the operating room and reduced trauma to the patient. To this last requirement one might add improved clinical results (often derived from better accuracy) and reduced complication rates resulting from the greater consistency of robotic (as compared to human) execution of precise tasks. For orthopaedic procedures involving bones, the authors further identify as crucial the ability of the system to register preoperative skeletal models with the actual bones in the operating room, to maintain this relationship once it is established, and to maintain accuracy in the presence of high reaction forces when cutting bone.

The authors classify robotic surgical systems along two axes: active versus passive, and positioning versus machining. They give as examples two systems—the Robodoc system (chapters 28 and 29) for hip surgery and the Northwestern knee replacement system (chapter 30)—that are described at length in this section. They then identify a number of other surgical procedures, including long bone osteotomies, spine surgery, and ligament reconstructions, that seem to be natural application areas for robotically assisted surgery. Finally, they discuss the advantages of computer and robotically assisted surgery. In addition to such obvious and direct benefits as improved surgical planning, greater accuracy in execution, potentially shorter duration of surgery, and lower complication rates, the authors make the very interesting point that the ability of clinical researchers to do well-controlled prospective studies will be greatly enhanced. By reducing random variability in surgical execution, these technologies will enable researchers to identify and isolate key factors affecting clinical outcomes and to incorporate the lessons learned into future computer-integrated surgical systems.

The next two chapters, "An Image-Directed Robotic System for Precise Orthopaedic Surgery," by Taylor et al., and "The Evolution of a Surgical Robot from Prototype to Human Clinical Use," by Mittelstadt et al., describe the initial development and subsequent evolution of an active robotic system, called Robodoc, for total hip replacement surgery. We have deliberately chosen to present these two chapters in order to illustrate the enormous amount of work that is required to progress from concept to prototype and then from prototype to a clinically useful system. Chapter 28 describes the requirements and overall architecture for this application and focuses primarily on the first-generation system that was developed as part of a joint study between IBM and the University of California at Davis. All of the issues identified by Stulberg and Kienzle in their introductory chapter, with the possible exception of shortening the time required for surgery, had to be addressed in this system and are discussed in chapter 28. This first-generation system was used in a veterinary clinical trial on 26 dogs in 1990. Had the project stopped at that point, the results would still have been very interesting and would have been well worth publishing in academic literature. The crucial next step, however, was the establishment of an effort by Integrated Surgical Systems to develop a second-generation system suitable for use on humans. A first clinical trial, involving 10 patients, was performed from November 1992 through February 1993. As this is written, a randomized clinical trial involving 300 patients at five sites is underway.[1] Chapter 29 describes the evolution of this system from a research prototype that functioned in a well-controlled research environment to a medical device that can be operated routinely in a hospital environment without engineering supervision by the system implementors. Anyone thinking this is a trivial task is urged to read the chapter.

The next two chapters, "A Computer-Assisted Total Knee Replacement Surgical System Using a Calibrated Robot," by Kienzle et al., and "Computer-Assisted Knee Arthroplasty," by Marcacci et al., describe robotic systems for assisting in total knee replacement surgery. Unlike Robodoc, the Kienzle system does not work by machining bone. Instead, the robot assists in locating the patient's femur and tibia and then positions a drill guide for the surgeon. The surgeon drills holes that are used to attach guide blocks to the patient's bones. The surgeon then uses the guide blocks to prepare the patient's bones to receive the implant. In contrast, the Marcacci system adopts the Robodoc approach of actively machining bone, although there are a number of differences between the systems, including the relative maturity of the systems. Knee surgery is not necessarily based exclusively on CT images. In an ultimate system, magnetic resonance images might be combined with CT images, gait analysis, and intraoperative force and 3D digitization to develop a complete biomechanical model of the patient. This model may then be used to develop an optimized surgical plan. Further, it is important to realize that many subsets of such an ultimate system are conceivable. For example, recent clinically tested (on 10 patients) work by Orti et al. (1993) uses only data acquired during the intervention with a 3D optical localizer in order to optimize placement of a graft for anterior cruciate ligament reconstruction.

It is interesting to note that both the hip surgery and knee surgery systems described above rely on temporarily implanted fiducial markers for preoperative-to-intraoperative registration. Chapter 33, "Computer-Assisted Spine Surgery Using Anatomy-Based Registration," by Lavallée et al., describes several markerless techniques applied to the problem of vertebra pedicle drilling using a variety of intraoperative sensors. Such registration methods clearly have very broad applicability beyond spine surgery.

The last chapter in this section, "Computer-Integrated Orthopaedic Surgery" by Rhademacher, Rau, and Staudte reviews many of the requirements of computer-assisted orthopaedic surgery and describes the interesting approach taken by the authors to exploit integrated CAD/CAM technology to manufacture custom "templates" that match a patient's bone. The authors go on to describe the first clinical use of their system for a triple osteotomy of a patient's pelvic bone.

NOTE

1. Tragically, Dr. Paul, who was founder and president of ISS, died in February 1993, just as the first clinical trial was ending. Those of us who knew him can attest to his extraordinary drive and vision, which played such an essential role in turning a possibility into a reality.

REFERENCE

ORTI, R., S. LAVALLEE, R. JULLIARD, P. CINQUIN, and E. CARPENTIER, 1993. Computer-assisted, knee ligament reconstruction. In *Proceedings of the IEEE EMBS Conference.* San Diego, November, pp. 936–937.

27 Computer- and Robot-Assisted Orthopaedic Surgery

S. DAVID STULBERG AND THOMAS C. KIENZLE III

ORTHOPAEDICS, the study of diseases of the musculoskeletal system, lends itself well to the application of computers and robotics. Many orthopaedic procedures involve the manipulation or "machining" of bones, the most inherently rigid structures in the human body. The skeletal system can readily be imaged using existing diagnostic techniques, such as CT scanning and MRI, and the data obtained can be converted to accurate computer simulation models. Because of their rigidity, the bones can reliably be immobilized and their location repeatably and consistently correlated to the computer model. Additionally, unlike soft tissues, the bones are able to withstand an applied force (e.g., from attached muscles, or from a drill or saw) without significant deformation. Thus, a computer model can be built that allows meaningful simulation of the natural motions of bones as well as their modification in operative procedures.

Current research in computer-assisted orthopaedic surgery focuses primarily on allowing the surgeon to better perform a difficult or inherently inaccurate aspect of a surgical procedure. To accomplish this, the bones in question are imaged and converted to a computer model (preferably 3D). The model allows the surgeon to view more of the affected area than is possible in the operating room, accomplish accurate preoperative planning, and test alternatives to derive the optimal surgical plan. Many researchers choose to take this one step further by employing a robot in the operating room to implement the results of the computer simulation. The use of a robot generally results in greater precision in implementing the computer-simulated preoperative plan than the surgeon can attain unaided. Because the size of most bones is generally much greater than the inherent error of high-precision imaging and robotic systems (typically less than 1 mm), the level of accuracy is sufficient for most orthopaedic procedures. However, the use of a robot in the operating room is still an emerging technology, and much work remains to be done to ensure that its benefits outweigh its risks.

Requirements

In order for a robot to be used in a computer-simulated orthopaedic procedure, several requirements must be met. The first set of requirements are those that would have to be met for any surgical robotic system:

1. The system must be safe for the patient and the surgeon. Because of the intimate contact required between the robot and the patient and surgeon during the operation, the strategies used in industry of isolating the robot from all human contact cannot be applied. Instead, fail-safe systems must be developed to restrict the robot's movements to only those approved by the surgeon.

2. The robot and imaging system must have sufficient accuracy for the task. Further, the reference frame used by the imaging system to describe the bones must be registered accurately to the reference frame of the robot.

3. The system must be able to be made sterile. Any part of the system that comes into contact with the surgeon, the patient, or the immediate area (the "sterile field") must be either draped or autoclaved.

4. The system must be ergonomically designed and carefully integrated into the operating room environment so that it becomes an easy-to-use tool for the surgeon and not a hindrance.

5. It is desirable that the system assist the surgeon in performing the surgery faster and with fewer and smaller incisions than are required for existing methods.

In addition to the requirements placed on any computer or robotic surgical system, there are further requirements specific to an orthopaedic system:

1. The involved bones must contain landmarks that enable their positions in the operating room to be registered with the computer model. The landmarks may be either natural or artificial (e.g., small pins placed percutaneously in the bone before the procedure).

2. The bones must be rigidly fixed in space from the time the first landmark is located until the last function on the bone is performed. Any motion of the bone during this period will directly induce an inaccuracy in the final result.

3. Since bone is a very hard tissue, special care must be taken to accommodate the large reactive forces present when it is cut or drilled. Otherwise, inaccuracies can be introduced due to the resulting relative motion between the bone and the cutter. A robot with sufficient stiffness must be used or a scheme employed to reduce the reactive forces (e.g., very high speed cutter or fixator between the cutter and bone).

Classification and examples

There are two fundamental ways to classify robot-based orthopaedic surgical systems. The first classification defines the system's interaction with the surgeon and patient and the second, the type of function it is to perform.

The first classification involves *active versus passive systems*. Active or "surgeon-replacing" systems are those in which the robot itself performs the final function, such as machining the bone to accept an implant or drilling screw holes. Passive or "surgeon-assisting" systems utilize the robot as a measuring device or an aid in accurately directing the surgeon. The surgeon, however, remains responsible for the actual resection, drilling, and positioning of the patient's bones and implants. Even a robot that actively moves to new positions can be considered, in this classification, as a passive system as long as it merely directs the surgeon's actions and does not directly operate on the patient. The differentiation between active and passive systems is important because the direct contact between the robot and the patient in an active system greatly increases the importance of safety considerations. On the other hand, a passive system requires further actions from the surgeon to complete the surgical goals—actions that have the potential to introduce inaccuracies in the final result.

The second classification involves *positioning versus machining systems*. Positioning systems are used in applications in which exactly locating a required modification is critical. In a positioning system, the robot might be used to identify the exact location of a resection or a drill hole or to indicate the placement of an implantable device. Machining systems are utilized where precision in preparing a surface with accurate contours or complex geometry is of paramount importance. For example, the robot might shape a cavity or make multiple resections of the bone. The distinction between these two types of systems is important mostly to the engineer, because, aside from the obvious differences in the end-effectors, machining tasks generally require a robot with high relative accuracy whereas positioning tasks need excellent absolute accuracy over a large work space.

An example of a system that falls into the categories of active and performs primarily a machining operation is the Integrated Surgical Systems (ISS) Robodoc system developed for performing total hip replacement (THR) surgery. In THR surgery, the head of the femur is replaced by an implant consisting of a metal ball and stem. The stem fits into a widened canal in the upper end of the femur (figure 27.1). The standard method for preparing the inside of the femur to accept the implant employs a broach (a rasp file shaped like the implant) to shape the femur. The implant is then affixed in the cavity using methylmethacrylate cement. Recently, however, there has been much interest in being able to bond the implant to the bone by direct bone ingrowth onto a coating on the implant. The researchers at ISS claim that by using a robot with a small rotary cutter they can machine the cavity more

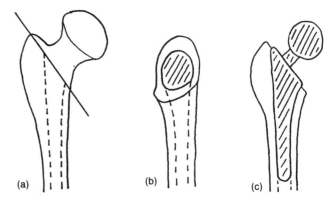

FIGURE 27.1 Total hip replacement. (A) Front view of femur indicating cut to be made (solid line) and cavity to be drilled (dotted lines). (B) Side view after femur is prepared. (C) Front view showing placed implant.

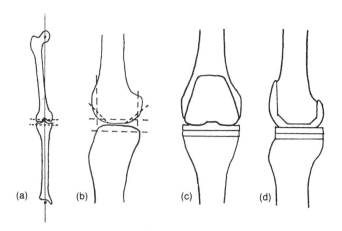

FIGURE 27.2 Total knee replacement. (A) Front view of femur and tibia showing correct alignment. (B) Side view of femoral and tibial cuts to be made. (C, D) Front and side views of prosthetic components in place.

accurately than with a broach and significantly increase the contact area between the implant and the bone. This, they believe, will facilitate the growth of bone onto the surface of the implant, giving a stronger bond and resulting in improved patient comfort and greater implant longevity. Although the positioning of the canal is important, the primary advantage of the ISS system is the accurate preparation of the inner surface of the bone to accept a preselected implant.

An example of a system that is passive and primarily performs positioning operation is the system the authors have been developing for performing total knee replacement (TKR) surgery. In TKR surgery, the articulating surfaces of the knee are replaced by metal and plastic implants (figure 27.2). The successful outcome of TKR surgery depends on the accuracy of implant orientation and on proper leg alignment. Currently, a system of jigs and rods is used by the surgeon to approximate the axis of the leg and to align the prosthetic components accordingly. By using CT-generated 3D models of the bones that provide information about the whole leg, it is easier for the surgeon to determine the optimal placement of the implant. In the operating room, this TKR system uses a robot to indicate to the surgeon where a cutting guide is to be located in order to achieve the correct implant positioning. The system does not actually cut or drill into bone; it leaves that task to the surgeon.

These two examples are illustrative of the more general opportunities for computer and robot assistance in orthopaedic surgical procedures. In essence, any proce-

dure that requires more accurate positioning of screws, holes, or pins in bone, more careful surface preparation of a bone, or more accurate alignment of bones or prosthetic components than is currently possible with standard techniques is a candidate for computer or computer and robotic assistance.

A general model of orthopaedic computer/or robot-assisted surgical systems includes several common aspects. First, such systems require an image acquisition system (a CT scanner, MRI machine, plain-film x-ray, or fluoroscope) to provide data unique to each patient. The acquired imaging data must then be processed by the computer, either in the form of a raw 2D image or as a reconstructed 3D model, to provide data with which the surgeon is able to simulate any surgical procedure desired. The computer can allow the surgeon to simulate the cutting or drilling of the patient's bones. The alignment of bones and the placement of prosthetic components can be simulated as well. The surgical procedure can be performed entirely on the computer, the results viewed, and the effects on the joints modeled. This process of simulated surgery and evaluation may be repeated as many times as necessary until the results are optimal—all before a single incision is made in the patient. Depending on the application, the image acquisition and computer planning steps can be performed in the operating room during surgery or preoperatively. With a robot as part of the system, the solutions found during the computer planning can be implemented directly and accurately during the actual surgery.

Opportunities for application

Numerous opportunities exist in orthopaedics for the application of computer/robotic systems to operative procedures. In addition to assisting first-time joint replacement operations described previously, a computer-robotic system may also be beneficial in repeat joint replacement surgery (revision arthroplasty). Not only can such a system help the surgeon plan the placement of the revision prosthesis; it can also aid the surgeon in the difficult task of identifying and removing the hardened cement left from the original procedure. The envelope of cement can be identified in the CT data, and a robot equipped with a high-speed rotary burr can carefully remove the residual cement.

An osteotomy is a procedure by which a surgeon can correct the alignment of a bone (thereby improving

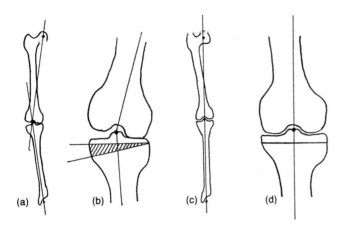

FIGURE 27.3 Tibial osteotomy. (A) Malalignment of femur and tibia. (B) Close-up of joint showing wedge of bone to be removed. (C, D) Postoperatively, alignment has been restored.

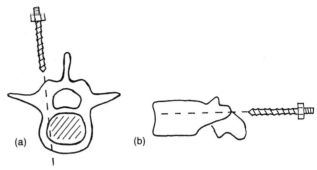

FIGURE 27.4 Pedicle screw placement. (A) Top view of a lumbar vertebra showing screw and trajectory (dotted line) through the pedicle (arrow). (B) Side view.

limb function) by cutting it and allowing it to reheal in a new position. For example, if the femur and tibia are sufficiently malaligned, either naturally or from previous trauma, the knee joint may be caused to wear unevenly. If this is recognized before the damage to the articular surfaces is too severe, a realignment of the bones that shifts the weight toward intact cartilage may be curative or at least delay the inevitable knee replacement surgery. To perform a high tibial osteotomy, the surgeon makes carefully planned cuts near the top of the tibia (usually removing a small wedge of bone) and then rejoins the two pieces of bone. The tibia is allowed to heal in its new alignment, changing the angulation of its top articular surface, and thus the dynamics of the knee (figure 27.3). A computer can be of obvious help in this process, by permitting more exact preoperative planning of the realignment and by facilitating the identification of the cutting planes by a robot in the operating room.

Another application that could benefit from the use of a high-accuracy robot is the placement of screws in the vertebrae of patients undergoing spinal fusion surgery. These screws are rigidly connected to a metal plate that serves to immobilize the involved vertebrae with respect to one another, thus allowing the surgeon to straighten a curved spine or to reinforce an unstable spine. The difficulty in such surgery is that the screw must be passed down the long axis of a thin cylinder of vertebral bone (the pedicle) with sufficient accuracy to prevent its protrusion out of its side (figure 27.4). Any mistake can threaten the integrity of a nearby nerve

root or even the spinal cord itself. Careful preoperative or intraoperative radiographic analysis can permit the surgeon to identify an acceptable trajectory for the screw. By using a computer to specify this trajectory, and a robot to aid in implementing it, the surgeon can more safely and securely introduce screws into this delicate area of the anatomy.

In anterior cruciate ligament (ACL) reconstruction surgery, a graft ligament, usually obtained from the patient's own patellar tendon, is inserted and affixed between carefully placed holes in the tibia and femur. The accurate placement of these holes determines the success of the restoration of function and the longevity of the repair. Currently, the operation is performed with the aid of an arthroscope that allows the surgeon to monitor the inside of the joint capsule as one hole is drilled in through the front of the tibia and another hole is drilled out through the side of the femur (figure 27.5). Ideally, the replacement ligament would pass through the original ACL's attachment sites. However, given the constraints of an arthroscopic procedure, these sites can be hard to identify and difficult to direct a drill through. The accuracy of the placement of these holes could be improved with preoperative planning performed on a computer using CT or MRI data and the correct knee kinematics verified with a software simulation. A robot could accurately indicate the precise location and orientation of the necessary holes in the operating room.

There are several other areas in orthopaedics that may benefit from the use of computer planning and robotic implementation. Joint replacement surgeries other than of the hip and knee may benefit from approaches similar to the THR and TKR systems described previously. In surgeries to correct scoliosis

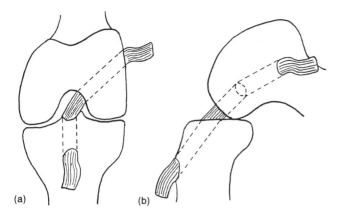

FIGURE 27.5 Anterior cruciate ligament replacement. (A) Front view of knee showing ligament graft passing through the front of the tibia, into the center of the joint, then out the side of the femur. (B) Side view.

(curvature of the spine), the final alignment of the vertebrae might be modeled before the spine is permanently fused. For difficult fractures, as for osteotomies, the final bone reconstruction and alignment might be modeled and the placement of the bony segments determined preoperatively. Limb-lengthening procedures may also benefit from computer modeling that aids the surgeon in calculating the required adjustments of the external fixator. In the future, robots might also aid the surgeon in performing microsurgery or in operating at remote or dangerous sites.

Orthopaedic computer-robotic systems could have future soft-tissue applications as well. In addition to ACL reconstructions, such a system could model and help implement the proper placement of grafts in other ligament reconstructions, ligament releases, and tendon transfers. A computer-robotic system might also aid in arthroscopic or percutaneous (through the skin) procedures by directing surgical instruments and by correlating preoperative 3D images to the area of interest during surgery.

Advantages

The advantages of computer- and robot-assisted surgical systems are numerous. Many of the procedures that will benefit greatly from computer assistance are those in which accuracy would be improved if the surgeon were able to view more of the involved bone than can be seen through the standard incision. In the ISS THR system, the CT model allows the surgeon to visualize

the inside of the femoral canal; in the authors' TKR system the surgeon benefits from being able to plan implant alignment with a model of the entire leg rather than trying to infer its structure from what is visible through a limited incision.

Another benefit previously mentioned is the flexibility inherent in simulating procedures on the computer. Not only can the procedure be repeatedly simulated until the surgeon is satisfied that the outcome will be optimal, but a computer simulation also is capable of allowing the surgeon to perform functions that are impractical if not impossible in the operating room. For example, by using a computer simulation, the surgeon could use contour-matching algorithms to approximate the original articular surfaces of a patient's joint and recreate them by accurately placing a prosthetic component. In the case of the TKR system, the computer allows representations of the prosthetic components to be superimposed over the model of the patient's bones. This allows the surgeon to match the implant closely with the natural knee (if appropriate) and simultaneously to achieve the correct alignment of the mechanical axis of the leg.

Ultimately, the preoperative planning step (which typically involves alignment of bones or placement of an implant based on bony landmarks) can be coupled with modeling of postoperative limb function. Models exist that can describe the effect on muscles and tendons resulting from any modification made to the bones and joints. Finite-element analysis can model the forces generated on natural and prosthetic articular surfaces. These simulations can ultimately be correlated with real and computer-modeled gait analysis and patient perception of the surgical outcome.

There are also some benefits that are not as immediately obvious. One advantage is a greatly increased ability to do prospective studies. With a computer system, the researcher or surgeon can control, or at least know, the exact positions of repaired bones and prosthetic devices. Even positioning that was previously unmeasurable or unknown can now be accounted for. For example, the placement of the tibial component in TKR surgery currently is determined partly by the surgeon "eyeballing" its location on the end of the resected tibia. Using a computer model, this placement could be more precisely related to identifiable bony landmarks (such as the intercondylar tubercles) that are removed when the top of the tibia is resected in preparation for the implant. New information regarding the surgical procedure can then be correlated with the patient's postoperative results to yield meaningful advances in clinical orthopaedic research. Further, once improvements in surgical procedure are identified, new releases of software can reflect these improvements and be of benefit not only to the most expert of surgeons but to all surgeons who employ the computer-robotic system. As new algorithms and systems for surgical procedures are developed, they can be readily demonstrated and taught to other surgeons using the computer to simulate the functional aspects of the surgery.

As the systems become more refined and ergonomic, other important benefits will be realized. As computer-simulated preoperative planning and robotic implementation are improved, the actual time a patient spends in the operating room will be reduced. This means not only a decrease in the cost of surgery but also a reduction in time the incision is open to contamination by infectious agents. Also, as the need to view the involved bones directly is lessened by presurgical imaging and computer modeling, the size of the incision can be decreased. The smaller incision will also decrease the possibility of infection and will allow for more rapid patient recovery and a smaller scar.

Because of the rigid and macroscopic nature of bones, the field of orthopaedics will see much of the early work with computers and robots in surgery. Despite the anticipated initial resistance to this new technology, it is easy to imagine a day when the use of a computer workstation is standard presurgical protocol and a surgical robot is a standard fixture in the orthopaedic operating suite. As these systems see increasing use in operating rooms, surgeons will begin to appreciate them for what they are: another useful tool at the surgeon's disposal.

28 An Image-Directed Robotic System for Precise Orthopaedic Surgery

RUSSELL H. TAYLOR, BRENT D. MITTELSTADT,
HOWARD A. PAUL, WILLIAM HANSON, PETER KAZANZIDES,
JOEL F. ZUHARS, BILL WILLIAMSON, BELA L. MUSITS,
EDWARD GLASSMAN, AND WILLIAM L. BARGAR

Background

AUGMENTATION OF HUMAN SKILL IN SURGERY

THE RESEARCH reported in this chapter represents a step in an evolving partnership between humans (surgeons) and machines (computers and robots) that seeks to exploit the capabilities of both to do a task *better* than either can do it alone. Recent advances in medical imaging technology (CT, MRI, etc.), coupled with advances in computer-based image processing and modeling capabilities, have given physicians an unprecedented ability to model and visualize anatomic structures in live patients and to use this information quantitatively in diagnosis and treatment planning. Further, advances in CAD/CAM technology have made it practical to use this data to design and precisely fabricate custom surgical implants for individual patients. One result is that the precision of image-based presurgical planning often greatly exceeds the precision of surgical execution. Typically, geometrically precise surgery has been limited to procedures (such as brain biopsies) for which a suitable stereotactic frame is available. The inconvenience and restricted applicability of these devices has led many researchers to explore the use of robotic devices to augment a surgeon's ability to perform geometrically precise tasks planned from CT or other image data.

The pioneering work in the use of general-purpose robots for surgery was that of Kwoh et al. [1] who used a six-axis industrial robot to replace a stereotactic frame in neurosurgery. In this case, the robot was mounted in a known position relative to the table of a CT scanner, and suitable geometric calibrations were performed. During surgery, the patient was scanned by CT and a desired placement for a biopsy needle probe was determined from the image data. The robot then positioned a passive needle guide appropriately, brakes were applied, and power was turned off. Finally, the surgeon inserted the needle through the guide into the patient's brain. The principal benefit gained was the greater convenience and faster positioning possible with the robot compared to the use of a stereotactic frame. A number of similar systems have been developed subsequently. The most successful to date is that of Lavallée et al. [2, 3], who used a stereopair of intraoperative radiographs to register the robot to the patient's CT data (and to the patient) and to plan needle paths that avoid blood vessels. More then 300 cases have been performed, although (again) the robot is turned off while the needle is inserted. Kelly et al. [4, 5] have implemented a specialized motorized stereotactic system for laser neurosurgery, in which an xyz table is used to reposition the patient's head relative to the focal point of a surgical microscope. More recently, Drake et al. [6] have reported several cases in which a general-purpose robot moved while in contact with the patient, although the motions were very simple and highly constrained. Further, these cases were performed on an exception basis, in which the surgeon had no practical alternative, so they involved somewhat more limited safety checking than would have been desirable for more routine use. Several other neurosurgery robots are in various stages of development (e.g., [7]).

A number of active robotic systems for augmentation of nonneurosurgical procedures have also been proposed or developed. For example, Davies et al. [8]

This paper is adapted from one published in the *IEEE Transactions on Robotics and Automation*, 10(3):261–275.

have developed a specialized robotic device to assist in laparoscopic prostatectomies, which has been used clinically. A number of groups (e.g., [9–12]) have developed a variety of other telerobotic devices for endoscopic and laparoscopic surgery. McEwen et al. [13] have developed and marketed a clinically qualified voice-controlled limb-positioning system for orthopaedics. Several groups (e.g., [14, 15]) have demonstrated in vitro robotic systems for positioning passive instrument guides for knee replacement surgery [14]. Of these applications, that of Davies comes closest to ours in the sense that it uses an active automatic device to perform a tissue removal operation. Important differences include an order-of-magnitude difference in the accuracy required for the application, the greater complexity of the shapes to be cut, the use of a general-purpose manipulator rather than a specialized device, and the greater degree of safety and consistency checking built into our system, which must move safely in a much less constrained volume.

PRECISE ORTHOPAEDIC SURGERY

Orthopaedic applications represent a particularly promising domain for the integration of image- and model-based presurgical planning, CAD/CAM technology, and precise robotic execution. For example, nearly half of the 300,000 total hip replacement operations performed each year use cementless implants. In these procedures, accurate preparation of the femoral cavity to match the implant shape, and accurate placement of the cavity relative to the femur, can significantly affect stress transfer, implant stability, and restoration of proper biomechanics, which in turn are important factors affecting efficacy. For example, Sandborn et al. [16] have reported that the size of gaps between bone and implant significantly affects bone ingrowth. Furthermore, the present manual broaching method for preparing the femoral cavity leaves considerable room for improvement. (Figure 28.1 shows a typical cementless implant and the corresponding broach used to make the hole for it. Figure 28.2 shows the use of a broach on a human patient. The procedure in a dog is essentially the same.) In one recent study, Paul et al. [17] found that only approximately 20% of the implant actually touches bone when it is inserted into a manually broached hole. The average gap between the implant and the bone was commonly 1–4 mm, and the overall hole size was 36% larger than

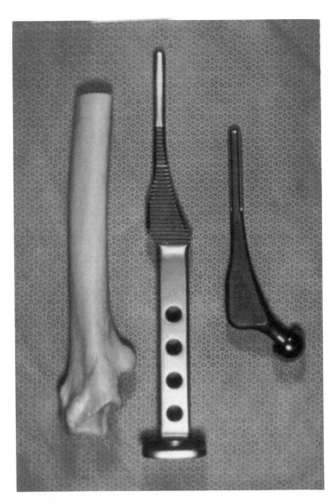

FIGURE 28.1 Typical cementless hip implant and instrumentation. A typical cementless hip implant. together with the broach used produce a corresponding hole in the patient's thigh in conventional manual surgery. Proper placement of the implant socket relative to the femur and accurate reproduction of the socket shape are very important to assure implant stability, uniform stress transfer, and restoration of the proper biomechanics.

the broach. Furthermore, the exact placement of the implant cavity relative to the bone (which affects restoration of biomechanics) depends on the surgeon's ability to line up the broach manually and to drive it the right distance into the femur. Driving the broach too far can split the femur. These considerations have led us to explore the use of robotic machining to prepare the femoral cavity for the implant. Initial feasibility studies by Paul et al. [18] demonstrated that a robot could successfully machine shapes in human cadaver bones and that preoperatively implanted calibration pins could be used to accurately register CT image and robot coordinates for a femur.

FIGURE 28.2 Manual broaching procedure. The use of a broach in a human cementless hip replacement. The procedure in a dog is essentially the same. One recent study [17] found that only approximately 20% of the implant actually touches bone when it is inserted into a manually broached hole. The average gap between the implant and the bone was commonly 1–4 mm, and the overall hole size was 36% larger than the broach.

Following those studies, we developed a complete planning and execution system suitable for use in an actual operating room. In vitro experiments with this first-generation system demonstrated an order-of-magnitude improvement in surgical precision, compared to manual broaching. One of the authors (Dr. Paul) conducted a veterinary clinical trial on dogs needing hip replacement surgery. This experience provided the basis for development of a second-generation system that is now in human clinical trials [19–21] (see also chapter 29).

Subsequent sections of this chapter will summarize the presurgical planning and surgical procedure followed for robotic hip replacement surgery and will discuss the requirements for robotic systems intended to augment human precision in surgery. After providing a brief overview of the system architecture, we will provide a fuller discussion of several key aspects of the system, including the image-based presurgical planning, geometric calibration, shape cutting, and safety checking mechanisms. Finally, we will discuss experience of the system in actual clinical use (on dogs) and some of the lessons learned.

Summary of procedure

Before surgery, three titanium pins are implanted through small skin incisions into the greater trochanter and condyles of the patient's femur. A CT scan is made of the leg. The presurgical planning system automatically locates the pins relative to the coordinate system of the CT images. The surgeon interactively selects an implant model and determines its desired placement relative to CT coordinates. This information is written to a diskette for use in surgery.

Key steps of the intraoperative procedure are shown in figure 28.3 for an in vitro test on a cadaver femur. Figure 28.4 shows the operating room scene during the first canine clinical trial in May 1990. Briefly, the procedure is as follows:

1. The robot is brought into the operating room and powered up. A sterile cutting tool is attached to a tool interface just below the force sensor, and the robot is covered with a sterile drape. The patient data diskette is loaded into the robot controller, and the robot is placed in a standby mode.

2. The patient is prepared and draped in the normal manner. Surgery proceeds normally until the acetabular component of the implant is implanted and the ball of the femur is removed.

3. The robot is brought up to the operating table, and the femur is rigidly attached to the robot base, using a specially designed fixator. The three titanium pins are exposed manually.

4. A ball probe "cutter bit" is inserted into the collet of the cutting tool. The top center of each pin is then located by a combination of manual guiding and autonomous tactile search by the robot. Although several modes of manual guiding are available, the most commonly used is force compliance. The surgeon simply pulls on the shaft of the cutter; the robot controller

(a)　　　　　(b)　　　　　(c)

(d)　　　　　(e)　　　　　(f)

FIGURE 28.3 Surgical procedure for hip surgery. (A) Fixated cadaver bone. (B) Manual guiding to approximate pin position. (C) Tactile search for a pin. (D) Cutting the shape. (E) On-line display. (h) Final result trial.

senses the forces exerted on the tool and moves the robot in the indicated direction.

5. The robot controller uses the pin location information to compute an appropriate transformation from CT coordinates to robot coordinates. The ball

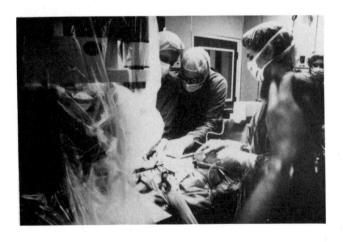

FIGURE 28.4 Operating room scene from first canine clinical trial in May 1990. The surgeon is Dr. Paul. The patient was a family pet needing hip replacement surgery.

probe is replaced by a standard cutting bit, and the robot cuts out the desired implant shape at the planned position and orientation relative to the pins. The surgeon monitors progress both by direct observation of the robot and patient and by looking at a graphic display depicting successive cuts.

6. When cutting is complete, the femur is unclamped from the fixator, and the robot is moved out of the way. The rest of the procedure proceeds in the normal way, with the added step of removing the locator pins from the patient.

Requirements and issues

HUMAN-MACHINE INTERACTION IN A SURGICAL SITUATION

Our goal is not to replace the surgeon. Instead, we are concerned with developing a surgical tool that can assist the surgeon by precisely executing a tissue removal task under the surgeon's supervision. Although the robot's geometric accuracy is much greater than the surgeon's, the surgeon's understanding of the total situation is clearly much greater than any computer's, and he or she is responsible for what goes on in the operating room. Suitable interfaces must be provided to allow the surgeon to monitor the robot's actions, pause execution at any time, initiate error recovery actions, and provide positional guidance to the robot. There is also the related problem of human-computer interaction in presurgical planning. Convenient and naturally understood interfaces must be provided to allow the surgeon to specify what implant shape is to be cut and where it is to go. Furthermore, the interfaces used intraoperatively to report progress of the surgery should be as consistent as possible with those used to plan it.

REGISTRATION OF PLAN DATA WITH INTRAOPERATIVE REALITY

The surgical plan is based on anatomic information derived from CT images taken prior to surgery. Reliable and accurate methods to locate the corresponding anatomic structures relative to the robot are essential if the plan is to be executed successfully.

VERIFICATION

It is very important to verify that the greater potential geometric accuracy offered by the use of a robotic surgical system is in fact achieved in practical use. Suitable methods must be developed for verifying the performance of individual system components and of the system as a whole.

OPERATING ROOM COMPATIBILITY AND STERILITY

It must be easy to incorporate the robot into a hospital's normal routine. It may be difficult for a hospital to dedicate an operating room to robotic surgery, and even if it does so, it is important that maintenance not be disruptive. These considerations led us to rule out some configurations (such as a Cartesian manipulator) suspended from the ceiling, that might otherwise have been attractive. Generally, the system should be easily brought into the operating room and set up as part of the normal presurgical routine. Similarly, removal, sterilization, and reattachment of the end-effector and other critical components should be easy, and suitable sterile drapes must be developed for the manipulator arm and other structural components that cannot be easily sterilized.

SAFETY, ERROR RECOVERY, AND BACKUP

Clearly, redundant safety mechanisms are very important for the protection of both the patient and the surgeon. Manual pause and emergency power-off functions are essential. Wherever possible, potential error conditions must be anticipated and checked for, and adequate recovery procedures must be available. Although the robot often may be able to continue with the procedure following a pause, it is also prudent to provide a reliable means of stopping the robot, removing it from the surgical field, and continuing the operation with manual backup. Because the surgeon must rely on the precision of the robot, it is extremely important that no single failure cause an undetected loss of accuracy. The system must monitor the position of the robot's cutting tool relative to the shape that it is supposed to cut and stop cutting if it strays out of the desired volume for any reason. It is especially important that systematic shifts (such as might arise from the bone slipping relative to the fixator) be detected promptly. A single misplaced cut can usually be repaired, but it may be much harder to correct for misplacing the entire cavity.

System architecture

The system (figure 28.5) consists of a presurgical planning component and an intraoperative (surgical) component. These components are summarized below and discussed at greater length in subsequent sections.

PRESURGICAL PLANNING

The presurgical planning component [22] permits the surgeon to select an implant model and size and to

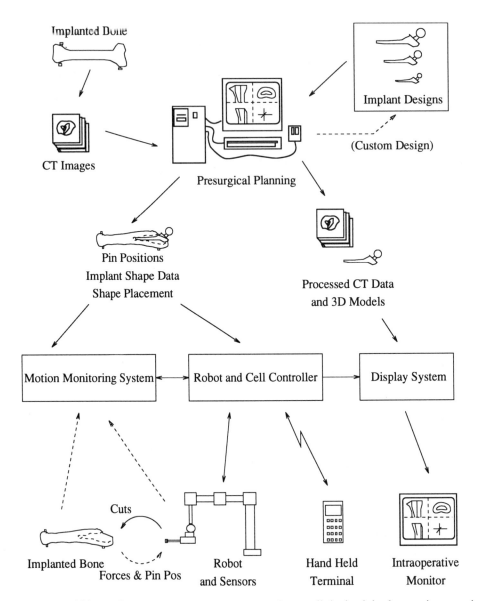

FIGURE 28.5   Architecture of hip replacement surgery system. The system consists of a presurgical planning component and a surgical component. In the system used for the veterinary clinical trial, the motion monitoring and robot control functions are subsumed within the robot controller.

specify where the corresponding shape is to be machined in the patient's femur. The system maintains a library of computer-aided design (CAD) models of implant designs and accepts CT data for individual patients. It automatically determines the CT coordinates of the preoperatively implanted locator pins and provides a variety of interactive graphics tools for the surgeon to examine the CT data, to select an appropriate model and size from the implant design library, and to manipulate the position and orientation of the selected implant shape relative to CT coordinates. The output consists of files containing (1) patient identification data, (2) the position of the locator pins relative to CT coordinates, (3) the implant specification, (4) the desired implant placement relative to CT coordinates, and (5) processed image and model data that will be used for a real-time animation of the progress of the surgery.

OPERATING ROOM SYSTEM

The operating room system (illustrated in figure 28.6) consists of several components. The five-axis *robot* is an IBM 7576 SCARA manipulator with an added pitch

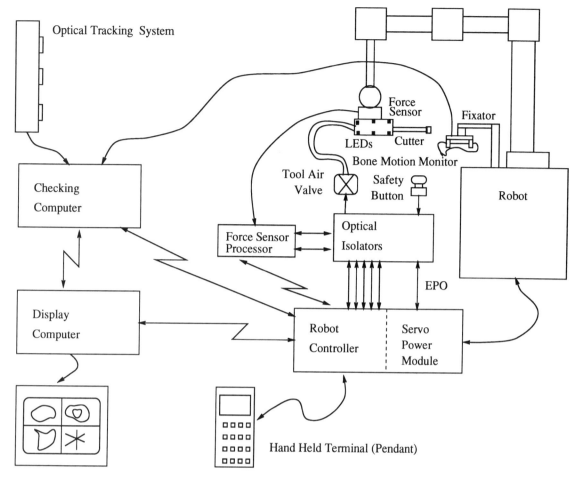

FIGURE 28.6 Operating room system architecture. The operating room system consists of (1) a surgical robot with its associated controller, tooling, and safety interlocks; (2) a fixator to hold the bone securely to the robot; (3) a redundant motion monitoring subsystem consisting of a checking computer, optical tracking system, and bone motion detector; and (4) a human-machine interface with an on-line display, display computer, and a hand-held terminal interfaced to the robot controller.

axis, a 6-degree-of-freedom force sensor, and a standard high-speed surgical cutting tool. During surgery, all but the robot's cutting tool is covered by a sterile drape; the cutting tool is sterilized separately. A sterile *fixator* rigidly attached to the robot's base holds the bone during the robotic part of the procedure. The robot controller provides servocontrol, low-level monitoring, sensor interfaces, and higher-level application functions implemented in the AML/2 language. During surgery, the force sensor is used to support redundant safety checking, tactile search to find the locator pins, and compliant motion guiding by the surgeon.

The *redundant motion monitoring subsystem* [23] relies on independent sensing to track the position and orientation of the robot end-effector during the cutting phase of the surgery, and checks to verify that the cutter tip

never strays more than a prespecified amount outside of the defined implant volume. It also monitors strain gauges, which can detect possible shifts of the bone relative to the fixation device. If either condition is detected, a "freeze motion" signal is sent to the robot controller. After motion is stopped, an application code in the robot controller queries the motion monitoring system for more information and then enters an appropriate error recovery procedure under the surgeon's supervision.

The *human-machine interface* includes an *on-line display system* that combines data generated in presurgical planning with data transmitted from the robot controller to show the progress of the cutting procedure superimposed on the CT-derived image views used in planning. A gas-sterilized *hand-held terminal* allows the surgeon to interact with the system during the course of the operation. This terminal supports manual guiding, motion enable, emergency power on/off, and menu selection functions. It may also be used to pace transitions from one major application step to the next and to select appropriate preprogrammed error recovery procedures should the need arise. Each of the major control components (robot control and motion checker) is able to freeze all robot motion or to turn off manipulator and cutter power in response to recognized exception conditions. If this happens, the surgeon must explicitly reenable motion from the handheld terminal.

Presurgical planning system

INPUT PROCESSING

One mundane but nevertheless essential task is to load the image data into the computer. The CT scanner used for the veterinary clinical trial of this system produced images on magnetic tape in GE 9800 format. The voxel size for typical scans was $0.39 \times 0.39 \times 1.5$ mm thick. Multiple cross-sectional images spaced 3 mm apart were taken throughout the proximal femur. In the vicinity of the locator pins, the images were spaced only 1.5 mm apart (i.e., they were contiguous). The input software includes facilities for tape reading, previewing image slices, selecting a region of interest to reduce the size of data sets, maintaining patient information, and other functions.

PIN LOCATION ALGORITHMS

A key problem [22, 24] is determining the location of the top center point of each locator pin relative to CT coordinates. This is by no means trivial. Although the density of the pins is much higher than that of bone, simple segmentation based on thresholding is complicated by "blooming" and other artifacts associated with the image formation process, so that the images are rather noisy. In particular, edge information is very unreliable.[1] The pins are not nicely aligned with the CT slices, and the CT voxels are not cubes. Even in the absence of noise, CT cross-sections that pass through the screw threads, hexagonal drive hole, and the pin head and shaft can produce images that are rather difficult to analyze. To overcome these problems, a robust three-phase method has been developed. In the first phase, simple density thresholding is used to dis-

tinguish the metallic "pin" voxels from surrounding "tissue" voxels. Unfortunately, blooming causes many "tissue" voxels to be mislabeled "pin," giving the pins a ragged, starburst appearance. These artifacts are cleaned up by first dilating and then eroding the binary thresholded image with standard 3D morphology filters, using spherical structural elements. This process also smooths out the screw threads and fills in the drive socket of the pin image. In the next phase, the approximate position and orientation of the pin are determined by calculating the first and second moments of the binary pin image

$$\mathbf{m}_1 = \frac{\sum_j \mathbf{p}_j}{\sum_j 1}$$

and

$$\mathbf{M}_2 = \frac{\sum_j (\mathbf{p}_j - \mathbf{m}_1)(\mathbf{p}_j - \mathbf{m}_1)^T}{\sum_j 1}$$

where the $\mathbf{p}_j$ are the coordinates of all voxels j classified "pin." Because the pin is cylindrically symmetric, two of the eigenvectors of $\mathbf{M}_2$ will be practically equal. The other eigenvector, $\mathbf{a}$, represents the principal axis of the pin.[2] In the third phase, a cross-sectional volume profile $h(d)$ is computed as a function of the distance d along the axis $\mathbf{m}_1 + d\mathbf{a}$ (figure 28.7). The intercept d_0 of the "leading edge" of the pin profile is computed, and the top center point p_{tc} of the pin then is readily computed thus:

$$\mathbf{p}_{\text{tc}} = \mathbf{m}_1 + d_0 \mathbf{a}$$

INTERACTIVE DOCKING SUBSYSTEM

The interactive docking subsystem integrates 3D image display and computer graphics techniques to support positioning of a 3D CAD model of the desired prosthesis shape relative to the CT image of the patient's anatomy. Because 3D perspective projections inherently distort distance and shape, we chose to use orthogonal 2D cross-sections to represent the 3D information. The interactive display screen is shown in figure 28.8. Three orthogonal sections through the CT data set representing the bone are shown, together with a simple graphic view showing the location of the three cutting planes relative to the data set. Standard resampling techniques are used to generate undistorted cross-sectional images, which may be displayed in one

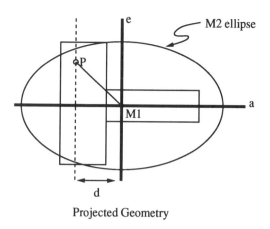

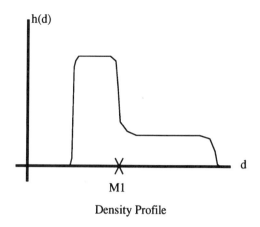

Projected Geometry   Density Profile

FIGURE 28.7   Projected pin profile.

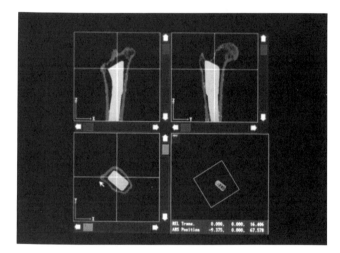

FIGURE 28.8   Presurgical planning display.

of three modes. *Gray-scale* mode simply displays the CT densities of each (resampled) voxel. *Color-map* mode uses different hues (red, blue, etc.) to represent different tissue classes (cortical bone, trabecular bone, etc.), which are presently computed by relatively simple intensity thresholding techniques.[3] *Surface contour* mode shows a graphic representation of boundaries between tissue types. This graphic data can be manipulated quickly and is very useful when the surgeon is identifying the desired cross-sectional views through the CT data,

In use, the surgeon typically selects boundary mode and uses the mouse to position and orient the cutting planes relative to the CT data. The surgeon then selects either gray-scale or color-map mode. Again using the mouse, the surgeon selects the desired implant model from a library of available designs, then manipulates

the position and orientation of the implant relative to the CT coordinate system. As this is done, the computer automatically generates the cross-sections corresponding to the selected orthogonal cross-sections and displays them superimposed on the corresponding 2D images. All manipulations, whether of the implant or of the cross-sectional CT views are specified relative to one of the three 2D views. Thus, complex 6D reorientations are accomplished by breaking them down into a sequence of simpler transformations. When the surgeon is satisfied, the coordinates of each locator pin, the implant specification, and the desired implant position and orientation relative to CT coordinates are written to a file.

In the future, we expect that the computer will assist the surgeon by computing and displaying appropriate "goodness-of-fit" measures and eventually by proposing optimized positions and custom implant designs. Even in its present state of development, however, this system has proved to be very effective and easy to use. The 2D cross-sectional displays are intuitively attractive to and easily learned by the orthopaedic surgeons who are the targeted end users. The restriction to one 2D rotation or translation at a time has similarly proved to be inconsequential, because our users tend to think of rotations and translations that are easily perceivable in a single display—namely, the ones that the system allows on a single interaction.

Geometric calibration

Geometric calibration (see, for example, [24–27]) is a crucial component of any practical robotic application, especially one in which geometrically accurate paths are an important factor. This is equally true of surgical applications. At the same time, it is important to define methods that are simple and robust, do not require elaborate equipment, and are appropriate for the accuracies required by the task. In this section, we will describe our approach to the trade-offs involved in meeting these requirements.

FIND PIN ROUTINE

The methods used in the calibration and in the actual surgical execution are very similar to methods earlier used in training a robot to copy pilot hole positions for automatic drilling of aircraft wing panels [28]. A ball probe "cutter" is inserted into the collet of the cutting tool, and the force sensor is used to determine points of contact with the object being located (typically, a cylindric pin). Points of contact are located by moving the ball to the proximity of the surface and then executing a slow, guarded motion in a specified direction. As soon as the force exceeds a specified threshold, the motion is stopped. Since there may be an unpredictable amount of overshoot, a sequence of very small steps x_i then are taken in the reverse direction, and the forces f_i along the motion direction are measured at each point. The apparent compliance is estimated by a straight-line approximation:

$$f_i = K(x_i - x_0)$$

The point x_0 where the force goes to 0 is assumed to be the contact point. Experience has shown that this method, although somewhat tedious, is in practice very robust. Repeatabilities of the order of 25 μm are routinely obtained. A cylindric object like a pin or cup is then easily located by finding three points on the top surface and three points on the side.

KINEMATIC MODEL

As stated earlier, the robot is a modified SCARA manipulator augmented by an extra "pitch" axis, which (in turn) carries a 6-degree-of-freedom force sensor and a high-speed revolute surgical cutter. The nominal kinematics are given by

$$\mathbf{p}_{tool} = \mathbf{p}_{wrist} + \mathbf{R}(\mathbf{z}, \theta_4)\mathbf{R}(\mathbf{y}, \theta_5)\mathbf{v}_c$$

where $\mathbf{R}(\mathbf{a}, \theta)$ is a rotation by angle θ about axis $\mathbf{a}$, and

$$\mathbf{p}_{wrist} = \mathbf{R}(\mathbf{z}, \theta_1)(l_1\mathbf{x} + \mathbf{R}(\mathbf{z}, \theta_2)l_2\mathbf{x}) + \theta_3\mathbf{z}$$

where l_1 = length of first link, l_2 = length of second link; θ_1 = first joint rotation; θ_2 = second joint rotation, θ_3 = sliding joint displacement; θ_4 = roll joint rotation, θ_5 = pitch joint rotation; and $\mathbf{v}_c$ = cutter displacement vector.

There are, of course, a number of error terms corresponding to link dimensional variations, encoder offsets, and the like. The calibration performed by the robot manufacturer characterizes these values quite well, and the local accuracy of the basic SCARA has proved to be sufficient for our purposes.[4] However, we were somewhat more concerned about the pitch motor and end-effector and therefore decided to develop an additional calibration procedure for these distal parts of the system. The crucial factor is the position of the tool tip, which is given by the following equation:

$$\mathbf{p}_{tool} = \mathbf{p}_{wrist} + \mathbf{R}(\mathbf{z}, \theta_4 + \Delta\theta_4) \cdot (\alpha\mathbf{x} + \mathbf{v}_{distal})$$

where

$$\mathbf{v}_{distal} = \mathbf{R}(\mathbf{x}, \beta) \cdot [\mathbf{R}(\mathbf{y}, \theta_5 + \Delta\theta_5)(\mathbf{v}_c + \Delta\mathbf{v}_c)];$$

$\Delta\theta_4$ = rotational misalignment of joint 4 with joint 5; α = displacement of pitch axis from roll axis; β = pitch axis tilt error term; $\Delta\theta_5$ = combined pitch offset and shaft alignment error; and $\Delta\mathbf{v}_c$ = cutter shaft displacement vector uncertainty.

Tool orientation is relatively less important, and no special efforts were required to calibrate it, aside from determining the angular offsets $\Delta\theta_4$ and $\Delta\theta_5$.

PARAMETER ESTIMATION

Our present calibration method uses a single vertical post rigidly mounted to robot's base. Essentially, the calibration works by repeatedly executing the "find pin" routine to measure the apparent position of the post for a number of different roll and pitch orientations. Because the post does not move, the post location and the unknown kinematic parameters $\alpha, \beta, \Delta\theta_4, \Delta\theta_5$, and $\Delta_{\mathbf{vc}}$ may be found by least-squares regression on the following linearized relation:

$$\begin{aligned}\mathbf{p}_{post} \cong \mathbf{p}_{wrist} &+ [\mathbf{R}_4 \cdot \mathbf{R}_5 \cdot (\mathbf{v}_c + \Delta\mathbf{v}_c)] \\ &+ [\beta\mathbf{R}_4 \cdot (\mathbf{x} \times \mathbf{R}_5 \cdot \mathbf{v}_c)] + [\Delta\theta_4\mathbf{R}_4 \cdot (\mathbf{z} \times \mathbf{R}_5 \cdot \mathbf{v}_c)] \\ &+ \Delta\theta_5[\mathbf{y} \times (\mathbf{R}_4 \cdot \mathbf{R}_5 \cdot \mathbf{v}_c)] + \alpha\mathbf{R}_4\mathbf{x}\end{aligned}$$

where $\mathbf{R}_4 = \mathbf{R}(\mathbf{z}, \theta_4)$ and $\mathbf{R}_5 = \mathbf{R}(\mathbf{y}, \theta_5)$.

Our experience with this calibration procedure has been good. A typical calibration run consisted of 28

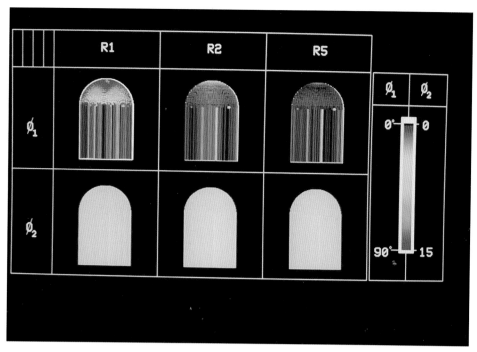

PLATE 1   Disparity images corresponding to the first view in figure 3.6 for methods (a) R1, (b) R2, and (e) R5, with disparity in ϕ_1 shown at the top and in ϕ_2 at the bottom. (See chapter 3.)

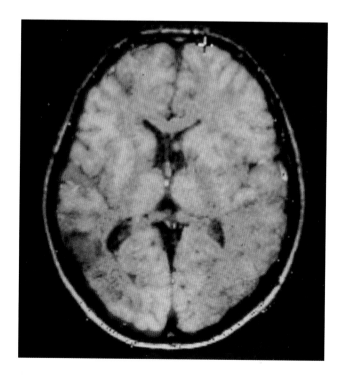

PLATE 2   Merged MRI/PET (FDG) for bilateral occipital ischemia. The bilateral hypometabolism shown by PET is only evident on the MRI scan as a unilateral lesion. (Reprinted with permission from Evans et al., 1992b.) (See chapter 6.)

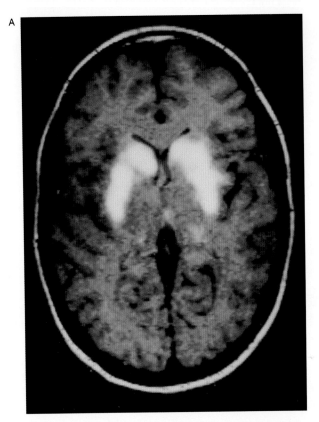

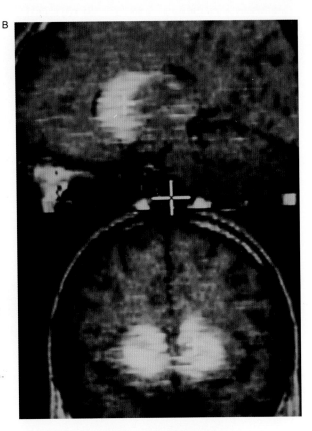

PLATE 3 MRI/PET merged images showing ^{18}F-labeled fluoroDOPA in normal brain. (Reprinted with permission from Evans et al., 1992b.) (See chapter 6.)

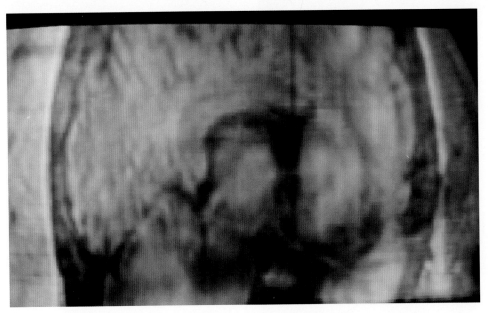

PLATE 4 Merged MRI/PET data set using 3D volume rendering for each data set before opacity-weighted compositing. A 3D sector was first removed before rendering. The PET data show glucose metabolism from an FDG scan. (Reprinted with permission from Evans et al., 19912a.) (See chapter 6.)

A

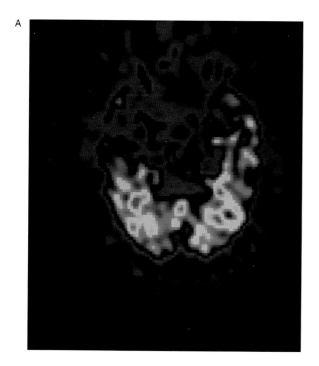

B

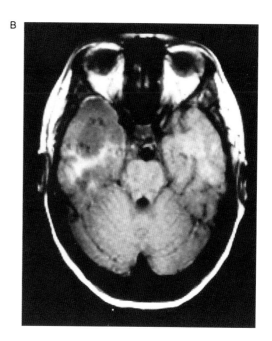

C

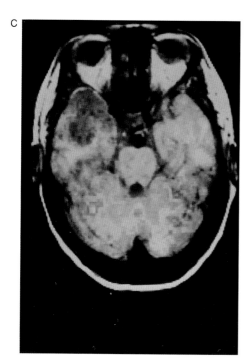

PLATE 5 Images of a temporal lobe oligodendrocytoma showing (a) the PET (FDG) image, (b) the corresponding MRI scan, and (c) the merged MRI/PET image. (See chapter 6.)

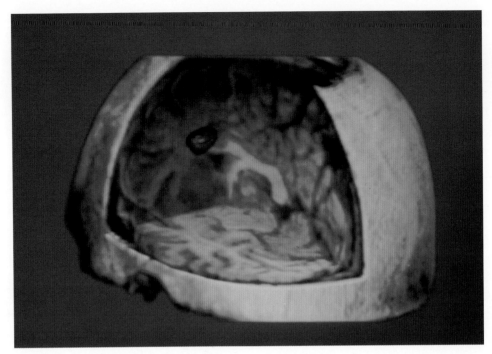

PLATE 6   Gradient-enhanced volume rendering of MRI following removal of a 3D sector to expose a PET activation focus in the anterior cingulate gyrus. The focus was one of four identified in response to a painful stimulus. (Reprinted with permission from Talbot et al., 1991.) (See chapter 6.)

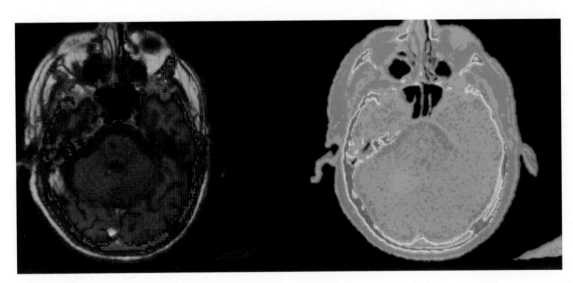

PLATE 7   Result of the 3D/3D registration between 2-mm-spaced CT section and 6-mm-spaced MRI images. The matching was based on the skin surface, and rms errors after convergence were 1.5 mm. From examination by radiologists, it was concluded that misregistration ranged between 1 and 2 pixels of MRI (i.e., between 1 and 2 mm). (See chapter 7.)

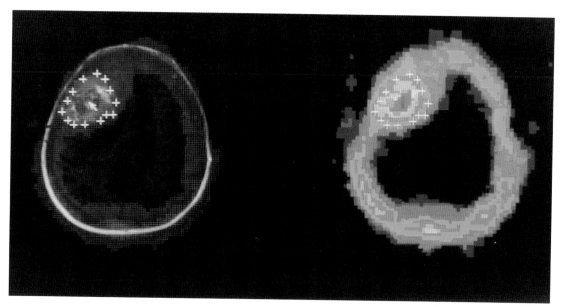

PLATE 8   Result of the 3D/3D registration between a volume of SPECT images (with a resolution of 64 × 64 × 64) with 6-mm-spaced MRI images. A composite image is constituted by an MRI section on which we superimpose the corresponding pseudo-color SPECT image computed in the volume of original SPECT images after registration. The matching was based on the skin surface using a range finder linked and calibrated with the SPECT image system. Rms errors after convergence of surface registration were 2 mm. The accuracy of the method was validated using known templates, and a mean error of 2.5 mm was reached, which is better than the voxel resolution of SPECT images. (See chapter 7.)

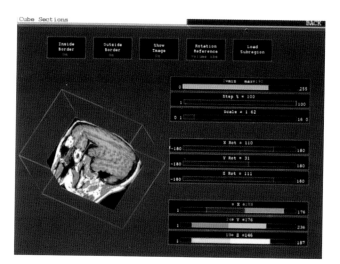

PLATE 9   Interactive orthogonal sectioning with 3D volume image visualization is achieved with the *Cube Sections* program. Color coding along the outside edges of the volume and the edges of the orthogonal images (left) correspond to sliders used to control interactive orthogonal sectioning (lower right). The cube is rotated using angle selection sliders (middle right). Selection boxes (top row) control visualization options, rotational coordinate systems, and subregion loading. (See chapter 10.)

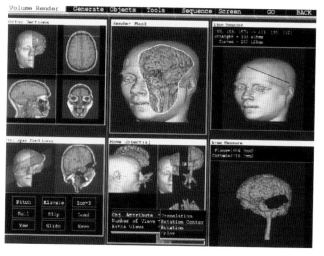

PLATE 10   Volume image editing and measurement in *Volume Render* of ANALYZE. Shown are interactive orthogonal (top left) and oblique (bottom left) sectioning, surgical simulation by "masking" (top center) and segmented object manipulation (bottom center), and selective measurement of curvilinear surface length (top right) and surface area (bottom right). (See chapter 10.)

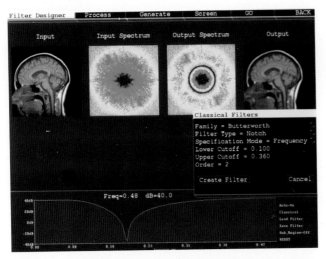

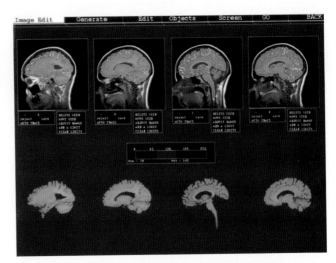

PLATE 11 Filtering in the frequency domain can be accomplished with the *Filter Designer* program. A Fourier transform can be applied to the original image data (upper left) to generate the spatial frequency spectrum (second from left). A frequency domain filter can be selected from standard filters (right middle) or interactively drawn (lower panel) and applied to the image spectrum, producing an output spectrum (second from right) and transformed into the spatial domain (right). (See chapter 10.)

PLATE 12 Semiautomated segmentation can also be invoked in the *Image Edit* program. A seed point is selected and a region is grown from the seed point, searching for voxels that drop outside of an interactively specified threshold range. The region's four-connected boundary interactively changes as the threshold is manipulated, providing immediate visual feedback on the location of the boundary and allowing the user to make the decision of the proper boundary to be used for segmentation. (See chapter 10.)

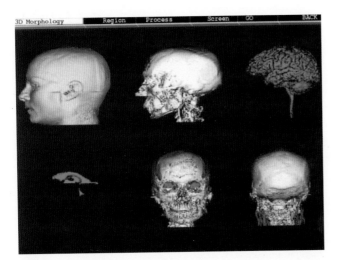

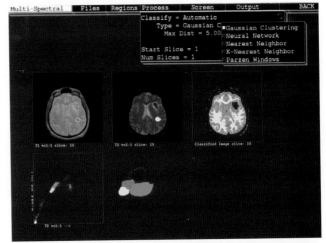

PLATE 13 The *3D Morphology* program provides advanced 3D morphological processing options, allowing a wide variety of advanced processing and segmentation techniques. One such technique is automated 3D segmentation of structures, as shown here for an MRI volume image of the head. Each of the rendered structures was automatically segmented using 3D morphological processing to build the object map used to render the skin, bone, brain, ventricles, eyes, and carotids (upper left to lower right). (See chapter 10.)

PLATE 14 The *Multi-Spectral* program provides investigative and automated methods for classification and segmentation of structures from image information with multiple spectral bands. For example, T_1-weighted and T_2-weighted MRI (upper left and center images) provide complementary information about the structures being imaged, forming a 2D feature space (lower left) that can be interrogated and automatically classified (lower right, upper right) for segmentation (See chapter 10.)

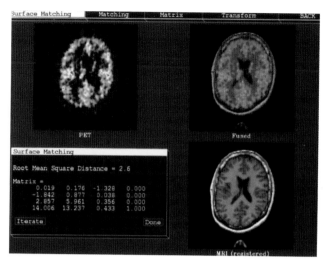

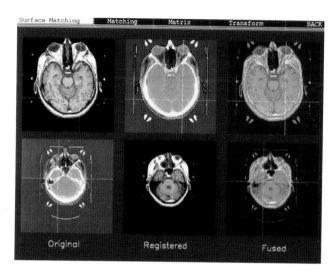

PLATE 15   Multimodality image fusion can be accomplished with the *Surface Matching* program. Surfaces of structures in two volume images can be automatically spatially correlated using a multiresolution approach to minimize Chamfer distances between the surfaces. Once a match is determined, the transformation matrix is computed (lower left), allowing application to one of the volume images to complete the spatial correlation. Here a PET image data set (upper left) is correlated to an MRI volume image (lower right), presented in a combined display (upper right). (See chapter 10.)

PLATE 16   Registration and fusion of MRI and CT head scan data, modalities often used together in various surgical planning procedures. Top row shows CT registered to MRI at one level; bottom row shows MRI registered to CT at another level. Note in fused images at right the appearance of all structures from both scans at both levels in good registration. (See chapter 10.)

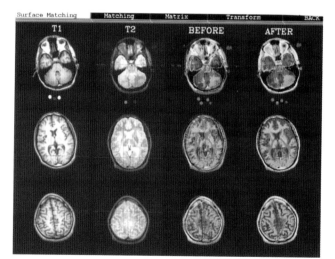

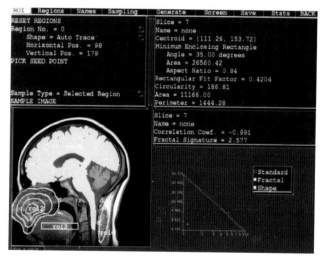

PLATE 17   Fusion is also useful to correlate spatially volume images from multiple scans within a single modality, differing either by time or technique. For example T_1-weighted MRI images (left column) can be spatially correlated with T_2-weighted MRI images (second column) by matching the surface of the skin. Once registered, the images can be displayed together (right column) for visualization of the complementary information from the two scans, or the correlated images can be passed on to other programs to take advantage of the correlated information. (See chapter 10.)

PLATE 18   Advanced measurement can be made using the functionality of the *Region of Interest* program. Fractal measurements are made at various scales, resulting in a plot of fractal signature (middle right) and the computation of fractal dimension for the image. Features of shape can be measured, including minimum enclosing rectangle, rectangle fit factor, circularity, centroid, area, and perimeter (upper right). (See chapter 10.)

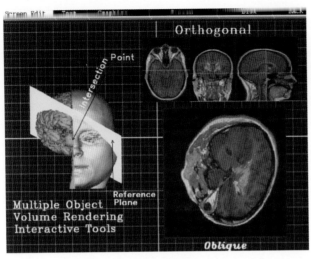

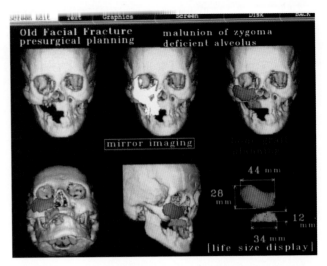

PLATE 19 The *Screen Edit* program provides interactive tools for composition of images, graphics, and text in preparation for presentation. Images from multiple sources can be displayed, cut, pasted, and resized on the screen, with a grid used for positioning. Text from multiple font types and in various colors, sizes, and angles is placed interactively on the screen. Graphic objects including arrows, frames, lines, circles, and disks can be integrated with the images. (See chapter 10.)

PLATE 20 Presurgical planning and subsequent postsurgical evaluation often require accurate quantitative assessment of components of the anatomy. Bone graft planning is shown using mirror imaging (upper row) and subsequent editing of the graft prostheses (upper right, lower left and middle), resulting in prostheses of accurate size and shape (bottom right). (See chapter 10.)

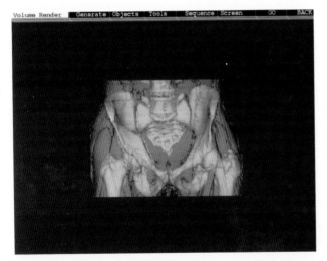

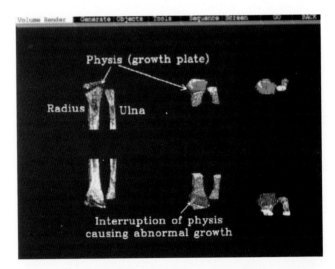

PLATE 21 In orthopaedic applications, it frequently is necessary to understand the soft tissue structure surrounding the skeletal structure of interest. In many biomechanics studies, the muscles, tendons, and ligaments are equally as important as the bone. From x-ray CT data, these soft tissue structures can be segmented with ANALYZE and rendered transparently on top of the underlying skeletal structures to visualize their relationship to the structure under examination. This image has been rendered using 24 bits of color to provide true-color transparency for the soft tissues. (See chapter 10.)

PLATE 22 The physis is the growth plate at the end of the long bones in the body and is responsible for the growth of these bones during childhood. Due to either trauma or pathologic disease, the physis may be damaged, causing no growth to occur in the area of interruption and irregular overall growth of the bone. These images have been rendered from an MRI scan of the end of the radius, depicting the bone and the physis. From this, the orthopaedic surgeon can determine the extent of damage, evaluate the current growth pattern, and plan a surgical approach to correct the problem. (See chapter 10.)

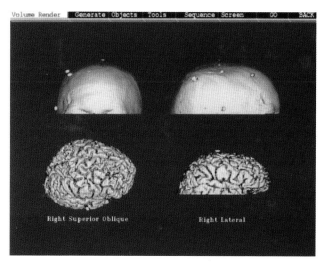

Right Superior Oblique   Right Lateral

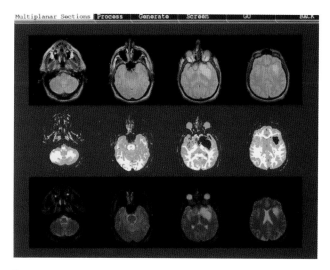

PLATE 23   These volume renderings of 3D-acquired MRI data depict the soft tissue and brain structure of an epilepsy patient used for neurosurgical planning. The green structures are fat beads used as markers of EEG electrode position indicating the electrical focus of the seizure activity (center marker). These can be visualized on the skin surface (top) and projected onto the brain surface (bottom) to map the seizure focus to a specific gyra in the brain structure preoperatively. (See chapter 10.)

PLATE 24   The *Multi-Spectral* classification techniques can be applied to multimodality images of the head for automated segmentation of various brain structures, including pathology such as the tumor shown here. Both T1-weighted (top row) and T2-weighted (bottom row) MRI, which have been spatially correlated using the *Surface Matching* program, are used to form a feature space in which the cluster corresponding to tumor tissue can be isolated. The voxels corresponding to this cluster can then be automatically identified (red) and segmented from other structures in the brain. The middle row contains the classified images, showing white and gray matter, cerebrospinal fluid, and a tumor. (See chapter 10.)

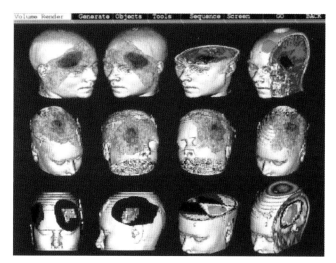

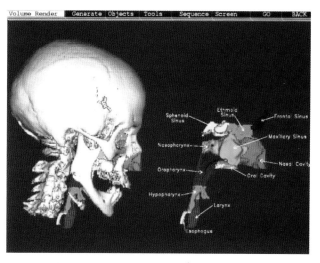

PLATE 25   Radiotherapy planning with ANALYZE, often used in conjunction with surgical planning. Top row shows 3D visualizations of dose distribution from two simulated external treatment beams, including dissections through target volume. Color spectrum represents magnitude of dose (purple-blue is low dose, orange-red is high dose). Center row shows 3D treatment plan using seven simulated intersecting treatment beams through tumor volume. Bottom row shows different 3D cutaways and dissections to visualize 3D treatment plan. (See chapter 10.)

PLATE 26   Using segmentation and volume-rendering techniques, images can be created for the purpose of anatomic education of surgeons and physicians. From cadaveric x-ray CT data of the head, the paranasal sinuses and other air spaces in the head can be segmented and rendered both with the skull for localization of familiar anatomy (left) and without the skull to visualize internal spaces (right). Each sinus and air space can be assigned a different color and examined individually or in relation to the other spaces or structures, with labels identifying each component. (See chapter 10.)

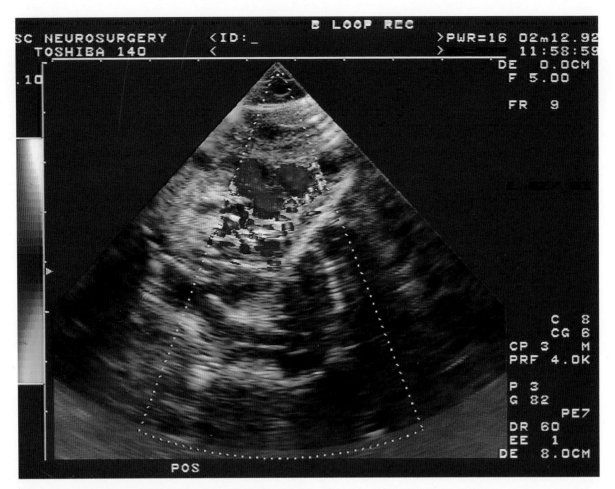

PLATE 27   Intraoperative B-mode sector scanning and color
Doppler imaging of a large arteriovenous malformation in a
26-year-old man. (See chapter 21.)

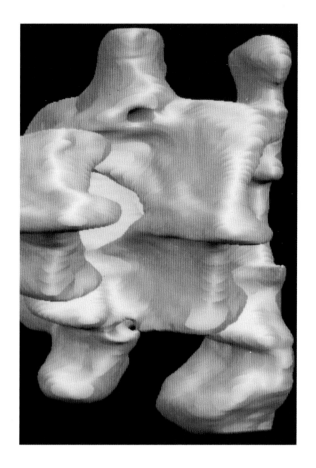

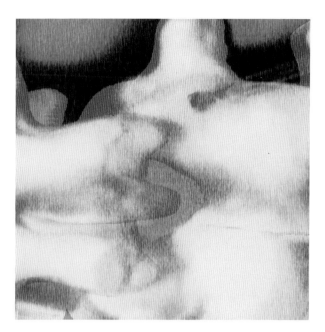

PLATE 28 (Left) Synthesis image computed from CT data (the image that would be produced by a video camera when the system is at the optimal location). (Right) On-line super-imposition between a reference synthesis imaged computed from CT data (in the red buffer) and the on-line video image that comes from the camera (in the green buffer). On this picture, both images match perfectly, so the guide rigidly fixed to the camera is coincident with the optimal trajectory defined on CT images. (See chapter 32.)

A

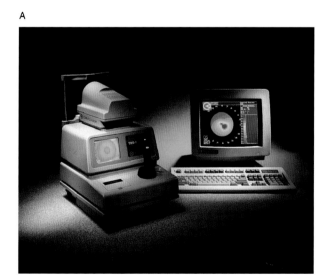

B

PLATE 29 (a) The Topographic Modeling System (TMS-1);

(b) The TMS-1 Light Cone. (See chapter 35.)

A

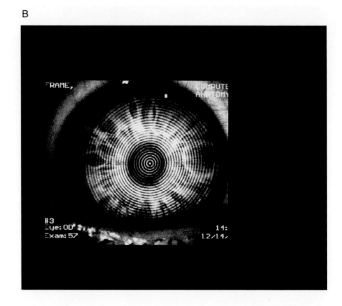

PLATE 30 (a) Reflected image from a normal cornea.
(b) Reflected image from an astigmatic cornea. (See chapter
35.)

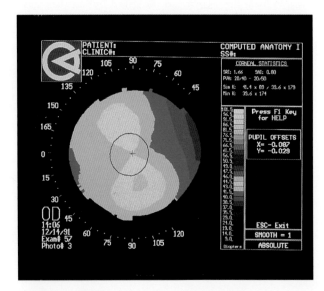

PLATE 31 Dioptric contour map of an astigmatic cornea.
(See chapter 35.)

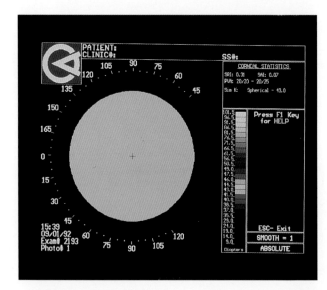

PLATE 32 Dioptric contour map of a ball in the spherical
system. (See chapter 35.)

A

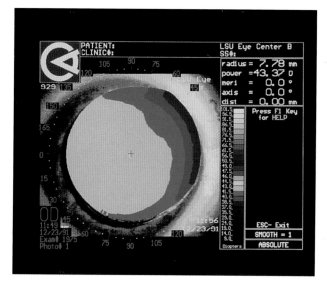

B

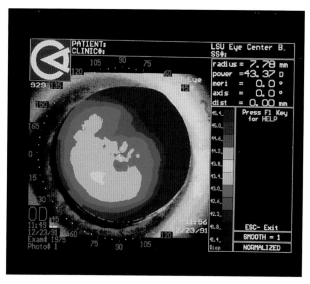

PLATE 33 TMS-1 absolute and normalized scale color-coded topographic maps of a normal cornea with 3 D of with-the-rule astigmatism characterized by the vertically oriented bow-tie pattern. (a) The absolute color scale (left) has fixed dioptric intervals that are 1.5 D in the central power range and 5.0 D in the high and low power ranges.

Each individual color always represents a specific power interval. (b) In the normalized color scale, the power intervals represented by individual colors are smaller and vary depending on the power range of the cornea being analyzed. (See chapter 35.)

A

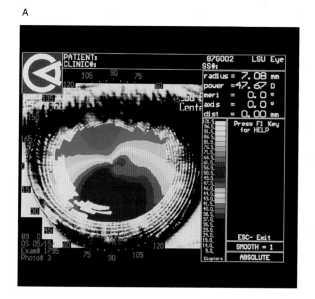

B

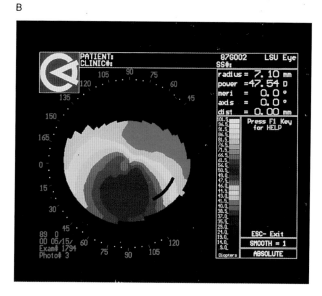

PLATE 34 Bilateral peripheral cones in the left (a) and right (b) eyes of a patient with keratoconus. (See chapter 35.)

A

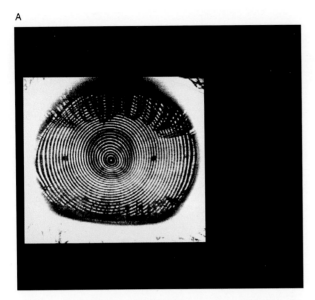

B

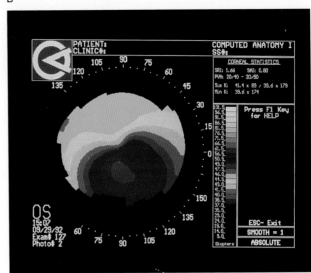

PLATE 35 Videokeratoscope image (a) and TMS-1 absolute scale color-coded topographic map (b) of the left eye of a patient with advanced keratoconus in the opposite eye, demonstrating that early changes noted with computer-assisted topographic analysis may not be detectable by visual inspection of the videokeratoscope mires. (See chapter 35.)

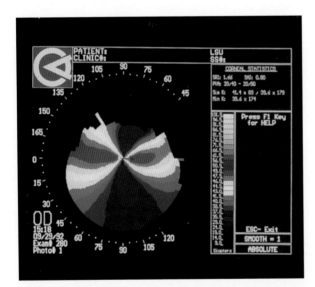

PLATE 36 An absolute-scale topographic map of a cornea with Terrien's marginal degeneration. The topography is characterized by marked flattening of the central cornea along a vertical axis with steepening of the inferior corneal periphery that extends into the mid-peripheral inferior oblique meridians. (See chapter 35.)

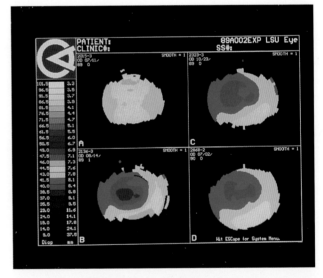

PLATE 37 Topographic analysis of an eye after area ablation with a VISX excimer laser for an attempted correction of 3.75 D. (Top left) Preoperative corneal topography. (Top right) Topography 5 weeks after PRK. (Bottom left) Topography 15 weeks after PRK. (Bottom right) Topography 52 weeks after PRK. (See chapter 35.)

A

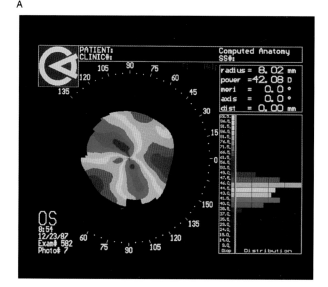

B

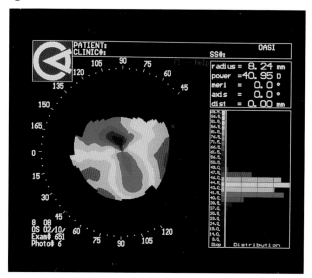

PLATE 38 (a) Absolute-scale color-coded topographic map of a cornea 9 months after penetrating keratoplasty. The map shows 8.0 D of astigmatism and paracentral surface irregularity superotemporal to the visual axis. (b) Absolute-scale color-coded topographic map of the same cornea 5 weeks after (a). Sutures are removed at 2 o'clock, 4 o'clock, and 7 o'clock. This result would not have been obtainable without the TMS-1 data map to identify the tight suture in the area off the keratometer major axis. (See chapter 35.)

A

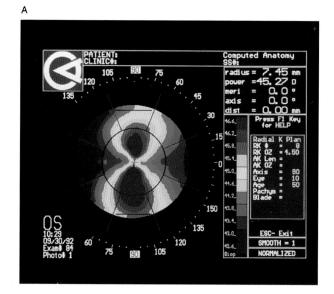

B

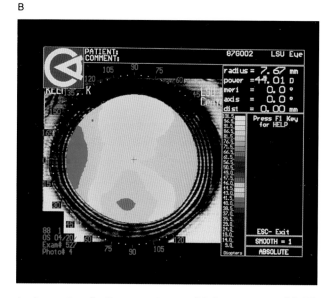

PLATE 39 (a) A patient with contact lens-induced corneal warpage caused by a superior riding rigid polymethyl methacrylate contact lens. Note that the topographic pattern is similar to that noted in keratoconus patients. This patient had no other findings consistent with keratoconus. (b) The topography returned to a normal pattern after contact lens wear was discontinued for a period of 5 months. (See chapter 35.)

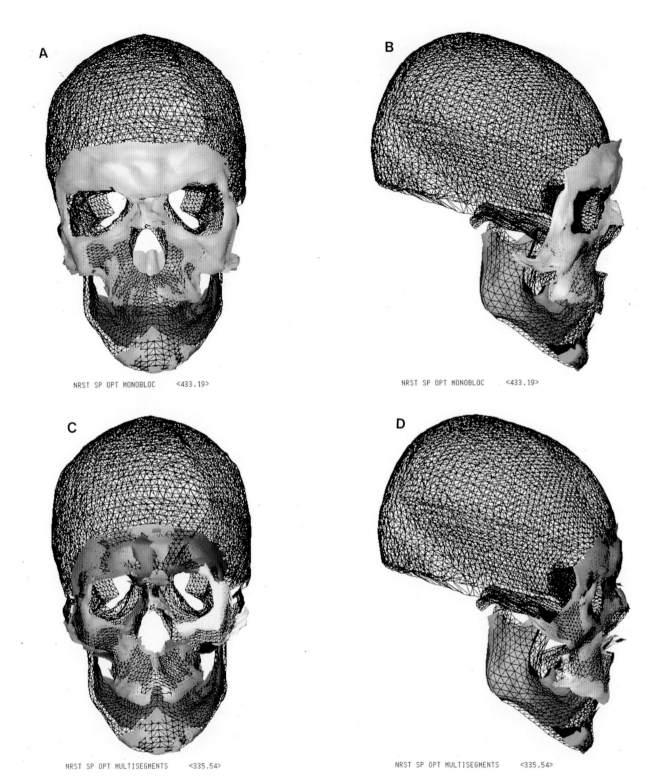

NRST SP OPT MONOBLOC   <433.19>

PLATE 40 Optimized osteotomy plans for a patient with Apert syndrome. (a, b) Optimized postoperative position of the midface for a monobloc osteotomy plan. (c, d) Optimized postoperative bone fragment positions for a multisegment osteotomy plan. The wire frame shows a superimposed normal form, and the solid segments show the bone fragment positions. Multiple segment plans permit a closer match to normal anatomy but often are more difficult to execute. (See chapter 52.)

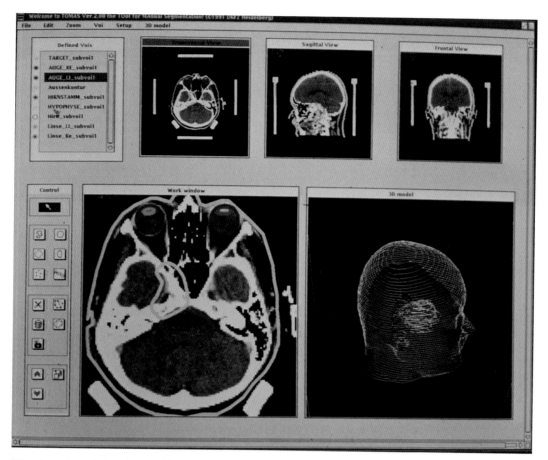

PLATE 41　User interface of the advanced image registration and segmentation program (module TOMAS in the VOXELPLAN software package) for the definition and 3D modeling of target volumes and organs at risk using CT and MRI data (Pross, 1993; Elliott, 1992). The target volume (brain tumor) is shown in yellow, the organs at risk (brain stem and eye lenses) in red and green, respectively. (See chapter 55.)

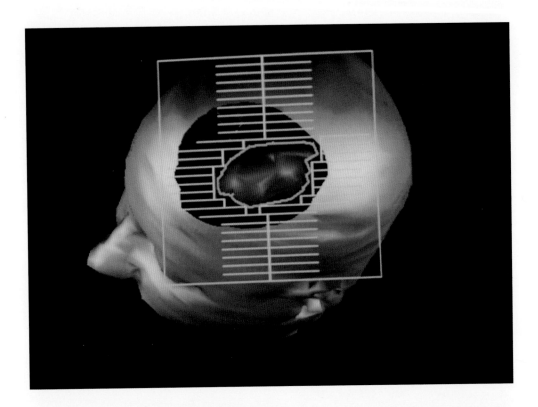

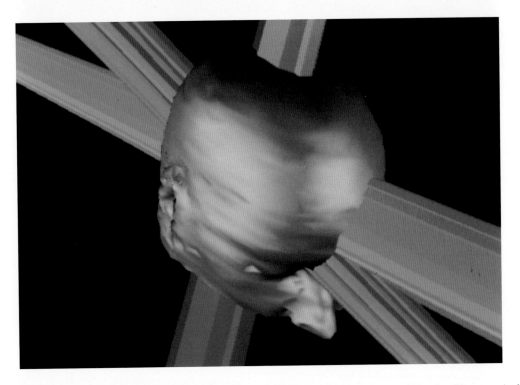

PLATE 42 (Top) Beam's-eye view for the design of radio-therapy treatment techniques (module VIRTUOS in the VOXELPLAN software package [Bendl, 1993]). The patient's surface (white) and the target volume (red) are shown from the direction of the beam. The program automatically fits the opening of a multileaf collimator (yellow) to the shape of the target volume (outlined in blue). (Bottom) Observer's-eye view of a conformal treatment technique with three noncoplanar irregularly shaped beams. (See chapter 55.)

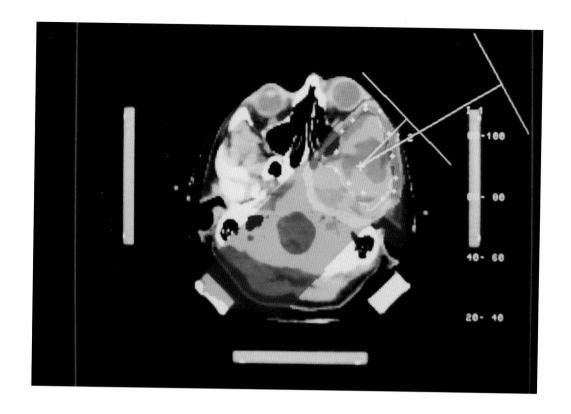

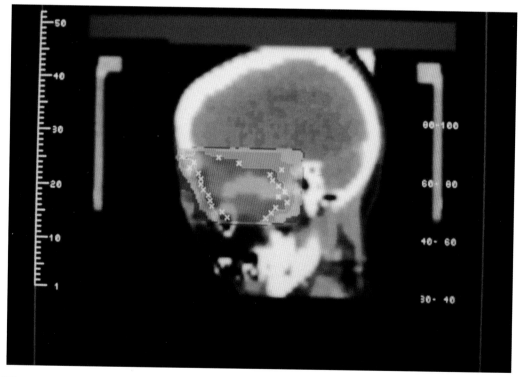

PLATE 43 3D treatment plan showing a transverse (top) and a multiplanar reconstructed sagittal section (bottom) for a patient with a brain tumor. The plan was reconstructed from 52 transverse CT images and shows the dose distribution (colored area) for a conformation treatment technique with two noncoplanar irregularly shaped beams (white crosses, target volume; red area, 80% isodose; green, 60–80%; light blue, 40–60% of maximum irradiation dose). (See chapter 55.)

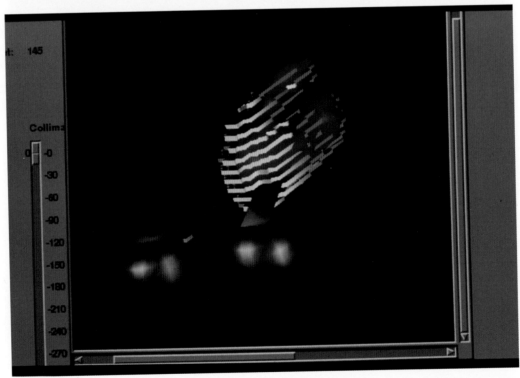

PLATE 44 (Top) Shaded surface display of a 3D treatment plan of a patient with a brain tumor (red, target volume; blue, optic nerve; violet, eyes; green, brain stem; yellow ribbons, 80% isodose indicating the treatment volume). (Bottom) Same plan as (a), but the brain stem is removed, showing that the target volume is not completely covered by the therapeutic dose at those parts close to the critical organ. (See chapter 55.)

poses, with roll angles varying through $\pm 90°$ and pitch angles varying from $2°–60°$. After reduction of the data, the average residual variation in the apparent position of p_{post} was typically approximately 0.1 mm. Over a series of nine calibration runs made during the canine clinical trial, the average residual variation ranged from 0.08 mm to 0.12 mm, and the maximum residual magnitude ranged from 0.16 mm to 0.33 mm, which is well within the required accuracy for this application. Further, because the wrist orientation does not change during the shape cutting phase, any remaining wrist calibration error simply causes the position of the hole to be shifted slightly in the patient's femur and does not affect the actual shape being cut.

Shape cutting

At present, we use a constant orientation cutting strategy. The shape is cut as follows:

1. An end mill (typically 7–9 mm in diameter) is placed in the collet of the cutting tool.
2. The cutter is oriented parallel to the long axis of the implant.
3. Successive transverse pockets (typically, approximately 2.5 mm deep) are cut to produce the rough shape of the implant. At the conclusion of this stage, the implant shape has a staircase appearance.
4. Successive longitudinal cuts are made to remove the excess material in the staircases. Although this produces a slightly scalloped surface finish, in practice it is easy to approximate the desired surface with a relatively small number of cuts. The residual height δh of any scallop will be given by the following equation:

$$\delta h = r_{\text{cutter}} - \sqrt{r_{\text{cutter}}^2 - \frac{d^2}{2}}$$

where r_{cutter} is the cutter radius and d is the distance between cuts. Solving for d gives

$$d = \sqrt{4r_{\text{cutter}}\delta h - 2(\delta h)^2} \cong 2\sqrt{r_{\text{cutter}}\delta h} \text{ for small } \delta h.$$

Thus, $r_{\text{cutter}} = 5$ mm and $\delta h = 0.05$ mm would require the finishing cuts to be 1 mm apart. These cuts are made without changing the cutter orientation.

5. If necessary, the end mill is replaced with a smaller-diameter ball cutter, and additional finishing cuts are made to sharpen the corners of the implant hole. Obtaining proper clearance for these cuts requires the cutter orientation to be changed slightly.

Changes in the implant designs during veterinary clinical testing rendered this step unnecessary.

One advantage of a constant-orientation cutting strategy is that it substantially eliminates the effect of unmodeled kinematic errors in the distal parts of the robot on the *shape* of the hole being cut, although they do still affect the *location* of the hole relative to the bone. Since the shape dimensional tolerances are in fact somewhat tighter than the positioning tolerances, maintaining a constant orientation is indeed valuable. More complex implant shapes, of course, may require full five-axis trajectories.

Intraoperative display

The presurgical planning system is also used in the operating room to provide displays showing the progress of the cutting phase of the surgery. During surgery, the planning system is connected to the robot controller via a standard serial communication line, and rechristened the "real-time monitor." Three orthogonal cross-sections through the 3D CT data set used to plan the surgery are displayed together with corresponding cross-sections of the shape to be cut, just as in presurgical planning. As each successive cutting stroke is made, the robot controller sends short messages to the display computer, which then changes the color of the portions of the cross-sectional images corresponding to the cutting stroke. Once a complete "layer" is cut out, that entire portion changes color yet again.

Safety-checking subsystems

REQUIREMENTS

Safety was a primary consideration in designing the system. The principal requirements were defined by the surgeon coauthors of this chapter, Dr. Paul and Dr. Bargar. These included the following.

1. *The robot must never "run away."* No single-mode hardware (or system) error may cause the application software to lose control of its motions. Furthermore, the application software must request only proper motions.

2. *The robot must never exert excessive force on the patient.* If forces on the cutter exceed expected values by more than a predefined threshold amount, then something may be wrong, and the robot must stop moving immediately.

3. *The robot's cutter must stay within a prespecified positional envelope relative to the volume being cut.* For hip replacement surgery, the main goal is to prevent a systematic shift in the placement or shape of the hole; a single gouge generally is reparable, although undesirable. Of course, other surgical procedures (such as brain surgery) may be less forgiving.

4. *The surgeon must be in charge at all times.* This is, of course, the fundamental dilemma. The surgeon has to trust the system to some extent. Nevertheless, the system must provide the surgeon with timely information about its status, and the surgeon must be able to pause motion at any time. Once robot motion is stopped, he or she must be able to further query the robot's status, to manually guide it, to select an appropriate recovery procedure to continue the surgery, or to completely terminate use of the robot and continue manually.

Robot controller checks

The robot controller routinely performs many safety and consistency checks, including monitoring position and velocity limits in the joint servos and monitoring of external signals. In addition to a basic power-enable relay (external to the controller), controller software provides facilities for disabling manipulator power, for "freezing" or pausing motion, for resuming interrupted motions, and for transferring control to application software recovery procedures. A safety time-out monitor turns off arm power if the controller does not affirmatively verify system integrity every 18 msec. Many conditions (externally signaled consistency checks, force thresholds, pushbutton closures, etc.) interrupt the application program, pause motion, or drop power under certain conditions. The surgeon can then use the hand-held terminal to query system status, to select local actions (such as manual guiding or withdrawal of the cutting tool), to continue the present motion, to discontinue or repeat the present step of the procedure, or to restart from an earlier stage of the procedure. One very common case is a simple surgeon-initiated pause to allow the surgical team to perform some housekeeping function like replacing an irrigation bottle or to allow the surgeon to make sure that all is well.

Force monitor checks

The microprocessor interface to a wrist-mounted force sensor computes forces and torques at the cutter tip. If any tip force component greater than approximately 1.5 kg/f is detected, the controller is signaled to pause motion. Forces greater than approximately 3 kg/f cause arm power to be dropped. Experiments in which a sudden large motion is commanded in the middle of cutting confirm that these checks are effective in detecting "runaway" conditions. They are also effective in detecting such conditions as the cutter stalling or being impeded by improperly retracted soft tissue.

Independent motion monitoring checks

We developed an independent checking subsystem to verify that the cutter step stays within a defined "safe" volume relative to the bone, essentially corresponding to the implant shape and an approach region. The checking system is implemented on a separate IBM PC/AT computer from the robot controller, in order to minimize the chances of common mode failures. The check requires two steps: (1) verification that the bone does not move relative to the fixator, which is rigidly attached to the robot's base, and (2) verification that the end-effector never strays from a defined volume in space.

We devised a strain gauge system for detecting motions of the bone relative to the fixator. Bench experiments demonstrated that motions on the order of 0.1 mm could be detected. However, experiments with the fixator indicated that even rather large forces (5 kg/f) produced only negligible (16 μm) motion, and the bone motion monitor was not used in any clinical tests. To verify end-effector motion, we used a Northern Digital Optotrak 3D digitizer, which is capable of tracking light-emitting diodes to an accuracy of better than 0.1 mm at a rate of approximately 1000 positions/ sec. We fabricated a rigid PC card with eight such beacons and affixed it to the robot's wrist, as shown in figure 28.9. An arbitrary coordinate system for the PC card was defined from the beacon positions, and the positions $\mathbf{b}_{pi}$ of the beacons relative to this coordinate system were measured. The Optotrak measures the positions $\mathbf{b}_{\sigma i}$ of these beacons in space, and computes a best estimate of the plate position $\mathbf{F}_p$ by regression from the relationship

$$\mathbf{b}_\sigma \cong \mathbf{F}_p \cdot \mathbf{b}_p$$

The robot-to-Optotrak and plate-to-cutter transformations, $\mathbf{T}_{ro}$ and $\mathbf{T}_{pc}$ are computed by ordinary least-squares estimation from data taken with the robot in

FIGURE 28.9 Robot's wrist during shape-cutting experiment. The LED beacon plates used by the motion monitoring system are clearly visible. The force sensor is just visible behind the top of the plates.

various known positions, using appropriate linearized models. Using these transformations, an estimate of the cutter coordinates $\mathbf{F}_{rc}$ relative to the robot may be obtained from the following relationship:

$$\mathbf{F}_{rc} = \mathbf{T}_{ro}^{-1} \cdot \mathbf{F}_p \cdot \mathbf{T}_{pc}$$

Constructive solid geometry (CSG) tree "check volumes" corresponding to implant and cutter selection were constructed from primitives bounded by quadric surfaces

$$\mathbf{p}_c^T \cdot \mathbf{Q}_i \cdot \mathbf{p}_c + \mathbf{q}_i \cdot \mathbf{p}_c + d_i \le 0$$

located 1 mm outside the furthest nominal excursions of the cutter when the shape is cut. Intraoperative checking is performed by reading the beacon plate coordinates from the Optotrak, computing the corresponding cutter position, and then checking to see if this position falls outside the check volume. If so, the checking subsystem signals an out-of-bounds condition through an optically isolated digital port to the robot controller, which pauses motion and then obtains more detailed information through a serial communications line.

To verify the performance of this system, we deliberately moved the cutter in a succession of very small steps through the boundary of the checking volume. We found that the system could detect when a motion

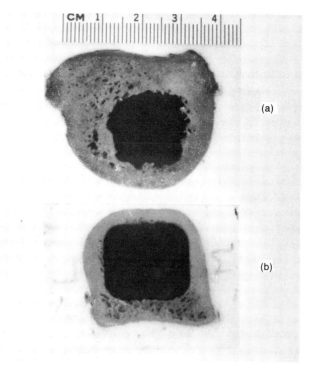

FIGURE 28.10 Comparative cross-sections. Sections of human cadaver bone (a) prepared with a manual broach and (b) machined with a robot. The measured midline dimensions of the machined sections are within 0.05 to 0.1 mm of nominal. Some surface irregularities are seen where the machined surface intersects chancellous bone; other chipping arises from the bone-sectioning process.

crossed a threshold to approximately 0.2 mm precision with constant orientation, and to approximately 0.4 mm with cutter reorientation. Checking rates of approximately 3–4 Hz were obtained using a slow (6-Hz 286) PC. At typical cutter speeds, the total excursion before motion is frozen is approximately 2 mm after accounting for all latencies.

Experience and discussion

IN VITRO

Extensive tests were conducted on plastic and cadaver bones and on foam test blocks, in order to verify basic system accuracy and to gain confidence in overall system behavior [23]. Figure 28.10 shows typical cross-sections produced by manual broaching and robotic machining. In one "bottom-line" experiment, three pins were implanted into a test fixture and located on CT images of the fixture. A number of foam blocks were then successively (and repeatably) clamped into a socket in the test fixture, which was placed at various poses within the work space of the robot. Test shapes were cut in the foam blocks, using steps 3 through 5 of the surgical procedure. The positions of these shapes and of the pins were then measured on a coordinate measuring machine with an accuracy of approximately 0.0125 mm (0.0005 in.). In a typical test run, the three blocks were cut for each of four separate poses (all combinations of left leg or right leg and 0° or 15° fixator pitch) for each of three separate CT scans, for a total of $3 \times 4 \times 3 = 36$ blocks. The total placement error of the test shapes was found to be 0.5 mm for a test fixture with pins placed at the distances they would be on a human. Similarly, the dimensions of test shapes machined in cadaver bone were measured with calipers accurate to 0.02 mm. Dimensional errors were less than 0.05 mm. Further tests, in which actual implant shapes were cut in both foam blocks and canine cadaver bones and an implant was then inserted into the hole, were also conducted. Although a dimensional study similar to [17] was not performed, the fit achieved

was qualitatively very good. The implant slipped into the hole with little effort and fit snugly. No gaps could be seen when the foam block was split longitudinally after insertion of the implant.

Cutting forces for bone machining were also measured. Typical results are shown in figure 28.11. The greatest force, which seldom exceeded 0.5 kg/f, typically was encountered when the cutter moved from the center "plunge" position to the first corner of a rectangular section of bone being removed. Forces would then drop off substantially as the cutter began moving along edges of the section, building up to somewhat smaller local maxima (approximately 0.3–0.4 kg/f) as successive corners of the shape were reached.

Except for bone motion detection, the redundant checking mechanisms discussed above were all integrated into the prototype surgical system and used in in vitro testing on cadaver bones. The most common "error" condition detected during these tests was excessive cutting force when the cutter plunged into unusually hard bone, which caused the controller to

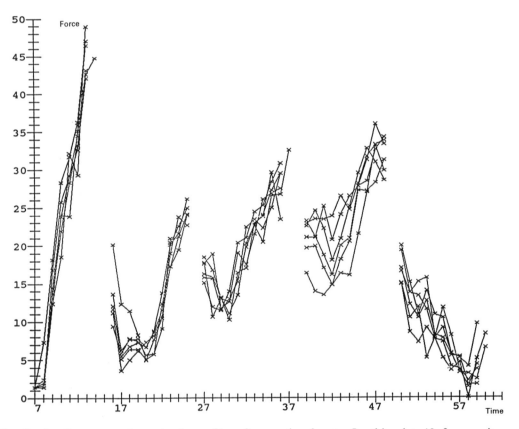

FIGURE 28.11 Cutting forces on cadaver dog bone. Plot of the magnitude of forces on the cutter tip for 5 typical cross-sectional cuts. In this plot 40 force units correspond to 1 pound (0.45 kg/f).

pause robot motion. Continuation from this condition was easily achieved by backing up the cutter 1–2 mm and restarting the current cut. Both the real-time monitor and the motion tracking system proved to be surprisingly useful in application debugging. Even though the display was essentially an animation, it provided useful information about exactly where the robot should be and what the controller thought it was doing. The motion tracker provided a useful consistency check to the calibration procedures. It also caught a real bug in the shape-cutting code that might otherwise have been very hard to find.

IN VIVO

A clinical trial on 26 dogs needing hip replacement surgery was conducted from May 1990 through September 1991. All procedures were successful, with no intraoperative complications or infections. There were no intraoperative or postoperative cracks or fractures, and (in the opinion of the surgeon) the implants were easily inserted and provided more mechanical stability than would normally be experienced with manual broaching of the femur. In contrast, cracking[5] was experienced in 5 of 15 cases in a manually broached control group, and the implant placement was not as good. Radiographs were used to compare placement of the implant in the femur for 15 cases in which the robot was used to prepare the femur with implant placement in 15 cases in which conventional manual broaching was done. It was found that, for the Techmedica cementless canine implants used in the study, conventional broaching often resulted in the proximal end of the implant being tilted more toward the medial direction of the femur (i.e., more in a varus orientation) than the surgeon judged to be optimal. Because of this possibility, the surgeon tended to select a slightly smaller implant design than he or she otherwise would have. In contrast, robotic machining consistently matched the implant axis with the axis of the proximal femur, enabling the surgeon to select the implant size that best matched the patient's internal bone geometry.

In surgery, the system worked very well. Although no systematic effort was made to compare surgical execution times, the total time of surgery was roughly comparable to that for manual broaching. Anecdotally, it was observed that the time required for robot machining was more consistent from case to case than the

time required for manual broaching. There were very few glitches, and there was little actual use of any of the error recovery capabilities of the system. This is as it should be. The force monitor occasionally froze motion when the cutter encountered an unusually hard section of cortical bone at the proximal end of the femur. In these cases, the surgeon simply restarted motion with the hand-held terminal. On two other occasions where the force monitor stopped motion (once when the cutter became entangled in some suture material and once when it got caught in an assistant's glove) it was necessary for the robot to withdraw from the bone. The surgical team cleared the entanglement and resumed the procedure with only a few cutting motions being repeated.

The veterinary surgeon (Dr. Paul) relied on the real-time monitor, in conjunction with his other senses, to provide positional status information. By listening to the cutter, he could tell when the cutter was in contact with hard bone. When he heard a change in pitch, he would look at display to verify that what he was hearing was consistent with where the robot was cutting. One interesting possibility for future work would be to automate such multisensory cross-checking.

The separate motion checking system was not used in vivo for dogs. The surgical field is rather crowded, because a technician must constantly irrigate the bone while the robot is cutting it. It proved to be very difficult to place the vision system sensors in the veterinarian's operating room so that they would always have a clear view of the end-effector. One possibility would have been to mount the cameras overhead. Another would have been to use the system for occasional spot checks of the robot. However, one consequence of the confidence gained from the in vitro tests was that the surgeon concluded that the additional redundancy gained was not worth the added complexity for veterinary cases. A different sensing solution altogether, based on monitoring of redundant joint encoders, was consequently adopted for the subsequent, human-qualified second-generation system [19–21] (see also chapter 29).

Conclusions

The system described in this chapter demonstrates the feasibility of adapting a general-purpose manipulator for use as a precise surgical tool. We have been able to demonstrate an order-of-magnitude improvement in the precision with which a surgeon can execute a critical step in hip replacement surgery. Beyond this, it may be worthwhile to recap how this system has addressed the general requirements discussed at the beginning of the chapter. We found that even very simple human-machine interaction technology can be surprisingly effective, although further improvements are desirable. The use of hands-on, force-compliant guiding for positioning the robot has been especially successful, because it enables the surgeon to position the robot in a way that is natural and intuitively simple. An animated information display showing the progress of the surgical procedure was useful, although this is again an area where considerable improvement can be made both in the presentation of information to the surgeon and in the incorporation of real-time sensing. One ultimate system might be some sort of head-up display showing the surgical plan superimposed on the actual patient, with the display being updated based on a combination of position tracking, cutter force data, acoustic sensing, and intraoperative imaging.

Model-to-reality registration was accomplished in this case by the use of landmark pins, which could be located easily both in CT images and in physical reality. Although their use in this particular surgery is acceptable, less invasive methods may often be desirable. One obvious choice is to register intraoperative radiographs to features on CT-derived models. Another would be to use a 3D digitizer such as the Optotrak to point out anatomical features, and then to provide real-time tracking of markers placed on the patient at the time of surgery (see, for example, [29]).

Verification of robot performance and of the methods chosen to register the plan to reality was an important issue, one that required as much time and effort as any other aspect of the system development and is discussed more fully in [24]. In this regard, experimental measurement of individual error sources and the bottom-line experiments described above went hand in hand. Similarly, the optical end-point check, though ultimately not used in the operating room, proved very useful in debugging the shape-cutting software. The related issue of safety was also paramount. The fact that our application required a robot to move a tool in contact with a patient motivated us to implement a number of redundant consistency checking mechanisms, which proved valuable both in application debugging and in actual surgery.

In implementing these redundant checking mechanisms, we encountered an important trade-off with the realities of operating room compatibility for a complex piece of equipment. The area around the patient is crowded, and it is often awkward to maintain the clear field of view required for optical checking equipment. This led the surgeon in this particular application to conclude that whatever extra safety may be gained by a completely independent visual check, compared to checks on the robot's encoders, does not justify the extra system and operating room complexity involved.[6] In other applications where an optical system is also taking a more active role, for example, in tracking the patient's anatomy, it may be desirable to permit its use for redundant safety checking as well.

In any case, it is clear that the system reported here represents only a step in the evolution of a human-machine partnership in the operating room, in which the complementary abilities of robotic devices and humans are exploited under the human's supervision to help provide a better result for the patient. Indeed, this process has continued for the hip surgery augmentation system we have described. The experience gained with veterinary patients provided the basis for development of a second-generation system [19, 20] for use on humans (see also chapter 29).

ACKNOWLEDGMENTS We wish to thank many people and groups who have contributed to this effort. Those deserving special mention include Techmedica, Inc. (implants), Bill Anspach of The Anspach Effort, Inc. (cutter tools), Steve Lamb of OSI Inc. (fixation system), Micro-Techmedical Corp. (sterile draping), Ken Honeycutt and Kip Harris of IBM Manufacturing Systems Products (robot consultation), Bob Olyha and Tony Castellano of IBM Research (interface electronics), and Jerry Krist and Leon Kehl of Northern Digital (optical tracking).

NOTES

1. Experiments by one of the authors [18, 24] with various materials showed that titanium and ceramic materials yielded the best contrast without excessive blooming. However, the resulting images were still far from clean. Titanium was chosen for reasons of biocompatibility and because it is more commonly used in orthopaedic implants than are ceramics.

2. This method would not work if the length of the pin shaft were such that all three eigenvectors had the same length. In this case, it would be necessary to use higher-order mo-

ments to disambiguate the axes. However, our locator pin design precludes this possibility.

3. The threshold values used to distinguish between different bone classes were qualitatively determined by the surgeon coauthor (Dr. Paul) and reflect his best judgment as to what is useful. Any such distinctions are to some extent arbitrary.

4. The specified repeatability of the robot we used is ± 0.05 mm in the xy plane and ± 0.02 mm in z. The robot's specified "xy region" accuracy is 0.2 mm over a 250-mm square. Over the rather shorter distances involved in machining a canine implant, the accuracy rapidly approaches the repeatability which, in our experience, was actually better than the specified value.

5. Fixed by wrapping cerclage wire around the affected bone.

6. As mentioned earlier, the next-generation robot [22] incorporates an additional, independent set of encoders to provide further redundancy.

REFERENCES

[1] KWOH, Y. S., J. HOU, E. JONCKHEERE and S. HAYATI, 1988. "A robot with improved absolute positioning accuracy for CT guided stereotactic surgery," *IEEE Transactions on Biomedical Engineering*, 35(2):153–161.

[2] LAVALLEE, S., 1989. Gestes medico-chirurgicaux assistes par ordinateur: Application a la Neurochirurgue stereotaxique. Doctoral thesis, University of Grenoble.

[3] LAVALLEE, S., 1989. A new system for computer-assisted neurosurgery. In *Proceedings of the Eleventh IEEE Engineering in Medicine and Biology Conference*, Seattle, November, pp. 926–927.

[4] KALL, B. A., P. J. KELLY, and S. J. GOERSS, 1985. Interactive stereotactic surgical system for the removal of intracranial tumors utilizing the CO_2 laser and CT-derived database. *IEEE Trans. Biomed. Eng.* Feb.:112–116.

[5] KELLY, P. J., B. A. KALL, S. J. GOERSS, and F. EARNEST, 1986. Computer-assisted stereotaxic laser resection of intra-axial brain neoplasms. *J. Neurosurg.* Mar.:427–439.

[6] DRAKE, J. M., M. JOY, A. GOLDENBERG, and D. KREINDLER, 1991. Robotic- and computer-assisted resection of brain tumors. In *Proceedings of the Fifth International Conference on Advanced Robotics*, Pisa, June, pp. 888–892.

[7] GLAUSER, D., P. FLURY, N. VILLOTTE, and C. W. BURCKHARDT, 1991. Conception of a robot dedicated to neurosurgical operations. In *Proceedings of the Fifth International Conference on Advanced Robotics*, Pisa, June, pp. 899–904.

[8] DAVIES, B. L., R. D. HIBBERD, A. TIMONEY, and J. WICKHAM, 1991. A surgeon robot for prostatectomies. In *Proceedings of the Fifth International Conference on Advanced Robotics*, Pisa, June, pp. 871–875.

[9] IKUTA, K., M. TSUKAMOTO, and S. HIROSE, 1988. Shape memory alloy servo actuator system with electric resistance feedback and application for active endoscopes. Presented at the IEEE Robotics and Automation Conference.

[10] STURGES, R. H., and S. LAOWATTANA, 1991. A flexible tendon-controlled device for endoscopy. In *Proceedings of the IEEE Robotics and Automation Conference*, Sacramento, pp. 2582–2591.

[11] GREEN, P., 1992. Advanced teleoperator technology for enhanced minimally invasive surgery. In *Proceedings of the Medicine Meets Virtual Reality Conference*, San Diego, June.

[12] WANG, Y., 1994. Robotically enhanced surgery. In *Proceedings of the Medicine Meets Virtual Reality Conference II*. San Diego, January.

[13] MCEWEN, J. A., C. R. BUSSANI, G. F. AUCHINLECK, and M. J. BREAULT, 1989. Development and initial clinical evaluation of pre-robotic and robotic retraction systems for surgery. In *Proceedings of the Second Workshop on Medical and Health Care Robots*, Newcastle-on-Tyne, September, pp. 91–101.

[14] GARBINI, J. L., R. G. KAIURA, J. A. SIDLES, R. V. LARSON, and F. A. MATSON, 1987. Robotic instrumentation in total knee arthroplasty. In *Proceedings of the Thirty-Third Annual Meeting, Orthopaedic Research Society*, San Francisco, January, p. 413.

[15] KIENZLE, T. C., S. D. STULBERG, M. PESHKIN, A. QUAID, and C. WU, 1993. An integrated CAD-robotics system for total knee replacement surgery. In *Proceedings of the 1993 IEEE Conference on Robotics and Automation*, Atlanta, May, pp. 889–894.

[16] SANDBORN, P. M., S. D. COOK, W. SPIES, and M. KOSTER, 1988. Tissue response in porous coated implants locking initial bone apposition. *J. Arthroplasty* 3:337.

[17] PAUL, H. A., D. E. HAYES, W. L. BARGAR, and B. D. MITTELSTADT, 1988. Accuracy of canal preparation in total hip replacement surgery using custom broaches. In *Proceedings of the First International Symposium on Custom-Made Prostheses*, Dusseldorf, October, pp. 153–161.

[18] PAUL, H. A., B. D. MITTELSTADT, B. L. MUSITS, W. L. BARGAR, and D. E. HAYES, 1988. Application of CT and robotic technology of hip replacement surgery. In *Proceedings of the First International Symposium on Custom-Made Prostheses*, Dusseldorf, October.

[19] PAUL, H., B. D. MITTELSTADT, W. BARGAR, B. MUSITS, R. TAYLOR, P. KAZANZIDES, J. ZUHARS, B. WILLIAMSON, and W. HANSON, 1992. A surgical robot for total hip replacement surgery. In *Proceedings of the IEEE Conference on Robotics and Automation*, Nice, May, pp. 606–611.

[20] KAZANZIDES, P., J. ZUHARS, B. D. MITTELSTADT, P. CAIN, F. SMITH, L. ROSE, and B. MUSITS, 1992. Architecture of a surgical robot. In *Proceedings of the 1992 IEEE Conference on Systems, Man, and Cybernetics*, Chicago, August.

[21] MITTELSTADT, B. D., P. KAZANZIDES, J. ZUHARS, P. CAIN, and B. WILLIAMSON, 1993. Robotic surgery: Achieving predictable results in an unpredictable environment. In *Proceedings of the Sixth International Conference on Advanced Robotics*, Tokyo, November 1–2, pp. 367–372.

[22] HANSON, W. H., H. A. PAUL, B. WILLIAMSON, and B. D. MITTELSTADT, 1990. Orthodock: A computer system for presurgical planning. In *Proceedings of the Twelfth IEEE Medicine and Biology Conference* Philadelphia, 12:1931–1932.

[23] Taylor, R. H., P. Kazanzides, B. D. Mittelstadt, and H. A. Paul, 1990. Redundant consistency checking in a precise surgical robot. In *Proceedings of the Twelfth IEEE Medicine and Biology Conference*, Philadelphia, pp. 1933–1935.

[24] Mittelstadt, B. D. (In Preparation) Doctoral thesis, University of California at Davis.

[25] Hollerbach, J. M., 1993. Advances in robot calibration. In *Proceedings of the Sixth International Symp. Robotics Research*. Cambridge, Mass: MIT Press.

[26] Everett, L. J., 1993. Models for diagnosing robot error sources. In *Proceedings of the 1993 IEEE Conference on Robotics and Automation*, Atlanta, May, 2:155–159.

[27] Goswami, A., A. Quaid, and M. Peshkin, 1993. Com-plete parameter identification of a robot from partial pose information. In *Proceedings of the 1993 IEEE Conference on Robotics and Automation*, Altanta, May, 1:168–173.

[28] Taylor, R. H., 1985. Method and apparatus to teach a robot the position and orientation of hole centerlines. U.S. Patent no. 4,4485,453.

[29] Taylor, R. H., C. B. Cutting, Y. Kim, A. D. Kalvin, D. Larose, B. Haddad, D. Khoramabadi, M. Noz, R. Olyha, N. Bruun, and D. Grimm, 1991. A model-based optimal planning and execution system with active sensing and passive manipulation for augmentation of human precision in computer-integrated surgery. In *Proceedings of the 1991 International Symposium on Experimental Robotics*, Toulouse, France. Berlin: Springer-Verlag.

29 The Evolution of a Surgical Robot from Prototype to Human Clinical Use

BRENT D. MITTELSTADT, PETER KAZANZIDES,
JOEL F. ZUHARS, BILL WILLIAMSON, PHILLIP CAIN,
FRED SMITH, AND WILLIAM L. BARGAR

CHAPTER 28 describes the first generation of our robotic surgical system for cementless total hip replacement (THR) surgery. This prototype was developed in a research environment and was intended for use only under the active supervision of the developing engineers. In fact, the 26 canine surgeries performed with the prototype system all required engineering assistance. Although appropriate for research, this level of support would be prohibitively expensive for a multicenter clinical trial.

In this chapter, we describe the design objectives for the two generations of the system and the changes that were implemented in the second-generation system to prepare it for use in multicenter clinical trials on human patients. These changes helped the system evolve from a prototype that could function only in a well-controlled, supervised research environment to a medical device that can be independently operated by surgical teams with varying levels of technical competence. The fundamental changes described in this chapter fall into three categories: system performance, system safety, and user interface. Changes in all three categories were applied to both the presurgical planning system and the surgical robotic system. Other categories of change that are equally important, but are not described herein, include technical documentation and manufacturability of the system.

Design objectives

CLINICAL PROTOTYPE FOR CANINE THR

The prototype was developed to confirm the theory that an image-directed robot could perform accurately the function of femoral canal preparation in THR surgery. There were two primary objectives in designing this system: to identify and implement the necessary functionality to achieve superior clinical outcomes and to provide adequate safety features.

Improving clinical outcomes for THR dictated high performance objectives for dimensional and placement accuracy in cavity preparation [1]. The safety features implemented in this system had to protect both the canine patient and the surgical team.

CLINICAL SYSTEM FOR HUMAN THR

The second-generation system was developed for multicenter clinical use on humans. The design objectives for this system included the following:

• The system must contain the same functionality as the prototype and meet the same specifications for dimensional and placement accuracy. The functional requirements include CT-based presurgical planning, identification of locator pin positions in the CT data and robot coordinate system, robot force control, and an emergency power-off function.

• Every component of the system, including the presurgical planning workstation, must function reliably when operated by nontechnical surgical teams.

• System performance with regard to accuracy of cavity preparation cannot depend significantly on the skill of the surgical team (i.e., clinical results should be relatively consistent between different teams of trained operating room staff).

• The system must be capable of detecting and responding to error conditions that have the potential of affecting system performance or patient safety.

• The technical documentation and system testing must comply with US Food and Drug Administration (FDA) requirements.

• The design must be manufacturable.

Our experience with the prototype enabled us to translate these design objectives into a set of system requirements. We then refined these requirements by performing a formal analysis of the potential failure modes for the entire system. This analysis involved identifying events that could cause an adverse effect, estimating the probable frequency of these events, and evaluating the severity of their effects on patient outcomes. The severity of the identifiable adverse events ranged from pain to loss of function.

We used the severity and frequency data from this analysis to determine which events must be specifically addressed by designing a hardware or software component to detect or prevent their occurrence. For example:

Event   Damage to the robot arm causes loss of accuracy.

Possible adverse effect   Inaccurate cavity preparation.

Hardware or software solutions   Implement startup diagnostics to determine whether the arm is ready for surgery.

Run a software routine to verify pin distance data by comparing the distances in CT data with the distances as computed by the robot.

Prevent the procedure from continuing if problems are detected.

System overview

When the design objectives were translated into requirements and specifications for the second-generation system, the basic structure, functionality, and procedural flow remained the same. The human clinical system, called the ROBODOC Surgical Assistant System,

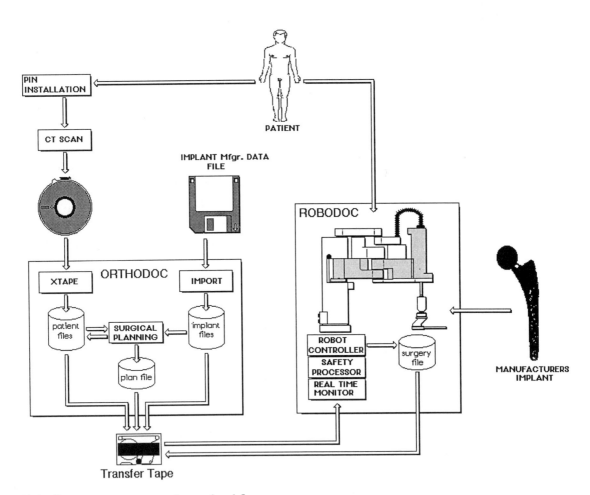

FIGURE 29.1   System components and procedural flow.

consisted of the same two main components, a presurgical planning system, now called the ORTHODOC Preoperative Planning Workstation (ORTHODOC), and a computer-controlled robot, now called the ROBODOC Surgical Assistant (ROBODOC), as shown in figure 29.1.[1]

The input to both generations of the presurgical planning system consists of a CT scan of the patient's femur and data supplied by implant manufacturers from which the system constructs implant models. ORTHODOC reads the CT data from a patient's scan and builds three orthogonal images and a 3D model of the bone. The surgeon develops a preoperative plan by selecting an appropriate model from a library of implants and manipulating it along with the images of the femur, to designate the appropriate placement of the implant in relation to the bone. The output from a preoperative planning session is written to a transfer tape that serves as ROBODOC input [2].

Both generations of ROBODOC (the operating room component of the system) consist of three physical units: (1) a five-axis SCARA robot, equipped with a high-speed rotary cutter; (2) an operating room (OR) monitor; and (3) a control cabinet, which houses the computers and electronic componentry. The second-generation system is shown in figure 29.2.

The ROBODOC control computer reads the preoperative plan, and the surgical robot machines a cavity for the selected implant in the specified position in the patient's femur. Dimensional accuracy of the cavity is a result of the robot's motion accuracy, but accurate cavity placement requires a means of registering the patient's anatomy in the preoperative plan (i.e., the femur in the CT scan) with the physical entity in the robot's work space. This registration is achieved by implanting three titanium locator pins in the femur prior to the CT scan. These pins provide a geometric frame of reference for preoperative planning and for femoral canal preparation.

Performance-related modifications

ORTHODOC WORKSTATION

The first-generation system was PC-based. Although the CT image data for canine patients was less than the 25 MB required for most human patients, updating the three orthogonal views of a bone model took approxi-

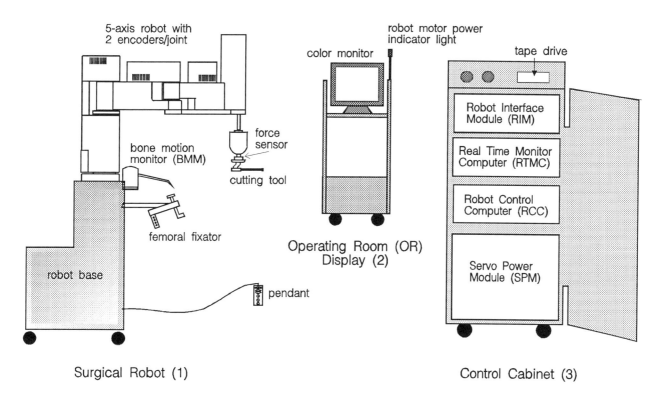

FIGURE 29.2 Components of the ROBODOC Surgical Assistant System.

mately 30 seconds. This relatively long delay between screen updates was tolerable for the prototype but unacceptable for clinical use in multicenter trials. The second-generation system was implemented on an International Business Machines (IBM) RS/6000, with 64 megabytes of RAM and two 200-megabyte hard drives. The IBM AIX operating system resides on one of these drives, and most of the application programs reside on the other. On the RS/6000, screens update in approximately 1 second. This performance enhancement enables surgeons to evaluate implant fit thoroughly by quickly viewing cross-sections through the bone and implant at all critical levels.

Support for longer implants

The second-generation system must support significantly longer implants (up to 220 mm for humans versus 120 mm for dogs) with the same degree of dimensional accuracy using the same diameter cutting tools as the prototype. To accomplish this, we made three significant modifications.

roll axis stiffness   The prototype had an industrial four-axis SCARA manipulator with a custom pitch axis. The roll axis was relatively compliant compared to the pitch axis (25 in.-lb./deg for roll and 150 in.-lb./deg for pitch), but the system was capable of maintaining the dimensional accuracy requirements because the forces were relatively low and the tool was relatively short.

For the human system, analysis indicated that to maintain accuracy, it was necessary to improve roll axis stiffness. The roll axis on the second-generation system was stiffened by moving the drive motor. On a standard SCARA robot, the roll axis drive motor is near the base of the arm (aligned with the theta-1 axis of rotation), and joint actuation is transferred from the motor to the shaft via two relatively long belts. Moving the drive motor to the end of the arm improved roll axis stiffness by a factor of six.

end-effector stiffness   The end-effector (cutter drive assembly) consists of four functional units: (1) a high-speed motor to drive the cutter; (2) disposable cutting bits; (3) cutter bearing sleeves, which support the shafts near the rotating end; and (4) a mounting assembly, which rigidly attaches the end-effector to the robot arm. The prototype was equipped with a standard surgical cutting system mounted on a detachable plate. In the operating room, the sterile assembly was installed with Allen wrenches.

To improve stiffness significantly for the second-generation system, the bearing sleeves and mounting assembly were redesigned. These changes involved using materials with enhanced mechanical properties and improving the mechanisms for attaching the bearing sleeves to the assembly and attaching the assembly to the robot arm.

calibration model   To accommodate longer implants, we had to improve the kinematic model for wrist-tool calibration. We found that several of the simplifying assumptions that had been applied to the prototype were invalid and the source of significant error with longer tools. For the second-generation system, we used the complete set of Denavit-Hartenberg (D-H) parameters to model the robot wrist joints and cutting tools.

Extension of robot vertical work space

The prototype had a vertical (z axis) work space of 250 mm. This range was adequate for all canine surgeries, but adequate for humans only when the angle of the femoral axis was less than 15° and the pin location probe was relatively flat during distal pin finding. To remove these constraints, we lengthened the effective z axis by 300 mm by adding a manually actuated motorized lift for raising the robot. This lift mechanism contains an encoder that monitors positional changes. In the second-generation system, the surgeon can adjust base height once to find the two distal pins and again to find the proximal pin and cut the implant cavity. This modification required calibration for misalignment between the robot z axis and the base-lift axis.

ROBODOC system integration

The prototype robot arm had a stepper motor "add-on" pitch axis, which did not facilitate coordinated motion between the joints. In addition, force feedback was obtained via a serial interface and could not easily be used for real-time force control.

The second-generation system contains a servo-driven direct-current motor pitch axis that is fully integrated by the robot manufacturer and therefore allows coordinated five-axis motion. The system architecture was redesigned [3] to accommodate high bandwidth, low latency, and acquisition of time-critical data including force feedback. This redesign facilitated improvements to the force control capabilities of the second-generation system [4]. Additional performance improvements were obtained by using a compiled general-purpose language (C++) instead of an interpreted robot-specific language (AML) [5].

Safety-related modifications

For the canine surgeries, all aspects of the procedure, from CT scanning through completion of the surgical procedure, were monitored by the developing engineers to ensure the proper performance of all steps. The second-generation system required significant safety-related enhancements to substitute for this level of supervision.

The safety systems in the second-generation system were designed to minimize the risk of injury to the patient and operating room staff, to provide both automated and manual controls, and to allow the system to function safely with limited technical supervision. Upgrading the system to make it safe enough for use on human patients required many hardware and software changes.

ORTHODOC DATA VALIDATION

To ensure that safety- and performance-related data are valid, software functions verify that the following items are correct prior to allowing the user to write a ROBODOC transfer file:

• *CT Scan protocol*   ORTHODOC performance (accuracy of pin finding and quality of image data) requires CT scanning with a specified protocol. This protocol prescribes a specific scan thickness, scan interval, and field of view. Software was developed to extract these data from the CT scan header file and confirm that the protocol was followed.

• *Pin data*   ORTHODOC verifies that three pins are located in the CT data. The software then checks the volume of the pins to ensure proper geometry and verifies that the pins are located in reasonable sites based on a simple model of the expected geometry.

• *Implant placement*   ORTHODOC verifies that implant placement is reasonable and prevents the surgeon from making gross placement errors.

BONE MOTION PREVENTION AND DETECTION DURING CT SCAN

Patient movement during the CT scan can cause significant errors in implant (cavity) placement. The system assumes that the relationship between the relative pin geometry (three points in space) and intended cavity placement is constant. Patient movement during the scan can distort this relationship. During the CT scan, canine patients were under general anesthesia and strapped to a special fixture to keep the bone relatively stationary. Because general anesthesia is not an option for the human clinical system, we developed two new system components, one for motion prevention and one for motion detection.

MOTION PREVENTION   The first component is a motion-prevention device that mounts on the CT table. It is designed to immobilize the leg while keeping the patient as comfortable as possible.

MOTION DETECTION   The system for detecting motion combines a special scan protocol with subsequent software checks. The protocol requires the CT technician to secure an aluminum rod to the thigh with Velcro straps and to position the region of interest so that the rod is present in the field of view for all scans through the bone. After the CT image data are loaded, ORTHODOC software evaluates the rod data to determine whether the rod moved during the CT scan. This evaluation is accomplished by first separating the rod pixels from the rest of the image and then computing a centroid for each scan plane. The set of centroids are then analyzed and compared to the expected model, which is a straight line. If detected motion exceeds the allowable threshold, ORTHODOC prevents the user from creating a ROBODOC transfer file, and the CT scan must be repeated. This motion detection system assumes that it is physically impossible to move the bone without shifting the rod.

DEDICATED ROBOT SAFETY PROCESSOR

Most of the safety components in the prototype ran on independent processors. To improve response time significantly, we added a digital signal processor board that functions as a dedicated safety processor [6]. This processor has a direct hardware interface to all safety-related hardware components, including the redundant encoders, force sensor, and bone motion monitor. The safety processor also has the ability to disable the power to the robot motors and the rotary cutting tool via a hardware relay.

The processor analyzes feedback data and compares the results to defined safety tolerances. Each exception condition has two safety thresholds: pause (or freeze) and stop (or emergency power off). The pause threshold is the lower (less urgent) of the two and allows the system to exhibit a more graceful response. When a pause threshold is exceeded, the system halts robot motion, deactivates the cutter, and displays a menu of recovery options on the OR monitor. When a stop threshold is exceeded, the safety processor removes power from the robot motors and cutter and signals the robot control computer to display an appropriate error screen.

ROBODOC ERROR DETECTION

To ensure patient safety and the accuracy of bone cavity preparation, the system must be capable of detecting a variety of error conditions that may occur during the surgical procedure, especially those having the potential to affect system performance negatively if left undetected. ROBODOC has three basic types of error checking: data-integrity checks, data-rationality checks, and detection of procedural errors.

DATA-INTEGRITY CHECKS   Data-integrity tests are used to detect corruption of critical data. For example, all relevant files on the hard drive are compared to backup copies every time the system is powered up. This check detects corruption of those files due to causes such as hard drive failure or unauthorized modification. As another example, checksums are used to validate the integrity of the implant-specific cut file that is read from the ROBODOC transfer tape. This file contains all the motion specifications necessary to machine the implant cavity and is therefore critical to the safety and performance of the system.

DATA-RATIONALITY TESTS   Data-rationality tests ensure that case-specific data, such as pin distances, are reasonable. For example, the software verifies that the interpin distance values, computed based on CT and robot coordinates, agree within a specified tolerance.

DETECTION OF PROCEDURAL ERRORS   The ROBODOC surgical procedure is designed to follow a specified sequence. The most common type of error condition is user error. Undetected procedural errors can compromise both safety and system performance. For example, when prompted to find the distal lateral pin, the surgeon might find the distal medial pin instead. Although this particular error would most likely be detected by the pin distance check described earlier, it is preferable to detect it as soon as possible so that corrective action may be taken immediately.

ROBODOC REDUNDANT POSITION CHECKING

To ensure patient and operator safety, the system needed a mechanism to track end-effector motion independently. The prototype had a vision-based system that tracked the position of the robot tool and verified that it remained within a specified volume during the cutting procedure. This system was judged to be too cumbersome for clinical use in hip replacement surgery.

We replaced this mechanism with a redundant set of position encoders, which are mounted on the output shaft of each robot joint. The safety processor and the robot control computer continuously monitor and compare output from both sets of encoders to verify that the reported positions are consistent within predefined safety limits. The pause and stop thresholds vary depending on whether the cutter is active. The thresholds are tighter when the robot is actively cutting and end-effector velocity must be slow.

ROBODOC SAFETY VOLUME   The safety volume–checking software was developed to prevent nonspecific run-time errors from causing the robot to cut beyond the boundaries of the intended cavity. This software uses implant-specific data files to define the envelope that encases an intended cavity. It verifies that commanded goal positions for the cutter are within this envelope prior to executing any motion commands.

ROBODOC BONE MOTION MONITOR

From the start of the pin-finding procedure to the completion of cavity preparation, the bone must remain stationary because movement of the femur would shift the robot's milling frame of reference and result in a distorted or malpositioned cavity. Both systems used a custom external fixation device (fixator) to immobilize the bone, but differences between canine and human anatomy required the fixator to be completely redesigned. The second-generation fixator is an assembly with interchangeable parts, which accommodate variations in patient anatomy and leg side. The fixator attaches to the bone with two halo pins at the knee and a proximal bone clamp. After attaching the fixator to the leg, the surgical team connects it to the robot base via an extension arm. Although the fixator was designed to immobilize the bone rigidly in relation to the robot, a change in the loading environment or improper installation may cause bone motion.

A prototype of a fixator-mounted bone motion detection system was developed for the first-generation system, but it was never used clinically. The second-generation system has a bone motion monitor (BMM) mounted on the robot base. It has a spring-loaded probe that securely attaches to the proximal femur. Two rotary encoders and a linear potentiometer measure 3D displacement of the probe relative to the robot base. The BMM is initialized prior to pin finding and continuously monitors the position of the bone until cavity preparation is complete. If motion exceeds a predefined threshold, the BMM interrupts the procedure and the OR monitor prompts the surgeon to reestablish the milling frame of reference by refinding the locator pins.

ROBODOC STARTUP DIAGNOSTICS

The prototype system did not include any startup diagnostics (other than computer memory tests) and relied on careful supervision to ensure that it would function properly for each canine surgical procedure. Because this level of supervision was not feasible for a multicenter clinical trial, startup diagnostic procedures were developed for the second-generation system.

The startup diagnostics verify that all safety- and performance-related components are functioning within specified tolerances. A hospital technician or member of the surgical team performs these procedures before the patient is anesthetized. If the system fails any of the diagnostic tests, surgery must be postponed until the problem can be diagnosed and corrected. ROBODOC software prevents the robotic procedure from continuing until the system has passed all the diagnostic tests.

In the prototype system, attention was focused primarily on quantifying the bottom-line performance specifications, which are the placement accuracy and dimensional accuracy of the implant cavity. The implementation of startup diagnostics required that appropriate component-level performance specifications be identified. This can be a difficult task because many sources of error do not affect the bottom-line performance in a straightforward manner. For example, the effect of a pin location error in the CT data or by the robot often depends on the direction of the error.

Performance specifications were identified for the following components and used in the implementation of startup diagnostics.

FORCE SENSOR To verify the accuracy of the force-sensing system, several readings are taken at different wrist configurations to determine the center of mass and weight of the attached diagnostic tool. The measured values are compared to previously determined values. The center of mass and weight parameters are subsequently used to compensate automatically for weight changes due to reorientation of the tool.

ROBOT XYZ ACCURACY To verify the xyz accuracy of the robot, the robot's ball probe performs a tactile search to locate physically six posts (known points) on a diagnostic fixture attached to the robot base. The approach for this procedure is the same as for pin finding [4]. The actual position of each post was determined initially using a coordinate-measuring machine. The respective post positions, as computed by the robot control computer, must match the actual positions within specified tolerances.

BMM ACCURACY After completion of the xyz test, the BMM probe is attached to the robot end-effector. The robot then executes a series of moves, pausing at predefined locations where output from the BMM is read. The system compares the positions reported by the BMM to robot-reported positions to verify that BMM accuracy is within specified limits.

ROBOT TOOL ACCURACY Accurate positioning and orientation of the robot tool is critical to the safety and success of the surgical procedure. After installing the cutter drive assembly and probe, a sterile diagnostic test checks the calibration parameters to verify that this tool has been properly installed. This test involves contacting a fixed point with multiple wrist configurations and then comparing the robot-sensed locations. Ideally, the robot-sensed locations should be identical as the point is fixed. In reality, there will be some variation in these positions owing to errors in robot accuracy, tool calibration, and the repeatability of the force-based point location strategy. This tool position error must be within a specified tolerance.

User interface modifications

ORTHODOC USER INTERFACE

During development of the first-generation system, significant effort was devoted to ensuring that the planning system (i.e., implant selection and placement) was easy for surgeons to use. Consequently, the second-generation system required few modifications to the planning system. The primary changes to the ORTHODOC user interface are the result of porting to the AIX operating system and adopting the X/Motif standard.

NEW ORTHODOC TOOLS

To make the preoperative planning system easier for end users to operate, new tools were added to facilitate CT data import, locator pin finding, and bone motion detection.

ROBODOC PENDANT AND OR MONITOR

The interface for the canine system included a standard industrial pendant with 32 software-programmable buttons for issuing commands to the robot and a limited amount of space (4 × 16 characters) for text.

The second-generation system was designed to interface directly with the surgical team. Because the technical ability of these end users typically is quite limited, the interface must be easy to operate, powerful, and responsive. The modified interface has the same two hardware components as its predecessor, but the pendant and OR monitor screens have been significantly refined.

A custom five-button pendant controls the robot and provides a means to respond to prompts and menus on the OR monitor. The OR monitor is a large, high-resolution color display. It prompts the surgical team to perform actions (e.g., install a cutting tool) and presents case-specific information for confirmation (e.g., the patient's name and implant type).

The surgeon or OR technician presses buttons on the pendant to select items from the screen. The buttons are labeled *up*, *down*, *select*, *pause*, and *stop*. The *up*, *down*, and *select* buttons are used to navigate through the menus. *Up* and *down* move a highlighted bar from one item to another, and *select* chooses the currently highlighted option.

The *pause* and *stop* buttons allow the surgeon to halt the procedure at any time. Pressing *stop* activates a relay that removes power from the robot motors and cutter (a hardware implementation). Pressing *pause* halts robot motion and turns off the cutter without removing motor power (a software implementation). Pressing *pause* also causes the OR monitor to display the Pause Menu, which contains a number of options, including one to resume robot motion. Thus, the *pause* button provides a convenient means of resuming the procedure. The Pause Menu also allows the surgeon to select certain approved procedural variations, such as moving a soft-tissue retractor, switching to a new nitrogen tank, or replenishing the irrigation system. The user interface of the second-generation system does not require any special technical skills to operate and provides the surgical team with an easy means of interacting with the system and controlling the robot.

ERROR RECOVERY AND EXCEPTION HANDLING

The user interface on the prototype provided few options for recovery from error and exception conditions. The second-generation system required an error-handling mechanism that would allow the surgical team to respond to a variety of exception conditions without engineering assistance.

The mechanism we implemented to handle these situations is a state-based software strategy, which controls the procedural flow using the values of state variables. The implementation includes preprocessor macros that delimit a section of code controlled by a state variable. The system will execute a section of code only if that section and one or more of its dependencies are in the unfinished state. After a section of code is executed, the state variables are set to the finished state.

This implementation of state variables facilitates error recovery and exception handling because the application defines a top-level entry point to the state analysis logic, which can be branched to at any time, from anywhere within the program. Error recovery from exceptions occurring either synchronously or asynchronously in relation to the flow of control can be performed by branching to this entry point. Branching to the top level causes the application to restart the most recent action as the state variable associated with its completion has not yet been set.

Sometimes recovery from an exception condition requires the surgical team to repeat a task that was previously complete. For example, if the BMM detects movement, the three locator pins must be refound because the bone motion exception handler resets the state variable for pin finding when bone motion is detected.

Human clinical experience

In October 1992, the US Food and Drug Administration (FDA) authorized use of the second-generation system in a single-center, 10-patient clinical trial. The purpose of this clinical evaluation was to prove that the system was safe for use by trained surgical teams. None of the patients suffered any intraoperative orthopaedic complications commonly associated with THR surgery, such as femoral fractures. Postoperative evaluations by an independent orthopaedist and postoperative review of x-ray films by an independent radiologist indicated satisfactory outcomes in all cases [7].

After reviewing the results of the first study, the FDA authorized a larger multicenter study in September 1993. This study, which is currently under way, will have a total patient population of 300 (150 in the control group and 150 in the study group). The patients will be randomly assigned to the groups, with the control group undergoing operations with standard surgical techniques. The purpose of this study is to determine the efficacy of the ROBODOC system, and initial results appear positive.

Figure 29.3 shows the ORTHODOC Preoperative Planning Workstation and figure 29.4 the ROBODOC Surgical Assistant System. The system in use during one of the first human surgeries is depicted in figure 29.5.

Conclusions

The canine surgeries demonstrated that the basic design of the prototype was appropriate for its intended

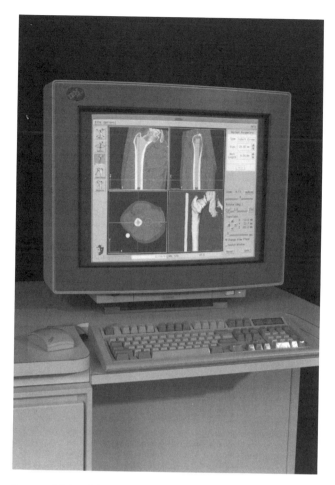

FIGURE 29.3   ORTHODOC Preoperative Planning Workstation.

function. In designing the second-generation system, efforts focused primarily on improving system performance, safety, and the user interface.

The performance-related modifications included improvements to system response time and support for a larger work piece (i.e., a human hip instead of a dog hip). In addition, improvements in the overall system performance were necessary for the proper operation of new safety features, such as the redundant position checking. These improvements were achieved by redesigning the system (i.e., better system integration).

The first-generation system included numerous safety features, such as force threshold checking and independent motion monitoring of the robot tool and bone. These features were retained in the second-generation system, although in many cases a new implementation was required to ensure OR compatibility. For example, the first-generation system included a

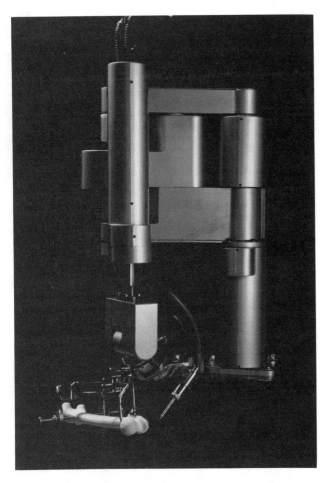

FIGURE 29.4   ROBODOC in a laboratory setting.

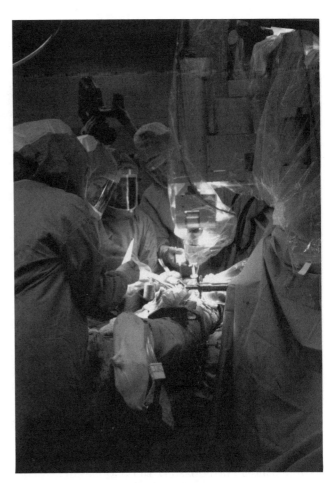

FIGURE 29.5   ROBODOC in the human operating room.

vision-based motion-monitoring system that was not used clinically due to space constraints and lack of an unobstructed view. The second-generation system includes a less obtrusive method based on a second set of position encoders located inside the robot arm. This system also introduces new safety features such as CT scan motion detection, startup diagnostics, data-integrity checking, and data-rationality tests.

The user interface modifications were necessary to allow the system to be used by trained OR personnel instead of by the system developers. ORTHODOC retained its icon-based graphic user interface, although with an X/Motif style. New icons were added to simplify auxiliary tasks such as loading the CT scan data, checking for motion, and finding the pins. The ROBODOC interface hardware was revised to provide a better display and a simpler hand-held pendant. Screen prompts direct the operating room staff through the surgical procedure. The state-based software enforces

the proper procedural flow at all times. Procedural variations are allowed for error recovery or temporary interruptions to the robotic procedure; however, the system prevents the OR team from skipping steps in the procedure. For example, the surgeon can elect to repeat pin finding but cannot cause the system to skip pin finding and start the cutting procedure.

The ROBODOC system is currently being used in a randomized, multicenter clinical trial authorized by the FDA. The purpose of this study is to determine the efficacy of the ROBODOC system for THR, but it will also provide valuable feedback on whether the performance, safety, and user interface modifications described here are sufficient for human clinical use.

ACKNOWLEDGMENTS   The authors acknowledge the contributions of all our colleagues at Integrated Surgical Systems, Inc., who have made this surgical robot a reality. We remember the late Dr. Howard A. Paul, who was responsible for the formation of ISS and who led the company through the first human surgeries. Dr. Russell H. Taylor, from the IBM T. J. Watson Research Center, was instrumental in the development of the first-generation system that predicated the work described here. We also appreciate the technical assistance we received from many sources, particularly Sankyo Seiki, IBM, JR-3, Delta Tau Data Systems, and Sutter General Hospital. We thank Emily Carbone for her assistance with this chapter.

NOTE

1. ROBODOC and ORTHODOC are trademarks of Integrated Surgical Systems, Inc., of Sacramento, California.

REFERENCES

[1] BLOEBAUM, R. D., D. M. RHODES, M. H. RUBMAN, and A. A. HOFMANN, 1991. Bilateral tibial components of different cementless designs and materials: microradiographic, backscattered imaging, and histologic analysis. *Clin. Orthopaed.* 268:179–187.

[2] HANSON, W. A., R. H. TAYLOR, H. A., PAUL, and W. WILLIAMSON, 1990. ORTHODOC—an image driven orthopaedic surgical planning system. In *Proceedings of the Twelfth IEEE Medicine and Biology Conference*, Philadelphia, 12:1931–2.

[3] KAZANZIDES, P., J. ZUHARS, B. D. MITTELSTADT, et al., 1992. Architecture of a surgical robot. In *Proceedings of the IEEE Conference on Systems, Man, and Cybernetics*, Chicago, October, pp. 1621–1624.

[4] KAZANZIDES, P., J. ZUHARS, B. D. MITTELSTADT, and R. H. TAYLOR, 1992. Force sensing and control for a surgical robot. In *Proceedings of the IEEE Conference on Robotics and Automation*, Nice, France, May, pp. 612–624.

[5] KAZANZIDES, P., B. D. MITTELSTADT, J. ZUHARS, P. CAIN, and H. A. PAUL, 1993. Surgical and industrial robots: Comparison and case study. In *Proceedings of the International Robots and Vision Automation Conference*, Detroit, April, pp. 10–19 to 10–26.

[6] CAIN, P., P. KAZANZIDES, J. ZUHARS, B. D. MITTELSTADT, and H. A. PAUL, 1993. Safety considerations in a surgical robot. *Biomed. Sci. Instr.* 29 April, pp. 291–294.

[7] BARGAR, W. L., J. K. TAYLOR, M. LEATHERS, and E. J. CARBONE, 1994. Preoperative planning and surgical technique for cementless femoral components using 3-D imaging and robotics: Report of human pilot study. In *Proceedings of the American Academy of Orthopaedic Surgeons Annual Meeting*, New Orleans, February, p. 110.

30 A Computer-Assisted Total Knee Replacement Surgical System Using a Calibrated Robot

THOMAS C. KIENZLE III, S. DAVID STULBERG,
MICHAEL PESHKIN, ARTHUR QUAID, JON LEA,
AMBARISH GOSWAMI, AND CHI-HAUR WU

Total knee replacement surgery

EVERY YEAR thousands of patients undergo total knee replacement (TKR) surgery in order to return to a more active and pain-free lifestyle. Currently, to install prosthetic knee components (figures 30.1, 30.2), a complex jig system of cutting blocks, alignment rods, and so forth is used to help the surgeon approximate the geometry of the bones and select the appropriate size and location of implants. This process, which relies heavily on an individual surgeon's experience with a given jig system, has prompted the search for a more accurate and repeatable system for the placement of total knee prosthetic components.

The purpose of TKR surgery is to replace the articular surfaces of the knee. Specifically, the end of the femur (thighbone) is replaced with a chrome-plated titanium component and the top of tibia (shinbone) is replaced with a polyethylene-topped titanium device. The patella (kneecap) is also resurfaced with a polyethylene component.

CONVENTIONAL JIG-BASED SYSTEMS

Before a conventional knee replacement surgery, a standard x-ray film of the whole leg (front view) is examined to determine the proper angle of the femoral component with respect to the shaft of the femur. This angle (usually approximately 7°) is chosen such that the tibia will be perpendicular to the ground and be directly under the hip joint.

During surgery, a hole is drilled at the end of the femur and a rod is placed down the center of the bone. A jig is placed on the rod, adjusted to the previously determined angle, and holes drilled into the bone where indicated by the jig. Guide pins are inserted in these holes, a cutting block is placed on the pins, and a cut is made that defines the horizontal plane of the femoral surface. A second jig is inserted on the rod, and the femoral component's remaining degrees of freedom are determined largely by inspection. The tibial component is placed in a similar manner, except that an alignment jig external to the leg is used to direct its positioning.

After all cuts are made, the prosthetic components then are tested in place and a polyethylene spacer chosen to maintain the proper ligament tension and full range of joint motion. The components then are cemented in place.

LIMITATIONS OF JIG-BASED SYSTEMS

It is currently believed that the accuracy of alignment of total knee components affects the surgical outcome for the patient and the longevity of the implant. Using the existing TKR jig systems, implants are oriented within 2° or 3° of the desired "natural" position. These jig systems introduce several sources of inaccuracy in alignment of the prosthetic components. One major source of error is that only the very ends of the involved bones are exposed during operation, forcing the surgeon to make decisions regarding the alignment of the

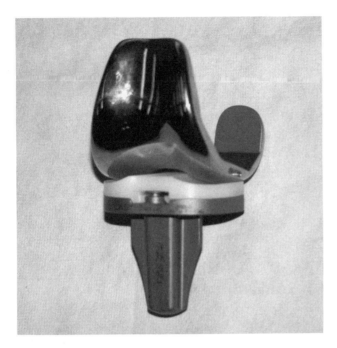

FIGURE 30.1 Prosthetic components used in total knee replacement surgery.

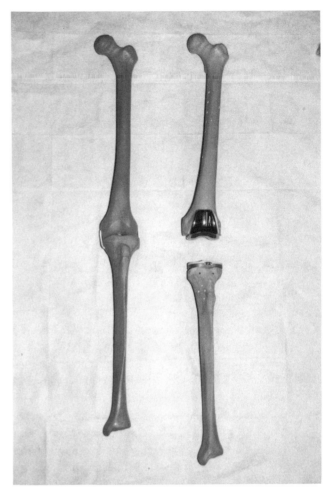

FIGURE 30.2 Femur and tibia before and after total knee replacement.

bones and joints based on very limited information. The preoperative x-ray film can help but still represents only a 2D projection of complex 3D structures.

A second source of error is the jig system itself, which represents a physical embodiment of an implant placement algorithm favored by the system's designer. Optimal placement of implants may not be achieved when the configuration of an individual patient's bones differ from those of the generalized model assumed by the jig system, or if the algorithm on which the system is based is suboptimal or obsolete.

Further, the existing jig systems, by necessity, direct a set of cuts in the bones based largely on local topography. It is hoped that these cuts will lead to the proper placement of the implants. A preferable approach would be to visualize the correct placement of the prosthesis, based on the overall geometry of the leg, and then determine the proper cuts required to achieve optimum placement.

MOTIVATION FOR ROBOTIC SYSTEMS IN TKR

An integrated system has been developed that uses a workstation displaying a 3D model of the patient's bones (obtained from a CT scan of the leg) and a modified industrial robot to direct the placement

of prosthetic components. The single focus of our computer-assisted TKR system is the accurate global positioning of components. In contrast, in previous work with computer-robotic total joint systems, such as Integrated Surgical Systems' (ISS) total hip replacement system [1], accurate machining of local surfaces has been of vital importance. In our TKR system, a graphics computer allows prosthesis placement decisions to be made by the surgeon based on a full view of the bones involved. A component placement algorithm can be implemented in software where it can be easily altered to accommodate an individual patient's bones or updated as better algorithms are developed. Finally, the intended component placement can be visualized and, if necessary, corrected well before any live bones are cut.

In addition to benefits from improved component placement, a computer-robotic system ultimately may allow for a smaller incision in the patient and require less time for surgery, which may both decrease complications due to infection and reduce the cost of surgery. Also, by using a computer to plan component placement and a robot to perform it, decisions made during the process are repeatable, can be accurately implemented and are readily available for systematic study of optimum component placement geometry.

System operation

To describe the computer-robotic system developed, it is easiest to step through the TKR procedure sequentially. The key steps are as follows:

Preoperative procedures
• Place five landmark pins in the patient's femur and tibia that will act as fiducial points for registration of the preoperative plan to the actual bones.
• Obtain a CT scan of the patient. Construct a 3D bone model from CT data, with reference frames based on the landmark pins and the femoral head.
• Using a graphics workstation, plan the placement of the femoral and tibial prosthetic components.

Surgical procedures
• Immobilize the bones using specially designed fixtures.
• Use the robot to determine the coordinates of the landmark pins on the femur, in order to register the femur to the preoperative plan.
• Use the robot to track the distal end of the femur as the femur is moved on a sphere about the femoral head. Infer the center of the femoral head for registration.
• Use the robot to guide the surgical cuts for placement of the femoral implant.
• Locate the landmark pins on the tibia.
• Use the robot to guide the surgical cuts for placement of the tibial implant.

LANDMARK PIN PLACEMENT

During a preoperative visit, the surgeon places four small landmark pins in the patient's bones at the knee to serve as fiducial markers to correlate (register) the CT and robot reference frames. Two pins are inserted into the lower end of the femur and two others into the

top of the tibia. Also during the preoperative office visit, a fiberglass tape cast is fit around the patient's ankle. Once hardened, the cast is removed carefully, and a landmark pin is placed in the cast over the medial malleolus (inner ankle bone). These pins provide five of the six fiducial markers necessary to define reference frames for the two bones. The sixth will be provided by the center of the femoral head (center of the hip socket).

CT SCAN AND PREOPERATIVE PLANNING

A CT scan is obtained of the patient's leg with the ankle cast (with pin) in place. Numerous slices (typically 75) of CT data are required in order to provide a sufficiently complete model of the bones. High CT resolution (slice spacing of 1.5 mm) is used in the vicinity of the landmark pins and the knee joint.

The CT data are read into a 486 personal computer with high resolution graphics. The CT representation is converted into a 3D model of the bones (figure 30.3). A 3D surface model of the bones is generated from the CT slices. Edge-detection algorithms are used to identify the boundaries between bone and soft tissue on each slice. Editing functions are provided to allow the user to modify the outlines. These 2D curves then are combined into surface models representing the tibia, the femur, and parts of the pelvis and foot.

When the 3D models of the bones have been built, the surgeon can begin preoperative planning. Graphic software allows the surgeon full freedom to simulate almost any function on the computer that could be

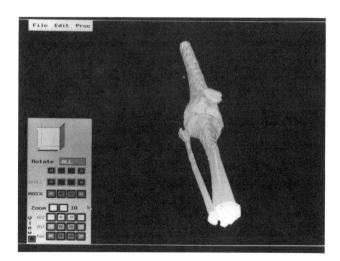

FIGURE 30.3 Three-dimensional bone reconstruction screen.

performed in the operating room. This includes, but is not limited to, moving the bones, rotating the joints, cutting and drilling the bones, and manipulating representations of any tools necessary during surgery. Further, the surgeon can view the bones from any angle and, ultimately, simulate the motion of the joint to verify the proper placement of the implant. A command file allows the surgeon to specify the sequence of steps to be performed in the preoperative plan. This flexible graphics system allows the surgeon to simulate the direct placement of the prosthetic components on the bones without introducing the approximations of a jig system. The exact criteria and algorithms for this direct process will be developed and refined based on numerous sources, including computer modeling, gait analysis, orthopaedic research, and surgical experience.

When the surgeon has determined the desired placement of the implant and has simulated the actions required to achieve it, location coordinates are stored for use by the robot controller. Included in this information are the locations and orientations, in the CT reference frame, of the six fiducial markers and of each planar cut to be made and hole to be drilled.

FEMORAL FIDUCIAL LOCATION

In the operating room, the patient's hip is immobilized with respect to the robot using a set of special fixtures. After making the opening incision, the surgeon places a custom-designed femoral clamp on the distal end of the femur (near the knee). The robot then is attached to the femoral clamp by means of a magnetic ball joint affixed to the robot's end-effector. (The end-effector is an integrated surgical tool, which is also equipped with drill and saw guides, a pin-finding probe, and attachment points for other accessories.) The first fiducial to be established is the location of the center of the femoral head. This point is determined by force-following the robot as the thigh is moved manually in a sphere centered at the hip joint. This process, referred to as *femur tracking* and described more fully later, estimates the center of the femoral head. Once this fiducial marker is established, the femoral clamp is disconnected from the robot and immobilized by a rigid fixturing arm. With the help of a small pin-finding probe attached to the end-effector, the robot is used to measure the coordinates of the final two femoral landmark pins. The robot, the surgical table, and fixturing for the pelvis, knee, and ankle are shown in figure 30.4.

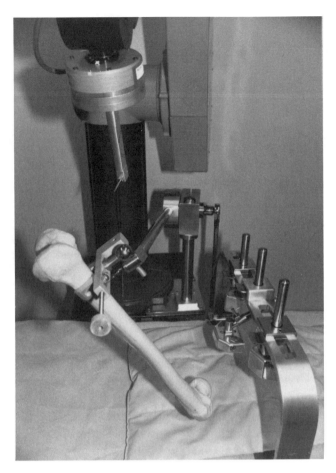

FIGURE 30.4 Robot, surgical table, and fixturing.

FEMORAL COMPONENT PLACEMENT

To orient the cuts for the femoral prosthetic component, a small cutting block needs to be placed on the bone. This defines the planes of the desired cuts. The robot is led to the approximate location. Using the three fiducial markers as reference points, the robot makes a small corrective movement to position a drill guide (built into the end-effector) where the holes for the block are to be placed. After double-checking the positioning, the surgeon drills the holes, leads the robot away from the knee, places guide pins in the holes, slides a cutting block onto the pins, and uses a bone saw resting on the cutting block to resect the bone.

TIBIAL FIDUCIAL LOCATION AND COMPONENT PLACEMENT

A similar procedure is used for the tibia, except that all the three tibial fiducial points are landmark pins. The tibia is immobilized using a rigid arm and a rod wedged in the intramedullary canal of the bone. The coordinates of the three landmark pins are located with the robot. The robot is again led to the approximate location of the holes to be drilled for a cutting block and allowed to make a small corrective movement. After drilling the holes and making the cuts, the surgeon continues the operation, from fitting the prosthetic components to closing the incision, in the conventional manner.

Fixturing

To allow the robot to align the resections accurately as specified by the graphics system, it is important that the patient's bones be held immobile with respect to the robot. There are several links that must be held as rigidly as possible: robot base to end of femur or tibia, surgical table to pelvis, surgical table to ankle, and robot base to surgical table. Each link has its own requirements and will be discussed briefly.

IMMOBILIZATION OF THE KNEE

The fixturing that immobilizes the distal femur and proximal tibia with respect to the robot base is the most crucial connection for the accuracy of the system. Any motion between these parts of the bones and the robot base will be directly translated into errors in landmark pin localization or guide hole location. A further requirement of this connection is that it have a high degree of freedom before being locked down because the knee has little freedom of movement once the pelvis and ankles have been connected to the table. For this reason, a 6–degrees of freedom fixturing arm with heavy-duty locking joints, similar in configuration to a spherical joint robot arm, is used (see figure 30.4).

Even with an extremely rigid fixturing arm, a major challenge remains to interface it to the bones. Only a relatively small area of bone is exposed and available for contact with an interfacing device. Further, this device must not interfere with the robot, landmark pins, cutting blocks, or bone saw. For the femur, a small bar clamp with pivoting jaws that grip the distal shaft of the bone is used. For the tibia, a rod is placed down the central canal and is firmly wedged. Both devices have a protruding post that allows connection to the end of the fixturing arm.

IMMOBILIZATION OF THE PELVIS AND ANKLE

The fixturing of the pelvis and ankle is less demanding than that of the knee, as a quarter of an inch of motion translates into less than a degree of rotation of the bone. However, there are no exposed bones to which clamps can be attached. Thus, sufficient clamping force must be applied to the ankle and pelvis with special fixtures to immobilize the underlying bone sufficiently, yet not to damage soft tissue.

In immobilizing the pelvis, the fixturing must allow full rotational range of motion of the hip joint so that the leg may be flexed by the surgeon (see femur tracking in a later section) while preventing any translational motion of the pelvis. A vacuum pack, a commercially available bag that hardens and molds to contour when air is removed, is used under the lower back of the patient during surgery to prevent pressure sore development without sacrificing rigidity. Downward pressure is applied to the pelvis at three points using anatomically contoured, foam-covered aluminum blocks attached to an adjustable pressure frame (or hipband) that connects to the surgical table (see figure 30.4).

Fiducial identification and registration

Crucial to the accuracy of the system as a whole is accurate registration of the femur and tibia to their images in the CT data on which preoperative planning was done. Therefore, it is essential that the locations of the fiducial markers be accurately determined in both the CT image and on the actual bones in the operating room.

LANDMARK PINS

The landmark pins must hold the thin cortical and the underlying soft trabecular bone of the knee joint without loosening and be small enough to be inserted through the skin as an office procedure. Further, they must be easily identified and accurately located both in CT images and in the operating room by the robot. The landmark pins are modified titanium screws with a chisel point machined into the tip and a recessed cone machined into the head. A drive tool allows the surgeon to insert the pins into the patient's bone.

The five landmark pins (four in the patient's bones and one affixed to the fiberglass ankle cast) are identified in the CT data, and their locations and orientations are stored in the computer. In the operating room, the robot finds each pin by having its pointer manually guided to the vicinity of the pin and then advancing slowly along the axis of the pin under force control until the end of the pointer is seated accurately in the bottom of the recessed cone.

CENTER OF THE FEMORAL HEAD

Assigning a third fiducial marker to the proximal femur presents a challenge. In most patients, the thigh is surrounded by sufficient soft tissue (muscle and adipose) to prevent any artificial fiducial on the skin surface from being consistently and reliably located with respect to the bone. Further, it is undesirable to subject the patient to the trauma of inserting a landmark pin anywhere but at the joint involved in the surgery. Therefore, the sixth fiducial point chosen is one that is never directly touched: the center of the head of the femur. It is found in the CT scan by identifying several points on the spherical face of the femoral head and calculating its center.

In the operating room, the robot must find the location of the center of the femoral head indirectly. With the robot clamped to the knee, the surgeon manually moves the entire leg (which is able to rotate only about the femoral head) through substantial arcs, while the attached robot samples positions. The center of the femoral head can then be inferred as the center of a sphere fit to the recorded positions.

Robot system and calibration

The robot system is based on a 6–degrees of freedom Unimation (Danburg, Ct.) PUMA 560 robot with a VAL controller and a six-axis end-point force sensor. Mounted on the force sensor is the surgical end-effector. A 486 personal computer communicates with the PUMA controller and serves as the system's high-level controller. A command file, distinct from that used in the graphics subsystem, allows the surgeon to define the steps of the procedure to be performed in the operating room. During the operation, the surgeon communicates with the robot system through pushbuttons on a hand-held control box that directs the sequencing of steps. Commands available in the command file include large passive movements of the robot by the surgeon (force following), small precise adjusting movements made by the robot, and programmed sequences that calibrate the end-effector, find locator pins, and identify the center of the femoral head.

Accuracy of the robot is critical to the successful implementation of the off-line strategies in a robotic surgery. Off-the-shelf robots are surprisingly inaccurate. Calibration is a practical way to improve the accuracy of a robot. In the rest of this section we describe motivation, theory, implementation, and performance of our calibration method. A more detailed description may be found in Goswanmi, Quaid, and Peshkin [2].

WHY IS CALIBRATION NECESSARY?

Because we program the robot off-line in order to implement preplanned surgical strategies, its *absolute accuracy*, in addition to its *repeatability*, is crucial for the success of the operation. Repeatability of a robot is the precision with which its end point achieves a particular pose under repeated commands to the same set of joint angles. The pose of a robot is expressed as a six-vector consisting of the position and orientation of its end point with respect to some reference coordinate frame.

Absolute accuracy represents the closeness with which the robot's actual pose matches the pose predicted by its controller. A robot may have high repeatability while having low absolute accuracy. Given the joint angles, the controller of a robot computes its end-point location and orientation. For this, it needs an accurate description of the robot that involves many physical parameters such as link lengths and joint offsets. These numeric parameters make up the kinematic model of the robot. The absolute accuracy of the robot depends on the accuracy of this model.

For various reasons, the numeric values of the kinematic parameters for a robot may not be correct. This may be due to manufacturing tolerances, deviations such as link and joint compliance, or time-dependent effects such as gear wear and component damage. Therefore, the nominal kinematic model that is programmed into the robot's controller cannot accurately compute the end-point pose from the joint angles. A practical approach to address this problem is to re-evaluate the parameters of a robot by using a calibration scheme. Periodic calibration of surgical robots is extremely important for safe and successful surgical procedures.

Our calibration scheme

The measuring device we used is known as a *telescopic ball-bar system*, manufactured by Automated Precision, Inc. It is relatively inexpensive, easy to use, and highly accurate. The heart of the system is a linear transducer (LVDT), with a maximum travel of 7.5 cm. The LVDT precisely measures the distance of the robot end point from a fixed location. The system setup is shown in figure 30.5.

The ball-bar has a magnetic chuck permanently mounted at one end and a removable high-precision steel sphere mounted at the opposite end. The removable sphere allows the insertion of extension rods, which permit the nominal length of the device to be increased in order to reach more of the robot's work space if desired. Additional magnetic chucks and steel

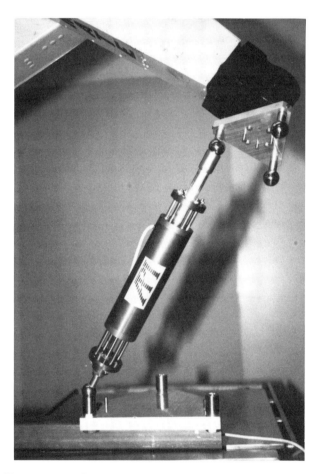

FIGURE 30.5 The calibration system with the ball-bar connected between one of three steel spheres attached to the robot end point and a magnetic chuck mounted on the table.

spheres mate with the ends of the device to form spherical joints. In our implementation, the sphere end of the ball-bar pivots around one of three stationary magnetic chucks mounted in the work space, while the chuck end of the ball-bar mates with one of the three steel spheres connected to the robot's moving end point.

The calibration system must read robot joint positions and LVDT lengths for various robot poses within the work space of the robot and within reach of the ball-bar. Simultaneously, using forward kinematics and the nominal robot kinematic model, the expected position of the robot end point can be calculated from the joint positions. This position gives us the expected location of the movable end of the ball-bar. The distance between the two ends is the expected ball-bar length. The difference between the expected ball-bar length and the actual length measured by the LVDT is the error due to incorrect robot kinematic parameters. We compute new parameters that minimize this error.

Our current method compensates only the static geometric errors of a robot because their contribution to the overall error is the largest. With a suitable model, our approach may be extended to include nongeometric parameters as well. The maximum number of *independent* kinematic parameters, N, of a robot is given by

$$N = 5n_r + 3n_p + 6 \qquad (1)$$

where n_r is the number of revolute joints and n_p is the number of prismatic joints in the robot. (In earlier literature, equation 1 was given as $N = 4n_r + 2n_p + 6$ because a conversion constant for each joint encoder was not included in the kinematic model, see [2].)

Regardless of the total number of physical parameters in the kinematic description of the robot, which may be much larger, N is the maximum number of parameters that can be identified by collecting data at the robot's end point alone. N is also the number of parameters sufficient to compute the end-point position and orientation from the robot's joint angles.

Allowing six parameters per link and two parameters per joint, a total of 54 parameters (for seven links and six joints) are required to describe the manipulator completely. According to equation 1, only 36 parameters may be identified. As mentioned earlier, these 36 are a sufficient set to compute endpoint pose from joint encoder outputs, even though they are not sufficient, for instance, to identify which specific manufacturing tolerances were exceeded in constructing the robot.

In practice, the computed distance from the end-point-mounted steel sphere to the fixed magnetic chuck will be different from the actual distance, as measured by the LVDT in the ball-bar. The difference, known as the *residual*, is determined at many data collection points scattered throughout the reachable work space. The aggregate sum-of-squares of the residuals (over all data collection points) is used as an objective function and is to be minimized by parameter estimation to ensure the best possible manipulator accuracy.

To identify all the independent parameters of a robot, one usually obtains both position and attitude data of the robot end point, which requires the use of a sophisticated measuring device. We have found that our simple (and less expensive) measuring device is equally capable of identifying all the robot parameters. Further details of our calibration method have been reported elsewhere [2].

Future work

Preparations are being made for extensive cadaveric testing to assess the accuracy of implant placement. Preliminary subsystem testing indicates that a goal of less than 1 mm of translational error and less than 1° of rotational error is achievable.

As the system evolves from the laboratory to the operating room, improvements to provide additional reliability, safety, and ease of use will be incorporated.

One improvement currently being developed is the use of the robot's end-effector as a cutting guide instead of as a drill guide. This will eliminate several manual steps in the procedure involving the cutting blocks and alleviate inaccuracies they introduce.

In the future, some components of this system could be adapted for other operations, including osteotomies, ligament reconstructions, and arthroplasty of joints other than the knee.

ACKNOWLEDGMENTS Support for this research was provided by Northwestern University, Northwestern Memorial Hospital, and National Science Foundation PYI grant DMC-8857854. Mike Brown, Dane Watkins, Rob Lentini, Boris Klovsky, and Amy Stock helped us with the fixturing prototypes. We would also like to thank James Bosnik of Drexel University for useful discussions, especially in regard to the idea of the robot end-point fixture. Kornel Ehmann of Northwestern University drew our attention to the use of the ball-bar for calibration purposes. Kam Lau of Automated Precision, Inc., was instrumental in making the ball-bar device available to us at a subsidized price.

REFERENCES

[1] PAUL, H. A., et al., 1992. A surgical robot for total hip replacement surgery. In *Proceedings of the 1992 IEEE International Conference on Robotics and Automation*, Nice, France, pp. 606–611.
[2] GOSWAMI, A., A. QUAID, and M. A. PESHKIN, 1993. Identifying robot parameters using partial pose information. *IEEE Control Systems Magazine* 13(5):6–14.

31 Computer-Assisted Knee Arthroplasty

MAURILIO MARCACCI, PAOLO DARIO, MARCO FADDA, GIAMPIERO MARCENARO, AND SANDRA MARTELLI

THE EMPLOYMENT of robotic technology in orthopaedics and particularly in robot-assisted knee replacement and reconstructive surgery aims mainly at improving the results of joint prosthesis implants. In fact, despite 10 years' experience with this type of surgery and the evolution of materials and designs that have recently taken place, most of the bad results depend on the lack of precision in the implantation technique [1, 2]. Although some causes of failure can probably be eliminated on implantation of the prosthesis by refining surgical technique, it is unthinkable that the prosthetic patterns presently available can give satisfactory results in surgical revisions or in cases of serious bone deformities [3].

In fact, the main obstacles to further improvement of the surgical results center on the following issues:

1. The prosthesis shape is based on a standard model that must be adapted to the constitution and individual kinematics (figure 31.1). It seems that the present generalizations need further improvement. In fact, joint kinematics of the knee with an implanted prosthesis still have not been completely clarified: The points that remain unclear involve the correlation between flexion and instantaneous rotation and concern the femoropatellar zones that are in contact during the bending range under load.

2. Furthermore, difficulties may arise in adjusting the patient's bone as precisely as possible to the standard prosthesis design. Human hands, however expert they may be, are liable to err in the fine preparation of the upper bone surfaces to the minimun acceptable tolerance.

3. In some cases, and usually in implant revision, it is difficult to make the prosthesis pattern correspond to deformed joint heads that have insufficient and irregular bone planes. The ideal is to model the prosthesis exactly in relation to the contact and support zones.

However, in this way the shape of the prosthesis surfaces becomes so complex as to make surgical preparation of the bone wall impossible.

To overcome these difficulties, we believe a robotic system assisting the surgeon is particularly suitable. This consists of a graphic workstation to which a robotic manipulator is connected, integral with the operating table and including a set of any safety systems and automatic controls. Such a system has numerous advantages: First, it permits accurate planning on an individual model of the joint that can, in future, also include simulation of the kinematics and dynamics of the joint. Using a computer lets the user consider a greater number of variables and individual parameters to simulate and solve particularly complex reconstructions. Finally, the use of manipulators when carrying out bone resections ensures accuracy to within a few tenths of a millimeter (both in the position and orientation of the surfaces) and provides an intelligent instrument that is simpler to use than those currently available.

Of course, various research themes still demand attention. The method for recognizing the patient's position in the robot's working area still is not satisfactory. An ideal matching should be absolutely precise, sensitive to the slightest change in instantaneous ratio and with trauma as slight as possible. Also, it is necessary to check the quality of the computer-assisted implant by means of further measurements, as well as to judge how much more accurate surgical preparation of the bone surfaces can be, compared to what can be done by humans. The apparatus that guarantees absolute safety of both the patient and the physicians needs to be completed. Finally, it is necessary to verify the utility of such a complex, costly system by a cost-benefit analysis.

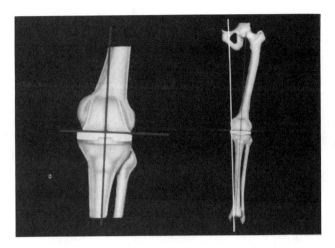

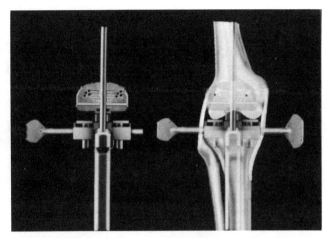

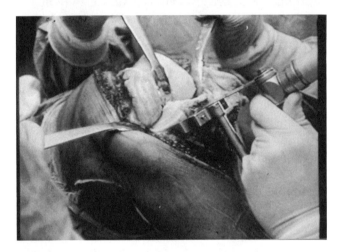

FIGURE 31.1 Standard implanted prostheses in clinical interventions at Istituti Ortopedici Rizzoli. In the total knee replacement, both tibial and femoral extremities are removed and reconstructed. Note that the shape and orientation of resections on tibia and femur are determined by the inner shape of the prosthesis.

Certainly, considering the present state of surgery, application of the robot may raise a few eyebrows. Nonetheless, in our opinion, the employment of robots not only in surgical technique but also in the study of osteoarticular physiology contributes greatly to our knowledge.

Description of the operation

The knee prosthesis is widely indicated in reconstructive surgery—that is, in patients suffering from arthosis, rheumatoid arthritis, and posttraumatic arthrosis. It has been shown that if the technique is correct, the results are positive in more than 85% of cases even 10 years after the operation [3].

Knee arthroplasty consists in the implantation of a tibial and a femoral component to replace the distal extremity of the femur and the proximal extremity of the tibia. The exact surgical procedure depends on the specific model of knee prosthesis chosen and requires the use of very complex, specific mechanical instrumentation (guides, positioning devices, cutting, and milling tools; figure 31.2).

In the past, the prostheses generally were fixed with acrylic cement at the bone heads, but current preference is given to a press-fit system, without cement, for fixation of the implant. When using this second technique, extreme precision is necessary in preparing the

FIGURE 31.2 Instrumentation (top) and execution (bottom) of resections for implantation of the knee prosthesis.

bone wall so that contact with the prosthesis is as extensive and stable as possible (figures 31.3, 31.4). For this reason, the use of mechanical instruments guided by a robot appears highly advantageous. The implantation technique provides for surgical exposure of the joint surface, carried out in accordance with ordinary criteria and techniques. When preparing the bone heads, use of the robot may change the technique currently in use: In fact, though at present complex instrumentation for achieving accurate cuts is in use, it is foreseen that the robot will execute resections autonomously in accordance with the presurgical planning [4].

The great difference between the manual and automated techniques is expected to be the precision in preparing the cuts and the exactness of joint reconstruction and limb alignment. Once the bones have been

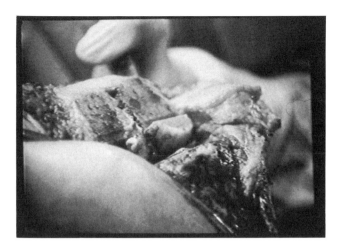

FIGURE 31.3 Resections for implantation of the knee prosthesis. The preparation of these surfaces is the most critical phase of the intervention.

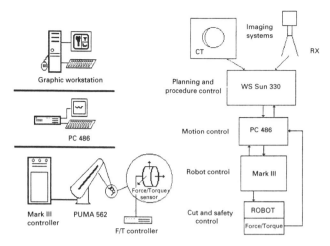

FIGURE 31.5 The present laboratory setup, including robots, workstation, control computers, and sensors.

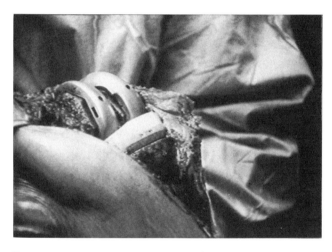

FIGURE 31.4 Implantation of knee prosthesis. In this picture, the reconstructed joint is shown and the stability of the prosthesis is tested.

prepared, the two components of a temporary removable prosthesis are implanted, and stability of the new joint is checked. Friction between the components of the joint is tested by flexing the knee, and shape of the resections (or the components themselves) is finely adjusted by the surgeon, if necessary.

Computer- and robot-assisted implementation

As mentioned earlier, the crucial point of knee prosthesis implantation is the execution of a succession of variably oriented flat surfaces that have to be identified on

the femur and tibia. It must be possible to plan position and orientation of these surfaces prior to the operation, and they must be clearly identifiable with reference to the limb's mechanical axis. To reproduce such a procedure automatically, we have furnished the laboratory with a SUN 330 graphic workstation (figure 31.5), two PUMA robots—different in size and load capacity—and a system of control computers as a link between the workstation, the robots and any safety systems fitted to them. Computer planning [4, 5] is a basic step in the procedure we are testing in our current laboratory project. This planning phase begins with the acquisition of a sequence of CT images of the limb, from which the 3D model of the joint is reconstructed (figure 31.6). Our system is voxel-based, and the acquisition, as well as the processing algorithms, always takes into account complete volumetric information of all the anatomic parts. This guarantees precise recognition of the different anatomic structures and their visualization in the way the surgeon is accustomed to evaluating them for the patient on whom he or she is operating. On the question of volumetric reconstruction, the surgeon can examine both the anatomic details and the mechanical characteristics of the knee to be treated. Selection of the prosthesis's position will be interactively made, because the surgeon will choose the size of prosthesis to implant and may change the proposed orientation should the automatically calculated standard prove unsatisfactory. It will, in future, also be possible to simulate the result of the implant in real time, according to the chosen specifications, in order to

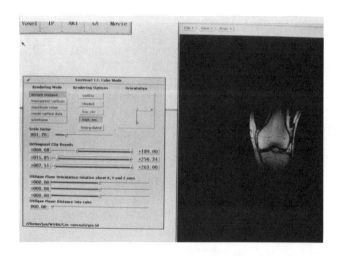

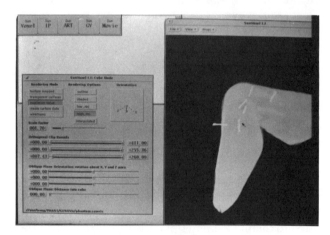

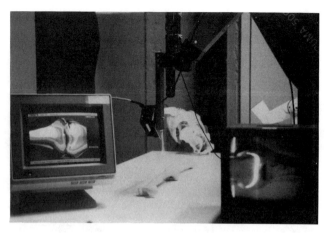

FIGURE 31.7 Experimental noninvasive matching using a laser range system. Tests are carried out on synthetic bones.

FIGURE 31.6 Planning on the SUN workstation. The model shown here is a reconstruction of a knee joint by SUN standard functions (standard image resolution: 0.5 mm; distance between two successive slices: 0.5 mm).

analyze in advance the kinematic behavior after implantation. Currently, this is checked during the operation, after carrying out the resections, with a temporary test prosthesis.

Accurate planning is already a particular characteristic of the computer-assisted operation, but the main advantage of a system combining computer planning and robot execution is that it gives to the surgeon the possibility to operate with the same precision as that planned. The most critical point of the procedure is the precise transformation of data from the SUN workstation, on which planning is performed, to the PUMA 560 robot, which is used to carry out the resections of the tibia and femur. The change of coordinates from the preoperative reference system on the CT scans of the limb to the intraoperative one in the robot's work space is currently in the implemental and verification phase.

Though we are investigating the possibility of noninvasive matching based on the use of a laser scanning system (figure 31.7) in order to identify the position of the exposed joint on the operating table, the most promising technique at the moment calls for the placing of individual artificial markers on the tibia and femur. The idea is to implant three small markers (length: 10–20 mm; head: 5-mm diameter) on the terminal part of the femur involved in the operation, which must therefore be exposed in the operating theater, and two markers on the proximal epiphysis of the tibia. The third reference necessary to identify it unambiguously may be placed externally, fixed to the ankle, where the skin is very thin and the bone very superficial. The procedure is composed of two phases: First, a CT scan of the bone is obtained and the markers are reproduced in the 3D model of the joint. Second, after the exposure of the joint, the robot, driven by a force-torque sensor, is put in contact with the markers and roughly aligned with its axis, and markers' positions and axes are automatically computed (figures 31.8, 31.9). Thus, the use of markers does not involve additional surgical aggression. Thanks to consolidated experience in the field of stereotaxis [7] and in prosthestic implants in the dog's hip [8, 9], we expect to maintain the precision of the planning in the execution phase.

The robot comes into action again after the matching phase, when the system is ready to make the resections. A high-speed osteotribe (approximately

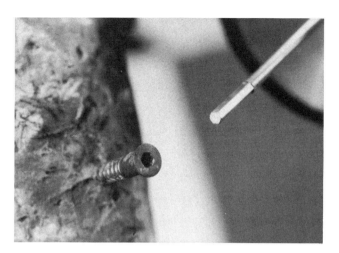

FIGURE 31.8 Trial marker and tool used for the matching phase. The probe is introduced in the hole until its bottom is reached, and tangential forces are cleared in order to align the probe and the marker's axis.

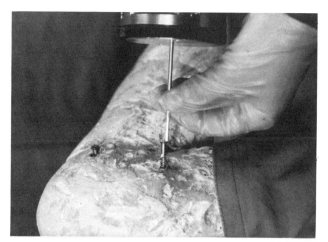

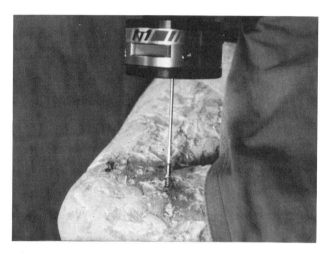

FIGURE 31.9 Example of the matching procedure on a phantom. Automatic search for markers' alignment and position for two successive markers.

80,000 rpm) replaces the matching probe on the robot's wrist (figure 31.10). As in the matching phase, a force-torque sensor is interposed between the osteotribe and the robot's joint in order to evaluate the reaction forces during sectioning (resolution along each axis better than 0.3 N). Present results show that standard reactions do not exceed 15 N, and a dangerous threshold for forces is set at 30 N during the cutting phase. This will contribute to increasing the safety of the patient, the robot manipulator, and the surgical instrument itself. At present, the trajectory the manipulator follows during execution is planned on the workstation, depending on analysis of the preoperative images according to an experimentally controlled strategy of advancement. The robot is controlled in position and carries out a succession of linear strokes until a perfectly smooth flat surface is described (figures 31.11 and 31.12). Further results are shown in figures 31.13 and 31.14.

During the automatic execution of knee interventions it is particularly important to check the position of the surgical instrument with respect to the numerous anatomic structures to be preserved. Delimitation of the volume of action given to the robot can be guaranteed by controlling it in position, but it must be supported by an intraoperative feedback in order to be compared with the strategy planned on the workstation. Additional dedicated mechanical constraints could be used to ensure complete safety of the operation.

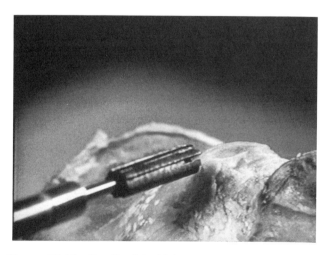

FIGURE 31.10 Details of the high-speed (80,000 rpm) osteotribe used for robot-assisted resection preparation.

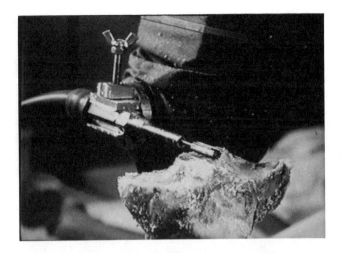

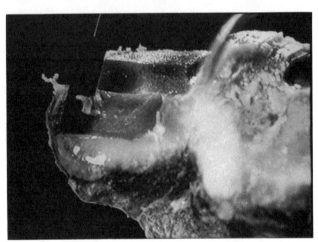

FIGURE 31.11 Automatic execution of knee resections using the high-speed osteotribe on a cow tibia (in vitro tests).

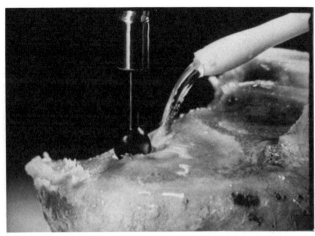

FIGURE 31.13 An example of trials for drilling holes on a cow tibia (in vitro tests). A submillimeter precision of positioning is achieved and the smoothness of the hole walls meets our requirements.

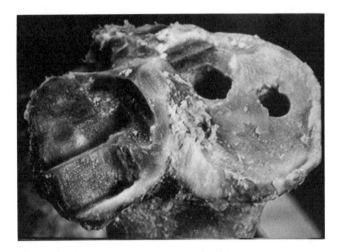

FIGURE 31.14 Examples of results obtained by the high-speed osteotribe mounted on the PUMA 560 robot, used without force feedback. In vitro tests are performed on a cow tibia. The smoothness of the surfaces and the sharpness of edges meet physicians' requirements.

Conclusions

The employment of a knee prosthesis implantation procedure assisted by a robot constitutes an important attempt at evolution in orthopaedic surgical technique and aims at achieving perfect recovery of limb functionality as well as a sufficiently long duration of the implant. The possibilities offered by a system consisting of a workstation for data and biomedical image pro-

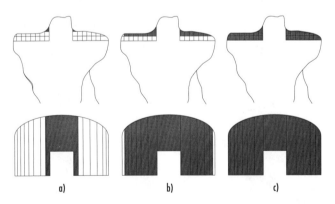

FIGURE 31.12 (a–c) An example of a possible strategy for the approximation of the tibial resection on a cow tibia (in vitro tests).

cessing, along with a connected robot manipulator, can already be appreciated in the experimental tests carried out in our laboratory even if, at present, only partial but significant aspects of the full programmed procedure are assessable. For example, computer planning of the operation can be effected by the surgeon in a period comparable to that already dedicated to preoperative study. In fact, automatic processing of the standard strategy does not require more than 10 minutes, and even possible future checking of the matching between the chosen prosthesis and the programmed resections will not need more than 5 minutes. Planning the operation at the computer workstation is therefore a technique that is easily used and flexible. As for the execution of flat surfaces with a robot manipulator, preliminary experiments show that surfaces obtained have both a finished level and dimensional precision on the order of a few tenths of a millimeter [10].

Today some problems remain to be solved by the scientific community. These concern, above all, the intrinsic safety of a manipulator's actions in the operating room. Although further investigations are needed, we believe that the evolution of automatic systems to assist the orthopaedic surgeon offer promise for important applications.

REFERENCES

[1] EWALD, F. C., M. A. JACOBS, R. E. MIEGEL, P. S. WALKER, R. POSS, and C. B. SLEDGE, 1984. Kinematic total knee replacement. *J. Bone Joint Surg.* 66-A(7):1032–1040.

[2] UEMATSU, O., H. P. HSU, K. M. KELLEY, F. C. EWALD, and P. S., WALKER, 1987. Radiographic study of Kinematic total knee arthroplasty. *J. Arthroplasty* 2(4):317–326.

[3] MARCACCI, M., R. BUDA, S. ZAFFAGNINI, A. VISANI, F. IACONO, and M. P. NERI, 1992. Press-fit vs. porous-coated knee prosthesis implant. Comparison of the results with a minimum follow-up of 3 years. In *Transactions of the Second Annual Conference of the European Orthopaedic Research Society*, Varese, Italy, September 27–30, p. 154.

[4] BELTRAME, F., P. DARIO, M. FADDA, M. MARCACCI, G. MARCENARO, G. MARTELLI, G. SANDINI, and A. VISANI, 1991. A laboratory for computer-assisted orthopaedic surgery. *Newsletter of the IEEE Robotics and Automation Society* 5(4):16–19.

[5] MARCENARO, G., F. BELTRAME, P. DARIO, M. FADDA, M. MARCACCI, S. MARTELLI, and A. VISANI, 1992. Computer planning of bone resections for knee prosthesis implantation. In *Proceedings of the Second International Conference on Automation Robotics and Computer Vision* (ICARCV), Singapore, pp. CV-2.3.1–2.3.5.

[6] LAVALLÉE, S., R. SZELISKI, and L. BRUNIE, 1991. Matching 3D smooth surfaces with 2D projections using 3D distance maps. In *Proceedings of S.P.I.E.: Geometric Methods in Computer Vision*, San Diego, July 25–26, pp. 322–336.

[7] LAVALLÉE, S., and P. CINQUIN, 1991. IGOR: Image guided operating robot. In *Proceedings of the Fifth International Conference on Advanced Robotics* (ICAR '91), Pisa, Italy, pp. 876–881.

[8] PAUL, H. A., B. MITTLESTADT, W. BARGAR, B. MUSITS, R. TAYLOR, P. KAZANZIDES, J. ZUHARS, B. WILLIAMSON, and W. HANSON, 1992. A surgical robot for total hip replacement surgery. In *Proceedings of the 1992 IEEE International Conference on Robotics and Automation*, Nice, France, pp. 606–611.

[9] TAYLOR, R. H., H. A. PAUL, C. B. CUTTING, B. D. MITTELSTADT, W. HANSON, P. KAZANZIDES, B. MUSITS, Y. Y. KIM, A. KALVIN, B. HADDAD, D. KHORAMABADI, and D. LAROSE, 1992. Augmentation of human precision in computer integrated surgery. *ITBM* 13(4):450–468.

[10] MARTELLI, S., M. FADDA, P. DARIO, M. MARCACCI, and A. VISANI, 1992. Analysis of the accuracy of a robotic procedure for knee arthroplasty. In *Proceedings of the Sixth Mediterranean Conference on Medical and Biological Engineering* (MEDICON '92), Capri, pp. 477–480.

32 Computer-Assisted Spinal Surgery Using Anatomy-Based Registration

STÉPHANE LAVALLÉE, JOCELYNE TROCCAZ,
PASCAL SAUTOT, BRUNO MAZIER,
PHILIPPE CINQUIN, PHILIPPE MERLOZ, AND
JEAN-PAUL CHIROSSEL

FOR MANY indications, the insertion of a linear tool inside a vertebra is required. This is often a delicate task. A first problem is to avoid damaging important adjacent structures such as nerves, spinal chord, and vessels (figure 32.1). A second problem is to achieve a medical objective with enough accuracy. For instance, in the case of important scoliosis, it is necessary to perform surgical spinal fixation. Some surgical techniques rely on strong fixation of screws inside the vertebral pedicles. The posterior parts of these screws then are attached one to the other by specific rods. Good fixation of the screws requires insertion in the vertebral body through the axis of the pedicle. More generally, the pedicle provides safe access to the vertebral body—for example, to inject osseous grafts or cements inside the vertebra in order to strengthen it, or to perform biopsy of a tumor inside the vertebral body. The exact location of the pedicle axis thus is required during the intervention. So far, surgeons only use a priori rules. For instance, the angle of insertion is more or less 20° relative to the sagittal plane. Such rules are based on anatomic studies (see [1, 2]), and so surgeons have only a statistical assessment, which does not take into account differences between patients, and important morphologic variations often are encountered.

Basically, in open surgery, the entry point of the surgical tool is usually easy to find as there is a direct visual access to it, but the direction of insertion inside the bone is much more difficult to estimate. It can be estimated that approximately 30% of transpedicular screws are incorrectly placed in lumbar vertebrae (e.g., see [3]). Of course, such percentages are strongly improved by some surgeons, but this represents a mean, and the problem becomes crucial for young surgeons. Also, for strongly deformed vertebrae and for vertebrae located in the thoracic or cervical region, good accuracy is much more difficult to achieve.

Most standard techniques require that the patients back be opened. Hence, a third problem is this need to perform a major operation though the intervention often is reduced to a single straight insertion. Percutaneous operations under radioscopic guidance are feasible; for instance, they are frequently used for nucleolysis (injection of an enzyme into an intervertebral disk). However, radioscopy provides a complex 2D projection of the scene, which is difficult to interpret, whereas real 3D information is required.

Considering the problems just listed, we have worked on the design of a computer-assisted surgical system based on the methodology we have been developing since 1985 [4–6]. The basic idea is to allow the surgeon to define a trajectory on medical images before effecting the intervention, using CT, and then to reproduce the selected trajectory in the operating room using specific guiding systems.

Our objective is twofold: First, the main requirement for a computer-assisted system is *to help the surgeon to perform the action accurately*. There are two ways to define this accuracy. It is the accuracy with which the objectives are defined, and thus it is limited by the information's accuracy (i.e., the images' resolution) and by the quality of the human-machine interface. Typically, a surgeon will have to define a surgical trajectory on a set of parallel CT images separated by

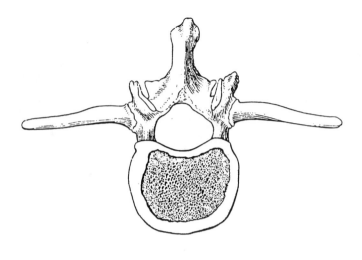

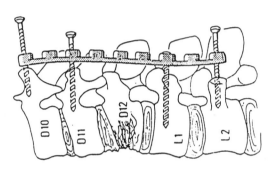

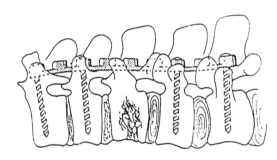

FIGURE 32.1 (Top) Anatomy of a vertebra. (Middle, bottom) Diagram of screws implanted in series of pedicles.

2 mm, with an image resolution of 0.5 mm. It is also the accuracy with which the defined strategy is reproduced through the system. This latter precision must be less than ± 1 mm.

For many interventions, such values are much better than the manual accuracy, because in a usual intervention the surgeon has mentally to integrate the geometry of preoperative images with the direct visualization of the scene. A direct consequence of improving the accuracy is to improve the reliability of the interven-

tion. This first objective is important mainly when the vertebrae do not have a normal shape (i.e., in cases of severe pathologic processes). Indeed, using a priori rules such as "the angle between the pedicle and the spineous process is $X°$" is impossible in such cases. Moreover, improving the accuracy and reliability should make it more feasible to perform interventions on cervical or thoracic vertebrae, which are more difficult to operate on than lumbar vertebrae. Indeed, because the pedicle is much smaller for these vertebrae, the risk of damaging adjacent structures is much higher.

A second objective is *to make the intervention less invasive*. Indeed, using intraoperative sensors such as x-ray systems or ultrasound imaging allows one to perform a linear insertion *percutaneously*. This means the aim is to replace a full opening of the back that exposes one or several vertebrae entirely by minimal surgery. The consequence of a less invasive operation is to reduce complication risks and intervention times. For instance, in some cases, the fixators that link the screws together are external to the skin of the patient. Thus far, a full opening of the back is necessary to implant the screws, whereas these fixators are fixed only temporarily and have to be withdrawn at some time.

In this chapter, we present several systems that we have designed to meet these requirements. First we introduce the experimental conditions used to demonstrate the technical feasibility of our approach. Then we present our modeling method of preoperative CT data, followed by how the surgeon defines the optimal trajectory on 3D images.

These two steps are common to all the systems described in the rest of the chapter. The next sections focus on the two last steps that are necessary to make an integrated system: first, the registration of the preoperative CT coordinate system with some intraoperative system and, second, the guiding system used by the surgeon to perform the action.

According to the choice of an intraoperative sensor, several registration methods can be used. The sensor can be a simple video camera, an x-ray imaging device, a 3D point localizer, or a 2D ultrasound probe localized in 3D.

In the same way, according to the choice of a guiding system, several methods enable the surgeon to make a surgical action that coincides with the surgical planning. The guiding system can be a guide fixed to a video camera, or it can be a 3D localizer mounted on the surgical tool, coupled with a dedicated screen user interface, alternatively, it can be a robot that positions a laser beam on which the surgical tool focuses. Both of the registration and the guiding systems prove to be accurate.

Experimental conditions

We have conducted in vitro experiments to assess the technical feasibility of the methods and systems described in this chapter. The most critical point is to test the system accuracy on the whole chain (from surgical planning to linear introduction inside the bone).

To define an accuracy test is not a simple task. One method would be to perform a CT examination of a cadaver or plastic vertebra, to define a trajectory that goes inside the pedicle, to use the complete system to make a hole inside the vertebra and, finally, to perform a new CT examination of the pierced vertebra that would allow comparison of the real trajectory with the planned trajectory. However, this comparison would imply registration between the two CT examinations, which would introduce inaccuracies that are not part of the system inaccuracies. For this reason, another accuracy test has been performed.

First, an isolated vertebra has been pierced with two tubular 3-mm holes. A 3D CT scan of this vertebra is obtained, and the positions of the hole axes $A1$ and $A2$ are defined interactively using the user interface presented in the section "Surgical Planning: Definition of a Trajectory." The accuracy test we chose has been to use the various registration techniques and guiding systems described in the following sections to compare the position indicated by the system with the position of the real hollow. Experiments will be described in a later section.

Information modeling

A set of CT sections is processed preoperatively. This modeling step is used for both surgical planning and registration. The main purpose is to extract a surface model of the operated vertebra.

For data modeling, many representations have been studied for volumes and surfaces. To model a volume given by a set of parallel sections, we use spline approximation in order to provide a C^2 continuous density function in each point [7]. However, in most cases, higher-level representation of data is necessary in our

methodology. Actually, a surface representation of operated structures is necessary for registration purposes (see the section "Registration").

3D SEGMENTATION

The most important and difficult step in data modeling is probably 3D segmentation. This step has been covered by many previous reports, and so it is not fully described here. One of the methods we have designed relies on solving a differential equation system based on the spline approximation of the volume [8]. A second method, the *snake-splines*, extends classic snakes to deform spline surfaces, with the possibility of local subdivisions and changes of topology (see [9, 10] and chapter 4). Cohen, Ayache, and Cohen [11] offer information on 3D snakes based on finite elements. The typical result of a 3D segmentation on CT images is shown in figure 32.2.

In some cases, significant noise occurs on images, as with automated 3D segmentation, which produces some artifacts. To correct such problems, we are building a user interface that enables one to modify the surface interactively, while it also can evolve automatically toward high-gradient regions. Whatever segmentation techniques are used, the result can be a dense set of 3D points that belong to the surface S of the vertebra.

OCTREE-SPLINES

Registration algorithms (presented later) rely on fast and accurate computations of Euclidean distances between the segmented surface S and 3D points of the space surrounding the surface. In fact, we must compute signed distances $\tilde{d}$: positive Euclidean distances outside the surface and negative distances inside the surface. If the surface S is discretized in n^2 points, the raw computation of the distance $\tilde{d}$ is an $O(n^2)$ process. As this computation will have to be performed during the intervention, it is necessary to speed up this process, so we precompute a 3D *distance map*, which is a function that gives the signed minimum distance to S from any point $\mathbf{q}$ inside a bounding volume V that encloses S. This distance map computation and storage is the last step of preoperative modeling.

The first representation that we studied was a uniform 3D distance map. At each point $\mathbf{q}$ on a regular grid of $\mathcal{N}^3$ points that describe V, the distance $\tilde{d}(\mathbf{q})$ is computed and stored.

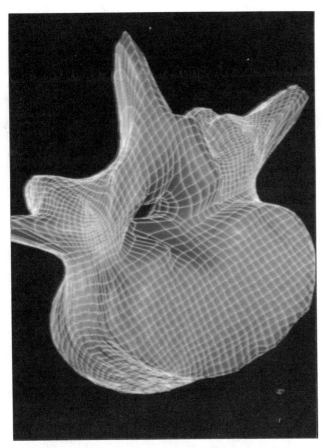

FIGURE 32.2 Result of 3D segmentation of a vertebra defined by a set of CT slices with spline-snakes. A sphere is roughly positioned on CT data around the vertebra, and the spherical surface then is attracted by edge points detected by standard filtering. The surface is more and more subdivided until it converges toward the final shape. The result of this spline-snakes processing is a parametric C^2 spline surface. An important characteristic is that the topology of the surface is automatically modified during the iterative process.

Looking for an improved trade-off among memory space, accuracy, speed of computation, and speed of construction, we developed a new kind of distance map, which we call the *octree-spline*. The intuitive idea behind this geometric representation is to have more detailed information (i.e., more accuracy) near the surface than far away from it. We start with the classic octree representation associated with the surface S [12] and then extend it to represent a continuous 3D function that approximates the signed Euclidean distance to the surface. This representation combines advantages of adaptive spline functions and hierarchic data structures. Using the octree-spline representation derived from a set of points of a surface S, the point-

to-surface distance is computed directly by looking at the node that contains the point in the octree-spline. Moreover, in the 3D/2D registration algorithm presented in section "X-Ray-Based Registration," it is necessary to compute the minimal signed distance $\tilde{d}_l$ to the surface along some projection lines. Precomputing lower bounds in each octree node and using a best-first search technique make the computation of these distances $\tilde{d}_l$ very efficient. (See chapter 7 or [13] for more details.) Typically, the result of the modeling step is a set of 200,000 surface points, which is used to build a six-level octree-spline.

Surgical planning: definition of a trajectory

Surgical planning relies on the user interface on the one hand and on optimization tools on the other. However, optimization procedures are used only when the information is too complicated to be handled interactively, and the result is always submitted to interactive validation. This step is the most important at the decision-making level, so it must be as interactive as possible.

We have built an interface that can process a volume of data in order to select and compute new sections in any direction. First, a cutting plane is interactively selected by the surgeon. Usually, this is a plane that is roughly axial. The position of the plane is interactively modified through the use of three cursors. A perspective view of the segmented model can be shown simultaneously with the intersection of the plane on the surface (this helps to locate roughly the plane in space). On some workstations, the reformatted image is computed at low resolution (64 × 64) in real time and at full resolution (512 × 512) when the user releases the mouse buttons. Once such a slice has been selected, the surgeon interactively draws a target point and a straight line through the pedicle axis. The trajectory is, in fact, a cylinder whose diameter is defined according to standard screw diameters. It then is possible to examine the selected trajectory by displaying slices that are orthogonal to the trajectory. Finally, the system can compute the maximal length of penetration of a tool inside the pedicle (that is, the distance between the entry point and the exit point on the vertebral surface). Such software is now common, and figure 32.3 shows a typical image of this user interface.

In the future, an optimization procedure will be added to help the surgeon select the optimal position of

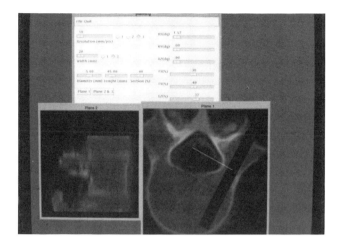

FIGURE 32.3 Interactive trajectory selection. First, the surgeon interactively selects an oblique slice in the volume of CT data. Then the surgeon interactively draws in the plane the trajectory he or she believes to be best (plane 1). Slices orthogonal to the current trajectory are automatically computed so the surgeon can check that the position of the optimal line is correct in three orthogonal slices. This process is repeated until the surgeon estimates that the screw will be placed ideally.

the tool. For instance, it is possible to find the position of a screw such that the minimum distance between the screw surface and the pedicle's exterior surface is maximal. Such a position may be incorrect, as many physical parameters are missing in this geometric optimization (e.g., the rigidity of bony structures at each voxel), but it can serve as a useful starting point for the interactive definition.

Registration

Preoperative and intraoperative registration are necessary to perform the previously defined surgical planning accurately. At this stage, the surgical trajectory is known in the coordinate system of the CT images, and a surface model of the vertebra is known in this coordinate system. The purpose is to estimate the location of the trajectory in the intraoperative coordinate system during the operation.

One widely used approach consists of adding material structures on the patient and leaving these landmarks during all image acquisitions and during the operation. This is the principle when a stereotactic frame is used in neurosurgery [14] or when pins are fixed to a patient's bones [15], or when balls are pasted on a patient's skin [16]. All these methods raise the prob-

lems of discomfort for the patient and organization between different medical departments. They may remain inaccurate and lack flexibility.

The solution that we propose considers registration among anatomic structures only. Our registration method is based on two points. First, an intraoperative sensor gives positional information about some reference anatomic structure (the vertebra). Then an algorithm performs a geometric matching between the surface S segmented in 3D on preoperative images and the structure segmented on intraoperative data. In this chapter, we show that this strategy can be applied using several types of intraoperative sensors that are readily available in operating theaters or are fairly inexpensive: video cameras, x-ray images, 3D pointers, or ultrasound images. The same matching algorithm is used for all but the video cameras. It is based on an iterative minimization of some distances between the surface S and the data. This algorithm can support data in the form of 3D points, contours of 2D projections, or both. The minimization is performed in a six-parameter space that represents the rigid-body transformations between two coordinate systems (three Euler angles and three translation components) [13].

VIDEO-BASED REGISTRATION

In a first approach, we designed a manual system that allows us to perform the registration and to guide the action at once. The principle of this method is shown in figure 32.4.

A video camera is fixed rigidly to a linear guide, and this set is carried by a six-axis passive manipulator (with no motors and no encoders). Using calibration procedures, the position of the guide defined by two points is estimated in the coordinate system of the video camera. Preoperatively, we use the volume of CT images to compute a virtual image that would be the video image created by the camera solidly linked to the guide if this guide were exactly coincident with the optimal trajectory defined on CT images. In the operating room, the posterior part of the vertebra must be visible and clean; then the virtual synthesis image is superimposed to the on-line video image of the camera. For instance, we use the green buffer to display the synthesis reference image and the red buffer to display the on-line video image. The surgeon manually moves the system carried by the passive manipulator in looking for a visual matching of both images. When both

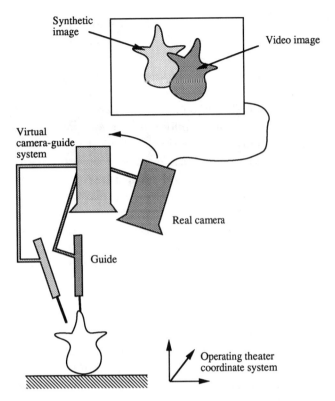

Synthetic image

Video image

Virtual camera-guide system

Real camera

Guide

Operating theater coordinate system

FIGURE 32.4 System made of a video camera and a linear guide. The registration process is made by moving the coupled system manually until the video image and a synthesis image computed from CT data are matched.

images are matched, then the guide is at the optimal location. Actually, as only one camera gives poor 3D information, we rely on the fact that the tip of the guide must be in contact with the surface of the vertebra. The experiments that we conducted on phantoms showed that this system allows us to reach a submillimetric registration. Color plate 28 shows the matching of the reference image with the video image. More details about this system are found elsewhere [17, 18].

The system is simple and accurate, and it enables us to control the registration in real time, which makes possible the detection and compensation of vertebral motion intraoperatively. However, we found it very difficult to manipulate the camera and the guide using the 6 degrees of freedom (dof) of a standard passive manipulator. A specific mechanical architecture would be necessary to help the surgeon obtain a good match (such as the decoupled passive manipulator described in Taylor et al. [19]). In the rest of this chapter, we present solutions for which the registration process is automated in order to overcome this drawback.

TRANSFORMATION AND PARAMETERS FOR AUTOMATED REGISTRATION

For automated registration, the problem we address is to estimate the transformation $\mathbf{T}$ between a coordinate system $\text{Ref}_{\text{intra}}$, associated with some intraoperative device, and the coordinate system Ref_{3D}, associated with the reference surface S and the CT images. $\mathbf{T}$ is also called the *final pose* of the structure S in $\text{Ref}_{\text{intra}}$. It can be defined by a translation vector: $\mathbf{t} = (T_x, T_y, T_z)^t$ and a 3×3 rotation matrix $\mathbf{R}$ defined by three Euler angles ϕ, θ, ψ. If we gather the six parameters of the transformation $\mathbf{T}$ into a six-component vector $\mathbf{p} = (T_x\, T_y\, T_z\, \phi\, \theta\, \psi)^t$ and use homogeneous coordinates, $\mathbf{T}(\mathbf{p})$ can be represented by a single homogeneous 4×4 matrix. The relation between a point $\mathbf{q} = (x\, y\, z\, 1)^t$ [or vector $\mathbf{v} = (x\, y\, z\, 0)^t$] in $\text{Ref}_{\text{intra}}$ and the corresponding point $\mathbf{r} = (X\, Y\, Z\, 1)^t$ [or a vector $\mathbf{u} = (X\, Y\, Z\, 0)^t$] in Ref_{3D} can be written as follows:

$$\mathbf{r} = \mathbf{T}(\mathbf{p})\mathbf{q}$$

or

$$\mathbf{u} = \mathbf{T}(\mathbf{p})\mathbf{v} \qquad (1)$$

X-RAY-BASED REGISTRATION

An x-ray device can provide intraoperative x-ray projections of the operated vertebra. Such a device made of an x-ray source and an image intensifier linked by a rigid arch is readily available, and it provides a video signal that can be digitized as any standard video signal. It irradiates the patient very reasonably: Irradiation problems are much more prevalent for the medical staff and the surgeon than for the patient, who undergoes x-ray irradiation only once or twice. Moreover, with our system, the surgeon does not have to operate under radioscopy throughout the intervention as just a few pictures are necessary. Note also that high-quality images are not necessary as these are not intended to be used for diagnosis but merely to exhibit some parts of the contours of the vertebra. To perform accurate registration, at least two projections are necessary; thus, we consider that we obtain $\mathcal{N}_P$ projections with $\mathcal{N}_P$ equal to two or more. Usually, the arch has to be installed in $\mathcal{N}_P = 2$ positions that make an angle ranging from $30°$–$90°$.

Four steps are necessary to obtain an accurate registration: The intrinsic calibration of the x-ray device, its extrinsic calibration, the segmentation of 2D edge points and, finally, the convergence of the 3D/2D matching algorithm.

INTRINSIC CALIBRATION OF THE X-RAY DEVICE Because one of our requirements is good accuracy in the recovered parameters of the registration, accurate sensor calibration is very important. Therefore, we cannot use approximations such as orthography or weak perspective (also called *scaled orthography*) for x-ray image calibration. Moreover, we must model any image distortions that deviate from the standard perspective model (severe nonlinearities usually proceed from the image intensifier). To take such *local* distortions into account with good accuracy, we have extended the biplanar method [20] to the *N-planes bicubic spline* (NPBS) *method*. By not limiting ourselves to the simplified-perspective, mathematic model, we can obtain an extremely accurate and simple process, employing a large number of calibration measurements and spline approximations of the calibration functions. To obtain such accurate calibration data, a plexiglass plate containing 10×10 metal balls is put more or less parallel to the image plane in two positions known with respect to one another. More details about the NPBS method are found elsewhere [21].

The result of this calibration process is a calibration function $\mathscr{C}_j(\mathscr{P}_i) = L_i$ that associates each pixel $\mathscr{P}_i$ of each projection j with a 3D line whose representation is known in a coordinate system Ref_j, associated to the x-ray device in position j.

EXTRINSIC CALIBRATION OF THE X-RAY DEVICE All views corresponding to the set of positions of the x-ray device must be registered in one absolute intraoperative coordinate system, $\text{Ref}_{\text{intra}}$: This is the purpose of the extrinsic calibration process. We must anticipate the use of a guiding system that will be a six-axis robot or a passive 3D localizer, both of which can be used to determine the location of a plexiglass calibration cage or plate that is put in the field of view of each projection and that contains reference metal balls. For each projection, the location of the calibration cage Ref_j is known in $\text{Ref}_{\text{intra}}$, and we have obtained a function $\mathscr{C}_j$ for each one of these N_P projections in Ref_j. Thus, by simple matrix products, we can gather all of these N_P functions into one general function valid for any pixel of any projection in $\text{Ref}_{\text{intra}}$. The result of this calibration process is, finally, a calibration function $\mathscr{C}(\mathscr{P}_i) = L_i$ that associates each pixel $\mathscr{P}_i$ of any projection with a

3D line whose representation is known in a coordinate system $\text{Ref}_{\text{intra}}$. Each line $L_i = (\mathbf{q}_i, \mathbf{v}_i)$ is given by a point $\mathbf{q}_i$ and a vector $\mathbf{v}_i$, which represent the set of points $\mathbf{q}_i + \lambda\mathbf{v}_i$. Another case of a calibration cage being carried by a robot and used to calibrate a pair of x-ray images has been described in Lavallée et al. [6].

EXTRACTION OF EDGE POINTS ON X-RAY IMAGES Given N_P projection images of the vertebra, we first select a set of M_P pixels $\{\mathscr{P}_i, i = 1 \ldots M_P\}$, that belong to the N_P edges of the vertebra. This means that we do not need to segment perfectly the projection contours of the surface S. Instead, only some pixels $\mathscr{P}_i$ that lie on the contours with high certainty need to be known. In a first step, interactive designation of these few contour points is used. If registration must be updated, a tracking algorithm can extract automatically edge points from the previous ones. (A standard search of pixels that have a local maximum gradient can be used.) Moreover, the next section shows that the matching algorithm can take the certainty of each contour point into account (e.g., this certainty can be proportional to the norm of the image gradient computed at each edge point). Automated 2D edge-points extraction remains to be investigated.

3D/2D MATCHING ALGORITHM Each pixel $\mathscr{P}_i$ corresponds to a 3D *matching line* L_i given in $\text{Ref}_{\text{intra}}$. The transformation of each line $L_i = (\mathbf{q}_i, \mathbf{v}_i)$ in $\text{Ref}_{\text{intra}}$ by $\mathbf{T}(\mathbf{p})$ into a line $l_i(\mathbf{p})$ in $\text{Ref}_{3\text{D}}$ is given by the following equation:

$$l_i(\mathbf{p}) = [\mathbf{T}(\mathbf{p})\mathbf{q}_i, \mathbf{T}(\mathbf{p})\mathbf{v}_i] = [\mathbf{r}_i(\mathbf{p}), \mathbf{u}_i(\mathbf{p})] \quad (2)$$

In the final pose $\mathbf{T}^*$, every matching line $l_i(\mathbf{p})$ is tangent to the surface S of the object. We have designed an algorithm that moves the surface S toward the matching lines (or, equivalently, that moves the rigid set of matching lines toward the surface) until S is in tangent contact with all these lines. This algorithm is based on a least-squares formulation.

We need a function that estimates the distance from any matching line to S. First, we define the *signed distance*, $\tilde{d}(\mathbf{r})$, between a point $\mathbf{r}$ and a closed surface S as $d_E(\mathbf{r})$ if $\mathbf{r}$ is exterior to S, and as the opposite of $d_E(\mathbf{r})$ if $\mathbf{r}$ is interior to S [$d_E(\mathbf{r})$ is the standard Euclidean distance from a point $\mathbf{r}$ to the surface]. Second, we define the signed distance between a line $l_i(\mathbf{p})$ represented in $\text{Ref}_{3\text{D}}$ and the surface S, $\tilde{d}_l[l_i(\mathbf{p})]$, as the minimum of $\tilde{d}(\mathbf{r})$ over all the points that belong to $l_i(\mathbf{p})$:

$$\tilde{d}_l[l_i(p)] \equiv \min_\lambda \tilde{d}[\mathbf{r}_i(\mathbf{p}) + \lambda \mathbf{u}_i(\mathbf{p})] \qquad (3)$$

Therefore, while the minimum unsigned distance along a line piercing the surface may be zero, the signed distance will be negative. The absolute value of $\tilde{d}_l[l_i(\mathbf{p})]$ thus indicates whether the line $l_i(\mathbf{p})$ is *close* and *tangent* to S. The energy minimized in a least-squares model, $E(\mathbf{p})$, is:

$$E(\mathbf{p}) = \sum_{i=1}^{M_P} \frac{1}{\sigma_i^2} [e_i(\mathbf{p})]^2 = \sum_{i=1}^{M_P} \frac{1}{\sigma_i^2} \{\tilde{d}_l[l_i(\mathbf{p})]\}^2$$

$$= \sum_{i=1}^{M_P} \frac{1}{\sigma_i^2} \left\{ \min_\lambda \tilde{d}[\mathbf{T}(\mathbf{p})\mathbf{q}_i + \lambda \mathbf{T}(\mathbf{p})\mathbf{v}_i] \right\}^2 \qquad (4)$$

where σ_i^2 is the variance of the noise of the measurement $\tilde{d}_l[l_i(\mathbf{p})]$. Given an initial estimate $\mathbf{p} = \mathbf{p}_0$ of the 3D/2D transformation parameters, we use the Levenberg-Marquardt algorithm to perform the iterative minimization of the energy $E(\mathbf{p})$.

To compute distances $\tilde{d}_l$ quickly, we use the octree-spline representation of distance maps introduced earlier. All details about the convergence and the robustness of the algorithm are presented in chapter 5 (see also [13]).

Note that in this application we can have good a priori knowledge of the rotation between the 3D images (Ref_{3D}) and the intraoperative coordinate system ($\text{Ref}_{\text{intra}}$): Indeed, the orientations of the patient during CT examination and during surgery are known with an accuracy of $\pm 30°$. Moreover, at the beginning of the algorithm, we first apply an initial translation between the centroid of the 3D points of the surface and the closest point from the projection lines associated with the centroids of the edge points for each projection. With such a good initialization, false local minima are unlikely to be reached.

Figure 32.5 shows a typical convergence obtained for two x-ray projections of the phantom used in our experiment.

REGISTRATION USING A 3D LOCALIZER

The registration method about to be described, which makes use of a 3D localizer, can be used in open surgery when the posterior surface of the vertebra is visible and clean. Several 3D localizers are commercially available, and different techniques are proposed and have been designed for surgery: mechanical passive manipulators with encoded six dof, [16, 22], optical sensors [19, 23], and ultrasound sensors [24].

In our application, we have chosen to use an optical sensor made of cameras watching infrared emitting diodes (Northern Digital system, Toronto, Canada) Sets of six diodes constitute rigid bodies, as shown on figure 32.6. The position and orientation of the three rigid bodies used in the system can be computed at a rate greater than 25 Hz, with an accuracy of ± 0.3 mm in three directions x, y, z for a volume of approximately 1 m^3.

ACQUISITION OF SURFACE POINTS USING A 3D POINTER
At the beginning of the operation, the surgeon fixes a reference rigid body to the spineous process. Gripping the rigid body using pliers that can be tightened with a little screw was found to provide adequate rigidity as no strength has to be applied to this reference rigid body during the intervention. This body defines the intraoperative coordinate system $\text{Ref}_{\text{intra}}$, and all coordinates of any other rigid body can be measured in this reference coordinate system (figure 32.7).

A second rigid body is provided with a sharp tip (figures 32.8, 32.9). Using a simple pivot calibration algorithm, the location of this tip is known in the coordinate system associated with the pointer rigid body; this pivot calibration algorithm looks for the invariant point of the transformations obtained when the tip is fixed in an arbitrary location and the rigid body is rotated around this point. Thus, the calibrated pointer enables one to measure coordinates of surface points by a simple manual or pedal contact switch (a force sensor that employs commercially available strain gauges can also be used to provide an automatic contact switch). This pointer is used to collect randomly some points on the posterior surface of the vertebra (see figure 32.8). Using simple transformations of coordinates, all the collected surface point coordinates are computed in the reference coordinate system $\text{Ref}_{\text{intra}}$. Note that motion of the vertebra during the point collection process does not affect the accuracy of the system as $\text{Ref}_{\text{intra}}$ is rigidly fixed to the vertebra.

REGISTRATION USING A 3D/3D MATCHING ALGORITHM
At that stage, the 3D data points are input in a 3D/3D matching algorithm with the octree-spline of the CT model. This matching algorithm is very similar to the 3D/2D matching algorithm presented earlier, but it is simpler. Using the notations introduced in previous sections, we look for the transformation $\mathbf{T}(\mathbf{p})$ between a surface S known in Ref_{3D} and a set of M_P points $\mathbf{q}_i$

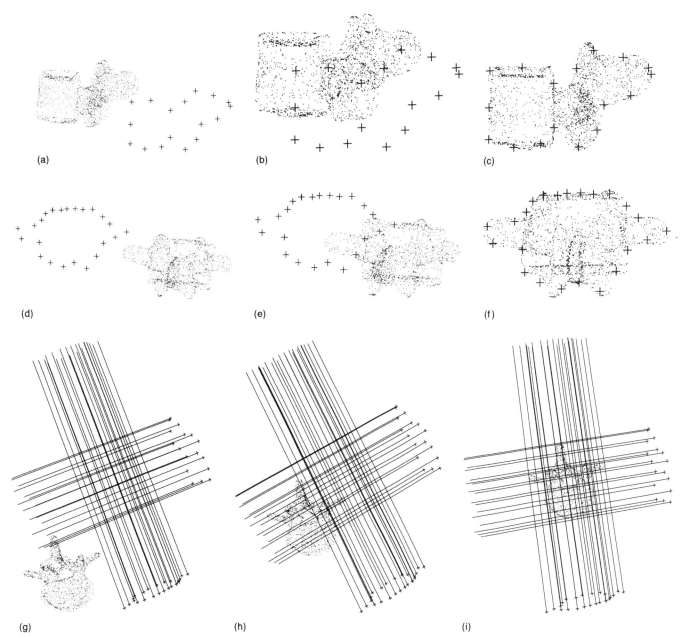

(a)   (b)   (c)

(d)   (e)   (f)

(g)   (h)   (i)

FIGURE 32.5 Typical convergence of the 3D/2D registration algorithm for the vertebra observed from two viewpoints. On each x-ray image (frontal and sagittal), the contour of the projection of the 3D surface model (set of points) converges toward the edge points interactively selected on the real projections (set of crosses). On the bottom, the convergence is observed in 3D: The projection lines corresponding to some edge pixels on the x-ray images come to fit the 3D surface. In the last iteration, all these projection lines are tangent to the 3D surface. For this case, convergence was reached in 10 iterations, requiring less than 1 sec on a workstation DEC 5000. The rms error is 0.5 mm at the end of convergence.

known in Ref$_{\text{intra}}$. The energy function (equation 4) now is replaced by the following:

$$E(\mathbf{p}) = \sum_{i=1}^{M_P} \frac{1}{\sigma_i^2}[e_i(\mathbf{p})]^2 = \sum_{i=1}^{M_P} \frac{1}{\sigma_i^2}\{\tilde{d}[\mathbf{T}(\mathbf{p})\mathbf{q}_i]\}^2 \qquad (5)$$

Given an initial estimate $\mathbf{p} = \mathbf{p}_0$ of the 3D/2D transformation parameters, we will use the Levenberg-Marquardt algorithm to perform the iterative minimization. The initial estimate is not too far from the true minimum of the energy function, as we have sufficient

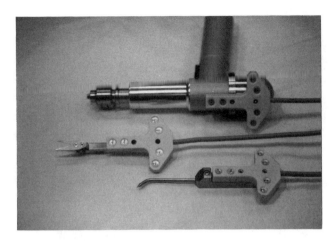

FIGURE 32.6 Set of three rigid bodies made of six infrared diodes. One rigid body is used as an absolute reference coordinate system fixed on the vertebra, a second is used as a pointing device to collect 3D surface points (it has a curved tip to make access to surfaces easier), and a third is mounted on a standard drill (or any other linear surgical tool).

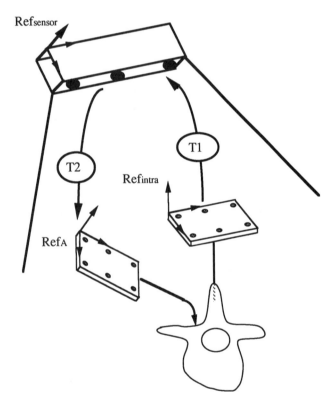

FIGURE 32.7 Reference rigid body fixed on the spineous process. The real optical sensor is used only as a relay so that coordinates of any rigid body Ref$_A$ are given in the coordinate system of the reference rigid body Ref$_{intra}$ by a simple matrix product $\mathbf{T_1T_2}$. Therefore, any motion of the vertebra is taken into account in real time.

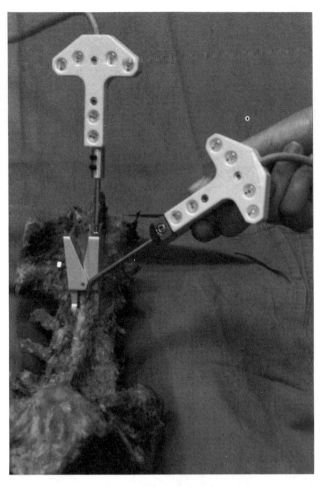

FIGURE 32.8 A pointer enables one to collect 3D coordinates of points that lie on the vertebral surface. Using a foot or manual switch, two acquisition modes are employed: Either points are digitized each time the pedal is pressed, or they are continuously recorded between two clicks.

a priori knowledge about the transformation $\mathbf{T(p)}$, and this prevents convergence in false local minima, which were found far from the true minimum in all our experiments.

Figure 32.10 shows a typical convergence obtained for the vertebra used in our experiment. Typical root mean square error of the surface matching is 0.5 mm.

REGISTRATION USING AN ULTRASOUND PROBE
(2.5D ULTRASOUND POINTER)

Instead of surface points digitization using a simple pointed rod that is put in contact with the vertebra, we designed a second system that makes use of a standard ultrasound probe to acquire contour points. The idea is

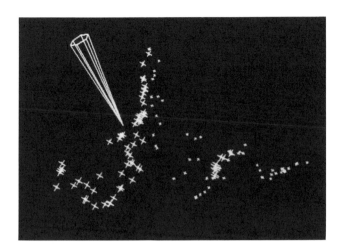

FIGURE 32.9 Surface points digitized with the 3D pointer are displayed in real time on a 3D view. The location of the pointer is also represented in 3D by an arrow. This enables one to control which regions of the vertebra have been digitized at any time. A full set of 3D points usually is digitized in less than 1 minute.

to install a rigid body with infrared diodes on the ultrasound probe and to calibrate the system so that the location of a pixel of any ultrasound image is known in the 3D space Ref_{intra}. To acquire surface points, the

video signal output from an ultrasound device is digitized at the same time that the location of the rigid body mounted on the probe is stored. In a first step, the operator, who does not need to be an ultrasound imaging specialist (there is no need for diagnosis), manipulates the probe freely and digitizes series of ultrasound images associated with their 3D locations. In a second step, the operator edits the images and segments interactively some contour points that lie on the surface that is digitized. The result is a set of 3D points in Ref_{intra}, arranged in little pieces of planar curves (figure 32.11). This whole system that encompasses the ultrasound image digitization and segmentation is named the *2.5D ultrasound pointer*.

Compared with the contact pointer previously described, a 2.5D ultrasound pointer has the major advantage of allowing percutaneous surface acquisition. At first glance, it might be considered unrealistic to make ultrasound images of bony structures, because ultrasound probes are used only for soft-tissue imaging. However, it is precisely because bony structures do not let ultrasound waves penetrate that we can easily obtain some points that lie on the bone surfaces. As reflections are generally the opposite with respect to normal surface vectors in this case of bony structures, some

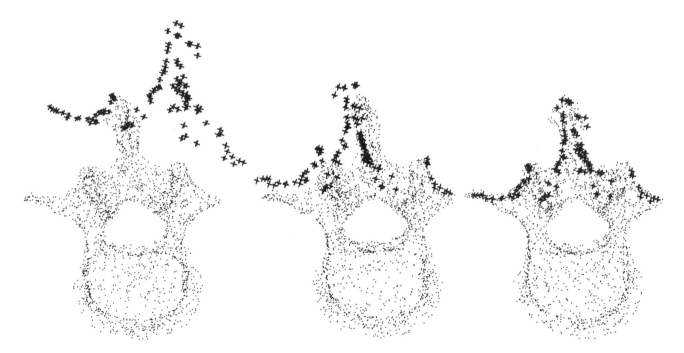

FIGURE 32.10 Typical convergence of the 3D/3D matching algorithm between the CT surface and some points acquired with the 3D pointer.

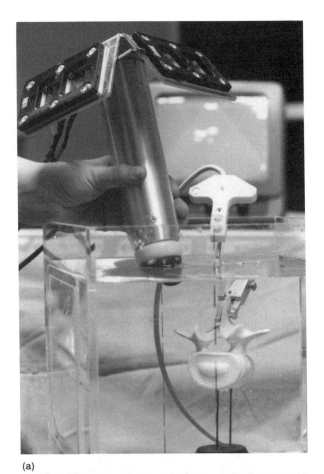

(a)

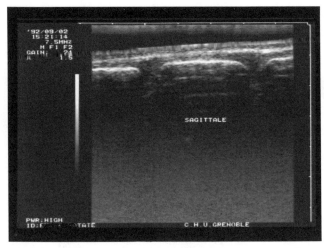

(c)

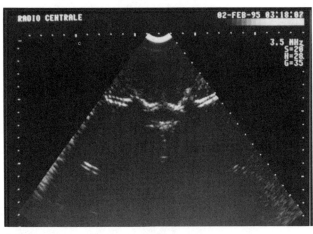

(d)

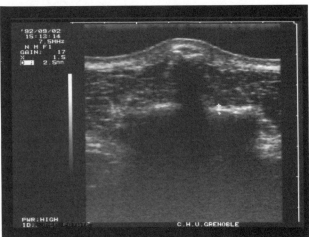

(b)

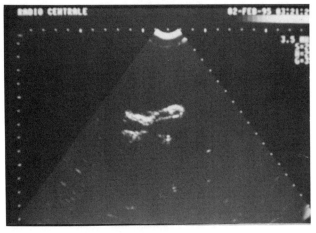

(e)

FIGURE 32.11 (a) Acquisition of ultrasound images of a phantom vertebra with a 2.5D ultrasound localizer. As the vertebra is close to the back skin, ultrasound images show the vertebra edges quite clearly. (b, c) Two images of a vertebra of a real patient. (d, e) Two images of the phantom vertebra used in our accuracy tests, on which we interactively segmented some contours that are likely to be surface points. Edges are appreciably thick, but a key point is to consider the upper part of these thick edges as the true edge as it corresponds to the front of the ultrasound wave.

parts of the surface are not seen on these images; fortunately, our 3D/3D registration algorithm needs only some random surface points.

A disadvantage of this system is that we need two steps to acquire the surface: first the digitization of 5 to 20 ultrasound images and then the interactive segmentation. In the future, we hope to perform an automated segmentation of surface points using the a priori knowledge contained in the surface model obtained with CT images.

At the end of 3D points acquisition with the 2.5D ultrasound pointer, the 3D/3D registration algorithm is started. A typical convergence is shown in figure 32.12. With our system configuration, rapid convergence is always achieved and residual errors of the surface matching usually are approximately 0.8 mm.

Care has been taken on calibration procedures so as to obtain such good accuracy with standard ultrasound probes. First, scaling factors of images were determined using known templates. We could check that distortions were very weak. Then the six-parameters transformation between an image coordinate system and the coordinate system associated with the rigid body mounted on the probe was determined using a known planar template, itself calibrated with the optical sensor. Such a procedure takes approximately 5 minutes and must be performed only if the rigid body is disassembled from the probe.

Note that all coordinates were acquired in the coordinate system Ref_{intra} of a reference rigid body mounted on the spineous process of the vertebra. We did not find that this reference rigid body substantially obstructed the acquisition of ultrasound images, and it offers the benefit that the system is completely insensitive to any vertebral motion. We believe this is feasible in percutaneaous surgery by fixing a small rigid body through the skin, on the spineous process, with a little screw. Although such a procedure might be considered a drawback, it brings a significant advantage of real-time tracking and, therefore, safe real-time checking.

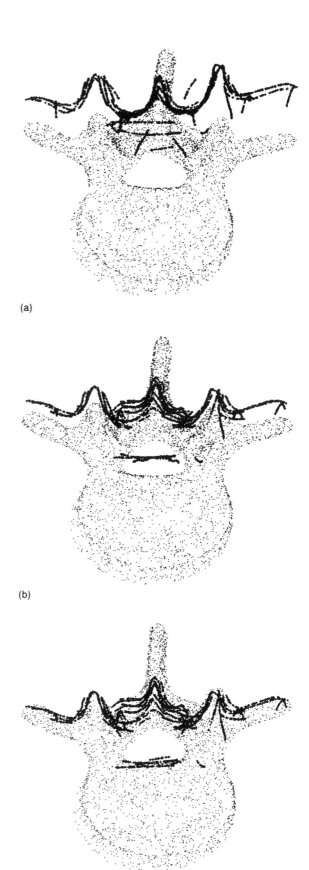

(a)

(b)

(c)

FIGURE 32.12 Typical convergence of the 3D/3D matching algorithm between the CT surface and some point acquired with the 2.5D ultrasound pointer. These points are arranged in pieces of curves. (a) The initial configuration. (b) Convergence after three iterations. (c) Final result after 10 iterations.

Performing the action with guiding systems

After registration, the optimal trajectory is known in the intraoperative coordinate system Ref_{intra}. A guiding system must help the surgeon reproduce this optimal trajectory accurately. According to the level of autonomy left to the surgeon, different kinds of guiding systems can be used, including passive, semiactive, and active [4]. Similar to the robotic system used in stereotactic neurosurgery [6], all the systems presented in this chapter for spinal surgery are considered semiactive because the trajectory is indicated by the system while the surgeon holds the tool in his or her hand. In fully passive systems, the surgeon would need to observe and interpret intraoperative medical information to decide whether the current tool position is suitable. In semiactive systems, intraoperative information given by the guiding system is not medical but technical. In active systems, the tool would be manipulated by the guiding system.

Video-based guiding system

In the first version of a guiding system designed for spinal surgery, described in the section "Video-Based Registration," the registration of the video images produces direct alignment of a guide with the optimal trajectory. At the time of the intervention, the system should be locked and the surgeon would have to introduce a linear tool inside the guide. However, the manipulator that carries the video camera and the guide is difficult to design as it must be safe, easy to handle, and able to be locked. Our current implementation of this manipulator has been found unsuitable.

Alignment using a 3D localizer

Using the 3D optical localization system presented earlier, we designed a method that enables us to position a tool exactly coincident with the optimal trajectory. The graphics display presented here corresponds to a minor extension of the work described in Adams, Mösges, et al. [16, 23].

ALIGNMENT PROCEDURE   First, a rigid body with infrared LEDs is mounted on the surgical tool, which may be any standard surgical drill, brace, or rigid needle (figure 32.6). The axis of the drill is calibrated in the coordinate system of the rigid body using a pivot cali-

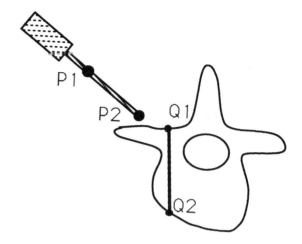

FIGURE 32.13   Points $\mathbf{P_1}$ and $\mathbf{P_2}$ define the drill axis. Points $\mathbf{Q_1}$ and $\mathbf{Q_2}$ define the optimal trajectory.

bration made with two different drill tips. Let $\mathbf{P_2}$ be the point at the tip of the drill and $\mathbf{P_1}$ be a point on the drill axis chosen at an arbirary distance of 30 mm from the tip. The 3D coordinates of $\mathbf{P_1}$ and $\mathbf{P_2}$ are computed in real time in the intraoperative coordinate system Ref_{intra}. Let $\mathbf{Q_1}\mathbf{Q_2}$ be the optimal trajectory defined by two points $\mathbf{Q_1}$ and $\mathbf{Q_2}$ in Ref_{intra} (figure 32.13). In the surgical planning, the point $\mathbf{Q_2}$ can easily be defined as a limit point that should not be passed during the introduction of any surgical tool (usually $\mathbf{Q_2}$ is a point on the anterior surface of the vertebral body). The drill is aligned with the optimal trajectory if and only if the distances between the drill points $\mathbf{P_1}$ and $\mathbf{P_2}$ and the optimal line $\mathbf{Q_1}\mathbf{Q_2}$ is zero. Now, in order to help the surgeon to reach optimal alignment, a graphic user interface has been designed. On the left part of the screen, we compute a view that is orthogonal to the optimal line. On that view, the optimal line $\mathbf{Q_1}\mathbf{Q_2}$ is reduced to a single point drawn as a red cross in the middle of the image. The drill point $\mathbf{P_2}$ is projected on that view and drawn as a green cross. The drill point $\mathbf{P_1}$ is projected on that view and drawn as a blue cross. For an arbitrary position of the drill, the three crosses are distinct (figures 32.14, 32.15).

To reach alignment easily, a two-step method usually is chosen by the operator. First, the surgeon aligns the tip of the drill on the optimal trajectory by looking for a fitting between the green and red crosses. The distance between the tip point $\mathbf{P_2}$ and the optimal line is computed and displayed in millimeters. A distance of 0.31 mm is reached in the case depicted in figure 32.16. Second, the surgeon aligns the orientation of the drill

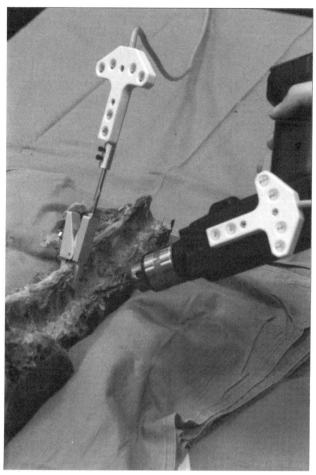

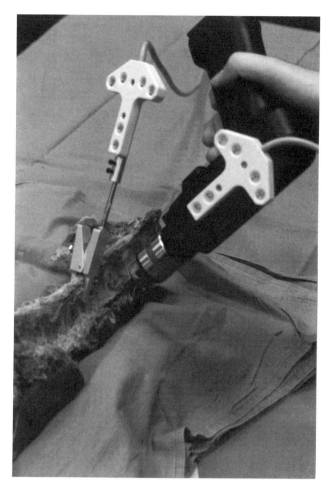

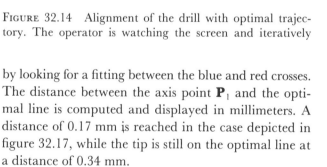

FIGURE 32.14   Alignment of the drill with optimal trajectory. The operator is watching the screen and iteratively positions the drill according to a best fit of three crosses on the screen.

by looking for a fitting between the blue and red crosses. The distance between the axis point $\mathbf{P}_1$ and the optimal line is computed and displayed in millimeters. A distance of 0.17 mm is reached in the case depicted in figure 32.17, while the tip is still on the optimal line at a distance of 0.34 mm.

We found that some other features were useful to display for the surgeon. First, the angle between the drill axis and the optimal line is computed and displayed in degrees. Then, the distance between the tip of the drill $\mathbf{P}_2$ and the limit point $\mathbf{Q}_2$ is computed and displayed in millimeters. Moreover, the amplitude of this depth is represented by a vertical color bar, the size of which is reduced as this distance between $\mathbf{P}_2$ and $\mathbf{Q}_2$ is reduced. Finally, on the right part of the screen, a 3D view represents the vertebral surface points, the optimal trajectory, and a drawing of the drill as an arrow. Although we can interactively change the point of view

and the scale of this view, we find it useful just for global representation and checking of abnormalities, but not as useful as the view with three crosses for the accurate-alignment procedure.

ACCURACY TEST WITH THE 3D LOCALIZER USING 3D/3D REGISTRATION BASED ON THE POINTING DEVICE   As described previously, we have conducted in vitro experiments to assess the accuracy of our method. The selected test has been to compare the position indicated by the system with the position of the real hollows made preoperatively inside the vertebra. In the experiment depicted in figures 32.16–18, the registration had been naturally performed with the method based on 3D surface points. Then a 3-mm-diameter drill was inserted in both 3-mm pedicular hollows. We then were able to compute the distances between the points lying on the axis of the inserted drill and the registered

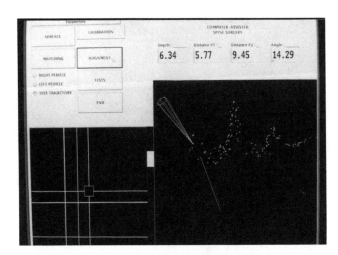

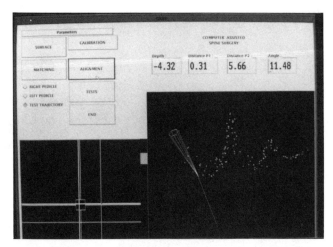

FIGURE 32.15   The drill is in an unaligned arbitrary position. On left, the drill points $\mathbf{P_2}$ and $\mathbf{P_1}$ appear as green and blue crosses, respectively. Both crosses are outside the central red square, which corresponds to the optimal trajectory. This view is, in fact, a scaled projection orthogonal to the optimal line (window is 512 × 512 pixels, but its real size is 25 × 25 mm). If a cross is inside the central square, it means that the corresponding point is within 1 mm of the optimal line. Exact values of distances in millimeters are also displayed. On the righthand 3D view, the tool represented as a cone does not fit the 3D optimal line.

FIGURE 32.16   The drill tip is on the optimal trajectory, but the orientation of the drill is not yet correct. On left, only the green cross that represents the tip point $\mathbf{P_2}$ is aligned with the optimal central red cross. On right, only the tip of the cone is on the 3D optimal line.

optimal line (see figure 32.18). In all our experiments, we acquired at least 50 points randomly digitized on the vertebral surface. The result for the mean and maximum distances ($\text{Error}_{\text{mean}}$ and $\text{Error}_{\text{max}}$) were as follows:

$$\text{Error}_{\text{mean}} = 0.5 \text{ mm}$$
$$\text{Error}_{\text{max}} = 0.9 \text{ mm} \tag{6}$$

These errors come from many sources, including 3D segmentation, sensor calibration, rigid-bodies calibration, drill and pointer calibration, 3D/3D registration, and mechanical play inside the 3-mm hollow. Such an accuracy meets our requirements.

Although we do not consider it an accuracy test, we conducted experiments in which the system is really used to drill the vertebra instead of passing through a premade hole. Figure 32.18 shows postoperative x-ray films after real drilling was performed with the system on a cadaver spine. According to surgeons, the result is visually correct: On frontal and sagital x-ray images, the drill seems to be inserted inside the middle of the pedicle. Interestingly, in these experiments, the surgeon could always drill within the 1-mm safety square

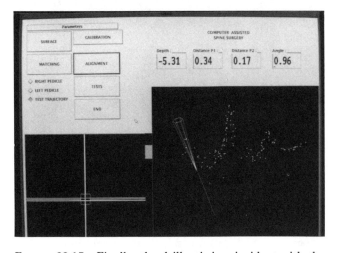

FIGURE 32.17   Finally, the drill axis is coincident with the optimal trajectory. On left, both green and blue crosses are fitting the optimal red cross. The vertical green bar of the middle screen indicates the depth of penetration—that is, how far the tip of the drill is from the limit point $\mathbf{Q_2}$ that must not be passed. On right, the cone is fitting the 3D optimal line.

represented on the screen, which means that this interface is highly efficient.

ACCURACY TEST WITH THE 3D LOCALIZER USING 3D/3D REGISTRATION BASED ON ULTRASOUND IMAGES   The

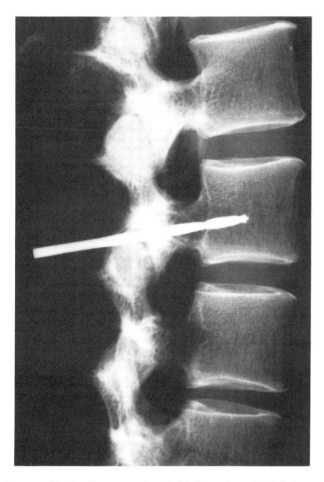 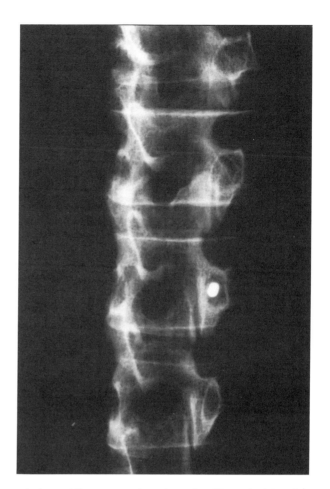

FIGURE 32.18 Postoperative (left) frontal and (right) sagittal x-ray films obtained with the technique that combines a 3D/3D registration based on the optical pointing device and the guiding system based on the 3D optical localizer. A drill has been inserted in a pedicle of a cadaver spine. Visually, the drill is correctly placed.

same accuracy test has been performed using the 2D ultrasound probe to extract surface points. In all our experiments, we acquired at least 10 ultrasound images randomly and, on each image, we segmented manually some pieces of curves that correspond to surface points of the vertebra. The result for the mean and maximum distances were as follows:

$$Error_{mean} = 0.6 \text{ mm}$$
$$Error_{max} = 1.0 \text{ mm} \tag{7}$$

Considering all the possible sources of inaccuracies with this system configuration, mainly due to ultrasound imaging, such very good values for overall accuracy were not expected. Nonetheless, all tests confirmed this result, which we consider to be the most important result presented in this chapter.

ALIGNMENT USING A SIX-AXIS ROBOT

In this section, we describe a robotic system that enables the surgeon to align a surgical tool with the optimal trajectory.

ALIGNMENT OF A SURGICAL TOOL WITH A LASER BEAM CARRIED BY THE ROBOT   In our robotic system designed for stereotactic neurosurgery, the reduction ratios of a six-axis robot have been modified so that its motions are slow. The robot positions a tube to a fixed location defined on images, after which the robot is stopped (motor's power is turned off) and the surgeon introduces a drill and a probe through the linear guide [6]. In the case of spinal surgery, the same safe system can be used. However, in some cases, it might be necessary to track some possible motions of the vertebra (which are not possible for the skull, as it is held in a stereotactic frame). In these specific cases, the robot cannot be fixed, requiring some motions close to the patient with a tool inserted in both the patient and the linear guide. This raises obvious safety problems that we have not yet solved. While we are working on this safety problem, we propose to use an optical solution.

The linear tube previously described can be replaced by a laser beam mounted on the end-effector of the robot. The robot positions the laser beam far away from the patient, thereby making the patient's skin unreachable by any part of the robot. A first considered solution was to use rigid bars around the patient but that raises accessibility problems in the work space. We found it more convenient to install the robot at a location where any part of it could not reach the patient. With this system, the surgeon uses a specific device to align a surgical tool with the laser beam, in position and orientation. The principle of such an alignment tool is shown in figure 32.19. Moreover, the maximal distance of penetration of a tool has been computed during the surgical planning (it is the distance between points Q_1 and Q_2, defined in figure 32.14). Thus, the surgeon can measure manually the distance of insertion of the surgical tool (drill or screw) and compare it with the maximal allowed distance.

ACCURACY TEST FOR THE ROBOT WITH 3D/2D REGISTRATION For an in vitro accuracy test, we used the registration method based on matching 2D projections with the 3D model (see X-Ray-Based Registration). Actually, we simulated x-ray images using video images for practical reasons. Nevertheless, x-ray devices and video cameras can be modeled in the exact same manner using the NPBS method [21]. We then used a six-axis PUMA 260 (Staubli, Faverges, France) robot carrying a 0.5-mW laser beam and calibrated it with the pair of cameras. Our intrinsic and extrinsic calibration procedures, although they are essential, are not described in this chapter; see Lavallée et al. [6] for similar work.

After registration between projection images and the 3D preoperative CT model, the robot is asked to align the laser beam with either hole axis corresponding to the left or right pedicle (figures 32.20, 32.21). We then visually determine whether the laser beam has passed through the 3-mm hole: Because the laser beam has an elliptic 3 × 1-mm section, when the laser goes perfectly

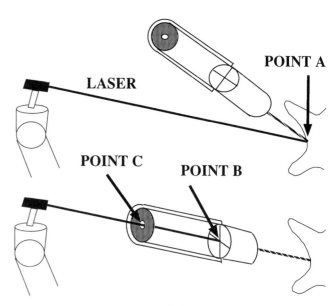

FIGURE 32.19 Alignment of a surgical tool with a laser beam: The robot positions a laser beam, and the surgeon holds an alignment device. First, the surgeon positions the tip of the tool on the impact made by the laser on the vertebra or on the skin (point A). Then the surgeon moves the orientation of the tool until the laser impact is aligned with a cross mounted on the back side of the tool (point B). Finally, when the tool is inserted, the orientation and position alignment is preserved through alignment of the laser beam with two points mounted on the back side of the tool, a cross (point B) and a hole (point C).

through the 3-mm-diameter hole, the red spot made by the laser on a black surface under the vertebra assumes the same size and shape as the section of the laser beam before entry in the vertebral hollow. The observed result is that in all our experiments, the matching was visually perfect, which corresponds to a submillimeter accuracy. If we move the vertebra, 1–4 sec are needed to perform a new registration using 3D/2D matching and to move the robot (no human intervention is required). This experiment has been performed for all positions of the vertebra for which the robot could align the laser beam with the pedicle, including, for instance, rotations of 180° of the vertebra around a vertical axis (several hundreds of cases). No difference has been detected for all these positions. Finally, the experiment has been conducted for both pedicles (left and right parts of the vertebra), and the exact same results apply for both cases.

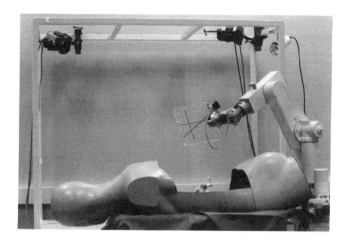
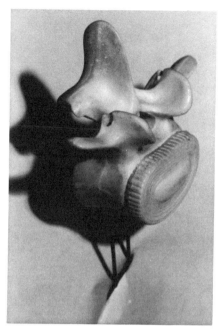

FIGURE 32.20 (Left) Photograph of robot experimental set-up. A phantom vertebra is placed inside an anatomic model, and a pair of video cameras simulate x-ray images and give projections of the vertebra. The robot holds a calibration plate and a laser beam aligned with a trajectory that had been defined such that it should go through the vertebral pedicle. (Right) The laser beam goes exactly through the linear hollow made in the vertebral pedicle before the experiment. Thus, a perfect bright red spot can be seen under the vertebra at the bottom of the picture. In this experiment, the laser source is at an approximate distance of 400 mm from the vertebra.

Discussion

Figure 32.22 displays a comparison of the four registration methods and the three guiding systems presented in this chapter. The criteria used for this comparison are discussed in the following sections. Numbers in parenthesis (x) refer to some items of this table that require detailed explanations.

REGISTRATION METHODS

First, all registration methods presented in this chapter are anatomy-based, which means that there is no need to fix or glue any material structure on the patient preoperatively. One of our major requirements is to make interventions possible *percutaneously*. This can be achieved through two methods: 3D/2D matching with x-ray images and 3D/3D matching using ultrasound images.

Accuracy of registration methods is obviously crucial. Surprisingly, similar accuracies have been obtained with x-rays, with the 3D pointing device, and with the 2.5D ultrasound pointer (1).

Only x-ray images allow us to *acquire intraoperative data automatically*. One need only position the x-ray device in two suitable locations and press one button. In contrast, the 3D pointer, the ultraound probe, and the video guiding system must be handled to digitize surface points.

Both x-ray images and random surface points with a 3D pointer are very *easy to acquire*, and no specific experience is required. Ultrasound images are more difficult to obtain (although no relevant medical information is required), and matching video images needs training.

Raw data acquired with a 3D pointer can be used directly for registration, whereas other methods require extraction of some edge points. However, 2D semiautomatic segmentation of edge points on x-ray imaging is investigated using the fact that our current implementations of matching algorithms can take false edge detections into account: In such a method, 2D segmentation and matching can be considered to be performed

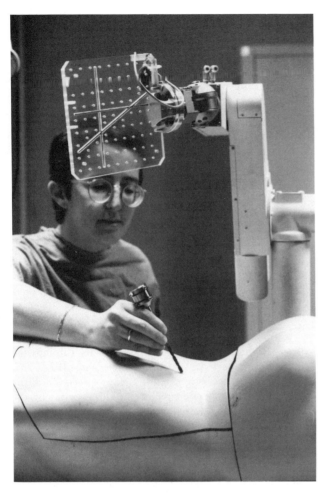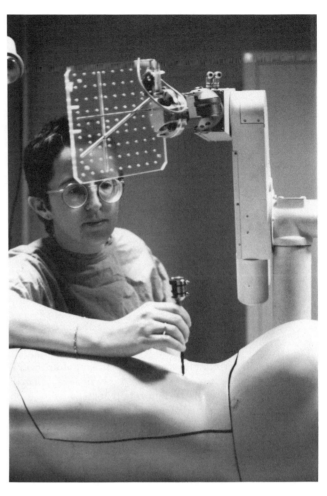

FIGURE 32.21 Alignment of a surgical tool, such as a drill, with the laser beam is shown according to the principle described in preceding figures. It enables one to envisage operations through the skin (percutaneous).

simultaneously (2). In the future, a similar idea could apply to ultrasound images, although this is much more complicated (2).

Once intraoperative data have been acquired, the matching algorithms are *fully automatic*. This obviously is not the case with the video guiding system.

In some applications, the required accuracy of these systems can tolerate some minor motions of the vertebra as the patient is under anesthesia. However, the *real-time tracking of motions* is necessary in most cases, at least for safety purposes. The ability of these systems to update registration intraoperatively can be seen from different points of view. A first approach is to remake a full registration each time the vertebra is considered to have moved. This is always possible but unsafe as patient movement is not easy to detect. However, in this category, an interesting possibility is to use two x-ray devices and to track edges on both images in real time. In fact, approximately 1 sec is usually required to track two contours and to obtain a 3D/2D matching convergence. The second approach, which is much more attractive, is to fix a reference rigid body on the vertebra at the beginning of the surgery and to track real-time motions of this reference rigid body using an optical sensor. This approach has been validated. With this method, all vertebral motions are taken into account, including breathing and motions of the vertebra displaced by surgical tools (3). Finally, with the video guiding system, note that a motion can be visually detected instantaneously by a mismatch between synthesis and true video images. However, this implies correction of such a motion by a new manipulation of the system, and therefore it cannot be considered a real-time system (4).

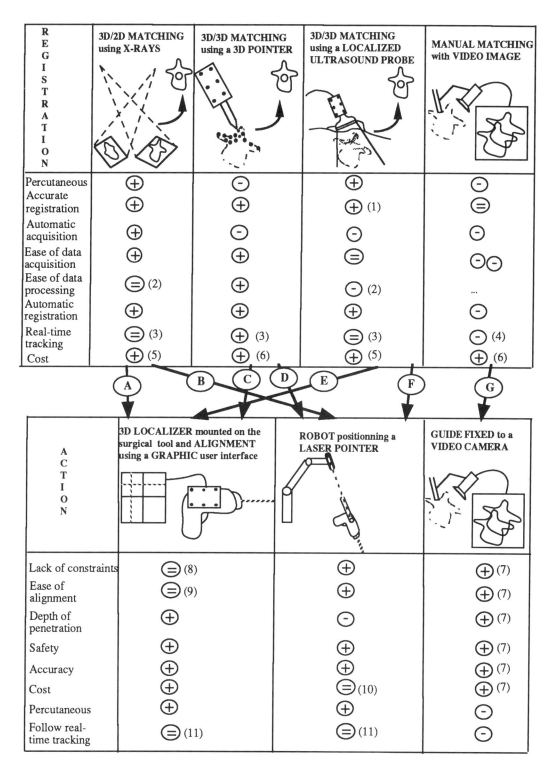

REGISTRATION	3D/2D MATCHING using X-RAYS	3D/3D MATCHING using a 3D POINTER	3D/3D MATCHING using a LOCALIZED ULTRASOUND PROBE	MANUAL MATCHING with VIDEO IMAGE
Percutaneous	⊕	⊖	⊕	⊖
Accurate registration	⊕	⊕	⊕ (1)	⊜
Automatic acquisition	⊕	⊖	⊖	⊖
Ease of data acquisition	⊕	⊕	⊜	⊖⊖
Ease of data processing	⊜ (2)	⊕	⊖ (2)	...
Automatic registration	⊕	⊕	⊕	⊖
Real-time tracking	⊜ (3)	⊕ (3)	⊜ (3)	⊖ (4)
Cost	⊕ (5)	⊕ (6)	⊕ (5)	⊕ (6)

A B C D E F G

ACTION	3D LOCALIZER mounted on the surgical tool and ALIGNMENT using a GRAPHIC user interface	ROBOT positionning a LASER POINTER	GUIDE FIXED to a VIDEO CAMERA
Lack of constraints	⊜ (8)	⊕	⊕ (7)
Ease of alignment	⊜ (9)	⊕	⊕ (7)
Depth of penetration	⊕	⊖	⊕ (7)
Safety	⊕	⊕	⊕ (7)
Accuracy	⊕	⊕	⊕ (7)
Cost	⊕	⊜ (10)	⊕ (7)
Percutaneous	⊕	⊕	⊖
Follow real-time tracking	⊜ (11)	⊜ (11)	⊖

FIGURE 32.22 Comparison of registration methods and guiding systems. (+, good; =, average; −, bad).

Finally, the cost of these systems is relatively low. The video guiding system and the 3D optical localization system are each inexpensive (6), and the x-ray and ultrasound systems, which are expensive, are always available in most standard surgical theaters and so they do not impose additional cost (5). Obviously, the marketing of such systems requires further consideration, which is outside the scope of this chapter.

GUIDING SYSTEMS

The advantages and disadvantages of the three guiding systems presented in this chapter are reviewed here. Note that the discussion about the video guiding system is ambiguous: If we assume that the video images have been registered, then the tube fixed to the camera is at a good location and the surgeon has only to insert a tool inside the guide. Such ease justifies the good score this system attains (see figure 32.22), but all considerations about registration with this system must be taken into account at this level (7). In the reminder of this section, we discuss only the use of the robotic system and the 3D localized tool.

The introduction of a robotic system or a 3D sensor into a surgical theater raises practical problems or *constraints*. Sterilization of these systems is possible, employing gas sterilization for the diodes or plastic bags to cover the robot. These systems do not clutter the operating room very much, as the cameras can be fixed on the lighting system and the robot can be fixed to the operating table above the bottom part of the back of the patient. However, a slight drawback of the optical system is that the field of view of the cameras must not be obstructed by the surgeon, the surgeon assistant, or any surgical tool (8). The use of these systems is limited in time compared to the entire operation's duration. For instance, use of the optical sensor requires approximately 1 min to collect surface points and only a few seconds to align the drill. Hence, even if the robot cannot suffer from possible obstruction such as might occur with the optical system, it does not make a significant difference.

Both systems are *easy to use for alignment*, even by a nonexperienced operator. However, with the optical digitizing localizer mounted on the surgical tool, the surgeon has to look at the screen of the computer to match crosses. With the laser pointer on the robot, the surgeon looks at crosses directly on the tool, which makes for a slightly easier alignment (9).

The depth of penetration of the tool inside the vertebra is taken into account automatically by the optical system, whereas this it is not true for the robot. However, with a manual measure, the depth can be known using alignment with the laser.

All systems are safe in the sense that they cannot produce any injury by themselves. Moreover, with semiactive systems, the action always is performed by the surgeon, who has the opportunity to decide whether something seems wrong at any time. The system brings information but does not constrain the surgeon to any action, and all the information used in standard nonassisted operations remains available.

The accuracy of these guiding systems has been shown to be submillimetric, which encompasses inaccuracies coming from all elements of the systems.

Intrinsically, guiding systems are *inexpensive*. A 3D digitizing system is made only of video cameras, appropriate lenses, a simple signal-processing board, and a triggering unit. A robot that carries a laser beam might be expensive if a standard six-axis robot is modified and used, but in fact it needs only four axes as a straight line is represented by four independent parameters in three dimensions, and no strength or load is applied on the robot, so no fast speed is required. Hence, the cost of such a system can be easily reduced (10). There are, however, some marketing issues that should be taken into account.

Both the 3D localizing system and the robotic system allow one to perform *percutaneous operations*. This is a significant feature and is obviously not the case with the video guiding system.

Because none of these systems is active, there is a need for the surgeon to react to any motion of the vertebra in the alignment process. Provided that real-time registration is used, the system can indicate a misalignment in real time as well as indicate the new alignment to perform, but it does not react physically (11).

REGISTRATION AND GUIDING SYSTEMS IN COMBINATION

In figure 32.22, arrows between the registration box and guiding systems box indicate which combinations are possible. Seven arrows are drawn, which shows that the methodology presented in this chapter is very versatile.

None of these combinations is found to be superior to all others. Each registration technique and each guiding system has its own advantages and drawbacks.

Thus, each surgeon can have the opportunity to select one system configuration according to his or her personal feelings. However, we can note that the number of devices used in each of these combinations ranges from one to three. Thus, we can construct three categories:

• *Single device*: Arrow C corresponds to a system that uses only a 3D localizer both for registration and action. Arrow G corresponds to a system that uses only a video camera and a passive manipulator.

• *Two-device combinations*: Arrows A, B, D, and F correspond to a system that uses two devices: Arrow A makes use of an x-ray device and a 3D localizer; arrow B, an x-ray device and a robot; arrow D, a 3D localizer and a robot; and arrow E, a 3D localizer and a 2D ultrasound probe.

• Three-device combinations: Arrow F corresponds to a system that uses three devices—a 3D localizer, a 2D ultrasound probe, and a robot.

EXTENSIONS

For all the applications mentioned in the first part of this chapter, the operation corresponds to a linear trajectory. In cases of osteotomies, the straight line must be replaced by a 3D plane. Thus, the surgical-planning software could easily take the definition of a cutting plane into account and, at the level of action, the 3D localizing system could be mounted on a saw or on a planar guide instead of a drill and the robot could carry a laser plane instead of a laser beam.

An important issue is to consider the use of active robots, as some other authors have done [15, 19, 25]. This brings obvious advantages in terms of accuracy, but the safety of such systems is a delicate problem.

Conclusion

In conclusion, this chapter has presented new systems for computer-assisted spinal surgery, based on our methodology of computer-assisted medical interventions. The clinical advantages of the general method are, first, to make the intervention more accurate than it is manually (thus more reliable), and second, in some configurations, to make it possible to envisage less invasive surgery by using percutaneous introduction. Moreover, these systems will enable one to confront clinical results with the surgical planning quantitatively, which should help to validate some possible sur-

gical planning optimization methods. Finally, interventions that are not practiced today because they are considered too dangerous for the patient (e.g., interventions on cervical and thoracic vertebrae) can be reconsidered with these systems.

A comparison of different techniques has been presented, but each technique has its own advantages and shortcomings. In our opinion, the choice of one technique over another is mainly a matter of personal preference for a particular user interface as they reach more or less the same accuracy. One surgeon might prefer to have a laser beam in his or her normal field of vision, whereas another might prefer a quantified measurement of the on-line misalignment on a screen (or output from a voice generator). We can, however, make an important distinction about the ability of these systems to facilitate percutaneous intervention, as this is a significant improvement for the patient. Either x-ray or ultrasound images, according to the availability of such devices in the surgical theater, are the preferred solution in this regard, compared to use of a 3D pointing device that can only digitize surface points by real contact.

In this paper, a submillimetric accuracy has been achieved for the entire process with three different systems that integrate some of the registration methods and guiding systems we have presented:

• System B: x-ray system, 3D/2D registration, robot positioning a laser guide
• System D: 3D pointer, 3D/3D registration, optical passive guide
• System E: ultrasound images, 3D/3D registration, optical passive guide

Many sources of possible inaccuracy are present at various levels, including 3D segmentation (essentially with the partial volume effect), definition of a straight line on CT data, intrinsic calibration of the robot, intrinsic calibration of the x-ray sensors, calibration of optical sensors and calibration of pointers, 2D segmentation of x-ray projection contours, 2D segmentation of ultrasound contours, 3D/2D matching, and 3D/3D matching. Our good results can be justified by the fact that these error sources are not cumulative and that most of the transformations are used in a subspace. For instance, the robot is used in a limited subspace (reconfigurations are prohibited), and the 3D/2D and 3D/3D matching algorithms are based on a least-squares criterion that absorbs some Gaussian noise.

The main feature of these systems is that they are based on the reproduction of preoperative surgical planning through accurate and automated registration procedures that are entirely anatomy-based.

This chapter has presented the technical feasibilty of our method. In the near future, we plan to begin clinical validation of the methods in patients. The systems do not constrain the surgeon to obtain a given trajectory, so the clinical validation will be performed on *easy* cases in which the surgeon has no real problems estimating whether the proposed trajectory is correct. Then, postoperative examination of screw implantation will validate the method. Such validation will require several months before delicate operations are performed (e.g., on cervical vertebrae). Extensions of this method to other clinical applications are also studied, which is straightforward in the field of orthopaedics.

ACKNOWLEDGMENTS   We thank Richard Szeliski and Lionel Brunie for their contribution to the work on matching algorithms. We also acknowledge Dr. Henri Graf, Prof. Jean Dubousset, Prof. Ashok Vazdev, and Prof. Guy Crouzet, for their advice on spine surgery and intervertebral punctures. Special thanks to Catherine Barbe, Delphine Henry, and Abbas Hijazi for their work on ultrasound calibration, Dr. Alain Herment and Dr. Sylvie Dalsoglio for their advice on ultrasound images, Prof. Max Coulomb and Dr. Frederic Combe for their help with CT images acquisition, Isabelle Marque and Frank Leitner for their work on 3D segmentation, Guillaume Champleboux for his work on x-ray calibration, and Eric Bainville for his work on 3D localizers.

REFERENCES

[1] OLSEWSKI, J. M., E. H. SIMMONS, F. C. KALLEN, F. C. MENDEL, C. M. SEVERIN, and D. L. BERENS, 1990. Morphometry of the lumbar spine: Anatomical perspectives related to transpedicular fixation. *J. Bone Joint Surg.* 72-A(4):541–548.

[2] KRAG, M. H., D. L. WEAVER, B. D. BEYNONN, and L. D. HAUGH, 1988. Morphometry of the thoracic and lumbar spine related to transpedicular screw placement for surgical spinal fixation. *Spine* 13(1):27–31.

[3] CASTRO, W. H. M., H. HALM, J. STEINBECK, and J. MALMS, 1993. Accuracy of pedicle screw placement in lumbar vertebrae. Presented at the Fourth Curacao Tropical International Orthopedic Congress, Curacao.

[4] LAVALLÉE, S., and P. CINQUIN, 1991. IGOR: Image guided operating robot. In *Proceedings of the Fifth International Conference on Advanced Robotics*, Pisa, Italy, pp. 876–881.

[5] LAVALLÉE, S., 1989. Geste Medico-Chirurgicaux Assistes par Ordinateur: Application a la Neurochirurgie Stereotaxique. Doctoral thesis, Grenoble University, France.

[6] LAVALLÉE, J., S. TROCCAZ, L. GABORIT, P. CINQUIN, A. L. BENABID, and D. HOFFMANN, 1992. Image guided robot: A clinical application in stereotactic neurosurgery. In *Proceedings of the IEEE International Conference on Robotics and Automation*, Nice, France, pp. 618–625.

[7] CINQUIN, P., 1987. Application des fonctions splines au traitement d'images numeriques, these d'etat. Doctoral thesis, Grenoble University, France.

[8] MARQUE, I., 1990. Segmentation d'Images Medicales Tridimensionnelles Basee sur une Modelisation Continue du Volume (in French). Doctoral thesis, Grenoble University, France.

[9] LEITNER, S., I. MARQUE, S. LAVALLÉE, and P. CINQUIN, 1991. Dynamic segmentation: Finding the edge with spline snakes. *Curves and Surfaces*, In P. J. Laurent, ed. Chamonix: Academic Press.

[10] LEITNER, F., and P. CINQUIN, 1991. Complex topology 3D objects segmentation. In *Proceedings of the S.P.I.E. Conference*, Boston, Vol. 1609.

[11] COHEN, I., N. AYACHE, and L. COHEN, 1991. Segmenting, visualizing and characterising 3D anatomical structures with deformable surfaces. In *Proceedings of the IEEE EMBS Conference*, Orlando, Fla., pp. 1183–1184.

[12] SAMET, H., 1989. *The Design and Analysis of Spatial Data Structures.* Reading, Mass.: Addison-Wesley.

[13] LAVALLÉE, S., R. SZELISKI, and L. BRUNIE, 1991. Matching 3-D smooth surfaces with their 2-D projections using 3-D distance maps. *S.P.I.E.: Geometric Methods in Computer Vision* 1570:322–336.

[14] KALL, B. A., P. J. KELLY, and S. J. GOERSS, 1987. Comprehensive computer-assisted data collection treatment planning and interactive surgery. *S.P.I.E.: Medical Imaging* 767:27–35.

[15] TAYLOR, R. H., H. A. PAUL, B. D. MITTELSTADT, E. GLASSMAN, B. L. MUSITS, and W. L. BARGAR, 1989. A robotic system for cementless total hip replacement surgery in dogs. In *Proceedings of the Second Workshop on Medical and Healthcare Robotics*, Newcastle, UK, pp. 79–89.

[16] MÖSGES, R., G. SCHLONDORFF, L. KLIMEK, D. MEYER-EBRECHT, W. KRYBUS, and L. ADAMS, 1989. Computer assisted surgery: An innovative surgical technique in clinical routine. In *Computer Assisted Radiology* (CAR '89), H. U. Lemke, ed. Berlin: Springer-Verlag, pp. 413–415.

[17] MAZIER, B., S. LAVALLÉE, and P. CINQUIN, 1990. Computer assisted interventionist imaging: Application to the vertebral column surgery. In *Proceedings of the Twelfth IEEE Engineering in Medicine and Biology Conference*, Philadelphia, pp. 430–431.

[18] MAZIER, B., S. LAVALLÉE, and P. CINQUIN, 1990. Chirurgie de la colonne vertebrale assistee par ordinateur: application au vissage pediculaire (in French). *ITBM* 11(5):559–566.

[19] TAYLOR, R. H., H. A. PAUL, C. B. CUTTING, B. MITTELSTADT, W. HANSON, P. KAZANZIDES, B. MUSITS, Y.

Y. Kim, A. Kalvin, B. Haddad, D. Khoramabadi, and D. Larose, 1992. Augmentation of human precision in computer-integrated surgery. *ITBM* (special issue on robotic surgery) 13(4):450–468.

[20] Martins, H. A., J. R. Birk, and R. B. Kelley, 1981. Camera models based on data from two calibration planes. *Comput. Graph. Image Proc.* 17:173–179.

[21] Champleboux, G., S. Lavallée, P. Sautot, and P. Cinquin, 1992. Accurate calibration of cameras and range imaging sensors, the NPBS method. In *Proceedings of the IEEE International Conference on Robotics and Automation*, Nice, France, pp. 1552–1558.

[22] Kosugi, Y., E. Watanabe, and J. Goto, 1988. An artic- ulated neurosurgical navigation system using MRI and CT images. *IEEE Trans. Biomed. Eng.* 35(2):147–152.

[23] Adams, L., A. Knepper, W. Krybus, D. Meyer- Ebrecht, G. Pfeiffer, R. Ruger, and M. Witte, 1992. Orientation aid for head and neck surgeons. *ITBM* (special issue on robotic surgery) 13(4):409–424.

[24] Reinhardt, H., H. Meyer, and E. Amrein, 1986. Robotik fur hirnoperationen (in German). *Polyscope Plus* (6):5–6.

[25] Davies, B. L., R. D. Hibberd, W. S. Ng, A. G. Timoney, and J. E. A. Wickham, 1991. A surgeon robot for prostatectomies. In *Proceedings of the Fifth International Conference on Advanced Robotics*, Pisa, Italy, pp. 871–875.

33 Computer-Integrated Orthopaedic Surgery: Connection of Planning and Execution in Surgical Intervention

KLAUS RADERMACHER, GÜNTER RAU, AND
HANS-WALTER STAUDTE

Motivation

USING IMAGING devices such as x-ray CT and computer-based image-processing systems, it is possible to record structures of a living organism in slices and to realize 3D reconstructions that can be visualized on a color graphic monitor. Some 3D image-processing systems also permit 3D planning of surgical interventions. Intraoperatively, there often are problems of 3D orientation because there is no adequate technical aid for a consequent 3D transfer of the individually planned steps of intervention. The accuracy of execution depends uniquely on the experience, the ability to think in 3D on the basis of a mental 3D model, and the manual skillfulness of the surgeon. Depending on the anatomic location of the intervention, this can result in severe risks.

In general, only freehand-guided and -positioned instruments, 2D images (with a drawing of surgical planning), and intraoperative biplanar x-ray imaging devices are available. For some interventions, standard tool guides and templates exist. Intraoperative positioning of these tool guides and templates in spatial relation to bone structure is carried out freehand. Even with those special devices that are adjustable to the anatomic conditions, the position is not exactly defined by the preoperative planning. Intraoperative measurements and repeated alignment under x-ray control leads to an increased exposure to radiation for the

medical staff as well as for the patient and it prolongs the duration of an intervention. Finally, it does not represent a sufficiently accurate and direct translation of the strategy of intervention defined during the preoperative phase of surgical planning. This situation may result, for example, in improper preparations of implant cavities in bone or imprecise osteotomies in the area of the extremities (Taylor et al., 1989). The precision and the high technologic standard of an individually designed implant is dramatically impaired by its freehand positioning during surgical intervention. For other even more complex and critical interventions such as those in the area of the spine or in pelvic surgery, no guide or positioning device is available.

Robots—the only technical answer?

For several years, international research activities have involved attempts to use modern robot technology with the aim of producing better tools and devices for quicker, more precise, and less straining surgical interventions. One major problem is the intraoperative localization and correlation among the reference systems of the object, the computer-based model, the environment, and the base of robot. To solve this problem of fusion (Taylor et al., 1989), different strategies and sensor concepts are pursued (Kosugi et al., 1988; Lavallée, 1989; Adams et al., 1990; Jacobi et al., 1990; Prasch et al., 1990; Martelli et al., 1991; Cinquin et al.,

1992; Taylor et al., 1992). Furthermore, the problem of intraoperative human-machine interaction (HMI) as well as the security and reliability of the overall system are central problems to be solved before robotics can be introduced into the surgical process (Rau and Trispel, 1982; Taylor et al., 1989).

The use of the technical system as such should require only a minimum of attention from the surgeon. The critical work process of surgical intervention within the physician-patient-machine system should not be charged additionally by time-consuming complex interactions with technical system components. This could be avoided by system integration effected through an ergonomic system design approach. By transferring the interaction with the complex technical system into a preoperative preparation and planning phase, the medical staff can be relieved of avoidable tasks during operation. The results of preoperative preparation and planning must be stored in a way that can be used easily during intervention.

Nevertheless, the special aspects of an ergonomic design of a medical work system, with its general as well as individual marginal conditions, have to be taken into account. Technical training of medical staff is possible only to a limited extend. The introduction of a robotic system into the operating theater probably will require an operating assistant with a special technical education. Apart from additional costs, this possibility leads to an additional human system component with additional interfaces and the necessity of interactions (human-human and human-machine) during surgical intervention. The number of interfaces (especially those between human and machine or human and human, respectively) always increases complexity, need of communication, and probability of error within a work system (Bernotat and Rau, 1980; Rau and Trispel, 1982). The design of efficient user interfaces with self-explanatory user guidance and optimized interaction sequences is one of the most important challenges in CIS.

The surgeon as the responsible medical expert must remain the highest hierarchic instance of the overall system. He or she must have total control of the process and must be able, even as a nontechnical user, to intervene at any moment in the ongoing process. At the same time, the surgeon wants to use the accuracy and precision (and, in very few cases, the speed) of the robot.

Safety and reliability of the system must be ensured by redundant sensor and control systems. Concerning intrinsic safety of the system, Davies et al. (1992) propose a very interesting concept of mechanically constraining the degrees of freedom and adapting the individual kinematic form of the motion axes to the specific task. Motion, in this case, is physically restricted to the limits of the planned work area. This concept would require different robots for different surgical interventions, which certainly would prevent a broad clinical application. A modular concept with multiple interchangeable subunits might be a solution to this problem, but this would lead to decreased accuracy. Another possibility is to use a robot with independent and redundant degrees of freedom and to brake or block mechanically the axes that are not needed for the specific mission or during different phases of intervention, respectively.

The analysis of surgical tasks and the synthesis and design of a kinematic configuration useful for a wide variety of surgical interventions will be essential for further work. Additionally, it should be mentioned that even very sophisticated preoperative simulations of an intervention will not prevent the need for an intraoperative change or modification of positioning or strategy in some cases. The intraoperative on-line modification and verification of a robot program will be very difficult for the medical staff. However, functionality on a lower level must be provided in some way. The surgeon should be able to use, but should not be forced to be absolutely dependent on, the technical support in any phase of intervention.

In summary, the use of robots in the operating room must be limited to interventions involving very complex 3D work through narrow accesses or that could not be realized without robotic support. In this context it should be noted that robots, on the one hand, and servomanipulators or remote manipulators, on the other, should be clearly distinguished from 6D coordinate-measuring devices (medical localizing systems) (Kosugi et al. 1988; Adams et al., 1990) or even automatic medical retractor holder systems that use auxiliary energy for locking mechanisms (McEwen et al., 1989). A *robot* is an automatic motion apparatus with several axes of which the movements are independently programmable and possibly sensor-guided with respect to sequences of movement, paths, or angles (Desoyer, Kopacek, and Troch, 1985). They are equipped with grippers, tools, or devices to perform positioning, handling, or manufacturing missions. Servomanipulators or remote manipulators are position- or force-controlled "passive robots" that are guided by the human operator (master). Areas of movement and restricted areas of collision could be programmed before operation and translated into variations of mechanical impedances in each degree of freedom depending on position, speed, or reacting forces. Regarding medical robotics, the different specifications should be clearly taken into account and compared with the specific requirements of each medical application.

Computer-integrated advanced orthopaedics

The aim of computer-integrated advanced orthopaedics (CIAO) is to enable medical staff to execute surgical interventions on bone according to the preoperative planning. The enhancement of precision and accuracy, shorter execution times, and additional technical support must not be traded for an additional loading of the intraoperative work process by complex technical systems or interactions (figure 33.1). The time for intraoperative measurement and alignment is minimized through a shift of these tasks into the preoperative planning phase. Work under x-ray control or with robotic systems is not necessary in most cases.

Nevertheless it should be possible to use a robot or servomanipulator as an intraoperative tool for geometrically difficult performances. In particular, the problem of a suitable user interface for the interaction of a nontechnical user with a complex technical system is one topic of our work. We try to avoid additional stress on the patient by avoiding, for example, preoperative (even invasive) fixation of reference markers or frames.

The central functional element in our approach is an individual template designed on the basis of preoperative CT image data. This individual template has so-called contact faces that copy without undercutting the complementary shape of segments of bone surface intraoperatively reachable by the surgeon. Hence, the template can be intraoperatively placed form-closed on the bone surface in exactly the predefined position and orientation. The region of bone structure relevant for surgical planning is scanned using x-ray CT. The 3D reconstruction and planning of intervention is performed by the physician using the 3D image-processing

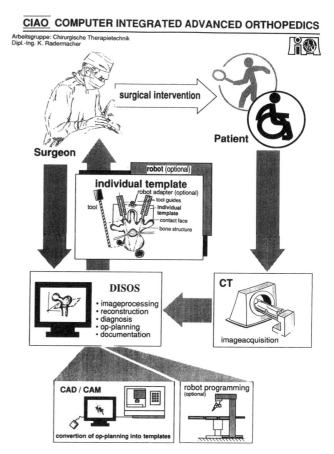

FIGURE 33.1 The concept of CIAO. (Reprinted with permission from Radermacher et al., 1993.)

system DISOS (Desktop Image-processing System for Orthopedic Surgery) developed especially within the CIAO project (figure 33.2). The results of segmentation of bone structure geometries and of surgical planning are documented in standard ASCII files.

DISOS is implemented on standard IBM PC hardware and is ergonomically designed especially with respect to the surgeon as a nontechnical user. An intuitive color, graphic user interface and an on-line help system allow the medical staff to perform diagnosis, image processing, and planning of surgical intervention without the need for any additional explanation or manual. It should allow maximum use of the medical expert's knowledge during diagnosis, segmentation, region of interest selection, correction of artifacts, verification of 3D reconstruction, and surgical planning of intervention. The data transmitted by DISOS contain, among other items, all necessary information about contours and surfaces of bony struc-

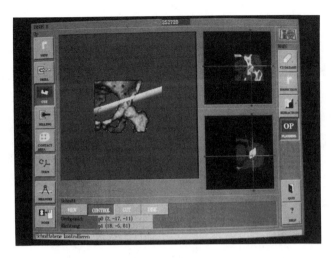

FIGURE 33.2   The DISOS system.

tures (including contact faces) and marker points with commentary labels and geometries describing the planning of the surgical intervention, needed for the following computer-aided design and manufacturing (CAD/CAM) procedure. Only for a final preoperative check does the doctor have to rejoin the preoperative process.

The surgical intervention itself is not weighed down by complex technology but may benefit maximally from it. Data are transmitted to the CAD/CAM system via a network or floppy disk.

Based on this data, contact face(s) are defined copying segments of the surface of the bone that are normally prepared during standard orthopaedic operations are defined on the CAD/CAM system. Individual templates are designed by inverting the surface normals of contact faces and connecting them with a rigid body representing the base of the individual template (figure 33.3). This basic rigid body of the template matching parts of the bone surface (a minimum of three intraoperatively identifiable contact points is possible only in very special cases) can be placed on the bone in a form-closed manner. Thus providing a hardware-based 3D/3D-surface-matching. Thereby, it is possible to identify and localize the bony structure very easily and quickly and to position tools exactly in the preoperatively defined position and orientation during intervention.

To define and reproduce exactly the position and orientation of cuts, bores, or sinkings on or into the

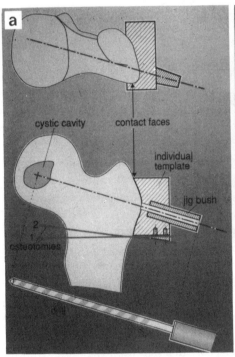

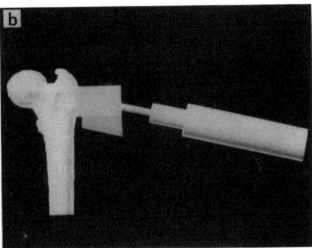

FIGURE 33.3   Principle of individual templates: (a) Template for the puncture and refilling of a cystic cavity in the femoral head, with an additional plug-in template for the second cut of an osteotomy for turning the cystic region out of the weight-bearing area. (Staudte, Radermacher, and Rau, 1993.) (b) CAD/CAM simulation.

454   ORTHOPAEDICS

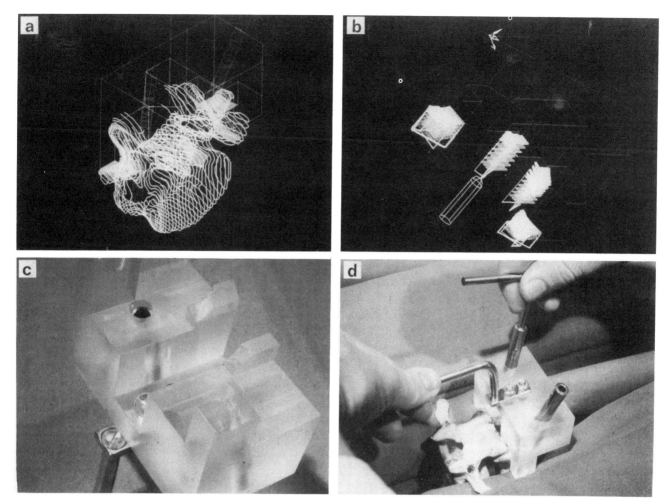

FIGURE 33.4 Procedure of transpedicle drilling, with an individual template. (a) Simulation of the intervention on the CAD/CAM system; definition of contact faces and in- dividual template. (b) Programming and simulation of NC manufacturing. (c) Individual template with contact faces. (d) Simulation of the intraoperative situation.

bone, we have merely to provide tool guides within or at the body of the individual template. Alternatively, we have to define reference points (bores) for the fixation of reusable standard tool guides. The positioning of these guides (and the tools) in 3D relationship to the bone is reproduced intraoperatively simply by putting the individual template on the natural surface of bone. Optional fixation of the template on bone by small pins or screws can be useful to avoid dislocation during work. Time-consuming efforts at measurement to align guides and tools can be shifted into the preoperative planning phase. Working under intraoperative biplanar x-ray control thus is markedly reduced.

Figure 33.4 shows the procedure of transpedicle drilling in a vertebra from the dorsal side. The bore hole is needed for fixation of a fixateur interne with

pedicle screws. These screws must be fixed exactly in the cortical bone of pedicles and vertebra from a dorsal portal of operation. Fixateur interne with transpedicle fixation are used, for example, in scoliosis therapy. The positioning of the bore holes conventionally must be performed under intraoperative biplanar x-ray control. Drilling is piloted by first introducing a thin metal probe into the estimated bore channel. Taking into account the direct neighborhood of the spinal cord and the roots of spinal nerves, this intervention implies a high risk. Neither the probe nor the drill or screws should injure these sensitive structures. Nonetheless, fixation of the screws in the cortical area of pedicles and vertebrae is essential for good anchoring. The drill jig of the individual template define exactly the position, orientation, length, and diameter of the bore hole (given that there is a known geometry of drilling tool) as it was planned during the preoperative planning phase.

After generation of the individual machining program, the template is manufactured on a numerically controlled milling machine or using the rapid prototyping process of stereolithography. In the case of a cutting manufacturing, semifinished material especially prepared for various classes of interventions can be used. Only the contact faces and the bore holes have to be applied individually. The semifinished products can be stored in a DISOS macro library. In this database, standardized tool guides, surgical fixation elements, fixateur-interne and -externe, holding systems, and even robotic and manipulator libraries could also be stored. Additionally, the storage of physiologic and pathologic bone structures and standard portals of surgical interventions may be useful. All components needed for the surgical intervention can be combined, adapted, and positioned during the phase of surgical planning in the coordinate system fixed relative to the computer model of bone. The reusable components are mounted preoperatively on the body of the individual template in the planned manner. Through this defined mechanical fixation in relation to the individual template and its contact faces, the position and orientation of each component in relation to bone is predefined by surgical planning. Intraoperatively, it can be reproduced simply by putting the template on bone. Initial experiments with anatomic preparations showed a maximal deviation from the optimal bore channel (according to the Magerl method) of less than 1 mm.

In some cases, it may be important to limit the depth of cutting in order to avoid damaging surrounding soft tissues. To realize, for example, an osteotomy of the vertebral body from a ventral portal, it must be ensured that the tip of the saw does not exceed in depth the dorsal surface of the vertebral body in order not to injure spinal cord. Ventral osteotomies can be applied for the correction of scoliosis. Conventionally, bone fusion holds the permanent correction of the pathologic curves. With the method of individual templates, even this irreversible loss of spinal function could be avoided. Hereby, the correction can be performed without the destruction of the intervertebral disks. To achieve this goal, the individual template is fixed on the ventral surface of the corresponding vertebra to avoid unvoluntary displacement. The position of the template is defined by its contact faces. A parallel

guide enabling parallel cutting in the predefined direction is connected with the template and the saw in the predefined manner (figure 33.5). A copying pin fixed at the saw is guided by a copying template describing the projected intersection curve of the cutting plane and the dorsal surface of the vertebra (see figure 33.5), and providing a cutting depth limited to the dorsal surface of the bone. A second individual template can be used to drill transpedicle-transcutaneous bore holes for a dorsal extern alignment and temporary fixation of the spine. Additional resorbable fixation at the vertebra's ventral face could be provided. These temporary fixations should stiffen the spine for approximately 3 months. After this time, the ventral fixation should be resorbed and the transpedicle extern could be removed. After 3–4 months, the spine would regain full motility. Experiments on anatomic preparations showed that it would be possible, by the use of individual templates, to correct a scoliosis of up to 45° (after Cobb) without a lasting stiffening of spinal segments.

Milling operations can be planned and executed precisely with the aid of individual templates. Apart from the contact faces defining the positioning of template in relation to bone, the template should consist of a 3D copying device reflecting the relevant geometries (areas or surfaces) that should be milled. Figure 33.6 shows the principle of such a 3D milling template. This guiding surface copies, for example, the marrow cavity of femoral bone but is radially expanded by the ratio of diameters of cam to milling head. Through 3D parallel guidance of the milling tool and a defined 3D relation of the components, the procedure provides an exact milling (or cleaning from cement) of the femoral cavity according to the plan of intervention. Fixation of bone in relation to the environment is not necessary; only the template must be fixed on bone.

These examples of individual templates represent only a small portion of the possible applications. Apart from osteotomies in the area of extremities or of skull, triple osteotomies for repositioning of pelvic bone (presented later), fixations in the area of lumbosacral joints (or spine in general), and geometrically limited 3D resections of cancerous bone tissue could benefit from this technique.

Robot-assisted surgery

For interventions requiring geometrically complex templates or small surgical portals, it appears useful to

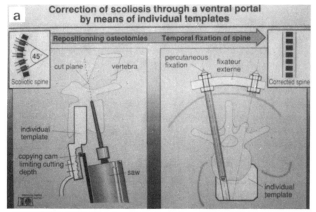

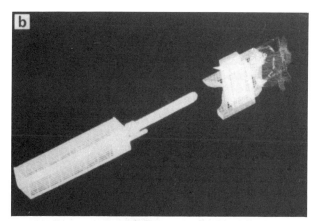

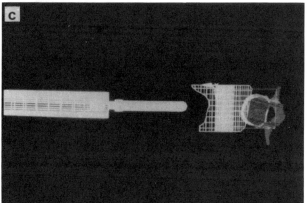

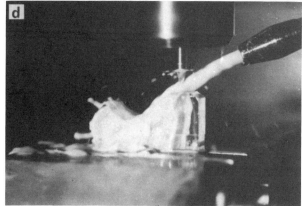

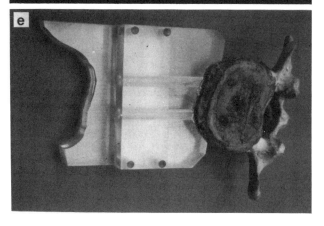

FIGURE 33.5 Individual template for ventral osteotomy of vertebra. (a) Principle of the surgical strategy. (b) CAD/CAM simulation of the intervention and design of template.

(c) NC manufacturing of template. (d) Realized template. (e) Copying pin in detail.

involve a robot or servomanipulator in the surgical procedure (figure 33.7). This necessitates the manufacture of only a basic individual template with its reference contact faces to the bony structure and a defined mechanical relation to a robot-hand coordinate system.

The gripper or hand of the robot of the CAD/CAM system is connected to the basic individual template.

The geometric relationship between the individual template and the robot-hand coordinate system or gripper stored in the macro database is preoperatively defined on the CAD/CAM system by the design of a rigid connection with defined reference points. It is described by the homogeneous (4×4) transformation $\mathbf{E_{IT}}$. The transformation $\mathbf{G_0}$ describes the individual

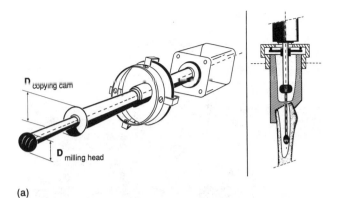

(a)

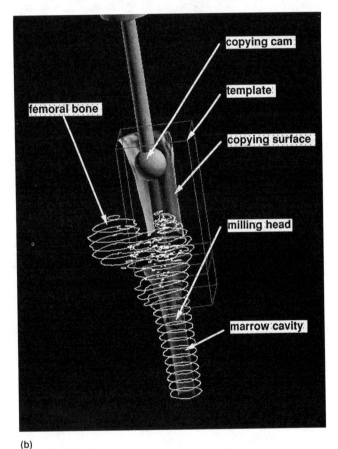

(b)

FIGURE 33.6 Principle of 3D milling of the marrow cavity of bone.

template in the bone coordinate system (in contact with bone) in the position preoperatively defined on CAD/CAM.

The simulated position of the bone structure in the coordinate system of the gripper $(E_{IT} * G_0^{-1})$ is defined as the base of the simulation, and programming of the tool paths of the whole working procedure is effected on CAD/CAM, even for different steps of intervention

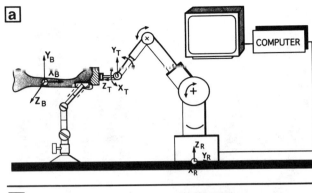

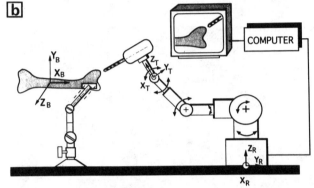

FIGURE 33.7 (a, b) Principle of an optional integration of a robot or manipulator within the surgical procedure.

with perhaps different tools x. The geometric relation E_x between the coordinate system of tool x and the gripper or hand coordinate system must be known and constant (this can be defined on CAD/CAM). The matrix $G_x(t)$ represents the time-dependent transformation between the bone coordinate system and the surgical instrument x (robot end-effector) preoperatively defined, calculated, and documented on CAD/CAM. The transform $[G_x(t) * E_x^{-1}]$ describes the time-dependent position of the robot hand in relation to the bone coordinate system, which also is calculated preoperatively (figure 33.8).

Apart from the necessity of redundant intraoperative sensing and control, the preoperative definition of restricted areas of motion can be provided and defined on CAD/CAM. The individual template, consisting of a basic body with contact faces and reference bore holes for fixation at the robot hand, is mounted on the hand or gripper of the robot before operation. The position of the robot's base coordinate system in the base coordinate system described by the homogeneous transform **Z** has to be defined. If the system includes, for example, infrared video cameras as redundant posi-

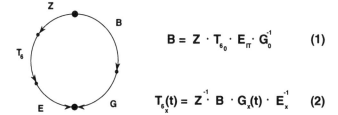

$$B = Z \cdot T_{6_0} \cdot E_\pi \cdot G_0^{-1} \qquad (1)$$

$$T_{6_x}(t) = Z^{-1} \cdot B \cdot G_x(t) \cdot E_x^{-1} \qquad (2)$$

Directed Transform Graph

FIGURE 33.8 Relations among the different coordinate systems described by homogeneous transformations. (Derived from Paul, 1981.)

tioning control, the system's base coordinate system may deviate from the robot's base coordinate system. If the robot base is defined as the system base, Z becomes the identity matrix. The overall system has to be calibrated before operation with an easy-to-use semiautomatic procedure.

Intraoperatively, the individual template is put on the bone in its predefined position by guiding the robot's hand (teach-in). The robot, guided by the surgeon, measures and calculates the position and orientation of the gripper described by the transform T_{60}, the template, and the bone in the system base coordinates described by B. Now the transformation between robot base and the bone is known, and it is possible to calculate and transform the tool path that was planned preoperatively. The time-dependent transform $T_x(t)$, describing the movement of the robot-hand coordinate system in relation to the robot's base coordinate system can be intraoperatively calculated for the different planned end-effectors x after B has been calculated. Before referring the coordinate systems by putting the template on the bone surface, the bony structure must be rigidly fixed by a special surgical holder system in relation to the system base coordinates (B = constant).

The translation of surgical work planned during the preoperative phase can be performed by the robot positioning a laser pointer (or other device) to indicate the position and orientation of bore holes, cutting planes, and so forth. In a further step, the robot could carry end-effectors such as drills, saws, or milling tools. The position of the end-effectors within the operating field could optionally be matched into the image of the CAD/CAM model displayed on a monitor in the operating room. This would provide an additional continuous method by which the surgeon could control the process.

One area of future research will be to realize a force-controlled servomanipulator that translates the preoperative planning into areas of variable mechanical impedance (i.e., to so-called virtual templates). Such an intelligent manipulator would be guided by the surgeon by hand and would offer resistance (change 6D impedance) at the limits of the planned work channel.

Experience

To verify the concept of CIAO, a series of feasibility studies with medical experts and engineering students have been performed, simulating the planning and execution of a surgical intervention on human bony preparations. Using two anatomic preparations of vertebrae, a ventral osteotomy and an intrapedicle drilling was simulated. Additionally, an anatomic preparation of a femur was used to simulate an osteotomy (2D cutting) and a 3D milling of femoral marrow. The bony structures were scanned on an x-ray CT. Data were transmitted to DISOS, where the surgeon planned his intervention. The results of segmentation, 3D reconstruction, and surgical planning were stored on a $3\frac{1}{2}$-in. floppy disk. The students transmitted the data to the CAD/CAM system. Individual templates were designed according to the markers and commentary labels transmitted together with geometric data and describing the surgeon's plan of intervention. The templates were manufactured of polymethylmethacrylate (PMMA) on a numerically controlled (NC) milling machine (in one case, we used stereolithography). Afterward, templates were given to the surgeon who performed the simulated intervention on the anatomic preparations. Times for execution and accuracy in all cases were much better than with unguided manual execution. Deviation of the tool from within region of interest was less than 1 mm in every case.

The first CIAO operation with individually designed and manufactured templates was carried out at District Hospital Marienhhe, Würselen, Germany. The surgical intervention on a 31-year-old woman, a triple osteotomy for repositioning the glenoid cavity of the left hip joint, was carried out with three independent templates for the three osteotomies (figure 33.9).

The patient was scanned on a CT scanner with a slice thickness of 2 mm and steps of 4 mm to minimize x-ray exposure of the pelvic region. Data were transmitted to DISOS. Segmentation, 3D reconstruction, and surgical planning were performed by the surgeon,

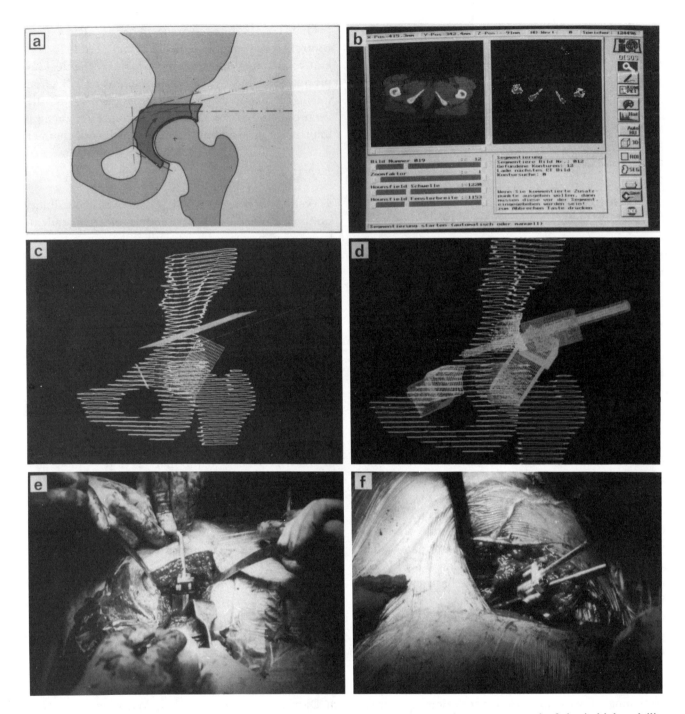

FIGURE 33.9 Triple osteotomy of pelvic bone. (a) Principle of triple osteotomy. (b) Image processing and surgical planning with DISOS. (c) Definition of cutting planes and bore holes in relation to bone on CAD/CAM system. (d) Computer-aided design of templates. (e, f) Intraoperative use of individual templates for ischial (e) and iliac (f) osteotomy.

(g, h) Intraoperative x-ray control of the ischial and iliac osteotomy. (i) Integration within the surgical environment. Individual templates on the instrument table. (k) Three independent templates (and Allen wrench for the intraoperative fixation of the reusable handles).

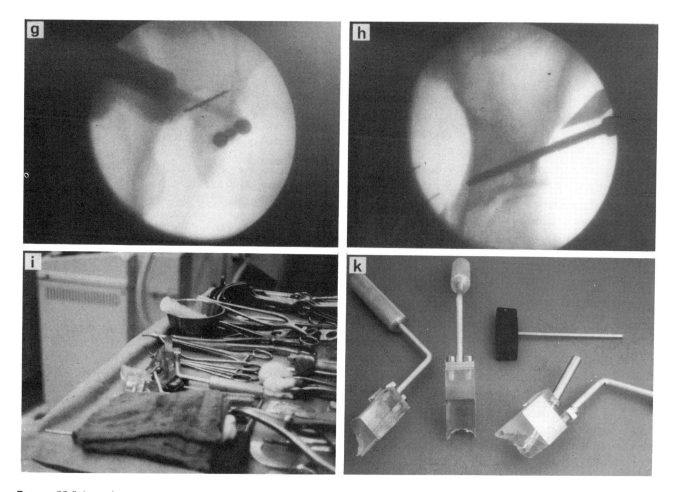

FIGURE 33.9 (cont.)

and the data were transmitted to the CAD/CAM system. On the CAD/CAM system, the cutting planes and the bore (for the repositioning and the refixation of bony structures) defined by the surgeon were used to design individual templates, which were adapted to the dorsal and the two ventral surgical portals. The templates were manufactured of PMMA on an NC milling machine. In the area of contact with surgical instruments, the templates have been armed with small panes of stainless steel. The jig for the bore also was made of stainless steel. The templates were cleaned and gas-sterilized and transmitted to the operating room together with the other surgical instruments. Reusable handles of aluminum were mounted intraoperatively.

The intraoperative x-ray control showed that definition of the cut planes by means of the templates was highly satisfying. It was superior to the first intraoperative approach by the surgeon when he initially tried to define the cut plane freehand in the conventional way.

The template with the jig bush for repositioning and the refixation of bony structures was very accurate as well. The bore hole passed approximately 10 mm above the glenoid cavity and the cutting plane 10 mm above the bore hole, according to the surgical plan.

The templates were readily accepted by the whole medical staff as a very common tool (see figure 33.9i); there was no sense of having something strange in the operating field, nor were the templates perceived as a completely new device.

Discussion

The concept of individual templates does not impose any burden on the surgical intervention or the patient beyond those in conventional procedures. It supports the surgeon in translating and executing the intervention exactly according to his or her preoperative planning, guiding the surgeon's instruments in the predefined 3D relationship to the bony structures. In addition, it releases the surgical team from avoidable tasks such as intraoperative x-ray imaging, calibration, and measurement.

The concept of task allocation within CIAO is to relieve the surgeon from those tasks that are not essentially based on his or her medical expertise and for which he or she is not really trained as an expert. Preoperatively, the planning of the intervention can be performed with our 3D image-processing system, DISOS, by a nontechnical user.

Nevertheless, the efficiency of the process must be optimized for clinical routine. The development of an integrated, high-performance, medical CAD/CAM system with a desktop manufacturing device will be one area for future development. Medical desktop manufacturing devices already are realized in the field of dentistry, where inlays can be designed and manufactured very efficiently by the dentist on desktop CAD/CAM systems on the basis of individual image data. High-performance, low-cost computer hardware, easy-to-use operating and application software, and a good knowledge of necessary features and interaction sequences during surgical planning (and programming), with resulting ergonomically designed self-explanatory user interfaces, will be essential for a broad acceptance of such systems in the medical field. DISOS already includes many functionalities for the definition of individual templates. The next step will be to integrate program components for the automatic generation of NC manufacturing programs.

Further investigations of the accuracy of the templates will be the aim of future work. Strategies for quality assurance in the phases of design, manufacturing, and mounting of components must be developed for each type of intervention. An application for robotics was not expressly indicated. The simulated or executed interventions could be performed satisfactorily with the intraoperatively easy-to-use individual templates. Nevertheless, the option to involve a robot or a servomanipulator in the surgical procedure is the subject of ongoing research.

ACKNOWLEDGMENTS We would like to thank Prof. Dr. R. Günther and his staff, especially Dr. M. Klein, Department of Radiology, as well as Prof. Dr. R. Repges and his staff at the Institute for Medical Statistics and Documentation, Aachen University Hospital, for their friendly and helpful cooperation. Thanks also to the support staff of the Helmholtz Institute for the excellent work performed on this project to date.

REFERENCES

ADAMS, L., W. KRYBUS, D. MEYER-EBRECHT, R. RUEGER, J. M. GILSBACH, R. MÖSGES, and O. SCHLÖENDORFF, 1990. Computer-assisted surgery. *IEEE Comput. Graph. Appl.* May:10:43–51.

BERNOTAT, R., and G. RAU, 1980. Ergonomics in medicine. In *Perspectives in Biomechanics*, H. Reul, Ghista, and G. Rau, eds. New York: Harwood Academic, pp. 381–398.

CINQUIN, P., J. DEMONGEOT, J. TROCCAZ, S. LAVALLÉE, G. CHAMPLEBOUX, L. BRUNIE, F. LEITNER, P. SAUTOT, B. MAZIER, A. PEREZ, M. DJAID, T. FORTIN, M. CHENIN, and A. CHAPEL, 1992. IGOR—image guided operating robot. Methodology, medical applications, results. *ITBM* 13(4):374–393.

DAVIES, B. L., R. D. HIBBERD, W. S. NG, A. G. TIMONEY, and J. E. A. WICKHAM, 1992. Mechanical constraints—the answer to safe robotic surgery? *ITBM* 13(4):426–436.

DESOYER, K., P. KOPACEK, and I. TROCH, 1985. *Industrieroboter und Handhabungsgerte* (in German). Munich: R. Oldenbourg Verlag.

FADDA, M., S. MARTELLI, M. DARIO, M. MARCACCI, A. VISANI, and S. ZAFFAGNINI, 1992. First steps toward robot-assist discectomy and arthroplasty. *ITBM* 13(4):395–408.

HÖHNE, K. H., H. FUCHS, and ST. M. PIZER, 1990. *3D-Imaging in Medicine*. Berlin: Springer-Verlag.

JACOBI, P., P. DANIEL, A. MUGLER, R. MORGENSTERN, H. DÖGE, and V. ROCKEL, 1990. Diagnosegesteuerte Therapierobotertechnik—medizinische und biomedizinische Aspekte (in German). *Z. Klin. Med.* 45(6):515–519.

KOSUGI, Y., E. WATANABE, J. GOTO, T. WATANABE, S. YOSHIMOTO, K. TAKAKURA, and J. IKEBE, 1988. An articulated neurosurgical navigation system using MRI and CT images. *IEEE Trans. Biomed. Eng.* 35(2):147–152.

LAVALLÉE, S., 1989. Geste medico-chirurgicaux assistes par ordinateur: Application a la neurochirurgie stereotaxique (in French). Doctoral thesis, Grenoble University, France.

MARTELLI, S., P. FADDA, M. DARIO, M. MARCACCI, G. P. MARCENARO, and A. VISANI, 1990. A laser scanner system for investigating non-invasive matching strategies in computer-assisted orthopedic surgery. In *Proceedings of the Annual International Conference of the IEEE EMBS* 13(4):1757–1758.

McEWEN, J. A., C. R. BUSSANI, G. F. AUCHINLECK, and M. J. BREAULT, 1989. "Development and initial clinical evaluation of pre-robotic and robotic retraction systems. In *Proceedings of the IEEE EMBS Eleventh Annual International Conference*, pp. 881–882.

PAUL, R. P., 1981. *Robot Manipulators*. Cambridge, Mass.: MIT Press.

PRASCH, J., 1990. Computerunterstüzte Planung von chirurgischen Eingriffen in der Orthopädie. iwb Forschungsberichte (diss., in German). Berlin: Springer-Verlag.

PREISING, B., T. C. HSIA, and B. MITTELSTADT, 1991. A literature review: Robots in medicine. *IEEE Eng. Med. Biol.* June:13–22, 71.

RADERMACHER, K., G. RAU, and H.-W. STAUDTE, 1993. CIAO—computer integrated advanced orthopedics. In

Proceedings of the Second European Conference in Engineering and Medicine, pp. 117–118.

RAU, G., and S. TRISPEL, 1982. Ergonomic design aspects in interaction between man and technical systems in medicine. *Med. Progr. Technol.* 9:153–159.

STAUDTE, H.-W., K. RADERMACHER, and G. RAU, 1993. Computerunterstützung in der operativen Orthopädie mit individuellen Bearbeitungsschablonen (Computer assistance in operative orthopedics using individual templates). In *Proceedings of the First German-Austrian-Swiss Congress of Orthopedics*, Munich, June 30–July 4.

TAYLOR, R. H., H. A. PAUL, B. D. MITTELSTADT, E. GLASSMAN, B. L. MUSITS, and W. L. BARGAR, 1989. Robotic Total Hip Replacement Surgery in Dogs. In *Proceedings of the IEEE EMBS Eleventh Annual International Conference*, pp. 887–889.

TAYLOR, R. H., H. A. PAUL, C. B. CUTTING, B. MITTELSTADT, W. HANSON, P. KAZANZIDES, B. L. MUSITS, Y. Y. KIM, A. KALVIN, B. HADDAD, D. KHORAMABADI, and D. LAROSE, 1992. Augmentation of human precision in computer-integrated surgery. *ITBM* 13(4):451–468.

Eye Surgery

EYE SURGERY IS an area in which computers are expected to play an increasingly important role. The three chapters included in this section reflect the transition from manual diagnosis and surgery toward more automated diagnosis and surgical planning and execution. The reader should realize that at the present time neither the hardware (computer power, stereo cameras, or microrobots) nor the software algorithms are fully developed. The lack of enthusiasm among eye surgeons for inclusion of robotics is due in part to the perceived difficulty and complexity of eye surgery. Therefore, automated diagnosis, surgical planning, and procedural execution are areas of active research.

Ophthalmic microsurgery can be classified into the specialties of cataract, keratorefractive, glaucoma, and vitreoretinal surgery. The first chapter, "Dexterity Enhancement for Surgery" by Charles, is a surgeon's look at the present state of technology and the clinical requirements for microsurgery. He identifies a critical need for more "dexterous" technology that can enhance the position capability and tactile feedback for microsurgeons. Charles distinguishes three phases for dexterity enhancement—namely, improving the performance of hand-held tools, better remote-actuated tools and, finally, full teleoperation. During teleoperation, the surgeon is in (constant) control of a microrobot that actually performs the procedure. Advantages stem from amplification of force feedback, scaling down of positioning commands, the introduction of low-pass filters to reduce surgeon hand tremor effects, and so on. The tool used by the surgeon (the "master") need not have the same geometry as the "slave" robot. Charles considers that the best master is a 6 degree-of-freedom wrist controller and that more complex masters, such as sensing gloves or exoskeletons, are unnecessary. An additional advantage of teleoperation is the ability to preset force, velocity, and position limits before initiating surgery. These in turn, limit the surgical space and increase the patient's safety.

The second chapter, "Computer-Assisted Eye Surgery" by Mammone et al., describes a topographic modeling system designed as an aid for surgery on the cornea (keratotomy, epikeratophakia, suture removal, suture adjustment, and excimer laser keratectomy). The system provides a contour map of the patient's corneal topography (radius of curvature). The depth from corneal vertex is obtained from triangulation between acquired and reference images and displayed in an optical power (dioptric) color map. These maps are displayed in real time by a 486 PC, which runs the image acquisition and analysis software. Although the primary role of the topographic modeling system is in diagnosis, it can also be used for surgical planning and simulation. The resident *Surgical Planning Screen* program overlays the surgical planning diagrams on the patient's color-coded topological map. An editor allows the surgeon to change the length or orientation of the proposed corneal cuts, while unforeseen geometric conflicts are detected and solved automatically by the program. The same computerized system can be used in postsurgical assessment, where subsequent corneal maps are stored and compared. Readers interested in related surgical planning work are referred to Hanna et al. (1988).

The third chapter, "Visual Monitoring of Glaucoma" by Lee and Brady, also focuses on the area of diagnosis, specifically for glaucoma. If untreated, glaucoma can lead to blindness. The current diagnostic procedure is based on manual measurements of the ocular fundus. An onset of glaucoma is associated with an increase in optical disk size over some months' time. The need to obtain repeated measurements over a long span and by several doctors leads to problems in both accuracy and repeatability, with variations of as much as 30%. Lee and Brady describe work toward an automated system used to detect the optical disk shape and surface curvature. This approach relies on stereo imaging, combined with shape from shading in order to detect the 3D profile of the optical nerve head (connected to the disk). The image integration algorithm is considered by the authors to be superior to either sparse binocular stereo depth measurements or surface reconstruction from a gradient of stereophotometry taken separately. Various subsequent clinical measurements can then be made, in the hope of achieving increased diagnostic accuracy and repeatability.

The problems of inaccurate measurement and poor repeatability are by no means limited to eye surgery. Indeed, they are common to other diagnostic areas, for which there is a need to compare sets of data taken at long time intervals. One example is in digital subtraction dental radiography, as described in the section on dentistry.

Readers interested in more technical detail on teleoperation and microrobotics should consult also chapters 13 and 16 in this book.

REFERENCE

HANNA, K. D., F. E. JOUVE, G. O. WANIG, and P. G. CIAILET, 1988. Computer simulation of arcuate keratotomy for astigmatism. *Refract. Corneal Surg.* 8:152–163.

34 Dexterity Enhancement for Surgery

STEVE CHARLES

MICROSURGERY for all surgical specialties began more than 50 years ago with the development of the operating microscope. Optical magnification enhances the visual efferent pathway for the surgeon, although little has been done to improve the tactile efferent pathway or the efferent dexterity or positioning system.

Having surveyed leading surgeons in ophthalmology and other specialties, it is the author's conclusion that there is a great need for electromechanical dexterity enhancement in all microsurgical specialties. Each expert believes that there are some procedures that can be performed by only a few microsurgeons. It also is believed that some procedures demand such a high level of dexterity that not even the best microsurgeons could perform them. The goal of dexterity enhancement technology is to improve positioning capability and tactile feedback for all microsurgeons.

Possible microsurgical applications

Microsurgical specialties traditionally include ophthalmic, otologic, and hand surgery, as well as neurosurgery. All surgical specialties are increasingly reliant on magnification for certain portions of the surgical procedure. Minimally invasive surgery can be broadly defined as surgery through existing portals, vascular channels, or small incisions.

Flexible or rigid endoscopic devices are used through oral, nasal, rectal, or vaginal approaches. Flexible endoscopes allow deeper access and usually have a 1–degree of freedom (dof), manual, crude bending mechanism at the tip. Rigid and flexible endoscopes have a lumen through which push-pull, flexible, cable-based instruments can be passed. Steerable, flexible catheters with balloons, lasers, or mechanical cutters are used for intravascular surgery. There is considerable similarity between small flexible endoscopic systems and catheter-based intravascular systems. Rigid endoscopes typically are used for arthroscopy. Long-shaft, rigid forceps, cautery, scissors, clip application instruments, and mechanical cutters are used through the lumina of arthroscopy systems. There are no commercially available precise micropositioning systems even with 1 dof available for minimally invasive surgical applications.

Ophthalmic microsurgery can be subdivided into the specialty areas of cataract, keratorefractive, glaucoma, and vitreoretinal surgery. Each subspecialty has evolving requirements for new downsized procedures that require electromechanical dexterity enhancement. Cataract surgery involves replacement of the cortex and nucleus of the crystalline lens with an implant material within the lens capsule. Restoration of variable focus after implantation means that very small openings in the lens capsule must be made and then sealed to restore mechanical and optical properties. Similarly, keratorefractive surgery would benefit from dexterity enhancement, as length, depth, and orientation of corneal incisions with a diamond knife require extreme accuracy for precise optical outcomes. Glaucoma surgery could be improved if we were able to perform microdissection of the aqueous humor drainage system. It is likely that small implantable drainage systems would then be micropositioned within the trabecular meshwork to lower the intraocular pressure and treat the glaucoma. Vitreoretinal surgery requires dexterity enhancement to remove 20 to 50-μm-thick membranes from the front and back surfaces of the retina in the macular region. Retinal vascular surgery has been accomplished by the author on several occasions but pushes the limit of human dexterity and therefore requires these electromechanical aids.

Otologic procedures are excellent candidates for dexterity enhancement. Stapedectomy procedures, acoustic neuroma dissections, and other middle ear procedures would likely benefit from improved positioning capability. It has been postulated by several experienced otologic surgeons that microscopic holes in the semicircular canals might benefit sufferers of Meniere's disease, a major cause of vertigo.

Neurosurgeons are increasingly using computer-assisted stereotactic procedures based on preoperative MRI and CT scanning to position a surgical instrument. This approach initiates the procedure in the proper location and approaches through the safest path but does nothing to enhance the accuracy of the intraoperative dissection. Closed endoscopy techniques with dexterity-enhanced dissection could reduce brain swelling and hemorrhage as well as improve the accuracy and safety of the procedure.

Hand surgery frequently involves the reanastomosis of small nerves and vessels. Lengthy hand, arm, and digit reimplantation procedures would be excellent candidates for enhanced dexterity.

Phases of dexterity enhancement

Simple methods to improve dexterity were studied before initiating the development of teleoperated, microsurgical robots. The author divides dexterity enhancement into three phases.

FIRST-ORDER DEXTERITY ENHANCEMENT

First-order dexterity enhancement includes all methods to improve the positioning performance of hand-held, hand-actuated tools. It was determined that although it could stabilize hand-held tool systems, mass degraded the dexterity of microsurgeons because of increased inertia, momentum, and weight-induced fatigue. Kinesthetic sense, pressure sense, and positioning ability were degraded by heavy instruments as well.

Some designers believe that tool handles should be circular cylinders, whereas the author stresses the use of contoured tool handles with an increasing cross-sectional area as distance increases in either direction from the normal tool-hand contact point. With this design, the instruments need not be held tightly for fear of dropping them. This is important as the reflex to catch a dropped instrument is so slow that the instrument will fall completely out of the surgeon's hand before it can be retrieved.

Hand-held tools normally contact the hand at two discrete points, the confluence of the first three digits and the second metacarpal joint and a point midway between the first and second metacarpal joints. The choice between these two contact points is determined by whether the instrument has a small-angle or near-right-angle formation with respect to the long axis of the forearm.

Hand-held tools are gripped at their center of mass to eliminate unnecessary torque loads. Many hand-held tools are actuated remotely and therefore require tubing, wire, or a fiber connection to the primary energy source. These cables interfere with dexterity in several ways. The cable has a hanging loop between the controller and the tool or, more typically, the loop lays on the surgical drape. Significant tool movement requires a force to overcome the mass and the flexibility of the loop as well as the dynamic friction at the tether–surgical drape contact. Any remotely actuated tools must have minimal moving mass and minimal friction to reduce vibratory load on the hand. The dynamics of the hand, glove, and tool system must be studied to rationalize instrument and even glove design.

Tools can be divided into those that require the surgeon's hand for actuation and those that only are positioned by the surgeon's hand. Tools that currently require the surgeon's force for operation include cutting tools and gripping instruments with two moving parts.

Tissue cutting can be accomplished mechanically or by vaporization. The latter is done with laser energy and is accompanied by a propagating acoustic effect, bubbles, and damage remote to the intended cutting point. Mechanical cutting tools work on three basic principles:

- Sharpness, defined as high pressure per unit area of the needle or blade brought about by small tissue-blade contact
- Shearing, either inclusive (with parallel blades) or exclusive (with nonparallel blades, such as scissors)
- Inertial cutting, entailing the use of high-speed cutter motion against stable tissue

Blade motion faster than the speed of sound brings about cavitation, streaming, and a propagating pressure wave with remote effects. Lasers and ultrasonic cutting are inappropriate for surgery near the retina, cochlea, semicircular canals, small vessels, and nerves.

SECOND-ORDER DEXTERITY ENHANCEMENT

Remote actuation is required for high-speed motion, radio-frequency energy, laser energy, infusion, vacuum, illumination, and other modalities that the hand cannot deliver. The author has studied the hand's capabilities and has determined that actuation motions as required by manual scissors and forceps greatly reduce the hand's positioning performance. Remote actuation can be defined as second-order dexterity enhancement.

Rotary motion is extremely difficult for the hand and degrades the stability of the tool tip. Telescopic motions are somewhat easier to accomplish than rotary or actuation functions but, again, these degrade positioning performance. Writinglike motions not requiring rotation or telescoping are the most precise motions of the human hand. Power-actuated, rotated, and telescoping hand-held tools will enhance dexterity but are still subject to first-order design constraints.

THIRD-ORDER DEXTERITY ENHANCEMENT

Third-order dexterity enhancement can be defined as full teleoperation. Robots are autonomous, preprogrammed positioners and are inappropriate in most types of microsurgery. Teleoperation systems are an extension of the operator in that the surgeon is always controlling the positioning process directly. Telemicrorobotic (TMR) systems can be divided into three components: the master (controller), the computer system, and the slave (manipulator). Autonomous robotic systems have very limited applications in microsurgery because of the change in geometry of the tissue that occurs as surgery is performed. Surgical procedures on bone systems offer the most potential for the use of robotic devices, but it remains possible for the tissue to move as the decompression or dissection process is being carried out.

In the general sense, the function of a TMR system is to match the dexterity attributes to the tool-tissue interface. It is crucial to understand the bandwidth characteristics of the human operator. Volitional positioning has a 5-Hz bandwidth, whereas a kinesthetic (position) feedback has a 15-Hz bandwidth. Vibration can be sensed to 10 KHz and frequency discriminated to 320 Hz.

The most important fundamental design criterion is to decide between hand-replica masters and slaves or wristlike masters and slaves. The author has determined that a wrist is the best choice for a dexterous positioner, rather than a full-motion hand utilizing digits independently. Exoskeleton masters and glove master systems have no application in microsurgical situations. The Utah/MIT hand, although exquisite, should not be used in microsurgery as its performance is significantly less than that of the human hand.

All microsurgery requires 6 dof. Hence, stylus, trackball, mouse, keyboard, and traditional joystick controllers are not appropriate for microsurgery. The author strongly believes that the master should look and feel like the handle of high-performance microsurgical tools.

Force reflection (feedback) means that forces (torques) encountered by the slave are electronically sent to actuators in the master. In the context of microsurgery, these forces would be scaled up in order to feel small forces (torques) that occur at the tool-tissue interface. This is in marked contrast to industrial, hazardous-environment, teleoperated systems in which the forces are typically scaled down to the master. High-fidelity telepresence would therefore demand a force-reflecting system in addition to a position-scaling system.

Position scaling is an obvious advantage of TMR systems. Simplistically, the master could be moved 1 mm and the slave 100 μm to provide 10:1 position downscaling. Position scaling must be variable to address the coarse to fine nature of microsurgical tasks. Traversing to reach the surgical target should be fast (1:1) to minimize operating time. A velocity-sensitive position-scaling paradigm is being studied that will allow fast traversing followed by precision downscaled motion as the target is approached. Performance of ± 10 μm appears to be the desirable criterion for microsurgery as cells are approximately 10–50 μm in size.

There is an intrinsic trade-off between range of motion (ROM) or work envelope and positioning performance in TMR system design. Large systems simply cannot be made to move precisely because of thermal coefficients, friction, inertia, and momentum. For this reason, it was decided that the surgeon would change the tools rather than investing the robot with sufficient ROM to pick up the tools from a tool carrier. The goal is to limit the work envelope of the robot to the dimensions required for a typical microsurgical space. The surgeon then would manually position the robot to begin the TMR portion of the procedure.

Velocity is the first derivative of position, and acceleration is the second. Performance envelopes among microsurgeons vary. Some surgeons err in the velocity domain, whereas others have deficits primarily in the position domain. Restated, some surgeons' movements are too fast, whereas others overshoot their mark or have a tremor despite appropriate velocities. Tremors can occur at rest, during motion, or intermittently. Tremors typically are in the 8- to 11-Hz region, slightly higher than the 5-Hz volitional positioning output bandwidth that allows low-pass filter paradigms.

Some surgeons have problems primarily in the force domain rather than the velocity domain. In the vernacular, they are heavy-handed but steady. Negative force scaling is an obvious advantage for soft tissue but a disadvantage for bone and cartilage. The surgeon's performance could be enhanced by providing enough force to remove bone or cartilage, if force gain is utilized, while at the same time providing a positioning boundary to avoid going beyond a thin bony layer and damaging soft tissue. The system must allow the surgeon to preset force, position, and velocity limits before initiating surgery. The robot teach pendant can be used to outline those areas that can be approached and those that must be avoided to set the position boundaries.

A survey of microsurgical tools reveals that there are a very limited number of discrete tasks performed by the microsurgeon. Tissue can be cut (pierced), gripped (lifted), aspirated, irrigated, coagulated, or vaporized. Shaft lengths vary depending on the task and specialty. In general, a 10- to 25-mm shaft length is needed for ocular surgery, 50- to 100-mm for ear surgery, and 100- to 160-mm for neurosurgery. The wide variety of tools currently available reflect surgeons' preference, commercial issues, and the absence of articulated instruments. Articulated instruments require new micromanufacturing and material science technologies. The current tools are made by crafts people, usually do not have interchangeable parts, and are constructed of 304 stainless steel. Ceramics, composites, and harder coatings are required to improve performance.

The feel of the master must be similar to that of the high-performance instruments used by surgeons currently. Hand-held tools are not gravity-compensated. A master could have limited or complete gravity compensation. In other words, it could be weightless or fall if left unsupported by the surgeon, as with manual instruments.

Masters for other teleoperation systems utilize position, rate, or force controllers. It is the author's belief that position controllers and position-driven slaves offer the best opportunity for microsurgery and most other telemicrooperated systems: This is called a *position-position loop*. Springlike behavior is not an attribute of hand-held tools but is an attribute of many controllers. The author believes that spring action of the master should be minimal for microsurgery. Dampening is velocity-dependent and can be demonstrated manually by the feel of stirring molasses. Slow movement is met with low resistance, but high-speed movement incurs great resistance. Although this approach could be employed as negative reinforcement for the surgeon who uses excessive velocities, it probably will result in an unnatural feel of the master and should be avoided.

The master could incorporate a gripper controller. Alternatively, gripping could be controlled by a proportional foot-pedal control, as patented by the author. The author believes that proportional foot-pedal control of actuation offers the greatest performance increase.

Manipulator architecture

Robots (slaves, manipulators) can have serial, parallel, or hybrid geometry. The full-functioned hand is hybrid in that there are serial joints and parallel function of the five digits. Fingers can oppose the action of one another (antagonists) or act in parallel as agonists. Surgery and other microtasks frequently rely on the stabilization of one hand by the other, demonstrating the human's intuitive use of parallel geometry. Serial manipulators have cumulative instability and error at the end-effector resulting from the summation of the individual joint instability. If the end-effector has sufficient ROM to overcome error for large joints, a feature known as *coarse-fine strategy*, it is analogous to the combined dynamics of the human arm and hand. Serial manipulators typically have increasingly smaller elements closer to the end-effector. For example, the shoulder must support the upper arm, forearm, and hand.

Manipulators can have gears, pulleys, tendons, hydraulics, and pneumatic or direct drive. As the goal is to minimize friction, inertia, momentum, and backlash, direct-drive manipulators offer the best performance for cellular-level surgery. Pneumatic systems are typically inaccurate for fine position control, although they are useful for certain force control applications. Hydraulic manipulators have friction, relatively high-moving mass, and the potential for leakage. Electromagnetic drives offer the best performance for telemicrorobots. Electrodynamic microrobots can have rotary or linear actuators. Choice of drivers depends on overall robot geometry, force, and bandwidth requirements.

Electric actuators include brush direct-current (DC) motors, brushless DC motors (BLDC), stepper motors, microsteppers, voice coils, galvanometers, and piezoelectric actuators. The author believes that voice coils, BLDC motors, and piezoelectric actuators offer the best performance for microsurgery.

Vision systems

The human visual system does not have diffraction-limited performance but has a maximum resolution of approximately 8 μm. This corresponds to 2000–4000 lines with typical displays. The human eye has a dynamic range of approximately 10^8, in contrast to 10^2 for CRTs, 10^3 for charge-coupled device (CCD) cameras, and even less for LCDs. Hence, because of limited resolution and dynamic range, an electronic imaging system should be used only if direct optical imaging is not possible. Stereo imaging is crucial for all forms of microsurgery, including endosurgery. Stereo not only provides depth perception but also improves the ability of the viewer to filter out near-field objects in the image system while concentrating on the far field. In addition, the brain provides considerable image enhancement when a stereo pair of low-contrast or noisy images are viewed.

Summary

Dexterity enhancement has a place in microsurgery. The challange is to better understand the surgeon manipulator-tool-tissue dynamics in order to improve performance. These systems must be developed by leveraging technologies developed for other industries to reduce costs and improve deliverability.

BIBLIOGRAPHY

BHATTI, P., P. H. MARBOT, and B. HANNAFORD, 1992. Pick and place operations with the mini-direct drive robot. The *IEEE Robotics and Automation Proceedings*, Nice, France.

BRENAN, C. J. H., P. G. CHARETTE, and I. W. HUNTER, 1992. Environmental isolation platform for microrobot system development. *Rev. Sci. Instrum.* 63(6).

BROOKS, T., 1990. Telerobotic response requirements. In *Proceedings of the 1990 IEEE Conference on Systems, Man and Cybernetics*, Los Angeles.

BROOKS, T., et al., 1987. Performance evaluation of a generalized six degree of freedom teleoperator (J.P.L. rep. no. 89-18). Pasadena, Calif.: Jet Propulsion Laboratory.

CHARETTE, P. G., I. W. HUNTER, and C. J. H. BRENAN, 1992. A complete high performance heterodyne interferometer displacement transducer for microactuator control. *Rev. Sci. Instrum.* 63(1).

HUNTER, I. W., et al., 1990. Manipulation and dynamic mechanical testing of microscopic objects using a tele-micro-robot system. *IEEE Control Systems Magazine* 10(2):3–9.

MARBOT, P. H., 1991. Mini direct drive robot for biomedical applications. Master's thesis, University of Washington, Seattle.

POURNARAS, C. J., R. D. SHERAT, J. L. MUNOZ, and B. L. PEFIG, 1991. New ocular micromanipulation for measurements of retinal and vitreous physiologic parameters in the mammalian eye. *Exp. Eye Res.* 53:723–727.

35 Computer-Assisted Eye Surgery

RICHARD J. MAMMONE, STEPHEN D. KLYCE,
MARTIN GERSTEN, AND XIAOYU ZHANG

THE INTRODUCTION of refractive corneal surgical procedures has spawned an interest in obtaining quantitative information about corneal topography. In radial keratotomy, for example, a number of radially placed incisions are made on the cornea, which causes the peripheral cornea to bow outward. The result is a flattening of the curvature of the central cornea, leading to a reduction in the refractive power of the surface. Myopia (near-sightedness) is corrected by the radial keratotomy procedure, offering an alternative to eyeglasses or contact lenses. Unfortunately, there is substantial variation in the amount of correction incurred by such procedures. Therefore, the need arose for a device that could assist the surgeon in evaluating preoperative and postoperative corneal topography.

Color plate 29 illustrates the Topographic Modeling System (TMS-1) manufactured by Computed Anatomy, Inc., New York. The TMS-1 provides the clinician with a detailed surface map of an individual's cornea. The device is currently being used in a number of institutions for postoperative and preoperative studies in corneal surgery. The instrument reflects a patterned light source off the cornea. The reflected image is digitized and processed for display. Color plate 30 shows the reflected image of the target from a normal and an astigmatic cornea, respectively. The instantaneous radii of curvature of the cornea are color-coded for display purposes. A more easily understood version of the color-coded dioptric map of an astigmatic cornea is shown in plate 31.

An appreciation of the advances occasioned by this new instrument can be obtained by reviewing the instruments that were available previously for measuring corneal topography. The two types of conventional clinical instruments are keratometers and photokeratoscopes. The underlying principles of these instruments will be discussed.

Principle of keratometry

The first attempt at measuring the radius of curvature appears to have been carried out by Scheiner in 1619 (Levene, 1963). In 1840, Kohlrausch placed a telescope at a known distance from the eye in order to measure the magnification of a reflected object (Stone, 1962). The magnification (actually a minification) is an approximate measure of the radius of curvature of the cornea. The cornea generally is modeled as a spherical convex mirror. The spherical approximation is very good for the central region of the cornea. However, as early as 1846, Senff (Stone, 1962) recognized the peripheral flattening of the cornea. His measurements showed that the cornea deviated from a sphere and was better approximated by an ellipsoid. The elliptic topographic model differs from the spherical corneal model primarily in the peripheral area. The periphery was considered optically unimportant because the iris obstructs most of the rays incident on this area. Therefore, modern keratometers measure the radius of curvature of only the central 3–4 mm of the cornea, which is nearly spherical. This limitation to the central 3–4 mm has allowed researchers to use the principle of keratometry.

As noted previously, the principle of keratometry approximates the cornea by a spherical mirror, as shown in figure 35.1. A target of height h is reflected at the mirror's surface. Typical targets (mires) consist of a small number of circles and crosshair patterns that reflect from the central area of the cornea. The reflection forms a virtual image of height y. The virtual image appears to lie in a plane, which is a distance $d + s$ from the target. The distance d between the target and the corneal apex usually is large relative to the focal length of the cornea. The distance to the focal plane of a sphere from its center is one half the radius R of the

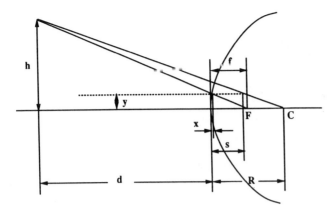

FIGURE 35.1   Principle of keratometry (Reprinted with permission from Mammone et al., 1990.)

sphere for rays making a small angle with the optical axis. A spherical surface will not focus parallel rays to a point. Instead, rays in the periphery will have shorter focal length than rays in the center. This generally undesired property is called *spherical aberration*. In the following discussion, we assume that the "focal plane" is located at different positions for each ring to correct for spherical aberration. The similar triangles in figure 35.1 yield the following equation:

$$\frac{y}{h} = \frac{R - s}{R + d} \simeq \frac{R - s}{d} \quad \text{for} \quad d \gg R \quad (1)$$

Also, for objects far away we have $s \simeq \frac{R}{2}$. Thus, solving for the spherical radius leads to the following:

$$R = \frac{2d}{h}y \quad (2)$$

The distances given by d and h are fixed for a particular instrument. Thus, there is a linear relationship between the measured height of the virtual image y and the radius of curvature R given by equation 2. Conventional keratometers measure the image height y with an optical doubler. The doubler forms two identical images that, when put in registration with each other, give a measure of the value for y. The doubler mechanism provides a measurement that is insensitive to the inevitable motion of the patient. The radius of curvature can then be obtained by using the principle of keratometry (see equation 2). The reading generally is expressed in units of optical power. The optical power F, measured in diopters, is expressed thus:

$$F = \frac{(n_c - 1)}{R} \quad (3)$$

where n_c is the keratometric index. The value of n_c generally is considered to be 1.3375 and takes into account the effect of the curvature of the back surface of the cornea. The value of F in diopters indicates the optical power of the corneal lens. This measurement method is used also in fitting contact lenses, whereby the curvature of the back surface of the contact lens is selected to fit the central curvature of the cornea. Because the cornea is not spherical, using the keratometer to fit contact lenses that ride on the peripheral corneal curvature does not always produce a good fit.

A keratometric measurement, or *K reading*, provides numbers in diopters that characterize the curvature of the central cornea alone. The keratoscope, on the other hand, is used to gain qualitative information about a much larger region of the cornea than that obtained with a keratometer. The keratoscope employs a target with a small number (10) of concentric rings. Because the reflected image must be viewed on axis, a cutout must be provided in the center of the target through which the cornea then is viewed. The camera view of the central area of the cornea is obstructed by the camera optics, and the diameter of this region will be determined by the required numeric aperture. Thus, no information is provided from the most central region of the cornea. By observing deviations in the ring patterns, one can be taught to recognize corneal surface shape anomalies such as abnormal flatness, steepness, or irregularity. However, interpretation of keratoscopic photographs has been difficult to teach and, importantly, it is not possible to perceive all topographic distortions that affect vision by visual inspection alone.

Owing to this limitation, there have been several attempts at transforming the photographic data obtained by a keratoscope into a numeric description (Ludlam and Wittenberg, 1966; Mandell and St. Helen, 1971). These attempts have had limited success. The major drawbacks include the lack of data from the central region of the cornea, the nonuniqueness of the corneal surface for a given image, curvature of the object field, calibration assumptions, and sampling errors. Several of these deficiencies have been overcome with the TMS-1, which is a combination and refinement of both the keratoscope and the keratometer, using a novel target and camera design. The hardware is closer to a keratoscope, whereas the software calculations for curvature more closely resemble a keratometer.

In 1882, Placido (Levene, 1963; Mandell, 1965) used a photographic camera to record the virtual

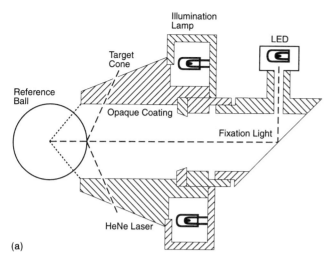

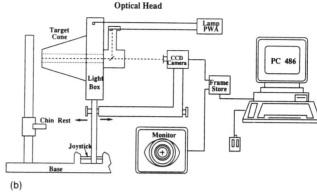

(a)

(b)

FIGURE 35.2 (a) Close-up of the unique TMS-1 cone-shaped target. (b) The keratoscope is focused with a joystick and video frames are captured by pressing a button on the joystick. (Reprinted with permission from Gersten, Mammone, and Zelvin, 1988.)

image of the keratoscope target. The target he used, which carries his name and is still in use today, consisted of concentric alternating black and white rings. The distorted image of the symmetric target gives the user a qualitative indication of the gross irregularities of the corneal surface. An improved target was suggested by Dekking (Knoll, 1961; Mandell and St. Helen, 1971) and further refined by Knoll (Knoll, 1961) and Mandell (Mandell and St. Helen, 1971). Knoll introduced a target that overcame some of the limitations of the Placido disk by allowing the rings to lie in different planes. Then more central rings are placed further away from the eye with the distances selected so as to provide a common image plane. This image plane formed the object plane of the camera. An aberration of reflective optics, called *curvature of field*, occurred because each object point was at a different distance from the reflective surface. The camera used was a telecentric optical system with a small optical aperture provided at the focal plane. The pinhole filters out all but the parallel rays from the camera's image.

Knoll's target still has some drawbacks. It is able to correct for field curvature but must be very large to cover the periphery of the cornea. Such a substantial distance requires the ring reflectors to be fairly large, which severely limits the number of usable rings. Also, the angle between the corneal apex and visual axis must be known a priori in order to reconstruct the corneal surface accurately. Furthermore, this measure-

ment is difficult to realize in practice, thus introducing additional uncertainties into the surface estimate. Finally, the photokeratoscope replaces the central region of the target with the camera lens, which eliminates the target in the area of most interest.

The target of the TMS-1 (see figure 35.2, plate 29) is much different from those used previously. A small cylinder with an internal opaque coating fits inside the orbital rim. The opaque coating is removed at predetermined spaced intervals so that the light from an internal source causes a series of 25–30 evenly spaced-illuminated rings to appear on the corneal surface. In the current model, the rings are spaced so as to form a noninverted virtual image of 25–30 rings. The target subtends an angle of more than 90° of the cornea by allowing the rings to be placed behind the apex.

Design of the Topographic Modeling System

The TMS-1, shown in figure 35.2, consists of an optical head for acquiring the 2D image of the illuminated rings, a 486-PC-style computer for storing and processing the image to obtain the curvature of the object cornea, and a video monitor for displaying the camera image in either the form initially acquired by the camera or as enhanced by computer processing. The keratoscope is mounted on a three-axis manual positioning platform, and its optical head contains the video camera, illumination lamp, dual-focusing gallium-arsenide lasers, and the target. The keratoscope generally is placed on a motorized table that can be raised or lowered to accommodate different patients by foot control.

The joystick and associated elevation ring are manipulated to adjust the location of the housing in three dimensions so as to position the video image of the corneal surface at a predetermined point on the optic axis of measurement. A pair of apertures are bored through the target cone at an angle to its central axis, and a pair of low-power helium-neon lasers are optically aligned with the aperture bores to provide beams whose intersection defines the predetermined point of focus on the cornea. When the cornea is near focus, the laser beams produce two visible light spots on the cornea. As the cone is brought closer to focus, the spots merge.

The video camera used is a charge-coupled device (CCD) camera. The CCD array guarantees a fixed, uniform sampling matrix of the image. The TMS-1 uses a telephoto lens with a small curvature of field to mitigate the effects caused by curvature of the object field. The field of view of the camera is selected to fit the average cornea's perimeter. This provides the maximum lateral resolution for the camera's CCD array. The rings are etched in the target so as to provide a uniform spacing for a 7.85-mm steel ball. The image from the camera is digitized and corrected for relative geometric and optical distortion.

The procedure for image acquisition appears to be easily assimilated into the clinic environment. The patient rests his or her chin on the chin rest and is asked to gaze at a reflected fixation spot of a centered LED light source. Adjusting the joystick forward and backward until the two laser beams form a single spot on the cornea places the corneal apex at a fixed distance from the cone. This method of fixating the cornea and aligning the instrument has been found to give measurements that are sufficiently reproducible for clinical use. There have been virtually no reports of the instrument causing patient discomfort in as much as the measurement is noninvasive and generally no contact is made with the patient's skin.

The new target has overcome many of the limitations of previously used targets. A wide field of view of the cornea is provided with high resolution. The system has a good alignment mechanism, incorporating the fixation point and two laser beams. These advantages come at the expense of a short working distance. To accommodate the short working distance used in the TMS-1, the principles of keratometry are revised by approximating the curvature of the human cornea with two models, spherical and elliptic

The spherical model

The TMS-1 acquires a digitized image that consists of a series of concentric rings. The inter-ring spacing of the corneal image is compared to the spacing of a reference image in order to obtain the surface topography. The first step in the computer processing of the image is to extract the ring positions along a semimeridian. The average width of a ring is approximately five samples in pixels. Each group of five pixels is fitted with a second-order polynomial. The positions of the peak of the quadratic polynomial is used as the center position of the ring. This process provides subpixel accuracy for the measurement of the ring positions (the y values).

The 2D array of data points extracted from the digital image are highly accurate estimates of the radial positions of the rings in a polar sampling grid. The array stores the sample from the center of the image first, then moves out to the peripheral ring. Data are obtained for 256 intervals in a counterclockwise direction. The resulting array consists of 256 entries in each row, one for every 1° increment around the digitized image. There are 25 or 30 columns in each matrix, representing the number of rings in the TMS-1 target cone. The 2D matrix is processed to provide the instantaneous radius of curvature at each point on the corneal surface given by one entry in the matrix. The processing is a point-to-point operation. Every point in the matrix will yield an estimate of the radius of curvature at that point. The ability to estimate the curvature from one measured point is based on the assumption that the surface is a sphere. The estimation procedure simply involves the similarity property of spheres. Thus, each coordinate on the surface of one sphere is proportional to that coordinate for a reference sphere. This point-to-point mapping will be similar to that given in equation 1, but correct point-to-point mapping can be obtained by the conventional principle of keratometry (see equation 2).

The exact expression corresponding to the principle of keratometry can be obtained by returning to figure 35.1. Consider the ray that is drawn to the focal point of the surface. We again allow the focal point to be at different locations for each ring to correct for spherical aberration. From the similar triangles, we have the following equation:

$$\frac{y}{h} = \frac{f - x}{f + d} \qquad (4)$$

where x is the sagittal depth of the incident point on the surface. The so-called principle of keratometry is obtained from equation 4 by assuming that $d \gg R - x$ for a sphere. However, the new cylindric target has dimensions that are small relative to those of the cornea. Thus, these terms cannot be neglected. Note that the exact solution for the focal length from equation 4 is as follows:

$$f = \left(\frac{d}{h}y + x\right) \Big/ \left(1 - \frac{y}{h}\right) \qquad (5)$$

Equation 5 requires both x and y coordinates for each point. In general, the sagittal depth x is not known but can be estimated. For a sphere of known radius R_{ref}, the values of the axial height y_{ref} and the sagittal depth x_{ref} are measured for each ring. Spheres of any radius will be similar:

$$\frac{R}{R_{\text{ref}}} = \frac{x}{x_{\text{ref}}} = \frac{y}{y_{\text{ref}}} = \text{constant} \qquad (6)$$

Thus, the sagittal depth is determined:

$$x = \frac{x_{\text{ref}}}{y_{\text{ref}}}y \qquad (7)$$

Substituting equation 7 into equation 5 and using the spherical approximation $f = \frac{R}{2}$ yields the estimate of the radius of curvature:

$$R = \frac{2(d/h + x_{\text{ref}}/y_{\text{ref}})y}{1 - y/h} \qquad (8)$$

Equation 8 is used to determine the initial estimate of the instantaneous radius for every point on the surface of the cornea, and it assumes that the cornea is spherical. The estimates are made relative to a reference sphere. In practice, the reference sphere is taken to be a 7.85-mm ball bearing. This estimation procedure performs very well with ball bearings or any other spherical surfaces. In contrast, a nonspherical surface target constructed according to the model given by Mandell and St. Helen (1971) is not estimated well by using equation 8. The resulting estimate fails to follow the change of the instantaneous radius away from the apex. Thus, the estimate given by equation 8 will be overly spherical. In the next section, we shall correct for the error introduced by the spherical assumption. A more general elliptic model will be used.

The estimate given by equation 8 provides a heuristic approach to studying asymmetries of the corneal surface. The error in the instantaneous radius of curvature as compared to the more exact elliptic method is generally within 0.3 D in the central region but 3–4 D in the periphery for normal corneas. The advantage of using equation 8 is that the spherical model can be computed very quickly.

Color plate 32 shows the dioptric map obtained from the spherical modeling system for an ellipse. This simple model has proved useful for initial diagnostic purposes. The dioptric powers are color-coded as indicated in the sidebar on the display screen. We have found that this form of color-coded display, which was originally suggested by Klyce (1984), is the most acceptable to clinicians.

Clinical studies

QUANTITATIVE DESCRIPTORS

The TMS-1 is widely used for clinical diagnosis with corneal topographic maps (Gersten, Mammone, and Zelvin, 1988, 1989; Mammone et al., 1990). As previously described, this device uses a 25- or 30-ring collimated videokeratoscope that provides a central fixation point as a reference for the computerized analysis of the instantaneous optical power. On each videokeratoscopic ring, 256 points are evaluated; therefore, the analysis includes thousands of individual locations and covers nearly the entire corneal surface from the visual axis to the far periphery. Color-coded contour maps, introduced by Klyce (1984) at the Lousiana State University Eye Center, and extended by Gersten (1989), provides both qualitative and detailed quantitative analysis of corneal topography. Warmer colors represent steeper curvatures, and cooler colors represent flatter curvatures. The instrument features operator-monitored automated digitization with resolution of approximately 500 lines per frame. Statistical procedures are utilized by the computerized algorithms to provide resolution on the corneal surface of less than 0.25 D. There are several color map displays. The absolute color scale, with dioptric power intervals of 1.5 D in the midrange (from 35.5 to 50.5 D) and 5.0 D beyond this range, is the most commonly used. In some instances, however, normalized color scales with dioptric intervals as small as 0.2 D can be used to demonstrate subtle variations in corneal topography. To augment the clinical utility and the applications of computer-assisted topographic analysis for research, the simulated keratometry value (Sim K), the surface asymmetry index (SAI), and the surface regularity index (SRI) developed by Klyce at LSU Eye Center also are provided during topographic analysis with the TMS-1 instrument.

The Sim K value (Wilson and Klyce, 1991a; Wilson et al., 1991b) provides the power and location of the steepest and flattest meridian from a reconstructed corneal surface analogous to values provided by the keratometer. This descriptor allows the clinician to correlate the topography seen on the color-coded map with another common parameter and obviates the need to obtain separate keratometric measurements. The spherocylindric Sim K value provides the power and location of the steepest meridian and the meridian 90° away. The nonspherocylindric Sim K value also provides the power and location of the actual flattest meridian, regardless of the angle between the steepest and flattest meridian. Prospective studies have demonstrated a high correlation between keratometry and spherocylindric Sim K values (Koch et al., 1989; Wilson et al., 1991b).

The SAI is a centrally weighted summation of differences in corneal power between corresponding points 180° apart on 128 equally spaced meridians that cross the 10 central photokeratoscopic mires (Klyce and Wilson, 1989; Wilson and Klyce, 1991a). For example, if the power on ring 4 at 5° is 44.0 and the power on ring 4 at 185° is 46.0, the difference, 2.0, is entered into the centrally weighted summation. Similar differences are entered for all corresponding pairs of points on the 10 central mires. SAI approaches zero for a perfectly radially symmetric surface and increases as the contour becomes more asymmetric. Because the normal cornea usually has a high degree of central radial symmetry, the SAI is a useful quantitative parameter for monitoring changes that occur in patients with contact lens–induced corneal warpage (Wilson et al., 1990b, 1991b) following penetrating keratoplasty, and in other corneal disorders that cause an alteration of corneal symmetry such as off-center keratoconus apices.

The SRI is determined from a summation of local fluctuations in power along 256 equally spaced hemimeridians on the 10 central mires (Wilson and Klyce, 1991b). This index approaches zero for a normally smooth corneal surface and increases directly with increasing irregular astigmatism. In a prospective clinical study (Wilson and Klyce, 1991b), there was a high correlation between the SRI and best spectacle-corrected visual acuity. The SRI value can be used to predict the optical performance that might be expected in a particular patient based on the corneal topography if other components of the visual system, such as the lens and the fovea, are functioning normally. This index would also be of value for predicting visual acuity after experimental refractive surgical procedures in animals.

CLINICAL EXAMPLES

Color-coded topographic maps and the quantitative descriptors provided by the TMS-1 instrument have made it possible to describe better the topography of normal corneas as well as to document corneal topographic changes that are caused by diseases and contact lens warpage or occur during surgical procedures or after surgical manipulations.

For patients with normal corneas, Dingeldein and Klyce (1989) reported considerable variations in corneal shape. Much like fingerprints, corneal shapes varied widely among individuals, but in each individual they were found to approximate mirror-image symmetry between the right and left corneas. In all eyes examined, the corneal surface was found to be aspheric, with the surface becoming progressively flatter from the center to the periphery (see color plate 33).

Corneal topographic assessment of large series of keratoconus patients has been performed using the TMS-1 instrument (Uusitalo, Lehtosalo, Klyce, 1989; Wilson, Lin and Klyce, 1991). Keratoconus is the most common ectatic dystrophy of the cornea. It is characterized by localized stromal thinning and a progressive alteration of corneal topography (see plate 34). In symptomatic patients, visual acuity is reduced by irregular astigmatism and stromal scarring. In this study, a detailed evaluation of corneal anterior surface shape was provided by the TMS-1 instrument (Wilson, Lin, and Klyce, 1991). The highest-quality image was selected for automated digitization and reconstruction to form a color-coded topographic map that allows inspection of the contour from the central to the peripheral cornea. Each color-coded topographic map was evaluated by using the TMS-1 movable cursor (see plate 35). The power, meridian, and distance in millimeters from the visual axis of the point on the cornea with the highest power was determined. This point was defined as the apex of the cone. The Sim K value for each cornea was determined, and a high correlation between the Sim K value and traditional keratometric measurements for either the total cylinder or the major cylinder axis was demonstrated.

In Terrien's marginal degeneration, progression of the corneal morphologic changes frequently is accompanied by the development of high astigmatism, usually against-the-rule. However, characterization of the corneal topography in these cases used to be limited to measurements using the keratometer or keratoscope; therefore, very little information regarding the overall topographic changes produced by the disorder was provided. To characterize the topographic changes, Wilson et al. (1991a) used the TMS-1 to construct a color-coded topographic map of the cornea (see plate 36).

A computerized algorithm also was developed to determine the power and location of the meridians of highest and lowest centrally weighted average power. The corneal topographic changes in the patients with Terrien's marginal degeneration were characterized by flattening over the areas of peripheral thinning produced by the disorder (Wilson et al., 1990a). The TMS-1 indicates that when thinning was restricted to the superior or inferior areas of the peripheral cornea, there was a relative steepening of the corneal surface approximately 90° away from the midpoint of the thinned area, which resulted in high against-the-rule or oblique astigmatism characteristic of the disorder.

In investigating the changes in corneal topography after excimer laser photorefractive keratectomy for myopia (Wilson et al., 1991a), the TMS-1 can be used to locate the center of the ablation with respect to the vertex normal and to provide the power at the center of the ablation. The central ablation power was determined, and distance from the vertex normal was measured on the preoperative and postoperative topographic maps. Inspection of plate 37 confirms the ability of the TMS-1 to locate the vertex normal reproducibly in an individual eye over an extended period of time. The location of the center of the ablation in relation to the center of the entrance pupil was also determined by TMS-1. The following information was provided: preoperative and postoperative uncorrected and best spectacle-corrected visual acuities for the eyes, the central ablation power for each eye over time, the correlation between the initial correction (change in central abla-

tion power from the preoperative value to the first postoperative measurement) and postoperative loss of effect (change in central ablation power from the first to the last postoperative measurement), and the net change in the central ablation power (change in mean central ablation power in diopters from preoperative to last follow-up measurement). This keratorefractive surgical procedure has been improved because of the diagnostic feedback provided by TMS-1 analysis in terms of centration of the corneal ablation over the pupil.

Postkeratoplasty astigmatism is a major problem following uncomplicated penetrating keratoplasty. In the past, only qualitative data were available from the keratoscope. Recently, Lin et al. (1990a,b) have used the TMS to quantify the amount of corneal surface irregularity after removal of a single running 10-0 nylon suture following penetrating keratoplasty (see plate 38). The SAI was estimated to assess irregular astigmatism. The lower the SAI, the more symmetric was the cornea and the lower was the level of irregular astigmatism. The study shows that following the removal of a single running 10-0 nylon suture, the change in corneal astigmatism is unpredictable. It also demonstrates that one cannot predict the changes in the mean corneal power.

Computer-assisted topographic analysis has provided new insights into the changes in corneal topography induced by contact lenses (Wilson et al., 1990b, 1991b). With the aid of the TMS-1, Wilson's group studied the corneal warpage shown in plate 39 and demonstrated that there frequently was a correlation between the position of the contact lens on the cornea and the altered topographic pattern.

Surgical planning and simulation

Recently, both Casebeer and Lindstrom independently evolved methods of obtaining an optimal refractive surgical result in the surgical treatment of myopia protocols based on patient-specific corneal topography, age, optical zone diameter, and the required refractive correction. Their methods involve the use of nomograms and formulas that allow the surgeon to select the optimal number, position, orientation, and length of the required corneal incisions.

The Casebeer and Lindstrom refractive surgical design methodologies have been implemented in software on the TMS-1. A computer program is used first to verify the patient's data and history. Updating and editing the patient's data may be performed at this time. Then a program defines and displays the refractive surgical plan in a numeric format based on these validated data. The surgeon may, at this point, wish to proceed to simulate and interactively edit the recommended design using the *Surgical Planning Screen* program, in which a surgical planning diagram is computed and overlaid on the patient's color-coded corneal topographic map (or videokeratograph). The surgical planning diagram shows the exact orientation and length of each incision in the visual context of the corneal topography and video image of the eye. Additionally, the surgeon may enter the corneal thickness measurements at selected points on the planning diagram. The surgical planning diagram may be edited, if necessary, using a mouse to adjust the position or length of incisions.

The *Surgical Planning Screen* program makes it possible for the surgeon preoperatively to visualize and validate better a proposed corneal refractive surgical procedure. The *Surgical Planning Screen* also provides the surgeon with important visual cues about the location of the proposed surgical incisions relative to observable landmarks on the limbus, sclera, and iris. Geometric surgical problems such as the unforeseen intersection of a radial (myopia) and transverse (astigmatic) corrective incision or the need to compute radial incisions symmetrically disposed about the major astigmatic axis are identified and solved automatically by the computer program.

Summary and conclusion

A new instrument has been introduced to provide a detailed map of the cornea. A number of clinical applications have been identified that illustrate the use of the instrument. The TMS-1 is rapidly becoming a necessary tool for corneal surgical procedures and as a diagnostic aid.

ACKNOWLEDGMENTS This work has been supported by the Center for Computer Aids for Industrial Productivity (CAIP) at Rutgers University with funds provided by the New Jersey Commission on Science and Technology and CAIP's industrial members, by National Eye Institute research grant EY03311, and by Computed Anatomy, Inc., New York, N.Y.

REFERENCES

DINGELDEIN, S. A., and S. D. KLYCE, 1989. The topography of normal corneas. *Arch. Ophthalmol.* 107:512–518.

GERSTEN, M., R. J. MAMMONE, and J. ZELVIN, 1988. Illuminated ring projection device. Patent no. 4,772,115, Sept. 20.

GERSTEN, M., R. J. MAMMONE, and J. ZELVIN, 1989. System for topographical modeling of anatomical surfaces. Patent no. 4,863,260, Sept. 5.

KLYCE, S. D., and S. E. WILSON, 1989. Methods of analysis of corneal topography. *Refract. Corneal Surg.*, 5:368–371.

KLYCE, S. D., 1984. Computer-assisted corneal topography, high-resolution graphic presentation and analysis of keratoscopy. *Invest. Ophthalmol. Vis. Sci.* 25:426–435.

KNOLL, H., 1961. Corneal contours in the general population as revealed by the photokeratoscope. *Am. J. Optom.* 38:389–397.

KOCH, D. D., G. N. FOULKS, C. T. MORAN, and J. S. WAKIL, 1989. The corneal EyeSys system. *Refract. Corneal Surg.*, 5:424–429.

LEVENE, J. R., 1963. The true inventor of the keratoscope and photokeratoscope. *Br. J. Hist. Sci.* 2:324–342.

LIN, D. T. C., et al., 1990a. An adjustable single running suture technique to reduce postkeratoplasty astigmatism. *Ophthalmology* 97:934–938.

LIN, D. T. C., S. E. WILSON, J. J. REIDY, S. D. KLYCE, M. B. McDONALD, M. S. INSLER, and H. E. KAUFMAN, 1990b. Topographic changes that occur with 10-0 running suture removal following penetrating keratoplasty. *Refract. Corneal Surg.* 6:21–25.

LUDLAM, W. M., and S. WITTENBERG, 1966. Measurements of the ocular dioptric elements utilizing photographic methods. *Am. J. Optom. Arch. Am. Acad. Optom.*, 43:249–263.

MAMMONE, R. J., M. GERSTEN, D. J. GORMLEY, R. S. KOPLIN, and V. L. LUBKIN, 1990. 3-D corneal modeling system. *IEEE Trans. Biomed. Eng.* 37:66–72.

MANDELL, R. B., 1965. Corneal topography. In *Contact Lens Practice, Basic and Advanced.* Springfield, Ill.: Charles C Thomas, chapter 3.

MANDELL, R. B., and R. ST. HELEN, 1971. Mathematical model of the corneal contour. *Br. J. Physiol. Optom.* 26:183–197.

STONE, J., 1962. The validity of some existing methods of measuring corneal contour compared with suggested new methods. *Br. J. Physiol. Optom.* 19:205–230.

UUSITALO, R. J., J. LEHTOSALO, and S. D. KLYCE, 1989. One-year follow-up of epikeratophakia for keratoconus. *Graefes Arch. Clin. Exp. Ophthalmol.* 227:401–407.

WILSON, S. E., and S. D. KLYCE, 1991a. Quantitative descriptors of corneal topography. *Arch. Ophthalmol.* 109:349–353.

WILSON, S. E., and S. D. KLYCE, 1991b. Advances in the analysis of corneal topography. *Surv. Ophthalmol.* 35.

WILSON, S. E., S. D. KLYCE, M. B. McDONALD, J. C. LIU, and H. E. KAUFMAN, 1991a. Changes in corneal topography after excimer laser photorefractive keratectomy for myopia. *Ophthalmology* 98:1338–1347.

WILSON, S. E., D. T. C. LIN, and S. D. KLYCE, 1991. Corneal topography of keratoconus. *Cornea* 10:2–8.

WILSON, S. E., D. T. C. LIN, S. D. KLYCE, and M. S. INSLER, 1990a. Terrien's marginal degeneration: Corneal topography. *Refract. Corneal Surg.* 6:15–20.

WILSON, S. E., D. T. C. LIN, S. D. KLYCE, J. J. REIDY, and M. S. INSLER, 1990b. Rigid contact lens decentration: A risk factor for corneal warpage. *J. C.L.A.O.* 16:177–182.

WILSON, S. E., D. T. C. LIN, S. D. KLYCE, J. J. REIDY, and M. S. INSLER, 1991b. Topographic changes in contact lens-induced corneal warpage. *Ophthalmology* 97:734–744.

36 Visual Monitoring of Glaucoma

SIMON LEE AND MICHAEL BRADY

THIS CHAPTER reports progress on a system to aid physicians in monitoring the development of glaucoma, a complex of eye diseases that annually cause blindness in an estimated 50,000 people in the United States. It is the second most common cause of blindness after diabetes. Approximately 2% of the British population older than 40 years suffers from glaucoma; 12.5% of all new cases of registerable blindness in Britain are due to this disease complex. Because of the lack of observable clinical features, glaucoma usually is treated fairly late, when irreversible nerve damage already has occurred. The earlier the diagnosis, the better is the prognosis; in most cases, blindness could be prevented if patients were treated at an early stage. However, current diagnostic methods are either not reliable or not sensitive enough for early detection. The need for automation is brought into sharp relief by intraobserver and interobserver variations in estimating clinically significant parameters, which can be as high as 25% and 35%, respectively (Rosenthal, Falconer, and Barret, 1980).

The medical background of glaucoma is sketched in the next section. Deformation ("cupping") of the optic nerve head surface is a reliable early sign of glaucoma. Unfortunately, this valuable information is not available at the present time due to the limitations of optic nerve head analysis systems. In this chapter, we describe an ophthalmologic image-processing system that integrates information provided by stereo vision and shape from shading to reconstruct the surface of the optic nerve head so that various clinical measurements can be made. First, the optic disk boundary has to be estimated; this enables the binocular stereo images to be registered. We then argue for feature-based stereo and describe the application of the algorithm derived by Pollard, Mayhew, and Frisby (the PMF algorithm) to matching blood vessel boundaries. The depth measurements that result from binocular stereo are accurate but sparse. We show that they are too sparse to support a reliable surface interpolation algorithm. We demonstrate how shape from shading, particularly stereophotometry, can be adapted to give dense esti-

mates of one component z_x of the surface z of the optic nerve head. In so doing, we propose the design of a novel binocular camera that is currently under construction in the United Kingdom. The gradient measurements computed by stereophotometry are dense but noisy. To achieve the goals of accuracy and density of depth measurement, the two sets of data are combined. The various physical measurements of the optic nerve head can then be computed accurately from the reconstructed surface. Potentially, the software we describe, together with the novel camera that is under construction to exploit the methods described herein, could be produced cheaply.

Medical background

Diseases in the glaucoma complex have in common an increase in intraocular pressure (IOP). For healthy eyes, IOP is normally between 10 and 20 mm Hg, though this varies from time to time and person to person. Glaucoma usually develops first as ocular hypertension, typically corresponding to a pressure rise exceeding 21 mm Hg. Initially, the patient has no loss of visual field. If IOP elevation persists, it may cause excavation of the optic nerve head, leading to loss of visual field. Without prompt treatment, blindness may ensue.

Let us review some simple anatomic features of the internal structure of the eye. The optic nerve is found just nasal to the posterior pole of the eye. It contains millions of nerve fibers that send messages from the photoreceptors to the brain. The optic nerve pierces the layers of the posterior eye nearly 3 mm medial to and very slightly above the posterior pole of the eye. The nerve fibers are separated from the adjacent retinal tissue and the choroid by the glial tissue. The extremity of the optic nerve in the interior of the eye is the *optic nerve head*, commonly known as the *optic disk*.

The optic nerve head refers to the tissues comprising the anterior termination of the nerve extending from the nerve head surface back to the *lamina cribrosa*, a large meshwork of connective tissue containing many pores through which the nerve fibers pass. The optic nerve head edge is located an average of 3.4 ± 0.3 mm from the fovea; the nerve head itself has an average horizontal diameter of 1.8 ± 0.2 mm and an average vertical diameter of 1.9 ± 0.2 mm. (The average diameter of an eyeball is approximately 23–25 mm.)

The internal nerve head surface generally is not flat. Almost all eyes have some form of physiologic excavation or *cupping* of the nerve head. The cup is an anatomic feature that is determined by the course of the nerve fibers as they pass from the retina into the optic nerve. The axons derive from the ganglion cells and travel through the inner part of the retina, forming the nerve fiber layer. When they reach the optic nerve head, they turn to exit the eye through the optic nerve, leaving a small depression in the center of the nerve head. Obliquity of the disk, size, vessels, and amount of glial and connective tissue determine the shape and size of the physiologic excavation of the optic nerve head. There are large variations in the size and shape of optic nerve heads. Owing to the large concentration of nerve fibers in this region, the rim may appear as an elevation, known as *papilla*. Figure 36.1 shows a stereo pair of gray-level images of an optic nerve head. The absence of the pigmented epithelium renders the color of the optic nerve head paler than the surrounding fundus; the light region is called the *pallor*. Blood vessels can be seen radiating out from the optic nerve head. The cupping of the optic disk can be seen clearly if the images are viewed stereoscopically.

Observation of the optic nerve head generally is regarded as fundamental to the management of any patient suspected of glaucoma (Douglas, Drance, and Schulzer, 1975; Radius, Maumenee, and Green, 1978; Pederson and Anderson, 1980; Motolko and Drance, 1981; Fazio et al., 1990). Typically, ophthalmologists take stereoscopic photographs of the fundus and attempt estimates of various physical measurements, including the depth, area, and volume of the optic cup, the cup-disk radii and area ratio, and the neuroretinal rim area. Stereoscopic photographs also allow assessment and comparison of the depth of the cup as well as of the 3D shape of the optic nerve head. In current practice, the boundaries of the optic nerve head and cup usually are drawn by hand on a transparency overlaid on the fundus photographs (Simpson et al., 1989a). The various area measurements then are obtained by counting the number of squares using a calibrated grid. Because the size of the optic nerve head is

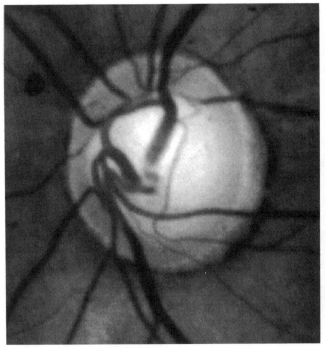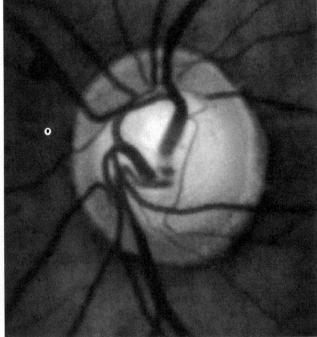

FIGURE 36.1   A stereo pair of fundus images.

governed by many physiologic factors, absolute measurements are not a completely reliable indicator of the disease. To differentiate pathologic from physiologic features, the patients' eyes are examined periodically, frequency varying from 3 months to 1 year. If, on successive examinations, there are changes in the shape of the optic nerve head, the disease is suspected.

Three-dimensional analysis of the optic nerve head has been hampered because it relies on subjective human interpretation of the fundus photographs and reproducibility is low even among expert observers. As noted earlier, clinical estimation of the parameters are inaccurate and highly variable (Lichter, 1976). This reduces the value of these measurements considerably, even though clinicians still use them to diagnose and follow up the disease (Sommer, Pollack, and Maumenee, 1979; Quigley et al., 1980; Simpson et al., 1989b). Consistency in the quantitative analysis of the optic nerve head is important. Eye patients are not necessarily examined by the same clinicians at each clinical visit, which usually take place at 6-month intervals. It is extremely difficult to follow up the disease and assess the progress with the tools currently available. Therefore, there is a need to analyze the fundus images objectively. Accuracy and reproducibility are the key attributes of any system for monitoring glaucoma.

The bottom line is that measuring and monitoring changes in the topography of the optic disk is key to assisting in the diagnosis and treatment of glaucoma. The challenges for computer vision are that the optic disk is small (1.8 mm in diameter) and lies at a distance of at least 25 mm from any imager, the albedo of the disk varies spatially, there is a sparse latticework of blood vessels, and there is considerable variation in healthy disks.

Previous work

Kottler, Rosenthal, and Falconer, (1974, 1976) took stereo fundus photographs using the Zeiss Fundus Camera with the Allen Stereo Separator.[1] An intensity-based stereo algorithm was used to compute the disparity between the stereo pair, and depth was calculated. Elliptic paraboloids then were fitted to the optic cup contours as computed. Their results were extremely prone to photographic conditions (Kottler, Rosenthal, and Falconer, 1974). Schwartz (1986) and Takamoto (Takamoto and Schwartz, 1985) also investigated stereo photography, either with the Zeiss Fundus Camera and the Allen Stereo Separator or with the Donaldson simultaneous stereo camera. The stereo correspondence problem was solved using manual photogrammetry, obtaining only approximately 300 measurements on each stereo pair. The main contribution of this semiautomatic method was to show that glaucomatous optic cups generally are deeper and wider than normal cups.

The Humphrey Retinal Analyzer simultaneously captures a stereo pair of images onto charge-coupled device (CCD) fundus cameras. Area-based stereo then is applied to the stereo pair, followed by surface interpolation. Dandona, Quigley, and Jampel (1989), concluded that the variability is large and speculated that the "... possible reason for this higher variability could be the relative lack of structural features available in the peripapillary retina for topographic mapping." Another commercial machine is the IMAGEnet system developed by Topcon. It acquires stereoscopic fundus images by digitizing slides and computes depth measurements by matching features on the optic nerve head. The surface reconstructed from the sparse data tends to be inaccurate as, inevitably, are all subsequent measurements.

The stereophotogrammetry technique of Algazi, Keltner, and Johnson (1985) combines area-based and edge-based stereo. The area-based stereo algorithm seeks the minimum average difference in image intensity as the best match for a 15 × 15 window. A "choice" algorithm was used to select depth measurements from either of the two stereo results on a pixel-by-pixel basis—if the two measurements were in reasonably good agreement, the depth measurement from area-based stereo is chosen because it was considered more accurate though prone to error; if the disagreement was large, the measurement from edge-based stereo was used. Two-dimensional polynomials then were used to fill in areas with missing data. The results obtained were noisy.

Because binocular stereo alone cannot provide dense and accurate depth measurements of the optic nerve head, structured light has been explored as an alternative. Structured light systems exploit triangulation between a light source radiating an appropriate pattern and a camera to provide range data of the object in the scene, the advantage being that depth measurements can be obtained from a featureless surface. In the simplest case, a single spot of light is projected onto the scene. The processing involved is simple but requires $O(n^2)$ operations to generate a depth map for an image of size $n \times n$ by scanning the spot across the whole scene.

Methods similar to this technique are employed in optical scanning microscopes and also in the Scanning Laser Ophthalmoscope, developed by Heidelberg Instrument, Inc. A laser beam is scanned across the fundus in two directions and focused onto a focal plane. By positioning a pinhole in the return light path (confocal detection), only light reflected from the section of the fundus lying at the focal plane of the scanning laser beam is detected by a camera. Currently, it takes approximately $\frac{1}{8}$ second to acquire a 256×256 image of a particular focal plane. To obtain depth measurements of the entire surface, successive measurements from multiple focal planes are needed. Dreher, Tso, and Weinreb (1991) and Weinreb, Dreher, and Bille (1989) reported the use of 32 equally spaced planes. A serious limitation of this method is that the eye has to remain still during the data acquisition interval, which is approximately 4 seconds in their case. Aligning the multiple planes can be a serious problem. To reduce the data acquisition time, the spatial resolution and the resolution of the depth measurements must be traded off.

If the single spot is extended to a slit of light, the data acquisition time is reduced to $O(n)$. Depth measurements along the stripe are computed, and the stripe can be swept across the scene to obtain denser depth measurements. To improve efficiency further, multiple stripes can be used. The data acquisition time is reduced to $O(\frac{n}{m})$ where m is the number of stripes projected. This method works well when there are no depth discontinuities and the object in the scene can be "seen" by both the light source and the camera. If these conditions are violated, some of the stripes seen by the camera will be broken and this will lead to ambiguous interpretation of the stripes. To overcome this problem, the Rodenstock Optic Nerve Head Analyzer, developed by G. Rodenstock Instrument, combined structured light and stereo. The Rodenstock analyzer consists of a stereoscopic video fundus camera, an illumination source that projects stripes onto the optic nerve head, a digital frame grabber, and a 16-bit microcomputer. The machine projects 14 stripes onto the fundus, approximately 10 of which fall onto the optic nerve head. The stripes then are matched in the stereoscopic images, from which approximately 1600 depth measurements can be computed. The method is promising, but severe practical problems must be resolved. Varma et al. (1988) pointed out that the surface reflectivity of the fundus is low and hence absorbs a large proportion of the incident light. The contrast of the stripes generally is poor, and they are totally invisible in some regions. Owing to the unavoidable movement of the eye, the stripes are not swept across the fundus to obtain additional depth measurements; therefore, the depth measurements are sparse and surface interpolation is required. Despite the initial success with this machine as reported by Capriolo et al. (1986; Capriolo, Millner, and Sears, 1987) and Mikelberg et al. (Mikelberg, Douglas, and Schulzer, 1984; Mikelberg et al., 1985; Mikelberg, Douglas, and Drance, 1988), Rodenstock terminated the project because of the technical problems.

Optic disk boundary detection

To measure parameters such as the cup-disk ratio and the neuroretinal rim area, it is necessary to delineate the optic disk boundary as accurately as possible. Repeatability is important as the measurements based on the disk usually are compared over time to detect structural changes of the optic nerve head. The optic disk boundary marks the position where the pigmented epithelial layer is absent, and so there is an intensity change at the disk boundary. Manual segmentation is time-consuming and impractical for mass image analysis. It is also subjective and depends on the skill and experience of the clinician. Intraobserver and interobserver variations can be large, especially when the contrast between the optic nerve head and the fundus is poor.

A number of practical considerations influence the design of an algorithm for determining the disk boundary. First, the physical size of the optic nerve head is 1.8 mm in diameter on average. It usually is magnified so that it occupies a significant area of the image. In the present work, the radius of the optic nerve head is 120 pixels on average. Second, fundus images usually are captured with the optic nerve head centered in the image. Third, the optic nerve head is lighter than the surrounding fundus owing to the lack of the pigmented epithelial layer. The intensity change is rapid over the disk boundary, but there are occasionally low-contrast regions that may cause ambiguity in defining the exact position of the boundary. Finally, a few blood vessels radiate out from the center of the optic nerve head to the fundus, crossing the optic disk boundary at right angles. This latter observation initially caused some difficulties with the active contour model that we use and necessitated a presmoothing process based on an application-specific morphologic structuring element (Lee and Brady, 1991b).

We used snakes (Kass, Witkin, and Terzopoulos, 1987) to determine the optic disk boundary. The behavior of the snake is controlled by internal and external energy functions (or forces). The internal energies serve as a smoothness constraint to resist deformation, whereas the external energies direct the snake toward the image features. To model a disk boundary snake, the appropriate energy functions have to be derived. For the internal energy, the disk boundary is modeled as a rubber band, and it interpolates across gaps in the boundary; more precisely:

$$E_{\text{smoothness}} = \int v_s^2(s)\, ds$$

where v_s is the first derivative of v with respect to arc length s.

If the location of the disk boundary is known, springs can be attached between points on the boundary and the corresponding points on the snake so that the snake can be pulled to the correct position. It is assumed that the disk boundary is the largest circular object in the image so that the outermost edge points of the Canny edge map correspond to the disk boundary. They can then be used to anchor the springs. In practice, the outermost edge points are not necessarily disk boundary points because there are gaps in the disk boundary, even in the morphologic closed image, mainly due to poor contrast. In addition, spurious edges may be present in the fundus background. To minimize the chance of anchoring springs to non–disk boundary edge points and thus pulling the snake to an incorrect position, the following constraints can be imposed:

1. The disk boundary is likely to be found within upper and lower limits from the center of the image. Edge points outside these limits are not accepted as potential boundary points and no springs should be anchored onto them.

2. Because the optic nerve head is lighter in color than the background, the image intensities on the inside of the edge (toward the center of the image) must be higher than outside the edge.

3. The edge orientation must be similar to that of a tangent to a circle centered at the image, at the corresponding position.

4. Edge segments with lengths shorter than a limit threshold are ignored. This prevents springs being anchored to spurious edges that satisfy constraints 1, 2, and 3.

The edge map is sampled at regular angle intervals and, if these constraints are satisfied, springs are attached to the edge points and the corresponding position of the snake. The image energy defines those features onto which the snake locks. The image features that correspond to the disk boundary are high-contrast edges. Because the disk boundary is known to be approximately circular, only edges with the appropriate sign should be allowed to contribute to the total energy function. The image energy is as follows:

$$E_{\text{image}} = \int T(I)\, ds$$

where

$$T(I) = \begin{cases} -D(G*I)^2 & \text{if } D(G*I) > 0 \\ 0 & \text{otherwise} \end{cases}$$

and where $D(G*I)$ is a directional second derivative of the image intensity function I in a direction perpendicular to the tangent of the snake.

The total energy to be minimized is

$$E_t = \int v_s^2\, ds + \varphi \sum_i (v_i - \bar{v}_i)^2 + \varsigma \int T(I)\, ds \quad (1)$$

Given an initial position for the snake, the disk boundary can be found by minimizing the total energy function of equation 1. A reasonable initial position for the snake is to place it anywhere between the upper and lower distance limits from the center of the image, as the disk boundary is most likely to be found in this region. Initially, the snake is set to be a circle. We follow Amini, Tehrani, and Weymouth, (1988) and minimize the snake energy function using dynamic programming. Two typical results are shown in figure 36.2.

Binocular stereo processing

Stereo matching commonly is classified as area-based or feature-based. Area-based stereo works by correlating small windows between the two images. Correlation usually is based on minimizing the difference

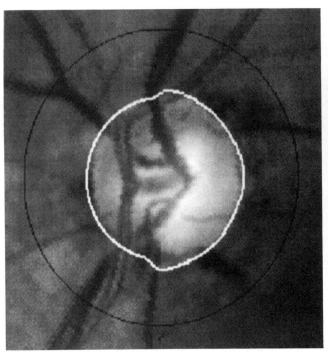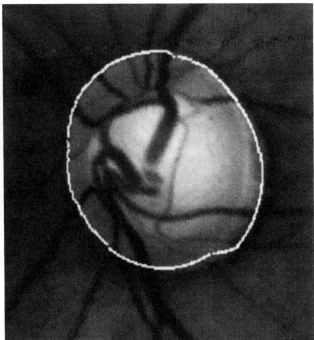

FIGURE 36.2   Two typical results using the disk boundary snake. The white curves are the identified disk boundaries. The initial position of the snake in (a) is the black circle.

between two putatively matching windows (Algazi, Keltner, and Johnson, 1985; Otto and Chau 1988). On the other hand, feature-based stereo first transforms the intensity images into feature descriptions, typically (though not always) using an edge detection process, and then computes disparity by matching them (Marr and Poggio 1979; Pollard, Mayhew, and Frisby, 1985).

Area-based stereo is particularly effective for densely textured surfaces (e.g., terrain images). Its main advantage is that, in principle, it produces dense depth measurements of the surface, as every window in the left image has a corresponding window in the right. However, area-based stereo is badly affected by noise when there are small image gradients, featureless surfaces, or low signal-to-noise ratio images. It implicitly assumes that the surface is smooth and continuous, and it is seriously affected by area foreshortening. Therefore, it also performs poorly when the surface gradient is large (e.g., discontinuities) and is best when the surface is flat and the two cameras are close together. The cost of computation is high, $O(MNmn)$ for $M \times N$ images and window size of $m \times n$. Because matching is based on raw intensity data, it is susceptible to image

noise. Unfortunately, several of the disadvantages just cited inevitably occur for optic disk image pairs.

Conversely, feature-based stereo matches only image features. Inevitably, the depth measurements obtained are fewer than for area-based stereo and sometimes can be sparse. On the other hand, feature-based stereo algorithms typically are faster because converting images to features reduces the quantity of data to be matched. It also copes better with large surface gradients and surface discontinuities than does area-based stereo, as these locations correspond typically to edges and so arise as features. Further, feature-based stereo is more accurate, because edge detection algorithms typically are accurate to better than one tenth of a pixel. Finally, robust feature-based algorithms have been reported and thoroughly tested (Pollard, Mayhew, and Frisby, 1985). For all these reasons, we use feature-based stereo, particularly the PMF algorithm.

In the special case that the optic axes of the cameras are parallel, the epipolars correspond to camera scan lines: hence, the points (x_R^i, y_R^i) in the right image that match a point (x_L, y_L) in the left image all satisfy $y_R^i = y_L$. This is not so when there is rotation between the cameras. For example, if the cameras are rotated relative to one another about the y axis so that the two camera axes converge, the epipolars are more complex and disparity is vector-valued. This is intrinsically the imaging geometry of the current situation. One way to deal with this situation is to make the epipolar lines explicit; then the search for matching points can be confined to epipolar lines. The calculation of depth must take the vertical component of disparity into account. To avoid this complication, one can try to rectify the stereo images by transforming them so that they are identical to those that would be taken with cameras whose axes are parallel and whose displacement is limited to the x direction. To evaluate the algorithm developed here before the novel camera system is available, existing fundus photographs, or pairs of photographs taken by moving a single fundus camera, are used. We rectify the stereo images, based on two assumptions:

- The background surface of fundus within the fundus images is flat except at the optic nerve head. This is a good assumption because the imaged area is only a small region (approximately 3 mm × 3 mm) of the spherical retinal surface.
- The disparity function over the "flat" fundus surface is constant or varies slowly. This assumption is true if the first assumption is true, parallel stereo geometry is assumed, and the surface is orthogonal to the camera axes. The camera axes usually converge, partly because of the optics of the eye and partly because of the camera orientation when the images are captured. We resample the images to simulate a rotation of the right image relative to the left about a vertical axis.

With these two assumptions, the stereo images can be rectified by matching the background of the fundus images. This enables the recovery of the in-plane transformation—that is, rotation and translation in the image plane—between the stereo pair.

The raw intensity images are used in the registration process. The left image is matched to the right image by translating and rotating the left image in the image plane. Matching is based on minimizing the sum of the differences in image intensity over the entire image. This simple method will be successful only if there are no abrupt changes in disparity so the center region corresponding to the optic nerve head, which was computed by the method sketched in the previous section, is first masked out. A typical result is shown in figure 36.3. It can be seen from the superimposed edge map

that edges in the fundus background are aligned. The unaligned edges in the center of the optic nerve head correspond to the disparity of blood vessel edges that lie close to the surface of the disk. The true disparity, D_{true} of any point in the surface is given by $D_{\text{true}} \approx D_{\text{background}} - D_{\text{register}}$, where $D_{\text{background}}$ is the disparity value of the fundus background and D_{register} is the relative disparity measured from the registered images. The approximation sign is used because it is assumed that the y component of disparity is zero, so only x disparity is measured. This may not be true because parallel stereo geometry cannot be guaranteed and $D_{\text{background}}$ can vary smoothly instead of having a constant value, as assumed. This acts as an offset to the relative disparity measured. Because depth is proportional to the reciprocal of disparity, depth cannot be computed from the disparity measured. Of course, this problem will be overcome in the new camera.

Image features extracted from the registered stereo pair are matched so that disparity can be measured. The feature-based stereo algorithm we chose is that developed by Pollard, Mayhew, and Frisby, (1985) because of its robustness and accuracy. PMF is a neighborhood support stereo algorithm that allows potential neighborhood matches to exchange support as long as they do not exceed a disparity gradient limit. Lee (1991), with Brady (1991a), provides more details. A fundus stereo pair is shown in figure 36.4. The two Canny edge maps of the registered stereo pair are superimposed and shown in the figure. It can be seen that the backgrounds of the two images are well aligned and that the epipolars are approximately parallel. The disparity map also is shown in figure 36.4. As described earlier, the measured disparity is not the true disparity, and depth of the optic nerve head cannot be computed due to the uncertainty in stereo triangulation. As is typical of such results, changes in the relative disparity function can be seen in the center of the optic nerve head, corresponding to the optic cup. The various clinical parameters discussed earlier cannot be measured directly from the stereo matching results. Even if the stereo geometry were known exactly and depth were calculated from disparity, it would be too sparse to measure the volume and such.

For this reason, we now consider how to reconstruct the surface of the optic nerve head from the sparse measurements provided by stereo alone. The problem of interpolating a surface through a set of data points

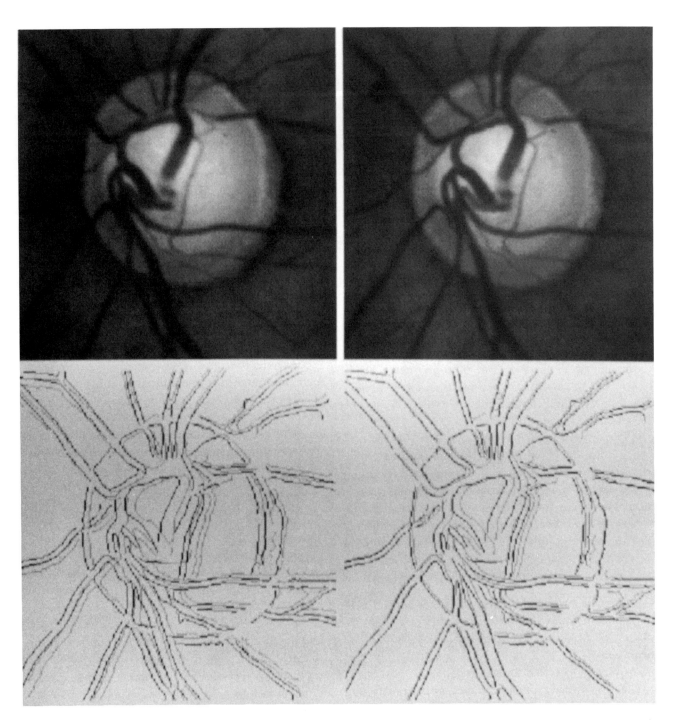

FIGURE 36.3   The top diagrams show the fundus stereo pair. Bottom left shows the superimposed edge maps before registration. Bottom right shows the superimposed edge maps after the stereo pair are aligned. It can be seen that the backgrounds are nearly in complete alignment.

usually is underconstrained—that is, there are many possible surfaces that pass through the given points. One solution is to interpolate the data using splines. An alternative is to treat surface reconstruction as an optimization problem. This is the approach of Grimson (1982), Terzopoulos (1983) and, more recently, Blake and Zisserman (1987). Smoothness constraints are imposed on the surface, and regularization is applied to the optimization problem. For example, Grimson (1982) suggested reconstructing the surface z as the

490   EYE SURGERY

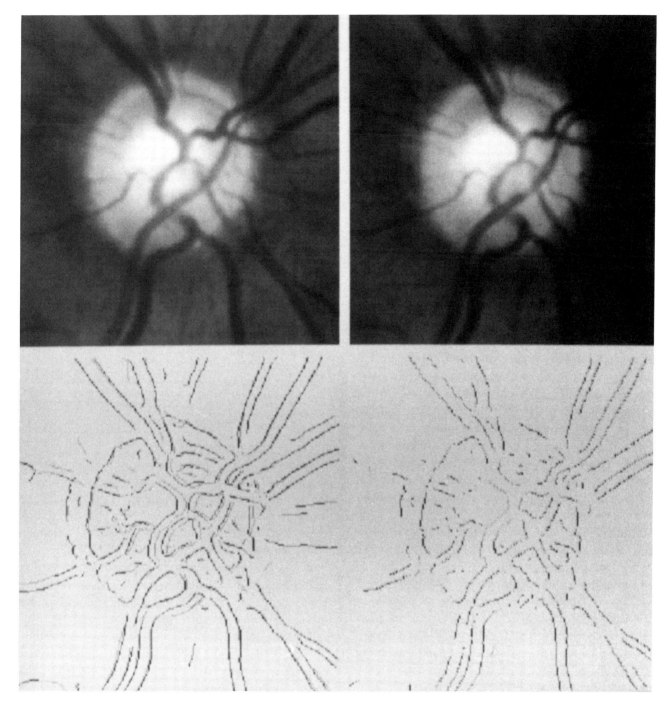

FIGURE 36.4 Result of binocular stereo. Top diagrams show stereo pair of fundus images. The Canny edge maps are superimposed and shown in bottom left. The disparity map of the feature-based stereo PMF algorithm is shown in the bottom right.

minimal solution to the quadratic variation in surface orientation:

$$\Theta\left(s\right) = \left\{ \iint \left(z_{xx}^2 + 2z_{xy}^2 + z_{yy}^2\right) dx\,dy \right\}^{1/2} \qquad (2)$$

where z denotes the surface and where, for example, z_{xx} is the second derivative of z with respect to x. The minimization problem was solved using conjugate gradient descent. The calculus of variations can be applied to the preceding optimization problem; the solution is the following biharmonic equation:

$$\nabla^4 z = z_{xxxx} + 2z_{xxyy} + z_{yyyy} = 0$$

As the results are typical of such methods, we illustrate the performance of Grimson's surface interpolation scheme on the sparse fundus depth data derived from the previous example. As noted earlier, relative disparity values, instead of depth measurements, are used. The disparity values computed from the discrete data are shown in figure 36.4. Later, we will plot the result as a surface; for now it can be seen that the central region of the disparity surface appears as a depression. Owing to the presence of the optic cup, the disparity in this region is smaller than that of the background. The disparity surface interpolated is qualitatively correct.

Because the fundus surface is smoothly shaded, very few features are available for matching, and this leads to sparse depth measurements. Not all edges related to rapid changes in surface orientation are detected, which provides insufficient constraint for accurate surface reconstruction. We have shown by experiment that the discrepancy between the interpolated surface and the actual surface can be large and is particularly serious near the edge of the cup where the edge information is lost. This has serious effects on the measurement of the clinical parameters such as the cup-disk ratio, as it requires the optic cup margin to be accurately located.

Although depth measurements of feature-based stereo alone provides insufficient constraint for accurate surface interpolation, it will be shown later that the sparse depth measurements provide valuable information for accurate surface reconstruction. Additional information about the surface (e.g. surface orientation) can be provided by other 3D depth modules, and more accurate reconstruction of the surface can be achieved.

Stereophotometry

When a surface is illuminated, the irradiating energy is partly absorbed and partly reflected over a solid angle of directions, from which it can be sensed. The radiation measured at a sensor is affected by several factors, most notably the reflectance and albedo of the surface; the surface orientation; the scene geometry; the distribution, intensity, and geometry of illumination sources; the position of the sensor; and the attributes of the opti-

cal system and sensor. Horn and Brooks (1989) provide a good introduction to the determination of shape from shading. In general, it is a difficult problem which, in applications such as this, can be made considerably easier by judicious choice of lighting. The complex reflectivity function simplifies considerably in the case of a surface whose reflectance function is Lambertian (perfect diffuser) and when there is a single collimated light source of strength E_s. In that case, the irradiance at the sensor is given by the following equation:

$$R(x,y) = \rho(x,y)\frac{E_s}{\pi}[\mathbf{n}(x,y)\cdot\mathbf{n}_s] \qquad (3)$$

where $\mathbf{n}(x,y)$ is the surface normal, $\mathbf{n}_s$ is the illumination direction, and $\rho(x,y)$ is the spatially varying albedo (an attenuation term). Image intensity $I(x,y)$ is proportional to the scene radiance $R(x,y)$; the constant of proportionality will be ignored in what follows as it does not affect the calculations. Conventionally, $\mathbf{n}(x,y)$ can be written as

$$\mathbf{n} = \frac{(-p, -q, 1)^{\mathrm{T}}}{\|(-p, -q, 1)\|}$$

where $p = \partial z/\partial x$, $q = \partial z/\partial y$, and z is the surface that we are attempting to measure.

Although questionable in many applications, the assumption of Lambertian reflectance seems appropriate for optic disk images. No direct evidence is available, as living tissue has a different reflectance characteristic than dead tissue (available, for example, pathologically). However, in our previous work on cataracts, a light source was focused on the optic disk and used to reflect and diffuse the light so that the lens was backlit. The polarization characteristics of the lens and fundus images exploited in that work strongly suggest that the reflectance of the cup is approximately Lambertian. The majority of shape-from-shading algorithms assume constant albedo, but this certainly is not the case in the present application.

It can be shown that to recover surface orientation for a Lambertian reflector, three illumination conditions suffice. This also allows the albedo $\rho(x,y)$ to be evaluated. Instead, we have developed a method that determines one component of the surface gradient z_x using just two light sources. This is important in applying stereophotometry to the optic nerve head because access is severely limited by the pupil of the eye. The novel fundus camera exploits the technique.

Suppose that the surface is Lambertian and that the two illumination sources are arranged such that the origins of the two reflectance maps are located on (say) the p axis. Let $I_1(x,y)$ and $I_2(x,y)$ be the image intensities of two images illuminated by sources 1 and 2, respectively:

$$I_1(x,y) = \rho \frac{E_{s_1}}{\pi} \frac{1 + p_{s_1}p + q_{s_1}q}{[(1 + p^2 + q^2)(1 + p_{s_1}^2 + q_{s_1}^2)]^1} \quad (4)$$

$$I_2(x,y) = \rho \frac{E_s}{\pi} \frac{1 + p_s p + q_s q}{[(1 + p^2 + q^2)(1 + p_s^2 + q_s^2)]^1} \quad (5)$$

To eliminate the surface albedo, we divide the first of these equations by the second to give the following:

$$M = \frac{I_1}{I_2}$$
$$= \frac{E_{s_1}}{E_s} \frac{(1 + p_{s_1}p + q_{s_1}q)}{(1 + p_s p + q_s q)} \frac{\sqrt{1 + p_s^2 + q_s^2}}{\sqrt{1 + p_{s_1}^2 + q_{s_1}^2}} \quad (6)$$

To further develop the design, we first choose to place the collimated illumination sources symmetrically (about a Cyclopean center), oriented in the x-z plane. Second, we arrange to illuminate the scene with equal-energy light sources (in practice, with the same light source). Then,

$$q_{s_1} = q_s = 0, \quad \text{and}$$
$$p_{s_1} = -p_s = p_s, \quad \text{and}$$
$$E_{s_1} = E_s = E_s$$

We find

$$M = \frac{1 + p_s p}{1 - p_s p}$$

so that

$$p = z_x = \frac{M - 1}{p_s(M + 1)} \quad (7)$$

In this way, the x component z_x of the surface gradient can be computed at each pixel. Of course, a similar method could then be used to compute the y component of the surface gradient by placing the two illumination sources symmetrically in the y-z plane; but in this application this is not a feasible proposition. Given z_x, the relative depth of points p in the surface can be found by integrating the surface gradient along some path from some origin (x_o, y_o) to the point p:

$$z_{el}(x, y_i) = z_{el}(x_o, y_i) + \int_{x_o}^{x} p \, dx \quad (8)$$

In the present case, we integrate along a path that is parallel to the x axis. Note that the integration requires knowledge of some $z_{el}(x_o, y_i)$ in each horizontal profile along which depth is integrated. Ideally, the relative depth calculated is independent of the choice of integration path—that is, when p is computed accurately and sufficiently, small steps are taken in the integration. Typically, the computed surface gradient z_x is prone to error, such as imaging noise and error in specifying the reflectance function, and the integrated depth, z, is no longer independent of the integration path. A surface integrability constraint (Horn and Brooks, 1986) can be imposed on the surface; but again this requires $q = z$, which is not available.

If the depth $z(x_o, y_i)$ is known at a point of each horizontal profile, the profiles can be tied together and the surface formed. The binocular stereo process described in the last section of this chapter provides a set of sparse, though accurate, depth measurements along edges, and these can be used as $z(x_o, y_i)$. Several binocular stereo measurements (we have found that the number varies from 5 to 15 on average) are available in each profile. Depth measurements from edges perpendicular to the epipolars are preferred because they are more accurate. In the rare case where there is no binocular stereo depth measurement within the profile, due to either sparse image features or lack of reliable vertical edges, it can be assumed that the depth function of regions outside the optic nerve head changes slowly relative to a neighboring profile. An error analysis of the surface gradient has been performed (Lee, 1991) but is omitted here for reasons of space.

Integrating surface gradients to give relative depths accumulates errors along the path of integration. Individual errors may be small, but the summed effect along an integration path can be large. In particular, a noise spike at one point seriously affects all subsequent depth estimates. It is important, therefore, that noise in the gradient map be filtered out. One way to do this is to smooth the surface gradient estimates with a Gaussian kernel; but this does not work well for optic disk data. First, it smooths out discontinuities at the edge of the disk, and second, the optimal value of the required Gaussian standard deviation is hard to estimate. Instead, we have developed a technique based on generalized least-squares fitting.

To develop the idea, we consider the one-dimensional case. Suppose we are given noise-corrupted 1D data, $\bar{p}(x)$. Our aim is to construct a best-fitting, smooth function $p(x)$. We begin by investigating the linear combination:

$$F = \int \left[(p - \bar{p})^2 + \alpha p_x^2 \right] dx$$

where α is a nonnegative weighting constant that controls the balance between faithfulness to the data and smoothness. The first term pulls $p(x)$ to conform to the data $\bar{p}(x)$, whereas the second resists severe deformation and requires $p(x)$ to be smooth. If α is small, the first term dominates, but if α is large, the second term dominates and the result will be a smooth curve, which, in the extreme case, is affected little by the given data. Note that higher derivatives of p could also be constrained; but we have not found this necessary. There is a more serious issue with which we must contend.

The second term penalizes the gradient of $p(x)$; it tries to keep $p(x)$ as flat as possible, and this causes oversmoothing in regions where the gradient is large. To preserve such large gradient regions, α can be varied according to the local gradient as the degree of smoothing is controlled by α. In essence, α should be small when the gradient is large and large when the gradient is small. In principle, one way to achieve this would be to set

$$\alpha(x) = \frac{\alpha_o}{\hat{g}(x)^2} \qquad (9)$$

where $\hat{g}(x)$ is an estimate of the gradient of the data. In practice, the data is corrupted by noise, so it is not possible to compute $g(x)$ accurately from the data, and hence it is impossible to obtain an accurate estimation of α. A possible choice for α is

$$\alpha(x) = \alpha_o e^{-p_x} \qquad (10)$$

Because the local gradient is large when there is a noise spike, this could give a poor choice of α; but the whole point of using generalized least squares was to suppress noise! Instead, we treat α as another functional and try to find the "best" α by minimizing some cost function. More precisely, we minimize the following:

$$F(p, \alpha) = \int \left[(p - \bar{p})^2 + \alpha p_x^2 + \gamma (\alpha - \bar{\alpha})^2 + \mu \alpha_x^2 \right] dx \qquad (11)$$

where γ and μ are nonnegative weighting constants; μ controls the smoothness of α, whereas γ prevents α deviating too much from its prior estimate $\bar{\alpha}$. It is possible to show (Lee, 1991) that the cost function $F(p, \alpha)$ is convex if α, μ, and γ are chosen appropriately.

Finally, to solve the minimization problem computationally, we must discretize the continuous problem, and to do this we use the finite element method. The total discretized cost is

$$F = \sum_{i=0}^{N} (p_i - \bar{p}_i)^2 + \sum_{i=1}^{N} \alpha_i (p_i - p_{i-1})^2$$
$$+ \gamma \sum_{i=0}^{N} (\alpha_i - \bar{\alpha}_i)^2 + \mu \sum_{i=1}^{N} (\alpha_i - \alpha_{i-1})^2$$

The minimum cost satisfies:

$$\frac{\partial F}{\partial p_i} = 0 \quad \forall i$$

$$\frac{\partial F}{\partial \alpha_i} = 0 \quad \forall i$$

This gives two set of equations:

$$(p_i - \bar{p}_i) + \alpha_i (p_i - p_{i-1}) + \alpha_{i+1} (p_i - p_{i+1}) = 0$$
$$2\gamma (\alpha_i - \bar{\alpha}_i) + (p_i - p_{i-1})^2 - 2\mu (\alpha_{i+1} - 2\alpha_i + \alpha_{i-1}) = 0$$

To solve for p_i and α_i, we can use an iterative scheme, such as the Jacobi:

$$p_i^{+1} = \frac{1}{1 + \alpha_i + \alpha_{i+1}} (\bar{p}_i + \alpha_i p_{i-1} + \alpha_{i+1} p_{i+1})$$

$$\alpha_i^{+1} = \frac{1}{2\gamma + 4\mu} \left[2\gamma \bar{\alpha}_i + 2\mu (\alpha_{i+1} + \alpha_{i-1}) - (p_i - p_{i-1})^2 \right]$$

This spatially varying filter performs significantly better than one that uses a constant value of α. The prior estimate $\bar{\alpha}$ is based on the values computed from a plastic model of the optic nerve head, for which the discontinuities are considerably more severe than are found in practice. Noise is well suppressed, and discontinuities are preserved. It has also been found by experiment that the results are relatively insensitive to the choice of μ and γ. The technique has been extended to two dimensions.

A typical experimental result is illustrated for the optic nerve head shown in figure 36.1. The fundus images were captured by a Zeiss Fundus Camera. Because the illumination is projected from the inside of the camera, the illumination angle cannot be changed without changing the viewpoint, so the requirement of fixed imaging geometry cannot be achieved. This introduces a stereoscopic effect between the two stereophotometric images and matching is not trivial. The

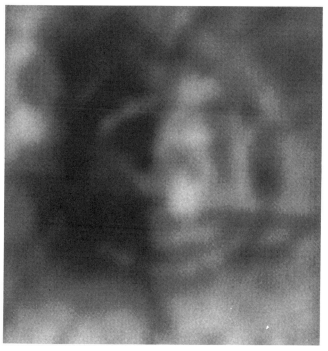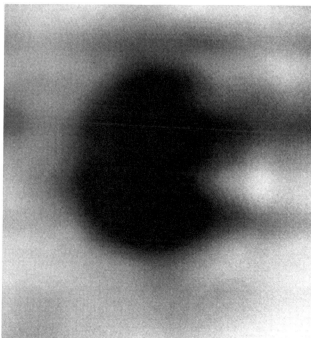

FIGURE 36.5   (Left) The gradient map of the fundus surface after smoothing. (Right) A shading representation of the reconstructed surface.

output of stereophotometry is shown in figure 36.5a. The gradient map was smoothed by the generalized least-squares algorithm. The surface was computed by integrating the surface gradient. The reconstructed surface is shown in figures 36.5b and 36.6. The depression seen at the center of the optic nerve head corresponds to the cupping of the optic nerve head. The results are noisy.

Integrating stereoscopic photography and stereophotometry

Stereo vision and shape from shading are complementary (Blake, Zisserman, and Knowles, 1985). Binocular stereo performs best in regions where the image intensity changes rapidly. On the other hand, stereophotometry performs best when the surface reflectance is homogeneous and the surface is smooth with no discontinuities. The optic nerve head contains regions of both types: The image intensity changes rapidly at the edges of blood vessels but slowly in the fundus background. This suggests that integrating depth measurements

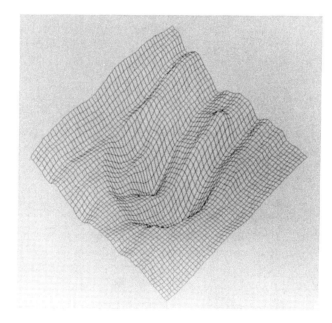

FIGURE 36.6   A 3D plot of the reconstructed surface of the optic nerve head shown in figure 36.5, right panel.

from the two processes may give a surface that is more accurate and reliable and for which the density of depth measurements is increased.

The depth of the reconstructed surface should be as close to the stereo depth data as possible, while its gradient should not deviate too much from that estimated by stereophotometry. To achieve this balance between the two sets of measurements, we first denote the discrepancy between the surface gradient z_x and the value estimated by stereophotometry by $f = z_x - p$. Because much of the noise in the gradient map is filtered by the generalized least-squares technique discussed in the previous section, we may assume that f is smooth. We minimize the weighted sum thus:

$$\mathscr{C} = \frac{1}{\sigma_s^2} \mathscr{P}(z) + \frac{\tau}{\sigma_{ps}^2} \mathscr{D}(z)$$

$$= \frac{1}{\sigma_s^2} \sum_{(i,j) \in \zeta} [z(\mathbf{x}_{i,j}) - \bar{z}_{i,j}]^2$$

$$+ \frac{\tau}{\sigma_{ps}^2} \int\int \left[\left(\frac{\partial f}{\partial x} \right)^2 + \left(\frac{\partial f}{\partial y} \right)^2 \right] dx\, dy \quad (12)$$

where ζ is the set of points at which there is a binocular stereo estimate, σ_s^2 is the variance of the binocular stereo depth measurements, σ_{ps}^2 is the variance of the stereophotometric gradient measurements, and τ is a nonnegative constant. Because $\mathscr{P}$ penalizes depth discrepancies between the reconstructed surface and the binocular stereo depth data, and $\mathscr{D}$ penalizes the smoothness of the deformation of the gradient function, τ is used to balance the relative contributions of the two terms. The first term $\mathscr{P}$ tries to pull the surface to the binocular stereo depth measurements; the second term $\mathscr{D}$ requires f to be smooth. If the variance of one set of measurements is large, the corresponding cost function will contribute less to the total cost, and the reconstructed surface is allowed to deviate from that particular set of measurements.

We will be able to estimate σ_s^2 and σ_{ps}^2 accurately when the novel camera is available. In the interim, these values need to be estimated. The accuracy of edge matching depends on the orientation of the edges; for edges making a small angle θ with the epipolar lines, the depth values computed are highly inaccurate. This observation can be incorporated into the surface reconstruction problem by multiplying σ_s^2 by $\frac{1}{\sin \theta}$.

The weighted sum then is expressed thus:

$$\mathscr{C} = \sum_{(i,j) \in \zeta} \frac{\sin \theta}{\sigma_s^2} [z(\mathbf{x}_{i,j}) - \bar{z}_{i,j}]^2$$

$$+ \frac{\tau}{\sigma_{ps}^2} \int\int \left[\left(\frac{\partial f}{\partial x} \right)^2 + \left(\frac{\partial f}{\partial y} \right)^2 \right] dx\, dy \quad (13)$$

The effect of the extra $\sin \theta$ term in equation 13 is that when the edges are perpendicular to the epipolar lines, the accuracy of the depth measurements $\bar{z}$ is believed to be high, and the first term then is weighted at its full strength with respect to the second term. When the angle becomes smaller, the accuracy of the depth measurements decreases, so the relative weighting decreases correspondingly. In the extreme case, the edges are parallel to the epipolar lines, such that stereo matching becomes impossible and the first term vanishes.

Assuming σ_s^2 and σ_{ps}^2 are constant across the image, we can write

$$\mathscr{C} = \sum_{(i,j) \in \zeta} \sin \theta [z(\mathbf{x}_{i,j}) - \bar{z}_{i,j}]^2$$

$$+ \tau_o \int\int \left[\left(\frac{\partial f}{\partial x} \right)^2 + \left(\frac{\partial f}{\partial y} \right)^2 \right] dx\, dy \quad (14)$$

where

$$\tau_o = \tau \frac{\sigma_s^2}{\sigma_{ps}^2}$$

We discretize these equations using a 2D nonconforming rectangular linear finite element. Values of the first and second derivatives within the (i,j)th element are simple functions of the nodal values.

$$u_y = u_{i,j} - u_{i,j-1}$$

$$u_x = u_{i,j} - u_{i-1,j}$$

$$u_{xx} = u_{i,j+1} - 2u_{i,j} + u_{i,j-1}$$

$$u_{xy} = u_{i,j} + u_{i-1,j-1} - u_{i,j-1} - u_{i-1,j}$$

The discretized total cost function then becomes

$$\mathscr{C} = \sum_{(i,j) \in \zeta} \sin \theta_{i,j} (z_{i,j} - \bar{z}_{i,j})^2$$

$$+ \tau \sum_{i,j} [z_{i,j+1} - 2z_{i,j} + z_{i,j-1} - (p_{i,j} - p_{i,j-1})]^2$$

$$+ \sum_{i,j} [z_{i,j} + z_{i-1,j-1} - z_{i,j-1} - z_{i-1,j}$$

$$- (p_{i,j} - p_{i-1,j})]^2 \quad (15)$$

The condition for $\mathbf{z}$ to be the minimum is

$$\frac{\partial \mathscr{C}}{\partial z_{i,j}} = 0 \quad \forall i,j \quad (16)$$

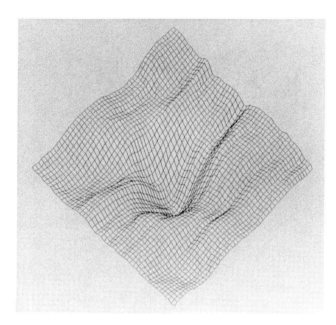

FIGURE 36.7 Result of integrating stereoscopic photographs and stereophotometry. The surface of an optic nerve head.

The total cost $\mathscr{C}$ is a quadratic function of z, so equation 16 is a set of linear simultaneous equations. A Jacobi iteration scheme was used to solve the equations. More efficient schemes, such as the Gauss-Seidel or the successive overrelaxation iteration scheme, can be used. Lee (1991) supplies details.

Figure 36.7 shows the result of integrating stereoscopic photography and stereophotometry of an optic nerve head. The stereo images are displayed in figure 36.3 and the surface is reconstructed by stereophotometry in figure 36.5. Because the disparity computed is relative disparity, real depth information cannot be recovered. Although information about edge orientation was incorporated into both surface reconstruction processes, the results shown are noisy and result from the limitations of the present imaging system. The cup depressions in the center of the two surfaces can be seen. The undulating appearance of the surface reconstructed from stereophotometry (due to mismatches) is rectified by the binocular stereo measurements. Unfortunately, because of the lack of "ground truth," the reconstructed surface cannot be compared with the actual fundus surface. However, we can conclude safely that the integrated surface is a more accurate representation of the original surface than either the surface interpolated from the sparse binocular stereo depth measurements or the surface reconstructed from the gradient measurements of stereophotometry. Because the shape of the optic nerve head is similar to that of the model, similar results can be confidently expected when the special imaging system is available.

Finally, we consider how to identify the cup margin. The definition of the cup margin is rather vague, different clinicians offering different criteria. For example, Simpson et al. (1989b) define the margin as the point where the surface curvature changes most rapidly. The Rodenstock Optic Nerve Head Analyzer defines the cup margin as 150 μm below the disk boundary. The latter method is better than the first because the surface near the cup margin can be smooth and thus the cup margin is ill-defined, especially in the nonglaucomatous cup and in the early stage of glaucoma. We adopt the latter definition. To delineate the cup margin, a plane is fitted by linear regression to the depth measurements corresponding to the disk boundary. The optic cup then is defined as the region that lies at a certain distance below this plane.

Four examples are shown in figure 36.8. For the plaster model, a plane is fitted to the background as there is no disk boundary in this case. The concavity is defined as the region that is one fifth of the maximum depth below the fitted plane. The boundary is marked as a black curve in the figure. It can be seen that the curve shown does not mark exactly the edge of the concavity because of the convention used to define the margin. In this case, a more accurate result can be obtained if surface curvature is used. However, the object is a model, and the margin of the concavity is not as well defined in the human optic nerve head.

In three images of the optic nerve heads shown, the white curves mark the disk boundary. A plane is fitted to the relative disparity measurements[2] of each boundary, and the cup margin is drawn as a black curve. There is a discrepancy between the marked margin and the margin perceived by manual examination of the stereo images.

NOTES

1. The Zeiss Fundus Camera is a monocamera. The Allen Stereo Separator consists of a motor-driven rotating glass prism that allows the viewing angle of the camera to change in a relatively short interval and without moving the camera.
2. Relative disparity is used instead of depth because of the limitations of the present imaging system.

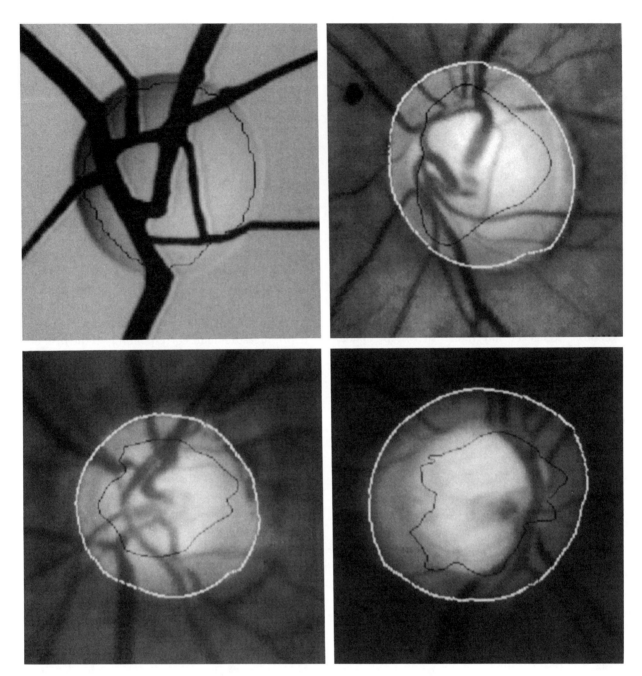

FIGURE 36.8 Four images derived from the detection of the concavity boundary. The white curves delineate the boundaries of the optic nerve head, and the black curves the boundary of the optic cup.

REFERENCES

ALGAZI, V. R., J. L. KELTNER, and C. A. JOHNSON, 1985. Computer analysis of the optic cup in glaucoma. *Invest. Ophthamol. Vis. Sci.* 26:1759–1770.

AMINI, A. A., S. TEHRANI, and T. E. WEYMOUTH, 1988. Using dynamic programming for minimization energy of active contour in the presence of hard constraints. In *Proceedings of the Second International Conference on Computer Vision*, pp. 95–99.

BLAKE, A., and A. ZISSERMAN, 1987. *Visual Reconstruction.* Cambridge, Mass.: MIT Press.

BLAKE, A., A. ZISSERMAN, and G. KNOWLES, 1985. Surface descriptions from stereo and shading. *Image Vis. Comput.* 3(4):183–191.

CAPRIOLO, J., U. KINGBEIL, M. SEARS, and B. POPE, 1986.

Reproducibility of the optic disc measurements with computerized analysis of stereoscopic video images. *Arch. Ophthalmol.* 104:1035–1039.

CAPRIOLO, J., J. M. MILLER, and M. SEARS, 1987. Quantitative evaluation of the optic nerve head in patients with unilateral vision field loss from primary open angle glaucoma. *Ophthalmology* 94:1484–1487.

DANDONA, L., H. A. QUIGLEY, and H. D. JAMPEL, 1989. Variability of depth measurements of the optic nerve head and peripapillary retina with computerized image analysis. *Arch. Ophthalmol.* 107:1786–1792.

DOUGLAS, R., S. M. DRANCE, and M. SCHULZER, 1975. The visual field and nerve head in angle-closure glaucoma. *Arch. Ophthalmol.* 93:409–411.

DREHER, A. W., P. C. TSO, and R. N. WEINREB, 1991. Reproducibility of topographic measurements of the normal and glaucomatous optic nerve head with the laser tomographic scanner. *Am. J. Ophthalmol.* 111(2):221–229.

FAZIO, P., T. KRUPIN, M. E. FEITL, E. B. WERNER, and D. A. CARRE, 1990. Optic disc topography in patients with low-tension and primary open angle glaucoma. *Arch. Ophthalmol.* 108:705–708.

GRIMSON, W. E. L., 1982. *From Images to Surface—A Computational Study of the Human Early Visual System.* Cambridge, Mass.: MIT Press.

HORN, B. K. P., and M. J. BROOKS, 1986. The variational approach to shape from shading. *Comput. Vis. Graph. Image Proc.* 33(2):174–208.

HORN, B. K. P., and M. J. BROOKS, 1989. *Shape from Shading.* Cambridge, Mass.: MIT Press.

KASS, M., A. P. WITKIN, and D. TERZOPOULOS, 1987. Snake: Active contour models. In *Proceedings of the First International Conference on Computer Vision*, pp. 259–268.

KOTTLER, M. S., A. R. ROSENTHAL, and D. G. FALCONER, 1974. Digital photogrammetry of the optic nerve head. *Invest. Ophthamol. Vis. Sci.* 13:116.

KOTTLER, M. S., A. R. ROSENTHAL, and D. G. FALCONER, 1976. Analog vs. digital photogrammetry for optic cup analysis. *Invest. Ophthamol. Vis. Sci.* 15:651–654.

LEE, S., 1991. Visual monitoring of glaucoma. Doctoral thesis, University of Oxford.

LEE, S., and J. M. BRADY, 1991a. Integrating stereo and photometric stereo to monitor the development of glaucoma. *Image Vis. Comput.* 9:39–44.

LEE, S., and J. M. BRADY, 1991b. Optic nerve head boundary detection. In *Proceedings of the British Machine Vision Conference*, pp. 359–362.

LICHTER, P. R., 1976. Variability of expert observers in evaluating the optic disc. *Trans. Am. Ophthalmol. Soc.* 74:532–572.

MARR, D., and T. POGGIO, 1979. A theory of human stereo vision. In *Proceedings of the Royal Society of London*, pp. 301–328.

MIKELBERG, F. S., P. J. AIRAKSINEN, G. R. DOUGLAS, M. SCHULZER, and K. WIJSMAN, 1985. The correlation between optic disc topography measured by the videoophthalmograph (Rodenstock Analyzer) and clinical measurement. *Am. J. Ophthalmol.* 100(3):417–419.

MIKELBERG, F. S., D. G. DOUGLAS, and S. M. DRANCE, 1988. Reproducibility of computerized pallor measurements obtained with the Rodenstock Disc Analyzer. *Graefes Arch. Clin. Exp. Ophthalmol.* pp. 269–272.

MIKELBERG, F. S., G. R. DOUGLAS, and M. SCHULZER, 1984. Reliability of optic disc topographic measurements recorded with a video-ophthalmograph. *Am. J. Ophthalmol.* 98(1):98–102.

MOTOLKO, M., and S. M. DRANCE, 1981. Features of optic disc in preglaucomatous eyes. *Arch. Ophthalmol.* 99:1992–1994.

OTTO, G. P., and T. K. W. CHAU, 1988. A "region-growing" algorithm for matching of terrain images. In *Proceedings of the Alvey Vision Conference*, pp. 123–128.

PEDERSON, J. E., and D. R. ANDERSON, 1980. The mode of progressive disc cupping in ocular hypertension and glaucoma. *Arch. Ophthalmol.* 98:490–495.

POLLARD, S. B., J. E. W. MAYHEW, and J. P. FRISBY, 1985. PMF: A stereo correspondence algorithm using a disparity gradient limit. *Perception* 14:449–470.

QUIGLEY, A. A., R. W. FLOWER, E. M. ADDICKS, and D. S. MCLEOD, 1980. The mechanism of optic nerve damage in experimental acute intraocular pressure elevation. *Invest. Ophthamol. Vis. Sci.* 19:155–157.

RADIUS, R. L., A. E. MAUMENEE, and W. R. GREEN, 1978. Pit-like changes of the optic nerve head in open-angle glaucoma. *Br. J. Ophthalmol.* 62:389–393.

ROSENTHAL, A. R., D. G. FALCONER, and B. BARRET, 1980. Digital measurement of pallor-disk ratio. *Arch. Ophthalmol.* 98:2027–2031.

SCHWARTZ, B., 1986. Changes in optics disc in ocular hypertension and glaucoma. *Jpn. J. Ophthalmol.* 30(2):143–153.

SIMPSON, A. J., S. LEE, K. J. HANNA, and A. J. BRON, 1989a. A method for measurement of neuroretinal rim area (tech. rep.). Oxford, Engl.: Visual Science Unit, Radcliffe Infirmary.

SIMPSON, A. J., B. C. REEVES, L. LINDSELL, and A. J. BRON, 1989b. Glaucoma conversion in the Oxford ocular hypertension trial (tech. rep.). Oxford, Engl.: Visual Science Unit, Radcliffe Infirmary.

SOMMER, A., I. POLLACK, and E. E. MAUMENEE, 1979. Optic disc parameters and onset of glaucomatous field loss. *Arch. Ophthalmol.* 97:1444–1448.

TAKAMOTO, T., and B. SCHWARTZ, 1985. Reproducibility of photogrammetric optic disc cup measurements. *Invest. Ophthamol. Vis. Sci.* 26:814–817.

TERZOPOULOUS, D., 1983. Multilevel computational processes for visual surface reconstruction. *Comput. Vis. Graph. Image Proc.* 24(1):52–96.

VARMA, R., W. C. STEINMANN, G. L. SPAETH, and R. P. WILSON, 1988. Variability in digital analysis of optic disk topography. *Graefes Arch. Clin. Exp Ophthalmol.* 226:435–442.

WEINREB, R. N., A. W. DREHER, and J. BILLE, 1989. Quantitative assessment of the optic nerve head with the laser tomographic scanner. *Int. J. Opthalmol.* 13:25–29.

Dentistry

Dentistry represents a relatively virgin, but quite promising, territory for computer-integrated surgical applications. The reduction in computing hardware costs, together with the widespread push for remote database access and x-ray image digitization have created the conditions for introducing computer methods in the provision of dental care. There are many opportunities for today's dental practitioner, as discussed by van der Stelt in his chapter, "Opportunities for Computer Usage in Dentistry." The author identifies various technologic needs in the three phases of dental care (diagnosis, treatment planning, and treatment execution). He shows how the chapters included in the section address these needs and what remains to be done in the future.

In the area of dental diagnosis, it is important to ensure that the procedures used are both standardized and repeatable. Standardization is required in order to ensure meaningful results when several specialists are consulted. Repeatability is needed to compare x-ray images taken at various times and determine the slow evolution of dental diseases. The second chapter by van der Stelt and Sanderink, "Direct Intraoral Digital Radiography in Dentistry," addresses the need for standardization through the use of digital intraoral radiography. Digital x-ray sensors have additional advantages over analog films, such as instant imaging, reduced radiation exposure, and the ability to store and transmit x-rays electronically.

In recent years, digitally stored x-rays have been used to subtract subsequent images and determine bone loss over time. However, this technique, called *digital subtraction radiology*, requires that identical x-ray source-patient geometry be maintained at every radiography session. The third chapter, "Robotic Control of Intraoral Radiography," by Dunn, Burdea, and Goratowski, shows how robotics can be used to orient the x-ray source in a controlled manner, following the patient's head position. The authors give initial experimental results using an industrial robot and an external 3D sensor placed outside the patient's mouth. The overall system accuracy is a function of robot and sensor accuracies and resolutions, as discussed by Burdea in chapter 16 of this book.

Computer simulations are used also in the treatment planning phase, when it is important to have a realistic model of the patient's mouth behavior. The fourth chapter, "Stress and Strain Trajectories in the Human Mandible Using a Servohydraulically Controlled Artificial Mouth," by Douglas et al., describes an experimental system for the modeling of stress and strain in the mandible under various dynamic conditions. The servo-controlled artificial mouth is useful as well in the design of surgical alloys and components and their computerized testing.

After all the preliminaries, we come to the actual treatment stage. In dentistry, this often requires the manufacture of precise dental restorations, such as crowns. The final chapter in this section, "CAD/CAM Automation and Expert Systems for Design and Fabrication of Dental Restorations," by Rekow and Nappi, introduces the use of modern CAD/CAM technology to the design and fabrication of dental restorations. The authors envision a central manufacturing location that can serve a multitude of remote dental offices in the most efficient and speedy way. Initial clinical trials have proved successful, and comparative tests are presently being conducted to assess the longevity of CAD/CAM restorations. A recently published report by Fortin et al. (1993) describes a CT-based system to help place dental implants very accurately.

The dental applications described in this section are each being developed separately by the respective research teams. In the future, these isolated components will become integrated into a complete automated system spanning all phases of dental care.

REFERENCE

FORTIN, T., J. L. COUDERT, P. SAUTOT, and S. LAVALLEE, 1993. Dental implant computer assisted surgical guide. In *Proceedings of the IEEE EMBS Conference*, San Diego, pp. 1617–1618.

37 Opportunities for Computer Use in Dentistry

PAUL F. VAN DER STELT

IN DENTISTRY, AS in many other medical areas, the role of the computer has become more important in the last two decades. Computer applications nowadays go beyond regular office management and database applications (Preston, 1993). Computer technology now is widely applied in dental practice and is no longer restricted to laboratory settings. More advanced computer applications are foreseen in the near future. This situation will stimulate the exchange of information, with regard to clinical needs and technical possibilities, between the research environment and the clinician or practitioner. In turn, this will further improve existing applications and will facilitate the development of new applications.

Three consecutive phases can be distinguished in the course of dental patient care: diagnosis, treatment planning, and finally the treatment itself (figure 37.1). The first phase regards the acquisition of data on the patient's medical and dental condition. The second phase relates to the use of this diagnostic information to recognize or exclude pathologic conditions and to make the most appropriate decision for correcting eventual pathologic conditions. The third phase is the treatment itself.

After the treatment phase has been completed, treatment effects must be evaluated. This is the start of a new cycle through the consecutive steps just described, beginning with the diagnostic phase and ending with the treatment phase. This may also include the decision not to perform active treatment as such.

In the reports cited throughout this chapter are some examples of computer applications in dentistry and the way computer technology is changing dental practice. An outline of the rationale for these exciting new developments is provided.

Computer applications in dental diagnosis

The diagnostic phase is perhaps the most important step in dental treatment. During this phase, information is obtained that is used to determine the direction of the steps that follow, including the decision to start active treatment or to wait for some time to see how the lesion or other pathologic condition develops. To ensure that the information obtained is reliable, the procedure to collect diagnostic information needs to be standardized and reproducible. *Standardized* means that the diagnostic procedure follows a systematic approach based on a model that describes the behavior and characteristics of the pathology to be traced (Halse and Molven, 1986; Dunn, 1992). Standardization ensures that in similar situations the diagnostic procedure will produce the same information. *Reproducible* relates to the fact that consecutive occurrences of the same diagnostic test produce results that are directly comparable. Reproducibility is required to compare pretreatment and posttreatment diagnostic information and to assess disease progress or treatment effects over some period of time. The progress of dental diseases, such as caries and periodontal bone resorption, tends to be slow. Hence, the time lapse between two consecutive examinations must be relatively long, typically some months to more than a year. This requires a high standard of reproducibility of the data acquisition system.

As in other human activities, the collection of diagnostic information is influenced by subjective factors. The dentist can be biased by the appearance of the patient. The chance that a disease process will be diagnosed correctly by the physician or dentist depends, to a large extent, on the subjective probability as used by the dentist to assess the reliability of his or her findings.

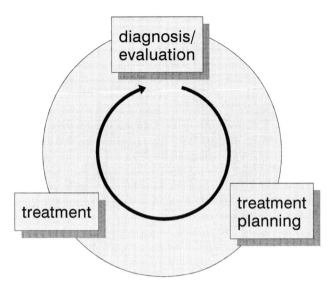

FIGURE 37.1 The three phases of dental patient care: diagnosis, treatment planning, and clinical treatment. When treatment is completed, the evaluation of treatment effects can be considered the start of a new cycle.

Perceptive and cognitive filters decrease the amount of information that is used effectively to reach a diagnosis. Computer technology can be a great help to decrease the subjectivity of the diagnostic process, thus improving both standardization and reproducibility (White, 1989; Mol and van der Stelt, 1992; van der Stelt, 1992).

Chapters 38 and 39 address the improvement of standardization and reproducibility in dental radiography. The computer applications described in that work show that during the exposure of the radiographic film as well as during the interpretation of the radiographic image, the conditions for the diagnostic process can be improved by the applied technology.

DIGITAL INTRAORAL RADIOGRAPHY

Intraoral digital radiography is a clear example of the fast-growing importance of computer-based diagnostic procedures in dentistry. Dose reduction, image enhancement, automated image analysis, and teleradiology are only a few of the advancements resulting from this new technology.

Teleradiology can be used in referral for second opinions and for advice of specialists on treatment planning. Prior approval for treatment from third-party insurance carriers is another application of teleradiology. (Farman, Farag, and Yeap, 1992). When

direct digital x-ray systems are more widespread in dentistry, it will be common practice among dentists to send radiographic images to colleagues using electronic mail systems or ISDN. The reasons for sending radiographic images might vary from patients moving to another region and therefore transferring to a new dentist, to consultation with experts, to approval by insurance companies. Teleradiology may also be applied within one dental practice, where more dentists or oral hygienists need access to the same patient database, including dental radiographs, or where one dentist is working on more than one surgical patient. A local network will provide access to the database containing all patient information, from numerous workstations within the same building (Dove et al., 1992).

It will take several years before filmless dental practice will become reality (if ever), but in the meantime many applications of digital radiography will become increasingly important. Digital radiography in dentistry still shows the typical characteristics of newly emerging technologies. Much research remains to be done to determine how this modality can be applied most effectively. It should be emphasized here that the diagnostic accuracy of computer-aided procedures must be determined before they can be considered a reliable support tool for clinical assessment in addition to professional experience. However, it already is clear that digital imaging techniques will provide us with new possibilities in diagnosis that cannot be achieved with film-based radiography (Dove et al., 1992).

Digital radiography also can contribute to the standardization of radiographic procedures. One example is in the application of geometric reconstruction techniques to obtain radiographs with similar projection geometry as for digital subtraction radiography. The use of digital image processing to correct the contrast or density of an image will improve standardization as well by making the image's density distribution comparable to that of a reference image (Ruttimann and Webber, 1986).

DENTAL ROBOTICS

Changes over time can be measured by subtraction radiography. Two images, each of which records the state of dentition at a specific time, are taken. Assuming that the normal anatomic structures do not change between the two films, the observed differences are indicative of expansion or resorption of the mineralized structures. An essential requirement is that the projection geometry of the pair of images be completely identical. If this is not the case, then the subtraction image represents not only structural changes over time but also the differences in the images resulting from different beam projections. Mechanical devices are used to provide a rigid connection among the x-ray source, the patient, and the film (Duckworth et al., 1983). This method, however, is inconvenient for the patient and cumbersome for the dentist. It restricts the use of subtraction radiography on a routine basis outside research laboratories.

Other radiographic procedures that require a strict imaging geometry have been described as well. An example of such a procedure is tomosynthesis, in which a finite set of radiographs is taken with the source at known locations and the projection data then are used to synthesize an arbitrary cross-section (Groenhuis, Webber, and Ruttimann, 1983; van der Stelt et al., 1986).

The high precision of positioning and repositioning the x-ray source with respect to the film and the patient is hardly feasible for a clinician. This problem can be solved by using a computer-controlled robot and patient position–sensing system. Such a system is able to be highly precise with regard to repeatability and measurement. Computer control will provide flexibility in the selection of different imaging procedures. A prototype system has been described to show the feasibility of this approach (Burdea et al., 1991; Levy et al., 1994). The accuracy of such a robot system should be well within the range required for producing standardized subtraction radiographs. A complete robotic system has been built and clinical trials remain to be performed before the idea proposed by Burdea and his colleagues can be fully validated.

Computer assistance in the understanding of jaw function

Computer systems are well suited for handling large amounts of data. This feature can be exploited to integrate diagnostic information contained in large data sets in order to understand the underlying relationships. This information can be used for decision support when the data sets consist of clinical data. Computer systems will integrate this information more effectively than do clinicians, thus increasing the reliability of the treatment planning procedure. Expert systems are just one example of applications wherein large data sets are used to provide clinical decision support (Stheeman, van der Stelt, and Mileman, 1992).

The information contained in the knowledge base is essential for the outcome of the inference process. If the information is incomplete or does not represent all appropriate diagnostic outcomes, then the expert system has no clinical value. Information in knowledge systems is based mostly on textbooks and epidemiologic data (White, 1989). Furthermore, logical relationships between disease patterns and symptoms can be defined in the system (Shortliffe, 1987). Extensive clinical trials are needed to collect the data. Computer simulations, however, may simplify the collection of complete sets of data required for the knowledge base.

In chapter 40, Douglas et al. describe a computer model of the human mandible that facilitates the investigation of strain and stress under various conditions. An artificial mouth was used to obtain accurate measurements in order to gather fairly complete information with regard to the stress distribution in the mandible during different load conditions. The use of models such as the one Douglas et al. describe is very useful for collecting comprehensive data sets. It is essential that the model be a good static and dynamic representation of the structures of interest. The accuracy of the simulation process is better when the conditions and structures contained in the model are described in great detail. However, to be manageable, the computer model must be an abstraction of the real world. In Chapter 40, there is a good description of how to construct a model that is an acceptable representation of the real world and yet not too complicated to be impractical.

Computer-aided manufacturing of dental restorations

Computer-aided design/computer-assisted manufacturing (CAD/CAM) is another interesting application of computer technology in dentistry, especially for the treatment phase (see chapter 41). CAD/CAM systems have been developed to produce crowns, inlays, and onlays. An optical device is used to scan the shape and size of the tooth that has been prepared for a crown or inlay restoration. These measurements replace the conventional dental impression procedure (Schultz et al., 1966). A computer is linked to the scanning device to calculate the 3D reconstruction of the space occupied

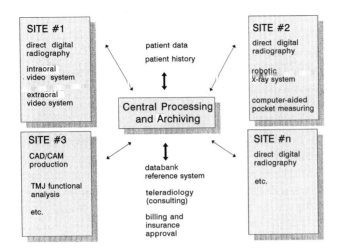

FIGURE 37.2 Possible integration of different computer-aided applications systems for diagnosis and treatment in dentistry. The system comprises not only subsystems for different specialized applications (e.g., CAD/CAM), but also several parallel subsystems for general dental tasks (patient registration, treatment charts, diagnosis, etc.).

by the restoration that is to be made. The computer controls a micromilling machine to grind a solid block of material according to the shape and size calculated by the computer program. The advantage of these systems is that the restorations can be made during one session. There is no need for temporary restorations. The price of these systems is still relatively high due to low volume of production. In a group practice, however, where several dentists will multiplex to it, such a system can be of great help in reducing the time required for a crown or inlay restoration with high quality and possibly lower costs. In this application, the need for standardization and the unique anatomic and functional characteristics of each patient present an interesting challenge.

Conclusion

From the work cited in this chapter, it is obvious that computer technology provides support to dental care. Many other applications exist that are not described herein—for example, systems to determine pocket depth, gingival attachment level, the temperature of the pocket, and biochemical and biophysical parameters such as PO_2 and PCO_2. Most systems monitor the data automatically, and a graphic representation of the measurements is produced to facilitate data interpretation.

Although the applications described in this chapter are stand-alone systems, in the future all applications need to be integrated into one system to facilitate the exchange of information more easily (figure 37.2). This will increase the utility in the dental operating theater. It is clear that much effort still is needed to develop, test, evaluate, and manufacture these integrated systems. Nevertheless, the automated systems already described demonstrate the feasibility of computer-aided diagnosis and treatment.

REFERENCES

BURDEA, G., S. M. DUNN, C. IMMENDORF, and M. MALLIK, 1991. Real-time sensing of tooth position for dental digital subtraction radiography. *IEEE Trans. Biomed. Eng.* 38:366–378.

DOVE, S. B., W. D. MCDAVID, U. WELANDER, G. TRONJE, and C. D. WILCOX, 1992. Design and implementation of an image management and communications system (IMACS) for dentomaxillofacial radiology. *Dentomaxillofac. Radiol.* 21:216–221.

DUCKWORTH, J., P. F. JUDY, J. M. GOODSON, and S. S. SOCRANSKY, 1983. A method for the geometric and densitometric standardization of intraoral radiographs. *J. Periodontol.* 54:435–440.

DUNN, S. M., 1992. An introduction to model-based imaging. *Dentomaxillofac. Radiol.* 21:184–189.

FARMAN, A. G., A. A. FARAG, and P. Y. YEAP, 1992. Communication in digital radiology. *Dentomaxillofac. Radiol.* 21:213–215.

GROENHUIS, R. A. J., R. L. WEBBER, and U. E. RUTTIMANN, 1983. Computerized tomosynthesis of dental tissue. *Oral Surg. Oral Med. Oral Pathol.* 56:206–214.

HALSE, A., and O. MOLVEN, 1986. A strategy for the diagnosis of periapical pathosis. *J. Endodon.* 12:534–538.

LEVY, G., G. BURDEA, S. DUNN, and R. GORATOWSKI, 1994. Robotic control for Dental Subtraction Radiography. In *Proceedings of MRCAS '94*, Pittsburgh, Penn, September 22–24, pp. 334–340.

MOL, A., and P. F. VAN DER STELT, 1992. Application of computer-aided image interpretation to the diagnosis of periapical bone lesions. *Dentomaxillofac. Radiol.* 12:190–194.

PRESTON, J. D., 1993. Computer applications in dentistry. In *Proceedings of the First International Conference on Computer in Clinical Dentistry*. Chicago: Quintessence Books.

RUTTIMANN, U. E., and R. L. WEBBER, 1986. A robust digital method for film contrast correction in subtraction radiography. *J. Periodont. Res.* 21:486–495.

SCHULTZ, L. C., G. T. CHARBENEAU, R. E. DOERR, C. B. CARTWRIGHT, F. W. COMSTOCK, F. W. KAHLER, JR., R. D. MARGESON, D. L. HELLMAN, and D. T. SNYDER, 1966. *Operative Dentistry*. Philadelphia: Lea & Febiger, pp. 131–204.

SHORTLIFFE, E. H., 1987. Computer programs to support clinical decision making. *J.A.M.A.* 258:61–66.

STHEEMAN, S. E., P. F. VAN DER STELT, and P. A. MILEMAN, 1992. Expert systems in dentistry: Past performance—future prospects. *J. Dent.* 28:68–73.

VAN DER STELT, P. F., 1992. Inference systems for automated image analysis. *Dentomaxillofac. Radiol.* 12:180–183.

VAN DER STELT, P. F., R. L. WEBBER, U. E. RUTTIMANN, and R. A. J. GROENHUIS, 1986. A procedure for reconstruction and enhancement of tomosynthetic images. *Dentomaxillofac. Radiol.* 15:11–18.

WHITE, S. C., 1989. Computer-aided differential diagnosis of oral radiographic lesions. *Dentomaxillofac. Radiol.* 18:53–59.

38 Direct Intraoral Digital Radiography in Dentistry

PAUL F. VAN DER STELT AND
GERARD C. H. SANDERINK

FOR MANY YEARS, film has been the only medium to register radiographic images on a permanent base. The rapid advances of computer technology in the last decade have considerably affected radiography in medicine as well as in dentistry. Four systems now are available commercially to acquire intraoral digital images comparable to conventional dental radiographs (table 38.1, figure 38.1). These systems have several advantages over conventional film-based radiography. However, there are drawbacks as well. In this chapter, film-based radiography and direct digital radiography will be compared, with special emphasis on the diagnostic performance of these imaging modalities. The possible directions for future developments will be discussed, including those of computer-aided diagnostic support and teleradiology.

Principles of direct intraoral digital radiography

In digital radiography, image acquisition is performed by means of a charge-coupled device (CCD) chip instead of the conventional x-ray film. The x-ray image that exists as spatially distributed intensity differences of the radiation after passing through the patient is acquired by the cells of the CCD chip and converted into an electronic signal that can be stored in a computer. In some systems, the x-ray image first is converted into a light image by a radiosensitive luminescent screen. The CCD chip then is activated by the light image. The width of the sensitive area of the CCD chip is approximately 20 mm and the height is between 24 and 29 mm. The number of pixels in this area ranges from 134×203 to 385×576. It is clear that the active area of the sensors is much smaller than conventional dental films. Only one molar or two bicuspids or front teeth can be imaged at the same time. This is a major drawback of direct digital radiography

at the moment, because lesions remain undetected when they fall outside the small image area.

The projection technique is similar in principle to the techniques used for film-based radiography. As in conventional dental radiography, specially designed aiming devices to facilitate reproducible registration of the sensor parallel to the teeth and perpendicular to the x-ray beam will give more standardized results (figure 38.2).

Digital images can be stored on disk. To accommodate many image files that are large, optical disks will be a better alternative, although prices are still prohibitive for routine applications.

Standard images have an eight-bit gray-level resolution. The images are displayed on a separate video monitor or on the screen of the computer monitor (figure 38.3). The monitor must be capable of reproducing the contrast and details of the digital images. Therefore, a super-VGA monitor is required when the images are displayed on the computer monitor screen.

Current systems

In the Trophy RadioVisioGraphy (RVG) system, the x-rays first hit the entrance screen (Mouyen et al., 1989; Mouyen, 1991). In this screen, radiation energy is converted into light energy. The light image is transferred to the CCD chip using a 2D array of optic fibers. The image may be slightly distorted at the borders because of the optic fiber (figure 38.4), but this distortion has no significant effect on the diagnostic image quality in normal situations (see also "Resolution," below).

The Flash-Dent system uses a set of small optical lenses to conduct the light of the entrance screen to the CCD image sensor (Flash-Dent, 1992). These optical components make the intraoral part of this system more bulky than the other systems. In both systems,

TABLE 38.1

Overview of commercially available intraoral digital x-ray systems

System and type of sensor	Dimensions (mm)
Trophy (France): RadioVisioGraphy (scintillation screen + fiberoptics + conventional CCD)	19 × 28
Villa (Italy): Flash-Dent (scintillation screen + lenses + conventional CCD)	20 × 24
Regam (Sweden): Sens-a-Ray (directly exposed CCD chip)	17 × 26
Gendex (Italy): Visualix (directly exposed CCD chip)	18 × 24
Dental film (for comparison)	
No. 1	24 × 40
No. 2	31 × 41

Note: For comparison, the dimensions of conventional dental films are given as well.

(a)

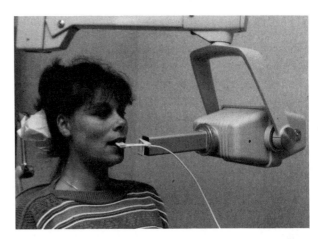

FIGURE 38.2 Intraoral digital imaging sensor utilizing a beam guiding instrument and rectangular open-ended tube to reduce radiation field size.

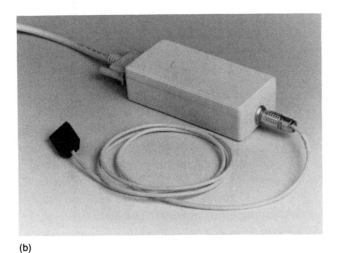

(b)

FIGURE 38.1 Complete intraoral digital radiography system (a) and the sensor (b).

the optical components protect the CCD chip from direct radiation, which could damage the electronic parts. It is, however, not known whether this risk also exists at low radiation doses, such as in diagnostic radiography.

The CCD sensor of the Regam system is radiation-resistant (Nelvig, Welander, and Wing, 1991). It is therefore possible to activate the sensor directly by the x-rays without intermediate light-emitting entrance screens. Another advantage is that the overall dimensions of the intraoral part are smaller than those of the other systems, whereas the sensitive area is the same or even larger. The Gendex Visualix system has a similar

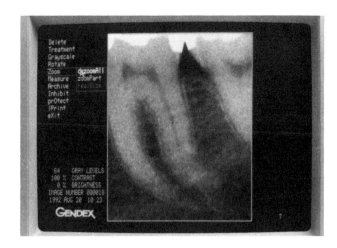

FIGURE 38.3 Example of a digital dental radiograph (zoom mode, using the full-screen height to display the image).

FIGURE 38.4 Distortion caused by the tapered fibers of an intraoral x-ray sensor system. Not all lines are straight and parallel.

design (Molteni, 1992). Table 38.1 gives an overview of the systems and their design.

Comparison with film

IMAGE CHARACTERISTICS

The image quality of dental film as used for intraoral radiographs is very high. It is questionable whether this high quality is necessary for most diagnostic tasks. The answer to this question is most important because image quality of most digital systems is less than that of dental film. Later the diagnostic performance of direct digital systems is addressed. In this section, some parameters for image quality are presented.

CONTRAST Film is an analog medium and therefore is able to render a continuous gray scale of an infinite number of gray levels. The gray level at a specific location of the film is given by the density, which is expressed as the negative logarithm of the ratio of the transmitted light intensities and the amount of incident light at that location:

$$D = -\log(I_t/I_i) \qquad (1)$$

where I_i is the intensity of the original light beam and I_t is the amount that passes through the film. In clinical radiographs, the range of gray levels extends from 0 (completely translucent) to 3 or 4 (completely black). Higher values have no clinical meaning, because the eye is not able to see gray-level contrasts at this level.

The density of digital images cannot simply be defined by measuring the amount of transmitted light. During the process of digitization, the spatial intensity differences in the x-ray image are converted into discrete numbers. These numbers normally range from 0 to 255, where 0 means completely black and 255 totally white. Therefore, density in a digital image is expressed as a number between 0 and 255.

It should be emphasized here that the number of gray levels displayed on the screen is sometimes less although the number of gray levels in the image file may be 255. The eye is capable of recognizing roughly 100 different gray levels, which means that the gray-level resolution of digital systems is not the limiting factor when small contrast differences must be detected. However, there are systems that use only 64 gray levels on the display side, which may be too low to show small details that have very little contrast.

As in standard film processing, care should be taken to use the full dynamic range of the digital imaging system. Underexposure or overexposure may result in a density distribution that does not cover all (or almost all) possible values between 0 and 255. It is clear that this will result in loss of information. The gray-level histogram can be easily utilized to check the full dynamic range of gray levels.

RESOLUTION In film-based radiography, the resolution of the system is affected by the size of the silver-bromide grains in the sensitive layer of the film. In digital systems, the spatial resolution depends on the number of pixels per millimeter in the CCD sensor and on the dimensions of the image memory. Because the number of pixels per row and column in the CCD chip generally is not the same as that of the image memory, aliasing may occur that will detoriate the effective resolution characteristics of the total system. Measurements of the performance of intraoral digital systems have shown that the effective spatial resolution is between 4 and 10 line pairs per millimeter (LP/mm), whereas conventional dental film is able to reproduce at least 10 LP/mm.

The connection between the input screen and the entrance surface of the CCD chip consists of tapered optic fibers or optical lenses. This connection may cause problems that are typical for this design. The optical components may produce distortion in the resulting digital image that cannot easily be corrected for (see figure 38.4). Especially when further image processing is required, the result may be degraded by these effects.

DOSE COMPARISON

Manufacturers of intraoral sensors always claim that these devices will give a considerable reduction of the patient dose. To some extent, this is true. However, most manufacturers take only the exposure time into account, though other factors are important as well. Among the most important are the field size and the number of exposures to give the required information.

EXPOSURE   Intraoral digital sensors are more sensitive to radiation than is conventional dental film. The relative exposure required to produce digital images is given in table 38.2. This table shows that intraoral sensors need an exposure that is only 30–40% of the exposure of E-speed film. However, this dose reduction can be obtained only when the digital system is used in standard mode. The high-resolution mode that some

TABLE 38.2

Relative exposure of intraoral digital imaging systems as compared to Kodak Ektaspeed (E-speed) film

System	Relative exposure (%)
E-speed film	100
Radiovisiography model 3200	40
High-resolution mode	160
Flash-Dent	40
High-resolution mode	80
Sens-a-Ray	40
Visualix	30

systems have requires a higher dose; for example, the Trophy RVG model 32000 in high-resolution mode requires a dose even higher than the dose for E-speed film.

BEAM SIZE   Because the size of the CCD sensor is smaller than that of intraoral film, the beam size can be further reduced in intraoral digital radiography. The beam size for conventional film-based radiography is approximately 28 cm^2 for a circular tube and 12 cm^2 for a rectangular tube. The field size can be reduced to approximately 19 × 29 mm (approx. 5.5 cm^2) for intraoral sensors. As a result, the dose for intraoral sensors will be lowered by a factor of 0.2–0.45. This does not take into account the number of radiographs that have to be retaken because of misalignment (cone cutting). The small field size will make it difficult to obtain the correct beam projection in all circumstances. However, the small field size will make less significant the dose increase due to retakes. Because of the limited size of the CCD sensors, it can be difficult to obtain a clear overview of the region of interest. Only two teeth are depicted at the same time in one image (and in the molar region, only one). In contrast, conventional films show four or five teeth on one image. Therefore, compared to conventional radiography, more images have to be obtained to show the same area. This reduces, to some extent, the effects of lower exposure and smaller beam size. It is difficult to estimate the number of digital exposures required to give the same information as a set of dental films. This depends largely on the diagnostic purpose of the radiographic survey. When only one tooth has to be examined, the number of images required is the same. When information about a full quadrant is needed, however, the number of digital images probably is six to eight, compared to four conventional films.

EFFECTIVE DOSE REDUCTION   The actual dose reduction when using intraoral digital sensors, as compared to conventional radiographs, depends on the dose per exposure as well as the field size and the number of images required for a specific radiographic examination. The relative dose for direct digital radiography can be estimated by the following:

$$D_{actual} = C_{exposure} \times O_{field} \times N_{dig/film} \times D_{film} \quad (2)$$

where D_{actual} = the dose of a set of digital images (unit: mSv); $C_{exposure}$ = the ratio of the dose per exposure for a digital radiographic image and the dose for a conventional radiograph; O_{field} = the size of the irradiated field for the digital radiograph as compared to the usual field size for conventional radiographs; $N_{dig/film}$ = the ratio of the number of images required to cover the same anatomic region or to produce the same amount of information as a set of conventional radiographs of that region; and D_{film} = the dose for a conventional radiograph of the same region of interest (unit: mSv).

Based on the values given for each of these parameters in the previous paragraphs and in table 38.2, the minimum and maximum relative dose for digital imaging can be estimated. The minimum dose (under ideal conditions) is, according to equation 2:

$$D_{actual} = 0.3 \times 0.2 \times 1 \times D_{film}(mSv)$$
$$= 0.06 \times D_{film}(mSv) \qquad (3)$$

A more pragmatic estimation for less ideal conditions gives:

$$D_{actual} = 0.4 \times 0.45 \times 2.0 \times D_{film}(mSv)$$
$$= 0.36 \times D_{film}(mSv) \qquad (4)$$

A dose reduction factor of 0.06–0.36 can therefore be realized when digital radiography is applied instead of conventional film techniques. Note that the high-resolution mode requires a higher exposure, resulting in a relative dose that is nearly one and a half times as high as the dose for a conventional radiographic examination.

Other factors may influence these results, and the effects of such factors are more difficult to estimate. The fact that errors are more easily (and therefore more effectively) corrected when direct intraoral radiography is used may increase the effect of dose reduction. On the contrary, the clinician may be tempted to make more exposures as a result of the instantaneous availability of digital images, whereas the time needed to develop conventional radiographs will discourage the dentist from taking more radiographs than necessary. More research is needed to gain more insight into these effects, because they determine the final dose reduction of digital radiography as compared to film-based radiography.

Diagnostic requirements

Several studies have been published concerning the diagnostic performance of intraoral digital radiographic systems. In most studies, the performance of the digital system is compared with conventional intraoral film, usually Kodak Ultraspeed (D-speed) film or Kodak Ektaspeed (E-speed) film. Digital systems can be very helpful during endodontic treatment in determining the length of the root canal, because there is no need to interrupt the endodontic procedure for film processing. Endodontic instruments, in order to reach the end of the root canal, are very thin. It is essential that the tip of the instrument in the image be recognized and located with respect to the end of the root canal. The RVG system in high-resolution mode is able to produce results that are comparable to those obtained using E-speed films. In normal mode, the image quality is slightly inferior (Shearer, Horner, and Wilson, 1991; Walker et al., 1991). In another study (Sanderink et al., 1992), the Visualix system did not perform as well as the RVG system and Ektaspeed film when no. 15 files were used. Using no. 10 files, the Visualix was slightly better than the RVG, but both systems were inferior to Ektaspeed film. These results show that image quality parameters do not simply predict the diagnostic performance of a system. In this case, the characteristics of contrast and resolution of both systems cause the differences in performance. The RVG system utilizes an intensifying screen to convert the x-ray image into a light image, which then is recorded by the CCD chip. The intensifying screen increases image contrast. The Visualix CCD chip is stimulated directly by the radiation, which produces images with lower contrast. Bar pattern tests show that resolution of the Visualix is better than that of the RVG. The lower resolution of the RVG system is demonstrated by the lower performance for no. 10 files as compared to no. 15 files. The resolution of the Visualix in principle is adequate to depict no. 10 files; these results are comparable to the performance of Kodak Ektaspeed film. However, the higher contrast of the RVG system gives it an advantage over the Visualix at lower spatial frequencies, as demonstrated by the results for the no. 15 files. Wenzel et al. (1991) found no difference between the RVG system and E-speed film for the detection of caries. Sanderink et al. (1992) found a lower image quality for the RVG system when using the normal mode, whereas for the high-resolution mode, the differences were not significant.

The magnification of digital images is very different from the magnification found in conventional radiographs. Normal exposure techniques in dentistry will produce radiographic images that have almost no magnification or distortion. The intraoral sensors in some systems, however, make use of tapered optical fibers or lenses to transduce the image on the input screen to the CCD and to reduce the size of the image to fit on the CCD chip. The display of the image on the monitor screen introduces another magnification factor. Electronic millimeter grids and rulers may help to show the amount of magnification with regard to sensor. These tools, however, do not help to compensate for distortion when object and sensor are not parallel or to show the magnification that occurs in other parts of the imaging chain.

Digital image processing

An important difference between film-based radiography and digital radiography is the option of computer-aided image processing that is provided by digital radiography. Image processing can be used for different purposes. The most important applications are image correction and image enhancement, digital subtraction radiography, image analysis, and image reconstruction.

IMAGE CORRECTION AND IMAGE ENHANCEMENT

The contrast and density of underexposed images can be corrected to some extent. Methods have been described to correct the density distribution of one image relative to a reference image (Ruttiman and Webber, 1986). These methods are very helpful to obtain standardized images. Contrast enhancement and edge enhancement appear to give better results for some diagnostic tasks (Wenzel et al., 1991).

SUBTRACTION RADIOGRAPHY AND IMAGE SEGMENTATION

One of the first applications of digital imaging in dental radiography was digital subtraction radiography. For subtraction radiography, a pair of images is required to be obtained at different times (e.g., to show disease progress). Subtraction radiography also is useful to monitor treatment effects.

The principle of subtraction radiography is that unchanged structures in the two images are canceled out, thus improving the visibility of changes that have occurred after the first image was made (Gröndahl and Gröndahl, 1983; Gröndahl, Gröndahl, and Webber, 1983). Anatomic structures that may hinder the detec-

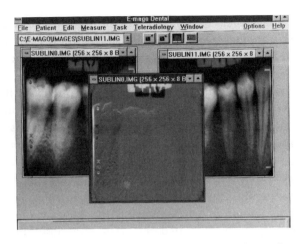

FIGURE 38.5 Example of an integrated imaging software package for digital radiography in dentistry. Several images can be viewed and analyzed at the same time. (Courtesy of E-mago/SOD.)

tion of bone changes in periodontal disease are removed. Only the loss of bone (or the growth of bone, when the defect is healing) will show up in the subtraction image.

Subtraction radiography requires two images having identical projection geometry. To obtain identical imaging geometry, mechanical devices usually are needed to connect the x-ray source, the patient, and the film rigidly. Generally, individual bite-blocks connected to the x-ray apparatus are used to position film-holding devices reproducibly in the mouth. This method is inconvenient for the patient and cumbersome for the dentist. Problems arise, however, when restorations are replaced. To overcome these problems, software-based methods have been developed that enable the reconstruction of an image according to the projection geometry of another image that serves as the reference image (Yen, Dunn, and van der Stelt, 1990; Dunn and van der Stelt, 1992) (figure 38.5).

IMAGE ANALYSIS

The usefulness of image segmentation based on the thresholding of density values is limited. The spatial distribution of the density values in the radiographic image represents the amount of absorption of radiation along the path between the focal spot and each position on the film. The radiation absorption depends on the thickness, type, and density of the material through which the radiation passes on its way to the film. This means that no simple relationship exists between the local density on the radiograph and the 3D structures in the object that is radiographed. More complicated image-processing techniques are needed to separate different entities in the radiographic image.

Image analysis is based mostly on higher-order information that is contained in the image. A priori knowledge is used in advanced image analysis applications. The interpretation and analysis of images can be improved by adding clinical information about the patient and general knowledge of anatomic structures and pathologic processes. This kind of image analysis is, in fact, a combination of image-based feature extraction and expert systems. The implementation of expert system techniques is essential to overcome the lack of information when only the local density distribution in the image is used to interpret the radiographic image. This approach more or less resembles the manner in which human observers interpret the radiographic image.

Several applications of advanced image analysis have been reported in the literature (Pitts and Renson, 1986; Mol and van der Stelt, 1991; van der Stelt and Geraets, 1991). The results of these procedures vary but appear very promising. The purpose of these applications is not to replace the clinician but rather to support him or her in making the diagnosis. Knowledge-based image analysis methods will suggest the most plausible diagnoses to the dentist, but it is the dentist who makes the final decision (Stheeman, van der Stelt, and Mileman, 1992).

IMAGE RECONSTRUCTION

Image reconstruction is another advantage of digital imaging over film-based radiography. The reconstruction of an image such that the projection geometry is similar to the projection geometry of a reference image has already been mentioned. Tomosynthesis is still being developed to make it feasible under clinical conditions. There is no doubt that this method will have great impact on the diagnostic information that can be obtained from radiography. A limited set of images will be sufficient to produce tomographic views of the object. No new radiographs will have to be taken to make other cross-sectional views when desired (Groenhuis, Webber, and Ruttimann, 1983; van der Stelt et al., 1986).

Clinical applications

At this moment, the main advantage of direct intraoral digital imaging is the fact that the images are instantaneously available. There is no need to wait for film processing. Misangulation of the x-ray beam can immediately be corrected while the x-ray tube and the CCD sensor are still in place. This makes it easier to find the correct angulation of the x-ray beam.

The overall density of underexposed images can be corrected digitally most of the time. Often overexposed images can be corrected as well. This will help reduce the number of retakes.

Clinical areas that may benefit from direct imaging capabilities are endodontics, oral surgery, and periodontology (Bragger, 1988; Bragger et al., 1989). Once larger CCD chips become feasible and more advanced image-processing facilities are available, then other clinical applications are conceivable, such as diagnosis of caries and the quantitative assessment of bone quality.

Subtraction radiography has been shown to be very useful for many clinical applications, among them the early diagnosis of caries (Halse, White, and Espelid, 1990), periodontal bone resorption and repair (Okano et al., 1990), and periapical bone lesions (Kullendorf et al., 1988). Several studies prove the usefulness of digital image processing for the evaluation of dental implants (Engelke, de Valk, and Ruttimann, 1990; Bragger et al., 1992; Jeffcoat, 1992). A more specific application is the use of image-processing techniques to quantify the structure of bone.

Future trends

It is clear that digital radiography in dentistry is still in its infancy. An important issue that has to be solved is the question of which standard to choose for dental digital imaging. Many standards exist, relating mostly to the file format and to communication protocols. It is not decided yet what information should be included in the image data file with regard to the sensor dimensions, the zoom factor, the image size, and possibly still other pertinent data. It is not necessary to define a separate imaging standard for dental radiography, but it is essential that industry and developers agree on how to implement the required information in the existing image file standards.

Only when these problems are solved can the development of advanced image interpretation procedures be effective. Now different standards will require too much programming effort to be useful.

In the future (perhaps the near future), the digital acquisition of images will be followed by computer-based image enhancement and image analysis. Several applications have already been developed and tested in the laboratory, aimed at the objective diagnosis of oral pathology. Among these applications are the automated detection of periapical radiolucencies, angular bone defects, proximal and occlusal caries defects, and the assessment of bone quality. Some of these procedures simply but effectively help the clinician to obtain measurements and gather diagnostic information; others are able to perform the diagnostic procedure rather independently. Systems that belong to this second group make use of methods known from expert systems and artificial intelligence (Stheeman, van der Stelt, and Mileman, 1992).

When the radiographic image is digitally formatted, it is easy to send it to another site by electronic mail or via the public phone system. Thereby, the dentist can access remote facilities for diagnostic support provided by expert centers. The expert can send his or her reply almost immediately back to the dentist, who can continue treatment. Another implementation is the office-wide availability of the same radiographic information. All radiographic images are stored on a central computer and are accessible in each of the operating theaters by a local area network within the dental office (Dove et al., 1992; Farman, Faraq, and Yeap, 1992; van der Stelt, 1992).

Conclusions

It is clear that the direct intraoral digital radiography systems now on the market are only the beginning of new developments. In terms of image quality, the systems provide a reasonable alternative to film-based radiography. The flexibility, however, of radiographic film with regard to the size of the sensitive area, and the convenient way of displaying multiple film-based images at the same time, remain superior to digital radiology.

There is a strong need for advanced image-processing techniques to support the interpretation of radiographic images. Computer technology will be able to support the diagnostic process to a large extent in the future.

Much clinical research is still needed before these systems can be introduced in general practice and used on a routine base.

REFERENCES

BRAGGER, U., 1988. Digital imaging in periodontal radiography. *J. Clin. Periodontol.* 15:551–557.

BRAGGER, U., W. BURGIN, I. FOURMOUSSIS, and N. P. LANG, 1992. Image processing for the evaluation of dental implants. *Dentomaxillofac. Radiol.* 21:208–212.

BRAGGER, U., L. PASQUALI, H. WEBER, and K. KORNMAN, 1989. Computer-assisted densitometric analysis for the assessment of alveolar bone density changes in furcations. *J. Clin. Periodontol.* 16:42–52.

DOVE, S. B., W. D. MCDAVID, U. WELANDER, G. TRONJE, and C. D. WILCOX, 1992. Development and implementation of an image management and communications system (IMACS) for dental maxillofacial radiology. *Dentomaxillofac. Radiol.* 21:216–221.

DUNN, S., and P. F. VAN DER STELT, 1992. Recognizing invariant geometric structure in dental radiographs. *Dentomaxillofac. Radiol.* 21:142–148.

ENGELKE, W., S. DE VALK, and U. RUTTIMANN, 1990. The diagnostic value of subtraction radiography in the assessment of granular hydroxyapatite implants. *Oral Surg. Oral Med. Oral Pathol.* 69:636–641.

FARMAN, A. G., A. A. FARAQ, and P. Y. YEAP, 1992. Communication in digital radiology. *Dentomaxillofac. Radiol.* 21: 213–215.

Flash-Dent (product brochure) 1992. Buccinasco, Italy: Villa Sistemi Medicali.

GROENHUIS, R. A. J., R. L. WEBBER, and U. E. RUTTIMANN, 1983. Computerized tomosynthesis of dental tissues. *Oral Surg. Oral Med. Oral Pathol.* 56:206–214.

GRÖNDAHL, H.-G., and K. GRÖNDAHL, 1983. Subtraction radiography for diagnosis of periodontal bone lesions. *Oral Surg. Oral Med. Oral Pathol.* 55:208–213.

GRÖNDAHL, H.-G., K. GRÖNDAHL, and R. L. WEBBER, 1983. A digital subtraction technique for dental radiography. *Oral Surg. Oral Med. Oral Pathol.* 55:96–102.

HALSE, A., S. C. WHITE, and I. ESPELID, 1990. Visualization of stannous treatment of carious lesions by subtraction radiography. *Oral Surg. Oral Med. Oral Pathol.* 69:378–381.

JEFFCOAT, M. K., 1992. Digital radiology for implant treatment planning and evaluation. *Dentomaxillofac. Radiol.* 21: 202–207.

KULLENDORF, B., K. GRÖNDAHL, M. ROHLIN, and C. O. HENRIKSON, 1988. Subtraction radiography for the diagnosis of periapical bone lesions. *Endodont. Dent. Traumatol.* 4:253–259.

MOL, A., and P. F. VAN DER STELT, 1991. Application of digital image analysis in dental radiography for the description of periapical bone lesions. *IEEE Trans. Biomed. Eng.* 38:357–359.

MOLTENI, R., 1992. Visualix, a new system for direct dental x-ray imaging: A preliminary report. *Dentomaxillofac. Radiol.* 21:222.

MOUYEN, F., 1991. The possibilities of the latest RVG 32000. *Dentomaxillofac. Radiol. Suppl.* 11:83.

MOUYEN, F., C. BENZ, E. SONNABEND, and J. LODTER, 1989. Presentation and physical evaluation of radiovisiography. *Oral Surg. Oral Med. Oral Pathol.* 68:238–242.

NELVIG, P., U. WELANDER, and K. WING, 1991. Sens-A-Ray: A new system for direct digital intraoral radiography. *Oral Surg. Oral Med. Oral Pathol.* 72:621–626.

OKANO, T., T. MERA, M. OHKI, I. ISHIKAWA, and N. YAMADA, 1990. Digital subtraction of radiographs in evaluating alveolar bone changes after initial periodontal therapy. *Oral Surg. Oral Med. Oral Pathol.* 69:258–262.

PITTS, N. B., and C. E. RENSON, 1986. Image analysis of biting radiographs: A histologically validated comparison with visual assessments of radiolucency depth in enamel. *Br. Dent. J.* 160:205–209.

RUTTIMAN, U. E., and R. L. WEBBER, 1986. A robust digital method for film contrast correction in subtraction radiography. *J. Periodont. Res.* 21:486–495.

SANDERINK, G. C. H., S. E. STHEEMAN, R. HUISKENS, and D. CHIN, 1992. An ROC-study on image quality in determining root-canal length, comparing RVG, Visualix and Ektaspeed film. *Dentomaxillofac. Radiol.* 21:222.

SHEARER, A. C., K. HORNER, and N. H. F. WILSON, 1991. Radiovisiography for length estimation in root canal treatment: an in vivo comparison with conventional radiography. *Int. End. J.* 24:233–239.

STHEEMAN, S. E., P. F. VAN DER STELT, and P. A. MILEMAN, 1992. Expert systems in dentistry: Past performance—future prospects. *J. Dent.* 20:68–73.

VAN DER STELT, P. F., 1992. Improved diagnosis with digital radiography. *Curr. Opin. Dent.* 2(4):1–6.

VAN DER STELT, P. F., and W. G. M. GERAETS, 1991. Computer-aided interpretation and quantification of angular periodontal bone defects on dental radiographs. *IEEE Trans. Biomed. Eng.* 18:334–338.

VAN DER STELT, P. F., R. L. WEBBER, U. E. RUTTIMANN, and R. A. J. GROENHUIS, 1986. A procedure for reconstruction and enhancement of tomosynthetic images. *Dentomaxillofac. Radiol.* 15:11–18.

WALKER, A., K. HORNER, J. CZAJKA, and N. H. F. WILSON, 1991. Quantitative assessment of a new dental imaging system. *Br. J. Radiol.* 64:529–536.

WENZEL, A., H. HINTZE, L. MIKKELSEN, and F. MOUYEN, 1991. Radiographic detection of occlusal caries in non-cavitated teeth. *Oral Surg. Oral Med. Oral Pathol.* 71:621–626.

YEN, L., S. M. DUNN, and P. F. VAN DER STELT, 1990. Finding invariant anatomical relationship in dental radiographs. *Proc. IEEE/EMBS* 12:2076–2077.

39 Robotic Control of Intraoral Radiography

STANLEY M. DUNN, GRIGORE C. BURDEA, AND
ROBERT GORATOWSKI

DENTAL RADIOGRAPHS are one of the most widely used diagnostic tools in dentistry. This remains true in spite of the inherent limitation that they provide only a 2D projection (i.e., view) of the area of interest. For many disease processes, this 2D view is sufficient to allow the practitioner to characterize the pathology and initiate a treatment plan. For example, to detect the presence or absence of lesions, one need only look for intensity changes in the film (or image, if it has been digitized).

However, as dental health has improved, the emphasis has shifted toward early detection of disease, which requires more exacting instruments. Nowhere is this more evident than in the diagnosis and treatment of periodontal disease. The goal is to be able to detect, as early as possible, small changes in the bony structure supporting the tooth. If such changes are not caught in time, the result can be tooth loss and continued oral health problems. Studies have shown that dental practitioners can detect disease earlier and with greater accuracy by looking at the differences between radiographs taken over time than by viewing a single radiograph. This "subtraction" technique can be done optically, by aligning films, or digitally, by digitizing each film and then subtracting corresponding picture elements to compute a difference image. With the advent of personal computers and low-cost imaging systems, most of the work can be done digitally.

This process presents a unique imaging problem. The two radiographs must enclose the same field of view of the mouth and must be taken with the same geometry. If they are not, then the radiographs cannot be subtracted meaningfully. The purpose of subtraction is to eliminate the anatomic features not of interest, the so-called *structured noise* in the image. If the imaging geometry is not the same, the visual appearance of the structured noise will differ and the difference between the images will not be zero, yielding a false positive difference.

The goal must be to produce standardized views of the area of interest. Much work to date has been done on mechanical devices to fix the object (i.e., the patient) and the imaging device (x-ray source) in position; a description of relevant work is given in the next section of the chapter. The goal of our research is to continue to study an approach to this problem that does not require fixing the patient in position relative to the x-ray source. The proposed approach is based on accurately positioning the x-ray source and then recognizing 3D properties of the objects of interest that are invariant in any view of the object. Once these invariants are recognized and measured in a digital image, the two digital images can be aligned to produce standardized digital images (radiographs). Then an accurate subtraction can be made to remove structured noise.

The impact of this result goes beyond its application to subtraction radiograpy. The same techniques can be used for programmable x-ray tube motion; with known position and orientation of the film (or CCD image sensor) in the patient's mouth, the x-ray source can be moved to a predefined sequence of positions in space relative to the film-recording device. In this way a desired set of projection images can be taken for tomosynthesis or other limited-angle 3D reconstruction techniques.

The section that follows gives some background on the problems of registering clinical radiographs. The

This chapter is based in part on the article, Real-Time Sensing of Tooth Position for Dental Digital Subtraction Radiography, by Grigore C. Burdea, Stanley M. Dunn, Charles H. Immendorf, and Madhumita Mallik (*IEEE Trans. Biomed. Eng.* 38(4):366–378, April 1991).

third section is a description of the mathematics of measuring 3D position. Results of preliminary studies showing the accuracy, reproducibility, and resolution of 3D measurements are shown in the section titled Experimental System and Results, and the final section contains concluding remarks.

Background and significance

Measuring the rate of change of bone loss is one way in which radiology is used to make a measurement of change over time. Two radiographs are taken, each of which records the state of the dentition at a specific time. Because the normal anatomic structure should not change between the two films, any observed differences are indicative of growth or decay in the bony structure. The early studies (Ortman et al., 1985; Rethman et al., 1985) used subtraction to detect lesions between teeth and in the supporting structure of the teeth. The more recent papers (Bragger, 1988; Bragger, Pasquali, and Kornman, 1988; Bragger and Pasquali, 1989; Bragger et al., 1989) cite applications of digital subtraction to measure bone loss and density in the supporting structure of the teeth. Showing the density changes in color (Bragger and Pasquali, 1989) improved the diagnosis agreement among observers. In all cases, however, the application papers point out the difficulty in making the initial measurements, the difficulty in reproducing the original imaging geometry, and the reasons these difficulties limit the usefulness of digital subtraction radiography. The same or similar problems arise in spatially disparate instead of time-disparate image sequences. The correspondence problem is difficult to solve, and the data acquisition should be examined first.

One of the earliest papers in the area, by Webber, Ruttiman, and Grondahl (1982), described the principle that the subtraction process removed "noise"—that is, the unchanged anatomy during the time between the two films. Webber and his colleagues already recognized the requirements of fixing the geometry to produce standardized radiographs, and used a template to fix the mouth in position. Mechanical devices to standardize the imaging geometry were used by Grondahl, Grondahl, and Webber (1983), McHenry and colleagues (1987), and Janssen et al. (1989a). These three studies all used subtraction in trials to quantitate bone loss. Janssen et al. (1989b) found that the digital subtraction system of measurement was the most sensitive to subtle change, in comparison to using a single radiograph or photographic subtraction, but that it required standardized geometry.

In the original subtraction paper by Webber, Ruttiman, and Grondahl (1982), the authors noted that there were four sources of error leading to improper registration of the pair of radiographs: tissue changes, film, x-ray energy, and inexact replication of imaging geometry. The first cannot be controlled, other than by assumptions on the localization of the changes. The second can be controlled by making sure the film type and processing chemicals are identical. Webber, Tzukert, and Ruttiman (1989) later studied the effects of x-ray energy and showed that the effects of energy can be controlled. The remaining problem is that of controlling the imaging geometry.

To date, most approaches to this problem have relied on a model of radiograph formation that utilizes a point projection of x-rays along straight lines through the tissue. The x-rays are attenuated along these diverging straight-line paths and form a distorted image on the film behind the hard tissue. As the source or the film move with respect to the tissue, the appearance of the tissue on the film is changed nonlinearly. Thus, in order to generate radiographs with the same appearance, it is important to reproduce the original imaging geometry. Following this line of reasoning, many studies of the subtraction technique have used mechanical fixtures (Webber, Ruttiman, and Grondahl, 1982; Grondal, Grondahl, and Webber, 1984; Jeffcoat, Jeffcoat, and Williams, 1984; McHenry et al., 1987; Janssen et al., 1989a,b), or compensatory algorithms (Jeffcoat, Jeffcoat, and Williams, 1984; van der Stelt, Ruttiman, and Webber, 1989), or both, to control the imaging geometry (i.e., the position of the point source and the attenuation paths through the tissue).

A good example of a mechanical standardization system for subtraction radiography is given in Jeffcoat, Jeffcoat, and Williams (1984). The x-ray source, the patient, and the film are connected using an occlusal stent and cephalostat. The mechanical connection of the source, object, and film should restrict any variations to in-plane translations and rotations. Matching three anatomic features in the two films allows the translations and rotations to be eliminated. The difficulty is twofold: First, the use of a mechanical fixture or fixed imaging geometry means that the field of view is restricted, which, in subtraction radiography, means that only a limited portion of the dentition can be imaged. Second, disease processes operate in 3D and not in 2D space.

The long-term goal of developing a practical dental digital subtraction radiography system calls for an image formation model and a methodology for using it. The model of invariant relations described by Dunn and van der Stelt (1992) requires only that the tissue of interest appear wholly contained in each of the two films. This is a much weaker constraint than the requirement that the imaging geometry be reproduced exactly, and it can be achieved with simple control of existing radiograph systems. If the location of the patient and the desired imaging geometry are known, then a control system can reposition the x-ray source. This control system to reposition the source need be accurate enough only to guarantee that the tissue of interest will appear on the film. In this chapter, we shall describe the design of such a position-sensing and control system and report on the accuracy of sensing the 3D position of the mouth.

Proposed robotic system for registering serial radiographs

Registering radiographs requires a system that provides good repeatability and accuracy for patient positioning. Present dental subtraction radiography positioning systems are mechanical, uncomfortable for the patient, and impractical for certain tooth positions. We propose to replace present mechanical systems with a sensorized system without a direct mechanical link to the x-ray source. This new system utilizes a robot arm as positioning device that tracks a magnetic sensor attached to the patient's mouth.

Industrial robot systems are presently used in many engineering fields due to their programming flexibility and excellent repeatability. An industrial robot can be viewed as a computer-controlled manipulator consisting of several rigid links connected in series by revolute or prismatic joints (Fu, Gonzalez, and Lee, 1987). One end of the chain of manipulator segments is attached to a fixed supporting base, while the other end is free and equipped with a tool. Most robots have 6 degrees of freedom (dof) and a wrist that can position and orient the attached tool. To adapt to changes in their environment, robots use external sensing data given by vision, touch, force, or other types of sensors. By using these sensor data, robots can change strategies, grasp or release objects, or avoid colliding with obstacles.

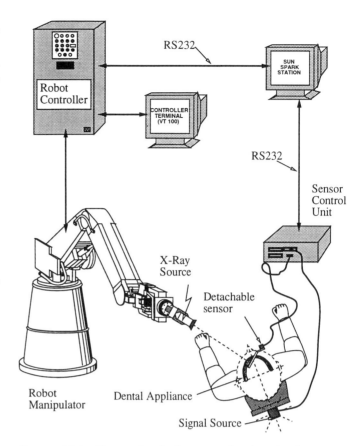

FIGURE 39.1 Proposed robotic system for dental subtraction radiography.

The proposed robotic dental subtraction radiographic system is shown in figure 39.1. The weight of the x-ray source (approximately 20 kg) is within the payload capability of several existing manipulators. The source is mounted directly on the robot wrist, at the end of the manipulator. The symmetry of the x-ray beam can be exploited by aligning the robot wrist rotation axis (roll) with the longitudinal axis of the x-ray source. Due to this symmetry, the rotation angle of the wrist becomes irrelevant. A robot with only 5 dof will suffice for this application, reducing the overall cost of the system.

In intraoral radiography the position of the robot wrist with the attached x-ray source has to change as a function of the patient position. If a sensor can provide the position and orientation of the targeted tooth, then the robot can orient itself to follow that sensor and the tooth. The system utilizes a 6-dof sensor that provides the position and orientation data (x, y, z, roll, pitch, and yaw) necessary to position the robot. A high sensor bandwidth allows for small motions of the patient head to be compensated by the robot in real time.

For real-time tracking of the dentition to be accomplished, the amount of computation performed by the robot controller must be reduced. One way to reduce the amount of computation is to maintain a fixed geometric relationship between tooth and sensor. This patented system (Burdea, Dunn, and Desjardins, 1992) utilizes a mouthpiece that serves as support for both the sensor and the x-ray film. Because the mouthpiece is rigid, the geometric relationship between the sensor and the tooth is fixed no matter how the patient turns his or her head. This relationship is computed off-line and stored in the memory of a host computer such as a PC or SUN workstation (Sun Microsystems Co., Sunnyvale, CA.) which is also part of the system. The host computer downloads the information to the robot controller at the time of subsequent radiographs. Although bone disease may alter the geometry of the mouth over time (many months), the presence of the mouth appliance ensures a constant positioning of the x-ray source versus the film. When very large changes in mouth geometry require a new mouth appliance, the process just described is repeated.

Sensor model

This section provides a model for the position-sensing mechanism as well as the robot target solution. The model is based on the homogeneous transformation technique first proposed by Denavit and Hartenberg (1955). This well-known technique utilizes matrix algebra to represent the spatial geometry of the robot arm with respect to a fixed-reference coordinate system. If the original coordinate system $OXYZ$ is rotated and translated in 3D space to form a new coordinate system $OUVW$, then the vector $\mathbf{p}$ can be transformed between the two coordinate systems through a homogeneous transformation matrix $\mathbf{T}$.

$$\mathbf{p}_{xyz} = {}^{xyz}\mathbf{T}_{uvw}\,\mathbf{P}_{uvw} \qquad (1)$$

$\mathbf{T}$ can be partitioned into two submatrices, namely, the rotation matrix expressing the orientation of the $OUVW$ system versus $OXYZ$, and the position vector of the origin of $OUVW$ in $OXYZ$. Its structure is expressed as

$$ {}^{xyz}\mathbf{T}_{uvw} = \begin{bmatrix} \mathbf{R}_{3\times3} & \mathbf{P}_{3\times1} \\ 0 & 1 \end{bmatrix} \qquad (2) $$

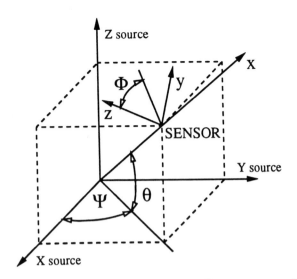

FIGURE 39.2 Sensor and source coordinate systems. (© 1991 IEEE, reprinted with permission.)

where $\mathbf{p} = [p_x, p_y, p_z]^T$. If a series of n rotations and translations are performed between multiple coordinate systems, then a composite homogeneous transformation matrix can be obtained by multiplying the sequence of homogeneous matrices ${}^{i-1}\mathbf{T}_i$, for $i = 1, 2, \ldots, n$.

The position sensor transmits six parameters. The first three are x, y, z, representing the translation between the sensor system of coordinates and its source system of coordinates, as shown in figure 39.2. The other three parameters are ψ, θ, and ϕ: ψ is the rotation of the x and y coordinates about the z axis, θ is the rotation of the z and the rotated x coordinates about the rotated y axis, and ϕ is the rotation of the rotated y and z coordinates about the rotated x axis (Polhemus, 1987).

With these six sensor parameters, the 4×4 transformation matrix ${}^{source}\mathbf{T}_{sensor}$, expressing the position and orientation of the sensor with respect to its source, is given by the following:

$$ {}^{source}\mathbf{T}_{sensor} = \mathbf{T}_{Z,\psi}\,\mathbf{T}_{Y',\theta}\,\mathbf{T}_{X'',\phi}\,\mathbf{T}_{trans} \qquad (3) $$

Another transformation, ${}^{sensor}\mathbf{T}_{tooth}$, expresses the position of the targeted tooth versus the sensor on the dental appliance. This transformation depends on the characteristics of the patient and therefore has to be determined for each patient once the dental appliance is built. The transformation that gives the position of the tooth of interest in source coordinates is as follows:

$$ {}^{source}\mathbf{T}_{tooth} = {}^{source}\mathbf{T}_{sensor}\,{}^{sensor}\mathbf{T}_{tooth} \qquad (4) $$

Although $^{sensor}\mathbf{T}_{tooth}$ is fixed (but patient-dependent), $^{source}\mathbf{T}_{sensor}$ will vary as a function of head position and orientation. In this way, $^{source}\mathbf{T}_{tooth}$ tracks the position of the patient's tooth with respect to the fixed system of coordinates of the source.

ROBOT MODEL

Consider a robot manipulator with n degrees of freedom; $n + 1$ orthonormal Cartesian coordinate systems are assigned to the robot links and base at the joint axes. The transformation $^{base}\mathbf{T}_{wrist}$ that expresses the position and orientation of the robot wrist with respect to the robot base (commonly known as the *arm matrix*) is as follows:

$$^{base}\mathbf{T}_{wrist} = {}^{base}\mathbf{T}_1 \cdots {}^{n-1}\mathbf{T}_{wrist} \qquad (5)$$

Another transformation that is needed is $^{wrist}\mathbf{T}_{x\text{-}ray}$ between the system of coordinates attached to the x-ray source and that attached to the robot wrist. To take advantage of the axial symmetry of the problem, $OX_{x\text{-}ray}Y_{x\text{-}ray}Z_{x\text{-}ray}$ is chosen so that $Z_{x\text{-}ray}$ points toward the wrist and is coaxial with the wrist. The origin of $OX_{x\text{-}ray}Y_{x\text{-}ray}Z_{x\text{-}ray}$ is located at a fixed distance L from the robot wrist, corresponding to the distance to the patient. $^{wrist}\mathbf{T}_{x\text{-}ray}$ then is fixed and given by the following:

$$^{wrist}\mathbf{T}_{x\text{-}ray} = \begin{bmatrix} 1 & 0 & 0 & 0 \\ 0 & -1 & 0 & 0 \\ 0 & 0 & -1 & L \\ 0 & 0 & 0 & 1 \end{bmatrix} \qquad (6)$$

To orient itself, the robot needs to know the patient position given in its own robot coordinates as $^{base}\mathbf{T}_{tooth}$. If the sensor source is placed at a fixed and known location versus the robot base, then the transformation $^{base}\mathbf{T}_{source}$ also is fixed and may be determined by measurements. The position of the patient with respect to the robot then is given thus:

$$^{base}\mathbf{T}_{tooth} = {}^{base}\mathbf{T}_{source}\,{}^{source}\mathbf{T}_{tooth} \qquad (7)$$

The alignment between the x-ray source and the targeted tooth is one of the keys to the reproducibility of the images. One possible solution is for the x-ray source to be aligned perpendicular to the plane of the film, so that the two systems $OX_{x\text{-}ray}Y_{x\text{-}ray}Z_{x\text{-}ray}$ and $OX_{film}Y_{film}Z_{film}$ coincide. This is shown in more detail in figure 39.3.

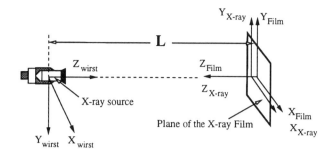

FIGURE 39.3   Alignment of x-ray source and targeted tooth plane.

The alignment condition sufficient to obtain the robot arm position is as follows:

$$^{base}\mathbf{T}_{x\text{-}ray} = {}^{base}\mathbf{T}_{tooth} \qquad (8)$$

or

$$^{base}\mathbf{T}_{wrist}\,{}^{wrist}\mathbf{T}_{x\text{-}ray} = {}^{base}\mathbf{T}_{tooth} \qquad (9)$$

from where:

$$^{base}\mathbf{T}_{wrist} = {}^{base}\mathbf{T}_{tooth}\,{}^{wrist}\mathbf{T}_{x\text{-}ray}^{-1} \qquad (10)$$

where

$$^{wrist}\mathbf{T}_{x\text{-}ray}^{-1} = {}^{x\text{-}ray}\mathbf{T}_{wrist}.$$

This equation represents the solution fed into the robot controller, which in turn determines the robot joint position based on inverse kinematics calculations (Fu, Gonzalez, and Lee, 1987). The solution given by this equation is a static one; to limit the adverse effects of the robot dynamics, it is necessary to have a high bandwidth in the control loop (here the bandwidth of the sensor and of the robot controller are the limiting factors), and relatively small and slow patient head motions. The overall process is shown in figure 39.4.

SOLUTION ACCURACY

The solution is correct to the extent that there are no errors in the overall system. Errors do exist, however, due to several factors such as robot control inaccuracies, sensor-tooth relationships, sensor errors, and errors in measurements that determine the fixed transformations $^{sensor}\mathbf{T}_{tooth}$ and $^{base}\mathbf{T}_{source}$. Such factors compound the overall positioning error, so that $OX_{x\text{-}ray}Y_{x\text{-}ray}Z_{x\text{-}ray}$ will not coincide with $OX_{film}Y_{film}Z_{film}$. The upper bound for the correctable positioning error is the limit with which a projective invariant can be measured in the film, as reported in the study by Dunn and van der

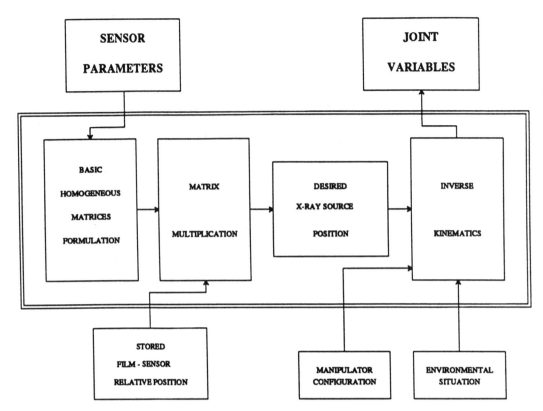

FIGURE 39.4 Inverse kinematics process. (© 1991 IEEE, reprinted with permission.)

Stelt (1992) (xy translation errors of 0–16 mm and rotation errors of 0°–16° about the x, y, or z axis).

To a first approximation the total error Δ_{total} in the solution may be expressed as a function of robot translation error Δ_{rtran}, robot rotation error Δ_{rrot}, and sensor translation error Δ_{stran}:

$$\Delta_{\text{total}} = \Delta_{\text{rtran}} + L \tan(\Delta_{\text{rrot}}) + \Delta_{\text{stran}} \quad (11)$$

Here the effects of the sensor rotation errors (which are small) have been neglected, as have the effects of the errors in measurements that determine the transformations $^{\text{base}}\mathbf{T}_{\text{source}}$ and $^{\text{sensor}}\mathbf{T}_{\text{tooth}}$. Special care must be taken to determine the fixed transformation $^{\text{base}}\mathbf{T}_{\text{source}}$, by precise measurements of the robot and source system of coordinates. Both Δ_{rtran} and Δ_{rrot} are functions of the robot arm's accuracy, which represents the difference between the commanded and actual positions of the robot. These errors vary from manipulator to manipulator and can be as large as 20 mm (Chen and Chao, 1987) (for changes in configuration from "lefty" to "righty") for Δ_{rtran} and 5° for Δ_{rrot}. The fact that in this application the work envelope is relatively small and the robot does not have to change its configuration also helps reduce the positioning errors. These errors can be further significantly reduced through robot calibration and compensation, to approximately 0.3 mm for Δ_{rtran}, for example (Chen and Chao, 1987).

The unknown Δ_{stran} represents the sensor errors, which have to be determined experimentally. If Δ_{stran} is 3 mm and the robot is calibrated so that Δ_{rrot} is 1° and Δ_{rtran} is 1 mm, then the total error Δ_{total} is 14.4 mm for $L = 600$ mm. This error is less than in the condition set up by Dunn and van der Stelt (1992). To verify that the sensor errors satisfy these conditions, a series of experiments were conducted as described in the following section.

Experimental system and results

A feasibility study has been performed at the Robotics Research Laboratory at Rutgers University to determine the accuracy with which we can measure the tooth position and orientation in real time (Burdea et al., 1991). A sensorized mouth appliance has been developed to maintain a fixed geometric relationship between sensor and tooth. This appliance consists of a dental mold, a rigid plastic connecting piece attached to the mold, and a sensor attached to the connecting piece. The plastic connection is designed to accommodate the attachment of the radiographic film at one end and that of the sensor at the other. The sensor is seated outside the mouth and allows the patient to close his or her mouth. This design allows the sensor to be used repeatedly for different patients; the only consumables are the plastic connection and the mouth appliance. The use of the plastic piece also allows the placement of the x-ray film at different locations in the mouth, affording a definite advantage over mechanical stents that allow the subtraction radiography of frontal teeth only. Of course, for different positions in the mouth there will be different connecting pieces. The connecting piece places the sensor away from the x-ray beam so that the sensor wires and electronics are not shown in the image on the film.

Two sets of measurements were taken, one using the Polhemus Isotrack (Polhemus, 1987) and a subsequent one using the Polhemus Fastrack (Polhemus, 1992). Both sensors utilize low-frequency magnetic field technology to determine their position and orientation in relation to a source reference frame. The Isotrack is capable of performing constant monitoring (maximum 60 times per sec) of the position and orientation of an object in 3D space (Polhemus, 1987). The newer Fastrack can perform up to 120 readings per second, with increased accuracy and reduced latency compared to the Isotrack. Data from the magnetic sensors are sampled by an electronic unit that is also connected to the sensor source. This electronic unit is in turn interfaced with a SUN Sparcstation I host computer over an RS232 serial line. The computer is used for programming, data transfer, and analysis.

The sensor and connecting piece were mounted on calibrated blocks and placed at known locations on a nonmetallic table. On the same table was rigidly mounted the sensor source, and the relationship between the block system of coordinates and the sensor system of coordinates was determined through measurements. This transformation then was used to determine the correct position and orientation of the sensor on the experimental table. The sensor readings were compared to the correct values measured off-line in order to determine sensor accuracy and repeatability. The latest data for the Fastrack are shown in figure

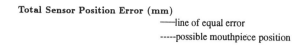

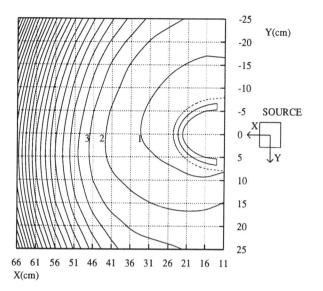

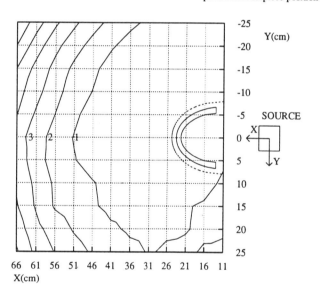

FIGURE 39.5 Fastrack sensor readings over the work envelope.

39.5, for a stationary sensor (the solid line represents the accuracy error data; the dashed line is the possible mouthpiece position). To suppress sensor noise, a number of 1000 readings were made and averaged for each sensor position.

Subsequently, the same series of tests was performed at different locations on the calibration table. These

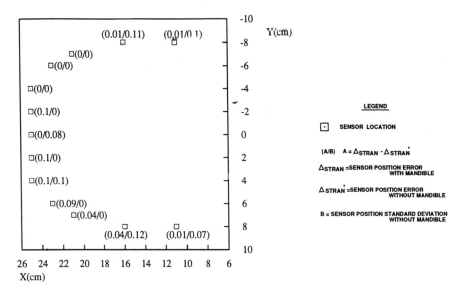

Euclidean Error (mm) of Sensor Measurements

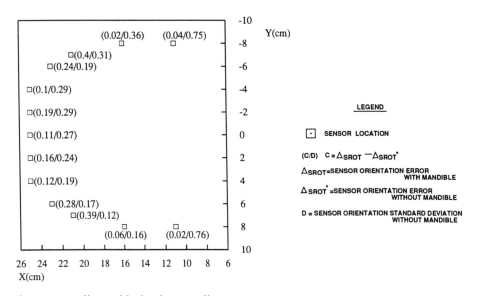

Total Orientation Error (degrees) of Sensor Measurements

FIGURE 39.6 Fastrack sensor readings with the dry mandible with orthodontic metal. (Top) Position errors. (Bottom) Orientation errors.

tests were made to determine whether there is significant degradation of sensor measurements as the distance between sensor and source increases. The optimum sensor range was determined to encompass a greater distance than the sensor will have from the source in the dental applications, when the source is fixed on the back of the x-ray chair or in some other convenient location. Within this range the sensor readings differ by at most 1 mm Euclidean translation and

1° total rotation when compared to the correct values. The larger errors are due to a relatively imprecise calibration table. Thus, the "correct" values had a built-in reading error of approximately 0.5–1.0 mm. According to its manufacturer, the sensor's measurements are not affected by x-rays.

The earlier experimental results on the Isotrack (Burdea, Dunn, and Desjardins, 1992) and the newer Fastrack sensor errors satisfy the constraints set out in the previous section. Under these conditions, Δ_{stran} is 2.5 mm or less for a sensor-to-source distance of 200 mm. This is within the optimal range for the application, so these results are very encouraging. Figure 39.5 shows the Fastrack position and orientation errors over the sensor work envelope.

A second set of measurements were performed to determine whether there is a significant degradation of sensor readings due to the presence of metal (i.e., restorations and orthodontic appliances) in the patient's mouth. An initial set of readings were done for all 6 dof with a dry mandible that had no metal using the Isotrack. These readings showed no difference in data whether the skull was interposed between the source and the sensor block or not (the difference was on the order of the sensor noise). Subsequently, the same mandible was fitted with orthodontic wire and 10 amalgam restorations and the same measurement procedure was applied. Then the same mandible was interposed between the Fastrack and its source. The measured translation error with the mandible present was Δ_{stran}, whereas the same error without the mandible was Δ_{stran^*}. The two sets of data were subtracted and the difference compared with the sensor noise standard deviation at that location. The results, illustrated in figure 39.6 (top), show that there is no significant change in sensor accuracy due to the metal in the mandible. The same test was repeated for sensor rotation errors as shown in figure 39.6 (bottom). The maximum $\Delta_{stran} - \Delta_{stran^*}$ was 0.1 mm, and the maximum noise standard deviation was 0.12 mm. This indicates that there is no adverse influence on sensor accuracy due to the presence of metal in the patient's mouth.

Conclusions

This chapter has described a sensorized dental appliance that allows accurate measurement of targeted tooth position without supplemental mechanical alignment. This sensorized appliance avoids direct mechanical contact with the x-ray source and therefore can be used to image posterior as well as anterior teeth. (Mechanical techniques apply to posterior teeth only.) Initial feasibility tests performed in 1991 at the Robotics Research Laboratory at Rutgers University had encouraging results. These tests were repeated in 1993 using a new-generation sensor with better accuracy. The first test results were thus reconfirmed.

The long-term goal of present research is to realize a complete system that integrates the robot manipulator with an x-ray source. The accuracy of this proposed system will be measured and compared with the model presented in this chapter to identify and eliminate any additional sources of error, including bent film and errors resulting from fitting the mouthguard to teeth that have drifted between radiographic examinations. Finally, results will be compared with measurements of the same bone structure made using present mechanical alignment techniques. Both techniques will benefit from image registration software commonly used today.

ACKNOWLEDGMENTS This research has been supported by National Institute of Dental Research grant 1-RO3-DE10230-01 and by grants from the University of Medicine and Dentistry of New Jersey and the Rutgers University Research Council.

REFERENCES

BRAGGER, U., 1988. Digital imaging in periodontal radiography. *J. Clin. Periodontol.* 15:551–557.

BRAGGER, U., and L. PASQUALI, 1989. Color conversion of alveolar bone density changes in digital subtraction images. *J. Clin. Periodontol.* 16:209–214.

BRAGGER, U., L. PASQUALI, and K. KORNMAN, 1988. Remodeling of interdental alveolar bone after periodontal flap procedures assessed by means of computer-assisted densitometric image analysis (CADIA). *J. Clin. Periodontol.* 15:558–564.

BRAGGER, U., L. PASQUALI, H. WEBER, and K. KORNMAN, 1989. Computer-assisted densitometric image analysis for the assessment of alveolar bone density changes in furcations. *J. Clin. Periodontol.*, 16:42–52.

BURDEA, G., S. DUNN, and P. DESJARDINS, 1992. Apparatus for taking radiographs used in performing dental subtraction radiography with a sensorized dental mouthpiece and a robotic system. U.S. Patent No. 5,113,424.

BURDEA, G., S. DUNN, C. IMMENDORF, and M. MALLIK, 1991. Real-time sensing of tooth position for dental digital subtraction radiography. *IEEE Trans. Biomed. Eng.* 38:366–378.

CHEN, J., and L. CHAO, 1987. Positioning error analysis for robot manipulation with all rotary joints. *IEEE J. Robot. Autom.* 6:539–545.

DENAVIT, J., and R. HARTENBERG, 1955. A kinematic notation for lower pair mechanisms based on matrices. *J. Appl. Mech.*, 77:215–221.

DUNN, S., and P. van der STELT, 1992. Recognizing invariant geometric structure in dental radiographs. *Dentomaxillofac. Radiol.*, 21:142–148.

FU, K., R. GONZALEZ, and C. S. G. LEE, 1987. *Robotics: Control, Sensing, Vision, and Intelligence.* New York: McGraw-Hill.

GRONDAHL, H., and K. GRONDAHL, 1983. Subtraction radiography for diagnosis of periodontal bone lesions. *Oral Surg.*, 55(2):208–213.

GRONDAHL, H., K. GRONDAHL, and R. WEBBER, 1983. A digital subtraction technique for dental radiography. *Oral Surg.* 55(1):96–102.

GRONDAHL, K., H. GRONDAHL, and R. WEBBER, 1984. Influence of variations in projection geometry on the detectability of periodontal bone lesions. *J. Clin. Periodontol.* 11:411–420.

JANSSEN, P., W. VAN PALENSTEIN HELDERMAN, and J. VAN AKEN, 1989a. The detection of in-vitro-produced periodontal bone lesions by conventional radiography and photographic subtraction radiography using observers and quantitative digital subtraction radiography. *J. Clin. Periodontol.* 16:335–341.

JANSSEN, P., W. VAN PALENSTEIN HELDERMAN, and J. VAN AKEN, 1989b. The effect of in-vivo-occurring errors in the reproducibility of radiographs on the use of the subtraction technique. *J. Clin. Periodontol.*, 16:53–58.

JEFFCOAT, M., R. JEFFCOAT, and R. C. WILLIAMS, 1984. A new method for the comparison of bone loss measurements on non-standardized radiographs. *J. Periodont. Res.* 19:434–440.

McHENRY, K., E. HAUSMANN, U. WIKESJO, R. DUNFORD, E. LYON-BOTTENFIELD, and L. CHRISTERSSON, 1987. Methodological aspects and quantitative adjuncts to computerized subtraction radiography. *J. Periodont. Res.* 22:125–132.

ORTMAN, L., R. DUNFORD, K. McHENRY, and E. HAUSMANN, 1985. Subtraction radiography and computer-assisted densitometric analyses of standardized radiographs. *J. Periodont. Res.* 20:644–651.

Polhemus Navigation Sciences Division, 1987. *Space Isotrak User's Manual.* Colchester, Vt.: McDonnell Douglas Electronics Co.

Polhemus Navigation Sciences Division, 1992. *Fastrack User's Manual.* Colchester, Vt.

RETHMAN, M., U. RUTTIMAN, R. O'NEAL, R. WEBBER, A. DAVIS, G. GREENSTEIN, and S. WOODYARD, 1985. Diagnosis of bone lesions by subtraction radiography. *J. Periodont. Res.* 56:324–329.

VAN DER STELT, P., U. RUTTIMAN, and R. WEBBER, 1989. Determination of projections for subtraction radiography based on image similarity measurements. *Dentomaxillofac. Radiol.*, 18:113–117.

WEBBER, R., U. RUTTIMAN, and H-G. GRONDAHL, 1982. X-ray image subtraction as a basis for assessment of periodontal changes. *J. Periodont. Res.* 17:509–511.

WEBBER, R., A. TZUKERT, and V. RUTTIMAN, 1989. The effects of beam hardening on digital subtraction radiography. *J. Periodont. Res.* 24:53–58.

40 Stress and Strain Trajectories in the Human Mandible Using a Servohydraulically Controlled Artificial Mouth

WILLIAM H. DOUGLAS, RALPH DELONG,
JOHN P. BEYER, BRAD LUNACEK, AND
MYER S. LEONARD

THERE ARE A number of reasons for developing and applying an artificial mouth in the study of dentofacial problems in biomaterials and biomechanics. These include the time, cost, and ethical problems involved in the execution of clinical trials. Two areas in particular can benefit from in vitro studies. The first of these is the testing of new biomaterials compositions whose properties may be challenged in an in vitro, clinically simulated environment. The second area of interest includes the assessment of design of appliances and the prosthetic replacement or rigid surgical fixation of fractured hard tissues. If a reasonable clinical simulation of the dentofacial structures can be attained in the laboratory, then significant advances can be made in the validation and development of new materials for dental and maxillofacial surgery.

In the design of an artificial mouth three criteria must be met (DeLong and Douglas, 1991):

1. Control of movement and forces involved in human incision and mastication
2. Provision of anatomic structures with the required form and physiologic properties
3. Provision of environmental factors, such as physiologic temperature, body fluids, and physiologic flora.

A full experimental implementation of an artificial mouth along these lines would be very difficult and probably is not achievable at present. However, such difficulties should not be used as a reason to lapse into extremely simple and unphysiological experimental models. At present, many of the main physiologic and anatomic parameters can be included in an in vitro simulation using an artificial mouth.

A large portion of the research done on dental biomaterials has been concerned with the wear of two articulated surfaces or materials. These studies have been responsible for the development of several experimental methods. For example, wear studies have resulted in a number of pin-on-disk systems (Harrison and Lewis, 1975; Powell and Dickson, 1975; Jaworzyn, Arundel, and Cantwell, 1978), which have difficulty in reproducing the dynamic force and movement of the mandibular teeth and generally do not include the anatomic forms of the teeth. Partial exceptions to these limitations are those systems that were designed to test artificial teeth and therefore use anatomic forms (Cornell et al., 1957; Thomson, 1965).

Experimental studies on the mandible, which have frequently addressed intraoral rigid fixation following surgical reduction of hard tissue fragments, have faced similar difficulties in providing good physiologic models. There has, however, been a clear pattern of progress and a tendency to move closer to the use of anatomic forms in the development of design and proof of appliances for rigid fixation of the mandible (Perren and Rahn, 1980). The chief aim in these studies has been to determine the areas of tensile and compressive strain in the horizontal plane of the mandible before and after rigid fixation of a vertical fracture. In this vein Champy et al. (1976) studied the flexion of a cantilever bar, and Luhr (1982) studied three-point bending, with special reference to the change in areas in tensile strain after the attachment of fixation plates. Champy also calculated bending moments in the mandible, which he found to be smallest anteriorly at the symphyseal line. Conversely, the same author determined the moments of torsion in 20 mandibles and found that the torsion was maximum anteriorly between the canines and minimal posteriorly. The work of Kroon et al. (1991) showed the application of composite mandibles with single-point loads to determine strain distribution relative to rigid surgical fixation designs. As indicated by this brief review, there is a clear trend toward better anatomic simulation in the assessment of mandibular strain under occlusal loading on the teeth.

In the present state of the art, two major areas must be addressed if the current trend toward better simulation in mandibular studies is to be continued. The first is the introduction of a more realistic simulation of the elevator muscles. It is common in the best of the present studies to apply a single load directly to the teeth. However, physiologically the force is applied directly to the mandible via the attachment of the elevator muscles and indirectly via the mandibular teeth when they occlude with the maxillary teeth. The second issue is the establishment of multiple-point loading of the teeth, consistent with the principles of dental occlusal contact. This should be achieved with the mandible not only in its centric position but also in its left and right lateral excursions (horizontal movements) as required by normal chewing. It should also include the mandible in the protrusive edge-to-edge position of the anterior teeth, which is adopted in the incision of food.

Such innovations would clearly have major implications for the determination of strain trajectories in the mandible, especially when it is recalled that the multiple intermaxillary dental contacts will produce changing force vectors as the mandible moves in the horizontal plane. Beginning with the artificial mouth concept of DeLong and Douglas (1991), it is the object of this chapter to resynthesize the principal mandibular forces and movements under servohydraulic control and, by coupling bonded strain gauges, to trace the resulting strain trajectories in a model of the human mandible.

Parameters of mandibular movement

DeLong and Douglas (1991) have reviewed the main parameters of the chewing cycle of the mandible (figure 40.1). They showed that the mandible is con-

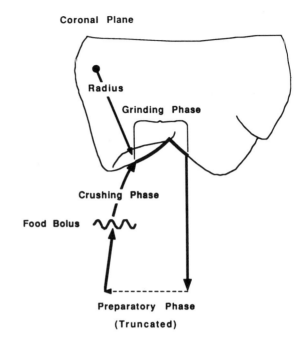

FIGURE 40.1   Three phases of chewing.

trolled by a neuromuscular feedback system and that chewing may be divided into three phases: the preparatory phase, the crushing phase, and the grinding phase. During the preparatory phase, the mandible drops down into position to crush the food bolus. At this stage, the mandibular-maxillary system is relatively flexible in the vertical plane. The only forces to be overcome are the weight of the mandible and the attenuation of the soft tissues. This is essentially an isotonic condition, and the mandible is controlled by position sensors (proprioception) in the muscles and other soft tissues. The servohydraulic equivalent of isotonicity is stroke control. Following this phase, the mandible crushes through the food to reach tooth-to-tooth grinding contact. In tooth contact, the mandibular-maxillary system is quite stiff in the vertical axis, the mandibular force is under isometric conditions, and a new kind of proprioception becomes active in the periodontal membrane. The servohydraulic equivalent of isometric control is load control. As the mandible glides to its centric home position, it is almost entirely controlled by the anatomy of the contacting teeth, which now become the major determinants of mandibular movement.

In summary, the chewing cycle involves, physiologically, an isometric-isotonic mode change. However, the major stresses are induced during the isometric

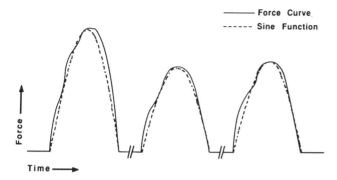

——— Force Curve
----- Sine Function

Force →

Time →

FIGURE 40.2 Representation of a masticatory force profile by a half sine function. (Reprinted with permission from Ahlgren and Owall, 1970.)

phase when the teeth are in contact. The crushing phase of chewing is subject to variable neuromuscular control depending on the consistency of the food. With very soft food the teeth will penetrate the food under mainly isotonic control. Conversely, with very hard food the mandible must induce isometric control to break the food. With food of intermediate consistency a mixed isometric-isotonic control will be induced. Therefore a full implementation of mandibular movement must be capable of resynthesizing three types of control: isometric, isotonic, and mixed. It should be noted, however, that it is under isometric (load) control that the challenging stress must be borne by the dentomandibular structures.

The actual reported values for the force of mastication vary between 9 and 180 N (Anderson, 1956; Nyquist and Owall, 1968; Ahlgren and Owall, 1970; DeBoever, 1978; Helkimo and Ingerwall, 1978; Gibbs, 1981; Lurell, 1985; Hagberg, 1986). The generally accepted value is less than 70 N. The magnitude of the force generated during human mastication as a function of time has been measured by placing strain gauges intraorally in dental restorations of several subjects (Nyquist and Owall, 1968; Ahlgren and Owall, 1970; Lurell, 1985). The shape of the force curve can be approximated by the positive half of a sine wave (figure 40.2). The duration of the forces during the grinding phase when the mandibular and maxillary teeth are in contact is from 0.25 to 0.33 sec (Helkimo and Ingerwall, 1978).

The action of bruxism, which is regarded as habitual and is found in only an estimated 8–12% of the population (Duckro et al., 1990), is performed in the absence of food. It is regarded as parafunctional and

differs from chewing in several respects. It does not involve a mode change and is performed entirely under isometric conditions in the vertical direction. The contact time is variable but generally much longer than the 0.25 seconds per cycle noted for chewing. Bruxing is a grinding back and forth action that is carried from the buccal through the centric position to the lingual position and back again. Typically, chewing stops at the centric position before the cycle begins again. The forces involved in bruxing generally are higher than those exerted in chewing. Bruxing is easier to simulate in the laboratory than chewing, and, as in chewing, the grinding isometric control is challenging to the teeth and mandibular support structures (Jent, Karlsson, and Hedegard, 1979).

Extended artificial mouth concept

The forces and mandibular movements involving the teeth that have been described so far are adequate if the study of stress and strain is to be limited to the crowns of individual teeth, or perhaps if it is extended slightly to include the crowns of several contiguous teeth in a quadrant of the dental arch. Experimental models based on such principles have been described by Douglas, Sakaguchi, and DeLong (1985) and by DeLong et al. (1985), using closed-loop servohydraulics. However, if the study of the distribution of stress and strain is to be extended to the complete dental arches and beyond to the skeletal mandibular support, then the experimental artificial mouth concept (DeLong and Douglas, 1991) must be extended by the following procedures:

1. The provision of an anatomically correct mandible with cortical bone and a spongy medulla and all the correct bony processes.

2. The addition of elevator muscles, especially the masseter-medial pterygoid sling and anterior fibers of the temporalis.

3. The addition of the full mandibular-maxillary occlusion, including the posterior and anterior segments. This should include lateral and protrusive excursions (horizontal movements) that create acceptable dental contacts.

4. Attachment of multiple strain gauges on the buccal surface of the mandible to trace strain distribution.

The extension of servohydraulics to simulate mandibular movement was first propounded theoretically by J. C. Ferre and his colleagues (Ferre et al., 1984a,b). They conceive of the mandible as an overhanging mechanically suspended structure. In the latter study, using what they call a physicomathematic approach and considering patterns of growth and comparative anatomy, they show that the temporomandibular joint (TMJ) is submitted to only minimal pressure under normal function. Ferre and his coworkers are in agreement on this point with Robinson (1946) and submit that the role of the TMJ is as a "centering pin" to guide the complex kinematics when the jaws are open and the teeth are out of occlusion. The corollary of the work of J. C. Ferre is that when the teeth are in contact, they are the main determinants of mandibular movement and force vectors.

Ferre notes that an examination of the anatomic arrangement and orientation of the masticatory musculature leads one to postulate the existence of a virtual muscular suspensory system of the mandible. The elevator muscles are seen to be opposed by the muscles that descend into the neck and make the mandible a suspensory system capable of fine control by sensors in the muscles, joints, and periodontal membranes under servo command. Essentially, as noted above, this command is isotonic (stroke control) when the teeth are out of contact and isometric (load control) when the teeth are in contact and the face is rigid in the vertical axis. The object of the present study is to extend the experimental realization of an artificial mouth (DeLong and Douglas, 1991) to include the overhanging suspensory mechanical concepts of J. C. Ferre and to determine the effects of such a structure on the stress and strain patterns transferred from the teeth and muscles into the mandible.

Materials and methods

Servohydraulic environment of the mandible

To resynthesize mandibular motion, it is necessary to reproduce movements in the horizontal and coronal (vertical) planes as discussed previously. The production of a controllable force with the required movements was accomplished using two closed-loop servohydraulic systems based on the Materials Testing Systems (Eden Prairie, Minn.) series 812 testing machines. The closed-loop control provides the necessary mechanism for both monitoring and controlling the prescribed force and motion. Load cells are used for both measure-

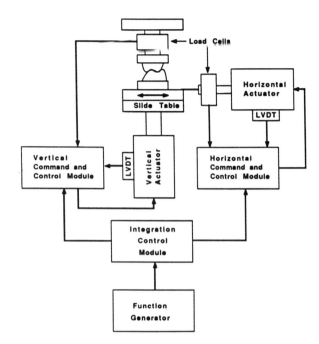

FIGURE 40.3 Control logic for the horizontal and vertical mechanical closed loops.

ment and control of the applied force (load control). Linearly variable differential transformers (LVDTs) built into the hydraulic actuators are used to monitor and control the movement. Each of the mechanical closed-loop systems consists of a testing fixture, a load cell, an LVDT, a hydraulic actuator mounted in a rigid frame, a command module, and a control module. The horizontal and vertical closed loops were coordinated by the integration control module. The overall logic is shown diagrammatically in figure 40.3.

The closed-loop system works by comparing measured actuator output to a predefined program. The program defines the desired force pattern for load control or the desired movement for stroke control. Any difference between the measured value and the program value is seen as an error. The error signal is used to correct the actuator output. The result is that the actuator follows a predefined path precisely. The force movement cycle is produced by operating the horizontal actuator in stroke control and the vertical axis in load control for bruxing (or by mode changing between load and stroke for chewing). A function generator is used to produce a waveform that determines the force profile of the occlusal force.

The maxillary element of the artificial mouth, like the maxilla of the biologic system, is stationary and acts as a reference point for mandibular movement. The maxillary element includes the load cell that is used for monitoring and controlling the occlusal force. The mandibular element consists of a universal joint that can be rotated in any direction and rests on a precise X-Y table. The Y table is positioned using a step motor to facilitate alignment and is not part of the closed-loop system. The X table describes motion in the coronal plane for lateral bruxing motions The Y table and step motor can also be made to move in the sagittal plane and produce a protrusive movement to bring the teeth edge to edge.

SIMULATION OF THE DENTOFACIAL ANATOMY

The experimental model used a composite (resin-inorganic intimate mixture) cast of the human mandible and maxilla, which had a spongy medulla and cortical plates and was supplied by Synthes, Inc. (Paoli, Pa.). The cranial parts were massively relieved posterior to the maxillary sinuses to accommodate an attachment that simulated the anterior fibers of the temporalis. The simulation of the anterior temporalis muscle was made up of simple metal parallel grips, lined by a compliant acrylic veneer, that could be clamped to the leading edge of the coronoid process. The masseter-medial pterygoid sling was simulated by a U-shaped trough lined by a compliant acrylic veneer, which was applied at the area of attachment of the masseter muscle, close to the angle of the mandible. Both of these simulated attachments were mechanically linked to the lower platform of the servohydraulic machine, and functioned as the mandibular elevators in the Ferre suspensory concept. Below the lower platform, a universal joint was attached that could accommodate any angle of the mandible in three axes.

Using Bioform plastic artificial teeth (Dentsuply International, Milford, Del.), 28 teeth were mounted in an acceptable prosthodontic occlusion using an acrylic denture resin. The positions of interdental contact were confirmed in centric and eccentric occlusion using traditional dental techniques. The experimental setup is shown in figure 40.4. The experimental arrangement allowed easy access to the buccal surfaces of the mandible, to which electric resistive strain gauges could be attached using recommended bonding techniques (M-bond 200 adhesive, Micromeasurements, Raleigh, N.C.) for accurate mapping of stress and strain patterns. The positioning of the strain gauges is shown in

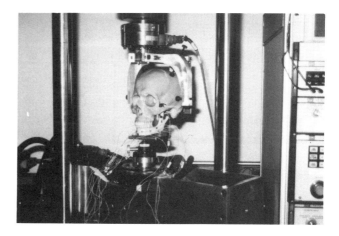

FIGURE 40.4 Servohydraulic environment of the artificial mouth. Experimental setup showing the mandible in the artificial mouth.

figure 40.5, where the x and y coordinates have the familiar meaning of analytic geometry and should not be confused with the nomenclature of X-Y tables. The major axis of the common mandibular fracture is in the vertical plane, and therefore compression and tensile opening of the fracture takes place in the horizontal (X) plane (at right angles to the fracture). Due to the surgical implications of this work, the majority of the gauges were fixed in the horizontal (X) direction. However, because the main axis of the teeth is in the vertical (Y) direction, a bonded strain gauge was attached in the Y direction at the base of the crown of each tooth and served as an indicator of the applied load to each tooth during the centric and eccentric positions of the mandible. Y-positioned gauges were also placed near the attachment of the simulated elevator muscles. The gauges were attached to conditioners that provided excitation voltage, amplification, and readout facilities. The outputs were attached to a computer-driven A–D data acquisition board. A 486 PC was utilized for data sampling and reduction of each individual strain, at each strain gauge position, under each condition of mandibular position and occlusal force. In all, 20 gauges were bonded in the Y (vertical) direction, and 68 gauges were bonded in the X (horizontal) direction.

This experimental arrangement provided the main parameters of the Ferre overhanging suspended model of the mandible with the appropriate dental occlusion and strain readout. The strain data were collected with occlusal dental contact under isometric control (load control). The mandible was examined in six positions

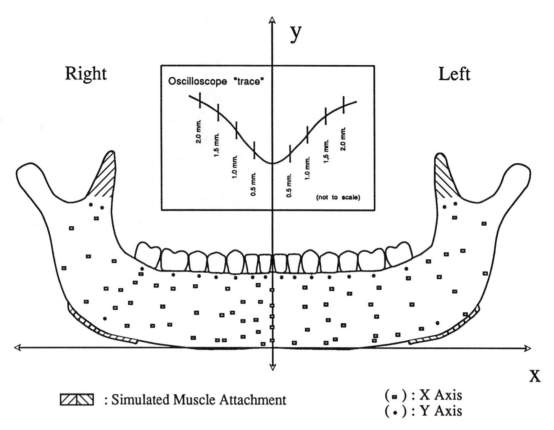

FIGURE 40.5   Drawing from an oral pantomograph of the experimental mandible showing the *x* and *y* positions of the strain gauges and the elevator muscles. The left and right lateral positions are also shown from 0.0 mm (centric occlusion) to 2.0 mm right and left.

in the horizontal axis: centric occlusion, four lateral positions (1 mm and 2 mm right and left lateral of centric), and one protrusive position with the anterior teeth edge to edge. At each mandibular position, a ramp load (maximum of 20 pounds) was applied to the mandible through the functional dentition. For this experiment, only the strains at 5 and 10 pounds of occlusal load were studied. In total 1056 measurements of strain were made. The data collected from the strain gauges of the experimental model were used to generate contour plots of mandibular strain using the software package Surfer 4 (Golden Software, Inc., Golden, Colo.), which also attempted to interpolate strain values between the experimentally measured values.

Results

The traces of the mandible in right and left lateral excursion on the cathode ray oscilloscope readout of the artificial mouth are shown as a drawing in figure 40.5. The lateral (or horizontal) movement of the

mandible is shown in the X direction and the vertical in the Y direction. Centric occlusion is the point of deepest interdigitation of the teeth and the point of closest approach of chin and nose. It can be seen that this point can be determined very accurately and reproducibly in the artificial mouth in repeated experiments. In horizontal movements away from centric occlusion, the vertical change in position of the mandible due to contact on the cuspal inclines of the teeth is also shown in figure 40.5. These movements can also be determined accurately and reproducibly in repeated experiments.

The data for Y strain could be reported simply as a histogram for the following mandibular positions: centric, anterior, and lateral positions 1 mm to the left and right. These are shown in figures 40.6–40.9, respectively, where the horizontal coordinate represents the positions of the individual teeth or the approximate attachments of the elevator muscles. Teeth are numbered according to the Federation Dentaire Internationale Annotation System (i.e., tooth no. 47 is the

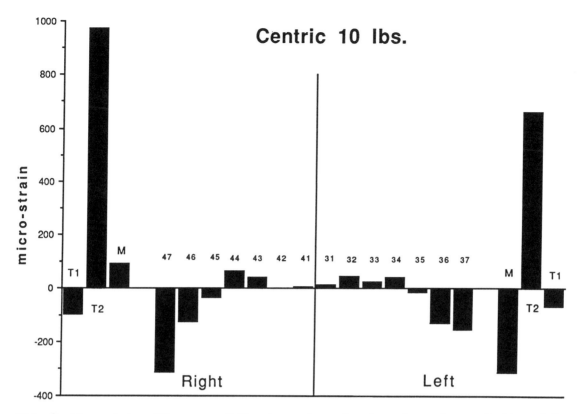

Centric 10 lbs.

FIGURE 40.6 Centric occlusion: Histogram of Y-strain values on the buccal surface of mandible, immediately below the teeth and muscle attachments. Positions of Y strains are plotted along horizontal axis.

lower right second molar). All four data sets represent values collected at 10 pounds of total occlusal load. Positive strain values correspond to regions on the buccal surface of the mandibular bone, just below the teeth, that are under tension. Negative strain values correspond to zones of compression.

The data for X-strain were reported on a 2D representation of the mandible, which was generated from a tracing of an oral pantomograph. This enabled a coordinate system to be developed for plotting the X-strain data, as already mentioned. Figures 40.10–40.13 are Surfer plots of the X-strain values from four different mandibular positions as previously presented: centric, anterior, and lateral positions 1 mm to the left and right of centric occlusion, respectively. The dark-gray zones represent areas of the buccal surface of the mandible that were under compression; the areas that are light gray in color represent tensile stresses.

Discussion

The functional strains as they appear are measured on the buccal surface and are of practical as well as theoretic importance. The restraining devices, such as plates and bars, that are used in postfracture rigid internal fixation are applied to the buccal surfaces of the mandible. It is the buccal strains that these devices resist as the fractured mandible is brought back to its physiologic rigidity. As noted previously, both Y strain and X strain were measured, and figure 40.5 should be consulted in the interpretation of the results. The Y strains, however, were used as an indication of the input forces generated by the elevator muscles and the contacting teeth.

Figure 40.6 shows a balanced distribution of dental centric occlusal contact. Not surprisingly, the posterior teeth (45–47, 35–37) show substantial compressive Y (vertical) strain with the maximum at the area of the second molar (47, 37). However, although the contacts were balanced, there do appear to be heavier Y stresses on the right side (c.f. the Y strains of teeth 47 and 37 in figure 40.6). This may be due to the heavier force application of the right temporalis and the changed direction of the masseter. However, these imbalances, apart from the Y strain, present a reasonably symmetric distribution.

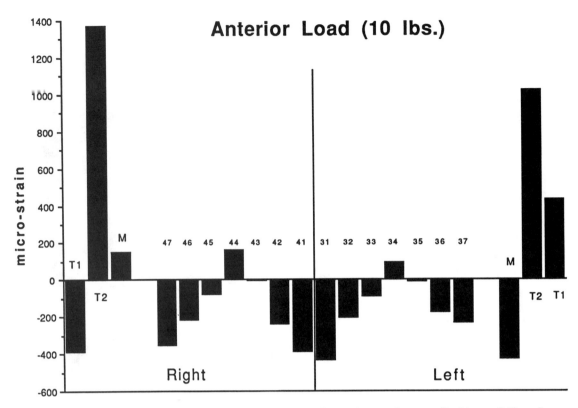

FIGURE 40.7   Anterior load: Histogram of Υ-strain values on the buccal surface of mandible, immediately below the teeth and muscle attachments. Positions of Υ strains are plotted along horizontal axis.

Figure 40.7, which presents the Υ strains with the mandible protruded as in food incision, shows major changes for the anterior teeth positions (41–43, 31–33). This is predictable, with the most compressive stress appearing at the anterior teeth due to the edge-to-edge position. It will be noted again that the right-side temporalis applies more force than the left. This imbalance aside, as with the centric position the distribution is quite symmetric. The molar and premolar positions in figure 40.7 call for special comment. In the protruded position of the mandible, these teeth come out of contact (disclusion); therefore, the Υ strains shown on the histogram for these teeth are the result of stress distribution from other anatomic locations in the mandible (i.e., the anterior teeth and the elevator muscles).

Figures 40.8 and 40.9 show the 1-mm left and right positions for the mandible. Figure 40.8 shows the effect of incisal guidance with the right anterior teeth and first premolar (32–34) showing tensile Υ strains. This is what would be expected, and inspires considerable confidence in the experimental model. However, the high compressive force on the right second molar (47) in figure 40.8 is puzzling and may be the result of

an interfering occusal contact on the right side as the mandible moves to the left. This is found from time to time in clinical experience. Yet, again, as found throughout with this model, there is somewhat more force applied on the right temporalis even with a left lateral movement. Figure 40.9 shows the right lateral position. The right canine and first premolar (43–44) show the tensile Υ strains expected for the guidance that these teeth perform. In this situation, the incisors are only minimally involved.

The X strains for the mandible in the centric position are shown in figure 40.10 and should be interpreted along with the data from figure 40.6. Immediately it can be seen that there is a considerable diversion from the expected symmetry. This may be due to the asymmetric pull of the right and left temporalis muscles (T_2). Most of the mandible is in tensile X strain, a finding that also applies to the lateral excursions shown in figures 40.12 and 40.13. This is in contrast to the tensile band theory (Champy, et al. 1976; Luhr, 1982), which submits that the entire upper part of the mandible is more likely to be in tensile strain when the lower portion of the body of the mandible is in compression.

536   DENTISTRY

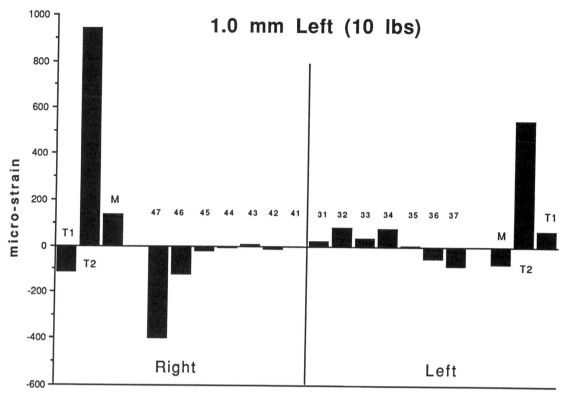

FIGURE 40.8   Lateral, 1.0 mm left: Histogram of Υ-strain values on the buccal surface of mandible, immediately below the teeth and muscle attachments. Positions of Υ strains are plotted along horizontal axis.

Our study could not generally confirm this theory. We found a tensile-compressive distribution of the tensile band only in the region of the mandible closely related to the masseter muscle. Because tensile X strain tends to destabilize mandibular fractures, this finding is of importance to the design of rigid fixation appliances.

Centric occlusion of the mandible, by definition, is a parameter related to the interdigitation of the upper and lower teeth. It appears that although the teeth may be balanced on the left and right sides of the mouth in the centric position, the distribution of strain in the mandible may not be balanced. This situation is demonstrated in figure 40.10, which shows more compressive strain on the patient's left side and more tensile on the right. Only in figure 40.13 are the tensile and compressive strains symmetrical; there, with the exception of the regions of the muscle attachments, the entire mandible presents tensile strain. Thus the conclusion from this experimental model is that centric occlusion of the teeth and symmetric distribution of mandibular strain are not the same, even though great experimental efforts were expended to make them coincide.

The asymmetry in the region of the temporalis is again shown in figure 40.11, which presents the mandibular position with the teeth edge-to-edge and the mandible protruded. The entire anterior region of the mandible under the incisor teeth shows compressive strain. This may be the condition that comes closest to the tensile band theory, if the two bilateral halves of the mandible may be considered independently. It is likely that in protrusion the anterior region of the mandible (in the area of the chin) will be depressed under the anterior forces that are shown in figure 40.7. Such depression of the mandible will result in compressive strains at the lower edge of the anterior region of the mandible. Figure 40.11 shows this condition, but it is far from a complete explanation, because the remainder of the strain distribution is rationalized only with difficulty.

At the very least, the present experimental study shows the general trends with respect to strain distribution, which appear to differ considerably from those postulated by accepted theory. A major reason for this difference is the inclusion of an acceptable dental occlusion with multiple contacts. It also appears to be

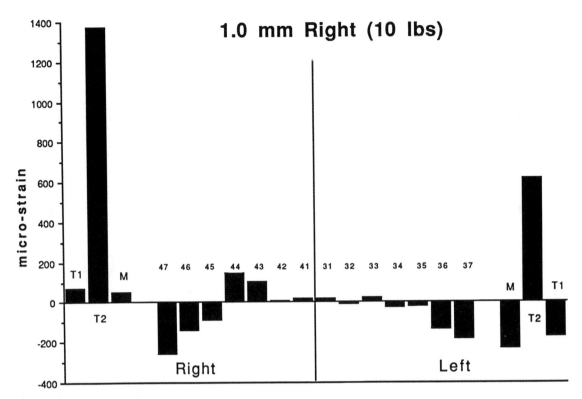

FIGURE 40.9 Lateral, 1.0 mm right: Histogram of Y-strain values on the buccal surface of mandible, immediately below the teeth and muscle attachments. Positions of Y strains are plotted along horizontal axis.

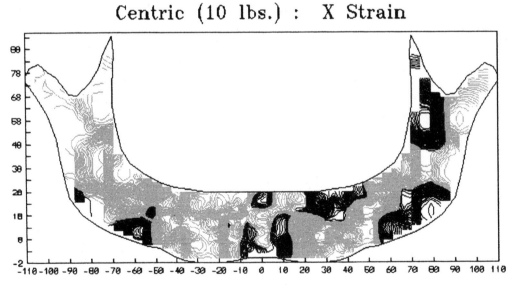

FIGURE 40.10 Contour plot of the X strains for centric occlusion (dark gray is compressive strain; light gray is tensile).

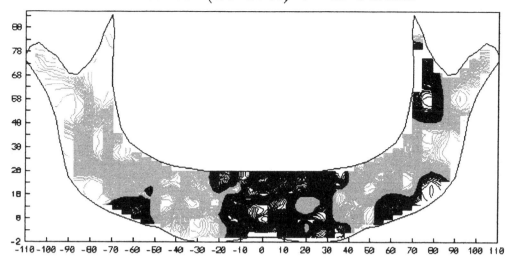

FIGURE 40.11 Contour plot of the *X* strains for anterior load (dark gray is compressive strain; light gray is tensile).

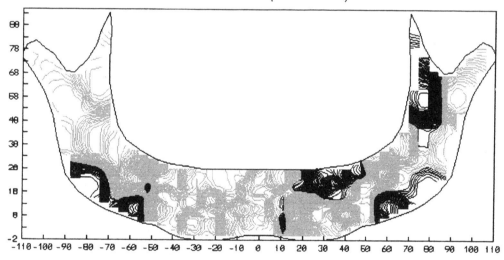

FIGURE 40.12 Contour plot of the *X* strains for lateral 1.0 mm left position (dark gray is compressive strain; light gray is tensile).

simplistic to design rigid internal fixation based on the theory that only tensile forces must be resisted in the alveolar region and that in the basal regions a ubiquitous compressive stress is always present to assist the stabilization of the fracture. It is clear that the distribution of the troublesome tensile strain is quite variable and changes as the function of the positions of the mandible and teeth.

Equally significant, the *Y* strains in the present study should be of importance in future finite-element studies. The *Y* strains may be used to develop boundary stresses, which should provide much more insight into mandibular strain than the finite-element models so far used. All of the present 3D finite-element studies, although sophisticated anatomically and in terms of material properties, seem to fail at the point of force

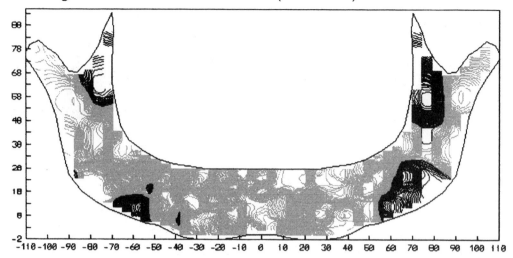

Right Lateral 1.0 mm (10 lbs.) : X Strain

FIGURE 40.13 Contour plot of the X strains for lateral 1.0 mm right position (dark gray is compressive strain; light gray is tensile).

input. They seem to ignore the fact that the dental occlusion involves multiple points of contact; frequently, sophisticated finite-element programs generate and publish solutions based on single-point force applications.

Although the experiments described in this chapter must be repeated with rigidly fixed simulated fractures, it appears that, for the greater part of the mandible, tensile strains are present to destabilize the fracture. Thus no assumption can be made that the compression will be present in all conditions.

ACKNOWLEDGMENT The authors acknowledge the support of A. O. Stifung in the execution of this work.

REFERENCES

AHLGREN, J., and B. OWALL, 1970. Muscular activity and chewing force: A polygraphic study of human mandibular movements. *Arch. Oral Biol.* 15:271–280.

ANDERSON, D. J., 1956. Measurement of stress in mastication. *J. Dent. Res.* 35(5):671–673.

CHAMPY, M., J. P. LODDE, J. H. JAEGER, and A. WILK, 1976. Osteosynthese mandibulaires selon la technique de Michelet: Bases biomecaniques. *Rev. Stomatol Chir. Maxillofac.* 77: 569–576.

CORNELL, J. A., J. S. JORDAN, S. ELLIS, and E. E. ROSE, 1957. A method of comparing the wear resistance of vari-

ous materials for artificial teeth. *J. Am. Dent. Assoc.* 54: 608–614.

DEBOEVER, J. A., 1978. Functional occlusal forces: An investigation by telemetry. *J. Prosthet. Dent.* 40(3):326–333.

DELONG, R., and W. H. DOUGLAS, 1991. An artificial oral environment for testing dental materials. *IEEE Trans. Biomed. Eng.* 38(4):339–345.

DELONG, R., R. L. SAKAGUCHI, W. H. DOUGLAS, and M. R. PINTADO, 1985. The wear of dental amalgam in an artificial mouth: A clinical correlation. *Dent. Mater.* 1(6):238–242.

DOUGLAS, W. H., R. L. SAKAGUCHI, and R. DELONG, 1985. Frictional effects between natural teeth in an artificial mouth. *Dent. Mater.* 1(3):115–119.

DUCKRO, P. N., R. C. TAIT, R. B. MARGOLIS, and T. L. DESIELDS, 1990. Prevalence of temporomandibular symptoms in a large United States metropolitan area. *J. Cranio. Pract.* 2:131–138.

FERRE, J. C., J. Y. BARBIN, J. J. HELARY, and J. P. LUMINEAU, 1984a. The mandible, an overhanging mechanically suspended structure: Considerations on the system of attachment and servo-command of the mandible. *Anat. Clin.* 6:3–10.

FERRE, J. C., J. Y. BARBIN, M. LAUDE, and J. L. HELARY, 1984b. A physicomathematical approach to the structure of the mandible. *Anat. Clin.* 6:45–52.

GIBBS, C. H., 1981. Occlusal forces during chewing and swallowing as measured by sound transmission. *J. Prosthet. Dent.* 46(4):443–449.

HAGBERG, C., 1986. Electromyography and bite force studies of muscular function and dysfunction in masticatory muscles. *Swed. Dent. J. Suppl.* 37:1–64.

Harrison, A., and T. T. Lewis, 1975. The development of an abrasion testing machine for dental materials. *J. Biomed. Mater. Res.* 9(3):341–353.

Helkimo, E., and B. Ingerwall, 1978. Bite force and functional state of the masticatory system in young men. *Swed. Dent. J.* 2:167–165.

Jaworzyn, J. M., P. A. Arundel, and J. Cantwell, 1978. Posterior composite restorations. *J. Dent. Res.* 57 (abstract no. 708):251.

Jent, T., S. Karlsson, and B. Hedegard, 1979. Mandibular movements of young adults recorded by intraorally placed light-emitting diodes. *J. Prosthet. Dent.* 42(6):669–673.

Kroon, F. M., M. Mathisson, J. R. Cordey, and B. A. Rahn, 1991. The use of miniplates in mandibular fracture: An in vitro study. *J. Craniomaxillofac. Surg.* 19(5):199–204.

Luhr, H., 1982. In *Oral and Maxillofacial Traumatology*, vol. 1, Chapter 5.2. E. Kruger and W. Schill, eds. Chicago: Quintessence, pp. 319–348.

Lurell, L., 1985. Occlusal forces and chewing ability in dentitions with cross arch bridges. *Swed. Dent. J. Suppl.* 26:1–45.

Nyquist, G., and B. Owall, 1968. Masticatory load registration during function. *Odont. Rev.* 19:45–54.

Perren, S. M., and B. A. Rahn, 1980. Biomechanics of fracture healing. *Can. J. Surg.* 23(3):228–232.

Powell, J. M., and G. Dickson, 1975. In vitro wear testing of restorative materials. *J. Dent. Res.* 54 (Special Issue A, abstract no. 708):356.

Robinson, M., 1946. The temporo-mandibular joint theory of reflex non-levers actions of the mandible. *J. Am. Dent. Assoc.* 33:1260.

Thomson, J. C., 1975. Attrition of acrylic teeth. *Dent. Pract.* 15:223–226.

41 CAD/CAM Automation and Expert Systems for Design and Fabrication of Dental Restorations

E. DIANNE REKOW AND BRUCE NAPPI

MILLIONS OF DENTAL crowns are placed in patients' mouths every year, restoring nonfunctional, broken, or decayed teeth to full function. The technique used to fabricate these crowns is the centuries-old, labor-intensive process of lost-wax casting (table 41.1). When a crown is needed because of decay or fracture of a tooth, a dentist prepares the tooth, removing all decay and creating a design of the remaining tooth structure that will (1) support the loads to which the tooth will be subjected during normal function, (2) integrate unique features of the material from which the crown is to be fabricated, and (3) maximize the self-retention of the crown on the tooth. An impression of the prepared tooth and the teeth adjacent to it is made. Another impression is made of the teeth in the opposite arch. A temporary crown is fabricated and placed on the prepared tooth, and the patient leaves the dental office.

Dental plaster is poured into the impressions, creating a 3D model of the patient's mouth. The portion of the model that has been prepared to receive the crown must be isolated and modified so that the model of that tooth can be removed and reinserted into the remainder of the model. This is necessary because a wax pattern of the crown must be created on that tooth, and proper design can only be accomplished if better access to the sides of the tooth is possible. This is accomplished through a multistep process that creates a die. In this process, (1) a pin is placed beneath the prepared tooth in the original model; (2) a second layer of plaster is added beneath the model, surrounding the pin, and allowed to dry; (3) cuts are made through the original layer of plaster on both sides of the prepared tooth; and (4) that segment is removed from the second layer of plaster, and excess plaster is removed to expose the area that will serve as the interface between the tooth

and the crown (called the *margin*). The die can be inserted into the indexed pinhole so that it is in its normal position in the dental arch, or it can be removed to facilitate creation of the wax pattern.

A technician creates the wax pattern of the crown on the die. Special care is taken to create a very close fit (to better than 100 μm) between the die and the wax around the margin. The chewing (occlusal) surface of the wax pattern is designed to provide the proper morphologic characteristics as well as the unique requirements for each patient so that the patient will be able to chew comfortably without any premature contacts between the restored and natural teeth. When the design in the wax is nearly complete, the die and wax pattern are reinserted into the model of the arch so that the side wall on the interproximal, cheek, and tongue sides of the restoration can be designed to follow the curvature of the adjacent teeth.

When the wax pattern is complete, a wax sprue is added and the wax is invested in a refractory material surrounded by a casting ring. After the investment hardens, the casting ring and its contents are placed in an oven, which burns away the wax. The casting ring is placed in a casting machine, where the material to be cast is melted in a crucible and cast into the void in the investment material using centrifugal force. The casting is recovered and the sprue removed, and then the restoration is polished. The patient must then return to the dentist's office. At that appointment, the temporary crown is removed and any debris from the cementing material is removed. This can be an unpleasant experience because the tooth may be quite sensitive. In most cases local anesthesia is administered at this juncture to minimize any pain the patient may otherwise experience. The prepared tooth is dried, and the restoration is glued onto the tooth.

TABLE 41.1

Steps required to create a dental restoration using the lost-wax casting technique

Take impression of prepared teeth.

Create the working cast:
- Pour plaster into impression material, creating the model.
  - Let plaster set.
  - Place indexing pin beneath prepared tooth.
  - Pour plaster base supporting model.
  - Let plaster set.

Create the die:
- Saw sections on both sides of prepared both through model portion of plaster (but not base portion of the paster).
- Remove the model section containing the prepared tooth.
- Remove excess plaster around the margin, isolating the margin and making it accessible.
  - Mark the margin with a red line.

Create the wax pattern:
- Using wax instruments, create a pattern of the desired restoration.
  - Add a sprue to the pattern.

Invest the wax pattern:
- Line a casting ring with expansion material.
- Attach a sprue to the base of the casting ring.
- Place the casting ring over the base.
- Mix investment material.
- Pour investment material into the casting ring.
- Let investment material harden.

Cast the restoration:
- Insert the casting ring into the oven and burn out wax pattern.
  - Place the casting ring into the casting machine.
  - Melt material from which the restoration is to be fabricated.
  - Pour molten material into the casting ring.
  - Recover casting from investment material.

Polish restoration.

When normal materials are used, the minimum time required for these operations is approximately 9 hours. Usually, however, a patient has appointments between 1 and 2 weeks apart, permitting time for the case to be sent to a laboratory, for the laboratory procedures to be completed, and for the case returned to the dentist. During this time, potential problems can arise. Temporary restorations seldom fit as well as permanent restorations, so the surrounding tissues can become inflamed and the prepared tooth may shift slightly. Both of these problems complicate the procedure for placing the final crown. Inflamed tissue is more sensitive and usually more resistant to anesthesia. Movement of the tooth can create problems in the fit of the cast crown. One of the greatest advantages of the automation available with new technologies is that it is now feasible to create a crown in less than one hour, permitting the patient's tooth to be prepared and the final crown fit into place, all in one appointment.

Recently, however, a focused effort has begun to integrate new, computer-based technologies into the design and fabrication processes. This chapter discusses some of the special considerations that provide interesting challenges in integrating new technologies, describes systems already available or under development, outlines criteria for measuring the clinical success of the systems, and reports how CAD/CAM-produced crowns are performing clinically.

Special considerations in implementing CAD/CAM

CAD/CAM techniques are state of the art in most industrial applications. At first glance, then, it would seem that the transfer of these technologies to dentistry should be straightforward and present no special problems. There are, however, a few differences between working in a live patient's mouth and operating in most industrial settings. These include the problems of access for data acquisition, the complexity of the design, and the precise fit requirements.

DATA ACQUISITION

Ideally, data that map the teeth should be acquired directly from the patient's mouth. With the current state of the art, impressions are used to capture the data. Unfortunately, the process of making the impressions and converting them to plaster models introduces errors on the order of approximately 25 μm (Craig, 1985). However, acquiring data directly from the mouth is not easy. In the posterior regions of the mouth, for patients with no joint limitations, the teeth are approximately 25 mm apart when the mouth is fully open. A number of automated instruments for acquiring data simply cannot fit into the space available, especially for the distal side of second molars. Furthermore, a patient can usually sit without movement for only approximately 1/8 sec (Slama, 1980). This further reduces the number of automated data acquisition techniques that are possible.

Additional consideration must be given to the fact that the mouth is a very humid environment, making the use of mirrors difficult. At least 50% of the teeth that are prepared have margins that are below the gingival border, thus visibility is limited due to the interference of surrounding tissues as well as the bleeding that usually accompanies tooth preparation. Unfortunately, it is the area of the margin that is most critical for the long-term success of any restoration.

COMPLEXITY OF THE DESIGN

Every dental crown created is unique. Each tooth is unique in size and shape. By the time a particular tooth needs a crown, it has been further "customized" by its unique history of previous restorations, decay pattern, and fractures. The occlusal surface that will be created to restore that tooth is also unique. Each crown must be morphologically like the tooth that is being restored: That is, every mandibular first molar has three buccal cusps and two lingual cusps; however, the relative positions of those cusps and the steepness of their inclines is uniquely determined by the functional movements of each patient. It is not simply a reflection of the tooth against which the restored tooth is to function. Furthermore, the geometry is complex, and there are no primitives that can be invoked to model the occlusal surfaces of posterior teeth. The complexity of the design is also complicated by the fact that a full 3D surface is required, with both its internal and external surfaces fabricated. This is particularly of interest because it makes fixturing the part during fabrication procedures an interesting challenge.

FIT REQUIREMENTS

The fit at the margins of any dental restoration is vital to its long-term success. Lack of an adequate fit is detrimental to both the tooth and the supporting soft tissues of the gums (the periodontal tissues). Generally, a good fit is taken to be 40–60 μm of gap between the margin of the tooth (where the restoration is supposed to fit) and where the edge of the restoration actually lies (Holmes, 1986).

System description

Given these special considerations of data acquisition, configuration, and fit requirements, the challenges of

applying technology to automate the production of dental restorations without compromising their quality are demanding. A number of systems (summarized in table 41.2) are currently either commercially available or under development. All share three functional components: data acquisition, restoration design, and fabrication (figure 41.1).

DATA ACQUISITION

The data required to design a restoration include a full 3D map of the tooth that has been prepared by the dentist, the areas where the restored tooth will contact the proximal tooth, and the configuration of the opposing or occluding teeth in their static, fully closed position as well as their path during functional excursions. Ideally, this information should be acquired directly from the mouth, to minimize the possibility of error. However, the data can be obtained from casts made from impressions of the mouth (which may, of course, incorporate some errors due to materials distortion), as in the first steps of the lost-wax casting technique. Dental CAD/CAM systems use two different technologies for data acquisition: optical and mechanical.

Optical data acquisition is either video-based or laser-triangulation-based. The video systems (manufactured by Siemens and by Sopha) project an array of calibrated lines onto the surface (Duret and Duret, 1986; Moermann and Brandestini, 1986). The reflection of these lines, deformed by the configuration of the surface upon which they are projected, is recorded by a charge-coupled device (CCD) sensor. The underlying configuration is extracted from the deformation information. The shortcoming of this technique is that it requires a consistent color of the surface to be mapped. Unfortunately, the prepared tooth is not likely to have a single color, because when it is prepared the surface is composed of a combination of enamel, dentin, and, in some cases, base filling materials (which could be composite or metal filling materials). Either the dentin or the enamel, or both, might be discolored from previous filling materials. To overcome this problem, a coating of titanium oxide powder is sprayed onto the prepared tooth. This provides the consistent (Lambertian) surface required but adds a layer of unknown thickness to the surface being mapped, creating an artificial surface that is imaged and then serves as the data on which the rest of the restoration must be designed and fabricated. Unless properly controlled, this artificial

Table 41.2

Comparison of dental CAD/CAM systems

System	Data acquisition technique	Fabrication technique	Degree of user interaction for restoration design	Restorative materials that can be fabricated	Availability in marketplace	Producer	Additional information
Siemens CEREC	Optical (intraoral or laboratory	Machining (grinding)	Some interaction required; no occlusion designed, created by clinician	Machinable ceramics and porcelains	Currently available	Siemens	Pelton and Crane A Siemens Company Dental Products Div. P.O. Box 7800 Charlotte, NC 28241
Sopha	Optical (laboratory only)	Machining (milling)	Some interaction required; occlusion design is included	Sopha millable ceramic; some metal alloys Titanium	Currently available	Sopha Bioconcept	Sopha Bioconcept 11835 W. Olympic Blvd. Suit 400 Los Angeles, CA 90064
Procera	3D copying via mechanical digitizer (laboratory only)	Electric Discharge Machining	User creates pattern to be copied; occlusion design created by lab procedures	Titanium	Currently available	Nobelpharam	Nobelpharma Procera Divisior 5101 S. Keeler Chicago, IL 60632
Titan	Mechanical contact digitizer (laboratory only)	Machining (milling)	Automatic; occlusion design created by lab procedure	Titanium	Currently available in Europe	DCS Alldent	DCS Groups Gewerbestrasse 15 4123 Allschivil 3 Switzerland
Cicero	Laser scanner (laboratory only)	Sintering and machining (milling)	Automatic; occlusion design is included	Powered ceramics and porcelains	Available in Europe 1993	Elephant Indust. BV	Elephant Industries BV Atoomeug 13 1627 Le Hoorn The Netherlands
DentiCAD	Mechanical robot arm intraoral or laboratory	Machining (milling)	Automatic; occlusion design is included	Machinable ceramics and porcelains; titanium and metal alloys	Available in Europe 1993	DentiCAD and BEGO	BEGO Bremmer Goldschlagerei Wilh. Herbst GmbH & Go Emil-Sommer-Strasse 7-9 D-2800 Bremen 41 Germany

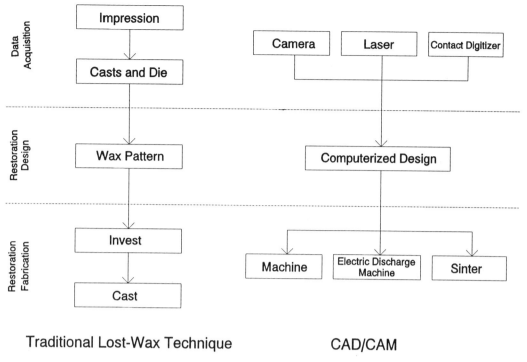

FIGURE 41.1   Traditional versus CAD/CAM operations for creating a dental restoration.

layer could significantly influence the fit of the restoration on the prepared tooth.

Laser-based optical systems have also been introduced. In most of these systems, an incident line or point is projected onto the surface to be mapped; the reflected location of the line or point is sensed by a CCD sensor and the x, y, and z coordinates of the point (or points on the line) are extrapolated (Jalkio, Kim, and Case, 1985). Unfortunately, these systems are impractical for use in the mouth due to the relatively long data acquisition times (greater than 1/8 second) and the need for a fixed distance between the sensor and the tooth during the digitizing process. Consequently, these systems can be used in dental CAD/CAM systems but require the use of stone models.

Mechanical systems for data acquisition rely on touching the surface to be mapped. The Titan digitizer is a specialized coordinate measuring machine that provides a point-by-point map of the surfaces of interest. Design limitations do not permit it to be used directly in the patient's mouth.

An alternative, under development for the Denti-CAD system, is a miniaturized linkage (figure 41.2); Marinaccio et al., 1992). It consists of a mounting post

that anchors the linkage to the teeth. Position sensors within the linkage establish the position of the tip relative to the mounting post. The precision of the linkage is better than 10 μm. This digitizer can be used directly in the mouth. The mounting post is attached to a tooth somewhere in the arch, away from the tooth to be restored. The dentist moves the pointer manually over the surface to be mapped. Each data point is digitized in 3D coordinates. As it is captured, each point is displayed on a computer monitor.

To begin, the DentiCAD user digitizes the adjacent and reference points from the occluding teeth, defining the space into which the external portion of the restoration must fit. Then the user establishes the general space in which the prepared tooth lies by arbitrarily digitizing a single point on each of the buccal, lingual, distal, and occlusal surfaces of that tooth. The entire prepared tooth surface is digitized by moving the probe at the end of the linkage over the surface of the tooth. There are no constraints in how the data must be acquired; it is ordered automatically by the software. Approximately 10–15 minutes are required to digitize the required surfaces completely. This is slightly longer than the time now required to take impressions

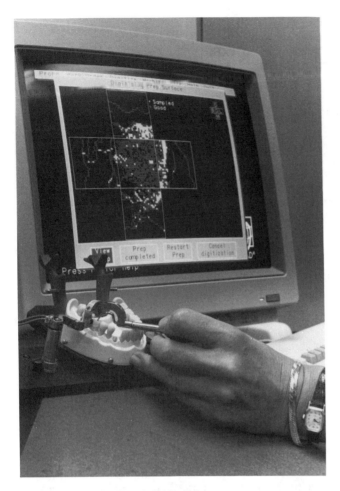

FIGURE 41.2   The Denti-CAD digitizer.

of the teeth. However, modifications to the software currently being investigated are expected to reduce this time to less than 5 minutes.

With any dental CAD/CAM system, when the data has been acquired, a 3D representation of the prepared tooth is created and displayed. With the DentiCAD system, this 3D image can be rotated on the screen, providing multiple views to verify that the desired information has been captured and the preparation design is acceptable. If changes to the prepared tooth are desired or needed, the linkage can be removed from the mounting fixture (but the fixture left in place), the tooth modified by the dentist, the linkage reinserted onto its mounting fixture, and the modified portion of the prepared tooth redigitized.

The DentiCAD mechanical digitizer offers at least two advantages over other data acquisition techniques. The primary advantage is that it is a technology and procedure that is already familiar to the dentist. The

activities involved in digitizing are essentially the same as those used to examine the teeth. Additionally, it is not necessary to place retraction cord to isolate the margins (this is required with optical systems or whenever impressions are made). The tip of the digitizing probe easily fits into the spaces created by the handpiece during preparation of the tooth; it is not necessary to visualize the margins or coat the teeth.

DESIGN BY EXPERT SYSTEM

Many of the dental CAD/CAM systems require the user to design the restoration interactively. Although this process capitalizes on the power of CAD, it requires an extremely knowledgeable user with training in dentistry and occlusal concepts. A major advantage the DentiCAD system offers is the artificial intelligence embedded in the CAD software. By integrating the decisions required for restoration design into the software, the system speeds the design process to under two minutes. Furthermore, no user interaction is required, so the user is free to pursue other tasks while the system operates. Consistency in design of the restoration is also made possible.

Each restoration is unique, determined by the configuration of the prepared tooth as well as the functional movements of the patient's jaw. Yet each tooth must be morphologically correct. The outcome of the design must be a restoration that is anatomically correct but, when in place on the prepared tooth, permits the patient to move through all possible positions without interference between the new restoration and other teeth. To accomplish this, a number of decisions must be incorporated into the design process. Figure 41.3 is a flowchart of design decisions incorporated into the DentiCAD software.

To begin the design process, the user acquires the required data as described in the previous section. The user also identifies the tooth to be restored, the type of restoration to be created (full crown, bridge, etc.), and the material from which it is to be fabricated. Three surfaces are defined: an internal configuration, an external configuration including the occlusal surface to the crest of convexity, and an external configuration from the crest of convexity to the margins. The internal

FIGURE 41.3   Decision flowchart for dental restoration design.

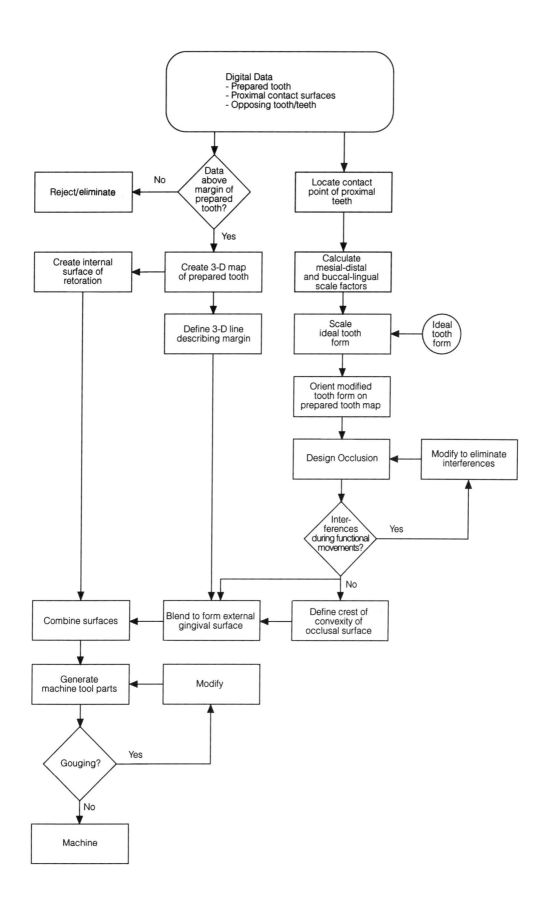

design reflects the configuration of the prepared tooth. The limit where the internal and external surfaces join is defined as the margin. On the prepared tooth, the margin is a well-defined line created by the dentist when the tooth is prepared. Data that are acquired from the tooth include data from below where the margin will be positioned, gingival to the area that the restoration is to cover. The software automatically establishes the margins by determining the inflection points of the array of curves defining that portion of the surface. Any data points beyond the margins are rejected.

The internal surface of the restoration is designed to follow exactly the configuration of the prepared tooth at the margins, but away from the margins a cement space is added. This permits a luting agent to be placed inside the restoration to hold the restoration to the tooth. Luting agents may function by either mechanical or chemical adhesion.

The external configuration of the restoration includes two portions, the occlusal surface to the crest of convexity of the restoration and the sides of the restoration (from the crest of convexity to the margins). The occlusal surface is derived initially from a database of ideal tooth forms. That form then is scaled to match the mesial-distal and buccal-lingual size of the available space. It is then reconfigured using splines and blending functions to integrate the functional movements of the patient obtained from the reference points digitized as part of the data acquisition steps.

The external configuration between the crest of convexity and the margins is created by defining a surface that blends the 3D line defined by the margin to the 3D line defining the crest of convexity. Figure 41.4 is an example of a DentiCAD automatically designed mandibular right first molar.

When the design is complete, the software of the dental CAD/CAM systems automatically creates the tool paths for fabrication. For milling operations, offset surfaces are created, accounting for the "problem" created by the machine tool being driven by specifying the position of the center of the cutter while the real surface of interest is established by the periphery of the cutter. With the DentiCAD system, the offset calculation includes antigouge checks as well so that as the cutter moves down the slope of one cusp toward the central groove (the buccal slope of the lingual cusp of a first molar, for instance) it does not cut away the rise of the slope of the cusp of the other side of the central groove.

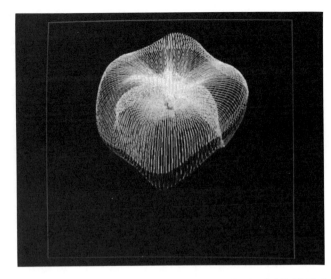

FIGURE 41.4 Crown designed by DentiCAD CAD/CAM expert system.

If gouging is detected, tooth paths are regenerated. If there is no gouging, the machine tool paths are automatically generated. The tool path commands include specification of spindle speed, feed rate, and depth of cut for the material selected.

FABRICATION

Dental CAD/CAM systems already available and under development fabricate restorations by machining (milling and grinding), electric discharge machining, and sintering combined with machining. The most popular technique is machining. The material of choice of many of the systems is ceramic. This poses some interesting challenges to the fabrication stage of restoration creation because the use of ceramic materials for dentistry has been limited by their brittle fracture initiating at surface flaws (Kelly et al., 1990; Anusavice, Hu, and Johhatie, 1991; Ellison et al., 1992; Scherrer and DeRijk, 1991). There, flaws are likely to be created by fabrication techniques.

Machining operations can remove 100 times more material per unit time than any alternative fabrication technique (Rekow, Thompson, and Yang, 1991). Grinding operations involve using a cutting tool made up of individual abrasive grains, with irregular, random shape, bound to a base (Niebel, Draper, and Wysk, 1989). Alternatively, in milling, the cutter geometry is regular and well defined.

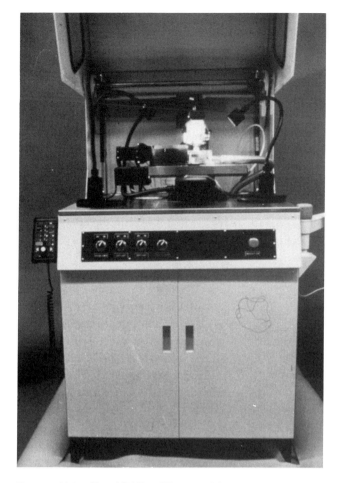

FIGURE 41.5 DentiCAD milling machine.

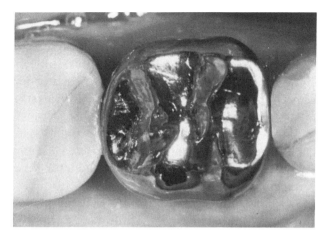

FIGURE 41.6 Finished DentiCAD restoration in place in dental patient.

Most information regarding machining ceramic materials deals with diamond grinding (Jahanmir et al., 1992). This is the technique used for fabrication with the CEREC system. Unfortunately the cutter selected for this system is a flat disk approximately 35 mm in diameter. This configuration severely limits the type of restoration that can be produced with that system.

Both the Sopha and DentiCAD systems utilize milling operations. (Figure 41.5 shows the DentiCAD milling machine.) Standard numerically controlled operations are employed. Both systems are capable of machining ceramics as well as metals. (Figure 41.6 shows a DentiCAD-produced titanium crown in place on a mandibular right first molar.)

Electric discharge machining (edm), used in the Procera system, was first used in the 1940s. Material is removed by thermal energy, generating a spark (Weller, 1984). A dielectric fluid provides a path for discharge of the fluid between an electrode tool and the workpiece. When sufficient voltage is applied, the dielectric fluid ionizes, passing current. The discharge area is focused, creating a local temperature above the melting point of the workpiece. A heat-affected layer of 2–130 μm remains after edm. The greatest disadvantage of edm is that the restorative material must be electrically conductive, making the use of aesthetic ceramic and porcelain materials almost impossible with this technique.

Sintering (used in the Cicero system) facilitates machining of materials that are otherwise very difficult to machine (porcelains, for instance; DeGamo, 1969). Powders (metal or nonmetallic powders) are compacted and heated to a specified temperature below a complete sintering temperature. This results in a part with sufficient strength to be handled and machined without difficulty. After it is machined to the desired configuration, the restoration is reheated to final sintering temperature. Because there is little dimensional change in the final sintering, a restoration prepared with this technique will properly fit the tooth.

Criteria for clinical success

There are three criteria for the clinical success of any restoration: fit (at the margin, interproximally, and occlusally), wear of the restorative material and the opposing teeth as they function against each other, and long-term clinical survival.

FIT

Fit at the margin is the most critical for clinical success (Christensen, 1966; Eden, 1979). If the interface between the restoration and the tooth is inadequate, the likelihood of recurrent decay rises quickly. If the restoration surface at the margin is rough or extends beyond the tooth surface, food debris accumulate, resulting in tissue irritation and inflammation, which often leads to periodontal disease and loss of the bone supporting the restored tooth.

In ideal laboratory conditions, fit at the margins of cast gold crowns (considered to be the most acceptable currently used restorative material) averages 48 μm around the periphery of the tooth (Holmes, 1986). The fit obtained with CAD/CAM-produced restorations has been reported to range from 23 μm (Rekow, Thompson, and Yang, 1991) to 150 μm (Peters and Bieniek, 1991; Reppel, Boening, and Walter, 1991).

Fit at the interproximal and occlusal surfaces is also important but is generally less critical than fit at the margins. When the interproximal fit is ideal, dental floss "pops" through the contact between the restored tooth and the one with which it is in contact (this translates to a gap of approximately 50 μm with a contact area of approximately 1 mm^2) (Jernberg, 1980). If the fit is too tight, it becomes difficult for the patient to maintain good oral hygiene, and tissue inflammation can result. If it is not tight enough, food becomes impacted between the teeth, resulting in tissue irritation and trauma. Unfortunately, to date, nothing is reported in the literature concerning the quality of interproximal fit of the CAD/CAM-produced restorations. Acceptable interproximal contact can be surmised, however, from the number of restorations that have been placed, some of which have now been functioning for more than 5 years.

Occlusal fit is critical for patient comfort (Ramfjord and Ash, 1971). If interferences occur during normal chewing motions, two things may happen. First, the patient may develop a reflex action, moving the jaw to avoid the contact. This may contribute to pathologies of the temporomandibular joint (TMJ). Alternatively, the patient may continue to function normally while the interferences cause excessive loading of the tooth, resulting in fracture or excessive wear of the opposing tooth or irritation and inflammation of the pulp of the restored or opposing tooth, which in turn could lead to the need for root canal therapy. Again, little is reported

explicitly in the literature about occlusal fit. In part this is because the clinician can adjust the occlusion in the patient's mouth using the dental drill to make it more comfortable. With CEREC-produced CAD/CAM restoration, the clinician is responsible for creating the occlusal surface of the restoration; it is not automatically created by the system. With other systems, the occlusion is created by a technician adding a layer of porcelain over a CAD/CAM-produced coping (the Titan system, for instance), by interactive operations of the system user (the Sopha systems), or completely automatically (the DentiCAD and Cicero systems). To date, there are no reports on the adequacy of the occlusal fit.

WEAR

For any dental restoration, surface smoothness is critical for prevention of plaque retention, for patient comfort and acceptance, and for avoidance of abrasion of opposing teeth (Clayton and Green, 1970; DeLong et al., 1989; Seghi, Rosensteil, and Bauer, 1991). Surface roughness of machined surfaces depends largely on the geometry of the cutters used to create the surfaces. However, the effects of machining parameters (feed rate, depth of cut, and spindle speed), machining environment (cutting fluids and what they contain), and cutter geometry are not well characterized (Jahanmir et al., 1992). Preliminary collaborative studies by the National Institute of Standards and Technology (NIST) and the University of Maryland suggest that the effects of these three sets of parameters are multifactorial (Rekow et al., 1992; Zhang et al., 1992). The studies conclude that for both ceramics and metals, the tribologic interactions on the interfaces between the cutting tool and the workpiece have a strong effect on the cutting mechanism. Additives to the cutting fluid can result in feed cutting forces increasing while the tangential cutting forces decrease. This combinational effect permits the cutting tool to stay in the cutting zone, significantly reducing tool vibration during machining and leading to better surface quality (Beale, 1990; Zhang et al., 1992; Zhang et al., 1993). Work in this area will continue with the objective of determining parametric equations relating machining parameters, machining environment, cutter geometry, and materials properties to quality of surface finish as well as to measures of surface and subsurface damage.

The first CAD/CAM-produced restorations were placed in 1986 (Moermann and Krejci, 1991). After 5 years, using US Public Health Service ratings (Ryge and Snyder, 1973), they received highest ratings for contour, color match, and lack of recurrent caries. Clinical data are becoming available on literally thousands of CEREC restorations that have been followed for at least 2 years. Overall, their performance is excellent (Bergmann, 1991; Bieniek and Peters, 1991; Bronwasser et al., 1991; Conforti, 1991; Magnusson, Oden, and Krystek, 1991; Otto, 1991). Far fewer clinical data are availale for the other systems. Some 2-year data have been reported for restorations produced using the Procera system (Bergman and Bessing, 1990) and, like the CEREC restorations, they have excellent results with respect to both longevity and tissue response. Two years, of course, is minimal for longevity of a restoration. Actual comparisons with cast gold restorations will be available only after 5 or 10 more years. However, early indications suggest that CAD/CAM-produced restorations are a viable alternative to traditional cast restorations.

Summary

CAD/CAM technology has created some exciting possibilities for restorative dentistry. Automation can produce restorations whose fit and performance compares favorably with that of traditional cast restorations, but that can be provided in a single visit to the dentist. The future for engineers and dentists alike, will be exciting challenging as they work to achieve advances, integrate new technologies as they develop (stereolithography, for instance), and enhance the systems, making them increasingly intelligent and operator-independent. New materials can be engineered to create more aesthetic, more toothlike restorations. Future developments, resulting from collaboration among engineers, material scientists, and dentists, will be very exciting.

ACKNOWLEDGMENT Development of the DentiCAD system was funded, in part, through NIDR grant R29 DEO8455. The authors also wish to thank Dave Gipe for his continuing technical and artistic support, and the design and development teams at Digital Dental Systems, Foster Miller, and Bego for their commitment and efforts.

REFERENCES

ANUSAVICE, K. J., S. HU, and JOHHATIE, B., 1991. Tensile stress in glass-ceramic crowns: Effect of flaws and cement voids. *J. Dent. Res.* (70) Abstr. 1343.

BEALE, D. S., 1990. A study of the cutting mechanism found in the machining of ceramics. Master's thesis, University of Maryland.

BERGMAN, B., and C. BESSING, 1990. A 2-year follow-up study of titanium crowns. *Acta Odontol. Scand.* 48:113–117.

BERGMANN, M., 1991. Swedish experiences with the CEREC method. In *International Symposium on Computer Restorations*, W. H. Moermann, ed. Zurich: Quintessence, pp. 309–314.

BIENIEK, K. W., and A. PETERS, 1991. Clinical evaluation of ceramic restorations machined by a CAD/CAM technique. In *International Symposium on Computer Restorations*, W. H. Moermann, ed. Zurich: Quintessence, pp. 327–336.

BRONWASSER, P., W. H. MOERMANN, I. KREJCI, and F. LUTZ, 1991. Marginal adaptation of adhesive CEREC-Dicor inlays. In *International Symposium on Computer Restorations*, W. H. Moermann, ed. Zurich: Quintessence, pp. 377–392.

CHRISTENSEN, G. J., 1966. Marginal fit of gold inlay castings. *J. Prosthet. Dent.* (16) 227–231.

CLAYTON, J., and E. GREEN, 1970. Roughness of pontic materials and dental plaque. *J. Prosthet. Dent.* 23:407.

CONFORTI, G. P., 1991. The CEREC system: Twenty months of clinical practice. In *International Symposium on Computer Restorations*, W. H. Moermann, ed. Zurich: Quintessence, pp. 337–338.

CRAIG, R. G., 1985. *Restorative Dental Materials*. St. Louis: Mosby.

DEGAMO, E. P., 1969. *Materials and Processes in Manufacturing*. New York: Macmillan.

DELONG, R., C. SASIK, M. R. PINTADO, and W. H. DOUGLAS, 1989. The wear of enamel when opposed by ceramic systems. *Dent Mater.* 5:266–271.

DURET, F., and E. DURET, 1986. Apparatus for taking odontological or medical impressions. U.S. Patent No. 4,611,288.

EDEN, G. T., 1979. Fit of porcelain fused to metal crown and bridge castings. *J. Dent. Res.* 58(12):2360–2368.

ELLISON, J. A., A. A. LUGASSY, J. C. STECOS, and M. P. MOFFA, 1992. Clinical trial of cast glass ceramic crowns: Seven-year findings. *J. Dent. Res.* (71) Abstr. 816.

HOLMES, J. R., 1986. Marginal fit of castable ceramic (DICOR) crowns. Master's thesis, University of North Carolina.

JAHANMIR, S., L. K. IVES, A. W. RUFF, and M. B. PETERSON, 1992. Ceramic machining: Assessment of current practice and research needs in the United States. NIST Special Publication SP-834.

JALKIO, J. A., R. C. KIM, and S. K. CASE, 1985. Three-dimensional inspection using multistripe structured light. *Optical Eng.* 24(6):966–974.

JERNBERG, G. R., 1980. The relationship between proximal tooth open contacts and periodontal disease. Master's thesis, University of Minnesota.

KELLY, J. R., R. GIORDANO, P. L. POBER, and M. J. CIMA,

1990. Fracture-surface analysis of dental ceramics: Clinically failed restorations. *Int. J. Prosthodont.* 3(5):430–440.

MAGNUSSON, D., A. ODEN, and I. KRYSTEK, 1991. Clinical evaluation of CEREC restorations. In *International Symposium on Computer Restorations*, W. H. Moermann, ed. Zurich: Quintessence, pp. 339–346.

MARINACCIO, P. J., B. NAPPI, K. M. CAPTAIN, and A. J. LANE, 1992. Contact digitizer, particularly for dental applications. U.S. Patent No. 5,131,844.

MOERMANN, W. H., and M. BRANDESTINI, 1986. Method and apparatus for the fabrication of custom-shaped implants. U.S. Patent No. 4,575,806.

MOERMANN, W. H., and I. KREJCI, 1991. Clinical and SEM evaluation of CEREC inlays after 5 years in situ, In *International Symposium on Computer Restorations*, W. H. Moermann, ed. Zurich: Quintessence, pp. 25–33.

NIEBEL, B. W., A. B. DRAPER, and R. A. WYSK, 1989. *Modern Manufacturing Process Engineering.* New York: McGraw-Hill.

OTTO, T., 1991. Clinical evaluation and experience with the CEREC method in a private practice after two years. In *International Symposium on Computer Restorations*, W. H. Moermann, ed. Zurich: Quintessence, pp. 347–354.

PETERS, A., and K. W. BIENIEK, 1991. SEM-examination of the marginal adaptation of computer-machined ceramic restorations. In *International Symposium on Computer Restorations*, W. H. Moermann, ed. Zurich: Quintessence, pp. 365–372.

RAMFJORD, S. P., and M. M. ASH, 1971. *Occlusion.* Philadelphia: Saunders.

REKOW, E. D., V. P. THOMPSON, D. SLATER-EL, and W. MUSOLF, 1992. CAD/CAM restoration surface finish as a function of machine tool parameters. *J. Dent. Res* 71 (abstr. 1399).

REKOW, E. D., V. P. THOMPSON, and H. S. YANG, 1991. Margin fit of CAD/CAM-produced crowns. *J. Dent. Res.* 70A (abstr. 1346):434.

REPPEL, P. D., K. BOENING, and M. WALTER, 1991. Festsitzender zahnersatz aus gefrastem/funkererodiertem Titan. *Dtsch Zahnaertztl Z* 4(11):756–758.

RYGE, G., and M. SNYDER, 1973. Evaluating the clinical quality of restorations. *J. Am. Dent. Assoc.,* 87:369–377.

SCHERRER, S. S., and W. G. DeRijk, 1991. Factors in the fracture resistance of posterior all-ceramic crowns. *J. Dent. Res.* (70) Abstr. 1342.

SEGHI, R. R., S. F. ROSENSTEIL, and P. BAUER, 1991. Abrasion of human enamel by different dental ceramics in vitro. *J. Dent. Res.* 221–225.

SLAMA, C. C., 1980. *Manual of Photogrammetry.* Falls Church, Va.: American Society of Photogrammetry.

WELLER, E. J., ed. 1984. *Nontraditional Machining Processes.* Society of Manufacturing Engineers.

ZHANG, G. M., T. W. HWANG, D. K. ANAND, and S. JAHANMIR, 1992. Tribological interactions in machining aluminum oxide ceramics. In *Proceedings of the Navy Tribology Workshop.* Annapolis, Md., pp. 9–13.

ZHANG, G. M., T. W. HWANG, D. K. ANAND, and S. JAHANMIR, 1993. Chemo-mechanical effects on the efficiency of machining ceramics. In *Proceedings of 1993 N.S.F. Design and Manufacturing Systems Conference*, Charlotte, N.C., pp. 421–428.

Minimal-Access Surgery

LAPAROSCOPIC surgery has seen remarkable growth over the last 5 years. In 1992, 70% of all gallbladder surgery in the United States, Europe, and Japan was done laparoscopically. By 2000, it is estimated that from 60% to 80% of abdominal surgeries will be performed laparoscopically [1]. Flexible endoscopy is also becoming more and more prevalent. This rapid explosion has, to a large extent, been driven by patient demand. Surgery done through small incisions often is much less traumatic than the same surgery done through large incisions. There is less postoperative pain, and the patient is able to resume normal activities much sooner than would be possible after open surgery. Unfortunately, these gains do not come without costs. What is better for the patient is often awkward for the surgeon, who has traditionally relied heavily on dexterity, tactile feedback, and excellent hand-eye coordination, and who now must operate using long sticks while looking at a television monitor showing video images coming from a camera that is usually pointed by an assistant. One is reminded of a remark (attributed to Winston Churchill) about the game of golf, to the effect that it is a game invented by the Devil, played with implements ill-adapted to the purpose. As we shall see, what is a problem for the surgeon represents an opportunity for the technologist, both to give back to the surgeon some of what has been lost and to provide new capabilities that can be used to develop better ways to help the patient.

As its title suggests, the first chapter in this section, "A Surgeon's Perspective on the Difficulties of Laparoscopic Surgery," by Michael Treat, describes some of the ways in which laparoscopic surgery, although advantageous for the patient, has complicated matters for the surgeon. The fundamental problem is that the surgeon's natural hand-eye coordination is severely degraded. Visualization problems include impaired depth perception when conventional monoscopic laparoscopes are used and the loss of the surgeon's ability to change his (or her) perspective simply by moving his head. Although stereo-optics and flexible, "chip on a stick" laparoscopes are very promising, Dr. Treat makes the point that trade-offs are involved. Stereoscopes have yet to match the image quality of the best monocular systems. Similarly, flexible scopes can be difficult and "unintuitive" to operate. It is proposed that a computer system, perhaps responsive to voice commands by the surgeon, to take over the detailed control of such flexible scopes would be very useful. Present-day laparoscopic instruments are characterized as "user-unfriendly," and computer-controlled teleoperated devices are proposed as one means to get around some of the dexterity limitations inherent in today's rigid sticklike instruments.

The second chapter, "Requirements and Possibilities of Computer-Assisted Endoscopic Surgery," by E. Schippers and V. Schumpelick, makes many of the same points, while also making some interesting broader comments about endoscopic surgery and placing laparoscopic abdominal surgery within the context of related developments in other surgical disciplines. As the authors point out, "laparoscopic surgery is not minor surgery; it is major surgery through a small incision." Although the reduced trauma to the patient has many advantages, there are also costs, both those associated with the equipment required and those associated with additional burdens placed on the surgeon. The authors provide a short description of laparoscopic cholecystectomy and then discuss a number of problems of endoscopic surgery. It is interesting to note that, whereas Treat discusses the dexterity limitations associated with laparoscopic instruments, Schippers and Schumpelick place greater emphasis on the tactile limitations, such as the surgeon's loss of direct contact with the organ in question. The difficulty of feeling a pulse is given as one example. The authors describe many of the same perspective, depth perception, and eye-hand coordination problems discussed by Dr. Treat, and also mention problems associated with image distortion and inaccurate color rendering by present-day video cameras. They also discuss the need for better systems for training surgeons and for on-line documentation of surgical cases.

The third chapter, "Perception and Manipulation Problems in Endoscopic Surgery," by Tendick et al., describes many of the same problems discussed in the previous two chapters, in this case from the perspective of experimental human factors research. Quantitative studies of the effects of such factors as stereo separation, viewpoint-hand alignment, and standard versus endoscopic instruments on task performance are presented. These studies clearly demonstrate that the difficulties described in the two previous chapters do indeed affect task performance. They also provide benchmarks that might be useful in assessing the effectiveness of new technology to address some of these problems.

The fourth chapter, "Robotically Assisted Laparoscopic Surgery: From Concept to Development," by Sackier and Wang, describes a telerobotic system designed specifically to replace the human surgical assistant whose job is to hold the camera during laparoscopic surgery. The robot, called AESOP by the authors, attaches to the rail of the operating table and has 4 active and 2 passive degrees of freedom. The surgeon uses a simple hand or foot controller to specify motion of the camera relative to the current field of view of the camera, thus addressing one of the requirements

described by Dr. Treat. Perhaps the most interesting thing about AESOP is that it has received regulatory approval and is being offered for sale. A number of other robotic systems for performing similar functions, with varying degrees of sophistication, are in various phases of development and commercial deployment [2, 3]. One very interesting device [3] tracks movements of the surgeon's head to replace the hand controllers used on many other systems. One salient characteristic of these systems is that they aim at performing a simple function alongside the surgeon in order to reduce the number of people required in the operating room. At the other extreme are complete "telepresence surgery" systems [4–7], in which a highly dexterous robotic system is interposed between the surgeon and the patient. In this scenario, most clearly described in [4], the surgeon will be seated at a control station, which may either be in the operating room or (eventually) at a great distance from the patient. However, the surgeon will be given the sensation of directly manipulating the patient's anatomy using conventional instruments.[1]

In the fifth chapter in this section, "A Telerobotic Assistant for Laparoscopic Surgery," Taylor et al. describe a system that resembles the simple scope-holding robots discussed earlier, in the sense that it is primarily intended to work cooperatively alongside the surgeon. Although the initial task set includes camera manipulation, the primary focus is the exploitation of machine capabilities that complement the surgeon's skills, rather than replacement of excess personnel in the operating room. Several interesting aspects of the system include an accurate, specially designed robot whose "natural" motions correspond with those commonly found in mimimally invasive surgery; force control; and computer image processing of the laparoscopic camera image in order to provide navigational information. It is interesting to note that the image processing and control capabilities of this system may make it somewhat less susceptible to communication delays in remote surgery than would be the case for pure teleoperation systems.

The sixth chapter, "A Clinically Applied Robot for Prostatectomies," by Davies et al., describes the development of a specialized system for one of the most common surgical procedures, namely transurethral resection of the prostate. When carried out manually with a conventional resectoscope, this procedure is time-consuming and tiring for the surgeon, and considerable training is required before proficiency is attained. In addition to its inherent interest as one of the first robotic assist systems for tissue removal to be applied clinically, this system is intriguing because of the several phases of development it went through. Initial feasibility studies were carried out using a potato and a conventional industrial robot, which was augmented with additional distal actuators to permit more accurate control of the cutter's trajectory. Once the desired cutting motions were determined, a completely passive mechanism was developed to constrain the cutter to the desired work volume. After this passive manipulation aid was used successfully on a number of patients, a motorized version was implemented and again applied clinically. In addition to describing these phases of development, the chapter discusses the use of intraoperative ultrasound in setting up the system for surgery, surgeon interfaces and human factors, and (briefly) safety.

The earlier chapters in this section focus primarily on systems dealing with rigid endoscopes, although many of the underlying technologies, software, and design considerations are equally applicable for nonrigid endoscopes. In contrast, the final chapter, "A Voice-Activated Tendon-Controlled Device for Endoscopy," by Sturges and Laowattana, focuses on the design of flexible endoscopes. The chapter includes an introduction describing many of the common design approaches to making flexible endoscopes. It proposes a very clever bead-and-chain approach for alternatively reshaping, stiffening, and advancing the tip of a flexible endoscope. An alternative actuator technology that holds considerable promise for flexible endoscopy is described by Ikuta elsewhere in this book (chapter 18). Finally, the Sturges chapter describes the authors' experiments with voice command and control, much along the lines suggested in Dr. Treat's introductory article.

NOTE

1. At the time of this writing (March 1994) the most fully developed of these systems appears to be that developed at SRI International by Green, Hill, and others (see [5, 8]). Unfortunately, no suitable chapter is available for inclusion in this collection, and Dr. Green's group has chosen to develop the system further before writing about it for external publication.

REFERENCES

[1] *World Medical Device and Diagnostic News*, August 5, 1992.
[2] GAGNIER, M., 1993. Oral presentation at Massachusetts General Hospital Symposium on Minimally Invasive Surgery, September 27–28.
[3] PETELIN, J. B., 1994. Computer-assisted surgical instrument control. In *Proceedings of the Medicine Meets Virtual Reality Conference II*, San Diego, pp. 170–173. Aligned Management Assoc., San Diego.
[4] SATAVA, R. M., 1993. High-tech surgery: Speculation on future direction. In *Minimally Invasive Surgery*, J. G. Hunter and J. M. Sackier, eds. New York: McGraw-Hill, pp. 339–347.
[5] GREEN, P., 1992. Advanced teleoperator technology for enhanced minimally invasive surgery. In *Proceedings of the Medicine Meets Virtual Reality Conference*. San Diego, June 4–7. Aligned Management Assoc., San Diego.
[6] HOLLAR, E., and H. BREITWEISER, 1994. Telepresence systems for application in minimally invasive surgery. In *Proceedings of the Medicine Meets Virtual Reality Conference II*. San Diego, pp. 77–80. Aligned Management Assoc., San Diego
[7] HUNTER, I., M. SAGAR, L. JONES, T. DOUKOGLOU, S. LAFONTAINE, and P. HUNTER, 1994. Teleoperated mocrosurgical robot and associated virtual environment. In *Proceedings of the Medicine Meets Virtual Reality Conference II*. San Diego, pp. 85–89. Aligned Management Assoc., San Diego.
[8] GREEN, P., 1993. Telepresence surgery. NSF Workshop on Computer-Assisted Surgery, Washington, D.C., February.

42 A Surgeon's Perspective on the Difficulties of Laparoscopic Surgery

MICHAEL R. TREAT

TRADITIONAL OPEN cholecystectomy (gallbladder removal done through a fairly large abdominal incision) is a well-respected, thoroughly understood procedure that was first done in the late 1880s. Over the next 100 years, this procedure was incrementally refined until it achieved an enviable safety record and success rate. Although open cholecystectomy had stood the test of time, in the late 1980s laparoscopic cholecystectomy overtook it with amazing rapidity. The reason for this revolutionary transformation was the obvious advantage that laparoscopic cholecystectomy had for patients, in terms of less postoperative pain and faster recovery to full function.

Laparoscopic cholecystectomy and open cholecystectomy are similar in that both procedures result in removal of a diseased gallbladder and the stones within the gallbladder. The difference between the two procedures is that the laparoscopic approach avoids the large incision required in the traditional approach. The large incision is avoided by the use of long (approximately 30 cm), thin (5- to 10-mm) instruments that are introduced into the abdominal cavity through small punctures in the abdominal wall. These instruments are basically long sticks with various grasping jaws, pincers, or scissors on the end. Visualization of the operative field is achieved by means of a laparoscope, which is essentially a close-focusing, wide-angle telescope. Like the other instruments, the laparosope is a long, thin, and rigid tube that is introduced through a small puncture in the abdominal wall. Space to maneuver the instruments in the abdominal cavity is obtained by insufflating carbon dioxide gas to lift the abdominal wall away from the organs.

Because of the limitations imposed on the surgeon by rigid, sticklike instruments and a rigid telescopic visual system, it is more difficult to perform laparoscopic surgery than it is to perform open surgery. Let us analyze the difficulties.

Difficulties with vision

The laparoscopic surgeon faces two main types of visual problems: impaired depth perception and difficulty in varying the perspective or point of view of the operative field. These visual problems are due to the inherent limitations of current telescope technology. This technology uses a rigid lens train to convey the internal image to a video camera mounted outside the patient.

DEPTH PERCEPTION

Impaired depth perception occurs because conventional laparoscopes are monocular. Stereoscopic laparoscopes are beginning to become clinically available. These systems employ dual optical pathways that are separated at the distal end (inside the patient) by enough distance to provide a stereo effect. These stereo systems are steadily improving, but at the present time the overall image quality (i.e., resolution and brightness) they provide is not quite as good as the best of the monocular systems.

Although stereo vision would seem to be a desirable goal, its actual clinical importance has not been proved. With experience, it is possible to use monocular vision to perform even complex tasks such as suture placement and knot tying. There are monocular visual cues that can provide the surgeon with some sense of depth. These cues include shadowing effects and the relative sizes of anatomic landmarks. However, many surgeons intuitively feel that having stereo vision would be helpful.

CHANGE OF PERSPECTIVE

In open surgery, the surgeon can change his or her perspective by tilting his or her head or by moving the entire body. In laparoscopic surgery, the rigid telescope is constrained to move in arcs of a sphere whose center is the point of the abdominal wall through which the telescope enters the abdomen. The perspective can be varied to some extent by movement of the telescope along its constrained arcs. However, to obtain a very different point of view requires removing the telescope from the abdominal cavity and putting it back through another entry point through the abdominal wall. This maneuver is feasible, but it is time-consuming and involves loss of vision while the telescope is being repositioned.

Making the telescope flexible or mounting the video camera directly on the end of a flexible shaft might eliminate the perspective problem, because the tip of the flexible scope could be positioned to achieve "around-the-corner" views not possible with a rigidly mounted camera. In fact, there is currently available a flexible laparoscope (patterned after conventional flexible gastroscopes or colonoscopes) that has its video chip on the end of a shaft with a steerable tip. Although this seems like a solution to the perspective problem, it introduces another problem. Using the flexible laparoscope is not as easy or intuitive as using the traditional rigid telescope, because the camera operator cannot simply point it where he or she wishes to look but must turn various dials on the instrument to adjust the direction in which the steerable tip is looking.

What would help in this situation is the use of a computer to relieve the human operator of the burden of having to work out the detailed control movements needed to position the tip to obtain the desired view. Ideally, the human surgeon could verbally instruct the scope as to what sort of view was wanted, and the scope would be intelligent enough to assume the proper configuration to provide the desired view.

Difficulties with instrumentation

Currently available laparoscopic instruments are user-unfriendly. They are too long to be handled with the same degree of ease as the tools used in open surgery. They lack the degrees of freedom that the surgeon's shoulder, arm and hand possess. They are constrained to move in spherical arcs determined by the site of entry through the abdominal wall; this constraint is a drawback when complex 3D tasks such as suturing are attempted. In addition, there is a fulcrum effect, resulting in the problem that instrument tip motion is not related in a constant way to motion of the operator's handle. As the instrument is advanced into the abdominal cavity, the location of the fulcrum changes, and small movements of the handle produce larger swings of the tip of the instrument.

A possible solution to the problem of user-unfriendly instruments is the use of computer-assisted positioning of surgical devices with more degrees of freedom than the "sticks" we are now using. The idea here is to use a computer to take over some of the functions of the surgeon's cerebellum in coordinating eye-hand movements. Such many-degree-of-freedom instruments would be difficult for a surgeon to control if he or she had to micromanage each joint of the device. The computer cerebellum might allow the human surgeon to control instruments with multiple joints operating at "unnatural" angles or around corners in ways that would normally be very difficult. In this scenario, the surgeon would operate wearing gloves and perhaps a shoulder harness that would be wired into the computer, which would translate the surgeon's upper-extremity movements into motions of the teleoperator arm. The computer would free the surgeon of having to micromanage the motion of the various joints of the arm and would allow to the teleoperator to mimic the surgeon's movements in a natural and intuitive way.

Laparoscopic surgery has made the patient's life easier but has complicated matters for the surgeon. It is hoped that by creatively applying technology we can make life a little easier for the surgeon as well.

43 Requirements and Possibilities of Computer-Assisted Endoscopic Surgery

E. SCHIPPERS AND V. SCHUMPELICK

FOR THOUSANDS of years, just about all surgery was necessarily "minimally invasive." Infections, pain, and shock made it very unlikely that the patient would survive any major surgical invasion. As medicine progressed, the introduction of sterile procedures, antibiotics, anesthesia, and intensive care made it possible for surgeons to perform much more significant interventions for physiologic reconstruction, functional replacement of organs, and anatomically correct reparation. Nevertheless, the collateral damage to the patient required by conventional surgical approaches is significant, and healing times are often long. As technology has progressed, the introduction of laparoscopic and endoscopic methods has greatly reduced the degree of invasiveness required to treat many conditions. Modern surgery is thus able more nearly to obey the ancient precept *Nil nocere suprema lex*, or "the highest rule is to do no harm."

This fundamental transformation in the way surgery is performed has taken place in a very short period of time—almost overnight. An example of the newer, less invasive methods is laparoscopic cholecystectomy, which uses modern instruments and microcameras to project images of the patient's anatomy onto a video monitor. The societal demand for shorter healing times has made laparoscopy the norm rather than an exception. These recent developments have brought abdominal surgery in line with other specialties such as neurosurgery, traumatology, gynecology, and urology, which for a decade have included endoscopy in the therapeutic codex.

In laparoscopy, as in the other disciplines, surgeons have to abandon the principle of diagnostic and therapeutic decisions made by means of the feeling of the organ "in their hands." Instead, they will have to devote themselves to the acquisition and perfection of new instrumental techniques. Videoendoscopic surgery thus complements the traditional surgery "of the eye and the hand" with an atraumatic procedure that avoids complications and unnecessary risks to the patient.

Laparoscopic surgery should not be considered minor surgery. It is major surgery done through small incisions. It is surgery carried out from a distance using long microinstruments under visual control inserted through 5- to 13-mm-wide trocars. It can be reproducible and precise, because the use of video monitors enlarges the level of detail of anatomic representation of the surgical scene. A major advantage of laparoscopic surgery is the reduction in trauma during the approach to the targeted organ, without compromise in terms of exposition of the introperative site. The trauma of the surgical intervention is further reduced by the fact that complex procedures are carried out delicately with the aid of microinstruments. It therefore becomes unnecessary to retract the abdomen in order to gain exposition to internal organs or to mistreat the intestine with hooks and towels.

These advantages are partially vitiated by the considerable effort required on the part of the surgeon (due to the nature of the procedure) and by higher equipment costs. Abdominal surgery, which, until recently, got by with sterilizable (traditional) instruments, now requires pricey, disposable, endoscopic ones. Laparoscopic surgery minimizes the trauma of the approach to the target organ but not the impact of the intervention itself on that organ. Thus, the term *endoscopic surgery* is more descriptive and to the point than the phase *minimally invasive surgery*.

Currently, endoscopic surgery comprises laparoscopic, thoracoscopic, endoluminal, and arthroscopic interventions. A survey of these procedures is given in

TABLE 43.1
Endoscopic surgery: Established procedures

Approach	Operation
Laparoscopic	Cholecystectomy, appendectomy, adhesiolysis, fundoplication, ulcer oversewing, proximal gastric vagotomy
Thoracoscopic	Sympathectomy, vagotomy, resection of bullae, pleurodesis, biopsy
Arthroscopic	Menisectomy, etc.
Endoluminal	Sphincterotomy, mucosectomy, ablation of polyps

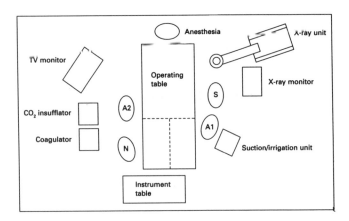

FIGURE 43.1   Arrangement of equipment and position of the operating team. (S, surgeon; Al, cameraman; A2, assistant; N, nurse.)

table 43.1. Other methods are either in the patient trials stage (reparation of hernias; resecting operations in the colorectal region) or in animal experimentation (resecting interventions on the liver and pancreas). This chapter surveys the modern spectrum of endoscopic surgery and its future applications, describing in detail the established laparoscopic cholecystectomy procedure. Subsequently, it outlines new requirements for surgeons and surgical instruments, current technology limitations, and the potential for improvements due to the use of computers.

Laparoscopic cholecystectomy

In a laparoscopic cholecystectomy procedure, the patient is first placed on an operating table that is permeable for x-rays. The surgical team then positions itself such that the surgeon and the camera operator are on the patient's left side, while the second assistant and the operating room nurse place themselves the patient's right side. Subsequently, the video monitor and instrument table are placed in the direct field of view of the operating team, so that coordinated actions can be carried out (figure 43.1).

The first incision is a curved one at the upper margin of the navel, in order to insert a cannula into the abdominal cavity. This allows pressurization of the abdominal cavity with carbon dioxide up to a pressure of 12–14 mm Hg. Next, an 11-mm trocar is inserted blindly for the forward-viewing endoscope. If the diagnostic view obtained establishes operability, then three additional trocars are placed under videoendoscopic control under the right costal arc (figure 43.2). The gallbladder is grasped with an atraumatic grasping forceps at the fundus and elevated in the direction of the right diaphragmal dome. Adherences with the

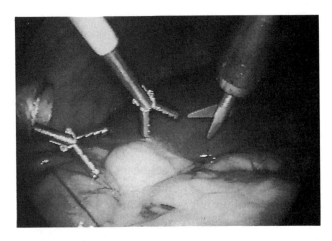

FIGURE 43.2   Three intraabdominal trocars for the introduction of fixation tongs and scissors.

neighboring organs (omentum, right colon flexure, duodenum) are separated bluntly or with a hook electrode. With a second grasping forceps, the infundibulum is grasped and stretched so that Callot's triangle is visible.

The next step is an incision of the peritoneum, followed by the dissection of the arteria and ductus cysticus. After this circular dissection and a clear identification of both structures (figure 43.3), they are occluded twice by clips and then divided between the clips. The preparation of the gallbladder is accomplished by stepwise detachment from the stretched structures with scissors or the hook electrode (figure 43.4). Occasional small visible vessels or bleedings in the gallbladder bed can be coagulated with high-frequency currents.

The extraction of the gallbladder takes place through

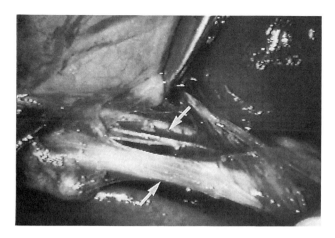

FIGURE 43.3 After dissection, identification of arteria cystica and ductus cysticus (arrows).

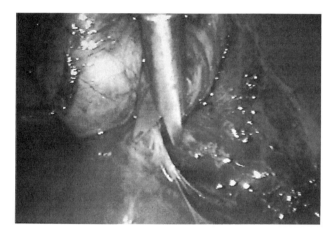

FIGURE 43.4 Preparation of the gallbladder with the scissors.

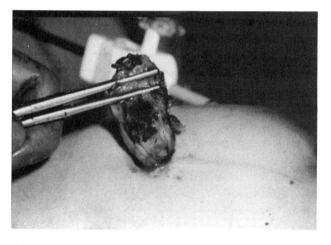

FIGURE 43.5 Extraction of the gallbladder through the incision at the umbilical margin.

the umbilical incision (figure 43.5). This means that the gallbladder is grasped with a strong pair of tongs at the infundibulum and then extracted under mild traction. If necessary, a tightly filled gallbladder is punctured percutaneously. After extraction the gallbladder bed is rinsed and hemostasis is accomplished. Next, a Robinson's drainage catheter is inserted into the gallbladder bed and the trocars are removed under visual control. The last step in the procedure is the release of the pneumoperitoneum and closure of the wound.

Problems of endoscopic surgery

SENSORY PROBLEMS

TACTILITY The direct examination of tissue consistency is extraordinarily helpful for the diagnostic differentiation between pathologic and healthy tissue as well as for therapy. In many cases the tactile sense is, in open surgery, the last decision parameter for determining the depth of penetration of the scalpel. The palpable pulsation of a blood vessel thus normally prevents its accidental opening. The abandonment of direct-contact open laparotomy and the interposition of long instruments used in minimally invasive surgery results in a considerable loss of sensory tactility. Moreover, in contrast to the open technique, an immediate manual compression is not possible due to the impediment of the closed abdomen. The considerable loss of time required for the necessary change of instruments can in this situation necessitate a change of procedure to open laparotomy in order to minimize intermediate bleeding.

Apart from the differentiation of the respective structures (e.g., ductus cysticus versus arteria cystica), the judgment of tissue consistency allows a demarcation of pathologic tissue from healthy organ structures. For example, intrapulmonary round lesions, which cannot be seen directly due to their location, can be localized through tactile palpation. The loss of such tactile feedback is a decisive disadvantage of the increasingly common resecting applications of endoscopic surgery. Even if the surgeon's tactile appreciation improves with practice and as surgical instruments improve, it cannot compare with the natural abilities of the surgeon's fingertips.

Future laparoscopic instruments will need sensing and control systems placed at their tips. These remote sensors will, ideally, replace the fingertip of the surgeon by measuring tissue consistency and pulsations and by transferring this information back to the surgeon's hand. Such tip sensors could be miniaturized ultrasound probes or piezoelectric films. The translation of ultrasonic changes at the target organ into sensory qualities at the joystick or at the tip of the instrument could be realized by means of computer-assisted simulation. These feedback sensations must correlate with the respective experiences of open surgery so that surgeons can adequately respond to the tactile feedback.

VISION Endoscopic surgery yields a further sensory handicap, which gains more and more importance especially in regard to the increasing use of reconstructive interventions: the restriction of the visual feedback. Factors that result in considerably reduced vision (compared to open surgery) include a limited field of view, peripheral image distortions, unnatural reproduction of colors, loss of illumination, and the projection of a natural 3D scene on 2D monitors.

The reduced field of view in endoscopic surgery cannot encompass the frequent changes of instruments as they pass through the abdominal cavity, because the camera sees only the target organ. This has led in the past to accidental organ lesions and other postoperative complications. Therefore, an additional camera depicting the whole body cavity and all intracavitary movements would be very helpful. A registered survey image would reduce the risk of dangerous movements considerably.

Distorted images and ineffectual color transmission also contribute substantially to a loss of accurate visual feedback. Compensating lenses can help minimize peripheral image distortion, but their optics further increase the loss of light. The light intensity is also considerably influenced by the illuminated organ itself, especially when severe bleeding occurs (hemoglobin has a large coefficient of light absorption). Conversely, when there is no bleeding and the organ surface is glossy, the large amount of light reflected can saturate the camera electronics and produce white spots on the monitor.

Variable illumination of the surgical site may also result from the (frequent) changes in the distance of the optics from the target organ (especially in complicated reconstructive interventions such as fundoplication). These movement, together with the reflective characteristics of the target organ surface, thus require frequent adjustments of the light intensity. To alleviate

this problem, it will be necessary to develop a computer-assisted intelligent light source that regulates its intensity in response to the specific situation. Such a tool will also be needed to compensate for color discrepancies in the image, which can lead to substantial problems of orientation in endoscopic surgery. A computer-assisted simulation could be very useful in this regard.

Current video systems provide a 2D image of the 3D anatomic space. This restriction poses two kinds of problems for the surgeon: problems of hand-eye coordination and difficulties with depth perception and spatial orientation. This loss of vision is compensated, at least in simple ablative interventions (such as cholecystectomy), by training and experience. However, more complex operations involving 3D reconstructions of parts of organs will, in the future, require a spatial image on the monitor screen. A stereo-endoscope that alternatively projects an image from a right and a left camera onto the monitor offers an answer to this problem. Viewed through shutter LCD glasses, the image becomes stereoscopic (3D). Many surgeons find wearing these glasses to be somewhat stressful, and there is a need for development of completely unencumbered systems.

INSTRUMENTAL PROBLEMS

The increasing use of endoscopic surgery has been very influential on the development of new instruments. At first, the miniaturization of commonly used surgical instruments was attempted. Some were newly developed (stapler applied through the trocar), and some were established instruments (trocars, scissors, and tongs). The increasing complexity of surgical intervention, however, imposed new demands in terms of instrument ergonomy and degrees of freedom. The main advantage of endoscopic surgery—preservation of the integrity of the abdomen—implies at the same time a considerable curtailment of the liberty of movement of the instruments. The rigid trocar necessary for the introduction of instruments further restricts mobility. The first real improvements have now been accomplished through the development of rotating and bendable instruments.

Further developments, up to the complete replacement of the surgical arm, aim to take the difficult position of the surgeon into consideration. The control of such intelligent, maneuverable systems must allow the surgeon to respond to any task events adequately by following the master-slave principle. This requires multifunctional instruments as well as on-line diagnostic information with respect to instrument and sensory feedback. The control of such a robotic arm or arms can only be realized in computer-assisted surgery, performed after intensive computer simulation training.

INSTRUCTION PROBLEMS

The unusual surgical approach, the reliance on restricted 2D video images, and the increased application of technical devices impose new dexterity demands on the surgeon and her or his assistants. Furthermore, certain conventional surgery techniques (such as the anastomosis and ligature) cannot be easily extended to endoscopy, and thus the new techniques require substantial training. The fast propagation of endoscopic surgery has led to a discrepancy between the number of experienced instructors and the number of surgeons driven by the competitive pressure to learn the new technique in a very short time. Therefore it is necessary to find new instructional approaches to supplement the traditional training on phantoms and animal models. Computer-based simulators similar to those used for flight training present one possibility for simulating operative procedures and monitoring the students' performance and errors.

DOCUMENTATION PROBLEMS

Surgical conscientiousness demands accurate documentation and quality control. The technology of videoendoscopy is uniquely suited to address these demands because the videotape recording allows a complete documentation of the procedure. To date, however, this potential is limited by the restrictions of storage capacities for the videotapes. The development of interactively accessible and reproducible computerized storage of image sequences could greatly simplify documentation.

Conclusion

Not only are current technical developments in modern endoscopic surgery fascinating, but the developmental potential is very promising. Never before have surgeons been so dependent on technology, and never before has there been such a need for cooperative and open-minded surgeons. Surgeons must be able to exploit technologies without losing control over what they do. Technology, however, should be able to serve the surgeon without compromising quality and potential for innovation. User and producer, surgeon and engineer, should always keep this mutual responsibility in mind.

44 Perception and Manipulation Problems in Endoscopic Surgery

FRANK TENDICK, RUSSELL W. JENNINGS,
GREGORY THARP, AND LAWRENCE STARK

IN TRADITIONAL surgery, it is usually necessary to cut through a lot of good tissue to get to the diseased area beneath. A large incision must be made through skin, muscle, and connective tissue to make room for conventional instruments and surgeons' hands. In endoscopic surgery, long thin instruments are inserted through small incisions or orifices to operate with minimal damage to healthy areas. The result is that patients may spend much less time in the hospital and can recover in a matter of days from some operations. *Endoscopy* is a general term for minimally invasive surgery of any area of the body (White and Klein, 1991), including the gastrointestinal tract (Cotton and Williams, 1982; Pearl, 1984), abdomen (laparoscopy) (Saleh, 1988; Semm, 1987), chest (thoracoscopy) (Boutin, Viallat, and Aelony, 1991), or joints (arthroscopy) (Johnson, 1986; Parisien, 1988). The clear advantage of fast recovery has led to an explosion of interest in endoscopy in the last several years, with new applications being developed continually.

Unfortunately, the surgeon's abilities are severely hampered by the limitations of current technology in endoscopy. Vision is limited by the narrow monoscopic field of view of the endoscope and by the transmission and video presentation of the endoscopic image. Other sensations, such as tactile sense and force feedback, are significantly reduced. Endoscopic instruments do not have the necessary degrees of freedom to allow performance of complex motions. Until endoscopic technology improves, the potential of endoscopy will not be realized.

This chapter is adapted from a paper that appeared originally in *Presence* 2(1):66–81, 1993.

Principles of endoscopy

An endoscope is basically a long tube through which an image of the surgical space inside the body is transmitted to the surgeon. This tube may be rigid for areas easily accessible through an incision, or flexible to extend through twisting paths, as in arteries or the gastrointestinal tract. In current systems, the image is presented on a video monitor. The image is passed through the tube, either by lens optics in a rigid endoscope or by fiberoptics in a flexible endoscope, to a charge-coupled device (CCD) video camera at the surgeon's end (Sivak, 1986; Classen et al., 1987; Knyrim et al., 1990). Alternatively, improvements in CCD technology have made it possible to locate the CCD array at the endoscope tip. A light source is transmitted to the endoscope tip through fiberoptics in all endoscopes. This technology is packed into a tube from a few millimeters to a centimeter in diameter.

For some operations, typically those requiring flexible endoscopes, instruments are passed through a channel in the endoscope. In operations where the surgical space is more easily accessible, as in laparoscopy, a rigid endoscope and multiple instruments are inserted through separate incisions. A wide range of instruments, including graspers, scissors, probes, staplers, and biopsy forceps, are used (White and Klein, 1991). These instruments all have only 1 degree of freedom (dof) at the tip, typically operated by a trigger handle. Instruments with nonmechanical elements include lasers, electrocoagulators, and irrigation-aspiration devices. This chapter will concentrate on the use of rigid laparoscopes and laparoscopic instruments, although most of the results are applicable to all endoscopic equipment and operations.

In many ways, endoscopic surgery is similar to tele-operation of a remote manipulator. The surgical environment cannot be sensed directly but only through the optics of the endoscope. Similarly, ease of manipulation and tactile sensation are limited by the surgeon's inability to access the surgical work space directly. Thus, although the surgeon is physically close to the patient, the surgical environment is effectively remote, with sensing and manipulation transmitted through the endoscope and long instruments. Solutions to the problems of remote manipulation exist for teleoperative applications in environments such as space or undersea. It is likely that similar solutions could be applied to endoscopy.

In this chapter, we attempt to identify the major problems of endoscopic technology, particularly in vision and manipulation. In watching experienced surgeons perform endoscopy, we observed two major problems. First, the lack of a stereoscopic view from the endoscope, and a lack of adequate monoscopic depth cues, forced the surgeons to grope forward and backward with instruments to gauge the relative depths of objects by touching them. This must be performed slowly enough to avoid damaging tissue on contact. Second, the fact that endoscopic instruments are constrained to pivot about the entry through the skin reduces their freedom of motion. This hampers the surgeon's ability to perform complex motions, as in suturing.

Vision in endoscopic surgery

There are many potential limitations to vision with a videoendoscope. These include limits in bandwidth, spatial resolution, contrast, and color fidelity of CCD, optical, and video technology (Pepper and Cole, 1978; Satava, Poe, and Joyce, 1988; Knyrim et al., 1989). There is a trade-off between image resolution and field of view for a given transmission bandwidth or array density of detectors.

There are also problems with endoscopes that are not inherent to video or optical technology. In particular, the monoscopic image provided by an endoscope does not give depth disparity information, which could be achieved with a stereoscopic view. The 3D positioning experiment described next evaluated the significance of this limitation.

METHODS IN THE 3D POSITIONING EXPERIMENT

One of the most obvious problems of sensing in endoscopy is the lack of stereoscopic vision when using conventional endoscopes. A simple experiment was designed to test surgeons' 3D positioning ability under a variety of viewing conditions, including endoscopic viewing and direct viewing with one or both eyes. In this experiment, paper markers suspended at different positions and heights by paper clips were plucked by surgeon subjects using either hand-held or endoscopic instruments (figure 44.1). The markers and paper clips were painted flat black; the bottom and sides of the experimental field were white. This created a high-contrast environment with minimal monoscopic depth

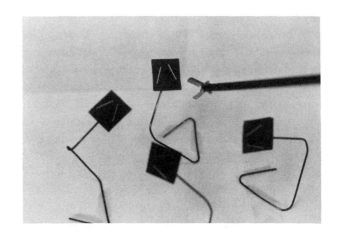

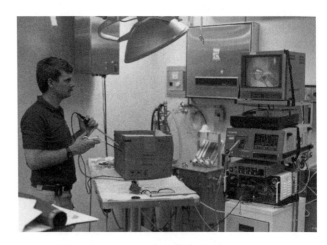

FIGURE 44.1 Three-dimensional positioning experiment. (Top) Endoscopic grasper is used to pluck black markers. (Bottom) Subject watches video monitor while performing task.

cues. Markers were 2 cm square, arranged within a circle of roughly 15 cm in diameter.

In the endoscopic viewing condition, the surgeon used a videoendoscope with a 10-mm-diameter tube, manufactured by Olympus, mounted with a model AR-T2 camera and CLV-10 xenon light source. The endoscopic view was displayed on a video monitor (see figure 44.1). Endoscope and instruments were inserted through holes in a box that held the experiment. In the direct viewing conditions, the top of the box was opened. When hand instruments (needle drivers) were used, the subjects reached in through the top of the box. The lid of the box was placed loosely over the subjects' arms when it was necessary to hide the subjects' view under nondirect viewing conditions.

Two surgical residents with experience in 50–100 laparoscopic operations were used as subjects. They were asked to pluck the four paper markers as quickly as possible. Three runs were timed under five visual conditions with both hand-held and endoscopic instruments. Subjects were given time to practice the task, and experiment order was randomized in order to reduce learning effects. Six target boards with different marker arrangements were used so that subjects would not memorize marker positions.

One subject performed two sets of three runs in all conditions except the limited-field-of-view conditions (described later), in which just one set was performed. The other subject performed one set under all conditions. Completion times for the subjects were similar in each condition, so the results in figure 44.2 were averaged. Thus, there were six trials for the limited-field-of-view conditions and nine trials for all other conditions.

Results of the experiment

Subjects performed the task while looking into the experiment box using both eyes (binocular direct condition; figure 44.2, left side), with one eye patched (monocular direct condition; figure 44.2, middle), or using the endoscope with the box closed (figure 44.2, right side). The loss of stereo view in the monocular direct condition accounted for only a part of the difference in performance between binocular direct and endoscopic viewing.

Three-factor fixed-effects analysis of variance (ANOVA) showed visual condition to be a significant factor ($p < .0001$). A posteriori Tukey tests (Zar,

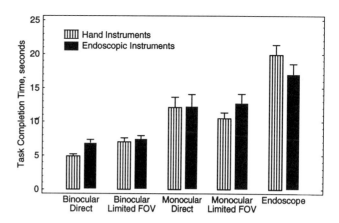

FIGURE 44.2 Effect of visual condition on performance of positioning task using hand-held or endoscopic instruments. Degradation of performance with endoscope is only partially explained by monoscopic view and limited field of view (FOV). Error bars represent standard error of the mean.

1984) showed each of the visual conditions—binocular direct, monocular direct, and endoscope—to be significantly different from the others at the 95% confidence level. Instrument condition was not a significant factor, although a two-tailed t test showed performance with hand and endoscopic instruments to be significantly different only in the binocular direct condition at the 95% confidence level. The subject factor was significant ($p < .05$) because one subject was slightly better in most conditions (Tendick, 1993). There was not significant interaction between subject and visual or instrument factors, however.

Because the narrow 30° field of view of the endoscope could also degrade task performance, two additional visual conditions with limited field of view were tried. The subjects' field of view was reduced to approximately 30° by a tube held in front of one or both eyes, respectively, in the monocular and binocular conditions. The limited field produced no significant change in performance in either case (see figure 44.2).

Discussion

Even when stereoscopic vision is lost, there are monoscopic depth cues that aid in the performance of 3D tasks. These include apparent size and perspective changes with depth, occlusion of far objects by closer ones, and brightness cues (because the single light source at the endoscope tip caused near objects to be much brighter). Although in some tasks monoscopic cues may be sufficient to allow performance as good as with stereo viewing (Liu, Tharp, and Stark, 1992), figure 44.2 shows that when the subject is limited to monoscopic vision, performance of the positioning task is slowed significantly.

It is also clear from figure 44.2 that poor performance with the endoscope is only partially explained by the loss of stereo, as shown by the difference between the monoscopic direct and endoscopic condition completion times. Limited spatial resolution, contrast, and color fidelity of the endoscopic image could reduce perception of monoscopic depth cues. The use of a stereo endoscope could thus improve performance. It is important to note, however, that these limitations of video technology can also reduce stereo performance compared to direct binocular viewing (Pepper, Cole, and Spain, 1983; Cole and Parker, 1989).

The contrast between black markers and the white background was chosen to simplify distinction of the markers. Within the body, there is much less contrast between shades of color of different tissues. Specular reflections from wet tissue and shiny instruments can also create confusing images. Stereopsis could therefore be a much more important cue in distinguishing tissues and instruments. Cole et al. (1990) showed that a cluttered environment greatly increases the need for stereo.

To create a useful stereo pair image, the two lenses in a stereo endoscope tip need some minimum separation. Because it is desirable to make the endoscope as narrow as possible, it is important to find the minimum lens separation that will give the surgeon an adequate perception of depth. This would require testing a stereo endoscope in a variety of representative surgical tasks, which has not yet been possible. However, there are some results from the teleoperations literature that may be relevant (Pepper, Cole, and Spain, 1983; McLaurin, Jones, and Mason, 1990). Kim et al. (1988) varied apparent interocular distance in a simulated teleoperated pick-and-place task using a head-mounted display. The task space was generated to appear centered at an optical distance of 40 cm. At this distance, most of the advantage of stereo viewing was gained with an interocular separation of only 2–4 cm (figure 44.3). Distance scales in endoscopic environments would be much smaller, so these results would have to be scaled appropriately. The steepness of the curve for small interocular distances in figure 44.3 shows that most of the benefit of stereo viewing occurs for relatively minimal ocular separation.

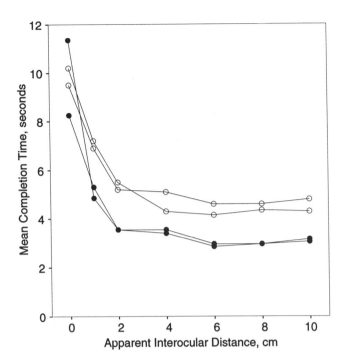

FIGURE 44.3   Mean completion time of a simulated pick-and-place task with stereo display as a function of apparent interocular distance. Data from two runs each by two subjects; each data point represents the average time for 20 targets per run. (Adapted from Kim et al., 1988).

Manipulation in endoscopic surgery

Because they pivot about the point of incision through the skin, endoscopic instruments have limited degrees of freedom. There are 3 dof of rotation possible at the insertion but only 1 dof of translation through the insertion hole, for a total of 4 dof. These make it possible to position the instrument tip anywhere within the radius of the instrument's length. Six degrees of freedom are necessary to translate arbitrarily and rotate a body in 3D space, so there are motions that the instruments cannot perform. What is lost is the ability to orient the instrument tip arbitrarily; the only rotation that can occur at the tip is about the long axis of the instrument.

In the 3D positioning experiment described earlier, this lack of orientation ability was not a problem. The only significant difference between performance with hand-held and endoscopic instruments was found with the binocular direct (see figure 44.2), wherein the difference was statistically significant at the 95% confidence level using the two-tailed t test. Subjects performed better in the familiar conditions of direct vision and hand instruments. There is no way for humans to

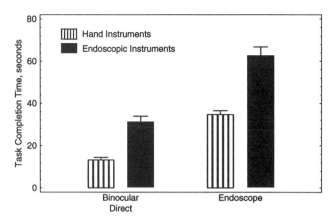

FIGURE 44.4   Time to tie a square knot with hand or endo-scopic instruments, using direct vision or endoscope. Unlike in the positioning task in figure 44.2, endoscopic instruments slow performance of this more complex task. Error bars represent standard error of the mean.

adapt to the missing degrees of freedom when using endoscopic instruments in more complex tasks, however. This was demonstrated in a test of knot-tying ability.

Two surgical resident subjects experienced in laparoscopic suturing performed a knot-tying task in which they drove a needle through a foam rubber pad and tied a square knot. Two visual conditions (binocular direct and endoscopic) and two instrument conditions (hand-held and endoscopic instruments) were used (figure 44.4). The subjects performed 11 runs total in each condition. As can be seen in figure 44.4, it took nearly twice as long to tie a square knot using endoscopic instruments under both visual conditions. Visual and instrument condition factors were both highly significant in this experiment (ANOVA $p <$ .0001). The reduced degrees of freedom of the endo-scopic instruments made it much more difficult to perform this complex task.

KINEMATICS OF ENDOSCOPIC MANIPULATION

The human arm has 7 dof that allow it to locate the hand in an arbitrary pose, with redundancy so that the arm may avoid obstacles or satisfy any of a number of optimization criteria (Hayward, 1988). This flexibility is lost when endoscopic instruments are used.

The serial joint arrangement of the arm gives it a large work space, and the parallel structure of the hand gives it excellent stiffness, damping, and rigidity properties (Hayward, 1988; Iberall and MacKenzie, 1989).

With lateral rotation and several flexing joints in each finger, there are more than 20 dof in the hand. Current endoscopic instruments do not allow the surgeon to take advantage of the unique properties of the hand.

Muscle tremor is a problem when performing fine tasks. The relatively low mass of the fingers and the good damping properties of the parallel structure in an instrument grasp reduce transmission of tremor to the instrument. Surgeons using hand-held instruments rest their wrist and forearm, whenever possible, on an available surface so that the large-magnitude tremor of the arm is not transmitted to the fingers and instrument. This is not usually possible with endoscopic instruments because the instrument handles stick out far from the patient.

There are many instrument grasps that surgeons use, with varying levels of power, dexterity, and precision (Anderson and Romfh, 1980). These grasps take advantage of different properties of the hand. For fine motion, surgeons commonly use a precision grasp, which is similar to gripping a pencil (Olszewski, 1984) (figure 44.5). The thumb, index finger, and middle finger provide a stable grasp. The instrument also rests on the skin between thumb and index finger for support. This area probably is important for force sensing; forces at the instrument tip acting about the fulcrum of support at the fingertips produce normal and tangential forces that could be detected by deformation in this compliant area.

The biomechanical properties of the hand influence the surgeon's strategies in performing basic movements. One of the most basic and essential motions in surgery is the driving of a suture needle. The driving motion is stabilized by lateral stiffness in the index and middle fingers, as will be demonstrated by a kinematic hand model in the next section. This stabilization is one example of an important use of hand properties in surgical manipulation that cannot be achieved with endoscopic instruments.

STIFFNESS AND THE PRECISION GRASP

Stability is an important factor when the hand and instrument contact tissue. The tissue may be relatively compliant, and the hand must maintain stiffness in some orientations to avoid deviation (e.g., when trying to make a straight cut). In the grasp shown in figure 44.5, there is significant stiffness in the index and middle fingers opposing abduction or adduction (lateral

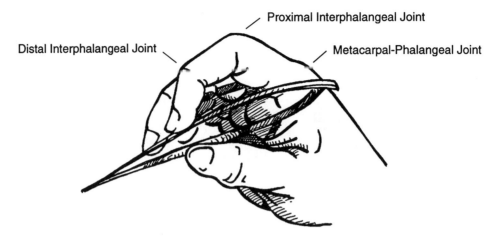

Distal Interphalangeal Joint

Proximal Interphalangeal Joint

Metacarpal-Phalangeal Joint

FIGURE 44.5   Surgeon's precision grasp.

motion). This is due to the action of the collateral ligaments at the metacarpophalangeal joints (Minami et al., 1985) and the interossei and lumbrical muscles (Spinner, 1984). The importance of this stiffness in constraining motion can be demonstrated with a kinematic model of the precision grasp.

THE MODEL   To develop the kinematic model, the grip transform method is used (Mason and Salisbury, 1985; Kerr and Roth, 1989). This method relates finger joint torques to fingertip forces and moments. These generalized forces (including both forces and moments) are transmitted through friction to the grasped object. For a particular grasp, these relationships are linear. If the finger joint torques are collected into a vector $\mathbf{T}$ and the generalized contact forces at the fingertips into $\mathbf{C}$, then they may be related by $\mathbf{T} = \mathbf{J}^T\mathbf{C}$, where $\mathbf{J}$ is the Jacobian matrix for the hand in this grasp. The contact forces produce net forces and torques on the grasped object, which are combined in a vector $\mathbf{F}$ and related by $\mathbf{F} = \mathbf{WC}$, where $\mathbf{W}$ is the grasp matrix. $\mathbf{W}$ is dependent on grasp location.

Through the principle of virtual work, velocities or infinitesimal displacements (in translation or rotation) of the finger joints, fingertips, and grasped object may be similarly related. Linear stiffness relationships between generalized displacements and forces can be expressed either in joint or object spaces. If $\mathbf{K}_\theta$ and $\mathbf{K}_o$ are defined to be stiffness matrices in joint and object spaces, respectively, they are related by the following equation (Tendick, 1993):

$$\mathbf{K}_o = \mathbf{W}\mathbf{J}^{-T}\mathbf{K}_\theta\mathbf{J}^{-1}\mathbf{W}^T$$

The model of the surgeon's precision grasp will show that lateral stiffness in joints of the index and middle fingers produces constraining stiffness in the object space.

The index and middle fingers and thumb were modeled. Flexion about two joints and lateral rotation about one joint were considered for each finger. See Spinner (1984) and figure 44.5 for diagrams of hand anatomy. In the index and middle fingers, flexion was modeled at the metacarpophalangeal (MP) and proximal interphalangeal (PI) joints but was assumed to be small at the distal interphalangeal joint. Lateral rotation (abduction-adduction) occurred at the MP joint. A thumb model was not necessary for the stiffness analysis described here but is included in Tendick (1993) for possible use in other analyses.

Matrix calculations were performed using Mathematica (Wolfram Research, 1991). The author's hand provided data for the model. Joint rotations and interjoint spacing were measured with protractor and calipers while the hand held a pencil in the precision grasp. Flexion and abduction-adduction axes on each finger were assumed to be orthogonal. Rotation was allowed to exist between the MP joints of the index and middle fingers, however, so that respective axes on the two fingers were not parallel. It is difficult to estimate the axes of joints externally, and estimation errors can propagate through the model. To reduce these errors, a 3D graphic image of the model was generated on a Silicon Graphics Iris 4D series workstation (figure 44.6). This graphic model was compared to an anatomic atlas (Rohen and Yokochi, 1983) and to the author's hand. Parameters were adjusted for anatomic

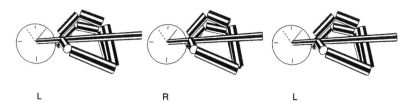

FIGURE 44.6 Stereogram of preferred orientations for precise motion, as computed from the grip transform model. The left-hand pair of images can be fused with a stereo viewer or by diverging the eyes; the right-hand pair may be fused by converging the eyes.

consistency and for fit with the actual hand when compared from many viewpoints. Simple stiffness measurements were performed to verify the validity of the model (Tendick, 1993).

Detailed derivation and parameters may be found in Tendick (1993). A stereogram graphic image of the model is shown in figure 44.6. A notable stiffness, due to the collateral ligaments and interossei and lumbrical muscles, opposes lateral rotation (abduction-adduction) at the MP joints in the index and middle fingers (see figure 44.5). These two joint stiffnesses account for stabilizing lateral stiffness in the instrument space. With stiffness defined in only two dimensions (one axis of two fingers) in finger joint space, the resulting linear stiffness can span at most two orthogonal directions in the instrument space (Strang, 1988). Using a 3×3 matrix $\mathbf{K}_o$ representing translational stiffnesses in the instrument space, this leaves one direction of translation unaffected.

This unconstrained direction (representing the eigenvector associated with the zero eigenvalue of $\mathbf{K}_o$) is shown as a solid line extending from the instrument tip in figure 44.6. It extends to approximately 1 or 2 o'clock on an imaginary clock face projected on a horizontal surface, for a right-handed surgeon with arm and third and fourth fingers resting on the surface. When a stereo pair image is fused in figure 44.6, it can be seen that this unconstrained direction is not confined to the horizontal plane but rises slightly toward the perimeter of the clock face.

DISCUSSION The advantage of this stiffness constraint to the surgeon is that it reduces the effect of perturbations orthogonal to a desired direction of precise force or motion. When driving a suture needle through tissue, surgery texts recommend that the incision be aligned so that the needle is pushed perpendicular to the incision and along the 1–2 o'clock to 6–7 o'clock axis on a clock face (Anderson and Romfh, 1980; Olszewski, 1984). This is the same as the unconstrained axis of the stiffness model. Rotation of the instrument between the fingertips, or by rotating the wrist, aids in cleanly driving the needle.

Of course, changing the posture of the arm and wrist will change the orientation of the hand and the unconstrained direction. This allows the surgeon some freedom to align the hand for best use of the constraint. Pronating the hand from the pose shown in figure 44.6 so that the index finger is nearly on top of the instrument would allow precise cutting with a scalpel.

Movements in other directions are possible. Figure 44.6 shows a second axis where there is relatively little stiffness (dashed line). This is the direction of the eigenvector of $\mathbf{K}_o$ associated with the smaller nonzero eigenvalue. In the linear stiffness model, the effect of MP joint lateral stiffness in this direction is less than one-hundredth of that of the third axis orthogonal to the first two (not shown). This third direction is the principal eigenvector of $\mathbf{K}_o$, which has the largest eigenvalue, where the greatest effect of lateral stiffness occurs. Cocontraction of antagonistic muscles allows some independent control of net force and total stiffness at thumb and finger joints. This allows the surgeon some freedom in constraining instrument motion.

Several simplifying assumptions were made in the stiffness model. Linear stiffness was assumed, although stiffness, particularly that due to ligament action, may not be linear. It was assumed that finger pads were compressed in holding the instrument, so that fingertip compliance would be negligible. More elaborate hand models will be important for optimal instrument design. Future models should include careful kinematic measurements from imaging data (An et al., 1979; Thompson and Giurintano, 1989) or cadaver studies (Hollister et al., 1992) and muscle, ligament, and tendon mechanical properties. Models should incorporate kinematics of contact and rolling (Cole, Hauser, and Sastry, 1989; Buchholz and Armstrong, 1992) and effective stiffness of changing grasp configuration (Cutkosky et al., 1987) to describe the interactions between hand and instrument.

Although the stiffness model is a limited example of the complexity of hand dexterity, it illustrates the significance of hand geometry. Passive stiffness from hand structure, active stiffness and damping from muscle co-contraction, and the advantages of a parallel rather than serial kinematic configuration of the hand make the hand a better tool for fine manipulation than the arm, even though the arm theoretically has enough degrees of freedom to move an instrument to any desired position and orientation. Current endoscopic instruments do not allow the surgeon to benefit from these advantages of the hand.

FORCE AND TACTILE SENSING

Force feedback is important for many types of surgical manipulation, including separating tissues, testing the strength or consistency of tissue, and guiding movement in cutting or suturing. In complex endoscopic operations when several instruments are in use simultaneously, some instruments may be out of view of the endoscope. Force feedback would be helpful to ensure that these instruments, for example, were still grasping tissue that was to be held away from the field of view (Coletta and Marcucci, 1992).

Forces at the tip of the endoscopic instrument are poorly transmitted to the surgeon's hand. Reaction forces at the tip can be negligible compared to friction at the instrument entry or forces needed to move the mass of the instrument and the unsupported hand and arm. The fulcrum effect of the long instrument handle can also reduce forces.

In conventional surgery, the surgeon may abandon instruments and use fingertips to distinguish bad tissue from good by touch or to feel what is going on beneath superficial tissue (Coletta and Marcucci, 1992). For example, the pulse of an artery may be felt externally. This tactile ability clearly is lost in endoscopy.

Conclusion

The work in this chapter attempts to identify some of the problems of current technology in endoscopic surgery. It is clear that there are problems to which teleoperation and robotics technology could be applied.

Whether complex teleoperation technology will be fully accepted in the operating room depends on whether improved performance can outweigh the disadvantages of greater cost and complexity. Although cost and patient comfort are significant factors in evaluating surgical procedures, the most important factor is patient outcome. Complex surgical technology must improve long-term outcome without increased likelihood of complications in order to be accepted.

Careful measurement of performance allows refinement of instruments and technique to optimize performance. Completion time was used as a measure of performance in these experiments, but other factors, such as accuracy or ability to perform a secondary task, should be tested as well. Experimentation can also measure parameters for optimal design of instruments (Charles and Williams, 1989). Objective evaluation of new instruments will ensure that appropriate technology is chosen for maximum efficiency and patient benefit.

ACKNOWLEDGMENTS   The authors are pleased to acknowledge partial support from the NASA Ames Research Center (Dr. Stephen Ellis, Technical Monitor) and from the Jet Propulsion Laboratory, California Institute of Technology (Dr. Antal Bejczy, Technical Manager). We thank Won Soo Kim for permission to include previous results.

REFERENCES

AN, K., E. CHAO, W. COONEY, and R. LINSCHEID, 1979. Normative model of human hand for biomechanical analysis. *J. Biomechs.* 12:775–788.

ANDERSON, R., and R. ROMFH, 1980. *Technique in the Use of Surgical Tools.* New York: Appleton-Century-Crofts.

BOUTIN, C., J. VIALLAT, and Y. AELONY, 1991. *Practical Thoracoscopy.* New York: Springer-Verlag.

BUCHHOLZ, B., and T. ARMSTRONG, 1992. A kinematic model of the human hand to evaluate its prehensile properties. *J. Biomech.* 25 (2):149–162.

CHARLES, S., and R. WILLIAMS, 1989. Measurement of hand dynamics in a microsurgery environment: Preliminary data in the design of a bimanual telemicro-operation test bed. In *Proceedings of the 1989 NASA Conference on Space Telerobotics,* pp. 109–118.

CLASSEN, M., K. KNYRIM, H. SEIDLITZ, and F. HAGENMULLER, 1987. Electronic endoscopy—the latest technology. *Endoscopy* 19:118–123.

COLE, A., J. HAUSER, and S. SASTRY, 1989. Kinematics and control of multifingered hands with rolling contact. *IEEE Trans. Autom. Contr.* 34(4):398–404.

COLE, R., J. MERRITT, S. FORE, and P. LESTER, 1990. Remote manipulator tasks impossible without stereo TV. In *Stereoscopic Displays and Applications*, J. O. Merritt and S. S. Fisher, eds. *SPIE* 1256:255–265.

COLE, R., and D. PARKER, 1989. Stereo TV improves manipulator performance. In *Three-Dimensional Visualization and Display Technology*, W. E. Robbins and S. S. Fisher, eds. *SPIE* 1083:18–27.

COLETTA, A., and L. MARCUCCI, 1992. Laparoscopic colectomy and its implications for the use of virtual reality in abdominal surgery. Paper presented at Medicine Meets Virtual Reality Symposium, San Diego, June 4–7.

COTTON, P., and C. WILLIAMS, 1982. *Practical Gastrointestinal Surgery*. Boston: Blackwell Scientific.

CUTKOSKY, M., P. AKELLA, R. HOWE, I. KAO, 1987. Grasping as a contact sport. In *Proceedings of the International Symposium on Robotics Research*, Santa Barbara., MIT Press.

HAYWARD, V., 1988. An analysis of redundant manipulators from several viewpoints. In *Robots with Redundancy: Design, Sensing, and Control*, A. K. Bejczy, ed. Italy: Springer-Verlag.

HOLLISTER, A., W. BUFORD, L. MYERS, D. GIURINTANO, and A. NOVICK, 1992. The axes of rotation of the thumb carpometacarpal joint. *J. Orthop. Res.* 10(3):454–460.

IBERALL, T., and C. MacKENZIE, 1989. Opposition space and human prehension. In *Dextrous Robot Hands*, S. T. Venkataraman and T. Iberall, eds. Berlin: Springer-Verlag.

JOHNSON, L. 1986. *Arthroscopic Surgery: Principles and Practice*. St. Louis: Mosby.

KERR, J., and B. ROTH, 1989. Special grasping configurations with dextrous hands. In *Proceedings of the 1986 IEEE International Conference on Robotics and Automation*, pp. 1361–1367.

KIM, W., A. LIU, K. MATSUNAGA, and L. STARK, 1988. A helmet mounted display for telerobotics. In *Proceedings of the 1988 IEEE Computer Society COMPCON*, pp. 543–547.

KNYRIM, K., H. SEIDLITZ, N. VAKIL, and M. CLASSEN, 1990. Perspectives in electronic endoscopy: Past, present and future of fibers and CCDs in medical endoscopes. *Endoscopy* 22(Suppl. 1):2–8.

KNYRIM, K., H. SEIDLITZ, N. VAKIL, F. HAGENMULLER, M. CLASSEN, 1989. Optical performance of electronic imaging systems for the colon. *Gastroenterology* 96:776–782.

LIU, A., G. THARP, and L. STARK, 1992. Depth cue interaction in telepresence and simulated telemanipulation. In *Proceedings of the SPIE Conference on Human Vision, Visual Processing and Digital Display*, Soc of Photo-Optical Instrumentation Engineers, Bellingham, Washington.

MASON, M., and J. SARISBURY, 1985. *Robot Hands and the Mechanics of Manipulation*. Cambridge, Mass.: MIT Press.

McLAURIN, A., E. JONES, and J. MASON JR., 1990. Three-dimensional endoscopy through alternating-frame technology. In *Stereoscopic Displays and Applications*. J. O. Merritt and S. S. Fisher, eds. *SPIE* 1256:307–311.

MINAMI, A., K. AN, W. COONEY, R. LINSCHEID, and E. CHAO, 1985. Ligament stability of the metacarpophalangeal joint: A biomechanical study. *J. Hand Surg. [Am.]* 10(2):255–260.

OLSZEWSKI, W., 1984. *CRC Handbook of Microsurgery*, vol. 1. Boca Raton, Fla.: CRC Press.

PARISIEN, J., 1988. *Arthroscopic Surgery*. New York: McGraw-Hill.

PEARL, R., 1984. *Gastrointestinal Surgery for Surgeons*. Boston: Little, Brown.

PEPPER, R., and R. COLE, 1978. Display system variables affecting operator performance in undersea vehicles and work systems (tech. rep. 269). Naval Ocean Systems Center, Monterrg, Ca.

PEPPER, R., R. COLE, and E. SPAIN, 1983. The influence of camera separation and head movement on perceptual performanance under direct and TV-displayed conditions. *Proc. Society for Information Display* 24:73–80.

ROHEN, J., and C. YOKOCHI, 1983. *Color Atlas of Anatomy*. New York: Igaku-Shoin.

SALEH, J., 1988. *Laparoscopy*. Philadelphia: Saunders.

SATAVA, R., W. POE, and G. JOYCE, 1988. Current generation video endoscopes: A critical evaluation. *Am Surg.* 54(2):73–77.

SEMM, K., 1987. *Operative Manual for Endoscopic Abdominal Surgery: Operative Pelviscopy, Operative Laparoscopy*. Chicago: Year Book Medical.

SIVAK, M., 1986. Video endoscopy. *Clin. Gastroenterol.* 15:205–215.

SPINNER, M., 1984. *Kaplan's Functional and Surgical Anatomy of the Hand*. Philadelphia: Lippincott.

STRANG, G., 1988. *Linear Algebra and Its Applications*. San Diego: Harcourt Brace Jovanovich.

TENDICK, F., 1993. Visual-manual tracking strategies in humans and robots. Doctoral dissertation, Graduate Group in Bioengineering, University of California at Berkeley.

THOMPSON, D., and D. GIURINTANO, 1989. A kinematic model of the flexor tendons of the hand. *J. of Biomech.* 22(4):327–334.

WHITE, R., and S. KLEIN, 1991. *Endoscopic Surgery*. St. Louis: Mosby Year Book.

Wolfram Research, 1991. Mathematica (Ver. 2.0). Champaign, IL: Wolfram Research.

ZAR, J. 1984. *Biostatistical Analysis*. Englewood Cliffs, N.J.: Prentice-Hall.

45 Robotically Assisted Laparoscopic Surgery: From Concept to Development

JONATHAN M. SACKIER AND YULUN WANG

LAPAROSCOPY WAS conceived at the turn of the century [1, 2] but found few early supporters. Its value as a diagnostic modality was promoted by a modest group of practitioners [3–6], but the use of monocular vision made it an uncomfortable procedure to perform. Certainly, advances in instrumentation and techniques led to widespread adoption for gynecologic operations as proposed by Steptoe [7] and Semm [8]. However, it was the addition of the video camera to the laparoscope that surely was the progenitor of the "laparoscopic revolution."

This simple addition meant that all on the operating team could follow the performance of an operation on a large television screen placed at a comfortable viewing distance. However, there were certain prices to pay for this advance. The 2D representation of the 3D human anatomy on a TV screen led to problems with depth perception, which are accommodated by either experience or the use of expensive 3D TV systems. With the absence of direct tissue contact, the surgeon has had to develop subtle modifications in technique to obtain tactile feedback, which the experienced laparoscopist can master.

Probably the most significant change, though, has been the requirement for someone other than the surgeon to control the laparoscope, effectively subjugating the surgeon's vision to another individual. The surgeon must, therefore, develop a "language" to command this individual to move the scope to the area under consideration. Invariably, the smallest movements of the scope-holding assistant—even the tremor from a heartbeat if greatly magnified—can lead to motion-induced nausea among the surgical team.

In these times of financial constraint, it is becoming progressively less likely that surgical assistants will be reimbursed. Therefore, one must employ an additional operating room technician or nurse to hold the camera, which leads to significant expense and the use sometimes of ill-trained personnel for this very important purpose. Ultimately, the result often is frustration on the part of the surgeon and delays in completing the operation. Additionally, if the person holding the telescope does not understand the importance of following instruments in and out of the abdomen through accessory cannulas then the potential for iatrogenic injury exists.

Some surgeons who operate single-handedly control the telescope themselves. This means that they do not have another hand free for the more important job of manipulating tissue graspers, which becomes extremely frustrating during delicate maneuvers such as suturing.

Early mechanical scope-holders

Mechanical scope-holders were created to address these problems. Such devices typically attach to the side of the operating table and reach up and over the surgical field through a series of mechanical linkages. The more advanced holders have pneumatically locking joints, whereby all the joints are held rigid or relaxed simultaneously by the press of a button. When the joints are rigid, the scope is held in a fixed position without any assistance. When the joints are relaxed, the surgeon can move the scope to a new viewing location. With a mechanical scope-holder, if the surgeon wishes to change the current view, he or she releases the surgical instruments, disengages the locking mechanism, moves the scope to a new position, reengages the locking mechanism, picks up instruments, and resumes the procedure. Although this technique does eliminate the need for extra personnel to hold the scope and allows the surgeon to control the view directly, it requires a

FIGURE 45.1 The robot AESOP. Note the computer control unit and positioning arm.

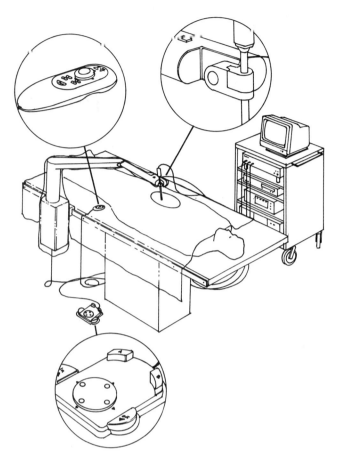

FIGURE 45.2 The operating-room environment, showing the positioner arm of the robot attached to the table, the hand and foot controls, and the computer that integrates all the functions of AESOP.

cumbersome, disruptive, and time-consuming process for the surgeon to change the field of vision.

A solution to these problems has been developed. A computer-controlled robot named *AESOP* (automated endoscope system for optimal positioning) holds the laparoscope and moves under direction of the surgeon (figure 45.1).

Construction of aesop

Figure 45.2 depicts AESOP in the operating-room environment and specifies the location of each component. The complete system is composed of the following parts: The chassis is an enclosure that houses the control computer, power system, system indicator lights, and power switch. The chassis plugs into a standard wall socket, which provides all the power necessary to operate AESOP. The control computer is connected to all of the sensors and actuators of the system and is responsible for interpreting the commands from the surgeon (who has a foot controller and a hand controller) into action by applying power to the actuators which position the robot. The program for the system is contained in the computer's read-only memory, which is a form of semiconductor device that provides unchangeable program storage. After these programs are entered initially at the factory, the program content remains unchanged even when the power is turned on and off.

The AESOP positioner is an electromechanical device that attaches to the rail of the surgical table. This device is attached to the laparoscope by a collar and collar-holder (see figures 45.1, 45.2) and holds and moves the laparoscope. The main structure of the positioner is made of machined and cast aluminum, and the joints include components such as bearings and gears, which are made of steel and plastic (figure 45.3). The positioner is widest (15 cm) where it attaches to the table and narrowest (3 cm) where it connects to the laparoscope.

The laparoscope is attached to the positioner by a disposable collar that is placed as close to the top of the laparoscope shaft as possible and snugly fits the instrument. It is made of a combination of sterilized plastic and stainless steel components. The collar-holder is a sterilized jaw that snaps into the positioner and clicks to the collar and is made of stainless steel.

To retain sterility once the positioner has been attached to the operating table, a disposable plastic

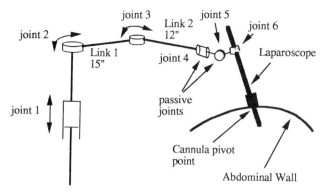

FIGURE 45.3 The joint structure of the positioner, collar-holder, and collar.

gown is passed over the scope. A hole in the gown allows the insertion of the sterile collar-holder while maintaining the integrity of the sterile field. The AESOP positioner is controlled by the surgeon by means of either a foot or hand controller. Because the hand controller is in the sterile field, it is made of a hermetically sealed plastic such that it may be sterilized by soaking.

Mode of operation

There are a number of ways in which AESOP may be used by the surgeon to position the scope. By grasping the positioner and depressing the disable button, AESOP functions as a manual scope-holder. When the disable button has been pressed, the joints become passive and the surgeon can move the positioner easily to any location. After releasing the disable button, the positioner becomes rigid once again. By using the foot or hand controller, the surgeon can move the laparoscope in, out, left, right, up, or down by applying pressure to the corresponding place on the controller. An important consideration is that all the commands are executed relative to the field of view on the video screen. Consequently, the commands are given with respect to the most natural and intuitive reference frame. The foot pedal is pressure-sensitive and maximum speed is governed. Therefore, commands are determined by how much pressure is exerted as well as the direction indicated by the command. As pressure on the pedal is increased, the speed with which the device moves is increased. If the maximum allowed speed of 3 inches per second is reached, increasing the pressure on the pedal has no further effect. Addition-

ally, commands can be combined so that by applying pressure appropriately, the surgeon can, for example, move the laparoscope diagonally up and to the left in one motion.

Another method of controlling the laparoscope is with memory buttons located on both the hand and foot controllers. If, during the performance of the procedure, the surgeon locates a view that is particularly useful, such as a panoramic view of the abdomen and the insertion points of all accessory cannulas, by the push of a button the position will be "remembered." Then, at any time during the procedure, by hitting the appropriate button, the laparoscope automatically will return to that programmed position. These buttons can be programmed and reprogrammed as many times as desired during a procedure.

Conclusions

The AESOP positioning system allows for smooth, fast, and efficacious control of the laparoscope during complex surgical procedures. It frees up the need for one additional person at the operating table and helps ensure the safety of the patient by allowing the surgeon to follow surgical instruments in and out of the field.

Since the term *robot* first appeared in Capek's play "Rossums Universal Robots" in 1920 (from the Czechoslovakian *Robota*, meaning "forced labor"), we have been intrigued and infatuated by an apparently human automaton—an intelligent and obedient but impersonal machine. This concept is especially appealing in the operating room where we frequently have to deal with communication problems with our assistants. Recently, the late Hap Paul [9] described the use of robotic assistants to create the medullary cavity for a cementless hip prosthesis. Although the introduction of this "robo-doc" met with much enthusiasm, there was some trepidation as well. Understandably, neither surgeons nor patients wish to have a machine perform what are deemed to be delicate medical interventions. However, the appeal of the AESOP device is that it actually returns to the surgeon control of her or his faculties and *enhances* the doctor's work rather than detracting from it, in essence providing the surgeon with a third arm!! Dr. Richard Satava [10, 11] recently published his view of future trends in surgery. It is our belief that the AESOP positioning device is the first step along the exciting road Dr. Satava has charted.

Afterword

Since this article was written, clinical use of AESOP has begun, and the US food and Drug Administration has granted permission to market AESOP commercially. The first clinical case was a laparoscopic cholecystectomy performed on August, 16, 1993, by Dr. Jonathan Sackier at The University of California at San Diego's Thornton Hospital. Since then, the system has been used by a number of general surgeons, gynecologists, and urologists at several sites around the United States.

Procedures performed include laparoscopic cholecystectomy, laparoscopic hernia repair, laparoscopic colectomy, and laparoscopic splenectomy. AESOP has assisted gynecologists in laparoscopic oophorectomy, laparoscopically assisted vaginal hysterectomy, hysteroscopic laparoscopic metroplasty, laparoscopic diagnosis with adhesiolysis, diagnostic laparoscopy, and laparoscopic salpingotomy. Urologists have used AESOP for laparoscopic nephrectomy, laparoscopic pelvic lymph node dissection, laparoscopic varicocele repair, and laparoscopic bladder neck suspension.

ACKNOWLEDGMENTS The authors would like to thank Amante Mangaser, Keith Laby, Steve Jordan, Jeff Wilson, Mark Phillips, and Joel Davis for their invaluable engineering contributions to this project.

REFERENCES

[1] OTT, D., 1909. Die direkte Beleuchtung der Bauchhole, der Harnblase, des Dickdarms und des Uterus zu diagnostichen Zwecken. *Rev. Med. Tchaque (Prague)* 2.27 90.

[2] KELLING, G., 1923. Zur coelioskopie. *Arch. Klin. Chir.* 126:226–229.

[3] KALK, H., and W. BRUHL, 1951. *Leitfaden der Laparoskopie.* Stuttgart: Thieme.

[4] RUDDOCK, J. C., 1937. Peritoneoscopy surgery. *Gynecol. Obstet.* 65:523–539.

[5] CUSCHIERI, A., 1974. Value of laparoscopy in hepatobiliary disease. *Br. J. Surg.* 61:318–319.

[6] BERCI, G., and A. CUSHIERI, 1986. *Practical Laparoscopy.* London: Baillierre Tindall.

[7] STEPTOE, P. C., 1967. *Laparoscopy in Gynaecology.* Edinburgh: Churchill Livingstone.

[8] SEMM, K., 1984. *Operationsehre fur endoskopische Abdominal Chirurgie: Operative Pelviskopie, operative Laparoskopie.* Stuttgart: FK Schattanuer Verlag GmbH.

[9] PAUL, H., 1992. Image-directed robotic surgery. In *Proceedings of the Medicine Meets Virtual Reality Symposium*, San Diego, June 4–7.

[10] SATAVA, R. M., 1993. Surgery 2001: A technologic framework for the future. *Surg. Endosc.* 7:111–113.

[11] SATAVA, R. M., 1993. High-tech surgery: Speculation on future directions. In *Minimally Invasive Surgery*, J. G. Hunter and J. M. Sackier, eds. Philadelphia: McGraw-Hill.

46 A Telerobotic Assistant for Laparoscopic Surgery

RUSSELL H. TAYLOR, JANEZ FUNDA,
BEN ELDRIDGE, DAVID LAROSE, STEVE GOMORY,
KREG GRUBEN, MARK TALAMINI, LOUIS KAVOUSSI,
AND JAMES ANDERSON

THE GOAL OF OUR work is to develop a new generation of "intelligent" surgical systems that can work cooperatively with a human surgeon to off-load routine tasks, reduce the number of people needed in the operating room, and provide new capabilities that complement the surgeon's own skills. An underlying premise of this work is that machine capabilities coupled with human judgment can accomplish many tasks better than either could do alone. A further premise is that such a partnership is synergistic with present trends toward geometrically precise, image-guided, and minimally invasive therapies in order to produce better clinical results, lower net costs through shorter hospital stays and recovery times, a reduced need for repeated surgery, and the like.

Most of the key enabling technology (3D imaging, modeling, visualization, real-time sensing, telerobotics, and system integration) is computer-based. The emergence of very powerful, affordable computer workstations together with scientific advances in imaging, modeling, and telerobotics means that critical cost and capability thresholds have been crossed, and the pace of research and clinical activity is increasing sharply.

Many of these systems take advantage of the increased precision with which computer-controlled mechanical devices can position and maneuver surgical instruments. This aspect of machine capability has been exploited in a number of orthopaedic and neurosurgical applications [1–6]. Some of the other work in this area has concentrated on exploiting computer and robotic technology in reducing fatigue, restoring hand-eye coordination, and improving dexterity of human surgeons, or reducing the number of personnel required in the operating room [7–14]. This dichotomy is by no means absolute. Some of these systems (e.g., [1]) clearly incorporate aspects of both types of functionality. The system described in this chapter similarly has aspects of both types of functionality. Although the initial application domain is laparoscopic surgery, using relatively simple tasks such as camera pointing and instrument positioning, the system is capable of operating both under the surgeon's direct control and more autonomously under the surgeon's supervision, while extracting targeting information from real-time images. We anticipate eventually applying this system to a very broad range of surgical tasks.

Robotic devices for endoscopic surgery

Laparoscopic surgery has seen remarkable growth over the last 5 years. In 1992, 70% of all gallbladder surgery in the United States, Europe, and Japan was done laparoscopically. By 2000, it is estimated that from 60 to 80% of abdominal surgeries will be performed laparoscopically [15]. Flexible endoscopy is similarly becoming more and more prevalent. Two salient characteristics of these procedures are that the surgeon cannot *directly* manipulate the patient's anatomy with his or her fingers and that the surgeon cannot *directly* observe what he or she is doing. Instead the surgeon must rely on instruments that can be inserted through a cannula or through the working channel of an endoscope. Often, an assistant must be responsible for pointing the camera while the surgeon performs the operation. The awkwardness of this arrangement has led a number

This paper is adapted from one to be published in *IEEE Engineering in Medicine and Biology Magazine*, Vol. 14, No. 3, May/June 1995.

of researchers to develop robotic augmentation devices for endoscopic surgery. Typical efforts include improved mechanisms for flexible endoscopes (e.g., [7], [16]), specialized devices for particular applications (e.g., [10]), voice control for existing mechanisms (e.g., [9]), full-blown "telepresence" systems [11, 12], and simple camera-pointing systems [13, 14, 17].

Of these efforts, the most ambitious in some ways is the telepresence surgical system of Green et al. at SRI International [11, 12], whose aim is to use a force-reflecting manipulator, stereo visualization, and other virtual reality technology to give the surgeon the sensation of performing open surgery.[1] Although the system reported in this chapter has some of the same capabilities as the SRI system and, indeed, may in some ways be better suited to remote telesurgery where time delays are large, our primary goal is somewhat different. We view surgical robotic devices as being most valuable in their ability to aid and augment the surgical team, allowing more efficient use of available surgical talent and enhancing the ability of surgeons to work quickly and accurately. Our goal is not so much telepresence surgery as the provision of an intelligent "third hand" operating under the surgeon's supervision that can off-load routine tasks, reduce the number of people needed in the operating room, and provide new capabilities (such as accurate targeting) that complement the surgeon's own abilities.

At the other extreme are systems whose goal is to do the very simple task of aiming a laparoscopic camera [13, 14, 17], thus possibly reducing the number of people required in the operating room, while leaving the responsibility for manipulating the patient's anatomy completely up to the surgeon.[2] These systems typically provide a very simple teleoperation interface that allows the surgeon directly to steer a robot holding a laparoscopic camera.

Our system, illustrated in figure 46.1, includes a specially designed, remote center-of-motion robot holding a laparoscopic camera or other instrumentation, a variety of human-machine interfaces, and a controller comprising robot-control, image-processing, and display functions. It has some aspects in common with the previously discussed scope-holding systems. In particular, we provide direct teleoperator control of camera positioning as one mode of operation, although perhaps with more flexibility and convenience in controlling the view and a richer set of human-machine interfaces. A crucial difference is that we provide alter-

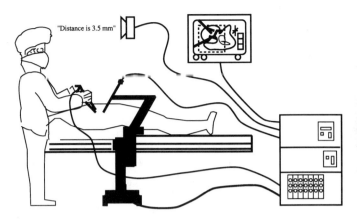

FIGURE 46.1   System overview.

natives to direct teleoperation to guide the system. In particular, the system is capable of capturing images from the camera and processing them to obtain geometric information about the patient's anatomy, which may then be used to assist in targeting the camera or other instruments held by the patient. Our eventual goal is a suite of functional capabilities including retraction, countertraction, hemostasis, suturing assistance, simple dissection, and so forth that a surgeon might reasonably expect a human assistant to perform, together with the ability to combine information coming from the camera with information obtained from other imaging modalities such as CT, MRI, ultrasound, or fluoroscopy, to target and control accurately therapeutic devices in ways that are better suited for machines than for people.

The present system prototype was developed as part of a joint study between IBM and the Johns Hopkins University Medical School. In subsequent sections, we describe the system's robot, the human-machine interfaces, and operational characteristics of the system.

Surgical robot

Manipulator design

Safety, control convenience, and flexibility for use in a wide variety of surgical applications were important factors in determining the manipulator design. In laparoscopic applications, rigid instruments are inserted into the patient's body through small cannulas inserted into the abdominal wall. This creates a fulcrum effect, so that there are really only four significant motion degrees of freedom (three rotations and depth of penetration) centered at the entry portals. Only very constrained lateral motions are acceptable.

If a robot is holding an instrument, it is very important that its motions obey these constraints. A conventional industrial robot can, of course, be programmed to move an instrument about such a fulcrum. Unfortunately, such motions usually require several manipulator joints to make large, tightly coordinated excursions, so that even relatively slow end-effector motions can require rapid joint motions. Any control or coordination failure can thus represent a potential safety hazard both for the patient and for the surgeon. Simply slowing down the actuators can cause the overall functioning of the robot to be painfully tedious. Consequently, we have a strong preference for manipulator designs that require only low-velocity actuation, that do not have motion singularities in the normal working volume, and that permit simple stable controls. Similarly, the motions required to perform a task should be reasonably intuitive for the surgeon. Even if the control computer is handling all the details, it is desirable not to surprise the surgeon with some unanticipated complex motion. Finally, we want a great deal of modularity to allow us to reconfigure the system for different procedures.

Our solution is to construct a kinematically redundant manipulator comprising a proximal translation component and a distal remote center-of-motion component providing angular reorientation about a fixed point and a controlled insertion motion passing through the remote motion center. Our present embodiment is shown in figure 46.2 and consists of three-axis linear xyz stage, a two-axis parallel four-bar linkage providing two rotations (R_x and R_y) about the remote motion center, and a two-axis distal component providing an insertion motion s and rotation R_z about the instrument axis, which passes through the remote motion center. Thus, the robot's distal 4 degrees of freedom (dof) are kinematically decoupled about the remote motion center, whose position may be translated in space by the proximal three-axis linear stage. For laparoscopic surgery, the remote motion center would be positioned to coincide with the point of entry into the patient's body. Similarly, for a frameless stereotaxy application involving multiple biopsies at a single puncture site, the remote motion center would again be positioned to coincide with the puncture site. The distal parts of the robot might then be used to aim a needle guide along multiple biopsy paths.[3]

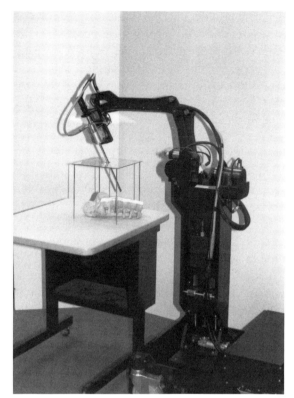

(a)

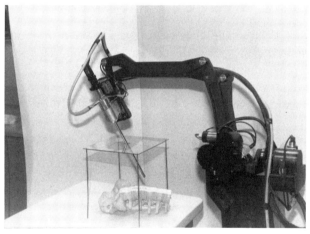

(b)

FIGURE 46.2 Remote center-of-motion robot. (a) The entire robot. The distal four axes. All motions are kinematically decoupled at the point where the laparoscopic instrument would enter the patient's body.

The range of motion of the present manipulator is ± 100 mm for the base x and y translations, ± 200 mm for the base z translation, $\pm 60°$ for the R_x and R_y rotation axes, $\pm 180°$ for the instrument rotation R_z, and ± 80 mm for instrument insertion s. The instrument carrier can be disconnected easily from the robot to facilitate cleaning and to provide a convenient sterile boundary. The instrument carrier will be sterilized before surgery, and the rest of the surgical robot will be covered with a sterile drape. Interchangeable collets in the instrument carrier accommodate cylindric instruments (such as laparoscopes) up to 17 mm in diameter.

The entire robot is on lockable casters and can be wheeled up to the operating table. This approach was chosen to provide maximum flexibility in positioning the robot and in allowing it to be easily introduced into and removed from the surgical field. We have also considered alternative designs in which the robot simply is mounted on the operating table rail.

Modularity has been emphasized in both the kinematic structure and the detailed implementation of the manipulator and controller. This should make it fairly simple to customize subassemblies as more experience is gained or new requirements emerge. For example, we are already considering design modifications to the four-bar linkage component to reduce bulk, further increase stiffness, and provide adjustability in the lengths of the links. Similarly, we have already implemented an additional motorized degree of freedom to rotate the camera "head" about the eyepiece of an angled-view laparoscope, thus making it possible to keep upright the image on the screen as the laparoscope is rotated about its axis.

The robot is designed to be nonbackdrivable. All linear axes are driven by direct-current (DC) motors acting through lead screws, and the major revolute axes (R_x and R_y) are driven by DC motors acting through a combined harmonic drive and worm gear transmission. One important safety consequence of kinematic decoupling and high-reduction drive trains is that only small, low-power motors are required and that no axis drive needs to be capable of any faster motion than is required for the corresponding task motions. A second safety consequence is that the mechanism will not move when the motors are deenergized. We can absolutely prevent unwanted motions or stop a runaway situation just by pulling the plug. Furthermore, because joint motions are relatively slow, there is more time available for safety monitoring and appropriate actions (such as shutting off power) should such intervention become necessary. The very high reduction ratio and nonbackdrivable transmission elements

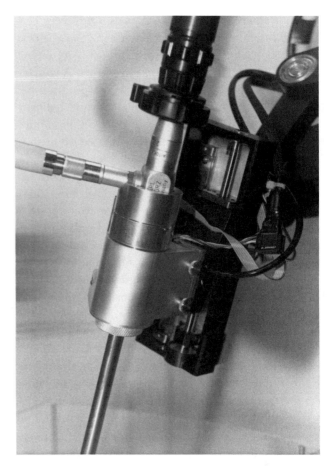

FIGURE 46.3   Detail of instrument carrier, showing force sensor.

cause any motion to stop very quickly when power is cut off.[4]

The robot has a 6-dof force-torque sensor placed just proximal to the instrument carrier, as shown in figure 46.3. This sensor allows the controller to monitor external forces exerted on the instrument during surgery and to take appropriate action (e.g., freeze) to prevent the robot from exerting excessive force on the patient. The force information provided by the sensor can also be integrated into the motion control law, giving the surgical robot the ability to comply with (i.e., move away from) external forces. This mode can be used to take hold of the instrument and manually guide the surgical robot (by exerting forces against the instrument) into the initial position for surgery or to move the surgical robot to a different portal during the procedure. We also anticipate future uses of this capability for tissue retraction and similar surgical tasks.

Low-level motion control, joint servoing, and basic safety monitoring are performed by a fast rack-mounted personal computer equipped with a combination of off-the-shelf and custom interface electronics. Higher-level control is performed by an IBM PS/2 workstation connected to the low-level controller through a shared memory interface.

Safety is a fundamental design goal for the system. Both computers, but especially the low-level controller, perform extensive consistency checks to verify system integrity. If any inconsistency or out-of-tolerance condition is detected, the controller turns off the robot power and initiates appropriate actions to notify the surgeon and application software. Additionally, the power-drive electronics incorporate a safety time-out feature as well as "power enable" interlocks. The controller software includes a real-time process that performs consistency checks every 5 msec. If a check fails, the controller can immediately disable manipulator power. If all checks are passed, the controller then reenables the safety time-out. If the safety time-out is not reenabled within 10 msec, manipulator power is automatically turned off, and appropriate status indicators are set. Our experience with this approach, both in industrial [18, 19] and surgical [20] robots, has shown that it provides a high degree of confidence in basic hardware and software integrity of the control system.

Although our present manipulator design is very well suited for "keyhole" surgeries, we have tried to insulate higher levels of application software from dependency on any particular kinematic structure, to an extent that goes somewhat beyond what is found in a typical industrial robot. Rather than simply specifying desired position goals for the surgical instruments and solving the corresponding kinematic equations, the control software sets up and solves nonlinear optimization problems to most closely achieve a desired instrument-to-patient relationship, subject to task and manipulator design constraints.

Consider a simple camera-pointing task in which the goal is to achieve a particular view of a body organ, using a rigid 30° angle-of-view laparoscope. In general, this is a 6-dof task. Unfortunately, the laparoscope is constrained by the cannula, so that only 4-dof (three rotations and insertion depth) are available. If the camera can be rotated on the eyepiece, then a fifth degree of freedom is available, but that is all.[5] Clearly, trade-offs are necessary based on what is most important for a particular task. For example, if one is simply aiming the camera for the purpose of viewing the patient's anatomy, one may wish to minimize apparent rotation about the axis of view at the expense of some variation in lateral displacement of the image or distance from the end of the laparoscope. On the other hand, if the intent is to project laser energy along the optical path of the laparoscope, then only very small lateral aiming errors can be tolerated, but image rotation may be less important.

It often is necessary to place bounds on the motion of different parts of the robot or surgical instruments and to guarantee that these bounds are rigorously enforced. For example, it may be very important to tell the robot to keep the end of the laparoscope out of the patient's liver. Similarly, we have thus far been assuming that no lateral motion of the cannula is permitted. If only the most distal four axes of the robot are being used and the remote center of motion is placed at the cannula, this constraint will be met trivially. However, there is a certain amount of "give" in the patient's abdominal wall, and there are some circumstances, such as stereo ranging or precise subsidiary motions for tissue manipulation, in which it would be desirable to use the proximal *xyz* stage to displace the cannula laterally by a small amount, so long as the patient's anatomy is not stretched too far.

Finally, additional motion capabilities can be added to the robot or instruments. For example, a steerable prism [21] can be added to the laparoscope to vary its angle of view. Alternatively, the rigid instrument may be replaced by some sort of steerable snake. In these cases, it is important to be able to take advantage of whatever manipulation capabilities exist without at the same time requiring that substantial software libraries be rewritten.

Our approach, described more fully elsewhere [21], is to express the problem of determining manipulator joint positions $\mathbf{q}(t)$ to achieve a desired motion task as a quadratic optimization problem:

$$\min \|\mathbf{A}(t) \cdot \mathbf{q}(t) - \mathbf{b}(t)\|$$

such that

$$\mathbf{C}(t) \cdot \mathbf{q}(t) \leq \mathbf{d}(t)$$

where $\mathbf{A}(t)$ and $\mathbf{b}(t)$ are derived from the relative weights of different goals to be achieved, propagated through the kinematic equations of the manipulator. Similarly, $\mathbf{C}(t)$ and $\mathbf{d}(t)$ express constraints that must be obeyed, again propagated through the kinematic equations of the manipulator.[6] The formulation permits task-step-dependent optimization criteria and constraints, such as "minimize image rotation" and "guarantee that the view axis passes within 0.5 mm of the defined target point," to be combined with standing instructions such as "minimize joint motion" and "guarantee that the remote motion center stays within 3 mm of the cannula center." It also is possible to have compound instructions such as "minimize the displacement of the remote motion center from the center of the cannula, but in all cases guarantee that the displacement never exceeds 3 mm." Weighting factors are used to specify the relative importance of different optimization criteria. If the constraints cannot all be satisfied, appropriate software exceptions are generated to be handled by higher levels of the application software.

It is useful to note that this formulation does not make assumptions about the number of degrees of freedom of the robot. In cases where redundant degrees of freedom are available, additional optimization criteria (typically, minimization of total joint motion or maximization of available free motion) are used to control how the extra freedom is to be used, subject to constraint satisfaction. In cases where insufficient degrees of freedom are available to force the optimization criterion to zero, the optimizer does the best it can, again subject to constraint satisfaction.[7]

In practice, this scheme has proved to be highly flexible and acceptably efficient, with typical solution rates of 15–20 Hz using a relatively slow (33-MHz 486) IBM PS/2 model 90. It has been implemented both for kinematically deficient (4 dof) and kinematically redundant (7 dof) manipulator configurations, including systems with somewhat different physical designs from our current robot [21].

Human-machine interfaces

During laparoscopic surgical procedures, the surgeon's gaze is most often centered on the television monitor displaying the live video image transmitted by the laparoscopic camera. This image is the surgeon's primary feedback about the patient's anatomy in relation to the surgical instruments and is frequently the basis for his or her communication with people assisting in the procedure. If the system is to function as an effective assistant rather than as a simple teleoperated slave, it is important that it have access to this important information source and communication channel. Consequently, the controller has the ability to capture and extract information from the laparoscopic images and to superimpose simple graphic overlays on the live video images. Typical overlays include cursors, simple graphic displays, and text that indicate distances and other quantitative information, icons and text describing system status, and so on. We are also considering, but have yet to implement, a number of other display functions, including peripheral display of patient status information, computer-enhanced presentation of the color video signal, and registration and overlay of preoperative models.

Similarly, a primary means by which the surgeon can instruct the system is to point to objects displayed on the video monitor. Although we have demonstrated the ability of the system to track visual markers on the surgical instruments, thus allowing the surgeon to designate anatomic features of interest simply by pointing at them directly [22], in practice it has proved much more convenient for the surgeon to use a mouse or joystick to position a cursor on the display screen. An obvious difficulty is that it can be inconvenient for the surgeon to let go of a laparoscopic instrument in order to grasp a conventional pointing device. Foot pedals are an often-suggested alternative but get mixed reviews from surgeons. Feet are inherently more clumsy than hands for precise tasks, and there are sometimes a number of other foot switches already in use, so that adding one more can be confusing. Our approach has been to provide a small (gas- or soak-sterilized) joystick device that can be clipped to a laparoscopic instrument and operated without requiring the surgeon to release the instrument (figure 46.4). We have evaluated a number of different designs; our current embodiment is functionally equivalent to a three-button mouse. It has a single TrackPoint joystick adapted from an IBM ThinkPad computer and three push-buttons in a package measuring approximately 35 mm across. We have also combined three such joysticks into a single surgeon interface that can be gas-sterilized or placed inside a sterile drape and clipped to a convenient position in the surgical field.

FIGURE 46.4 Instrument-mounted joystick.

Synthesized speech has proved to be extremely useful as a means of providing information and short instructions to the surgeon. On the input side, speech recognition systems are just beginning to be reliable and fast enough to be useful as a hands-off command interface. In an earlier embodiment of the system [22], we constructed such an interface using an experimental speech recognition system developed at IBM Research.[8] As expected, we learned that speech recognition is clearly the most convenient modality for many surgeon inputs but that it cannot substitute for pointing in many situations *and* recognition accuracy and response time are critical to surgeon acceptance. We are planning to apply these lessons to the present system in the near future, using recent product-level IBM speech recognition systems as the basis.

As with all aspects of the system, we have empasized modularity in designing these interfaces and, to the extent possible, have tried to insulate application software from detailed dependencies on any particular

hardware embodiments or configuration. One obvious advantage of this approach is the ability to take advantage of the rapid evolution of new technology in this field, such as head-mounted displays, haptic interfaces, and other virtual reality devices, and we have already begun to explore some of these possibilities. Another advantage is that the modularity also tends to improve system robustness, both from a software engineering viewpoint and by making it easy to provide redundant interfaces. For example, if a speech synthesizer fails, the same information can be displayed (albeit more annoyingly) as text superimposed on the video monitor.

Operating modes

DIRECT TELEOPERATION

In direct teleoperation, the surgeon interactively controls the motion of the robot by directly commanding individual motions. Perhaps the most direct form is force compliance. The surgeon grasps the laparoscopic instrument and pulls on it; the controller responds to the force-torque values sensed by the force sensor in the robot's "wrist" and moves the robot in the direction that the surgeon is pulling. Two modes are provided: One uses the proximal xyz stage to translate the remote motion center, and the other uses the distal four axes to control instrument orientation and insertion.[9]

In other modes, the surgeon uses the instrument-mounted joystick to specify motions of the laparoscope or other instruments held by the robot. When a single joystick is used, one of the push-buttons is used to select pairs of motion directions (e.g., xy, zR_z, R_xR_y) to be controlled by the joystick. When multiple joysticks are active, this multiplexing is not needed. We provide two basic joystick-controlled modes. In the anatomy-centered viewpoint mode, a particular anatomic feature remains centered in the camera's field of view. The sensation to the surgeon looking at the television monitor is one of flying about an imaginary sphere centered on this feature, zooming in and out (i.e., shrinking or enlarging the sphere's radius) or rolling about the camera's axis of view. Most often, the anatomic feature is located by triangulation from a pair of video images, as discussed in the next section. The viewpoint displacement mode is used to move the camera to view different parts of the patient's anatomy. In this mode, the sensation is more nearly one of flying through the patient's anatomy.

VISION-GUIDED OPERATION

The surgeon has the ability to designate anatomic features of interest by pointing at them. As discussed earlier, the most normal pointing method is the instrument-mounted joystick to control a cursor superimposed on the video display, although other modes also are possible. Once a feature has been designated, the controller has the ability to determine the 3D position of the anatomic feature by image processing. When a monoscopic video source such as a standard (nonstereo) laparoscopic camera is in use, the controller captures one image, moves the robot to displace the camera a small amount perpendicular to the view axis, and acquires a second image. Multiresolution correlation [23] is used to locate the feature in the second image, and the feature's spatial position is computed by triangulation.[10]

Once the feature's position is determined, the controller can easily solve an aiming problem and move the robot so that the feature is centered in the camera's field of view. If desired, additional correlation steps can be performed to home in on the feature, although this has not proved to be important in practice. One useful capability that we have demonstrated is the ability to designate a viewpoint and save it for later recall. For example, the surgeon may define two or three views of the anatomy being observed, together with views of the entry portals for hand-held surgical instruments, and then instruct the controller by menu selection about which view is desired.

We are presently developing facilities for combining multiple anatomic feature positions determined by stereo image processing into a simple "terrain model" of the patient's anatomy and then for using this model for a variety of enhanced displays and manipulation control capabilities.

GUIDED AUTONOMY: ASSISTANT FUNCTIONS

One of the key attributes of a good assistant is the ability to perform simple tasks autonomously under the general supervision of the surgeon. An important goal for our surgical robot is that it be able to do much the same thing. The system should be able to perform a simple task without requiring detailed control by the surgeon. Vision-guided camera pointing is one example of such a function. The surgeon simply designates the anatomic feature to be viewed, and the robot automatically centers the feature. In fact, in the case of angled-view laparoscopes, the robot usually can do a better job than can an average human assistant, as the controller is not confused by coordinate transformations and the robot is both more accurate and steadier than a human.[11]

We have begun to explore applications in which the robot positions a surgical instrument rather than a simple diagnostic laparoscope. In many of these applications, the robot positions a therapeutic laparoscope so that a surgical instrument inserted into the working channel will be accurately placed on a particular anatomic feature. One such example is shown in figure 46.5. In this example, a small pellet represents a gallstone that has spilled out of a broken gallbladder during a cholecystectomy and must be retrieved. The surgeon selects the point-and-grab mode from a menu by pushing a button; the controller uses the speech synthesizer to inform the surgeon that it is in the point-and-grab mode and asks the surgeon to designate the feature to be grabbed (in this case, the pellet). The surgeon uses the instrument-mounted joystick to point at the pellet and pushes a button. The controller acquires a stereo pair of images, locates the anatomic feature, and shows the surgeon where it thinks the feature is. The controller then uses the speech synthesizer to ask the surgeon to confirm that it has located the feature correctly and waits for permission to move the robot. After the surgeon confirms the desired motion by pushing a button, the controller moves the robot so that the laparoscope's working channel is properly aligned with and at the correct standoff distance from the pellet. The surgeon then inserts an appropriate tool through the working channel and grasps the pellet.

In the future, we anticipate extending this capability to a number of different assistant tasks, such as biopsy sampling, multiple drug injections, retraction, hemostasis, and suturing. In some of these cases, we anticipate developing specialized instruments, possibly with additional controlled degrees of freedom, to operate with the robot. In other cases, relatively simple off-the-shelf instruments can be used.

Such assistant capabilities tend to follow a common general paradigm. The surgeon will select a specific action to be performed and will designate the appropriate anatomic target. The system will locate the designated target accurately, obtain confirmation if needed, and maneuver the instrumentation into position, often performing additional subsidiary sensing

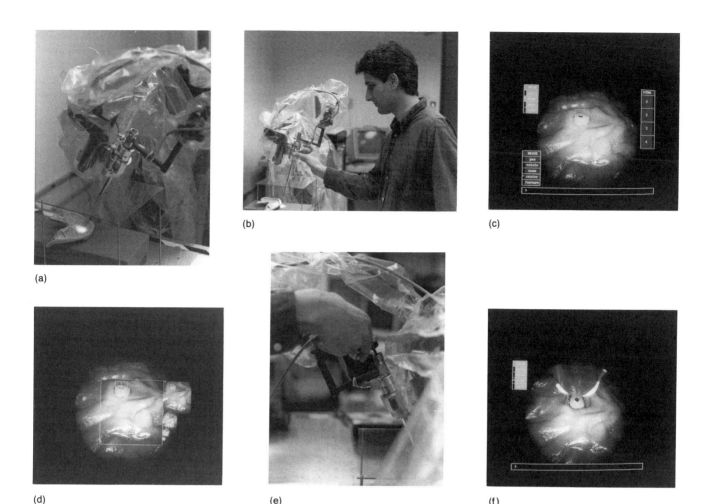

(a)

(b)

(c)

(d)

(e)

(f)

FIGURE 46.5 In vitro demonstration of point-and-grab application: (a) The experimental setup, consisting of the surgical robot holding a Storz theraputic laparoscope with a 6-mm working channel, a rubber simulation of patient anatomy, and a small target to be grasped by a surgical instrument inserted into the working channel of the laparoscope. In this picture, the robot is draped as it would be in surgery. (b) Force-compliant manual guiding of the robot. The robot enters this mode whenever the surgeon depresses two buttons on opposite sides of the instrument carrier. (c) The display monitor after the surgeon has designated the target using the instrument-mounted joystick to place cursor crosshairs on the image of the target. (d) The scene just after the computer has located the target by multiresolution correlation. This view shows the correllation window tree. Normally, this display is used for debugging and would be suppressed in production use. (e) Insertion of the instrument into the working channel. (f) The scene during the pickup operation. The pellet appears to be off-center but is lined up with the working channel of the scope.

and control. It will then perform the desired task under the surgeon's general supervision, again often performing additional sensing and control steps on its own, within constraints determined for the task. It should be noted that this paradigm has many potential advantages for remote surgical applications, in which delays can make simple teleoperation impractical. We are beginning to explore such applications.

An additional extension is the incorporation of anatomic models obtained from preoperative imaging, such as CT or MRI, or from other intraoperative modalities such as fluoroscopy or ultrasound. One of the key advantages of the robot, relative to a human, is that it is very accurate and stable. This makes it a natural candidate for brachytherapy, biopsies, and other frameless stereotaxy applications. Again, we are beginning to explore such applications.

Conclusion

We have described a robotic system designed to function as an intelligent third hand in laparoscopic and

FIGURE 46.6　In vivo evaluation of system in a pig. Shows in vivo cholecystectomy performed by Dr. Talamini on a pig at Johns Hopkins University. The procedure shown is a "non-survival" evaluation, in which euthanasia was performed immediately at the conclusion of the procedure, without the pig ever waking up from anesthesia. A survival procedure would be similar, except that proper sterility precautions (such as draping the robot) would be taken.

other general surgical procedures. The system includes a specially designed robot, a variety of human-machine interfaces, image-processing capabilities, and a modular controller that supports a number of operating modes. Although considerable work remains to be done, our early experiences with the system prototype are already very encouraging. At the present time, the prototype system described here is working well in our laboratory at IBM Research. A second system has been installed at Johns Hopkins University Medical School, where in vivo preclinical testing has begun (figure 46.6). Initial surgical feedback has been very positive, and we are beginning to consider additional ways to exploit the precise positioning and image guidance capabilities of the system.

ACKNOWLEDGMENTS　We wish to thank a number of people at IBM Research and elsewhere who contributed substantially to this work. Dr. Michael Treat of Columbia Presbyterian Medical Center provided useful input and feedback during early phases of this project. As co–principal investigator of the joint study between IBM and Johns Hopkins University (JHU) Medical School, which provided a context for much of this work, Dr. Jim Anderson of the JHU Radiology Department offered significant technical input in defining directions as the project evolved. David Grossman and John Karidis were key participants in many conceptual design discussions for the remote center-of-motion manipulator, and Jerry McVicker contributed early designs of key components. Bob Lipori, Jay Hammershoy, Bob Krull, and other members of IBM Research's Central Scientific Services (CSS) built the prototype manipulator which, notably, worked as soon as it was assembled and wired up. Bob Olyha of CSS developed key electronic components and interfaces and so should share the credit for the unusual ease with which the present robot was debugged. Nils Bruun, Dieter Grimm, and other CSS members designed and built an earlier remote center-of-motion robot with a very different mechanical design that nevertheless proved very useful for software and control system development. MIT Cooperative students Nick Swarup and John DeSouza contributed to various aspects of human-machine interface and software development. Ted Selker and Joe Rutledge of IBM Research contributed early TrackPoint prototypes for use in developing the instrument-mounted joystick. Finally, we owe special thanks to Mr. John Tesar of Karl Storz Endoscopy, US, who provided the laparoscopic Cameras and instruments used in developing the system.

NOTES

1. We have seen a very impressive videotape of a one-armed "open" implementation of the system working in vitro, and (at the time of this writing) Dr. Green's group is reportedly working on a two-armed version suitable for clinical use.
2. This idea was proposed by Dr. Michael Treat, of Columbia Presbyterian Medical Center, in 1989 or 1990. It may well have occurred to others at about the same time. It has some obvious attractions as an entry-level application as it is relatively simple, does not directly challenge the surgeon, and does not require a fundamental change in other aspects of the surgical procedure.
3. We have also speculated on possible uses of the robot for more open surgeries. In an open-tissue machining application, for example, the instrument carrier either could be replaced by a specialized cutting tool or could be adapted to hold such a tool so that the tip of the cutter was located at the remote motion center.
4. One potential difficulty is the problem of what to do after a "safety freeze" that occurs while the robot is holding an instrument inserted in the patient. Because the robot will become rigid rather than floppy, as would be the case if backdrivable actuators were used, it will not be possible for the surgeon simply to grasp the robot to withdraw the instrument. Instead, the surgeon would loosen the collet in the instrument carrier and withdraw the instrument, after which the robot can be wheeled away. Alternatively, the entire instrument carrier can be disconnected from the ro-

bot using the quick-release mechanism provided. One significant advantage of this approach is that it avoids possible damage to the patient caused by the uncontrolled instrument motions such as can result if the robot simply becomes floppy or continues to move because of inertia after a safety freeze is initiated. If additional passive compliance is needed, the most appropriate place to provide it is either in the laparoscopic instrument itself or in the instrument carrier.

5. This camera rotation is redundant if a $0°$ laparoscope is used. However, for angled-view scopes it can be used to rotate the image to maintain some preferred view orientation.

6. In our present solution method, we do not attempt to minimize the *integral* error (i.e., the value of $\min \|\mathbf{A}(t) \cdot \mathbf{q}(t) - \mathbf{b}(t)\|$ integrated over time t). Instead, we solve the minimization problem for multiple time steps, using linearized expressions for $\mathbf{A}(t), \mathbf{b}(t), \mathbf{C}(t)$, and $\mathbf{d}(t)$. See [21] for a more detailed discussion.

7. It is interesting to note that functions developed on a system with 7 dof (three proximal rotations, instrument insertion, instrument rotation, camera-view angle, and camera rotation) were successfully ported to the 4-dof distal portion of our present robot in just a few days. Furthermore, the trade-offs made by the optimization software proved to be very sensible, so that the apparent performance of system functions remained acceptable.

8. "Computer Assisted Surgery at IBM Research," videotape showing excerpts of past and current work on computer-assisted surgery at the IBM T. J. Watson Research Center, depicts the interface. Queries should be directed to Russell H. Taylor, Manager of Computer Assisted Surgery Research, IBM T. J. Watson Research Center, PO Box 704, Yorktown HYS, NY 10598.

9. Although we have yet to implement such a mode, it would also be straightforward to implement a remote force controller, in which the surgeon exerts forces on a detached 6-dof "force joystick." In this case, the center-of-motion compliance could be set to produce teleoperation modes analogous either to the anatomy-centered viewpoint or the viewpoint displacement modes described later.

10. If a stereo laparoscope is available, then one may dispense with the subsidiary motions. We are exploring the acquisition of such a laparoscope and have already demonstrated the use of the image-processing software for a simulated biopsy experiment using two standard TV cameras.

11. One of the principal goals of a current IBM/Johns Hopkins joint study is to obtain quantitative in-vivo verification of this claim. At the time this is written, these measurements have not been performed. Preliminary experiments at IBM with a $30°$ angle-of-view laparoscope using a pumpkin as a patient have, however, shown this to be the case.

12. "TrackPoint," "ThinkPad," and PS/2 are registered trademarks of International Business Machines, Armonk, New York.

REFERENCES

[1] KELLY, P. J., A. KALL, S. GOERSS, and F. EARNEST, 1986. "Computer-assisted stereotaxic laser resection of intra-axial brain neoplasms. *J. Neurosurg.* March: 427–439.

[2] BENABIB, A. L., P. CINQUIN, S. LAVALLEE, J. F. LEBAS, J. DEMONGEOT, and J. DE ROUGEMONT, 1987. Computer-driven robot for stereotactic surgery connected to CT scan and magnetic resonance imaging. In *Proceedings of the American Society for Stereotactic Functional Neurosurgery*, pp. 153–154.

[3] KWOH, Y. S., J. HOU, E. JONCKHEERE, and S. HAYATI, 1988. A robot with improved absolute positioning accuracy for CT guided stereotactic surgery. *IEEE Trans. Biomed. Eng.* February: 153–161.

[4] LEWIS M. A., and G. A. BEKEY, 1992. Automation and robotics in neurosurgery: Prospects and problems. In *Neurosurgery for the Third Millenium*, M. L. J. Apuzzo, ed. American Association of Neolological Surgeons.

[5] PAUL, H., B. MITTELSTADT, W. BARGAR, P. KAZANZIDES, B. WILLIAMSON, J. ZUHARS, R. TAYLOR, and W. HANSON, 1992. Accuracy of implant interface preparation: Hand-held broach vs. robot machine tool. In *Proceedings of the Orthopaedic Research Society*, Washington, D.C.

[6] KIENZLE, T. C., S. D. STULBERG, M. PESHKIN, A. QUAID, and C. WU, 1993. An integrated CAD-robotics system for total knee replacement surgery. In *Proceedings of the 1993 IEEE Conference on Robotics and Automation*, Atlanta, pp. 889–894.

[7] IKUTA, K., M. TSUKAMOTO, and S. HIROSE, 1988. Shape memory alloy servo actuator system with electric resistance feedback and application for active endoscopes. Presented at the IEEE Robotics and Automation Conference.

[8] CHARLES, S., R. E. WILLIAMS, and B. HAMMEL, 1989. Design of a surgeon-machine interface for teleoperated microsurgery. *Proc. IEEE EMBS Conf.*, pp. 883–884.

[9] STURGES, R., 1989. Voice controlled flexible endoscope [videotape]. Pittsburgh: Carnegie-Mellon University.

[10] DAVIES, B. L., R. D. HIBBERD, A. TIMONEY, and J. WICKHAM, 1991. A surgeon robot for prostatectomies. In *Proceedings of the Fifth International Conference on Advanced Robotics*, Pisa, pp. 871–875.

[11] GREEN, P., 1993. Telepresence surgery. *Presented at the National Science Foundation Workshop on Computer Assisted Surgery*, Washington, D.C., February.

[12] GREEN, P., 1992. Advanced teleoperator technology for enhanced minimally invasive surgery. In *Proceedings of the Medicine Meets Virtual Reality Symposium*, San Diego, June 4–7.

[13] WANG, Y., 1993. Automated endoscopic system for optimal positioning [advertising brochure]. Computer Motion, Inc.

[14] WANG, Y., 1994. Robotically enhanced surgery. In *Proceedings of the Medicine Meets Virtual Reality Symposium II*, San Diego, January 27–30.

[15] *World Medical Device and Diagnostic News*, August 5, 1992.

[16] STURGES, R. H., and S. LAOWATTANA, 1991. A flexible tendon-controlled device for endoscopy. In *Proceedings of the IEEE Robotics and Automation Conference*, Sacramento.

[17] Gagnier Oral Presentation at Massachusetts General Hospital Symposium on Minimally Invasive Surgery, September 27–28, 1993.

[18] TAYLOR, R. H., and D. D. GROSSMAN, 1983. An integrated robot systems architecture. *IEEE Proc.*, July. (7): 842–855.

[19] IBM Corporation, *AML/2 Manufacturing Control System User's Guide*, 1986.

[20] TAYLOR, R. H., H. A. PAUL, KAZANZIDES, B. D. MITTELSTADT, W. HANSON, F. ZUHARS, B. WILLIAMSON, B. L. MUSITS, E. GLASSMAN, and W. L. BARGAR, 1991. Taming the bull: Safety in a precise surgical robot. In *Proceedings of the 1991 International Conference on Advanced Robotics*, Pisa, Italy, June.

[21] FUNDA, J., R. TAYLOR, K. GRUBEN, and D. LaROSE, 1993. Optimal motion control for teleoperated surgical robots. In *Proceedings of the 1993 SPIE International Symposium on Optical Tools for Manufacturing and Advanced Automation*, Boston, September.

[22] R. H. TAYLOR, J. FUNDA, D. LaROSE, and M. TREAT, 1992. An experimental system for computer assisted endoscopic surgery. In *Proceedings of the IEEE Satellite Symposium on Neurosciences*, Lyons, France, November.

[23] MORAVEC, H. P., 1980. Obstacle avoidance and navigation in the real world by a seeing robot rover. Doctoral thesis, Stanford University.

47 A Clinically Applied Robot for Prostatectomies

BRIAN L. DAVIES, ROGER D. HIBBERD, ANTHONY G. TIMONEY, AND JOHN E. A. WICKHAM

WE WERE FIRST approached in the summer of 1988 by the Institute of Urology in London, under its director Mr. John Wickham, to look into the possibility of robotizing a transurethral resection of the prostate (TURP). This did not strike us immediately as the most obvious candidate for a robotic surgical procedure! However, it has turned out, perhaps fortuitously, to be a relatively straightforward and safe robotic application with the method that we have adopted. Unlike such applications as neurosurgery, the prostate is a fairly forgiving gland in which the accuracies required are not particularly high. Provided the cutting instrument is correctly prepositioned by the surgeon, we found it possible to constrain mechanically the motions to operate safely within the desired volume. In the unlikely event of a total failure of the system and all its safety sensors, the cutter would be mechanically prevented from moving beyond the volume of tissue that was to be subsequently removed.

Initially, the range of the parameters of the process were investigated by conducting a preliminary feasibility study using a standard six-axis Unimation Puma 560 (Unimation Inc, Danbory, Ct.) robot. In defining the problem, one of the major difficulties was assessing the surgeons' requirements in engineering terms. One difficulty is that urology surgeons do not traditionally have a quantitative approach and are not accustomed to specifying the size of the gland in millimeters but rather will classify it in qualitative terms as *big, medium,* or *small.* Considerable preliminary investigation was necessary to determine sizes, weights, and forces that could be used for engineering specifications.

Another difficulty was communication. Both urology surgeons and roboticists have a large vocabulary of special terms, so that it required much effort and iteration to achieve a mutual understanding that resulted in a satisfactory engineering specification!

Conventional TURP

The prostate gland is a roughly chestnut-sized gland located between the base of the penis and the bladder neck (figure 47.1) [1]. The urinary tract can become blocked with adenomatous tissue, which is usually benign. It is estimated that a 40-year-old man has a 29% chance of undergoing TURP in his lifetime [2]. Although in the past, outflow obstruction was removed by an open procedure, more recently TURP is most commonly undertaken as a minimally invasive procedure that is regarded as safe [3]. In TURP, a rigid endoscope (typical diameter, 8.5 mm) is inserted down the center of the penis through the urethra and located at the verumontanum near the base of the penis. In addition to a rod lens, the endoscope contains channels for illumination, irrigation, and suction, as well as room for a diathermic cutting loop. The procedure now accounts for 38% of all major surgical procedures carried out by American urologists and is second only to cataract extraction as the major operation causing expenditure under Medicare [4]. It is regarded as a complex procedure and, for a surgeon to achieve proficiency, requires that more TURP procedures be carried out during training than any other urologic operation.

The working element of the resectoscope consists of a tungsten wire loop. Under direct endoscopic vision, a high-frequency current is applied to the loop and the obstructing tissue is removed in "chips" by successive cuts. The resection continues until all the tissue is removed, forming a cavity that approximates to an asymmetric truncated cone. Hemostasis is effected by sealing the blood vessels with a high-frequency coagulating current. During the procedure, the operator's vision through the endoscope is maintained by continuous inflow of a nonelectrolytic, hypoosmolar irrigating

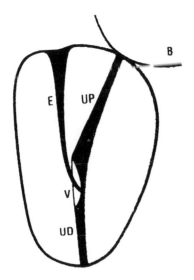

FIGURE 47.1 Sagittal view of a normal prostate gland.

TABLE 47.1
Preoperative dimensions of prostate gland

	Mean (mm)	Range (mm)
Length	41	29–59
Width	52	48–80
Anteroposterior diameter	35	33–60

solution into the resectoscope. The irrigant and chips of tissue pass into the bladder, from which they are removed at intervals using a suction bulb. The volume to be resected is roughly conical in form, with the apex of the cone at the verumontanum v (see figure 47.1) and the base circle at the bladder neck. The verumontanum forms the junction between the urinary duct and the ejaculatory duct. This is a visible landmark used by the surgeon to locate the start position for TURP. Distal to the verumontanum is the sphincter mechanism. Neither the sphincter nor the verumontanum must be cut in a prostatectomy. Damage to the sphincter mechanism during prostatectomy results in incontinence and occurs in up to 4% of patients [5]. Thus, the area for resection must be confined to the area between the bladder neck (proximally) and the verumontanum (distally). Only adenomatous tissue should be removed from the prostate, and typically only 38% of the preoperative transrectal ultrasound weight is resected [6]. The actual dimensions of the prostate, measured by the authors in a preoperative transrectal ultrasound assessment, were as shown in table 47.1.

Feasibility study using a standard industrial robot

To determine whether a robotic prostatectomy was feasible and to investigate the nature of problems to be encountered, it was decided to carry out a preliminary feasibility study using a standard six-axis Unimation Puma industrial robot. However, the complex trajectory described previously is difficult to achieve using a standard 6-degrees-of-freedom (dof) robot, and it was found necessary to add two additional frameworks to the conventional robot to achieve the appropriate motions. The outer framework was hung on the fifth (pitch) axis of the Puma and carried the external framework, which, in turn, held the cutter assembly. The combination of these five axes enables the cutter to be positioned and oriented correctly. The sixth (rotation) axis then was used to carry a high-speed rotary cutter, mounted in an endoscope, held on the inner framework so that the cutter could reciprocate through its stroke length. The inner frame could thus reciprocate and rotate with reference to the external frame.

The feasibility of performing the required procedure was demonstrated by cutting the appropriate near-conical shape from a potato mounted in a perspex box, as shown in figure 47.2. Potatoes are the traditional medium used by junior surgeons to best simulate pros-

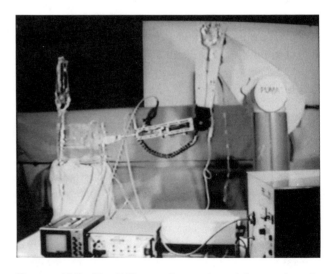

FIGURE 47.2 Feasibility study conducted by cutting the appropriate near-conical shape from a potato mounted in a perspex box.

tatic tissue when undergoing training in TURP. An artificial penis was mounted on the box and the endoscope with cutter was passed down the center. Saline solution was used for irrigation, and a separate suction tube was used for removing fluid and particles of debris. A video camera was attached to the eyepiece of the endoscope which, together with high-intensity illumination, permitted the cutting process to be displayed on a monitor. The cutter swept out a wide angle that varied from 60° above the horizon to 30° below and required careful programming of the sequence of cuts to avoid any singularity points in the robot motion. These singularities may lead to unpredictable motions in some positions, with disastrous consequences.

To provide a realistic feasibility study, the software was written to allow full control by the surgeon. Before commencing the procedure, the surgeon inserted the cutter down the center of the penis to the start position, using the view through the endoscope as a guide. The coordinates of the size of the robot trajectory then were selected by the surgeon, and the sequence of cuts to produce the shape was generated automatically. The surgeon had the ability to intervene at any point based on viewing the procedure on the monitor and could select further sequences of cuts to enlarge the resected aperture. Thus, the surgeon could control the whole procedure, using his or her experience and judgment, but was relieved of the necessity of making awkward physical motions, thus avoiding the back and neck strain prevalent among many urologists. The whole sequence of cuts could be performed within 5 minutes, compared to normal procedures, which can take more than an hour. This reduction in surgery duration could lead to an added benefit because it is not necessary to cauterize until the end of the procedure. This would be advantageous as well because it could minimize the amount of irrigant absorbed, which could further enhance the safety of the procedure.

Thus, the feasibility study was believed to demonstrate successfully the viability of using a robotizied procedure. However, it was considered that the use of an unconstrained conventional robot, without the benefit of safety features, was not acceptable for patients. Therefore, it was decided to build gradually toward the use of a special-purpose robot for prostatectomies by constructing a custom-made safety frame that could be manually operated by the surgeon and then subsequently implement a motorized version of the frame containing safety software.

The manual safety frame

To avoid the necessity of using 7 dof and a standard robot to produce the complex shape required in TURP, a special frame was designed (figures 47.3, 47.4) with only three motions [7]. The reciprocating cutter is located inside an endoscope that is carried on a circular arc that, in turn, is mounted on a ring which is free to rotate through 360°. The arc, together with the ring, is arranged to give a conical motion of the cutter pivoted about the tip of the resectoscope. A series of indent locations on both the arc and the frame of the ring allow incremental motions to be made, which permit controlled cuts to be taken in sequence (figure 47.5).

FIGURE 47.3   Specially designed manual safety frame.

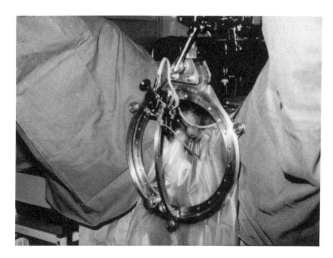

FIGURE 47.4   Safety frame in position for surgery.

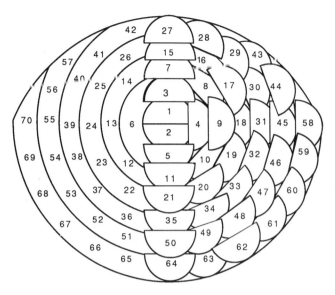

FIGURE 47.5 Typical sequence of cuts at the bladder neck.

The addition of a metal shield, clamped to the ring, provides a physical stop for the cutter, thus preventing any cuts being taken outside the predefined range. Thus, the frame acts as a safety fixture that prevents the surgeon from inadvertently cutting outside a predefined volume.

The sequence for the operating procedure is first to place the patient in a lithotomy position (i.e., with legs in stirrups) to allow access for the frame and the surgeon. A preliminary examination is carried out, and the frame then is positioned and oriented to allow the resectoscope to be clamped without disturbing its alignment. The resection is accomplished by the surgeon using electrocautary. Hemostasis is achieved generally at the end of the procedure, with the resectoscope freed from the frame. Using the current design of frame, a volume of up to 60 ml can be resected.

To date, a safety-frame TURP has been carried out on 40 patients presenting to the St. Peter's group of hospitals with the symptoms of prostatic outflow obstruction. The patients were assessed by outpatient uroflowmetry, for which a flow rate of 15 ml/sec or less indicates obstruction. Pressure flow studies were used also to confirm outflow resistance. Transrectal ultrasound estimation of prostate dimensions and volume were obtained. Detailed results are shown in Timoney et al. [8]. Postoperative assessment was carried out on discharge, after 6 weeks, and at 3 months, 6 months, and 1 year. The preoperative and postoperative flow

rates of 10.0 and 22.2 ml/sec using the frame compared favorably with those found by Neal et al. [9] in a study of 205 patients undergoing traditional TURP who showed a preoperative and postoperative flow rate of 9 and 18 ml/sec, respectively. Thus, it would appear that the outcome after a frame prostatectomy is similar to that after conventional TURP.

The robotized version of the safety frame

Having satisfied ourselves that the geometry of the frame was correct, the manual frame was then redesigned using similar kinematics, and each motion was motorized (figures 47.6, 47.7). A continuous-flow re-

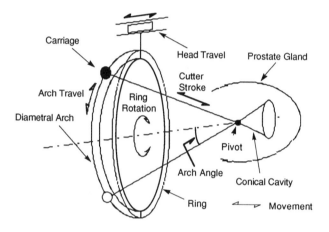

FIGURE 47.6 A 3D schematic of the motorized frame.

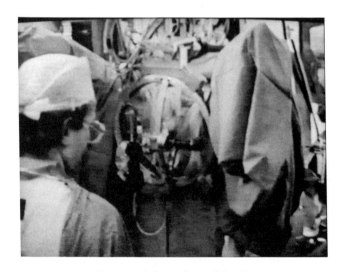

FIGURE 47.7 Motorized frame in position for surgery.

sectoscope with rack-and-pinion drive was mounted onto the arc and driven by a direct-current (DC) motor. All the motors are rare-earth permanent magnet motors with integral optical position encoders and an epicyclic gearbox and are driven by a control system that is monitored by an IBM PC. Software has been written for the PC to allow the surgeon to specify the size of the prostate and its shape at three different cross-sections, using information obtained from an ultrasound inspection carried out beforehand. An automatic curve-fitting routine then is used to define the combined motions of the motors to produce the required curved trajectory of the cutter or the sequence of single-axis motions that approximate the required shape. Safety checks are incorporated throughout the software to ensure that at no time can the motor-encoder system be asked to move the cutter outside the predefined limits of the prostate. In addition, a physical clamp system, attached to the arc drive, ensures that even if the motor should attempt to move the cutter outside the predetermined conical shape, it will be physically prevented from doing so and the motor controller will cut out. The system is under continuous control of the surgeon who can observe the procedure on a monitor via a camera attached to the endoscope. The motions can be interrupted at any time, incorporating inherently safe techniques for shutdown, and the procedure completed manually. In this way, a special-purpose, robotized device has been constructed that is inherently safe. For safety reasons, it is not intended that any form of expert system will be involved. Instead, the knowledge, skill, and judgment of the surgeon are available at each stage, and a conscious decision and keyboard input are required from the surgeon before a new motion is made. This ensures that the surgeon maintains complete control of the operation and can assure himself or herself that everything is performing satisfactorily.

Servo control is provided by two master controller boards, one of which drives two slave controller boards while the other drives an input-output (I/O) unit. Each master controller has a program (written in BASIC) resident in its memory. These programs interact with a human interface program (written in Turbo Pascal) running on the IBM PC through RS232 links. The human interface program receives instructions from the surgeon. Several pages were designed to achieve the following tasks:

- Formation of a 3D ellipsoid digital model of the prostate
- Formation of a patient's database, including both preoperative and postoperative records
- Selection of a mode of cutting (overlapping cone method or barrel-shaped method)

To ensure safety of the operation, the obvious solution is to have a total backup system, but this is not economically viable. A suitable alternative would be to have a selective backup. This is ensured by providing reliable hardware functionality and following existing safety requirements. Equipment such as an uninterruptible power supply is essential, from which the motorized frame and computer system would draw their power. Hard limit stops are installed to prevent movements physically from extending beyond a predetermined limit for the patient concerned if the software should fail. Another issue for consideration is the inclusion of safe recovery procedures in the event of system failures or unexpected interruption of the operation, so that the operation can be resumed if possible or else can be terminated safely and gracefully.

Figure 47.8 illustrates the use of two backup systems running in parallel with the main system, which is the IBM computer. They communicate with each other on the computer bus, forming a triangular interchecking loop. Each backup system is similar to the main system in that it will have a safety monitor, a kinematic model of the motorized frame, error recovery procedures, and a communication protocol all embedded in its software. Independently, each receives feedback from the sensors mounted on the motorized frame.

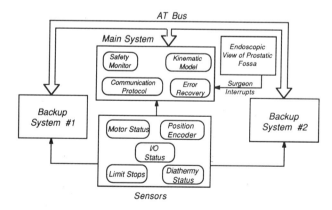

FIGURE 47.8   Layout of the control system.

Sizing the prostate

It is crucial that the enlarged, adenomal portion of the prostate (the target for the motorized frame) be sized sufficiently accurately. Only then can a safe automatic cutting and motion sequence be generated fully so that only the adenomal, and not the prostatic, capsule is resected. The current sizing method, when applying the manual frame, is transrectal ultrasound scanning. This procedure is carried out preoperatively. Successive transverse scans at 5-mm intervals are taken from the bladder neck toward the verumontanum. In each scan, the anteroposterior height (AP diameter) and the width of the prostate are noted. These dimensions are used to plan the extent of the arch, the ring, and the head movements. Successive conical resections enable the cavity to be matched to the prostate shape and size.

Although transrectal ultrasonography worked well in the case of the manual frame, because it was done manually it substantially increased the overall operative time. Furthermore, it did not give accurate measurements of the prostate for a frame TURP, partly because the axis of entrance to the prostate was not well defined and partly because the location of the verumontanum could not be obtained positively.

Ultrasound scans can also be done transurethrally, but this requires the patient to be anesthetized; hence it is not appropriate, or desirable, for use in a preoperative procedure. However, a transurethral probe can be used in the motorized frame at the start of an operation when a semiautomated scan can be carried out.

The motorized frame is mounted in position following a preliminary cystoscopy, and a systematic setup procedure is undertaken (figure 47.9). The ultrasound probe then is introduced onto the carriage of the frame via a bracket that locates the sensor proximal to the verumontanum section.

The distance from the verumontanum to the bladder neck is determined first under direct endoscopic vision. Using the same setup and under the supervision of the surgeon, the head of the motorised frame is advanced until the bladder neck is reached. The ultrasound image is fed back onto a frame grabber in the IBM computer, and an image is reproduced on either the main screen or a secondary screen of the IBM computer. A light pen is provided for the surgeon to outline the capsule (adenoma) boundary, this outline is employed by the user interface to establish a 3D model of the prostate and subsequently to determine the extent of the resection. The user interface directs the head to move the ultrasound probe at 5-mm intervals from the bladder neck toward the verumontanum, stopping at each interval for light-pen input. The input from the light pen is a digitized *x-y* coordinate used by the user interface for further numeric analysis to form an ellipsoid model of the prostate.

The initial setup is not disturbed during the preliminary examination of the prostate to determine its length and cross-section nor during the replacement of the ultrasound probe by the resectoscope. This ensures a common reference for both the cutting and imaging activities, which is necessary for a repeatable and reliable robotic operation.

The surgeon-computer interface

An important area for consideration when implementing software in an operating room is the interface between the computer and the user—in this case, the surgeon. Because the software is going to be used by nonengineering personnel who may not be familiar with computers or electronically programmable systems, the human-computer interface should be designed in such a way that one can become acquainted with it in a relatively short time of perhaps only a few practice occasions. Also, the way data are presented and the way they are input into the software routine must be simple, effective, and yet flexible, allowing no chance for erroneous data input. The operating-room environment is a complex one, with many distractions, and correct decisions must be made in emergencies on the basis of a very easy-to-use human-computer interface.

Software structure

To further enhance the underlying structured approach to programming (for which the Pascal language was used), the software for the prostate robot divides its task into a series of components, conveniently presented as pages of screen display. To facilitate future expansion, the design of the software has been as comprehensive as possible. Figure 47.10 shows the screen display under normal operating conditions. The pages of screen display handle the following tasks:

- Providing easy control of each axis of the frame
- Setting up the system for operation

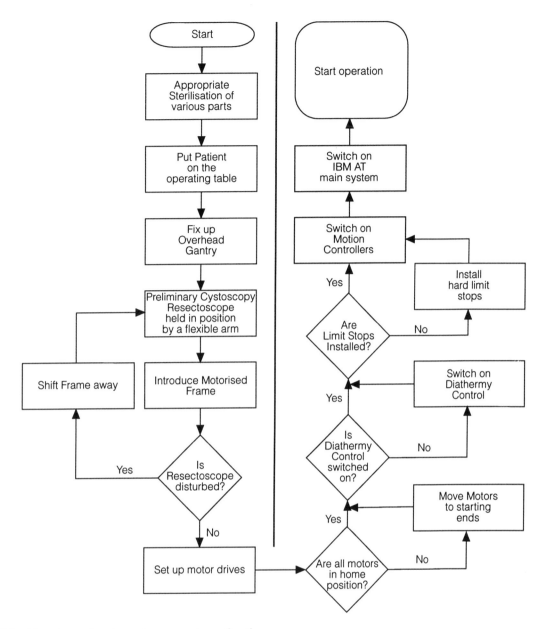

FIGURE 47.9 Flowchart showing setup procedures for the motorized frame.

• Storing patients' particulars for database purposes (both preoperative and postoperative results can be stored for statistical studies)

• Generating the desired cut sequence based on results of ultrasound sizings

• Giving safety observations

The software for the prostate robot uses a non-overlay global definition block, in which variables that are safety-related and are employed to control the operation are declared. This allows a more systematic and central control of important parameters. Switching from one page to another can be easily controlled by a series of tests that ensure the availability and correctness of data before the next page is entered. As is typical of imperative languages, there is a logical sequence neatly interwoven into the page displays. This logical sequence is clearly spelled out and will contribute to reduced chances of logical sequence errors.

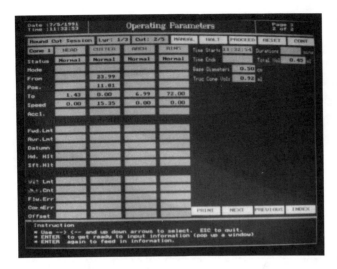

FIGURE 47.10 Sample pop-up window requesting information in prostate robot software.

File reading and writing operations are kept to a minimum within the execution of a page display. They appear only at the entry and exit points of the page. This not only speeds up data processing but also provides easy verification of data. However, this process is memory-intensive.

Considerations for the user

Clinical experience reaffirmed that simplifying the job of the surgeon must be a primary issue in the design of the software. The introduction of a computer system into the operating room should be done with care because it is to be used by the surgeon or the surgeon's assistant, in addition to the normal scope of work. The time factor should be regarded as crucial; a task should not involve too many steps or take too long to achieve its end. The user must be trained in the operation of the automated system.

Software for the prostate robot should incorporate the following:

• Task accomplishment is self-driven, using pull-down menus and pop-up windows where appropriate to provide simple and effective explanations (figure 47.10).

• Mouse-driven selection and keyboard-driven selection should be considered.

• Only a handful of keys (on the keyboard) should be used frequently to avoid difficulties in getting used to their assigned functions. For this reason, a key

should not be assigned for more than one function unnecessarily.

• Graphic presentation of 3D models is desirable as it gives the user a tangible grasp of the information captured by the computer.

• When a decision is asked of the user, the answer is confirmed twice. This allows for a change of mind.

• Even when an action is under way, having received the user's decision, there is always an interrupt mechanism to provide for a change of mind.

These suggestions aim to reduce the work required from the surgeon and hence the likelihood that he or she will commit a mistake.

Results

The first stage of the development of the motorized frame has now been completed. Successful resections have been accomplished using the hot-loop diathermy on potatoes. Improvements to the system have been made and preliminary clinical trials have been successfully carried out using the motorized frame. The appropriate levels of sterilization are achieved by mounting the motor-encoder system to the frame when the frame has been sterilized and set up preoperatively. The motors and other equipment then are shrouded in a sterile sheath. This procedure is considered necessary because the frame is very close to the operating site and it is not feasible simply to cover it with sterile cloth drapes. A partial resection has been carried out on 5 patients to date, the remainder of the procedure being completed manually with excellent results. The complexity of the operating-theater environment should not be underestimated. It is very difficult to simulate the environment of an actual operation in a laboratory or even in the theater itself.

The next phase of development for the motorized frame is to develop further fault-tolerant software; to duplicate sensors for the frame suitably and adequately, and to devise a quick and reasonably accurate way of obtaining transurethral ultrasound data of the prostate adenoma, with reference to an easily identifiable datum. The use of transrectal ultrasonography for intraoperative monitoring of the process will also be investigated. Additional kinematic configurations will be investigated to determine whether it is possible to mount the motor-encoder system remote from the operating site by using additional power transmission elements. This would then simplify sterilization measures. Following these activities, it should be possible for the complete procedure to be carried out robotically without difficulty.

Conclusions

The safety of surgical robots is of paramount importance, and some suggestions have been made concerning methods of achieving adequate safety. A case study has been presented of this approach applied to a prostatectomy. A special-purpose kinematic system was designed based on a preliminary feasibility study. This safety frame then was constructed and applied clinically to 30 patients, using the surgeon to move each axis within the physical constraints of the frame. The results of these tests confirmed the validity of the kinematic approach and demonstrated the necessary sequence of procedures. The kinematic geometry then was used to construct an automated system based on robotic principles. This robotic system has now been applied to 5 patients to produce a partial resection automatically, on the basis of preoperative ultrasonography. The first patient was treated in April 1991. This represents a world first in robotically removing substantial quantities of tissue from a human patient. The refinement of the procedures, together with the use of transurethral ultrasound for preliminary sizing of the prostate, should soon result in a totally automated procedure using an inherently safe system.

REFERENCES

[1] McNeal, J. E. 1989. Anatomy and embryology. In *The Prostate*, J. Fitzpatrick and R. Krane, eds. Churchill Livingston Press, Edinburgh.

[2] Glynn, R. J., E. W. Campion, G. R. Bouchard, and J. E. Silbert, 1985. The development of benign prostatic hyperplasia among volunteers in the normative aging study. *Am. J. Epidemiol.* 121:78–82.

[3] Mebust, W. K., H. E. Holtgrewe, A. T. K. Cockett, P. C. Peters, and the Writing Committee, 1989. Transurethral prostatectomy: Immediate and postoperative complications. A cooperative study of 13 participating institutions evaluating 3,885 patients. *J. Urol.* 141:243–247.

[4] Holtgrewe, H. L., W. K. Mebust, J. B. Dowd, P. C. Peters, and C. Proctor, 1989. Transurethral prostatectomy: Practice aspects of the dominant operation in American urology. *J. Urol.* 141 (2):248–253.

[5] Fowler, F. T., et al., 1988. Symptom status and quality of life following prostatectomy. *J.A.M.A.* 259:3018–3022.

[6] Miyazaki, Y., A. Yamaguchi, and S. Hara, 1983. The value of transrectal ultrasonography in preoperative assessment for transurethral prostatectomy. *J. Urol.* 129:48–50.

[7] Davies, B. L., R. D. Hibberd, A. Timoney, and J. E. A. Wickham, 1989. A surgeon robot for prostatectomies. In *Proceedings of the Second International Conference on Robotics in Medicine*, Newcastle, U.K.

[8] Timoney, A. G., W. S. Ng, B. L. Davies, R. D. Hibberd, and J. E. A. Wickham, 1991. Frame prostatectomy: The first stage of a robotic procedure. *J. Endourol.* 15:2.

[9] Neal, D. E., P. D. Ramsden, L. Sharples, A. Smith, P. H. Powell, R. A. Styles, and R. J. Webb, 1989. Outcome of elective prostatectomy. *Br. Med. J.* 299:767–771.

48 A Voice-Actuated, Tendon-Controlled Device for Endoscopy

ROBERT H. STURGES, JR., AND
SCHITT LAOWATTANA

ENDOSCOPES HAVE been playing a significant role in reducing invasive surgery for a large number of patients. The field of endoscopy is evolving rapidly. More sophisticated endoscopes with a higher level of performance are being developed and introduced every year. Currently, there are five basic types of endoscopes (Miller, 1986): conventional structure, rod lens telescope, gradient optic, fiberoptic, and microchip sensor. The conventional structure is based on the telescopes used for astronomy; by adding a distal prism at the tip, the user can vary the field of view. An object lens and a relay lens form a real inverted image for endoscopists. The rod lens telescope yields better resolution and light transmission through a series of glass rods interspersed with spaces filled with air. External reflection and chromatic aberration are reduced by using a blooming glass and a flint glass. For very small target areas, the gradient optic can be used as it consists of a single glass element with different refractive indices. However, it has poor light transmission as well as some limitations in viewing angle (45–60°).

Each of these three endoscopes has a rigid structure, which limits its length of operation. To obtain longer lengths of operation, particularly for esophagoscopy and colonoscopy, more flexible endoscopes, such as the fiberoptic type, are required. In this type, refraction in a fiber bundle transmits light from a light source to the target area. Images are transmitted back through another fiber bundle, which is arranged in a coherent or parallel manner. In the microchip sensor endoscope, another flexible type, the optical elements are replaced entirely by microchip sensors and electronic wiring. With adequate light from a noncoherent fiberoptic bundle, video images are created for storage as well as for viewing in diagnosis through a monitor. Such a viewing system is called an *indirect video system* and has 25% less resolution compared with a direct video sys-

tem. However, comparative studies show that flexible endoscopes detect an average of three times as many polyps and cancers as do rigid endoscopes.

Although the fiberoptic and microchip sensor endoscopes are more flexible than the other three types, their stems (made of long rubber or plastic tubes) still are positionally uncontrollable over most of their length. Figure 48.1 is a diagram of the human colon, which is composed of a set of labyrinthine and reverse bends. The five major parts are the rectum and sigmoid, descending, transverse, and ascending colon. The smallest radius of curvature is approximately 2–3 cm, located at the bending portion between the rectum and the sigmoid colon. The transverse colon, which is 40–50 cm long, is the largest and most mobile part of the colon. It extends between the right and left colic flexures, forming a loop that is directed downward and forward. Because the transverse colon is suspended posteriorly by the soft living tissue called the *transverse mesocolon*, its movements always are affected by the breathing process and other movements in the intestinal cavity. Use of a colonoscope is impeded by peristaltic action of the gastrointestinal (GI) tract, which is continuously attempting to expel the device. Involuntary motions of the GI tract create difficulties in acquiring a target and in using the array of diagnostic and therapeutic tools that are deployed through a channel in the stem. The GI tract also may cramp, thus trapping the device inside the colon. High mechanical flexibility is required for the endoscope to traverse the colon without creating potentially damaging interacting forces. However, the very compliance required in this stem makes maneuvering the endoscope around the bends of the colon extremely difficult. So-called alpha (α) loops often are created by the endoscopist to help advance the stem at the reverse bends (e.g., at the junctions of the sigmoid-descending colon

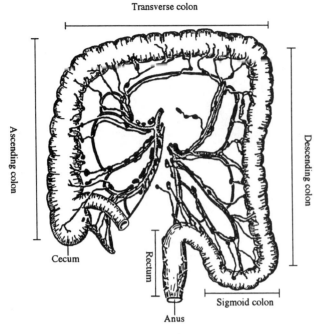

Figure labels: Transverse colon, Ascending colon, Descending colon, Cecum, Rectum, Sigmoid colon, Anus

FIGURE 48.1 Diagram of the human colon.

and the descending-transverse colon). Twisting and retracting the stem are required for making such loops. Hence, high interacting forces between the endoscope and the wall of the colon are inevitable.

Steering systems at the tip of the endoscope provide two directional controls—up-down and left-right—which are manually operated through two concentric knobs. In this respect, flexible endoscopes can be considered in the class of teleoperated manipulators, with limited degrees of freedom and direct mechanical master-slave coupling. This manual procedure, which bears no particular relation to the resulting motions, has the potential to damage the surrounding tissue. Successful operation and manipulation of these medical devices requires great proficiency as well as a great deal of time. These skills have obviously been mastered by endoscopists worldwide. However, the length of endoscopes still is limited to approximately 1 m, which leaves 80% of the digestive tract unexplored, regardless of which end is entered.

Major objectives for a new endoscope

As pointed out earlier, there are many difficulties in operating current endoscopes that may result in discomfort or risk to the patient. To simplify the endoscopic procedure, we propose a safer, more precisely controllable device. The major objectives of the new device are defined as follows:

• The motion of the endoscope stem must be smooth and should match the labyrinthine paths of the colon. Hence, a highly flexible stem is required.

• Integrated with suitable control systems, the endoscope stem is required to minimize the interacting force with the wall of the colon.

• A human-machine interface (i.e., a voice-controlled command system) is needed that frees the hands of the endoscopist.

Most of the current research on endoscopes is directed toward enhancing vision systems and acquiring wider tip angles. Unfortunately, the fundamental problem of steadily predictable motion has not been resolved completely. This chapter focuses on our approach to this problem: a flexible tendon-controlled bead chain that forms a semipassively controllable spine.

Advanced approaches for stem control

For better insertion and retraction, the stem could be actively controllable. The stem would consist of a number of serial rotational joints with a prismatic joint at its base. With the specified positions and orientations of these joints, the stem would traverse the colon easily, avoiding extensive contact with the surrounding tissue. This could be done through the mapping or shifting method that has been implemented in redundant manipulators by transferring tip trajectories to the next joint and consecutively to the rest of the joints. Tip trajectories would be generated in real time through a manual or automatic steering system that points the tip in the desired direction. While the stem is advanced, the succeeding joint then moves toward the position and orientation of the preceding joint in the previous step. This steering strategy is called *snake motion*. We will describe briefly three applications of this approach.

The redundant degrees of freedom in snake robots (e.g., Toshiba snake robots [Asano et al., 1983; Asano, 1984; Obama, Ozaki, and Asano, 1985; Tsuchihashi, Wakahara, and Asano, 1985]) have been used for obstacle avoidance. Hence, the reachable working space, which may be highly cluttered, could be accessed by their end-effectors. However, some of the disadvantages associated with these robots include requiring more, continuous degrees of freedom and operating at slower speeds. Tracking of the position and velocity trajectory, as well as the position and orientation of the snake tip and stem, are computed relative to the joint displacement and the rate of the prismatic joint. Such computations are not trivial, and the difficulty depends on the current configuration of the snake stem. Trajectory planning also requires a well-modeled environment. Furthermore, miniaturization of the overall system to realize an application in endoscopes is difficult to achieve.

In the snake motion scheme, a number of small actuators installed at each joint perform the mapping operation. The complexity of the mechanical arrangements for these miniactuators and the computation of the mapping operation increase exponentially with the length of the stem for most practical applications. Algorithms employed in planning the trajectory, which are based on pseudoinverse Jacobians (Klein and Huang, 1983), are proportional to n^3, where n is the number of degrees of freedom. A model of an active endoscope stem utilizing snake motion has been demonstrated using a shape memory alloy (SMA) servo actuator system (Ikuta, Tsukamoto, and Hirose, 1988). The control algorithms demonstrated the tractability of trajectory planning for limited degrees of freedom. SMA (Schetky, 1984) is an alloy that can be stretched or deformed rapidly by changing its temperature. The stem of this prototype endoscope consists of five 2D rotational joints, each of which is 13 mm in diameter and 40 mm long. These joints are driven by a pair of antagonistic wires of titanium-nickel, a stable type of SMA, through an electric resistance feedback control system. Changing of resistances because of the SMA wire deformation is not completely reversible. This hysteresis between the forward and backward paths is approximately 10%; therefore, position control is inaccurate. Moreover, the speed of advancing and retracting the device is limited by the heating and cooling rates of the SMA. The time, t, that an SMA wire takes to heat to a temperature, T, above the ambient temperature, T_a, is given by the expression:

$$t = \beta \ln \left[1 - \left(\frac{T - T_a}{T_0} \right) \right]^{-1} \qquad (1)$$

where T_0 is the maximum temperature the SMA wire would reach when heated by current and β is the time constant $K\phi^n$ where ϕ is the wire diameter and K and n are function terms depending on which types of alloy are used to make such an SMA wire.

The dominant parameters in equation 1 for determining the speed of deformation is the time constant β. For example, a 0.25-mm Ti-Ni wire with 22 N lifting capacity has a β of 3.15. A cluster of smaller wires of the same type and lifting capacity will deform faster than a single wire. However, a larger cross-section would be required for such a cluster. Wire spacing, another crucial factor, must be properly allocated for an airflow system to remove heat from the wires efficiently. Hence, the trade-off between overall size of the SMA actuator system and the deformation time should be carefully considered.

Another type of snake robot called the *ORM* (the Norwegian word for a snake, Pieper, 1968) was developed for the Stanford Artificial Intelligence Project. The positional control of each joint is binary, providing only two states: θ_0 or $-\theta_0$, where θ_0 is a constant. In case of n links, there would be 2^n possible configurations. Consequently, the tip could be placed at 2^n points. Sufficient links are required for the robot to place its tip close to any arbitrary point within its working space. Such a robot would have a high level of difficulty traversing inside a small, highly labyrinthine and reverse path such as the human colon.

One of the more important problems with utilizing the snake motion scheme in endoscopy is that the snake tip must glide through the environment while the stem duplicates the trajectory of the tip. Moreover, changes in the GI tract that occur over time must be accommodated, but there is only a limited knowledge of these changes. To eliminate the difficulties and limitations found in such snake motion schemes, we propose a simpler, semipassive approach that we call *slide motion*.

Slide motion scheme

In the slide motion scheme, the stem consists essentially of two major parts: one or two *spines* and an endoscope *conduit*, which is a covering tube for the spine. Using control methods that will be described shortly, the spine can be made temporarily flexible or stiff. The endoscope conduit is an elastomer tube and has a specified degree of passive stiffness so that it can be pushed forward over the stiffened spine without buckling. This outer tube also is radially stiff so that its circular cross-section can be maintained during bending. A lubricant is supplied at the contacting layer between the spine and the flexible conduit so that the relative sliding motion between them can be realized while minimizing the thrust forces. The distal end is flexed by the endoscopist to observe and point in the desired directions. A typical steering system is driven by two pairs of cables through a series of bent washers. Such a system provides four directions of steering (i.e., up-down and left-right), as shown in figure 48.2. However, experienced endoscopists often steer the distal end in just one plane (up-down *or* left-right) while rotating the endoscope stem to obtain the other degree of freedom. This degree of freedom is considered to be plane-redundant, but it aids in achieving the circular steering space more easily. Figure 48.3 also shows a cross-section of an endoscope with one spine for controlling the stiffness. In its initial position, the spine is advanced to its maximum limit (approximately 5 cm) and made rigid. The conduit then is inserted into the colon up to the first substantial curve. While the spine is sufficiently stiff, the flexible conduit moves incrementally relative to the spine and within the predetermined axial travel limits, using the spine as a guide. The flexible conduit is inserted further at the same forward rate that the spine is retracted; thus, the spine is relatively stationary with respect to the patient's GI tract. The total forward insertion distance of the endoscope is equal to the spine axial travel limits. Such limits would be adjusted to

meet the specific requirements for the radius of curvature at each bend of the colon. Figure 48.1 shows that the four bends are located at the connections among the rectum and sigmoid, descending, transverse, and ascending colon. In most patients, the actual configuration of the colon is not completely guaranteed a priori. Reverse bends with angles exceeding 360° are found in some patients who have congenital abnormalities.

When the incremental forward motion of the flexible conduit is complete, the spine is relaxed and pushed forward to its maximum limit. The maximum limit can be obtained because the conduit assumes the shape of the colon through gentle static contact. These motionless contacts form intermittent position constraints that serve as a guide for the relaxed spine. Reaction forces from the GI walls direct toward the center line of the GI tract, which aids the motion of the spine inside. The spine is advanced to its maximum limit while the flexible conduit remains stationary with respect to the patient. The spine then is stiffened in its new position. Advancement of the conduit and spine now is repeated cyclically; the endoscope is advanced no more than the spine axial travel limit with each cycle.

By reversing this procedure, the endoscope can be removed from the colon while minimizing the relative motion between the endoscope and the colon. During the removal of a conventional endoscope, the relative motion is prominent, which causes stress at the curves of the colon along the length of the conduit. The situation becomes worse if a colon wall segment arrests its normal peristaltic action and cramps around the device, resisting removal. Attempting to remove the stem against these high interacting forces will significantly increase the risk of trauma. Therefore, minimizing

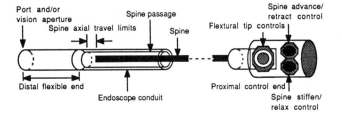

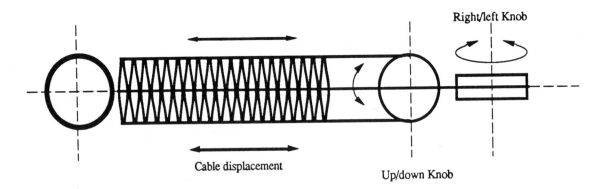

FIGURE 48.3 Cross-section of an endoscope having a spine with controllable stiffness.

the relative motion and interacting forces is a major advantage.

The stiffened spine inside the flexible conduit resists the involuntary motions of the colon. Thus, the distal end of the endoscope can be positionally supported. This support provides the stable platform required for visual or therapeutic procedures in the colon. From a safety viewpoint, the spine can be relaxed immediately if peristaltic action or cramping is observed. Hence, critical damage to tissues is avoided. Moreover, the flexible conduit will not buckle or bend severely and will maintain a more accurate position as it is constrained by the stiffened spine. In some situations, when the stable platform is not required, the spine can be removed and replaced by other therapeutic or diagnostic devices. This design for multiple functions along the inside path reduces the dimension of the stem.

In some industrial and space applications, contact with the environment is not possible. For these applications, two spines could be utilized. One spine serves as a spinal cord that mechanically connects the conduit. The other movable spine can then be advanced or retracted to its maximum limit by using the first spine and the case as a guide. Because the maximum-limit motion includes the steerable tip, the curve commanded by the master is copied by one or the other locking spines. Once the second spine has reached its maximum limit, it can be stiffened and the first spine relaxed so that the process can be repeated. These applications will most likely require indirect remote control from a master station, such as that used with modern teleoperators.

From the foregoing discussion of the operational scenarios for a slide motion endoscope, we can derive the robotic control needs of such a device: 3 degrees of active freedom, continuous over their motion range, plus 1 continuous and 1 binary dof for each locking spine. The common 3 dof include the two orthogonal steering axes at the tip (pitch and yaw) and the one advance-retract axis, which moves the endoscope base with respect to the world coordinate frame. The locking spine degrees of freedom are limited to motions relative to the sheath of the endoscope. Thus, all controlled motions are interrelated in the cyclic manner mentioned earlier: Tip steering and advance-retract motion are mutually exclusive. Stable tip location is guaranteed only if advancement and retraction occur with an equal and opposite spine motion. Automatic control of these motions in a diagnostic scenario re-

quires visual or tactile sensing of the lumen (the open passage of the esophagus or colon), as well as sensitivity to resisting forces in the advance-retract motion axis. Although the acquisition of such feedback is routine, control strategies for steering and moving remain a subject for future research. Similarly, details of the implementation of teleoperator type controls are beyond the scope of this chapter.

Central tendon-locking spine

A central tendon-locking spine consists of a set of cylindric beads strung on a flexible cable. One of the simplest shapes is a cylindric bead with a hemispheric head and an inverted conical tail. All beads are free to rotate on adjacent beads around their centers. In the presence of a cable tension force, these beads slide axially along the cable until the positional constraints at both ends of the bead chain are satisfied. Consequently, increasing the cable tension force creates friction forces between beads and ultimately increases the apparent stiffness of the entire bead chain. Therefore, pulling the cable stiffens the bead chain, and relaxing the cable tension force loosens it. The bead chain with a continuous cable is shown in figure 48.4. When a tensile force is applied to the tendon, it is highly desirable that the configuration of the bead chain not be altered or at least that the reaction forces transverse to the beads be very small.

Frictional losses incurred from bead to bead along the chain reduce the locking strength of the joints near the tip. It is desirable to reduce this parallel, cable-to-bead interface friction, μ_{cb}. To improve the locking strength, however, the normal surface coefficient of friction, μ, must be as great as possible between each bead. Some materials (e.g., unglazed ceramics and high-durometer elastomers) have values of μ approaching 1. The tensile reaction forces encountered in the previously defined geometry preclude the use of these

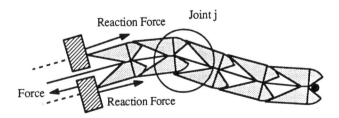

FIGURE 48.4 Bead chain with a continuous cable.

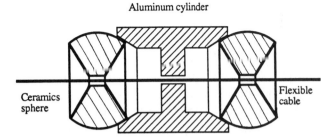

FIGURE 48.5 Sequential chain with alternating bead shapes.

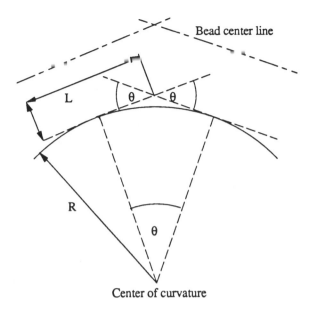

FIGURE 48.6 Minimum radius of curvature.

materials. In any event, it is difficult to make ceramic beads with this geometry. An equivalent locking chain can be realized by alternating sets of spherical and cylindric beads strung on a flexible cable, as shown in figure 48.5. These two parts are both axially and end-to-end symmetric. A suitable combination of materials can provide a higher surface coefficient of friction than any single material; for example, the surface coefficient of friction between aluminum and ceramic is almost 0.5 but for aluminum alone is 0.2.

Bead geometries and physics of flexible bead chains

In this section, we examine how bead design affects spine performance requirements, which include spine curvatures, diameter, stiffness, and stability. As indicated in figure 48.6, the effective minimum radius of curvature, R, for the bead chain is the distance from the center of curvature to one side (not the center line). R depends on the rotational displacements available at each joint and the effective bead length, L. The locking strength also depends on the geometry and the friction coefficient.

For performance consistency and ease of manufacture, the bead geometry in figure 48.4 is selected to be as simple as possible. Standard part shapes with conventional linear or circular profiles are desired. Recall that a pull on the tendon should result in locking the chain into position without causing it to move.

Assume that L is the effective length of each bead and θ is the maximum joint angle at each bead interface. As shown in figure 48.6, the minimum bend radius R is determined by the following equation:

$$R = \frac{L \tan\left(\frac{\theta}{2}\right)}{2} \qquad (2)$$

To advance the stem at the reverse bend between the rectum and the sigmoid colon, R must be approximately 2 cm. L and θ then determine the number of beads, N, at each bend. For example, if the same R and larger L and θ are selected, N will then be reduced. The selection of parameters affects how closely the bead chain can approximate a circular arc, which is a significant factor affecting the clearance between the inside diameter of the endoscope and the bead chain.

A cylindric bead with a hemispheric head, referred to simply as a *cylindric geometry* (figure 48.7), is bored conically at the tail with a half-angle called a *leg angle*, θ_L. For the bead leg to sit perfectly on the adjacent bead at the maximum rotation, the leg angle must be equal to θ. If the inside (ID) and outside (OD) diameters are large enough, some diagnostic or therapeutic tools could be placed *inside* the bead chain. To prevent interference among such tools and the tendon cables, two cables can be placed *outside* the bead chain. This configuration will be discussed in the section, "Integrating Voice Control for Endoscopic Control."

In case of a single cable, all beads are strung on a flexible cable that is fixed to the bead located at the tip. Analysis of the motion of any pair of beads shows that pulling the inside cable with a tension force, F, will cause one bead to rotate onto the other, resulting in a positive displacement of the cable. This displacement, d, can be calculated as a change in length $a - b$ of figure 48.7. The rotational angle, α, varies between 0

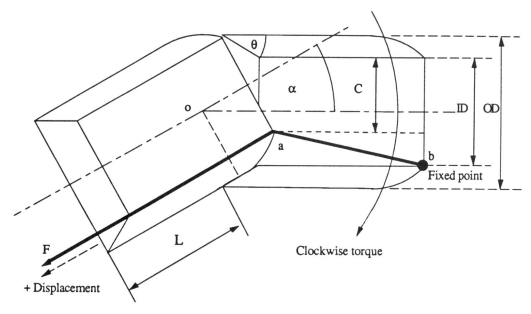

FIGURE 48.7   Cylindric geometry.

and θ_L and can be divided equally among n subintervals for the purposes of analysis. Hence,

$$\Delta\alpha = \frac{\theta}{n} \quad \text{(a constant step size)}$$

Cable work for each pair of beads can be obtained as

$$\text{Cable work}_i(\alpha) = F\Delta d_i(\alpha) \quad i = 0,\ldots,n \quad (3)$$

where displacement $\Delta d_i(\alpha)$ occurs at α_i for small $\Delta\alpha$.

The clockwise torque, $\tau_i(\alpha)$, at each step size $(\Delta\alpha)$ provides the cable work for a positive displacement, as shown in figure 48.7:

$$\tau_i(\alpha) = \frac{\text{Cable work}_i(\alpha)}{\Delta\alpha} \quad (4)$$

Cable displacements will not occur if the torque in equation 4 does not exceed the threshold torque resulting from surface friction, such that

$$\text{Resisting torque}_i(\alpha) = k\mu_i(\alpha)F \quad (5)$$

where k is a geometric constant that is a function of θ_L,

$$k = \frac{\pi}{4}(1 + \cot^2\theta_L)$$

and $\mu_i(\alpha)$ is the static surface coefficient of friction required for locking two beads together at position i.

We equate equations 4 and 5 to obtain the threshold friction coefficient that will just lock the beads together:

$$\mu_i(\alpha) = \frac{\Delta d_i}{k\Delta\alpha_i} \quad (6)$$

as $n \to \infty$

$$\frac{\partial d_i(\alpha)}{\partial\alpha_i} = k\mu_i(\alpha) \quad (7)$$

Let μ_s be the surface coefficient of friction between the selected materials. The locking position between two beads can then be obtained as a set of angles:

$$\left\{ \sum_{i=1}^{n} \alpha_i \,\middle|\, \mu_i(\alpha) < \mu_s \right\} \quad (8)$$

We will see that this set will vary with geometry and material properties. For example, table 48.1 shows the computation of $\mu_i(\alpha)$ for a leg angle of 30° and selected values of radii of curvature, ODs, and clearance.

The clearance, C, of figure 48.7 is the effective ID formed at the maximum rotational angle $(\alpha = \theta)$. C is a function of ID, OD, θ_L, and α. The larger value of clearance makes possible the placement of some diagnostic and therapeutic tools inside the beads. The lower limit on C is restricted by the OD of the cable. Notice that the clearance is always reduced for any bead angle α. Table 48.1 shows maximum values of the computed $\mu_i(\alpha)$ for various cases. Cases A and B are for the larger values of C; cases C, D, E, and F are at the lower limit.

TABLE 48.1

Static surface coefficient of function [$\mu_i(\alpha)$] for the cylindric geometry

C_{min} (mm)	Case	R (mm)	OD (mm)	ID (mm)	L (mm)	Max. $\mu_i(\alpha)$
14.28	A	25.40	25.40	22.72	12.11	0.62
	B	38.10	25.40	22.72	18.92	0.62
1.59	C	7.62	6.35	3.29	2.29	0.41
	D	12.70	6.35	3.29	5.01	0.41
	E	25.40	6.35	3.29	11.82	0.41
	F	38.10	6.35	3.29	18.62	0.41

C_{min} = minimum clearance; Case = case used in design analysis; R = radius of curvature;
OD = outside diameter; ID = inside diameter; L = effective length.

Plots of d and μ with respect to α are shown in figure 48.8. Note the strong nonlinear displacement relation for large beads and the requirement for high coefficients of friction for locking. As indicated in figure 48.8b, there are some α angles in the interval where $\mu_i(\alpha)$ exceeds 0.2, the value for aluminum. At these positions, the bead chain cannot lock; consequently, beads having the cylindric geometry are not suitable for use in flexible-stiff spines. In addition, for any $\mu_i(\alpha)$ curve that is not continuous (as depicted in figure 48.8b), it is impossible to predict the direction of the bead's motion or the resulting chain configuration for certain initial angles (usually between ·20 and 30°) when the spine is stiffened.

To improve the locking ability over the entire rotational range, the geometry can be varied to reduce the turning moment. This can be achieved by removing the material from the point where the cable bends from the spherical center. The cable can also be brought closer to the center line by reducing the inside diameter.

The conical bore aligned with the inside diameter (ID-based geometry) is shown in figure 48.9. The conical bore is at the head rather than the center of its spherical surface, so that its apparent opening is always greater than or equal to the ID of the mating bead. This geometry maximizes the bore throughout the chain. The contact point at $\alpha = 0°$, g, on the spherical surface is determined by θ_L and the bead OD, as shown in figure 48.9. The actual thickness of the bead wall is represented as t. To maintain the normal sphere-to-core contact between the beads, the apparent diameter of the conical bore on the spherical surface must be

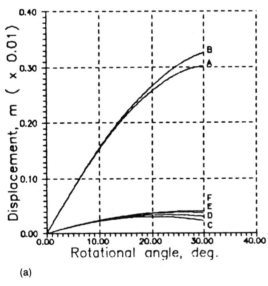

(a)

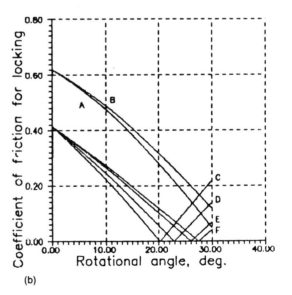

(b)

FIGURE 48.8 Plots of $d_i(\alpha)$ and $\mu_i(\alpha)$ versus α for cylindric geometry.

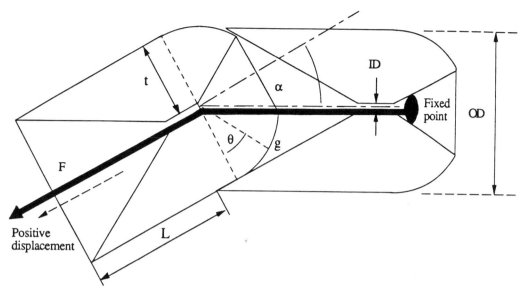

FIGURE 48.9 ID-based geometry.

smaller than the circle described on the core of its mating bead. Thus, the ID of the beads is constrained as follows:

$$ID < OD - 2t_m \qquad (9)$$

where t_m is the minimum value of the bead wall thickness such that the ID-based geometry could be realized. By the geometry in figure 48.9:

$$t_m = OD \sin^2\left(\frac{\theta_L}{2}\right) \qquad (10)$$

Figure 48.10 shows a plot of d and μ versus α for the ID-based geometry. Parameters used for these calculations, using equations 3–7, are given in table 48.2. From table 48.2, ID-based geometry for the large beads cannot be used, as equation 8 is not satisfied. Figure 48.10 shows that the plot of friction coefficients versus α does not vary. Changing the radius of curvature, R, affects only the effective length, L. There is no relationship between L and the characteristics of the displacement in ID-based geometry. Moreover, the friction coefficients are almost constant in the region $0 \le \alpha \le \theta$.

Smaller beads with such a geometry have also been examined. The results are shown in table 48.3 and figure 48.11. The small ID-based geometry provides the lowest μ (<0.2). The ID-based geometries, unlike the cylindric geometry, do not suffer from the problem of discontinuous curves, and the bead's motion can always be predicted. Hence, the small ID-based geome-

try can be utilized for the beads in the flexible-stiff spine. Some improvements to enhance its stability will be discussed in the next section.

Tendon-locking spine analysis

ARRANGEMENT OF SPINES

The tendon-locking spine is constructed by placing a number of small, ID-based-geometry beads over a cable. Two possible arrangements for the single tendon-locking spine are shown in figure 48.12. Double spines, used where touching the environment is not desired (as described earlier), are conceptually similar to the single tendon-locking spine arrangements.

In figure 48.12a, the locking spine and other diagnostic or therapeutic tools lie together inside the outer tube. To allow the spine to move easily, another cover sleeve wrapped around the spine is required. The alternative arrangement separates the cover sleeve from the outer tube while maintaining a parallel mechanical connection. This design avoids mechanical interaction between the spine and the medical equipment in the stem.

JOINT STRENGTH

From table 48.3, the parameter set G ($R = 2.5$ cm and OD = 0.6 cm) of an ID-based geometry is selected based on its μ and small dimensions. A practical endo-

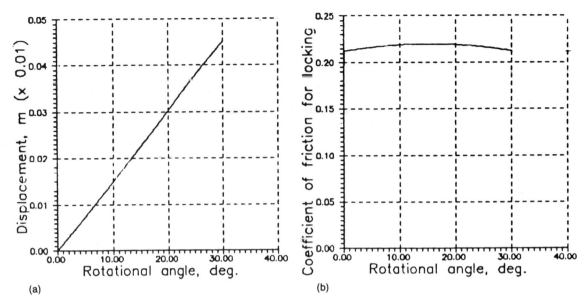

FIGURE 48.10 Plots of $d_i(\alpha)$ and $\mu_i(\alpha)$ versus α for the ID-based geometry.

TABLE 48.2

Static surface coefficient of function $[\mu_i(\alpha)]$ for the ID-based geometry

$C_{\min}$ (mm)	Case	R (mm)	OD (mm)	ID (mm)	L (mm)	Max. $\mu_i(\alpha)$
14.28	A	25.40	ID-based geometry cannot be used*			
	B	38.10	ID-based geometry cannot be used*			
1.58	C	7.62	6.35	1.69	0.90	0.21
	D	12.70	6.35	1.69	3.62	0.21
	E	25.40	6.35	1.69	10.43	0.21
	F	38.10	6.35	1.69	17.24	0.21

$C_{\min}$ = minimum clearance; Case = case used in design analysis; R = radius of curvature; OD = outside diameter; ID = inside diameter; L = effective length.

*The condition $\delta \leq \theta_L$ must be satisfied in order to make the ID-based geometry. See text.

TABLE 48.3

Static surface coefficient of function $[\mu_i(\alpha)]$ for the small ID-based geometry

R (mm)	Case	OD (mm)	ID (mm)	t (mm)	L (mm)	Max. $\mu_i(\alpha)$
12.70	A	6.35	0.36	2.99	6.81	0.045
	B	6.35	0.50	2.93	6.81	0.062
	C	6.35	0.61	2.87	6.81	0.076
	D	6.35	0.94	2.71	6.81	0.120
25.40	E	6.35	0.27	3.04	13.62	0.034
	F	6.35	0.42	2.97	13.62	0.053
	G	6.35	0.53	2.91	13.62	0.067
	H	6.35	0.83	2.76	13.62	0.104

R = radius of curvature; Case = case used in design analysis; OD = outside diameter; ID = inside diameter; t = bead wall thickness; L = effective length.

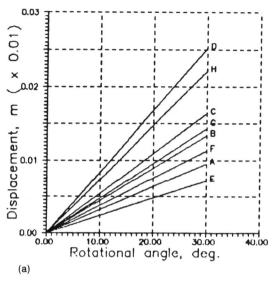

FIGURE 48.11   Plots of $d_i(\alpha)$ and $\mu_i(\alpha)$ versus α for the small ID-based geometry.

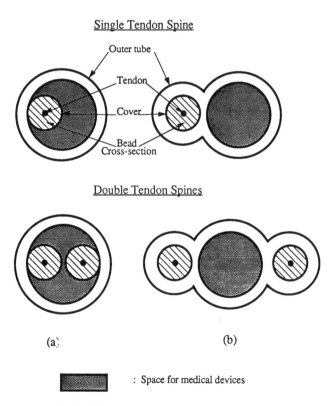

FIGURE 48.12   Two arrangements for spines.

scope of 1.5 m long requires approximately 100 beads. When the beads are at relative angles other than 0, the friction at the contacting points reduces the tension force in the cable from the base to the tip of the stem.

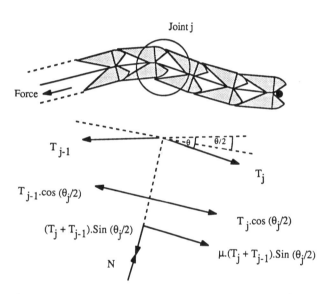

FIGURE 48.13   Diagram of force equilibrium at each joint.

The iterative equation for computing the cable force at each joint (j) (as indicated in figure 48.13) is determined from the geometry:

$$F_j = \frac{F_{j-1}\left(1 - \mu_{cb}\tan\left(\frac{\theta_j}{2}\right)\right)}{\left(1 + \mu_{cb}\tan\left(\frac{\theta_j}{2}\right)\right)} \qquad (11)$$

Applying equation 11 to long chains shows that the cable force decreases along the bead chain. From

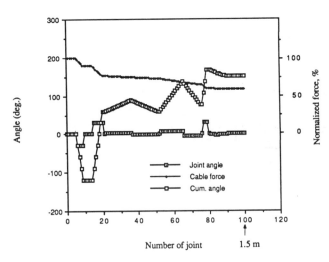

FIGURE 48.14 Plot of reduction in cable force for a stem configured as in figure 48.1, approximating a normal colon.

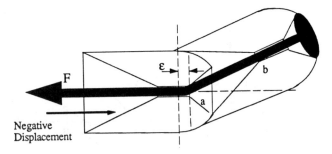

FIGURE 48.15 Stability improvement on the small ID-based geometry.

bench tests, a cable force between two adjacent beads produces a measured turning torque within 0.5% of the predicted value. This reduction is a function of the cumulative angle between each bead and hence will vary with stem configuration. Figure 48.14 shows the predicted reduction in cable tension progressing from the base to the stem, where it is flexed into the configuration of the colon shown in figure 48.1.

POSITIONAL STABILITY

The stability of the flexible-stiff spine depends on the internal turning torque, which attempts to rotate the beads toward the axis of zero rotational angle ($\alpha = 0°$), because this is less than the resisting torque resulting from the frictional force. If the frictional force is not sufficient to prevent relative rotation, the bead will rotate to minimize α. If the bead rotation resulting from cable tension causes α to increase, the chain will develop a kink spontaneously, with the beads alternately rotating. This condition corresponds to the lowest potential energy, which occurs as α tends toward 0. As indicated by figure 48.11, a positive displacement occurs as the beads are departing from the axis of zero rotational angle. The surface coefficient of friction, μ, can be expected to decrease as a result of wear along the contacting surfaces, and the entire bead chain could, therefore, become tangled. This unstable configuration may create appreciable displacement between the stem and the colon, which obviously could damage the tissue.

To improve the stability of the chain, an offset parameter, ε, is introduced to obtain a negative cable displacement (a change in line a-b) while rotating the bead from 0° to θ. The offset parameter changes the relative position of the cable bend point with respect to the ideal center of the spherical head of the bead. This negative displacement corresponds to the lowest potential energy, which occurs as the rotation tends toward 0°. Therefore, the kinking of the bead chain could be avoided. A larger value of ε would provide a more stable margin; the practical value of ε depends on the expected rate of wear. Figure 48.15 shows such an improvement for enhancing positional stability.

Integrating voice control for endoscopic control

OVERVIEW

Recently, speech recognition has been successfully implemented in several applications, especially those performed by operators whose hands and eyes are ever busy. For example, some industrial applications that use speech recognition are as follows:

• Reporting specific defects of assembled parts. General application commands are Pass and Fail. Specific words depend on types of assembled parts and processes (e.g., Solder Bridge for an incomplete solder path).
• Controlling equipment in manufacturing and assembly processes. For example, Reverse Frame and Speed Frame Up commands change the direction or increase the speed of part-handling machines.
• Auditing inventory parts.

In addition to these implementations in industry, speech recognition has begun to play a vital role in alleviating the chronic shortage of skilled operators and practitioners in the medical community. Applications of speech recognition in this area require a relatively large vocabulary and both speaker-dependent and speaker-independent modes. In brief, a speaker-independent system can recognize the speech of any person. Such a system is more difficult to build than a speaker-dependent system because a set of reference patterns suitable for a specific person may not work well for others.

Medical-related activities that already have integrated speech recognition systems include dictating routine medical reports (e.g., laboratory tests, electrocardiographic records, and x-ray data), recording and reviewing patient status as well as surgical procedures, and retrieving information from database systems. However, there is no evidence to date of using speech recognition to control medical devices in endoscopic procedures. As described previously, endoscopic procedures require mastery by highly skilled practitioners. It is clear that hand-eye coordination is crucial in determining the smoothness and success of such procedures. Thus far, no one has discovered a shortcut for becoming skilled in this art; a long, time-consuming practice is required.

Of equal importance to our mechanical design and control of the slide motion scheme is the way that users would communicate with this new equipment. Our choice of a voice-actuated human-machine interface was selected to reduce the degree of complexity in hand-eye coordination. Moreover, the voice actuator makes it possible for a single endoscopist to perform a procedure alone, whereas at the present time an assistant often is needed.

The performance of speech recognition–voice actuation depends on three factors. The first and second factors are word recognition accuracy and word-grouping constraints. These topics are beyond the scope of this chapter. More relevant information can be found in Lee (1988). The third factor is application design and integration, which is described in the following section.

GAIT GENERATION AND FUNCTIONAL VOCABULARY

Currently, there are several mobile robots that imitate the gaits of biologic systems (e.g., insect, crab). The slide motion scheme produces a new gait, similar to an earthworm. For safety and performance at speed, the new endoscope should slide into the colon or esophagus with the maximum rate of progress while minimizing

contact forces on the GI wall. The so called rule-based approach suitably generates a constant pattern of gait resulting from a specific type of environment. Examples of mobile robots using such a gait-generating approach are the Ohio State University Hexapod and Tokyo Institute of Technology Quadrupeds.

An earthworm gait for the slide motion scheme is mechanically generated by the steering mechanism and the locking spine. Choices of functional vocabularies should be selected such that their meanings to both gait-generating mechanisms and to users are compatible. Therefore, it is clear that the selected functional vocabularies must be designed in the control level of the steering and locking mechanism. Two control modes—semiautomatic and fully automatic—are required.

In semiautomatic mode, the endoscopist synchronizes the movement of the steering mechanism and the advancement of the conduit. The endoscopist determines advancing directions by giving voice commands to the steering mechanism (i.e., Up-down or Left-right) together with specified values of angular displacement (0–180°). Subsequently, the conduit is commanded to move forward. The coordinate frame at each image is shown in figure 48.16. The y axis points forward and perpendicular to the image. The initial position of the endoscope tip is located at point O $(0, 0, 0)$. With the Up-down and Left-right commands, the angular displacement is measured by the angle difference between the steering axis and the x-z plane and y-z plane, respectively, in the counterclockwise direction. With this set of coordinate frames, the initial position of the tip is at 90° of angular displacement in both planes. It also is possible to transform the angular displacement into the 2D Cartesian coordinates of the image such that the user can specify directly the desired location of the endoscope tip.

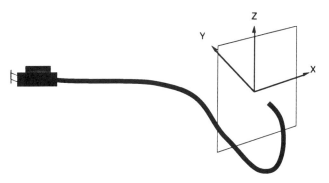

FIGURE 48.16   Coordinates at the image.

The maximum forward conduit displacement constraint is determined by the smallest reverse bend between the rectum and sigmoid colon. The process of moving the conduit (which consists of stiffening the locking spine, incrementally advancing the conduit over the stiff spine, and relaxing and pushing the spine to catch up to the tip of the conduit), can be achieved automatically by a single voice command, Forward.

Note that while the person in the loop is necessary for advancing the endoscope, retraction of the equipment can be done automatically, without any supervision from the endoscopist, either by relaxing the locking spine and slowly pulling the equipment out or by reversing the automatic process of advancing the endoscope while relaxing the tip-steering tendons. The latter case is mechanically possible because the reverse path is given and no steering action is needed.

We have installed a voice-actuated system (VCS 1000) into a personal computer (27 MHz). Communication is affected through a serial port at 9600 baud. Two miniservos (FUTABA FP-S128) with an output torque of 3.5 kg-cm drive the endoscope steering system. The miniservos were mounted on a conventional endoscope, as shown in figure 48.17. There are four separate word groups in our command vocabulary:

FIGURE 48.17   Driving unit for the steering mechanism.

Set 1	Yes-no	Confirmation of actions
	Display	Menu of operation
	Memory	Record of information
	Function	Enter
Set 2	Numbers (0–9)	Angular displacement
Set 3	Up-down	Direction of movement
	Left-right	
	Forward-backward	
	Faster-slower	Speed
	Begin-stop	Start/stop motion
Set 4	Open-close	Special function (e.g., cutting)
	On-off	Turn on-off equipments

In the fully automatic control mode, the movement of the endoscope into the colon is accomplished by voice command only. Conduit insertion distance is estimated by the positioning of the prismatic joint drive. Such information approximates the location of the endoscope tip with reference to the colon. The incremental step size in moving backward or forward subsequently is selected based on the current position of the tip with respect to the GI tract. We anticipate the future use of passive stereo imaging of the lumen to determine the direction for advancing stem motion.

Discussion

As mentioned earlier, one limitation of the continuous cable configuration is the loss of cable tension as a result of the friction between the cable and the beads. To maintain the cable force at a specified level (i.e., sufficient locking strength at each joint), the continuous cable could be replaced by a series of electric resistance wires, as shown in figure 48.18. These resistance wires are preloaded initially by stretching them, which causes the bead chain to be normally rigid. When an electric current is passed through these wires, their longitudinal expansion decreases the original interacting forces between the beads. Hence, the beads separate from one another, allowing rotational motion at the interfaces; the bead chain then becomes flexible. We are currently investigating the relationships between these parameters for practical operation.

By combining this design with the concept of the alternating bead shape sequential chain, an ideal bead chain could be realized. While stiff, the alternating sequential chain certainly increases the joint rigidity, which is due to the increase in the surface coefficient of friction between the two different materials. A small reduction in the cable force is obtained from the chain, which consists of electric wire segments. Small reductions can be controlled by adjusting the length of the wire segments. The combination of the alternating sequential chain and the electric wire segments is highly recommended for the flexible-stiff spine. In some applications where miniaturization is not required, the joint strength and rigidity can be accomplished more easily

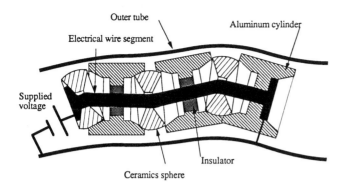

Outer tube

Aluminum cylinder

Electrical wire segment

Supplied
voltage

Insulator

Ceramics sphere

FIGURE 48.18   Beads on electric wire segments.

(e.g., by employing high-strength hydraulic locking devices).

In the design of the bead geometry, the most critical design constraint is reduction of the internal turning torque resulting from the input work. This work, as a function of α, can be minimized by reducing the cable displacement. Moreover, the lowest potential energy must occur at $\alpha = 0°$; hence, the bead chain that is composed of large, hollow-section beads yielding positive displacements will likely not be stable.

Conclusion

Recently, several designs and analyses of multiple-degrees-of-freedom robots have been introduced in the robotics literature. Such robots have flexible structures that can approximate the morphology and functionality of snakes. However, trajectory planning of snake robots becomes computationally and mechanically more burdensome as the number of degrees of freedom increases. Furthermore, miniaturizing the overall system for some medical applications, as in endoscopy, is difficult to achieve. The primary issues in control include command system design to free the hands of the endoscopist and sequencing techniques to ensure reliable motion of the stem.

We propose a novel semipassive concept called the *slide motion scheme* that can produce complicated stem configuration with only a few degrees of freedom. We believe that although the snake motion scheme is a viable solution for applications such as obstacle avoidance, the slide motion scheme offers certain advantages. With the latter scheme, no massive computations for mapping positions and orientations are required, and the mechanical arrangements for the actuators are simpler. Our choice of a voice-actuated human-machine

interface was selected to reduce the degree of complexity in hand-eye coordination. Moreover, the voice actuator makes it possible for a single endoscopist to perform a procedure alone, whereas currently an assistant often is needed.

We have seen that the ID-based geometry represents the most advantageous bead design for implementing the flexible-stiff spine, as joint strength and stability are enhanced. This scheme not only provides efficient motion control through simple hardware but also offers the potential for greater ease of performing endoscopic procedures. Our ongoing research seeks suitable control schemes for semiautomatic and fully automatic systems. A prototype for this scheme is currently being developed.

REFERENCES

ASANO, K., 1984. Control system for a multijoint inspection robot. In *Proceedings of the 1984 National Topical Meeting on Robotics and Remote Handling in Hostile Environments*, Gatlinburg, Tenn., April 23–27, pp. 375–382.

ASANO, K., M. OBAMA, Y. ARIMURA, M. KONDO, and Y. HITOMI, 1983. Multijoint inspection robot. *IEEE Trans. Ind. Elect.* IE-30(3):277–281.

IKUTA, K., M. TSUKAMOTO, and S. HIROSE, 1988. Shape memory alloy servo actuator system with electric resistance feedback and application for active endoscopes. In *Proceedings of the IEEE Conference on Robotics and Automation*, Philadelphia, pp. 427–430.

KLEIN, C., and C. HUANG, 1983. Review of the pseudoinverse for control of kinematically redundant manipulators. *IEEE Trans. Systems, Man Cybern.*, March, vol. 13, no. 2, pp. 245–250.

LEE, K. F., 1988. Large vocabulary speaker-independent continuous speech recognition: The SPHINX System. Doctoral thesis, Computer Science Department, Carnegie-Mellon University, Pittsburgh.

MILLER, R. A., 1986. Endoscopes instrumentation evolution, physical principles and clinical aspects. *Br. Med. Bull.* 42(3):223–225.

OBAMA, M., F. OZAKI, and K. ASANO, 1985. A locomotive inspection robot turbine building interior inspection in nuclear power plants. *Proc. 2nd Int. Conf. on Advanced Robotics*, Tokyo, pp. 355–362.

PIEPER, D. L. 1968. The kinematics of manipulators under computer control. Memo no. A.I. 72, Department of Computer Science, Stanford University.

SCHETKY, L. McD., 1984. Shape memory effect alloys for robotic devices. *Robotic Age* 6(7):13–17.

TSUCHIHASHI, T., Y. WAKAHARA, and K. ASANO, 1985. A computer aided manipulation system for multijoint inspection robot. *Proc. 2nd Int. Conf. on Advanced Robotics*, Tokyo, pp. 363–369.

Ear, Nose, and Throat Surgery

EAR, NOSE, AND throat surgery (ENT) is a wide field, a trilogy that has in common one anatomic feature: its functional surface is the mucous membrane of the upper respiratory tract. Most other characteristics of the subdisciplines (otology, rhinology, and laryngology, including head and neck surgery) differ, and they confront the surgeon with very specific demands. The challenge to introduce computer-based methods for planning and execution of surgery has varied widely among the subdisciplines, ranging from enthusiasm in the sector of otology, where anatomy (e.g., in the middle cranial fossa) is most complicated, through critical anticipation in the field of rhinology, where endoscopic minimally invasive procedures have long been used, to skepticism in laryngology and head and neck surgery.

The two major objectives of surgery in the region of the throat and the larynx are correction of vocal disorders due to functional impairment or infection and the resection of tumors of the upper respiratory tract. For both objectives, surgeons increasingly use lasers, and microsurgery is the method to control these effectors. The flexibility of the vertebral column in the neck region, the soft tissues affected, and the motion imposed on them by breathing complicate the modeling of pathologic processes. Thus far, in this region, computers have been used only for surgical planning and for therapy proposal. ESTher, the expert system for therapy proposal for cancers of the larynx [1], is one example of a knowledge-based system used for such purposes. The integration of computer vision into the digital op-

erating microscope may open the way for model-based execution of therapy using a computer-guided laser beam.

The chapters in this section focus on otology and rhinology. Christ et al., in the chapter "Indications and Requirements for Computer-Assisted Surgery of the Middle Cranial Fossa and the Temporal Bone," point out that imaging has dramatically improved diagnostic precision for tumors and infections of this region. Therapeutic activities, however, are still manual labor. The surgeon guides a drill through solid compact bone, taking care to preserve structures such as the vestibular labyrinth, the cochlea, the facial nerve, and the ganglion geniculi. Damage would cause balance disorders, deafness, or facial palsy. The authors describe the use of a passive mechanical localizer that can guide the surgeon to a tumor that can be deeply located and as small as 2 mm in diameter. For this procedure, the authors see advantages in cases of anatomic malformations and tumors or cholesteatoma, as well as for training of less experienced surgeons. Problems that must be solved include intersection with the operating microscope and matching of information generated by different imaging modalities.

In the second chapter, Kainz et al. report on "Indications and Requirements for Computer Integrated Paranasal Sinus Surgery." In particular, they describe functional endoscopic sinus surgery, a very delicate procedure that aims at restoring the mucous membrane of the nasal cavity and the paranasal sinuses when it is afflicted by infectious disease. This is "keyhole" surgery at its best in a critical region where the eye, the brain, and major blood vessels can be damaged. The authors point out the anatomic peculiarities of this area, which has a high rate of variation. They discuss conventional surgical planning and its disadvantages. The common techniques used for microscopic and endoscopic interventions are outlined. The authors clearly describe the demands for computer integration, which include freehand manipulation by the surgeon (rather than robotic guidance) and frameless registration.

Clinical experience with a navigation system for ENT is documented in the chapter by Klimek, Mösges, and Schlöndorff. "Long-Term Experience with Different Types of Localization Systems in Skull-Base Surgery" sketches the way from mechanical localizers equipped with potentiometers to infrared detection of patient and instrument. The authors report on large-scale clinical trials that have been carried out with their system and present encouraging results. They are optimistic that such systems can cope with the specific demands of a discipline that, of all surgical branches, has the shortest duration of in-house care. Many of these interventions are now carried out under local anesthesia and on an outpatient basis. Such localization systems are advancing current trends in medical practice by reducing the level of invasiveness required for surgical intervention.

Recently, several important articles on research and clinical applications of CIS in ENT have appeared. Although it proved impractical to include these articles in this book, they warrant brief discussion here. Nitsche et al. [2] report on ENT applications of a sonic digitizer that is thoroughly described by Reinhardt in chapter 23 of this book. Clinical application in ENT has thus far been limited to 20 endonasal interventions. Zinreich et al. [3] recently published an article on technical features and clinical applications of the ISG Viewing Wand localizer, in which the authors briefly address ENT surgery. Because the system was designed for neurosurgery, crucial ENT requirements such as free-hand operation and maneuverability of the patient's head are not fully met.

Research on two robotic systems for use in ENT surgery has recently been published. Blanshard et al. [4] describe experiments carried out with a mechatronic tool for microdrilling in stapedotomy. It has not, however, been used clinically on humans. Another robotic application in otology is reported by Kavanaugh [5], who describes experiments using a robotic drill to simulate mastoidectomy. His results are promising enough that one can speculate about the possibility of a robot carrying out the temporal bone dissection. In 1984, this vision was the driving force behind the Aachen CIS explorations that finally resulted in development of the passive systems just described. Now, in 1994, with increased imaging precision, high-performance control computers, and the possibility of designing appropriate task-specific robots, it seems plausible to begin considering evolution from passive to active systems in ENT surgery.

REFERENCES

[1] HAUX, R., J. HOEFENER, J. INGENERF, R. REPGES, M. RICHTER, R. MÖSGES, G. SCHLOENDORFF, and B. SCHMELZER, 1989. Knowledge-based decision support for laryngeal tumour diseases: Design and structure of the ESTHER systems. In *Expert Systems and Decision Support in Medicine*, O. Rienhoff, U. Piccolo, and B. Schneider, eds. Berlin: Springer, pp. 225–234.

[2] NITSCHE, N., M. HILBERT, G. STRASSER, H. P. TUEMMLER, and W. ARNOLD, 1993. Application of a non-contact computerized localising system in paranasal surgery. *Otorhinolaryngol. Nova* 3:57–64.

[3] ZINREICH, S. J., S. A. TEBO, D. M. LONG, H. BREM, D. E. MATTOX, M. E. LOURY, C. A. VANDER KOLK, W. M. KOCH, D. W. KENNEDY, and R. N. BRYAN, 1993. Frameless stereotaxic integration of CT imaging data: Accuracy and initial applications. *Radiology*, pp. 735–742.

[4] BLANSHARD, J., P. N. BRETT, M. GRIFFITHS, K. KHODABANDEHLOO, and D. BALDWIN, 1992. A mechatronic tool for microdrilling a stapedotomy. In *Proceedings of the First Conference On Mechatronics in Medicine*, Malaga, pp. 11–21.

[5] KAVANAGH, K. T., 1994. Applications of image-directed robotics in otolaryngologic surgery. *Laryngoscope*.

49 Indications and Requirements for Computer-Assisted Surgery of the Middle Cranial Fossa and the Temporal Bone

CLAUS PETER CHRIST, C. TONI HAID,
STEPHAN R. WOLF, AND LUDGER KLIMEK

SURGICAL INTERVENTIONS of the skull base are known to be extremely difficult and dangerous and set a high operative standard for every surgeon working thereon. From the earliest operations in this area, physicians have sought assistance in order to reduce complications and render such operations safer.

First, conventional x-ray films and, later, so-called modern imaging techniques such as CT or MRI supported the surgeon in his or her work, aiding the surgeon's pursuit of a safe route through the complicated topographic anatomy. However, there remains a discrepancy between the orientation using those images displayed on the lightbox in the operating theater and the orientation in the actual operative sites. Even experienced surgeons sometimes run into trouble when attempting to delineate the exact anatomic position of their surgical instrument, especially in cases of anatomic variations, malformations, or intraoperative bleeding (Adams et al., 1990).

The computer-supported coupling of an imaging technique (CT or MRI) with a 3D position–recognition system now offers a new and powerful possibility for intraoperative identification and location of anatomic structures in real time. Computer-assisted surgery (CAS) was developed in 1987 at the University of Aachen (Schlöndorff et al., 1987) and was used predominantly to increase intraoperative safety during endonasal surgery of the paranasal sinuses. To our knowledge, the work reported in this chapter reflects the first time that a prototype of this computer-supported localizer system has been tested in operations of the internal auditory canal and the cerebello-

pontine angle via the enlarged middle cranial fossa approach.

Materials and method

Surgical interventions of the temporal bone area can be separated into operations of the middle ear, the inner ear, the internal auditory canal, and the cerebellopontine angle. We chose operations of the internal auditory canal and the cerebellopontine angle to determine what advantages, if any, a surgeon receives when using the computer-supported localizer system (see chapter 51).

The topographic anatomy of the temporal bone region is a challenge for every imaging system. Function-preserving surgery requires protection of important functional structures (e.g., facial nerve, middle ear, labyrinth, or cochlea). Most of these structures are surrounded completely by bone. The surgeon must work through more or less compact bone supported only by his or her anatomic experience and conventional imaging systems. Tumors and chronic diseases such as a cholesteatoma can destroy anatomic landmarks and reduce orientation possibilities in the operative field.

In a pilot study, 12 patients with acoustic neuromas have been operated on via the enlarged middle cranial fossa approach (Wigand et al., 1982) with support of the CAS system. The surgical procedure began with a craniotomy of the temporal bone to reach the temporal lobe of the brain, which has to be removed by a retractor. After the superior semicircular canal was identified, an enlarged middle cranial fossa approach was effected,

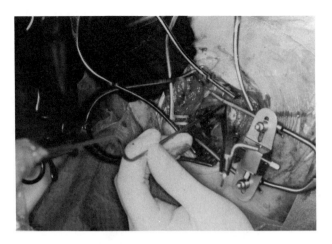

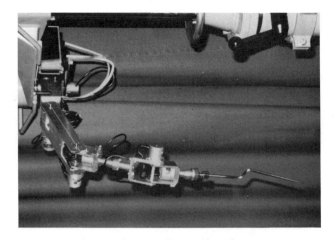

FIGURE 49.1 Intraoperative site during acoustic neuroma surgery, using the enlarged middle cranial fossa approach. Tip of the digitizer is on a bony structure, supposed to be the cranial wall of the internal auditory canal (right ear).

FIGURE 49.2 Mechanical measuring arm with digitizer (prototype of the CAS equipment).

removing the bone above the internal auditory canal (figure 49.1). This difficult approach allows maximum preservation of important anatomic structures such as the labyrinth, cochlea, facial nerve, and ganglion geniculi (Wigand et al., 1982).

As previously mentioned, the demanding topographic anatomy sets a high standard for the surgeon. Aside from an exact positioning of the craniotomy, the reliable recognition of anatomic landmarks (e.g., the superior semicircular canal, the internal auditory canal and its fundus, and the cochlea) is essential to ensure development of the operative site and preservation of functional inner ear structures (Auerbach and Wigand, 1987). Therefore, we sought answers to the following questions:

- Is the CAS system able to identify even small anatomic structures reliably?
- Is the resolution of the currently used imaging procedures sufficient?
- Can the CAS system increase the safety and quality of the operation?
- Does the CAS system help to reduce operating time?

Results

The equipment used for registering anatomic structural position intraoperatively—a measuring arm and digitizer (figure 49.2)—was borrowed from surgery of the paranasal sinuses with only minor alterations (Schlön-

dorff et al., 1987). The mechanical arm was easily maneuverable and had an exact and reliable function. Even in the depths of the middle cranial fossa, it was possible to point to anatomic structures from all directions. Using the information processed by the CAS system and represented by images on the computer screen, rapid and certain recognition of important anatomic landmarks (e.g., superior semicircular canal, internal auditory canal, cochlea, cerebellopontine angle) was possible (figures 49.3, 49.4). Exact localization of these structures by direct comparison of the computer screen image with the actual operative site status showed a difference of approximately 1 mm.

A special vector function, already installed in the prototype, was shown to be particularly reliable in processing information from the plane perpendicular to the digitizer. By this means, the level of important anatomic structures was shown in relation to the surgical instrument. Especially with the aid of this function, anatomic structures can be rapidly approached and surely preserved (Adams et al., 1990).

Nonetheless, it became obvious during the intraoperative application that the resolution of the processed images needed to be improved if the desired detailed reproduction of the inner ear structures is to be achieved. Therefore, intensive work is being carried out to integrate the latest CT technology into the CAS system. The resolution of such CT images, produced using such equipment as the Somatom HiQ S (Siemens, Erlangen, Germany), is approximately 0.4 mm. Hence, display of the finest anatomic structures with high resolution is possible. In addition, 3D presenta-

FIGURE 49.3 Enlarged middle cranial fossa approach during removal of an acoustic neuroma (left petrous bone). Tip of the digitizer on the supposed superior semicircular canal.

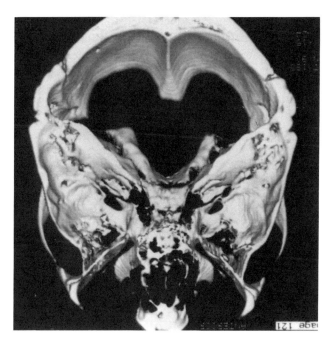

FIGURE 49.5 Three-dimensional reconstruction of the skull base using the Somatom HiQ S (Siemens, Erlangen, Germany).

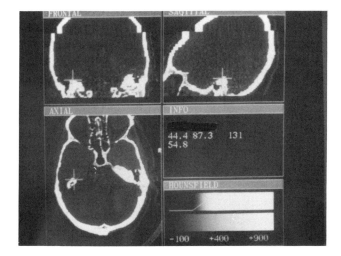

FIGURE 49.4 Tip of the digitizer, represented in the form of a cross in three dimensions on the computer screen, as an intraoperative control of the anatomic position in real time (same patient as in figure 49.3).

tions can be calculated, which lead to further improvements in the 3D orientation (figure 49.5).

Conclusions

Reliable recognition of important anatomic landmarks is an essential requirement for function-preserving surgery in complex anatomic regions such as the middle cranial fossa and the petrous bone (Auerbach and Wigand, 1987). Within an accuracy of approximately

1 mm, the prototype of the CAS system used in our study supported detection of these structures. The results of other studies, predominantly involving endonasal surgery of the paranasal sinuses, can be confirmed (Mösges and Schlöndorff, 1988; Mösges et al., 1989). Using the operative microscope together with the mechanical measuring device produced little intraoperative interference, but even this should be avoidable in the near future when a nonmechanical measuring system employing infrared transmission can be introduced into the system. Integration of the latest CT technology, affording high resolution of the finest anatomic structures, and further improvements of the resolution of the presented images pave the way for routine application of computer assistance during ear and skull-base surgery, in order to increase safety and quality of operations and simultaneously avoid time-consuming preparations.

The experiences in this study are easily transferrable to other interventions in the temporal bone area. Especially in cases of malformations of the middle ear or extensive destruction of important anatomic landmarks by tumors or cholesteatomas, CAS can provide vital information about the exact positioning of the surgical instrument intraoperatively in real time. Computer-supported imaging techniques offer additional support to every young surgeon trying to learn his or her way through the middle and inner ear.

REFERENCES

[1] ADAMS, L., W. KRYBUS, D. MEYER-EBRECHT, R. RÜGER, J. GILSBACH, R. MÖSGES, and G. SCHLÖNDORFF, 1990. Computer-assisted surgery. *IEEE Comput. Graph. Appl.* 10(3):43–51.

[2] AUERBACH, G., and M. E. WIGAND, 1987. Chirurgisch-anatomische Orientierungshilfen für den erweiterten transtemporalen Zugang zum Kleinhirnbrückenwinkel. *HNO* 35:381–389.

[3] MÖSGES, R., and G. SCHLÖNDORFF, 1988. A new imaging method for intraoperative therapy control in skull-base surgery. *Neurosurg. Rev.* 11:245–247.

[4] MÖSGES, R., G. SCHLÖNDORFF, L. KLIMEK, D. MEYER-EBRECHT, W. KRYBUS, and L. ADAMS, 1989. CAS—computer assisted surgery—an innovative surgical technique in clinical routine. In *Computer Assisted Radiology '89*, H. U. Lemke et al. eds. Berlin: Springer, pp. 413–415.

[5] SCHLÖNDORFF, G., R. MÖSGES, D. MEYER-EBRECHT, W. KRYBUS, and L. ADAMS, 1987. CAS (computer assisted surgery): Ein neuartiges Verfahren in der Kopf- und Halschirurgie. *HNO* 37:187–190.

[6] WIGAND, M. E., C. T. HAID, M. BERG, and G. RETTINGER, 1982. The enlarged transtemporal approach to the cerebello-pontine angle: Technique and indications. *Acta Otorhinolaryngol.* (Italy) 2:571.

50 Indications and Requirements for Computer-Integrated Paranasal Sinus Surgery

JOSEF KAINZ, LUDGER KLIMEK,
HEINZ STAMMBERGER, AND RALPH MÖSGES

ENDONASAL SURGERY has become standard treatment for diseases of the paranasal sinuses. The endonasal approach is no longer the exception as there are only a few pathologies that must be treated via the external approach. However, this has not always been so. From their introduction before the turn of the century until the late 1970s, endonasal procedures were considered extremely risky and, in many hospitals, were abolished because of the level of danger. The renaissance of these procedures began when visual aids such as the microscope, the endoscope, and magnifying glasses were introduced and used in combination with newly developed functional surgical techniques [1, 2]. Heermann [3] began using the surgical microscope for endonasal procedures in 1954. Others have since reported very important work on endoscopic surgery [4–6].

Currently, the endonasal approach is used for a variety of pathologic processes that can be reached via the nasal cavity. Indications include recurrent and chronic sinusitis, nasal and sinus polyposis, mucoceles and retention cysts of any paranasal sinus, mycoses, Eustachian tube obstruction, removal of foreign bodies, dacryocystorhinostomies, closure of cerebrospinal fluid (CSF) fistulas, excision of small neoplasms in the area of the nose and paranasal sinuses, decompression surgery in endocrine orbitopathy, posttraumatic optic nerve decompression, and the transnasal approach to the pituitary gland.

Extensive statistics have proved that complications of endonasal surgery for inflammatory paranasal sinus disease are rare and no more frequent than when the external approach, is used. However, a 2% complication rate is widely accepted [2, 7–10]. These complications are orbitoocular, vascular, and encephalomeningeal. This residual complication rate often is attributable to poor intraoperative orientation. Especially when paranasal sinus procedures are carried out endonasally, orientation often is reduced by bleeding and resulting impaired view. Anatomic variations from the norm can render surgery dangerous in cases of missing bony coverings over highly sensitive structures (e.g., optic nerve, internal carotid artery) or if these structures bulge outward into the sinus cave. Moreover, procedures based on topographic landmarks are limited when tumors or preceding surgery have destroyed these landmarks. To prevent the surgeon from violating critical structures, it is necessary at any given time, that he or she be aware of the topographic relationship between the instrument and vulnerable structures.

Special anatomic considerations in endonasal surgery

ROOF OF THE ANTERIOR ETHMOID

The roof of the anterior ethmoid, swinging up anteriorly from its more or less horizontal course to form the posterosuperior wall of the frontal recess, is a preferred area for CSF leaks. Here the anterior ethmoid artery (AEA) presents with an extraordinary course: Coming from the orbit, it has to pass through the anterior ethmoid (in the so-called orbitocranial canal) on to the anterior cranial fossa to reach finally the nasal cavity (figure 50.1). Exactly at the exit of the AEA, where it leaves the dome of the ethmoid sinus roof medially to reach the ethmoid sulcus in the olfactory fossa (figure 50.2), we could localize a place of least resistance in the skull base [11–13]. The following special anatomic features proved to be contributing structures in this anatomic findings.

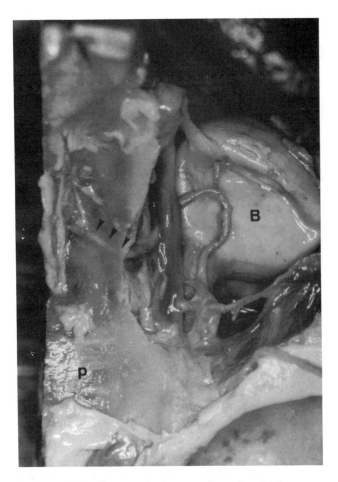

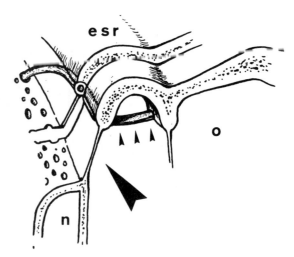

FIGURE 50.2 Schematic drawing of the ethmoid sinus roof (esr) presenting the place of least resistance in the anterior skull base (large arrowhead). The most critical area for lesions to occur is in the vicinity of the anterior ethmoid artery, where it leaves the dome of the ethmoid medially to reach the ethmoid sulcus in the olfactory fossa after having passed through the anterior ethmoid (small arrowheads). (o, orbit; n, nasal cavity.)

FIGURE 50.1 Course of the anterior ethmoidal artery, which stems from the ophthalmic artery and passes into the anterior ethmoid foramen. It then swings across the anterior ethmoid in a bony canal (canalis orbitocranialis, indicated by arrowheads). In this case, the bony canal lies directly under the ethmoid sinus roof. The artery reaches the anterior cranial fossa (olfactory fossa), where it is embedded in a bony groove (ethmoid sulcus) and runs forward to the cribroethmoid foramen to reach finally the nasal cavity. (B, eyeball; p, posterior.)

First, there are striking differences in the thickness of the bony walls at different areas of the roof of the anterior ethmoid. The bony wall of the ethmoid sulcus (0.05 mm) is 10 times thinner than the ethmoid sinus roof (0.5 mm). As the os ethmoidale is "open" superiorly—at least in its anterior two thirds—the roof of these open cells and spaces is formed by the os frontale, which covers the open spaces like a dome with its foveae ethmoidales. This frontal bone is considerably thicker and harder than the surrounding bony ethmoid structures. The dome, the highest point of the ethmoid roof, can be as high as 16 mm above the level of the cribriform plate. In this area, therefore, the ethmoid labyrinth is bordered medially by the very thin lateral lamella of the cribriform plate. This fragile bony lamella, into which the ethmoid sulcus is carved, represents the lateral wall of the olfactory fossa (figure 50.3).

Different classifications have been used to evaluate the anatomic variations in shape and size of the olfactory fossa. Of great clinical consequence is the classification according to vertical extension, created by the anatomist Keros [14] (figure 50.4a). His type 1 includes those cases in which the olfactory groove is only 1–3 mm deep; these comprise 12% of cases. Type 2 is the most common, accounting for 70% of all cases. Here the level of the cribriform plate lies 4–7 mm under the ethmoid sinus roof (ESR). This type is surgically less favorable, because over a wider area a very thin and vulnerable bone builds up the roof. Through this lamella, the dura can easily be injured and penetration into the anterior cranial fossa may occur. Type 3 is found in approximately 18% of all cases. Here, the cribriform plate lies 8–16 mm below the ESR. The very thin bony lamella just described is even larger, and therefore this type is the most dangerous for the surgeon.

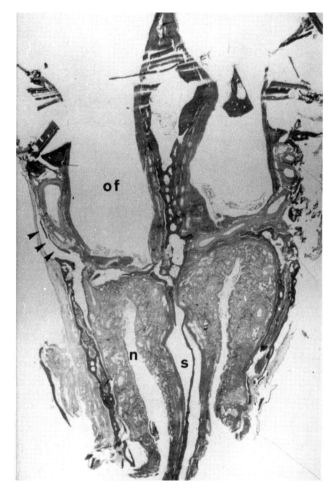

FIGURE 50.3 Histologic section in the coronal plane through the anterior skull base at the critical area, which we described as a place of least resistance (arrows). (s, septum; n, nasal cavity; of, olfactory fossa.) (van Gieson's stain, × 1.)

According to our anatomic dissections, a direct correlation with these three types could be demonstrated by our classification according to horizontal extension [12] (figure 50.4b). The narrower the fossa, the deeper it usually is, which may herald more danger for the surgeon.

In a series of 40 skull dissections [12], we found the length of the ethmoid sulcus to vary from 3 to 10 mm on the left (average, 5.6 mm) and from 3 to 16 mm on the right side (average, 6.3 mm). The length of the orbitocranial canal varied from 4 to 13 mm on the left (average, 7.7 mm) and from 5 to 15 mm on the right (average, 7.95 mm). In 40% of all cases, bony dehiscences of the canal were present. Thus, a partially or totally open semicanal (semicanalis ethmoidalis) is

formed with a bony dehiscence usually on the inferior aspect of the canal.

The dura mater in most areas of the skull is in only loose contact with the bone, except in the vicinity of the olfactory fossa. Performing dissections on an anatomic specimen, it is impressive to see that the lateral lamella of the cribriform plate not only is fractured very easily by minimal trauma but, especially in the vicinity of the AEA, has a tendency for chip fractures [13]. Here, the dura is fixed very tightly to the bone, especially at the entry and exit points of the AEA and its branches and where the olfactory nerves (fila olfactoria) penetrate the cribriform plate. In most of our cases, the AEA was running intradurally during its course through the olfactory fossa.

Coronal CT scans demonstrate those anatomic features uncovering the place of least resistance in the anterior skull base (figure 50.5). The anatomic details of the height, width, and configuration of this superior labyrinth vary greatly. Additionally, there are differences between the right and the left sides.

Encephalomeningeal complications often occur if missing landmarks render orientation difficult. A typical indication for the use of localizing systems is a preoperated patient with massive nasal polyposis. Especially in the ethmoid region, anatomy can be difficult to identify in these cases because of extensive scarring and many adhesions. The insertion of the middle turbinate as an important landmark often is missing because turbinectomy was part of radical previous surgery (figure 50.6). The dura then often is injured at a typical weak point, which we describe as a place of least resistance in the skull base [12]—namely, the medial part of the roof of the anterior ethmoid, especially where the AEA leaves the dome of the ESR medially to reach the ethmoid sulcus in the olfactory fossa. Missed diagnosis of a CSF leak can result in life-threatening conditions such as meningitis or brain abscess.

ANTERIOR ETHMOID ARTERY

The AEA stems from the ophthalmic artery and passes into the anterior ethmoid foramen. Then it swings across the anterior ethmoid in a bony canal (canalis orbitocranialis) (see figures 50.1, 50.2). This bony canal sometimes is directly under the ESR, but frequently there is a distance of 1–3 mm between the ESR and the canal, which then has a bony mesentery. The artery reaches the anterior cranial fossa between

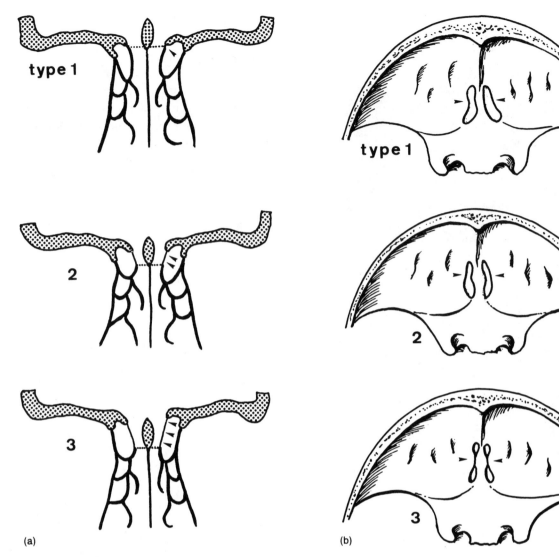

(a)   (b)

FIGURE 50.4   Schematic drawing of the anterior skull base at the critical area, presenting a classification of the anatomic variations of the olfactory fossa relative to the ethmoid sinus roof into three types (see text). (a) Classification according to the vertical extension [14]. Arrowheads indicate lateral lamella of the cribriform plate (place of least resistance at the anterior skull base; see text). (b) Classification according to the horizontal extension of the olfactory fossa [12]. For type 1, the horizontal extension at the narrowest point (arrowhead) of the fossa is wider than 2 mm, for type 2 it is wider than 1 mm, and for type 3 it is less than 1mm.

the anterior and middle third of the olfactory fossa. It is embedded in a bony groove (ethmoid sulcus) as it runs forward to the cribroethmoid foramen and distributes into its branches.

Injury of the AEA results in bleeding into the nasal cavity but might also result in intraorbital bleeding if the vessel retracts into the orbit, producing massive orbital hematoma with compression of the optic nerve. This can result in immediate blindness if decompression cannot be achieved under emergency conditions.

POSTERIOR ETHMOID CELLS   At the posterior part of the anterior skull base, the vulnerable anatomic features are at the lateral walls of the sphenoid sinus (figure 50.7) and the posterior ethmoid cells (figure 50.8) hiding the optic nerve and the internal carotid artery [15, 16]. Posterior ethmoid cells with a bulging optic canal have long been known as Onodi (Grünwald) cells (see figure 50.8). Lang [17] found Onodi cells in 12% of 53 specimens investigated, whereas we found them in 42% [16]. The average bulging of the optic canal

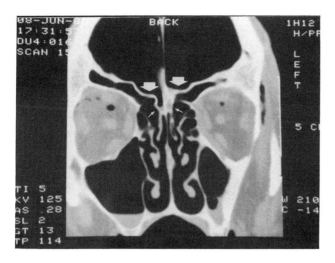

FIGURE 50.5 Coronal CT scan of a cadaver head demonstrating the critical area at the anterior skull base (small arrows) on both sides, presenting the orbitocranial canal (anterior ethmoid artery) on the left side and demonstrating different height of the ethmoid sinus roof (large arrows).

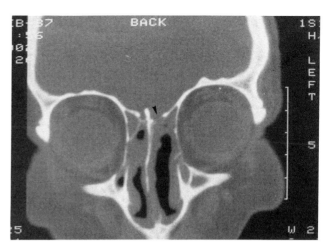

FIGURE 50.6 Coronal CT scan of a patient with CSF leak resulting from an iatrogenic lesion of the ethmoid sinus roof exactly at the area we described as a place of least resistance at the skull base (arrowhead). This patient, in another hospital, underwent a total endonasal sphenoethmoidectomy for polyps, with resection of the middle turbinate. The lateral lamella of the cribriform plate (arrowhead) is missing.

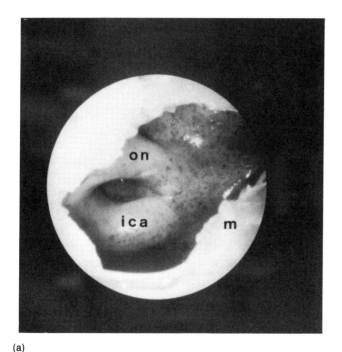

(a)

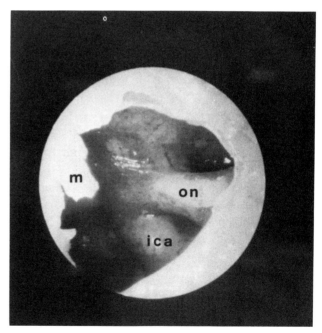

(b)

FIGURE 50.7 Endoscopic view of the sphenoid sinus on the right side (a) and on the left side (b) presenting maximal bulging of both the optic nerve (on) and the internal carotid artery (ica). (m, medially.)

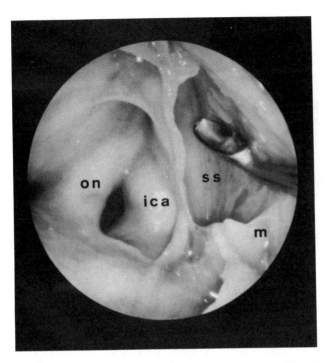

FIGURE 50.8 Endoscopic view of a posterior ethmoid cell, showing bulging of the optic nerve (on) and an extraordinary bulging of the internal carotid artery (ica). (ss, sphenoid sinus; m, medially.)

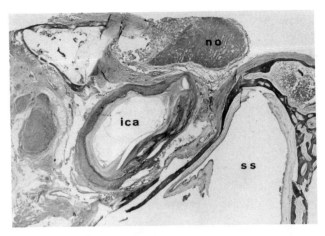

(a)

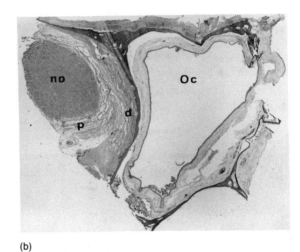

(b)

FIGURE 50.9 Histologic sections through the optic nerve (no) and the internal carotid artery (ica) at the level of the sphenoid sinus (a) and at the level of an Onodi cell (b). (Hematoxylin-eosin stain, ×15.) (ss, sphenoid sinus; Oc, Onodi cell; p, pia mater; d, dura mater.)

into the paranasal sinus was, according to this study, 3.2 mm, but maximum bulging was 14 mm! The mean thickness of the bony wall was 0.28 mm. Dehiscences in the bony wall of the optic canal were found in 12% of cases. Histologic serial sections demonstrate the microanatomic features of this key area (figure 50.9). Figure 50.7 shows a maximal bulging of the optic canal and the internal carotid artery into the sphenoid sinus on both the right and left sides. This is a rare condition; a moderate bulging of the optic canal, the so-called tuberculum nervi optici, is, found more frequently.

For the ENT surgeon, the topographic anatomy of the most posteriorly located cells of the posterior ethmoid is of utmost importance. These cells often pneumatize further laterally than the sphenoid sinus. Sometimes ethmoid cells have even developed above the sphenoid sinus. The surgeon must realize that the anterior wall of the sphenoid sinus need not be exactly behind the most posterior recess of the posterior ethmoid cell. According to the pneumatization of Onodi cells, the anterior wall of the sphenoid sinus need not take a frontal course but may run anteromedially to posterolaterally. If the surgeon must open the sphenoid sinus anteriorly on the endonasal transethmoid way, the anterior sinus wall has to be identified as far medially and inferiorly as possible. After the ground lamella of the middle turbinate has been perforated, it may be a severe mistake to follow the lamina papyracea posterolaterally when looking for the sphenoid sinus behind an Onodi cell. This is the area where the optic nerve can be damaged most easily. As CT scans in the coronal plane demonstrate these bulgings of the optic nerve and internal carotid artery very well (figure 50.10), CT scans are mandatory in preoperative evaluation.

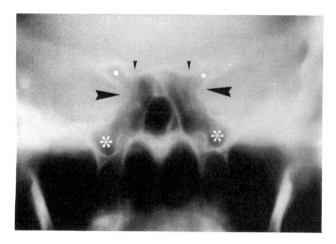

FIGURE 50.10 Coronary CT scan presenting the bulging of the optic canal (small arrowheads) and the internal carotid artery (large arrowheads). The recess between these two protrusions is called the *lateral superior recess* (small asterisks); the other recess between the maxillary nerve and the N. canalis pterygoidei is called the *lateral inferior recess* (large asterisks).

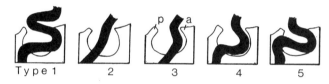

FIGURE 50.11 Schematic drawing of the five types of carotid loop: double-siphon (type 1), arcus type (2), V-type (3), U-type (4), and omega type (5). (p, processus clinoideus posterior; a, processus clinoideus anterior.)

INTERNAL CAROTID ARTERY

There are variations of the internal carotid artery (ICA) in relation to the sphenoid sinus [18, 19]. Five different types of carotid loop are identified according to its curvature in the area of the cavernous sinus at the lateral wall of the sphenoid sinus: These are the double-siphon, arcus type, V-type, U-type, and omega type (figures 50.11, 50.12). We have to differentiate between two typical bulgings of the ICA into the sphenoid sinus at its lateral wall (figure 50.13). The anterior prominence is located inferior and posterior to the tuberculum nervi optici at the lateral wall of the sphenoid sinus in 78% of patients. The posterior prominence lies far back in the sphenoid sinus, also at its lateral wall, in 25% [18]. The bulging can extend up

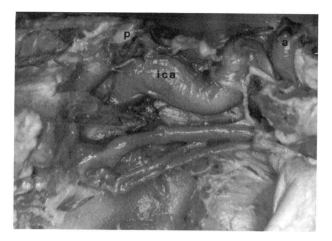

(a)

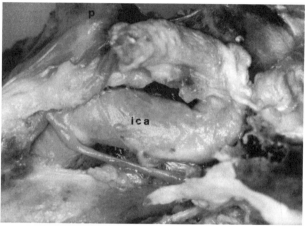

(b)

FIGURE 50.12 Internal carotid artery (ica) in the area of the cavernous sinus (cadaver head). (a) V-type carotid loop. (b) Omega type (carotid loop). (p, processus clinoideus posterior; a, processus clinoideus anterior.)

to 7 mm. The bony-wall thickness at the point of the largest prominence can be very thin (0.1 mm); in 12% of all cases, there are bony dehiscences. These bulgings of the ICA are larger in more curved types of the artery (omega and U-type) and smaller in less curved types (arcus and V-type) [18].

Vascular complication can be fatal if the ICA is injured, [5, 9, 20–22], as this vessel is a major provider of the blood supply to the brain, and its path through the skull base traverses a lengthy course in bony canals where it is reached by the surgeon for revision surgery if it is injured. If massively pneumatized Onodi cells

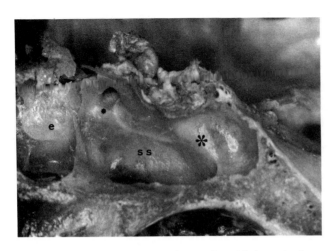

FIGURE 50.13 Lateral wall of the sphenoid sinus (cadaver head). The internal carotid artery (ica) presents with two bulgings. Both anterior (small asterisk) and posterior (large asterisk) protrusion of the ica into the sphenoid sinus (ss) are demonstrated. (e, ethmoid.)

are present and the ICA is bulging into these posterior ethmoid air cells (see figure 50.8), the ICA can be injured in this region.

Surgical planning

Currently, there are four different imaging techniques that are used widely for evaluating the paranasal sinuses: plain-film sinus radiographs, conventional tomography, CT, and MRI. For special questions regarding the vascular anatomy (e.g., in highly vascularized tumors), digital subtraction angiography (DSA) and magnetic resonance angiography (MRA) will come into use.

With plain radiographs, only gross disease in the major paranasal sinuses can be identified. With conventional tomography and more especially with CT, superior and more versatile pictures are achieved. CT allows one to detect even minor opacifications of diseased cells. Decalcified bony structures by inflammatory changes or malignant infiltration with bony destruction can be identified on CT using density measurements. High-resolution CT is required if small changes are to be detected (e.g., if a small bony defect in the roof of the ethmoid as a source of a CSF leak is suggested).

MRI allows for particularly accurate differentiation of soft-tissue structures such as tumor tissue, inflamma-

tory changes, or retained secretions. It is very useful in identifying mycotic infections of the paranasal sinuses. Furthermore, it has the advantage over CT of being able to provide direct sagittal views. However, the inability of MRI to image bony structures directly renders CT the standard investigative technique for paranasal sinus imaging. It is a general rule in our departments that every patient scheduled for an endonasal procedure must have a preoperative tomogram or CT scan.

Three-dimensional reconstructions can be valuable if they represent and highlight details of anatomic structures and spatial relationships more readily to the surgeon. Color coding of the gray-shaded density scale (according to Hounsfield units in CT) may be useful in this attempt. Rotation and translation of objects must be possible. Cuts into volumetric bodies and removal of objects are required to allow a view of internal surfaces from any angle desired.

Many available systems suffer from poor imaging dynamics. Standard use of such systems in operative planning requires that the systems allow for real-time imaging behavior—that is, it must be possible to turn objects in split seconds on the monitor, as the surgeon during paranasal sinus procedures is accustomed to moving his or her position or that of the patient to improve visualization. A zoom function to enlarge optional details on the monitor should be basic for examination of small pathologic processes and critical regions. Matrices of 512×512 pixels and 1024×1024 pixels should be visualized with 1-pixel resolution. Tissue differentiation options (i.e., the selection of special Hounsfield windows) are necessary in paranasal sinus surgery.

Most important to us is ease of interaction between the surgeon and the image workstation. Neither a time-consuming image preparation (e.g., for segmentation in 3D imaging) nor complicated user interfaces will be accepted by surgeons. Software should be menu-driven and self-explanatory.

Microscopic and endoscopic surgery

CAS systems can be used in addition to visual aids such as the endoscope and microscope. We have gained experience in the use of the Aachen CAS system that is described in detail in chapter 51 of this book [23–26]. This system can be applied in two ways in endoscopic paranasal sinus surgery.

In the first method of application, the position of the endoscope is exactly determined with the help of the CAS system. Several endoscopes were fitted into special mountings, and the established dimensional data of these endoscopes were integrated into the CAS software so that every endoscope can be used as a measuring instrument in the CAS system. Thus far, hardware and software components exist to combine CAS with rigid endoscopes of 2.7 mm and 4 mm in diameter (Karl Storz Endoscopy America, Inc., Kennesaw, Ga.). The surgeon views questionable structures through the endoscope and can display cuts at a given distance behind these structures on the monitor. Thereby, the surgeon gains knowledge of distant surfaces that is especially helpful while opening ethmoid cells near the skull base.

In the second method of application, a measuring probe is used in addition to an endoscope. The surgeon points at questionable structures and compares the endoscopic findings with the image displayed on the CAS monitor. The combination of CAS and a microscope is similar to this second method of application. Other approaches include directly superimposing tomographic image information from CT and MRI or DSA onto a microscopic or endoscopic picture [27].

Discussion

Endonasal surgery in the vulnerable region near the skull base requires safe and thorough action. Most complications occur because the surgeon is not aware of the exact position of the instrument he or she is using. For endonasal surgery, a localizing system should be used whenever the previously described critical regions may affected by surgical manipulation. Surgeons are thus released from time-consuming exposure of topographic landmarks, and the duration of surgery decreases. The surgical procedure is rendered safer and perhaps even more thorough. Especially in ethmoid surgery, overlooked diseased ethmoid cells or fissures can be the cause of persistent or recurring problems [1]. CAS systems allow all pathologic processes to be visualized in the image source (e.g., CT or MRI).

Solutions to the problem of intraoperative localization were found in combining preoperatively generated image data with sophisticated 3D coordinate-measuring devices. Such systems have been mainly described for navigation in neurosurgery, working either with electromechanical [27–32] or ultrasonic coordinate mea-

surement [23, 34, 35]. Automated surgical robots [36–38] are contrasted to these freehand navigation systems. We believe that interactive frameless devices suit the special needs of endonasal surgery in a highly effective manner.

REFERENCES

[1] STAMMBERGER, H., 1991. *Functional Endoscopic Sinus Surgery*. Philadelphia: B. C. Decker.

[2] WIGAND, M. E., 1981. Transnasale, endoskopische Chirurgie der Nasennebenhöhlen bei chronischer Sinusitis. III. Die endonasale Siebbeinausräumung. *HNO* 29: 287–293.

[3] HEERMANN, H., 1958. Über endonasale Chirurgie unter Verwendung des binokularen Mikroscopes. *Arch. Klin. Exp. Ohr. Nas. Kehlkopfheilk.* 171:295–296.

[4] MESSERKLINGER, W., 1969. Die normalen Sekretwege in der Nase des Menschen. *Arch. Klin. Exp. Ohr. Nas. Kehlkopfheik.* 195:138.

[5] DRAF, W., 1978. *Endoskopie der Nasennebenhöhlen*. Berlin: Springer.

[6] WIGAND, M. E., and W. STEINER, 1977. Endonasale Kieferhöhlenoperation mit endoskopischer Kontrolle. *Z. Laryngol. Rhinol.* 56:421.

[7] FREEDMANN, H. M., and E. B. KERN, 1979. Complications of intranasal ethmoidectomy: A review of 1000 consecutive operations. *Laryngoscope* 89:421–434.

[8] STANKIEWICS, J. A., 1989. Complications of endoscopic sinus surgery. *Otolaryngol. Clin. North Am.* 22(4):749–759.

[9] RAUCHFUSS, A., 1990. Komplikationen der endonasalen Chirurgie der Nasennebenhöhlen. Spezielle Anatomie, Pathomechanismen, operative Versorgung. *HNO* 38:309–316.

[10] STAMMBERGER, H., and W. POSAWETZ, 1990. Functional endoscopic sinus surgery. Concept, indications and results of the Messerklinger technique. *Eur. Arch. Otorhinolaryngol.* 247:63–76.

[11] KAINZ, J., A. DIE, 1987. Ethmoidalis anterior in ihrem Verlauf am Siebbeindach: Eine kritische Stelle bei der frontobasalen Fraktur. *Acta Chir. Austr.* 19:400–401.

[12] KAINZ, J., and H. STAMMBERGER, 1989. The roof of the anterior ethmoid: A place of least resistance in the skull base. *Am. J. Rhinol.* 4:191–200.

[13] KAINZ, J., and G. WOLF, 1990. Morphologische Besonderheiten der vorderen Rhinobasis in ihrer Bedeutung für die Traumatologie des kraniofacialen Überganges. *Acta Chir. Austr.* 22:78.

[14] KEROS, P., 1965. Über die praktische Bedeutung der Niveau-Unterschiede der Lamina cribrosa des Ethmoids. *Laryngol. Rhinol. Otol.* 41:808–813.

[15] KAINZ, J., W. ANDERHUBER, and G. WOLF, 1991. The optic nerve and internal carotid artery at the skull base: Places of hazard during sinus surgery. *Surg. Radiol. Anat.* 13:15.

[16] KAINZ, J., and H. STAMMBERGER, 1992. Danger areas of the posterior rhinobasis. An endoscopic and anatomical-surgical study. *Acta Otolaryngol.* 112:852–861.

[17] LANG, J., 1988. *Klinische Anatomie der Nase, Nasenhöhle und Nebenhohlen. Grundlage für Diagnostik und Operation.* Stuttgart: Thieme.

[18] KAINZ, J., L. KLIMEK, and W. ANDERHUBER, 1993. Vermeidung vaskulärer Komplikationen bei der endonasalen Nasennebenhöhlen-Chirurgie. Teil 1-Anatomische Grundlagen und chirurgische Bedeutung. *HNO.*

[19] KRAYENBÜHL, H., and M. B. YASARGIL, 1979. Zerebrale Angiographie für Klinik und Praxis. Stuttgart: Thieme.

[20] ASHIKAWA, R., H. KAITO, T. OKIHISA, Y. MITAMI, et al., 1964. On nasal bleeding from the intracranial internal carotid artery. *Otorhinolaryngol. Tokyo,* 7:512–523.

[21] GHORAYEB, B. Y., D. R. KOPANIKY, and J. W. YEAKLEY, 1988. Massiv posterior epistaxis. A manifestation of internal carotid injury at the skull base. *Arch. Otolaryngol. Head Neck Surg.* 114:1033–1037.

[22] MANIGLIA, A. J., 1989. Fatal and major complications secondary to nasal and sinus surgery. *Laryngoscope* 99:276–283.

[23] ADAMS, L., W. KRYBUS, D. MEYER-ELBRECHT, R. RÜGER, J. M. GILSBACH, R. MÖSGES, and G. SCHLÖNDORFF, 1990. Computer-assisted surgery. *IEEE Comput. Graph. Appl.* 10(3):32.

[23] ROBERTS, D. W., J. W. STROHBEIN, J. F. HATCH, W. JURRAY, and H. KETTENBERGER, 1986. A frameless stereotaxic integration of computerized tomographic imaging and the operating microscope. *J. Neurosurg.* 65:545–549.

[24] KLIMEK, L., M. WENZEL, R. MÖSGES, and M. BARTSCH, 1991. Computergeschützes Verfahres zur intraoperativen Orientierung bei Orbitaeingriffen. *Ophtalmo-Chir.* 3:177–183.

[25] KLIMEK, L., R. MÖSGES, and M. BARTSCH, 1991. Indications for CAS (computer-assisted surgery). Systems as navigation aids in ENT surgery. In *Proceedings of the Computer Assisted Radiology '91.* Berlin: Springer-Verlag, pp. 358–361.

[26] SCHLÖNDORFF, G., D. MEYER-EBRECHT, R. MÖSGES, W. KRYBUS, and L. ADAMS, 1987. CAS—computer-assisted surgery. *Arch. Otorhinolaryngol.* Suppl. 2:45.

[27] LABORDE, G., J. GILSBACH, A. HARDERS, L. KLIMEK, A. NACHTSHEIM, and W. KRYBUS, 1992. CAL—a computer assisted localizer for preoperative planning of surgery and intraoperative orientation. *Acta Neurochir.* (in press).

[27] MÖSGES, R., and G. SCHLÖNDORFF, 1988. A new imaging method for intraoperative therapy control in skull base surgery. *Neurosurg. Rev.* 11.245–247.

[28] GUTHRIE, B. L., and J. R. ADLER, 1991. Frameless stereotaxy: Computer-assisted neurosurgery. In *Perspectives in Neurological Surgery,* D. L. Barrow, ed. vol. 2, St. Louis: Quality Medical Publications.

[29] KOSUGI, Y., E. WATANABE, and J. GOTO, 1980. An articulated neurosurgical navigation system using MRI and CT images. *IEEE Trans. Biomed. Eng.* 35(2):147–152.

[30] MÖSGES, R., G. SCHLÖNDORFF, L. KLIMEK, D. MEYER-EBRECHT, W. KRYBUS, and L. ADAMS, 1989. CAS—computer-assisted surgery. An innovative surgical technique in clinical routine. In *Proceedings of CAR '89,* H. U. Lemke, ed. Berlin: Springer, pp. 413–415.

[31] REINHARD, H., H. MEYER, and E. AMREIN, 1988. A computer-assisted device for the intraoperative CT-correlated localization of brain tumors. *Eur. Surg. Res.* 20:51–58.

[32] WATANABE, E., Y. MAYANAGI, T. HANAMURA, S. MANAKA, S. YOSHIMOTO, and K. TAKAKURA, 1989. Multimodality stereotactic guiding system (neuronavigator). In *Abstract Proceedings of the Tenth Meeting of the World Society for Stereotactic and Functional Neurosurgery,* Maebashi, Japan.

[33] WATANABE, E., T. WATANABE, and S. MANAKA, et al., 1987. Three-dimensional digitizer (neuronavigator): New equipment for computed-tomography guided stereotaxic surgery. *Surg. Neurol.* 27:543–547.

[34] FRIETS, E. M., J. W. STROHBEIN, J. F. HATCH, and D. W. ROBERTS, 1989. A frameless stereotactic operation microscope for neurosurgery. *IEEE Trans. Biomed. Eng.* 36:608–617.

[35] ZWEIFEL, H. J., H. F. REINHARDT, G. A. HORSTMANN, and E. AMREIN, 1990. CT/MRI-korrelierte Stereometrie mit Ultraschall für Hirnoperationen. *Ultraschall Med.* 11:72–75.

[36] DRAKE, J. M., M. JOY, A. GOLDENBERG, and D. KREINDLER, 1990. Computer- and robot-assisted resection of thalamic astrocytomas in children. *Neurosurgery* 29(1):27–33.

[37] KWOH, Y. S., J. HOU, E. A. JONCKHEERE, and S. HAYATI, 1988. A robot with improved absolute positioning accuracy for CT guided stereotactic brain surgery. *IEEE Trans. Biomed. Eng.* 35(2):153–160.

[38] YOUNG, R. F., 1987. Application of robotics to stereotactic neurosurgery. *Neurol. Res.* 9:123–128.

51 Long-Term Experience with Different Types of Localization Systems in Skull-Base Surgery

LUDGER KLIMEK, RALPH MÖSGES, AND
GEORG SCHLÖNDORFF

SKULL-BASE surgery is characterized by a variety of important neural and vascular structures in a narrow operating field. Therefore, several special surgical instruments have been developed, and the use of operating microscopes and endoscopes for visual support has become routine in many departments. With the application of new microsurgical techniques and availability of functional monitoring equipment, skull-base surgery has reached a new dimension. Excellent understanding about the anatomic features of the lesion, its extent, and endangered healthy adjacent structures is required for optimum outcome. The importance of preoperative imaging has been remarked by various authors. However, the necessary link between the imaging information and intraoperative findings has been inadequate thus far.

Intraoperative imaging can be achieved by linking the operating table with the CT scanner. However, this technique requires a great deal of apparatus and therefore has only been employed in only a few places in the world [1]. Currently, intensive research is being done on interactive image processors that support intraoperative orientation on the basis of preoperative imaging data. Four generations of systems developed by the authors have been used in skull-base procedures over the last 6 years until 1993.

Method

Computer-assisted-surgery (CAS) consists of a high-capacity computer that processes CT or MRI data in real time connected to a measuring device for determination of position. For practical application, a diagnostic CT or MRI examination is performed. Data are transmitted either by flexible disks or via a fiberoptic network (e.g., a picture archiving and communication system [PACS] installation).

From these tomographic imaging data, the computer calculates a 3D reconstruction and displays the tip of the instrument as a reticle into this model. To correlate the coordinate system of the created 3D model with the actual position of the patient's skull relative to the measuring probe, four reference points have to be defined. These markers must be visible on the CT and MRI images and likewise be identifiable during the operation. For this, we use radiopaque plastic markings for CT and hollow wooden bodies filled with vaseline or gadolininium-DTPA for MRI. These are attached to the patient's skull for imaging and replaced afterward with color markings.

Intraoperatively, the position of the instrument in the region of interest and its presentation on the screen are directly related—that is, the display image dynamically moves to the chosen cut in the monitor presentation. The surgeon gets precise orientation instantaneously (i.e., at a rate of 20 slices/sec) as determined by the motion of the digitizer. Thus, he or she has a means of checking position that comes close to intraoperative CT or MRI monitoring.

MECHANICAL MEASURING SYSTEMS

Three generations of mechanical position-measuring devices were developed; followed by an optical infrared system.

In a first attempt, we applied a commercial robot arm. However, because this device was developed to be applied in mechanical workshops, it was cumbersome to handle owing to its reaction forces. Moreover, its accuracy and range were insufficient.

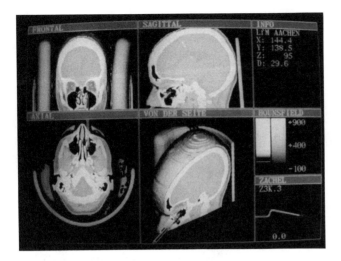

FIGURE 51.1 Image display on the CAS monitor screen.

Therefore, we developed an appropriate measuring device which has 6 degrees of freedom [2, 3]. Digital increment encoders have been applied for shaft angle measurement. The pulse signals of the six rotary encoders are evaluated by 16-bit counters. A dedicated 68008 microcomputer calculates the position of the measuring probe from the measured angles and the given arm lengths. The system was developed with 3D imaging (figure 51.1).

A third generation of mechanical systems was developed to achieve better intraoperative handling [4] (figure 51.2). Counterbalanced arm elements allow for easy movements in every position. The 68008 was replaced by a PC-486.

With the mechanical systems, a registration procedure has to be carried out at the beginning of each operation. This is achieved by tipping the patient's markings with the stylus. Thereby, the markers' coordinates are adjusted to the coordinates of the markings in the MRI or CT images, establishing the correlation of the position of the patient's skull relative to the measuring arm. This registration has to be repeated after every displacement of the skull intraoperatively. The accuracy of the latest generation devices was proved to be within 0.6 mm in a measuring volume of $0.36\,m^3$ [5].

OPTICAL POSITION MEASUREMENT

In the optical measuring system (figure 51.3) the position of the instrument relative to the operative site is determined by infrared diodes attached to the skull [6].

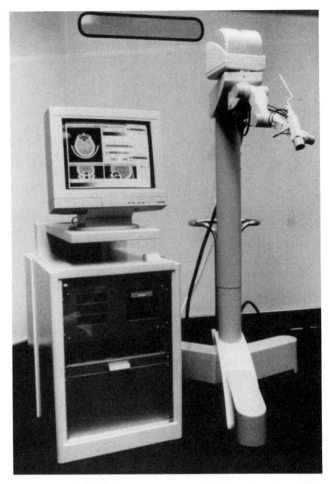

FIGURE 51.2 The Aachen device for CAS with electro-mechanical measuring arm (coordinate digitizer).

The instrument handle is equipped with five diodes as well. The diodes are detected by three cameras. As the geometric arrangement of these diodes is known, the position can be calculated by triangulation. Even if one camera is screened off during surgery, measurement remains possible. No calibration of the system is required because the cameras are self-adjusting. This allows for movement of the patient intraoperatively. Accuracy was proved to be within 1 mm.

Results

The system has been used for a variety of otorhinolaryngologic [7], neurosurgical [8], ophthalmologic [4], and other procedures. In skull-base surgery, 257 cases have been handled by 12 surgeons in 6 hospitals. Paranasal sinus surgery for infectious or tumorous lesions of the anterior and posterior ethmoid, the sphenoid, and

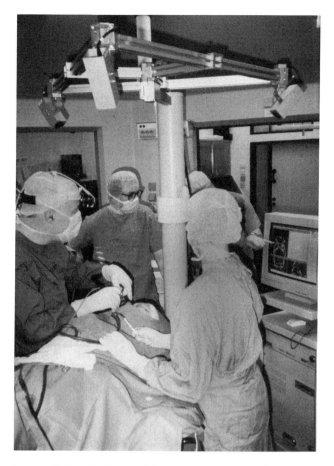

FIGURE 51.3 Optical position measurement for CAS.

frontal sinus has been documented for 177 cases (69%). In orbital surgery, the system was used for 31 procedures (12%), including such operations as tumor resection and foreign body extraction. Surgery of cerebellopontine angle tumors mainly via the transtemporal approach accounted for 26 (10%) of the skull-base cases (mainly performed by Prof. T. Haid, Erlangen, Germany); of these, 23 (9%) were for rare indications.

Surgeons reported that the localizing aid avoided time-consuming exposure of topographic landmarks. In addition, the duration of surgery decreased in several cases.

The commercial robot arm, which was used in a first attempt intraoperatively in 12 skull-base procedures, was found to be too cumbersome to handle. An inaccuracy of more than 3 mm was judged unacceptable for skull-base procedures, as was the low movement range.

The majority of procedures were performed with the second and third generation of mechanical measuring systems ($n = 229$). Three-dimensional imaging was

shown to be highly effective in both preoperative surgical planning and intraoperative orientation. After several hardware and software alterations, the mechanical arm system reached an accuracy of 0.6 mm. With the use of counterbalanced arm elements, a nearly power-free movement of the measuring probe was achieved. However, the mechanical linkage to the instrument and the need for a calibration procedure after every displacement of the patient made us search for additional measurement possibilities.

The infrared system was only recently applied in the operating room so that only 16 cases have been performed thus far. To date, it has proved to be very useful for endoscopic procedures. Its continuous registration function allows for movement of the patient during measurement so that it can be used even for procedures under local anesthesia.

In microscopic surgery, the infrared diodes sometimes became screened off by the microscope, indicating that further improvements in the arrangement of the infrared cameras are necessary before the system can be used with the microscope equally effective as with the endoscope.

Discussion

Until to now, localization problems in skull-base surgery were solved mainly by plain x-ray films or fluoroscopy. Intraoperative imaging ultrasonography [9, 10] rarely is applicable because of covering bony structures. Intraoperative CT or even MRI remains the exception, although tomographic imaging techniques such as CT or MRI provide the most accurate imaging information and best tissue differentiation. A solution for the localization problem was found in combining preoperatively generated image data with different sophisticated 3D coordinate-measuring devices and modern computer graphics.

Methods based on the application of sonar techniques or electromagnetic fields were rejected because of distortions from environmental influences (changes in temperature or reflections in the sonar technique, distortions of the field when bringing metallic bodies into the measuring space in the electromagnetic technique). Such influences cannot be recognized easily as measurement errors [11, 12]. Electromechanical 3D coordinate-digitizing devices for navigation in neurosurgery have been reported by some authors [13–15], whereas infrared measurement is new.

We believe that interactive frameless devices used in a passive way, such as those developed by our group, can fit the special needs of skull-base surgery in a highly effective manner. Such systems follow the principle of feedback control; that is, they still grant the surgeon free action. The surgeon makes the decision of whether to rely on the path delineated by the computer. The computer documents the deviation from the ideal course that the surgeon then must justify. Considering ethical and psychological aspects as well as safety regulations, these systems represent a transitional stage between conventional surgery and robotic surgery.

The CAS system can be easily installed in every operating room and can be transported for use in different departments. In a routinely equipped setting, the system can be used without additional expense. In some cases, an additional CT or MRI investigation is needed because the primary imaging was performed without the registration markers but, with routine use of the system, this duplication of tasks can be easily avoided.

Thus far, no statements regarding the reduction of operative complications using CAS are possible due to the wide field of applications and the number of different procedures performed. Surgeons have reported that they gain time by avoiding the intraoperative search for landmarks.

Aside from on-line localization assistance intraoperatively, CAS provides valuable information for pre-surgical planning by 3D imaging and further image processing. Special options such as zoom and tissue differentiation provide additional information. Systems such as CAS open new perspectives for lowering risks and raising effectiveness in skull-base surgery for lesions affecting both the intracranial and extracranial space.

REFERENCES

[1] LUNSFORD, L. D., 1982. A dedicated system for the stereotactic operation room. *J. Appl. Neurophysiol.* 45:374–378.

[2] MÖSGES, R., and G. SCHLÖNDORFF, 1989. A new imaging method for intraoperative therapy control in skull base surgery. *Neurosurg. Rev.* 11:245–247.

[3] SCHLÖNDORFF, G., R. MÖSGES, D. MEYER-EBRECHT, W. KRYBUS, and L. ADAMS, 1989. CAS (computer-assisted surgery). Ein neuartiges Verfahren in der Kopf- und Halschirurgie. *HNO* 37:187–190.

[4] KLIMEK, L., M. WENZEL, R. MÖSGES, and M. BARTSCH, 1991. Computergestütztes Verfahren zur intraoperativen Orientierung bei Orbitaeingriffen. *Ophtalmo-Chir.* 3:177–183.

[5] ADAMS, L., W. KRYBUS, D. MEYER-EBRECHT, et al., 1990. Computer-assisted surgery. *IEEE Comput. Graph. Appl.* 10(3):43–51.

[6] KRYBUS, W., A. KNEPPER, and L. ADAMS, et al., 1991. Navigation support for surgery by means of optical position detection. In *Proceedings of the CAR '91*, H.U. Lemke, M. L. Rhodes, C. C. Jaffe, and R. Felix, eds. Berlin: Springer-Verlag, pp. 362–366.

[7] KLIMEK, L., R. MÖSGES, and M. BARTSCH, 1991. Indications for CAS (computer-assisted surgery) systems as navigation aids in ENT surgery. In *Proceedings of the CAR '91*, H. U. Lemke, M. L. Rhodes, C. C. Jaffe, and R. Felix, eds. Berlin: Springer-Verlag, pp. 358–361.

[8] LABORDE, G., J. GILSBACH, and A. HARDERS, 1993. CAL —a computer assisted localizer for preoperative planning of surgery and intraoperative orientation. *Acta Neurochir.* (in press).

[9] GOODING, G. A. W., M. S. B. EDWARDS, and A. E. RABKIN, et al., 1983. Intraoperative realtime ultrasound in the localization of intracranial neoplasms. *Radiology* 146:459–462.

[10] KNAKE, J. E., R. BOWERMAN, and S. SILVER, et al., 1985. Neurosurgical applications of intraoperative ultrasound. *Radiol. Clin. North Am.* 23(1):73–90.

[11] ZWEIFEL, H. J., H. F. REINHARDT, and G. A. HORSTMANN, et al., 1990. CT/MRI-korrelierte Stereometrie mit Ultraschall für Hirnoperationen. *Ultraschall Med.* 11:72–75.

[12] ROBERTS, D. W., J. W. STROHBEIN, J. F. HATCH, et al., 1986. A frameless stereotaxic integration of computerized tomographic imaging and the operating microscope. *J. Neurosurg.* 65:545–549.

[13] KELLY, P. J., 1986. Computer-assisted stereotaxis: New approaches for the management of intracranial intra-axial tumors. *Neurology* 36:535–541.

[14] REINHARDT, H., H. MEYER, and E. A. AMREIN, 1988. Computer-assisted device for the intraoperative CT-correlated localisation of brain tumors. *Eur. Surg. Res.* 20:51–58.

[15] WATANABE, E., T. WATANABE, and S. MANAKA, et al., 1987. Three-dimensional digitizer (Neuronavigator): New equipment for computed-tomography guided stereotaxic surgery. *Surg. Neurol.* 27:543–547.

Craniofacial Surgery

Despite the relatively small number of major craniofacial reconstructions performed each year, craniofacial surgery has long been an extremely productive application area for the development of computer-assisted surgical methods. As is pointed out in the introductory chapter in this section, "Applications of Simulation, Morphometrics, and Robotics in Craniofacial Surgery," by Cutting, Bookstein, and Taylor, much of the initial impetus for CT-based 3D modeling and visualization of patient anatomy came from this field. A simple slice-by-slice presentation of CT data is much less useful to a craniofacial surgeon, who is primarily concerned with shape, than it is to a neurosurgeon. The first author of this chapter, Court Cutting, is a craniofacial surgeon who has participated in the evolution of computer-based planning and execution methods over the past decade. The chapter combines a historical perspective of this evolution, a summary of requirements for such systems, and a report on the authors' own approach to meeting these requirements.

The chapter identifies two major paradigms in craniofacial reconstruction; reconstruction of deficient areas with prosthetic materials, and cutting the bones of the face apart and repositioning the fragments, possibly with the use of bone graft material to fill in the resulting gaps between bone fragments. The crucial problems in the first paradigm include modeling the patient's skull, determining the desired implant shape, and fabricating the implant from a suitable biocompatible material. As the chapter details, the fact that implanted materials do not grow with the patient, together with biocompatibility and fabrication issues,

remain significant challenges. The crucial problems for the second paradigm include (again) modeling the patient's skull, determining where the bones are to be cut apart and how they are to be rearranged relative to one another, and then actually achieving the desired realignment intraoperatively. The development of good models of what is normal, to be used in planning, is described as a very important goal. There is great difficulty associated with actually carrying out planned procedures accurately. One consequence is that most osteotomy strategies that are performed are simple, involving only a few bone fragments.

The chapter discusses at some length the work of Cutting, Bookstein, and Grayson to develop statistically meaningful models of normal skull anatomy and to use those models to develop optimal osteotomy strategies. Highlighted are the work of Cutting's group at New York University and more recent joint work between NYU and IBM Research to develop a complete computer-integrated planning and surgical augmentation system.

In the second chapter of this section, "Simulation of Surgical Procedures in the Craniofacial Region," Klimek, Klein, and Mösges make many of the same points concerning the importance of 3D modeling and planning. One interesting topic is that surgical planning eventually may involve rather detailed simulation and analysis of individual surgical steps, especially where soft tissues are concerned. The authors describe their own planning system and report their experiences with the use of stereolithography in the fabrication of patient skull models for production of custom prosthetic implants. They also briefly discuss the use of video montage techniques in surgeon-patient communication. As is often the case, the nontechnical challenges (e.g., whether the patient can sue if the desired result is not exactly achieved) are often as great as the technical problems that must be overcome.

The third chapter, "Craniofacial Surgical Planning and Evaluation with Computers," by Vannier, Marsh, and Tsiaras, describes the work of another pioneering group that has been very influential in the development of computer-based methods for planning craniofacial procedures.

It should be noted that many of the systems described elsewhere in this book also have significant craniofacial application. For example, the systems of Udupa and Gonçalves (chapter 3) and of Robb and Hanson (chapter 10) comprise significant surgical simulation capabilities for craniofacial applications. Similarly, in chapter 11 Waters describes some initial methods for predicting how soft tissues will react and deform, which is a crucial element in developing more sophisticated planning systems that can predict facial appearance.

52 Applications of Simulation, Morphometrics, and Robotics in Craniofacial Surgery

COURT B. CUTTING, FRED L. BOOKSTEIN, AND
RUSSELL H. TAYLOR

THIS CHAPTER focuses on computer-assisted methods for craniofacial surgery, including the use of CT-based modeling and mathematic analysis of facial structures to plan surgical procedures and the use of real-time sensing and robotics to assist the surgeon in accurately executing the surgical plan. We begin with a historic review of surgical planning and discuss the impact that 3D medical imaging has had on the craniofacial community. Surgical planning from plain radiographs, commonly referred to as *cephalometric surgical planning*, then is discussed, as this is the most widely used tool for planning such procedures at present. The first generation of "cut-and-move" 3D CT-based surgical simulators then is reviewed, with attention paid to their strengths and weaknesses. We digress briefly into custom prosthetic methods for craniofacial surgical procedures and contrast them with the autogenous material reconstructive methods currently used most widely.

Next we discuss 3D surface morphometrics in detail. The applications of anatomic modeling, homology mapping, and statistics to 3D CT-based surgical planning are described. This leads to a description of our current second-generation CT-based surgical planner, which incorporates numeric optimization as its hallmark. Some hint then is given as to what elements will be found in future generations of craniofacial surgical planning software systems.

As surgical planning software advances, progressively more precise surgical plans will be developed. It is not possible to execute these plans with any degree of precision using current surgical methods. The final section of the chapter will be devoted to the applications of robotic methods to the execution of craniofacial surgical procedure. Our present approach, illustrated in figure 52.1, integrates optimization-based presurgical planning with an intraoperative system to assist the surgeon in precise plan execution. The key elements of this intraoperative system are a sensing system for tracking the relative positions of bone fragments in the operating room and a passive manipulation aid, or "robot," to help the surgeon position the fragments.

Review of 3D image-based medical modeling for craniofacial surgical planning

The construction and visualization of 3D medical models derived from medical images grew as a logical consequence of the movement from traditional x-ray films to electronic imaging modalities such as CT, MRI, ultrasonography, laser surface scanners, and so forth. Because many of these modalities, especially CT and MRI, usually produce images of 2D "slices" through the patient, it was natural for computer-oriented individuals in the field to stack these slices and produce 3D medical images. The first such software was produced by Gabor Herman and his associates [1–4]. Since then, an extensive body of literature has developed in this field, which will not be reviewed here. The reader is referred to other chapters in this book and to Udupa and Herman [5] for a more complete review and bibliography. Here, we will limit ourselves to a few observations concerning the synergy between developments in this field and craniofacial surgery.

Three-dimensional CT-based modeling and visualization (3D CT) first came into prominence in its application to craniofacial surgery. At first, this seemed strange, given the widespread use of CT in other more

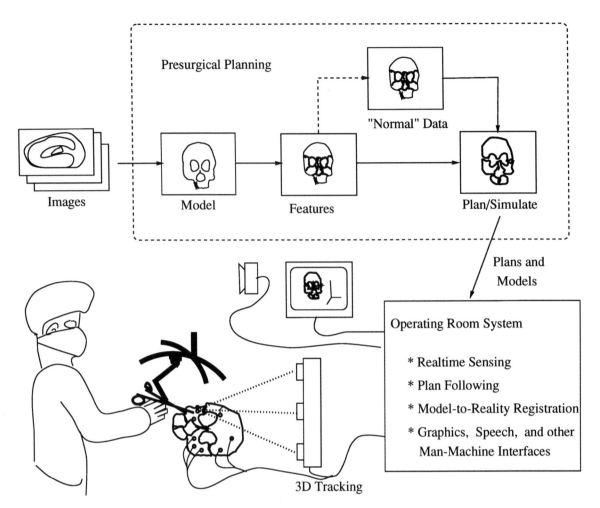

FIGURE 52.1 Computer-integrated craniofacial surgery. This shows the overall structure of our system, which consists of presurgical planning and intraoperative execution components. Although details will vary, this structure is typical of an emerging family of computer-integrated systems for craniofacial and other information-intensive surgical procedures.

life-threatening areas. In retrospect, it is now very clear why craniofacial surgery was so important in the development of 3D CT: The craniofacial surgeon must focus on the skull in its entirety rather than on small sections at a time. It is essential for the surgeon to consider relationships among distant parts of the skull. The midface must be moved with respect to the forehead and mandible, often skipping over a large number of CT slices in a single contemplated motion. For this reason, the "slice-at-a-time" approach, which is so useful in tumor following, does not work well in shaping operations considered by the craniofacial surgeon. Craniofacial surgery has figured so prominently in the early development of 3D CT also because this modality focuses on bone. The high radiodensity of bone relative to soft tissue makes it fairly easy to use simple thresholding to determine which image volume elements in an image correspond to bone.[1] Pioneers in the applications of 3D computer imaging to craniofacial surgery were Drs. Jeffrey Marsh and Michael Vannier at Washington University in St. Louis. Their textbook [6] provides a fuller discourse and an extensive bibliography.

As we will see in subsequent sections, the analysis of shape is a crucial element in quantitative planning of craniofacial surgeries. One consequence of this is the increasing importance of boundary representation methods that preserve topological connectivity information. A number of medical modeling systems are beginning to provide such interfaces, although there is no universally accepted standard. For example, Udupa et al. [7–10] use a standard voxel-defined surface representation. In contrast, the system developed by our group and discussed later in this chapter uses a winged-edge surface representation first developed by Baumgart [11] for computer-aided design and computer vision applications. In our system, 3D images are input and converted to a standard volumetric representation using the QSH software developed by Noz and Maguire [12], segmented, and converted to a winged-edge boundary representation using the Alligator algorithm developed by Kalvin et al. [13, 14].

Custom prosthetics

There are currently two major paradigms in craniofacial surgical reconstruction. The first is reconstruction of deficient skeletal areas with the onlay of prosthetic materials. The second is cutting the existing bone within the face and moving it into new positions, frequently requiring the placement of bone grafts in the gaps that result between fragments. In this section, we discuss the first paradigm.

Surgeons have long sought to use materials molded of an inert substance to effect changes in facial shape. This usually involves carving an implant material to the desired shape and then placing it over a deficient area in the underlying cranial bone. With the development of 3D image-based modeling, it became possible to describe the shape of these implants very precisely. The usual procedure involves the application of mirror-imaging methods. For example, if a patient has lost a section of his or her cheekbone following tumor resection or trauma, mirror imaging of the normal side, superimposed across the abnormal side, yields a subtraction image of what is missing. A 3D computer model of the desired implant is created, and various computer-aided design/computer-aided manufacturing (CAD/CAM) methods may be used to create a precision custom implant [15–20].

Unfortunately, in most congenital craniofacial anomalies, there is not a "normal" side to mirror. In many common malformations (such as Apert, Crouzon's, and Treacher Collins syndromes, and hypertelorism) the deformities are bilaterally symmetric. Similarly, in hemifacial microsomia or plagiocephaly, although the site of pathology is unilateral, the opposite side may exhibit changes that are more deformed than the side of the primary pathologic process. Mirror imaging in

such cases often is useless. In the future, overlays of an appropriately scaled and registered normal form may be of some use in generating a subtractive image for the specification of a custom implant. In these deformities, however, it will still be necessary to reduce or reposition abnormally projecting segments of bone to effect their correction.

The principle obstacle to the development of the custom implant paradigm has been the development of satisfactory biomaterials. Biomaterial substitutes are frequently used in other surgical disciplines such as orthopaedics, where the implants may be placed in a sterile surgical environment. Unfortunately, though, the surgical field in craniofacial procedures often is contaminated with nasal and oral secretions, which are laden with bacteria. This has traditionally made the use of foreign implants in the face difficult. Recently, hydroxyapatite materials have led to new interest in such implants. These substances are similar to the mineral structures in normal bone and are much better tolerated than materials used in the past. They are unfortunately quite brittle and difficult to shape by hand in an operating room. A means of accurately preforming such implants from preoperative images is therefore highly desirable.

The complexity of 3D biologic implants often is difficult to reproduce with conventional numerically controlled machine tools. The new generation of 3D "solid printing" processes (stereolithography, selective laser sintering, computer-controlled extrusion, etc.) will further propel this area forward, as they are capable of producing very complex shapes with reasonably high accuracy. Although in some cases it may be possible to "print" an implantable device directly, biocompatibility and materials limitations will more commonly be met by using the 3D printer to produce a mold or model that, in turn, can be used to produce the actual device.

Currently, the reconstruction of craniofacial malformations using autogenous material remains the dominant paradigm. Such a reconstruction uses the native material of the patient that is perfused with blood vessels. This makes the result of such a reconstruction as resistant to infection as any other portion of the patient's body. As discussed earlier, it will always be necessary to reduce or at least move overprojecting sections of the patient's skeleton to effect the result. This will never be done by custom implants alone. Perhaps the biggest objection to the implant paradigm is that it will never be useful in the growing face: For reasons of psychosocial development, surgeons no longer put off facial reconstruction until adulthood. The psychological devastation created by forcing a patient to grow up through adolescence with major facial malformations has prompted surgeons to perform these corrections earlier and earlier in childhood. Custom implants will not grow with the patient.

Despite these reservations, we expect custom implants to become an increasingly important part of craniofacial surgical reconstruction. The development of better biomaterials with improved software and hardware for the production of custom implants will make this option increasingly attractive over time.

The cephalometric tradition in surgical planning

Craniofacial surgical procedures are most often planned with tracings made from 2D radiographs. Frontal and lateral radiographs are taken and the silhouette lines of bony skull edges are traced onto paper. Cutouts then are made of the desired osteotomy fragments and are manipulated accordingly. This 2D surgical planning has been computerized using a digitizer tablet [21, 22]. The cephalometric tradition is very well established in orthodontics and orthognathic surgery. For this reason, standards have been developed that quantitate the position of landmarks in their relationships to one another for a number of ages, races, and sexes. These numeric standards have been used as ideals in surgical planning. The clinician would move the bone fragment cut out in his or her plain-paper surgical simulation until it more closely approximated normal. Measurements would be taken as a result and then compared to the ideal, and another cycle would be started. These hand-done optimization cycles were repeated until a surgical plan was derived that would yield the most normal-looking face for the patient. This 2D optimization cycle has been computerized [23, 24].

The deficiencies of 2D cephalometric surgical planning have led to the development of 3D cephalometrics. Two-dimensional cephalometric planning becomes useless in attempting to consider the result of rotations. For example, consider the result of rotating a palate fragment in an axis perpendicular to a frontal plane view. If one then switches to the lateral view, the cutout that has been prepared is no longer correct. The lateral view cutout has undergone a shape change that can no longer be appreciated. The situation becomes even more difficult if the axis of rotation is not perpendicular to the plane of either of the traditional posteroanterior or lateral cephalometric views. This situation is most commonly encountered in treatment of hemifacial microsomia (figure 52.2).

In slightly more advanced systems, landmarks seen in the two cardinal cephalometric views may be located in three dimensions by triangulation [25]. This allows a 3D model of the patient's skull to be constructed from such landmarks. A surgical planning system has been written that operates on these 3D landmark data [23, 26, 27].

Automated optimization of bone fragment position to best fit normal form has become an essential element in 3D cephalometric software. Three-dimensionalization of the Bolton standards produces the appropriate age-matched ideal form defined in numeric terms [25]. The sum-of-square distances from landmarks on an individual patient to the corresponding ideal landmarks provides a figure of merit for bone fragment positioning. Standard mathematic programming techniques [28, 29] may be used to compute a 6–degree of freedom (dof) bone fragment motion that minimizes this figure of merit, as an initial suggestion to the surgeon for use in surgical planning [23, 26, 27].

It is essential that the clinician modify every automatically generated optimized plan to account for biologic variables. Placement of bone grafts in gaps leads to varying degrees of resorption. Similarly, it frequently is known that a section of the patient's facial bones will not grow normally after the operation. Thus, overcorrections to allow for resorption and future abnormal growth must be made in developing a surgical plan. Further, soft tissues attached to bone fragments may constrain the fragments' movement. For all these reasons, automated optimizations to best fit an ideal should be regarded only as a starting point in surgical planning. Automated optimization remains an extremely useful "first guess" in surgical planning, despite this caveat.

First-generation 3D CT-based craniofacial surgical planners: Simulators

The development of 3D CT systems and the tradition of cephalometric surgical planning naturally led to the development of CT-based surgical simulation. Preoperative and postoperative 3D images often would suggest an improved surgical design in retrospect (figure

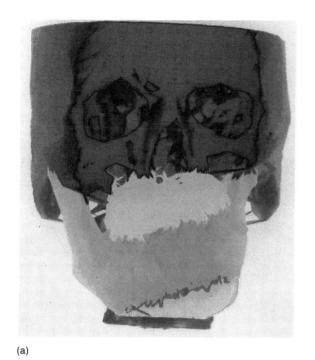

(a)

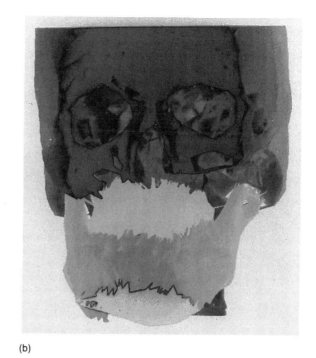

(b)

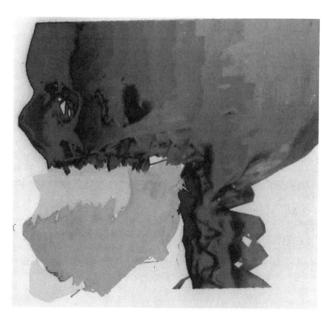

(c)

(d)

FIGURE 52.2 Surgical simulation for patient with hemi-facial microsomia. (a, c) Positions of the bone fragments preoperatively. (b, d) Movements required to correct the patient's condition. Note the truly 3D axes of rotational movements. It is not practical to plan these movements simply from anterior and lateral x-ray views.

52.3). The first generation of "cut-and-move" 3D CT-based surgical simulators soon followed. The first attempt at 3D CT-based surgical simulation was performed by Marsh, Vannier, and Warren using commercial CAD/CAM software [30]. This soon gave way to the development of custom programs specifically designed to simulate craniofacial surgery [23]. A greatly simplified user interface proved to be extremely helpful, as craniofacial surgeons are considerably less sophisticated computer users than are the engineers who

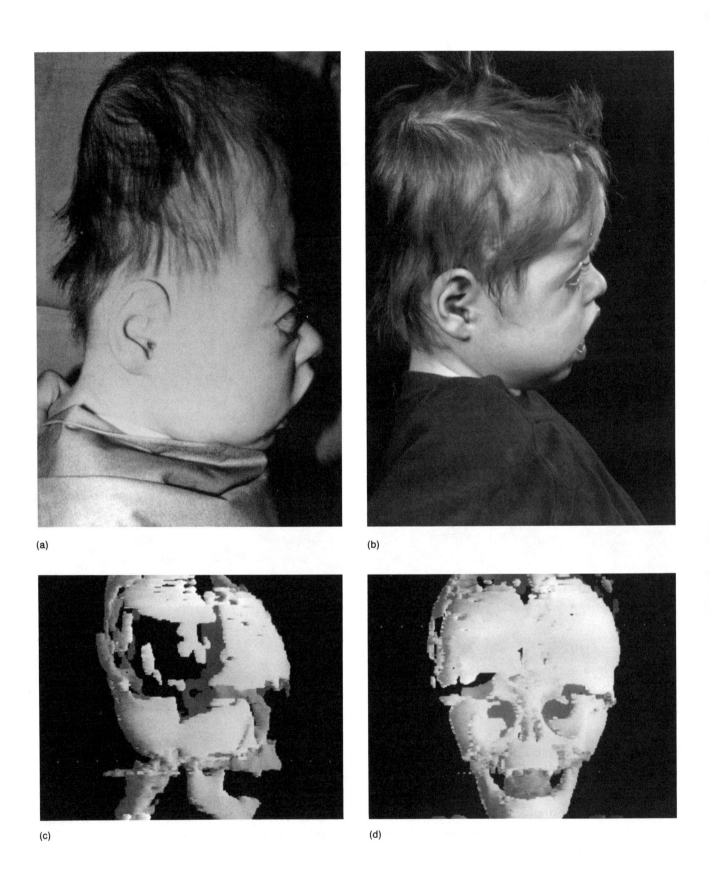

(a)

(b)

(c)

(d)

are the most frequent users of commercial CAD/CAM programs. Since then, a relatively large number of these cut-and-move surgical simulators have been developed (e.g., [8, 10, 31–35]).

As this first generation of CT-based craniofacial surgical simulation programs is now relatively mature, it is possible to criticize the programs' advantages and disadvantages. Their principle advantage has been in allowing the clinician to design an unusual osteotomy set to solve a particular problem, arising most commonly in cranial vault reshaping. Here, the problem may frequently be stated as "How can I reproduce the most normal-looking skull with the fewest number of bone fragments?" These simulation programs allow the clinician in such circumstances to design any number of different osteotomies and compare the simulations visually. Current CT-based simulations are far less useful in quantitative than in qualitative decision making. In procedures in the midface and mandible, the question often is not where to cut the bones but how far the fragment should be moved. In the lower regions of the face, for example, the position of nerves, arteries, and lines of easy fracture often determine where the cuts will probably be made, but how much to move the fragments remains mysterious. The absence of numeric standards in 3D CT-based simulations have rendered these programs essentially useless in this type of planning.

Morphometric analysis of CT-based 3D models

The 3D cephalometric simulations described earlier continue to be our most valuable tool in making these determinations. This may seem surprising, given that CT-based data sets are far richer than that of 3D cephalometrics. What is lacking is a standard, ideal, 3D normative model, based on analysis of 3D skull surface data.

FIGURE 52.3 Turricephaly correction. (a, b) Preoperative and postoperative views. (c, d) Graphic renderings of postoperative CT scans showing the correction. Although the patient's appearance is much better, too many fragments were used, leading to skeletal instability. A secondary bone-grafting procedure was required. Better preoperative planning software could have facilitated production of a more efficient surgical design, possibly avoiding or reducing the extent of the secondary procedure.

Until recently, the measurement of shape has been done almost exclusively through the use of landmarks (i.e., points that may be unambiguously located in 2D or 3D images [or physically on specimens] and that may be homologously matched between individuals). Changes in a landmark's position relative to others in a constellation of landmarks may be used to compute changes in shape of the object. Such landmark-based morphometrics have a long history and are reviewed extensively elsewhere [37]. They have been used widely in cephalometrics.

With the advent of 3D CT, it has become essential that morphometrics extend beyond landmarks and into curves and surfaces. These regions of the form that exists between landmarks carry much information that hitherto has been ignored. In this section, we will discuss our recent research into the morphometrics of curves and surfaces, particularly as it relates to the planning of craniofacial surgical procedures.

Fundamental to any morphometric system is the notion of homology first discussed at length by D'Arcy Thompson [38]. In examining differences in shape among different individuals, or in the same individual at different times, it is necessary to establish a one-to-one correspondence for homology between points on the different samples. Such a one-to-one correspondence can be established only if there is a regularity of structure between individuals. This regularity must be defined and understood as a crucial first step in defining any homology mapping.

In biology, the study of the regular appearance of structure among different individuals is called *anatomy*. Human anatomy has been studied for centuries, and the regular structures that occur routinely in different individuals are extremely well codified. However, anatomy is a fund of knowledge that usually is completely foreign to computer scientists and engineers. This deficiency must be remedied as anatomy will be at the very heart of the next level of software hierarchy beyond the low-level image-processing operators common to current 3D medical imaging.

The morphometric system on which we have embarked is based on our concept of *ridge curves* [39, 40]. The ridge curves to which we refer form a common link between the anatomy and the differential properties present in 3D medical images. In the skull, these ridges are very regular and have assigned anatomic names (figure 52.4). Aside from having a regular anatomic identity, ridges are formed from connected surface

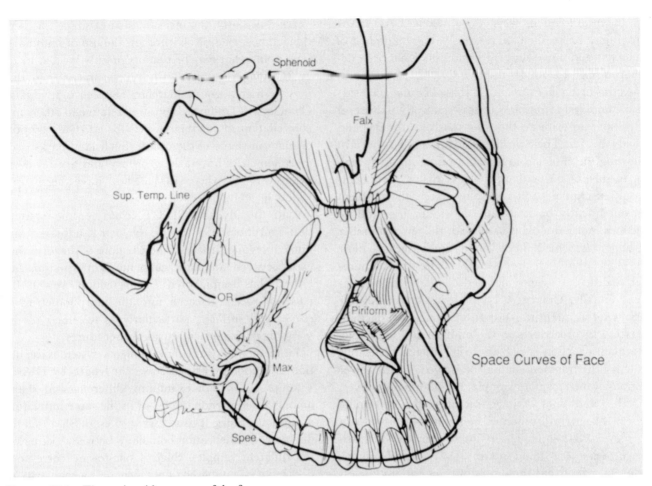

FIGURE 52.4   The major ridge curves of the face.

points, each of which is a local maximum of one of the principle curvatures along the line perpendicular to the ridge. These differential geometric properties make it possible to find these lines automatically on a surface extraction from 3D volume data [40]. From a biologic viewpoint, ridge curves usually arise on bone as a result of the pull of muscle insertions on the bone. They also occur where muscle groups come together, producing a sharp crest or ridge within the bone. It is this biologic consideration that causes us to focus on ridge curves rather than other differential geometric lines, such as the umbellic lines used by Felix Kline in his study of Apollo Belvedere [41]. It should be noted that ridge curves are features of surfaces that are the main focus in craniofacial surgery. It should also be noted that the system we are using differs in several ways from those that would be natural to an anthropologist. For example, suture lines between separate bones would seem, to an anthropologist, to make good

surface separating lines but because the sutures are frequently impossible to see on 3D CT or MRI scans, we have not used them.

Landmark definitions too are compromises between image processing and anatomy. Junctions between suture lines, which are useful in anthropology, are not useful for our application, again because they cannot be readily identified from CT image data. We have chosen to define landmarks in this ridge curve–based morphometric system as points on ridges that are local maxima of curvature, torsion, or their product. Although this definition gives landmarks the requisite 3D uniqueness, the resulting points often may not correspond to anthropologic landmarks that are close to them. An advantage of defining landmarks this way is that they lie on ridges and divide ridge curves into subsections. Further, connecting landmarks between ridges with geodesic lines allows the surface of the skull to be patched out into standard regions (figure 52.5).

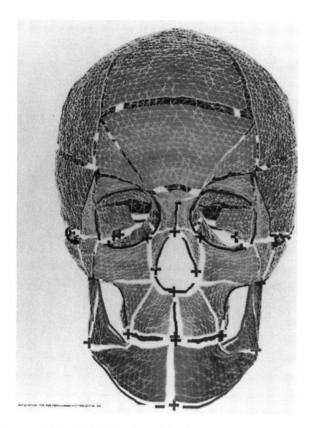

FIGURE 52.5 CT-derived model of sample skull "patched out" in standard format. Patches are shown slightly "exploded." Ridge curves are shown as heavy solid lines and landmarks as crosses.

We have also defined several landmarks as local maxima or minima of Gaussian curvature in the middle of a ridgeless section of surface. These isolated landmarks, such as the boss points in the anterolateral forehead, make useful subdivision points over a large area of otherwise featureless skull. The patched-out skull surface model forms the basis of the one-to-one homology map among individuals that we have been seeking.

A more complete topological map of our current patching scheme of aesthetically significant surfaces is shown in figure 52.6. In this scheme, there exists a hierarchy of three different types of surface points: landmarks, ridge points, and otherwise featureless surface points between landmarks and ridges. This hierarchy has been intuitively commonplace to surgeons and artists since the inception of these disciplines. The relationship among all of these points must be considered if one is to reshape a human skull to achieve a more normal facial appearance.

Our system begins by establishing the homology map between the raw surface data segmented from a patient's volume scan and this standard homology map. We begin by performing a surface segmentation of the original volume data and placing it in a topologically connected surface data structure [14]. The ridge curves then are extracted on this raw surface model using a combination of a priori knowledge of structure and differential geometric operators [40]. Local curvature and torsion maxima then are identified on these ridges to locate the landmarks. Recent work with these operators in our group, principally by David Dean [42], has shown that curvature seems to be a much more regular feature than torsion in identifying landmarks. A geodesic line is found between neighboring landmarks on different ridge curves, as dictated by the homology map in figure 52.4. It should be noted that this geodesic line is one that continually decreases in distance in approaching its target point. Therefore, it is not guaranteed to be the line of minimum surface distance between the two points. The search for this line could be quite exhaustive. The "geodesic finder" subroutine may proceed in two directions over a sharp ridge. The routine is guided in the direction of a geodesic specified on the homology map. The individual skull is thus homology-mapped, and only the aesthetically significant outer surface of the skull is extracted and each point identified. The rest of the raw surface data from the inside of the skull then is discarded. This is desirable in the craniofacial surgical application, whereas it would be extremely undesirable in other applications. Further, it should be noted that other homology mappings of the inner surface of the skull are also important, particularly in craniofacial syndromology. For the purposes of surgical planning, however, they are irrelevant and are not considered. At this point, we may look at the homology map pictured in figure 52.4 as having been warped to the specific geometry of the individual under study.

It is essential to develop a sensible statistical strategy for dealing with the homology-mapped data. Most necessary for use in optimizing surgical simulation programs is the generation of an average form from a large number of normal individuals. Before one begins using such an average form as a target for optimization, one must carefully examine the sample that will be used to form the average. We are currently using normal skulls from the Hamman-Todd morgue skeleton collection of the Cleveland Museum of Natural History, collected

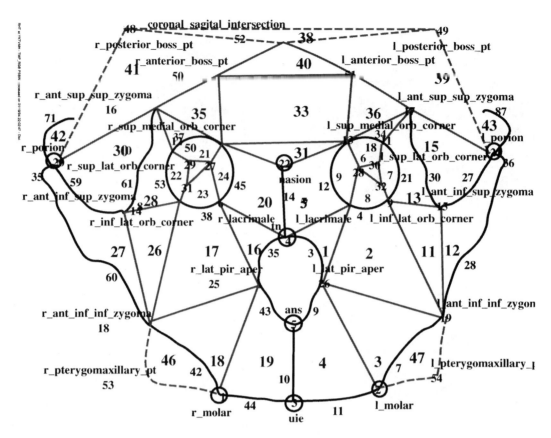

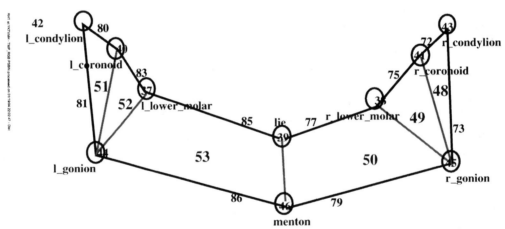

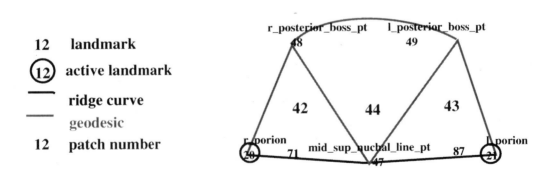

12	landmark
(12)	active landmark
▬	ridge curve
▬	geodesic
12	patch number

largely during the 1930s and 1940s from Caucasians aged 18–55 years. This collection is extremely well catalogued, and the individuals are not known to have suffered from any type of facial deformity. Our current use of this sample as a target for optimization can be criticized from a number of viewpoints. As the population of Cleveland during that time was not ethnically heterogeneous, the average may be skewed to people of Northern and Eastern European origin. It should be noted, however, that the patients treated in a craniofacial surgical unit are much more severely abnormal than any minor ethnic difference among Caucasians. We freely admit that it would be preferable to use a collection of "beautiful" skulls as targets for optimization. However, the radiation dose required to collect this information from normal individuals cannot be ethically justified at this time. Similarly, it should be noted that the definition of *beautiful* is a matter of fashion that changes with time. In recent years, radically different body shapes have been alternately in and out of fashion. There is also some interesting work in the psychology literature which suggests that what people perceive as beautiful may simply be an average [41, 42]. Clearly, further work is needed to define the appropriate sample databases for optimization programs.

Once the target sample has been selected, it is necessary to generate an average form. For landmarks, this issue has been exhaustively studied and is reviewed elsewhere [35]. Points on ridges and on surfaces between landmarks may not be averaged using the same methods. It should be noted that such points require several parameters to define them as there is no 3D uniqueness property that defines them in the direction of the ridge on surface. For example, a point between landmarks on a ridge must be localized with respect to its relative position between the landmarks. As this point is not unique with respect to its neighbors on the ridge, for statistical purposes it is considered to be deficient by a coordinate in the direction of the ridge. This means that statistical operations are not performed in the direction of a tangent to the ridge. Similarly, for surface points in the middle of a "patch," two parameters are required with respect to the corner points of the patch to fix its location. There is no 3D

uniqueness to this point with respect to any of its neighbors in the plane tangent to the surface at that point. Thus it is considered to be deficient by two coordinates for statistical purposes, leaving only the information in the direction normal to the surface for statistical processing.

In practice, ridges and surfaces are averaged as follows: ridges are scaled and superimposed at their landmarks. A piecewise cubic spline interpolant is constructed for each sample. The data are then recut to produce an equally spaced subdivision of each ridge as a function of arc length. These points then are averaged as a first pass. The first pass violates the concept of the deficient coordinates alluded to earlier. Although this has the desirable property of damping any random oscillations in amplitude in an individual sample, the length of the oscillation increases in the resulting average, as a direct result of considering the deficient coordinate. It should be noted that the first pass also is much smoother than any of its samples. The first-pass average then is used to generate cutting planes that are perpendicular to this average at equally spaced intervals as a function of arc length. Each plane is used to recut each of the original spline samples to determine the intersection of each sample with the plane. The "proper" average is constructed as an average at each of these planar intersections in sequence. For surface points, only the data in the direction of the surface normal are to be averaged. A linear Coon's surface [43] is constructed for each surface patch, and the surface is divided into a roughly equally spaced set of subdivisions. The normal line then is constructed from each of these subdivisions on each sample Coon's surface, and the distance is measured between the Coon's surface and the actual surface intersection on the sample. These deviations between the Coon's surface estimate and the actual surface are averaged for each parametric point in the model, allowing the generation of an average surface lofting over the Coon's surface. Details of the implementation of these algorithms are explained elsewhere [40, 45].

It is not sufficient to describe the geometry of an average without some discussion of variability about that average. Recently, the chi square statistic has been applied to probability statements about group differences between ridge curve segments [42]. This allows one to make probabilistic group determinations based on considerations of an entire ridge curve subsegment or surface patch at a time. More sophisticated

FIGURE 52.6 A more complete topological abstraction of the midface.

statistical comparisons between ridge and surface sections between landmarks are possible and are the subject of ongoing work in our group.[2]

This leads us to syndromology, which is a well-known study in the cephalometric tradition. What are the morphometric descriptors that distinguish various craniofacial anomaly syndromes? We are presently developing syndromologic shape criteria based on surface morphometrics, in a manner analogous to earlier work on landmark-based morphometrics [37]. Aside from aiding in differential diagnosis, such shape considerations of common syndrome groups will be useful in answering questions that identify the osteotomy set most likely to be useful in the treatment of a particular syndrome.

The most important application of this comprehensive morphometric system will be in the automated detection of radiologic abnormalities. As this field advances, we expect extensive automated homology mapping of each individual compared with a normal model to be performed on every volume scan. An extensive multivariate morphometric computation then will be performed on the data, and statistically significant deviations in shape will be shown in various colors on a workstation for further examination by the radiologist. This futuristic vision of the marriage of morphometrics to image processing is discussed in greater detail elsewhere [46].

Surgical planning and optimization with 3D models

A strategy for optimization of bone fragment position may be derived directly from considerations of 3D morphometrics as just described. In the earlier section on cephalometrics, we discussed optimization of bone fragment position by adjusting the fixed variables of rigid motion in an effort to minimize a landmark-based error term. For landmarks, this was the sum-of-squares distances between each landmark on the patient and those landmarks on the target data set. In 3D surface morphometrics, there are two other types of error terms based on ridge points and surface regions. For ridge lines between landmarks, we seek to minimize the sum-of-squares areas between the patient's ridge and the homologous ridge on the normative data set. For surface regions, the appropriate term is a volume difference between the surface on the patient and that of the ideal. These landmark ridge and surface error terms must be blended to produce a single figure of merit for

the error of fit between a patient's bone fragments and the ideal form. We are currently exploring empirically the different blending functions. It seems to us that the standard deviations that evolve from the consideration of variability described previously could be used to establish weighting factors for the optimization at each point, although this has not yet been accomplished.

Recently, we have extended our surgical planning software to make it capable of automatically suggesting appropriate osteotomy sequences for midface and mandibular craniofacial surgical procedures. In these regions of the face, standard osteotomies have evolved that avoid injuries to vital structures while providing the easiest separation between bones. If all of these osteotomies are considered together, a very complex multisegment design results. The program begins by optimizing the position of all of these small bone fragments with respect to the normal form. Then, one by one, osteotomy lines are removed from the plan in order of increasing impact on facial shape. A hierarchy of surgical plans then is evolved which balances surgical complexity against facial shape. The clinician may select the osteotomy design with the fewest number of pieces that still produces a relatively normally shaped face.

As one might expect, designs with the most bone fragments tend to produce the most normal shapes. The problem with such multisegment plans is that that they are very difficult to carry out in the operating room, as it is very difficult with standard instrumentation to position precisely many small fragments relative to one another and then to achieve rigid fixation of these fragments. For cranial vault osteotomies, in which there is considerably more flexibility in determining where osteotomies are to be placed, this decision continues to be left to the clinician. Examples of optimized osteotomies for the correction of craniofacial malformations are shown in color plate 40.

The future of craniofacial surgical planning software

It is obvious that the optimizing craniofacial surgical simulator just described leaves a number of deficiencies unresolved. The most notable of these are in automated osteotomy selection, soft-tissue prediction, and considerations of growth. In this surgical simulator, automatic location of osteotomy sites is provided only in the midface and mandible where "standard" osteotomy lines have been defined. In the future, an algorithmic strategy for the solution of cranial vault reshaping cases, such as that depicted in figure 52.3, will evolve. One characteristic of cranial vault reconstruction is that segments from one portion of the patient's cranium may be moved to quite a different portion to correct a defect. Similarly, a portion of cranium may be split into inner and outer pieces, which may be used separately as appropriate. We speculate that one possible strategy might start by identifying a large section of the patient's cranium requiring correction. The system would then seek to find the portion of the actual skull that most nearly approximates the desired shape. This potential osteotomy fragment would then be pruned until some numeric tolerance for normality is achieved. A decision would be made on whether to move the fragment whole, thus leaving a new hole to be filled, or to split it into inner and outer parts. The process would then be repeated, with interactive guidance from the surgeon, until a complete plan is devised. In an alternative, related strategy, the surgeon might designate a set of osteotomies for the patient's cranium. The system would then start with the largest fragment and attempt to match as much of it as possible to some portion of the desired shape. The system would propose pruning off sections from this fragment until some numeric tolerance for normality is achieved, thus creating more fragments for potential use. The process would be repeated until a complete plan is achieved.

Accurate prediction of the soft-tissue changes that will accompany overlying bone movements is absent from the current craniofacial surgical planners. It is laudable that one of the current surgical simulators [47] attempts to perform a soft-tissue prediction following a movement of underlying bones. Although this report is encouraging, further extensive work will be required. The most obvious approach is to model the overlying soft tissue using finite elements. The physical parameters for the elements will have to be adjusted based on feedback from the empiric results of many prior procedures. At first, the model may be simply a thin skin over homogeneous tetrahedral soft tissue. It may be necessary to sophisticate the model progressively into separate fat and muscle soft-tissue components as well as to provide another layer for the periosteum over the bone, possibly adjusting for variable levels of skin thickness over the soft tissue. This can be done only after many postoperative scans have been compared with the preoperative starting forms. Once

the character of the model as well as the parameter of the finite elements has been established, it will be necessary to fold this data into the optimization loop. The real goal of craniofacial surgery is not to optimize skull shape but to optimize the shape of the overlying face. As a result, the rigid motion of a bone fragment should be adjusted, a finite-element computation made, and then the facial surface evaluated to determine an error of fit to a normal face. Given the time-consuming nature of such a complex finite-element computation, each iteration in the optimization loop will be costly.

Perhaps the greatest deficiency in current surgical simulation software systems is their inability to predict growth. For psychosocial reasons, it is very important that the craniofacial surgeon correct these deformities in early childhood. Surgical planning must become 4D. It is necessary to gain some estimate of the growth predictors of the face in designing a surgical procedure. Just as in the case of soft-tissue prediction discussed earlier, this will require much longitudinal evaluation of postoperative patients. For soft-tissue prediction, a single pair of preoperative and postoperative scans will not be all that is required to adjust finite-element parameters. To correct for growth, a large number of longitudinal samples of postoperative patients will be needed. The cost in radiation load of 3D CT scanning makes this impractical. Furthermore, longitudinal studies of normal children, although somewhat useful, clearly have limitations in modeling growth processes that are already abnormal and in predicting long-term outcomes. We expect that surface scanners that use only light striping will provide low-cost 3D surface models for postoperative follow-up in the near future [48–51]. However, these scanners show only the skin surface and provide merely indirect information about underlying structures. If relatively inexpensive MRI scanners should become available for routine use at every craniofacial clinic, it may become more practical to obtain the large-scale longitudinal studies that are needed to develop good predictive models for such patients.

Use of robotic techniques for precise execution of craniofacial surgical procedures

To this point, we have discussed software that develops precise rigid motion specifications for bone fragments in craniofacial surgical procedures, without any regard for actual execution of this plan. Early in the evolution of craniofacial surgery, it was realized that multisegment osteotomies would be required to attain the desired reconstructive flexibilities [52, 53]. Difficulties with positioning the fragments accurately and fixing them into position led to the abandonment of this multisegment approach. As the years have passed, numerous technical innovations have made multisegment designs more approachable. The new precision bone saws allow osteotomies to be made with ease and great precision. On the rigid fixation side, screw and plate systems have been evolved that provide rigid 3D fixation of fragments. We expect in the near future that this will be replaced with resorbable bone fragment fixation materials that will be as easy to apply as squeezing a toothpaste tube.

Very little progress has been made, however, in positioning bone fragments accurately. This is particularly important, as the "artistic" method frequently breaks down in craniofacial surgery. In performing craniofacial surgery, an incision usually is made from ear to ear across the top of the scalp and the soft tissue peeled down away from the bone. The need to leave vital structures attached to this soft tissue envelope usually provides very limited access to most of the areas of the midface. For example, the need to leave the optic nerve connected to the soft-tissue globe makes it difficult to visualize the cheekbones through more than a small aperture through the soft tissue. Similarly, during the operative procedure, the soft tissues become quite swollen. In assessing the result of a bone fragment movement, the soft tissue is pulled over the bone and one is usually forced to make a judgment about facial shape by looking at a swollen skin envelope. Because of these difficulties, freehand positioning of bone fragments, even by a very good surgeon, is seldom more accurate than approximately 5 mm, relative to the planned positions.[3] This lack of precision is a serious limitation on the results that can be achieved. Improvement in accuracy of plan execution by at least a factor of two, and preferably a factor of five, is required.

Currently, intermediate occlusal splints are used in our unit for the performance of multisegment midface osteotomies. Occlusal splints are plastic bite plates placed between the teeth that establish a rigid relationship between the upper and lower jaws. What usually is done is that the midface is osteotomized into one large fragment. An intermediate splint then is placed between the teeth using the lower jaw as a reference to position one small segment of the upper midface. This

midface then is fixed into position and cut away from the rest of the midface fragment mask. The splints are changed and another segment of this larger piece is fixed into position and cut away. Multiple such splints are used until the final splint containing only the palate section is positioned and fixed into place.

This technique has its limitations. First, it is extremely time-consuming. Second, the surgeon is required to start with a large one-piece osteotomy, which usually causes steady bleeding from the inner nose that may not be easily controlled. This bleeding continues through multiple courses of splint changes and fixation operations until the procedure is completed. The result often is significant blood loss, which must be replaced through transfusions. The method also is unsatisfactory in that the soft-tissue envelope frequently will not allow the rest of a large bone fragment to reach the position desired to properly place a single cheekbone. For example, in Apert syndrome, there is so much midface concavity that one cheekbone would have to project 5–6 cm out from the face in order to position the opposite cheekbone correctly. The tightness of the soft-tissue envelope about the midface section makes this impossible.

These difficulties could be greatly alleviated if we could make the planned cuts in any convenient order and accurately assemble bone fragments one at a time relative to one another and to the skull fragment, again in whatever order is most convenient. For example, such a system would allow the surgeon to start with the bone fragments that involve the least bleeding, thereby minimizing blood loss. Similarly, soft-tissue constraints on intermediate configurations could be avoided.

To do this, the crucial intraoperative requirements are the ability to track and report accurately to the surgeon the actual position of bone fragments relative to one another and to the skull base and to report this information to the surgeon, and the ability to assist the surgeon in manipulating the fragments into the desired configuration and then to hold them in place while the surgeon affixes them to one another. Of these, the ability to track and report accurately relative bone fragment positions is perhaps the most important. A number of methods have been used by various groups to establish 3D position in the operating room, including mechanical linkages (e.g., [54–56]), sonic localizers (e.g., [57]), and optical tracking (e.g., [58]).

We have explored an electromagnetic rigid motion–sensing system [24]. In principle, small orthogonal sensing coils could be placed on each bone fragment, allowing measurement of relative rigid motion with respect to the skull base. One advantage of this approach is that these devices are relatively unaffected by (nonmetallic) obstructions between the transmitter and sense coils. However, a serious drawback is potential distortion caused by eddy currents, magnetic fields, or similar environmental influences in the operating room. The problem is exacerbated by the fact that these distortions may not be readily apparent to the surgeon or to the computer that is reading the sensors. These considerations led us to concentrate on optical tracking.

The principal geometric sensor in our present system is an Optotrak 3D optical digitizer manufactured by Northern Digital Corp. (Toronto, Canada), which uses three CCD line scan cameras to track active LED beacons. This system is fast and accurate, is much less readily confused by stray light than similar lateral cell–based devices, and (unlike electromagnetic field 6D sensors) is unaffected by metal or magnetism in the operating theater. The model in our laboratory is capable of producing 1000 3D positions per second to an accuracy of approximately ±0.1 mm and of returning up to eight 6D positions computed from sets of 3D beacon positions with an additional overhead of nearly 10 msec beyond the 3D sampling time.

Typically, three or four noncollinear beacons are attached to each (future) bone fragment by means of percutaneous K-wires before any osteotomies are done, as shown in figure 52.7. The position of the skull then is determined (see later), as is the position of each beacon relative to the skull, and hence to its corresponding bone fragment. Once this step is completed, the osteotomies may be performed in any order; the relative 6D positions of two bone fragments may be computed by measuring the corresponding beacon positions.

The registration of the model of the patient's skull derived from preoperative images with the actual skull in the operating room is a crucial step. The most straightforward method uses a calibrated pointing device comprising a number of beacons whose positions are measured continuously by the Optotrak, as shown in figure 52.8. The surgeon uses this device to point to a number of predetermined anatomic landmarks on the patient's skull. The 6D registration transformation can then be computed by minimizing the sum-of-squares distance between corresponding model and actual landmarks. In practice, it is necessary to account

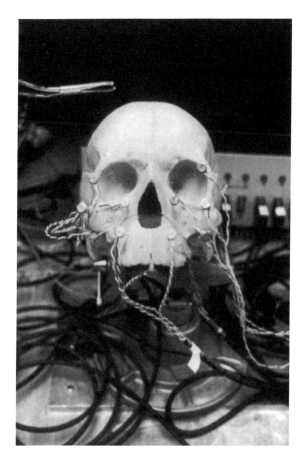

FIGURE 52.7 Plastic skull model with optical beacons. In surgery, the beacons would be affixed to the patient's skull with percutaneous K-wires. One beacon is flashed at a time, and its position is sensed by three line scan cameras in a commercially available 3D digitizer manufactured by Northern Digital, Inc. This device can track the 3D position of the beacons with an absolute accuracy better than ±0.1 mm, at repetition rates in excess of 1000 beacons per second. The position and orientation of a bone fragment may be computed from the position of any three noncollinear beacons affixed to the fragment.

for possible patient head motion during this procedure by simultaneously measuring the positions of beacons affixed to the skull and beacons affixed to the pointing device.

An alternative method measures ridge lines on the skull rather than simple point landmarks. By tracing out the ridge lines while simultaneously monitoring the rigid motions of the skull base, it is possible to generate a ridge map of the skull in the coordinate system of the beacon tracking system. A ridge-based optimization, much like that discussed in the section Surgical Planning and Optimization with 3D Models, can be

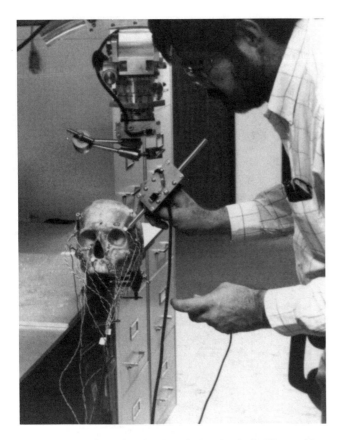

FIGURE 52.8 Locating landmarks on the skull. The position of the tip of the digitizer wand relative to the beacons on the wand has previously been calibrated. The positions of the beacons mounted to the skull are continuously monitored to provide a base coordinate system for the landmark location. Once the skull has been located, the positions of the beacons relative to the preoperative skull coordinate system may be computed.

performed to define the registration transformations relating the patient, the tracking device coordinate system, and the preoperative CT-based model.[4] Similarly, multiple surface points can be digitized by dragging the stylus across bony surfaces, and the surface-based optimization described previously can also be used. In fact, just as in surgical planning, we anticipate using an appropriate weighted optimization combining landmark, ridge curve, and surface point data. The advantage of such methods is that a single erroneous measurement is much less likely to introduce any significant error in the 6D registration than is the case with simple landmark-based registration. An additional advantage is that ridge curves can often be located more rapidly and consistently than can point landmarks.

A simple human-machine interface uses a variety of modalities (graphics, synthesized voice, tonal cues, etc.) to provide feedback to the surgeon about the relative position of bone fragments compared to the surgical plan. This is an area where rapid technologic progress is being made, driven by very rapid advances in computer graphics, entertainment applications, and virtual reality. In our experience [59], simple tonal cues and "slider-style" graphic displays work extremely well so long as repositioning can be done one degree of freedom at a time (see later). They are *much* less effective if multiple, coupled degrees of freedom must be dealt with simultaneously. For this purpose, a 3D rendering is needed. We have found that even simple line drawing–perspective animations can be very helpful in such situations and can provide useful feedback even where the realignment can be done one degree of freedom at a time. We are exploring the use of more powerful intraoperative graphic renderings.

The next essential component is a mechanical positioning device to assist in repositioning one bone fragment relative to another and then to hold the desired alignment while the surgeon applies screws and plates or other fastening devices to hold them together. The surgeon in our group (Dr. Cutting) initially sought the use of an active robotic device that could automatically accommodate small motions in skull-base position. Several problems arose with this approach. The first was the difficulty of specifying an appropriate motion trajectory. The presence of vital structures all around the anatomy being manipulated made certain motion trajectories permissible, whereas others could be quite devastating. Along with this concern was deciding how strong a robot should be. The permissible amount of force that could be applied safely in a given direction was difficult to specify. Finally, the possibility of the robot making undesired motions raises obvious safety problems. In principle, every one of these difficulties can be handled. However, we found ourselves wondering whether, in this particular application, a simpler passive manipulation aid might be just as good.

The defining characteristic of a passive manipulation aid is that the surgeon provides all the motive force. Although this certainly simplifies safety considerations, compared with an active device, it also creates additional demands on the mechanical design. Generally, the manipulation aid should interfere as little as possible with the surgeon's tactile appreciation for what is happening to the patient while preserving the desired alignment once it is achieved. Although a low-impedance 6-dof clamping device is relatively easy to design (e.g., the Retract-robot produced by Elmed, Inc., of Addison, Illinois or the more sophisticated device described in [60]), such devices can be difficult to use as alignment aids. Generally, it is much easier to align an object 1 dof at a time rather than all at once. Once a degree of freedom has been aligned, it is important that subsequent motions to align other degrees of freedom not disturb the work that has already been accomplished. Furthermore, the degrees of freedom of the manipulation aid should be naturally and intuitively tied to the task at hand. In practice, these considerations rule out most conventional kinematic structures commonly used with industrial robots.

Our approach [59, 61–63] is to develop manipulation aids with manually actuated (or computer-controlled) brakes to provide selective locking of *orthogonally decoupled* degrees of freedom resolved in a tool frame located at a work point as close as possible to the reorientation centroid of the bone fragment being manipulated. In such a mechanism, the revolute axes are all mutually perpendicular and intersect at the work point. Each motion axis of the mechanism only affects 1 rotational or translational degree of freedom of a bone fragment or other object rigidly held at the work point. This permits the surgeon to work on only 1 or 2 dof at a time without disturbing those that have already been aligned.

Our present implementation (figure 52.9) consists of a three-axis *coarse positioning system*, a 6-dof *fine positioning system*, and a standard 6-dof *adjustable tooling clamp* (Retract-Robot, Elmed Inc.). The fine positioning system consists of three counterbalanced linear stages carrying a conventional z axis and crossed goniometer-cradle x and y axes with a rotation center approximately 150 mm from the mechanism. One advantage of the coarse-fine structure is that it permits relatively large work volumes while limiting the inertia with which the surgeon must cope. The modularity is similarly very useful for experimentation. In this implementation, manual braking is used for all axes. Earlier experiments [57] showed the feasibility of using computer-actuated brakes, especially when coupled with tonal cues to the surgeon. In this case, however, we decided to use the simplest approach, even at the cost of the minor inconvenience of manually turning a locking screw.[5]

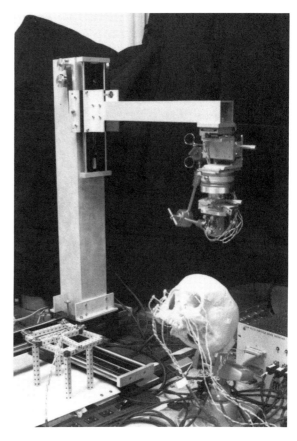

FIGURE 52.9   Passive manipulation aid for surgery. The manipulation aid consists of three coarse positioning axes, a six-axis remote-center-of-motion fine positioner, and an adjustable instrument holder. The coarse positioning axes are used to position the fine positioner's center of motion at the desired center of motion of a bone fragment. Because the fine positioner motions are orthogonally decoupled at the remote center, each rotational and translational degree of freedom may be realigned independently and locked by the surgeon.

The actual use of the mechanism for relocating a bone fragment to a desired pose relative to another bone fragment is straightforward. The coarse axes of the manipulator are adjusted so that the center of rotation of the fine manipulator coincides with the desired center of motion of bone fragment B_i. The bone fragment is grasped by bone forceps, which are rigidly affixed to the manipulator by means of an adjustable clamp (Retract-Robot, Elmed Inc., 1990), and a motion coordinate system aligned with the goniometer axes is computed. In a typical alignment strategy, the realignment is done by first unlocking all "fine-motion" degrees of freedom and manipulating the fragment into its approximate desired position, with

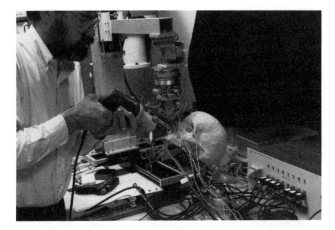

(a)

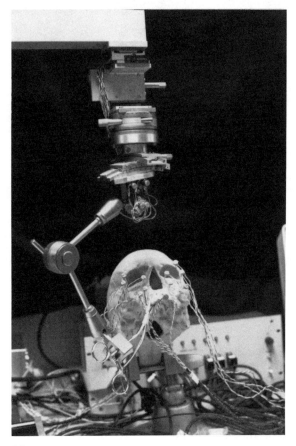

(b)

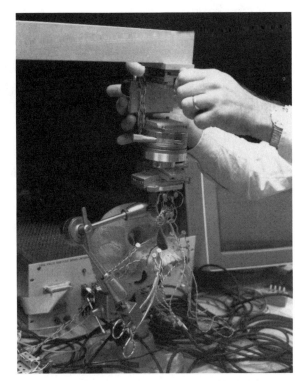

(c)

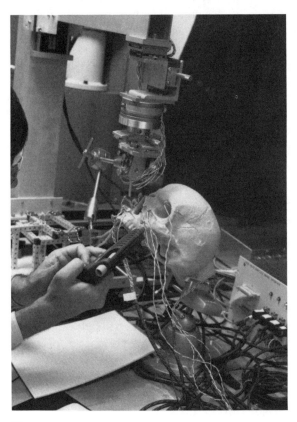

(d)

FIGURE 52.10 Midface osteotomy procedure on a plastic skull model. (a) Cutting a bone fragment. (b, c) Fine alignment of bone fragment. (d) Reattaching the bone fragment. Alignment errors of approximately 0.7 mm in translation and 1 degree in rotation were achieved in preliminary experiments. Work is now underway at New York University to develop a clinical version of this system.

the surgeon relying on his or her own tactile feedback information to verify that there is no undesired obstruction. All degrees of freedom then are locked, after which each degree of freedom is successively unlocked, brought into alignment, and locked.

In practice, this scheme has worked well in the laboratory. Alignments within 0.3 mm and 0.5 degrees, as measured by the optical tracking system in bench-top experiments, are typically achieved in approximately 2–3 minutes for the final alignment phase. In another "bottom-line" experiment on a plastic skull (figure 52.10), multiple point landmarks were digitized. Skull registration was performed by pointing to three landmarks on the teeth. A bone fragment was cut free, repositioned relative to the skull base, and reaffixed with hot melt glue; and the landmark points were remeasured. The resulting bone fragment landmark positions, relative to the skull-base landmarks, were within 0.7 mm and 1 degree of the desired values. Work is now underway at New York University to develop a clinical version of this system.

Conclusion

In this chapter, we have sketched a view of the present state and possible near-term evolution of computer-integrated craniofacial surgery. Crucial components include 3D modeling and simulation based on CT images, morphometric analysis of 3D surfaces both to produce good normative models and to produce optimized plans for individual patients, and a variety of intraoperative robotic technologies to assist the surgeon in precisely executing planned procedures. Advances in planning and execution are synergistic. As better analysis and simulation tools become available, it will be possible to develop better surgical plans. On the other hand, an otherwise excellent plan that cannot be carried out is of limited use. The development of better intraoperative tracking and manipulation aids is likely to increase significantly the usefulness of and demands on surgical planning software. Both planning and execution systems are still in their infancy. As crucial cost, computer performance, and technology thresholds are crossed in the coming decade, today's innovation will become tomorrow's standard practice. Further, craniofacial surgery is likely to continue to be a driving application for research that, in turn, will be useful in many other information-intensive surgical areas, such as orthopaedics and neurosurgery, in which

model-based analysis and planning, coupled with accurate surgical execution, can have significant benefits for patients. We are excited about the future.

ACKNOWLEDGMENTS We would like to thank the many members of our research team who have participated in various phases of this work and who indeed are coauthors of many of the articles that report our progress. In particular, key people from New York University include Deljou Khorramabadi, Betsy Haddad, David Dean, David Kim, and Marilyn Noz. At IBM, key people include Alan Kalvin, Yong-Yil Kim, Nils Bruun, Bob Olyha, Dieter Grimm, and Dave LaRose. We also thank Dr. Bruce Latimer, Director, Laboratory of Physical Anthropology, Cleveland Museum of Natural History, for access to the Hamman-Todd morgue skeletal collection.

NOTES

1. In fact, simple threshold-based segmentation does not work particularly well for regions of the skull in which there are thin bony plates. In these regions, partial voluming effects can lead to false holes, or "pseudoforamina." This problem has led to much more sophisticated segmentation methods, which are also applicable in orthopaedics and other clinical areas. These methods will not be discussed further here but represent another example of how craniofacial applications have motivated much more broadly applicable image-processing and modeling research.

2. It should be noted that 3D color graphics will be absolutely critical in reporting results of this kind of very complex statistical processing. Few clinicians or anthropologists will be interested in examining the voluminous tables of data such computations will generate. Some type of graphic summation of these computations will be essential.

3. We are not aware of any quantitative postoperative studies measuring freehand positioning on actual patients. Only a relatively few sites (New York University in particular) today attempt the sort of quantitatively accurate planning that would make such a study meaningful. The positioning accuracy quoted represents the best judgment of the surgeon author (Dr. Cutting) regarding what can be achieved freehand.

4. One further refinement that we are considering makes multiple traces of the digitizing stylus in directions orthogonal to the ridge curves at a number of points along the curves. In this case, once approximate alignment is known, an observed trace path can be "registered" in the two coordinates perpendicular to the direction of the ridge curve, with a corresponding trace predicted from the preoperative model derived from patient CT.

5. It should be noted that the fact that the motions are all kinematically decoupled makes a tremendous difference. The 6-degree-of-freedom adjustable clamp, in contrast, is either floppy or rigid. It has proved relatively difficult to tighten it without moving it slightly. Fortunately, a few

millimeters of displacement during tightening can easily be accommodated in the actual fine-adjustment process, which takes place with the clamp rigidly locked.

REFERENCES

[1] HERMAN, G., and H. LIU, 1977. Display of three-dimensional information in computed tomography. *J. Comp. Assist. Tomogr.* 1:155.

[2] HERMAN, G., and H. LIU, 1979. Three-dimensional display of human organs from computed tomograms. *Comput. Graphics Image Proc.* 9:1.

[3] HEMMY, D., D. DAVID, and G. HERMAN, 1983. Three-dimensional reconstruction of craniofacial deformity utilizing computed tomography. *Neurosurgery*, 13:534.

[4] HEMMY, D., G. HERMAN, D. DAVID, et al., 1983. Three-dimensional reconstruction of the skull and facial bones utilizing computer tomography in craniofacial surgery. In *Proceedings of the Eighth International Congress of Plastic and Reconstructive Surgery*, Montreal, pp. 275–276.

[5] UDUPA, J., and G. HERMAN, 1991. *3D Imaging in Medicine*. Boca Raton, Fla.: CRC Press.

[6] MARSH, J., and M. VANNIER, 1985. *Comprehensive Care for Craniofacial Deformities*. St. Louis: Mosby.

[7] UDUPA, J., G. HERMAN, P. MARGASAHAYAM, L. CHEN, and C. MEYER, 1986. A turnkey system for the display and analysis of 3D medical objects. *SPIE Proc.* 671:154.

[8] UDUPA, J., and D. ODHNER, 1990. Interactive surgical planning: High speed object rendition and manipulation without specialized hardware. In *Proceedings of the First IEEE Conference on Visualization in Biomedical Computing*, IEEE Press, Piscatoway, W.J. p. 330.

[9] UDUPA, J., and G. HERMAN, 1992. Boundaries in multidimensional digital scenes: Theory and algorithms (tech. rep. MIPG182). Philadelphia: Medical Image Processing Group, University of Pennsylvania.

[10] UDUPA, J., H. HUNG, D. ODHNER, and R. GONCALVES, 1992. 3DVIEWNIX: A data-, machine-, and application-independent software system for multidimensional data visualization and analysis. *SPIE Proc.* Vol. 1653.

[11] BAUMGART, B. G., 1974. Geometric modelling for computer vision. Doctoral thesis, Stanford University.

[12] NOZ, M. E., and G. Q. MAGUIRE, 1988. QSH: A minimal but highly portable image display and processing toolkit. *Comput. Methods Programs Biomed.* 27:229–240.

[13] KALVIN, A. D., C. B. CUTTING, B. HADDAD, and M. NOZ, 1991. Constructing topologically connected surfaces for the comprehensive analysis of 3-D medical structures. In *Proceedings of the SPIE Medical Imaging Conference V*, Soc. Photo-Optical Inst. Eng., Bellingham. Wash.

[14] KALVIN, A. D., 1991. Segmentation and surface-based modelling of objects in 3D biomedical images. Doctoral thesis, New York University, New York, 1991.

[15] FELLINGHAM, L., J. VOGEL, C. LAU, and P. DEV, 1986. Interactive graphics and 3-D modelling for surgical planning and prosthesis and implant design. *Proceedings of the Nat. Comp. Graphics. Assn.*, 3:132–142.

[16] KAPLAN, E., 1987. 3-D CT images for facial implant design and manufacture. *Clin. Plast. Surg.* 14;663

[17] RHODES, M., R. KUO, and S. ROTHMAN, 1987. An application of computer graphics and networks to anatomic model and prosthesis manufacturing. *IEEE Comput. Graph. Appl.* 7(2):12.

[18] TOTH, B., W. STEWART, and L. F. ELLIOT, 1987. Computer designed prostheses for orbitocranial reconstruction. In *Craniofacial Surgery*, D. Marchac, ed. Berlin: Springer-Verlag.

[19] TOTH, B., D. ELLIS, and W. STEWART, 1988. Computer designed prosthesis for orbitocranial reconstruction. *Plast. Reconstr. Surg.*, 81:315.

[20] ZONNEVELD, F., S. LOBREGT, J. VAN DER MEULEN, and M. VAANDRAGER, 1989. Three-dimensional imaging in craniofacial surgery. *World J. Surg.* 13:328.

[21] CUTTING, C., F. BOOKSTEIN, B. GRAYSON, and J. G. MCCARTHY, 1984. Computer aided planning of orthognathic surgery. In abstracts of the Plastic Surgery Research Council Meeting, Detroit.

[22] BHATIA, S., and J. SOWRAY, 1984. A computer aided design for orthognathic surgery. *Br. J. Oral Maxillofac. Surg.* 22:237.

[23] CUTTING, C., F. BOOKSTEIN, B. GRAYSON, L. FELLINGHAM, and J. MCCARTHY, 1986. Three-dimensional computer assisted design of craniofacial surgical procedures: Optimization and interaction with cephalometric and CT-based models. *Plast Reconstr. Surg.*, 77:877.

[24] CUTTING, C., B. GRAYSON, E. BOOKSTEIN, L. FELLINGHAM, and J. G. MCCARTHY, 1986. Computer-aided planning and evaluation of facial and orthognathic surgery. *Clin. Plast. Surg.* 13:449.

[25] GRAYSON, B., C. CUTTING, F. BOOKSTEIN, H. KIM, and J. G. MCCARTHY, 1988. The three-dimensional cephalogram: Theory, technique, and clinical application. *Am. J. Orthod. Dentofacial Orthop.*, 94:327.

[26] CUTTING, C., B. GRAYSON, F. BOOKSTEIN, L. FELLINGHAM, and J. G. MCCARTHY, 1987. Three-dimensional computer-aided design of craniofacial surgical procedures. In *Craniofacial Surgery*, D. Marchac, ed. Berlin: Springer-Verlag, p. 17.

[27] CUTTING, C., 1991. Applications of computer graphics to the evaluation and treatment of major craniofacial malformations. In *3D Imaging in Medicine*, J. Udupa and G. Herman, eds. Boca Raton, Fla.: CRC Press, pp. 163–189.

[28] LUENBERGER, D., 1973. *Linear and Non-Linear Programming*, London: Addison Wesley.

[29] LAWSON, C. F., and R. J. HANSON, 1974. *Solving Least Squares Problems*. Englewood Cliffs, N.J.: Prentice-Hall.

[30] MARSH, J., M. VANNIER, W. G. STEVENS, J. WARREN, D. GAYOU, and D. DYE, 1985. Computerized imaging for soft tissue and osseous reconstruction in the head and neck. *Clin. Plast Surg.*, vol. 12, p. 279.

[31] BREWSTER, L., S. TRIVEDI, H. TUY, and J. UDUPA, 1984. Interactive surgical planning. *IEEE Comput. Graph. Appl.*, vol. 4, p. 31.

[32] YOKOI, S., T. YASUDA, Y. HASHIMOTO, J. TORIWAKI, M. FUJOKA, and H. NAKAJIMA, 1986. A craniofacial surgical

planning system. In *Proceedings of the National Computer Graphics Association*, vol. 3, p. 93.

[33] McEwen, C., I. Jackson, and R. Robb, 1987. Personal communication to Dr. C. Cutting concerning craniofacial surgical simulation additions to the Mayo Clinic ANALYZE software.

[34] Altobelli, D. E., R. Kikinis, J. B. Mulliken, H. Cline, W. Lorensen, F. Jolesz, 1991. Three-dimensional imaging in medicine: Surgical planning and simulation of craniofacial surgery. In *Proceedings of the International Conference of the IEEE Engineering in Medicine and Biology Society*, Vol. 13, pp. 289–290.

[35] Udupa, J., 1986. Computerized surgical planning: Current capabilities and medical needs. In *Proceedings of the Society of Photo-Optical Instrumentation Engineers*, Bellingham, Washington, p. 474.

[36] Yasuda, T., Y. Hashimoto, S. Yokoi, and J. Toriwaki, 1990. Computer system for craniofacial surgical planning based on CT images. *IEEE Trans. Med. Imag.*, p. 270.

[37] Bookstein, F. L., 1991. *Morphometria Tools for Landmark Data—Geometry and Biology*. New York: Cambridge University Press.

[38] Thompson, D., 1961. On the theory of transformations, or the comparison of related forms. In *On Growth and Form*, J. T. Bonner, ed. Cambridge, Engl.: Cambridge University Press, pp. 268–325.

[39] Bookstein, F. L., and C. B. Cutting, 1988. A proposal for the apprehension of curving craniofacial form in three dimensions. In *Craniofacial Morphogenesis and Dysmorphogenesis*, A. Burdi, K. Dryland-Vig, and K. Ribbens, eds. Ann Arbor: University of Michigan, pp. 127–140.

[40] Cutting, C., F. Bookstein, B. Haddad, D. Dean, and H. Kim, 1993. A spline-based approach for averaging three-dimensional curves and surfaces. In *Proceedings of the Society of Photo-Optical Instrumentation Engineers*, SPIE, Bellingham, Wash., pp. 29–44.

[41] Hilbert, D., and S. Cohn-Vossen, 1952. *Geometry and the Imagination*. New York: Chelsea Publishing.

[42] Dean, D., 1993. The middle Pleistocene homo. Doctoral thesis, Department of Anthropology, The City University of New York.

[43] Langlois, J., and L. Roggman, 1990. Attractive faces are only average. *Psychol. Sci.*, p. 115.

[44] Langlois, J., L. Roggman, L. Musselman, and S. Acton, 1991. A picture is worth a thousand words: Reply to "On the difficulty of averaging faces." *Psychol. Sci.*, p. 354.

[45] Rogers, D., and J. Adams, 1976. *Mathematical Elements for Computer Graphics*. New York: McGraw-Hill.

[46] Bookstein, F. L., and C. B. Cutting, 1991. A proposal for an automated synthesis of morphometrics and image analysis for solid medical images. In *Proceedings of the IEEE Workshop on Technology Requirements for Biomedical Imaging*, Washington, D.C., May 21.

[47] Altobelli, D., R. Kikinis, J. Mulliken, H. Cline, W. Lorensen, and F. Jolesz, 1993. Computer-assisted three-dimensional planning in craniofacial surgery. *Plast. Reconstr. Surg.*, 92:576.

[48] Arridge, S., J. Moss, A. Linney, and D. James, 1985. Three dimensional digitization of the face and skull. *J. Maxillofac. Surg.*, 13:136.

[49] Moss, J., A. Linney, S. Grinrod, S. Arridge, and J. Clifton, 1987. Three-dimensional visualization of the face and skull using computerized tomography and laser scanning techniques. *Eur. J. Orthodont.*, 9:247.

[50] Cutting, C., J. G. McCarthy, and D. Karron, 1988. Three-dimensional input of body surface data using a laser light scanner. *Ann. Plast. Surg.*, 21:38.

[51] Vannier, M., T. Pilgram, G. Bhatia, and B. Brunsden, 1991. Facial surface scanner. *IEEE Comput. Graph. Appl.*, 17:72.

[52] Obwegeser, H., 1969. Surgical correction of small or retrodisplaced maxillae: The "dish-face" deformity. *Plast. Reconstr. Surg.*, 43:351.

[53] Converse, J., and D. Telsey, 1971. The tripartite osteotomy of the mid-face for orbital expansion and correction of the deformity in craniostenosis. *Br. J. Plast. Surg.*, 24:365.

[54] Adams, L., J. M. Gilsbach, W. Krybus, D. Meyer-Ebrecht, R. Mösges, and G. Schlondorff, 1990. CAS—a navigation support for surgery. In *3D Imaging in Medicine*. Berlin: Springer-Verlag, pp. 411–423.

[55] Kosugi, Y., E. Watanabe, J. Goto, T. Watanabe, S. Yoshimoto, K. Takakura, and J. Ikebe, 1988. An articulated neurosurgical navigation system using MRI and CT images. *IEEE Trans. Biomed. Eng.*, 35:147–152.

[56] Vander Kolk, C., S. Zinreich, B. Carson, N. Bryan, and P. Manson, 1992. An interactive 3D-CT surgical localizer for craniofacial surgery. In *Craniofacial Surgery*, A. Montoya, ed. Bologna, Italy: Monduzzi Editore, p. 25.

[57] Reinhardt, H. F., and H. J. Zwelfel, 1990. Interactive Sonar-operated device for stereotactic and open surgery. *Stereotactic Funct. Neurosurg.*, 54 + 55:393–397.

[58] Adams, L., A. Knepper, W. Krybus, D. Meyer-Ebrecht, G. Pfeiffer, R. Rueger, and M. Witte, 1991. Navigation support for surgery by means of optical position detection and real-time 3D display. *Proc. Comput. Aided Radiol. 91*.

[59] Taylor, R. H., C. B. Cutting, Y. Kim, A. D. Kalvin, D. Larose, B. Haddad, D. Khoramabadi, M. Noz, R. Olyha, N. Bruun, and D. Grimm, 1991. A model-based optimal planning and execution system with active sensing and passive manipulation for augmentation of human precision in computer-integrated surgery. In *Proceedings of the 1991 International Symposium on Experimental Robotics*, June 25–27. Toulouse, France: Springer-Verlag.

[60] McEwen, J. A., C. R. Bussani, G. F. Auchinleck, and M. J. Breault, 1989. Development and initial clinical evaluation of pre-robotic and robotic retraction systems for surgery. In *Proceedings of the Second Workshop on Medical and Health Care Robots*, International Advanced Robotics Program, Newcastle-on-Tyne, pp. 91–101.

[61] Taylor, R., J. Funda, D. LaRose, Y. Kim, N. Bruun, N. Swarup, C. Cutting, and M. Treat, 1992. A passive/

active manipulation system for surgical augmentation. In *Proceedings of the First International Workshop on Mechatronics*, Malaga, Spain, October.

[62] TAYLOR, R. H., A. PAUL, C. B. CUTTING, B. MITTELSTADT, W. HANSON, P. KAZANZIDES, B. MUSITS, Y. KIM, A. KALVIN, B. HADDAD, D. KHORAMABADI, and D. LaROSE, 1992. Augmentation of human precision in computer-integrated surgery. *Innovation Technol. Biol. Med.* 13(4): 450–468.

[63] CUTTING, C., R. H. TAYLOR, F. BOOKSTEIN, A. KALVIN, B. HADDAD, Y. KIM, M. NOZ, and J. McCARTHY, 1991. Comprehensive three-dimensional cephalometric system for the planning. In *Proceedings of the Fourth Biannual Meeting of the International Society of Cranio-Maxillofacial Surgery*, Santiago de Campostella, June 13–16.

53 Simulation of Surgical Procedures in the Craniofacial Region

LUDGER KLIMEK, HANS-MARTIN KLEIN, AND RALPH MÖSGES

THE SIMULATION of intervention into complex systems, for the purpose of risk evaluation, is standard in technologic science. It can be found as an integral part of pilot's training using flight simulators, as well as in the automobile industry. Such methods have not, as yet, gained popularity in surgical disciplines. This may be due in part individual anatomic variations that explain the necessity for models to be custom-made before any surgical procedure can be realistically simulated. The individual manufacture of suitable models incurs high costs and technical ability.

The basic information about the constructional components of the patient's anatomy is highly accurately achieved using modern tomographic imaging facilities such as high-resolution CT or MRI. Plastic skull models, crafted using milling techniques and computer-assisted manufacturing (CAM) methods are already commercially available. In orthopaedic surgery or facial reconstructive surgery of extensive bony defects, these methods are used to manufacture individual prostheses.

At Aachen University of Technology, different methods for manipulating 3D volume data on screen have been developed. The technique of stereolithography is used for the manufacture of custom-made plastic patient models. Moreover, computer-aided video montage is used prior to facial plastic surgery.

Problems at issue

An analysis of the operating site is essential for every preoperative plan. Intraoperative action demands the analysis and identification of structures adjacent to the pathologic site. Target points have to be defined and the trajectory of surgical instruments determined in regard to sensitive structures in their path.

Experienced surgeons will complete this simulation mentally. They will combine their knowledge of the normal anatomy in the region of interest with the individual results of the patient's previous physical examination and clinical status, adding knowledge gained by imaging methods. Processing of this information leads to the resulting individual case strategy.

Surgeons usually gain their knowledge of anatomy during medical school and specialty training by cadaver dissection, by studying surgical textbooks, and while assisting experienced colleagues in the operating room. The surgeon thus has a mental model of the region in question. This knowledge includes a certain number of anatomic norm variations. As it can never be possible to predict the patient's status, it becomes necessary to ascertain early individual's anatomy to preplan each surgical phase. For this purpose, clinical examination and the different imaging methods come into play.

All classic image representation techniques in medicine are disadvantaged by the fact that they reproduce only a 2D picture of 3D reality. Conventional x-rays produce a superimposed image of all visible structures. CT and MRI systems offer 2D cuts of the object examined. Potentially, all data concerning the 3D structure of an examined object can be obtained using a sequence of adjacent slices. Surgeons are used to reconstructing mentally the 3D information from the 2D tomographic images. However, a demand exists for 3D reconstructions to plan difficult procedures, especially in the fields of traumatology and tumor surgery of the head and neck. Surgery planning for complex surgical procedures in these fields can benefit from 3D models of the patient's individual anatomy [1–8]. Such reconstruction makes it much easier to "get the feel" of the mutual relationship of affected structures. Three-dimensional models are available either as monitor reconstructions or molded reproductions of the patient's anatomy.

Surgical planning on screen

Real simulation of an intraoperative procedure is attained only if suitable manipulation of the patient's model is possible, in anticipation of the procedure's course of events [9]. Fundamental manipulations of a 3D patient model [10] are as follows:

- Three-dimensional rotation and translation of parts or of the complete volumetric entity
- Calculation of cross-sections, either in the main axes or of any slice
- Cutting open a volumetric entity
- Measurements by way of model (distances, surfaces, and volume)
- Mirroring across any symmetric axis
- Enlargements and reductions in an object's size
- Removal of objects

Surgical planning in the true sense demands further manipulation of the patient model [10]:

- Definition of a cutaneous incision and path to lesion
- Interactive simulation of the effect of surgical instruments (forceps, suction, lasers, and ultrasonic disintegrators)
- Calculation of the effect of local change on the entire object
- Functional calculations (movement, oscillative properties)

For clinical application, a high rate of calculation is necessary to allow the manipulation of objects in real time. As of today, however, few medical workstations allow interactive real-time processing of a 3D patient model [11]. Processing of this type means the manipulation of a millionfold units of data per second, for which reason settled architecture is needed for the data-processing system itself [2, 8, 11–18]. We have examined the prerequisites and possibilities for such use, using both a PC-based system as well as the CAS-system's image-processing workstation.

MANIPULATION OF 3D SURFACE RECONSTRUCTIONS

Nearly all medical 3D reconstructions are based on sectional imaging techniques such as CT and MRI. There are several different concepts available for 3D recon-

struction of tomographic image data [6, 19–25]. We used a self-constructed PC-based system (80386/387, 33 MHz) for simple surface reconstructions of CT data. This system allows for further image manipulation for the purpose of actual operative planning with options for measurements. For data transport, a picture archiving and communication system (PACS) was used, as has been described by several groups [13, 26, 27].

Exemplarily, the planning of a reconstructive operation in a case of trauma with subsequent primary care shall be demonstrated. Image data were generated using a SOMATOM DRH computer tomograph (Siemens, Germany). Slice thickness and slice feed totaled 2 mm. Reconstruction of the preoperative site and image manipulation, with removal of dislocated fragments and a previously placed Paladur prosthesis, are shown in figure 53.1a. Repositioning of fragments and the implantation of a measured prosthesis were simulated. The defect first was symmetrically mirrored on its axis (figure 53.1b). Using the resulting data, a measured prosthesis was calculated and fitted into the defect (figure 53.1c).

SURGICAL PLANNING USING MULTIPLANAR 3D RECONSTRUCTIONS

The CAS system acts as an intraoperative localization aid [28]. Its intraoperative use is described in detail in chapter 51. The presently employed computer system is based on the VME-bus. The central processing unit (CPU) module is an Eltec Eurocom-5 equipped with an MC 68020 processor and 68681 coprocessor. The most important task of the CPU is the generation of the voxel model and the transformation of the coordinates of the 3D coordinate digitizer. For mass storage, 360-MB and 80-MB hard disks are used.

Capacity is sufficient for the storage of 128 CT or MRI images. As usual, the images are displayed in gray shades, whereas graphic and alphanumeric information—such as the coordinate digitizer's position or pull-down menus—are superimposed in arbitrary colors via a color look-up table.

For the display of the 3D model, special hardware was developed, the 3D coordinate transformer. It takes only 90 msec for the visualization of a 512^2 image, independent of the specific transform coefficients (angle of the sectional views, zoom factors, etc.). The system presents the operative field by three perpendicular sec-

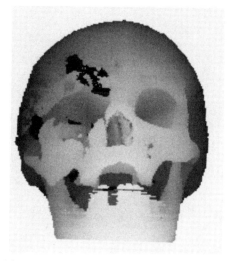

(a)

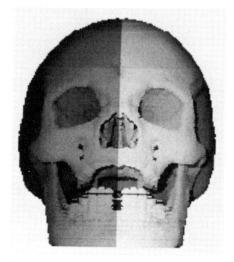

(b)

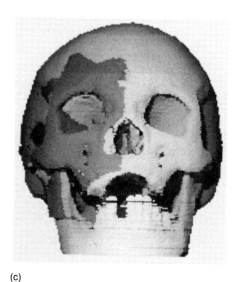

(c)

FIGURE 53.1 Planning a reconstructive procedure after surgery with insufficient primary treatment. Computer tomograph was made using a SOMATOM DRH (Siemens, Germany); 2-mm slice thickness, 2-mm slice feed. Reconstruction of the preoperative site with simulated removal of primarily placed Paladur prosthesis. (b) Axis-symmetric mirror image of opposite side. (c) View after simulated repositioning of fragments and fitting of custom-made prosthesis.

tional views through the volume of interest. The position of a measuring probe inside this volume is marked by a cross-hair cursor on each sectional view.

Both intraoperative imaging and preoperative surgical planning can gain substantially from this form of depiction. The system's high image frequency of 12 pictures per second is close to the eye's fusion frequency, making it possible to forge through the surgical field of operation. Viewing a visual surface in this manner, the dynamics of the images can supplant the third dimension. The corresponding perpendicular cross-sections complete the 3D model when static images are shown (figure 53.2).

In addition, optional oblique cuts through the 3D model are possible. Thereby the examiner can look into the operative site from all sides and in all layers. For better orientation in this kind of presentation, a 3D surface reconstruction is displayed. Application has shown that fading in this perspective view of

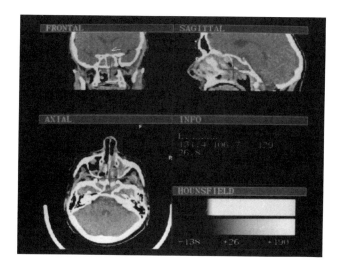

FIGURE 53.2 Depiction on a CAS screen of three orthogonal cross-sections (frontal, sagittal, and axial) in a patient with retrobulbar tumor.

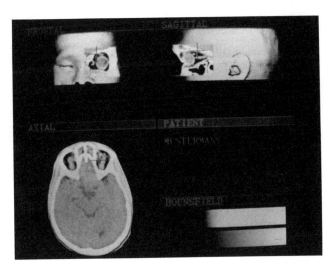

FIGURE 53.3 3D surface depiction on a CAS screen, with cutout of the region of interest (orbit).

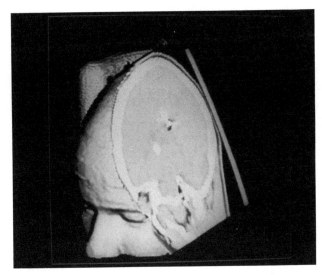

FIGURE 53.4 3D surface reconstruction, projected on a CAS screen in conjunction with contour depiction. This augmented surface view facilitates orientation if oblique cross-sections that have been chosen.

the patient's residual skull onto the sectional surface (figure 53.3) is helpful and eases orientation whenever a surgical incision is placed oblique to the main axes (figure 53.4).

Using the image workstation for presurgical planning, the measurement of any distance is possible. Aside from this easily operated basic function, zones of interest can be interactively changed. With the image-zoom function, the user can call up optional details enlarged on the monitor.

If the CAS system is placed in the operating room, every step of the surgical procedure can be simulated ahead of time on screen. In this case, a further option proved helpful, the so-called look-ahead function, which allows a preview into deeper-lying planes of view. The surgeon can request that a cut be shown that is beyond the actual surface being worked at, to view an area any distance away from the tip of the measuring probe. Thereby, the surgeon can visualize structures at certain distances ahead of his or her instrument with millimeter precision.

Easy handling of the interactive elements is critical if such systems are to become popular in preoperative planning. This is valid for the graphic user surface as well as for manipulative elements, such as mouse, trackball, joystick, or touch-screen. The CAS-system provides a Windows (Microsoft Corporation) user surface, which is easy to learn. A mouse with three keys is employed as the interface. Even computer-inexperienced surgeons will easily acquire handling procedures.

MODEL MANUFACTURING

The use of 3D images for preoperative surgical planning could be exhibited in numerous fields of study. A major benefit may be an improved perception of complex bony relationships. Logical sequelae of 3D representation is the manufacture of custom plastic models, using batch files of 3D organ reconstructions [12, 29–32].

Plastic models for preoperative simulation of the procedure are produced using the CAM technique. CAM also requires that a mathematic volume model of the object be manufactured with the image model, to serve as source data for steering the fabricating device. Especially in bony skull defects, individual prostheses are manufactured exactly according to the defect. This individual prosthesis manufacturing may be the most important area of application for CAM in plastic surgery of the head. Thus far, milling machines have been used to produce skull models or implant prostheses, but milling tools have limited abilities to reproduce complex anatomic structures. Even if five-axis milling systems are used, the problem of collisions between tool and object is not yet controlled.

For several years, a few companies have been offering model manufacturing services using CT batch files [33, 34]. The object is crafted of polyurethane foam by a multiaxis, computer-controlled milling apparatus.

Steering data for the mill is derived from the 3D object's zone coordinates. However, the exactness of models produced in this manner is limited by several factors. The use of easily milled but very porous and soft polyurethane foam allows great inexactness. Furthermore, undercutting as well as collision between milling apparatus and object are problems inherent in the manufacture of complex milled objects. In turn, no milling application is more complex than the crafting of basal skull regions.

Here an alternative is offered by stereolithography. With stereolithography, arbitrary models can be produced by stratifying thin layers with the highest accuracy. This technique has only lately been inaugurated into medical use. However, it has already found widespread application in manufacturing [35]. A liquid plastic monomer is polymerized in layers by an ultraviolet laser and is hardened. Using the laser beam in this procedure, an $x - y$ scanner traces the vectors of the structures computed earlier from the CT information. The hardened layer is lowered on a platform into a vat, where it is overlaid with a fine polymer layer, which again is being traced by the laser beam in conformity with the given path, and where it is hardened. In this way, a finely worked model is produced [35, 36].

A variety of unit systems for stereolithography are obtainable from various commercial suppliers. We use a unit from 3D Systems (Darmstadt, Germany) that has been set up for the manipulation of data from the industrial arena, especially computer-aided design (CAD). The maximum length of the object edges is 254 mm (10 inches). The ultraviolet laser operates at a wavelength of 325 nm, and its "life span" is a minimum of 2000 operating hours.

Unfortunately, there are still no routinely established production methods available for stereolithographic techniques in medicine. Therefore, we have developed hardware and software components with which to interface to tomographic imaging systems such as CT and MRI [36]. First, the conversion into an object-oriented representation is necessary, as is usual in CAD. In a so-called slicing technique, a series of slices is computed from these data sets, and it is conveyed to the actual control computer of the lithographer random-access memory [35].

A great variety of plastic materials already are available for the manufacturing process. The photohardening ability of the material is the determining factor in whether the stereolithography technique can be used. Polymers, chemical urethanes, epoxy resins, or polycarbonates that have been modified using acrylic groups, as the latter can be easily combined and may form polymers by activated photoreactions, are the plastic materials most commonly used to date [35].

The clinical advantage of the system can be explained using the example of a 10-year-old patient who suffered from a congenital melanotic neuroectodermal tumor located in his upper jaw on the right side. The size of the temporarily inoperative, locally aggressive tumor was reduced by radiochemotherapy in the first year of life. At the age of 1 year, complete resection of the tumor was performed [37]. The resulting large bony defect was temporarily covered by a polymethyl methacrylate prosthesis (Palacos). A stereolithographic model has been prepared for planning the reconstructive plastic reoperation.

Altogether, 79 CT scans were created and reconstructed in 3D (figure 53.5a). The segmentation required for the reconstruction was automatically performed using density thresholds for the osseous parts. Differentiation between alloplastic implant and bone must be effected interactively on screen.

The time spent computing the surface of the child's skull as the basis of the transfer to the stereolithography computer totaled 70 minutes. Subsequent slicing (single-slice computation) took nearly 59 hours. An immediate dependence on the size of the available operational store and processing speed, which has had a superproportional impact on objects with a data volume of more than 2 MB, had appeared in preliminary trials. For geometrically true preparation of filiform structures, the instability of the model existing during the polymerization must be taken into account. To get any deformations under control, computation of adequate supporting structures is required. Subsequent model manufacturing took another 60 hours.

The created model of the cranial bone and the alloplastic prosthesis revealed excellent detail retention and dimensional accuracy (figure 53.5b). Using the individual skull model of the child, the reconstructive procedure could be highly accurately prepared.

The individual manufacture of custom prostheses and implants to cover bony defects using stereolithographic techniques could be of great importance in the future. The tissue compatibility of different plastic monomers is the subject of current investigations among several groups.

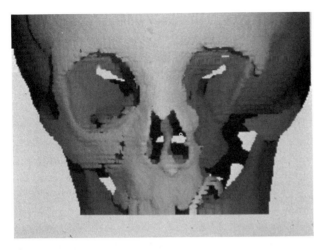

(a)

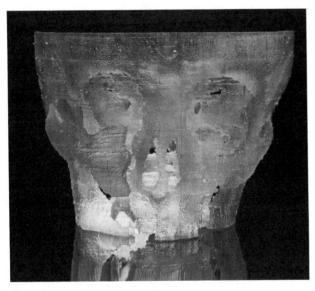

(b)

FIGURE 53.5 (a) Planning an operative revision after prior tumor resection. 3D reconstruction after simulated removal of original prosthesis. (b) Stereolithographic model of same patient, prior to plastic reconstruction of defect.

COMPUTER-ASSISTED VIDEO MONTAGE

Especially in facial plastic surgery, it is desirable to demonstrate the expected result (i.e., the postoperative appearance) to the patient before the procedure. For a long time, only verbal explanations, sketches, and photomontages were available for this purpose, although these were largely abstract. Computer-assisted processing of video data has opened new vistas for patient information. Using video montage, the corrections are made on a patient's video still picture that anticipate the desired surgical result with astonishing realism. The patient can express his or her expectations concerning facial portions to be changed more concisely. The system consists of readily available components: a VHS Camcorder and an Apple Macintosh-2 computer with video interface [38].

To begin, a video batch file of the patient's frontal and side aspect is recorded by the Camcorder. The image data are relayed to a personal computer. A static frontal as well as side picture of the patient is chosen from the image series. Using this portrait, prospective surgical steps can be easily and quickly acted out by means of a menu-controlled electronic mouse. This can be done in a few minutes, in cooperation with the patient. Possible corrections the patient may desire can be taken into account, and directly integrated into the operative therapy.

This system has been experimentally used prior to nasal plastic surgery (figure 53.6). However, for medicolegal reasons, such systems remain problematic. Can the patient sue, on the grounds of an unfulfilled contract, if the simulated result could not be accomplished? For this reason, we do not use this system routinely.

Discussion

Facial plastic surgery is predestined as a field for operative preplanning using 3D depiction and model manufacture because of the complexity of anatomic structures involved. Valuable information for therapeutic planning can be gained by simple manipulation such as cutting out, moving, exchanging, enlarging, or enhancing the contrast of object portions on monitor reconstructions. In addition, structures in a certain area can be measured.

Complex simulations, such as the effect of surgical instruments on different tissue types or the results of vessel ligation, are not yet possible with the CIS methods now in use. Currently, the most realistic surgical simulation is possible on plastic models of a patient's skull. The operative procedure and effects of partial action on the surgical result can be judged realistically using such plastic models.

At present, the models are being manufactured by two methods mainly—the milling technology and stereolithography. The tools used in milling operations generally have limited capabilities of motion, which

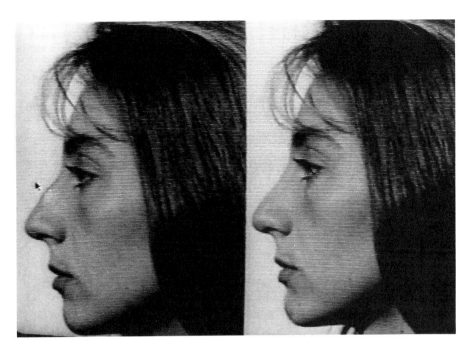

FIGURE 53.6 Video simulation of the operative result after facial plastic surgery. Left frame shows video still picture of patient's face; right frame depicts simulation of prospective nasal plastic surgery.

essentially depend on the number of axes available. With an increase in the degrees of freedom, the complexity of path control will increase to a superproportional degree. Utmost precision with complicated structures is required for medical applications. There is no currently foreseeable solution to the problems of milling operations.

Stereolithography imposes on the user far fewer restrictions regarding the object geometry. For the first time, it has thus become possible to construct closed cavities such as paranasal sinuses, middle and inner ear structures, and the complete internal anatomy in an all-enclosed cranium. Our trial appears promising for true-to-scale reproductions of bony structures. However, the reproduction of complex soft tissue does not appear to be possible in the near future.

One can surmise that practical simulation will become as popular in surgical training of the future as it is now in routine aviation. Quality control with consequences for physicians' licensing is conceivable, by way of repeated practice of surgical skills using such simulators. Skill with such simulators may even be an element of general course requirements for relicensing.

ACKNOWLEDGMENTS Primary tomographic information for the reconstructions shown was generated by the Department of Diagnostic Radiology (Prof. R. Günther, M.D., Director) and Department of Neuroradiology (Prof. A. Thron M.D., Director). Technical prerequisites for the clinical use of CAS systems were made possible by Dr.-Ing. W. Krybus, Dipl.-Ing. L. Adams, and Dipl.-Ing. R. Rüger of the Institute of Technical Measurements, Aachen (Prof. Dr. Ing. Meyer-Ebrecht, Institute Director). CAS research was sponsored with funds from the Ministry of Science and Research, State of North-Rhine-Westfalia (proj. no. IV. B7-400 098 86) and Federal Ministry of Research and Technology (proj. no. 01 KN 88012). For the support of current system improvements, we thank the following companies: Karl Storz, Tuttlingen, and Bodenseewerk Gerätetechnik GmbH Überlingen.

REFERENCES

[1] GREVERS, G., C. WILIMZIG, T. VOGL, and G. LAUB, 1990. Weiterentwicklung der 3D-KST-Rekonstruktionstechnik im Kopf-Hals-Bereich. *Laryngorhinootologie* 69:653–656.
[2] HEMMY, D. C., D. J. DAVID, and G. T. HERMAN, 1983. Three-dimensional reconstruction of craniofacial deformity using computed tomography. *J. Neurosurg.* 13:534–541.
[3] MARSH, J. L., M. W. VANNIER, W. G. STEVENS, J. O. WARREN, D. GAYOU, and D. M. DYE, 1985. Computerized imaging for soft tissue and osseous reconstruction in the head and neck. *Clin. Plas. Surg.* 12:297–291.
[4] McSHAN, D. L., A. SILVERMAN, D. M. LANZA, L. E. REINSTEIN, and A. S. GLICKMAN, 1979. A computerized three-dimensional treatment planning system using interactive color graphics. *Br. J. Radiol.* 52:478–481.

[5] SCHAD, L. R., R. BOESECKER, W. SCHLEGEL, G. HART-MANN, V. STURM, L. G. STRAUSS, and W. J. LORENZ, 1987. Three dimensional image correlation of CT, MR, and PET studies in radiotherapy treatment planning of brain tumors. *J. Comput. Assist. Tomogr.* 11(6):948–954.

[6] SCHELLHAS, K. P., M. EL DEEB, C. H. WILKES, R. K. CHECK, J. W. LARSEN, K. B. HEITHOFF, and H. M. FRITTS, 1988. Three-dimensional computed tomography in maxillofacial surgical planning. *Arch. Otolaryngol. Head Neck Surg.* 114:438–442.

[7] VANNIER, M. W., J. L. MARSH, and J. O. WARREN, 1983. Three-dimensional computer graphics for craniofacial surgical planning and evaluation. *Comput. Graph.* 17:263–274.

[8] ZINREICH, S. J., 1988. 3-D CT for cranial, facial and laryngeal surgery. *Laryngoscope* 98:1212–1219.

[9] WEISBURN, B., A. S. PATNAIK, and L. L. FELLINGHAM, 1986. An interactive graphics editor for 3D surgical simulation. *Proc. SPIE Conf. PACS* 4:483–485.

[10] MÖSGES, R., 1992. Die Methodik computergestützten Operierens dargestellt am Beispiel Hals- Nasen- Ohrenärztlicher Eingriffe. Habilitation Thesis, RWTH: Aachen Technical University.

[11] AMELING, W., 1989. Digitale Bildverarbeitung in der Medizin, Texturanalyse und 3D-Rekonstruktion. *Biomed. Tech.* (Berlin) 34:1–7.

[12] DEV, P., L. L. FELLINGHAM, A. VASSILIADIS, S. T. WOOLSON, D. N. WHITE, and S. L. YOUNG, 1986. 3D graphics for interactive surgical simulation and implant design. *Proc. SPIE Conf. PACS* 507:52–57.

[13] FASEL, B., F. VOSSEBÜRGER, and D. MEYER-EBRECHT, 1989. High speed networks for PACS—introduction and comparison. In *CAR '91: Computer Assisted Radiology,* H. U. Lemke, M. L. Rhodes, C. C. Jaffee, and R. Felix, eds. Berlin: Springer, pp. 557–580.

[14] HERMAN, G. T., and H. K. LIU, 1979. Three-dimensional display of human organs from computed tomograms. *Comput. Graph. Image Proc.* 9:1–21.

[15] JANICKE, S., W. WAGNER, F. SCHWEDEN, and P. MEINZER, 1990. 3-D imaging of the skull base: A critical comparison of different techniques illustrated by clinical cases. *Rev. Neuroradiol.* 3(Suppl. 4):24.

[16] UDUPA, J. K., 1982. Interactive segmentation and boundary surface formation for 3D digital images. *Comput. Graph. Imag. Proc.* 18:213–235.

[17] UDUPA, J. K., 1986. Computerized surgical planning: Current capabilities and medical needs. *Proc. SPIE Conf. PACS* 4:474–482.

[18] UDUPA, J. K., G. HERMAN, 1991. *3D Imaging in Medicine.* Boca Raton, Fla.: CRC Press.

[19] AMELING, W., 1985. Digitale Bildverarbeitung und Echokardiographie. 3D-Rekonstruktion und Texturanalyse. *Fortschr. Echokardiogr.,* 3–15.

[20] HÖHNE, K. H., 1987. 3D-Bildverarbeitung und Computer-Graphik in der Medizin. *Info Spek* 10:192.

[21] ROBB, R. A., and C. BARILLOT, 1989. Interactive display and analysis of 3-D medical images. *IEEE Trans. Med. Imag.* 8(3):217–226.

[22] SCHNEIDER, W., 1989. *Verfahren zur Erzeugung, Veränderung und Darstellung von dreidimensionalen Modellen natürlicher Objekte.* Heidelberg: Dr. Alfred Hüthing Publishers.

[23] SCHUBERT, R., W. J. HÖLTJE, U. TIEDE, K. H. HÖHNE, 1991. 3D-Darstellung für die Kiefer- und Gesichtschirurgie. *Radiologe* 31:467–473.

[24] TOENNIES, K. D., G. T. HERMAN, and J. K. UDUPA, 1989. Surface registration for the segmentation of implanted bone grafts. In *CAR '89: Computer Assisted Radiology,* H. U. Lemke, M. L. Rhodes, C. C. Jaffee, and R. Felix, eds. Berlin: Springer, pp. 381–385.

[25] TUY, H. K., and J. K. UDUPA, 1983. Representation, display and manipulation of 3D discrete scenes. In I. K. Udupa, ed. *Proceedings of the Sixteenth Hawaii International Conference on System Sciences 2,* Springer, New York, 397–406.

[26] ASTINET, F., M. LANGER, A. KERN, W. ZENDEL, O. GUCKELBERGER, and R. FELIX, 1991. PACS—experiences and future developments. In *CAR '91: Computer Assisted Radiology,* H. U. Lemke, M. L. Rhodes, C. C. Jaffee, and R. Felix, eds. Berlin: Springer, pp. 398–406.

[27] INOUYE, T., 1985. Research and development activities towards computer assisted radiology in Japan. In *CAR '85,* Computer Assisted Radiology, H. U. Lemke, M. L. Rhodes, C. C. Jaffee, and R. Felix, eds. Berlin: Springer, pp. 623–627.

[28] SCHLÖNDORFF, G., R. MÖSGES, D. MEYER-EBRECHT, W. KRYBUS, and L. ADAMS, 1989. CAS (computer assisted surgery) ein neuartiges Verfahren in der Kopf- und Halschirurgie. *HNO* 37:187–190.

[29] ALDINGER, G., A. FISCHER, and N. KURTZ, 1984. Computergestützte Herstellung individuell anatomischer Endoprothesen. *Z. Orthop.* 122:733.

[30] ALDINGER, G., and A. WEIPERT, 1991. 3D-basierte Herstellung von Hüftgelenken: Das Aldinger-System. *Radiologe* 31:474–480.

[31] RHODES, M. L., Y. M. AZZAWI, E. S. CHU, W. V. GLENN, and S. L. G. ROTHMANN, 1985a. Anatomic model and prosthesis manufacturing using CT images. In *Proceedings of the NCGA: Networks Computer Graphics and Application Conference.* In: M. L. Rhodes, ed. Mosby, St. Louis, 3:110–124.

[32] RHODES, M. L., Y. M. AZZAWI, E. CHU, A. T. PANG, W. V. GLENN, and S. L. G. ROTHMAN, 1985b. A network solution for structure models and custom prostheses manufacturing from CT data. In *CAR '85: Computer Assisted Radiology,* H. U. Lemke, M. L. Rhodes, C. C. Jaffee, and R. Felix, eds. Berlin: Springer, pp. 404–411.

[33] KLIEGIS, U., R. NEUMANN, T. KORTMANN, W. SCHWESIG, R. MITTELSTÄDT, H. WEIGEL, and W. ZENKER, 1989. Fast three-dimensional visualization using a parallel computing system. In *CAR '89: Computer Assisted Radiology,* H. U. Lemke, M. L. Rhodes, C. C. Jaffee, and R. Felix, eds. Berlin: Springer, pp. 747–751.

[34] SCHMITZ, H. J., T. TOLXDORFF, J. HONSBROCK, T. FRITZ, and U. GROSS, 1989. 3D-based computer assisted manufacturing of individual alloplastic implants for cra-

nial and maxillofacial osteopiastles. In CAR '89: Computer Assisted Radiology, H. U. Lemke, M. L. Rhodes, C. C. Jaffee, and R. Felix, eds. Berlin: Springer, pp. 390–393.

[35] CIESLAK, W., 1988. Stereolithographie. Grenzen und Möglichkeiten einer neuen Technologie. *Laser Magazine 3.*

[36] KLEIN, H. M., W. SCHNEIDER, J. NAWRATH, T. GERNOT, E. D. VOY, and R. KRASNY, 1992. Stereolithographische Modellfertigung auf der Basis dreidimensional rekonstruierter CT-Schnittbildfolgen. *Fortschr. Röntgenstr.* 156.

[37] VOY, E. D., and R. MERTENS, 1984. Neue therapeutische Aspekte beim seltenen, sogenannten kongenitalen melanotischen Ektodermaltumor im Kiefer-Gesichts-Bereich. *Fortschr. Kiefer Gesichtschir.* 31:76–79.

[38] SCHMELZER, B., B. WAELKENS, P. CAUWENBERGE, and R. MÖSGES, 1991. Computer-gesteuerte Videomontagen zur Operationsvorbereitung bei plastischen Kopf- und Halseingriffen. *Arch. Otorhinolaryngol. Suppl.* 2:311.

54 Craniofacial Surgical Planning and Evaluation with Computers

MICHAEL W. VANNIER, JEFFREY L. MARSH, AND
ALEXANDER TSIARAS

COMPUTERS ARE USED more frequently for surgery today than at any time in the past. We predict that the future role of computers in surgery will expand until their contribution to the success of many procedures is essential. Students who enter the medical profession today will never know a time without computers in surgery. They will accept the technology and enhance it beyond our modest ambitions; much of the change will occur during our lifetimes and even before the start of the coming century.

The use of computers for surgical planning began with orthopaedic and craniofacial applications more than 10 years ago. The diagnosis and treatment of craniofacial disorders are based to a significant degree on radiologic imaging, especially CT and MRI. In the past 10 years, digital computer-based 3D reconstruction imaging of CT and, more recently, MRI scans has become a valuable tool for the evaluation of craniofacial deformities. The computer graphics methods that serve as the basis for 3D reconstruction imaging have evolved rapidly, and dramatic improvements in terms of image quality, efficiency, versatility, ease of use, and reduction in the cost of systems have been realized. Virtually all modern CT and MRI scanners possess some form of 3D reconstruction imaging capability, and manufacturers now offer a wide range of products in this area. The acceptance of these systems for study of craniofacial anomalies is widespread. These intrinsically quantitative 3D imaging methods have enabled the development of objective measurement protocols for the study of skull form and volume change.

Computer-based imaging for simulation surgery implies graphic display and manipulation of anatomy, typically derived from volumetric medical imaging methods such as CT and MRI. This process closely parallels that of flight simulation for training of pilots, battlefield simulation for modern armies, and visual

entertainment in television and motion pictures by special effects generation. In fact, medical researchers in simulation surgery have borrowed heavily from technology developed originally for engineering, training, and entertainment applications. This trend will continue, and laboratory curiosities will become available as tools for the surgeon. It is becoming less and less important today that the operator of medical simulation systems be knowledgeable and skilled at the intrinsics of the hardware and software he or she uses. User-friendly graphic interactive interfaces between humans and computers, often considered as a vital part of virtual reality systems, will have a central role in surgical simulation systems of the future. Surgery is nearing the end of its beginning, and we will not soon see the beginning of the end in the development of this technology and its applications.

Surgical planning

The planning of surgical procedures has become practical because critical pathologic information is now available preoperatively, principally as a consequence of CT and MRI (Fujino, 1992). These techniques are effective in gathering high-contrast volumetric data with resolution at or below the surgeon's ability to perform operative manipulations. Many surgical procedures may use, but do not require, such extensive preoperative planning. The ability of current imaging methods to classify and discriminate pathologic soft tissues is good but not excellent; with present technology, imaging is not entirely reliable in distinguishing neoplastic or infected tissues from adjacent normal structures that are indirectly altered. In addition, many soft-tissue structures are continuously deformable and can change significantly from the time that they are imaged to the time when operative interventions take place. In addition, their size, shape, and orientation changes during the operative intervention, so that images can be used only as a general guide to document the preoperative size, position, and relationship of tissues (Adams et al., 1990).

Despite these limitations, there are cases where surgical planning with geometric precision is both desirable and effective. The first real applications of quantitative surgical planning were in orthopaedic cases, but the use of 3D scanning for evaluation of craniofacial anomalies has stimulated rapid development and adoption of computerized surgical planning hardware and software. Craniofacial deformities are uncommon and often complex anomalies, both developmental and acquired in origin, that affect an individual's facial appearance and can interfere with normal function (Vannier and Marsh, 1992). The principal goal of craniofacial surgical intervention is normalization of facial appearance; the procedures are based on the premise that normalization of underlying skeletal anatomy will result in normal or approximately normal facial appearance.

The planning of these surgical procedures has traditionally been based on cephalometric radiographs obtained with a standardized imaging fixture under controlled conditions. The substitution of CT for cephalometric skull radiography became practical when high-quality 3D reconstructions of the skull could be obtained with suitable geometric accuracy, typically imprinted on hard copy in a life-size film format. In much the same way, cephalometric radiographs and life-size CT reconstruction images are used to develop measurements that then are employed in procedures to aid in the displacement or reorientation of the facial skeletal components after they have been freed from their normal attachments through osteotomies.

The planning processes for other surgical procedures that are formally planned—including stereotactic procedures, especially in neurosurgery, placement of custom implants in orthopaedic surgery, and other similar scenarios—parallel the planning of craniofacial surgical procedures. The technology to support these activities includes a means of gathering geometrically precise and accurate volumetric data, an interactive display and manipulation workstation or computer system, a means of interactively manipulating the images and separating them into component parts, reference standards for normative measurements, and a means of documenting the results of the procedure,

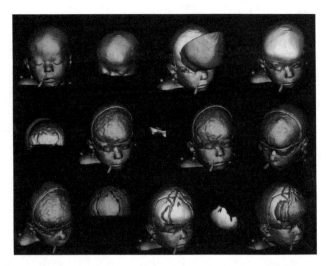

FIGURE 54.1 Surgical planning for orbital advancement in patient with unicoronal synostosis. The frontal bone has been removed to expose the dura. The affected ipsilateral harlequin orbit has been advanced to achieve symmetry with the "normal" contralateral orbit. Skull recontouring has been done with onlay of the fragmented frontal bone. This figure outlines the steps involved in the surgical correction of this unilateral skull deformity. The images were obtained using CT scans and volumetric rendering on a Silicon Graphic workstation. The surgical procedure was simulated in a stepwise fashion, in much the same way it is conducted in the operating room.

usually in hard copy on film, print, or transparency (Vannier, Marsh, and Warren, 1984).

Display and manipulation workstations

Interactive workstations are becoming commonplace in research laboratories where images are handled. This technology has been adapted for use in the planning and evaluation of surgical procedures through the development of visualization software augmented by specific tools that allow interactive manipulation of CT and MRI data volumes and their separation into multiple subvolumes that can be moved with respect to one another (Fujioka, 1988; Yasuda, Yokoi, and Toriwaki, 1988). Specific tasks that are analogous to the maneuvers used by surgeons in their intraoperative manipulation of the patient can be accomplished using these interactive tools (Marsh, Vannier, and Stevens, 1985; Cutting et al., 1986).

The workstations are tied to a computer network that transmits CT or MRI scan data into their local storage. The first step, typically, is resampling and iso-

674   CRANIOFACIAL SURGERY

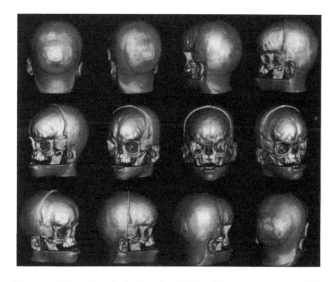

FIGURE 54.2 Surgical plan for child with syndromal cranio-synostosis and hypotelorism, including bimaxillary osteotomies, separation of both orbits, and exposure of the frontal dura. The frontal bone has been removed to reveal the dura covering the frontal lobes of the brain. All of the skin and facial musculature covering the facial bones has been removed and the orbits exenterated to reveal the underlying skull surface.

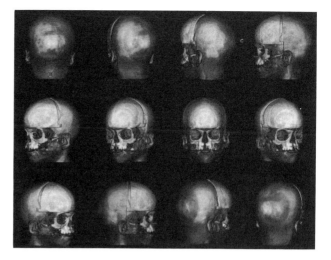

FIGURE 54.3 The surgical plan for the procedure to correct the hypotelorism has been performed and the frontal bone replaced. Note that the orbits are now separated and tilted to obtain a more normal relationship.

tropic representation of the data. A threshold is set and there is surface display of the patient's external soft-tissue surface; at a higher threshold setting, the underlying skeletal components can be extracted. The workstations provide a platform on which software tools are implemented and applied to the discrete volumetric voxel data sets that represent the preoperative scans from the patient. The workstations allow definition of subvolumes, displacement of individual subvolumes with respect to one another, and visualization of intermediate results at each step in the procedure (Vannier, Marsh, and Warren, 1983; Schellhaus et al., 1988).

This application is analogous to the use of engineering workstations in computer-aided design (CAD) and computer-aided manufacturing (CAM). Each design engineer makes use of a set of interactive tools to manipulate the size, shape, and relationship of individual discrete objects and object assemblies. The computer maintains a complete mathematical representation of the objects and assemblies in a mathematically precise form. The representation of data in the CAD/CAM environment is an important determinant of the ultimate functionality of these units. In particular, modern CAD/CAM systems all incorporate some form

of solid modeling, usually using boundary representation or a hybrid representation for internally stored objects and their various components and attributes. The engineer is able to perform a large range of manipulations on the stored objects, permitting an almost unlimited range of shapes to be generated. The ultimate result of the CAD/CAM process is a final, discrete manufactured object or object assembly.

Simulation of surgical procedures closely parallels this work and, in some instances, an amalgam of CAD/CAM and computer visualization or medical computer graphics software has been adapted to the specific needs of simulated surgery. The principal reasons for not employing CAD/CAM systems directly in medicine include the fact that medical data sets consist primarily of volumetric data that generally do not possess regular, well-defined subobjects or surfaces. Medical image data are irregular and very highly detailed, with structure at every level from the most minute resolution element, the individual voxel, to groups of voxels in the entire scanned object. In addition, human soft tissue is continuously deformable and not easily modeled using the rigid constructs that are typically incorporated in CAD/CAM systems.

Modeling

The modeling of biologic objects, and especially body regions or individual organs, is an essential step in the

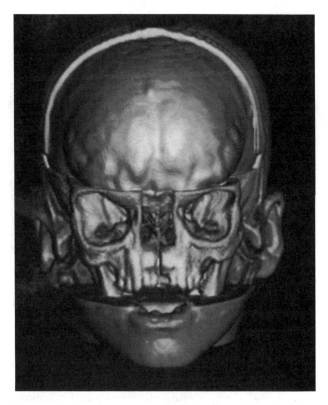

FIGURE 54.4 An enlargement of the frontal surgical plan shows the detailed anatomy and complex geometry of the facial skull.

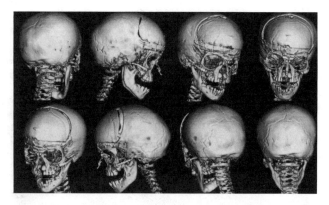

FIGURE 54.5 Actual postoperative 3D CT skull reconstruction images (same case as figure 54.2) after bilateral orbital translocation and frontal bone recontouring. Bone plate fixation has been used frontally, at the orbital margins, and at both zygomata. Postoperative 3D CT scanning permits comparison of the surgical results with the preexisting plan for verification and validation.

planning of craniofacial or orthopaedic or other types of surgery (Zonneveld et al., 1989; Vannier and Marsh, 1992). We can represent a body region mathematically with an internally stored database, and this data can be rendered onto a display screen for interactive analysis, hard-copied as individual images on film, replicated as a physical 3D object. In some cases, the representation of the object scanned, typically voxels, must be altered through resampling or surface extraction to achieve a representation suitable for the intended manipulations. The transformation of solid-object representations is implemented but carries specific limitations and drawbacks. The principal concern with biologic objects derives from their high dimensionality, the presence of noise within the measurements, partial volume averaging, and the presence of a high degree of structure and irregularity at all resolution levels.

Mathematical modeling is typically performed using a hybrid solid modeler that uses both voxel and boundary representations. Typical boundary representations are either of the *nurbs* (nonuniform rational b-splines)

or *faceted* (usually as planar polygons such as triangles) type. The voxel representation is closest to the original form of CT or MRI data and is well suited to the needs of biomedical surface or volumetric display methods. The nurbs or exact representation of surfaces is mathematically precise and efficient, especially for regularly shaped regions or objects. Nurbs representations have desirable mathematical properties that allow interactive manipulation and efficient storage and computations. Faceted boundary representations are amenable to computer graphics display using interactive workstations. Modern interactive design and display computer graphics systems incorporate special hardware that accelerates the display list processing of planar polygons, giving remarkable performance that cannot be achieved for interactive applications in near real time by any other representation. As a consequence of the trade-offs among volumetric, faceted, and nurbs formats, we are often faced with the problem of maintaining multiple internal representations of the same object to enjoy the advantages of each.

Physical modeling of objects has been demonstrated using subtractive milling techniques with standard multiaxis machine tools (Alberti, 1980; Brix, Hebbinghaus, and Meyer, 1985; Zonneveld et al., 1991; Kärcher, 1992) or through rapid prototype manufacturing using techniques such as stereolithography (Lill et al., 1991; Wolf, Lindner, and Ewers, 1992). Many examples of biomedical objects have been manufactured and applied in selected instances. The applications of physical models include the use of life-size replicas of scanned objects such as a patient's skull to perform mock surgery or as a teaching device, and the fabrication of custom implants or appliance (Zonneveld and Noorman van der Dussen, 1992). The principal drawbacks associated with physical modeling are the cost, complexity, and time required to produce highly detailed life-size objects.

Conclusion

Virtually any surgical procedure can be simulated; however, this does not imply that the simulation will be accurate, complete, or useful, or that it can be accomplished efficiently. In fact, simulation of a surgical procedure can be more complex, awkward, and difficult than the procedure itself, especially when the surgeon involved has relatively little computing experience.

ACKNOWLEDGMENTS The collaboration and assistance of Steven Senft, Ph.D., Robert H. Knapp, B. M., R. T., Roberta Yoffie, R. T., and Barry Brunsden are gratefully appreciated. The work was supported in part by the National Institute of Dental Research grant NIH-DE08909.

REFERENCES

ADAMS L., W. KRYBUS, D. MEYER-EBRECHT, et al., 1990. Computer-assisted surgery. *IEEE Comput. Graph. Appl.* 5: 43–50.

ALBERTI, C., 1980. Three-dimensional CT and structure models. *Br. J. Radiol.* 53:261.

BRIX, F., D. HEBBINGHAUS, D. MEYER, 1985. Verfahren und Vorrichtung für den Modellbau im Rahmen der orthopädischen und traumatologischen Operationsplanung. *Röntgenpraxis* 38:290.

CUTTING, C., F. L. BOOKSTEIN, B. GRAYSON, et al. Three-dimensional computer-assisted design of craniofacial surgery procedures: Optimizations and interaction with cephalometrics and CT-based models. *Plast. Reconstr. Surg.* 77:877–885.

FUJINO, T, ed., 1992. *Proceedings of the Inagural Congress of the International Society for Simulation Surgery.* Kanagawa, Japan: Keio University.

FUJIOKA, M., S. YOKOI, T. YASUDA, Y. HASHIMOTO, J. TORIWAKI, H. NAKAJIMA, 1988. Computer-aided interactive surgical simulation for craniofacial anomalies based on 3D surface reconstruction CT images. *Radiat. Med.* 6: 212–214.

KÄRCHER, H. Three dimensional craniofacial surgery: Transfer from a three-dimensional model (Endoplan) to clinical surgery: A new Technique (Graz). *J. Craniomaxillofac. Surg.* 20:125–131.

LILL, W., P. SOLAR, C. ULM, M. MATEJKA, 1991. CT-assisted three-dimensional modeling of the maxillofacial region: Reproducibility and applications. *Z. Stomatol.* 88(2): 77–84.

MARSH, J. L., M. W. VANNIER, W. G. STEVENS, 1985. Computerized imaging for soft tissue and osseous reconstruction in the head and neck. *Plast. Surg. Clin. North Am.* 12: 279–291.

SCHELLHAS, K. P., M. EL DEEB, C. H. WILKES, et al., 1988. Three-dimensional computed tomography in maxillofacial surgical planning. *Arch. Otolaryngol. Head Neck Surg.* 114:438.

VANNIER, M. W., J. L. MARSH, 1992. Craniofacial imaging: Principles and applications of three-dimensional imaging. *Lippincott's Reviews: Radiology* 1(2):193–209.

VANNIER, M. W., J. L. MARSH, J. O. WARREN, 1983. Three-dimensional computer graphics for craniofacial surgical planning and evaluation. *Comput. Graphics* 17:263–273.

VANNIER, M. W., J. L. MARSH, J. O. WARREN, 1984. Three-dimensional CT reconstruction images for craniofacial surgical planning and evaluation. *Radiology* 150:179–184.

WOLF, H. P., A. LINDNER, R. EWERS, 1992. Konstruktion eines 3-dimensionalen Schaedelmodelles aus CT-Scans mittels Stereolithographie. *Z. Stomatol.* 89:10.

YASUDA, T., S. YOKOI, J. TORIWAKI, 1988. A simulation system for brain and plastic surgeries using CT images. In *Proceedings of the Ninth International Conference on Pattern Recognition,* Rome, pp. 1282–1286.

ZONNEVELD, F. W., S. LOBREGT, J. C. H. VAN DER MEULEN, et al. 1989. Three-dimensional imaging in craniofacial surgery. *World J. Surg.* 13:328f.

ZONNEVELD, F. W., M. F. NOORMAN VAN DER DUSSEN, 1992. Three-dimensional imaging and model fabrication in oral and maxillofacial surgery. *Oral Maxillofac. Surg. Clin. North Am.* 4(1):19–33.

ZONNEVELD, F. W., M. F. NOORMAN VAN DER DUSSEN, U. KLIEGIS, P. F. G. M. VAN WAES, 1991. Volumetric CT-based model milling in rehearsing surgery. In *Proceedings CAR '91,* H. U. Lemke, M. L. Rhodes, C. C. Jaffe, and R. Felix, eds. New York: Springer, pp. 347–353.

Radiotherapy

FOR THE MAJORITY of tumor patients, cancer therapy entails radiotherapy, either as the primary therapeutic modality or in conjunction with surgery or chemotherapy. Radiotherapy is not surgery in the strictest sense. Usually no blood is shed; sterility often is not a problem; and there is no surgeon who leaves the battlefield with the confidence of having gained another victory over an evil disease. Yet terms such as *radiosurgery* and *gamma knife* are commonly used, and many of the underlying planning and registration problems are very similar to those for more mechanical forms of CIS. For these reasons, we have chosen to include a section with some recent developments in radiotherapy.

Radiotherapy can be carried out in two ways: as external radiotherapy, using fractionated irradiation or single-dose delivery as in radiosurgery, or as brachytherapy, to destroy the tumor by close contact with radioactive seeds. Brachytherapy, in turn, may be applied using an intracavitary or interstitial approach. Only in the latter case is sterility an issue. However, most elements of the radiotherapy chain are identical for all methods. Therefore, considerations concerning patient fixation, treatment planning, the transfer of treatment parameters to the patient, and patient positioning apply to both external radiotherapy and to brachytherapy. For the actual radiation treatment, however, different image-guided computer-assisted methods have been developed. The so-called afterloading technique for brachytherapy is discussed briefly by Kall (chapter 25). Refined patient positioning and increased accuracy for the placement of one or more hollow probes containing the ionizing material can be achieved with the help of a localizer. A description of

the procedure and the clinical results obtained with this method can be found in Mösges et al. (1991).

In "Requirements in Computer-Assisted Radiotherapy," Schlegel has analyzed requirements for computer assistance in external radiotherapy. Two major difficulties exist: geometric precision and computational performance. Increased precision is needed for the detection of the position of the patient during imaging and during irradiation. Localizers with real-time capability can improve the reproducibility of fractionated radiotherapy. Treatment planning should be performed in 3D, including the simulation of the therapeutic process and its visualization. New treatment techniques such as conformal external radiotherapy can improve the exact delivery of the required dose to the target volume. Linking the elements of the radiotherapy chain by computer integration could significantly improve treatment for the majority of cancer patients.

In the second chapter of this section, "Motion Planning in Stereotaxic Radiosurgery," Schweikard, Adler, and Latombe describe an interactive system to assist radiosurgeons in planning radiation beam therapies. This is one specific solution to the "inverse dosimetry problem" delineated previously by Schlegel: how to deliver a calculated dose to a target volume without irradiating healthy tissue beyond tolerance. The system does not automatically optimize beam paths. Instead, it leaves it up to the radiotherapist to choose which treatment plan to follow out of several proposals based on 2D imaging. The software has been evaluated using clinical cases as references. The results demonstrate that planning time can be reduced and energy deposition can improve. However, it seems necessary to link all elements of the radiotherapy chain into an integrated software system.

The integration of preoperative imaging, planning, and intraoperative registration is the topic of the chapter by Troccaz et al., "Conformed External Radiotherapy." The authors describe a method using a mechanical localizer that carries an ultrasound probe for precise registration of the target with the reference system of the accelerator. The automatic registration of the patient model based on preoperative images with intraoperative sonography represents a major advance.

The preoperative model is created by automatic 3D segmentation that adapts to complex topology. With intraoperative movement of the probe, a set of equations is created for 3D/3D registration, permitting conformal irradiation to be performed. The system is now entering clinical evaluation.

REFERENCE

Mösges, R., B Korves, J. Ammon, and B. Kremer, 1991. Computer-assisted positioning for after-loading with iridium 192. *HNO*, pp. 429–432.

55 Requirements in Computer-Assisted Radiotherapy

WOLFGANG SCHLEGEL

WHEN ANALYZING further possibilities for the improvement of cancer therapy, it has to be considered that for approximately 18% of cancer patients (i.e., for 265,000 patients per year in Europe) the inability to control the locally growing tumor is the cause of death. Currently, there are two major reasons for the failure in local tumor control:

1. There may be a *geometric miss* of parts of the target volume, resulting in a partial underdosage in radiotherapy and a subsequent tumor recurrence proceeding from the underdosed area. Geometric misses may be caused not only by incomplete knowledge of the shape of the tumor and of tumor extensions, but also by patient movement during irradiation and by the inability to position the patient accurately at the irradiation unit (figure 55.1).

2. Depending on the location and the shape of the tumor, it may be impossible to reach a radiation dose in the tumor volume that is sufficiently high to kill all tumor cells. The reason for such an underdosage on the whole is that radiosensitive healthy tissue existing in the neighborhood of the tumor would be overdosed if a sufficiently high dose were applied to the whole tumor volume. Irreparable damage to this sensitive healthy tissue would occur and cause severe side effects. The problem exists especially for radioresistant tumors in the neighborhood of radiosensitive organs (figure 55.2).

The problem of achieving cure free from side effects can be understood by considering the relationship between the applied radiation dose, the tumor control probability (TCP), and the normal tissue complication probability (NTCP), as shown in figure 55.3. When higher doses in the target volume can be achieved while at the same time sufficiently sparing organs at risk, it should be possible to reach significantly higher probabilities for complication-free survival for those patients suffering from local cancer disease (Suit et al., 1988). The required procedure is an irradiation technique that results in a dose distribution closely matching the shape of the target volume (figure 55.4). Such techniques are called *conformal radiotherapy*. The feasibility of conformal radiotherapy requires the optimization of all processes of the radiotherapy chain.

The chain of radiotherapy: Current practice and future requirements

Radiotherapy can be thought of as a chain consisting of different independent processes (figure 55.5). To increase the probability of patient cure, we must optimize all these processes; this can be achieved using computer assistance. This chapter describes the current state of the art in radiotherapy and discusses the requirements for the optimization of the various steps it involves.

Patient fixation systems

To obtain undistorted, artifact-free tomographic images that can later be used for the detection of tumor volume and for dose planning, imaging must be performed with the patient immobilized. Furthermore, a radiotherapy treatment of a tumor can be effective only if the irradiation beam hits the tumor tissue throughout the entire irradiation procedure. Displacement between tumor geometry and irradiation field, caused by misalignment of the patient or by movement during irradiation, may cause severe underdosage of the tumor tissue or overdosage of neighboring anatomic structures. Especially for radiotherapy with high doses, adequate fixation systems are extremely important.

For the head and neck region, numerous fixation systems have been developed in recent years that ensure patient immobilization to a greater or lesser extent (see, e.g., Graham et al., 1991; Schlegel et al., 1992; figure 55.6). To improve repositioning of the patient and to minimize patient movement during irradiation,

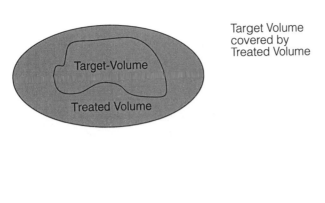

Target Volume covered by Treated Volume

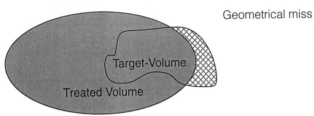

Geometrical miss

FIGURE 55.1 The problem of geometric miss of the target volume: If parts of the target volumes are missed (due to incomplete detection of the target volume, to errors in locating, positioning, and irradiating the target, or to patient movement during irradiation), tumor recurrences may evolve from the underdosed area.

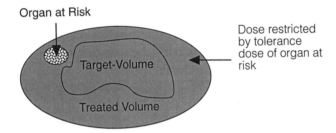

Organ at Risk

Dose restricted by tolerance dose of organ at risk

FIGURE 55.2 The problem of underdosage on the whole: In many cases, radiosensitive tissues (organs at risk) are close to the target volume. Conventional radiotherapy techniques often result in an inclusion of the organ at risk in the treatment volume, thus limiting the absolute dose that can be applied to the tumor tissue.

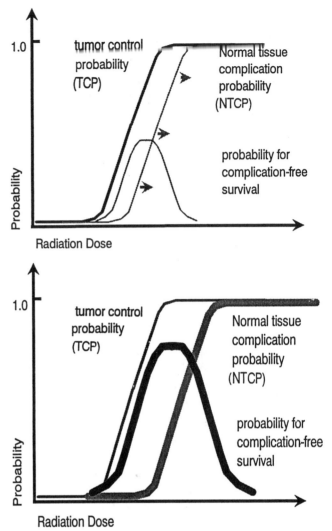

FIGURE 55.3 If the dose to the tumor tissue is increased, the probability for local tumor control (TCP) also increases along a sigmoidal curve. On the other hand, the probability that side effects will occur (NTCP, normal tissue complication probability) will simultaneously increase. The probability of complication-free tumor control is a product of TCP and (1 − NTCP). The resulting function shows a maximum at a certain dose. (b) The maximum probability for complication free tumor control can be raised, if the NTCP curve is shifted to the right. This can be achieved by improved sparing of critical tissues.

computer vision methods have recently been developed and are now undergoing experimental and clinical evaluation (Menke, Mack, and Schlegel, 1993). Complete immobilization for the treatment of brain tumors still can be achieved only with stereotactic frames, which are invasively screwed to the patient's skull. The disadvantage of fixation with stereotactic frames, however, is that the fixation cannot be reproduced from day to day within a fractionated radiotherapy procedure. The radiobiological advantages of fractionated irradiation thus cannot be utilized. For other parts of the body, patient fixation is even more difficult than for the head and neck region; satisfying solutions are still completely lacking.

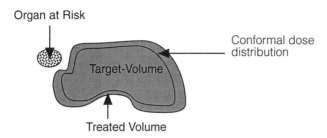

Organ at Risk

Conformal dose distribution

Target-Volume

Treated Volume

FIGURE 55.4   Conformal treatment techniques result in a spatial dose distribution which closely matches the shape of the target volume. Organs at risk are spared, even if they are nearby, and the dose to the target volume can be raised.

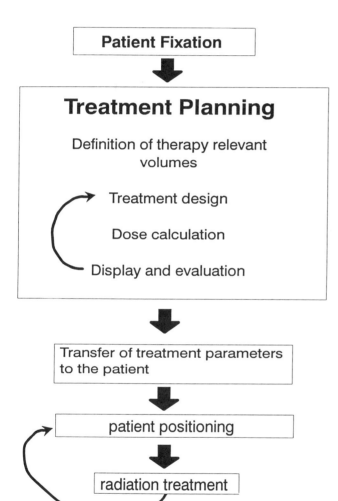

Patient Fixation

Treatment Planning

Definition of therapy relevant volumes

Treatment design

Dose calculation

Display and evaluation

Transfer of treatment parameters to the patient

patient positioning

radiation treatment

FIGURE 55.5   Radiotherapy can be considered as a chain of independent processes. There are two loops in this chain: The processes of treatment design, dose calculation and dose display and evaluation has to be repeated, until the dose distribution is optimized. The processes of patient positioning and irradiation has to be repeated 20–30 times. Such a fractionation gives normal tissue a better chance to recover from radiation exposure.

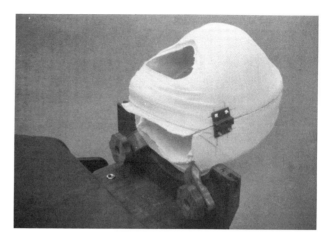

FIGURE 55.6   Relocatable patient fixation system for the irradiation of tumors located in the head and neck area.

TREATMENT PLANNING

DEFINITION OF THERAPY-RELEVANT VOLUMES   There are two classes of therapy-relevant volumes: target volumes and organs at risk (Landberg, 1993; Quast, 1993).

Gross tumor volume, clinical target volume, and planning target volume   The target volume concept as used in radiotherapy has recently been revised (Landberg et al., 1992; figure 55.7). The radiotherapeutic planning process starts with the detection of the location, form, and extent of the gross tumor volume (GTV), which by definition is the gross palpable or visible or demonstrable extent and location of malignant growth. Clinical experience indicates that around the GTV there is generally subclinical involvement—that is, individual malignant cells, small cell clusters, or microextensions —that cannot be detected by the staging procedure. The GTV and this surrounding volume of local subclinical involvement together make up the clinical target volume (CTV). To ensure that all tissue included in the CTV will receive the prescribed dose, one must irradiate a geometrically larger volume than the CTV. The probability of movements of the tissue containing the CTV as well as movements of the patient and variations in beam geometry characteristics has led to the concept of the planning target volume (PTV). After the identification of the GTV, the radiotherapist must define the PTV. PTV definition is problematic because it requires an estimation of the importance of the possible variations in the selected beam arrangement, as

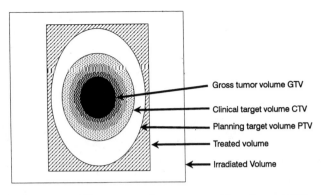

Gross tumor volume GTV

Clinical target volume CTV

Planning target volume PTV

Treated volume

Irradiated Volume

FIGURE 55.7   The target volume concept (Landberg, 1993).

well as consideration of anatomic location, the use of immobilization devices, and so forth.

Organs at risk   Organs at risk (OARs) are normal tissues whose radiation sensitivity may significantly influence treatment planning. According to their radiation sensitivity, OARs are subdivided into three classes: those where radiation lesions are fatal (class I), moderate (class II) or mild (class III). In addition, for treatment optimization the type of organ function (parallel or serial) must be taken into account.

Requirements in the definition of therapy-relevant volumes
The importance of the definition of therapy-relevant volumes in radiotherapy must not be underestimated. Tumor tissue that is not included the target volume will be underdosed with high probability; organs at risk that are not taken into account during this process probably will not be considered in the evaluation of treatment plans and will eventually be overexposed. Errors or approximations made during this step will strongly influence the effectiveness of treatment planning and the outcome of the whole radiotherapeutic process.

In modern radiotherapy planning systems, methods of digital image manipulation, image processing, locating, viewing, and comparison of the many images associated with a patient, and especially image segmentation tools are still insufficient or even missing. For future systems, improved methods of tissue characterization will be needed during the phase of determination of the clinical target volume and of the planning target volume. In this context, the physiologic and biochemical basis of MRI suggests that it will be more useful than CT for displaying GTVs and defining CTVs

for certain radiotherapy patients, most notably those with central nervous system involvement (Bradley et al., 1984). However, MRI may be severely lacking in geometric accuracy (Schad, Lott, et al., 1987); such accuracy is, of course, critical in precision radiotherapy planning. The inability of MRI to provide electron density information is a second important impediment to the usefulness of MRI, used alone, radiotherapy planning. Because the use of CT used planning avoids the latter two limitations, the best way to make use of the exceptional imaging capabilities of MRI is to integrate MRI with CT-assisted radiotherapy planning (Fraas and McShan, 1987; Schad, Boesecke, et al., 1987). Therefore, 3D image registration methods, which allow radiotherapists to combine MRI, CT, PET, and DSA imaging within the process of target definition, are an important tool.

The precise 3D geometry of therapy-relevant volumes must be included in the treatment planning process. The commonly used method for extracting this 3D information is interactive manual segmentation of CT or MR scans. The number of images comprising a 3D image used for 3D radiotherapy planning may vary from 20 to 60. As many as 10 or perhaps even more structures may need to be outlined on each of these images. This segmentation process requires enormous effort to be expended for each patient. To make the process easier and faster, 3D image segmentation and modeling tools that are as automated as possible must be developed and included in treatment planning systems. A research project funded by the European Community (COVIRA, computer vision in radiology) is currently focusing on this demand (Elliott, Knapman, and Schegel, 1992). An example of a user interface for an advanced 3D image segmentation program is shown in color plate 41.

TREATMENT DESIGN   Once the anatomic structures of interest have been delineated and modeled in 3D, the best possible directions from which to aim radiation beams at the target volume must be selected. To concentrate the radiation dose to the target volume while sparing other regions, it is necessary to direct multiple beams of radiation from various angles at the target to permit the best possible separation between the target volume and critical structures. The so-called beam's-eye view technique (Goitein and Abrams, 1983) provides an effective computer graphic tool for selecting optimum directions, sizes, and shapes of beams by projecting 3D anatomic information into a coordinate system defined according to the geometry of the beam. The result is the representation of contours outlining the patient's anatomic structures in 3D perspective as if they are being viewed from the source of radiation along the central ray of the beam.

With the help of 3D computer graphics, it is possible to match the shapes of the beams to the target volume from every incidence angle, to ensure that critical organs will not be touched by primary beams over the whole length of the irradiation field (see plate 42). Especially for this phase of therapy planning, an appropriate user interface is essential.

Realizing the potential benefits of 3D computer graphics for the radiotherapy simulation process will require software that performs a superset of the functions used in conventional practice while retaining the ambience of the traditional methods. For the process of treatment design, a system must be used that faithfully reproduces the function and the feel of a physical simulator so that an experienced radiotherapist can use the system with essentially no retraining (Sherouse and Mosher, 1987; Bendl et al., 1993). Some special requirements should be considered.

DOSE CALCULATION   After treatment techniques have been defined, the irradiation dose within the patient must be calculated according to the physical laws of interaction of radiation with matter. Numerous algorithms have been developed in the past for calculating the irradiation dose within the patient's body, on the basis of more or less empiric models. Prerequisite for these calculations is the accurate knowledge of the physical beam characteristics of the irradiation units, the patient's geometry, and the distribution of electron densities within the human body. As has been pointed out previously, the individual patient-related parameters (geometry and electron densities) can be extracted with high accuracy from CT data only. A remaining problem is that most dose calculation methods either are inaccurate (causing dose calculation errors in irregularly shaped fields or inhomogeneous media of up to 10%–15%) or are much too slow for practical use (Schlegel, 1985). This latter problem can arise when computers with insufficient performance capability are used.

Thus one important requirement for the future is the development of better models for dose calculation in radiotherapy (Ahnesjö, 1993; Bortfeld, Schlegel, and

Rhein, 1993). Furthermore, there is a need for modeling the physical effects of radiation on tissue for situations that cannot be assessed by dosimetric measurements. Dose calculation methods based on the Monte Carlo simulation are the solution for that problem; however, the speed of such calculations has still to be increased by a factor of 1000 to be of value for clinical application.

DISPLAY AND EVALUATION OF TREATMENT PLANS   To confirm that a certain treatment technique will lead to the desired result (complete dose coverage of the target volume, sparing of organs at risk), dose calculation results must be displayed and evaluated quantitatively. For large target volumes it can sometimes be difficult even for an experienced radiotherapist to select the best of several competing treatment plans, even if consideration is given to the dose distribution in only one or a few planes. The selection process becomes far more difficult if the entire spatial distribution of the radiation dosage is to be considered in judging the merits of a given plan. If the analysis must be done on a slice-by-slice basis, the radiation oncologist can be overwhelmed by the amount of data that must be assimilated.

Current systems rarely have the ability to display all the data needed to develop a 3D plan in one image (see plates 43, 44). Such techniques could be very valuable in understanding 3D dose distributions. Methods to display simultaneously 3D dose distributions and the relevant anatomy are being investigated (Schlegel et al., 1992; Bendl et al., 1993; Schiemann et al., 1993).

It is obvious that all the steps in radiotherapy involve a degree of uncertainty, of which the radiotherapist should be aware when judging a certain treatment plan. Thus, in addition to the problem of 3D display of target volumes, organs at risk, and neighboring anatomic structures and that of 3D dose distribution, another important issue will be the visualization of the uncertainties of the treatment procedure (e.g., caused by dose calculation uncertainty, the inability to reproduce patient position, or patient movement during the treatment).

QUANTITATIVE EVALUATION AND BIOLOGICAL TREATMENT PLANNING   Users ask for treatment planning systems providing at least quantitative evaluation of dose distributions by calculating minimum and maximum dose levels, integral doses, or dose volume histograms in the target volume or organs at risk (Becker et al.,

1989; Becker and Bamberg, 1993). Quantitative parameters must be defined in order to describe the quality of a treatment plan. Knowledge-based systems are needed to provide information concerning doses tolerated by certain healthy tissue structures and for mapping of morphology and radiotolerance data onto individual 3D patient images.

OPTIMIZATION The conventional way of finding an optimal treatment plan is *forward planning*: During a treatment planning session, the definition of the treatment technique, calculation of dosage, and evaluation of treatment plans are repeated until an acceptable plan has been found (figure 55.8). In clinical practice, all optimizations of treatment plans are currently performed by such an interactive trial-and-error procedure. Cumbersome interactions and extremely long dose calculation times often prevent the user from carrying out many iterative steps and may lead to inadequate plans.

If the optimum treatment for an individual patient is to be determined by iterative optimization, the time required for each iteration loop must be minimized. The need for short calculation times (with the aim of real-time response in dose calculation) urgently motivates the further acceleration of dose calculation in radiotherapy planning. Geometric preoptimization definition of objective functions and fast dose calculation have to be combined to form a self-optimizing treatment planning system that requires only minor interactive corrections by the radiotherapist.

For target volumes with convex shapes that are not too close to organs at risk, it will not be difficult for an experienced planner to define conformal treatment techniques. In most cases, multiple fixed-field treatment techniques with irregularly shaped beams will lead to a good result. However, problems arise in target volumes with concave shapes. It has been shown that horseshoe-shaped target volumes, for example, can be treated with dynamic techniques such as using biaxial moving beam techniques combined with dynamic field shaping, or using eccentric moving beams. However, trial-and-error planning for such cases is a heuristic and very time-consuming approach, making the performance of therapy very cumbersome. It is clear that such techniques will never be accepted in clinical practice.

A completely different approach to conformal treatment planning, especially for complex-shaped targets,

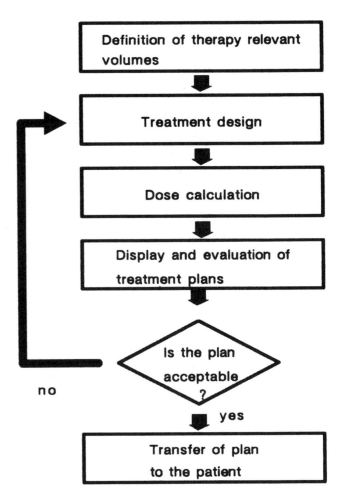

FIGURE 55.8 The principle of iterative optimization in radiotherapy treatment planning (forward planning).

has recently been suggested by Brahme (1988). This approach is called *inverse planning* (figure 55.9). In inverse planning not only is the shape of the collimator adapted to the target contour in every position of the gantry, but the intensity also varies within the beams. A simple example of the irradiation problem presented by concave-shaped target volumes, as shown in figure 55.10, demonstrates that irradiation beams with non-uniform intensity may be used to solve the problem. The question in such cases, however, is how the beam intensity modulation can be determined for a given target volume of arbitrary shape and a given number of stationary beams. Practical solutions for the calculation of the intensity modulation functions were proposed first by Brahme, using a convolutional approach, and later by Webb (who used the optimization method of simulated annealing [Webb, 1989]) and by Bortfeld

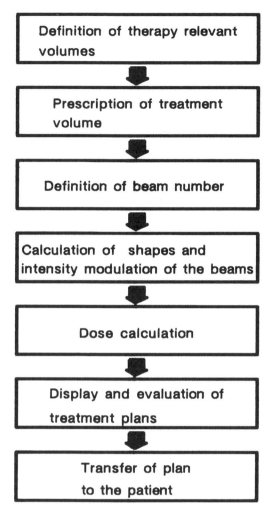

Definition of therapy relevant
volumes

⬇

Prescription of treatment
volume

⬇

Definition of beam number

⬇

Calculation of shapes and
intensity modulation of the beams

⬇

Dose calculation

⬇

Display and evaluation of
treatment plans

⬇

Transfer of plan
to the patient

FIGURE 55.9   The principle of inverse planning.

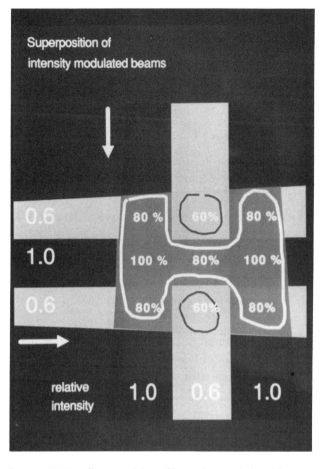

Superposition of
intensity modulated beams

0.6   80 %   60%   80 %

1.0   100 %   80%   100 %

0.6   80%   60%   80%

relative
intensity   1.0   0.6   1.0

FIGURE 55.10   Superposition of intensity-modulated beams, showing that intensity modulation can be used to create conformational dose distributions as well as for target volumes with concave shape.

et al. (who applied 3D image reconstruction methods to conformation radiotherapy in analogy to CT [Bortfeld et al., 1990]). An open question is how the intensity-modulated beams will be generated in practice. Scanning beams or dynamic compensators would fulfill the requirements but are not yet available (Schlegel, 1993).

TRANSFER OF TREATMENT PARAMETERS TO THE PATIENT

Once treatment planning is accomplished, it is of great importance that the parameters defined during the treatment planning phase be accurately reproduced while the patient is actually irradiated. Current systems scarcely support the radiotherapist as far as this transfer of treatment planning parameters to the

patient is concerned. Radiotherapists commonly use anatomic landmarks within the images as a geometric reference; often these markers cannot be accurately reproduced and therefore cause errors of up to several centimeters (Blanco, López-Bote, and Desco, 1987; Reinstein and Meek, 1987). Correlation of digital reconstructed radiographs (either from CT or MRI) with x-ray simulation radiographs and treatment verification films could be used to solve this problem.

For radiotherapy of lesions in the head and neck region, the more precise technique of stereotactic localization and positioning is used (Schlegel et al., 1992). As in stereotactic neurosurgery, a patient-related 3D coordinate system must be introduced that can be accurately reproduced, either on the basis of artificial or favorably anatomic landmarks. The coordinates of the

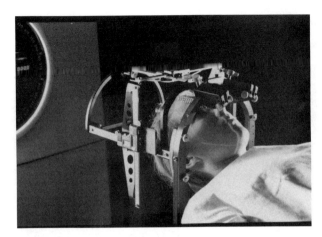

FIGURE 55.11 Stereotactic positioning of a patient at a linear accelerator for sterotactically guided radiosurgery. The patient's head is fixed in a stereotactic frame (Riechert-Mundinger System) and the isocenter is adjusted with the help of a stereotactic target positioner using laser indicators.

isocenter can then be calculated during treatment planning and accurately adjusted at the linear accelerator, for example with the help of stereotactic target positioners (figure 55.11).

TREATMENT TECHNIQUES

One result of the introduction of 3D treatment planning systems has been a change from the conventional coplanar treatment techniques to techniques with a more complex irradiation geometry. Two features of 3D radiotherapy should be emphasized: *field shaping* and *noncoplanar radiation geometry*.

Field shaping is made possible by *multileaf collimators* (MLCs), which allow irradiation beams to be shaped to the form of the target volume. There are MLC systems available that are adjusted manually according to templates corresponding to the shape of the tumor from different viewing angles according to the "beam's-eye view," and there are computer-controlled MLC systems that are adjusted electronically according to the precalculated beam contours (figure 55.12). MLC-equipped irradiation units are just now becoming available, and it is anticipated that MLCs will become a standard feature of radiotherapy, tremendously facilitating conformal therapy in the near future (Webb, 1993).

For a long time, radiotherapy made use only of beams that were perpendicular to the patient's longitudinal axis. The reason for this restriction was that in

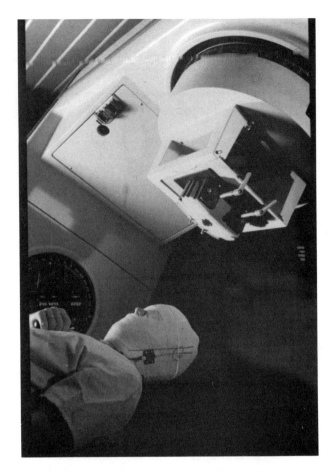

FIGURE 55.12 Treatment situation for a patient treated with conformational high-precision radiotherapy. The manual multileaf collimator is attached to the accessory holder of the Linac and adjusted to the precalculated shape of the target volume.

conventional 2D planning it was not possible to calculate dose distributions for longitudinal oblique beam incidence. The second important technique that is enabled by 3D treatment planning is that of *noncoplanar beam geometry*. For many tumor locations, noncoplanar techniques are much better suited to spare organs at risk than are coplanar techniques (Schlegel, 1993). The *convergent beam technique* makes extensive use of such noncoplanar beams (figure 55.13). Many fixed or moving beams enter the body from many different oblique directions and cross in the target volume. With such an irradiation geometry, a very high dose with a steep dose gradient to surrounding healthy tissue can be reached (Hartmann et al., 1985). This technique is also the basis of *radiosurgery*, a technique using small circular or irregularly shaped moving beams to administer a

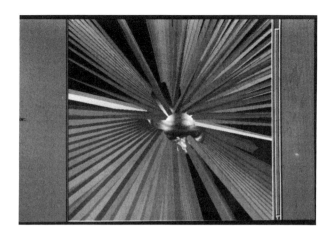

Figure 55.13 Observer's-eye view of a convergent beam irradiation technique showing the beam geometry of 126 beams being distributed over a hemisphere. The beams have a common intersection point at the isocenter that is assumed to coincide with the center of the tumor.

high dose to a circumscribed brain lesion in a single session with the help of stereotactic fixation and guidance systems.

Conclusions

The field of computer-assisted radiology has a major impact on medical diagnostics: The advanced tomographic imaging systems such as CT and MRI, which are based on computer technology, have initiated a revolution in medical imaging, enabling earlier and more differentiated recognition of disease processes, especially Malignancies. Radiotherapy up to now has been relatively neglected as attention has focused on the sensational achievements of diagnostic imaging. In this context, it should be emphasized that patients will benefit from improved diagnostics only if efficient therapies can be offered that are able to cure the detected disease. Therefore, we should concentrate our efforts on the application of modern computer technology to the field of radiotherapy. It can be expected that computer-aided radiotherapy will significantly contribute to improved quality of life for cancer patient. For those patients suffering from locally growing tumors, the introduction of advanced computer-aided planning and irradiation techniques is the only short-range prospect with a high probability of improving cure rates.

For these goals to be reached, however, all processes involved in the radiotherapy chain must be analyzed

and optimized. The most urgent problems in this context can be summarized as follows:

1. To improve the precision of radiotherapy, especially for tumors located in the body, advanced fixation, positioning, and verification tools must be developed. Satisfying solutions can be expected only from system that combine the ability to reproduce the patient's position with the ability to detect and correct patient movement and organ movement during the irradiation. Development of such systems will be achievable only by integration of real-time imaging techniques into the irradiation procedure.

2. A large portion of radiotherapy treatment planning will have to be performed in 3D in the future; thus, 3D imaging modalities as CT and MRI must be considered an indispensable prerequisite in this context. The new and exciting developments in 3D medical imaging must be completely integrated into the radiotherapy chain to achieve a more refined definition of target volumes and organs at risk. The resulting improved information about malignant growth and surrounding healthy anatomic structures will provide a much more realistic basis for computer-assisted treatment planning. Real-time 3D simulation of the irradiation geometry, faster and more precise dose calculation algorithms, and new optimization tools will result in the determination of safer and more effective treatment techniques.

3. The immobilization and patient positioning problem has been solved in an elegant way for tumors in the brain and the head and neck region by applying stereotactic fixation and positioning methods. However, these methods cannot be applied for all other tumor sites. The missing link between computer simulation and the treatment situation itself is probably the weakest point in the radiotherapy chain. X-ray radiotherapy simulators are only a subjective tool and cannot fill this gap unless the digital imaging methods and image-matching processes of simulator images and digital reconstructed radiographs are introduced to make the transfer of planning parameters to the patient a more objective process. Utilizing the imaging capability of the radiotherapy beam itself, real-time electronic portal imaging will be the method of choice in the future, providing an interface between treatment planning and the treatment and serving as a verification tool for patient positioning and dose delivery.

4. Computer-controlled conformal treatment techniques enabling the safe and reproducible delivery of

improved physical dose distributions will complete the radiotherapy chain.

Radiotherapy of the near future will be performed as a computer-controlled, conformal, 3D procedure that comprises solutions to all the problems discussed in this chapter. Because nearly 50% of all cancer patients are undergoing radiotherapy, many thousands of patients every year could benefit from such comprehensive computer-assisted radiotherapeutic procedures.

ACKNOWLEDGMENTS I gratefully acknowledge contributions of my colleagues Jürgen Proß (plate 41), Rolf Bendl (plates 42, 44 and figure 55.13) and Otto Pastyr (figure 55.11 and 55.12).

REFERENCES

AHNESJÖ, A., 1993. Dose calculation methods for multidimensional treatment planning. In *Three-Dimensional Treatment Planning*, P. Minet, ed. Liège: European Association of Radiology, pp. 277–288.

BECKER, B., and M. BAMBERG, 1993. Design of a medical expert system for biological radiotherapy planning. In *Three-Dimensional Treatment Planning*, P. Minet, ed. Liège: European Association of Radiology, pp. 213–220.

BECKER, G., R. LOHRUM, T. WERNER, J. BÜRKELBACH, G. NÉMETH, R, BOESECKE, W. SCHLEGEL, and W. J. LORENZ, 1989. Presentation and evaluation of 3D dose distributions in radiotherapy planning. In *Computer-Assisted Radiology: CAR '89*, H. U. Lemke, ed. Berlin: Springer, pp. 254–261.

BENDL, R., J. PROSS, M. KELLER, J. BÜRKELBACH, and W. SCHLEGEL, VIRTUOS: A Program for VIRTUal radiotherapy simulation. In *Computer-Assisted Radiology: CAR '93*, H. U. Lemke, ed. Berlin: Springer, pp. 676–682.

BLANCO, S., M. A. LÓPEZ-BOTE, and M. DESCO, 1987. Quality assurance in radiation therapy: Systematic evaluation of errors during the radiation execution. *Radiother. Oncol.* 8: 256–261.

BORTFELD, T., J. BÜRKELBACH, R. BOESECKE, and W. SCHLEGEL, 1990. Methods of image reconstruction from projections applied to conformation radiotherapy. *Phys. Med. Biol.* 35:1423–1434.

BORTFELD, T., W. SCHLEGEL, and B. RHEIN, 1993. Decomposition of pencil beam kernels for fast dose calculations in three-dimensional treatment planning. *Med. Phys.* 20:311–318.

BRADLEY, W. G., V. WALUCH, R. A. YADLEY, and R. R. WYCOFF, 1984. Comparison of CT and MR in 400 patients with suspected disease of the brain and cervical spinal cord. *Radiology* 152:695–702.

BRAHME, A., 1988. Optimization of stationary and moving beam radiation therapy techniques. *Radiother. Oncol.* 12: 129–140.

ELLIOTT, P. J., J. M. KNAPMAN, and W. K. SCHLEGEL, 1992. Interactive image segmentation for radiation treatment planning. *IBM Systems J.* 31:620–634.

FRAAS, B. A., and D. L. McSHAN, 1987. 3-D Treatment Planning: Overview of a clinical planning system. In *The Use of Computers in Radiation Therapy*, I. A. D. Bruinvis, ed. Amsterdam: North Holland, pp. 273–276.

GOITEIN, M., and M. ABRAMS, 1983. Multi-dimensional treatment planning: I Delineation of anatomy. *Int. J. Radiat. Oncol. Biol. Phys.* 9:777–787.

GRAHAM, J. D., A. P. WARRINGTON, S. S. GILL, and M. BRADA, 1991. A noninvasive relocatable stereotactic frame for fractionated radiotherapy and multiple imaging. *Radiother. Oncol.* 21:60–62.

HARTMANN, G. H., W. SCHLEGEL, V. STURM, B. KOBER, O. PASTYR, and W. V. LORENZ, 1985. Cerebral radiation surgery using moving field irradiation at a linear accelerator. *Int. J. Radiat. Oncol. Biol. Phys.* 20:1185–1192.

LANDBERG, T. G., A. WAMBERSIE, J. CHAVAUDRA, J. DOBBS, G. HANKS, K. A. JOHANNSON, T. MÖLLER, J. PURDY, A. AKANUMA, J. P. GERARD, J. C. HORIOT, and N. SUNTHARALINGAM, 1993. Definitions of volumes. In *Three-Dimensional Treatment Planning*, P. Minet, ed. Liège: European Association of Radiology, pp. 7–16.

LANDBERG, T. G., A. WAMBERSIE, J. CHAVAUDRA, J. DOBBS, G. HANKS, K.-A. JOHANNSON, T. MÖLLER, J. PURDY, A. AKANUMA, J.-P. GERARD, J.-C. HORIOT and N. SUNTHARALINGAM, eds. 1994. Prescribing, recording and reporting beam therapy, ICRU Report No. 50.

MENKE, M., T. MACK, and W. SCHLEGEL, 1993. Modification of planned 3D dose distributions by patient set-up errors. In *Three-Dimensional Treatment Planning*, P. Minet, ed. Liège: European Association of Radiology, pp. 323–334.

PROSS, J., 1993. TOMAS: A tool for manual segmentation of 3D images for radiotherapy planning. In *Three-Dimensional Treatment Planning*, P. Minet, ed. Liège: European Association of Radiology, pp. 323–334.

QUAST, U., 1993. Target volume concept and tolerance dose concept clearing dose specification in ICRU report no. 50. In *Three-Dimensional Treatment Planning*, P. Minet, ed. Liège: European Association of Radiology, pp. 17–25.

REINSTEIN, L. E., and A. G. MEEK, 1987. Workshop on geometric accuracy an reproducibility in radiation therapy. *Int. J. Radiat. Oncol. Biol. Phys.* 13: 809–810.

SCHAD, L., R. BOESECKE, W. SCHLEGEL, G. HARTMANN, V. STURM, L. STRAUSS, and W. LORENZ, 1987. Three-dimensional image correlation of CT-, MR- and PET studies in radiotherapy treatment planning of brain tumors. *J. of Comp. Assist. Tomog.* 11:948–954.

SCHAD, L., S. LOTT, F. SCHMITT, V. STURM, and W. V. LORENZ, 1987. Correction of spatial distortion in MR imaging: A prerequisite for accurate stereotaxy. *J. Comput Assist. Tomogr.* 11:499–505.

SCHLEGEL, W., 1985. The use of computers in radiotherapy treatment planning. In *Tutorial Notes of CAR '85*, H. U. Lemke, ed. Berlin: Springer, pp. 47–68.

SCHLEGEL, W., 1993. Impact of 3D treatment planning on treatment techniques. In *Three-Dimensional Treatment Planning*, P. Minet, ed. Liège: European Association of Radiology, pp. 131–142.

SCHLEGEL, W., O. PASTYR, R. BOESECKE, T. BORTFELD, G. BECKER, L. SCHAD, G. GADEMANN, and W. J. LORENZ, 1992. Computer systems and mechanical tools for stereotactically guided conformation therapy with linear accelerators. *Int. J. Radiat. Oncol. Biol. Phys.* 24:781–787.

SCHIEMANN, T., B. DIPPOLD, R. SCHMIDT, A. POMMERT, M. RIEMER, R. SCHUBERT, U. TIEDE, and K. H. HÖHNE, 1993. 3D-Visualisation for radiotherapy treatment planning. In Computer Assisted Radiology 93, H. U. Lemke, K. Inamura, C. C. Jafe, and R. Felix, eds. Berlin, Heidelberg, New York: Springer, pp. 669–675.

SHEROUSE, G. W., and C. E. MOSHER, 1987. User interface issues in radiotherapy CAD software. In *The Use of Computers in Radiation Therapy*, I. A. D. Bruinvis, ed. Amsterdam: North Holland, pp. 429–436.

SUIT, H. D., J. BECHT, J. LEONG, M. STRACHER, W. WOOD, L. VERHEY, M. GOITEIN, 1988. Potential for improvement in radiation therapy. *Int. J. Radiat. Oncol. Biol. Phys.* 14: 777–785.

WEBB, S., 1989. Optimization of conformal radiotherapy dose distributions by simulated annealing. *Phys. Med Biol.* 34:1349–1369.

WEBB, S. 1993. *The Physics of Three-Dimensional Radiation Therapy: Conformal Radiotherapy, Radiosurgery, and Treatment Planning.* Bristol, Engl.: IOP Publishing.

56 Motion Planning in Stereotaxic Radiosurgery

ACHIM SCHWEIKARD, JOHN R. ADLER, AND
JEAN-CLAUDE LATOMBE

Background

STEREOTAXIC radiosurgery is a precision procedure that uses an intense, focused beam of radiation as an ablative surgical instrument. The treatment uses the spatial information provided by CT and MRI for targeting. Several leading medical schools worldwide have recently reported dramatic success with this technique in the treatment of brain tumors [1] and malformations [2]. In addition to being safer than conventional operations, stereotaxic radiosurgery is much less expensive.

Although radiosurgical procedures have been used in a limited way for more than 20 years, it was only with the advent of CT and MRI that many new applications for radiosurgery were developed. By coupling stereotaxic precision localization with a sharply collimated beam, specialized instrumentation makes it possible to target a biologically ablative dose of ionizing radiation to a well-circumscribed brain lesion. With an accuracy approaching 1 mm, a very large, "necrosing" dose of radiation (1000–5000 rad) is delivered at a single sitting. Radiosurgical treatment often supplants a major operation and is typically done on an outpatient basis. It allows treatment for many brain lesions that are otherwise inoperable.

Presently there are three types of radiosurgical techniques, distinguished by the radiation source used:

1. Static beam of heavy charged particles (protons or helium ions) generated by a synchrocyclotion [3]
2. Static array of 201 ^{60}Co sources (gamma-knife) [4]
3. Photon beam produced by a standard medical linear accelerator moved by a gantry [5].

These techniques are discussed and compared in various publications (e.g., see [6]). Radiophysical and clinical studies suggest that under most circumstances the three techniques are comparable. However, due to their greater flexibility and relatively low cost, linear accelerator techniques (LINAC) are the most widespread. During treatment, the accelerator moves around the patient's head along a predefined path, so that the radiation is concentrated by crossfiring at a target volume (often a tumor) from multiple directions, and the amount of energy deposited in normal tissues is relatively small.

The overall stereotaxic radiosurgery treatment consists of the following steps:

1. A metal frame, called a *stereotaxic frame*, is attached under local anesthesia to the patient's skull using screws or pins. The position of the frame with respect to the jointed mechanism is adjusted by means of a micrometric system. Hence, it is known with high precision.

2. CT and magnetic resonance images are obtained and analyzed with the frame attached. The locations of both the tumor and the critical structures are determined with respect to the frame.

3. A path for the radiation beam is planned based on this spatial information, and the intensity of the beam along this path is selected. The dose distribution corresponding to this path is computed by a dosimetry program. This program embeds a model of the fluence of the radiation beam through the brain tissues and integrates this fluence over time at every point of interest. The results are visualized on a graphic display. If the surgeon finds the distribution acceptable, the treatment proceeds to step 4; otherwise, another path is generated.

4. The gantry moves the activated beam along the path accepted by the surgeon.

This procedure is quite long; steps 1, 2, 3, and 4 require on the order of 30 minutes, 1–2 hours, 2–3 hours, and 1–2 hours, respectively.[1] The patient is conscious throughout all steps, and the stereotaxic frame, which remains attached to the patient's head (since the correspondence between the images and the gantry must be maintained), is painful. Shortening the procedure would reduce the patient's discomfort. Furthermore, it could save time for the surgeon and allow the treatment of more patients with the same equipment. In this context, various computer techniques can be applied. In particular, in step 2, image interpretation techniques can be used to locate regions of interest automatically. Several such techniques have been reported in the literature (e.g., see [7, 8]). Meanwhile, in step 3, planning techniques could be used to generate appropriate beam motions. The latter objective is the topic of this chapter.

Many of the brain tumors considered inoperable involve the skull base and are adjacent to critical structures such as the optic nerve and chiasm, the carotid artery, and the brain stem. Although radiosurgery has proved to be a valuable and oftentimes curative treatment for these lesions, their close proximity to such important and extremely radiation-sensitive areas is problematic. Because damage to these structures can result in such severe side effects as paralysis or blindness, the path of the beam must be selected so as to irradiate them minimally. Finding the best trajectory for a radiation beam is further complicated by the typically irregular shape such tumors assume. Despite the complexity of treatment planning, it is currently done manually. Given that the problem is largely one of geometric reasoning, it would seem reasonable that it might be done better and faster by computer; that hypothesis is investigated in this chapter.

The planning problem considered here has recently been termed the "inverse dosimetry problem" [9, 10]. Given a spatial map of the brain and a treatment plan, the goal of the direct dosimetry problem is to compute energy deposition in brain tissues. This problem is currently solved by dosimetry programs embedding models of the fluence of the radiation beam as it travels through tissues. Meanwhile, the inverse problem is how to deliver a specific dose of radiation to a target volume without, at the same time, irradiating healthy tissue beyond tolerance [10]. Previous research sought to find a mathematic solution of this problem by solving an integral equation: Given the desired dose distribution and the equation expressing the dose received at any one point as the integral over time of the fluence of the radiation beam, solve this integral for the fluence of the beam throughout the treatment. The approach is promising, and progress has been reported over the last few years [10–14]. However, existing results still apply only to simple dose distributions in two dimensions. It seems that it will be extremely difficult to handle realistic 3D dose distributions. Furthermore, the integral equation does not take into account some important parameters. For example, treatment plans may be generated that are too complicated to execute or that are even infeasible due to mechanical constraints in the system moving the radiation beam.

Our approach to radiosurgical planning is different. It derives from geometric computation techniques developed for robot motion planning [15]. We treat the critical brain structures as "obstacles" that the radiation beam is not allowed to traverse. Hence, we represent them as volumes obstructing beam access to and exit from the tumor. Our planner computes an explicit representation of all the allowed motions of the beam when it crossfires at the tumor. From this representation, it extracts connected arcs of maximal length, making it possible for the beam to strike the tumor from many different directions and thus reduce the dose received by healthy tissues (other than the critical structures). These arcs define the path of the beam generated by the planner. The intensity of the beam along this path is computed in a straighforward manner by assuming no attenuation of the fluence of the beam when it travels through brain tissues. Our planner could likely be improved by using a better model of the fluence of the beam and applying inverse dosimetry technique, such as those evoked in the previous paragraph, to select the intensity of the beam along every computed arc.

In its current form, our planner solves a purely geometric problem. The user (typically the surgeon) defines interactively the number of arcs to be computed, as well as parameters constraining these arcs (e.g., the minimal length of each arc, the minimal angle between the planes containing any two arcs). Hence, our planner is mainly a computational tool to assist the surgeon in exploring several possible treatment plans. It guarantees that the arcs it generates satisfy the constraints defined by the input parameters, and it is complete (that is, it always finds such arcs if they exist). However, these properties are not sufficient to guarantee the optimality of the selected treatment. In fact, because it seems impossible to propose a comprehensive optimality criterion taking all parameters into account (desired dose distribution, duration of treatment, patient's medical history), we believe that providing the surgeon with an interactive tool to explore the range of possible treatment plans is currently the most suitable way to proceed.

Our planner has been developed for a specific LINAC system based on the Brown-Roberts-Wells stereotaxic localization, which is available at the Stanford Medical Center (see the next section). We present preliminary experimental results obtained with this planner on two recorded cases and compare these results with the manually planned treatments that were actually performed. Although still preliminary, these results and similar ones obtained on nine other recorded cases indicate that motion-planning software can both significantly reduce energy deposition in critical tissues and dramatically shorten the duration of step 3 for complex cases.

Very different image-guided robotic systems have been developed for other types of surgical applications [16, 17]. The system in Lavallée et al. [16] is used for inserting electrodes or radioactive seeds into a patient's brain with high accuracy; the electrode or seed is moved to an appropriate entry position by a 6-degree-of-freedom (6-dof) robot and then moved into its final placement in the brain by the surgeon. A robotic system designed to create femoral cavities that are precisely shaped and positioned for inserting uncemented prostheses is described in Paul et al. [17]. Motion-planning techniques could also be beneficial to the development of these systems. However, the planning issues they raise are different from those of radiosurgery.

LINAC system

Although there are several LINAC-based systems [6], one of the most frequently used devices is based on the Brown-Roberts-Wells stereotaxic localization [18, 19]. The experimental work reported in this chapter has been carried out with such a system, which is described here. In the rest of the chapter, this system will be referred to as the LINAC system.

The radiosurgical equipment used in our work is depicted in figure 56.1. It consists of a floor stand (couch) with four joints and a gantry with a revolute joint moving a 6-MeV photon source generating a circular beam. The position of the floor stand can be adjusted with three prismatic joints. Its orientation in the horizontal plane is set by a revolute joint about the axis

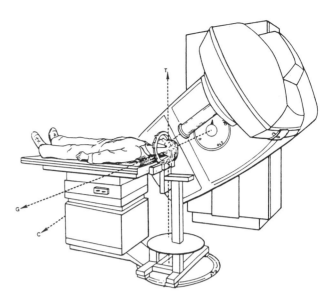

FIGURE 56.1 Schematic of radiosurgical equipment [19].

designated by T in figure 56.1. The linear accelerator can be moved by rotating the gantry about the axis denoted by G. The beam central axis is denoted by C. The three axes T, G, and C always intersect in one point. While the accelerator is rotated, the floor stand joints remain fixed, so that the beam can span only vertical angular sectors. The radius of the beam generated by the accelerator can be adjusted by inserting a lead collimator into the accelerator. The beam can be turned on and off during the motion.

The standard treatment using this equipment is the following. Assume first that the tumor is approximated[2] as a ball $\mathscr{T}$. The prismatic joints in the floor stand are adjusted such that the intersection point of T, G, and C coincides with the center of $\mathscr{T}$. The beam radius is set to the radius of $\mathscr{T}$. The revolute joint of the floor stand (axis T) is set to a fixed angular position α_1. In this position the gantry is moved around G between two orientations β_1 and β_1', while the beam is activated. In this way, the beam spans a vertical angular sector whose apex is the center of $\mathscr{T}$. Furthermore, throughout the motion, $\mathscr{T}$ is inside the beam. The floor stand revolute joint then is set to a new angular position α_2, and a second arc (β_2, β_2') is generated by moving the gantry, and so on. The standard motion procedure described in Lutz, Winston, and Maleki [18] consists of four such arcs. The angle between any two planes containing these arcs should be large enough so that the volumes swept by the beam when it moves along the various arcs have a small intersection outside $\mathscr{T}$. It is thus ensured that the dose inside $\mathcal{T}$ largely exceeds the dose absorbed by surrounding tissues. Energy deposition can be computed by a standard dosimetry program currently in clinical use at Stanford. If this computation shows too large a dose to critical regions, the four-arc path is modified by changing the floor stand angles, the gantry motion ranges, or the beam intensity along each arc. When the tumor is aspheric, it is approximated as a collection of nonintersecting spheres. Each sphere is treated independently as described earlier.

The planner presented later directly applies to this system and generates standard four-arc paths. However, it has the potential to be more general. In particular, with the same system kinematics, it can generate paths with an arbitrary number of arcs, which allows a better distribution of energy in the brain, especially when the tumor and critical structures are adjacent to one another. Extensions (not described in this chapter) would also allow the planner to deal with a less constrained mechanical gantry. This is important because, as reported elsewhere [20, 6], better energy deposition can be achieved by using a system with more versatile kinematics. In fact, we plan to replace our current gantry by a robot arm allowing arbitrary 5-dof motions of the linear accelerator and we plan to extend our planner to this new system (see the conclusion).

Geometry of the beam configuration space

Our planning approach is mainly geometric. We explicitly represent the set of all orientations of the beam where it crossfires at the tumor without intersecting any of the critical regions in the brain. From this representation we extract a set of circular arcs defining a possible path of the beam. In this section, we show how a set of valid orientations of the beam can be generated. Arc computation will be described in the next section.

BEAM CONFIGURATION SPACE

Let us assume that the tumor is modeled as a target ball of radius r centered at the coordinate origin O. A *configuration* of the radiation beam is defined as the orientation of its central axis C when this axis goes through O. In the following, we assume that the energy distribution along the beam is constant; hence, any two opposite orientations of the beam are equivalent. We can then represent a beam's configuration by the two antipodal points where its central axis intersects the unit sphere S^2 centered at O. The set of all beam configurations—that is, the beam's *configuration space*—is thus represented as the sphere S^2 with antipodal points identified.

The kinematics of our LINAC system constrains the beam configuration to move along arcs of great circles of S^2 contained in vertical planes. A path of the accelerator is thus defined as a series of such arcs.

Our planning techniques treat critical regions as obstacles that should not be intersected by the beam. This leads to precomputing the map of each critical region into S^2 as a set of forbidden configurations called *C-obstacles*. The complement of the C-obstacles in S^2 is called the *free space*.

C-OBSTACLES

Let $C_i, i = 1, \ldots, m$, denote the critical regions of the brain. Each region C_i maps into S^2 as follows:

We grow C_i isotropically by the radius r of the target ball (i.e., the radius of the beam); this yields a grown region C_i'. Intuitively, C_i' is obtained by moving a ball of diameter r to all placements where it is in contact with C_i, without overlapping it; C_i' is equal to C_i enlarged by the volume swept out by the ball. More formally, we have

$$C_i' = C_i \oplus B_r = \{c + b \mid c \in C_i, b \in B_r\}$$

where B_r is the ball of radius r centered at the coordinate origin O, and $\oplus$ denotes the Minkowski set sum.

Hence, if the beam central axis does not cross the enlarged region C_i', then the beam does not intersect C_i. The central projection of C_i' from O into S^2 gives the C-obstacle corresponding to C_i. Note that each C-obstacle consists of two antipodal regions.

COMPUTATION OF FREE SPACE

The following simple technique can be used to compute an approximation of free space:

Let $C_i, i = 1, \ldots, m$, be polyhedra approximating the critical regions, and D_r be a polyhedron bounding the ball B_r. (In our implementation, D_r is simply a cube of edge length $2r$ centered at O.) We construct each C_i' as $C_i \oplus D_r$, rather than $C_i \oplus B_r$. C_i' is then a polyhedron whose computation is studied elsewhere [21, 22]. This approximation yields a particularly simple projection

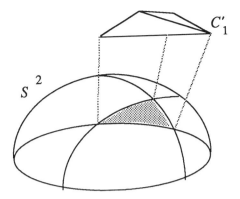

FIGURE 56.2   Construction of free space.

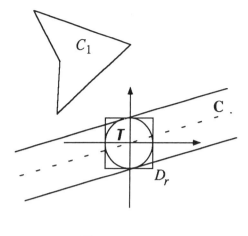

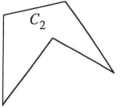

(a)

of C'_i into S^2. Indeed, each edge E of C'_i maps to an arc of a great circle that is the intersection of the plane containing O and E with S^2. The set of edges of all grown regions C'_i thus determines a collection of great circles that partition S^2 into an arrangement of regions (figure 56.2). The free space is the union of a subset of these regions.

Let n be the total number of vertices of the polyhedra $C_1, \ldots, C_m$. Let the number of vertices of the polyhedron D_r be small enough to be considered $O(1)$. The grown regions C'_i can be computed in $O(n)$ time using the algorithm described in [22]. They have a total of $O(n)$ vertices and thus yield $O(n)$ great circles in S^2, forming an arrangement of $O(n^2)$ regions. This arrangement can be computed in $O(n^2)$ time by a topological sweep algorithm [23].

Example   Free space computation is illustrated in figure 56.3 with a simple 2D example. (The beam configuration space is then the unit circle S^1.) In figure 56.3a, C_1 and C_2 are polygons approximating critical regions, C is the beam central axis at some arbitrary free configuration of the beam, and D_r is the bounding square containing the target disk $\mathcal{T}$. In figure 56.3b, C'_i and C'_2 are the grown regions corresponding to C_1 and C_2. Each grown region is projected into S^1 as two antipodal arcs (the C-obstacles). The complement of these arcs—that is, the two antipodal arcs shown in bold lines—represents free space.

In the following, we assume that C-obstacles and free space have been computed using the preceding approximation. They are therefore bounded by arcs of great circles.

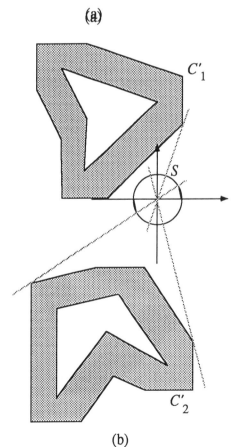

(b)

FIGURE 56.3   Computation of free configurations in a 2D example (see text).

Computation of vertical free arcs

In this section, we show how free arcs defining the path of the LINAC system can be extracted from the free space computed as above. In the next subsection we keep our presentation independent of the kinematic limitations of this system. In the following two subsections, we then explicitly deal with these limitations by focusing on the generation of free vertical arcs.

CHARACTERIZATION OF GREAT CIRCLES

Let g be any great circle of S^2. We can represent g by two antipodal points of a sphere DS^2, the *dual sphere* of S^2, defined as the extremities of the two opposite unit vectors erected at O and normal to the plane containing g.

Let e be an edge (arc of great circle) of a C-obstacle, and let u and v be its endpoints. Let $G(u)$ be the set of all great circles of S^2 containing u. This set maps into DS^2 as a great circle $n(u)$. In the same way the great circles of S^2 containing v map to a great circle $n(v)$ of DS^2. The two circles $n(u)$ and $n(v)$ partition DS^2 into four regions. Two of these regions represent the set of great circles in S^2 that intersect the arc e. The other two regions represent the great circles in S^2 that do not intersect e.

Consider the C-obstacle edges in S^2. The set of great circles corresponding to the endpoints of these edges partition DS^2 into an arrangement A of regions. Let R be any such open region of dimension 2, and let p be any point in R. The great circle of S^2 corresponding to p intersects a possibly empty set of C-obstacle edges. By construction of the great circles forming A, when p moves in R, this set remains constant. We denote it by $\sigma(R)$. We called R a *regular region* of DS^2 and $\sigma(R)$ the *characteristic set* of R.

The arrangement A is created by $O(n)$ great circles. It contains $O(n^2)$ regions and can be computed in $O(n^2)$ time (as previously, n is the total number of vertices of the critical regions). The characteristic set of any region in A can be computed in $O(n)$ time. The characteristic set undergoes minor changes between two adjacent regular regions. These changes can be computed in constant time; thus it is possible to generate all characteristic sets in $O(n^2)$ time.

However, the LINAC system can move the beam source only along arcs of vertical great circles. Al-though the computation of A and the characteristic sets can be useful for a more versatile mechanical system, it is too general for the present purpose.

FREE VERTICAL GREAT CIRCLES

Vertical great circles of S^2 are represented by points of the horizontal circle H of DS^2. The intersection points of H with the circles of the arrangement A decompose H into arcs. Let $L = (s_1, s_2, \dots)$ be the sorted list of these arcs. All vertical great circles represented by points in the same arc s_i intersect the same C-obstacle edges (possibly none). Let $r(s_i)$ denote the number of C-obstacle edges intersected by the great circle of S^2 represented by any point of s_i; $r(s_i)$ is equal to the size of the characteristic set of the region of A containing s_i (although it can be computed more directly). If $r(s_i) = 0$, then all points in s_i represent free great circles of S^2. By scanning the list L of arcs of H, we can identify all arcs s where $r(s)$ reaches 0 and report the sublist of these arcs, which represents all free vertical great circles of S^2.

As mentioned earlier, this computation does not require the precomputation of the characteristic sets of the regions of A. The intersections of H with the circles generating A can be computed in $O(n)$ time. The sorted list L is thus produced in $O(n \log n)$ time. The number $r(s_1)$ can be computed directly in $O(n)$ time. The arcs s_1 and s_2 are separated by a point where H intersects a great circle of A. By analyzing this intersection, one can compute $r(s_2)$ from $r(s_1)$ in constant time. In the same way, each new number $r(s_i)$ can be computed in constant time from $r(s_{i-1})$. Hence, the list of arcs s verifying $r(s) = 0$ is generated in $O(n \log n)$ time.

FREE VERTICAL ARCS OF GIVEN LENGTH

In many cases, however, there are no free vertical great circles, or the existing ones do not have sufficient angular distance between them (see the section on the LINAC system). Therefore, it may be more interesting to compute vertical great circles in which free arcs have a cumulated length greater than some specified value K. When the accelerator is moved along such a circle, the beam must alternately be turned on and off.

The vertices of the free space in S^2 map to a collection of great circles of DS^2. These circles partition H into a list $L' = (s'_1, s'_2, \dots)$ of arcs ($L \subseteq L'$). Consider any arc s_i' in this list. All vertical great circles of S^2 represented by the points of s_i' intersect the same C-obstacle edges *in the same order*. We decompose every arc s_i' into subarcs such that when a point p varies from one extremity of any subarc to the other, the total length of free arcs in the great circle of S^2 represented by p increases or decreases monotonically. Each subarc of H thus contains at most one connected segment representing great circles containing free arcs with total length greater than the given threshold K.

The number of segments thus extracted from H is polynomial in n. The computation also requires polynomial time. It involves finding the zeros of polynomial equations. We will not discuss this issue here, because the implemented planner makes use of an approximate technique based on discretizing H (see the section on implementation).

One may alternatively consider great circles containing a connected free arc whose length is greater than some value. The computation of such great circles can be done using a technique very similar to that outlined previously.

Path planning

A path of the LINAC system consists of a series of arcs (connected or not) contained in different vertical great circles. We consider the path planning problem defined by four parameters: the radius r of the target ball approximating the tumor, the number k of great circles, the minimal cumulative length K of the free arcs in each great circle, and the minimal angle ω between the planes of any two great circles. The planner uses the value of r to compute free space. Then it generates a path as follows:

We give an arbitrary orientation to the horizontal great circle H of DS^2. Let $(s_1^\kappa, s_2^\kappa, \dots)$ be the sorted list of the arcs of H representing the vertical great circles of S^2 whose free arcs have a total length greater than K. We must find a series of k points $p_1, \dots, p_k$ in these arcs such that the angle $\omega(p_i, p_j)$ between the vertical planes containing the great circles represented by any two points p_i and p_j is larger than ω. [Note that $\omega(p_i, p_j)$ is equal to the angular distance between p_i and p_j in H.]

Assume that the points p_i have been computed. If none coincides with an endpoint of an arc s_j^κ, then we can move all the points p_i simultaneously, in the direc-

tion opposite to that of H, until one reaches an endpoint of an arc s_j^κ. Therefore, to compute the points p_i, we can assume that one point coincides with the first endpoint of an arc s_j^κ (the arc being oriented as H).

We begin by placing the point p_1 at the first endpoint of an arbitrarily selected arc s_{j1}^κ. We then move in the direction of D and place p_2 within an arc s_{j2}^κ (possibly, equal to s_{j1}^κ), such that the angular distance between p_1 and p_2 is minimal but larger than ω. After p_1 and p_2 are placed, the remaining points are positioned in the same way. Whenever a new point is positioned, it is also verified that the point's angular distance to p_1 is greater than or equal to ω. If no appropriate placement is found for any point p_2 through p_k, then p_1 is selected at the first endpoint of another arc and the construction is repeated.

If the planner terminates successfully, it provides a set of k great circles satisfying the input constraints, along with the free arcs in each great circle. If it fails to find a path, one can modify the constraints—that is, the values of r, k, K, and ω. It is easy to show that the planner is complete. If there exist k vertical great circles, each containing free arcs of total length K (or more), whose planes make angles greater than or equal to ω, the planner is guaranteed to return such circles; otherwise it returns failure.

Assume that the arcs s_j^κ in H have already been computed. Let q be the number of these arcs. For a given position of p_1, the placement of every point p_i takes $O(\log q)$ time. The placement of all points, if possible, thus takes $O(k \log q)$ time. In case of successive failures, the process is repeated up to q times, yielding a total planning time of $O(kq \log q)$. If $K = 2\pi$ (i.e., if we are interested only in great circles), then $q \in O(n)$. If $K < 2\pi$, then q has a higher-degree polynomial dependence on n.

Alternatively, a problem can be defined so that each great circle contains a connected free arc of length greater than or equal to K. The selection of the points p_i is done as described already.

Implementation

An interactive planner based on the techniques described in the previous sections has been implemented to compute appropriate multiarc paths for our LINAC system. The software is written in C language and runs on a Silicon Graphics workstation. The planner has been connected with dosimetry and imaging software already in use with the stereotaxic system at Stanford Medical Center.

CT and magnetic response images give the anatomy of the brain in parallel axial cross-sections separated by 3–5 mm. The critical regions in each cross-section are delineated by polygons. These polygons are then "thickened" by the distance between cross-sections, yielding a polyhedral approximation of every critical region. Currently, the delineation operation in each cross-section is done manually.

The planner is interactive. The user (typically the surgeon) sets the parameters r, k, K, and ω. The planner generates a path made of multiple arcs satisfying the constraints entailed by these parameters, if such arcs exist. The dose distribution corresponding to this path is computed and visualized. The user can modify the input parameters iteratively to get different paths and hence different treatment plans.

The planning algorithm works as described in the section on path planning, with the difference that the horizontal great circle H in DS^2 is discretized into N equidistant points (typically, $N = 128$). For every point p in the discretization of H, the planner computes the set of free arcs in the great circle of S^2 represented by p and the total length (or maximal length) of these arcs. This leads the planner to compute each arc s_j^κ as a list of point instead of as a continuous segment. The rest of the planner operates in the same way as detailed earlier. The implemented planner is resolution-complete: If there exist arcs satisfying the input contraints, it is guaranteed to find them, provided that N is small enough. The value $N = 128$, used in our experiments, led to satisfactory results.

The planner either returns a path (set of arcs) or indicates failure. If it returns a path, the dosimetry program is run and computes the energy deposition in the brain tissue that will result from the execution of this path. If the surgeon does not find this distribution acceptable, the planner is called back with different parameters. If the planner fails to return a path, it can also be called back with different parameters.

The planner incorporates several straightforward improvements. For example, when it finds a path, it can iteratively rotate the k vertical planes containing the planned arcs to maximize the minimal length of free arcs in each one. When it fails to find a path satisfying the constraints, it can find, by bisection, the maximal ω for which there is a path.

Currently, we assume in the planner that the fluence of the beam is constant throughout tissues and is perfectly focused. (However, the dosimetry program used to evaluate plans incorporates a more sophisticated state-of-the-art model of the beam fluence.) The fluence is set by the planner to the same value along the k arcs, proportional to the inverse of the total length of these arcs. A potential improvement of the planner, which we have not yet explored would be to allow for a different beam intensity along each arc. This could be done by using results obtained with the inverse dosimetry problem (see, e.g., [10]). In fact, since the general form of this problem seems extremely complex, one could use our planner to generate a set of arcs defining a class of treatment plans and then use inverse dosimetry techniques to select an optimal or quasi-optimal plan in that class.

An important issue not investigated so far is tumor representation. An almost spherical tumor can be well represented by a single target ball, but this ball is not necessarily the one that achieves the best geometric match with the tumor. Actually, because the radiation beam is not perfectly focused, and there is some dose fall-off in the vicinity of the target ball, it is often suitable to approximate the tumor by a smaller ball. When the shape of the tumor is more complicated, one may represent it by several balls; a distinct path can be generated for each ball. For the same reasons as detailed previously, these balls should be separated by some space. To simplify the use of our planner and improve the generated treatment plan, a geometric method for approximating tumors by a given number of balls was implemented. This method is based on an algorithm described in Welzl [24] for finding the smallest sphere containing a set of points in space. However, this work is not well developed and requires additional research. Ultimately, we see tumor representation an integral part of the planning problem.

Experiments

To carry out a preliminary evaluation of the planner, we ran it on 11 cases that had previously been treated with the LINAC system at the Stanford Medical Center. In each case, the dose distribution for the treatment computed by the planner was compared to the distribution for the original treatment, which had been generated manually. Comparison was done at a large number of critical points (only a subset of them are given below). Although a more global (volumetric) evaluation could be useful, we do not think that it would yield significantly different results. We report 2 representative cases below, taken from our 11 experimental cases.

To make comparison with manual planning realistic, the planner was run with $k = 4$ and an initial value of ω equal to the standard $45°$. We also requested the planner to find great circles containing a connected free arc of length greater than some K. When the planner found a path, this path was automatically optimized as explained earlier. When the planner failed, ω was determined by bisection. In all cases, the planner took on the order of $1-2$ min to generate a treatment (including C-obstacle computation).

The planner was also used to generate paths with more than four vertical arcs. Interestingly, this usually led to relatively small dosimetric improvements. On the other hand, limited additional experiments have shown that in some cases the restriction to vertical arcs impairs dose distribution (see the conclusion).

Our experiments with tumors of complex shape (i.e., whose representation requires several target balls)

have been very limited so far. Although encouraging, the results are not yet significant, and no such case is reported below.

Case 1

Figure 56.4 shows the CT image of an axial cross-section of the brain. A single critical region (brain stem) is delineated by a polygon B. The tumor is designated by T. Both the manually generated path and the computed path consist of four connected arcs in different planes. They were generated for a tumor approximated by one sphere of radius 10 mm.

Figure 56.5 shows the energy deposition computed by the dosimetry program in four cross-sections distant by 3 mm for the manually generated path. Figure 56.6 shows the deposition computed for the path generated by the planner. In both figures, doses are shown as gray levels in steps of 200 centiGray (cGy; 1 Gray = 1 joule/kg).

Quantitative dose values are given in table 56.1 for both paths, at the vertices of the brain stem B in five

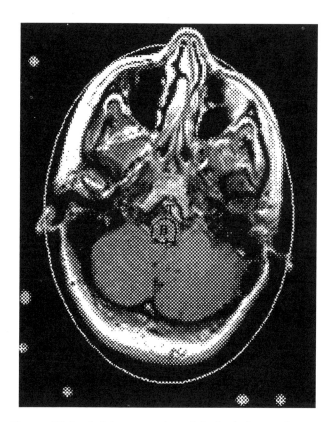

FIGURE 56.4   Axial cross-section of the brain in case 1.

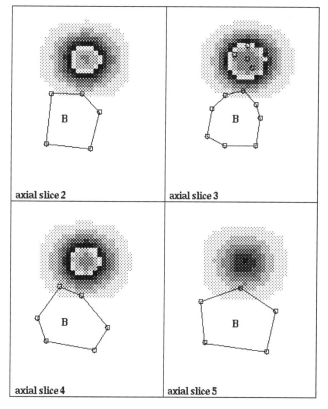

FIGURE 56.5   Dose distribution for the manually planned treatment in case 1.

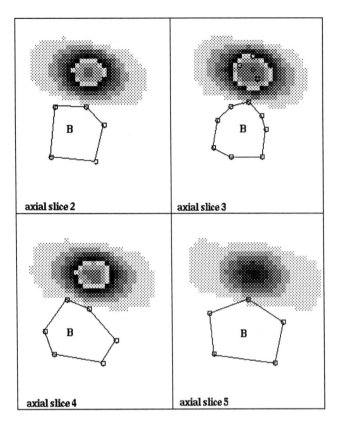

B		**B**
axial slice 2		axial slice 3
B		**B**
axial slice 4		axial slice 5

FIGURE 56.6 Dose distribution for the automatically planned treatment in case 1.

cross-sections. The first column contains point labels. The second and fourth columns show the dose values for the manually planned path and the computed path, respectively, in centiGray. The third and fifth columns show these values as a percentage of the dose deposited at the center of the sphere approximating the tumor. A nonzero dose is computed in some vertices of B for the automatically planned path, despite the fact that nowhere along this path does the beam intersect B. In fact, the beam is not perfectly focused, and the dose close to the theoretic cylinder modeling the beam is not exactly null. The dosimetry program makes use of a model of the beam that takes this into account. If the surgeon considers that the dose received by some areas in the critical structures is too high, he or she can rerun the planner using a smaller target ball.

An elevated relative dose is obtained for vertices close to the tumor, mainly at points BrStem. 5.1, BrStem. 4.2, and BrStem. 3.1. Table 56.1 shows that the dose at these points is reduced in the computed path by 46%, 55%, and 76% respectively, relatively to the manually planned path. The table shows a substantial dose reduction ratio at all other vertices, but these reductions are less critical because the doses for the manually generated paths are significantly lower.

CASE 2

Figure 56.7 shows the CT image of an axial cross-section of the brain for case 2. Two critical regions B (brain stem) and OC (optic nerve and chiasm) are delineated by polygons. The tumor is designated by T. Again both the manually generated path and the automatically computed path consist of four connected arcs in different planes. The tumor was approximated by a single sphere.

Figures 56.8 and 56.9 show energy distribution computed by the dosimetry program in the cross-section shown in figure 56.7 for the manually and the automatically planned treatments, respectively. Table 56.2 compares dose values at the vertices of the critical regions.

Conclusion

This chapter describes a planner developed to help a surgeon generate satisfactory paths for a radiation beam used in radiosurgery. Using geometric techniques, this planner avoids irradiating critical regions of the brain. Experiments on 11 cases indicate that it reduces the path planning time involved in radiosurgery and improves energy deposition.

The main obstacles to clinical use of the planner is its insufficient integration with other software components and its lack of a user-friendly interface. Actually, the work presented in this chapter is a first step aimed at demonstrating the usefulness of a computer-based planner in radiosurgery. We will soon replace our current LINAC system with a more versatile one using a general 5-dof gantry. We are currently developing an integrated software package for this new system, which will include medical imagery, treatment planning, and dosimetry simulation.

We envision that significant future progress can be achieved in the following two directions: First, for some locations of a tumor (relative to critical regions), the constraints of our LINAC system seriously reduce the quality of the radiosurgical treatment. Better treatment could be achieved by using a system allowing arcs in both vertical and nonvertical planes. Such a

TABLE 56.1
Comparison of energy doses in the brain stem (case 1)

Point labels	Manually planned motion		Computed motion	
	Dose (cGy)	Percentage of dose at center	Dose (cGy)	Percentage of dose at center
BrStem.1.1	177.8	8.9	80.9	4.1
BrStem.1.2	76.7	3.8	10.8	0.5
BrStem.1.3	13.7	0.7	0.0	0.0
BrStem.1.4	14.5	0.7	0.0	0.0
BrStem.1.5	42.5	2.1	1.4	0.1
BrStem.2.1	161.0	8.0	23.9	1.2
BrStem.2.2	121.7	6.1	25.8	1.3
BrStem.2.3	60.7	3.0	1.6	0.1
BrStem.2.4	33.2	1.7	0.0	0.0
BrStem.2.5	32.6	1.6	0.0	0.0
BrStem.3.1	239.5	12.0	55.0	2.8
BrStem.3.2	60.3	3.0	0.5	0.0
BrStem.3.3	68.5	3.4	1.7	0.1
BrStem.3.4	37.0	1.9	0.0	0.0
BrStem.3.5	144.2	7.2	18.6	0.9
BrStem.3.6	90.9	4.5	6.0	0.3
BrStem.3.7	38.7	1.9	0.0	0.0
BrStem.3.8	38.5	1.9	0.0	0.0
BrStem.4.1	163.2	8.2	19.4	1.0
BrStem.4.2	242.6	12.1	106.6	5.4
BrStem.4.3	43.8	2.2	1.2	0.0
BrStem.4.4	30.6	1.5	0.0	0.0
BrStem.4.5	30.0	1.5	0.0	0.0
BrStem.4.6	40.6	2.0	0.3	0.0
BrStem.5.1	313.4	15.7	165.6	8.4
BrStem.5.2	88.2	4.4	50.2	2.5
BrStem.5.3	8.0	0.6	0.0	0.0
BrStem.5.4	11.1	0.6	0.0	0.0
BrStem.5.5	89.9	4.5	30.1	1.5

system would make manual planning harder, but this difficulty could be eliminated by an automatic planner. Automatic planning might motivate the development of even more flexible radiosurgical systems.

Second, in the longer term, faster and more reliable image interpretation techniques should make it possible to connect image acquisition directly to beam control. This could make it possible to eliminate the painful stereotaxic frame attached to the patient's head. It could also allow the application of radiosurgery to the destruction of tumors in parts of the human body that are more difficult to localize in space, such as the liver and pancreas [25].

Our current research program is oriented toward these two directions. We are also investigating techniques for automatically extracting a set of target volumes (e.g., balls, ellipses) from a given tumor, a problem that we have overlooked thus far.

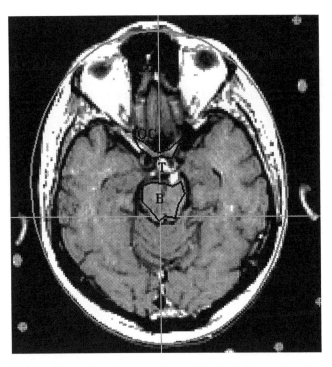

FIGURE 56.7 Axial cross-section of the brain in case 2.

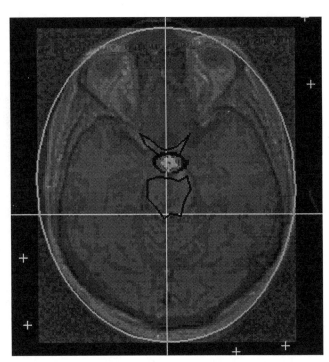

FIGURE 56.9 Energy deposition for the automatically planned treatment (case 2).

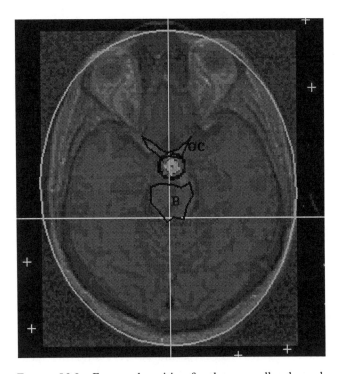

FIGURE 56.8 Energy deposition for the manually planned treatment (case 2).

Stereotaxic radiosurgery of brain tumors is one instance of so-called bloodless surgery, in which there is markedly growing interest. We expect that computer-based motion-planning techniques such as those described earlier, together with image interpretation techniques, will facilitate further development of this safer, less painful, and more cost-effective type of surgery.

ACKNOWLEDGMENTS This work was funded in part by the Sheikh Hassan M. Enany Gift Fund. The authors thank Rick Cox, Bill Haneman, Paul Hemler, Todd Koumrian, and David Martin from the Stanford Medical Center for making their radiosurgical dosimetry program available to them and discussing various aspects of treatment planning.

NOTES

1. These durations and other information are given here to help the nonspecialist reader apprehend the motivation for the work described in this chapter.
2. Approximating a tumor by a target ball (or a set of balls) is a delicate issue that will be briefly addressed in the section on implementation.

TABLE 56.2

Comparison of energy doses in case 2

Point labels	Manually planned motion		Computed motion	
	Dose (cGy)	Percentage of dose at center	Dose (cGy)	Percentage of dose at center
OptNerve.3	27.8	1.4	0.0	0.0
OptNerve.3	173.3	8.7	24.3	1.2
OptNerve.3	159.8	8.0	14.5	0.7
OptNerve.3	46.3	2.3	0.0	0.0
OptNerve.3	57.4	2.9	0.4	0.0
OptNerve.3	35.9	1.8	0.0	0.0
OptNerve.3	140.9	7.0	4.1	0.2
OptNerve.3	199.0	9.9	29.1	1.5
BrStem.3	146.7	7.3	3.3	0.2
BrStem.3	200.5	10.0	7.9	0.4
BrStem.3	70.0	3.5	0.5	0.0
BrStem.3	24.8	1.2	0.0	0.0
BrStem.3	21.7	1.1	0.0	0.0
BrStem.3	17.8	0.9	0.0	0.0
BrStem.3	19.4	1.0	0.0	0.0
BrStem.3	17.9	0.9	0.0	0.0
BrStem.3	24.0	1.2	0.0	0.0
BrStem.3	31.1	1.6	0.0	0.0
BrStem.3	116.0	5.8	8.1	0.4
BrStem.3	104.0	5.2	0.6	0.0
Chiasm.3	322.1	16.1	229.8	11.5
Chiasm.3	404.3	20.2	219.0	11.0
Chiasm.3	364.9	18.2	248.3	12.4
Chiasm.3	135.3	6.8	6.1	0.3
Chiasm.3	174.0	8.7	23.5	1.2

REFERENCES

[1] BERNSTEIN, M., and P. H. GUTIN, 1981. Interstitial irradiation of brain tumors: A review. *Neurosurgery* 9:741–750.

[2] BETTI, O. O. et al., 1989. Stereotactic radiosurgery with the linear accelerator: Treatment of arteriovenous malformations. *Neurosurgery* 24(3):311–321.

[3] LARSSON, B. et al., 1958. The high-energy proton beam as a neurosurgical tool. *Nature* 182:1222–1223.

[4] LEKSELL, L., 1968. Cerebral radiosurgery I: Gamma thalamotomy in two cases of intractable pain. *Acta Chir. Scand.* 13:585–595.

[5] HARTMANN, G. H., 1955. Cerebral radiation surgery using moving field irradiation at a linear accelerator facility. *Int. J. Radiat. Oncol. Biol. Phys.* 11:1185–1192.

[6] PODGORSAK, E. B. et al., 1988. Dynamic stereotactic radiosurgery. *Int. J. Radiat. Oncol. Biol. Phys.* 14:115–126.

[7] COHEN, I., L. COHEN, and N. AYACHE, 1992. Using deformable surfaces to segment 3D images and infer differential structures. In *Lecture Notes in Computer Science 558*, Sandini, ed. New York: Springer, pp. 648–652.

[8] LEITNER, F., and P. CINQUIN, 1991. Dynamic segmentation: Detecting complex topology 3D objects. In *Proceedings of the IEEE International Conference on Engineering in Medicine, Biology, and Society*, Orlando, Fla., pp. 295–296.

[9] KOOY, H. M., and N. H. BARTH, 1990. The verification of an inverse problem in radiation therapy using Monte Carlo simulations. *Int. J. Radiat. Oncol. Biol. Phys.* 18:433–439.

[10] BARTH, N. H., 1990. An inverse problem in radiation therapy. *Int. J. Radiat. Oncol. Biol. Phys.* 18:425–431.

[11] BRAHME, A., J. ROOS, and I. LAX, 1982. Solution of an integral equation encountered in rotation therapy. *Phys. Med. Biol.* 27:1221–1229.

[12] CORMACK, A., 1987. A problem in rotation therapy with x-rays. *Int. J. Radiat. Oncol. Biol. Phys.* 13:623–630.

[13] CORMACK, A., and R. CORMACK, 1987. A problem in rotation therapy with x-rays II: Dose distributions with an axis of symmetry. *Int. J. Radiat. Oncol. Biol. Phys.* 13:1921–1925.

[14] BRAHME, A., 1988. Optimization of stationary and moving beam radiation therapy techniques. *Radiother. Oncol.* 12:127–140.

[15] LATOMBE, J.-C., 1991. *Robot Motion Planning.* Boston: Kluwer.

[16] LAVALLÉE, S. et al., 1992. Image-guided operating robot: A clinical application in stereotactic neurosurgery. In *Proceedings of the IEEE Conference on Robotics and Automation,* Nice, France, pp. 618–624.

[17] PAUL, H. A. et al., 1992. A surgical robot for total hip replacement surgery. In *Proceedings of the IEEE Conference on Robotics and Automation,* Nice, France, pp. 606–611.

[18] LUTZ, W., K. R. WINSTON, and N. MALEKI, 1988. A System for stereotactic radiosurgery with a linear accelerator. *Int. J. Radiat. Oncol. Biol. Phys.* 14:373–381.

[19] WINSTON, K. R., and W. LUTZ, 1988. Linear accelerator as a neurosurgical tool for stereotactic radiosurgery. *Neurosurgery* 22(3):454–464.

[20] PIKE, B., E. B. PODGORSAK, and T. M. PETERS, 1987. Dose distributions in dynamic stereotactic radiosurgery. *Med. Phys.* 14(5).

[21] LOZANO-PÉREZ, T., 1983. Spatial planning: A configuration space approach. *IEEE Trans. Comput.* 32(2):108–120.

[22] GUIBAS, L., and R. SEIDEL, 1986. Computing convolution by reciprocal search. In *Proceedings of the ACM Symposium on Computational Geometry,* pp. 90–99.

[23] EDELSBRUNNER, H., and L. GUIBAS, 1989. Topologically sweeping an arrangement. *J. Comput. System Sci.* 35:165–194.

[24] WELZL, E., 1991. Smallest enclosing disks (tech. rep. B 91-09). Institut für Informatik, FU Berlin.

[25] GUTHRIE, B., and J. ADLER, 1991. Frameless stereotaxy: Computer-interactive neurosurgery. *Perspect. Neurol. Surg.* 2(1):1–22.

57 Conformal External Radiotherapy: Preliminary Results in the Treatment of Prostatic Carcinoma

JOCELYNE TROCCAZ, YANN MENGUY,
MICHEL BOLLA, PHILIPPE CINQUIN,
PATRICK VASSAL, NOUREDDINE LAIEB,
LAURENT DESBAT, ANDREE DUSSERRE, AND
SYLVIE DAL SOGLIO

THE PURPOSE OF computer-assisted medical intervention strategies is to help surgeons and physicians use multimodal images, in a rational and quantitative way, to plan and perform medical interventions [1]. Conformal radiotherapy has to deliver a specific dose to a tumoral target volume with high precision, concurrently sparing as much as possible organs at risk. In fact, external irradiation may suffer from a lack of accuracy for any of the following reasons:

1. The gross tumor volume and the organs at risk are not accurately defined.

2. There is a lack of planning tools for preparing the irradiation plan—that is, efficient computation and visualization tools allowing a 3D display of the target, the organs at risk, and the dose distribution, and mathematic tools for dose delivery optimization.

3. The location of the gross tumor volume during the radiation treatment is not well-known. This can result from limitations at the simulation stage, during which the target is not always visible (e.g., the prostate), or from patient set-up based on the use of marks on the patient's skin that are not fixed with respect to the organs.

As a consequence, the radiation oncologist may choose inadequate irradiation fields and simplify the ballistics. This is the reason why computer-assisted methods are required for irradiating small tumors that are well localized and do not move during irradiation, where high precision and high dose may enhance local control, quality of life, and overall survival. Such methods may be particularly useful when using external irradiation during the boost, to treat localized (T_1/T_2) or locally advanced (T_3/T_4) prostatic carcinoma. The aims are to conform the dose specification accurately to the anatomic boundaries of the planning target volume (taking full advantage of 3D imaging systems), to optimize the ballistics, to increase the dose, and finally to maximize the therapeutic ratio between tumor control probability and normal tissue complication probability. In this chapter, we present the first results of this approach on a dummy prostate.

Technical approach

As explained previously, our system is intended to make a correct set-up of the patient possible for irradiation, according to the planning target volume and ballistics, both preoperatively defined. It relies on the automatic registration of preoperative images (CT or MRI) and intraoperative images (ultrasonography). We call *intraoperative* the images acquired in the irradiation room when the treatment occurs. The registration stage makes it possible to determine the actual position and orientation of the planning target volume with respect to the reference system of the accelerator. Thus,

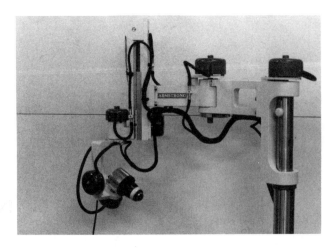

FIGURE 57.1 The passive arm.

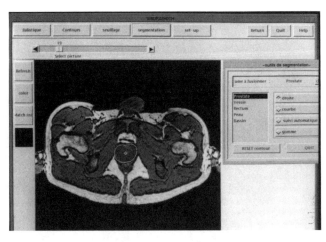

FIGURE 57.2 Preoperative image processing.

it results both in patient set-up modification and in correction of the ballistics. The system is made up of software and hardware. The former is concerned with preoperative and intraoperative image processing (calibration of the sensors, acquisition, and treatment) and includes the automatic registration of images. The latter mainly consists of an ultrasonic probe, a six-axis encoded motorless arm (figure 57.1), calibration objects, and a workstation and its real-time video digitizing board. This system is intended to be used with any standard linear accelerator.

ACQUISITION OF MULTIMODAL INFORMATION AND MODELING

PREOPERATIVE IMAGE PROCESSING A preoperative CT (or MRI) examination of the patient is performed. These images are interactively segmented in order to get a 3D surface representation of the organs (at least the prostate) in the preoperative reference system. The segmentation of the prostate is necessary for the registration of preoperative and intraoperative data. The segmentation of critical organs may be used to optimize the dose delivery.

In the current implementation of the system, a user interface (figure 57.2) enables the operator to segment any of the relevant 2D sections to model the prostate and the critical organs. Extracting the contours can be manual or automatic (using standard filtering), or both, depending mainly on the image quality. To obtain a dense set of data, a linear interpolation is performed between two contours extracted in two successive sections.

In the near future, this "2.5D" segmentation will be replaced by a direct 3D segmentation such as the spline-snakes method presented in Leitner and Cinquin [2]. It is an extension of the classic spline approximation used to model a volume as a C^2 continuous function of the density in each point. The snake-splines segmentation process entails iteratively deforming an initial surface (e.g., sphere) under the attraction of edge points detected by filtering. The result is a parametric C^2 spline surface. An important characteristic of this approach is that it can adapt to an object of complex topology (e.g., a vertebra).

INTRAOPERATIVE IMAGE PROCESSING The basic idea is to obtain a 3D localization of intraoperative ultrasonic images with respect to the irradiation system by means of a localizing device (the encoded arm). The patient is intraoperatively positioned on the couch, and a set of ultrasonic images is acquired. As we will see in the following, the ultrasonic probe is calibrated with respect to the end-effector of the arm. In other words, the transform existing between the ultrasonic image reference system and that of the end-effector is known. Each time an image is acquired, the position of the end-effector with respect to the reference system of the arm is stored. Therefore, the 3D position of the echographic plane is known for each acquisition. Because the arm is also calibrated with respect to the irradiation system, ultrasonic images are localized in the

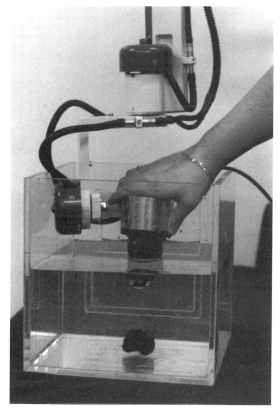

(a)

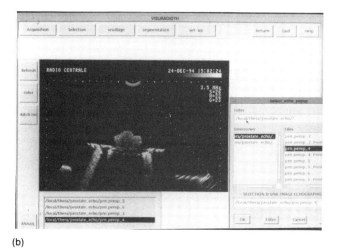

(b)

FIGURE 57.3 Intraoperative image acquisition (a) and segmentation (b) of a dummy prostate.

accelerator reference system (let us call it $R_{isocenter}$). These images are interactively segmented (figure 57.3) to provide a set of points belonging to the prostate external surface whose coordinates are now known with respect to the isocenter of the linear accelerator.

Description of the localizing device The localizing device is aimed at providing 3D localization (position and orientation) of the ultrasonic probe, thus that of the intraoperative images. Three possible types of localizing systems exist: optical, ultrasonic, and mechanical. The optical solution entails tracking with a set of cameras the movements of infrared emitters fixed to the instrument whose position must be known [3]. In the sonic solution, the position of the instrument is computed by measuring the traveling time of sound impulses between emitters fixed to the instrument and receivers (microphones) [18]. The mechanical solution, which we have chosen, consists of having an articulated encoded arm on which the instrument is fixed. The internal position sensors of the arm, or encoders, allow for continuous computation of the position and orientation of the instrument. The arm has a six-axis passive (SCARA) architecture. The first three joints (two rotations and a translation) allow the end-effector to be positioned in the work space; the last three joints (three rotations) define the orientation of the end-effector (figure 57.4). Such an architecture has two chief advantages: It is very easy to move the end-effector because the weight is self-supported by the arm and because the arm moves between two parallel planes, avoiding collision with the environment (in particular, the patient) is very easy. The end-effector has been designed so that different objects (calibration objects, ultrasonic probe) can be plugged into it in an accurate and repeatable way.

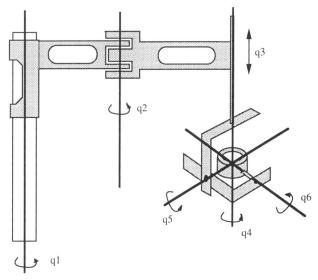

FIGURE 57.4 The SCARA arm.

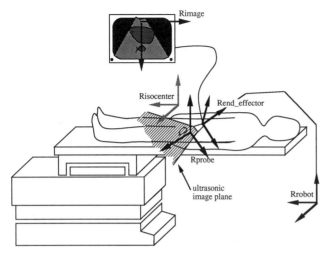

FIGURE 57.5 The different intraoperative reference systems.

FIGURE 57.6 Extrinsic calibration of the arm: The calibration object.

Calibration of the intraoperative localizing device The calibration stage is necessary to define intraoperative data in the accelerator reference system. This requires the determination of four rigid transforms (figure 57.5):

1. R_{robot} to $R_{\text{end-effector}}$ (intrinsic calibration of the arm): This transform is a function of the arm configuration. It depends on the arm model, whose parameters have to be determined once. This is done by fixing a laser beam on the end-effector and collecting a set of measurements for which the laser spot intersects a small plate. The spot coordinates are acquired by means of a video camera, and the corresponding encoder's readings of the arm are stored simultaneously. Finally, the arm parameters are estimated using a nonlinear least-squares minimization.

2. R_{robot} to $R_{\text{isocenter}}$ (extrinsic calibration of the arm): This step is based on the use of the patient alignment system of the accelerator. This system consists of three orthogonal laser planes. A calibration object (figure 57.6) is fixed on the arm end-effector, and the arm is moved so that one laser plane passes through two slits (1.5 mm large) in the object. This is performed for the three laser planes and allows the computation of the transform.

3. R_{image} to R_{probe} (intrinsic calibration of the probe): The purpose of this calibration is to determine the transform from pixel coordinates to millimetric coordinates. This is done by acquiring the image of a calibration object and determining the scaling factors. Including a more complex model based on the use of a

spline function would allow us to take into account local distortions in the image [4].

4. R_{probe} to $R_{\text{end-effector}}$ (extrinsic calibration of the probe): This is done by moving the arm and observing the resulting motion of the probe. This gives a system of the form $AX = XB$, where A (B) is the transform corresponding to the end-effector (probe) motion, and X is the unknown transform relating R_{probe} to $R_{\text{end-effector}}$. A is easily computed from the encoder readings. B is computed from the registration of two sets of points acquired for two positions of the arm by means of a noniterative least-squares fitting algorithm [5]. Two such equations, and therefore two arm movements, are necessary to solve this system (see [6]).

STRATEGY DEFINITION

In the case of radiotherapy, strategy definition means irradiation planning. It includes the definition of the planning target volume and the choice of the ballistics. This stage has been made easier by the recent development of powerful graphic workstations that allow for computation and visualization of 3D dose distribution. Nevertheless, there is still a need for the development of better dose optimization tools.

Some preliminary results have been obtained. That is the case, for example, in Schweikard, Adler, and

Latombe [7], who apply classic path-planning tools used in the field of robotics to find a ballistics for which the beams intersect as little as possible some critical organs. This purely geometric approach has been developed in the context of arc therapy in stereotactic radiosurgery. Despite the fact that it does not find the optimal solution to the dosimetric problem, it may be able sensitively to decrease the dose received by critical anatomic regions of the brain.

A more complex problem is the resolution of the inverse dosimetry. Indeed, because the classic method is iterative, nothing can be said about the optimality of the dosimetric solution. We are currently investigating that problem with different approaches. One of them relies on an algebraic formulation of the inverse problem that takes advantage of regularization methods such as the one successfully applied to image reconstruction [8, 9]. Solving the inverse problem will lead naturally to the increasing use of dynamic multibeam irradiation. The work described by Podgorsak et al. [10] was a first step toward dynamic irradiation. Executing more general coordinated trajectories of the system gantry and couch as a result of the optimization process will require a full automation of the accelerator. Much attention must be given to the safety problems.

REGISTRATION OF MULTIMODAL INFORMATION

At the registration stage, we have a set of 3D points representing the prostate in the preoperative reference system and a much more restricted set of 3D points belonging to the prostate surface expressed in $R_{\text{isocenter}}$. The following step consists in the automatic registration of these two sets of points. The problem is to find the rigid transform (six position and orientation parameters), between the preoperative and intraoperative reference systems that allows us to superimpose data acquired in these two modalities. It is done by using the 3D/3D registration approach introduced in Lavallée, Szeliski, and Brunie [11], which is close to

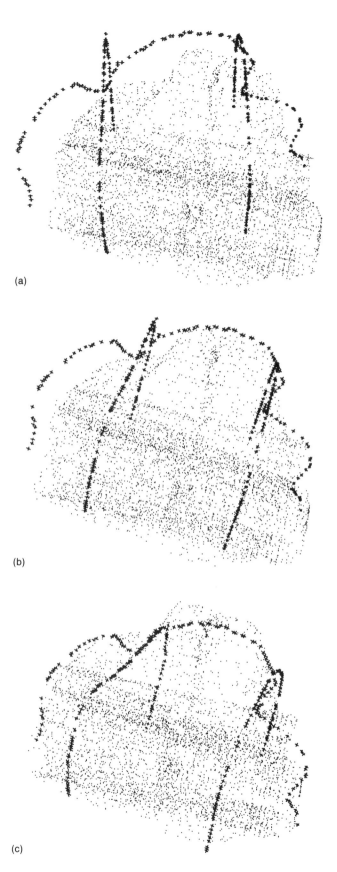

(a)

(b)

(c)

FIGURE 57.7 Convergence of the 3D/3D registration algorithm: One set of points segmented on relatively registered ultrasound images is matched with the prostate surface segmented on CT images (a) before registration, (b) during registration; and (c) after registration.

the one described in Brunie et al. [12] (see also chapter 5 in this book). It is based on a least-squares minimization of the distance between the two sets of points. Figure 57.7 shows some steps of the distance minimization. To compute distance to the preoperative 3D surface quickly and accurately, we represent a precomputed distance map as an octree-spline whose resolution increases near the surface. Let us note, first, that only a small number of ultrasonic images are necessary and that they can be located in any direction. Second, the contours segmented on them need not be connected (a small set of accurate points is preferable to a less precise complete contour).

Performance of action

Before irradiating the patient, it is necessary to take into account the set-up position and orientation errors. Because the registration has been done, the actual position and orientation of the prostate with respect to $R_{\text{isocenter}}$ is known. The planning target volume and the ballistics, preoperatively defined, are mapped in $R_{\text{isocenter}}$ by applying to them the transform found by the registration algorithm. The target is translated to the isocenter by means of the 3 translational degrees of freedom of the couch. The ballistics are modified to counteract the orientation errors in patient positioning (figure 57.8). This corresponds to new values for the isocentric rotation of the couch, for the isocentric rotation of the gantry, and for the rotation of the collimator. Note that small orientation errors may result in large couch displacements, depending on the direction of the error vector (figure 57.9). This last point motivates the development of planning tools that make it possible to compute the collision-free configurations of the system couch and gantry. Such tools are classically used in robotics [13]. They will be absolutely necessary for multibeam dynamic irradiation.

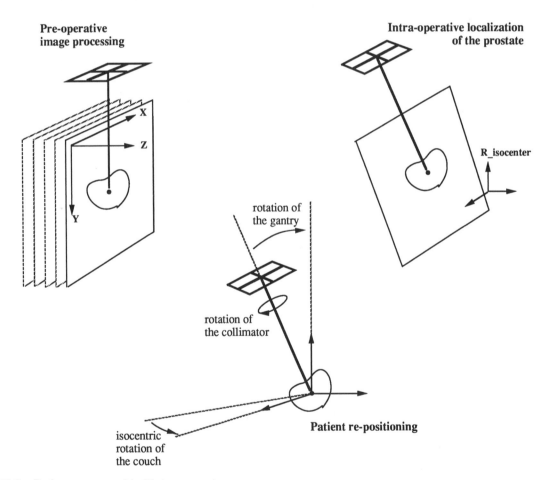

FIGURE 57.8 Patient set-up and ballistics correction.

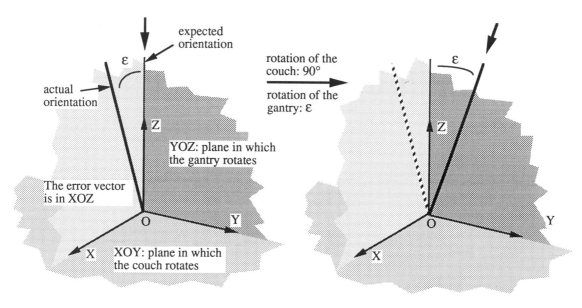

FIGURE 57.9 Small errors may cause large displacements.

DISCUSSION

The same registration process can be used for anatomic structures other than the prostate. For example, pelvic bone surfaces can be detected on CT and MRI, and some surface points can be acquired with ultrasound images. The set-up is corrected only for errors exceeding a given threshold. Our approach could be used to register preoperative 3D data with preoperative 2D portal digital data (see [12] for the 3D/2D image registration). In this case, the registration can be performed on the pelvic bones with respect to which the prostate is fixed. This would allow the global 3D correction of the patient set-up. The portal imaging device will certainly become a standard element of irradiation systems within the next decade, because it has the advantage of enabling in vivo dosimetry.

At the present time, our system has been tested on a dummy prostate made of agar-agar, carbon, and propanol [17]. This prostate includes metallic seeds that can be seen on CT images. The accuracy of the whole system has been evaluated on the simulator of the linear accelerator. The position of the seeds can be measured once the set-up correction proposed by the system has been executed, by means of simulation images (x-ray images). The accuracy of the system is evaluated by comparing their position, relative to the isocenter, to the expected one computed from preoperative images (see [12] for a more precise explanation of a

similar experiment). The accuracy obtained was on the order of 1.5 mm. The next stage will be to validate the approach for use on patients for the prostatic boost before each fraction. This can be done by delineating the irradiation fields on the patient's skin after the set-up correction proposed by the system is made. Before performing any treatment, a conventional simulation with retrograde cystography and impregnation of the rectum will be performed. The classic simulation films will be used to verify the adequacy of the correction proposed by our system. Another way to achieve a more accurate measurement is by placing some radio-opaque seeds in the prostate of a phantom and comparing their position to the expected one. The expected accuracy is to less than 3 mm. When this quality control is achieved, the next step will be to improve the ballistics by increasing the number of fields (see the section on registration of information) and to assess acute tolerance and late morbidity according to European Organization for Research and Treatment of Cancer (EORTC) criteria of this cohort of patients. This will make it easier to conduct a dose escalation study (up to 75 Gy) for advanced T_3/T_4 prostatic carcinoma.

Conclusion

Prostate cancer is the second most common form of malignant disease in men, after bronchus carcinoma.

Individual screening with rectal examination, serum PSA, and endorectal ultrasound enable us, more frequently than in the past, to diagnose clinically localized prostatic carcinoma. Prostatectomy and external irradiation are the two ways to perform radical treatment for clinical stages T_1 and T_2. They can be combined to give better long-term results: If there is no need to increase the dose, a higher precision may decrease the normal tissue complication probability and improve quality of life. Conversely, definitive irradiation is the only treatment for locally advanced T_3/T_4 prostatic carcinoma; in these stages, there is an increase in tumor control probability when the specified dose to the prostate is 70 Gy or greater, but the use of long-term treatment sequelae (grade 3 or more) may become harmful. Conformal radiotherapy thus offers a good opportunity to optimize dose to the tumor volume and to maximize the therapeutic ratio between improved local control and reduced morbidity, which may have an impact both on quality of life and overall survival. This technique must be tested carefully by physicians, physicists, and computer scientists, and must be checked via a quality-control assurance program before becoming a routine procedure in clinical practice.

ACKNOWLEDGMENTS This research is financially supported by Digital Equipment Corporation, SIEMENS AG, La Ligue Nationale contre le Cancer (comité Isère) and INSERM grant no 920 901. Special thanks to Stéphane Lavallée for his fruitful contribution to this project.

REFERENCES

[1] CINQUIN, P., J. DEMONGEOT, J. TROCCAZ, S. LAVALLÉE, G. CHAMPLEBOUX, L. BRUNIE, F. LEITNER, P. SAUTOT, B. MAZIER, A. PEREZ, M. DJAID, T. FORTIN, M. CHENIN, and A. CHAPEL, 1992. IGOR, image-guided operating robot: Methodology, medical application, results. *Innov. Tech. Biol. Med.* 13(4):374–394.

[2] LEITNER, F., and P. CINQUIN, 1991. Complex topology 3D objects segmentation. *SPIE* 1609:295–296.

[3] ADAMS, L., A. KNEEPER, W. KRYBUS, D. MEYER-EBRECHT, G. PFEIFER, R. RUGER, and M. WITTE, 1992. Orientation aid for head and neck surgeons. *Innov. Tech. Biol. Med.* 13(4):409–424.

[4] CHAMPLEBOUX, G., S. LAVALLÉE, P. CINQUIN, 1992. A new approach for accurate calibration of cameras and range imaging sensors: The NPBS method. In *Proceedings of the IEEE Conference of Robotics and Automation*, Nice, Trance, pp. 1552–1557.

[5] ARUN, K. S., T. S. HUANG, and S. D. BLOSTEIN, 1987. Least square fitting of two 3D points sets. *IEEE Transactions on Pattern Analysis and Machine Intelligence* PAMI-9 (5): 698–700.

[6] WANG, C. C., 1992. Extrinsic calibration of a vision sensor mounted on a robot. *IEEE Trans Robotics Autom.* 8(2):161–175.

[7] SCHWEIKARD, A., J. ADLER, and J. C. LATOMBE, 1992. Motion planning in stereotactic radiosurgery. (tech. rep. STAN-CS-92-1441), Stanford University.

[8] DESBAT, L., 1989. Regularization parameter estimation. In *Proceedings of the Colloquium "Errors, Uncertainties and Bias in Astronomy,"* C. Jaschek and F. Murtagh eds. Strasbourg: Cambridge University Press, pp. 313–316.

[9] DESBAT, L., and P. TURLIER, 1991. Measurement optimization in tomography. In *Proceedings of the Thirteenth International Association for Mathematics and Computers in Simulation World Congress on Computation and Applied Mathematics*, Trinity College, Dublin, pp. 1523–1524.

[10] PODGORSAK, E. B., 1988. Dynamic stereotactic radiosurgery. *Int. J. Radiat. Oncol.* 14(1):115–126.

[11] LAVALLÉE, S., R. SZELISKI, and L. BRUNIE, 1991. Matching 3D smooth surfaces with their 2D projections using 3D distance maps. *SPIE: Geometric Methods in Computer Vision*, 1570:322–336.

[12] BRUNIE, L., S. LAVALLÉE, J. TROCCAZ, PH. CINQUIN, and M. BOLLA, 1993. Pre- and intra-radiotherapy multimodal image registration. *Radiother. Oncol.* 29:244–252.

[13] BELLIER, C., C. LAUGIER, E. MAZER, and J. TROCCAZ, 1991. A practical system for planning safe trajectories for manipulator robots. In *Proceedings of the Second International Workshop on Experimental Robotics*, R. Chatila, ed. Toulouse: LAAS.

[14] VAN HERK, M., 1992. An electronic portal imaging device: Physics, development, and application. Doctoral thesis, Universiteit van Amsterdam.

[15] YU, C., and F. KRISPEL, 1992. Imagerie en temps réel avec accélérateur linéaire Mevatron. *Bull. Cancer/Radiother.* 79:271–277.

[16] BIJHOLD, J., J. V. LEBESQUE, A. M. HART, and R. E. VIJLBRIEF, 1992. Maximizing setup accuracy using portal images as applied to a conformal boost technique for prostatic cancer. *Radiat. Oncol.* 24:261–271.

[17] BURLEW, M. M., E. L. MATSEN, J. A. ZAGZEBSKI, R. A. BANJAVIC, and S. W. SUM, 1980. A new ultrasound tissue-equivalent material. *Radiology* 134.

[18] REINHARDT, H. F., G. A. HORSTMANN, and O. GRATZI, 1994. Ultrasonic stereometry in microsurgical producures for deep-seated brain tumors and vascular malformations. *Neurosurgery.*

The High-Tech Operating Room

THE CLOSING CHAPTER of this book, "The Vision of Image-Guided Computerized Surgery," by Jolesz, Kikinis, and Shtern, presents the views of some of the most forceful proponents in the emerging field of CIS. The authors describe their vision of the so-called high-tech operating room. The main concept is image-guided surgery, which has been extensively discussed by many authors in this book.

Jolesz, Kikinis, and Shtern characterize five key aspects of the high-tech operating room. Although the authors' detailed breakdown is slightly different from that we proposed in our general introduction, we would like to show how those five issues have been addressed in this book.

The first issue is *visualization of surgery*. Information derived from a variety of imaging modalities is necessary to define targets and follow any changes in real time during surgery. Mösges and Lavallée have described a wealth of medical information in chapter 1. In chapter 2, Greinacher has detailed how multimodal data can be integrated through the use of picture archiving and communication systems. Udupa and Gonçalves (chapter 3) and Ayache et al. (chapter 4) have detailed some of the most efficient techniques of image modeling. However, real-time data acquisition, processing, and manipulation is clearly an issue that calls for further research work. Similarly, Jolesz, Kikinis, and Shtern advocate for the development of 3D real-time interactive display systems. Such 3D display methods have been presented by Udupa and Gonçalves, Pom-

mert et al., and Robb and Hanson in chapters 3, 9, and 10, respectively. Up-to-date technologies for interactive manipulation have been described in the section Human-Machine Interfaces (chapters 12–15).

The second issue is *localization*. The registration section of this book (chapters 5–7) addresses the problem of collecting all the available and necessary data in order to build a unique patient model and to correlate this model with the surgical physical space. Real-time updating of registration during surgery applied to deformable structures remains an issue. The use of the registered patient model for accurate surgical planning is a crucial and unavoidable step that has been covered by several of the technology chapters (chapters 8–11). Also, many of the applications chapters propose implementations adapted to particular cases. For instance, the optimization of surgical planning is detailed for craniofacial applications in chapter 52 by Cutting, Bookstein, and Taylor and for radiotherapy in chapter 56 by Schweikard, Adler, and Latombe. Similarly, the use of the registered model during surgery with passive navigation systems is critical. A description of the basic technologies is presented in chapter 1, and many applications that use navigation aids are detailed in the clinical sections of this book, in chapters 22, 23, 32, and 51.

The third requirement discussed in the final chapter is *access*. The authors stress the importance of achieving minimally invasive surgery. This trend has also been detailed in chapter 1, and many systems described in this book aim at achieving that goal. However, many problems have to be faced. The technical issues are related mainly to human-machine interfaces, which are addressed in chapters 12–15. The seven chapters of the section Minimal-Access Surgery also focus on these problems and propose some solutions.

Intraoperative and postoperative automated *control of surgery* is the fourth requirement. The authors mention instances of on-line monitoring of energy transfer during some therapeutic procedures through the use of ultrasound or MRI, as well as robotic aids for controlling surgery. Although this book does not thoroughly discuss the first point, the second is covered largely by the robotics sections and it also is more specifically ad-dressed in the safety section (section introduction and chapter 19). For instance, the companion chapters by Taylor and Mittelstadt and their colleagues (chapters 28 and 29) present efficient real-time and redundant control of robotics action in the section on orthopaedics.

Last but not least, *integration* is considered to be a major challenge. No system can pretend to meet every requirement of every application. However, we hope this book has demonstrated that there now exist several systems that have successfully integrated a computation with a variety of technologies to meet the specific requirements of particular clinical applications.

58 The Vision of Image-Guided Computerized Surgery: The High-Tech Operating Room

FERENC A. JOLESZ, RON KIKINIS, AND
FAINA SHTERN

CONVENTIONAL freehand surgical procedures have certain fundamental limitations. Their execution has depended, to greater or lesser degree, on hand-eye coordination. The main problem is that visible light does not penetrate far past the exposed surface, and therefore the surgeon cannot visually comprehend the complete 3D information necessary to fully appreciate volumes. This is the main reason that surgical approaches are typically described in terms of advance through tissue layers rather than in terms of volumes, even in those cases (e.g., tumor removal) in which the excision of a target volume is the ultimate goal of the procedure. It has now become apparent that visually guided freehand procedures compare poorly to precise stereotactic localization, in which navigation through exact coordinates can be preplanned and then accurately executed.

The deficiencies in direct visualization can be reduced by complementing the surgeon's eyes with imaging modalities that reveal both surfaces and volumes in the context of anatomy. This 3D information can then be utilized to provide localization coordinates and guidance for passive and active devices to perform a given intervention. Although diagnostic imaging techniques now are widely used to establish 3D reference frames, and various types of precision therapeutic equipment are available or under development, it is the integration of these technologies and their control by computers that will lead to the realization of the vision of the computerized surgical theater of the future [1].

A system of image-guided computerized stereotactic surgical intervention comprises five major components: visualization, localization, access, control, and integration. These components must be combined and integrated into the operating room environment to provide a framework for new therapeutic strategies. The ultimate goal is to utilize high technology to reduce the invasiveness and risk of surgical techniques and to provide a more comprehensive approach to surgery.

Visualization

Visualization for conventional surgery is limited by the reflective character of visible light. Other serious shortcomings result from the physiology of the human visual system, including limited spatial resolution due to the constraints of the human stereoscopic visual configuration. Moreover, the ability to discern contrast (and therefore tissue characteristics) is based on the absorption and reflection of light and color. The use of operating microscopes can improve spatial resolution, and multiple stereoscopic views can be obtained by taking advantage of observer head and body motion. Even with these corrections, human visualization should be complemented (and in some cases even replaced) by the use of modern imaging modalities such as ultrasonography (US), CT, MRI, single photon emission computerized tomography (SPECT), and positron emission tomography (PET). Although each of these systems provides some degree of tissue characterization, the ability to present contrast between various tissues and to distinguish normal from pathologic anatomy varies according to the physical principles of the image acquisition system. This modality-dependent tissue characterization explains why imaging systems are utilized diagnostically and complementarily.

Tissue characterization ability (or contrast) is not the only feature that distinguishes among these imaging modalities. Spatial and temporal resolution are also important features, particularly if images are to be used not only for diagnosis but also for monitoring interventional procedures. Methods also differ in their ability to display 2D or 3D images without spatial distortion, which may be a factor in their suitability for use in stereotactic localization.

For monitoring and controlling surgical interventions, two important attributes of imaging modalities should be distinguished: target definition and the ability to demonstrate therapy-induced changes in real time. In tumor therapy, for example, the most important condition for target definition is exact localization of the lesion, including a precise definition of tumor margins. Because diagnosis can be executed preoperatively, multiple modalities often are utilized (e.g., CT and MRI, or MRI and PET). This so-called image fusion can improve on the tissue characterization of a single modality by adding features detectable only with another modality [2–4]. It also is possible that one imaging method will be used for diagnosis and a different one will be used to monitor therapy. In cases where destructive energy is employed during surgery, monitoring and control techniques are required that are sensitive to the physical changes occurring during the time span of the procedure. When tissue volumes are treated with thermal energy (e.g., interstitial laser therapy, focused ultrasound surgery, or cryosurgery), visualization is not restricted to target definition but is used also to follow the temporal and spatial dispersion of heat energy within the tissue. Some imaging modalities (CT and US) are capable of demonstrating the irreversible changes induced by thermal energy deposition; MRI parameters are sufficiently temperature-sensitive to detect and localize thermal changes even before they produce any significant tissue damage.

The visualization requirements for surgery include real-time or near-real-time image display and the unlimited manipulation of images within the 3D workspace. Cross-sectional image representation, even with multiplanar reformatting, is not sufficient. Only when 3D reconstructed images are displayed with real-time speed and can be interactively manipulated will the operator be able to command the entire visualization process through the computerized control of image acquisition, reconstruction, and display. The use of virtual reality is only one potential avenue to permit freedom of navigation within the 3D data sets. Operator-controlled image display methods, with or without motion-sensitive manipulative devices, should provide an operator-dependent, position-independent

perception of the virtual reality and its relationship to the real object. Image-controlled surgical interventions require a user-friendly environment that will not restrict the surgeon's ability to achieve interactive speed while manipulating both the displayed virtual images and the real object.

The real-time display of 3D data requires that the various steps of the image processing be fully automated [5]. Near-real-time image processing is imperative if the visualization is to be used for the construction of virtual reality. This can be accomplished only with very powerful computers utilizing large-capacity parallel processors. Although these computing demands increase expenses compared to conventional low-tech surgery, the benefits gained contribute not only to the visualization process but also to other important components of high-tech computerized surgery.

Localization

Localization in 3D space is a critical step for image-guided surgery. After the target is defined, the spatial coordinates describing the target volume are registered within a reference frame. This reference frame can be identical with that of the imaging system or, alternatively, the spatial coordinates of the target can be defined in relationship to anatomic or fiducial landmarks. In the latter case, when the patient is repositioned (e.g., from an imaging system to the operating room, or from one imaging system to another), it is sufficient to register only these landmarks within the new reference frame, as long as their spatial relationship with the target is stable.

The registration process usually involves matching the reference frames of one or more imaging modalities with the patient's anatomy and subsequently transferring these coordinates to the operating theater. In conventional stereotactic neurosurgery, this is accomplished by using rigid frames attached to the patient's head. This technique not only causes patient discomfort but also lengthens the procedure and is unsuitable for accessing all lesions. Traditional head-frame-based stereotactic surgery is being replaced by a frameless approach. The frameless stereotactic approach is feasible only with the use of sensors, active or passive mechanical arms, and various registration methods in combination with complex computational techniques [6–8]. Frameless stereotactic procedures generally are performed using retrospective data sets acquired previously for diagnostic purposes, in which case registration of the spatial data with patient anatomy is performed in the operating room [9–11].

The need for registration can be avoided or the process simplified if the interventional procedure can be performed within an imaging system, provided that anatomic landmarks are visible. Localization during real-time US-guided biopsy is a good example of this approach. Another example is the utilization of an operating table locked to the reference frame of an imaging system (e.g., CT or MRI), allowing localized procedures to be executed without need for registration outside the imaging field. The introduction of more accessible (or "open") MRI systems may offer an ideal way to localize and guide procedures simultaneously without the need for table repositioning. Registration can be obtained using image data exclusively. Anatomic structures, such as surfaces, can be utilized for computerized registration methods that are in turn used in image fusion techniques that match images derived from different modalities to one another. Various devices and tools can be used for both registration and localization purposes. Whether they take the form of markers, pointers, needles, operating microscopes, or other instruments, their common feature is that they provide x, y, and z coordinates. This spatial information, provided on the cross-sectional, reformatted, or 3D-reconstructed images, can be used for defining surgical incisions or trajectories for needle penetration, or for guiding the path of endoscopes within the body [3, 9, 11–13].

Optical or electromagnetic sensors can be attached to any tool or instrument that requires spatial guidance. The advantage of sensors over mechanical arms is that they can be used for freehand procedures. The utility of either type of sensor is somewhat limited, however. There must be an uninterrupted pathway between the optical sensor and the light-emitting source. In the case of electromagnetic sensors, the presence of metals within the operating volume may cause significant spatial distortions and prevent precise localization.

Mechanical arms with various degrees of freedom can also be used for localization and for guiding needle insertion or other procedures. The flexible arms can be positioned according to the image-derived coordinates or according to anatomic and fiducial landmarks. When the flexible arm is in position, it can be fixed to guide the needle through the predetermined trajectory. In contrast to such passive systems, actively moving robotic arms have the advantage of being controllable by computers working directly from the image data, and therefore both the localization and the advance through the trajectory can be performed in one continuous procedure [11, 12, 14–16].

Surgical planning, which is essentially trajectory optimization, is an integral part of image-guided interventional procedures. Following target definition and correct spatial registration within the appropriate reference frame, single or multiple trajectory options can be tested in the context of anatomy. The trajectories are more or less complex depending on the requirements of the procedure (whether biopsy, surgical removal, radiotherapy, etc.). In a complex surgical planning environment, algorithms for image manipulation should be available to allow interactive manipulation of various components of the anatomy, translation and rotation of the structures, and demonstration of different views, planes, surfaces, volumes, and access directions. Computerized surgical planning, combined with interactive visualization tools, provides a virtual environment capable of modeling surgical situations and approaches, enabling intervention strategies to be optimized [6, 7, 9, 10, 13, 17].

Access

The invasiveness of a surgical procedure is determined primarily by the accessibility of the target structure. Optimization of surgical strategies is therefore directed toward minimizing tissue damage caused by passage through normal tissues. With the increasing use of preoperative image data and intraoperative visualization tools (e.g., endoscopes, laparoscopes, and US), surgical incisions can be positioned optimally, explorations are limited, and the size of operational volumes has decreased. There has been a revolution in surgical instrumentation as well, and further improvements in the mechanical and physical properties of the therapeutic devices can be expected. Particularly interesting is the use of interstitial thermal surgery (laser or cryosurgery) in which the treatment device can be introduced via a needle or endoscope or through a small incision [18, 19]. Focused ultrasound surgery is even less invasive, as the thermal effects develop within the body with no effect on the surrounding tissues (this is referred to as *no-access surgery*).

The fundamental problems with minimally invasive or reduced-access surgery, however, remain limited visualization, difficult localization, and lack of control beyond the smaller-sized operational volumes. It is difficult to appreciate the full extent of anatomy through a small incision or exploration or via an endoscope. The invisibility of anatomic landmarks makes localization and registration difficult, and the limited access hampers the control of bleeding or other complications if they occur beyond the operational volume.

To overcome these problems, minimally invasive procedures should be enhanced and complemented by image data that provide information beyond the visible surfaces and the limited explored volume. In addition, tools and instruments used in minimally invasive surgical procedures should be equipped with sensors or, alternatively, the procedures should utilize computer-controlled mechanical arms. With these developments, minimally invasive surgical approaches will dominate the surgery of the future.

Control

As has been demonstrated in the past few years, information provided by imaging modalities can be exploited to control the mechanical, thermal, or chemical effects of various therapeutic methods. Surgical robots have already been introduced (primarily in orthopaedic surgery), and other image-guided mechanical devices are under development. Although human operators exhibit more degrees of freedom than robots, and manually performed procedures can be more complex, robotic devices offer the advantages of much greater precision and speed and the potential for automation [14–16].

One extremely important aspect of control is the measurement of energy deposition into tissues during therapeutic procedures. Ultrasound guidance has been used for controlling interstitial laser therapy, cryosurgery, and focused ultrasound surgery of tumors. Within its limits of spatial and contrast resolution, US is able to depict irreversible tissue damage caused by these interventions. MRI is superior to US monitoring in terms of improved demonstration of anatomy, better detection of tumor margins, and inherent sensitivity to thermal changes within tissue. Using MRI is possible to demonstrate reversible as well as irreversible temperature changes, thereby avoiding undesired heating or freezing of normal tissues. MRI data can also be used for the feedback control of energy-producing devices that can be turned on and off according to the signal generated within or outside the treated target volume. Other procedures, such as ethanol injection, may also be controllable on the basis of magnetic resonance images acquired in real time during the procedure.

Integration

The integration of imaging systems, therapeutic devices, and computers in the operating room environment, along with anesthesia machines, specialized lighting, and other equipment, is a major challenge. Even more difficult will be achieving a near-real-time operational control of these complex devices while still allowing the human operator to perform surgical procedures in an interactive way. The development of appropriate user interfaces will be critical. Real-time image acquisition and image processing will have to be integrated with display techniques permitting rapid visualization both directly and through a simulated virtual reality. Eventually, the integration of image acquisition, visualization, localization, and therapeutic devices will enable an operator-controlled precise stereotactic procedure with limited invasiveness.

Real-time monitoring of destructive energy deposition is mandatory for treating tissue volumes. This can be achieved with imaging guidance when the procedure is executed within the imaging system, allowing spatial and temporal control and the potential for automatic feedback control supervised by the operator. Mechanical devices with or without robotic arms can also be fully controlled through image-derived information, whether the images are used in careful preplanning of the trajectories or in real time. The breakthroughs expected in surgery will change the therapeutic approach but will also require education and training of surgeons, anesthesiologists, and radiologists.

Conclusion

Advances in technology have resulted in substantial changes in surgery. Minimally invasive surgical approaches have been developed, and the use of endoscopic as well as cross-sectional imaging techniques has increased. For a more complete exploitation of high-tech therapeutic devices, computers and modern imaging modalities will have to be combined within a new operating room milieu. In this new environment, visualization, localization, access, and control will be fully integrated and adapted to the needs of the human operator performing the procedure. It is anticipated that the use of advanced technologies will result not only in reduced invasiveness of surgical interventions but also in better outcomes. It also is expected that, despite the high initial cost of the tools necessary to create this environment, overall expenses will eventually be reduced because of the higher efficiency of these new procedures and the shorter hospitalization and recovery times that will be required.

REFERENCES

[1] JOLESZ, E. A., and F. SHTERN, 1992. The operating room of the future. *Invest. Radiol.* 27(4):326–328.

[2] EVANS, A. C., S. MARRETT, J. TORRESCORZO, S. KU, and L. COLLINS, 1991. MRI-PET correlative analysis using volume of interest (VOI) atlas. *J. Cereb. Blood Flow Metab.* 11:869–878.

[3] LEVIN, D. N., C. A. PELIZZARI, G. T. Y. CHEN, et al., 1988. Retrospective geometric correlation of MR, CT, and PET images. *Radiology* 169:817–823.

[4] PELIZARRI, C. A., G. T. Y. CHEN, D. R. SPELBRING, R. R. WEICHSELBAUM, and C. T. CHEN, 1989. Accurate three-dimensional registration of CT, PET, and/or MRI images of the brain. *J. Comp. Assist. Tomogr.* 13:20–26.

[5] CLINE, H. E., W. E. LORENSEN, R. KIKINIS, and F. A. JOLESZ, 1990. Three-dimensional segmentation of MR images of the head using probability and connectivity. *J. Comput. Assist. Tomog.* 14(6):1037–1045.

[6] APUZZO, M. L., and J. K. SABSHIN, 1983. Computed tomographic guidance stereotaxis in the management of intracranial mass lesions. *Neurosurgery* 12:277–285.

[7] BROWN, R. A., 1979. A computerized tomography-computer graphics approach to stereotaxic localization. *J. Neurosurg.* 50:715–720.

[8] ROBERTS, D. W., J. W. STROHBEHN, J. F. HATCH, et al., 1986. A frameless stereotaxis integration of computerized tomographic imaging and the operating microscope. *J. Neurosurg.* 65:545–549.

[9] KELLY, P. K., 1986. Computer-assisted stereotaxis: New approaches for the management of intracranial intra-axial tumors. *Neurology* 36:535–541.

[10] KELLY, P. J., B. A. KALL, S. GOERSS, 1986. Results of computer-assisted stereotactic laser resection of deep-seated intracranial lesions. *Mayo Clin. Proc.* 61:20–27.

[11] ZINREICH, S. J., D. DEKEL, B. LEGGETT, et al., 1990. Three-dimensional CT interactive "surgical localizer" for endoscopic sinus surgery and neurosurgery. *Radiology* 177:217.

[12] KOSUGI, Y., E. WATANABE, J. GOTO, et al., 1988. An articulated neurosurgical navigation system using MRI and CT images. *IEEE Trans. Biomed. Eng.* 35(2).

[13] ZAMORANO, L., C. CHAVANTES, M. DUJOVNY, et al., 1989. Image-guided stereotactic laser resection of intracranial lesions: Endoscopic and laser technique. *Neurosurgery: State of the Art Reviews* 4(suppl.):105–118.

[14] KWOH, Y. S., J. HOU, E. A. JONCKNEERE, et al., 1988. A robot with improved absolute positioning accuracy for CT-guided stereotactic brain surgery. *IEEE Trans. Biomed. Eng.* 35(2).

[15] TAYLOR, R. H., J. FUNDA, D. LAROSE, and M. TREAT, 1992. An experimental system for computer-assisted endoscopic surgery. IEEE Satellite Symposium on Neuroscience and Technology. Lyons.

[16] TAYLOR, R. H., H. A. PAUL, C. B. CUTTING, B. MITTELSTADT, W. HANSON, P. KAZANZIDES, B. MUSITS, Y. Y. KIM, A. KALVIN, B. HADDAD, D. KHORAMABADI, and D. LAROSE, 1992. Augmentation of human precision in computer-integrated surgery. Innovations Technologie on Biologie et Medicine Special Issue on Computer Enhanced Surgery. Vol. 13, no. 4.

[17] LAVALLÉE, S., and P. CINQUIN, 1990. Computer-assisted medical interventions. Proceedings of the Nato Advanced Workshop in Travemuende, June 1990. In *3D Imaging in Medicine*, K. H. Hoehne, H. Fuchs, and S. M. Pizer, eds. (Nato ASI Series F: Computer and Systems Sciences, vol 60.) New York: Springer, pp. 301–312.

[18] MATSUMOTO, R., F. A. JOLESZ, A. M. SELIG, and V. M. COLUCCI, 1992. Interstitial Nd:YAG laser ablation in normal rabbit liver: Trial to maximize the size of laser-induced lesions. *Lasers Surg. Med.* 12:650–658.

[19] MATSUMOTO, R., K. OSHIO, and F. A. JOLESZ, 1992. Monitoring of laser- and freezing-induced ablation in the liver with T_1-weighted MR imaging. *J. Magnetic Resonance Imaging* 2:555–562.

CONTRIBUTORS

ADLER, JOHN R. Department of Neurosurgery, School of Medicine, Stanford University, Stanford, California

ANDERSON, JAMES. Department of Radiology, Johns Hopkins University School of Medicine, Baltimore, Maryland.

AYACHE, NICHOLAS. Project EPIDAURE, INRIA, Sophia-Antipolis, France

BAJURA, MICHAEL. Department of Computer Science, University of North Carolina, Chapel Hill, North Carolina

BARGAR, WILLIAM L. Sutter Hospital, Sacramento, California

BENABID, ALIM LOUIS. Service de Neurochirurgie, La Tronche, France

BEYER, JOHN P. Minnesota Dental Research Center for Biomaterials and Biomechanics, University of Minnesota, Minneapolis, Minnesota

BOLLA, MICHEL. Service de Radiothérapie, La Tronche, France

BOOKSTEIN, FRED L. University of Michigan, Ann Arbor

BRADY, MICHAEL. Robotics Research Group Department of Engineering Science, University of Oxford, Oxford, England

BRETT, PETER N. AMARC, University of Bristol, Bristol, England

BRUNIE, LIONEL. TIMC-IMAG, Faculté de Médecine de Grenoble, Sophia-Antipolis, France

BUCKINGHAM, R. O. AMARC, University of Bristol, Bristol, England

BURDEA, GRIGORE C. Center for Computer Aids for Industrial Productivity, Rutgers University, Piscataway, New Jersey

CAIN, PHILLIP. Integrated Surgical Systems, Inc., Sacramento, California

CHARLES, STEVE. The Center for Retinal Vitreous Surgery, Memphis, Tennessee

CHIROSSEL, JEAN-PAUL. Department of Neurosurgery, Grenoble Hospital, Grenoble, France

CHRIST, CLAUS PETER. University Department of Otorhinolaryngology, Nürnberg, Germany

CINQUIN, PHILIPPE. TIMB-IMAG, Faculté de Médecine de Grenoble, La Tronche, France

COHEN, ISAAC. Project EPIDAURE, INRIA, Sophia-Antipolis, France

COHEN, LAURENT. Project EPIDAURE, INRIA, Sophia-Antipolis, France

COLLINS, D. L. McConnell Brain Imaging Unit, Montreal Neurological Institute, Montreal, Quebec, Canada

CUTTING, COURT B. New York University Hospital, New York, New York

DAL SOGLIO, SYLVIE. Service de Radiologie, La Tronche, France

DARIO, PAOLO. Instituti Ortopedici Rizzoli, Lab. Biomeccanica, Bologna, Italy

DAVIES, BRIAN L. Centre for Robotics, Imperial College of Science, Technology and Medicine, London, England

DELONG, RALPH. Minnesota Dental Research Center for Biomaterials and Biomechanics, University of Minnesota, Minneapolis, Minnesota

DESBAT, LAURENT. TIMC-IMAG, Faculté de Médecine, La Tronche, France

DOUGLAS, WILLIAM H. Minnesota Dental Research Center for Biomaterials and Biomechanics, University of Minnesota, Minneapolis, Minnesota

DUNN, STANLEY M. Department of Biomedical Engineering, College of Engineering, Rutgers University, Piscataway, New Jersey

DUSSERRE, ANDREE. Service de Radiothérapie, La Tronche, France

ELDRIDGE, BEN. IBM T. J. Watson Research Center, Yorktown Heights, New York

EVANS, ALAN C. McConnell Brain Imaging Unit Montreal Neurological Institute, Montreal, Quebec, Canada

FADDA, MARCO. Instituti Ortopedici Rizzoli, Lab. Biomeccanica, Bologna, Italy

FUCHS, HENRY. Department of Computer Science, University of North Carolina, Chapel Hill, North Carolina

FUKUSHIMA, TAKANORI. Department of Neurological Surgery, University of Southern California, Los Angeles, California

FUNDA, JANEZ. IBM T. J. Watson Research Center, Yorktown Heights, New York

GABORIT, LINE. TIMC-IMAG, Faculté de Médecine de Grenoble, La Tronche, France

GERSTEN, MARTIN. Department of Ophthalmology, New York University, New York, New York

GILLIES, G. T. Department of Biomedical Engineering, University of Virginia, Charlottesville, Virginia

GLASSMAN, EDWARD. IBM T. J. Watson Research Center, Yorktown Heights, New York

GLEASON, P. LANGHAM. Division of Neurosurgery, Harvard Medical School, Boston, Massachussetts

GOMORY, STEVE. IBM T. J. Watson Research Center, Yorktown Heights, New York Gonçales, Roberto J.

GONÇALVES, ROBERTO J. Medical Imaging Processing Group, Department of Radiology, University of Pennsylvania, Philadelphia, Pennsylvania

GORATOWSKI, ROBERT. Department of Electrical and Computer Engineering, Rutgers University, Piscataway, New Jersey

GOSWAMI, AMBARISH. Department of Mechanical Engineering Northwestern University, Evanston, Illinois

GRADY, M. S. Department of Neurological Surgery, University of Washington, Seattle, Washington

GREINACHER, CHRISTIAN F. C. Siemens Medical Engineering Group, Erlangen, Germany

GRUBEN, KREG. Johns Hopkins University School of Medicine, Baltimore, Maryland

GRUEN, PETER. Department of Neurological Surgery, University of Southern California, Los Angeles, California

HAID, C. TONI. University Department of Otorhinolaryngology, Nürnberg, Germany

HANSON, DENNIS P. Department of Physiology and Biophysics Biomedical Imaging Resource, Mayo Foundation, Rochester, Minnesota

HANSON, WILLIAM. IBM Palo Alto Science Center, Palo Alto, California

HIBBERD, ROGER D. Centre for Robotics, Imperial College of Science, Technology and Medicine, London, England

HIROSE, SHIGEO. Department of Mechanical Engineering Science, Tokyo Institute of Technology, Tokyo, Japan

HOFFMANN, DOMINIQUE. Service de Neurochirurgie, La Tronche, France

HÖHNE, KARL HEINZ. Institute of Mathematics and Computer Science in Medicine, University Hospital Eppendorf, Hamburg, Germany

HOWARD, M. A. III. Department of Neurological Surgery, University of Washington, Seattle, Washington

IKUTA, KOJI. Center of Robotic Systems in Microelectronics, University of California, Santa Barbara, California

JENNINGS, RUSSELL W. University of California, San Francisco, California

JOLESZ, FERENC A. Department of Radiology, Harvard Medical School, Boston, Massachusetts

KAINZ, JOSEF. Department of Otorhinolarygology, University ENT Hospital Medical Faculty at Karl-Franzens-University, Graz, Austria

KALL, BRUCE A. Mayo Clinic, Rochester, Minnesota

KAVOUSSI, LOUIS. The Johns Hopkins University School of Medicine, Baltimore, Maryland

KAZANZIDES, PETER. Integrated Surgical Systems, Sacramento, California

KELLY, PATRICK J. Department of Neurosurgery, New York University Hospital, New York, New York

KHODABANDEHLOO, KOOROSH. AMARC, University of Bristol, Bristol, England

KIENZLE, THOMAS C. III. Department of Orthopaedic Surgery, Northwestern University Medical School, Evanston, Illinois

KIKINIS, RON. Department of Radiology, Harvard Medical School, Brigham and Woman's Hospital, Boston, Massachussetts

KLEIN, HANS-MARTIN. Department of Diagnostic Radiology, University Hospital, Aachen, Germany

KLIMEK, LUDGER. Department of Otorhinolaryngology, Head and Neck Surgery, Aachen University Hospital, Aachen, Germany

KLYCE, STEPHEN D. Lions Eye Research Laboratories, LSU School of Medicine, Baton Rouge, Lousiana

LAIEB, NOUREDDINE. TIMC-IMAG, Faculté de Médecine, La Tronche, France

LAOWATTANA, SCHITT. Department of Medical Engineering, Carnegie Mellon University, Pittsburgh, Pennsylvania

LaROSE, DAVID. IBM T. J. Watson Research Center, Yorktown Heights, New York

LASKO HARWILL, ANN. Formerly of VPL Research, Inc., Foster City, California

LATOMBE, JEAN-CLAUDE. Robotics Laboratory, Department of Computer Science, Stanford University, Stanford, California

LAVALLÉE, STÉPHANE. TIMC-IMAG, Faculté de Médecine de Grenoble, La Tronche, France

LEA, JON. Department of Mechanical Engineering, Northwestern University, Evanston, Illinois

LEE, SIMON. Robotics Research Group, Department of Engineering Science, University of Oxford, Oxford, England

LEITNER, FRANÇOIS. Faculté de Médecine de Grenoble, La Tronche, France

LEONARD, MYER S. Minnesota Dental Research Center for Biomaterials and Biomechanics, University of Minnesota, Minneapolis, Minnesota

LUNACEK, BRAD. Minnesota Dental Research Center for Biomaterials and Biomechanics, University of Minnesota, Minneapolis, Minnesota

MAMMONE, RICHARD J. Center for Computer Aids for Industrial Productivity, Rutgers University, Piscataway, New Jersey

MARCACCI, MAURILIO. Instituti Ortopedici Rizzoli, Lab. Biomeccanica, Bologna, Italy

MARCENARO, GIAMPIERO. Instituti Ortopedici Rizzoli, Lab. Biomeccanica, Bologna, Italy

MARRETT, T. S. McConnell Brain Imaging Unit, Montreal Neurological Institute, Montreal, Quebec, Canada

MARSH, JEFFREY L. Cleft Palate and Craniofacial Deformities Institute, St. Louis Childrens Hospital Washington University School of Medicine, St. Louis, Missouri

MARTELLI, SANDRA. Instituti Ortopedici Rizzoli, Lab. Biomeccanica, Bologna, Italy

MAZIER, BRUNO. TIMC-IMAG, Faculté de Médecine de Grenoble, La Tronche, France

MENGUY, YANN. TIMC-IMAG, Faculté de Médecine , La Tronche, France

MERLOZ, PHILIPPE. Department of Orthopaedics, Grenoble Hospital, Grenoble, France

MITTELSTADT, BRENT D. Integrated Surgical Systems, Sacramento, California

MONGA, OLIVIER. Project EPIDAURE, INRIA, Sophia-Antipolis, France

MÖSGES, RALPH. Department of Ear, Nose and Throat Diseases and Plastic Head and Neck Surgery, University Hospital, Aachen, Germany

MUSITS, BELA L. IBM T. J. Watson Research Center, Yorktown Heights, New York

NAPPI, BRUCE. Foster Miller, Inc, Waltham, Massachusetts

NEELIN, P. McConnell Brain Imaging Unit, Montreal Neurological Institute, Montreal, Quebec, Canada

OHBUCHI, RYUTAROU. Department of Computer Science, University of North Carolina, Chapel Hill, North Carolina

PAUL, HOWARD A. Integrated Surgical Systems, Sacramento, California

PESHKIN, MICHAEL. Department of Mechanical Engineering, Nortwestern University, Evanston, Illinois

POMMERT, ANDREAS. Institute of Mathematics and Computer Science in Medicine, Hamburg, University Hospital Eppendorf, Germany

QUAID, ARTHUR. Department of Mechanical Engineering, Northwestern University, Evanston, Illinois

RADERMACHER, KLAUS. Helmholtz Institute for Biomedical Engineering, Aachen, Germany

RAU, GÜNTER. Helmholtz Institute for Biomedical Engineering, Aachen, Germany

REINHARDT, HANS F. Neurosurgical University Clinic Department for Stereotaxy and Computer Assisted Neurosurgery, Basel, Switzerland

REKOW, E. DIANNE. Department of Orthodontics, University of Medicine and Dentistry of New Jersey, Newark, New Jersey

RIEMER, MARTIN. Institute of Mathematics and Computer Science in Medicine, University Hospital Eppendorf, Hamburg, Germany

RITTER, R. C. Department of Physics, University of Virginia, Charlottesville, Virginia

ROBB, RICHARD A. Department of Physiology and Biophysics Biomedical Imaging Resource, Mayo Foundation, Rochester, Minnesota

ROSEN, JOSEPH M. Department of Surgery, Dartmouth Medical School and Thayer Engineering, Hanover, New Hampshire

SACKIER, JONATHAN M. School of Medicine, University of California, San Diego, California

SANDERINK, GERARD C. H. Department of Oral Radiology, Academic Center for Dentistry, Amsterdam, The Netherlands

SATAVA, RICHARD. Defense Advanced Research Projects Administration, Arlington, Virginia

SAUTOT, PASCAL. TIMC-IMAG, Faculté de Médecine de Grenoble, La Tronche, France

SCHIPPERS, E. Department of Surgery, Aachen, Germany

SCHIEMANN, THOMAS. Institute of Mathematics and Computer Science in Medicine, University Hospital Eppendorf, Hamburg, Germany

SCHLEGEL, WOLFGANG. German Cancer Research Center, Heidelberg, Germany

SCHLÖNDORFF, GEORG. Department of Otolaryngology, Aachen University Hospital, Aachen, Germany

SCHUBERT, RAINER. Institute of Mathematics and Computer Science in Medicine, University Hospital Eppendorf, Hamburg, Germany

SCHUMPELICK, V. Department of Surgery, Aachen, Germany

SCHWEIKARD, ACHIM. Robotics Laboratory, Department of Computer Science, Stanford University, Stanford, California

SHERIDAN, THOMAS B. Department of Mechanical Engineering, Massachusetts Institute of Technology, Cambridge, Massachusetts

SHTERN, FAINA. Chief, Diagnostic Imaging Research Branch, National Cancer Institute, National Institutes of Health, Rockville, Maryland

SMITH, FRED. Integrated Surgical Systems, Inc. Sacramento, California

STAMMBERGER, HEINZ. Department of Otorhinolarygology, University ENT Hospital Medical Faculty at Karl-Franzens-University, Graz, Austria

STARK, LAWRENCE. University of California, Berkeley, California

STAUDTE, HANS-WALTER. Department for Orthopaedic Surgery, District Hospital Marienhöhe, Würselen, Germany

STULBERG, S. DAVID. Department of Orthopaedic Surgery, Northwestern University Medical School, Evanston, Illinois

STURGES, ROBERT H. JR. Department of Medical Engineering, Carnegie Mellon University, Pittsburgh, Pennsylvania

SZELISKI, RICHARD. Digital Equipment Corporation, Cambridge Research Lab, Cambridge, Massachusetts

TALAMINI, MARK. Johns Hopkins University School of Medicine, Baltimore, Maryland

TAYLOR, RUSSELL H. IBM T. J. Watson Research Center, Yorktown Heights, New York

TENDICK, FRANK. University of California, San Francisco, California

THARP, GREGORY. University of California, Berkeley, California

THULL, BERNHARD. Helmholtz Institute for Biomedical Engineering, Aachen, Germany

TIEDE, ULF. Institute of Mathematics and Computer Science in Medicine, University Hospital Eppendorf, Hamburg, Germany

TIMONEY, ANTHONY G. Institute of Urology, Middlesex Hospital, London, England

TREAT, MICHAEL R. Columbia Presbyterian Medical Center, New York, New York

TROCCAZ, JOCELYNE. TIMC-IMAG, Faculté de Médecine de Grenoble, La Tronche, France

TSIARAS, ALEXANDER. Mallinckrodt Institute of Radiology, Washington University School of Medicine, St. Louis, Missouri

TSUKAMOTO, MASAHIRO. Department of Mechanical Engineering Science, Tokyo Institute of Technology, Tokyo, Japan

UDUPA, JAYARAM K. Medical Image Processing Group, Department of Radiology, University of Pennsylvania, Philadelphia, Pennsylvania

VAN DER STELT, PAUL F. Department of Oral Radiology, Academic Center for Dentistry, Amsterdam, The Netherlands

VANNIER, MICHAEL W. Mallinckrodt Institute of Radiology, Washington University School of Medicine, St. Louis, Missouri

VASSAL, PATRICK. TIMC-IMAG, Faculté de Médecine, La Tronche, France

VON PICHLER, CLETUS. Helmholtz Institute for Biomedical Engineering, Aachen, Germany

WANG, YULUN. Computer Motion, Inc., Goleta, California

WATANABE, EIJU. Department of Neurosurgery, Tokyo Metropolitan Police Hospital, Tokyo, Japan

WATERS, KEITH. Digital Equipment Corporation, Cambridge Research Lab, Cambridge, Massachussetts

WICKHAM, JOHN E. A. Institute of Urology, Middlesex Hospital, London, England

WILLIAMSON, BILL. Integrated Surgical Systems, Sacramento, California

WOLF, STEPHAN R. University Department of Otorhinolaryngology, Nürnberg, Germany

WU, CHI-HAUR. Department of Electrical Engineering and Computer Science, Northwestern University, Evanston, Illinois

ZHANG, XIAOYU. Center for Computer Aids for Industrial Productivity, Rutgers University, Piscataway, New Jersey

ZUHARS, JOEL F. Integrated Surgical Systems, Sacramento, California

INDEX

Head-mounted display (HMD). *See*
    Display, head-mounted
Head tracking, 233, 252
Head-up display. *See* Display, head-up
Hemifacial microsomia, 644
Hierarchically linked objects, 240
Hip surgery. *See also* Rizzoli orthopaedic
    robot; ROBODOC
  femoral head puncture, 454
  prosthesis, 374, 400, 456–458
  total hip replacement (THR), 372, 374
  validation, 405
Holography, 304
Homogeneous transformation matrix, 522
Homology matching, 100, 102, 106, 647.
    See also Registration
Host computer, 525
Hough space, 82
Human error, xii, 311
Human factors, 201, 203–219, 223–229,
    241, 556–557. *See also* Ergonomics
Human-machine communication, 201,
    208–209, 284, 452, 586–587. *See also*
    Computer-aided surgery; Display;
    Ergonomics; Human factors; Tele-
    surgery; Visualization
Human performance
  compared to machines, xi–xii, 311, 391
  measurement, 218–219, 568–571
  strain, 205–206, 219
Humphrey Retinal Analyzer, 485
Hydraulic servomanipulator, 227
Hydroxyapatite, 643
Hyperthermia, 364

I

IGOR (Image Guided Operating Robot)
  accuracy, 349
  angiograms use with, 345, 346
  architecture overview, 344–345
  background, 343
  clinical experience, 350
  discussed, 350
  geometry, 519–520
  preoperative imaging, 345–350
  projection geometry, 505
  reconstruction, 515
  registration, 348–350, 483, 486 (*see also*
      Registration)
    preoperative-to-intraoperative, 349
    x-ray-to-operating room, 348–349
  segmentation (*see* Segmentation)
    finite element approach, 4
    snake approach, 4, 487
  safety, 349–350
  surgical planning, 346–348
IMAGEnet system, 485
Image, xiv, 3, 145, 247, 300
  acquisition, 148, 302–303, 430, 435–437,
      545, 547
  classification, 38, 63, 148
  coordinate systems, 34

distortion, 348, 511, 514 (*see also*
    Calibration)
edge detection, 60–62, 160, 487, 489
editing, 181
filtering, 35, 60
  Canny-Deriche filter, 61
  Laplacian zero-crossings, 60
fusion of images (*see* Registration)
geometry, 514–515
gray-level, 35
inertia moments, 90
interpolation, 36, 42
  shape-based interpolation, 36
interpretation, 161 (*see also* Registration;
    Segmentation)
masking, 37
modalities (*see* CT; MRI; PET; SPECT;
    Ultrasound; X-ray)
partial volumes, 155
pixel, 33, 225, 233–234, 250, 476,
    485–486, 488, 493, 509, 511
processing, 155, 157–158 (*see also*
    Registration; Segmentation)
  intraoperative, 708
  morphological operators, 148, 181
registration (*see* Registration)
scanner, 319
volume measurements, 33, 149
voxel, 33, 323
Image-Guided Operating Robot (IGOR).
    See IGOR
Implants
  craniofacial, 643, 666
  dental, 502
  orthopaedic, 374–375, 380, 400, 418, 425,
      456–458
Inaccuracy, 637
Induction heating, 363–365
Infection, 378
Information systems, 21–22, 307, 316. *See*
    also PACS
Infrared diodes, 636
Inlays, 505
Input-output (i/o) tools, 202
INRIA, 90
Instruction, 565
Intensity-based stereo algorithm, 485
Internal auditory canal, 621
Internal carotid artery (ICA), 631
Intraocular pressure (IOP), 467, 483
Intraoperative monitoring, 312, 720
Intraoperative systems, xiv. *See also* CAS
    systems; Craniofacial surgery; ENT
    surgery; Neurosurgery; Orthopaedic
    surgery; Localizer systems; Minimal
    access surgery; Navigation systems;
    Radiotherapy; Robot, surgical; Spine
    surgery; Telesurgery systems, etc.
Intraoral digital sensor, 512, 514
Intraoral digital radiography, 509, 512,
    515–516. *See also* X-ray
Inverse dosimetry. *See* Radiotherapy
    treatment planning

ISG viewing wand localizer, 304, 620
Isometric control, 530–533
Isotonic control, 530–532
Iterative closest point algorithm, 89

J

Jig systems, 409
Johns Hopkins University (JHU), 590
Joystick, 227, 234, 272, 280–281, 476, 586

K

Keratoconus, 478
Keratometry, 473–479. *See also*
    Keratorefractive surgery; Keratoscope
Keratorefractive surgery, 467. *See also*
    Keratometry
Keratoscope, 473, 474–475, 479. *See also*
    Keratometry
Knee surgery, 372, 375–376. *See also*
    Arthroscopy; Orthopaedic surgery
  anterior cruciate ligament (ACL)
      reconstruction, 372, 376
  total knee replacement (TKR), 372, 374,
      380, 409–410, 417–419
  jig-based systems, 409–410
  robotic systems for (*see* Northwestern
      TKR system; Rizzoli orthopaedic
      robot)
Knoll's target, 475
Knowledge base, 505
K reading, 474

L

Labyrinth, 621
Lambertian reflectance, 492–493, 545
Lamina cribrosa, 483
Laminar flow, 308
Landmarks. *See* Registration
Laparoscope. *See* Endoscope; Endoscopic
    surgery; Laparoscopic surgery
Laparoscopic cholecystectomy, 202, 555,
    556, 559, 562–563, 580. *See also*
    Laparoscopic surgery
Laparoscopic surgery, 217, 219, 223,
    555–556, 561. *See also* Laparoscopic
    cholecystectomy; Minimal access
    surgery
  advanced displays for, 564
  advanced sensors for, 564
  described, 559, 561–562, 567–568, 577
  depth perception as a limitation
    qualitative discussion, 559–560, 564
    quantitative study, 568–570
  education and documentation needs for,
      565
  information management requirements,
      565
  instrumentation limitations
    dexterity, 560, 564
    fulcrum effect, 560, 570–571
    tactility, 560, 563, 574